Oxford Dictionary of
National Biography

Volume 54

Oxford Dictionary of National Biography

IN ASSOCIATION WITH

The British Academy

From the earliest times to the year 2000

Edited by
H. C. G. Matthew
and
Brian Harrison

Volume 54
Taylour–Tonneys

OXFORD
UNIVERSITY PRESS

OXFORD
UNIVERSITY PRESS

Great Clarendon Street, Oxford OX2 6DP

Oxford University Press is a department of the University of Oxford.
It furthers the University's objective of excellence in research, scholarship,
and education by publishing worldwide in

Oxford New York

Auckland Bangkok Buenos Aires Cape Town
Chennai Dar es Salaam Delhi Hong Kong Istanbul Karachi
Kolkata Kuala Lumpur Madrid Melbourne Mexico City Mumbai Nairobi
São Paulo Shanghai Taipei Tokyo Toronto

Oxford is a registered trade mark of Oxford University Press
in the UK and in certain other countries

Published in the United States
by Oxford University Press Inc., New York

© Oxford University Press 2004

Illustrations © individual copyright holders as listed in
'Picture credits', and reproduced with permission

Database right Oxford University Press (maker)

First published 2004

British Library Cataloguing in Publication Data
Data available

Library of Congress Cataloging in Publication Data
Data available: for details see volume 1, p. iv

ISBN 0-19-861404-7 (this volume)
ISBN 0-19-861411-X (set of sixty volumes)

Text captured by Alliance Phototypesetters, Pondicherry
Illustrations reproduced and archived by
Alliance Graphics Ltd, UK
Typeset in OUP Swift by Interactive Sciences Limited, Gloucester
Printed in Great Britain on acid-free paper by
Butler and Tanner Ltd,
Frome, Somerset

LIST OF ABBREVIATIONS

1 *General abbreviations*

AB	bachelor of arts
ABC	Australian Broadcasting Corporation
ABC TV	ABC Television
act.	active
A$	Australian dollar
AD	*anno domini*
AFC	Air Force Cross
AIDS	acquired immune deficiency syndrome
AK	Alaska
AL	Alabama
A level	advanced level [examination]
ALS	associate of the Linnean Society
AM	master of arts
AMICE	associate member of the Institution of Civil Engineers
ANZAC	Australian and New Zealand Army Corps
appx *pl.* appxs	appendix(es)
AR	Arkansas
ARA	associate of the Royal Academy
ARCA	associate of the Royal College of Art
ARCM	associate of the Royal College of Music
ARCO	associate of the Royal College of Organists
ARIBA	associate of the Royal Institute of British Architects
ARP	air-raid precautions
ARRC	associate of the Royal Red Cross
ARSA	associate of the Royal Scottish Academy
art.	article / item
ASC	Army Service Corps
Asch	Austrian Schilling
ASDIC	Antisubmarine Detection Investigation Committee
ATS	Auxiliary Territorial Service
ATV	Associated Television
Aug	August
AZ	Arizona
b.	born
BA	bachelor of arts
BA (Admin.)	bachelor of arts (administration)
BAFTA	British Academy of Film and Television Arts
BAO	bachelor of arts in obstetrics
bap.	baptized
BBC	British Broadcasting Corporation / Company
BC	before Christ
BCE	before the common (*or* Christian) era
BCE	bachelor of civil engineering
BCG	bacillus of Calmette and Guérin [inoculation against tuberculosis]
BCh	bachelor of surgery
BChir	bachelor of surgery
BCL	bachelor of civil law
BCnL	bachelor of canon law
BCom	bachelor of commerce
BD	bachelor of divinity
BEd	bachelor of education
BEng	bachelor of engineering
bk *pl.* bks	book(s)
BL	bachelor of law / letters / literature
BLitt	bachelor of letters
BM	bachelor of medicine
BMus	bachelor of music
BP	before present
BP	British Petroleum
Bros.	Brothers
BS	(1) bachelor of science; (2) bachelor of surgery; (3) British standard
BSc	bachelor of science
BSc (Econ.)	bachelor of science (economics)
BSc (Eng.)	bachelor of science (engineering)
bt	baronet
BTh	bachelor of theology
bur.	buried
C.	command [identifier for published parliamentary papers]
c.	*circa*
c.	*capitulum pl. capitula*: chapter(s)
CA	California
Cantab.	Cantabrigiensis
cap.	*capitulum pl. capitula*: chapter(s)
CB	companion of the Bath
CBE	commander of the Order of the British Empire
CBS	Columbia Broadcasting System
cc	cubic centimetres
C$	Canadian dollar
CD	compact disc
Cd	command [identifier for published parliamentary papers]
CE	Common (*or* Christian) Era
cent.	century
cf.	compare
CH	Companion of Honour
chap.	chapter
ChB	bachelor of surgery
CI	Imperial Order of the Crown of India
CIA	Central Intelligence Agency
CID	Criminal Investigation Department
CIE	companion of the Order of the Indian Empire
Cie	Compagnie
CLit	companion of literature
CM	master of surgery
cm	centimetre(s)

Cmd	command [identifier for published parliamentary papers]
CMG	companion of the Order of St Michael and St George
Cmnd	command [identifier for published parliamentary papers]
CO	Colorado
Co.	company
co.	county
col. *pl.* cols.	column(s)
Corp.	corporation
CSE	certificate of secondary education
CSI	companion of the Order of the Star of India
CT	Connecticut
CVO	commander of the Royal Victorian Order
cwt	hundredweight
$	(American) dollar
d.	(1) penny (pence); (2) died
DBE	dame commander of the Order of the British Empire
DCH	diploma in child health
DCh	doctor of surgery
DCL	doctor of civil law
DCnL	doctor of canon law
DCVO	dame commander of the Royal Victorian Order
DD	doctor of divinity
DE	Delaware
Dec	December
dem.	demolished
DEng	doctor of engineering
des.	destroyed
DFC	Distinguished Flying Cross
DipEd	diploma in education
DipPsych	diploma in psychiatry
diss.	dissertation
DL	deputy lieutenant
DLitt	doctor of letters
DLittCelt	doctor of Celtic letters
DM	(1) Deutschmark; (2) doctor of medicine; (3) doctor of musical arts
DMus	doctor of music
DNA	dioxyribonucleic acid
doc.	document
DOL	doctor of oriental learning
DPH	diploma in public health
DPhil	doctor of philosophy
DPM	diploma in psychological medicine
DSC	Distinguished Service Cross
DSc	doctor of science
DSc (Econ.)	doctor of science (economics)
DSc (Eng.)	doctor of science (engineering)
DSM	Distinguished Service Medal
DSO	companion of the Distinguished Service Order
DSocSc	doctor of social science
DTech	doctor of technology
DTh	doctor of theology
DTM	diploma in tropical medicine
DTMH	diploma in tropical medicine and hygiene
DU	doctor of the university
DUniv	doctor of the university
dwt	pennyweight
EC	European Community
ed. *pl.* eds.	edited / edited by / editor(s)
Edin.	Edinburgh

edn	edition
EEC	European Economic Community
EFTA	European Free Trade Association
EICS	East India Company Service
EMI	Electrical and Musical Industries (Ltd)
Eng.	English
enl.	enlarged
ENSA	Entertainments National Service Association
ep. *pl.* epp.	*epistola(e)*
ESP	extra-sensory perception
esp.	especially
esq.	esquire
est.	estimate / estimated
EU	European Union
ex	sold by (*lit.* out of)
excl.	excludes / excluding
exh.	exhibited
exh. cat.	exhibition catalogue
f. *pl.* ff.	following [pages]
FA	Football Association
FACP	fellow of the American College of Physicians
facs.	facsimile
FANY	First Aid Nursing Yeomanry
FBA	fellow of the British Academy
FBI	Federation of British Industries
FCS	fellow of the Chemical Society
Feb	February
FEng	fellow of the Fellowship of Engineering
FFCM	fellow of the Faculty of Community Medicine
FGS	fellow of the Geological Society
fig.	figure
FIMechE	fellow of the Institution of Mechanical Engineers
FL	Florida
fl.	*floruit*
FLS	fellow of the Linnean Society
FM	frequency modulation
fol. *pl.* fols.	folio(s)
Fr	French francs
Fr.	French
FRAeS	fellow of the Royal Aeronautical Society
FRAI	fellow of the Royal Anthropological Institute
FRAM	fellow of the Royal Academy of Music
FRAS	(1) fellow of the Royal Asiatic Society; (2) fellow of the Royal Astronomical Society
FRCM	fellow of the Royal College of Music
FRCO	fellow of the Royal College of Organists
FRCOG	fellow of the Royal College of Obstetricians and Gynaecologists
FRCP(C)	fellow of the Royal College of Physicians of Canada
FRCP (Edin.)	fellow of the Royal College of Physicians of Edinburgh
FRCP (Lond.)	fellow of the Royal College of Physicians of London
FRCPath	fellow of the Royal College of Pathologists
FRCPsych	fellow of the Royal College of Psychiatrists
FRCS	fellow of the Royal College of Surgeons
FRGS	fellow of the Royal Geographical Society
FRIBA	fellow of the Royal Institute of British Architects
FRICS	fellow of the Royal Institute of Chartered Surveyors
FRS	fellow of the Royal Society
FRSA	fellow of the Royal Society of Arts

FRSCM	fellow of the Royal School of Church Music
FRSE	fellow of the Royal Society of Edinburgh
FRSL	fellow of the Royal Society of Literature
FSA	fellow of the Society of Antiquaries
ft	foot *pl.* feet
FTCL	fellow of Trinity College of Music, London
ft-lb per min.	foot-pounds per minute [unit of horsepower]
FZS	fellow of the Zoological Society
GA	Georgia
GBE	knight or dame grand cross of the Order of the British Empire
GCB	knight grand cross of the Order of the Bath
GCE	general certificate of education
GCH	knight grand cross of the Royal Guelphic Order
GCHQ	government communications headquarters
GCIE	knight grand commander of the Order of the Indian Empire
GCMG	knight or dame grand cross of the Order of St Michael and St George
GCSE	general certificate of secondary education
GCSI	knight grand commander of the Order of the Star of India
GCStJ	bailiff or dame grand cross of the order of St John of Jerusalem
GCVO	knight or dame grand cross of the Royal Victorian Order
GEC	General Electric Company
Ger.	German
GI	government (*or* general) issue
GMT	Greenwich mean time
GP	general practitioner
GPU	[Soviet special police unit]
GSO	general staff officer
Heb.	Hebrew
HEICS	Honourable East India Company Service
HI	Hawaii
HIV	human immunodeficiency virus
HK$	Hong Kong dollar
HM	his / her majesty('s)
HMAS	his / her majesty's Australian ship
HMNZS	his / her majesty's New Zealand ship
HMS	his / her majesty's ship
HMSO	His / Her Majesty's Stationery Office
HMV	His Master's Voice
Hon.	Honourable
hp	horsepower
hr	hour(s)
HRH	his / her royal highness
HTV	Harlech Television
IA	Iowa
ibid.	*ibidem*: in the same place
ICI	Imperial Chemical Industries (Ltd)
ID	Idaho
IL	Illinois
illus.	illustration
illustr.	illustrated
IN	Indiana
in.	inch(es)
Inc.	Incorporated
incl.	includes / including
IOU	I owe you
IQ	intelligence quotient
Ir£	Irish pound
IRA	Irish Republican Army
ISO	companion of the Imperial Service Order
It.	Italian
ITA	Independent Television Authority
ITV	Independent Television
Jan	January
JP	justice of the peace
jun.	junior
KB	knight of the Order of the Bath
KBE	knight commander of the Order of the British Empire
KC	king's counsel
kcal	kilocalorie
KCB	knight commander of the Order of the Bath
KCH	knight commander of the Royal Guelphic Order
KCIE	knight commander of the Order of the Indian Empire
KCMG	knight commander of the Order of St Michael and St George
KCSI	knight commander of the Order of the Star of India
KCVO	knight commander of the Royal Victorian Order
keV	kilo-electron-volt
KG	knight of the Order of the Garter
KGB	[Soviet committee of state security]
KH	knight of the Royal Guelphic Order
KLM	Koninklijke Luchtvaart Maatschappij (Royal Dutch Air Lines)
km	kilometre(s)
KP	knight of the Order of St Patrick
KS	Kansas
KT	knight of the Order of the Thistle
kt	knight
KY	Kentucky
£	pound(s) sterling
£E	Egyptian pound
L	lira *pl.* lire
l. *pl.* ll.	line(s)
LA	Lousiana
LAA	light anti-aircraft
LAH	licentiate of the Apothecaries' Hall, Dublin
Lat.	Latin
lb	pound(s), unit of weight
LDS	licence in dental surgery
lit.	literally
LittB	bachelor of letters
LittD	doctor of letters
LKQCPI	licentiate of the King and Queen's College of Physicians, Ireland
LLA	lady literate in arts
LLB	bachelor of laws
LLD	doctor of laws
LLM	master of laws
LM	licentiate in midwifery
LP	long-playing record
LRAM	licentiate of the Royal Academy of Music
LRCP	licentiate of the Royal College of Physicians
LRCPS (Glasgow)	licentiate of the Royal College of Physicians and Surgeons of Glasgow
LRCS	licentiate of the Royal College of Surgeons
LSA	licentiate of the Society of Apothecaries
LSD	lysergic acid diethylamide
LVO	lieutenant of the Royal Victorian Order
M. *pl.* MM.	Monsieur *pl.* Messieurs
m	metre(s)

m. *pl.* mm.	membrane(s)
MA	(1) Massachusetts; (2) master of arts
MAI	master of engineering
MB	bachelor of medicine
MBA	master of business administration
MBE	member of the Order of the British Empire
MC	Military Cross
MCC	Marylebone Cricket Club
MCh	master of surgery
MChir	master of surgery
MCom	master of commerce
MD	(1) doctor of medicine; (2) Maryland
MDMA	methylenedioxymethamphetamine
ME	Maine
MEd	master of education
MEng	master of engineering
MEP	member of the European parliament
MG	Morris Garages
MGM	Metro-Goldwyn-Mayer
Mgr	Monsignor
MI	(1) Michigan; (2) military intelligence
MI1c	[secret intelligence department]
MI5	[military intelligence department]
MI6	[secret intelligence department]
MI9	[secret escape service]
MICE	member of the Institution of Civil Engineers
MIEE	member of the Institution of Electrical Engineers
min.	minute(s)
Mk	mark
ML	(1) licentiate of medicine; (2) master of laws
MLitt	master of letters
Mlle	Mademoiselle
mm	millimetre(s)
Mme	Madame
MN	Minnesota
MO	Missouri
MOH	medical officer of health
MP	member of parliament
m.p.h.	miles per hour
MPhil	master of philosophy
MRCP	member of the Royal College of Physicians
MRCS	member of the Royal College of Surgeons
MRCVS	member of the Royal College of Veterinary Surgeons
MRIA	member of the Royal Irish Academy
MS	(1) master of science; (2) Mississippi
MS *pl.* MSS	manuscript(s)
MSc	master of science
MSc (Econ.)	master of science (economics)
MT	Montana
MusB	bachelor of music
MusBac	bachelor of music
MusD	doctor of music
MV	motor vessel
MVO	member of the Royal Victorian Order
n. *pl.* nn.	note(s)
NAAFI	Navy, Army, and Air Force Institutes
NASA	National Aeronautics and Space Administration
NATO	North Atlantic Treaty Organization
NBC	National Broadcasting Corporation
NC	North Carolina
NCO	non-commissioned officer
ND	North Dakota
n.d.	no date
NE	Nebraska
nem. con.	*nemine contradicente*: unanimously
new ser.	new series
NH	New Hampshire
NHS	National Health Service
NJ	New Jersey
NKVD	[Soviet people's commissariat for internal affairs]
NM	New Mexico
nm	nanometre(s)
no. *pl.* nos.	number(s)
Nov	November
n.p.	no place [of publication]
NS	new style
NV	Nevada
NY	New York
NZBS	New Zealand Broadcasting Service
OBE	officer of the Order of the British Empire
obit.	obituary
Oct	October
OCTU	officer cadets training unit
OECD	Organization for Economic Co-operation and Development
OEEC	Organization for European Economic Co-operation
OFM	order of Friars Minor [Franciscans]
OFMCap	Ordine Frati Minori Cappucini: member of the Capuchin order
OH	Ohio
OK	Oklahoma
O level	ordinary level [examination]
OM	Order of Merit
OP	order of Preachers [Dominicans]
op. *pl.* opp.	opus *pl.* opera
OPEC	Organization of Petroleum Exporting Countries
OR	Oregon
orig.	original
OS	old style
OSB	Order of St Benedict
OTC	Officers' Training Corps
OWS	Old Watercolour Society
Oxon.	Oxoniensis
p. *pl.* pp.	page(s)
PA	Pennsylvania
p.a.	per annum
para.	paragraph
PAYE	pay as you earn
pbk *pl.* pbks	paperback(s)
per.	[during the] period
PhD	doctor of philosophy
pl.	(1) plate(s); (2) plural
priv. coll.	private collection
pt *pl.* pts	part(s)
pubd	published
PVC	polyvinyl chloride
q. *pl.* qq.	(1) question(s); (2) quire(s)
QC	queen's counsel
R	rand
R.	Rex / Regina
r	recto
r.	reigned / ruled
RA	Royal Academy / Royal Academician

RAC	Royal Automobile Club		Skr	Swedish krona
RAF	Royal Air Force		Span.	Spanish
RAFVR	Royal Air Force Volunteer Reserve		SPCK	Society for Promoting Christian Knowledge
RAM	[member of the] Royal Academy of Music		SS	(1) Santissimi; (2) Schutzstaffel; (3) steam ship
RAMC	Royal Army Medical Corps		STB	bachelor of theology
RCA	Royal College of Art		STD	doctor of theology
RCNC	Royal Corps of Naval Constructors		STM	master of theology
RCOG	Royal College of Obstetricians and Gynaecologists		STP	doctor of theology
RDI	royal designer for industry		*supp.*	supposedly
RE	Royal Engineers		suppl. *pl.* suppls.	supplement(s)
repr. *pl.* reprs.	reprint(s) / reprinted		s.v.	*sub verbo* / *sub voce*: under the word / heading
repro.	reproduced		SY	steam yacht
rev.	revised / revised by / reviser / revision		TA	Territorial Army
Revd	Reverend		TASS	[Soviet news agency]
RHA	Royal Hibernian Academy		TB	tuberculosis (*lit.* tubercle bacillus)
RI	(1) Rhode Island; (2) Royal Institute of Painters in Water-Colours		TD	(1) *teachtaí dála* (member of the Dáil); (2) territorial decoration
RIBA	Royal Institute of British Architects		TN	Tennessee
RIN	Royal Indian Navy		TNT	trinitrotoluene
RM	Reichsmark		trans.	translated / translated by / translation / translator
RMS	Royal Mail steamer		TT	tourist trophy
RN	Royal Navy		TUC	Trades Union Congress
RNA	ribonucleic acid		TX	Texas
RNAS	Royal Naval Air Service		U-boat	*Unterseeboot*: submarine
RNR	Royal Naval Reserve		Ufa	Universum-Film AG
RNVR	Royal Naval Volunteer Reserve		UMIST	University of Manchester Institute of Science and Technology
RO	Record Office		UN	United Nations
r.p.m.	revolutions per minute		UNESCO	United Nations Educational, Scientific, and Cultural Organization
RRS	royal research ship		UNICEF	United Nations International Children's Emergency Fund
Rs	rupees		unpubd	unpublished
RSA	(1) Royal Scottish Academician; (2) Royal Society of Arts		USS	United States ship
RSPCA	Royal Society for the Prevention of Cruelty to Animals		UT	Utah
Rt Hon.	Right Honourable		*v*	verso
Rt Revd	Right Reverend		v.	versus
RUC	Royal Ulster Constabulary		VA	Virginia
Russ.	Russian		VAD	Voluntary Aid Detachment
RWS	Royal Watercolour Society		VC	Victoria Cross
S4C	Sianel Pedwar Cymru		VE-day	victory in Europe day
s.	shilling(s)		Ven.	Venerable
s.a.	*sub anno*: under the year		VJ-day	victory over Japan day
SABC	South African Broadcasting Corporation		vol. *pl.* vols.	volume(s)
SAS	Special Air Service		VT	Vermont
SC	South Carolina		WA	Washington [state]
ScD	doctor of science		WAAC	Women's Auxiliary Army Corps
S$	Singapore dollar		WAAF	Women's Auxiliary Air Force
SD	South Dakota		WEA	Workers' Educational Association
sec.	second(s)		WHO	World Health Organization
sel.	selected		WI	Wisconsin
sen.	senior		WRAF	Women's Royal Air Force
Sept	September		WRNS	Women's Royal Naval Service
ser.	series		WV	West Virginia
SHAPE	supreme headquarters allied powers, Europe		WVS	Women's Voluntary Service
SIDRO	Société Internationale d'Énergie Hydro-Électrique		WY	Wyoming
sig. *pl.* sigs.	signature(s)		¥	yen
sing.	singular		YMCA	Young Men's Christian Association
SIS	Secret Intelligence Service		YWCA	Young Women's Christian Association
SJ	Society of Jesus			

2 Institution abbreviations

All Souls Oxf.	All Souls College, Oxford
AM Oxf.	Ashmolean Museum, Oxford
Balliol Oxf.	Balliol College, Oxford
BBC WAC	BBC Written Archives Centre, Reading
Beds. & Luton ARS	Bedfordshire and Luton Archives and Record Service, Bedford
Berks. RO	Berkshire Record Office, Reading
BFI	British Film Institute, London
BFI NFTVA	British Film Institute, London, National Film and Television Archive
BGS	British Geological Survey, Keyworth, Nottingham
Birm. CA	Birmingham Central Library, Birmingham City Archives
Birm. CL	Birmingham Central Library
BL	British Library, London
BL NSA	British Library, London, National Sound Archive
BL OIOC	British Library, London, Oriental and India Office Collections
BLPES	London School of Economics and Political Science, British Library of Political and Economic Science
BM	British Museum, London
Bodl. Oxf.	Bodleian Library, Oxford
Bodl. RH	Bodleian Library of Commonwealth and African Studies at Rhodes House, Oxford
Borth. Inst.	Borthwick Institute of Historical Research, University of York
Boston PL	Boston Public Library, Massachusetts
Bristol RO	Bristol Record Office
Bucks. RLSS	Buckinghamshire Records and Local Studies Service, Aylesbury
CAC Cam.	Churchill College, Cambridge, Churchill Archives Centre
Cambs. AS	Cambridgeshire Archive Service
CCC Cam.	Corpus Christi College, Cambridge
CCC Oxf.	Corpus Christi College, Oxford
Ches. & Chester ALSS	Cheshire and Chester Archives and Local Studies Service
Christ Church Oxf.	Christ Church, Oxford
Christies	Christies, London
City Westm. AC	City of Westminster Archives Centre, London
CKS	Centre for Kentish Studies, Maidstone
CLRO	Corporation of London Records Office
Coll. Arms	College of Arms, London
Col. U.	Columbia University, New York
Cornwall RO	Cornwall Record Office, Truro
Courtauld Inst.	Courtauld Institute of Art, London
CUL	Cambridge University Library
Cumbria AS	Cumbria Archive Service
Derbys. RO	Derbyshire Record Office, Matlock
Devon RO	Devon Record Office, Exeter
Dorset RO	Dorset Record Office, Dorchester
Duke U.	Duke University, Durham, North Carolina
Duke U., Perkins L.	Duke University, Durham, North Carolina, William R. Perkins Library
Durham Cath. CL	Durham Cathedral, chapter library
Durham RO	Durham Record Office
DWL	Dr Williams's Library, London
Essex RO	Essex Record Office
E. Sussex RO	East Sussex Record Office, Lewes
Eton	Eton College, Berkshire
FM Cam.	Fitzwilliam Museum, Cambridge
Folger	Folger Shakespeare Library, Washington, DC
Garr. Club	Garrick Club, London
Girton Cam.	Girton College, Cambridge
GL	Guildhall Library, London
Glos. RO	Gloucestershire Record Office, Gloucester
Gon. & Caius Cam.	Gonville and Caius College, Cambridge
Gov. Art Coll.	Government Art Collection
GS Lond.	Geological Society of London
Hants. RO	Hampshire Record Office, Winchester
Harris Man. Oxf.	Harris Manchester College, Oxford
Harvard TC	Harvard Theatre Collection, Harvard University, Cambridge, Massachusetts, Nathan Marsh Pusey Library
Harvard U.	Harvard University, Cambridge, Massachusetts
Harvard U., Houghton L.	Harvard University, Cambridge, Massachusetts, Houghton Library
Herefs. RO	Herefordshire Record Office, Hereford
Herts. ALS	Hertfordshire Archives and Local Studies, Hertford
Hist. Soc. Penn.	Historical Society of Pennsylvania, Philadelphia
HLRO	House of Lords Record Office, London
Hult. Arch.	Hulton Archive, London and New York
Hunt. L.	Huntington Library, San Marino, California
ICL	Imperial College, London
Inst. CE	Institution of Civil Engineers, London
Inst. EE	Institution of Electrical Engineers, London
IWM	Imperial War Museum, London
IWM FVA	Imperial War Museum, London, Film and Video Archive
IWM SA	Imperial War Museum, London, Sound Archive
JRL	John Rylands University Library of Manchester
King's AC Cam.	King's College Archives Centre, Cambridge
King's Cam.	King's College, Cambridge
King's Lond.	King's College, London
King's Lond., Liddell Hart C.	King's College, London, Liddell Hart Centre for Military Archives
Lancs. RO	Lancashire Record Office, Preston
L. Cong.	Library of Congress, Washington, DC
Leics. RO	Leicestershire, Leicester, and Rutland Record Office, Leicester
Lincs. Arch.	Lincolnshire Archives, Lincoln
Linn. Soc.	Linnean Society of London
LMA	London Metropolitan Archives
LPL	Lambeth Palace, London
Lpool RO	Liverpool Record Office and Local Studies Service
LUL	London University Library
Magd. Cam.	Magdalene College, Cambridge
Magd. Oxf.	Magdalen College, Oxford
Man. City Gall.	Manchester City Galleries
Man. CL	Manchester Central Library
Mass. Hist. Soc.	Massachusetts Historical Society, Boston
Merton Oxf.	Merton College, Oxford
MHS Oxf.	Museum of the History of Science, Oxford
Mitchell L., Glas.	Mitchell Library, Glasgow
Mitchell L., NSW	State Library of New South Wales, Sydney, Mitchell Library
Morgan L.	Pierpont Morgan Library, New York
NA Canada	National Archives of Canada, Ottawa
NA Ire.	National Archives of Ireland, Dublin
NAM	National Army Museum, London
NA Scot.	National Archives of Scotland, Edinburgh
News Int. RO	News International Record Office, London
NG Ire.	National Gallery of Ireland, Dublin

NG Scot.	National Gallery of Scotland, Edinburgh
NHM	Natural History Museum, London
NL Aus.	National Library of Australia, Canberra
NL Ire.	National Library of Ireland, Dublin
NL NZ	National Library of New Zealand, Wellington
NL NZ, Turnbull L.	National Library of New Zealand, Wellington, Alexander Turnbull Library
NL Scot.	National Library of Scotland, Edinburgh
NL Wales	National Library of Wales, Aberystwyth
NMG Wales	National Museum and Gallery of Wales, Cardiff
NMM	National Maritime Museum, London
Norfolk RO	Norfolk Record Office, Norwich
Northants. RO	Northamptonshire Record Office, Northampton
Northumbd RO	Northumberland Record Office
Notts. Arch.	Nottinghamshire Archives, Nottingham
NPG	National Portrait Gallery, London
NRA	National Archives, London, Historical Manuscripts Commission, National Register of Archives
Nuffield Oxf.	Nuffield College, Oxford
N. Yorks. CRO	North Yorkshire County Record Office, Northallerton
NYPL	New York Public Library
Oxf. UA	Oxford University Archives
Oxf. U. Mus. NH	Oxford University Museum of Natural History
Oxon. RO	Oxfordshire Record Office, Oxford
Pembroke Cam.	Pembroke College, Cambridge
PRO	National Archives, London, Public Record Office
PRO NIre.	Public Record Office for Northern Ireland, Belfast
Pusey Oxf.	Pusey House, Oxford
RA	Royal Academy of Arts, London
Ransom HRC	Harry Ransom Humanities Research Center, University of Texas, Austin
RAS	Royal Astronomical Society, London
RBG Kew	Royal Botanic Gardens, Kew, London
RCP Lond.	Royal College of Physicians of London
RCS Eng.	Royal College of Surgeons of England, London
RGS	Royal Geographical Society, London
RIBA	Royal Institute of British Architects, London
RIBA BAL	Royal Institute of British Architects, London, British Architectural Library
Royal Arch.	Royal Archives, Windsor Castle, Berkshire [by gracious permission of her majesty the queen]
Royal Irish Acad.	Royal Irish Academy, Dublin
Royal Scot. Acad.	Royal Scottish Academy, Edinburgh
RS	Royal Society, London
RSA	Royal Society of Arts, London
RS Friends, Lond.	Religious Society of Friends, London
St Ant. Oxf.	St Antony's College, Oxford
St John Cam.	St John's College, Cambridge
S. Antiquaries, Lond.	Society of Antiquaries of London
Sci. Mus.	Science Museum, London
Scot. NPG	Scottish National Portrait Gallery, Edinburgh
Scott Polar RI	University of Cambridge, Scott Polar Research Institute
Sheff. Arch.	Sheffield Archives
Shrops. RRC	Shropshire Records and Research Centre, Shrewsbury
SOAS	School of Oriental and African Studies, London
Som. ARS	Somerset Archive and Record Service, Taunton
Staffs. RO	Staffordshire Record Office, Stafford

Suffolk RO	Suffolk Record Office
Surrey HC	Surrey History Centre, Woking
TCD	Trinity College, Dublin
Trinity Cam.	Trinity College, Cambridge
U. Aberdeen	University of Aberdeen
U. Birm.	University of Birmingham
U. Birm. L.	University of Birmingham Library
U. Cal.	University of California
U. Cam.	University of Cambridge
UCL	University College, London
U. Durham	University of Durham
U. Durham L.	University of Durham Library
U. Edin.	University of Edinburgh
U. Edin., New Coll.	University of Edinburgh, New College
U. Edin., New Coll. L.	University of Edinburgh, New College Library
U. Edin. L.	University of Edinburgh Library
U. Glas.	University of Glasgow
U. Glas. L.	University of Glasgow Library
U. Hull	University of Hull
U. Hull, Brynmor Jones L.	University of Hull, Brynmor Jones Library
U. Leeds	University of Leeds
U. Leeds, Brotherton L.	University of Leeds, Brotherton Library
U. Lond.	University of London
U. Lpool	University of Liverpool
U. Lpool L.	University of Liverpool Library
U. Mich.	University of Michigan, Ann Arbor
U. Mich., Clements L.	University of Michigan, Ann Arbor, William L. Clements Library
U. Newcastle	University of Newcastle upon Tyne
U. Newcastle, Robinson L.	University of Newcastle upon Tyne, Robinson Library
U. Nott.	University of Nottingham
U. Nott. L.	University of Nottingham Library
U. Oxf.	University of Oxford
U. Reading	University of Reading
U. Reading L.	University of Reading Library
U. St Andr.	University of St Andrews
U. St Andr. L.	University of St Andrews Library
U. Southampton	University of Southampton
U. Southampton L.	University of Southampton Library
U. Sussex	University of Sussex, Brighton
U. Texas	University of Texas, Austin
U. Wales	University of Wales
U. Warwick Mod. RC	University of Warwick, Coventry, Modern Records Centre
V&A	Victoria and Albert Museum, London
V&A NAL	Victoria and Albert Museum, London, National Art Library
Warks. CRO	Warwickshire County Record Office, Warwick
Wellcome L.	Wellcome Library for the History and Understanding of Medicine, London
Westm. DA	Westminster Diocesan Archives, London
Wilts. & Swindon RO	Wiltshire and Swindon Record Office, Trowbridge
Worcs. RO	Worcestershire Record Office, Worcester
W. Sussex RO	West Sussex Record Office, Chichester
W. Yorks. AS	West Yorkshire Archive Service
Yale U.	Yale University, New Haven, Connecticut
Yale U., Beinecke L.	Yale University, New Haven, Connecticut, Beinecke Rare Book and Manuscript Library
Yale U. CBA	Yale University, New Haven, Connecticut, Yale Center for British Art

3 Bibliographic abbreviations

Adams, *Drama*   W. D. Adams, *A dictionary of the drama*, 1: *A–G* (1904); 2: *H–Z* (1956) [vol. 2 microfilm only]

AFM   J O'Donovan, ed. and trans., *Annala rioghachta Eireann / Annals of the kingdom of Ireland by the four masters*, 7 vols. (1848–51); 2nd edn (1856); 3rd edn (1990)

Allibone, *Dict.*   S. A. Allibone, *A critical dictionary of English literature and British and American authors*, 3 vols. (1859–71); suppl. by J. F. Kirk, 2 vols. (1891)

ANB   J. A. Garraty and M. C. Carnes, eds., *American national biography*, 24 vols. (1999)

Anderson, *Scot. nat.*   W. Anderson, *The Scottish nation, or, The surnames, families, literature, honours, and biographical history of the people of Scotland*, 3 vols. (1859–63)

Ann. mon.   H. R. Luard, ed., *Annales monastici*, 5 vols., Rolls Series, 36 (1864–9)

Ann. Ulster   S. Mac Airt and G. Mac Niocaill, eds., *Annals of Ulster (to AD 1131)* (1983)

APC   *Acts of the privy council of England*, new ser., 46 vols. (1890–1964)

APS   *The acts of the parliaments of Scotland*, 12 vols. in 13 (1814–75)

Arber, *Regs. Stationers*   F. Arber, ed., *A transcript of the registers of the Company of Stationers of London, 1554–1640 AD*, 5 vols. (1875–94)

ArchR   *Architectural Review*

ASC   D. Whitelock, D. C. Douglas, and S. I. Tucker, ed. and trans., *The Anglo-Saxon Chronicle: a revised translation* (1961)

AS chart.   P. H. Sawyer, *Anglo-Saxon charters: an annotated list and bibliography*, Royal Historical Society Guides and Handbooks (1968)

AusDB   D. Pike and others, eds., *Australian dictionary of biography*, 16 vols. (1966–2002)

Baker, *Serjeants*   J. H. Baker, *The order of serjeants at law*, SeldS, suppl. ser., 5 (1984)

Bale, *Cat.*   J. Bale, *Scriptorum illustrium Maioris Brytannie, quam nunc Angliam et Scotiam vocant: catalogus*, 2 vols. in 1 (Basel, 1557–9); facs. edn (1971)

Bale, *Index*   J. Bale, *Index Britanniae scriptorum*, ed. R. L. Poole and M. Bateson (1902); facs. edn (1990)

BBCS   *Bulletin of the Board of Celtic Studies*

BDMBR   J. O. Baylen and N. J. Gossman, eds., *Biographical dictionary of modern British radicals*, 3 vols. in 4 (1979–88)

Bede, *Hist. eccl.*   *Bede's Ecclesiastical history of the English people*, ed. and trans. B. Colgrave and R. A. B. Mynors, OMT (1969); repr. (1991)

Bénézit, *Dict.*   E. Bénézit, *Dictionnaire critique et documentaire des peintres, sculpteurs, dessinateurs et graveurs*, 3 vols. (Paris, 1911–23); new edn, 8 vols. (1948–66), repr. (1966); 3rd edn, rev. and enl., 10 vols. (1976); 4th edn, 14 vols. (1999)

BIHR   *Bulletin of the Institute of Historical Research*

Birch, *Seals*   W. de Birch, *Catalogue of seals in the department of manuscripts in the British Museum*, 6 vols. (1887–1900)

Bishop Burnet's History   *Bishop Burnet's History of his own time*, ed. M. J. Routh, 2nd edn, 6 vols. (1833)

Blackwood   *Blackwood's [Edinburgh] Magazine*, 328 vols. (1817–1980)

Blain, Clements & Grundy, *Feminist comp.*   V. Blain, P. Clements, and I. Grundy, eds., *The feminist companion to literature in English* (1990)

BL cat.   *The British Library general catalogue of printed books* [in 360 vols. with suppls., also CD-ROM and online]

BMJ   *British Medical Journal*

Boase & Courtney, *Bibl. Corn.*   G. C. Boase and W. P. Courtney, *Bibliotheca Cornubiensis: a catalogue of the writings ... of Cornishmen*, 3 vols. (1874–82)

Boase, *Mod. Eng. biog.*   F. Boase, *Modern English biography: containing many thousand concise memoirs of persons who have died since the year 1850*, 6 vols. (privately printed, Truro, 1892–1921); repr. (1965)

Boswell, *Life*   *Boswell's Life of Johnson: together with Journal of a tour to the Hebrides and Johnson's Diary of a journey into north Wales*, ed. G. B. Hill, enl. edn, rev. L. F. Powell, 6 vols. (1934–50); 2nd edn (1964); repr. (1971)

Brown & Stratton, *Brit. mus.*   J. D. Brown and S. S. Stratton, *British musical biography* (1897)

Bryan, *Painters*   M. Bryan, *A biographical and critical dictionary of painters and engravers*, 2 vols. (1816); new edn, ed. G. Stanley (1849); new edn, ed. R. E. Graves and W. Armstrong, 2 vols. (1886–9); [4th edn], ed. G. C. Williamson, 5 vols. (1903–5) [various reprs.]

Burke, *Gen. GB*   J. Burke, *A genealogical and heraldic history of the commoners of Great Britain and Ireland*, 4 vols. (1833–8); new edn as *A genealogical and heraldic dictionary of the landed gentry of Great Britain and Ireland*, 3 vols. [1843–9] [many later edns]

Burke, *Gen. Ire.*   J. B. Burke, *A genealogical and heraldic history of the landed gentry of Ireland* (1899); 2nd edn (1904); 3rd edn (1912); 4th edn (1958); 5th edn as *Burke's Irish family records* (1976)

Burke, *Peerage*   J. Burke, *A general [later edns A genealogical] and heraldic dictionary of the peerage and baronetage of the United Kingdom* [later edns *the British empire*] (1829–)

Burney, *Hist. mus.*   C. Burney, *A general history of music, from the earliest ages to the present period*, 4 vols. (1776–89)

Burtchaell & Sadleir, *Alum. Dubl.*   G. D. Burtchaell and T. U. Sadleir, *Alumni Dublinenses: a register of the students, graduates, and provosts of Trinity College* (1924); [2nd edn], with suppl., in 2 pts (1935)

Calamy rev.   A. G. Matthews, *Calamy revised* (1934); repr. (1988)

CCI   *Calendar of confirmations and inventories granted and given up in the several commissariots of Scotland* (1876–)

CCIR   *Calendar of the close rolls preserved in the Public Record Office*, 47 vols. (1892–1963)

CDS   J. Bain, ed., *Calendar of documents relating to Scotland*, 4 vols., PRO (1881–8); suppl. vol. 5, ed. G. G. Simpson and J. D. Galbraith [1986]

CEPR letters   W. H. Bliss, C. Johnson, and J. Twemlow, eds., *Calendar of entries in the papal registers relating to Great Britain and Ireland: papal letters* (1893–)

CGPLA   *Calendars of the grants of probate and letters of administration* [in 4 ser.: *England & Wales, Northern Ireland, Ireland*, and *Éire*]

Chambers, *Scots.*   R. Chambers, ed., *A biographical dictionary of eminent Scotsmen*, 4 vols. (1832–5)

Chancery records   chancery records pubd by the PRO

Chancery records (RC)   chancery records pubd by the Record Commissions

CIPM	Calendar of inquisitions post mortem, [20 vols.], PRO (1904–); also Henry VII, 3 vols. (1898–1955)
Clarendon, Hist. rebellion	E. Hyde, earl of Clarendon, The history of the rebellion and civil wars in England, 6 vols. (1888); repr. (1958) and (1992)
Cobbett, Parl. hist.	W. Cobbett and J. Wright, eds., Cobbett's Parliamentary history of England, 36 vols. (1806–1820)
Colvin, Archs.	H. Colvin, A biographical dictionary of British architects, 1600–1840, 3rd edn (1995)
Cooper, Ath. Cantab.	C. H. Cooper and T. Cooper, Athenae Cantabrigienses, 3 vols. (1858–1913); repr. (1967)
CPR	Calendar of the patent rolls preserved in the Public Record Office (1891–)
Crockford	Crockford's Clerical Directory
CS	Camden Society
CSP	Calendar of state papers [in 11 ser.: domestic, Scotland, Scottish series, Ireland, colonial, Commonwealth, foreign, Spain [at Simancas], Rome, Milan, and Venice]
CYS	Canterbury and York Society
DAB	Dictionary of American biography, 21 vols. (1928–36), repr. in 11 vols. (1964); 10 suppls. (1944–96)
DBB	D. J. Jeremy, ed., Dictionary of business biography, 5 vols. (1984–6)
DCB	G. W. Brown and others, Dictionary of Canadian biography, [14 vols.] (1966–)
Debrett's Peerage	Debrett's Peerage (1803–) [sometimes Debrett's Illustrated peerage]
Desmond, Botanists	R. Desmond, Dictionary of British and Irish botanists and horticulturists (1977); rev. edn (1994)
Dir. Brit. archs.	A. Felstead, J. Franklin, and L. Pinfield, eds., Directory of British architects, 1834–1900 (1993); 2nd edn, ed. A. Brodie and others, 2 vols. (2001)
DLB	J. M. Bellamy and J. Saville, eds., Dictionary of labour biography, [10 vols.] (1972–)
DLitB	Dictionary of Literary Biography
DNB	Dictionary of national biography, 63 vols. (1885–1900), suppl., 3 vols. (1901); repr. in 22 vols. (1908–9); 10 further suppls. (1912–96); Missing persons (1993)
DNZB	W. H. Oliver and C. Orange, eds., The dictionary of New Zealand biography, 5 vols. (1990–2000)
DSAB	W. J. de Kock and others, eds., Dictionary of South African biography, 5 vols. (1968–87)
DSB	C. C. Gillispie and F. L. Holmes, eds., Dictionary of scientific biography, 16 vols. (1970–80); repr. in 8 vols. (1981); 2 vol. suppl. (1990)
DSBB	A. Slaven and S. Checkland, eds., Dictionary of Scottish business biography, 1860–1960, 2 vols. (1986–90)
DSCHT	N. M. de S. Cameron and others, eds., Dictionary of Scottish church history and theology (1993)
Dugdale, Monasticon	W. Dugdale, Monasticon Anglicanum, 3 vols. (1655–72); 2nd edn, 3 vols. (1661–82); new edn, ed. J. Caley, J. Ellis, and B. Bandinel, 6 vols. in 8 pts (1817–30); repr. (1846) and (1970)
DWB	J. E. Lloyd and others, eds., Dictionary of Welsh biography down to 1940 (1959) [Eng. trans. of Y bywgraffiadur Cymreig hyd 1940, 2nd edn (1954)]
EdinR	Edinburgh Review, or, Critical Journal
EETS	Early English Text Society
Emden, Cam.	A. B. Emden, A biographical register of the University of Cambridge to 1500 (1963)
Emden, Oxf.	A. B. Emden, A biographical register of the University of Oxford to AD 1500, 3 vols. (1957–9); also A biographical register of the University of Oxford, AD 1501 to 1540 (1974)
EngHR	English Historical Review
Engraved Brit. ports.	F. M. O'Donoghue and H. M. Hake, Catalogue of engraved British portraits preserved in the department of prints and drawings in the British Museum, 6 vols. (1908–25)
ER	The English Reports, 178 vols. (1900–32)
ESTC	English short title catalogue, 1475–1800 [CD-ROM and online]
Evelyn, Diary	The diary of John Evelyn, ed. E. S. De Beer, 6 vols. (1955); repr. (2000)
Farington, Diary	The diary of Joseph Farington, ed. K. Garlick and others, 17 vols. (1978–98)
Fasti Angl. (Hardy)	J. Le Neve, Fasti ecclesiae Anglicanae, ed. T. D. Hardy, 3 vols. (1854)
Fasti Angl., 1066–1300	[J. Le Neve], Fasti ecclesiae Anglicanae, 1066–1300, ed. D. E. Greenway and J. S. Barrow, [8 vols.] (1968–)
Fasti Angl., 1300–1541	[J. Le Neve], Fasti ecclesiae Anglicanae, 1300–1541, 12 vols. (1962–7)
Fasti Angl., 1541–1857	[J. Le Neve], Fasti ecclesiae Anglicanae, 1541–1857, ed. J. M. Horn, D. M. Smith, and D. S. Bailey, [9 vols.] (1969–)
Fasti Scot.	H. Scott, Fasti ecclesiae Scoticanae, 3 vols. in 6 (1871); new edn, [11 vols.] (1915–)
FO List	Foreign Office List
Fortescue, Brit. army	J. W. Fortescue, A history of the British army, 13 vols. (1899–1930)
Foss, Judges	E. Foss, The judges of England, 9 vols. (1848–64); repr. (1966)
Foster, Alum. Oxon.	J. Foster, ed., Alumni Oxonienses: the members of the University of Oxford, 1715–1886, 4 vols. (1887–8); later edn (1891); also Alumni Oxonienses … 1500–1714, 4 vols. (1891–2); 8 vol. repr. (1968) and (2000)
Fuller, Worthies	T. Fuller, The history of the worthies of England, 4 pts (1662); new edn, 2 vols., ed. J. Nichols (1811); new edn, 3 vols., ed. P. A. Nuttall (1840); repr. (1965)
GEC, Baronetage	G. E. Cokayne, Complete baronetage, 6 vols. (1900–09); repr. (1983) [microprint]
GEC, Peerage	G. E. C. [G. E. Cokayne], The complete peerage of England, Scotland, Ireland, Great Britain, and the United Kingdom, 8 vols. (1887–98); new edn, ed. V. Gibbs and others, 14 vols. in 15 (1910–98); microprint repr. (1982) and (1987)
Genest, Eng. stage	J. Genest, Some account of the English stage from the Restoration in 1660 to 1830, 10 vols. (1832); repr. [New York, 1965]
Gillow, Lit. biog. hist.	J. Gillow, A literary and biographical history or bibliographical dictionary of the English Catholics, from the breach with Rome, in 1534, to the present time, 5 vols. [1885–1902]; repr. (1961); repr. with preface by C. Gillow (1999)
Gir. Camb. opera	Giraldi Cambrensis opera, ed. J. S. Brewer, J. F. Dimock, and G. F. Warner, 8 vols., Rolls Series, 21 (1861–91)
GJ	Geographical Journal

Gladstone, *Diaries* — *The Gladstone diaries: with cabinet minutes and prime-ministerial correspondence*, ed. M. R. D. Foot and H. C. G. Matthew, 14 vols. (1968–94)

GM — *Gentleman's Magazine*

Graves, *Artists* — A. Graves, ed., *A dictionary of artists who have exhibited works in the principal London exhibitions of oil paintings from 1760 to 1880* (1884); new edn (1895); 3rd edn (1901); facs. edn (1969); repr. [1970], (1973), and (1984)

Graves, *Brit. Inst.* — A. Graves, *The British Institution, 1806–1867: a complete dictionary of contributors and their work from the foundation of the institution* (1875); facs. edn (1908); repr. (1969)

Graves, *RA exhibitors* — A. Graves, *The Royal Academy of Arts: a complete dictionary of contributors and their work from its foundation in 1769 to 1904*, 8 vols. (1905–6); repr. in 4 vols. (1970) and (1972)

Graves, *Soc. Artists* — A. Graves, *The Society of Artists of Great Britain, 1760–1791, the Free Society of Artists, 1761–1783: a complete dictionary* (1907); facs. edn (1969)

Greaves & Zaller, *BDBR* — R. L. Greaves and R. Zaller, eds., *Biographical dictionary of British radicals in the seventeenth century*, 3 vols. (1982–4)

Grove, *Dict. mus.* — G. Grove, ed., *A dictionary of music and musicians*, 5 vols. (1878–90); 2nd edn, ed. J. A. Fuller Maitland (1904–10); 3rd edn, ed. H. C. Colles (1927); 4th edn with suppl. (1940); 5th edn, ed. E. Blom, 9 vols. (1954); suppl. (1961) [see also *New Grove*]

Hall, *Dramatic ports.* — L. A. Hall, *Catalogue of dramatic portraits in the theatre collection of the Harvard College library*, 4 vols. (1930–34)

Hansard — *Hansard's parliamentary debates*, ser. 1–5 (1803–)

Highfill, Burnim & Langhans, *BDA* — P. H. Highfill, K. A. Burnim, and E. A. Langhans, *A biographical dictionary of actors, actresses, musicians, dancers, managers, and other stage personnel in London, 1660–1800*, 16 vols. (1973–93)

Hist. U. Oxf. — T. H. Aston, ed., *The history of the University of Oxford*, 8 vols. (1984–2000) [1: *The early Oxford schools*, ed. J. I. Catto (1984); 2: *Late medieval Oxford*, ed. J. I. Catto and R. Evans (1992); 3: *The collegiate university*, ed. J. McConica (1986); 4: *Seventeenth-century Oxford*, ed. N. Tyacke (1997); 5: *The eighteenth century*, ed. L. S. Sutherland and L. G. Mitchell (1986); 6–7: *Nineteenth-century Oxford*, ed. M. G. Brock and M. C. Curthoys (1997–2000); 8: *The twentieth century*, ed. B. Harrison (2000)]

HJ — *Historical Journal*

HMC — Historical Manuscripts Commission

Holdsworth, *Eng. law* — W. S. Holdsworth, *A history of English law*, ed. A. L. Goodhart and H. L. Hanbury, 17 vols. (1903–72)

HoP, *Commons* — *The history of parliament: the House of Commons* [*1386–1421*, ed. J. S. Roskell, L. Clark, and C. Rawcliffe, 4 vols. (1992); *1509–1558*, ed. S. T. Bindoff, 3 vols. (1982); *1558–1603*, ed. P. W. Hasler, 3 vols. (1981); *1660–1690*, ed. B. D. Henning, 3 vols. (1983); *1690–1715*, ed. D. W. Hayton, E. Cruickshanks, and S. Handley, 5 vols. (2002); *1715–1754*, ed. R. Sedgwick, 2 vols. (1970); *1754–1790*, ed. L. Namier and J. Brooke, 3 vols. (1964), repr. (1985); *1790–1820*, ed. R. G. Thorne, 5 vols. (1986); in draft (used with permission): *1422–1504*, *1604–1629*, *1640–1660*, and *1820–1832*]

IGI — *International Genealogical Index*, Church of Jesus Christ of the Latterday Saints

ILN — *Illustrated London News*

IMC — Irish Manuscripts Commission

Irving, *Scots.* — J. Irving, ed., *The book of Scotsmen eminent for achievements in arms and arts, church and state, law, legislation and literature, commerce, science, travel and philanthropy* (1881)

JCS — *Journal of the Chemical Society*

JHC — *Journals of the House of Commons*

JHL — *Journals of the House of Lords*

John of Worcester, *Chron.* — *The chronicle of John of Worcester*, ed. R. R. Darlington and P. McGurk, trans. J. Bray and P. McGurk, 3 vols., OMT (1995–) [vol. 1 forthcoming]

Keeler, *Long Parliament* — M. F. Keeler, *The Long Parliament, 1640–1641: a biographical study of its members* (1954)

Kelly, *Handbk* — *The upper ten thousand: an alphabetical list of all members of noble families*, 3 vols. (1875–7); continued as *Kelly's handbook of the upper ten thousand for 1878* [1879], 2 vols. (1878–9); continued as *Kelly's handbook to the titled, landed and official classes*, 94 vols. (1880–1973)

LondG — *London Gazette*

LP Henry VIII — J. S. Brewer, J. Gairdner, and R. H. Brodie, eds., *Letters and papers, foreign and domestic, of the reign of Henry VIII*, 23 vols. in 38 (1862–1932); repr. (1965)

Mallalieu, *Watercolour artists* — H. L. Mallalieu, *The dictionary of British watercolour artists up to 1820*, 3 vols. (1976–90); vol. 1, 2nd edn (1986)

Memoirs FRS — *Biographical Memoirs of Fellows of the Royal Society*

MGH — Monumenta Germaniae Historica

MT — *Musical Times*

Munk, *Roll* — W. Munk, *The roll of the Royal College of Physicians of London*, 2 vols. (1861); 2nd edn, 3 vols. (1878)

N&Q — *Notes and Queries*

New Grove — S. Sadie, ed., *The new Grove dictionary of music and musicians*, 20 vols. (1980); 2nd edn, 29 vols. (2001) [also online edn; see also Grove, *Dict. mus.*]

Nichols, *Illustrations* — J. Nichols and J. B. Nichols, *Illustrations of the literary history of the eighteenth century*, 8 vols. (1817–58)

Nichols, *Lit. anecdotes* — J. Nichols, *Literary anecdotes of the eighteenth century*, 9 vols. (1812–16); facs. edn (1966)

Obits. FRS — *Obituary Notices of Fellows of the Royal Society*

O'Byrne, *Naval biog. dict.* — W. R. O'Byrne, *A naval biographical dictionary* (1849); repr. (1990); [2nd edn], 2 vols. (1861)

OHS — Oxford Historical Society

Old Westminsters — *The record of Old Westminsters*, 1–2, ed. G. F. R. Barker and A. H. Stenning (1928); suppl. 1, ed. J. B. Whitmore and G. R. Y. Radcliffe [1938]; 3, ed. J. B. Whitmore, G. R. Y. Radcliffe, and D. C. Simpson (1963); suppl. 2, ed. F. E. Pagan (1978); 4, ed. F. E. Pagan and H. E. Pagan (1992)

OMT — Oxford Medieval Texts

Ordericus Vitalis, *Eccl. hist.* — *The ecclesiastical history of Orderic Vitalis*, ed. and trans. M. Chibnall, 6 vols., OMT (1969–80); repr. (1990)

Paris, *Chron.* — *Matthaei Parisiensis, monachi sancti Albani, chronica majora*, ed. H. R. Luard, Rolls Series, 7 vols. (1872–83)

Parl. papers — *Parliamentary papers* (1801–)

PBA — *Proceedings of the British Academy*

Pepys, *Diary* — *The diary of Samuel Pepys*, ed. R. Latham and W. Matthews, 11 vols. (1970–83); repr. (1995) and (2000)

Pevsner — N. Pevsner and others, Buildings of England series

PICE — *Proceedings of the Institution of Civil Engineers*

Pipe rolls — *The great roll of the pipe for . . .*, PRSoc. (1884–)

PRO — Public Record Office

PRS — *Proceedings of the Royal Society of London*

PRSoc. — Pipe Roll Society

PTRS — *Philosophical Transactions of the Royal Society*

QR — *Quarterly Review*

RC — Record Commissions

Redgrave, *Artists* — S. Redgrave, *A dictionary of artists of the English school* (1874); rev. edn (1878); repr. (1970)

Reg. Oxf. — C. W. Boase and A. Clark, eds., *Register of the University of Oxford*, 5 vols., OHS, 1, 10–12, 14 (1885–9)

Reg. PCS — J. H. Burton and others, eds., *The register of the privy council of Scotland*, 1st ser., 14 vols. (1877–98); 2nd ser., 8 vols. (1899–1908); 3rd ser., [16 vols.] (1908–70)

Reg. RAN — H. W. C. Davis and others, eds., *Regesta regum Anglo-Normannorum, 1066–1154*, 4 vols. (1913–69)

RIBA Journal — *Journal of the Royal Institute of British Architects* [later *RIBA Journal*]

RotP — J. Strachey, ed., *Rotuli parliamentorum ut et petitiones, et placita in parliamento*, 6 vols. (1767–77)

RotS — D. Macpherson, J. Caley, and W. Illingworth, eds., *Rotuli Scotiae in Turri Londinensi et in domo capitulari Westmonasteriensi asservati*, 2 vols., RC, 14 (1814–19)

RS — Record(s) Society

Rymer, *Foedera* — T. Rymer and R. Sanderson, eds., *Foedera, conventiones, literae et cuiuscunque generis acta publica inter reges Angliae et alios quosvis imperatores, reges, pontifices, principes, vel communitates*, 20 vols. (1704–35); 2nd edn, 20 vols. (1726–35); 3rd edn, 10 vols. (1739–45), facs. edn (1967); new edn, ed. A. Clarke, J. Caley, and F. Holbrooke, 4 vols., RC, 50 (1816–30)

Sainty, *Judges* — J. Sainty, ed., *The judges of England, 1272–1990*, SeldS, suppl. ser., 10 (1993)

Sainty, *King's counsel* — J. Sainty, ed., *A list of English law officers and king's counsel*, SeldS, suppl. ser., 7 (1987)

SCH — Studies in Church History

Scots peerage — J. B. Paul, ed. *The Scots peerage, founded on Wood's edition of Sir Robert Douglas's Peerage of Scotland, containing an historical and genealogical account of the nobility of that kingdom*, 9 vols. (1904–14)

SeldS — Selden Society

SHR — *Scottish Historical Review*

State trials — T. B. Howell and T. J. Howell, eds., *Cobbett's Complete collection of state trials*, 34 vols. (1809–28)

STC, 1475–1640 — A. W. Pollard, G. R. Redgrave, and others, eds., *A short-title catalogue of . . . English books . . . 1475–1640* (1926); 2nd edn, ed. W. A. Jackson, F. S. Ferguson, and K. F. Pantzer, 3 vols. (1976–91) [see also Wing, *STC*]

STS — Scottish Text Society

SurtS — Surtees Society

Symeon of Durham, *Opera* — *Symeonis monachi opera omnia*, ed. T. Arnold, 2 vols., Rolls Series, 75 (1882–5); repr. (1965)

Tanner, *Bibl. Brit.-Hib.* — T. Tanner, *Bibliotheca Britannico-Hibernica*, ed. D. Wilkins (1748); repr. (1963)

Thieme & Becker, *Allgemeines Lexikon* — U. Thieme, F. Becker, and H. Vollmer, eds., *Allgemeines Lexikon der bildenden Künstler von der Antike bis zur Gegenwart*, 37 vols. (Leipzig, 1907–50); repr. (1961–5), (1983), and (1992)

Thurloe, *State papers* — *A collection of the state papers of John Thurloe*, ed. T. Birch, 7 vols. (1742)

TLS — *Times Literary Supplement*

Tout, *Admin. hist.* — T. F. Tout, *Chapters in the administrative history of mediaeval England: the wardrobe, the chamber, and the small seals*, 6 vols. (1920–33); repr. (1967)

TRHS — *Transactions of the Royal Historical Society*

VCH — H. A. Doubleday and others, eds., *The Victoria history of the counties of England*, [88 vols.] (1900–)

Venn, *Alum. Cant.* — J. Venn and J. A. Venn, *Alumni Cantabrigienses: a biographical list of all known students, graduates, and holders of office at the University of Cambridge, from the earliest times to 1900*, 10 vols. (1922–54); repr. in 2 vols. (1974–8)

Vertue, *Note books* — [G. Vertue], *Note books*, ed. K. Esdaile, earl of Ilchester, and H. M. Hake, 6 vols., Walpole Society, 18, 20, 22, 24, 26, 30 (1930–55)

VF — *Vanity Fair*

Walford, *County families* — E. Walford, *The county families of the United Kingdom, or, Royal manual of the titled and untitled aristocracy of Great Britain and Ireland* (1860)

Walker rev. — A. G. Matthews, *Walker revised: being a revision of John Walker's Sufferings of the clergy during the grand rebellion, 1642–60* (1948); repr. (1988)

Walpole, *Corr.* — *The Yale edition of Horace Walpole's correspondence*, ed. W. S. Lewis, 48 vols. (1937–83)

Ward, *Men of the reign* — T. H. Ward, ed., *Men of the reign: a biographical dictionary of eminent persons of British and colonial birth who have died during the reign of Queen Victoria* (1885); repr. (Graz, 1968)

Waterhouse, *18c painters* — E. Waterhouse, *The dictionary of 18th century painters in oils and crayons* (1981); repr. as *British 18th century painters in oils and crayons* (1991), vol. 2 of *Dictionary of British art*

Watt, *Bibl. Brit.* — R. Watt, *Bibliotheca Britannica, or, A general index to British and foreign literature*, 4 vols. (1824) [many reprs.]

Wellesley index — W. E. Houghton, ed., *The Wellesley index to Victorian periodicals, 1824–1900*, 5 vols. (1966–89); new edn (1999) [CD-ROM]

Wing, *STC* — D. Wing, ed., *Short-title catalogue of . . . English books . . . 1641–1700*, 3 vols. (1945–51); 2nd edn (1972–88); rev. and enl. edn, ed. J. J. Morrison, C. W. Nelson, and M. Seccombe, 4 vols. (1994–8) [see also *STC, 1475–1640*]

Wisden — *John Wisden's Cricketer's Almanack*

Wood, *Ath. Oxon.* — A. Wood, *Athenae Oxonienses . . . to which are added the Fasti*, 2 vols. (1691–2); 2nd edn (1721); new edn, 4 vols., ed. P. Bliss (1813–20); repr. (1967) and (1969)

Wood, *Vic. painters* — C. Wood, *Dictionary of Victorian painters* (1971); 2nd edn (1978); 3rd edn as *Victorian painters*, 2 vols. (1995), vol. 4 of *Dictionary of British art*

WW — *Who's who* (1849–)

WWBMP — M. Stenton and S. Lees, eds., *Who's who of British members of parliament*, 4 vols. (1976–81)

WWW — *Who was who* (1929–)

Taylour, Lord **William Desmond** (1904–1989), archaeologist, was born at Pennington House, Milford Road, Lymington, Hampshire, on 3 January 1904, the younger son of Geoffrey Thomas Taylour, fourth marquess of Headfort (1878–1943), a landowner, later senator of the Irish Free State, and fellow of the Linnean Society, and his wife, Rose (Rosie; d. 1958), an actress ('a teacher of music') at the Gaiety Theatre, London, daughter of Charles Chamberlain Boote, a comedian, of Luton, Bedfordshire, and his wife, Marie. Taylour was brought up at Headfort, co. Meath, and then followed his elder brother, Terence Geoffrey Thomas, who later succeeded as fifth marquess, to Harrow School (1917–21). However, while his brother went up to Oxford, Lord William Taylour, as he was styled, though passionate about archaeology, was encouraged to pursue a career, first in the diplomatic service (1921–2), and then in banking on Wall Street, New York. He returned to London where he was the business manager of the interior design company belonging to Maria Louisa Arnold.

During the Second World War Taylour served in the North African campaign, reaching the rank of captain in the 2nd Derbyshire yeomanry (TA). At the end of hostilities he was a member of the Allied Control Commission for Germany until 1947. Taylour then turned to archaeology; he described himself as 'a latecomer in the field' (W. D. Taylour, *The Mycenaeans*, rev. edn, 1983, 6). He was admitted to read archaeology and anthropology at Trinity College, Cambridge, in 1947; he achieved a first class in part one (1949), and an upper second in part two (1950). Among the archaeological influences on him were Grahame Clark, the then Disney professor, and Glyn Daniel, then lecturer in archaeology.

Taylour had been brought up as a Roman Catholic, like his mother. While he was at Cambridge, his sister, Lady Millicent, introduced him to Father Gilbey, the Roman Catholic chaplain in the University of Cambridge. Gilbey's talks at Fisher House were to influence Taylour's thinking. A contemporary at St Edmund House, a Roman Catholic residence, recalled Taylour as 'A very good Catholic in a balanced kind of way … he would attend Mass in the Chapel not every day, but every other day' (Stewart). Taylour served as treasurer to the Cambridge University Catholic Association, and was later made a knight commander of the order of St Gregory the Great.

Taylour's earliest archaeological work in the Mediterranean was in 1948 at Sabrathah in Tripolitania working under Kathleen Kenyon and J. B. Ward-Perkins, the director of the British School at Rome. After graduating Taylour wrote a doctoral dissertation on Mycenaean pottery in Italy (doctorate awarded 1955). He took part in the joint Ashmolean Museum and Sydney University excavation of Myrtou-Pighades on Cyprus under the direction of Joan Du Plat Taylor (1950–51); he was responsible for the publication of the Iron Age pottery.

Taylour visited Greece in 1949. After the completion of the work on Cyprus, Taylour worked on the renewed British excavations at Mycenae in 1952 and 1953 under the direction of Alan John Bayard Wace, publishing the work

in the area round the Perseia spring in the *Annual of the British School at Athens* (1955). Taylour's interest in the links between Greece and Italy during the Late Bronze Age brought an opportunity to work with Carl William Blegen (1887–1971) of the University of Cincinnati on the Bronze Age site at the 'palace of Nestor' (Ano Englianos) in western Messenia. Taylour joined the excavations for six seasons (1953–5, 1957–9), and was responsible for the excavation of some of the more significant tombs; his findings were published in *The Palace of Nestor at Pylos in Western Messenia*, volume 3 (1973).

Recognition of Taylour's contribution to Late Bronze Age Greece was confirmed by his election as a fellow of the Society of Antiquaries of London (1958). His doctoral dissertation was published as *Mycenaean Pottery in Italy, and Adjacent Areas* (1958). Taylour's archaeological career then took a dramatic turn. British involvement with the excavation of Mycenae had drawn to a close with Wace's death in 1957 as well as the uneasy political situation over Cyprus. A committee (consisting of C. Martin Robertson, the chairman of the British School at Athens, Elisabeth B. Wace, and Taylour) was established to supervise the work at Mycenae, and in 1959 Taylour resumed the excavations in conjunction with the Greek Archaeological Society, working first with John Papademetriou, and then, after his death in 1963, with George E. Mylonas (1964, 1966, 1968, 1969).

The discovery of further Linear B tablets was announced promptly in *Antiquity* (1961), and Taylour contributed to J. Chadwick, ed., *The Mycenae Tablets, III* (1963). Among the other finds was what was later recognized as a cult site within the walls of the acropolis, promptly announced in the *Illustrated London News* (1969–70) and *Antiquity* (1969–70). The clay figures from this complex were described by him as 'perfectly hideous' (*Daily Telegraph*). The complexity of the site at Mycenae, and the protracted excavations, called for a new approach to the publication of the finds, announced in the *Annual of the British School at Athens* (1969). In fact the first volume, prepared by Taylour, in the monograph series Well built Mycenae: Helleno-British Excavations within the Citadel at Mycenae, 1959–1969, did not appear until 1981. Further volumes in the series, with Taylour acknowledged as co-author, include *The South House and Annexe* (vol. 9), *The Temple* (vol. 10; 1999), and *The Room with the Fresco* (vol. 11). The research for this ongoing work is supported by the Mediterranean Archaeological Trust, established by Taylour. Taylour's research trips included driving groups of students to Greece and showing them various sites along the way.

Taylour also directed the excavation, over six seasons, of the Bronze Age site of Hagios Stephanos in southern Laconia (1959 to 1977). The preliminary results were published in the *Annual of the British School at Athens* (1972). The finds from the site demonstrated the link between Crete and the Greek mainland. Taylour's love of Late Bronze Age Greece is revealed in *The Mycenaeans* (1964), a book Glyn Daniel had to persuade him to write. A revised second edition appeared in 1983 which took account of the cult site at Mycenae. The volume was translated into Italian (1966).

In his later years Taylour continued to work on the publication of the Mycenae excavations, and his last research trip to Greece was made in 1988. The development of lung cancer took its toll, and Taylour died at his home, St Aubyns, Woodlands Road, Great Shelford, Cambridgeshire, on 2 December 1989. He never married. Ironically, Taylour's death coincided with a conference in Athens on the archaeological work of Wace and Blegen; the subsequent volume, Carol Zerner, ed., *Wace and Blegen: Pottery as Evidence for Trade in the Aegean Bronze Age, 1939–1989* (1993), was dedicated to Taylour, acknowledging his work establishing links between mainland Greece and Italy.

As a field archaeologist Taylour was 'a striking figure with his distinctive Egyptianizing headdress (to protect his bald head), shorts, and bush shirt (with the contents of the pockets carefully organized)' (*Annual Report of the British School at Athens*, 1988–9, 41). He has been described as 'an aristocratic scholar of the old school ... something of Lord Peter Wimsey in Lord William Taylour' (*Daily Telegraph*). DAVID GILL

Sources Burke, *Peerage* (1999) · *Antiquaries Journal*, 70 (1990), 526 · *Annual Report of the British School at Athens* (1988–9), 40–41 · *Daily Telegraph* (7 Dec 1989) · I. Stewart, 'Lord William Taylour, 1904–1989', address given at Trinity College chapel, Cambridge, 28 April 1990 · J. Du Plat Taylor, *Myrtou-Pighades: a late bronze age sanctuary in Cyprus* (1957) · J. M. Bulloch, 'Peers who have married players', *N&Q*, 169 (1935), 92–4 · b. cert. · d. cert.
Archives American School of Classical Studies, Athens, papers · FM Cam., antiquity · priv. coll., Mycenae archive, field notes
Likenesses photograph, repro. in Stewart, 'Lord William Taylour' · photographs, British School at Athens
Wealth at death £983,107: probate, 13 Feb 1990, *CGPLA Eng. & Wales*

Te Kooti Arikirangi Te Turuki (*c.*1832–1893), Maori fighter and religious leader, was born about 1832 at Te Pa-o-Kahu, Turanganui-a-Kiwa (Poverty Bay), New Zealand, the second of four surviving children of Hone Te Rangipatahi and Turakau (Heni), of the Rongowhakaata tribe. His line of descent was collateral to the senior Ngati Maru chiefs, a *hapu* ('subtribe') of Rongowhakaata. His birth was predicted by the seer Toiroa of Nukutaurua, who foresaw the birth of two (or three) children. If the first born, the child of Te Turuki, died, and the younger, the child of Te Rangipatahi, lived, then evil would come to the land. That child Toiroa named Arikirangi, dedicating him to the Maori god of war and humankind, Tu-matauenga.

Te Kooti was baptized (before April 1852) by the Anglican mission. This name was probably a transliteration of Coates, lay secretary of the Church Missionary Society. In 1868, after his escape from Chatham Island (Wharekauri), he adopted the ancestral name Te Turuki as a statement of spiritual rebirth.

Te Kooti had many wives. About 1857 he married Irihapeti, daughter of Te Waaka Puakanga of Te Whanau-a-Ruataupare *hapu* of Turanga. They had one son, Wetini, born *c.*1860. During his imprisonment on Wharekauri, Te Kooti legally married Maata Te Owai on 27 July 1867. He had another son, born on Wharekauri on 28 October 1866;

the child's name and mother are unknown. After his escape he took other wives: Te Mauniko Te Waru, Oriwia Nihipora Kunaiti (*d.* 1931), Huhana Tamati (*c.*1850–1898), Honia (Nia) Te Whiu, Makurata Hineore (Makurata Himiona; *d. c.*1930), Tamaku, and Heni Kumekume (*d.* 1898). Heni, his favourite wife, remained with him from 1868 until his death.

Oral narratives record that Te Kooti's father rejected him as a youth, burying him alive in a *kumara* ('sweet potato') storage pit. He was adopted by Te Turuki, his father's elder kinsman. He attended the Anglican mission at Whakato, in Turanga, where he mastered literacy from the scriptures, but failed to become a lay preacher. As supercargo on Maori-owned trading vessels, he visited Auckland where he attended the Wesleyans' Native Institution. He associated with young men at Turanga who raided settlers, seeking *utu* ('compensation') for grievances: principally illegal land purchases. In particular, he contested the sale of a Ngati Maru block, defined later as 'Matawhero 4', part of which was acquired by the trader John Harris in 1843. Te Kooti's attack on Matawhero, after his escape in 1868, created his notoriety which lingers.

In 1865 civil war came to Poverty Bay in the wake of missionaries for a new faith, Pai Marire. Te Kooti fought alongside the government's troops at the siege against the Pai Marire at Waerenga-a-Hika in November. Regardless, he was arrested 'on suspicion of being a spy' (Binney, *Redemption Songs*, 48); the charge was unproven. In March or April 1866 he was re-arrested, probably after Harris informed the agent for the general government, Donald McLean, that Te Kooti and his elder brother Komene 'ought to be got rid of' as 'known thieves'; Harris reiterated Te Kooti was 'a spy' (Binney, *Redemption Songs*, 52). He was sent without trial, despite his letter to McLean requesting one, to Wharekauri on 5 June 1866.

Te Kooti led the escape of the prisoners (163 men, 64 women, and 71 children) from Wharekauri on 4 July 1868. There, during the fever of tuberculosis, he experienced visions and heard the 'Voice of God' (Binney, *Redemption Songs*, 67). He developed a new faith, based in the scriptures, known as *Ringatu* ('Upraised Hand'): worshippers raised their right hands at the end of prayers. They identified with the children of Israel, exiled in their own land. Their escape was characterized by precision and 'moderation' (Binney, *Redemption Songs*, 82).

The prisoners landed at Whareongaonga, south of Poverty Bay, on 9 July 1868. Government messengers sent by the resident magistrate, Reginald Biggs, demanding the surrender of their arms, reached them on 12 July. As Biggs had been responsible for their extended detention on Wharekauri, while he tried to obtain land cessions at Turanga, he was not trusted. Te Kooti stated that they would not fight unless pursued on their journey through the Urewera Mountains to Tauranga on Lake Taupo.

Burdened with children and goods, their journey was slow. On 20 July Te Kooti ambushed militia troops blocking their passage at Paparatu. After two further victories Te Kooti sought the shelter of Puketapu ('holy mountain') at the edge of the Urewera. There he requested right of passage to Taupo from the Maori king, Tawhiao, but was rejected. With nowhere to go, Te Kooti turned back and struck at Matawhero on 9 November 1868.

The attack targeted those whom he blamed for his illegal exile or who had sold his tribal land during this exile. Biggs and his family were killed; they were living on the contested land at Matawhero, which the trader, George Read, had bought from Harris, and fenced in 1867, accepting the 'risk' (Binney, *Redemption Songs*, 109). Thirty Europeans (including children of mixed descent) died; the adult males had fought for the militia. Te Kooti executed about twenty-two Maori, including Paratene Pototi, who had hustled him into exile in 1866. He took about 300 Turanga Maori prisoners as he withdrew on 17 November.

Military pursuit followed, culminating in the siege of Nga Tapa (1–6 January 1869). Overwhelmed, Te Kooti and about 270 others escaped at night. About 120 males, largely 'unarmed Turanga natives' (Binney, *Redemption Songs*, 145), were captured and executed, while 80 (mostly women and children) were made prisoners.

From 1869 Te Kooti bore a price on his head: £1000, increased to £5000 in 1870. He lost two further sieges—in October 1869 and March 1870—but escaped. He failed to gain the support of the Maori king, although he was sheltered by Tuhoe in the Urewera. In May 1872 he took sanctuary with Ngati Maniapoto in the King Country, ending the New Zealand wars. There, King Tawhiao set the condition that he cease fighting. In 1873, Te Kooti accepted, and supervised the carving of the meeting-house, Tokanganui-a-Noho, built for Tawhiao at Te Kuiti: the earliest of the celebrated meeting-houses decorated by Te Kooti.

On 12 February 1883, at the insistence of the chief Rewi Maniapoto, Te Kooti was formally pardoned. He was ostensibly free, but in February 1889 was stopped as he attempted to return home to Turanga. Arrested by armed forces, he was convicted of 'unlawful assembly' (Binney, *Redemption Songs*, 410). Sent to prison, he was released on surety orders, later found illegal. The supreme court judge ruled: 'No one had a right to stop him' (Binney, *Redemption Songs*, 416). The government took the case to the Court of Appeal in 1890, where the judges' panel reinstated the original verdict. His case has become a famous study of legal rights.

Te Kooti is remembered as a skilled composer, adapter, and singer of *waiata* ('songs'). He was a prophet, and his sayings are quoted, including those which predict his successor, one greater than he. From 1873 he committed himself to peace and the pursuit of justice through law. He developed the teachings, prayer book, and sacred days of the Ringatu faith.

Some descriptions of Te Kooti exist, although he refused to be photographed. In 1892 he was described as 5 feet 8 inches tall. He had a straggling grey beard, and the first two fingers on his left hand were missing, severed at Te Porere, Taupo, in October 1869. His left ear was pierced, and he wore a *pounamu* ('greenstone') earring of indigenous origins. Other descriptions noted the name Rikirangi tattooed on his breast, with further names on his arms. He

suffered from asthma. The 1892 description noted: 'Kindly face. Very intelligent' (Binney, *Redemption Songs*, 480).

On 27 February 1893 Te Kooti left the King Country for Wainui, near Ohiwa harbour, where the government had granted 600 acres, on condition that Te Kooti never return to Turanga. He was fatally injured on 28 February, when a cart, in whose shade he was resting, upended and fell. Te Kooti died on 17 April 1893 at Te Karaka, Ohiwa. It is not known where he is buried. His body was stolen and interred at Maromahue, near Ohiwa, but was removed and hidden by his followers. In death, as in life, Te Kooti remains a contested figure.   JUDITH BINNEY

Sources J. Binney, *Redemption songs: a life of Te Kooti Arikirangi Te Turuki*, rev. 2nd edn (1997) · J. Binney, 'Te Kooti Arikirangi Te Turuki', *DNZB*, vol. 1 · J. Binney and G. Chaplin, *Ngā Mōrehu: the survivors*, rev. 3rd edn (1990)
Archives Archives New Zealand, Wellington, New Zealand Maori Affairs (MA) department, papers, MA 23/8(a–c) · Auckland Museum, letters · Hawke's Bay Museum, Napier, diary · NL NZ, Turnbull L., letters, MS-papers-390 · NL NZ, Turnbull L., notebook, MS-papers-3091 | Archives New Zealand, Wellington, New Zealand Army Defence (AD), Chatham Island prisoners, AD31/14–16 · NL NZ, Turnbull L., Donald McLean papers, MS-papers-32 | FILM New Zealand Film Archive, Wellington, 'The Te Kooti trail', R. Hayward, 1927 | SOUND Radio New Zealand Archives, 'The upraised hand', H. Williams, 1986
Likenesses T. Ryan, two pencil sketches, 1887, NL NZ, Turnbull L. · T. Ryan, oils, 1891; photograph, Hawke's Bay Museum, Napier · H. Hill, pen and ink, March 1892, NL NZ, Turnbull L.

Te Mahanga (*fl.* 1805). *See under* Exotic visitors (*act. c.*1500–*c.*1855).

Te Rauparaha (d. 1849), Maori chief and war leader, was said to have been born shortly before Captain James Cook visited New Zealand, perhaps in 1768, at Te Taharoa, south of Kawhia, on the west coast of the North Island of New Zealand. He was the fifth child of the chief, Werawera of Ngati Kimihia *hapu* ('clan, descent group') of the Ngati Toarangatira people (then a small tribe commonly known as Ngati Toa). His mother was Parekowhatu, a high-ranking woman of Ngati Huia *hapu* of the numerous and powerful Ngati Raukawa people of Maungatautari. Despite his own junior rank, Te Rauparaha early displayed leadership in the wars that had been raging from his childhood between the Waikato tribes and those of Kawhia. As a youth he took Marore as his first wife, but eventually had at least seven other wives and many children. One wife, Te Akau of Tuhourangi, was the widow of a high chief of Ngati Raukawa, Hape-ki-tuarangi; Te Rauparaha was later recognized as heir to Hape's *mana* ('authority') within Ngati Raukawa. As a youth he was plagued with disease which made him wild and restless, but by early adulthood he was showing his brilliance as a military tactician.

Although Te Rauparaha took part in many previous wars and exploits and was the most important leader of his people by 1819, the first expedition which brought his fame to the wider Maori world was the exploratory expedition he joined at Kawhia, which had set out from Hokianga that year under Nga Puhi and Te Roroa leadership. Te Rauparaha was motivated by the ongoing, bitter

Te Rauparaha (d. 1849), by John Alexander Gilfillan, c.1842

wars with Waikato, to explore for a new homeland as far south as Wellington and southern Wairarapa. At Omere overlooking Cook Strait, a European vessel was seen, and Te Rauparaha discussed with other chiefs the advantages of bringing his people south to Kapiti. There had been fighting with the local people wherever the expedition's passage was resisted, but Te Rauparaha was careful to save some of the chiefs for peacemaking and arranged a marriage alliance with Ngati Apa.

When Te Rauparaha returned home, the situation at Kawhia had worsened. He began to promote the idea of a migration to his people, and to their kin and allies: Kapiti had abundant food, Europeans to trade with, and they would be near the sources of greenstone, precious to all Maori. Te Rauparaha travelled the land, seeking, at first unsuccessfully, allies to join him. As another Tainui army approached he abandoned Kawhia. The epic journey, full of hazard since Te Rauparaha was bringing the vulnerable non-combatants with him, was broken for a year at Taranaki while food supplies were grown and a major battle was fought with pursuing Waikato forces; in the later stages of the migration there was fighting with other peoples that attempted to prevent their passage. Te Rauparaha and his allies from Kawhia, escorted by a large force of sections of Te Ati Awa, Ngati Tama, and Ngati Mutunga from northern Taranaki, arrived on the Kapiti coast about 1821.

Despite peacemaking and marriage alliances, the local people were afraid that Te Rauparaha's migration would take all their land and resources by force, and a plot was hatched to kill him. He was invited by the Muaupoko people to their settlement at Ohau, Papaitonga, to accept the gift of a canoe. Trusting in his local alliances, he went with a small party of his eldest children and stepchildren. They were attacked as they slept, and all were killed save Te Rauparaha, who escaped naked. Grieved and enraged at his loss, Te Rauparaha began a bitter battle against the local peoples, particularly Muaupoko, destroying their *pa* ('fortifications') built on platforms in the Horowhenua lake. There were many other battles. Some of his Taranaki allies returned home at this time, and for security Te Rauparaha moved his people to the island of Kapiti. All the local peoples combined to attack him on Kapiti itself but Te Rauparaha and his allies defeated them in a major battle known as Waiorua, probably about 1824. This battle established Te Rauparaha's claim in the district and his fame spread over the whole country. Groups from Taranaki and Maungatautari migrated successively to join him over the next decade, and eventually the whole district, including Wellington, was carved up and shared among his allies, while the original local people were driven inland to forest and mountain refuges, or forced to share their lands and resources. Many were killed or enslaved.

The people of the northern South Island had been among those who attacked Te Rauparaha and his allies on Kapiti, and eventually he turned his attention to them. Tribal groups in the northern South Island were defeated in a number of expeditions, and allies of Te Rauparaha settled in their territory and subjugated many of the survivors. Some Ngai Tahu were defeated in the struggle, and in retaliation their kin of Kaiapoi killed Te Pehi Kupe, the *ariki* ('person of supreme rank') of Te Rauparaha's people, Ngati Toa, and other chiefs, about 1829. In 1830 Te Rauparaha hired a European vessel, the *Elizabeth*, and used it to kidnap the Ngai Tahu paramount chief, Te Maiharanui, and carry him off to Kapiti where he was killed and eaten as *utu* ('payment') for the dead of Ngati Toa. During 1831 and 1832 Te Rauparaha carried out another major campaign against Ngai Tahu, taking their *pa* at Kaiapoi and Akaroa, both with great loss. Ngai Tahu later retaliated in a number of campaigns; in one of these Te Rauparaha barely escaped capture at Lake Grassmere.

Tensions built among the various allies of Te Rauparaha on the Kapiti coast, and about 1834 a major war erupted among them. By this time Te Rauparaha's authority over his conquest and over the lands his allies occupied had begun to erode. It had slipped further, and another battle was being fought in 1839 when the first New Zealand Company officials arrived in the *Tory*. They were in a hurry to buy land, and when Te Rauparaha claimed ownership from Rangitikei to Cloudy Bay and the South Island's west coast, they believed him, and 'purchased' vast lands from him and a few other chiefs in both main islands to which many others had rights, in deeds he signed but which were not adequately translated to him. In 1840, so sought after was he by officialdom as the greatest chief in Cook Strait that he signed the treaty of Waitangi twice.

Te Rauparaha later agreed he had sold the Nelson district, but emphatically denied the sale of the Wairau valley. Before the commission set up by the colonial government to inquire into the company's purchases could consider Wairau, in 1842 and 1843 company officials, desperate for land for their settlers, decided to force the issue. Te Rauparaha escorted their surveyors off his land and burnt their huts. The police magistrate from Nelson and company officials recruited volunteers and attempted to arrest Te Rauparaha; shooting began, and the company's troop was defeated with heavy loss. One of the Maori dead was Te Rauparaha's kinswoman, wife to his nephew, Te Rangihaeata, and Te Rauparaha could not prevent his nephew from killing the European prisoners. Company officials and European settlers demanded his trial and execution, but in his inquiry in 1844 Governor FitzRoy cleared Te Rauparaha of blame. Relations between governors, officials, and Te Rauparaha were afterwards fraught with suspicion. When war erupted in the Hutt valley in 1846, Te Rauparaha was suspected of fomenting it and Governor George Grey had him arrested and held without trial on the *Calliope* for ten months; he was then permitted to live in Auckland. He was allowed home to Otaki in January 1848, where he lived with his son, Tamihana. His last years were spent there, supporting the missionary Octavius Hadfield, in building the famous church, Rangiatea. However, he did not adopt Christianity. He died at Otaki on 27 November 1849 and was buried near Rangiatea, but afterwards his kin carried his body away secretly to Kapiti.

In the face of adversity, Te Rauparaha succeeded in establishing a new homeland for his people. In achieving this, he radically changed the tribal map of New Zealand, at a heavy cost to his opponents. In the literature he has been vilified as a model of savage treachery; such views were nourished by European ignorance of Maori cultural norms, and maintained by a need to justify inequitable dealings in land.

ANGELA BALLARA

Sources 'He pukapuka tataku tenei i Nga Mahi A Te Rau-paraha nui'; 'Na tana tamaiti tupu ake, na Tamihana te Rauparaha i tuhituhi kei wareware', MS history of his father written by Tamihana Te Rauparaha, NL NZ, Turnbull L., fMS 220 • P. Burns, *Te Rauparaha: a new perspective* (1980) • W. T. L. Travers, *The stirring times of Te Rauparaha* [n.d., c.1872] • Otaki minute books, native land court, NL NZ, Turnbull L., MSS microfilm collection 06, vols. 1–11 • Nelson minute books, native land court, NL NZ, Turnbull L., MSS microfilm collection 06, vols. 1–4 • old land claims files, National Archives of New Zealand • I. Wards, *The shadow of the land* (1968) • P. Te Hurinui Jones and B. Biggs, *Nga Iwi o Tainui* (1995) • W. Wakefield, diary, 1839–42, MS/TS ATU • E. J. Wakefield, *Adventure in New Zealand*, 2 vols. (1845) • E. Dieffenbach, *Travels in New Zealand*, 2 vols. (1843)

Likenesses J. A. Gilfillan, drawing, c.1842, NL NZ, Turnbull L. [*see illus.*] • E. I. Abbott, portrait, June 1845, Hocken Library • G. F. Angas, double portrait, oils (with son Katu), South Australian Museum, Adelaide • J. A. Gilfillan, pencil sketch, Hocken Library

Teach [Thatch], **Edward** [*known as* Blackbeard] (d. **1718**), pirate, grew up in Bristol, according to most recent assessments. If true, he would have seen the steady rise of successful privateers during the wars with France after 1689. But his initial name and place of origin remain uncertain.

One early unconfirmed source gave his family name as Drummond; another suggested that he was born in Jamaica. Whatever the reality it was from Jamaica, using the name Edward Teach or some similar variation, that he apparently sailed aboard a privateer during the War of the Spanish Succession. When that conflict ended in 1713 many sailors, including Teach, refused to give up this relatively free and profitable existence for the harsh discipline and arbitrary treatment found in the merchant marine or the Royal Navy. Instead they turned to piracy, swelling the ranks of Caribbean buccaneers to several thousand persons. Many of the pirate bands operated out of New Providence (modern Nassau) in the Bahamas, raiding shipping throughout the Atlantic and as far away as the Red Sea, then frequently selling their stolen goods in British North America, where Atlantic ports chafed under increasingly restrictive imperial trading laws. Colonial officials from New York to Charlestown, South Carolina, were often willing to tolerate, and even protect, ships carrying unauthorized goods, if crews would sell hard to obtain items at reasonable prices and then linger in town to spend their cash in local establishments.

In 1716 Teach joined the crew of Benjamin Hornigold, one of the most skilled and ruthless of the Bahama pirates, and within months he proved such an aggressive figure that Hornigold put him in charge of a captured sloop. The two men terrorized shipping in the western Atlantic together, returning occasionally to New Providence for supplies. One of their richest prizes, taken in the eastern Caribbean late in 1717, was the *Concorde*, a large French vessel under Captain d'Ocier which had entered the African trade after a wartime sojourn in Rio de Janeiro. Apparently, this 300 ton ship, measuring 104 feet and carrying twenty guns, had been built by the English in 1710 and named the *Concord*, but when the French seized it the following year they modified the hull and altered the name. When Hornigold granted Teach command of the vessel the young pirate changed the name again, calling it *Queen Anne's Revenge*, and added another twenty guns. Now in command of a heavily armed vessel Teach reputedly bested the *Scarborough*, a British man-of-war sent from Barbados to destroy him, and went on to plunder at least eighteen ships in the next six months, usually sailing in consort with several smaller boats. His reputation spread rapidly, and he cultivated his flamboyant image as a fierce fighter, impetuous leader, and constant womanizer. Though no confirmed likeness survives, contemporary accounts and popular prints portrayed him as a tall, rugged man with a massive beard, which he decorated with ribbons (and even slow-burning hemp fuses on occasion) to heighten his fearsome appearance.

Dismayed by the rise of rampant piracy in their Atlantic dominions, the British government took measures to suppress it. George I appointed Woodes Rogers, a former privateer from Bristol, to be the new governor of the Bahamas, instructing him to make war on brigands in the Caribbean and to grant pardons to any who would voluntarily surrender. Teach's wealthy former mentor, Hornigold, accepted a pardon from Rogers when he arrived at

Nassau, but Teach, now known to the public and feared as Blackbeard, followed a different course. In May 1718, in the boldest gambit of his brief career, he brazenly ordered his flotilla, including Stede Bonnet's *Revenge*, David Harriot's *Adventure*, and a captured Spanish sloop, to blockade the busy port of Charlestown. In scarcely a week the brigands seized eight or nine vessels and ransomed their prizes to local authorities for a much needed chest of medicine before escaping by sea to the protection of North Carolina's treacherous outer banks.

In early June, in the shallow waters of Topsail inlet (now Beaufort inlet), *Queen Anne's Revenge* ran aground, as did the smaller *Adventure*. The move may have been on purpose so that Blackbeard and a select crew of loyal men could transfer the accumulated booty to another vessel and abscond, leaving Bonnet and other irate pirates to fend for themselves. In September Bonnet and his crew were captured near the mouth of the Cape Fear River by a force from Charlestown, and by the end of the year Bonnet and forty-eight other pirates had been tried in that port and publicly hanged. Meanwhile Blackbeard entered Pamlico Sound and put in at North Carolina's new village of Bath Town, where he obtained a pardon from Governor Charles Eden and married the daughter of a planter. But captain and crew were not easily reconciled to land, and within months they were at sea again, laying hold of a heavily laden French ship and claiming that it had been found adrift without a soul on board.

In Virginia, Governor Alexander Spotswood was locked in controversy with his council and saw an attack on Blackbeard as a way to upstage his opposition. He suspected Governor Eden and his Bath neighbour, Tobias Knight (North Carolina's secretary, chief justice, and collector of customs), of protecting the notorious pirate and sharing in his spoils. So Spotswood put a price of £100 on Blackbeard's head and financed an expedition south by land and sea to expose the supposed corruption. On 22 November 1718 Lieutenant Robert Maynard, commanding two sloops and fifty-four well-armed men, engaged the pirate force in a bloody seaboard battle at North Carolina's Ocracoke inlet. Having pledged neither to give quarter nor to seek it Blackbeard died fighting, and Maynard suspended his severed head from the bowsprit. The victors carried more than a dozen captured pirates back to Virginia, where they were hanged on gibbets along the path from James River to Williamsburg, later known as Gallows Road. If they left behind any treasure, its whereabouts remains a mystery, but in November 1996 divers at Beaufort inlet located the possible remains of *Queen Anne's Revenge* in 20 feet of water, prompting a flurry of fresh interest in Blackbeard and the brief heyday of Atlantic piracy.   PETER H. WOOD

Sources D. Botting, *The pirates* (1978) · S. C. Hughson, *The Carolina pirates and colonial commerce, 1670–1740* (1894) · D. Defoe, *A general history of the pyrates*, ed. M. Schonhorn (1972) · R. E. Lee, *Blackbeard the pirate: a reappraisal of his life and times* (1974) · H. L. Osgood, *The American colonies in the eighteenth century*, 4 vols. (1924), 1.525–52 · H. F. Rankin, *The pirates of colonial North Carolina* (1960) · M. Rediker, *Between the devil and the deep blue sea: merchant seamen, pirates, and the Anglo-American maritime world* (1987) · North Carolina Maritime Museum website

Teacher, William (1810/11–1876), wine and spirit merchant, was probably born in Paisley, the son of a sailor called Teacher and his wife, Margaret Frame. William's father was lost at sea before his first birthday, and his mother worked in a cotton mill at Bridge of Weir, near Paisley. After a cursory education of probably no more than six months in the parish school, Teacher started work in the mill at the age of seven as a 'piecer'. At eleven, he was apprenticed to a tailor, Robert Barr, who inculcated a spirit of self-improvement in his pupil. After his apprenticeship he returned to mill work but got into trouble because of involvement with the radical reform movement, and he subsequently went to work for a Mrs MacDonald, who ran a grocer's shop in Anderston, a fast developing industrial district of Glasgow. Teacher suggested Mrs MacDonald take out a licence for the sale of spirits. The reform of the Scottish excise in 1823 had reduced spirit duty and this, together with the growing industrial population, offered a buoyant market for whisky retailers. Teacher's former trade was renowned for its 'drinking usages' and heavy whisky consumption; this may also have influenced his choice of business.

Teacher married his employer's daughter, Agnes MacDonald, on 2 June 1834 and ultimately took over the running of the business. In 1836 he opened a second 'dram' shop at 50 Cheapside, Glasgow, and over the next twenty-five years increased his licensed premises to eighteen. Multiple retailing was a new development in the whisky trade and at the time of his death Teacher was probably its largest multiple retailer. Nicknamed 'Old Thorough', he managed the shops in a unique style: excessive drinking was discouraged, 'treating' (the purchase of drinks for friends) was prohibited, and smoking was banned (a ban not lifted by his descendants until 1926). This style has been attributed to his strict Victorian principles but it may also have been a reaction to the temperance movement and to the fact that the town council acquired, and utilized, local police powers to curb an excess of licensed premises well before other Scottish cities. Keeping respectable premises reduced the likelihood of losing one's licence.

The shops, which were 'the apple of his eye' (Bergius, 14), required a varied stock and this prompted Teacher's move into wholesaling in 1851 at 347 Argyle Street, Glasgow. Expansion required new headquarters in 1864 and the firm moved to 17 St Enoch Square where it remained until 1873 when the site was taken over for the building of St Enoch Station. A new building covering 14, 16, and 18 St Enoch Square was commissioned at a cost of £8000 and remained the headquarters until 1991.

Teacher and his wife had eleven children. The eldest, a son, died of scarlet fever at seventeen. Two other sons died in infancy. This left William junior (1836–1880) and Adam (1839–1898) as the first and second in seniority. They developed the business on the foundations laid by the 'dram' shops, opening branches in Manchester (1866) and London (1876), registering the blend Highland Cream (1884), and building a malt distillery, Ardmore (1898).

Teacher was a member and treasurer of the Unitarian church, a minority religion in presbyterian Scotland. Members tended to be freethinkers who stood out against the mainstream. He supported Chartism and later movements for toleration and freedom. He entertained people of note in the world of letters, including Harriet Martineau, Henry and Millicent Fawcett, and Ralph Waldo Emerson. Teacher was a director of the Glasgow Trade Society and a commissioner for income tax. He died from haematemesis on 27 December 1876 at the family home, Rowmore, Row, Gareloch, Dunbartonshire.

RONALD B. WEIR

Sources G. E. Cousins, *A family of spirit: William Teacher and his descendants, 1830–1875* (1975) · W. M. Bergius, *Reminiscences, 1893–1938* [n.d., 1939?] · E. Chisnall, *The spirit of Glasgow: the story of Teacher's whisky* (1995) · H. C. Craig, *The Scotch whisky industry trade record* (1994) · d. cert.
Archives William Teacher & Sons, 2 Glasgow Road, Dumbarton
Likenesses photographs, William Teacher & Sons, Dumbarton
Wealth at death £98,343 14s. 4d.: confirmation, 28 Feb 1877, CCI

Tealby [née Bates], **Mary** (1801/2–1865), animal welfare organizer, is a figure about whose early life nothing is known, except that she had a brother, the Revd Edward Bates. In the autumn of 1860 she established what later became known as the Battersea Dogs' Home.

She was the widow of Robert Chapman Tealby, a timber merchant. In 1860, already an active supporter of the Royal Society for the Prevention of Cruelty to Animals (RSPCA), she was living in Victoria Road, Holloway, London. The *Islington Gazette* reported on 6 October 1860 her view, having found so many starving dogs in that district alone, that 'the aggregate amount of suffering amongst those faithful creatures throughout London must be very dreadful indeed'. Concerned with the fate of dogs dying 'of lingering starvation' in the streets (*An Appeal*, 6) she established secure premises in St James's Road, Holloway, where dogs could be exercised and lost dogs retrieved by their owners. As the rules made clear the home was to be neither a permanent home for 'old, worn out favourites' nor a hospital, but a 'temporary refuge to which humane persons may send *only* those lost dogs so constantly seen *in the streets*' (*Annual Report*, 1865, 7).

The first meeting of the committee running the home was held on 27 November 1860 at the premises of the RSPCA in Pall Mall, with the Revd Edward Bates as honorary secretary and Mary Tealby in the chair. Tealby was not a wealthy woman and much of the committee's early work focused on essential fund-raising. She was also active in visiting the premises regularly, and by 1861 had become a life governor of the home. The last meeting she attended was in December 1864.

Mary Tealby died on 3 October 1865 in Biggleswade, Bedfordshire, from cancer and exhaustion, aged sixty-three. She and her brother were buried in the same grave in the churchyard of St Andrew's, Biggleswade. The dogs' home committee recorded their loss, declaring Mary Tealby to be a 'kind-hearted and generous lady' (*Annual Report*, 1865, 4). For many years to come the reports of the dogs' home—subsequently moved to Battersea—were dedicated to her as 'the foundress and unwearied benefactress' (ibid., 1893).

HILDA KEAN

Sources G. Costelloe, *The story of the Battersea Dogs' Home* (1979) · *An appeal for the home for lost and starving dogs by a member of the society* (1861) · *Annual report of the Temporary Home for Lost, Starving Dogs at Hollingsworth St, St James' Road, Holloway* (1865) · minutes of the Home for Lost and Starving Dogs, 1860–67, Battersea Dogs' Home archive, London · *The Dogs' Home Battersea, 1860–1960*, Battersea Dogs' Home (1960) · *Islington Gazette* (6 Oct 1860), 3 · *The Queen* (28 Sept 1861), 49–50 · earl of Harrowby, *Our moral relation to the animal kingdom* (1862) · gravestone, St Andrew's churchyard, Biggleswade, Bedfordshire · d. cert. · *Annual report of the Battersea Dogs' Home* (1893) [archive of Battersea Dogs' Home] · private information (2004)
Wealth at death under £100: probate, 10 Feb 1866, CGPLA Eng. & Wales

Teale, Thomas Pridgin (1831–1923), surgeon, the eldest son of Thomas Pridgin Teale, surgeon, and his wife, Frances Ann, daughter of the Revd Charles Isherwood, curate-in-charge of Brotherton, Yorkshire, was born in Leeds on 28 June 1831. He was the son, grandson, and nephew of Leeds surgeons. His father was a distinguished FRS, the inventor of the 'long anterior flap' method of amputation of the leg, and the author of what was a standard work on hernia. The name Pridgin, a corruption of Prujean, is an indication of Teale's Huguenot descent through his paternal grandmother.

Teale was educated first at Leeds grammar school, and from the age of thirteen to eighteen at Winchester College. He matriculated at Brasenose College, Oxford, in 1849, and became BA (1852), MA (1855), and BM (1856). He received his medical training at King's College, London, of which he was later elected an honorary fellow. After a short period of continental travel and study, he began to practise in Leeds in 1856. In 1862 he married his cousin Alice (d. 1891), daughter of the Revd William Henry Teale, rector of Devizes; they had four sons and four daughters. Second, in 1899, he married Mary Jane Elizabeth, second daughter of Daniel Charles Jones, of Tamworth; they had no children.

Teale was elected surgeon to the Leeds General Infirmary in 1864 and practised there for twenty years before being appointed to the consulting staff. In collaboration with his colleague Thomas Clifford Allbutt, Teale was a pioneer in 'team work' in medicine, and in the surgical treatment of scrofulous neck. At the instigation of Allbutt, Teale undertook the experiment of removing enlarged tuberculous glands before suppuration had occurred; his example was soon generally followed. Teale, like his father, was expert in the treatment of vesical calculus, and their joint experiences at the Leeds General Infirmary in this branch of surgery covered a period of almost eighty years. He also performed lithotrities and ovariotomies, carrying out the latter operation at a time when it was unpopular with many in the medical profession. At the Leeds Infirmary, despite the doubts of some senior colleagues, he also practised antiseptic surgery, and was one of the most successful champions of the new technique. He was an advocate of ether anaesthesia, as opposed to all other methods, and chloroform was vigorously excluded from his practice. As lecturer and teacher by the bedside, Teale, though no orator, made a strong impression by his earnestness, directness, simplicity, enthusiasm, and reliance upon personal experience.

Teale's interests extended to sanitation. He invented new fireplaces and new pokers and taught the virtues of ventilation. He lectured to the Royal Institution on domestic hygiene, and wrote *Dangers to Health: a Pictorial Guide to Domestic Sanitary Defects*, which passed through four editions (two in 1879, and one in both 1881 and 1883) and was translated into French, Spanish, and Italian, and into German by Princess Helena (Princess Christian of Schleswig-Holstein). In 1888 Teale was elected FRS. He was for many years examiner in surgery at the University of Oxford, and from 1876 to 1901 he was a member of the General Medical Council.

Teale published papers on general surgical subjects and ophthalmology. He designed a suction curette for the extraction of soft cataract and demonstrated the value of atropine in the treatment of iritis. He also added much to the science of surgery, and practised the craft with hands which, for deftness, gentleness, exquisite delicacy of touch, and effective movement, were unsurpassed in his day. Teale died at his home, North Grange, Headingley, Leeds, on 13 November 1923, and was survived by his wife.   B. A. BRYAN

Sources C. A., *PRS*, 96B (1924), xxi–xxv · J. R. Kaye, 'J. Pridgin Teale', *Journal of the Royal Sanitary Institute*, 44 (1923–4), 332–3 · Foster, *Alum. Oxon.* · CGPLA Eng. & Wales (1924) · DNB
Archives U. Leeds, Brotherton L., notebook on Parisian hospitals
Likenesses T. Earle, bust, 1867, Leeds General Infirmary · E. Edwards, photograph, 1867, Wellcome L. · W. Hanson, photograph, Wellcome L. · photograph, repro. in C. A., *PRS* · photograph, RS
Wealth at death £61,364 13s. 3d.: probate, 8 Feb 1924, CGPLA Eng. & Wales

Teall, Sir Jethro Justinian Harris (1849–1924), geologist, was born at Northleach, Gloucestershire, on 5 January 1849, the only (and posthumous) son of Jethro Teall, a landowner of Sandwich, Kent, and his wife, Mary, daughter of Justinian Hathaway of Northleach. He was educated at Northleach grammar school and later at Berkeley Villa School, Cheltenham, where he developed a fondness for science. He entered St John's College, Cambridge, in 1869, intending to read mathematics. But with his interest in geology further stimulated by his tutor, Thomas Bonney, Teall turned from mathematics to science, attending Adam Sedgwick's last course of lectures. Teall obtained a first in the natural sciences tripos of 1872, and graduated BA in 1873 and MA in 1876.

In 1874 Teall was the first recipient of the Sedgwick prize for geology, endowed in memory of the late professor. The following year (1875) he was elected to a fellowship at his college, which he held until his marriage in 1879 to Harriet Cowen, daughter of George Roberts Cowen of Nottingham. After graduating, Teall lectured

under the university extension scheme and also undertook private petrographic research. His earlier petrological papers included 'Notes on the Cheviot andesites and porphyrites' (1883), 'The metamorphosis of dolerite into hornblende-schist' (1885), 'On the origin of banded gneisses' (1887), 'The sequence of plutonic rocks' (1892), and 'On the plutonic rocks of Garabal Hill and Meall Breac' (1892, with John Dakyns). Teall also published mineralogical papers such as 'On granite containing andalusite from the Cheesewring, Cornwall' (1887), 'On the occurrence of rutile-needles in clays' (1887), and 'Notes on some minerals from the Lizard' (1888).

Developing contemporary German lines of enquiry, Teall was one of the first British geologists to study the mineralogical changes induced by stresses within the earth's crust, and to deal with the natural history and genesis of many important metamorphic minerals. His study of the conversion of dolerite into hornblende schist initiated a celebrated long-running debate about the 'Scourie Dykes' of the north-west highlands.

Teall was particularly interested in the crystallization of magmas. His study of Garabal Hill near Loch Lomond, for example, based on mapping of an igneous complex and the microscopic and chemical study of rocks from different parts of the rock mass, enabled him to deduce the order of crystallization of different minerals as the magma cooled. He concluded that the basic minerals preceded the acidic in crystallization. Teall's extensive study of British igneous rocks led him to publish his greatly admired *British Petrography* (1888), a beautifully illustrated work that remains a monument to his scientific ability, his broad outlook, and his clear interpretation of geological phenomena. His wife was responsible for some of the fine illustrations.

In 1888, by then regarded by many as Britain's leading petrographer, Teall accepted Archibald Geikie's invitation to join the Geological Survey of Great Britain, and at once undertook work connected with the detailed investigations then being undertaken in Scotland. This led to the publication in official memoirs of important petrographic investigations connected with the Lewisian Gneisses, the Torridon Sandstone, and the post-Cambrian igneous rocks. In 1901 Teall succeeded Geikie as director of the survey, a position he held until his retirement in 1914. He had the task of revitalizing and reorganizing the institution in the light of the recommendations of a government committee of inquiry into the survey's activities, held in 1900. Given that he had had no previous senior administrative experience, Teall was remarkably successful in his new role. Indeed, his administration left a lasting impression on the survey. The scope of its activities was enlarged, its scientific status upheld, and its utility and educational value enhanced.

Teall was elected fellow of the Geological Society in 1873, and served as secretary (1893–7) and president (1900–02). For his presidential addresses he chose to speak on the history of petrology, yielding an important early study of the history of the discipline. He was elected a fellow of the Royal Society in 1890 and was president of the Geologists'

Association (1898–1900). The Geological Society awarded him the Bigsby medal (1889) and subsequently its highest award, the Wollaston medal (1905); the Académie des Sciences of Paris awarded him the Delesse prize (1907). Teall received doctorates from Oxford, Cambridge, Dublin, and St Andrews, and he was knighted in 1916. He died at his home, 174 Rosendale Road, Dulwich, London, on 2 July 1924, being survived by his wife and two sons.

Teall was a scrupulous scientist with wide scientific sympathies. He was judicious in his conclusions, not bound by theories, and paid careful regard to any piece of evidence, however small. Thus his published works hold an important and honoured place in the geological literature, and many of them, such as his presidential addresses to the Geological Society and the Geologists' Association, significantly influenced the development of British petrography and petrology.   DAVID OLDROYD

Sources 'Eminent living geologists: Jethro Justinian Harris Teall', *Geological Magazine*, new ser., 5th decade, 6 (1909), 1–8 · J. S. F. [J. S. Flett], *PRS*, 97B (1924–5), xv–xvii · J. E. Marr, 'Sir Jethro Justinian Harris Teall: born 5th January, 1849. Died 2nd July 1924', *Geological Magazine*, 61 (1924), 382–4 · J. S. F. [J. S. Flett], *Quarterly Journal of the Geological Society*, 81 (1925), lxiii–lxv · E. B. Bailey, *Geological survey of Great Britain* (1952) · J. S. Flett, *The first hundred years of the geological survey of Great Britain* (1937) · D. R. Oldroyd, *The highlands controversy: constructing geological knowledge through fieldwork in nineteenth-century Britain* (1990) · CGPLA Eng. & Wales (1924) · DNB
Archives BGS, geological survey corresp. | U. Birm., Lapworth MSS
Likenesses W. Stoneman, photograph, 1918, NPG · photograph, repro. in Flett, ed., *First hundred years*, plate VI · photograph, repro. in 'Eminent living geologists', *Geological Magazine*, facing p. 1 · photograph, BGS
Wealth at death £11,038 13s.: resworn probate, 14 Aug 1924, CGPLA Eng. & Wales

Teare, Alfred James (1879–1969), trade unionist and politician, was born on 31 October 1879 at 122 Buccleuch Street, Barrow in Furness, Lancashire, the third of the four children of Manx parents, Robert Teare, a house painter then working in the shipyards, and his wife, Mary Ann Callow. Little is known about his early life, though in old age he remarked that when left an orphan he suffered hardships. When still a child he returned to live in Douglas, and was educated at the Tynwald Street elementary school. He left school in 1892 and served his apprenticeship as a printer in the offices of the *Mona's Herald* and *Manx Sun*. Completing his apprenticeship in 1897, he joined the Typographical Association and became a member of the Manx Socialist Society, founded in 1895 as a discussion and propaganda group. What he remembered best about his early political life was his activity for the society's food and clothing fund, which provided free dinners, boots, and clothes for impoverished children in the early 1900s.

From 1899 to 1902, during the Second South African War, Teare was a member of the Isle of Man Volunteers. On 19 November 1902 he married Annie Blackburn (1880–1954), daughter of a Douglas herbalist, with whom he had two daughters. His interests included various sporting and musical activities, and membership of the Isle of Man Choir. He was also a lifelong member of the Baptist church. In 1908 he became secretary of the new Manx

branch of the Independent Labour Party, which was not a great success, perhaps partly because he left the island to work in Bradford. He returned in 1911 to work as a linotype operator for the *Isle of Man Times*.

The Manx suffered great hardship during the First World War: the cost of living early in 1917 was nearly 80 per cent above the 1914 level, while wages had risen scarcely at all. In March Teare chaired a meeting of seventy unskilled workers in Douglas, and on his advice a second meeting agreed to join the Workers' Union, an organization not confined to any particular industry and including all grades of workers. Though himself a skilled craftsman, Teare became the key figure in the rapid expansion of unskilled unionism, first as Douglas branch secretary and then as island union secretary. By 1918 the Workers' Union branch had over 1000 members, of which 500 were in Douglas, and had established a 56-hour maximum working week and a wage of 28s. as the norm for general workers.

Food prices were a major concern. In June 1918 Lord Raglan, the island's governor, announced that the subsidy which cut the cost of a 4 lb loaf from 1s. to 9d. would be discontinued. Protest meetings and calls for a general strike resulted. Teare chaired a strike committee including, besides the Workers' Union, representatives of the seamen, shop assistants, tailors, and the Douglas Trades Council. On July 4–5 the island was brought to a standstill, and Raglan reinstated the subsidy. Following this mobilization of organized labour, Raglan resigned, income tax was introduced, and under a new governor the island was able to embark on an era of social reform.

The Manx Labour Party, founded early in 1918 with a constitution modelled closely on that of the British Labour Party, also owed a great deal to Teare's initiative and judgement. In 1919 he was appointed as the first working-class JP in the island, a month before he was elected in South Douglas as one of the first four Labour members of the House of Keys.

Teare's achievements in 1917–19 were the basis for a long life as a leading labour activist. In 1921 he became full-time organizer for the Workers' Union in the Isle of Man; in the opinion of Richard Hyman, the union's historian, the island was one of its most successful districts. In 1929 the Workers' Union was absorbed into the larger, more centralized Transport and General Workers' Union (TGWU). Teare retained his position as union organizer until a second strike in 1935 highlighted differences with Harry Pugh, the Liverpool district organizer, and led to Teare's resignation. He later claimed that the strike had been unnecessary.

Teare was a member of the Manx legislature for forty-three years, in the Keys until 1951 and in the legislative council until 1963. There was no such position as official leader of the Manx Labour Party, but he was widely regarded as the island's outstanding Labour leader. He held many important positions, was a member of the governor's war cabinet in 1939–45, and took an especial interest in unemployment, housing, and issues of social welfare. In 1946 he was awarded the MBE. He was also, from

1933 to 1965, a member of Douglas town council, latterly as an alderman and freeman of the borough. In 1963 he published *Reminiscences of the Manx Labour Party*, a booklet characterized, unlike many politicians' memoirs, by a modest, unassuming tone and enthusiasm for the efforts of others. He suffered considerable ill health throughout his life, but survived until the age of ninety. He died at White Hoe Hospital, near Douglas, on 17 December 1969, and was buried in Douglas borough cemetery on 20 December.

Alfred Teare led the foundation of the two major labour organizations in the Isle of Man, the Workers' Union branch (later the TGWU) and the Manx Labour Party, and did sterling work for both as well as for the wider community. A moderate and practical socialist, he was described in 1951 as 'the Manx Ernest Bevin' (Teare papers, Manx National Heritage Library). As he said in 1935, his whole object in life was to give a helping hand to those less fortunate than himself.   ROBERT FYSON

Sources A. J. Teare, *Reminiscences of the Manx Labour Party* (Douglas, 1962) · R. Fyson, 'Labour history', *New history of the Isle of Man*, 5: *The modern period, 1830–1999*, ed. J. Belchem (2000), 279–310 · R. Hyman, *The workers' union* (1971) · A. Fletcher, biographical sketch, *Manx worthies*, ed. D. Kelly (2003) · A. Teare, letter to Richard Hyman, 21 June 1965, U. Warwick Mod. RC, MSS 51/3/1/50 · 'The great strike', *Manx Quarterly*, 20 (April 1919), 237–57 · Teare papers, Manx National Heritage Library, Douglas [incl. Douglas Workers' Union minute bk, 1917–1921] · private information (2004) [Anne Fletcher, granddaughter] · b. cert. · D. Kermode, *Offshore island politics: the constitutional and political development of the Isle of Man in the twentieth century* (2001) · U. Warwick Mod. RC, TGWU papers [incl. Workers' Union] · *Mona's Herald* (23 Dec 1969) · *Isle of Man Examiner* (18 Dec 1969)

Archives Manx National Heritage Library, Douglas, family papers

Likenesses photograph, *c*.1959, repro. in Teare, *Reminiscences of the Manx Labour Party*, 1 · group portrait, photograph (Douglas Branch Workers' Union Committee), U. Warwick Mod. RC, TGWU papers; repro. in *Annual Report* [Workers' Union] (1919), 28 · photograph, Manx Museum, Douglas; repro. in Fyson, 'Labour history', 293

Wealth at death under £2000: will, 1969/630, Isle of Man general registry, Douglas

Tearle, Sir **Godfrey Seymour** (1884–1953), actor, was born in New York on 12 October 1884, of theatrical stock on both sides. He was the elder son of (George) Osmond *Tearle (1852–1901), actor, and his second wife, Marianne Levy (*d.* 1896), actress, daughter of F. B. Conway, American actor and manager. Godfrey Tearle and his younger brother Malcolm, who also became an actor, were therefore familiar with the atmosphere of the playhouse from babyhood. Tearle had his first speaking part when he was nine, in his father's touring Shakespearian company, which was well known in the English provinces and a famous training ground for young actors; after 1899 he remained with the company until his father's death in 1901, when he was nearly seventeen. He was educated privately and at Carlisle grammar school in Cumberland. With such antecedents and training and great natural gifts Godfrey Tearle might well have been expected to make an early leap to the head of his profession. He had inherited from his father a notably fine voice and he had

learned from him how to use it to the best advantage; he trod the stage with a natural authority. Yet it seemed that in his early manhood he failed to make the impression that might have been expected either upon the public or upon the theatre managers, for he was kept year after year playing important but never quite leading parts.

The First World War helped to retard Tearle's career, and it was not until J. B. Fagan invited him to appear as Othello at the Royal Court Theatre in 1921 that London playgoers were given their first chance to see what he could do in one of the great classical parts. It was a performance of beauty and emotional power that fell only just short of greatness. But here, too, he was unlucky: in that post-war decade the classics were out of fashion. Although he now took rank as a leading London actor his talents were wasted on run-of-the-mill comedies and he was not given another chance to appear in Shakespeare until 1930, when he was cast as Horatio in an all-star special performance of *Hamlet* at the Haymarket. To many in the audience it seemed that here was an actor whose full quality had not been recognized. As a result he was invited to play Hamlet at the same theatre, which he did in 1931, but without notable success. He had to wait until 1946, when he acted Antony opposite Dame Edith Evans's Cleopatra at the Piccadilly, and until 1948 when he repeated his Othello at Stratford upon Avon with the added authority of twenty-five years, before he could bring it truly home to critics and playgoers that he had the stuff of greatness in him.

It was said of Tearle by some among his multitude of friends that the only reason why he was not a great actor was that he was too nice a man, and although this was intended as a witticism it may well have been the truth. He lacked the core of hardness, the dedicated purpose, the ruthless ambition, that carries men to the top of the tree and this streak of softness showed sometimes in the characters he played. It was impossible for Tearle to be convincingly cruel, as was seen when in 1950 he took over the part of the father in *The Heiress*. He went through all the motions of cruelty, but the character remained almost benign. Nevertheless Tearle was a superbly well-endowed actor. It was remarked that he had an ability to suggest, as some actors of an older day had learned to suggest, magnificence borne in on the senses of an audience by his mere presence and sheer authority, so that he seemed a little larger than life. This made him an ideal hero of romance and he was much in request for such parts when he returned to the stage after his three years in the army in the First World War. Perhaps the most striking of these roles was Boris Androvsky in the spectacular and very popular stage version at Drury Lane in 1920 of the novel *The Garden of Allah* by Robert Hichens.

Tearle won a prize in a sweepstake that amounted to several thousand pounds and he used the money to go into management at the Apollo; everybody wished him well for he was very popular, but his first production failed outright and his second, *The Fake* (1924) by Frederick Lonsdale, did only moderately, and the money was lost. It was not in his nature to repine. A chance to become a prosperous actor–manager had been missed, but engagements continued to flow in. He appeared in films from 1906, when he was Romeo in a one-reel film; other credits included *The Thirty-Nine Steps* (1935), *One of our Aircraft is Missing* (1942), and *The Titfield Thunderbolt* (1953). On stage or film, in England or America, at headquarters or on tour, he pursued his career, rising to opportunities for distinction when they came his way, yet never going out of his way to seek for them, except perhaps in 1938 when he made his second and more successful appearance as actor–manager, presenting at the Lyric *The Flashing Stream*, the first play by Charles Morgan. Though Tearle's career was not that of an ambitious man, it was that of a man of excellent gifts and a high sense of professional integrity, and when it was rewarded in 1951 with a knighthood there was a general sense of satisfaction. He had been the first president of Equity in 1932. Tearle's first marriage, to Mary Malone, actress, was dissolved. He married second, in 1932, Stella Freeman (*b.* 1910), actress, who died in 1936; his third marriage in 1937 to Barbara Mary Palmer, actress, was also dissolved. During the last years of his life, Searle was a close friend of the actress Jill *Bennett (1929?–1990). He died at 18 Bentinck Street, London, on 8 June 1953. He had no children.   W. A. DARLINGTON, *rev.* K. D. REYNOLDS

Sources J. Parker, ed., *Who's who in the theatre*, 6th edn (1930) · *The Times* (10 June 1953) · L. Halliwell, *The filmgoer's companion*, 5th edn (1976) · private information (1971) · personal knowledge (1971) · *CGPLA Eng. & Wales* (1953)
Likenesses photograph, 1914, Hult. Arch. · D. Farson, photographs, Hult. Arch. · Sasha, photographs, Hult. Arch.
Wealth at death £13,641 15s. 10d.: probate, 1 Aug 1953, *CGPLA Eng. & Wales*

Tearle, (George) Osmond (1852–1901), actor, was born at Adelaide Street, East Stonehouse, Plymouth, on 8 March 1852, the son of George Tearle, a colour sergeant in the Royal Marines, and his wife, Susan Lavers Treneman. After serving in the Crimean War and the Second Opium War his father retired on pension to Liverpool. Educated there at St Francis Xavier's College, Tearle took part in amateur theatricals, and in 1868 in 'penny readings' with T. H. Hall Caine. Inspired by Barry Sullivan's acting he took to the stage, and made his début at the Adelphi Theatre, Liverpool, on 26 March 1869, as Guildenstern in *Hamlet*. In 1870, on Sullivan's recommendation, he became leading man at the Theatre Royal, Aberdeen. At Warrington in 1871 he appeared for the first time as Hamlet, a character which he played in all some 800 times. Early in 1874 he was a prominent and popular member of the Belfast stock company. After six years' provincial probation he made his first appearance in London at the Gaiety on 26 March 1875, as George de Buissy in Campbell Clarke's unsuccessful adaptation of *Rose Michel*, and later played at the same house Charles Courtly in Boucicault's *London Assurance*. Afterwards he toured with Mrs John Wood's old comedy company as Charles Surface and Young Marlow.

At Darlington in 1877 Tearle set up his own travelling company. On 30 September 1880 he made his American début at Wallack's Theatre, New York, as Jaques in *As You Like It*, and he remained there for two years as the leading actor of the stock company. After spending the summer of 1882 in England, he reappeared at the Star Theatre, New York, in April 1883 as Hamlet, and subsequently toured in the United States as Wilfred Denver in *The Silver King*. In 1883 Tearle married an actress, Marianne Levy (*d.* 1896), the widowed daughter of the New York theatrical manager F. B. Conway. Tearle had previously been divorced by his first wife, Mary Alice Rowe, who was also an actress. He had a son and a daughter from his first marriage and two sons from his second; all three sons, most notably Godfrey *Tearle, had theatrical careers.

In 1888 Tearle returned to England and organized his Shakespearian touring company. In 1889, and again in 1890, he conducted the festival performances at Stratford upon Avon, producing in the first year *Julius Caesar* and *1 Henry VI* and in the second *King John* and *The Two Gentlemen of Verona*. His travelling company changed its bill nightly, and had a repertory of thirteen plays. It was deemed an excellent training ground for the stage novice. Tearle last appeared in London at Terry's Theatre on 4 July 1898, as Charles Surface to Kate Vaughan's Lady Teazle. His last appearance on the stage was at Her Majesty's Theatre, Carlisle, on 30 August 1901, as Richelieu. He died the following week, on 7 September, at Byker, Newcastle upon Tyne, and was buried on the 11th at Whitley Bay, Northumberland, beside his second wife.

As a Shakespearian actor Tearle combined the incisive elocution of the old school and the naturalness of the new. A man of commanding physique and dignified presence, he was well equipped for heroic parts. In later life he subdued his declamatory vigour, and played Othello and King Lear with power and restraint. He gained no foothold in London, but in America and the English provinces he won a high reputation.

W. J. LAWRENCE, *rev.* NILANJANA BANERJI

Sources *The Era* (14 Sept 1901) · C. E. Pascoe, ed., *The dramatic list*, 2nd edn (1880) · P. Hartnoll, ed., *The concise Oxford companion to the theatre* (1972) · P. Hartnoll, ed., *The Oxford companion to the theatre*, 3rd edn (1967) · *Era Almanack and Annual* (1893–6) · R. J. Broadbent, *Annals of the Liverpool stage* (1908) · T. A. Brown, *History of the New York stage from the first performance in 1732 to 1901*, 3 vols. (1903) · J. A. Hammerton, *The actor's art* (1897) · R. M. Sillard, *Barry Sullivan and his contemporaries: a histrionic record*, 2 vols. (1901) · *The Stage* (12 Sept 1901) · Hall, *Dramatic ports.* · b. cert.
Likenesses Chancellor & Son, photograph (as Coriolanus) · Forbes & Co, lithograph · J. S. Virtue & Co., photograph (as King John) · print, Harvard TC
Wealth at death £233: probate, 13 June 1902, *CGPLA Eng. & Wales*

Teck. For this title name *see* Mary Adelaide, Princess, duchess of Teck (1833–1897).

Tecumseh (*c.*1768–1813), leader of the Shawnee Indians, was probably the son of Puckeshinwa, a Shawnee, and Methoatske, a Creek (or part Creek) woman. He fought with the British-supported native alliance led by Little Turtle, which defended the Old North-West against three successive American armies between 1790 and 1794. Tecumseh's own confederacy may have been inspired by Little Turtle's early successes.

Defeat in 1794, subsequent land treaties, shortage of game for food, and addiction to white manufactures left

Native American society split. Older chiefs counselled accommodation while younger warriors favoured resistance, and many were receptive to the revival religion initiated in 1805 by Tecumseh's brother Tenskwatawa (also Elskwatawa, Laubewausikaw). He experienced a revelation from the Great Spirit, who blamed native suffering on apostasy and acculturation, and who promised to dispose of the oppressors and restore native prosperity once he had been placated. Fearing religious mania, the governor of Indiana, William Henry Harrison, demanded the Delawares require that the 'pretended prophet' (Tenskwatawa) stop the sun (letter quoted in Esarey, 1.182–4). The total eclipse of 16 June 1806 secured Tenskwatawa's reputation. Thousands of Native Americans soon attended his gathering near Greenville, Ohio. Tecumseh, who was by this time a band chief advocating common native ownership of all native land to stop further sales, appealed to the revival's converts as well as to young warriors who opposed land alienation. This directly challenged the American policy of rapidly extinguishing native title and turning the indigenous people from semi-nomads to sedentary farmers.

Americans paid scant attention to Tecumseh's pronouncements, but demands from the 'war hawks' for retaliation against Canada led the British to revitalize their Indian alliances. Given the prophet's influence, Governor General Sir James Craig invited him to come to Canada to talk; Tecumseh appeared instead, and impressed British agents with both his revolutionary ideas and his reliability. He was one of only a handful of native people to whom the British confided their fear of war and wish for native allies. This left Tecumseh a broker of British promises, strengthening his confederacy. Peace was threatened in 1809 when, at Fort Wayne, Indiana Territory, Governor Harrison began negotiations for 3 million acres of native land. Tecumseh shrewdly announced that his followers would kill the signatory chiefs, in a stroke which was reassuring to his followers, and gave the British no reason for fear and the Americans no cause for comfort. Harrison linked subsequent raids to the prophet's revival, which was by this time based in Tippecanoe, Indiana Territory. He invited Tenskwatawa to talks at Vincennes in August 1810. However, Tecumseh appeared there instead, and again expounded his confederation's goals and demanded that the land be returned. Harrison thereafter understood that Tecumseh, not the prophet, was the 'great man of the party' (letter quoted in Esarey, 1.459–69).

In November 1810 Tecumseh visited Fort Malden, Amherstburg, Upper Canada, and declared his men ready to fight once they had received British supplies. The agent, Matthew Elliott, sensing danger, requested instructions. Faced with other similar reports, the British reduced arms supplies to the Indians, although some considered this short-sighted, given that war was near, and thought that native hostility towards the Americans should be fostered.

Continued depredations persuaded Harrison that the native people needed chastisement. He demanded of Tecumseh the surrender of the thieves and murderers he was allegedly harbouring. Instead Tecumseh arrived in Vincennes on 27 July with 300 followers. Both sides there repeated old demands. Harrison, however, was relieved to hear Tecumseh's talk of taking his unification message south. Rightly thinking the prophet 'deficient in judgement' (Esarey, 1.548–51), Harrison organized an expedition to his village at Tippecanoe, where, on 7 November, Tenskwatawa launched a rash and unsuccessful attack which left his followers scattered and years of effort squandered.

Tecumseh, unaware, continued his journey south, but few southern warriors joined him. In February 1812 he visited Fort Malden and requested essential food, clothing, and supplies.

Harrison was initially confident that he had killed native resistance at Tippecanoe, but he faced renewed violence in the spring, even though the confederation was in ruins. As war neared, Tecumseh visited Fort Wayne, talking peace but simultaneously moving his men to Canada. In July they fought alongside the British, and their signal successes in early hostilities restored many vacillating native people to the king's standard. Their anticipation of easy triumph was too optimistic, however. American naval victories on the Great Lakes by September 1813 forced Major-General Henry Procter to order the dismantling of forts and burning of buildings around Amherstburg preparatory to retreat. Procter, commanding the 41st regiment, was pressed by Tecumseh to stand at Moraviantown, Upper Canada, where on 5 October 1813 he faced Harrison's stronger force. There are various accounts of Tecumseh's death that day and of how he predicted the end. Native resistance survived him but was not decisive. An Ottawa chief summarized the Indian dilemma, saying, 'Since our Great Chief Tecumtha has been killed we do not listen to one another, we do not rise together' (speech of 6 Oct 1914, Record Group 10, Public Archives of Ottawa, Indian Affairs, F12).

Peace brought a return to the status quo before hostilities, but made native alliances superfluous. The British prime minister, Lord Liverpool, asked, 'Are we honour bound to do more for them?' (Horsman, 256). With punitive American treaties stripping away their lands, the answer was evident.

No native resistance in North America was successful in the long run. The same combination of factors that conspired against other attempts to stem the white advance were at play here. None the less, Tecumseh's visionary realization that his brother's revival provided an opportunity to energize and unite dispirited nations over a wide area to resist surrender of their land, his brilliant manipulation of both Britain and the United States in working toward this goal, and his retention of the respect of native and white people, friend and foe, in peace and war confirms Harrison's characterization of him as 'one of those uncommon geniuses, which spring up occasionally to produce revolutions and overturn the established order of things' (letter quoted in Esarey, 1.548–51).

HERBERT C. GOLTZ

Sources L. Esarey, ed., *Messages and letters of William Henry Harrison*, 2 vols. (1922) · *Michigan pioneer and historical collection*, 40 vols. (1877–1929) · *American state papers, class II, Indian affairs*, 2 vols. (1832–4) · C. Carter, ed., *The territorial papers of the United States*, 27 vols. (1934) · W. H. Wood, ed., *Select British documents of the war of 1812*, 3 vols. (1920–28) · B. Drake, *The life of Tecumseh and his brother, the prophet* (1841) · H. C. Goltz Jr, 'Tecumseh, the prophet and the rise of the northwest Indian confederation', PhD diss., University of Western Ontario, 1973 · G. C. Chalou, 'The red pawns go to war: British–American Indian relations, 1810–1815', PhD diss., Indiana University, 1971 · J. Sugden, *Tecumseh's last stand* (1985) · R. Horsman, *Matthew Elliott, British Indian agent* (1964) · J. Mooney, *The ghost-dance religion and the Sioux outbreak of 1890* (1896) · R. D. Edmunds, *Tecumseh and the quest for Indian leadership* (1984)

Archives NA Canada, MG 19, RG 8, RG 10 · PRO, Co 42/89, 146–52, 160, 165 | Detroit Public Library, Burton collection · National Archives and Records Administration, Washington, DC, War Department, secretary's office, letters sent, Indian affairs · Wisconsin Historical Society, Madison, Draper MSS

Teddeman, Sir Thomas (*c.*1620–1668), naval officer, was a son of Thomas Teddeman (*d.* after 1658), sometime mayor of Dover, Kent. Captain Henry Teddeman was his brother. In August 1652, on the outbreak of war with the Dutch, Teddeman was appointed lieutenant of the *Royal Sovereign*, the largest ship in the navy, which suggests that he had some powerful patrons. His naval service was brief, however, for in 1653 he was commanding a small privateer, the *Speedwell* of Dover, of four guns and 40 tons, against the Dutch. After the war he probably pursued a mercantile career for several years, but in 1657 he was appointed captain of the *Victory*. Early in March 1660 he was appointed captain of the *Tredagh* for the summer guard, no doubt by the influence of Edward Mountagu (later earl of Sandwich), and he acted as Mountagu's election agent at Dover, a seat which Mountagu won in 1660. Teddeman commanded in *Tredagh* (soon renamed the *Resolution*) in the Mediterranean, where on 31 May off Algiers he encountered six Spanish ships which he chased into Gibraltar and under the guns of the forts. However, in December the ship's company petitioned to the king against him, and Sir William Coventry commented sarcastically, 'what Teddyman and his officers are may appear by their impeaching each other' (Longleat House, Wiltshire, Bath papers, Coventry MS 98, fol. 66). Teddeman survived an investigation and in May 1661 was appointed to the *Fairfax*.

In command of the *Kent* in 1663, Teddeman carried the earl of Carlisle to Archangel on an embassy to Russia. In May 1664 he transferred to the *Revenge*, and in 1665, in the *Royal Katherine*, he was rear-admiral of the Blue squadron, with the earl of Sandwich, in the action off Lowestoft, for which he was knighted on 1 July. Following this success, in August he led a disastrous attempt to capture a Dutch East India Company fleet, rumoured that year to be returning from Smyrna and Batavia with exceptionally rich cargoes. This fleet had followed its normal wartime route round Shetland and was heading into the North Sea when it was ordered to take refuge; the ships anchored in Bergen, then under neutral Danish rule. A plot was then hatched whereby the Danes and English agreed to share the plunder, but no final orders had been given to each side when Teddeman's squadron arrived off Bergen on 10 August.

Sir Thomas Teddeman (*c.*1620–1668), by Sir Peter Lely, *c.*1665–6

Fearing lest he should be trapped by an approaching Dutch rescue force, Teddeman attacked on 12 August but, faced by a wind off the land, could not send in his fire-ships. The commander of the Danish fort, lacking instructions to the contrary, sided with the Dutch. After three and a half hours of battle Teddeman's squadron retreated in confusion, having suffered 500 or 600 casualties against fewer than 100 on the Dutch side. In the same year Teddeman was among those summoned to parliament in connection with the abuse of regulations concerning prize goods.

Happier times arrived in 1666; as vice-admiral of the blue, in *Royal Katherine*, Teddeman was involved in what was known as 'the four-day fight', when between 1 and 4 June English vessels engaged a Dutch fleet in the channel. The Dutch lost six or seven ships and 2000 killed or wounded, the English lost more heavily but felt themselves to have put up a better fight. He was vice-admiral of the white in the 'St James fight' on 1 July, also against the Dutch, off North Foreland, which resulted in a brilliant and decisive English victory. In October 1667, the year in which he commanded the Dover squadron, Teddeman discussed the matter of discipline in the fleet with Samuel Pepys, who knew him well; Teddeman lamented its bad state, while praising his patron Sandwich. The following year Pepys found him languishing in a house in Old Street, Clerkenwell, very ill of a fever—'a good man, a good seaman, and stout' he remarked in his diary (Pepys, *Diary*, 9.164). Teddeman died on 12 May 1668. His funeral on 15 May, which Pepys attended, was held at Loriners' Hall, Moorgate, and he was buried the same day at St Mary's, Rotherhithe, Surrey. Nothing is known of Teddeman's wife or children, beyond a passing reference by Sir Thomas Allin, who met Teddeman's son-in-law at sea early in 1668.   ANITA McCONNELL

Sources C. R. Boxer, 'Review of *De Retourvloot van Pieter de Bitter (1664–1665) door J. C. M. Warnsinck*', *Mariner's Mirror*, 15 (1929), 322–4 · J. D. Davies, *Gentlemen and tarpaulins: the officers and men of the Restoration navy* (1991) · B. Capp, *Cromwell's navy: the fleet and the English revolution, 1648–1660* (1989) · Pepys, *Diary*, vols. 1, 3, 5–9 · parish register, Rotherhithe, St Mary, 15 May 1668, LMA [burial] · W. L. Clowes, *The Royal Navy: a history from the earliest times to the present*, 7 vols. (1897–1903), vol. 2, pp. 256, 266, 278, 427 · Bodl. Oxf., MS Rawl. A. 226, fol. 152 · *CSP dom.*, 1651–2 · PRO, ADM 2/1735, fols. 76, 97v; ADM 2/1745, fol. 18v; ADM 3/273, fol. 73 · PRO, HCA 25/10 · *The journal of Edward Mountagu, first earl of Sandwich, admiral and general at sea, 1659–1665*, ed. R. C. Anderson, Navy RS, 64 (1929) · *The journals of Sir Thomas Allin, 1660–1678*, ed. R. C. Anderson, 2, Navy RS, 80 (1940), 16

Likenesses P. Lely, portrait, *c.*1665–1666, NMM [*see illus.*]

Tedder, Arthur William, first Baron Tedder (1890–1967), air force officer, was born at Glenguin (now Glengoyne), a distillery about 20 miles north of Glasgow, on 11 July 1890, the youngest of the three children of Arthur John Tedder (1851–1931), an excise and revenue official, and his wife, Emily Charlotte Bryson (1854–1936). His father was knighted in 1909 for his work on Lloyd George's old age pension scheme and served as commissioner of customs and excise from 1911 to 1918.

Croydon and Cambridge, 1902–1913 His father's excise duties ensured for Tedder a varied education: at Lerwick in the Shetlands (1895–8), Elgin, near the Moray coast (1899–1901), and Whitgift School, Croydon, south London (1902–9). There he developed a lifelong love of drawing in coloured pencils, especially landscapes and buildings—humans more rarely. At heart an all-weather countryman, he excelled in military exercises with the Officers' Training Corps (OTC), becoming a crack shot and reaching the rank of cyclist-sergeant. A natural navigator, he learned to read the stars easily. Indoors, he learned to play the piano, and even his earliest letters are fluent and witty; sometimes, however, his quick tongue cut more sharply than he intended.

Tedder's talents flourished at Magdalene College, Cambridge (1909–13), under the benign influence of two devoted teachers, A. C. Benson and F. R. Salter. He remained active in the OTC, added rowing to his enthusiasms, climbed about on college roofs, and yet relished small group conversation, helped by a pipe, never by alcohol. Benson and Salter perceived a quality of mind superior to that indicated by a moderate history degree (second-class honours, division two) awarded in June 1912. They encouraged him to study German at an institute in Berlin during the summer vacation, return to Magdalene in October for a fourth year, and prepare himself for a diplomatic career.

At that institute Tedder met (Wilhelmina) Rosalinde St Clair Maclardy (1891–1943), the Sydney-born daughter of a printer, William McIntyre St Clair Maclardy (b. 1852), and his wife, Wilhelmina Rosalinde Foster (1863–1904). Out of their love emerged a capacity for constant application vainly sought by his parents and teachers. During the next

Arthur William Tedder, first Baron Tedder (1890–1967), by unknown photographer, *c.*1943

thirty years, whenever they were apart, the couple wrote almost daily to each other. Shaw's plays, emphasizing self-discipline and constant effort, deeply influenced them; so too did the notions of theosophy, a movement seeking some universal truth supposed to be common to all religions.

Encouraged by Rosalinde, Tedder wrote an essay in 1913 for which he received the prince consort prize at Cambridge. A revised version, published by Cambridge University Press in 1916 as *The navy of the Restoration from the death of Cromwell to the treaty of Breda: its work, growth and influence*, remains highly regarded. Some credit is owed to his uncle Henry, librarian at the Athenaeum, who discussed the essay with him, contributed much to the bibliography, and saw it through the press.

Fiji and the army, 1914–1915 Tedder abandoned his diplomatic prospects in 1913 and, although he applied (unsuccessfully) for a position at Queensland University, Brisbane, an academic career did not appeal either. In a restless mood he accepted a three-year probation as a Colonial Office cadet in Fiji and left England in February 1914. Rosalinde returned to Sydney in June, and the couple considered marrying in Fiji. By August, however, Tedder had decided that its European society was petty, his prospects were poor, and the climate would wither her. The outbreak of war cleared his path: eager now to join the regular army, he resigned, resisting strong official pressure to remain at his post. After a month in Sydney with Rosalinde he returned to England in December.

Commissioned as a second lieutenant in the Dorsetshire regiment in January 1915, Tedder joined the 3rd (reserve) battalion at Wyke Regis, near Weymouth. A serious knee injury in February condemned him to dogsbody duties in Wyke until July, then at a base camp in Calais until October, when he was allowed home to continue his agitation for a transfer to the Royal Flying Corps (RFC). Rosalinde, meanwhile, had returned to England, in response to Tedder's urgent plea: they married in June 1915. Later they had two sons and a daughter.

Wartime airman, 1916–1919 The RFC accepted Tedder in January 1916, now that he was fully mobile again, and during that year his progress was astonishing. Promoted captain in March, he was taught to fly in April, and joined 25 squadron (equipped with the FE 2b, a two-seater with its engine placed behind the crew) on the western front in June. On 21 June he wrote to Rosalinde that an anti-aircraft gun 'put a shrapnel bullet through the nacelle of my aircraft, in one side and out the other, cutting one of the petrol pipes and passing down between my legs. Petrol came pouring out in a continuous stream over my right foot' (Tedder MSS). Amazingly, flames did not appear, and so a career that had barely begun did not end in agony. When appointed flight commander in August, Tedder immediately had all his aircraft painted Cambridge blue. He was promoted major in command of 70 squadron for six months from January 1917. His new squadron flew the Sopwith 1½ Strutter, the RFC's first aircraft with a machine-gun firing through the propeller arc and the observer seated *behind* the pilot.

Although he was an excellent navigator and a competent pilot with 25 squadron, never flinching from combat and carrying out such varied tasks as reconnaissance, photography, escort, and bombing raids with thoughtful determination, Tedder's main strength was seen on the ground with 70 squadron when his duties prevented him from flying regularly. Older than most pilots and more thoroughly educated, his diligence and literary skill enabled him to shift paper swiftly and pacify higher command. He also had the calm temperament and good humour needed to see men through times of heavy casualties—of which there were many.

On all his aerodromes, Tedder created Cambridge-like oases of comfort and gossip, neatly decorated and comfortably furnished, for himself and men of similar tastes. While he preferred quiet chat, serious music, and solitary walks, he cheerfully played the latest songs from the shows and took an active part in all sports. Hugh Trenchard, head of the RFC in France (a man who made or marred numerous careers), noticed him favourably; so too did Wilfrid Freeman, an officer who later helped him into high command and sustained him there.

In July 1917, at Shawbury, Shropshire, Tedder had his first taste of tasks in which he later specialized: large-scale training in air fighting, gunnery, and artillery observation. In May 1918 he was sent to Cairo to organize similar training, but his ship was torpedoed on leaving Marseilles. He was rescued by a Japanese destroyer—a distinction, he later claimed, unmatched by any other senior British

officer. Having been promoted lieutenant-colonel in July 1918, he adroitly handled discontent over the demobilization shambles at the end of the war. He returned to England in March 1919, rejected an offer to resume his Colonial Office career in April, was granted a permanent commission as a squadron leader in August, and took command of 207 squadron at Bircham Newton, Norfolk, in February 1920.

Constantinople, 1922–1923 By September 1922, when the Chanak crisis (a Turkish challenge to British control of the Dardanelles) threatened to escalate into war, Tedder had so impressed Trenchard that his was one of three squadrons sent from England to Constantinople in support of a strong naval and military force. He remained there for nine hard months, helping to ensure that the threat remained dormant. During that time he revived the reputation he had won on the western front. It was founded on sensible, consistent discipline; a practical concern to improve living conditions; a readiness to share information with all ranks; and plenty of realistic training. Throughout a sensitive period he avoided incidents, not only with Turks, Greeks, or Russians, but also with senior British naval or army officers or French allies. His excellent performance confirmed Trenchard's good opinion, and in July 1923 he was selected for the Royal Naval Staff College course at Greenwich the following October—naval because the RAF's own college had opened only the previous year, and the infant service was desperately short of staff-trained officers.

Student, trainer, teacher, 1923–1936 At Greenwich Tedder wrote thoughtful essays—on anti-shipping bombs, warplane design, cloud-flying problems—and in January 1924 he was promoted wing commander. From Greenwich, he took command in September of a flying training station at Digby, Lincolnshire. His practical ideas to improve flying standards impressed Freeman (now commandant of the Central Flying School). So did his efforts to make Digby a place where officers and men were content as well as busy: planting bushes and flowers, cleaning and painting buildings, encouraging sports and hobbies—creating, as he tried to do wherever he served, a well-disciplined family atmosphere.

In January 1927 his reward was a senior Air Ministry appointment: deputy director of training. An even higher mark of favour came in January 1928, when he was sent to study for one year at the Imperial Defence College, near Buckingham Palace. There officers of all three services and civil servants who were specially promising considered matters of high policy—advised, at intervals, by government ministers and senior politicians. Thus primed, Tedder was appointed a member of the directing staff at the RAF Staff College, Andover (1929–30), and, on promotion to group captain, deputy commandant (1931). He developed his talent for cogent argument, on paper or across a table, and wrote—among much else—three excellent studies of the Gallipoli campaign, focusing particularly on inter-service co-operation when attempting a landing upon a hostile shore. These were problems that would concern him deeply a decade later.

After commanding an air armament school at Eastchurch, Essex (1932–4), Tedder returned to the Air Ministry in April 1934 as director of training and was promoted air commodore in July. Until September 1936 he was responsible for flying, armament, and navigation training, with an interest in the effective use of weapons, and kept in touch with designers, manufacturers, and government departments. These were years of reorganization and expansion to face the prospect of another war, and on his initiative civilian schools took over elementary flying training, leaving service schools free to concentrate on advanced training and so provide operational squadrons with better-prepared crews.

Singapore, 1936–1938 Tedder went to Singapore in October 1936 as head of an enormous command stretching from Burma to Hong Kong and on to Borneo. Appointed CB in February 1937 and promoted air vice-marshal in July, he reformed the air staff organization, visited every unit, improved relations with other services, sought sites for new airfields, helped to devise and conduct realistic tri-service exercises to counter a possible Japanese attack, and resisted the endless social rituals that for some officers in all services were preferable to military duties.

Director-general of research and development, 1938–1940 In July 1938 Freeman (now air member for research and development) had Tedder brought back to England to take up a new Air Ministry appointment as director-general of research and development. Until December 1940 he and Freeman (closely watched by other senior officers in the Air Ministry, as well as by politicians and Treasury officials) worked with managing directors, chief designers, and senior trade union officials of aircraft manufacturers and their suppliers to provide Britain with aircraft, weapons, and other equipment capable of resisting the Luftwaffe and carrying the war to Germany.

Their task was complicated by a revolution in the design, construction, equipment, and production of aircraft. It was a revolution so profound that several promising ventures failed for technical reasons (for example, the Westland Whirlwind, a twin-engined, cannon-armed fighter that was a particular favourite of Tedder's), while others (notably Whittle's jet engine) were not pressed forward with sufficient urgency—even though Tedder himself was among Whittle's supporters.

A further complication came in May 1940, when the entire aircraft business was detached from the Air Ministry and made part of a new Ministry of Aircraft Production under the control of Lord Beaverbrook. In Tedder's opinion, Beaverbrook supposed that improvisation gave better results than organization, set unrealistic targets as opposed to making rational plans, and preferred exhortation to argument, threats to persuasion.

Mediterranean campaigns, 1940–1943 Tedder consequently became desperate to escape, and Freeman, who had himself returned to the Air Ministry as vice-chief of the air staff, supported a request in November 1940 from Arthur

Longmore, head of Middle East command in Cairo, for Tedder to be appointed his deputy. But Prime Minister Churchill (advised by Beaverbrook) preferred instead Owen Boyd. Unfortunately, Boyd fell into Italian hands *en route* for Cairo and Churchill relented. Tedder, promoted air marshal, arrived in Cairo in December and succeeded Longmore in May 1941. He quickly impressed Charles Portal—chief of the air staff from October 1940—with his abilities, and at Portal's request sent him regular and brutally frank reports on the Mediterranean scene as he saw it, to which Portal replied in kind. By October 1941 he had earned the confidence of Claude Auchinleck, the army commander, whose support, allied to that of Portal and Freeman, prevented Churchill from sacking him over a dispute about air strengths on the eve of operation Crusader (November 1941). Portal threatened resignation, and Freeman refused, as he put it, to play either Judas or Brutus.

Tedder gradually assembled an outstanding team, headed by Peter Drummond (his deputy) and Grahame Dawson (in charge of repair and maintenance) in Cairo, with Arthur Coningham (field commander), assisted by Thomas Elmhirst (responsible for administration and supply) from February 1942; in March 1943 he recruited as his chief scientific adviser Solly Zuckerman, a biologist who transformed himself after 1939 into an expert on the effects of bombing. Tedder frequently left his office—as in his squadron commander days—to talk to all ranks and became 'the most unstuffy of great commanders, who could be found sitting cross-legged, jacketless, pipe smouldering, answering questions on a desert airstrip' (*The Times*, 5 June 1967). He was knighted (KCB) in January 1942, promoted air chief marshal in July, and awarded a GCB in November.

Success in the desert war, achieved by November 1942, commended Tedder to an American general, Dwight D. Eisenhower, newly arrived in north-west Africa as supreme allied commander, and to Carl A. Spaatz, head of American air forces there. They formed a triumvirate which did much to balance increasingly tense relations with Bernard Montgomery, an exceptional but single-minded British field commander, who became increasingly reluctant to discuss hopes and fears with fellow commanders, preferring instead to declare his own intentions. As head of Mediterranean air command (from February 1943) Tedder recast Anglo-American air power into an effective shape, ending early setbacks in Tunisia and helping to bring about a complete victory there in May 1943, followed by the conquest of Sicily in August, and the invasion of Italy in September.

Rosalinde had joined Tedder in Cairo in June 1942, to do welfare work, but she was killed on 4 January 1943 in an aircraft accident at Heliopolis airfield, near Cairo. On 26 October 1943 Tedder married Marie (Toppy) de Seton Black (1907–1965); they had a son, born in May 1946. Toppy, recently divorced from Captain Ian Reddie Hamilton Black RN, was the younger daughter of Colonel Sir Bruce Gordon Seton, ninth baronet, of Abercorn, Linlithgow, and his wife, Elma.

Overlord and after, 1944–1945 In December 1943 Tedder was appointed Eisenhower's deputy for operation Overlord, launched in June 1944 to liberate occupied Europe and assist the Soviet Union to overthrow Hitler. Advised by Zuckerman, Tedder persuaded Eisenhower to require a prolonged, systematic attack on French, Belgian, and west German marshalling yards controlling railway systems serving the invasion area. It would be easy for the Germans to move reinforcements and heavy weapons quickly if they had the use of undamaged railways. Therefore, if the allies were not to be swept back into the sea, the German build-up must be delayed and disorganized. Churchill, fearing the political consequences of French and Belgian civilian casualties, urged President Roosevelt to cancel the plan, but Roosevelt supported Eisenhower. About 7000 civilians died, many fewer than were killed by ground fighting after D-day.

From August 1944, after the breakout from Normandy, this 'transportation plan' envisaged the paralysis of Germany's industrial, commercial, and agricultural life by inhibiting all movement. Raw materials are useless unless they can be shifted to factories, turned into weapons (or something equally vital), and carried to where they are needed; similarly, harvested crops are of little value unless they can be moved from where they are grown to where they are eaten; and synthetic oil, essential to military operations, cannot be produced without coal, which must be transported from where it is mined to a refinery.

Although Arthur Harris, commanding British night bombers, preferred to continue his destruction of German cities and Spaatz (now commanding American day bombers) preferred to focus on aircraft factories, oil targets, and their defending fighters, Tedder gradually won significant support from both men as well as co-operation from the immense allied tactical air forces. It was less than he thought ideal, but perhaps as much as he could obtain without fracturing the façade of Anglo-American unity, which he and Eisenhower were determined to maintain. Together they received the German surrender at Rheims on 7 May 1945. Tedder then went as Eisenhower's representative to Berlin, where he and Marshal Zhukov, the Russian commander, shared the honour and satisfaction of receiving a formal surrender, shortly after midnight on 9 May; Spaatz and General de Lattre de Tassigny, on behalf of the United States and France, witnessed this dramatic ceremony.

Two principles had guided Tedder's years of command throughout the Mediterranean and north-west European campaigns. First, the need for close relations with the United States at whatever cost to British influence over grand strategy: British industry could not provide sufficient weapons (ground or air) to avoid defeat, let alone achieve victory. American supplies were already essential for the desert war in 1941 and American manpower would become so for the Overlord campaign. Second, the need for centralized control of air power: Tedder insisted on this, overcoming strong opposition from naval and army commanders. Air superiority, he argued, must be sought before close support at sea or on land could be offered; and he must be the judge (advised by his field commanders) of where and when that support could best be offered.

Chief of the air staff, 1946–1949 Tedder achieved five-star rank (marshal of the Royal Air Force) in September 1945, succeeded Portal as chief of the air staff on 1 January 1946, and was elevated to the peerage. During that same year he received honorary doctorates from several British universities, and in May he was granted the freedom of London. In June he was appointed chairman of the chiefs of staff committee, working with Montgomery (army) and John Cunningham (navy). Montgomery detested all committees and despised his colleagues, who returned the sentiment with interest. The work got done, often by deputies, but harmony was not restored until November 1948, when the prime minister, Attlee, found Montgomery another important position.

In August 1947 Tedder organized exercise Thunderbolt, a four-day study of the strategic air offensive between 1943 and 1945. Those officers still serving who had helped to direct that offensive were required to revive their memories and even to take part in scripted reconstructions of significant episodes. They were helped by secret documents, especially reports by the British bombing survey unit, prepared under Zuckerman's direction (unsurprisingly, they supported the transportation plan) and four excellent lectures, 'Air power in war', which Tedder had delivered at Cambridge earlier that year (published in 1948). Two equally elaborate exercises followed: Pandora (on scientific and technical aids to air war) in May 1948 and Ariel (on manpower problems) in April 1949.

Tedder's air force had responsibilities stretching from Germany to Hong Kong via the Middle East, but, following massive demobilization in 1945–6, too few skilled long-service personnel to cope with them properly; and, although the day of piston-engined warplanes was clearly ending, funds were unavailable, in peacetime, for the rapid development of their jet successors. By 1948 many demands exacerbated these problems: the Berlin airlift, unrest in Malaya, and especially concern over the Middle East (to safeguard oil supplies, protect sea links with the Far East, and provide for effective defence in the event of Soviet aggression).

Tedder supervised reforms in organization, recruitment drives, and the restoration in 1948 of a radar based defence system for Britain, linked to an enlarged Fighter Command. Above all he encouraged the closest relations with American airmen, quietly preparing, from 1946 onwards, bases in England for their strategic bombers and attempting to standardize equipment and training. But he also supported Attlee's decision that Britain must have her own nuclear weapons, and planning began in 1948 for a British jet bomber force capable of carrying them.

Tedder was succeeded on 1 January 1950 by John Slessor, an outstanding officer, widely regarded as the obvious heir. On most service issues they agreed, but in method and temperament they differed markedly. As early as 1947 Tedder had tried, but failed, to remove Slessor from contention; he failed again in 1949. Ralph Cochrane was his choice, but Slessor's superior merits (strongly supported backstage by Trenchard, Portal, and Freeman) got him home—and he immediately offered Cochrane the position of vice-chief, which he accepted.

Washington, 1950–1951 After a few weeks as a BBC governor, Tedder was pressed back into uniform by Attlee in April 1950 as chairman of the British Joint Services Mission in Washington, DC. Although he was weary of life at the top military table, he accepted the appointment—for no more than twelve months, from May—because the Americans respected, trusted, and even liked him. His main task was to help translate NATO (founded in April 1949) into a practical military organization. When the Korean War broke out in June 1950 he occupied a key position as a conduit through whom military authorities in Washington and Whitehall could privately explain what they really expected of each other.

To his everlasting joy Tedder learned in November 1950 that he had been elected chancellor of Cambridge University, succeeding Jan Christian Smuts, whom he regarded as the greatest man he ever met. Nothing in Tedder's public life, not even appointment as chief of the air staff, gave him more satisfaction than this elevation, the highest to which a devout 'Cantab' can aspire: he was, moreover, the first Magdalene man to be so honoured. This news strengthened his determination to resist strong pressure, American and British, to stay on in Washington. On his return to England in May 1951 he was restored to the BBC, as vice-chairman, and took up other demanding tasks: director of the Distillers Company, chairman of Standard Motors (from 1954), and president of Surrey County Cricket Club (an office in which patronage gave more pleasure than any he commanded in Whitehall or Washington).

The Malcolm clubs One service interest remained paramount. The Malcolm clubs, founded for airmen in Algiers in July 1943, were the pride and joy of his second wife, Toppy, and Tedder shared her enthusiasm wholeheartedly. No military operation received more passionate attention. The clubs offered civilized comfort, such as Tedder had sought for men under his command ever since 1915, but they were an unofficial organization, with no Air Ministry backing, and were held to compete with (rather than complement) the activities of the Navy, Army, and Air Force institutes. During the 1950s the Tedders stubbornly resisted efforts to close them, mustering influential allies and raising funds. The clubs were not allowed to expand on a scale the Tedders thought desirable, but fourteen outlived them: seven in Germany, three in Bahrain, three in the Far East, and one in England.

During the last twenty years of his life Tedder made numerous speeches, all carefully prepared, to gatherings of peers, schoolboys, chemists, cricketers, academics, medics, engineers, and military persons. He spoke regularly in debates on defence issues in the House of Lords between 1953 and 1962 and vehemently opposed the Anglo-French/Israeli assault on Egypt in October 1956: 'A tragic mistake and a folly because it was the wrong action at the wrong time and in the wrong way' (*Hansard 5L*, 12 Dec 1956).

With Prejudice Until he was sixty Tedder's youthful appearance, helped by an unlined face and a full head of neatly groomed dark brown hair, was often remarked upon. A small, slim man, he had large eyes, a long straight nose, and, less fortunately, outstanding ears. In April 1960 he suffered a stroke in Los Angeles. His recovery was slow and his ability to write (or, much worse, to draw) declined. Although he gradually became chairbound he remained mentally alert and even cheerful, but on 3 January 1965 Toppy died suddenly.

In the circumstances the completion of Tedder's Second World War memoirs, *With Prejudice* (begun in 1962, published by Cassell in October 1966), was remarkable. He received essential help from the historian David Dilks (who gathered vast amounts of material) and from his secretary, Marjorie Grover (who sorted and filed it most efficiently); Zuckerman and other friends offered detailed criticism, but the finished work—lucid, detailed, outspoken—is Tedder's. He died at his home, Well Farm, Woodmansterne Lane, Banstead, Surrey, on 3 June 1967. He lived just long enough to know that his book had attracted scholarly, as well as popular, attention throughout the English-speaking world. Many readers must regret that he found neither time nor strength to cover his whole life.

Tedder's elder son, Arthur Richard Brian Tedder (1916–1940), air force officer, was killed in action over France on 3 August 1940. Tedder's younger son, **John Michael Tedder**, second Baron Tedder (1926–1994), organic chemist, was born on 4 July 1926 in London and educated at Dauntsey's School in Wiltshire. He read natural sciences at Magdalene College, Cambridge. After research on fluorine chemistry and a Birmingham PhD, he was a chemistry lecturer at Sheffield University (1955–64), specializing in valence theory, pioneering gas chromatography in the quantitative analysis of complex organic mixtures, and working on the halogenation of hydrocarbons. He married on 17 April 1952 Peggy Eileen Growcott, younger daughter of Samuel George Growcott of Birmingham; they had two sons and one daughter. He was Roscoe professor of chemistry at Queen's College, Dundee (1964–9), and Purdie professor of chemistry at St Andrews (1969–89), and used mass spectrometry to investigate the reaction of neutral intermediates with organic molecules. In 1966 he published *Basic Organic Chemistry*, a textbook which pioneered a mechanistic approach to the teaching of organic chemistry, and which was translated into many languages and ran into a number of editions. After succeeding his father in 1967 he spoke in the Lords on science, technology, and higher education. His career was truncated by Parkinson's disease, then Alzheimer's, and he died on 18 February 1994 at Stratheden Hospital, near Cupar, Fife. He was survived by his wife and three children, and succeeded as third baron by his elder son, Robin John Tedder (b. 1955). VINCENT ORANGE

Sources [Lord Tedder], *With prejudice: the war memoirs of marshal of the Royal Air Force, Lord Tedder* (1966) • Lord Tedder [A. W. Tedder], *Air*

power in war (1948) · Lord Tedder [A. W. Tedder], 'Air, land and sea warfare', *Journal of the Royal United Service Institution*, 91 (1946), 59–68 · Lord Tedder [A. W. Tedder], 'The problem of our future security', *RAF Quarterly*, 19 (1948), 8–18 · V. Orange, *Tedder: quietly in command* (2003) · A. C. Mierzejewski, *The collapse of the German war economy, 1944–1945: allied air power and the German national railway* (1988) · A. C. Mierzejewski, 'Intelligence and the strategic bombing of Germany: the combined strategic targets committee', *International Journal of Intelligence and Counter-Intelligence*, 3 (1989), 83–104 · S. Cox, 'An unwanted child: the struggle to establish a British bombing survey', *The strategic air war against Germany, 1939–1945: report of the British bombing survey unit* (1998), xvii–xli · S. Cox, '"The difference between white and black": Churchill, imperial politics and intelligence before the 1941 crusader offensive', *Intelligence and National Security*, 9 (1994), 405–47 · Lord Zuckerman, 'Marshal of the RAF Lord Tedder (1890–1967): the politically sensitive airman', *Six men out of the ordinary* (1992), 65–98 · D. Richards, *Portal of Hungerford* (1977) · J. Terraine, *The right of the line: the Royal Air Force in the European war, 1939–1945* (1985) · S. Zuckerman, *From apes to warlords* (1978) · W. Jackson and Lord Bramall, *The chiefs: the story of the United Kingdom chiefs of staff* (1992) · E. J. Kingston-McCloughry, *The direction of war: a critique of the political direction and high command in war* (1955) · W. W. Rostow, *Pre-invasion bombing strategy: General Eisenhower's decision of March 25, 1944* (1981) · S. Ritchie, *Industry and air power: the expansion of British aircraft production, 1935–1941* (1997) · R. G. Davis, 'RAF–AAF higher command structures and relationships, 1942–45', *Air Power History*, 38 (1991), 20–28 · C. Foxley Norris, 'Marshal of the Royal Air Force Lord Tedder', *The war lords: military commanders of the twentieth century*, ed. M. Carver (1976), 485–99 · V. Orange, *Coningham* (1990) · J. Kent, *British imperial strategy and the origins of the cold war, 1944–49* (1993) · R. Owen, *Tedder* (1952) · W. M. Aitken, ed., *A history of 207 squadron* (1984) · *The Times* (5 June 1967) · priv. coll., Tedder MSS · d. cert. · Burke, *Peerage* [John Tedder] · *WWW* [John Tedder] · *The Independent* (24 Feb 1994) · *The Times* (25 Feb 1994) · *Daily Telegraph* (8 March 1994)

Archives priv. coll., MSS · Royal Air Force Museum, Hendon, department of research and information services, logbook, diaries, and staff college lectures | Christ Church Oxf., corresp. with Portal · IWM, corresp. with Tizard · King's Lond., Liddell Hart C., corresp. with Sir B. H. Liddell Hart | FILM BFI NFTVA, documentary footage · BFI NFTVA, news footage · IWM FVA, actuality footage · IWM FVA, documentary footage · IWM FVA, news footage | SOUND IWM SA, oral history interview

Likenesses A. Robitschek, 1942, priv. coll. · photographs, 1942–53, Hult. Arch. · H. Carr, oils, 1943, IWM · H. A. Freeth, chalk drawing, 1943, IWM · R. Tollast, chalk drawing, 1943, Churchill College, Cambridge · photograph, *c.*1943, IWM [*see illus.*] · W. Stoneman, photograph, 1946, NPG · H. Carr, oils, 1949, Magd. Cam. · W. Bird, photograph, 1961, NPG · Artzybasheff, portrait, repro. in *Time* (9 Nov 1942), cover · Hayden, caricature, repro. in *Flight* (1 Nov 1945), 477 · photograph, repro. in *Life* (31 Jan 1944), cover

Wealth at death £34,082: probate, 22 Aug 1967, *CGPLA Eng. & Wales* · £143,440.65—John Tedder: resworn confirmation, 1998, *CCI* (1994)

Tedder, Henry Richard (1850–1924), librarian, was born on 25 June 1850 at 2 Victoria Grove, Kensington, London, the eldest child of six boys and four girls born to William Henry Tedder (1821–1909) and Elizabeth Ferries (*d.* 1907), shopkeepers. Their second son, Sir Arthur John Tedder, a civil servant, was the father of Arthur William Tedder, first Baron Tedder of Glenguin, marshal of the RAF. Henry and Arthur were educated privately and abroad until 1869. Henry worked for Herbert Spencer, assisting in the editing of *The Principles of Sociology* (1877–96). Spencer continued to have a strong influence on Tedder throughout his life and appointed Tedder as an administrator of the Spencer Trust on his death.

Henry Richard Tedder (1850–1924), by George Hall Neale, 1914

It may have been Spencer who introduced Tedder to John Emerich Edward, Baron Acton of Aldenham, who employed Tedder as librarian in 1873–4 to produce the catalogue of his great private collection, published in 1874. Acton was an active member of the Athenaeum and it was on his recommendation that Tedder was appointed to assist the now ailing Spencer Hall in 1874, and to take over as librarian on Hall's death in 1875. Tedder was to remain librarian until 1914, combining his duties with those of secretary of the club from 1888 onwards. On his retirement in 1914 Rudyard Kipling composed the poem 'To a Librarian' in his honour.

In 1877 a correspondence in *The Times*, started by Edward W. B. Nicholson, librarian of the London Institution, led to the first meeting of the embryonic Library Association (LA) at the London Library on 9 April 1877. Tedder and Nicholson were appointed joint honorary secretaries and organized the first Library Association conference held in October of that year, attended by Melville Dewey, who also influenced Tedder.

Tedder was active on both sides of the debate concerning the revision of the Public Libraries Act of 1855, as a result of his membership of the Metropolitan Free Libraries Association. This led to his resignation as secretary of the Library Association in 1880 and some animosity toward him from the provincial public librarians, who saw him as the representative of a London clique opposed to public libraries. Nevertheless, in both 1880 and 1881 he was invited to report on the administration of Cambridge University Library, and he continued to edit the LA's *Monthly Notes*. By 1889 financial difficulties in the LA led to Tedder's appointment as treasurer, a post over which he had a virtual monopoly from 1889 to 1924. He was elected president in 1897.

Tedder's efficiency as an organizer and contributor led to involvement in many other projects. Among these was the *Dictionary of National Biography*, for which Tedder wrote 185 signed articles, principally concerning printers and booksellers. In 1882 he wrote the entry 'Libraries' for the *Encyclopaedia Britannica* and in 1885 he co-operated with Michael Kearney on the entry 'Romance'. Kearney witnessed Tedder's marriage on 1 January 1887 to Alice Callan (1860–1915), daughter of Daniel Callan. From 1894 to 1914 Tedder contributed over forty signed articles to Palgrave's *Dictionary of Economics*. He was treasurer of the Gibbon commemoration committee, and served on the committee of the London Library from 1884 to 1909. In the 1890s he worked on several schemes for the education of librarians, advocating women librarians and administering the first professional examinations for membership of the LA.

In 1902 Tedder was elected to the Royal Historical Society in recognition of his work on the bibliography of national history. A. W. Pollard acknowledged him as the man who first put the idea of the *Short-Title Catalogue* (1926) into his head. Tedder served as treasurer of the Royal Historical Society from 1904 to 1924 and vice-president in 1923. He also served on the royal commission on public records from 1910 to 1916. Ill health resulting from war work and his wife's death in 1915 led to a reduction in his activities. Although he was married on 12 December 1916 to Violet Anns (1877–1954), daughter of Frederick Anns, and continued in his posts as treasurer for the LA and the Royal Historical Society, he was prevented from completing the centenary history of the Athenaeum by his death at his home, 25 Montserrat Road, Putney, London, on 1 August 1924. SARAH DODGSON

Sources R. J. Busby, 'Henry Richard Tedder FSA 1850–1924: a study in libraries and London institutional life', fellowship diss., Library Association, 1974 · H. R. Tedder, *Librarianship as a profession* (1884) · J. McCabe, *A biographical dictionary of modern rationalists* (1920) · *CGPLA Eng. & Wales* (1924) · b. cert. · d. cert.
Archives Athenaeum, London · Library Association, London | CUL, letters to Lord Acton · King's AC Cam., letters to Oscar Browning
Likenesses G. Hall Neale, oils, 1914, Athenaeum, London [*see illus.*]
Wealth at death £7800 6s. 1d.: probate, 3 Oct 1924, *CGPLA Eng. & Wales*

Tedder, John Michael, second Baron Tedder (1926–1994). *See under* Tedder, Arthur William, first Baron Tedder (1890–1967).

Teedyuscung (*c*.1700–1763), leader of the Delaware Indians, was born near Trenton, New Jersey, son of a Lenape called Old Captain Harris. While Unami Delaware was his first language, his training in native traditions was patchy and he spoke English fairly well. As a young adult on the fringes of colonial society he sold baskets and brooms to support himself.

About 1730 Teedyuscung and his father migrated to the Forks of the Delaware (later Easton, Pennsylvania); there they joined other refugees in new—and for the first time self-consciously 'Delaware'—villages. In this fluid environment his speaking talents made him a leader, though he had no hereditary claim to office. The formative event of his political career was Pennsylvania's fraudulent acquisition of the Forks in the 'walking purchase' of 1737, which by late 1749 forced the region's Delawares westward to the Susquehanna and Ohio countries. Teedyuscung's family found refuge at the nearby Moravian mission of Gnadenhütten, where, on 12 March 1750, he was baptized Gabriel. A week later his wife, a Munsee Delaware, was baptized Elisabeth; with two of the couple's six children she remained a practising Christian, and lived with Moravians intermittently until her death in 1762. But Teedyuscung—known for hard drinking and emotional outbursts—left Gnadenhütten, and for the most part Christianity, in 1754.

That year, at the urging of Iroquois leaders eager to populate the strategic upper Susquehanna valley, Teedyuscung led approximately seventy Gnadenhütten emigrants to Wyoming (later Wilkes-Barre, Pennsylvania). He soon emerged as the self-described 'king' of the area's several hundred diverse inhabitants. During the Seven Years' War his diplomacy defended their land against four powerful foes: Pennsylvania (whose behaviour in the walking purchase he repeatedly denounced), the Iroquois (whose characterization of the Delawares as dependent 'women' he repudiated), backcountry white settlers (against whom he briefly warred in 1755–6), and the Connecticut-based Susquehanna Company (whose claims the Iroquois and Pennsylvania also contested). In all this Teedyuscung found common cause with Pennsylvania Quakers who criticized their government's policies, and, despite a drinking problem that publicly embarrassed him at important councils, brokered negotiations between the British and the Delawares and other Indians of the Ohio country.

Teedyuscung died in Wyoming valley on 19 April 1763, when an arsonist burned his house around him as he slept and then torched the rest of the main Wyoming Delaware town. Circumstantial evidence inculpates the Susquehanna Company; within two weeks of his murder its settlers occupied the ground on which his home had stood.

DANIEL K. RICHTER

Sources A. F. C. Wallace, *King of the Delawares: Teedyuscung, 1700–1763* (1949) · J. Miller, 'Teedyskung', *ANB* · J. H. Merrell, *Into the American woods: negotiators on the Pennsylvania frontier* (1999) · F. Jennings, *Empire of fortune: crowns, colonies and tribes in the Seven Years' War in America* (1988) · C. H. Sipe, *The Indian chiefs of Pennsylvania* (1927), 326–70

Teeling, Bartholomew (1774–1798), Irish nationalist, was born at Lisburn, co. Antrim, the eldest son of Luke Teeling, a linen merchant, and his wife, Mary, the daughter of John Taaffe of Smarmore Castle, co. Louth. He had at least two younger brothers, **Charles Hamilton Teeling** (1778–

1850), newspaper proprietor, and George. The family business prospered in the 1780s, and Luke Teeling became a figurehead in the Catholic business community in Antrim. In December 1792 he attended the Catholic Convention as one of the Antrim delegates and spoke passionately in favour of demanding full Catholic emancipation from the British government, now that the Catholic position had been strengthened by the support of Belfast's United Irishmen, with whom Luke was in close contact. His speech was enthusiastically received and the motion carried, but the convention secured only extension of the franchise to Catholics, in the Relief Act of 1793.

Bartholomew was educated in Dublin at the academy of the Revd W. Dubourdieu, a French protestant minister, where he became proficient in French. Before the age of twenty he joined the United Irishmen and his family became ever more closely associated with the movement. In the summer of 1795 Charles travelled through Antrim, Derry, Tyrone, Fermanagh, Leitrim, and Westmeath, drumming up support for the Catholic Defenders. Bartholomew made his own recruiting journey on foot through Ireland and was influential enough to become a member of the national executive committee of the United Irishmen soon after it was set up towards the end of 1796. By then both his brother and his father were in gaol, having been arrested on 16 September 1796 by Lord Castlereagh on suspicion of treason. Luke was confined in Carrickfergus prison until 1802 but Charles appears to have escaped, for, according to his own account, he was on the run together with his brother-in-law, John Maginnis, and Alexander Lowry early in 1797.

As one of the representatives of Ulster United Irishmen, Bartholomew attended a United Irish meeting in Dublin in early June 1797 to discuss plans for a rising. On returning to Ulster, he and his fellow delegates met resistance from their military leaders in Antrim, who refused to act without guaranteed assistance from the French. Learning that warrants had been issued for their arrest, Teeling and his fellow militants fled Ireland. He travelled via England to Hamburg, where he arrived on 13 July with instructions to check that the Dutch fleet under the command of General Hoche was preparing to set sail for Ireland. He reassured the United Irish leadership in Ulster that all was in order, but by the autumn the situation had dramatically changed, following Hoche's sudden death and the defeat of the Dutch fleet at the battle of Camperdown. Teeling's letter from Paris, where he was then based, to inform his Dublin contacts of the two disasters was crucially intercepted by the Irish authorities.

In Paris, Teeling's friend Theobald Wolfe Tone procured him a commission in the French army. In the summer of 1798 Teeling, together with Tone's brother Matthew, was sent to join General Humbert's force at Rochefort, one of three fleets preparing to invade Ireland. Appointed aide-de-camp and interpreter to Humbert, Teeling set sail with more than a thousand men who made up Humbert's attack and landed at Killala on 22 August. A misguided campaign ensued: Humbert marched his troops southwards to capture the garrison at Castlebar, thereby losing precious time, and doubled back via Collooney to Ballinamuck, where they met the crown's forces under Cornwallis. The battle on 8 September was short and Humbert soon surrendered. Teeling and Matthew Tone were taken to Dublin, where they were court-martialled and sentenced to death. Although Humbert intervened on Teeling's behalf and praised him for his attempts to prevent the rebel troops from pillaging and carrying out revenge attacks, the lord lieutenant denied the plea for mercy. Teeling was hanged at Arbour Hill prison in Dublin on 24 September 1798. A century later a memorial to him was erected at Carricknagat, near Collooney, where he had distinguished himself in battle on 5 September.

Charles Teeling remained in Ulster during the 1798 rising and its aftermath, and in 1802 he settled at Dundalk as a linen bleacher. In the same year he married a Miss Carolan of Carrickmacross, co. Monaghan. Later he became proprietor of the *Belfast Northern Herald* and moved to Newry, where he established the *Newry Examiner*. From 1832 to 1835 he also owned and edited a monthly periodical, the *Ulster Magazine*. In 1828 he published his *Personal narrative of the 'Irish rebellion' of 1798*; a *Sequel* appeared in 1832. His history is particularly valuable for its description of the Catholic Defender movement in Ulster before 1798 and its relations with the United Irishmen, as well as for its description of the rising in Ulster. Teeling also published an alternative account of the battle of the Diamond in 1795 between the Catholic Defenders and protestant Peep o' Day Boys that led to the formation of the Orange order. Teeling died in Dublin in 1850. His eldest daughter Mary married Thomas O'Hagan, first Baron O'Hagan, in 1836.   C. L. FALKINER, *rev.* S. J. SKEDD

Sources C. H. Teeling, *History of the Irish rebellion of 1798*, new edn (1972) · C. H. Teeling, *Sequel to personal narrative of the 'Irish rebellion' of 1798* (1832) · R. R. Madden, *United Irishmen* · M. Elliott, *Partners in revolution: the United Irishmen and France* (1982) · M. Elliott, *Wolfe Tone: prophet of Irish independence* (1989) · L. M. Cullen, 'The political structures of the Defenders', *Ireland and the French Revolution*, ed. H. Gough and D. Dickson (1990), 117–38 · *Correspondence of Charles, first Marquis Cornwallis*, ed. C. Ross, 3 vols. (1859), vol.2, pp. 389, 402
Likenesses J. H. Lynch, lithograph (after miniature), NG Ire.; repro. in Madden, *United Irishmen*

Teeling, Charles Hamilton (1778–1850). *See under* Teeling, Bartholomew (1774–1798).

Teerlinc [*née* Bening or Benninck], **Levina** (*d.* 1576), painter, was one of the daughters of Simon Bening, or Benninck (1483?–1561), the finest Bruges illuminator of the sixteenth century. She was presumably trained in her father's workshop, and came to England, into royal service, about 1545. She was by then married to George Teerlinc, who became a gentleman pensioner, while she was granted in November 1546 an annuity of £40 p.a., which continued until her death. The Teerlincs lived in more than one London parish, and Levina, for a painter, enjoyed an unusual degree of social status. In the new year's gift list of 1563 she is described as 'gentlewoman' and by her son, in 1595, as 'sworne as one of the privye chamber to the Quenes Majestie' (Strong, *Renaissance Miniature*, 54).

In that role Teerlinc annually presented a miniature. In

1553 she gave Mary I 'a smale picture of the Trynite' (Strong, *Renaissance Miniature*, 55), and nine more miniatures are recorded in the surviving new year's gift lists between 1559 and 1576. These were either portraits of the young queen or of her in a group with, for example, her knights of the Garter or on progress. As early as 1551 Teerlinc was sent to the Princess Elizabeth 'to drawe owt her picture' (ibid.). No signed or documented work by her is known and what can be assembled as an *œuvre* emerges from the few surviving miniatures between 1545 and 1575. The most important of these is that depicting the royal maundy (priv. coll.) and an early portrait of Elizabeth I (Royal Collection). Others can be more speculatively added to that nucleus, both miniatures and illuminations, but there can be no certainty that they are by her.

Based on this possible *œuvre*, Levina Teerlinc's style is that of the illuminators in the Ghent–Bruges tradition, although the portrait miniatures attributed to her show the influence of Lucas Hornebolt, her predecessor, and—in terms of composition—Hans Eworth. Their most characteristic feature is a head attached to a too small, spindly body. Their technique is awkward, thin, and often cursory, which is perhaps surprising in light of the regard in which she was held, as suggested by her very high salary. Resident in Stepney, she died on 23 June 1576.

ROY STRONG, *rev.*

Sources R. Strong and V. J. Murrell, *Artists of the Tudor court: the portrait miniature rediscovered, 1520–1620* (1983) [exhibition catalogue, V&A, 9 July – 6 Nov 1983] · R. Strong, *The English Renaissance miniature* (1983), 54–64

Teesdale, Sir Christopher Charles (1833–1893), army officer and courtier, was the son of Lieutenant-General Henry George Teesdale (1799–1871), of South Bersted, Sussex, and Rose Budd Dobree of Guernsey. He was born at Grahamstown, Cape Colony, on 1 June 1833. He entered the Royal Military Academy at Woolwich in May 1848, and received a commission as second lieutenant in the Royal Artillery on 18 June 1851. He went to Corfu in 1852, was promoted to first lieutenant on 22 April 1853, and in 1854 was appointed aide-de-camp to Colonel William Fenwick Williams, British commissioner with the Turkish army in Asia Minor during the Crimean War.

Teesdale, with Dr Humphry Sandwith, another member of the British commissioner's staff, accompanied Williams to Erzurum, and thence to Kars, where they arrived on 24 September 1854, a year before it was besieged by the Russian army. Williams returned to the headquarters of the Turkish army at Erzurum, leaving Teesdale at Kars to establish what discipline and order he could. During the whole winter Teesdale, aided by his interpreter, a Mr Zohrab, worked incessantly to secure the well-being of the troops. Support having arrived at Kars in March 1855, Teesdale returned to Erzurum, rejoined Williams, and was made a major in the Turkish army. In a letter from the Foreign Office dated 7 March 1855, the British government commended Teesdale's efforts to avert a repetition of the previous year's famine at the Kars garrison.

On 1 June 1855 a courier from Colonel Henry Atwell Lake informed Williams of the formidable Russian army assembled at Gumri, and the indication of a speedy advance upon Kars. On the following day Teesdale started with Williams and Sandwith for Kars, arriving there on 7 June. On the 9th Teesdale, with Zohrab his interpreter, went to his post at the Tahmasp batteries, and on the 12th he made a reconnaissance of the Russian camp. On the 16th the Russians, 25,000 strong, attacked early in the morning, but were repulsed by artillery fire. Two days later the Russians established a blockade of Kars, and shortly afterwards intercepted communication with Erzurum. The garrison of Kars was continually occupied in skirmishes with the enemy, and in the task of strengthening the fortifications. On 7 August an attack was made by the Russians, who were again beaten off.

Teesdale lived in Tahmasp Tabia with General Kmety, a Hungarian soldier for whom he acted as chief of staff. He was constantly engaged in harassing the Cossacks with parties of riflemen, or in menacing and attacking the Russian cavalry with a company of rifles and a couple of guns. In September the weather deteriorated, provisions grew scarce, cholera broke out, and desertions became frequent. At 4 a.m. on 29 September the Russian general, Muravyov, attacked the heights above Kars and on the opposite side of the river. At Tahmasp the advance was heard and preparations made to meet it. The guns were charged with grapeshot. Teesdale, returning from his rounds, flung himself into the most exposed battery in the redoubt, Yuksek Tabia, the key of the position. The Russians advanced steadily to effect a surprise; but they were received with crushing artillery fire. Some Russian troops penetrated the defences, but Teesdale assisted in organizing the defence, rallied his Turkish gunners, and the Russians were denied success. He prevented Turkish troops from massacring the Russian wounded, and he led two bayonet charges against advancing Russians. The battle of Kars lasted seven and a half hours. Near midday the Russians were driven off in great disorder but, having failed to capture Kars, resumed its siege.

Teesdale, who was hit by a piece of spent shell and received a severe contusion, was most favourably mentioned in dispatches. On 12 October General Williams wrote: 'My aide-de-camp, Teesdale, had charge of the central redoubt and fought like a lion.' After the battle Teesdale was decorated with the third class of the order of the Mejidiye, and promoted to lieutenant-colonel in the Turkish army.

Cholera, famine, and severe cold debilitated the garrison and there were nightly desertions. Selim Pasha's large army was expected in November to relieve the besieged troops, but never came. On 24 November 1855 it was considered impossible to hold out any longer, and Teesdale was sent with a flag of truce to the Russian camp to arrange for a meeting of the generals and to discuss terms of capitulation; these were arranged the following day, and on the 28th the garrison laid down its arms, and Teesdale and the other English officers became prisoners of war. They were hospitably treated by the Russians, and started on 30 November for Tiflis, which they reached on 8 December. In January 1856 Teesdale accompanied General

Williams to Ryazan, about 180 miles from Moscow. After having been presented to the tsar in March, they were given their liberty and returned to England.

Teesdale was made a CB on 21 June 1856, though still a lieutenant of Royal Artillery. He was also made an officer of the Légion d'honneur, received the medal for Kars, and on 25 September 1857 was awarded the Victoria Cross for acts of bravery at the battle of 29 September 1855. He was also decorated by the tsar.

From 1856 to 1859 Teesdale continued to serve as aide-de-camp to Williams, who had been appointed commandant of the Woolwich district. On 1 January 1858 he was promoted to be second captain in the Royal Artillery, and on the 15th of the same month to be brevet major in the army for distinguished service in the field. His gallantry recommended him to the prince consort, who was seeking to surround his eldest son with good influences, and on 9 November 1858 he was appointed equerry to the prince of Wales, a position which he held for thirty-two years. From 1859 to 1864 he was again aide-de-camp to Williams during his term of office as inspector-general of artillery at headquarters in London. He continued to rise in the army, becoming regimental colonel in 1882 and major-general in 1887. He was appointed aide-de-camp to Queen Victoria in 1877, and in 1887, on the occasion of the queen's jubilee, he was made KCMG.

In 1890 Teesdale resigned the appointment of equerry to the prince of Wales, and was appointed master of the ceremonies and extra equerry to the prince, positions which he held until his death. He retired from the army active list with a pension on 22 April 1892. He died, unmarried, on 1 November 1893 at his home, The Ark, South Bersted, Sussex, from a paralytic stroke, a few days after his return from a small estate he had in Germany. He was buried on 4 November in South Bersted churchyard.

R. H. VETCH, *rev.* K. D. REYNOLDS

Sources W. A. Lindsay, *The royal household* (1898) · Boase, *Mod. Eng. biog.* · H. Sandwith, *Narrative of the siege of Kars* (1856) · *The Times* (2 Nov 1893) · *The Times* (6 Nov 1893) · H. A. Lake, *Kars and our captivity in Russia* (1856) · *LondG* (26 Oct 1855) · *LondG* (10 Nov 1855) · *LondG* (11 Dec 1855)
Archives Royal Artillery Institution, Woolwich, London, papers, MD/1125
Likenesses photograph, 1856 (with Sir William Williams), NPG · P. Sebah, carte-de-visite, *c.*1863, NPG · W. & D. Downey, woodbury-type photograph, NPG; repro. in *The Cabinet Portrait Gallery*, 2 (1891) · D. J. Pound, line engraving (after photograph by Watkins), BM, NPG · portrait, Royal Collection
Wealth at death £15,141 13s. 9d.: probate, 23 Dec 1893, *CGPLA Eng. & Wales*

Teft, Elizabeth (*bap.* **1723**), poet, the daughter of Joshua and Eliza Teft, was baptized at Rothwell, Lincolnshire, on 27 October 1723. She was a member of the middling ranks, although not well off financially, a pious Anglican, and (in the wake of the second Jacobite rising) a convinced Hanoverian supporter. What is known about her comes almost entirely from the volume she published (apparently at her own risk, since no publisher's name appears) in 1747 as *Orinthia's Miscellanies, or, A Compleat Collection of Poems*. She had already had a poem printed in the

Gentleman's Magazine in June 1741, about her fantasy of solving her money problems with a lottery win. This provoked other *Gentleman's* contributors to reply, and she in turn answered one of them in July 1742. These magazine poems reappear in her volume.

Teft was *au fait* with the current literary scene (the works of Pope and of Richardson, for instance), and was also able to quote figures from the past, such as the seventeenth-century poet Henry King. She evidently moved in circles which appreciated her work: she writes of friendships and love affairs among this group, and several poems are written by request. The first in the volume reports how a female friend had urged her not to hide her light under a bushel, but to publish for the glory of God. (This counterbalances her own statement that she wanted the money.) Teft visited Cley in Norfolk (and wrote a rollicking poem about the hostess of an inn there) as well as London. In London she made a visit to Bedlam (the Bethlem Hospital) and attended a synagogue; equally a tourist in both places, she was repelled by Judaic worship only less than by the public exhibition of the insane. She may have worked for her living, since she says, 'my Character secures my Bread' (Teft, 153–4).

Some of Teft's most interesting poems discuss the status of women, the inequities of marriage and of education. In one poem, having complained of women's lack of access to the classical languages, she insists that she has no desire to change her own gender. She complains that women are denied a stake in their country, so that feelings of patriotism or an interest in politics are deprived of both a foundation and an outlet, and reduced to something little better than instinct. She writes fervently of her religious faith, and frankly about her unalluring personal appearance.

Nothing is known of her later life.   ISOBEL GRUNDY

Sources E. Teft, *Orinthia's miscellanies, or, A compleat collection of poems* (1747) · *GM*, 1st ser., 11 (June 1741) · *GM*, 1st ser., 11 (Oct 1741) · *GM*, 1st ser., 12 (June 1742) · *GM*, 1st ser., 12 (July 1742) · Blain, Clements & Grundy, *Feminist comp.* · *IGI*

Tegart, Sir Charles Augustus (1881–1946), police officer in India, was born in Londonderry on 5 October 1881, the second son of Joseph Poulter Tegart, Church of Ireland clergyman, and his wife, Georgina Johnston. His father was rector of Dunboyne, co. Meath. Educated at Portora Royal School, Enniskillen, and Trinity College, Dublin, Tegart joined the Indian police in June 1901. He was assigned to Bengal, and, after training and probation, became superintendent of Patna.

Tegart transferred to Calcutta in 1906 with the rank of acting deputy commissioner to direct the special branch of the Bengal criminal investigation department, an élite unit, renamed the intelligence branch (IB) in 1913, when it employed 50 officers and 127 men. Following the province's unpopular administrative partition in 1905, Bengal endured a wave of political violence, organized by militant Indian nationalists; terrorist attacks between 1907 and 1917 numbered over 200. Undercover work engrossed Tegart. Tall, lean, and blue-eyed, he could never have passed for a Bengali, despite fluency in the language, but he donned false beard and turban to visit rough areas at night as a Sikh taxi driver. His special talent was for recruiting and managing informers, whom he met alone in unlikely places at high risk to himself. Colleagues sometimes complained that he played his cards too close to his chest; Tegart answered that his best agents confided in him as an individual. A tough disciplinarian, he yet enjoyed friendly relations with subordinates, British and Indian, who respected his courage. He received the king's police medal in 1911 and was made an MVO in 1912. Promotion to deputy commissioner came a year later.

In the eyes of Bengali insurgents the First World War offered ideal conditions for a rebellion. Refused permission to enlist, Tegart remained in India, monitoring plots to import armaments from Germany. The police operation culminated in a raid on 9 September 1915, when the key figure in the German scheme, J. N. Mukherji, was killed in an exchange of gunfire, allegedly by Tegart himself, who was now more than ever a marked man. In June 1916 his favourite assistant, B. K. Chatterjee, became the eleventh Bengal IB officer to be murdered since the start of the war. Tegart gave his Indian staff the freedom to return to normal police units without dishonour; none took the option. Conscious of the ostracism suffered by native policemen, he thought they deserved better pay and housing. From August 1916 the Bengal government fully utilized emergency powers; with 804 terrorist suspects interned by June 1917, political crime fell sharply, allowing Tegart to go to Europe and join the army. He was nevertheless recalled to India in November 1917 to advise Sir Sidney Rowlatt's inquiry into sedition. 'He appears to treat the whole thing as a game', remarked Rowlatt (Curry, 7). Cheerful banter, fearless bravado, and delight in the chase all contributed to the emergent legend of 'Tegart of the Indian police'. He even used a small bomb as a paperweight: one day, supposing it no longer live, he threw it across the office in jest and destroyed part of the wall. Annie Besant, of the Indian National Congress, accused him of punching suspects and threatening one with a gun; the Bengal government concluded that these allegations were baseless.

After serving in France with the Royal Field Artillery later in 1918 and then in the Rhineland with the occupation army, Tegart undertook intelligence work in Britain and Ireland (1919–23). As a Unionist, he deplored the outcome of the Anglo-Irish War. His marriage to Kathleen Frances Herbert took place on 7 June 1922; they had no children.

Tegart's return to Calcutta as commissioner of police in 1923 followed the recrudescence of terrorism. The governor of Bengal, Lord Lytton, thought an Irishman might have insight into revolutionary nationalism. In fact, Tegart gave it little credence—young Bengalis were so emotional, he judged, that a few evil men could easily manipulate them. His presence raised morale in the European community. Known to friends as Mike, he captained the Calcutta A team at polo and drove around in an open car with his Staffordshire bull terrier perched on the hood behind him. Radical nationalists saw him as the insolent embodiment of an oppressive police state. A businessman called Ernest Day who bore a resemblance to Tegart was shot dead by mistake in January 1924. After the reintroduction of internment in 1925 police quelled the terror campaign within two years. Non-political violent crime also halved during Tegart's term of office. A CIE from 1917, he became a knight in 1926. Subsequent honours included CSI (1931), LLD (1933), and KCIE (1937).

When emergency powers lapsed in April 1930, released detainees made an audacious foray on Chittagong. Internment resumed, and Tegart set about tracking down terrorist suspects once more. A bomb thrower in Dalhousie Square, Calcutta, narrowly failed to assassinate him on 25 August 1930. Soon afterwards he commanded an assault on rebels hiding in the French enclave of Chandannagar. Having arrived in Britain on leave in 1931, he resigned from the police on being appointed to the Council of India (1932–6), the body advising the secretary of state in London. He was forthright in voicing his opinions, using a lecture to the Royal Empire Society on 1 November 1932 to accuse the Calcutta Corporation of employing known terrorists as schoolteachers.

The Colonial Office wanted Tegart to be inspector-general of the Palestine police in 1937. He refused but joined Sir David Petrie in visiting the mandate (December 1937 – January 1938) to advise on dealing with Arab guerrillas. Staying to oversee implementation of their report, he did not finally leave until May 1939. By then, a 2 metre high barbed-wire fence ('Tegart's wall') ran all along the frontier with Lebanon and Syria and some fifty fortified police stations ('Tegarts') had been built. His survival of an ambush on 31 December 1938 seemed further proof of a charmed life.

During the Second World War Tegart worked for the Ministry of Supply until 1942, assessing factories to decide allocation of resources. He then became head of the intelligence (anti-black market) bureau of the Ministry of Food. Despite suffering from arthritis and heart disease, he chose not to retire, dying suddenly at his home, the Croft House, Warminster, Wiltshire, on 6 April 1946. His wife survived him.   JASON TOMES

Sources J. Curry, *Tegart of the Indian Police* (1960) • M. Silvestri, '"An Irishman is specially suited to be a policeman": Sir Charles Tegart and revolutionary terrorism in Bengal', *History Ireland*, 8/4 (2000), 40–44 • *The Times* (8 April 1946) • C. Tegart, *Terrorism in India* (1932) • R. Popplewell, *Intelligence and imperial defence: British intelligence and the defence of the Indian empire, 1904–1924* (1995) • P. Griffiths, *To guard my people: the history of the Indian police* (1971) • m. cert. • CGPLA Eng. & Wales (1946)

Archives St Ant. Oxf., Middle East Centre, corresp. and papers relating to Palestine • U. Cam., Centre of South Asian Studies, corresp. and papers | BL OIOC, files relating to security in Bengal

Likenesses W. Stoneman, photograph, 1937, NPG • photograph, repro. in Curry, *Tegart*, frontispiece • photograph, repro. in Silvestri, 'An Irishman', 41

Wealth at death £16,114 15s. 10d.: probate, 20 July 1946, CGPLA Eng. & Wales

Tegetmeier, William Bernhardt (1816–1912), naturalist and journalist, was born on 4 November 1816 at High Street, Colnbrook, Buckinghamshire, the eldest of three sons of Godfrey Conrad Tegetmeier (*d.* 1841), a surgeon

William Bernhardt Tegetmeier (1816–1912), by Cameron Studio

who had emigrated from the American colonies, and Sarah, widow of Carl Luer and daughter of a Dr Norman of Langport in Somerset. The family moved to London when Tegetmeier was twelve, and he was apprenticed in 1831 to his father for five years. From 1833 to 1837 he attended lectures at University College, London, taking honours five times. His training then continued at University College Hospital, where he acted as clinical clerk to John Elliotson. For about two years Tegetmeier assisted Frederick Gee in Brackley, Northamptonshire, but he revolted from the drudgery of provincial medical practice.

In 1841 Tegetmeier returned to London, where he attended John Hoppus's lectures on mental philosophy at University College and practised as a mesmeric healer. He also briefly taught at a boys' school. In 1845 he became lecturer on domestic economy at the Home and Colonial Society's training college, and married Anne Edwards Stone (1826–1909), mistress of the infant department of the practising school attached to the college. Both were instantly dismissed as a result, but Tegetmeier was subsequently reinstated and held his position until 1866. He began to write schoolbooks, notably a *Manual of Domestic Economy* (1858; 14th edn, 1894) which was widely used in industrial schools for girls. The Tegetmeiers lived in north London and had four daughters (two predeceasing their parents) and one son.

From an early age Tegetmeier was an enthusiastic breeder of poultry and pigeons, both fancy and racing, and he became the leading authority on these birds and

many other aspects of natural history. In 1853 some of his earliest writing on these subjects appeared in the *Cottage Gardener* and as a short book, *Profitable Poultry*. Tegetmeier's best-known works, the *Poultry Book* (1867; enlarged, 1873) and *Pigeons* (1868; enlarged, 1873), included coloured plates by his friend Harrison Weir. He also published standard works on pheasants and game birds. In 1855 Tegetmeier came to the attention of Charles Darwin, who was studying pigeons and other domestic birds as part of the research which led to the *Origin of Species* (1859) and *Variation of Animals and Plants under Domestication* (1868). Tegetmeier introduced Darwin to the institutions of the fancy, took him to shows, and answered numerous queries in correspondence.

Tegetmeier was also a keen apiarist. After he moved from Wood Green to Muswell Hill in 1856, he built observation hives in the garden and experimented on interbreeding and hive formation. His most significant finding, announced at the 1858 meeting of the British Association for the Advancement of Science, involved the much debated question of how bees built their cells in the form of perfect hexagons. Tegetmeier showed that bees actually constructed cylindrical cells; only when raised up in contact with one another did these cells gain their characteristic mathematical regularity. Darwin extended these experiments and cited them in the *Origin*, recognizing that Tegetmeier had given a physical, material explanation to a phenomenon which many naturalists had seen as evidencing divine design. For his part, Tegetmeier became a convinced evolutionist, and always prided himself on his connection with the celebrated naturalist.

With the success of his books, Tegetmeier increasingly turned to journalism as his chief source of income. In 1859 he began to write on natural history for the weekly *Field*, and within a few years became its chief correspondent on poultry and pigeons. Over a period of nearly fifty years Tegetmeier wrote thousands of articles, notes, and reviews on a wide variety of subjects. From 1882 he became principal leader writer and a frequent reviewer for *The Queen*, the leading women's weekly newspaper. Here Tegetmeier received extensive assistance from his wife and drew on his own knowledge of domestic economy. He was a firm tory, profoundly opposed to the campaign for women's rights and all extensions of the suffrage from 1832 onwards. He believed in a deity, but was not a Christian.

'Old Teg', with his bushy beard, broad-brimmed hat, and immoderate enthusiasm for pigeons, poultry, cock-fighting, book-collecting, bee-keeping, and scientific zoology, became celebrated as one of the notable eccentrics of metropolitan journalism. In 1857 he was a founder of the Savage Club, whose members included George Augustus Sala, G. A. Henty, and Gustave Doré. Through burlesque and satire, the Savages celebrated the bohemian literary culture which flourished during the mid-Victorian expansion of periodical publishing.

Tegetmeier died in Hampstead on 19 November 1912, and was buried in Marylebone cemetery, Finchley, on 23

November. 'If he was not a great man', an obituarist wrote, 'he was, at any rate, a great character' (*Daily Telegraph*, 21 Nov 1912).   J. A. SECORD

Sources E. W. Richardson, *A veteran naturalist: being the life and work of W. B. Tegetmeier* (1916) • W. B. Tegetmeier, 'How I became a naturalist', *The Tatler* (13 April 1904) • J. A. Secord, 'Nature's fancy: Charles Darwin and the breeding of pigeons', *Isis*, 72 (1981), 163–86 • *The correspondence of Charles Darwin*, ed. F. Burkhardt and S. Smith, [13 vols.] (1985–) • *CGPLA Eng. & Wales* (1913)
Archives CUL, letters to Darwin
Likenesses H. Herkomer, etching, 1879, repro. in Richardson, *Veteran naturalist*, frontispiece • Cameron Studio, photograph, NPG [*see illus.*] • portraits, repro. in Richardson, *Veteran naturalist*
Wealth at death £7330 6s. 10d.: probate, 8 Jan 1913, *CGPLA Eng. & Wales*

Tegg, Thomas (1776–1846), publisher, was born on 4 March 1776 at Wimbledon, Surrey, the son of Thomas Tegg (1740?–1781) and his wife, Hannah, née Veargitt (1747–1785). His father, a prosperous grocer, died in 1781. His mother remarried the following year, but she died shortly thereafter, in November 1785, leaving Thomas a nine-year-old orphan.

Thomas Tegg's deceased parents must have left enough money for him to attend boarding-school at Galashiels, Selkirkshire, Scotland, where he spent four happy years, due in large measure to a kindly schoolmaster. However, this pleasant period in his life altered dramatically when he became an apprentice to a tyrannical and drunken bookseller at Dalkeith, Alexander Meggett. Unable to endure his employer's abuse, he ran away, and for several years lived by his wits and hard work, taking different jobs, sometimes with booksellers, throughout the British Isles and Ireland. Just short of his twentieth birthday he decided to go to London to make his fortune in the book trade. There he won and lost several jobs before being hired by John and Arthur Arch, Quaker booksellers in Gracechurch Street.

With an unexpected legacy of £200 in 1800 Tegg found a business partner and initiated 'Tegg and Dewick', a bookselling business at 6 Westmorland Buildings, Aldgate. He also now felt able to marry Mary Holland (1781–1852) in St Bride's Church on 30 April that same year. Unfortunately the business failed, leaving Tegg nearly bankrupt. Nevertheless he qualified for a licence as a country auctioneer, which allowed him to travel throughout Britain buying odd lots of books to sell later at auction. His wife served as clerk and cashier. This venture proved so successful that he continued holding nightly auctions in London for many years.

Between 1801 and 1804 Tegg entered into partnership with Castleman. Their shop, the Eccentric Book Warehouse, was located at 122 St John's Street, West Smithfield, London. They not only sold books at retail, but also held auctions and published semi-lurid Gothic tales as chapbooks with such titles as *Albani, or, The Murder of his Child*; *Almagro and Claude, or, Monastic Murder Exemplified in the Dreadful Doom of an Unfortunate Nun*; and *Domestic Misery, or, The Victim of Seduction*. In 1804 Tegg severed his connection with Castleman and went into business for himself at 111 Cheapside, premises he kept for the next twenty years. In 1824 he acquired the Old Mansion House at 73 Cheapside, the location of the firm for the rest of his life.

From the outset Tegg's publishing business, as distinct from auctions and the sale of stationery, divided itself into three main categories. He issued many reprints of books which had gone out of copyright; he purchased remainders, sometimes with the copyrights, from other publishers, and sold them at greatly reduced prices; and he produced a number of original works, often on commission. Tegg wrote:

> My line is to watch the expiration of copyright and then produce to the public either current works at a cheaper rate, or to revive works of merit which have been lost to the public by the perversity of authors, by bungling of the first publishers, or by excessive price; and I have in this way disinterred a number of good books, which, in my management, have had a great sale.   (Tegg, *Extension of Copyright*)

At a time when Dr Samuel Johnson's *Dictionary* was selling for 5 guineas Tegg came out with an edition at 2 guineas. He published several abridgements of Blackstone's legal *Commentaries*, one of which sold for as little as 4s. 6d. Other standard works he reissued included Adam Smith's *Wealth of Nations*; ten volumes of John Locke's works; Burton's *Anatomy of Melancholy*; Hooker's *Ecclesiastical Polity*; and the writings of Bishop Butler. In general Tegg opposed copyright, since it interfered with his reprint business. He was dismayed at the prospect of an even longer term for copyright if Sergeant Talfourd and his supporters prevailed: an extension from twenty-eight to forty-two years, or seven years beyond the life of an author, whichever was the longer term.

Authors targeted Tegg for opprobrium. Thomas Carlyle wrote to the House of Commons:

> May it please your honourable house, to forbid all Thomas Teggs, and other extraneous persons … to steal from him his small winnings, for a space of sixty years, at shortest. After sixty years, unless your honourable house provides otherwise, they may begin to steal.   (*Parliamentary Debates, Commons*, 9 Sept 1838)

Tegg lost this struggle, and copyright was extended in 1842, but by then he was resigned to watching others struggle to produce cheap reprints of standard and popular works.

A second part of Tegg's business involved acquiring and subsequently selling remainders, the dead stock of others. One of the attractions of these transactions was that the expenses were usually borne by the original publishers who had either fallen on hard times or suffered bad luck. Certainly, opportunism marked Tegg throughout his career. The panic of 1825–6 devastated publishers and printers who owned the copyrights to Sir Walter Scott's novels. Tegg predictably took advantage of this and hastened to a sale by Hurst and Robinson where he bought 'the best of Scott's novels' at 4d. a volume. In this instance he acquired only the leftover stock, not the copyrights.

The firm of Colburn and Bentley became one of Tegg's best sources for remainders during the turbulent years from 1829 to 1832. At the conclusion of their partnership, Tegg agreed to buy the remainders of twenty-seven works from them, among which were: *Adventures of an Irish Gentleman*, *Adventures of Perkin Warbeck*, *Caleb Williams*, *Basil Barrington*, *Clarence*, *Country Curate*, *Denounced*, *The English at Home*, *The English Army in France*, *Gertrude*, *Hope Lesley*, *Journal of the Heart*, *Midsummer Medley*, *Mussulman*, and *Tales of an Indian Caliph*.

In 1834 John Murray reluctantly concluded that he had to dispose of the remaining volumes of his Family Library, and so turned to Thomas Tegg. In what became the largest outlay of his career, Tegg paid £8000 for 355,000 volumes of the library. According to their agreement, Tegg did not acquire the copyrights of the Murray volumes, but he did get all the leftover bound stock; the stereotype plates; woodcuts; copies bound in boards; and copies in quires.

In addition to reprinting out-of-copyright books and selling remainders, Tegg became a major publisher of new books. Some were little more than extended pamphlets, while others were multi-volume editions. When news reached London of Horatio Nelson's death at Trafalgar in 1805, Tegg hastily commissioned someone to do a biography with a woodcut portrait, 5000 copies of which were sold for 6*d*. each. Tegg also produced 4000 copies of a life of Napoleon Bonaparte at 6*d*. Both were at the low end of the price scale, whereas his monumental *London Encyclopedia* (1825), in twenty-two super royal octavo volumes, commanded many guineas.

Representative samples among his entirely new publications include: *Collection of Gothic Tales and Romances* (1811); *Comic Song Book* (1817); *A New Chronology, or, Historical Companion* (1811); *Handbook for Emigrants* (1839); *Present for Apprentices* (2nd edn, 1848); and *Treasury of Wit and Anecdote* (1842).

Thomas Tegg was the head of a large family of twelve children, and did what he could to further the business interests of his sons. Two of them, James and Samuel, emigrated to Australia in 1834 and established bookstores in Sydney and Hobart Town. Besides selling books, they published original Australian works and distributed new books imported from their father in London. Thomas was uncertain which, if any, of his sons would want to continue his publishing enterprise, especially after James died unexpectedly in Australia in 1845. **William Tegg** (1816–1895), publisher, was born in Cheapside on 29 May 1816. He was articled to an engraver before joining his father's firm. In his will Thomas provided that William could select £5000 worth of books from the firm's stock prior to the rest being sold at auction. With this legacy William decided to carry on the business, although on a more modest scale and without the flamboyance of the founder.

Throughout his life Thomas Tegg took great pride in his accomplishments and would not let others forget his humble origins. He characterized himself as 'the broom that swept the booksellers' warehouses', and boasted in 1838, 'I have published more books, and sold them at a cheaper rate, than any bookseller in Britain' (letter to the editor of *The Times*). His reputation, on the other hand, rested on his exploitation of the reprint and remainder trade. To appreciate Tegg's achievement it is instructive to

compare his publishing output with that of a major firm like that of George Routledge. After fifty years in business from 1836 to 1888, Routledge estimated that he had issued approximately 5000 works, an average of two every week. Similarly, Tegg claimed to have published 4000 titles after forty years (1800–40), also averaging two volumes per week. An even more revealing comparison is their respective net worth at the time of their deaths: Routledge's estate had a value of £80,000, while Tegg's amounted to £90,000.

Thomas Tegg died in Wimbledon on 21 April 1846 while his youngest son, twenty-year-old Alfred Byron Tegg, was at Pembroke College, Oxford. According to the *Gentleman's Magazine*, Alfred 'was so affected by the shock of his father's death, that his own followed shortly after, and their bodies were deposited on the same day on the grandfather's coffin in Wimbledon churchyard' (*GM*).

Tegg's obituary reiterated the theme of his hard-won success: 'Mr. Tegg's early career was one of struggling and difficulty, and his life presents a striking illustration of how much can be accomplished by perseverance and earnestness of purpose' (*GM*).

In 1847 William moved the firm to 12 Pancras Lane, London. Three years later it was relocated to 85 Queen Street where it remained until 1860, when it returned to 12 Pancras Lane for another twenty-three years. William continued the practice of reprinting standard works, buying up remainders, and commissioning new publications, particularly schoolbooks, children's literature, humour, reference works, and practical manuals. He borrowed the pseudonym Peter Parley to write books for the young, and his series Talks with Animals ran through twelve editions. From 1854 to 1875 he was a member of the common council of the City of London.

In 1883 William moved to 12 Doughty Street, and retired from the business in 1890. He died in London on 23 December 1895 and was survived by his wife, Mary Ann.

JAMES J. BARNES and PATIENCE P. BARNES

Sources DNB · J. J. Barnes and P. P. Barnes, 'Reassessing the reputation of Thomas Tegg, London publisher, 1776–1846', *Book History*, 3 (2000), 45–60 · *Memoir of the late Thomas Tegg: abridged from his autobiography by permission of his son, William Tegg* (1870) · *GM*, 2nd ser., 25 (1846), 650 · H. Curwen, *A history of booksellers, the old and the new* (1873) · R. A. Gettmann, *A Victorian publisher: a study of the Bentley papers* (1970) · S. Bennett, 'John Murray's Family Library and the cheapening of books in early nineteenth-century Britain', *Studies in Bibliography*, 29 (1976), 139–76 · Boase, *Mod. Eng. biog.*, 3.907 · P. A. H. Brown, *London publishers and printers, c.1800–1870* (1982) · *Publishers' Circular*, 64 (4 Jan 1896), 6 · private information (2004) [Michael Crellin; Gwen Crellin, a descendant of the Tegg family] · T. Tegg, *Extension of copyright* (1840), 1 [letter to Lord John Russell in pamphlet form] · *Parliamentary debates, Commons*, 42 (9 Sept 1838), 1072

Archives BL, corresp. with William Hone, Add. MSS 40120, 40856, 41071, *passim* · JRL, Methodist Archives and Research Centre, letters, mostly to James Everett

Wealth at death under £90,000: 20 Aug 1847, will

Tegg, William (1816–1895). *See under* Tegg, Thomas (1776–1846).

Teichman, Sir Eric (1884–1944), diplomatist and traveller, whose original name of Erik Teichmann was changed by deed poll in 1906, was born at Eltham, Kent, on 16 January 1884, the youngest of the six children of Emil Teichmann, merchant, of Chislehurst, Kent, and his wife, Mary Lydia, daughter of Frederick Augustus Schroeter, a London fur merchant. His father, originally from Ansbach, then part of Prussia, settled in England in the 1860s and became senior partner in a fur trading company. Eric Teichman was educated at Charterhouse School and at Gonville and Caius College, Cambridge, and represented the university against Oxford in the point-to-point steeplechase of 1903. After taking an ordinary degree by way of the medieval and modern languages tripos in 1904, he spent nearly two years studying on the continent and travelling extensively in Russia. In December 1906 he passed the competitive examination to join the consular service, and in January 1907 he went to Peking (Beijing) as a student interpreter. Although he was already suffering severely from arthritis and a few years later was badly injured in a riding accident, he never allowed this to interfere with his love for riding, shooting, and exploration. He travelled much in central Asia and spent most of the early part of his career on special service on the Tibetan border and in the loess highlands of the north-west, regions upon which he became the acknowledged authority.

In June 1919 Teichman was appointed CIE and promoted assistant Chinese secretary in Peking, serving under Sidney Barton. In 1921 he returned to London to work in the Foreign Office; while there he met and married Ellen Cecilia, widow of Major Douglas Scott Niven, and daughter of Marmaduke John Teesdale, of Walton on the Hill, Surrey. There were no children; his wife survived him.

Teichman returned to Peking in 1922 to replace Barton as Chinese secretary; he remained in that post until his retirement in September 1936. He was appointed CMG in 1927 and KCMG in 1933, and was given the local rank of counsellor of embassy in 1927. Between September 1935 and January 1936 he journeyed home through central Asia in order to carry out a special mission to Urumchi on the way. He travelled from Suiyuan to Kashgar by motor-truck, crossed the Pamir and the Karakoram ranges to Gilgit by pony and on foot, and then travelled by air to Delhi. He then wrote *Journey to Turkistan* (1937), his 'swan song of Asiatic travel'. He had previously published *Travels of a Consular Officer in North-West China* (1921) and *Travels of a Consular Officer in Eastern Tibet* (1922), and in 1938 he published *Affairs of China*. He had been awarded the Murchison grant by the Royal Geographical Society in 1925. His publications were of great value to contemporary students of east Asia. In February 1942 he agreed to go out again for one year as adviser to the British embassy at Chungking (Chongqing). He again travelled home through central Asia but published no record of this journey. On his return for the last time from China he was appointed GCMG in 1944. On 3 December of the same year he was shot dead by an American soldier whom he disturbed poaching in the grounds of his Norfolk home at Honingham Hall.

J. T. PRATT, *rev.* FRANK DIKÖTTER

Sources *The Times* (5 Dec 1944) · private information (1959) · personal knowledge (1959) · *CGPLA Eng. & Wales* (1945)
Archives University of Bristol Library, special collections, letters
Likenesses Miss Jacobs, crayon drawing, Honingham Hall, Norfolk
Wealth at death £138,654 2s. 6d.: probate, 15 June 1945, *CGPLA Eng. & Wales*

Teignmouth. For this title name *see* Shore, John, first Baron Teignmouth (1751–1834).

Teilo [St Teilo, Eliau, Eliud] (*supp. fl. c.*550), holy man and supposed bishop, was the founder of the episcopal church of Llandeilo Fawr in Dyfed. By the twelfth century he had been appropriated by the expanding see of Llandaff and erroneously turned into its second bishop. Along with David and Padarn, Teilo of Llandeilo was one of the most important saints in south-west Wales, although by the eleventh century his church had fallen within the sphere of the kingdom of Morgannwg in the south-east, which facilitated its eventual appropriation by Llandaff. His feast day is celebrated on 9 February. As a hypocoristic of a type very well attested among Irish and British saints of the sixth century, but only rarely thereafter, the name Teilo is good evidence for the saint's floruit, and for the antiquity of his cult. Although there are passing notices of Teilo in the twelfth-century lives of other Welsh saints, the main surviving accounts of his alleged life and deeds are two related versions of the *Vita sancti Teiliaui*. This life was composed as part of the ecclesiastical propaganda in the Book of Llandaff, compiled under Bishop Urban in the early twelfth century and intended to provide the episcopal church with a demonstrable early history. Consequently the information supplied about Teilo is of uncertain reliability at best. Much of the text seems to be a rewriting of material from a (lost) life of St David with the intention of elevating the position of Teilo and therefore, of course, that of the church of Llandaff. There is also a Middle English metrical life of Telyou preserved in BL, Egerton MS 2810, folios 94–99, which is based on the earlier *Vita* and was possibly composed at Gloucester.

The earlier version of the life of Teilo (traditionally attributed to Geoffrey, brother of Bishop Urban) states that he was of noble parentage, while the second version, contained in the Book of Llandaff, adds that he was born at 'Eccluis Gunniau', near Penally in Dyfed, and names his parents as Ensig ap Hydwn Ddu and Gwenhaf ferch Llifonwy, thus making him the uncle of St *Euddogwy. This link to Euddogwy (Oudoceus) was probably intended to provide Teilo with a suitable connection to his successor to the bishopric of Llandaff and casts suspicion over the whole genealogical scheme. Both versions claim that Teilo was a disciple of St Dyfrig *archipresul*, whom, it is claimed, he was to succeed as bishop of Llandaff. However, Rhigyfarch's life of St David, composed *c.*1090, has Eliud as disciple of David, perhaps suggesting that the connection to Dyfrig was also a later invention at Llandaff. The *Vita sancti Teiliaui* also contains an elaborate description of the alleged journey of David, Teilo, and Padarn to Jerusalem, as well as an account of Teilo's visit to Brittany, including Dol. His death, at or near Llandeilo, is said to have led to a three-way conflict over possession of his body between the churches of Penally, Llandeilo, and Llandaff, which was resolved by its miraculous multiplication into three bodies—though the author of the life clearly regarded the one preserved at Llandaff as the original!

The information about the saint contained in this life has been coloured by the interests of Llandaff to such an extent that its reliability as a source for hagiographical (never mind historical) information about the original Teilo, patron of Llandeilo Fawr, is uncertain. However, evidence for the earlier history, or at least the existence, of his cult and episcopal church has been preserved in the marginalia entered into the so-called Lichfield gospels during the eighth and ninth centuries, when the manuscript was still housed at Llandeilo. These include land grants to 'God and St Teilo' (that is, his church) as well as manumissions and other documents witnessed by the 'bishop of Teilo'. In addition, the text in the Book of Llandaff entitled *Braint Teilo* ('The privilege of Teilo'), which was probably originally composed in the late tenth or early eleventh century, describes the privileges and immunities granted to the church of Teilo by the kings of Morgannwg (Glamorgan), and demonstrates that by that time the church of Teilo was located within the sphere of Morgannwg—a precondition of its eventual appropriation by Llandaff. The topographic evidence for the cult of Teilo in Wales further demonstrates that the appropriation of the saint and his church by Llandaff was a late development, since it is focused on Llandeilo and not Llandaff. The dedications are therefore concentrated in western Carmarthenshire (around Llandeilo) and western Pembrokeshire (in Penally and Daugleddyf), with extensions in Glamorgan (four dedications), Monmouthshire (four), Brecknockshire (two), and also in Radnorshire and Cardiganshire (with one dedication each). The distribution closely mirrors that of St David's cult, possibly reflecting the earlier association between these two important south-west Welsh saints. According to his Llandaff life, Teilo visited Brittany and consequently it is not surprising to find dedications to him there, especially in Cornouaille, including the church and parish of Landelau and the church of Landêliau in Plévin.   DAVID E. THORNTON

Sources A. W. Wade-Evans, ed. and trans., *Vitae sanctorum Britanniae et genealogiae* (1944) · J. G. Evans and J. Rhys, eds., *The text of the Book of Llan Dâv reproduced from the Gwysaney manuscript* (1893) · P. C. Bartrum, ed., *Early Welsh genealogical tracts* (1966) · E. Owen, *A catalogue of the manuscripts relating to Wales in the British Museum* (1900), 816–17 · W. Davies, 'Braint Teilo', *BBCS*, 26 (1974–6), 123–37 · D. Jenkins and M. E. Owen, 'The Welsh marginalia in the Lichfield gospels [pt 1]', *Cambridge Medieval Celtic Studies*, 5 (1983), 37–66 · D. Jenkins and M. E. Owen, 'The Welsh marginalia in the Lichfield gospels [pt 2]', *Cambridge Medieval Celtic Studies*, 7 (1984), 91–120 · G. H. Doble, *Lives of the Welsh saints*, ed. D. S. Evans (1971) · E. G. Bowen, *The settlements of the Celtic saints in Wales*, 2nd edn (1956)

Telfair, Charles (1778–1833), naturalist, was born at Belfast and arrived in Mauritius as a naval surgeon on one of the British blockading ships in 1810. He settled there, practised as a surgeon, and served as government secretary at Bourbon (Réunion), and private secretary to Sir Robert Farquhar at Mauritius. He also held the posts of guardian of vacant estates and secretary to the vice-admiralty court, and became something of a sugar 'baron', introducing the first horizontal roller mill at the Bel-Ombre factory in 1819. He became a correspondent of Sir William Jackson Hooker, sent plants to Kew, became honorary supervisor of the botanical garden at Pamplemousses, Mauritius, 1826–9, and established a botanical garden at Réunion. He also collected bones of an extinct bird, the solitaire, from Rodriguez, which he forwarded to the Zoological Society, London, and to the Andersonian Museum, Glasgow. From 1829 to 1833 Telfair was president of the Société d'Histoire Naturelle at Port Louis, a society which he co-founded. In 1830 he published *Some account of the state of slavery at Mauritius since the British occupation in 1810, in refutation of anonymous charges … against government and that colony.*

Telfair was married to Annabella Chamberlain. He died at Port Louis, Mauritius, on 14 July 1833 following a short but painful illness, and was buried in the cemetery there. Hooker commemorated him by the African genus *Telfairia* in the cucumber family. His wife, who died at Port Louis on 23 May 1832, also communicated specimens of Mauritius algae to W. J. Hooker and drawings to *Curtis's Botanical Magazine* (1826–30).

G. S. BOULGER, rev. ANDREW GROUT

Sources W. H. Harvey, 'Notice of a collection of algae, communicated to Dr Hooker by the late Mrs Charles Telfair, from "Cap Malheureux", in the Mauritius', *Journal of Botany*, 1 (1834), 147–57, esp. 149–51 · G. Rouillard and J. Guého, *Le Jardin des Pamplemousses, 1729–1979* (1983) · E. Nelmes and W. Cuthbertson, eds., *Curtis's Botanical Magazine: dedications, 1827–1927* [1931], 14–16 · H. E. Strickland and A. G. Melville, *The dodo and its kindred* (1848), 52 · F. A. Stafleu and R. S. Cowan, *Taxonomic literature: a selective guide*, 2nd edn, 6, Regnum Vegetabile, 115 (1986), 205–6 · Desmond, *Botanists*, rev. edn · A. MacGregor and A. Headon, 'Re-inventing the Ashmolean: natural history and natural theology at Oxford in the 1820s to 1850s', *Archives of Natural History*, 27 (2000), 369–406 · *Sugar in Mauritius*, Public Relations Office of the Sugar Industry, 4th edn (1987), chap. 1
Archives AM Oxf., corresp. · RBG Kew, letters · RBG Kew, plant specimens
Likenesses oils, Royal Society of Arts, Port Louis, Mauritius; repro. in Nelmes and Cuthbertson, *Curtis's Botanical Magazine dedications*, 15
Wealth at death died in debt: *Asiatic Journal*, new ser., 13/2 (March 1834), 173

Telfair, Edward (c.1735–1807), merchant and politician in the United States of America, was born at Town Head, Lanark, of unknown parentage. He attended Kirkcudbright School on the Solway Firth, but nothing is known of his early life. He entered the mercantile business and at age twenty-three his firm sent him to Virginia as its agent. He moved from Virginia to Halifax, North Carolina, and in 1766 to Georgia, presumably to join his brother William who had established himself as a merchant in Savannah three years earlier. Edward and his brother affiliated with Basil Cowper in a new firm, Cowper and Telfairs. The brothers also established a separate partnership, William and Edward Telfair & Co. Their business experience and acumen soon made the Telfairs prosperous. Like other merchants Edward Telfair acquired extensive land grants. His properties, including a sawmill in St George parish, made him known throughout the province. St Paul's parish (later Augusta) elected him to the Commons house in 1768. On 18 May 1774 he married Sarah (Sally) Gibbons of Savannah and the marriage produced three sons, Josiah, Thomas, and Alexander, and three daughters, Mary, Sarah, and Margaret.

Like other Savannah merchants Telfair opposed British efforts to tax internal colonial trade during the 1760s and early 1770s. He attended the protest meeting at Tondee's Tavern on 10 August 1774 and was elected to the extra-legal provincial congress that met on 18 January 1775. News in the spring of 1775 of the fighting between British troops and Massachusetts's militia men at Lexington heightened revolutionary fervour in Georgia, and Telfair was one of those who broke into the royal magazine in Savannah and took out a powder supply, sending some to the American patriot army surrounding Boston. Despite that bold action Telfair hesitated to declare for independence. Both his brother, William, and his partner, Cowper, remained loyal to the crown. For his reluctance to take the oath of allegiance to the American patriot association prescribed by the continental congress, the Georgia council of safety listed Telfair's name among those whose going about was considered dangerous to the liberties of the people. After Georgia joined the other twelve colonies in a bid for independence, Telfair cast his lot with the friends of congress. The Georgia electorate forgave his tardiness and elected him to the continental congress in 1777 and continued to do so annually thereafter until he declined to accept the honour in 1785. In congress he served inconspicuously on the commerce committee, and on behalf of Georgia signed the articles of confederation, which would bind the former colonies until the adoption of the constitution. In addition to his service in congress, Burke county (formerly St George parish) elected him to the Georgia legislature in 1783.

In 1786, with the war over and the capital moved from Savannah to Augusta, Telfair served his first term as governor of the state. Over the opposition of the Savannah authorities he had an armed guard remove the public records to Augusta. He was re-elected under the new state constitution of 1788 and served two further terms from 1789 until 1794. As governor he welcomed President George Washington to Georgia in May 1791, and entertained him at his mansion, The Grove, in Augusta. His refusal to recognize the right of a citizen of South Carolina to sue the sovereign state of Georgia, despite the 1793 ruling of the United States supreme court in the *Chisholm v. Georgia* case, led to the adoption of the eleventh amendment to the federal constitution forbidding citizens of one state to file suit against a different state. A remarkable feature of his administration was his signing of huge land grants to individuals so far in excess of the legal limits that the total exceeded the land available.

After his last term as governor Telfair returned to Savannah, retired from political life, and devoted his energies to his business until his death there on 17 September 1807.

He was buried in Bonaventure cemetery, Savannah. Telfair left his considerable fortune to his wife and children. His daughter Margaret helped build Hodgson Hall, the library of the Georgia Historical Society, as a memorial to her husband, William Brown Hodgson. His daughter Mary, who never married, endowed the Telfair Academy of Arts and Sciences in Savannah among other benefactions. At her death in 1875 her estate was worth $700,000.

EDWARD J. CASHIN

Sources E. M. Coulter, 'Edward Telfair', *Georgia Historical Quarterly*, 20 (June 1926), 2.99–124 · W. Harden, 'Basil Cowper's remarkable career in Georgia', *Georgia Historical Quarterly*, 1 (March 1917), 24–35 · J. F. Cook, *The governors of Georgia* (Huntsville, AL, 1979), 68–70 · K. Coleman and C. S. Gurr, eds., *Dictionary of Georgia biography*, 2 vols. (Athens, GA, 1983), 2.965–6 · Edward Telfair papers, collection 791, Georgia Historical Society, Savannah, Georgia
Archives Georgia Historical Society, Savannah, letter-book
Wealth at death left wife, sons, and daughters equal shares of his estate; personal property inventoried at $5474; inventory of his son Alexander's estate a few years later amounted to $60,492: probate court records, Chatham county courthouse, Savannah, Georgia, 1807

Telfer, James (1800–1862), poet and novelist, was born on 3 December 1800 in Southdean, Roxburghshire, the son of John Telfer and his wife, Isabella, *née* Taylor, a domestic servant. His father was a shepherd, and Telfer at first supported himself in the same line of work, but through a process of self-education he eventually gained a post as schoolmaster at Castleton, Roxburghshire; after 1834, he was auxiliary schoolmaster at a small country school at Saughtrees, Liddesdale, Roxburghshire, where he remained until his death. Never earning more than £20 a year, he none the less married Janet Beattie, supported a family, and from time to time continued to write.

Telfer's interest in writing was spurred on by a youthful acquaintance with James Hogg, who befriended and encouraged him. His first book was *Border Ballads and other Miscellaneous Pieces* (1824), dedicated to Hogg, and to some degree imitative of him. Some of the poems are marred by conventionalized sentimental diction, but the poems that make use of Scots dialect are often remarkable for their pace, intensity, and humour. Of these, several combine folkloric subjects with a wit and charm reminiscent of Burns: 'The Gloamyne Buchte' deals with a young couple's tryst being interrupted by the appearance of a bizarre supernatural creature who sings a fantastic song about stealing children, and 'The Kerlyn's Brocke' is a wild and delightful evocation of a witches' sabbath. Though forgotten today, these are minor gems that, along with lyrics like 'Love has stown my wits away', deserve a place in anthologies of the period.

Telfer also published a novel, *Barbara Gray, or, The Widow's Daughter* (1835), which was popular enough to be reprinted in a collection of his work in 1852. Though uneven and sometimes prolix, *Barbara Gray* is still worth reading, being animated primarily by angry social protest against rapacious landowners in rural Scotland—a stronger theme than the mature Telfer was comfortable with, for he wrote in the preface to the reprinted edition that he hoped he would not be accused of a 'design to promote discontent'. (This may have been politic, for the 1852 volume is dedicated to the duke of Northumberland.) The novel's bleak conclusion emphasizes the helplessness of the poor, a condition with which Telfer was quite familiar. The vicious landowner's persecution and seduction of Barbara Gray seems inspired by the novels of Richardson, as does her slow descent into misery and death thereafter. But despite its melodrama and its darkness, *Barbara Gray* is also a skilful tale of love and loss set amid an often beautifully evoked highland landscape. It suggests that Telfer might have developed into a capable and original novelist, but he published no other books of fiction. He died of apoplexy on 18 January 1862 at his home in Saughtrees.

RAYMOND N. MACKENZIE

Sources C. Rogers, *The modern Scottish minstrel, or, The songs of Scotland of the past half-century*, 4 (1857) · d. cert.

Telford, Thomas (1757–1834), civil engineer, was born on 9 August 1757 at Glendinning sheep farm in the parish of Westerkirk, Eskdale, Dumfriesshire, the second son, the first of the same name having died in infancy, of John Telford, an Eskdale shepherd, and his wife, Janet Jackson (*d.* 1794). Four months later his father died and Telford was brought up by his mother.

Early life The close knit Eskdale community, in particular Telford's mother's brother Thomas, believed to have been factor to Sir James Johnstone of Westerhall, helped to support the family. Although brought up in poverty, Telford is said to have been so full of fun and humour that he was known as 'Laughing Tam' (Smiles, 296). He gained a good basic education at Westerkirk parish school, interspersed with occasional farm work. At school he met the younger generation of leading local families, and formed a close friendship with Andrew Little, later a schoolmaster in Langholm, his subsequent correspondence with whom until 1803 represents the main source of information on his early life.

On leaving school about 1772 Telford was at first apprenticed to a stonemason at Lochmaben, from whom he is believed to have run away after being badly used, and then to Andrew Thomson at Langholm, working on the simple buildings of that remote locality. Langholm Bridge, probably built about 1778, is said to bear Telford's mason's mark, and he is reputed to have carved the Pasley family memorial and headstone to his father's grave which still exist in Westerkirk churchyard. Whenever an opportunity arose, Telford diligently gleaned knowledge from books borrowed from Eskdale's scanty shelves, for example, on literature and poetry from the elderly Miss Pasley of Craig, who befriended him. In 1780, having mastered such mason-work as Eskdale could provide, he went to Edinburgh to improve his prospects and presumably worked on its New Town or possibly at Ramsey Lane where his reputed mason's mark was found during demolition of a building in 1973. While there, in his spare time, he learned to draw and studied the architecture of the locality, sketching and admiring the Gothic splendour of

Thomas Telford (1757–1834), by Samuel Lane, 1820–22

Melrose Abbey and Roslin Chapel, a style which later influenced much of his own work.

In February 1782 Telford's restless ambition drove him to seek more challenging and better paid work in London where, through John Pasley, an eminent merchant and relative of Miss Pasley, he met architects Robert Adam and Sir William Chambers and obtained employment as a stonemason on the building of Somerset House. The following year he seriously considered, but decided against, entering into business with a fellow stonemason, Mr Hatton, to contract for work at Somerset House. While in London Telford was consulted by Sir James Johnstone of Westerhall about alterations to his house in Eskdale and was instructed in the matter by his brother, William Pulteney (1729–1805). Pulteney, who had changed his name on marrying the heiress of the earl of Bath, was impressed by Telford's work and personality and employed him on the restoration of Sudborough rectory, Northamptonshire, in 1783–4. Other commissions followed and within a decade a close friendship had developed between them to the extent that Telford was known in Shrewsbury as 'young Pulteney'. His career owed much to Pulteney's powerful patronage.

In 1784 the funding for building Somerset House stalled

and Telford obtained employment in Portsmouth, working on the dockyard commissioner's house and chapel designed by Samuel Wyatt. Before long he was superintending the contract, his first important position of independence and responsibility. While at Portsmouth he widened his knowledge by observing harbour and dock work under construction, and studying limes and mortars from copies of the lectures of Joseph Black and Antoine François de Fourcroy, adding to the compilation of useful data which became his vade-mecum. Telford was a freemason and in a letter of February 1786 wrote that he was about to direct the fitting up of a lodge room to his plans at The George inn. On completion of the dockyard buildings later in the year Telford went to Shropshire at Pulteney's invitation (he was then an MP for Shrewsbury) to undertake the restoration of Shrewsbury Castle as an occasional residence. In July 1787, with a reference from Robert Adam, he became clerk of works for the new county gaol at a salary of £60 per annum. Soon afterwards he was operating as county surveyor of public works, a post which he held for life, later through his able deputy, Thomas Stanton, at Ellesmere, directing work on public buildings including at least forty-two bridges.

Telford lived in and practised as an architect from Shrewsbury Castle during and after restoring it in the Gothic style. Other work upon which he was engaged in 1787–93 included the county infirmary, private houses, street improvements, drainage, and the following church work: restoration of St Mary's, Shrewsbury, and All Saints', Baschurch, the new churches of St Mary Magdalen, Bridgnorth, which Pevsner calls 'a remarkable design, of great gravity inside and out, and apparently done in full awareness of recent developments in France' (Pevsner, Shropshire), St Michael's, Madeley, and, almost certainly, the basic plan for St Leonard's, Malinslee. In 1788 at Pulteney's request Telford advised on St Chad's, Shrewsbury, accurately predicting its fall just before the event actually occurred. He also superintended the excavation of the ruins of the Roman city of Uriconium, on Pulteney's estate near Wroxeter, the plan and sections for which, in Archaeologia, 1789, represent his earliest-known published drawings. In 1793 he added greatly to his knowledge of architecture and antiquities from a study tour of Bath, Oxford, London, and other cities.

In 1790, at Pulteney's instigation as a director of the British Fisheries Society, Telford's lifelong connection with the society began. He advised on the improvement of numerous harbours and settlements in northern Scotland including Lochbay, Tobermory, Ullapool, Keise, Staxigo, Broad Haven, Wick, Sarclet, Clyth, Lybster, Forse, Dunbeath, Helmsdale, Brora, and Portmahomack. The largest, Pulteneytown, at Wick, executed to his designs over several decades, with its impressive Argyll Square, still survives as a fine testimonial to his architectural and planning skills. In 1796 Telford tested and soon after used at Lochbay pier a newly patented aluminous hydraulic cement, later known as Roman cement, which set very quickly. His support for and extensive use of the cement influenced its nationwide adoption for many years in

facing, pointing, and brick-jointing mortars. Telford's work for the society led to his involvement in governmental surveys of the highlands in 1801–2 and to his wide-ranging recommendations for improvement which resulted in the setting up of commissions for making the Caledonian Canal and highland roads and bridges. In 1834 the society made Telford a present of inscribed silverware 'in grateful acknowledgement of the numerous and valuable professional services gratuitously rendered during a long course of years' (Dunlop, 59).

Canals Telford's engineering career developed from 1793 on his appointment as 'General Agent, Surveyor, Engineer, Architect and Overlooker' (Gibb, 28) to the important 68 mile Ellesmere Canal, joining the rivers Mersey, Dee, and Severn. The canal, now a thriving leisure facility, still makes use of many buildings and structures designed and built under Telford's direction. The most remarkable is Pontcysyllte cast-iron aqueduct over the Dee, based on his embryo sketch design of March 1794, except for the piers, but not developed until after the iron trough concept had been proved operationally at Longdon-on-Tern aqueduct on the Shrewsbury Canal in 1795–6. At Pontcysyllte, with the support and approval of William Jessop, Telford deviated from traditional bulky masonry construction by building eighteen upright masonry piers and forming nineteen arches with cast-iron ribs supporting an iron trough with 1 in. thick sides, 1007 ft long and 126 ft high. The ironwork was made and erected by William Hazledine, the masonry was built by John Simpson, and the whole supervised by Matthew Davidson. The result, the supreme engineering achievement of the canal age, was still in service in 2003. Sir Walter Scott thought it 'the most impressive work of art he had ever seen' (ibid., 35). A misleading attempt by Hadfield in 1993 to question the traditional attribution of the concept and design of the aqueduct to Telford is incompatible with authoritative early evidence.

The 60 mile Caledonian Canal constructed across the highlands of Scotland in 1804–22 was engineered by Telford and Jessop jointly until 1812, afterwards solely by Telford, basically with the same team that built Chirk and Pontcysyllte aqueducts. Davidson superintended work at the eastern end and John Telford, succeeded by Alexander Easton, at the western end. Simpson was the main contractor, with John Wilson and John Cargill working as his foremen masons. In engineering terms the 100 ft wide ship canal, with its twenty-eight huge locks and deep summit cutting at Laggan, was then the most advanced in the world. In making it, innovation abounded in the use of iron railways, machinery, equipment, steam engines for pumping and dredging, and in lock construction, notably at Beauly where a 55 ft depth of mud was preconsolidated before excavating the lock-pit.

Despite its hard-won achievement and provision of much-needed work (in 1811, 1385 men were employed), the Caledonian Canal was in other respects one of Telford's less successful projects. Costs escalated with high inflation and unforeseen difficulties, additional funding was in short supply, and some workmanship, for example at Banavie and Fort Augustus locks, proved defective. A. E. Penfold attributed the latter to a lack of close site supervision arising from a management structure favouring the contractors. The canal, which eventually opened in 1822, had a depth of 12 ft instead of 20 ft, had cost about twice the estimate, and had taken eighteen years instead of seven to cut. By then, through no fault of Telford's, the reasons for creating it had largely evaporated and, relative to its capacity, the canal, although important locally, has never been much used, except in 1918 when there were 6254 passages associated with mine-laying in the North Sea. The canal is now a major tourist attraction.

In Sweden the Trollhätte Canal, comprising the western end of the Gotha Canal, had been completed in 1800 under the direction of its promoter, Count von Platen, and engineer, Samuel Bagge. From 1808 Telford, at the invitation of the king of Sweden, acted as consulting engineer for its 114 mile eastwards extension from Lake Vänern to the Baltic at Söderköping, with at first Bagge and later Lagerheim superintending operations in Sweden. In 1808, with his assistants William Hughes and Hamilton Fulton, Telford met and surveyed the line with von Platen, provisionally fixing lock sites, sizes, and other details. It was the start of a close friendship which lasted until von Platen's death in 1829. Construction commenced in 1809 and four years later 7000 men were employed, including John Wilson and James Simpson from 1813, but there were delays and the canal was not completed until 1832. Telford's guidance was transmitted to von Platen in a voluminous correspondence. In 1809 Telford was made a knight of the Swedish royal order of Vasa in recognition of his valuable services, his letters from Sweden afterwards being addressed to 'Sir Thomas Telford'. His international reputation was now such that he was also consulted by the Russian government on canal navigation schemes.

Telford worked in various capacities on at least thirty-three canal projects in Great Britain and on the Welland Canal in Canada and the Panama Canal, and was involved with eleven river navigation projects. He also investigated the development of fast canal boats and in 1832-3 hundreds of experiments were made at the Adelaide Gallery, London, by his chief assistant, John Macneill, in an unsuccessful attempt to compete with steam locomotion on railways.

Telford was the last of the great canal engineers of the industrial revolution. Of his later projects, Harecastle Tunnel, on the Trent and Mersey Canal, was one of the most remarkable feats in tunnelling history. More than 2920 yards long, it was constructed, in exact accordance with his plans under the supervision of resident engineer, James Potter, in less than three years from fifteen shafts. The Birmingham Canal improvement, engineered to his characteristically direct line and level by means of the best practice and a prodigious cutting at Smethwick, saved 8 miles in length and offered maximum benefit to its users in other ways. This, too, ranks as one of the finest canal engineering projects. Similarly, the Birmingham and Liverpool Junction Canal effected a 12 mile saving in length, but required long cuttings up to 90 ft deep in what turned out to be slip-susceptible marl, and a diversion at Shelmore to avoid Lord Anson's game preserves which involved a mile-long embankment up to 60 ft high. Both features presented Telford with great problems as his health declined, problems which were eventually overcome under William Cubitt's direction. To the north, Telford's canal–seaport warehouse interchange at Ellesmere Port, greatly used for over a century, represented a peak of efficiency for the time.

Road making Telford's main achievements in road making were the London to Holyhead and Bangor to Chester roads as engineer to the Holyhead road commissioners from 1815, and the Glasgow to Carlisle, Lanarkshire, and highlands of Scotland roads as engineer to the highland roads commissioners from 1803. These long-distance arteries of the heyday of coaching declined in use from the 1840s as the railway network developed, to be resurrected in the twentieth century as Telford's vision of mechanical propulsion was fulfilled by the motor vehicle. Abroad, for Tsar Alexander I, Telford advised on the 100 mile Warsaw to Brzesc major road towards Moscow, completed in 1825. Unexecuted or partially executed improvements on roads which he surveyed for the government or others included the Carlisle to Portpatrick, Birmingham to Liverpool, Carlisle to Edinburgh, London to Milford Haven and south Wales, and the Great North Road from London via York and Edinburgh to Inverness.

Between 1803 and 1821, with the valuable assistance of John Rickman, James Hope, and John Mitchell, respectively, secretary, agent, and chief inspector to the highland road commissioners, Telford was responsible for the provision of about 1200 miles of new or improved roads in the highlands, with 1100 bridges. These works opened up Scotland west and north of the Great Glen, in Telford's own words, 'advancing the country at least a century' (Smiles, 389). His connection with the Holyhead and Scottish roads continued through inspections for the rest of his life. In terms of construction his major roads were commodious, well-drained and incorporated a hand-pitched stone foundation beneath a layer of conventional road metal. Unlike J. L. McAdam's roads, they were properly engineered to improved lines and gentle gradients, and, although more expensive initially, facilitated traction and reduced maintenance costs. Sir Henry Parnell considered the Holyhead Road to be 'a model of the most perfect road making that has ever been attempted in any country' (Parnell, 35). Much of it is still in use and considered 'a long-lasting memorial to Telford's skill and vision' (Penfold, *Engineer*, 58).

Bridge building Throughout his lifetime Telford designed, built, or advised on, thousands of masonry bridges, including 1100 to a standard specification on highland roads alone in 1803-21. His bridges ranged from simple culverts to the sophisticated 150 ft elliptical span of Over bridge, Gloucester (1826-30). His first major bridge was erected over the Severn at Montford in 1790-92 using convict labour. Six years later it was followed by Bewdley

Bridge, which, with its segmental arches and classical balustrades in a gentle arc, is considered 'one of the most elegant bridges in England' (Ruddock, 154). Telford's finest Scottish bridges include Dunkeld (1805–9), also with its extrados on the arc of a great circle, and his *ne plus ultra* of architectural experimentation and excellence of construction, Dean bridge, Edinburgh (1829–32), with its intricately achieved slenderness. Gibb considered the bridges at Broomielaw, Glasgow (1833–5), and Dean, 'a fitting crown to Telford's creative life' (Gibb, 261). Both were constructed by John Gibb under the competent supervision of resident engineer Charles Atherton. In construction terms, from 1790 Telford developed, and by example widely influenced, the beneficial adoption of hollow piers and spandrels in large-span bridges, which resulted in a stronger structure, facilitated internal inspection, and reduced weight on foundations. Telford's architectural experience enabled him to impart grace and beauty to the appearance of many of his bridges.

Telford's innovative practice was also most effectively applied to cast-iron road bridges. Buildwas Bridge (1796), probably the second major iron bridge to be completed in Britain, differed considerably in concept from Coalbrookdale iron bridge in that Telford modelled it on the principles of timber rather than masonry construction. In applying this more appropriate concept, particularly if its iron was as ductile as that which he used later, he achieved a bridge of half the weight of that at Coalbrookdale with a considerably increased span. Four years later Telford, with a young associate, James Douglass, made a very bold proposal for a 600 ft cast-iron arch over the Thames to replace London Bridge. From 1800 it was promoted in a superb Malton aquatint, later issues of which were dedicated by Telford to George III. Expert opinion on the practicability of the proposal, widely canvassed under Telford's direction by a parliamentary committee, varied greatly and although the project was seriously considered for many years it was not implemented, in Skempton's opinion because of 'the unprecedented scale of the project, coupled with lack of knowledge of and agreement on the technical factors involved' (Penfold, *Engineer*, 79).

In 1810 Telford, drawing on his previous experience and experiments, designed an economical prefabricated, lozenge-lattice spandrel arch for use at locations where it would be more expensive or impractical to construct in masonry. At least nine arches with standardized spans of 105 or 150 ft were cast and erected by Hazledine in 1812–30, of which those at Craigellachie, Chester (Eaton Hall), Holt Fleet, and Birmingham (Galton) are still in use, as is another at Tewkesbury of larger span. The prototype at Bonar Bridge over Dornoch Firth, erected in 1812, lasted until 1891. Of Telford's cast-iron bridges, Rolt aptly commented, 'No other man has ever handled cast iron with such complete assurance and understanding, his exact knowledge … enabling him to achieve that perfection of proportion which gives strength the deceptive semblance of fragility' (Rolt, xiii).

Suspension bridges Telford's creation on the Holyhead Road of the elegant Menai wrought-iron suspension bridge, with an unprecedented span of nearly 580 ft, was his greatest work and the most outstanding bridge development of the early nineteenth century. Its final form evolved from his experimentally based proposal of 1814–18 for Runcorn Bridge, further experimental work, and an almost continuous design process, to its triumphal opening in 1826. In 1814 Telford had correctly anticipated modern practice in envisaging parallel wire main cables, but eventually opted for flat chain-bar links as being more practicable to achieve and maintain at that time. The masonry, which is of exceptional quality, was executed by John Wilson. Hazledine manufactured the ironwork, the testing and fixing of which under the supervision of resident engineer William Provis, his brother John Provis, and Thomas Rhodes, was at the forefront of technology. Nearly 36,000 bars and plates, including all those used in the bridge, were tested to about twice their design load. A relatively minor but significant drawback of the bridge, which gave Telford an anxious time in 1825–6, was that its deck undulated in strong winds, but fortunately only moderately during his lifetime. (This was adequately remedied at moderate cost under Provis's direction in 1839.)

Telford's experimental results were widely propagated in leading textbooks and in 1828 Provis published a magnificently illustrated account of the Menai Bridge project dedicated to Telford. In 2003 the Institution of Civil Engineers and American Society of Civil Engineers recognized both bridges as 'international civil engineering landmarks'. The project led to a surge in suspension bridge building and exercised a fundamental influence on the practice and development of I. K. Brunel, J. L. Clark, J. M. Rendel, and others between 1818 and 1840, establishing this type of bridge in its true role as the most economic means of achieving the largest spans. From about 1840, according to J. A. Roebling in 1867, because suspension bridges were not considered rigid enough for railway use, Telford's great achievement was mistakenly left unappreciated and greatly undervalued. The Menai Bridge was tastefully reconditioned in 1940. Conwy suspension bridge, created by means of the identical technology, also opened in 1826, still has its original ironwork. Telford's other suspension bridge projects included his controversial Clifton Bridge proposal of 1830, in which he envisaged possible deck undulation being inhibited by means of smaller spans, at the same time offering an opportunity for two splendid Gothic revival towers rising dramatically from the floor of the gorge. The design is understood to have received general approval, but it failed to attract sufficient funding.

Railways and steam carriages Telford believed that a fundamental disadvantage of carriage by railway, as distinct from canals and tramways, was that all traffic would have to be handled by the company owning the line, thus creating monopolies to the disadvantage of the user. He considered that steam power could best be applied to land transport in the form, not of railways, but of self-propelled vehicles operating on roads. He supported the setting up of and gave evidence to a parliamentary select committee in 1831, which reported that steam carriages were practicable and safe and should be protected from high tolls. By 1833 Telford was a leading promoter in a steam carriage company intended to operate on the London to Holyhead road and took part in an experimental journey on the London to Birmingham section in Dance's steam carriage. The size of the engine proved to be insufficient and the carriage only reached Stoney Stratford, 57 miles from London, at an average speed of 7 m.p.h. High tolls, opposition from vested interests, mechanical shortcomings, and Telford's death in the following year, all contributed to the demise of this initiative.

Railway projects on which Telford acted as engineer or advised included the Stratford and Moreton line (1821–6), operated with horse traction, and the Clarence (1828–9), Newcastle and Carlisle (1829), and Liverpool and Manchester (1827–9) railways; the latter's directors had offered him the post of engineer in 1825 but he declined, possibly out of loyalty to some of the canal companies by whom he was employed. During construction, following some difficulties, he inspected this work with George Stephenson in connection with a £100,000 exchequer loan and was instrumental in persuading the company to abandon the idea of fixed engines and inclined planes in favour of a level line suitable for locomotive haulage. Important railway proposals which he planned, but which were not executed, included the Glasgow to Berwick line (1810), to be operated with horse traction and steam-powered inclined planes; the London to Dover (1824), locomotive operated; East and West India docks (1828); and the Glasgow, Forth, and Clyde Canal to Broomielaw (1829), which was mainly in tunnel.

Other engineering works and public service Telford made an important contribution to the drainage of the English fens. In 1818–21, jointly with the elder John Rennie, he advised on the execution of the Eau Brinck Cut which bypassed the meandering Ouse above King's Lynn. The cut, the width of which had been specified by Joseph Huddart, proved to be insufficient and soon afterwards it was widened at Telford's instigation with most beneficial effects. Telford also worked on the Nene outfall cut from Wisbeach to Crab Hole in the Wash, executed in 1827–30 for about £200,000. It was on this work, while visiting Crab Hole with the younger John Rennie, that he was soaked to the skin in a storm and caught a severe chill. On his way back to London, Telford was taken with a violent diarrhoea at Cambridge, where he was confined for a fortnight and nearly died. His health never fully recovered and the complaint returned from time to time with increasing severity until his death. Rennie found Telford 'a most agreeable facetious companion' (Rennie, 201). Telford's most important achievement in this field, made possible by the Nene outfall cut, was the drainage of about 48,000 acres of the North Level. For this work, carried out in 1830–34 for about £150,000, he was the sole engineer.

Telford advised on or acted as engineer for the improvement of more than 100 harbours, docks, or piers, including many in Scotland for the highland road commissioners using forfeited estates funds. In addition to the British Fisheries Society harbours already mentioned,

these included, between 1801 and his death, those at Aberdeen, Peterhead, Ardrossan, Glasgow, Fraserburgh, Dundee, Leith, Belfast, Holyhead, Howth and Dunmore, Greenock, and Dover. At St Katharine's Dock in the Port of London, on a restricted and awkwardly shaped site which had required the demolition of more than 1250 houses and the excavation of 27 acres, in 1826–8 Telford designed an entrance lock giving access to a basin interconnecting two irregular-shaped docks. This arrangement enabled each dock to be cleaned out separately without interrupting shipping operations. The loss of water through lockage was compensated for by an ingenious arrangement of pumps which delivered water from the river into either the lock or basin as required. The work, which was the most advanced of its kind, was executed under the diligent supervision of Rhodes as resident engineer.

Telford advised on numerous water supply schemes, one of the earliest, in 1799–1802, being a piped supply to Liverpool pumped by steam engines from springs at Bootle. In 1806 he was appointed engineer of the Glasgow waterworks and, in association with James Watt, completely reorganized its defective and impure supply. An innovative feature was a cast-iron main with flexible joints specially invented by Watt to enable water to cross the Clyde. In 1810–22 Telford was consulted on Edinburgh water supply and in association with local engineer James Jardine was involved in the construction of Glencorse Reservoir, with what was then one of the tallest earth dams in Britain. With characteristic attention to detail, all the pipes in the main leading into the city were proved at a pressure equal to that of a column of water from 300 to 800 ft high; they are still in service. *The Scotsman* in 1825 considered these works 'the most extensive, perfect and complete ever executed in modern times' (Paxton, 17). In 1827–34 Telford, with assistants John Macneill and James Mills, was engaged on his largest water supply project, to supply London with much-needed pure water. In 1834 Telford proposed to bring it in from the Verulam near Watford and the Wandle at Beddington at an estimated cost of £1.177 million. Although not implemented, according to Smiles, these proposals strongly stimulated the water companies and eventually led to great improvements.

Between 1823 and 1830 Telford superintended the design and provision of highland churches and manses at many sites from Islay northwards to the Shetland Islands. In 1823–4, as superintending surveyor to the highland churches commission, he prepared plans, specifications, and estimates for standardized structures based on the proposals of his three surveyors, of which those of William Thomson for the churches were closest to the form finally adopted. The basically austere structures, most of which still exist, are often enlivened by a touch of Telford's architectural artistry. He estimated that the churches were capable of containing 22,000 persons without inconvenience.

After Waterloo severe economic depression spread over Britain and in 1817 the exchequer bill loan commission was created to assist the financing of worthwhile public works projects in order to provide employment. Telford was appointed its adviser on all works requiring the information of a civil engineer and during the first ten years of the commission's existence he recommended nearly £1 million of assistance which was duly authorized. It was a time-consuming and important task. At least twenty projects had come under his review by 1829, those receiving more than £20,000 being the Regent's Canal (part), Rennie's Southwark Bridge, the Gloucester and Berkeley Canal, Portsmouth and Arundel Canal, the Tay ferry at Dundee, Portleven harbour in Cornwall, Kingston Bridge, the Liverpool and Manchester Railway, and the Ulster Canal. James Mills frequently acted as his surveyor.

Publications and poetry Telford's publications consisted mainly of engineering reports, but he wrote authoritative articles for the *Edinburgh Encyclopaedia*, of which he was a leading shareholder. These were 'Bridge', with co-author Alexander Nimmo (first published 1812), 'Civil architecture' (1813), 'Navigation inland', also with Nimmo (1821, partly written in 1814), and almost certainly 'Jessop' (1817); altogether they amounted to over 300 pages with eighty-two plates and were particularly influential before 1830 when the whole encyclopaedia was issued. Telford's early technical publications included his *Experiments … on Mr. James Parker's Cement* (1796), articles in the *Philosophical Magazine* on the proposed iron arch replacement for London Bridge (1801), canals (1803), and his highlands report (1803), and 'Canals' in J. Plymley's *General View of the Agriculture of Shropshire* (1803). Telford's novel proposal to suspend arch bridge centering by means of radiating iron stays in *A Journal of Natural Philosophy* (1813) encouraged the design of catenarian and stay suspension bridges. His compilation, *General Rules for Repairing Roads*, widely circulated from 1819, and from 1833, Parnell's *Treatise on Roads*, propagating the road-making practice applied on the Holyhead Road, together exercised a fundamental influence for over a century.

Telford's most important publication, despite its shortcomings as a personal narrative, was his autobiographical *Life* (1838), edited by John Rickman; it was written from 1831 as his health, hearing, and new commitments declined. Although its magnificent atlas of engraved plates and its appendices constituted an invaluable record of his practice and achievement, the book was not very successful commercially at a price of 8 guineas. By the time it was eventually published, four years after his death, the nation was in the grip of railway expansion and it was to some extent outdated as a working manual. The unsold stock was bought by James Walker, who succeeded Telford as president of the Institution of Civil Engineers, and copies were awarded as Telford premium prizes for many years.

Telford's enjoyment of the books lent to him by Miss Pasley marked the start of his lifelong love of poetry and an almost excessive admiration for literary ability. This interest led to his friendship with the Revd Archibald Alison, author of an essay *Taste* in 1790, whom he had met at Sudborough rectory about 1783, and who had introduced him to Thomas Campbell. Rickman introduced him to Robert Southey. All became his close friends. His earliest-

known printed poetical work was an eight-verse poem in W. Ruddiman's *Weekly Magazine, or, Edinburgh Amusement* on 5 May 1779, which ended:

> Lang may ye sing, weel may ye phrase,
> Hae routh and plenty a' your days;
> And I shall gar a' our green braes
> Ken weel your name,
> I'm sure ye still sall hae the praise
> O'ESKDALE TAM.

This poem was closely followed by *Eskdale*, first published separately at London in 1781, probably for the Pasleys, prefaced by his introduction as a 'stonemason … a young man of no education but common reading, assisted by some books lent him by neighbouring gentlemen'. It was reprinted on several occasions and was well thought of by Southey. At least twelve poems are known to have been written by Telford during his lifetime, many of which are mentioned by Samuel Smiles. The last known was a tribute to some verses by his fellow Eskdaleman, Sir John Malcolm, in 1831. Telford sometimes initialled his writings TT, but his usual signature was Thos. Telford. From about 1806 he did not join the letters o and s. The most widely circulated was a manuscript poem to Robert Burns, which Dr Currie considered of 'superior merit' to other poems found among the poet's papers: he printed twenty-six verses of it in many editions of Burns's works from 1801.

Professional connections and character Telford was the first president of the Institution of Civil Engineers in 1820–34. Soon after taking office he established the valuable tradition of recording the proceedings and discussions of meetings and the substance of papers read. His diligent and invaluable fostering of the institution as a forum for engineering knowledge included such activities as encouraging membership, provision of a library of books and drawings, urging members to present papers, and even chasing up and making good the subscriptions of Gotha Canal engineers Lagerheim, Edström, and others. His position as parliament's engineer gave him considerable influence with the political establishment and he was the driving force behind the obtaining of the institution's royal charter in 1828. In his will he left the institution his largest bequest, of more than £3000, and his books, drawings, and papers. His next two largest bequests were to the parish libraries at Westerkirk and Langholm. Telford's contribution to the institution was fundamental to its early development. He was elected to fellowship of the Royal societies of Edinburgh and London in 1803 and 1827 respectively.

Telford never married and according to John Rickman 'lived life as a soldier always in active service' (*Life of Thomas Telford*, 283). From 1800 he needed a permanent base in London and lived in rooms at the Salopian Coffee House, Charing Cross, until taking possession in 1821 of 24 Abingdon Street, where he lived until his death. From 1800, for more than thirty years, Telford's contact with the Revd Archibald Alison and his family was probably the nearest approach to home life that he ever enjoyed. Little of Telford's character is to be gleaned from his publications, but the opinions of some of his contemporaries are informative. Rickman stated that Telford's most distinguishing character trait was a benevolence which made him accessible to all who came to him for information. His pupil, Joseph Mitchell, recounted his master's 'great delight in his work. The perfect good faith and honour of all his transactions, his clear conscience, and his cheerful temper cast a halo of happiness throughout our establishment' (Mitchell, 102). In 1793 Catherine Plymley wrote after meeting Telford that he was 'an excellent architect and a most intelligent and enlightened man. His knowledge is general, his conversation very animated, his look full of intelligence and vivacity' (Penfold, *Engineer*, 2). She also praised the liberality and cheerfulness of his charitable donations.

Southey wrote of Telford, 'there is so much intelligence in his countenance, so much frankness, kindness and hilarity about him flowing from the never-failing well spring of a happy nature, that I was upon cordial terms with him in five minutes' (Southey, 7). Telford was not a lover of concert music: he wrote, 'the melody of sounds is thrown away upon me, one look, one sentence from Mrs. Jordan has more effect upon me than all the fiddlers in England' (Gibb, 294). Sir David Brewster wrote of Telford's apparent sternness of manner which created difficulties at times in his relationships, and belied the genuine benevolence and kindness of his nature. His comment was that Telford's

> quick perception of character, his honesty of purpose, and his contempt for all other acquirements, save that of practical knowledge and experience which was best fitted … have enabled him to leave behind him works of inestimable value … which have not been surpassed either in Britain or in Europe. (Brewster, 46)

Telford died on 2 September 1834 at 24 Abingdon Street, of a bilious derangement. He was buried in Westminster Abbey.

Lasting influence With hindsight, a more theoretical approach would have benefited Telford's structural design practice, but his reliance on experimental and practical procedures was the best available means of achieving the desired result at the time. An essential factor in his immense achievement was his sound judgement in selecting capable and reliable assistants and contractors, to whom he was able to devolve responsibility without losing control. Under his direction they translated his designs into effect often at, and even extending, the frontiers of engineering technology and knowledge. Telford's beneficial influence is most alive today through his many surviving works, modern contract procedures, and the Institution of Civil Engineers as a forum of engineering excellence. Of Telford's surviving works, although leisure interest in his canals is increasing, his roads and bridges, for which he was aptly dubbed by Southey 'Colossus of Roads' and 'Pontifex Maximus' (Smiles, 476), now make the greatest contribution to society. L. T. C. Rolt, who was also the biographer of George Stephenson and Isambard Brunel, believed that Telford's 'achievement was as great as theirs and of equal historical significance' (Rolt, xi). Smiles, Rolt, Penfold, and others have all helped to restore his reputation from its low ebb during the 'railway mania'

era. He has a lasting modern memorial in the new town, Telford, which was created in Shropshire in the 1950s. Telford was undoubtedly one of the greatest civil engineers of all time. ROLAND PAXTON

Sources *The life of Thomas Telford: civil engineer, written by himself*, ed. J. Rickman (1838) · [R. Southey], review, *QR*, 63 (1839), 403–57 · [D. Brewster], *EdinR*, 70 (1839–40), 1–47 · S. Smiles, *Lives of the engineers*, 2 (1861) · A. Gibb, *The story of Telford* (1935) · L. T. C. Rolt, *Thomas Telford* (1958) · *Thomas Telford, engineer* [Ironbridge 1979], ed. A. Penfold (1980) · A. E. Penfold, *Thomas Telford, 'Colossus of roads'* (1981) · R. Southey, *Journal of a tour in Scotland in 1819* (1929) · J. Mitchell, *Reminiscences of my life in the highlands*, 1 (1883) · H. Parnell, *A treatise on roads* (1833) · C. Hadfield, *Thomas Telford's temptation* (1993) · R. A. Paxton, 'Review of "Thomas Telford's temptation"', *Institution of Civil Engineers Panel for Historical Engineering Works Newsletter* (Dec 1993), 6–7 · A. R. B. Haldane, *New ways through the glens* (1962) · A. Maclean, *Telford's highland churches* (1989) · J. Dunlop, *The British Fisheries Society, 1786–1893* (1978) · [R. Buckle], *The Institution of Civil Engineers presents a bicentenary exhibition in honour of … Thomas Telford* [1957] [exhibition catalogue, London, 1957] · T. Ruddock, *Arch bridges and their builders, 1735–1835* (1979) · *To Sir John Malcolm upon receiving his miscellaneous poems — a poem by Thomas Telford*, ed. R. A. Paxton (1971) · *Three letters from Thos. Telford*, ed. R. A. Paxton (1968) · J. Rennie, *Autobiography of Sir John Rennie, FRS* (1875) · J. A. Roebling, *Annual report of Covington and Cincinatti Bridge Company* (1867) · Institution of Civil Engineers, *A collection of works of art and objects of historical interest* (1950) · A. W. Skempton, *British civil engineering, 1640–1840: a bibliography of contemporary printed reports, plans, and books* (1987) · private information (2004) · Inst. CE, Telford papers

Archives British Waterways Archive, Gloucester, manuscript plans · HLRO, corresp., reports, and papers · Inst. CE, corresp., notebooks, and papers · Ironbridge Gorge Museum Trust, corresp. and papers · NA Scot., letter-books, corresp., reports, and papers · NL Scot., corresp., diary, and papers · PRO, corresp., reports, and papers · Shrops. RRC, corresp., reports, and papers | Birm. CA, corresp. with Boulton and Watt · Inst. CE, corresp. with Andrew Lettle and Lettle family · Ironbridge Gorge Museum Library and Archives, Telford, corresp., accounts, plans, family papers of his assistant James Thomson · NL Scot., papers relating to Greenock harbour

Likenesses H. Raeburn, oils, 1812, Lady Lever Art Gallery, Port Sunlight · S. Lane, oils, 1820–22, Inst. CE [*see illus.*] · G. Patten, oils, 1829, Kelvingrove Art Gallery, Glasgow · H. Meyer, engraving, *c.*1830 (after portrait), Ironbridge Gorge Museum Trust · W. Raddon, engraving, pubd 1831 (after S. Lane), NPG · P. Hollins, marble bust, exh. RA 1832, Inst. CE · W. Brockedon, pencil and chalk drawing, 1834, NPG · E. H. Baily, memorial statue, 1839, Westminster Abbey · D. A. Francis, bronze medallion, 1928, Westerkirk · A. Zydower, sculpture, 1957 · W. C. Edwards, line engraving (after S. Lane), NPG · J. F. Skill, J. Gilbert, W. Walker, and E. Walker, group portrait, pencil and wash (*Men of science living in 1807–8*), NPG · oils (as young man), Shrewsbury Borough Museum

Wealth at death over £16,600; also property amounting to 70 per cent more: Telford, *Life*

Temperley, Harold William Vazeille (1879–1939), historian, was born at 2 Newnham Terrace, Cambridge, on 20 April 1879, the third son of Ernest Temperley (*c.*1849–1889), a fellow, bursar, tutor, and lecturer in mathematics at Queens' College, Cambridge, and his wife, Marion (*d.* 1900), daughter of Thomas Wildman DD, episcopalian chaplain at Callander. After Sherborne School, he went up to King's College, Cambridge, in 1898 to read history, heading the tripos in both parts (1900 and 1901). Following his failure to gain a fellowship at King's, he went to Leeds University as a lecturer for one year in 1903, prior to accepting an invitation from the master of Peterhouse, Sir

Adolphus William Ward, to take up a fellowship at that college in 1905.

Temperley began as a historian of eighteenth- and nineteenth-century British constitutional history: his rejected fellowship dissertation for King's College had been 'The office of prime minister under the Hanoverian dynasty'. His first book—*Life of Canning* (1905)—was an eloquent but unsubtle whig eulogy on his (coalition tory) subject. By the outbreak of the First World War, however, Temperley's interests had shifted to Europe and British foreign policy. He travelled extensively in Austria–Hungary and the Balkans before 1914. Initially sympathetic to Hungarian liberal nationalism, Temperley soon became the advocate of the 'subject peoples' of the empire, particularly the Slovaks and the Serbs. This enthusiasm culminated in his *History of Serbia* (1917) which should be understood primarily as a sentimental homage to a gallant wartime ally. He retained a fascination with the 'rejuvenating' qualities of the 'Near East' for the rest of his life.

At the outbreak of the war Temperley volunteered for the Fife and Forfar yeomanry; he narrowly missed the Gallipoli landings because he had typhoid fever. The rest of his war service was spent at the War Office, where he was given the task of preparing papers on the historical, political, and statistical background to the various territorial disputes in the Balkans. After the armistice he undertook several official missions to the area, served on the boundary commission on Albania, and as an adviser to the British delegation to the Paris peace conference in 1919. Throughout this period he showed himself a passionate adherent of the Yugoslav and Albanian causes against Italian territorial pretensions.

Temperley's European sympathies and historical interests were in many ways an extension of his classic British whiggery. Already in 1905 he had praised Canning as the 'man who first foresaw and promoted the growth of national liberty on the Continent of Europe'. Like Canning he was an enthusiastic believer in the power of public opinion, which he believed could be used to shame oppressive regimes into granting minority rights. In *A History of the Peace Conference of Paris* (6 vols., 1920–24), which he edited, he had described the war as 'a conflict between the principles of freedom and of autocracy [which] began in 1688' (1.xxiii). Revealingly, his editorial guidelines had spoken of the Versailles settlement as the establishment of 'the reign of law above that of force' and reminded contributors that: 'What is desired is less a summary of ascertained fact than an indication of how far each measure or set of events arrested or retarded the establishment of this great guiding principle' (Fair, 149).

It was in the 1920s and early 1930s that Temperley's career really took off, and he became Britain's foremost exponent of diplomatic history during its interwar heyday. In 1919 he was made reader in modern history at the University of Cambridge, and professor of modern history in 1930. Under his guidance undergraduate history at Peterhouse flourished. He founded the *Cambridge Historical Journal* in 1923, perhaps his most lasting contribution to the

discipline, which helped to establish the study of modern British and European history, particularly in the nineteenth and twentieth centuries. He also served as Seeley librarian. In 1927 he published his best-selling and frequently reprinted textbook, co-authored by A. J. Grant, *Europe in the Nineteenth Century, 1789–1914*, which was used by generations of sixth-formers and undergraduates. At the same time Temperley was active in forging international links, particularly through his presidency of the International Congress of Historians (1933–8).

This was also the period when Temperley matured as a scholar. His large-scale study, *The Foreign Policy of Canning, 1822–1827* (1925), though overwhelmingly laudatory of its subject, lacked the youthful exuberance of the earlier eulogy; it was also much less critical of Canning's rival Castlereagh. Similarly, his last major work, *England and the Near East: the Crimea* (1936), made a conscious attempt to be fair to the Russians, and even to his long-time *bêtes noires*, the Turks; it was originally conceived as a much larger enterprise which would take the story down to the Congress of Berlin in 1878. Temperley's scholarly prestige and political experience made him the obvious choice to co-edit the official documents on the origins of the First World War with G. P. Gooch and the assistance of Lillian M. Penson. It strengthened his hand in the interminable disputes with the Foreign Office about the selection and doctoring of documents; his guileless patriotism dictated that the British cause could only be helped by the unvarnished truth. The upshot was *British Documents on the Origins of the War, 1898–1914* (13 vols., 1926–38). At about the same time Temperley published—again with Lillian Penson—two further important edited collections: *Foundations of British Foreign Policy from Pitt, 1792, to Salisbury, 1902*, and *A Century of Diplomatic Blue Books, 1814–1914* (both 1938).

Temperley neither expounded nor possessed an entirely coherent philosophy of history. His Rankean insistence on the study of the broadest possible range of (diplomatic) records, especially those of foreign powers, deeply influenced a whole generation of research students, such as C. W. Crawley, Patrick Bury, and, for a while, Herbert Butterfield; in *Frederic the Great and Kaiser Joseph* (1915) he acknowledged his 'obligation to German scholarship' at a time when it was not fashionable to do so. Simultaneously, however, Temperley was a fervent believer in 'imaginative insight' and the value of literature as a historical source and inspiration; this found expression in his pamphlet *Foreign Historical Novels* (1929). From the very outset Temperley was a passionate advocate of the 'lessons of history': his early works make explicit reference to contemporary concerns. And although he became markedly less present-minded in his later historical works, he spent the very last years of his life in a profitless quest to apply Canning's principle of only intervening in Europe with commanding force to the challenge of the Third Reich. On the other hand Temperley also claimed (in his inaugural lecture at Cambridge in 1930) that history should not be used to:

demonstrate a belief in the progress of humanity, in the truth of Christianity, or even the existence of God. All such attempts serve only to make history the handmaid of science or of dogma or of philosophy. History should be studied for herself alone. (*Research and Modern History*, 1930, 18)

Perhaps, as his would-be biographer Herbert Butterfield surmised, it was the Romantic in him that loved the past for its own sake.

Historically Temperley was a whig of organicist Burkeian sympathies; while he venerated the grand narrative of British constitutional development, he was never prescriptive of continental internal affairs. His contemporary politics were broadly Liberal, though he did vote for the Labour Party on at least one occasion in the 1920s and later developed an intense sympathy for Neville Chamberlain. He was a passionate defender of the League of Nations. He shared the prejudices of his time about race, and was a great propagator of national stereotypes. By contrast he vigorously supported the campaign for women's degrees at Cambridge. This may have been the result of his first marriage to the strong-minded Gladys Bradford (1885–1923). The daughter of Job Bradford, barrister, she was a sometime fellow of Newnham and a published historian in her own right. They were married on 19 July 1913, and had one son. After her tragic early death in 1923, he married in 1929 his cousin Dorothy Vazeille Temperley, sometime headmistress of a girls' school in South Africa, and daughter of Arthur Temperley, prebendary of Lincoln Minster; they had no children.

Temperley was a gregarious—often anarchic—figure who delighted in a keen sense of paradox in history. He was capable of great personal generosity, as well as sentimental outbursts. He was also unpredictable and prone to long abstruse feuds with libraries, archives, ministries, pupils, and colleagues. It may well be that the tense exchanges with the Foreign Office over the edition of documents deprived him of a knighthood. He was certainly disappointed not to have been awarded the regius professorship in 1927. Nevertheless he collected a very diverse list of honours, including honorary degrees from Durham and St Andrews, fellowship of the British Academy (1927), and corresponding membership of the Polish, Czech, Romanian, and Norwegian national academies; he was also invested with numerous foreign decorations. In 1938 Temperley was elected master of Peterhouse, which he remained until his early death following a coronary thrombosis at the master's lodge, Peterhouse, on 11 July 1939. He was survived by his wife.   BRENDAN SIMMS

Sources CUL, Butterfield MSS · J. D. Fair, *Harold Temperley: a scholar and Romantic in the public realm* (1992) · M. Faissler, 'Harold Temperley', *Some historians of modern Europe*, ed. B. Schmitt (1942) · J. D. Hargreaves, 'Some notes on Gooch and Temperley', *History*, new ser., 39 (1954), 68–75 · M. Cowling, *Religion and public doctrine in modern England*, 1 (1980) · DNB · CGPLA Eng. & Wales (1939)

Archives CUL, corresp. and papers relating to him · Peterhouse, Cambridge, papers · PRO, Foreign Office papers · Thorney House, Somerset, MSS | BL, corresp. with Sir Sydney Cockerell, Add. MS 52755 · BL, corresp. with Macmillans, Add. MS 55081 · BLPES, Webster MSS · CAC Cam., corresp. with C. B. A. Behrens · CUL, corresp., mainly letters to R. W. Seton-Watson [some copies] · King's AC Cam., letters to Oscar Browning · King's Lond., Liddell Hart C.,

corresp. with Sir B. H. Liddell Hart · NL Wales, Davies papers | SOUND BL NSA, recorded lectures

Likenesses H. Smith, oils, c.1940–1941, Peterhouse, Cambridge · Ramsey & Muspratt, photographs, NPG

Wealth at death £13,313 5s. 11d.: resworn probate, 13 Sept 1939, CGPLA Eng. & Wales

Tempest family (*per. c.*1500–1657), gentry, were established at Bracewell near Skipton in Craven from an early date. The marriage of Richard Tempest to the heir of the Bowling family of Bowling in Bradforddale in 1497 or 1498 established the family with a second sphere of influence in the central West Riding. For a period in the first half of the reign of Henry VIII, **Sir Richard Tempest** (*c.*1480–1537) secured a pre-eminence in the central West Riding. After his death in the Fleet prison in 1537, while under investigation by the council for malfeasance, his two elder sons were unable to maintain their father's standing and, in the third generation, the family's reputation and status were considerably diminished.

The success of the family was based primarily on the marriage of Richard Tempest, son of Sir Nicholas Tempest (*d.* in or after 1483) and his wife, Margaret, or Cicely, Pilkington, to Rosamund (1475/6–1554), the only child of Tristram Bowling of Bowling, in 1497 or 1498. By his daughter's marriage settlement Bowling disinherited his brothers and an illegitimate son of the Bowling name in favour of Richard Tempest. The same settlement envisaged that if Tempest's uncles died without male heirs Tempest would also inherit Bracewell and the family's other Craven estates, and this eventuality came to pass with the death of his uncle Sir Thomas Tempest in 1507. A second factor was Tempest's acquaintance with both Henry VII and Henry VIII. While never one of the inner circle of minions, Tempest was an esquire to both monarchs. He was a participant in the jousts to celebrate the birth of Henry, prince of Wales, in 1511 and took part in other court tournaments in 1516. He was one of the knights dubbed at Tournai on Christmas day 1516; he was named as a knight of the body in 1519 and 1521. In the absence of the younger men in 1519 Tempest was one of the four esquires whose duties included lying on the king's pallet, that is, in the guardroom to the privy chamber. He was in the entourage which met Charles V in 1520 and François I at the Field of Cloth of Gold later that summer. While he does not appear holding household offices after 1521 (and it is noteworthy that in 1522–3 he served on the Scottish borders and not in France), it may be assumed that he exploited his proximity to the king to establish a stranglehold over large parts of the West Riding and Lancashire through his monopoly of the stewardships of the duchy of Lancaster. In the 1520s he was also receiver of the lands of the third earl of Derby during the latter's minority. He served as sheriff of Yorkshire in 1516–17. His acquisition of these offices was aided by the early death of Sir John Savile of Thornhill in 1505. The latter's son, Sir Henry Savile (1499–1558), clearly begrudged Tempest's holding offices late his father's and a series of disputes developed between the two men.

Reports of Tempest's misdoings occurred throughout

his adult life and came to destroy his reputation. There were reports of his using strong-arm tactics and retaining the king's tenants in Bradford about 1503. It was reported that his servants had murdered the king's under-keeper of woods at Barnoldswick before 1513. By 1536 no fewer than nine murders were attributed to members of the Tempest household, although in most cases the evidence implicating Tempest is tendentious. It is hardly surprising that in 1533 an unknown writer suggested to Cromwell that the government of Yorkshire would be improved if Tempest (and others, including Savile) were removed from the commission of the peace. Complaints by Savile to the council in winter or spring 1536 prompted a major enquiry into Tempest's conduct. Savile's accusations included the claim that Tempest was corruptly granting waste land in the manor of Wakefield and had peculated coat and conduct money intended for troops in the Anglo-Scottish war of 1532–3. Some wrongdoing was amply demonstrated, but Tempest was also able to show that Savile habitually employed similar methods. The council's prosecution was halted by the outbreak of the Pilgrimage of Grace in which Tempest's conduct was decidedly lacklustre. He kept himself out of the hands of the commons, but his contribution was disappointing, and during December 1536 the decision was made to transfer the constableship of Sandal Castle to Savile. After Tempest went to London in June 1537 he was imprisoned, probably to answer the charges brought against him by Savile, and died in the Fleet prison in August.

While Tempest was not directly a victim of the pilgrimage his younger brother **Nicholas Tempest** (d. 1537) of Bashall near Clitheroe was tried and executed at Tyburn for his involvement. Tempest is named (with Sir Stephen Hamerton) as the one of the gentry captured by the north Craven commons on 21 October 1536. He led a column of the rebel commons to Whalley Abbey which opened its doors to him after being threatened with the burning of its barns. He was executed for his association with the dissolved monastery at Sawley. In December 1536 the abbot and convent sent to Tempest asking for his aid. They were destitute and Tempest sent them some victuals out of charity. For this act he was executed, on 25 May 1537. He was married to Beatrice, daughter of John Bradford of Heath in Yorkshire.

Sir Richard's elder son, **Sir Thomas Tempest** (c.1500–1545), was knighted at Jedburgh in 1523 by the third duke of Norfolk, was sheriff of Yorkshire in 1542–3, and saw action on the Scottish borders in the latter year. By 1511 he was married to Margaret Tempest, the heir of Sir Thomas Tempest; he was her cousin's son. In this way the unentailed Lincolnshire lands of the family which descended to the heirs-general were brought back into the possession of the male line. By virtue of his Lincolnshire lands Tempest appears on Lincolnshire commissions of the peace and sewers in the early 1530s. In Yorkshire Sir Thomas seems to have been as willing as his father to use violence. In 1522 he was almost certainly responsible for the murder of John Warde, an estate officer of the prioress of Esholt, after he had stopped Tempest hunting in the

prioress's woods, and he also had John Jepson assassinated in Wakefield at Easter 1536 after he had complained about Sir Richard to the council. Following his father's death he made little impression on county society, and died without issue. The estates then passed to Sir Richard's second son, **Sir John Tempest** (c.1500–1565), who was knighted at Kelso in September 1545. He too was active on the borders in the early 1540s, but was captured by the Scots and ransomed in 1542–3. He recovered some of his father's offices, including the stewardships of Bradford and Wakefield and the constableship of Sandal Castle, and was sheriff of Yorkshire in 1546. Late in life he married Anne, the daughter of William Lenthall of Henley-on-Thames. He was her third husband; she was first married to Sir Thomas Tempest of the co. Durham family, a lawyer who was a member of the council of the north from 1525 to his death in 1544. After Sir Thomas's death she married George Smith of Esshe and Nunstainton, co. Durham, who died in 1547. She had married Sir John by 1550. From the mid-1550s Sir John begins to appear in the records as borrowing heavily from London merchants and others. It was reported that by 1564 his total liability on bonds was £7000; he also owed two London creditors £2740 on mortgage. In 1564 a syndicate of relatives redeemed the larger part of the Tempest family estate from Sir John's mortgagees and made sales of some of the estates to try to settle his debts. It seems that his agreement to their settlement was coerced, for in a chancery bill Tempest complained of being arrested on the various bonds he had entered into, and of having been imprisoned for a period in York Castle. The remaining lands were entailed on Sir Richard Tempest's nephew **Richard Tempest** (1536–1583), the son of Nicholas, who was MP for Aldborough, Yorkshire, in 1572, with Sir John being reduced to the status of an annuitant out of the estates. At about this time Archbishop Young of York referred to Sir John as 'a ruler of men and service [but] not able to rule himself or his men' (E. B. Tempest, 504). It is not known why he became so indebted. His wife had died by 1563 and he did not remarry. He died in November 1565.

The impression made on county society by the succeeding generation of Tempests seems to have been limited. Richard Tempest did not sit in parliament again after 1572, and following his cousin's death continued to sell parts of the family estates, probably in an attempt to escape Sir John's debts. In 1569 he was captured while leading a force of 200 men against the northern rising, but refused to join the rebels. He served on the commission of the peace from about 1577, having been earlier named as a 'meet councillor' and a protestant by Sir Thomas Gargrave in his assessment of the Yorkshire gentry. Tempest's will, drawn up in February 1583, does not, however, suggest strong religious convictions. He was married twice, to Helen or Eleanor, daughter of John, eighth Baron Scrope of Bolton, and to Elizabeth, daughter of Thomas Wentworth of Elmsall, who survived him, and whom he named as his executor. But he had no children from either marriage, and when he died, by September 1583, his heir was his younger brother Robert Tempest (c.1539–1601).

The last adult male of the family was another Richard Tempest, who served as a colonel of horse to Charles I and saw action in the royalist army in Yorkshire. He was captured early in 1643 and held at Manchester, but was again in arms for the king in 1644 (when he surrendered in York on 16 July) and once more in 1648. He died in 1657, having sold the remaining family estates in order to disinherit his daughter. As a result there are no known personal papers or estate archive.   R. W. HOYLE

Sources Tempest pedigrees, BL, Add. MS 40670 [collection by Mrs E. B. Tempest] · T. D. Whitaker, *The history and antiquities of the deanery of Craven*, 2 vols. (1878), vol. 1, pedigree, facing p. 96 · R. W. Hoyle, 'The fortunes of the Tempest family of Bracewell and Bowling in the sixteenth century', *Yorkshire Archaeological Journal*, 74 (2002), 169–89 · W. Brown, H. B. McCall, and J. Lister, eds., *Yorkshire Star Chamber proceedings*, 4 vols., Yorkshire Archaeological Society, 41, 45, 51, 70 (1909–27) · E. B. Tempest, 'Nicholas Tempest, a sufferer in the Pilgrimage of Grace', *Yorkshire Archaeological Journal*, 11 (1891), 247–78 · P. R. Newman, *Royalist officers in England and Wales, 1642–1660: a biographical dictionary* (1981), 368 · HoP, *Commons, 1558–1603*, 3.480–81 · [F. W. Dendy and C. H. Hunter Blair], eds., *Visitations of the north*, 4 pts, SurtS, 122, 133, 144, 146 (1912–32) · E. B. Tempest, 'The Tempest family at Bowling Hall', *Bradford Antiquary*, new ser., 1 (1900), 491–511

Tempest, Sir John (c.1500–1565). *See under* Tempest family (*per. c.*1500–1657).

Tempest, Dame Marie [*real name* Mary Susan Etherington] (1864–1942), actress, was born on 15 July 1864 in the Marylebone Road, London, the daughter of Edwin Etherington (1838–1880), stationer, and his wife, Sarah Mary Castle. She took her stage name from the woman she called her godmother, Lady Susan Vane-Tempest: the lack of baptismal records serves to emphasize how far Tempest was her own invention. Her background contained an element of mystery on which she liked to play; her father was the illegitimate son of a man described only as 'a tall blond soldier', who probably financed Tempest's education. She attended Midhurst School, an Ursuline convent at Thildonck, Belgium, a private school in Paris, which gave her fluency in French, and the Royal Academy of Music, where she studied singing under Manuel García and won bronze, silver, and gold medals. By the age of twenty-one she had made her operatic début in Franz Suppé's *Boccaccio* at the Comedy Theatre and was to play leading roles for the rest of her life.

Tempest's own account of her early ambitions, however, dwells less on the opportunities offered her by this expensive training than on the struggle to use it and be valued for doing so. When she first mentioned a desire to act, her 'Grandmamma Etherington', according to her own account, managed to produce Gladstone to dissuade her:

> He spoke of the Greek drama, and then of the monkish Mysteries and Moralities, of Restoration drama and then, clearly introduced by the grand preamble, he spoke of the advent of women on the stage. He frowned as he suggested the depravity of the life I wished to live.   (Bolitho, 14)

Dame Marie Tempest (1864–1942), by Sir William Nicholson, 1903

Most of Tempest's contemporaries in the theatre, especially actresses, had to contend with profound suspicion from the Victorian bourgeoisie. Many also encountered a patronizing male refusal to take their aspirations seriously; this underlies the failure of Tempest's four-year marriage (begun in 1885) to Alfred Edward Izard, a fellow student at the academy, with whom she had a son in 1888; he expected her, she remarked acidly, to be 'both Patti and Mrs Beeton' (ibid., 33).

The risk of trivialization was exacerbated for Tempest by a talent rooted in a comic style that seemed the gracefully spontaneous product of good manners. Memoirs speak of her 'world-renowned' curtsey (*DNB*) and the elegant way she would pass a teacup, as if she merely played herself. Her career, however, was marked by hard work and careful planning. Her approach to a role was not primarily intellectual but grounded in the physical attributes of a character; by constant repetition she gained the effect of unstudied ease. She was acerbic when identified with the characters she played; when, for instance, a theatre manager kitted out her dressing-room in frilled chintz, she pointed out 'I consider [it] my work place. Kindly take all this nonsense away' (Smith, *Look Back*, 257).

The move from opera singer to comic actress took several years. In London she had considerable success in light opera by Hervé and André Messager, creating the title role in *Dorothy* in 1887, before moving to New York for five years. On her return in 1895 she was engaged by George Edwardes for principal roles in musical comedy at Daly's Theatre. While less demanding musically, the very frivolity of Edward Morton's *San Toy*, and Owen Hall's *A Greek Slave* and *The Geisha Girl*, meant that they were dependent for their success on the charm and energy of the cast. In the latter production Tempest set her own stamp on the role of O Mimosa San, a comic Madame Butterfly who sings about the romance between a goldfish and a naval officer:

> Her small inside he daily fed
> With crumbs of the best digestive bread.
> 'This kind attention proves', said she,
> 'How exceedingly fond he is of me.'
> (Holledge, 36)

In 1900 Tempest decided to concentrate on acting, and in 1901 constructed a showcase for herself of two carefully contrasted roles: the sophisticated and scheming heroine in *Becky Sharp*, an adaptation of *Vanity Fair* by Robert Hichens and her second husband, Cosmo Charles Gordon-Lennox, whom she married in 1898, and the exuberant working-class Polly Eccles in Robertson's *Caste*. Both allowed her to abandon sentimental whimsy for an earthier, more vivacious relationship with the audience. Later she explored a more complex range of feeling: when she appeared in Alfred Sutro's *The Barrier* in 1907 Max Beerbohm described her as 'one of the very few English actresses equipped for emotion' (Beerbohm, 329).

Tempest's reputation was well established when in 1914 she embarked on a nine-year tour encompassing North America, Australia, New Zealand, South Africa, India, China, Japan, and the Philippines. On her return she shrewdly revived a comedy favourite, *The Marriage of Kitty*, which Gordon-Lennox had written for her. On his death in 1921 she married the actor William Graham Browne, her constant adviser until his death in 1937. In 1925 they appeared together as the Blisses in Noël Coward's *Hay Fever*. Tempest suggested Coward direct the play himself, and their partnership proved fruitful. Judith Bliss allowed Tempest to create a witty, middle-aged persona for herself, an ironic observer of her own 'Celebrated Actress Glamour' (Coward, 19). It demonstrated her ability to laugh at the Victorian vehicles in which she had made her name and bring her talent to bear on the new, more brittle comic style of the 1920s. In 1927 Coward wrote a similar role for her in *The Marquise*, a costume play in which she played a middle-aged woman delightedly amused at the antics of two lovers duelling over her.

In 1935 Tempest celebrated her golden jubilee on the stage at a special Drury Lane matinée attended by the king and queen. The £5000 raised endowed a Marie Tempest ward at St George's Hospital, one of many charities for which she worked energetically. Two years later she was made a DBE, but the year was marred for her by the death of Browne. In 1938 she created the role of Dora Randolph in Dodie Smith's play *Dear Octopus*, once more a shift into a new style. For the first time, Tempest played an old, rather than older, woman, the linchpin of a middle-class family. Smith's avowed intent was to offer a warm and attractive image of family life; staged as it was during the Munich crisis, the play took on an elegiac, lamplight quality. Its success, Smith remarked, was in no small measure owing to the resonance Tempest had brought to it, a fact which became apparent when she saw the New York production: 'One must see Lucille Watson as Dora to see exactly how good Marie Tempest is' (Grove, 121). However, Tempest's

memory was giving her problems, and her co-ordination was no longer perfect. Although her discipline was such that this was not apparent on stage, this was to be her last important role. It is sad that personality clashes led Dodie Smith in her autobiography to echo Victorian patronage, quoting producer Binkie Beaumont's assertion that 'the technique for which she was so famous emanated entirely from her husband' (Smith, *Look Back*, 252). Tempest's technique was the result of effort, not natural skill, but she was her own woman. She died on 14 October 1942 in London.   FRANCES GRAY

Sources H. Bolitho, *Marie Tempest* (1936) · *DNB* · D. Smith, *Look back with astonishment* (1979) · J. Holledge, *Innocent flowers* (1981) · N. Coward, *Hay fever* (1983) · D. Smith, *Dear octopus* (1938) · P. Hare, *Noel Coward* (1995) · M. Beerbohm, *Last theatres* (1970) · V. Grove, *Dear Dodie: the life of Dodie Smith* (1996)
Archives Metropolitan Toronto Reference Library, notebook, album, and address book
Likenesses J. E. Blanche, oils, 1903, Garr. Club · W. Nicholson, oils, 1903, NPG [*see illus.*] · W. Nicholson, oils, 1908, priv. coll. · W. Nicholson, oils, 1908 (*Souvenir de Marie*), Gallery of Modern Art, Dublin · J. O. de Ban, lithograph, *c*.1910, V&A · Stage Photo Co., photograph, *c*.1930–1939, NPG · G. Anthony, photograph, 1935, NPG · Histed, photogravure (as young woman), NPG · G. Sheringham, pencil drawing, Garr. Club · photographs, Trinity College of Music, Jerwood Library, Mander and Mitchenson Theatre Collection · photographs on postcards, NPG

Tempest, Nicholas (*d.* 1537). *See under* Tempest family (*per. c*.1500–1657).

Tempest, Pierce (1653–1717), printseller, was the sixth son of Henry Tempest of Tong in Yorkshire and his wife, Mary Bushall; his eldest brother, John, was the first baronet. This background gave him the entrée to the circles of virtuosi in London where he spent his entire career, although he maintained his link with York, and was particularly close to Francis Place and William Lodge, both of whose work he published.

Tempest was in London by November 1678, when he established himself in the Strand as a publisher of prints, one of the most important of his day. The range of his production, which still awaits full investigation, was very varied; the mezzotints he published are all datable to between about 1683 and 1688. Tempest seems never to have put an address on his plates, and his advertisements and letters give such a motley collection of addresses as to suggest that he preferred dealing from home to keeping a shop. His most important publications were the six sets of bird and animal designs engraved by Place and Griffier from 1686 onwards from newly commissioned drawings by Francis Barlow, and the famous series entitled *The Cries of London* drawn by Marcellus Laroon and engraved by John Savage; this began with forty plates in 1687 and expanded to seventy-four by the summer of 1689. After 1700 Tempest published fewer plates, though he kept his older ones in print. He now turned his attention to dealing in old master prints and drawings, and became a friend and supplier to such important collectors as the Talmans. In 1709 he published a translation of Cesare Ripa's *Iconologia* (1593) illustrated by Isaac Fuller the younger.

Tempest died on 1 April 1717 and was buried in St Paul's,

Covent Garden. In his will he asked his brother Nicholas to supervise the education of his illegitimate only child, George (a task that his brother refused). The will was proved on 24 April by Hannah Williams, the mother and guardian of George.

F. M. O'DONOGHUE, rev. ANTONY GRIFFITHS

Sources Tempest family record book, Broughton Hall, Yorkshire · S. Shesgreen, *Criers and hawkers of London: engravings and drawings by Marcellus Laroon* (1990) · A. Griffiths and R. A. Gerard, *The print in Stuart Britain, 1603–1689* (1998), 244–5, 260 [exhibition catalogue, BM, 8 May – 20 Sept 1998] · Burke, *Peerage*
Likenesses F. Place, mezzotint (after E. van Heemskerk), NPG, BM · J. Savage, portrait (after M. Laroon), repro. in *Cries of London* (1687–9), plate 73

Tempest, Sir Richard (c.1480–1537). *See under* Tempest family (*per.* c.1500–1657).

Tempest, Richard (1536–1583). *See under* Tempest family (*per.* c.1500–1657).

Tempest, Sir Thomas (c.1500–1545). *See under* Tempest family (*per.* c.1500–1657).

Temple. For this title name *see* Osborne, Dorothy [Dorothy Temple, Lady Temple] (1627–1695); Chamber, Anna [Anna Grenville-Temple, Countess Temple] (1709?–1777); Grenville, Richard, second Earl Temple (1711–1779).

Temple, Anna Grenville-, Countess Temple. *See* Chamber, Anna (1709?–1777).

Temple, Charles Lindsay (1871–1929), colonial official and author, was born on 20 November 1871 at Simla, India, the son of Sir Richard *Temple, bt (1826–1902), administrator in India, and his second wife, Mary Augusta (d. 1924), daughter of Charles Robert Lindsay of the Bengal civil service and his wife, Rhoda Charlotte. Temple was connected through his immediate family, and his mother's relationship with the earls of Crawford, to the intellectual, social, and political élite of the period. After attending Sedbergh School (1882–9) he entered Trinity College, Cambridge, in 1890 to read engineering but left the following year due to recurring bouts of ill health. In spite of considerable intellectual ability he abandoned a university career, instead joining the Hampstead literary set where he developed his linguistic and anthropological interests. Finding no lasting satisfaction there, he decided to seek his fortune in Brazil. Between 1893 and 1896 he rapidly learnt Portuguese, travelled, traded, and ran his own coffee plantation in Cuyaba. Dissatisfied with limited success, he travelled to London, gaining a Royal Geographical Society diploma in surveying in 1896 before returning to Brazil in the hope of building a major road between Para and Cuyaba. Thwarted by the vacillation of the local authorities he gave up this plan, gained a post with the consular service, and served in Para and Manaos (1898–1901).

In August 1901, seeking faster promotion, Temple transferred to the colonial service. Because of the reputation he had built in Brazil, he was appointed to the newly formed political service for Northern Nigeria as a third-class resident—higher than the normal starting rank of assistant resident. Between 1901 and 1910 he enhanced his reputation through exceptional work as resident-in-charge of the important provinces of Bauchi, Sokoto, and Kano, as well as becoming chief examiner in the Hausa language. Following his services to the Northern Nigerian lands committee, Temple was made a CMG in 1909. In 1910 he was appointed chief secretary with a dormant commission to administer the protectorate in the absence of the governor. Temple acted, with great success, as governor from January to August 1911 and from June to October 1912. Following the amalgamation of Nigeria in January 1914, he served under Sir Frederick Lugard, the governor-general, as lieutenant-governor of the northern provinces, and held this office until his retirement due to ill health in 1917.

Temple's wife, Olive Susan Miranda MacLeod (1880–1936) [see Temple, Olive Susan Miranda], whom he had married on 28 April 1912, shared his sense of adventure and his intellectual interests. Olive went on tour with Charles, taking an active interest in his administrative and anthropological activities. They both wrote books and articles on Nigeria as well as making photographic and phonographic recordings of the local communities, presenting useful collections to the Royal Geographical Society and to the social anthropologist Sir James George Frazer.

As one of the most able administrators of the first two decades of British control in Northern Nigeria, Temple had an important influence on the formative years of indirect rule. He frequently had fierce clashes with Lugard over the application of this policy, particularly objecting to Lugard's capricious style of administration which he felt undermined hard won reforms. Early accounts of Temple are largely critical but subsequently available sources have led to a reassessment of his significance to the colonial history of Nigeria. Of these sources, his wife's papers, which give a particularly detailed and vivid account of Temple's time in Nigeria, make clear that he was a very ambitious man determined to make a name for himself as a liberal, scientific, and modern administrator. Other contemporary accounts demonstrate that he largely achieved this, and would have been appointed governor of Uganda in 1917 had ill health not intervened. During Charles's sick leave (from 1916) and recuperation the Temples stayed in Cape Province, and it was here that he wrote *Native Races and their Rulers* (1918). In this book Temple explained and justified his conception of indirect rule from the basis of a social Darwinist world-view, as well as making a satirical and cryptic attack on Lugard's style of administration. Finding South Africa uncongenial, the Temples moved to Granada, Spain, where they remained until Charles died of kidney failure on 9 January 1929. He was buried in Granada. C. J. F. ALDERMAN

Sources C. J. F. Alderman, 'British imperialism and social Darwinism: C. L. Temple and colonial administration in Northern Nigeria, 1901–1916', PhD diss., Kingston University, 1996 · M. Perham, *Lugard*, 2: *The years of authority, 1898–1945* (1960) · D. J. M. Muffett, *Concerning brave captains* (1964) · I. F. Nicolson, *The administration of Nigeria, 1900–1960* (1969) · A. H. M. Kirk-Greene, *The principles of native administration in Nigeria: selected documents, 1900–1947*

(1965) • G. Brenan, *South from Granada* (1963) • P. D. Curtin, *Imperialism: selected documents* (1972) • K. Tidrick, *Empire and the English character* (1990) • R. Heussler, *Yesterday's rulers: the making of the British colonial service* (1963) • R. Heussler, *The British in Northern Nigeria* (1968) • J. M. Carland, *The colonial office in Nigeria, 1898–1914* (1985) • M. Crowder, *West Africa under colonial rule* (1981) • M. Crowder, *The story of Nigeria* (1966) • K. Robinson and F. Madden, *Essays in imperial government* (1963) • *Colonial Office List* (1902–16) • *CGPLA Eng. & Wales* (1929) • Burke, *Peerage* • *The Sedberghian* (March 1929)

Archives Bodl. RH, historical notes on Bauchi and Kano, MSS Afr. s. 1531, 5–6 • Bodl. RH, topographical and anthropological sketches, notes, and photographs, MSS Afr. s. 2000; t. 37 • NRA, priv. coll., corresp. relating to his travels in Brazil • PRO, Colonial Office MSS, CO 446, 584, 585, 586, 763, 764, 658 • PRO, Foreign Office MSS, FO 566, 779, 789, 812, 820, 804 • RGS, corresp. | Dunvegan Muniments, Isle of Skye, Macleod MSS, section 4, ref. 2123/1–4 • Dunvegan Muniments, Isle of Skye, Olive Macleod MSS, sections 4 and 5, *passim*

Likenesses photograph, repro. in Perham, *Lugard*

Wealth at death £1871 19s. 7d.: resworn probate, 3 April 1929, *CGPLA Eng. & Wales*

Temple [*née* Lamb], **Emily Mary** [Amelia], **Viscountess Palmerston** (1787–1869), political hostess, was born on 21 April 1787, the fifth surviving child of Elizabeth *Lamb, *née* Milbanke, Viscountess Melbourne (*bap.* 1751, *d.* 1818). She was ostensibly and legally the child of Peniston Lamb, first Viscount Melbourne (1745–1828), but her natural father was probably George O'Brien *Wyndham, third earl of Egremont (1751–1837). She received her formal education (such as it was) from governesses, but learned the skills for her future life as a political hostess from her adored mother and her mother's close friend, Georgiana, duchess of Devonshire. She also acquired their loose interpretation of sexual morality, a firm sense of family, and the 'Devonshire House drawl', a distinctive mode of pronunciation common to the whig aristocracy. She enjoyed a particularly close relationship with two of her four brothers, William *Lamb, later second Viscount Melbourne, and Frederick *Lamb, later Baron Beauvale and third Viscount Melbourne. (Her only sister, Harriet, died in 1803.)

The charming, coquettish Emily Lamb made her society début in 1804, and her elegant figure, grey eyes, dark hair, and translucent complexion won her many male admirers. Women, especially those of an age to be her rivals in the marriage market, were less taken with her. Lady Melbourne was ambitious for all her children, and encouraged the suit of the young, handsome, rich whig peer Peter Leopold Louis Francis Nassau Cowper, fifth Earl Cowper (1778–1837). The couple were married on 20 July 1805 at Melbourne House in London. But Cowper was dull. Having so much, he lacked ambition, and despite the hopes of the whig grandees he never came to anything as a politician; it was only the sparkle of his wife that kept him from fading completely into obscurity. As early as December 1805 Lady Harriet Cavendish (no admirer of Lady Cowper) observed that:

> He is never with her and affects great indifference and neglect, though I believe he really cares for her as much as he can for anything and she seems tolerably contented,

Emily Mary Temple, Viscountess Palmerston (1787–1869), attrib. E. Butler Morris, *c.*1867

> though I hear she is reduced to rejoice when he comes home drunk, as he talks to her more then than at any other time. (Cavendish, 139)

Although initially much in love with her husband, Emily Cowper was not one to put up with such treatment for long. She followed her mother's dictum and provided her husband with an indisputable heir—George, Viscount Fordwich, born in June 1806—and then (her husband complaisant) proceeded on her merry way through a throng of admirers, suitors, and lovers. The paternity of her four further children—Emily, William, (Charles) Spencer, and Frances, born between 1808 and 1820—was a matter for speculation then and is now, but William bore a striking physical resemblance to his mother's most consistent lover, Henry John *Temple, third Viscount Palmerston (1784–1865), who was also supposed to be the father of her youngest child, Frances.

After Lady Melbourne's death in 1818 Emily assumed responsibility for her brothers, and much of her energy was directed towards the management of (or interference in) their affairs. William's tormented marriage with Lady Caroline Lamb and the wreckage of his political career in the 1820s was a matter of lasting concern, and with Frederick, a career diplomat, she maintained a regular political and social correspondence. She also inherited her mother's role as a leader of fashionable society, becoming (with Lady Jersey and Madame de Lieven) one of the 'lady patronesses' of the society balls held at Almack's, and a regular member of the court of George IV. By the late 1820s she had established herself as a hostess to the Canningite whigs, which grouping included both her brother William and her lover Palmerston, at the Cowper mansion, Panshanger, in Hertfordshire. When the widowed Melbourne became home secretary in 1830 and then prime minister in 1834, Lady Cowper naturally assumed the role of his hostess; her ties to the ministry were cemented by Palmerston's position as foreign secretary. She sincerely mourned the death of Lord Cowper, on 27 June 1837, barely a week after the accession of Queen Victoria, and consequently played little public part at the court during the first year of Victoria's reign, though she offered advice to Melbourne on his handling of the young queen. The marriages of her children, especially her daughters, were also a major preoccupation: her namesake, Lady Emily, had inherited all her mother's liveliness, and it was something of a surprise to society at large when in 1830 she decided to marry the earnest, evangelical tory Anthony Ashley-Cooper, later seventh earl of Shaftesbury. Despite considerable personal attractions, her younger daughter, Lady Frances, was more difficult to suit, and Frances was still unmarried when, on 16 December 1839, Emily Cowper and Palmerston were finally married. Lady Frances (who did not like Palmerston) was not amused. The queen, young love embodied, felt sure the match between the elderly couple would make Albert smile, but she gave them a condescending blessing because Palmerston 'is quite alone in the world, and *Lady C.* is a very clever woman, and *much* attached to him' (*Letters of Queen Victoria*, 1st ser., 1.255). But if Victoria and Albert represented the love match of the century, Emily and Palmerston ran them a close second. 'What is the use', Palmerston was to write, 'of People being Married, if they are to pass their Lives away from Each other?' (Reynolds, 6). At the age of sixty-two Emily refused to travel alone with 'Poodle' Byng, an old admirer, lest it arouse Palmerston's jealousy.

The wife of the foreign secretary had important social obligations, for in addition to any political entertaining she might undertake on behalf of the ministry, she was expected to receive and entertain the diplomatic corps in London and in the country, and she was required to present the wives and daughters of the corps at court. Lady Palmerston threw herself into the part with gusto, but the ministry was on its last legs, and when it fell in September 1841 she and Palmerston took themselves off on a tour of his Irish property. A period out of office she considered beneficial, for it would allow the whig party, 'grown supine and tired', to 'start up like a Giant refreshed' (*Letters of Lady Palmerston*, 257).

Lady Palmerston was soon established, in office and out of it, as the première political hostess in London. Her regular Saturday parties during the season at 5 Carlton House Terrace and, from 1855, at Cambridge House, Piccadilly (which conveniently had two gates, facilitating the arrival and departure of her guests' coaches), were packed with politicians, diplomats, and courtiers, peers, bishops, and office-seekers, as well as a smattering of carefully selected journalists, notably John Delane of *The Times*, and the inevitable array of débutantes with their ambitious mamas. The point about Lady Palmerston's 'drums' was that everybody who counted, or who aspired to count, went to them.

They served to bolster the governments in which Palmerston was involved, and to forge support for him in opposition, but they were not restricted to his political colleagues. In a time of great fluidity of political parties and personal allegiances, at Lady Palmerston's everyone could meet. Only when Palmerston suffered personal indignity or when party feeling ran particularly high did Lady Palmerston exclude his opponents from her soirées, and then only for a few days. But the huge Saturday night parties for hundreds were only part of her role. More intimate gatherings, dinners (often preceding a big evening party), and country house parties at the Palmerstons' Hampshire home, Broadlands, were directed with aplomb by Emily, to explicitly political ends. She was a great believer in the power of social influence, and when a contentious vote was forthcoming in the house she would declare 'Stay! we will have a party!' (Airlie, *Lady Palmerston*, 2.43). Few political men cared to admit the power of such influence, the insinuating charm of social recognition, the frisson from hearing the latest political gossip at first hand, the satisfaction of wives and daughters at being invited to balls and parties at Cambridge House; fewer still admitted that their votes in the house, or their acceptance or refusal of office, could be affected by the warmth of Lady Palmerston's greeting, or the heartiness of her husband's; but Palmerston's friends and enemies alike acknowledged the importance of his wife's hospitality in maintaining his position.

Emily Temple entertained indefatigably for her husband for twenty-five years. As importantly, she was his friend and confidante: Henry Greville thought that 'no other human being than his wife share[d] his confidence' (*Diary of Henry Greville*, 4.259). She was not a political thinker, but had a firm grasp of the realities of the political system and its operation. She had learned her political loyalties at her mother's knee; family, not ideology or party, was her ultimate master, and in her eyes Palmerston could do no wrong. As an intelligence gatherer with sources in Britain and all over continental Europe she had no equal. She had a reputation for indiscretion, but it was always calculated:

> She always understood full well what she was telling, to whom she was telling it, when and where it would be repeated, and whether the repetition would do harm or good … no one ever knew from or through Lady Palmerston what Lord Palmerston did not wish to be known. (*The Times*, 15 Sept 1869)

After the deaths of her brothers William and Frederick, in 1848 and 1853, she inherited the Lamb estates, at Brocket Hall in Hertfordshire, Melbourne in Derbyshire, and elsewhere. The Palmerstons' health failed slowly but inevitably in the 1860s, but the parties went on, and Emily continued to listen to Palmerston from the ladies' gallery of the House of Commons, or anxiously to await his late-night return from the house. Palmerston died, still in office as prime minister, at Brocket on 18 October 1865. Emily was devastated, but consoled herself with her children and grandchildren. She moved out of Cambridge House into 21 Park Lane in January 1866, and divided her time between Brocket, Broadlands, London, and her children's houses. London society continued to call on Lady Palmerston until her death at Brocket on 11 September 1869; six days later she was buried next to her husband in Westminster Abbey.   K. D. REYNOLDS

Sources The letters of Lady Palmerston, ed. T. Lever (1957) · Mabell, countess of Airlie, In whig society, 1775–1818 (1921) · Mabell, countess of Airlie, Lady Palmerston and her times, 2 vols. (1922) · The Lieven–Palmerston correspondence, ed. Lord Sudley (1943) · K. Bourne, Palmerston: the early years, 1784–1841 (1982) · K. D. Reynolds, Aristocratic women and political society in Victorian Britain (1998) · Hary-O: the letters of Lady Harriet Cavendish, 1796–1809, ed. G. Leveson-Gower and I. Palmer (1940) · A. Hayward, The Times (15 Sept 1869) · J. Ridley, Lord Palmerston (1970) · The letters of Queen Victoria, ed. A. C. Benson, Lord Esher [R. B. Brett], and G. E. Buckle, 9 vols. (1907–32) · Lady Enfield, memoir, in Leaves from the diary of Henry Greville, ed. A. H. F. Byng, countess of Strafford, 4 vols. (1883–1905) · F. E. Baily, The love story of Lady Palmerston (1938) · The Times (18 Sept 1869) · L. G. Mitchell, Lord Melbourne (1997) · GEC, Peerage · m. cert. [Henry John Temple] · d. cert.

Archives BL, family corresp., Add. MSS 45548–45556, passim; MS 45911 · BL, papers · Hatfield House, Hertfordshire, diaries · U. Southampton L., family corresp. | BL, letters to fourth Lady Holland, Add. MS 52125 · BL, corresp. with Lord Holland, Add. MS 52001 · BL, corresp. with Princess Lieven, Add. MSS 47368–47369 · Hants. RO, letters to Lord Malmesbury · PRO, corresp. with Lord John Russell, PRO 30/22

Likenesses T. Lawrence, oils, c.1803, Broadlands, Hampshire; repro. in Baily, Love story · Hoppner-Jackson, portrait, c.1810, repro. in Letters, ed. Lever · J. R. Swinton, oils, c.1840, Broadlands, Hampshire; repro. in Baily, Love story · J. Lucas, oils, c.1850, Broadlands, Hampshire; repro. in Letters, ed. Lever · attrib. E. B. Morris, drawing, c.1867, Broadlands, Hampshire [see illus.] · M. Gauci, lithograph (after J. Lucas), BM · H. Hering, carte-de-visite, NPG · F. Holl, stipple (after J. R. Swinton), BM · portraits, repro. in Letters, ed. Lever

Wealth at death under £120,000: probate, June 1870, CGPLA Eng. & Wales · £8000: probate, 3 Aug 1870, CGPLA Ire.

Temple, Frederick (1821–1902), archbishop of Canterbury, was born on 30 November 1821 on Santa Maura, one of the Ionian Islands. He was son of Octavius Temple (1784–1834), major in the 4th foot, sub-inspector of militia in the Ionian Islands, and resident at Santa Maura. William Johnson *Temple was his grandfather. Frederick Temple claimed to belong to the Stowe branch of the Temple family, of which Richard *Grenville, third duke of Buckingham and Chandos, was the head. His mother was Dorcas (1786–1866), daughter of Richard Carveth of Probus, Cornwall.

Family and education Temple was the thirteenth of fifteen children, seven of whom died young. The family returned to England in 1830 to a farm at Axon, near Culmstock in Devon. His father died on 13 August 1834 in Sierra Leone, where he had been made governor the year before, having failed as a farmer. With a government pension of £100 per annum Frederick's mother, despite having no formal education herself, educated her three youngest children until they went to school, although much of their time was spent in farm labour. She thus exercised an unusual influence over all her children, especially Frederick, who never forgot his debt to her for his early education and remained close to his mother for the rest of her life. She joined him and his sisters in Oxford in the autumn of 1843 and as soon as he had a home to offer in Rugby in 1857, he shared it

Frederick Temple (1821–1902), by Sir Hubert von Herkomer, 1896

with her and his youngest sister, Jennetta. His mother lived there until her death on 8 May 1866; this marked Temple's first real separation from her.

On 29 January 1834 Temple entered Blundell's School, Tiverton, and remained there until 25 March 1839. From the first he showed great ability and industry. In half a year he passed through the lower to the upper school, two and a half years being the usual period required. In 1838 he won the Blundell scholarship, and entered Balliol College, Oxford, on 9 April 1839, a gift of £50 (probably from Sir Thomas Acland) enabling him to avail himself of the scholarship. Throughout his undergraduate days he was forced to live very economically. He went up to Oxford a first-rate mathematician, winning the Powell prize during his first year and later the senior exhibition from the Mercers' Company. In addition, during the three years following he so much improved his limited knowledge of classics that he was proxime accessit (second) for the Ireland university scholarship in March 1842. In May 1842 he was the first person to obtain without the help of any private tuition (owing to the kindness of his tutors, particularly Robert Scott) a double first class in classics and mathematics. He had several distinguished tutors, such as Robert Scott; A. C. Tait, to whose friendship and wisdom he owed much; Benjamin Jowett, who was only four years his senior, and became one of his most intimate friends; and W. G. Ward, who was his mathematical tutor. Among his friends and contemporaries were A. H. Clough, Constantine Prichard, A. P. Stanley, J. D. Coleridge, Matthew Arnold, and R. R. W. Lingen. He was much impressed by the deep religious tone of Newman and Pusey, and though naturally much interested in the theological discussions arising out of the publication of the Tracts for the Times, he was never strongly influenced by them.

Temple went up to Oxford a tory, and so remained while he was an undergraduate. But Oxford enlarged his outlook, and his views gradually settled into the Liberalism which characterized his later life. In 1846 he was on Gladstone's Oxford election committee. When the case to deprive Ward of his degrees (after he had published a strong defence of Roman Catholicism in *The Ideal of a Christian Church*), was brought before convocation at Oxford on 13 February 1845, Temple voted in the minority against the censure and also against his degradation; later, in 1847, he signed the memorial against Bishop Hampden's condemnation. In November 1842 he was appointed lecturer in mathematics and logic, and was afterwards elected fellow of Balliol and, in 1845, junior dean of his college, during which time he was one of the few Englishmen to read much German philosophy, particularly that of Kant. He was ordained deacon in 1846, and in 1847 priest, by Bishop Samuel Wilberforce of Oxford.

Schoolmaster and educationist When Tait left Balliol for Rugby in June 1842, he had vainly offered Temple a post there, but Temple then felt that his first duty was to his college. On 1 May 1848, however, he left Oxford on the advice of Sir J. P. Kay Shuttleworth to undertake work under the committee of council on education, first as examiner in the education office at Whitehall until the end of 1849, then as principal of Kneller Hall, between Whitton and Twickenham, a training college for workhouse schoolmasters. At the end of 1855, after the failure of Kneller Hall, Temple was made inspector of training colleges for men, having been regarded for some years as an authority on educational matters. He was invited by the Oxford University commission, set up in August 1850, to give evidence in writing, and proposed several reforms, including the opening up of fellowships and the creation of new professorships, which were afterwards put into effect. To the *Oxford Essays* of 1856 he contributed an essay on national education, and in June 1857, in conjunction with Thomas Dyke Acland, was chiefly responsible for persuading the University of Oxford (followed soon after by Cambridge) to institute (21 June 1858) the associate in arts examination which later developed into the Oxford and Cambridge local examinations.

On 12 November 1857 Temple was appointed headmaster of Rugby School, where he had undoubted success, exercising influence on both masters and boys as a stimulating intellectual teacher and an earnest religious man. Notable among his reforms were those to increase the staff, to enlarge and systematize the teaching of history and to relate this to the other disciplines, to make English language and literature a 'form' subject throughout the school (from 1865), and to introduce natural science, music, and drawing into the regular curriculum (from 1864). Before he left he obtained money to build a new quadrangle, containing a music school and drawing school, two science lecture rooms, two laboratories, and six good classical classrooms. He also made the game of rugby football less barbarous, and during his time the chapel was enlarged to meet the increased numbers of pupils. While headmaster he gave evidence to the Newcastle royal commission on popular education in 1860, and in 1861 before the public schools commission under Lord Clarendon, which led to the Public Schools Act of 1868. He was subsequently, on 28 December 1864, appointed a member of the Taunton royal commission on endowed schools, on which he was very influential. Its report was issued in March 1868; chapter 2, on the kinds of education desirable, and chapter 7, containing the recommendations of the commissioners, were drafted by him. These chapters, together with his Oxford essay, give Temple's mature views on secondary education.

Bishop of Exeter On 23 July 1869 Gladstone offered Temple the deanery of Durham. He refused this, but in September of the same year Gladstone boldly offered him a choice of four bishoprics, and he accepted the see of Exeter, on account of his west country background. His appointment raised a storm of opposition on the grounds that he had been a contributor to the notorious *Essays and Reviews* (1860), even though his own essay, 'The education of the world', was little open to exception and was based on a sermon originally given at Rugby and later before Oxford University. However, since the volume had no editor, the contributors took equal responsibility for it, those with benefices (Rowland Williams and H. B. Wilson) being condemned by convocation for heresy (a sentence reversed by the privy council). Temple had, moreover, supported J. W. Colenso's appeal to the privy council in 1865. Lord Shaftesbury and E. B. Pusey united to oppose his consecration, and it was doubtful beforehand whether the dean and chapter of Exeter would act on the *congé d'élire*. Ultimately, of the twenty-three members entitled to vote, thirteen were in favour, six against (including some of the most senior clergy), and four were absent. When the confirmation took place in Bow church, two of the beneficed clergy of the diocese appeared in opposition, led by Bishop Trower, subdean of the cathedral. Urged on many sides by friends and opponents to make some declaration as to his orthodoxy, he firmly refused to break silence until after his consecration, which took place on St Thomas's day, 21 December 1869, in Westminster Abbey. Consecrating him were the bishops of London (Jackson), acting for Archbishop Tait, who was ill; St David's (Thirlwall); Worcester (Philpott); and Ely (Browne), who nevertheless refused to present him. He was enthroned on 29 December 1869. After his consecration he withdrew his essay from future editions of *Essays and Reviews*, as was announced to convocation in February 1870. To quote a letter of 11 February 1870 from J. B. Lightfoot to E. W. Benson, 'he was courageous in refusing to withdraw his name when it was clamorously demanded, and not less courageous in withdrawing it when the withdrawal would expose him to the criticism of his advanced friends'.

Two main ideas led to Temple's change from youthful toryism to Liberalism: first, the need to raise the condition of the working classes, and secondly, the conviction that their amelioration could be effected only by enabling them to help themselves. A strong advocate of educational reform, he was also a social reformer, as is evidenced by his strong and persistent advocacy of temperance; nevertheless, he was firmly convinced that neither education nor temperance would be effective without religion. As bishop of Exeter he had an early opportunity of putting his views into practice. The Elementary Education Act was passed in 1870, making it necessary for churches to improve and add to their schools. At a meeting at Exeter in September 1870, by his words and his example in subscribing £500, Temple persuaded the diocese to raise a large sum for the purpose. It was also necessary to deal with senior schools in the diocese of Exeter. His letter to the mayor of 5 February 1872 on the endowed schools commissioners' proposals carried such weight that his main points were eventually adopted. They embodied a system of exhibitions, whereby the poorest child might rise from elementary to senior school and so to university, and also the establishment of two schools for the secondary education of girls. In 1904 a royal commission under Professor Sadler found that there was a higher percentage of children receiving secondary education in Exeter than in any other British city, and attributed it to a great extent to Temple's efforts. In Plymouth, too, he was instrumental in founding secondary schools.

Temple had from as early as 1862 taken part in the temperance movement, which had come into prominence partly through the report of the committee of convocation of Canterbury in 1869. When as bishop he took the chair in Exeter on 23 January 1872 at a meeting of the United Kingdom Alliance, the proceedings were so unruly as to require the intervention of the police, and a bag of flour struck him in the chest. Soon afterwards, however, he was always enthusiastically received at his frequent public addresses on the subject. He later became chairman of the Church of England Temperance Society (CETS) and president of the National Temperance League, and was made an honorary member of the Rechabite Order in 1883. At Canterbury he reorganized the diocesan branch of the CETS and spoke on temperance as late as 1900 in the House of Lords.

Despite the size of his diocese, which comprised Devon and Cornwall, Temple visited most of the parishes, in many of which a bishop had not been seen for long, and soon realized the need to divide the diocese. Lady Rolle's donation in 1875 of £40,000 to the endowment fund gave a great impetus to the scheme, and in 1876 a bill to create the diocese of Truro was passed, which included a transfer of £800 per annum from the Exeter endowment.

In 1874 Temple was petitioned by the chancellor of the diocese (Archdeacon Phillpotts, son of the previous bishop) to inquire into the legality of the erection of a new reredos in the cathedral. As visitor and ordinary he gave sentence for its removal. After appeal by the dean and chapter, the dean of arches reversed this judgment, but the privy council, on appeal from Phillpotts on 25 February 1875, reversed the judgment of the court of arches, in so far as it limited the bishop's visitatorial jurisdiction over the cathedral, but maintained it on two points,

namely the non-requirement of a faculty and the legality of the figures. When a similar question was raised in regard to the reredos in St Paul's in April 1888 by the Church Association, circumstances had changed following the Public Worship Regulation Act of 1874. The privy council ruled there was nothing illegal in the figures, and the legislature had granted to the bishops discretionary power to stop proceedings. Accordingly, as bishop of London, Temple refused to allow the case to proceed. His veto was later upheld by the House of Lords. His speeches while bishop of Exeter—in the House of Lords on the University Tests Bill (14 July 1870) and on the bill for opening churchyards to nonconformists (15 May 1876)—showed him true to his liberal principles. During his episcopate he became the University of London delegate to the governing body of Rugby School in 1871, and for the last ten years of his life was its chairman. He was also governor of Sherborne School and ultimately also of Winchester and Charterhouse. At Canterbury he maintained close links with King's School. At Jowett's prompting, in 1884 he delivered at Oxford the Bampton lectures, on the relation between religion and science. Among his hearers on one occasion were Matthew Arnold and Robert Browning; many younger men who heard him, including Cosmo Gordon Lang, never forgot the impression which he made, partly by his vigorous arguments and still more by his direct and forceful personality.

Marriage and family On 24 August 1876 Temple, then aged fifty-five, married Beatrice Blanche, fifth daughter of William Saunders Sebright Lascelles and Lady Caroline Georgiana Howard (daughter of the sixth earl of Carlisle). Lacking his intellectual powers, she offered him simple companionship throughout his later years. They had two sons, Frederick Charles (1879–1957), who served in the Indian Civil Service as an engineer from 1908 to 1936 and was regional controller of fuel and power in Britain from 1942 to 1946, and William *Temple (1881–1944), who, uniquely, followed his father as archbishop of Canterbury in 1942.

Bishop of London On 27 January 1885 Gladstone, on E. W. Benson's advice, offered Temple the see of London. A public meeting in the Guildhall at Exeter on 27 February 1885, which led to many testimonials, proved how completely the bishop had won his way. Of the 700 clergy of the diocese who had protested against his election in 1869, 654 signed a memorial of regret on 31 July 1885 at his departure. He was enthroned at St Paul's in April 1885 and threw himself with his accustomed vigour into the work of the diocese and into all the great ecclesiastical and social questions of the day. In accordance with his views on self-government, he introduced on 1 June 1885 a plan to allow the clergy to elect their own rural deans. Besides delivering his episcopal charges, he gave addresses in turn at the several ruridecanal chapters and held his first diocesan conference in 1886. He spoke on subjects including the relation of the church to the poor in London and the growth of scepticism and indifference (1888), and dealt with the archbishop's judgment in the trial of Edward King, bishop of Lincoln (upheld by the privy council in

1892). On this case, he had been leading adviser to Archbishop Benson. He reorganized lay work in the diocese, forming a new organization of readers on 21 March 1891. He also added to the number of suffragan bishops, reviving the ancient title of bishop of Marlborough in 1886. In 1887 it was mainly due to his energy and advocacy that the church's memorial of Queen Victoria's jubilee took the permanent form of Church House, in Dean's Yard, Westminster. While at Exeter he piloted through the House of Lords the Pluralities Act Amendment Bill, which became an act of parliament in 1885. The Clergy Discipline Act passed in 1892 owed much to his efforts.

In 1888 Temple was a member of the Cross royal commission on education, never missing a sitting, and was a prime mover of the Education Bill of 1890. In the summer of 1889 he gave valuable evidence before a commission presided over by Lord Selborne with reference to a teaching university for London, and as a member of another commission under Lord Cowper offered a defence of the collegiate system and of denominational institutions in the university. He gave evidence on 6 July 1894 before the secondary education commission, of which James Bryce was the chairman. He continued to be actively engaged in the reform of elementary education for the rest of his life, serving on the parliamentary subcommittee on aid to diocesan schools in 1897. He also served on the royal commission on the blind, the deaf and the dumb in 1885, and in the same year played a leading part in the royal commission on housing of the working classes in 1885. While bishop of London, he gave land to enlarge Bishop's Park, Fulham, originally given by Bishop Jackson in 1884, which was opened by the chairman of the London county council on 22 December 1893. Later, when archbishop of Canterbury, he handed over a field adjoining Lambeth Palace for use as a recreation ground. This was put in order by the London county council and opened on 24 October 1901.

At the time of the dockers' strike, from 14 August to 14 September 1889, Temple's return to London from his holiday, after prompting by Cyril Bickersteth of the Christian Social Union, led the lord mayor to intervene and form the so-called Mansion House conciliation committee (which also included Cardinal Manning), by means of which a compromise was ultimately reached. It was remarked at the time that Temple was undiplomatic and showed little sympathy with the dockers, whose demands he considered unreasonable.

Archbishop of Canterbury On 22 October 1896 Temple was nominated by Lord Salisbury to the archbishopric of Canterbury, even though his eyesight and physical strength were already failing. He was given a public farewell in St Paul's on 23 December 1896, and a meeting to commemorate his London episcopate took place at the Guildhall on 18 January 1897, which the lord mayor and corporation of the City of London attended in state. At least 1500 persons were present, and many presentations were made to the archbishop and his wife. He had previously been honoured by the diocese with the presentation of a pastoral staff in November 1891.

Temple was enthroned in Canterbury Cathedral on 8 January 1897 and was older than any of his predecessors. His first public task was to issue the responses to Pope Leo XIII's pronouncement on Anglican orders on 19 February 1897, from which he 'cut out all the thunder'. With the consent of the ecclesiastical commissioners he sold Addington Park in July 1898, the country residence of the archbishops since its purchase by Archbishop Manners Sutton; with part of the proceeds of the sale he bought a house in the precincts of Canterbury known as the Old Palace, which he had converted by Caröe into a suitable residence. The memorial stone was laid on 28 May 1899. On 21 June 1897 Temple attended the service in St Paul's to commemorate the sixtieth year of Queen Victoria's reign, and on 23 June he was the principal figure on the steps of St Paul's to receive the queen after her progress through the city. He also preached at the service of thanksgiving for her eightieth birthday on 24 May 1899. In 1897 he presided at the fourth Lambeth conference of bishops of the Anglican communion, called to celebrate Augustine's landing at Ebbs Fleet in 597 and beginning with a service there on 2 July. On the following day he received in Canterbury Cathedral the 194 members of the conference at an inaugural service, and delivered an address from the chair of Augustine. The conference was dismissed on 1 August 1897, Temple having proved himself, against many expectations, to be a remarkable chairman and leader. On 3 August he led a pilgrimage of more than one hundred bishops to Glastonbury. The encyclical letter, a summary of the resolutions arrived at by the conference, was drafted in the course of a night entirely by himself, with characteristic emphasis on purity and temperance. With only slight modification it was adopted by the conference and published. On 26 May 1898, at the invitation of Dr James Paton, convener of the committee on temperance of the Church of Scotland, the archbishop paid a visit to the general assembly, and delivered an address chiefly on temperance. He visited Scotland a second time at the request of Bishop Wilkinson for the dedication on 31 July 1902 of the chapter house added to St Ninian's Cathedral, Perth, in memory of Bishop Charles Wordsworth. During the six years of his archbishopric he made two visitations of his diocese. In his first charge of October 1898 he dealt with the practice of confession and the unity of ceremonial, together with the questions of 'the doctrine of the Holy eucharist', 'improper objects of worship', and 'prayers for the dead'. The second charge was entirely devoted to the Education Bill of 1902.

In 1899 the lawfulness of the use of incense and of processional lights was referred to the archbishops of the two provinces for judgment. The hearing took place at Lambeth on 8, 9, and 10 May, and the opinion, which was drafted solely by Temple without consultation, was delivered by Temple at Lambeth on 31 July 1899. He decided that the two practices were neither enjoined nor permitted by the law of the Church of England. This resulted in a solemn protest led by the duke of Newcastle on 19 January 1900. The third question on the reservation of the blessed sacrament, referring only to the southern province, was brought before the archbishop of Canterbury alone, and he decided 'that the Church of England does not at present allow reservation in any form'.

Temple, who had been made an honorary LLD of Cambridge on 20 January 1897, received the honorary freedom of the city of Exeter on 22 January 1897, and of the borough of Tiverton on 3 October 1900. In January 1901 he officiated at the funeral of Queen Victoria in St George's Chapel, Windsor. Although he was infirm, he crowned Edward VII in Westminster Abbey on 9 August 1902 and, after doing homage, had to be helped to his feet by the king. He received the collar of the Victorian order.

Temple spoke for the last time in the House of Lords on 4 December 1902, when A. J. Balfour's Education Bill came up for the second reading. Earl Spencer, as leader of the opposition, spoke against the bill, and the archbishop followed in its favour. Before completing his speech, however, he was taken ill and had to leave the house. He received his final communion in the presence of his family and four leading bishops on 11 December 1902. He died at Lambeth Palace on 23 December 1902, and was buried in the cloister garth of Canterbury Cathedral.

Although Temple accomplished much through his unusual vigour of mind and body, his personality could be considered greater even than his work. He had extraordinary force of character, shrewd common sense, and a simplicity which distinguished him from his most able contemporaries. He did not consider Christian doctrine to be at the heart of Christian faith and, like S. T. Coleridge, considered Christianity a life, not a speculation. He went straight to the point with a directness which sometimes earned for him the reputation of brusqueness, and even a lack of sensitivity. Those who worked with him closely, however, soon came to regard this as a superficial view of his character. With his strength he combined a tenderness of feeling and warmth of affection which were often noticeable, in spite of his apparent lack of spirituality, in his public utterances. His devotion to his mother, who lived with him until the day of her death, and to whose opinions he always reverently deferred, had a deep influence on his character. Though tricks of oratory were utterly alien to his nature, his sermons in Rugby School chapel (of which three volumes were published) had a lasting effect on those who heard them, both masters and pupils. He had a particular sympathy for laymen and introduced lay representation into local church assemblies. In the latter part of his life he spoke most frequently on foreign missions, temperance, and the education controversy. On these subjects the fire of his younger days never died away, despite his failing health. On other matters, particularly those involving administration, he could be less than enthusiastic, as his successor, Randall Davidson, observed. Although he was a man of his times, as his passion for temperance amply testifies, Temple made his mark on the English church and nation, most particularly in the field of educational reform.

H. M. Spooner, rev. Mark D. Chapman

Sources M. D. Chapman, 'F. Temple', *Biographisch-Bibliographisches Kirchenlexikon*, 10 (1995) • E. G. Sandford, ed., *Memoirs of Archbishop Temple, by seven friends*, 2 vols. (1906) • P. Hinchliff, *Frederick Temple, archbishop of Canterbury* (1998) • A. C. Benson, *The life of Edward White Benson*, 2 vols. (1899) • D. L. Edwards, *Leaders of the Church of England, 1828–1944* (1971) • E. Carpenter, *Cantuar* (1971) • J. B. Hope, *Rugby since Arnold* (1967) • F. A. Iremonger, *William Temple, archbishop of Canterbury* (1948) • A. M. G. Stephenson, *Anglicanism and the Lambeth conferences* (1978) • L. Creighton, *Life of Mandell Creighton* (1904) • L. Campbell and E. Abbott, *Life of Benjamin Jowett* (1897) • G. K. A. Bell, *Randall Davidson, archbishop of Canterbury*, 3rd edn (1952) • Gladstone, *Diaries* • S. Green, 'Archbishop Frederick Temple on meritocracy, liberal education and the idea of a clerisy', *Public and private doctrine: essays in British history presented to Maurice Cowling*, ed. M. Bentley (1993)

Archives LPL, corresp. and papers; letter-book; corresp. and papers relating to work as bishop of London • priv. coll., corresp. • PRO • Rugby School, Warwickshire, sermons • U. Birm. L., letters | BL, corresp. with Arthur James Balfour • BL, corresp. with W. E. Gladstone, Add. MSS 44368–44569, *passim* • Bodl. Oxf., letters to H. D. Acland, H. W. Acland, and S. A. Acland • Bodl. Oxf., letters to Samuel Wilberforce, etc. • LPL, corresp. with E. W. Benson • LPL, letters to A. C. Tait • St. George's Chapel, Windsor, letters to H. J. Ellison • Trinity Cam., letters to Henry Sidgwick

Likenesses M. S. Morgan, engraving, pubd 1831, NPG • J. Tissot, watercolour, 1869, Rugby School, Warwickshire • T. Woolner, bust, *c*.1871, Rugby School, Warwickshire • G. F. Watts, oils, exh. RA 1880, Rugby School, Warwickshire • H. von Herkomer, oils, 1896, Fulham Palace, London [*see illus.*] • F. W. Pomeroy, monument, 1905, St Paul's Cathedral, London • T. Brock, medallion, Rugby School, Warwickshire • G. Frampton, bronze bust, Sherborne School, Dorset; replica, Rugby School, Warwickshire • H. Furniss, caricature, pen-and-ink sketch, NPG • F. C. Gould, sketches, NPG • S. P. Hall, group portrait, watercolour (*The Bench of Bishops, 1902*), NPG • H. von Herkomer, oils, second version, LPL • E. A. F. Prynne, oils, bishop's palace, Exeter • Spy [L. Ward], caricature, repro. in *VF* (6 Nov 1869) • Spy [L. Ward], caricature, chromolithograph, NPG; repro. in *VF* (11 Sept 1902) • cartes-de-visite, NPG • chromolithograph, NPG; repro. in *VF* (6 Nov 1869) • photographs, NPG • prints, NPG • woodcuts, NPG

Temple, George Frederick James (1901–1992), mathematician and Roman Catholic priest, was born on 2 September 1901 at 134 Wornington Road, North Kensington, London, the only son of James Temple (*d*. in or before 1917), railway inspector for the Great Western Railway, and his wife, Frances (Fanny), *née* Compton. His parents were English country folk from Oxfordshire. There is no record of previous scientific activity in the family. He went to Northfields elementary school and Ealing county school, which he left after less than five years because of the death of his father. His subsequent progress resulted from a combination of brilliance, diligence, and good fortune. In 1918 he enrolled at Birkbeck College. In the following year he was received into the Roman Catholic church. His faith formed his life. He had close friendships with a number of Dominicans and Benedictines, loving liturgy and theology, especially Aquinas.

In 1919 Temple became part-time research assistant in the Birkbeck physics department. He took the general honours BSc in 1922, and then became steward in the physics department and began to publish papers on A. N. Whitehead's theory of gravitation. At that time the differential geometry of Einstein's general relativity theory of gravitation was seen as forbidding, and Whitehead's alternative seemed attractive. Whitehead himself was on the point of leaving the chair at Imperial College and invited Temple there in 1924 as demonstrator in mathematics.

Three more papers on general relativity were accepted by the University of London for a PhD in 1926. Whitehead's successor, Sydney Chapman, recognized Temple's ability and recommended him for an 1851 Exhibition scholarship. He spent the year 1928–9 at Imperial, working on the new wave mechanics of the atom. His mathematical character was now clear. He had an ability to find interesting problems before they were fashionable, to see through to the simplicity of the essentials, and to write a few important papers before seeking a new topic.

In 1928 Paul Dirac published his equation for the electron, which removed an unexplained anomaly in the fit of wave mechanics with experiment, conformed with the requirements of relativity, and yet was not of the expected mathematical form. Temple saw this as a challenge. He spent the second year of his 1851 research studentship at Trinity College, Cambridge, working under Sir Arthur Eddington, who had reacted in the same way to Dirac's equation. Temple answered the challenge by deriving Dirac's results in a more abstract algebraic way. Two highly original papers clarified the whole situation and established Temple as a first rank mathematician.

Temple left Cambridge in 1930 to become an assistant professor at Imperial College, and on 2 September the same year he married Dorothy Lydia Carson (1898–1979), eldest daughter of Thomas Ellis Carson, shipping office manager of Liverpool. Their marriage was exceedingly happy, and Temple's achievements owed an enormous debt to his wife's love and support. There were no children of the marriage.

In 1932 Temple was appointed to a chair at King's College, London, where he remained until 1953. The department was at a low ebb but once he was joined by J. G. Semple in 1936 they were able to turn it, over twenty years, into a leading research department. Two principal themes initially interested Temple. The success of the algebraic approach led him to an investigation of symbolic representation of algebraic forms which might prove useful in abbreviating the heavy algebra of general relativity. Quantum theory continued to exercise him until he concluded in 1935 that his earlier doubts were valid and that the theory contained a calamitous paradox. Characteristically he did not search for some modification of the theory or of his proof to avoid the paradox but simply gave up all work on it. His mathematics had to issue in the same kind of certainty that he enjoyed in Aquinas's theology.

The Second World War found Temple seconded to the Royal Aircraft Establishment at Farnborough, working both on supersonic aerodynamics and on various practical problems, notably 'shimmy', the wheel wobble of aircraft on landing. His ability to get to the essentials was shown over the de-icing of bombers' wings. He realized that any such equipment would mean a smaller bomb load, more bombers, and so increased losses from anti-aircraft fire. He concluded by advising better use of meteorology. He became an acknowledged expert in supersonic flight. The inadequacy of the mathematical foundations there and his quest for precision led him after the war to the use of generalized functions which, in a paper published in the *Journal of the London Mathematical Society* in 1953, he showed were equivalent to the distributions of Laurent Schwartz. This easy transition between pure and applied mathematics was another continuing characteristic.

On returning to King's in 1945 Temple (who was elected FRS in 1943) continued research over a wide field. He was principal scientific adviser to the minister of civil aviation from 1948 to 1950 and chairman of the Aeronautical Research Council from 1961 to 1964. He was appointed CBE in 1955. He was one of a group of leading scientists who led the foundation of the International Union of Theoretical and Applied Mechanics in 1948. He served as treasurer from 1952 to 1960, president from 1960 to 1964, and vice-president from 1964 to 1968.

In 1953 Temple succeeded Sydney Chapman as Sedleian professor of natural philosophy at Oxford. He used his relative freedom from administration to codify his previous work. Then in 1960 he used generalized functions to understand the geometric theories of de Rham, Whitney, and Hodge in several papers of great beauty and depth. He had long taken an interest in the history of mathematics and after his retirement from Oxford in 1968 he commenced work on *100 Years of Mathematics*. This was not published until 1981. That it read like an authoritative survey of the century but included only the development of those fields in which he had worked made the book a monument to the breadth of his interests.

Following the death of his wife in 1979 Temple continued his long association with the Benedictines. He was admitted to Quarr Abbey, at Ryde, Isle of Wight in 1980. His solemn profession as a monk was in 1982 and he was ordained priest in 1983. He was diligent at liturgy and prayer and studied hard at theology and mathematics, the latter in a new field for him, the foundations. His aim was typically precise and ambitious: to construct a new theory from which the more usual bases for mathematics, set theory and logic, could be deduced and their consistency assured. His exposition was in manuscript form at his death at Kite Hill Nursing Home, Wootton Bridge, Isle of Wight, from prostate cancer on 30 January 1992. He was buried at Quarr Abbey. All his life he was a man of unfailing courtesy, wit, and kindness, though capable of trenchant criticism. His learning was recognized by four honorary doctorates and by the Sylvester medal of the Royal Society.

C. W. KILMISTER

Sources MS notes as FRS, RS · C. W. Kilmister, *Memoirs FRS*, 40 (1994), 385–400 · *The Independent* (4 Feb 1992) · *The Times* (5 Feb 1992) · *WWW*, 1991–5 · personal knowledge (2004) · private information (2004) · b. cert. · m. cert. · d. cert.

Likenesses photograph, repro. in Kilmister, *Memoirs FRS*, 384 · photograph, repro. in *The Times* · portrait, repro. in *The Independent*

Temple, Georgina Cowper- [*née* Georgina Tollemache], **Lady Mount-Temple** (1821?–1901), religious enthusiast, was born on 8 October, probably in 1821 in Ireland, the ninth daughter and twelfth child of Admiral Richard Delap Halliday (1772–1837), who in 1821 assumed the

Georgina Cowper-Temple, Lady Mount-Temple (1821?–1901), by Robert Thorburn

name and arms of Tollemache, and his wife, Elizabeth Stratford (d. 1861), daughter of John, third earl of Aldborough. At the time of Georgina's birth her father was still a serving naval officer. With three brothers and seven surviving sisters she would have felt the stimulation of a full family life and the influence of a religious father of a strong evangelical persuasion. After his death in 1837, Georgina lived quietly in London with her mother at 11 Chesham Place and at Brighton. She was slight of figure and tall, her hair golden brown, with an aquiline nose and light warm grey eyes. She married the Hon. William Francis Cowper (1811–1888) [see Temple, William Francis Cowper-], apparent son of the fifth Earl and Countess Cowper, at St George's, Hanover Square, on 21 November 1848; his father was actually almost certainly Lord Palmerston, whom Lady Cowper subsequently married. Her marriage was one of complete happiness, finding in her husband a man sharing her own religious fervour with whom she could join in his philanthropic work. At the start she owned to feeling out of her element, so different was the world of gaiety and brilliance at the Palmerston's Broadlands to the quiet life of faith and prayer at home. In their Curzon Street house, where D. G. Rossetti took exception to rose-garlanded chintzes, the firm of William Morris & Co. was called in when the staircase needed renovation.

John Ruskin was introduced to Mrs Cowper in 1853, having first seen her in Rome in the winter of 1840. In 1863 spiritualism and possibly occult phenomena brought them more intimately together. Ruskin was suffering from the complexity of his obsession for Rose La Touche and found in Mrs Cowper a ready sympathizer, sensitive to a mind in great distress. His letters to his tutelary power during the following decade demonstrate the claims he made on her never-failing loyalty. He called her Philé, Egeria, and Isola. He dedicated his second edition of Sesame and Lilies (1871) to her.

Lady Palmerston died in 1869; Broadlands, inherited by her son, who changed his name to Cowper-Temple, became Georgina's home, the centre of religious activity and philanthropic work, and also a refuge to their many friends. According to Leicester Warren there were no clocks or fixed hours: breakfast when one rose, luncheon when hungry, and dinner on returning home. Mrs Cowper-Temple was a vegetarian and total abstainer. Older now, though still upright and stately, her silvered hair suggested a halo; her eyes seemed those of a mystic while her countenance was one of deep serenity, though Arthur Benson observed that her smile was the sort that comes of having been told daily for many years that your smile is like a sunset or a strain of music. Her long plain dress of black merino worn with a high white mob cap bore resemblance to an abbess of the past. A necklace of little silver cherubs with a tiny ladder was her only ornament, sometimes relieved by a bunch of lilies of the valley at the neck. Giving herself unsparingly for all who came to her, she numbered among her friends not only clergymen, including F. D. Maurice, Charles Kingsley, bishops, and curates, but those from other walks of life, such as Charlotte Yonge, Louisa, Lady Waterford, the George Macdonalds, Louisa, Lady Ashburton, Thomas Carlyle, and Augustus Hare. The first annual religious conference at Broadlands was held in the Orangery and under the cedars in the park in July 1874. Here Mrs Cowper-Temple, as high priestess, found common ground with Quakers, spiritualists, Shakers, budding theosophists, nonconformists, ritualistic curates, and members of the Church Army: all were welcome. Working there on his predella for Dante's Dream, Rossetti found the company all on the parsonic tack (1876) and made a portrait drawing of his hostess (unlocated).

Georgina's husband was raised to the peerage as Baron Mount-Temple in 1880 and died in 1888. Lady Mount-Temple presented Rossetti's Beata Beatrix to the National Gallery in memory of her husband. She left Broadlands and their house at 1 Cheyne Walk, moving to no. 9, but living predominantly at Babbacombe Cliff, Torquay, built for them by W. E. Nesfield. Here she died on 17 October 1901 after five weeks' illness. Her funeral took place at Romsey Abbey on 21 October; a window erected to her memory there celebrates her work among the fishermen at Torquay, as does a statue raised in gratitude on Babbacombe Downs. At her death she left almost all her possessions to Mme Juliet Deschamps, whom she had adopted as a child in 1869. Other bequests went to the Church Army and the Victoria Street Society of Protection of Animals from Vivisection. In 1909 Mme Deschamps, who had inherited Rossetti's Blessed Damozel (Sancta Lilias), gave it to the Tate Gallery in memory of Georgina Mount-Temple.

VIRGINIA SURTEES

Sources E. D. H. Tollemache, *The Tollemaches of Helmingham and Ham* (1949) · L. A. Tollemache, *Old and odd memories* (1908) · E. Clifford, *Broadlands as it was* (1890) · *The works of John Ruskin*, ed. E. T. Cook and A. Wedderburn, library edn, 39 vols. (1903–12), vols. 35–6 · M. L. Warren, *Diaries*, 2 (privately printed, Taunton, 1924), 308–16 · V. Surtees, 'Ruskin and Rossetti at Broadlands', *Hampshire County Magazine* (Aug 1981) · *John Ruskin to Lord and Lady Mount-Temple*, ed. J. L. Bradley (1964) · *Letters of Dante Gabriel Rossetti*, ed. O. Doughty and J. R. Wahl, 4 vols. (1965–7), vol. 3 · L. P. Smith, *Unforgotten years* (1938) · *The Times* · m. cert. · d. cert.
Archives U. Southampton L., Mount Temple archive | U. Southampton L., Broadlands collection
Likenesses E. Clifford, watercolour, 1887, SUL, Broadlands collection · G. F. Watts, red and white chalk and charcoal drawing, 1896, Watts Gallery, Compton, Surrey · R. Thorburn, miniature, Helmingham Hall, Suffolk [*see illus.*] · carte de visite · photogravure photograph (after E. Clifford), repro. in Cook and Wedderburn, eds., *Works of John Ruskin*, vol. 37, facing p. 36 · print (after R. Thorburn), NPG
Wealth at death £8792 17s. 1d.: probate, 24 Jan 1902, *CGPLA Eng. & Wales*

Temple, Henry, first Viscount Palmerston (1672/3–1757), politician, was the second but eldest surviving son of Sir John *Temple (1632–1705), speaker of the Irish House of Commons, and his wife, Jane (d. 1708), the daughter of Sir Abraham Yarner, muster-master general of Ireland. On 21 September 1680, when he was about seven years old, he was appointed, jointly with Luke King, chief remembrancer of the court of exchequer in Ireland. Later, on King's death, the grant was renewed to Temple and his son Henry for life (6 June 1716); it was then worth nearly £2000 per annum.

About 1689 Temple entered Eton College, and in 1693 he progressed to King's College, Cambridge, where he matriculated as a fellow-commoner that Easter. He married, probably on 10 June 1703, Anne (d. 1735), the daughter of Abraham Houblon, a founding director of the Bank of England. The couple had three sons and two daughters.

As the principal representative of the Irish Temples, Henry Temple was created an Irish peer as Baron Temple and Viscount Palmerston on 12 March 1723. A supporter of the Walpole administration and its successors, he was successively MP for East Grinstead, Sussex, from 1727 to 1734, for Bossiney, Cornwall, from 1734 to 1741, and for Weobly, Herefordshire, from 1741 to 1747. Palmerston did not hold formal office other than his Irish sinecure, but in 1730 was among the members of parliament whom Walpole consulted during the debates on Dunkirk, when the ministry's majority was threatened, and in 1734, on the government's behalf, he offered Dr William Webster a crown pension of £300 per annum if he would turn the *Weekly Miscellany* into a ministerial paper. Sir Charles Hanbury Williams wrote several skits upon 'Little Broadbottom Palmerston', while William Oliver, in his *Practical Essay on Warm Bathing* (1751), claimed Palmerston's cure at Bath in 1736 of a severe illness as proof of the efficacy of the water.

Over two years after the death of his first wife, Palmerston remarried, on 11 May 1738. His new wife was Isabella (d. 1762), the widow of Sir John Fryer, bt, and the daughter of Sir Francis Gerard, bt. There were no children from the marriage. Palmerston's eldest son and heir, Henry (c.1704–1740), was by this time himself widowed, having married Elizabeth Lee on 18 June 1735. Elizabeth had died at Montpellier in October 1736. She was the stepdaughter of the poet Edward Young, and the couple were probably alluded to as Philander and Narcissa in Young's 'Night Thoughts' (1742). The younger Henry Temple died on 18 August 1740, leaving a son, also Henry *Temple (1739–1802), by his second wife, Jane (d. 1789), the daughter of Sir John Barnard. This Henry Temple was father of Henry *Temple, third Viscount Palmerston, the prime minister.

Palmerston displayed the common interest of his aristocratic generation in cultural affairs. With regard to his own property, he added the garden front to his house at East Sheen, and greatly improved the mansion of Broadlands, near Romsey, Hampshire. The volume of *Poems on Several Occasions* (1736) by Stephen Duck includes 'A Journey to Marlborough, Bath', inscribed to Palmerston. Part of the poem describes a feast given by the peer annually on 30 June to the threshers of the village of Charlton, between Pewsey and Amesbury, Wiltshire, in honour of Duck, a native of that place. Palmerston's bequest of a piece of land continued to help support the dinner.

Among his other activities, Palmerston was a correspondent of the duchess of Marlborough, and some angry letters passed between him and Swift in January 1726, as Swift resented the treatment he and his friends had received from the Temple family. He helped Bishop Berkeley in his scheme concerning the island of St Kitts, and he presented to Eton College in 1750 four large volumes on heraldry, which had been painted for Henry VIII by John Tirol. He died at Chelsea on 10 June 1757, aged eighty-four, and was succeeded by his grandson Henry.

W. P. COURTNEY, rev. MATTHEW KILBURN

Sources J. Lodge, *The peerage of Ireland*, rev. M. Archdall, rev. edn, 5 (1789), 240–44 · R. S. Lea, 'Temple, Henry', HoP, *Commons, 1715–54* · GEC, *Peerage*, new edn, vol. 2 · J. H. Plumb, *Sir Robert Walpole*, 1 (1956); repr. (1972), 214–15 · *The correspondence of Jonathan Swift*, ed. F. E. Ball, 3 (1912), 297–302 · Nichols, *Lit. anecdotes*, 5.162 · *The works of … Sir Chas. Hanbury Williams*, ed. H. Walpole and E. Jeffrey, 3 vols. (1822) · D. Lysons, *The environs of London*, 4 vols. (1792–6) · W. Sterry, ed., *The Eton College register, 1441–1698* (1943)
Archives U. Southampton L., family and estate papers | TCD, corresp. with William King
Wealth at death regular income from sinecure in Ireland and estates in Surrey (East Sheen) and Hampshire (Broadlands); family pictures and marble tables, and house in St James's Square to be heirlooms: *DNB*; GEC, 10.294

Temple, Henry, second Viscount Palmerston (1739–1802), politician and traveller, was born on 4 December 1739, the only son of Henry Temple (c.1704–1740), joint chief remembrancer of the Irish court of exchequer, and his second wife, Jane Barnard (d. 1789), daughter of Sir John *Barnard (c.1685–1764), lord mayor of London in 1738. He inherited the viscountcy from his grandfather, Henry *Temple, first Viscount Palmerston, in 1757. He was educated at Clare College, Cambridge, from 1757 to 1759 and embarked on three tours in England before he was twenty-one, visiting several aristocratic houses as well as Birmingham, Newcastle, Leeds, and other commercial centres, and thereby established a taste for travel which stayed with him all his life. On coming of age he acquired an income of £7000 per annum from his family properties, half the sum coming from Irish estates in co. Sligo and a few properties in Dublin. He was a typical English absentee landlord, disliked the country and saw it as a land of bogs and barren mountains—'the most dreary waste I ever yet beheld', he wrote (Connell, 352). His income from Ireland rose to £6000 per annum out of a total of £12,000 after his mother's death on 28 January 1789.

Palmerston took his seat in the Irish House of Lords on 22 October 1761 but he never spoke there. His political ambitions, such as they were, were centred on England and on 28 May 1762 he was elected for the Cornish pocket borough of East Looe, then the property of John Buller, through the good offices of Henry Bilson Legge, who was chancellor of the exchequer in the duke of Newcastle's administration. He was a desultory attender and a very occasional speaker in the house, preferring the delights of foreign travel to the boring duty of political life. He supported the preliminaries of the peace of Paris in December 1762 and his neighbour Hans Stanley, member for Southampton, recommended him to George Grenville on 9 December 1764 as a man 'highly worth your seeking' (Grenville MSS). Palmerston nevertheless spoke against Grenville on the issue of general warrants on 29 January 1765, and Horace Walpole remarked with approval that he was 'a young man of sense' (Walpole, *Memoirs*, 2.45). Rockingham, who was on the lookout for talent, offered him a seat at the Board of Trade in December 1765 with a salary of £1000 per annum, and he accepted despite his declaration that 'My views … have never been directed towards the attainment of any public employment' (Rockingham MSS). He remained in office in the subsequent ministry of Chatham, being transferred to the Admiralty board in September 1766. He retained that office under Grafton and North until December 1777, and was then promoted to the Treasury board where he stayed until the fall of North in March 1782.

Despite Palmerston's early promise, his political career took second place to his travels. He visited Paris in 1762 and was presented to the French royal family at Versailles, and in 1763 embarked on a grand tour of Europe which lasted eighteen months, visiting France, Switzerland, Rome, Naples, and northern Italy. He met John Wilkes in Paris, called on Voltaire at Ferney, and was introduced by Sir William Hamilton to classical antiquities at Naples. He returned to his house, Broadlands, in Hampshire, with a collection of antique marbles and sculptures. He had met his future first wife at Spa and they were married on 6 October 1767. She was Frances Poole (1733–1769), daughter of Sir Francis Poole, second baronet, who had died in 1763, and his wife, Frances Pelham, who was a granddaughter of Sir John Pelham. Their marriage was happy, but on 1 June 1769 Frances died after giving birth to a stillborn daughter.

Palmerston had lost his seat at East Looe at the general election of 1768. His former patron Bilson Legge was dead

and Buller had other plans for the borough, but his friend Hans Stanley invited him to become his colleague at Southampton, a more populous constituency. He was elected without undue expense, but at the next election in 1774 he found a safer refuge in the government borough of Hastings through the favour of Lord North. He supported North's American policy but spoke rarely: he was hampered by a stammer. On seventeen occasions between 1768 and 1774 he had intervened briefly in debates in parliament, but only one speech is recorded in the years 1774 to 1780, one between 1784 and 1790, and none thereafter. He had become a spectator rather than a participant.

Palmerston's reaction to his wife's death was to embark on his foreign travels once more. He spent five months in the autumn of 1770 mainly in Switzerland and he also continued his social life at home. He had been elected to Almack's in 1765 and the Society of Dilettanti in 1766, and he became a member of the Catch Club in 1771, where he enjoyed singing rounds and catches in the evenings. He also became intimate with Garrick, Reynolds, and Gibbon, and with Sir Joseph Banks, the president of the Royal Society, to which he was elected in 1776. He was a pallbearer at the funerals of the two former. He was not a gambler, except for small, nominal stakes at cards, but he spent large sums on the refurbishment and rebuilding of Broadlands by Capability Brown after 1768 and by Henry Holland after 1788. He remarried on 7 January 1783. His second wife was Mary Mee (1754–1805), daughter of Benjamin Mee of Bath, who was a substantial city merchant in Fenchurch Street. He was not, however, financially successful and ended dependent on Palmerston's financial assistance.

Palmerston's second marriage was a love match like his first. His wife was a sociable, witty, and affectionate woman and they had two sons and three daughters. They carried on an extensive social life at their London houses at Sheen and Hanover Square. A contemporary remarked that no schoolboy was 'so fond of a breaking-up as Lord Palmerston is of a junket and pleasuring. [Their life is made a] toil of pleasure' (C. Burney, *Memoirs of Doctor Burney*, ed. F. d'Arblay, 3 vols., 1832, 3.271–2). After 1790 they dined occasionally with the prince of Wales at Brighton and also with his estranged wife, Caroline, at Blackheath, and after they met Emma Hamilton in Paris in 1791 she became a frequent visitor and companion.

Palmerston drifted away from his former partisanship with Fox after the French Revolution. He had supported the Fox–North coalition in 1783 against Shelburne, and voted against Pitt on the Regency question in 1788–9 and over the Ochakov affair in 1792, but his travels in France in 1791 made him aware of the violent tendencies of the revolution. The Palmerstons arrived in Paris two weeks after the flight to Varennes and stayed three months, during which time he attended most of the debates in the constituent assembly, witnessing the increasingly hostile tone against the royal family. He saw the riot at the Champ de Mars on 17 July and with his wife waited on Louis XVI and Marie Antoinette at Versailles five days before the mob broke in and massacred the Swiss guards. They left

Paris soon afterwards and retreated to Naples, where they spent twenty-six 'idyllic' months before returning home.

Palmerston supported Pitt thereafter. He deplored the failure of Lord Fitzwilliam's viceroyalty of Ireland in 1795 but shared the view of his wife that the 'feebleness of character, duplicity and I may add treachery' of the duke of Portland was to blame (Connell, 373). When the Irish rising led to expectations of a union with Britain, Palmerston, foreseeing the abolition of the Irish House of Lords, and apparently fearing that as an Irish peer he would be disqualified from sitting in the Commons, solicited a British peerage, but he was unsuccessful, Pitt no doubt regarding him as too recent a convert to his policies.

Palmerston's attitude was also influenced by the falling off of his income from his Irish estates during the troubles of the 1790s. By 1799 his total debts exceeded £30,000 and he had to sell two English properties and mortgage Broadlands. He had sustained his membership of the House of Commons after 1784 by purchase, Treasury support being no longer forthcoming under Pitt. In 1784 he bought a seat at Boroughbridge from the duke of Newcastle for £2685—substantially below the normal market price—but in 1790 Newcastle refused to return him again because of his support of the opposition and he moved to Newport, Isle of Wight, for £4200. In 1796 he secured his return at Winchester through the duke of Portland's good offices, but by the end of that parliament he had decided to give up any further search. On 3 November 1801, he wrote to his wife:

> I have sat in seven Parliaments and do not now find myself desirous of throwing away a great sum of money for the satisfaction of continuing any longer, nor in the situation in which I now stand would it be either proper or even justifiable for me to do so. (Connell, 448)

He resolved to make a further attempt to secure a British peerage. In his draft letter to Addington he reminded him of this point and stated that he had always acted as 'an independent man and a zealous supporter of our constitution as it at present exists. ... Favours of a lucrative kind I have not solicited' (ibid., 448). Again, however, he was disappointed and five months later he died of an 'ossification of the throat' on 16 April 1802 at Hanover Square, London. His wife survived him less than three years, dying of cancer on 20 January 1805 at Broadlands. She was buried alongside him in a vault in Romsey Abbey, where there is a monument to them by Flaxman. Their eldest son was Henry John *Temple, third Viscount Palmerston (1784–1865), the prime minister.   E. A. SMITH

Sources B. Connell, *Portrait of a whig peer* (1957) · L. B. Namier, 'Temple, Henry', HoP, *Commons, 1754–90* · A. Aspinall and R. G. Thorne, 'Temple, Henry', HoP, *Commons, 1790–1820* · GEC, *Peerage* · *Life and letters of Sir Gilbert Elliot, first earl of Minto, from 1751 to 1806*, ed. countess of Minto [E. E. E. Elliot-Murray-Kynynmound], 3 vols. (1874) · H. Walpole, *Memoirs of the reign of King George the Third*, ed. G. F. R. Barker, 4 vols. (1894) · *The last journals of Horace Walpole*, ed. Dr Doran, rev. A. F. Steuart, 2 vols. (1910) · *Chatham correspondence* · *DNB* · BL, Grenville MSS · Rockingham MSS
Archives BL, political journal, Add. MSS 48587–48589 · LUL, drafts of speeches · U. Southampton L., corresp., diaries, and travel journals | BL, Grenville MSS · NL Scot., corresp. with first earl of Minto and countess of Minto · PRO, Pitt MSS, 30/8 · U. Nott., Portland MSS
Likenesses A. Kauffmann, oils, 1765, Broadlands · T. Heaphy, portrait, 1801, Broadlands

Temple, Henry John, third Viscount Palmerston (1784–1865), prime minister, was born on 20 October 1784 at 4 Park Street (later 20 Queen Anne's Gate), Westminster; he was the eldest of the five children of Henry *Temple, second viscount (1739–1802), and his second wife, Mary (1754–1805), daughter of Benjamin Mee, a London merchant later resident in Bath. He had one brother, William (1788–1856), British minister at Naples for twenty-three years, and two surviving sisters, Elizabeth (1790–1837), wife of Laurence Sulivan, and Frances (1786–1838), who married admiral of the fleet Sir William Bowles. His father, a follower of Charles James Fox, was an English MP for forty years. Although this amiable dilettante devoted himself chiefly to society and travel, his friendships, especially with the diplomat James Harris, first earl of Malmesbury, were important for his elder son. Mary, Viscountess Palmerston, is a rather colourless figure beside her much older husband—equally well meaning, but never quite at ease among the aristocracy.

Beginnings, 1784–1806 From childhood Henry John Temple displayed an enviable degree of emotional security; relations with both parents were warmly affectionate, self-sufficiency and good humour lifelong characteristics. Always close to his siblings, he furthered his brother's career and the careers of his sisters' husbands. The children accompanied their parents on an extended continental tour in 1792–4; an Italian tutor succeeded a French governess. The foundations were laid of excellent French and good Italian; later he added good Spanish and some knowledge of German. On the family's return, he was sent to Harrow School (1795–1800), where a school song commemorates 'Temple's frame of iron': he flourished in what was in many ways a schoolboy republic—no place for weaklings—became a monitor, and was chosen to 'declaim', that is, to deliver orations in Latin and English.

The next stage in Temple's education was not unusual for young men of good abilities from aristocratic families: three years at Edinburgh University (1800–03), lodging and studying with the political economist Dugald Stewart. The mental and moral philosophy, exalting common sense, and simplified Smithian economics that his host taught made an indelible impression. In the 'Autobiographical sketch' of his middle age, composed for his mistress and future wife, he ascribed 'whatever useful knowledge and habits of mind I possess' to his time in Scotland (Bulwer, 1.367). Temple's Edinburgh companions were mainly Englishmen of his own sort; they devoted some of their leisure to a largely English volunteer corps.

If the Scottish universities offered more relevant instruction than Oxford and Cambridge could provide, the English universities' social superiority was unshaken. Temple, from 1802 Lord Palmerston, went up to St John's, Cambridge, in October 1803, where he formed his closest friendships. He chose the college himself for its 'remarkably good society ... the best in the university', listing the

Henry John Temple, third Viscount Palmerston (1784–1865), by Francis Cruikshank, *c.*1855

peers' sons (*Letters*, ed. Bourne, 5–6). His letters to one friend, Laurence Sulivan, who married his sister Elizabeth, are a valuable source. Although his Cambridge studies were less demanding, the tutors at St John's, like Dugald Stewart, rated him highly; he took his MA (27 January 1806) without examination, a nobleman's privilege. Palmerston's university life centred on clubs in which he was a leading light: the Speculative, a forerunner of the Cambridge Union, with a membership drawn exclusively from St John's and Trinity, and an even smaller Saturday Club of Johnians which met weekly to dine and talk. He also enrolled in his college's own volunteer corps; afterwards his participation in amateur soldiering continued with the command of the South-West Hampshire militia for some years. The main purpose of his eighteen months at Cambridge was to launch his career as a supporter of William Pitt the younger. The influence of Burke, sustained by the course of recent history, was paramount: the young Palmerston awarded him 'the palm of political prophecy' (ibid., 97). His Cambridge contemporaries were mostly Pittites; he did not consider joining his father's political friends. While still an undergraduate, he stood (February 1806) for the university seat vacated by Pitt's death, finishing close behind two other youthful aristocrats, Lord Henry Petty and Viscount Althorp, later the third Earl Spencer.

Parliament and office: the first phase, 1806–1830 Lord Malmesbury, Palmerston's guardian until his majority, was instrumental in finding him a constituency. Elected for Horsham in November 1806 and unseated on petition

(20 January 1807), he narrowly failed (May 1807) to secure one of the Cambridge University seats at the general election and was returned the next day for Newport, a pocket borough on the Isle of Wight. Malmesbury's influence had already brought his protégé minor office as a lord of the Admiralty (3 April 1807) when in October 1809 it presented him with the opportunity of entering Spencer Perceval's cabinet. Perceval gave him three choices: chancellor of the exchequer or secretary at war in the cabinet, with the option of a junior lordship of the Treasury until he had proved himself in parliament and felt able to take the chancellorship. Palmerston had been identified as a coming man, although not on the strength of his first undistinguished contributions to debate (he made his maiden speech on 3 February 1808). A salutary caution, an enduring trait, held him back. Unready for such rapid promotion, he pleaded a fear of failing in the house. He accepted the secretaryship at war and retained it under five prime ministers, outside the cabinet until 1827. He entered upon his duties at the War Office on 27 October 1809 and was sworn of the privy council on 1 November 1809.

Predictions of a great future were quickly forgotten; Palmerston's reputation was that of a competent administrator and adequate performer on the treasury bench. He revealed an appetite for hard work, improving departmental organization and accounts, and made Sulivan permanent head of the office. He showed courage and humanity when an unbalanced half-pay officer, Lieutenant Davies, shot at and slightly wounded him (8 April 1818), paying for the man's legal defence. Like many Pittites, now labelled tories, he was a good whig at heart. In confrontations with successive commanders-in-chief, he insisted on the rights of a minister accountable to the Commons. Claims to be acting in the spirit of the constitution since the revolution of 1688 were really prompted by the growing pressure of public opinion on the unreformed parliament.

In the political vocabulary of the day, Palmerston was a 'Catholic', and supported Catholic emancipation from 1812 after finally winning one of his university's seats on 27 March 1811, which he held until 1831. On another front, he kept a low profile as Liverpool's ministry passed the repressive legislation of the troubled years 1816–20. He dated his emergence as a Liberal from the mid-1820s, talking by then of the 'stupid old Tory party' (Bourne, *Palmerston*, 248). He was not an adherent of Canning, who on becoming prime minister offered him the governorship of Jamaica, hardly complimentary to someone whom Liverpool had invited to govern India. Promotion to the cabinet as postmaster-general with an English peerage had also been turned down. There were personal reasons for declining India but, clearly, he thought better of his political prospects at home than others did. Canning put him into the cabinet (April 1827), where he remained, still secretary at war, until 1828. Promised the Home Office or the exchequer in Canning's ministry, he got neither; the need to accommodate others kept him in his old post. George IV, who disliked Palmerston's independence at the War Office, suggested Jamaica, and denied him the exchequer under Goderich (August 1827). Canning gave him another chance of ruling India, again declined.

Breaking with the 'pig-tails' or 'illiberals'—names he applied to conservative tories—Palmerston resigned (May 1828) with the Canningites from Wellington's government over its refusal to sanction an instalment of parliamentary reform, the transfer of East Retford's representation to Manchester. He had yet to show the promise that carried him to the Foreign Office. Canning noticed his reluctance to speak in cabinet on business not directly related to his own department, but discerned his potential. The house was surprised on 1 June 1829 by Palmerston's eloquent and persuasive attack on the government for deferring to the Holy Alliance in Portugal and Greece. At the same time he acknowledged the necessity of more or less friendly relations with its component powers. His advocacy of constitutionalism and nationalism was always subject to the retention of 'an influence both with the free and the despot' (*Letters*, ed. Bourne, 232). Canning's policy before it was his, it took account of political and military facts. Virtually all British politicians were liberals by continental standards; parliamentary monarchy rested on an unshakeable consensus. On the other hand, Britain's military weakness, a consequence of the pervasive libertarianism that ruled out conscription, obliged her to work with continental powers.

This speech and others on foreign policy over the following years impressed the whig leader, Lord Grey: Palmerston is a classical instance of the late developer in politics. Wellington twice attempted to win him back. The duke's enemies on the far right also approached Palmerston; they sounded him about joining an eccentric coalition of ultras and the bolder whigs. His cautious, unspecific commitment to parliamentary reform and his dislike of the government's stance abroad stopped him from rejoining Wellington; he treated the ultras' overtures as 'comical'. If the latter perceived that he was a man for coalitions, he saw himself as a decided Liberal.

Life outside politics For many years Palmerston was best known as a man about town, living in London at 12 and then 9 Stanhope Street from 1811 until his marriage. Men and women found it difficult to resist the charm of this handsome man—a lively, amusing talker, much in demand. Well read, he was faithful to eighteenth-century tastes in the arts. A considerable womanizer, nicknamed Cupid, he took mistresses from society and women from the *demi-monde*; they co-existed with a liaison ending, after thirty years, in matrimony. Proud of his virility, he recorded sexual successes and failures in his pocket diaries, methodical in this as in other matters. To a woman calling herself Emma Murray, later Mrs Mills (*d*. 1860), he paid a regular allowance for two decades. One of her children by aristocratic lovers bore the names Henry John Temple Murray (1816–1894); Palmerston helped to educate him and several of her natural or foster children. Murray served uneventfully in the consular service, where his putative father had placed him.

A similar tolerance marked Palmerston's relationship, which began between 1807 and 1809, with Emily, *née* Lamb

[*see* Temple, Emily (1787–1869)], Lord Melbourne's sister, wife of the fifth Earl Cowper. He is credited with the paternity of three of her five surviving children supposedly by Cowper: William Francis Cowper-*Temple (1811–1888), created Baron Mount-Temple, to whom Palmerston left his estates with the stated wish that he should assume the name and arms of Temple; Emily (1810–1872), Palmerston's favourite, wife of Anthony Ashley-*Cooper, seventh earl of Shaftesbury (1801–1885), whose second son, Evelyn Ashley (1836–1907), succeeded his childless uncle in the Temple property, again in accordance with Palmerston's wishes; and Frances (1820–1880), who married Viscount Jocelyn, the third earl of Roden's heir. In addition, Palmerston believed he had fathered Lady Cowper's stillborn boy in 1818. If she was, in Creevey's words, one of the 'most … profligate women in London', her first husband's complaisance protected her; Palmerston was sometimes jealous of other lovers. After a short widowhood she married him on 16 December 1839; if their vows were not strictly observed, at least on his side, they were nevertheless a devoted couple. Under Melbourne's genial influence even Queen Victoria thought the union good for both parties. Her physical beauty wore well. Irrepressible spirits and the sense of fun preserved in her letters made her popular. Not particularly clever, she helped Palmerston with her social gifts. For more than half a century she was a leading hostess; those who deplored her morals seldom declined her invitations.

Womanizing, until desire outran performance, was only one of Palmerston's recreations. As late as 1863 a shady Irish journalist, O'Kane, cited the then prime minister as co-respondent in his divorce. The case was dismissed, and with it a claim for £20,000 damages, for want of proof that the O'Kanes were married. The greatest prizes in racing eluded a patron of the turf whose enthusiasm was the subject of friendly caricature. He hunted into old age, turning out in the rain with Napoleon III's staghounds in his seventies. 'Rien ne perce un habit rouge', he joked (Earl of Malmesbury, *Memoirs of an ex-Minister*, new edn, 1885, 455). The pleasantly barbed jest to traditional foes evokes the man. He provided good sport, too. Declining, as premier, to gratify an aspirant to the peerage, he directed his secretary to 'gild the pill' with an invitation to a day's shooting. The Palmerstons' hospitality—in London, at 94 Piccadilly from 1855, at Broadlands in Hampshire, and Brocket in Hertfordshire (Emily's property)—was politically important.

This lifestyle was expensive. Palmerston inherited substantial debt; his net income from all sources except government stock was about £8000. Well over half his acreage then lay in Ireland: valuable properties in Dublin and more than 10,000 acres on the coast of Sligo, populated with small tenants largely reliant on harvest labour in England to pay their rents. Palmerston set himself to improve their condition and his rental amid difficulties that were often too much for west of Ireland landlords. Borrowing to build a harbour, roads, and schools, and to drain boglands, he nearly doubled his Irish income by 1840 to over £11,000. When the great famine of 1845–9 struck, the estate shipped destitute families to North America; he and his agent incurred severe criticism for taking this course, to which there was, in their view, no economic alternative. Holdings, enlarged by emigration, were still small as the receipts climbed back towards pre-famine levels. From prudence and humanity he respected the tenant right, which he famously denounced as 'land-lords' wrong' (Hansard 3, 177, 27 Feb 1865, 823). Subject to the agent's approval, tenants were permitted to sell, or bequeath, the occupancy of holdings; an almost universal custom in Ireland that effectively limited rent.

On coming into his inheritance Palmerston prepared an ambitious development plan for each of his four estates in England and Ireland, and always practised the 'progressive improvement' at which, as a statesman, he exhorted people to aim. In Hampshire and Yorkshire he spent £100,000 in twenty years on buying land, besides the outlay on improvements. Debt swollen by this expenditure absorbed a large slice of his income in the 1820s. If not a necessity, an official salary eased his position until late in life. He lost heavily in the stock exchange crash of 1825, although one venture, in Welsh slate quarrying, eventually repaid him handsomely with an annual return of nearly £10,000 in the 1860s.

The Foreign Office, 1830–1834, 1835–1841 Evicted by the Cambridge tories in May 1831, Palmerston took refuge at Bletchingley, Surrey (18 July 1831), a seat which disappeared in the Reform Act. He was returned for South Hampshire on 15 December 1832, but lost the seat in 1834; elected for Tiverton on 1 June 1835, he held that seat until his death. As foreign secretary (22 November 1830) he was the most successful and popular of whig ministers under Grey and Melbourne. Yet his methods, and his manner, made colleagues and chiefs nervous: his reappointment on 18 April 1835 was probably due to Melbourne's concern for his small majority. In November 1830 he expected to be chancellor of the exchequer and leader in the Commons in the coalition out of which the nineteenth-century Liberal Party grew. But the whigs preferred Althorp, and Palmerston went to the Foreign Office which Lansdowne had refused. By liberalism he understood the development of liberties with deep roots in most of Europe: 'equitable laws', security of property and person, and 'something to say in the management of their community'. Naturally, countries differed in the evolution of their 'social habits' and institutions, yet not so as to preclude the application of 'similar formulae … with slight variations' (7 May 1832, Beauvale MS 60463). He was as much a man of ideas as Gladstone or Salisbury. His political philosophy, in and after 1830, allowed for growth.

During the Reform Bill's passage, Palmerston agreed that 'Divide et impera should be the maxim of government for these times', with extremists isolated by 'fair concessions', and was inclined to think the £10 household franchise too high, if anything (30 June 1832, Beauvale MS 60463). The tories exasperated him by their stupidity: reactionaries at court and in the Lords risked alienating public opinion permanently from monarchy and aristocracy. This fear overcame his reluctance to support a large creation of peers if the Lords did not give way. Subsequently, he held up a triumph of evolutionary change to other states. He considered household suffrage and shorter parliaments possible in his lifetime, and found the Chartist demand for one man one vote harmless because it ignored realities. 'The word constitution all over Europe means a parliament', he reminded a foreign ambassador in the 1860s, looking as ever for the adoption of the British model. By his death parliamentary institutions had been established almost everywhere on the continent outside Russia and Turkey. Their existence was a tribute to Britain's envied stability and the flexible political settlement she enjoyed from 1832: 'All countries', wrote Palmerston next year, '… are, and always have been in a state of transition' (Bourne, Palmerston, 372).

Between Britain and Russia Palmerston saw at work 'the same principle of repulsion … that there was between us and Buonaparte'; the political systems were mutually antagonistic (28 Feb 1834, Bligh MSS). The Anglo-Russian co-operation, sought wherever British interests made it advisable, could never remove that underlying hostility. Ideological considerations, however, ranked below the prosperity on which everything depended. From that angle, it did not matter whether the powers were 'despotical … or constitutional', he said at the 1857 election. 'That which concerns us … is that … whether they be free or enslaved, commercial intercourse shall not be interrupted but … as free … as the prejudices of … different nations permit' (The Times, 28 March 1857). What was 'miscalled protection' had no place in his scheme of things. Example and persuasion were the best means of diffusing British liberalism, political and economic, in Europe: 'generous sympathy' did not justify interference in the internal affairs of another state, so long as its people acquiesced in the existing order.

Palmerston's foreign policy relied on playing off rival powers against one another to secure Britain's freedom of action, with the aim of deploying her 'moral weight' on the side of peoples struggling for liberty, meaning 'rational government' in his sense (21 March 1839, Beauvale MS 60466). No other course was open to a liberal Britain in Europe. As he had to tell his countrymen after the sharpest reverse that his diplomacy met (over the Schleswig-Holstein question): 'Ships sailing on the sea cannot stop armies on land' (The Times, 24 Aug 1864). In the wider world, the British mission was to 'extend, as far and as fast as possible, civilization', forcibly if treaties proved ineffectual.

Palmerston built his policy in Europe and further afield round an uneasy relationship with France: 'the best ally for us', he held. France alone constituted a potential danger to his country's insular security, but educated Frenchmen measured the regimes of Louis Philippe and Napoleon III against Britain's standards of freedom and self-discipline. Strategy and political kinship aligned Britain with France. It was often felt that he leant too far towards the old enemy. He had to begin by warning British envoys, whose mental habits reflected the long French wars, how important it was not only to be on good terms with her 'but to appear to all Europe to be so'. British economic and maritime strength joined to France's military capability commanded the conservative powers' respect.

In practice, British diplomacy was much less straightforward than Palmerston contrived to make it seem. With the France of Louis Philippe, he exploited situations that favoured their intervention, from Greece to the Low Countries. In doing so, he endeavoured to avoid a breakdown in relations with the conservative powers. During the suppression of the 1830–31 rising in Poland he wanted the tsar to regard their differences as occurring between friends, and to know that Britain was not bound to revolutionary France. This attitude helped him to continue Canning's work and establish an independent Greece guaranteed by Russia as well as the Western allies. To that achievement he added a leading part in the arduous negotiations that erected the Belgian kingdom. French troops drove out the Dutch; British and French warships blockaded the coast of the Netherlands, and Palmerston displayed extraordinary patience and resource at the London conference (1830–31) in obtaining international recognition for the new state. Austria, Prussia, and Russia gave a reluctant consent to the outcome of a popular revolution. They could take comfort from the tone in which he informed the French that the Belgians' initial choice of a king, a son of Louis Philippe, meant war. French feelings were soothed by the arrangement that a substitute with British royal connections, Leopold of Coburg, should marry the excluded prince's sister.

With these successes behind him, Palmerston promoted the constitutional cause boldly in the Iberian peninsula; France was a collaborator, but also a rival. Instrumental in expelling the reactionary Don Miguel from Portugal, Britain assisted with the defeat of the first Carlist rebellion in Spain. Diplomacy was backed up by British sea power and volunteers, who were aided by their government. Palmerston was the moving spirit in the Quadruple Alliance (1834) between Britain, France, and the two peninsular monarchies, conceived as 'a Western Confederacy of free states … a political and moral power'.

At the other end of the Mediterranean, Britain and France came close to war over the future of the Ottoman empire. Palmerston worsted the French in the Near East by enlisting the other powers against her Egyptian protégé, Mehmet Ali. Turkey's survival was a British and European interest. Egyptian forces retreated before the amphibious operations of British and Austrian squadrons and the revolt they raised in occupied territory. Rear-Admiral Charles Napier's threat to bombard Alexandria (November 1840) completed Mehmet Ali's rout; he renounced the conquests of years. Some in the cabinet objected to combining with the conservative powers: Palmerston countered by intimating his readiness to resign. His belief that Louis Philippe would not incur the risks of war was vindicated: 'Governments', he said, 'seldom take the first step in war unless they have either right or might on their side', and the French had neither. He dominated his colleagues, prepared 'with all my heart and soul' to accept responsibility for armed conflict, if it came to that. The Straits convention (1841) committed the great powers to preserving the Ottoman empire: 'We have been waging war … without burning priming', he commented (20 Sept 1840, 24 Nov 1840, Beauvale MS 60467). Closure of the straits to foreign warships in peacetime underpinned the commitment. The isolation of France had given Russia an inducement to relax pressure on a supposedly moribund empire. Yet Palmerston's fundamental distrust of Russia remained; nor did he think France had any alternative whenever Britain chose to invoke the liberal alliance.

The First Opium War (1839–42), always associated with him, further enhanced Palmerston's reputation, and brought Britain Hong Kong. He handled the Chinese question with notable success in domestic politics. The tories criticized him for being drawn into war by traders in opium, legal under the British flag but illegal in China. The vision of a huge oriental market vanquished their scruples when they took office in 1841. Palmerston was understandably gratified by this conversion, attributed to the prevailing depression at home, and sure that 'These Asiatic triumphs … will relieve embarrassment of all kinds' (*Letters*, ed. Bourne, 275). His second term at the Foreign Office left him widely admired in and out of parliament.

Opposition, 1841–1846, and the Foreign Office under Russell, 1846–1852 Palmerston was glad of an interval in his departmental labours; he drove himself hard. The small Foreign Office staff complained bitterly of his demands; before his marriage he often worked into the early hours. His behaviour in opposition did nothing to reassure colleagues, whose reservations he had increasingly disregarded in making policy, although at home he moved with his party towards free trade and voted for the Maynooth Bill in 1845. He attacked the tories for being too conciliatory towards France, and employed strong language about the surrender of territory to America in the Ashburton treaty (1842). This outspokenness revealed his impatience to take foreign affairs out of the hands of 'a set of geese'; he assailed his successor, Lord Aberdeen, in leading articles written for the *Morning Chronicle*. 'Palmerston and War' were linked in men's minds as Peel's ministry neared its end. Loath to form a government in December 1845, Lord John Russell discovered an excuse in objections to Palmerston as foreign secretary, voiced by the third Earl Grey, and in his refusal to take another post. There was no keeping Palmerston from the Foreign Office when Russell succeeded Peel in July 1846. He replied to charges that his policy had 'a *tendency* to produce war' by pointing out that it had advanced British interests without a major conflict, if not quite peacefully (*Letters of Queen Victoria*, ed. A. C. Benson and Lord Esher, and G. E. Buckle, 1st ser., 1907, 2.69).

The contrast between Palmerston's vocal championship of European liberalism and a realistic appreciation of where Britain's advantage lay was sharper than ever. Anglo-French relations, improved under Aberdeen, deteriorated again with the affair of the Spanish marriages. Britain accused her ally of breaking a promise not to marry a French prince to the young Queen Isabella II, or to her sister and heir, until the queen had married and borne children. Isabella's union to a Spanish cousin assumed to be impotent was celebrated simultaneously with her sister's to the duc de Montpensier (October 1846). Nevertheless, Britain and France co-operated in the forcible restoration of constitutionalism in Portugal in 1847 under the provisions of the Quadruple Alliance, an episode that repaired some of the damage done by the Spanish marriages. Palmerston followed it up with an initiative to exploit the liberal tide flowing in Europe. A cabinet minister, Lord Minto, was sent to Switzerland and Italy with instructions to encourage the 'progressive system of internal improvement' exemplified by the reforming pope, Pius IX. The liberals' victory in the Swiss civil war that year was made possible by the absence of foreign intervention, averted largely by Palmerston's tactics in holding off collective action by the powers until the Catholic cantons had been defeated. To Austrian protests at what looked like gratuitous interference in Italy, he replied: 'Prince Metternich thinks he is a conservative in clinging obstinately to the *status quo* ... We think ourselves conservatives in preaching and advising everywhere concessions, reforms and improvements, where public opinion demands them' (A. J. P. Taylor, *The Italian Problem in European Diplomacy*, 1934, 32).

The revolutions of 1848 demonstrated the intelligence of whig foreign and domestic policies. But the failure of continental liberalism to consolidate its gains ensured the success of reaction, which in France took the form of a Bonapartist revival. Palmerston's response to the democratic republic that displaced the monarchy in February 1848, and to Louis Napoleon Bonaparte's election as its president in December, was pragmatic. He stayed close to the power that was potentially more dangerous and more helpful to Britain than any other. 'What business is it of ours', he enquired, 'whether the French nation thinks proper to be governed by a King, an emperor, a president or a consul?' (*Hansard 3*, 102, 2 Feb 1849, 206–7). The prince president proved easier to work with than Louis Philippe. He was an Anglophile, which had an important bearing on Palmerston's future. Russell and other colleagues were slower to realize that this Bonaparte was very different from his uncle Napoleon I. Palmerston was dismissed on 19 December 1851 for having approved, in conversation with the French ambassador, of the coup that made Louis Napoleon dictator.

Palmerston's removal had been discussed at intervals for several years. Queen Victoria and her husband did not share his view that revolutions might be judged on their merits. They complained of the dispatches sent off before he had received royal comments that were often full and pointed. The cabinet admired and resented Palmerston's mastery of his portfolio and his independence. His growing populism disconcerted them. Though for him property and education qualified a man to vote, he considered 'no set of men ... too ignorant to understand their own interests and ... manage their own affairs ... the knowledge requisite ... is speedily acquired by ... taking part in

them' (Webster, 1.272). His language in reproving governments for their slowness to change imperilled the practical co-operation integral to his policy. Attacked in parliament in July 1849, he had argued that encouragement of liberals entitled Britain to the gratitude of a future Europe, while the preservation of normal relations with states opposed to liberalism safeguarded the peace so necessary to his country.

If sometimes provocative towards great powers, Palmerston was overbearing when small states offended. On 17 June 1850 the Lords condemned his employment of the Mediterranean Fleet to collect relatively modest compensation due to, among others, a Gibraltarian Jew of dubious repute, David Pacifico. The Commons upheld him after he had delivered the most famous of his speeches (25 June 1850), 'extraordinary and masterly', admitted W. E. Gladstone, one of his sternest critics in the debate. Speaking for four and a half hours, with scarcely a note, Palmerston rose to parliamentary heights no one had thought him capable of scaling, and with a conclusion which became one of the best-known flights of parliamentary oratory in that century:

> I therefore fearlessly challenge the verdict which this House ... is to give ... as the Roman, in days of old, held himself free from indignity, when he could say *Civis Romanus sum*; so also a British subject, in whatever land he may be, shall feel confident that the watchful eye and the strong arm of England will protect him against injustice and wrong. (*Hansard 3*, 112, 25 June 1850, 444)

The claim had no basis in international law, and was patently unenforceable against powerful countries. It was a declaration of equality with nations strong enough to behave in the same way towards inferiors; as such it went down very well with the public. His colleagues' misgivings were an open secret. But Palmerston had been prudent where it mattered. Britain's moral support did not save Sardinia from being crushed by Austria in 1849, when she tried to set up the constitutional kingdom of Northern Italy that Palmerston wanted to see. He urgently advised the Sardinians against war. Nor was the British fleet ordered to prevent the Neapolitan Bourbons from reconquering Sicily, where the revolutions of 1848 began, although Britain and France insisted on a delay for negotiations. By the end of 1849 reaction had prevailed in Italy, the German lands, and Hungary; in the last Russian intervention was decisive. Sending British and French warships to stiffen Turkey in her refusal to surrender Hungarian refugees pleased domestic opinion, but did not disguise the abandonment of Hungary.

Russell could no longer tolerate the contradictions of Palmerstonian policy. After, as before, the Greek debate Palmerston would not be shifted from the Foreign Office to another post, with or without the lead in the house. A few weeks ahead of his dismissal, he flaunted his antagonism to authoritarian regimes. Stopped by the cabinet from meeting the exiled Hungarian patriot Kossuth, he received a London radical deputation and failed to rebuke them for violently hostile references to the Austrian and Russian emperors. This was the occasion on which he said that Britain's role called for 'a good deal of judicious bottle-holding'; a sporting metaphor made famous in *Punch* (6 December 1851). Russell's hesitancy is explained by his awareness of the esteem in which Palmerston was held by tories and radicals on the back benches: 'both would be ready to receive him as leader', the premier had told the queen.

Coalition, war, and the first premiership, 1851–1858 The expulsion of Palmerston, who refused to exchange the Foreign Office for the Irish viceroyalty, had the predicted effect of upsetting the government (20 February 1852). He led the attack on its Militia Bill, voted down as an inadequate response to public anxiety about national defences against a Bonapartist France. This display of patriotic vigilance was not needed for his popularity, which had grown with his fall. The tories had always hoped he might be persuaded to return to them: Lord Derby made repeated offers, which did not include his old department, during the minority government formed on the resignation of the divided whigs. Prepared to enter a coalition, Palmerston would not join a tory administration as such; ties of two decades to the whigs were reinforced by the prospective partners' reluctance to give up agricultural protection and by his distaste for their bigots. He thought the leadership of his own party was within his grasp, surmising that on a secret vote they would prefer him to Russell. On reflection, he accepted the Home Office (28 December 1852) in the whig and Peelite ministry that replaced Derby's. Busying himself with prison reform, factory legislation, and public health in a spirit of humanitarianism and efficiency, he carried his objections to Russell's plans for a wider franchise to the length of resigning on 16 December 1853. It was too soon to strengthen the 'democratic element' in the state; the question had failed to arouse much interest. He did not persist with his resignation; nor did he again oppose parliamentary reform openly. Russell's bill was dropped after its introduction.

Kept out of the Foreign Office, Palmerston advocated resistance to fresh Russian pressure on Turkey, and continued to insist that war (March 1854) could have been averted by more resolute diplomacy and a better understanding with France. The Turkish fleet's destruction at Sinope the previous December excited such indignation that the cabinet feared his resignation on an unrelated question would bring them down. Helped by his hints to newspapers, the public identified him with their desire to stand up to Russia. His realism did not desert him: the imminent struggle 'must as far as we are concerned have a very limited range' (*Letters*, ed. Bourne, 308). That did not prevent him from conceiving a grand design for the 'circumvallation' of Russia, her borderlands distributed between neighbouring countries and independent Poland. The aim was to make the world a safer place for liberalism, and the sultan. Lord Aberdeen commented that the plan would mean a thirty years' war. Official British war aims were restricted to keeping Russia out of Turkey. When Palmerston took over, he did not ask the cabinet to reconsider his visionary project, although he adverted to it with selected individuals.

The revelation of military weakness in the Crimea made Palmerston prime minister. Losses inflicted by the enemy were much smaller than the mortality from exposure and disease, for which incompetence and neglect were blamed. The home secretary escaped the censure visited upon Aberdeen and others. At the end of 1854 Russell questioned Aberdeen's leadership, and proposed Palmerston for the War Office. Personal ambition rather than concern for the country were thought to have prompted him: Palmerston spoke contemptuously in cabinet of such opportunism. Appreciation of this solidarity made him their choice to lead the Commons when Russell resigned in January 1855, unable to withstand J. A. Roebuck's motion for an inquiry into the conduct of the war. After a majority of 157 had swept Aberdeen aside, the two party chiefs, Russell and Derby, could not induce Palmerston, for whom press and public were clamouring, to serve under either. Warned not to show herself unwilling to send for him, the queen lamented that he would redraw the map of Europe.

The circumstances of his accession to power (6 February 1855) at seventy set the tone of Palmerston's premiership. The outcry that greeted the plight of the Crimean army seemed, briefly, to have undermined the position of the aristocracy. Palmerston followed Aberdeen because his reputation qualified him to restore confidence in the ability of his class to rule an ever more urban, industrial, and imperially minded state. He had much radical goodwill: A. H. Layard of the Administrative Reform Association declared that if anyone could change the existing system of government for the better, it was Palmerston, who had been deterred from making Layard a junior minister only by strenuous representations from, among others, Gladstone. Radicals, argued Palmerston, often mistook the whole trend of contemporary Britain. The social process was one of levelling up: 'it is an aristocratic movement. I am delighted to see the humbler classes raising themselves in the scale of society' (*Hansard 3*, 136, 1 March 1855, 2165). It was sound policy to proclaim the openness of his class and its diminishing distance from those below. A start on civil service reform furnished proof of the ministry's intentions; at the same time he reassured parliament, more nervous than he was of the Administrative Reform Association, by opposing Layard's attempt to force the pace. The latter's motion of 15 June 1855 was lost by a huge margin.

The pressing requirement was for a leader who could hold his own in the Commons and bring to the higher direction of the war qualities which the peace-loving Aberdeen did not possess. The foreign secretary, Lord Clarendon, was as nearly a technocrat as was possible at that period; he owed a great deal to Palmerston, whose subordinate he had been as minister to Spain, and never lost the habit of looking for instructions. The new war minister, Lord Panmure, was uninspired and slow to act; successive British commanders in the Crimea disappointed. Palmerston's experience enabled him to infuse unwonted energy into the military machine: the logistics of the campaign were soon at least adequate. Strategy was determined by the need to capture Sevastopol before launching any further large-scale attacks, though he was ready with ideas for widening the invasion. He had public opinion with him, but, his cabinet colleague Sir George Cornewall Lewis noted, the Commons did not believe there was 'a real national interest in supporting Turkey' (G. C. Lewis, diary, 20 July 1855, NL Wales, Harpton Court Collection, 3569). Gladstone and two other Peelites left the cabinet almost at once, ostensibly in protest at proceeding with the inquiry into the war, in reality because their enthusiasm for the war did not match Palmerston's. In May the tories decided to turn the ministry out. Aided by Peelites and radicals, they got its majority down to three on the loan urgently needed to keep Turkey fighting (20 July 1855). Tory cross-voting rescued Palmerston and the bill. The public registered its disapproval of his treatment so strongly that the second reading ten days later went unopposed. Even before Sevastopol fell, in September, he was likened to a dictator, controlling the house through his hold on opinion outside.

Doubts about the war in cabinet and parliament obliged Palmerston to persist with inherited peace negotiations at Vienna while operations continued. Russell, the British plenipotentiary, virtually gave away the allied case, and then criticized in the house terms to which he had agreed. He was forced to resign in July. A people who exaggerated the British part in its fall rejoiced at the taking of Sevastopol; the French assault carried the fortress. When Napoleon III tired of the war, Palmerston had no option: it was all he could do to hold the emperor to proposals drafted without consulting Britain. In the treaty of Paris (30 March 1856) the allies settled for the containment of Russia on terms little changed since the combatants had been close to agreement before the war. The cost of the war to Russia and the internal reconstruction on which she embarked left Napoleon free to pursue his aims in Italy, with Palmerston's discriminating assistance.

Initially, the cabinet comprised five Peelites and nine whigs, or Liberals, as they now tended to call themselves. After the rapid departure of some Peelites (21 February 1855) and the absorption of the rest, it was a Liberal government. M. T. Baines's elevation to the cabinet in December 1855, representing the provincial middle class, was one step to advertise the administration's broad outlook. Palmerston went too far for many when he unsuccessfully tried to modernize the Lords by introducing life peers. His colleagues were dubious; tories and Peelites denounced the innovation. There was also criticism of Palmerston's religious policy, designed to conciliate the rising power of nonconformity and improve relations between church and chapel. Advised by the leading evangelical layman, his stepdaughter's husband, Lord Shaftesbury, he favoured evangelicals for preferment—men congenial to nonconformists. Privately, he explained this bias as a '*political* duty' (Steele, 167); his own inclinations ran to broad-churchmen like A. C. Tait, whom he appointed bishop of London in 1856. That year ministers endorsed a Church Rates Bill to exempt nonconformists, which passed its second reading. It did not go on to the Lords and certain

defeat, but indicated a wish to please the moderate majority in the chapels. He rejected suggestions that he was not a reformer: 'Failure, at first, is an unavoidable incident to free discussion' (*Hansard 3*, 143, 25 July 1856, 1465). The unbroken prosperity of the war years underwrote his policies. The 'war ninepence' on income tax did not lift it above 1s. 4d. in the pound, and Lewis at the Treasury borrowed extensively at low rates. Only its economic well-being, Palmerston observed, had made the country 'stick to the war'.

The opposition to Palmerston, like his support, cut across parties. Russell resented his exile from the cabinet, which the prime minister was in no hurry to end. These assorted enemies banded together to defeat the government on 3 March 1857 on Richard Cobden's motion censuring the resort to force against China. Palmerston defended the controversial decisions of Sir John Bowring, governor of Hong Kong, in accordance with his practice of standing by the man on the spot. Recent consultations between Britain, France, and the United States about their posture in the Far East had prepared the ground. The three envisaged armed negotiation with China and Japan. Seizure at Canton (Guangzhou) of the *Arrow* (October 1856), a vessel flying the British flag although its Hong Kong registration had expired, afforded a pretext, reinforced by other instances of Chinese disregard for the letter and spirit of the treaty signed in 1842. Palmerston depicted Bowring, 'essentially a man of the people', as an example of middle-class achievement and the victim of factional politics. He met the opposition victory with a dissolution. The polls bore out immediate reactions in the City and the main provincial towns. A number of tory candidates protested their regard for Palmerston, and tendered him 'a general support'. At one stage *The Times* listed returns as for or against the prime minister rather than Liberal or Conservative. The election was a personal triumph.

Palmerston's national standing had already allowed him to carry off set-backs elsewhere. Ferdinand II of Naples, whose methods the British used the Congress of Paris to deplore, defied an Anglo-French note and joint naval demonstration, making the allies look mildly ridiculous. Palmerston fared no better in disputes with the United States that arose from Crimean War recruiting inside her borders, and from conflicting interests in Central America. Britain submitted to the dismissal of her minister in Washington and three consuls; the navy in Central American waters was instructed to avoid an incident. The Commons approved this caution decisively (30 June 1856); no one wanted disruption of the vital transatlantic trade. There was much less concern about war with Persia in 1856–7, largely at the Indian taxpayers' expense. Russia was in no condition to help Persia, whose encroachment upon Afghanistan, the buffer against the arrival of Russian expansion at the Indian frontier, elicited the successful British action.

Except in India, where he favoured the annexation of princely states before the mutiny, Palmerston preferred influence to territory. He was not tempted by Napoleon III's idea that Britain should take Egypt and France

Morocco. British interests and Western civilization were best served by maintaining local regimes and opening their lands to trade: 'Let us try to improve all these countries by the general influence of our commerce', he commented, 'but let us all abstain from a crusade of conquest which would call down ... the condemnation of ... other civilized nations' (H. E. Maxwell, *The Life and Letters of ... [the] Fourth Earl of Clarendon*, 1913, 2.300–01). The Anglo-Moroccan treaty of 1856 exemplified the desired arrangement: abolition of most restrictions on imports; tariffs fixed at 10 per cent, for revenue, not protection; and the benefits of extraterritoriality for British residents. In the era of 'informal empire', this was the pattern of agreements with China, Japan, and other states where guarantees of most favoured nation status did not suffice.

If economic penetration sometimes called for the employment of force, the extirpation of the slave trade depended upon it. Few doubted Palmerston's sincerity in declaring that its suppression was one of the 'great objects always before him in life' (Gladstone, *Diaries*, 5.495). At the Foreign Office he constructed a network of treaties with European governments that permitted the Royal Navy to intercept suspected slavers wearing foreign colours, and deliver them for adjudication in their own courts or before mixed commissions representing both signatories. When Portugal held out against the imposition of this control, Palmerston secured an act of parliament (1839) providing for unilateral enforcement; Brazil was similarly coerced. Along the west and east African coasts treaties outlawing the traffic were pressed on local rulers; the effect was to establish British paramountcy in those regions. It was Palmerston who gave substance to the international declaration of intent to abolish the slave trade (1815). The United States' attitude left ample scope for its perpetuation, and in the 1850s France revived it under another name. Not until after the outbreak of the civil war did Washington bring America into line. Protracted negotiations were necessary before the French halted 'free emigration' in black Africa in exchange for access to indentured labour from India for their sugar colonies.

Britain's inability to coerce the United States and France was a reminder of her limitations. So was Palmerston's discomfiture when France and Russia overcame Anglo-Turkish resistance to uniting the Romanian principalities, Ottoman tributary states. At Osborne (August 1857) the emperor and Palmerston devised a formula to cover the latter's retreat. Napoleon did not want to lower the prime minister in the eyes of his countrymen at an awkward moment: British weakness had again been exposed, this time in India. Palmerston welcomed the news of the mutiny: 'distressing by reason of ... individual sufferings ... but not really alarming ... it may tend to our establishing our power upon ... a firmer basis'. The recapture of Delhi within four months seemed to indicate that the British were not facing a 'real war' (*Panmure Papers*, 2.399, 466). He did not foresee the partisan war that prolonged the insurrection.

The rapid growth of newspaper circulations after 1855 added to the pressure of public opinion on MPs. While Palmerston made the most of this development, he considered that newspapers finished by reflecting opinion, however hard they tried to mould it. He could not ride the storm that blew up on the Conspiracy to Murder Bill and turned him out on 19 February 1858. The attempted assassination of Napoleon in January by conspirators based in Britain had produced strongly worded French demands, diplomatic and military, for changes in her law. Palmerston found French anger 'perfectly natural'. If war resulted, France would have 'a plausible ... cause which all Europe will admit to be just' (Broadlands MS, CAB/89). The cabinet baulked at his proposal to deport aliens suspected of plotting against foreign governments: the bill making conspiracy to commit murder outside the jurisdiction a felony instead of a misdemeanour was only a gesture, but on its second reading the same combination that had beaten Palmerston in 1857 carried the motion, which convicted him of going beyond conciliation to appeasement. Bystanders jeered as he went home. The political price of the French alliance had risen too high for a nation sensitive to any hint of dictation by another power. His resignation appeared to terminate Palmerston's political life.

The reconstruction of Liberalism, and the second administration, 1859–1865 *The Times* attributed Palmerston's overthrow to underlying discontent at his failure to broaden the ministry's composition in line with the shift towards a more popular Liberalism. There was evidence of a reforming administration: besides the Divorce Act (1857), a landmark in social legislation of which Palmerston was proud, a cabinet committee under his chairmanship outlined a reform bill lowering the £10 franchise to £6 or £8. Parliament endorsed, overwhelmingly, ministers' handling of the banking crisis in November 1857. On the debit side, filling a cabinet vacancy in December with a friend, Lord Clanricarde, discredited by allegations about his personal character, suggested indifference to the respectable voter. It offended Liberals who were neither old-style whigs nor radicals—often businessmen and lawyers from midland and northern seats, not hostile to aristocratic leadership, only disappointed in their expectations of Palmerston.

No one supposed Derby's incoming minority government would last long. Palmerston confounded those who had written him off by taking readily to opposition. Too sanguine of ousting Derby at first, he realized that the road back lay through the Liberal members who had seen in him something more than a 'traditional politician' (*The Times*, 1 March 1858). He promised them that his next ministry would be more representative of a changing party. Tory misjudgements assisted his recovery. The government's Reform Bill united Liberals of all shades by leaving the £10 franchise untouched and removing urban 40 shilling freeholders from the counties, where the party relied on them. The election which Derby called in the spring of 1859 after being beaten on these points was overshadowed by the war between France, allied to Sardinia, and Austria, impending for months, which raised the prospect of a European struggle. Tory policy appeared likely to align Britain with Austria when technological advances had jeopardized naval superiority over France. Fear of war worked to Palmerston's advantage. He had maintained contact with Napoleon, paying him a well-publicized visit in November 1858. Earlier, in Paris, the emperor assured him that in modernizing her fleet France did not mean to overtake her neighbour. As war approached, Palmerston strove to calm the distrust of Napoleon, although he shared it, and overrode the friends of Austria in his party. He countered the government's Austrian leanings, which caused panic on the stock exchange, with a pro-French neutrality. Freeing Italy from Austrian hegemony, attractive though that was, had a lower priority than peace.

With the navy in transition, Palmerston pointed out, the country was in no state to take on France. A Palmerston government offered an assurance of peace. Reconstruction of the Liberal Party after an election which it won, with a reduced majority, proceeded on the basis of continued neutrality, parliamentary reform, and a more broadly based ministry than his last. Liberal MPs meeting at Willis's Rooms on 6 June 1859 sealed the accord. Palmerston and Russell pledged themselves to serve under each other if sent for: like most of those present, Russell privately conceded that the international situation required Palmerston at the helm, but recognition of his standing placated the former leader. When a vote of confidence had disposed of the tories (10 June 1859), Austrian sympathies inspired a royal attempt to impose Lord Granville as premier, easily and politely frustrated by other leading Liberals. In forming a ministry (he took office on 12 June 1859), Palmerston cast his net widely: the old whig element in the cabinet fell from twelve out of fifteen in February 1858 to eight out of sixteen; there were half a dozen former Peelites and, a novelty, two radicals. As advised, he enlisted the ablest men he could—hence the Peelite representation. He justified his exclusion of old friends by the necessity of putting together a comprehensive Liberal administration. It was understood that the proximity of war had handed Palmerston 'a power no one dreamed he would have again' (Sir E. Bulwer-Lytton, quoted in Steele, 30).

Ironically, Cobden and John Bright now looked on Palmerston as their best hope for peace. Refusing his invitation to enter 'the citadel of power', Cobden undertook to support the government so long as his close associate, Milner Gibson, sat in cabinet. Gladstone, who voted with the tories in June, could not bear to be left out. Palmerston was persuaded to substitute the exchequer for the India Office, where he had meant to marginalize a formidable opponent. The relationship of Palmerston and Gladstone was central to this ministry; the elder proved the stronger of two strong men. Gibson and Gladstone backed Palmerston and his foreign secretary, Russell, when the cabinet opposed a defensive pact between Britain, France, and Sardinia to safeguard the last's territorial gains in 1859. The premier and his supporters fell back on the Anglo-French commercial treaty which Cobden helped to negotiate. Afraid of France, government and public were eager to share the credit for events in Italy.

France confined Austria to Venetia; Sardinia turned a blind eye to Garibaldi's expedition to Sicily in May 1860, and her troops completed the conquest of the Papal States and Naples. Britain's contribution to uniting Italy was almost entirely diplomatic. The exception was her refusal to join France in preventing Garibaldi from crossing the Straits of Messina, where Napoleon did not like to act alone. Fearful of a continental coalition, he was always anxious to have Britain with him; her friendship was, too, confirmation of his claim to be a liberal. 'I cannot see', remarked Palmerston, 'the use of representing the ... emperor as a deep deceiver ... an inveterate enemy ... he professes the fixed desire of being our faithful ally' (Steele, 250). Taking Napoleon at his word, he urged France to refrain from intervening when nationalists ignored the terms of the Franco-Austrian armistice (July 1859) in handing over the central Italian duchies and the Romagna to Sardinia. This supporting role made Palmerston an apologist for the emperor. He sought to mitigate the offence in the French appropriation of Savoy and Nice: Napoleon's 'noble enterprise' beyond the Alps was substantially intact. The government kept up diplomatic pressure for the evacuation of Rome, where France had protected the papacy since 1849. Palmerston's Italian policy embraced 'English and Protestant interests' (Palmerston to Russell, 17 Sept 1861, ibid., 266), and envisaged shrinking the pope's residual territory to its modern dimensions. For that Napoleon was not prepared, although he withdrew his garrison.

Anglo-French co-operation extended round the world. The second and third China wars, begun in 1856, ended with the British and French occupation of Peking (Beijing) (1860); British marines landed with the French in Mexico in 1861; and French warships participated in the British-led bombardment of Japanese defences in 1864. Disliking these 'combined operations' with rivals, Palmerston saw them as unavoidable if international jealousy of Britain's global presence was to be contained. Distrust of France remained strong: the volunteer movement was a spontaneous reaction to deep-seated fears; if of small military value, in Palmerston's view, it provided a useful indication of the national mood. Public opinion upheld him in spending millions to confirm naval superiority; he maintained that the mutual respect essential to the successful working of the French, or any comparable, alliance, required Britain to be safe from attack. It took France's attitude to the *Trent* incident, all that an ally could wish, to relax British suspicions.

Washington's surrender of Confederate emissaries taken off a British ship encouraged Napoleon and a cross-section of British opinion to press for joint mediation in the American Civil War. Palmerston was torn between lifelong opposition to slavery and the attraction of a permanently divided United States, the probable outcome of a brokered settlement. He resisted Gladstone's bid to pre-empt a cabinet decision by his Newcastle speech of October 1862, hailing the Confederacy as an emergent nation: but spoke and voted with Russell and Gladstone when mediation was rejected in November. Gladstone had the impression that this result did not displease the premier, much less eager to intervene than the emperor. The tide had turned against the Confederacy, and the North was amassing a formidable power, military and naval.

Differences over Poland and Schleswig-Holstein strained the French alliance in 1863–4. Napoleon's suggested European congress to consider the Polish question in the context of a wholesale revision of the Viennese treaties alarmed other powers; it seemed to imply further French expansion. Short of war, it was the only way to help the rebels in Russian Poland, whose sufferings excited Western compassion. Russell's language in replying to the French proposal gave considerable offence. The emperor derived understandable satisfaction from the humiliation of British diplomacy in the next European crisis, over Schleswig-Holstein. Despite a verbal intimation (*Hansard 3*, 172, 24 July 1863, 1252) that the Danes might count on Britain, Palmerston was critical of them, saying afterwards: 'They were wrong in the beginning, and have been wrong in the end' (Guedalla, *Gladstone and Palmerston*, 290). If the Baltic kingdom, with its strategic location, was a significant British interest, the treatment of the German element in Schleswig and the duchy's incorporation in Denmark were undeniable breaches of treaty obligations. But both parties in Britain condemned Austrian and Prussian occupation of the duchies on Germany's behalf. The Danes' obduracy—'they are not an intelligent race' said Palmerston (Connell, 383)—and German awareness that there was nothing to fear from anyone entailed the failure of Britain's efforts at the London Conference of 1864. The cabinet's resolution, by a single vote, on physical intervention only if the Danish capital were threatened, underlined British helplessness.

Yet the public did not hold this signal reverse against Palmerston: the crowd cheered as he left the Commons after answering the tory censure of his policy. He had done what was expected of him. He had spoken, undiplomatically, of Russia's 'inheritance of triumphant wrong' in Poland (*Hansard 3*, 169, 27 Feb 1863, 935), and informed the Austrian and Prussian envoys that their governments were guilty of the bloodshed over the duchies. Britain's circumstances and her policy excluded 'great sacrifices … of men and money', he told his constituents (*The Times*, 24 Aug 1864). Even if the French had been ready to move, Palmerston was apprehensive of a demand for payment in German territory. As a substitute for force, he urged *The Times* to sustain a warlike tone in its editorials: Bismarck was unimpressed. There was no question, however, of withdrawing from Europe: the alliance with France survived. At times Palmerston had felt that war between these uneasy allies might be near: but, like Louis Philippe and Napoleon, he exerted himself to control national feeling. Gladstone's tribute should be remembered: 'he [Palmerston] … was entirely above flattering … the most vulgar appetites and propensities of the people' (Ramm, *Political Correspondence, 1876–1886*, 2.1). His reward, and Britain's, was a greater say in Europe than would otherwise have been theirs.

The British headed the contemporary expansion of Europe and America into other continents. Dealings with 'weaker and less civilized' countries went through stages outlined by Palmerston in 1864: initial willingness to sign a trade treaty, followed by breaches of faith, violence, Western protests and reprisals until the eventual 'display of superior strength' (5 Oct 1864, Broadlands MS, PM/J/1). Force, and its intimation, were not absent from the striking growth of British trade and investment in Latin America, which outstripped progress in the Pacific. Suppression of the mutiny secured the accelerating profitability of India. On a political plane, Palmerston won the domestic argument about his country's methods in the East: critics were 'doing their best to take the bread out of the mouths of our working classes' (*Hansard 3*, 175, 31 May 1864, 973). But empire brought an obligation to improve the lot of subject peoples. Palmerston contrasted his colleague Sir Charles Wood's oversight of Indian administration with the Russian record in Poland: 'The result … makes England a bright example for other countries' (19 April 1864, Hickleton MS A4/63/146). He seems to have accepted without question the establishment of responsible government in the settler colonies, but did not look for the severance of their remaining, and voluntary, ties with Britain; they were the fullest expression of a liberal empire.

Those colonies were not far ahead in their adoption of democracy. Cobden's reference to the prime ministerial Palmerston as 'the Feargus O'Connor of the middle classes' (J. Morley, *The Life of Richard Cobden*, 1881, 2.416) was near the mark. Palmerston pioneered the kind of politics often associated with Gladstone and Joseph Chamberlain. At intervals he went on the stump, and in the 1860s made speeches aimed specifically at a working class whose self-respect and respect for other classes were qualifying more of them for membership of the political nation. He amused a Glaswegian audience by claiming to be a working man himself; at Lambeth he talked of social mobility and was criticized in the press for overstating it. He preached a popular capitalism: increasing wages and returns on capital went hand in hand; employers should not treat the workforce as 'machines … to produce so much profit … but … rational beings' (*The Times*, 7 Nov 1856). There is an obvious contrast here with his position on parliamentary reform after the 1860 bill, on which he and Russell agreed before coming into office. Lack of interest outside Westminster compelled them to abandon the measure in an unfriendly house. Although Palmerston saw no reason to repeat the attempt until opinion had ripened, he promoted 'bit by bit reform', which gave four new constituencies to the industrial north of England in 1861. The evolving political system to which he imparted its distinctive character was well described as 'an aristocratico-democratic representative constitution' (G. C. Lewis, *A Dialogue on the Best Form of Government*, 1863, 82).

The Palmerston of these years voted for the Liberation Society's church rate bills, and expressed sympathy with nonconformist complaints of the Anglican monopoly in university government. In deference to Peelite high-churchmen in the cabinet, he made fewer evangelical appointments while pointing to their reception by church people and nonconformists. Baronetcies for parliamentary representatives of nonconformity proclaimed their acceptability in the party he led. An essentially political investment in nonconformist goodwill paid: the most militant of nonconformists found it hard to depict Palmerston as an enemy; greater harmony between church and chapel helped the Liberals at the 1865 election. The familiar tory cry of 'the Church in danger' sounded unconvincing in that atmosphere; even E. B. Pusey urged his adherents to vote for a minister who had done much to strengthen the establishment.

Religion divided Palmerston and Gladstone more than anything else. 'There was a greater storm in the cabinet … than I ever heard before' (15 Nov 1862, Glynne–Gladstone MS 29/1), wrote Gladstone when the premier stood firm on denying Samuel Wilberforce the archbishopric of York. Their published correspondence suggests that their better-known disagreements were not caused by serious policy differences. Palmerston believed the chancellor was using his financial responsibility to become 'master of the cabinet' (Connell, 291), and asserted his own authority as first lord of the Treasury. Gladstone's acceptance from the outset that modernization of the fleet was imperative foreshadowed the outcome of their repeated arguments over the naval estimates, in particular. Palmerston joked about the many contemplated resignations of his colleague, who came closest to leaving on the fortifications loan (1860). Sure of the cabinet, he faced his challenger with lasting relegation to the back benches beside radicals whose opinions on most subjects, defence included, were not his. That summer he quietly welcomed the Lords' action in throwing out repeal of the paper duties: he disliked the sacrifice of revenue, and contrived to prevent the ensuing controversy about the Lords' power from developing into an unwanted crisis. Gladstone got his way the next year, by inserting the repeal in a unified finance bill which the peers could not reject. Cutting expenditure, once defence spending reached its peak, had Palmerston's blessing. In all his long experience, keeping taxes low was vital to political health. The two men compromised on direct versus indirect taxation: Palmerston was for halting the decline in income tax at 5d. in the pound, not the 4d. reached by 1865, since it was levied upon those who could comfortably afford to pay, and concentrating reductions upon the fiscal burdens of the vast majority.

'Progressive improvement' had many aspects. Palmerston befriended the extension of the Factory Acts, and obliged pressure groups with royal commissions on a variety of social problems. But his constructive influence did not owe a great deal to legislation. Gladstone linked Palmerston with the Liberals' goal in declaring that they had set themselves to remove 'any occasion … of conflict between classes' (The Times, 2 June 1865). In saying of Palmerston 'he devoted more time and ability to … understanding the people than any democratic politician of his age', the Daily News (25 Oct 1865) recognized that his ministries were a conscious introduction to a new era. If not a good party man, he fashioned the instrument which

served Gladstone well: a Liberalism whose unifying idea and function—social harmony in the pursuit of ordered change—he had redefined and emphasized. Disraeli and, with more success, Lord Salisbury tried to acquire this Palmerstonian inheritance.

The last months of Palmerston's life saw an electoral victory in July 1865 which considerably increased his majority. In Ireland Fenianism confronted him: no surprise to someone who had insisted on stationing there, at a quiet time, 'a sufficient Saxon force to make any movement on the part of the Celts perfectly hopeless, and sure to bring immediate destruction on those who take part' (Panmure Papers, 2.446). If the harshness is unexpected, he may be said to have taken a more realistic view of Irish unrest than was usual then. He did not live to meet the new parliament. A robust constitution, which had withstood gout and lesser ailments, was perceptibly weakening during 1865; he died from pneumonia at Brocket on 18 October of that year. 'Die, my dear Doctor, that's the last thing I shall do!' were said to be his last words (E. Latham, Famous Sayings, 1904, 12). Given a state funeral, he was buried at Westminster Abbey, the last of many honours—dying a knight of the Garter (1856), lord warden of the Cinque Ports (1862), and rector of Glasgow University (1863). His Irish peerage became extinct.

Posthumous reputation There is a wide measure of disagreement about Palmerston. The official life begun by his friend Sir Henry Bulwer was completed and revised by Evelyn Ashley, Shaftesbury's son. They presented him as an authentic Liberal, without doing justice to his perception of change and adaptation to it. Shorter nineteenth-century studies drew on Bulwer and Ashley. The publication of Morley's Gladstone in 1903 lent authority to the contention of diverse critics in his lifetime that the real Palmerston was distinctly conservative in domestic politics, if a liberal in Europe. Variations on that theme prevailed until lately. In the 1960s one scholar summed him up as an 'ill-considered Tory hack, rising by unorthodox methods, in association with … but not by the will of Whiggery … [to] a sort of Caesarian supremacy' (D. Southgate, The Passing of the Whigs, 1962, 295). Another, in an influential book, wrote that Palmerston's policies 'involved crude belligerence abroad, and class fear at home' (J. Vincent, The Formation of the Liberal Party, 1857–1868, 1966, 146). A different Palmerston appeared in Webster's classic account of his diplomacy and Bourne's exhaustively researched biography, neither of which got beyond 1841. A recent study of the two administrations (E. D. Steele, Palmerston and Liberalism, 1855–1865, 1991) has argued that they reflected the thinking of a statesman who was not merely liberal but genuinely progressive by contemporary standards.   DAVID STEELE

Sources P. Guedalla, Palmerston (1926) · H. C. F. Bell, Lord Palmerston, 2 vols. (1936) · C. Webster, The foreign policy of Palmerston, 1830–1841: Britain, the liberal movement and the Eastern question, 2 vols. (1951) · D. G. Southgate, 'The most English minister …': the policies and politics of Palmerston (1966) · J. Ridley, Lord Palmerston (1970) · K. Bourne, Palmerston: the early years, 1784–1841 (1982) · E. D. Steele, Palmerston and liberalism, 1855–1865 (1991) · The letters of the third Viscount Palmerston to Laurence and Elizabeth Sulivan, 1804–1863, ed.

K. Bourne, CS, 4th ser., 23 (1979) · *Gladstone and Palmerston: being the correspondence of Lord Palmerston with Mr Gladstone, 1851–1865*, ed. P. Guedalla (1928) · B. Connell, ed., *Regina v. Palmerston: the correspondence between Queen Victoria and her foreign and prime minister, 1837–1865* (1962) · *The Greville memoirs, 1814–1860*, ed. L. Strachey and R. Fulford, 8 vols. (1938) · Gladstone, *Diaries* · W. H. L. E. Bulwer, *The life of John Henry Temple, Viscount Palmerston*, ed. E. M. Ashley, 3 vols. (1870–74) · A. E. M. Ashley, *The life of Henry John Temple, Viscount Palmerston, 1846–1865*, 2 vols., 2nd edn (1876) · *The political correspondence of Mr Gladstone and Lord Granville, 1868–1876*, ed. A. Ramm, 2 vols., CS, 3rd ser., 81–2 (1952) · *The political correspondence of Mr Gladstone and Lord Granville, 1876–1886*, ed. A. Ramm (1962) · *The Panmure papers, being a selection from the correspondence of Fox Maule*, ed. G. Douglas and G. D. Ramsay, 2 vols. (1908) · BL, Beauvale MSS · U. Southampton L., Broadlands archives · Clwyd RO, Glynne-Gladstone MSS · BL, Bligh MSS, Add. MS 41285 · University of York, Hickleton MSS

Archives BL, letter-books, letters received, accounts, Add. MSS 48417–48586, 49963–49969 · BL, letters from his wife, notebook, and mathematical notes, Add. MSS 45553–45554, 59853 · CUL, corresp. relating to election as MP for University of Cambridge · Duke U., Perkins L., letters and memoranda · NA Canada, corresp. relating to Canada · NL Scot., corresp. · Royal Archives, Brussels, letters and notes · St John Cam., papers · U. Mich., Clements L., letters · U. Southampton L., political corresp. and papers | All Souls Oxf., corresp. with Sir Charles Richard Vaughan · Alnwick Castle, Northumberland, letters to Henry Drummond · BL, corresp. with fourth earl of Aberdeen, Add. MS 43069 · BL, Beauvale MSS · BL, corresp. with J. D. Bligh, Add. MSS 41268–41285 · BL, letters to Lord Broughton, Add. MS 46915 · BL, corresp. with W. E. Gladstone, Add. MSS 44271–44273 · BL, corresp. with Sir Robert Gordon, Add. MS 43218 · BL, letters to third earl of Hardwicke, Add. MSS 35424, 35648–35678, *passim* · BL, corresp. with first Baron Heytesbury, Add. MSS 41560–41563 · BL, letters to third Lord Holland and Lady Holland, Add. MSS 51599–51603 · BL, corresp. with fourth Lord Holland and Lady Holland, Add. MSS 52001–52002, 52125 · BL, letters to R. B. Hoppner, Egerton MS 2343 · BL, letters to sixth Baron Howard de Walden, Add. MS 45176 · BL, Lamb papers · BL, corresp. with Prince Lieven and Princess Lieven, Add. MSS 47263, 47366 · BL, letters to second earl of Liverpool, Add. MS 38194 · BL, corresp. with third Viscount Melbourne, Add. MSS 60460–60473 · BL, letters to C. P. Moraes Sarmento, Add. MS 63174 · BL, corresp. with Sir Charles Napier, Add. MSS 40019–40041 · BL, corresp. with Sir Robert Peel, Add. MSS 40222–40588 · BL, corresp. with comte de Puisaye, Add. MS 7985 · BL, corresp. with first marquess of Ripon, Add. MS 43512 · BL, corresp. with first earl of Ripon, Add. MS 40862 · BL, corresp. with Sir George Shee, Add. MSS 60337–60342 · BL, letters to second Earl Spencer · BL, corresp. with Lord Strathnairn, Add. MS 42797 · BL, corresp. with Laurence Sulivan, Add. MSS 58782–58783 · BL, corresp. with eleventh earl of Westmorland, Microfilm/509/2 · BL, corresp. with Charles Wood, Add. MS 49531, *passim* · BL OIOC, corresp. with J. C. Hobhouse, MS Eur. F 213 · BL OIOC, corresp. with Sir John McNeill, MS Eur. D 1165 · BL OIOC, corresp. with Sir G. B. Robinson, MS Eur. F 142 · Bodl. Oxf., letters to Michael Bruce; letters to fourth earl of Clarendon; letters to Benjamin Disraeli; letters to Henry Fox; letters to sixth Baron Howard de Walden; corresp. with Lord Kimberley · Bodl. Oxf., Clarendon MSS · Borth. Inst., letters to Sir Charles Wood · Bucks. RLSS, letters to twelfth duke of Somerset · Claydon House, Buckinghamshire, letters to W. E. Nightingale · Cumbria AS, Carlisle, corresp. with Sir James Graham · Derbys. RO, letters to Sir R. J. Wilmot-Horton · Devon RO, letters to Sir Thomas Dyke Acland; letters to Earl Fortescue; letters to twelfth duke of Somerset · East Riding of Yorkshire Archives Service, Beverley, letters to Thomas Grimston and Charles Grimston · Flintstone RO, Hawarden, Glynne-Gladstone MSS · Hants. RO, letters to James Harris, first earl of Malmesbury · Harrowby Manuscript Trust, Sandon Hall, Staffordshire, corresp. with earls of Harrowby · Harvard U., Houghton L., letters to Sir John Bowring · HLRO, corresp. with Speaker Brand · Lambton Park, Chester-le-Street, co. Durham, corresp. with first earl of Durham · LPL, corresp. with Charles Blomfield; corresp. with A. C. Tait · Lpool RO, letters to fourteenth earl of Derby · NA Scot., letters to eleventh earl of Dalhousie; corresp. with Sir Andrew Leith Hay · NL Scot., letters to Sir G. Baillie Hamilton; corresp. with second earl of Minto · NL Wales, letters to Sir George Cornewall Lewis · NMM, letters to second earl of Minto; letters to Sir Charles Napier · Norfolk RO, corresp. with Sir Henry Lytton Bulwer · NRA Scotland, priv. coll., corresp. with tenth earl of Wemyss · priv. coll., letters to Spencer Perceval · PRO, corresp. with Stratford Canning, FO 352 · PRO, dispatches to and from first Baron Cowley and second Baron Cowley, FO 519 · PRO, corresp. with first Earl Granville and second Earl Granville, PRO 30/29 · PRO, letters to Lord Hammond, FO 391 · PRO, corresp. with Sir Henry Pottinger, FO 705 · PRO, corresp. with Lord John Russell, PRO 30/22 · RIBA BAL, letters to T. L. Donaldson · Royal Arch., Melbourne MSS · Sheff. Arch., letters to James Stuart-Wortley · St Deiniol's Library, Hawarden, letters to fifth duke of Newcastle · Staffs. RO, letters to first Baron Hatherton; corresp. with second duke of Sutherland and duchess of Sutherland · Trinity Cam., letters to Lord Houghton · U. Durham L., corresp. with second Earl Grey, letters to third Earl Grey · U. Durham L., corresp. with Viscount Ponsonby · U. Nott. L., corresp. with fourth duke of Newcastle and fifth duke of Newcastle · U. Southampton L., corresp. with John Wilson Croker relating to military and political matters; letters to Lord Shaftesbury; letters to duke of Wellington · UCL, letters to Lord Brougham; corresp. with Sir Edwin Chadwick · W. Sussex RO, corresp. with Richard Cobden; letters to duke of Richmond · W. Yorks. AS, Leeds, corresp. with first marquess of Clanricarde · Wilts. & Swindon RO, corresp. with Sidney Herbert and Elizabeth Herbert · Woburn Abbey, Bedfordshire, corresp. with Lord George William Russell · Yale U., Beinecke L., letters to Colonel Wylde

Likenesses T. Heaphy, watercolour drawing, 1802, NPG · T. Heaphy, drawing, 1804, Buscot Park, Oxfordshire · T. Lawrence, portrait, c.1810–1820, Broadlands · J. Partridge, oils, 1850; on loan to the Palace of Westminster, London, 1979 · F. Cruikshank, oils, c.1855, NPG [*see illus.*] · R. C. Lucas, wax relief, 1856, NPG · G. Vivian, photograph, 1858, NPG · F. Grant, oils, 1862, Gov. Art Coll. · E. B. Morris, oils, 1863, Dover town hall · J. Lucas, oils, 1866, Trinity House, London · J. Partridge, oils, c.1884–1845, NPG · J. Gilbert, group portrait, pencil and wash (*Coalition Ministry, 1854*), NPG · R. Jackson, marble statue, Westminster Abbey · M. Noble, marble bust, Reform Club, London · M. Noble, statue, market place, Romsey, Hampshire · J. Partridge, group portrait, oils (*Fine art commissioners*), NPG · J. Phillip, group portrait, oils (*House of Commons, 1860*), Palace of Westminster, London · D. Wilkie, group portrait, oils (*Queen Victoria's first council, 1837*), Royal Collection · T. Woolner, bronze statue, Parliament Square, London

Wealth at death under £120,000: probate, 22 Dec 1865, CGPLA Eng. & Wales

Temple, James (1606–c.1674), regicide, was the only surviving son of Sir Alexander Temple (c.1582–1629) of Etchingham in Sussex, and his first wife, Mary Penyston, daughter of John Somer of Kent. Alexander Temple was MP for Sussex in 1625–6. James Temple was educated at Lincoln's Inn from 1622, although his attendance was irregular, and he was not called to the bar. His absence may have been caused, in part, by his participation in the duke of Buckingham's fateful military campaign to the island of Ré in 1627, during which his elder brother was killed. Before April 1629 he married his stepsister Mary, daughter of John Busbridge of Etchingham, Sussex. They had five sons and a daughter. In the years following the death of his father in 1629 Temple forged friendships with many future parliamentarians, such as Sir Thomas Pelham, one of the most prominent puritan grandees in Sussex, with whom Temple and his family lived in the early 1640s. Upon the outbreak of civil war, Temple was made captain of a troop of horse under his uncle, William Fiennes, Viscount Saye and Sele, and subsequently served as captain of Tilbury Fort, a position which his father had earlier held. His most significant military contribution, however, occurred in Sussex, where he served on parliament's county committee, and where, as governor of Bramber Castle, he played a prominent part in the defence of the town against royalist troops. After the introduction of the New Model Army in 1645, he served as governor of Arundel Castle.

Temple was returned to parliament as a recruiter MP for Bramber in September 1645, and quickly emerged as a supporter of the political independents. He was among the members who fled to the safety of the army in the wake of the presbyterian disturbances in the summer of 1647, and thereafter played a prominent part in attempts to undermine the work of the presbyterians, not least in terms of policy in Ireland. He was nominated as a parliamentary commissioner for Munster in late 1647, although he may never have left England, where his services were certainly valuable in 1648 when Tilbury Fort assumed a position of strategic importance during the second civil war in Essex.

After Pride's Purge in December 1648 Temple quickly emerged as an opponent of negotiated settlement with the king, and was named to the high court of justice to try Charles I. He attended every day of the trial and signed the death warrant [see also Regicides]. In the months after the execution of the king he played an active part in the work of parliament, not least on the committee for plundered ministers, although he also remained occupied by his work as governor of Tilbury. During late 1649 and early 1650, however, suspicions began to emerge regarding his financial propriety, as well as his work as guardian of the Catholic Sir Charles Shelley, heir to one of Sussex's most prominent recusant families. His fall from favour eventually resulted in his removal as governor of Tilbury, in September 1650, following allegations of mismanagement, and thereafter he played little part in Westminster affairs. He sat in none of the parliaments of the protectorate, and probably opposed the Cromwellian regime. When he returned to Westminster during the brief restoration of the Rump in 1659, it was as a republican sympathizer, albeit one opposed to the army.

Temple probably absented himself from parliament after the readmission of those members who had been removed at Pride's Purge, and as a regicide almost certainly feared for his safety after the return of Charles II. He fled from London, travelling under an alias, but was arrested in Warwickshire in mid-June 1660. He was held prisoner in the Tower until being tried along with the other regicides in the following October. At his trial he acknowledged having signed the death warrant, but claimed to have played little part in the deliberations, and even the prosecuting counsel admitted that 'there are some worse than he', although he also added that 'he is

bad enough' (State trials, 5.1217). Having surrendered himself according to the proclamation of 4 June, however, Temple was able to plead for his life, and so avoided execution. Subsequently, in 1662 when a bill was prepared to allow the remaining regicides to be executed he appeared before the House of Lords and submitted a petition in which he offered an elaborate excuse for his role in the death of Charles I. He claimed that he had been urged by two royalists, Stephen Goffe and Henry Hammond, not to refuse to participate in the trial, in order that he could gain intelligence on the work of the commissioners and 'from time to time to give them an account'. He also claimed to have 'often applied himself to that cruel tyrant and usurper Cromwell with tears in his eyes, begging of him not to bring such a blot of bloody stain upon the Protestants as to execute his sacred majesty' (Seventh Report, HMC, 156). Temple further suggested that his favour to the royal cause was the reason for his fall from power in the early 1650s. Although an implausible tale, he nevertheless received support from a number of royalists, but to no avail. He was transferred to a prison on Jersey in 1662, and probably died there some time around 1674.

J. T. PEACEY

Sources T. Prime, Some account of the Temple family (1899) · J. A. Temple and H. M. Temple, The Temple memoirs (1925) · C. H. Firth and R. S. Rait, eds., Acts and ordinances of the interregnum, 1642–1660, 3 vols. (1911) · JHC, 4–8 (1644–67) · CSP dom., 1638–68 · Seventh report, HMC, 6 (1879) · J. G. Muddiman, The trial of King Charles the First (1928) · State trials, vol. 5 · R. Mollet, A chronology of Jersey (1949) · M. A. E. Green, ed., Calendar of the proceedings of the committee for compounding … 1643–1660, 5 vols., PRO (1889–92) · CSP Ire., 1647–60 · J. T. Peacey, 'Temple, James', HoP, Commons, 1690–1715 [draft]

Temple, Sir John (1600–1677), judge and historian, was born in Ireland, the eldest son of Sir William *Temple (1554/5–1627), provost of Trinity College, Dublin, and Martha (d. in or after 1627), daughter of Robert Harrison of Derbyshire. His father was knighted by Viscount Grandison in 1622. After graduating BA (1617) and MA (1620) from Trinity College, Dublin, John Temple entered Lincoln's Inn in 1620 and then spent some time travelling abroad. On 22 June 1627 he married Mary (d. 1638), daughter of Dr John *Hammond (c.1555–1617) of Chertsey, Surrey, and his wife, Mary Harrison (d. 1650). They had four sons and three daughters before Mary's death at Penshurst, Kent, in November 1638.

Temple was a gentleman pensioner by the time he was knighted during the king's coronation visit to Scotland in 1633. At court in England, Temple was the friendly associate of Robert Sidney, second earl of Leicester, on whose behalf he lobbied assertively for the post of secretary of state during the earl's absence on embassy to France. Later he conducted Leicester's end of negotiations for appointment as lord lieutenant of Ireland. Temple was in the north of England with the king in the spring of 1639; he wrote several accounts of developments there to the earl. He was consistently solicitous of Leicester's often straitened financial situation. In the teeth of some opposition in the Irish parliament, Temple was created master of the rolls of Ireland on 31 January 1641, in succession to Sir Christopher Wandesford, having purchased the office. He did not leave to take up his appointment until August. On his arrival he was admitted a privy councillor at Dublin Castle.

When the Irish rising broke out in October 1641 Temple was of the greatest service to government in provisioning the city of Dublin. On 23 July 1642 he was returned MP for Meath, and resided at Staplestown, co. Carlow. In the struggle between crown and parliament Temple's inclinations drew him to the side of the latter, and, in consequence of the vehement resistance he offered to the cessation, he was in August 1643 suspended from his office by the lords justices Borlase and Tichborne, acting on instructions from Charles I, and, with Sir William Parsons, Sir Adam Loftus, and Sir Robert Meredith, imprisoned in Dublin Castle. He was charged with having written in May and June two scandalous letters against the king, which had been used to allege that Charles favoured the rebels. His imprisonment lasted nearly a year; he was then exchanged for Sir Thomas Malet, who was being held by parliament. In 1646 he was recruited to a vacant seat for Chichester in the English House of Commons, receiving at the same time its special thanks for his services to the English interest in Ireland at the beginning of the rising. Shortly afterwards he joined the Westminster committee responsible for overseeing Irish affairs.

Also that year, Temple published his *History of the Irish Rebellion* which made an immediate and great sensation. As the work of a professed eye-witness, and one whose position entitled him to speak with authority, its statements were received with unquestioning confidence, and the work did much to inflame popular indignation in England against the Irish, and to justify the severe treatment afterwards meted out to them by Cromwell. But its deliberate exaggeration of the blood-letting which took place in 1641 was just one aspect of the book's partisan intent. Temple was an important member of an 'Irish independent' interest which aimed to prevent any reconciliation between parliament and the marquess of Ormond, the lord lieutenant who had negotiated a truce with the rebels in September 1643. By stoking the fires of retributive rage against Catholic atrocity, Temple probably hoped to implicate Ormond as an accessory to massacre after the fact (an undertaking made more explicit with the publication of Adam Meredith's *Ormonds Curtains Drawn*, in which Temple may well have had a hand). Temple also saw the manipulation of opinion in England for a war of imperial conquest in Ireland as a way of undermining the principal rival to the Irish independents for dominance in planter affairs in the south, Murrough O'Brian, Lord Inchequin, who was an ally of leading Westminster presbyterians.

Publication of Temple's history of the rebellion coincided with the appointment of Philip Sidney, Lord Lisle, eldest son of the second earl of Leicester, as the new lord lieutenant of Ireland in January 1646. This appointment was part of a strategy which also involved the disavowal of a joint Anglo-Scottish solution to the continuing Irish question. Inasmuch as it also encouraged the adoption of a scorched earth policy of total conquest, Temple's tract accorded well with the desires of the adventurers who had a substantial stake in the complete subjugation of the Irish. Temple was appointed to Lisle's privy council, accompanying him to Ireland in 1647. When Lisle's commission ended in April 1647, Temple returned with him to England. Resuming his place at Westminster, Temple proceeded to harry Inchequin's agent, Sir Philip Perceval, recently returned as a recruiter member, in a campaign of vilification which coincided with the impeachment of the eleven members by independents in the lower house friendly to the interests of the army.

In 1647, after the conclusion of the peace between Ormond and the English parliament, Temple was appointed a commissioner for the government of Munster, and on 16 October the following year he was made joint commissioner with Sir William Parsons for the administration of the great seal of Ireland. But, having supported the majority in favour of pursuing further the peace talks with the king then being held at Newport on the Isle of Wight, Temple was purged from the House of Commons in December 1648. He appears to have held aloof from the Commonwealth regime until 21 November 1653, when he was appointed as a commissioner for the settlement of the estates belonging to delinquents in Ireland. In 1655 he went to Ireland with a highly commendatory letter from Cromwell to Lord Deputy Fleetwood and his council of state in a successful bid to regain the office of master of the rolls. In September that year he and Sir Robert King, Benjamin Worsley, and others were appointed to a commission for letting and setting of houses and lands belonging to the state in the counties of Dublin, Kildare, and Carlow; on 13 June 1656 Temple was appointed a commissioner for determining disputes over the land settlement arising among the adventurers. For these services, so it is said, he received on 6 July 1658 a grant of two leases for twenty-one years: one comprised the town and lands of Moyle, Castletown, and Park, adjoining the town of Carlow, amounting to about 1490 acres, in part afterwards confirmed to him under the Act of Settlement on 18 June 1666; the other was made up of certain lands in the barony of Balrothery West, co. Dublin, to which were added those of Lispoble in the same county on 30 March 1659 for a similar term of years. He obtained license to go to England for a whole year or more on 21 April 1659.

At the Restoration, Temple was confirmed in his office of master of the rolls, sworn a member of the privy council, and appointed a trustee for the army officers who had remained loyal to Ormond and the Stuarts in 1649. On 4 May 1661 he and his eldest son, William *Temple (1628–1699), were elected to represent co. Carlow in the Irish parliament. On 6 May he obtained, for the payment of a fine of £540, a reversionary lease from the queen mother, Henrietta Maria, of the park of Blandesby or Blansby, Pickering, Yorkshire, for a term of forty years. That summer he wrote several letters to the earl of Leicester describing his fears for a renewed outbreak by the Irish Catholics, encouraged as they were, in Temple's estimation, by the king's repeated interventions on their behalf for the restoration of property they claimed they had been deprived of wrongfully. Temple himself received a confirmation in perpetuity of his lands in co. Dublin, including those of Palmerstown, under the Act of Settlement in 1666; to these were added on 20 May 1669 others in counties Kilkenny, Meath, Westmeath, and Dublin. Other grants followed. On 3 May 1672 he received 144 acres formerly part of Phoenix Park, and on 16 November 1675 certain lands, fishings, and so on, in and near Chapelizod. He was appointed vice-treasurer of Ireland in 1673, but died on 12 November 1677. He was buried beside his father in Trinity College near the campanile, having that year donated £100 to the college for building works. He was survived by two sons, William and John *Temple (1632–1705), and two daughters. Temple's *History* was reprinted in 1679, helping once more to fan the flames of partisan politics in England. A decade later, James II's Irish parliament of 1689 ordered the book to be burnt by the hand of the public hangman. ROBERT DUNLOP, *rev.* SEAN KELSEY

Sources M. W. Henning and P. Watson, 'Temple, Sir John', HoP, *Commons, 1660–90*, 3.535–6 · *Report on the manuscripts of Lord De L'Isle and Dudley*, 6, HMC, 77 (1966) · J. Adamson, 'Strafford's ghost: the British context of Viscount Lisle's lieutenancy of Ireland', *Ireland from independence to occupation, 1641–1660*, ed. J. Ohlmeyer (1995), 128–159 · F. E. Ball, *The judges in Ireland, 1221–1921*, 1 (1926), 338–40 · PRO, 11/353, fols. 334–5 · IGI
Archives BL, letters to earl of Essex, Stowe MSS 200–212 · CKS, letters to second earl of Leicester
Likenesses C. Johnson, portrait, Berkeley Castle, Gloucestershire
Wealth at death made gifts of nearly £6000; devised several bequests in connection with English trading community at Smyrna worth several hundred dollars: will, PRO, PROB 11/353, fols. 334–5

Temple, Sir John (1632–1705), lawyer and politician, was born on 25 March 1632, the second son of Sir John *Temple (1600–1677) of Dublin and Ballycrath, co. Carlow, master of the rolls in Ireland, and his wife, Mary (d. 1638), daughter of Dr John *Hammond. He was probably educated at Bishop's Stortford grammar school and then entered Pembroke College, Cambridge, on 30 January 1647, and Gray's Inn on 4 May 1650. He returned to Ireland in 1653 and from 1654 he practised in the Irish court of chancery. In 1657 he spent over three months in England, during which time he was called to the bar, on 17 November 1657. Following the Restoration, on 10 July 1660, he was appointed solicitor-general for Ireland. In the elections to the Irish parliament in 1661 Temple was returned for the borough of Carlow, and on 6 September 1661 he was chosen temporary speaker of the Irish House of Commons in the absence of Sir Audley Mervin.

Temple married, on 4 August 1663, Jane (d. 1708), daughter of Sir Abraham Yarner of Dublin, the muster-master general. They had four sons and seven daughters. He was knighted on 15 August 1663 and in January 1664 Lord Lieutenant Ormond wrote that he was a young man of 'extraordinary parts' (*CSP Ire., 1663–5*, 349). His legal career was

now well established, and after 1664 his combined earnings from chancery and the solicitor-general's office did not fall below £1000 p.a. until 1687. In 1666–9 his income benefited from work generated by the Irish land settlement. Temple was now settled in Ireland as the confidante of Irish politicians like Ormond. He rented a house near the King's Inns and built a house at Palmerston, near to the lord lieutenant's residence. Temple was rarely away from Ireland, visiting England in winter 1670–71 and summer 1675. In 1678 Ormond wrote that Sir John 'gives us very usefully very much of his pains, and I think must afford us more in the quality of Speaker' (*Ormonde MSS*, new ser., 4.167), should the Irish parliament be summoned, but that he was reluctant to take on the office. Lord Orrery described him in July 1679 as 'one of the ablest and honestest lawyers in his majesties dominions' (MacLysaght, 218). Temple was again in England in August–October 1679 when there were rumours that he would be appointed attorney-general in England 'at the mediation of my Lord of Essex' (*Ormonde MSS*, new ser., 5.225). This appointment fell through, according to one account, because Charles II 'would never trust any of the blood of a rebel' (Thompson, 198–9), a reference to his father.

In 1680 Lord Chamberlain Arlington reportedly feared that Temple's links with whig politicians such as the earl of Essex, and his failure to obtain the attorney's post would make him obstructive. Judging from his correspondence with Ormond this does not seem to have been the case. Temple was reappointed solicitor-general following the accession of James II, but the gradual introduction of more Roman Catholics into legal office saw him isolated. The appointment of a more vigorous attorney-general, Sir Richard Nagle, also cut into his employment. With an annual rent roll of £1960 Temple was now in a position to enjoy the fruits of astutely invested profits from his legal career. In late July 1687 he left for England and did not return until May 1688. The revolution saw him back in England as a key adviser on Irish policy to William III. Temple was attainted by the Irish parliament of James II, but on 30 October 1690 he was named attorney-general in Ireland. He did not resume his Irish practice, but he was resident in Ireland in 1691–2. Ill health and business apparently made him return to England in autumn 1692, although others thought this a ruse to avoid involvement in the new Irish parliament. Temple continued in office until he was removed in summer 1695.

Despite rumours to the contrary, Temple did not become master of the rolls in Ireland, an office which his brother, Sir William, held under a life patent. Sir William instead surrendered the office in 1696 and it was granted to William Berkeley, the future fourth Lord Berkeley of Stratton, who that same year married Sir John's youngest daughter. One of her elder sisters married the third Baron Berkeley of Stratton and then the first earl of Portland, while another married Sir Basil Dixwell, second baronet. In retirement Temple lived at East Sheen, Surrey, where he died on 10 March 1705. He was buried at Mortlake, Surrey, on 16 March. He was survived by his wife, who died on 25 June 1708, two sons, and four daughters. Most of his estates in England and Ireland were settled on his two sons, the elder of whom, Henry *Temple, was created Viscount Palmerston on 12 March 1723.

STUART HANDLEY

Sources *The early essays and romances of Sir William Temple … with The life and character of Sir William Temple, by his sister Lady Giffard*, ed. G. C. Moore Smith (1930) · J. Lodge, *The peerage of Ireland*, 3 (1754), 321–2 · T. C. Barnard, 'Lawyers and the law in later seventeenth-century Ireland', *Irish Historical Studies*, 28 (1992–3), 273–6 · T. Prime, *Some account of the Temple family* (1899), 55–68, 107 · *Herald and Genealogist*, 3 (1866), 400, 404 · Venn, *Alum. Cant.* · *Calendar of the manuscripts of the marquess of Ormonde*, new ser., 8 vols., HMC, 36 (1902–20), vols. 4–7 · *CSP Ire.*, 1660–70 · *CSP dom.*, 1685; 1690–91; 1695–6 · E. MacLysaght, ed., *Calendar of the Orrery papers*, IMC (1941), 218 · E. M. Thompson, ed., *Correspondence of the family of Hatton*, 1, CS, new ser., 22 (1878), 198–9 · *The manuscripts of his grace the duke of Portland*, 10 vols., HMC, 29 (1891–1931), vol. 3, pp. 503–4 · *The correspondence of Henry Hyde, earl of Clarendon, and of his brother Lawrence Hyde, earl of Rochester*, ed. S. W. Singer, 2 (1828), 241–2
Archives NL Ire., corresp. with duke of Ormond

Temple [*née* MacLeod], **Olive Susan Miranda** (1880–1936), traveller and author, was born on 18 February 1880, the second of the two daughters of Sir Reginald MacLeod of MacLeod (1847–1935), twenty-seventh chief of clan and *rentier*, and his wife, Lady Agnes Mary Cecilia (*d.* 1921), eldest daughter of Stafford Henry *Northcote, first earl of Iddesleigh (1818–1887), politician and author. Her elder sister was Dame Flora *MacLeod (1878–1976). The twenty-fifth chief had encumbered his estates, giving aid during times of famine, and consequently the land-based fortune of the MacLeods had dwindled to the point where poverty had driven them from their seat of 800 years, Dunvegan Castle, on the island of Skye. Olive's father was therefore faced with the task of building his own fortune if the MacLeods were to retain their historic pre-eminence. Sir Reginald achieved this through his investments in the City of London, the great success of which eventually returned the family to Dunvegan. These early lessons in social responsibility and the realities of economic survival may well have helped to forge Olive's remarkable character which was to fascinate all who met her.

Olive MacLeod grew up in a warm and intellectually stimulating atmosphere, but her heart was always set on adventure. At first this was by proxy through her relationship with Boyd Alexander (1873–1910), the African traveller and ornithologist whom she met in 1908. Olive, who had many admirers, was uncertain about Alexander's proposal of marriage, and he, a shy and lonely man, took her procrastination very badly. In his frustration Alexander began to plan a further trip to Africa, and it was only shortly before he was due to leave on 12 December 1908 that she finally agreed to marry him. At this point it was too late for Alexander to change his plans, and he proceeded to Africa, hoping to marry Olive on his return. Sadly, however, he was killed on the shores of Lake Chad on 3 May 1910 by hostile local inhabitants. Olive could not help but feel that if she had agreed to the marriage earlier, Alexander would not have died so tragically. Her friend Violet Asquith, who had also recently lost a fiancé, added to Olive's turmoil by persuading her that she was, to all intents and purposes, a widow. She consequently adopted

Olive Susan Miranda Temple (1880–1936), by unknown photographer

the dress and demeanour of a bereaved wife—much to the fascination of the sensationalist publications of the period. Her family detested Violet Asquith's influence, feeling that such hysteria was alien to Olive's real nature. Therefore, they fell with relief on Olive's plan to travel to Africa to place a stone on Alexander's grave, and her doting father arranged for her to be escorted by Captain and Mrs Amaury-Talbot (he had experience of Southern Nigeria as a district commissioner, later becoming an official anthropologist, and his wife published *Women's Mysteries of a Primitive People: the Ibidios of Southern Nigeria* in 1915). However, the romance of this journey only fuelled the interest of sensation-hungry journalists who covered the story in lurid detail—with at one point Olive's death being incorrectly announced in most papers. In fact she travelled over 3700 miles through Africa, passing many places previously unvisited by a white woman. She also made useful recordings of many matters of botanical, ethnological, and zoological interest, publishing them later in her first book, *Chiefs and Cities of Central Africa* (1912).

During that journey Olive MacLeod met Charles Lindsay *Temple (1871–1929), then chief secretary and acting governor of Northern Nigeria. Though Temple entertained Olive and her party at his residence, he refused her permission to travel up-country thinking the area too unsettled to be traversed by a white woman. Undeterred, Olive planned her own journey in secret, ignoring Temple's instructions. When he found out he was furious, but also fascinated by this enigmatic Scotswoman. Olive must have been equally intrigued for when, back in London, she heard that Temple was home on leave she went to some effort to contrive a meeting. Their marriage followed shortly afterwards, on 28 April 1912. Olive lived with Temple in Nigeria during the remainder of his service as well as travelling throughout Africa with him during his periods of leave. She continued to develop her interests in all aspects of African life, learned Hausa (the lingua franca of Northern Nigeria), and, during her visits to London, presented several serious papers, including one to the anthropological section of the British Association. She also published the data which she had gathered on Northern Nigeria between May 1912 and October 1916, taking full advantage of her privileged access to official documents, in her encyclopaedic compilation *Notes on the Tribes, Provinces, Emirates and States of the Northern Provinces of Nigeria* (1919). In addition, her private papers reveal a detailed knowledge and understanding of administrative life as well as an amused contempt for the first governor-general of Nigeria, Sir Frederick Lugard.

In 1917 Olive Temple travelled with her husband to South Africa, and from there to Granada where they lived until Charles's death on 9 January 1929. The anthropologist and travel writer Gerald Brenan (1894–1987), who knew the Temples during their time in Spain, was struck by the gravity and weight of Olive's character, by her liberal broad-mindedness and painful honesty, but above all by her strong sense of responsibility. However, Brenan is probably incorrect in his suggestion that Olive totally subsumed her nature and ambitions under those of her husband—such was the coincidence of their intellectual and artistic interests, to say nothing of the distinctly patrician outlook that they both unconsciously possessed. Following her husband's death, Olive returned to Britain, spending much of her time in Kent. She died on 16 May 1936 at Carmen de los Fosos, Granada, only a year after her much loved father, and was buried beside her husband in the cemetery near their house. Olive Temple was survived by an adopted daughter, Mary Edith Northcote.

C. J. F. ALDERMAN

Sources C. J. F. Alderman, 'British imperialism and social Darwinism: C. L. Temple and colonial administration in Northern Nigeria, 1901–1916', PhD diss., Kingston University, 1996 · H. Callaway, *Gender, culture and empire: European women in colonial Nigeria* (1987) · J. Alexander, *Whom the gods love* (1977) · G. Brenan, *South from Granada* (1957); pbk edn (1963) · *CGPLA Eng. & Wales* (1936) · private information (2004) [Conrad Swan] · will, 22 April 1934

Archives Bodl. RH · NRA, priv. coll., corresp. and papers relating to Boyd Alexander, Charles Temple, and northern Nigeria | Dunvegan Castle, Isle of Skye, Macleod MSS, sections 4 and 5, *passim*

Likenesses photograph, priv. coll. [*see illus.*] · portrait, repro. in Alexander, *Whom the gods love*

Wealth at death £17,730 6s. 7d.: probate, 13 July 1936, *CGPLA Eng. & Wales*

Temple, Sir Peter, second baronet (*bap.* 1592, *d.* 1653), politician, was baptized at Stowe, Buckinghamshire, on 15 October 1592, the eldest of four sons of Sir Thomas Temple, first baronet (1567–1637), of Stowe, and his wife, Hester (*d.* 1656), daughter of Miles Sandys. Sir Peter's grandfather John Temple, who also had lands in Leicestershire and Warwickshire, acquired the freehold of Stowe in 1590; Sir Thomas purchased the baronetcy in 1611. Peter Temple bought a knighthood in February 1609 and inherited both baronetcy and estates on the death of his father in February 1637. He was already twice married. His first wife, Anne, daughter of Sir Arthur Throckmorton of Northamptonshire, whom he married on 5 July 1614, died in childbirth in January 1620, leaving an infant daughter, Anne. His second marriage, on 20 May 1630, was to Christian (*b.* in or before 1596, *d.* 1655), daughter and coheir of Sir John Leveson of Staffordshire; they had a son, Sir Richard *Temple, third baronet (1634–1697), of Stowe, and two daughters, Frances and Hester.

Temple held a number of posts in Buckinghamshire: he was high sheriff in 1634–5; JP for the town of Buckingham and its MP in the Short and the Long parliaments; and a member of the county committee in 1643. As sheriff he had the misfortune to be responsible for the assessment and collection of ship money from a particularly recalcitrant county. Arrears were still outstanding in July 1636 despite several summons by the privy council, though the final shortfall was small. Although he was not very active in the Long Parliament, Temple supported the parliamentarian cause, but was probably inhibited by the divided allegiance of his family; his wife and some of her relatives were royalists. However, he used his influence to help his relations, including recusants threatened with sequestration. He served as colonel of a parliamentarian regiment but was no republican. He was appointed to the high court of justice to try the king but did not appear, and resigned his commission after Charles was executed. In 1652 an informant alleged that Temple had said he hoped to see the king in England soon and that the Commons had murdered the late king. He denied the charge and seemingly no proceedings were taken against him.

Another reason for Temple's political inactivity may have been his financial problems. For several generations the Temple family had incurred debts, partly to acquire land. Sir Peter was permanently short of money despite an income of £700 a year from the dowry lands of his first wife, a dowry of £3000 from his second, and £800 annually from his father. His father, with whom he shared a mutual hostility, accused him of wasting money in gambling, drinking, and other extravagances; Sir Peter claimed he never received the full marriage settlement promised in 1614. His reduced rental income as his tenants' and his own property were pillaged added to his problems. By 1647 his creditors launched a joint legal suit which continued for six years. For much of the time he was unable to travel openly for fear of being seized for debt; in 1650 he thwarted an attempt in parliament to have his whole estate sold, arguing that 'selling my whole estate and the utter undoing of me and my posterity after me' was 'contrary to right' (Gay, 'Debt settlement', 257). Finally, in August 1653, an agreement was reached that a group of his creditors should administer the estate except Stowe Manor House and some of its lands for ten years, or longer if Temple still lived. The income, apart from an allowance for his widow and son, would repay his debts of £24,000. The agreement was nullified by Temple's sudden death on 12 September 1653; he was buried at Stowe. Despite his financial problems he was well regarded by some: Sir John Lenthall said, 'he was in his lifetime accounted a person of great credit and integrity, and enjoyed a plentiful estate both real and personal' (ibid., 256). He left a number of papers, including personal correspondence and two manuscript books of medical and culinary recipes.

JOAN A. DILS

Sources Keeler, *Long Parliament*, 358 · E. F. Gay, 'The rise of an English country family', *Huntington Library Quarterly*, 1 (1937–8), 367–90 · E. F. Gay, 'The Temples of Stowe and their debts: Sir Thomas Temple and Sir Peter Temple, 1603–1653', *Huntington Library Quarterly*, 2 (1938–9), 399–428, esp. 412–16, 418–19, 432–4, 436 · E. F. Gay, 'Sir Richard Temple, the debt settlement and estate litigation, 1653–1675', *Huntington Library Quarterly*, 6 (1942–3), 255–91, esp. 256–7, 259–60 · GEC, *Baronetage*, 1.82 · C. G. Bonsey, ed., *Ship money papers*, Buckinghamshire RS, 13 (1965), ix–xiv · parish register, Stowe, 1568–1790, Bucks. RLSS, PR201/1/1 · HoP, *Commons, 1558–1603*, 3.481 · HoP, *Commons, 1660–90*, 3.536 · *JHC*, 7 (1651–9), 76, 79, 108 · R. Gibbs, *Worthies of Buckinghamshire* (1888), 377 · A. Steele Young and V. F. Snow, eds., *The private journals of the Long Parliament*, 3: *2 June to 17 September 1642* (1992), 88, 482 · *Journal of Sir Samuel Luke*, ed. I. G. Philip, 1–3, Oxfordshire RS, 29, 31, 33 (1950–53), 3.198 · A. M. Johnson, 'Buckinghamshire, 1640–1660: a study in county politics', MA diss., University of Swansea, 1963, 63 · *Eighth report*, 1, HMC, 7 (1907–9), 19
Archives Bucks. RLSS, legal papers · Hunt. L., corresp. and papers | Hunt. L., Stowe MSS
Wealth at death £6000—p.a.: HoP, *Commons, 1660–90* · no value given; lands valued at £3800; plus income from manor house at Stowe; plus debts of nearly £26,000: Gay, 'Sir Richard Temple'

Temple, Peter (*bap.* 1599, *d.* 1663), regicide, was baptized at St Botolph, Sibson, Leicestershire, on 14 October 1599, the third son of Edmund Temple (*d.* 1616) of Temple Hall, Sibson, and his wife, Elizabeth, the daughter of Robert Burgoine of Wroxhall, Warwickshire. As a younger son he was apprenticed as a linen draper, but inherited the Temple Hall estate when his older brothers, Paul and Jonathan, died. He married Phoebe, the daughter of Edmund Gayring of London and they had three sons, all baptized at St Botolph, Sibson: John on 21 March 1625, Edmund on 3 November 1638, and Peter on 10 June 1635.

In 1642 Temple was chosen as a member of the committee for the short-lived east midlands association of Leicestershire, Derbyshire, Nottinghamshire, Rutland, Northamptonshire, Bedfordshire, and Huntingdon under Thomas, Lord Grey of Groby. He was a captain of a troop of horse and was chosen as a member of the county's militia committee in January 1643. He became sheriff of Leicestershire on 19 January 1644, and in this capacity he acted against the Baptists. In 1645 he was involved in raising funds to supply the Scottish army in Leicester and its vicinity, but he had an undistinguished career as a military man. He was accused of cowardice and of trying to dissuade Lord Grey from fortifying Leicester, and was absent from the city when it was besieged, leaving for London immediately prior to the arrival of the royalist forces (29

May 1645). He also served as governor of Cole Orton in the county. He was elected to parliament as a recruiter MP for Leicester borough on 17 November 1645 following the disablement of the previous member, Thomas Cooke, and, in order to take up the seat, was created a burgess. On election he took the oaths of supremacy and allegiance.

There was a considerable presence from Leicestershire in the organization and membership of the high court of justice to try Charles I. Temple was named as a commissioner of the court, and attended regularly. He was absent from only two of the sessions and signed the king's death warrant on 29 January 1649 [*see also* Regicides]. He was subsequently chosen to sit on the committee for compounding at Goldsmiths' Hall on 13 June 1649 and a month later was voted £1500 from the sequestrations from Leicestershire in reparation for war expenses. By January 1650 he had received £1200 of this and despite information from the county commissioners that they could not pay the remainder it was ordered to be paid from the Michaelmas rents. In December 1650 the council of state called on him to return to his duties as militia commissioner for Leicestershire. The gifts registered to Temple from the mayor and corporation in 1650 describe him as a colonel.

Little overt evidence is available about Temple's religious profession, though he seems to have suppressed the supporters of adult baptism. In October 1649, as a JP in Leicestershire, he convicted Samuel Oates of the heresy of baptizing adults, contrary to the parliamentary ordinance of 2 May 1648. In February 1650 the mayor and aldermen of the corporation of Leicester requested his advice in coping with the publications and activities of Ranters in the city—Jacob Bauthumley was a Leicestershire shoemaker and Abiezer Coppe's 'Fiery Flying Roll' was being distributed. Temple was sent one of the Ranters' publications 'of a very dangerous consequence [which] lets open a very wide dore to Atheism and profanes' (Leics. RO, Hall MSS, xii, no. 642, 18 Feb 1650).

At the recall of the Rump Parliament in 1659 Temple returned to power in London and was given lodgings in Whitehall. At the Restoration he was excluded from pardon by the Act of Oblivion and subsequently from the Indemnity Bill of 29 August 1660. He surrendered on 12 June 1660 and was one of the nineteen regicides named by Ludlow whose future would be decided by parliament. He was prepared to admit his part in the execution of Charles I, but denied that this was a confession of 'guilt', a variation on the argument whereby the regicides denied the clause in the indictment which accused them of acting from self-interest and malice. He was convicted and condemned to be hanged, but pleaded the benefit of the king's proclamation. He was imprisoned in the Tower and died there of dropsy on 20 December 1663. His estate of Temple Hall was bestowed on James, duke of York.

SARAH BARBER

Sources DNB · *JHC*, 3 (1642–4), 354, 576, 638 · *JHC*, 6 (1648–51), 267 · *JHC*, 8 (1660–67), 61, 63, 139 · C. H. Firth and R. S. Rait, eds., *Acts and ordinances of the interregnum, 1642–1660*, 2 (1911), 1133–6 · M. A. E. Green, ed., *Calendar of the proceedings of the committee for compounding … 1643–1660*, 1, PRO (1889), 144, 166 · *CSP dom.*, 1650, 468 · parish register, Sibson, 1061–1812, Leics. RO [transcripts] • H. Hartopp, ed., *Register of the freemen of Leicester*, 1 (1927) • *Records of the borough of Leicester*, 4: *1603–1688*, ed. H. Stocks (1923) • Leics. RO, Hall papers, xi, xii • R. Pye and J. Ennis, *A more exact relation of the siege laid to the town of Leicester* (1645) • *A narration of the siege and taking of the town of Leicester* (1645) • P. Temple and others, *An examination examined, being a full and moderate answer to Major Innes relation concerning the siege and taking of the town of Leicester* (1645) • R. L. Greaves, 'Temple, Peter', Greaves & Zaller, *BDBR*

Archives Leics. RO, Leicester corporation, Hall MSS

Temple, Sir Richard, third baronet (1634–1697), politician, was born on 28 March 1634, the only son of Sir Peter *Temple, second baronet (*bap.* 1592, *d.* 1653), of Stowe, Buckinghamshire, and his second wife, Christian (*b.* in or before 1596, *d.* 1655), daughter and coheir of Sir John *Leveson (1555–1615), of Trentham, Staffordshire. Temple entered Gray's Inn on 6 November 1648 and was admitted to Emmanuel College, Cambridge, a few weeks later on 23 December.

In 1653 Temple succeeded to a substantial, but heavily indebted estate, with a rent roll estimated at £3029, but with over £1500 absorbed by fixed charges. Despite being under age Temple was returned to parliament for Warwickshire in 1654, served as a justice of the peace, and soon acquired household office as carver to the protector. In April 1655 he contracted smallpox and at one point was 'in extremity of sickness and likely to die' (Gay, 289). In October 1656 he made a settlement with his father's creditors, paying £7000 for a debt of £19,468. He sat for Buckingham in Richard Cromwell's parliament, making his first recorded speech on 2 February 1659. Temple was indignant when the army expelled the Rump in October 1659 and he welcomed George Monck's intervention from Scotland. On 26 January 1660 he visited the army, then at Stony Stratford, and quarrelled with some of its republican elements. He was ordered into the custody of the Rump for suggesting the county petition for a free parliament, being released upon the return of the secluded members. He sat in the Convention of 1660 for Buckingham, where he was perceived by Lord Wharton as a 'friend', and possibly as a supporter of modified episcopacy. In August 1660 he applied for preferment to the secretary of state, William Morrice, only to receive a discouraging reply. Worse still, following the lapse of parliamentary privilege, he was committed to a debtors' prison at the suit of his half-sister, Lady Baltinglas.

Despite this drawback Temple retained his seat in the parliamentary elections of April 1661, earning the nickname Sir Timber Temple for his promise of wood for a new town hall in his constituency. Temple was created a knight of the Bath on 18 April 1661, mainly as an attempt to demonstrate royal favour to his relative Sir Richard *Leveson, and hence obtain the Trentham estate from the childless knight. Temple was very active in the Commons as both a speaker and committee man, and as early as 1661 was probably an opponent of the court. At first he joined the opposition to the earl of Clarendon headed by the earl of Bristol and was clearly in sympathy with Bristol's support for the declaration of indulgence, as a consistent proponent of moderation in church matters. However,

Sir Richard Temple, third baronet (1634–1697), by unknown artist, *c*.1670s

Temple's attempt in 1663, through Bristol, to offer his services to Charles II as a parliamentary undertaker, floundered upon his oppositionist stance and an angry Charles II reported his actions to the Commons. Temple survived this setback, but at the cost of his local offices. In 1664 he opposed repeal of the coercive clause in the Triennial Act and, following Bristol's disgrace, he joined the opposition grouping headed by the duke of Buckingham. He supported such measures as the ban on the import of Irish cattle and the attack on Clarendon. In 1668 he promoted a triennial bill and seems to have supported an anti-Clarendon ministry which would adopt a moderate religious policy. On 9 May 1668 Temple received leave of the house to go to France for the recovery of his health. He spent much of his time in Montpellier, taking the waters, and did not return to England until October 1669.

In 1669 Buckingham engaged Temple to support the court, and on 28 November 1670 Andrew Marvell reported that Temple was one of a group of MPs who 'openly took leave of their former party, and fell to head the King's business' (*Poems and Letters*, 1.305). Contemporaries accounted for his new stance by reference to his financial difficulties and his desire to atone for his service to the protector. He still defended nonconformists, but his court stance led him to join the political faction headed by the earl of Arlington. This connection led to his appointment as a commissioner for plantations on 19 June 1671 and then as a commissioner of customs on 23 March 1672, a post worth £2000 p.a. During the next three years Temple paid off most of the money he had borrowed between 1656 and 1667. His improved financial position may also account for his marriage, on 25 August 1675, to Mary (*b.* after 1640, *d.* 1727), daughter of Henry Knapp of Rawlins, Oxfordshire. Temple received a portion of £4000 and possession of Woodcote. Their first child, Richard *Temple, the future first Viscount Cobham, was born on 24 October 1675. They had three other sons and six daughters.

Temple spent the next few years as a spokesman for the court, but although he spoke often he was described in 1673 as one of 'the worst heard that can be in the House' (Airy, 1.132). In 1676 Wiseman noted to Lord Treasurer Thomas Osborne, first earl of Danby, that 'your Lordship every day speaks with him. I hope he will spoil no more votes' (Browning, 3.98), and in 1677–8 his salary at the customs of £1200 was augmented by a pension from the excise. In 1678 he defended Danby from the charges which led to his impeachment, and as a result of his adherence to the court, and the personal intervention of his erstwhile patron, Buckingham, he lost his seat at Buckingham in the election of February 1679. In the election of August 1679 he was returned with Danby's son, Lord Latimer. In this parliament he spoke in favour of the bill uniting protestants, but his stance on the Exclusion Bill was unclear, and possibly designed to weaken the bill. In September 1679 John Verney reported that Temple had been accused of being a Catholic; the accusation evidently persisted because in 1681 Temple took the matter before the courts, and one of his accusers, William Burton, was sentenced to the pillory. In 1683–4 Temple was able to secure a new charter for Buckingham which named him as steward.

Temple retained his customs post until the accession of James II, when he objected to the new monarch collecting the customs duties without parliamentary sanction and was dismissed. As a consequence his finances were hit and he borrowed more, but in April 1686 he was granted a pension of £1200 p.a. for 'good services to the late and present king' (*Calendar of Treasury Books*, 8.697). However, this latest spell of royal favour did not survive his negative response to the three questions and his consequent loss of local office including the stewardship of Buckingham.

Temple was a late adherent to the cause of William of Orange, joining the prince on 12 December 1688 after James II had fled, 'but those as goes in now signifies little but are rather laughed at' (Verney and Verney, 2.469). Having been returned to the convention for Buckingham on 9 January 1689 Temple again showed himself to be an active speaker from his 'uppermost seat' (Schwoerer, 172), and he supported the abdication and vacancy resolutions and the declaration of rights. In early February 1689 it was reported that Temple and his Buckinghamshire neighbour, Richard Hampden, were 'for a Commonwealth and against kingly government' (Hunt. L., Stowe MSS, STT 410), but in fact Temple had renewed his connection with Danby and was soon to be recognized as a court tory. He was appointed to the customs commission in April, prompting one correspondent to opine: 'I find he will be vicar of Bray still, let who will reign, and though all hates him yet he gets what he aims at' (Verney and Verney, 2.471). In debate he supported the ministry's attempts to obtain adequate war supplies and defended the privileges

of the Commons from encroachment by the Lords. In 1693 he published *An Essay on Taxes* in which he argued against the monthly assessment or land tax as destructive of the estates of the peers and gentry, and against a general excise. Having recovered from a serious illness in April 1694 he lost his customs place in the following August. Shrewsbury condemned him for 'corruption, disaffection, neglect, and in short being good for nothing' (*CSP dom.*, 1694–5, 181), but he was a victim of a change in court managers away from Danby (now marquess of Carmarthen) and towards the emerging whig Junto. Temple moved into opposition and in 1696 contributed to the debates on the price of guineas and Fenwick's attainder, which he opposed. Temple died on 10 May 1697 at Stowe and was buried there on the 15th.   STUART HANDLEY

Sources HoP, *Commons, 1660–90* · HoP, *Commons, 1690–1715* [draft] · G. Davies, 'The political career of Sir Richard Temple (1634–1697) and Buckingham politics', *Huntington Library Quarterly*, 4 (1940–41), 47–83 · E. F. Gay, 'Sir Richard Temple, the debt settlement and estate litigation, 1653–1675', *Huntington Library Quarterly*, 6 (1942–3), 255–91 · C. Roberts, *Schemes and undertakings: a study of English politics in the seventeenth century* (1985), 57–77 · L. G. Schwoerer, *The declaration of rights, 1689* (1981) · O. G. Knapp, *A history of the chief English families bearing the name of Knapp* (1911), 85–6 · F. P. Verney and M. M. Verney, *Memoirs of the Verney family during the seventeenth century*, 2nd edn, 4 vols. in 2 (1907), vol. 2, p. 290 · GEC, *Peerage* · *The poems and letters of Andrew Marvell*, ed. H. M. Margoliouth, 2nd edn, 1 (1952), 305 · O. Airy, ed., *Essex papers*, CS, new ser., 47 (1890), 132 · A. Browning, *Thomas Osborne, earl of Danby and duke of Leeds, 1632–1712*, 3 vols. (1944–51) · *CSP dom.*, 1654 · G. Lipscomb, *The history and antiquities of the county of Buckingham*, 4 vols. (1831–47), vol. 3, p. 110

Archives BL, Stowe MSS, political papers, speeches, etc., *passim* · Bodl. Oxf., speeches · Bucks. RLSS, legal papers · Hunt. L., corresp. and papers · U. Reading, Rural History Centre, daybook | Hunt. L., Stowe MSS

Likenesses portrait, *c.*1670–1679; Sothebys, 18 March 1981, lot 25 [*see illus.*]

Temple, Richard, first Viscount Cobham (1675–1749), politician and landowner, was born on 24 October 1675, the first child of Sir Richard *Temple, third baronet (1634–1697), of Stowe, Buckinghamshire, and MP for Buckingham, and his wife and first cousin, Mary (*b.* after 1640, *d.* 1726), the daughter of Henry Knapp of Rawlins, Oxfordshire. He was baptized at St Paul's, Covent Garden, on 1 November 1675. His father had inherited substantial debts on his accession to the title and Buckinghamshire estates in 1653. Consequently the young Temple was directed towards a career that could help to maintain the family's status in their home county without further burdening their landed resources. On 30 June 1685, when not yet ten years old, he was commissioned as an ensign in Prince George of Denmark's regiment. Despite his youth he was court-martialled (with Lord Churchill, later the duke of Marlborough, as presiding officer) on 21 June 1686 at Hounslow for refusing to obey a superior officer. He was dismissed from the regiment, but was recommissioned on 1 May 1687, and was promoted captain in 1689. He was probably the 'Temple major' attending Eton College in 1687; 'Temple minor' was probably his younger brother Purbeck (1676–1698).

Richard Temple, first Viscount Cobham (1675–1749), by Sir Godfrey Kneller, c.1710–13

Temple entered Christ's College, Cambridge, on 31 October 1694 as a fellow-commoner. He did not take a degree and his military career seems to have taken precedence, as he was listed as a captain in Captain Ventris Columbine's regiment of foot in the Flanders army list of 1695. He served with them at the siege of Namur. Sir Richard Temple died on 10 May 1697, and his son succeeded to the baronetcy and estates. The pressures of maintaining a growing family, among other demands, had prevented the debts of the second baronet from being fully redeemed and, although income from the estates has been estimated at an average of £2200 per annum for the first ten years of Temple's ownership, average outgoings stood at 87 per cent of this sum. Temple was returned to the Commons for Buckingham in the by-election following his father's death. In the Commons he was a whig and a supporter of the court of William III, and in August 1701 was foreman of the grand jury at the Buckinghamshire assizes that petitioned the king to pursue war with France over the Spanish succession, and call a new parliament. When war came Temple returned to his military career, and on 10 February 1702 he was appointed colonel of his own regiment of foot.

While he was initially stationed in Ireland, Temple's war was fought mainly in the Netherlands. He was promoted to the rank of major-general in 1706 and played a leading role at the siege of Lille in 1708, for which he was rewarded with the task of presenting news of the capture of the town to Queen Anne.

Temple was also recognized as a loyal political ally by Marlborough and Lord Godolphin. He had been unable to stand for election at Buckingham in 1702 as he was serving with the army, and Marlborough gave him leave to campaign in person for the Buckinghamshire by-election in November 1704. Temple represented Buckinghamshire until the election of 1708, and then returned to his former seat of Buckingham, where he remained until 1713. He maintained a whig stance, voting for the naturalization of the Palatines in 1709, and for the impeachment of Henry Sacheverell in 1710.

Temple continued to receive promotions in the army: his rank of major-general was confirmed on 1 January 1709, and he was promoted lieutenant-general a year later. On 24 April 1709 he received the colonelcy of the Earl of Essex's regiment of dragoons. After the formation of Robert Harley's ministry Temple's position weakened. On 7 December 1711 he voted in the Commons for 'No Peace without Spain', and in April 1712 was omitted from the list of general officers intended for service in that summer's campaign in Flanders. In 1713 he was cashiered and stripped of his regiment. He was defeated at Buckinghamshire in the 1713 election and failed to be returned on petition. He retired to his estate at Stowe, where he initiated the remodelling of the three garden terraces south of the house into a single parterre according to French taste. Charles Bridgeman was employed to design the garden, but Temple himself (or his foreman John Lee) was probably responsible for the innovation of the ha-ha, a trench that marked the boundary of the garden without the rural vista's being interrupted by a wall, and similar to the trenches which Temple employed during warfare.

The accession of George I brought Temple's rehabilitation. On 19 October 1714 he was appointed envoy-extraordinary and plenipotentiary to the imperial court at Vienna and created Baron Cobham. The title enhanced his status by emphasizing his collateral descent from the medieval English nobility, although the new Lord Cobham was not the lineal representative of any previous holder of the title. He seems not to have been expected to undertake a lengthy diplomatic posting and returned during 1715. In September that year he married Anne Halsey (d. 1760), whose father was Edmund Halsey, proprietor of the Anchor Brewery in Southwark. Anne Halsey brought her husband a £20,000 settlement and family connections with London business interests.

Cobham continued to be in favour with the ministries of George I. He was appointed constable of Windsor Castle in 1716, and on 6 July that year he was sworn of the privy council. On 23 May 1718 he was created Viscount and Baron Cobham, with a special remainder in both titles to his younger sisters and the heirs male of their bodies, first his second surviving sister Hester, who had married Richard Grenville of Wooton, neighbouring Stowe; and then his third surviving sister Christian, the wife of Sir Thomas Lyttleton of Hagley in Worcestershire. In 1719 Cobham was appointed leader of the British expedition against Spain, co-ordinated with that of the French forces under the duke of Berwick, which sailed from Spithead on 21

September. Cobham's original plan was to attack Corunna, but rather than face the town's defences he sailed instead into Vigo Bay, taking the town of Vigo and destroying the Spanish military stores there.

Although Robert Walpole's ministry presented few opportunities for military adventures Cobham remained in favour. In 1721 he was appointed colonel of the King's Own Horse and in 1722 comptroller of accounts for the army, and from 1723 he was governor of Jersey for life. The post was not entirely a sinecure as some correspondence survives relating to his duties, although he never visited the island.

Cobham was devoting an increasing amount of energy to developing the gardens and house at Stowe. In 1717 he opened the New Inn on the outskirts of the grounds to accommodate tourists. The special remainder to the peerages created in 1718 accepted that Lady Cobham would have no children and expressed Cobham's desire to found a dynasty based on the amalgamated Temple and Grenville estates in Buckinghamshire. Bridgeman extended the gardens further south, adding an octagonal lake, while Sir John Vanbrugh contributed ornamental buildings. As was intended by Cobham the gardens began to attract visitors: the antiquarian Sir John Evelyn described them in 1725 as 'very noble'. A further phase of expansion in the second half of the 1720s enclosed and remodelled the land to the west of the house.

It may have been Cobham's dynastic ambitions that led him to break with Walpole in 1733. Recognized by Vanbrugh as a good judge of poetry Cobham had been a friend of Alexander Pope since 1725, and so had some connections with the literary opposition to Walpole. His wife's family brought him extensive connections with mercantile interests which felt Walpole's ministry insufficiently active in protecting British trading interests. However, his decision to oppose Walpole's Excise Bill in 1733 remains unexplained. On 14 June, the day after parliament was prorogued, Cobham was dismissed from the colonelcy of the King's Own Horse. From then on reconciliation with Walpole was impossible.

Stowe gradually became a centre for Walpole's opponents. The 1734 elections brought four young relatives of Cobham into the Commons. One of them, his nephew and eventual heir, Richard *Grenville (later Grenville-Temple), was elected for Buckingham under Cobham's direct influence. The others were George *Lyttelton (another nephew) and Thomas Pitt (Lyttelton's brother-in-law) in Okehampton and William Pitt (the brother of Thomas and eventual brother-in-law of Richard Grenville) at Old Sarum. Cobham and his kinsmen gradually evolved a strategy by which 'Cobham's cubs' would claim the role of representatives of the patriot whig tradition, attacking Walpole as the centre of corruption in the body politic. From 1735 Cobham began courting Frederick, prince of Wales, and was rewarded in 1737 when Frederick visited Stowe and began to co-ordinate his political activity with that of Cobham's protégés.

During this period Cobham further expanded the gardens at Stowe. The Elysian Fields to the east of the house were laid out during the 1730s by William Kent, who set aside Bridgeman's formal design principles. There, Cobham added ornamental buildings which iconographically set forth his political creed. Chief among these was the Temple of Ancient Virtue, which included busts of four Greek heroes of liberty to contrast with the headless statue outside its ruined neighbour, the Temple of Modern Virtue, popularly believed to represent Walpole.

Cobham's political strategy involved alliances with whomsoever opposed Walpole. These included disaffected whigs who, like the earl of Chesterfield, disliked long-standing opposition leaders such as John Carteret and Sir William Pulteney, and eventually also tory leaders such as Sir William Wyndham, who was trusted by Lyttelton, William Pitt, and the prince of Wales. Cobham's literary connections extended through Pope to Lord Bolingbroke, whose ideas were current in opposition circles and successfully articulated the idealized form of government that patriots hoped the post-Walpole age would bring. This alliance of interests helped strengthen Cobham's campaign for more assertive action against Spanish incursions on English trade, which was always a theme of his opposition in the 1730s and was redoubled in January 1739 when Cobham opposed Walpole's Spanish Convention, which accepted £95,000 in compensation for British merchants whose goods had been seized by Spanish ships without guaranteeing that the payment would actually be made. Although Cobham's negotiations with the disaffected duke of Argyll failed to create the united patriot opposition he hoped for, enough talents were ranged against Walpole to weaken the credibility of the ministry.

The fall of Walpole brought Cobham some of the rewards he sought. He was restored to his regiment and promoted in rank. For many of his supporters, however, his accepting restoration to the army conflicted with his refusal to allow them into the ministry. Cobham's continued opposition was based on his personal antipathy to Carteret, his opposition to Carteret's support for British subsidy for Hanoverian troops, and reluctance to make common cause against the man and his policy with Walpole's allies—Henry Pelham and Thomas Pelham-Holles, duke of Newcastle. Furthermore, the reconciliation between the prince of Wales and his father, George II, ended the alliance with the reversionary interest. A party that had been able to portray itself as the combination of traditional whiggery and a reinvigorated patriotism was soon unable to show itself as anything other than another family connection whose support could be bought by concessions from the ministry.

The growing respect for the debating and administrative skills of William Pitt shown by Cobham's party (now much larger than in the 1730s) gradually changed the nature of Cobham's patronage. Discussions among the opposition in 1743 and 1744 showed that Pitt, Lyttelton, and others placed more emphasis upon winning office than on campaigning for the reduction of British military involvement in Europe, as Cobham wished. Cobham took part in the negotiations that led to the foundation of the broad-bottom ministry in 1744 and won a new regimental command and a Treasury place for his nephew George *Grenville. However, by 1744 Cobham was increasingly viewed as Pitt's representative rather than his party leader. Henry Pelham's priority was to obtain the skills and following of Pitt, and, as George II would not at this stage employ Pitt, taking Cobham's nominee into the ministry was a means to an end. Cobham's decisions over policy reflected his age and his reluctance to take great political risks. While many still took their lead from him, it was Pitt's manoeuvring in and out of opposition as much as Cobham's decision to support the Pelhams in or out of office that won the Cobham connection their share in the Pelham ministry as reconstituted in 1746. Cobham's politics, since 1733 founded to some extent on nostalgia, were now overtaken by practicalities, and he effectively retired from national concerns.

Cobham devoted his remaining political energies to Buckinghamshire affairs. His palace and gardens at Stowe were further enlarged and beautified under Lancelot 'Capability' Brown, head gardener from 1741 and then clerk of works. Cobham became sponsor of the second and subsequent editions of the guide to Stowe first published by Benton Seeley in 1744, recognizing that it helped maintain the fame of the gardens. Cobham's scheme for the amalgamation of the Temple and Grenville estates was assured by managing both Stowe and his political interest in Buckinghamshire in consultation with and through his nephew Richard Grenville.

Cobham died at Stowe on 13 September 1749 and was buried there five days later. He was succeeded in the peerages created in 1718 by his sister Hester Grenville, and in the baronetcy by a distant cousin, William Temple, who had earlier agreed not to contest the breaking of the entail on Stowe in return for his debts being paid. Cobham's widow, Anne, survived him until 20 March 1760. Through his own military and political career, careful financial management, the development of the Stowe estate, and latterly the adoption of a younger generation of politicians, Cobham successfully founded a dynasty whose influence would be felt in British politics for the rest of the eighteenth century. Although much altered, the landscape gardens of Stowe remain a monument to the aspirations and ideology of Cobham and his protégés in their heyday of the 1730s. MATTHEW KILBURN

Sources L. M. Wiggin, *The faction of cousins: a political account of the Grenvilles, 1733–1763* (New Haven, CT, 1958) · J. V. Beckett, *The rise and fall of the Grenvilles: dukes of Buckingham and Chandos, 1710 to 1921* (1994) · M. Bevington, *Stowe: the garden and the park*, 3rd edn (1996) · GEC, *Peerage* · E. Cruickshanks and S. N. Handley, 'Temple, Sir Richard, fourth baronet', HoP, *Commons, 1690–1715* · G. Clarke, 'Grecian taste and Gothic virtue: Lord Cobham's gardening programme and its iconography', *Apollo*, 97 (1973), 566–71 · L. Colley, *In defiance of oligarchy: the tory party, 1714–60* (1982) · M. Mack, *Alexander Pope: a life* (1985) · *The Marlborough–Godolphin correspondence*, ed. H. L. Snyder, 3 vols. (1975) · P. Lawson, *George Grenville: a political life* (1984) · D. Stroud, *Capability Brown*, new edn (1984) · L. Edye, ed., *The historical records of the royal marines*, 1 (1893) · W. Sterry, ed., *The Eton College register, 1441–1698* (1943)

Archives BL, corresp., Add. MSS 57820, 57807, 57837 · Hunt. L., corresp. and papers | Hunt. L., Stowe MSS

Likenesses G. Kneller, oils, *c.*1710–1713, NPG [*see illus.*] · W. Kent, portrait, *c.*1720–1729, Stowe School, Buckinghamshire; repro. in *Apollo* (June 1973) · P. Scheemakers, marble bust, *c.*1740, V&A; repro. in *Apollo* (June 1973) · J. B. van Loo, portrait, *c.*1740, Hagley Hall, Worcestershire; repro. in *Apollo* (June 1973) · J. B. van Loo, portrait, *c.*1740, Stowe School, Buckinghamshire; repro. in J. M. Robinson, *Temples of delight — Stowe landscape gardens* (1994), 34 · oils, *c.*1740 (after J. B. van Loo), NPG; repro. in *Apollo* (June 1973) · G. Bickham, line engraving, 1751 (after oil painting; after J. B. van Loo, *c.*1740), BM, NPG

Wealth at death estate yielded £4000 p.a.; owned £32,000 of South Sea Company stock; £500 p.a. as governor of Jersey; wife's fortune of £20,000 since 1715; total annual income est. at £7000 p.a. by end of life: Beckett, 18, 19, 28

Temple, Sir Richard, first baronet (1826–1902), administrator in India, was born at Kempsey, near Worcester, on 8 March 1826, the elder son and heir of Richard Temple (1800–1874), a country gentleman and active local magistrate, and his first wife, Louisa Rivett-Carnac, of a famous Anglo-Indian family. From Thomas Arnold's Rugby School, in 1844 he entered the East India Company's college at Haileybury, and passed out top, going to India in January 1847.

Temple gained his formative experience in settlement work in the North-Western Provinces, recording the rights of cultivators. His rise was swift. James Thomason, the lieutenant-governor, whose biographer Temple became, made him joint magistrate of the extensive Allahabad district, responsible for police, revenue, and settlement in a tract with over half a million people, south of the Jumna. He married on 27 December 1849 Charlotte Frances (*d.* 1855), daughter of Benjamin Martindale of the Bengal civil service; they had five children. Temple's wife persuaded him that 'distinction could be won by the pen … as well as … in the field' (Temple, 1.49). A regular contributor to the *Calcutta Review*, he subsequently edited this influential quarterly, in which Indian policy was debated—under cover of a transparent anonymity—for a largely official readership. Later in 1850 he accepted the renewed offer of a post in the recently conquered Punjab from John Lawrence, who enlisted his literary skills in drafting the historic first report of the Punjab commission. Temple went on to draft the next report, and the Punjab code of civil procedure. Lord Dalhousie, the formidable governor-general, thought highly of him. Temple was made secretary in July 1854 to Lawrence as chief commissioner, and had established his reputation when ill health and family considerations drove him home in 1856. He returned to India in 1857.

Temple was destined to be an outstanding representative of the 'Punjab school' of Indian administration which grew up round John Lawrence with Thomason as a seminal influence. He sympathized with the evangelicalism of his mentors; Thomason's 'saintly presence' (Temple, 1.41) deeply impressed him. He shared their preoccupation with the welfare of the peasant as the primary justification of British rule, its best security in the long run, and the foundation of economic and social progress. Yet for all his devotion to Lawrence—'we suited each other to perfection' (ibid., 1.71)—Temple possessed an urbanity and a

Sir Richard Temple, first baronet (1826–1902), by Sir Benjamin Stone, 1897

wide culture lacking in the older man. He adapted the spirit of the Punjab school to the bureaucratic politics of the centre, and to the old regulation-bound presidencies of Bengal and Bombay, where it was rarely possible to carry matters with a high hand. He remained at Lawrence's side until the latter left the Punjab. As commissioner of Lahore in 1859–60, Temple helped to contain the 'white mutiny' among the company's European troops, and dealt skilfully with Muslim and Sikh unrest, which he later described as 'the after-swell … to a tornado' (ibid., 1.108). His grasp of Indian problems, exhibited before James Wilson, financial member of the viceroy's council, took him to Calcutta in 1860 as special assistant to Wilson and his successor. There opened up 'a vista of promotion without end' (ibid., 1.118). The early death of Wilson weakened Temple's position, but viceregal patronage and the friendship of Bartle Frere made him acting chief commissioner of the new Central Provinces in 1862. The character of 'Temple's raj' and the arrival of Lawrence as viceroy secured his confirmation. His administration reports depict the pattern of post-mutiny improvement, from reinforced security of tenure for the cultivator to the formation of an educational department and the beginnings of local self-government.

Lawrence rewarded his protégé with rapid advancement: he was made resident at Hyderabad in April 1867, foreign secretary in the central government in January

1868, and financial member of council from April 1868 to April 1874. His first wife had died in 1855, and on 28 January 1871 he married Mary Augusta (d. 1924), daughter of Charles Robert Lindsay of the Bengal civil service, with whom he had two children, including Charles Lindsay *Temple. Mary Temple received the Imperial Order of the Crown of India in 1878; her charm and intelligence assisted a very ambitious man. As India's finance minister under three viceroys—Lawrence, Lord Mayo, and Lord Northbrook—he is best remembered for his championship of income tax, which he and Lawrence favoured for reasons of equity. The British official and business communities joined with wealthy Indians in attacking a modest impost. Although Northbrook abandoned the tax as not worth the resentment it excited, Temple's career was unaffected. Seconded to oversee famine relief in Bengal in January 1874, he was instrumental in organizing the distribution of food with an efficiency and liberality that resulted in an insignificant mortality. Appointed lieutenant-governor of Bengal in April 1874, he continued the reforming labours of another member of the Punjab school, Sir George Campbell, at a more moderate pace. He enjoyed the confidence of Lord Salisbury, the secretary of state for India; they discussed a wide range of Indian questions in an exceptionally interesting correspondence. Temple was made CSI in 1866, KCSI in the following year, and GCSI and CIE in 1878; he was created a baronet in 1876, an unusual honour for an Indian civil servant. In January 1877 a new viceroy, Lord Lytton, sent Temple to the famine in southern India. Criticized for being over-generous in the Bengal famine, Temple now erred on the side of stringency: the 'Temple ration' and other measures deterred large numbers from seeking relief. While the policy was Lytton's, it was Temple who carried it out; its rigour, however, was modified by pressure from the secretary of state and the Madras government, supported by expert opinion. Nevertheless, an estimated 3.5 million deaths exposed the limitations of British rule.

Temple achieved the distinction of governing Bombay—to which he was appointed in April 1877—as well as Bengal. 'One cannot help seeing', he wrote, '… a new mental force … springing up in Indian politics, which must add to our already numerous anxieties': Western education acted upon important elements of the population, such as the Maratha Brahmans in the Bombay presidency, whose disaffection lay close to the surface (Temple to Salisbury, 28 Jan 1878, Salisbury MSS). He was accessible and conciliatory to educated Indians, and later endorsed Lord Ripon's extension of local self-government: 'some risk must be borne … the Government is so strong that it can afford to be trustful' (R. Temple, *Oriental Experience*, 1883, 125). The British were not so strong, however, that they could ignore Russia's Asiatic expansion and its impact upon Indians, especially if it reached the Middle East. Temple welcomed Disraeli's decision to bring Indian troops to the Mediterranean and threw himself into organizing their dispatch: 'the pulse of Baghdad is felt at Bombay' (Temple to Salisbury, 9 Feb 1878, Salisbury MSS).

A Palmerstonian Liberal by upbringing and conviction,

Temple transferred his allegiance to the tories: he left Bombay prematurely to contest East Worcestershire, unsuccessfully, at the 1880 election. A member of the London school board (1884–94), its vice-chairman (1885–8), and chairman of its finance committee, he represented Evesham (1885–92) and Kingston upon Thames (1892–5) in the Commons. Parliamentary fame eluded him, but his journal-letters (now in the British Library), written to his wife, illuminate the life and work of the late Victorian house. A privy councillorship on 8 February 1896 sweetened the retirement of a loyal back-bencher and tireless committee man. A stream of books and articles, mainly on Indian subjects, had marked his final homecoming: *India in 1880* (1880), *Men and Events of my Time in India* (1882), *Oriental Experience* (1883), *Cosmopolitan Essays* (1886), and short lives of Lawrence (1889) and Thomason (1893). *Life in Parliament* (1893), *The House of Commons* (1899), his autobiography (1896), and the *Progress of India, Japan and China in the Century* (1902) followed. *Letters and Character Sketches from the House of Commons* appeared posthumously (1912). The Royal Society elected him to its fellowship in 1897, and he was awarded the honorary degrees of DCL at Oxford (1880), LLD at Cambridge (1883), and LLD at McGill (1884); the last was conferred when he visited Canada as president of the British Association's economic and statistical section at its Montreal conference. Temple died at his London home, Heath Brow, Hampstead Heath, on 15 March 1902, and was buried at Kempsey, Worcestershire, where he owned about 1000 acres. His eldest son, from his first marriage, Colonel Richard Carnac *Temple, succeeded to the baronetcy.

Physically unprepossessing, Temple was a cartoonist's delight. His enemies had always fastened on the ambition and vanity laid bare in his autobiography. The portrait in John Beames's *Memoirs of a Bengal Civilian* (1961) exemplified this hostility. Temple was nevertheless an extremely capable administrator, inspired by ideals to which he held tenaciously. DAVID STEELE

Sources R. Temple, *The story of my life*, 2 vols. (1896) · G. R. G. Hambly, 'Sir Richard Temple and the government of India, 1868–1880: some trends in Indian administrative policy', PhD diss., U. Cam., 1961 · M. Naidis, 'Sir Richard Temple: literary proconsul', *South Atlantic Quarterly*, 65 (1966), 82–94 · R. B. Smith, *Life of Lord Lawrence*, 2 vols. (1883) · T. R. Metcalf, *The aftermath of revolt: India, 1857–1870* (1965) · E. C. Moulton, *Lord Northbrook's Indian administration, 1872–1876* (1968) · B. M. Bhatia, *Famines in India: a study in some aspects of the economic history of India, 1860–1945* (1963) · Hatfield House, Hertfordshire, Salisbury MSS · *The Times* (18 March 1902)
Archives BL, parliamentary journal, letters, and character sketches, Add. MSS 38916–38928 · BL OIOC, corresp. and papers, MSS Eur. F 86 · Suffolk RO, Ipswich, letters | Balliol Oxf., letters to Sir Louis Mallet · BL, corresp. with H. Bruce, Add. MS 43994 · BL OIOC, Lord Lawrence MSS; Northbrook MSS; Lytton MSS · CUL, corresp. with Lord Mayo · Hatfield House, Hertfordshire, Salisbury MSS · NRA, priv. coll., letters to duke of Argyll · U. Newcastle, letters to Sir Charles Trevelyan
Likenesses T. Brock, marble statue, *c*.1884, Bombay town hall · B. Stone, photograph, 1897, NPG [*see illus.*] · Maull & Fox, photograph, NPG · Spy [L. Ward], caricature, chromolithograph, NPG; repro. in *VF* (15 Jan 1881)
Wealth at death £56,644 18s. 6d.: probate, 6 Aug 1902, CGPLA Eng. & Wales

Temple, Sir Richard Carnac, second baronet (1850–1931), army officer and oriental scholar, was born at Allahabad, India, on 15 October 1850, the elder son of Sir Richard *Temple, first baronet (1826–1902), a civil servant, of The Nash, Kempsey, Worcestershire, and his first wife, Charlotte Frances (*d*. 1855), daughter of Benjamin Martindale. He was educated at Harrow School and at Trinity Hall, Cambridge (of which in 1908 he was elected an honorary fellow), and in 1871 he obtained a commission in the Royal Scots Fusiliers and went with them to India.

Transferred to the Indian army in 1877, Temple was first posted to the 38th Dogras, and with them took part in the Second Anglo-Afghan War (1878–9). He next served in the 1st Gurkha regiment. Having been mentioned in dispatches for his services in the Afghan campaign, he was selected in 1879 for the post of cantonment magistrate in the Punjab, where his lifelong study of Indian history, folklore, and ethnology was initiated: witness his *Legends of the Panjâb* (3 vols., 1883–90) and contributions to *Panjab Notes and Queries*. On 18 March 1880, while stationed with a detachment of his regiment at the penal settlement of Port Blair in the Andaman Islands, he married Agnes Fanny (*d*. 10 Sept 1943), second daughter of Major-General George Archimedes Searle, Madras staff corps. They had one son and two daughters.

The outbreak in 1885 of the Third Anglo-Burmese War brought Temple once more on active service, and led in 1887 to his being placed in charge of King Thibaw's capital on Thibaw's deposition. From Mandalay he was promoted in 1891 to be president of the municipality and port-commissioner of Rangoon, where he raised and commanded the Rangoon naval volunteers and other volunteer forces. The last nine-and-a-half years of his service were as chief commissioner of the Andaman and Nicobar islands.

After succeeding to the baronetcy in 1902 Temple retired in 1904, having reached the rank of lieutenant-colonel in 1897, and entered upon the most fruitful period of his literary activities. His editorial publications included *A Geographical Account of the Countries Round the Bay of Bengal, 1669–1679* by Thomas Bowrey (1905), *The Travels of Peter Mundy, in Europe and Asia, 1608–1667* (5 vols., 1907–28), and *The Diaries of Streynsham Master, 1675–1680* (1911). In 1913 he was president of the anthropological section of the British Association, and in 1925 he was elected a fellow of the British Academy. For his services in India he was appointed CIE in 1894, and, for work connected with the joint committee of the St John Ambulance Association and the British Red Cross Society during the First World War, CB in 1916. He was also a bailiff grand cross of the order of St John of Jerusalem (1927). He contributed to the Pitt Rivers collection and to those of other museums.

In his later years, from 1921 until his death, Temple was greatly inconvenienced by domestic troubles and ill health, which led to an enforced exile, mostly at Territet in Switzerland. There, in touch with many devoted friends, he continued his literary activities, including the editorship of the *Indian Antiquary*, of which he had been sole editor since 1892. He had an exceptional range of oriental knowledge and interests, worked very hard, and enjoyed it. He died at Hôtel Bonward, Territet, Vaud, Switzerland, on 3 March 1931, survived by his wife, and was succeeded as baronet by his son, Richard Durand Temple DSO (1880–1962).

R. E. ENTHOVEN, *rev.* M. G. M. JONES

Sources R. E. E., 'Sir Richard Temple, bt., 1850–1931', *PBA*, 17 (1931) • Burke, *Peerage* (1959) • personal knowledge (1949) • *WWW* • *CGPLA Eng. & Wales* (1931)
Archives BL OIOC, papers, MS Eur. F 98 • Royal Anthropological Institute, London, annotations to an Andamanese grammar • SOAS, papers
Likenesses W. Stoneman, photograph, 1925, NPG
Wealth at death £3478 7s. 6d.: probate, 20 April 1931, *CGPLA Eng. & Wales*

Temple, Sir Thomas, first baronet (*bap.* 1614, *d.* 1674), colonial governor, was born at Stowe, Buckinghamshire, and baptized there on 10 January 1614, the second son of Sir John Temple of Stanton Bury, Buckinghamshire, and his first wife, Dorothy Lee (*d.* 1625). A member of a prestigious but chronically indebted gentry family, he fought as an officer on the parliamentary side during the civil war, although he claimed after the Restoration that he disapproved of the imprisonment of Charles I and had participated in efforts to set the king free.

During the interregnum a family connection with William Fiennes, Viscount Saye and Sele, was crucial in gaining for Temple and two partners a Cromwellian grant of 'the Contrie and Territories called Laccady and that part of the Country Called Nova Scotia', recently captured from the French, by patent dated 9 August 1656 (PRO, CO 1/13, no. 11). Temple was named to govern Nova Scotia and set out in 1657 for Boston, where he would in fact reside for most of the rest of his life, with only occasional visits to Nova Scotia, as in the spring and summer of 1659, and London. The seeming grandeur of his position and pretensions was, in reality, a poor disguise for the fragility of his circumstances, and he faced serious rivals for both the contested territory and the trade of Acadia, or Nova Scotia. The fiction of English control was based on a superficial conquest of Acadian settlements in 1654, and the population remained overwhelmingly American Indian, while the small colonial presence consisted mainly of Acadian French. French military and diplomatic rejoinders, while intermittent, always posed a threat, while rivals also existed in England, especially during the two years immediately following the Restoration. Temple had returned to London by February 1662 to defend his interests, and there secured elevation to the rank of baronet on 7 July 1662 and a new proprietary grant with a royal commission as governor of the notional colony.

Temple then returned to Boston to enjoy for a few more years whatever proceeds he could realize from the Acadian fur trade, offset by an annual payment of £600 by which a powerful English rival had to be bought off. Trading arrangements had depended on English investors, for whom he initially acted as a glorified agent. In New England, however, his commercial naïvety contrasted with the acumen of the Boston merchants, who were glad to use his English connections for their own profit. Advancing him loans, the merchants used their status as his creditors to lay claim to consignments of furs, the principal commodity yielded by the Nova Scotia trade. By about 1667 a succinct contemporary verdict of his position was that 'T. Temple dwells idly at Boston and is fooled by them' (PRO, CO 1/21, no. 174).

Temple also bore the expense of defending Nova Scotia during the Anglo-French war of 1666–7, and suffered a disastrous blow when the crown agreed by the treaty of Breda 1667 to restore the territory to France. He delayed the hand-over effectively enough that he was reportedly described by Charles II, to a French diplomat, as 'un coquin', a rogue (Colbert de Terron to Louis XIV, 24 Jan 1669, Archives du Ministère des Affaires Étrangères, correspondance politique, Angleterre, 94, fols. 28–9), but surrendered his interests in 1670. In Boston he had become a substantial property owner and a prominent member of the Congregational North Church. For the puritan divine Cotton Mather, Temple was 'as fine a Gentleman as ever set foot on the American strand' (Mather, 103). Now, however, he was harassed by creditors and had to sell off his properties. He eventually returned to London, where he died on 27 March 1674, leaving an insolvent estate. He was buried the next day at Ealing, Middlesex. Temple's efforts to rescue his persistently chaotic financial affairs had seemed to be verging on success by 1666, but ultimately fell victim to the characteristic uncertainties of imperial enterprise in the disputed territories of north-eastern North America.

JOHN G. REID

Sources PRO, CO 1, vols. 12–30 • correspondance politique, Angleterre, Archives du Ministère des Affaires Étrangères, Paris, vol. 94 • Massachusetts archives, vol. 2, Massachusetts State Archives • *CSP col.*, vols. 1, 5, 7 • *The memorials of the English and French commissaries concerning the limits of Nova Scotia or Acadia*, 2 vols. (1755) • *Suffolk deeds*, 14 vols. (Boston, 1880–1906) • *Records of the Suffolk county court*, 2 vols. (1933) • C. Mather, '*Parentator*: memoirs of remarkables in the life and the death of the ever-memorable Dr. Increase Mather, who expired, August 23, 1723', *Two Mather biographies: Life and death and Parentator*, ed. J. Scheick (1989) • B. Bailyn, *The New England merchants in the seventeenth century* (1955) • A. H. Buffinton, 'Sir Thomas Temple in Boston: a case of benevolent assimilation', *Publications of the Colonial Society of Massachusetts*, 27 (1932), 308–19 • E. F. Gay, 'The Temples of Stowe and their debts: Sir Thomas Temple and Sir Peter Temple, 1603–1653', *Huntington Library Quarterly*, 2 (1938–9), 399–438 • R. R. Johnson, *John Nelson, merchant adventurer: a life between empires* (1991) • J. G. Reid, *Acadia, Maine, and New Scotland: marginal colonies in the seventeenth century* (1981) • H. Ryder and others, 'Temple, Sir Thomas', *DCB*, vol. 1 • *DNB*
Wealth at death Suffolk, Massachusetts, county court judged that Temple's estate 'will prove insolvant'; Temple expected royal compensation for surrendering interests in Nova Scotia, but none paid: *Records of the Suffolk county court*; Johnson, *John Nelson*, 21–2

Temple, Sir William (1554/5–1627), college head, was a son of Anthony Temple (*d.* 1581) and grandson of Peter Temple of Derset and Butlers Marston, Warwickshire. He was educated at Eton College, and at King's College, Cambridge, where he gained a scholarship. After entering King's in 1573 he was elected a fellow by 1576 and graduated BA in the following year, receiving his MA by 1581.

Temple supplicated for incorporation as MA at Oxford on 11 July 1581.

Temple quickly made a name for himself as a follower of the logical teachings of Petrus Ramus (Pierre de la Ramée), and his adherence to the controversial Ramist 'method' soon led him into a polemical battle with Everard Digby, a fellow of St John's College, Cambridge, who published a defence of Aristotelianism, the *Theoria analytica*, in 1579. Digby followed this treatise by an even more contentious work of 1580, *De duplici methodo*, which attacked the Ramist revision of dialectical method. It proved the first in a pamphlet war and was quickly followed by Temple's *Ad Everardum Digbeium Anglum admonitio de unica P. Rami methodo reiectis ceteris retinendis* (1580), written under the pseudonym of Franciscus Mildapettus of Navarre—in reference to Ramus's connection with the Collège de Navarre. The third pamphlet in 1580 was a rejoinder by Digby: *Everardi Digbei Cantabrigiensis admonitioni Francisci Mildapetti*, entered in the Stationers' register for 3 November. This in turn occasioned Temple's *Pro Mildapetti de unica methodo defensione contra diplodophilum commentatio* (1581), which ended the correspondence between the two.

The Ramist debate, 1580–1584 The core of the debate lay in the Ramist redefinition of dialectic in the sixteenth century. Ramus transferred two parts of Ciceronian rhetoric—invention and disposition—to dialectic. By thus placing the finding and arrangement of arguments in dialectic, rather than rhetoric, Ramus and his followers undermined current trends in Aristotelian logic. Likewise their emphasis on a single method, applicable to all subjects, which was based on division into dichotomies, challenged the Aristotelian double method. Digby spent much of his initial pamphlet on the various types of double method one could find in a repetitious critique of the Ramist single method. Temple was quick in his *Admonitio* to demonstrate how deeply indebted Digby was to the scholastic method. In his dedicatory epistle to his patron, Philip Howard, first earl of Arundel, he decried the decline of dialectic and in typical humanist fashion outlined the history of the decline with copious reference to Aristotelian commentators, rather than Aristotle himself—a favourite humanist argument. In his view, dialectic should no longer be thought of as a subject solely of use in the schools but rather its true application to everyday life beyond the ivory towers was lauded. Since Ramist dialectic, with its rhetorical semblance, was essentially concerned with persuasion, Temple argued that it would be vitally useful in all areas of political and social life.

The acrimony of the dispute was not only engendered by the generational conflict involved (Temple was younger than Digby), but was also exacerbated by the differing religious affiliations of the main protagonists. Temple, as his later career demonstrates, was very much a moderate puritan. Digby, on the other hand, became embroiled in a controversy concerning his religious outlook in the later 1580s, when William Whitaker, master of St John's College, argued for his deprivation from his fellowship on the grounds that he was a suspected Catholic and eventually won, forcing Digby to leave St John's.

Though it seems unlikely that Digby was indeed Catholic his interpretation of theological doctrines of predestination was in direct conflict with those of the puritan wing of the Church of England.

In his *Pro Mildapetti* Temple was not content to attack Digby but produced a thoroughgoing defence of Ramism. An English translation of the title of this work demonstrates its scope: *A dissertation of William Temple of King's College, Cambridge, on behalf of a defense of Mildapet concerning the unipartite method, directed against the lover of the double way, to which is added an explanation of some questions in physics and ethics, along with a letter concerning the dialectic of Ramus, addressed to Johannes Piscator of Strasbourg*. His section on physics, primarily concerned with its relationship with logic, was directed against George Liebler, a professor of natural philosophy at Tübingen, who advocated the Aristotelian method. More extensive attacks were launched on Theodore Zwinger's interpretations of Aristotelian ethics and Johann Piscator's logical investigations, thus extending the debate to include authors who tried to hold the middle ground in the war between Ramus and Aristotle. However, the main target was the German theologian and teacher Piscator, who was Calvinist and based in Strasbourg, but also had links with Herborn and Wittenberg. Temple's debate with Piscator proved lucrative for a number of printers. The Wéchel press in particular played a part in bringing it to a wider audience by publishing in 1582 an edition of Piscator's *Animadversiones* (republished by them in 1583, 1586, 1587, and 1593). In the same year the Wéchels also produced an edition of Temple's *Epistola de dialectica*. The Wéchel press also published other works connected with Temple's interventions in the Ramist debate. He continued his critique of Aristotelian physics in 1584 by writing a preface for a pro-Ramist work by James Martin of Dunkeld, Perthshire, whose book *De prima simplicium et concretorum corporum generatione disputatio*, first published in England at Cambridge in 1584, was republished by the Wéchels in 1589. Again, Temple in fact demonstrated more interest in logic than in physics itself, contenting himself with a denunciation of Aristotelian physics and a strong recommendation of Ramist-style contemporary commentators. Both treatise and preface elicited a response from Andreas Libavius who, like Piscator, attempted to take a moderate stance in the current Aristotelian–Ramist conflict.

Temple continued his debate with Piscator in an important work of 1584: *P. Rami dialecticae libri duo, scholiis G. Tempelli Cantabrigiensis illustrati*, published at Cambridge and later at Frankfurt in 1591. Along with this extensive commentary on the Latin text of Ramus's *Dialecticae libri duo*, the work contained not only Temple's condemnation of Piscator's theories grouped under twenty-nine heads, but also an attack on Porphyry, the author of the *Isagoge*, a well-known introductory text to Aristotelian logic. The themes of the pamphlets were continued in this work which, yet again, advocated the Ramist single method in no uncertain terms. James Mullinger exaggerated the importance of this work, the first English edition of the Latin text for eight years, by claiming that it was 'probably in the possession of every Cambridge scholar'—an assertion not supported by the findings of the university inventory lists (Mullinger, 406). The consequences of Temple's decision to address the dedication to Sir Philip Sidney were to radically transform his life, leading him away from his former educational appointments at King's (where he ceased to be fellow in 1583) and as headmaster of the Lincoln free school (from the early 1580s), to become secretary to a number of extremely influential men in late Elizabethan England.

Public career, 1585–1609 Sidney's contacts with the Wéchels may have made him an even more attractive potential patron to Temple. In November 1585 Temple was appointed Sidney's secretary. He travelled with him to the Low Countries following Sidney's appointment as governor of Flushing. This pleasant working relationship was terminated only on 17 October 1586, when Sidney died in Temple's arms as a result of injuries received at the battle of Zutphen on 22 September. He left his secretary £30 a year in his will. Temple, in his turn, wrote a number of elegies in the Cambridge memorial volume for Sidney. A more fitting tribute to Sidney was Temple's unpublished Ramist commentary on the former's *An Apologie for Poetrie* (1595)—the *Analysis tractationis de poesi contextae a nobilissimo viro Philippo Sidneio equite aurato*. Internal evidence suggests that this work was written prior to Sidney's death, possibly early in Temple's employment. Described by a modern commentator as 'an outstanding example of Tudor practical criticism' (Webster, 11), it demonstrates how texts were read using a Ramist schema.

On Sidney's death Temple found employment with William Davison, principal secretary, and then with Sir Thomas Smith, clerk of the privy council. From 1594 to 1601 he was secretary to Robert Devereux, second earl of Essex, and through his influence was elected as MP for Tamworth, Warwickshire, in 1597. Though previously it has been suggested that he may have travelled to Ireland with Essex in 1599, comments in a later work indicate that he did not accompany the earl. His association with Essex proved a liability following the earl's plot to overthrow Elizabeth I in 1601, and though Temple protested his innocence he failed to convince Sir Robert Cecil, principal secretary. For some years Temple was cast out into a political wilderness and despite his dedication of his 1605 work on the Psalms to Henry, prince of Wales, he remained in obscurity until his elevation as provost of Trinity College, Dublin, in November 1609. Some time before 1600 he married Martha (d. in or after 1627), daughter of Robert Harrison of Derbyshire; they had two sons, including Sir John *Temple (1600–1677), and three daughters.

Provost of Trinity College, Dublin, 1609–1627 Temple's appointment as provost may well have been on the strength of his *Logicall Analysis of Twentye Select Psalmes Performed by W. Temple* (1605), which, with the more extensive Latin version of 1611, *Analysis logica triginta psalmorum*, proved to be the last of his published works. The vice-chancellor of Trinity, Luke Challoner, with James Ussher, professor of theological controversies, may well have felt

that the application of Ramist themes to theology accorded well with what they were attempting to do in the Dublin college. Inherent in the work, and indeed in the 1611 edition, which Temple judiciously dedicated to the first earl of Salisbury (Cecil), was his theological leaning towards a moderate puritan position, which would also have recommended him to the establishment at Trinity. His puritan stance was equally evident in his dealings with George Abbot, archbishop of Canterbury, when the latter remonstrated with Temple in 1613 over the self-evident puritanism at Trinity. Temple's defence of Trinity at this point, coupled with his obvious dislike of the use of surplices within the college, strengthens today's perception of him as a moderate puritan. In memoranda on the subject he asserted repeatedly his conformist nature but it is equally clear that his view of the matter differed markedly from that of Abbot.

As provost Temple proved an effective administrator, at least in his first years in the post, travelling to England in 1616 on college business. He produced the first set of statutes, now unfortunately only partially extant, and responded to the increasing growth of the college by regulating the position of officers. His decision to divide the fellows into two groups—senior fellows, with voting rights, and junior fellows, who had no say in the election of the provost—was to prove controversial, as indeed was his tendency to appoint family members to lucrative posts. By the last year of his provostship there was widespread discontent within the college, particularly with his policy concerning the disposal of college lands in Ulster, and following his death attempts were made to recover college revenues from his widow. Given that as a layman Temple could not avail himself of the preaching positions that usually helped finance the office of provost, he was forced to augment his salary by taking political positions. By 1610 he had been made a master in chancery and in the 1614 parliament he held the seat for Dublin University. He was knighted on 4 May 1622 by the lord deputy, Sir Oliver St John, for his activity in Irish politics. Temple wrote his will on 21 December 1626, and died at Trinity College on 15 January 1627, aged seventy-two; he was buried in the old chapel near the provost's seat. His long reign as provost proved a crucial period in the consolidation of the new colonial college in Ireland and as the author of the first extant set of statutes his decisions proved influential for centuries to come.   ELIZABETHANNE BORAN

Sources S. Akester, 'The life and works of Everard Digby (c.1551–1605)', DPhil diss., U. Oxf., 1980, 198–247 · J. P. Mahaffy, *An epoch in Irish history: Trinity College, Dublin, its foundation and early fortunes, 1591–1660* (1903), 145–91 · J. Freundenthal, 'Beiträge zur Geschichte de englischen Philosophie', *Archiv für Geschichte der Philosophie*, 5 (1892), 1–41 · H. L. Murphy, *A history of Trinity College Dublin from its foundation to 1702* (Dublin, 1951), 51–64 · C. Maxwell, *A history of Trinity College, Dublin, 1591–1892* (Dublin, 1946), 28–9, 44, 49 · J. Lodge, *The peerage of Ireland*, rev. M. Archdall, rev. edn, 5 (1789), 233–5 · L. Jardine, *Francis Bacon: discovery and the art of discourse* (1974), 1–65 · J. W. Binns, *Intellectual culture in Elizabethan and Jacobean England: the Latin writings of the age* (1990), 316–21 · J. Webster, *William Temple's analysis of Sir Philip Sidney's 'Apology for poetry'*, Medieval and Renaissance Texts and Studies, 32 (New York, 1984) · W. Gilbert, *Renaissance concepts of method* (New York, 1960), 202–9 · W. S. Howell, *Logic* and rhetoric in England, 1500–1700 (New York, 1961), 194–206 · J. B. Mullinger, *The University of Cambridge: from the royal injunctions of 1535 to the accession of Charles the first* (1884), 405–9 · H. Kearney, *Scholars and gentlemen: universities and society in pre-industrial Britain, 1500–1700* (1970), 61

Archives TCD, corresp. and papers as provost

Temple, Sir William, baronet (1628–1699), diplomat and author, was born in London on 25 April 1628 at the Blackfriars home of his father, Sir John *Temple (1600–1677), lawyer and master of the rolls in Ireland, and his wife, Mary Hammond (d. 1638); he was baptized at St Anne Blackfriars on 30 April. Temple spent much of his childhood living with his uncle, the Laudian theologian Dr Henry Hammond, at Penshurst, Kent. He subsequently attended Bishop's Stortford School, probably from about 1639 to 1643, and was admitted a fellow-commoner of Emmanuel College, Cambridge, on 31 August 1644. There he became a pupil of the Platonist Ralph Cudworth. Temple left Cambridge, probably in 1647, without taking his degree, but having used his time at university to become a moderately accomplished tennis player.

Dorothy and Ireland In 1648 Temple set out for the continent to complete his education. On the Isle of Wight, during a break in his journey, he met Dorothy *Osborne (1627–1695), daughter of Sir Peter Osborne of Chicksands (1584–1653), and her brother, who were travelling to St Malo to meet their father, then the royalist governor of Guernsey. Temple seems to have immediately fallen in love with the spirited Dorothy, especially when she took the blame for some graffiti scrawled on a window pane by her brother, and they began a lengthy courtship, much of it conducted by correspondence. One half of it—Dorothy's letters to him—survived, their unaffected charm ensuring their abiding popularity after being first published in 1888. In reality the obstacles in the couple's way were considerable. Temple was abroad for most of the following five years: he was in France, where he learned the language, from 1648 until winter 1651, and after a brief return to England he travelled for much of 1652 in Germany, the Netherlands, and Flanders, developing a particular liking for Brussels and forming an ambition to become English resident there if Charles II were to be restored. During this journey Temple began his literary output, producing his earliest essays (heavily influenced by Montaigne) and romances. Moreover, his travels gave him a tolerant, cosmopolitan mentality (and a good grasp of languages) that were both to influence his diplomatic career and to shape his later writings. He was in Ireland briefly in 1654 before returning to London, where he engaged 'in the usual entertainment of young and idle men' (Moore Smith, 6). Both families, too, opposed any marriage between William and Dorothy, each believing that more prestigious matches could be found. Although they probably became engaged in February 1652 the marriage did not take place until Christmas day 1654, and in the interval Dorothy was permanently scarred by an attack of smallpox that briefly threatened her life. They lived initially with Hammond relatives at Reading, where their first son, John, was born on 18 December 1655, but

Sir William Temple, baronet (1628–1699), by Sir Peter Lely, c.1660

moved in May 1656 to Ireland, living alternately in Sir John Temple's house in Dublin and on an estate that William acquired in co. Carlow.

Public life in England Temple's opposition to the Commonwealth led to a deliberate decision not to seek public office until the Restoration. His political career therefore began in earnest in March 1660 when he was elected to the Irish Convention for Carlow; he was returned for the seat once more in the legitimate parliament of May 1661. Later that summer he went to England as part of a parliamentary delegation to the king, not returning to Ireland until late in 1662. Probably in September 1663 Temple took his family back to London to stay, and at some point in the first half of 1665 he purchased a house on the site of the old priory at Sheen, in Surrey, developing a garden praised extravagantly by John Evelyn. By then his household had acquired another permanent member, his sister Martha (1638–1722), who had been widowed after thirteen days of marriage to Sir Thomas Giffard in April 1662; she became the earliest chronicler of her brother's life and character. To her,

> he was rather tall than low, his shape when he was young very exact. His hair a dark brown curl'd naturally, & while that was esteemed a beauty nobody had it in more perfection. His eyes grey but very lively … His humour naturally gay, but a great deal unequal, sometimes by cruel fits of spleen and melancholy, often upon great damps in the weather, but most from the cross & surprising turns in his business, & cruel disappointments he met with so often in … the contributing to the honour and service of his country … He grew lazy, & easier in his humour as he grew older, though it had been observed to be a part of his character

never to seem busy in his greatest employments. (Moore Smith, 27–8)

A lover of music, art, good wine, and conversation, his one excess, according to Lady Giffard, was an over-indulgence in fruit; hence the orangery that Evelyn commented upon, and the occasion when he gorged so many peaches at Brussels that he tactfully had to refuse the opportunity to go to Antwerp by boat. He lived off about £500 a year for much of his life, giving him cause to regret, at least implicitly, his father's longevity: in 1675 he informed the earl of Danby that he was worried about the cost of keeping his family at The Hague, because 'if I had money of my own to make use I should not lie in any pain, but that cannot be expected of [a] man whose father still keeps the estate of the family' (Egerton MS 3325, fol. 33). Although Lady Giffard claimed that his religion was firmly Anglican, his reputation for scepticism was sometimes interpreted as atheism (indeed, Gilbert Burnet regarded him as a Confucian), and this caused him some difficulties with a hostile bishop of Ely when he stood for election at Cambridge in 1679.

Munster and the triple alliance On the outbreak of the Second Anglo-Dutch war in 1665 Temple made overtures to the secretary of state, Arlington, for a diplomatic position, and was supported by the recommendation of the lord lieutenant of Ireland, the duke of Ormond, whose initial coldness towards him had been rapidly overcome. On 22 June he was appointed special ambassador to the prince-bishop of Munster, Christopher-Bernard von Galen, England's sole ally in the war, and undertook three days of successful negotiations (in Latin) with the militaristic prelate which led to the briefly threatening invasion of Gelderland by Munster forces in the autumn. Having canvassed Arlington shamelessly for it Temple was given the position that he had long craved—the residency at Brussels—on 8 October 1665, and was created a baronet on 31 January 1666. In April he went back to Munster in a futile attempt to prevent von Galen withdrawing from the war. Temple's three days with the bishop in the previous year had given him a misplaced confidence in von Galen's sincerity (although he knew all too well that the bishop's promised English subsidies had fallen well into arrears), and despite being liberally wined and dined Temple's anger at being duped and concern that he might be detained culminated in a hair-raising horseback escape to Dusseldorf.

When the French invaded the Spanish Netherlands in May 1667, at the outbreak of the war of devolution, Temple hastily dispatched Dorothy to England but stayed on in Brussels himself. He visited Breda briefly during the peace negotiations of July 1667 that ended the Anglo-Dutch War, but had no influence on the treaty signed there. In September 1667 he visited The Hague, where he met Johan de Witt, grand pensionary of Holland. Almost immediately the two men were greatly impressed with each other. Temple, who had been convinced for some time that England's rightful diplomatic alignment should be an alliance with the Netherlands against French expansionism, shared de Witt's natural concern about the potential

French threat to his country, and strongly advocated a pro-Dutch policy in his reports to Arlington. Temple's stance coincided with a change in attitude at Charles II's court, where alarm about French intentions in Flanders were supplanting the king's innate francophilia.

In these circumstances Temple was appointed special ambassador to the Netherlands, serving there from 17 to 28 December 1667 and (after a brief return to England for discussions) again from 3 January to 13 February 1668. His instructions empowered him to sound de Witt on a military alliance between England and the United Provinces for the defence of the Spanish Netherlands and to broker an agreement between France and Spain. In reality Temple was preaching to the converted, for de Witt had already secured the agreement of the states of Holland to such a scheme, and on 9 January he also had a favourable hearing from the states general. Moreover, the adherence of the Swedes was also virtually guaranteed beforehand. Temple's real successes were the speed with which he conducted his negotiations, his ability to convince de Witt of the trustworthiness of Charles II and Arlington, his winning over Castel Rodrigo, the governor of the Spanish Netherlands, and his insistence on signing the treaty without waiting for London to discuss the potentially problematic commercial clauses. His willingness to speak frankly and effectively to postpone discussion of contentious issues, along with unheard-of speed within the byzantine Dutch system of government, ensured that the treaty was completed within five days. The speed of Temple's actions disconcerted the French and, seemingly, Charles II too, but Temple's policy was followed through, and the ratifications of the treaty were exchanged on 8 February. Temple's reward from the states general was a gold chain and medal valued at 6000 guilders. Temple returned briefly to Brussels before going as English ambassador-extraordinary to the congress of Aix-la-Chapelle, officially from 2 April to 2 July 1668, although he did not arrive at Aix until 18 April.

Ambassador to the Netherlands On 12 June 1668 Temple arrived in London, and shortly afterwards was appointed the first resident ambassador in the Netherlands since 1627, landing at Rotterdam on 16 August to take up his post, which carried a salary of £7 a day. By now his relationship with de Witt was a strong personal friendship as well as a diplomatic duty, but Temple also spent an increasing amount of time with William of Orange. He had no inkling of the changes of attitude in England, where almost from the very first Charles II had been seeking to rebuild relations with the French, a process that culminated in the secret treaty of Dover (1670).

Temple's time at The Hague was taken up primarily by a succession of negotiations with the Dutch over difficult colonial and commercial issues, with the Spanish over their payment of subsidies to Swedish troops (as set out in the triple alliance), and with the Treasury commission in London over attempts to increase his allowance; Dorothy had to make a trip in person to secure the latter, from £7 to £10 a day. Arlington's letter to him of 1 September 1670, recalling him to London, came as a complete shock to

Temple, but was a clear sign of the change of policy that had been implemented at Dover. He landed at Great Yarmouth on 16 September, and on his return to London he found the attitude towards him of the king and the ministers, even Arlington, noticeably cold. He retained the title of ambassador in name only; given the public perception of him as the leading advocate of the triple alliance his dismissal would have been a clear indication of the abandonment of that policy. In the event it was his wife's return home, of all things, that precipitated the public breach with the Netherlands and the destruction of the alliance. In August 1671, in an incident deliberately engineered by Charles and the French, the yacht *Merlin* that had been sent to bring Dorothy and her family home demanded that an entire Dutch fleet should dip its topsails to salute it. When Charles II praised her courage (she had insisted that the *Merlin*'s captain should attempt to enforce the salute) Temple philosophically replied that '[although] I had made the alliance with Holland … my wife was like to have the honour of making the war' (*Works*, 3.502–3).

First retirement and return to diplomacy From 1670 to 1674 Temple lived in retirement at Sheen, spending much time and effort in attempting to extract back pay and expenses from the Treasury. He also returned to his writing. Probably his most enduring and famous work, *Observations upon the United Provinces of the Netherlands*, was written in autumn 1672 and published in London in the following year. Despite its unapologetic advocacy of his discarded alliance policy the work is a lively, detailed survey of the nature of the country, particularly strong on the workings of its complex system of government, and also reveals many of Temple's strengths and weaknesses as a writer. Lively and perceptive observations, many drawn from his own recollections, give the piece its attractiveness: his tendencies to digress, and to emphasize his own correctness and expertise, still grate. At much the same time Temple wrote his *Essay upon the Original and Nature of Government*, which ignored the fashionable theory of social compact, argued that society was founded on the family, that climate accounted for differences between nations, and that laws were merely customs sanctioned by lengthy usage. *An Essay upon the Advancement of Trade in Ireland* was published in 1673, having been written some years earlier for the ministry, and in October 1673 he made another attempt to revive the triple alliance policy in the paper *Upon the Conjuncture of Affairs in October 1673*.

When the war policy, in turn, was abandoned—along with the ministers who had supported it, like his erstwhile patron, Arlington—Temple was the obvious choice to attempt to rebuild Charles II's relations with the Dutch. In February 1674 Temple returned to the Netherlands as ambassador to finalize the peace treaty ending the Third Anglo-Dutch War. Shortly afterwards he turned down the position of ambassador-extraordinary to Spain, and on 27 May was appointed ambassador-extraordinary to The Hague, where he arrived in July. On 13 December 1675 he was additionally appointed one of the English plenipotentiaries to the congress to Nijmegen, and was in attendance

there between June 1678 to March 1679. Temple's continued prominence in this period can be attributed largely to his successful transition from the patronage of the fallen Arlington to that of the new chief minister, the earl of Danby, whose attempt to build a foreign policy more acceptable to a sensitive and recalcitrant parliament could only benefit from the support of the leading English champion of Dutch interests. The transition was made easier by the fact that Danby, the former Thomas Osborne, was a friend from his youth (despite having been a relation and former suitor of Dorothy).

Temple was partly responsible for arranging the marriage between William of Orange and Mary, daughter of James, duke of York. He had always been impressed by William, seeking ways in which he could help restore him to his family's offices since as early as 1666, and in 1674 he claimed that William 'by his personal qualities cannot fail if he lives of making a great figure in the world' (BL, Add. MS 70948, fol. 84). A close friendship developed between the two men, supplanting that between Temple and the murdered de Witt, and Sir William's dispatches from 1674 to 1679 are full of praise for the prince. The relationship proved its worth as the idea of the marriage developed, and three years of delicate negotiation (Dorothy sometimes acting as go-between) finally culminated in the ceremony on 4 November 1677. Ten days later Temple's father died, and he succeeded to his office of master of the rolls in Ireland (having held the reversion since 1664), thereby almost trebling his annual income.

In July 1678 Temple was hastily sent to The Hague once more. Despite the fact that the Nijmegen treaties were about to be signed the French had suddenly announced that they did not intend to return any of the towns they had conquered in the Low Countries. Temple and the states general hastily contrived a new treaty, signed on 25 July, by which the Dutch and English pledged joint action unless the French withdrew. The French eventually complied, and Temple went on to Nijmegen, where the final treaty was concluded—a treaty that he called 'the hardest pinch of business that ever befell me in my life' (*Ormonde MSS*, new ser., 4.174), and one that he disapproved of, believing that it was too generous to the French.

During this period Temple twice refused the position of secretary of state. It was first offered in 1677 when it was thought that Henry Coventry would resign, then for a second time in January 1679. On the latter occasion Temple pleaded ill health and turned it down, saying that he was 'so honest a man as never to make so ill a bargain for so good a master, which would be like selling him very dear, a horse that I knew to be old and resty' (*Buckinghamshire MSS*, 400). In reality Temple's unwillingness to work alongside the other secretary, Sir Joseph Williamson, seems to have been at least equally responsible. Early in 1679 he proposed restructuring the privy council to Charles II and became a member of the new body (which contained equal numbers of court and country members) on 21 April. In reality this proved a sop to public opinion: Charles effectively ignored the new council, to Temple's disappointment. Temple was elected MP for Cambridge

University in October 1679, a parliamentary seat being seen as essential if he was to be a candidate for secretary of state. Personal tragedy also struck the Temples in 1679, with the death of their daughter Diana of smallpox at the age of fourteen: 'an incurable wound', Temple called it, 'which I will hope I may live sometimes to forget but never to remember without the most sensible trouble and grief' (*Ormonde MSS*, new ser., 5.376).

In summer 1680 it was proposed that Sir William should go to Spain as ambassador-extraordinary. Despite initial reluctance he agreed to go, partly because he saw it as a way of escaping the political turmoil in England (or so he told Ormond). In the meantime he was a regular speaker for the court in the second Exclusion Parliament, but his inexperience and irregular attendance ensured that he was generally regarded as an ineffectual parliamentarian. The first part of his *Miscellanea* was published in the same year. The dramatic political realignments of January 1681, the culmination of the rise to pre-eminence of Temple's political opponent (but personal friend) Halifax, led to his removal from the privy council (on the 24th), and he also lost the Spanish embassy. His only subsequent political appointment came on 14 March 1683, when he became a commissioner for the remedy of defective titles in Ireland. Although James II was polite enough to Temple after his accession his long-standing suspicion of Sir William's close friendship with William of Orange militated against any return to office during James's reign.

Second retirement   In 1680 Temple bought an estate near Farnham, Surrey, for £2000, and on its completion in 1686 he renamed it Moor Park (after the countess of Bedford's seat in Hertfordshire, whose gardens he had long admired) and made Sheen over to his eldest son, John. Temple played no part in the events of 1688, despite being known to be closer to William of Orange than almost anyone in England, and again turned down an offer of a secretaryship of state. His son John was a more enthusiastic advocate of the change of regime, but in reality, it proved to be his nemesis: in April 1689 John filled his pockets with stones and drowned himself at London Bridge within a week of being appointed secretary-at-war by William III. According to a much later account from a family member, John had been ill for some time with 'a tetter on his hand which stuck in and is thought to have disordered his senses' (*Egmont Diary*, 3.311–12). He believed he was not up to the job of secretary, but William had insisted on it, and the final straw came when Major-General Hamilton, whom he had recommended as an intermediary to the Jacobite lord lieutenant of Ireland, Tyrconnell, promptly defected. Therefore it was into a gloom-ridden Temple household, later in 1689, that the young Jonathan Swift arrived as a new secretary. Relations between Temple and Swift were initially strained, but gradually improved, and Temple helped his young protégé with the revision of the 'Tale of a Tub'. Partly thanks to Swift's support several of Temple's important works were published in the 1690s, notably the second parts of his *Miscellanea* (1690; including his essay 'Ancient and modern learning') and *Memoirs of what Past in Christendom, from … 1672 to … 1679* (1691), as well as his *Introduction to the History of England* (1695), which was riddled with factual inaccuracies and interpretative distortions. He also returned to poetry, producing translations and imitations of Virgil and Horace.

Although William III occasionally visited Moor Park to consult him informally (as in 1692–3 over the Triennial Bill), Temple effectively remained withdrawn from public affairs in the 1690s. As Lady Giffard noted, his health had deteriorated since the 1670s, with frequent attacks of gout (he had been troubled by fevers and eye problems even earlier than this, during his residency at The Hague) but he was determined not to consult doctors, hoping 'to die without them and trusted to the advice but chiefly to the care of his friends' (Moore Smith, 29–30). He was seriously ill in 1693, and Dorothy's death on 7 February 1695 also seems to have affected him deeply. He resigned his post as master of the rolls in Ireland on 29 May 1696, although he had always discharged this office through a deputy. He died at Moor Park at 1 a.m. on 27 January 1699, according to Swift, and was buried on 1 February alongside Dorothy and Diana at Westminster Abbey, although his heart was buried beneath a sundial at Moor Park. By his will, dated 8 March 1695, he left some of his Irish lands to Esther Johnson, Lady Giffard's servant and Swift's Stella, and by a codicil dated 2 April 1697 he left £100 to Swift himself. Temple was survived by his two granddaughters, Elizabeth and Dorothy, the children of John, the suicide, and his French widow Marie Duplessis; the baronetcy became extinct with his death.

Reputation   As both a statesman and a writer Temple's posthumous reputation enjoyed more than a century of almost unchallenged acclaim followed by a dramatic decline from which it has never really recovered. Contemporaries had been divided in their assessment: Burnet was damning, calling him 'a vain man, much blown up in his conceit, which he showed too indecently on all occasions … he was a corrupter of all that came near him, and he delivered himself up wholly to study ease and pleasure' (*Burnet's History*, 2.70). Temple's subsequent literary standing owed much to Swift, who published many of his letters, memoirs, and miscellanea in 1700–09 and immortalized Temple as the hero of *The Battle of the Books*. He gained further plaudits from Dr Johnson, the combined efforts of two such literary giants seeming to immortalize Temple as one of the great pioneers of English prose style, despite occasional negative voices (notably that of Hume). T. P. Courtenay's equally positive *Memoirs of the Life, Works and Correspondence of Sir William Temple, Bart.* (1836) prompted Macaulay's devastating critique which condemned Temple as a second-rate thinker, writer, and statesman— hence his famously acid remark that Temple was almost universally famous without anybody knowing very much about him. An edition of his early essays and romances by G. C. Moore Smith (1933) and a magisterial but rather dull biography by H. E. Woodbridge (1940) only partly rehabilitated Temple's literary reputation, and as late as 1970 R. C. Steensma could claim that Temple was still generally seen as 'a bumbling amateur scholar and an unfortunate diplomat' (Steensma, 137). The enduring popularity of Dorothy's letters to him ensured that to many general readers of the twentieth century Temple was known only as a distant and somewhat lightweight object of affection, to whom Dorothy had been initially attracted by his innate gullibility. The likes of Steensma and Samuel Holt Monk (1963) at least partly restored Temple to a position as an important, but not particularly seminal, figure in the tradition of the English essay, his particular contribution being the development of the apposite use of the paragraph. Monk and Cynthia Marburg (1932) also set Temple in the context of the seventeenth century *libertin* tradition, stressing the impact of his early visits to France, the influence of the likes of Montaigne and the Epicureans, and the powerful streak of scepticism that these influences imparted to his writings and his public life.

Temple's reputation as a statesman undoubtedly benefited from hindsight's casting him as a forward thinking advocate of alliance with the Dutch and opposition to France—the policy that England finally adopted twenty years after his failed triple alliance. The centrality of francophobia to foreign policy making until Waterloo and beyond ensured that Macaulay, for example, could praise Temple's policy, regardless of his limited opinion of him as both a writer and a statesman. Sir Keith Feiling was less critical and less overtly whiggish in his treatment; even so he eulogized Temple as 'candid and courageous, human and humane', whose boldness and 'sanguine pressure' had brought about the triple alliance (Feiling, 153, 254). Then, in 1982 A. C. Elias damagingly suggested that Temple had deliberately altered the text of many of his manuscript letters before their eventual publication by Swift, his suggested purpose being to downplay Arlington's part in creating the triple alliance and to exaggerate his own. Elias also suggested that far from eulogizing Temple, Swift secretly despised him. Elias presented a picture of Temple as a thoroughly second-rate diplomat and writer that was, in essence, not too far removed from Macaulay's verdict. Shortly afterwards, K. H. D. Haley at least partly redressed the balance, stressing Temple's position as a diplomat rather than a statesman, and the relatively limited room for manoeuvre that the former position entailed: 'he had to remain fundamentally an agent, not a deviser of policy' (Haley, 314), but even in such an essentially reactive position his achievements were considerable. As Haley rightly pointed out, possessing the confidence of de Witt and William of Orange simultaneously was no mean feat, even if it meant that Temple was inevitably (and ultimately fatally) seen by some of his colleagues, and above all by Charles II, as a man who was too friendly to the Dutch, whoever happened to control their state. Haley also challenged Elias's attack on Temple's 'modification' of his letters, noting that a diplomat writing many dispatches under heavy pressure of time would naturally wish to tidy them up before they appeared in print, and that many of the supposedly suspicious omissions or insertions detected by Elias were entirely explicable when set in context.

Most critics of the nineteenth and twentieth centuries were irritated by Temple's overt vanity both as statesman and writer. In his letters and works he constantly presented himself as an honest plain speaker, albeit one who could be excessively fawning towards those whom he wished to impress—Arlington had to reprimand him for the extravagance of his compliments, which extended on hearing of his appointment to Brussels to likening the secretary of state to 'some saint, to whom they [the Flemish] profess a more particular devotion' (PRO, SP 77/33, fol. 293). His attempts at self-deprecation, as in the dedication of the second part of his *Miscellanea*—*has qualescunque nugas* ('these trifles, such as they are')—have tended to leave exactly the opposite impression. He can appear somewhat authoritarian, as in his statement, reported by his sister, 'that no body should make love after forty, nor be in business after fifty' (Moore Smith, 29)—his own retirement from diplomacy at almost exactly that age therefore seemingly part of some predetermined master plan. Conversely, his love of leisure, and determination not to let his work dominate his life, hardly fits well with the obsessive work ethic prevalent in government service since such terms as 'professionalization' and 'meritocracy' became fashionable. He could certainly be wildly over-optimistic and over-reliant on first impressions, as in his hopelessly mistaken opinion of bishop von Galen, was often less well informed than he would have liked or than he claimed to be (as in the case of the abandonment of the triple alliance), and was too inclined to the dramatic gesture (his sudden bursts of action, madcap journeys, and dramatic last-minute treaties perhaps compensating for the seeming indolence that Lady Giffard noted). On the other hand, his attitude to public life was characterized as much by what he was not as by what he was. Above all he was not corrupt, either by contemporary or later standards—although typically for Temple he was loud and self-righteous in proclaiming the fact. In both his political and literary careers, he showed himself a keen and perceptive student of human nature, and this, perhaps, shaped both his strengths and his weaknesses: as a statesman he was a capable and reliable subordinate for the likes of Arlington and Danby, rather than an independent power broker; as a writer he was readable, intelligent, and stylish, rather than deeply profound. As a participant in one of the greatest love stories of the seventeenth century, however, Temple is always likely to retain a kind of immortality.

J. D. DAVIES

Sources K. H. D. Haley, *An English diplomat in the Low Countries: Sir William Temple and John de Witt, 1665–72* (1986) • H. E. Woodbridge, *Sir William Temple: the man and his work* (New York, 1940) • D. Osborne, *Letters to Sir William Temple*, ed. K. Parker (1987) • *The early essays and romances of Sir William Temple … with The life and character of Sir William Temple, by his sister Lady Giffard*, ed. G. C. Moore Smith (1930) • R. C. Steensma, *Sir William Temple* (New York, 1970) • *The works of William Temple*, 4 vols. (1754) • PRO, state papers foreign, esp. SP 77 (Flanders) and 84 (Holland) • H. H. Rowen, *John de Witt* (Princeton, 1978) • W. Temple, *Observations upon the United Provinces of the Netherlands*, ed. G. N. Clark (1932) • R. Faber, *Sir William Temple, the brave courtier* (1983) • *Manuscripts of the earl of Egmont: diary of Viscount Percival, afterwards first earl of Egmont*, 3 vols., HMC, 63 (1920–

23), vol. 3, pp. 311–12 · E. R. Edwards and G. Jagger, 'Temple, Sir William', HoP, *Commons, 1660–90*, 3.544–5 · N. Luttrell, *A brief historical relation of state affairs from September 1678 to April 1714*, 6 vols. (1857) · letters to Arlington, BL, Add. MS 35852 · correspondence with Danby, BL, Egerton MS 3325 · *Burnet's History of my own time*, ed. O. Airy, new edn, 2 vols. (1897–1900) · letters to Danby, BL, Add. MS 70948 · correspondence, 1665–80, BL, Add. MSS 9796–9804 · will, PRO, PROB 11/450, fols. 46–7 · A. C. Elias, *Swift at Moor Park* (Philadelphia, 1982) · Evelyn, *Diary*, 4.163, 576 · *Calendar of the manuscripts of the marquess of Ormonde*, new ser., 8 vols., HMC, 36 (1902–20), vols. 4–5 · *The manuscripts of the earl of Buckinghamshire, the earl of Lindsey … and James Round*, HMC, 38 (1895) · T. P. Courtenay, *Memoirs of the life, works and correspondence of Sir William Temple*, 2 vols. (1836) · K. Feiling, *British foreign policy, 1660–72* (1930) · J. Miller, *Charles II* (1991) · R. Hutton, *Charles the Second: king of England, Scotland and Ireland* (1989) · S. Pincus, *Protestantism and patriotism: ideologies and the making of English foreign policy, 1650–68* (1996) · G. M. Bell, *A handlist of British diplomatic representatives, 1509–1688*, Royal Historical Society Guides and Handbooks, 16 (1990) · instructions, etc, BL, Add. MS 56244 · letters to the earl of Essex, BL, Stowe MSS, esp. MSS 203–11 · S. H. Monk, ed., *Five miscellaneous essays by Sir William Temple* (1963) · C. Marburg, *Sir William Temple: a seventeenth century 'Libertin'* (1932) · GEC, *Baronetage*, 4.25–6 · Venn, *Alum. Cant.*, 1/4.213 · J. L. Chester, ed., *The marriage, baptismal, and burial registers of the collegiate church or abbey of St Peter, Westminster*, Harleian Society, 10 (1876) **Archives** BL, corresp. and MSS, Harley MSS · BL, corresp. and papers, Add. MSS 9796–9801, 9803–04 · PRO, SP 77, 84 · Staffs. RO · Trinity Cam. · U. Southampton L., letter-books, MS 62 · Yale U., Beinecke L., corresp. and papers | BL, letters to Lord Arlington, Add. MS 35852 · BL, corresp. with Lord Danby, Egerton MS 3325 · BL, letters to Lord Essex, Stowe MSS 200–211, *passim* · BL, letters to Sir William Trumbull · Bodl. Oxf., corresp. with Sir John Williamson **Likenesses** P. Lely, portrait, *c.*1660, Broadlands [*see illus.*] · P. Lely, oils, priv. coll.; copy, NPG · G. Netscher, oils, NPG · oils (after P. Lely), NPG **Wealth at death** bequeathed leases of lands in Yorkshire and Armagh to sister, and of those in Clownes to nephew John; Moor Park estate divided into four equal parts, one to sister, one to each granddaughter, and the fourth part divided 3:2 between brothers Sir John Temple and Henry Temple; granddaughter Elizabeth received inlaid cabinet, gold watch, and all gold and silver left in chest; codicil bequeathed £100 to Jonathan Swift: will, PRO, PROB 11/540, fols. 46–7

Temple, William (*bap.* 1705, *d.* 1773), clothier and writer on economics, was born at Trowbridge, Wiltshire, where he was baptized on 3 August 1705, the son of William Temple (*d.* 1736), a clothier, and his wife, Elizabeth. He was brought up a General Baptist as a member of the Conigre church, which during his early life was moving into Arianism, and he was almost certainly educated at the dissenting academy associated with the church. He was in business as a clothier on his own account by 1724 and left off trade about 1756.

Temple's first published work was a eulogistic obituary of his father, contributed to the *Gloucester Journal* in 1736. In 1738 trade depression led to weavers' riots in west Wiltshire. Their complaints, particularly of lowered rates for weaving and of truck payments, were vividly and sympathetically presented by Country Commonsense (Thomas Andrews of Seend) in an 'Essay on riots' in the *Gloucester Journal*. Temple's reply also appeared in the *Journal* and was reprinted as a pamphlet, *The Case as it now Stands between the Clothiers, Weavers and other Manufacturers*, under the pseudonym Philalethes. In this work Temple adopted a tone which was a sorry contrast to the measured statement of the 'Essay on riots'. He bitterly attacked the justices who supported prosecutions for truck payments, he complained of the idleness and drunkenness of the workpeople, and he argued that high prices and low wages were necessary to make them industrious. Weavers were the object of his particular scorn, 'the most feeble, weak, and impotent of all the manufacturers'; putting a child apprentice to a weaver meant that he could obtain 'a comfortable subsistence with scarce any human abilities' (W. Temple, *The Case as it now Stands*, 1739, 12, 13).

It was at the same period that Temple entered into controversy with John Smith, the author of *Chronicon rusticum-commerciale, or, Memoirs of Wool* (1747). In 1739 he replied to Smith's anonymous pamphlet *The Grazier's Complaint*, which complained of the low price of English wool, with a characteristic piece of detailed argument to show the greater advantage to the country gained by working up the wool into cloth; this appeared in the *Sherborne Mercury* under the pseudonym Weaver on 6 February 1739. Smith's *Chronicon rusticum-commerciale* provoked a *Refutation* by Temple of one of its principal arguments, that English wool was underpriced compared with Spanish. This pamphlet appeared in 1750, as did a rejoinder by Smith 'in answer to Mr. Temple's (pretended) Refutation'. Early in 1751 Temple had the last word in an *Epistle* to Smith, subtitled *An Expostulatory Address to him upon his Forgery and Chicanery*. This pamphlet announced proposals for printing *A Discourse upon Wools* by Temple, but it is not known to have been published.

In 1758 Temple's controversial skills were deployed against William Bell, who had received a Cambridge prize for a *Dissertation on Populousness* which advocated the renunciation of commerce in favour of a purely agricultural society. Temple's *Vindication of Commerce and the Arts* appeared under the pseudonym I. B., MD.

In his later years Temple was a supporter of John Wilkes; he held a fête in his garden to celebrate Wilkes's release from prison in 1770, sent £20 towards his expenses in 1772, and in his will left him £500 'for his strenuous exertions in the cause of liberty'. He died at Trowbridge on 16 May 1773 of a paralytic stroke and was buried at St James's Church, Trowbridge, on 20 May.

Temple left no living children, and his wife, Grace, had died in 1769. Also in his will he left £2000 to the City of London to found a professorship at Gresham College; the holder was to expound the views expressed in the *Vindication*, which was summarized under seven headings in the will, beginning: '1. That all mankind are naturally inclined to indolence'. The will provided that Temple's papers should be edited and a digest printed and sold at a moderate price, one copy being given gratis to each corporation in England. His library of 1500 volumes was left to Gresham College. In fact, for reasons unknown, none of the provisions of the will was acted upon.   K. H. ROGERS

Sources J. de L. Mann, 'Clothiers and weavers in Wiltshire during the eighteenth century', *Studies in the industrial revolution*, ed. L. S.

Presnell (1960), 66–96 · *Gloucester Journal* (29 June 1736) · [T. Andrews], 'Essay on riots', *Gloucester Journal* (19 Dec 1738) · I. B. [W. Temple], *A vindication of commerce and the arts* (1758) · *Salisbury Journal* (30 April 1770) · *Bath Chronick* (27 Feb 1772) · *Bath Chronick* (20 May 1773) · parish registers, Wilts. & Swindon RO, WSRO 608 · rate book, Wilts. & Swindon RO, WSRO 714/24 · *VCH Wiltshire*, 3.122–3
Archives Wilts. & Swindon RO, letter · Wilts. & Swindon RO, pattern and account book
Wealth at death £3345 legacies; plus annuities of £40; freehold and copyhold property in Trowbridge: will

Temple, William (*bap.* 1798, *d.* 1837). *See under* Bewick, Thomas, apprentices (*act.* 1777–1828).

Temple, William (1881–1944), archbishop of Canterbury, was born on 15 October 1881 at the bishop's palace, Exeter, the younger son of Frederick *Temple (1821–1902), archbishop of Canterbury, and his wife, Beatrice Blanche (1845–1915), daughter of William Lascelles, son of the second earl of Harewood.

Family and schooling His father was almost sixty when William was born; he had been a fellow of Balliol College, Oxford, and headmaster of Rugby School before becoming bishop of Exeter and later bishop of London and archbishop of Canterbury. His mother was closely related to many members of the upper aristocracy. Academically, ecclesiastically, and socially Temple was thus born into the élite of the late Victorian establishment; he remained genially loyal to it throughout life, yet without any sense of its confining his own enthusiasms or behaviour. He was loyal above all to the legacy of his father. Educated at Rugby, where his godfather John Percival was headmaster, and then at Balliol, where Edward Caird was master, he developed loyalties which embraced both: he later wrote Percival's biography, while Caird's neo-Hegelian idealism provided the philosophical inspiration for many of his academic writings. At both Rugby and Balliol, and then throughout life, R. H. Tawney was a close friend. 'I think *anything* is possible to him' (Iremonger, 36), his final school report, in 1900, concluded. His intellectual grasp already embraced the classics, philosophy, music, and poetry, but it excelled in the self-confidence of his own interpretation more than in academic precision, though his judgement was never careless. He was fat and cheerful, with an uproarious laugh that went on and on, a photographic memory, and already troublesome attacks of gout. He changed very little thereafter.

Oxford, Repton, and the First World War At Oxford, Temple obtained firsts in both halves of the classics course and was president of the Oxford Union, but more revealing than these conventional achievements was the marvellous essay on Robert Browning that he read to a Balliol society, more gripping than almost anything he wrote later (except the *Readings in St John's Gospel*). 'To Browning', he insists, 'the climax of history, the crown of philosophy, and the consummation of poetry is unquestionably the Incarnation' (*Religious Experience*, 51), and he judged the depiction of John in 'A Death in the Desert' to be Browning's greatest writing. For Temple himself that centrality of the incarnation, true for him already as an undergraduate, remained true for every period of his life. He went on

William Temple (1881–1944), by Philip A. de Laszlo, 1934

to be for six years a fellow of Queen's College, Oxford, lecturing ostensibly on Plato's *Republic* but in reality on his own mix of Greek and Christian themes. The intense personal reading of his ten Oxford years grounded the work of the rest of his life, but in this period too his political and ecumenical interests developed. He became very closely associated with the Student Christian Movement (SCM), declared himself a socialist, was elected president of the Workers' Educational Association, and in 1908 was ordained by the archbishop of Canterbury, Randall Davidson. He had aspirations to be a priest (and a bishop!) since childhood, and the career of a philosophy don had limited attractions. Two years earlier the bishop of Oxford had declined to ordain him on account of Temple's admitted doubts about the historicity of the virgin birth and physical resurrection, doubts which by 1908 Davidson believed had been largely overcome.

In 1910 Temple became headmaster of Repton School, Derbyshire, in 1914 rector of St James's, Piccadilly, London, and in 1919 a canon of Westminster. In this decade he wrote ten books, mostly collections of sermons, edited the newspaper *Challenge* (1915–18), and was a secretary of the National Mission of Repentance and Hope (1916) as well as the youngest member of the archbishops' commission on church and state. He became chairman and joint leader with H. R. (Dick) Sheppard of the Life and Liberty movement—which aimed to gain a wider freedom for the church from the state—as well as a card-carrying member of the Labour Party. Life and Liberty shows Temple at his most oratorical moment. 'We demand liberty for the

Church of England' (Hastings, *History of English Christianity*, 63), he declared at a Queen's Hall meeting in July 1917. Helpful as the delegation of various administrative powers by parliament to a new church assembly in the Enabling Act of 1919 undoubtedly was, it was hardly the 'freedom of the Church' for which Temple had campaigned so rhetorically. Moreover, it is likely that Davidson would have secured much the same result if no Life and Liberty movement had ever existed.

These multiple activities suggest some uncertainty on Temple's part as to what he wanted to do, coupled with frenetic activity, much stimulated by the war and even, perhaps, by his lack of direct involvement in it. Headmastering quickly seemed a mistake, despite the fine sermons he gave at Repton and the impact on the upper sixth of listening to his reading Browning in his study. His marriage on 24 June 1916 to Frances Gertrude Acland Anson (1890–1984) helped to stabilize his life. His mother had lived with him in Oxford, Repton, and London, until her death on Good Friday 1915. Frances Anson was the daughter of Frederick Anson and granddaughter of Sir Thomas Acland, a friend of Temple's father, and his mother had hoped that he would marry her. Frances took over Temple's mother's role in his life with remarkable fidelity. They had no children.

It is symbolic that Temple stayed up late on the night before his wedding putting the final touches to his first major book, *Mens creatrix* (1917). His life was always dominated by the immediate requirements of work. It seems unlikely that any of Temple's wartime activities had as much effect as admirers claimed or hoped for, but his own position as someone in the public eye, possessing at once the confidence of the church's leadership and that of reformist circles, was much enhanced. It was crucial for Temple's future that Randall Davidson liked and admired the son of his predecessor as archbishop, even if at times he found Temple's impetuosities hard to understand. It was clearly important that so able and influential a man be found an adequate job which really suited. Late in 1920, when Temple was still only thirty-nine, Lloyd George offered him the diocese of Manchester, where he remained until translation to the archbishopric of York in 1929.

Bishop of Manchester Manchester suited Temple, though he stood in every way in contrast with his formidable predecessor, Bishop E. A. Knox. Knox had been an unmitigated protestant, tory, and autocrat. Temple was none of these things, and his time in the diocese was distinguished by its lightness of touch in which the intellectual life, breadth of churchmanship, and social concern were all allowed to flourish. Knox had refused to divide an overlarge diocese; Temple saw that division was essential and founded the separate diocese of Blackburn (1926). While showing himself a thoroughly pastoral bishop, for whom parish visiting had a high priority, he was nevertheless drawn at Manchester into various forms of wider leadership. He wrote his second major book, *Christus veritas* (1924), together with half a dozen other works including

his *Life of Bishop Percival* (1921). In 1924 he chaired the inter-denominational Conference on Christian Politics, Economics, and Citizenship (COPEC) at Birmingham, a project into which he had put much work. In 1925 he became chairman of the commission on Christian doctrine appointed by the archbishops, and he remained in that position until its report was completed in 1937. In 1926 he was the principal preacher at a Cambridge University mission and greatly influenced, among others, a young undergraduate named Michael Ramsey. Also in 1926 he took a leading part in an unsuccessful, and probably unhelpful, intervention in the coal strike. Internationally he was assuming an increasingly authoritative role in the burgeoning ecumenical movement. He took an active part both in the first World Conference on Faith and Order, held at Lausanne in 1927, and in the International Missionary Council's conference in Jerusalem at Easter 1928, where he was clearly the leading intellectual figure and chiefly responsible for the writing of its message. It was not surprising that when a new archbishop of York was needed a few months later, following Cosmo Gordon Lang's translation to Canterbury, Temple seemed the obvious candidate. He was enthroned early in January 1929.

Archbishop of York Temple's thirteen years at York were by far the most important and effective in his life. He and his wife loved Bishopthorpe and used it for much formal and informal entertaining, including the housing of numerous evacuees when the Second World War began. He was now properly placed to exercise the sort of national and international leadership for which he was naturally suited, whether lecturing in American universities, preaching at the opening session of the disarmament conference in Geneva (1932), or chairing the General Advisory Council of the BBC. The continuous round of preaching, lecturing, and presiding in parishes, university missions—the Oxford mission of 1931 was particularly memorable—and ecumenical gatherings was heavy enough in itself. Yet he found time to write his three most enduringly important books, *Nature, Man and God* (1934), compiled from the Gifford lectures given in Glasgow between November 1932 and March 1934, *Readings in St John's Gospel* (1939 and 1940), and *Christianity and Social Order* (1942). He also became the unchallenged leader of the international ecumenical movement. Already in 1929 he was elected chairman of the Faith and Order continuation committee, and he continued to head Faith and Order, with its annual committee meetings held—until prevented by the war—at various places in Europe up to his death. The following year he chaired the Committee on Christian Unity at the Lambeth conference. By the mid-1930s, working closely with J. H. Oldham and Wim Visser't Hooft, he had become the principal public sponsor of the idea of a world council of churches, a plan adopted at two international conferences in 1937: that of Life and Work at Oxford in July and that of Faith and Order (chaired by Temple) a month later in Edinburgh. At a subsequent meeting in Utrecht in May 1938 he was elected chairman of the provisional committee of the world council 'in process of formation', and at home in September 1942 he inaugurated the British Council of Churches with a service in St Paul's, becoming its president.

Probably Temple's most important contributions in the social field in these years were to commission, with the help of a special committee and the Pilgrim Trust, an impressive report on unemployment, *Men without Work* (1938), and to convene and chair the Malvern conference (January 1941) on church and society, the latter being at once a follow-up to COPEC and a first attempt to plan theologically the guidelines for a post-war world, for which T. S. Eliot, Richard Acland, Dorothy L. Sayers, and Donald Mackinnon were among the principal speakers. It is noticeable that in these cases he provided a forum for others rather than for himself. He had become notably less interventionist. The young radical had turned into a fairly cautious senior statesman. Indeed, given the acute international, and national, crises of the 1930s it might seem that Temple avoided committing himself or providing a personal lead in regard to most of them. Unlike many archbishops of Canterbury he was never keen to participate in House of Lords debates, though he frequently broadcast and wrote letters to *The Times*. On very diverse tacks several of his fellow bishops—notably George Bell of Chichester, Hensley Henson of Durham, Arthur Headlam of Gloucester, and Archbishop Lang himself—took up quite outspoken positions on the great issues of the time in a way that Temple, for whatever reason, failed to do. His response was chiefly to press ahead with cementing international Christian fellowship. He did, however, make very clear his disagreement with the widespread pacifism of the peace movement led by his former ally Dick Sheppard.

Archbishop of Canterbury With the war any impression of indecisiveness disappeared. Temple's profound national loyalty and moral restraint were well fitted for church leadership at such a time. This was shown at once on the outbreak of war by a BBC radio address, which did much to produce a Christian consensus behind the war effort. When Lang retired from Canterbury in 1942 there was no imaginable alternative to Temple, though Churchill did not like his lack of bellicosity. He was enthroned in Canterbury Cathedral on 23 April 1942 and spent rather more time at Canterbury than his immediate predecessors had, as Lambeth Palace had been devastated by air raids, but he insisted on continuing to occupy a part of it that had been left relatively undamaged. He travelled incessantly around the country, often speaking several times in a single day. The demands upon his attention multiplied, but his staff remained minute. As a result his attacks of gout grew incredibly painful and severe. Temple appealed insistently for anything possible to be done to help save Europe's Jews. At the domestic political level he was largely responsible for ensuring church support for R. A. Butler's Education Act of 1944, about which he spoke frequently in the Lords, thus helping to inaugurate a revolution in the church's relationship to state education. *The Church Looks Forward* (1944), the only book of his Canterbury period, is a fairly slight collection of sermons and speeches. Throughout the summer of 1944 his gout grew worse, aggravated by one engagement after another, until early in October he was taken by ambulance from Canterbury to rest in the Rowena Court Hotel in Westgate-on-Sea, where he died on 26 October. After cremation five days later, his ashes were buried in the cloister garth at Canterbury Cathedral, next to the grave of his father.

While the range of Temple's concerns as revealed in his thirty-four books and seventy pamphlets was almost limitless, three in particular require consideration if his achievement is to be properly evaluated: first, the philosophical and theological; second, the social; third, the ecumenical. The first has at least a certain chronological priority.

The philosophical theologian Temple began his adult life as a lecturer in philosophy, preoccupied with mind, value, purpose, personality, and ethics. While he often spoke of history, it was essentially the idea of history—its Hegelian role, a discoverable all-embracing providence—that he had in mind; it was to the authority of philosophers, rather than historians, that he still appealed. On past history itself, oft-repeated generalities about Palestine, Greece, and Rome, the supposed divergent character of southern and northern Europe, and the like reflected his early education rather than history in all its complexity as increasingly interpreted by twentieth-century historians. He never quite gave up the hope of providing a 'theological philosophy' which would start with mind, end with Christ, and somehow satisfy both believers and academic philosophers. It remained his belief that this was 'the only Philosophy which has any hope of being altogether satisfactory' (*Nature, Man and God*, 44). *Mens creatrix* was conceived as mostly philosophy, and *Christus veritas* as mostly theology, but it was hard to see any real line of division. His power as a Christian writer and his weakness as a convincing philosopher both derived from the very security of his own faith in God and the divinity of Christ, about which, he affirmed, he had never had the slightest doubt. Even his early contribution 'The divinity of Christ' to an otherwise somewhat 'modernist' collection of essays, *Foundations*, by young Oxford dons (1912) was actually remarkably orthodox. Even on the virgin birth, about which he had hesitated at Oxford, he reached absolute certainty in 1916 while attending an orchestral concert in the Queen's Hall. Temple's most mature contribution to theological philosophy was, undoubtedly, his Gifford lectures. Dedicated to the memory of Edward Caird and still recognizably making use of the idealist approaches fashionable thirty years earlier, it also represented an attempt to refashion them in a more 'realist' manner. It is noticeable, for instance, that terms like 'nature', 'natural theology', and 'natural law', nowhere to be found in *Mens creatrix*, litter the pages of his later writings. 'It is our task', he could also claim, 'consciously and deliberately to construct a "synthesis" of the classical and medieval "thesis" with the modern "antithesis", and this in some fundamental respects will resemble the "thesis" more closely than the "antithesis"' (ibid., 80). He had long admired Aquinas, whose *Summa theologiae* he read in its entirety, and adopted some almost Thomist stances, but his cast of mind remained inherently different.

If the central concern throughout his intellectual life was to portray a 'Christocentric metaphysic' convincingly, Temple saw this as a theology of incarnation more than redemption, and as Catholic rather than protestant. Yet the cross was pivotal in his Christology. He had grown up a loyal son of his father, product of Rugby and Balliol, a liberal Victorian protestant, confident that Oxford idealism provided a satisfactory tool for the construction of a philosophical theology. Over the years he, like the Church of England as a whole, had moved steadily in a more Catholic direction under the influence of Bishop Charles Gore, Father Herbert Kelly of Kelham, T. S. Eliot, even Cosmo Gordon Lang, and, latterly, Thomist philosophers like Jacques Maritain. However, the temper of the 1930s and the threat of war also had an impact on Temple: the more strident voices of Karl Barth and Reinhold Niebuhr contributed to an existentialist sense of crisis to which he was not temperamentally sympathetic but which could hardly be avoided. He realized that he could no longer lead the younger generation of theologians and that it now seemed inappropriate to try to 'make sense' of everything in a way he had previously sought to do. In such circumstances it was natural to turn more deliberately towards the one system on offer on the Catholic side which did still try to provide a Christian synthesis. He wrote in the last year of his life:

> No one is equal to St Thomas as a map-maker of the spiritual and moral world. If our need is, as I think, first and foremost for such a map, we do well to go back to him, making such modifications as our own survey may dictate. (*Religious Experience*, 236)

In the preface to *Mens creatrix*, Temple admitted to three decisive influences: St John's gospel, Plato, and Robert Browning. He recognized his own thinking as highly intuitive: 'I never know the processes which it has followed. Often when teaching I have found myself expressing rooted convictions which until that moment I had no notion that I held' (*Nature, Man and God*, ix). He thought this reflected a Platonic or Johannine mind. To John he returned continually, and his most influential spiritual work was, unquestionably, *Readings in St John's Gospel*. It was in no way a work of modern biblical scholarship, in which he was remarkably little interested. Here, as elsewhere in his best writing, what impresses most is a deeply personalist spirituality and profound devotion to Christ of a very traditional kind. It remains a meditative masterpiece.

Social concerns Temple's social thought was never sharply separated from philosophy and theology, but aimed at action, not just by himself, but in leading or inspiring large collective initiatives. Most of this was educative rather than in any way directly political. Youthful liberal enthusiasm, the example of bishops B. F. Westcott and C. Gore, and growing social concern within the SCM, in which Temple took a very active part, all brought him to commit himself to what he called socialism. At the pan-Anglican congress of 1908 he boldly declared, 'The alternative stands before us—Socialism or Heresy; we are involved in one or the other' (Fletcher, 180). For Temple as for Westcott 'socialism' meant in reality no more than serious social concern. In the same year he became president of the Workers' Educational Association, though he did not join the Labour Party until ten years later, and left it in 1921. 1924 was the year of the first Labour government; it was also the year of Temple's COPEC conference. He left the Labour Party just as the COPEC preparations were beginning, probably recognizing the danger of their being stigmatized as party political. In fact the COPEC programme remained close to Labour's. Its ten commissions working across three years produced some impressive reports, though the conference itself, only one week long and attended by 1500 delegates, could do little but endorse the commissions' recommendations about such matters as housing, education, and unemployment. There was nothing very novel here and nothing immediately effective. What remained important was the extent to which church people, especially the clergy, were being re-educated by Temple to accept such matters as being of major Christian concern.

When he moved from education to intervention within the political process Temple was less sure-footed. Probably he learned from the coal dispute of 1926. He was profoundly reluctant ever to oppose government policy in public, and held that it could not be for him, as a bishop, to argue how principles should be put into practice; his role was only to elucidate the so-called 'middle axioms', derived from general principles, according to which precise policy might be formulated. It is not clear that this approach was convincing, but it seemed safe enough. He also wanted facts to be made better known, as was done effectively in the report *Men without Work* (1938). Occasionally he seemed to go further, as in his controversial opinions on banking and credit.

Temple's last important book, probably his most influential, was *Christianity and Social Order* (1942), at once short and clear. Over 140,000 copies were quickly sold, and it was reprinted thirty years later with a preface by Edward Heath. It and the Malvern conference (1941) together did much to ensure that British Christians welcomed the welfare state as it developed after the war, along lines being proposed in the war years by William Beveridge, R. H. Tawney, Stafford Cripps, and R. A. Butler—all Temple's friends. Temple was the first person to use the term 'welfare state' in print (in 1941). William Temple College (later the William Temple Foundation) was opened in 1947 by Bishop Leslie Hunter to continue this side of Temple's work.

Ecumenism Temple's third special concern was the ecumenical movement. As a young man he had attended the Edinburgh International Missionary Conference of 1910 as a steward, selected by the SCM. Of the seven major international ecumenical conferences held before his death he was absent from only two: Stockholm in 1925 and Tambaram in 1938. Continually involved, almost throughout his adult life, in SCM activities, he became the organization's most regular speaker at the annual Swanwick conferences. Generations of its leaders became his faithful followers. After 1929 as chairman of Faith and Order he soon became international ecumenism's most powerful patron and spokesman, even if others had to do most of the spadework. He was always an admirable chairman of meetings, a highly convincing public speaker, and a constructor of formulas which satisfied all sides of an argument, what he called 'my parlour trick of fitting everybody's pet point into a coherent document when they thought they were contradicting one another' (Iremonger, 396). Moreover, as archbishop of York he held a higher ecclesiastical position than anyone else in the first rank of the movement, at least after the death of Archbishop Söderblom in 1931. In May 1933 he invited to Bishopthorpe an informal group of ten people representing the various different international ecumenical bodies then in existence, out of which developed a new sense of shared leadership; at another informal meeting at Princeton two years later he took the lead in proposing an 'interdenominational, international council representing all the churches', and in July 1937 he chaired the meeting of the so-called committee of Thirty-Five at Westfield College, which formulated the precise proposal for a world council of churches, subsequently accepted by the Oxford and Edinburgh conferences that summer. The next year at Utrecht he was elected chairman of the provisional world council's central committee.

Temple's enthronement sermon at Canterbury was devoted largely to 'the great new fact of our era': that is to say, 'this world-wide Christian fellowship, this ecumenical movement' (*The Church Looks Forward*, 2–3). Christian unity, schemes of reunion (notably that of south India), and the ecumenical movement generally provide the principal themes running through his one Canterbury book, *The Church Looks Forward* (1944). For Temple the final challenge was whether he could lead both the Church of England and the ecumenical movement, especially at a time when England was at war. What seems certain is that for him the one real ground for a renewed hope in the circumstances of the time had come to lie in the development of a 'world-wide Christian fellowship' signified by the World Council of Churches, lack of communion between any two Christians being 'the fundamental anomaly' (ibid., 12). It is unlikely that the world council would have been proposed, agreed to, and brought into provisional existence without his combination of authority and persuasiveness. Yet his contribution remained essentially one of an imaginative presidency. In theological terms he offered little in interpretation as to what the world council would actually signify in relation to the nature of the church. Perhaps he was too contented an Anglican to see the point in this. Thus he showed no animus against Roman Catholicism but, equally, until his final Canterbury years, rather little interest in it, or in Eastern Orthodoxy. The impression given is that in the latter part of his life, while the advance of the ecumenical movement had become the most significant thing within it, he was too busy, often too tired, to reflect sufficiently on what it must entail. Yet, all the more remarkably, he suggested in 1944 that he should pay a personal visit to Pope Pius XII.

Evaluation Bishop Hensley Henson, who dissented from nearly all Temple's policies, declared him 'felix opportunitate mortis, for he has passed away while the streams of opinion in Church and State, of which he has become the outward symbol and exponent, were at flood, and escaped the experience of their inevitable ebb' (*Letters*, ed. Braley, 159). Others have repeated this opinion, but it is not well founded. If Temple had lived into the post-war world, he would have possessed an unparalleled authority and would have seen almost all he stood for realized in the policies of the Labour government and the inauguration in 1948 of the World Council of Churches. Any 'ebb' in popularity of the ideas for which he had been the symbol and exponent came a full thirty years later. In his character there was an evenness about him which altered very little. Certainly he became more cautious in the expression of his opinions: the establishment man gained ground on the liberal, the Catholic on the protestant. What remains striking, however, is the consistency of his concerns from about 1908, when he was ordained, until his death. His life of John Percival is revealing, coming as it did at a hinge point in his own career. Percival represented the Rugbeian tradition, derived from Thomas Arnold and his father, in which he was himself brought up: liberal protestant yet somewhat authoritarian in manner, almost nationalist, almost puritan too in its ruggedness. Temple was invited to write Percival's biography as a natural heir. He could not refuse, and he did his best. Nevertheless, while he shared many of Percival's concerns, his temperament, viewpoint, and mode of behaviour as a bishop were strikingly different.

It has been said that Temple was a man of ideas but was poor in the evaluation of people. Michael Ramsey even called him a 'hopeless' judge of character (Chadwick, 118). Doubtless a kindly optimism about others at times misled him, yet he was very good at picking out and advancing younger men of outstanding ability. Many of the ablest figures in the church of the next generation had been brought forward by him: Geoffrey Fisher, Leslie Hunter, Michael Ramsey himself, Wim Visser't Hooft, and Oliver Tomkins among others. He was capable of showing and instilling affection even through the briefest of meetings. His humour was infectious, like his laugh. His photographic memory, whereby he could literally call to mind every word of a book he had recently read, was extraordinary. The clarity and speed with which he wrote memoranda or answered letters were also outstanding. There have been more convincing philosophical theologians, more effective social reformers, greater preachers, more single-minded ecumenists, but no one who combined all these skills to so high a degree and who so steadily matched his leadership with the hour. His ceaseless activity on so many fronts was possible only because of a remarkable inner calm, a prayerfulness, cheerfulness, and lack of pomposity which all who encountered him experienced.

Weaknesses there were. Perhaps the most serious was a reluctance, of which Temple may have been unaware, to take up an unpopular position. In this he was very different from his great contemporary, George Bell, bishop of Chichester. While often able to engineer a consensus where it had seemed impossible, he shrank from taking sides where there were truly unbridgeable divisions. Above all, he avoided any sustained disagreement with government policy. He cherished the Church of England as a national institution, and he wanted to be a national leader of it. He thought, somewhat loosely, in terms of nations and their varying characters. He cherished his Englishness, delighting in English literature and government as much as in a church which, he claimed, 'has never failed to be utterly, completely, provokingly, adorably, English' (*Religious Experience*, 90). He was never—at least after Life and Liberty—a party leader, though often able, well ahead of the generality, to articulate a position at which the church would later arrive. He at times looked like a prophet and was acclaimed as such, but in the bitter international conflicts and political uncertainties of the 1930s he failed to be prophetic or to steer opinion when he alone might have been able to do so. Once the war came he could give an assured public leadership once more. 'We stand at the bar of history, of humanity, and of God' (Iremonger, 566–7), he declared in regard to action to save the Jews, in what was probably his finest House of Lords speech on 23 March 1943. The government, however, ignored every proposal he made. Unlike Bell, he refused to criticize a policy of obliteration bombing. His uncomplicated attitude to issues relating to the war may be illustrated by a letter to the Ministry of Labour and National Service, in which he wrote, 'I regard conscientious objection as completely wrong', but added, 'I regard the recognition of it as one of the glories of our country' (*William Temple: Some Lambeth Letters*, 50).

In and after his death Temple's reputation was immense, enhanced by a widespread feeling that he was irreplaceable. One major biography, by his long-standing friend and colleague from Life and Liberty days, F. A. Iremonger, was published in 1948. It was knowledgeable and extensive, but its author was too close to Temple to evaluate his life with fully convincing authority. There have been other smaller books and various studies of aspects of his thought, but no large-scale reappraisal. The general estimation of his importance has probably declined. His approach to theological philosophy was already out of fashion in his lifetime, while the very achievement of many of his more practical goals, especially within the ongoing history of the ecumenical movement, obscured Temple's pioneering role. Yet it would be hard to think of any other twentieth-century ecclesiastical figure whose impact on history has been comparable, certainly in England, possibly in the world. He represented in himself so much of the transformation in Christian consciousness characteristic of the century. Again, as one of the leading figures of the British society of his generation, he deserves to be placed in the company of Winston Churchill, Bertrand Russell, or George Bernard Shaw—among whom he might well be judged the most balanced in mind, the most consistent throughout a long career, and, certainly, the most personally loved.   ADRIAN HASTINGS

Sources F. A. Iremonger, *William Temple, archbishop of Canterbury* (1948) · J. Kent, *William Temple: church, state and society in Britain, 1880–1950* (1992) · A. Hastings, 'William Temple', *The English religious tradition and the genius of Anglicanism*, ed. G. Rowell (1992), 211–26 · *William Temple: some Lambeth letters*, ed. F. S. Temple (1963) · A. M. Ramsay, *From Gore to Temple* (1960) · O. Thomas, *William Temple's philosophy of religion* (1961) · J. Fletcher, *William Temple: twentieth century Christian* (1963) · R. Craig, *Social concern in the thought of William Temple* (1963) · J. F. Padgett, *The Christian philosophy of William Temple* (1974) · A. Suggate, *William Temple and Christian social ethics today* (1987) · S. C. Spencer, 'The decline of historicism in William Temple's social thought', DPhil diss., U. Oxf., 1990 [incl. the only full bibliography of Temple's writings] · A. Hastings, *A history of English Christianity, 1920–1990*, 3rd edn (1991) · W. Temple, *Nature, man and God* (1934) · *Religious experience and other essays and addresses by William Temple*, ed. A. E. Baker (1958) · W. Temple, *The church looks forward* (1944) · *Letters of H. H. Henson*, ed. E. F. Braley (1951) · O. Chadwick, *Michael Ramsay: a life* (1990) · *WWW* · *CGPLA Eng. & Wales* (1945)

Archives Borth. Inst., corresp. and papers as Archbishop of York · Canterbury Cathedral, archives, notes for addresses · Canterbury Cathedral, papers · LPL, corresp. and papers | BL, corresp. with Lord Cecil, Add. MS 51154 · BL, corresp. with Macmillans, Add. MSS 55100–55101 · BL, letters to Albert Mansbridge, Add. MSS 65254, 65255B · Bodl. Oxf., corresp. with J. L. Myers; corresp. with Lord Selborne and Lady Selborne; letters to Sir Alfred Zimmern · Lancs. RO, letters to T. H. Floyd · LPL, Bell papers; Davidson papers; corresp. with Arthur Headlam; Lang papers; corresp. with Edwin Palmer; letters to H. R. L. Sheppard; letters to Mervyn Stockwood; Frederick Temple papers | FILM BFI NFTVA, current affairs footage · BFI NFTVA, documentary footage · BFI NFTVA, news footage | SOUND BL NSA, 'Out of the wilderness', xx (1822082.1) · BL NSA, other sound recordings

Likenesses J. W. Nichol, oils, 1915, Repton School; copy, 1915, Queen's College, Oxford · J. W. Nichol, oils, 1917, Queen's College, Oxford · T. C. Dugdale, oils, 1929, LPL · T. C. Dugdale, oils, 1929, Man. City Gall. · P. A. de Laszlo, oils, 1934, LPL [*see illus.*] · photographs, *c.*1940, Hult. Arch. · H. Coster, photograph, 1942?, NPG · O. Birley, oils, 1943, Bishopthorpe Palace, York · K. Hutton, double portrait, photograph, 1943 (with William Beveridge), Hult. Arch. · W. Stoneman, photograph, 1943, NPG · P. A. de Laszlo, study for portrait, Balliol Oxf. · photograph, NPG

Wealth at death £28,584 15s. 7d.: probate, 5 Feb 1945, *CGPLA Eng. & Wales*

Temple, William Francis Cowper-, Baron Mount-Temple (1811–1888), politician, was born William Francis Cowper at Brocket Hall, Hertfordshire, on 13 December 1811. He was the son of Emily Mary Lamb (1787–1869) [see Temple, Emily Mary], sister of William Lamb, second Viscount Melbourne and prime minister. His legal father was her first husband, Peter Leopold Louis Francis Nassau Cowper, fifth Earl Cowper (1778–1837). But he was very probably the illegitimate son of Henry John *Temple, third Viscount Palmerston (1784–1865), who became his stepfather in 1839 (on his mother's marriage to him) and whose estates he inherited. There was a striking physical resemblance between them, but no conclusive evidence has been found. Like his nephew Evelyn Ashley, Palmerston's secretary, Cowper was a moderate evangelical. In later life he was spasmodically vegetarian and moved on the fringe of the mesmerism movement.

W. F. Cowper was educated at Eton College, where as he

William Francis Cowper-Temple, Baron Mount-Temple (1811–1888), by unknown photographer

afterwards remarked he learned no English whatever, and in 1827 entered the Royal Horse Guards as a cornet; he was promoted lieutenant in 1832, captain (unattached) in 1835, and brevet major in 1852. In 1835 he became private secretary to his uncle, Lord Melbourne, at that time prime minister, and was returned to parliament as member for Hertford, which he continued to represent until 1868. In 1841 he was appointed a junior lord of the Treasury, and when the whigs returned to office in 1846 he became a lord of the Admiralty. He held this post until March 1852, and again from December 1852 to February 1855, when he was made under-secretary for home affairs. Six months later he was appointed president of the Board of Health and was sworn of the privy council; in February 1857 he was transferred to the newly created vice-presidency of the committee of council on education, and on 24 September 1857 resumed the presidency of the Board of Health, holding both offices together until March 1858. In 1858 he passed the Medical Practitioners Act establishing the General Medical Council, and his speech explaining its provisions was published in the same year. In August 1859 Cowper became vice-president of the Board of Trade, and in February 1860 commissioner of works, an office he continued to hold until 1866.

In this capacity Cowper did much useful work; in 1862 he carried the Thames Embankment Bill, and in 1863 the Courts of Justice Building Bill. He initiated the practice of distributing for charitable purposes flowers from the London parks, and was keenly interested in the efforts to check enclosures. In 1866 he carried the Metropolitan

Commons Bill, the first measure which empowered a local authority to undertake the care and management of a common as an open space, and in February 1867 he became first president of the Commons Preservation Society, which had been started in 1865. In 1869, as chairman of the select committee on the enclosure acts, he was instrumental in preserving many rural commons, and to his action in 1871 was largely due the failure of the attempt to enclose Epping Forest. Cowper also waged war with many of his neighbours in the New Forest over the same question. His action may have been stimulated by his friend John Ruskin, and in 1871 Cowper and Thomas Dyke Acland were the original trustees of Ruskin's Guild of St George.

In 1866 Cowper ceased to be first commissioner of works when the Conservatives under Derby returned to power, and he was not included in Gladstone's first administration in 1868. He represented South Hampshire from 1868 until his elevation to the peerage in 1880. His mother died on 11 September 1869, and Cowper inherited under Palmerston's will many of his estates in Ireland and Hampshire, including Broadlands, at Romsey. By royal licence, dated 17 November 1869, he assumed the name Temple in addition to Cowper.

In the parliament of 1868–74 Cowper-Temple took an important part in the debates on education. As first vice-president of the committee he had interested himself in the subject, and an address he delivered at Liverpool in October 1858 was published in the same year by the National Association for the Promotion of Social Science. On 11 March 1870 he led a large deputation to Gladstone from the National Education Union; on 14 June 1870 the cabinet accepted his amendment (the famous 'Cowper-Temple amendment', clause 14) to the Elementary Education Bill to exclude from rate-built schools all denominational formularies and thus, somewhat uncertainly, providing for non-denominational religious instruction. On 16 June Gladstone announced Cowper-Temple's success (and his own defeat) 'to an eager and agitated House'. On 25 May 1880 Cowper-Temple was, on Gladstone's recommendation, created Baron Mount-Temple of Mount-Temple, co. Sligo. During his later years he confined himself mainly to philanthropic activity, advocating such measures as the Criminal Law Amendment Act of 1885.

Cowper married, first, on 27 June 1843, Harriett Alicia (1821/2–1843), daughter of Daniel *Gurney of North Runcton, Norfolk; she died aged twenty-one on 28 August following, and on 21 November 1848 he married Georgina (1821?–1901), daughter of Admiral Richard Delap Tollemache, formerly Halliday (1772–1837) [see Temple, Georgina Cowper-]. She died aged seventy-nine on 17 October 1901, a prominent spiritualist and a friend of Ruskin. With neither wife had he any children; the title became extinct on his death, and the property he inherited from Lord Palmerston passed to his nephew, Evelyn Ashley. He died at Broadlands on 16 October 1888 and was buried at Romsey on the 20th. A. F. POLLARD, *rev.* H. C. G. MATTHEW

Sources GEC, *Peerage* · *The Times* (17–23 Oct 1888) · Gladstone, *Diaries* · W. G. Collingwood, *The life of John Ruskin* (1900) · G. W. E.

Russell, *A short history of the evangelical movement* (1915) · J. Murphy, *The Education Act, 1870* (1972) · K. Bourne, *Palmerston: the early years, 1784–1841* (1982)
Archives U. Southampton L., family and estates papers; corresp. and papers; corresp. | BL, corresp. with W. E. Gladstone, Add. MSS 44374–44788, *passim* · BL, corresp. with Lord Holland, Add. MSS 51558–51559 · Chatsworth House, Derbyshire, Chatsworth MSS · Chatsworth House, Derbyshire, letters to sixth duke of Devonshire · Herts. ALS, letters to E. B. Lytton · NL Scot., letters from George Macdonald, MS 9745 · U. Southampton L., Broadlands MSS · U. Southampton L., Broadlands MSS, letters from Moriz, Count Esterházy · U. St Andr. L., corresp. with James Forbes · UCL, corresp. with Sir Edwin Chadwick
Likenesses photograph, NPG [*see illus.*]
Wealth at death £76,123 6s. 1d.: probate, 4 Jan 1889, *CGPLA Eng. & Wales*

Temple, William Johnson (*bap.* **1739**, *d.* **1796**), Church of England clergyman and essayist, was baptized on 20 December 1739 in Berwick upon Tweed, the eldest of the five children of William Temple (1710–1774), collector of customs for Berwick upon Tweed, merchant, and mayor of Berwick (1749–50 and 1753–4), and his wife, Sarah (*d.* 1747), younger daughter of Alexander Johnston, merchant, of Newcastle upon Tyne. She brought to the marriage, along with other property, the farmed estate of Allerdean, some 4 miles south-west of Berwick, which Temple inherited.

About 1751 Temple seems to have begun attending the free grammar school established by the Berwick corporation. He left Berwick in autumn 1755 for the University of Edinburgh, where he struck up the lifelong friendship with his fellow student James Boswell which is his main claim to fame. He next went to Trinity Hall, Cambridge, on 22 May 1758. As early as 2 May 1759 he was admitted to the Middle Temple and took his name off the books at Trinity Hall on 20 November 1761. He seems to have spent the next eighteen months mainly in London. His father had become bankrupt by the end of 1762 and Temple had drawn on his own (Johnston) funds to give the creditors 5s. in the pound. Now considerably impoverished, when he was readmitted to Trinity Hall as a fellow-commoner on 22 June 1763 he had the church rather than the bar in mind. At Cambridge he made the acquaintance of Thomas Gray and a circle of the poet's young admirers.

On 28 June 1765 Temple graduated LLB. He was ordained priest on 21 September 1766 and on the following day was instituted to the rectory of Mamhead, about 10 miles from Exeter, on the presentation of his cousin once removed Wilmot Vaughan, fourth Viscount Lisburne. On 6 August 1767 Temple married Anne Stow (*bap.* 1741, *d.* 1793), youngest daughter of William Stow (1692?–1753), like Temple's father twice mayor of Berwick, and his first wife, Anne Blake, sister of Sir Francis Blake FRS of Twisell Castle, some 9 miles south-west of Berwick. The Temples had eight children, of whom one, Francis (1770–1863), ended up as an admiral, and another, Octavius (1784–1834), became lieutenant-governor of Sierra Leone.

When the Temples settled at Mamhead in October 1767, the living was worth only £80 a year. There were quarrels with the Lisburnes, as well as marital friction and money troubles, all of which made Temple so depressed that he seemed suicidal to Norton Nicholls in 1771. Nevertheless, Temple read the proofs of Boswell's *Account of Corsica* in 1767, visited Edinburgh in 1770 and 1773, when he met some of the literati, and received visits from Boswell at Mamhead in 1769 and 1775. In 1774 his 100-page *Essay on the Clergy* was published, which highlighted the social role of the clergy, defining a clergyman as 'a private and public teacher of religion and virtue' (p. 18), which drew from David Hume, who had seen the book in proof, the insulting counter-definition of 'a person appropriated to teach hypocrisy & inculcate vice' (Temple to Boswell, 15 Feb 1774, *Correspondence*, 1.340). In 1775 he made a new friend, the poet and dramatist Edward Jerningham, and began a rather tepid correspondence with him which lasted until 1793.

In Boswell's opinion, Temple excelled in writing 'characters' of men and books, such as the well-known portrait of Gray, which first appeared in Temple's letter to Boswell of 3 September 1771, a month after Gray's death. Boswell sent it to the *London Magazine* where it was published anonymously and without authority in March 1772 (41.140) before being incorporated by William Mason with slight alterations in his life of Gray (1775) and then used by Johnson in his account of Gray in the *Lives of the Poets* (1779–81). The character of Gray seems to have been typical of the remarks on authors which Temple wrote down in his 'green book', unfortunately lost, which impressed Boswell so much that it induced Temple to plan a volume of letters on literary and moral subjects addressed to Boswell. The work never materialized. A much longer and later sketch cuts a hero down to size—*The character of Dr Johnson, with illustrations from Mrs Piozzi, Sir John Hawkins, and Mr Boswell*, published anonymously by Dilly in 1792. Though Temple asserts that Johnson's learning and talents have been overrated by his partial admirers, he cannot avoid praising the 'piety and good sense' of the *Rambler* essays, and the 'noble' dictionary.

On 9 September 1776 Temple was collated to the vicarage of St Gluvias near Penryn in Cornwall, a living worth over £300 a year, but in the long run this advancement did little to curb his inveterate complaining about his lot. In 1779 he published anonymously *Moral and Historical Memoirs*, a 424-page book of eleven essays, staunchly whig and critical of absolute monarchy, but in the years that followed he was never able to complete the several works on Italian and church history he had planned. In the early 1780s he did much to further in Cornwall the movement for more equal representation in parliament, corresponding with the Yorkshire reformer Christopher Wyvill on the matter, and in the early 1790s he took the lead in founding the Cornwall County Library. He travelled to London in May 1790 with his daughter Nancy, paying a strained visit to Boswell and his daughter Veronica, and in August–September 1792 Boswell, Veronica, and her younger sister Euphemia visited the Temples in Cornwall. In 1789 Temple had welcomed the storming of the Bastille, but in December 1790 he was converted to the anti-French position after reading Burke's *Reflections on the Revolution in France*. By the end of 1791 even parliamentary reform was suspect, and by 1794 France had become for him a country whose 'inhabitors ought to be wiped from the face of the Earth' (Temple to Boswell, 6 Dec 1791 and 30 Jan 1794, MSS Yale C2915, C2954).

During a visit of nearly two months to St Gluvias in 1794 Norton Nicholls secured Temple's consent to the marriage of his daughter Nancy to the Revd Charles Powlett, which Temple had previously opposed. Despite earlier friction, father and daughter spent three apparently enjoyable months in Suffolk as Nicholls's guests in 1795. Temple died at St Gluvias on 13 August 1796 of a severe abdominal complaint similar to that which had carried off his wife in 1793, whose age then is given as forty-six in the St Gluvias burial register and on the family gravestone in the churchyard, where Temple too was buried. Though both believed this, the evidence points to her having died aged fifty-two (Correspondence, 1.132, n. 4). Temple bequeathed all his property, including the estate of Allerdean when sold, to be divided equally among his children, apart from a legacy of £20 a year to his widowed sister Sarah Forster. Nancy was to be given £1000 of her share at the time of her marriage.

Boswell's role in his correspondence with Temple became known in 1856, when the majority (97) of his surviving letters to Temple were published. But it was not until the twentieth century that the letters from Temple to Boswell were discovered, 338 in all. Temple told Boswell as much about his family, professional, and financial troubles as Boswell told him about his own, and was equally frank about his sexual needs and difficulties, as when, after his wife's death, he revealed his attraction to Susan Frood, the vicarage housekeeper, and the unsavoury attempts of Charles Powlett and Nancy to destroy Susan's reputation (Temple to Boswell, various letters June 1793 to 3 Nov 1794, MSS Yale University).

In the religious sphere his letters show Temple deserting his Socinian and almost sceptical stance of 1763 for the orthodoxy of his middle and later years, while in the political dialogue he moved from his initial whig republicanism to the conviction that 'our own present Government' was 'the wisest and best that mankind in any age or any country in the world were ever blessed with' (Temple to Boswell, 11 Dec 1792, MS Yale C2930). The correspondence as a whole provides

> an extraordinarily vivid and comprehensive picture of literary, professional, domestic, and intellectual life over a period of almost forty years. That period saw its share of differences and debates, long separations and less than successful reunions, grief, disappointment and disillusion; but what survived, indeed triumphed over, every vicissitude, is finally a friendship that held firm against all the tests time sent its way.　(Correspondence, 1.lix)

THOMAS CRAWFORD

Sources The correspondence of James Boswell and William Johnson Temple, ed. T. Crawford, 1 (1997), vol. 6 of The Yale editions of the private papers of James Boswell, research edn · W. J. Temple, letters to James Boswell, Yale U., Beinecke L., MSS C2644–C2981 · Diaries of William Johnston Temple, 1780–1796, ed. L. Bettany (1929) · Letters of James Boswell, ed. C. B. Tinker, 2 vols. (1924) · J. Boswell, letters to W. J. Temple, Morgan L. · L. Bettany, ed., Edward Jerningham and his friends: a series of eighteenth century letters (1919) · The Yale editions of the private papers of James Boswell, trade edn, ed. F. A. Pottle and others, 14 vols. (1950–89) · F. Brady, James Boswell: the later years, 1769–1795 (1984) · F. A. Pottle, The literary career of James Boswell (1929) · F. A. Pottle, Pride and negligence: the history of the Boswell papers (1982) · Berwick upon Tweed parish register, Berwick RO, MS M98 [baptism]
Archives Yale U., Farmington, Lewis Walpole Library, letters
Wealth at death approx. £8000—incl. Allerdean, Northumberland, valued at £6000; £1043 from brother's estate in India; £500 in Berwick Turnpike Trust: will, PRO, PROB 11/1282; BL OIOC Madras wills and testaments, 1785–6; PRO, PROB 11/1252; will [Robert Temple]; Yale U., MS Yale C2790; Crawford, ed., The correspondence, 1.404

Templeman, Peter (1711–1769), physician and secretary of the Society of Arts, the eldest son of Peter Templeman (d. 1749), a solicitor in Dorchester, Dorset, and his wife, Mary, daughter of Robert Haynes, was born on 17 March 1711, probably in Dorchester and educated at the Charterhouse. Proceeding to Trinity College, Cambridge, in June 1728, he graduated BA with distinction in 1731, and then planned to take holy orders—perhaps with a scholarly career in mind. Deciding on a medical career instead, he took himself off to the Netherlands in June 1735, and the next year enrolled in the University of Leiden, where he attended the lectures of Hermann Boerhaave, but is not listed as having taken a degree. Unless he obtained an MD elsewhere by purchase, 'Dr Templeman', as he was subsequently styled, would seem to have been merely a courtesy usage.

Going to London in 1739 with the intention of building a medical practice, Templeman soon had that intention subverted by his insistent scholarly leanings and preference for the company of men of learning, which combined with a generous allowance from his father to reinforce a disinclination for the active socializing in fashionable circles that was the standard way of securing a remunerative clientele. Much more in character was his joining with a number of fellow spirits in 1741 to form a small medical club, which held its meetings once a fortnight at an inn. Among its members were John Fothergill and a friend whom Templeman had made at Leiden, Matthew Maty. It was to the influential Fothergill that Templeman chose in 1750 to put the idea of starting a society to obtain for its members advance news from all over Europe of improvements in medical practice and knowledge— what would later be known as an abstracts service. Though that suggestion came to nothing, in 1753–4 Templeman published an example of what he had had in mind in the form of translations from French (a language of which he had a complete command) of select papers on matters relating to medicine read before the Académie Royale des Sciences in Paris. Further translating and editing work, not confined to medicine, followed.

In June 1756 Maty was appointed to the inaugural staff of the British Museum as keeper of its department of printed books. Doubtless with his friend's encouragement, Templeman also applied for a post in the museum, and was rewarded in December 1758 with the keepership of the reading-room. But in contrast to Maty's position, this proved to be not nearly as congenial as he had imagined, requiring him to spend six hours of each working day cooped up in a dark and damp room at the beck and call of readers and with next to no opportunities of pursuing any scholarly work of his own. Worse, the promised apartment within the museum, into which he had looked forward to moving his wife, Frances (d. 1762), and their daughter, he found unacceptably sub-standard, and the outside lodgings allowance that replaced it was not nearly adequate. After his repeated protests had left the trustees quite unmoved, he felt compelled to seek a supplementary means of livelihood and in March 1760 competed successfully for the post of secretary of the recently founded Society of Arts, Manufactures, and Commerce. The museum did not require its staff to work for it exclusively and one of the unsuccessful candidates had in fact been Maty, whose lighter museum duties would have made it easy for him to hold the two posts in tandem. The different character of Templeman's post, however, permitted much less leeway; the trustees soon took exception to the lengthy absences from it which his new post entailed and after seven months terminated his employment.

The Society of Arts proved a haven by comparison, and during the nine years Templeman worked for it his abilities were at last fittingly harnessed and to good effect. His most concrete achievement was a projected 'historical register' which, though he failed to complete it, became in later hands the first two volumes of the society's *Transactions*. He was still hard at work on this in May 1769 when deteriorating health made it necessary for him to be relieved of his duties and sent on indefinite leave. For at least two years would-be successors had been covetously eyeing his post and waiting for it to fall vacant, and on 22 September 1769 their hopes were at last realized when Templeman succumbed to a particularly acute attack of the asthma that had troubled him for most of his life. He was buried on 28 September in St Martin-in-the-Fields, alongside his wife, who had predeceased him in 1762— and 'without pomp', as he had specially requested in his will.   D. E. ALLEN

Sources Nichols, *Lit. anecdotes*, 2.299–302 · W. C. Smith, 'Dr. Peter Templeman and his appointment as secretary of the society in 1760 [pts 1–3]', *Journal of the Royal Society of Arts*, 108 (1959–60), 462–6, 630–33, 771–3 · H. T. Wood, *A history of the Royal Society of Arts* (1913), 24–5 · D. G. C. A. [D. G. C. Allan], 'The origin and growth of the society's archives, 1754–1847', *Journal of the Royal Society of Arts*, 106 (1957–8), 623–9 · D. G. C. Allan and J. L. Abbott, eds., *The virtuoso tribe of arts and sciences* (1992) · A. E. Gunther, *The founders of science at the British Museum, 1753–1900* (1980), 8–13 · R. W. Innes Smith, *English-speaking students of medicine at the University of Leyden* (1932), 230 · *GM*, 1st ser., 39 (1769), 463
Archives RSA, transactions
Likenesses W. Evans, stipple, 1799, Wellcome L. · R. Cosway, oils, RSA; repro. in Allan and Abbott, eds., *The virtuoso tribe*, 81

Templer, Ethel Margery, Lady Templer (1904–1997). *See under* Templer, Sir Gerald Walter Robert (1898–1979).

Templer, Sir Gerald Walter Robert (1898–1979), army officer, was born at Colchester, Essex, on 11 September 1898, the only child of Lieutenant-Colonel Walter Francis Templer of the Royal Irish Fusiliers and later of the army

Sir Gerald Walter Robert Templer (1898–1979), by Harold Speed, 1955

pay department and his wife, Mabel Eileen, daughter of Major Robert Johnston, from co. Antrim, of the army pay department in India.

Education and early career After attending private schools in Edinburgh and Weymouth, Templer went, in January 1912, to Wellington College, where, as a small boy who was not good at games, his life was made unhappy by bullying. He entered the Royal Military College, Sandhurst, in December 1915, and left in July 1916 with no distinction. Being then under the age of nineteen, he was not allowed to join a battalion on active service and had to spend a year in Ireland before he joined the 1st battalion, the Royal Irish Fusiliers, in France in November 1917. After the war he went with the battalion to Persia, Iraq, and Egypt, before returning to Dover, England, in 1922. There he became a noted athlete, gaining his army colours as a hurdler and being chosen as a reserve for the 1924 Olympics team. On 8 September 1926 he married Peggie Davie [*see below*], daughter of Charles Davie, a retired solicitor from Devon, and his wife Beatrice (*née* Walrond). They had a daughter and a son.

Templer was still a platoon commander when he gained entry to the Staff College, Camberley, in 1927. While a student there, he transferred to the loyal (north Lancashire) regiment on so-called accelerated promotion to captain; he stayed with the regiment in Aldershot in 1930 for a few months before being posted as general staff officer, grade 3 (GSO3), to the 3rd division on Salisbury Plain. There he fell foul of his GSO1 who wrote an adverse report, recommending his removal from the army. When Templer refused to accept it, the general, Harry Knox, tore it up and wrote a favourable one himself. Templer's next appointment was as GSO2 at northern command, York, where his relations with his GSO1, Harold Alexander, were cordial.

In 1935 Templer, still a captain, commanded a company, first in the 2nd battalion of the Loyals on Salisbury Plain and then, as a brevet major, with the 1st battalion in Palestine, where the Arab population was causing trouble for the British. There were only two battalions in Palestine at that stage and Templer's company was charged with supporting the police in a large area of the north. He revelled in the independence and responsibility this gave him. His performance gained him both a mention in dispatches and the DSO, an exceptional award for a company commander.

In 1936 he returned to a staff appointment in England, and in 1937 he became a royal Irish fusilier again, when the fusiliers' 2nd battalion was resuscitated; but he never served with the fusiliers at regimental duty. In 1938, at last a substantive major and now a brevet lieutenant-colonel, he became a GSO2 in the military intelligence directorate at the War Office, responsible for preparing plans for intelligence in wartime, including the formation of an intelligence corps and for the organization of clandestine operations. His imagination and the thoroughness of his staff work made a major contribution in these fields.

The Second World War   When war broke out Templer went to general headquarters in France as a GSO1 under the head of intelligence, Major-General F. N. Mason-Macfarlane, and acted as his chief of staff when the latter was ordered by Viscount Gort on 16 May 1940 to take command of an *ad hoc* force to link up with the French on the western flank of the British expeditionary force. On his return from France on 27 May, he was charged with raising the 9th battalion of the Royal Sussex regiment, and in November he was promoted to command the 210th infantry brigade at Weymouth under the 3rd division of B. L. Montgomery. In May 1941 he went as brigadier, general staff, to 5th corps and in April 1942 he was promoted major-general to command the 47th (London) division at Winchester. Five months later he was promoted again to command 2nd corps district at Newmarket, at forty-four the youngest lieutenant-general in the army, but very short of active service command. When it appeared that his corps was never going to engage in active fighting, he asked to be allowed to revert in rank to major-general and be given command in an active theatre of war.

Templer's request was granted, and on 31 July 1943 he took over command of the 1st division, resting in north Africa. His chance to see action at last came in October, when he was transferred to the command of 56th division in the British 10th corps in the US Fifth Army in Italy. It had just crossed the Volturno River near Capua and was struggling through the rain-soaked hills on the far side. In the first week of November the division had closed up to the German positions south of the River Garigliano and was ordered to throw them off Monte Camino. Conditions of weather and terrain were severe, and the attack failed, 201st guards brigade, which had borne the brunt and suffered heavy casualties, justifiably feeling that the higher command had underestimated the force needed. Templer was not popular with the guards for some time after that. A month later the assault was renewed in greater strength, notably in artillery support, and was successful, as was the division's crossing of the Garigliano in mid-January 1944. Attempts to expand the bridgehead did not, however, get far and were called off, just as the need to reinforce the landing at Anzio became urgent. One of Templer's brigades was sent there on 30 January and he followed with the rest of the division on 12 February. He was heavily involved in beating off German counter-attacks, at one time also assuming command of 1st division, whose commander was wounded.

After four weeks in the bridgehead, in which it suffered heavy casualties, 56th division was relieved and sailed for Egypt to rest and refit, before returning to Italy in July. On 26 July Templer was transferred to the command of 6th armoured division which was leading the advance as the Germans withdrew towards Florence. Two weeks later, as he was driving up to the front, a lorry, in which was a looted piano, pulled off the road to let him pass and blew up on a mine. Debris struck his back, crushing one vertebra and damaging two others. In great pain, he was removed to hospital and returned to England in plaster in September. His short active war service was at an end. When he had recovered he was employed for a time by the Special Operations Executive before, in March 1945, being appointed to the staff of his erstwhile instructor at the Staff College, Montgomery (now field marshal), at Twenty-First Army group, as director of civil affairs and military government in Germany. As the war drew to an end, and as it ended in May, with a staff of only fifty officers, he controlled and directed a population whose economic and social structure had collapsed. He flung himself into the task with all his accustomed energy and directness, one incident becoming notorious. Exasperated by the failure of the mayor of Cologne, Konrad Adenauer, to take practical steps to improve the physical conditions of his city, while he concentrated on political matters, Templer ordered his dismissal. Adenauer bore him no grudge and although, when he became chancellor, he would never see Templer socially, he would send him a case of the best hock whenever he visited London.

High commissioner in Malaya   Templer moved to join Montgomery at the War Office, first in March 1946 as director of military intelligence, and then in 1948 as vice-chief of the Imperial General Staff; he remained in that post with Montgomery's successor, Sir William Slim, until June 1950, when, promoted general at the age of fifty-two, he took over eastern command. He had expected this to be his last post, and it might well have been, had not Sir Henry Gurney, high commissioner in Malaya, been ambushed and killed by communists in October 1951. The suggestion had already been made that a soldier should be appointed to bring both military operations and civil government under one head. The colonial secretary, Oliver Lyttelton, accepted Slim's recommendation of Templer for this post, having first tried to obtain the services of General Sir Brian Robertson and then Slim himself.

Templer's success in Malaya, where he arrived in February 1952, was to compensate for all his previous disappointments. The basis of it was the Briggs plan, proposed and initiated by Lieutenant-General Sir Harold Briggs, brought in from retirement as director of operations in April 1950. He had not, however, been able to obtain the authority and full co-operation from all branches of the administration, including the police, to implement it effectively. Briggs had left in December 1951, and Templer provided all the authority, drive, and imagination that had been lacking. His arrival was not greeted with universal enthusiasm, many fearing that he would concentrate on security to the neglect of political development. However, probably his greatest contribution to the success of the long struggle against the communists in Malaya was his insistence on rapid progress to independence and the assumption of political responsibility, including that for security, by the Malay, Chinese, and Indian inhabitants of the federation.

By the summer of 1954 such progress had been made that Templer could recommend that his place should be taken by his civilian deputy, Sir Donald MacGillivray, and this was effected in October. The chief of the Imperial General Staff (CIGS) Field Marshal Sir John Harding, had recommended Templer as his successor, and wished him to spend a year as commander-in-chief of the British army of the Rhine in order to gain some first-hand experience of NATO beforehand; but this was blocked by the foreign secretary, Sir Anthony Eden, who objected to such a short tenure at a crucial period of German rearmament, not, as some suggested, because of Templer's brush with Adenauer.

Chief of the Imperial General Staff In September 1955 Templer became the army's professional head as chief of the Imperial General Staff (CIGS). At that time the situation in the Middle East was of major concern to the chiefs of staff and to Eden's Conservative administration. In December Templer was sent to try to persuade the young King Hussein that Jordan should join the Baghdad pact. The pro-Egyptian faction, supported by the Palestinian element, strongly opposed this, forcing a series of political crises, starting while Templer was in Amman, which culminated in March 1956 with the dismissal of the British general John Glubb from the Jordanian Arab Legion.

Templer's whole period as CIGS was an unhappy one for him, including, as it did, the fiasco of Suez and the reductions in the size of the army resulting from the decision of Harold Macmillan to work towards the end of conscription. At heart an imperialist and a dedicated infantryman, Templer regarded with extreme distaste the abandonment of imperial responsibilities and the reductions in infantry which flowed from them. He was never much interested in the defence problems of Europe and had an instinctive dislike of alliances. He had a keen sense of duty, and faced the unpleasant task of cutting down the army, reinforced by the knowledge that his subordinates knew that he would be as fair and just in his decisions as he would be relentless and vigorous in seeing that they were promptly and obediently executed, after he had fought every one of them tooth and nail with the defence secretary, Duncan Sandys, whom he loathed. Exacting in his demands on himself, he demanded high standards in others. A martinet in appearance and manner, his displeasure—even his presence—was intimidating. He became a field marshal in 1956.

Templer's principal activity after leaving active duty in 1958 was the foundation and support of the National Army Museum. He was tireless in raising the money and in badgering government departments and other authorities to lend their support to the project, which owed its success mainly to him. He was constable of the Tower of London (1965–70), HM lieutenant of Greater London (1967–73), and colonel of the Royal Horse Guards (1962–9) and, after their amalgamation with the 1st (Royal) Dragoons, of the Blues and Royals (from 1969 to his death). He was appointed OBE in 1940, CB in 1944, CMG (1946), KBE (1949), KCB (1951), GCMG (1953), GCB (1955), and KG (1963). He held honorary doctorates from Oxford and St Andrews, as well as numerous other honours. He died at his home, 7 Sloane Court West, Chelsea, London, on 25 October 1979. His funeral took place in St George's Chapel, Windsor Castle, on 2 November and his ashes were buried in the churchyard of St Michael's, Wilsford, Wiltshire.

Templer was survived by his widow, **Ethel Margery [Peggie] Templer** [*née* Davie], Lady Templer (1904–1997), and their two children. For many years Lady Templer 'made a successful career as an officer's wife, resolutely in the background' (*The Times*, 7 April 1997), running social clubs for her husband's men, and served as a lieutenant-colonel in the St John Ambulance brigade in the Second World War. In Malaya she came into her own, learning to speak and broadcast in Malay, and founding the Lady Templer Hospital in Kuala Lumpur. Her women's organization apparently caused the communists to warn against her, observing 'This woman bandit is cunning' (ibid.). Lady Templer died on 24 March 1997, and her ashes were buried with those of her husband.   MICHAEL CARVER

Sources J. Cloake, *Templer, tiger of Malaya: the life of Field Marshal Sir Gerald Templer* (1985) · R. Clutterbuck, *The long, long war* (1966) · private information (2004) · personal knowledge (2004) · *The Times* (7 April 1997) · *CGPLA Eng. & Wales* (1980)
Archives NAM, papers | Bodl. RH, corresp. on medical matters as high commissioner, Federation of Malaya, mainly with Dr H. M. O. Lester · CAC Cam., corresp. with Sir E. L. Spears | FILM BFI NFTVA, news footage · IWM FVA, actuality footage · IWM FVA, documentary footage · IWM FVA, news footage · IWM FVA, propaganda film footage (Central Office of Information) | SOUND BL NSA, documentary footage · IWM SA, oral history interview
Likenesses W. Stoneman, two photographs, 1942–5, NPG · H. Speed, oils, 1955, Federation Regiment, Malaya, Officers' Mess [*see illus.*] · T. Cuneo, group portrait, oils, 1958 (*Visit of the queen and Prince Philip to the Staff College*), Staff College, Camberley, Surrey ·

M. Gerson, photograph, 1966, NPG · group portrait, photograph, 1972, Hult. Arch. · double portrait, photograph, 1973 (with Nat Cohen), Hult. Arch. · J. Gunn, oils, priv. coll. · C. Leeds, charcoal sketch, priv. coll. · sketch, priv. coll.

Wealth at death £115,322: probate, 4 March 1980, *CGPLA Eng. & Wales* · £183,077—Ethel Margery (Peggie) Templer: probate, 18 Aug 1997, *CGPLA Eng. & Wales*

Templeton, James (1802–1885), carpet manufacturer, was born on 7 July 1802 in Campbeltown, Argyll, Scotland, the son of Archibald Templeton, a farmer, and his wife, Ann Harvey.

Templeton began his career in Glasgow, working for a wholesale merchant. He was later employed by a Liverpool merchant house and spent more than three years on their behalf in Mexico. On his return to Glasgow he gained experience in the cotton industry before moving to Paisley, where he used his accumulated savings to found a shawl-making business in 1829. During the 1830s he became interested in weaving chenille, which Paisley manufacturers had begun to use in the production of shawls. Templeton and William Quigley, a weaver he employed, devised an improved method of weaving chenille, and in July 1839 they obtained a patent for the process. However, realizing that the same method might be used to create a new type of carpet, Templeton bought out Quigley's interest in December that year. He married Mary (1807–1889), the daughter of John Stewart, a cotton spinner, and his wife, Margaret, *née* Tod, on 1 December 1831. Two sons and two daughters were born in Paisley, another son and daughter later in Glasgow.

Templeton returned to Glasgow in 1839 and began to manufacture chenille carpets in King Street (later renamed Redan Street), using premises rented from a cotton-thread manufacturer. His object was to provide a cheaper substitute for the traditional hand-tufted Axminster carpets which, together with imported oriental or Turkey carpets, catered for the top end of the market. The pile yarn for the surface of the chenille carpet was woven in a weft loom, in a manner similar to the weaving of a piece of cloth, and then cut into narrow strips which resembled striped caterpillars in appearance. The strips, each one of which constituted a line of pile, were then woven in a setting loom to the warp threads forming the base of the carpet. This was more efficient than the time-consuming process used in Axminster production, where pieces of yarn constituting the pile had to be tied to each pair of warp threads by hand.

The Glasgow factory produced both seamless carpets to fit a particular room, and strips of carpeting woven on looms less than a yard wide which were subsequently sewn together to make a whole carpet. A wide range of colours was employed in the pattern and the carpet surface had a rich appearance closely resembling a traditional Axminster.

Templeton's younger brother Archibald and his brother-in-law Peter Reid became partners in James Templeton & Co. in 1843, but Templeton was the dominant figure. Reid handled the accounts, and by 1850 Archibald

Templeton had departed to run the London office and warehouse.

After the first three years of operations the firm was consistently profitable and grew steadily in size. Competition from new chenille carpet producers, which emerged when the original patent expired, was countered by emphasis on high quality and attractive designs. Templeton recruited a large team of designers, and his carpets won prize medals at a succession of international trade exhibitions. In 1856, when the original factory burnt down, he purchased a former cotton mill in William Street (later renamed Templeton Street) and production was soon resumed. Sales continued to grow, and by 1870 the firm's capital exceeded £102,000—a sevenfold increase since 1851.

Templeton also began making the cheaper and more popular Brussels carpeting during the 1850s. In 1855 production was transferred to a new factory in Crownpoint Road, and in partnership with his eldest son, **John Stewart Templeton** (1832–1918), Templeton established a separate firm, known as J. and J. S. Templeton & Co., to control operations.

During the 1870s sales of chenille carpets and carpeting began to decline and profits also fell. Attempts to mechanize the weaving process met with only partial success. It was relatively simple to devise a weft power-loom, but the problem of producing an efficient setting power-loom had not been fully solved when Templeton retired in 1878, at the age of seventy-six. Nevertheless, his firm then ranked as the second largest producer of chenille carpets and carpeting, with a quarter of the British output.

Templeton's public life centred on the Free Church of Scotland. He was an elder of St John's Free Church, Glasgow, and in later life regularly attended St George's Free Church. He held no public offices and in politics he was a staunch Liberal. A number of local charities benefited from his generosity, and he left a legacy of £500 to the Glasgow Ladies Auxiliary Society for the Outdoor Blind. He was a benevolent employer. He instituted a Sunday school for his young male employees, and he remembered thirty-seven of his long-serving weavers by name in his will. His wife supported his efforts, holding cookery classes for female workers and publishing a book on simple cookery for working-class households.

Templeton died of angina pectoris at his home, 2 Claremont Terrace, Glasgow, on 27 August 1885 at the age of eighty-three. He was buried in the Glasgow necropolis. His wife died on 27 October 1889.

It was left to John Stewart Templeton, assisted by his brother James Templeton junior, to establish the Glasgow enterprise at the forefront of the British carpet industry. The mechanization of chenille weaving was perfected and power-looms were installed under licence from their American inventors to weave spool Axminster carpeting, which offered another cheaper substitute for traditional Axminsters. Price cuts were initiated, substantially boosting sales and profits, and in the process transforming chenille and Axminster production into a major sector of the carpet industry. Meanwhile the other Glasgow branch had become a leading producer of Brussels and Wilton carpeting. By the eve of the First World War the Templeton enterprise had become the largest in the British carpet industry, rivalled only by John Crossley & Sons of Halifax.

JAMES NEVILLE BARTLETT

Sources F. H. Young, *A century of carpet-making, 1839–1939: James Templeton & Co.* (1944) • *Glasgow Herald* (27 Aug 1885) • J. N. Bartlett, *Carpeting the millions: the growth of Britain's carpet industry* (1978) • D. Bremner, *The industries of Scotland: their rise, progress, and present condition* (1869) • will and personal inventory, Sheriff's court, Glasgow • *Glasgow Herald* (9 Oct 1918) • m. cert. • d. cert. • b. cert. [J. S. Templeton] • m. certs. [J. S. Templeton] • d. cert. [J. S. Templeton] **Wealth at death** small bequests to thirty-seven weavers employed for twenty years or more; £500 to Glasgow Ladies Auxiliary Society for the Outdoor Blind: will and inventory, Sheriff's Court, Glasgow

Templeton, John (1766–1825), naturalist, was born at Bridge Street, Belfast, co. Antrim, Ireland, the son of James Templeton (*d.* 1790), a wholesale merchant, and Mary Eleanor, daughter of Benjamin Legg of Malone. He was a 'delicate' boy:

> my experience was … for many years very precarious during some of the infantile diseases. I have heard that the lamp of life was so nearly extinguished that final hope was exhausted, and I was left until a coffin should be prepared. (Deane, 33)

He was educated at the school established by David Manson (1726–1792), an innovative schoolmaster and brewer, whose pupils were taught 'to read and understand the English tongue, without the discipline of the rod, by intermixing pleasurable and healthy exercise with their instruction' (Manson, 3).

The Templetons' business evidently prospered, and John Templeton may be described as a man of independent means; if he had any role in running the family business, the fact is never mentioned by biographers. After his father's death he lived in the family's country house, Orange Grove, about 2 miles from Belfast, renaming it Cranmore (*crann mór*, great tree) after the sweet chestnut (*Castanea sativa*) trees that still survive two centuries later. He had become a keen gardener about 1786, and in 1793 laid out an elaborate garden at Cranmore. Templeton's interest in botany arose in 1790, according to Thomas Dix Hincks, from a need to eradicate weeds from Cranmore. He became an extraordinary plantsman, growing exotic and native plants, raising trees from seeds, and experimenting by cultivating tender plants outdoors; he was probably the first to grow *Camellia* and *Fuchsia* in the open air in Ireland. Hincks stated that Templeton contributed information to Thomas Martyn's edition of Philip Miller's *The Gardener's and Botanist's Dictionary* (1807).

Templeton's political views were liberal. He supported parliamentary reform, Catholic emancipation, and the ideals of the United Irishmen although he did not agree with their methods. Among his close friends was a founder of the Society of United Irishmen, Thomas Russell, who was executed on 10 October 1803 at Downpatrick. A. Wilson wrote that 'among the little group [of Belfast citizens] whose liberal interest raised the whole outlook of the community none was a more remarkable

personality than John Templeton' (Wilson, 104). He was a co-founder of the *Belfast Monthly Magazine* (1808–14), and regularly contributed articles on natural history and meteorology. An active supporter of learned societies as well as philanthropic organizations, Templeton was one of the promoters of the Belfast Academical Institution and a member of its first board of visitors. He joined the Belfast Society for Promoting Knowledge (founded in 1788 as the Belfast Reading Society) and helped compile catalogues (1793 and 1818) of its library, later the Linen Hall Library. Templeton was appointed curator of the society's museum which was handed over in 1833 to the Belfast Natural History Society; he was made an honorary member of that society soon after its formation in 1821. He was a member of the Irish Harp Society, vice-president of the Belfast Literary Society (1803), and an associate of the Linnean Society of London (1794).

Templeton was a careful observer and a painstaking and accurate artist; he was interested in all aspects of the natural world. As a young man he went fowling but gave it up after observing the suffering of a wounded bird. He was also keen on fishing and his illustration of the extinct Lough Neagh char is a unique record. His extant diaries (1806–25, in the Ulster Museum, Belfast) record the general weather and temperature at 8 a.m. daily, the flowering of plants, the planting of crops, and the calling of birds. While Templeton rarely ventured outside Ulster, he made frequent excursions by himself and with fellow naturalists around the north of Ireland to collect plants; among those known to have accompanied him are Robert Brown (1773–1858) and Dr William Jackson Hooker (1785–1865). Brown chose an Australian shrub belonging to the bean family (Fabaceae) to name *Templetonia* after his friend.

Templeton visited London on several occasions and, according to Hincks, following his second visit to London, Sir Joseph Banks offered him a grant of land and salary if he would go to New Holland. Templeton declined because of his 'attachment to his aunt and sisters … as well as to his native country' (Hincks, 406). On 21 December 1799 he married Katherine Johnson (*c.*1773–1868), daughter of another Belfast merchant, Robert Johnson. The couple had five children; their only son, Robert (1802–1892), studied medicine and became an expert entomologist and conchologist. Templeton died in Belfast on 15 December 1825 and was buried in Clifton Street burying-ground.

Templeton's most memorable discovery was the hybrid Irish rose, which he named *Rosa x hibernica*, at Holywood, co. Down, about 1795, yet this rose is only one of many plants and animals he recorded. He published papers on peat bogs, bird migration, and acclimatizing plants, but his observations remain essentially unpublished, incorporated in the copious manuscripts, often beautifully illustrated with sketches and watercolour paintings of native plants and animals, that are extant. Robert Lloyd Praeger described him as 'the most eminent naturalist Ireland has produced' (Praeger, 165) but added that little is known about him. Templeton was certainly influential during his lifetime, especially in his native city within scientific, literary, and social circles. He was a painstaking, comprehensive observer of a diverse range of plants and animals, and an accomplished all-round naturalist, but published little of substance.   E. CHARLES NELSON

Sources T. D. Hincks, 'Memoir of the late John Templeton, Esq.', *Magazine of Natural History*, 1 (1828), 403-6 · *Magazine of Natural History*, 2 (1828), 305-10 · A. Wilson, 'John Templeton', in *Centenary volume, 1821-1921*, Belfast Natural History and Philosophical Society, ed. A. Deane (1924), 104-5 · R. L. Praeger, *Some Irish naturalists: a biographical note-book* (1949), 163-5 · R. Nash and H. Ross, *Dr Robert Templeton Roy. Art., 1802-1892, naturalist and artist* (1980) · C. D. Deane, 'John Templeton and Orange Grove', *The Ulster countryside* [Belfast 1983], ed. J. Forsyth and R. H. Buchanan (1983), 29-34 · J. Killen, 'John Templeton — the Gilbert White of Ireland and the friend of everyman', *Linen Hall Review*, 9/3/4 (1992), 4-7 · D. Manson, *A new pocket dictionary* (1762)
Archives NHM, notes and drawings · Royal Irish Acad., list of Irish plants · Ulster Museum, Belfast, corresp. and papers | National Botanic Gardens, Dublin · NHM, letters to Sowerby family · RBG Kew, W. J. Hooker MSS · TCD, department of botany, J. T. Mackay MSS · TCD, Sirr MSS

Templeton, John (1802-1886), singer, was born on 30 July 1802, at Riccarton, near Kilmarnock, Ayrshire, the son of Robert Templeton. He had a fine voice as a boy and took part in concerts in Edinburgh with his eldest brother, a singer and teacher. In 1822 he became precentor to the Rose Street Secession church, then under John Brown. Intending to become a professional singer, he went to London and studied under Jonathan Blewitt, Thomas Welsh, De Pinna, and Tom Cooke.

In July 1828 Templeton made his stage début at Worthing, Sussex, as Dermot in *The Poor Soldier*, and, after some appearances in the provinces, made his London début on 13 October 1831 as Belville in William Shield's *Rosina* at Drury Lane. This was followed, on 20 February 1832, by his portrayal of Raimbaut in the first performance in England of Meyerbeer's *Robert le diable*. In 1833 he took the part of Don Ottavio in Mozart's *Don Giovanni* at Covent Garden at five days' notice. That same year Maria Malibran chose him as her tenor for Bellini's *La sonnambula*, at Covent Garden, and he continued to be her leading tenor until her premature death in 1836. After their final performance together on 16 July 1836 Malibran gave him the jewelled betrothal ring which she always wore as Amina. Bellini was so pleased with Templeton's performance of the part of Elvino that he once embraced him and promised to write a part that would immortalize him. Templeton played the leading tenor roles in the first performances in English of Rossini's *Le siège de Corinthe* (1836), Mozart's *Die Zauberflöte* (1838), and Donizetti's *La favorite* (1843). He visited Paris in 1842 with Balfe, and met Auber. The following year he started touring the provinces giving lecture recitals on Scottish, English, and Irish folk-songs, and in 1845-6 he went on a tour of America with his 'Templeton Entertainment'. He retired to New Hampton, near London, in 1852, and died there at his home, Tempé Villa, on 2 July 1886. He had four brothers, all of whom were singers.

Templeton's voice was of very fine quality and exceptional compass. Cooke called him 'the tenor with the additional keys'. His chest voice ranged over two octaves, and he could sustain A and B♭ in alt with ease. His weakness was an occasional tendency to sing flat. He had a repertory of thirty-five operas, in many of which he created the chief parts. He also wrote a few songs, one, 'Put off! Put off!' on the subject of Queen Mary's escape from Lochleven. *A Musical Entertainment*, his reminiscences and commentaries, was published in Boston in 1845.

                J. C. HADDEN, *rev.* ANNE PIMLOTT BAKER

Sources *New Grove* · D. Baptie, ed., *Musical Scotland, past and present: being a dictionary of Scottish musicians from about 1400 till the present time* (1894) · Grove, *Dict. mus.* · [W. H. H. Husk], ed., *Templeton & Malibran: reminiscences of these renowned singers, with original letters & anecdotes* [1880] · *CGPLA Eng. & Wales* (1886)
Likenesses C. Baugniet, lithograph, pubd 1844, BM · Maclure & Macdonald, lithograph (after A. Keith), NPG · portrait, repro. in *London Figaro* (10 July 1886), 12 · two portraits, repro. in Husk, ed., *Templeton and Malibran*
Wealth at death £290 18s. 0d.: probate, 26 July 1886, *CGPLA Eng. & Wales*

Templeton, John Stewart (1832-1918). *See under* Templeton, James (1802-1885).

Templewood. For this title name *see* Hoare, Samuel John Gurney, Viscount Templewood (1880-1959).

Tenby. For this title name *see* George, Gwilym Lloyd-, first Viscount Tenby (1894-1967).

Tench, Watkin (*bap.* **1758**, *d.* **1833**), marine officer and author, was baptized on 10 November 1758 in the parish of St Mary on the Hill, Chester, probably the fifth of five children of Fisher Tench (*d.* 1784?) who 'between the years 1760 and 1770 … kept an academy for dancing, and a most respectable boarding-school' in Bridge Street (Hemingway, *History of Chester*, 1831, 33), and his wife, Margaret (*d. c.*1794). The range of Tench's knowledge—Latin and French language and literature, English literature (especially Shakespeare and Milton), travel writing, and social theory—suggests a grammar school education and a socially and culturally ambitious home life. Time spent over the border in Wales possibly influenced his subsequent interest in cross-cultural relations. One of his books is dedicated to Welsh magnate Sir Watkin Williams Wynn (1772-1840), in 'gratitude to a family, from whom I have received the deepest obligations' (Tench, *First Four Years*, 126). These obligations may have included his commission as a second lieutenant of marines in 1776. He was promoted first lieutenant in 1778, captain in 1782, major in the army in 1794, and lieutenant-colonel in 1798.

Tench served in the American War of Independence from 1777 to 1783 (he was a prisoner of the French in Maryland for part of 1778). At some point in the 1780s he lived in the West Indies. On 13 May 1787 he sailed for New Holland on the convict transport *Charlotte*, arriving at Botany Bay on 7 January 1788. He left the colony on 18 December 1791, reaching Spithead on 19 June 1792. On 22 October 1792 he married Anna Maria Sargent (1766–1847), daughter of Robert Sargent and his wife, Hannah Hill, of Stoke Damerel, near Plymouth. After the outbreak of war (February 1793) between Britain and revolutionary France, Tench joined the Channel Fleet. His ship, the *Alexander*, was captured on 6 November 1794 and he spent six months as a prisoner, first on French ships in Brest harbour, then in the town of Quimper in Brittany. From 1802, after further service with the Channel Fleet, he was on shore duties. He was promoted lieutenant-colonel in the Royal Marines in 1804, colonel in the army in 1808, colonel-commandant en second in the Royal Marines in 1809, major-general in 1811, and lieutenant-general in 1821, and from 1819 was commandant of the Plymouth division of Royal Marines. He retired in 1827 and died on 7 May 1833 at the home of his brother-in-law Daniel Little at Devonport, Devon; he was buried at Devonport.

Tench's first two books—*A Narrative of the Expedition to Botany Bay* (1789) and *An Account of the Settlement at Port Jackson* (1793)—together provided an astute and lively narrative of the first four years of the colony of New South Wales. His third book, *Letters written in France to a friend in London between the month of November 1794 and the month of May 1795* (1796), reported on the volatile circumstances which followed the fall of Robespierre. Tench may also have had a hand in the composition of an imaginary-voyage narrative, *Fragmens [sic] du dernier voyage de La Perouse* (Quimper, 1797).

Anglican in religion and liberal whig in politics, Tench was a man of strong convictions but—within gentlemanly limits—an enquiring mind. 'Enlightened' was a favourite word, and he was proud to serve a Britain defined by its limited monarchy, protestant religion, the rule of law, ideals of public service, and commercial and intellectual innovation. He wished to see these values spread, those of 'despotism' (and 'democracy') resisted: 'had I been a Frenchman I should have struggled as hard for the Revolution of 1789, as I should have resisted with all my might that of 1792' (Tench, *Letters from Revolutionary France*, 100). His commitment to the spread of enlightened British principles was, however, matched by a feeling for the distinct strengths of other peoples and systems which frequently led him to doubt the practicability or propriety of British policy in practice. He was passionately opposed to slavery in the West Indies, conscious in certain respects of the destructive impact of colonization on the Aboriginal people of New South Wales, and keen that Britain should accept the post-Jacobin French Republic of 1795.

GAVIN EDWARDS

Sources W. Tench, *Sydney's first four years: being a reprint of 'A narrative of the expedition to Botany Bay' and 'A complete account of the settlement at Port Jackson'*, ed. L. F. Fitzhardinge (1979) · W. Tench, *Letters from revolutionary France*, new edn (2001) · M. C. Flynn, 'Watkin Tench', *Australian literature, 1788–1914*, ed. S. Samuels, DLitB, 230 (2001), 381–5 · *GM*, 1st ser., 103/1 (1833), 476 · L. F. Fitzhardinge, 'The origin of Watkin Tench: a note', *Royal Australian Historical Society Journal and Proceedings*, 50 (1964), 74–7 · *Army List* · *IGI* · will, PRO, PROB 11/1818, sig. 413

Archives Mitchell L., NSW, collection · Mitchell L., NSW, MS letters
Likenesses photographs (after portraits), priv. coll. · photographs, Mitchell L., NSW

Tenducci, Giusto Ferdinando (*c*.1735–1790), singer and composer, was born in Siena; his principal singing teacher was the castrato Caffarelli (Gaetano Majorano) and he received his musical education at the Naples conservatory (*c*.1744–1750). He made his début as a soprano castrato at Cagliari in 1750, during the marriage celebrations of the duke of Savoy, and from 1752 sang in various Italian cities and at Dresden. Having come to London in autumn 1758 as second man at the King's Theatre, he appeared first in Galuppi's *Attalo*, in which he introduced an aria by Caffarelli. Charles Burney believed that in Cocchi's *Ciro riconosciuto* (16 January 1759) he showed 'a much better voice and manner of singing' (Burney, *Hist. mus.*, 4.471) than the first man. After his second London season the opera company was in financial difficulties and Tenducci spent eight months in debtors' prison before a benefit concert was held for him in January 1761. He sang at the Salisbury festivals in 1762–4 and each summer from 1761 to 1764 at Ranelagh Gardens, where he performed some of his own songs and where Lydia Melford, in Tobias Smollett's *Humphrey Clinker*, thought herself in paradise because he warbled so divinely. In February 1762 he was engaged at Covent Garden to create the role of the young hero, Arbaces, in *Artaxerxes*, Thomas Arne's very successful English opera. Arbaces' air 'Water Parted from the Sea' remained one of his favourite songs. He returned to Italian opera at the King's in 1764–5, when he created the title role in *Adriano in Siria* by J. C. Bach, who became a close friend.

In summer 1765 Tenducci moved to Dublin and had considerable success at the Smock Alley Theatre as a singer and adapter of operas, including George Rush's *The Royal Shepherd*, *Artaxerxes*, and the pasticcio *Pharnaces*. He played Young Meadows in Arne's *Love in a Village* with libretto by Isaac Bickerstaff, and sang in Tommaso Giordani's *L'eroe cinesi* (7 May 1766), the first *opera seria* to be staged in Ireland. In August 1766 he was secretly married by a Catholic priest to Dorothea (*b*. *c*.1750), the daughter of Thomas Maunsell, an influential barrister. They eloped and the story of the ensuing melodrama was told by Dorothea in *A True and Genuine Narrative of Mr. and Mrs. Tenducci*. Hounded by her enraged relatives, he was imprisoned, released, re-imprisoned, and finally freed on bail when he became seriously ill. However, her family eventually relented, Tenducci renounced the 'errors of Popery' (*GM*) on 27 June 1767, and they were married in a protestant ceremony in July. Tenducci taught and gave concerts in Dublin until the couple moved in June 1768 to Edinburgh, where he sang for the Edinburgh Musical Society. His programmes included Scottish songs and inspired George Thomson's life work on Scotland's traditional airs. In 1844 Thomson wrote:

> the most judicious charmingly expressive singer of Scottish songs I ever had the pleasure of listening to was Signor Tenducci, whose passionate feeling and exquisitely touching

Giusto Ferdinando Tenducci (c.1735–1790), by Thomas
Gainsborough, c.1773–5

expression of the melody was not more remarkable than his
marked delivery of the words.   (Hadden, 21)

In August 1769 Tenducci drew a quarter's salary in
advance and disappeared to London. His wife, having performed with him in Edinburgh, sang in his place until
December and was then employed by the Musical Society
at 3 guineas a week. In February 1770 she joined Tenducci,
who had sung at Covent Garden in December, and she
made her only London appearance in *Amintas* (his arrangement of *The Royal Shepherd*) for his benefit at the Haymarket in May. That year he also sang in the York oratorios, at the Three Choirs Meeting, and at the Salisbury Festival, where Elizabeth Harris found his wife 'a genteel well
behav'd young woman' (Burrows and Dunhill, 602). He
also became a professional member of the Noblemen and
Gentlemen's Catch Club. He performed in Italian operas
at the King's in 1770 and 1771, when Burney found him 'so
much improved, during his residence in Scotland and Ireland, as not only to be well received as first man on our
stage, but, afterwards, in all the great theatres of Italy'
(Burney, *Hist. mus.*, 4.497). On 26 February 1771 the *Gazetteer* claimed that Tenducci, £1000 in debt, had attempted
to abscond to Italy 'with his wife and *her* child'. The couple
left for Italy at the end of the opera season, and that
November Horace Mann wrote to Horace Walpole of
Tenducci's success in Florence. Over the next five years he
sang in many operatic centres, notably Rome, Venice, and
Naples. Casanova reports an encounter with Tenducci,
who introduced him to his wife and claimed to have
fathered two children, whom the castrato said must be his
since he acknowledged them as such. In Italy, in winter
1772–3, Dorothea left Tenducci for William Kingsman,

and in February 1776 her marriage to Tenducci was
annulled on the grounds of his impotence. By this time,
Dorothy was already married to Kingsman and the following month Elizabeth Harris wrote of recent divorces,
including that of Mr and Mrs Tenducci: 'she has been married sometime, and has two children' (Burrows and
Dunhill, 884).

Tenducci reappeared on the London stage in February
1777, singing at Drury Lane and in oratorios at Covent Garden. Financial difficulties drove him to France, where
Mozart met him with J. C. Bach in August 1778 and wrote a
scena for him. Tenducci returned to London in 1779 and
was active mainly as a concert singer; he performed in the
Bach–Abel concerts at Hanover Square, in provincial festivals, and in the 1785 Handel concerts at Westminster
Abbey. In 1783–4 he sang in *Artaxerxes* and other English
operas at the Smock Alley Theatre, Dublin, and in an English translation of J. C. Bach's adaptation of Gluck's *Orfeo
ed Euridice*, with Mrs Billington as his Euridice. His final
London stage appearances were in that opera, in Italian, at
the King's Theatre in spring 1785. About this time he published his *Instruction of Mr. Tenducci to his Scholars* and in
March 1786 he announced his retirement from public performance to concentrate on teaching. His final benefit
concert, in commemoration of J. C. Bach, consisted of
unpublished music by his friend. Tenducci moved to Italy,
possibly because he was again in debt, and died in Genoa
on 25 January 1790.

OLIVE BALDWIN and THELMA WILSON

Sources G. W. Stone, ed., *The London stage, 1660–1800*, pt 4: 1747–
1776 (1962) · C. B. Hogan, ed., *The London stage, 1660–1800*, pt 5: 1776–
1800 (1968) · *GM*, 1st ser., 37 (1767), 379 · *Gazetteer* (26 Feb 1771) · *Gazetteer* (1 March 1776) · *Public Advertiser* (13 Jan 1761) · *Public Advertiser*
(15 March 1786) · *Public Advertiser* (4 May 1786) · *Scots Magazine*, 52
(1790), 153 · C. Sartori, *I libretti italiani a stampa dalle origini al 1800*, 7
vols. (Cuneo, 1990–94) · T. J. Walsh, *Opera in Dublin, 1705–1797: the
social scene* (1973) · D. Tenducci, *A true and genuine narrative of Mr. and
Mrs. Tenducci in a letter to a friend at Bath* (1768) · G. F. Tenducci, preface, *Orpheus and Eurydice* (1785) · minutes book of the Edinburgh
Musical Society, vol. 3, Edinburgh Public Library music department · J. C. Hadden, *George Thomson, the friend of Burns: his life and
correspondence* (1898) · C. S. Terry, *John Christian Bach* (1967) · A. Rees
and others, *The cyclopaedia, or, Universal dictionary of arts, sciences, and
literature*, 45 vols. (1819–20), vol. 35 · Burney, *Hist. mus.*, vol. 4 ·
R. Fiske, *English theatre music in the eighteenth century* (1973) · Walpole, *Corr.*, vols. 23, 38 · *The letters of Mozart and his family*, ed. and
trans. E. Anderson, rev. S. Sadie and F. Smart, 3rd edn (1985) · 'Tenducci, Giusto Ferdinando', *The catalogue of printed music in the British
Library to 1980*, ed. R. Balchin, 56 (1986), 47–8 · T. Smollett, *The expedition of Humphrey Clinker* (1771) · J. O'Keeffe, *Recollections of the life of
John O'Keeffe, written by himself*, 1 (1826) · W. T. Parke, *Musical memoirs*,
2 (1830) · T. Wilkinson, *The wandering patentee, or, A history of the Yorkshire theatres from 1770 to the present time*, 1 (1795) · D. Lysons and
others, *Origins and progress of the Meeting of the Three Choirs* (1895) ·
B. Matthews, ed., *The Royal Society of Musicians of Great Britain: list of
members, 1738–1984* (1985) · H. J. Gladstone, G. Boas, and H. Christo-
pherson, *Noblemen and Gentlemen's Catch Club* (1996) · *Music and theatre in Handel's world: the family papers of James Harris, 1732–1780*, ed.
D. Burrows and R. Dunhill (2002) · G. Casanova, *History of my life*,
trans. W. R. Trask, 12 vols. (1997), vol. 10

Likenesses T. Gainsborough, oils, c.1773–1775, Barber Institute of
Fine Arts, Birmingham [*see illus.*] · T. Beach, oils, 1782, Garr. Club ·
T. Beach, oils, 1782, priv. coll. · J. N[ixon], aquatint caricature, 1789,
BM · E. Harding, line engraving, 1796 (after J. Nixon), Harvard TC ·

J. Bruscett, portrait · W. Dickinson, engraving (after T. Beach, 1782), BM · J. Finlayson, engraving (after J. Bruscett), BM, Harvard TC · T. Gainsborough, oils · J. Nixon, pen and wash drawing, V&A, Coke collection · engraving, repro. in G. F. Tenducci, *Instruction of Mr. Tenducci to his scholars* (1785?), title-page

Wealth at death see *Scots Magazine*

Tenison, Edward (*bap.* 1673, *d.* 1735), bishop of Ossory, baptized at Norwich on 3 April 1673, was the only surviving child of Joseph Tenison of Norwich, and Margaret Mileham. After attending St Paul's School, London, under Dr Gale he entered Corpus Christi College, Cambridge, as a scholar on 19 February 1691. He graduated BA in 1695, and proceeded LLB (1697) and DD (1731), the last two at Lambeth. He was apprenticed to his uncle, Charles Mileham, an attorney at Great Yarmouth, but soon abandoned the law for the church. In 1697 he was ordained deacon and priest, and was presented to the rectory of Wittersham, Kent, which he resigned a year later on being presented to the rectory of Sundridge in the diocese of Rochester; this he held jointly with the adjacent rectory of Chiddingstone.

On 24 March 1705 Tenison was made a prebendary of Lichfield, resigning in 1708 on being appointed archdeacon of Carmarthen. On 19 March of the following year he became a prebendary of Canterbury. His first publication, a paper on 'The husbandry of canary seed', appeared in *Philosophical Transactions* for 1713. In 1715 he acted as executor to his cousin Archbishop Thomas Tenison (1636–1715) and became involved in litigation concerning dilapidations, about which he commented in *The True Copies of some Letters* (1716). The inheritor, in 1714, of a considerable estate from his uncle Edward Tenison of Lambeth, he was to lose heavily as an investor in the South Sea Company six years later.

In 1730 Tenison became chaplain to the duke of Dorset, lord lieutenant of Ireland, who in 1731 nominated him to the bishopric of Ossory. In the following year he published an edition of two books of Lucius Columella's *De re rustica*, which, together with several sermons on the necessity of public spirit and the Bangorian controversy, comprise his principal literary endeavour. He married a second cousin, Ann (*d.* 1750), daughter and coheir of Nicholas Sayer of Pulham St Mary, Norfolk, and niece of Archbishop Tenison. The couple had five daughters and one son, Thomas (1702–1742), who became a prebendary of Canterbury in 1739.

Tenison died in Dublin on 29 November 1735 and was buried in the city's St Mary's Church. He bequeathed money for the education of the poor, the promotion of Irish agriculture, and, in a codicil of 23 January 1735, a sum of £200 to Corpus Christi College, Cambridge.

J. H. LUPTON, *rev.* PHILIP CARTER

Sources H. Cotton, *Fasti ecclesiae Hibernicae*, 1–2 (1845–8) · Venn, *Alum. Cant.* · *GM*, 1st ser., 5 (1735), 737 · Nichols, *Illustrations* · C. M. Tenison, 'Tenisoniana', *Miscellanea Genealogica et Heraldica*, 3rd ser., 2 (1896–7), 33

Likenesses G. Kneller, oils, 1720, CCC Cam. · G. Vertue, line engraving, 1731 (after G. Kneller), BM, NPG

Tenison, Eva Mabel [*pseuds.* Michael Barrington, Nauticus, Historicus] (**1880–1961**), historian and novelist, was born on 31 May 1880 in Liverpool, the eldest of three children of Charles McCarthy Tenison (formerly Collins; 1850–1915), barrister, and his wife, Elizabeth Isabel (*d.* 1940), third daughter of William Crompton Ashlin, of Claughton, Birkenhead. Of Anglo-Irish descent, her father was granted by royal licence in 1890 the right to bear the name and arms of Tenison as representative of the family of Archbishop Tenison.

Eva Mabel Tenison, known to her friends as Mab and to others as E. M. T., was educated privately and spent part of her youth in Australia and Tasmania. In 1904 she published a novel, *The King's Fool*, under the pen-name of Michael Barrington. It received favourable reviews and was followed in 1909 by *The Knight of the Golden Sword*, a novel about Claverhouse. This was the precursor of her biography *Grahame of Claverhouse, Viscount Dundee* (1911), on which she had been working since 1905. It received high praise from thirty-two journals. As with all her work, her aim was to put the record straight and to correct inaccuracies that had been perpetuated by established historians. In 1912 Tenison and two aunts took a lease of Yokes Court, Frinsted, near Sittingbourne, Kent, and in that year, with Adeline, duchess of Bedford, she campaigned vigorously and successfully for the release of royalist political prisoners in Portugal. When the First World War broke out she wrote, hastily, *Chivalry and the Wounded* (1914) to inspire members of the St John Ambulance Brigade. Four thousand copies were distributed throughout the empire. In 1922 this was revised and republished, under her own name, as *A Short History of the Order of St John of Jerusalem*. Her brother Lieutenant-Commander Julian Tenison RN fell in action in 1917. She dedicated her novel *Alastair Gordon, RN* (1921) to his memory.

Also under the Barrington name, Tenison published two historical novels, *Antagonists of Destiny* (1948), about James VIII and III (James Francis Edward Stuart, the Old Pretender), and *The Invisible Army* (1948), set in the days of Charlemagne. In the 1920s there appeared under her own name *Louise Imogen Guiney* (1923), a biography of the American poet. The year 1933 saw publication of the first volume of Tenison's *magnum opus*, *Elizabethan England, being the History of this Country 'in Relation to all Foreign Princes'*. It was based on original manuscripts, many hitherto unpublished, and sixteenth-century printed matter, and embraced a survey of life and literature of the period. Work started on this Herculean task in the 1920s and the book was published privately over thirty years, mainly by subscription. Each volume is sumptuously illustrated with portraits, maps, plans, and facsimiles and with a large portfolio of documents and maps. *Elizabethan England* was thoroughly researched, and the author kept in close contact with Spanish scholars. As her conclusions contradicted received opinions, the work was not popular in academic circles. The *Mariner's Mirror* obituary of Tenison claimed that:

> The work abounds in fresh discoveries and resulting appraisals, any one of which, if made by a writer in the

public eye, would have been trumpeted in the Sunday newspapers and expounded in the *English Historical Review*. The Tenison discoveries have been received in studied silence, but are beginning to be incorporated in current works.

Tenison had scant regard for the scholarship of many of her contemporaries: she was particularly critical of Sir Sidney Lee, editor of the *Dictionary of National Biography*, and pointed out numerous errors for which she held him responsible.

Yokes Court burnt down in 1952. Volumes 11 and 12 were yet unpublished and the manuscripts were destroyed. After finding refuge at Hedingham Castle, Castle Hedingham, Halstead, Essex, Tenison, then in her seventies, set out to reconstruct them, adding two slimmer volumes of addenda and corrigenda. She also published her most esoteric book, *Blaye, Rudel and the Lady of Tripoli* (1953), under the Barrington pseudonym.

Among Tenison's major works are interspersed small volumes of verse and monographs on people whom she admired, such as Lord Kitchener and her friend the duke of Alba and Berwick, as well as an unpublished autobiography. She was awarded the order of St John and was a corresponding member of the Real Academia de la Historia. She contributed many patriotic articles to journals such as the *Mariner's Mirror*, *Khaki*, and *The Patriot* under the pseudonyms Nauticus and Historicus.

In her youth Tenison was exceptionally beautiful, a beauty retained in old age, when she resembled (in the recollection of the present writer) a small Dresden shepherdess, dressed in fashions of the nineteenth century. She was in the great tradition of the eighteenth-century gentleman scholar; her reclusiveness deliberately concealed her sex from the academic world. Tenison died at Hedingham Castle in August 1961, and was buried in Castle Hedingham cemetery.   ROBERT INNES-SMITH

Sources University of Kent, Canterbury, Templeman Library, E. M. Tenison MSS · *Mariner's Mirror*, 48 (1962), 1–3 [obit.] · P. Gibbs, *Pageant of the years* (1946) · Burke, *Gen. Ire.* · priv. coll., E. M. Tenison MSS · personal knowledge (2004) · Castle Hedingham parish council and burial board
Archives priv. coll. · University of Kent, Canterbury, Templeman Library
Likenesses bust · photograph (as young woman), priv. coll. · photographs
Wealth at death £24,704 15s. 2d.: probate, 15 Nov 1961, *CGPLA Eng. & Wales*

Tenison, Richard (1642–1705), Church of Ireland bishop of Meath, was born at Carrickfergus, co. Antrim, the eldest son of Major Thomas Tenison. His father, who apparently was second cousin to Dr Thomas Tenison, archbishop of Canterbury, seems to have settled in Ulster shortly before the Irish rising and was bailiff or sheriff of Carrickfergus in 1645. Richard Tenison attended a local school in Carrickfergus before he was sent into the care of Francis Radcliffe at St Bees School, Cumberland. He was admitted to Trinity College, Dublin, on 2 November 1659 at seventeen. There is no record of Tenison receiving any degree in the college registers but he was referred to as MA in some contemporary documents. He was appointed to the mastership of Trim Diocesan School, where he taught with considerable success before taking holy orders. By 1666 he had married a woman whose name is unknown, his eldest surviving son, Henry, being born in that year.

Tenison was appointed chaplain to Arthur Capel, earl of Essex, shortly after Essex had been appointed lord lieutenant of Ireland in 1672. Essex awarded him the sinecures of the rectories of Laracor and Augher, the vicarages of Donaghmore and St Peter's, Drogheda, and the deanery of Clogher. In February 1682 Tenison was consecrated at Christ Church, Dublin, as bishop of Killala, and during the same year was awarded a DD by Trinity College. He had married Anne (d. 1696), daughter of John Norbury, by 1684, the year in which Richard, the first of their five sons, was born. By 1688 Tenison and John Vesey, archbishop of Tuam, were the only prelates in the province of Connaught. Along with Vesey he gave 'encouragement to the Protestants as long as they remained without imminent danger of their own lives' (Mant, 1.697) before they were finally forced to remove to England in that year. Tenison settled in London, where he was employed as lecturer alongside Henry Hesketh in the parish of St Helen, Bishopsgate. He was probably placed in this position with the aid of Thomas Tenison, who was at that time rector of St Martin-in-the-Fields and St James's, Piccadilly.

After the Williamite victory Tenison returned to Ireland, where he was presented to the see of Clogher on 26 February 1691. Hesketh was nominated to replace him as bishop of Killala but was never consecrated. Tenison was among the group of Church of Ireland reforming bishops in the 1690s associated with William King and Nathaniel Foy. While bishop of Clogher he completed substantial repairs to the bishop's palace at his own expense, and obtained a reputation for preaching 'by which he reduced many dissenters to the church' and in one visitation confirmed about 2500 people (Harris, 2.191). In June 1697 he was translated to the bishopric of Meath. During the following year he became vice-chancellor of Trinity College, Dublin, and was later elected a privy councillor. He died probably in co. Meath on 29 July 1705 and was buried in the chapel of Trinity College. Tenison did not publish any major scholarly work save for five of his sermons. His will benefited the poor of Navan and Kells and bequeathed £200 to set up a fund for the support of orphans and widows of clergymen, an example that he desired others would emulate. He was survived by his six sons, two of whom, Henry and Richard, sat as MPs in Irish parliaments; his sons Norbury and Thomas were named as beneficiaries of Archbishop Tenison's will. His offspring were the forerunners of the Hanbury-Tenison family of Lough Bawn, co. Monaghan.   H. T. WELCH

Sources J. B. Leslie, *Clogher clergy and parishes* (1929) · W. Harris, ed., *The whole works of James Ware concerning Ireland, revised and improved, including 'The writers of Ireland'*, 2 vols. (1764) · H. Cotton, *Fasti ecclesiae Hibernicae*, 4 vols. (1878) · R. Mant, *History of the Church of Ireland, from the Reformation*, 2 vols. (1840) · Burke, *Gen. Ire.* (1976) · Foster, *Alum. Oxon.* · admissions book, TCD, MUN V/23/1, fol. 32 · Burtchaell & Sadleir, *Alum. Dubl.* · *The story of St Bees, 1583–1939: a souvenir of the 350th anniversary of the opening of St Bees School* (1939) · *DNB* · A. Acheson, *A history of the Church of Ireland, 1691–1996* (1997)

Archives NL Ire. | TCD, corresp. with William King
Wealth at death gave £200 for widows and orphans of clergy: *DNB*

Tenison, Thomas (1636–1715), archbishop of Canterbury, was born at Cottenham, Cambridgeshire, on 29 September 1636 and baptized there on 2 October, the son of John Tenison (1599–1671), curate of the parish, and Mercy, eldest daughter of Thomas Dowsing of Cottenham.

Education and early career In 1637 John Tenison became rector of Mundesley, Norfolk, and in 1641 of Topcroft, Norfolk, but, as a royalist, he was ejected from Mundesley during the interregnum, while retaining the latter. A kinsman of Sir Thomas Browne of Norwich, the future archbishop was educated at Norwich School, where at the age of twelve he was reportedly deeply shocked by Charles I's execution, later calling it 'an execrable murther' (Tenison, *Argument*, 25). In April 1653 he entered Corpus Christi College, Cambridge, as a Parker scholar. Here he was probably influenced by the Cambridge Platonists, who sought to lift religion from a dispute over theological niceties to a set of universal principles. A particular influence among them was Ralph Cudworth, who refuted Thomas Hobbes's *Leviathan*. Among Tenison's fellow students were his future episcopal colleagues John Tillotson, Richard Kidder, Robert Grove, Simon Patrick, and James Gardiner. Tenison graduated BA in 1657, but with Anglican prospects so uncertain he, like others, briefly studied physick instead of seeking orders. In 1659, however, the deprived Bishop Brian Duppa of Salisbury secretly ordained him at Richmond upon Thames: Anglican ordinations were still forbidden. Reportedly meticulous rather than brilliant as a student, Tenison proceeded MA in 1660 (incorporated at Oxford in June 1664), became a fellow of Corpus in March 1662, and proceeded BD in 1667 and DD in 1680.

Briefly rector of Bracon Ash (1661–2), near Norwich, Tenison resigned it in favour of his father in 1662, when Francis Wilford, the new dean of Ely and master of Corpus, presented him to the prestigious parish of St Andrew the Great, Cambridge (1662–7). Here he made an impact on both town and university. In particular he won considerable reputation during the plague for being the only college fellow to remain in residence, and at great personal risk, but fortified by 'a preservative powder … administered in wine' (*Masters' History*, 191), he constantly cared for his stricken parish throughout the crisis; when he resigned in 1667 his parishioners gave him a handsome commemorative silver tankard.

The year 1667 was significant for Tenison. He married Anne (*d.* 1714), daughter of Richard Love (*d.* 1661), the former dean of Ely and master of Corpus Christi. He also became rector of Holywell with Needingworth, Huntingdonshire, a parish in the gift of the earl of Manchester, whose chaplain he had been for some years. Methodical as ever, Tenison drew up a terrier of land belonging to the church and established a charity for the poor. Meanwhile he became chaplain to the king, but, more important, he was also making his name as a writer. In 1670 he published *The Creed of Mr Hobbes examin'd*, dedicated to Manchester. Reportedly a more succinct critique of Thomas Hobbes

Thomas Tenison (1636–1715), by Robert White, before 1702

than Cudworth's, it was a popular work, perhaps partly instrumental in Oxford University's condemnation of *Leviathan* in 1683. He followed this with *A Discourse on Idolatry* (1677), the first of many contentious pamphlets attacking Rome, and *Baconia* (1678), an academic work praising Bacon's work and placing him ahead of Copernicus, Galileo, and Harvey. In 1673 it may have been his kinship with Sir Thomas Browne that led to his becoming upper minister at St Peter Mancroft, Norwich, the centre of religious life in the city, a post he held for only eighteen months. After Browne's death Tenison edited his papers, which he published in 1685.

St Martin-in-the-Fields Tenison's reputation as parish priest in Cambridge and Huntingdonshire and as a controversialist led to further promotion; he was recommended to the lord chancellor, Heneage Finch, first earl of Nottingham, for the living of St Martin-in-the-Fields in October 1680. Here Tenison was joining Nottingham's distinguished London circle of churchmen, including John Tillotson, John Sharp, Edward Stillingfleet, Simon Patrick, and Richard Kidder. St Martin's itself was a large, prestigious parish at the centre of the capital's life. As pastor he was also extremely busy—in a randomly chosen month there were seventy-seven baptisms, 144 burials, and four marriages; communions were at least monthly. The diarist John Evelyn was concerned about his busy life. After applauding his preaching and his 'most holy conversation' he feared for his health: 'the insuperable pains he takes and care of his parish will I fear wear him out' (Evelyn, 4.307).

Tenison remained in this key parish for eleven years,

years of considerable turbulence, and contributed significantly to London's vibrant ecclesiastical life. For instance, in 1681 'devout young men' of the parish formed a society for a life of regular prayer meetings and strict rules as to behaviour (Spurr, 133). His own parishioners included many leading national figures. Those he attended at their deaths included Edward Turberville, the informer, and in 1687 Nell Gwyn. He was heavily criticized for preaching at the latter's funeral and, at the height of anxieties about the advance of popery under James II, for distributing in her name charity money among poor papists. Most significant of all was the duke of Monmouth, a regular worshipper at St Martin's. During his confinement at the Tower after his rebellion it was to Tenison that he turned for spiritual counsel. In July 1685 Tenison joined bishops Thomas Ken and Francis Turner, and George Hooper, rector of Lambeth, for the duke's last hours before execution. Though reportedly speaking more gently than the others, he failed, as they did, to persuade him to be reconciled to his wife and to admit his guilt as a rebel. He too had to refuse Monmouth the sacrament, and with them attended him on the scaffold. Hostile though he was to popery, Tenison would not countenance open rebellion.

Tenison's incumbency of St Martin's coincided with a phenomenal increase in its population, rising from 19,000 in 1660 to 38,000 ten years later and 69,000 in 1685. Little wonder that he concurred with parliament's further division of the parish in establishing St James-in-the-Fields, now St James's, Piccadilly. (St Anne-in-the-Fields, now St Anne's, Soho, had already been hived off in 1678.) Tenison retained both St Martin's and St James's until his preferment to the bishopric of Lincoln. He also set up a chapel of ease in Swallow Street (now Regent Street), and later moved a wooden former Catholic chapel from Hounslow Heath to Conduit Street for Anglican use; this later became St George's, Hanover Square. A bibliophile himself, he recognized that clergy and tutors for the nobility in his parish needed free access to books; in 1684, at his own expense and advised by John Evelyn and Christopher Wren, he built a library, the first public library in London, in which he deposited many books and manuscripts. With education as another lifelong interest, he was an early pioneer of charity schools, establishing St Martin's free school for the poor in 1683, and another in St James's parish a few years later. With a Renaissance spirit he took personal care in searching out efficient teachers and intelligent, needy pupils whom he encouraged to enter university. Near the end of his life he founded a school for poor girls in Lambeth, in which his wife showed 'constant and prudent care' (will, PRO, PROB 11/550, sig. 3), and a charity school in Croydon in 1714.

Roman controversy and revolution As vicar of St Martin's, Tenison was at the epicentre of the increasingly heated Romanist debates and convulsions of the 1680s. Suited to the role, he entered fully into the constant pamphleteering. He may have remembered the interregnum with horror, but the increasing identification of the monarchy with Romanism, subtle under Charles II, overt under James II, propelled Tenison energetically into the fray.

Catholics came to recognize him as a leading opponent; this was so much the case that his colleague, Simon Patrick, had to warn him of the danger he was courting. As early as 1678 he had published *A Discourse on Idolatry*, antipapist in substance, though academic in style. Once at St Martin's, however, time for scholarship was shorter, and his later pamphlets were less well researched and increasingly contentious. His sermon at St Sepulchre's, London (1681), entitled 'Concerning discretion in giving alms', degenerated into a vituperative attack on Catholic institutions, in particular charities, and caused much animosity. This was followed by *A Discourse Concerning a Guide on Matters of Faith* (1683), a work on the question of authority, on where a true basis for religious truth could be found; this he republished in 1687. With James II's accession in 1685 the controversy intensified, and St Martin's became more than ever the Anglican bastion. When James tried to silence John Sharp, rector of St Giles-in-the-Fields, in 1686, Tenison threw himself into the struggle, and possibly played a major part in his restoration. In 1687 he published *The Difference betwixt Protestant and Socinian Methods*, defending Anglicanism against false Catholic claims, and with William Claggett he published a bibliography of the controversy, *The Present State of the Controversie between the Church of England and the Church of Rome*. In the same year he contributed *The Tenth Note, on Holiness* in a reply, with other leading churchmen, to Bellarmine's century-old fifteen notes of the true church. Even more significant was his impassioned public debate the following September with Andrew Pulton, master of the Jesuit College at the Savoy. In this high-profile encounter Tenison led the Anglican side. He was now noted as an effective and potent protagonist of the Anglican church, a dangerous role at the time, and again contributed to the increasing flood of pamphlets. Converts too became highly prized: Tenison, for instance, constructed a special liturgy at St Martin's for receiving John Taffe, a former Irish Capuchin, into the Anglican church.

Tenison was a leader of the London agitation following the second declaration of indulgence (27 April 1688). After a gathering of London clergy Archbishop William Sancroft invited him to attend the bishops' meetings at Lambeth on 11 May, and again more crucially on 18 May, when they decided to petition the king. On the following Sunday, 20 May, like many others, Tenison refused to read the declaration. Throughout the crisis until the bishops' acquittal he was the vital link between them and the clergy. Though Tenison was thus a potent force as leader of the London clergy, little is known of his part in the discussions which later led to James's abject capitulation to the Anglican bishops in what has become known as 'the Anglican Revolution' (Goldie, 108). Tensions rose. On 30 September, when a Jesuit preacher at the Savoy, probably Pulton, attacked Anglicanism, the crowds publicly dragged him from his pulpit. Tenison, as a leading Anglican apologist, preached his reply at a crowded service at St Martin's.

After James's departure Tenison, fully backing the new

regime, was still at the heart of affairs. Though the revolution ended the controversy's intensity Tenison edited and published, as editor, *Popery not Founded on Scripture* and a translation of La Placette's *Of the Incurable Scepticism of the Church of Rome*. In the weeks before the Convention, which eventually offered William and Mary the throne, he was closely in touch with political and church leaders.

Comprehension With the incoming regime ecclesiastical affairs took a new turn with a revived attempt by Daniel Finch, second earl of Nottingham, secretary of state, and senior moderate clergy to effect a rapprochement between the established church and dissenters. On 14 January 1689 Tenison was one of several moderates, including John Tillotson, Simon Patrick, and William Lloyd, who met at the house of the dean of St Paul's, Edward Stillingfleet, to discuss the possibility of making concessions. A twin package was proposed: a comprehension bill to bring most dissenters, principally presbyterians, back into the church, and a toleration bill to allow the rest to worship elsewhere. Finch introduced these in the Lords in February 1689. When the comprehension bill failed the following May, Tenison joined the commission appointed by William III to review the liturgy, canons, and ecclesiastical courts with comprehension in mind. His earlier work, *An Argument for Union* (1683), had already identified him as a leading protagonist for comprehension and protestant union, and now in 1689 he published anonymously *A Discourse Concerning the Ecclesiastical Commission Opened in the Jerusalem Chamber* to promote its cause. Typically conscientious, he attended seventeen of the eighteen sessions, and was on the eventual informal subcommittee, suggesting suitable alterations to the prayer book; meticulous as usual, he set about collecting words in the liturgy that gave most offence. Tenison's eagerness for comprehension, and, in particular, his reported lack of support for episcopal reordination of dissenting ministers, antagonized many.

The commission's debates were on the whole dignified, but convocation, meeting on 21 November to discuss its proposals, was not. All attempts by Tenison and others to persuade members to agree on comprehension were met with hostility, and the proposals came to nothing. Convocation was adjourned in December and later dissolved with parliament without passing any judgment on the commission's proposals. Tenison was acutely disappointed. Though he briefly considered raising the issue again in the mid-1690s he never tried to challenge the verdict. The bid for comprehension had failed. Like others, he, however, accepted occasional conformity as a suitable, though unsatisfactory, compromise, much to the hostility of tories and high-churchmen.

Archdeacon, diocesan bishop, and primate Already Tenison was highly respected for his work in Cambridge and at St Martin's, and for his leadership of the London clergy in James's reign, so it was not surprising that Gilbert Burnet recommended him, with nine others, to William III for early preferment. Consequently the crown, using its prerogative, appointed him archdeacon of London; Bishop

Henry Compton of London instituted him on 26 October 1689. Tenison retained his incumbencies at St Martin's and St James's. Apart from his annual visitations, there is little evidence of his personal activities in his brief spell as archdeacon.

Further preferment followed late in 1691, when William nominated Tenison to the important see of Lincoln; Tillotson, with the bishops of London, Worcester, and Ely assisting, consecrated him in Lambeth Palace chapel on 19 January 1692. Lincoln was a huge diocese of five archdeaconries and fifty deaneries, sadly neglected by his scholarly predecessor, Thomas Barlow. Tenison, with his usual energy and zeal, at once sought to restore order, root out slackness, and keep a firm eye on the clergy. His first visitation between April and June lasted at least five weeks, during which he travelled over 400 miles. His spell at Lincoln was brief. Though further preferment came too soon for him to achieve notable results, he laid solid foundations for his successor, James Gardiner.

In 1693 Tenison was offered the archbishopric of Dublin, but despite pressure from the Irish episcopate he refused, possibly on his wife's advice. Tillotson died on 22 November 1694, recommending Tenison as his successor at Canterbury. Though other names were suggested, principally Edward Stillingfleet and John Hall, others pressed for Tenison 'as less high in his notions and temper' (Carpenter, 132), and William appointed him on 6 December. In many ways he was an admirable compromise. Already respected for his previous work he had been helped by the first earl of Nottingham, worked closely with the second over comprehension, and was now adviser to the Sunderland family. Naturally opinions were divided. To some he was recognized as a person of great learning, piety, and moderation, who had already been marked out by Romish priests and Jesuits. Tories, like Thomas Hearne, however, noted that he lacked sense and judgement, and that he would be a tool of the whigs. Formally elected on 15 January 1695 he was enthroned at Canterbury in person on 16 May, the first primate since the Reformation to be thus installed. Meanwhile he had been in constant attendance at the bedside of Queen Mary prior to her death on 28 December 1694. Subsequently he gave spiritual counsel to the bereft king, and probably persuaded him to put aside his mistress Elizabeth Villiers. Tenison preached at Queen Mary's funeral on 5 March 1695.

Reform and discipline of the church Tenison became primate at the end of fifty years of political and ecclesiastical turmoil. He immediately set out to improve the reputation of the clergy, which in an age of cynicism and immorality was low. In 1695 he revived the archbishop's court, summoned Thomas Watson, bishop of St David's, to answer charges of simony, and deprived him of his see. His predecessor, Tillotson, and Queen Mary had already planned in 1694 the issue of eighteen royal injunctions for the strict enforcement of the canons of 1604, which their deaths late that year had prevented. Tenison continued the policy and persuaded King William to issue the injunctions, which he amplified with his own *Rules and Orders*. He aimed to establish a well-educated, competent, and loyal clergy, and to keep pluralities within the bounds of the law. To achieve the first he reinforced ordination procedures, laid down by canons 34 and 35, to ensure that candidates were men of integrity and of sufficient educational standard. He himself was reportedly tough examining his own Canterbury ordinands and in interrogating future incumbents before institution. He also tackled the problem of pluralities and non-residence, then a major church abuse. In the Canterbury diocese he insisted on strict adherence to canon law, but he was equally exacting elsewhere. He used his special primatial authority for issuing dispensations, and with the help of his chaplain, Edmund Gibson, he meticulously investigated each petition for plurality. Apart from demanding a certificate of consent from relevant diocesan bishops he often made his own additional enquiries. On one occasion in January 1712 he was in conflict with the queen herself. When she legitimately used the royal prerogative to issue a dispensation for plurality Tenison protested. In a long, respectful, but vehement letter of criticism he dubbed her 'the nursing mother' of the church and himself its 'watchman or shepherd' (Carpenter, 164). Significantly, the archbishop had his way.

The Canterbury diocese and All Souls College, Oxford Like earlier primates Tenison was eager to make Canterbury a model for other dioceses. Immediately after installation he carried out his primary visitation during which he confirmed almost 4000 candidates. This was unusual, for few archbishops visited and confirmed in the Canterbury diocese. Some, like Sancroft, sent other prelates to deputize every few years, but others, such as Gilbert Sheldon and John Tillotson, failed to do even this. One incumbent, Thomas Brett, tory though he was, was appreciative. Tenison, he wrote, 'has done more than any other of his predecessors for these hundred years' (Brett, 245). Not only did he visit and confirm 'very frequently', he made sure the ceremonies were not 'in a hurry or huddle' (ibid., 244) as elsewhere, but administered with decorum in small groups at a time with questions and answers made audible. 'Nothing could be more solemn, decent and regular' (ibid., 245). Similarly he broke with tradition by personally conferring priests' and deacons' orders five times in twenty years. This was rare then for archbishops, who normally conferred only episcopal orders. In his last years, when confined to Lambeth through ill health, he continued to show concern for the Canterbury clergy's welfare. In 1706 he gave the cathedral a handsome throne carved by Grinling Gibbons.

As archbishop Tenison was also visitor of All Souls College, Oxford, a role he took seriously. In 1698 he ended a long-running dispute over the election as warden of Leopold Finch (son of the second earl of Winchilsea and a kinsman of Nottingham's) by declaring the wardenship vacant and personally reappointing Finch to the post. Four years later he was at odds with Finch's reforming tory successor, Bernard Gardiner, over the warden's right of veto in fellows' elections, especially in cases of non-residence. Tenison again acted decisively. Through his vicar-general he carried out, in 1710, a rare formal visitation of the college—performed by only archbishops Cranmer and Whitgift before—and annulled the warden's right of veto.

Reformation of manners As archbishop Tenison eventually gave energetic support to the movement which sprang up in the 1690s to combat the flood of vice seen as engulfing society. He knew Restoration London only too well. Unlike some bishops, however, he had initial misgivings over supporting the growing number of interdenominational societies for the reformation of manners, principally because they gave the lead in combating sin to civil magistrates rather than to the clergy. His circular letter to the bishops in April 1699, following the king's proclamation on the subject, emphasized the duty of the clergy to catechize parishioners thoroughly and thus imbue them with the faith. Only thus would true moral reformation take place, and other methods would be rendered unnecessary.

Tenison campaigned in other ways for moral reform. He hoped to tighten the lax procedures concerning marriage. In the 1690s he was partly responsible for drafting two acts designed to help eradicate clandestine marriages by insisting on marriage only by banns or licence. Both by letter and by injunction he requested the bishops' support, especially in preventing the common abuse whereby officials issued blank marriage licences. The press and stage were also in his sights. In 1698 he unsuccessfully introduced a bill to outlaw blasphemous and scandalous publications, and he hoped for strict government surveillance of the theatre; though unsuccessful in this he and Dean Thomas Sherlock of St Paul's managed to get one playhouse closed. As late as 1711 the queen herself was still appalled by the 'looseness and corruption of manners' and 'the neglect of wholesome discipline' (Brown, 338), and in August 1711 she wrote to Tenison requesting the bishops' support.

Patronage and politics On becoming primate Tenison strove to continue the moderate consensus achieved thus far by Nottingham and Tillotson, 'a dogged rearguard action to prevent the church ... from becoming the battlefield of political faction', as it, in fact, did under Queen Anne (Bennett, 'William III', 105). Tenison himself tried to project impartial churchmanship, even taking care to use Caroline ceremonies and devotions in his chapel at Lambeth. After Queen Mary's death William III set up a commission of the two archbishops and four other prelates to recommend preferments. With his presence essential for a quorum and holding the casting vote Tenison's authority was paramount. Despite his earlier London friendship with John Sharp, now archbishop of York, differences in personality and Tenison's suspicion of him as a high-churchman created friction between the two men: decisions were often made in Lambeth without Sharp's participation. By 1698, with William's political situation deteriorating, the preferments commission hardly met, and Tenison soon found himself in the eye of a political storm. Whigs and tories both entered the fray. Whigs, for instance, pressed the archbishop for the preferment of William Talbot to Worcester, only to find that he went to the poor see of Oxford. Tory ecclesiastics, led by three discontented prelates, Henry Compton, Jonathan Trelawny, and Thomas Sprat, and the mercurial Francis Atterbury, pressed for a sitting convocation, still in abeyance since 1689. This Tillotson and Tenison had consistently advised William to avoid, but now the old policy of moderation was in ruins. Late in 1700 William bowed to pressure and allowed convocation to sit and debate.

Now Tenison was at the centre of conflict, exposed to every shaft of tory venom. Predictably the lower house, energized by Atterbury and led by its prolocutor for 1701, George Hooper, was in no mood for courtesies. Apart from discussion of the book *Christianity not Mysterious* by the deist John Toland, much heated debate centred on the lower house's claim to independence, especially its right to continue sitting and debating beyond the primate's formal notice of prorogation. From the first Hooper consistently ignored Tenison's order to adjourn, and the house often continued sitting, eventually adjourning itself. On one occasion, when Tenison summoned Hooper to appear in the upper house, Tenison, ironically, adopted highchurch tones in lecturing him on episcopal authority over lower clergy. They took little notice. Frequent angry verbal altercations followed between the two men until convocation's final session in June. Parliament was soon prorogued and then dissolved, and with it convocation. Tenison had remained firm against a hostile and bitter lower house, but not without being appalled by the vehemence of tory attacks, even being branded in 1702 as a servile party hack bullying his fellow ministers of the gospel for whig ends.

With William III's death Tenison's fortunes and influence diminished noticeably, for Queen Anne already distrusted whigs. In seeking ecclesiastical advice Anne turned not to Tenison, but to the moderate tories Nottingham and Sharp. Though Tenison perforce crowned her, it was Sharp who she insisted preach at the coronation. Nevertheless Tenison remained politically active until beset by illness. At least until September 1710 Anne invited him, when fit enough, to join ministers at weekly meetings of the formal cabinet council. Until mid-1709, when his health declined further, he was frequently in the Lords; in 1703 and 1704, for instance, he led ten prelates vigorously into opposition against the occasional conformity bills of 1703 and 1704, which, largely owing to him, were rejected. Later he spoke fervently in favour of the Anglo-Scottish union.

As to patronage, however, Tenison was marginalized; only in 1705, with Lord Treasurer Godolphin's support, did he manage to get his protégé William Wake appointed to Lincoln. Until then all appointments went to highchurchmen, such as Hooper and William Beveridge. Even during the whig ascendancy after 1708, and despite personal approaches to the queen, his influence was negligible; even whig ministers in their temporary supremacy could not deliver the appointments that Tenison wanted, with the one exception of Charles Trimnell to Norwich

(1709). Indeed in 1708 Anne appointed two tories, Sir William Dawes and Offspring Blackall, secretly in her closet, without either prelates or whig ministers knowing. Tenison broke with tradition the following February by absenting himself from their consecration at Lambeth, supposedly on grounds of ill health.

Throughout both reigns Tenison was a passionate supporter of the new regime and a continuing protestant succession. He attended both Mary and William at their deaths, and crowned Anne. His sermon at Mary's funeral provoked the bitter criticism of the non-juror Thomas Ken for failing to persuade her to confess her shortcomings in supplanting her father. Tenison maintained a dignified silence. When Anne's only surviving child died in 1700 Tenison strongly supported the passage of the Act of Settlement (1701), thus ensuring the Hanoverian succession. From then onwards, as perhaps its leading protagonist, he frequently corresponded with Electress Sophia of Hanover, even sending her a chaplain and Anglican prayer books. His support for a protestant succession was but part of his passionate vendetta against Catholicism. Under William III he had already been involved in government surveillance of suspicious messages from abroad, and, unusually for a bishop, he had voted for the attainder of Sir John Fenwick in 1696. In 1706, using royal authority, he requested bishops to list all advowsons and schools in Catholic hands. Tenison maintained his vigorous antipapist pursuit into his last years.

Meanwhile, running battles in convocation continued. Autocratic again and now sick and impatient, when a new convocation met in 1708 he instantly prorogued it without even allowing prayers. In the tory years that followed (1710–14) the tables turned. The firebrand Atterbury won election as prolocutor in 1711, and secured the exclusion of the archbishop from automatic presidency of convocation. For Tenison, already marginalized, this was another calculated slight. Perhaps he lacked sufficient leadership, imagination, and even sense of humour to make the lower house amenable, but with convocation as a focus of the reign's running political and ecclesiastical battle, the gulf was unbridgeable.

During this tory spell the phalanx of whig prelates maintained a defiant front against the ministry, benevolently but firmly disciplined by Tenison, though himself too sick to attend. All new episcopal appointments went to the tories, but Tenison need not have worried over the succession. The extremism of the Occasional Conformity Act (1711) and Schism Act (1714), placing further restrictions on nonconformists, mostly whig in their politics, ensured that most new prelates joined the Hanover tories, thus ensuring with the whigs the Hanoverian succession.

Theological conflict Remembering Cromwellian dissensions Tenison, as archbishop, was eager to keep theological peace while religious and political passions raged so fiercely. He dealt autocratically with any hint of heterodoxy; private thinking must not become public. Socinianism had recently revived in the writings of Stephen Nye and Thomas Firmin. In 1695 he drew up 'Directions … for the preserving unity in the church and the purity of the

Christian faith concerning the Holy Trinity', which he persuaded the king to issue under royal seal; judges again were to assist. Later still in 1711 he noted that a new Dutch translation of the Book of Common Prayer had been printed by a Dutch Socinian and lacked a trinitarian ascription. He ordered its total suppression and a new edition to be printed.

With William Whiston, the eccentric Lucasian professor of mathematics at Cambridge, Tenison was equally autocratic. Whiston was banished from the university in 1710 and deprived of his chair for his anti-trinitarian essay 'De trinitate' in his *Sermons and Essays* (1709), the book being condemned by convocation. He appealed to Tenison, who promptly laid it before convocation, this time formally, which infuriated Whiston, honest and well intentioned as he was. Whiston again appealed to Tenison after being refused communion in London; the archbishop again dealt with this curtly and formally without quiet sympathy, which might have yielded better results. In 1710, however, in a dispute over the possible rebaptism of dissenters, Tenison refused to condemn lay conduct of the rite. Though in this he followed traditional church teaching, his attitude incurred the hostility of high-church bishops and clergy of the lower house.

Tenison had little time for the nonjurors, who refused to swear allegiance to William and Mary. He failed to understand them. A youthful Stuart supporter in Cromwellian times, he, however, had no difficulty at all in owing allegiance to William and Mary rather than James II. Later experience had made him firmly whig. For him having a protestant sovereign was the church's only security. His lengthy correspondence with the nonjuror Robert Nelson over a possible rapprochement came to nothing. While Jacobitism was still a potent force, he was too convinced a whig and too cautious a prelate to risk negotiations with so small a group.

The Society for the Propagation of the Gospel in Foreign Parts and the church overseas Tenison was the first archbishop to take sustained personal interest in the church's mission overseas, and positively encouraged Thomas Bray in founding the Society for the Propagation of the Gospel in Foreign Parts (1701). Once called 'the prime instrument for energetic Imperial Anglicanism' (Schlenther, 131), the society initially aimed to win American colonists of dissenting stock back to the church, and only then to convert native Americans. Tenison himself presided over its first meeting at Lambeth Palace and, annually re-elected as president, he chaired many of its later meetings at St Martin-in-the-Fields. He was often directly involved in its activities. When four Iroquois native American sachems (princes) went to London in April 1710, he showed particular interest, presiding over a special committee concerning them. Two years later he wrote warmly to them addressing them as 'My Lords', and provided money out of his own purse for the mission that followed (Tenison to sachems, 29 May 1712, BL, Stowe MS 119, fol. 73).

Though it was the bishop of London who officially licensed missionaries Tenison, even as late as 1710, insisted on vetting their credentials himself and meeting them before departure. He encouraged missionaries to send him reports and messages from as far afield as America, St Helena, and Tenerife. Always an educational enthusiast he was elected vice-chancellor of William and Mary College, Virginia, and later bequeathed books to a proposed college in Barbados.

Tenison was much concerned with the lack of episcopal oversight in the American colonies. Earlier attempts to supply bishops by William Laud and at the Restoration had failed. In 1705 Tenison brought the matter to the queen's attention. Possible candidates were named, a bishop's house bought in New Jersey, and a draft bill (1712) presented to parliament, but progress was too slow. Anne's death brought the scheme to a halt, and no more was done for decades. Tenison, however, bequeathed £1000 for two protestant bishoprics. Certainly his work for the Society for the Propagation of the Gospel was substantial; a contemporary spoke of his practical wisdom as president, putting 'a stop to many indirect motions and steps made to put us out of the way' (Kennett, 123).

Nor was Tenison's overseas concern confined to Anglicans. In March 1698 he welcomed Tsar Peter of Russia with his priests to hold discussions and to witness an ordination; in 1701 he entertained a Greek patriarch at Lambeth. King Frederick I of Prussia's request for advice about introducing the Anglican liturgy and episcopacy into his kingdom, however, met with a lukewarm response.

Ireland and Scotland The Irish church interested Tenison. In November 1690 he served on William III's commission to eradicate its considerable abuses, and in 1693 he was pressed to accept the archbishopric of Dublin, which he refused. Later the Irish episcopate asked him, once installed at Lambeth, to keep informal oversight over their church, which he did, especially during William's reign. Though Tenison left no obvious impression on the Irish church, his close contact with it was beneficial. He was instrumental in having conscientious men appointed to bishoprics, and his frequent contact by letter with most Irish prelates, especially Narcissus Marsh, archbishop of Dublin, did much to raise morale at a difficult time. Simultaneously he kept English government officials in Ireland sympathetic to the church's needs, while his influence at Whitehall helped curb the illegal activities of Irish presbyterians, then increasing in strength with the influx of French Huguenots and Scottish immigrants.

Scottish episcopalians after the revolution of 1688 felt beleaguered by, and indeed suffered from, the presbyterian nature of the religious settlement in that country. Tenison took his duty seriously and stoutly supported them by presenting William III with a detailed memorandum of grievances and by writing to Scottish ministers about their poverty. He also took an active part in the commission negotiating for Anglo-Scottish union (1702–5). He regularly attended its meetings, gladly approved the outcome, and led crucial episcopal support for the bill in the Lords. He fended off tory taunts that he, as archbishop, was voting for presbyterian government of the Scottish church. He viewed the matter pragmatically: to him the

Church of Scotland was 'as true a protestant church as the Church of England, though he could not say it was so perfect' (McCormick, 759–60). Nevertheless, as part of the Union package in February 1707 Tenison introduced a bill for the security of the Church of England to safeguard its doctrine and liturgy, as a parallel to the Kirk Act for Scotland. Largely through his efforts—though he was too ill to attend the debates—the United Kingdom parliament went further in 1712, passing a Toleration Act for Scotland, thus ensuring the Scottish episcopalian church a definite legal basis.

Last years, decline, and death In later years Tenison's friends affectionately dubbed him Old Totius, a nickname derived from his official title Totius Angliae Primas. Even so, after George I's accession Tenison still felt isolated and impotent, for Charles Townshend needed tory support for his ministry. Tenison disapproved not only of the new royal court, but the church too with its 'motley bench and motley synod' (Sykes, *William Wake*, 2.99). 'All our Church matters are at sixes and sevens', he expostulated (ibid., 100). Though John Wynne and Richard Willes, both whigs, were raised to the episcopate, Tenison took no part in choosing them. In fact, in his last years he had little contact with his fellow bishops, except formally through chaplains. His relations with them were now poor, as they adjusted to the new regime.

For years Tenison had suffered from gout. As early as 1704 he had missed some meetings of the cabinet council. Early in 1707, rudely cajoled by Lord Somers, the leading whig, over episcopal appointments and in great pain, he visited the queen, only to be rebuffed. In June that year he complained of being 'very lame' and unable to 'go abroad' (Sykes, *Queen Anne*, 441). He last attended a normal session of the Lords in March 1709, and presided over his last consecration of bishops (Philip Bisse and John Robinson) on 19 November 1710; at the five remaining consecrations of his life other bishops presided in his place. Even so, with remarkable resilience he had a firm grip on life. His health was precarious enough in 1711 for tory circles to suggest the apparently imminent succession to Canterbury of the tory John Robinson. At Christmas 1713 the end was again reported near, but, cheating the tories, his tenacious grip on life lasted long enough for him to see the Hanoverians safely installed. Meanwhile his mind was still sharp to the end. Even as late as 1711 to 1714 he was often writing to William Wake over pastoral minutiae in the diocese of Lincoln. He rallied to take centre stage among the fourteen men appointed as regency commissioners in the Lords on 5 August 1714 when George was declared king. Sick though he was he actually crowned the new monarch on 20 October, and ironically it was his antagonist, Atterbury, who bore the crown from the altar for him. In 1715 with other prelates he issued a condemnation of the Jacobite rising. Eventually Old Totius died at Lambeth Palace on 14 December 1715 and was buried simply, as he wished, in the chancel of Lambeth parish church in the following week. Wake was rapidly appointed his successor two days later. Tenison's wife, Anne, had died a year earlier. They had no surviving children.

Assessment and subsequent reputation Tenison was vilified in his lifetime, by James II as 'that dull man' with 'languid oration' (Carpenter, 405) and by Jonathan Swift as 'the dullest good for nothing man I ever knew' (Forster, 1.180n.). Yet his friend Evelyn wrote that he had not met 'a man of a more universal and generous spirit, with so much modesty, prudence and piety' (Evelyn, 5.66). His underlying qualities were already apparent before becoming primate. Meticulous both academically and administratively he was a devoted, courageous, and conscientious pastor in Cambridge, Holywell, and St Martin's. An effective preacher who drew crowds of listeners and a potent and marked controversialist against Catholics in the 1680s, he was an enthusiast for comprehension in 1689. A bibliophile, he opened libraries and founded schools, three of which, in Kennington, Croydon, and Lambeth, still bear his name. He was a dynamic bishop of Lincoln.

Once Tenison became primate these underlying qualities were still apparent, though they were soon to be obscured. Even in his last years he still concerned himself with the details of pastoral care in his own see and in the wider church. He worked to improve the quality of the clergy and the moral standards of the nation. He supported episcopalians in Scotland and Ireland, and cultivated a deep interest in the church's mission overseas, both as first president of the Society for the Propagation of the Gospel and in promoting the need for bishops in the American colonies. Theologically he would brook no public debate of apparently wayward theological ideas, and remained hostile towards Catholicism.

Though at first, while he tried to keep tempers cool, the future promised well, Tenison quickly fell victim to the hideous religious and political passions that soon flared up. Thereafter, weakened by illness, often in acute pain, and drained of energy by the political and religious kaleidoscope of Anne's reign, he cut a beleaguered, lonely, almost dreary, figure in the confusing, battering world around him. Marginalized by the queen and court, even harassed by whigs for supposed inactivity in promoting their men and cause, he was later ignored by George I's administration. The vigorous activist of the 1680s had become the enfeebled, almost solitary figure of the 1700s. Nevertheless, despite his sickness he remained active in mind, and maintained a vigorous correspondence in pursuit of his objectives. It was as late as 2 December 1715, a few days before his death, that he made the important codicil to his will bequeathing funds for American bishoprics. A generous man with a reportedly strong Fenland country accent, he made numerous legacies at his death. Devoted to the 1688 revolution and the Hanoverian succession, he experienced his participation in George I's coronation as indeed a crowning moment. Old Totius may have been to some 'a dull and prosaic man'; he was also 'by any account … a great primate' (Bennett, *Tory Crisis*, 20), even if his true greatness was partly obscured.

WILLIAM MARSHALL

Sources E. Carpenter, *Thomas Tenison, archbishop of Canterbury* (1948) · E. G. Rupp, *Religion in England, 1688–1791* (1986) · G. V. Bennett, *The tory crisis in church and state, 1688–1730: the career of Francis*

Atterbury, bishop of Rochester (1975) · G. V. Bennett, *White Kennett, 1660–1728, bishop of Peterborough* (1957) · G. V. Bennett, 'William III and the episcopate', *Essays in modern church history*, ed. G. V. Bennett and J. D. Walsh (1966), 104–31 · N. Sykes, 'Episcopal administration in England in the eighteenth century', *EngHR*, 47 (1932), 414–46 · N. Sykes, 'Queen Anne and the episcopate', *EngHR*, 50 (1935), 433–64 · G. S. Holmes, *British politics in the age of Anne* (1967) · N. Sykes, *William Wake, archbishop of Canterbury, 1657–1737* (1957) · *Memoirs of the life and times of Thomas Tenison, archbishop of Canterbury* (1716?) · N. Sykes, *From Sheldon to Secker: aspects of English church history, 1660–1768* (1959) · bishop of London's register, 1675–1715, GL, MS 9531/17 · Archbishop Tenison's registers 1, 2.1, 2.2, LPL · GL, Archdeacon of London MSS, 09057/2, 09060A/4, 09059/6, 9811/1 · parish register, St Andrew's, Cambridge, Cambs. AS, P23/1/1 · parish register, Holywell, Cambs. AS, Huntingdon, Huntingdon 2280 · *Masters' History of the college of Corpus Christi and the Blessed Virgin Mary in the University of Cambridge*, ed. J. Lamb (1831) · T. Brett, *An account of church government*, 2nd edn (1710) · G. Holmes, *Augustan England* (1982) · G. S. Holmes, *The making of a great power: late Stuart and early Georgian Britain, 1660–1722* (1993) · E. Gregg, *Queen Anne* (1980) · Venn, *Alum. Cant.* · A. T. Hart, *John Sharp, archbishop of York* (1949) · G. V. Bennett, 'Robert Harley, the Godolphin ministry, and the bishoprics crisis of 1707', *EngHR*, 82 (1967), 726–46 · *JHL*, 15–20 (1691–1718) · G. Hennessy, *Novum repertorium ecclesiasticum parochiale Londinense, or, London diocesan clergy succession from the earliest time to the year 1898* (1898) · Evelyn, *Diary* · B. S. Schlenther, 'Religious faith and commercial empire', *The Oxford illustrated history of the British empire: the eighteenth century*, ed. P. J. Marshall (1998), 128–50 · T. Tenison, *An argument for union* (1683) · J. Forster, *The life of Jonathan Swift* (1875) · E. Calamy, *An historical account of my own life, with some reflections on the times I have lived in, 1671–1731*, ed. J. T. Rutt, 2 vols. (1829) · *The letters and diplomatic instructions of Queen Anne*, ed. B. C. Brown (1935) · T. Tenison, *Baconiana* (1679) · F. Blomefield and C. Parkin, *An essay towards a topographical history of the county of Norfolk*, [2nd edn], 11 vols. (1805–10), vol. 6 · Tenison commonplace book, V&A NAL, MS F48.D40 · T. E. S. Clarke and H. C. Foxcroft, *A life of Gilbert Burnet, bishop of Salisbury* (1907) · *Remarks and collections of Thomas Hearne*, ed. C. E. Doble and others, 11 vols., OHS, 2, 7, 13, 34, 42–3, 48, 50, 65, 67, 72 (1885–1921) · *State papers and letters addressed to William Carstares*, ed. J. M'Cormick (1774) · *Memoirs of Thomas, earl of Ailesbury*, ed. W. E. Buckley, 2 vols., Roxburghe Club, 122 (1890) · W. Newton, *The life of the right reverend Dr White Kennett, late lord bishop of Peterborough* (1730) · private information (2004) [Norwich School; Archbishop Tenison's School, Kennington] · will, PRO, PROB 11/550, sig. 3, fols. 19v–25r · M. Goldie, 'The political thought of the Anglican revolution', *The revolutions of 1688*, ed. R. Beddard (1991), 102–36 · C. Rose, *England in the 1690s: revolution, religion and war* (1999) · T. Tenison, *A discourse concerning the ecclesiastical commission opened in the Jerusalem chamber* (1689) · J. Boulton, 'The poor among the rich: paupers and the parish in the West End, 1600–1724', *Londinopolis: essays in the social and cultural history of early modern London*, ed. P. Griffiths and M. S. R. Jenner (2000), 197–225 · J. Spurr, 'The church, the societies and the moral revolution of 1688', *The Church of England, c.1689–c.1833: from toleration to tractarianism*, ed. J. Walsh, C. Haydon, and S. Taylor (1993), 127–42 · letter of Archbishop Tenison introducing a missionary to the 'Sachim' of North America, BL, Stowe MS 119, fol. 73 · observations on the Dutch translation of the Book of Common Prayer, BL, Stowe MS 117, fols. 51–65 · J. Gregory, *Restoration, reformation and reform, 1660–1828: archbishops of Canterbury and their diocese* (2000) · E. Carpenter, *The protestant bishop, being the life of Henry Compton, 1632–1713, bishop of London* (1956)

Archives LPL, corresp., papers, collections · NL Wales, letters · PRO, estate papers, C111/65 · V&A NAL, commonplace book | Bodl. Oxf., letters to Gilbert Burnet · LPL, corresp. relating to American affairs · LPL, corresp. with and relating to United Society for the Propagation of the Gospel · TCD, corresp. with William King

Likenesses M. Beale, oils, 1681–8, Bishop's House, Lincoln · attrib. M. Beale, portrait, c.1692, CCC Cam. · oils, 1695 (after engraving by R. White, c.1695–1702), NPG · attrib. S. Dubois, oils, c.1700, LPL · R. White, print, before 1702, BM [*see illus.*] · portrait, 1795, St Paul's/Sion College, London · circle of Kneller, portrait · oils, Knole, Kent

Tennant, Charles (1768–1838), chemical manufacturer, born on 3 May 1768 at Laigh Corton Farm, near Ayr, Ayrshire, was the sixth of thirteen children of John ('Auld Glen') Tennant (1726–1810), a farmer, and his second wife, Margaret McClure (1738–1784). The Tennants moved to Ochiltree, and after his education at home and Ochiltree parish school, Charles was apprenticed to a hand-loom weaver at Kilbarchan. After he had studied bleaching methods at Wellmeadow, he started his own bleachfield at Darnley about 1788 with a friend from Paisley. Bleaching then consisted of boiling or 'bucking' the cloth in weak alkali and finally 'crofting' or exposing it in the open air for some days. This second process was gradually replaced by using chlorine dissolved in water; later dilute potash ley was used in place of the water, the resulting liquid being known as 'eau de Javelle'.

On 17 October 1795 Tennant married Margaret Wilson (1765–1843) at Paisley Abbey; there were nine children of this marriage. In 1798 he took out a patent to make strong bleaching solution cheaply by passing chlorine into a well-agitated mixture of lime and water. Certain Lancashire bleachers infringed his patent and Tennant took legal proceedings against them. The proceedings revealed, however, that this method had been in use for some years before the patent had been granted and it was

Charles Tennant (1768–1838), by John George Murray (after Andrew Geddes)

consequently declared void. In 1799 Tennant took out another patent to manufacture bleaching powder by passing chlorine over slaked lime, a process probably largely developed by his partner, Charles Mackintosh. He then moved to St Rollox, near Glasgow, where with his partners he established a factory to produce the powder commercially. Soda ash and other alkali products were also made, and St Rollox eventually grew into one of Europe's largest chemical works.

Outside business, Tennant was politically active and a strong supporter of free trade and the Reform Bill. He managed to improve Glasgow's water supply and also encouraged railway development, becoming chief promoter of the Garnkirk and Glasgow Railway, which opened in 1831. Charles Tennant was a handsome man with a determined mouth and chin, deep-set eyes, and bushy eyebrows. He was hard-working, shrewd, kind, and quiet. Modestly he refused to be considered for a knighthood just a few months before his death from erysipelas at his home, 195 West George Street, Glasgow, on 1 October 1838. He was buried at Glasgow necropolis on 8 October. His estate was valued at more than £94,000.

CHRISTOPHER F. LINDSEY

Sources N. Crathorne and others, *Tennant's stalk: the story of the Tennants of the glen* (1973), 55–98 · T. Webster, '*Tennant v. Slater*', in T. Webster, *Reports and notes of cases and letters patent for inventions*, 1 (1844), 125–6 · W. Carpmael, 'Tennant's patent', *Law reports of patent cases*, 1 (1843), 177–9 · J. R. Hume, 'The St. Rollox chemical works, 1799–1964', *Industrial archaeology*, 3 (Aug 1966), 185–92 · S. Blow, *Broken blood: the rise and fall of the Tennant family* (1987), 17–53
Archives Tennant Trust, The Glen, Innerleithen, Borders | Ches. & Chester ALSS, United Alkali MSS · Lpool RO, letters to Muspratt family · Mitchell L., Glas.
Likenesses A. Geddes, oils, 1830–39, Tennant Trust, The Glen, Innerleithen, Scottish Borders · P. Park, plaster bust, c.1838, Kelvingrove Art Gallery and Museum, Glasgow · P. Park, Carrara marble statue, 1841, Glasgow necropolis · J. F. Skill, J. Gilbert, W. Walker and E. Walker, group portrait, pencil and wash, c.1856 (*Men of science living in 1807–8*), NPG · A. Geddes, oils, Kelvingrove Art Gallery and Museum, Glasgow · J. G. Murray, mezzotint (after A. Geddes), NPG [*see illus.*] · W. Walker and G. Zobel, engraving (*Men of science living in 1807–8*; after J. F. Skill, J. Gilbert, W. Walker, and E. Walker), NPG
Wealth at death £94,237 18s. 1d.: NA Scot., SC 36/48/27, fol. 622

Tennant, Sir Charles, first baronet (1823–1906), industrialist, was born on 4 November 1823, in Glasgow, second son and third and youngest child of John Tennant (1796–1878), chemical manufacturer, of St Rollox, Glasgow, and Robina Arrol. His parents never married. Robina Arrol had two children from an earlier liaison. Educated at Ayr Academy and a private school at Tillicoultry, he was sent at the age of sixteen to Liverpool for commercial training before entering the St Rollox chemical works in 1843. This had been established in 1799 by his grandfather, Charles *Tennant (1768–1838), to produce bleaching powder, but by the 1820s had become the largest alkali works in Britain, accounting for one-third of national output.

The Tennant interests underwent some decline as the competitive situation favoured other areas with cheaper

Sir Charles Tennant, first baronet (1823–1906), by John Singer Sargent, 1901

coal or easier access to salt deposits. Nevertheless, Tennant reinvigorated the enterprise after 1850. He was masterful in negotiations, and was one of the earliest capitalists to recognize that large-scale business required skills of public presentation: he was highly effective at shareholders' meetings, disclosing enough to create the illusion of participation but withholding information so that he always kept control. His successes attracted the almost superstitious regard of his fellow citizens, and he formed a coterie of Glasgow capitalists who trusted his judgement and were eager to share in his initiatives.

Until the 1880s Tennant's business career was characterized by shrewd, dauntless expansion and great rewards. His successes began with the erection of a large works at Hebburn-on-Tyne. Tennant then brought his fellow alkali makers together to form the Tharsis Sulphur and Copper Company, incorporated at Glasgow in 1866, to take over pyrite mines in southern Spain. He initiated a bold programme of development. Tharsis acquired seven metal-extraction companies in Britain by 1872, and because of its by-products, Tennant became interested in metallurgical technology. In 1872 he led the formation of the Steel Company of Scotland, intending to use the iron component in the Tharsis pyrites; but the metallurgical techniques proved inadequate, and the Steel Company turned instead to conventional supplies of pig iron and scrap. The Tharsis pyrites contained tiny components of gold, which Tennant and his associates were keen to recover. The Cassel Gold Extraction Company, which was formed largely at his behest in 1884, acquired the rights to a cyanide process which raised the level of gold recoverable from 55 per cent to 95 per cent. It enjoyed a decade of high prosperity before a decision of the chief justice of the Transvaal in 1896 overturned its patents. Tennant and his associates also acquired several gold-mining companies near Mysore in India. He was the chief initiator of Nobel's Explosives Ltd, a British company formed in 1876 to exploit the patents of Alfred Nobel, and served as its chairman. Additionally he took on the chairmanship of the Union Bank of Scotland and a directorship of the North British Railway.

Although he continued to accumulate massive riches, Tennant's business interests suffered from strategic errors in the last quarter-century of his life. This was partly because, for all his amiability and generosity, he was an irritable, impressionable, and sometimes unreasonable man. Thus he was offered an opportunity to adopt the Solvay process of alkali manufacture, which by the 1880s was outstripping in efficiency the Leblanc process used at the St Rollox works. Instead, Tennant persuaded his fellow Leblanc producers that their by-products, especially bleaching powder, would compensate for the inferiority of their process, and in 1890 he rallied some forty-five businesses, including the St Rollox works, into the United Alkali Company under his presidency. It engaged in deadly competition with Brunner, Mond & Co., until in 1926 the two were among the companies that merged to form Imperial Chemical Industries. Another misjudgement by Tennant and his supporters injured Tharsis. In 1896 they rejected an overture from German chemists and metallurgists to erect a plant in the Rhineland to process pyrites, and were thus excluded from many new developments. Tharsis had accumulated reserves of £500,000 by 1899, but failed to buy new mines to ensure its survival. Tennant's retirement as its chairman in 1906 was overdue. After the Steel Company of Scotland declined to near bankruptcy, Tennant retired as chairman in 1894, thereafter serving as honorary president.

In 1853 Tennant bought The Glen estate in Peeblesshire. He remodelled the house into a baronial mansion resembling Glamis, and improved the grounds extensively. He also amassed a notable library and a collection of pictures, including ten by Reynolds, six by Romney, five each by Gainsborough and Turner, and three by Constable. His judgement as a collector was warped by comparing his possessions with other people's, although he found a real and almost naïve pleasure in sharing his collection with others. He enjoyed praise, and was flattered by his appointment as a trustee of the National Gallery in 1894. The Glen was a scene of boundless hospitality, where the intimacies of Victorian family life were relieved of its most irksome restraints. 'It is impossible to exaggerate the charm of the place,' wrote Sir Algernon West, 'A happier or cleverer family never made a country house more delightful' (West, 2.208). W. E. Gladstone, visiting in November 1890, noted that his host 'bubbles with contentment' (Diaries, 12.333). Three of Tennant's daughters were active in the Souls group, among whom he was nicknamed the Bart. He was one of the earliest provincial industrialists to become a major metropolitan figure, and

held magnificent parties at his great house in Grosvenor Square: 'the gorgeous home was ablaze with lights and alive with flunkeys; the drawing rooms full of people … The dining room groaned with silver plate and heaps of roses', wrote his guest John Addington Symonds, who described Tennant as 'a kind old man, but not of excellent manners & awfully rich' (Letters, 2.250, 3.734).

Tennant married first, on 2 August 1849, Emma (1821–1895), daughter of Richard Winsloe, of Mount Nebo, Taunton. They had six sons and six daughters. After her death he married, in November 1898, Marguerite Agaranthe (1868–1943), daughter of Colonel Charles Miles, MP for Malmesbury (1882–5). They had four daughters, the third of whom was the politician Katharine *Elliot, later Baroness Elliot of Harwood.

Tennant was elected as Liberal MP for Glasgow at a by-election in 1879. In the general election of 1880 he outraged his lowland neighbours by standing for his local constituency of Peebles and Selkirk, and beating by thirty-two votes the tory member. He retained this seat until 1886, when he was defeated by fifty votes. He unsuccessfully contested the Partick division of Lanarkshire in 1890, but made no further attempt to enter the House of Commons, in which he was never prominent. On Gladstone's recommendation he was created a baronet in July 1885. He opposed the introduction of death duties by W. V. Harcourt in 1894, and his economic views changed so far that in 1904 he became a member of the tariff commission associated with Joseph Chamberlain and W. A. S. Hewins.

Tennant died after the haemorrhage of a chronic gastric ulcer, on 4 June 1906, at Broad Oaks, Byfleet, Surrey, and was buried close to The Glen in Traquair churchyard. In appearance he was lithe, dapper, dexterous, and alert. 'He took his own happiness with him and was self-centred and self-sufficing: for a sociable being, the most self-sufficing I have ever known,' wrote his daughter Margot *Asquith, countess of Oxford and Asquith. 'He advanced on his own lines rapidly and courageously, not at all secretively, almost confidingly; yet he was rarely taken in.'

RICHARD DAVENPORT-HINES

Sources N. Crathorne and others, Tennant's stalk: the story of the Tennants of the glen (1973) · S. Blow, Broken blood: the rise and fall of the Tennant family (1987) · S. G. Checkland, The mines of Tharsis: Roman, French, and British enterprise in Spain (1967) · M. Asquith, The autobiography of Margot Asquith, 1 (1920), 5–6 · The Times (6 July 1906), 4 · Sir A. West, Recollections, 2 (1899), 208 · The letters of John Addington Symonds, ed. H. M. Schueller and R. L. Peters, 3 vols. (1967–9), vol. 2, p. 250; vol. 3, p. 734 · Gladstone, Diaries

Archives NA Scot., SC 42/20/16 · NRA, priv. coll., corresp. and papers | BL, letters to W. E. Gladstone, Add. MSS 44461–44524, passim · Bodl. Oxf., corresp. with Margot Asquith · NL Scot., corresp. with Lord Rosebery

Likenesses cartoon, c.1865, Mitchell L., Glas. · D. Macnee, oils, c.1870, priv. coll.; repro. in Crathorne and others, Tennant's stalk · oils, c.1870, priv. coll.; repro. in Blow, Broken blood · photograph, c.1900, repro. in Blow, Broken blood · J. S. Sargent, oils, 1901, priv. coll. [see illus.] · H. J. Brooks, group portrait, oils (Private view of the Old Masters Exhibition, Royal Academy, 1888), NPG · F. Verheyden, caricature, watercolour study, NPG; repro. in VF (9 June 1883) · J. W. Watt, lithograph, NPG

Wealth at death £3,151,974 18s. 1d.: DSBB

Tennant, Sir David (1829–1905), politician in Cape Colony, born at Cape Town on 10 January 1829, was the eldest son of Hercules Tennant, civil commissioner and resident magistrate of Uitenhage, and his first wife, Aletta Jacoba, daughter of Johannes Hendricus Brand, member of the court of justice at the Cape, and sister of Sir Christoffel Brand, first speaker of the Cape house of assembly.

After being educated at a private school in Cape Town, Tennant was admitted on 12 April 1849 attorney at law of the supreme court, and practised also as a notary public and conveyancer and in the vice-admiralty court of the colony, with much success. In 1856 he published a second and revised edition of his father's *Notary's Manual for the Cape of Good Hope*. For many years he was registrar of the diocese of Cape Town and legal adviser to the bishop; during his tenure of office there the prolonged litigation concerning Bishop Colenso took place. On 3 May 1849 he married Josina Hendrina Arnoldina (*d*. 1877), daughter of Jacobus François du Toit of Stellenbosch, a descendant of a French protestant family settled at the Cape since 1685; they had two sons and a daughter. On 8 October 1885 in London he married as his second wife Amye Venour, elder daughter of Sir William Bellairs (1828–1913) of Strawberry Hill, Twickenham, lieutenant-general, and his first wife, Emily Craven Gibbons.

In May 1866 Tennant was returned to the house of assembly of the Cape of Good Hope as member for Piquetberg, representing it until his retirement in 1896. On 18 June 1874 he was unanimously elected speaker of the house of assembly in succession to his uncle, Sir Christoffel Brand, holding the position unopposed for nearly twenty-two years. His rulings were seldom questioned and he exercised great but fair-minded influence in the house. In 1893, when he was accorded a special vote of thanks for his services in the chair, the prime minister, Cecil Rhodes, bore witness to 'the firmness and impartiality with which he had maintained the dignity and rights of the house'. He retired on a pension on 26 February 1896.

Tennant was closely identified with the educational life of the colony, and for some years was a member of the council of the University of the Cape and chairman of the South African College council. He was justice of the peace for Cape Town, Wynberg, and Simonstown, and served on several government commissions. He was knighted by patent on 4 October 1877, and was created KCMG on 25 May 1892. On his retirement from the speakership he acted as agent-general for the colony in London although he had not acquired the requisite business aptitude for the position. He resigned on 31 December 1901. He died on 29 March 1905 at his home, 39 Hyde Park Gate, London, and was buried in Brompton cemetery. He was survived by his second wife.   CHEWTON ATCHLEY, *rev.* LYNN MILNE

Sources *The Times* (31 March 1905) · *The Times* (3 April 1905) · *Cape Argus* (30 March 1905) · *Cape Times* (31 March 1905) · *Argus Annual and Cape of Good Hope Directory* (1896) · Burke, *Peerage* (1905) · *DSAB* · Burke, *Gen. GB* (1914) · *CGPLA Eng. & Wales* (1905) · private information (1912)
Likenesses W. Greter, oils; known to be in family possession in 1912 · photographs, National Library of South Africa, Cape Town · portrait, Parliament House, Cape Town

Wealth at death £12,672 17*s*. 11*d*.: probate, 1 May 1905, *CGPLA Eng. & Wales*

Tennant, Henry (1823–1910), railway administrator, was born at Countersett on the shores of Semmerwater, near Bainbridge in Wensleydale. Little is known about his background, but his family were strong Quakers, and he undertook his education at Ackworth, the well-known Quaker school near Pontefract. At the age of sixteen he started his working life as a bookkeeper with the firm of Messrs Charles Bragg & Co. at Newcastle upon Tyne, and two years later was appointed to the staff of the infant Brandling Junction Railway on Tyneside, where he soon became chief clerk. In 1844, as George Hudson engineered the Newcastle and Darlington Junction Railway, Tennant secured the post of chief clerk to the general manager, but he left in 1846 to become accountant and traffic manager of the Leeds and Thirsk Railway. On 17 February 1847 he married Mary Jane Goundry (*d*. 1900), also a Quaker. There were no children from the marriage.

Mounting the ladder of success rapidly as the youthful railway industry threw up opportunities for capable, ambitious young men, Tennant became general manager of the line in 1848. Inevitably, he was soon involved in the negotiations which led the Leeds Northern (as it became known) to amalgamate with the York, Newcastle and Berwick, and York and North Midland railways to form the North Eastern Railway (NER) in 1854. Tennant immediately became accountant of the new line and held the post until 1870 when he became general manager.

From 1854 to 1870 Tennant was active in forging, and implementing, the policies which led the NER to absorb the remaining significant independent railways in the area until in contemporary perception it had the district to itself, and was the most complete railway monopoly in the country. He was particularly noted for helping to define its pricing policies and for masterminding the complex scheme of finance by which the ordinary stocks and shares of the constituent railways of the NER were merged into a new class of North Eastern ordinary shares known as 'consols'. The scheme served as a model for the reorganization of other railway companies' stocks as the course of railway amalgamation proceeded apace.

On the retirement of William O'Brien as general manager in 1870, Tennant was appointed to succeed him, and he held the job until his retirement from executive management in 1891 at the age of sixty-eight. Over the years of his reign the NER evolved into the most powerful of Britain's provincial railways. Its ordinary stocks paid the high dividend of 10 per cent in the early 1870s, and, while the line was subject thereafter to the diminishing returns which beset the industry as a whole, it had a reputation under Tennant for financial strength and sound administration, though not great flair. He brought to the job a skill in handling figures and a reputation for conducting negotiations with shrewdness and a cool, unemotional, and unhurried style. These qualities recommended him to the York City and County Bank, whose board of directors he chaired for a while. Inevitably, he was, in the early railway age (and later), a frequent witness and contributor to many railway parliamentary contests, select committees, and inquiries of the time. In the 1880s he was also closely involved with the evolution of a progressive labour relations policy for the NER, as the impact of militant general unionism on Tyneside made itself felt, and demanded a response.

On his retirement in 1891, Tennant was elected a director of the NER and was granted the sum of £10,000 in recognition of his services to the growth of the railways in the north-east over the preceding forty years, as well as in anticipation of a continuing consultative contribution to the management of the line. His service on the board continued to the end of his long life, and he was appointed joint deputy chairman in 1905. While his influence on executive management inevitably waned, he remained prominent in the work of the company, and his reputation earned him appointments on the boards of other railways. He also directed ventures in which the NER had a stake, such as the Forth Bridge Company and shipping lines; these investments protected its share of continental traffic around 1900. At various times he acted as an arbitrator for the Board of Trade and the Irish Office on transport matters.

For much of his professional life Tennant lived unostentatiously in the city of York. His retirement from executive railway management in 1891 enabled him to expand his involvement in the local community. He made an active contribution to the York Liberal Association and local Liberal politics, and put in a long stint as a city JP. His contribution to education in York was particularly notable. He took an interest in the schooling of working-class children, making his motto 'For every child an equal opportunity'. He was elected to the York school board in 1889 after a stiff political campaign, and served as vice-chairman of the board and later as a co-opted member of the York education committee (from which he retired only in 1906). He was active in the temperance movement, and in 1892 when the North Eastern Temperance Union was forged out of a number of regional bodies, he was elected its president and remained so until his death. For his service to railways, but doubtless also his contribution to Liberal politics and values in York, he was offered, but declined, a knighthood in 1907 from Sir Henry Campbell-Bannerman.

Tennant died at his home, Holgate Hill House, York, on 25 May 1910. He was buried in the Quaker burial-ground at Heslington, York, on the 28th. An obituary in the *Yorkshire Gazette* mourned the loss of a 'Great Railway Administrator and Educationist'. Tennant was, indeed, both these things and very much a man of the north.

R. J. IRVING

Sources York City Library, Henry Tennant MSS, Box Y.379.153 · *Yorkshire Gazette* (28 May 1910) · W. W. Tomlinson, *The North Eastern railway: its rise and development* [1915]; repr. with new introduction by K. Hode (1967) · *Yorkshire Gazette* (3 Nov 1906) · R. J. Irving, *The North Eastern Railway Company, 1870–1914: an economic history* (1976) · *CGPLA Eng. & Wales* (1910) · R. J. Irving, 'Tennant, Henry', *DBB*
Likenesses portrait, repro. in Tomlinson, *The North Eastern railway*

Wealth at death £174,000 0s. 4d.: probate, 30 June 1910, *CGPLA Eng. & Wales*

Tennant, Sir James (1789–1854), army officer in the East India Company, second son of William Tennant, merchant, of Ayr, and his wife, Wilhelmina Ramsay, daughter of Dr William *Dalrymple, was born at Ayr on 21 April 1789. He was educated at the Royal Military College, Marlow, and at the Royal Military Academy, Woolwich (1804–5), and sailed as cadet of the East India Company on 31 August 1805 in the East India fleet which accompanied the expedition of Sir David Baird and Sir Home Popham to the Cape of Good Hope. The company cadets and recruits, under Lieutenant-Colonel Wellesley, Bengal establishment, took part in the capture of Cape Town. Tennant arrived in India on 21 August 1806, and was commissioned lieutenant, Bengal artillery, antedated to 29 March for his Cape service.

In 1810 Tennant commanded a detachment of artillery on service on the 'vizier's dominions'. On 1 January 1812 he was appointed acting adjutant and quartermaster to Major G. Fuller's detachment of artillery, and on 15 January marched from Bauda with the force under Colonel Gabriel Martindell to attack Kalinjar, a formidable fort on a large isolated hill 900 feet above the surrounding level. Kalinjar was reached on 19 January; by 28 January the batteries opened, and on 2 February, the breaches being practicable, an unsuccessful attempt was made to storm. On 3 February the fort surrendered. Tennant was employed throughout this and the following year in various minor operations in the districts bordering on Bundelkhand.

On 27 December 1814, with two 18-pounders and four mountain guns of the 3rd division, Tennant joined Sir David Ochterlony at Nahr, on the north-north-east side of the Ramgarh Ridge, to take part in the operations against Nepal. In March 1815 Tennant ascended the Ramgarh Ridge, with the force under Lieutenant-Colonel Cooper, and, bringing up his 18-pounders with great labour, opened fire on Ramgarh, which soon surrendered, Jorjori capitulating at the same time. Taragarh (11 March) and Chamha (16 March) were reached and taken. All the posts on this ridge having been successively reduced, the detachment took up the position assigned to it before Malaun on 1 April. Malaun was captured by assault on 15 April before the 18-pounders, which were dragged by hand over the hills at the rate of 1 or 2 miles a day, had arrived; these guns were eventually left in the fort.

Tennant was promoted second captain in the regiment and captain in the army on 1 October 1816, and first captain in the Bengal artillery on 1 September 1818. His next active service was in the Pindari and Anglo-Maratha wars of 1817–19. He joined the centre division under Major-General T. Brown of the marquess of Hastings's grand army at Sikandra in the Cawnpore district, but as it was moving forward to Mahewas on the River Sind in November 1817, it was attacked by cholera. He took part in some of the operations, as captain and brigade-major of the 2nd division of artillery, and received a share of the Deccan prize-money for general captures. He was brigade-major of artillery in the field in 1819 and 1820. He was selected to command the artillery at Agra on 23 December 1823, and on 31 December was nominated first assistant secretary to the military board.

On 28 May 1824 Tennant was appointed assistant adjutant-general of artillery. In November 1825 he accompanied the commandant of artillery, Brigadier-General Alexander Macleod, to Agra; there, and at Mathura, the commander-in-chief, Lord Combermere, assembled his army for the siege of Bharatpur. The siege began in the middle of December; on 24 December the batteries opened fire, breaches were found practicable on 18 January 1826, and this formidable place was carried by assault. Tennant, who, as assistant adjutant-general of artillery, had managed the artillery, was thanked by the commandant in regimental orders (21 January 1826). Tennant's 'methodical habits and mathematical talent rendered labour easy to him which would have been difficult to others'. In February he accompanied Combermere to Cawnpore and to the presidency. Tennant married on 7 April 1828 Elizabeth Louisa (1803/4–1882), eldest daughter of Charles Pattenson, Bengal civil service. Lieutenant-General James Francis Tennant CIE FRS (1829–1915), Royal Engineers, was their son.

Tennant was promoted major on 3 March 1831. He was appointed agent for the manufacture of gunpowder at Ishapur on 28 April 1835 (confirmed on 28 July) and he ceased to be assistant adjutant-general of artillery. On 11 April 1836 he became a member of the special committee of artillery officers. He was promoted lieutenant-colonel on 18 January 1837, and in consequence vacated the agency for gunpowder.

For his services on the committee of artillery officers Tennant received the thanks of the government of India. On 21 March 1837 he was posted to command the 4th battalion of artillery. On 28 November 1842 he was given the command of the Cawnpore division of artillery. On 17 November 1843 he was appointed to command, with the rank of brigadier-general, the foot artillery attached to the army of exercise assembled at Agra under Sir Hugh (afterwards Lord) Gough. This force left Agra for the Gwalior campaign on 16 December, crossing the River Chambal on 21 December. In spite of great exertions, Tennant and the heavy ordnance got considerably behind. Gough did not wait for his heavy guns, and the battle of Maharajpur (29 December) was rather riskily fought without them (see Gough's dispatch, *LondG*, 8 March 1844).

On 10 February 1844 Tennant was again appointed commandant of the artillery at Cawnpore. On 3 July 1845 he was promoted colonel in the army, and was sent report on field magazines of the upper provinces. He, however, resigned this appointment, to the regret of the government, and resumed his command at Cawnpore. In 1846–7 Tennant was associated with Colonel George Brooke, Bengal artillery, on a committee at Simla, on the equipment of mountain batteries. Their experience of the Nepal war, 1814–16, led to valuable minutes. On 2 September 1848 Tennant was appointed brigadier-general to command the Marwar field force. He was then attached to the army of the Punjab to command the artillery with the rank of

brigadier-general. He commanded it at the battle of Chilianwala (13 January 1849) and was mentioned in dispatches. He also commanded it at the battle of Gujrat (21 February 1849), mentioned in dispatches. He received the thanks of parliament, of the government of India, and of the court of directors of the East India Company. He was made a CB on 5 June 1849.

On 13 March 1849 Tennant resumed his appointment at Cawnpore, and on 19 December was transferred to Lahore as brigadier-general commanding. On 30 January 1852 he was given command of the cis-Jhelum division of the army. He was made a KCB on 8 October 1852. He died at Mian Mir, Lahore, on 6 March 1854. His wife survived him. Tennant's attainments were of a very high order, and in Stubbs's view 'he was better acquainted with the details of his profession than perhaps any officer in the regiment'.

R. H. VETCH, *rev.* ROGER T. STEARN

Sources BL OIOC · dispatches, *LondG* [various dates] · F. W. Stubbs, ed., *History of the organization, equipment, and war services of the regiment of Bengal artillery*, 1–2 (1877) · F. W. Stubbs, ed., *History of the organization, equipment, and war services of the regiment of Bengal artillery*, 3 (1895) · V. C. P. Hodson, *List of officers of the Bengal army, 1758–1834*, 4 (1947) · Ross of Bladenburg, *The marquess of Hastings* (1893) · H. T. Prinsep, *History of the political and military transactions in India during the administration of the marquess of Hastings*, 2 vols. (1825) · J. G. Duff, *A history of the Mahrattas*, 3 vols. (1826) · V. Blacker, *Memoir of the operations of the British army in India during the Mahratta War of 1817, 1818 and 1819* (1821) · J. N. Creighton, *Narrative of the siege and capture of Bhurtpore* (1830) · T. Seaton, *From cadet to colonel: the record of a life of active service*, 2 vols. (1866) · E. J. Thackwell, *Narrative of the Second Seikh War, in 1848–49* (1851) · T. A. Heathcote, *The military in British India: the development of British land forces in south Asia, 1600–1947* (1995) · Boase, *Mod. Eng. biog.* · P. Moon, *The British conquest and dominion of India* (1989)

Tennant, James (1808–1881), mineralogist and mineral and shell dealer, was born on 8 February 1808 at Upton, near Southwell, Nottinghamshire, the third child of John Tennant, excise officer, and his wife, Eleanor (*née* Kitchen). By 1819 his parents had moved to Mansfield, and he was educated at schools both there and at Derby. In October 1824 he was apprenticed as shop assistant to John Mawe, mineral dealer, of 149 Strand, London. Mawe had been a great traveller and his shop was a resort for men of science from all over the world. Here Tennant gained his acquaintance with minerals. Mawe also sold turned ornamental marbles worked in Derbyshire, business which Tennant continued after Mawe's death.

Tennant attended lectures at his mechanics' institute and, later, those given by Michael Faraday at the Royal Institution. Faraday was a Mawe customer; he bought minerals there for use in his experiments. When Mawe died in 1829 his widow, Sarah, maintained the business, with Tennant now as resident manager. In 1838 Tennant was elected a fellow of the Geological Society, and was appointed to assist John Phillips (1800–1874) as lecturer in geological mineralogy at King's College, London, on Faraday's recommendation. 'His class here [became] the largest in the kingdom' (*ILN*, 12 March 1881).

Sarah Mawe had been created mineralogist to Queen Victoria on her accession. In February 1840 Tennant purchased the Mawe business and, on 15 October 1840, he inherited this title. The business lay only three doors from Somerset House, home of the Geological Society of London from 1828 to 1860, which helped to extend his circle of customers. By 1844 Tennant's shop was already 'too well known to require comment' (G. A. Mantell, *Medals of Creation*, 2.987).

From 1850 to 1867 Tennant was also lecturer on mineralogy and geology to the gentlemen cadets in the practical class of the Royal Military Academy, Woolwich. In 1852–3 he was paid £2 a day to arrange and catalogue minerals in the British Museum. In 1853 he was made professor of geology at King's, but he resigned in 1869 on becoming keeper of the extensive collection of minerals of Angela, Baroness Burdett-Coutts (1814–1906). However, he retained his mineralogy lectureship at King's until his death. His pupil John Ruskin later said that Tennant's classes were 'the best practical teaching I know of' (*Works*, 26.451). In 1848 Tennant had purchased the 6000 specimens of the Stowe collection of minerals and fossils, made by the duke of Buckingham, for £68 5s. He disposed of many of the best specimens before trying to sell the remainder. These were bought by Ruskin in 1867 for £3000. But Ruskin considered he had been swindled and sued Tennant. After he had paid legal fees of £1000, Ruskin received £1000 back and further specimens to the value of £500 in an out-of-court settlement.

Tennant's practical knowledge of minerals was extensive. By 1849 he possessed the finest collection of diamonds as crystals in England. He exhibited minerals and fossils for educational purposes at the Great Exhibition of 1851. In 1852 he encouraged emigrants to new countries to look for minerals other than gold, especially diamonds, and he superintended the recutting of the Koh-i-noor diamond and other crown jewels. When there was debate over the first diamonds found in South Africa in 1867, he correctly maintained their genuineness. By 1860 he was selling models of Waterhouse Hawkins's reconstructions of extinct animals, including dinosaurs. Collections to illustrate Lyell's *Elements of Geology* were offered by 1866.

Tennant was an early member of the Geologists' Association, helping with its first field excursions in 1860. He was elected its third president (1862–4). He was an enthusiast for technical education, which he supported by giving liberally from his own resources. In 1869 he was elected freeman of the Turners' Company and, in May 1873, master. He persuaded the company to offer annual prizes for excellence in turning. Tennant's private collection of fossils was offered for sale in 1875. He died, unmarried, on 23 February 1881 at his home at 149 Strand, London. He was buried at Camberwell old cemetery, London, on 28 February. After his death an extensive selection from his private collection was purchased by the British Museum. His vast stocks were sold off in a series of auctions which lasted from 1881 to 1972. He was author of a number of educational works and also active as publisher, bookseller, and as a popular lecturer encouraging his favourite science.

H. S. TORRENS

Sources *Geological Magazine*, new ser., 2nd decade, 8 (1881), 238–9; repr. in *Quarterly Journal of the Geological Society of London*, 38 (1882), 48–9 • H. S. Torrens and M. A. Taylor, 'Geological collectors and museums in Cheltenham, 1810–1988', *Geological Curator*, 5 (1988–94), 173–213, esp. 176 • *ILN* (12 March 1881), 253–4 • *Nature*, 23 (1880–81), 418 • F. J. C. Hearnshaw, *The centenary history of King's College, London, 1828–1928* (1929) • G. S. Sweeting, *The Geologists' Association, 1858–1958* (1958) • A. C. Stanley-Stone, *The Worshipful Company of Turners of London* (1925) • W. T. Stearn, *The Natural History Museum at South Kensington: a history of the British Museum (Natural History), 1753–1980* (1981) • *The works of John Ruskin*, ed. E. T. Cook and A. Wedderburn, library edn, 39 vols. (1903–12), vols. 26, 29 • J. Tennant, letter, *ILN* (31 Jan 1852) • advertisement, *Salopian Monthly Illustrated Journal* (Aug 1875) • G. A. Mantell, diary, NL NZ, Turnbull L. • *CGPLA Eng. & Wales* (1881) • *DNB* • *IGI* • *The Times* (26 Feb 1881) • *The Times* (28 Feb 1881)

Archives King's Lond. • NHM

Likenesses Rogers, portrait; formerly in the collection of Lady Burdett Coutts in 1898; copy known to be in the Strand vestry in 1898 • wood-engraving (after photograph by H. N. King), NPG; repro. in *ILN* (12 March 1881)

Wealth at death under £10,000: resworn probate, Nov 1882, *CGPLA Eng. & Wales* (1881)

Tennant, Margaret Emma Alice. *See* Asquith, Margaret Emma Alice, countess of Oxford and Asquith (1864–1945).

Tennant [*née* Abraham], **Margery Mary Edith Josephine Pia** [May] (1869–1946), factory inspector, was born on 5 April 1869 in Rathgar, co. Dublin, the only daughter of Dr George Whitley Abraham, lawyer, and his wife, Margaret Curtin.

May Abraham was educated privately, mainly by her father, and never achieved any formal qualification. Although brought up a Roman Catholic, she later joined the Anglican church. Her father died in 1887 and May moved to London, arriving with an introduction to Emilia, Lady Dilke. Lady Dilke was, at that time, a leader of the Women's Trade Union League, which campaigned to organize women workers and to investigate the health risks to industrial workers caused by dangerous substances. Her niece, Gertrude Tuckwell, had recently resigned as her secretary and May Abraham was offered both that job and the post of treasurer to the league. She soon became involved in the league's efforts to organize women, developing a particular interest in the need for legislation to protect women laundry workers.

When public concern about the conditions suffered by industrial workers led, in 1891, to the setting up of the royal commission on labour, May Abraham was one of four women assistant commissioners appointed at the same time to investigate industrial issues concerning women. The women assistant commissioners' report, which highlighted the appalling conditions under which so many women worked, led directly to a decision by W. E. Gladstone's final government to appoint women factory inspectors. Accordingly, in 1893, May Abraham became the first woman factory inspector appointed in England. Two years later she was the superintending inspector of five women and in 1896 she published *The Laws Relating to Factories and Workshops, Including Laundries and Docks*, designed to clarify the legislation relating to industry.

In August 1893 May Abraham was appointed to the committee of inquiry as to chemical works and two years later joined the committee on dangerous trades, which was

Margery Mary Edith Josephine Pia Tennant (1869–1946), by unknown photographer

chaired by Harold John (Jack) Tennant (1865–1935), the youngest son of Sir Charles *Tennant and his first wife, Emma; he had been elected Liberal MP for Berwickshire in 1895. Described by her friend Violet Markham as beautiful and gracious, with dark hair, dark grey-blue eyes, and an enchanting smile, May attracted the attention of Jack Tennant and on 8 July 1896 they were married.

May Tennant continued with her work as a factory inspector until her resignation, just before the birth of her first son in 1897. As her family of four sons and one daughter grew she continued to work in a voluntary capacity, attending meetings of the dangerous trades committee until 1899 and taking on, in 1898, chairing of the industrial law committee. In 1909 she was appointed a member of the royal commission on divorce.

On the outbreak of the First World War in 1914, May Tennant's involvement in public affairs increased. She was a founder member, later treasurer, of the Central Committee on Women's Employment. Set up in 1914, this committee continued to campaign on behalf of unemployed women for the next twenty years. In 1917 she was appointed director of the women's division of the national service department. When this was disbanded six months later she joined the Health of Munition Workers Committee. She was made a Companion of Honour in recognition

of her war work, but the war also brought her personal tragedy when her eldest son, Henry, was killed in action in 1917. Her husband died in November 1935.

May Tennant continued with her voluntary work after the war and became chair of the maternal mortality committee set up in 1928 to reduce the risks to women in childbirth and she later became involved in efforts to improve the training of midwives. From 1941 to her death in 1946 she campaigned actively for the Royal Air Force Benevolent Fund.

Shortly before the First World War, May Tennant and her husband bought and rebuilt a large country house, Great Maytham, at Rolvenden in Kent. It was here that she developed her expertise as a gardener, becoming a recognized authority on gardening matters and a well-known figure in the Royal Horticultural Society. Great Maytham was to become her main residence and she died in a house on the estate on 11 July 1946 after some years of illness.

SERENA KELLY

Sources V. R. Markham, *May Tennant: a portrait* (1949) • M. D. McFeely, *Lady inspectors: the campaign for a better workplace, 1893–1921* (1988) • *The Times* (12 July 1946) • *DNB*
Archives NMM, corresp. with Dame Katherine Furse
Likenesses photograph, repro. in Markham, *May Tennant* [see illus.]
Wealth at death £26,509 2s.: probate, 1 Jan 1947, *CGPLA Eng. & Wales*

Tennant [*née* Eroles], **Mariquita Dorotea Francesca** (1811–1860), social reformer, was born on 1 November 1811, the daughter of Don Antonio Eroles of Barcelona, an army officer. Her sister, Rosa Florentina Eroles, married Francis Beaufort Edgeworth (d. 1841), the half-brother of the novelist Maria Edgeworth. Mariquita Eroles was married twice, firstly to David Reid (1807–1835), fourth son of Andrew and Janet Reid of Lyonsdown near Barnet. They lived in Florence and had a daughter, Mary. After David Reid's death in November 1835 his widow remained in Florence, where she married the Revd Robert John Tennant (d. 1842), Anglican chaplain to the British congregation there. The marriage, which may have been the occasion for her conversion from Catholicism to Anglicanism, was short-lived. Robert Tennant died in July 1842, and after remaining a few months more in Florence, Mariquita Tennant joined her widowed sister at the Edgeworth's family home, Edgeworthstown, in Ireland.

By the end of 1848 Mariquita Tennant was living at The Limes, a medieval house belonging to her sister, situated near St Andrew's Church in the village of Clewer, near Windsor. On 29 December 1848 she gave refuge to a young woman called Marianne George who had been abused by her stepfather, the father of her four children. Tennant intended simply to remove her from her surroundings and train her as a servant, but the rector of Clewer, Thomas Thellusson Carter (1808–1901), was anxious to provide a safe refuge for other women in moral danger. Not only was Windsor a garrison town, but two railway companies were bringing their lines into the town, and there were many itinerant workers. Mariquita Tennant therefore offered to help any women wishing to escape from the beerhouses and brothels of Clewer Fields, a notorious slum area not far from Windsor Castle. On 14 June 1849 she admitted two more young women to her house. Both had sought refuge in Clewer Fields but, hearing of Mariquita Tennant, they approached her and were taken to The Limes. Others followed, so that very soon there were more than a dozen, with numbers continuing to increase.

Clearly Mariquita Tennant could not cope with so many women single-handedly: many of them were unruly and some violent. Within a strict disciplinary framework she endeavoured to teach them basic domestic skills interspersed with religious instruction. As the work proceeded she began to cherish the notion of founding a religious sisterhood (of which she would be the self-styled lady superior), similar to that founded by E. B. Pusey at Park Village West. To that end she adapted the Park Village rule to suit her own needs. That the sisterhood never became a reality was due to the lack of reliable volunteers. Indeed, her only really committed helper was Charlotte Julia Weale (1829–1918), who came to Clewer in February 1850 for a period of six months. During her time at the Clewer house of mercy Charlotte Weale kept comprehensive notebooks detailing the case histories of the women, the daily timetable, and religious instructions. She also kept copies of correspondence between Tennant and supporters of her work, such as Elizabeth Herbert (1822–1911) and W. E. Gladstone, in whom Mariquita Tennant found a kindred spirit. Their mutual concern for a young woman called Emma Clifton led Tennant (despite her poor health) to travel to London and personally seek her out in the hope of bringing her back to Clewer—a mission which ultimately proved fruitless.

It is clear from Charlotte Weale's writings that Mariquita Tennant was not an easy person to work with, which is probably why none of her helpers stayed very long. This, in addition to the difficulty of establishing and maintaining order and discipline within the house, took its toll on Mariquita Tennant's health. There was also the stress of finding alternative accommodation, The Limes having been a temporary measure. But in February 1851 the house of mercy finally moved to a large house in Hatch Lane, Clewer, called Nightingale Place, which had a 15 acre estate. By this time Tennant had already resolved to resign, and finally left in April 1851.

Following her retirement from the house of mercy, Mariquita Tennant withdrew to her private home, Trinity House, in Windsor, where she lived with her daughter Mary in increasingly poor health. When well enough she attended Holy Trinity Church close by, and shortly before her death she opened a meeting-room in Bier Lane not far from Clewer Fields, which was known as Our Room. She died on 21 February 1860 at 9 Claremont Road, Clewer, after a short illness, prematurely aged and worn out. She was buried in Clewer churchyard within sight of The Limes. A visitor to Clewer in 1864 described her gravestone as representing an open coffin containing a Bible and a cross on top of an empty shroud, with the words 'Non est hic, sed resurrexit' (Not here, but risen) carved inside the open lid. This ornate memorial was later replaced with a simple stone cross.

Mariquita Tennant was an enigmatic woman whom history has bypassed. She was a pioneer in the great wave of moral rescue work begun in the mid-nineteenth century and later undertaken by the religious communities which sprang from the Oxford Movement. The Clewer house of mercy which she left behind in Hatch Lane evolved quite differently under the wise, gentle, but firm guidance of Harriet Monsell (1811–1883). Nor was the quasi-sisterhood envisioned by Mariquita Tennant in any way like the Community of St John Baptist which took over her work. But though she cannot claim to have founded a religious community, she can rightly be credited with the foundation of a religious work in the house of mercy; she was the forerunner of all who followed at Clewer.

VALERIE BONHAM

Sources V. Bonham, *A place in life: the Clewer House of Mercy, 1849–83* (1992) • T. T. Carter, *The first ten years of the house of mercy, Clewer* (1861) • C. Weale, *Open letter* (1850) • T. T. Carter, *Harriet Monsell: a memoir* (1884) • Gladstone, *Diaries* • private information (2004) • *Windsor and Eton Express* (25 Feb 1860) • d. cert.
Archives Community of St John Baptist, Clewer | LPL, Gladstone MSS • Oxon. RO, Wilberforce visitation questionnaire, Oxford diocese
Likenesses oils, Community of St John Baptist, Clewer, near Windsor, Berkshire • photograph (in later life), Community of St John Baptist, Clewer, near Windsor, Berkshire
Wealth at death under £200: administration, 19 March 1860, *CGPLA Eng. & Wales*

Tennant, Smithson (1761–1815), chemist, was born on 30 November 1761 at Selby, Yorkshire and baptized there in the abbey church on 3 December. He was the only child of the Revd Calvert Tennant, absentee rector of Great Warley in Essex and fellow of St John's College, Cambridge, and his wife, Mary, daughter of William Daunt, a Selby surgeon-apothecary. Tennant's father died in 1772 and his mother in 1781, leaving him with sufficient inheritance to live his life as he wished. After passing through grammar schools at Scorton, Tadcaster, and Beverley, Tennant attended the chemistry lectures of Joseph Black at the University of Edinburgh in 1781. In October 1782 he entered Christ's College, Cambridge, to study chemistry and botany, first as pensioner and later as fellow-commoner.

In the summer of 1784 Tennant travelled to Denmark and Sweden, where he met the chemist Karl Scheele, and two years later he toured France and the Low Countries. On 13 January 1785, with the support of his Cambridge colleagues, he was elected a fellow of the Royal Society and in 1786 he transferred with his friend Busick Harwood to Emmanuel College. During this period Tennant was befriended by William Hyde Wollaston, a medical student at Gonville and Caius College, who was to become his business associate in 1800.

Shortly after receiving his MB degree in 1788, Tennant took up residence at 4 Garden Court, Temple, in London and indulged his interests in natural philosophy. His first scientific paper, on the decomposition of fixed air, which confirmed by analysis the presence of carbon in the gas, was published in the *Philosophical Transactions* for 1791. In 1792–3 he toured the continent again, and on his return to England attended the London hospitals prior to taking his Cambridge MD degree in 1796. With no interest in pursuing a medical practice, Tennant settled instead into a career as a gentleman chemist. He published an important paper in 1797 which demonstrated that diamond has the same chemical composition as charcoal. About this time he purchased 500 acres of newly enclosed land near Shipham in Somerset, where he carried out experiments in agricultural chemistry during the few months each year he resided there.

In 1800 Tennant entered into a business partnership with Wollaston, who had then recently abandoned his London medical practice to establish a chemical business. The two men agreed to share expenses and profits from the purification of alluvial platinum ore and the manufacture of various organic substances important to the textile industry. Owing principally to Wollaston's discovery of a method for the production of malleable platinum, and profitable sales of the pure metal, the business flourished and Tennant's accumulated profit at the time of his death was about £3000. From the residues of the platinum purification process, Tennant isolated and characterized the two new metals osmium and iridium. Publication of these discoveries, which established Tennant's fame as a chemist, earned for him the Royal Society's Copley medal for 1804. Thereafter Tennant's contribution to the business became almost negligible as he became more interested in political economy and discourse with the Whig political figures connected with John Whishaw and Holland House.

In 1812 Tennant gave a short series of informal lectures on mineralogy to his friends in his home; in 1813 he was elected professor of chemistry at Cambridge, and the following year he delivered a course of lectures. In September 1814 he set out on a tour of the southern provinces of France. He was killed in an accident on 22 February 1815 near Boulogne, when a bridge over which he was riding collapsed; he was buried a few days later in the public cemetery at Boulogne.

Tennant never married, and left an estate valued at £5000. He published a total of nine scientific papers (seven of which are listed in the Royal Society's *Catalogue of Scientific Papers*), mostly on topics in chemical analysis, and was an early member (1799) of London's Askesian Society. His biographer described him as 'tall and slender, with a thin face and light complexion, of striking and agreeable appearance, with expressive features and strong marks of intelligence' (Whishaw, 91).

MELVYN C. USSELMAN

Sources [J. Whishaw], 'Some account of the late Smithson Tennant, Esq.', *Annals of Philosophy*, 6 (1815), 1–11, 81–100 · D. McDonald, 'Smithson Tennant, FRS, 1761–1815', *Notes and Records of the Royal Society*, 17 (1962), 77–94 · A. E. Wales, 'Smithson Tennant, 1761–1815', *Nature*, 192 (1961), 1224–6 · D. C. Goodman, 'Tennant, Smithson', *DSB* · *Catalogue of scientific papers*, Royal Society, 5 (1871), 931 · L. F. Gilbert, 'W. H. Wollaston MSS at Cambridge', *Notes and Records of the Royal Society*, 9 (1951–2), 311–32 · M. C. Usselman, 'The platinum notebooks of William Hyde Wollaston', *Platinum Metals Review*, 22 (1978), 100–06 · M. C. Usselman, 'William Wollaston, John Johnson and Colombian alluvial platina', *Annals of Science*, 37 (1980), 253–68 · *DNB* · M. C. Usselman, 'Smithson Tennant: the eccentric eighth professor of chemistry', *Transformation and change: three centuries of chemistry at Cambridge*, ed. M. Archer (2003)

Archives CUL, Wollaston MSS · Royal Swedish Academy of Science, letters to Berzelius

Wealth at death £5000: administration, PRO; McDonald, 'Smithson Tennant', 90

Tennant, Stephen James Napier (1906–1987), aesthete, was born on 21 April 1906 at Wilsford Manor, near Amesbury, Wiltshire, the fourth son of Edward Priaulx Tennant, first Baron Glenconner (1859–1920), landowner and member of parliament, and his wife, Pamela Adelaide Genevieve Wyndham (1871–1928), a writer. Of his parents, Tennant was perhaps inevitably more attached to his mother, a romantic 'Soul' who would greet visitors to the Glenconners' Scottish baronial pile with her brood arranged about her 'in a sort of photographic pose' (Hoare, 7). But she was more at home at Wilsford Manor, the arts and crafts house she had created in 1906, the year of her youngest son's birth. Wilsford would become an extension of Stephen Tennant's personality, a constant reminder of his childhood in a life which remained essentially childlike. There his mother recorded his baby talk, the flowers speaking his name, 'Stephen, Stephen', as he passed; and acknowledged that 'what may be self-centred in later life is prettily cloaked in childhood' (ibid., 9). It was a sense of idyll destroyed by the death of the Glenconners' eldest son, Edward, a budding poet, in the First World War. Just as the aftermath of war influenced his generation, so Stephen Tennant's later relationship with the war poet Siegfried Sassoon seemed invested with the memory of his dead brother and the world before war.

Unsuited to formal schooling, Tennant was educated at home, his artistic talent encouraged by Pamela (he later illustrated her compendia *The Vein in the Marble*, 1925, and *The White Wallet*, 1928). In 1922 he attended the Slade School of Fine Art, where he met the artist Rex Whistler. The two shared a passion for Edgar Allen Poe and P. B. Shelley, but it was through Cecil Beaton's lens that Tennant's flamboyant imagination would create his fantastic self-image. Like his mother before him, Tennant adopted a romantic pose, becoming the visual epitome of the 'bright young people', a largely tabloid press response to post-war aristocratic hedonism. He was photographed by Beaton in his silver-foil bedroom in Smith Square: made up, marcell-waved, and clad in a pinstripe suit with his brother's leather flying jacket over his shoulders, he seemed a parody of a City gentleman and a wartime flying ace, an outrageous simulacrum of the masculinity which the war had sapped. The *Daily Express*'s 'William Hickey' column, written by Tom Driberg, avidly recorded his party entrances: 'The Honourable Stephen Tennant arrived in an electric brougham wearing a football jersey and earrings' (Hoare, 105).

If the bright young people's antics were essentially infantilist, then Tennant was part Peter Pan, part Dorian Gray—a glittering androgynous figure invested with an

Stephen James Napier Tennant (1906–1987), by Sir Cecil Beaton, 1927

almost alien sexuality. He remained inordinately attached both to his mother (who, two years after her first husband's death in 1920, had married Lord Grey of Falloden, the former foreign secretary), and to his nanny, Rebecca Trusler. When he half-seriously proposed marriage to Elizabeth Belloc-Lowndes, Tennant stipulated that Nanny should accompany them on their honeymoon. On the deaths of these two controlling influences (Lady Grey in 1928, Trusler a year later), Tennant was left to his life of fantasy. Into the emotional breach stepped Siegfried *Sassoon (1886–1967), with whom he had begun a relationship in 1927, and who watched as Tennant's friends—including the incongruous figure of William Walton—were persuaded to act out his eighteenth-century *fêtes galantes* in full costume and make-up on the lawns of Wilsford. 'It was very amusing, and they were painted up to the eyes, but I didn't quite like it', Sassoon wrote in his diary (Hoare, 92); yet he had become obsessed by their fantastic ringmaster.

'It was a tremendous *coup de foudre*', recalled Peter Quennell, 'Sassoon was like the worthy vicar of a parish coming to town and meeting this great society beauty' (Hoare, 132). The pair 'honeymooned' in Bavaria, for the health of the now tubercular aesthete, and in Sicily. Tales of Sassoon being sent back to their hotel to fetch Tennant's pearls led Edith Sitwell to dub the pair 'the Old Earl and Little Lord Fauntleroy' (ibid., 132). But Tennant's precarious physical and mental state was a source of real concern, and in 1932 he was sent to the Cassell Hospital at Penshurst in Kent, where he received psychoanalysis and where Sassoon attempted to direct his friend's treatment with the help of Sir Henry Head. But Tennant was growing

tired of Sassoon's attentions, and, dismissing his lover, returned to Wilsford alone.

Tennant now began a period of restlessness. He travelled to the south of France searching for passion and inspiration in the Vieux Port of Marseilles, where he sketched *matelots* for his putative masterpiece, *Lascar: a Story of the Maritime Boulevards*, 'a restless glittering book, about men who have no homes' (Culme, 16). He received encouragement from Virginia Woolf, E. M. Forster (a particular and loyal friend), Elizabeth Bowen, Rosamond Lehmann, and, most notably (for the contrast it presented), his beloved friend, the American writer Willa Cather; but as Cather told him, 'Nobody ever wrote a masterpiece by resolving to do so' (ibid., 172). Cyril Connolly was less forgiving: 'Essentially he is an adolescent exhibitionist acting out the role of grand *écrivain méconnu*' (Hoare, 298). Constantly rewritten in jewel-coloured inks, *Lascar* remained unpublished. Yet Nancy Mitford could not resist putting Tennant in her own novel *Love in a Cold Climate* (1949) as the character Cedric Hampton, who drives the tyrannical Uncle Matthew to an insane rage when encountered by the station bookstall dressed in a suit edged in contrasting colours, for which crime he is shaken 'like a rat'. 'You'd never think', as Cedric said afterwards, 'that buying *Vogue Magazine* could be so dangerous. It was well worth it though, lovely Spring modes' (ibid., 281).

During the Second World War Tennant retreated to a flat in Bournemouth when Wilsford was taken over by the Red Cross. Although he wrote a cogent preface, 'The room beyond', to Cather's *On Writing* (1947), his depressive state had by now deteriorated to the extent that he received electroconvulsive therapy and insulin coma treatment at clinics in Scotland and Middlesex. He returned to Wilsford exhibiting what V. S. Naipaul, his later tenant, diagnosed as 'accidie' (Hoare, 361).

Tennant now obsessively redecorated his childhood home, covering the Syrie Maugham décor of the 1930s with flock and velvet and littering the floors with paintings and letters like confetti; he turned the grounds into an English Côte d'Azur with sand, palms, and tropical lizards. Here, at Wilsford, he held court to guests brought by Beaton to visit this 'last professional beauty', as Osbert Sitwell had called him (Hoare, 337); Truman Capote complained of being served soup with candied violets in it, and Christopher Isherwood, having been subjected to a particularly intense session of poetic reverie, told Beaton, 'That kind of talk scares the shit out of me.' But for a new generation Tennant acquired a certain mythic status: David Hockney, Patrick Procktor, and Kenneth Anger came to pay homage, and Philip Core wrote that Tennant's 'mania for tinselled detritus' had anticipated 'the amphetamine glitter taste of the 1960s' (Core, 177); Caroline Blackwood could compare him only to the rock star David Bowie. Wreathed in his own legend, Tennant had become the stuff of footnotes and anecdotes, as the painter Michael Wishart described him, 'resembling a rainbow, exquisite and rarely seen … Stephen's unique beauty still hung around him like an old-timer at the stage door, hoping for employment' (Wishart, 164–5). When the present writer visited Tennant at Wilsford in 1986, the house had remained largely untouched since the war, filled with Venetian gilt mirrors, rare animal skins, straw hats, and, perhaps, its occupant's portrait in the attic. With his long hennaed hair and turquoise rings on elegant hands, Tennant himself resembled an exotic Edwardian hostess who had somehow survived into a modern age.

On 28 February 1987 Tennant's languid reign at Wilsford came to an end with his death there; and on 4 March his ashes were interred in the neighbouring churchyard at St Michael's, Wilsford-cum-Lake, where his mother had been buried. The following October the three-day auction of his house and contents propelled Tennant into the spotlight once more. For all his self-obsession, there was yet something innocent and wonderful about Stephen Tennant: he had dedicated himself to a life as art, and in that unique creation he undoubtedly succeeded.

PHILIP HOARE

Sources P. Hoare, *Serious pleasures: the life of Stephen Tennant* (1990) · H. Vickers, *Cecil Beaton* (1985) · S. Blow, *Broken blood: the rise and fall of the Tennant family* (1987) · N. Crathorne and others, *Tennant's stalk: the story of the Tennants of the glen* (1973) · [J. Culme], *The contents of Wilsford Manor* (1987) [sale catalogue, Sothebys, London, 14–15 Oct 1987] · P. Core, *Camp: the lie that tells the truth* (1984) · M. Wishart, *High diver* (1977) · J. Moorcroft Wilson, *Siegfried Sassoon: the making of a war poet* (1998) · *CGPLA Eng. & Wales* (1987) · b. cert. · d. cert. · Burke, *Peerage* (1999)

Archives priv. coll., journals · Ransom HRC | Bodl. Oxf., corresp. with Sybil Colefax · Hugo Vickers Archive, Wyeford, Ramsdell, Hampshire | FILM BBC WAC · priv. coll., home footage · priv. coll., interview, H. Pembroke and N. Haslam, *c.*1980s

Likenesses C. Beaton, photograph, 1927, Sothebys, Cecil Beaton archive [*see illus.*]

Wealth at death £814,971: administration, 20 Aug 1987, *CGPLA Eng. & Wales*

Tennant, William (1784–1848), scholar of oriental languages and poet, son of Alexander Tennant, merchant and farmer, and Anna Watson, was born in Anstruther, Fife, on 16 May 1784. He lost the use of both feet in childhood, and used crutches throughout his life. After receiving his elementary education at the burgh school in Anstruther, where he was a contemporary of Thomas Chalmers (1780–1847), he studied at St Andrews University for two years (1799–1801), but he was forced to leave early for financial reasons. On returning to his parental home in 1801 Tennant steadily pursued his literary studies. For a time he acted as clerk to his brother Alexander, a corn factor, first in Glasgow and then at Anstruther. Owing to a crisis in business his brother disappeared, and Tennant suffered a short period of imprisonment for his brother's debts at the instance of the creditors. He began the study of Hebrew about this time, while continuing to increase his knowledge of classical languages.

While at St Andrews, Tennant made some respectable verse translations and a Scottish ballad, 'The Anster Concert' (1811): although a piece of light verse, based on the medieval poem 'Christ's kirk on the green', it demonstrates his interest in native verse traditions. With *Anster Fair*, published anonymously in 1812 by William Cockburn in Anstruther, Tennant instantly achieved greatness. Based on the Fife folk-song 'Maggie Lauder', it combines

William Tennant (1784–1848), by unknown artist

local folk tradition with Italian elements drawn principally from Tasso's *Orlando Furioso*, and is composed in the style of a mock epic. Following publication Tennant received the praise of Alexander Fraser Tytler, Lord Woodhouselee, and a revised edition, published at Tennant's own expense, was issued in 1814 and won from Lord Jeffrey a warm reception in the *Edinburgh Review*; he described it there both as 'eminently original' and 'bold and vigorous' and referred to Tennant as a 'kind of prodigy' (Jeffrey). Six editions of the poem appeared in the author's lifetime.

Tennant's father's house had long been a centre of literary activity—a focal point for gatherings of visitors and townsfolk with literary interests and a desire for self-improvement—and Tennant's own literary aspirations were encouraged by this atmosphere. In 1813 he formed, along with Captain Charles Gray, Matthew Conolly (his biographer), and others, the Anstruther Musomanik Society, the members of which, according to their code of admission, assembled to enjoy 'the coruscations of their own festive minds' (Conolly, *Memoir*, 213). The main purpose of the society was to recite verse, much of which was composed expressly for the meetings. Honorary members of proved poetic worth, including James Hogg, were admitted, Sir Walter Scott assuring the members, on receipt of his diploma in 1815, of the pleasure the award gave him, and of his best wishes for their healthy indulgence in 'weel-timed daffing' (ibid.).

In 1813 Tennant was appointed parish schoolmaster of Dunino, 5 miles from St Andrews. The close proximity of the university and its library gave him the opportunity not only to develop his Hebrew scholarship, but also to gain a knowledge of Arabic, Syriac, and Persian, and here he also became acquainted with scholars such as Hugh Cleghorn. In 1816, through the influence of Burns's friend George Thomson and others, Tennant became schoolmaster at Lasswade, Midlothian. In 1819, the year in which his edition of Allan Ramsay's poems was published, he was elected teacher of classical and oriental languages at the Dollar Academy, Clackmannanshire, and held the post with distinction until 1834, when Jeffrey, then lord advocate for Scotland, appointed him professor of Hebrew and oriental languages in St Mary's College, St Andrews, where Tennant established a reputation for being a talented and well-liked lecturer.

None of Tennant's later literary work, however, lived up to the initial promise of *Anster Fair*. In 1822 he published *The Thane of Fife*, a serious attempt at epic poetry concerning the Danish invasion of the ninth century. The first part of the poem was so poorly received that he never completed it. In 1823 appeared *Cardinal Beaton*, a tragedy in five acts, and in 1825 *John Baliol*, a historical drama. Tennant returned to the formula of the mock epic in 1827, with his *Papistry Storm'd, or, The Dingin Doon o' the Cathedral*. Written entirely in Scots, it concerned the destruction of St Andrews Cathedral at the Reformation, and is another example of his local patriotism, which combined comic elements with an indebtedness to the verse style of Sir David Lindsay. He published a number of works which reflected his interest in oriental languages, including five 'Hebrew Idylls', contributed to the *Scottish Christian Herald* in 1836–7, and a *Syriac and Chaldee Grammar*, which became a popular textbook. In 1830 Tennant became a contributor to the *Edinburgh Literary Journal*, publishing prose translations from Greek and German, and discussing with Hogg the value of issuing a new metrical version of the Psalms, in a correspondence which was published in 1830.

William Tennant retired, owing to ill health, in 1848, but continued to write and to research. He died, unmarried, at Devon Grove, Clackmannanshire, on 14 October 1848, and was buried at Anstruther, where an obelisk monument with a Latin inscription was raised to his memory.   T. W. BAYNE, rev. RICHARD OVENDEN

Sources M. F. Conolly, *Memoir of the life and writings of William Tennant* (1861) · *The comic poems of William Tennant*, ed. A. Scott and M. Lindsay (1989) · G. Angeletti, 'Hogg's debt to William Tennant: the influence of "Anster Fair" on Hogg's poetry', *Studies in Hogg and His World*, 6 (1995), 22–32 · F. Jeffrey, 'Tennant's "Anster Fair"', *EdinR*, 24 (1814–15), 174–82 · W. Tennant, letter to Walter Scott, 1815, NL Scot., MS 866, fol. 3 · W. Tennant, letters to Archibald Constable & Co., 1813–23, NL Scot., MS 332, fols. 1–32 · M. F. Conolly, *Biographical dictionary of eminent men of Fife* (1866) · Chambers, *Scots.* (1835) · T. Constable, *Archibald Constable and his literary correspondents*, 2 (1873); repr. (New York, 1975), 207–9 · bap. reg. Scot.

Archives Mitchell L., Glas. · NL Scot., letters · U. Edin. L., reading notes | Glos. RO, letters to Daniel Ellis · NL Scot., letters to Archibald Constable

Likenesses F. Croll, stipple and line engraving, NPG; repro. in *Hogg's Weekly Instructor* · oils, Scot. NPG [*see illus.*] · pencil and watercolour drawing, Scot. NPG

Wealth at death £503 4s. 6d.: probate, NA Scot., SC 64/42/8/315–18

Tennent, Gilbert (1703–1764), Presbyterian minister in America, was born on 5 February 1703 in Vinnescash, co.

Armagh, Ireland, the first of five children born to William Tennent (1673–1746), a Presbyterian minister, and Katherine Kennedy (d. 1753); William *Tennent junior was his brother. Both parents were Scottish Presbyterians who had emigrated to Ireland. In 1718 the family moved to America, where William Tennent served congregations in New York and Pennsylvania. Having been educated at the University of Edinburgh, William Tennent taught his son Gilbert so effectively that in 1725 he graduated MA of Yale College without having earned the bachelor's degree. In addition the elder Tennent impressed upon his eldest son his understanding of experiential Christianity, which he would pass on to numerous other young men at the 'log college' that he established.

After a period of spiritual struggle, Gilbert Tennent had an intense religious experience in 1723. Feeling called to the ministry, he was licensed to preach in 1725 and ordained in 1726 in New Brunswick, New Jersey, where he ministered to a Presbyterian congregation until 1743. The spiritual indifference of his parishioners discouraged him until he became acquainted with Theodorus Jacobus Frelinghuysen, the Dutch Reformed minister of congregations in the New Brunswick area. Frelinghuysen had brought with him from his native East Friesland the beliefs and practices of continental pietism. He preached pungent sermons to impress upon impenitent sinners the perils of their condition, and stressed the need for a conversion experience, which was to be followed by pious living. These beliefs coincided with what Gilbert Tennent had learned from his father. When Gilbert Tennent adopted Frelinghuysen's methods he noticed more obvious responses.

Tennent felt so deeply the need to awaken Presbyterians from their spiritual stupor that he carried his message beyond the bounds of his own parish, to pastorless congregations and the congregations of pastors of whose apparent lack of spirituality he did not approve. Little is known of Tennent's family life. His first wife, who remains nameless, died in 1740. In 1742 he married Cornelia Clarkson, *née* Bancker de Pyster (d. 1753).

When the English evangelist George Whitefield arrived in 1739 Tennent introduced him to evangelistic 'New Light' colleagues in the middle colonies. In 1740 his intensity led him to preach at Nottingham, Pennsylvania, on 'The danger of an unconverted ministry', an extremely censorious condemnation of many of his ministerial colleagues. In the same year he accompanied Whitefield on a preaching tour in New England, and in 1741 he followed up alone on Whitefield's ministry there. Tennent's evangelism led to numerous spiritual revivals during what has been called 'the first great awakening of religion'. In a backlash against the New Lights' perceived exaggerated emphasis on emotional experiential religion, officials of the synod of Philadelphia expelled Tennent and his allies in 1741. The ejected Presbyterians joined their colleagues to the north and formed the rival New York synod. The two remained separate until 1758, and it was largely through Tennent's increasing moderation and his efforts to reach out to his former adversaries that the synods were able to reunite.

A major reason for Tennent's shift was his awareness of Count Ludwig von Zinzendorf's Moravians, who came to America in 1741. The Moravians concentrated on experience without a firm doctrinal base. As the Moravians enjoyed some success, Tennent began to speak against them. Tennent denied that he had changed his emphasis. His explanation was that when he left New Brunswick in 1743 to become the minister of a congregation of White-field's supporters in Philadelphia that became the Second Presbyterian Church, his members needed more instruction than exhortation. Tennent also changed his style of preaching. As a revivalistic awakener, he spoke almost extemporaneously. In Philadelphia he read his sermons from his manuscript. No longer did he rebuke so harshly his fellow ministers, nor did he inject himself into their congregations.

When Gilbert Tennent's father's log college closed, Tennent joined other New Lights in establishing a new college, first at Elizabethtown, Pennsylvania, and later at Princeton, New Jersey; he served as a trustee from 1746 until his death. Following the death of his second wife, from 1753 to 1755, he embarked with Samuel Davies on a tour of the British Isles to raise funds for the institution. In addition he became a staunch supporter of efforts to defend Pennsylvania against the incursions of the Spaniards and the French, and published sermons on the subject in the late 1740s and 1750s. Some time before 1762 he married Sarah Spoffard (d. 1764), with whom he had three children, one son and two daughters; all four survived him.

Gilbert Tennent was one of British America's best-known clergymen, but his active ministry took its toll on his health. His declining health and some parishioners' dissatisfaction with his formal style of preaching led his congregation to call for an assistant, which led to a controversy that afflicted him during the last two years of his life. He died in Philadelphia on 23 July 1764, and was buried beneath the centre aisle of the Second Presbyterian Church, which he had served for twenty-one years. At a later date his body was moved to the cemetery of Abington Presbyterian Church, Pennsylvania.

JOHN B. FRANTZ

Sources M. J. Coalter, *Gilbert Tennent, son of thunder: a case study of continental pietism's impact on the first Great Awakening in the middle colonies* (New York, 1986) · M. J. Coalter, 'Gilbert Tennent, revival workhorse in a neglected awakening theological tradition', *Religion in New Jersey life before the civil war*, ed. M. R. Murrin (Trenton, 1985) · M. J. Coalter, 'The radical pietism of Count Zinzendorf as a conservative influence on the awakener, Gilbert Tennent', *Church History*, 49 (1980), 35–46 · M. J. Coalter, 'Tennant, Gilbert', *ANB* · W. B. Sprague, 'Gilbert Tennent', *Annals of the American pulpit*, 3 (1859), 35–41 · A. Alexander, *The log college: biographical sketches of William Tennent and his students, together with an account of the revivals under their ministries* (1968), 23–67 · L. J. Trinterud, *The forming of an American tradition: a re-examination of colonial Presbyterianism* [1949] · M. E. Lodge, 'The Great Awakening in the middle colonies', PhD diss., U. Cal., Berkeley, 1964 · J. Tanis, *Dutch Calvinistic pietism in the middle colonies: a study in the life and theology of Theodorus Jacobus Frelinghuysen* (The Hague, 1967) · B. F. Le Beau, *Jonathan Dickinson and the formative years of American Presbyterianism* (Lexington, Kentucky, 1997)

Archives Hist. Soc. Penn., papers · Presbyterian Historical Society, Philadelphia, papers · Presbyterian Study Center, Montreat, North Carolina, family records · Princeton Theological Seminary, New Jersey, Speer Library, papers · Princeton University, New Jersey, Firestone Library, family papers

Likenesses attrib. G. Hesselius, oils, Princeton University, New Jersey

Wealth at death £300 to son for education; also provided for daughters: Sprague, 'Gilbert Tennent'

Tennent, Hamilton Tovey- (1782–1866), army officer in the East India Company, born at Garrigheugh, Comrie, Perthshire, on 20 August 1782, was the second son of John Tovey of Stirling and his wife, Hamilton, daughter of Sir James Dunbar of Mochrum and Woodside, third baronet, judge-advocate of Scotland, and his wife, Jacobina, *née* Hamilton. He was educated at Stirling, and on 28 December 1798 was commissioned as lieutenant in the Bombay military service. In 1801 he was posted to the 24th regular native infantry at Goa and was employed on active service against the Marathas. In 1805, while serving under Lord Lake at the siege of Bharatpur, he was severely wounded in an assault on the town. On 17 January 1811 he was promoted captain. In 1813 he was placed in command of Ahmednagar, and appointed brigade major at Poona. After more service against the Marathas he was appointed in 1819 private secretary to Mountstuart Elphinstone, governor of Bombay. He was promoted major on 19 January 1820, and accompanied Elphinstone on his tour through the province until November 1821, when he was compelled by the effect of his wounds to return to England. He retired from the service on 24 April 1824, being promoted lieutenant-colonel. In 1832 he succeeded to the estates of his cousin, James Tennent, of The Pynnacles, Great Stanmore, Middlesex, and of Overton, Shropshire, and assumed his surname and arms. In 1836 he married Helen, only daughter of General Samuel Graham, lieutenant-governor of Stirling Castle. They had no children. Tovey-Tennent was a large contributor to charitable objects. Among other gifts he presented a site for a new church at Stanmore in 1854, and contributed £1000 to erect a school at Stirling. He died at The Pynnacles, on 4 March 1866. He was succeeded in his estates by his nephew, James Tovey-Tennent.

E. I. CARLYLE, *rev.* M. G. M. JONES

Sources *GM*, 4th ser., 1 (1866), 608 · *GM*, 4th ser., 2 (1866), 693 · Burke, *Gen. GB* (1871) · Dodwell [E. Dodwell] and Miles [J. S. Miles], eds., *Alphabetical list of the officers of the Indian army: with the dates of their respective promotion, retirement, resignation, or death … from the year 1760 to the year … 1837* (1838) [Bombay presidency] · T. E. Colebrooke, *Life of the Honourable Mountstuart Elphinstone*, 2 vols. (1884), vol. 2

Wealth at death under £20,000: resworn probate, Oct 1866, *CGPLA Eng. & Wales*

Tennent, Sir James Emerson, first baronet (1804–1869), traveller and politician, third son of William Emerson (d. 1821), merchant, of Belfast, and Sarah, youngest daughter of William Arbuthnot, of Rockville, co. Down, was born at Belfast on 7 April 1804 and was educated at Trinity College, Dublin, which awarded him an honorary degree of LLD in 1861. In 1824 he travelled abroad. An enthusiast in the cause of Greek freedom, he visited Greece and met Lord Byron. His impressions of the country appeared in 1826 in *A Picture of Greece in 1825, Letters from the Aegean* (2 vols., 1829), and *The History of Modern Greece* (2 vols., 1830). These works received mixed notices.

On 28 January 1831 Emerson (as he was then known) was called to the bar at Lincoln's Inn, where he had become a student on the advice of Jeremy Bentham, but it is doubtful if he ever practised his profession. On 24 June 1831 he married Laetitia, only daughter and heir of William Tennent, a wealthy banker at Belfast, of Tempo Manor, co. Fermanagh. In 1832 when his father-in-law died he assumed his name and arms, in addition to his own, by royal licence, and succeeded to estates in counties Sligo and Fermanagh.

Tennent was elected member of parliament for Belfast on 21 December 1832. He supported Lord Grey's administration until 1834 when he joined Lord Stanley's and Sir James Graham's followers, and with them afterwards supported Peel. He favoured free trade and thought that some of the burdens of agriculture should be relieved and that tenants should be legally entitled to security of tenure if they made improvements.

At the election in 1837 Tennent was defeated at Belfast, but on petition was seated in 1838. In 1841 he was re-elected, but was unseated on petition. In 1842 he regained his seat, and that year performed the most important service of his parliamentary career as the chief promoter of the Copyright of Designs Bill, which extended protection against copying to those who had devised designs, such as those for wallpapers and textiles, to complement that accorded to inventors under the patent legislation. This was of very considerable importance to manufacturers and helped to ensure the success of the Great Exhibition of 1851, since manufacturers could safely put their products on display. He was secretary to the India board in 1841–3, and remained a member of the House of Commons until July 1845, when he was knighted.

From 1845 to 1850 Tennent was civil secretary to the colonial government of Ceylon. On 31 December 1850 he was gazetted governor of St Helena, but he never took up the appointment. After his return home he again sat in parliament as member for Lisburn from 10 January to December 1852. In 1852 he was permanent secretary to the poor-law board and that year was made secretary to the Board of Trade. On his retirement on 2 February 1867 he was created a baronet.

Tennent described his stay in Ceylon in *Ceylon: an Account of the Island* (2 vols., 1859), a work which went through five editions in eight months. It contained a vast amount of information arranged with clarity and precision, and received generally good reviews. In 1861 he republished part of it as *Sketches of the Natural History of Ceylon*. He published two other works on the country, in 1860 and, in 1867, *The Wild Elephant and the Method of Capturing and Taming it in Ceylon*. He was elected a fellow of the Royal Society on 5 June 1862. He died suddenly at his home, 66 Warwick Square, Belgrave Road, London, on 6 March 1869, and was buried in Kensal Green cemetery on 12 March. His widow died on 21 April 1883; they had two daughters, Ethel Sarah and Edith Laetitia Anna, and a son, Sir William Emerson Tennent, second baronet, who was born on 14 May 1835. He was called to the bar at the Inner Temple on 26 January 1859, became a clerk in the Board of Trade in 1855, accompanied Sir William Hutt to Vienna in 1865 to negotiate a treaty of commerce, and was secretary to Sir Stephen Cave in the mixed commission to Paris (1866–7) for revising the fishery convention. He died at Tempo Manor, co. Fermanagh, on 16 November 1876 and the baronetcy became extinct.

G. C. BOASE, *rev.* ELIZABETH BAIGENT

Sources *The Times* (8 March 1869) · *The Times* (15 March 1869) · *The Times* (17 Nov 1876) · Burke, *Peerage* · *Dod's Parliamentary Companion* · [H. T. Ryall], ed., *Portraits of eminent conservatives and statesmen*, 2 vols. [1836–46] · Allibone, *Dict.* · *CGPLA Eng. & Wales* (1869)

Archives NRA, priv. coll., corresp. and papers relating to Ceylon · PRO NIre., corresp. and papers | BL, corresp. with Sir Robert Peel, Add. MSS 40413–40600 · BL OIOC, letters to marquess of Tweeddale · Bodl. Oxf., letters to Benjamin Disraeli · Bucks. RLSS, letters to first Baron Cottesloe · Lpool RO, letters to fourteenth earl of Derby · U. Durham L., corresp. with third Earl Grey

Likenesses lithograph, pubd 1852, NPG · R. A. Artlatt, stipple (after G. Richmond), BM, NPG; repro. in Ryall, *Portraits of eminent conservatives*, no. 12 · P. Macdowell, marble bust, Belfast Corporation · portrait, repro. in *ILN*, 3 (1843), 293

Wealth at death under £6000: probate, 1 May 1869, *CGPLA Eng. & Wales*

Tennent, William, junior

Tennent, William, junior (1705–1777), Presbyterian minister, was born on 3 June 1705 in co. Armagh, Ireland, the second of five children of William Tennent senior (1673–1746), clergyman and educator, and Katherine Kennedy (d. 1753), daughter of the well-known Presbyterian minister Gilbert Kennedy. Both parents were Scots-Irish.

William Tennent went to America in 1718 with his parents, three brothers, and one sister. He attended the so-called 'log college', established by his father, at Neshaminy, Pennsylvania, and continued his preparation for the ministry in New Brunswick, New Jersey, under the tutelage of his more famous elder brother, Gilbert *Tennent (1703–1764), who served Presbyterian congregations in that area. Possibly because of the pressure William Tennent put upon himself to do well in his studies, he became ill. For six weeks, he hovered between death and life. Thereafter, he steadily improved to the extent that after about a year he recovered.

Restored to good physical and mental health, William Tennent was licensed to preach. When his younger brother John died in 1732, William was asked to serve his congregation at Freehold in Monmouth county, New Jersey, on a trial basis. Evidently he proved satisfactory, for in the following year, 1733, he was ordained and installed as the congregation's regular minister, a position that he held for the next forty-four years.

William Tennent was steady in pastoral visitation and preaching to his and other congregations to which he was invited. His theology was moderately Calvinistic, including the doctrines of God's omnipotence, human depravity, and the atonement of Christ. His sermons were well received, not only by his parishioners but also by students at the College of New Jersey who were said to have travelled 20 miles on foot to attend services in his church. At least two of his sermons were published during his lifetime. Unlike his brother Gilbert, William often attempted to avoid controversy. When young clergymen asked him to resolve their dispute about whether faith or repentance came first in a sinner's conversion, he listened to their arguments and then suggested to his devout parishioners that the issue did not matter, because they had both.

Still, William Tennent could take firm stands. When New Jersey's Governor William Franklin attempted to transform the Presbyterian College of New Jersey (later Princeton University), of which Tennent was a trustee and vice-president, into a public institution, Tennent resisted vigorously and effectively.

In the controversy that temporarily ruptured the Presbyterian church during the 'Great Awakening of Religion' in the mid-1700s, William Tennent was a New Sider who participated in 'revivals of religion'. He went on evangelistic tours with Presbyterian ministerial colleagues Samuel Blair, to Virginia, and John Rowland, to Maryland. He supported George Whitefield, the English evangelist who preached throughout British America. When the 'log college' ministers formed their 'New Side' New Brunswick presbytery and New York synod, he became a member, and was one of their most prominent ministers. During the colonists' controversy with Great Britain, he prayed for the Americans but kept politics out of his pulpit.

So engrossed was the young William Tennent in his ministry that he overlooked personal matters. He entrusted the land around his parsonage to an incompetent manager, who led him into debt. A friend, Isaac Noble, suggested that a wife could more capably manage his finances and incidentally provide 'conjugal' enjoyment. Tennent replied that he lacked the skills necessary for courtship. When Noble recommended and introduced Tennent to his sister-in-law, widow Catherine van Burgh Noble, William met, proposed to, and married her within a week, on 23 August 1738. The couple had six children, three of whom lived to adulthood. Son William (III) Tennent became the minister of the Presbyterian congregation in Charles Town, South Carolina. Two other sons became physicians, one of whom died before his father.

In appearance William Tennent was impressive, a tall man, over 6 feet, thin, with bright penetrating eyes, a long nose, and a narrow face. In later life he is said to have worn a white wig. Normally he was serious but was able to relax and be pleasant with friends. He died on 8 March 1777, probably in Freehold. A large congregation attended his funeral. He was buried under the floor of the church in which he preached at Freehold. Presumably his wife and two sons survived him.   JOHN B. FRANTZ

Sources A. Alexander, 'Memoir of the Rev. William Tennent, Jr.', *The log college: biographical sketches of William Tennent and his students together with an account of the revivals under their ministries* (1968), 97–131 · E. Boudinot, *Memoirs of the life of William Tennent, formerly pastor of the Presbyterian church of Freehold in New Jersey in which is contained, among other interesting particulars, an account of his being three days in a trance and apparently lifeless* (1828) · W. B. Sprague, 'William Tennent (second)', *Annals of the American pulpit*, 3 (1859), 53–62 · M. J. Coulter,

Gilbert Tennent, son of thunder: a case study of continental pietism's impact of the first Great Awakening in the middle colonies (1986) · T. J. Wertenbaker, *Princeton, 1746–1896* (1946) · C. H. Maxson, *The Great Awakening in the middle colonies* (1920); repr. (Gloucester, MA, 1958) · M. J. Westercamp, *Triumph of the laity: Scots-Irish piety and the Great Awakening, 1625–1760* (1988) · M. J. Coulter, 'Gilbert Tennent: revival workhorse in a neglected awakening theological tradition', *Religion in New Jersey before the civil war*, ed. M. R. Murrin (1985) · L. J. Trinterud, *The forming of an American tradition: a re-examination of colonial Presbyterianism* [1949] · G. S. Klett, *Presbyterians in colonial Pennsylvania* (1937) · H. E. S., 'Tennent, William', *DAB* · M. A. Noll, 'Tennent, William (1673–1746)', *ANB*
Wealth at death comfortable: Alexander, 'Memoir of William Tennent'

Tenniel, Sir John (1820–1914), artist and cartoonist, was born on 28 February 1820 at 22 Gloucester Place, New Road, Bayswater, London, the third son of John Baptist Tenniel (1793–1879), a fencing and dancing master of Huguenot origins, and his wife, Eliza Maria (d. 1864), of Liverpool. Living in genteel poverty in Kensington, his parents could not afford much formal education for their six children. Tenniel, the third son, attended a local primary school and then became the pupil of his athletic father, who taught him fencing, dancing, riding, and other gentlemanly arts. At the age of twenty, while fencing with his father, the button of his opponent's foil fell off and he suffered a cut that blinded his right eye—an injury that he concealed from his father for the rest of his life in order to spare him any pangs of guilt.

A rather introverted youth, Tenniel preferred reading, sketching, and attending the theatre to sporting pursuits. Encouraged by a family friend, John Martin, the well-known painter of heroic biblical scenes, he became fascinated by religious paintings and visited art galleries and museums in London, where he copied works into a sketchbook. Although he admired the liturgy and vestments of the Roman Catholic church, he strongly resented the dogma and authoritarianism of this faith and prized the relative freedom of the Anglican church. Endowed with a near-photographic memory, he learned to memorize an image and then replicate it at home. At the age of sixteen he sold his first oil painting at the Society of British Artists and in 1837 he exhibited another painting—*Captain Peppercull Interceding for Nigel with Duke Hildebrand*. As a student or probationer at the Royal Academy Schools he had to copy old masters and learn the rudiments of human anatomy in the life class. Discouraged by the old-fashioned curriculum and the lack of instruction, he sought more congenial company in the Clipstone Street Art Society near Fitzroy Square, which he joined in the mid-1840s. There he befriended the illustrator Charles Keene, and found the freedom to draw from live models (both nude and costumed) and to paint in oil. He also sketched the Elgin marbles at the British Museum, under the tutelage of Sir Frederick Madden, and knights in armour at the Tower of London.

Tenniel's artistic career may be divided into four stages, which tended to overlap in his maturity. First he painted classical subjects with a romantic sensibility derived in

Sir John Tenniel (1820–1914), by Frank Holl, c.1883

part from German painting. Second, he drew black and white decorative initials and small figures in medieval costume that mocked the prevailing cult of Gothicism. Third, he became the magisterial political cartoonist of *Punch*, the leading comic weekly of the Victorian era. And last, he illustrated such books as S. C. Hall's *The Book of British Ballads* (1842); *Aesop's Fables* (1848); Thomas Moore's *Lalla Rookh* (1861); Richard Barham's *The Ingoldsby Legends* (1864, originally illustrated by George Cruikshank and John Leech); and, most famously, Lewis Carroll's two classics, *Alice's Adventures in Wonderland* (1865) and *Through the Looking-Glass, and What Alice Found There* (1872). He read every work carefully before drawing the characters and tried to take as few artistic liberties with the text as possible.

Early career At the outset Tenniel showed a Pugin-like nostalgia for the chivalric and Christian values of an imagined golden age of medieval culture. In 1845 he submitted a 16 foot high design to the Fine Arts Commission in the competition for the frescoes in the new House of Lords. Tenniel's late entry consisted of a coloured sketch and an unfinished cartoon entitled *The Spirit of Justice*. Although the commissioners honoured him with a premium of £200, much controversy surrounded the award and they eventually opted for Daniel Maclise's design on the same subject. Asked to paint a smaller fresco for the House of Lords, Tenniel designed *A Song for St. Cecilia's Day* (1846) for which he earned £400 and this was added to the upper waiting hall or the hall of poets. The prize money paid for his first visit to Europe, notably Munich, where he studied the paintings of the Nazarene school. In 1848,

when Chartist agitators poured into London to present their third petition, Tenniel and his new friend, the incomparable comic artist John Leech, enrolled as special constables to patrol the streets at night. Fearful for their own safety in the depths of south London, they were much relieved to encounter no potential rioters on their beat.

Punch years Somewhat disenchanted by his attempts at fresco painting, Tenniel was hungry for a steady income. Fortunately, the two main founders of *Punch, or, The London Charivari*, Douglas Jerrold and Mark Lemon, admired the illustrations he had done for the Revd Thomas James's new edition of *Aesop's Fables* and he was hired in November 1850 to replace the gifted artist Richard Doyle, who had resigned in protest over *Punch*'s anti-Catholic bias. At the outset Tenniel drew only initial letters, titles, and 'small cuts' for the pocket book and almanac. His first title-page appeared in volume 20 (January 1851) along with several preface designs featuring Mr Punch. Evidently, Tenniel made the leap from high art to cartooning with some misgivings but showed barely a break in stride. Many years later—in the 1880s—a friend took him to task for being too serious in his cartoons. To this gentle chiding he retorted that critics who denied him 'everything but severity, "classicality", and dignity' failed to realize that he did have 'a very keen sense of humour and ... my drawings are sometimes really funny!' (Spielmann, 403). Like a great jazz pianist brought up on the keyboard works of Bach and Handel, he continued to draw on classical imagery and many of his cartoons reflected a half respectful and half parodic attitude towards tradition. If he lacked the irreverence of Harry Furniss, his 'senior cartoons' or 'big cuts' in *Punch* could be droll or whimsical and almost as didactic as a leader in *The Times*.

Although Tenniel's early and lasting preference for drawing his designs on a woodblock with a 6H pencil may have deprived his cartoons of the sharp lines made possible by etching on steel, he did achieve more bite with his wood-engraving technique. He also had the good fortune to work with two outstanding teams of engravers—Joseph Swain and his son, Joseph Blomley Swain, and the brothers Edward and George Dalziel, who followed his instructions with skill and goodwill. Throughout his career he relied entirely on his powerful memory to capture his subjects—a habit that deprived some cartoons of a certain liveliness or freshness. At the same time some of his small cuts and book illustrations harked back to the Gothic-revival Eglinton tournament of 1839 that Doyle and Leech had caricatured so cleverly. If, as Roger Simpson has pointed out, Tenniel's 'serious medievalizing art failed to contribute very much to the creation of a new Victorian domestic iconography', he did 'revolutionize and propel into dominance ... a minor facet of early Victorian comic art ... the comic history piece', that combined 'scholarship, draftmanship, and a capacity for self-parody' (Simpson, 71).

Promoted in 1861 to a junior partnership with Leech at a

salary of £500, Tenniel began to produce political cartoons every week. When Leech died suddenly in 1864, Tenniel assumed his large mantle, and wore this with distinction until he retired at the end of 1900. Altogether he produced some 2165 big cuts, not to mention all the smaller
designs, compared with Leech's output of 720. At the end
of his career he reckoned that only six numbers of *Punch*
over the course of fifty years lacked one of his major or
minor works.

A compulsive worker, Tenniel lived rather austerely
until his marriage in 1854 to Julia Giani, an Italian from
Liverpool. He settled with his bride at 10 Portsdown Road,
Maida Hill, where they enjoyed only two years together.
Julia died of tuberculosis on 23 January 1856 aged only
thirty-one. Her death devastated Tenniel, who continued
to mourn and never remarried. Instead, he invited his
mother-in-law, Eve, to become his housekeeper and she
remained in this capacity until she died twenty-three
years later. Although a keen amateur actor, he did not
indulge in the bohemian nightlife of comic artists and
writers who dined and wined heavily in London's clubs
and restaurants. A private and taciturn man, Jackides—
his nickname at *Punch*—emulated Leech by saying little at
the boisterous round table dinners of the staff every Wednesday—usually held in Bouverie Street, Whitefriars—
when they planned the next week's first cartoon or big
cut. On these occasions Tenniel rarely proposed a topic
but calmly smoked his monogrammed churchwarden
pipe while his colleagues decided the issue. Courted by
London's leading hostesses, he much preferred private
dinner parties. If some friends thought that he resembled
Don Quixote, they all praised his exquisite manners and
'sunny wholesome disposition' (Lucy, 379). During his
long tenure at *Punch* he took only two holidays (one to Italy
in the autumn of 1878 and the other to Paris for the 1889
exhibition). As for exercise, he enjoyed riding in London
parks and rowing with friends up the Thames on a summer's day.

Some sympathetic critics have noted a certain severity
and coldness in Tenniel's cartoons after the 1860s. As
Simpson observes, he 'reduc[ed] the vibrant tradition of
Hogarth and Gillray to a cold, righteous imperial iconography' (Simpson, 9). But this stricture does not allow for
the dramatic change in tastes between the Hanoverian
and Victorian ages. After all, James Gillray and his contemporaries did not have to worry unduly about any constraints in matters scatological and sexual that forced Victorian cartoonists to temper their jokes so severely. If
Tenniel's political cartoons lacked vibrancy and warmth,
they possessed a magisterial quality best exemplified by
his famous double-page cut *Dropping the Pilot*, which
blended *gravitas* with all the punch of a telegram announcing the Kaiser's dismissal of Bismarck in 1889 (*Punch*, 29
March 1890, 98, 150–51).

The number and quality of the animals in his big cuts
made Tenniel seem like the Landseer of Victorian cartooning. His elephants, tigers, lions, horses, cats, dogs, and
other animals were in a class of their own, partly because
he spent hours at the zoo observing feral creatures in

motion and at rest. Tenniel's images of statuesque female
icons also impressed viewers, especially younger men.
Second only to Queen Victoria, whom he revered, the
woman most prized by Tenniel was Britannia, whom he
depicted as a full-breasted Pallas Athene dressed either in
armour or a soft Grecian robe and wielding a two-handed
sword. Tenniel was not alone in seeing her as the tran-
scendent symbol of British virtue, wisdom, and power.

Despite their dignified quality some of Tenniel's cartoons partook of the dominant prejudices of the day. His
depiction of Jews included such standard antisemitic features as the hooked nose and the dark, oily locks of the
Shylock–Fagin variety that were not confined to *Punch*.
And yet he did not distort Benjamin Disraeli's features any
more than those of his great rival, William Gladstone.
Tenniel also endowed some African chieftains or warriors
with such racialized traits as thick lips and big bellies (for
example, *Time's Waxworks*, *Punch*, 31 Dec 1881, 81, 307). But
when it came to the Irish—especially Fenians or republican separatists wedded to physical force—he delighted
in simianizing rebel Paddy. Indeed, his Fenian apemen
rank among the fiercest images of political violence ever
to appear in the serio-comic format. By means of low fore-
heads, pointed ears, snub noses, high upper lips, receding
chins, prognathous jaws, and sharp fangs, he turned these
agitators into Calibans or gorilla–guerrillas (as in *The Irish
Frankenstein*, *Punch*, 20 May 1882, 82, 235).

Illustrating *Alice* Much impressed by Tenniel's work in
Aesop's Fables, Charles Dodgson (Lewis Carroll) asked the
artist to illustrate his *Alice* books. If this choice proved
felicitous, the writer and artist did not enjoy a happy marriage. And after enduring Carroll's constant interventions
while working on *Through the Looking-Glass*, Tenniel
resolved to end his collaboration. But if the measure of
success for a book illustrator is to make it impossible for
readers to imagine any other characters than those
drawn, then his ninety-two contributions deserve to be
called superb. Who can think of Alice without conjuring
up Tenniel's angelic girl with the unruly mane of hair, the
smock and pinafore, and the striped stockings? And the
same question can be posed of corpulent Father William
going through his perpetual motions, the Caterpillar, the
Mock Turtle, the March Hare, the Cheshire Cat, the Jabber-
wock, the ugly Duchess, and Tweedledum and Tweedle-
dee, and so on down the line. As Michael Hancher has
made clear, the quest for the sources of Tenniel's marvellous menagerie of persons and creatures in the *Alice* books
reveals many connections between 'high' and 'low' art.
Suffice to say that the designs for *Alice* derived not just
from such contemporaries as Leech, Doyle, Du Maurier,
and Grandville but also from Flemish and Italian painters
of the Renaissance. The endearingly pathetic figure of the
White Knight with his flowing moustache and prominent
nose, sitting insecurely astride a horse laden with a bunch
of carrots and turnips as well as a bellows and fire-tongs,
evokes those foolhardy knights who became mired in the
mud of the Eglinton tourney some thirty years before.
Needless to say, the White Knight's long drooping moustache resembled that on the artist's upper lip as well as

Van Dyck's equestrian portrait of Charles I (National Gallery, London).

Later years Honoured by Gladstone with a knighthood in 1893, Tenniel was as well known as many of the politicians he drew. Seeking to distance himself from Gillray's ribald and scurrilous prints, he cultivated respectability and embraced the label of cartoonist rather than caricaturist. As David Low put it, he aspired to attain 'a high standard of gentlemanly decorum' and his commitment to 'discretion ... tact and ambiguity' meant that his cartoons caused no offence (Low, 20–21). For this reason his best big cuts possessed a dignified, even Olympian, quality that fell out of fashion before his death. Besides producing weekly cartoons for *Punch* Tenniel also painted a number of watercolours on classical or romantic themes. He also drew a revealing pen-and-ink self-portrait (1889; National Portrait Gallery, London). Thirty-seven folders of Tenniel's drawings are in the Houghton Library at Harvard University.

After his retirement, Tenniel's many friends at *Punch* and among the social and political élite gave him a lavish testimonial dinner at the Hotel Metropole on 12 June 1901 chaired by Arthur Balfour (then leader of the House of Commons) and attended by other prominent politicians and dignitaries. The glowing tributes and the cheering of the guests when Tenniel rose to reply to the toasts so overwhelmed the guest of honour that he could barely mumble a few words before sitting down in acute embarrassment.

Tenniel spent his last years as a semi-invalid drawing and painting until the sight in his left eye failed altogether. Owing to a hip injury his devoted sister, Victoria, could no longer care for him in the large house they had shared for so long in Maida Hill. Reluctantly, they moved in 1909 to a new convenience flat at 52 FitzGeorge Avenue, West Kensington, which he found too small and noisy. He died there on 25 February 1914, three days shy of his ninety-fourth birthday. Modest to the end he left instructions for cremation at Golders Green and burial of his ashes in Kensal Green cemetery, which took place on 4 March 1914.

The Times awarded Tenniel not only a long obituary that praised his ability to capture 'the joys and sorrows of his countrymen' but also an editorial entitled simply, 'The cartoonist' (*The Times*, 3 March 1914). Here the writer predicted that his political cartoons would be as fresh fifty or a hundred years hence as they were on the day of publication, adding that they comprised 'the most attractive textbook of modern history' for the younger generation. Not even 'the gravest student of history' should neglect his pictorial jokes that owed as much to public opinion and the editorial policy of *Punch* as they did to the artist's own imagination.

A founding member of the Arts Club (in 1863), Tenniel was elected to the more exclusive Garrick in 1873 and he also belonged to the Royal Institute of Painters in Water Colours. In his will he left the modest sum of £10,509 to be divided among a few relatives, close friends, and

retainers. Tenniel's black and white cartoons set a standard of artistic merit and irony with a comic turn that left their mark on many contemporary cartoonists. Along with Leech and Sambourne his many memorable cuts helped to make *Punch* into a national, indeed, imperial, institution.

L. PERRY CURTIS JUN.

Sources R. Engen, *Sir John Tenniel: Alice's White Knight* (1991) · R. Simpson, *Sir John Tenniel: aspects of his work* (1994) · F. Sarzano, *Sir John Tenniel* (1948) · M. H. Spielmann, *The history of 'Punch'* (1895); facs. edn (1969) · M. Hancher, *The Tenniel illustrations to the 'Alice' books* (1985) · C. Monkhouse, 'The life and works of Sir John Tenniel', *Easter Art Annual* (1901) · F. Morris, 'John Tenniel, cartoonist', PhD thesis, University of Missouri, Columbia, 1985 · R. D. Altick, *'Punch': the lively youth of a British institution, 1841–1851* (1997) · R. G. G. Price, *A history of Punch* (1957) · S. Houfe, *John Leech and the Victorian scene* (1984) · H. Furniss, *The confessions of a caricaturist*, 2 vols. (1901) · H. W. Lucy, *Sixty years in the wilderness*, 1 (1909) · H. G. Wells, *Experiment in autobiography* (1934) · D. Low, *British cartoonists, caricaturists and comic artists* (1942) · J. Ruskin, *The art of England* (1884), 161–97 · H. S. Marks, *Pen and pencil sketches* (1894) · *Punch*, 146 (4 March 1914) [Sir John Tenniel suppl.] · *Punch*, 20–121 (1851–1901) · E. Hodnett, *Image and text* (1983), 167–95 · *The Times* (27 Feb 1914) · *The Times* (3 March 1914) · *WW* · W. Jerrold, *Douglas Jerrold and Punch* (1910) · W. Jerrold and R. M. Leonard, *A century of parody and imitation* (1913) · [G. Dalziel and E. Dalziel], *The brothers Dalziel: a record of fifty years' work ... 1840–1890* (1901) · G. S. Layard, *The life and letters of Charles Samuel Keene* (1892) · d. cert.

Archives Harvard U., Houghton L., drawings

Likenesses G. J. R., pencil drawing, 1844, NPG · J. Tenniel, self-portrait, oils, 1882, Aberdeen Art Gallery · F. Holl, oils, c.1883, NPG [*see illus.*] · J. Tenniel, self-portrait, pen and ink, 1889, NPG · Elliott & Fry, photographs, NPG · Elliott & Fry, two cartes-de-visite, NPG · H. Furniss, caricatures, pen-and-ink sketches, NPG · Spy [L. Ward], chromolithograph caricature, NPG; repro. in *VF* (26 Oct 1878) · E. Ward, oils, Reform Club, London

Wealth at death £10,683 10s. 3d.: probate, 16 March 1914, CGPLA Eng. & Wales

Tennyson, Alfred, first Baron Tennyson (1809–1892), poet, was born on 6 August 1809 at Somersby rectory, Lincolnshire, the fourth child (there were to be eight sons and four daughters in fourteen years) of the Revd Dr George Clayton Tennyson (1778–1831), rector of Somersby, and his wife, Elizabeth (*bap.* 1780, *d.* 1865), daughter of the Revd Stephen Fytche, vicar of Louth, Lincolnshire.

The family Tennyson's father, though not strictly disinherited, had been reduced in favour and fortune much below his younger brother, and Tennyson's youth was overshadowed by this family feud between the Tennysons of Somersby and the grandparents, of Bayons Manor (16 miles away), with their favoured son (later Charles Tennyson-*D'Eyncourt; 1784–1861). Tennyson's wife, Emily, was to write, in her reminiscences for her two sons, of this 'caprice on the part of your great-grandfather', whereby Dr Tennyson

> was deprived of a station which he would so greatly have adorned and put into the Church for whose duties he felt no call. This preyed upon his nerves and his health and caused much sorrow in his house. Many a time has your father [the poet] gone out in the dark and cast himself on a grave in the little churchyard near wishing to be beneath it. (Lincoln MS; compare H. Tennyson, *Memoir*, 1.15)

The black blood of the Tennysons was all too familiar. The oldest surviving brother (George had died in infancy) was smallness and emptiness of life sometimes overwhelmed me. (Lincoln MS, 'Talks and Walks'; H. Tennyson, *Memoir*, 1.40)

Schooling, juvenilia, and Lincolnshire In 1815 Tennyson left the village school and—staying with his grandmother in Louth—became a pupil at Louth grammar school, where his elder brothers Frederick and Charles had started in 1814. Tennyson: 'How I did hate that school! The only good I ever got from it was the memory of the words, "sonus desilientis aquae", and of an old wall covered with wild weeds opposite the school windows' (H. Tennyson, *Memoir*, 1.7). In 1820 he left Louth, to be educated at home by his learned, violent, and often drunken father—who believed in him. 'My father who was a sort of Poet himself thought so highly of my first essay that he prophesied I should be the greatest Poet of the Time' (Trinity Notebook, 34).

Tennyson was to recall ruefully his youthful ambitions and poetical models. It was the mouthability of poetry, the urge to roll it aloud, that drew him.

> The first poetry that moved me was my own at five years old. When I was eight, I remember making a line I thought grander than Campbell, or Byron, or Scott. I rolled it out, it was this: 'With slaughterous sons of thunder rolled the flood'—great nonsense of course, but I thought it fine. (H. Tennyson, *Memoir*, 2.93)

He was much moved by the death of Byron in 1824: 'I was fourteen when I heard of his death. It seemed an awful calamity; I remember I rushed out of doors, sat down by myself, shouted aloud, and wrote on the sandstone: "*Byron is dead!*"' (ibid., 69).

> Before I could read, I was in the habit on a stormy day of spreading my arms to the wind, and crying out 'I hear a voice that's speaking in the wind', and the words 'far, far away' had always a strange charm for me.

Tennyson spoke of the three-book epic ('à la Scott') written in his 'very earliest teens'. 'I never felt so inspired—I used to compose 60 or 70 lines in a breath. I used to shout them about the silent fields, leaping over the hedges in my excitement' (Trinity Notebook, 34; H. Tennyson, *Memoir*, 1.11–12).

Tennyson's prodigious excitement is evidenced in the play he wrote (1823-4) in imitation of Elizabethan comedy, *The Devil and the Lady*, a wondrous pastiche, alive in its ambivalent erotic deploring, its vistas of space, its anatomizing of old age, and its grim humour. Duller, placatingly conventional, there was published in April 1827, by J. and J. Jackson, booksellers of Louth, *Poems by Two Brothers* (three brothers, since Frederick supplied four poems for this volume by Charles and Alfred); it earned them £20 (more than half in books) and courteous flat notices in the *Literary Chronicle* (19 May 1827) and the *Gentleman's Magazine* (June). Tennyson's unoriginal contributions were written 'between 15 and 17' (1893 reissue of 1827, quoting Tennyson). Wisely, he did not include any of them in later editions of his works.

But the Lincolnshire of Tennyson's young days was alive in his late poems, notably those in dialect, 'wonderful studies in English vernacular life' as Richard Holt Hutton called them (Hutton, 380). Tennyson's gruff gnarled humour here found its local habitation and intonation,

Alfred Tennyson, first Baron Tennyson (1809–1892), by Julia Margaret Cameron, 1865 [*The Dirty Monk*]

Frederick *Tennyson (1807–1898); irascible, he was to live, mostly in Italy, in expatriate eccentricity. The next senior was Charles (later, from 1835, as the condition of an uncle's bequest, Charles Turner, often known as Charles Tennyson *Turner (1808–1879), an exquisite poet, praised by Coleridge); he was for many years addicted to opium and vulnerable to alcohol (it was long before he arrived at his serenity). A younger brother, Edward, succumbed in 1832 to insanity, which proved incurable throughout his long life (he died in 1890, only two years before his famous brother). Arthur for a while in the 1840s collapsed into alcoholism. Then there was the brother who rose from the hearthrug and introduced himself, 'I am Septimus, the most morbid of the Tennysons' (C. Tennyson, *Alfred Tennyson*, 199). Of him, Tennyson wrote to his uncle Charles in 1834:

> At present his symptoms are not unlike those with which poor Edward's unhappy derangement began—he is subject to fits of the most gloomy despondency accompanied with tears—or rather, he spends whole days in this manner, complaining that he is neglected by all his relations, and blindly resigning himself to every morbid influence. (Received 15 Jan 1834, *Letters*, 1.106)

Morbid influence, not blindly resigned to but contemplated with creative courage, informs much of Tennyson's deepest work, unhappiness current or unforgettable, misery unutterable that yet found itself uttered.

> In my youth I knew much greater unhappiness than I have known in later life. When I was about twenty, I used to feel moods of misery unutterable! I remember once in London the realization coming over me, of the *whole* of its inhabitants lying horizontal a hundred years hence. The

audible in his own recorded reading of the best of them, 'Northern Farmer: New Style', 'founded', as Tennyson said, on a single sentence: 'When I canters my 'erse along the ramper [highway] I 'ears "proputty, proputty, proputty"' (*Poems*, 2.688).

Cambridge, Arthur Hallam, and early accomplishments In November 1827 Tennyson entered Trinity College, Cambridge, where Charles had just joined Frederick. He was unhappy there at first (and often subsequently—see the bitter sonnet that he chose not to publish, 'Lines on Cambridge of 1830'): 'The country is so disgustingly level, the revelry of the place so monotonous, the studies of the University so uninteresting, so much matter of fact—none but dryheaded calculating angular little gentlemen can take much delight' in algebraic formulae (18 April 1828, *Letters*, 1.23). But fortunately he came to know some well-rounded larger gentlemen, foremost among them Arthur Henry *Hallam (1811–1833) [*see under* Hallam, Henry (1777–1859)], whom Tennyson met about April 1829. Hallam had entered Trinity College the previous October. The friendship, deepening into love, of Hallam and Tennyson was to be one of the most important experiences of Hallam's short life and of Tennyson's long one.

A further flowering at Cambridge: in October 1829 Tennyson was elected a member of the Apostles, an informal debating society to which most of his Cambridge friends belonged (such eminent, though not pre-eminent, Victorians as John Kemble, Richard Chenevix Trench, Richard Monckton Milnes, and James Spedding). Then in June 1829 he won the chancellor's gold medal with his prize poem on the set subject *Timbuctoo*. Reworking an earlier poem (as he was so often to do with consummate re-creative imagination), this on Armageddon, 'altering the beginning and the end' to bend it on Timbuctoo, 'I was never so surprised as when I got the prize' (Lincoln MS, 'Materials for a Life of A. T.'; H. Tennyson, *Memoir*, 2.355). The surprise was the greater in that the winning poem was, unprecedentedly, not in heroic couplets but in blank verse. At the heart of the poem is a mystical trance such as fascinated Tennyson lifelong. Hallam, happily worsted, wrote with characteristic generosity and acumen: 'The splendid imaginative power that pervades it will be seen through all hindrances. I consider Tennyson as promising fair to be the greatest poet of our generation, perhaps of our century' (A. H. Hallam to Gladstone, 14 Sept 1829, *Letters of Arthur Henry Hallam*, 319).

Then in December 1829 (or, it may be, April 1830), Hallam met Tennyson's sister Emily, with whom he was soon to fall in love. In the summer of 1830 Tennyson visited the Pyrenees with Hallam. (More than thirty years later, in June 1861, Tennyson was to return there with his family and to write 'In the Valley of Cauteretz', in lasting love of Hallam.) Hallam and Tennyson were to visit the Rhine country in the summer of 1832. In the autumn of 1832 the engagement of Hallam to Tennyson's sister was to be reluctantly recognized by Hallam's family.

Poems, Chiefly Lyrical was published by Effingham Wilson in June 1830; some of Tennyson's most enduring notes, elegiacally lyrical, with his riven sensibility ('Supposed

Confessions of a Second-Rate Sensitive Mind Not at Unity with Itself'), are especially manifest in the volume's most remarkable achievements, 'Mariana', 'A spirit haunts the year's last hours', and 'The Kraken'.

Tennyson's father, after marital separation and then a return to protracted illness and weakness, died in March 1831. Tennyson left Cambridge without taking a degree. His choice of life? His uncle Charles wrote on 18 May 1831 to Tennyson's grandfather, the Old Man of the Wolds:

> We discussed what was to be done with the Children. Alfred is at home, but wishes to return to Cambridge to take a degree. I told him it was a useless expense unless he meant to go into the Church. He said he would. I did not think he seemed much to like it. I then suggested Physic or some other Profession. He seemed to think the Church the best and has I think finally made up his mind to it. The Tealby Living was mentioned and understood to be intended for him.

Then, reverting to the matter: 'Alfred seems quite ready to go into the Church although I think his mind is fixed on the idea of deriving his great distinction and greatest means from the exercise of his poetic talents' (*Letters*, 1.59–61).

Poetic talents needed the support of financial talents. Fortunately, from his aunt Russell he received £100 a year (this continued into the 1850s), and when his grandfather died in 1835, there came to Tennyson about £6000. Even though most of this was lost in a bad investment, there was to be the civil-list pension of £200 a year that began in 1845 (he drew it until he died), and his straits were never as dire as he liked to maintain.

The poetic talents were Arthur Hallam's focus in the *Englishman's Magazine*, in August 1831: 'On Some of the Characteristics of Modern Poetry, and on the Lyrical Poems of Alfred Tennyson'. W. B. Yeats was to praise this essay as

> criticism which is of the best and rarest sort. If one set aside Shelley's essay on poetry and Browning's essay on Shelley, one does not know where to turn in modern English criticism for anything so philosophic—anything so fundamental and radical—as the first half

of Hallam's piece (*The Speaker*, 22 July 1893; Yeats, 277). Of Tennyson's art, Hallam's essay remains the most compactly telling evocation, prescient too. Hallam limned five characteristics:

> First, his luxuriance of imagination, and at the same time his control over it. Secondly his power of embodying himself in ideal characters, or rather moods of character, with such extreme accuracy of adjustment, that the circumstances of the narration seem to have a natural correspondence with the predominant feeling, and, as it were, to be evolved from it by assimilative force. Thirdly his vivid, picturesque delineation of objects, and the peculiar skill with which he holds all of them *fused*, to borrow a metaphor from science, in a medium of strong emotion. Fourthly, the variety of his lyrical measures, and exquisite modulation of harmonious words and cadences to the swell and fall of the feelings expressed. Fifthly, the elevated habits of thought, implied in these compositions, and imparting a mellow soberness of tone, more impressive, to our minds, than if the author had drawn up a set of opinions in verse, and sought to instruct the understanding rather than to communicate the love of beauty to the heart. (Jump, 42)

Hallam's acute praise was welcome but not to everybody—Tennyson was already becoming 'the Pet of a Coterie', according to Christopher North (John Wilson) in *Blackwood's Magazine* in May 1832 (Jump, 50). In February 1832 the notoriously scathing Christopher North had praised Tennyson highly, albeit with caveats, in *Blackwood's*, but then in May he followed this with a wittily severe—not indiscriminate—review of the 1830 volume, this to 'save him from his worst enemies, his friends' (Jump, 51). Tennyson, pricked though not bridled by such reviewers, was exacerbatedly thin-skinned and always self-critical, often revising talent into genius—or expunging: the volume of 1830 included twenty-three poems that he did not subsequently reprint, as well as seven not collected in his two-volume *Poems* (1842) though reprinted later. The poems of 1830 that he did reprint, he—unusually—grouped as 'Juvenilia', justly in some cases, unjustly (protectively) for such a great poem as 'Mariana'.

Fertile, Tennyson issued in December 1832 *Poems* (published by Edward Moxon, the title-page dated 1833). Among its feats were 'The Lady of Shalott', 'Mariana in the South', 'Œnone', 'The Palace of Art', 'The Lotos-Eaters', and 'A Dream of Fair Women'. There were some failures subsequently acknowledged: seven poems never reprinted, and seven not collected in *Poems* (1842) though reprinted later. A venomous review by J. W. Croker (*Quarterly Review*, April 1833) drew blood but was a spur: the best of the poems were to be made even better, duly revised for republication, ten years later, but the painful rewording process began at once. As his Cambridge friend Edward FitzGerald wrote on 25 October 1833:

> Tennyson has been in town for some time: he has been making fresh poems, which are finer, they say, than any he has done. But I believe he is chiefly meditating on the purging and subliming of what he has already done: and repents that he has published at all yet. It is fine to see how in each succeeding poem the smaller ornaments and fancies drop away, and leave the grand ideas single. (*Letters of Edward FitzGerald*, 1.140)

It is heartening that in October 1833 Tennyson could be so actively creative in new and newly improved poems. For it was on 1 October that there was sent to him the news of the sudden death of Arthur Hallam, stricken on 15 September by apoplexy while visiting Vienna. His body was brought back by sea to Clevedon, on the Bristol Channel, 'Among familiar names to rest', 'And in the hearing of the wave' (*In Memoriam*, XVIII and XIX).

The blow, not to Tennyson alone, but to his sister Emily, to both families, and to Hallam's many friends and admirers, was profound, 'a loud and terrible stroke' (reported the Cambridge friend Charles Merivale) 'from the reality of things upon the faery building of our youth' (from H. Alford, 11 Nov 1833, Merivale, 135). The sense of the Tennyson family loss is audible in a letter by Frederick of 18 December 1833:

> We all looked forward to his society and support through life in sorrow and in joy, with the fondest hopes, for never was there a human being better calculated to sympathize with and make allowance for those peculiarities of temperament and those failings to which we are liable. (*Letters*, 1.104)

Yet in the first stricken month, Tennyson set to write poems that later became some of the finest sections of *In Memoriam* (the earliest is dated 6 October 1833, none being published until seventeen years after Hallam's death), as well as soon drafting 'Ulysses', 'Morte d'Arthur', and 'Tithonus' (this last not published until 1860, the other two 1842)—three great poems prompted by the death of his Arthur, and all finding extraordinarily compelling correlatives, in ancient worlds, for his feelings personal and universal, ancient and modern.

'The Two Voices' belongs to 1833, and was said by Tennyson's son to have been 'begun under the cloud of this overwhelming sorrow, which, as my father told me, for a while blotted out all joy from his life, and made him long for death' (H. Tennyson, *Memoir*, 1.109). But Tennyson had longed for death before Hallam died, and a draft of 'The Two Voices' was in existence three months earlier, in June 1833, when his friend J. M. Kemble wrote to W. B. Donne:

> Next Sir are some superb meditations on Self destruction called *Thoughts of a Suicide* wherein he argues the point with his soul and is thoroughly floored. These are amazingly fine and deep, and show a mighty stride in intellect since the *Second-Rate Sensitive Mind*. (*Poems*, 1.570)

Suicide appears, often enacted and sometimes discussed, in an extraordinary number of Tennyson's poems over the years, where it is complemented not only by suicidal risks but by martyrs and by the military (as in 'The Charge of the Light Brigade'). Mary Gladstone was to record 'a plan he had of writing a satire called "A suicide supper"', and that Tennyson 'would commit suicide' if he believed that death were annihilation (*Mary Gladstone*, 8 June 1879, 160).

On 14 February 1834 Tennyson replied to a request from Hallam's father to contribute to a memorial volume:

> I attempted to draw up a memoir of his life and character, but I failed to do him justice. I failed even to please myself. I could scarcely have pleased you. I hope to be able at a future period to concentrate whatever powers I may possess on the construction of some tribute to those high speculative endowments and comprehensive sympathies which I ever loved to contemplate; but at present, though somewhat ashamed at my own weakness, I find the object yet is too near me to permit of any very accurate delineation. You, with your clear insight into human nature, may perhaps not wonder that in the dearest service I could have been employed in, I should be found most deficient. (*Letters*, 1.108)

In Memoriam A.H.H. (1850) was duly to render such dearest service—to Hallam, to Tennyson himself, and to all his readers then and since, to all those who, like Queen Victoria and whatever their beliefs, have found, in its mourning and in its recovery, lasting consolation.

Tennyson, afraid (with good cause) of the spite which—like Keats before him, and similarly with some class animus—he precipitated in reviewers, tried in 1834 to placate Christopher North, and tried in early March 1835 to discourage John Stuart Mill from writing about the poems.

> I do not wish to be dragged forward again in any shape before the reading public at present, particularly on the score of my old poems most of which I have so corrected (particularly Œnone) as to make them much less imperfect. (To James Spedding, *Letters*, 1.130)

Fortunately, Mill went ahead, and discerningly praised in Tennyson

> the power of *creating* scenery, in keeping with some state of human feeling; so fitted to it as to be the embodied symbol of it, and to summon up the state of feeling itself, with a force not to be surpassed by anything but reality.   (*London Review*, July 1835; Jump, 86)

Love, marriage, and lifelong faith It was in 1834 that Tennyson fell in love with Rosa Baring, of Harington Hall, 2 miles from Somersby. It was to be a brief and frustrated love (she was rich, she was a Baring, she was—it seems—a coquette), but it was never to fade from his memory. It was less the joys of this young romance than the pains of disillusionment, following promptly in 1835-6, that had a lastingly valuable presence within his writing, for the pressures of social snobbery—long known from the Tennyson v. Tennyson-D'Eyncourt feud—and of 'The rentroll Cupid of our rainy isles' ('Edwin Morris'), 'This filthy marriage-hindering Mammon' ('Aylmer's Field'), are acidly etched in 'Locksley Hall', 'Edwin Morris', and *Maud*, all written or inaugurated between 1837 and 1839. Tennyson was the better able to gauge this amatory excitement of his because of his soon coming to love, deeply, Emily Sellwood [*see* Tennyson, Emily Sarah (1813-1896)]. He had first met her in 1830, the daughter of a solicitor in Horncastle (5 miles from Somersby). In May 1836 Emily's sister Louisa married Tennyson's older brother Charles (now curate of Tealby in Lincolnshire), and Tennyson was to date his love for Emily from this wedding, where he glimpsed the happy bridesmaid as his future happy bride. In 1838 the engagement was recognized by her family and his, but was broken off in 1840, partly because of financial insecurity ('owing to want of funds', their son was to write (H. Tennyson, *Memoir*, 1.150)), but also because of Tennyson's religious unorthodoxy and spiritual perturbation. It was not until 1849 that his correspondence with Emily was renewed. Then the honest faith and the honest doubt evinced within *In Memoriam* (to be published in May 1850) played a large part in overcoming Emily's doubts, and she and the poet were wed on 13 June 1850. The service was at Shiplake-on-Thames where Tennyson's friend Drummond Rawnsley was vicar.

This was to be a happy marriage, clearly seen in 'The Daisy', about Tennyson's visit to Italy with Emily in 1851 (a delayed honeymoon), and in the lovely late tribute, 'June Bracken and Heather', written in 1891, the year before he died, and constituting the dedication of his final and posthumous volume. Equably hierarchical and reciprocally loving, warmly embracing the double duty of family claims and the claims of art, their life together was a joy. It was sadly darkened by the stillbirth of their first child on 20 April 1851, and by the grievous loss of their son Lionel (b. 16 March 1854), dead in his thirties (April 1886), but it was blessed with the lifelong self-abnegating dedication of their son Hallam *Tennyson (1852-1928). Their home was at first Chapel House, Montpelier Row, Twickenham. In November 1853 they moved to Farringford (Freshwater, Isle of Wight), which Tennyson bought in 1856. Among the many notable visitors to Farringford was Garibaldi, in April 1864. In April 1868 the foundation stone was laid of Tennyson's second home, Aldworth, at Blackdown, Haslemere.

Emily Tennyson was judged incomparable by Edward Lear:

> I should think, computing moderately, that 15 angels, several hundreds of ordinary women, many philosophers, a heap of truly wise & kind mothers, 3 or 4 minor prophets, & a lot of doctors and school-mistresses, might all be boiled down, & yet their combined essence fall short of what Emily Tennyson really is.   (2 June 1859, Noakes, 167)

More two-edgedly, FitzGerald granted that she was

> a Lady of a Shakespearian type, as I think AT once said of her: that is, of the Imogen sort, far more agreeable to me than the sharp-witted Beatrices, Rosalinds, etc. I do not think she has been (on this very account perhaps) as good a helpmate to AT's Poetry as to himself.   (7 Dec 1869, *Letters of Edward FitzGerald*, 3.177)

Benjamin Jowett praised her: 'overflowing with kindness—but also in a certain way very strong', 'his friend, his servant, his guide, his critic'. 'It was a wonderful life—an effaced life like that of so many women' (Harvard MS, Catalogue, 19-20). 'One of the most beautiful, the purest, the most innocent, the most disinterested persons whom I have ever known': 'she was probably her husband's best critic, and certainly the one whose authority he would most willingly have recognized' (H. Tennyson, *Memoir*, 2.466-7).

His wife was of unique importance to Tennyson's religious self. She trusted Charles Kingsley, who in September 1850 described *In Memoriam* as

> altogether rivalling the sonnets of Shakespeare.—Why should we not say boldly, surpassing—for the sake of the superior faith into which it rises, for the sake of the proem at the opening of the volume—in our eyes, the noblest English Christian poem which several centuries have seen?   (*Fraser's Magazine*; Jump, 183)

Aubrey de Vere characterized Emily, a few months after the marriage:

> Her great and constant desire is to make her husband more religious, or at least to conduce, as far as she may, to his growth in the spiritual life. In this she will doubtless succeed, for piety like hers is infectious, especially where there is an atmosphere of affection to serve as a conducting medium. Indeed I already observe a great improvement in Alfred. His nature is a religious one, and he is remarkably free from vanity and sciolism. Such a nature gravitates towards Christianity, especially when it is in harmony with itself.   (14 Oct 1850, Ward, 158-9)

Gruffer, there are Tennyson's words to Gladstone's daughter Mary (4 June 1879): 'We shall all turn into pigs if we lose Christianity and God' (*Mary Gladstone*, 157). 'T. loves the spirit of Christianity, hates many of the dogmas', reported William Allingham in January 1867 (Allingham, 149). He respected the breadth and latitude of F. D. Maurice. In October 1853 Maurice was forced to resign from his professorship in London for arguing that the popular belief in the endlessness of future punishment was superstitious. Tennyson abominated the belief in eternal torment, and he had recently asked Maurice (who had agreed) to be godfather to Hallam Tennyson. 'To the Rev. F. D. Maurice' is a verse invitation that glowingly revives the Horatian epistle, and bears comparison with such classics of the kind as Ben Jonson's 'Inviting a Friend to Supper'.

In April 1869 Tennyson attended the meeting to organize the Metaphysical Society, which he joined and which flourished until 1879. In his seventies he said to Allingham, in July 1884: 'You're not orthodox, and I can't call myself orthodox. Two things however I have always been firmly convinced of—God,—and that death will not end my existence' (Allingham, 329). The very late poems, 'The Ancient Sage' (1885), on Lao-Tse, and 'Akbar's Dream' (1892), on what was then called Mohammedanism, seek to realize—under the influence of Benjamin Jowett—'The religions of all good men', in support of the conviction that 'All religions are one'.

Two months before he died, Tennyson talked with John Addington Symonds:

> He told me he was going to write a poem on Bruno, and asked what I thought about his [Bruno's] attitude toward Christianity. I tried to express my views, and Hallam got up and showed me that they were reading up the chapter of my 'Renaissance in Italy' on Bruno. Tennyson observed that the great thing in Bruno was his perception of an Infinite Universe, filled with solar systems like our own, and all penetrated with the Soul of God. 'That conception must react destructively on Christianity—I mean its creed and dogma—its morality will always remain.' Somebody had told him that astronomers could count 550 million solar systems. He observed that there was no reason why each should not have planets peopled with living and intelligent beings. 'Then,' he added, 'see what becomes of the second person of the Deity, and the sacrifice of a God for fallen man upon this little earth!' (29 Aug 1892, *Letters of John Addington Symonds*, 3.744)

From *Poems* (1842) to *The Princess* (1847) Between 1832 and 1842 Tennyson published no volume-length work. The span has been mildly melodramatized into 'the ten years' silence', but he wrote much during this period, founding and building *In Memoriam*, creating his exquisite 'English Idyls' (most notably, 'Edwin Morris' and 'The Golden Year'), and he rewrote with depth and passion. At the urging of his friend Richard Monckton Milnes, he reluctantly sent to *The Tribute* (September 1837) a true though as yet unperfected poem, 'Oh! that 'twere possible', which was to be 'the germ' of the amazing monodrama of madness, *Maud* (1855).

Life was taxing. On the death of Dr Tennyson in 1831 the family had been allowed by the incoming rector to continue to live in the rectory at Somersby, but then, in 1837, they had to move to High Beech, Epping Forest. 'His two elder brothers being away' (Frederick in Corfu and then Florence—for good; and Charles settled at Grasby, Lincolnshire), it was on Alfred that there 'devolved the care of the family and of choosing a new home' (H. Tennyson, *Memoir*, 1.149–50; 'My mother is afraid if I go to town even for a night; how could they get on without me for months?', to Emily Sellwood, 10 July 1839, *Letters*, 1.171). Then in 1840 they had to move to Tunbridge Wells, and in 1841 to Boxley, near Maidstone. The engagement to Emily Sellwood was broken off in 1840. Then there was the

investing by Tennyson in 1840–41 of his invaluable small fortune (about £3000) in a scheme for wood-carving by machinery, which had collapsed by 1843. These were among the things that made much of life a misery. 'I have drunk one of those most bitter draughts out of the cup of life, which go near to make men hate the world they move in' (H. Tennyson, *Memoir*, 1.221). FitzGerald reported of Tennyson, to Tennyson's brother Frederick, on 10 December 1843 that he had 'never seen him so hopeless' (*Letters of Edward FitzGerald*, 1.408). In 1843–4 Tennyson received treatment.

> The perpetual panic and horror of the last two years has steeped my nerves in poison: now I am left a beggar but I am or shall be shortly somewhat better off in nerves. I am in a Hydropathy Establishment near Cheltenham (the only one in England conducted on pure Priessnitzan principles) … Much poison has come out of me, which no physic ever would have brought to light.   (To FitzGerald, 2 Feb 1844, *Letters*, 1.222–3)

The hydropathy was endured near Cheltenham; Tennyson then lived, first, at 6 Bellevue Place, and then at 10 St James's Square, Cheltenham.

In an unpublished poem ('Wherefore, in these dark ages of the Press'), Tennyson spoke of 'this Art-Conscience', a surety which, along with courage, steadied and secured him. This, with more than a little help from his friends, who encouraged him, pressed him. On 3 March 1838: 'Do you ever see Tennyson? and if so, could you not urge him to take the field?' (R. C. Trench to R. M. Milnes, Reid, 1.208). 'Tennyson composes every day, but nothing will persuade him to print, or even write it down' (Milnes, 1838, Reid, 1.220). Another Cambridge friend, G. S. Venables, urged him in August/September 1838:

> Do not continue to be so careless of fame and of influence. You have abundant materials ready for a new publication, and you start as a well-known man with the certainty that you can not be overlooked, and that by many you will be appreciated. If you do not publish now when will you publish? (*Letters*, 1.163–4)

On 25 November 1839 FitzGerald all but gave up:

> I want A. T. to publish another volume: as all his friends do: especially Moxon, who has been calling on him for the last two years for a new edition of his old volume: but he is too lazy and wayward to put his hand to the business. (*Letters of Edward FitzGerald*, 1.239)

Then there was the American threat. To the importunate FitzGerald Tennyson wrote *c*.22 February 1841: 'You bore me about my book: so does a letter just received from America, threatening, though in the civilest terms that if I will not publish in England they will do it for me in that land of freemen' (*Letters*, 1.188). Long after, to Allingham, Tennyson recalled this provocation:

> I hate publishing! The Americans forced me into it again. I had my things nice and right, but when I found they were going to publish the old forms I said, By Jove, that won't do!—My whole living is from the sale of my books. (Allingham, 168, 27 Dec 1867)

So at last, in May 1842, Tennyson issued *Poems* (Moxon). The first volume selected the best of 1830 and 1832, together with a few poems written *c*.1833; the second volume consisted of new poems, some soon famous, such as

'Locksley Hall', and some among his greatest: 'Morte d'Arthur', 'Ulysses', 'Break, break, break', and 'St Simeon Stylites'.

By June 1845 Tennyson had set to work on his long poem about university education for women, *The Princess*. The plan had formed in 1839, at a time when there was in Cambridge and elsewhere a renewed sympathy with women's claims, one that remembered Mary Wollstonecraft's *Vindication of the Rights of Woman* (1792) and gained a new impetus from Anna Jameson's *Characteristics of Women* (1832), later known as *Shakespeare's Heroines*. Jameson herself acknowledged many of the old ideals of womanhood. What marriage would be, once women's intellectual rights were respected: this was then the central woman question. Tennyson's poem, ever apt, is a vivid reflection of the age's humanely troubled concern. Like Tennyson himself, it is liberal in spirit, conservative in upshot. Progressive, perhaps, for as T. S. Eliot said of Whitman and Tennyson, 'Both were conservative, rather than reactionary or revolutionary; that is to say, they believed explicitly in progress, and believed implicitly that progress consists in things remaining much as they are' (T. S. Eliot, 'Whitman and Tennyson').

FitzGerald divined that this new poem was both a symptom and a cause of Tennyson's improved state of mind. In September 1845, through the good offices of (among others) Henry Hallam, Tennyson was granted by Sir Robert Peel a civil-list pension of £200 a year, for life. The following year, with his publisher Edward Moxon, he visited Switzerland (August 1846), 'the stateliest bits of landskip I ever saw' (A. Tennyson to FitzGerald, 12 Nov 1846, *Letters*, 1.264). The mountainscape was soon to rise within *The Princess* (published December 1847).

FitzGerald thought *The Princess* 'a wretched waste of power at a time of life when a man ought to be doing his best' (FitzGerald to Frederick Tennyson, 4 May 1848, *Letters of Edward FitzGerald*, 1.604). Carlyle was even less sympathetic: 'very gorgeous, fervid, luxuriant, but indolent, somnolent, almost imbecil' (25 Dec 1847, *Collected Letters*, 22.183). Yet here are three of Tennyson's finest lyrics— 'Tears, idle tears', 'Now sleeps the crimson petal, now the white', and 'Come down, O maid, from yonder mountain height'. The Prologue presents a group of young friends at a country-house fête; they speak of women's rights, and then tell, each in turn ('a sevenfold story'; 'Prologue', 198), the tale of a princess who founds a university for women; her plans are broken by an irruption of men and then by an eruption of love. Tennyson's subtitle, 'A Medley', is truthful, and defensive. The poem, locally fine, is happy not to have to be a whole, whether politically or personally. It was for the poet a relief and a release from the pains of his 1840s. He duly felt obliged to recast it more substantially than any other of his long poems.

In 1848 Tennyson visited Ireland and Cornwall, taking up again a projected Arthurian enterprise, and in 1849 the correspondence with Emily Sellwood was renewed. Tennyson now was granted his *annus mirabilis*. For 1850 was to see, first, the publication of *In Memoriam* (anonymously, in the last week of May); next, his wedding, in June; and then in November his appointment as poet laureate.

Hereafter Tennyson was to be, though he enjoyed denying it, secure. Secure in reputation, though the passing judgements were sometimes harsh—'that fierce light which beats upon a throne' (Dedication to *Idylls of the King*) beats too upon the poet's throne. Secure, too, in finances: with strong sales and with publishers of integrity (Moxon through to Macmillan, with Ticknor doing the distinctly unusual thing for an American publisher of the time and honourably paying up), he stayed the course and stayed in print. In the last year of his life he earned more than £10,000, and he left an estate worth more than £57,000 (Martin, 578).

In Memoriam (**1850**) In 1842 Tennyson's sister Emily, after eight years of quasi-widowed fidelity to Arthur Hallam, had married Captain Richard Jesse RN. Comments on this were harshly unjust, but Tennyson was not, and he gave his sister in marriage. He must, though, have been aware that the changed relation of the Tennysons to the Hallams might cast a shadow on the poem that was becoming *In Memoriam*, which he chose not to publish until 1850, when it closed with the wedding of a different sister of Tennyson's (Cecilia) to a family friend (Edmund Lushington) who could not but call up Arthur Hallam.

Tennyson had written what became sections of *In Memoriam* within a month of Hallam's death (September 1833).

> The sections were written at many different places, and as the phases of our intercourse came to my memory and suggested them. I did not write them with any view of weaving them into a whole, or for publication, until I found that I had written so many.   (H. Tennyson, *Memoir*, 1.304)

On 30 November 1844 Tennyson wrote to his aunt Russell:

> With respect to the non-publication of those poems which you mention, it is partly occasioned by the considerations you speak of, and partly by my sense of their present imperfectness: perhaps they will not see the light till I have ceased to be. I cannot tell, but I have no wish to send them out yet.   (*Letters*, 1.231)

On 29 January 1845 FitzGerald wrote to W. B. Donne:

> A. T. has near a volume of poems—elegiac—in memory of Arthur Hallam. Don't you think the world wants other notes than elegiac now? Lycidas is the utmost length an elegiac should reach. But Spedding [their Cambridge friend] praises: and I suppose the elegiacs will see daylight—public daylight—one day.   (*Letters of Edward FitzGerald*, 1.478)

The day dawned: it was in part the loving respect in which the poem (passed on to her, in manuscript or in proof, by her cousin) was held by Emily Sellwood, soon to be Emily Tennyson, in April 1850 that fortified Tennyson's confidence in the poem that he published (anonymously) next month, and that was to win him, immediately and despite the mild fiction of anonymity, the laureateship and incontestable fame.

Tennyson had used the octosyllabic quatrain rhyming *abba* in his patriotic poems of 1832–3.

> As for the metre of *In Memoriam* I had no notion till 1880 that Lord Herbert of Cherbury had written his occasional verses

in the same metre. I believed myself the originator of the metre, until after *In Memoriam* came out, when some one told me that Ben Jonson and Sir Philip Sidney had used it.
(H. Tennyson, *Memoir*, 1.305-6)

(For 1880, read 1870; see letter of 8 August 1870, *Letters*, 2.553-4.)

It is rather the cry of the whole human race than mine. In the poem altogether private grief swells out into thought of, and hope for, the whole world. It begins with a funeral and ends with a marriage—begins with death and ends in promise of a new life—a sort of Divine Comedy, cheerful at the close. It is a very impersonal poem as well as personal.
(Knowles, 182)

George Eliot saw the poem under a different aspect: 'Whatever was the immediate prompting of *In Memoriam*, whatever the form under which the author represented his aim to himself, the deepest significance of the poem is the sanctification of human love as a religion' (*Westminster Review*, Oct 1855; G. Eliot, 191).

Both human love and divine love faced the challenge not only of the ages but of the aeons. In 'Parnassus', written three years before he died, Tennyson was to imagine the two powers that were now seen to tower over all poetic aspirations: 'These are Astronomy and Geology, terrible Muses!' *In Memoriam* did not stand in need of or in dread of Darwin's *Origin of Species*, for the poem preceded the work of science by nine years. Moreover Tennyson owed much not only to Charles Lyell and his *Principles of Geology* (1830-33), which he mentioned to Milnes in 1836 (*c*.1 Nov, *Letters*, 1.145), but to William Buckland and his school of thought. Yet *In Memoriam* became imaginatively central to the Darwinian evolutionary controversy, in a world where the Victorians feared that the ape in the zoo might suddenly ask 'Am I my keeper's brother?' Tennyson threw off epigrams that he did not publish, one being 'Darwin's Gemmule', and another 'By a Darwinian' (both 1868), and he published 'By an Evolutionist' in 1889.

By January 1851 *In Memoriam* was already in its fourth edition. Tennyson never issued an edition with his name on the title-page, but from 1870 it appeared in collected editions of his works. The poem was to be on everyone's lips and in most hearts, validating not only honest doubt but honest faith, a consolation of philosophy for the age. In March 1889 F. W. H. Myers acknowledged what the poem had effected:

It is hardly too much to say that *In Memoriam* is the only speculative book of that epoch—epoch of the 'Tractarian movement', and much similar 'up-in-the-air balloon-work'—which retains a serious interest now. Its brief cantos contain the germs of many a subsequent treatise, the indication of channels along which many a wave of opinion has flowed, down to that last 'Philosophie der Erlösung', or Gospel of a sad Redemption—'To drop head foremost in the jaws / Of vacant darkness, and to cease'—which tacitly or openly is possessing itself of so many a modern mind. (*Nineteenth Century*; Jump, 399)

Queen Victoria's poet laureate In November 1850 Tennyson was appointed poet laureate, Wordsworth having died in April (and Samuel Rogers having declined).

The night before I was asked to take the Laureateship, which was offered to me through Prince Albert's liking for my *In*

Memoriam, I dreamed that he came to me and kissed me on the cheek. I said, in my dream, 'Very kind, but very German'. In the morning the letter about the Laureateship was brought to me and laid upon my bed. I thought about it through the day, but could not make up my mind whether to take it or refuse it, and at the last I wrote two letters, one accepting and one declining, and threw them on the table, and settled to decide which I would send after my dinner and bottle of port. (Knowles, 167)

Tennyson's character and his convictions (political and national), as well as his versatility, enabled him to be imaginatively duteous in the exercise of his responsibilities, the most felicitous of the poets laureate. The next year, there followed his first such publication (dated March 1851), his deftly loving dedication, 'To the Queen', heading the seventh edition of his *Poems*.

Aware that the poet laureate should express his convictions but should also be careful not to harness his office to his own party political judgements, Tennyson on occasion published pseudonymously—for instance a run of patriotic poems during the invasion scare from France in early 1852. 'Among the most enthusiastic national defenders are Alfred Tennyson and Mrs. A. T.', wrote their friend Franklin Lushington on 8 February 1852:

At least they have been induced by Coventry Patmore to subscribe five pounds apiece for the purchase of rifles to teach the world to shoot—which appears to me a rather exaggerated quota for the laureate to contribute out of his official income, his duty being clearly confined to the howling of patriotic staves. (*Letters*, 2.26)

Tennyson differentiated such staves from his first independent publication as laureate later the same year: his *Ode on the Death of the Duke of Wellington* (published on the day of the funeral, 18 November 1852) is a noble foursquare paean, much called on in later years when a great national loss has been felt, as at the death of Winston Churchill. Written, Tennyson insisted, from genuine admiration of the man, it was a true laureate ode, though not requested by the queen.

In January 1862 Tennyson published the verse dedication to open a new edition of *Idylls of the King*, in memory of Albert, prince consort, who had died in December 1861. (Tennyson was to conclude *Idylls of the King*, in the Imperial Library edition of 1873, with a complementary or married tribute, 'To the Queen', beginning 'O loyal to the royal in thyself'.) There followed, in April 1862, his first audience with Queen Victoria, at Osborne, Isle of Wight:

I went down to see Tennyson who is very peculiar looking, tall, dark, with a fine head, long black flowing hair and a beard—oddly dressed, but there is no affectation about him. I told him how much I admired his glorious lines to my precious Albert and how much comfort I found in his 'In Memoriam'. He was full of unbounded appreciation of beloved Albert. When he spoke of my own loss, of that to the Nation, his eyes quite filled with tears. (Queen Victoria's journal, 14 April 1862, Dyson and Tennyson, 69)

There was humour, too, in their relation. 'She was praising my poetry; I said "Every one writes verses now. I daresay Your Majesty does." She smiled and said, "No! I never could bring two lines together!"' (Allingham, 150, 18 Feb 1867). A later audience, in August 1883 when Tennyson was in his seventies, was movingly set down by the queen:

> After luncheon saw the great Poet *Tennyson* in dearest Albert's room for nearly an hour;—and most interesting it was. He is grown very old—his eyesight much impaired *and he is very shaky on his legs.* But he was very kind. Asked him to sit down … When I took leave of him, I thanked him for his kindness and said I needed it, for I had gone through so much—and he said you are so alone on that 'terrible height, it is Terrible. I've only a year or two to live but I'll be happy to do anything for you I can. Send for me whenever you like.' I thanked him warmly.   (Queen Victoria's journal, 7 Aug 1883, Dyson and Tennyson, 102)

'Asked him to sit down': for a sardonic rendering of such an audience, see Max Beerbohm's caricature, *Mr. Tennyson reading 'In Memoriam' to his Sovereign* (Beerbohm). There, it is less the poet's vigorous left arm than his splayed legs that should establish his taking his liberty. But two royal profiles face his singular one.

Maud (1855), and Idylls of the King (1859–1885) In July 1855 Tennyson published *Maud, and Other Poems*. Notable among the other poems was 'The Charge of the Light Brigade'. The charge, at Balaklava in the Crimea, had taken place on 25 October. Tennyson's periodical publication in *The Examiner* (9 Dec 1854) had stirred not only the nation but the troops to whom copies were sent.

'This poem of *Maud or the Madness* is a little *Hamlet*, the history of a morbid, poetic soul, under the blighting influence of a recklessly speculative age'; 'The peculiarity of this poem is that different phases of passion in one person take the place of different characters' (*Poems*, 2.517–18).

Tennyson's acquaintance with Dr Matthew Allen, the wood-carving financial speculator who was also a mad-doctor (the poet John Clare was in his care for a while), was one experiential base for the poem—Tennyson visited his asylum near High Beech. What also courses through the poem is the black blood of the Tennysons. The poem aroused controversy, some of it low: 'Sir, I used to worship you, but now I hate you. I loathe and detest you. You beast! So you've taken to imitating Longfellow. Yours in aversion' (reported in letter of 8 Jan 1856, *Letters of Dante Gabriel Rossetti*, 1.281–2). George Eliot reviewed it anonymously: 'its tone is throughout morbid; it opens to us the self revelations of a morbid mind, and what it presents as the cure for this mental disease is itself only a morbid conception of human relations' (*Westminster Review*, Oct 1855; G. Eliot, 192). The poem was accused of craving war (the protagonist leaves at the end for the Crimea) and of fomenting sin. 'If an author pipe of adultery, fornication, murder and suicide, set him down as the practiser of those crimes'. Tennyson: 'Adulterer I may be, fornicator I may be, murderer I may be, suicide I am not yet' (Lincoln MS, draft 'Materials for a Life of A. T.'; C. Tennyson, *Alfred Tennyson*, 286). It remained one of the poems that Tennyson was most moved to read aloud. Its sense of all that may impede marriage, or darken it, lived on in the two long narrative poems, of sombre power, that Tennyson published together in 1864: 'Enoch Arden' and 'Aylmer's Field'.

Tennyson's Arthurian interests were lifelong: from the early lyrical poems, 'The Lady of Shalott', 'Sir Galahad',

and 'Sir Launcelot and Queen Guinevere', through the deeply contemplative 'Morte d'Arthur', to the elongated linking of narratives that became *Idylls of the King*. (A long *I* in *Idylls*; no article, not 'The Idylls of the King'; and an intimation that the series did not, though Hallam Tennyson uses the word, constitute an epic.)

> From his earliest years he had written out in prose various histories of Arthur … On Malory, on Layamon's *Brut*, on Lady Charlotte Guest's translation of the *Mabinogion*, on the old Chronicles, on old French Romance, on Celtic folklore, and largely on his own imagination, my father founded his epic.
> (*Poems*, 3.255)

In 1848 Tennyson visited Ireland and Cornwall, taking up again his projected Arthurian enterprise. It was not until 1855 that he decided the shaping, and in 1859 the first four *Idylls* were published, *Enid* (later *The Marriage of Geraint* and *Geraint and Enid*), *Vivien* (later *Merlin and Vivien*), *Elaine* (later *Lancelot and Elaine*), and *Guinevere*. A revision and expansion of *Morte d'Arthur*, as *The Passing of Arthur*, was published in 1869, with a note: 'This last, the earliest written of the Poems, is here connected with the rest in accordance with an early project of the author's' (*The Holy Grail and Other Poems*, '1870'). *Gareth and Lynette* was published in October 1872, and the Imperial Library edition of Tennyson's *Works* (1872–3) then brought together the series (with a new epilogue: 'To the Queen'), virtually complete except for *Balin and Balan* (written 1874, published 1885).

Victorian Arthurianism was sometimes moral, sometimes romantic, sometimes both. In *The Return to Camelot: Chivalry and the English Gentleman*, Mark Girouard noted that after the 1830s Tennyson's dealings with Arthurian material changed. 'The 1850s were, indeed, studded with Arthurian projects', and Tennyson more and more shaped inspiring models for 'modern members of the ruling class' (Girouard, 180, 184). But Tennyson had aspirations larger than the political, the passing. 'As for the many meanings of the poem my father would affirm "Poetry is like shot-silk with many glancing colours"'. On his eightieth birthday, he said: 'My meaning … was spiritual. I took the legendary stories of the Round Table as illustrations. I intended Arthur to represent the Ideal Soul of Man coming into contact with the warring elements of the flesh' (*Poems*, 3.258–9).

Deaths in the family, honours, and the peerage Tennyson's mother died in February 1865. There is no recovering just what she meant to her son, though she is to be glimpsed, as a gracious silence, in the record of early life, her piety being praised in 'Isabel': 'The queen of marriage, a most perfect wife'. Then in April 1879 came the death of Charles, the brother whom Tennyson loved best ('altogether loveable, a second George Herbert in his utter faith', Tennyson wrote to James Russell Lowell, on 18 November 1880; *Letters*, 3.199), and whom he hauntingly commemorated in 'Frater Ave atque Vale' and in 'Prefatory Poem to My Brother's Sonnets' (1879, opening Charles's *Collected Sonnets*, 1880).

But the immitigable grief was the grievous loss of Tennyson's son Lionel (*b.* 1854). In February 1878 Lionel had married Eleanor Locker. As is clear from a notebook of Lionel's, of 1874-6, in which he set down epigrams, observations, squibs, and light verse, he had a levity light-years away from the gravity of his elder brother, Hallam. Lionel made fretful his protective parents, with his dashing ways, his nattiness of garb, and his very unTennysonian stammer or stutter.

Lionel Tennyson's work for the India Office took him to India in 1885, where he contracted fever, 'hung between life and death for three months and a half' (H. Tennyson, *Memoir*, 2.323), and then, in April 1886, died in the Red Sea on his way home. Tennyson was desolate, but he strove to share his wife's Christian fortitude—in her words, 'The loss to us is indeed unspeakable but infinite Love and Wisdom have ordained it' (26 Oct 1886, *Letters*, 3.343). Tennyson was to realize such family tragedy, both personal and everywhere, in one of his finest poems of saddened gratitude: 'To the Marquis of Dufferin and Ava'. His love of Lionel lived on in his love of his grandsons: first, Eleanor's and Lionel's Alfred B. S. Tennyson (b. 1878—see the endearing playfulness of the dedication to *Ballads and Other Poems*, 1880, and 'To Alfred Tennyson My Grandson'); and then their Charles Tennyson (b. 1879) who lived to a great age, nearly 100, to honour his grandfather in works biographical and editorial.

Honours came to Tennyson with and following the laureateship. In June 1855 he received an honorary DCL at Oxford; the occasion was graced by the affectionate impudence of the cry (adapting the opening of 'The May Queen'), 'Did your mother call you early, dear?' In 1869 he became an honorary fellow of Trinity College, Cambridge (where neither he in the past nor his son Hallam in the immediate future proceeded to a degree). In March 1880 he was invited to stand for the lord rectorship of Glasgow University, but withdrew when he learned that the election was conducted along party lines. He had in 1865 refused the offer of a baronetcy, and again in 1873, 1874, and 1880. Then in September 1883 he accepted a barony, acknowledging to the queen 'This public mark of your Majesty's esteem which recognizes in my person the power of literature in this age of the world' (c.1 Oct 1883, *Letters*, 3.265).

As well as the honour to literature and to Tennyson, and the affectionate respect in which he held the queen, he would have been moved by this chance to score, with dignity, off the rival branch of the family, who—half a century earlier—had elevated themselves to the name Tennyson-D'Eyncourt. 'I am very glad we have changed our name, as it gives us a good position', had written Edwin Tennyson-D'Eyncourt: 'Besides which it will keep us in a great measure clear of the Somersby Family who really are quite hogs' (1 Aug 1835, *Letters*, 1.135).

Closer to home, Tennyson and his wife justly saw the peerage as a bequest to their self-abnegating son. In 1873 and again in 1880, Tennyson had even put to Gladstone a proposal (as to the baronetcy then offered) that breached all precedent:

I am still much of the same mind—except that many of my friends having reproached me as for a wrong done to my

family in declining the Baronetcy for myself, I feel still more than I did that I would fain see it bestowed on my son Hallam *during my lifetime*, if that could be done without embarrassment to you.   (3 Nov 1880, *Letters*, 3.198)

In 1883 Emily said of the accepted barony: 'That Hallam should inherit the duties belonging to this distinction is a cause of deep thankfulness to me' (27 Sept 1883, ibid., 3.264). She declared herself thankful 'that he should have an honourable career marked out for him when his work for his father has ceased' (C. Tennyson, *Alfred Tennyson*, 472). It would be to underrate Hallam Tennyson to say that he owed his becoming governor-general of Australia to his father's peerage, but presumably the title was no hindrance. Three months after his father took his seat in the House of Lords (March 1884), Hallam married Audrey Boyle; the couple duly lived with his parents, and continued the life of loving service.

Friendships Tennyson and Edward FitzGerald had been friends since their Cambridge days, and the two rather enjoyed their amiable friction. 'He spoke of Edward Fitz-Gerald—had not seen him for years before his death; Fitz-Gerald could not be got to visit. "But no sort of quarrel?" "O no! fancy my quarrelling with dear old Fitz!"' (Allingham, 320, 1883). One of Tennyson's finest late poems, 'To E. FitzGerald', alive throughout its 56-line single sentence, recalls the last visit by Tennyson and his son Hallam to FitzGerald in 1876. The poem breathes friendship, and it generously delights in FitzGerald's great translation imitation, *The Rubáiyát of Omar Khayyám*. FitzGerald's affectionate scepticism had its bracing side. Of the elegies that became *In Memoriam*, he wrote to W. B. Donne on 27 February 1845:

We have surely had enough of men reporting their sorrows: especially when one is aware all the time that the poet wilfully protracts what he complains of, magnifies it in the Imagination, puts it into all the shapes of Fancy: and yet we are to condole with him, and be taught to ruminate our losses and sorrows in the same way. I felt that if Tennyson had got on a horse and ridden twenty miles, instead of moaning over his pipe, he would have been cured of his sorrows in half the time. As it is, it is about three years before the Poetic Soul walks itself out of darkness and Despair into Common Sense.   (*Letters of Edward FitzGerald*, 1.486)

Tennyson's exquisite verse epistle 'To E. L., on His Travels in Greece' (published 1853) is a tribute to Edward Lear's artistic pencil and writer's pen. Lear set Tennyson's poems to music, and he worked lifelong on illustrations of the poems; on 19 February 1886, two years before he died, he wrote to Ruskin that although 'nearly always in bed' he could 'even go on working at my 200 Tennyson illustrations begun in 1849' (Lear, 276). These appeared posthumously in *Poems by Tennyson Illustrated by Lear* (1889). In person, there had been increasing tensions. 'AT was most disagreeably querulous and irritating and would return, chiefly because he saw people approaching', Lear wrote in his diary of June 1860, but Frank Lushington

would not go back, and led zigzagwise toward the sea—AT snubby & cross always. After a time he would not go on—but led me back by muddy paths (over our shoes,) a short cut home—hardly, even at last avoiding his horror,—the villagers coming from church … I … believe that this is my last visit to Farringford:—nor can I wish it otherwise all things considered.   (Noakes, 176)

It was Emily Tennyson in whom Lear delighted.

Tennyson's friendship with F. T. Palgrave, with whom he visited Portugal in August 1859 (and Derbyshire and Yorkshire in 1862), led to his assisting Palgrave in selecting poems for the most famous, most influential, and best of anthologies, *The Golden Treasury* (1861). Palgrave dedicated it to Tennyson, and—faced with Tennyson's refusal to have his own poems in it—included no living poets. The particular advice and recommendations of Tennyson survive and are of enduring interest—not least because, of the great English poets, Tennyson is the one who was least willing to expatiate as a literary critic. His summary judgements are shrewdly content to remain pith and gist: 'One plods over Wordsworth's long dreary plains of prose— one knows there's a mountain somewhere' (Allingham, 294, 2 Sept 1880).

W. E. Gladstone had played a part in securing a pension for Tennyson in 1845: 'it appears established that, though a true and even a great poet, he can hardly become a popular, and is much more likely to be a starving one' (24 Feb 1845, Parker, 3.441). Gladstone showed his historical and critical acumen in 1859:

> Mr. Tennyson is too intimately and essentially the poet of the nineteenth century to separate himself from its leading characteristics, the progress of physical science and a vast commercial, mechanical, and industrial development. Whatever he may say or do in an occasional fit, he cannot long either cross or lose its sympathies.   (*Quarterly Review*, Oct 1859; Jump, 248)

Gladstone published in the *Nineteenth Century* (January 1887) an important reply to Tennyson's onslaught (dramatized, but …) on the age in 'Locksley Hall Sixty Years After'. Tennyson and Gladstone had long enjoyed a wary but genuine friendship. They agreed in loving Arthur Hallam and his memory; they agreed that Tennyson was a true poet; and they agreed to a cruise together to Norway and Denmark in September 1883, during which the offer of a barony was prompted and precipitated. But they disagreed about Gladstone's politics, which were both Liberal and liberal, and particularly about Ireland. Four months before Tennyson died, he sent someone a letter: 'Sir, I love Mr. Gladstone but hate his present Irish policy' (28 June 1892, *Letters*, 3.446). Nor was it only Ireland, for the Franchise Bill of 1884 seemed to Tennyson a grave mistake. He fired a warning sonnet across Gladstone's bows. 'Statesman, be not precipitate in thine act', he boomed, or so the first unauthorized printing ran—and then perhaps decided that he had himself been precipitate in according to Gladstone the tribute of the word Statesman, for the poem as printed in the *Memoir* reads 'Steersman …', which better fits not only the navigating metaphor of the poem but Tennyson's reservations as to Gladstone's statesmanship.

Tennyson's admiration for Benjamin Jowett is best articulated in 'To the Master of Balliol' (written 1890, published 1892). Jowett had long been a close friend of the family. Both men were robust; the anecdote that is either Benjamin Jowett or *ben trovato* has Jowett saying of a new poem that Tennyson recited, 'I think I wouldn't publish that, if I were you, Tennyson'; whereupon the poet retorted, 'If it comes to that, Master, the sherry you gave us at luncheon was beastly' (Martin, 433). Jowett's 'Notes on Characteristics of Tennyson' cannot be bettered for their sympathetic acumen (Ricks, *Tennyson and His Friends*, 186–7):

> Absolute truthfulness, absolutely himself, never played tricks.
> Never got himself puffed in the newspapers.
> A friend of liberty and truth.
> Extraordinary vitality.
> Great common sense and a strong will.
> The instinct of common sense at the bottom of all he did.
> Not a man of the world (in the ordinary sense) but a man who had the greatest insight into the world, and often in a word or a sentence would flash a light.
> Intensely needed sympathy.
> A great and deep strength.
> He mastered circumstances, but he was also partly mastered by them, *e.g.* the old calamity of the disinheritance of his father and his treatment by rogues [Dr Allen and the wood-carving scheme] in the days of his youth.
> Very fair towards other poets, including those who were not popular, such as Crabbe.
> He had the high-bred manners not only of a gentleman but of a great man.
> He would have wished that, like Shakespeare, his life might be unknown to posterity.
> In the commonest conversation he showed himself a man of genius. He had abundance of fire, never talked poorly, never for effect. As Socrates described Plato, 'Like no one whom I ever knew before'.
> The three subjects of which he most often spoke were 'God,' 'Free-Will,' and 'Immortality,' yet always seeming to find an (apparent) contradiction between the 'imperfect world,' and 'the perfect attributes of God.'
> Great charm of his ordinary conversation, sitting by a very ordinary person and telling stories with the most high-bred courtesy, endless stories, not too high or too low for ordinary conversation.
> The persons and incidents of his childhood very vivid to him, and the Lincolnshire dialect and the ways of life.
> Loved telling a good story, which he did admirably, and also hearing one.
> He told very accurately, almost in the same words, his old stories, though, having a powerful memory, he was impatient of a friend who told him a twice-repeated tale.
> His jests were very amusing.
> At good things he would sit laughing away—laughter often interrupted by fits of sadness.
> His absolute sincerity, or habit of saying all things to all kinds of persons.

Tennyson's voice, character, and appearance   Thackeray stated, in the early summer of 1841: 'Perhaps it is Alfred Tennyson's great big yellow face and growling voice that has had an impression on me. Manliness and simplicity of manner go a great way with me, I fancy' (*Letters and Private Papers*, 2.26). In his readings, the poet himself evoked 'the poet' who 'Read, mouthing out his hollow oes and aes, / Deep-chested music' ('The Epic'). Thrillingly chanting *Maud*, 'The Charge of the Light Brigade', 'Northern Farmer: New Style', a song from *Idylls of the King*, and other verses, Tennyson's voice has been preserved for posterity thanks to an emissary of Thomas Edison's in May 1890.

Allingham relished Tennyson and 'his own sonorous manner, lingering with solemn sweetness on every vowel sound—a peculiar *incomplete* cadence at the end. He modulates his cadences with notable subtlety' (Allingham, 158, 25 Aug 1867). FitzGerald exulted in the harsher music, reporting of 'St Simeon Stylites': 'this is one of the Poems A. T. would read with grotesque Grimness, especially at such passages as "Coughs, Aches, Stitches, etc.", laughing aloud at times' (FitzGerald's notes at Trinity College, Cambridge).

Tennyson's eminent contemporaries paid affectionate tribute not only to his voice but to his character, appearance, and garb. FitzGerald noted on 23 May 1835: 'I will say no more of Tennyson than that the more I have seen of him, the more cause I have to think him great. His little humours and grumpinesses were so droll, that I was always laughing' (*Letters of Edward FitzGerald*, 1.162).

Carlyle described Tennyson to Emerson in August 1844, as

One of the finest looking men in the world. A great shock of rough dusty-dark hair; bright-laughing hazel eyes; massive aquiline face, most massive yet most delicate, of sallow-brown complexion, almost Indian-looking; clothes cynically loose, free-and-easy;—smokes infinite tobacco. His voice is musical metallic,—fit for loud laughter and piercing wail, and all that may lie between; speech and speculation free and plenteous: I do not meet, in these late decades, such company over a pipe! (*Collected Letters*, 18.169)

Six months later Jane Welsh Carlyle remarked that

Alfred is dreadfully embarrassed with women alone—for he entertains at one and the same moment a feeling of almost adoration for them and an ineffable contempt! Adoration I suppose for what they *might be*—contempt for what they *are!* The only chance of my getting any right good of him was to make him forget my *womanness* ... he smoked on all the same—for *three* mortal hours!—talking like an angel—only exactly as if he were talking with a clever *man*—which—being a thing I am not used to—men always *adapting* their conversation to what they *take to be* a womans taste—strained me to a terrible pitch of intellectuality. (31 Jan 1845, *Collected Letters*, 19.16–17)

Arthur Hugh Clough said: 'I like him personally better than I do his manner in his verses; personally he is the most unmannerly simple big child of a man that you can find' (13 Nov 1856, *Correspondence of Arthur Hugh Clough*, 2.522).

Nathaniel Hawthorne gave a detailed account of his impressions of the poet on 30 July 1857:

Tennyson is the most picturesque figure, without affectation, that I ever saw; of middle-size, rather slouching, dressed entirely in black, and with nothing white about him except the collar of his shirt, which methought might have been clean the day before. He had on a black wide-awake hat, with round crown and wide, irregular brim, beneath which came down his long black hair, looking terribly tangled; he had a long, pointed beard, too, a little browner than the hair, and not so abundant as to encumber any of the expression of his face. His frock coat was buttoned across the breast, though the afternoon was warm. His face was very dark, and not exactly a smooth face, but worn, and expressing great sensitiveness, though not, at that moment, the pain and sorrow which is seen in his bust ... I heard his voice; a bass voice, but not of a resounding depth; a voice rather broken,

as it were, and ragged about the edges, but pleasant to the ear. His manner, while conversing with these people, was not in the least that of an awkward man, unaccustomed to society; but he shook hands and parted with them, evidently as soon as he courteously could, and shuffled away quicker than before. He betrayed his shy and secluded habits more in this, than in anything else that I observed; though, indeed in his whole presence, I was indescribably sensible of a morbid painfulness in him, a something not to be meddled with. Very soon, he left the saloon, shuffling along the floor with short irregular steps, a very queer gait, as if he were walking in slippers too loose for him.   (Hawthorne, 351–3)

Julia Margaret Cameron, in 1862, caught Tennyson's prescience as well as the comedy of his so loathing celebrity-invading, a loathing strong in such poems as 'To —, After Reading a Life and Letters' and 'The Dead Prophet' (1885), pieces dealing with what Tennyson saw as the invasion of the Carlyles' privacy by the biographer James Anthony Froude.

He was very violent with the girls on the subject of the rage for autographs. He said he believed every crime and every vice in the world were connected with the passion for autographs and anecdotes and records,—that the desiring anecdotes and acquaintance with the lives of great men was treating them like pigs to be ripped open for the public; that he knew he himself should be ripped open like a pig; that he thanked God Almighty with his whole heart and soul that he knew nothing, and that the world knew nothing, of Shakespeare but his writings; and that he thanked God Almighty that he knew nothing of Jane Austen, and that there were no letters preserved either of Shakespeare's or of Jane Austen's, that they had not been ripped open like pigs. Then he said that the post for two days had brought *him* no letters, and that he thought there was a sort of syncope in the world as to him and to his fame.   (J. M. Cameron letter, Taylor, 2.193)

Henry James described Tennyson for William James some seventeen years later, on 29 March 1877:

He is very swarthy & scraggy & strikes one at first as much less handsome than his photos.: but gradually you see that it's a face of genius. He had I know not what simplicity, speaks with a strange rustic accent & seemed altogether like a creature of some primordial English stock, a 1000 miles away from American manufacture. (James and James, 1.283)

And finally, Thomas Hardy, in 1880,

often said that he was surprised to find such an expression of humour in the Poet-Laureate's face, the corners of his mouth twitching with that mood when he talked; 'it was a genial human face, which all his portraits belied'; and it was enhanced by a beard and hair straggling like briars, a shirt with a large loose collar, and old steel spectacles. (Hardy, 178)

Tennyson had the good fortune to be the neighbour on the Isle of Wight, and then the friend, of the greatest of Victorian portrait photographers, Julia Margaret Cameron. He valued her photographs of him, liking best the one he dubbed 'The Dirty Monk' (1865). As to portraits: FitzGerald, on 5 June 1871, wrote to Emily Tennyson, of Samuel Laurence's, painted about 1840:

Very imperfect as it is, it is nevertheless the *best* painted Portrait I have seen; and certainly the *only* one of old Days. 'Blubber-lipt' I remember Alfred once called it; so it is; but still the only one of old Days, and still—the best of all, to my thinking. I like to go back to Days before the Beard, which makes rather a Dickens of A. T. in the Photographs—to my mind. (*Letters of Edward FitzGerald*, 3.290–91)

On this portrait see *Letters*, 3.290n. For the representations by Cameron (photographs), by Thomas Woolner (medallion and busts), by James Spedding and D. G. Rossetti (drawings), by G. F. Watts (paintings), and the statue by Hamo Thornycroft, see David Piper, *The Image of the Poet: British Poets and their Portraits* (pp. 166–80).

Tennyson's plays and final years Tennyson wrote to Allingham on 29 July 1865: 'To own a ship, a large steam-yacht … and go round the world—that's my notion of glory' (Allingham, 118–19). In his old age he enjoyed a series of cruises delightful and calmative: in 1883, a fortnight on the *Pembroke Castle* (Scotland, Norway, and Denmark); in 1887, to Devon and Cornwall; in 1888, on Lord Brassey's yacht in and about the channel; and in the last two years of his life, 1891 and 1892, to Jersey. He had travelled in 1880 to Venice, Bavaria, and the Tyrol, with Hallam Tennyson. The sacred elegiac poem 'Crossing the Bar' was written in October 1889 while crossing the Solent. According to his son, when Tennyson showed him this poem, 'I said "That is the crown of your life's work." He answered, "It came in a moment"'. A few days before his death Tennyson said to his son, 'Mind you put my "Crossing the Bar" at the end of all editions of my poems' (H. Tennyson, *Memoir*, 2.366–7).

Extraordinary fecundity, energy, and variety continued to characterize Tennyson. He returned to earlier accomplishments: nearing seventy, in May 1879 he published, after repeated piracies, *The Lover's Tale*, which had been omitted from *Poems* (1832) despite Arthur Hallam's protests: 'You must be pointblank mad … Pray—pray—pray—change your mind again' (20 Nov 1832, *Letters of Arthur Henry Hallam*, 688). He also created anew: in December 1880, *Ballads and Other Poems*; in November 1885, *Tiresias, and Other Poems*; in December 1886, *Locksley Hall Sixty Years After*; and in December 1889, *Demeter and Other Poems*.

Tennyson's youthful dramatic extravaganza, *The Devil and the Lady*, and his mature masterpiece in monodrama, *Maud*, had given no notice that he would embark as a playwright during the last two decades of his life. Back in the 1830s his art in the dramatic monologue had been assuredly inaugurative and diverse, with the impassioned utterances of Ulysses, Tithonus, and St Simeon Stylites rivalling the simultaneous feats of Browning in different veins—but the stage, the Victorian stage?

It was in June 1875 that Tennyson published *Queen Mary*, initiating this new misguided phase. Henry James, no great hand at the stage himself, noted that

Great surprise, great hopes, and great fears had been called into being by the announcement that the author of so many finely musical lyrics and finished, chiselled specimens of narrative verse, had tempted fortune in the perilous field of the drama.

James saw that Tennyson 'has not so much refuted as evaded the charge that he is not a dramatic poet. To produce his drama he has had to cease to be himself' (*The Galaxy*, Sept 1875; H. James, 165–6). A production followed in April 1876, and then in December 1876 ('1877') the publication of his second historical drama, *Harold*. Henry Irving and Ellen Terry did their best for *The Cup* in July 1881. *The Promise of May*, his only published work in prose, was produced in November 1882. As though anticipating T. S. Eliot's *Murder in the Cathedral*, he wrote *Becket*. 'I gave Irving my *Thomas à Becket*', Tennyson said in 1880, and he meant 'gave':

He said it was magnificent, but it would cost £3000 to mount it,—*he* couldn't afford the risk. If well put on the stage, it would act for a time, and it would bring me credit—but it wouldn't pay. The success of a piece doesn't depend on its literary merit or even on its stage effect, but on its *hitting* somehow. (Allingham, 287, 5 Aug 1880)

Irving procrastinated for years, but six months before Tennyson's death he agreed to produce it, and did so in February 1893.

Strong of constitution, Tennyson lived to a great age. In his nerve-shattered thirties (the 1840s) he had despairingly resorted to water cures, and intermittently throughout his life he had a fear of blindness, but it was not until a few years before he died that ill health came upon him. In 1888 he suffered severe rheumatic illness, from which he did not recover until May 1889; in 1890–91 there was perilous influenza; and then in July 1892 he entered what was to be his last illness, bronchitis, influenza, neuralgia.

Death and posthumous reputation On 6 October 1892, having recently reached his eighty-fourth year, Tennyson died at Aldworth. That day, Queen Victoria recorded:

A fine morning—I heard that dear old Ld Tennyson had breathed his last, a great national loss. He was a great poet, and his ideas were ever grand, noble, elevating. He was very loyal and always very kind and sympathising to me, quite remarkably so. What beautiful lines he wrote to me for my darling Albert, and for my children and Eddy [her grandson the duke of Clarence and Avondale]. He died with his hand on his Shakespeare, and the moon shining full into the window, and over him. A worthy end to such a remarkable man. (Queen Victoria's journal, Dyson and Tennyson, 140)

Tennyson was buried in Westminster Abbey on 12 October. The grave is next to that of Browning, and in front of the monument to Chaucer. On 28 October 1892 there was posthumously published *The Death of Œnone, Akbar's Dream, and Other Poems*. He left £57,206 13s. 9d.—this, and royalties to come, from poems that have lasted.

Such was the sense of national loss that the abolition of the office of poet laureate was solemnly mooted when Tennyson died. It was not until 1 January 1896, more than three years later, that a successor was announced: Alfred Austin, poetaster laureate.

Emily Tennyson died on 10 August 1896. In October 1897 Hallam Tennyson published, in two volumes, *Alfred Lord Tennyson: A Memoir*. To this he had devoted the five years since the poet's death, amassing, cutting, and (on occasion) shielding, towards the classic Victorian form, a life and letters. Indispensable, the *Memoir* is capacious and honourable, at its best in breathing a sense of what it was like in the immediate vicinity of Tennyson during the second half of his life, a memoir quite as much duly as unduly reticent.

In due course there came the expected 'reaction against Tennyson'. Samuel Butler, his grim comic nose in the wind, had started to jeer as soon as the breath was out of Tennyson's body:

I see they packed the volume of Shakespeare that he had near him when he died in a little tin box and buried it with him. If they had to bury it they should have either not packed it at all, or, at the least, in a box of silver-gilt. But his friends should have taken it out of the bed when they saw the end was near. It was not necessary to emphasize the fact that the ruling passion for posing was strong with him in death.

A little later he went on, 'It seems that it was not the copy actually in bed with Tennyson when he died that was buried with him, but another copy, let us hope of the same edition, and equally well bound, was substituted for it' (Butler, 254, 257).

Imminent Edwardians ousted eminent Victorians. Some lovers of Tennyson tried to reform things from within: Harold Nicolson in 1923 brilliantly rescued many of the true poems by conceding that much of Tennyson must go—while insisting that the essential Tennyson, 'a morbid and unhappy mystic', could and would stay. Here, of all things, was an English *poète maudit*, more, a *poète lauréat maudit*. French symbolism, in the person of Verlaine, had judged *In Memoriam* harshly: 'When he should have been broken-hearted, he had many reminiscences'—for all the world as if reminiscences were not one deep and honourable way of attending to a broken heart. It was W. B. Yeats who enjoyed giving English currency to Verlaine's gibe (*The Oxford Book of Modern Verse*, 1936, ix).

It was left to T. S. Eliot, who warmed wittily and deeply to Tennyson, to insist in 1936 on the needed obvious: 'Tennyson is a great poet, for reasons that are perfectly clear. He has three qualities which are seldom found together except in the greatest poets: abundance, variety, and complete competence' (T. S. Eliot, 'In Memoriam', 328).

Pressed by an anthologist for a biographical paragraph in 1837, Tennyson had sent only the 'dry dates': 'I have no life to give—for mine has been one of feelings not of actions—can he not miss me out altogether?' (13 July 1837, *Letters*, 1.154). But the life that truly he gave was one that realized feelings, his own and ours. The qualities of his poetry are most vividly commemorated, appreciated, and placed in the criticism by his contemporaries: by Matthew Arnold, Walter Bagehot, Arthur Hallam, Gerard M. Hopkins, and R. H. Hutton. Supremely, by Walt Whitman (*The Critic*, 1 Jan 1887; Jump, 349–50):

To me, Tennyson shows more than any poet I know (perhaps has been a warning to me) how much there is in finest verbalism. There is such a latent charm in mere words, cunning collocations, and in the voice ringing them, which he has caught and brought out, beyond all others—as in the line 'And hollow, hollow, hollow, all delight', in 'The Passing of Arthur'.

CHRISTOPHER RICKS

Sources *Letters of Alfred Lord Tennyson*, ed. C. Y. Lang and E. F. Shannon, 3 vols. (1982–90) · *The Tennyson archive*, ed. C. Ricks and A. Day, 31 vols. (1987–93) [Tennyson MSS in facs., incl. the great collections at Harvard U., Houghton L.; at the Tennyson Research Centre, Lincoln; and at Trinity Cam.] · *The poems of Tennyson*, ed. C. Ricks, rev. edn, 3 vols. (1987) · C. Ricks, ed., *Tennyson and his friends* (1992) [exhibition catalogue, Harvard U., Houghton L.] · *Poems and plays: the Eversley edition*, ed. H. Tennyson, 9 vols. (1907–8) · H. Tennyson, *Alfred Lord Tennyson: A Memoir*, 2 vols. (1897) · H. Tennyson, ed., *Tennyson and his friends* (1911) · C. Tennyson, *Alfred Tennyson* (1949) · H. Dyson and C. Tennyson, *Dear and Honoured Lady* (1969) · F. T. Palgrave, ed., *The golden treasury* (1861), ed. C. Ricks (1991) · J. Jump, ed., *Tennyson: the critical heritage* (1967) · R. B. Martin, *Tennyson: the unquiet heart* (1980) · C. Ricks, *Tennyson*, 2nd edn (1989) · A. Thwaite, *Emily Tennyson: the poet's wife* (1996) · W. Allingham, *Diary* (1907) · S. Butler, *Notebooks*, ed. G. Keynes and B. Hill (1951) · *The collected letters of Thomas and Jane Welsh Carlyle*, 18, ed. C. de L. Ryals and K. J. Fielding (1990); 22, ed. C. de L. Ryals and K. J. Fielding (1995) · *Correspondence of Arthur Hugh Clough*, ed. F. L. Mulhauser, 2 vols. (1957) · W. Ward, *Aubrey de Vere: a memoir* (1904) · G. Eliot, *Essays*, ed. T. Pinney (1963) · *The letters of Edward FitzGerald*, ed. A. M. Terhune and A. B. Terhune, 4 vols. (1980) · *Mary Gladstone (Mrs Drew): her diaries and letters*, ed. L. Masterman (1930) · *Letters of Arthur Henry Hallam*, ed. J. Kolb (1981) · F. E. Hardy, *The early life of Thomas Hardy* (1928) · H. James, *Views and reviews*, ed. L. R. Phillips (1908) · W. James and H. James, *The correspondence of William James*, ed. I. K. Skrupskelis and E. M. Berkeley, 1 (1992) · N. Hawthorne, *The English notebooks 1856–1860*, ed. T. Woodson and B. Ellis (1997) · R. H. Hutton, *Literary essays* (1888) · J. Knowles, 'Aspects of Tennyson II (a personal reminiscence)', *Nineteenth Century*, 33 (1893), 164–88 · V. Noakes, *Edward Lear*, 2nd edn (1979) · [E. Lear], *Selected letters*, ed. V. Noakes (1988) · C. Merivale, *Autobiography* (1899) · C. S. Parker, *Sir Robert Peel*, 3 vols. (1899) · T. W. Reid, *Monckton Milnes*, 2 vols. (1890) · *Letters of Dante Gabriel Rossetti*, ed. O. Doughty and J. R. Wahl, 1 (1965) · *Letters of John Addington Symonds*, ed. H. M. Schueller and R. L. Peters, 3 vols. (1969) · H. Taylor, *Autobiography*, 2 vols. (1885) · *The letters and private papers of William Makepeace Thackeray*, ed. G. N. Ray, 2 (1945) · W. B. Yeats, *Uncollected prose*, ed. J. P. Frayne, 1 (1970) · M. Beerbohm, *The Poets' Corner* (1904) · T. S. Eliot, 'Whitman and Tennyson', *Nation and Athenaeum* (18 Dec 1926) · T. S. Eliot, 'In Memoriam', *Selected essays*, rev. edn (1951) · M. Girouard, *The return to Camelot: chivalry and the English gentleman* (1981) · J. Killham, *Tennyson and The Princess: reflections of an age* (1958) · H. Nicolson, *Tennyson: aspects of his life, character and poetry* (1923) · D. Piper, *The image of the poet: British poets and their portraits* (1982)

Archives Harvard U., Houghton L. · Tennyson Research Centre, Lincoln · Trinity Cam. | SOUND Tennyson Society, Lincoln

Likenesses J. Spedding, drawing, c.1831, NPG · S. Laurence, oils, c.1840, NPG · D. G. Rossetti, drawing, 1855, Col. U. · T. Woolner, plaster relief, 1856, NPG · G. F. Watts, portrait, c.1863–1864, NPG · J. M. Cameron, photograph, 1865, NPG [*see illus.*] · J. M. Cameron, photographs, NPG · bust, Trinity Cam.

Wealth at death £57,206 13s. 9d.: probate, 16 Dec 1892, CGPLA Eng. & Wales

Tennyson, Charles. *See* Turner, Charles (1808–1879).

Tennyson [*née* Sellwood], **Emily Sarah**, **Lady Tennyson** (1813–1896), secretary and manager for her husband, Alfred, Lord Tennyson, was born on 9 July 1813 in Market Place, Horncastle, Lincolnshire, the eldest of the three daughters of Henry Sellwood (1782–1867) and his wife, Sarah, *née* Franklin (1788–1816), a younger sister of Sir John Franklin, the sailor and explorer. Sellwood himself was born in Berkshire and had come to Horncastle before 1808. He married in 1812 into the remarkable family of a Spilsby grocer. Their connections and his own energy helped him to become prominent in Horncastle, where he practised as a solicitor for forty years. Her uncle John Franklin's two strong wives, Eleanor Porden and Jane Griffin, influenced Emily's idea of what women could be and

Emily Sarah Tennyson, Lady Tennyson (1813–1896), by George Frederic Watts, 1865

do. Her own particular talent was for music and she composed and played all her life. But it was her marriage to Alfred *Tennyson (1809–1892), poet laureate, which gave her the chance to make use of all her skills and virtues. Benjamin Jowett wrote to her son that Julia Margaret Cameron used to say that, though unknown, Emily Tennyson was as 'great' as her husband and that 'the poet himself was aware that these words were truly spoken'. Jowett wrote, 'It was a wonderful life—an effaced life, like that of so many women … He could never have been what he was without her'.

Emily Sellwood first saw Tennyson when she was nine years old and he was a boy, outside her house while their two fathers discussed business. Somersby, where the Revd George Clayton Tennyson was vicar, was only 7 miles from Horncastle. Emily described the Tennysons as 'among our neighbours we had as friends'. Only three when her mother died, Emily was extremely close to her father. The girls were educated first by 'some ladies' in Horncastle, and it is likely that it was when they were with the Misses Bousfield of Far Street that they made friends with Alfred Tennyson's sisters: Mary, Emily, Matilda, and Cecilia. Emily Sellwood later attended boarding-schools in Brighton and London.

It was soon after Emily left school that she stayed overnight at Somersby for the first time in April 1830. Six years later Tennyson's elder brother Charles married Emily's youngest sister, Louisa; Tennyson's poem 'The Bridesmaid' celebrates his feelings. This first Tennyson–Sellwood marriage was full of stress and was one of many reasons why Henry Sellwood did not encourage Alfred and

Emily to marry in the late 1830s, although they were informally engaged. The poet's gloomy material prospects and worrying heredity, his despair following the death of his friend Arthur Hallam, and his religious doubts made Tennyson write to Emily: 'I fly thee for my good, perhaps for thine'. There was no contact for seven years until they met in Kent in 1847 at the home of Tennyson's sister Cecilia and her husband, Edmund Lushington. Tennyson's poems *The Princess* and *In Memoriam* and the reconciliation of Charles and Louisa all had a good deal to do with Emily's eventual agreement to marry.

Emily Sellwood married Alfred Tennyson on 13 June 1850 at Shiplake, near Henley-on-Thames. The ceremony was performed by the Revd Drummond Rawnsley, the husband of Emily's cousin Catherine (*née* Franklin). Emily was nearly thirty-seven and Alfred nearly forty-one. Tennyson said the peace of God came into his life when he married. Emily's devotion, faith, tolerance, flexibility, and managerial skills transformed his life.

There was a first, stillborn, son in 1851. Then, in 1852 and 1854, the two boys, Hallam *Tennyson (1852–1928) and Lionel, were born. Emily taught them herself until they went to school in 1865 but Tennyson was also actively involved in their upbringing. Emily said that those days when the boys were young were the happiest period of her life. It was also the healthiest period. So often portrayed (for example by Virginia Woolf and Thomas Hardy) as a woman who spent her entire life on a sofa, she was able to scramble over rocks and give the boys rides on her back. She had been delicate as a girl and her ill health in later life (after some sort of breakdown in 1874) may have been caused by gynaecological problems as well as overwork.

The family settled at Farringford, Freshwater, on the Isle of Wight, in 1853. In 1868 they built a house, Aldworth, Sussex, near Haslemere, and came to divide their time between the two houses, with some travel in the summers. Emily's full powers came into play with her marriage. She devoted the rest of her life to her poet and his work. She answered his letters (sometimes for six or seven hours a day), protected him from criticism, corrected his proofs, set his poems (more than twenty of them) to music, ran the households and their farm, and lent a sympathetic ear to his constant fussing and grumblings as well as his reading aloud. She herself read French, German, and Italian but had no Greek or Latin. One of her greatest pleasures was to listen to Tennyson's *viva voce* translations of Homer.

Some observers (notably Anne Gilchrist) thought Emily's attitude ill-conceived. 'Mrs Tennyson, watching him with anxious, affectionate solicitude … surrounds him ever closer and closer with the sultry perfumed atmosphere of luxury and homage in which his great soul droops'. But most people, including Tennyson himself, felt she was his perfect partner. Her faith in God ('as clear as the heights of the June-blue heaven') sustained them both and enabled them to cope with the death of Lionel in 1886 on the way home from India. (It had been Emily's idea that he should go.)

Lady Tennyson (as she became in 1883) spent her

remaining years, after the poet's death in 1892, helping their son Hallam to write the two-volume *Memoir* of Tennyson's life. Much of it was written by Emily herself, based closely on her journals. She died of 'congestion of the lungs' on 10 August 1896 at Aldworth and was buried four days later in Freshwater church on the Isle of Wight. The best-known portrait of her was painted by G. F. Watts. It is in the Usher Gallery in Lincoln. An earlier (apparently more accurate) portrait by Millais remains in the family. Both show her physical delicacy, which her strong character so triumphantly overcame.   ANN THWAITE

Sources A. Thwaite, *Emily Tennyson: the poet's wife* (1996)
Archives Harvard U., Houghton L. · Lincoln Central Library, Tennyson Research Centre, corresp. · Yale U., Beinecke L.
Likenesses J. Millais, watercolour?, 1854?, priv. coll. · G. F. Watts, charcoal drawing, c.1858, Watts Gallery, Compton · G. F. Watts, oils, 1865, Usher Art Gallery, Lincoln [*see illus.*] · Cameron Studio, photograph, 1890 (with husband and son), NPG · photographs, Lincoln Central Library

Tennyson, Frederick

Tennyson, Frederick (1807–1898), poet, was born at Louth in Lincolnshire on 5 June 1807, the second son of George Clayton Tennyson (1778–1831), rector of Bag Enderby and Somersby, and his wife, Elizabeth Fytche (*bap.* 1780, *d.* 1865). Frederick grew up in the Somersby rectory, together with his brothers Alfred *Tennyson (1809–1892) and Charles (1808–1879) [*see* Turner, Charles], four other brothers, and four sisters. While his younger brothers received much of their early education at home, Frederick, as the oldest surviving son (the Tennysons' first child had died in early infancy), was sent away to school: first to the grammar school in Louth in 1814, and then from 1818 to 1826 to Eton College, where he was captain of the school.

From Eton Frederick went first to St John's, then to Trinity College, Cambridge, closely followed by his younger brothers Charles and Alfred. His university career was interrupted in 1828 when he was rusticated for three terms. Having failed to attend chapel, he superciliously accused the chancellor, Christopher Wordsworth (brother of William), of hypocrisy at the disciplinary hearing. Frederick's punishment for this act of insolence set him at odds with a father whose health had been seriously undermined by heavy drinking. The two came to blows on 20 February 1829—in an incident that required the presence of the village constable; the constable was the Tennysons' next-door neighbour, a fact often not mentioned in accounts of this incident. After gaining his BA degree in 1832 and spending a few footloose years in and around Somersby, Frederick went to live in Florence, managing to support a comfortable lifestyle with income from inherited property in Grimsby. In 1839 he married Maria Giuliotti (*d.* 1884), daughter of the chief magistrate of Siena.

The confusingly titled *Poems by Two Brothers* (1827) had contained a handful of poems by Frederick, in addition to those by Alfred and Charles. Frederick continued to write poetry, but his collection *Days and Hours* (1854) was so little noticed that he published no more poetry until an old man. The greater part of his life was dedicated to pursuing

his love of music—in Florence he frequently invited a small orchestra to play at his home—and mysticism. Like his sister Mary he was a keen reader of Swedenborg. After leaving Italy in 1859 and moving to St Ewold's, Jersey, he helped to edit and promote an arcane and astrological book about masonry—*Veritas* (1874)—by his friend Henry Melville.

The work produced in Tennyson's last years—*The Isles of Greece* (1890), an epic based on fragments of Sappho and Alcæus, *Daphne* (1891), and *Poems of the Day and Year* (1895)—was no more noticed than the earlier volume (part of which was contained in the 1895 title). Four lyrics included in the second edition of Palgrave's *Golden Treasury* showed Frederick at his best, but did not encourage discovery of his other work. He outlived both Alfred and Charles, and spent his final years in South Kensington, London, at 14 Holland Villas Road, the home of his oldest child, Julius, by then a captain in the army, and reputed to be the strongest man in uniform. Frederick Tennyson died at home on 26 February 1898.

Edward FitzGerald's opinion of his friend Frederick's poetry, as expressed in a letter to E. B. Cowell in 1871, has been borne out by posterity: 'There is a monotony and total want of dramatic faculty in the stories (for stories mostly the book consists of) which will confine them to very few readers, and to those few readers' shelves.'
                                                                    MICHAEL THORN

Sources C. Tennyson, *The Tennysons: background to genius* (1974) · H. Tennyson, *Alfred Lord Tennyson: a memoir by his son*, 2 vols. (1897) · C. Tennyson, *Alfred Tennyson* (1949) · R. B. Martin, *Tennyson: the unquiet heart* (1980) · N. Page, ed., *Tennyson: interviews and recollections* (1983) · M. Thorn, *Tennyson* (1992)
Archives Indiana University, Bloomington, Lilly Library, personal papers, corresp., and family papers · Lincoln Central Library, Tennyson Research Centre
Likenesses J. M. Cameron, photograph, c.1865, Lincoln Central Library, Tennyson Research Centre · R. Taylor & Co., woodengraving (after photograph), BM; repro. in *ILN* (26 Sept 1891)
Wealth at death £1085 14s. 3d.: resworn probate, April 1899, *CGPLA Eng. & Wales* (1898)

Tennyson, Hallam

Tennyson, Hallam, second Baron Tennyson (1852–1928), biographer and governor-general of Australia, was born on 11 August 1852 at Twickenham, Middlesex, eldest son of the poet laureate, Alfred *Tennyson, first Baron Tennyson (1809–1892), and his wife, Emily Sarah, *née* Sellwood (1813–1896). The Tennysons were a close family and, as boys, Hallam and his brother Lionel were doted upon by their middle-aged parents. Emily Tennyson was reluctant to let either son leave her care for formal schooling. The boys were often dressed in identical tunics with lace fineries, scarlet stockings, and strapped slippers. Charles Dodgson photographed them in 1857, remarking that they were the most beautiful boys he had ever seen. Alfred, Lord Tennyson described his eldest son as a 'noble child' (Martin, 378). Educated at home by his mother and a series of tutors, Hallam then briefly attended a preparatory school at Bailey Gate in Dorset run by Charles Kegan Paul, a former chaplain at Eton who thought the boy 'accurate' rather than brilliant at his studies (ibid.). From 1866 to 1872 he

Hallam Tennyson, second Baron Tennyson (1852–1928), by Cameron Studio, *c.*1890

attended Marlborough College and matriculated at Trinity College, Cambridge in 1872. In 1877 he was admitted to the Inner Temple.

Hallam Tennyson occupied a particularly important place in his father's life. He travelled with him around Europe taking nineteen summer tours between 1874 and 1892, and was closely involved in all his father's literary affairs, acting as secretary, confidant, occasional amanuensis, and warden of the poet's privacy. Hallam Tennyson's own literary aspirations were modest; he produced some prize-winning poetry at Marlborough, contributed articles to magazines, published an edition of *Jack and the Beanstalk*, illustrated by Randolph Caldecott, and edited two poetry collections.

Tennyson was summoned home to assist after his mother's breakdown in health in 1874, and devoted himself to his family thereafter. He became a councillor of the Imperial Federation League in 1883 and through this activity both embraced his father's strong interests in strengthening empire ties and extended his own reputation in government circles.

In 1883 Hallam Tennyson became engaged to Audrey Georgina Florence Boyle (1853/4–1916), and they were married at Westminster Abbey on 25 June 1884. Audrey, daughter of the diplomat Charles Boyle and his wife, Zacyntha, was the only daughter in a family of six sons. She joined the close-knit Tennyson family and accepted her husband's filial occupations without demur, although she often found her position difficult. The couple lived at Farringford and were constantly 'on call' to the poet and his wife. Their first son, Lionel Hallam, was born in 1889

after five years of marriage, followed by (Alfred) Aubrey (1891–1918), and Harold Courtenay (1896–1916).

Tennyson continued to act as his father's efficient private secretary until the latter's death in 1892. Succeeding as second baron, Tennyson then began immediately on his father's biography. With his father's friends Henry Sidgwick and Francis Palgrave, he sorted over 40,000 letters. At the poet's direction, more than three-quarters of his letters were destroyed under the supervision of Lady Tennyson. The resulting two-volume biography, *Alfred Lord Tennyson: a Memoir by his Son* (1897), is a conscientious work of guarded commemoration. Hallam Tennyson was tall, fair, bearded, well-proportioned in youth, with dark eyes and a good speaking voice. Contemporaries regarded him as highly conventional, careful, systematic, and devoted beyond the call of duty. His fidelity was motivated by open admiration of a man whom he saw as embodying the very best in his countrymen. On his deathbed, Lord Tennyson expressed regret at making a 'slave' of his son (H. Tennyson, 775).

Hallam Tennyson continued working from Farringford, serving as a magistrate, and on the councils of Marlborough College and the Gordon Boys' Home. In 1896, after his mother's death and freed from filial duties, he actively sought selection for service in the empire. Joseph Chamberlain invited him to consider the position of governor of South Australia in mid-1898. After initial hesitation Tennyson accepted the post in January 1899, arriving with his family in Adelaide in April that year.

The new governor's lack of experience was soon offset in colonial minds by his lack of ostentation, which was applauded, although gubernatorial remunerations remained an issue. Tennyson complained frequently about the costs of official entertaining and maintaining his establishment. His diligence, however, was noted and his family was fêted; Lady Tennyson and her young sons were regarded with affection.

Tennyson defended state governors' rights to deal directly with the British government. He promoted the dispatch of the HMCS *Protector* to China during the Boxer uprising of 1899–1900. With his British patriotism aroused by the Second South African War (1899–1902), he marched with the volunteer South Australian contingent in October 1899, bidding them farewell on the troopship *Medic*. While state governor, he designed the South Australian seal and flag and endowed a Tennyson medal for students. He was awarded an honorary LLD degree from Melbourne and Adelaide universities, and the honorary colonelcy of the 7th Victorian light horse and the South Australian artillery.

In July 1902, following Lord Hopetoun's unanticipated resignation, Lord Tennyson became Australia's acting governor-general and then, from January 1903 to January 1904, a period he designated, governor-general. He was created GCMG on 25 June 1903.

As governor-general Tennyson adopted a unifying position in Australia, although his personal enthusiasm for imperial federation occasionally blinded him to Australia's own priorities. A later commentator remarked that

'Tennyson's tour of duty [saw] the consolidation of the office of governor-general as an institutional framework which assisted in maintaining the Imperial connection' (Cunneen, 43).

Lord Tennyson and his family returned to England in 1904, taking up residence again at Farringford. He refused the governorship of Madras, preferring to remain with his sons in England, although he retained an active interest in empire settlement schemes. He was made a privy councillor in 1905, and received honours from the universities of Oxford and Cambridge. In 1907 and 1908 he edited and published nine volumes of his father's poetry and in 1911 produced another memoir, *Tennyson and his Friends*. His leisure pursuits included yachting, geology, and playing golf. After 1913 he served as deputy governor of the Isle of Wight.

Tragedy struck in 1916, when Harold, Tennyson's youngest son, was killed in action and his wife, Audrey, aged sixty-two, died from pneumonia. In March 1918 Aubrey, Tennyson's middle son, was also killed in action. Lionel Tennyson was wounded three times but survived. On 27 July 1918 Lord Tennyson was married by special licence at the parish church of South Stoneham, in Hampshire; his second wife was Mary Emily Hickens (*b.* 1855), a widow, daughter of Charles Prinsep, former advocate-general of Bengal.

Hallam, Lord Tennyson, died at his home, Farringford, Freshwater, Isle of Wight, on 2 December 1928 and his funeral was held at the parish church, Freshwater, Isle of Wight on 5 December. Lionel Tennyson succeeded his father as third baron.   SUZANNE L. G. RICKARD

Sources NL Aus., Lord Tennyson's papers, MS 1963 · R. B. Martin, *Tennyson: the unquiet heart* (1980) · H. Tennyson, *Alfred Lord Tennyson: a memoir by his son*, 2 vols. (1897) · C. Cunneen, *Kings' men* (1983) · *Audrey Tennyson's vice-regal days: the Australian letters of Audrey Lady Tennyson to her mother Zacyntha Boyle, 1899–1903*, ed. A. Hasluck (1978) · *Lady Tennyson's journal*, ed. J. O. Hoges (Charlottesville, VA, 1981) · J. A. La Nauze, *Alfred Deakin: a biography*, 2 vols. (1965) · P. Serle, *Dictionary of Australian biography*, 2 vols. (1949), vol. 2, p. 413 · *AusDB*, vol. 12 · *DNB* · H. T. Burgess, ed., *The cyclopedia of South Australia*, 1 (Adelaide, 1907), 165 · *Town and Country Journal* [Sydney] (11 Feb 1899) · *Town and Country Journal* [Sydney] (15 April 1899) · *The Times* (3 Dec 1928), 19c · *The Times* (6 Dec 1928), 19 · NL Aus., Lady Tennyson's papers, MS 479 · Venn, *Alum. Cant.* · d. cert.
Archives Lincoln Central Library, Tennyson Research Centre, papers · Mitchell L., NSW, corresp. and papers · NL Aus., corresp. and papers, MS 1963 | BL, letters to Mary Gladstone, Add. MS 46244 · BL, letters to W. E. Gladstone, Add. MSS 4484–4526, *passim.* · BL, corresp. with Macmillans, Add. MSS 54980–54986 · Harvard U., Houghton L., letters to D. L. Thomson · NL Aus., corresp. with Alfred Deakin · NL Aus., Lady Audrey Tennyson's papers, MS 479 · NPG, letters to George Frederic and Mary Watts · NRA, priv. coll., corresp. with Alfred, Lord Tennyson, and Charles Tennyson D'Eyncourt · U. St Andr. L., corresp. with Wilfred Ward | SOUND State Library of South Australia, Adelaide, sound recording, GRG 26/2/13
Likenesses Cameron Studio, photograph, *c*.1890, NPG [*see illus.*] · T. Roberts, oils, 1902, Parliament of Australia, Canberra · B. Riviere, oils, 1908, NL Aus. · T. Roberts, oils, 1914, Historical Monuments Commission, New Parliament House, Canberra · portraits, NL Aus., Pictorial Collection
Wealth at death £146,338 4s. 4d.: probate, 14 Feb 1929, CGPLA Eng. & Wales

Tennyson-D'Eyncourt, Sir Eustace Henry William. *See* D'Eyncourt, Sir Eustace Henry William Tennyson-, first baronet (1868–1951).

Tenterden. For this title name *see* Hales, Sir Edward, third baronet and Jacobite earl of Tenterden (1645–1695); Abbott, Charles, first Baron Tenterden (1762–1832); Abbott, Charles Stuart Aubrey, third Baron Tenterden (1834–1882).

Tenzing Norgay [*known as* Sherpa Tenzing] (1914–1986), mountaineer, was born in late May 1914 at Tsa-chu, in the Kharta valley of Tibet, the son of Ghang-La Mingma (*d.* 1949) and his wife, Kinzom. He was the eleventh of thirteen children. His family lived at Thami, in the Solu Khumbu region of Nepal, and his mother was in Tibet visiting relatives when he was born. After the 1950s, perhaps for political reasons, he sometimes identified Thami as his birthplace. In either case he was a Sherpa, a member of an ethnic group that had migrated from eastern Tibet to Solu Khumbu in the sixteenth century. At birth he was named Namgyal Wangdi, but a lama at the Rongbuk monastery, probably his uncle the Zatul Rimpoche, said he should be renamed Tenzing Norgay, which meant 'wealthy fortunate follower of religion'. Tenzing was sent to the Thami monastery at a young age to become a monk, but he ran home after a monk hit him. He had no other formal education and remained illiterate throughout his life. He helped his family grow potatoes, barley, and tsampa (a maize), as well as tend sheep and yaks near Mount Everest, known locally as Chomolungma ('Goddess mother of the world').

Tenzing heard stories about Everest from Sherpas who had been porters with the British expeditions in the 1920s, and he developed an ambition to climb the peak that was very unusual among Sherpas. Although lamas taught that Chomolungma was the abode of gods, Tenzing recalled, 'What I wanted was to see for myself; find out for myself. This was the dream I have had as long as I can remember' (Tenzing, *Man of Everest*, 41). Sherpa inheritance patterns also forced younger sons such as Tenzing to seek their fortune away from home. At the age of thirteen he ran away to Katmandu, but returned after six weeks. At the age of eighteen, in 1932, he left for Darjeeling, India, where he hoped to become a porter on the next Everest expedition in 1933. He was not chosen but stayed in Darjeeling to work as a servant and manual labourer. In 1935 he married Dawa Phuti (*d.* 1944). They had two daughters and a son, who died young. Eric Shipton chose him as a porter for the 1935 Everest expedition, and he returned to Everest in 1936 and 1938. He carried loads to 27,200 feet, and in 1938 the Himalayan Club awarded him one of the first 'tiger medals' for high-altitude porters.

In 1939 Tenzing went on an expedition to the Hindu Kush, and he remained on the north-west frontier of India for the duration of the war as a cook for the Chitral scouts. After his first wife's death he returned to Darjeeling in 1945 and married Ang Lahmu (*d.* 1965). In 1947 he joined

Tenzing Norgay [Sherpa Tenzing] (1914–1986), by unknown
photographer, 1953 [on Chukhung Peak, 3 April 1953]

Earl Denman, a Canadian, on a maverick expedition to
Everest. He was Professor Giuseppe Tucci's personal assistant for a year in Tibet in 1948, and went on H. W. Tilman's
journey to western Nepal in 1950. After the war, he
worked for many British, Swiss, and French mountaineering expeditions, including an attempt on Nanga Parbat
and the ascent of Nanda Devi east in 1951. Tenzing
assumed increasing responsibility and often served as sirdar, or head porter.

In 1952 Tenzing was chosen as sirdar for the Swiss Everest expedition and made a full member of the climbing
team. His relationship with the Swiss was warmer and less
hierarchical than it had been with the British, and he
became very close friends with his climbing partner, Raymond Lambert (1915–1997), a Swiss guide. On 28 May 1952
Tenzing and Lambert reached 28,250 feet, the highest elevation ever. In the autumn of 1952 Tenzing returned to
Everest with the Swiss, but did not reach as high.

In 1953 Colonel John Hunt, leader of the British Everest
expedition, also invited Tenzing to be sirdar and member
of the climbing team. At a crucial point Tenzing persuaded the exhausted and heavily laden Sherpa porters to
force a route up the Lhotse face to the south col. Tenzing
and Edmund Hillary, a New Zealand bee-keeper, made the
first ascent of Mount Everest (29,028 feet) on 29 May 1953.
Afterwards Tenzing adopted 29 May as his date of birth
(the actual date was unknown). On the summit he buried
an offering to the gods and said a prayer, and Hillary took a
famous photograph of him flying the flags of the United
Nations, Britain, Nepal, and India from his ice axe.

News of their ascent was publicly announced on 2 June

1953, the day of Queen Elizabeth II's coronation. Controversy soon surrounded Tenzing's nationality (Nepali or
Indian?), and the question of who reached the summit
first. Posters of Tenzing dragging Hillary to the top
appeared in Nepal and India. Despite a joint statement
that they reached the summit together, and Tenzing's
admission in his autobiography (*Man of Everest*, 268) that
Hillary had been first on the rope, the issue has remained
contentious. Tenzing was given the Nepal tara and numerous honours and awards in Nepal, India, Switzerland,
France, Italy, the Soviet Union, and the United States. In
Britain the queen gave Tenzing the George Medal, a comparatively obscure but high civilian award for gallantry,
while Hillary and Hunt received knighthoods. The prime
minister of India, Jawaharlal Nehru, had refused to allow
Tenzing to be given a British knighthood (Hansen, 'Confetti of empire').

Nehru appointed Tenzing permanent director of field
training of the new Himalayan Mountaineering Institute
in Darjeeling. After Tenzing and other Sherpas were
trained as mountaineering instructors in Switzerland, the
Indian government opened the institute on 4 November
1954. Nehru told Tenzing, 'Now you will make a thousand
Tenzings' (Tenzing, *After Everest*, 53). Tenzing built Ghang-
la, a new home in Darjeeling, and was famous but not rich.
After one of his sisters died in 1956, he took responsibility
for raising her five children. In 1961, having separated
from his second wife, he married Daku (1938–1992), and
they had three sons and a daughter. Tenzing also bred
many Lhasa terriers at his home. Over time his position at
the institute became largely honorary, and he often led
trekking groups in the Himalayas or travelled abroad to
visit friends. He sometimes travelled to promote Darjeeling tea, and the government of West Bengal paid for his
children's education. In 1976 he was forced to retire from
the institute, which he resented. Despite the promise of a
job for life, early retirement with an inadequate pension
compelled the elderly Tenzing to continue shepherding
American tourists through the Himalayas and Tibet. In
later years members of his family also climbed Everest,
including his nephew Gombu in 1963 and 1965, his son
Jamling in 1996, and his grandson Tashi in 1997.

Tenzing published two authorized autobiographies
with ghost writers. *Man of Everest* (1955), written with
James Ramsey Ullman (1909–1971), concerns his early life
and was widely translated. It appeared in the USA as *Tiger
of the Snows*. Rabindranath Mitra, a friend in Darjeeling,
was an intermediary between Tenzing and Ullman. Tenzing also published *After Everest* (1977) with Malcolm
Barnes. Tenzing disowned a controversial book by Yves
Malartic that was based on brief airport conversations.
Wary of the intense political pressures that he came
under in 1953, Tenzing tried to avoid politics or controversial issues. He stood 5 feet 8 inches tall, possessed a wide
and famously infectious smile, and was known for his
humility and simple dignity.

Late in life Tenzing was unhappy and began drinking
excessively. He suffered for several years from a bronchial

condition, from which he died on 9 May 1986 at Darjee-ling. He was cremated on 14 May and his ashes were buried in a large state funeral at the Himalayan Mountaineering Institute. A statue of Tenzing standing on the summit of Everest was unveiled at his grave in Darjeeling in 1997.

PETER H. HANSEN

Sources Tenzing Norgay, *Man of Everest* (1955) · Tenzing Norgay, *After Everest* (1977) · *The Statesman* (10 May 1986) · *Times of India* (10 May 1986) · *New York Times* (10 May 1986) · *The Guardian* (10 May 1986) · *The Times* (10 May 1986) · *The Rising Nepal* (10 May 1986) · *Alpine Journal*, 92 (1987) · *Himalayan Journal*, 43 (1985–6) · P. Hansen, 'Debate: Tenzing's two wrist watches: the conquest of Everest and late imperial culture, 1921–1953: comment', *Past and Present*, 157 (1997) · P. Hansen, 'Confetti of empire: the conquest of Everest in Nepal, India, Britain and New Zealand', unpublished essay · *Reputations: Hillary and Tenzing: Everest and after*, video, 1997, BBC · *The adventurers: Hillary and Tenzing, climbing to the roof of the world*, video documentary, 1997, Public Broadcasting Service · W. Unsworth, *Everest*, another edn (1991) · private information (2004) [T. Tenzing, E. Hillary, J. Hunt, C. Wylie]
Archives Princeton University Library, James Ramsey Ullman MSS · RGS, Everest expedition archives | FILM BFI NFTVA, *Reputations*, BBC2, 18 June 1997 · BFI NFTVA, documentary footage | SOUND BL NSA
Likenesses C. Hewitt, photograph, 1953, Hult. Arch. · photograph, 1953 (with Edmund Hillary), Hult. Arch. · photograph, 1953, RGS [*see illus.*] · photograph, 1953, NPG; *see illus. in* Hunt, (Henry Cecil) John, Baron Hunt (1910–1998) · T. Lansner, photograph, 1983, Hult. Arch. · statue, 1997, Himalayan Mountaineering Institute, Darjeeling · photographs, RGS

Teonge, Henry (1621–1690), Church of England clergyman and diarist, was born at Wolverton, Warwickshire, on 18 March 1621, the son of George Teonge (*d.* 1662), rector of Wolverton, and his wife, Dorothy Nicholls. He was educated at Warwick School before entering Christ's College, Cambridge, in 1639, graduating BA in 1643. He served as rector of Alcester between about 1650 and 1670, when he moved to Spernall. Financial difficulties compelled him to seek additional employment in the navy, and in May 1675 he became chaplain of the frigate *Assistance* (under Captain William Houlding), ordered to join Sir John Narbrough's fleet in the Mediterranean. He served on her until she paid off in November 1676. A period ashore in London and Spernall only encouraged Teonge's creditors, and he judiciously returned to sea in April 1678, joining Captain Anthony Langston's *Bristol* for another voyage to the Mediterranean, where he transferred to the *Royal Oak* on 16 January 1679. After his return to England in June of the same year Teonge never returned to sea, and he lived in comparative obscurity at Spernall until his death. He married first Jane, and they had three sons and a daughter; following her death in 1682, he married Penelope Hunt at Spernall on 21 October 1686. Teonge died at Spernall, where he was buried on 21 March 1690; he was survived by his second wife.

Teonge's posthumous fame rests solely on his diary of his two naval voyages. Full of interest in his surroundings and lively good humour, the diary is one of the most important descriptions of seagoing life in the seventeenth century. It frequently displays rather greater concern for the wardroom meals than for the spiritual well-being of the crew, together with a remarkably self-deprecating

honesty on Teonge's part. On his first going to sea he admitted that all his possessions were in 'an old sack' (*Diary*, 26 May 1675) and that he was only able to obtain the essentials for his voyage by pawning his cloak and selling his horse. The social aspects of naval life proved irresistible to the impoverished, ageing chaplain, and the rituals of toasting, songs, and party games were recorded in exhaustive detail. Teonge noted with relish the officers' dinner on 29 May 1678, the king's birthday:

> an excellent salad and eggs, a fillet of veal roasted, a grand dish of mackerel, and a large lobster—so hard is our fare at sea: and all washed down with good Margate ale, March beer, and, last of all, a good bowl of punch. (ibid., 29 May 1678)

The nature of Teonge's diary, and the disappearance of the manuscript for almost a century after its first publication in 1825, led to persistent suggestions that it might have been a forgery. Confirmation both of Teonge's existence and of the sequences of events which he recorded came from the Admiralty records in the Public Record Office, and the re-emergence of the manuscript itself at a Sothebys sale in 1918 put the matter conclusively to rest.

J. D. DAVIES

Sources *The diary of Henry Teonge*, ed. G. E. Manwaring (1927) · J. D. Davies, *Gentlemen and tarpaulins: the officers and men of the Restoration navy* (1991)
Archives NMM, journal
Wealth at death £66: will and inventory, Manwaring, ed., *The diary*

Ternan [St Ternan] (*fl.* 6th–7th cent.), holy man, was an obscure saint venerated mainly in north-east Scotland. His feast day, 12 June, is the same as that of the (equally obscure) Irish St Torannán. The two may well be identical, since the Irish martyrologies describe him as living 'across the sea', linking him with *Alba*, Scotland, and specifically with Banchory-Ternan, while at least one Scottish source calls Ternan 'archbishop of Ireland'. His dedications are mostly in Mearns (Kincardineshire) and Aberdeenshire, notably at Arbuthnott, Slains, and Banchory-Ternan, but with a scattering in the Western Isles as well. His bell and some corporeal relics were preserved at Banchory-Ternan until the Reformation.

The main source for legends concerning Ternan is the early sixteenth-century *Breviarium Aberdonense*. The lessons for his feast day locate his birthplace in Mearns (perhaps at Arbuthnott), and associate him with St Palladius (patron of Fordoun, a few miles west of Arbuthnott) and St Machar of Aberdeen. They also connect him with an otherwise unknown king or nobleman called Convecturius (perhaps from Gaelic *coinmedoir*, collector of tribute), a heathen whom he allegedly converted. Ternan's baptism by St Palladius (*fl.* 431) is told in the lessons for the latter's feast day, and is also mentioned by the chronicler John Fordun. However, he is also said to have studied under Pope Gregory the Great (*r.* 590–604), to have been ordained by him, and then to have brought back to Scotland a bell given to him by the pope; this was the bell preserved at Banchory-Ternan. A fragmentary foundation legend of Laurencekirk (also in Mearns), preserved in a late eleventh-century Canterbury source, calls St Ternan *archipontifex Hiberniae*, knows that he is said to have resuscitated three dead men, and describes how he had a disputation with Archbishop Laurence, Augustine's successor at Canterbury, on the paschal question at or near Fordoun, in which he accepted Laurence's arguments.

None of this helps to establish Ternan as a historical figure separate from the Irish Torannán; he is probably a legendary transposition of the latter, introduced into eastern Scotland after the Gaelic conquest of the Picts in the ninth century. His cult became important and popular, causing him to be associated with other saints with dedications in the same area.   ALAN MACQUARRIE

Sources *Breviarium Aberdonense* (1509–10) [Propria Sanctorum, 12 June] · *Johannis de Fordun Chronica gentis Scotorum / John of Fordun's Chronicle of the Scottish nation*, ed. W. F. Skene, trans. F. J. H. Skene, 2 (1872), bk 3, chap. 9 · W. J. Watson, *The history of the Celtic place-names of Scotland* (1926), 298–300 · A. Macquarrie, 'An eleventh-century account of the foundation legend of Laurencekirk, and of Queen Margaret's pilgrimage there', *Innes Review*, 47 (1996), 95–109 · *Félire Óengusso Céli Dé / The martyrology of Oengus the Culdee*, ed. and trans. W. Stokes, HBS, 29 (1905) · R. I. Best and H. J. Lawlor, eds., *The martyrology of Tallaght*, HBS, 68 (1931) · *Félire húi Gormáin / The martyrology of Gorman*, ed. and trans. W. Stokes, HBS, 9 (1895)

Likenesses J. Sibbald, manuscript, 1471–84, Paisley Museum and Art Gallery, Arbuthnott Book of Hours; repro. in Dowden, *The bishops of Scotland: being notes on the lives of all the bishops, under each of the sees, prior to the Reformation*, ed. J. H. Thomson (1912), facing p. 96 · J. Sibbald, manuscript, 1491, Paisley Museum and Art Gallery, Arbuthnott Missal; repro. in Dowden, *The bishops of Scotland: being notes on the lives of all the bishops, under each of the sees, prior to the Reformation*, ed. J. H. Thomson (1912), facing p. 98

Ternan [*married name* Robinson], **Ellen Lawless** [Nelly] (**1839–1914**), actress, but chiefly remembered as the inamorata of Charles *Dickens, was born on 3 March 1839 at 11 Upper Clarence Place, Maidstone Road, Rochester, Kent, the third of four children of the actors Thomas Lawless *Ternan (1790–1846) [*see under* Jarman, Frances Eleanor] and his wife, Frances Eleanor, *née* *Jarman (1802–1873). Ellen (usually known as Nelly) had two elder sisters, Frances Eleanor and Maria Susanna, and a younger brother who died in infancy. The three girls were put on the stage as 'infant phenomena', Frances with outstanding success, Nelly making her first appearance in Sheffield at the age of three; she was the least theatrically gifted of the sisters. After the early death of their father in 1846 they were obliged to earn their living, touring the north of England, Ireland, and Scotland with their mother. W. C. Macready, who acted with Mrs Ternan, took an interest in the family and gave some assistance. Nelly's first adult engagement was in a burlesque at the Haymarket in 1857, and it was after this that she was engaged by Charles Dickens, with her mother and Maria, to perform with his amateur company in *The Frozen Deep* in Manchester.

Nelly was eighteen, Dickens forty-five. The history of their relationship remains obscure in some respects, but there is no doubt that he fell passionately in love with her and changed the pattern of his life to accommodate this passion. He separated from his wife and gave substantial financial support to the Ternan family; and according to Kate, his clear-eyed daughter, who was the same age as Nelly, his attentions were at first a source of elation and

Ellen Lawless Ternan (1839–1914), by unknown photographer

pride to the Ternans. He trusted Nelly's judgement, sometimes showing her his work at proof stage. He praised her pride and self-reliance, and referred to her as his 'magic circle of one' and his Darling, 'drearily missed' during a separation. He used variants of her name in his novels: Estella, Bella, and Helena Landless. The relationship was known to a small group of intimates, but kept profoundly secret from the public on whose favour Dickens depended.

Nelly Ternan left the stage in 1860, and either lived in France or travelled there with Dickens over a period of several years. In 1865 she and her mother were returning from abroad with him when their train was derailed; although Nelly was injured, Dickens was at pains to conceal her presence. He joined her frequently at Slough, and later at Nunhead, both places where he had taken houses under a false name. He also made plans to take her to the United States with him in 1867, but was dissuaded by the fear of scandal. It is believed, though not proven, that a son was born to them, who died in infancy; and that Nelly's situation caused her some pain and guilt.

Dickens left Nelly £1000 in his will and set up a private trust fund which freed her from the necessity of working again after his death in 1870. She travelled abroad, then on 31 January 1876, in the parish church at Kensington, she married a clergyman twelve years her junior, George Wharton Robinson (1850–1910); she presented herself as much younger than her real age, thereby cancelling out the years of her association with Dickens. She helped her husband to run a boys' school in Margate, and gave birth to a son and a daughter. Her last years were spent at Southsea, where she was reunited with her sisters. It is notable that, although all three sisters knew Dickens intimately, they were neither asked for nor gave any account of their relations with him, and that no letters survive. For many years his admirers denied the fact of his attachment to Nelly Ternan, and, even when the weight of evidence made this position untenable, some continue to insist that the affair was unconsummated: a view that hardly fits with what is known of Dickens or of Victorian mores, or with her own silence on the subject. Nelly Ternan was remembered as a clever and charming person, forceful of character, undomesticated, and interested in literature, the theatre, and politics; but she remains an enigmatic figure. She died from cancer at 18 Guion Road, Fulham, London, on 25 April 1914 and was buried in the Highland Road cemetery, Southsea, in her husband's grave. There are no living descendants.

Her eldest sister, **Frances Eleanor Trollope** (1835–1913), was born in August 1835 on a paddle-steamer in Delaware Bay during her parents' tour of America. After a successful career on the stage she went to Florence to study opera singing, and became governess to Bice (Beatrice), the daughter of the widowed Thomas Adolphus *Trollope (1810–1892). On 29 October 1866 she married her employer. They lived in Italy for many years. She wrote a number of novels, several of which, including *Aunt Margaret's Trouble* (1866) and *Mabel's Progress* (1867), were serialized anonymously by Dickens in *All the Year Round*. After her husband's death in 1892 she wrote the life of her mother-in-law, Frances *Trollope (1779–1863). During her last years her sister Nelly lived with her in Southsea, and she died there on 14 August 1913.

The third Ternan sister, **Maria Susanna Taylor** (1837–1904), also appeared on the stage until her marriage, on 9 June 1863, to William Rowland Taylor, the son of a prosperous Oxford brewer. Shortly after her mother's death she left her husband, and at the age of forty enrolled at the Slade School of Fine Art to learn to paint. She made her home in Rome and travelled adventurously in north Africa; and she worked as an artist and journalist, writing for the London *Standard* for more than twelve years. She returned to England in 1898 and died in Southsea on 12 March 1904.   CLAIRE TOMALIN

Sources C. Tomalin, *The invisible woman: the story of Nelly Ternan and Charles Dickens* (1990) · *The letters of Charles Dickens*, ed. M. House, G. Storey, and others, 8 (1995) · m. cert. [Frances Eleanor Trollope] · m. cert. [Maria Susanna Taylor] · J. Sutherland, *The Longman companion to Victorian fiction* (1988) · d. cert. [Frances Eleanor Trollope] · *CGPLA Eng. & Wales* (1904) · UCL, Katharine Longley archive
Archives priv. coll. | Princeton University, New Jersey, Trollope MSS · Theatre Museum, London, Morley MSS · Theatre Museum, London, Trollope MSS · University of Illinois, Trollope MSS
Likenesses photograph, *c*.1858, priv. coll.; repro. in Tomalin, *Invisible woman*; priv. coll. · drawing, UCL, Katharine Longley archive · group portrait, photograph (with sisters), V&A; repro. in Tomalin, *Invisible woman* · photograph, V&A [*see illus.*] · photographs, UCL, Katharine Longley archive
Wealth at death £1241 5*s.* 10*d.*: probate, 2 June 1914, *CGPLA Eng. & Wales* · £1264 1*s.* 1*d.*—Frances Eleanor Trollope: probate, 13 Oct 1913, *CGPLA Eng. & Wales* · £530 14*s.* 9*d.*—Maria Susanna Taylor: probate, 16 May 1904, *CGPLA Eng. & Wales*

Ternan, Thomas Lawless (1790–1846). *See under* Jarman, Frances Eleanor (1802–1873).

Terne, Christopher (1620/21–1673), physician, son of Nathaniel Terne of Chatham, Kent, was born at Rochester, Kent. After schooling at Rochester he was admitted to St John's College, Cambridge, as a pensioner on 4 April 1636, aged fifteen, graduating BA in 1640 and MA in 1643. He entered the University of Leiden on 22 July 1647, and there graduated MD. In May 1650 he was incorporated first at Cambridge and then at Oxford. Terne was examined as a candidate at the College of Physicians on 10 May 1650, and was elected a fellow on 15 November 1655. He was elected assistant physician to St Bartholomew's Hospital, London, on 13 May 1653 and held office until 1669. He married Susan, daughter of Henry Borne.

Terne was appointed lecturer on anatomy to the Barber-Surgeons' Company in 1656, and in 1663 Samuel Pepys heard him lecture 'upon the Kidnys, urethers, and yard, which was very fine' (Pepys, 4.59). Terne's 'Praelectio prima ad chirurgos' and his other lectures (nos. 1917–21), written in a beautiful hand, are preserved in the Sloane collection in the British Library. The lectures, dated 1656, begin with an account of the skin, going on to the deeper parts, and were delivered contemporaneously with the dissection of a body on the table. Several volumes of notes of his extensive medical reading are preserved in the same collection (nos. 1887, 1890, and 1897), together with an important essay entitled 'An respiratio inserviat nutritioni?'. He delivered the Harveian oration (1662–3?) at the College of Physicians, in which, as in his lectures, he spoke with the utmost reverence of William Harvey. The oration exists in manuscript (Sloane MS 1903). Terne also wrote some Latin verses on Christopher Bennet, which were placed below his portrait in the *Theatrum Tabidorum*. He was elected a fellow of the Royal Society on 8 October 1662. Terne died at his house in Lime Street, London, on 1 December 1673, and was buried in St Andrew Undershaft.

Terne's daughter Henrietta (d. 1712) married the physician Edward *Browne. Terne's library was sold on 12 April 1686 with that of Dr Thomas Allen. See *Bibliothecae medicae, sive, Catalogus libolum … Christ. Terne* (1686).

     NORMAN MOORE, rev. MICHAEL BEVAN

Sources Venn, *Alum. Cant.* · Munk, *Roll* · Pepys, *Diary*, 4.59 · M. Hunter, *The Royal Society and its fellows, 1660–1700: the morphology of an early scientific institution*, 2nd edn (1994)

Terrick, Richard (1710–1777), bishop of London, was born probably at York and was baptized in York Minster on 20 July of that year. He was the eldest son of Samuel Terrick (d. 1719), prebendary of York, and his wife, Ann, née Gibson (d. 1764), widow of Nathaniel Arlush of Kedlington, Yorkshire. Although his early schooling is apparently unrecorded he matriculated as pensioner at Clare College, Cambridge, on 30 May 1726; he graduated BA in 1729 and MA in 1733. He was a fellow of the college from 1731 to 1738; the latter year, in which he resigned his fellowship, was probably the date of his marriage to Tabitha (1712/13–

1790), daughter of William Stainforth, rector of Simonburn, Northumberland. Terrick was ordained deacon in the diocese of Ely on 24 December 1732 and priest two years later. Of a clerical family, it is probable that he was from an early age destined for a career in the church; his younger brother Samuel (d. 1761) followed him to Cambridge and was subsequently a prebendary of Durham.

Terrick quickly acquired valuable connections. He was preacher at the Rolls Chapel from 1736 to 1757, and from 1739 to 1742 he served as chaplain to the speaker of the House of Commons, Arthur Onslow. He was a canon of Windsor from 1742 to 1749 and chaplain to George II from 1745 to 1757. He became vicar of Twickenham on 30 June 1749 and on 7 October of the same year he was installed as prebendary of Ealdland and canon-residentiary at St Paul's Cathedral.

Partly through the influence of William Cavendish, fourth duke of Devonshire, but more particularly due to the personal decision of George II, Terrick was nominated to the bishopric of Peterborough on 7 June 1757 and consecrated at Lambeth on 3 July. At this point he relinquished his preferments, with the exception of Twickenham. One of his first acts as bishop was to issue a letter to his clergy urging a more devout observance of Good Friday. According to Horace Walpole, who despised Terrick as a timeserver and on one occasion reportedly insulted him by addressing him, after his elevation to the bench, as plain 'Mr Terrick' (N&Q), Terrick deserted the duke of Devonshire and transferred his allegiance to John Stuart, third earl of Bute, in expectation of preferment on the accession of Bute's affectionate pupil the future George III. If so he was not disappointed. The death of Richard Osbaldeston on 13 May 1764 created a vacancy for the see of London. The prime minister, George Grenville, was solicited for the vacancy by William Warburton, bishop of Gloucester, and Thomas Newton, bishop of Bristol. However, as Grenville tactfully explained to Warburton, George III had intended that Terrick should succeed Osbaldeston ever since the latter's appointment in 1762 (Smith, 2.314). On his translation Terrick informed Grenville that he had increased the income of Peterborough from 1000 guineas to 'eleven hundred pounds clear' (ibid., 2.313). He was confirmed as bishop on 6 June 1764 and resigned the vicarage of Twickenham, which he estimated as '£200, clear about £140' (ibid.). On 11 July 1764 he was sworn of the privy council.

There was never any doubt but that Terrick would be a loyal ministerial adherent in the House of Lords. In February 1764 he pledged his support to the ministry of George Grenville (Tomlinson, 88–9). As bishop of London his pastoral responsibilities included the North American colonies, and he strongly supported the work of the Society for the Propagation of the Gospel in those areas; he preached the annual sermon before the society in 1764. He gave general support to the policy of taxing the American colonies and, ultimately, of using force to suppress the rebellion. Terrick was not one of the opponents of the repeal of the Stamp Act in 1766 and he seems to have shared the view of several of his fellow bishops that

repeal, by allaying colonial discontent, would render more acceptable the long-standing Anglican aspiration to establish a resident bishop in the colonies. He was listed as a supporter of North's administration in 1774 and 1775 (Debrett, 7.17; London Evening-Post, 7 Oct 1775).

He shared much of the anti-Catholicism of his time, forbidding the intrusion of mural paintings into St Paul's Cathedral on the grounds that such a practice was 'Popish' (Sykes, 236) and instituting diocesan inquiries into the alleged growth of Catholic numbers. In 1765 Horace Walpole noted, 'I see by the papers that the Bishop of London is suppressing Mass-houses' (Walpole, Corr., 30.209). However, he did not oppose the Quebec Act, which granted limited toleration and legal rights to francophone Catholics in Canada, in 1774. By contrast he spoke and voted in the House of Lords against the Dissenters Relief Bill on 19 May 1772 and appears to have colluded with several dissenting critics of the bill to help to secure its rejection in the upper house (Ditchfield, 54, 76). He devoted considerable time and money to the refurbishment of the chapel of Fulham Palace and was a generous benefactor of Clare College, Cambridge. Though never a distinguished scholar he published six separate sermons and acquired a reputation as a conscientious, if not a particularly inspiring, diocesan. There is also evidence that he was a more than competent preacher; Alexander Carlyle, for instance, heaped praise upon his preaching and his reading of prayers. It was probably for these reasons that he remained on close terms with George III, who, according to Walpole, consulted him about the surreptitious marriages of the dukes of Cumberland and Gloucester (Walpole, Corr., 23.483). On the death of Archbishop Drummond of York in 1776 the king offered the vacancy to Terrick, who declined it on grounds of age and ill health.

Terrick died at Fulham Palace on 31 March 1777 and was buried on 8 April in All Saints' churchyard, Fulham. The monument to him in that church was probably more accurate than many eulogies to the dead when it singled out his 'great experience and sound judgment, his candour, moderation and benevolence' (Nichols, Lit. anecdotes, 9.584). There was nothing in the exercise of his benevolence that challenged either Anglican doctrinal orthodoxy or Anglican hegemony in the state. It is a measure of the success of his career that his daughter Elizabeth (d. 1804) married Nathaniel *Ryder [see under Ryder, Sir Dudley], who became the first Baron Harrowby, and that his widow was reported to have bequeathed a fortune of £30,000 on her death in 1790 (GM, 1st ser., 60/1, 1790, 186).

G. M. DITCHFIELD

Sources Venn, Alum. Cant., 1/4.215 · Fasti Angl., 1541–1857, [Bristol], 117 · Fasti Angl., 1541–1857, [St Paul's, London], 4, 32 · Fasti Angl., 1541–1857, [York], 53, 68 · N&Q, 4th ser., 7 (1871), 104 · GM, 1st ser., 34 (1764) · GM, 1st ser., 47 (1777) · GM, 1st ser., 60 (1790) · GM, 1st ser., 63 (1793) · GM, 1st ser., 64 (1794) · D. Lysons, The environs of London, 2 (1795), 348–9 · The Grenville papers: being the correspondence of Richard Grenville … and … George Grenville, ed. W. J. Smith, 2 (1852) · Additional Grenville papers, 1763–1765, ed. J. R. G. Tomlinson (1962) · G. M. Ditchfield, 'The subscription issue in British parliamentary politics, 1772–1779', Parliamentary History, 7 (1988), 45–80 · N. Sykes, Church and state in England in the XVIII century (1934) · Nichols, Lit.

anecdotes, vols. 4, 9 · *Autobiography of the Rev. Dr. Alexander Carlyle … containing memorials of the men and events of his time*, ed. J. H. Burton (1860) · J. Debrett, *The history, debates and proceedings of both houses of parliament, 1743–1774*, 7 vols. (1792) · *London Evening-Post* (1775)
Archives LPL, American correspondence · LPL, corresp. and papers | BL, Hardwicke MSS · BL, Newcastle MSS · BL, Liverpool MSS · Harrowby Manuscript Trust, Sandon Hall, Staffordshire, letters to first Lord Harrowby · Harrowby Manuscript Trust, Sandon Hall, Staffordshire, letters to Nathaniel Ryder · Westminster College, Cambridge, Cheshunt Foundation, corresp. with Selina, countess of Huntingdon
Likenesses N. Dance, oils, 1764, LPL · N. Dance, portrait, c.1765, Fulham Palace, London · B. West, oils, 1766, Sandon House, Staffordshire · E. Fisher, mezzotint, 1770 (after N. Dance, c.1765) · N. Dance, portrait, 1773, LPL · J. Freeman (after N. Dance, c.1765), Clare College, Cambridge · J. Hoppner, portrait, Fulham Palace, London · Stewart, oils (after N. Dance), Fulham Palace, London
Wealth at death considerable: will, PRO · widow bequeathed £30,000 on her death, 1790: *GM* 60, 186

Terrien De Lacouperie, Albert Étienne Jean Baptiste

(*d.* 1894), philologist, born in Normandy, was a descendant of the Cornish family of Terrien, which emigrated to France in the seventeenth century during the civil war, and acquired the property of La Couperie in Normandy. His father was a silk merchant and Terrien De Lacouperie, after accompanying him to Hong Kong, followed his father into the silk trade. After almost all of his property was destroyed in a typhoon, he returned to Europe. Opposition to the republic made him decide to settle permanently in England rather than his native France, and he eventually became a British subject. He turned his attention entirely to the study of oriental languages, in which he had become interested in Hong Kong, where he had acquired an intimate knowledge of the Chinese language. In 1867 he published in Paris a philological work, entitled *Du langage: essai sur la nature et l'étude des mots et des langues*, which attracted considerable attention. He became interested in the progress made in deciphering Babylonian inscriptions, and by the resemblance between the Chinese characters and the early Akkadian hieroglyphics. The comparative philology of the two languages occupied most of his later life, and he was able to show an early affinity between them.

In 1879 Terrien De Lacouperie went to London, and in the same year was elected a fellow of the Royal Asiatic Society. In 1884 he became professor of Indo-Chinese philology, as applied to the languages of south-eastern Asia, at University College, London. He took a particular interest in the derivations of the languages of Chinese indigenous groups, and collected materials on their vocabulary and grammar, including those of the Lolos people of western China. He published his findings in *The Languages of China before the Chinese* in London in 1887. The Lolos material had originally been collected by Edward Baber of the British consular service, who was a close friend. Lacouperie also wrote extensively for the *Journal of the Royal Asiatic Society* and other publications on the relationship between Babylonian and Chinese characters, the origins of Asiatic languages, other related philological subjects, and Buddhism. From 1886 he edited the *Babylonian and Oriental Record*. His last years were largely occupied by a study of

the *I Ching* (*Yi Jing*) (Book of changes), the oldest work in the Chinese language. Its meaning had long proved a puzzle both to native and to foreign scholars. Lacouperie demonstrated that the basis of the work consisted of fragmentary notes, chiefly lexical in character, and noticed that they bore a close resemblance to the syllabaries of Chaldea. In 1892 he published the first part of an explanatory treatise entitled *The Oldest Book of the Chinese*, in which he stated his theory of the nature of the *I Ching* and gave translations of passages from it. The treatise, however, was not completed before his death.

Terrien De Lacouperie's services to oriental study were recognized by an honorary LittD from the University of Louvain and, for a time, a small pension from the French government. When that was withdrawn his friends tried, unsuccessfully, to obtain him an equivalent from the English ministry. He was twice awarded the prix Julien by the Académie des Inscriptions et Belles-Lettres for his services to oriental philology. Terrien De Lacouperie died of typhoid fever at his home, 136 Bishop's Road, Fulham, on 11 October 1894, leaving a widow, Antoinette de la Brunetière. He also edited the 'Babylonian and Oriental Record' from 1886.   E. I. CARLYLE, *rev.* JANETTE RYAN

Sources *The Times* (15 Oct 1894) · *The Athenaeum* (20 Oct 1894), 531 · R. K. D., *Journal of the Royal Asiatic Society of Great Britain and Ireland* (1895) · *The Times* (30 Aug 1894) · J. S. Cotton, *The Academy* (20 Oct 1894), 308–9 · *CGPLA Eng. & Wales* (1895)
Wealth at death £255 16s. 1d.: administration, 19 June 1895, *CGPLA Eng. & Wales*

Terrington. For this title name *see* Woodhouse, Vera Florence Annie, Lady Terrington (*b.* 1889, *d.* in or after 1956).

Terriss, Ellaline [*real name* (Mary) Ellaline Lewin; *married name* (Mary) Ellaline Hicks, Lady Hicks] (**1871–1971**), actress, was born (Mary) Ellaline Lewin on 13 April 1871 at the Ship Hotel, Stanley, Falkland Islands, the eldest of the three children of William Charles James Lewin [*see* Terriss, William (1847–1897)], actor, and his wife, Isabel Lewis (Amy Fellowes; *d.* 1898). She was among the most successful musical comedy actresses of the late Victorian and Edwardian periods. She was educated privately. As a girl she had no ambition to go on the stage although she made a single appearance in a pantomime at the Alexandra Theatre, Liverpool, on 1 January 1887 when she 'danced a hornpipe with much success' (Broadbent, 319–20). Her career began in earnest when, having played Mary Herbert in Alfred Calmour's one-act play *Cupid's Messenger* at home as a treat for her father, she was summoned by telegram by Herbert Beerbohm Tree to take the part at the Haymarket Theatre, London, on 14 February 1888.

This led to a three-year engagement with Charles Wyndham at London's Criterion Theatre. Terriss then moved to the Princess's Theatre, London, appearing first as Arrah Meelish in Dion Boucicault's *Arrah-na-pogue* on 29 August 1891. She went on to play leading parts at the Court Theatre where, *inter alia*, she appeared in a one-act musical duologue, *His Last Chance*, with (Edward) Seymour *Hicks (1871–1949). After a brief courtship they were married on 3 October 1893; their solitary wedding breakfast was Irish stew and burgundy. Their partnership—described as 'one

Ellaline Terriss (1871–1971), by Barraud, 1889

of the happiest, both private and professional, the theatre has known' (*Richmond Times*, 3) despite Hicks's perennial lack of thrift—was commemorated by an exhibition at the British Theatre Museum in 1971.

Terriss was the heroine of Oscar Barrett's Christmas pantomime *Cinderella* at the Lyceum Theatre, London, in 1894, which transferred to Abbey's Theatre, New York. On her return she appeared as the original Thora in W. S. Gilbert's *His Excellency* at the Lyric Theatre in October 1894.

At the Gaiety Theatre, London, in 1895, Terriss played Bessie Brent in the trend-setting *Shop Girl*, by H. J. W. Dam and Ivan Caryll 'the very first musical comedy' (Macqueen-Pope, 318), followed in May by J. T. Tanner's *My Girl* and Dora Wemyss in the *Circus Girl* by J. T. Tanner and W. Paling. Terriss's greatest successes were here, until 1898, and at other London theatres, the Vaudeville (1900–05) and the newly built Aldwych and Hicks (later Globe) theatres (1905–10) in leading parts in musical plays. Many of these were scripted by Hicks, including the *Runaway Girl* (1898), the *Cherry Girl* (1903), the *Catch of the Season* (1904), the *Beauty of Bath* (1906), the *Gay Gordons* (1907), and the *Dashing Little Duke* (1909); the best loved among them, and one of her own favourites, was *Bluebell in Fairyland* (1901), in which she sang the 'Honeysuckle and the Bee'. This was revived in 1905 for the opening of the Aldwych and was brought back to the Prince's Theatre in 1916. Among her other roles she was also acclaimed as Phoebe Throssell in J. M. Barrie's *Quality Street* at the Vaudeville (1902).

However, life was darkened for a time in 1897 when Terriss's first child died shortly after his birth, her father was stabbed to death by a deranged actor outside the Adelphi Theatre, London, and her mother died shortly

afterwards. She and Hicks adopted an Irish girl, Mabel, at about this time. Their own daughter, Betty, was born in 1904.

The couple lost money in the building of three London theatres: the Aldwych, the Hicks, and the Queen's. From 1911 they toured theatres and music halls in Britain and abroad, although Ellaline returned to the London stage for some dozen productions, finally playing Mrs Thornton in Hicks's *Miracle Man* at the Victoria Palace in May 1935. She also made recordings of her most popular songs, and appeared in films including *Blighty* (1926), *Land of Hope and Glory* (1926), *Atlantic Glamour*, *A Man of Mayfair*, and *The Iron Duke* (1934). She and Hicks were among the first performers to go to France in 1914 to entertain the troops. In 1940 they went to the Middle East with the Entertainments National Service Association (ENSA).

In later years Terriss took up painting and was tutored in South Africa, where she and Hicks spent much of the Second World War, by the marine artist George Pilkington, and an exhibition of her work was held at Foyle's Art Gallery, London, in February 1959. Her husband, who was knighted in 1935, died on 6 April 1949.

Terriss was 'an actress of great freshness and sweetness' (*The Times*, 17) and was regarded as a 'perfect type of English beauty' with a 'Dresden shepherdess air of delicacy' (*Daily Telegraph*) but was known also for her warmth and kindness. She wrote two volumes of autobiography, *Ellaline Terriss by Herself and with Others* (1928) and *Just a Little Bit of String* (1955). Ellaline Terriss died at the Holy Family Nursing Home, Hampstead, London, on 16 June 1971 following a hip fracture.   C. M. P. TAYLOR

Sources E. Terriss, *Just a little bit of string* (1955) • E. Terriss, *Ellaline Terriss, by herself and with others* [1928] • S. Hicks, *Hail fellow, well met* (1949) • S. Hicks, *Me and my missus* (1939) • S. Hicks, *Twenty-four years of an actor's life* (1910) • *The Times* (17 June 1971) • *Richmond Times* (18 June 1971) • *Stage and Television Today* (24 June 1971) • *Daily Telegraph* (17 June 1971) • *The Guardian* (17 June 1971) • J. Parker, ed., *Who's who in the theatre*, 10th edn (1947) • R. J. Broadbent, *Annals of the Liverpool stage* (1908) • Biographical File, Theatre Museum, London • P. Cliffe, 'Ellaline Terriss', *This England* (winter 1990), 54–6 • W. Macqueen-Pope, *Gaiety: theatre of enchantment* (1949) • A. E. Wilson, *The Lyceum* (1952) • *The Era* (18 Dec 1897) • A. J. Smythe, *The life of William Terriss* (1898) • P. Hartnoll, ed., *The Oxford companion to the theatre*, 2nd edn (1957) • m. cert.

Archives FILM BFI NFTVA, performance footage | SOUND BL NSA, 'Tribute to Ellaline Terriss', BBC Radio, 7 July 1971, NP1740R • BL NSA, performance recordings

Likenesses Barraud, photograph, 1889, NPG [*see illus.*] • A. Ellis, photograph, 1894, NPG • A. Ellis, photograph, NPG • Ellis & Walery, photograph, NPG • Ellis & Walery, two postcards, NPG • S. Georges Ltd, photograph, NPG • P.M., pen-and-ink sketch (as young girl), NPG • D. Pusinelli, portrait • A. Tofts, portrait • Vaughan & Freeman, photograph, NPG

Terriss, William [*real name* William Charles James Lewin] (1847–1897), actor, was born on 20 February 1847 at 7 Circus Road, St John's Wood, London, the youngest of the three sons of George Herbert Lewin, a barrister (a connection of Mrs Grote, the wife of the historian of ancient Greece, and a grandson of Thomas Lewin, private secretary to Warren Jenkins), and his wife, Mary, *née* Friend. He began his formal education at Christ's Hospital in April

William Terriss (1847–1897), by Boning & Small

1854, and remained there for two years before transferring successively to a school at Littlehampton, Windermere College, and Bruce Castle School, Tottenham, from the last of which he ran away. At the age of sixteen he embarked on a career in the merchant navy, the duration of which, though greatly expanded in his recollections in later life, was only a fortnight. He did, however, retain his uniform, and was thus attired when he arrived aboard a private carriage at Weston-super-Mare Station on the last day of February 1865. The manner of his arrival, combined with his appearance and bearing, resulted in Lewin being mistaken for Queen Victoria's second son, Prince Alfred. Alert to the advantages of the error, Lewin sustained his role until he left the town to the cries of 'Long live Prince Alfred!' Brief though they both were, Lewin's experiences at sea and 'role-playing' as Prince Alfred prefigured his career as an actor specializing in nautical melodrama.

Lewin, who had been only ten when his father died, swiftly disposed of his small inheritance; his elder brothers set about finding a career for him, and he tried tea planting in Assam, where Thomas Lewin was deputy commissioner of Chittagong, and medicine at St Mary's Hospital, where Friend Lewin was a houseman. Neither

career lasted, but at St Mary's he took part in a programme of amateur dramatics held at the Royal Gallery of Illustration in Regent Street (27 April 1867). Encouraged by this experience, he secured engagements in Birmingham, the first—unpaid—as a necessarily acrobatic double for the leading man in Boucicault's *Arrah-na-pogue* and the second—paid—as Chowser in the same author's *The Flying Scud*. Now intent on a theatrical career, Lewin—in consultation with his brother Friend and a London street directory—lighted upon Terriss as his stage name and set about securing an engagement with the Bancrofts, opposite whom the Lewins had lived in St John's Wood. Not for the first—or last—time Terriss used his disarmingly frank manner to good effect, and emerged with the part of Lord Cloudwrays in the forthcoming revival of T. W. Robertson's *Society* at the Prince of Wales Theatre (21 September 1868). The Bancrofts did not retain Terriss's services for the next production (Robertson's *School*), and the actor took the only offer available to him, at Astley's Amphitheatre, to which his accomplishment as a horseman made him well-suited. It was at Margate that Terriss's prowess as a swimmer so impressed the young Isabel Lewis (*d.* 1898), who acted under the stage name of Amy Fellowes, that she effected an introduction, as a consequence of which the couple were married, at Holy Trinity Church by Portland Road Station on 15 September 1870. The sparsity of representatives from both families may have been indicative of their lack of enthusiasm for the match, but, undiscouraged, the newly-weds set off for their honeymoon—a bus ride to Richmond.

Before long Terriss took his young bride on a far more ambitious expedition, to the Falkland Islands via Montevideo, which was in a state of revolution. The final leg of the journey to the Falklands was fraught with difficulties (a water-logged vessel, 200 miles off course, without operational pumps) and might have ended in disaster but for Terriss's remarkable powers of leadership in a crisis. During a sojourn of only five months in the Falkland Isles, Terriss busied himself with sheep farming, breaking in horses, and building and sailing a raft, and became a father—to a daughter, Ellaline *Terriss, who began her long life at the Ship Hotel, Stanley, on 13 April 1871. The return voyage aboard a whaler was not lacking in incident, with the crew mutinying and electing Terriss as captain.

In the summer of 1871 the Terriss family settled into a house on Barnes Common, which was to be their base for the next twelve years. Terriss resumed his stage career at Drury Lane, where his roles included Silvius in Adelaide Neilson's benefit performance of *As You Like It*, but the wanderlust reclaimed him, and he took his family to Lexington, Kentucky, where he was involved in a short-lived horse-breeding venture. By the autumn of 1872 the Terriss family was back in Barnes, where Tom was born on 28 September, his father having begun his third assault on the stage a week earlier at Drury Lane as Master Graeme—resplendent in tartan kilt—in Andrew Halliday's *The Lady of the Lake*, in which Clement Scott commended his natural and manly declamation. Other successes during the

1870s included Doricourt in *The Belle's Stratagem* (at the Strand Theatre, 29 November 1873, for 250 performances), Captain Molyneux in Boucicault's *The Shaughraun* (at Drury Lane, 4 September 1875, and the Adelphi, 18 November 1876), and Squire Thornhill in *Olivia*, W. G. Wills's adaptation of Goldsmith's *The Vicar of Wakefield* (at the Court Theatre, 28 March 1878), with Ellen Terry in the title role.

The connection with Ellen Terry was maintained when Terriss joined Henry Irving's Lyceum company to play M. de Château Renaud in *The Corsican Brothers* (20 September 1880). During his first engagement Terriss's roles included Sinnatus in Tennyson's *The Cup*, Cassio, Mercutio, and Don Pedro (in *Much Ado about Nothing*). At the Lyceum, Terriss, who ranked second only to Ellen Terry, enjoyed a unique relationship with Irving, who would countenance remarks and agree to suggestions 'to put the lime[light] on me' (Rowell, 27) which would have been unthinkable from any other actor. Well proportioned, his face blessed with handsomely regular features, gallant of bearing, and forthright, if sometimes uncomprehending, in his delivery of Shakespearian verse, Terriss was the perfect foil and contrast to Irving. In 1883–4 he accompanied Irving on his American tour, but in 1884–5 he remained at the Lyceum Theatre during Mary Anderson's tenure. As Romeo, whom he had already played to the Juliet of both Ellen Wallis (Drury Lane, 1874) and Adelaide Neilson (Haymarket, 1879), Terriss was again the perfect physical embodiment, though judges seeking the soul and the poetry of the young Montague found him wanting. On 27 May 1885 Terriss and Ellen Terry, with Irving now playing Dr Primrose, appeared in a revival of *Olivia*.

At the end of 1885 Terriss entered into a new phase of his career, when he moved to the Adelphi Theatre to play Lieutenant David Kingsley in *Harbour Lights*, by G. R. Sims and Henry Pettitt, which enjoyed an uninterrupted run of 513 nights. His performance was hailed as the most perfect impersonation of a British sailor since T. P. Cooke—an achievement which must have been enriched by Terriss's own adventures at sea. There followed a succession of roles—Frank Beresford in *The Bells of Haslemere* (25 July 1887), Jack Medway in *The Union Jack* (19 July 1888), and Eric Normanhurst in *The Silver Falls* (29 December 1888)—in which Terriss could display his personal accomplishments to advantage, sometimes in scenes which paralleled episodes in his own life. In 1889 he toured the United States with Jessie Millward (1861–1932), his leading lady and constant companion since the mid-1880s. Their repertory included *Othello* and a Shakespeare recital, as well as contemporary works.

After a revival of *Harbour Lights* at the Adelphi Theatre, Terriss returned to Irving's Lyceum company, where his most important roles were Claudio in *Much Ado about Nothing* (5 January 1891), the King in *Henry VIII* (5 January 1892), Edgar in *King Lear* (10 November 1892), and Henry II in Tennyson's *Becket* (6 February 1893). During 1893–4, together with Jessie Millward, who had joined the Lyceum company (where she too had served an apprenticeship), he accompanied Irving on a lengthy North American tour.

Terriss and Jessie Millward returned to the Adelphi Theatre on 6 September 1894, when he was the original Gerald Austen in *The Fatal Card*, by Haddon Chambers and B. C. Stephenson. The English première of *The Girl I Left behind Me*, by Franklin Fyles and David Belasco, was staged on 13 April 1895, to be followed by *One of the Best*, by George Edwardes and Terriss's son-in-law, Seymour Hicks, on 21 December 1895. G. B. Shaw, whose review was headed 'One of the worst', wrote: 'Mr Terriss continues to retain his fascination even in tartan trousers; and he rises fully to such heights as there are in the trial scene and the degradation scene' (*Saturday Review*, 28 Dec 1895). Shortly afterwards, Shaw wrote *The Devil's Disciple* as a vehicle for Terriss, who, having dozed during Shaw's reading of his work, dismissed it as unsuited to Miss Millward and himself. Instead, on 23 December 1896 Terriss and Jessie Millward appeared to great acclaim in a revival of Douglas Jerrold's prototypical nautical melodrama *Black-Eyed Susan*. The Adelphi Theatre then played host to William Gillette's *Secret Service*, initially with an American company, then with an English cast including Terriss as Lewis Dumont, a northern spy in the Confederate capital of Richmond, and Jessie Millward as a loving and protective, though not completely unsuspicious, southern belle.

Jessie Millward could not protect Terriss from the fate which awaited him at the stage door of the Adelphi Theatre on the evening of 16 December 1897. For some time she had been troubled by nightmares, in particular one in which Terriss was calling out 'Sis! Sis!' from a locked room, the door of which she burst open to catch him as he fell. On the ill-fated night Terriss and John Henry Graves left her flat for the theatre where, just before seven o'clock, Terriss was stabbed three times by an out-of-work actor, Richard Archer Prince. Jessie Millward arrived in time to witness the dreadful scene and to hear Terriss's last words: 'Sis! Sis!'. Terriss's death was as sensational as melodrama; at the ensuing trial, Prince, who had harboured a long-standing sense of grievance against Terriss, was pronounced insane and committed to Broadmoor Criminal Lunatic Asylum. Terriss's death left behind the traditional figure of the bereft heroine, except that in his case there were two: his wife and Jessie Millward. It was Jessie Millward who, in defiance of the custom of the day, whereby women attended funerals only most exceptionally, was present at the funeral service on 21 December at Brompton cemetery, accompanied by Sir Henry Irving. Her wreath was inscribed 'To my dear comrade'. Mrs Terriss remained at the family home, The Cottage, 2 Bedford Road, Bedford Park. In his death, as in his life, Terriss's loved ones displayed a generosity of spirit to each other. Mrs Terriss did not outlive her husband long, and died the following year; after a period of intense desolation, Jessie Millward resumed her career, and eventually (in 1907) married the Scots actor John Glendinning. Of Terriss's three children, his daughter Ellaline survived her one hundredth birthday on 13 April 1971 by three months.

Terriss was accorded an unusual memorial in the form of a new lifeboat house on the Grand Parade, Eastbourne, built by subscriptions raised by the *Daily Telegraph*; he also had a theatre at Rotherhithe briefly named after him. On the centenary of his death, a memorial plaque to Terris was unveiled by Sir Donald Sinden at the Adelphi Theatre, where Terriss's ghost is said to haunt the scene of his death. A good-looking and athletic man, gallant in bearing, his performances in Shakespeare were creditable though not outstanding, but in a succession of melodramatic (often nautical) roles he was unsurpassed, the last and probably the finest flowering of a tradition which the theatre was about to cede to the cinema. Whether there would have been a place for Terriss in that new world will remain an unanswerable question.

RICHARD FOULKES

Sources A. J. Smythe, *The life of William Terriss* (1898) · G. Rowell, *William Terriss and Richard Prince: two characters in an Adelphi melodrama* (1987) · J. Millward, *Myself and others* (1923) · E. Terriss, *Just a little bit of string* (1955) · S. Hicks, *Me and my missus* (1939) · C. E. Pascoe, ed., *The dramatic list*, 2nd edn (1880) · D. Mullin, ed., *Victorian actors and actresses in review: a dictionary of contemporary views of representative British and American actors and actresses, 1837–1901* (1983) · G. Rowell, 'Mercutio as Romeo: William Terriss in *Romeo and Juliet*', *Shakespeare and the Victorian stage*, ed. R. Foulkes (1986) · *The Stage* (23 Dec 1897) · *The Era* (18 Dec 1897) · *The Era* (25 Dec 1897) · *The Times* (18 Dec 1897) · *Era Almanack and Annual* · G. B. Shaw, *Our theatre in the nineties*, 1 (1931) · m. cert. · *CGPLA Eng. & Wales* (1898) · *DNB*

Archives Theatre Museum, London

Likenesses Barraud, woodburytype photograph, c.1885, NPG; repro. in *The Theatre* · Bassano, photograph, NPG · A. Beardsley, pen-and-pencil caricature, V&A; repro. in *Pall Mall Budget* (9 Feb 1893) · Boning & Small, carte-de-visite, NPG [see illus.] · photographs, repro. in Smythe, *Life of William Terriss* · photographs, repro. in Rowell, *William Terriss and Richard Prince* · photogravure (as Henry VIII), NPG

Wealth at death £18,809 12s. 2d.: resworn probate, Sept 1898, *CGPLA Eng. & Wales*

Terrot, Charles (1758–1839), army officer, was born at Berwick upon Tweed on 1 May 1758, eldest son of Charles Terrot, captain of invalids and commander of the garrison, and Elizabeth Pratt, of an established local family. He entered the Royal Military Academy, Woolwich, on 15 March 1771. He was commissioned second lieutenant on 1 March 1774 and in 1776 volunteered for service in North America; he first saw action at Three Rivers on 8 June when the Americans were forced to withdraw to Ticonderoga. In June 1777 he joined General Burgoyne's army on its advance from Canada. After the taking of Ticonderoga on 6 July, he took command of the artillery there, and helped beat off an American attack in September.

After Burgoyne's surrender at Saratoga, Terrot returned to Canada. On 7 July 1779 he was promoted first lieutenant and in 1780 went to Niagara where he remained for nearly four years and was employed chiefly as an assistant military engineer. The defences of the place were fully repaired under his supervision. In 1782 he surveyed the country between lakes Erie and Ontario with a view to its purchase by the government from the Native Americans. He conducted the subsequent negotiations with the indigenous peoples to their satisfaction and to the considerable advantage of the government. On 8 March 1784 he was promoted captain-lieutenant and returned to England. In 1791 he volunteered for service in India and

arrived at Madras on 10 October as quartermaster to a force of two artillery companies. He subsequently joined Lord Cornwallis's army and in February 1792 took part in the siege of Seringapatam until peace terms were agreed with Tipu Sultan. On 26 March he moved with the army marching to Madras which was reached in May.

On the opening of the war with France, Terrot, still acting as quartermaster, took part in the attack on Pondicherry which, after a brief bombardment, was successfully concluded on 23 August 1793. On 25 September he was promoted to captain and returned to England to command no. 3 company, 1st battalion Royal Artillery, at Portsmouth. On 1 March 1794 he was made brevet major for his services and became commander of the artillery at Portsmouth and of the south-west district. He married Eleanor Bell on 29 April 1795 at Berwick upon Tweed; they had three children. He was made a brevet lieutenant-colonel on 1 January 1798. The following year he served during the Helder expedition, landing on 27 August, and joining in the action at Bergen on 19 September under the duke of York, at Alkmaar on 2 October, and at Beverwijk on the 6th. On the conclusion of hostilities he returned to England in November only to be shipwrecked off Yarmouth in company with Anthony Farrington and, like him, lost all his baggage.

Terrot was promoted major in the regiment on 12 November 1800 and lieutenant-colonel on 14 October 1801. After a period of regimental duty he was promoted colonel, Royal Artillery, on 1 June 1806. In July 1809 he joined the expedition to the Scheldt and directed the artillery at the siege of Flushing which surrendered on 15 August. He was briefly involved in a demand for the city's church bells, or cash in lieu, as outdated tradition required. This was refused both by the city and by the British government and was never attempted again.

Terrot became a major-general on 4 June 1811 and in 1814 was sent to command the artillery at Gibraltar in succession to Major-General John Smith. The latter, however, owing to the death of the governor, had succeeded to the command of the fortress, and refused to be relieved. Having vainly awaited developments, after three months Terrot successfully sought permission to return to England. He resigned his appointment and retired on 23 September 1815 on a pension of £700 a year backdated to 25 June 1814. He was promoted to lieutenant-general on the retired list on 12 August 1819 and to full general on 10 January 1837. He died in Newcastle upon Tyne on 23 September 1839.
R. H. VETCH, rev. P. G. W. ANNIS

Sources PRO, WO 76/359 · J. Kane, *List of officers of the royal regiment of artillery from the year 1716 to the year 1899*, rev. W. H. Askwith, 4th edn (1900) · F. Duncan, ed., *History of the royal regiment of artillery*, 3rd edn, 2 vols. (1879) · J. H. Lefroy, 'Lieut. General Charles Terrot', *Minutes of the Proceedings of the Royal Artillery Institution*, 16 (1889) · *Army List* (1814) · *GM*, 2nd ser., 12 (1839), 548 · F. W. Stubbs, ed., *History of the organization, equipment, and war services of the regiment of Bengal artillery*, 3 vols. (1877–95) · [J. Squire], *A short narrative of the late campaign of the British army etc., with preliminary remarks on the topography and channels of Zeeland* (1810) · J. C. Smith, *Chronological epitome of the wars in the Low Countries from the peace of the Pyrenées in*

1659, to that of Paris in 1815 (1825) • C. Stedman, *The history of the origin, progress, and termination of the American war*, 2 vols. (1794) • A. Dirom, *A narrative of the campaign in India which terminated the war with Tippoo Sultan in 1792* (1793) • J. T. Jones, *Journals of sieges carried on by the army under the duke of Wellington in Spain*, ed. H. D. Jones, 3rd edn, 3 vols. (1846) • E. Cust, *Annals of the wars of the eighteenth century*, 5 vols. (1857–60) • IGI • N&Q, 7th ser., 3 (1887), 256

Terrot, Charles Hughes (1790–1872), Scottish Episcopal bishop of Edinburgh, born at Cuddalore, India, on 19 September 1790, was a descendant of a Huguenot family. His father, Elias Terrot, a captain in the Indian army, was killed at the siege of Bangalore within weeks of his son's birth. His mother, whose maiden name was Mary Fonteneau, returned to England and settled with her son at Berwick upon Tweed. From the age of nine he was educated at the home of the Revd John Fawcett of Carlisle, and later attended Carlisle grammar school. In 1808 he entered Trinity College, Cambridge, and graduated BA in 1812. He was elected a fellow of his college in 1813 and in the same year was ordained deacon.

Ordained priest in 1814 by the bishop of Chester, Terrot became minister of the episcopal congregation at Haddington, a position formerly held by his uncle, the Revd William Terrot. This was a 'qualified chapel' of Scottish episcopalians who had conformed to the Hanoverian dynasty in the early eighteenth century and thus qualified for legal toleration. They were not in communion with the bishops of the Scottish Episcopal church, having adopted the English Book of Common Prayer and being staffed by clergymen ordained in the Church of England. Terrot led this congregation into union with the Scottish Episcopal church in 1815, a union made possible by the Scottish episcopalians' renunciation of Jacobitism in 1788 and their adoption of the Thirty-Nine Articles in 1804. While at Haddington, Terrot devoted his leisure to poetry, winning the Cambridge University Seatonian prize in 1816 for his poem 'Hezekiah and Sennacherib'. In 1817 he went to Edinburgh as colleague to James Walker (later bishop of Edinburgh), with whom he shared the charge of St Peter's, Roxburgh Place. Terrot was married in 1818 to Sarah Ingram (d. 1855), daughter of Captain Samuel Wood of Minlands, near Berwick upon Tweed. They had fourteen children, six of whom predeceased Terrot. His eldest daughter, Sarah Anne Terrot, was the third woman to join the Sisterhood of the Holy Cross (Park Village Sisterhood), founded by Edward Pusey in 1845. She nursed British forces in the Crimea with Florence Nightingale, and was afterwards awarded the Royal Red Cross. From 1829 to 1833 Terrot was in sole charge of St Peter's, and in 1833 he became one of three clergy at St Paul's, York Place, Edinburgh. In 1837 he was appointed dean of Edinburgh and Fife, in 1839 rector of St Paul's, and in 1841 bishop of Edinburgh and Pantonian professor at the theological college (while retaining the charge of St Paul's).

On the death of William Skinner (1778–1857), bishop of Aberdeen, Terrot was elected primus of the Scottish Episcopal church. As primus he found it difficult to sympathize with the former non-juring tradition in Scottish Episcopacy, preferring the southern high-church tradition that looked to the Church of England. But he was a force for unity when the tensions between the Anglicizing and the formerly non-juring traditions of Scottish Episcopalianism, together with Anglo-Catholicism, erupted in controversies over the eucharist and the Scottish communion office in the late 1850s and 1860s. In 1859 he married a widow, Charlotte Madden (d. 1862). Terrot remained primus until a paralytic stroke compelled his resignation in 1862. An excellent mathematician, he was for fourteen years a fellow of the Royal Society of Edinburgh. He was also a member of the Architectural Society of Scotland. Besides numerous charges and sermons, Terrot edited the Greek text of the epistle to the Romans, with an introduction, paraphrase, and notes (published 1828), and translated the Lutheran Johann Ernesti's *Institutio interpretis novi testamenti* (1761) in two volumes entitled *Principles of Biblical Interpretation* (1832–3). Terrot died on 2 April 1872 at Edinburgh, and was buried in the city's Calton cemetery.

GEORGE STRONACH, *rev.* ROWAN STRONG

Sources W. Walker, *Three churchmen* (1893) • *Edinburgh Almanac* (1828) • *Edinburgh Almanac* (1832) • *Edinburgh Almanac* (1834) • Dundee University, Brechin Diocesan Archives, Terrot MSS • *Scottish Ecclesiastical Journal* (1857–72) • *The Scotsman* (3–4 April 1872) • *Scottish Guardian* (15 May 1872) • *Proceedings of the Royal Society of Edinburgh*, 8 (1872–5), 9–14 • private information (1898) • Register of the College of Bishops, NA Scot. • R. Strong, *Alexander Forbes of Brechin* (1995) • P. Nockles, '"Our brethren of the north": the Scottish Episcopal church and the Oxford movement', *Journal of Ecclesiastical History*, 47 (1996), 655–82

Archives BL, letters to W. E. Gladstone, Add. MSS 44357–44394, *passim* • NA Scot., Scottish Episcopal church MSS • U. St Andr. L., corresp. with James David Forbes • University of Dundee, Brechin diocesan archives • University of Dundee, corresp. with Alexander Forbes

Likenesses carte-de-visite, NPG • engraving, repro. in Walker, *Three Churchmen*

Wealth at death £11,558 12s. 11d.: inventory, 4 May 1872, NA Scot., SC 70/1/175/761

Terry, Charles Sanford (1864–1936), historian and musician, was born at Newport Pagnell, Buckinghamshire, on 24 October 1864, the elder son of Charles Terry, a physician there, and his wife, Ellen Octavia, daughter of Octavius Thomas Prichard, physician, of Abingdon Abbey, Northamptonshire. Both his grandfathers and two of his great-grandfathers were medical men. He was educated at St Paul's Cathedral choir school, King's College School, London, Lancing College, Sussex, and at Clare College, Cambridge, where he obtained a second class in the historical tripos of 1886. From 1890 to 1898 he was lecturer in history at Durham College of Science, Newcastle upon Tyne. Thereafter he became lecturer in history in Aberdeen University. In 1903 the lecturership was raised to a chair, which he held until his retirement in 1930. In 1901 he married Edith, eldest daughter of Francis Allfrey, brewer, of Newport Pagnell; there were no children of the marriage. He died at his home, Westerton of Pitfodels, near Aberdeen, on 5 November 1936.

Among those Englishmen who have served Scotland, Terry takes a high place. He was not greatly concerned with the ideas which give rise to history, or with personalities: his interest lay in the pure course of events, which he set forth not only with sound scholarship, but with a remarkable clarity and conciseness and the power of marshalling intricate masses of detail into a lucid and balanced narrative. These gifts, with his warm and attractive personality, made him an excellent and popular teacher. His considerable bulk of published work includes several useful collections of material concerning the various Jacobite movements and an important edition of the *Albemarle Papers, 1746–1748* (2 vols., 1902). His most valuable historical work, however, deals with the seventeenth century in Scotland. The chief of it is contained in his *Life and Campaigns of Alexander Leslie, First Earl of Leven* (1899) and *John Graham of Claverhouse, Viscount of Dundee* (1905), and in his editorial work on *The Cromwellian Union* (1902) and *Papers Relating to the Army of the Solemn League and Covenant* (2 vols., 1917). These books, exploring involved and neglected material, served to undermine a number of classic misstatements: and at a time when Scottish history was only too commonly seen with narrow scope, he dealt with Scotland always as part of Europe.

Terry was also a very fine musician, with a special interest in Johann Sebastian Bach. His *Bach: a Biography*, published in 1928 (revised edn, 1933), was received with enthusiasm in Germany, and still holds a pre-eminent place. He also wrote on the Bach family, and his other editorial and critical work on J. S. Bach includes important editions of the *Chorals* (3 parts, 1915–21), *Original Hymn-Tunes for Congregational Use* (1922), and *Cantata Texts, Sacred and Secular* (1926), and critical analyses for the Musical Pilgrim series, founded in 1924. His editions remain useful, 'if used with caution' (*New Grove*). He also contributed to the third edition of Grove's *Dictionary of Music*. At Aberdeen he virtually created the university choral and orchestral society, acting for many years as its conductor.

Terry received honorary doctorates of music from the universities of Oxford and Edinburgh, and other honorary degrees from Glasgow, Aberdeen, Durham, and Leipzig. This German degree (PhD) was conferred upon him in 1935 on the occasion of the 250th anniversary of the birth of Bach. He was elected an honorary fellow of Clare College in 1929. His widow gave his Bach library to the Royal College of Music. A photograph of him in old age, of admirable liveliness, is reproduced in volume 24 of the *Aberdeen University Review*.

A. M. MACKENZIE, *rev.* H. C. G. MATTHEW

Sources Grove, *Dict. mus.* (1940) · *The Times* (6 Nov 1936) · *New Grove* · private information (1949)
Likenesses J. B. Souter, pencil drawing, Royal College of Music, London · A. Sutherland, oils, U. Aberdeen, King's College · photograph, repro. in *Aberdeen University Review*, 24 (1937), facing p. 124
Wealth at death £1579 13s. 3d.: confirmation, 21 Jan 1937, CCI

Terry, Daniel (1789–1829), actor and playwright, was born in Bath and educated first at Bath grammar school and then at a private school at Wingfield, Wiltshire, under Revd Edward Spencer. For five years he was a pupil of the architect Samuel Wyatt, but, after acting the part of Heartwell in *The Prize* at Bath, Terry left him to join the company at Sheffield under the management of the elder Macready. His first appearance was as Tressel in *Richard III*, and he went on to play Cromwell in *Henry VIII* and Edmund in *King Lear*. Towards the close of 1805 he joined Stephen Kemble in the north of England. When Kemble's company broke up in 1806 he went to Liverpool. His success there recommended him to Henry Siddons, who brought him out in Edinburgh (29 November 1809) as Bertrand in William Dimond's *The Foundling of the Forest*.

At that period Terry's figure is said to have been well formed and graceful, his countenance powerfully expressive, and his voice strong, full, and clear, though not melodious. He is also credited with stage knowledge, energetic and appropriate action, good judgement, and an active mind. On 12 December 1809 he was Antigonus in *The Winter's Tale*, on 8 January 1810 Prospero, and on 29 January Argyle in Joanna Baillie's *The Family Legend*. Scott, who contributed a prologue which Terry delivered, spoke well of this performance. On 22 November Terry played Falstaff in *Henry IV*. On 15 January 1811 he was the first Roderick Dhu in *The Lady of the Lake*, adapted by Edmund John Eyre; on 6 March he played Polonius; on the 18th he repeated Roderick Dhu in *The Knight of Snowdoun*, a second version, by Thomas Morton, of *The Lady of the Lake*, not much more prosperous than the former; and on the 23rd, for his benefit, was Falstaff in *The Merry Wives of Windsor*. He was Lord Ogleby in *The Clandestine Marriage* on 18 November 1811.

Terry made his first appearance in London in this part, at the Haymarket, on 20 May 1812. During that season he played Shylock, Job Thornberry, Sir Anthony Absolute, Major Sturgeon in *The Major of Garratt*, Dr Pangloss in *The Heir-at-Law*, Don Caesar in *A Bold Stroke for a Husband*, Megrim in *Blue Devils*, Harmony in *Everyone has his Fault*, Sir Edward Mortimer in *The Iron Chest*, Leon in *Rule a Wife and have a Wife*, Gradus in *Who's the Dupe?*, Romaldi in *The Tale of Mystery*, Barford in *Who Wants a Guinea?*, Selico in *The Africans*, Heartall in *The Soldier's Daughter*, Bustleton in *Manager in Distress*, Octavian, and Iago—a remarkable list for a first season. He created some original characters in unimportant plays, the only part of note being Count Salerno in Eyre's *Look at Home* (15 August 1812), founded on Moore's *Zeluco*. Terry was announced to reopen, on 14 November, the Edinburgh theatre as Lord Ogleby, but was ill and did not appear until the 23rd. The following day he played Shylock.

On 8 September 1813, as Leon in *Rule a Wife and have a Wife*, Terry made his first appearance at Covent Garden, where, except for frequent migrations to Edinburgh and summer seasons at the Haymarket, he remained until 1822. Among the parts he played in his first season were Sir Robert Bramble in *The Poor Gentleman*, Dornton in *The Road to Ruin*, Ford, Sir Adam Contest in *The Wedding Day*, Ventidius in *Antony and Cleopatra*, Shylock, Churlton, an original part in James Kenney's *Debtor and Creditor* (26 April 1814), and Sir Oliver in *The School for Scandal*.

On 12 March 1816 *Guy Mannering*, a musical adaptation by Terry of Scott's novel, was seen for the first time; this appears to have been the first of Terry's adaptations from Scott. At the Haymarket he appeared as Periwinkle in *A*

Bold Stroke for a Wife, Hardcastle, Hotspur, Sir George Thunder, Sir Pertinax McSycophant, Sir Fretful Plagiary, Eustace de Saint-Pierre, Lord Scratch in *The Dramatist*, and in many other parts. In 1815, meanwhile, he had, by permission of the Covent Garden management, supported Sarah Siddons in Edinburgh, where he played Macbeth, Wolsey, King John, and the Earl of Warwick.

On 2 October 1817 his acting at Covent Garden of Frederick William, king of Prussia, in Abbott's *The Youthful Days of Frederick the Great* raised Terry's reputation to the highest point it attained, and on 22 April 1818 he was the first Salerno in Shiel's *Bellamira*. In Jameson's *Nine Points of the Law*, at the Haymarket on 17 July, he was Mr Precise, and in *The Green Man*, on 15 August, he exhibited what was called a perfect piece of acting as Mr Green. At Covent Garden on 17 April 1819 he was the first David Deans in his own adaptation of *The Heart of Midlothian*. Later that season he played Sir Sampson Legend in *Love for Love*, Buckingham in *Richard III*, Prospero, Sir Amias Paulet in *Mary Stuart* (adapted from Schiller), and Lord Glenallan. He was announced for Jonathan Oldbuck in his own and Pocock's adaptation of *The Antiquary* on 25 January 1820, but illness seems to have prevented his playing the part, which was assigned to John Liston. On 17 May Terry was the first Dentatus in Sheridan Knowles's *Virginius*. At the Haymarket during the summer seasons he played a great round of comic and other characters, including Hardy in *The Belle's Stratagem*, Peachum in *The Beggar's Opera*, Falstaff in 1 *Henry IV*, Old Hardcastle, Sir Peter Teazle, Dr Pangloss, Polonius, Lear, Sir Anthony Absolute, Pierre in *Venice Preserv'd*, and Rob Roy. Among many original parts, in pieces by Kenney, T. J. Dibdin, and others, Terry was Sir Christopher Cranberry in *Exchange No Robbery*, by his friend Theodore Hook, on 12 August 1820.

Having quarrelled with the management of Covent Garden on a question of terms, Terry made his first appearance at Drury Lane on 16 October 1822, when he spoke an occasional address by Colman and played Sir Peter. He afterwards acted Crabtree, John Dory in *Wild Oats*, Cassio, Belarius in *Cymbeline*, Kent in *King Lear*, Dougal in *Rob Roy*, Solomon in *The Stranger*, and Grumio, and on 4 January 1823 was the first Simpson in John Poole's *Simpson and Co.* At the Haymarket on 7 July he was the first Admiral Franklin in Kenney's *Sweethearts and Wives*, and on 27 September the first Dr Primrose in a new adaptation by T. J. Dibdin of *The Vicar of Wakefield*. The season 1823–4 at Drury Lane saw him as Bartolo in *Fazio*, Lord Sands, Menenius in *Coriolanus*, and the first Antony Foster in a version of *Kenilworth* (5 January 1824). The following season he appeared as Orozembo in *Pizarro*, Justice Woodcock in *Love in a Village*, Adam in *As You Like It*, Moustache in *Henri Quatre*, Hubert in *King John*, and Rochfort in an adaptation of *The Fatal Dowry*. Among his original roles were Zamet in *Massaniello* (17 February 1825) and Mephistopheles in *Faustus* (16 May), the latter one of his best parts. In 1825, in association with his friend Frederick Henry Yates, he became manager of the Adelphi, and opened on 10 October in a piece called *Killigrew*. This was followed on the 31st by Edward Fitzball's

successful adaptation of *The Pilot*, in which Terry was the Pilot. He also appeared in other parts.

Terry's financial affairs had meanwhile become so involved that he had to retire from management. Under the strain of the collapse which followed, his mental and physical powers gave way. After leaving the Adelphi he retired temporarily to the continent, and was then re-engaged at Drury Lane to play Polonius and Simpson. Finding himself unable to act, and his memory quite gone, he threw up his engagement. On 12 June 1829 he suffered a stroke, and died later that month.

Terry married his first wife in Liverpool and on 25 June 1815 married Elizabeth Wemyss *Nasmyth (1793–1862) [*see under* Nasmyth family], the daughter of the painter Alexander *Nasmyth. Mrs Terry—who, after Terry's death, married the lexicographer Charles Richardson—was herself an artist, and took some share in the decoration of Scott's home, Abbotsford. Terry left, by his second marriage, a son named Walter, after Scott (who promised to look after the boys' fortunes), and a daughter, Jane.

Terry, who was almost as well known in Edinburgh as in London, was highly respected in both places. His friend Sir Walter Scott thought highly of his acting in tragedy, comedy, pantomine, and farce. While escaping from the charge of ranting, he was best in scenes of vehemence, and was wise enough not to attempt parts of tender emotion. In comedy he excelled in old men, and in characters of amorous dotage, such as Sir Francis Gripe, Don Manuel, or Sir Adam Contest, he was excellent. His Falstaff was good. His chief fault was uneasiness. He disapproved of the starring system, and was conscientious enough not to pose as a star.

Terry's idolatry of Scott led him to imitate both his manner and his calligraphy. Scott, who corresponded freely with him on most subjects, declared that, were he called upon to swear to any document, the most he could do was to attest it was his own writing or Terry's. Terry had caught, according to Lockhart, the very trick of Scott's meditative frown, and imitated his method of speech so as almost to pass for a Scot. Scott lent him money for his theatrical speculations, and gave him excellent advice. Being intimate with the Ballantynes, Terry had a financial stake in their printing and publishing business, and when the firm became bankrupt Scott was saddled with his liability of £1750. Terry's architectural knowledge was of great use to Scott, who consulted him while building Abbotsford; he also consulted Terry on many literary questions, especially in regard to plays, and seems to have trusted him with revising *The Doom of Devorgoil* for the stage. It seems likely that Terry was responsible for many of the numerous adaptations of Scott that saw the light between the appearance of *Waverley* and the actor's death. He also compiled *The British Theatrical Gallery* (1825), a collection of full-length portraits with biographical notes.

JOSEPH KNIGHT, rev. KLAUS STIERSTORFER

Sources J. G. Lockhart, *Memoirs of the life of Sir Walter Scott*, 7 vols. (1837–8) · *Dramatic Magazine*, 1 (1829), 189–90 · 'Memoirs of Mr Daniel Terry', *Theatrical Inquisitor, and Monthly Mirror*, 5 (1814), 131–2 ·

Oxberry's Dramatic Biography, new ser., 1/5 (1827), 73–83 · G. G. Cunningham, ed., *Lives of eminent and illustrious Englishmen*, 8 vols. (1835–7) · *New Monthly Magazine*, new ser., 27 (1829), 452 · *The biography of the British stage, being correct narratives of the lives of all the principal actors and actresses* (1824) · Genest, *Eng. stage* · J. C. Dibdin, *The annals of the Edinburgh stage* (1888) · T. S. Munden, *Memoirs of Thomas Shepherd Munden, by his son* (1844) · A. Lang, *The life and letters of John Gibson Lockhart*, 2 vols. (1897) · W. C. Russell, *Representative actors* (c.1875) · G. B. Bryan, *Stage lives: a bibliography and index to theatrical biographies in English* (1985)

Archives NL Scot., corresp. with Sir Walter Scott

Likenesses H. W. Pickersgill, oils, c.1813, Scot. NPG · W. Nicholson, watercolour drawing, exh. 1816, Scot. NPG · S. De Wilde, watercolour drawing (as Barford in *Who wants a guinea?*), Garr. Club · J. P. Knight, oils, Garr. Club · portrait (as Leon in *Rule a wife and have a wife*), repro. in *Theatrical Inquisitor*, 1 · prints, BM, NPG

Terry, Edward (1589/90–1660), travel writer, was born at Leigh, Kent, possibly the son of Richard Terry (d. 1647), landowner. He attended Rochester School before matriculating from Christ Church, Oxford, on 1 July 1608, aged eighteen. He graduated BA on 26 November 1611 and proceeded MA on 6 July 1614. The East India Company engaged him as a chaplain and in February 1616 he sailed in the flagship of the fleet. Having taken in the Cape of Good Hope and seen its Khoi-Khoi (Hottentot) inhabitants, near the Comoro Islands they overtook a Portuguese carrack which fired on the leading ship and refused to parley. In the ensuing fight at close quarters with the flagship, the English commander was killed and the disabled carrack was run ashore and burnt by her crew. After arriving at Surat in September Terry accepted an engagement as chaplain to Sir Thomas Roe, and the next February he joined the ambassador near Ujjain, Malwa (Madhya Pradesh). They followed the emperor, Jahangir, and his vast entourage to Mandu some 60 miles further south. Here Terry shared a room with Thomas Coryate and later a tent when, in October, Jahangir moved again towards Ahmadabad, Gujarat. At Ahmadabad in May 1618 Terry survived an epidemic which killed several of Roe's suite; in September Roe, mission accomplished, and the survivors (one in four according to Terry) left for Surat. They sailed for home in February 1619, arriving in The Downs that September.

Terry had spent slightly over twenty-seven months in India, seeing only parts of Gujarat and Malwa, but an enquiring mind and linguistic ability enabled him to compile a historically valuable account of the entire Mughal dominions and their varied inhabitants. He learned some Persian, the language of the court, and some Arabic, that of the learned. He found Hindustani 'a smooth tongue and easie to be pronounced' (Purchas, 1905, 1474). Mutually ignoring political and religious differences, he and the Jesuit in charge of Portuguese affairs at court conversed in Latin: Father Corsi was 'a very great intelligencer, knowing all news that might be had' (Terry, 444). In 1622 Terry presented a manuscript account to Charles, prince of Wales, which was transmitted to Samuel Purchas who published an edited version in part two of the 1625 edition of *Purchas his Pilgrimes*. Terry's own *A Voyage to East India* (1655) is a revision of this manuscript, expanded probably at least seven times, mainly by religious disquisition. It contains a full-length engraving of Jahangir, and some copies include a version of the important map (BL, K115/22) drawn by William Baffin and engraved by Renold Elstrack from information accumulated by Roe, whose sources included Terry.

Terry returned for a period to Christ Church and was afternoon lecturer at Carfax, Oxford, in 1621 and 1622. Anthony Wood asserts that he then obtained a 'small cure' (Wood, *Ath. Oxon.*, 3.505–7), and by 1625 or 1626, when his son James was born, Terry had married. Whether this was to Elizabeth, his wife in 1660, is not clear; it is possible he was the Edward Terry who married Elizabeth Bland on 17 January 1630 at St Margaret Moyses, London. On 26 August the previous year he had become rector of Great Greenford, Middlesex. A second son, Edward, was born in the early 1630s. Terry remained at Great Greenford during the 1640s and 1650s, apparently acceptable to the authorities. His *Pseudeleutheria, or, Lawlesse Liberty* (1646) was a sermon preached before the lord mayor at St Paul's on 16 August that year, while *The Merchants and Mariners Preservation and Thanksgiving* (1649) was a sermon preached to his old employers, the East India Company, at St Andrew Undershaft. Following the Restoration he published *A Character of His Most Sacred Majesty King Charles the IId* (1660) in the hope, Wood claimed to have heard from James Terry, of obtaining the deanery of Windsor, but he died at Greenford on 8 October that year. He was buried in the chancel of his church on 10 October. His wife, Elizabeth, died in 1661, and was buried at Greenford on 22 August. Terry was briefly succeeded as rector by his second son and namesake, who had been a fellow of University College, Oxford, and rector of Amersham, but he was ejected in 1662. James Terry was also ejected from his rectory of Michelmersh, Hampshire. Both brothers were subsequently licensed as nonconformist ministers. Edward Terry's account of his voyage continued to receive attention: his narrative was appended to *The Travels of Pietro della Vale* (1665); a French translation appeared in 1663 and was reissued in 1696; and there were two Dutch translations in 1707 and 1727. MICHAEL STRACHAN

Sources E. Terry, *A voyage to East India* (1655) · S. Purchas, *Hakluytus posthumus, or, Purchas his pilgrimes*, bk 2 (1625); repr. Hakluyt Society, extra ser., 15 (1905) · W. Foster, *Early travels in India* (1921); repr. (New York, 1975) · Foster, *Alum. Oxon.* · Wood, *Ath. Oxon.*, 2nd edn, 2.253; 3.505–7 · *The embassy of Sir Thomas Roe to the court of the great mogul, 1615–1619*, ed. W. Foster, Hakluyt Society, 2nd ser., 1–2 (1899); rev. edn (1926) · M. Strachan, *Sir Thomas Roe, 1581–1644: a life* (1989) · *Walker rev.*, 480 · *DNB* · P. S. Seaver, *The puritan lectureships: the politics of religious dissent, 1560–1662* (1970), 113 · R. C. Prasad, *Early English travellers in India* (1965); 2nd rev. edn (1980) · M. Strachan, *The life and adventures of Thomas Coryate* (1962) · *CSP col.*, vols. 2–4, 6, 8 [East Indies]; contd as E. B. Sainsbury, *A calendar of the court minutes ... of the East India Company*, ed. W. Foster, 11 vols. (1907–38) · L. E. Pennington, ed., *The Purchas handbook: studies of the life, time and writings of Samuel Purchas*, 2 vols., Hakluyt Society, 2nd ser., 185–6 (1997) · *IGI*

Likenesses R. Vaughan, line engraving (aged sixty-four), BM, NPG; repro. in Terry, *Voyage to East India* (1655)

Terry, Edward O'Connor (1844–1912), actor and theatre proprietor, was born on 10 March 1844 at 42 Gibson Street, Lambeth, London, the son of John Terry, a painter and actor, and his wife, Emblen Ann, *née* Middleton. Terry was already an experienced amateur actor when he swiftly

Edward O'Connor Terry (1844–1912), by Lock & Whitfield, pubd 1879

quit a commercial career to appear professionally, on a 'stage' made from 9 inch planks laid upon trestles, at the Mechanics' Institute, Christchurch, Hampshire, on 15 August 1863 with the dishonest manager of an impoverished 'fit-up' company. Minor roles at a series of provincial theatres followed. In 1866–7 he appeared in Charles Calvert's company at the Prince's Theatre, Manchester, where his parts included one of the three sisters in *Macbeth*, the Clown in *Antony and Cleopatra*, and the Second Citizen in *Julius Caesar*, and received some acclaim from the *Morning Post*.

This led to Terry's London début, at the Surrey Theatre on 14 September 1867, as Finnikin Fusselton in *A Cure for the Fidgets*. Thereafter he played at the Lyceum and, from 1868, the Strand, taking leading parts in burlesques and comedies, before joining John Hollingshead's company at the Gaiety Theatre in 1876. Here, one of the celebrated Gaiety Quartet, with Nellie Farren, Edward W. Royce, and Kate Vaughan, he was to 'take burlesque to its highest peak' (Pope, 164). After leaving the Gaiety in 1885, and a period touring in the provinces as Montague Joliffe in A. W. Pinero's *In Chancery* and Chevalier Walkinshaw in the same author's *The Rocket*, Terry returned to London and leased the Olympic Theatre. He opened there on 16 December 1886 as Mr Chuffey in *The Churchwarden*, which he had adapted from a German farce.

Terry opened his own 800-seat theatre, Terry's, in the Strand, London, on 17 October 1887. Theatre and fittings were designed by Walter Emden to reassure the public after the recent destruction by fire of the Paris Opéra Comique and the theatre in Exeter. There, 'the most amusing theatre in London' (*The Times*, 3 April 1912), Terry was to earn his fortune, primarily by productions of plays by Pinero. *Sweet Lavender*, which opened on 21 March 1888, with Terry as Dick Phenyl, ran originally for 670 performances and is said to have earned him more than £50,000. Among other successes, Terry's saw the first legitimate production of Frances Hodgson Burnett's own adaptation of *Little Lord Fauntleroy*, on 15 May 1888. The theatre closed on 8 October 1910, shortly after Terry had sold it. It was subsequently converted to a picture house, and was pulled down in 1923.

Terry took productions abroad, notably to Australia, Canada, and South Africa, as well as making many provincial tours. His last runs in London were in 1909–10 at His Majesty's Theatre, as Crabtree in *The School for Scandal* and as Uncle Gregory in W. G. Robertson's *Pinkie and the Fairies*. He played the Club Servant in the royal command performance of Bulwer-Lytton's *Money* on 17 May 1911 at Drury Lane, and Brown in T. W. Robertson's *David Garrick* at the gala performance at His Majesty's Theatre on 27 June 1911.

Terry was regarded as an 'incomparable eccentric character' (Archer, 151) and as a 'past master of the art of comic despair' (*South African News*, 24 Jan 1903). His voice was particularly memorable, 'with the shrill staccato notes of a piccolo which would suddenly run down through a whole gamut of strange sounds into the deep grunt of a bassoon' (*The Times*, 3 April 1912). He was kind, genial, and a keen churchman. In 1889 he lectured to the church congress at Cardiff on the tensions between stage and church. He was treasurer of the Royal General Theatrical Fund between 1896 and 1911, when he became chairman. In the 1880s and 1890s he was a member of the Richmond board of guardians and, for a period, a member of the Barnes school board. From 1897 until his death he was the ruling councillor of the Barnes Habitation of the Primrose League. He was a churchwarden at Barnes parish church and held office in various other local organizations. He was a council member or trustee of a range of national as well as local charities, and became a magistrate for Surrey in 1906. Prominent in freemasonry, he was in 1889 the grand treasurer of all England. He was one of the founders, in 1898 at Barnes, of the Edward Terry Lodge.

Terry's first wife, Ellen Dietz (c.1849–1897), whom he had married in 1870 and with whom he had a son and (probably) two daughters, died in 1897. On 24 October 1904 he married Florence Edgecombe, *née* Rendle, the widow of Sir Augustus Harris, the one-time lessee of Drury Lane Theatre. Terry died from cancer on 2 April 1912 at his home, Priory Lodge, Church Road, Barnes, and was buried on 6 April in Brompton cemetery.

C. M. P. TAYLOR

Sources E. Terry, 'In the days of my youth', *M. A. P.* (10 Jan 1903) • *The Stage* (4 April 1912) • *The Era* (6 April 1912) • E. Reid and H. Compton, eds., *The dramatic peerage*, rev. edn [1892] • J. Parker, ed., *The green room book, or, Who's who on the stage* (1908) • W. Macqueen-Pope, *Gaiety: theatre of enchantment* (1949) • W. Trewin, *The Royal General Theatrical Fund* (1989) • b. cert. • m. cert. [Florence Harris] • d. cert. • *Era Almanack and Annual* (1895) • J. P. Wearing, *The London stage, 1900–*

1909: a calendar of plays and players, 2 vols. (1981) · J. P. Wearing, *The London stage, 1910–1919: a calendar of plays and players*, 2 vols. (1982) · G. Rowell, *Theatre in the age of Irving* (1981) · P. Hartnoll, ed., *The Oxford companion to the theatre* (1951) · A. Hyman, *The Gaiety years* (1975) · C. E. Pascoe, ed., *The dramatic list*, 2nd edn (1880) · *Reminiscences of J. L. Toole*, ed. J. Hatton, 2 vols. (1889) · W. Archer, *The theatrical 'World' of 1894* (1895) · *The Times* (3 April 1912) · *Richmond and Twickenham Times* (6 April 1912) · *Richmond Herald* (6 April 1912) · *Evening Standard* (2 April 1912) · playbills, Man. CL

Archives Richmond Central Library, London · Theatre Museum, London

Likenesses Lock & Whitfield, photograph, pubd 1879, NPG [*see illus.*] · photograph, Theatre Museum, London · photograph, repro. in *Daily Sketch* (3 April 1912)

Wealth at death £44,056 14s. 6d.: probate, 17 Aug 1912, CGPLA Eng. & Wales

Terry, Dame Ellen Alice (1847–1928), actress, was born in Smithford Street, Coventry, Warwickshire, on 27 February 1847, the fifth and third surviving child of the actors Benjamin Terry (1818–1896) and his wife, Sarah Ballard (1819–1892), who were then on tour. Benjamin Terry was of Irish descent, the son of a publican; his wife was of Scottish descent, the daughter of a Wesleyan minister in Portsmouth. Several children of the large Terry family distinguished themselves on stage: the eldest daughter, Kate, Marion *Terry, Florence, and the youngest son, Fred *Terry. Ellen was originally named Alice Ellen, but by the time of her first marriage she had reversed these names.

Early acting career Trained by her parents, Ellen went on the stage as a child, her first part being the boy Mamillius in Charles Kean's production of *The Winter's Tale*, on 28 April 1856, at the Princess's Theatre in London. Under Kean's management of the Princess's, which ended in 1859, she also played Puck in *A Midsummer Night's Dream* (1856), Arthur in *King John* (1858), and Fleance in *Macbeth* (1859). Her salary was initially 15s. a week, rising to 30s. during *A Midsummer Night's Dream*. Mrs Kean gave her further training, concentrating especially on the child's voice so that she could easily be heard in the gallery of the theatre. During the summer, when the Princess's was closed, her father successfully organized a drawing-room entertainment of two short plays, which she acted at the Royal Colosseum, Regent's Park, London, and then on tour.

By 1859 Ellen Terry was already an experienced juvenile actress with a reputation for fresh, high-spirited comedy. In that year she played in Tom Taylor's comedy *Nine Points of the Law* at the Olympic Theatre, and then in 1861 joined the company of the Royalty Theatre in Soho, which included W. H. Kendal, David James, and Charles Wyndham. While in London she lived with her family at 92 Stanhope Street, near Regent's Park. In 1862 she became a member of J. H. Chute's well-known stock company at the Theatre Royal, Bristol, which also performed at the Theatre Royal, Bath. Here she stayed until 1863, when she went to London again to play in J. B. Buckstone's company at the Theatre Royal, Haymarket, in a repertory that included Shakespeare, Sheridan, and modern comedy.

Marriage to G. F. Watts During the run of Taylor's hit comedy *Our American Cousin* at the Haymarket, in which she

Dame Ellen Alice Terry (1847–1928), by Barraud, pubd 1888

played Mary Meredith, Ellen Terry abruptly left the stage to prepare for her marriage with the celebrated artist George Frederic *Watts (1817–1904). They were married on 20 February 1864 at St Barnabas, Kensington, and went to live in Little Holland House, Kensington, the residence of Mrs Thoby Prinsep. Watts was forty-seven, and Ellen Terry a week short of her seventeenth birthday. The disparity between their ages and temperaments was marked, and the young Mrs Watts was regarded with suspicion and perhaps hostility by the circle of married ladies, including Mrs Prinsep, who had appointed themselves protectresses of their adored 'Signor' as they termed him. The marriage lasted less than a year, and in 1865 the shocked young wife, who did not wish the separation forced upon her, found herself back with her family. In some respects the marriage was an artistic success if a personal failure. Ellen Terry added to her acquaintance a number of cultured and important people, among them Browning, Tennyson, Gladstone, Disraeli, and the photographer Julia Margaret Cameron, and was widely exposed to the arts. She and her husband entered into a productive if short-lived artistic relationship. He had painted her in 1862 in *The Sisters*, when she sat for him with Kate; she now happily modelled for the paintings *Watchman, what of the Night*, *Choosing*, *Ellen Terry*, and *Ophelia*. For many years after the marriage she was a cult figure for poets and painters of the later Pre-Raphaelite and Aesthetic movements, including Oscar Wilde. Tall, slender, with beautiful flaxen hair, grey eyes, full red lips, finely framed features, graceful of carriage and movement, fresh and always young, Ellen Terry was as much an art object as an actress.

Resumption of acting, relationship with E. W. Godwin, and birth of children Compelled to return to the stage, in which she now took little pleasure, to earn her living, Ellen Terry in 1867 joined the company at the Queen's Theatre, Long Acre, under the management of Alfred Wigan. Here she acted for the first time with Henry Irving, in Garrick's adaptation of *The Taming of the Shrew, Kathrine and Petruchio*, she playing the former and he the latter; both, she said, performed badly. In the summer of 1868 she left the stage once more, to live with the architect, interior designer, and essayist Edward William *Godwin (1833–1886), in the Hertfordshire countryside on Gusterwood Common. She had met Godwin while acting in Bristol, and resumed the acquaintance in London. Godwin had been widowed in 1865. His knowledge of colours and fabrics, his interest in oriental design, and his preference for simplicity of style permanently influenced Ellen Terry's taste and her choice of design schemes for her own residences and of materials for her own clothing and stage costumes. After her return to the stage and their separation Godwin continued to design costumes for her. She, however, was to remain away from the theatre for six years; during this time she bore Godwin two children: Edith Ailsa Geraldine *Craig, born on 9 December 1869, and (Edward Henry) Gordon *Craig, born on 16 January 1872. After her daughter's birth, Godwin designed and built a house for his new family at Fallows Green, Harpenden, Hertfordshire, and Ellen Terry lived there until 1874. Godwin became preoccupied with problems arising from his architectural practice and was often away from home; he also suffered increasing financial difficulties. Concerned for the future security of her small children, Ellen Terry left Hertfordshire in 1874 and went back to work in the theatre. A chance encounter in the Hertfordshire countryside with her old friend the playwright Charles Reade had led to an engagement at the Queen's Theatre in Reade's drama *The Wandering Heir*, at a handsome salary of £40 a week; she replaced Mrs John Wood in the leading part on 27 February 1874.

Ellen Terry toured in a trio of Reade plays and then distinguished herself as Portia in the Bancrofts' production of *The Merchant of Venice* at the Prince of Wales's Theatre in 1875. The separation from Godwin occurred in this year, while she was living in a house on Taviton Street, off Gordon Square. After several more roles at the Prince of Wales's, including Blanche Haye in a revival of T. W. Robertson's *Ours* in 1876, she joined John Hare's company at the Court Theatre. When she was with Hare, she moved with her children from lodgings in Camden Town to Rose Cottage at Hampton Court. Her greatest success with Hare was as Olivia in W. G. Wills's eponymous adaptation of *The Vicar of Wakefield*; it was a role that she also played at Henry Irving's Lyceum. On 21 November 1877, having received a divorce from Watts, she married the actor (formerly soldier) Charles Clavering Wardell (1839–1885) at St Philip's, Kensington. Wardell, whose stage name was Kelly, was thirty-eight, and the two had met while acting together in

Reade's plays in 1874. They went to live, with the children, at 33 Longridge Road, Earls Court. The marriage lasted less than three years—they were separated in 1881—but it was at least the cause of a reconciliation with her mother and father, whom she had not seen since her alliance with Godwin.

Professional and personal relationship with Henry Irving In July 1878, Henry *Irving (1838–1905), who had entered into a lease for the Lyceum Theatre, called on Terry at Longridge Road; they had not met since 1867. The outcome was a contract at the Lyceum at a salary of 40 guineas a week and an annual benefit performance; her touring salary, for much of her Lyceum career, was a generous £200 a week. Her first part at the Lyceum was Ophelia, on 30 December 1878, the day Irving inaugurated his new management with *Hamlet*. Irving was employing a leading lady, an experienced actress of thirty-one, who already possessed a considerable reputation, a devoted audience following, and a memorable recent appearance as Portia. Ellen Terry was to remain with Irving for twenty-four years, undertake frequent provincial tours and seven tours to America with the Lyceum company, and play a total of thirty-six parts. Eleven of these were in Shakespeare; she also acted in plays by Tennyson, Bulwer-Lytton, Reade, Sardou, and other contemporary playwrights, such as W. G. Wills, who were commissioned by Irving to write for the Lyceum. Irving's repertory consisted mostly of Shakespeare and Victorian romantic melodrama, with the occasional comedy, and of course Terry did not have, since Irving was an absolute if benevolent dictator, a free choice of parts.

Certainly Terry achieved her greatest distinction in Shakespeare, especially in Shakespearian comedy. Her Shakespearian parts at the Lyceum were Ophelia, Portia (*The Merchant of Venice*, 1879), Desdemona (*Othello*, 1881), Juliet (*Romeo and Juliet*, 1882), Beatrice (*Much Ado about Nothing*, 1882), Viola (*Twelfth Night*, 1884), Lady Macbeth (*Macbeth*, 1888), Queen Katherine (*Henry VIII*, 1892), Cordelia (*King Lear*, 1892), Imogen (*Cymbeline*, 1896), and Volumnia (*Coriolanus*, 1901). She also played Lady Anne in a scene of *Richard III* for Irving's benefit performance in 1879. Her last appearance at the Lyceum was as Portia on 19 July 1902, but she did tour the provinces with Irving and the Lyceum company in the autumn of that year. Of her principal non-Shakespearian roles at the Lyceum, her most successful and critically esteemed were Queen Henrietta Maria in Wills's drama *Charles I* (1879), Camma in Tennyson's short tragedy *The Cup* (1881), Margaret in the immensely popular and long-running Wills version of *Faust* (1885), Nance Oldfield in Reade's romantic comedy of the same name (1883), and Olivia (*Olivia*, 1885).

Ellen Terry's close association with Irving over such a long period of time may also have involved a sexual relationship. Some contemporaries and later biographers declared that they were lovers. Irving was separated, but not divorced from his wife. Terry was separated from Wardell in 1881; he died in 1885. Irving was godfather to both her children. They were close to one another, not only professionally at the Lyceum, but also in private life. They went on holidays together, and Irving wrote her letters that can only be described as tender, loving, and committed. Yet there is no decisive evidence of a physical love affair, only a possibility which some see as a probability, some as a certainty. Terry had a great admiration for Irving as an actor and as a hard worker, although she could clearly perceive his faults.

The stage after Irving Terry's lengthy and famous correspondence with George Bernard Shaw, which was especially prolific between 1895 and 1900, and much of which consisted of his advice on her acting and his attempts to woo her away from the Lyceum, represented an affectionate relationship of another kind, for they met only occasionally until the rehearsals for *Captain Brassbound's Conversion* in 1906. Her replies reveal a great deal about both her art and her personality.

During the Lyceum years Ellen Terry changed residence more than once. In 1889 she moved to 22 Barkston Gardens, Earls Court, but, still remaining fond of the country and remembering the house at Harpenden, she lived from time to time, when she was not required in London or on tours, in a series of rural dwellings. One of them was a small public house at Uxbridge, the Audrey Arms, in which she was required by the terms of her lease to act as publican. Evidently she kept the beer so poorly that she had virtually no customers. In 1896 she occupied Tower Cottage by the town gate in Winchelsea, Sussex, and in 1900 acquired her last country home, Smallhythe, a fifteenth-century farmhouse just south of Tenterden, Kent. It is now owned by the National Trust and functions as an Ellen Terry museum, library, and archive. She moved her London residence in 1902 from Barkston Gardens to 215 King's Road, Chelsea.

In 1889 Terry's son Teddy joined the Lyceum company as an actor in a drama of the French Revolution, Watts Phillips's *The Dead Heart*; he had earlier walked on when the company was on tour in Chicago. He remained with the Lyceum, and acted in the provinces, until 1897, when he left the stage to study drawing and produce his first woodblock engravings. His sister, Edy, who also appeared at the Lyceum for several years from 1887 in small parts, became much more interested in costume design than acting. She designed costumes for her mother and for productions staged by Lily Langtry and Mrs Brown Potter in the early years of the twentieth century.

After she finally left the Lyceum, Ellen Terry did not lack invitations to act, although her age now restricted the kind of parts she could play. Her best post-Lyceum role was her first, Mistress Page in *The Merry Wives of Windsor*, under the management of Herbert Beerbohm Tree, at His Majesty's on 10 June 1902. Her performance was a triumph, and with Tree playing Falstaff and Madge Kendal as Mistress Ford the play ran for 156 performances. In 1903 Terry made a financially unfortunate move into management when she took the Imperial Theatre for a season, chiefly to introduce the designing and directing talents of her son to an as yet unknowing and uncaring professional world. Ibsen's *The Vikings at Helgeland* opened in April 1903,

with set and lighting design and properties as well as direction by Craig, and the costumes, designed for a large cast, by his sister. Their mother acted the role of the fierce and warlike Hiordis, in which she was miscast. There were tensions between actors and director and between director and business manager, and the public did not come. *The Vikings* was withdrawn after only thirty performances, and the big losses were only partially recompensed by a cheaply and hastily mounted *Much Ado about Nothing* which then toured successfully in the provinces. It was the only occasion when this formidably talented family collaborated on an event of major theatrical significance. After this Craig left England for Europe, his own career as a designer and theorist, and Isadora Duncan. Edy founded the feminist-oriented Pioneer Players in 1911, directed plays for them, and looked after her mother. The relationship between mother and daughter was not an easy one.

Ellen Terry remained active in the theatre for a few more years, despite increasing health problems. She created the part of Alice in J. M. Barrie's *Alice Sit-by-the-Fire* at the Duke of York's Theatre in 1905, and, finally submitting to Shaw's constant hounding, took a part in one of his plays: Lady Cecily Waynflete in *Captain Brassbound's Conversion* at the Royal Court in 1906. Soon after this, on 12 June 1906, an Ellen Terry jubilee performance, marking her fifty years on the stage, was organized at Drury Lane by the theatrical profession. It raised for the actress a much needed £6000. Enrico Caruso, Paoli Tosti, Nellie Melba, and a host of leading actors, actresses, and entertainers went through a substantial and varied programme. Like a grand and beautiful divinity, Terry herself finally appeared on the stage in an act of *Much Ado about Nothing* (performed by no fewer than twenty-two members of the Terry family) to the worshipful plaudits of a packed house. Later in 1906 she played Hermione in Tree's production of *The Winter's Tale* at His Majesty's. She toured America in 1907 with *Captain Brassbound's Conversion*, and took the role of Aunt Imogen in W. Graham Robertson's fairy play *Pinkie and the Fairies* at His Majesty's in 1908. She still did provincial tours, including one of the Shaw play, and in 1910–11 visited America once more with a programme of lectures on and recitations from Shakespeare. On this tour she visited a recording studio and recorded five passages from Shakespeare, the only extant evidence of the sound of her voice. She later gave her Shakespeare programme in Britain and visited New Zealand and Australia with it in 1914–15. There followed scenes from Shakespeare performed in music-halls under the management of Oswald Stoll, and her last Shakespearian part was the Nurse in *Romeo and Juliet* (1919) at the Lyric, Shaftesbury Avenue. She also appeared in at least five films, and her last stage role was Susan Wildersham in Walter de la Mare's fairy play *Crossings*, on 19 November 1925 at the Lyric, Hammersmith. She had been on the stage for sixty-nine years.

Marriage to James Carew, honours, and death On 22 March 1907 in Pittsburgh, Pennsylvania Ellen Terry married her third husband, the American actor James Carew (1876–1938), whom she met at the Royal Court and with whom she toured America in *Captain Brassbound's Conversion*.

Carew was thirty-one. The marriage broke up amicably in 1910. The Chelsea house was given up in 1921; for some years Terry's financial condition had been poor and her financial affairs disorganized, and she moved, in worsening health, to a flat in Burleigh Mansions, St Martin's Lane. St Andrews University conferred an honorary LLD upon her in 1922, and in the new year's honours list of 1925 she was made a dame grand cross of the British empire, only the second actress to be so honoured. In 1927 she suffered an attack of bronchial pneumonia. On 21 July 1928 she died at Smallhythe of a cerebral haemorrhage. After a ceremony at Smallhythe church on 24 July, her body was taken to the crematorium at Golders Green, Middlesex, and another ceremony took place that evening at St Paul's, Covent Garden. Her ashes were interred in St Paul's in August 1929, and a memorial tablet was unveiled by Sir John Martin-Harvey.

A great actress Aside from the great appeal of her Aesthetic and Pre-Raphaelite image, Ellen Terry found her way into the hearts of her public by her liveliness, irrepressible spirits, and sense of fun in high comedy; her warmth, sincerity, trustfulness, and depth of romantic feeling in love scenes; her transparent innocence and beauty of mind in most characterizations; and her power to arouse the deepest pathos. She was a beautiful woman, and until late in her career never seemed to grow old; a sense of happy, everlasting youth invested her on stage. It is not surprising that her greatest part was Beatrice, and all the critics agreed that she would have made a superb Rosalind. She never played the part because Irving, although he did put on plays for her sake, such as *Olivia*, which offered little for him and a great deal for her, did not think fit to produce *As You Like It* and demean himself in, probably, the small part of Jaques. By the time she left the Lyceum she was too old for Rosalind. Terry's Margaret in *Faust* combined her ability to portray tenderness, innocence, and love as well as to arouse sorrow because of her suffering; this combination also made her Desdemona and Imogen effective. She was not, despite her best efforts, capable of tragedy. She admitted herself that she lacked stamina for long speeches; she also lacked physical force and the ability to sustain strong emotion. Her very personality was not suited to tragedy. In her hands Lady Macbeth was a fragile, devoted wife easily crushed by the weight of her husband's ambition and estrangement from her. The sleep-walking scene was played for pathos rather than tragic power. Volumnia was a 'true woman', as one critic put it, busying herself with the domestic tasks of a Victorian household.

From the point of view of acting technique, Ellen Terry was noted for grace, charm, and lightness; words such as 'gliding', 'floating', and 'dancing' were used to describe her stage movement, in which she tended to restlessness. Her voice was distinct, melodious, and musically pitched, with a noticeable vibrato in moments of deep emotion. Early in her career she was afflicted with stage fright on first nights; later she had difficulty remembering lines, a problem that grew much worse toward the end and severely hampered her in the playing of new parts. She worked extremely hard in preparing a role, sometimes filling several copies of a play with extensive marginalia and underlinings, giving herself specific instructions on textual emphasis, pace, pitch, volume, and movement, as well as comments on character. She always appeared natural on the stage; sometimes it seemed as if she were not acting at all, but merely being Ellen Terry. Indeed, her method was to absorb parts into herself, to possess a character rather than change herself into one.

None of her faults seemed to matter. In a real sense she was beyond serious criticism, the acerbic Henry James being the only critic who steadily gave her bad reviews, and even he occasionally dwindled into praise, notably when reviewing her Imogen. She was one of the very few English actresses to be adored by her public. They respected and admired Irving, a great artist but not a lovable man; they doted on Terry. She was not a tragic actress, and like Irving disliked the new drama represented by Ibsen and his followers. She did not, like Eleanora Duse, whom she much admired, venture into new dramatic territory. Her acting range may have been limited, but within it she was incomparable.　　　　　　　　MICHAEL R. BOOTH

Sources *Ellen Terry's memoirs*, ed. E. Craig and C. St John (New York, 1932) [with notes and biographical chapters by eds.] · E. Terry, *The story of my life* (1908) · *Ellen Terry and Bernard Shaw: a correspondence*, ed. C. St John (1931) · R. Manvell, *Ellen Terry* (1968) · J. Parker, ed., *The green room book, or, Who's who on the stage* (1909) · W. G. Robertson, *Time was: the reminiscences of W. Graham Robertson* (1931) · B. Stoker, *Personal reminiscences of Henry Irving*, 2 vols. (1906) · E. G. Craig, *Ellen Terry and her secret self* (1932) · C. St John, *Ellen Terry* (1907) · C. Hiatt, *Ellen Terry and her impersonations* (1908) · L. Irving, *Henry Irving: the actor and his world* [1951] · J. Martin-Harvey, *The autobiography of Sir John Martin-Harvey* (1933) · b. cert. · m. cert. [G. F. Watts] · m. cert. [C. C. Wardell] · d. cert. · J. Parker, ed., *Who's who in the theatre*, 11th edn (1952)

Archives BL, letters, Add. MS 46473 · Ellen Terry Memorial Museum, Smallhythe, Kent, corresp. · Hunt. L., letters · Russell-Cotes Art Gallery and Museum, Bournemouth, papers · University of Washington, corresp. and papers | BL, corresp. with George Bernard Shaw, Add. MSS 43800–43802, 46172g · Bodl. Oxf., letters to various members of the Lewis family · LMA, letters to Ida Donisthorpe [copies] · NYPL, corresp. with Edward Craig · Theatre Museum, London, letters to lord chamberlain's licensee and others; letters to Peter McBride | FILM BFI NFTVA, current affairs footage | SOUND BL NSA, performance recordings

Likenesses photograph, 1856 (as Mamillius), NPG · G. F. Watts, oils, 1862 (with her sister), Eastnor Castle, Herefordshire · J. M. Cameron, photograph, 1864 · G. F. Watts, oils, *c*.1864, NPG · G. F. Watts, oils, 1864, Watts Gallery, Compton, Surrey · G. F. Watts, oils, *c*.1864–1865, NPG; repro. in G. F. Watts, *Watchman, what of the night* · J. Forbes-Robertson, oils, 1876, NPG · W. Brodie, marble bust, 1879, Royal Shakespeare Memorial Theatre Museum, Stratford upon Avon · A. L. Merritt, oils, 1883, Garr. Club · J. S. Sargent, oils, 1888–9, Tate Collection · J. S. Sargent, oils, 1889, NPG · J. Collier, group portrait, oils, 1904, Garr. Club · C. J. Becker, pencil drawing, 1913, Royal Shakespeare Memorial Theatre Museum, Stratford upon Avon · W. G. Robertson, oils, 1922, NPG · C. Roberts, chalk drawing, 1923, NPG · Barraud, photograph, NPG; repro. in *Men and Women of the Day* (1888) [*see illus.*] · A. Broom, group portrait, photograph, NPG · J. M. Cameron, photograph, U. Texas, Gernsheim Collection · E. G. Craig, pen, ink, and wash drawing (as Mrs Page in *The Merry Wives of Windsor*), V&A · E. M. Hale, oils, Russell-Cotes Art Gallery, Bournemouth · HM, caricature, pen-and-ink drawing (with Irving), Theatre Museum, London · C. G. Manton, group portrait, watercolour (*Conversazione at the Royal*

Academy, 1891), NPG • W. G. Robertson, oils (after his pastel drawing), Ellen Terry Memorial Museum, Smallhythe Place, Kent • Window & Gore, cabinet photographs, NPG • oils (as Portia), Garr. Club • pencil drawing, Garr. Club • photographs, Theatre Museum, London • plaster cast of death mask, NPG • prints, BM, NPG, Harvard TC

Wealth at death £22,231 1s. 2d.: probate, 12 Oct 1928, *CGPLA Eng. & Wales*

Terry, Fred (1863–1933), actor, was born in London on 9 November 1863, the youngest son of Benjamin Terry (1818–1896), actor, and his wife, Sarah Ballard (1819–1892), actress, daughter of a Scottish minister at Portsmouth. Among his elder sisters were the actresses Kate Terry, Ellen *Terry, Marion *Terry, and Florence Terry; Fred, after education in London, France, and Switzerland, sustained the family tradition by going on the stage at the age of sixteen. He 'walked on' in a celebrated revival of Bulwer-Lytton's *Money*, with which the Bancrofts opened their management of the Haymarket Theatre on 31 January 1880. After experience on tour Terry appeared at the Lyceum Theatre in July 1884 in the revival by Henry Irving of *Twelfth Night*, as Sebastian to the Viola of his sister Ellen, whom he resembled remarkably. 'I don't think,' Ellen Terry wrote in later years, 'that I have ever seen any success so unmistakable and instantaneous.' More touring followed, in Britain and in the United States of America, but from the summer of 1887 the young actor, with his fine voice and presence, was found consistently in London. He was successful as Dr William Brown in Hamilton Aidé's *Dr Bill* at the Avenue Theatre (February 1890), and in a variety of parts for H. Beerbohm Tree at the Haymarket Theatre between 1890 and 1894. These included D'Aulnay in W. S. Gilbert's *Comedy and Tragedy* (1890), John Christison in H. A. Jones's *The Dancing Girl* (1891)—Julia Emilie *Neilson (1868–1957), daughter of Alexander Ritchie Neilson, of London, whom he married later in that year, was in the cast—and Laertes in *Hamlet*. Early in 1896 he was touring with John Hare in the United States; in June of the same year he was Charles Surface in the revival at the Lyceum by Johnston Forbes-Robertson of Sheridan's *The School for Scandal*.

Don Pedro in *Much Ado about Nothing* (St James's Theatre, 1898), and Squire Thornhill in W. G. Wills's *Olivia* (Lyceum, June 1900) were among the numerous performances that preceded Terry's own venture into management with his wife. This took place at the Haymarket on 30 August 1900; Terry, superbly made up, appeared as Charles the Second in Paul Kester's *Sweet Nell of Old Drury*, one of two parts with which his name became inseparably connected. During the next twenty-seven years Terry and Julia Neilson kept almost entirely to romantic-historical plays. (His great-nephew Sir John Gielgud was to recall that Terry and Neilson 'took the theatre dreadfully seriously. This made them extremely good in rubbish. They performed in very fustian plays' (Gielgud, 12). Much of their time was spent in the provinces, but from 1905 to 1913 they had annual London seasons of six months at the New Theatre. During these they introduced to London such plays as Orczy-Barstow's *The Scarlet Pimpernel* (1905), with Terry in his other famous part of Sir Percy Blakeney; *Dorothy o' the Hall* by Paul Kester and Charles Major (1906); and *Henry of Navarre* (1909) by William Devereux. Terry retired from the stage in 1927.

Terry, who could be a character actor of high skill, is likely to be remembered best for his command of the romantic flourish and for his manliness, gaiety, and unfailing Terry charm, qualities evident in his various performances of Benedick (not seen in central London) and of Charles Surface. Off-stage his kindness and jollity were remarked on, as was his violent temper. Gielgud recalled that 'He used to make [his wife's] life hell at rehearsals and his company was terrified of him' (Gielgud, 18). In 1918, when his portrait as Sir Percy Blakeney, painted by Frank Daniell, was presented to him by the British theatre managers whose theatres he visited (some sixty in number), it was stated that he had never appeared in a variety theatre or acted for the cinema. He died at his home, 4 Primrose Hill Road, St Pancras, London, on 17 April 1933. He had a son, Dennis Neilson-Terry, whose early death in 1932 cut short a promising stage career, and a daughter, Phyllis Neilson-Terry, an actress of distinction. It was unfortunate that Terry never used his powers to the full. He was equipped technically and physically for more testing work than the cape-and-sword parts in which he established his name, but once he was accepted as an actor of the romantic-historical school he did not attempt to escape from the convention. All his productions were set in the same popular mould.

J. C. TREWIN, *rev.* K. D. REYNOLDS

Sources *Ellen Terry's memoirs*, ed. E. Craig and C. St John, rev. edn (1933) [with notes and biographical chapters by eds.] • *The Times* (18 April 1933) • J. Parker, ed., *Who's who in the theatre*, 6th edn (1930) • J. Gielgud, J. Miller, and J. Powell, *An actor and his time*, new edn (1996) • *CGPLA Eng. & Wales* (1903)

Archives Richmond Local Studies Library, London, letters to Douglas Sladen

Likenesses A. Ellis, photograph, 1894, NPG • C. Buchel & Hassall, lithograph, 1916, NPG • F. Daniell, portrait, 1918 (as Sir Percy Blakeney), priv. coll. • Ellis & Walery, postcards, NPG • Histed, photogravure photograph, NPG

Wealth at death £20,521 3s. 9d.: probate, 18 July 1933, *CGPLA Eng. & Wales*

Terry, John (c.1555–1625), Church of England clergyman, was born at Long Sutton, Hampshire. He entered Winchester College in 1572, when his age was given as fourteen, and matriculated from New College, Oxford, on 10 January 1575, when he was said to be aged nineteen. He was elected a fellow in 1576, graduated BA on 12 November 1578, and proceeded MA on 15 June 1582. Having been ordained by John Piers, bishop of Salisbury, he resigned his fellowship on being presented to the living of Stockton, Wiltshire, by Bishop Thomas Cooper of Winchester in 1590. At about this time Terry married Mary White of Stanton St John, sister to John White, the noted puritan rector of Dorchester; the baptism of their eldest son, Stephen, was recorded on 20 August 1592.

Terry was strongly antipathetic to Roman Catholicism. His book *The Triall of Truth* (1600) violently attacked from a

Calvinistic standpoint such 'anti-Christian' doctrines as transubstantiation and justification by works. Special venom was reserved for the reverencing of images, bogus miracles, and the papal supremacy. A second part of this work was published in 1602, and a third in 1625. In his will, dated 25 April 1625, Terry asked for burial in the churchyard of Stockton, as near as possible to the parsonage. He made bequests to five sons, and to the poor of Stockton and of his birthplace, Long Sutton, and he also left money to finance religious instruction for the young people of Stockton. He died on 10 May and was buried three days later, when his funeral sermon was preached by John Antram, the parson of neighbouring Langford. He is commemorated by a memorial in Stockton church, which gives his age at death as seventy. STEPHEN WRIGHT

Sources Wood, *Ath. Oxon.*, new edn, 2.410 · *Reg. Oxf.*, vol. 2/1–3 · T. Miles, 'History of the parish of Stockton', *Wiltshire Archaeological and Natural History Magazine*, 12 (1870), 192–215 · T. F. Kirby, *Winchester scholars: a list of the wardens, fellows, and scholars of … Winchester College* (1888) · *Hist. U. Oxf.* 4: *17th-cent. Oxf.*, 575 · R. C. Hoare, *The history of modern Wiltshire*, 1/2: *Hundred of Heytesbury* (1822) · PRO, PROB 11/146, sig. 73

Wealth at death not large: PRO, PROB 11/146, sig. 73

Terry, Joseph (1793–1850), confectioner, was born on 11 November 1793 at Pocklington, Yorkshire, the son of Thomas Terry, a farmer, and his wife, Elizabeth Dales. After serving an apprenticeship, he opened an apothecary's shop in Walmgate, York. In 1823 he married Harriet, the daughter of William Atkinson, of Leppington Grange, near York; they had five sons and three daughters. Harriet was the sister-in-law of Robert Berry, of the confectioners Bayldon and Berry, in St Helen's Square, York, since 1767. After Berry's death, Joseph joined his son in the euphonious partnership of Terry and Berry. By 1830 he was in sole charge of the business, making cakes and sugar confectionery, marmalade, mushroom ketchup, and medicated lozenges.

During the 1830s Terry established retail agencies in no fewer than seventy-five towns, mostly in northern England and the midlands, but also in London and Luton. In 1836 he helped to form an association in London to protect the consumer against the adulteration of the products of confectioners and lozenge makers. A roly-poly of a man, bald on top, but with plentiful side hair and mutton-chop whiskers, he died at West Huntington, York, on 8 June 1850, survived by his wife.

Joseph Terry's second son, **Sir Joseph Terry** (1828–1898), was born in York on 7 January 1828, and educated at St Peter's School. He then joined the family firm, which in 1851 had 127 employees. After an interregnum when it was run by executors, Joseph and his two younger brothers took control of the firm in 1854. That year he married Frances, the daughter of Dr Joseph Goddard of London; they had three sons before she died in 1866.

Always the dominant partner, Joseph Terry put his abundant energies into expanding the firm. In 1864 he transferred manufacturing to a new site in York, where he erected a steam-powered factory. Two years later there were 400 different items in the price list. In 1871 he married Margaret, the daughter of William Thorpe of Aldborough House, Malton, Yorkshire, with whom he had a son and three daughters.

Their eldest son, Thomas, a partner after 1880, built up exports to Australia and New Zealand. During that decade the firm received a number of exhibition awards for its confectionery. Since at least the 1860s it had been making chocolate products, but its reputation in these lines grew only after Joseph Terry built a separate chocolate factory in 1886. It was incorporated as Joseph Terry & Sons Ltd in 1895, when it had 300 employees.

On York city council from 1860, Terry served as sheriff of York in 1870, and was later lord mayor four times; he was knighted in 1887. He assisted all the main societies and associations in York, from the school of art to the city's cricket club and the asylum. His craggy and bearded face hid a genial and benevolent disposition. He was a freemason, a member of the York Sunday school committee, and president of the York Conservative Association. However, he overexerted himself in a by-election in the city, and died of heart failure at the Royal Station Hotel on 12 January 1898. He was buried at York cemetery on 15 January 1898. He was survived by his wife. T. A. B. CORLEY

Sources *Terry's of York, 1767–1967*, Joseph Terry and Sons (privately printed, London, [1967]) · Burke, *Gen. GB* (1954) · *VCH Yorkshire* · *Yorkshire Herald* (12 Jan 1898) · *The Times* (13 Jan 1898) · *Yorkshire Gazette* (15 Jan 1898) · Boase, *Mod. Eng. biog.* · *Yorkshire Gazette* (23 April 1892) · *Yorkshire Life* (May 1967) · M. Colbeck, *Made in Yorkshire* (1992) · E. Baines, *History, directory, and gazetteer of the county of York*, 2 (1822) · W. White, *History, gazetteer, and directory of the West-Riding of Yorkshire*, 2 vols. (1837–8) · d. cert. · d. cert. [Sir Joseph Terry]

Likenesses miniature, c.1849, repro. in *Terry's of York*, Joseph Terry

Wealth at death £38,959 10s. 2d.—Sir Joseph Terry: probate, 1898

Terry, Sir Joseph (1828–1898). *See under* Terry, Joseph (1793–1850).

Terry, Marion Bessie (1852?–1930), actress, the fifth surviving child of the actors Benjamin Terry (1818–1896) and Sarah Ballard (1819–1892), was born possibly on 13 October 1852, although no record of her birth has been traced.

She was known as Polly within the family. With her favourite sister, Florence, she was educated at Sunnyside, Kingston upon Thames, a genteel boarding-school for girls. Her first stage appearance was as Ophelia in a *Hamlet* supervised by the dramatist Tom Taylor at the Theatre Royal, Manchester, on 21 July 1873. Like all the young Terry girls—Kate, Florence, and Ellen *Terry were also actresses of distinction—she was of a striking appearance, with golden-brown hair and matching eyes, and she immediately exhibited the remarkable family talent for the stage. Marion was swiftly transported to London's West End and Henry Neville's management of the Olympic, to play Isabelle in John Maddison Morton's farce *A Game of Romps* on 4 October 1873. Later in the same management she played the first of her many refined and aristocratic ladies, Lady Valeria in Morton's comedy *All that Glitters is not Gold*. Her second Shakespearian part, at the Olympic, was Hero in *Much Ado about Nothing* in 1874. After a season with Ada

Marion Bessie Terry (1852?–1930), by Barraud, pubd 1891

Swanborough at the Strand she was engaged at the Haymarket and appeared in four of W. S. Gilbert's plays, the most notable being *Engaged* in 1877, in which she created with great success the sweetly tender but thoroughly materialistic Belinda Treherne. In 1879 she joined the Bancroft company at the Prince of Wales's and then the Haymarket, performing Blanche Haye in *Ours* and Bella in *School*, two of the Bancrofts' profitable revivals of T. W. Robertson's comedies.

By this time Marion Terry was an established actress, and continued to play leading roles in contemporary dramas and comedies. In 1884 she replaced her sister Ellen, who was ill, as Viola in *Twelfth Night* at the Lyceum. In 1887 she joined Beerbohm Tree's new company at the Comedy and later the Haymarket, and in 1888 she toured the provinces with Henry Irving in another part of Ellen's, Margaret in *Faust*. In the 1890s she again followed in her sister's footsteps and toured with the Lyceum as Rosamund in Tennyson's *Becket*, as Portia, and again as Margaret. She played in most of the leading managements of the late Victorian and Edwardian periods, distinguishing herself as Mrs Erlynne in Wilde's *Lady Windermere's Fan* at the St James's in 1892, and appearing in significant new plays by Henry Arthur Jones, Henry James, and James Barrie. In 1900 she acted Rosalind and Portia at the Stratford festival, and in 1908 and 1909 toured in America and Canada. By 1923, when she played the Principessa della Cercola in Somerset Maugham's *Our Betters* at the Globe, she had been on the stage for fifty years. It was her last part; worsening arthritis and other ailments forced her from

the theatre. In her final years she lived at 2 Alexandra House, St Mary's Terrace, Paddington; previously she resided for some years at 32 Buckingham Palace Mansions. She died at home on 21 August 1930 of a cerebral haemorrhage. A memorial service was held at St Paul's, Covent Garden, on 26 August, and she was buried at St Albans cemetery on the same day. She never married and had no known liaisons.

Always in the shadow of her older and more famous sister Ellen, Marion Terry was nevertheless at the top of her profession, which she took with the greatest seriousness. Her reputation came from her beauty, poise, rich voice, natural refinement, devotion to hard work, and ability to create a wide range of convincing characters from the high comedy of the modern repertory, a comedy of sets and costumes as elegant as the actress herself. Unlike Ellen, she performed little Shakespeare, and appeared in only a handful of his plays. She possessed all the charm and grace of her sisters, but not Ellen's power of pathos, and she was not a tragic actress. She was sometimes accused of over-intellectuality, but her strength was in the sparkle, charm, and sweet emotional simplicity of good comic writing and character creation. Off the stage she was reserved, believing that the all too public life of the actress should be kept entirely apart from her private life, and she firmly adhered to the accepted moral and social standards of her time.   MICHAEL R. BOOTH

Sources J. Parker, ed., *Who's who in the theatre*, 6th edn (1930) · M. Steen, *A pride of Terrys* (1962) · *Ellen Terry's memoirs*, ed. E. Craig and C. St John (New York, 1932) [with notes and biographical chapters by eds.] · *The Times* (22 Aug 1930) · D. Mullin, ed., *Victorian actors and actresses in review: a dictionary of contemporary views of representative British and American actors and actresses, 1837–1901* (1983) · T. E. Pemberton, *Ellen Terry and her sisters* (1902) · d. cert.
Likenesses Barraud, photograph, pubd 1891, NPG [*see illus.*] · H. Edwin, silhouette drawing, 1895, NPG · photograph, repro. in Steen, *A pride of Terrys*, facing p. 145
Wealth at death £12,136 4s. 5d.: resworn administration, CGPLA Eng. & Wales (1930)

Terry, Sir Richard Runciman (1864–1938), choirmaster and music scholar, was born on 3 January 1864 at Ellington, Northumberland, the elder son of Thomas Terry, a schoolmaster, and his wife, Marion Jane Ballard Runciman, daughter of Walter Runciman, of Dunbar, and sister of Walter, later first Lord Runciman of Shoreston. Educated in Northumberland and St Albans and at Battersea grammar school, where he latterly assisted with teaching, he spent a year in Oxford (1887–8) and two years in Cambridge, where he sang in the choir of King's College under the direction of A. H. Mann, whose techniques of choral training proved an important model.

Terry left Cambridge in 1890 without completing a degree to teach music at Elstow School near Bedford, a post which was followed by an appointment as organist of St John's Cathedral, Antigua, in 1892. He returned from the West Indies late in 1893, and taught briefly in Margate (1894) and at St John's School, Leatherhead (1894–5). This was a time of spiritual crisis, and he was received into the Roman Catholic church in 1896. In that year he went to teach music at Downside School, Somerset, attached to

Sir Richard Runciman Terry (1864–1938), by Philip Hagreen, 1919

the Benedictine monastery there, and set about reviving the school choir. In this he had outstanding success, and the achievements of the choir were widely fêted. Terry's connections with the music antiquarian William Barclay Squire at the British Museum, and new contacts with the historian Edmund Bishop and Edmund Ford, prior (later abbot) of Downside, fired his passion for the music of William Byrd and other pre-Reformation English composers who were then largely unknown. He transcribed quantities of pre-Reformation music from original sources, and the school choir gave the first modern performances of many works, including William Byrd's mass for five voices (1899).

On the strength of his choral work at Downside, Terry was appointed by Cardinal Vaughan to direct the new choir of Westminster Cathedral, taking up the post early in 1902. He married Mary Lee (1879/80–1932), daughter of Jasper Stephenson, a farmer, on 14 September 1909; they had a son and a daughter. By 1909 the choir's repertory was dominated by Renaissance polyphony, including both continental and English works, which he transcribed in hastily written pencil scores that survive in the cathedral choir library. Through its inclusion in the liturgy, music either unknown or dismissed as dry and dull reached a wide public; however, little was recorded for the gramophone. Terry also engaged with contemporary composers, and both Gustav Holst and Ralph Vaughan Williams wrote for the cathedral choir. He compiled the influential *Westminster Hymnal* (1912), where some of his own music appears under the pseudonym Laurence Ampleforth in the first edition, and wrote on Roman Catholic

church music. In 1916 he was appointed editor of the ten-volume series Tudor Church Music, funded by the Carnegie Trust of the United Kingdom. However, in 1922, because of his lack of progress with the project and criticism of his editorial standards, he was ousted by his collaborators, led by Percy C. Buck, and resigned ostensibly on grounds of ill health.

Terry resigned his post at Westminster Cathedral in 1924, and for much of his later life was engaged in adjudicating, editing, writing, and lecturing; his work was especially concerned with sea-shanties, which he collected and studied, influenced by his Northumbrian roots. He was awarded an honorary DMus by Durham University in 1911, and was knighted in 1922. He died in the Princess Beatrice Hospital, Kensington, London, on 18 April 1938. Subsequent scholarship has extended the perspective of the informative but adulatory monograph by Hilda Andrews published in 1948. His reputation rests on his skills as an outstanding choir trainer, and on his revival of Renaissance polyphony, especially Latin liturgical music by English composers, which was one of the pioneering achievements of the early music movement. JOHN HARPER

Sources H. Andrews, *Westminster retrospective: a memoir of Sir Richard Terry* (1948) · T. Day, 'Sir Richard Terry and 16th century polyphony', *Early Music*, 22 (1994), 297–307 · D. Molloy, 'Richard Terry and Westminster Cathedral: the remaking of an English Catholic tradition', MMus diss., University of East Anglia, 1992 · E. Roche, '"Great learning, fine scholarship, impeccable taste": a fiftieth anniversary tribute to Sir Richard Terry (1865–1938)', *Early Music*, 16 (1988), 231–6 · R. Turbet, 'An affair of honour: *Tudor church music*, the ousting of Richard Terry, and a trust vindicated', *Music and Letters*, 76 (1995), 593–600 · R. Turbet, 'A monument to enthusiasm and industry: further light on *Tudor church music*', *Music and Letters*, 81 (2000), 433–7 · T. E. Muir, '"Hark an awful voice is sounding!" Redefining the English Catholic hymn repertory: *The Westminster hymnal* of 1912', MA diss., U. Durham, 2001 · b. cert. · m. cert. · d. cert.

Archives SOUND BL NSA, performance recording

Likenesses P. Hagreen, oils, 1919, unknown collection; copyprint, NPG [*see illus.*] · photograph, 1923, repro. in Andrews, *Westminster retrospective*, frontispiece

Wealth at death £2021 10s. 8d.: probate, 26 July 1938, *CGPLA Eng. & Wales*

Terry-Thomas. *See* Stevens, Thomas Terry Hoar (1911–1990).

Tertis, Lionel (1876–1975), viola player, was born in West Hartlepool on 29 December 1876, the elder son and oldest of three children of Polish immigrants Alexander Tertis, a Jewish minister, and his wife, Phoebe Hermann. Three months later the family moved to Spitalfields, where he went to the board school. His first instrument was the piano and he gave a concert when he was six. At thirteen he left home to earn a living as a pianist, and saved enough to enter in 1892 Trinity College of Music, where he had violin lessons under B. M. Carrodus, continuing the piano under R. W. Lewis for three intermittent terms.

In 1895, after six months at Leipzig Conservatorium, Tertis entered the Royal Academy of Music and studied the violin under Hans Wessely, changing to the viola in 1897. He had to teach himself, fell in love with the instrument, and dedicated his life to raising the neglected viola

Lionel Tertis (1876–1975), by George Herbert Buckingham Holland, 1962

to full recognition as a solo instrument. Two of his friends were so inspired by his playing that they composed works for him: E. York Bowen wrote a concerto and two sonatas, and Benjamin Dale a suite.

In 1897 Tertis joined the Queen's Hall Orchestra under Henry Wood, who promoted him to principal viola. He returned to the Royal Academy of Music as a sub-professor in 1899 and was appointed full professor of the viola in 1901. He left the orchestra in 1904 to concentrate on solo work, and by 1908 had made such a reputation that the Royal Philharmonic Society engaged him to play Bowen's concerto, and in 1911 the orchestrated version of Dale's suite under Artur Nikisch. It was in 1911 too that he gave his first performance of Bach's chaconne, and his monumental interpretation became unsurpassed by any violinist. In 1913 Tertis married Ada Bell (d. 1951), daughter of the Revd Hugh Gawthrop.

During the First World War Tertis became involved with many distinguished Belgian refugee musicians, including the violinist Eugène Ysaÿe, who invited him to play Mozart's sinfonia concertante with him under Henry Wood. He played informal chamber music at Muriel Draper's house in Chelsea with many great artists, including Pablo Casals, Alfred Cortot, Jacques Thibaud, Artur Rubinstein, and Harold Bauer. He later toured America with the Bauer Piano Quartet and played the first performance of Ernest Bloch's suite in Washington.

Meanwhile the era of recording had opened, and, accepted as the greatest exponent of the viola, Tertis made countless recordings between 1920 and 1933, from which a selection was reissued by EMI on long-playing records in 1966 and 1974, and others by the Pearl Company in 1981. One of the highest moments in his career was in 1924 at the Royal Albert Hall, when he performed Mozart's sinfonia concertante with Fritz Kreisler, whom he admired beyond any other violinist. He had triumphed in his task, the viola had come into its own, and none had helped him more than the composers. After Bowen and Dale came Sir Arnold Bax, Ralph Vaughan Williams, Gustav Holst, Sir Arthur Bliss, and Sir William Walton. John Ireland, Sir Edward Elgar, and Frederick Delius all sanctioned his arrangements of their works. He returned to the Royal Academy of Music from 1924 to 1929 to teach the viola and direct the chamber music. During this time he trained the Griller Quartet.

In 1937 fibrositis compelled Tertis to give up playing in public, and he then directed his unabated energies (with the co-operation of the outstanding lutenist Arthur Richardson) to the creation of the ideal viola. The first was completed in 1938, and Richardson made over a hundred himself. By 1965 there were over 600 Tertis models in existence, and in 1973 makers were producing them in seventeen countries.

In 1940 Tertis returned to the concert platform, giving charity concerts and demonstration recitals on the Tertis model viola. He published numerous arrangements for the viola and also wrote an autobiography, *Cinderella No More* (1953), which he revised and enlarged as *My Viola and I* (1974). In 1956 he went to America to demonstrate the new viola, and two years later to South Africa. In 1959 he married the cellist Lillian Florence Margaret Warmington, daughter of Harold Henry Warmington, solicitor. He finally retired in 1964. He succeeded in his mission because of his amazing virtuosity on the large viola, hitherto unused, and because of the magnetism that seemed to flow out of that immensely strong figure, rooted to the platform like an oak tree. One became inevitably drawn into the very heart of the music he was performing.

Tertis was appointed CBE in 1950. He was also FRAM and an honorary fellow of Trinity College, London (1966). He won the Kreisler award of merit (1950), the gold medal of the Royal Philharmonic Society (1964) and of the Worshipful Company of Musicians, and the Eugène Ysaÿe medal and diploma of honour of the Ysaÿe Foundation, Brussels (1968). He died at 42 Marryat Road, his Wimbledon home, on 22 February 1975.   BERNARD SHORE, *rev.*

Sources L. Tertis, *My viola and I* (1974) · *Times Educational Supplement* (14 Dec 1974) · personal knowledge (1986) · *The Times* (25 Feb 1975) · *CGPLA Eng. & Wales* (1975) · W. Forbes, 'Tertis, Lionel', *New Grove*

Archives SOUND BL NSA, performance recordings

Likenesses E. Kapp, drawing, 1933, U. Birm. · G. H. B. Holland, oils, 1962, NPG [*see illus.*] · H. Coster, photographs, NPG

Wealth at death £9741: probate, 20 May 1975, *CGPLA Eng. & Wales*

Tesdale, Thomas (*bap.* 1547, *d.* 1610), benefactor, was baptized on 13 October 1547 at Stanford Dingley, Berkshire, the son of Thomas Tesdale (1507–1556), farmer and trader, and his second wife, Joan (*d.* 1548), daughter of William

Knapp of Harcourt, Berkshire, and widow of Richard Foster of Stanford Dingley. Following his father's death Tesdale was brought up by his uncle Richard Tesdale, a saddler of Abingdon, Berkshire, and was the first scholar admitted to John Roysse's reconstituted free school there in 1563. By the age of twenty he had taken over the malt-making side of the family business and in June 1567 married Maud (1545–1616), the daughter of Reginald Stone of Henley-on-Thames, Oxfordshire, and widow of Edward Little of Abingdon. None of their children survived infancy.

Tesdale was active in the public life of Abingdon and in 1580 became both a principal burgess and master of Christ's Hospital. He was elected mayor in 1581 but declined to serve as he had left the borough on moving to Ludwell Manor near Kidlington, Oxfordshire. Soon after 1586 he moved to Glympton near Woodstock, Oxfordshire, where he rented the manor house and successfully engaged in the production of woad for dyeing, in addition to other agricultural enterprises. He became a wealthy man. He died at Glympton on 13 June 1610 and was buried at Glympton church, where he was commemorated by a black marble tombstone with a brass figure and inscription. Following his widow's death in 1616 a fine alabaster monument to husband and wife was erected close by his original tombstone.

Tesdale's will dated 31 May 1610 made generous provision for his widow and other relatives as well as a number of bequests to Abingdon charities; he also left £5000 to establish places at any Oxford college for six scholars and seven fellows from Abingdon School. He stated a preference for Balliol, but although the six scholars eventually took their places there it was not for long. There were similar connections between other schools and foundations at other Oxford colleges, like that between Reading and St John's College according to Sir Thomas White's bequest. Tesdale's generosity was part of a wider pattern of collegiate expansion during the early seventeenth century. There were protracted delays in finalizing the arrangements and when in 1623 Richard Wightwick, rector of East Illsley, Berkshire, offered to supplement Tesdale's bequest, the Abingdon corporation petitioned James I to allow its transfer from Balliol to found a new college. With the assistance of George Abbot, archbishop of Canterbury, one of Tesdale's three feoffees to uses, and the approval of the chancellor of the university, William Herbert, third earl of Pembroke, whose name it took, Broadgates Hall was refounded as Pembroke College on 29 June 1624.   JOHN PLATT

Sources Fuller, *Worthies* · *Hist. U. Oxf.* 4: 17th-cent. *Oxf.* · D. Macleane, *A history of Pembroke College, Oxford*, OHS, 33 (1897) · *DNB* · H. Savage, *Balliofergus; or, A commentary upon the foundation, founders, and affaires, of Balliol colledge* (1668)
Likenesses double portrait, oil on wood, *c*.1590 (with wife, Maud), Pembroke College, Oxford · English school, oils, *c*.1600, Pembroke College, Oxford · W. Sonmans?, oils, 1670, Bodl. Oxf. · J. Taylor, oils, 1684, Christ's Hospital, Abingdon

Tesimond, Oswald (1563–1636), Jesuit, was born in Northumberland, or possibly York, in 1563 and was educated in York in 'Le Horse Fayre' free school along with Guy Fawkes and John and Christopher Wright. He entered the English College, Rome, on 9 September 1580 but joined the Society of Jesus on 13 April 1584 by leave of the cardinal protector, Moroni. After studying theology at Messina he taught philosophy there and at Palermo. It is not known when he was ordained but he was sent to the Madrid seminary, leaving in November 1597 to go on the English mission. He landed at Gravesend on 9 March 1598. He assisted Edward Oldcorne in Worcestershire and Warwickshire for eight years. On 28 October 1603 he was professed of the four vows.

Tesimond is chiefly remembered for his role in the Gunpowder Plot. It seems certain that Robert Catesby revealed the plot to Tesimond, and Tesimond revealed it to the Jesuit superior, Henry Garnet, under the seal of confession about 23 July 1605 with the object of seeking his advice. Tesimond went to the conspirators on 6 November 1605 at Huddington (Worcestershire), after their flight from London, to give the usual consolations of religion to the conspirators seen as a group of Catholics in dire spiritual need. Thomas Wintour at his execution cleared the Jesuits and particularly Tesimond from any charge of counselling or advising in the plot. Although in his hand, Tesimond's so-called narrative of the Gunpowder Plot—in poor Italian but one of the two most complete accounts (both are at Stonyhurst College)—was probably based on the work in Latin of a secular priest. It was sent to Rome for the better information of the Jesuit authorities.

The proclamation for Tesimond's arrest on 15 January 1606 described him as

> of a reasonable stature, black hair, a brown beard cut close on the cheeks and left broad on the chin, somewhat long-visaged, lean in the face but of a good red complexion, his nose somewhat long and sharp at the end, his hands slender and long fingers, his body slender, his legs of a good proportion, his feet somewhat long and slender. (Morris, 1.144)

Successfully handing off an attempt by a pursuivant to arrest him in London he holed up in papist houses in Essex and Suffolk until he was able to take a small boat to Calais with a cargo of dead pigs, of which he passed as the owner. After some time at St Omer he moved south. Sir Edwin Rich reported his recent arrival in Naples in a letter to James I of 5 October 1610 warning him against accepting a gift of poisoned clothing which Tesimond was supposed to be sending him.

Tesimond became prefect of studies and consultor at Messina from 1617, a post he held for some years, with a spell at Rome from 10 January until 10 December 1621, when he returned to Messina. In 1626 he was in the professed house at Naples as confessor in the church. After holding other offices in the province he died in Naples on 23 August 1636 and was buried there.

FRANCIS EDWARDS

Sources T. M. McCoog, ed., *Monumenta Angliae*, 1: *English and Welsh Jesuits, catalogues, 1555–1629* (1992) · T. M. McCoog, ed., *Monumenta Angliae*, 2: *English and Welsh Jesuits, catalogues, 1630–1640* (1992) · H. Foley, ed., *Records of the English province of the Society of Jesus*, 6 (1880), 144 · H. Foley, ed., *Records of the English province of the Society of*

Jesus, 7/2 (1883), 767 · J. Morris, ed., *The troubles of our Catholic fore-fathers related by themselves*, 1 (1872), 143–83 · F. Edwards, *Guy Fawkes: the real story of the Gunpowder Plot?* (1969) · *The Gunpowder Plot: the narrative of Oswald Tesimond alias Greenway*, ed. and trans. F. Edwards (1973) · M. Nicholls, *Investigating Gunpowder Plot* (1991) · A. Fraser, *The Gunpowder Plot: terror and faith in 1605* (1996) · F. Edwards, 'The Stonyhurst narratives of the Gunpowder Plot', *Journal of the Society of Archivists*, 4 (1970–73), 96–108 · *The condition of Catholics under James I: Father Gerard's narrative of the Gunpowder Plot*, ed. J. Morris (1871) · PRO, SP 14/57/n.92

Archives Stonyhurst College, Lancashire, unfinished autobiography | Archivum Romanum Societatis Iesu, Rome, Fondo Gesuitico, letters to General SJ, 18.X.1603, 651/655 · Archivum Romanum Societatis Iesu, Rome, MSS Anglia and catalogues of provinces of Sicily and Naples, Anglia A series · Stonyhurst College, Lancashire, C. Grene collectanea, MSS, C, H. 176–188, A.iv.4 [narrative]

Tessier, Isabelle Emilie de (b. 1850/51). *See under* Ally Sloper group (act. 1867–1923).

Tessimond, Arthur Seymour John (1902–1962), poet, was born on 23 June 1902 at 32 Devonshire Road, Claughton, Birkenhead, the son of George Arthur Tessimond, a bank inspector, and Amy Evans. As a child he felt misunderstood and starved of parental affection. He was sent to school at Charterhouse, which he entered at the age of fourteen; but he ran away when he was sixteen, only to return home after two weeks. In the following year he went to Liverpool University, where he studied for four years, during which time he became engaged to be married. After leaving university he taught for two years; but, when his engagement broke up, he moved to London and worked in bookshops and at other occupations, before turning to advertising copywriting, with which he stayed for the rest of his working life.

At the beginning of the Second World War Tessimond gave up his home and his job and avoided the authorities, having decided that he would be 'intensely miserable' as a soldier and 'useless and even dangerous to others' (Nicholson, xvii). Later he registered and found that he was medically unfit for military service. In 1945 he inherited £4000 from his father—then a considerable sum: he spent half of it on sessions with four or five psychoanalysts, and the rest on 'nightclub hostesses, striptease girls and models' (ibid., xviii).

Tessimond came to attention as a poet through his work in *New Signatures*, an influential anthology edited by Michael Roberts in 1932. The anthology is seen as heralding the left-wing poetic movement of the 1930s, and its principal contributors were W. H. Auden, C. Day-Lewis, and Stephen Spender from Oxford, and Julian Bell, John Lehmann, and William Empson from Cambridge. Lehmann, who was instrumental in getting the anthology published by the Hogarth Press, for which he worked, had met Tessimond in London. Tessimond also contributed in the following year to the companion and more avowedly political anthology *New Country*, where his own apolitical poetry seemed out of place beside that of Auden, Day-Lewis, and Spender.

None the less, Tessimond's poems in these anthologies were decidedly modern for their day. Michael Roberts saw the contributors to *New Signatures* as offering an 'urban poetry, the poetry of the machine age' (*New Signatures*, 1932, 8); and he remarked that the 'poems of Mr. Tessimond show that a generation has appeared which spontaneously delights in those things which their predecessors ... tried so hard to admire' (ibid., 14). He instances Tessimond's 'La marche des machines', with its subtitle 'Suggested by Deslav's Film'; and Tessimond seemed to share with other contributors a predilection for industrial imagery, as manifested in Stephen Spender's better-known 'The Express'. Yet Tessimond did not include 'La marche des machines' in any of the three collections of his poetry published in his lifetime; and its subject matter was not typical of his work.

Tessimond's early poems owed a good deal to imagism and very little to the left-wing literary movement that dominated the 1930s. The notable orientation of his early work is aesthetic (as a young man he had written to Ezra Pound, asking his advice). Yet Tessimond was not a devoted modernist, and his later poetry became more conventional in conception and more commonsense in outlook. He came closest to the social poetry of the 1930s in poems that capture the feel of everyday experience, as in his much anthologized poems 'The British' and 'England (autumn 1938)'—nostalgic but unillusioned summings-up of a world about to be brought to an end by the Second World War:

> The generous smile of music-halls,
> Bars and bank-holidays and queues;
> The private peace of public foes;
> The truce of pipe and football news.
> ('England (autumn 1938)', *Voices in a Giant City*, 1947)

Tessimond published only three volumes of poetry in his lifetime: *The Walls of Glass* (1934); *Voices in a Giant City* (1947); and *Selection* (1958). After his death three further volumes appeared: *Not Love perhaps* (1978); *Morning Meeting* (1980); and *The Collected Poems* (1985), which included translations from the French poet Jacques Prévert, along with original poems not previously collected.

Voices in a Giant City takes its title from the poems it contains about the ordinary people of London—'The Man in the Bowler Hat', 'The Intellectuals', 'The Prostitute', 'The Smart-boy'; and this could be seen as the subject matter to which Tessimond responded most readily. In keeping with this were his extensive and highly esteemed translations of Prévert, whose delight in the ordinary Tessimond seemed somewhat to share.

An underlying preoccupation of many of Tessimond's poems is the limitations of the self and the sometimes tortured relation of the self to others and particularly to the opposite sex. After the breaking-off of his engagement, Tessimond never married, and he seems to have been involved in many unhappy relationships. Many of his poems are about love and happiness—happiness that cannot be chosen, and love that comes by fate, often bringing unhappiness.

In the latter part of his life, Tessimond was subject to manic depression, and this led to his being given shock treatment, which affected his memory. He was found dead of a cerebral haemorrhage in his flat at 4A Joubert Mansions, Jubilee Place, Chelsea, London, on 15 May 1962. He had been dead for two days. A few days before, he is said to have given away all his money to his latest girl-friend; however, his estate was valued at probate at just over £920. His body was cremated.   A. T. TOLLEY

Sources H. Nicholson, 'Introduction', *The collected poems of A. S. J. Tessimond* (1993) • A. T. Tolley, *The poetry of the thirties* (1975) • J. Lehmann, *The whispering gallery* (1955) • I. Hamilton, ed., *The Oxford companion to twentieth-century poetry in English* (1994) • b. cert. • d. cert.
Wealth at death £920 8s. 2d.: probate, 1962, CGPLA Eng. & Wales

Testwood, Robert (*c.*1490–1543), musician and protestant martyr, is of unknown parentage. For seven years he was educated and trained in music as a boy chorister of the Chapel Royal of Henry VII. Thereafter he made his career in the profession of church music, as both singer and specialist choir-trainer in the elaborate polyphony of the period. He became master of the choristers successively at the collegiate church of St Mary, Warwick, by Michaelmas 1523; at the parish church of St Botolph, Boston, at Whitsun 1524; and early in 1529 at Thomas Wolsey's Cardinal College, Ipswich. There the dean was able to laud him as 'a very synguler cunnynge man', giving such excellent service in training the boys that 'I thynke verely there be no better children within the rea[l]me of England' (PRO, SP 1/53, fol. 197v). At some stage he married, though his wife's name is not known.

Following the dissolution of Ipswich College in 1530 Testwood found short-term employment in London. During his service at Ipswich he may have made the acquaintance of Wolsey's servant Thomas Cromwell, to whom he wrote about 1532 for assistance. By now, however, 'for his knowledge in music he had so great a name' that the choirmen of St George's Chapel, Windsor, sought his engagement (*Acts and Monuments*, 5.465), and thus about 1533 Testwood was admitted a lay clerk of one of the finest liturgical choirs in the kingdom. As well as singing he also composed; no work is now known, though Thomas Morley listed him in 1597 among the composers whose works he had perused.

By this time, and perhaps during his sojourn in London, Testwood had embraced some basic tenets of Lutheranism, so becoming an intriguing example of the penetration of reformist ideals among the middle ranks of church laity. He supported fervently Henry VIII's moves towards the royal supremacy, and in May 1534 made himself useful to Cromwell by taking a leading part in denouncing to the king's council two among the more conservative of the canons of Windsor, report of whose treasonous words led to their imprisonment and deprivation. He expressed his opinions not only in conversation at the clergy dining tables but also in the chapel itself. Not a reticent individual, but rather a 'merry-conceited man' (*Acts and Monuments*, 5.468), he exhorted pilgrims to the shrines of Henry VI and John Schorne to abstain from idolatry, slighted and damaged an image of the Virgin Mary, and scorned and mocked the ceremonies of Relic Sunday.

With the appointment of Simon Heynes as a canon of Windsor in December 1535 Testwood gained an ally among the residentiaries, but found himself increasingly the object of the attention of dangerous adversaries among those more conservative, especially Thomas Magnus, an influential man at court, whose devotional poem in praise of the Virgin Mary exhibited in the chapel Testwood twice plucked down. Further, by loudly altering the words of a duet he was singing in chapel, he denied the capacity of the Virgin to act as redeemer or intercessor between man and God. At a meeting of the Order of the Garter held at Windsor a few days later an exasperated chapter procured Thomas Howard, duke of Norfolk, to summon Testwood and berate and revile him 'as though he would have sent him to hanging by and by' (*Acts and Monuments*, 5.470).

Foxe believed that Testwood by now was known personally to Thomas Cromwell as 'his special friend' (*Acts and Monuments*, 5.467), and that it was through this connection that during the 1530s he was spared from any serious molestation for his evangelical beliefs. After Cromwell's execution in July 1540 such protection was withdrawn, and as a member of the illustriously royal foundation of the College of St George, Windsor, Testwood (like his fellow lay clerk John Marbeck) was more vulnerable than most to the revenge of Cromwell's enemies. In autumn 1540 John London, now canon of Windsor, alluded at his dining table to the evil reputation of the St George's singing men for harbouring heretical opinions, provoking Testwood to a dangerous confrontation. By early 1543 the political climate was right for a conservative strike against sacramentarian heretics, and London and two other canons accumulated a book of accusations against some dozen people of Windsor and delivered it to Stephen Gardiner, bishop of Winchester and a privy councillor. On 15 March 1543 searchers commissioned by Gardiner entered the houses of Testwood and three other suspects, and in each found writings repugnant to the terms of the Act of the Six Articles of 1539. When John London reported to the king, Henry appeared 'astonied and sore angry' at the revelation of such 'abominable heresies' (*LP Henry VIII*, 18/2, no. 546, p. 324).

All four were arrested; disabled by gout, Testwood was held in Windsor, and though apparently released from custody following interrogation was all but confined to his house by his condition. The respite was brief. In May 1543 the King's Book was published, expounding the principles of belief underpinning Henry's Church of England, and the king himself was not averse to procuring a public demonstration of the fate, under law, potentially awaiting any whose temerity extended to an inability to conform. About the middle of July, as easy targets, the Windsor suspects were rearrested; on 21 July, still on crutches, Testwood was committed with them to gaol. They were charged with heresy, and their trial took place in Windsor on 26 July following.

The substance of the indictment against Testwood was his having been both heard and seen to mock the elevation of the sacrament at the moment of consecration, so denying the doctrine of transubstantiation. He did not deny reports that by averting his eyes at the critical moment he declined ever to accord to the consecrated elements their usual reverence. Slight though it was, this sufficed to procure his conviction for heresy, and at Windsor on 28 July 1543 the sentence of death by burning was executed on him and two others. Within days Henry was regretting their execution; his reported sigh of 'Alas, poor innocents' (*Acts and Monuments*, 5.496) was supported by the consequent conviction of London and others for perjury. ROGER BOWERS

Sources *The acts and monuments of John Foxe*, ed. J. Pratt, [new edn], 5 (1877), 464–94 · R. Bowers, 'The cultivation and promotion of music in the household and orbit of Thomas Wolsey', *Cardinal Wolsey: church, state, and art*, ed. S. J. Gunn and P. G. Lindley (1991), 178–218, esp. 198–9, 205 · D. MacCulloch, *Thomas Cranmer: a life* (1996), 297–315 · T. Morley, *A plain and easy introduction to practical music*, ed. R. A. Harman (1952), 321 · *LP Henry VIII*, 5, no. 1764; 7, no. 828; 8, no. 1001; 10, nos. 997, 1119; 18/1, no. 292; 18/2, no. 546 (p. 324) · S. L. Ollard, *Fasti Wyndesorienses: the deans and canons of Windsor* (privately printed, Windsor, 1950), esp. 84, 59 · R. A. Leaver, ed., *The work of John Marbeck* (1978), 176–86, 209–28

Tetley, Henry Greenwood (1851–1921), industrialist, was born in Bradford, Yorkshire, on 20 September 1851, the son of Samuel Tetley, a stuff merchant, and his wife, Catherine. After working for over twenty years at the big textile firm of S. C. Lister & Co. and having risen to be head of the silk department, in 1893 he accepted the offer of a post in Essex with Samuel Courtauld & Co., makers of silk mourning crape. The firm's profits had recently slumped badly, and it had become evident that drastic change was needed in order to modernize production and sales methods as well as to regain profitability. Tetley was brought in to reorganize the manufacturing end of the business. He in turn introduced a new sales manager, Thomas Paul Latham, from Manchester. Both became directors in 1895. These two men, wholly outsiders to a family firm, were to direct its destiny for the next quarter-century, with Tetley as the driving force.

Tetley set about reforming production methods with much gusto. Old machinery was scrapped; the isolation of the company in Essex was broken down as new managers were imported from the textile areas of northern England and as production was started in Lancashire; new lines of coloured fabrics were developed. Losses were turned into profits. But the level of profitability was still only moderate and by 1904 it had become evident that a plateau had been reached. It was then that Tetley succeeded in the first of two striking business gambles. First, he persuaded his fellow directors that Samuel Courtauld & Co. should buy the patent rights to the new viscose process, a British invention for making what was then called artificial silk and later became known as rayon, the first successful man-made fibre. In July 1904 the patents were bought for approximately £25,000. Tetley made it clear to the board that the aim was to find a new source of profits for the company. To that end a new factory was set up, in Coventry. Sundry teething problems, technical and managerial, were overcome, and the profitability that followed was remarkable: a 6 per cent dividend in 1904 had become 30

per cent in 1911 and 50 per cent in 1912. Some part of this bounteous distribution arose from the second of Tetley's business gambles: the purchase in June 1909 for approximately £31,000 of the American rights to the viscose process and the establishment of an American subsidiary which started rayon production inside the US tariff barrier in 1911. The way in which he acquired the American rights represented so shrewd a piece of opportunism as to be not far from sharp practice. He had earlier made an agreement for technical co-operation with the holders of the French viscose rights, and in 1906 an international consortium came into being. In 1908–9 the holder of the American rights sought technical help and entry into the consortium. Tetley was entrusted with the task of negotiating with him on the consortium's behalf. He proceeded to exploit the fact that Courtauld & Co. were far the most successful members of the consortium by simply buying up the rights for his own company, leaving thereby some very aggrieved Frenchmen to be mollified by Latham. The profits being earned by the parent company and its American subsidiary were so big that in 1913 a new company, Courtaulds Ltd, was floated with an issued capital of £2 million. A series of bonus issues raised it to £12 million by 1920. Courtaulds had become the world's largest rayon producer. Tetley was primarily responsible for that achievement, and in 1917 he appropriately became chairman of the company.

By all accounts, Tetley was an aggressive man with a furious temper. He had a relentless energy for business, trampling on obstacles and people in the course of putting his ideas into practice. While he was periodically precipitate and sometimes bombastic, his partnership with Latham provides a good example of the co-operation of opposites. His unswerving devotion to matters of business is apparent in numerous letters; always lucid and straightforward, they bombarded colleagues and subordinates with orders, plans, and demands for information. Tetley was a self-made man whose efforts brought him a fortune, but neither his will nor his correspondence suggest any noteworthy outside interests. The date of his marriage, the identity of his wife, Charlotte, and details of his family life remain unknown. He served as president of the Silk Association but took no part in public affairs. He maintained a house in London, at 17 Avenue Road, Regent's Park, and died at his country residence, Alderbrook, Cranleigh, in Surrey, on 21 August 1921. No *Times* obituary marked his death, but two months later his substantial wealth was noted among the wills recorded in that paper. Apart from some small legacies and bequests to such patriotic or charitable institutions as his trustees might select, the bulk of his fortune went to his wife, Charlotte, and his children. D. C. COLEMAN

Sources D. C. Coleman, *Courtaulds: an economic and social history*, 3 vols. (1969–80) · D. C. Coleman, 'Tetley, Henry Greenwood', *DBB* · *The Times* (11 Oct 1921), 13c
Archives Courtaulds plc, London, company archives · Essex RO, Chelmsford, early records of Courtaulds plc
Likenesses photograph, repro. in Coleman, *Courtaulds*, vol. 2

Wealth at death £1,917,819—gross: *The Times*; will

Tetlow, Norman (1899–1982), mechanical engineer, was born on 7 February 1899 at Oldham, Lancashire, the eldest in the family of three sons and two daughters of James Tetlow, textile manager and owner of the Oldham Velvet Company, and his wife, Emily Goodwin. He was educated at Manchester secondary school, Oldham, and entered Manchester University as an engineering student in 1915. His studies were interrupted by service with the Royal Flying Corps (between 1917 and 1919), and he graduated BSc (Hons) in 1923. Thereafter mechanical engineering became a lifelong career, first in industrial employment and later as a private consultant. In 1926 he married Nell (*d*. 1963), daughter of John Gregson, butcher; they had one son.

In the 1920s there was an established demand for centrifugal pumps for a great variety of purposes, such as irrigation, mine drainage, and boiler feeding. This was subsequently augmented by the growing needs of the petroleum industry in response to the changing pattern of road, sea, and air transport and of power generation. Among the leading manufacturers of such pumps was the long-established firm of Mather and Platt of Manchester (later incorporated within Weir Pumps) whose employ Tetlow entered. He became keenly interested in this specialized branch of engineering and was acknowledged as a leading authority on the design and construction of such pumps.

Tetlow's expertise assumed a new significance during the Second World War, when German air raids made the transport of petrol and fuel oil by road difficult and dangerous. This led to the construction of an extensive pipeline system linking the principal oil ports with major airfields in Britain. Its operation was dependent on the availability of powerful, high-pressure centrifugal pumps, and Tetlow—as estimating and commercial manager of the centrifugal pump department of his firm—became closely involved with the pumps' manufacture and installation.

The system was only the prelude, however, to a project even more critical to the outcome of the war. While planning the invasion of Europe a major problem was how to supply adequate fuel to the vast mechanized forces to be landed in Normandy. In 1943 Lord Louis Mountbatten raised the possibility of laying a submarine pipeline across the channel. This was referred to A. C. *Hartley, chief engineer of the Anglo-Iranian Oil Company, who at first pronounced it impossible. Nevertheless, a successful prototype was laid under the Bristol Channel from Swansea to north Devon and thus was born the highly successful PLUTO project (Pipelines Under the Ocean). The first pipeline—of 3 inch diameter steel pipe welded in 4000 ft lengths and wound on huge drums—from Sandown to Cherbourg was laid in August 1944 and seventeen others were subsequently laid to supply the allied armies as they advanced into Flanders and on to the Rhine. The network eventually extended to more than 1100 miles, and for months delivered more than a million gallons of fuel daily. The success of this project, ultimately the responsibility of Sir Donald Banks, director-general of the petroleum warfare department, depended on many technological factors, but none more vital than the three major pumping stations—with which Tetlow was particularly concerned—at Sandown, Shanklin, and Dungeness.

After the war Tetlow set up as a private consultant, retaining his specialized interest in the pumping and transport of oil. This provided new technological and economic problems as the size of major pipelines increased—up to 36 inches in diameter—and he found a particular demand for his services in connection with large new installations in Iran. Tetlow also retained his interest in the well-being of the engineering profession. He was a member of all three professional bodies and served on the council of the Institution of Mechanical Engineers in 1956, and as chairman of its north-western branch.

His colleagues remembered Tetlow not only as a capable and original engineer but also as a man with a pleasing and gifted personality. His first wife died in 1963, and in 1970 he married Sophia, daughter of Hugh Brooks, director of Oldham Brewery Co., and former wife of the Revd Frederick Tattersall. They met through their common interest in painting, as Tetlow had a strong artistic streak, expressed in sketches and water-colours. Possessed of a keen sense of humour and a ready wit, he also had a great gift for friendship. He spent his last years at Holt, Norfolk, and died in Kelling Hospital, Norfolk, on 13 February 1982.   TREVOR I. WILLIAMS, *rev.*

Sources *The Times* (23 Feb 1982) · archives, Institution of Mechanical Engineers, London · *CGPLA Eng. & Wales* (1982) · *DNB*
Archives Institution of Mechanical Engineers, London
Wealth at death £132,966: probate, 11 May 1982, *CGPLA Eng. & Wales*

Teulon, Samuel Sanders (1812–1873), architect, was born on 2 March 1812 at Hillside, Crooms Hill, Greenwich, the eldest of the four sons of Samuel Teulon (*b*. 1785), cabinet-maker (later a surveyor) of Greenwich, and his wife, Louisa Sanders from Rotherhithe. His father's family was of Huguenot origin and he retained an allegiance to this French connection. In 1835 Teulon married Harriet Bayne (*d*. 1866), with whom he had six sons (two died in infancy and the eldest became principal of Chichester Theological College) and four daughters.

Teulon attended the Royal Academy Schools and was then articled to the architects George Legg and George Porter, before starting his own practice in London in 1838. He spent much of 1841–2 travelling and sketching on the continent with, among others, Ewan Christian and Horace Jones, both later architects of distinction.

Teulon developed a vigorous and idiosyncratic Gothic style: indeed he has come to be regarded as the chief among the rogue architects of the mid-Victorian Gothic revival (cf. H. R. Goodhart Rendel, *Journal of the Royal Institute of British Architects*, 56, 1949, 251). He obtained few commissions for public buildings because, after his early success, he declined to enter the competitions, but he acquired connections with the landed and wealthy,

Samuel Sanders Teulon (1812–1873), by unknown photographer, 1872

Archives Essex RO, Colchester, reports, accounts, and plans relating to Great Birch rectory · priv. coll., drawings · RIBA, nomination papers

Likenesses photograph, 1872, RIBA BAL [see illus.] · photograph, RIBA BAL

Wealth at death under £30,000: probate, 1873, CGPLA Eng. & Wales

Teviot. For this title name see Rutherford, Andrew, earl of Teviot (d. 1664); Livingstone, Thomas, Viscount Teviot (c.1651–1711); Kerr, Charles Iain, first Baron Teviot (1874–1968).

Tew, Thomas (d. **1695**), pirate, was a sea-captain from a respectable Rhode Island family when, in 1692, he bought an interest in the sloop *Amity*, which was being fitted out in Bermuda as an 8-gun privateer. In December 1692 he sailed in command of the *Amity*, in company with George Dew in another sloop, with a commission from Isaac Richier, the lieutenant-governor of Bermuda, to sail to the Gambia and attack the French factory at Goree, England being at war with France. However, a storm separated the *Amity* from her consort in mid-Atlantic, and, with almost certain premeditation, Tew decided to turn pirate, round the Cape, and head for the Indian Ocean. In the strait of Bab al-Mandab at the mouth of the Red Sea, the *Amity* took an Arab ship laden with so much treasure that when it was divided up at St Mary's Island off Madagascar, where they arrived on 19 October 1693, each of Tew's sixty men received £1200.

The *Amity* was careened and reprovisioned at St Mary's, and then, on 23 December, Tew and most of his men set sail for home, arriving at Rhode Island in April 1694 with '£100,000 in gold and silver and a good parcel of Elephants' teeth, bought up by the merchants of Boston' (Pringle, 137). Out of this immense booty the backers of the venture received about £45,000, Tew's share amounting to £8000.

Tew spent summer 1694 at Newport, while the *Amity* was refitted; then he bought for £300 a new privateering commission from Colonel Benjamin Fletcher, the governor of New York, and sailed again in November. In June 1695 the *Amity* joined Captain Avery's pirate fleet in the Red Sea, where some time towards the end of that year, Tew was killed by a shot from the *Fateh Mohammed* as he attempted to take her.

Tew's activities were condoned by Governor Fletcher, who profited by them, and whose parties were attended by Tew's wife and two daughters in rich silks and jewels looted from the East. Indeed Fletcher, who found Tew 'a man of courage and activity … a very pleasant man' (Jameson, 167), once 'openly caressed [the pirate] and presented him with a gold watch to encourage him to make New York his port of return' (Pringle, 150). Tew's pirate flag featured a hand and sword.   RANDOLPH COCK

including the royal family, and as a result designed several spectacular country houses. Clients valued his highly individual command of the Gothic language and came to respect him as a reliable man of business. Among the most notable of his houses were: Shadwell, Norfolk (1856–60), for Lady Buxton; Tortworth Court, Gloucestershire (1849–53), built for the second earl of Ducie; Bestwood Park, Nottinghamshire (1862–4), for the tenth duke of St Albans; and Elvetham Hall, Hampshire (1859–62), for Lord Calthorpe. All these are in the most energetic high Victorian style, with a rich multiplicity of towers and gables, and a studiously observed asymmetry. His many churches are equally eclectic, with frequent use of the patterned brickwork and polychromy more often associated with William Butterfield. The most striking surviving examples are: at Burringham, Lincolnshire (1856–7); his vigorous recasting of St Mary's, Ealing (1863–74); Huntley, Gloucestershire (1861–3), with clear echoes of Burges at Cardiff Castle; Hunstanworth, co. Durham (1862–3); Leckhampsted, Berkshire (1859–60); St Mark's, Silvertown, in London's docklands (1862); St Thomas's, Wells (1856–7); as well as Woodchester, Gloucestershire (1862–3); and his two essays in neo-Romanesque at Hawkley, Hampshire (1865), and Oare, Wiltshire (1857–8). His masterpiece was St Stephen's, Rosslyn Hill, Hampstead (1869–75), finished after Teulon's death by Ewan Christian. Teulon's most prominently sited non-ecclesiastical work is the Buxton memorial fountain (1861–6) in Victoria Tower Gardens, Westminster, a richly decorated structure with Gothic arches and a much repaired spire of iron and enamel.

Teulon died on 2 May 1873 in his house, Tensleys, The Green, Hampstead, and was buried under a simple tomb in Highgate cemetery. He left a substantial estate of nearly £30,000.   JEFFREY RICHARDS, rev. M. J. SAUNDERS

Sources M. J. Saunders, 'Samuel Sanders Teulon, 1812–1873: a pragmatic rogue', *The architectural outsiders*, ed. R. Brown (1985), 132–52 · M. J. Saunders, *The churches of S. S. Teulon* (1982) · *The Ecclesiologist* · *The Builder* · two sketchbooks, RIBA BAL · Principal Registry of the Family Division, London, 1872 (2) 387 · Bedfordshire County RO, Russell MSS, R4/4140 etc. · *CGPLA Eng. & Wales* (1873) · *Dir. Brit. archs.* · d. cert. · private information (2004)

Sources D. Defoe, *A general history of the pyrates*, ed. M. Schonhorn (1972) · P. Pringle, *Jolly Roger: the story of the great age of piracy* (1953) · J. Franklin Jameson, ed., *Privateering and piracy in the colonial period: illustrative documents* (1923) · J. Rogoziński, *The Wordsworth dictionary of pirates* (1997) · D. Cordingly, *Life among the pirates* (1995) · P. Gosse, *The pirate's who's who* (1924) · D. Marley, *Pirates and privateers of the Americas* (1994)

Te Wherowhero, Potatau (*c.*1775–1860), Maori king and war leader, was born in the late eighteenth century, possibly between 1770 and 1780, and probably in central Waikato in the North Island of New Zealand. He was the eldest son of the Waikato war leader and *ariki* ('personage of supreme rank') Te Rauangaanga (*fl.* 1790–1820) of Ngati Mahuta, a Tainui tribe (that is, descended from the crew of the founding canoe, Tainui), and his wife, Parengaope, a woman of very high rank of Ngati Koura, also a Tainui descent group. Te Wherowhero was known by another name in youth, now forgotten, and took the name Te Wherowhero early in the nineteenth century, possibly to commemorate one of the first red blankets (used as cloaks) obtained from Europeans, or in another version, to commemorate a red *kaka* feather cloak he wore at the time of one of his military victories. Later still, he took the additional name Potatau. Through his senior lines of descent from the chiefs and commanders of many founding canoes, especially Tainui and Te Arawa, Te Wherowhero's rank was virtually supreme among Maori; only the Te Heuheu family of Taupo were his rivals in terms of seniority of lineage. Because of his *ariki* status, great care was taken in his education. He was trained in the Te Papa-o-Rotu *whare wananga* ('school of learning') at Whatawhata as a *tohunga* ('priest, sage'), learning the esoteric lore of his people taught only to a privileged few, and was also trained as a warrior. He was to become a superb duellist, using traditional weapons. He had at least four wives, and three surviving children.

As a young man Te Wherowhero gradually took over from his father the role of leader of his people in war, especially against the Kawhia tribe, Ngati Toa, and their Ngati Koata and Ngati Rarua allies. He assisted to drive Ngati Toa out of Kawhia about 1820, and is said to have instigated the killing of Te Rauparaha's wife, Marore. He followed the Kawhia tribes to Taranaki; his side was defeated in a disastrous battle on the plain of Motunui because they had ignored his orders and attacked rashly; he himself fought and won a famous series of duels using only a digging tool. He then took his forces to Pukerangiora *pa* ('fortification') in Taranaki and successfully rescued an expedition of allies of Waikato which had been under siege in the pa. Back in Waikato, he led the resistance to the attacks of the northern, musket-armed Nga Puhi people at Matakitaki in 1822; the guns produced panic and the Waikato side was disastrously defeated, but Te Wherowhero led the defence, at one stage fighting alone. After these wars he lived at Orongokoekoea in the upper Mokau district of Ngati Maniapoto, where his senior wife gave birth to his eventual heir, Matutaera, later known as Tawhiao. Te Wherowhero led in many other battles in Hauraki and Whangarei during the warrent period before 1831, and led a large force to Taranaki to obtain *utu* ('payment') for his previous defeat, taking the Pukerangiora *pa* with great loss. It is said that Te Wherowhero killed 150 prisoners with his own hand before fatigue forced him to stop. Subsequently, he failed to take the Ngamotu *pa* near the future site of New Plymouth, but led

Potatau Te Wherowhero (*c.*1775–1860), by George French Angas, pubd 1847

further expeditions against Taranaki in the mid-1830s, finally making peace in 1836. His last 'military' exploit was to escort with a large force the people of Tamaki, Ngati Whatua, and others, to their homes in the late 1830s (they had taken refuge from Nga Puhi attacks in the upper Waikato region), guaranteeing their safety by remaining for several years at Te Awhitu.

In 1840 Te Wherowhero refused to sign the treaty of Waitangi, probably on the grounds that its hurried and unceremonious presentation to him compromised his *mana* ('authority and prestige'), but he was a friend to the nascent European settlement at Auckland and to successive governors. The huge feast he gave to Auckland Maori at Remuera in 1844, and his message to Hone Heke's northern forces that he would stand by the governor if they attacked Auckland, made Governor Robert FitzRoy acutely aware that the small European community was reliant on his goodwill. Governor George Grey also cultivated Te Wherowhero's friendship and requested him to move to Mangere, closer to Auckland; he also had a cottage at Pukekawa, on the site of the future Auckland domain, and another home at Kohimarama, later a suburb of Auckland. In 1849 Te Wherowhero signed an agreement to provide Auckland with military protection.

In 1845 the chief Pirikawau, friend and functionary of George Grey, visited England, and afterwards reported that the governor had told Queen Victoria that Te Wherowhero, the chief of Waikato, was the most powerful of all the Maori chiefs. This was not strictly true. Te Wherowhero was not the chief of the whole of Waikato, nor was he the only important contemporary war leader of that district. He was the ruling chief of his own power-ful tribe or *hapu*, Ngati Mahuta, and because of his *ariki* sta-tus was greatly reverenced in a number of others, espe-cially Ngati Apakura, Ngati Hinetu, and Ngati Maniapoto. But when Maori began to be interested in the idea of set-ting up a king, Te Wherowhero was the man they eventu-ally turned to. Not only did his lineage provide him with senior kin links to all the most important canoe areas and tribes, but his people's lands were fertile and rich in abun-dant resources, enabling him to carry out without strain the inevitable duties of hospitality the position would require. He himself was reluctant. By then approaching, if not in his eighties, he shrank from assuming the burden of resisting the pressure of the colonial government to acquire his people's most fertile lands, by taking those people and their lands under his authority. He feared, rightly, that European suspicion of the title 'Maori king' would cause an irreparable breach, since officials were inclined to see the move as potentially treasonable. (He himself saw no clash in having Queen Victoria as sover-eign, with the governor to rule the colonists and himself as king for the Maori people.) Nevertheless, when no less than seven great meetings had confirmed his election, he accepted, and was ritually 'crowned' with a Bible and anointed as king on 2 May 1859 at Ngaruawahia by Wir-emu Tamihana Tarapipipi Te Waharoa of Ngati Haua, one of the most important leaders of the King movement. He was known as King Potatau Te Wherowhero, a form of address that became a title handed on to his successors.

Potatau Te Wherowhero was Maori king for just over a year. His main activity in that time was to oppose the more extreme element among his supporters, who attempted to prevent government officials from functioning within the king's hegemony. As king he had returned to the Wai-kato to live, but he threatened to return to Mangere, Auck-land, unless his supporters desisted from hindering the government mail from passing up and down the Waipa River. He died at Ngaruawahia on 25 June 1860; his *tangi-hanga* ('funeral ceremonies'), delayed to allow the many who wished to pay him respects to assemble, took place on 5 July, when his son was anointed as his successor. Like many great chiefly contemporaries, his body was buried secretly, at night.

Te Wherowhero was remarkable for his rank, his prow-ess as a war leader and duellist in troubled times, but his main early importance lies in his protection of the nas-cent colony. Later, his reluctant acceptance of the role of first Maori king saw the beginning of one of the most remarkable movements for unification and self-determination among the Maori people.

ANGELA BALLARA

Sources *Te Kingitanga: the people of the Maori King movement* (AUP, 1996) · P. Te H. Jones, *King Potatau* (Wellington, 1960) · P. Te H. Jones, 'Maori kings', *The Maori people in the nineteen-sixties*, ed. E. Schwimmer (Auckland, 1968) · J. E. Gorst, *The Maori king* (1864) · B. Y. Ashwell, *Letters to the Church Missionary Society*, Auckland Insti-tute and Museum [typescript] · E. Ramsden, letters received from 'Princess' Te Puea Herangi and Alex McKay, NL NZ, Turnbull L., Micro MS 534 · *Te Hokioi* [Maori language newspaper] · *Te Paki o Matariki* [Maori language newspaper]

Likenesses G. F. Angas, engraving, pubd 1847, NL NZ, Turnbull L. [*see illus.*] · G. F. Angas, oils?, repro. in *The New Zealanders illustrated, or, Savage life and sources*

Tewkesbury, Alan of (*b*. before 1150, *d*. 1202), abbot of Tewkesbury and compiler of a manuscript collection, was successively canon of Benevento (1171?–1174); monk (1174–9), then prior (6 August 1179 – early June 1186) of the Benedictine monastery of Christ Church, Canterbury; and abbot (from June 1186) of the Benedictine abbey of Tewkesbury in Gloucestershire, from which office he takes his name. He is known principally for the important collection of letters relating to the Becket controversy which he assembled as a monument to the new martyr of Canterbury. Of his origins very little is certainly known. Gervase of Canterbury described him as English; Marga-ret Harris has suggested that he may have been an orphan taken into the care of Christ Church, Canterbury, during the great famine of 1149—which would make him almost certainly a Kentish man, and explain his later return to the monastery. Contemporaries called him master, testi-fying to education in the schools (perhaps in Paris), but his career before entry into the novitiate at Canterbury in 1174 has not been traced, except for Gervase's report that he had been a canon in the cathedral church of Benevento in southern Italy, by which time he must already have been at least twenty-one. Stubbs's speculation that he had been given that prebend by Archbishop Lombard (1171–9), who had served Archbishop Thomas of Canterbury at an earlier stage in his career (1163–8), has not been con-firmed, but it remains a possibility, although no point of contact has been established between them (Stubbs, lviii, n.1).

Alan's character and experience must have commended him to the monks at Canterbury, however, since he was the unanimous choice of the community for the office of prior on 6 August 1179, after only five years' monastic experience (against the wishes of Archbishop Richard of Canterbury), and his steadfast defence of the monastery's rights in opposition to Archbishop Baldwin led to his 'exile' to Tewkesbury in 1186 (abbatial benediction, 15 June), where he remained as abbot until his death on either 6 or 7 May 1202. He was buried in the ambulatory of the abbey church. Although a small collection of letters and sermons survives from his hand, Alan is principally renowned for his successful opposition to Archbishop Baldwin's proposal to found a college of secular canons in honour of saints Stephen and Thomas of Canterbury at Hackington and for the compilation of the largest collec-tion of letters relating to the cause of St Thomas. Known as 'Prior Alan's collection', it was compiled at Canterbury between *c*.1174–6 and 1180–84 from earlier propagandist collections, John of Salisbury's second letter collection, and the disorderly residue from Becket's exiled chancery. In its most extensive form it comprised 598 items (BL, Cot-ton MS Claudius B.ii), arranged in chronological order and prefaced by John of Salisbury's life of St Thomas, supple-mented by Alan's own prologue and 'additions'.

For the greater part of his life, therefore, Alan was an exemplary monastic superior, defending monastic rights at Canterbury, Coventry (he wrote a letter to Pope Clement III supporting the monks in their quarrel with Bishop Hugh), and Tewkesbury, and opposing slackness; and in his later years he became increasingly engaged in public affairs both ecclesiastical and secular, acting as papal judge-delegate from time to time, securing the favour of Prince John, both as earl of Gloucester and as king, and serving as itinerant justice in midland and western counties in the first year of John's reign (1199–1200). Despite the fragmentary character of the surviving evidence (the annals of Tewkesbury, for example, contains only two references to him, his election and his death, the former misdated by one year), he emerges as a man of courage and conviction. Gervase of Canterbury gives a graphic account of his confrontation with Henry II over the election of a new archbishop of Canterbury in 1184; and his letters reveal both his continuing commitment to his mother house of Canterbury and his growing disenchantment with the community which squandered (as he saw it) the advantages won by Becket's martyrdom.

A. J. Duggan

Sources M. A. Harris, 'Alan of Tewkesbury and his letters, I–II', *Studia Monastica*, 18 (1976), 77–108, 299–351 · Alan of Tewkesbury, 'Epistolae', *Patrologia Latina*, 190 (1854), 1477–88 · *Materials for the history of Thomas Becket, archbishop of Canterbury*, 2, ed. J. C. Robertson, Rolls Series, 67 (1876), xliii–xliv, 299–301, 323–52 · A. Duggan, *Thomas Becket: a textual history of his letters* (1980), 85–145 · *The correspondence of Thomas Becket*, ed. and trans. A. J. Duggan, 2 vols., OMT (2000), 1.lxxx–ci [for MS sources] · M. Gullick, 'A twelfth-century manuscript of the letters of Thomas Becket', *English Manuscript Studies, 1100–1700*, 2 (1990), 1–31 · D. Knowles, C. N. L. Brooke, and V. C. M. London, eds., *The heads of religious houses, England and Wales*, 1: 940–1216 (1972), 34, 73 · *The historical works of Gervase of Canterbury*, ed. W. Stubbs, 2 vols., Rolls Series, 73 (1879–80), 1.293, 306, 310–31 *passim*, 335; 2.391 · *Ann. mon.*, 1.53–4, 56; 2.244; 4.391 · W. D. Macray, ed., *Chronicon abbatiae de Evesham, ad annum 1418*, Rolls Series, 29 (1863), 103 · W. Stubbs, ed., *Chronicles and memorials of the reign of Richard I*, 2: *Epistolae Cantuarienses*, Rolls Series, 38 (1865), 331, 356–7, 374 · *Chronica magistri Rogeri de Hovedene*, ed. W. Stubbs, 4, Rolls Series, 51 (1871), 126 · D. Royce, ed., *Landboc, sive, Registrum monasterii beatae Mariae virginis et sancti Cenhelmi de Winchelcumba*, 2 (1903), 301 · F. Barlow, *Thomas Becket* (1986), 7
Archives BL, Cotton MS Claudius B.ii

Tewson, Sir (Harold) Vincent (1898–1981), trade unionist, was born at Bradford, Yorkshire, on 4 February 1898, the youngest in the family of three sons and two daughters of Edward Tewson, a nursery gardener, and his wife, Harriet Watts. He left elementary school at fourteen and became an office boy at the headquarters of the Amalgamated Society of Dyers (later the Dyers', Bleachers', and Textile Workers Union, and eventually part of the Transport and General Workers Union). In 1916 he joined the army as a private in the West Yorkshire regiment and served on the western front. His courage and tenacity soon brought him promotion, and within a year he had achieved the commissioned rank of lieutenant, and in 1917 he won the MC. He ended his military career as a brigade staff officer and left the army with many commendations. He never lost his regard for the armed forces and throughout his life he carried a distinctive military bearing, not least in his straight-back walking style.

Sir (Harold) Vincent Tewson (1898–1981), by Lafayette, 1932

On demobilization after the First World War Tewson returned to trade union life as a clerical assistant of the Dyers' Union, then a strong and influential organization in the textile industry. His special field was in the area of piece-work price lists and in negotiations dealing with piece-rate wages. He gained a reputation for meticulous detail—perhaps another reflection of his military experience—and in assisting the union's membership during a period of slump and great depression in the textile trades.

It was the experience in those years of depression and mass unemployment which politicized Tewson, and he soon joined the radically inclined Independent Labour Party and became the youngest member of Bradford city council at the age of twenty-five. In 1926, following the general strike of that year, he left Yorkshire for London to join the full-time staff of the TUC as secretary of its newly formed organization department. He quickly established a close friendship with another newcomer to the TUC, Walter Citrine, and the two men worked together in a strong partnership. In 1929 he married a fellow employee of the TUC, Florence Elizabeth, the daughter of William Francis Moss, a printer. His wife became a JP and they had two adopted sons.

In 1931 Tewson was appointed assistant general secretary to Citrine and he remained a close, industrious, and effective lieutenant until, finally, he succeeded Citrine as TUC general secretary in 1946. He was knighted in 1950. Tewson remained general secretary through to 1960. It was then that he faced his greatest challenge—working with the newly elected government of Clement Attlee after Labour's landslide victory of 1945. It was a unique experience for the TUC leadership, since they had never before worked with a majority Labour administration. Tewson, very much the 'insider', had no experience of working life outside the trade union bureaucracy. He lacked Citrine's drive, imagination, and acute sense of political power-broking. He was hesitant, over-cautious, and suspicious of change. The Attlee government was not at ease with the TUC general secretary, nor he with them. This left him exposed to the powerful influences of those members of the TUC general council whose sense of political power-dealing was well developed, especially Arthur Deakin of the Transport Workers, Tom Williamson of the General and Muncipal Workers Union, and the miners' leader, Sir William Lawther. Between them they dominated the TUC, and its general secretary, in the decade after the Second World War.

Even so Tewson played an important role in the crucial post-war period, when the Attlee government asked the trade unions to operate a policy of voluntary pay restraint. It was a period of considerable social and industrial tension, as Britain tried to settle into a post-war ambience of economic planning, extensive nationalization of key industries, rehousing, and general post-war reconstruction. Food and clothing rationing was still in existence when the government asked the unions to operate pay restraint. The union leadership was itself unsure of how to exercise such a policy and the TUC was called on to play a vital role in leadership. Tewson applied himself with great dedication to this task. And in later years, even after his retirement, he claimed this period as his most significant achievement as TUC general secretary. The pay policy was a voluntary operation without legislative backing. It operated from 1948 to 1950, and at the same time the unions asked the government to produce a matching policy on profits and prices. Eventually the policy broke down, partly because of the economic effects of the Korean War, when prices rose rapidly. The TUC tried to modify its policy, but at the 1950 September congress the wage restraint policy was defeated by a narrow majority.

Tewson then turned his attention to the development of trade union affairs on the international scene. He played a major role in establishing the Anglo-American and the British productivity councils and was a member of the Economic Planning Board from 1947 to 1960. The Anglo-American productivity councils were especially influential in helping British industry to adapt to more effective management systems in the 1950s. Along with these activities Tewson played a strong role in helping to establish the International Confederation of Free Trade Unions (ICFTU), with its headquarters in Brussels. At the end of the war the Americans, French, British, and Soviets agreed to set up a new trade union international, the World Federation of Trade Unions (WFTU), but this soon broke up in fierce political argument, notably between the Americans and Russians. Tewson himself became highly critical of the functioning and methods of the WFTU. He deprecated the 'public polemics which had been used by members of the Bureau to express their views' (V. L. Allen, *Trade Union Leadership*, 1957, 299). But the general thrust of his criticisms reflected the view, already well-formed by many Western trade union leaders, that the WFTU was essentially a communist, indeed a Soviet, front organization. He criticized the way the WFTU bureaucracy spent money, particularly on delegations to countries with dubious credentials, as well as the style and content of WFTU publications, in which the bias in favour of communist countries and organizations had become all too apparent. It was scarcely a surprise to anyone when the organization broke up and the non-communist group began preparations to form the ICFTU, Tewson serving as secretary of a commission which brought the new organization into being in 1949.

Tewson was president of the ICFTU from 1953 to 1955 and remained an active figure in the leadership until his retirement in 1960. Yet they were never easy years. He frequently found himself in conflict with some of the American trade union leaders, especially George Meany, president of the American equivalent to the TUC. Meany was anxious to push the anti-communist offensive on the trade union front with a vigour, and sometimes a crudity, that upset Tewson. He also objected to American tactics in trying, single-handed, to set up trade union groups in British colonies. The result, often, was severe tension between the two men, Meany regarding Tewson as too cautious and old-fashioned. It was an issue that was never wholly resolved. Tewson retained his interest in international affairs after his retirement and in 1961 he was appointed to sit on the Zanzibar commission of inquiry. He was also a part-time member of the London Electricity Board from 1960 to 1968 and of the Independent Television Authority from 1964 to 1969.

Tewson was not an innovator; his cautious, over-careful temperament curbed that. But he brought stability and predictability to the TUC at a time when that institution was undergoing enormous new pressures in post-war Britain. His manner, style, dress, and even speech was in the same conservative, unadventurous, and moderate mode. His philosophy was exemplified in an interview for his local paper (*Barnet Press*, 10 Feb 1978) a few years before his death. He told the story of his first strike experience, in the textile industry before the First World War. It lasted six weeks, he explained; 'we wanted another 18 pence and we settled for a bob [a shilling]. That's what it's always been about—patience, compromise, moderation'. Tewson died in Letchworth, Hertfordshire, on 1 May 1981.

GEOFFREY GOODMAN

Sources *The Times* (2 May 1981) · *Free Labour World* (1981) · *Barnet Press* (10 Feb 1978) · personal knowledge (2004) · TUC and ICFTU reports, Trade Union Congress Library · *DNB*
Likenesses Lafayette, photograph, 1932, NPG [*see illus.*] · P. Cade, group portrait, photograph, Hult. Arch.
Wealth at death £1859: probate, 5 Aug 1981, *CGPLA Eng. & Wales*

Tey, Josephine. See MacKintosh, Elizabeth (1896–1952).

Teyoninhokarawen. See Norton, John (1770–1831?).

Teyte, Dame **Margaret** [Maggie] (1888–1976), singer, was born on 17 April 1888 at Wolverhampton, the eighth of nine children of Jacob James Tate and his second wife, Maria Doughty. The composer and songwriter James William *Tate was her brother. There were also two sons of a previous marriage. Jacob Tate was a prosperous wine merchant and a keen amateur musician who had once journeyed to Leipzig in order to take piano lessons with Theodor Leschetizky. Maria Tate was also musical, and sang. When the family moved to London in 1898 Maggie began to have some music lessons, at first in piano and theory at the Royal College of Music. She was invited to sing, as an amateur, at a church charity concert in 1903, and aroused the interest of her accompanist, a young man of social as well as musical background named Walter Rubens, the brother of Paul Rubens who composed musical comedies. She was in effect adopted by the Rubens family, who divined her promise and introduced her to Lady Ripon, the musical hostess and friend of Jean De Reszke.

In 1904 Maggie was sent by her English patrons to study with De Reszke in Paris for two years, and at once impressed him with what seems to have been from the first a pure timbre and easy emission of tone. She quickly absorbed both the vocal training of De Reszke and the general artistic atmosphere of Paris. In 1906, when not yet eighteen, she made her first public appearances in a Mozart festival organized by Reynaldo Hahn and Lilli Lehmann, at which she sang in scenes from *Le nozze di Figaro* (as Cherubino) and *Don Giovanni* (as Zerlina), still using the original spelling of her surname, which she was soon to change in order to preserve its correct pronunciation in France. On 7 February 1907 she made her stage début at Monte Carlo as Tyrcis in Offenbach's *Myriame et Daphné* (a new version of the first act of *Les bergers*), as Zerlina, and as Rosa in Saint-Saëns's *Le timbre d'argent*. On her twentieth birthday she made her first appearance at the Paris Opéra-Comique, as Glycère in *Circé* by the brothers Hillemacher, and appeared there also in other roles, including that of Mignon.

Teyte's chance came when she was chosen to succeed Mary Garden in the role of Mélisande in Debussy's *Pelléas et Mélisande*, and coached for the part by the composer himself (her first performance was on 13 June 1908). Debussy also accompanied her, both at the piano and as conductor, in performances of his own songs, and from that time French song in general, and the music of Debussy in particular, became the centre of her artistic career, at least in its more serious aspect. On her return to England in 1910 she sang Mélisande and her Mozart roles (adding to them Blonde in *Die Entführung aus dem Serail*), besides such leading parts as Madam Butterfly, Gounod's Marguerite (in *Faust*), and Offenbach's Antonia (in *The Tales of Hoffmann*), with the Beecham Opera Company and later with its successor, the British National Opera Company (BNOC), both at Covent Garden and on provincial tours.

For three consecutive seasons (1911–14) Maggie Teyte sang with the Chicago Opera Company, both in Chicago itself and on tour in Philadelphia and New York; among her parts with this company was the title role in Massenet's *Cendrillon*, which was the sole occasion that she sang in the same production as Mary Garden, the Prince Charming. At Boston, where she was a member of the Opera Company from 1914 to 1917, her Mimi and Nedda were specially admired; but America was not to see her Mélisande until as late as 1948. In England, after the First World War, she continued her appearances as Mimi, Butterfly, Hansel, and the Princess in the BNOC's first performances of *The Perfect Fool*, a satirical opera by Gustav Holst, but for a while she also made frequent sallies into operetta and musical comedy (*Monsieur Beaucaire*, *A Little Dutch Girl*, *Tantivy Towers*), and was at one time in some danger of being regarded as a lightweight artist.

It was therefore fortunate that in the mid-thirties Teyte's career should have received a fresh impetus from an unexpected source. Joe Brogan, a great admirer of her art who was the founder of the Gramophone Shop in New York, had been campaigning for some authentic Debussy recordings from her, and in 1936 succeeded in persuading HMV to make an album. Maggie Teyte, accompanied by Alfred Cortot, made a recording that became famous. Thereafter her status as an interpreter of French song was indisputable, and during the next decade she made many further records of Fauré, Hahn, and other French composers with Gerald Moore as accompanist, as well as a few orchestrally accompanied songs by Berlioz, Duparc, and Ravel. Her London and New York recitals became notable events, and in 1948 her Mélisande was at last seen in America, at the New York City Center, some forty years after her first appearance in the part. In 1951 she sang Belinda in *Dido and Aeneas* by Purcell, to the Dido of Kirsten Flagstad, at the Mermaid Theatre (then located in Acacia Road, St John's Wood), and on 17 April 1955 (her sixty-seventh birthday) she gave what proved to be her farewell concert at the Royal Festival Hall, still in remarkably good voice.

Maggie Teyte was small and slight, with a personality that was often charming, always downright, and sometimes abrasive. She was twice married. Her first marriage, to Eugène de Plumon, a French lawyer, took place in 1909. They divorced in 1915 and in 1921 she married Walter Sherwin Cottingham, son of Walter Horace Cottingham, a Canadian-American millionaire; they were divorced in 1931. There was no child of either marriage.

Throughout Teyte's long career the quality of voice remained inimitable and unmistakable: it was a very pure sound, always under perfect control, with softly floated head-notes devoid of shrillness, and with an uncommonly free and fearless use of the chest register, which gave strong character and humour to such renowned performances of hers as that of 'Tu n'es pas beau' from Offenbach's *La périchole*. She could still sound fresh and youthful even in Ravel's taxing *Shéhérazade* at the age of sixty. Although her French accent was not flawless (containing certain exotic intonations that were said to have charmed Debussy), she showed an acute sensibility to the colour and meaning of the phrase, and in such songs as Debussy's 'Chansons de Bilitis' she was hardly surpassed. A slightly excessive use of the downward portamento occasionally introduced a sentimental touch into otherwise immaculate interpretations, but her combination of natural gifts, spontaneity, and musical taste secured for her a unique position in her chosen field which was eventually, if belatedly, recognized in official circles. In 1943, at a dinner given in her honour in London, she received the croix de Lorraine accompanied by a letter from General de Gaulle; she was made a chevalier of the Légion d'honneur in 1957 and appointed DBE in 1958.

Maggie Teyte died in a London nursing home, after a long illness, on 26 May 1976.

DESMOND SHAWE-TAYLOR, rev.

Sources M. Teyte, *Star on the door* (1958) · G. O'Connor, *The pursuit of perfection: a life of Maggie Teyte* (1979) · personal knowledge (1986) · *CGPLA Eng. & Wales* (1976) · D. Shawe-Taylor, 'Teyte, Dame Maggie', *New Grove*
Likenesses J. Lavery, oils, 1907, NPG
Wealth at death £4646: probate, 17 Aug 1976, *CGPLA Eng. & Wales*

Thaarup, Aage Gjerfing (1906–1987), milliner, was born on 29 April 1906 in Copenhagen, Denmark, in a lower-middle-class family of moderate means. He was the second of four brothers. After a conventional high- and commercial-school education he was employed as a trainee salesman in the millinery department of Fornesbeck, the largest Copenhagen department store. He then received an educational grant, which he supplemented by extracurricular fashion drawing and English teaching, and worked for a brief period in Berlin and at a Paris couture milliner, Maison Lewis. He returned to Copenhagen but, unable to settle, left for London in 1928.

A period as a traveller with a wholesale hat firm having proved disappointing, Thaarup borrowed £200 and went to India in 1929, accumulating during the voyage the basis of a smart society clientele associated with the viceregal court. On his return to London in 1932, with £300 further borrowed capital, he opened a small salon at 4 Berkeley Street. By 1935 he was established as the most fashionable and innovative milliner in London with a royal and international society clientele. He also made hats for film and stage productions.

Thaarup's creativity lay in his sense of form and the suitability of the hat for the personality of the wearer, the outfit, and the occasion for which it was intended. His sewing skills were minimal and he consistently stressed his reliance on the craft of his assistants. Nevertheless, with an enterprise then unusual in the London fashion accessory trade, after becoming a limited company and moving to larger premises in Grosvenor Street, he began to export hats to Lord and Taylor in New York and, less successfully, to Paris. Publicity was sustained by fashion shows, such as a surrealist-inspired display in New York in 1936, as well as others in collaboration with the newly formed Fashion Group of London. The wit and originality of these shows inspired his nickname, the 'Mad Hatter'. His house in Bywater Street, Chelsea, became a centre for the artistic intelligentsia, several of whom were to contribute to his artistically innovative magazine *Pinpoints*, of which four numbers were issued (1938–9).

Being both lame and a Danish national, Thaarup was not directly involved in the war. However, the abnormal trading conditions forced his business into administration in 1940–42. Hats were nevertheless unrationed and were popular accessories, and as trade revived Thaarup organized touring fashion exhibitions as well as beginning a small wholesale trade. Popular innovations were '6 o'clock hats' for semi-formal wartime entertaining and miniature hats as gift tokens. His post-war popularity was confirmed by hats made for Queen and Princess Elizabeth for prestige royal occasions such as the victory parade in 1946 and for the trooping of the colour in 1950, but Thaarup appears never to have become a royal warrant holder.

In 1947, participating in the post-war export drive, Thaarup launched Aage Thaarup (Export and Wholesale) Ltd. In 1948 he became president of the Associated Millinery Designers of London. Despite a series of worldwide promotional tours and the innovative introduction of a 'Teen and Twenty' range of hats, the firm which had merged with Aage Thaarup Ltd was bankrupt by 1955 with debts of £16,500 and assets of £6500, which *The Times* ascribed to overtrading, the long credit customary in the fashion industry, and inadequate financial supervision; Thaarup's generosity to friends and family also probably played a part in the collapse. It is perhaps characteristic of his ebullient and optimistic personality that after the bankruptcy hearing, with help from friends, he spent the weekend at the Ritz.

Sponsored by friends, Thaarup continued to work for the next ten years. He was based first at 132 King's Road, Chelsea, where he was assisted by students, several of whom became successful milliners in their own right, and from 1960 in Hanover Square, where he remained until retirement in 1965. He then lived for some years at Flat 2, 104 Elm Park Gardens, Chelsea.

Small, spare, and sprightly, witty and articulate with a slight Danish accent, conventional in dress but with an enduring affection for flowing bow-ties, Thaarup remained on the fringes of the fashion world until he died of heart disease, on 11 December 1987 at St Stephen's Hospital, Chelsea. He never married. His autobiography, *Heads and Tales* (1956), outlined his career. Examples of his work have survived in the Victoria and Albert Museum, London, and the Museum of Fashion, Bath, as well as other collections. M. GINSBURG

Sources A. Thaarup and D. Shackell, *Heads and tales* (1956) · *The Times* (12 Oct 1955) · *British Millinery* (Nov 1955) · *The Times* (14 Dec 1987) · personal knowledge (2004) · *LondG* (10 June 1955), 3551 · d. cert.
Archives V&A, department of textiles and dress, artefacts, scrap books
Likenesses T. Gidal, two photographs, 1940, Hult. Arch. · photographs, repro. in Thaarup and Shackell, *Heads and tales*

Thach, Nathaniel (b. 1617), miniature painter, was the son of Richard Thach (d. 1652), a freeman of the Salters' Company, and his wife, Priscilla, whom he married on 27 June 1616. Nathaniel was baptized on 4 July 1617 in his grandfather's church, All Saints', Barrow, in Suffolk; there were two further surviving children, Thomas and Margaret. Priscilla Thach was the daughter of the Revd Richard Cradock (1562–1630) and the sister of John Cradock (b. 1595), who married Dorothy Braughton (3 August 1630); John Cradock succeeded his father in 1630 as rector of Barrow and fathered Mary *Beale (bap. 1633, d. 1699), the painter, who was thus first cousin to Nathaniel Thach.

The Thaches lived in London, in the parish of St Martin-in-the-Fields. By early 1644 Nathaniel Thach had left London. He may, like Alexander Cooper, the miniaturist, have lived and worked abroad, for a time perhaps at the expatriate Stuart court at The Hague, for he was described in the will of his uncle John Cradock (dated 2 April 1644) as 'late of London Picture drawer' (Edmond, 108). As such he was bequeathed by Cradock, who was an accomplished amateur and freeman of the Painter–Stainers' Company, 'all my empastered rounds' (ibid.)—presumably, that is, vellums stretched on cards stiffened with gesso on both sides, ready for painting. By 2 December 1652, when his father's will was drawn up, there was no reference to his being resident abroad in the bequest to him of £10, so he had probably returned to London, but it was his sister Margaret, and his uncle Thomas who executed and supervised the will, not the sons (ibid., 116).

The only evidence as to how Thach learnt the art of miniature is circumstantial, in that most of his known sitters are associated with the extended circle around Elizabeth of Bohemia in The Hague, in which Alexander Cooper and his former master Peter Oliver also seem to have worked. However slight the inferential value of that association Thach's miniatures are almost always derived from paintings in large encountered on the continent, and iconographically have little in common with the progressive streams of the English tradition in the 1640s and 1650s, as represented especially in the work of Samuel Cooper. The Woman in a Masque Costume of 1649 (V&A) is a copy after a painting identified as a portrait of Elizabeth of Bohemia's twelfth child, the Princess Sophia, and attributed to Gerrit Honthorst's royal pupil the talented Princess Louise Hollandine. The sitter is shown in a feathered head-dress, apparently as a native princess of Virginia, an iconography rooted in the international court masque of the pre-war period and viewed increasingly as illegitimately frivolous in Britain and the Netherlands in the 1640s.

Stylistically Thach's hand combines elements of the polychrome stipple associated with Peter Oliver and John Hoskins but the stroke is greatly elongated into a loose hatch, somewhat like that of the early Cooper or Matthew Snelling. Thach, as the scion of a relatively wealthy household in London and connected through his Suffolk background to a circle of keen connoisseurs of painting, should, however, not be seen as a regular limner like Oliver, Hoskins, or Cooper but as a skilled amateur, practising the art as a courtly accomplishment as recommended in treatises on civility such as The Compleat Gentleman (1634) by Henry Peacham.

Works by Thach are in the Royal Collection, the Mauritshuis in The Hague, and the Musée Carnavalet in Paris, as well as the Victoria and Albert Museum, London, where in addition to the signed Woman in Masque Costume there is on loan an unsigned but exceptionally beautiful Charles II, after a portrait by Adriaen Hanneman of 1648 or later. It is certainly attributable to Thach but was formerly given to David Des Granges (Murdoch, 85), evidently by analogy with versions of the same Hanneman portrait produced by Des Granges in quantity for distribution to supporters when Charles was in Scotland in 1651. At Ham House there is a portrait of similar date formerly identified as Henrietta Maria, again formerly attributed to Des Granges, and again also probably by Thach (ibid., 313). The identifiable works thus seem to cluster narrowly at the end of the 1640s and very early 1650s. The latest date, 165[?] (the final figure is unfortunately illegible) appears on the signed version of the Charles II after Hanneman in the Mauritshuis; both stylistically and circumstantially, however, it clearly belongs with the others of this group.

JOHN MURDOCH

Sources M. Edmond, 'Bury St Edmunds: a seventeenth century art centre', Walpole Society, 53 (1987), 106–18 · J. Murdoch, Seventeenth-century English miniatures in the collection of the Victoria and Albert Museum (1997)

Thacher, Thomas (1620–1678). See under Thatcher, Peter (1587/8–1641).

Thackeray, Anne Isabella. See Ritchie, Anne Isabella, Lady Ritchie (1837–1919).

Thackeray, Francis (1793–1842), author, was the sixth son of William Makepeace Thackeray (1749–1813), of the Bengal civil service, and his wife, Amelia (d. 1810), third daughter of Lieutenant-Colonel Richmond Webb. He entered Cambridge in 1810, graduated BA from Pembroke College in 1814 and MA in 1817. He became curate of Broxbourne in Hertfordshire. In 1829 he married Mary Ann Shakespear (d. 1851). He died at Broxbourne on 18 February 1842, leaving two sons, the Revd Francis St John Thackeray and Colonel Edward Talbot Thackeray, VC, and one daughter, Mary. He enjoyed a good relationship with his nephew William Makepeace Thackeray, the novelist, whom he saved from gambling debts on more than one occasion and who called his uncle 'saintly Francis, lying at rest under the turf' (Ray, 166).

Thackeray was famous in the family for his invention and narration of fairy tales. Of his published works, the most interesting is A History of William Pitt, Earl of Chatham (1827). Macaulay, in reviewing the work in the Edinburgh Review for 1834, criticized the author for his extravagant praise of his hero. The life, however, was painstaking, and contained a good deal of fresh information from the state paper office. He also wrote A Defence of the Clergy of the Church of England (1822), and, in 1831, Order Against Anarchy as a reply to Paine's Rights of Man. His Researches into the ecclesiastical and political state of ancient Britain under the Roman emperors was published posthumously in 1843.

E. I. CARLYLE, rev. MYFANWY LLOYD

Sources GM, 2nd ser., 17 (1842), 559 · 'Pedigree of Thackeray [pt 2]', Herald and Genealogist, 2 (1865), 440–55, esp. 447–8 · Venn, Alum. Cant. · G. N. Ray, Thackeray, 2 vols. (1955–8), vol. 1

Thackeray, Frederick Rennell (1775–1860), army officer, the third son of Frederick Thackeray (1737–1782), physician, of Windsor, and his wife, Elizabeth (d. 1816), daughter of Abel Aldridge of Uxbridge, was born in Windsor, Berkshire, and baptized on 16 November 1775. His father's sister was the wife of Major James Rennell of the Bengal Engineers, the geographer. George *Thackeray was his younger brother, and William Makepeace *Thackeray, the novelist, his first cousin once removed.

After attending the Royal Military Academy, Woolwich, Thackeray was commissioned second lieutenant, Royal Artillery, on 18 September 1793, and was transferred to the Royal Engineers on 1 January 1794. He served at Gibraltar from 1793 until 1797, when he went to the West Indies, having been promoted first lieutenant on 18 June 1796. He took part, on 20 August 1799, in the capture of Surinam under Sir Thomas Trigge. In 1801 he was aide-de-camp to Trigge at the capture of the Swedish West Indian island of St Bartholomew on 21 March, the Dutch island of St Martin on 24 March, the Danish islands of St Thomas and St John on 28 March, and Santa Cruz on 31 March.

On 18 April 1801 Thackeray was promoted second captain. He returned to England in 1802, and in 1803 went again to Gibraltar. He was promoted first captain on 1 March 1805, and again returned to England. In February 1807 he was sent to Sicily, and joined the expedition under Major-General McKenzie Fraser to Egypt; he returned to Sicily in September. In 1809 Thackeray was commanding royal engineer with the force under Lieutenant-Colonel Haviland Smith detached by Sir John Stuart (when he made his expedition to the Bay of Naples) from Messina on 11 June to make a diversion by an attack on the castle of Scylla. The siege was directed by Thackeray with such skill that, although raised by a superior force of French, the castle was untenable, and had to be blown up.

In March 1810 Thackeray was sent from Messina by Sir John Stuart with an ample supply of engineer and artillery stores to join Colonel John Oswald in the Ionian Islands, to besiege the fortress of Santa Maura. Its position on a long narrow isthmus of sand made it difficult of approach, and it was well supplied and contained casemated barracks sufficient for its garrison of 800 men under General Camus. Oswald landed on 23 March. No enfilading batteries could be erected; but after the British direct batteries had opened fire the siege works were pushed gradually forwards, until on 15 April Thackeray pointed out the necessity for carrying by assault an advanced trench held by the enemy which would enable him to reconnoitre the approach to, and the position for, the breaching battery, and he proposed to turn the trench, when taken, into an advanced parallel of the attack. The operation was carried out successfully; the enemy were driven out of the trench at the point of the bayonet by Lieutenant-Colonel Moore of the 35th regiment; large working parties were at once sent in, and, by Thackeray's judicious and indefatigable exertion, the trench on the morning of 16 April 1810 was converted into a lodgement from which the attackers could not be driven by the fire of the enemy, while the British infantry and sharpshooters were able so greatly to

harry the artillery of the place that in the course of the day it surrendered. Thackeray was mentioned in dispatches. Oswald also wrote to thank him. Thackeray received on 19 May 1810 a brevet majority in special recognition of his services.

Thackeray sailed in July 1812 with the Anglo-Sicilian army under Lieutenant-General Frederick Maitland, and landed at Alicante in August. He took part in the operations of this army, which, after Maitland's resignation in October, was successively commanded by Generals Mackenzie, William Clinton, Campbell, and Sir John Murray, who arrived in February 1813. On 6 March Thackeray marched with the allied army from Alicante to attack Suchet, and was at the capture of Alcoy. He took part in the battle of Castalla on 13 April, when Suchet was defeated. On 31 May he embarked with the 14,000 strong army, which carried a powerful siege train and ample engineer stores, for Tarragona, where they disembarked on 3 June. Thackeray directed the siege operations, and on 8 June a practicable breach was made in Fort Royal, an outwork. Thackeray objected to an assault on this work before everything was ready for the construction of a parallel and advance from it. All was prepared on 11 June, and instructions were given for an assault after a vigorous bombardment. But Murray, having received intelligence of a French advance, counter-ordered the assault and raised the siege. For this he was court-martialled at Winchester, and found guilty of an error of judgement. Murray seems at the time of the siege to have blamed Thackeray for delaying the attack, for on the arrival of Lieutenant-General Lord William Bentinck to take command on 18 June, Thackeray wrote to him indicating that an attempt had been made to attach blame to him for the termination of the siege of Tarragona, and requesting Lord William as an act of justice to investigate his conduct before Sir John Murray left, and while all the relevant persons were still present. This letter was sent to Murray, who exonerated Thackeray (reply of Murray, dated Alicante, 22 June).

Thackeray was promoted lieutenant-colonel, Royal Engineers, on 21 July 1813. He had moved, at the end of June, with Lord William Bentinck's army to Alicante, and was at the occupation of Valencia on 9 July, and at the investment of Tarragona on 30 July. He took part in the other operations of the army under Bentinck and his successor, Sir William Clinton. During October and November Thackeray was employed in rendering Tarragona once more defensible. In April 1814, by Wellington's orders, Clinton's army was broken up, and Thackeray returned to England in ill health.

At the beginning of 1815 Thackeray was appointed commanding royal engineer at Plymouth; in May 1817 he was transferred to Gravesend, and on 26 November 1824 he went to Edinburgh as commanding royal engineer of Scotland. He was promoted colonel in the Royal Engineers on 2 June 1825, and was made a CB, military division, on 26 September 1831. In 1833 he was appointed commanding royal engineer in Ireland. He was promoted major-general on 10

January 1837, when he ceased to be employed. He had married at Rosehill, Hampshire, on 21 November 1825, Elizabeth Margaret Carnegie, third daughter of William *Carnegie, seventh earl of Northesk; they had three sons and five daughters.

Thackeray was made a colonel-commandant of the corps of Royal Engineers on 29 April 1846, was promoted lieutenant-general on 9 November 1846, and general on 20 June 1854. He died at his residence, The Cedars, Windlesham, Bagshot, Surrey, on 19 September 1860, and was buried at York Town, Farnborough, Hampshire. Thackeray's wife and children survived him.

R. H. VETCH, *rev.* ROGER T. STEARN

Sources A. P. Burke, *Family records* (1897) · PRO, War Office records · *LondG* · Institution of Royal Engineers, Chatham, Royal Engineers Records · J. Philippart, ed., *The royal military calendar*, 3rd edn, 5 vols. (1820) · *Annual Register* (1860) · T. W. J. Connolly, *History of the royal sappers and miners*, 2nd edn, 2 vols. (1857) · W. F. P. Napier, *History of the war in the Peninsula and in the south of France*, new edn, 6 vols. (1886) · H. Bunbury, *Narratives of some passages in the great war with France, from 1799 to 1810* (1854) · A. J. Guy, ed., *The road to Waterloo: the British army and the struggle against revolutionary and Napoleonic France, 1793–1815* (1990) · R. Muir, *Britain and the defeat of Napoleon, 1807–1815* (1996) · Boase, *Mod. Eng. biog.* · *CGPLA Eng. & Wales* (1860)
Likenesses F. Barswell, oils, Royal Engineers HQ Mess, Chatham, Kent
Wealth at death under £8000: probate, 13 Nov 1860, *CGPLA Eng. & Wales*

Thackeray, George (1777–1850), college head, was born at Windsor on 10 October 1777 and baptized at the parish church on 23 November 1777. He was the fourth and youngest son of Frederick Thackeray (1737–1782), a physician of Windsor, and his wife, Elizabeth (*d.* 1816), daughter of Abel Aldridge of Uxbridge. Frederick Rennell *Thackeray was his elder brother. George became a king's scholar at Eton College in 1792, and a scholar of King's College, Cambridge, in 1796, where he graduated BA in 1802, MA in 1805, and BD in 1813. He was a fellow of King's from 1800 to 1803, when he married (9 November 1803) a Miss Carbonell. He was ordained, and in 1801 was appointed assistant master at Eton, becoming lower master in 1809. On 4 April 1814 he was elected provost of King's College, and in the same year obtained the degree of DD by royal mandate.

Following the death of his first wife, Thackeray married, in 1816, Mary Ann, eldest daughter of Alexander Cottin of Cheverells, Hertfordshire. Her death, in 1818, cast a gloom over Thackeray's subsequent life. He devoted much of his time to collecting rare books, and 'there was not a vendor of literary curiosities in London who had not some reason for knowing the provost of King's'. He directed the finances of the college with great ability, and during his provostship an extensive building programme was carried out. But he was chiefly remembered as an obstinate opponent of reform, invoking his sole right, under the founder's statutes, to initiate business at college meetings to prevent the abolition of the privilege whereby Kingsmen could graduate without examination. He held the appointment of chaplain-in-ordinary to George III and to the three succeeding sovereigns.

Thackeray died in Wimpole Street, London, on 21 October 1850, and he was buried in a vault in the ante-chapel of King's College. His daughter, Mary Ann Elizabeth, bequeathed Thackeray's library to King's College on her death.

E. I. CARLYLE, *rev.* M. C. CURTHOYS

Sources *GM*, 2nd ser., 34 (1850), 664–5 · Venn, *Alum. Cant.* · D. A. Winstanley, *Early Victorian Cambridge* (1940); repr. (1955)
Likenesses F. Joseph, oils, King's Cam. · R. J. Lane, lithograph (after F. Joseph), BM, NPG

Thackeray, Thomas James [Tom] (1796–1877), playwright, army officer, and agriculturist, was born on 5 September 1796 in Madras, India, the elder son of Thomas Thackeray (1767–1852) of Bath, a surgeon on the Madras establishment of the East India Company, and his first wife, Frances (Fanny) Ward (*d.* 1800), daughter of the Revd Henry Ward of Stevenage, Hertfordshire. He entered Eton College in January 1810, went up to St John's College, Cambridge, as a pensioner on 15 October 1814, and was awarded the degree of MB in 1820. After an interval he was commissioned, on 26 March 1824, as ensign in the 2nd Somerset militia. Eventually he rose to the rank of captain, on 10 January 1842, which rank he retained until his retirement on 11 August 1855. He lived for a time at Clench Wharton, Norfolk, but he was a fluent speaker of French and spent much of his adult life resident in Paris.

Thackeray began his writing career in the drama—a not uncommon part-time occupation for army officers—with *The Barber Baron* (Haymarket, 8 September 1828), a farce about a Strasbourg barber who wins a château by lottery. William Farren and John Reeve won praise as baron and comic porter, though an otherwise hostile *Times* was determined to consign to 'just oblivion … such a piece of unsuited and unmitigated dulness' (10 Sept 1828). It was published by Thomas Richardson in 1830, and was followed by an unpublished melodrama, *The Castle of Wolfenstein* (Olympic, November 1828), and *The Executioner* (Coburg, February 1829), published in *Richardson's New Minor Drama* (vol. 3, 1830). For the summer season at the Haymarket in 1830 Thackeray wrote *The Force of Nature* and (with Charles Shannon) the farce *My Wife, my Place*. He instinctively turned to foreign models for inspiration, especially in the former play, which, set in Paris, was considered 'striking and effective' in situation (*The Times*, 17 July 1830). A historical drama, *Gustavus of Sweden, or, The Masked Ball* was licensed in 1833, but his best success was probably *The Mountain Sylph* (1834), a largely versified 'romantic ballet opera', with music by John Barnett. This was almost Thackeray's last venture into drama in Britain, though *L'abbaye de Penmarc'h*, a three-act melodrama written jointly with Pierre Tournemine, was performed in Paris at the Théâtre de la Porte-Saint-Antoine (2 February 1840) and published in that city.

Thackeray's intimate knowledge of the contrasts between the theatre in London and Paris made his advice invaluable to the growing number of dramatists who sought radical theatrical reform in Britain in the 1830s. His pamphlet *On Theatrical Emancipation, and the Rights of*

Dramatic Authors (1832) showed the unequivocal superiority of conditions for French (and Belgian) authors compared to British, who, lacking copyright protection and fair remuneration, laboured under a state-sustained monopoly in London which restricted not only the number of theatres but also the class of drama that each was permitted to perform. Thackeray's evidence underpinned the case of the anti-monopoly agitators, whose ally in parliament, Edward Bulwer-Lytton, chaired the select committee (1832) inquiring into the state of the drama, the immediate result of which was reform of dramatic copyright in 1833.

Thackeray was also an agriculturist and published extensively on the subject, exclusively in French, from 1846 to the late 1850s. A history of the Royal Agricultural Society, England, appeared in 1848, but his special interests included drainage, barn construction, the use of farmyard dung and artificial fertilizers, and the benefits of deep ploughing. His large-scale *Registre du cultivateur, ou, Livre complet de tous ses comptes* (8 vols., Paris, 1850–57) detailed the work of a farmer on a month-to-month basis.

Thackeray's other writings, on the army and firearms, were exclusively in English. This included a two-volume treatise on the military organization and administration of France (1856); but his best-known work was the manual for soldiers on the principles of rifle-firing over various distances (1854; 3rd edn, 1861), the foundation of which was a series of three lectures he delivered at the Guildhall, Bath, in 1853 (separately published, 1853).

Thackeray was a man of means, his father having left him well off. As described by Mrs William Bayne, '[h]e was a most agreeable man of the world, and had a fair share of good looks' (Mrs R. Prynne and Mrs W. Bayne, xxx). He had a considerable circle of friends, including several authors, such as James Robinson Planché, Thomas J. Serle, and Edward Bulwer-Lytton. However, in 1840 his involvement, as an agent of Bulwer's, in attempted burglary at the Paris dwelling of Bulwer's estranged wife to recover certain papers and also to suborn witnesses against her, astonished all who knew him, including his second cousin the novelist William Makepeace Thackeray, who commented: 'What the juice have Tom Thackeray and Lawson [his accomplice] been about?—they are both gentlemen and I can't conceive what could bring them to meddle with such dirty work' (*Letters and Private Papers*, 1.434). Lady Bulwer's double civil action against them in Paris aroused much public interest in that city and in London. Both defendants were acquitted, none of the prosecution evidence having been heard, on the grounds that Lady Bulwer could not sue for civil redress without her husband's permission, which not surprisingly he refused to give. The judgment was confirmed on appeal. The scandal was conceivably the cause of the apparent delay in Thackeray's promotion to captain.

Tom Thackeray was unmarried. He died in France at his home at 83 rue du Faubourg St Honoré, Paris, on 21 February 1877.   JOHN RUSSELL STEPHENS

Sources W. F. Prideaux, 'Bibliographical note on Dickens and Thackeray', *N&Q*, 10th ser., 3 (1905), 131–2 • F. Boase, 'Thomas James Thackeray', *N&Q*, 11th ser., 3 (1911), 215 • Boase, *Mod. Eng. biog.*, 6.673–4 • *The letters and private papers of William Makepeace Thackeray*, ed. G. N. Ray, 4 vols. (1945–6) • *The Times* (10 Sept 1828), 2 • *The Times* (17 July 1830), 3 • *The Times* (23 March 1840), 5 • *The Times* (30 March 1840), 3 • *The Times* (27 July 1840), 5 • J. R. Planché, *Recollections and reflections*, rev. edn (1901) • Mrs R. Prynne and Mrs. W. Bayne, *Memorials of the Thackeray family* (privately printed, 1879) • private information (2004) [archivist, Eton College] • E. B. Watson, *Sheridan to Robertson: a study of the nineteenth-century London stage* (1926) • 'Barnett, John', Grove, *Dict. mus.* (1927) • A. Nicoll, *Early nineteenth century drama, 1800–1850*, 2nd edn (1955), vol. 4 of *A history of English drama, 1660–1900* (1952–9), 412, 614 • *Catalogue général des livres imprimés de la Bibliothèque Nationale*, 185 (1959) [bibliography of works pubd in Fr.] • *CGPLA Eng. & Wales* (1877)

Wealth at death under £14,000—effects in England: will, 12 March 1877, *CGPLA Eng. & Wales*

Thackeray, William Makepeace (1811–1863), novelist, was born on 18 July 1811 at Calcutta, the only child of Richmond Thackeray (1781–1815), secretary to the board of revenue in the East India Company at Calcutta, and Anne Becher (1792–1864), second daughter of John Harman Becher, a writer for the East India Company, and his wife, Harriet.

Ancestry and early life Harriet Becher, after the birth of Anne's younger sister (also Harriet), appears to have abandoned husband and children to elope with Captain Charles Christie under whose 'protection' she lived until his death in 1805. She then married Captain Edward William Butler of the Bengal artillery in October 1806, John Becher, her legal husband, having died in 1800. The novelist got to know his grandmother as Mrs Butler when he stayed with her in Paris in 1834–5, and when she lived with him in 1840–41 and again in 1847, the year she died. She is said to have been the model for Miss Crawley in *Vanity Fair*. Anne Becher was brought up by her paternal grandmother, also Anne Becher, whose severe evangelical beliefs did not preclude ambition for a marriage of wealth and position for Anne. When Anne fell in love with Henry Carmichael-Smyth (1780–1861), an ensign of the Bengal Engineers, her grandmother intervened, finally persuading Anne that the young man had died and sending the bereaved girl to India in April 1809 in the company of her sister Harriet, their mother, and Captain Butler. Anne was a beautiful woman and very successful in Calcutta social circles where Richmond Thackeray joined many others suitors, prevailing and marrying her on 13 October 1810. Her sister Harriet had married Captain Allan Graham eight months earlier.

The novelist's father, Richmond, second son of William and Amelia Thackeray, was born at South Mimms on 1 September 1781 and went to India at the age of sixteen to assume his duties as writer. By 1804 he had fathered a daughter by a native mistress, the mother and daughter being named in his will. Such liaisons being common among gentlemen of the East India Company, it formed no bar to his courting and marrying Anne Becher. The novelist's great-grandfather Thomas Thackeray (1693–1760), headmaster of Harrow School, chaplain to Frederick, prince of Wales, and, from 1753, archdeacon of Surrey,

William Makepeace Thackeray (1811–1863), by Samuel Laurence, 1852

had sixteen children. Thomas's fourth son, also Thomas (1736–1806), was a surgeon at Cambridge, and one of his sons, William Makepeace (1770–1849), was a physician at Chester. The youngest son of Thomas the archdeacon, also named William Makepeace (1749–1813), married Amelia Richmond and fathered Richmond, the novelist's father. Amelia was third daughter of Colonel Richmond Webb, who was related to General John Richmond Webb, of Wijnendale fame, described in *Henry Esmond*. The novelist chose the Webb crest of arms as his own because it 'was prettier and more ancient' (*Letters and Private Papers*, 3.446); and he is said to have credited the Webbs with introducing 'wits … into the family' which was otherwise a 'simple, serious' one (F. Bradley-Birt, *'Sylhet' Thackeray*, 1911, 16).

Five months after William Makepeace Thackeray's birth, Richmond was promoted to the post of collector of the house tax at Calcutta and of the Twenty-four Pergunnahs, a district south of Calcutta. The family may have set up house at the collector's residence at Alipore, though Richmond's will refers to 'the house in Chowringhee in which I reside' (Ray, *Uses of Adversity*, 61). Some time in 1812 Richmond invited a new acquaintance home to dine: Captain Henry Carmichael-Smyth, Anne's supposedly deceased lover. He had been informed by Mrs Becher, who had returned all his letters, that Anne no longer cared for him. Mrs Fuller (the novelist's granddaughter) wrote, 'After a while the situation became so impossible that Richmond Thackeray had to be told; he listened gravely, said little, but was never the same to Anne again' (*Letters*

and Private Papers, 1.cxiv; Ray, *Uses of Adversity*, 63). Thackeray's fiction is dotted with accounts of parental interference in young love.

Richmond Thackeray died on 13 September 1815 leaving an estate worth £17,000. His will directed annuities drawn from the estate of £450 to his wife, £100 each to his sister, Augusta, his son, William Makepeace, and his illegitimate daughter, Sarah, and about £30 in total to Sarah's mother and an old servant. Young William Makepeace was sent at the age of five to England in December 1816, while his mother Anne remained to marry Henry Carmichael-Smyth in the winter of 1817–18. The couple returned to England in 1819.

Thackeray was accompanied on his journey to England by a former colleague of his father, by his cousin Richmond Shakespeare, and by a native servant, Lawrence Barlow. When the ship stopped at St Helena, Barlow took Thackeray to see a man walking in a garden; 'that is Bonaparte!' said the servant. 'He eats three sheep every day, and all the little children he can lay hands on!' (Ray, *Uses of Adversity*, 66). William was taken in very briefly by his aunt Charlotte Sarah (Richmond's sister) and her husband, John Ritchie.

Early education   In the winter of 1817–18 Thackeray attended a school at Southampton

> of which our deluded parents had heard a favourable report, but which was governed by a horrible little tyrant, who made our young lives so miserable that I remember kneeling by my little bed of a night, and saying, 'Pray God, I may dream of my mother!'   (Ray, *Uses of Adversity*, 70)

In the following year he entered a school at Chiswick where he remained until December 1821, after which he was enrolled at Charterhouse School. Summers he spent with the Bechers at Fareham until the return of his mother and Major Carmichael-Smyth in 1819. Though he never returned to India, the India connections of the families that made up the Fareham circle are evident in many accounts of returned East India men, including Jos in *Vanity Fair* and Colonel Newcome in *The Newcomes*. Only one work, *The Tremendous Adventures of Major Gahagan* (1838), is set in India. Thackeray's treatment in the Chiswick school and at Charterhouse, which he attended from 1822 to 1828, may have been better than at the first school at Southampton, but his recollections of school tyrannies and the terrors of school boyhood show up repeatedly in his fiction. His portraits of Miss Tickletoby, Dr Birch, and Dr Swishtail and his descriptions of Slaughterhouse and Blackfriars schools suggest that flogging and fagging were the primary agents of instruction. His recollections were that he had been 'licked into indolence', 'abused into sulkiness', and 'bullied into despair' (ibid., 97). He must have felt keenly the difference between his treatment in England, even among his well-intentioned relatives, and what he had known in India where he was attended by numerous servants and played with by his mother and aunt. Among Thackeray's most convincing fictional portraits are those of young or misfit boys in school, like Dobbin in *Vanity Fair*, and of the loneliness of boys like Henry

Esmond. However, the few surviving letters from Southampton and Chiswick, written under the censoring eyes of schoolmasters, do not betray the pain and misery portrayed in Thackeray's fiction.

Thackeray's academic achievements at Charterhouse were not outstanding, though his natural abilities caused him to rise through the ranks respectably (Ray, *Uses of Adversity*, 84–6). He was quite near-sighted and, having no spectacles, was unable to take a very active role in games—though, apparently for the amusement of older boys, he and a schoolmate, George Venables, were put to a fight in which the latter flattened the future novelist's nose (*Letters and Private Papers*, 2.256).

Thackeray spent the summers with his mother and Major Carmichael-Smyth at Addiscombe, near Croydon, until 1825, when they moved to a house named Larkbeare near Ottery St Mary and Exeter, the setting for much of *Pendennis*. The rector of nearby Clyst Hydon, the Revd Francis Huyshe, became a close family friend and was probably the model for Pendennis's would-be mentor, Dr Portman. In his final two years at Charterhouse Thackeray was a member of the first form and received 'instruction' directly from Dr Russell, who, Thackeray complained, refused to acknowledge any of his efforts or achievements and singled him out for put-downs. Thackeray's parodies of Russell began while in school and show up in much of his fiction. In the end Thackeray's formal education was weak, including little if any mathematics and involving a rote approach to classics that did little for the understanding. But Thackeray was a voracious reader and a keen observer of his surroundings. Perhaps the most ingrained notion Thackeray carried away from Charterhouse was a sense of class distinctions; for though the public schools mixed the sons of the very wealthy with those of lesser families, there was a keen sense of community that separated those at public schools from all others. There is more than a little truth in the notion that the *Book of Snobs* was 'written by one of them'; for though Thackeray was able to see and depict pretension and overreaching English snobbism, he never 'forgot his place' or the codes learned in public school that separated him from less privileged men.

Thackeray's aunt Harriet Graham and her husband both died, leaving a daughter, Mary Graham, who from 1820 lived with the Carmichael-Smyths and as a younger sister to William. She played a Laura Bell to Thackeray's Pendennis and eventually married Colonel Charles Carmichael, the major's brother. Mary and her husband lent Thackeray £500 when hard times struck in 1841, a debt that hung as heavily over him as Pen's debt to Laura in *Pendennis*.

Years in Cambridge and Germany Illness in his last year at Charterhouse, during which he reportedly grew to his full 6 feet 3 inches, postponed Thackeray's matriculation at Trinity College, Cambridge, until February 1829. Thackeray was 'coached' for college by the well-intentioned Major Carmichael-Smyth. It was appropriate to William Thackeray's paternal family background that he should

try to think of himself as a potential scholar. The Thackeray side of the family was well-known for its scholars, from the archdeacon, his great-grandfather, to his great-uncles and cousins the physicians, to his cousin Elias, a vicar, and two of his cousins, the provost and vice-provost of King's College, and his cousin by marriage, a professor of political economy. Though Thackeray entered late, he was determined, perhaps under some pressure from his mother's expectations, to read for an honours rather than a pass degree. Thackeray apparently saw little of his tutor, William Whewell, but his private tutor, Henry Fawcett, found Thackeray a ready enough scholar at first. Like Pendennis, he seems to have applied himself with some enthusiasm, studying from eight in the morning to three every day, but before long he decided that private reading would suit his ends better than assiduous attendance at lectures.

Cambridge distractions soon eroded study time and energy, but it was not all wine parties and debates and outings. Thackeray read widely: histories (Gibbon, Hume, Smollett), modern novels and poems—making a special effort with Shelley, whose *Revolt of Islam* impressed him. And he began to write. He had published a couple of poems and a translation the year before in the *Western Luminary*, a Devon newspaper, but at Cambridge his contributions to *The Snob* and, after the long vacation, to its replacement, *The Gownsman*, began to develop his talents in parody and humour. Having arrived in late February, his first contribution to *The Snob* was his famous 'Timbuctoo', a parody (not submitted, of course) of the prize competition, which Tennyson won that year. By mid-May he was working closely with *The Snob*'s editor, William Williams, contributing six more pieces by the end of term in June.

Thackeray's relatives in Cambridge welcomed him with open arms, but he found their company staid. When he applied to his cousin the vice-provost for advice about his progress toward the end of his first term, it was suggested he hold over and not take the first-year examinations. In the end he did take them—five days of eight-hour exams on mathematics and classical authors. He had been sick before the exams and yet made it to the top of the fourth class 'where clever "non-reading" men were put, as in a limbo' (*Letters and Private Papers*, 1.76).

In the company of William Williams, just graduated and serving supposedly as Thackeray's mathematics coach for the summer, Thackeray went to Paris to learn French and extend his education with continental experience. Williams soon abandoned Thackeray, who discovered for himself museums, artists' studios, and Frascati's gambling opportunities. By the account he sent home, the first visit to Frascati's was a brush with evil that taught him the lesson to avoid gambling, whereas in truth it seems to have whetted his taste for play, which by the end of his second year at Cambridge landed him some £1500 in debt. Thackeray returned to Cambridge in October, where distractions continued to outweigh the honours curriculum in maths and classics. It is not known exactly when Thackeray decided that further pursuit of an honours degree was a waste of time, but the decision formed a part of his break for independence from his mother, to whom he wrote the next year:

> You seem to take it so much to heart, that I gave up trying for Academical honours—perhaps Mother I was too young to form opinions but I did form them—& these told me that there was little use in studying what could after a certain point be of no earthly use to me ... that three years of industrious waste of time might obtain for me mediocre honours wh. I did not value at a straw[. I]s it because I have unfortunately fallen into this state of thinking that you are so dissatisfied with me[?]   (*Letters and Private Papers*, 1.138)

Only four contributions to *The Snob's* successor *The Gownsman* and two letters home offer evidence of Thackeray's second-year activities at Cambridge. But his circle of acquaintance included important friendships with Henry Alford, John Allen, Henry Nicholson Burrows, Charles Christie, William Hepworth Thompson, and John Hailstone—all members of a debating society formed in imitation of the Apostles (Ray, *Uses of Adversity*, 128). His other friends included James Spedding, John Mitchell Kemble, A. W. Kinglake, William Brookfield, Richard Monckton Milne, and Alfred Tennyson. His best friends in the autumn term were John Allen, who influenced him to affirm his religious beliefs, and Edward Fitzgerald, a shy man who shared Thackeray's love of literature and who influenced him to doubt his beliefs. Fitzgerald graduated in December, leaving the field to Allen, who lost out to faster men, including Harry Matthews, the prototype of Bloundel in *Pendennis*, who seems to have led Thackeray into gambling dissipation in the Lent and Easter terms.

At the examinations that year Thackeray ended in the second class, dashing any hopes of an honours degree. At the Easter break he announced he would spend the vacation with a friend named Slingsby in Huntingdonshire, but instead went to Paris with Edward Fitzgerald, an outing about which, he years later remarked, 'my benighted parents never knew anything' (Ray, *Uses of Adversity*, 126). There is some evidence to believe that Thackeray contracted a venereal disease at this time. In October 1859 he wrote in a familiar strain, 'My old enemy gives me rather serious cause for disquiet—not the spasms—the hydraulics—a constant accompaniment of those disorders is disordered spirits' (*Letters and Private Papers*, 4.154; C. M. Jones, 'The medical history of William Makepeace Thackeray', ibid., 4.453–59). It is clear that he spent time in Paris with a woman ten or twelve years his senior whom he met at a masquerade ball. The experience may have been the inspiration for Pendennis's infatuation with both Emily Fotheringay, who was ten years his senior, and with Fanny Bolton—with the sexual element reduced to resisted temptation. Another apparently sanitized account of the meeting with Mlle Pauline appeared in *Britannia* on 5 June 1841. Thackeray left Cambridge without a degree in June 1830.

Seeking a career Thackeray's bid for independence at the age of nineteen still entailed getting permission from his mother for his next venture: an extended stay in Germany, learning the language, reading, and getting to know societies other than his own. Intending to join the English society of Dresden, he ended at Weimar for six months, dressed in the uniform of a cornetcy of Devon yeomanry obtained for him by Major Carmichael-Smyth. He reported home on falling in love with two young ladies who abandoned him for better prospects; on meeting Goethe and the intellectual circle presided over by his daughter-in-law, Ottilie von Goethe; on studying German and things in general with Dr Friedrich August Wilhelm Wiessenborn; and on reading and translating Schiller's poetry. He undertook several writing projects but placed none.

Thackeray illustrated Schiller's poem about Pegasus in harness, drawing the winged horse with a cart, an image to which he returned repeatedly as indicative of his own relationship to high art. In Germany, Thackeray was, for the first time in his life, free to follow his own bent, and he cut a relatively successful figure of some grace and significance. Though German philosophy may have been too heavy for him, he was already imbibing the wisdom, scepticism, tolerance, and suspended judgement of Weimar's rather relaxed society. Though still a somewhat self-centred would-be English rake, he was already showing the tendencies of mind that led him to Victor Cousin's philosophy of uncertainty, which he read in 1832 (Colby, 27) and Montaigne's amused, detached observations of life in the *Essays*, which Thackeray read and reread throughout his life. On his return to England in the early summer of 1831, Thackeray spent a few weeks at Larkbeare before taking up law studies at the Middle Temple in June. He read law, clerked, attended dinners, and disparaged his work in letters home and to Edward Fitzgerald who occasionally came up to London to roam the streets and go to plays with him. He remained in this routine for nearly a year, during which his passion for the theatre and for reading fiction and history were developed more assiduously than the law. Losing any real ambition for the law, and without entrée to the circles of society which his expected fortune and his public school education led him to expect, he spent the year of his maturity in a variety of 'ungentlemanly' pursuits as bill discounter, desultory journalist, and artist. His friendship with Harry Kemble that year provided more dissipation, gambling, raucous nights—resulting in repeated entries in his diary vowing reform. His friendship with the editor of *Fraser's Magazine*, William Maginn, dates from 1832, when Maginn took him to a 'common brothel where I left him, very much disgusted & sickened' (Ray, *Uses of Adversity*, 156), but it is not clear that he was always to react so.

On coming of age on 18 July 1832 Thackeray's first business was to pay old gambling debts, a painful act which did not cure his craving for cards and dice. Nevertheless, with a fortune remaining at between £15,000 and £20,000, there was no reason for him to apply himself seriously to any profession that did not completely appeal to him. With the passage of the Reform Bill Thackeray joined Charles Buller in the campaign for a seat in parliament from Cornwall, which he undertook in spite of his allegiance to the tories and Wellington. Thackeray next spent several months in Paris, enjoying the independence of his inheritance, casting about pleasurably but without purpose, recording feelings of guilt and unhappiness in his diary.

Early in 1833 Thackeray purchased the *National Standard* for which he and James Hume, as sub-editor, provided the bulk of copy. After ten months the venture ended in failure, but Thackeray had joined the Garrick Club and got to know the London literati to whom he would return after yet another venture into France to take up his next 'real' profession: painting. His first attempt to study painting in Paris came in 1833, while he styled himself Paris correspondent for the *National Standard*, but it appears that his literary and artistic careers were both undertaken as fulfilments of pleasure by a man of some fortune. However, by December 1833 a series of bank failures in India wiped out the bulk of Thackeray's inheritance, leaving him without income. The *Standard* failed early in 1834, and Thackeray's second opportunity to study art materialized in September when his grandmother Butler moved to Paris and gave him a room. Embarking on what was supposed to be a three-year apprenticeship in the ateliers of a French artist, and thanking God for making him poor, Thackeray appears to have applied himself happily and seriously to his studies only to discover, within a year, that his talent for comic drawings would never develop into satisfactory art. This was a bitter disappointment to a man who had sacrificed a great deal of social pretension to follow a trade generally considered no better than 'a hair-dresser or a pastry-cook, by gad', as Major Pendennis remarks of Clive Newcome's parallel decision in *The Newcomes*. By the summer of 1835, virtually penniless, disgusted with his talent, with the vulgarity of his artist friends, with the moral degradation of his gambling cronies, one of whom committed suicide, and with his own repeated failures to reform or succeed, Thackeray's bohemian sojourn reached a nadir of depression.

Apprenticeship and marriage But then Thackeray met Isabella Gethin Shawe (1816–1893), second daughter of Matthew Shawe, a colonel, who had died after extraordinary service, primarily in India, and his wife, Isabella Creagh. Isabella was living with her mother and sister on a pension in Paris. It was unlikely that any mother would encourage such a suitor as Thackeray, who, having moved from Mrs Butler's to a dingy den, consorted with painters and gamblers, without profession or expectations. Yet his love for Isabella appears to have focused Thackeray's attention on his condition and given him a purpose and drive that had hitherto been lacking. Through a sudden new industry Thackeray determined to win and wear Isabella as his wife. With the backing of his friend John Bowes Bowes, Thackeray published his first book—*Flore et Zéphyr*, a collection of captioned lithographs—which gained neither attention nor money. Then his stepfather became a major underwriter for a new journal of radical politics, the *Constitutional and Public Ledger*; this enabled Thackeray, as Paris correspondent, with an income of 8 guineas a week, to propose to Isabella in April 1836, and marry on 20 August.

The marriage was, from all accounts, a very happy one, though beset by problems. The mother-in-law, never happy about losing her daughter, especially to Thackeray, proved a virago, serving amply as prototype for the gallery of horrid mothers-in-law in Thackeray's fiction. Then the *Constitutional* failed, leaving the future novelist—now responsible for a small family—without support except what could be gained by freelance writing. He took his bride to London and began ten years of heavy hack work, living from hand to mouth and suffering one domestic and financial disaster after another. Three daughters were born, Anne Isabella, later Lady *Ritchie (1837–1919), a novelist in her own right, in 1837, Jane (who died at eight months) in 1838, and Harriet Marian ('Minnie', later the wife of Leslie Stephen) [see Stephen, Harriet Marian] in 1840. Jane's death, Minnie's birth, and an apparent genetic tendency brought on serious depression in Isabella. This was compounded by feelings of worthlessness as mother, wife, and housekeeper and by neglect from Thackeray; finding he could get no work done at home, he spent more and more time away, researching for his travel narratives and writing essays and stories, primarily for *Fraser's Magazine*. From the demise of the *Constitutional* in July 1837 to the end of 1840 Thackeray published ninety magazine pieces and his first book, *The Paris Sketch Book*; he also signed a contract for a book in two volumes on Ireland. During the same time two books of reprints were published, though without benefit to his purse (*The Yellowplush Correspondence* in Philadelphia and a pamphlet on George Cruikshank). Perhaps this frantic activity kept Thackeray from noticing anything special about his shy wife's condition, but in mid-August 1840, on his return from a two-week trip in the Low Countries gathering materials for a guidebook never written, he was alarmed by his wife's languor and depression.

Two radical changes then affected Thackeray's life: he turned his attention from his work to his ailing wife, and his sense of guilt appears finally to have produced a profound effect on his personality and behaviour well beyond repeated self-recriminations in a diary. His attention to Isabella and his daughters and his acceptance of his part in creating their condition and his responsibility for their future raised his consciousness about their restraints and vulnerabilities, their worth and potential, and about the self-important self-centredness of his own life as well as that of ordinary men, his peers, whose birthright was to enjoy life and use wives and other women kinsfolk as superior servants. Beginning with *The History of Samuel Titmarsh and the Great Hoggarty Diamond* (serialized from September 1841), his narratives of young men pursuing normal courses of self-fulfilment depict more and more accurately the women who suffered and supported them. Sam Titmarsh's fortunes flare and funk, leaving him chastened and dependent on his resourceful, strong, and loving wife, whose economic contribution to the family equals her husband's. Mary Titmarsh may be based in part on Isabella, but unlike the novelist's wife she proved more resilient and sensible than her husband. Arthur Pendennis, the 'hero' of Thackeray's second major work and the narrator of most of his subsequent books, constitutes a major study of masculine self-absorption, learning and relearning and then forgetting to understand the cruelties to women that passed as ordinary behaviour for sons, lovers, husbands, and fathers.

In September Thackeray took the ailing Isabella to Ireland, hoping that the company of her mother and sister Jane would help restore her spirits. During the crossing Isabella threw herself from a water-closet into the sea, from which she was eventually rescued; it was no longer possible to avoid recognition of her mental breakdown. The Irish sojourn, originally planned as a research trip for *The Irish Sketch-Book*, turned into a domestic battle with the mother-in-law from which Thackeray and Isabella fled after four weeks. In debt to his grandmother and indebted in incalculable ways to his children's nurse, Brodie, who gave up wedding plans to continue caring for the distressed family, Thackeray was also in receipt of an advance from Chapman and Hall for an Irish book which he had been unable to research or write. He returned to his parents in Paris, where he managed, over the next six months, to write ten magazine pieces, a small book (*The Second Funeral of Napoleon*), a serial novelette (*The History of Samuel Titmarsh*), and several chapters of a novel never finished (*The Knights of Borsellen*). From November 1840 to February 1842 Isabella was in and out of professional care, her condition waxing and waning, but in the long run deteriorating until she was placed with Dr Puzin at Chaillot, where she lapsed into a stable, detached condition, unaware of the world around her.

The experience of his mother-in-law's cruelties in contrast to the support of Brodie, his own mother, and Mary Graham Carmichael created in Thackeray deep understanding of women's capacities for cruelty, devotion, generosity, and demands. These insights are apparent in his complex portraits of women such as Amelia Sedley and Helen Pendennis, who exact dreadful tolls from the men they control through helpless love; of women like Blanche Amory, Becky Sharp, and Beatrix Esmond, who exercise control through imperious sexuality; and of women such as Ethel Newcome and Laura Pendennis, whose native intelligence and humour are the objects of male repression and societal control. All these women have secret depths, intelligence, and emotional complexities that Thackeray reveals in ways that some readers have taken to be inconsistency of characterization.

In the six years from the manifestation of Isabella's insanity at the end of 1840 to the start of the serial publication of *Vanity Fair* in January 1847, Thackeray published 386 magazine pieces and three books, all under pseudonyms. There are over twenty known pseudonyms, the most famous and clearly differentiated being George Savage Fitzboodle, Michael Angelo Titmarsh, Major Gahagan, Ikey Solomons, and Charles James Yellowplush. Thackeray's use of pseudonyms allowed him to develop a remarkable range of ventriloquist voices and a habit of presentation which dominated the later works, written in the person of Pendennis, an admitted *alter ego* who undergoes subtle analysis and complex criticism by the 'author'

whose defences of Pendennis are full of apparently deliberate holes. Some would argue that this is a clumsy and inept narrative technique, allowing readers to equate Pendennis with his creator and to conclude, therefore, that Pen's false starts and contradictions represent Thackeray's lack of control over his medium. To those who hold a more charitable view, that Thackeray presents an ironic vision above and beyond that of his narrator, the effect is a sense of ever-increasing narrative complexity and subtlety, a finer and sharper criticism of social conventions.

Having placed his wife in the care of Dr Puzin in 1842 Thackeray returned to London, leaving his daughters for the next four years with his mother in Paris. London was where he could earn by writing what was needed to support his family and make his way in the world. At first he lived in the family house at 13 Great Coram Street, which he shared uneasily with his cousin Mary and Charles Carmichael. His first contribution to *Punch* appeared, but almost immediately he undertook the long deferred research trip to Ireland, spending five months there. Though he had reviewed the Irish novelist Charles Lever rather roughly, their meeting was cordial and their friendship lasted for life. Thackeray dedicated *The Irish sketch-book* to Lever, who reviewed it admiringly in the *Dublin Review*, though he obviously had reservations about the portrait of Ireland, and he later caricatured Thackeray as Elias Howle in *Roland Cashel*. Willingness to tilt irreverently at older, better-known novelists had already landed Thackeray in hot water with Edward Bulwer, later Lord Lytton; for in *Yellowplush* (1837) he lampooned Bulwer's inflated literary style and attributed to him grossly inflated self-aggrandizement. When the *Yellowplush* papers were reprinted in New York in 1852, Thackeray wrote a preface apologizing for the unfairness of the portrait and wrote Bulwer a letter at the same time. In 1855 a collection of Thackeray's *Miscellanies* published both in London and on the continent of course included the Bulwer lampoons again. Apologies aside, Thackeray never actually recanted his attitude toward Bulwer's style.

On his return to London Thackeray gave up the house, moving first to a hotel and then to fourth-floor lodgings in Jermyn Street. He next undertook travel in Belgium to revive the project abandoned in 1839 when he returned to find his wife in deep depression, but again the guide to the Low Countries failed to emerge. During this time Thackeray lived the life of an ineligible bachelor, frequently invited to dinners, but always on the verge of loneliness, and he revived the theatregoing, club-haunting, late-night life of his days before marriage. The only real difference was that now he was writing for his life, seriously committed to the grind of 'odious magazinery', driven by want and ambition.

Thackeray had written a short novel, *Catherine*, in 1838, published a collection of *Comic Tales* in 1840 and another novelette, *The history of Samuel Titmarsh*, in 1841, but he wanted to write a full-length novel. It had to be serialized, however, since he could not afford the time to write it all before being paid, and he had not yet convinced publishers to provide significant advances.

Barry Lyndon *Barry Lyndon*, begun in January 1844 in *Fraser's Magazine*, was a potential novel always in danger of being discontinued. Written in the style of Fielding's *Jonathan Wild*, it represents a major advance over his early fiction in characterization, narrative technique, plot construction, and complexity of themes, but readers of *Fraser's Magazine* were apparently unprepared to distinguish easily between a ruffian's bragging autobiographical voice and that of a satirical author exposing both the egoism of the character and the chicanery of the society in which he bilked and was bilked. The narrative voice in the novel represents a brilliant ventriloquist act, demonstrating the skills Thackeray had been honing in earlier works through using a variety of well-defined pseudonyms. In writing both *Catherine* and *Barry Lyndon* Thackeray was also trying to upstage the popular Newgate or crime fiction that he thought unrealistically and perhaps dangerously glamourized the lives of the criminal heroes. He particularly disapproved of Bulwer's exploitation of false sentiment on behalf of noble highwaymen. *Barry Lyndon* was to have exposed the real unlikeable greed, cruelty, lack of conscience, and vulgarity of the criminal mind. Readers' understandable dislike of the narrator, Barry himself, extended inappropriately to the author, and the magazine's editors asked Thackeray to shut the story down after ten instalments. *Barry Lyndon* remains, however, a critically acclaimed and highly regarded first novel. It is the story of an Irish lad who grows up with a colossal ego and quick temper, who fights duels, cheats at cards, suffers repeated well-deserved set-backs in the English and then the Prussian army, and rises to wealth through a fortune-hunter's marriage, after which his cruelties to his wife and his stepson are not redeemed by his maudlin sorrow for the death of his own son. Ending in prison, he pens his memories, appealing without self-consciousness for sympathy and admiration.

One reason why Thackeray was willing to shut *Barry Lyndon* down was that in August, at three days' notice, he undertook a three-month trip to the Mediterranean with stops in Spain, Greece, Turkey, the Holy Land, and Egypt, recounted in frequent essays 'From our fat contributor' in *Punch* and more meditatively in *Notes of a Journey from Cornhill to Grand Cairo* (1846). Comical recollections survive of Thackeray's severe difficulties in writing *Barry Lyndon*, 'Fat contributor', and *Cornhill to Cairo* while fighting bedbugs and seasickness. The cockney's view of the world, a chief element in his Paris and Irish travel books, dominates the writing; for Thackeray acknowledged to himself that visitors bring as much of their view of the world with them as they find on their travels, and he eschewed pontification. Back in London, in April 1845 he moved to slightly better bachelor quarters in St James's Street, where he was visited by his mother and children in June. And in October he had Isabella, now thought to be incurable, installed in Camberwell with a Mrs Bakewell, in whose care she remained for the rest of her life. One more move, in June 1846, to Young Street, put Thackeray in a

house to which he invited his parents and to which he brought his daughters to stay. His parents, however, chose to remain in Paris out of the reach of the major's London creditors, though Thackeray paid the debts in 1848, clearing the way for their return to England when they chose.

Although Thackeray continued to contribute heavily to *Fraser's Magazine* and regularly to the *Foreign Quarterly Review* and the *Morning Chronicle*, *Punch* was increasingly in the 1840s his periodical affiliation. The magazine's weekly staff dinners were important in his life until he resigned in December 1851 over differences with the editors and with his chief staff rival, Douglas Jerrold, about editorial policy in treating political issues, particularly Catholic emancipation and the character of Louis Philippe. *Punch* published his next two major works, which gained him genuine first-class popular standing and prepared the way thematically for *Vanity Fair*. The first was a comprehensive and exhaustive analysis of 'The Snobs of England. By one of themselves' (March 1846 to February 1847); the other was a series of parodies of the novelists G. P. R. James, Charles Lever, Mrs Gore, Edward Bulwer, Benjamin Disraeli, and James Fenimore Cooper, entitled *Punch's Prize Novelists* (April to October 1847).

Major novels and relations with publishers Nothing Thackeray had written thus far, however, quite prepared readers for the panoramic scope, protean voice, or seriousness of comic vision incorporated in *Vanity Fair*, begun in January 1847 and running for nineteen months as the first publication to bear the name William Makepeace Thackeray on the title-page. Of all Thackeray's works *Vanity Fair* is the one that has been most discussed and most frequently adapted for stage and film. It is almost always cited as his best work, though some readers and critics give *Henry Esmond* that honour.

Vanity Fair chronicles the rise and fall of Becky Sharp's fortunes, the fall and rise of Amelia Sedley's fortunes, and the roles played in their lives by a variety of men. George Osborne, a young 'padded booby', as Becky says, who loses his inheritance by marrying Amelia, but then wishes to run away with Becky, is killed at the battle of Waterloo and mourned for fifty chapters by the silly Amelia. Rawdon Crawley, a not too bright but basically good-hearted soldier who loses his inheritance by marrying Becky, ends by reluctantly accepting the governorship of an island in exchange for his wife's honour. In the wings is William Dobbin, awkward, devoted, and the only true gentleman in the book who finally 'wins and wears' Amelia, though he seems aware that the pay-off is not worth the effort. The subtitle, 'A Novel without a Hero', gives ample warning that there are no very intelligent, very elegant, very noble, or very admirable characters in the book; it does not, however, advertise the brilliance, dexterity, humour, skill, or intelligence of the narrator—or, rather, narrators. Although Thackeray does not use the first-person form with a named narrator, the presence of a story-teller with a chameleon's colouring and a showman's skills is inescapable. Unlike many Victorian novelists with palpable narrators who frequently intrude in the story to make sure the reader is 'getting it', the narrator of *Vanity Fair* appears to toy with the reader, offering obviously erroneous and contradictory directions; the reader must therefore accept responsibility for pointing morals, if any, independently of the comic untrustworthy narrator.

Thackeray's primary publishers in the 1840s had been Chapman and Hall who, besides the Irish and Mediterranean travel books, published four Christmas volumes. It is rumoured that *Vanity Fair* was turned down by five or more publishers before Bradbury and Evans, the proprietors of *Punch*, agreed to publish it in the same format and style that they used for their star author, Charles Dickens. Though the novel's initial print run and sales were under 5000 copies, and though Thackeray complained that popularity did not match critical success, 1847 proved a watershed year, separating Thackeray's struggling hack work from the success that brought publishers begging to his door. He made £1200 plus a share of profits from *Vanity Fair*, and each novel thereafter earned him more than the previous one until the last years of his life when his income exceeded £7000 a year. Bradbury and Evans subsequently published Thackeray's three other major serial novels: *Pendennis* (1848–50), *The Newcomes* (1853–5), and *The Virginians* (1857–9).

Pendennis, a twenty-three-month serial, begun in August 1848 but interrupted for three months at the end of 1849 because of Thackeray's nearly fatal illness (most probably cholera or typhoid), chronicles the youth, education, and launched writing career of Arthur Pendennis, son of a country squire, formerly an apothecary. Four major episodes in Arthur's life drive the plot: his first innocent, passionate, hopelessly absurd passion for an actress, the Fotheringay, much older than himself; a second, somewhat cold-blooded play-acted love passage with Blanche Amory, more suitable by education and social status but artificial in manners and character; there follows Arthur's briefly glorious and ultimately ignominious career as a college student at Oxbridge; and then a third, tawdry and nearly tragic liaison with a porter's daughter, Fanny Bolton. In *Pendennis* Thackeray used a limited omniscient narrator who plays very few of the narrative games employed in *Vanity Fair*. And though many critics have found easy parallels between Arthur's biography and that of the author, it seems clear that Pendennis, who in the main has a love of truth and hatred of lies, is yet the world's worst at remembering lessons learned. Though Pendennis is rewarded at the end by marriage to his childhood playmate, Laura Bell, there is much to suggest that Thackeray is already shifting his satirical and critical mode and gaze from the obvious vanities and hypocrisies of society to the subconscious, more habitual injustices and cruelties of conventional behaviour, particularly as played out in domestic circles between husbands and wives, parents and children, and among siblings. Pendennis, who lacks the ability to see such subtleties, is chosen narrator for two later novels (*The Newcomes* and *The Adventures of Philip*), in which he plays the role of wise, observant arbiter of intelligent common sense and good intentions;

time and again, however, Thackeray exposes the narrator, Pendennis, for the insensitive boor that he is. Thackeray's apprenticeship in this type of narration began with the pseudonymous works of his youth. The only difference between Barry Lyndon and Arthur Pendennis is that Pendennis is well mannered, polite, educated, and conventionally married to a conventional woman. But he is just as egotistical, self-centred, self-satisfied, and content in his male-dominated world as was Barry.

The major force in Thackeray's writing career was his third publisher, George Smith. In his first approach in 1849 Smith offered Thackeray £1000 for his next book, sight unseen, but Thackeray was already committed and counter-offered a Christmas book, *The Kickleburys on the Rhine*. In 1852 Smith signed the novelist to a contract for a novel in three volumes, stipulating that he could publish nothing else in the six months before or after publication. Smith, known as the prince of publishers, was generous with his money and ruthless in his control. Thackeray, who from 1847 to 1851 had averaged fifty-nine magazine publications a year in addition to two major serials, in 1852 had but one publication, *The History of Henry Esmond*.

It is on *Esmond* that Thackeray's fame as a historical novelist primarily rests. The first, three-volume edition was printed in an antique typeface and with antique spelling. Set during the reign of Queen Anne, the novel focuses attention on the English revolution and on the conflicts over succession caused by William III and Anne having no surviving children. Like Barry Lyndon, who writes his life's history while in prison at the end of his life, the narrator and main character, Henry Esmond, writes his memoirs in the twilight of his years on his estate in Virginia, a property he came to after all the events worth telling about his life have taken place. Orphaned, one might say, three times, Henry grows up vulnerable and sensitive to slights and grateful for attention. He adores his first spiritual leader, the Jesuit Father Holt; but his allegiances turn protestant under the priest's successor, Rachel Castlewood, who for at least the first quarter of the novel plays the role of mother in his life. A man of loyalties, Henry waxes political in college, goes to war, and serves the Jacobite cause, not so much because of personal convictions, readers are led to believe, but in order to impress Rachel's daughter Beatrix. The novel is both controversial and psychologically subtle and complex because it is clear that Rachel Castlewood, though married to Lord Castlewood and playing the mother role, is in love with Henry by the end of the first volume. Clearly Henry does not know that, and, perhaps as clearly, Rachel is in denial, even after the death of Lord Castlewood. But after spending all of volume two and most of volume three in love with Rachel's daughter Beatrix, Henry finally recognizes the daughter for the vixen that she is and declares for and marries the mother, retiring to Virginia. Perhaps the most intriguing thing about Henry's life is his successive discoveries that what he thought was true, wonderful, and good proves to be false, disappointing, and even evil. Truth, he seems to conclude, is very elusive and naught but grief comes from accepting the truths of others. However, even the truth of self-reliance seems uncertain in this novel, where Thackeray once again plays off the narrator's insights against the reader's suspicions, giving readers one of the most thought-provoking and unsettling among Victorian novels. Thackeray's amateur knowledge of the period was so extensive that he contemplated writing a history in the style of Macaulay's *History of England*, and he was asked by a publisher to edit a multi-volume correspondence of Horace Walpole.

However restrictive, the contract with Smith for *Esmond* said nothing about delivering lectures, and Thackeray had already planned a series on eighteenth-century English humorists, which he began delivering in London and other major cities in England and Scotland, making more money from them than from his occasional writings in previous years. On publication of *Esmond* he took his lecture tour to America for five months, visiting New York, Boston, Providence, Philadelphia, Baltimore, Washington (where he dined with outgoing President Millard Fillmore and incoming President Franklin Pierce and lobbied on behalf of international copyright), Richmond, Charleston, and Savannah. The lectures were published in England as soon as the contractual time of silence expired. On a second tour of America two and a half years later he lectured on the four Georges, adding Albany and Buffalo to the itinerary in the north and Mobile, New Orleans, St Louis, and Cincinnati in the south and west. Thackeray's wealth was accumulating, and he invested in railways on both sides of the Atlantic and in the transatlantic cable, demonstrations of which were thought promising in the 1850s, though the first success came three years after Thackeray's death.

Thackeray's encounters with American publishers, who had republished his early work at will, were remarkably different from those by Charles Dickens and later Anthony Trollope who both lost their tempers over their lack of control of American publications. Thackeray, acknowledging that half a loaf was better than no loaf, laughed and befriended James Fields in Boston, George Putnam in Philadelphia, and, in New York, the Appletons and the biggest pirates of them all, the Harper Brothers—negotiating courtesy contracts and recording his unpleasant thoughts on the matter of authors' rights only in letters home.

Under their previous contract Bradbury and Evans published *The Newcomes*, another twenty-three-month serial that began in July 1854. It chronicles the affairs of a 'most respectable family' of merchants, bankers, and petty aristocrats. The respectability is primarily one of manners and appearances, and the novel reveals in great detail intense intra-family jealousies, rivalries, fights, and outward politeness. The central character is, ostensibly, Clive Newcome, who plays at becoming an artist and plays at aspiring to the hand of his very elegant cousin Ethel Newcome, but whose pliable nature and lack of ambition nearly destroy his attractiveness as a handsome, well-intentioned, charming young man. A major role is also played by Clive's father, Thomas, the East Indian merchant and half-brother to the establishment Newcomes.

Thomas, indulgent of Clive to a fault, presses his son to marry Rosie McKenzie (who brings along her termagant mother), though Clive is never in love with her. Thomas is, however, in love with Rosie and appears to live out his own youthful failure to marry the girl he loved through the marriage he arranges for his son. Although the novel is on its surface about the men, it is easy to see that *The Newcomes* is a major exploration of the marriage market (particularly through Lady Kew's efforts to find an appropriately wealthy buyer for her niece, Ethel) and of the cruelties and injustice of the role of women in Victorian society. One reaches this conclusion, for the most part, by ignoring the opinions expressed by Pendennis, the narrator, and seeing the reality of the situations described. Thackeray paints a remarkably sympathetic portrait of Clara, who marries the tyrannical and abusive Barnes Newcome and then runs away with Jack Belsize. That the decision to break her marriage vows is a traumatic experience for Clara is abundantly clear, but that she is fully justified in taking her situation into her own hands in a country with no laws to protect her is equally clear.

Family life The result of Isabella's illness was that Thackeray lived the rest of his life as a *de facto* widower, though unable to remarry or have any 'normal' relationship with a woman. His letters show that he developed an extraordinary number of confidential relations with women who were emotional supports to him. Most remarkable among his relationships were two which threatened or promised to be more than friendships: the first with Jane Octavia, the wife of his close college friend William Brookfield; the second with Sally Baxter, an American girl twenty years his junior. The first relationship had all the potential for a serious affair, but was kept under a strict restraint that exacerbated the emotional pressures. Having given up hope of a cure for Isabella, Thackeray and Jane—a partial invalid apparently troubled by doubts about her husband eleven years her senior—began a friendship that could have been innocent enough. Though much of their correspondence was destroyed or snipped, it is clear that the 'brother sister' love under which they conducted their relations threatened to boil over in 1851, when William Brookfield finally barred Thackeray from further visits to or correspondence with Jane. Thackeray, declaring his aggrieved innocence, nursed his bruised ego vicariously in *The History of Henry Esmond*, which he had just begun, chronicling the demise of the loveless marriage of Frank and Rachel Castlewood and the latter's suppressed and initially unacknowledged love for Esmond. Thackeray may have indulged a modicum of revenge in having Esmond displace his love for Rachel on to her daughter Beatrix, a 'betrayal' Rachel perforce suffered in silence. Be that as it may, the emotional trauma of the Brookfield relationship, like that of his wife's mental breakdown, left Thackeray not only more melancholy but wiser and tenderer in his understanding of both men and women and of thwarted desires.

The second relationship—with Sally Baxter, whom he met while visiting Mr and Mrs Baxter during his stay in

New York in 1852—was far more playful, though Thackeray wrote to his mother, of all people, about his surprise and pleasure in discovering, at his age, that the foolish emotions of young love were still available to him. Though again in New York in 1855, when Sally married Frank Wade Hampton of South Carolina, Thackeray declined to attend, apparently because of real though of course unjustified feelings of jealousy.

Thackeray's confidantes included Mrs Anne Procter, who had been a principal support to him in his troubles with Isabella and to whose husband, Bryan Procter (Barry Cornwall), he dedicated *Vanity Fair*. More important were Jane Elliot and her unmarried sister Kate Perry, whom Thackeray met while writing *Vanity Fair* in 1846. Their friendship, by Kate's account, sprang up 'like Jack's bean stalk in a pantomime, which rushed up sky high without culture; and, thank God, so remained till his most sad and sudden end' (*Letters and Private Papers*, 1.cxxv). These two ladies were true confidantes, bolstering Thackeray during his emotional involvement with Jane Brookfield and in the trials and challenges of single parenting. With many other women, to whom less intimate letters survive, Thackeray developed social friendships that apparently thrived on his charming, gallant, but utterly safe status as a 'single man' who was married. The condition lent piquancy and restraint to relationships that supplied his genuine need for and interest in feminine companionship.

While *The Newcomes* was being written Thackeray and his daughters moved to Onslow Square, Brompton, in May 1854, after nine years at Young Street. Thackeray's plan to provide his parents with a home in his own house was abandoned after a four-month experimental visit in 1857, and another house was found for them two years later. Henry Carmichael-Smyth was a complex, energetic, somewhat eccentric, and erratic character, constantly developing schemes for investments and inventions, which Thackeray found irritating. And his mother, whose love always entailed a demand for some control and for conformity to her religious views, was easier to deal with in small doses and at a distance. A remarkable exchange of letters with his mother and daughter includes stern reproaches to the grandmother for attempting to indoctrinate Anne and Minnie in her strict beliefs during Thackeray's visit to America in 1852 (see *Letters and Private Papers*, 3.85–7, 93–6, 140–41, 4.168–70). Anne was fifteen by then, shared many of Thackeray's liberal ideas, and was highly critical of the Old Testament—or at least of the prevailing interpretations of an angry avenging God. But Thackeray wished to live at peace with his mother, and most biographers claim that he never really achieved full independence from her influence, though it exerted itself only in her presence and in her relatively narrow sphere.

Thackeray doted on his daughters and had a special affinity with Anne, who, he was afraid, was 'going to be a man of genius' (*Letters and Private Papers*, 2.240). His fears did not prevent his employing her as a secretary, her handwriting appearing in the manuscripts from *The Newcomes* onwards. Nor did he stand in the way, though he did not take a positive hand, when Anne submitted a story anonymously to Smith for the *Cornhill*, and he failed utterly to conceal his pride when it was accepted. He both feared that Anne and Minnie would be unable to secure husbands and feared that they would. They focused his energies from their birth to his own death, for he frequently said that all his work was aimed at restoring his lost patrimony. In March 1860 Thackeray purchased 2 Palace Green, Kensington, and after having it completely rebuilt, the family moved in during March 1862. When his house, furnishings, wine, books, and copyrights were sold in 1864 after his death, each girl received nearly £10,000. Major Carmichael-Smyth died in 1861; Mrs Carmichael-Smyth died in 1864.

Literary relations   From the time Thackeray joined the Garrick Club in 1833, clubs featured prominently in his social life. Even when he was hardest at work, he seldom wrote in the evening, when he usually dined out in the home of friends or at a club. Talk was a necessary ingredient of Thackeray's 'research' for his writing, and he made acquaintances wherever he travelled. The Garrick and the Reform were his favourite clubs, though he belonged to the Athenaeum, the Century (in New York), and to several debating societies like the Eccentric, the Shakespeare, and the Rationals. Of Thackeray's writing friends Francis Sylvester Mahoney (Father Prout), Bryan Procter (Barry Cornwall), Jack Sheehan, and Jacob Omnium figure most pleasantly in his letters. He worked closely with illustrators George Cruikshank, John Leech (a friend since Charterhouse days), Richard Doyle, and Frederick Walker.

Thackeray's relationship with Charles Dickens has been controversial among critics since the 1840s, no critic able to refrain from championing one side or the other. Although in an often repeated lecture for charities Thackeray praised Dickens in fulsome terms for four pages, he could not stop himself from adding 'I may quarrel with Mr. Dickens's art a thousand and a thousand times, I delight and wonder at his genius' ('Charity and humour', *Harper's New Monthly Magazine*, 7, June 1853, 88). Privately he objected to Dickens's overblown writing style, and he remarked once that Dickens was cool to him because he had 'found him out' as a poseur. And though Dickens wrote a moving memorial full of praise for Thackeray, published in the *Cornhill Magazine* just a month after Thackeray's death, he could not refrain from saying that 'We had our differences of opinion. I thought that he too much feigned a want of earnestness, and that he made a pretence of under-valuing his art, which was not good for the art that he held in trust' (February 1864, 130). They were too different and too similar to ever really like each other.

At first Thackeray got on fairly well with Dickens's chief supporter, John Forster, though he caricatured him in his letters to friends—a circumstance that became known to Forster, who of course objected, with Dickens acting as his second. In 1847 club gossip led to a flare-up over Forster's supposed remark that Thackeray was 'false as Hell', but after a reconciliation it was Forster who brought Dr

Elliotson to Thackeray when he fell seriously ill in 1849. A remark three months later in *Pendennis*, however, opened the famous 'dignity of literature' controversy that revealed the deep rifts in thought, temperament, and—one would have said at the time—breeding that separated Thackeray from Dickens and Forster, whose claims to social status rested entirely upon their literary efforts. Thackeray, on the other hand, had family ties that bestowed status apart from his literary reputation. Comments by Forster on the desirability of state support for artists and against the passage in *Pendennis*, which Forster said disparaged the profession of writing, led to a response by Thackeray and counters by Forster (the relevant documents are reprinted in the Garland edition of *The History of Pendennis*, New York, 1991). Another reconciliation ensued, but soreness remained. Then in May 1858 rumours spread about Dickens's separation from his wife, Kate, and Thackeray contradicted one rumour about Dickens's having an affair with his sister-in-law Georgina by blurting out 'no such thing—its with an actress' (*Letters and Private Papers*, 4.86). Dickens, when he heard the story, thought Thackeray was spreading a tale of him and an actress—which, though true, was not his business to discuss. This episode was still rankling in each author's thoughts when the famous 'Yates affair' broke out a month later. Young Edmund Yates published an unflattering description of Thackeray, questioning his honour and veracity, to which Thackeray objected. Dickens and Forster stood by Yates, who was nevertheless deprived of his club membership at the Garrick and subsequently lost appeals to the club membership and in court. No further connection was made between the two novelists until, the week before he died, Thackeray approached Dickens on the steps of the Reform Club and shook his hand.

Thackeray's normal relations with his writing colleagues were cordial, but the differences with Douglas Jerrold over the virulence of *Punch* satire did not end with Thackeray's resignation from the staff in 1851: in an 1855 *Quarterly Review* essay on the drawings of his old friend John Leech, Thackeray remarked off-handedly that *Punch* without Leech would be worthless. The remark, meant to praise Leech, naturally offended the rest of the staff. Thackeray's success led to renewals of school friendships with members of the aristocracy such as Lord Houghton (Richard Monckton Milnes), and he made many new friends among the social élite. These have fuelled the notion that he disparaged his profession to curry favour with the upper classes, an idea he denied and which, though still widely accepted, withstands little scrutiny.

Later works and final years Though Smith made offers for the remaining large serials, Thackeray remained with Bradbury and Evans for one more novel. *The Virginians* (1857–9) is a sequel to *Esmond*, and recounts the adventures of Henry Esmond's grandsons in the period of the American Revolution. But then *The Virginians* failed to earn expected profits (it is not true that the publisher lost any money), and Thackeray felt free to switch publishers. Early in his career Thackeray had made a bid to be editor of the *Westminster Review*, and in the mid-1850s he had proposed a periodical to George Smith and then withdrawn; so it is not very surprising that Thackeray readily agreed to edit Smith's *Cornhill Magazine*, which began publication in January 1860, or that he took his duties seriously—agreeing to read all submissions, writing prospectuses and letters of acceptance and rejection, though drawing the line at reading proofs for any but his own writings. Thackeray did much of the work at home with the help of an amanuensis and a courier for messages to and from Smith's office and home. The work was onerous and demanding enough to occasion friction between editor and publisher, but the letters show a deep personal regard and respect between the two. Thackeray sponsored Smith's nomination to the Reform Club, and the families exchanged social visits, particularly after Smith's marriage.

Smith's contract with Thackeray to edit the *Cornhill Magazine* was tied to others under which Thackeray contributed fiction—*Lovel the Widower* (1860), *The Adventures of Philip* (1861–2), and *Denis Duval* (1864)—and editorial essays (*The Roundabout Papers*). This prevented him from writing for any other publisher the rest of his life; Smith even prevented Thackeray from offering a short piece to *Punch* as a conciliatory move.

Thackeray's later fiction is seldom written about and less often admired. *The Adventures of Philip* adopts again Arthur Pendennis as narrator to chronicle the story of a not terribly brilliant, not terribly industrious, not terribly sensitive young man's struggle through adversity, including a corrupt and sycophantic father, to success in a writing career and in love. Philip's story follows a trajectory similar to Thackeray's own life, but the interest of the story must lie in finding Pendennis to be an unreliable narrator whose expressed values and approbation of characters is frequently insensitive in ways of which Thackeray must have expected readers to disapprove. Many readers, unwilling to grant this view, find the later novels weak, bland, and tedious in spite of the smooth dexterity of Thackeray's writing style. *Lovel the Widower* is a fictional reworking of a play, *The Wolves and the Lamb*, and is frequently seen as a filler that Thackeray produced to fulfil his contract with George Smith. Returning to historical fiction with *Denis Duval*, which was truncated at his death, Thackeray set his last novel among the French Huguenots in England in the latter half of the eighteenth century. Both *Esmond* and *Duval* are first-person narrations requiring what would appear to be a first-hand knowledge of current events at the time. The first editor of *Denis Duval*, appending comments to the unfinished book, remarked on the care with which Thackeray prepared his work, referring to his

> many most careful notes, and memoranda of inquiry into minute matters of detail to make the story true. How many young novelists are there who haven't much genius to fall back upon, who yet, if they desired to set their hero down in Winchelsea a hundred years ago for instance, would take the trouble to learn how the town was built, and what gate led to Rye (if the hero happened to have any dealings with that place), and who were its local magnates, and how it was governed? And yet this is what Mr. Thackeray did though his

investigation added not twenty lines to the story and no 'interest' whatever: it was simply so much conscientious effort to keep as near truth in feigning as he could.   (*Cornhill Magazine*, 9, June 1864, 656)

Thackeray was a large man, 6 feet 3 inches, and weighing over 15 stone. His height kept him from looking rotund, but his round face with its flattened nose, near-sighted squint, and high forehead lent itself to self-caricature. As a young man he affected a monocle and later signed many of his drawings with a pair of spectacles with crossed temples. By the age of forty he had white hair, parted on the left and worn over his ears and collar. The fullest recorded description of his appearance occurs in Edmund Yates's unpleasant lampoon, but a number of photographs and drawings show him in the typical unsmiling Victorian dignity which was required by long exposure times and which belied the constant humour of his writings from beginning to end. His health worsened during the 1850s and he was plagued by the recurring stricture of the urethra that laid him up for days at a time. He worsened matters by over-eating and drinking and avoiding exercise, though he enjoyed horseback riding and kept a horse.

On 23 December 1863, after returning from dining out and before dressing for bed, Thackeray suffered a stroke and was found dead on his bed in the morning. His death at the age of fifty-three was entirely unexpected by his family, friends, and reading public. An estimated 7000 people attended his funeral at Kensington Gardens. He was buried on 29 December at Kensal Green cemetery.

Posthumous reputation From the publication of *Vanity Fair* in 1847–8 to the First World War Thackeray's reputation grew steadily. Never the best-seller that Dickens was, he was more highly regarded than Dickens by readers such as Charlotte Brontë and Jane Welsh Carlyle and by reviewers like Robert Bell and Lady Eastlake. From the beginning, however, there were detractors who preferred writers whose characters were less ambiguous and whose grasp of moral conventions was more comfortable.

Charles Dickens and other critics such as John Forster (Dickens's first biographer), Michael Sadleir (in his biography of Bulwer-Lytton, 1931) and, more recently, John Carey (*Thackeray: Prodigal Genius*, 1977) have thought that Thackeray had a thin skin, being able to dish out but not receive criticism, and that this characteristic revealed itself significantly as an uneasy social position in English society, which, after *Vanity Fair*, lionized him as a writer but distrusted him as an outsider with bohemian connections. The result, such critics aver, was to tone down his satire against the upper classes, with whom in his later years he allegedly curried favour.

A very different view cites evidence that Thackeray's pedigree, particularly on his father's side—a family of professionals, doctors, academics, and clergy as well as East India officials with sufficient family wealth to pay for public school and a Cambridge education—ushered him with some grace and comfort into the manners of the upper classes. It is a view that acknowledges Thackeray as

a thinker whose experiences and philosophy led to a profound change of heart and mode of thinking from an ordinary privileged young man to a sensitive and hurt but keen-eyed observer of social and domestic injustices. It was less the success of *Vanity Fair* and the responsibilities of single parenthood and much more the thoughtful incorporation of Comte's positivism and Victor Cousin's tolerance and eclecticism that informed the subtle exposure of ordinary greed and insensitivity in the male-dominated society and legal system that was England in the 1850s.

Thackeray was capable of exposing the hypocrisy of conventional socially acceptable behaviour, but he had an unusual capacity to distrust his own and other people's best views. His ability to create detailed realistic images combined with an ability to detect sham or self-deception in the best-intentioned acts led one reviewer to compare Thackeray to a fly settling on a good dinner. Readers of a more philosophical bent appreciated his reluctance to impose a moral imperative. He was a man of principles and honour whose sense of guilt about his self-indulgences was balanced by a sense of honesty in acknowledging his appetites. His own and his characters' moral dilemmas and self-directed humour have endeared and repelled readers, according to their tastes, from the beginning.

Biographers accounting for Thackeray's development as a writer, whether they think of the later works as a decline or as more subtle and complex narratives and social criticism, generally point to major turning points: Thackeray's marriage and loss of one child and then of his wife (1836–44), the success of *Vanity Fair* (1847–8), the nearly fatal illness during the writing of *Pendennis* (1849), and the break with the Brookfields (1852). Without a doubt Thackeray was changed by these events, but it is not obvious that he increasingly became the complacent toothless lion and bland purveyor of harmless fiction—as argued by critics who prefer the biting, rollicking satire of the early works culminating in *Vanity Fair*. It has been argued that with time he became a shrewder, more subtle, and more philosophical exposer of the ordinary treacheries of conventional society.

Thackeray stands alone among male Victorian novelists in the estimation of feminist critics in the last quarter of the twentieth century who delighted in reading against the grain of Victorian conventions on gender and found Thackeray subtly in harmony with their criticism of those conventions.

There is no comprehensive bibliography: the longest listing of periodical and book materials—Lewis Melville's in *Thackeray: a Biography*, volume 2 (1910)—is augmented and corrected by E. Harden, *A checklist of contributions by William Makepeace Thackeray to newspapers, periodicals, books, and serial part issues, 1828–1864* (1996), while the most detailed description of Thackeray's separately published books is Henry S. Van Duzer's *A Thackeray Library* (1919). Gordon Ray's four-volume collection of Thackeray's letters in the 1940s (*William Makepeace Thackeray: Letters and Private*

Papers) and his two-volume biography in the mid-1950s (*The Uses of Adversity* and *The Age of Wisdom*) brought Thackeray a burst of attention and new appreciation. Ray's remains the standard biography, while his study of the living prototypes for Thackeray's fiction, *The Buried Life* (1952), adds significantly to knowledge of Thackeray's circle of acquaintance. The economics and logistics of Thackeray's professional affairs with publishers are detailed in Peter Shillingsburg's *Pegasus in Harness* (1992) and his methods of composition are described in Edgar Harden's *The Emergence of Thackeray's Serial Fiction* (1979) and his *Thackeray's English Humourists and Four Georges* (1985). The record of Thackeray's meticulous attention to detail is continued in *Annotations for selected works of William Makepeace Thackeray*, edited by Edgar Harden (1990); Harden's two-volume *Thackeray the Writer* (1998–2000); and R. D. McMaster's *Thackeray's Cultural Frame of Reference* (1991). Evidence of Thackeray's interest in historical details about London in the second and third decades of the nineteenth century, the period of *Vanity Fair*, is traced by Joan Stevens in 'Vanity Fair' and the London skyline (*Costerus*, new ser., 2, 1974, 13–41). Stevens shows the historical and geographical accuracy of the novel, though it is notoriously and deliberately anachronistic in its description of dress. Thackeray's carelessness and capacity for error are recorded by John Sutherland in *Victorian Fiction: Writers, Publishers, Readers* (1995). Two supplementary volumes of letters were compiled by Harden (1994).

Thackeray's novels have been the subject of a number of film adaptations, beginning with *Vanity Fair* in 1911. A version of 1935 entitled *Becky Sharp* (or *Lady of Fortune* in the United States) starred Miriam Hopkins, Cedric Hardwicke, and Nigel Bruce. In 1975 Stanley Kubrick made a highly acclaimed motion picture of *Barry Lyndon*, employing cutting-edge cinematography but apparently completely missing the point that Thackeray intended readers to see through Barry's self-aggrandizement to the criminal heart. However beautiful and innovative as a film, Kubrick's Barry is rather romanticized, like the fictional criminals Thackeray was writing against.

By the end of the twentieth century Thackeray was overshadowed by much more successful resurgences of interest in Anthony Trollope, the Brontës, George Eliot, and even more so, Charles Dickens. In spite of Hollywood and BBC adaptations and new biographies—*Thackeray* by D. J. Taylor (1999) and *William Makepeace Thackeray: a Literary Life* by P. Shillingsburg (2001)—Thackeray's works do not now attract the public they deserve. Except for *Vanity Fair* they are not often taught in schools. Thackeray's realism, detached tolerance, and failure to assert expected Victorian moral imperatives may explain some of this neglect. The historical weight of his later novels may have alienated some modern readers, yet his skill in speech, his vivid characters, and his philosophical stance deserve more appreciation.   Peter L. Shillingsburg

Sources *The letters and private papers of William Makepeace Thackeray*, ed. G. N. Ray, 4 vols. (1945–6) [with 2 vol. suppl., ed. E. F. Harden (1994)] · G. Ray, *William Makepeace Thackeray: the uses of adversity* (1955) · G. Ray, *William Makepeace Thackeray: the age of wisdom* (1958) · G. Ray, *The buried life: a study of the relation between Thackeray's fiction and his personal history* (1952) · P. Shillingsburg, *Pegasus in harness: Victorian publishing and W. M. Thackeray* (1992) · E. Harden, *The emergence of Thackeray's serial fiction* (1979) · E. Harden, *Thackeray's 'English humourists' and 'Four Georges'* (1985) · J. Sutherland, *Thackeray at work* (1974) · R. A. Colby, *Thackeray's canvass of humanity: the author and his public* (1979) · J. Dodds, *Thackeray: a critical portrait* (1941) · G. Tillotson, *Thackeray the novelist* (1954) · A. Monsarrat, *An uneasy Victorian: Thackeray the man* (1980) · I. Ferris, *William Makepeace Thackeray* (1983) · C. Peters, *Thackeray's universe* (1987)

Archives BL, corresp., literary MSS and papers · BL, Add. MSS 43484, 43738, 46891-46910, 47229; RP 3278, 3407, 3630 (iv) · Boston PL, letters and papers · FM Cam., literary papers and letters · Harvard U., Widener Library · Harvard U., Houghton L., letters and papers · Hunt. L., letters, drawings, and literary MSS · King's School, Canterbury, letters, sketches and literary MSS · Morgan L. · NL Scot., letters · NYPL, Berg Collection, letters, drawings, and literary MSS · Princeton University, New Jersey, Parrish Collection, letters and literary MSS · Princeton University, New Jersey, Taylor Collection, letters and MSS · Ransom HRC, corresp. papers, and literary MSS · Trinity Cam., letters, corresp., literary MSS, and artwork · U. Leeds, Brotherton L., letters · University of Rochester, New York, Rush Rhees Library, corresp., literary MSS and papers · Yale U., Beinecke L. | BL, letters to Lord Broughton, Add. MS 47229 · BL, letters to Royal Literary Fund, loan 96 · BL, corresp. with George Smith, RP 4894 · Bodl. Oxf., letters to F. M. Evans · Morgan L., corresp. with George Smith · NL Scot., letters to Blackwoods · NL Scot., letters to John Brown · NL Scot., corresp. with George Smith and Mrs Proctor · NRA Scot., priv. coll., letters to John Swinton · Trinity Cam., letters to Lord Houghton

Likenesses G. Chinnery, group portrait, pencil and wash, 1814, Harris Museum and Art Gallery, Preston · J. S. Deville, bust, 1820, priv. coll. · J. Spedding, pencil sketch, 1829, priv. coll. · J. Spedding, pencil sketch, 1831, priv. coll. · D. Maclise, pencil drawing, 1832, Garr. Club · D. Maclise, pencil drawing, 1833, Garr. Club · W. M. Thackeray, self-portrait, pen, 1834, Hunt. L. · W. M. Thackeray, self-portrait, pen and wash, 1834, Athenaeum Club, London · D. Maclise, group portrait, lithograph, pubd 1835, V&A; repro. in *The Fraserians* · miniature, c.1835, Morgan L. · F. Stone, oils, c.1839, NPG · D. Maclise, pencil drawing, c.1840, NPG · A. D'Orsay, pencil sketch, 1848, priv. coll.; repro. in *Letters*, ed. Ray, vol. 2, p. 386 · R. Doyle, pencil and watercolour drawing, 1848, Scot. NPG · R. Doyle, pencil drawing, 1848, BM · sketch, 1850-59, priv. coll. · S. Laurence, chalk drawing, 1852, priv. coll.; repro. in *Letters*, ed. Ray, vol. 3, p. 89 [*see illus.*] · S. Laurence, drawings, 1852; replicas, BM · F. Holl, stipple, pubd 1853 (after S. Laurence), BM, NPG · C. Martin, pencil drawing, 1853, BM · J. H. Whitehurst, daguerreotype, 1855, Boston PL · photograph, 1856, Boston PL · E. Landseer, pen, ink, and wash caricature, 1857, NPG · S. Laurence, sketch, 1862, repro. in Monsarrat, *Uneasy Victorian*, jacket; priv. coll. · Brucciani & Co., plaster cast of death mask and right hand, 1863, NPG · E. Goodwin Lewis, chalk drawing, 1863, Kensington Public Library · photograph, 1863, priv. coll. · J. E. Boehm, plaster statuette, 1864, NPG · J. Durham, plaster bust, 1864, NPG · J. Gilbert, oils, 1864, Garr. Club · S. Laurence, oils, c.1864 (after drawing, 1862), NPG · C. Marochetti, bust, c.1866 (later altered by E. O. Ford), Poet's Corner, Westminster Abbey · N. N. Burnard, marble bust, c.1867, NPG · S. Laurence, oils, 1881, Reform Club, London · W. Lockhart Bogle, oils, 1893, Trinity Cam. · L. Jennings, marble bust, 1911, Thackeray Memorial, Calcutta · J. E. Boehm, plaster cast (after bust by J. S. Deville, 1824-5), NPG · W. M. Thackeray, self-portrait, pencil drawing, Walsall Museum and Art Gallery · W. M. Thackeray, self-portrait, watercolour, Hunt. L. · H. Watkins, photograph, NPG · carte-de-visite, NPG · photographs, repro. in *Letters*, ed. Ray, vol. 4, p. 275 · portraits, repro. in *Letters*, ed. Ray · portraits, repro. in Ray, *William Makepeace Thackeray: the uses of adversity*, 110

Wealth at death under £20,000: administration, 5 March 1864, *CGPLA Eng. & Wales*

Thackrah, Charles Turner (1795–1833), surgeon, was born on 22 May 1795 in Leeds and baptized at St John's Church, Briggate, Leeds, on 13 July 1795, the son of George Thackrah (1770–1820), a chemist and druggist, and his wife, Alice Leader (1771–1828). In addition to residences in Leeds, his family had connections in the nearby village of Shadwell. Thackrah originally intended to fulfil his mother's wish that he should have a career in the clergy, and he studied under several local clergymen. However, in 1814 he enrolled as a pupil at the Leeds Infirmary, and in 1815 he moved to London, where for two years he attended lectures at Guy's Hospital, studying under Sir Astley Cooper. In October that year he joined the physical society at Guy's. In March 1816 Thackrah applied to practise as an apothecary, but was refused permission as he was not yet twenty-one; after a wait of three months he was admitted to the Society of Apothecaries. Thackrah's premature attempt to take the apothecaries' examination was illustrative of the tremendous drive and self-belief which characterized his approach to his medical studies and his later career. Thackrah contracted tuberculosis while in London, and, though his poor health did not diminish his ambition, it caused him much suffering and depression throughout the remainder of his life.

On returning to Leeds in 1817 Thackrah established a private practice and supplemented his income by becoming town surgeon, with responsibility for the care of the town's paupers. In 1818 he wrote a prize-winning essay on the properties of the blood, particularly the process of coagulation, which brought him into dispute with William Hey, the dominant figure at Leeds Infirmary. The argument was resolved in Thackrah's favour after experiments at a local slaughter-house. The essay was published in 1819 and posthumously with a biographical memoir in 1834. In 1821 Thackrah's prestige in Leeds grew after he was invited to give the inaugural address at the Leeds Philosophical and Literary Society, for which he acted as joint secretary from 1819 to 1822. In 1823 and 1824 he gave public lectures on physiology at the Philosophical Hall. He became a member of the Royal College of Surgeons in 1821. In 1823 Thackrah's growing reputation was tarnished when it was revealed that he was the father of an illegitimate child, Charles Turner Thackrah Wailes, who was born following an affair with a patient. He acknowledged his son in his will with a legacy of £200. In the spring of 1824 Thackrah married Mary Henrietta, daughter of J. Scott of Wakefield, with whom he had one daughter, Mary Henrietta, born in 1825; mother and child both died in 1828. In 1830 he married Grace, daughter of A. Greenwood of Dewsbury Moor.

Thackrah also had ambitions as a teacher, in the tradition of his own mentor, Astley Cooper. He began by taking on a few apprentices, before establishing his own school of anatomy at 9 South Parade. Things did not go entirely smoothly. His attempts to have the school recognized by the Royal College of Surgeons were constantly refused, and his efforts to promote the school met with hostility from some of his colleagues at the Leeds Infirmary, particularly when he championed junior members'

accusations of misconduct among senior staff. The dispute came to a head in 1827 when one of Thackrah's pupils was successfully prosecuted for an assault on the sub-apothecary at the infirmary, following an argument at a clinical session conducted by the senior surgeon, Samuel Smith. Thackrah sought to defend his student's actions in the local press, claiming that his student was provoked by Smith, whom he accused of conducting a personal attack on himself. Thackrah did little to help his cause with the verbose and arrogant style of his letter, which included a list of all his achievements and publications. Smith replied with an equally vitriolic letter challenging Thackrah to a public contest in dissection, to which Thackrah responded disdainfully by saying that one of his students could attend in his place. After this confrontation Thackrah continued with his teaching and his research, which included a study of cholera. By the time the Leeds medical school was founded in 1831, his rift with the local medical establishment had healed; though not a founder of the school, Thackrah was invited to teach and to merge his school with the new institution.

However, it is not as a pioneer of medical education that Thackrah is best remembered, but for his writings on occupational disease. Some commentators have suggested that Thackrah's interest in preventive medicine and occupational diseases was stimulated by a meeting with Robert Owen in Leeds in 1815, yet there is no evidence that the two actually met. Thackrah's knowledge of occupational disease came from several years of careful observation, commencing with his appointment as town surgeon and aided by local investigations undertaken by his students. In 1831 Thackrah summarized his observations in a treatise, *The Effects of the Principal Arts, Trades on Health and Longevity*, in which he detailed diseases associated with more than 150 occupations. He also advised on how such diseases could be prevented with reference to diet, alcohol abuse, posture, exercise, pollution, and ventilation. In particular Thackrah studied the impact of the new textile factories on workers' health. Among workers in the flax-spinning industry he observed that the dusty atmosphere of workshops was associated with a high incidence of respiratory disease. However, his greatest criticism of the new factory system was directed towards the exploitation of children. His treatise was well received by factory reformers and was quoted by Michael Sadler when introducing the Ten Hours Bill in March 1832; in the same year Thackrah shared a platform with Robert Oastler in support of the Ten Hours Movement. The treatise was to remain the standard work on occupational diseases for the next sixty years.

In 1833 Thackrah bought an estate in Shadwell, in response to his wife's concerns over his failing health. Commenting on his last days, his pupil H. Y. Whytehead wrote:

> Bodily suffering, and the entreaties of his dearest friends, were insufficient to induce him to relax his ardour in the pursuit of fame. His health was manifestly declining, and the short intervals of repose, in which he indulged when nature could endure no more, only served to protract his sufferings.

A pulmonary affection was superadded to his original visceral disease. (Whytehead, 18–19)

Thackrah died of tuberculosis on 23 May 1833.

CLARE HOLDSWORTH

Sources A. Meiklejohn, *The life, work and times of Charles Turner Thackrah, surgeon and apothecary of Leeds, 1795–1833* (1957) · J. Cleeland and S. Burt, 'Charles Turner Thackrah: a pioneer in the field of occupational health', *Occupational Medicine*, 45 (1995), 285–97 · H. Y. Whytehead, 'A biographical memoir of Mr Thackrah', in *An inquiry into the nature and properties of the blood, in health and disease*, rev. T. G. Wright (1834)
Archives U. Leeds Library
Likenesses C. Milnes, oils, 1823, U. Leeds, medical school · C. H. Schwanfelder, miniature, c.1823, U. Leeds., medical and dental library
Wealth at death £4000

Thackwell, Sir Joseph (1781–1859), army officer, born on 1 February 1781 at Rye Court, Worcestershire, was the fourth son of John Thackwell JP (d. 1808), of Rye Court and Moreton Court, Worcestershire, and his wife, Judith, daughter of J. Daffy of Maysington, descended from the Egyoke family. Apparently educated mostly at Worcester, he was commissioned cornet in the Worcester provisional (later fencible) cavalry in June 1798, became lieutenant in September 1799, and served with it in Ireland until it was disbanded in April 1800. On 23 April 1800 he became cornet by purchase in the 15th light dragoons, and lieutenant, on 13 June 1801. After the treaty of Amiens (March 1802) he was placed on half pay, but was brought back to the regiment on its augmentation in April 1804 prior to the resumption of war; he became captain on 9 April 1807. The 15th, converted to hussars in 1806, formed part of Lord Paget's hussar brigade in 1807, and was sent to the Peninsula in 1808, under Sir John Moore. It played the principal part in Paget's brilliant cavalry action at Sahagun (21 December 1808), helped cover the retreat to Corunna, and with the rest of the army was evacuated in January 1809. It then served in England, largely in support of the civil power. In April 1810 it served against Sir Francis Burdett's supporters, and escorted him to the Tower. In 1811 and 1812 it served against Luddites and other disaffected people in Nottinghamshire, Lancashire, and Yorkshire.

In January 1813 Thackwell embarked with the 15th for the Peninsula, landing at Lisbon in February. It formed part of the hussar brigade attached to Graham's corps and at the passage of the Esla, on 31 May, Thackwell commanded the leading squadron which surprised a French cavalry picket and took thirty prisoners. He took part in the battle of Vitoria (21 June 1813)—when he was wounded in the right shoulder—and in the subsequent pursuit, in the battle of the Pyrenees at the end of July, and in the blockade of Pamplona (October 1813). He was also present at Orthes, Tarbes, and Toulouse. On 1 March 1814, after passing the Adour, he was in command of the leading squadron of his regiment, and had a creditable encounter with the French light cavalry, for which he was recommended by Sir Stapleton Cotton, though in vain, for a brevet majority. He served with the 15th in the 1815 campaign. It was in Grant's brigade which was on the right of the line at Waterloo (18 June). Its share in the battle was described by Thackwell himself (see H. T. Sibthorne, *Waterloo Letters*, 1891). After several engagements with the French cavalry, it suffered severely in charging an infantry square towards the end of the day. Thackwell had two horses shot under him and was wounded in the left arm. He lay all night where he fell, was found next day and taken to hospital, and had his arm amputated close to the shoulder. He obtained his majority in the regiment on the day of Waterloo.

In 1816 the 15th returned to England and was stationed in the north, again serving in support of the civil power. In October 1816, at a riot in Birmingham, Thackwell was hit on the head by a stone or brickbat, and knocked unconscious for several hours. On 21 June 1817 he was made brevet lieutenant-colonel. On 16 August 1819 at St Peter's Field, Manchester (the Peterloo massacre), the 15th charged and dispersed the crowd. Thackwell succeeded to the command of the 15th on 15 June 1820. In October 1831 the 15th suppressed reform riots in Nottingham and its vicinity, and were thanked by the county magistrates. He was an efficient and humane commander, and in the 15th courts martial and floggings were rare. In November 1831 he arranged to exchange to half pay with Lord Brudenell, who reportedly paid between £35,000 and £40,000 for command of the 15th. After holding his command for twelve years, and having served thirty-two years in the regiment, Thackwell was placed on half pay on 16 March 1832. He was made KH in January 1834.

Thackwell married, on 29 July 1825, Maria Andriah (d. 21 June 1874), eldest daughter of Francis Roche of Rochemount, co. Cork (uncle of Lord Fermoy); they had four sons and three daughters.

On 10 January 1837 Thackwell became colonel in the army, and on 19 May he obtained, by exchange, command of the 3rd (King's Own) light dragoons. He went with it to India, reaching Calcutta in November 1837, but soon left it to command, with the local rank of major-general, the cavalry of the army of the Indus in the Afghan campaign of 1838–9. He was present at the siege and capture of Ghazni, and he commanded the second column of that part of the army which returned to India from Kabul in the autumn of 1839. He was made CB in July 1838, and KCB on 20 December 1839. He commanded the cavalry division of Sir Hugh Gough's army in the short campaign against the Marathas of Gwalior at the end of 1843, and was mentioned in Gough's dispatch after the battle of Maharajpur. In the First Anglo-Sikh War he commanded the cavalry at Sobraon (10 February 1846), and led it in file over the entrenchments on the right, doing work (as Gough said) usually left to infantry and artillery. He was promoted major-general on 9 November 1846.

When the Second Anglo-Sikh War began Thackwell was appointed to command the 3rd division of infantry; but on the death of Brigadier Cureton in the action at Ramnagar on 22 November 1848 he was transferred to the cavalry division. After Ramnagar the Sikhs crossed to the right bank of the Chenab. To enable his own army to follow them Gough sent a force of about 8000 men under Thackwell to pass the river higher up, and help to dislodge the Sikhs from their position by moving on their left flank and rear. Thackwell found the nearer fords impracticable, but crossed at Wazirabad and on the morning of 3 December camped near Sadulapur. He had orders not to attack until he was joined by an additional brigade; but he was himself attacked towards midday by about half the Sikh army. The Sikhs drove the British pickets out of three villages and some large plantations of sugar cane, and so secured for themselves a strong position. Their artillery kept up a heavy fire until sunset, and they made some feeble attempts to turn the British flanks, but there was very little fighting at close quarters. In the course of the afternoon Thackwell received authority to attack if he thought proper; but as the enemy was strongly posted, he considered it safer to wait until next morning. By morning the Sikhs had disappeared, and it is doubtful whether they had any other object in their attack than that of gaining time for a retreat. Gough expressed his 'warm approval' of Thackwell's conduct, but there were some signs of dissatisfaction in his dispatch of 5 December. An officer of fifty years' service is apt to be over-cautious. This was not the case with Gough himself, but Chilianwala (13 January 1849) went far to justify Thackwell. He commanded the cavalry at Chilianwala, but actually directed only the left brigade. At Gujrat (21 February 1849) he was also on the left, and kept in check the enemy's cavalry when it tried to turn that flank. After the battle was won he led a vigorous pursuit until nightfall. In his dispatch of 26 February 1849 Gough said: 'I am also greatly indebted to this tried and gallant officer for his valuable assistance and untiring exertions throughout the present and previous operations as second in command with this force'. He received the thanks of parliament and, on Wellington's recommendation, the GCB (5 June 1849).

In November 1849 Thackwell was appointed colonel of the 16th lancers. In 1854, with war against Russia apparently imminent, Thackwell tried unsuccessfully to gain employment on active service with the cavalry. Instead he was temporary inspecting general of cavalry from April 1854 to February 1855, during the absence of the duke of Cambridge. On 20 June 1854 Thackwell was promoted lieutenant-general. In 1853 he bought Aghada Hall and estate, co. Cork, and he spent most of his last years shooting and improving his property. In early 1856 Lord Hardinge recommended him for a baronetcy but Palmerston refused, claiming it would create 'an inconvenient precedent' (Wylly, 356). He died on 8 April 1859 at Aghada Hall. His wife survived him.

All Thackwell's sons became army officers. His second son, Major-General William de Wilton Roche Thackwell (1834–1910), commissioned in 1853, served in the Crimea and the 1882 Egyptian campaign. Thackwell's third son, **Osbert Dabitôt Thackwell** (1837–1858), was commissioned ensign on 25 June 1855 and became lieutenant on 23 November 1856. He was lieutenant in the 15th Bengal native infantry when it mutinied at Nasirabad on 28 May

1857. He became interpreter to the 83rd foot, was in several engagements, and distinguished himself in the defence of Neemuch. He was at the siege of Lucknow and, after its capture, was killed in the street on 20 March 1858.

Thackwell's youngest son, Francis John Roche Thackwell, captain, Royal Irish Lancers, died in 1869 from wounds received from a tiger.

E. M. LLOYD, *rev.* ROGER T. STEARN

Sources H. C. Wylly, ed., *The military memoirs of Lieut.-General Sir Joseph Thackwell* (1908) · *GM*, 3rd ser., 6 (1859), 540–41 · *Annual Register* (1859) · *Dod's Peerage* (1858) · Burke, *Gen. GB* (1937) · R. Cannon, ed., *Historical record of the fifteenth, or king's regiment of light dragoons, hussars* (1841) · G. E. F. Kauntze, *Historical record of the third, or king's own light dragoons* (1857) · E. J. Thackwell, *Narrative of the Second Seikh War, in 1848–49* (1851) · Lord Hardinge and Lord Gough, dispatches, *LondG* (1845–6) · *Gloucestershire Chronicle* (8 May 1897) · *Gloucestershire Chronicle* (29 May 1897) · Marquess of Anglesey [G. C. H. V. Paget], *A history of the British cavalry, 1816 to 1919*, 1 (1973) · R. Muir, *Britain and the defeat of Napoleon, 1807–1815* (1996) · H. C. B. Cook, *The Sikh wars: the British army in the Punjab, 1845–1849* (1975) · A. Babington, *Military intervention in Britain: from the Gordon riots to the Gibraltar incident* (1990) · J. A. Norris, *The First Afghan War, 1838–1842* (1967) · T. A. Heathcote, *The military in British India: the development of British land forces in south Asia, 1600–1947* (1995) · P. Spear, *The Oxford history of modern India, 1740–1947* (1965) · *WWW*, 1897–1915 · D. Read, *Peterloo: the 'massacre' and its background* (1958) · J. Marlow, *The Peterloo massacre* (1969) · R. Whalmsley, *Peterloo: the case re-opened* (1969)

Likenesses T. H. Wilson, lithograph, BM · engraving, repro. in Wylly, ed., *Military memoirs*, frontispiece · oils, NAM

Wealth at death under £10,000: probate, 19 July 1859, *CGPLA Eng. & Wales*

Thackwell, Osbert Dabitôt (1837–1858). *See under* Thackwell, Sir Joseph (1781–1859).

Thane, John (1747?–1818), dealer in prints, medals, and manuscripts, may have been the child born in Westminster on 12 August 1747, the son of Peter and Susan Thane. His elder sister, Susanna, survived him. Thane collected the writings of the numismatist and printseller Thomas *Snelling (1712–1773) and published them as *Snelling on the coins of Great Britain, France and Ireland … containing seventy copper plates* (1762–74) with an excellent portrait drawn and engraved by himself. On 25 November 1770 Thane married Snelling's daughter Mary Lord (b. 1739). Her death may have ended this brief marriage, for about 1776 he married Elizabeth Seymour Flack (d. 1824). She, with four sons, Thomas, William, Charles, and John, and three daughters, Ann Charlotte, Elizabeth, and Maria, outlived him.

In 1772–5 Thane was living at 24 Gerrard Street, Soho, London, and from here he published regular catalogues of his retail stock of prints. He was a friend of Joseph Strutt, engraver and antiquary, who lived for a time in Thane's household; Thane published Strutt's *Regal and Ecclesiastical Antiquities of England* in 1773. By 1781 Thane had moved to Rupert Street near by, where he dealt in manuscripts, coins, and medals, becoming well known for his expert knowledge of these, besides pictures, and other objects of virtu as well as prints. In 1781 he took on a second shop with the printseller Anthony Torre: they insured the contents of this 'shop and the Warerooms communicating in the brick dwelling of Mr Greenwood auctioneer situate no. 28 Haymarket' for £1000. The new outlet was probably dedicated to modern prints, for from about this time Thane became a significant publisher of contemporary pictures in stipple. He guided the formation of several notable print collections including that of the banker William Esdaile. He himself was particularly interested in antique portraits and autographs. The collection of some 2000 portraits assembled by John Nickolls and sold at his death to Dr John Fothergill were sold at Fothergill's death in 1780 to Thane for either £150 or 200 guineas (sources differ); he broke up the volumes and disposed of the portraits to the principal collectors of the time.

Thane edited and published *British autography: a collection of facsimiles of the handwriting of royal and illustrious personages, with their authentic portraits*, issued in three volumes, probably in 1788–93. A memorial portrait of Thane by John Ogborne after William Redmore Bigg was used as a frontispiece to the second edition. Thane died in May 1818, probably at his home, Spur Street, Leicester Fields, London; he was buried on 10 May at St Anne's, Soho. Between November 1818 and May 1821 his extensive stock of prints, coins, and medals, diverse items, and lastly his copperplates, went through the salerooms in London and Paris, contributing to an estate valued at nearly £14,000.

TIMOTHY CLAYTON and ANITA MCCONNELL

Sources parish register, St Anne's, Soho, City Westm. AC [baptism, burial] · F. H. W. Sheppard, ed., *The parish of St Anne, Soho*, Survey of London, 34 (1966), 393 · Nichols, *Illustrations*, 5.436–7 · Nichols, *Lit. anecdotes*, 2.160; 3.620, 664; 5.668; 9.740 · will registers, Bank of England, 1818, vol. 9 K–Z, no. 2101; 1841, vol. 58 K–Z, no. 12085 · GL, MS 11936, no. 44394, Sun Fire office insurance policy no. 437859 · will, PRO, PROB 11/1605, sig. 294
Likenesses group portrait, line engraving, pubd 1798 (after *Sketches taken at print sales* by P. Sandby), BM · J. Ogborne, line engraving (after W. R. Bigg), NPG; repro. in E. Daniell, *Supplement to John Thane: British autography* (1854)
Wealth at death under £14,000: will registers, Bank of England, London, 1818, vol. 9 K–Z, no. 2101

Thanet. For this title name *see* Tufton, Sackville, ninth earl of Thanet (1769–1825).

Thankerton. For this title name *see* Watson, William, Baron Thankerton (1873–1948).

Thatcher [Thacher], **Peter** (1587/8–1641), Church of England clergyman, was the eldest of at least three sons of Peter Thatcher of Queen Camel, Somerset. He matriculated from Queen's College, Oxford, in May 1603 aged fifteen, graduated BA from Corpus Christi College in 1608, and proceeded MA in 1611. In 1616 he became vicar of Milton Clevedon, Somerset, sufficiently close to Queen Camel for it to be possible that he retained family connections there, and about the same time he married Anne Allwood, perhaps of a Somerset family; their second son was **Thomas Thacher** (1620–1678). By 1621 he was one of a circle of 'much respected friends and brethren in the ministry' in Somerset (Bernard, sig. A5r), some at least of

whom were Calvinists looking for further reformation in the ceremonies of the established church. In 1623 he moved to Salisbury as rector of St Edmund's, and he found there an opportunity to promote a much wider reformation.

Thatcher had been invited by a determined group in the St Edmund's vestry who gradually acquired authority in the town and pushed through a programme of social and civic reform. He voiced his support for their campaign 'to reform the drunkenness, idleness, running to the alehouse and other such courses, which have been and are the bane of our poor in Sarum'. He found 'God's providence' at work in the plague epidemic of 1627 which scattered the opponents of the godly and so facilitated action for 'the public good' of the city (PRO, SP 16/527/4; Hants. RO, 44M69, L37/38). His aspirations were shared by other clergy in the west country, notably John White of Dorchester, with whom Thatcher had close contact, but he never acquired White's civic dominance in his own town. He appears readily to have yielded first place to the ambitious lawyer, Henry Sherfield, Salisbury's recorder, and to John Ivie, a Salisbury councillor.

Sherfield's disgrace before Star Chamber in 1633, following his iconoclastic attack on a painted window in St Edmund's Church, brought a check to local reform and to Thatcher's prospects. Archbishop William Laud had criticized him in Star Chamber as one who 'hath not read all the divine service in a whole year together' (Emlyn, *State-Trials*, 1.404). Within a month of Sherfield's death, in January 1634, Thatcher was writing to Sir Robert Harley in search of a safer berth, but he turned down what must have been the tempting offer of the living of Brampton Bryan, Herefordshire, perhaps because his wife died on 23 March. According to Cotton Mather, Thatcher also contemplated following his second son, Thomas, and brother Anthony, whose emigration to New England he helped to finance in 1635; but that similarly came to nothing. He married Alice Batt (1604/5–1669), daughter of a parishioner, on 14 April 1635 and apparently lived quietly with his family in St Edmund's, where he died between 1 February 1641, when he made his will, and 28 February, when the vestry elected his successor. On 19 October the same year his widow married Francis Dove, another member of the St Edmund's reforming caucus and brother of a Long Parliament MP for the city.

Thatcher left no publications, and the fate of any manuscripts is unknown. He left £50 each to his nine surviving children (six sons, three of them young and perhaps children of Alice, and three daughters), but his chief legacy was his library: more than a hundred volumes in Latin and English of biblical and devotional writings, ranging from Calvin and Beza through Thomas Cartwright to John Davenant and Nicholas Byfield, all carefully listed in a schedule to his will and bequeathed to Thomas in New England. The inheritance perhaps helped Thomas Thacher achieve greater prominence in urban reformation than his father: from 2 January 1644 as cleric–physician at Weymouth, Massachusetts, and from 1669 as pastor of the

Third (Old South) Church in Boston, also in Massachusetts. He was the author of *A Brief Rule*, one of the first medical tracts published in New England, giving advice against smallpox, which was published in 1678. With his first wife, whom he married on 11 May 1643, Thomas had five children; he married in 1664 Margaret Sheafe, widow, of Boston. He died in 1678.   PAUL SLACK

Sources P. Slack, 'Poverty and politics in Salisbury, 1597–1666', *Crisis and order in English towns, 1500–1700*, ed. P. Clark and P. Slack (1972), 164–203 · Foster, *Alum. Oxon.* · will, PRO, PROB 11/187, sig. 112 · *Churchwardens' accounts of S. Edmund and S. Thomas, Sarum, 1443–1702* (1896), 172–3 · J. Eales, *Puritans and roundheads: the Harleys of Brampton Bryan and the outbreak of the English civil war* (1990), 55 · *The manuscripts of his grace the duke of Portland*, 10 vols., HMC, 29 (1891–1931), vol. 3, pp. 32–3 · C. Mather, *Magnalia Christi Americana*, 7 bks in 1 vol. (1702), bk 3, p. 149 · S. Emlyn, ed., *A complete collection of state-trials*, 3rd edn, 6 vols. (1742), vol. 1, p. 404 · R. Bernard, *The faithfull shepherd* (1621), sig. A5r · PRO, SP 16/527/4 · Sherfield papers, Hants. RO, Jervoise of Herriard Park papers, L37/38 · M. P. Clark, 'Thomas Thacher', *American writers before 1800: a biographical and critical dictionary*, ed. J. A. Levernier and D. R. Wilmes (1983), 1441 · *William Whiteway of Dorchester: his diary, 1618 to 1635*, Dorset RS, 12 (1991), 142 · parish register, Salisbury, St Edmund, Wilts. & Swindon RO · P. Cash, 'Thacher, Peter', *ANB* · *IGI*
Wealth at death £473 15s. 0d.—in cash gifts: will, PRO, PROB 11/187, sig. 112

Thaun, Philip de (*fl.* 1113×19–1121×35), Anglo-Norman poet, was probably from the seigneurial family of Than, or Thaon, near Caen. He is the earliest known Anglo-Norman poet. It is possible that he moved from Normandy to England in the late eleventh century with his uncle Hunfrei de Thaun, chaplain to Yun, who was seneschal dapifer to Henry I, and is usually identified with Eudo or Odo Dapifer, who died on 29 February 1120. Hunfrei is named at the beginning of the *Cumpoz*, which Philip sent to him for comment and correction. The family de Thaun did not survive beyond the fifteenth century. P. Meyer disputed Philip's seigneurial background, and saw no reason to suppose that Philip was more than a simple cleric who, like Wace, travelled to England to make his services available to the court (Meyer, 34.367).

Philip de Thaun's first work was the *Cumpoz*, or *Compuz* ('Computus'), called in Wright's edition *Liber de creaturis*. It was written between 1113 and 1119 as a clerics' aid to calculate the moveable feasts of the church calendar. Written in rhyming hexasyllabic couplets, and interspersed with edifying exhortations, its principal sources appear to have been Bede, William de Conches, and Chilperic of St Gall's *De compoto*. There are four manuscripts of the *Cumpoz* in England, and three in the Vatican Library.

Between 1121 and 1135 Philip de Thaun translated the first French version extant of the bestiary *Physiologus* (*Li bestiaire*) and dedicated it to his queen, Adeliza of Louvain, wife of Henry II. *Li bestiaire*, written in rhyming hexasyllabic couplets except for the final 303 octosyllabic lines (ll.2891–3194), comprises a prologue, 35 chapters on animals, 3 on precious stones, and an epilogue. There are three extant manuscripts of *Li bestiaire*. Although Philip's manuscript source is unknown, he appears to have made few alterations to the general substance of the Latin bestiary tradition, with its descriptions of animal properties

and its typological interpretation of the animal *exempla*. Presumably the ordering of the *exempla* and the addition of material from Isidore of Seville were done by his source. Philip was, however, responsible for the translation into French and for its (somewhat pedestrian) versification. While not a literary masterpiece, this very early French translation of the *Physiologus*, composed for the edification and enjoyment of the court, has become, by the primacy of its date of composition, an important source of information for the language of Anglo-Norman England.

Also attributed to Philip de Thaun, although its sole manuscript (Paris, Bibliothèque Nationale, fonds fr. 25407) contains no dedication identifying him or a patron, is a hexasyllabic translation-adaptation of the *Sibylla Tiburtina*, supplemented with material from the *Libellus de Antichristo* by Adso of Montier-en-Der, and entitled *Le livre de Sibile* (*c.*1239). The attribution to Philip of an alphabetical lapidary, an apocalyptic lapidary, and the *Débat de l'âme et du corps* is less certain.   JEANETTE BEER

Sources P. de Thaon, *Comput* (*MS BL Cotton Nero A. V.*), ed. I. Short, Anglo-Norman Texts, plain text ser., 2 (1984) · P. de Thaon, *Le bestiaire*, ed. E. Walberg (1970) · P. de Thaon, *Der computus des Philippe von Thaon*, ed. E. Mall (1873) · P. de Thaon, *Le livre de Sibile*, ed. H. Shields (1979) · T. Wright, ed., *Popular treatises on science, written during the middle ages* (1841) · P. Meyer, 'Les bestiaires', *Histoire littéraire de la France*, ed. P. Meyer, 34 (1914), 362–72 · H. Shields, 'Oral techniques in written verse: Philippe de Thaon's *Livre de Sibile*', *Medium Aevum*, 49 (1980), 194–206 · L. Morini, 'A proposito del *Livre de Sibile* di Philippe de Thaon', *Medioevo-Romanzo*, 8/2 (1981–3), 259–69 · P. E. Bennett, 'Some doctrinal implications of the *Comput* and *Bestiaire* of Philippe de Thaun', *Épopée animale, fable, fabliau: actes du IVe colloque de la Société internationale renardienne* [Evreux 1981], ed. G. Bianciotto and M. Salvat (Paris, 1984), 95–105 · X. Muratova, 'The decorated manuscripts of the bestiary of Philippe de Thaon', *Proceedings of the Third International Beast Epic, Fable and Fabliau Colloquium* (1979), 217–46
Archives Bibliothèque Nationale, Paris, fonds fr. 25407

Thayendanegea. *See* Brant, Joseph (1743–1807).

Thayre, Thomas (*fl.* 1603–1625), medical practitioner, about whom little is known, describes himself as a 'chirurgian' in July 1603, but as his name does not occur among the members of the Barber–Surgeons' Company, and as he uses no such description in 1625, he was probably one of the numerous irregular practitioners of the period, and no sworn surgeon. He published in London in 1603 *Treatise of the Pestilence*, dedicated to Sir Robert Lee, lord mayor 1602–3. The cause of the disease, the regimen, drugs, and diet proper for its treatment are discussed. Ten diagnostic symptoms are described, and some theology is intermixed. The general plan differs little from that of Thomas Phaer's *A Treatise on the Plague*, and identical sentences occur in several places. These passages have suggested the untenable view that the works are identical, and Thayre a misprint for Phayre. A similar resemblance of passages is to be detected in English books of the sixteenth century on other medical subjects, and is usually to be traced to several writers independently adopting and slightly altering some admired passage in a common source. Thayre published a second edition in 1625 entitled

An Excellent and Best Approved Treatise of the Plague, dedicated to John Gore, lord mayor 1624–5. The work shows little medical knowledge, but preserves some interesting particulars of domestic life, and, though inferior in style to the writings of Christopher Langton and even of William Clowes, contains a few well put and idiomatic expressions. NORMAN MOORE, *rev.* MICHAEL BEVAN

Sources T. Thayre, *Treatise of the pestilence* (1603) · T. Thayre, *An excellent and best approved treatise of the plague* (1625)

Theakston, Joseph (1772–1842), sculptor, was born in Spurriergate, York, and was baptized on either 14 December 1772 or 21 December 1772 in St Michael's, Spurriergate, the son of John and Sarah Theakston of York. His father having died while he was still a child, his mother apprenticed him in 1786 to John Fisher the elder, a local sculptor. In 1794 he completed his apprenticeship, moved to London, and became a pupil of John Bacon the elder, whose work exerted upon him a formative stylistic influence. He then spent several years working as an assistant to John Flaxman and Edward Hodges Baily. From 1818 until his death twenty-four years later he was employed by Francis Chantrey to carve the draperies and other accessories of the latter's statues and groups.

Although his individual contributions to Chantrey's works are mostly unrecorded, Theakston's dominant role in the execution of two colossal stone statues of George Granville Leveson-Gower, first duke of Sutherland, from small models by Chantrey, is actually recorded: the first (1834–6) stands on the duke's estate at Trentham Park, Staffordshire, and the second (1836–8), height (including base) *c.*106 ft, is on Ben Bragghie, Golspie, Sutherland. (The one in Scotland is signed 'Theakston Fab. Chantrey Auct.'.) Theakston's contemporary reputation is well summed up in his obituary in *The Times*:

> He was perhaps the ablest drapery and ornamental carver of his time, as he was certainly the most rapid … few could imagine the rapidity of his execution from his quiet manner of handling his tools … When he began to carve a statue, he knew perfectly well what was required of him, and cut away the superfluous marble at once. He had not to try again and again, like most other artists … he may be said never to have struck the chisel with the hammer in vain. (25 April 1842)

As Peter Cunningham, the son of Chantrey's foreman and secretary Allan Cunningham, put it: 'He was a consummate master in making marble convey the qualities and surfaces of silks and satins, velvets and ermines' (*The Builder*, 14 Feb 1863). Besides assisting Chantrey, he produced busts and monumental and ornamental works of his own, and exhibited occasionally at the Royal Academy from 1809 to 1837. In 1829 he was paid £1000 for a sculptured marble chimney-piece and clock-frame for the grand hall in Buckingham Palace. Joseph Theakston died where he had lived at 9 Belgrave Place, London, on 14 April 1842, aged sixty-nine, and was buried on the 21st alongside his wife at Kensal Green cemetery in London.

E. I. CARLYLE, *rev.* TERRY CAVANAGH

Sources *The Times* (25 April 1842), 7 · *GM*, 2nd ser., 17 (1842), 672 · *Art Union*, 4 (1842), 99 · R. Gunnis, *Dictionary of British sculptors, 1660–1851*, new edn (1964) · A. Yarrington, I. D. Lieberman, A. Potts, and M. Baker, 'An edition of the ledger of Sir Francis Chantrey RA at the Royal Academy, 1809–1841', *Walpole Society*, 56 (1991–2), esp. 284, 299–300 [whole issue] · P. Cunningham, 'New materials for the life of Sir Francis Chantrey', *The Builder*, 21 (1863), 112 · Graves, *RA exhibitors* · Redgrave, *Artists* · IGI

Theal, George McCall (1837–1919), historian and civil servant, was born on 11 April 1837 at Saint John, New Brunswick, where his United Empire Loyalist forebears had settled. He was the eldest of the nine children of William Young Theal, a doctor, and his wife, Mary, *née* Bell. Theal's schooling at the Cockaigne Academy and at St John Grammar School gave him the normal grounding of a classical education. Significantly, a favourite book was Gibbon's *Decline and Fall of the Roman Empire*. After spending time in the United States and west Africa, he was *en route* for Australia with friends when he decided to stay in South Africa. Frontier newspapers, schoolteaching, some months at the diamond fields, and five years at the Lovedale mission occupied his early years in South Africa. He published two early works: *South Africa as it is* and a *Compendium of the History and Geography of South Africa* which, by 1877, had reached a third edition. He also collected oral records, subsequently published as *Kaffir Folk Lore*.

The years from 1877 to 1881 were crucial for South Africa: widespread frontier resistance was quelled, and Carnarvon's imperially propelled federation project failed. They were also decisive years for Theal. He moved from the eastern Cape to Cape Town and lost his close association with the indigenous people among whom he had worked as missionary and as government appointee. His early sympathy for the conquered peoples disappeared in his later work. Excited by the records of the past that he encountered in his official duties, he became a zealous archivist and dedicated historian.

Theal was appointed colonial historiographer in 1891. This was a decade after his bitter disappointment when the Sprigg government appointed the Revd H. C. V. Leibbrandt to the recently created post of librarian to the house of assembly and keeper of the archives. Theal's consolation was an unwelcome, but better paid and mercifully short, appointment as magistrate at Tamacha. He returned to Cape Town as a clerk in the native affairs department. It was part of his work to prepare summaries of documents and investigate disputes. In addition, he was instructed to search out and prepare for publication documents relating to issues of current concern. His four volumes of *Basutoland Records* (three published) and his nine volumes on the *Records of South East Africa* resulted from such work. Successive Cape governments backed him in his wider commitment to search for, transcribe, translate if necessary, and prepare for publication the records of Cape Colony. To this end he was permitted to spend long years working in repositories in Britain and in Europe. The most notable result was the thirty-six volumes of *Records of the Cape Colony* from 1793 to January 1828. Theal knew foreign languages and drove himself hard; his work was not faultless, but his achievement remains impressive. Long before the age of photocopying, his work equipped scholars in South Africa with some, at least, of the documents necessary for historical research.

Writing history flowed from his archival work. Here, too, he achieved and maintained a prodigious productivity. He studied the ethnography of the indigenous people and published the results. More impressively, he achieved an eleven-volume survey of the South African past which brought the story almost up to his own day, as well as a host of smaller histories. He drew on earlier works, but none of his predecessors had attempted quite so broad a canvas. The chronological span of his publications extends from 1871 to the 1960s, when reprints of some of his compilations were issued.

In 1904 the Cape government decided to retire all civil servants over sixty years of age. After vigorous protests and a parliamentary select committee, Theal received a pension based on his salary as civil service clerk, but he retained the title and emoluments of colonial historiographer until his death. He continued to work assiduously. One of his later tasks was to prepare for publication the manuscript of G. W. Stowe's work *The Native Races of South Africa*. Theal's ideas were disseminated widely when some of his works were translated into Dutch, and his writing became the basis of school textbooks. He was utterly convinced of his own impartiality and accuracy, and he vaunted his own merits. He omitted annotations from his historical writing and claimed that this was the result of his desire to avoid expense and delay. He has been condemned by late twentieth-century historians for his own self-congratulation—however wide his interests, his sympathies were extremely narrow, and his accuracy has not escaped unscathed the scrutiny of later scholars. Like other historians of his day, writing in other places, he saw history as a progressive movement. For him the theme of progress lay in the achievements of the white population of South Africa, both Boer and colonial British, who in establishing themselves and subjugating the indigenous peoples, made possible the inevitable triumph of civilization over barbarism. Always concerned to defend the white colonist or trekker, Theal berated unpopular officials and humanitarians. He conspicuously failed to see that there was 'another side' to frontier issues, and simplified complex movements to the point of caricature. For example to him the upheavals in the interior subsequently called the mfecane resulted simply from the savagery of Shaka, whom Theal called the 'Attila of South East Africa'. He similarly dismissed the cattle killing as the 'madness' of the Xhosa, whose leaders perpetrated 'a blunder such as a child would not have made'.

Theal received honorary doctorates from Queen's University, Kingston, Ontario, in 1895 and from the University of the Cape of Good Hope in 1899. The criticisms of his own day were muted and his evident sympathy for the trekkers won him the lasting esteem of many Afrikaner historians. But since 1930, if not earlier, the castigation of Theal has become an academic industry, and his errors and misrepresentations have been frequently subjected to withering attack. Placed alongside the burgeoning studies of black polities and of the experience of indigenous peoples, Theal's work appears now to be at best superficial and smug, at worst callous. Yet historians, like others, are entitled to be judged by the standards of their own context. His presentation of South African history was guided by what he judged to be the crucial needs of his own times—co-operation among the white inhabitants of South Africa and the development among them of a shared sense of identity.

Described as tall and massive, with grey eyes that betokened humour, Theal apparently possessed an air of essential simplicity and charm. He spent his last years at Wynberg. An Episcopalian by birth, he became a Presbyterian by choice, but served as an elder in the Dutch Reformed church at Wynberg. He died in Wynberg on 17 April 1919, survived by two children, Martin William and Hannah Catherine Hester. His wife, Mary, *née* Stewart, had died on 23 November 1911. He was buried in the Dutch Reformed church cemetery at Wynberg. Friends collected funds and commissioned an oil portrait to serve as his memorial. The painting, by Professor E. Roworth, is now housed in the South African Library at Cape Town.

B. M. NICHOLLS

Sources D. Schreuder, 'The imperial historian as colonial nationalist', *Studies in British imperial history: essays in honour of A. P. Thornton*, ed. G. Martel (1986) · C. C. Saunders, *The making of the South African past: major historians on race and class* (1988) · K. Smith, *The changing past: trends in South African historical writing* (1988) · R. F. M. Immelman, *George McCall Theal: a biographical sketch, with notes and bibliography* (1964) [repr. from the C. Struik re-issue of *Basutoland records*] · M. Babrow, 'A critical assessment of George McCall Theal', MA diss., University of Cape Town, 1962 · C. J. Muller, 'George McCall Theal', *Standard encyclopaedia of southern Africa*, ed. D. J. Potgieter, 10 (1974) · A. J. Böeseken, 'Theal', *DSAB* · C. C. Saunders, 'Theal of Lovedale', *History in Africa*, 8 (1981) · C. Saunders, 'Pre-Cobbing mfecane historiography', *The mfecane aftermath*, ed. C. Hamilton (1995), 21–34 · I. D. Bosman, *Dr George McCall Theal as die Geskiedskrywer van Suid-Afrika* (1932) · C. C. Saunders, 'The making of an historian: the early years of George McCall Theal', *South African Historical Journal*, 13 (1981) · J. F. Preller, 'The Leibbrandt appointment', *South African Archives Journal*, 1 (1959)
Likenesses E. Roworth, oils, South African Library

Theed, William, the elder (1764–1817). *See under* Theed, William, the younger (1804–1891).

Theed, William, the younger (1804–1891), sculptor, was born at Trentham, Staffordshire, the son of the sculptor and painter **William Theed the elder** (1764–1817). William Theed the elder entered the Royal Academy Schools in 1786 and began his career as a painter showing classical subjects and portraits at the Royal Academy exhibitions from 1789. In 1790 he went to Italy, and from 1791 he was working in Rome, where his close friends were the artists John Frearson and Henry Howard. He is said to have married a French woman, Mlle Rougeot, in Naples which he visited in 1795. After returning to England in 1796 he worked as a modeller for the Staffordshire firm of Wedgwood (1800–1804) and afterwards as a designer for the silversmiths Rundell and Bridge (1804–17). His sculptures include *Thetis Returning from Vulcan with Arms for Achilles* (exh. RA, 1812; Royal Collection) and the relief on the monument to Thomas Westfaling (1817) in St Mary's Church, Ross-on-Wye, Herefordshire. He was elected an associate of the Royal Academy in 1811 and Royal Academician in 1813.

After receiving some instruction in art from his father, the younger Theed worked for several years in the studio of the sculptor E. H. Baily. On 15 January 1820 he was admitted as a student to the Royal Academy Schools, where he won a silver medal in 1822. He also won a silver palette from the Society of Arts in 1820 for a figure of Hercules, and two years later he gained its silver Isis medal. In 1826 Theed went to Rome, where he is said to have studied under the Danish sculptor Bertel Thorvaldsen and the Italian Pietro Tenerani, as well as with John Gibson and R. J. Wyatt. He developed a close friendship with Gibson and later acted as a contact between Gibson and some of his patrons in England. Theed worked in a studio at 9 via degli Incurabili, near the piazza del Popolo, where he executed some classicizing ideal works—such as *A Nymph Preparing her Bow for the Chase* (marble, 1837; priv. coll.)—and many portrait busts, including those of the duke of Lucca and the prince and princess of Capua (all exh. RA, 1839). In 1844–5, after nearly twenty years in Rome, he received the commission which marked a turning point in his career, when Prince Albert, the prince consort, asked Gibson to send designs by sculptors working in Rome for statues to be placed in Osborne House, Isle of Wight. Two designs by Theed were accepted, *Narcissus at the Fountain* and *Psyche Lamenting the Loss of Cupid* (both marble, 1847; Royal Collection).

Theed returned to London in 1848 and soon established a highly successful professional practice. He was presumably married by about this date: his wife, Mary (*b. c.*1815), and a son, Edward (*b. c.*1850), were both mentioned in the census returns of 1881. At the Great Exhibition of 1851 he showed three works, the *Narcissus*, *Prometheus* (marble, 1851; priv. coll.), and *The Prodigal's Return* (marble version, 1850; Usher Gallery, Lincoln), the last a life-size elaborately carved narrative group, which heralded Theed's mature style as a sculptor of naturalistic set pieces. He made further works for the prince consort, notably *Sappho* (marble, 1851; Royal Collection), some busts after the antique, and a series of mythological reliefs for the reception rooms of Buckingham Palace. His *The Bard* (marble, 1858; Mansion House, London), a subject from Thomas Gray's poem of the same name, was one of sixteen statues by leading sculptors commissioned by the corporation of London for the Egyptian Hall in the Mansion House. In the mid-1850s Theed made a series of twelve bas-reliefs illustrating scenes from Tudor history (bronze, cast by Elkingtons, *c.*1852–8) for the prince's chamber in the Palace of Westminster.

The mainstay of Theed's production, however, lay in the field of portraiture, and he received commissions for many major commemorative statues during his career. They included James Watt (bronze, 1857; Piccadilly Gardens, Manchester, after Chantrey), Sir Isaac Newton (bronze, 1858; St Peter's Hill, Grantham), and Edmund Burke (marble, 1858; St Stephen's Hall, Palace of Westminster, London). For St George's Hall, Liverpool, he made the statues of Edward Stanley, fourteenth earl of Derby (marble, 1869) and Henry Booth (marble, *c.*1874), and for Manchester town hall Charles Pelham Villiers (marble,

1876), John Bright (marble, 1878), and William Ewart Gladstone (marble, 1879). His principal church monuments were those to Sir James Mackintosh (marble, 1855) and Sir Herbert Benjamin Edwardes (marble, 1868) in Westminster Abbey and to Henry Hallam (marble, 1862) in St Paul's Cathedral, and the memorial to the seventeenth-century benefactor Humphrey Chetham (marble, 1853) in Manchester Cathedral. This last, a richly carved seated figure, portraying the subject in Jacobean dress, was reproduced in Parian ware ceramics with several other designs by the sculptor. Theed's portrait busts included those of John Gibson (marble, 1852; Conwy parish church, north Wales; replicas, *c.*1868, RA and NPG), Sir Henry Holland (marble, 1873; NPG), Victoria Mary Louisa, duchess of Kent (marble, 1861), Queen Victoria (bronze, 1864), and Prince Albert (marble, 1862) (the last three all Royal Collection, several versions).

As Theed was one of the sculptors most favoured by the prince consort, it was appropriate that he should be chosen by Queen Victoria in 1861 to take the death mask of the prince. In the following years Theed executed several notable memorial statues of Prince Albert, including those at Balmoral Castle (marble, 1863; bronze replica, 1867) and Coburg, Bavaria (bronze, 1865), and replicas for Sydney, Australia (bronze, 1866), Grimsby (bronze, 1879), and Bishop's Waltham (Royal Albert Infirmary) (terracotta replica made by J. M. Blashfield, 1865; destroyed). In 1868 he completed for the queen a romantic double portrait statue representing the royal couple in Anglo-Saxon costume (marble, 1863–7; Royal Collection). Also known as *The Parting*, the group, which symbolizes Anglo-German ties and the royal couple's future reunion, again displays the bravura handling of historical costume in which Theed came to excel. The sculptor's crowning achievement was his group *Africa* (marble, 1865–71), one of four colossal allegories of continents placed on the outer corners of the Albert Memorial in Hyde Park. Centred on a figure of an Egyptian queen seated on a camel, the work consists of a variety of figures representing the different African peoples together with symbols of African culture and history.

Despite his early immersion in the studios of the neoclassical sculptors in Rome, Theed developed into a versatile and eclectic sculptor who was equally at ease with classicizing ideal works, historical realism, and modern life portraiture. His successful practice and large output—he showed more than eighty works at the Royal Academy between 1824 and 1885—was underpinned by the extensive patronage of the English royal family. He died of old age on 9 September 1891, at his home, Campden Lodge, Campden Hill, Kensington, London.

MARTIN GREENWOOD

Sources DNB · R. Gunnis, *Dictionary of British sculptors, 1660–1851* (1953); new edn (1968) · J. Turner, ed., *The dictionary of art*, 34 vols. (1996), vol. 30, p. 703 · Graves, *RA exhibitors* · *The Athenaeum* (19 Sept 1891), 393 · B. Read, *Victorian sculpture* (1982) · E. Darby and N. Smith, *The cult of the prince consort* (1983) · R. Ormond, *Early Victorian portraits*, 2 vols. (1973) · H. Le Grice, *Walks through the studii of the sculptors at Rome*, 2 vols. (1841), vol. 1, pp. 60–61 · S. C. Hutchison, 'The Royal Academy Schools, 1768–1830', *Walpole Society*, 38 (1960–

62), 123–91, esp. 173 · D. Brumhead and T. Wyke, *A walk round Manchester statues* (1990) · P. Atterbury, ed., *The Parian phenomenon* (1989) · d. cert. · *CGPLA Eng. & Wales* (1891) · J. Ingamells, ed., *A dictionary of British and Irish travellers in Italy, 1701–1800* (1997), 934 · W. Sandby, *The history of the Royal Academy of Arts*, 1 (1862), 382–3 · Redgrave, *Artists*, 2nd edn, 426–7 · census returns, 1881

Archives CUL, letters to Joseph Bonomi · NL Scot., corresp. mainly with Lord Rutherford · RA, Gibson papers and corresp.

Likenesses Caldesi & Co., carte-de-visite, NPG

Wealth at death £40,751 8s. 3d.: resworn probate, Nov 1893, *CGPLA Eng. & Wales* (1891)

Theinred [Theinred of Dover] (*fl. c.*1150), music theorist, has been plausibly identified with the Tenredus mentioned by John of Salisbury in his *Metalogicon* as a grammarian. He was, apparently, an ecclesiastic, though no biographical data have been discovered. His name suggests an Old Norse or Anglo-Saxon origin. His only known work, *De legitimis ordinibus pentachordorum et tetrachordorum*, survives in a single copy (Bodl. Oxf., MS Bodley 842, fols. 1–44v); it remains unedited. Theinred's name, life, date, and treatise (title, content, and incipit) have long been the victims of numerous errors, distortions, and fictions—a plague of misinformation that has haunted even very recent publications.

The treatise, which displays an intimate knowledge of plainchant, is addressed to Alveredus of Canterbury (otherwise unknown), and is divided into three books, with a proœmium. Book 1 treats primarily intervals and their proportions; following Boethius, the discussion is notable only for its thoroughness. Book 2 deals principally with issues of consonance and dissonance; in it Theinred discusses the admissibility of thirds and sixths in organum, and compares the relative consonance of the pure thirds (5:4, 6:5) to the ditonus and semiditonus (81:64, 32:27). In this, he anticipates the work of Walter of Odingham. Book 3 is an extended and original discussion of the problem of chromatically altered tones (beyond the B♭ accepted by Guidonian theory) in plainsong. Tacitly rejecting modal theory altogether, Theinred completely reworks species theory. He recognizes no pre-existing scale or gamut—though he assumes the diatonic system—and defines species strictly in terms of internal intervallic arrangement. Through various permutations Theinred derives complexes that include the seven diatonic pitches and also B♭, E♭, and F♯. This material is presented not in music notation, but in letter notation, modified for the chromatic tones. Some thirty items from Gregorian chant are cited, classified by their usage of these altered tones.

Although the historical significance of his work cannot be fully assessed until it is better known, it is clear that Theinred's approach, views, and criticism of then prevailing thought are unique in medieval music theory, throwing fresh light on several issues crucial to the development of Western music. JOHN L. SNYDER

Sources Theinred of Dover, 'De legitimis ordinibus pentachordorum et tetrachordorum', Bodl. Oxf., MS Bodley 842 · J. L. Snyder, 'The *De legitimis ordinibus pentachordorum et tetrachordorum* of Theinred of Dover', PhD diss., Indiana University, 1982 · J. L. Snyder, 'A road not taken: Theinred of Dover's theory of species', *Journal of the Royal Musical Association*, 115 (1990), 145–81 · J. L. Snyder, 'Theinred of Dover on consonance: a chapter in the history of harmony', *Music Theory Spectrum*, 5 (1983), 110–20 · Guido d'Arezzo, *Micrologus de disciplinis artis musicae, Scriptores ecclesiastici de musica sacra potissimum*, ed. M. Gerbert, 3 vols. (St Blasien, 1784), 2–24 · *Hucbald, Guido, and John on music: three medieval treatises*, ed. C. V. Palisca, trans. W. Babb (1978), 57–83 · C. C. J. Webb, 'Tenred of Dover', *EngHR*, 30 (1915), 658–60 · *Ioannis Saresberiensis episcopi Carnotensis Metalogicon libri IIII*, ed. C. C. I. Webb (1929) · *The metalogicon of John of Salisbury: a twelfth-century defense of the verbal and logical arts of the trivium*, trans. D. D. McGarry (1955)

Archives Bodl. Oxf., Bodley 842, fols. 1–44v

Thellusson, Peter (1737–1797), merchant, was born in Paris on 27 June 1737, the third son of Isaac de Thellusson (1690–1755), banker in Paris and minister of Geneva at the court of France (1730–44), and his wife, Sarah, daughter of Abraham Le Boullenger, of Leiden. The family of Thellusson was of French origin, but took refuge at Geneva during the French wars of religion. Isaac's second son, George (1728–1776), and his partner, Jacques Necker, the future minister of Louis XVI, built up in Paris a first-class banking house.

On 6 January 1761 Thellusson married Ann, second daughter of Matthew Woodford of Southampton, and sister of an MP; they had three sons and three daughters. His eldest son, Peter Isaac Thellusson (1761–1808), MP from 1795, was on 1 February 1806 created Baron Rendelsham in the Irish peerage.

Peter Thellusson was sent to England to complete his education in 1761 and was naturalized by act of parliament in the same year. He set up as a merchant banker in London, with help from his brother George and from Pierre Naville, a London merchant from Geneva, who had married his sister. He was agent for his brother's Paris house, as well as for Vandenyver & Cie and other great houses of Paris, Geneva, and Amsterdam. He insured in London French ships sailing to the East Indies; in 1779 he helped to invest £100,000 from Geneva in the Irish tontine. He thus was a typical member of the 'Huguenot International'. He also engaged in business on his own account, trading chiefly with the West Indies, and speculated on the stock exchange. In the early years of the French Revolution, he was the chief London correspondent of Greffulhe and Montz, who had taken over the Thellusson–Necker bank. In connection with them, he speculated on specie and on assignats, and he received large sums which were exported from France by or for the émigrés. He thus amassed a considerable fortune, and, among other landed property, purchased the estate of Broadsworth in Yorkshire.

Thellusson died on 21 July 1797 at his seat at Plaistow, near Bromley in Kent. By his will, dated 2 April 1796, he left £100,000 to his wife and children. The remainder of his fortune, valued at £600,000 or £800,000, he assigned to trustees to accumulate during the lives of his sons and his sons' sons, and of their issue existing at the time of his death. On the death of the last survivor the estate was to be divided equally among the three eldest male lineal descendants of his three sons then living. If there were no heir, the property was to go to the extinction of the national debt. At the time of Thellusson's death he had no great-grandchildren, and in consequence the trust was limited to the life of two generations. The will was generally seen as absurd, and the family endeavoured to get it set aside. On 20 April 1799 the lord chancellor, Alexander Wedderburn, Lord Loughborough, pronounced the will valid, and his decision was confirmed by the House of Lords on 25 June 1805. As it was calculated that the accumulation might reach £140 million, the will was regarded by some as a peril to the country, and an act—often called the Thellusson Act—was passed in 1800 prohibiting similar schemes of bequest. A second lawsuit arose in 1856, when Charles Thellusson, the last grandson, died. It was decided in the House of Lords on 9 June 1859. As George Woodford Thellusson, Peter's second son, had no issue, the estate was divided between Frederick William Brook Thellusson, fifth Baron Rendlesham (1840–1911), and Charles Sabine Augustus Thellusson (1822–1885), grandson of Charles, Peter's third son. In consequence of mismanagement and the costs of litigation, they succeeded to only a comparatively moderate fortune.

E. I. CARLYLE, rev. FRANÇOIS CROUZET

Sources H. Lüthy, La banque protestante en France de la révocation de l'édit de Nantes à la Révolution, 2 vols. (1959–61) · Burke, Peerage · GEC, Peerage · Burke, Gen. GB · GM, 1st ser., 67 (1797), 624, 708, 747 · GM, 1st ser., 68 (1798), 1082 · Annual Register (1797), 148 · Annual Register (1859), 333 · D. C. A. Agnew, Protestant exiles from France, chiefly in the reign of Louis XIV, or, The Huguenot refugees and their descendants in Great Britain and Ireland, 3rd edn, 2 vols. (1886) · J. L. de Lolme, General observations on the power of individuals to prescribe by testamentary dispositions, the particular future uses to be made of their property; occasioned by the last will of the late Mr Peter Thellusson of London (1798) · J. F. Hargrave, A treatise on the Thellusson Act: 39 and 40 Geo. III.c.98 (1842) · F. Vesey, Case upon the will of the late Peter Thellusson [1799]
Archives W. Yorks. AS, Doncaster archives department
Wealth at death approx. £700,000: DNB

Thelwall, Algernon Sydney (1795–1863), Church of England clergyman and teacher of elocution, was born in Cowes, Isle of Wight, the eldest son of John *Thelwall (1764–1834), the political reformer, and his wife, Susan Vellum (d. 1816). Educated by private tuition, he was admitted a pensioner at Trinity College, Cambridge, in 1813 and, having been elected a scholar in 1816, graduated BA as eighteenth wrangler in 1818. He was admitted at the Middle Temple in 1816, but was ordained priest in 1819, becoming English chaplain and missionary to the Jews in Amsterdam from 1819 to 1826. Returning to England he became curate of Blackford, Somerset, in 1828, marrying on 11 November 1828, at Islington, Georgiana Anne, eldest daughter of a Mr Tahourdin.

Thelwall was a prominent evangelical, whose published Sermons (1833) revealed a greater awareness of the importance of the church in its corporate capacity than had been common among evangelicals of the preceding generation. His polemical works included a scriptural refutation of Irvingism (1834) and an exposure of the iniquity of the opium trade with China (1839). He was a founder of the Trinitarian Bible Society, and was secretary from 1846 to 1851. During 1842–3 he was minister of the Bedford Chapel, Bloomsbury, and was curate of St Matthew's, Pell Street, from 1848 to 1850 and again during 1852–3, but he

never held a benefice. A determined anti-Catholic, he contributed attacks on Tractarianism to the series of Brighton Protestant Tracts, and came to wider notice as reporter of the proceedings of the protestant committee convened in 1845 to oppose a state grant to the Catholic seminary at Maynooth.

From 1850 until his death Thelwall was lecturer in elocution and public reading at the theological department of King's College, London. His The Reading Desk and the Pulpit (1861) argued for the importance to clergymen of his subject. Thelwall died at his home, 43 Torrington Square, London, on 30 November 1863. Three of his sons were admitted at Trinity College, Cambridge. M. C. CURTHOYS

Sources GM, 3rd ser., 16 (1864), 128 · Venn, Alum. Cant. · Boase, Mod. Eng. biog. · D. W. Bebbington, Evangelicalism in modern Britain: a history from the 1730s to the 1980s (1989) · J. Wolffe, The protestant crusade in Great Britain, 1829–1860 (1991) · GM, 1st ser., 98/2 (1828), 462

Thelwall, Sir Eubule (c.1557–1630), lawyer, was the fifth son of John Wyn Thelwall (c.1528–1586) of Bathafarn Park, Llanbedr, Denbighshire, and Jane (1525–1585), daughter of Thomas Griffith of Pant-y-llondu, Llanasa, Flintshire.

Thelwall was educated at Westminster School and at Trinity College, Cambridge, where he graduated BA in 1577. He was incorporated at Oxford, where he proceeded MA in 1580, and looked set for an academic career until his enrolment at Gray's Inn in 1590, when he must have been over thirty. Thanks to leases of lands from his family's patron, the countess of Warwick, he was already a man of some means when called to the bar in 1599, and he gradually built up an extensive estate in the lordship of Ruthin, Denbighshire, of which he became recorder in 1604. Appointed an associate bencher of Gray's Inn in 1612, master in chancery and clerk of the alienations office in 1617, and a full bencher at his inn in 1623, he may have owed much of his preferment to his Gray's Inn colleague Francis Bacon. He was knighted on 29 June 1619.

One of Thelwall's first acts as a chancery master was to secure an increase in the fees his department was allowed to charge, buying Bacon's support with a gratuity of £1200. This bribe came to light during Bacon's impeachment in 1621, when both Thelwall's actions and the remit of his office were attacked in parliament by Sir Edward Coke. Presumably as a result of this mauling, Thelwall took care to secure himself a Commons seat (for Denbighshire) in 1624, when he attempted to procure the abolition of the subpoena office, whose fees would have reverted to the chancery masters. He was noticeably slower to leap to the defence of his superior, Lord Keeper John Williams, when the latter faced impeachment charges, which may explain why Williams supported a rival candidate for the Denbighshire election in 1625.

Denied a seat on this occasion, Thelwall was returned for Denbighshire again in 1626, when he filed a petition against Lewis Bayly, bishop of Bangor, in whose diocese he lived, accusing the latter of simony, embezzlement, assault, and fornication, and of nominating unqualified men 'and others … that understand not the [Welsh] language' to benefices (Bidwell and Jansson, 3.5); the investigating committee did not report before the dissolution, at which time one of his enemies reported a rumour that Thelwall had been arrested. He played a more constructive role in the Commons during the sessions of 1628 and 1629, seeking to smooth the passage of the subsidy bill and the petition of right, steering the Denbighshire copyholders' bill through committee, and making an impassioned speech for a better preaching ministry:

> I think it is time to complain of ministers when I, that have a dozen or fourteen of them within ten mile of me round about, the least of their benefices to the value of £50 *per annum*, may ride my horse a month and not hear a sermon. I believe they are not busied as they should be, and therefore it is time to think of a reformation. (Cole, 3.436)

If somewhat ruthless in his professional dealings, Thelwall was also noted for his charitable works. At Gray's Inn he supervised the building of the chapel and paving of the courts, while at Jesus College, Oxford, of which he became president in 1621, he secured the first proper set of statutes for the college, and was said to have invested nearly £5000 of his own money in the chapel and library, in addition to donations he solicited from other Welsh alumni.

Thelwall never married, and at his death on 8 October 1630 his estate was divided between his financier brother Sir Bevis Thelwall and several nephews. He was buried in the chapel of Jesus College, which still owns a portrait of him as a child.   SIMON HEALY

Sources J. P. Ferris and A. D. Thrush, 'Thelwall, Sir Eubule', HoP, *Commons, 1604–29* [draft] · *Hist. U. Oxf.* 4: *17th-cent. Oxf.* · W. P. Griffith, *Learning, law and religion: higher education and Welsh society, c.1540–1640* (1996) · W. Notestein, F. H. Relf, and H. Simpson, eds., *Commons debates, 1621*, 7 vols. (1935) · W. B. Bidwell and M. Jansson, eds., *Proceedings in parliament, 1626*, 4 vols. (1991–6) · R. C. Johnson and others, eds., *Commons debates, 1628*, 6 vols. (1977–83) · G. E. Aylmer, *The king's servants: the civil service of Charles I, 1625–1642* (1961)
Likenesses oils (as a child), Jesus College, Oxford
Wealth at death approx. £10,000: will, PRO, PROB 11/158, fols. 310–11

Thelwall, John (1764–1834), political reformer and lecturer, was born on 27 July 1764 at Chandos Street, Covent Garden, the son of Joseph Thelwall (1731–1772), a silk mercer. He was a sickly child, suffering from asthma and a tendency to stammer. After his father's death his mother continued the silk business, and in 1777 John left his boarding-school at Highgate to work for the family firm. He found this irksome, and preferred to continue his education by self-tuition through wide reading, for which he was frequently reproached by his mother. Personal dissatisfaction and uncongenial family life (his elder brother drank heavily, and may have been mentally ill) was reflected in his restless and short-lived attempts to find a career. John tried to become a painter, then made a fruitless attempt to 'get upon the stage'. He was apprenticed to a master tailor, but quickly abandoned the trade to make a further attempt to study as a painter. In 1782 he was articled as clerk to the attorney John Impey of Inner Temple Lane. Once again, however, he found himself more attracted to a literary life than to the duties required of him by the legal profession. After three and a half years studying for the bar, his articles were cancelled and in 1786 he

John Thelwall (1764–1834), attrib. John Hazlitt, c.1800–05

'launched into the world as a literary adventurer' (J. Thelwall, xviii). He had already published in journals during the early 1780s. In 1787 his *Poems on Various Subjects* appeared to some praise from the *Critical Review*, and he also became editor and principal contributor to the *Biographical and Imperial Magazine*. With other journalism, and some private tuition, he managed to support himself and his mother (whose silk business had by now failed).

Thelwall began his career as a political lecturer by speaking at public debating societies, especially the Society for Free Debate, which met in Coachmakers' Hall. All shades of political opinion were canvassed at debates: Thelwall was at first 'decidedly ministerial' in his sympathies, but the early progress of the French Revolution encouraged a more critical and reformist attitude to the establishment. In 1790 he was a poll clerk at the Westminster election, and in this capacity met and impressed the veteran reformist John Horne Tooke, whom Thelwall subsequently regarded as his 'intellectual and political father' (C. B. Thelwall, 76). On his birthday, 27 July 1791, he married Susan Vellum, whom he had met in 1789, while convalescing in Rutland. He settled with her near Guy's and St Thomas's hospitals. Here he attended the anatomical lectures given by Henry Cline (whom he had known since 1787), William Babington, and others. At this time he was a close friend of the surgeon and republican Astley Cooper. Between October 1791 and 1793 he was a 'most conspicuous' member of the Physical Society at Guy's Hospital, a distinguished group that met for lectures on and discussion of advanced medical and scientific issues. On 26 January 1793 he presented to the society a lecture entitled 'Animal vitality', which speculated on the vital principal of life, and 'controverted' John Hunter's theory that this principle was inherent in the blood. The lecture was a great success: it was discussed at five subsequent meetings of the Physical Society, and published as *An Essay towards a Definition of Animal Vitality* (1793).

From 1792 Thelwall had divided his time between scientific interests and his commitment to the rapidly expanding movement for parliamentary reform. When in November 1792 government agents closed the Society for Free Debate, Thelwall resolved to 'assert and vindicate' the right to political discussion (C. B. Thelwall, 98). He offered a reward in hope of finding a room for debate and, from November 1793, commenced his political lectures at Compton Street and subsequently at the large meeting-room at Beaufort Buildings, Strand. His central place in metropolitan reformist circles is suggested by his affiliations with various reformist groups. He attended the Society of the Friends of the Liberty of the Press and joined the moderate Friends of the People at Southwark. He was acquainted with members of the long-established Society for Constitutional Information, and in October 1793 Joseph Gerrald introduced him to the more broadly based, working-class reform movement in the *London Corresponding Society, founded in January 1792 by the shoemaker Thomas Hardy. 'Citizen' Thelwall quickly became the most prominent and articulate member of the reform movement, calling in his speeches for universal suffrage and an end to the war with France. His witty, upbeat presence as a public speaker is evoked by his 'libel of the Bantum Cock', which (implicitly) compared George III to a cock on a farmyard dunghill. The radical publisher Daniel Isaac Eaton was charged with seditious libel for publishing Thelwall's satire in *Politics for the People*, but he was acquitted and the prosecution ridiculed for glossing Thelwall's remarks about the cock with the phrase 'meaning our lord the king'. Thelwall claimed that audiences of 750 people attended his lectures, but his outspoken opinions and his popularity also brought the attentions of government agents and informers (including James Walsh, who in August 1797 would spy on Samuel Taylor Coleridge and William Wordsworth at Nether Stowey). Thelwall could be self-dramatizing and given to exaggeration, but he responded to a genuine threat of violence when he decided to make his hat 'cudgel proof', and deliberately walked down the middle of the street to avoid attack.

In the belief that the London Corresponding Society was about to call a general convention (similar to the French revolutionary administration), the British government arrested the leaders of the reform movement. On hearing of Thomas Hardy's arrest, on 12 May 1794, Thelwall observed to a friend: 'Affairs are at a sad crisis, citizen' (C. B. Thelwall, 153). The following day Thelwall was arrested at Beaufort Buildings; his papers and books were confiscated, and he was imprisoned in the Tower of London. He remained in the Tower over the summer months until, on 6 October, he was indicted with the others on a capital charge of treason and moved to the 'Common Charnel House' of Newgate gaol (J. Thelwall, xxviii). After the trials of Hardy and Horne Tooke, Thelwall was tried at the Old Bailey from 1 to 5 December and—like his two friends—acquitted. This outcome 'electrified' the court room, and brought loud applause from the crowd gathered outside. The charges against the other reformists were dropped, and the prisoners were released.

While Thelwall emerged as a hero of the reform movement, he also continued his literary career. In 1793 he published *The Peripatetic*, a 'political-sentimental' compendium of prose and verse that he later claimed was Wordsworth's pattern for his dramatic poem *The Excursion* (1814). During his imprisonment in 1794, he wrote the verses published in *Poems Written in Close Confinement* (1795). After a brief respite following his trial, Thelwall resumed his political activities and published his lectures in his own journal, *The Tribune* (1795–6). His prolific output of pamphlets included *The Natural and Constitutional Rights of Britons* (1795), *Peaceful Discussion* (1795), *The Rights of Nature* (1796), and *Sober reflections on the seditious and inflammatory letter of the Right Hon. Edmund Burke to a noble lord* (1796). Although in 1795 he had retired from the London Corresponding Society, he maintained his support for the society's principles and, on 26 October and 12 November 1795, spoke at the mass meetings called by the society in Copenhagen Fields, Islington. His stature as a leader of the reformists is suggested by James Gillray's satirical cartoon of him in 'Copenhagen House', and by Edmund Burke's wry observation that the mass gatherings of reformists constituted 'the Thelwall festival'.

On 29 October 1795 the king's carriage was attacked at the opening of parliament, an incident used by the government as a pretext for the introduction of the 'two bills' or 'Gagging Acts'. The Seditious Meetings' Bill, passed into law on 18 December 1795, suppressed public meetings and effectively prevented Thelwall's lectures at Beaufort Buildings. Undeterred, and at considerable personal risk, he continued his political career under the guise of lectures on classical history. During 1796 he made a lecture tour of East Anglia, speaking at Norwich, Yarmouth, Wisbech, and King's Lynn. He was nearly captured by a press-gang at Yarmouth, and was 'successively attacked' on other occasions when he tried to speak. 'Such was the conclusion of [my] political career', Thelwall wrote in 1801 (J. Thelwall, xxx).

Like Thelwall in London, Coleridge had delivered numerous political lectures at Bristol during 1795. The two had corresponded since April 1796, and in the summer of 1797 Thelwall's walking tour through the west country of England brought him to Nether Stowey, where he arrived on 17 July. For ten days Thelwall, Coleridge, and William and Dorothy Wordsworth (recently settled at Alfoxden House) formed a 'most philosophical party' walking in the Quantock coombes. They read Wordsworth's play *The Borderers* in Alfoxden Park, and enjoyed a high-spirited dinner at which an informer, the servant Thomas Jones, was also present. The conversation was reported and, within a few days, Thelwall's old adversary James Walsh—Coleridge's 'Spy Nosy'—arrived at Stowey, only to find that Thelwall had already left.

Thelwall, impressed by Coleridge's and Wordsworth's

life of literary retirement, hoped to settle at Stowey too. But, like the poets, he had not forgotten politics entirely: in Coleridge's well-known anecdote, Thelwall claimed that the Quantocks was 'a place to make a man forget that there is any necessity for treason!' (S. T. Coleridge, *Table Talk*, 1, 24 July 1830, 181). Seemingly embarrassed by Thelwall's notoriety, and anxious to consolidate his friendship with the Wordsworths, Coleridge put him off. Thelwall eventually settled with his family at a farm in Llys-wen, on the banks of the River Wye, near Brecon. Here the one-time champion of the reform movement commenced a life of farming and literary composition, describing himself as the 'new Recluse'.

In 1801 Thelwall published his *Poems Chiefly Written in Retirement*. 'To the Infant Hampden' and 'Lines Written at Bridgwater' deserve comparison with Coleridge's blank verse 'conversation poems' of the later 1790s. After failing as a farmer, he resumed his lecturing career in November 1801, speaking now about elocution and the 'Science of human speech'. At Edinburgh in 1804 he responded to critical remarks by Francis Jeffrey in the *Edinburgh Review* by opening a pamphlet war with his *Letter to Francis Jeffrey on Certain Calumnies and Misrepresentations in the 'Edinburgh Review'*. Soon afterwards he settled at Bedford Place, where he taught speech therapy and elocution, and in 1809 he established an institute in Lincoln's Inn Fields, where he continued to practise as an elocutionist. His *Letter to Henry Cline* (1810) alluded to his early friendship with the surgeon, to 'treasured remembrances of anatomical and physiological facts', and outlined his system and some successful cases he had treated. In seeking the 'enfranchisement of fettered organs' through speech therapy, Thelwall merged the scientific and political ideals that had formed two aspects of his career in the 1790s; as he wrote in his *Letter to Henry Cline*, 'the medical man and the philanthropist will not be insensible to the value of this new science'.

In 1816 his first wife, Susan, died, leaving him four children to support, the eldest of whom was Algernon Sydney *Thelwall. His Institute of Elocution flourished until 1818, when, following the end of the Napoleonic wars, the call for a parliamentary reform movement had revived. Thelwall returned to the cause, purchasing and editing a journal, *The Champion*, in which he published a series of powerful denunciations of the Peterloo massacre (16 August 1819). He married, about 1819, Henrietta Cecil Boyle and reopened his elocution school at Brixton. From now on Thelwall resumed his career as an itinerant lecturer, appearing at literary and philosophical societies throughout the country. His subjects included 'elocution, history, the classics, polite literature, impediments of speech &c.' (Britton, 1.185); a representative course, dated 16 August 1832, comprised ten 'Lectures, Elocutionary & Critical, on Milton in Particular, & the English Poets in General'. On 25 January 1834 Thelwall wrote cheerfully from Bristol, saying he was 'as animate as ever' on the platform. He also mentioned, however, an 'unpleasant symptom of the chest', that he was 'less & less able to bear the exertion of walking', and that he still endured his 'astmha [*sic*], or whatever it is'. Three weeks later, on 17 February 1834, Thelwall died at Bath. His second wife survived him.

Coleridge's sense that 'Citizen John Thelwell had something good about him' (24 July 1830, *Table Talk*, 1.180) was echoed in other nineteenth-century memoirs. Thelwall's reputation was enhanced from the 1960s by the work of E. P. Thompson, and the bicentenary in 1994 of his trial for treason occasioned widespread interest in his political, scientific, literary, and medical careers.

NICHOLAS ROE

Sources *Public characters of 1800–1801* (1801), 177–93 · J. Thelwall, 'Memoir', *Poems written in retirement* (1801) · J. Britton, *The autobiography of John Britton*, 1 (privately printed, London, 1850), 180–86 · Mrs Thelwall, *The life of John Thelwall* (1837) · C. Cestre, *John Thelwall* (1906) · E. P. Thompson, *The making of the English working class* (1963) · E. P. Thompson, 'Disenchantment or default? A lay sermon', *Power and consciousness*, ed. C. C. O'Brien and W. D. Vanech (1969) · D. Rockey, 'John Thelwall and the origins of British speech therapy', *Medical History*, 23 (1979), 156–75 · A. Goodwin, *The friends of liberty: the English democratic movement in the age of the French Revolution* (1979) · P. J. Corfield and C. Evans, 'John Thelwall in Wales: new documentary evidence', *BIHR*, 59 (1986), 231–9 · N. Roe, *Wordsworth and Coleridge: the radical years* (1988) · N. Roe, 'Coleridge and John Thelwall: the road to Nether Stowey', *The Coleridge connection*, ed. R. Gravil and M. Lefebure (1990) · N. Roe, *The politics of nature: Wordsworth and some contemporaries* (1992) · N. Roe, 'Coleridge and John Thelwall: medical science, politics and poetry', *The Coleridge Bulletin*, new ser., 3 (spring 1994), 1–23 · E. P. Thompson, 'Hunting the Jacobin fox', *Past and Present*, 142 (1994), 94–140 · S. T. Coleridge, *Table-talk*, ed. C. Woodring, 2 vols. (1990)
Archives NL Scot., letters to Robert Anderson
Likenesses H. Richter, stipple, pubd 1794, NPG · J. Gillray, portrait, 1795 (*Copenhagen House*), BM · attrib. J. Hazlitt, oils, c.1800–1805, NPG [*see illus.*] · stipple, BM; repro. in J. Baxter, *A new and impartial history of England* [1796]

Theobald (c.1090–1161), archbishop of Canterbury, was born at Thierville (Eure) in Normandy, some 5 kilometres north of the abbey of Le Bec-Hellouin, in the valley of the Risle and within the lordship of Brionne.

Family and early monastic career Theobald's father was reputed to have been a knight, presumably in the service of the count; and, accordingly, was of a similar social standing to Herluin, the founder of Bec. The author of a brief life of Theobald, perhaps Miles Crispin, the precentor of Bec who died about 1150, considered his lineage distinguished, but does not name his parents. Robert de Torigni describes Theobald as noble and honourable. Theobald's father was a neighbour, and perhaps a kinsman, of Gilbert Beket, the father of Theobald's successor at Canterbury. He had several children. One of the younger sons, *Walter, was made by Theobald his second-in-command at Canterbury. Four of Theobald's nephews, Guillaume, Gilbert, Roger, and Lechard, together with their tutor, the clerk Thomas d'Évreux, witness a charter of his from 1150–53. The first of these, named as Guillaume de Thierville, is found as a clerk in Bishop Bartholomew of Exeter's household about 1172.

A date for Theobald's birth about 1090, when Robert Curthose was duke of Normandy, would suit the information that he was very old when he died and also produce a likely chronology. The author of his life states that he was very well educated in the liberal arts, but does not claim him as an alumnus of the abbey. He entered the monastery of Bec when the noble Guillaume de Montfort of Montfort-sur-Risle was abbot (1093–1124), the 266th of his 346 admissions, and so, perhaps, about 1117, when he would be about twenty-seven. The biographer adds that Theobald spent many years as a claustral monk, ten years as prior, and was elected abbot on the death of Boso in June 1136. But he obtained the office only with difficulty. Archbishop Hugh of Rouen first withheld consent because he had not been consulted, then the benediction because Theobald, like his predecessors, would not make a profession of canonical obedience. In the end Peter the Venerable, abbot of Cluny, who was on a visit to Normandy, secured a compromise, a verbal profession. According to the life, the archbishop thereafter loved him dearly. But it seems as though the abbey, perhaps because Theobald soon deserted it, was not so indulgent.

Archbishop of Canterbury William de Corbeil, archbishop of Canterbury, died on 21 November 1136, at a time when King Stephen's authority was crumbling in both England and Normandy under attacks from Scotland and Anjou and internal rebels, mostly in support of his rival to the throne, Henry I's daughter, the empress Matilda, widow of the emperor Heinrich V and the wife of Geoffrey, count of Anjou. By November 1138, however, Stephen had weathered the storm and could spare time for Canterbury. His younger brother, Henry de Blois, bishop of Winchester, who was administering the vacant diocese and coveted the arch-see, had been negotiating with Pope Innocent II for permission to be translated. In June 1138 a papal legate, Alberic, cardinal-bishop of Ostia, arrived in England; and after a visitation of the dioceses he summoned a general council to Westminster for 11 December. In his mandate to the diocese of Canterbury he listed the appointment of a new archbishop among the business to be transacted. He recognized the right of the monks to elect, but also mentioned the interest of the bishops and the king in the matter.

Stephen had in fact clearly decided to thwart his brother's vaulting ambition; and with the pope's and the legate's connivance—and, presumably, the support of some of the leading bishops—staged a *coup de théâtre*. Theobald went to London on the invitation of the king and queen; and at the very end of the council, on 24 December, when Henry of Winchester had absented himself for some business at St Paul's, Theobald was elected archbishop. The procedure is variously described and the parts played by the several constituent actors are uncertain. But there seems to have been no overt opposition to the abbot's election. It could be that Theobald's relative obscurity served him well. On 8 January 1139 the legate, assisted by most of the provincial bishops, consecrated him archbishop at Canterbury. Meanwhile the pope had summoned the English prelates to a general council (the Second Lateran Council) to be held at Rome in Lent; and Theobald set off with four of his suffragans and four abbots. Before August he returned with a pallium. But Innocent had found a novel way of checking Canterbury's pretensions to a primacy: on 1 March he named Henry de

Blois, bishop of Winchester, his standing legate in the kingdom. He was also offering an olive branch. But Henry never forgave his brother for his treachery; and his ambition to create a third ecclesiastical province in England, based on Winchester, became an additional threat to Theobald.

Household government Theobald was not only an ambitious man but also a brave one. The almost inevitable civil war in England and Normandy, which was about to begin, ensured a tense political situation and an insoluble problem of loyalty. Henry of Winchester's legation (1139–43) and ambitions were a recipe for a similar anarchy in the English church. And the monks of Christ Church, Canterbury, who had been feuding with William de Corbeil over how the collegiate church of St Martin at Dover should be reformed, and continued to behave unlawfully in the two years' vacancy after his death, offered an immediate challenge to Theobald's authority. Although the incomer was, like his illustrious predecessors, Lanfranc and Anselm, a monk of Bec, he was also a man of a new age. He appointed his brother Walter as archdeacon of Canterbury at the earliest opportunity, brought over his nephews (*nipoti*), and recruited a household of clerks, which, distinguished though it might be, was not the traditional family of a monk-bishop. Indeed, its brilliance must have been an unexpected outcome of the arrival of a hitherto obscure abbot. Among the stars of this alma mater of three future archbishops and six bishops were Roger de Pont l'Évêque, Thomas Becket of London, John of Canterbury (later archbishop of Lyons), Bartholomew, the future bishop of Exeter, William of Northolt, John of Pagham, and William de Vere. Most of these were masters of arts; by 1145 Theobald had also attracted the Italian master of laws, Vacarius, and by 1147–8 John of Salisbury, both in their different disciplines scholars and figures of European importance.

Although the purpose of the household was utilitarian—to protect and exercise Theobald's rights as an ordinary, metropolitan, primate, landowner, and first minister of the king—and was not intended to form a public school, it soon became, backed by Canterbury's fine library, one of the most distinguished academies that the English church ever produced. Several of its members remembered fondly the idyllic days they had passed there. It was a stimulating and also a competitive society. The archbishop worked hard to advance his clerks; and he had his favourites. When he promoted his brother Walter from the archdeaconry to the suffragan see of Rochester early in 1148, he gave Roger de Pont l'Évêque the vacant office. And, probably in 1152, he and some of Roger's friends, led by Thomas Becket, smothered a serious homosexual scandal in which the archdeacon was involved. In 1154 Theobald obtained for Roger a great prize, the archbishopric of York. After that Theobald doted on Becket, while John of Salisbury became his devoted confidential secretary.

The monks of Canterbury There is every reason to think that Theobald's administration was efficient and progressive. With one of the greatest stylists of the age, John of

Salisbury, drafting his diplomatic and legal correspondence, and humbler chancellors and scribes producing his charters, the literary and business documents produced were much influenced by the practices of the papal curia and the English royal court. Moreover, this household of bright young men was in general out of sympathy with 'musty' monastic culture; and its recruitment indicates how the once insubordinate abbot was changing into an authoritarian bishop. Theobald took a sincerely benevolent interest in all monastic and canonical communities within his diocese and province; but he opposed their exemption from episcopal control and deplored, and sometimes withstood, even disregarded, the growing habit of 'undisciplined' monks appealing to the pope against episcopal authority. The prior of the cathedral chapter, Christ Church, in 1138 was Jeremiah, who, as sub-prior, had been a thorn in William de Corbeil's flesh, and had been promoted illegally *sede vacante*. Theobald, at first impressed by this firebrand, allowed the monks to recolonize St Martin's, Dover, and used Jeremiah as his agent in the reform of the diocese. But by 1143 he had had enough, deposed him, and, although forced to reinstate him by Innocent II and his legate, Henry of Winchester, made life so uncomfortable for him that, with the solace of 100 marks to acquit the debts he had incurred by his appeal, Jeremiah resigned and retired to St Augustine's. When his replacement, Walter Durdent, a pious and learned monk, was elected bishop of Coventry in 1149, Theobald made a bad mistake by promoting his chaplain, Walter Parvus, to be prior of Christ Church. This man's mismanagement created so much havoc that Theobald, the son of a knight, had to use military force to restore order. He captured and imprisoned monks engaged in appealing to Rome, confiscated the priory's archives, and in 1152 arrested Walter at Lambeth and had him imprisoned at Gloucester. In his place he promoted the sub-prior Wibert, with whom he collaborated in reforming the chapter's administration.

As Theobald was abbot of Christ Church, he suffered few restraints on his inherent authority. St Augustine's, however, was far from domestic. Dedicated to the apostle of the English and the founder of the see, the burial place of the saint and of the first ten archbishops, it was not only the standing rival of Christ Church, but also claimed total exemption from the archbishop's jurisdiction. It had, moreover, in 1120 and 1139 obtained papal confirmation of its portfolio of forged papal bulls granting it independence and much besides. It was only with difficulty that William de Corbeil had obtained a profession of obedience from Hugh of Trottiscliffe, elected abbot in 1126; and a rebel group of monks, led by Hugh's nephew, the sacrist, William—William the Devil to Christ Church monks—and supported by the prior, Silvester, quarrelled with Theobald over a number of matters, mainly financial and administrative.

In 1144 Pope Lucius II decided most of the points at issue in the archbishop's favour. And in September 1149, when the prior and sacrist refused to observe the interdict placed on England by Eugenius III and Theobald, the archbishop, supported by the pope, excommunicated the two

by name and had them publicly flogged at the door of Northfleet church before releasing them from his sentence. When Abbot Hugh died in 1151, Silvester, who paid the king 500 marks for custody of the abbey and a free election, secured the promotion and was succeeded as prior by William. Theobald, alleging simony, naturally withheld confirmation and benediction for as long as possible from his old enemy. But on 28 August 1152 he bowed to Eugenius's mandate, and, while reserving his rights, blessed Silvester without receiving a profession. But he did not let go. At Henry II's great council on 17 July 1157 at Northampton, Theobald proved that Abbot Hugh had made a profession to William de Corbeil. Whereupon Silvester, in the presence of six bishops, submitted.

Metropolitan and legate Theobald had restored order to his own see, city, and diocese. In his province, however, his metropolitan rights were at first largely nullified by Henry of Winchester's legation. Until the end of 1143 Theobald had to accept second place in the English church, and, although both he and Henry were monks, and had a common belief in the freedom of the church, their individual interests were often in conflict. Theobald's subordination did, however, shield him from having to take a leading part in dealing with Stephen's arrest of Roger, bishop of Salisbury, and the latter's episcopal kin in June 1139, and in contesting the king's traditional interference in the appointment to bishoprics and abbeys. The efforts made by Stephen and Henry to appoint first their nephew Waldef, and then William fitz Herbert (consecrated by Henry at Winchester in 1143), to the see of York, in the latter case provoking bitter opposition from the Cistercian order and its candidate, Henry Murdac, and extending the disorder in the church, also spared Theobald a powerful rival in the north.

After his legation lapsed on the death of Innocent II on 24 September 1143, Henry failed to get its renewal from Celestine II or his three successors, who employed legates *a latere*; nor could Theobald, despite repeated attempts, obtain one until Eugenius III rewarded him for his loyalty early in 1150. To judge by the terms of its renewal by Adrian IV in 1155, Theobald, on account of his prudence, steadfastness, probity, knowledge, and virtue, was granted a delegation of papal powers throughout the kingdom, including the right to convene councils, and, should he think fit, correct all errors and make ordinances. Theobald wasted no time. In March 1151 he held a legatine council in London, attended by the king, his eldest son, Eustace, and the nobility, which promulgated eight canons condemning the present ills in the kingdom, in particular, attacks on church property and illegal imposts on the clergy. The guilty were to be punished by anathema.

Until his own legation lapsed with the death of Adrian IV on 1 September 1159 and the subsequent papal schism, Theobald rebuilt and defended his metropolitan authority, even if only with powers delegated from Rome. He defeated, aided by some luck, Henry of Winchester's attempt to compensate for his lost legation by creating a province of 'western England', with Winchester as his metropolitan see. Eugenius III disliked Henry and favoured Theobald. The archbishop also successfully withstood the attempts of the Welsh bishops, led by Bernard of St David's, to create an independent province. Bernard's successor, David fitz Gerald, in 1148, at the start of his long tenure of the see, made an elaborate profession of obedience to Canterbury. Ireland, however, was removed from Canterbury's sphere of influence. Theobald consecrated Patrick to Limerick in 1140. But in 1152 the papal legate, Giovanni Paparo, completed the reform of the Irish church into four provinces, with the primacy going to Armagh.

As for Canterbury's primacy within Britain, in 1143–4 Theobald, during a visit to Pope Celestine II, obtained with the help of the papal chancellor, the Englishman Robert Pullen, some sort of a confirmation, although in 1148 at Rheims, Eugenius III indicated that it did not cover York. Uncertainty over its extent is shown between 1143 and 1155 by Theobald's secretariat's styling the archbishop, seemingly indifferently, 'primate of the whole of Britain', 'primate of the whole of England', 'primate of England', and 'primate of the English'. And in 1154, on the death of Archbishop William of York, Theobald, presumably acting as papal legate, consecrated his archdeacon, Roger de Pont l'Évêque, to the see without requiring a written profession. This evasion ensured that he and Roger remained on good terms.

Coping with civil war Theobald was no less successful in his dealings with the English rulers and the civil war. The attempts made first by Henry I's daughter, Matilda, and her husband, and then by their son, Henry, to drive Stephen out of Normandy and England, which began seriously in 1139, caused problems for the nobles and prelates in both dominions. On his election to Canterbury in 1138 Theobald had done homage and sworn fealty to Stephen, who had been crowned by his predecessor in 1135. The church, hostile to hereditary claims in its own polity, usually accepted *de facto* kings, and judged all types of ruler according to how they treated ecclesiastical rights. But it may be presumed that the church had a prejudice against female rulers, especially if, as with the empress, they were imperious. Theobald as a pure Norman was committed to the continuing unity of the duchy and kingdom, but would have regarded the Angevins as hereditary enemies. Basically, however, the church was self-interested and opportunistic. Hence, although Theobald was sensible of a primary allegiance to Stephen, whom he knew the papacy had recognized, he did not consider that those factors overrode all other considerations, or that they extended to Stephen's sons.

A month after Stephen was captured by Matilda's supporters at Lincoln on 2 February 1141, Henry of Winchester recognized the empress as his lady, and swore fealty conditional on her acceptance of him as her principal adviser. Theobald, however, more principled—as even William of Malmesbury acknowledged—insisted that he must first obtain Stephen's permission; and, when he visited him in his prison at Bristol, Stephen allowed him to bow to necessity. In the next six months the archbishop

was regularly, but probably not constantly, in Matilda's company. He was there on midsummer day, when the Londoners ejected her and her entourage from the city before she could be crowned. He remained after the legate had changed sides and adhered to Stephen's queen. And he was with her in September when she attacked Henry in Winchester and was then herself beset by the queen and her troops. Theobald, like Matilda, escaped only with difficulty, and suffered the indignity of being manhandled and robbed, while Earl Robert of Gloucester, Matilda's half-brother and the real leader of her party, was captured by the royalists. Whereupon, both Henry of Winchester and Theobald started the negotiations that led in November to the exchange of Stephen for Robert. Theobald was at the legatine council at Westminster on 7 December when Stephen was reinstated. And at Christmas he crowned Stephen and the queen at Canterbury. The civil war continued until 1149; but after Matilda returned to Normandy in 1148, never to return, the fighting and disorder gradually subsided.

The end of Stephen's reign and accession of Henry II Stephen, a kindly man, apparently showed no resentment for Theobald's temporary apostacy: he had yielded to *force majeure* in the interests of the church; and Theobald accepted that Stephen was the legitimate monarch with the traditional rights in the English church. The archbishop's frequent meetings with the popes, together with the proliferation of appeals from English ecclesiastical courts to the papal curia, did, however, make the papacy for a time the effective head of the English church. This was, inevitably, unwelcome to Stephen, and made life difficult for Theobald. When the king refused to allow the archbishop to attend Eugenius's general council at Rheims on 21 March 1148 and sent three 'safe' bishops instead, Theobald—making his way there by swimming rather than sailing, as the admiring pope exclaimed—was punished for his defiance by the confiscation of his temporalities. In return, Eugenius suspended all those English prelates who had not attended, and, except for Henry of Winchester, delegated their absolution to Theobald. Moreover, at the end of the council the pope was about to excommunicate Stephen when Theobald begged for him to be spared.

In April 1148 the archbishop returned to England, was expelled by the king, and sojourned in Flanders. There he added to his offences by consecrating at St Omer his friend, Gilbert Foliot, abbot of Gloucester, to the bishopric of Hereford after securing the consent of Geoffrey, count of Anjou, whose adherents were in control of those parts. Eugenius supported Theobald by putting an interdict on England, and the archbishop, never daunted, returned again to the kingdom and was reconciled to the king. Gilbert Foliot, on Theobald's instruction, then swore fealty to Stephen. Adroitness was almost becoming double-dealing. In 1150 Theobald was rewarded with a papal legation.

By this time Stephen, in imitation of the Capetians in France, wanted to have his elder son, Eustace, crowned king and thus have the dynasty confirmed. He met, however, with determined opposition from Eugenius and

Theobald, who, while remaining outwardly correct, had become sympathetic to the Angevin cause, and, while waiting on events, insisted on the maintenance of the *status quo*. Theobald refused Stephen's demand at the Council of London in April 1152 for the coronation, escaped again to Flanders when threatened with violence by royalists, but made his peace with the king in August. In January 1153 Henry, Matilda's and Geoffrey's son, by then duke of Normandy and, in the right of his wife, duke of Aquitaine, invaded England; and the death first of the queen and then of Eustace robbed Stephen of the will to continue the struggle. It had become obvious to most involved that some settlement would have to be made. Theobald and his clerks were active in the negotiations that led at Winchester on 6 November to Stephen's recognition of Henry as his associate ruler and heir. Stephen died on 25 October 1154 while Henry was abroad. The church and the barons respected the treaty, and on 19 December Theobald crowned Henry king.

The old archbishop of Canterbury was accepted and at first honoured by the new young king. Theobald baptized his second son, Henry, born on 28 February 1155. But his attempt to repeat the success he had had in the church, when he contrived the election of his archdeacon to the archbishopric of York on 28 February 1154, by procuring for his next archdeacon, Thomas Becket, the royal chancellorship in January 1155, was less rewarding. Becket had acquired a grander master and eagerly entered a new world, and if Theobald had hoped to use him as a means of exerting influence within the king's government, he was to be disappointed. Nevertheless, relations between the old primate (whose health was beginning to fail, causing him to be increasingly reliant on John of Salisbury for the conducting of routine business) and the new king were generally good. Occasional friction, arising from the two men's concern to protect their respective interests, was offset by a matching willingness to minimize differences.

Last days, death, and achievement Although Theobald was in poor health when Pope Adrian IV died on 1 September 1159, he took an active part in the recognition of Alexander III by the kings of France and England in the schism that followed. To his Council of London in June 1160, which considered the matter and advised the king, he was carried in a litter. His last days were clouded by the failure of both the king and his chancellor, who were together in his Normandy, to visit him. And he complained bitterly of his former clerk's ingratitude. He died in his palace at Canterbury on 18 April 1161, comforted by John of Salisbury, and was buried shortly afterwards in his cathedral in the chapel of the Holy Trinity, behind the altar on the north side, with Archbishop Lanfranc's tomb on the south. While the cathedral was being repaired in 1180, after the great fire of 1174, Theobald's tomb was discovered and opened. Although a little shrunken, the archbishop's body was intact and rigid, so that some people hailed him as a saint. He was reburied in a lead chest in the nave before the altar of St Mary, and the old marble tomb was replaced above him.

For a tyro Norman abbot of relatively humble background, with, apparently, no experience of English conditions and without influential patrons, whether ecclesiastical or secular, Theobald's achievements are remarkable. Once he had escaped from the authority of Henry of Winchester, he led the English church adroitly through a most difficult period while defending Canterbury resourcefully against all its rivals. He provided a nursery for the church's future leaders; and he also worked consistently to preserve the unity of the kingdom and to restore the Anglo-Norman empire. Despite these successes, his character remains elusive. Gervase, with his treatment of Christ Church priors in mind, calls him impetuous. Adventurous and resolute would be kinder. A scholar and a patron of scholars and able clerks, a friend of monks and religious communities, a brave and ambitious performer, yet flexible and skilful in avoiding danger, he had, perhaps, a set of qualities that did not make either for greatness or for popularity. But Henry of Huntingdon, a contemporary who had seen him in action, thought him, unlike his predecessor at Canterbury, entirely praiseworthy. Theobald's misfortune was to be overshadowed by the grandeur of his own creation, his successor, Thomas Becket.   FRANK BARLOW

Sources 'Chronicon Beccense', *Beati Lanfranci ... Opera omnia*, ed. Luc d'Achery (Paris, 1648), 1–31 • 'Compendium vitae venerabilis Theobaldi quinti abbatis Becci, postea archiepiscopi Cantuariensis', *Beati Lanfranci ... opera omnia*, ed. Luc d'Achery (Paris, 1648), 51–2 • *The historical works of Gervase of Canterbury*, ed. W. Stubbs, 2 vols., Rolls Series, 73 (1879–80) • John of Worcester, *Chron.* • *The letters of John of Salisbury*, ed. and trans. H. E. Butler and W. J. Millor, rev. C. N. L. Brooke, 2 vols., OMT (1979–86) [Lat. orig. with parallel Eng. text] • John of Salisbury, *Historia pontificalis: John of Salisbury's memoirs of the papal court*, ed. and trans. M. Chibnall (1956) • William of Malmesbury, *The Historia novella*, ed. and trans. K. R. Potter (1955) • *Letters and charters of Gilbert Foliot*, ed. A. Morey and others (1967) • J. C. Robertson and J. B. Sheppard, eds., *Materials for the history of Thomas Becket, archbishop of Canterbury*, 7 vols., Rolls Series, 67 (1875–85) • R. Howlett, ed., *Chronicles of the reigns of Stephen, Henry II, and Richard I*, 4, Rolls Series, 82 (1889) • Henry, archdeacon of Huntingdon, *Historia Anglorum*, ed. D. E. Greenway, OMT (1996) • D. Whitelock, M. Brett, and C. N. L. Brooke, eds., *Councils and synods with other documents relating to the English church, 871–1204*, 2 (1981) • A. Saltman, *Theobald, archbishop of Canterbury* (1956) • F. Barlow, *Thomas Becket*, [2nd edn] (1997) • C. R. Cheney, *English bishops' chanceries, 1100–1250* (1950) • W. L. Warren, *Henry II* (1973)

Theobald, Sir Henry Studdy (1847–1934), barrister and art collector, was born in Calcutta on 7 June 1847, the only son of William Theobald (1798–1870) and his second wife, formerly Mrs Balfour, *née* Bishop. Each parent had one child by a previous spouse. William Theobald was a member of the Calcutta bar and author of a number of legal works.

When about four, Theobald was taken to Germany, where he boarded with a family in Frankfurt am Main. He received a good elementary education at the *Gymnasium* there, and then spent a year at a Dickensian English preparatory school. At thirteen he entered Rugby School, where he was impressed by the headmaster, Frederick Temple, but thought little of the general educational standard.

Theobald entered Balliol College, Oxford, in 1866. His academic achievements there included a Taylorian scholarship in German with French in 1868, a first class in classical and a second class in mathematical moderations (1868), and a first class in *literae humaniores* (1870). In 1871 he was elected a fellow of Wadham College, where fellowships had recently become open to graduates of other colleges. He was one of several distinguished lawyers to hold the Wills legal exhibition, and in addition to lecturing in the college he became senior bursar in 1881. The bursar's post, which he held until 1888, was challenging, since Wadham was then in straitened circumstances caused by the agricultural depression. In 1909 the college elected him to an honorary fellowship.

Theobald intended to make a career at the chancery bar, and in 1867 joined the Inner Temple, where he was subsequently a tutor in real property law and a bencher. He was called to the bar in 1873. After a year working with a special pleader, he entered the chambers of Horace Davey, and subsequently undertook drafting and other work for H. B. Buckley, later Lord Wrenbury. In the early stages of his career he held several posts giving him experience of legal administration. He was clerk to the commission on unreformed municipal corporations, which reported in 1880, counsel to the statute law revision committee, and, in 1884, secretary to the committee on chancery business, which reported in 1886. At the request of Lord Selborne he drafted the Lunacy Act of 1890. This established detailed, some would say over-detailed, procedures for the administration of mental institutions.

During this period Theobald published several legal works. *A Concise Treatise on the Construction of Wills* was first published in 1876. The work quickly became a standard treatise, and by the beginning of the twenty-first century it had reached its sixteenth edition. He was also joint author, with J. H. Balfour Browne, of *The Law of Railway Companies* (1881), which went into four editions, and wrote *The Law of Land* (1902).

In 1899 Theobald became a queen's counsel. However, he failed to establish himself as an advocate, and in 1907 accepted the position of master in lunacy. His responsibility in this office was to make arrangements for administering the affairs of chancery lunatics, persons with substantial property which they were alleged to be incapable of managing themselves because of mental disorder. Two years after his appointment, he became blind as a result of a detached retina, but he continued in his post and carried out his duties with astuteness and sensitivity until his retirement at the end of 1922, after which he was knighted.

While a student at Oxford, Theobald started to collect prints and drawings. As a member of the Burlington Fine Arts Club, he was on the organizing committee for an exhibition of English mezzotints held in 1902. He was acquainted with Whistler, and owned a number of his drawings and sketches, which eventually passed to the National Museum, New York. He developed a special interest in the work of John Crome, and in 1906 he published *Crome's Etchings: a Catalogue and an Appreciation, with some Account of his Paintings*. Following the loss of his sight, most of his collection was sold in 1910 through Christie, Manson, and Woods in London and H. G. Gutekunst in Stuttgart, and realized record-breaking prices. However, an important set of plates of mezzotints by David Lucas of Constable's landscapes, and related correspondence, were purchased privately for the Fitzwilliam Museum, Cambridge, and Theobald himself presented the Crome etchings to the Castle Museum at Norwich.

Theobald married twice. His first wife, whom he married on 19 December 1885, was Anne, daughter of Edward Rogers, a merchant, of Wolverhampton. She died in 1918, in her early seventies. Two years later, on 10 April 1920, Theobald married Winifred Sarah Jackson (1877–1937), daughter of Thomas William Jackson, a postmaster; she gave him her devoted care. He had no children.

In retirement Theobald remained active, in spite of his disability. He published *The Law Relating to Lunacy* in 1924 and a second edition of *The Law of Land* in 1929. He also wrote a brief collection of reminiscences, published posthumously in 1935 under the title *Remembrance of Things Past*. These show that he had a wry sense of humour, and a wide circle of friends. He died at his home, 57 Bedford Gardens, Kensington, London, on 8 June 1934, from coronary thrombosis, and was cremated three days later at Golders Green crematorium.

SHEILA DOYLE

Sources H. S. Theobald, *Remembrance of things past* (1935) · *The Times* (21 Oct 1918), 11; (1 Jan 1923), 12, 16; (9 June 1934), 19; (11 June 1934), 16; (12 June 1934), 19; (13 June 1934), 21; (16 July 1934), 17 · I. Elliott, ed., *The Balliol College register, 1833–1933*, 2nd edn (privately printed, Oxford, 1934), 51 · *Wadham College Gazette* (1899), 76; (1909), 229–30; (1910), 312–13; (1922), 37; (1923), 67; (1934), 193–4 · *Solicitors' Journal*, 78, 430 · J. Foster, *Men-at-the-bar: a biographical hand-list of the members of the various inns of court*, 2nd edn (1885) · *The later letters of John Stuart Mill, 1849–1873*, 3 (1972), 1261 · m. certs. · d. cert.
Likenesses photograph, repro. in *The Times* (11 June 1934), 19 · photographs, repro. in Theobald, *Remembrance of things past*, frontispiece
Wealth at death £185,062 10s. 6d.: probate, 12 July 1934, *CGPLA Eng. & Wales*

Theobald, James (*bap.* **1688**, *d.* **1759**), merchant and antiquary, was baptized at St Mary's, Lambeth, Surrey, on 21 June 1688, the eldest surviving son of Peter Theobald (1656–1742) and his wife, Elizabeth (*b.* 1662), the daughter of Thomas Gleane. He was apprenticed to his father in the Barber–Surgeons' Company from 1704 until 1712, and, together with his brother Peter (1694–1778), became a freeman of the City on 4 July 1727. They were both elected court assistants in 1745, James was master in 1750, and Peter became warden in 1753. On 22 March 1715 James married Sarah, the daughter of Josiah Kingsman of Horndon-on-Hill, Essex (to whose son William Peter Theobald was apprenticed). Of their three daughters, only Martha (*b.* 1716), the eldest, reached maturity; a son, James, was baptized at Lambeth on 9 May 1720.

The Theobalds were prominent timber merchants. James's grandfather, Daniel, had been a Southwark shipwright; his father, who was importing Norwegian timber by the 1680s, built up a thriving trade at Lambeth, and was joined by his two sons before 1722. In 1733 they provided the trustees for Georgia with a large model of a Dutch sawmill, which was shipped to the colony. From 1728 they acted as trustees to Archbishop Tenison's girls' charity school at Lambeth and to Peterson's charity in St Saviour's parish, Southwark, where James acquired property, including the local workhouse. In a document for 1727 the two brothers are named as lords of the manor of Old Paris Garden, Southwark. Theobald Street, Southwark, commemorates the family.

From 1723 Theobald lived at Belvedere House in Lambeth. By 1739 he had moved to Surrey Street, off the Strand, and in 1743 inherited considerable property from his father in London, Surrey, and Leicestershire. The following year he purchased as his country residence Hill House, which he renamed Waltham Place, at White Waltham in Berkshire. From 1728 to 1734 he was the duke of Chandos's main financial intermediary, enabling John Wood to build Queen Square in Bath; he also lent the contractor Ralph Allen capital to resurface St Bartholomew's Hospital with Bath stone between 1730 and 1732. As a governor and committee member of Thomas Coram's Foundling Hospital, he made manuscript corrections in July 1740 to a report entitled *A Sketch of the General Plan for Executing the Purposes of the Royal Charter*.

James and Peter Theobald's private Bank of England drawing office accounts, dating from 1727, reveal extensive Scandinavian trading. James owned wharves, docks, warehouses, and a timber yard in Southwark. He ran his own company (1742–9), served as a bank director (1743–56), and held bank stock. (Peter was also a director, from 1756 to 1768.) They joined the Russia Company in 1741, and James became a governor of the Merchant Seamen's Corporation in June 1747.

Theobald was elected fellow of the Royal Society on 4 November 1725; he later served as council member and auditor (1728–42). He supplied the society with its firewood and helped to reorganize and conserve its museum collections. In February 1742 he was awarded the society's Copley silver medal for his work on a committee set up in December 1736 to produce the medal. An influential member, he made 121 introductions and signed thirty-two certificates between 1727 and 1757. He also communicated a considerable amount of material about Scandinavian natural history and antiquities to the society and the Society of Antiquaries (to which he was elected on 23 November 1726). In particular he summarized and read an account of Swedenborg's *Principia rerum naturalium* (1734) to the Royal Society at three meetings held in 1737 and 1738.

Theobald served as joint secretary to the Society of Antiquaries from 3 January 1728 to 1735, and became an honorary member of the Spalding Gentlemen's Society on 28 June 1733. He was elected a vice-president of the Society of Antiquaries in November 1750, and was a leading force in procuring the society's deed of incorporation in 1751 and implementing numerous innovative changes (1733–54). In 1754 the society published his questionnaire, designed to obtain factual data about antiquities, natural history,

agriculture, and manufactures on a parochial basis; he himself compiled the histories of eighteen parishes in ten counties between 1755 and 1758, illustrating them with his own pen and wash drawings. His handwritten account of Margate in 1756, with well-executed sketches of the church, the harbour, and a horse-drawn bathing machine, is bound up with the society's library copy of John Lewis's history of the Isle of Thanet (1736). When Henry Baker suggested that members should record significant contemporary events for posterity, Theobald wrote some useful accounts of the York Street Watergate (May 1757) and the Arundel marbles, followed, in June 1758, by 'An account of the rise and progress of the Society of London for the Encouragement of Arts, Manufactures & Commerce' (Society of Antiquaries of London, Ants. Papers 1758), on which Thomas Mortimer's anonymous *Concise Account of the Society of Arts* (1763) was largely based. This manuscript, which was rediscovered in 1994, is a valuable source of additional information about the society, which Theobald joined in December 1754 and of which he became vice-president on 5 February 1755; his brother Peter and son James were also active members. Theobald's antiquarian miscellany (BL, Add. MS 45663) is a good indicator of his wide interests.

Theobald was a pallbearer at the funeral of his friend Sir Hans Sloane in January 1753 and a Sloane trustee; he had presented Sloane with seventy-nine specimens for his natural history collections. Theobald also promoted the career of the naturalist George Edwards, who singled him out as one of his earliest patrons. Theobald's magnificent lustre chandelier, presented in 1754, forms the centrepiece of Barber–Surgeons' Hall. His impressive collection of natural history objects, coins, medals, prints, and drawings was auctioned in 1768. Peter Theobald's house at Kew Green later became the herbarium of the Royal Botanic Gardens.

Theobald's second marriage, on 18 March 1735, to Elizabeth, the daughter of James Whitchurch and a niece of Baron Scrope, brought a dowry of £10,000. In 1749 he also inherited the Somerset manors of Nunney Castle and Nunney Mawdley from the Whitchurch family, and in 1754 he bought Grays Thurrock Manor, Essex. He died on 20 February 1759, and his widow, Elizabeth, on 18 June 1759, in Surrey Street.   JOHN H. APPLEBY

Sources J. H. Appleby, 'James Theobald, FRS (1688–1759), merchant and natural historian', *Notes and Records of the Royal Society*, 50 (1996), 179–89 · D. G. C. Allan and J. H. Appleby, 'James Theobald's "missing" MS history of the Society of Arts and his "chronological register" of the present age', *Antiquaries Journal*, 76 (1996), 201–14 · parish register (baptism), St Mary, Lambeth, 21 June 1688 · Royal Society of Arts, *Minutes of committees*, vol. 1 of Royal Society of Arts, *Minutes of the Society* · Barber–Surgeons' Company, court minute books, GL, Guildhall MSS 5257/7–9 · Peter Theobald's will, proved, 5 Feb 1743, PRO, PROB 11/724/59 · trusteeship of Tenison's girls' charity school, Lambeth, LMA, MS A/ATG 15–16, 1728 · James and Peter Theobald's joint 1727 bill as lords of Old Paris Garden Manor, PRO, C11/68/8 · J. Evans, *A history of the Society of Antiquaries* (1956) · will, PRO, PROB 11/844, sig. 76

Archives BL, antiquarian miscellany, Add. MS 45663 · JRL, English MS 19 · S. Antiquaries, Lond., church notes and drawings | Essex RO, Chelmsford, Grays Thurrock manor, court book · Hunt.

L., Brydges corresp. • S. Antiquaries, Lond., account of Society of London for the Encouragement of Arts, Manufactures, and Commerce

Wealth at death very considerable estate and property in Southwark, Lambeth, Grosvenor Square, Burlington Street; first and second wives' dowries; Bank of England drawing office account and bank stock: will, PRO, PROB 11/844, sig. 76

Theobald, Lewis (*bap.* **1688**, *d.* **1744**), literary editor and writer, the son of Peter Theobald (*d.* 1690), an attorney, and his second wife, Mary, was born in Sittingbourne, Kent, and baptized there on 2 April 1688.

Early years and education His godfather was Lewis *Watson, Baron Rockingham, and when Peter Theobald died in September 1690 Lewis was taken into the Rockingham household and educated with the sons of the family, chiefly by the Revd James Ellis, 'a very able schoolmaster', who ran a highly respected school in Isleworth, Middlesex, 'purely for grounding young Gentlemen, noblemen's sons or Gentlemen of some Rank, in Classick Learning, & fitting them for the University' (*Reliquiae, Remarks,* 11.341; 2.9). Ellis gave Theobald a thorough grounding in Greek and Latin and, equally important, instilled in him a lifelong love of the scholarship that made classical literature accessible to modern readers. Theobald did not, however, attend university; he was apprenticed to an attorney, which contributed significantly to his skills as an editor of Shakespeare. His clerkship was before the act of 1729 regulating the training and practice of attorneys (2 Geo. II c. 23), when attorneys' bills were still written in court hand and clerks required the ability to read and write secretary script.

Life as a man of letters As an attorney Theobald might have prospered, but, as he acknowledged to Rockingham's daughter Lady Monson, 'If I have not made all the Advantages, which might have accrued from so favourable a Situation in Life, it is, that Nature had not done her Part, and all Soils are not equally susceptible of Improvement' (dedication, *The Happy Captive: an English Opera,* 1741, sig. A2r). Instead he set up as a man of letters while maintaining a desultory practice at law, settling in London, where he married and had a son, Lewis (the date of his marriage and his wife's name are unknown), and lived in Wyan's Court, Great Russell Street, in the parish of St Giles-in-the-Fields. In 1707, when he may still have been an apprentice-clerk, he published *A Pindaric Ode on the Union of Scotland and England* and *Naufragium Britannicum,* a poem dedicated to the memory of Admiral Sir Cloudesley Shovell. The following year his *Persian Princess, or, The Royal Villain,* a tragedy written 'before I was full Nineteen Years Old' (dedication, *Persian Princess,* 1715, sig. A5v), was performed at Drury Lane. There were two performances, and the theatre managers granted him an unusual second night's benefit.

Theobald became a writer for Bernard Lintot, and his first production, *The Life and Character of Marcus Cato of Utica* (1713), drew upon the success of Joseph Addison's *Cato* (1713) and was followed by a translation of Plato's *Phaedo* (1713), which Cato is said to have read on the last night of his life. These works probably initiated his friendship

with Addison and were followed by another translation, *Monsieur Le Clerc's Observations upon Mr. Addison's Travels through Italy* (1715). Anticipation of Alexander Pope's translation of Homer produced *A Critical Discourse upon the Iliad of Homer … by Monsieur de la Motte* (1714). Theobald also contracted with Lintot to translate the seven tragedies of Aeschylus, but the translation was never published. In April 1714 he undertook to translate into blank verse with annotations Homer's *Odyssey* (book 1, 1717), Sophocles' *Electra* (1714), *Oedipus tyrannus* (1715), *Oedipus Coloneus, Trachiniae,* and the satires and epistles of Horace (all unpublished). After breaking with Lintot he continued with Aristophanes' *The Clouds* (1715) and *Plutus, or, The World's Idol* (1715), translated into colloquial prose and printed for Jonas Brown. Although he failed to establish himself with the public by these translations, those from Greek drama were 'highly esteemed' by Richard Porson (*Reliquiae,* 3.137 n. 1).

Theobald also published more poetry: *The Mausoleum, a Poem: Sacred to the Memory of her Late Majesty Queen Anne* (1714) was dedicated to Charles Boyle, fourth earl of Orrery, his most consistently generous patron (and, in the 1690s, the antagonist of Richard Bentley in the Phalaris controversy). Apart from passing tributes to Addison and Pope, both of whom Theobald admired at this time, the poem is unremarkable. On the other hand, *The Cave of Poverty, a Poem: Written in Imitation of Shakespeare* (1715) is interesting for its use of the stanza of *Venus and Adonis* at a time when Shakespeare's poems were generally neglected. Theobald also launched *The Censor,* a tri-weekly periodical that ran from 11 April to 17 June 1715 (no. 30), ceased publication, and then resumed 1 January to 30 May 1717 (no. 96), with a second, collected edition in three volumes (1717).

The Shakespearian literary criticism found in *The Censor* is important for its emphasis on language and character at the expense of neo-Aristotelian concerns with plot and poetic justice. No. 7 (25 April 1715) is the first examination of *King Lear* in relation to its source in Holinshed's *Chronicles* (1577). Succeeding essays address the affective power of Shakespeare's language, psychology and motive of characters in relation to the moral significance of their actions, and the idea of poetic justice in relation to *hamartia* and the tragic emotions of pity and fear. *The Censor's* radical independence from neo-Aristotelianism, anticipating the shift of critical focus in the late eighteenth century and beyond, is evident in no. 70 (2 April 1717):

> it is not to be expected that a Genius like *Shakespear's* is to be judg'd by the Laws of *Aristotle,* and the other Prescribers to the Stage; it will be sufficient to fix a Character of Excellence to his Performances, if there are in them a Number of beautiful Incidents, true and exquisite Turns of Nature and Passion, fine and delicate Sentiments, uncommon Images, and great Boldnesses of Expression.

Such enthusiasm for figurative language, unusual for its time, is desirable in an editor of Shakespeare and fundamental to Theobald's later success with conjectural emendation.

About 1715 Theobald began an association with John Rich's theatre in Lincoln's Inn Fields, and in February 1716

The Perfidious Brother was produced. The play involved Theobald in controversy, because a watchmaker, Henry Mestayer, had given him a preliminary version of the play and then claimed that Theobald had plagiarized his work. Theobald believed that he had 'created [the play] anew: For even where the Original Matter is continued, I have brought it to Light, and drawn it as from a *Chaos*' (preface, *Perfidious Brother*, 1715, sig. A3r). Mestayer subsequently published a version of the play (1716), ironically dedicated to Theobald. Although Theobald evidently proceeded in good faith, the controversy is regrettable. His association with Rich's theatre had two benefits: he became assistant (and lifelong friend) to John Stede, Rich's prompter, and librettist for a series of operatic pantomimes, often loosely based on classical themes, in which Rich played the leading role of Harlequin.

As assistant to Stede, Theobald acquired precise knowledge of theatrical production and of dramatic manuscripts, especially prompt books, which led eventually to speculation about the nature of manuscript copy for Shakespearian quarto and folio texts. His activities as librettist gave him irregular but significant income in a life of fleeting affluence and financial crisis. Rich himself acknowledged that his 'Theatre has of late ow'd its Support in great Measure' to pantomime (*Rape of Proserpine, or, The Birth and Adventures of Harlequin*, 1727, dedication, v–vi), and, indeed, the first two nights of *The Rape of Proserpine* brought in a staggering £420 11s. The popular appeal of pantomime may well have suggested alternative principles of dramatic art to those rules prescribed by neo-Aristotelianism, or at least have reinforced Theobald's readiness to accept Shakespeare's neglect of them. Theobald had revised *Richard II* in 1719 as a neo-Aristotelian experiment, believing that its 'Beauties … would have stronger Charms if they were interwoven in a regular Fable … maintaining the *Unity* of *Action*, or supporting the *Dignity* of the *Characters*' (*Richard II*, 1720, preface, sig. A2r), but the play's minimal success in the theatre gave no support to this theory.

Theobald as textual critic Theobald's interest in Shakespeare was ultimately centred not on adaptation but on the recovery and explication of his 'genuine' text, and when Pope's *Shakespear* (1725) appeared with a declaration that he had 'discharg'd the dull duty of an Editor' to his 'best judgment' (1.xxii), Theobald was prompted to publish *Shakespeare restored, or, A specimen of the many errors as well committed, as unamended, by Mr. Pope in his late edition of this poet* (1726), the first critical book devoted to Shakespeare and evidently the product of much previous study. Apart from his title, Theobald is polite to Pope and, despite 'a Veneration, almost rising to Idolatry, for the Writings' of Shakespeare, declares that he 'would be very loth even to do *him* Justice at the Expence of *that other* Gentleman's Character' (Theobald, *Restored*, iii). He insists, however, that it is the duty of an editor,

> Wherever he finds the Reading suspected, manifestly corrupted, deficient in Sense, and unintelligible … to exert

every Power and Faculty of the Mind to supply such a Defect, to give Light and restore Sense to the Passage, and, by a reasonable Emendation, to make that satisfactory and consistent with the Context, which before was so absurd, unintelligible and intricate.   (ibid., v)

Shakespeare Restored devotes 132 pages to cruces in *Hamlet* and an appendix of 62 compressed pages to other plays. Theobald recognizes that successive editions were generally printed from their immediate predecessors, with the consequence that 'the more the Editions of any Book multiply, the more the Errors multiply too' (Theobald, *Restored*, ii–iii). He inaugurates scholarly study of Shakespearian grammar and usage by means of parallel passages. Because he had the plays by heart, he was familiar with recurring patterns of imagery. His belief that Shakespeare wrote secretary script, 'the universal Character in our Author's Time' (Theobald, *Shakespeare*, 5.273n.), and his own 'Acquaintance with Stage-Books' (Theobald, *Restored*, 138) allowed him precisely to visualize manuscript copy and the kinds of misreading such copy might induce in a printed text. A principal test of conjectural emendation was that a proposed reading should be consistent with 'the Traces of the Letters' (that is, with the *ductus litterarum*) of secretary script and Elizabethan orthography (ibid.). These considerations are brought to bear on his famous emendation of the first folio's (1623) 'and a Table of greene fields' found in the Hostess's description of the death of Falstaff (*Henry V*, II.iii.16–17) '— for his Nose was as sharp as a Pen, and *a' babled* of green Fields' (Theobald, *Restored*, 138).

Shakespeare Restored establishes many of the editorial principles and techniques found in Theobald's *Shakespeare* (1733). It also fully exposed the inadequacies of Pope's *Shakespear*. Pope's initial printed response was in 'Fragment of a Satire' (1728), where he gave Theobald the sobriquet 'pidling *Tibbalds*' (l. 14). He also included him among the swallows and eels in *Peri Bathous* (1728), but his most sustained ridicule occurs in *The Dunciad Variorum* (1729). Pope's caricatures of Theobald are often self-portraits deriving from Pope's own experience as a translator and editor (Seary, 87–97), but the thrust of his attack is on Theobald's attention to the minutiae of texts, which he attempts to represent as proof of dullness. He sought also to represent Theobald's antiquarianism as evidence of lack of taste, because 'he laboured to prove *Shakespear* … conversant in such authors as *Caxton* and *Wynkin*, rather than in *Homer*' (A. Pope, *Dunciad*, 1.162–3n.). Theobald's commentary does, of course, make full use of 'The Classicks of an Age that heard of none' (ibid., 1.128), but his concern in his explication of Shakespeare with 'all such reading as was never read' (ibid., 1.166) marks the beginning of modern scholarship devoted to Renaissance English literature.

Theobald responded good-humouredly to Pope's satire, declaring 'I ought to be very well satisfied with my Share of *Honours* in his Kingdom of *Dullness*' and resolving to assert 'the Legality of my Master's Title to those Dominions, in which he exercises so free a Sway, and from whence he so unsparingly dispenses his *Promotions*' (*Daily Journal*, 17 April 1729). This he accomplished with further corrections of Pope's second edition of *Shakespear* (1728). He also began an extended commentary in the manner of *Shakespeare Restored*. During this work he was solicited by William Warburton to engage in a lengthy correspondence devoted to textual criticism as part of Warburton's manoeuvres to raise himself from his obscurity as a clergyman in the provinces. Meanwhile, a noble patron, probably the earl of Orrery, had presented Theobald with a manuscript of *Cardenio* by Shakespeare and Fletcher. Theobald acquired another two manuscripts and revised the play as *Double Falshood, or, The Distrest Lovers* (1728). Although enemies suggested that the play was a forgery, it was successful on stage, earning Theobald much-needed benefit nights. (Modern consensus is that *Double Falshood* is based on a lost play by Shakespeare and Fletcher.)

Public demand for an edition of Shakespeare by the author of *Shakespeare Restored* was now mounting. After the death of the poet laureate, Laurence Eusden, in 1730, an attempt was made to assist Theobald financially, when he 'would fain sit down to my little studies with an easy competency'. Sir Robert Walpole, Lord Gage, and Frederick, prince of Wales, recommended him for the laureateship, although 'after standing fair for the post at least three weeks' he finally 'had the mortification to be supplanted by Keyber' (letter, December 1730, Nichols, *Illustrations*, 2.617). At a time when 'the Severity of a rich Creditor' had stripped him 'so bare, that I never was acquainted with such Wants, since I knew the Use of Money' (letter, November 1731, Jones, 280), Jacob Tonson, the chief proprietor of Shakespearian copyrights, signed a contract (26 October 1731, Bodl. Oxf., MS Rawl. D. 729), and in January 1734 Theobald's edition was published in seven volumes, and, with profits in excess of 1100 guineas, made Theobald the best paid of the early editors of Shakespeare. Among the subscribers were the prince and princess of Wales and most of the principal nobility. Theobald was vindicated from the aspersions of Pope. Even the *Grub-Street Journal*, which had been hostile, granted him 'the title, he so incontestably possesses, of the best English critic' (*Grub-Street Journal*, 229, 16 May 1734). His text, with 1356 explanatory notes, was the most popular in the eighteenth century and reached nine editions by 1773.

The years immediately following publication of his *Shakespeare* were the apex of Theobald's career. However, by 1737 his financial situation was again precarious, when Hogarth published his engraving of *The Distrest Poet* with the poet writing verses with a title alluding to Theobald's early poem, *The Cave of Poverty*, and Pope's verse portrait in *The Dunciad* as a motto. (There is no known portrait of Theobald, but George Steevens speculated that Hogarth had caught his likeness (see Richardson).) In 1741 he was again appealing to the public for support at a benefit night of *Double Falshood*. His last scholarly project was an edition of Beaumont and Fletcher in collaboration with Thomas Seward and John Sympson, published posthumously in 1750. He had continued to support a life of scholarship

with a series of plays, adaptations, operas, and entertainments, of which the most successful was *Orpheus and Eurydice (with the Metamorphoses of Harlequin)* (1740).

Theobald died of jaundice at his house in Wyan's Court on 18 September 1744, attended by John Stede. According to Stede,

> He was of a generous spirit, too generous for his circumstances; and none knew how to do a handsome thing, or confer a benefit, when in his power, with a better grace than himself. He was my antient friend of near 30 years acquaintance. Interred at Pancras the 20th, 6 o'clock P.M. I only attended him. (Nichols, *Illustrations*, 2.745n.)

There is no record of Theobald's burial in the parish registers. Beginning on 23 October, his library, which included the first folio (1623) and 29 pre-1623 quartos, was sold by auction over four nights in 631 lots, of which perhaps lot 460 is the most tantalizing:

> One hundred ninety-five old English Plays in Quarto, some of them so scarce as not to be had at any Price, *to many of which are Manuscript Notes and Remarks of Mr. Theobald's*, all done up neatly in Boards, in single Plays. (*Catalogue of the Library of Lewis Theobald, esq. Deceas'd* [1744])

Influence and reputation Theobald made fundamental contributions to English scholarship and print culture. Although he adapted plays for the stage, his edition of Shakespeare marks a profound revolution in attitudes: first, Shakespeare clearly becomes an author to be studied, in addition to being heard on the stage; second, what Shakespeare wrote takes precedence over the taste of his editor, literary fashions, grammar, usage, and predilections of later readers. Recovery of Shakespeare's 'genuine' text is established in Theobald's preface and notes for the first time as a specifically scholarly activity, separated as far as possible from literary criticism, which, in his then novel opinion, could only be practised when the text was reliable:

> The Science of Criticism, as far as it affects an Editor, seems to be reduced to these three Classes; the Emendation of corrupt Passages; the Explanation of obscure and difficult ones; and an Inquiry into the Beauties and Defects of Composition. This Work is principally confin'd to the two former Parts ... the proper Objects of the Editor's Labour. The third lies open for every willing Undertaker. (preface, Theobald, *Shakespeare*, 1.xl–xli)

Separation of textual scholarship from literary criticism was essential not only for cultural history but for cultural continuity, which could only be effected by a reliable text with notes explaining obscurities of thought, allusions, and figurative language in the context of its times.

Theobald's work was not always fully appreciated by his successors, and Johnson's denigration of him in his preface to *Shakespeare* (1765) is to be regretted by all but the most uncritical of Johnson's adulators. Even Malone corrected Shakespeare's anachronisms, which Theobald refused to do. The chief fault of his edition is that it is based on Pope's, although he knew that the first quarto or folio texts were the basis of all succeeding editions. His choice of copy was, however, owing to legal regulation of copyright and required by Jacob Tonson. The range of his scholarship and the acumen and tact with which he applied it to the recovery and illumination of Shakespeare's texts have led modern critics and editors to characterize Theobald as 'the best all-round editor of Shakespeare in [his] period or any other' (Vickers, 1) and 'one of the finest editors of the last three centuries' (G. Taylor, in Wells, 54).   PETER SEARY

Sources L. Theobald, *Shakespeare restored, or, A specimen of the many errors as well committed, as unamended, by Mr. Pope in his late edition of this poet* (1726) · *The works of Shakespeare … with notes*, ed. L. Theobald, 7 vols. (1733) · P. Seary, *Lewis Theobald and the editing of Shakespeare* (1990) · R. F. Jones, *Lewis Theobald: his contribution to English scholarship, with some unpublished letters* (1919) · C. Corbett, *Catalogue of the library of Lewis Theobald, esq. deceas'd* [1744] · L. Theobald, *Double falshood, or, The distrest lovers* (1728) · Nichols, *Illustrations*, vol. 2 · *Reliquiae Hearnianae: the remains of Thomas Hearne*, ed. P. Bliss, 2nd edn, 3 vols. (1869) · *Remarks and collections of Thomas Hearne*, ed. C. E. Doble and others, 2, OHS, 7 (1886) · *Remarks and collections of Thomas Hearne*, ed. C. E. Doble and others, 11, OHS, 72 (1921) · J. Freehafer, 'Cardenio, by Shakespeare and Fletcher', *Publications of the Modern Language Association of America*, 84 (1969), 501–13 · S. Kukowski, 'The hand of John Fletcher in *Double falshood*', *Shakespeare Survey*, 43 (1991), 81–9 · G. H. Metz, ed., *Four plays ascribed to Shakespeare … an annotated bibliography* (1982) · Lincoln's Inn Fields theatre accounts, 1724–5, BL, Egerton MS 2265 · Lincoln's Inn Fields theatre accounts, 1726–7, BL, Egerton MS 2266 · Bernard Lintot's accounts, BL, Add. MS 38729 · W. Richardson, *A portrait of this useful critick* (1794), bound in vols. 1–2 of *The plays of William Shakespeare* (1793) [BL, shelfmark 681. f. 1, 2] · W. Van Lennep and others, eds., *The London stage, 1660–1800*, 5 pts in 11 vols. (1960–68) · B. Vickers, ed., *Shakespeare: the critical heritage*, 2: *1693–1733* (1974) · S. Wells and others, *William Shakespeare: a textual companion* (1987) · *Daily Journal* (17 April 1729) · 'articles of argument' between Lewis Theobald and Jacob Tonson for publishing an edition of Shakespeare, 26 Oct 1731, Bodl. Oxf., MS Rawl. D. 729 · *Grub-Street Journal*, 229 (16 May 1734) · parish register, Sittingbourne, CKS [Sedingbourn the register of mariages, baptisinges, & burialls from the year of our Lord 1561], 338/1 [baptism] · Rockingham's accounts, Lincs. Arch.

Archives Folger, corresp. | BL, letters to William Warburton, Egerton MS 1956

Wealth at death valuable library

Theodore of Tarsus [St Theodore of Tarsus] (**602–690**), archbishop of Canterbury and biblical scholar, was a figure of exceptional importance for the establishment and growth of the church in early England; as Bede said of his archbishopric, 'Never had there been such happy times since the English first came to Britain' (Bede, *Hist. eccl.*, 4.2). Bede is the principal source for Theodore's later career, from the time he was first approached about the archbishopric of Canterbury in 667; many details of his earlier career can be gleaned from the corpus of biblical commentaries which record his teaching at the school of Canterbury.

Education in the Near East and at Constantinople Theodore was born in Tarsus (now Gözlü Kule in south-eastern Turkey) in 602, in the Greek-speaking province of Cilicia. Nothing is known of his earliest education, nor of Tarsus itself, which lies buried far beneath the present-day Turkish city. Antioch on the Orontes (then in Syria, now Antakya in south-eastern Turkey) was the largest city in the vicinity of Tarsus: a flourishing Christian city, which from the fourth century onwards housed a distinctive school of Christian exegetes, including Diodorus of Tarsus, and his two influential pupils, Theodore of Mopsuestia (*d.* 428) and John Chrysostom (*d.* 407). The biblical exegesis of this Antiochene school was characteristically literal (as opposed, that is, to the allegorical approach of Alexandrine exegetes such as Origen): its approach was historical and philological and had resort to such disciplines as grammar, rhetoric, philosophy, and medicine in its attempt to elucidate the sacred text. The fact that the biblical exegesis of the Canterbury commentaries is wholly Antiochene in character, especially in its resort to the disciplines of rhetoric, philosophy, and medicine, and that John Chrysostom is the patristic authority most frequently quoted in the Canterbury commentaries, suggests that Theodore received his early training at Antioch. Furthermore, Antioch was at that time a city bilingual in Greek and Syriac, so it may be presumed that Theodore first came into contact with Syriac Christianity in Antioch. At several points in the biblical commentaries, Syriac words are quoted; particularly interesting is the fact that the commentaries, in explaining the 'cucumbers and melons' of Numbers 11: 5, contain the observation that 'cucumbers are called *pepones* when they grow large … in the city of Edessa they grow so large that a camel can scarcely carry two of them' (Bischoff and Lapidge, 1.413). This observation implies that Theodore had travelled at some stage to Edessa, which lies about 150 miles northeast of Antioch (it is now Sanliurfa in south-eastern Turkey). Edessa was the principal centre of Syriac-speaking Christianity from the second century onwards; the great exegete Ephrem (*d.* 373) taught in Edessa, and Theodore's younger contemporary, Jacob of Edessa (*d.* 708), won renown as a biblical scholar and exegete. It is not certain how much experience the young Theodore had acquired of Syriac Christianity: Ephrem is once quoted by name in the Canterbury commentaries (although the text in question was also available in Greek translation); and the commentaries contain various explanations which have striking parallels with Syriac texts such a the 'Book of the cave of treasures' (which is not known to have been translated into Greek). These parallels can best be explained on the assumption that Theodore had some (perhaps rudimentary, probably only spoken) knowledge of Syriac, and that he had spent time in Edessa in contact with Syriac exegetes. In any case, Syria was twice invaded during the early seventh century: in 613 by Persian armies (who were subsequently defeated by the armies of the Byzantine emperor Heraclius), and in 637 by the Arabs. Theodore's presence is next attested in Constantinople, and it is possible that he went there as a refugee from one of these invasions. The Canterbury commentaries contain various remarks on the habits of the Persians, which implies that Theodore had the opportunity of observing them close at hand.

Theodore's presence in Constantinople is confirmed by a statement in the Canterbury biblical commentaries to the effect that 'Theodore reports that in Constantinople he saw the Twelve Baskets woven from palm-branches and preserved as relics' (Bischoff and Lapidge, 42). From other sources it is known that these relics were housed in a shrine at the foot of the famous Porphyry Column which stood at the centre of the Forum of Constantine (the column is still standing in present-day Istanbul, where it is known as the Cemberlitas, though the shrine has disappeared). Constantinople in the time of the emperor Heraclius (r. 610–41) was an imperial city of culture and learning, which attracted scholars from all parts of the empire; in particular, it housed a university and several famous libraries. Heraclius had invited to Constantinople the great polymath Stephen of Alexandria, who gave lectures on philosophy and medicine and was known to be teaching there in 619 or 620; but in Heraclius's time Constantinople was also home to the historian Theophylact Simocatta, the poet George of Pisidia, and the anonymous author of the *Chronicon Paschale*. The intellectual complexion of the Canterbury commentaries suggests that Theodore's scholarly orientation was derived from his period of study in Constantinople, particularly his interest in philosophy, rhetoric, medicine, computus, astronomy, and astrology. Stephen of Alexandria was expert in all these fields, and it is striking that several medical explanations in the Canterbury commentaries have precise parallels in Stephen's *scholia* or lecture notes, which may suggest that the young Theodore attended the lectures of the great polymath.

A Greek monk at Rome   Theodore's presence is next attested in Rome, where he was living as a Greek monk at the time he came to the notice of the pope who appointed him to the vacant archbishopric of Canterbury. The circumstances which took Theodore from Constantinople to Rome are unknown. There were at that time a number of communities of oriental monks living in Rome, many of them refugees from the Arab invasions of Syria and north Africa. One of these communities housed Greek-speaking monks from Cilicia; it was located *ad aquas Salvias* (now the Tre Fontane, outside the southern gate of Porto San Paolo) and dedicated to St Anastasius, a soldier who had been martyred by the Persians in 628. It is highly likely that Theodore belonged to this monastery: he was Cilician in origin and the earliest attestations of the cult of St Anastasius in England can be linked with him. During the 640s the community of Cilician monks was actively engaged, on the pope's behalf, in the monothelete controversy. In an effort to end several centuries of theological wrangling, the emperor Heraclius and the patriarch of Constantinople issued in 633 a formulation to the effect that there was only 'one will' in Christ, and this formulation was made a matter of imperial policy in 638. Although Pope Honorius I (r. 625–38) expressed initial support, subsequent popes were adamant in their opposition to the imperial policy. Their opposition was articulated at Rome by the Greek theologian Maximus the Confessor and was promulgated by the Lateran Council of 649 under the presidency of Pope Martin (r. 649–53). The *acta* of the Lateran Council were drawn up by various communities of Greek monks resident in Rome, including the Cilician

monks of St Anastasius. It is likely that Theodore participated in the drafting of these *acta* (indeed the list of witnesses to them includes the name of one *Theodous monachus*, who is arguably identical with the later archbishop of Canterbury). In any event, the consequences of the Lateran Council were dire. Because the promulgation of its *acta* was in opposition to imperial policy, Pope Martin was arrested, taken to Constantinople, and tried and condemned for treason, as was Maximus the Confessor, the principal architect of the Lateran *acta*, who was condemned, mutilated, and exiled to the Black Sea, where he died in 662. The theological differences between pope and emperor were not settled until the Sixth Ecumenical Council of 680.

Appointment as archbishop of Canterbury   In 664 the archbishopric of Canterbury fell vacant through the death of Deusdedit; his successor, one Wigheard, went to Rome to collect the pallium, but died there of the plague in 667. At this point, Pope Vitalian (r. 657–72) sought the advice of one of his trusted counsellors, Hadrian, then abbot of a small monastery near Naples, concerning the vacancy. After declining the post himself, Hadrian suggested the name of Theodore, who (as Bede recounts) was then living as a monk in Rome. Vitalian was hesitant about appointing Theodore (his hesitancy becomes comprehensible in light of Theodore's involvement with the Lateran Council of 649 for the death of Maximus had taken place only a few years before Wigheard's arrival in Rome). However, this hesitancy was overcome on the condition that Theodore should be tonsured after the manner of western monks (Greek monks shaved their heads completely) and that Hadrian should accompany him to England. When Theodore's hair had grown and been tonsured in the shape of a crown, he was consecrated by Vitalian on 26 March 668, and set out for England on 27 May of the same year. He arrived in England on 27 May the following year (669) to begin his archbishopric. He was then aged sixty-seven.

Ecclesiastical administration, theology, canon law, and liturgy   Theodore set about his administrative responsibilities with the urgency of an old man in a hurry. As soon as Hadrian arrived in England in 670, the two of them undertook a comprehensive tour of the archdiocese. The archbishopric itself had been vacant for five years before Theodore's arrival and a number of other bishoprics were similarly vacant (there were only three English bishops in office when he arrived). He moved swiftly to fill the vacancies, making appointments to Rochester, Dunwich, and Winchester. Because the bishop of York, Ceadda, had been appointed uncanonically, he was deposed by Theodore, and Wilfrid appointed in his stead; Theodore subsequently appointed Ceadda to the see of Lichfield. With the English episcopate thus restored to strength, Theodore summoned a national synod, which met under his presidency at Hertford in September 672 or 673. This synod (the *acta* of which are fully reported by Bede, *Hist. eccl.*, 4.5) made certain provisions which had a long-lasting effect on the structure of the English church: for example, that national synods should be convoked twice-yearly at a place called 'Clofesho', and that the number of dioceses should expand as the number of the faithful increased. The intention behind this last stipulation was that very large (and wealthy) dioceses, such as that of Bishop Wilfrid in Northumbria, should be broken up into smaller, more manageable units. This intention inevitably brought Theodore into conflict with Wilfrid; but on this particular issue, Theodore's will prevailed. On the pretext of a quarrel with King Ecgfrith of Northumbria, Theodore in 677 deposed Wilfrid; the vast Northumbrian see was broken up into three dioceses: Deira (with its see at York), Bernicia (with its see at either Lindisfarne or Hexham), and Lindsey. Wilfrid went to Rome to appeal to the pope; his grievance was heard by a synod of Italian bishops in October 679. After the death of King Ecgfrith in 685, Theodore effected a reconciliation with Wilfrid by appointing him to the Deiran see. The reconciliation was announced in a letter sent from Theodore to various authorities in England; in his life of Bishop Wilfrid, Stephen of Ripon preserves the text of Theodore's letter to Æthelred, king of the Mercians (r. 675–704). This letter is one of the few surviving texts composed by Theodore himself.

One of Theodore's principal administrative concerns was with orthodox belief. This concern is seen in his response to the initiative taken by Pope Agatho (r. 678–81) to effect a reconciliation between the papacy and the Byzantine emperor on the monothelete controversy. Pope Agatho decided to canvass the opinion of the western churches; to this end he sent to England a legate named John, precentor of St Peter's in Rome. Theodore in turn summoned an English synod which met at Hatfield on 17 September 679 (the Hatfield in question is arguably that in Yorkshire). The synod was asked to endorse the *acta* or stipulations of the Lateran Council of 649; as Bede (Bede, *Hist. eccl.*, 4.17 [15]) reports the *acta* of the Synod of Hatfield, their wording was closely based on the wording of the earlier council, particularly in respect of their credal statement. It is an intriguing irony that Theodore (and his English church) was being asked by the papal legate to endorse the *acta* of an earlier council in which he himself had participated. His participation is adverted to by Pope Agatho in a letter to the Byzantine emperor (Constantine IV), dated 27 March 680, in which Agatho explains that it had been his intention to invite Theodore 'the philosopher and archbishop of Great Britain' to join the papal party at the ecumenical council which was to convene in Constantinople in the attempt to resolve the controversy (Lapidge, *Theodore*, 23). The pope evidently knew that Theodore was one of the few living theologians who had participated in drafting the *acta* of the Lateran Council of 649 and that he would have had an unrivalled knowledge of the doctrinal complexities; but by then Theodore was seventy-eight years old and too tired to make the journey to Rome and on to Constantinople. After so much hatred and bloodshed, the Sixth Ecumenical Council, which met at the emperor's palace in Constantinople in 680, formally condemned the imperial policy of monotheletism.

Theodore was also deeply concerned with matters of canon law and ecclesiastical legislation. Bede reports that many of the *acta* promulgated by Theodore's first synod at Hertford were drawn by him from a *liber canonum*; and various evidence indicates that this book was a copy (modified) of the second recension of the collection of conciliar canons and papal decretals compiled by Dionysius Exiguus (*fl.* 525). The same collection of canons also formed the basis of teaching in canon law at the school of Theodore and Hadrian in Canterbury; excerpts from it also constitute the second book of the *Iudicia* which have been transmitted under Theodore's name. In their present form, these *Iudicia* present the responses given *viva voce* by Theodore to various questions put to him by one Eoda (otherwise unknown) on matters of private penance; the answers were subsequently edited by an unidentified 'disciple of the [North]umbrians' (*discipulus Umbrensium*). The first book of the *Iudicia* is concerned with private penance, the second with canon law. It is interesting that many of Theodore's judgements on matters of penance were informed by his experience as a Greek monk; in particular, St Basil is quoted by name five times (the text in question being the three canonical letters to Amphilochius of Iconium), but other Greek authorities such as Gregory of Nazianzus and the pseudo-Dionysius are quoted as well. Theodore's opinions on private penance as collected in the *Iudicia* were widely influential, not only in England, but in Ireland and on the continent. Theodore here played a pivotal role in the transmission of eastern ideas to the Latin west.

Another sphere in which Theodore played a role of this sort is that of liturgy—in particular, in the widespread use of the litany of the saints in public and private worship. Although the form of the litany, with its Greek invocation to the Lord to have mercy (*Kyrie eleison*), followed by petitions to individual saints to pray for the petitioner, is wholly familiar today, it is not attested in the Latin west before the eighth century. In fact the earliest Latin version of such a prayer is found in a prayerbook written probably at Worcester in the later eighth century (now BL, Royal MS 2 A.XX); but it is clear that this Latin litany is a translation of a Greek litany of the saints in a form found in another (but later) Anglo-Saxon manuscript (BL, Cotton MS Galba A.xviii). Because the form of the litany of the saints, with its characteristic long list of petitions to individual saints, is first found in Greek and Syriac manuscripts from the patriarchate of Antioch, the most reasonable hypothesis is that Archbishop Theodore brought with him to England a small prayerbook containing (among other Greek prayers) a litany of this sort, which was subsequently copied into the Galba manuscript, but also translated into the Latin form found in the Royal manuscript. In any event, the form soon spread from England to Ireland and the continent, and had become commonplace by the Carolingian period.

Scholar and teacher It was perhaps in the field of scholarship that Theodore made his most important contribution to Anglo-Saxon culture. Bede reports that, because Theodore and Hadrian were extremely learned in sacred and secular literature, 'they attracted a crowd of students into whose minds they daily poured the streams of wholesome learning' (Bede, *Hist. eccl.*, 4.2); he goes on to specify instruction not only in scripture but also in metre, astronomy, and computus, and adds that in his own day (731) some of their students survived who were as fluent in Greek and Latin as in their native English. One of these students was Aldhelm; among others Bede names Albinus (Hadrian's successor as abbot of St Peter's and St Paul's in Canterbury), Tobias (bishop of Rochester), and Oftfor (bishop of Worcester). With the exception of Aldhelm, none of these students has left any writings. In any event, the nature of the instruction given by Theodore and Hadrian is revealed in a substantial corpus of biblical commentaries and glosses which can be shown to have originated in their Canterbury school as notes taken by the English students from the *viva voce* instruction of the two great Mediterranean masters. In particular, a set of commentaries on the Pentateuch and gospels reveals the extraordinary range of learning which they brought to bear on the biblical text. It would appear that the teaching was conducted by comparing the Latin text of the Vulgate Bible with that of the Greek Septuagint and Greek New Testament (various comments point to meanings in the Greek text which are misrepresented in Jerome's Latin), and then illustrated by reference to a huge range of patristic authorities. These authorities are for the most part Greek ones. Although reference was made on occasion to a few Latin fathers, such as Augustine, Jerome, and Isidore, the majority of these references are to Greek exegetes: Basil of Caesarea, Clement of Alexandria, Cosmas Indicopleustes, Ephrem (in Greek), Epiphanius of Salamis, John Chrysostom, and Flavius Josephus. (Various other Greek fathers were borrowed from but not quoted by name and reference is occasionally made to patristic texts which have not survived.) The underlying intention of these commentaries was to extract the literal meaning of the biblical text: to explain the flora and fauna mentioned in the Bible, minerals and precious stones, the customs of the Jews, the topography of the Holy Land, and the paraphernalia of everyday life in biblical times. This method of interpretation is usually characterized as 'Antiochene'; its deployment in the Canterbury commentaries is wholly unusual in western medieval exegesis, but is explicable in light of Theodore's background. As in earlier Antiochene exegesis, reference is frequently made to scholarly disciplines such as philosophy, rhetoric, and medicine and it is clear that Theodore had unusual expertise in these fields.

In addition to these commentaries on the Pentateuch and gospels, there is a huge (but as yet unprinted) corpus of glosses on the remaining books of the Bible preserved in numerous medieval manuscripts, which, when printed, will reveal how Theodore (and Hadrian) approached the remainder of the sacred text. In addition, a substantial corpus of medieval manuscripts preserves glosses to other patristic texts (notably Sulpicius Severus, Rufinus, Gildas, Isidore, Jerome, Cassian, Orosius, Gregory the Great, as well as various canons and papal decretals, and the rule of St Benedict) which manifestly derive from the teaching of Theodore and Hadrian at the Canterbury school. In their most accessible form, these glosses are preserved in the famous Leiden glossary, a manuscript copied *c.*800 at St Gallen from batches of glosses derived from the Canterbury school, and now in Leiden (Bibliotheek der Rijksuniversiteit, Voss. lat. Q. 69); but related materials are preserved in a large number of (unprinted) manuscript glossaries.

The biblical commentaries and glosses are the record of Theodore's (and Hadrian's) oral teaching. A small corpus of writings composed by Theodore himself survives. There is, for example, a brief poem in octosyllables ('Te nunc, sancte speculator') addressed by Theodore to Hædde, bishop of Winchester. The trochaic rhythm of these octosyllables is wholly distinct from that of other octosyllables composed in Ireland and England (for example by Aldhelm), and would appear to have been modelled by Theodore on that of Greek anacreontic hymns (also octosyllabic in form) with which he was familiar in his youth. So unusual is this form in surviving Anglo-Latin literature that three such hymns preserved in the ninth-century Book of Cerne (including the well-known hymn 'Sancte sator suffragator') can confidently be attributed to Theodore as well. Another work which is very probably by Theodore is an unprinted Latin *Passio sancti Anastasii*, an account of the Persian martyr Anastasius, who was the patron saint of the monastery of Cilician monks *ad aquas Salvias* in Rome. It has been shown that this Latin translation was produced from a copy of the Greek *passio* which had an interlinear, word-by-word gloss. Its Latin is not coherent, therefore, and it was probably this incoherent *passio* of St Anastasius which Bede 'corrected as best he could' (Bede, *Hist. eccl.*, 5.24). Finally, Theodore was almost certainly the author of the *Laterculus Malalianus*, a Latin work based partly on the Greek *Chronographia* of John Malalas (*d.* 578) and partly consisting of original exegesis of the life of Christ, from conception to death. The work draws on many of the same Greek fathers cited in the Canterbury biblical commentaries (notably Epiphanius and Ephrem the Syrian), and shares much of their scholarly orientation, particularly an interest in medicine and chronology.

Given that Theodore was some sixty-seven years old when he arrived in England, his scholarly output is astonishing. Knowledge of this output will be considerably refined when more of the works attributable to him (particularly the biblical glosses and the *Passio sancti Anastasii*) are available in print. But it may be no exaggeration to say that the school of Canterbury, under his direction between 670 and 690, represents the apogee of biblical scholarship in the Latin west between late antiquity and the twelfth century and that he was one of the greatest scholars ever to adorn the see of Canterbury.

Death and commemoration Theodore died on 19 September 690, aged eighty-eight. He was buried in the cathedral at Canterbury and his tomb was inscribed with a metrical epitaph consisting of nineteen elegiac distichs, composed—to judge from its diction—by Aldhelm. The tomb and the inscription have been destroyed by successive reconstruction at Canterbury; the epitaph is known because Bede preserved eight lines of it in his *Historia ecclesiastica* (5.8). An unprinted life of Theodore by the eleventh-century hagiographer, Goscelin, is preserved in two contemporary manuscripts; but the historical information contained in this life is derived wholly from Bede and adds nothing to our understanding.

MICHAEL LAPIDGE

Sources Bede, *Hist. eccl.* · M. Lapidge, ed., *Archbishop Theodore* (1995) · B. Bischoff and M. Lapidge, *Biblical commentaries from the Canterbury school of Theodore and Hadrian* (1994) [incl. Pentateuch glosses, vol. 1, pp. 291–385] · M. Lapidge, 'The school of Theodore and Hadrian', *Anglo-Saxon England*, 15 (1986), 45–72

Theodosius [Flavius Theodosius; *known as* Count Theodosius] (*d.* **376**), Roman general, conventionally known as Count Theodosius from an extraordinary military command that he held in Britain in 367–8, as *comes* (general, or 'count'); he is also called Theodosius the elder to distinguish him from his second son, the emperor Theodosius (*r.* 379–95). Since the younger Theodosius was born *c.*346 at Cauca (Coca) in Spain (where he owned land after his father's death) and since kinsmen are recorded in 408 as influential landowners in Spain, it is likely that Count Theodosius himself came from a Spanish propertied family. His wife's name was Thermantia. The family was evidently Christian but is unlikely to have been rich and well-connected before his time, since he (unusually for landed gentry in the late-Roman period) chose a military career and seems to have lacked higher education and the younger Theodosius, even according to a sympathetic source, was only 'moderately cultured' (Pichlmayr, 48.11–12). Nothing is known of Theodosius's early career (which was 'distinguished', according to the contemporary historian Ammianus Marcellinus), unless it is implied by a panegyrist's allusion to 'land victories in Batavia [modern Netherlands] and defeat of the Saxons by sea' (Pacatus, 5.2) which might belong to the emperor Valentinian I's recovery of the Rhine frontier in 366, but are more likely to relate to the ill-defined campaigns of 367–8.

In June 367 Valentinian had received news of a concerted attack upon Britain by its neighbours, the so-called 'Barbarian conspiracy' of which Ammianus Marcellinus gives the only real account. Archaeological evidence in confirmation has often been sought, but continues to be elusive, while Ammianus Marcellinus's account is geographically vague and leaves questions unanswered; that he was writing in the reign of Theodosius's son probably forced him to panegyrize the father. The invaders were Picts from north of the Clyde–Forth isthmus, Scots from Ireland, and 'Attacotti' of unknown origin; meanwhile north-German Franks and Saxons were attacking 'the Gallic areas' (the channel coast of Gaul or possibly of Britain). The Roman coastal commander had been killed, and his colleague, the general (*dux*) who commanded the land garrison of Britain, had been eliminated. The obscure *areani* who collected military intelligence beyond the frontiers had changed sides, a 'province' had been overrun, and many soldiers had deserted their units. To retrieve these disasters, Theodosius was sent to Britain with the rank of *comes* and a small army consisting of four infantry units from the strategic reserve.

Theodosius landed at Rutupiae (Richborough, Kent) and advanced towards London, the capital, rounding up enemy raiding parties as he went. At London, his base for the winter of 367–8, he successfully offered an amnesty to Roman deserters and recruited a new head of the civil administration (the *vicarius*) and a new *dux* of the British garrison. Ammianus Marcellinus gives no details of the fighting that restored Roman authority in 368: his principal episode is the arrest and execution of a criminal exiled to Britain who was now plotting to seize power. This episode remains mysterious, perhaps because Theodosius forbade further investigation, but also because the victim Valentinus was brother-in-law of the Maximinus who later became Valentinian's praetorian prefect and chief civil minister. Theodosius is also said to have 'restored cities and forts, and protected the frontiers with garrisons and outposts' (Ammianus Marcellinus, 28.3.3, 28.3.7), perhaps appropriate to a refurbishment of the fixed defences like that which was being directed by Valentinian on the Rhine and Danube frontiers; but possible pieces of evidence—such as fort repairs and the drafting of new garrisons, the strengthening of town walls with towers, the deployment of 'signal towers' on the north Yorkshire coast—have not been dated conclusively to 368. Theodosius is also said to have created a new province called Valentia; this certainly existed thereafter, but its location remains uncertain. The mysterious *areani*, who probably operated north of Hadrian's Wall, were disbanded.

Theodosius's achievement was genuine—his subsequent career proves that—but it cannot be quantified. On his return to the imperial court he was promoted to joint commander-in-chief (*magister equitum*) and operated successfully against the German Alamanni in the Black Forest in 370, and again in 372, when he commanded the cavalry advance guard in Valentinian's penetration of the Main valley. He may also have campaigned on the Danube. Then in 373 he achieved another independent command, this time in Mauretania (modern Algeria), where Roman rule was threatened by a major internal revolt. Its leader was a Moorish chieftain called Firmus who had killed his pro-Roman brother Sammac in a dispute over the succession to their father 'King' Nubel, thereby upsetting the equilibrium in Mauretania between the Romanized cities and farmers, protected by static garrisons and a small mobile reserve, and the necessary loyalty of the native tribal chieftains. Theodosius sailed from Arles with a small army, with which he arrested incompetent local officials and punished disloyal units with savage reprisals; then in a brilliant series of campaigns (373–4), which combined long marches and pitched battles against heavy numerical odds, and by judicious diplomacy and terrorism, he broke up Firmus's coalition of tribes and procured his betrayal. Firmus, who had once denounced Theodosius to his own (Theodosius's) men as a 'brutal executioner', killed himself rather than fall into his hands alive.

Theodosius was now congratulated as the 'physician of Africa's recovery' by the orator Symmachus, who exclaimed that his fame would never yield to 'envy'. This qualification may have been added to the letter (Symmachus, x.1) when it was published, for Theodosius fell from power when his patron Valentinian suddenly died of a stroke, on 17 November 375, in distant Pannonia (modern Hungary). Theodosius, who was then still in Africa, was arrested and taken to Carthage where, after receiving baptism, he was beheaded in December 376. Contemporaries understandably tell us almost nothing about the execution for 'treason' of an emperor's father. Ammianus Marcellinus is entirely silent. However, it seems unlikely that Theodosius was actually planning a coup. The order for his execution must have come from the imperial court where his colleague Merobaudes, joint commander-in-chief (*magister peditum*), was taking other precautions against a possible usurpation. But even if the execution was a matter of business for Merobaudes, he gained personally by removing a rival.

The younger Theodosius, who was then a *dux* on the Danube frontier, retired to Spain; but after the death of Valentinian's younger brother, the eastern emperor Valens, in battle against the Goths on 9 August 378, Valentinian's son Gratian recalled Theodosius to take command. Soon afterwards, on 19 January 379, Theodosius was promoted to the vacant eastern throne, where he founded a dynasty which lasted another two generations in both the east (until 450) and the west (until 455). Count Theodosius, therefore, as the new dynasty's 'divine' ancestor, was duly honoured posthumously in panegyric and by the erection of public statues.   R. S. O. TOMLIN

Sources *Sexti Aurelii Victoris liber de caesaribus*, ed. F. Pichlmayr, rev. edn, rev. R. Gruendel (Leipzig, 1966), 11–12 · Pacatus, *Panegyric to the Emperor Theodosius*, ed. and trans. C. E. V. Nixon, 5 (1987), 2 · Ammianus Marcellinus, *History*, ed. and trans. J. C. Rolfe, 3 vols., rev. edn (1971), 27.8, 28.3, 29.5, 30.7.9–10 · Symmachus, *Q. Aurelii Symmachi quae supersunt*, ed. O. Seeck, 1 (1883) · A. R. Birley, *The fasti of Roman Britain* (1981), 333–9 · P. Bartholomew, 'Fourth-century Saxons', *Britannia*, 15 (1984), 169–85 · S. S. Frere, *Britannia: a history of Roman Britain*, 3rd edn (1987), 339–48 · P. Salway, *Roman Britain* (1981), 374–96 · A. S. Esmonde Cleary, *The ending of Roman Britain* (1989), 44–6 · J. Matthews, *The Roman empire of Ammianus Marcellinus* (1989), 367–76 · A. H. M. Jones, J. R. Martindale, and J. Morris, *The prosopography of the later Roman empire*, 1: AD 260–395 (1971) [s.v. Theodosius 3]

Therry, John Joseph (1790–1864), Roman Catholic priest, son of John Therry and his wife, Eliza, *née* Connolly, was born at Cork. He was educated privately and at St Patrick's College, Carlow, under Dr Doyle. Ordained priest in 1815, he was assigned to parochial work in Dublin, and then in Cork, where he became secretary to the bishop, Dr Murphy. His interest in Australia was aroused by the transportation of Irish convicts.

Therry was one of the two official Catholic chaplains sent out by the Colonial Office to New South Wales in December 1819 under the pressure of radical demand, the increasing influence of the Irish hierarchy, and the somewhat diffident promptings of Bishop Poynter, vicar apostolic of the London district. He reached Sydney in May 1820 on the convict ship *Janus*. At first he ministered in a temporary chapel in Pitt Street, and at Parramatta often in the open air. His colleague Philip Conolly proceeded to

Van Diemen's Land, and for five seminal years Therry was the only Roman Catholic priest on the mainland: thus he earned the sobriquet the Patriarch of the Roman Catholic church in New South Wales. On 29 October 1821 Governor Macquarie laid the foundation-stone of St Mary's Chapel in Hyde Park, the first church on the site of Sydney's Roman Catholic cathedral. Therry was a devoted pastor, popular, energetic, and restless, who travelled great distances to serve his scattered people. He was respectful of authority, but impatient at any curtailment of what he considered to be his legal or social rights as a priest. Pious, zealous, and obstinate, he could be quarrelsome and difficult, particularly in matters concerning the considerable property he managed to accumulate in order to ensure the future of his church. He came into collision with the governor, Sir Ralph Darling, in 1827 and was for a time deprived of his salary as chaplain, but his pastoral and educational work continued with unabated vigour. In 1833 he became subordinate to the first Catholic vicar-general in the colony, the English Benedictine William Bernard Ullathorne, and then in 1835 to the first bishop, John Bede Polding, who sent him in 1838 as vicar-general to Van Diemen's Land (which became Tasmania during his ministry). There his long residence was characterized by a complex dispute on financial matters with the first bishop, Robert Willson.

Therry returned to live in Sydney during 1856 and became priest at St Augustine's, Balmain, where he died rather suddenly on 25 May 1864; he was buried in the crypt of St Mary's Cathedral, Sydney.

C. A. HARRIS, *rev.* JOHN EDDY

Sources *AusDB* · H. N. Birt, *Benedictine pioneers in Australia*, 2 vols. (1911) · E. M. O'Brien, *Life and letters of Archpriest John Joseph Therry* (1922) · J. H. Cullen, *The Catholic church in Tasmania* (1949) · P. J. O'Farrell, ed., *The Catholic church and community in Australia: a history* (1977) · J. Waldersee, *Catholic society in New South Wales, 1788–1860* (1974) · B. H. Fletcher, *Ralph Darling: a governor maligned* (1984)
Archives Mitchell L., NSW
Likenesses portrait, probably Catholic Institute of Sydney, Sydney
Wealth at death estate incl. great tracts of land: will, *AusDB*

Therry, Sir Roger (1800–1874), judge in Australia, was born on 22 April 1800 at Cork, Ireland, the third son of John Therry, a barrister and excise commissioner, and his wife, Jane, *née* Keating. The landed prosperity of the Terry (later Therry) family of Cork had declined since the seventeenth century.

After schooling at Clongowes College, Therry entered Trinity College, Dublin, in December 1818. He did not complete his degree but read law, and was called to the bar in Ireland (1824), though he did not practise. Having been admitted to Gray's Inn in November 1822, he was called to the English bar in 1827. He practised little there, but was a law reporter and, in 1827, private secretary to George Canning, whose published speeches he edited. Favourably noticed by William Huskisson, Therry accepted his offer to become commissioner of the court of requests (a small debts court) in New South Wales.

With his wife, Anne (*d.* 1874), the daughter of P. Carley (or Corley) of Clones, co. Monaghan, and the widow of

John Reilly of Dublin, whom he had married on 9 August 1827, Therry reached Sydney in November 1829. His permitted private practice in the supreme court was spectacularly successful. He was well regarded by Governor Bourke, and was made a crown grants commissioner (1833) and acting attorney-general (1839).

Committed to Roman Catholic causes, and known as an Irish supporter of O'Connell's Catholic emancipation efforts, Therry found advancement to higher public office difficult in a colony where religious intolerance flourished. His successful defence of a newspaper publisher, in defamation proceedings by the influential landowner James Mudie, was another handicap. Mudie's *Felonry of New South Wales* (1837) unreasonably attacked Therry and his religious sympathies. Injured by the publication, Therry complained at being passed over for judicial appointments.

Having been drawn to politics, in 1835 Therry stood unsuccessfully for election as chairman of quarter sessions. He was seen as Bourke's protégé, and the defeat embarrassed him and the governor equally. As acting attorney-general, Therry was *ex officio* a legislative councillor, and his speeches were commended. On the introduction, in 1843, of a limited franchise, Therry had a narrow victory in the seat of Camden after a campaign marred by sectarian rancour. He was a self-styled 'liberal', and his political views so prevaricated that one journalist dubbed him an 'Anythingarian'.

In 1845 Therry went to Melbourne as resident judge for Port Phillip, where he was received by a hostile press and a suspicious bar. Maintaining his composure, he disarmed critics by his judicial stature. He was promoted to the supreme court at Sydney in 1846, and at first found his colleagues unfriendly; however, his urbanity overcame their reserve, and his soundness as a lawyer strengthened the bench. He excelled as primary judge in equity, no decree of his ever being reversed. On responsible government (1856) the judges took *ex officio* places in the legislative council, a duty Therry relished. In February 1859, wearied by judicial overwork, he resigned on a pension, and the following month, after a huge public farewell dinner, he and his wife left Australia.

In England, Therry published his *Reminiscences* (1863), a useful account of early colonial Australia. The first edition sold out in England, but much of a second edition, printed just as Australian criticisms of the book's personalities became known, was withdrawn. Finding their native Ireland unappealing, the Therrys, in failing health, spent much time at French spas. Therry was knighted in 1869, and became a valetudinarian at Bath. He died on 17 May 1874 at his London home, 21A Hanover Square, and was buried in the Roman Catholic cemetery at Kensal Green. One son and two daughters survived him, as did Lady Therry by ten days.   J. M. BENNETT

Sources R. Therry, *Reminiscences of thirty years' residence in New South Wales and Victoria* (1863); facs. edn with introduction by J. M. Bennett (1974) · C. H. Currey, 'Therry, Sir Roger', *AusDB*, vol. 2 · [F. Watson], ed., *Historical records of Australia*, 1st ser., 15–20 (1922– 4) · *CGPLA Eng. & Wales* (1874) · m. cert. · *Home News for Australia* (2 June 1874)
Archives Mitchell L., NSW | Mitchell L., NSW, Sir Richard Bourke MSS · Mitchell L., NSW, Macarthur MSS · NL Ire., Sir Richard Bourke MSS
Likenesses C. Summers, marble bust, 1870, Mitchell L., NSW · A. Debenham, oils, Mitchell L., NSW
Wealth at death under £7000: probate, 9 June 1874, *CGPLA Eng. & Wales*

Thesiger, Alfred Henry (1838–1880), judge, was born on 15 July 1838, the fourth and youngest son of Frederick *Thesiger, first Baron Chelmsford (1794–1878), the lord chancellor, and his wife, Anna Maria (d. 1875), youngest daughter of William Tinling of Southampton. His brothers included Frederic Augustus *Thesiger, second Baron Chelmsford (1827–1905). He was educated at Eton College before matriculating on 15 May 1856 at Christ Church, Oxford, where he graduated BA in 1860 and MA in 1861. Both at school and at college he excelled at cricket and rowing, while battling against ill health. He became a student of the Inner Temple and was called to the bar in 1862. On 31 December 1862 he married Henrietta, the second daughter of the Hon. George Handcock, fourth son of the second earl of Castlemaine; they had no children.

Thesiger joined the home circuit, and quickly built up a large London practice. For a time he was postman of the court of exchequer, and on 3 July 1873 he became a queen's counsel. His later practice lay chiefly in commercial and compensation cases. In January 1874 he was elected a bencher of his inn, and on 10 September 1877 attorney-general to the prince of Wales. In 1876 he was a member of the commission on the fugitive slave circular, and in 1877, on the recommendation of Lord Cairns and to public surprise, he was appointed to succeed Sir Richard Paul Amphlett as a lord justice of the Court of Appeal, at the age of thirty-nine. He was duly sworn of the privy council. During his brief time on the bench he showed industry and judicial ability, and was remembered for his slight and youthful appearance. He died at 5 South Eaton Place, Eaton Square, London of blood poisoning on 20 October 1880 and was buried in Brompton cemetery. He was survived by his wife.

J. A. HAMILTON, *rev.* HUGH MOONEY

Sources *Law Times* (23 Oct 1880), 419, 433 · *The Times* (21 Oct 1880) · J. Haydn, *The book of dignities: containing rolls of the official personages of the British empire* (1851) · E. Foss, *Biographia juridica: a biographical dictionary of the judges of England … 1066–1870* (1870) · *CGPLA Eng. & Wales* (1880)
Likenesses Lock & Whitfield, woodburytype photograph, NPG; repro. in T. Cooper, *Men of mark: a gallery of contemporary portraits* (1880) · J. E. Millais, chalk drawing, Inner Temple, London · wood-engraving (after photograph by Surrey Photographic Company), NPG; repro. in *ILN* (17 Nov 1877)
Wealth at death under £80,000: probate, 9 Dec 1880, *CGPLA Eng. & Wales*

Thesiger, Ernest Frederic Graham (1879–1961), actor, was born in London on 15 January 1879, third of the four children (three sons and one daughter) of the Hon. Sir Edward Pierson Thesiger (1842–1928) and his wife, Georgina Mary Stopford (d. 1906). His father was a clerk assistant in the House of Lords and his grandfather Frederick

*Thesiger, first Baron Chelmsford (1794–1878), had been lord chancellor. He went to a private school at Weybridge, Surrey, and then to Marlborough College, where he professes to have been lonely and unhappy, and in 1896, at the age of seventeen, he persuaded his father to set aside his plans for his son to follow a conventional civil service career and allow to him to study at the Slade School of Fine Art. He trained there for four years: his fellow students included Augustus John (whom he thought conceited) and Wyndham Lewis. His father was a talented musician who became a friend of the composer Percy Grainger, and Thesiger himself attended some classes at the Guildhall School of Music. For ten years he followed the profession of painter, 'oblivious of the fact', as he writes in his memoirs, 'that my pictures were mostly bought out of kindness' (Thesiger, 40). He enjoyed travel in Europe and life in London, where his privileged family connections, combined with his own charm, courtesy, and ready wit, gave him access to a wide social circle. He married Janette Mary Fernie Ranken (d. 1970) on 29 May 1917. They had no children.

Thesiger's love of acting was fostered in amateur performances while he was still a student at the Slade, and he often took part in amateur theatricals at Christmas parties in his uncle's house in Knaresborough Place, London. Becoming aware that he would never make his fortune as a painter, and encouraged by his success on the amateur stage, in 1909 he arranged an introduction to the actor–manager Sir George Alexander, who gave him his first professional part and 'took the trouble to try to teach me to act' (Thesiger, 89). Engagements followed with Charles Hawtrey and Beerbohm Tree, who gave him his first Shakespearian role as Roderigo in Othello. From the beginning he was happier in contemporary roles, confessing that he found '"tradition" very hampering' (ibid., 105).

Thesiger was on holiday in France when the First World War broke out. Returning to England he joined the Queen Victoria rifles as a private soldier; he was injured in France before he reached the front line and he was discharged in 1915, resuming his acting career almost immediately. His first major success followed with his appearance as Bertram Tully in W. W. Ellis's farce A Little Bit of Fluff, which opened in October 1915 and ran for nearly three years. From then until shortly before his death Thesiger was in almost continuous employment as an actor, playing mostly on the West End stage, but appearing regularly at the Malvern Festival and, occasionally in the post-war years, in the Edinburgh Festival. In 1955 he visited Moscow, playing Polonius to Paul Scofield's Hamlet. His film career began in 1932 in The Old Dark House and he subsequently appeared in numerous films.

Although he appeared from time to time in works by Shakespeare and other Elizabethan and Restoration dramatists, he was most at home interpreting the characters created by contemporary English dramatists, and he created roles in plays by Arnold Bennett, Eden Philpotts, James Barrie, Somerset Maugham, George Bernard Shaw, John Galsworthy, and others. As in his personal life he preferred the deployment of reason, wit and intelligence to grand displays of passion, and in his memoir he comments on the difficulty of appearing to be natural on the stage (Thesiger, 97–8). He found Shaw the most congenial and helpful of the dramatists in whose plays he appeared; early in the rehearsals for Saint Joan (1924), in which he was to play the Dauphin, he was told by Shaw, 'You already know as much about the part as I do' (ibid., 142).

As well as painting and collecting Victorian glassware, he maintained a lifelong interest in embroidery and needlework. At the end of the First World War, with official encouragement, he set up a short-lived needlework school as an occupation for those who were physically or emotionally disabled by the war, and he published Adventures in Embroidery in 1941. In the last year of his life, and the fiftieth year of his acting career, he was awarded the order of commander of the British empire. Thesiger died at his home, 8 St George's Court, Gloucester Road, London, on 14 January 1961.   MICHAEL ANDERSON

Sources The Times (16 Jan 1961) · Who was who in the theatre, 1912–1976, 4 vols. (1978) · WWW, 1961–70 · E. Thesiger, Practically true (1927) · Burke, Peerage (1939)
Archives Theatre Museum, London, corresp. with George Bernard Shaw and Charlotte Shaw
Likenesses W. B. E. Ranken, oils, 1918, Man. City Gall. · E. Schilsky, bronze bust, 1925, V&A · W. R. Flint, chalk drawing, c.1945, BM · K. Pollak, photograph, NPG · J. S. Sargent, charcoal drawing, repro. in Thesiger, Practically true · photograph, NPG · photographs, repro. in Thesiger, Practically true
Wealth at death £46,525 1s.: probate, 10 April 1961, CGPLA Eng. & Wales

Thesiger, Frederic Augustus, second Baron Chelmsford (1827–1905), army officer and courtier, was born on 31 May 1827, the eldest of the seven children of Frederick *Thesiger, first Baron Chelmsford (1794–1878), lawyer, tory MP and lord high chancellor, and his wife, Anna Maria (d. 1875), youngest daughter of William Tinling. His brothers included Alfred Henry *Thesiger (1838–1880).

Thesiger's career before Africa Thesiger was educated at Eton College, and was commissioned by purchase as second lieutenant in the rifle brigade on 31 December 1844. He purchased an exchange to the Grenadier Guards as ensign and lieutenant on 28 November 1845. Promoted lieutenant and captain on 27 December 1850, he served in Ireland as aide-de-camp to the lord lieutenant from February to November 1852, and remained from 8 January 1853 to 5 August 1854 as aide-de-camp to the general officer commanding in Ireland. On 31 May 1855 he joined his battalion in the Crimea. He served as aide-de-camp to the commander of the 2nd division from 18 July to 29 September 1855, and as deputy assistant quartermaster-general from 8 November 1855 to 24 January 1856. He was present at the siege and fall of Sevastopol. On 2 November 1855 he was made brevet major, and was awarded the Mejidieh (fifth class).

On 28 August 1857 Thesiger was promoted captain and lieutenant-colonel in the Grenadier Guards. Wanting further action, he unconventionally exchanged on 30 April 1858 into the 95th foot, then involved in the suppression of the Indian mutiny. He joined his regiment in India in

Frederic Augustus Thesiger, second Baron Chelmsford (1827–1905), by Lock & Whitfield, pubd 1882

November 1858 and was present at Koondrye, the last action in which the Rajputana field force was engaged.

Thesiger remained in India for the next sixteen years. From 13 July 1861 to 31 December 1862 he was deputy adjutant-general of the British troops in the Bombay presidency, and was made brevet colonel on 30 April 1863. His administrative talents were recognized, and Sir Robert Napier selected him to be deputy adjutant-general of the Abyssinian expeditionary force from 21 January to 10 June 1868. He was present at the capture of Magdala. His tireless and efficient service was rewarded by being made CB on 14 August 1868 and by serving as aide-de-camp to the queen from 15 August 1868 to 14 March 1877. When Napier was appointed commander-in-chief in India, he insisted on Thesiger being made adjutant-general, which he was from 17 March 1869 to 15 March 1874.

On 1 January 1867 Thesiger married Adria Fanny (d. 1926), the eldest daughter of Major-General John Heath of the Bombay army. They had four surviving sons (two died in infancy). The eldest, Frederic John Napier *Thesiger (1868–1933), became viceroy of India.

In 1874 Thesiger returned to England, initially to command the camp at Shorncliffe (from 1 October 1874 to 31 December 1876) as colonel on the staff, and then to command the 1st infantry brigade at Aldershot (from 1 January 1877 to 1 February 1878) as brigadier-general. On 15 March 1877 he was promoted major-general. In 1877 he declined the post of deputy adjutant-general, Horse Guards, wanting a command in India. Also, his limited private income, on which the purchase of commissions had been a heavy burden, made the expense of a home command difficult.

He was selected in 1878 as general officer commanding in South Africa with the task of ending the Cape Frontier War against the Gcaleka (Xhosa) and Ngqika Xhosa.

Character and shortcomings Hitherto Thesiger had enjoyed a successful career, though one with an emphasis on the prosaic staff and administrative duties in which he excelled, rather than on experience of commanding an army in the field. He was typical of the privileged, conservative military establishment, with its emphasis on gentlemanly values, discipline, and sport. He appeared courteous and modest, with a considerate yet firm manner to subordinates. He set an example of calmness under fire, and of participation in field sports. Frugal and teetotal, he attempted to end drunkenness in his command, and to combat idleness among young officers induced them to study further. Tall and lean, with a long, thin, hooked nose and restless, watchful dark eyes under black bushy eyebrows, he tended to be somewhat introspective and withdrawn, though he was able to adopt a genial manner in company. He was a keen amateur actor, a good public speaker despite his sharp, rather jerky, delivery, and an accomplished clarinettist. Subordinates appreciated his decency and high character, which made him popular among them.

Although industrious, conscientious, and brave, Thesiger was never more than a prosaic product of the army system, and lacked the military flair and vision to overcome its deficiencies. Operations in South Africa during 1878–9 showed his shortcomings. He championed stereotyped military tactics, and with his patron, the duke of Cambridge, deplored recent army reforms and the advanced ideas of generals like Sir Garnet Wolseley, who chose a talented staff including trained intelligence officers. Thesiger in 1878 recruited his staff from those officers who had served him at Aldershot. So his staff's processing of intelligence remained inadequate, while his inability to delegate meant that he spent time and energy on tasks proper to his subordinates. His diffident manner discouraged discussion with his staff, though he too often allowed his habitually swift decisions to be swayed by contrary advice. And while he did study in advance the methods of the various enemies in South Africa, he underrated their fighting ability.

The war against the Xhosa When Thesiger took up his command at King William's Town on 4 March 1878 with the local rank of lieutenant-general (which he held from 25 February 1878 to 16 July 1879), only the Ngqika Xhosa were still in the field. They were ensconced in the broken and forested country of their traditional stronghold, known as the Pirie bush. Thesiger mistakenly deployed several strong columns to try to trap the Ngqika in a pincer movement and bring them to battle, but the Ngqika evaded pitched encounters. The failure of five offensives between March and April 1878 at last persuaded Thesiger to accept colonial advice and divide the area of operation into eleven areas, each patrolled by a mobile mounted force. This proved successful, thanks to the leadership of Lieutenant-Colonel Evelyn Wood and Major Redvers

Buller. Resistance was effectively over by mid-June 1878, though mopping-up operations continued until August.

On 9 August Thesiger set up his headquarters in Pietermaritzburg to prepare for the invasion of Zululand. The mission in South Africa of the high commissioner, Sir Bartle Frere, was to create a confederation of the British colonies in the interests of imperial security and economy. Neighbouring African polities were perceived as potential obstacles to this. The Cape Frontier War of 1877–8 had been fought to remove one such hindrance, while Thesiger's annexation of Port St John's on 31 August 1878, which overawed the Mpondo people between the Cape and Natal, overcame another. The militarily powerful Zulu kingdom (with some 29,000 warriors) continued the greatest challenge, but Frere was confident that a swift, relatively minor campaign would neutralize it.

Thesiger, who succeeded as Baron Chelmsford on 5 October 1878, faced strategic constraints. When he advanced into Zululand he would leave his own frontiers inadequately protected, while his dependence on slow-moving and vulnerable supply trains would limit the manoeuvrability and size of the five columns—totalling 17,929 men, of whom 5476 were British regulars—converging on oNdini, King Cetshwayo's chief residence.

With the danger of Zulu counter-raids in mind, Chelmsford selected invasion routes in sectors considered vulnerable to Zulu attack. The advance across the lower Thugela River by no. 1 column, under Colonel Pearson, would protect the coastal plain; that over the Buffalo River at Rorke's Drift by no. 3 column, under Colonel Glyn, central Natal; and that across the Blood River by no. 4 column, under Colonel Wood, the Transvaal. To improve the defence of the Natal middle border and to strengthen no. 3 column, which he decided to accompany, Chelmsford broke up no. 2 column, under Colonel Durnford. Part remained on garrison duty above the middle Thugela, and the rest moved up to support no. 3 column. He kept no. 5 column, under Colonel Rowlands, in a defensive role on the Phongolo River to protect the Transvaal from the Pedi people, with whom hostilities were continuing, and to cover no. 4 column's northern flank from both the Zulu and the equivocal Swazi.

The British invasion of Zululand began on 11 January 1879. Chelmsford's hopes for a rapid, co-ordinated advance were rapidly dashed by deficient staff work, unreliable maps, insufficient cavalry for reconnaissance, and the rain-sodden, broken terrain. The Zulu directed their main army against no. 3 column and dispatched a smaller force against no. 1 column. Local irregulars confronted no. 4 column.

On 20 January no. 3 column set up camp at Isandlwana Mountain. The camp was left unentrenched because it was intended only as a temporary staging post. The following day Chelmsford sent out a strong reconnaissance in the direction of the Qudeni Forest on his south-eastern flank. It met some resistance, and early on 22 January Chelmsford set out to reinforce it. Since over half of no. 3 column was now committed in the Qudeni area, he ordered up Durnford with part of no. 2 column to

reinforce the camp. However, because Chelmsford did not anticipate that the Zulu might attack the camp during his absence, he neglected to leave specific orders for its defence. To his subsequent relief, Major Clery on his own initiative instructed Lieutenant-Colonel Pulleine, the senior officer in camp until Durnford's arrival, to act strictly on the defensive.

Durnford upset these orders by advancing to prevent Chelmsford from being attacked in the rear by the small decoy Zulu forces he observed, and by requiring Pulleine to move up in his support if required. Durnford's patrols provoked the Zulu army of nearly 20,000 men into an attack, and the rapidly deploying Zulu outflanked the extended British firing line and overran the camp, killing 1357 of the 1768 defenders. The Zulu reserve continued into Natal and attacked the hastily fortified British depot at Rorke's Drift, which its greatly outnumbered garrison desperately and successfully defended.

Chelmsford, meanwhile, had been inexcusably out of communication for much of the day as he scouted ahead with a small party: not until late afternoon did he finally credit reports that his camp was under attack. He then acted decisively to recapture it, and the Zulu withdrew. Chelmsford retired with the demoralized remnant of his force into Natal and relieved Rorke's Drift.

Chelmsford under siege The defeat at Isandlwana shattered Chelmsford's invasion plans. The heavy loss of life, weapons, ammunition, and transport meant that he could make no further advance until his forces had been reinforced and fresh transport assembled. Meanwhile, no. 1 column was blockaded by Zulu forces at Eshowe while no. 4 column withdrew to a strongly defended position at Khambula. Chelmsford's health and morale temporarily broke down, and he turned particularly to Wood and Buller at Khambula to retrieve the situation with a number of successful mounted raids.

Chelmsford convened a court of inquiry into the loss of the camp at Isandlwana. Its report, submitted on 29 January, attributed most of the blame to Durnford and to the poor performance of the Natal native contingent: this expedient version passed into the official account.

Despite much public criticism of Chelmsford, the British government stood by him and sent out the reinforcements he requested. By the end of March he felt strong enough to attempt the relief of Eshowe. He was determined to avoid the mistakes which had led to the Isandlwana disaster, and organized effective forward reconnaissance and followed regular laagering procedures. On 1 April the 5670 troops under his command routed the Zulu force of about 10,000 men before his laager at Gingindlovu and then evacuated the Eshowe garrison. Meanwhile, the real turning point of the war had occurred at Khambula where, on 29 March, Evelyn Wood routed the main Zulu army.

Chelmsford was embarrassed by the growing numbers of troops at his disposal and was uncertain how best to use them for his second invasion of Zululand; while his commissariat and transport department—which had already proved itself unequal to the demands placed upon it—all but broke down under the strain. He eventually decided to employ two widely spaced columns. The 1st division of 7500 men, under Major-General Crealock, would advance on oNdini north along the coast, while the 2nd division of 5000 men, under Major-General Newdigate, would advance on oNdini from the north-west in co-operation with Wood's force of 3200 men, renamed the flying column. A believer in the active defence, Chelmsford also ordered diversionary raids by colonial forces across the exposed Natal–Zululand border. This brought him into conflict with Sir Henry Bulwer, the lieutenant-governor of Natal, who correctly feared raids would invite retaliation.

This shrill contest between the military and civil authorities in Natal was the last straw for the British government, which already perceived Chelmsford to be demoralized, uncertain of his strategy, and unable to bring the increasingly expensive war to a speedy conclusion. Its solution was to create a single, unified command in southern Africa under Wolseley, which would subordinate both Bulwer and Chelmsford and sideline Frere. Chelmsford learned on 16 June of Wolseley's appointment, which spurred him to bring the war to a decisive conclusion.

On 31 May the 2nd division began its laboured advance into Zululand to rendezvous with the flying column. Chelmsford was criticized for having become overcautious as he laagered every night and frequently halted to build supply depots and bring up supplies. The death on patrol on 1 June of the prince imperial of France, an observer on Chelmsford's staff, damaged his reputation further, as did his disagreements with the efficient Major-General Clifford, whom the duke of Cambridge had specifically selected as inspector-general of the lines of communication. War correspondents were critical. Chelmsford required a crushing victory to restore his credit, and this he achieved at Ulundi on 4 July, when his 5124 troops, drawn up in a hollow square, irrevocably broke the Zulu army of 15,000 men or more.

Highly resentful of Wolseley's appointment, Chelmsford resigned his command on 9 July and left him to complete the pacification of Zululand. Chelmsford was coolly received in England. Yet, despite his many detractors, some stood by him, especially Queen Victoria. Though she was unable to ensure that he was ever again offered an active command, she conspicuously favoured him with honours and attention.

On 19 August 1879 Chelmsford was made GCB (he had been made KCB in 1878), and on 1 April 1882 he was promoted to the permanent rank of lieutenant-general. He was appointed lieutenant of the Tower of London, a position he held from 4 June 1884 to 29 March 1889. He became a full general on 16 December 1888, and was placed on the retired list on 7 June 1893. In 1898 he was appointed colonel of the Sherwood Foresters (Derbyshire regiment), and was transferred to the 2nd Life Guards in 1900. The queen also appointed him gold stick at court; Edward VII retained him as such, and made him GCVO in 1902.

Chelmsford died on 9 April 1905 at the United Service Club, 116 Pall Mall, London, following a sudden seizure while playing billiards, and was buried at Brompton cemetery. His conduct of the Anglo-Zulu War has long been criticized. Despite some attempts to rehabilitate his reputation, modern scholars confirm the earlier adverse judgements on his generalship.   J. P. C. LABAND

Sources J. P. C. Laband, ed., *Lord Chelmsford's Zululand campaign, 1878–1879* (1994) · J. Mathews, 'Lord Chelmsford: British general in Southern Africa, 1878–1879', DLitt and Phil diss., University of South Africa, 1986 · G. French, *Lord Chelmsford and the Zulu war* (1939) · S. Clarke, ed., *Zululand at war: the conduct of the Anglo-Zulu war* (1984) · J. Mathews, 'Lord Chelmsford and the problems of transport and supply during the Anglo-Zulu war of 1879', MA diss., University of Natal, 1979 · J. P. C. Laband, *Kingdom in crisis: the Zulu response to the British invasion of 1879* (1992) · P. Gon, *The road to Isandlwana: the years of an imperial battalion* (1979) · W. H. Clements, *The glamour and tragedy of the Zulu war* (1936) · R. Coupland, *Zulu battle piece: Isandhlwana* (1948) · I. Knight, *Brave men's blood: the epic of the Zulu War, 1879* (1990) · I. Knight, *Zulu: Isandlwana and Rorke's Drift* (1992) · J. Laband and J. Mathews, *Isandlwana* (1992) · D. R. Morris, *The washing of the spears* (1966) · *The Times* (10 April 1905) · *Army List* · *DNB* · *CGPLA Eng. & Wales* (1905)

Archives NAM, corresp. and papers | NAM, letters to Charles Pearson · Natal Archives Depot, Pietermaritzburg, Sir Theophilus Shepstone MSS, corresp. with Sir E. Wood · Natal Archives Depot, Pietermaritzburg, Government House, Natal, MSS · PRO, War Office MSS, MSS relating to the Anglo-Zulu war · Royal Arch., Duke of Cambridge MSS · University of Natal, Durban, Killie Campbell Africana Library, Wood MSS

Likenesses photograph, 1878, NAM · J. N. Crealock, four pen and watercolour drawings, 1878–9, Sherwood Foresters Museum, The Castle, Nottingham · M. B., lithograph, pubd 1879, NPG · group portrait, photograph, 1879 (with staff), NAM · photograph, 1881–9, NAM · H. Brown, portrait; known to be in the 2nd Life Guards, 1912 · H. Brown, portrait, priv. coll. · Elliott & Fry, cabinet photograph, NPG · Judd & Co., lithograph, NPG; repro. in *Whitehall Review* (8 March 1879) · Lock & Whitfield, woodburytype photograph, NPG; repro. in T. Cooper and others, *Men of mark: a gallery of contemporary portraits* (1882) [see illus.] · Spy [L. Ward], caricature, chromolithograph, NPG; repro. in *VF* (3 Sept 1881) · engraving, repro. in *ILN* (23 Aug 1879) · wood-engravings, NPG; repro. in *ILN* (1897)

Wealth at death £68,304 3s. 10d.: probate, 23 May 1905, *CGPLA Eng. & Wales*

Thesiger, Frederic John Napier, first Viscount Chelmsford (1868–1933), viceroy of India, was born at 7 Eaton Square, London, on 12 August 1868, the eldest son of Frederic Augustus *Thesiger, second Baron Chelmsford (1827–1905), and his wife, Adria Fanny (d. 1926), daughter of Major-General John Heath, of the Bombay army. He was educated at Winchester College and at Magdalen College, Oxford, playing cricket for the university, as captain in 1892. Having gained a first in law, he was elected to a fellowship at All Souls (1892–9), and called to the bar (Inner Temple) in 1893. On 27 July 1894 he married Frances Charlotte (1869–1957), eldest daughter of Ivor Bertie Guest, first Baron Wimborne. They had four daughters and two sons, of whom the elder was killed in Mesopotamia in 1917. Thesiger served on the London school board (1900–04), was elected to the London county council in 1904, and became an alderman in 1913. In 1905 he succeeded to his father's title. He was governor of Queensland (1905–9) and New South Wales (1910–13) and, briefly, officiating governor-general of Australia (1909–10). He dealt successfully with a constitutional crisis over a dissolution in 1907,

Frederic John Napier Thesiger, first Viscount Chelmsford (1868–1933), by Sir Gerald Kelly, 1922–3

and assisted the first Labour government in New South Wales.

Chelmsford became viceroy of India in April 1916, after serving in India as a captain in the 4th Dorset territorials, chosen—other candidates being unwilling to leave England—as a safe man to succeed Lord Hardinge, who was suspected of becoming headstrong. Tall, good-looking, and dignified, Chelmsford looked the part; his task was to keep India quiet, and supportive in troops, supplies, and money, especially as the débâcle of the Mesopotamia campaign (1917) showed up weaknesses in the army leadership and ordnance. He instituted army reforms, including King's commissions for Indians, war conferences, a central publicity board, and an Indian industrial commission. He secured an Indian war loan to Britain by linking it to the resolution of the very long-running dispute over protective tariffs: a differential duty on cotton imports. Indentured emigration was banned in the same spirit of rallying public opinion by 'standing up for Indian rights'.

On constitutional questions Hardinge's legacy included suggestions for post-war rewards; his remarks about provincial autonomy had been rebuffed, and most Indian politicians were not then raising very radical demands, but the influential Round Table group, including India Office officials, talked of steps towards Indian self-government, which Chelmsford concluded he was expected to propose. Following a line he claimed he had favoured in 1915 he asked his first executive council to consider the ultimate goal of British rule and the first steps to be taken towards it. Sir Reginald Craddock, the home member of the government of India, wanted as little reform as possible, but proposals were sent to London in November 1916 for Indianization of the public services, more representative and independent local government, increased provincial autonomy even at some cost to efficiency, and legislative councils with majorities elected mainly on the basis of enlarged territorial constituencies. In the India Office, Sir William Duke's committee added the important proviso that the provincial legislatures must also have some measure of responsibility.

In August 1917, after Edwin Montagu had succeeded Sir Austen Chamberlain as secretary of state, the British government (responding to Chelmsford's urgent pleas) finally authorized a declaration of the goal of British government of India. Its two key terms were 'responsible government' and 'progressive realization'. Chelmsford, assuming they implied a partial transfer of power to Indians at the provincial level (or diarchy) as a first step, saw his role as persuading as many as possible of the senior officials in India, and hence influential opinion in Britain, to accept the reforms by ensuring the proposals were practical, and Montagu's inventiveness was kept in check. Montagu painted Chelmsford as over-cautious and unconstructive. The latter's contribution was not originality, but was as important as that of Montagu in ensuring that reforms were introduced in 1919, transitional to Indian self-government. The Indian princes, too, were organized into a representative council. Also important were Chelmsford's consultative style of government (unfamiliar in India, but assisted by procedural reforms), and his commitment to making the new central legislature work, trying to carry it with him on political and fiscal policy.

Chelmsford's government managed to subdue the terrorist threat in Bengal and elsewhere, and devised strategies on political agitation as Indian self-government became the admitted goal and nationwide nationalist organization was ever more effective. Chelmsford's greatest failure was the handling of the Punjab disturbances in 1919. In many areas, serious disturbances accompanied a campaign against legislation to extend wartime powers to impose restrictions on 'terrorists', measures also invoked against mainstream politicians. In the Punjab wartime upheavals and outdated political policies made for an explosive situation; after the arrest of local leaders, and the exclusion of Gandhi, exceptional violence was met (and exacerbated) by exceptional force. Worst was the massacre of hundreds from a peaceful crowd in Amritsar ordered by General Reginald Dyer, contrary to rule because intended (as Dyer later admitted) to set an example. Once fully publicized during 1920, this marked a turning point in Britain's relations with Indians. Chelmsford was culpable in not curbing the tendencies of Punjab policy and the atmosphere of panic in 1919, and arguably for continuing martial law regulations (extended because of war with Afghanistan) and then acting too slowly and judiciously. After a committee of inquiry Dyer was forcibly retired, as was one civil officer; several other military and civil offenders were censured. But when Dyer was lionized in Britain, including by the House of Lords, as the 'saviour of the Punjab', Chelmsford failed to make his own condemnation convincing. His instincts were conciliatory (shown also after the Afghan War, against strong opposition from London), but they led him into an impasse from which he could not escape, unable as he was to make what he called 'flamboyant' gestures.

Unpopular with Europeans in India for being too radical, and with many Indians for representing a discredited regime, and himself impatient with Indian leaders who refused to co-operate in his reforms, Chelmsford lost much of his effectiveness and enjoyment in office in the final months before the end of his term in April 1921. However, under the able guidance of the home member, Sir William Vincent, his government was able to establish policies to manage the first great Gandhian campaign, which began in 1920. Chelmsford was also well pleased with the first session of the new legislative assembly.

On his return to England he resumed his interest in education, also expressed in India through a major educational review and a Calcutta University commission. Chelmsford chaired the University College, London, committee (1920–32), and the statutory body appointed in 1923 to draft revised statutes for Oxford University. He led the Indian delegation to the League of Nations in 1922—India, already represented in the imperial war cabinet and war conferences, had anomalous international status—and secured India's place in the International Labour Organization as one of the eight principal industrial nations, and as a member of the governing body. Allowing his Indian colleagues latitude to criticize South African treatment of Indians, or to explain Indian interests in the opium question, he sought to demonstrate that the delegation was not a mere mouthpiece of the British government. Indian interests also featured in Chelmsford's decision in 1924 to join the first Labour government as first lord of the Admiralty.

Chelmsford was created viscount in 1921, and made KCMG (1906), GCMG (1912), GCSI and GCIE (1916), and GBE (1918). He was sworn of the privy council in 1916. He received honorary degrees from the universities of Birmingham (1927), Oxford (1929), Edinburgh and Sheffield (1932), and an honorary fellowship of Magdalen College, Oxford (1917). He was again elected to a fellowship of All Souls in 1929, and warden in 1932. He died suddenly of a heart attack at Ardington House, near Wantage, Berkshire, on 1 April 1933, and was succeeded in his titles by his younger son, Andrew Charles Gerald (1903–1970). His wife survived him. Honourable, loyal, clever, well liked, and

respected by friends and colleagues, Chelmsford was a public servant whose achievements have been underrated; he himself considered, with good cause, that he was one of the architects of a new India. P. G. ROBB

Sources *The Times* (3 April 1933) • *Oxford Magazine* (27 April 1933) • DNB • P. G. Robb, *The government of India and reform, 1916–21* (1976) • P. G. Robb, *The evolution of British policy towards Indian politics, 1880–1920* (1992) • K. J. Schmidt, 'India's role in the League of Nations, 1919–1939', PhD diss., Florida State University, 1994 • *Report on Indian constitutional reforms*, Command 9109 (1918) • E. S. Montagu, *An Indian diary*, ed. V. Montagu (1930) • A. Rumbold, *Watershed in India, 1914–1922* (1979) • CGPLA Eng. & Wales (1933)

Archives BL OIOC, papers relating to India | All Souls Oxf., letters to Sir William Anson • BL OIOC, letters to Sir Harcourt Butler • BL OIOC, corresp. with Lord Willingdon • BL OIOC, letters to Sir William Lawrence • BL OIOC, corresp. with J. S. Meston • CUL, corresp. with Lord Hardinge • NA Scot., corresp. with Lord Lothian • PRO, corresp. with Ramsay MacDonald, PRO 30/69/1/190 • Trinity Cam., Montagu MSS • U. Birm. L., corresp. with Austen Chamberlain • U. Cam., Centre of South Asian Studies, Verney MSS

Likenesses W. Stoneman, photograph, 1921, NPG • photograph, c.1921, NPG • G. Kelly, oils, 1922–3, unknown collection; copyprint, NPG [see illus.] • G. Kelly, oils, c.1923, All Souls Oxf.

Wealth at death £26,452 7s. 3d.: probate, 24 May 1933, CGPLA Eng. & Wales

Thesiger, Sir Frederick (d. 1805), naval officer in the British and Russian services, was the eldest son of John Andrew Thesiger (d. 1783), and his wife, Miss Gibson (d. 1814) of Chester. After several voyages in the service of the East India Company he entered the Royal Navy as a midshipman under Sir Samuel Marshall. In 1782 when Admiral Sir George Rodney sailed for the West Indies, Thesiger was appointed acting-lieutenant on board the *Formidable*. Sir Charles Douglas, captain of the fleet, later recommended his appointment as aide-de-camp to Rodney. Thesiger continued in the West Indies under Admiral Hugh Pigot, Rodney's successor, and afterwards accompanied Douglas to America. After the peace of 1783 he returned to England.

With the outbreak of war between Russia and Sweden in 1788, Thesiger obtained permission to enter Russian service. In 1789 he took command of a 74-gun ship and quickly distinguished himself in a naval engagement at Svenskund in Finland, where he obliged the Swedish admiral on board the *Gustavus* to strike to him. In June 1790 he took part in the desperate action fought off the island of Bornholm. Although the victory went to the Russians, Thesiger was the only survivor of the six British captains in Russian service. He was rewarded with the insignia of the order of St George by the Empress Catherine herself.

In 1796 Sir Frederick commanded a ship in the Russian squadron which came to the Downs to co-operate with the English fleet in the blockade of the Texel. After Catherine's death in 1796 Thesiger grew discontented with her successor, Paul, and tendered his resignation. He was detained in St Petersburg for a year, and finally departed without receiving his arrears of pay or his prize money.

Thesiger arrived in England when her maritime supremacy was threatened by the armed neutrality of

Russia, Denmark, and Sweden. Because of his knowledge of the Baltic and the Russian navy Thesiger was frequently consulted by Earl Spencer, the first lord of the Admiralty. When war broke out he was promoted commander and served Lord Nelson as an aide-de-camp at the battle of Copenhagen (2 April 1801). At the crisis point of the battle Thesiger volunteered to proceed to the crown prince with the flag of truce. Knowing that celerity was important, he took his boat through the Danish fire, avoiding a safer but slower route. During subsequent operations his knowledge of the Baltic coast and of the Russian language proved of great value.

Thesiger returned to England bearing dispatches from Sir Charles Morice Pole, and received a flattering reception from Lord St Vincent. He was promoted post captain, and obtained permission to assume the rank of knighthood and to wear the order of St George. After the rupture of the treaty of Amiens he served as British agent for the prisoners of war at Portsmouth. Sir Frederick died, unmarried, at Elson, near Portsmouth, on 26 August 1805.   E. I. CARLYLE, rev. RICHARD H. WARNER

Sources *Short sketch of the life of Captain Sir F. Thesiger* (1806) · *Obshchii morskoi spisok* [General naval list] (1885–1907) · R. C. Anderson, 'British and American officers in the Russian navy', *Mariner's Mirror*, 33 (1947), 17–27 · R. C. Anderson, 'Great Britain and the rise of the Russian fleet in the eighteenth century', *Mariner's Mirror*, 42 (1956), 132–46 · R. C. Anderson, *Naval wars in the Baltic during the sailing-ship epoch, 1522–1850* (1910); repr. as *Naval wars in the Baltic, 1522-1850* (1969) · V. A. Divin and others, eds., *Boevaia letopis' russkogo flota* [Chronicle of the battles of the Russian fleet] (Moscow, 1948) · F. F. Veselago, *Kratkaia istoriia russkogo flota* [A short history of the Russian fleet] (1939)

Thesiger, Frederick, first Baron Chelmsford (1794–1878), lord chancellor, was born at 1 Fowkes Buildings, Tower Street, London, on 15 July 1794, the third and youngest son of Charles Thesiger (d. 1831), comptroller and collector of customs in the island of St Vincent in the West Indies, and his wife, Mary Anne (d. 1796), daughter of Theophilus Williams of London. His paternal grandfather, John Andrew Thesiger (d. 1783), was a native of Saxony, who settled in England about the middle of the eighteenth century, and was employed as amanuensis to the marquess of Rockingham.

Thesiger was sent at the age of seven to Dr Charles Burney's school at Greenwich. He was destined for the navy, in which his uncle, Sir Frederick *Thesiger, afterwards Nelson's aide-de-camp at Copenhagen, was a distinguished officer, and went in 1806 to Gosport naval academy. After a year at Gosport he joined the frigate *Cambrian* as a midshipman in 1807 and was present at the seizure of the fleet at Copenhagen; but shortly afterwards left the navy on becoming heir to his father's West Indian estates by the death of his last surviving brother, George. He was sent to school for two more years and then in 1811 went out to join his father at St Vincent. A volcanic eruption on 30 April 1812 entirely destroyed his father's estate and considerably impoverished his family. It was then decided that he should practise as a barrister in the West Indies.

Thesiger entered Gray's Inn on 5 November 1813, and

read successively in the chambers of a conveyancer, an equity draughtsman, and of Godfrey Sykes, a well-known special pleader. Sykes thought his talents would be thrown away in the West Indies, and on his advice, though without family connections there, Thesiger resolved to try his fortune in England. On 18 November 1818 he was called to the bar, joining the home circuit and Surrey sessions. In two or three years, after the removal of his chief competitors, Turton and Broderic, he attained the leadership of these sessions. He also became by purchase one of the four counsel of the palace court of Westminster. The legal experience which he gained through a succession of small civil and criminal cases gave him a good deal of useful knowledge, and his defence in 1824 of Hunt, the accomplice of the famous murderer John Thurtell, brought him to public attention. An action of ejection, which was tried three times in Chelmsford in 1832, was so important in further enhancing his reputation that when he was eventually raised to the peerage, he chose as his title the name of that circuit town.

On 9 March 1822 Thesiger married Anna Maria Tinling (d. 9 April 1875); they had three daughters and four sons, including Frederic Augustus *Thesiger and Alfred Henry *Thesiger.

In 1834 Thesiger became a king's counsel and was leader of his circuit for the next ten years. His name became very prominent in 1835 as counsel for the petitioners before the election committee which inquired into the return of O'Connell and Ruthven for Dublin. After an unsuccessful contest in 1840 at Newark against Wilde, the solicitor-general, he was returned to parliament as Conservative member for Woodstock on 20 March. In 1844, owing to differences of opinion with the duke of Marlborough, he ceased to represent Woodstock, and was elected for Abingdon, and at the general election of 1852 he was returned for Stamford by the influence of Lord Exeter.

On 8 June 1842 Thesiger was created DCL by the University of Oxford, and on 19 June 1845 was elected a fellow of the Royal Society. On 15 April 1844 he was appointed solicitor-general in succession to Sir William Webb Follett and was knighted. The breakdown of Follett's health left him almost all the work of both law officers, and on Follett's death he became attorney-general on 29 June 1845, retiring on the fall of the Peel administration on 3 July 1846. Had the ministry lasted another fortnight, he would have succeeded to the chief-justiceship of the common pleas (which became vacant on 6 July by the death of Sir Nicholas Tindal, and was given to Wilde). Instead, he returned to his private practice at the bar, and in parliament acted with Lord George Bentinck.

Thesiger became attorney-general again in Lord Derby's first administration from February to December 1852. When Lord Derby formed his second administration, and Lord St Leonards refused because of his advanced age to join, Thesiger became lord chancellor on 26 February 1858 and was created Baron Chelmsford (1 March 1858) and a privy councillor. His chancellorship was short, since the government fell in June 1859. His chief speech while in office was an opposition to the removal of Jewish disabilities, on which subject he had repeatedly been the principal speaker on the Conservative side in the House of Commons. He was very much opposed to the idea of Jews in parliament, as well as to the establishment of the Roman Catholic hierarchy in England.

After his resignation Thesiger remained active in judicial work, both in the House of Lords and the privy council. He constantly found himself in collision with Lord Westbury. The two men did not get on personally and Lord Chelmsford opposed Lord Westbury vigorously in relation to the hardship inflicted under the new Bankruptcy Act of 1862 on the officials of the former insolvent court. Chelmsford resumed office again under Lord Derby in 1866, but was somewhat summarily set aside in 1868 by Disraeli when Lord Derby ceased to be prime minister. He died on 5 October 1878 at his house, 7 Eaton Square, London.

Thesiger was, after the death of Follett, probably the most popular leading counsel of his day. As a lawyer he was ready and painstaking, and was a good cross-examiner, although not renowned for his intellectual abilities. Politically, he was right-wing and Conservative; however, as a judge he seems to have remained independent and principled on the whole. Two incidents are reported which, although dubious, did not seem to cast a shadow on his career. The first involved being sued by a client for settling a case without consultation. However, Lord Chelmsford defended himself successfully. The second concerned his purported appointment of a friend (though only barely qualified as a barrister) to the position of master in chancery. In the end he was defeated and outvoted: the friend was never appointed. On balance, he will be remembered as a sound and fair judge; and there is little evidence that these reported incidents damaged his judicial reputation in any way.

J. A. HAMILTON, rev. SINÉAD AGNEW

Sources E. Foss, *Biographia juridica: a biographical dictionary of the judges of England … 1066–1870* (1870) • J. B. Atlay, *The Victorian chancellors*, 2 (1908), 79–111 • Burke, *Peerage* (1980) • Boase, *Mod. Eng. biog.* • [T. T. Shore], ed., *Cassell's biographical dictionary* (1867–9), 481 • C. Knight, ed., *The English cyclopaedia: biography*, 5 (1858) • *Law Journal* (12 Oct 1878), 625 • *Law Times* (12 Oct 1878), 405 • *Men of the time* (1875), 234–5 • L. C. Sanders, *Celebrities of the century: being a dictionary of men and women of the nineteenth century* (1887), 247 • *A dictionary of contemporary biography* (1861) • J. Foster, *The register of admissions to Gray's Inn, 1521–1889, together with the register of marriages in Gray's Inn chapel, 1695–1754* (privately printed, London, 1889), 416 • Ward, *Men of the reign*, 177–8 • *Life of John, Lord Campbell, lord high chancellor of Great Britain*, ed. Mrs Hardcastle, 2 (1881), 357 • T. A. Nash, *The life of Richard, Lord Westbury*, 2 (1888), 38

Archives NRA, priv. coll., personal corresp. | BL, corresp. with Sir Robert Peel, Add. MSS 40452–40602 • Bodl. Oxf., letters to Benjamin Disraeli • Lpool RO, letters to fourteenth earl of Derby • NRA, priv. coll., letters to S. H. Walpole • PRO, letters to Lord Cairns, PRO 30/51 • PRO, letters to Lord John Russell, PRO 30/22 • Som. ARS, letters to Sir William Joliffe

Likenesses W. Walker, mezzotint, pubd 1847 (after E. U. Eddis), BM • E. U. Eddis, oils, c.1859, Abingdon Guidhall, Oxfordshire • H. Gales, group portrait, watercolour, 1868 (*The Derby cabinet of 1867*), NPG • F. Sargent, pencil drawing, c.1870–1880, NPG • Elliott & Fry, photograph, 1882, NPG • W. Holl, stipple (after G. Richmond), BM • Judd & Co., lithograph, repro. in *Whitehall Review* (8 March 1879) • Lock & Whitfield, woodburytype photograph, probably NPG • D. J. Pound, engraving (after photograph), repro. in *Ann. Gift.*, 1 (1859), 21 • D. J. Pound, line engraving (after photograph by Mayall), NPG; repro. in *Illustrated News of the World* • Spy [L. Ward], caricature, repro. in *VF* (3 Sept 1881) • carte-de-visite, NPG • photograph, repro. in T. Cooper, *Men of mark: a gallery of contemporary portraits*, 1 (1876), 16 • portrait, repro. in *Green Bag*, 13 (1901), 301 • portrait, repro. in *VF*, 2 (1870), pl. 39 • wood-engraving (after photograph), repro. in *ILN*, 73 (1878), 360 • wood-engravings, repro. in *ILN* (1879)

Wealth at death under £60,000: resworn probate, May 1879, *CGPLA Eng. & Wales* (1878)

Thew, Robert (1758–1802). *See under* Boydell, John, engravers (*act.* 1760–1804).

Theyer, John (*bap.* 1598, *d.* 1673), antiquary, was baptized at Brockworth, Gloucestershire, on 5 November 1598, the son of John Theyer (*d.* 1631) and his wife, Jane, and grandson of Thomas Theyer of Brockworth. He entered Magdalen College, Oxford, in 1613, but did not graduate. After three years there he practised common law at New Inn, London, where the mother of Anthony Wood, the future antiquary, proposed to send her son to qualify under him as an attorney. Although Wood did not go, he became a lifelong friend.

In 1628, at Theyer's marriage to his wife, Susan, he was given by his father a small estate at Cooper's Hill, Brockworth. From his grandmother's brother, Richard Hart, last prior of Llanthony Secunda, Gloucestershire, Theyer had inherited a valuable library of manuscripts. The Theyers, who had a son, John, made Cooper's Hill their home, and were visited by Wood, who made use of the library.

In 1643 Theyer was in Oxford, serving in the king's army, and presented to Charles in Merton College garden a copy of his *Aerio mastix, or, A vindication of the apostolicall and generally received government of the church of Christ by bishops* (1643). On 6 July that year he was created MA by the king's command, on account of his literary and ecclesiastical achievement. According to Wood he became a Roman Catholic about this time, and began, but did not finish, 'A friendly debate between protestants and papists'. His estate was sequestered by parliament, and he was pronounced one of the most 'inveterate' delinquents with whom they had to deal. His family was almost destitute until his discharge was obtained on 4 November 1652.

Theyer died at Cooper's Hill on 25 August 1673, and was buried in Brockworth churchyard on 28 August. The collection of 800 manuscripts on which his reputation was almost exclusively founded went to his grandson Charles Theyer (*b.* 1651), who had matriculated from University College, Oxford, in 1668 and who was probably the lecturer of Totteridge, Hertfordshire, who published *A Sermon on her Majesty's Happy Anniversary* (1707). After the collection had passed to the London bookseller Robert Scott, a partial catalogue was prepared by William Beveridge, later bishop of St Asaph, and William Jane in 1678 (BL, Royal MSS appendix, 70); 312 were bought by Charles II, the last large collection to enter the royal manuscripts.

CHARLOTTE FELL-SMITH, rev. ROBERT J. HAINES

Sources I. Gray, 'John Theyer, 1598–1673', in I. Gray, *Antiquaries of Gloucestershire and Bristol*, Bristol and Gloucestershire Archaeological Society Records Section, 12 (1981), 43–4 · *The life and times of Anthony Wood*, ed. A. Clark, 1, OHS, 19 (1891), 130 · parish registers, Brockworth, Glos. RO, P62 · S. E. Bartlett, 'History of the manor and advowson of Brockworth', *Transactions of the Bristol and Gloucestershire Archaeological Society*, 7 (1882–3), 161–4 · Foster, *Alum. Oxon.*

Archives BL, catalogue of royal and king's MSS, 26 · Bodl. Oxf., Wood D45 · Bodl. Oxf., Ballard 65

Thicknesse [*née* Ford], **Ann** (1737–1824), writer and musician, was born on 22 February 1737 near the Temple, London, the only child of Thomas Ford (*d.* 1768), clerk of the arraigns, and his wife, formerly Miss Champion. Her father made sure that she had an unusually extensive education, which he claimed had cost him at least £400 a year and included private lessons from singer and actor Susanna Cibber. A spirited and unconventional woman, Ford proved to be a talented musician who played several instruments and sang. In 1758 Frances Greville described her to Charles Burney as 'the most pleasing singer I ever heard … I would rather hear her than any Italian I have yet heard' (Highfill, Burnim & Langhans, *BDA*, 5.365).

At first Ford performed only within domestic settings, as was deemed suitable for a woman of her class. She gave musical entertainments in her father's house, attended by leading professional and amateur musicians, as well as playing and singing at gatherings of fashionable society in London and Bath. In 1760 she was painted by Thomas Gainsborough, a fellow enthusiast for the viola da gamba and resident of Bath. She also attracted the attention of William Villiers, third earl of Jersey, a married man who apparently offered her an annuity of £800 to be his mistress. Ford refused and, resolutely determined to be independent, left her father's house for that of a friend, Elizabeth Thicknesse, aiming to support herself by performing in public, an unacceptable step for a woman of her class. Her father had her arrested and brought back to the family home. Nothing daunted, she left again and announced a series of five subscription concerts at the Little Theatre in the Haymarket, the first of which she gave on 18 March 1760. This series raised £1500 in subscriptions, despite the efforts of the rejected earl of Jersey to detract from her enterprise. Her outraged father surrounded the theatre with runners in an attempt to prevent the first concert but Charles Bennet, third earl of Tankerville, one of Ford's aristocratic supporters, ensured that they were dispersed.

In early 1761 Ford published *A Letter from Miss F—d, Addressed to a Person of Distinction*, in which she attempted to clear her name of malicious rumour by making public her treatment by Jersey, who denied her accusations in his response, *A Letter to Miss F—d*. Ford argued that she had found 'many sensible people of the opinion, that a young woman may sing in public, or … be a public singer, with virtue and innocence' (*Letter from Miss F—d*, 17–18) and that performing in public was merely 'to repeat, for my own advantage, what I so often did, and to as large an assembly, at your house, and for your L—d—p's amusement' (ibid., 29). Her original letter sold 500 copies in five days and both letters gained wider distribution when they

Ann Thicknesse (1737–1824), by Thomas Gainsborough, 1760

were summarized in the *Gentleman's Magazine* (January and February 1761). Despite the scandal Ford continued her public performances, playing the water-tuned musical glasses at Thomas Sheridan's lectures and, from 15 October 1761, giving a series of appearances at the Spring Gardens room, singing English airs and playing the musical glasses, English guitar, and viola da gamba. In this year of remarkable determination and achievement she also published the first known method for the musical glasses, *Instructions for Playing on the Musical Glasses*, and *Lessons and Instructions for Playing the Guitar*, which included several pieces for the guitar, almost certainly composed by Ford herself.

In November 1761 Ford left London with Elizabeth Thicknesse for Landguard Fort in Suffolk, where Elizabeth's husband, Philip *Thicknesse, was lieutenant-governor. On 27 September 1762, six months after Elizabeth's death, Ford married Philip at Felixstowe, Suffolk. The couple had two children, John and Charlotte. There is no record of Ann Thicknesse performing again in public, although the memory of her musical career is evoked in a 1790 Gillray cartoon of Philip Thicknesse ('Lieutenant Gover Gall-Stone'), in which Ann is depicted playing the musical glasses.

The Thicknesses moved frequently, living in Hertfordshire, Monmouthshire, Hythe, and Bath, and were enthusiastic travellers. In 1775 they embarked on an eighteen-month journey (with viola da gamba, two guitars, a violin, and a parakeet); this was described in Philip Thicknesse's *A Year's Journey through France and Part of Spain*, which was published in 1777 with illustrations that are almost certainly by Ann. She herself turned to writing, publishing her *Sketches of the Lives and Writings of the Ladies of France* in three volumes between 1778 and 1781. In 1792 Philip Thicknesse died suddenly while he and Ann were travelling through France to Italy. Ann was arrested and confined in a convent but released in July 1794, after proving that she was capable of providing for herself. Her later publications included a novel, *The School for Fashion* (1800). When she made her will in 1818 she was living in Edgware Road in London with her close friend Sarah Cooper. She died on 20 January 1824.   SOPHIE FULLER

Sources *A letter from Miss F—d, addressed to a person of distinction* (1761) · P. Gosse, *Dr Viper: the querulous life of Philip Thicknesse* (1952) · Highfill, Burnim & Langhans, *BDA*, 5.364–6 · M. Rosenthal, 'Thomas Gainsborough's *Anne Ford*', *Art Bulletin*, 80 (1998), 649–65 · S. McVeigh, *Concert life in London from Mozart to Haydn* (1993) · A. H. King, 'The musical glasses and glass harmonica', *Proceedings of the Royal Musical Association*, 72 (1945–6), 97–122 · P. Coggin, '"This easy and agreeable instrument": a history of the English guitar', *Early Music*, 15 (1987), 205–18 · earl of Jersey [W. Villiers], *A letter to Miss F—d* (1761) · [A. C. H. Seymour], *The life and times of Selina, countess of Huntingdon*, 2 vols. (1844) · M. I. Wilson, 'Gainsborough, Bath and music', *Apollo*, 105 (1977), 108–9 · S. L. Sloman, 'Gainsborough in Bath, 1758–59', *Burlington Magazine*, 137 (1995), 509–12 · M. Rosenthal, 'Testing the water: Gainsborough in Bath in 1758', *Apollo*, 142 (Sept 1995), 49–54 · *DNB*

Likenesses T. Gainsborough, oils, 1760, Cincinnati Art Museum, Ohio [*see illus.*] · T. Gainsborough, oils, c.1760, BM · G. Cipriani, portrait, AM Oxf.

Thicknesse, George (*bap.* 1714, *d.* 1790), schoolmaster, was baptized on 22 November 1714 at Farthingoe in Northamptonshire, one of the sons of John Thicknesse (c.1670–1725), rector of Farthingoe, and Joyce, daughter of the Revd Thomas Blencowe, rector of Thenford, Northamptonshire, and niece of Sir John Blencowe; Philip *Thicknesse was a younger brother. George Thicknesse was admitted scholar of Winchester College in 1726 and matriculated as a fellow-commoner from King's College, Cambridge, in 1738 but did not graduate—and presumably did not reside—as he had already, in 1737, become chaplain (or usher) of St Paul's School, London. In 1744 he was elected surmaster, and in 1748 high master. The appointment of a nongraduate must relate to the catastrophic decline of the school under his predecessor, George Charles, who was dismissed for brutality; the school had only thirty-five boys when Thicknesse succeeded him.

Under Thicknesse, St Paul's rapidly recovered in numbers and reputation. According to his eccentric and admiring brother Philip he relied on reasoning and never used the rod, but discouraged any tendency in the boys to poetry and declined to meet Dr Johnson, as 'he deemed him only a poet' (Thicknesse, 3.49). He certainly retained the affection of his pupils, especially Philip Francis, who called him 'the wisest learnedst, quietest and best man he ever knew' (*Memoirs of Sir Philip Francis*, 2.279) and, though occasionally reprimanded, he retained also the trust of the governing body, the Mercers' Company. In

1758 Thicknesse suffered what may have been a brief mental breakdown. He retired, on a pension of 100 guineas a year, in 1769 and spent the rest of his life in Warwickshire, first in the house of a Winchester school friend at Mollington and later at Arlescote House, near Edgehill. There he died, unmarried, on 18 December 1790; he was buried, in accordance with his instructions, on the north side of Warmington churchyard, 'in a plain coffin' with 'no mound or … gravestone or monument' (Thicknesse, 3.48). His pupils, however, placed a marble bust of him by John Hickey, with an inscription by Philip Francis and Edmund Burke, in St Paul's School in 1792.

J. H. LUPTON, *rev.* ARTHUR HUGH MEAD

Sources M. F. J. McDonnell, *A history of St Paul's School* (1909) · M. McDonnell, ed., *The registers of St Paul's School, 1509–1748* (privately printed, London, 1977), 443–4 · P. Thicknesse, *Memoirs and anecdotes of Philip Thicknesse*, 3 vols. (privately printed, London, 1788–91) · J. Parkes and H. Merivale, *Memoirs of Sir Philip Francis*, 2 vols. (1867) · acts of court of the Mercers' Company, 1748–69, Mercers' Hall, London · R. J. W[alker], 'George Thicknesse, high master', *The Pauline* [magazine of St Paul's School, London], 13 (1895), 207–10 · A. H. Mead, *A miraculous draught of fishes: a history of St Paul's School* (1990) · T. F. Kirby, *Winchester scholars: a list of the wardens, fellows, and scholars of … Winchester College* (1888) · *GM*, 1st ser., 60 (1790), 1153 · *GM*, 1st ser., 84/2 (1814), 629 · Nichols, *Lit. anecdotes*, 1.426n.; 9.251–6

Likenesses J. Hickey, marble bust, 1792, St Paul's School, London

Wealth at death had pension of 100 guineas p.a. from governors of St Paul's School; also £50 p.a. under will of William Holbech from 1771; in 1785 Philip Francis gave £20; in 1786 William Perry, another former pupil, offered rent-free accommodation; lacked private means: Thicknesse, *Memoirs*, 3.52

Thicknesse, Philip (1719–1792), travel writer, born at Farthingoe, Northamptonshire, on 10 August 1719, was the seventh son (there were also two daughters) of John Thicknesse (c.1670–1725), rector of Farthingoe, and grandson of Ralph Thicknesse of Balterley Hall, Staffordshire. His mother, Joyce Blencowe, was niece of Sir John Blencowe, justice of the common pleas and baron of the exchequer. Of the seven sons, three died in infancy. The surviving four all achieved positions of some influence: Thomas (1706–1742) was a clergyman, a Whitehall preacher, and a candidate for the provostship of King's College, Cambridge, in January 1742; Ralph (1709–1742) was an assistant at Eton College and published an edition of *Phaedrus, with English Notes* in 1741, but died suddenly while playing the violin at Bath; George *Thicknesse (*bap.* 1714, *d.* 1790) was, successively, chaplain, surmaster, and high master of St Paul's School.

Education and early travels Philip was placed at Aynhoe School after the death of his father in 1725, but soon moved with his mother to London, where he became a gratis scholar at Westminster School through the kindly intervention of the headmaster, Dr Robert Friend, whose family were neighbours of the Thicknesses in Northamptonshire. However, Thicknesse was very unhappy at Westminster, and repeated truancy led to his removal from the school. He was then apprenticed to Marmaduke Tisdale, a London apothecary, but left fairly rapidly after becoming

Philip Thicknesse
(1719–1792), by
Nathaniel Hone,
1757

too fond of Tisdale's choicest cordials. Thicknesse had read an account of Georgia by General James Oglethorpe, and—aged only sixteen—contrived to join the general, with a group of Scots and German emigrants as well as the Wesley brothers, on board the *Simmonds* and the *London Merchant*, which set sail for America on 20 October 1735. They reached Savannah on 2 February 1736. Despite building himself a wooden cabin on an island in a creek, and living 'a true Robinson Crusoe line of life' (Thicknesse, *Memoirs*, 31), Thicknesse abandoned life in Georgia after seeing a vision of his mother while playing the flute on the banks of the creek, and sailed back to England in 1737. He was then given a job in the offices of the Georgia colonists in Old Palace Yard, but was soon dismissed for giving too frank an account of settler life. He failed to obtain a commission in Oglethorpe's projected Georgia regiment, probably because of his tactlessness, but Sir Robert Walpole helped procure him a commission as captain in an independent company at Jamaica. There, he was involved in British attempts to quell the guerrilla activities of runaway slaves in the mountains, and encountered many hair-raising ambushes and near-fatal skirmishes. While in Jamaica he formulated his lifelong conviction that slavery, provided it involved humane treatment of the slaves, was a natural state of affairs.

Return to England and first marriage Probably because he had fallen out with his fellow officers, Thicknesse applied for a six-month leave of absence from Jamaica and returned to London at the end of 1740. Through the good offices of Thomas Townshend (a scholar of King's College, Cambridge, where Philip's brother Thomas was then a fellow), he was appointed captain-lieutenant in a marine foot regiment with headquarters at Southampton. He soon became embroiled in a tavern brawl followed by a duel with another former Jamaica officer who publicly accused Thicknesse of having fled from the enemy slaves. Also while stationed at Southampton, Thicknesse met Maria Lanove (d. 1749), daughter of a prosperous Huguenot refugee and heir to £40,000. In 1742 they eloped and married after he abducted her from a protective cohort of

soldiers in Southampton High Street. Once she was pregnant, Thicknesse was appointed to the seventy-gun *Ipswich* under Admiral Medley, bound for Gibraltar. After a year in the Mediterranean, he returned to England on half pay. He fell out with his parents-in-law, and he and Maria moved to Bath. With time on his hands, Thicknesse threw himself into the social whirl of Bath, and began to enjoy gambling. However, early in 1749 Maria and their children (by now numbering three) contracted a type of diphtheria; she and two of the children died, leaving only one surviving daughter, Anna. Maria's parents died shortly thereafter, her father in his sleep, her mother by hurling herself out of a window onto some iron railings at the very spot in Southampton High Street where Thicknesse had abducted Maria. Thicknesse spent much of the rest of his life in a fruitless attempt (involving an unsuccessful appeal to the House of Lords) to get hold of the fortune to which he believed himself entitled by this unfortunate sequence of events. In the meantime, he did inherit £5000 on his father-in-law's death. A distant relative, Captain Rigg, took Thicknesse and his daughter to live with him in Queen Square, Bath. It was at this time in his life that Thicknesse began to suffer from gallstones and to assuage the pain through the liberal use of laudanum, to which he was thereafter addicted, and the praises of which he was always eager to sing, in person and in print. He especially recommended it to men over fifty, whom he urged to take ten to twenty drops of strong laudanum daily. No doubt Thicknesse's own addiction exacerbated his quarrelsome tendencies.

Second marriage and further quarrels A widower for less than a year, Thicknesse married on 10 November 1749 Lady Elizabeth Touchet (1725–1762), eldest daughter and heir of Lord Audley, the sixth earl of Castlehaven. Her father, whose family were long-standing Roman Catholics, raised strong objections to the marriage, but she nevertheless brought a dowry of £5000. With £1200 of this, Thicknesse in February 1753 bought the lieutenant-governorship of Landguard Fort in Suffolk, built by Charles I in 1628 at the mouth of Harwich harbour. At Landguard, Thicknesse soon became involved in wrangles about authority and precedence with various local notables and military personnel. In 1762 he began a long feud with Colonel Vernon of the Suffolk militia, later Lord Orwell. Thicknesse purchased a printing press and produced broadsheets designed to sabotage Lord Orwell's election hopes, which were distributed in Ipswich. The final straw came when Thicknesse made Lord Orwell the mocking present of a cannon-shaped piece of flotsam. Following the infamous 'affair of the wooden gun', Thicknesse was tried at Bury St Edmunds for libel in March 1753. Found guilty, he spent three months in the king's bench prison (where he made many friends), was fined £100, and had to provide security in the form of two friends for £500 each and £1000 himself, to guarantee that he would keep the peace for seven years. Amazingly, he was allowed to resume command of Landguard Fort on his release, even though he had also, as part of his campaign against Lord Orwell, attempted to blackmail Lord Bute into supporting him, by threatening to publish some papers of Lady Mary Wortley Montagu (Bute's late mother-in-law). These endeavours are inaccurately represented in *A Narrative of what Passed between General Sir Harry Erskine and Philip Thicknesse, Esq.* (1766).

Third marriage and visit to France The feud with Lord Orwell was contemporaneous with turbulent events in Thicknesse's personal life: in late March 1762 his wife Elizabeth died, having given birth to a baby boy on 29 June 1760. She had been attended in her delivery and long illness by a close friend, Ann Ford (1737–1824) [see Thicknesse, Ann], an accomplished singer and viola da gamba player, who had been involved in a scandalous affair with the aged earl of Jersey in 1761. She and Thicknesse married on 27 September 1762. Their marriage was to last until his death thirty years later. Philip and Elizabeth had produced six children, two of whom died in infancy. The survivors were two girls and two boys. There is confusion over the names of the surviving girls: Charlotte (*b.* 1751) certainly survived, since Thicknesse recalls (in *A Year's Journey*, 1777) having placed her in a convent. One of the other two, Elizabeth (*b.* 1750) or Joyce (*b.* 1753), also survived. Elizabeth's surviving sons were George (1757–1818), later Lord Audley, baron of Castlehaven, and Philip (*b.* 1760). In 1784, following a very public feud with his father, George assumed the surname of Touchet.

While he and his third wife remained at Landguard, Thicknesse continued to embellish the whimsical Felixstowe Cottage, a former fisherman's hut a few miles from Landguard, where they spent the summer months. (An account of the cottage, with a print claiming to be 'copied from one of the earliest Productions of Gainsborough', was published in the *Harwich Guide* in 1808, and reprinted in the *Gentleman's Magazine* in November 1809.) Eventually tiring of the project, Thicknesse sold the cottage to Lady Dowager Bateman for £400 and took his family to France in April 1766. There he deposited Charlotte (Elizabeth, according to Nichols, *Lit. anecdotes*, 9.261) in the convent at Ardres, where she seems to have spent the rest of her life, and had her looks ruined by smallpox. Thicknesse published an account of the French journey, entitled *Observations on the Customs and Manners of the French Nation* (1766), much of which takes issue with Smollett's hostile account of France and the French in *Travels through France and Italy* (1766). Thicknesse relates suggestively that 'an English lady of fashion who resides here [Paris], to whom I lent Smollet's Travels, says, he certainly lodged at ale-houses, and conversed with the lowest class of mechanics that frequent such houses' (Thicknesse, *Observations*, 91). Capitalizing fully on his trip, Thicknesse also published in 1768 *Useful Hints to those who Make the Tour of France*, which contains more attacks on Smollett.

On their return to Britain the Thicknesses lived briefly at Quoit, Monmouthshire, where Ann had inherited a small estate. Thicknesse erected a monument to John Wilkes on a mountain there, before they sold up and moved in 1768 to the livelier environment of Bath, 'to complete the education of his children' (Nichols, *Lit. anecdotes*, 9.262). Thicknesse bought a house in the fashionable

Crescent and hobnobbed with the leading lights of Bath society. He befriended but then antagonized the comic playwright Samuel Foote, who ridiculed Thicknesse as 'Dr Viper' in his play *The Capuchin* (1776), a rewriting of Foote's earlier *A Trip to Calais* (1775). The name stuck and was used by Thicknesse's enemies, such as James Makittrick Adair, in the years that followed. Thicknesse was also mocked as the character of Graham in Richard Graves's satirical novel *The Spiritual Quixote* (1773). In 1774 Thicknesse sold the house in the Crescent for £2000, and based the family at his cottage at Bathampton, which he extended and landscaped in eccentric style, constructing a hermit's grotto in the garden and making ornamental use of ancient skeletons dug up on the plot.

Continental visit, travel writings, and quarrels On the final collapse of his hopes of inheriting a substantial legacy from his first wife's mother (the House of Lords threw out his case in 1775), Thicknesse once again took his family (now comprising eight children) to the continent, spending most of the year 1776 abroad, and leaving his two youngest daughters (aged ten and thirteen) in a convent to complete their education. The travellers excited much attention in France and Spain, since their pet monkey, Jacko, insisted on riding postilion, dressed in a red jacket and boots. The family were made especially welcome by the monks at the hermitages and convent of Montserrat, where they also enjoyed the botanical richness of the landscape: Thicknesse later put the earl of Coventry in touch with Père Pascal, one of the monks, which led to another public quarrel once Thicknesse discovered that Père Pascal had sent the earl numerous botanical samples for which he remained unremunerated. Thicknesse produced an account of the trip in *A Year's Journey through France, and Part of Spain* (2 vols., 1777). It was a lucrative venture, securing an advance of £580 and boasting a subscription list of 430 worthies, including the duchess of Cumberland, Henry Pelham, David Garrick, and Thomas Gainsborough. Samuel Johnson pronounced it 'entertaining' (Boswell, 3.235). It is a saner and more sentimental travelogue than his earlier exercises in the genre.

Having returned to Bathampton, Thicknesse continued to work on the cottage (renamed the Hermitage of St Catherine in honour of Montserrat), such that it became a popular tourist attraction for people visiting Bath. A monument to Chatterton (the first in Britain) became the garden's centrepiece in 1784, and gained a further gruesome interest after Thicknesse buried his eldest daughter Anna underneath it, 'as she was virtuous, dutiful, and not void of some genius' (Thicknesse, *Memoirs*, 407). In 1778 Thicknesse published *The New Prose Bath Guide*, containing a wealth of practical information on household management and leisure pursuits at Bath: and in 1780 *The Valetudinarian's Bath Guide, or, The Means of Obtaining Long Life and Health*, in which he recommends not only the Bath waters and 'Wine, and Drinking to excess' (Thicknesse, *Valetudinarian*, 45), but also frequent inhalation of 'the breath of young women' (ibid., 18) as conducive to long life and good health. This recipe earned him a few lines of mockery in Thomas Mathias's satirical poem *The Pursuits of Literature* in 1794 (lines 167–70). In 1784 Thicknesse published *A Year's Journey through the Pais Bas, and the Austrian Netherlands*, describing a rather quarrel-ridden tour performed during the preceding months. Also during the early 1780s he consolidated his enmity with James Makittrick Adair, a Bath physician with whom he traded accusations of quackery; and contrived to fall out with Thomas Gainsborough after thirty years of friendship. Thicknesse has a fair claim to have 'discovered' Gainsborough in 1754, recognizing his talents as a local painter in Suffolk, and encouraging him to move to Bath, where he first became a successful portrait painter. In 1788 he published *A Sketch of the Life and Paintings of Thomas Gainsborough*, much of which describes their trivial quarrel (over an unfinished portrait and a viola da gamba).

Memoirs By this time Thicknesse had fallen out with his two sons from his second marriage, not least because they had recently inherited fortunes from the earl of Castlehaven. The younger, Philip, bought the Hermitage from his father, who later tried unscrupulously to swindle and defame him over the transaction. Young Philip also made an unfortunate marriage to a Bath milliner, a Miss Peacock. Meanwhile, his brother Lord Audley seduced and ruined a Miss Walkins at Bristol, who died in 1780. In 1782 Thicknesse published a bitter pamphlet denouncing his son entitled *Queries to Lord Audley*, and in the meandering and digressive *Memoirs and anecdotes of Philip Thicknesse, late governor of Landguard Fort, and unfortunately father to George Touchet, Baron Audley* (3 vols.; 2 vols. in 1788, vol. 3 in 1791), he more extensively berates both his 'wretched and undutiful sons' (Thicknesse, *Memoirs*, 274). Volume 3, in which his vitriol is especially concentrated, is an extremely rare book since Lord Audley and Philip bought and destroyed all the copies they could find. Thicknesse inserted the following clause into his will, and published it in volume 3 of the *Memoirs*: 'I leave my right hand, to be cut off after death, to my son, Lord Audley, and desire it may be sent him in hopes that such a sight may remind him of his duty to God, after having so long abandoned the duty he owed his Father who once affectionately loved him' (Gosse, 271).

Thicknesse's *Memoirs* attracted a great deal of attention. The *Gentleman's Magazine* commended its sensible approval of slavery (*GM*, 1788). It prompted James Gillray (perhaps encouraged by a Captain Crookshanks with whom Thicknesse had, unsurprisingly, fallen out) to execute one of his more personally offensive cartoons, 'Lieutenant-Governor Gall-Stone Inspired by Alecto, or, The Birth of Minerva'. The rather Goya-esque scene features Thicknesse surrounded by skeletons, demons, books, and manuscripts, symbolizing his obsessions, quarrels, addictions, and literary outrages. In 1790 his old antagonist Dr Adair published *Curious Facts and Anecdotes, not Contained in the Memoirs of Philip Thicknesse*, a vituperative satire on the 'duncical' (Adair, 34) activities and deranged feuds of the 'Censor General of Great Britain' (ibid., title-page). Adair alleges that Thicknesse 'sent a letter to a person and his wife with *human excrement*, insinuating that Dr Adair was the author of the epistle and the

present' (ibid., 62). The *Memoirs* themselves are disarmingly frank about Thicknesse's opportunistic and often rather calculated showdowns. In the dedication he wrote:

> if … it be true, that I quarrel with three out of four of my friends, I find that turns up more profitable than living well with them. … I know not what I should have done to make both ends meet, in my old age, if it had not been for the *repeated kindnesses* of my enemies. … I can at any time muster ten or a dozen knaves and fools, who will put an hundred pounds or two into my pocket, merely by holding them up to public scorn. (Gosse, 274)

Final journey In 1789 Thicknesse published a pamphlet entitled *Junius Discovered*, in which he claimed (erroneously) to have identified the mysterious satirist as Horne Tooke. Also in this year he and Ann moved to Sandgate, near Hythe, where they converted a barn into a house with a spectacular view of the sea. However, Ann reports that 'the daily sight of the Continent soon became *infectious*' (*Harwich Guide*; reprinted *GM*, 1809, 1015), and, nothing daunted by the early stages of the French Revolution, they made a brief trip to Paris, from where Thicknesse sent lively accounts of political developments to the *Gentleman's Magazine*. After a brief return to England, they departed more wholeheartedly in 1792, planning to reside in Italy; but Thicknesse died of a seizure in the carriage just outside Boulogne, on 19 November 1792. Ann Thicknesse was arrested as a foreigner and confined in a convent for eighteen months until after Robespierre's execution. Thicknesse was buried in the protestant cemetery at Boulogne, where Ann erected a monument to his memory. It bears a plangent epitaph celebrating his 'eminent virtues' and paying tribute to the 'memory of a man with whom she lived thirty years in perfect felicity' (Nichols, *Lit. anecdotes*, 9.288). She lived until 1824.

Assessment As a notorious public figure and as a private citizen, Thicknesse is an enigma. Capable of immuring his daughters in convents and quarrelling irreconcilably with his sons, he was also apparently adored by his three wives. Easily the most irascible individual within the arena of late eighteenth-century print culture, he was nevertheless celebrated by, among others, the *Gentleman's Magazine* (to which he was a contributor of gossipy essays) as 'a man of probity and honour, whose heart and purse were always open to the unfortunate' (*GM*, 1792), and 'a man of great sensibility' (ibid., 1789). His twentieth-century biographer observes that 'to anyone who has made a close study of Philip Thicknesse, there come occasions when he can but marvel that nobody ever shot him or bludgeoned him to death' (Gosse, 214). His publications were varied and peculiar, testifying to his opportunistic exploitation of the literary marketplace. His travel accounts (their abuse of Smollett aside) are some of his more measured publications: casual treatises on man-midwifery, deciphering, gout, and fraudulent automatons exhibited by foreigners in London represent the more bizarre range of his interests. From the early 1760s he contributed gossip paragraphs to the *St James's Chronicle* under the pen-name of A Wanderer, and to the *Gentleman's*

Magazine under the signature Polyxena. Many of his books were reviewed by the *Monthly Review* and the *Critical Review* (with which latter journal he conducted a long-standing feud), in whose pages he became something of a comic celebrity. Thicknesse may be considered one of the greatest self-publicists of the eighteenth century. A correspondent to the *Gentleman's Magazine* in 1791 describes an encounter with him at a hotel in Boulogne, and remarks:

> (when he chose) he could shew himself the Gentleman, the Philosopher, and the Man of Letters; and for eccentricity of genius few stand superior to him: as a Traveller, he will be remembered by many in Spain as one of *monkey-driving* memory. (*GM*, 1791)

KATHERINE TURNER

Sources P. Gosse, *Dr Viper: the querulous life of Philip Thicknesse* (1952) · P. Thicknesse, *Memoirs and anecdotes of Philip Thicknesse, late governor of Landguard Fort, and unfortunately father to George Touchet, Baron Audley*, 2nd edn (1790) · Nichols, *Lit. anecdotes*, 9.251–88 · *GM*, 1st ser., 58 (1788), 631–2 · *GM*, 1st ser., 59 (1789), 642 · *GM*, 1st ser., 61 (1791), 1018–19 · *GM*, 1st ser., 62 (1792), 1154 · *GM*, 1st ser., 79 (1809), 1012–16 · E. Hinchliffe, *Barthomley: in letters from a former rector to his eldest son* (1856) · T. Wright, ed., *The works of James Gillray* (1873), 116–17 · GEC, *Peerage* · P. Thicknesse, *Observations on the customs and manners of the French nation, in a series of letters, in which that nation is vindicated from the misrepresentations of some late writers* (1766) · P. Thicknesse, *Useful hints to those who make the tour of France, in a series of letters, written from that kingdom* (1768) · P. Thicknesse, *A year's journey through France, and part of Spain*, 2 vols. (1777) · P. Thicknesse, *The valetudinarian's Bath guide, or, The means of obtaining long life and health* (1780) · P. Thicknesse, *Useful hints to those who travel into France or Flanders, by the way of Dover, Margate, and Ostend* (1782) · J. M. Adair, *Curious facts and anecdotes, not contained in the memoirs of Philip Thicknesse, esq.* (1790) · J. Boswell, *The life of Samuel Johnson*, 2 vols. (1791)

Archives Hunt. L., letters to John Cooke

Likenesses T. Gainsborough, oils, *c.*1730–1735, City Art Museum, St Louis, Missouri · N. Hone, enamel miniature, 1757, NPG [*see illus.*] · J. Gillray, caricature, etching, NPG; repro. in Wright, ed., *Works of James Gillray* · J. Gillray, etching, BM, NPG; repro. in Adair, *Curious facts* · W. Hoare, chalk drawing, BM · caricature, etching, NPG · drawing (after portrait by W. Hoare), BM · portrait, repro. in Gosse, *Dr Viper*, facing p. 80 · portrait, repro. in Thicknesse, *Memoirs*, 3, prefatory plate

Thierry, Charles Philippe Hippolyte de (1793–1864), self-proclaimed sovereign chief of New Zealand, was the eldest son of Charles Antoine de Thierry and his wife, Mary Louise, the daughter of Antoine Adrien de Laville. He was born in April 1793, probably at Grave, in the Netherlands, where the family found itself having fled France. The revolution had made continued residence there impossible for his father, a French merchant mariner turned equerry at the French court. In November 1794 the family arrived in England, where his father assumed the title of baron. After a peripatetic childhood, Thierry was engaged on two diplomatic missions. He afterwards married Emily Rudge (*d.* 1856), probably on 8 May 1819 at Gloucester; they had five children. That year, on 26 May, Thierry matriculated from Magdalen Hall, Oxford, and claimed to have then transferred to Queens' College, Cambridge, but he did not graduate.

At Cambridge in 1820 Thierry met two Maori chiefs with the missionary Thomas Kendall, and then conceived the idea of founding an empire in New Zealand. Kendall returned to New Zealand and in 1822 purportedly bought 40,000 acres near Hokianga for Thierry, who based on this purchase a claim to all the land from Auckland to the north cape of the North Island. He applied to Earl Bathurst, then secretary of state, for confirmation of this grant, but was met with the response that New Zealand was not a British possession. He then tried the Dutch and French governments without success.

Proceeding to form a private company to carry out his plans, Thierry returned from France in 1826, fleeing from creditors, and set up an office in London, where he slowly acquired some little support. In 1827 he went to the United States to enlarge his sphere of action, and thence by the West Indian islands to Panama, where he expressed interest in cutting a canal. In 1835 he arrived in Tahiti. Here he issued a proclamation asserting his intention to establish his authority as sovereign chief of New Zealand by force. This threat carried some weight, since, although opposed by the British consul, he had recruited a military force in Tahiti. In 1837 he arrived in New South Wales, where he recruited about sixty colonists and sailed in the *Nimrod* to the Bay of Islands. Having summoned a meeting of chiefs at Mangunga, he explained his schemes and his title to the land he claimed; the chiefs refused to recognize his title, and showed alarm at his statement that he expected his brother to follow him with 500 persons. He also made a formal address to the white residents of New Zealand, in the course of which he announced that he came as neither an invader nor a despot, but to govern within the bounds of his own territories, and proceeded to expound a scheme of settlement and administration which showed him both communistic and paternal. He stated that he had brought with him a surgeon to attend the poor, and a tutor and governess to educate the settlers' children with his own. But, despite this solemn bravado, Thierry and his party had supplies for only two or three weeks, and his potential threat to British interest was quickly discounted. Ultimately, through the intervention of a missionary, two of the chiefs agreed to grant Thierry some land near Hokianga on condition he repudiate his larger claim. The rest of his party dispersed after rioting, and thus his grand scheme ended in failure, although he continued to send inflated accounts to France indicating success.

New Zealand was proclaimed a British colony in the treaty of Waitangi in 1840, thus thwarting Thierry's ambitions of a French colony. In 1850 he left for the California goldfields, then spent two years on the French consulate staff in Honolulu before returning to Auckland, where his wife died in 1856. By 1860 he had begun to achieve some financial success, but he died suddenly in Auckland on 8 July 1864. C. A. HARRIS, *rev.* JANE TUCKER

Sources J. D. Raeside, 'Thierry, Charles Philippe Hippolyte de', *DNZB*, vol. 1 · J. D. Raeside, *Sovereign chief: a biography of Baron de Thierry* (Christ Church, New Zealand, 1977) · P. Adams, *Fatal necessity: British intervention in New Zealand, 1830–1847* (1977) · P. Mennell, *The dictionary of Australasian biography* (1892) · G. W. Rusden, *History of New Zealand*, 1 (1883) · *New Zealander* (4 July 1864) · *New Zealander* (16 July 1864)

Archives Auckland Public Library · Mitchell L., NSW | NL NZ, Turnbull L., Buick MSS

Likenesses J. I. McDonald, watercolour, 1903, NL NZ, Turnbull L. · photograph (after portrait), NL NZ, Turnbull L.

Thimbleby [*alias* Ashby], **Richard** (1614–1680), Jesuit, was born in Lincolnshire, the fifth son of Richard Thimbleby esquire (*d.* 1623), of Irnham, Lincolnshire, and his wife, Mary, daughter of Edward Brookesby esquire, and grand-daughter of Lord Vaux of Harrowden. He entered the novice college at Watten in 1631 and was admitted to the Society of Jesus in 1632, and was professed of the four vows in 1646. After having taught philosophy and theology at Liège he was made minister and consultor at the English College, St Omer, in 1642. He was sent on the English mission about 1648, being attached to the residence of St Dominic in Lincolnshire, of which he became superior. He was rector of the house for novices at Watten from 1666 until 1672, during which time he gave spiritual exercises at the convent of the blue nuns in Paris, and acted as confessor there. He was the author of *Purgatory Surveyed* (1663), reprinted, with a preface, by Father W. H. Anderdon in 1874. It is, in part, a translation of Étienne Binet's *De l'estat heureux et malheureux des ames souffrantes du purgatoire* (1625), with his own additions. He was also the author of *Some generall observations upon dr Stillingfleet's book … with a vindication of St. Ignatius Loyola and … the Jesuits* (1672), a response to Edward Stillingfleet's *Discourse Concerning … Idolatry* (1671). He died at the English College, St Omer, on 7 January 1680.   THOMPSON COOPER, *rev.* RUTH JORDAN

Sources T. M. McCoog, *English and Welsh Jesuits, 1555–1650*, 1, Catholic RS, 74 (1994), 107 · G. Holt, *St Omers and Bruges colleges, 1593–1773: a biographical dictionary*, Catholic RS, 69 (1979), 261 · A. de Backer and others, *Bibliothèque de la Compagnie de Jésus*, new edn, 1, ed. C. Sommervogel (Brussels, 1890), 602–3 · A. Kenny, ed., *The responsa scholarum of the English College, Rome*, 2, Catholic RS, 55 (1963), 449–50 · T. H. Clancy, *English Catholic books, 1641–1700: a bibliography*, rev. edn (1996), 158 · J. Gillow and R. Trappes-Lomax, eds., *The diary of the 'blue nuns' or order of the Immaculate Conception of Our Lady, at Paris, 1658–1810*, Catholic RS, 8 (1910), 16, 18–19, 421–2 · A. Hamilton, ed., *The chronicle of the English Augustinian canonesses regular of the Lateran*, 2 vols. (1904–6), vol. 1, pp. 125, 130–33; vol. 2, pp. 149, 151–5 · G. Oliver, *Collections towards illustrating the biographies of the Scotch, English and Irish members of the Society of Jesus*, 2nd edn (1845), 47 · Gillow, *Lit. biog. hist.*, 5.540 · H. Foley, ed., *Records of the English province of the Society of Jesus*, 2 (1875), 643; 5 (1879), 597; 7 (1882–3), 768

Thimelby [*née* Aston], **Gertrude** (1617–1668), poet, was one of ten children, and the fourth daughter, of Sir Walter Aston, later Baron Aston of Forfar (1584–1639), and Gertrude Sadler. Her mother was granddaughter of Sir Ralph Sadler, treasurer-general to Edward VI, and the family divided its time between the Aston estate at Tixall, in Staffordshire, and the Sadler mansion at Standon Lordship, near Ware, Hertfordshire. The Astons were Roman Catholic, and it is suggested that under them 'Tixall was the refuge of hunted priests' (Hamilton, 1.136).

In 1645 Gertrude married Henry (*d.* 1655), third son of Sir John Thimelby. She and her husband probably lived at Corby, near Irnham, in Lincolnshire (Clifford, xxv). Henry's eldest brother, John, lived at Irnham. A report written in 1676 records that nearly 41 per cent of the population of Irnham was Catholic, and further evidences the many fines paid for recusancy by the Thimelby family from about 1575 to about 1681 (Trappes-Lomax, 164–9).

Though Thimelby's extant poems number only nineteen (by Clifford's attribution seventeen were found together in manuscript and two among loose sheets) the quality of her poems suggests a larger *œuvre*. They chronicle the happy and sad occasions of an aristocratic and close-knit Roman Catholic community; their tone is at once that of a woman who loves her family and friends and that of one who enjoys writing. Thimelby's command of the conventions of occasional poetry is obvious; more remarkable are those poems that, rather, take command of conventions with fresh and insightful results.

The role of her father in Thimelby's education as a poet is implied in her elegy for him. Lord Aston was a long-time patron and friend of Michael Drayton; noting their 'long and cordial intimacy' Clifford suggests that 'Drayton composed several of his poems at Tixall' and even credits him with the Aston family's 'poetic impulse' (Clifford, xviii–xix). While Thimelby was not a contemporary of Drayton it seems reasonable to conclude that she had access to the collections dedicated to her father. Clifford notes as well Lord Aston's apparent close friendship with William Herbert, third earl of Pembroke (ibid., xx), of a well-known literary family. Clifford further suggests that Thimelby (and her siblings) seem to have been intimate with Crashaw, Fanshaw, and Caryl and may have been known to Sandys, Waller, and Davenant (ibid., xxviii). Among the family letters collected by Clifford many refer to poems received or desired suggesting a lively circulation of manuscripts. Finally Clifford notes sixty or seventy volumes of poetry in the library at Tixall that were published during the latter part of the seventeenth century (ibid., xi).

In 1655, following the deaths of her husband and then her infant son, Thimelby entered the monastery of St Monica in Louvain, Flanders, where her sister-in-law Winifred Thimelby was prioress. The closeness of the Aston and Thimelby families, demonstrated not only by Gertrude's marriage to Henry and her brother Herbert's marriage to Henry's sister Katherine but also by surviving correspondence (edited by Arthur Clifford in the nineteenth century), suggests that Thimelby's was a retreat to religious and familial comfort. She professed in 1658 and died in Louvain in 1668. Although Latz cites a letter from Winifred Thimelby to the family in England reporting Gertrude's death, the cause is not noted (Latz, 32).

DONNA J. LONG

Sources A. Clifford, ed., *Tixall poetry* (1813) · D. L. Latz, 'Neglected writings by recusant women', in D. L. Latz, *Neglected English literature: recusant writings of the 16th–17th centuries* (Salzburg, 1997), 11–48 · T. B. Trappes-Lomax, 'The owners of Irnham Hall, co. Lincoln and their contribution to the survival of Catholicism in that county', *Lincolnshire Architectural and Archaeological Society* (1962), 167–77 · A. Hamilton, ed., *The chronicle of the English Augustinian canonesses regular of the Lateran*, 2 vols. (1904–6)
Archives Hunt. L., MS 904

Thirkell [*née* Mackail; *other married name* McInnes], **Angela Margaret** (1890–1961), novelist, was born at 27 Young Street, Kensington, London, on 30 January 1890, the eldest child of John William *Mackail (1859–1945), classical scholar and, from 1905, Oxford professor of poetry, and his wife, Margaret, only daughter of Edward Burne-*Jones. Her childhood at Pembroke Gardens, Kensington, was surrounded by writers and artists: her godfather was J. M. Barrie, and Rudyard Kipling was a cousin who encouraged her early attempts at verse. Even at an early age, she was a keen observer of distinctions of social degree: as a girl, when asked to hand round cakes at a tea-party given by a wealthy patron of her grandfather, she protested 'I'm not a servant' (Strickland, 18). She was educated at Claude Montefiore's nearby Froebel Institute, and the newly formed St Paul's Girls' School at Hammersmith, where she won prizes for literature before leaving for a finishing school in Paris. On returning to England, she met James Campbell McInnes (1874–1945), a concert singer sixteen years her senior, and the couple married six weeks later on 5 May 1911. McInnes had lived with his lover, Graham Peel, a composer of popular songs, for many years, and, when the couple's first son was born in January 1912, he was named Graham for him. A second son, who was to become the novelist Colin *MacInnes, was born in 1914, but by this time the marriage had soured: as Thirkell was later to remark, 'Marriage is not a cure for alcoholism' (Strickland, 33). When her third child, Mary, died in infancy in May 1917, she blamed the death on the physical assaults she had endured during her pregnancy. The subsequent divorce on grounds of McInnes's adultery and cruelty was widely reported in the press. On 13 December 1918 she married a young Tasmanian engineer, George Lancelot Allnutt Thirkell (1890/91–c.1940), and in January 1920 they sailed for Australia with her two sons.

While struggling with domesticity on a small income, Thirkell gave birth to a third son, Lancelot George, and a combination of depression and financial necessity encouraged her to begin writing. In June 1921 'An interview with J. M. Barrie' appeared on the women's page of the Australian weekly The Forum, beginning a steady stream of articles, short stories, and pieces for Australian journals and radio. In 1929 she sailed to England, ostensibly on holiday, taking her youngest son, Lance, with her, but failed to return. Her son Colin joined her a few weeks later, while Graham remained with his stepfather in Melbourne.

Once in England, Thirkell began earning her living as a journalist, becoming friends with the Punch journalist E. V. Lucas, and contributing regularly to the Fortnightly Review. Three Houses, a book of childhood reminiscences, appeared in 1931 to enjoy a quiet success. However, she would become known for her novels of polite manners, adapting the somewhat narrow world of Trollope's Barsetshire, where retainers were faithful yet comic, and young couples dutifully paired off in the last chapter. The first, Ankle Deep (1932), enjoyed large sales and an even greater popularity in America than England, a trend which continued throughout her career. It was followed by High Rising later that year, in which The Times detected an 'underlying impulse of "feminism"', but Mrs Thirkell's heroines have their pudeur and would shrink from such a word' (Strickland, 78). High Rising introduced Thirkell's alter ego and best-loved character, Laura Morland, a talented hack writer of improbable thrillers. In 1934 she left Barsetshire briefly to write Trooper to the Southern Cross, a disguised account of her travels around Australia, under the pseudonym Leslie Parker, and The Demon in the House, a collection of short stories parodying Coventry Patmore's Angel in the House. In the same year she published Wild Strawberries, her third Barsetshire novel, which was a predictable success on both sides of the Atlantic, prompting Punch to declare her 'the uncontested heiress of the English novel of pastoral England' (ibid., 91). The failure of O, these Men, these Men!, a sombre portrait of a woman married to a violent and unfaithful drunk, convinced Thirkell that her public wanted 'another strawberry soufflé' (ibid., 92).

Thirkell's Barsetshire novels created a cast of characters who progressed from one novel to the next, a shrewd strategy engendering a devoted readership. Until the outbreak of the Second World War, she produced saleable confections by the year, and Pomfret Towers (1938) was a particular success. She has been described by her admirers as a witty social historian, and by her critics as a snob, and the thin line dividing the two can be traced in the development of her novels. Cheerfulness Breaks in (1940) offended many by what seemed a sneering portrait of working-class evacuee children, and the New Statesman hoped that, come the revolution, 'the tweeded dummies of this pygmy Barsetshire will be the first to burn' (Strickland, 131). More disturbingly, Cheerfulness was initially not accepted by Thirkell's American publisher, who found it antisemitic. She made reluctant revisions, protesting apparently without irony that 'my Jewish characters are no more representative of Jews than Fagin' (ibid., 130).

After the war, Thirkell's light wit further soured as her high-tory sensibilities were outraged by the Attlee administration and the foundation of the welfare state. Novels such as Private Enterprise (1946) emphasized the necessity of preserving the old social order, and Thirkell's political opinions were with increasing clumsiness placed in the mouths of her characters. She was with difficulty persuaded to delete a potentially libellous lampoon of the chancellor of the exchequer, Sir Stafford Cripps, from Love amongst the Ruins (1948). Though the Conservatives returned to power in 1951, celebrated in Happy Returns (1952), Thirkell failed to regain the popularity she had enjoyed during the thirties.

She died at Birtley House, Bramley, near Guildford, of aplastic anaemia on 29 January 1961, a day before her seventy-first birthday, and was buried at Rottingdean, Sussex, beside her Burne-Jones grandparents. Her last novel, Three Score and Ten (1961), was completed by C. A. Lejeune. Two omnibus collections of her novels appeared in 1966 and 1967, and an Angela Thirkell Society continues to pay her tribute.   KATHERINE MULLIN

Sources M. Strickland, Angela Thirkell: portrait of a lady novelist (1977) • A. Thirkell, An autobiographical sketch (1956) • T. Gould, Inside outsider: the life and times of Colin McInnes (1993) • V. Kenny, 'A refined look at Australia: Angela Thirkell as trooper to the southern cross', *Aspects of Australian fiction*, ed. A. Brissenden (1990), 97–112 • L. R. Collins, *English country life in the Barsetshire Novels of Angela Thirkell* (1994) • *The Times* (30 Jan 1961) • J. Shattock, *The Oxford guide to British women writers* (1993) • Blain, Clements & Grundy, *Feminist comp.* • C. Buck, *Bloomsbury guide to women's literature* (1993) • J. Todd, ed., *Dictionary of British women writers* (1989) • P. Schlueter and J. Schlueter, eds., *An encyclopedia of British women writers* (1988) • *DNB* • *CGPLA Eng. & Wales* (1961) • b. cert. • m. certs. • d. cert.

Archives U. Leeds, Brotherton L., corresp. and papers incl. literary MSS | BL, letters to Ian Robertson, Add. MS 69036 • Bodl. Oxf., letters to Violet Milner • Royal Society of Literature, London, letters to the Royal Society of Literature

Likenesses J. Collier, oils, 1912, National Gallery of Victoria, Melbourne, Australia • W. Stoneman, photograph, 1957, NPG • H. Coster, photographs, NPG • oils, repro. in Strickland, *Angela Thirkell*, frontispiece

Wealth at death £74,656: probate, 13 March 1961, *CGPLA Eng. & Wales*

Thirkleby [Thurkilbi], **Roger of** (*d.* 1260), justice, was the son and heir of Thomas of Thirkleby, a man of no great importance who took his name from a hamlet of that name, in the parish of Kirby Grindalythe in the East Riding of Yorkshire. It is not clear how Roger came to work in the courts, only that by Michaelmas term 1230 he was a clerk of the bench, and by the end of 1231 he was the clerk of the bench to justice William of Raleigh. A clerk called Roger who worked for William of York was probably Roger of Whitchester rather than Roger of Thirkleby, but it is nevertheless a possibility that Thirkleby owed his introduction to the royal service to William, a fellow Yorkshireman. In 1235 or 1236 he renounced his clerical orders and married Letice, daughter of Peter of Edgefield of Norfolk, and widow of William de Roscelin.

Thirkleby apparently remained as a clerk until Trinity term 1242, when he was promoted to justice. However, he was mentioned as a justice in a single final concord of the previous term, and had already served as an eyre justice, on the circuit of William of York, and as a puisne justice on eyres held between January 1240 and November 1241, after which he undertook gaol deliveries in Norfolk and Suffolk before receiving his promotion. He continued as a puisne bench justice until 1249, although he spent much of his time away on eyre in the counties. He was chief justice on three eyres in the south-west in 1243 and 1244, and then from 1245 to 1252 he and his colleague Henry of Bath were the leading eyre justices. He led groups of justices on the brief circuit of 1245, the major country-wide visitation of 1246 to 1249, and a brief circuit of 1251 to 1252, before withdrawing from eyres to concentrate on work at the bench. He had succeeded Bath as senior justice there early in Michaelmas term 1249, remaining until Trinity 1251, except for a visit to the continent with Richard, earl of Cornwall, and others in Hilary term 1250, after which he went on eyre. He returned to the bench, again as senior justice, in Michaelmas term 1252, receiving a salary of 100 marks p.a. In Hilary 1256, however, he again returned to eyres to complete work on a lengthy country-wide circuit which had been begun in 1252, taking over a group of justices earlier led by Simon of Wauton. The eyres were

brought to an end in 1258, first by famine and then by political uncertainty. Thirkleby returned as senior justice of the bench in Michaelmas term 1258, remaining in that office until his death, which occurred shortly before 13 June 1260, when his name suddenly disappeared from the feet of fines (though the *Flores historiarum* incorrectly says that he lived until about 24 August). In all he took part in fifty-one eyres, in thirty-eight of them as chief justice. Many of his eyre rolls have survived, including thirteen from the eyres of 1246 to 1249, the most impressive group of eyre rolls to survive for any justice up to that time. His service as a justice of assize is also reflected in two assize rolls of his, covering the years from 1249 to 1260, which have likewise survived, as have a number of his bench rolls. His clerk, by 1257, was Robert of Beverley, from his native East Riding of Yorkshire.

It is difficult to assess the work and influence of a justice living at a time from which no law reports survive, but it is clear from contemporary opinions and the length of his career that Thirkleby was a great judge. The death of Matthew Paris a year earlier than Thirkleby has denied us his obituary of a man with whom he was personally acquainted, but the author of the *Flores historiarum* considered him to be second to none in the kingdom in justice and the laws of the land. His judgements are mentioned in a number of thirteenth-century treatises, including the *Summa magna* attributed to Ralph Hengham. Paris records Thirkleby's disapproval of the introduction of a particular legal principle from the church courts into the lay civil courts, likening it to the pollution of a stream with a poison. He is not known to have taken a significant part in politics, although in 1252 a speech reported by Paris shows his resentment of the power of the Poitevin faction at court, and he was able to work with the reformers who were in power after 1258, since in 1259 he was one of those appointed to sell the king's wardships and choose sheriffs.

As a man of property Thirkleby's first recorded action was in 1233, when he secured exemption from suit of local courts and service on juries in respect of his lands in Thirkleby, Kirby Grindalythe, Newton, and Swaythorpe in the East Riding of Yorkshire. In the course of his career he added to his ancestral estates in the county, mainly in the area of the upper Derwent valley and the wolds, in such places as Wintringham, North Duffield, Knapton, East Heslerton, Gilling, Helperthorpe, Rudston, Weaverthorpe, Lowthorpe, East Lutton, and Sledmere, and also at Paull, Ottringham, and Keyingham in Holderness. In 1247 and 1250 he received grants of free warren over his demesnes in Thirkleby, Helperthorpe, and Duffield, and in 1253 the grant of a weekly market in Driffield. Thirkleby's marriage gave him life interests in Norfolk to which he added by lease and purchase, acquiring property in Erpingham, Pulham St Mary, Caister St Edmunds, Tuttington, Mattishall, Bodham, and Heckingham. Like his close colleague Henry of Bath, he also came to have interests in the Holland area of Lincolnshire, then being reclaimed from the fens, at Gedney, Fleet, Whaplode, Sutton, and Holbeach; his holdings included much marsh land. Among minor interests was property in Leicestershire, at Hallaton, and he had town houses in Bury St Edmunds and Westminster. The heir of Thirkleby's wife was Thomas de Roscelin, the son of her first marriage; she and Roger seem to have had no surviving children, since his ultimate heir was his brother Thomas who, although he held no administrative office, often witnessed royal charters and was therefore probably a royal counsellor. As his executors Thirkleby appointed Simon, abbot of Langley, Thomas of Heslerton, and Master Roger of Heslerton.

DAVID CROOK

Sources *Curia regis rolls preserved in the Public Record Office* (1922–), vol. 16 · C. A. F. Meekings, 'Martin Pateshull and William Raleigh', *BIHR*, 26 (1953), 157–80 · C. A. F. Meekings, *King's bench justices, 1239–58* [forthcoming] · D. Crook, *Records of the general eyre*, Public Record Office Handbooks, 20 (1982) · Paris, *Chron.*, vol. 5 · *Ann. mon.*, vol. 1 · H. R. Luard, ed., *Flores historiarum*, 3 vols., Rolls Series, 95 (1890) · F. Blomefield and C. Parkin, *An essay towards a topographical history of the county of Norfolk*, [2nd edn], 11 vols. (1805–10) · Chancery records · court of common pleas, feet of fines, PRO, CP 25/1 · plea rolls, PRO, KB 26, JUST 1
Wealth at death substantial landed estate

Thirlby, Styan (*bap.* 1691, *d.* 1753), textual critic and theologian, was baptized on 7 January 1691 at St Margaret's, Leicester, the son of Thomas Thirlby (*d.* 1701), vicar of St Margaret's, Leicester, and his wife, Mary (1663–1723), eldest daughter of Henry Styan of Kirby Frith. He was educated at the Leicester Free School, where, according to the head usher, the Revd John Kilby, 'his self-conceit was censured as very offensive.—He thought he knew more than all the school' (Nichols, *Lit. anecdotes*, 4.264). He was admitted to Jesus College, Cambridge, as a sizar on 10 April 1707 and graduated BA in 1710/11.

In 1710 Thirlby engaged in controversy, publishing *The University of Cambridge vindicated from the imputation of disloyalty … also, from the malicious and foul aspersions of Dr. B—ly, late master of Trinity College*, a 'violent and intemperate pamphlet' in which he 'abuses Bentley without measure or decency' (Monk, 1.289). This was followed by involvement in the renewed Arian controversy in *An Answer to Mr. Whiston's Seventeen Suspicions Concerning Athanasius* (1712), a work generally considered (according to a correspondent of Dr Charles Ashton, the master of Jesus College) to be beyond the powers of such a young man in its knowledge of ecclesiastical history and of the church fathers, and leading Ashton's correspondent ('A. M.') to declare Thirlby 'the greatest Young Man that has appeard these many years' (Smith, 222). On 16 October 1712 he was elected to a fellowship at Jesus, taking his MA in 1714.

Thirlby settled into the life of a fellow, and

> From his mental abilities no small degree of future eminence was presaged; but the fond hopes of his friends were unfortunately defeated, by a temper which was naturally indolent and quarrelsome, and by an unhappy addiction to drinking … being sometimes in a state of intoxication for five or six weeks together. (Nichols, *Lit. anecdotes*, 4.264, 267)

He did, however, continue his studies in divinity and published what was to be his *magnum opus*, a folio edition of Saint Justin Martyr's *Apologiae duae et dialogus cum Tryphone*

Judaeo cum notis et emendationibus (1722), with the Greek text and a Latin translation in parallel columns. In his preface he again attacks Bentley 'in so extravagant a style that he makes the reader, at the very outset of his work, doubt whether the editor was in a sane mind' (Monk, 2.167). His performance cost him the support of Ashton.

From study of divinity Thirlby proceeded to medicine, becoming (in Johnson's phrase) 'a nominal physician'; he also lived briefly with the duke of Chandos, serving as librarian, but 'is reported to have affected a perverse and insolent independence, so as capriciously to refuse his company when it was desired' (Nichols, *Lit. anecdotes*, 4.266). He then took up civil law, obtaining an LLD in 1728, and gave sporadic lectures, having Sir Edward Walpole as one of his students. This acquaintance led to a lifelong friendship and his moving to London, living in Walpole's house for a period. In May 1741 Walpole also procured him a sinecure as king's waiter in the Port of London custom house, worth about £100 a year, after which he lived in lodgings.

From his undergraduate years Thirlby was interested in the text of Shakespeare. He bought editions of Shakespeare from Nicholas Rowe (1709) to William Warburton (1747), making extensive marginalia, most of which are acute, some intemperate. Warburton's reference in his preface to *Shakespear* (1747) to (unpublished) letters from Pope urging him to edit Shakespeare (1.xix n.) produced: 'You might as well have said See my arse in a band box' (Folger Shakespeare Library, PR 2752 1747a c. 2). Theobald visited him in Cambridge early in 1729; their conversation included speculation about Shakespeare's 'foul papers' being manuscript copy for certain plays, as appears from Theobald's recognition, after Thirlby, that a passage in *Love's Labour's Lost* (V. ii. 817–22) is Shakespeare's first draft of matter that receives its final version later in the scene (ll. 837–54) (Seary, 144). Thirlby also gave Theobald 'the Liberty of collating his Copy of *Shakespeare*, mark'd thro' in the Margin with his own Manuscript References and accurate Observations' (*Works of William Shakespeare*, ed. Theobald, 1.lxv) and sent him (7 May 1729) a list of seventy proposed emendations, not all of which were accepted (Folger, MS W.b. 74, fols. 65r–67v). In his edition, Theobald has fifty-two references to Thirlby. Johnson also had access to Thirlby's marginalia in Warburton's *Shakespear* (1747), when preparing his *Shakespeare* (1765), and has forty-two citations. Thirlby never published his own projected edition of Shakespeare 'and consequently exerted only a dislocated subterranean influence upon the editorial tradition, as his orphaned conjectures were adopted (often without acknowledgement) by others' (Taylor, 54).

Thirlby died unmarried in London on 19 December 1753, leaving a simple will (11 January 1751): 'I give all I have to the Honble M^r. Edwd. Walpole to do all I can to enable him to pay himself what I owe him' (PRO, PROB 11/807). Probably his legacy consisted of books.

PETER SEARY

Sources Nichols, *Lit. anecdotes*, 4.264–71 · parish register, Leicester, St Margaret, 7 Jan 1691, Leics. RO [baptism] · J. Nichols, *The history and antiquities of the county of Leicester*, 4 (1807–11), 239, 614 · admissions register, Jesus College, Cambridge, College Archives,

COL.1.2 • J. R. Tanner, ed., *Historical register of the University of Cambridge … to the year 1910* (1917) • J. H. Monk, *The life of Richard Bentley, DD*, 2nd edn, 2 vols. (1833) • S. Thirlby, letter to L. Theobald with list of proposed emendations, 7 May 1729, Folger, W.b. 74, fols. 65r–67v • *The works of William Shakespeare*, ed. L. Theobald, 7 vols. (1733) [annotated copy with marginalia by S. Thirlby, Folger, PR 2752 1733 c.2] • *The works of Shakespear*, ed. W. Warburton and A. Pope, 8 vols. (1747) [annotated copy with marginalia by S. Thirlby, Folger, PR 2752 1747a c.2] • C. Spencer and J. W. Velz, 'Styan Thirlby: a forgotten "editor" of Shakespeare', *Shakespeare Studies*, 6 (1972), 327–33 • J. H. Smith, 'Styan Thirlby's Shakespearean commentaries: a corrective analysis', *Shakespeare Studies*, 11 (1978), 219–41 • 'A. M.', author of a letter to Charles Ashton, Master of Jesus College, March 1711/March 1712, Jesus College Archives [excerpt printed by J. H. Smith, p. 222] • A. Sherbo, *The birth of Shakespeare studies: commentators from Rowe (1709) to Boswell-Malone (1821)* (1986) • *The works of Shakespeare … with notes*, ed. L. Theobald, 7 vols. (1733) • *The works of Shakespeare … the genuine text*, ed. W. Warburton and A. Pope, 8 vols. (1747) • P. Seary, *Lewis Theobald and the editing of Shakespeare* (1990) • G. Taylor, 'General introduction', in S. Wells, G. Taylor, J. Jowett, and W. Montgomery, *William Shakespeare: a textual companion* (1987) • will, PRO, PROB 11/807

Wealth at death most valuable legacy was library: will, PRO, PROB 11/807

Thirlby, Thomas (*c*.1500–1570), bishop of Westminster and of Ely, was born in Cambridge where his father, John (*d*. 1539), was town clerk. His mother, Joan (*d*. 1557), was the daughter of William Campion of London. Thomas was the first of their three children, probably born a few years earlier than 1506 as claimed in his memorial at Lambeth, since by 1521 he had graduated BCL from Trinity Hall, Cambridge. As an undergraduate there he had upset his upstairs neighbour, the future martyr Thomas Bilney, by the too-frequent playing of his recorder. These musical interludes did not impede his studies, as he was duly elected a fellow of his college, and proceeded to doctorates in civil and canon law in 1528 and 1530.

Early employments Anne Boleyn and her family were said to have been among Thirlby's early patrons, though evidence for this is lacking. The royal physician William Butts was certainly a helpful friend; but the obvious agent of Thirlby's advancement was Stephen Gardiner, the king's secretary and the master of Trinity Hall. From 1528–9 Thirlby was much engaged in legal business on behalf of Cambridge University; in 1530/31 he was its auditor. In 1532 he occurs as official to the archdeacon of Ely, and in the same year he received his first benefice, the rectory of Ribchester, Lancashire. By 1533 he had come to Thomas Cromwell's notice, and was regarded as sympathetic to Henry VIII's plans for a change of wife. The king made Thirlby his chaplain, probably at the instance of Thomas Cranmer (who had known Thirlby since Cambridge, and whose evangelical opinions Thirlby at this time shared).

In May 1533 Thirlby was at court when the news came from Dunstable that Cranmer had put the king and queen asunder. Thirlby was then attached to the embassy sent to France to explain the king's matrimonial adjustment (28 May – 1 September). On his return he was recommended by Cromwell for further preferment; by 24 May 1534 (when Cranmer so addressed him) he was archdeacon of Ely. The archbishop wrote scornfully of Thirlby's 'ambitious mind' in some administrative concern (*Miscellaneous Writings*, 292) but, according to the later testimony of Ralph Morice, 'there was no man lyvyng could more frendelie esteme any man of hymself' as did Cranmer of Thirlby, to whom his generosity was proverbial (Ellis, 26). Also in 1534 Thirlby was made provost of St Edmund's College, Salisbury. In February 1535 he became a member of Doctors' Commons, and practised in the court of arches. On 12 June 1537 he was collated to the prebend of Yetminster Prima in Salisbury Cathedral. During 1537, as a member of the council of the north, he was closely associated with the duke of Norfolk in restoring order after the Pilgrimage of Grace; he was present at the final examination of the rebel leader, Robert Aske. He was back at court in time to attend the baptism of the future Edward VI on 15 October. Five days later he was granted a canonry in the royal free chapel of St Stephen in Westminster.

During 1537 Thirlby had been among those who advised on the drafting of the doctrinal statement called the Bishops' Book. Early in the following year he was short-listed for further diplomatic service. From April to August 1538, with Gardiner and Sir Francis Bryan, he was engaged in a mission to France to promote alliance through marriage treaties (particularly between Henry VIII's daughter Mary and the duc d'Orléans). Thirlby was embarrassed by his poor grasp of French, especially as spoken by François I. The embassy was totally eclipsed by a Franco-imperial concordat to which England was not a party. Thirlby and his colleagues responded sluggishly to their recall, though Gardiner would bear the brunt of Henry's displeasure. Returning through Kent in September Thirlby adroitly fielded questions about the recent destruction of Thomas Becket's shrine. On 1 October he was appointed to a heresy commission. On 23 December 1539 he was made master of St Thomas's Hospital, Southwark, which he was obliged to surrender to the crown in the following month.

Bishop and ambassador In July 1540 Thirlby was prolocutor of the lower house of the convocation of Canterbury when the king's marriage to Anne of Cleves was annulled. On this occasion he was already called 'elect' of Westminster, though it was not until 17 December following that the new diocese of Westminster was created and, by the same patent, Thirlby was appointed its bishop. He had Middlesex for his territory and Westminster Abbey for his cathedral; he was consecrated on 19 December in Henry VII's chapel there. He took his seat in the House of Lords on 16 January 1541. As the first and only bishop of Westminster Thirlby was rarely at home in the former abbot's house (now the deanery). He never conducted a visitation, and was not present in the abbey for the two main state occasions held there when it was a cathedral—the coronation of Edward VI and that king's funeral. In the absence of its bishop the diocese functioned well enough; but the administration was in part handled by those who also served the parent diocese of London, by which Westminster was easily reabsorbed at the end of Thirlby's episcopate.

By April 1541, if not before, Thirlby was dean of the Chapel Royal, a post he retained into Mary's reign. From

June 1542 he occurs as a privy councillor. These promotions gave him status to head a mission, and he was duly sent to the emperor Charles V, then in northern Spain, as Henry VIII's mind turned again towards alliance against France. This embassy, for which Thirlby was paid from 30 June to 10 October, laid the foundations for the treaty of the following year, and the war with France that resulted. In 1543 he was appointed to negotiate a marriage between Prince Edward and Mary, queen of Scots, a union beyond even Thirlby's skill to accomplish. He played a leading part in shaping the King's Book of *Necessary Doctrine* in 1543. In July 1544 he was appointed a counsellor of state during the king's absence in the French war. In 1545 Thirlby, with Sir William Petre and others, represented England at the imperial Diet of Bourbourg; when these meetings ended in July, Thirlby remained as resident ambassador to the imperial court. For the next three years he followed Charles V through the climacteric of his reign, and was present at the battlefield of Mühlberg (24 April 1547) where the advance of protestantism was decisively checked.

The reign of Edward VI Meanwhile Henry VIII had died in January, pointedly excluding Thirlby and Gardiner from the council he intended to govern in Edward VI's minority. It was expected that Thirlby would be replaced as ambassador by Sir John Mason in April 1547, but he served a further year. On 14 April 1548 Edward formally notified the emperor that Thirlby had been recalled, and that Sir Philip Hoby would succeed him. Charles, writing from Augsburg on 8 June, replied that the returning ambassador had 'always acted with great modesty and discretion in the discharge of his duty' (*CSP Spain*, 1547–9, 270–71). Hoby felt that Thirlby's 'politique and wise sorte for serche of intelligence' had been 'so well and wittely guided' that he was himself unworthy to take his place (BL, Harley MS 523, fols. 108–108v).

Thirlby was home in time to attend discussions on liturgical reform held at Chertsey in September 1548. At the debate in the Lords in December he took exception to changes made to the eucharistic policy document agreed at Chertsey, from which he found omitted all mention of 'adoration' and 'oblation'. He was in turn criticized by Protector Somerset for breaking the common front to which the latter considered the bishops were committed. Somerset spoke to the king of his disappointment at Thirlby's conservatism, to which the young monarch allegedly replied: 'I expected … nothing else but that he, who had been so long time with the emperor as ambassador, should smell of the *Interim*' (Robinson, *Original Letters*, 2.646). Thirlby voted against the third reading of the Uniformity Bill on 15 January 1549, though he complied with the law as subsequently enacted. On 12 April he was again named to a heresy commission.

In February 1550 the privy council, now led by Warwick, decided the diocese of Westminster should be dissolved. This was chiefly to allow more scope for the reformist Nicholas Ridley, who had been designated bishop of London. Thirlby was therefore required to surrender his see on 30 March. On 1 April Ridley became bishop of the reunited metropolitan diocese, while Thirlby was translated to Norwich. He was enthroned on 28 April; after that he rarely if ever entered his diocese. He was by no means in disgrace, for he was regularly employed in government business in the remaining years of Edward's reign. On 18 January 1551 he was appointed to a further heresy commission, in May he was sent to negotiate with the Scots, and during 1552 he was at least nominally involved in several of the financial commissions.

Councillor of Queen Mary On 2 April 1553 Thirlby was sent back to Brussels as resident. Audience with the emperor was delayed until early June, when Charles was reported to be frail but alert. The failing health of Thirlby's own sovereign was by this time of more concern; news of Edward's death reached Brussels on 11 July. Queen Mary retained Thirlby in post, but brought him back to attend her first parliament. On 25 October he was admitted to the privy council, and was expected to belong to its innermost circle. He returned to Brussels on 29 December, and in January 1554 he received Cardinal Pole there on his way to England as legate. Thirlby had his final audience with Charles V on 1 May, returning to England to assist at the queen's marriage with the emperor's son Philip in Winchester Cathedral on 25 July. The queen had given Thirlby the superior see of Ely, to which he was elected on 30 July, and where he was enthroned by proxy on 24 September. His appointment was ratified by papal provision on 21 June 1555, the bull being among those that Thirlby himself, along with Viscount Montagu and Sir Edward Carne, went to Rome to receive. This embassy left Calais on 27 February and, after a meeting with Henri II, proceeded south in a leisurely way, learning of the death of two successive popes and finding time to inspect a giant tortoise at Ferrara. The ambassadors were eventually received by Paul IV on 8 June, and had a final audience on the 16th. Thirlby received a gold cross from the pope; the more substantial achievement was papal confirmation of the deal that Pole had made with parliament in the previous December, the necessary financial preconditions to the reunion with Rome. Carne remained in Rome as resident; Montagu and Thirlby returned by Venice, and were back in London on 24 August.

In his absence Thirlby had been thought likely to succeed the earl of Bedford as lord privy seal. On his return he was promoted to the 'select' group of eight privy councillors who had particular responsibility to liaise with the now absent King Philip. In October he took temporary custody of the great seal when Gardiner became ill. In November, following Gardiner's death, the queen proposed Thirlby as 'most worthy' to become lord chancellor in his place (*CSP Venice*, 1555–6, 257). Philip, however, preferred Paget, and Archbishop Heath emerged as compromise candidate. It was the only time Thirlby came close to the high political office for which he would seem to have been so admirably qualified. A less welcome prominence fell to him when he was required to perform the ritual degradation of Cranmer at Oxford on 14 February 1556. There is no reason to doubt that his execution of this duty was reluctant and tearful.

It was expected that Thirlby would return to Brussels later in 1556; in fact he remained in England and was engaged in occasional public duties. He never resided in his diocese of Ely, relying on the capable chancellor, John Fuller, who had previously served him at Norwich. But he continued to be employed as a diplomat, his final mission coming when England sought to conclude the war with France to which the queen's marriage had led. Thirlby was (with the earl of Arundel and Dr Nicholas Wotton) employed in the negotiations at Cercamp from October 1558; from there they moved to Brussels and then to Cateau Cambrésis, where the treaty was concluded on 3 April 1559. Thirlby had thus been abroad yet again when his monarch died. Queen Elizabeth had issued a new commission to Thirlby and his colleagues five days after her accession, renewed in January 1559.

Deprivation and captivity Beyond the completion of this work Thirlby felt unable to adapt his conscience once more to serve a new regime. He returned to the Lords in April 1559 when parliament was already in session. He was reckoned the keenest opponent of the reformist cause. He voted against the Uniformity Bill, and refused the oath of supremacy which the subsequent legislation required. On or by 5 July he and the other dissenting bishops were deprived of their sees. Their open hostility to the religious settlement, and their refusal to attend prayer book services, eventually provoked harsher treatment. On 3 June 1560 Thirlby was taken to the Tower of London; in his absence there he was excommunicated on 25 February 1561. In September he and the other prominent Catholic prisoners were permitted to associate in specified groups of four. In September 1563, when plague made London unhealthy even for state prisoners, Thirlby and the former secretary John Boxall were released to house arrest in Archbishop Parker's custody. Parker's immediate concern was the risk of infection; but after a period of quarantine Thirlby (with his manservant and boy) joined the archbishop's household. In this honourable and not uncongenial captivity Thirlby passed his final years. He died at Lambeth Palace on 26 August 1570 and was buried two days later in the parish church there. His coffin was opened in 1783 and the body was exhibited in a good state of preservation.

Thirlby was of the last generation of episcopal diplomats; to his competence in his lay capacity (once he had mastered the French language) there are many testimonies. His employments abroad left him little opportunity to influence ecclesiastical affairs at home. His absence undoubtedly contributed to the failure of Westminster to survive as a diocese; it is unfortunate that Thirlby's name should principally be linked to that abortive scheme.

C. S. KNIGHTON

Sources Venn, *Alum. Cant.*, 1/4.220 • Cooper, *Ath. Cantab.*, 1.287–90 • *Fasti Angl., 1300–1541*, [Salisbury], 101 • *Fasti Angl., 1300–1541*, [Monastic cathedrals], 19 • *Fasti Angl., 1541–1857*, [Ely], 7, 37, 69 • *LP Henry VIII*, vols. 7, 12–21 • *CSP Venice, 1534–58* • *CSP Spain, 1538–58* • *CSP for., 1547–59* • *APC, 1542–58* • G. M. Bell, *A handlist of British diplomatic representatives, 1509–1688*, Royal Historical Society Guides and Handbooks, 16 (1990), 20, 50–52, 54, 77, 79, 164, 180, 289 • T. F. Shirley, *Thomas Thirlby: Tudor bishop* (1964) • H. Ellis, ed., *Original letters of eminent literary men of the sixteenth, seventeenth, and eighteenth centuries*, CS, 23 (1843), 25–6 • H. Robinson, ed. and trans., *The Zurich letters, comprising the correspondence of several English bishops and others with some of the Helvetian reformers, during the early part of the reign of Queen Elizabeth*, 1, Parker Society, 7 (1842), 20 • H. Robinson, ed. and trans., *Original letters relative to the English Reformation*, 1 vol. in 2, Parker Society, [26] (1846–7), 185, 430–31, 645, 646 • *Miscellaneous writings and letters of Thomas Cranmer*, ed. J. E. Cox, Parker Society, [18] (1846), 115n., 224, 244, 246, 292–3 • *Correspondence of Matthew Parker*, ed. J. Bruce and T. T. Perowne, Parker Society, 42 (1853), 122, 192–5, 203, 215, 217 • D. MacCulloch, *Thomas Cranmer: a life* (1996), 136, 396, 398, 458, 521, 591–2 • BL, Harley MS 523, fols. 108–108v • BL, Add. MS 5825, p. 36 • P. Yorke [earl of Hardwicke], ed., *Miscellaneous state papers, 1501–1726*, 2 vols. (1778), vol. 1, pp. 62–102 • F. Godwin, *A catalogue of the bishops of England, since the first planting of Christian religion in this island* (1601), 225–6 • *The diary of Henry Machyn, citizen and merchant-taylor of London, from AD 1550 to AD 1563*, ed. J. G. Nichols, CS, 42 (1848), 75, 93, 102–3, 194, 203, 237, 249 • administration of wills, PRO, PROB 6/2, fol. 51

Archives City Westm. AC, act book as bishop of Westminster | CUL, episcopal records, Ely diocesan records, G/1/8, fols. 23–42v, 46–50v • GL, episcopal registers, Westminster, MS 9531/12, part 1, fols. 242–275 • Norfolk RO, episcopal registers, Norwich, Reg. /12/18, fols. 1–5v, 1–82 [sic]

Likenesses oils, Trinity Hall, Cambridge

Wealth at death see administration, PRO, PROB 6/2, fol. 51

Thirlwall, (Newell) Connop (1797–1875), historian and bishop of St David's, born in Mile End Old Town, London, on 11 February 1797, was the third son of the Revd Thomas Thirlwall, and his wife, Susannah Connop (d. 1842) of Mile End, the widow of an apothecary.

The father, **Thomas Thirlwall** (d. 1827), Church of England clergyman and author, was the son of Thomas Thirlwall (d. 1808), vicar of Cottingham, near Hull, who claimed descent from the barons of Thirlwall Castle, Northumberland. The younger Thomas, after holding some small benefices in London, was presented in 1814 to the rectory of Bower's Gifford in Essex, where he died on 17 March 1827. He was a man of fervent piety, and the author of several published works, including *Diatessaron, seu, Integra historia domini nostri Jesu Christi, ex quatuor evangeliis confecta* (1802).

Education and early career Connop Thirlwall showed such precocity that when he was only eleven years of age his father published a volume of his compositions called *Primitiae*, a work in after years so odious to the author that he destroyed every copy that he could obtain. The preface by his father says that

> at a very early period he read English so well that he was taught Latin at three years of age, and at four read Greek with an ease and fluency which astonished all who heard him. His talent for composition appeared at the age of seven.

He briefly attended Bancroft's School and from 1810 to 1813 was a day scholar at Charterhouse, where he was friendly with George Waddington, George Grote, and J. C. Hare. After leaving school he seems to have worked alone for a year, entering Trinity College, Cambridge, as a pensioner in October 1814.

While an undergraduate Thirlwall found time to learn French and Italian, and, besides acquiring a considerable reputation as a speaker at the union, was secretary of the society when the debate was stopped by the entrance of

(Newell) **Connop Thirlwall** (1797–1875), by Herbert Watkins, 1858

the proctors (24 March 1817), who, by the vice-chancellor's command, ordered the members to disperse and on no account to resume their discussions. A few years later, when Thirlwall spoke at the Speculative Society, a debating society in London, John Stuart Mill recorded that he was the best speaker he had heard up to that time, and that he had not subsequently heard any one whom he could place above him (Mill, 125). In 1815 he obtained the Bell and Craven scholarships, and in 1816 was elected scholar of his own college. There he was especially friendly with, and influenced by, William Whewell. In 1818 he graduated BA. He was twenty-second senior optime in the mathematical tripos, and also obtained the first chancellor's medal for proficiency in classics. In October of the same year he was elected fellow of his college.

Thirlwall was now able to realize what he called 'the most enchanting of my daydreams' (Stokes, 32), and spent several months on the continent. The winter of 1818–19 was passed in Rome, where he formed a close friendship with Bunsen, then secretary to the Prussian legation, at the head of which was Niebuhr; a meeting between Thirlwall and the historian cannot be definitely established.

Thirlwall had at this time developed a dislike for the profession of a clergyman and, pressured by his family, he entered Lincoln's Inn in February 1820 in pupillage with Basevi, Disraeli's uncle. He was called to the bar in the summer of 1825 and practised for two years on the home circuit. Much of his success in later life may be traced to his legal training; but the work was always distasteful to him, though relieved by foreign tours, by intellectual society, and by a return to more congenial studies whenever

he had a moment to spare. In 1824 he translated two tales by Tieck, and began his work on Schleiermacher's critical essay on St Luke's gospel. Both these were published (anonymously) in the following year, the second with a critical introduction, remarkable not only for thoroughness, but for acquaintance with modern German theology, then a field of research virtually untrodden by English students. In October 1827 Thirlwall abandoned law and returned to Cambridge. The prospect of the loss of his fellowship at Trinity College, which would have expired in 1828, probably determined the precise moment for taking a step which he had long meditated. He was ordained deacon before the end of 1827, and priest in 1828; his motivation seems to have been the opportunity for literary study.

At Cambridge Thirlwall at once undertook his full share of college and university work. Between 1827 and 1832 he held the college offices of junior bursar, junior dean, and head lecturer; in 1828, 1829, 1832, and 1834 he examined for the classical tripos. Thirlwall attracted around him a dazzling group of young men; they formed the Cambridge Conversazione Society, which was immediately dubbed 'the Apostles' (it had twelve members). In 1828 the first volume of the translation of Niebuhr's history of Rome appeared, the joint work of himself and Julius Charles Hare. This was attacked in the *Quarterly Review* (January 1829), and Thirlwall contributed to Hare's elaborate reply a brief postscript which is worthy of his best days as a controversialist. In 1831 the publication of *The Philological Museum* was started with the object of promoting 'the knowledge and the love of ancient literature'. Hare and Thirlwall were the editors, and the latter contributed to it several masterly essays. It ceased in 1833. In 1829 Thirlwall held for a short time the vicarage of Over, and in 1832, when Hare left college, he was appointed assistant tutor. His lectures were as thorough and systematic as Hare's had been desultory.

In 1834 Thirlwall's connection with the educational staff of Trinity College was rudely severed when—true to his liberalism—he supported the admission of dissenters to Cambridge degrees. He replied to a pamphlet by T. Turton in a *Letter on the Admission of Dissenters to Academical Degrees*; it argued that 'Cambridge colleges are not theological seminaries' or even 'schools of religious instruction' and he attacked college divinity lectures and compulsory chapel. This publication is dated 21 May 1834, and five days later Christopher Wordsworth, master—perhaps influenced by H. J. Rose—wrote to the author, calling upon him to resign his appointment as assistant tutor. Thirlwall immediately obeyed and, as the master had added that he found 'some difficulty in understanding how a person with such sentiments can reconcile it to himself to continue a member of a society founded and conducted on principles from which he differs so widely', Thirlwall addressed a circular letter to the fellows, asking each of them to send him 'a private explicit and unreserved declaration' on this point. Most desired to retain him, but several—including Whewell with whom he quarrelled publicly on the matter—did not acquit him of rashness; a few did not condemn the master's action.

On Thirlwall's return, in November 1834, from a continental visit Lord Brougham offered him the valuable living of Kirby Underdale in Yorkshire. He accepted without hesitation, and went into residence in July 1835. He had had little experience of parochial work, but he proved himself both energetic and successful in this new field; he was sometimes helped by W. H. Thompson.

He was elected to the senate of London University; when in London for meetings he met many Cambridge friends and in 1838 they formed the Sterling Club, for the exchange of (mainly liberal) ideas. At Kirby Underdale Thirlwall completed his *History of Greece* (8 vols., 1835–44), originally published in the *Cabinet Cyclopaedia* of Dr Dionysius Lardner. This work entailed prodigious labour. At Cambridge, where the first volume was written, he used to work all day until half-past three, when he left his rooms for a rapid walk before dinner, at that time served in hall at four; in Yorkshire he is said to have worked sixteen hours a day in his study. By a curious coincidence he and George Grote, his friend and schoolfellow, were writing on the same subject at the same time, unknown to each other. On the appearance of Grote's first two volumes in 1846 Thirlwall welcomed them with generous praise, and when the publication of the fourth volume in 1847 enabled him to form a maturer judgement, he told the author that he rejoiced to think that his own performance would 'for all highest purposes, be so superseded' (Grote, 174). Grote in the preface to his work bore testimony to Thirlwall's learning, sagacity, and candour. Portions of Thirlwall's history were translated into German by Leonhard Schmitz in 1840, and into French by A. Joanne in 1852.

Bishop of St David's In 1840 Lord Melbourne offered the bishopric of St David's to Thirlwall. He had read his translation of Schleiermacher, and formed so high an opinion of the author that he wished to appoint him to Norwich in 1837, but was dissuaded by episcopal comment. In 1840 he took a stronger line, effectively pressing Thirlwall onto a reluctant Archbishop Howley, whose agreement to what was bound to be a controversial appointment he secured in advance. Tractarians, unsurprisingly, were scandalized, but the appointment was not challenged.

Thirlwall brought to the larger sphere of work as a bishop the thoroughness which had made him successful as a parish clergyman. Within a year he read prayers and preached in Welsh; he later encouraged the eisteddfod. He visited every part of his large and, at that time, little-known diocese; inspected the condition of schools and churches; and by personal liberality augmented the income of small livings. It has been estimated that he spent £40,000 while bishop on charities of various kinds. After a quarter of a century of steady effort he could point to the restoration of 183 churches; to 30 parishes where new or restored churches were in progress; to many new parsonages; and to a large increase in education. Yet he was not personally popular. He was moody and unwilling to make the usual politenesses. He instituted priests without a word of encouragement. He was sarcastic with his colleagues and rude to his servants. Popular rumour had it that his dog was trained to know and bite curates. His friends were almost all in England and he relished his visits to London to stay with Monckton Milnes and visit the Metaphysical Society. His almost reclusive existence at Abergwili was lightened from 1862 by an intense but apparently platonic friendship with a spirited and talented beauty, Elizabeth Johnes of Dolau Cothi, Pumpsaint, some 20 miles from Abergwili. Their correspondence was published after Thirlwall's death in *Letters to a Friend* (1881).

Thirlwall took a lively interest in the events of the day, and in all questions affecting not merely his own diocese but the church at large. On such he elaborated his decision unbiased by considerations of party, of his own order, or of public opinion. His seclusion from such influences gives a special value to his eleven triennial charges, which are, in fact, an epitome of the history of the Church of England during his episcopate, narrated by a man of judicial mind, without passion or prejudice, and fearless in the expression of his views. On controversial issues he often took the opposite side to the Anglican episcopate. He supported the grant to Maynooth (1845); the abolition of the civil disabilities of the Jews (1848); and, in a powerful and memorable speech, the disestablishment of the Irish church (1869). He was the only bishop to vote for the repeal of the corn laws in 1846. But he was a strong supporter of the Ecclesiastical Titles Act. Though broad church in his interest in German theology and in his support for comprehension, his theological views did not advance. He quarrelled with Rowland Williams when the latter was vice-principal at Lampeter (Thirlwall's appointment), and Thirlwall's signature made unanimous the bishops' condemnation of *Essays and Reviews* (1860), a position Thirlwall defended in his *Charge* (1863). But he declined to prevent Bishop Colenso from preaching in his diocese, or to urge him to resign his bishopric.

Thirlwall was a regular attendant at convocation, a member of the royal commission on ritual (1868), and chairman of the Old Testament Revision Company. In May 1874 he resigned his bishopric and retired to Bath, blind and partially paralysed. He died unmarried at 59 Pulteney Street, Bath, on 27 July 1875. He was buried on 3 August in Westminster Abbey, in the same grave as George Grote. His funeral sermon, which was preached by Dean Stanley, formed the preface of the posthumous volume of Thirlwall's *Letters to a Friend* (1881). In 1884 the Thirlwall prize (for the best thesis involving historical research) was instituted at Cambridge in the bishop's memory. Thirlwall's life was one of paradox: a notable scholar whose early liberalism turned to theological caution; a priest who disliked the clergy; and a broad-church bishop preaching comprehension, whose sarcasm inspired few among his flock and revulsion among the many non-Anglicans in his diocese.

J. W. CLARK, rev. H. C. G. MATTHEW

Sources J. C. Thirlwall, *Connop Thirlwall* (1936) · A. P. Stanley, ed., *Letters to a friend* (1881) · D. Forbes, *The liberal Anglican idea of history* (1952) · *Remains ... of Connop Thirlwall*, ed. J. J. S. Perowne, 3 vols. (1877–8) · L. Stokes, *Letters, literary and theological* (1881) · I. Ellis, *Seven against Christ: a study of 'Essays and reviews'* (1980) · *Church Quarterly Review*, 16 (1883) · J. S. Mill, *Autobiography* (1873) · H. Grote, *The personal life of George Grote* (1873)
Archives Bodl. Oxf., letters · NL Wales, corresp.; letters | BL, corresp. with W. E. Gladstone, Add. MSS 44388–44425, *passim* · Bodl. Oxf., corresp. with Sir Thomas Phillipps · Bodl. Oxf., letters to William Wilberforce · JRL, letters to E. A. Freeman · LPL, corresp. with A. C. Tait · NL Wales, letters to Johnes family · Trinity Cam., corresp. with W. Whewell
Likenesses drawing, 1808 · S. Lawrence, portrait, *c.*1840 · H. Watkins, photograph, 1858, NPG [*see illus.*] · photograph, 1863, repro. in Thirlwall, *Connop Thirlwall* · E. Edwards, photograph, *c.*1864, NPG; repro. in E. Edwards, *Portraits of men of eminence in literature, science and the arts, with biographical memoirs*, ed. L. Reeve and E. Walford, 6 vols. (1863–7) · F. Holl, oils, *c.*1865, Abergwili Palace, Carmarthen · photograph, 1874, repro. in Thirlwall, *Connop Thirlwall* · E. Davis, bust, 1876, Westminster Abbey · E. Davis, marble bust, Trinity Cam. · oils, U. Wales, Lampeter · portrait (aged eleven)
Wealth at death under £16,000: probate, 8 Sept 1875, *CGPLA Eng. & Wales*

Thirlwall, Thomas (*d.* 1827). *See under* Thirlwall, (Newell) Connop (1797–1875).

Thirning, William (*d.* 1413), justice, probably came from Thirning in Huntingdonshire, where his name occurs in connection with the manor of Hemingford Grey. Thirning served on various commissions before becoming a serjeant in 1383. In 1377 he was on the commission of peace for the county of Northampton, and on 20 December of that year was a commissioner of oyer and terminer in Bedfordshire. In June 1380 he was a justice of assize for the counties of York, Northumberland, Cumberland, and Westmorland. He was appointed a king's serjeant in 1388, and a justice of the common pleas on 11 April of the same year; he became chief justice of that court on 15 January 1396. In 1392 he was one of the commissioners appointed by the king to inquire into the shortcomings of the government of the city of London. In the parliament of January 1398, when the judges were asked for their opinions on the answers for which their predecessors had been condemned in 1388, Thirning replied that declaration of treason not yet declared was a matter for parliament, but that had he been a lord of parliament, if he had been asked, he would have replied in the same manner.

Thirning's attitude on this occasion did not prevent him from taking a leading part in the process of deposing Richard II in 1399. He was one of the persons appointed to obtain Richard's renunciation of the throne on 29 September, and was one of the commissioners who on the following day pronounced the sentence of deposition in parliament. According to Walsingham, Thirning advised Henry of Lancaster to abandon his idea of claiming the throne by right of conquest, the chief justice arguing that such a claim would have made all tenure of property insecure. Although doubt has been thrown on the composition of the delegation, it seems almost certain that Thirning was one of those sent to interview Richard in the

Tower of London on 29 September and obtain his renunciation of the throne; and after the estates had pronounced sentence of deposition on 30 September Thirning was one of the commissioners sent the following day to announce the sentence to Richard. According to Walsingham, when the sentence was read Richard refused to renounce the spiritual honour of king. Thirning then reminded him of the terms in which on 29 September he had confessed that he was deposed on account of his demerits. Richard demurred, saying it was simply that his government had not been acceptable to the people. Thirning, however, insisted, and Richard only smiled and asked to be treated honourably. On 3 November Thirning pronounced the judgment of the king and peers against the accusers of Thomas, duke of Gloucester. The leniency of the judgment, according to Walsingham, caused some ill feeling among the people.

Thirning continued to be chief justice throughout the reign of Henry IV, and was reappointed on the accession of Henry V in 1413. He must have died very soon after, for his successor, Richard Norton (*d.* 1420), was appointed on 26 June of the same year, and in Trinity term of that year Thirning's widow, Joan, brought an action of debt.

C. L. Kingsford, *rev.* Anthony Tuck

Sources Baker, *Serjeants* · G. O. Sayles, ed., *Select cases in the court of king's bench*, 7 vols., SeldS, 55, 57–8, 74, 76, 82, 88 (1936–71), vols. 6–7 · 'Annales Ricardi secundi et Henrici quarti, regum Angliae', *Johannis de Trokelowe et Henrici de Blaneforde ... chronica et annales*, ed. H. T. Riley, pt 3 of *Chronica monasterii S. Albani*, Rolls Series, 28 (1866), 155–420 · C. Given-Wilson, ed. and trans., *Chronicles of the revolution, 1397–1400: the reign of Richard II* (1993) · G. O. Sayles, 'The deposition of Richard II: three Lancastrian narratives', *BIHR*, 54 (1981), 257–70 · *RotP* · *Chancery records* · C. M. Barron, 'The quarrel of Richard II with London, 1392–7', *The reign of Richard II: essays in honour of May McKisack*, ed. F. R. H. Du Boulay and C. M. Barron (1971), 173–201

Thistlethwayte [*née* Bell], **Laura Eliza Jane Seymour** (1831?–1894), courtesan and lay preacher, was the daughter of Captain Robert H. Bell of Bellbrook, Glenavy, co. Antrim, and his second wife, Laura Jane Seymour, an illegitimate daughter of the third marquess of Hertford. She is believed to have been born at Glenavy, probably on 18 October 1831. After an unsupervised childhood, she left home at an early age to become a shop-girl and prostitute in Belfast, where she also appeared briefly and unsuccessfully on the stage. A move to Dublin about 1846 secured her finances to the extent that she was able to drive in Phoenix Park in her own carriage. It is difficult to establish the identities of her clientele, but she was reputed to have had an association with Dr William Wilde, the father of Oscar, and it is alleged that at this time she made the acquaintance of an unnamed official at Dublin Castle.

About 1849 Laura Bell moved to London, where she worked as a shop-girl in Jay's General Mourning House in Regent Street, whence she was removed by the Nepalese envoy, Prince Jang Bahadur, who set her up in a house in Wilton Place. He was recalled shortly afterwards, having lavished large sums of money upon her. Continuing her life as a courtesan in London and Paris, she drew much attention and admiration for her golden hair, blue eyes, beautiful figure, and sparkling demeanour by riding and driving a smart equipage in Hyde Park. Several lovers were attributed to her in this period, including Arthur Thistlethwayte who died in the Crimea in 1854, the brother of her future husband. There is also evidence that she was a friend of Sir Edwin Landseer, and may have had some hand in the modelling of one of the lions on his monument to Nelson in Trafalgar Square.

On 21 January 1852 Laura Bell retired from her profession and married (Augustus) Frederick Thistlethwayte (1830–1887), a rich army subaltern, the son of Thomas Thistlethwayte and his second wife, Tryphena Bathurst, daughter of Henry Bathurst, bishop of Norwich. They first lived at 100 Westbourne Terrace, and moved in 1856 to 15 Grosvenor Square. The marriage was not a success, and there were no children. She was a spendthrift, and ran up huge debts, for which her husband was obliged more than once to deny responsibility, even going to court to limit his liabilities. In an unlikely turn of events, Laura Thistlethwayte became a lay preacher. There is no evidence of a conversion experience, and little to explain her actions. She declared herself to be a Methodist, and was invited to preach in Plymouth Brethren chapels and in the Polytechnic in London. Her greatest triumphs were in the Dingwall area of Scotland, where she had rented property from Lady Ashburton, and where her beauty, her jewellery, and her preaching held audiences spellbound; but she fell foul of the Free Church ministers and was held at arm's length by society.

In London, Laura Thistlethwayte held dinner parties for politicians and public figures, which gatherings her husband did not always attend, despite their almost exclusively male composition. In 1864 she began an extensive correspondence with William Ewart *Gladstone, who was the executor of the late duke of Newcastle's will. Her connection with Newcastle may have dated from his period as chief secretary in Dublin in 1846; he had also been a guest at her dinner parties. The correspondence with Gladstone (printed in appendices in volumes 7 and 12 of the Gladstone Diaries) lasted until her death in 1894, and reveals, in its first seven years, an intense intimacy potentially dangerous for the politician who addressed her as his 'Dear Spirit'. Eventually Gladstone resolved to encourage her to mend her marriage, which had come close to complete breakdown, although he did not discontinue his visits to her house or end the correspondence. She persisted in making Gladstone gifts which she would not allow him to return, and which were to prove an embarrassment when she and her husband were sued for debts in 1878 and 1879. She became importunate in her demands for his attendance at social occasions when he was occupied with politics, and after this period the correspondence was continued on a more level tone. Their relationship was to be the subject of much salacious speculation, which was refuted by Gladstone's sons on evidence provided by him shortly before his death.

Frederick Thistlethwayte died on 7 August 1887 from a self-inflicted shot wound: he had been accustomed to summoning his servants by firing his pistol. His widow retired to Woodbine Cottage, Fortune Green Lane, Hampstead, where she died on 30 May 1894. She left her estate, some £41,000, to Lord Edward Pelham-Clinton, the second son of the duke of Newcastle, with the condition that after his death the funds were to be used to provide 'a retreat for clergymen of all denominations, true believers and literary men' at Woodbine Cottage; the foundation never came into existence. She was buried in Paddington Green cemetery, beside her husband.   J. GILLILAND

Sources Gladstone, Diaries · archives, Wallace Collection · J. Gilliland, Gladstone's 'dear spirit', Laura Thistlethwayte (privately printed, Oxford, 1994) · H. C. G. Matthew, Gladstone, 1809–1874 (1986) · H. C. G. Matthew, Gladstone, 1875–1898 (1995) · archive, LPL · J. F. Burns, 'From whoredom to evangelism', Lisburn Historical Society Journal, 2 (1979) · Lady St Helier [S. M. E. Jeune], Memories of fifty years (1909) · H. J. Coke, Tracks of a rolling stone (1905) · Men, women and things: memories of the duke of Portland (1937) · Memoirs and correspondence of Dr Henry Bathurst, lord bishop of Norwich, ed. T. Thistlethwayte (1853) · The letters and memories of Sir William Hardman … second series, 1863–1865, ed. S. M. Ellis (1925) · m. cert. · d. cert.
Archives Wallace Collection, London | BL, Gladstone MSS · LPL, Gladstone MSS
Likenesses R. Buckner, portrait, 1871, priv. coll. · A. B. Clayton, portrait, priv. coll. · E. J. A. Girard, miniature (Laura Bell?), Wallace Collection, London · photograph, Lambeth Manuscript Archive · photograph (after R. Buckner), Somerset House, London, Witts Collection
Wealth at death £41,357 11s. 0d.: resworn probate, April 1895, CGPLA Eng. & Wales

Thistlethwayte, Robert (bap. 1690, d. 1744), college head and subject of sexual scandal, was the third son of Francis Thistlethwayte (b. 1658) of Winterslow, Wiltshire, where the Thistlethwayte family had held the manor since the sixteenth century, and of Compton Valence, Dorset. His mother was Mary, daughter and coheir of Robert Pelham of Compton Valence; she was buried on 26 September 1690, presumably dying as a result of the birth. Robert was baptized at Winterslow on 16 December 1690. His early education is unknown. He matriculated with his elder brother Francis at Wadham College, Oxford, on 2 December 1707, graduating BA in February 1712 and MA in June 1714. He became scholar of the college in 1711 or 1712, and fellow in 1715. On 27 May 1716 he was ordained deacon, but he evidently postponed becoming priest until 4 June 1721. Two years later he succeeded his uncle, Gabriel Thistlethwayte, as rector of Winterslow. In December 1723 he was elected, at a remarkably young age, warden of Wadham College against a rival candidate, Robert Nash. Thomas Hearne commented:

> both these gentlemen are Whigs, but Nash being looked upon as the cunninger man and more able than the other to do mischief to the college, they unanimously struck in for Thistlethwayte, especially since the Tory side could not carry it for one of themselves. (Oxford Historical Society, 50, 1907, 148)

To comply with college statutes Thistlethwayte had to proceed to the degrees of BD and DD. A dispensation to take the degrees early passed the university's convocation by a majority of two votes (ibid., 234). He became prebendary of Westminster in 1730, and, at about the same time, chaplain to George II. He inherited a family property, Westbarn Grange, Witham Friary, near Frome, Somerset, and was probably responsible for its rebuilding.

Thistlethwayte's wardenship of a college that was, and had been for some time, at a low ebb would doubtless have been undistinguished had he not become involved in accusations of sexual impropriety, which led him to resign. On 3 February 1739 an undergraduate, Philip French, was found by his colleagues in great distress; he eventually revealed that he had been sexually assaulted by the warden. His father was sent for and counsel's opinion sought. French resisted strenuous attempts by Thistlethwayte and others to get him to drop the charges. On 19 February the vice-chancellor, the decidedly tory master of Balliol College, Theophilus Legh, acting as a justice of the peace, bound over French to make good his allegation at the next assize and ordered Thistlethwayte himself to appear there on a bond of £200. Thistlethwayte resigned the wardenship on 22 February, and left Oxford six days later. There were rumours that he had committed suicide; alternatively, that he was about to marry 'Carew Reynold's sister … a buxom lass with a small fortune and that [he] hopes to wipe off the stain by this means' (Hants. RO, MS 9M73/9627/3). He did not appear at the assize, held on 9 March, when the grand jury found a true bill against him. He resigned his Westminster prebend on 25 April, and his Winterslow benefice at about the same time. On 5 July he was at Dover, where he drew up his will, evidently *en route* for the continent. Meanwhile George Baker, a scholar of Wadham College, proceeded to a further accusation of homosexual activities against John Swinton, fellow of the college. This accusation was dismissed by the vice-chancellor, but led to the publication of a pamphlet, *A faithful narrative of the proceedings in a late affair between the Rev. Mr. John Swinton, and Mr. George Baker* (1739), which included an account of the evidence against Thistlethwayte in lascivious detail. Robert Langford, the college butler, told of repulsing several attempts to kiss and fondle him, until Langford had 'wondered why gentlemen of his fortune did not provide themselves with women, or wives'; Thistlethwayte answered that 'he would not give a farthing for the finest woman in the world; and he loved a man as he did his soul'. William Hodge, a barber, similarly claimed to have been attacked while he was shaving the warden (*Faithful Narrative*, 15–18). A burlesque poem, *College-Wit Sharpen'd*, added to the amusement of the reading public by recycling the same material.

Thistlethwayte seems to have spent the next four years in exile, probably at Boulogne, where he died in or about January 1744. He was buried at St Mary the Virgin, Dover, on 4 February 1744. The will drawn up in 1739 was proved on 16 February 1744. His nephew, Alexander Thistlethwayte (MP for Hampshire, 1751–61), inherited Westbarn Grange; in addition Thistlethwayte left cash bequests totalling some £6000.   C. S. L. DAVIES

Sources *A faithful narrative of the proceedings in the late affair between the Rev. Mr John Swinton, and Mr George Baker … to which is prefix'd a particular account of the proceedings against Robert Thistlethwayte* (1739) · *College-wit sharpen'd, or, The head of a house with a sting in the tail … the Wadhamites: a burlesque poem* (1739) · R. B. Gardiner, ed., *The registers of Wadham College, Oxford*, 2 vols. (1889–95) · G. Wyndham, letters to James Harris, Hants. RO, Malmesbury papers, 9M 73/9627/1–15 · C. Cohen, *So great a cloud: the story of All Saints, Winterslow*, pt 1 (privately printed, Winterslow, Wilts., 1995)
Archives Wadham College, Oxford, convention book, MS 2/3 | Hants. RO, George Wyndham letters, 9M73/9627
Wealth at death freehold ownership of Westbarn Grange, Witham Friary, Frome, Somerset, and cash bequests of approx. £6500: will, PRO, PROB 11/732

Thistlewood, Arthur (*bap.* 1774, *d.* 1820), radical and revolutionary, was baptized at Horsington parish church, near Horncastle, Lincolnshire, on 4 December 1774. He was the illegitimate son of William Thistlewood, a stock breeder, and Ann Burnet, a small shopkeeper. He probably attended Horncastle Free Grammar School and subsequently trained as a land surveyor. However, in 1795 he is recorded as a grazier of Tupholme, and subsequently he was an ensign in the 1st West Yorkshire militia, July 1798 to February 1799; for a similarly short period in 1803 he held a commission in the 3rd Lincolnshire militia. Claims for his first marriage differ: he may have married a Miss Bruce of Bawtry in 1791/1792, or Jane Worsley of Lincoln in January 1804. Both women are said to have been wealthy, with a fortune reverting to their family after death in childbirth within two years of marriage. A son, Julian, credited to both the 1804 marriage and an illicit liaison, was accepted by Susan Wilkinson, a Horncastle butcher's daughter whom Thistlewood married in 1808. About this time he is said to have inherited a large estate which he sold in return for an annuity, but the purchaser went bankrupt almost immediately. An attempt at farming was also a financial disaster.

Information concerning Thistlewood's early life is confused and some picaresque details should probably be discounted, including his service as a captain with the French grenadiers. This seems to have been his own invention, of which he made much after arriving around 1810–11 in London, where he quickly made the acquaintance of leading radicals, especially the circle round the agrarian reformer Thomas Spence. There he found an ideological framework for his embittered personal experience of financial difficulty and thwarted aspirations: 'The Mammonites have swayed us too long, we must have no property mongering jugglers, they have always entailed misery on the most industrious and useful people in every nation' (J. Watson to A. Thistlewood, 24 July 1818, PRO, HO 42/178). In 1811 he was secretary to a committee for the defence of an Irish radical journalist charged with libelling Castlereagh, Peter Finnerty. In 1812–13 he was closely involved with a shadowy group that proposed to send an emissary to Paris inviting Napoleon to invade Britain and restore the Saxon constitution. Thistlewood's role was to finance the enterprise out of a rumoured windfall of £10,000 in a chancery case, but the plan folded when the money did not materialize. Ostensibly bizarre, the aim is intelligible within the context of English radicalism's

There was no immediate crackdown by the government, largely because of the need to keep intact its intelligence network, but early in 1817 habeas corpus was suspended and warrants issued for the arrest of the leading Spenceans. Thistlewood remained at liberty until May, when he was arrested while preparing to leave for America with his family. Along with Watson and two other Spenceans he was charged with high treason. Watson was acquitted in June 1817, however, when the crown's chief witness was exposed as a pimp, perjurer, and plausible *provocateur*, and the case against the others was withdrawn. Throughout the remainder of 1817 their activities continued, but with Watson increasingly inclined towards open constitutionalism and Thistlewood to a *coup d'état* to expedite their objectives. Fresh plans were devised for destabilizing the capital, with St Bartholomew's fair on 6 September the cloak to proceedings. Emissaries were sent into the country and plans made to storm the Bank of England. The plot was real enough— the home secretary, Sidmouth, compared it directly to the Despard conspiracy—but it was defeated by a combination of deft official action and the over-optimism of the protagonists.

The failure prompted Thistlewood to air the idea of an attack on the privy council 'in the manner of Despard' (J. Shegoe to N. Conant, 18 Sept 1817, PRO, HO 42/170). A further action was planned for 11 October, which dissolved in circumstances approaching farce. Fearful of police surveillance, most of the Spencean circle reverted to tavern-based agitation and publication. Thistlewood struck off on a course of his own, challenging Sidmouth to a duel over the non-return of confiscated property. The dispute had already been the subject of *An interesting correspondence between Thistlewood and Sidmouth concerning the property detained, in consequence of an arrest, on a charge of high treason* (1817). The challenge resulted in May 1818 in a twelve-month gaol sentence for threatening a breach of the peace. This Thistlewood served, in circumstances of some severity, in Horsham gaol.

After his release Thistlewood organized with Watson a lavish London reception for Hunt on 5 September 1819, after 'Peterloo'. Their involvement compromised Hunt's constitutional stance and this, along with a dispute about radical tactics after Peterloo, led to a damaging public dispute between them. A few days before Peterloo, Thistlewood had proposed a rising. He now began to formulate what would become known as the Cato Street conspiracy [see Cato Street conspirators (*act.* 1820)]. He visited the provinces, while the Spenceans intensified agitation in London. Though the key conspirators included a spy, George Edwards, the wider web of those implicated in Cato Street will never be clear: the London Irish community and a number of trade societies, notably shoemakers, were prepared to lend support, while unrest and awareness of a planned rising were widespread in the industrial north and on Clydeside.

Thistlewood intended to assassinate the cabinet at the home of the earl of Harrowby, where the cabinet was

Arthur Thistlewood (*bap.* 1774, *d.* 1820), by Cooper, pubd 1820 (after Abraham Wivell)

long tradition of Saxon constitutionalism, and the plan was scrutinized closely by the government. Thereafter Thistlewood's activities are well documented in official papers. One spy presciently observed that he was 'quite the gentleman in manners and appearance … from his past life, his present pursuits, principles and low connections etc he seems to be a second edition of Colonel Despard' (J. Smith to J. Beckett (Home Office), 8 Feb 1813, PRO, HO 42/136). In 1814 he visited a number of Jacobin émigrés in Paris, among them William McCabe, the United Irish agent.

The peak of the Spenceans' influence came in late 1816, when they briefly secured the leadership of the parliamentary reform movement in London. Henry Hunt was invited by them to address a mass meeting at Spa Fields on 2 December, but agreed to do so only on condition that explicitly Spencean material in their address was deleted. To this the organizing committee, of which Thistlewood and Dr James Watson were leading members, agreed, primarily because it was their intention to use the occasion to foment widespread unrest in the capital that might signal the commencement of a general rising to the country at large. Ground had been laid for this by extensive agitation among taverns and barracks in the capital, and via an extensive correspondence with provincial centres where radicals held themselves in readiness. McCabe returned clandestinely for the meeting. In the event the majority of Hunt's audience remained peaceable, but a sizeable element were responsible for several hours of rioting in the City, while a small force with Thistlewood at its head marched on the Tower of London and demanded its surrender. Only at nightfall was order restored.

advertised as going to dine on 23 February 1820. The advertisement, however, was an official hoax. The conspirators were apprehended in a loft in Cato Street by Bow Street Runners and a detachment of guards around 8.30 that night. In the struggle that followed, one police officer, Richard Smithers, was killed with a rapier by Thistlewood, who then escaped, only to be captured the following morning. In all, thirteen conspirators were arrested and charged with high treason. Two turned king's evidence, which removed the need for the crown to call Edwards as a witness. The case against one prisoner was dropped. After three days' trial, on 17, 18, and 19 April, Thistlewood was found guilty and sentenced to a traitor's death. Five conspirators were transported, while Thistlewood and four others were hanged, publicly decapitated, and buried at Newgate on 1 May 1820.

MALCOLM CHASE

Sources PRO, Home Office MSS · State trials, vols. 32–33 · G. T. Wilkinson, *An authentic history of the Cato Street conspiracy* (1820) · M. Chase, *The people's farm: English radical agrarianism, 1775–1840* (1988) · I. McCalman, *Radical underworld: prophets, revolutionaries, and pornographers in London, 1795–1840* (1988) · I. J. Prothero, *Artisans and politics in early nineteenth-century London: John Gast and his times* (1979) · J. Belchem, '*Orator Hunt*' (1985) · D. Johnson, *Regency revolution: the case of Arthur Thistlewood* (1975) · J. Stanhope, *The Cato Street conspiracy* (1962) · C. Emley, 'Thistlewood, Arthur', *BDMBR*, vol. 3, pt 2 · A. Smith, 'Arthur Thistlewood: a Regency republican', *History Today*, 3 (1953), 846–52 · T. M. Parssinen, 'The revolutionary party in London, 1816–20', *BIHR*, 45 (1972), 266–82
Archives Essex RO, Chelmsford, papers relating to his examination for attempted murder of the cabinet · PRO, Home Office MSS · PRO, Treasury solicitor's MSS
Likenesses W. Holl, group portrait, stipple, pubd 1817 (*Spa Fields rioters*; after G. Scharf), BM, NPG; *see illus. in* Watson, James (1766–1838) · Cooper, mixed-method engraving, pubd 1820 (after A. Wivell), NPG [*see illus.*] · Wivell, engraving, 1820, City Westm. AC · lithograph, pubd 1820, BM · stipple, pubd 1820 (after A. Wivell), BM, NPG · prints, NPG

Thistlewood, Thomas (1721–1786), slave owner and diarist, was born on 16 March 1721 at Tupholme, Lincolnshire, the second son of Robert Thistlewood (1675–1727), a farmer, and his wife, Jane, *née* Langstaffe (1696–1738). After attending schools in Ackworth, Yorkshire, he learned agriculture and worked as a farm-hand for several Lincolnshire farmers. In 1745 he left Lincolnshire to travel to India as purser of supercargo on a ship belonging to the East India Company. He returned to England in 1748, but decided to migrate to Jamaica, and arrived in Kingston on 24 April 1750. He later moved to Westmoreland parish in the far west of the island, where he remained for the rest of his life, working until 1767 as a slave overseer before buying a livestock and provision pen called Breadnut Island.

Although he was successful on his own terms, becoming a landowner and the owner of thirty-six slaves as well as serving as a vestryman and JP, Thistlewood's life would have occasioned little comment were it not for the fortuitous preservation of a remarkable diary that he kept faithfully throughout his residence in Jamaica. This diary and other writings fill eighty-four notebooks (now in the Lincolnshire Archives) and provide a penetrating account of

life lived mainly among slaves of African descent in early Jamaica. Although Thistlewood eventually established a rich social life among fellow white inhabitants, he spent most of his time, especially in his first decade in Jamaica, when he was particularly receptive to African cultural survivals, among the black population. In his diaries he details his involvement with slaves, noting work routines, punishments meted out, sexual encounters, and frequent social interactions. The portrait of Jamaica that his diaries reveal shows a brutalized slave population, living in conditions of extreme flux, uncertainty, and trauma, who nevertheless were able to fashion lives for themselves that were not entirely controlled by their masters' dictates. Thistlewood notes in dry, flat, serviceable, and completely unreflective prose many episodes of horrifying brutality and sexual exploitation. He proved adept at using both brutality and sexual opportunism as a means of maintaining control of slaves. His diaries also show, moreover, the extent to which fear and violence were the underlying principles underpinning the survival of a system in which white people were heavily outnumbered by resentful slaves. Thistlewood found this out in 1760 when caught in the middle of Tacky's revolt—a multi-parish uprising of slaves that white inhabitants managed to put down only after considerable difficulties and which greatly threatened the stability of the island. Thistlewood's control over his slaves was particularly tested in this revolt, but he managed to keep his cool in the middle of utmost danger.

Most Jamaican white men lived lives of excess, and were widely famed, as the historian Edward Long noted, for their immoderate passions and appetites. Thistlewood did not share their predilection for gluttony and alcoholism, but he did share their enthusiasm for fornicating with black and coloured women, and his diaries provide remarkable detail about his very active sexual life. Although he remained a serial philanderer until his death, he became devoted to one slave in particular, Phibbah, with whom he lived, virtually as man and wife, for over thirty-four years. Even though her life can be re-created only from Thistlewood's perspective, Phibbah—an illiterate house slave who had managed by the time of her death to acquire considerable property and become herself a slave owner—is the most fully realized slave presented through the diary. It seems clear that, although she and Thistlewood enjoyed a relationship marked by mutual affection, Phibbah also gained from her association with Thistlewood protection for her family and was able to build a family estate to pass to her descendants. Unfortunately the only child that Phibbah and Thistlewood had together, John, died before he could inherit this property or the property that Thistlewood acquired. At Thistlewood's death, on 30 November 1786 at Breadnut Island, he was comfortably placed, and left an estate worth £2408 sterling as well as land worth over £600. He was buried on 1 December in the Anglican churchyard at Savanna-la-Mar, Jamaica.

The main value of Thistlewood's copious diaries lies in the light they shed on slavery in eighteenth-century

British America. That might have disappointed Thistlewood, who fancied himself as an Enlightenment man in the tropics, and who would have thought his claim to later distinction rested with his importance as a skilled horticulturist. By the time of his death he was prosperous and respected among the white population and was treated with a wary caution by slaves. The diaries show him as both brutal and tender, and point to the complex social codes that governed the relationship between white masters and African slaves in eighteenth-century slave societies.   TREVOR BURNARD

Sources Lincs. Arch., Monson deposit, Monson 31/1–86 · D. Hall, *In miserable slavery: Thomas Thistlewood in Jamaica, 1750–86* (1989) · T. Burnard, 'Thomas Thistlewood becomes a Creole', *Varieties of southern history: new essays on a region and its people*, ed. B. Clayton and J. Salmond (1996), 99–118 · P. D. Morgan, 'Slaves and livestock in eighteenth-century Jamaica: Vineyard Pen, 1750–51', *William and Mary Quarterly*, 52 (1995), 47–76 · E. Long, *The history of Jamaica*, 3 vols. (1770)
Archives BL, meteorological journals kept at Bread Nutt Island, Add. MSS 18275/A–B [copies] · Lincs. Arch., journals and papers mostly relating to time in Jamaica
Wealth at death £2408 0s. 4d. [£3371 5s. 1d. local currency]: Jamaica Archives, inventiones, vol. 71, fol. 200, 1787

Thoday, David (1883–1964), botanist, was born on 5 May 1883 at Honiton, Devon, the eldest of the six children of David Thoday (1858–1922), an elementary schoolmaster, and his wife, Susan Elizabeth, daughter of Charles Bingham. Both his parents came from villages in the Cambridgeshire fenland, where his grandfathers were skilled rural craftsmen, his father from Willingham and his mother from Guyhirne. In 1884 Thoday's father, a man of strong personality, evangelical in religion and radical in politics, moved to London, where he continued to teach in elementary schools and later became a headmaster. Thoday was educated at Tottenham grammar school (1894–8) and at Tottenham Pupil Teachers' Centre. The principal of the latter institution, T. E. Margerison, encouraged him to apply to university and in 1902 he was awarded a scholarship by Toynbee Hall and was admitted to Trinity College, Cambridge, as a subsizar. At the same time he joined the Cambridge Day Training College, intending to become a schoolteacher.

The lectures of H. Marshall Ward, A. C. Seward, and the plant physiologist F. F. Blackman, attracted Thoday to botany and, after being placed in the first class in part one of the natural sciences tripos (1905), he was awarded a senior scholarship and in 1906 he obtained a first class in part two (botany). He was awarded the Walsingham medal in 1908. Later, in 1933, he proceeded to an ScD.

Thoday remained at Cambridge for five more years, first as a research student under Blackman, and from 1909 to 1911 as university demonstrator. During this period he worked on various physiological problems and published several papers, of which the best-known was on Sachs's 'half leaf' method of measuring photosynthesis, a method which Thoday materially improved. On 15 June 1910 he married Mary Gladys (d. 1943), daughter of John Thorley Sykes, cotton broker, of Denbighshire. She was a

botanist of some distinction, who had collaborated with him in some of his research, being placed in the first class in both parts of the natural sciences tripos at Girton College, Cambridge; she was a research fellow of Newnham College from 1909 to 1912.

In 1911 Thoday became lecturer in physiological botany at Manchester University, where his wife was honorary research fellow; he moved in 1918 to the chair of botany at the University of Cape Town. For a botanist with Thoday's breadth of interest South Africa offered wonderful opportunities. He soon embarked on physiological, anatomical, and taxonomic studies on the xerophytic plants in which South Africa's seasonally dry climate is so rich: he became particularly interested in the ericoid (small-leaved) shrubs and the functional significance of their reduced leaf areas.

Although Thoday greatly enjoyed his years at Cape Town, he decided for family reasons to resign his chair and in 1923 he became professor of botany at the University College of North Wales, Bangor, where he remained until he retired in 1949, his wife acting as honorary lecturer there. In spite of the difficulties posed by the very small and poorly funded department at Bangor, problems exacerbated by the influx of evacuated students from University College, London, Thoday built up an efficient teaching department and managed to continue his research on the water relations and tissue differentiation of plants. In collaboration with Miss A. J. Davey he also studied contractile roots. Among the many papers he wrote at Bangor the most notable was perhaps the series on the succulent *Kleinia articulata*, which included work on their peculiar acid metabolism.

After retiring in 1949 Thoday spent two years in Egypt as professor of plant physiology at Alexandria, but political difficulties in Egypt led to his return to Britain in 1952 and he returned to Bangor in 1953 where he worked on the interaction of host and parasite in Loranthaceae (mistletoes) until he was nearly eighty and had become crippled with rheumatism.

Thoday had an unusually clear analytical mind and great experimental ingenuity; he had a flair for designing simple but effective apparatus, including the widely used Thoday potometer and Thoday respirometer. Although he had comparatively few students, he had great influence on botanical teaching and research, especially through his *Botany: a Text-Book for Senior Students* (1915) and his presidential address to section K of the British Association (1939), in which he put forward ideas on the differentiation of plant tissues which were in some respects ahead of his time. Thoday was elected FRS in 1942 and received an honorary DSc from the University of Wales in 1960.

Thoday was a rather small man, always extremely neat in appearance, and with a modest and unassuming manner. Music, for which he had a critical and discriminating taste, was his chief leisure interest, but he was also deeply concerned with political affairs. He fully supported his wife's work in the cause of peace (she was also a convinced suffragist) and he gave generous help to refugees.

The Thodays had four sons of whom the third, John Marion Thoday, became professor of genetics at Cambridge in 1959. Thoday died at his home in Haulfre Park Crescent, Llanfairfechan, Caernarvonshire, on 30 March 1964.

P. W. RICHARDS, rev.

Sources W. Stiles, *Memoirs FRS*, 11 (1965), 177–85 · private information (1981) · personal knowledge (1981) · *CGPLA Eng. & Wales* (1964) **Archives** U. Wales, Bangor, corresp. and papers **Likenesses** M. Alexander, pencil drawing, U. Wales, Bangor, school of plant biology · photograph, repro. in Stiles, *Memoirs FRS* **Wealth at death** £12,456: probate, 17 June 1964, *CGPLA Eng. & Wales*

Thom, Alexander (1801–1879), printer and writer, was born on 18 April 1801 in Scotland (his place of birth may be Findhorn, or Bervie, or Aberdeen). His father, **Walter Thom** (1770–1824), journalist and author, was born at Bervie, Kincardineshire. He moved to Aberdeen where he wrote a *History of Aberdeen* (1811), and *Pedestrianism* (1813) celebrating particularly the athletic feats of Captain Robert Barclay Allardice. In 1813 he went to Dublin as editor of *The Correspondent*, later becoming editor and joint proprietor of the *Dublin Journal*, a newspaper financially dependent on government patronage. Its circulation declined drastically in the 1820s to about 300 copies per issue. He was a founder member of the Association for the Suppression of Mendicity in Dublin in 1818. He also contributed to Brewster's *Encyclopaedia*, to Sinclair's *Statistical Account of Scotland*, and to Mason's *Statistical Account of Ireland*. He died in Dublin on 16 June 1824.

Alexander Thom went to Dublin in 1813 with his father and entered the printing business in 1816, working in the newspaper office. In 1824 he obtained, through the influence of Sir Robert Peel, the contract for printing for the Post Office of Ireland. In 1838 he obtained the contract for the printing for all royal commissions in Ireland. He took over the printing and publishing of the official *Dublin Gazette* in 1851, and in 1876 was appointed to the post of queen's printer for Ireland. In 1844 he founded the work by which he was subsequently known, the *Irish Almanack and Official Directory*, which in a short time superseded all other publications of the kind in the Irish capital. Its superiority to its predecessors was due to its inclusion of many valuable statistics relating to Ireland. Thom continued personally to supervise its publication until 1876 when he disposed of the copyright to his son-in-law, Frederick Pilkington. In 1862 he produced a valuable related work, *Thom's British Directory and Official Handbook of the United Kingdom*, the last edition of which was published in 1873. In 1860 he published at his own expense for gratuitous distribution *A collection of tracts and treatises illustrative of the natural history, antiquities, and the political and social state of Ireland*, two volumes which contain reprints of the works of Ware, Spenser, Davis, Petty, Berkeley, and other writers on Irish affairs in the seventeenth and eighteenth centuries. In 1848 he became a founder member of the Dublin Statistical Society (later the Statistical and Social Inquiry Society of Ireland), of which he was vice-president from 1871 to his death.

Thom, who was twice married, died at his residence, Donnycarney House, Coolock, near Dublin, on 22 December 1879. He was buried in Mount Jerome cemetery, Harold's Cross, Dublin. His second wife, Sarah Mackay (*née* McCulloch) survived him until 1903, and bequeathed his historical library of 4000 volumes to the National Library of Ireland.

C. L. FALKINER, rev. C. J. BENSON

Sources W. N. Hancock, *Journal of the Statistical and Social Inquiry Society of Ireland*, 8/56 (1880), 5–8 · J. W. Hammond, 'The founder of *Thom's Directory*', *Dublin Historical Record*, 8/2 (1945–6), 41–56 · 'Select committee on journals, bills, and printed papers', *Parl. papers* (1835), 18.129–380, nos. 61, 392 · *Scottish Notes and Queries*, 12 (1898–9), 117 · B. Inglis, *The freedom of the press in Ireland, 1784–1841* (1954), 177 · *CGPLA Ire.* (1880) · *Irish Times* (Dec 1879) · copy of will of Sarah Thom, 8 May 1903, NA Ire., T2269 **Wealth at death** under £100,000: probate, 27 Jan 1880, *CGPLA Ire.*

Thom, Alexander (1894–1985), aerodynamicist and archaeologist, was born on 26 March 1894 in Carradale Mains, Argyll, the elder son (there were no daughters) of Archibald Thom, farmer, and his wife, Lily Stevenson Strang of Glasgow. The family moved in 1901 to Dunlop, Ayrshire, where Thom went to school, afterwards attending Kilmarnock Academy, from about 1907. He studied civil engineering at the Royal Technical College in Glasgow and at the University of Glasgow (BSc 1915), where he won the George Harvey prize and also studied archaeology. In 1917 he married Jeanie Boyd (d. 1975), daughter of Allan Kirkwood, farmer. They had two sons and a daughter. The younger son, Alan, an aerodynamicist, was killed in a flying accident in 1945; the other, Archibald S. Thom, followed his father as a lecturer in engineering at Glasgow University.

After working as a structural engineering designer Thom was a draughtsman with aircraft firms before becoming a lecturer at the University of Glasgow in civil engineering and aeronautics (1922–39). He built the first wind tunnel in Scotland and obtained his PhD in 1926 and DSc in 1929 from Glasgow University, both for theoretical and experimental studies of flow around cylinders in various configurations.

Thom worked throughout the Second World War at the Royal Aircraft Establishment, Farnborough, where he commissioned and ran the high-speed tunnel for testing early Spitfires. In 1945 Thom was elected professor of engineering science at Oxford and a fellow of Brasenose College. He took over a small department and greatly expanded it, his research centring on a method of calculation of flow problems. Initially he used a small mechanical calculator to solve each problem, a laborious process later rapidly accomplished by computer. He was an active member of the Aeronautical Research Committee for many years.

In parallel with his academic work Thom spent every summer accurately surveying megalithic sites on the west coast of Scotland, an activity which combined happily with his skill as a yachtsman. On his retirement in 1961 he returned to his home at Dunlop and devoted himself to analysis and further surveys of megalithic circles and aligned stones, from the Orkneys to as far south as the well-known Carnac site in Brittany, with over 2000 stones.

The results of these labours over a period of fifty years were many papers and five influential books, the last two of which were completed by his son. These, particularly *Megalithic Sites in Britain* (1967), drew attention to the probable astronomical significance of the megalithic remains. By statistical analysis of his surveys he deduced that their builders had employed a common unit of measurement, the megalithic yard of 0.83 m., not in simple circles but in circular arcs centred on right-angled triangles. Some sites he considered to be astronomical calendars, others lunar observatories, showing the scientific abilities of prehistoric man.

Thom's ideas remain contentious, and although he presented his theories fully supported by data and lucidly explained, their comprehension requires a knowledge of mathematics, statistics, surveying, astronomy, and archaeology—not a common combination. However, he is regarded as the founder of the subject of 'archaeoastronomy'. Thom's work was recognized by honorary degrees from the universities of Glasgow (LLD, 1960) and Strathclyde (DSc, 1976). He was a member of the British Astronomical Association, and a fellow of the Royal Astronomical Society, the Society of Antiquaries of London, and the Society of Antiquaries of Scotland. Above all, Sandy Thom was esteemed by his colleagues; he was truly egregious, a kind man and a good skipper, whether of a yacht's crew, a survey party, or a department. Thom died in Belford Hospital, Fort William, on 7 November 1985.

S. S. WILSON, rev.

Sources A. S. Thom, 'A personal note about my late father, Alexander Thom', *Archaeoastronomy*, 7 (1985), 32–41 • R. L. Menitt, 'Some observations on Alexander Thom', *Archaeoastronomy*, 7 (1985), 42–8 • [A. Burl], *Antiquity*, 60 (1986), 136–7 • *The Times* (11 Nov 1985) • personal knowledge (1993) • private information (1993) [A. S. Thom] • d. cert.

Thom, James (b. c.1785). *See under* Thom, James (1802–1850).

Thom, James (1802–1850), sculptor, was born on 17 April 1802 at Skeoch Farm near Lochlee in Tarbolton parish, Ayrshire, and baptized at Tarbolton church on 19 April, the second of three sons of James Thom, a farm worker, and his wife, Margaret Morrison. His mother had been a frequent visitor to the home of the Burns family at Mossgiel and often recalled these visits in the presence of her family. They later moved to Meadowbank in the adjoining parish of Stair, where Thom attended a small local school. With his younger brother, Robert (1805–1895), he was apprenticed to a firm of builders in Kilmarnock, Howie and Brown, where he was later employed as an ornamental carver. It was while renovating a tombstone in Crosbie kirkyard, Troon, in 1827 that he attracted the attention of David Auld, a barber in Ayr and custodian of the Burns monument at Alloway. On Auld's suggestion Thom carved a bust of Robert Burns from the copy of the portrait by Alexander Nasmyth that hung at the Burns monument. So impressed was Auld by the bust that he encouraged the sculptor to attempt a more ambitious work, and in 1828 Thom carved a life-size statue of Burns's Tam O'Shanter (Burns monument, Alloway). This was hewn without any

preliminary sketches, directly from a block of rough-grained sandstone supplied from a neighbouring quarry. It was followed soon afterwards by the companion statue of Souter Johnnie (Burns monument, Alloway), for which a subscription was raised locally to meet the costs.

Before placing the statues at the Burns monument, Auld exhibited them in Ayr in July 1828 with great success. Afterwards he took them to Edinburgh—where they received the praise of Sir Walter Scott—and Glasgow. In April 1829 they went to London where the critics at once hailed them as inaugurating a new era in sculpture. They were seen as works of untutored genius unconstrained by academic convention and perfectly capturing the spirit of Burns's poetry. The homely naturalism of the pair's clothing—particularly Tam's circular cap and knitted stockings—and their expressive attitudes and humour were much admired. Sixteen replicas of the figures were said to have been ordered as well as small-scale reproductions carved by Thom and his brother Robert. Moreover, 1 shilling admission was charged to see the works, and the net profit raised from the exhibitions was said to have been nearly £2000; this was divided equally between the sculptor, Auld, and the trustees of the Burns monument. Thom in addition received a special award of 20 guineas from the board of manufacturers in Scotland.

Encouraged by his successes, Thom made companion statues of the Landlord and Landlady from the same poem (Burns monument, Alloway; versions at the Cottage of Souter Johnnie, Kirkoswald, Ayrshire). He also carved a group representing *Old Mortality and his Pony* (1830) from Scott's novel, a figure based on Burns's song 'Willie brew'd a peck o' maut', and statues of Burns (1830) and Sir William Wallace (freestone, 1830; Wallace Tower, Ayr). In 1835 a second exhibition of Thom's work was organized in London though this did not meet with the success of the earlier venture.

About 1836 Thom went to America. Some of his works had been sent there for exhibition and sale but his agent had kept the proceeds. Recovering a portion of the money, Thom decided to remain in America and he settled at Newark, New Jersey, where in the following years he executed many replicas of his best-known works. They included the Tam and Souter figures, *Old Mortality and his Pony* (version at Laurel Hill cemetery, Philadelphia), a statue of Burns, as well as ornamental garden pieces. He is also credited with discovering the freestone quarries at Little Falls, New Jersey; these provided the materials for his architectural carvings at Trinity Church, New York. Having amassed a considerable fortune, he purchased a farm at Ramapo, Rockland county, New York, where he built a house to his own designs. He is said to have abandoned sculpture in his last years and died of consumption in his lodging house in New York city on 17 April 1850. He married and had a son, James Crawford Thom (b. 1835), who became an artist, and a daughter, Ada Crawford Thom.

Thom was one of a group of Scottish so-called 'mason sculptors' (others were John Greenshields, Robert Forrest, David Anderson, and John Currie) who enjoyed a vogue in the early nineteenth century for genre works and familiar subjects from Scottish history and literature. Their direct and often humorous approach to everyday subject matter—extending a distinct tradition in local stone carving—significantly influenced the development of mainstream sculpture in both Britain and America during the mid-nineteenth century.

Another artist of the same name, **James Thom** (*b. c.*1785), subject painter, was born in Edinburgh. He studied art in his native city, and between 1808 and 1815 exhibited in Edinburgh some thirteen pictures, of which one or two were historical, three were portraits, and the rest of domestic subjects (including two designs for vignette illustrations to Burns). In 1815 he sent two pictures to the British Institution, and about that time moved to London where he had some success. In 1825 his *Young Recruit* was engraved by A. Duncan.

MARTIN GREENWOOD

Sources *DNB* · W. S. Lanham, *The history of James Thom, the Ayrshire sculptor* [n.d., 1950x59?] · R. L. Woodward, 'Nineteenth century Scottish sculpture', PhD diss., U. Edin., 1979, 249–52 · R. Gunnis, *Dictionary of British sculptors, 1660–1851* (1953); new edn (1968) · J. McBain, 'James Thom, sculptor', *Annual Burns Chronicle and Club Directory*, 25 (Jan 1916), 61–71 · *Ayr Advertiser* (23 April 1896) · *GM*, 2nd ser., 34 (1850), 98 · *The Athenaeum* (19 June 1830), 379 · 'The Ayrshire sculptor', *New Scots Magazine*, 1 (Dec 1828), 33–9 · Thieme & Becker, *Allgemeines Lexikon*
Likenesses W. Tannock, portrait, exh. RA 1830

Thom, John Hamilton (1808–1894), Unitarian minister, was born on 10 January 1808 in Newry, co. Down, where his father, John Thom (1776–1808), who had come from Scotland in 1800, was a Presbyterian minister; his mother was Martha Anne (1779–1859), daughter of Isaac Glenny of Newry. In 1823 he entered the Belfast Academical Institution. He was profoundly impressed by reading the sermons of the American minister William Ellery Channing (1780–1842), with their Unitarian theology and Romantic eloquence, but his Unitarian commitment never entirely escaped the more exalted view of Jesus characteristic of his Arian teachers in Belfast. Nor was he exposed to the rigorous necessarianism of Joseph Priestley (1733–1804) and Thomas Belsham (1750–1829), which so deeply affected many of his English colleagues, especially those trained at Manchester College, York.

In 1828 Thom became minister of the Ancient Chapel, Toxteth Park, just outside Liverpool, but in 1831 the early death of John Hincks (*b.* 1804), minister of Renshaw Street Chapel, Liverpool—whose brother William Hincks (1794–1871) had earlier occupied that pulpit and whose father, Thomas Dix Hincks (1767–1857), was Thom's teacher—brought him to that important post. Congregational minutes indicate considerable opposition: John Finch (1784–1857), an Owenite iron merchant, protested against the 'aristocratical' way in which the invitation was issued by the pew owners; others worried about Thom's youth or, with John Hincks in mind, his delicate health.

The objections were overcome, but the early years of Thom's tenure were difficult. Some members complained of his 'stile and manner', others that his sermons were too abstract and inattentive to practical, ethical questions.

John Hamilton Thom (1808–1894), by Robinson & Thompson, early 1860s

Many years later, Thom conceded his immaturity; but at the time he took on his critics with a startling imperiousness, pleading his ignorance of the workaday world, insisting on his entire freedom, and lecturing the congregation on the proper duties of minister and flock. With strong support from congregational leaders, among them William Rathbone (1787–1868), he survived the criticism and remained at Renshaw Street as minister—with a three-year leave in 1854–7, during which he was replaced by William Henry Channing (1810–1884), the son of his American inspirer—until he retired from loss of voice in 1866. On 2 January 1838 he married Hannah Mary Rathbone (1816–1872), the second daughter of William Rathbone, whose eventually futile opposition to the match was based on concern about Thom's health and its possible implications for his daughter's financial prospects. There were no children.

The denomination in England became generally aware of Thom in 1839 when, in *Unitarianism Defended*, the Liverpool ministers—Thom, James Martineau (1805–1900), and Henry Giles (1809–1882)—answered one by one thirteen lectures by local Anglican ministers determined to confute Unitarianism. The brilliance of the defence made a great impression, but Thom's and Martineau's lectures contain hints of the subversion that the 'new school'—in the leadership of which they were joined by John James Tayler (1797–1869) and Charles Wicksteed (1810–1885)—visited on post-Priestleyan rational religion over the next thirty years, rejecting materialism and necessity, subordinating the nexus of religion and science, and questioning the authority of the Bible as testimony.

Thom's views were reinforced by Joseph Blanco White (1775–1841), the former Spanish priest and once an influential figure at Oriel College, Oxford, who lived his last years in Liverpool; in 1845 Thom published a life of Blanco White, based on White's own accounts. He had written a memoir of his predecessor, John Hincks, in an edition of his sermons (1832) and was to publish a biographical account of his friend Tayler incorporating his letters (1872). Eventually Tayler and Martineau moved to London as professors and successive principals at Manchester College, but Thom remained in Liverpool, where his relative leisure allowed him to edit the *Christian Teacher* in 1839–44 and to take the lead in the shared editorship of its greatly influential successor, the *Prospective Review* (1845–55).

The conflict between the 'new school' of Thom and his friends and the 'old school' of the Priestleyans came to a head in 1866 in a conservative resolution insisting on a broadly worded commitment to historical Unitarianism as a qualification for membership in the British and Foreign Unitarian Association. Although the new school was probably in a minority among Unitarian ministers and laymen at the crucial meeting, long-standing Unitarian resistance to anything resembling a creed assured the overwhelming defeat of the resolution. Martineau and Thom were less successful in their next initiative, to submerge the Unitarian identity and name in the Free Christian movement.

Members of the new school led a revolution in taste as well as in doctrine. Although nearly everyone in their generation had been deeply affected by Romantic poetry, and while there was general sympathy with the Gothic revival so dramatically embodied in new Unitarian churches built in mid-century, the new school carried the Romantic impulse to the very centre of their thought and into their language. The reservations of Thom's early hearers were soon swept away, and the diary of George Holt (1790–1861), one of the great Liverpool Unitarian merchants, repeatedly records his dissatisfaction with preaching elsewhere compared with Renshaw Street. L. P. Jacks (1860–1955), a later minister there, continued to regard Thom as the finest preacher of them all, though many readers a century later may find his sermons (the best-known of several collections is *Laws of Life after the Mind of Christ*, 1882, 1886) highly convoluted (yet precise) in rhetoric and too self-conscious in the deliberate, lapidary creation of verbal beauty. Although privately Thom could reveal a sly sense of humour, in public he was an awe-inspiring figure, and it was said in Liverpool that merely seeing him enter the pulpit did one as much good as hearing a sermon from anyone else.

Thom exercised wide influence in another area of Unitarian activity where there was little disagreement. The domestic mission movement—aimed not at proselytizing but at reclaiming the dignity and self-worth of the poorest of the poor—was begun in Boston by the American minister Joseph Tuckerman (1778–1840). On a tour of England in 1833–4, Tuckerman made a particular impression in Liverpool, and while missions were established in almost every major town starting in London, the mission in Liverpool, established in 1836, may have been the best-known of them all. Much of this fame was owing to the death of its first missionary, the Revd John Johns (b. 1801), from cholera in 1847. Thom did not himself go regularly into the slums: ministers confided that task to missionaries thought to have special abilities, and their reports provided the texts on which ministers could descant in drawing support from their wealthy and comfortable hearers. The methods of the movement meshed superbly with the

way in which Thom and his friends saw religion, as well as social improvement, as an intensely individual experience—in his words, 'heart acting on heart, conscience on conscience, soul on soul, man on man' (*Religion, the Church, and the People*, 1849, 25). Thom and Martineau never abandoned that view, though all about them the rage grew for collective solutions, legislative intervention, and even socialism.

After his retirement, Thom remained in Liverpool and in regular attendance at Renshaw Street. Clad in immaculate broadcloth and conveyed in a smart brougham, he was a daunting presence for the youthful Jacks, who knew that he was constantly being judged by, and against, his distinguished predecessor: Thom once rebuked him for derogating from ministerial dignity by riding a bicycle. Thom died of old age and exhaustion at his residence, Oakfield, in Sefton Park, Liverpool, on 2 September 1894, and was interred on 7 September in the burial-ground at the Ancient Chapel, Toxteth Park.   R. K. Webb

Sources *Christian Life* (8 Sept 1894) · *The Inquirer* (8 Sept 1894) · A. Holt, *Walking together: a study in Liverpool nonconformity, 1688–1938* (1938) · R. K. Webb, 'John Hamilton Thom: intellect and conscience in Liverpool', *The view from the pulpit*, ed. P. T. Phillips (1978), 210–43 · L. P. Jacks, *The confession of an octogenarian* [1942] · U. Lpool L., special collections and archives, Rathbone MSS · A. Holt, *A ministry to the poor: being the history of the Liverpool Domestic Mission Society, 1836–1936* (1936) · Lpool RO, Ullet Road Church Records · d. cert.
Archives Lpool RO, corresp., papers, and sermons · U. Lpool, Sydney Jones Library, journal, family corresp., and papers | DWL, letters to James Martineau · Lpool RO, letters to Anne Holt
Likenesses Robinson and Thompson, photograph, 1860–64, repro. in J. Thom, *A spiritual faith* (1895) [*see illus.*] · Robinson and Thompson, photograph, 1892, U. Lpool · oils, Ullet Road Church, Liverpool · photograph, Liverpool City Libraries; repro. in Webb, 'John Hamilton Thom', 210
Wealth at death £23,872 7s. 5d.: probate, 26 Nov 1894, *CGPLA Eng. & Wales*

Thom [Tom], **John Nichols** [*alias* Sir William Courtenay] (*bap.* **1799**, *d.* **1838**), impostor and lunatic, was baptized on 10 November 1799 at St Columb Major, Cornwall, the only son (he had one sister) of William Thom (or Tom), a small farmer and innkeeper, and his wife, Charity, whose maiden name was Bray. Charity Thom showed symptoms of insanity by 1816 and later died in the county lunatic asylum. Thom was educated at Bellevue House Academy, Penryn, and at a school in Launceston, run by Richard Cope, the local Congregational minister, on narrow religious lines, which left a lasting impression on his mind. He was clerk to a solicitor at St Columb (1817–20) and, after a few months as an innkeeper at Wadebridge, he became clerk to Lubbocks, wine merchants, in Truro. He married in February 1821 Catherine Fisher (*b. c.*1775), daughter of William Fulpitt of Truro, a comfortably off fisherman turned market gardener, and, using his wife's money, took over Lubbocks on the retirement of the partners. Thom appeared a friendly, diligent tradesman, better educated than most. Almost 6 feet tall, swarthy, and well built, he was a fine cricketer, reputedly one of the best wrestlers in Cornwall, and well known locally for his feats of strength.

Although Thom said little about his religious and political beliefs, in 1821 he secretly joined the Spencean Society, which advocated the nationalization of land. On 19 June 1828 Thom's business premises in Truro burned down, and although they were insured and rebuilt he showed signs of incipient insanity and was under treatment for much of 1829–31. In May 1832 he vanished when on a visit to Liverpool to sell a cargo of malt; he reappeared in September at Canterbury, where he falsely claimed he had been travelling in the Near East. He had probably been living in London, masquerading as Squire Thompson and taking an interest in the cause of distressed Jews. He had grown his hair and beard extravagantly long and, calling himself Count Moses Rothschild, he lodged at The Rose inn. Here he showed a talent for duplicitous self-advertisement, financing the largesse he distributed to the credulous mob by loans on which he promised repayment with interest.

Styling himself a knight of Malta, Thom assumed the name of Sir William Courtenay and claimed the earldom of Devon; the real earl lived in France and surprisingly never confronted Thom's imposture. He also claimed the Kentish estates of Sir Edward Hales, sixth baronet, who had died without issue in 1829, and bought some of his clothes from his valet. At the general election of December 1832, standing for Canterbury as an independent, Thom capitalized on the enthusiasm for reform and, promising to abolish tithes, taxes on shopkeepers, primogeniture, placemen, and corporate bodies, he polled a respectable 375 votes (the winner polled 834). However, a few days later he secured only four votes in the county election for East Kent. He then published *The Lion*, a weekly broadsheet (March–May 1833), which amid much scurrilous nonsense acutely attributed the cause of the prevailing popular unrest to heavy taxation and exorbitant rents. Unfortunately, Thom was indicted for perjury in his defence of some smugglers at Rochester, and at Maidstone assizes (25 July 1833) he was sentenced to three months' imprisonment and seven years' transportation. After his wife arrived from Cornwall to relate his previous insanity, he was placed in the county lunatic asylum at Barming Heath, where for four years he was a model patient. His father, backed by Thom's former employer (now MP for Truro), petitioned the home secretary, Lord John Russell, for his release, which was granted on 3 October 1837.

Persisting in his claim to be the rightful earl of Devon, Thom refused to return to Cornwall with his family, and for three months lodged near Canterbury with George Francis, a blinkered snob deluded by Thom's aristocratic pretensions and impressed with his biblical exegesis. Thom aimed to whip up the rural working classes against the unfair distribution of wealth, low wages, lack of employment, and the harsh operation of the poor law. Closely resembling the traditional likeness of Christ, and mouthing messianic and apocalyptic prophecies, he gathered about forty followers, armed them with cudgels, and, mounted, with pistols, on a white horse, with a flag bearing a lion as emblem, he led them about the countryside. A

warrant charged him with enticing away the labourers of a local farmer, and on 31 May 1838 Thom shot Nicholas Mears, one of the constable's party serving the warrant, cruelly mangling the dying man with his sword. When two companies of the 45th regiment marched from Canterbury that afternoon to arrest him, Thom retired to Bossenden Wood, threatening his followers with death if they fled. In a fight only lasting a few minutes, Thom, having shot one of the officers, Lieutenant Bennett, was himself killed, along with eight of his followers; three more died of their wounds a few days later. Of those captured, three were subsequently sentenced to transportation and six to a year's hard labour. Thom was buried on 5 June in Hernhill churchyard, where no mark or memorial was allowed over his grave.

Thom's paranoia, with its delusions of grandeur and sartorial extravagance, was accompanied by considerable clarity of thought and a commanding presence, all of which gulled his illiterate and ignorant followers (and indeed some of the Canterbury well-to-do). In the aftermath of the final incident in Thom's life, the government of Lord Melbourne came under fire for releasing him from his asylum, and the established church was attacked for its lack of influence locally.   BASIL MORGAN

Sources P. G. Rogers, *Battle in Bossenden Wood* (1961) · *An essay on the character of Sir W. Courtenay and the causes of his influence over the public mind*, 3rd edn (1833) · Canterburiensis, *The life and extraordinary adventures of Sir William Courtenay, knight of Malta, alias John Nichols Tom* (1838) · R. Matthews, *English messiahs: studies of six English religious pretenders, 1656–1927* (1936) · J. F. Thorpe, *History of the Canterbury riots* (1888) · B. Reay, *The last rising of agricultural workers: rural life and protest in nineteenth-century England* (1990) · DNB
Archives CKS, Knatchbull MSS
Likenesses H. Hitchcock, watercolour · prints, NPG

Thom, Walter (1770–1824). *See under* Thom, Alexander (1801–1879).

Thom, William (1710–1790), author and Church of Scotland minister, was born at New Monkland, near Glasgow. Nothing is known of his parents or his early life. He was educated at Glasgow University, where he studied under the celebrated moral philosophy professor Francis Hutcheson. Thom received his MA in 1732 and was licensed by the presbytery of Hamilton in 1738, but he did not receive a call to the ministry until 1746; during that period he was described by another young minister, Alexander Carlyle, as having had 'great sway' among the other young men of the Literary Society (*Autobiography*, ed. Burton, 52). In May 1746 Thom was presented to the parish of Govan, Lanarkshire, by the professors of Glasgow University, who held the patronage of the parish. The call was opposed by the parishioners, probably because of their dissatisfaction with the principle of patronage and Thom's association with members of the modernizing or moderate faction within the church, and the ordination was delayed until 25 February 1748.

During a ministry of more than four decades Thom worked effectively to overcome that opposition. Although his call had been sponsored by the moderate leadership of

Glasgow University, in a series of more than twenty controversial sermons and tracts, most published anonymously, he would gradually align himself with their ecclesiastical opponents in the orthodox or popular party. His 1766 *Short History of the Late General Assembly* announced his opposition to ecclesiastical patronage, the principal dividing line between moderate and popular clergyman, despite the fact that he owed his own position to that practice. He also began a lengthy dispute with his patrons at Glasgow University, in part because they refused to augment his stipend; he developed his case in a series of six critical pamphlets, in which he first displayed the sarcastic wit for which he became famous. Yet there were serious issues involved. In *The Motives which have Determined the University of Glasgow to Desert the Blackfriar Church* (1764), Thom criticized the professors for attending their own chapel rather than hearing a local orthodox preacher, John Gillies. More substantively, his *Defects of an University Education, and its unsuitableness to a Commercial People* (1761) criticized the classical curriculum at the university for devoting excessive attention to such rarefied subjects as the metaphysics of morals—implicitly criticizing his former teacher Francis Hutcheson—instead of a practical education based upon the mechanical arts and history.

Thom also became a strong advocate of the interests of farmers and weavers, who formed the bulk of the congregants in his parish, reflected in his 1771 *Letter of Advice to the Farmers, Land-Labourers, and Country Tradesmen in Scotland*. In a series of five or more anonymous pamphlets beginning with his 1770 *Seasonable Advice to the Landholders and Farmers in Scotland*, he also became Scotland's most prominent promoter of their emigration to America. Like other popular party ministers, he expressed considerable sympathy for the position of the American colonies during their war for independence, about which he published three sermons. He married Grizel Scot on 22 October 1753, and they had four children before her death in 1760. On 17 April 1780 he married Agnes, daughter of John M'Kechnie, merchant in Glasgow. William Thom died at Govan on 8 August 1790; his second wife died in 1817.

Since his death Thom has been known principally for his eccentricity and wit. Only recently have historians come to appreciate his prominent role as a critic of the classical style of education at Glasgow University, which helped inspire the development of the practically orientated Anderson's Institution, the forerunner of the University of Strathclyde, founded in 1796 by the popular party adherent John Anderson. Because most of his works appeared anonymously, Thom's prominent influence in encouraging emigration from Scotland to America during the 1770s was not recognized for two centuries. Thom's career highlights the developing ties that emerged in eighteenth-century Scotland among popular presbyterianism, the growing artisan class, and a keen interest in America.   NED C. LANDSMAN

Sources *Fasti Scot.* · *The works of the Rev. William Thom, late minister of Govan* (1799) · 'Thom of Govan pamphlets', NL Scot., Colquhoun of Luss MSS · W. I. Addison, *A roll of graduates of the University of Glasgow

from 31st December 1727 to 31st December 1897* (1898), 604 · *Autobiography of the Rev. Dr. Alexander Carlyle … containing memorials of the men and events of his time*, ed. J. H. Burton (1860); repr. as *Anecdotes and characters of the times*, ed. J. Kinsley (1973), 52 · R. B. Sher, 'Commerce, religion and the Enlightenment in eighteenth-century Glasgow', *Glasgow*, ed. T. M. Devine and G. Jackson, 1: *Beginnings to 1830* (1995), 312–59, esp. 342–50 · R. K. Donovan, 'Evangelical civic humanism in Glasgow: the American war sermons of William Thom', *The Glasgow Enlightenment*, ed. A. Hook and R. B. Sher (1995), 227–45 · U. Glas., Thom MSS
Archives U. Glas.

Thom, William (1798?–1848), poet and weaver, was born in Aberdeen, probably on 12 March 1798. He hardly knew his father, who may have been a merchant or an architect. Run over by a nobleman's carriage at an early age, Thom was lamed for life; his widowed mother was offered compensation of 10s. by the occupant of the carriage. Educated only at a dame-school, Thom became an autodidact. At the School Hill Factory in Aberdeen, he worked simultaneously as a weaver and as a student, delighting especially in Scottish songs and poems. He also became adept at this time at playing the flute.

Thom married when he was aged about twenty, but the couple separated after only a few years. By 1837, when he briefly gave up weaving, Thom was living with Jean Whitecross, a Kirriemuir woman, with whom he had four children. A very poor man, Thom struggled to feed himself and his family by itinerant bookselling and flute playing. Jean Whitecross died in 1840, by which time the family had settled in Inverurie and Thom had returned to weaving. It was really at this point that his career as a poet began. He was already well known in his own community for songwriting, but, early in 1841, one of his poems, 'The Blind Boy's Pranks', was published in the *Aberdeen Herald*, and, soon after, in many other Scottish newspapers. The poem secured Thom a valuable patron, J. A. Gordon, a former English MP and laird of Knockespock. Gordon's English connections were extremely useful to Thom; he spent the summer of 1841 at his patron's house in London.

In 1844 Thom brought out a short-lived journal, the *Inverurie Gossamer*, and, by subscription, *Rhymes and Recollections of a Hand-Loom Weaver*, which contained the powerful 'Whisperings for the unwashed'. One thousand copies of the book were distributed and Thom received donations from admirers amounting eventually to several hundred pounds. It was said these admirers included Scottish merchants living in Calcutta. By this time Thom had formed a relationship with Jean Stephen (1821–1848), of Inverurie, with whom he had three children. Literary success and this new relationship did not prevent Thom becoming the victim of his own personal weaknesses; he spent fewer and fewer hours at his loom and became a hard drinker. Between late 1844 and late 1847 Thom and his family lived in London. He was welcomed by Lady Blessington, Dickens, and Jerrold. Smith, Elder & Co. republished his volume of poetry and waited for another. It never came. Though Thom formed close friendships with such literary-minded working men as George Julian Harney and Thomas Cooper, he did not heed their urgings to work at his poems. Offers of publication in journals were spurned, his relationship with Gordon collapsed, and his money ran out; in poor health, Thom left for Dundee in late 1847. He died, probably of tuberculosis, on 29 February 1848, at Hawkhill, Dundee, and was buried in the western cemetery, Dundee. One month later Jean Stephen, too, was dead; a public appeal eventually raised well over £300 for their three children. Thom identified closely with the Paisley weaver-poet Robert Tannahill and, like him, was a tragic figure. Mostly he wrote in the Scottish dialect rather than standard nineteenth-century English, producing both lyrics and protest verse about the sufferings of the poor. He was undoubtedly a poet of greater talent than most of his early and mid-Victorian working-class colleagues.   STEPHEN ROBERTS

Sources W. Thom, *Rhymes and recollections of a hand-loom weaver* (1844); another edn, ed. W. Skinner (1880) · O. Ashton and S. Roberts, *The Victorian working class writer* (1999) · R. Bruce, *William Thom, the Inverurie poet: a new look* (1970) · T. Royle, *The mainstream companion to Scottish literature* (1993) · B. Maidment, ed., *The poorhouse fugitives: self-taught poets and poetry in Victorian Britain* (1987) · *The collected letters of Thomas and Jane Welsh Carlyle*, 23, ed. C. de L. Ryals and K. J. Fielding (1995)
Archives U. Aberdeen L., special libraries and archives, letters and papers relating to him | BL, Royal Literary Fund archive, MSS
Likenesses engraving, repro. in Thom, *Rhymes and recollections*, front · engraving, repro. in *Illustrated Magazine*, 4 (Nov 1844)

Thomas [Thomas of Bayeux, Thomas (I) of York] (*d.* 1100), archbishop of York, was of Norman descent and was archbishop from 1070 until his death in 1100. He was the son of a priest; a Durham obituary book records his parents' names as Osbertus and Muriel; such commemoration indicates his lifelong *pietas* (devotion) towards them. Thomas received a good education. He and his brother *Samson (bishop of Worcester, 1096–1112) were among the promising young clerks for whom Bishop Odo of Bayeux paid to study at Liège and other cities; his studies may have taken him as far afield as Germany and Spain. In Normandy, he may also have been a pupil of Lanfranc, the future archbishop of Canterbury. In due course, Bishop Odo appointed him treasurer of Bayeux Cathedral. Thomas also served William I in England as a royal chaplain; he may have been a ducal chaplain in Normandy before 1066.

Archbishop of York The northern metropolitan see of York became vacant on the death on 11 September 1069 of the last Anglo-Saxon archbishop, Ealdred. On 23 May 1070, the day before the Council of Windsor, the king named Thomas of Bayeux to succeed; but no steps towards his consecration were taken until Lanfranc was consecrated archbishop of Canterbury on 29 August 1070. Thereafter, Thomas travelled to Canterbury, but, before he would consecrate him, Lanfranc required Thomas 'after the custom of his predecessors' to give him a written profession of obedience reinforced by an oath of loyalty. Dissatisfied by the evidence that Lanfranc cited, Thomas refused on the grounds that the rights of the church of York forbade him to do otherwise; he left Canterbury without consecration. Upon hearing of these events, William I was angry. Lanfranc hastened to court, where he calmed the king's anger and won round the Normans who were present by an explanation of his case; according to the Canterbury account, the English fully supported Lanfranc. The king first cajoled and then browbeat, by threat of exile for himself and his family, a reluctant Thomas, so that, in late 1070 or early 1071, he returned to Canterbury for consecration. He made a profession of obedience to Lanfranc personally, with the reservation that he would not repeat such a profession to Lanfranc's successors until he had publicly received proof that his own predecessors had so done, and had rightly so done. His profession was probably made only verbally and not altogether according to the written formula that was prepared at Canterbury. In any case, no text of Thomas's first profession survives. Lanfranc proceeded to his consecration. (For these events, the Canterbury account in Lanfranc, *Letters*, 38–43 should be compared with the York account in Hugh the Chanter, *History of the Church of York*, 4–7.)

Relations with Rome In autumn 1071 Thomas travelled to Rome in company with Lanfranc and Remigius, bishop of Dorchester. During their visit, each archbishop received his pallium from Pope Alexander II. However, the York sources, especially Hugh the Chanter, were studiously silent about the visit, for which Canterbury evidence predominates. On the second day of the bishops' audience with the pope, in the course of other business, charges were made that neither Thomas nor Remigius had come canonically to the episcopate—Thomas because he was a priest's son and Remigius because he had purchased it by services rendered to the king. Each surrendered his ring and staff and they threw themselves upon the papal mercy. When Lanfranc pleaded for them on the grounds of their learning and experience and of the king's need of them, Alexander allowed Lanfranc in his own presence to restore the bishops' insignia. During the audience Thomas advanced two claims on behalf of the church of York: first, as against Lanfranc's insistence upon the primacy of Canterbury, that the churches of Canterbury and York were equal in status to each other and that, by ordinance of Pope Gregory the Great, neither should be in any way subject to the other, save that precedence for the time being should belong to whichever archbishop was senior by consecration; and second, that the three bishops of Dorchester, Worcester, and Lichfield rightly owed obedience to York, not Canterbury. After long argument, Alexander ruled that the whole matter should be heard in England and there settled by the bishops and abbots of the whole kingdom. According to William of Malmesbury, Alexander wished to avoid offending either archbishop (*Vita Wulfstani*, 25).

The matter was duly considered at a council held at Eastertide (*c.*8 April 1072) in the king's chapel in his castle at Winchester, and again at Pentecost (27 May) in the royal vill at Windsor; on both occasions, the papal legate Hubert was present. The evidence continues to come mainly from the Canterbury side: Lanfranc's report to Pope Alexander on events up to Easter 1072, together with the concord on the primacy which was formulated at Winchester and confirmed at Windsor, and Archbishop Thomas's second profession of obedience which followed. As at Rome, so at Winchester there was a prolonged debate during which, on the issue of the primacy, Lanfranc maintained the irrelevance of the dispositions of Pope Gregory I because he referred to the churches of London and York, not Canterbury and York. Lanfranc claimed that other arguments of Thomas were thin and weak. According to Lanfranc, King William rebuked Thomas gently and patiently for the weakness of his arguments. Thomas replied that he had not hitherto appreciated the strength of the precedents and arguments that Canterbury could deploy. He suppliantly besought Lanfranc to banish from his mind any rancour that the conflict might have engendered and to agree to a settlement that offered a few gracious concessions to York; he probably had in mind those which, given his dearth of suffragans other than Durham, would permit him to function as a metropolitan. Such, in Lanfranc's report, was the genesis of the concord adopted at Winchester.

The concord, of which Lanfranc sent the pope a copy, had the form of a judgement made with the king's agreement and in his presence by the bishops and abbots to whom the pope had referred the matter. As regards the relations of Canterbury and York, it recognized the vindication of the view that York should be subject to Canterbury and should obey the directions of its archbishop as primate of the whole of Britain in all matters relating to the Christian religion. The archbishop of York and his suffragans must obey the primate's summons to a council, wherever convened, and must also obey his lawful instructions. On the death of an archbishop of Canterbury, the archbishop of York should come to Canterbury and duly consecrate his successor, with the help of the other suffragans of the church of Canterbury, as his own primate; if the archbishop of York died, his successor should, however, come for consecration to Canterbury or to wherever the archbishop of Canterbury might direct. In one respect, Lanfranc did not get his way: as in 1070, he had pressed for what he considered the ancient right of the archbishop of Canterbury to require from the archbishop of York a public oath as well as a profession of obedience; 'out of love for the king' (probably in fact because of the king's refusal), Lanfranc waived the oath in Thomas's case but reserved the position of his own successors who might wish to exact one. As regards jurisdiction over the three disputed dioceses, this was tacitly denied to the archbishop of York; the limit of his province was set to the north of the diocese of Lichfield and mostly at the River Humber, although by compensation he was given jurisdiction northwards 'to the furthest limits of Scotland'. Thomas soon afterwards made an absolute profession of obedience to Lanfranc and his successors as archbishops of Canterbury and of due obedience to their just and canonical commands, adding the comment that when making his earlier profession he was uncertain on this matter and had promised obedience to Lanfranc unconditionally but to his successors conditionally. For Thomas's lifetime, the issue of the primacy was settled.

Relations with Canterbury So far as the authority of Canterbury is concerned, Thomas in general honoured the spirit and the letter of the settlement of 1072. Only two incidents call for notice. In perhaps 1086, according to the unsupported story of Hugh the Chanter, Lanfranc and Thomas accompanied King William to the Isle of Wight before his last crossing to Normandy. The king was told by someone unspecified of the York tradition that the concord of 1072 was a forgery of the Canterbury monks which they had fraudulently sealed. The king promised to decide the matter judicially if he returned to England. In 1093 there is an irreducible conflict of evidence about Thomas's stand when he consecrated Anselm archbishop of Canterbury. According to Hugh the Chanter, Thomas demurred to a petition that he consecrate Anselm 'primate of all Britain' and required the phrase 'metropolitan of Canterbury' to be substituted (*Hugh the Chanter*, 12–15). At Canterbury, Eadmer slightly more probably has Thomas objecting to the words 'metropolitan of all Britain' with its implicit denial of York's metropolitan status but agreeing to 'primate of all Britain' (*Historia novorum*, 42–3). For the rest, during Lanfranc's lifetime Thomas was present at the Council of London (1074 or 1075) which settled the precedence of the two archbishops and other prelates at church councils. In 1081, at Lanfranc's Council of Gloucester, upon the king's order and with Lanfranc's consent, Thomas consecrated William of St Calais to be bishop of Durham. Lanfranc and Thomas corresponded amicably upon pastoral matters. When the see of Canterbury was vacant from 1089 to 1093, Thomas was to the fore in consecrating bishops—Ralph Luffa of Chichester (1091), Herbert de Losinga of Thetford (1091), and Hervey of Bangor (1092); but there is no sign of his taking advantage to press the claims of York. Hugh the Chanter cited a letter of Pope Urban II which, if genuine, probably dates from 1093 or 1094, summoning Thomas to account for his having in 1072 wrongly subjected his church to the archbishop of Canterbury (*Hugh the Chanter*, 10–13); there is no record that Thomas responded.

Thomas was only occasionally able to exercise the jurisdiction to the north which the concord of 1072 assigned to him. His best opportunity was in 1073, when Earl Paul of Orkney sent a clerk, Ralph, for episcopal consecration. Thomas arranged the ceremony at York on 3 March but required two further consecrators. Making no reference to his one suffragan of Durham, he wrote to Lanfranc with somewhat exaggerated deference, requesting the help of two bishops. He undertook to give no grounds for the suspicion once expressed by Bishop Remigius of Dorchester that he would claim a precedent for his own jurisdiction over him or his brother of Worcester. Lanfranc dispatched bishops Wulfstan of Worcester and Peter of Chester, whom he advised to keep Thomas's letter as a record of his undertaking. Hugh the Chanter claimed that, commanded by Malcolm III and Queen Margaret of Scotland, Bishop Fothad of St Andrews came to York, where he professed canonical subjection to the church and its archbishops.

To the south, Thomas had no lasting success. Prevented

in 1072 from claiming bishoprics for his province, he could still claim 'appurtenances' of his diocese that he had already sought but not secured at Rome in 1071. With support from Odo of Bayeux, he claimed twelve vills at Worcester which Archbishop Ealdred had retained after surrendering the see in 1062; but in 1072 the king's court decided against him. Bishop Remigius of Dorchester's transfer of his see to Lincoln occasioned greater difficulties, for Thomas claimed that the region of Lindsey, together with Lincoln, Stow, Louth, and Newark, belonged to his diocese. In 1092, when Remigius planned the consecration of his new cathedral, Thomas issued a prohibition, which Remigius ignored. William II, allegedly bribed by Remigius, allowed the consecration to go ahead; but when most of the bishops had assembled for it, Remigius's sudden death led to a postponement. When, on the day after his own consecration, Anselm of Canterbury was about to consecrate Remigius's successor, Robert Bloet, Thomas warned Anselm to consecrate him as bishop of Dorchester, not Lincoln. According to Hugh the Chanter, after a bribe of £3000 King William in 1094 arranged a concord to settle the matter: Thomas (it was said unwillingly) surrendered his claim to Lincoln, Lindsey, Stow, and Louth, and received in return the abbeys of Selby and St Oswald at Gloucester.

Secular affairs and diocesan reform Thomas seems to have been of exemplary loyalty to kings William I and II, but he took little known part in secular affairs. In 1088 he was at Salisbury during the trial for treason of Bishop William of St Calais; beforehand, he refused to counsel William, and during the trial he upheld the ruling of the king's court that William must do right to the king before being reinvested with his fief. But on William's deathbed in 1095, Thomas gave him the viaticum.

Thomas appears to best advantage in ordering his diocese, which, when he arrived, had been devastated by warfare, especially the Conqueror's harrying of the north in 1069. To his clergy, he showed a liberality that his successors deemed excessive. At York itself, in 1070 he found in the ruined cathedral only three of the meagre establishment of seven canons; he recalled the fugitives and created more canons. Having re-roofed and rehabilitated the old Anglo-Saxon cathedral, he rebuilt the refectory and dormitory to provide for a common life. Perhaps in the early 1080s, he built a new cathedral. He appointed a provost and recovered and increased the endowments. Perhaps in the early 1090s, Thomas deemed that better stewardship of cathedral property would result from the establishment of separate prebends for the canons. Having already appointed a master of the schools, he proceeded to introduce, on the Norman model, a dean, precentor (chanter), and treasurer. To assist with the oversight of his vast diocese, he appointed archdeacons.

Of Thomas's character, contemporaries were unanimous in their praise. A handsome and dignified man, he was agreeable in any company, whether engaged in serious business or honest fun; he inspired both respect and liking. He was a man of acknowledged piety and humility; and his observance of celibacy was unquestioned. He was

a considerable musician who composed many hymns; he insisted that ecclesiastical chanting should be solemn and not effeminate. He was a good Latinist, who composed William the Conqueror's epitaph on his tomb at Caen. He was well versed in many branches of knowledge. His sterling reputation was widely known on the continent. Three of his kin became bishops: his brother Samson, who had also been treasurer of Bayeux and a royal chaplain, and at whose consecration Thomas assisted, became bishop of Worcester (1096–1112); Samson's sons Thomas and Richard became respectively archbishop of York (1109–14) and bishop of Bayeux (c.1108–1133).

Death In 1100 Thomas heard at Ripon that William II had died on 2 August. He hastened to London, where he was indignant on finding that Henry I had already been crowned; since Anselm of Canterbury was abroad, he wished to implement his claim to officiate. But Thomas, who was weakened by sickness and age, was easily persuaded that the peace of the kingdom had demanded haste. He returned to the north after mid-September and on 18 November died at either York or Ripon. He was buried in York Minster near his predecessor Ealdred; Hugh the Chanter cited his epitaph (*Hugh the Chanter*, 20–21).

H. E. J. COWDREY

Sources *Hugh the Chanter: the history of the church of York, 1066–1127*, ed. and trans. C. Johnson (1961) · *Willelmi Malmesbiriensis monachi de gestis pontificum Anglorum libri quinque*, ed. N. E. S. A. Hamilton, Rolls Series, 52 (1870) · *The Vita Wulfstani of William of Malmesbury*, ed. R. R. Darlington, CS, 3rd ser., 40 (1928) · *The letters of Lanfranc, archbishop of Canterbury*, ed. and trans. H. Clover and M. Gibson, OMT (1979) · J. Raine, ed., *The historians of the church of York and its archbishops*, 3 vols., Rolls Series, 71 (1879–94) · *Eadmeri Historia novorum in Anglia*, ed. M. Rule, Rolls Series, 81 (1884) · Ordericus Vitalis, *Eccl. hist.* · John of Worcester, *Chron.* · [J. Stevenson], ed., *Liber vitae ecclesiae Dunelmensis*, SurtS, 13 (1841) · D. Whitelock, M. Brett, and C. N. L. Brooke, eds., *Councils and synods with other documents relating to the English church, 871–1204*, 2 (1981) · R. C. van Caenegem, ed., *English lawsuits from William I to Richard I*, SeldS, 1, 106 (1990) · J. E. Burton, ed., *York, 1070–1154*, English Episcopal Acta, 5 (1988) · Pope Alexander II, 'Epistolae et diplomata', *Patrologia Latina*, 146 (1853)

Thomas [Thomas (II) of York] (*d.* 1114), archbishop of York, came of a notable clerical family, being the son of *Samson (*d.* 1112), treasurer and possibly dean of Bayeux and then bishop of Worcester from 1096 until his death, brother of Richard, bishop of Bayeux (c.1108–1133), and nephew of Archbishop *Thomas (I) of York (1070–1100). To distinguish him from his uncle he is commonly known as Thomas (II) of York or Thomas the younger. It was to the first Archbishop Thomas that he owed his promotion as provost of the collegiate church of Beverley in 1092. He was introduced as a clerk at the king's court, where he became a royal chaplain. On 27 May 1108, six days after the death of Archbishop Gerard, Thomas was appointed archbishop of York by Henry I. According to Hugh the Chanter, the king had been intending to confer on him the vacant bishopric of London, but, at the request of Dean Hugh and other members of the York chapter who were then at court, he was appointed to York instead. It was a popular appointment with the chapter, as Thomas had been educated at York; Hugh asserts that the canons, given a free choice in 1100, would have elected him to succeed his uncle. Hugh records that Thomas's popularity with the York chapter was partly due to certain characteristics that he shared with his late uncle; almost certainly he would have been expected to be sympathetic to the stance taken by York in response to the demands of the archbishops of Canterbury that the northern archbishops make written profession of obedience to them. Indeed, Hugh states that Thomas 'knew the rights and wrongs of the case' (*Hugh the Chanter*, 27). The archbishop-elect then attended Anselm's council held at London (28 May 1108) to which his predecessor had been travelling at the time of his death, and associated himself with Anselm's reforms.

Almost immediately the question of the primacy was raised. The monks of Christ Church, Canterbury, put pressure on Archbishop Anselm (*d*. 1109) to summon Thomas in order to receive consecration and make profession. The dean and chapter of York, however, wrote to Thomas to forbid him to go to Canterbury or to make such profession. Thomas declared that he would take the advice of the king, and journeyed to the royal court at Winchester. Henry I was inclined to support York's claims and ordered Thomas not to make profession. Anselm, however, wrote to Thomas demanding that he accept consecration and fixing a day for the ceremony; and he threatened that he would himself perform episcopal functions within the diocese of York should Thomas refuse. Thomas contrived to delay, excusing himself from the journey on the grounds that the chapter of York had forbidden him to make profession, and that his predecessor, Gerard, had so impoverished the see that he could not afford to travel. There followed an interchange of letters: from Anselm forbidding Thomas to go to Rome for his pallium; from Anselm to the pope requesting him to withhold the pallium until Thomas had been consecrated; from Thomas to Anselm explaining that his chapter had forbidden him to make profession; and from the chapter to Thomas threatening to denounce him should he do so. On Anselm's behalf the bishops of London and Rochester attempted to persuade Thomas to act as the archbishop wished. Thomas received them at Southwell, explaining that he had communicated all this to the king, who was then in Normandy. The king then wrote to Anselm ordering him to stop his demands until he should return to England. He also sent the dean of York to Rome with letters explaining the situation, and asking the pope to send a legate to England to decide the case, since Thomas was unable, for various reasons, to travel to Rome. The pope agreed, and sent Cardinal Odalric (Ulric) with the pallium and instructions concerning the dispute.

Thomas's prevarication succeeded in postponing the matter until after the death of Archbishop Anselm, who on his deathbed still warned Thomas against exercising episcopal authority before he had been consecrated; and the king, having received the papal envoys in Normandy, sent them ahead to England. When he himself returned he was approached by the monks of Canterbury, and he ordered them to wait until Whitsun for an answer. On 13 and 14 June 1109 he received at court the various parties,

including the archbishop-elect and the papal legate. But the king was no longer inclined to support York; as Hugh the Chanter realized, he had done so in the past partly in order to oppose Anselm rather than from firm conviction of the rightness of York's cause. Henry now changed his mind, and ordered Thomas to make profession. He commanded the bishops, and members of Thomas's own family, to use their influence with him, and, under pressure to resign if he did not make profession, Thomas capitulated: he made a vague profession to an unnamed archbishop of Canterbury, and was consecrated by the bishop of London on 27 June 1109 in the presence of six bishops. In response to requests by the bishops of Norwich and Durham, the king declared that the profession had been made in response to a royal command, rather than as the result of a legal sentence.

Following his profession and consecration Thomas journeyed north with Cardinal Odalric, and received his pallium from the legate at York on 1 August. Thomas was under pressure to consecrate Turgot (*d*. 1115) as bishop of St Andrews, without the profession of obedience that Archbishop Gerard had demanded, and this he did in York on the same day. Thomas spent three days in York before accompanying the cardinal south as far as the River Trent. As they parted the archbishop was astounded to receive a summons from the legate to the Roman curia to answer charges of having made his profession contrary to the decrees of the Roman church. However, he and others present persuaded the cardinal that the profession had been forced upon him by the king, and the summons was withdrawn.

Thomas also consecrated, with written profession, Michael, bishop of Glasgow, and later Ralph Nowell (*d*. 1144), bishop of Orkney, and Wimund, bishop of Man and the Isles. As archbishop he was credited with the creation of two prebends in the church of York, possibly those of Fridaythorpe and Sherburn in Elmet, and he granted the canons the vill of Helperby to hold in common. He granted to the collegiate church of Southwell the liberties enjoyed by the churches of York, Beverley, and Ripon, and aided the same church in its construction work by ordering the men of Nottinghamshire to make their Pentecostal procession to the church of Southwell rather than that of York. His period of office saw the introduction of the regular canons to the diocese of York, both to Bridlington and in 1113 to the ancient minster church of Hexham, where the hereditary priest, Eilaf, was expelled, and replaced by canons drawn from Huntingdon. Thomas allegedly tried to remove the bones of St Eata to York to compensate for York's lack of relics, but was thwarted in his attempts by a vision of the saint himself. He endowed the Augustinian priory of Hexham with a generous amount of land, rents, and allowances, as well as with books and ornaments.

Thomas (II) was a corpulent man; Hugh the Chanter states that he was 'full-bodied and fatter than he should have been' (*Hugh the Chanter*, 49), and that this explained both his lack of action and his submission over the matter of the profession of obedience: his corpulence would have prevented him tolerating the discomforts of exile. His overweight may have been a factor in his early death. Hugh notes as another characteristic of Thomas that he maintained his virginity. During his period as provost of Beverley, Thomas had suffered an illness and was allegedly told by his doctors that his life could only be saved by breaking his lifelong vow of chastity. His friends, according to William of Newburgh, attempted to persuade him to this course of action by introducing a woman secretly into his household. Thomas, however, refused both medical advice and the well-meaning assistance of his friends, and recovered after he had prayed to St John of Beverley. But the illness returned at a later date, and Thomas died at Beverley on either 19 or 24 February 1114. He was buried in York near to the tomb of his uncle. Walter Daniel, in his life of Ailred, abbot of Rievaulx, recorded that Thomas's death was seen in a vision by the young Ailred, son of Eilaf, the priest ousted from Hexham by Thomas; when he announced the event to his disbelieving family several days before news of it arrived in Hexham, his father drew laughter by commenting 'truly he has died, who lives a bad life' (*Life of Ailred*, 72).

Thomas's rule at York was a brief one, but he clearly had the affection and trust of the York canons who remembered him as a man 'agreeable both in morals and manners' despite his capitulation over his profession of obedience (*Hugh the Chanter*, 27). Similar epitaphs were given by Richard of Hexham and William of Newburgh, and Symeon of Durham praised Thomas's chastity and probity. JANET BURTON

Sources Hugh the Chanter: the history of the church of York, 1066–1127, ed. and trans. C. Johnson (1961) · Eadmeri Historia novorum in Anglia, ed. M. Rule, Rolls Series, 81 (1884) · Willelmi Malmesbiriensis monachi de gestis pontificum Anglorum libri quinque, ed. N. E. S. A. Hamilton, Rolls Series, 52 (1870) · 'Epistolae Anselmi', ed. F. S. Schmitt, S. Anselmi Cantuariensis archiepiscopi opera omnia, 3–5 (1938–61) · R. Howlett, ed., Chronicles of the reigns of Stephen, Henry II, and Richard I, 1, Rolls Series, 82 (1884) · J. E. Burton, ed., York, 1070–1154, English Episcopal Acta, 5 (1988) · 'Historia regum', Symeon of Durham, Opera, vol. 2 · Florentii Wigorniensis monachi chronicon ex chronicis, ed. B. Thorpe, 2 vols., EHS, 10 (1848–9) · J. Raine, ed., The priory of Hexham, 1, SurtS, 44 (1864) · D. Nicholl, Thurstan: archbishop of York, 1114–1140 (1964) · F. Barlow, The English church, 1066–1154: a history of the Anglo-Norman church (1979) · The life of Ailred of Rievaulx by Walter Daniel, ed. and trans. M. Powicke (1950) · Chronica magistri Rogeri de Hovedene, ed. W. Stubbs, 1, Rolls Series, 51 (1868)

Thomas. *See* Brown, Thomas (*d.* 1180).

Thomas (*fl. c.*1170). *See under* Thomas (*fl.* 1170–1180).

Thomas [Tumas] (*fl.* **1170–1180**), poet, was a Norman clerk, and author of a romance, *Tristan*, in which he names himself twice (as Thomas and Tumas) and whom his German imitator Gottfried von Strassburg (1210) calls 'Thômas von Britanje'. His romance survives in the form of ten fragments, drawn from six manuscripts (M. Benskin discovered an important fragment in Carlisle in 1994), and is estimated to have comprised a little over 12,000 lines in all. Its contents can be largely reconstructed from the Norse translation, the *Tristrams Saga* (1226). Thomas was conscious of the co-existence of rival versions of the legend in the hands of a variety of story-tellers and

rejected the idea of a total synthesis in favour of following his own course. This involved criticizing certain choices and showing confidence in the Welsh latimer and story-teller Breri (Bledhericus). Thomas makes powerful use of a training in dialectic and rhetoric and appears as a pessimistic, and frequently ironic, commentator on the vicissitudes of earthly love. His language is not markedly Anglo-Norman and it is likely that he settled in England from Normandy. His romance contains a eulogistic description of London. Thomas is certainly writing after Wace's *Brut* (1155) and, arguably, after Chrétien de Troyes's *Cligés* (probably dating to the 1170s or early 1180s). His frequently posited presence at the court of Henry II and Eleanor of Aquitaine, particularly at the time of the estrangement and the revelation of Henry's adultery with Rosamund Clifford, must remain mere supposition. At all events, Thomas's *Tristan* cannot convincingly be read as an endorsement of *fin' amor*.

The **Thomas** (*fl. c.*1170), poet, who, as 'mestre Thomas', wrote the romance of *Horn* has, since Söderhjelm's demonstration in 1886, been distinguished from the author of *Tristan*. It is true that he, too, is sophisticated and erudite, had an excellent clerkly training, shares many clerical prejudices, displays Latin influence, maintains a generally aristocratic tone, and is particularly sympathetic to music (he seems to have been an excellent harpist). At the end of the *Horn*, which is itself apparently a sequel to an earlier work on Aalof (Horn's father), Thomas leaves to his son Wilmot (Gilemot), who is presented as an excellent young poet, the task of composing a work on Hadermod (Horn's son). This suggests a date at the end of his professional career which might be put at *c.*1170. The linguistic evidence suggests that Thomas was an immigrant to England. Anglo-Norman features of his language are relatively slight and there are clear signs of south-western origin, suggesting that he or his parents originated in the Loire valley. He may have studied at Poitiers. He has some knowledge of English, and seems to know Brittany and Dublin. The *Horn* is filled with the spirit of the crusades and of the *chanson de geste* and is written in rhymed *laisses* of alexandrines. TONY HUNT

Sources B. H. Wind, 'Nos incertitudes au sujet du Tristan de Thomas', Mélanges de langue et de littérature du moyen âge et de la Renaissance offerts à Jean Frappier (1970), 2.1129–38 · M. Blakeslee, 'The authorship of Thomas's Tristan', Philological Quarterly, 64 (1985), 555–72 · W. Söderhjelm, 'Sur l'identité du Thomas auteur du Tristan et du Thomas auteur du Horn', Romania, 15 (1886), 575–96 · The romance of 'Horn' by Thomas, ed. M. K. Pope, 2, Anglo-Norman Text Society, 12–13 (1964), 1–2, 121–4

Thomas (*fl. c.*1177). *See under* Ely, Richard of (*fl.* 1177–1189).

Thomas [Thomas of Galloway], **earl of Atholl** (*d.* **1231**), magnate, was the younger son of *Roland, lord of Galloway (*d.* 1200), and Helen (*d.* 1217), daughter of Richard de Morville, lord of Lauderdale and Cunningham and constable of the Scottish king. He had one brother and two sisters who survived to adulthood: *Alan, who succeeded in 1200 to the lordship of Galloway; Ada, wife of Walter Bisset of Aboyne; and Dervorguilla, wife of Nicholas de

Stuteville of Liddel in Cumbria. A marriage to an unidentified wife, contracted before c.1207–8, produced a son old enough to serve as a hostage in England in 1213. Before January 1210 he married Isabella, elder daughter of Henry, earl of Atholl, and received the title of earl. With her he had two sons, but only the younger, Patrick [see below], survived childhood. Maduff, 'son of the earl', a witness to a charter of Isabella in her widowhood, may be the son of the first marriage, or illegitimate. Thomas had one certain bastard, Alan.

The extent of Thomas's inheritance in Galloway is unknown, but from 1204–5 it furnished him with a fleet of galleys. In that year he entered the service of King John, who hired the vessels for use in the abortive Normandy campaign and for the 1206 expedition to Poitou. This service brought property in northern and western England, apparently lost when he returned to Scotland c.1209. It was probably in the period 1205–9 that Thomas committed the rape at York for which he was pardoned in 1212 at the request of the Scottish king. In 1211 Earl Thomas served against the MacWilliams in Ross, and in 1212 he began a series of operations in Ulster directed against Áed Ó Néill, the MacWilliams' ally, which culminated in 1214 in his construction of a castle at Coleraine. Scottish and English policies here coincided, and an initial small grant of land in Ulster from John was enlarged in June 1215 into a substantial lordship centred on Coleraine. This, and a grant of the custody of Antrim Castle, were unsuccessful moves designed to win the earl's support in John's conflict with the barons—he is not known to have played any part in the civil war in England of 1215–17.

In June 1219 Earl Thomas gave homage and fealty to Henry III and received confirmation of his Irish possessions, but in July 1222 was ordered to surrender Antrim, and by 1224 Coleraine had been destroyed by Ó Néill. The mounting threat to Ulster from Hugh de Lacy, who was trying to recover the lordship there of which John had dispossessed him, saw English attempts to retain Earl Thomas's interest in Ireland, with cash payments and temporary grants of land being made until his possessions in Ulster could be restored. When the crown reached an accommodation with the Lacys in 1226, an apparently ineffective attempt was made to safeguard the earl's possessions. His inability to defend his Irish lands in the early 1220s arose from Earl Thomas's commitment to his brother's venture into Manx politics. In 1221 his galleys destroyed a Hebridean fleet off the Irish coast and slew Diarmait Ó Conchobhair, claimant to the kingship of Connacht, which was held by an ally of Henry III, and in 1228 Earl Thomas was again active in the Isles, joining Alan's invasion of Man in support of the exiled King Ragnvald. But Earl Thomas gave no further aid after Ragnvald's death in 1229, and by July 1230 his ships were once more in English service, probably for Henry III's expedition to Brittany and Bordeaux. Earl Thomas's death, possibly as the result of a tournament accident, and his burial in Coupar Abbey are recorded in 1231. In 1252 Patrick, son of Constantine of Goswick, a knight of the earl of Dunbar, was pardoned by Henry III for the killing of Thomas of Galloway. Isabella survived him for an unknown number of years, but was dead before 1242. From about 1233 to perhaps about 1237, the earldom was held by Alan Durward, possibly through exercise of the wardship of the heir, Patrick, and in 1237 an unnamed earl of Atholl, perhaps Durward, witnessed the treaty of York.

The career of **Patrick**, fifth earl of Atholl (c.1222–1242), who was a minor in 1231, was brief. In 1242 he was about to enter his inheritance, when his murdered body was found in his burnt-out lodgings in Haddington. No satisfactory explanation for his murder presents itself, but his Comyn kinsmen accused John Bisset and his uncle, Walter Bisset of Aboyne, husband of Patrick's aunt, Ada. While the Comyns claimed that control of Patrick's paternal lands in Galloway and Ireland was the motive, their accusations may have been prompted by territorial rivalry in Scotland. This was believed by many contemporaries, including Alexander II, who was reluctant to act until he was forced to banish Walter Bisset by the earls of Buchan and Dunbar. Atholl passed to Patrick's maternal aunt, Forueleth, and her husband, David Hastings. RICHARD D. ORAM

Sources Scots peerage, 1.419–23 · K. J. Stringer, 'Periphery and core in thirteenth-century Scotland: Alan, son of Roland, lord of Galloway and constable of Scotland', Medieval Scotland: crown, lordship and community: essays presented to G. W. S. Barrow, ed. A. Grant and K. J. Stringer (1993), 82–113 · A. A. M. Duncan, Scotland: the making of the kingdom (1975), vol. 1 of The Edinburgh history of Scotland, ed. G. Donaldson (1965–75), 178, 179n., 246n., 529–30, 543–6 · D. E. Easson, ed., Charters of the abbey of Coupar-Angus, 2 vols., Scottish History Society, 3rd ser., 40–41 (1947) · A. Young, 'The political role of Walter Comyn, earl of Menteith, during the minority of Alexander III of Scotland', SHR, 57 (1978), 121–42, esp. 122–3 · A. O. Anderson and M. O. Anderson, eds., The chronicle of Melrose (1936), no. 1894

Thomas [Thomas of Eccleston] (fl. c.1231–c.1258), Franciscan friar and chronicler, was the author of one of the chronicles which is one of the chief sources of information about the early growth of the Franciscan order. The order's origins are well documented, but for its expansion and development these chronicles are of special value. Jordan of Giano was an Italian friar who went on the first mission to Germany and provides a vivid and reliable account of the formation of the German province. Salimbene, also an Italian, was an inveterate gossip, an Italian Matthew Paris, full of precious detail and wild prejudice. Thomas was an Englishman who witnessed the formation of the English province and met many of the great figures among the early Franciscans, including two future ministers-general, Alberto da Pisa and Haymo of Faversham. Much of his chronicle consists of notes and anecdotes; but he was a careful, observant witness, crucial to what is known of the early Franciscans, and not only in England; he draws many vivid vignettes of life in the order, specifically so that his friend Brother Simon, and doubtless other friars, could judge their own lives 'by the example of those who were better'; and could find no less edification in their own order than in reading of the wonderful deeds of other orders (De adventu, ed. Little, 1).

Thomas is known only from his *Tractatus de adventu Fratrum Minorum in Angliam et dilatione et multiplicatione ipsorum in ea* ('A treatise on the coming of the Friars Minor to England, and the spreading and multiplication of the friars in England'). The prefatory letter is addressed by 'frater Thomas' to 'fratri Simoni de Esseby', presumably the guardian of a Franciscan convent. In John Bale's autograph notebook, the mid-sixteenth-century *Index Britanniae scriptorum*, Thomas was originally called Thomas of Esseby, probably by confusion with Simon: but Bale saw his mistake and changed 'de Esseby' to 'de Eckleston'. Bale knew and annotated a copy of the book (now Bodl. Oxf., MS Lat. misc. c.75, formerly Phillipps 3119) which gives the author no such toponym, unless it has been cut away by a binder; and Bale's unsupported word is of little value. None the less Brother Thomas is now commonly known as Thomas of Eccleston; and if that was truly his place of origin, he presumably came from Eccleston in Cheshire or from one of the four Ecclestons in Lancashire.

Thomas himself relates that while still in secular habit he saw a group of English friars who had entered the order in Paris: this presumably occurred after the dispersal of the University of Paris in 1229. He may have seen them in Oxford; but it is certain only that he studied at Oxford when he was himself a friar. It may be that his reminiscence of the early friars walking fervently to lectures through 'bitter cold and deep mud' reflected his own experience—but it is not specifically referred to himself or to Oxford (*De adventu*, ed. Little, 27). The book itself cannot be earlier than 1257–8, but, as it fails to note significant events of those years, it may be dated with some confidence to c.1257–8. Thomas says that he had been collecting material for twenty-six years, which takes the date back to c.1231–2, quite soon, that is, after 1229: it may reasonably be concluded that the twenty-six years represent the author's years as a friar, and that he entered the order c.1231–2.

Thomas's weakness as a chronicler is his lack of interest in chronology: the book is arranged by themes—on the first arrival of the friars in 1224, on the first division of the friars into separate houses, on the first reception of novices, and so forth, concluding with chapters on the succession of ministers-general and the provincial ministers of England, and a final gathering of disconnected anecdotes. It is very difficult to deduce dates from it; it lacks the order and clear narrative of the contemporary chronicle of Jordan of Giano on the friars in Germany. Nevertheless it has great value, for Thomas had been an assiduous and careful note-taker, and could be remarkably observant. He had sat at the feet of some of the leading friars of the period: he probably knew Agnellus of Pisa, first minister provincial in England; he certainly knew his successor, Albert of Pisa, minister from 1236 to 1239, then briefly minister-general and the most notable of the early Italian Franciscans to visit Britain. When Albert arrived he held a provincial chapter in Oxford and made trial of the English friars. He later rebuked the friars at Oxford for the most modest indulgence; and ordered a new cloister at Southampton to be demolished because it caused annoyance to the townsfolk. In spite of this Albert came greatly to respect the English province. Thomas has also preserved a precious summary of one of Albert's sermons and vignettes of his conversation. Thus: 'We should greatly love the Friars Preachers, because they have profited our order in many ways and occasionally taught us how to avoid future perils' (*De adventu*, ed. Little, 82). Of Albert's sermons to English novices, Thomas preserves two parables against presumption and hasty zeal: for the latter, telling the story of a young ox who found his elders ploughing rather too slowly for his taste. So they asked him to help them, and when he was set under the yoke he ploughed with great energy half a furrow, at which point he was exhausted. The older oxen told him that they ploughed at a more moderate pace, so that they could keep going steadily.

Albert's successor, the English friar Haymo of Faversham, also followed Albert as minister-general of the order, inspiring changes which made him almost a second founder of the order. Of his personal qualities almost nothing would be known, were it not for Thomas's description of Haymo's conversion to the order in Paris, and of his conduct at a provincial chapter: 'such was his zeal for poverty that he sat in the refectory ... in a thoroughly vile and torn habit on the ground, with the humblest folk' (*De adventu*, ed. Little, 86). Thomas is thus a vivid witness of the links between the English province and the government of the order in the 1230s and early 1240s; and it has been shown that his account of the general chapters of 1230, 1232, and 1239, and of the role of the ministers-general, Elias and John Parenti, though not without its prejudices, is essentially reliable and evidently based on the reports of eyewitnesses. The value of his evidence is very apparent by comparison with scholars' ignorance of the politics of the Dominican order in the 1230s—or of the development of the Franciscan province in France.

ROSALIND B. BROOKE

Sources *Fratris Thomae vulgo dicti de Eccleston tractatus de adventu Fratrum Minorum in Angliam*, ed. A. G. Little (1951) · *Tractatus Fr. Thomae vulgo dicti de Eccleston de adventu Fratrum Minorum in Angliam*, ed. A. G. Little (Paris, 1909) · Thomas of Eccleston, *The coming of the Friars Minor to England and Germany, being the chronicles of Brother Thomas of Eccleston and Brother Jordan of Giano*, trans. E. G. Salter (1926), 1–126 · Emden, *Oxf.*, 1.623–4 · R. B. Brooke, *Early Franciscan government: Elias to Bonaventure*, Cambridge Studies in Medieval Life and Thought, new ser., 7 (1959), 27–45 · A. G. Little, 'Chronicles of the mendicant friars', *Franciscan papers, lists, and documents* (1943), 25–41 · A. Gransden, *Historical writing in England*, 1 (1974), 488–94 · Bale, *Index*, 437

Thomas [Thomas of Brotherton], **first earl of Norfolk** (1300–1338), magnate, was the fifth son of *Edward I (1239–1307) and the first from Edward's second marriage, to *Margaret (1279?–1318), daughter of Philippe III, king of France (d. 1285); he was thus the elder of the two half-brothers of *Edward II (d. 1327).

Acquiring an estate, 1300–1312 Thomas was born, unexpectedly, at Brotherton, Yorkshire, on 1 June 1300, as his mother was travelling to Cawood, where her confinement was to occur. The chronicler Rishanger reports that the delivery was initially difficult, but that in her suffering Margaret called on St Thomas of Canterbury for aid, as was customary for pregnant women, and gave birth without difficulty. Hence the child was named Thomas of Brotherton in honour of Thomas Becket, and for his own place of birth. Rishanger goes on to demonstrate Thomas's patriotism, saying that when he was first nursed by a French woman he screamed and vomited up her milk, so that people feared for his life. When he was given an English wet-nurse, however, he immediately recovered and drew refreshment from her. But, despite Rishanger's optimism, Thomas grew to become a man of modest achievement, in his capacity as first a younger brother and then an uncle of the king.

In 1306 Edward I promised, on behalf of himself and his eldest son, Edward, to provide Thomas with an inheritance worth 10,000 marks a year, as had been stipulated in the contract drawn up by Pope Boniface VIII when Edward married Margaret. He also promised Thomas the lands of Roger (IV) Bigod, earl of Norfolk, valued at 6000 marks, if the earl died without a direct heir, since his estate would then pass to the crown under the terms of a settlement made in 1302. Bigod did indeed die later in 1306, and his lands came into royal custody. Thomas's elder half-brother, Edward II, held the estate until 1310, when he gave Thomas and his younger brother, *Edmund of Woodstock, joint custody for their support and maintenance. It was said that Edward I had hoped to bestow the earldom of Cornwall on either Thomas or Edmund, but Edward II's elevation of Piers Gaveston thwarted that intention. Instead, Thomas was created earl of Norfolk in December 1312, obtained the Bigod estate as his father had promised, and received the office of marshal.

Servant of Edward II, 1313–1322 Edward II summoned Thomas to parliament for the first time in January 1313, though as he was only twelve years old his role in government and politics was largely honorific at this stage. Edward similarly summoned him to serve in Scotland in 1313, but remitted the service shortly afterward. Nevertheless, Thomas was called on to perform military service in Scotland and elsewhere continuously thereafter. He served with his brother Edmund as executor of their mother's will after her death on 14 February 1318. Later that year Thomas and Edmund were among the royalists witnessing the treaty of Leake. The same year the young Edward Balliol, who was later to claim the Scottish throne, was assigned to the household of Thomas and Edmund. The following year Edward II named Thomas keeper of the realm when he departed for war in Scotland. As keeper Thomas summoned the mayor of London to appear before himself, the bishop of Winchester, and the earl of Pembroke on 24 March, to hear complaints about his conduct of elections in London. Thomas ordered the disputants to resolve their conflict or appear before him at Westminster the following day; after withdrawing to talk the matter over the mayor and citizens reached an agreement. On 15 July 1319 Edward II knighted Thomas, along with many others, when they mustered at Newcastle in preparation for a campaign in Scotland. When Edward travelled to France to perform homage, from 19 June to 22 July 1320, Thomas accompanied him with a large retinue. At some point during these years Thomas married his first wife, Alice, the daughter of Roger Hales, the coroner of Norfolk. The match was a remarkably obscure one for a member of the royal family, but all the signs are that Thomas was a less than dynamic personality, who is seldom if ever recorded as acting on his own initiative.

Thomas actively supported his half-brother during the baronial rebellion of 1321–2. In March 1321 he tried to arrange negotiations with the earl of Hereford, who had broken with the king and assembled troops to plunder the lands of the Despensers, but the attempt failed. In April Thomas sat in place of the king in judgment on the younger Hugh Audley, accused of having broken his contract of 1317 to stay in attendance on the king. In October Edward dispatched Thomas with the earls of Pembroke and Richmond to Leeds Castle, Kent, after Sir Bartholomew Badlesmere's men refused entry to the queen, thereby precipitating civil war. Thomas and his brother Edmund later joined the royal army in 1322 as it moved toward the Welsh marches to confront the baronial rebels.

Political haverings, 1323–1329 After the rebellion Thomas apparently fell out of favour temporarily. In August 1323 he surrendered the lordship of Chepstow in Wales, which formed part of the Bigod inheritance, to the king's favourite, Hugh Despenser the younger, for life for the modest rent of £200 a year. In the following year he released Despenser from the rent, as well as from any actions arising out of waste, sales, or destruction committed by Despenser, for only £800. Then Edward II temporarily confiscated the office of marshal because of Thomas's failure to have someone execute the office on his behalf in Lancashire, when royal justices arrived there to hold the king's pleas. Thomas offered a fine of £100 to recover the office, which Edward pardoned, taking the opportunity, however, to administer a verbal rebuke to his half-brother, saying that if Thomas failed to perform his duties properly, he would be punished.

Edward's attitude towards Thomas changed in 1326. As fears of an invasion from France by Queen Isabella heightened, Edward had to rely on a close coterie of supporters. In January he gave Thomas a gift of £200 out of the issues of the bishopric of Norwich, then in royal custody. He also appointed Thomas one of the supervisors of the array in Norfolk and Suffolk, and in May amplified his authority by naming him captain and principal surveyor of the array in a broad swath of eastern counties from Lincolnshire to Essex. Edward also granted Thomas a number of favours, such as the lands of contrariants, wardships, and markets.

Despite these incentives, Thomas deserted Edward. He may have been in communication with Isabella, Roger Mortimer, and his own brother Edmund while they were overseas, for their invasion force landed at Thomas's property of Orwell on 24 September 1326. Thomas met them there, along with Henry, earl of Lancaster, and they spent the night at Thomas's castle. At his command, his men plundered manors belonging to the younger Despenser. Thomas accompanied the queen and her army in their pursuit of Edward II and the Despensers across England, and was present at the baronial council in Bristol that on 26 October declared Prince Edward keeper of the realm. The following day Thomas and Edmund were among the nobles who sat in judgment on the elder Despenser, and they both acted as judges in the trial of the younger Despenser in November. In the summons to the first parliament of the new regime Thomas and Edmund headed the list of nobles, and both sat on the council headed by Henry of Lancaster to watch over the young king.

At first fully supportive of Isabella and Mortimer, Thomas sat on a number of commissions of oyer and terminer, and served as an overseer of the justices of the peace in Norfolk and Suffolk during 1327. He was summoned to serve against the Scots, and participated in the ill-fated Stanhope campaign, which ended in humiliation for Edward III. His own contribution to the campaign may not have amounted to much more than the composition of a brief description of the privileges he claimed in his capacity of earl marshal. In return for his support for the regime he recovered Chepstow, received lands forfeited by the Despensers worth 1000 marks, and obtained an important wardship, as well as other favours. The high point of his involvement came in 1328, when his son Edward married Beatrice, daughter of Roger Mortimer. Edward III and his mother attended the celebrations at Hereford, which included a tournament.

Soon after the wedding, however, Thomas participated in Henry of Lancaster's brief rebellion against the government. Although Thomas and Henry had apparently fallen out over the murder of Sir Robert Holland by Lancaster's followers in October, Thomas met with a group of dissident magnates in London at the beginning of December, and was reconciled with Lancaster when the latter arrived. The nobles and prelates, including Thomas and Edmund, entered into a sworn confederation for the stated benefit of reforming the king and realm, but Thomas and Edmund deserted the rebels and returned to the king's side, whereupon the rebellion collapsed. Nevertheless, Thomas found himself out of favour at court, and witnessed only a few charters in these years.

Servant of Edward III, 1330–1338 By 1330, however, Thomas was again being employed by the crown. On Saturday 17 February 1330, he and Edmund accompanied Edward III's wife, Philippa, on her coronation march from London to Westminster, holding her bridle on either side of her palfrey and dressed merely as grooms. That summer Thomas travelled to Gascony on royal business, and he was a member of a delegation sent to negotiate with Philippe VI of France the following year. In June 1331 he participated in a tournament in Stepney in the King's Company. Edward placed him on several judicial commissions, and in 1332 appointed Thomas one of the keepers of the peace in Norfolk and Suffolk. Responding to unrest in Ireland, Edward in 1331–2 ordered Thomas to restore order on his own lands (pre-eminently the lordship of Carlow) or risk having them seized should a royal army be brought to Ireland,

and he summoned Thomas to serve there, though the expedition never materialized. Thomas participated in the Scottish campaign which culminated in the battle of Halidon Hill on 19 July 1333, where he commanded a contingent of royal forces. In the next few years Edward showed his confidence in his uncle by calling on Thomas to serve in Scotland, to consult about the defence of the realm, and to protect Wales from invasion by the Scots. Edward also appointed him a captain of the array in England and Wales, and named him keeper of Perth (1337).

During the 1330s, Thomas also entered into several land transactions that did not work to his advantage. In 1332 he surrendered to the king most of the Despenser manors which he had received in 1327, in part fulfilment of Edward I's promise of lands worth 10,000 marks. Edward III then regranted them to Thomas for life, on condition that on Thomas's death they would pass to William de Bohun, a royal favourite. Bohun at some point gained possession of the lands in return for a rent of £800, but in 1336, in a deal strikingly similar to the one he made with the younger Despenser over Chepstow, Thomas remitted payment of the rent. In 1333 Thomas granted to William Montagu, another royal favourite, all of his lands in Ireland and some of his English property for a period of fifteen years. This grant was made as part of a proposed marriage between Thomas's daughter Alice and William's son William, and the lands were to revert to William and Alice on the elder William's death. Alice, however, married Edward Montagu, William senior's brother. These actions do not speak well either of Thomas's financial acuity, or of his ability to protect his own interests generally, and he seems to have been taken advantage of by both his half-brother and his nephew, as they sought to provide estates for their favourites. Nor was he able to control his own household, so that in 1337 Edward found it necessary to appoint Constantine Mortimer to restore it to order, having first caused Thomas to appear before himself to hear complaints about the unruliness and destructiveness of his followers. In this, as in other matters, Thomas completely submitted himself to Edward's rule. At about the same time Thomas once again lost the office of marshal, though he recovered it before he died.

Thomas's only son, Edward, died in 1337. He himself died the following year, probably in September, and was buried at Bury St Edmunds. His first wife had died by 1330, and Thomas married as his second wife, not much more impressively, Mary, widow of Sir Ralph Cobham and daughter of Sir Piers Brewes, who outlived him and died c.1361. His eldest daughter, Margaret *Brotherton, married John, Lord Seagrave, and inherited the earldom of Norfolk. Thomas's estates were divided between Margaret and Alice. Margaret, in particular, was to show a strength of character sadly lacking in her father.

SCOTT L. WAUGH

Sources GEC, *Peerage* · F. Palgrave, ed., *The parliamentary writs and writs of military summons*, 2 vols. in 4 (1827–34) · *RotP*, vols. 1–2 · *Chancery records* · Rymer, *Foedera*, new edn · *Chronicon Galfridi le Baker de Swynebroke*, ed. E. M. Thompson (1889), 21, 42, 43, 196, 217–20 · *Adae Murimuth continuatio chronicarum. Robertus de Avesbury de gestis* *mirabilibus regis Edwardi tertii*, ed. E. M. Thompson, Rolls Series, 93 (1889), 35, 46, 57 • *Willelmi Rishanger … chronica et annales*, ed. H. T. Riley, pt 2 of *Chronica monasterii S. Albani*, Rolls Series, 28 (1865), 438–9 • W. Stubbs, ed., *Chronicles of the reigns of Edward I and Edward II*, 2 vols., Rolls Series, 76 (1882–3) • *Thomae Walsingham, quondam monachi S. Albani, historia Anglicana*, ed. H. T. Riley, 2 vols., pt 1 of *Chronica monasterii S. Albani*, Rolls Series, 28 (1863–4), vol. 1 • H. R. Luard, ed., *Flores historiarum*, 3 vols., Rolls Series, 95 (1890), vol. 3, pp. 109, 199, 233, 302, 334 • N. Denholm-Young, ed. and trans., *Vita Edwardi secundi* (1957) • M. Prestwich, *Edward I* (1988), 131 • N. Fryde, *The tyranny and fall of Edward II, 1321–1326* (1979), 5, 51, 107, 136, 183, 185–7, 194, 207, 208, 217, 222, 231, 236, 269 • J. R. Maddicott, *Thomas of Lancaster, 1307–1322: a study in the reign of Edward II* (1970), 5, 23, 71, 201, 265, 290, 299 • J. R. S. Phillips, *Aymer de Valence, earl of Pembroke, 1307–1324: baronial politics in the reign of Edward II* (1972), 11, 19, 172, 183, 190–91, 201, 216, 221, 226, 228, 260, 284 • R. Nicholson, *Edward III and the Scots: the formative years of a military career, 1327–1335* (1965), 16, 36, 71–2, 128, 129, 132, 139, 194, 211, 238–9 • Tout, *Admin. hist.*, 1.256–7; 2.43, 95 (n. 3), 252 (n. 2); 3.4, 189, 326, 410; 4.446 • *CPR, 1338–40* • *CCIR, 1337–9* • *CIPM*, 10, no. 121

Thomas, ninth earl of Mar (*c.*1330–1377). *See under* Donald, eighth earl of Mar (1293–1332).

Thomas [Thomas of Woodstock], **duke of Gloucester** (**1355–1397**), prince, was the seventh (but fifth surviving) son of *Edward III (1312–1377) and *Philippa of Hainault (1310?–1369). He was born at Woodstock on 7 January 1355, and on 22 February Edward III celebrated his son's birth with a great feast and a tournament there. At about the same time he was baptized. Thomas Hatfield, bishop of Durham, was one of his godfathers, and raised him from the font: perhaps he was named Thomas in his godfather's honour. Another godfather was Thomas de la Mare, the abbot of St Albans. Thomas was by some way the youngest of Edward's sons: he was almost twenty-five years younger than *Edward, the Black Prince, and more than twelve years younger than Edward's fifth son, *Edmund of Langley. In a sense therefore he belonged to a different generation from his elder brothers, who took a leading part in politics and war during their father's reign. He was closer in age to his nephew Richard II than to Richard's father, the Black Prince, and his political and military career was to be played out mainly in Richard's reign.

Early life and marriage During his infancy Thomas remained with his mother, who was given an allowance for his maintenance by the king in 1358, though in the first year of his life he had a nurse—possibly a wet-nurse—called Alesia Vang, wife of Marmaduke Vang of Somerset. By 1366 he had his own household, but otherwise little is known of his life until the 1370s. As the king's youngest son he would of course depend on royal patronage for a suitable marriage, and for sufficient income to maintain his estate as he came to manhood. On 3 April 1374 he was granted a group of manors which formed part of the inheritance of Humphrey (IX) de Bohun, earl of Hereford and Essex, who had died in the previous year. The grant stated that he 'will take to wife' Eleanor, the elder of Humphrey's two daughters and coheirs, who was born *c.*1365. Their marriage probably took place in the early summer of 1374: on 1 June *John of Gaunt, duke of Lancaster, issued instructions for the delivery of a goblet and a silver ewer to 'the lady of Woodstock on the day of her marriage' (*John of Gaunt's Register*, 2, no. 1431). On 10 June 1376 Thomas was appointed constable of England, an office that had been hereditary in the Bohun family, and on 24 August the king came to Pleshey, the centre of the Bohun lands in Essex, and granted his son an annuity of 1000 marks (£666 13s. 4d.) to maintain his estate as constable. The income was to be derived from several Bohun manors, including Pleshey and High Easter, which were placed in Thomas's custody until his wife came of age and could receive livery of her inheritance. Pleshey was to become Thomas's principal residence. The revenue from these manors, however, amounted to no more than £243, and the remaining £423 13s. 4d. was assigned on the exchequer until the following year, when the custody of the Bohun lordships of Brecon, Hay, Huntington, Caldicot, and Newton in the Welsh marches was granted to him during the minority of the heiresses.

Edward III had evidently decided that the Essex lands of the Bohun family should pass to Thomas, but Eleanor's younger sister, Mary, was entitled to half the inheritance, and was thus an attractive marriage prospect. At Edward's death in 1377, however, Mary was still unmarried, and in May 1380, when the inheritance was formally partitioned and Thomas and Eleanor given livery of her share, Thomas was also granted custody of Mary's purparty. Froissart suggests that Thomas was responsible for bringing Mary up, and that he hoped to persuade her to become a member of the order of Poor Clares so that the whole Bohun inheritance would devolve upon him and Eleanor, but, while Thomas was on campaign in France in 1380, his elder brother John of Gaunt in effect abducted Mary from Pleshey, and married her to his son Henry, earl of Derby (the future *Henry IV). Henry's marriage to Mary undoubtedly took place in 1380, though how much more of Froissart's story is true cannot be determined with any certainty. Mary and Henry were given livery of her share of the inheritance on 22 December 1384, and Thomas thus had to relinquish control of the estates assigned to her, including Brecon and Hay. Mary's marriage had serious long-term consequences for Thomas. It left him 'dependent on Crown grants rather than on inherited resources' for the rest of his life (Goodman, *Loyal Conspiracy*, 90), and may also have provoked a breach with Gaunt which was never fully healed. Furthermore relations between Thomas and Henry of Derby never seem to have been especially close. They disputed the partition of the Bohun inheritance throughout Richard II's reign until Thomas's death, and they were at odds over the issue of Richard's possible deposition at the end of December 1387.

Military career Thomas played no part in the military expeditions to France in the last years of his father's reign, and apparently he did not identify with either side in the political crisis of 1376. Thomas's lack of military and political experience in his late teenage years is surprising. His elder brother Edmund of Langley had been with his father on the Rheims campaign in 1359–60 when he was only eighteen, and was created earl of Cambridge when he was twenty-one; but there is no evidence that Edward III had an earldom in mind for Thomas in 1376, when he reached the same age. In the political climate of that year, the grant of an earldom to the king's youngest son, with its accompanying endowment in lands or annuities, might have been difficult, but his father's failure to honour him may have contributed to his belief, which was to strengthen in Richard II's reign, that he received less than his due as Edward III's son.

However, his father knighted him at his last Garter ceremony on 23 April 1377 (though he did not receive the order itself until 1380) and, by virtue of his marriage to the heiress of the hereditary constable of England, Thomas successfully claimed the right to carry the sceptre and the dove at the coronation of Richard II on 16 July 1377. On the eve of the coronation he was created earl of Buckingham, with an income of £1000 a year to maintain his estate. This income, however, was not derived from land, but from the revenues of alien priories, which were in the king's hands during the war with France. Thomas thus had a vested interest in the continuation of the war.

War was to be Thomas's principal preoccupation over the next three years. Like his elder brothers he was excluded from the continual councils which had responsibility for administration during Richard II's minority, though he may have had some informal influence over government. During the summer of 1377 a Franco-Castilian fleet was active in the English Channel, and, according to Froissart, Thomas and his brother Edmund prevented the fleet from landing a force at Dover. In November he put to sea with a force of about 3600 sailors and 4000 men-at-arms and archers, but his attempt to engage the Castilian fleet at Sluys ended when his own ships were dispersed by a storm. He had better luck in December, when he pursued the Castilians down the channel and captured eight of their ships off Brest. In April 1378 the duke of Brittany leased Brest to the English, and Thomas was one of the commanders appointed to receive it from the duke.

Thomas's next expedition, the most substantial of his career, was also to Brittany, being intended to bolster the position of the pro-English duke. On 3 May 1380 he engaged to serve for one year with a force of over 5000 men, almost half of whom were members of his own retinue. His army moved overland from Calais and reached Brittany in late September, where he laid siege to Nantes. The duke, however, made peace with Charles VI of France, and Thomas had to lift the siege. After overwintering in Brittany, he returned to England, reaching Falmouth on 3 May 1381. Although the expedition achieved little, no blame could be laid at Thomas's door: as in 1375, the military commanders in the field in Brittany had to abandon their expedition in the face of a political agreement to which they were not party. He had some difficulty in obtaining payment of all the sums due to him from the exchequer for the expedition: even in 1388 the crown was still in debt to him. After his return to England, Froissart suggests that Thomas spent some time on his wife's estates in Wales, though it is also possible that he was at Pleshey during the peasants' revolt, preparing to take military action against the rebels in Essex. On 28 June he

took a force to Billericay to disperse the rebels there, and he was subsequently appointed a justice of the peace in Essex and Cambridgeshire to deal judicially with the rebels in those counties. In mid-July he was in Gloucester, suppressing local disturbances there.

Thomas's frustrating military career continued after the revolt. When the truce with Scotland expired in February 1384, Thomas and Gaunt were appointed joint leaders of an expedition to Scotland. The two lords crossed the border at Easter, and did some damage in south-east Scotland, but the expedition ran short of food and returned to England. Walsingham criticized the expedition as one of the most expensive and wasteful for many years. In 1385 Thomas brought a retinue of 400 men-at-arms and 800 archers to the king's campaign in Scotland. The expedition never engaged the enemy in battle, but on 6 August, 'at the king's first entry into Scotland', Richard created Thomas duke of Gloucester, with an annuity of £1000 in addition to his annuity as earl of Buckingham. His title and his annuity were formally confirmed in parliament in November. Apart from £60 from the fee farm of Gloucester, the whole of this new annuity was assigned on the customs of London, Boston, Hull, Lynn, Ipswich, and Yarmouth, but Thomas soon complained that he was unable to receive the full amount from these sources. Although he was now a duke, he still lacked a substantial territorial endowment: he relied for the greater part of his income, estimated at about £2500 a year, on assignments on the customs and the alien priories. His landed estate still amounted to little more than Eleanor's share of the Bohun inheritance, attenuated by her mother's dower.

Political strains, 1385–1387 The impression of a nation united in arms, and led by its king on the verge of adulthood, which the expedition of 1385 to Scotland provided, only served to disguise for a time the growing tension between the king and some of the nobility, including Thomas. Although Thomas had some grounds for feeling that he had not received the rewards he was entitled to, his brother Edmund, now duke of York, was similarly ill-endowed, and had not been able to make as good a marriage. Edmund's character was, however, in Froissart's words, 'soft and peaceable', but neither term could be applied to Thomas, who seems to have been a much more forceful person, discontented, overbearing, and ambitious, and able to inspire fear as well as respect. To some extent, therefore, Thomas's personality explains his political stance after 1385, but none the less his grievances had substance, and his hostility to those round the king was apparently widely shared, not just by some of his fellow nobles, but also, it seems, by many of the gentry class who were represented among the Commons in parliament.

Some hint of the growing tension between the king and Thomas came at the Salisbury parliament in April 1384, when a Carmelite friar accused Gaunt of treason. There was no truth in the accusation, but, according to Walsingham, Thomas rushed into the king's chamber and threatened to attack or kill anyone—even the king—who suggested that Gaunt was a traitor. The Carmelite friar may have had some connection with Robert de Vere, earl of

Oxford, one of the king's leading favourites, who was becoming increasingly unpopular with some of the nobility. De Vere's favour with the king brought him substantial rewards in the form of landed property, and this must have been especially galling to Thomas, whose income still depended heavily on exchequer annuities which he could not always obtain. Furthermore, the centre of the de Vere inheritance in East Anglia was Hedingham Castle, less than 20 miles from Pleshey, and de Vere's rapid rise in the king's favour must have seemed a threat to Thomas's position in Essex.

Thomas's hostility to the king had its roots not just in his concern for his wealth and territorial position, but also in his belief, shared by other nobles such as the earl of Arundel, that the king's wish to negotiate a peace settlement with France was misguided. John of Gaunt, however, was more sympathetic to Richard's foreign policy, and, as long as Gaunt remained in England, Thomas was perhaps unwilling to engage in open opposition to the king. In July 1386, however, Gaunt left for Castile, and Thomas now seems to have assumed the leadership of those who were opposed to the king, and who sought the removal of de Vere and other favourites from the court. When parliament met in October 1386, the Commons were faced with a demand from the chancellor, Michael de la Pole, for an unprecedentedly large grant of tax to pay for the defence of the realm against the French invasion that had been threatening since the summer. The Commons refused to consider a grant of tax until the chancellor was dismissed, but Richard declined to meet parliament and retreated to his palace at Eltham, Kent. Thomas and some of his associates may initially have been planning an attack on de Vere, but they now associated themselves with the Commons' initiative against de la Pole. At the express wish of both Commons and Lords, Thomas and the bishop of Ely, Thomas Arundel, confronted the king at Eltham. According to Henry Knighton they reminded Richard of his duty to attend parliament; they went on to complain about the damage done to the realm by the evil counsellors around the king, and they concluded by pointing out to Richard that a king who allowed himself to be alienated from his people by evil counsellors, and was unwilling to be guided by law and by the wise advice of the Lords, risked deposition. The implicit threat was enough to bring Richard round [see Lords appellant]. He agreed to meet parliament and to dismiss de la Pole, who was subsequently impeached by the Commons, with Thomas acting as one of the judges appointed from among the Lords. Parliament then established a commission of government, of which Thomas was a member, to oversee the government for one year from 19 November.

Thomas's hand can perhaps be seen in the decision of the commission in December 1386 to reject overtures for peace with France, and begin preparations for the renewal of the war. The king, however, had been deeply offended by the establishment of the commission, and in the summer of 1387 he consulted his judges about his rights. They told him that those who had imposed the commission on him against his will should be punished as traitors. This opinion served to raise the political stakes substantially, and in the autumn of 1387 Thomas, together with the earls of Arundel and Warwick, prepared a pre-emptive strike against the king. On 14 November they marched to Waltham Cross, Hertfordshire, where in the presence of a group of mediators they formally submitted an appeal (or accusation) of treason against de la Pole, de Vere, and three other associates of the king, Alexander Neville, archbishop of York, Sir Nicholas Brembre, the mayor of London, and Sir Robert Tresilian, chief justice of the king's bench. The mediators agreed to arrange a meeting with the king, and on 17 November the three lords came into the king's presence at Westminster Hall, where they repeated their intention to proceed against de la Pole, de Vere, and the others by way of an appeal. Richard agreed that the appeal should be heard in the parliament which would assemble in February 1388.

The Merciless Parliament De Vere's response to these events, however, was to raise an army in Cheshire and confront the three lords in the field. Thomas, perhaps supported by Arundel, seems to have suggested deposing Richard immediately, but was restrained by Warwick, who argued that their first concern must be to defeat de Vere. Accordingly they left London to march northwards, and were joined at Huntingdon on 12 December by the earls of Derby and Nottingham. The five lords, known as the lords appellant, routed de Vere's army at Radcot Bridge on 20 December. De Vere escaped, but the appellants marched victorious to London, and with 500 armed men at their backs they confronted Richard in the Tower on 30 December. According to the chronicle of Whalley Abbey, they deposed Richard for three days, but then reinstated him because they could not agree on a successor. This account is given some support from Thomas's confession in 1397 in which he says that the lords agreed to Richard's deposition for two or three days, but then restored him to the throne. The story may well be true: it was widely believed at the time that Thomas had designs on the crown, and he even went to the lengths of denying any such intention at the opening of parliament in February. According to the Whalley chronicler, Derby opposed Thomas's claim, as he had every reason to do. He and his father, John of Gaunt, had a better title to the throne as Richard's nearest male heirs, and it is difficult to see how Thomas could have held on to the crown in face of the superior right of the house of Lancaster.

At the opening of the so-called Merciless Parliament, on 3 February 1388, Thomas and his co-appellants formally presented their appeal of treason against de la Pole, de Vere, and the three other accused. The essence of the charges against them was that they had accroached royal power and had used their influence over the king to persuade him to accept their unwise counsel. All were convicted and all but Neville, who was sentenced to loss of his temporalities, were condemned to death, though de la Pole, Neville, and de Vere had already escaped overseas. Thomas and his colleagues then turned their attention to a group of officials and chamber knights who had enjoyed the king's favour, notably the king's former tutor, Sir

Simon Burley. These men were impeached, and most were condemned to death. The death sentence on Burley, however, divided the appellants and aroused opposition elsewhere. Thomas, together with Arundel and Warwick, was determined to have Burley executed, but Derby and Nottingham were inclined to spare him, and so was the duke of York, who had a bitter disagreement with his brother over Burley's fate. The two accused each other of lying, and were only calmed down by the king. The pleas for mercy failed, however; the Commons supported Thomas's insistence that Burley should die, and he was executed on 5 May. The dispute over Burley had exposed the fragile nature of the appellants' coalition, and had made Thomas appear an extremist, albeit one who enjoyed the support of the Commons in parliament. Richard did not forget Thomas's stance over Burley's fate.

Thomas reaped some personal rewards from his political dominance. He and his fellow appellants voted themselves £20,000 to cover their 'expenses' in bringing the 'traitors' to justice, though the money was paid only gradually over the following years. He sought to strengthen his own territorial position by petitioning to have his annuities secured on lands forfeited by those who had been convicted in the Merciless Parliament, but although the petition was accepted nothing was done about it, and he did not manage to use his period of political dominance to diminish substantially his dependence on exchequer annuities. He did, however, succeed in obtaining £1920 of the sums still owed to him for the Breton expedition of 1380: £635 6s. 8d. of this was derived from the sale of de Vere's forfeited goods.

The appellants' political ascendancy continued for some months after the end of the Merciless Parliament, but in foreign affairs they were largely unsuccessful. As in the autumn of 1386, Thomas and Arundel sought to implement a more vigorous policy towards France, but Arundel's naval expedition in the summer and autumn achieved little, and a Scottish invasion in August culminated in the defeat of a locally raised English force at Otterburn. After these set-backs Thomas could see some advantage in responding favourably to the peace initiatives instigated by the duke of Burgundy in December 1387, and he accepted Burgundy's proposal for a truce. None the less, the military failures of the summer damaged the appellants' standing in public opinion, and by the beginning of 1389 their influence was waning. Hostility towards Richard's favourites had brought them together in the first place, and once the favourites were removed the essential reason for their coalition disappeared. On 3 May 1389 Richard II formally resumed responsibility for government, and Thomas was removed from the council.

France and Ireland, 1389–1397 Thomas's political exile did not last long. With Gaunt returning to England in November, Richard had no wish at this stage to risk a confrontation with his former opponents, and Thomas was restored to the council by 10 December 1389. He could not expect, however, to enjoy any real influence with the king, and in 1391 his thoughts turned to a crusade in north-east Europe. His nephew Henry, earl of Derby, had acquitted himself with distinction there in the previous year, and Thomas was perhaps motivated by a desire to emulate his success. Accordingly he assembled an expedition which left England for the Baltic in September 1391, but he was driven back by a storm at the entrance to the Skagerrak, and after trying to seek landfall successively in Denmark, Norway, and Scotland he eventually reached the English coast at Tynemouth: another expedition had ended in failure and frustration, and his debts for the expedition now had to be paid, though the king made him a gift of £500 towards his expenses.

On 29 April 1392 Richard II declared that he intended to appoint Thomas lieutenant in Ireland for five years. Indentures were sealed, and Thomas began to make preparations for his departure. He received a total of £6333 6s. 8d. in advances from the exchequer, and spent almost £1250 on the purchase of artillery and on wages and rewards for his retinue. However, on 23 July his appointment was cancelled. No reason was given for its cancellation, but it is possible that the king wanted him to join Gaunt in the peace negotiations with France which were about to resume. Thomas may not have been unhappy to have his appointment countermanded, judging by the view he formed of Ireland when he went there with the king in 1394; on the other hand it was one more set-back to a career that had been notable so far for its frustrations. Much of the debt to the crown that he had incurred in preparing for the expedition was eventually remitted.

In 1393 Thomas and Gaunt led the English delegation to a peace conference at Leulinghem, near Calais, which concluded a provisional peace treaty between England and France. Rumours that peace might be agreed contributed to an outbreak of unrest in Cheshire in 1393. Thomas held the office of justice of Chester, and the leaders of the rising believed that Thomas shared responsibility with Gaunt for the progress of the negotiations. There is no evidence, however, that Thomas sympathized with the rebels' fears that peace would put an end to their careers as soldiers: indeed, according to Walsingham he mustered his retinue and was ready if necessary to help his brother put down the rising. On the other hand both Froissart and the French author of the *Chronicque de la traïson et mort de Richart Deux roy Dengleterre* suggest that Thomas was opposed to a settlement with France. Thomas had discovered during the Merciless Parliament that he stood high in favour with the Commons, and he may have been anxious not to be identified too closely with a peace policy that, as a debate in the parliament of January 1394 showed, was not popular with the Commons. If this is true, then his inclusion as one of the English envoys at the 1393 peace conference may be explicable in terms of his status rather than his opinions: the dukes of Burgundy and Berri represented France, and thus it was necessary for Richard II to send two royal dukes to represent him. Yet there is no other evidence that he was opposed to the general tenor of the negotiations in 1393. Indeed, he may have felt he would have more room for manoeuvre at home if his brother Gaunt was to be duke of a greatly enlarged Aquitaine: Jean de Grailly and Sir Richard Stury, who spoke about Thomas to Froissart during the latter's visit to England in 1395, thought that this was true. Perhaps the evidence would permit the conclusion that Thomas was unenthusiastic about peace with France rather than openly hostile, and went along with the negotiations in which his elder brother took the lead.

The provisional agreement of 1393 between England and France brought an end to the war for the time being, and in 1394 Richard II turned his attention to Ireland. He planned the largest royal expedition there for almost two hundred years, and Thomas was one of the nobles who agreed to accompany the king. The expedition landed at Waterford on 1 October 1394, but Thomas did not stay long in Ireland. Richard sent him back to England as his envoy at the parliament that opened in January 1395, and, according to Froissart, Thomas was unimpressed with the country. He described it as very poor, with a poor and wretched people, and he thought that military action there was futile: Ireland, he said, was a country 'neither of conquest nor of profit', and anything 'conquered in one year would be lost the next year' (Œuvres, 16.5). The king made him a grant of part of the land in Leinster to be vacated by the Ó Broin family, but there is no evidence that Thomas believed the grant was anything more than nominal.

If there is any truth in the story presented by Froissart, relations between Thomas and those around the king seem to have become strained during 1395. When Froissart visited England in that year, he spoke at length to Jean de Grailly about the duke. Grailly described Thomas in terms that were not unflattering but suggested a certain wariness on the part of the court towards him. Grailly said that he had 'a most wonderful head', but that he was proud and arrogant, though well-loved by the commons of England. His part in the execution of Sir Simon Burley had not been forgotten. Grailly also suggested that after the death of Richard II's queen in 1394 Thomas hoped that the king might marry his own daughter *Anne of Woodstock, countess of Stafford (c.1382–1438), who had been widowed two years earlier, but the king had rejected the idea on the ground that she was too close a kinswoman. Later that year Robert le Mennot (Robert the Hermit) visited England, and spent two days and nights at Pleshey with the duke and his family. He too reported his impressions to Froissart. He had no doubt that Thomas was opposed to attempts to bring the war to an end, and set himself to persuade the duke to change his mind, but even his powerful advocacy of an Anglo-French crusade to save eastern Christendom from the Turks failed to move the duke. According to Froissart, Thomas held the French in contempt and his heart was hardened against peace. Froissart believes that Robert the Hermit probably related his conversation with Thomas to the king, for both Richard and the French seem to have been anxious to find out what Thomas was thinking.

Froissart gives the impression that he was well informed about comings and goings at Pleshey, and about Thomas's opinions. He suggests that Thomas preferred to reside at Pleshey, rather than at court in the company of his two brothers, and he paints a picture of the duke as a jealous, brooding figure, ready to tell anyone who visited him what he thought of the king and those round him. It is likely that Thomas did indeed spend much time at Pleshey in 1395 and the first six months of 1396, though he also had a 'hall' in London, which was well equipped with tapestries, furnishings, plate, and other household goods at the time of his forfeiture in 1397. He must have spent some time there as well as at Pleshey. He enjoyed little real power or influence at court, however, and his lack of enthusiasm for peace with France set him apart from his brothers as well as from the king. On the other hand he still enjoyed royal patronage. In 1390 Richard II granted him the reversion of the lordship of Holderness, worth £600 a year, and when the reversion fell in at the death of Queen Anne in 1394 Thomas gained possession and his dependence on exchequer annuities was thus reduced. He was also granted the custody of the inheritance of his late son-in-law, the earl of Stafford, and he was wealthy enough in these years to endow his newly founded college of secular priests at Pleshey with manors from his inheritance.

Arrest and death In the early summer of 1397 Richard II seems to have decided to launch a pre-emptive strike against Thomas and two of his co-appellants in 1387–8, the earls of Arundel and Warwick. At first he hoped to secure them by a trick, inviting them to a banquet in London on 10 July at which they would be arrested. Thomas declined the invitation on the ground that he was too ill to travel from Pleshey: only Warwick turned up, and was arrested after dinner. Arundel was persuaded by his brother the archbishop of Canterbury to surrender himself, but Richard resolved to go to Pleshey in person and arrest Thomas. According to Walsingham he assembled a large force of Londoners, household knights, and a group of nobles. They set out from London under cover of darkness and arrived at Pleshey early in the morning of 10 July. Thomas, who Walsingham says was gravely ill, was woken and came down to meet the king accompanied only by a few priests from his college. The two exchanged courtesies, and Richard then arrested the duke. He was given a short time to bid farewell to his family and household, and then left the castle under armed escort. The earl of Kent and Sir Thomas Percy took him to Calais, where he was imprisoned. The author of the continuation of the *Eulogium historiarum sive temporis* gives a harsher account of the exchanges between Thomas and the king: Thomas apparently begged the king to spare his life, but Richard replied that he would have the same mercy he had shown to Burley—a sentiment that has the ring of truth about it.

Richard's motives for arresting Thomas and his fellow appellants have been variously interpreted both by contemporary chroniclers and by modern historians. Some of the former, for instance the French author of the *Traïson*, maintain that Thomas was involved in a plot against the king. There is no evidence for this, but it may well be true, as Froissart suggests, that Richard felt threatened by his uncle's hostility to the *rapprochement* with France that followed the twenty-eight-year truce between the two countries in 1396. Thomas had shared the Commons' objections to Richard's proposal in January 1397 for a joint Anglo-French expedition against Milan, and he may, as the author of the *Traïson* suggests, have felt that the return of Brest to the duke of Brittany in the previous year had been unwise and unnecessary. It is likely that Richard moved against the former appellants for fear that if he did not, they might move against him. If there was any suggestion of a plot, it existed only in Richard's mind.

Richard intended to charge the three former appellants with treason for their 'riding against the king' in 1387. When parliament assembled, heavily guarded, at Westminster on 17 September 1397, Thomas, Arundel, and Warwick were formally appealed of treason. Arundel and Warwick both stood trial in parliament: Arundel was condemned to death and executed, while Warwick, though convicted, was reprieved and sentenced to exile in the Isle of Man. When the order was given for Thomas to be brought before parliament, however, the earl of Nottingham, who was earl marshal and captain of Calais, replied that he could not produce him because he was dead: 'By order of my most excellent lord the king, I held this duke in my custody in the lord king's prison in the town of Calais; and there, in that same prison, he died' (*RotP*, 3.378).

Both contemporaries and modern historians have accepted that Thomas was murdered in Calais. The evidence that he was seriously ill in 1397 might argue for a death by natural causes, perhaps hastened by the rigours of imprisonment, but such a suggestion flies in the face of what everybody thought at the time, and would require the assumption that the subsequent account of his murder was an invention. Thomas was almost certainly murdered on the instructions of the earl of Nottingham, who in turn must have been acting on orders from the king. In the first parliament of Henry IV's reign one of Nottingham's valets, John Hall, was charged with Thomas's murder, and his confession was read out in parliament. Hall said that Nottingham had told him he had been commanded by the king to murder Thomas; he went to a house in Calais where some of his accomplices produced the duke and took him to a side chamber in the house. Thomas was allowed to confess himself to a chaplain, and he was then told to lie on a bed. A feather bed was placed over him, and he was suffocated. Parliament was told that he had died on 25 or 26 August, but Sir William Rickhill's account of his mission to Calais to procure Thomas's political confession makes it clear that he was still alive on 8 September: he may have been murdered that night.

On 24 September parliament found Thomas guilty of treason, and all his lands and property were forfeited to the crown. On the following day the king ordered that a confession obtained from Thomas by Sir William Rickhill, one of the king's judges, should be read in full parliament. In his confession, made to Rickhill at Calais on 8 September and written in English, Thomas admitted that he was one of those who imposed the commission of 1386 on the king, and 'along with others, took upon myself royal powers' (*RotP*, 3.379). He went on to confess that, along with others, he came armed into the king's presence, discussed giving up his homage to the king, and agreed to depose him 'for two or three days' (Given-Wilson, 81), after which he was restored. He concluded by swearing that after he renewed his oath to the king in 1388 he had never been guilty of fresh treasons, and asked the king for mercy and grace. Rickhill then asked him if he had anything else to add to what he had written, and he said that he now remembered that he had told the king 'that, if he wished to be a king, he should stop begging to save the life of Simon Burley' (Given-Wilson, 83).

The events in Calais were no doubt planned in advance by the king, with the co-operation of the earl of Nottingham. Although Richard II had arrested Thomas and prepared a charge of treason against him, he could not have been confident of obtaining a conviction had Thomas been produced to stand trial in parliament. John of Gaunt, as high steward of England, would have presided over his trial, and, whereas Gaunt seems to have had little compunction about passing the death sentence on Arundel, he would probably have been very reluctant to do so on his own brother. Furthermore, Thomas was still popular with the common people, and however effectively Sir John Bussy, the speaker, managed the Commons in parliament, there remained the risk of popular demonstrations in Thomas's favour. Thomas's murder, in the side room of a Calais house, was thus a political necessity for Richard, and his confession gave legitimacy to his conviction for treason.

On 14 October Richard ordered the earl of Nottingham to deliver Thomas's body to Richard Maudeleyn, a royal clerk, who was instructed to hand the body over to Thomas's widow for burial in Westminster Abbey. It was buried in the chapel of St Edmund and St Thomas, well away from the burial places of Thomas's royal kindred; but his widow requested in her will that his body should be moved to the chapel of Edward the Confessor, to lie beside his mother and father, and after her death in October 1399 Henry IV carried out her instructions. Walsingham's account of Thomas's death concludes with a eulogy which perhaps encapsulates the opinion of many who did not share the king's suspicions of him. He was, says Walsingham, 'the best of men … in whom was placed the hope and solace of the whole community' (*Historia Anglicana*, 2.226), and 'who always worked for the advantage of the realm and the honour and benefit of the king' ('Annales Ricardi secundi', 221).

Personality and possessions Following Thomas's conviction for treason the exchequer drew up an inventory of his forfeited possessions at Pleshey. The inventory survives, and provides detailed evidence for the duke's tastes and interests. Pleshey must have been a residence of some magnificence. Thomas possessed fifteen tapestries which hung in the great hall and various chambers. Their subjects were mainly scenes from romances such as the stories of Charlemagne and Godfrey de Bouillon, and the battle between Gawain and Lancelot. There were religious subjects, too, such as the nativity of Christ, the presentation and purification of the Virgin Mary, and from the Old Testament the story of Judith and Holofernes. He had sixteen beds with hangings of gold and silk: one was of white satin embroidered in gold with the arms and crest of the duke. His chapel was richly equipped: one cope, valued at £60, was made of cloth of gold, lined with satin, and embroidered with various beasts and birds and the emblem of the Garter; there were also forty-two books in the chapel, including Bibles, missals, psalters, and antiphoners, a martyrology, and a little book of prayers covered in black and white velvet and embroidered with swans, the badge of the Bohun family. Elsewhere in the castle he had a library of eighty-four books, including a copy of the Wycliffite translation of the Bible into English, made *c*.1382. This survives, and is now BL, Egerton MS 617. Possession of a Wycliffite translation of the Bible need not imply any interest in Wyclif's theology or sympathy with Lollardy: there is no evidence that Thomas's piety was anything other than conventional, and it is significant that the English Bible was not listed in the inventory among the books in his chapel. Some of the devotional works belonged to his wife, and may have been inherited from her Bohun forebears. Her religious interests perhaps went deeper than those of her husband: in her will she described a crucifix as 'her favourite possession' and she left her daughter Joan a book with the psalter and other devotions, 'which book', she said, 'I have often used' (Nichols, 177).

In his 'hall' in London, Thomas also had a number of books, but it is difficult to judge how far the books he had in London and at Pleshey genuinely represent his literary taste. In London he had, among other books, one 'written in French called *Meistre des Istories*' (CIM, 1392–1399, no. 372), a book of the 'Lives of the church fathers', the romance of Godfrey de Bouillon, a Bible in Latin and another in French, and a copy of the *Golden Legend*. At Pleshey he had books in English, French, and Latin; books of romances, such as the *Romance de la rose*, *Ector de Troye*, *Le romance de Lancelot*, and *La gest de Fouke filtz Waryn*, and devotional works in French such as a book of the miracles of Our Lady. He also had a book of the gospels glossed in English. He had a French translation of Livy, 'a little book called the Flour de Histories' (probably *Flores historiarum*), and two copies of Trivet's chronicle. He owned a number of law books, including copies of the English statutes and two large books of civil law, and also a copy of Giles of Rome's *De regimine principum*, which may have been the copy that Burley forfeited in 1388. The devotional works and the romances, mainly in French, perhaps testify to his real interests, which were probably those of most of his fellow nobles at the end of the fourteenth century. Assuming that he read the books at all, he must have been bilingual in English and French, with English probably as his mother tongue, and he could probably read Latin. He is known to have written a treatise on the office of constable, which he had held since 1376 and evidently took seriously, but it is not listed among his books at Pleshey. This treatise, *The Ordenaunce and Forme of Fightyng within*

Listes, exists in both an English and an Anglo-Norman version, but the earliest text of the English version exists in a late fifteenth-century manuscript (BL, Lansdowne MS 285), and it is likely that Thomas's original text was the Anglo-Norman version.

The inventory reveals his taste in books, tapestries, plate, and vestments; but his physical appearance is less easy to establish. There is a miniature portrait of him in the book of benefactors of the abbey of St Albans (BL, Cotton MS Nero D.vii). It shows him bearded, with the Bohun swan in the background; but the manuscript is late fifteenth-century, and the portrait is probably not a likeness. Nothing but the matrices remain of the monumental brass that was once on his tomb in Westminster Abbey, though there is an engraving of it in Sandford's *Genealogical History of the Kings of England* (1677), which shows that it was very elaborate. It had representations not just of Thomas and his wife, but of members of his royal kindred, including his father, Edward III. His pride in his royal birth is well expressed in this memorial. He and his wife had one son, Humphrey, and three daughters, Anne (*b. c*.1382), Joan, who died unmarried on 16 August 1400, and Isabel (*b*. 1386), who became a nun in the Minoresses in London and took her vows on 23 April 1402, her sixteenth birthday. Humphrey was born about 1381, and was taken to Ireland by Richard II in 1399. When news of Henry Bolingbroke's landing in England reached Ireland, Richard II had him lodged in Trim Castle in the lordship of Meath. In August 1399 Bolingbroke ordered him to be returned to England, but he died on the way back, possibly in a shipwreck off Anglesey or possibly of plague at Chester. Anne thus became Thomas's sole heir. She married first Thomas, earl of Stafford, who died in 1392, and then in 1398, without royal licence, his brother Edmund, who was killed at the battle of Shrewsbury in 1403. Her third husband was Sir William *Bourchier, later count of Eu. She died on 16 October 1438. Thomas's wife, Eleanor, died on 3 October 1399. Walsingham says that she died of a broken heart after suffering the loss of her husband and her only son: Shakespeare's portrayal of the grief-stricken duchess in act I of *Richard II* may not be far from the truth. She was buried in St Edmund's Chapel in Westminster Abbey; her monumental brass, showing her in widow's dress, survives.

ANTHONY TUCK

Sources BL, Add. MS 32097, Add. MS 40859A; MS Cotton Nero D.vii; MS Cotton Titus B.xi; MS Egerton 617 · PRO, exchequer queen's remembrancer accounts various, E101 · PRO, exchequer of receipt, issue rolls, E403 · *Chancery records* · *RotP*, vol. 3 · L. C. Hector and B. F. Harvey, eds. and trans., *The Westminster chronicle, 1381–1394*, OMT (1982) · *Knighton's chronicle, 1337–1396*, ed. and trans. G. H. Martin, OMT (1995) [Lat. orig., *Chronica de eventibus Angliae a tempore regis Edgari usque mortem regis Ricardi Secundi*, with parallel Eng. text] · *Thomae Walsingham, quondam monachi S. Albani, historia Anglicana*, ed. H. T. Riley, 2 vols., pt 1 of *Chronica monasterii S. Albani*, Rolls Series, 28 (1863–4) · 'Annales Ricardi secundi', *Johannis de Trokelowe et Henrici de Blaneforde … chronica et annales*, ed. H. T. Riley, pt 3 of *Chronica monasterii S. Albani*, Rolls Series, 28 (1866), 155–280 · F. S. Haydon, ed., *Eulogium historiarum sive temporis*, 3 vols., Rolls Series, 9 (1858–63), vol. 3 · *Œuvres de Froissart: chroniques*, ed. K. de Lettenhove, 25 vols. (Brussels, 1867–77) · B. Williams, ed., *Chronicque de la traïson et mort de Richart Deux, roy Dengleterre*, EHS, 9

(1846) • [J. Nichols], ed., *A collection of … wills … of … every branch of the blood royal* (1780) • C. Given-Wilson, ed. and trans., *Chronicles of the revolution, 1397–1400: the reign of Richard II* (1993) • *John of Gaunt's register*, ed. S. Armitage-Smith, 2 vols., CS, 3rd ser., 20–21 (1911) • T. Twiss, ed., *Monumenta juridica: the Black Book of the admiralty*, 1, Rolls Series, 55 (1871) • R. Gough, *The history and antiquities of Pleshy* (1803) • F. Sandford, *A genealogical history of the kings of England* (1677) • M. R. James and E. G. Millar, *The Bohun manuscripts*, Roxburghe Club (1936) • Viscount Dillon and W. H. St John Hope, 'Inventory of the goods and chattels belonging to Thomas, duke of Gloucester', *Archaeological Journal*, 54 (1897), 275–308 • A. Goodman, *The loyal conspiracy: the lords appellant under Richard II* (1971) • A. Goodman, *John of Gaunt: the exercise of princely power in fourteenth-century Europe* (1992) • N. Saul, *Richard II* (1997) • A. Tuck, *Richard II and the English nobility* (1973) • J. Sherborne, *War, politics and culture in fourteenth-century England*, ed. A. Tuck (1994) • J. S. Roskell, *The impeachment of Michael de la Pole earl of Suffolk in 1386* (1984) • J. J. N. Palmer, *England, France and Christendom, 1377–99* (1972) • J. Tait, 'Did Richard II murder the duke of Gloucester?', *Historical essays by members of the Owens College, Manchester*, ed. T. F. Tout and J. Tait (1902), 193–216 • R. L. Atkinson, 'Richard II and the death of the duke of Gloucester', *EngHR*, 38 (1923), 563–4 • M. V. Clarke, 'Forfeitures and treason in 1388', *Fourteenth century studies*, ed. L. S. Sutherland and M. McKisack (1937), 115–45 • R. Holt, 'Thomas of Woodstock and events at Gloucester in 1381', *BIHR*, 58 (1985), 237–42 • *Adae Murimuth continuatio chronicarum. Robertus de Avesbury de gestis mirabilibus regis Edwardi tertii*, ed. E. M. Thompson, Rolls Series, 93 (1889) • GEC, *Peerage*, new edn, 5.719–29
Archives BL, Lansdowne MS 285
Likenesses miniature, 15th cent., BL, Cotton MS Nero D.vii, fol. 110 • engraving (after monumental brass), repro. in Sandford, *Genealogical history*, 230; destroyed, formerly in Westminster Abbey

Thomas [Thomas of Lancaster], **duke of Clarence** (1387–1421), prince and soldier, was the second son of *Henry IV, born in London in the autumn of 1387 to Mary de Bohun (*b. c.*1369), Henry's first wife. As children he and his brothers moved around the Lancaster and Bohun castles and after the death of their mother in 1394 lived for a time in the households of John of Gaunt and Margaret, the countess marshal. He was knighted on 12 October 1399, on the eve of his father's coronation, and appointed steward of England. He became a knight of the Garter in 1400.

The danger that Ireland would be swept into the Welsh revolt led Henry IV to appoint Thomas king's lieutenant there from 18 July 1401 with a salary of £8000 per annum, but no more than a fraction of this was effectively paid and by August 1402 he found himself reduced to impotence in Dublin.

By November 1403, with more than a year's salary in arrears, Thomas returned to England and served briefly the following year in the relief of Coety Castle in Glamorgan. In February 1405 he replaced the indisposed earl of Somerset as admiral of the fleet to guard the sea off Dover for a quarter of a year. In March 1406 he again indented for service in Ireland for twelve years, his salary as lieutenant being now fixed at £6000 p.a. He deferred sailing for another two years until persuaded to accept a commission for three years at a salary of £4666, the first payment being allocated on specific revenues with the promise that he would be paid his arrears. He reached Dublin on 2 August 1408, arrested the earl of Kildare, and conducted a

campaign in Leinster before holding a parliament at Kilkenny in January 1409. But in March his father's illness gave him the occasion to return and he remained at court with his retinue, resisting the urging of his brother Henry [*see* Henry V] to resign his office and the refusal of the council to pay him his second year's salary unless he returned to Ireland. Thomas clung to his lieutenancy for its status and as a source of income, yet his cavalier attitude to his duties there brought reprimands from the council which, under Prince Henry, governed England in the years 1410–11.

By 1411, despite being the king's favourite son, Thomas had still no title, few lands, and little military experience. All three came in the next two years. On 16 August 1410 he had a papal dispensation to marry Margaret Holland, the widow of the recently deceased John Beaufort, earl of Somerset, although this was obstructed by Somerset's brother, Bishop Beaufort, until May 1412. By his marriage he then gained control not only of his wife's lands to the value of £1400 p.a. but also the custody of Somerset's heirs and their inheritance. On 9 July following he himself was created earl of Aumale and duke of Clarence with an annuity of 2000 marks. Wealth and title were prerequisites for the major military command which he was now given. He had urged acceptance of the treaty of Bourges (18 May 1412) by which the duke of Orléans and other Armagnac lords offered to vest Henry IV with Aquitaine in return for military assistance against the duke of Burgundy, and when it became clear that the king could not himself lead the expedition Clarence was appointed its commander on 8 June. This was a snub to Prince Henry, who saw himself supplanted in his father's favour and his succession jeopardized. The rift between the brothers became common knowledge and a cause for alarm. Many regarded Thomas as the more kingly and warlike figure, and the army of 4000 men which he led through western France devastated the land with impunity to south of the Loire. Meanwhile the Armagnac lords had made peace with the duke of Burgundy and had to buy off the English army with a large ransom of 210,000 écus at the treaty of Buzançais (14 November 1412). The expedition was a preliminary to Henry V's subsequent invasion and brought Clarence honour and profit. Having wintered in Bordeaux he returned in April 1413 following Prince Henry's succession to the throne.

Whatever their previous differences Henry V now made Thomas his partner in the enterprise of war. Clarence mustered one of the largest companies (of 240 men-at-arms and 720 archers) in 1415 at Southampton where, before sailing, he presided at the trial of Cambridge, Scrope, and Grey. But at Harfleur he was among those who succumbed to dysentery and had to return to England before the march to Agincourt. He took part in the ceremonial reception of the emperor Sigismund in 1416 and briefly acted as keeper of the realm when Henry V attended the tripartite conference at Calais in September. When, on 1 August 1417, he landed at Touques with Henry V he embarked on a period of sustained campaigning which ended only with his death. He immediately displayed his mettle at the siege of Caen, where he led the scaling party and captured the Abbaye aux Hommes, saving it from destruction. His men were given leave to plunder the town, from which the inhabitants were driven, and Clarence sent to the mayor of London for English settlers, thus initiating an occupation that was to last until 1450. Moving south he took Alençon and joined the king for the winter siege of Falaise. Following its surrender in February 1418 Clarence was granted the *vicomtés* of Auge, Orbec, and Pont Audemer for life; in his move to occupy these he reduced a series of fortresses along the line of the Risle including Harcourt and Bec-Hellouin. With reinforcements for his company brought over from England in June, he was present at the sieges of Louviers and Pont de l'Arche, and by 1 August was encamped outside Rouen at the Porte Cauchoise. In his company were his stepson Henry Beaufort, earl of Somerset, and Edward Holland, count of Mortain, both recent arrivals, in their teens, who fell victim to the disease in the encampment. Following the fall of Rouen in January 1419 the English advance carried him to Vernon and Mantes, and he was at Meulan in May and June for Henry V's fruitless negotiations with the duke of Burgundy. The seizure of Pontoise on 31 July by John Holland, earl of Huntingdon, enabled Clarence to conduct a daring *chevauchée* to the walls of Paris which precipitated the flight of Charles VI to Troyes.

The treaty of Troyes in May 1420 proved to be only an interlude in the continuing campaign, and from July to November Clarence was occupied in the sieges of Montereau and Melun where he was joined by his Beaufort stepsons whom his wife had brought to France in the previous year. Throughout the conquest of Normandy, Clarence had operated under the eye of Henry V in what had been predominantly a war of sieges. When the king left for England early in 1421 Clarence was given supreme command. To forestall the advance of a Franco-Scottish force into south-west Normandy, and eager to win the renown in battle which had hitherto evaded him, he led a small army into Maine and Anjou, but was intercepted at Baugé on the return from Angers. Ill-informed of the size and movements of the enemy, but hoping to win advantage by surprise, he resolved on an immediate attack, discounting the advice of his lieutenants Huntingdon and Gilbert Umfraville to consolidate his own force and position. On 22 March, in confused hand-to-hand fighting, Clarence was killed and Huntingdon and his two Beaufort stepsons were captured. His body was recovered from the field by men of Thomas Montagu, earl of Salisbury, who conducted the retreat. He was buried in Canterbury Cathedral where his widow erected a tomb with the effigies of her two husbands in St Michael's Chapel.

Clarence was a bold and spirited commander whose reputation attracted a war retinue both numerous and distinguished. He saw soldiering in terms of personal valour and fame and had none of his brother's intellectual approach to war and politics. Almost certainly he felt overshadowed by his elder brother and denied opportunities

for service. Before 1417 he had received few material rewards, for in his will of that date he provided for his debts, the wages of his retinue, and his funeral expenses to be paid from the ransom money due from the count of Angoulême of which 123,000 écus was still outstanding. By 1421 he was almost certainly richer, both from the spoils of France and the payment of £4838 from the arrears of his annuities, but he had amassed no fortune and bought no further lands. He had no legitimate children and his French fiefs reverted to the crown. His widow died on 30 December 1439.   G. L. HARRISS

Sources J. H. Wylie, *History of England under Henry the Fourth*, 4 vols. (1884–98) · J. H. Wylie and W. T. Waugh, eds., *The reign of Henry the Fifth*, 3 vols. (1914–29) · J. Lydon, *The lordship of Ireland in the middle ages* (1972) · A. J. Otway-Ruthven, *A history of medieval Ireland* (1968) · R. A. Newhall, *The English conquest of Normandy, 1416–1424: a study in fifteenth-century warfare* (1924) · C. T. Allmand, *Lancastrian Normandy, 1415–1450* (1983) · N. H. Nicolas, ed., *Proceedings and ordinances of the privy council of England*, 7 vols., RC, 26 (1834–7), vol. 1 · E. F. Jacob, ed., *The register of Henry Chichele, archbishop of Canterbury, 1414–1443*, 2, CYS, 42 (1937) · F. S. Haydon, ed., *Eulogium historiarum sive temporis*, 3 vols., Rolls Series, 9 (1858) · B. Williams, ed., 'Chronique de Normandie', *Henrici quinti, Angliae regis, gesta, cum chronica Neustriae, Gallice*, EHS, 12 (1850) · T. Walsingham, *The St Albans chronicle, 1406–1420*, ed. V. H. Galbraith (1937) · 'The chronicle of John Strecche for the reign of Henry V, 1414–1422', ed. F. Taylor, *Bulletin of the John Rylands University Library*, 16 (1932), 137–87 · G. L. Harriss, *Cardinal Beaufort: a study of Lancastrian ascendancy and decline* (1988) · *Chancery records* · PRO, DL 28/1/2 · J. D. Milner, 'The English enterprise in France, 1412–13', *Trade, devotion and governance: papers in later medieval history* [Manchester 1989], ed. D. J. Clayton and others (1994), 80–101 · Westminster Abbey Muniments, 12163
Archives PRO, muster roll 1195, E101 · PRO, warrants for issues and indentures for service, E404 · Westminster Abbey, muniments, receiver-general's accounts 6–9 Henry V, 12163
Likenesses alabaster effigy, Canterbury Cathedral
Wealth at death £300 p.a. from own lands; £1400 p.a. from wife's lands: Westminster Abbey, receiver-general's accounts, 6–9 Henry V, 12163

Thomas ab Ieuan ap Rhys. *See* Tomas ab Ieuan ap Rhys (*c*.1510–*c*.1560).

Thomas ap Roger Vaughan (*c*.1400–1469). *See under* Vaughan family (*per. c*.1400–*c*.1504).

Thomas ap Watkyn Vaughan. *See* Vaughan, Sir Thomas (*fl. c*.1456), *under* Vaughan family (*per. c*.1400–*c*.1504).

Thomas de Hibernia (*d. c*.1270). *See under* Hibernicus, Thomas (*c*.1270–*c*.1340).

Thomas of Ashborne. *See* Ashbourne, Thomas (*fl.* 1371–1397).

Thomas of Beverley. *See* Beverley, Thomas of (*d.* after 1225).

Thomas, St, of Canterbury. *See* Becket, Thomas (1120?–1170).

Thomas of Eccleston. *See* Thomas (*fl. c*.1231–*c*.1258).

Thomas of Erceldoune [*called* Thomas the Rhymer] (*fl.* late 13th cent.), supposed author of poetry and prophecies, is the subject of a romance dating from the fourteenth century and of a celebrated border ballad, both describing his dealings with the fairy queen. The contemporary evidence relating to him, however, is limited to two charters.

The historical evidence In the first, undated, charter (Cartulary of Melrose, BL, Harl. MS 3960, fol. 109a), 'Thom*e* Rimor de Ercildun' is the last of the named witnesses when Peter de Haga, lord of Bemersyde, promises to pay half a stone of wax annually to the chapel of St Cuthbert of Old Melrose. The hand is of the second half of the thirteenth century, corresponding to the dates of other personages in the charter. Peter de Haga was probably the third of that name, attested 1240–80; a date for the charter between 1260 and 1280 seems likely. Ercildun—there are innumerable variant spellings—is now known as Earlston, a village north of Melrose (Borders), close to the Eildon Hills; in the romance *Thomas of Erceldoune* the tryst between Thomas and the queen takes place at the Eldo(u)ne tree, as it does in some versions of the ballad.

The second charter, from the cartulary of the Trinity House of Soutra (NL Scot., MS Adv. 34.4.1), states that 'Thomas de Ercildo*un*, filius *et* heres Tho*m*e Rymour de Ercildo*un*' cedes all his heritable property in Earlston to Soutra, and is dated 2 November 1294. It may be that the elder Thomas of Ercildun is now dead, or he may conceivably have entered a monastery, having renounced his property.

Given that neither charter accords Thomas the title *miles*, it may be assumed that Thomas was below the rank of knight. Alexander Nisbet in 1702 (Nisbet, 157) is the first to refer to Thomas as a knight: 'Sir Thomas Learmont (who is well known by the Name of Thomas the Rymer, because he wrote his Prophesies in Rhime)'. The surname Learmont (Leirmont, Lermont) is first given to Thomas in Hector Boece's *Scotorum historiae* (1527). The second charter suggests that Thomas's son and heir did not inherit the byname Rymour. Opinion is divided as to whether Rymour is an ordinary surname or refers to poetic prowess. From 1229 onwards the word is well attested both as a surname and as denoting a profession or ability.

Poetic reputation For Thomas's abilities as a poet no certain evidence survives. He has, however, been associated with the Middle English romance *Sir Tristrem*, which is thought to have been written late in the thirteenth century. It survives only in the Auchinleck manuscript (NL Scot., MS Adv. 19.2.1.), compiled *c.*1330–1340. The dialect of the poem remains problematic; while Sir Walter Scott thought it was composed in a Scottish dialect, it has been suggested that it is in a northern English or even non-northern dialect. Thomas is mentioned five times as the source of the story. The most detailed allusion occurs at the beginning of the poem:

> I was at Ertheldoun
> With Tomas spak y there;
> Ther herd y rede in roune
> Who Tristrem gat and bare ... Bi yere

> Tomas telles in toun
> This aventours as thai ware.
> (NL Scot., MS Adv. 19.2.1, 1ff.)

This personal encounter with Thomas may be an invention to affirm the veracity of the author. Chronologically, that Thomas should be the source of a late thirteenth-century romance is not inconceivable. However, *Sir Tristrem* is generally regarded as a truncated adaptation of the Anglo-Norman romance of *Tristan* of Thomas of Britain (*fl. c.*1150?–1175); it may be that the author confused two Thomases.

Thomas of Erceldoune is associated with *Sir Tristrem* by Robert Mannyng of Brunne in the prologue to his *English Chronicle* (completed in 1338). The passage begins:

> I see in song, in sedgeyng tale
> of Erceldoun & of Kendale.
> (*Story of England*, lines 93–4)

The latter poet is referred to later in the same work as Thomas of Kendale. Mannyng praises the 'geste' of *Sir Tristrem* as a superlative work:

> if men it sayd as made Thomas;
> but I here it no man so say.
> (ibid., ll. 100–01)

The lines are obscure; it is not certain whether the Thomas referred to is Thomas of Erceldoune, nor whether Mannyng believes him to be the author of the poem.

The romance In the later middle ages Thomas gained a reputation as a prophet as well as a poet. The origins of his prophetic gifts are described in the romance entitled *Thomas of Erceldoune*, thought to date from 'not earlier than the first half of the fourteenth century, and probably rather later' (Nixon, 2.45). It survives in five manuscripts: 1 the Thornton manuscript (Lincoln Cathedral Library, MS 91, formerly A.5.2), in a hand which is in all probability that of Robert Thornton of Ryedale in the North Riding of Yorkshire (*d.* 1456x65)—watermarks place the manuscript between 1419 and 1450, 2 CUL, MS Ff.5.48, mid-fifteenth century, 3 BL, Cotton Vitellius MS, E.x, mid-fifteenth century, 4 BL, Lansdowne MS, 762, first half of the sixteenth century, 5 BL, Sloane MS, 2578, *c.*1547. Some independent value attaches to a version resembling the Sloane text printed in London in 1652, *Sundry Strange Prophecies of Merlin, Bede, Becket and Others*.

The three fifteenth-century manuscripts are all in English dialects. There is however a northern substratum in all the texts, with a number of words mainly or exclusively Scottish in origin; Nixon concludes that the romance is of northern provenance, the evidence pointing to the eastern border country.

The romance consists of three sections, or 'fyttes'. On a May morning Thomas sees a huntress, whom he takes to be the queen of heaven. The lady informs him she is from a different country, whereupon Thomas asks leave to lie with her. He is warned that she will forfeit her beauty in consequence, but Thomas persists, promising eternal constancy. He lies with her seven times, and then the woman is transformed into the Loathly Lady. She tells Thomas to take his leave of middle earth for a year and takes him through a secret entrance in 'Eldone Hill'. For three days they travel through dark floods, until they arrive at a garden, where Thomas is forbidden to eat the fruit, lest the devil seize him. Thomas has a vision of the four ways that lead to heaven, paradise, purgatory, and hell. A fifth way leads to the lady's own country. The lady is afraid of what will happen if the king finds out that Thomas has lain with her, and imposes a taboo: Thomas is to speak to no one in the land but herself. She is then transformed back into her beautiful self. They enter the castle, and behold great revelry. The lady informs Thomas that she must take him back. He believes he has been there only three days, but she assures him that it has been three years or more (in the Cambridge manuscript, seven years). The following day the fiend is to 'feche his fee', and she is afraid he will choose Thomas because of his size and beauty. She takes him back to the Eldone tree.

In the second fytte, Thomas asks the lady for a gift, a token of their encounter. She gives him the gift of the tongue that will never lie, and prophesies a series of events, which take up virtually the whole of the second and third fyttes. The events referred to in the second fytte are historical, ranging in date from the battle of Falkirk (1298) to the battle of Otterburn in 1388. The events referred to in the third fytte cannot be linked satisfactorily with historical data. Repeatedly the lady desires to take her leave, but Thomas detains her with his thirst for knowledge. Finally Thomas takes pity on the weeping queen. With a promise to return if she can, she blows her horn and leaves.

The prolixity of motifs in the first fytte of *Thomas of Erceldoune* is such that it cannot be traced back to a single literary source; the fairy mistress theme, the disappearance into fairyland, the Loathly Lady, and the miraculous passage of time are widespread motifs, particularly in Celtic literature. Perhaps the first fytte was intended as a poetic justification of the prophecies that follow; however, the manuscripts all preserve three fyttes.

The ballad In the ballad *Thomas the Rhymer*, or *Thomas Rymer* (Child, 37), the hero is called True Thomas. Child printed five versions of varying length, the oldest of which were collected by Scott and Jamieson from Anna Brown of Falkland (Child, 1.317–29; 4.454–5). Mrs Brown learned her ballads before 1759 from her mother's side of the family. There has been much dispute as to the priority of the ballad and the romance *Thomas of Erceldoune*, part of a wider debate concerning the communal or individual origins of folksong.

The ballad closely resembles in plot the first fytte of the romance. Thomas, lying on a 'grassy bank' or 'Huntlie bank' espies:

> a lady fair,
> Coming riding down by the Eildon tree.

He takes her to be the queen of heaven, but she tells him she is 'but the queen of fair Elfland'. He mounts up behind her and they ride off, Thomas promising to serve her for seven years. They ride over land and water for forty days and nights, until they come to a 'garden green'. In most versions Thomas is not permitted to eat of the fruit, which is accursed, but, in a version printed by Scott, Thomas eats of an apple which 'will give the tongue that can never lie'. The queen shows Thomas 'fairlies three', the roads that lead to heaven, hell, and to Elfland, whither they are bound. There Thomas is forbidden to speak, at the risk of not returning to his own country. The ballad ends abruptly with a description of Thomas's green uniform and the statement that he was not seen on earth until seven years passed. The return of Thomas and his fairy mistress to earth is not described in the ballad. In the twentieth century the ballad has been collected from the oral tradition in Scotland and in North Carolina. Duncan Williamson (*b.* 1928), an Argyll traveller now settled in Fife, concludes his performance of the ballad with prophecies relating to the world wars and the construction of the Caledonian Canal.

Prophet and poet Although no sources contemporary with Thomas's lifetime attribute prophecies to him, during the fourteenth and fifteenth century his dual reputation as prophet and poet became well established. In Sir Thomas Gray of Heaton's *Scalacronica* (*c.*1362) Thomas is coupled with Merlin. Blind Hary the minstrel, in his *Schir William Wallace* (*c.*1470–1480), describing the rescue of Wallace from prison in Ayr in 1296 or 1297, says that Thomas Rimour was then at Fail, a Trinitarian priory nearby, and attributes prophecies concerning Wallace to him. Fail, however, is not attested before 1335.

A further source dating Thomas to the late thirteenth century is Walter Bower's *Scotichronicon*, written in the 1440s: in 1285, 'that rustic seer Thomas, he of Ersildon' (Bower, 5.428–9) predicted to Patrick, seventh earl of Dunbar (*d.* 1308), the violent death of Alexander III, prophesying the arrival before noon the next day of a calamitous wind that would affect all Scotland. The story is repeated by John Mair (Scotus, *Historia majoris Britanniae*, 1521) and by Boece in his *Scotorum historiae* (1527).

A number of the prophecies told to Thomas by the fairy queen in the romance have fourteenth-century analogues. British Library, Harley MS 2253 (southern or southwestern dialect, *c.*1340) attributes on folio 127 some seventeen prophecies to Thomas de Essedoune, who had been questioned by 'La countesse de Donbar', perhaps the wife of the earl of March to whom Thomas prophesied in 1285, possibly 'Black Agnes' (*d.* 1369) who defended Dunbar Castle in 1337. One of the prophecies, 'When laddes weddeþ louedis', is echoed in the Sloane and Cotton manuscripts of the romance (ll. 650–56), and in British Library, Arundel MS 57 (completed in 1340, in Canterbury), which on folio 8 attributes a number of obscure sayings to Thomas de Erseldoune.

The prophetic legend In the centuries that followed, Thomas of Erceldoune became a convenient peg on which to hang predictions. Nixon lists five manuscripts of the fifteenth–seventeenth centuries which have some prophecies in common with the romance, and four further manuscripts containing variants. The process of expansion culminates in BL, Sloane MS 1802 (*c.*1600), which bears the title 'The haill Prophecie of Scotland, Ingland,

and su(m part) of France and Denmark. Prophecyit be Meruellous Merling, Reid, Berlingtonn, Thomas Rymour, Waldhaue, Eitraine, Benester, and Sibilla all according in one, conteining mony strange and meruellous things'. This manuscript is closely related to the earliest printed version, published by Robert Waldegrave in 1603. There were twelve further editions between 1680 and 1786; chapbook versions were published in 1820 and 1840.

In the witch trial of Andro Man (1598), Andro is assured by the queen of Elfin that he will know all things 'as Thomas Rymour did' (Chambers, 220). Bessie Dunlop, tried in 1576, is taken to meet the queen of Elfame by her medium Thom Reid, who died at the battle of Pinkie (1547). The queen is said by Bessie to be Thom's mistress. Perhaps, under torture, Bessie confused her Thomases. The witch trials are the first dated sources to identify Thomas's mistress as the queen of Elfin.

Seventeenth-century sources add to the legend: Patrick Gordon's rhymed history of Bruce (1615) refers to Thomas Rymour's death in old age in 1307. Thomas Dempster's unreliable *Historia ecclesiastica gentis Scotorum* (1627) records that Thomas drew inspiration from Eliza of Haddington (north of Berwickshire), a nun and poetess, who was blessed with visions because of her devotion to the Virgin Mary, and wrote a book of poetic prophecies. Thomas not only knew her writings but consulted her. Dempster dates her to 1284.

Walter Scott's *Minstrelsy of the Scottish Border* (1802) records a host of local traditions and prophecies relating to Thomas the Rhymer. Further traditions are noted by Chambers, Murray, and Geddie. These are by no means confined to the borders area, but were extant in many parts of the highlands and Aberdeenshire; some oral traditions persist among the Scottish travelling people to this day. The legend of Thomas and his otherworld sojourn continues to inspire authors, among them Theodor Fontane (whose ballad was set to music by Carl Loewe), Rudyard Kipling, James Branch Cabell, W. H. Auden, Nigel Tranter (*True Thomas*, 1981), and Ellen Kushner (*Thomas the Rhymer*, 1990). A family called Learmont claiming descent from Thomas existed in Berwickshire until c.1840; the Russian poet Mikhail Lermontov (1814–1841) believed that he was descended from Thomas the Rhymer.   CYRIL EDWARDS

Sources *Thomas of Erceldoune*, ed. I. Nixon, 2 vols. (1980–83) • J. A. H. Murray, ed., *The romance and prophecies of Thomas of Erceldoune*, EETS (1875) • F. J. Child, ed., *The English and Scottish popular ballads*, 5 vols. (1882–98) • A. Lupack, ed., *'Lancelot of the laik' and 'Sir Tristrem'* (1994) • R. Chambers, *Popular rhymes of Scotland*, new edn (1870) • DNB • J. Russell, *The Haigs of Bemersyde* (1881) • W. P. Albrecht, *The Loathly Lady in 'Thomas of Erceldoune'* (1954) • D. Buchan, *The ballad and the folk* (1972) • J. G. Lockhart, *Memoirs of the life of Sir Walter Scott*, [2nd edn], 10 vols. (1839) • W. Scott, *Minstrelsy of the Scottish border*, 2 vols. (1802) • J. Geddie, *The Rhymer and his rhymes* (1920) • Melrose cartulary, BL, Harley MS 3960 • Soutra cartulary, NL Scot., Adv. MS 34.4.1 • NL Scot., Auchinleck MS Adv. MS 19.2.1 • Lincoln Cathedral Library, MS 91 • CUL, MS Ff.5.48 • BL, Cotton Vitellius MS E.x • BL, Lansdowne MS 762 • BL, Sloane MS 1802 • BL, Sloane MS 2578 • BL, Harley MS 2253 • BL, Arundel MS 57 • A. Nisbet, *An essay on additional figures and marks of cadency* (1702) • H. Boece, *Scotorum historiae a prima gentis origine* (Paris, 1527) • The *story of England by Robert Manning of Brunne*, AD 1338, ed. F. J. Furnivall, 2 vols., Rolls Series, 87 (1887) • *Sundry strange prophecies of Merlin, Bede, Becket and others* (1652) • *Scalacronica, by Sir Thomas Gray of Heton, knight: a chronical of England and Scotland from AD MLXVI to AD MCCCLXII*, ed. J. Stevenson, Maitland Club, 40 (1836) • *Hary's Wallace*, ed. M. P. McDiarmid, 2 vols., STS, 4th ser., 4–5 (1968–9) • W. Bower, *Scotichronicon*, ed. D. E. R. Watt and others, new edn, 9 vols. (1987–98), vol. 5 • Joannes Major Scotus, *Historia Maioris Britanniae* (1521) • *The whole prophecie of Scotland, England, and somepart of France and Denmark* (1603) • P. Gordon, *The famous historie of the renowned … Prince Robert, surnamed the Bruce* (1615) • *Thomae Dempsteri Historia ecclesiastica gentis Scotorum, sive, De scriptoribus Scotis*, ed. D. Irving, rev. edn, 2 vols., Bannatyne Club, 21 (1829)

Archives NL Scot., MS Adv. 19.2.1 • School of Scottish Studies, Edinburgh, papers, prints, tapes • Vaughan Williams Memorial Library, London, Cecil Sharp House, papers, prints, tapes

Thomas of Lancaster, second earl of Lancaster, second earl of Leicester, and earl of Lincoln (c.1278–1322), magnate, was the eldest son of *Edmund, earl of Lancaster and Leicester (1245–1296), second surviving son of *Henry III, and of Blanche (d. 1302), widow of Henri, king of Navarre, and daughter of Robert, count of Artois, son of Louis VIII of France. On his father's side Thomas was thus the grandson of Henry III, the nephew of Edward I, and the cousin of Edward II, and on his mother's side, the grandson of Louis VIII of France and grandnephew of Louis IX: a position close to the two royal families of England and France which does much to explain both his political role and his political pretensions. Since his parents married between 18 December 1275 and 18 January 1276, and he was still a minor in 1297, he was probably born c.1278.

Early career Under Edward I, Thomas's place in the royal family brought him rapid promotion. He first appears in 1290, when plans were being made for his marriage to Béatrice, daughter of Hugues, son of the duke of Burgundy. But these fell through, and in 1294, by the autumn of that year, he had married Alice [*see below*], daughter and heir of Henry de Lacy, earl of Lincoln, securing part of the Lacy inheritance with the promise of the remainder on Lacy's death. It was thanks to the king that the marriage settlement excluded collateral heirs to the two Lacy earldoms of Lincoln and Salisbury, to Lancaster's advantage, and, a little later, that his own earldom of Derby was successfully defended against the claims of the disinherited John de Ferrers. Towards the end of the reign he also received numerous minor gifts from Edward and, in 1307, the valuable franchise of return of writs. In return he gave loyal service to his uncle and benefactor. He first served on the Falkirk campaign of 1297–8 (in the course of which he was knighted), fought at Falkirk in 1298, was present at Caerlaverock in 1300, and accompanied Prince Edward to Perth in 1304–5 and on campaign again in 1306–7. The king's obvious fondness for his nephew may have owed something to the unmartial ways of his own son and heir. But this did not separate Lancaster from the prince, with whom he remained on friendly terms.

Edward II and Gaveston, 1307–1312 Although Edward II's accession in July 1307 rapidly led to the marshalling of baronial opposition to the new king, it marked no break in

Thomas of Lancaster, second earl of Lancaster, second earl of Leicester, and earl of Lincoln (*c.*1278–1322), manuscript painting [right, with St George]

Lancaster's close relationship with his cousin. The political goodwill evident in the first few months of the reign, which allowed Edward to recall his favourite, Piers Gaveston, from exile and to secure a tax grant from parliament, was soon dissipated by the two issues which were to dominate Edward II's early years: the intolerable conduct of Gaveston, and the king's misgovernment, exemplified among much else by purveyance—the forcible levying of foodstuffs to feed the royal household and armies. But Lancaster's alignment with the king's opponents on these issues was by no means immediate, and for the first eighteen months of the new reign he enjoyed Edward's favour and company. He was with him in the north in the weeks following the old king's death, travelled south with him after Edward's cancellation of the current Scottish campaign, dined with him fairly frequently, and benefited from numerous royal grants. Of these, the grant of the stewardship of England, made to Lancaster and his heirs in the summer of 1308, was the most important and the most portentous. Unlike his father-in-law, Henry de Lacy, he had no part in the Boulogne declaration of January 1308, which complained about 'the oppressions ... committed against the people' (Phillips, 316), nor in the exiling of Gaveston, which followed in the summer. It was only in the winter of 1308–9, as the other earls made their peace with the king in the gratifying absence of Gaveston, that

Lancaster began to move in the opposite direction. There was no dramatic break with Edward, nor are the causes of their separation at all clear. But from November 1308 he ceased to witness royal charters, the flow of favours to him dried up, and he moved north to his own estates.

By the spring of 1309 Lancaster's alienation was beginning to be transformed into a more positive support for reform. In March or April he was present with a very large retinue, and in company with some of the other earls, at a tournament at Dunstable. There, complaints may have been formulated about purveyance, judicial malpractices, and other abuses, which were subsequently petitioned against in the April parliament. Redress was offered in the Statute of Stamford, drawn up at the Stamford parliament in July, which was the price paid by Edward for Gaveston's recall in June. Although Lancaster had previously shown the favourite no hostility, he opposed his return, unlike most of the other earls; indeed, one chronicle reports that he became the 'captain' of the dissenters. For reform, and against the king's friend, he had thus begun to identify with both the main lines of opposition to Edward.

These now began to converge. The opprobrious behaviour of Gaveston after his return (Lancaster's nickname of 'Churl' was one of several which the favourite is said to have coined for the earls about this time), together with the military successes of the Scots and the emergence of purveyance as the overriding grievance against Edward's government, all combined to generate a virtually united demand for reform. Lancaster became its spokesman. In the parliament which opened in February 1310 he presented a petition of grievances to the king, and in March Edward agreed to appoint *lords ordainer to reform the realm. The work of the twenty-one men subsequently elected bore fruit with the publication of the ordinances in August 1311 and of a second, supplementary, set, mainly directed at the royal household, in November. For most of the intervening period Edward was campaigning in the north, mainly to keep Gaveston out of harm's way. The ordaining earls, including Lancaster, refused to serve there. But it was the death of Henry de Lacy in February 1311, rather than politics, which most directly affected Lancaster at this time, for it brought him two new earldoms, an overwhelmingly dominant position among the landed aristocracy, and perhaps a reinforcement of his emerging leadership. He and the earl of Warwick, both among the more intransigent reformers, are said to have presented the second ordinances to the king, and one chronicle even spoke of 'the ordinances of the earl of Lancaster'. For the remainder of his life his adherence to these reforms was to remain his chief principle of action.

The ordinances were in the first place a means to good government. They sought to strengthen the king's finances, to answer the complaints which, on matters such as purveyance, had often arisen from financial weakness, and to prevent future abuses by demanding 'the consent of the baronage in parliament' for a wide range of royal initiatives (*Statutes of the Realm*, 1.158–60). In all this they represented both a set of restraints on Edward's kingship and a popular programme, 'a remedy for the poor and oppressed', as the bishops termed them (*Councils and Synods*, 2/2.1369); though the programme was one which could not be enforced without the conciliar checks which the ordainers had failed to put in place. But the ordinances were also an indictment of Gaveston, whose activities were seen to epitomize the disregard for law and custom which lay at the heart of Edward's misrule. They therefore called once again for the favourite's exile; yet events were to show that, with Gaveston out of the way, the opposition would disintegrate. The negative principle of common hostility to a favourite that the ordinances embodied counted for more than their positive call for reform.

In deference to the ordinances Gaveston went abroad in October 1311, but, in their defiance, he was back in England again by Christmas. At York, in January 1312, the king revoked the ordinances and restored the favourite to full power. After Gaveston had been excommunicated by Archbishop Robert Winchelsey, the leading ecclesiastical ordainer, Lancaster took the initiative in the baronial reaction which followed. He demanded from the king Gaveston's surrender and renewed exile, and when these demands were predictably ignored he and other magnates moved north in pursuit of the royal party. In early May Gaveston was captured in Scarborough Castle, after having allowed himself to become separated from Edward. A truce was then made, whose favourable terms for the prisoner probably owed much to some arrangement between the earl of Pembroke, a moderate among the ordainers, and the king. Gaveston was travelling south in Pembroke's charge to meet Edward when he was seized at Deddington in Oxfordshire by the earl of Warwick, Lancaster's close partner. He was led off to Warwick, 'tried' before a court in which Lancaster and Warwick were the chief judges and the exile of Gaveston decreed in the ordinances the main point of law, and then executed, on 19 June 1312, on Lancaster's land near Kenilworth. Lancaster had thus been the initiator of Gaveston's prosecution and a chief party to his quasi-judicial murder—a role which demonstrated his detestation of Gaveston, his regard for the ordinances, and his willingness to use violence against the one and in defence of the other.

The break-up of the baronial coalition, 1312–1314 Gaveston's death permanently alienated Edward from Lancaster and divided the ordainers; for in its wake Pembroke and Earl Warenne, both among the more conciliatory reformers, were drawn back towards the king. Lancaster's position was more fortuitously weakened in May 1313 by the death of his ally, Archbishop Winchelsey, after which clerical backing for the ordinances was largely withdrawn. Yet he retained considerable bargaining power, thanks to his possession of the extremely valuable jewels and horses captured during Gaveston's pursuit in the north. It was in the interests of Lancaster to present the jewels as illicitly taken from the royal treasury by Gaveston, though in fact they are more likely to have been entrusted to him in his official role as royal chamberlain. After a period in July 1312 when civil war was very close, negotiations began in September for the transfer of the king's goods. Lancaster and his followers wanted a pardon, the maintenance of

the ordinances, and the condemnation of Gaveston—which would have amounted to the ordinances' endorsement—as 'the enemy of the king and the realm' (Stubbs, 211); the king wanted the return of the jewels and military aid against the resurgent Scots. Eventually, in February 1313, the jewels were returned, and the barons pardoned in October, though without Edward's recognition, either explicit or implicit, of the ordinances. Lancaster remained on his estates for most of this time, conducting negotiations through intermediaries, and the final royally inclined compromise reflected his own shortcomings as a leader. Possessing a programme, he lacked not only the means but also the will to enforce it.

But Edward's feeble victory did nothing to solve his real problems, which lay in Scotland. The Scots' siege of Stirling from the summer of 1313, and the fall of other English-held castles, had committed the king to a northern campaign in 1314. Writs for the summoning of an army were issued in December 1313, but Lancaster and three other earls—Warwick, Arundel, and Warenne—refused to serve, arguing that the summons had not been decided on in parliament, as the ordinances decreed. This legalistic point covered both a deeper sense of disgruntlement with Edward's government and also the concealed but continuing tensions resulting from Gaveston's death. Three other ordaining earls—Pembroke, Gloucester, and Hereford—all joined Edward's army, highlighting Lancaster's increasingly isolated position as the ordinances' defender. But his isolation at least meant that he was not directly associated with the greatest English military disaster of the middle ages, which occurred when Edward II was defeated by Robert I at Bannockburn in June 1314.

Government and the court, 1314–1318 Edward's humiliation at Bannockburn was interpreted as a divine judgment in favour of the ordinances. The battle forced Edward into immediate dependence on Lancaster, and during the next two years his leading role in government, for the first and last time, gave him the chance to implement all that he stood for. Yet his position perhaps owed as much to his lands, wealth, and following as to the apparently providential vindication of his programme seen in the victory of the Scots. 'By the size of his patrimony', says the *Vita Edwardi secundi*, 'you may assess his power.' His actual patrimony, consisting of the three earldoms of Lancaster, Leicester, and Derby, lay largely in Lancashire, in Leicestershire and Warwickshire (centred on Kenilworth Castle), and in Staffordshire and Derbyshire (centred on Tutbury Castle), with an outlying castle and estate at Dunstanburgh, in Northumberland. To these were added, on Henry de Lacy's death, the two earldoms of Lincoln and Salisbury, and extensive new lands in Yorkshire, Lancashire, Lincolnshire, and north Wales. Among the Yorkshire holdings was the castle of Pontefract, which was to become Lancaster's favourite residence.

The significance of these estates lay partly in their contiguity. Stretching as they did across south Lancashire, south Yorkshire, and the north midlands, they gave Lancaster lordship over a wide swathe of territory which spanned almost the breadth of England. But, of course, it was their profitability that mattered most. Their total value was probably about £11,000 a year, of which about £6500—considerably more than half—came from the Lacy inheritance. An income of this size made Lancaster by some way the richest of the earls and enabled him to build up the retinue on which his power came partly to depend. His following, like his estate, was abnormally large. At its maximum, in the middle years of the reign, it contained about fifty knights; but, since many of these commanded sub-retinues of their own, and since Lancaster could also array troops directly from his lands, the total military force at his command was much greater than this. Attracted by Lancaster's wealth and by the generous fees that he was able to offer, its leading members were spread across the area of his own landed dominance. As he drifted into political isolation, and even without a party behind him, his retinue made him a force to be reckoned with.

It was Lancaster's misfortune that power became available to him at a time when its constructive use was peculiarly difficult. After Bannockburn the north lay open to Scottish attack, and Edward's financial problems, compounded by the ruinous famine of 1315–17, hindered any attempt at effective defence, or indeed at effective government. These were years of national demoralization. Lancaster's remedy, predictably, was the full enforcement of the ordinances. It was a sign of the turnaround in his political fortunes that these were confirmed by the king both at the York parliament of September 1314, the first after the battle, and at the Westminster parliament of January 1315. Then followed a purge of the royal household, the resumption of royal grants, and a wholesale change of sheriffs: all measures envisaged in the ordinances, closely associated with Lancaster, and largely designed to put the king's finances on a sound footing. If Lancaster's policies here were a means to the more effective prosecution of the Scots, he was also personally involved throughout 1315 in the formulation and execution of policy towards Scotland, taking steps to finance the keeping of the north and to consult the northern clergy and magnates to this end. In August, when Carlisle was under siege, he was appointed as 'superior captain' of the king's northern forces, and in October he was planning a large expedition to the north: a plan thwarted by the famine's depletion of the country's military resources and by a revolt on his own estates, led by his former retainer, Adam Banaster. He thus had a central role in the country's government and defence. Yet it was one qualified by his own separation from the king, both geographically (he retired from Westminster in the spring of 1315) and emotionally (for the death of Gaveston still came sharply between them). Pembroke remained Edward's more trusted confidant, and Lancaster the never quite dominant outsider.

Chief councillor, and relations with the king Formal domination Lancaster did eventually achieve, for at the Lincoln parliament of January 1316 he was appointed as the king's chief councillor. He accepted his new role in the hope that reform might continue, but he reserved his right to withdraw if Edward refused to follow his and the council's

advice. His unwillingness to commit himself here was of a piece with his continuing reluctance to reside at Westminster: from April onwards he was once again on his own north midland estates. Yet he remained the champion of the ordinances. A new committee, which included Lancaster, was set up to reform the royal household, the ordinances themselves were republished in the counties in March, and a further resumption of royal grants followed in April. He continued, too, to be consulted about Scottish affairs and he was associated with Edward's plans for a new Scottish campaign in the summer of 1316. But his relationship with the king was heading for disruption. At York in August 1316 they quarrelled violently, particularly over the king's unwillingness to enforce the ordinances, and in November their differences were exacerbated by the triumph of the queen's candidate over Lancaster's in the election to the see of Durham. The almost simultaneous appointment of the earl of Arundel as captain of the northern forces, after the campaign's cancellation in October, marked Lancaster's supersession, in the king's counsels as much as in the north.

Political isolation Lancaster was now politically isolated. The earl of Warwick, his partner in the prosecution of Gaveston, had died in August 1315, and the other earls were close to the king. From this point onwards, for nearly two years, he was to remain an external critic of Edward's government, a one-man opposition whose political leverage lay almost solely in his wealth and following. His refusal to attend meetings of the council—at Clarendon in February 1317, at Westminster in April, and at Nottingham in July—was symptomatic of an increasingly deep alienation from Edward's regime. It was rooted in personal and constitutional grievances, both deriving primarily from the composition of the court. The years 1316–17 saw the rise of a powerful court party, headed by five barons—the two Hugh Despensers, father and son, Hugh Audley the younger, Roger Damory, and William Montagu. Three of the five—the younger Despenser, Audley, and Damory—had founded their fortunes on marriage to the sisters and coheirs of the earl of Gloucester, killed at Bannockburn. But all had grown rich on royal patronage and stood to lose from the enforcement of the ordinances, whose demand for a resumption of past royal grants and the consent of the baronage in parliament to future ones would have left them dispossessed. It was in their interests as well as his own that Edward, in December 1316, unsuccessfully sought to overthrow the ordinances by seeking papal absolution from his oath to maintain them.

Lancaster's opposition to these men was partly one of political principles: their nourishment from the king's largesse was an affront to the ordinances and a drain on the king's finances, in the desperately difficult economic and military circumstances created by the famine and the Scots. They were, too, at the centre of the small council meetings which Edward was using, in place of parliament and contrary to the ordinances, to determine military policy. But his hostility—that of an 'out' protesting against the favours enjoyed by the 'ins'—was also bitterly personal. More personal still was his opposition to Earl Warenne, a figure on the fringes of the court, who had abducted his wife, supposedly with the support of the other courtiers, in April 1317 (see below). But Lancaster's particular objections to the court and to Edward's methods of government, voiced in a letter which he wrote to the king about July 1317, had no means of making their mark; especially since even the more moderate of Edward's friends, including former ordainers such as Pembroke and Hereford, had been retained by the king on generous terms. That was why he now began to take the law into his own hands. In October 1317 he may have supported the attack by a Northumbrian freebooter, Sir Gilbert Middleton, on the new bishop of Durham, Louis Beaumont, and his brother Henry, an unpopular courtier whom the ordainers had sought to eject, as they made their way towards Durham for Louis's consecration. At any rate, several of those in Middleton's gang are found in Lancaster's service shortly afterwards. More certainly, about the same time he used his retinue to seize castles held by Damory and Warenne. But he also called in the Scots, both against the Beaumonts and against Damory, so qualifying his claim to be taking a stand on principle. To ally with the kingdom's enemies in order to purge the court suggested a peculiar sense of priorities.

Despite these antagonisms, there were good reasons for Edward and his friends to seek a reconciliation with Lancaster. The size of his following, a matter for public comment and criticism in 1317, added another element of instability to an already dangerously unstable political situation; the attacks on the courtiers had shown how the retinue could be used to forward by violence ends unattainable by other means; while the continuing successes of the Scots, who in the spring and summer of 1318 advanced as far as south Yorkshire, made it imperative to secure the military support of Lancaster and his private army. So it was that from November 1317 attempts began to be made to bring Lancaster and Edward together, largely through the mediation of Pembroke, Hereford, the Kentish baron Bartholomew Badlesmere, and, especially, of the bishops. Pembroke and Badlesmere had already promoted Lancaster's arguments by securing the consent of the avaricious Damory to restraints on Edward's patronage. Aired more generally, however, this issue was to prove an almost intractable stumbling-block in the negotiations with Lancaster which followed. The two sides were far apart. Lancaster wanted the full observance of the ordinances, the removal of the king's 'evil counsellors', their trial in parliament for wrongfully receiving the king's grants, and an immediate resumption of those grants. All this was anathema to the courtiers, who stood to lose everything from Lancaster's demands. The negotiations swayed backwards and forwards, but eventually bore fruit in a treaty made at Leake, in Staffordshire, in August 1318. It marked the measure of Lancaster's defeat. A new standing council was to be set up; but on it Lancaster was represented only by a banneret. The ordinances were to be maintained; but the guarantors

for their maintenance included some of the leading courtiers. About the resumption of royal grants and the removal of evil councillors nothing whatever was said.

Following the treaty of Leake, at the York parliament of October and November, a limited resumption and a limited reform of the royal household were both put in hand. But there was otherwise little movement in Lancaster's direction. Why had he conceded so much? The answer almost certainly lies in the private inducements offered to him by the king and the court to modify his demands. In November some of the leading courtiers acknowledged large debts to him, and these payments are likely to have been the price of peace. More remarkably, in the same month he came to terms with his wife's abductor, Earl Warenne, in a coercive settlement which gave him all Warenne's lands in Yorkshire and north Wales, and which was almost certainly connived at by Edward and his friends. The position of the chief courtiers had been preserved, their chief opponent satisfied, and Warenne abandoned, along with Lancaster's principles.

The rise and fall of a party leader, 1319–1322 In conciliating Lancaster, Edward's mediators had sought to make possible the united campaign against the Scots which was eventually launched in 1319. It was planned at the York parliament of May 1319, where Lancaster was present in a newly co-operative mood. As steward of England, he there petitioned for the right to appoint the steward of the royal household, which would have given him the power to regulate household expenditure: a prime reforming objective. To judge by the tract on the steward's office, probably drawn up under his auspices in 1321, he intended to go further and to ground on the stewardship a wider claim to a general supervisory role in government. That these claims went unrecognized, however, did not prevent his participation in the new campaign, with a very large force, though it was a mark of his continuing wish for independence that his men apparently took no pay from the king, leaving their leader free from the contractual disciplines and obligations that pay would have implied.

Despite Lancaster's service the campaign of 1319 was a disaster. In September the English army laid siege to Berwick, but its leaders immediately fell to quarrelling. Edward's foolish promise of patronage to the younger Despenser and to Damory, once the town had been taken, alienated Lancaster, who withdrew his troops when it became known that the Scots had slipped past the besiegers and were devastating Yorkshire. Lancaster himself was rumoured, almost certainly unjustly on this occasion, to be in collusion with the Scots, with whom a truce had to be made in December, after the renewal of border raids. All the old divisions were reopened. Lancaster refused to attend a parliament at York in January 1320, and the growing strength of the courtiers, who were once again receiving generous grants from Edward, seemed to herald a return to the politics of 1316–18. In the spring of 1320 the success of a mission to the papal curia in obtaining Edward's absolution from his oath to the ordinances gave the king a degree of political emancipation which he had not known since 1311, though Pembroke's continuing influence at court seems to have nullified the effects of Edward's new-found freedom. Lancaster meanwhile remained in the north, at Pontefract, once again in isolation.

What drew Lancaster back to the political stage was the radical realignment of forces brought about by the rise of the Despensers to supremacy at court and the consequent breakup of the old court party. During 1319 the two Despensers had come to dominate the court, controlling access to the king, monopolizing his ear, and directing the royal household. Their hold over Edward gave full play to their territorial ambitions, notably in south Wales, where the younger Despenser's share of the Clare inheritance was greatly enlarged in the last months of 1320 by the illicit take-over of Gower and other lands. This challenged the interests of the remaining marcher lords, among whom were some of the other leading members of the court, including Hereford (who also had a claim to Gower), Damory, and Audley. Hereford took the lead in resisting, and in February 1321 appealed to the one magnate with both the power and the motive to counter the Despensers: Thomas of Lancaster. Their alliance was probably sealed in a meeting between them at Pontefract. In April disturbances broke out in the marches; and in May, after Hereford's request to the king for the removal of the younger Despenser from court and his temporary surrender to Lancaster had been refused, the barons began the systematic devastation of the lands of the Despensers and their allies.

Although Lancaster was clearly regarded as the barons' leader, he took no part in the ravaging of the Despensers' lands. He may have found some difficulty in weighing in on the side of men such as Damory who had formerly been his enemies, while he was also violently at odds with another renegade courtier, Bartholomew Badlesmere, perhaps because Badlesmere's appointment as steward of the household in 1318 usurped a position which Lancaster regarded as within his gift. His role at this stage, therefore, was a passive one, and confined to the organization of a coalition against the court. To this end he convened two meetings in the north in May and June 1321. At the first, held at Pontefract, he tried to secure the active backing of fifteen northern lords against the Despensers, but they were unwilling to do more than join with Lancaster in a league for their mutual defence. At the second, held at Sherburn in Elmet, a larger gathering assembled, in response to the request of the northerners and again under Lancaster's auspices. It included the northerners themselves, the marchers, and a substantial body of Lancastrian retainers, which outnumbered either of the other two parties. But in its main purpose the assembly was a failure. The northerners again refused to join up, and it was mainly Lancaster's own men who set their seals to an indenture of mutual alliance against the Despensers. Two other pieces of business came before the meeting. First, it was presented with a general bill of grievances, which, invoking the ordinances, enumerated both the complaints of the marchers and other more general instances of Edward's misgovernment. Second, an indictment was drafted against the Despensers, to be put before the parliament that had been summoned for July.

These northern meetings represented an attempt by Lancaster to extend the quarrel of the marchers and to build a great coalition against the Despensers. But the northerners were too circumspect to commit themselves to a cause that was not their own, perhaps particularly since Lancaster's own commitment was more a matter of theory than practice. After the meeting he remained at Pontefract, while his marcher allies moved south, continuing to devastate the Despenser lands before they finally entered London at the start of August. With civil war near, and Pembroke pressing Edward to yield, the king rapidly conceded the Despensers' exile. But this was the most temporary of victories, for by Michaelmas the younger Despenser had once more rejoined the court.

Defeat and execution Edward was now well placed to take the offensive. The first move in his campaign came in October, when he laid siege to Badlesmere's castle at Leeds in Kent, on the pretext that the queen had been refused entry there. The marchers, in co-operation with Badlesmere, wished to raise the siege, but Lancaster forbade them to do so and, it seems, refused to receive the unfortunate Badlesmere when the marchers subsequently retreated to Pontefract. This willingness to elevate a private quarrel over a public cause was not the only mark of his deficiencies as a leader. They were shown, too, by the desertions from his retinue which began to multiply about this time, as men became conscious of the risks involved in what seemed likely to be an armed confrontation with the crown. Lancaster's awareness of his weakness here, and of the need to draw in more support, was indicated by a further northern meeting which he convened at Doncaster in November. To it he summoned not only the marchers and the northerners but also a large number of other men whose unimpeachable royalist record suggested how desperately wide he was now having to cast his net. The meeting produced a further petition against the Despensers, later sent to the king, and an appeal by Lancaster himself for the backing of the city of London. Shortly afterwards he sought help again from the Scots, this time going beyond the working partnership of 1317, to enter into a formal alliance with Robert I.

By this stage Edward was moving with an army towards the marches. He was foiled for a time in his attempts to cross the Severn and had to tolerate further attacks by his opponents on Despenser manors. But in late January he was able to reach the west bank of the Severn at Shrewsbury and to secure the surrender of a large party of marchers, to whom Lancaster had offered no active help. Others of the marchers under Hereford then withdrew to Lancaster at Pontefract. Lancaster meanwhile had laid siege to the royal castle at Tickhill, in Yorkshire, whose constable had been acting as Edward's spy. The siege brought a crucial change in Edward's strategy, for he promptly turned away from the marches and towards the north. Lancaster's forces were now falling apart, and there was a general reluctance to rally to a failing cause. On 10 March, weakened further by the treacherous desertion of Robert Holland, his chief henchman and recruiting officer, he was unable to prevent the royalists crossing the Trent at Burton. Retreating northwards, probably towards his castle at Dunstanburgh, Lancaster and his small army were intercepted on the River Aire at Boroughbridge on 16 March. In the battle which followed Lancaster was captured, and on 22 March 1322, after what amounted to a show trial, he was executed at Pontefract.

Cult and character Like Simon de Montfort, whose lands he inherited and whose career superficially resembles his own, Thomas of Lancaster came to be regarded as a saint. Within six weeks of his death miracles were reported from his tomb at Pontefract and an armed guard was sent by the king to close the church where his body lay. In 1323 there were riots as crowds of people tried to gain access to the place of his execution to pray and make offerings. In 1327, after Edward II's deposition, the Commons asked the new king to press for his canonization; and, even after the political circumstances which had given rise to the cult had passed into history, popular veneration for Lancaster persisted. On the eve of the Reformation his hat and belt were still preserved at Pontefract as respective remedies for headaches and the dangers of childbirth.

A large part of this contemporary reputation derived from Edward II's vices rather than Lancaster's virtues. As Edward's rule degenerated, first into misgovernment by the Despensers before 1322, and then into something approaching tyranny, any leader dying in opposition to the regime might have expected popular acclaim. Yet there was more than this to Lancaster's fame. From 1311 onwards he had consistently identified himself with the ordinances, though not above all else: he gave priority to private profit at the treaty of Leake in 1318 and to personal antagonism towards the Despensers in his last years. In placing the ordinances at the centre of his political life, with whatever qualifications, he came to stand, not just for constitutional restraints on the crown and its patronage, but for the redress of popular grievances and the reform of widespread abuses. On matters such as purveyance and the malpractices of royal justice, the ordinances had offered relief, not primarily to barons, but to the politically unimportant. Much of the vigour of his cult lay here.

In many ways, however, Lancaster was an unconvincing and unaccomplished idealist. A harsh landlord, much petitioned against for his breaches of law and equity, and quick to resort to violence, he was not a man to inspire either affection or loyalty. His childless wife left him in 1317, the northerners failed to respond to his call in 1321, and even his retinue mostly broke and ran in the months before Boroughbridge. Although he partnered Archbishop Winchelsey in captaining the ordainers, in general he lacked the backing of the bishops and schoolmen which had given justice and reflected glory to Simon de Montfort's cause. This was as much a failure of political leadership as of personality. For most of his career he remained an outsider in politics, apparently by his own choice, preferring residence in his northern castles to the king's company at Westminster. In so doing he maintained his integrity at the expense of his influence, relying for his political weight more on his estates and manpower than to any engagement with government. When he turned to the Scots for help in 1317 and 1322, or disdained to receive Bartholomew Badlesmere in his final months, he showed that he lacked political judgement. Man of principle though he was, it was not only the intensely difficult circumstances of his career which set limits to his political effectiveness, but also, and perhaps primarily, his own inadequacies.

Alice Lacy The abduction of Lancaster's wife, **Alice Lacy**, *suo jure* countess of Lincoln, and countess of Lancaster and Leicester (1281–1348), by Earl Warenne was only one episode in what was an adventurous career. Probably born at her father's castle of Denbigh, Alice played no discernible part in Thomas of Lancaster's life and, like many medieval women, came into her own only after her husband's death. According to the Meaux chronicle, her abduction by Warenne was carried through, not from lust, but merely to spite her husband, who had stood with the royal council in 1314 in attempting to prevent Warenne from divorcing his wife, Joan de Bar, in order to marry his mistress, Maud Nerford. Alice's separation from Lancaster, however, did not protect her from the consequences of his death in opposition to the king in 1322. After his fall both she and her mother were imprisoned at York. There Alice was threatened with burning by the two Hugh Despensers, father and son—a characteristic instance of their casual brutality—until she surrendered to their will. She lost her great inherited lordship of Denbigh (which she never regained) and most of her other estates, but she was allowed to keep her title of countess of Salisbury and Lincoln, together with a life interest in lands worth 500 marks.

Alice's brief fling with Warenne (if such it was) led to no lasting liaison, and by November 1324, after her release from prison, she had taken as her second husband Ebulo Lestrange of Knockin, in Shropshire, a minor baron of the Welsh marches. He had formerly sided with Lancaster in the pursuit of Gaveston, though there appears to have been no regular connection. The marriage was a sign that she had salvaged enough from the wreck of her first husband's career—including the custody of Lincoln Castle and £20 from the earl's third penny in the county—to make her an attractive match. His wife's property served to shift Lestrange's main interest to Lincolnshire, though he spent a large part of his later career campaigning in Scotland, where he died in September 1335. Alice was one of his executors.

Alice did not remain husbandless for long. At the end of 1335 or the beginning of 1336 she was abducted from her ancestral castle of Bolingbroke in Lincolnshire, probably with her own connivance and despite having taken a vow of chastity in her widowhood, by Sir Hugh de Freyne, a Herefordshire knight, royal keeper of the castle and town of Cardigan, and steward of Cardiganshire since 1330. After facing down Edward III's brief anger (and orders for their imprisonment), the couple made their peace with the king and were married early in 1336. His new wife's title and lands brought Freyne a personal summons to parliament for the first and last time in November 1336. He died shortly afterwards, in December 1336 or January 1337, at Perth. Alice did not marry again and died childless in October 1348, aged sixty-six. She was buried at the side of her second husband at the Premonstratensian house of Barlings, in Lincolnshire. Her many manors and lordships, most of which she had gathered together again after the débâcle of Boroughbridge, fell to the house of Lancaster, under the terms of the original marriage settlement made with her first husband some fifty-four years earlier.   J. R. MADDICOTT

Sources PRO, accounts various, E 101 · Duchy of Lancaster, ministers' accounts, PRO, DL 29 · *Chancery records* · W. Stubbs, ed., *Chronicles of the reigns of Edward I and Edward II*, 2 vols., Rolls Series, 76 (1882–3) · *Chronicon Henrici Knighton, vel Cnitthon, monachi Leycestrensis*, ed. J. R. Lumby, 2 vols., Rolls Series, 92 (1889–95) · H. R. Luard, ed., *Flores historiarum*, 3 vols., Rolls Series, 95 (1890) · *Nicolai Triveti annalium continuatio*, ed. A. Hallius [A. Hall] (1722) · N. Denholm-Young, ed. and trans., *Vita Edwardi secundi* (1957) · *Thomae Walsingham, quondam monachi S. Albani, historia Anglicana*, ed. H. T. Riley, 2 vols., pt 1 of *Chronica monasterii S. Albani*, Rolls Series, 28 (1863–4), vol. 1 · J. R. Maddicott, *Thomas of Lancaster, 1307–1322: a study in the reign of Edward II* (1970) · R. Somerville, *History of the duchy of Lancaster, 1265–1603* (1953) · J. R. S. Phillips, *Aymer de Valence, earl of Pembroke, 1307–1324: baronial politics in the reign of Edward II* (1972) · A. Luders and others, eds., *Statutes of the realm*, 11 vols. in 12, RC (1810–28), vol. 1 · F. M. Powicke and C. R. Cheney, eds., *Councils and synods with other documents relating to the English church, 1205–1313*, 2 (1964) · GEC, *Peerage*
Likenesses manuscript painting, Bodl. Oxf., MS Douce 231, fol. 1 [*see illus.*]

Thomas of Lancaster. *See* Thomas, duke of Clarence (1387–1421).

Thomas of Newmarket. *See* Newmarket, Thomas (*fl.* 1371–1384).

Thomas of Woodstock. *See* Thomas, duke of Gloucester (1355–1397).

Thomas of York. *See* York, Thomas of (*b. c.*1220, *d.* before 1269).

Thomas the Rhymer. *See* Thomas of Erceldoune (*fl.* late 13th cent.).

Thomas Wallensis [Thomas the Welshman] (*d.* **1255**), bishop of St David's, was, by his own account, of Welsh origin. He became a Franciscan friar, and was a canon of Lincoln in 1235, a regent master in theology at Paris in 1238, and one of the first four Franciscans to teach at Oxford, being expert in Greek. Before 27 May 1238 Robert Grosseteste offered him the archdeaconry of Lincoln with a prebend, writing that he preferred Thomas's claims above all others although he was still young. In 1243 Thomas took an active part in the dispute which arose between Grosseteste and the abbot of Bardney. Matthew Paris ascribes the origin of the suit against the abbot to the archdeacon. He was elected to the poor bishopric of St David's on 16 July 1247, and he accepted it at Grosseteste's

urging, and out of love for his native land. He was consecrated on 26 July 1248 at Canterbury. In 1252–3 he visited the Roman curia, and on 10 October 1253 issued an important set of statutes for his cathedral and its chapter. He was present at the parliament in London at Easter 1253, and joined in excommunicating all violators of Magna Carta. He died on 11 July 1255.

MARY BATESON, *rev.* MARIOS COSTAMBEYS

Sources J. C. Davies, ed., *Episcopal acts and cognate documents relating to Welsh dioceses, 1066–1272*, 1, Historical Society of the Church in Wales, 1 (1946) · T. Jones, ed. and trans., *Brut y tywysogyon, or, The chronicle of the princes: Peniarth MS 20* (1952) · R. W. Southern, *Robert Grosseteste: the growth of an English mind in medieval Europe* (1986)

Thomas, Sir Alfred Brumwell (1868–1948), architect, was born in London, the son of Edward Thomas, a district surveyor working in Rotherhithe. He was articled to W. Seckham and at the same time studied at Westminster School of Art and at the Architectural Association in London. He commenced practice about 1894, initially with his father, under the name of E. Thomas & Son, but later worked independently, adding the invented name Brumwell as a distinguishing feature.

Thomas achieved notable success in competitions for large public buildings, beginning with Belfast city hall in 1896. In this palatial building, completed in 1906, he displayed his ability to design on a grand scale, working freely in the English baroque style; his design featured towers and domes on the exterior and spacious interiors replete with rich marbles and carved woodwork. One of the most important examples of the baroque revival anywhere in the British Isles, this magnificent building was a perfect expression of the prosperity and civic pride of Belfast at the turn of the century and still forms the centrepiece of the city.

During the building of the city hall Thomas was invited by the sculptor F. W. Pomeroy in 1903 to collaborate on the adjacent Dufferin memorial, to be sited within its grounds; Thomas was responsible for the Portland stone base and canopy designed in an Italian Renaissance style to harmonize with the main building. Later, in 1922–4, he masterminded a scheme for remodelling the entire grounds around the city hall, which culminated in the creation of the garden of remembrance which contains the city's war memorial erected to his design in 1925–7.

Thomas's other main competition successes—Woolwich town hall (1899–1908) in south-east London and Stockport town hall (1903–6) in Cheshire, both of which were contemporary with Belfast—were designed in a similar idiom and faced in the same material, Portland stone. Following the completion of Belfast city hall, Thomas was knighted in 1906. Other buildings by him included the West of England Eye Infirmary at Exeter, a public library in Lewisham Way, Deptford, London (1911–14), the Skefco ball bearing works at Luton (1919), a war memorial at Dunkirk, and Clacton town hall, Essex (1931).

At the age of forty-six Thomas volunteered in the First World War and he served from 1914 to 1916, during which he attained the rank of major. In his professional life he was a member of the council of the Royal British Colonial Society of Architects, a fellow of the Royal Institute of British Architects, and sometime president of the Architectural Association. Of well-groomed and handsome appearance (judging from his portrait of 1906) he appears to have been of likeable character, remembered with obvious affection by his obituarists. In particular, he had many friends in Northern Ireland and visited Belfast fairly frequently up to the time of his retirement from practice in 1938.

For some years Thomas lived in the Temple, London, and during the Second World War he was twice bombed out. He died unmarried on 22 January 1948 at Holloway Sanatorium, Virginia Water, Surrey, in his eightieth year.

PAUL LARMOUR

Sources A. S. Gray, *Edwardian architecture: a biographical dictionary* (1985), 347–8 · J. G. Gamble, *RIBA Journal*, 55 (1947–8), 271–2 · *The Builder*, 174 (1948), 134 · *Belfast News-Letter* (26 Jan 1948) · A. Service, 'Thomas, Sir Alfred Brumwell', *The dictionary of art*, ed. J. Turner (1996) · [D. Dixon and others], *The city hall of the county borough of Belfast* (1906) · *WWW* · B. Thomas, 'Belfast city hall: forty years after', *Belfast News-Letter* (1 Aug 1946), 3 · d. cert. · *CGPLA Eng. & Wales* (1948)

Likenesses photograph, *c.*1906, repro. in [Dixon and others], *City hall*

Wealth at death £3709 13s. 1d.: administration with will, 23 March 1948, *CGPLA Eng. & Wales*

Thomas [*married name* Cudlip], **Annie Hall** (1838–1918), novelist, was born on 25 October 1838 at Aldborough in Norfolk, the only daughter of Lieutenant George Thomas, a naval officer in charge of the coastguard station there. She was educated at home, and began writing in order to support herself after her father's death in 1856. Her first published work, 'A Stroll in the Park', appeared in the first issue of *London Society*, in 1862. During her long and prolific career she published more than seventy popular novels (all appearing under her maiden name), and she also contributed stories and sketches to publications including *St Paul's Magazine*, *Temple Bar*, *All the Year Round*, and many American journals. William Tinsley, in his *Random Recollections of an Old Publisher* (1900), described Thomas as 'a bright, merry, light-hearted girl, a writer of bright, easy-reading fiction, of which she could write acres in a short time'; she boasted 'of being able to write a three-volume novel in about six weeks' (Tinsley, 2.248–9).

Although there was some speculation in her social circle that Annie Thomas might marry W. S. Gilbert, she married the Revd Pender Hodge Cudlip on 10 July 1867. Gilbert may have made reference to his unsuccessful suit in one of the Bab Ballads, with the line, 'Henceforth she'll only marry curates' (Tinsley, 2.248). Pender Cudlip, from Porthleven in Cornwall, was curate of Yealmpton in Devon at the time of their marriage; they later moved to Sparkwell, near Plympton, also in Devon. In a letter to A. C. Swinburne (*c.*1 May 1871), the painter Simeon Solomon mentioned meeting Thomas at Torquay: 'I have ... been staying with ... Miss Annie Thomas the novelist now Mrs Pendercudlip (I beg to state that *I* did not pend her cudlip, I would scorn the action)' (*Swinburne Letters*, 2.142).

In an anonymous article for *Blackwood's* (September 1867), Margaret Oliphant attacked writers of sensation fiction, including Annie Thomas and Mary Elizabeth Braddon, for the immorality and literary inferiority of their work. Although Oliphant notes that Thomas's *Played out* (1866) and *Called to Account* (1867) 'are neither immoral ... nor *horsey*, which is akin to immoral', her immense popularity combined with her 'very small amount of literary skill' provoked Oliphant's scorn, as did an article in the *Revue des Deux Mondes* which described Thomas as a representative English novelist (Oliphant, 272, 261, 260–61). Charlotte Yonge shared Oliphant's distaste for Thomas's writing; in a letter to her cousin Mary Yonge (22 December 1869), she sharply criticizes Thomas's sympathetic depiction of an unmarried woman with a son, who had passed herself off as a widow: 'I cannot think how Mr. Cudlip could let her write such a book' (Foster, 341).

Thomas's novels, unlike those of her contemporary Braddon, however, have not found favour with modern critics. *The Feminist Companion to Literature in English* describes her stories as 'feeble' and 'pompously told', 'silly' and 'slight', containing just enough 'mild spice to keep the pages turning' (Blain, Clements & Grundy, *Feminist comp.*, 1073–4), while John Sutherland notes that 'her novels are unpretentious but not so bad as to be wholly unenjoyable' (Sutherland, 165).

Annie Thomas died on 24 November 1918 at Wingfield House, Stoke, Plymouth; her husband had died some years before. She may have been in some financial difficulty in her final years, as she is listed as an applicant to the Royal Literary Fund (Cross, 43). Certainly personal tragedy had afflicted her; in the preface to her novel *Blotted out* (1876), she apologizes for 'the shortcomings of the third volume ... The first portion of it was written while my two dear sons were dying, the latter half immediately after their death' (Wolff, 1.326). Her son-in-law, Major William Price Drury (1861–1949), however, was a Royal Marine, and the author of several nautical novels.

MEGAN A. STEPHAN

Sources R. L. Wolff, *Nineteenth-century fiction: a bibliographical catalogue based on the collection formed by Robert Lee Wolff* (1981), 1.326 · W. Tinsley, *Random collections of an old publisher* (1900), 2.248–50 · M. Oliphant, 'Novels', *Blackwood*, 102 (1867), 263 · *WWW*, 1916–28 [CD-ROM] · F. Hays, *Women of the day: a biographical dictionary of notable contemporaries* (1885) · Allibone, *Dict.* · *The Swinburne letters*, ed. C. Y. Lang, 2 (1959–62), 142 · N. Cross, *The Royal Literary Fund, 1790–1918: an introduction to the fund's history and archives with an index of applicants* (1984), 43 · Blain, Clements & Grundy, *Feminist comp.*, 1073–4 · S. Foster, 'Unpublished letters of C. M. Yonge', *N&Q*, 215 (1970), 339–41 · *Wellesley index* · J. Sutherland, *The Longman companion to Victorian fiction* (1988) · m. cert. · d. cert.

Thomas, Arthur Goring (1850–1892), composer, was born on 20 November 1850 at Ratton Park, Sussex, the youngest son of Freeman Thomas of Ratton Park and his wife, Amelia, eldest daughter of Colonel Thomas Frederick. As a child Thomas showed exceptional musical abilities, and at the age of ten demonstrated remarkable powers of extemporization. He was educated at Haileybury College and intended for a career in the civil service, but ill health prevented this and he decided on the serious study of music. In 1873 he went to Paris, where, on the advice of the composer Ambroise Thomas, he studied for two years with Emile Durand. In 1875 he returned to England and on 13 September 1877 began a three-year course at the Royal Academy of Music. He studied under Arthur Sullivan and Ebenezer Prout and won the Lucas composition medal in 1879 and again, with his dramatic scena *Hero and Leander*, in 1880. He also received lessons in orchestration from Max Bruch. A student composition, the anthem 'Out of the deep', for soprano, chorus, and orchestra, was performed at a concert of the academy on 19 June 1878. His first attempt at opera, *Don Braggadocio*, to a libretto by his brother, was never completed, but part of *The Light of the Harem* was successfully performed by the academy on 7 November 1879. In 1881 his choral ode *The Sun-Worshippers* was performed at the Norwich festival and published in London.

These achievements led to a commission for an opera from the impresario Carl Rosa, which Thomas fulfilled with *Esmeralda*, to a libretto by Theodor Marzials and Alberto Randegger based loosely on Victor Hugo's *Notre-Dame de Paris*, and dedicated to the soprano Pauline Viardot. *Esmeralda* was first performed by the Carl Rosa company at Drury Lane on 26 March 1883 and immediately became popular. Performances of the work in German translation at Cologne (14 November 1883) and Hamburg (27 September 1884) were exceptionally well received. It was revived at Covent Garden on 12 July 1890, sung in French and with the original happy ending altered by the composer to a tragic one.

In 1885 the Carl Rosa company produced a second opera by Thomas, *Nadeshda*, with a libretto adapted by Julian Sturgis from a Russian story. The first performance took place at Drury Lane on 16 April with Alwina Valleria in the title role, and it was performed in Dublin on 27 August of the same year. It was also given in a German version at Breslau in 1890. An orchestral *Suite de ballet* was performed at Cambridge by the University Musical Society, for which it was composed, on 9 June 1887, and a duet for soprano and mezzo-soprano, 'The Dawn' ('Aurora is Waking'), was performed at the Birmingham festival in 1891.

In addition, Thomas composed many songs and vocal duos, some of which were fashionable in the late 1880s and early 1890s, and three further dramatic vocal scenas. An unfinished comic opera, *The Golden Web*, was completed by S. P. Waddington and produced posthumously at the Royal Court Theatre, Liverpool (15 February 1893), and at the Lyric Theatre, London (11 March 1893). Another unfinished work, the cantata *The Swan and the Skylark*, was completed by Charles Villiers Stanford and performed at the Birmingham festival in 1894.

Esmeralda and *Nadeshda* achieved for Thomas the position of leading British musical dramatist of his day and a high reputation in Germany. His music shows predominantly French lyrical influences and a talent for elegant melody and sensitive orchestration, but it is less successful in sustaining dramatic interest throughout the complicated plots. Contemporary critics commented on the naturalness and flexibility of the recitatives, which, in contrast to his generally conservative style, were considered advanced. Shortly after Thomas's death, George Bernard Shaw assessed his position thus: 'He always seemed to be dreaming of other men's music—mostly Frenchmen's; so that he spent his life on elaborating, with remarkable facility and elegance, what Gounod and his disciples had done before' (Shaw, 2.141).

Thomas's character was considered charming and modest, and Maude Valérie White, a fellow pupil at the Royal Academy of Music, described him as 'quite exceptionally attractive and agreeable' (White, 138). However, his naturally fragile mental state was disturbed by the pressure of expectation to produce further works equal in effect to *Esmeralda* and *Nadeshda*, and was further upset by a serious accident a few months before his death. Suffering from depression, Thomas committed suicide by throwing himself in front of a fast train at West Hampstead Station on 20 March 1892, and was instantly killed. He was buried in Finchley cemetery. A memorial concert was held at St James's Hall, London, on 13 July 1892. Most of the leading operatic singers of the day took part, and, as a result, the Goring Thomas scholarship was founded at the Royal Academy of Music.   ROSEMARY FIRMAN

Sources J. W. Klein, 'Tragic, forgotten pioneer: Arthur Goring Thomas', *Music Review*, 36 (1975), 180–86 · J. Spencer, 'Thomas, Arthur Goring', *New Grove* · J. Dibble, 'Thomas, Arthur Goring', *New Grove*, 2nd edn · A. Loewenberg, *Annals of opera, 1597–1940*, 3rd edn (1978) · M. V. White, *Friends and memories* (1914), 138 · G. B. Shaw, *Music in London, 1890–94*, 3 vols. (1932) · *The Times* (22 March 1892) · Brown & Stratton, *Brit. mus.*, 408 · H. Klein, *Thirty years of musical life in London, 1870–1900* (1903) · N. Burton, 'Opera, 1865–1914', *The Romantic age*, ed. N. Temperley (1981), 330–57 · J. W. Klein, 'English opera abroad', *Musical Opinion*, 66 (1942–3), 44–6 · E. Walker, *A history of music in England*, rev. J. A. Westrup, 3rd edn (1952) · W. B. Squire, 'Thomas, Arthur Goring', Grove, *Dict. mus.*

Archives BL, musical MSS and papers, Add. MSS 36739–36742 · Royal College of Music, London | FM Cam., letters to W. Barclay Squire

Likenesses photograph, 1886?–1889, repro. in Klein, *Thirty years of musical life in London* · F. I. Thomas, chalk drawing, 1889, NPG

Wealth at death £9368 0s. 9d.: administration, 30 June 1892, *CGPLA Eng. & Wales*

Thomas, Bertram Sidney (1892–1950), explorer and Arabist, was born on 13 June 1892 at Avon Villa, Springfield Road, Pill, near Bristol, the son of William Henry Thomas, master mariner, and his wife, Eliza Ann, *née* Thomas. His education at the local village school was supplemented by private tuition; at the age of sixteen he was accepted for employment in the Post Office and seemed set for a modest career in this or other branches of the home civil service. Although he had achieved no academic or sporting distinction at school he had shown some aptitude for music, which remained an interest and solace to him throughout his life.

As with many of his generation the outbreak of the First World War provided Thomas with his first experience of overseas travel and a wider horizon. He survived two years with the North Somerset yeomanry in Belgium, and in 1916 was transferred to the Somerset light infantry in Mesopotamia, for the last two years of the war. He then was fortunate enough to be spotted as a man of talent by Sir Arnold Wilson, the British acting civil commissioner in the Persian Gulf. This was the turning point in Thomas's career. He held a number of civilian posts under Wilson and distinguished himself as political officer at Shatra during the Iraqi uprising in 1920. He also derived from Wilson his initial fascination with exploration—a fact which he acknowledged in the dedication of his later and most famous book, *Arabia felix*, where he recorded that it was to Wilson's 'advice and encouragement in the years 1918–1931 [that] my journeyings in Arabia owe their inspiration … he set my feet upon the rock, and ordered my goings'.

Wilson's successor in the gulf, Sir Percy Cox, retained Thomas in his position as a political adviser to the Arab leaders serving under the provisional British administration. He was appointed OBE and transferred to Transjordan as assistant to the chief British representative at the court of Amir Abdullah. He became in 1924 financial adviser (and later first minister) in the sultanate of Muscat, and it was during this period that his serious journeys of exploration began, with trips to the interior of Muscat that contributed substantially to the geographical and ethnological knowledge of the region.

Thomas developed an ambition to make the first crossing of the 'empty quarter' (the Rub' al Khali) of Arabia. He recognized that if he applied for official permission to do this he was likely to be refused. As he subsequently admitted in *Arabia felix*, 'my plans were conceived in darkness, my journeys heralded only by my disappearances, paid for by myself and executed under my own auspices'. While other British officials in the gulf escaped from the heat of the summer to the hill stations in India, Thomas worked through the gruelling gulf summers and stored up his leave until the winters—the only possible season to explore the desert. In the winter of 1927–8, for instance, he made a 600-mile journey through the southern borderland of the area that he wished to penetrate. On these trips he dressed as a Bedouin, eschewed tobacco and alcohol, and spoke only Arabic.

Finally, in October 1930, Thomas slipped away in the middle of the night from the port of Muscat and (hitching a lift, by arrangement, on a passing British warship) arrived at Dhufar, on the Indian Ocean (southern) coast of Arabia, from where he intended to commence his south–north crossing of the 'empty quarter'. After waiting some months for his guides (who were involved in desert hostilities) he eventually set out with a small camel caravan but no promise of protection from the warring and predatory tribes of the interior. He emerged fifty-eight days later at Doha, on the Persian Gulf. The Royal Geographical Society in London promptly awarded him their founder's medal, and other learned societies around the world followed suit.

One person dismayed at Thomas's achievement was the rival Arabian explorer Harry St John Philby, who had been awaiting the consent of the Saudi Arabian ruler to make his own attempt at the crossing. Philby subsequently made the first east–west crossing, and explored the empty quarter in greater depth than Thomas had attempted and achieved greater fame in the process. Thomas none the less enjoyed considerable success with his subsequent books about Arabia, which included *Alarms and Excursions in Arabia* (1931), *Arabia felix* (1932), and *The Arabs* (1937). He was also much in demand as a lecturer on both sides of the Atlantic and received degrees and honorary degrees from a number of leading universities, including Cambridge. It was at this time (1933) that he married Bessie Mary, daughter of Surgeon-Major Edmond Hoile, with whom he had one daughter.

Thomas, continuing his career of public service, was a public relations officer in Bahrain for part of the Second World War (1942–3). He went on to be (1944–8) the first director of the Middle East Centre for Arabic Studies, initially in Palestine and later in the Lebanon; these services were recognized by a CMG in 1949. He died on 27 December 1950, in the house where he was born.

Thomas's first crossing of the empty quarter, albeit by the shortest and easiest route, assured him a permanent place in the history of European exploration of Arabia. He was admired by T. E. Lawrence (who wrote a preface to one of his books) and by his successor Wilfred Thesiger, who found twenty years later that Thomas was remembered by the Bedouin as an honourable, brave, and tolerant man. His refusal to compromise either his Christian faith or his loyalty to British interests was never held against him by the Arabs and brought him respect from his compatriots.

JOHN URE

Sources DNB · B. S. Thomas, *Arabia felix* (1932) · J. Keay, *Royal Geographical Society history of world exploration* (1991) · W. Thesiger, *Arabian sands* (1959) · CGPLA Eng. & Wales (1951)
Archives U. Cam., faculty of oriental studies, corresp. and papers | BLPES, letters to C. G. Seligman · St Ant. Oxf., Middle East Centre, corresp. with Cecil Edmonds · St Ant. Oxf., Middle East Centre, letters to H. St J. B. Philby
Likenesses photograph, 1930, RGS
Wealth at death £12,754 1s. 7d.: probate, 10 Sept 1951, CGPLA Eng. & Wales

Thomas, (Walter) Brandon (1848–1914), actor and playwright, was born on 24 December 1848 at 101 Mount Pleasant, Liverpool, the eldest of the three children of Walter Thomas (d. 1878), a bootseller, and his wife, Hannah Morris. He was educated at private schools to the age of twelve: first at the Mechanical Institute, Liverpool, and then at Plumb's House boarding-school, near Prescot. In September 1861 he became a shipwright and was then indentured as a joiner. Having learned bookkeeping, he took a clerkship with timber merchants in Liverpool and Bootle from 1865 until 1875, and then found a similar post in Hull, where his family had moved five years previously. Thomas supplemented his income with a little journalism, but his passion was the theatre. His first opportunity to perform publicly was at Baker Street schoolroom, Hull, where he sang and recited at Saturday temperance evenings. He was introduced to William and Madge Kendal, on tour in 1876, as a potential future actor.

In 1879 Thomas left for London and joined the Hare-Kendal team at the Court Theatre. He made a pseudonymous début there, as Mr Brandon, in G. W. Godfrey's *The Queen's Shilling*. Under the same management at the St James's he played a variety of small parts and, during the

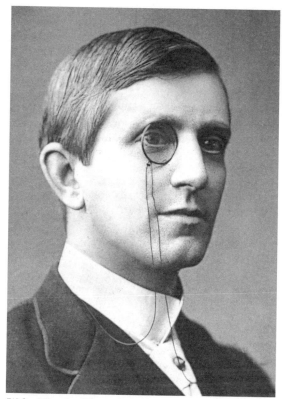

(Walter) Brandon Thomas (1848–1914), by unknown photographer, c.1895

off-seasons, gained provincial touring experience. In September 1885 he embarked on a gruelling but successful nine-month American tour with Rosina Vokes. On his return, though in continuing demand as singer and reciter at private At Homes and working men's clubs, he sought primarily to broaden his acting experience. He was well cast ('natural and true', said *The Theatre*) in Pinero's *Sweet Lavender* (Terry's, 21 March 1888) as the banker Geoffrey Wedderburn, his first important West End part. His speciality was Scots characters, such as Tammy Tamson in his own *A Highland Legacy* and Macphail in Pinero's *The Cabinet Minister* (Court, 23 April 1890). In 1891 Thomas successfully invested £1000 in a syndicate backing an experimental triple bill, comprising the première of his own play *The Lancashire Sailor*, coupled with *A Commission* and Cecil Clay's *A Pantomime Rehearsal* (Terry's, 6 June). He took prominent roles in all three and logged 152 performances. Pinero, considering him for casting as Cayley Drummle in *The Second Mrs Tanqueray* in 1893, was impressed by his 'vein of sympathetic kindly geniality' (*Collected Letters*, 143); and Shaw praised his effectiveness as Sir Lucius in *The Rivals* (Court, 11 November 1895) 'mainly by not doing what is expected of him' (Shaw, 1.254).

Thomas's début as a playwright, with *Comrades* (Court, 16 December 1882), was generally regarded as promising. Several other pieces followed, including *The Colour Sergeant* (Princess's, 26 February 1885), *A Highland Legacy* (Strand, 17 November 1888)—his earliest play, dating from the 1860s, described by *The Times* as 'a little masterpiece'— and, least successfully, *The Gold Craze* (Princess's, 30 November 1889). But nothing in Thomas's career foreshadowed the phenomenal success of *Charley's Aunt*, a farcical comedy written for W. S. Penley as the Oxford undergraduate cajoled by two friends into impersonating an aunt (from Brazil, 'where the nuts come from') to act as chaperone for their respective sweethearts. First performed at Bury St Edmunds (29 February 1892) and toured through the provinces, it opened in London on 21 December at the Royalty and transferred to the Globe on 30 January, where on 19 December 1896 it completed a record 1469 performances. Continually revived in Britain and elsewhere, it was performed in London at Christmas every year from 1904 to 1930 (excepting 1906 and 1927). Thomas hoped posterity might remember him as a great actor, but he was destined to be known only as the author of *Charley's Aunt*. Though the plot is relatively slight, it is a clever, energetic piece, and deserves its status as a minor classic.

Thomas's acting career continued to flourish, notably as Pius X in Hall Caine's *The Eternal City* (His Majesty's, 1902) and John of Gaunt in *Richard II* (Her Majesty's, 1903). He also went on writing moderate successes, such as *The Queen of Brilliants* (Lyric, 8 September 1894) and *No 22a Curzon Street* (Garrick, 2 March 1898), but *A Judge's Memory* (Terry's, 13 March 1906) was not well received. He acted Colonel and Sir Francis Chesney, his role in the original *Charley's Aunt*, for the last time during the 1913–14 Christmas season at the Prince of Wales's.

An essentially clubbable man, Thomas belonged to the Hogarth, Eccentric, Savage, and Garrick. Between 1883 and 1903 he was a volunteer in the Artists' Rifles. Of soldierly bearing, but slim build, he stood just under 6 feet tall. Not from affectation, but owing to poor eyesight, he sported a monocle, which became a kind of trade mark.

On 22 December 1888, two days before his fortieth birthday and following long opposition on religious grounds from her Jewish family, Thomas married Marguerite Blanche Leverson (d. 1930). After his death she supervised revivals of his most famous play. There were three children, the two eldest of whom—Amy (1890–1974) and Jevan Brandon-Thomas (1898–1977)—pursued theatrical careers, partly sustained by performing in *Charley's Aunt*. Thomas died at his home, 47 Gordon Square, Bloomsbury, on 19 June 1914, and was buried on the 22nd in Brompton cemetery.   JOHN RUSSELL STEPHENS

Sources J. Brandon-Thomas, *Charley's aunt's father: a life of Brandon Thomas* (1955) · A. Nicoll, *Late nineteenth century drama, 1850–1900*, 2nd edn (1959), vol. 5 of *A history of English drama, 1660–1900* (1952–9) · A. Nicoll, *English drama, 1900–1930* (1973) · J. Shattock, ed., *The Cambridge bibliography of English literature*, 3rd edn, 4 (1999) · J. P. Wearing, *The London stage, 1890–1899: a calendar of plays and players*, 2 vols. (1976) · J. P. Wearing, *The London stage, 1900–1909: a calendar of plays and players*, 2 vols. (1981) · *The Times* (20 June 1914) · *The Times* (23 June 1914) · *The Theatre*, 4th ser., 9 (1887), 170 · *The Theatre*, 4th ser., 11 (1888), 265 · *The collected letters of Sir Arthur Pinero*, ed. J. P. Wearing (1974) · G. B. Shaw, *Our theatres in the nineties*, rev. edn, 3 vols. (1932) · H. G. Hibbert, *A playgoer's memories* (1920) · *The Theatre*, 4th ser., 10 (1887), 51 · *ILN* (31 March 1888) · *Men and women of the time* (1891)

Likenesses photograph, 1892, repro. in Brandon-Thomas, *Charley's aunt's father* • photograph, *c.*1895, Theatre Museum, London [*see illus.*] • Barraud, photograph, repro. in *The Theatre*, new ser., 9 (Jan–June 1887) • M. Beerbohm, caricature, repro. in Brandon-Thomas, *Charley's aunt's father* • A. S. Mallett, Allen & Co., lithograph • photographs, repro. in Brandon-Thomas, *Charley's aunt's father*

Wealth at death £1315 18*s.* 4*d.*: probate, 25 Feb 1915, *CGPLA Eng. & Wales*

Thomas [*née* Macnamara], **Caitlin** (1913–1994), writer, was born on 8 December 1913 at 12 Hammersmith Terrace, west London, the last of the four children of Francis Macnamara (1884–1946), romantic Irishman, and his first wife, Mary (Yvonne) Majolier (1886–1973), half-French daughter of Edouard Majolier, corn broker, and his Irish wife, Susan Cooper. Nicolette *Devas was an elder sister. The Macnamaras were a protestant landowning family in co. Clare, Ireland. Francis, with ambitions to be a poet and bohemian, abandoned wife and children when Caitlin was an infant, embracing cultural and political ventures (they included a 'Republic of Macnamaraland') that failed to mature. Her childhood was spent largely at Blashford, Hampshire, bordering the New Forest. At the age of sixteen she ran away to London with a daughter of Augustus John, intent on being a dancer, and had a brief career as a chorus girl. A conviction that she possessed artistic talents, and was marked out for the success that her father was never able to achieve, was unshaken by her failure to do more than paint a little and write poems for friends to admire.

As a young woman Caitlin lived in England and in Ireland, where her father turned the family house at Ennistimon, derelict since the troubles, into an unsuccessful hotel. She found it easy to attract men. Augustus John painted her and seduced her, and they were still lovers when she met the poet Dylan *Thomas (1914–1953) in London in 1936, soon after her return from Paris, where she had been living with another painter. Caitlin and Dylan married on 11 July 1937, and she soon encountered the rigours of artistic penury. There were three children: Llewelyn Edouard (*b.* 1939), Aeronwy Bryn Hart (Aeron; *b.* 1943), and Colm Garan Dylan (*b.* 1949). Her husband often abbreviated her name, which she pronounced with a short 'a', to Cat.

A volatile woman, Caitlin both enjoyed her status as the poet's wife and resented the domestic drudgery that went with it. Both she and her husband drank heavily and were intermittently unfaithful. Marriage became another reason for not writing, although during the Second World War she filled notebooks with an incipient autobiography which she planned to call 'Story of a woman'. Nothing came of this, or of the poems she continued to write in the last years of the marriage, at the Boat House in Laugharne, west Wales, where she responded to her husband's absences in London and America by seducing local men. In 'Self Portrait', a surviving poem evidently of this period, she describes herself as an idealist reduced to the commonplace (Ferris, *Caitlin*, 242–3), and signs herself Catnag Thomas.

It took Dylan Thomas's death in 1953 to provoke Caitlin into writing a book that provided a public reputation to set against the private perception, among acquaintances, of a woman enraged with life, and deeply resentful of her role as an adjunct to a famous, feckless husband. Published in 1957 as *Leftover Life to Kill*, its account of her marriage to Thomas, together with glimpses of her sexual activities on Elba, where she stayed after his death, was vivid and outrageous.

Publishers encouraged Caitlin to write more, and she did her best to oblige, offering a darker view of her marriage in 'Am I the perfect fool?', where anger with Dylan Thomas was mingled with affection. It was not seen as marketable; nor was 'Year of disgrace', the diary of her stay on another island, Procida. The manuscripts accumulated, but her only other published work was *Not quite Posthumous Letter to my Daughter* (1963), a series of malevolent observations about men and money addressed to Aeronwy. A thread of feminist feeling can be detected in her writings, not least in private correspondence, where she could be savagely humorous; but it was swallowed up by her appetite for rancour.

Settled in Rome from 1957, where she took up with a small-time film actor, Giuseppe Fazio, Caitlin divided her energies between her writing—verse as well as autobiography—and furious attacks on the Dylan Thomas copyright trustees, a pursuit that cost her a small fortune in fruitless attempts to overturn their policy of prudent management. She was an alcoholic for years but overcame this; an unfinished work, 'Jug', was written at an addiction clinic. A book-length typescript blamed alcohol for her downfall. Rewritten more than once, it did the rounds of publishers for decades; *Double Drink Story* was finally published in 1997.

In 1963, aged forty-nine, Caitlin had a son by Fazio, Francesco; he was one of the few unalloyed pleasures of her second life in Italy as an eccentric Englishwoman, which lasted, with occasional trips to Britain, for thirty-seven years. Her belief in her gifts remained, though she once admitted to being 'the biggest misfit of the age' (Ferris, *Caitlin*, 231). She died in Catania, Sicily, where she and Fazio had lived since 1983, on 1 August 1994, and was buried at Laugharne on 10 August alongside her husband, as she had requested.   PAUL FERRIS

Sources personal knowledge (2004) • private information (2004) [family] • P. Ferris, *Dylan Thomas*, rev. edn (1999) • P. Ferris, *Caitlin: the life of Caitlin Thomas* (1993) • C. Thomas, *Leftover life to kill* (1957) • C. Thomas, *Not quite posthumous letter to my daughter* (1963) • N. Devas, *Two flamboyant fathers*, pbk edn (1985) • C. Thomas, *Double drink story: a life with Dylan Thomas* (1997) • b. cert. • b. cert. [Mary Majolier] • *CGPLA Eng. & Wales* (1994)

Archives priv. coll., MSS and letters | Ransom HRC, corresp. with H. McAlpine

Likenesses A. John, oils, *c.*1930, NMG Wales • A. John, oils, *c.*1937, Glynn Vivian Art Gallery, Swansea • A. Devas, oils, *c.*1942, Tate collection • group portrait, photograph, 1953, Hult. Arch. • T. West and L. Butt, group portrait, photograph, 1966, Hult. Arch. • F. R. Bunt, group portrait, photograph, 1968, Hult. Arch. • A. John, four drawings, NMG Wales • A. John, two portraits, oils, NMG Wales

Wealth at death under £125,000: probate, 15 Dec 1994, *CGPLA Eng. & Wales*

Thomas, Cecil Walter (1885–1976), sculptor and medal-list, was born in London on 3 March 1885 at 24 Hedley Road, Shepherd's Bush, the son of John Thomas, a seal engraver, and his wife, Alice Sophia, *née* Ings. He was apprenticed to his father, and then studied at the Slade School of Fine Art, Heatherley's School of Art, and the Central School of Arts and Crafts, London, where he graduated with honours. Thomas specialized in gem-engraving, working in the family studio while also under-taking commissions for Fabergé.

The use of portraiture in cameos developed into Thomas's interest in coins and medals for which he is best-known. His early training meant that he was one of the few twentieth-century British medallists capable of engraving directly into the die. His first extant medal is a small military style medallet for Sesame House (bronze uniface, 1899; BM). Other early works include the seal for London county council, and many lyrical cast-bronze medals including *Sir Henry Irving* (1905) and the *Surrey Rose Club* (1909). The latter is described as 'an example of the romanticism, informed by continental *art nouveau*, of Thomas' early work' (Attwood, *Artistic Circles*, 60). Thomas's Oxford millenary medal (1912), struck in silver, bronze, and lead (BM), typifies his interpretation of the English arts and crafts movement, with its use of medi-eval iconography and attention to lettering. Cecil Thomas first exhibited at the Royal Academy, London, in 1909 and was a regular exhibitor thereafter. He also showed for many years at the Royal Miniature Society's annual exhib-ition and was made an associate of that society in 1914, and a fellow in 1915. Other group exhibitions later included the Grosvenor Gallery, London, Walker Art Gal-lery, Liverpool, Manchester City Galleries, Paris Salon, and shows in America.

While serving as a staff officer in the trenches in the First World War, Thomas was spotted describing tactics to the men in his command by means of sand models and transferred to intelligence duties. He was severely wounded, but took up medal-making again almost imme-diately. Thomas volunteered to serve again through the Second World War, including three years in the reconnais-sance model-making unit, Medmenham, and was demo-bilized at the age of sixty.

After the First World War, Thomas began to make larger sculpture in stone and bronze, including many church memorials, notably at Toc H Guild Church, Tower Hill, London. Other commissions included portraits of Arch-bishop Most Reverend Lord Davidson of Lambeth (1933; Canterbury Cathedral) and Bishop Talbot (Southwark Cathedral). He also made the bronze memorial bas-relief to the St John Ambulance Brigade (St John's Gate, Clerken-well, London). Upon returning to London in 1919 he rented and later owned Kensington House and studios (now Dora House), 108 Old Brompton Road, South Kens-ington, where he lived and worked until his death. He married in 1930 Dora Margaret (*d.* 1967), younger daughter of Alderman George Pearson, and they had one son, Anthony. A great craftsman, Thomas was a loyal member of the Art Workers' Guild and became master in 1946.

Throughout his career Cecil Thomas was considered a reliable artist to commission for heraldic work and por-traits, and was on the Royal Mint's panel of preferred art-ists. Although he won the competition outright for design-ing the first coinage of Elizabeth II, only his 6*d.* and florin coins were produced for Britain. He was asked to tidy the other designs used; this rankled. Almost as a consolation his crowned effigy of the queen was used on some of the Commonwealth coinage, for example in the West Indies, Fiji (1953–65), and in Hong Kong, Mauritius, and Nigeria. He continued to design royal portraits on official medals, including the coronation medal (1953), an effigy used again in New Zealand in 1975 for the queen's service medal. He was appointed OBE in 1953. When asked in 1966 to design the decimal currency, he refused—disgusted by his previous unsatisfactory experience.

Themes for medals ranged from privately commis-sioned portraits of children and young women to the duke of Edinburgh's prize, the Art Workers' Guild medal, Grant Medical College India prizes, the Halford trophy (1953), medals for parochial readers, and for Shell/BP. Des-pite his numerous official commissions Thomas was never wholly deferential. Recalling Edward VIII's sitting at Dora House in 1937 Thomas complained that forty min-utes of the hour allotted to him were taken up with his royal sitter answering telephone calls from 'all his wretched women' (BM, 1978 12.20.21). In his later years Thomas carried out a number of large bronze groups for New Zealand at King's College, Auckland, the public park, Dunedin, and at Virginia water reserve, Wanganui. A devout Anglican and a freemason, Cecil Thomas valued propriety almost to the point of primness. In later life he attended St Bride's and St Mary the Boltons near his home. His pleasures were modest but he was sociable, enjoying the company of people of all ages, and thoroughly enjoyed parties at Dora House. He worked regular hours to the end of his life despite failing health, sculpting as often by touch and memory but stopping in the early evening with his current assistant to sip an aperitif, always Dubonnet with Ritz crackers.

After his wife Dora died in 1967 Thomas created the Dora Trust devoted to advancing British sculpture. From about 1970 he made a room in his house available to the then struggling Royal Society of British Sculptors for their office and received their gold medal in 1973. After his own death in London on 16 September 1976, and through the generosity of his son, Anthony, the whole house and stu-dio became the society's headquarters and exhibition space. Thomas's studio collection of medal plasters and proofs are now in the department of coins and medals, British Museum.   FRANCES SIMMONS

Sources *The Times* (20 Sept 1976) · P. Attwood, 'Thomas, Cecil', *The dictionary of art*, ed. J. Turner (1996) · D. Buckman, *Dictionary of art-ists in Britain since 1945* (1998), 1182 · P. Attwood, *Artistic circles: the medal in Britain, 1880–1918* (1992), 60 [exhibition catalogue] · J. Johnson and A. Greutzner, eds., *The dictionary of British artists, 1880–1940* (1976), vol. 5 of *Dictionary of British art*; repr. (1994), 498 · L. Brown, *A catalogue of British historical medals, 1760–1960*, 3 vols. (1980–95) · L. Forrer, ed., *Biographical dictionary of medallists*, 6 (1916), 69–72 · b.

cert. • Thieme & Becker, *Allgemeines Lexikon* • *The Times* (31 Aug 1977), 14f • BM, department of coins and medals
Likenesses C. W. Thomas, self-portrait, plaster bas-relief, 1972, BM • cast bronze bas-relief, Art Workers' Guild, London
Wealth at death £28,551: *The Times* (31 Aug 1977)

Thomas, Christopher James (1807–1894), soap boiler, was born on 16 August 1807 in Llangadog, Carmarthenshire, the eldest of nine children (seven sons and two daughters) of Thomas Thomas (1776–1856), wholesale grocer and butter merchant, and Anne (1785–1842), daughter of Christopher James, grocer of Melingriffith, Glamorgan, and his wife, Mary. Both parents were Welsh.

Thomas's education was disrupted. He attended Taliesin School in Merthyr Tudful, but left at twelve to help run the family business while his father was away, though he returned briefly just before his fourteenth birthday. By 1830 he had moved to Bristol to work in the family soap business at the Red Lion Yard, 7 Redcliffe Street, after his uncle Jones, in one of his 'unaccountable fits' (Somerville, 29) had threatened to discharge the men and close the house.

In 1831 Thomas Thomas bought out John Jones, who was replaced by Christopher. Thomas Thomas retired in 1841 and the firm amalgamated with the soap boilers Fripp & Co. as Thomas, Fripp, and Thomas. In 1856 the four surviving brothers, Christopher, Thomas, Herbert, and Charles, bought out the Fripps and the company was renamed Christr. Thomas & Bros. In February 1844, at Lewins Mead Unitarian Chapel, Christopher married Mary (1813–1893), the daughter of Samuel Lang, a Bristol ironmonger, and his wife, Protheria. After several moves the couple settled at Drayton Lodge, Durdham Park, Bristol. They had six children.

The technical progress of the firm owed much to the brothers' willingness to seek out and adopt new ideas, and they took out several patents: for 'Improvements in the manufacture of soap' in 1852, for example, and 'the extraction of glycerine from lyes' in 1879. The firm also pioneered the use of silicate of soda to fill soaps, patenting their method in 1855 and 1862. Christopher and Charles travelled widely in Europe and America. A visit to the Palazzo Vecchio in Florence apparently inspired the design of the chimneys of the Broad Plain works, rebuilt in 1882. Like other soap boilers Christr. Thomas & Bros. adopted brand names. In the 1870s they introduced the good quality Sinclair's Cold Water Soap and the cheaper Magic Arizonic Soap which was sold beyond their usual territory by a Mr Harrison, 'a thorn in the side of many Northern makers' (Somerville, 50). Christopher Thomas retired in 1877 on a pension of £600, and in 1881 he transferred his interest in the Broad Plain works to the other partners. The entry in *Kelly's Directory* for Bristol in 1894, the year of his death, shows how much the firm had diversified during his life, from just soap boilers to 'manufacturers of composite and paraffin candles, silicate of soda, glycerine & refiners of Edible Cotton seed Oil' as well.

From 1845 until 1887 Thomas served as Liberal councillor for the St Philip's ward of Bristol. In 1874 he was elected mayor, the council being influenced in their choice by his 'wide reading and cultivated mind' (Somerville, 26) which the councillors thought made him best suited to preside over the visit to Bristol that year of the British Association. He served on the Bristol city docks committee from 1848 until 1878, and was a member of the Bristol chamber of commerce from 1853 until 1877. He was president of the Anchor Society in 1853 and of the Bristol and Gloucester Archaeological Society in 1878. He was chairman of the Bristol and South Wales Union Railway which opened in 1863, and one of its ferries was named after him.

Thomas died on 2 January 1894 in Bristol, less than three months after his wife, Mary. His memorial in Lewins Mead Unitarian Chapel, where he was an active worshipper, is a fitting tribute, recording that 'he here bore testimony to the simple truths of the Unitarian belief whereon his heart was ever stayed'. Thomas's only son William died as a child and none of his five daughters was directly involved in the business, though the youngest, Anna Louise, married the brother of one of the directors. However, his brothers' descendants continued the family's involvement in the business until its take-over by W. H. Lever in 1912–13.

NANCY COX

Sources J. Somerville, *Christopher Thomas, soapmaker of Bristol* (1991) • *Mathews Annual Directory for … Bristol* (1866) • *Kelly's directory of the city of Bristol* (1894) • *The Times* (5 Jan 1894)
Archives Bristol RO • priv. coll. • Unilever, archives | Bristol RO, Lewins Mead Unitarian Chapel minutes
Likenesses photograph, c.1850, priv. coll.; repro. in Somerville, *Christopher Thomas* • photograph, c.1874, priv. coll.; repro. in Somerville, *Christopher Thomas*
Wealth at death £36,917 15s. 1d.: probate, 16 Feb 1894, CGPLA Eng. & Wales

Thomas, Sir Dalby (c.1650–1711), merchant and writer, was the eldest son of William Thomas (c.1599–1668), a sea captain and merchant, and his second wife, Susanna (b. c.1629), the daughter of John Dalby of Stepney, Middlesex. His father was a prominent figure in Stepney, and left him a very respectable estate, including property both there and in Berkshire. Thomas was able to advance himself further by marrying, on 9 May 1673, Dorothy (c.1656–1722), the daughter of John Chettle of Blandford St Mary, Dorset, a match which produced at least two offspring, a son, Dalby, and a daughter, Susanna.

Thomas soon established himself as a colonial merchant, taking particular interest in the West Indies. In March 1688 he was granted permission to recover wrecks off the coast of Hispaniola, and the following month he was ordered to investigate the activities of treasure hunters in that area. He was also prominent as a lobbyist at court, and attempted to obtain the repeal of a new duty on sugar which threatened the livelihoods of his colleagues in the plantation trade. Failure to achieve this objective led to the publication of his first major work, *A Historical Account of the Rise and Growth of the West Indian Colonies* (1690), which displayed a thorough knowledge of both planting and shipping. The tract championed the establishment of a common factory and credit bank to encourage the development of West Indian commerce, and also called for the creation of a council of trade composed of experienced merchants, rather than the peers and gentry who dominated the lords of trade.

Having displayed great energy in the cause of the colonists, Thomas found further opportunities for expounding his views on mercantile affairs. Alongside Hugh Chamberlain, he put forward one of the many schemes for the revival of the English fishing industry, which, it was later claimed, received the approval of a Commons select committee appointed in January 1692 to review the matter. In December 1693 they made another attempt to impress parliament, publishing *A Proposal ... for the Erecting and Managing of a Trade by a General Fishery*, as well as *A Supplement*. Thomas again argued for the creation of a bank to encourage commercial development, although on this occasion his scheme was to be founded on landed securities. However, the scheme was not adopted.

Thomas found greater success in the pursuit of personal advancement. In March 1694 he gained appointment as a commissioner for the Million Act lottery, in which capacity his name appeared twice more in print the following year with advertisements concerning the exchange of blank tickets. It has also been suggested that he may have been the author of another publication of 1695, *Some Thoughts Concerning the Better Security of our Trade and Navigation* (Appleby, 177). In that year he was given co-responsibility for the collection of the glass duties, and his familiarity with government revenue probably encouraged him to draft the *Propositions for General Land Banks*, in which he betrayed a deep antipathy to the 'monied directors' at the recently created Bank of England. Not surprisingly, he was one of the commissioners appointed in 1696 to receive subscriptions for the new land bank, but the experiment failed through lack of investment. He met with further disappointment in 1697 when his bid to administer the leather duties was rebuffed, but he was chosen to manage the Malt Act lottery, and to oversee the collection of the stamp taxes.

In June 1698 Thomas was again at the forefront of national debate on trade when he appeared at Westminster on behalf of the Royal African Company. The following year he was appointed an assistant of that company, his experience of the West Indian slave trade an obvious recommendation for that post. Although prominent in the City, he soon found himself humbled before the Commons, who questioned him on 25 February 1699 concerning rumours that bribes had been paid to MPs to obstruct the passage of a bill to ban the distilling of spirits from corn. After prevaricating under interrogation before the house, he was found guilty of complicity in the scandal and placed in the custody of the serjeant-at-arms, presumably for the rest of the session. He was no stranger to controversy, having been arraigned on charges of manslaughter several years before. Disgrace before parliament was doubtless a factor behind the subsequent curtailment of his career in government finance, and his reputation was further tarnished by allegations that he embezzled public funds. In early 1700 he was preoccupied with setting his estate in order and obtaining the passage of a private act to sell off the Islington lands which he had

settled on his marriage. Such a move may have reflected temporary financial difficulties, perhaps linked to his decision to take up residence in Low Leyton, Essex. He was undoubtedly most eager for favour at the court of Queen Anne, and petitioned in June 1702 to become a commissioner of prizes. However, despite a reminder to the new ministry that he was 'long conversant in business', he did not secure the post, and such failure may have led him to accept the potentially hazardous office of agent-general of the African Company on the Gold Coast (Shaw, 17.40). Whether he was motivated by greed (the post carried an annual salary of £1000) or pride, the appointment brought him the recognition of the queen, who knighted him on 1 August 1703, shortly before his departure for Africa.

Even for a businessman of Thomas's experience and qualities, the Gold Coast proved too great a challenge. The company's position was already undermined by interloping English traders, while foreign competition and native unrest conspired to render his task impossible. His correspondence back to England demonstrated the obduracy with which he met these difficulties, but he was forced to trade with the English free merchants, such was the weakness of the company's settlements. He was bitterly criticized for this, and for other aspects of his governance, but some of his initiatives were astute, most notably his alliance with the Asante. One of his last letters back to England, written in September 1710, was later published to alert parliament to the desperate plight of the company, but Thomas did not live to see any improvement in its affairs. He died at his post in 1711, and by his will, proved in May 1711, left the bulk of his estate to his wife. His son, Dalby, who served as a lieutenant in the Royal Navy, did not long survive him, but his widow lived until 1722, and his daughter, Susanna, until 1731. Both women were buried at Hampton, Middlesex, where Susanna had displayed her piety by erecting a new vicarage.   PERRY GAUCI

Sources W. A. Shaw, ed., *Calendar of treasury books*, 8–27, PRO (1923–55) · K. G. Davies, *The Royal African Company* (1957) · will of William Dalby, PRO, PROB 11/328, sigs. 147–8 · will of Sir Thomas Dalby, PRO, PROB 11/521, sig. 116 · IGI · J. O. Appleby, *Economic thought and ideology in seventeenth-century England* (1978) · JHC, 11 (1693–7), 22 · JHC, 12 (1697–9), 510, 528 · J. L. Chester and G. J. Armytage, eds., *Allegations for marriage licences issued by the dean and chapter of Westminster, 1558 to 1699; also, for those issued by the vicar-general of the archbishop of Canterbury, 1660 to 1679*, Harleian Society, 23 (1886), 215 · J. L. Chester and G. J. Armytage, eds., *Allegations for marriage licences issued by the bishop of London*, 2, Harleian Society, 26 (1887), 96 · G. W. Hill and W. H. Frere, eds., *Memorials of Stepney parish* (privately printed, Guildford, 1890–91), 218, 222, 238 · J. L. Chester and J. Foster, eds., *London marriage licences, 1521–1869* (1887), 1331 · D. Lysons, *An historical account of those parishes in the county of Middlesex which are not described in 'The environs of London'* (1800), 81, 84, 88 · *The manuscripts of the House of Lords*, new ser., 12 vols. (1900–77), vol. 4, p. 77; vol. 10, p. 167 · *CSP dom.*, 1690–1, 471; 1700–02, 581
Archives PRO, letters concerning official business, PRO T70
Wealth at death wealthy, but may have overreached himself at times; bequeathed £5000

Thomas, David [*pseud.* Dafydd Ddu Eryri] (**1759–1822**), poet and schoolmaster, was born in Y Waunfawr, Caernarvonshire, the son of Thomas Gruffydd (1716–1781), a weaver, and his wife, Mary Humphreys (1714–1794). His early education was sketchy. In 1774 he was taught for eight months by John Morgan, the curate of Llanberis, where he met Abraham Williams (Bardd Du Eryri; 1755–1828), who introduced him to Welsh poetry and loaned him books and some of the manuscript collections he had inherited from the scholar–cleric Dafydd Ellis (1736–1795), curate at Llanberis before John Morgan. Thomas followed his father's craft for some years, later teaching in his home village and nearby areas.

In Caernarfon, Thomas met the poet Robert Hughes (Robin Ddu yr Ail o Fôn; *d.* 1785), who had moved to the town in 1783 after having worked for twenty years in London as a legal clerk. Hughes was a co-founder of the London Gwyneddigion Society. From him Dafydd Ddu heard of the social and literary meetings enjoyed by the Welsh literati in London and he sent out his own invitation to a meeting of poets at his home in Betws Garmon. From this developed the 'school of Dafydd Ddu', whose members were popularly known as Dafydd Ddu's chicks. He won the main prize for an *awdl* (a long poem in selected strict metres) in the St Asaph and Llanrwst eisteddfods of 1790 and 1791, held under the auspices of the Gwyneddigion. These poems were accepted as templates for the form, and the poet's prestige as a mentor of authority was now assured, with his influence extending beyond Caernarvonshire.

Dafydd Ddu could write fluently in the free, alliterative metres, but he was mainly concerned to refurbish the native strict metres. He emphasized correctness of language, style, and metre, with tight control of imagination, circulated his own bardic grammar among his disciples, and travelled extensively to further his aims. He would even legislate on content, such was his desire to offer clear guidance to bardic pupils. As a poet his work has outlived its appeal, but he brought valuable influence to bear at a time when knowledge of *cerdd dafod*, the unique strict-metre system, had deteriorated and there was a real need for a bardic teacher of unchallengeable authority. His work as a critic makes him an important link between his idol, Goronwy Owen (1723–1769), the leader of the eighteenth-century neo-classical revival, and the early eisteddfod poets of the nineteenth century. On 4 November 1803 he married Elinor Thomas; they had no children. A collection of his poems, including some by others, *Corph y gaingc*, was published in 1810, a second edition appearing posthumously in 1834.

David Thomas died as the result of a riding accident, at Llanrug, where he was living, on 30 March 1822. He was buried there on 2 April.   E. G. MILLWARD

Sources G. T. Roberts, 'Dafydd Ddu o Eryri a'i gysylltiadau llenyddol', MA diss., U. Wales, Bangor, 1929 · G. R. Hughes, *Taliesin*, 28 (July 1974), 55–69 · H. L. Williams, *Safonau beirniadu barddoniaeth yng Nghymru yn y bedwaredd Ganrif ar Bymtheg*, 21–32 · T. Parry, *Trafodion Cymdeithas Hanes Sir Gaernarfon*, 41 (1980), 59–81
Archives BM, MSS · NL Wales, corresp. and papers · NL Wales, letters and poems
Likenesses portrait, repro. in *Corph y gaingc* (1810)

Thomas, David (1813–1894), Congregational minister, was born at one of two neighbouring farms, Vatson North or Vatson South, in the parish of East Williamston, near Saundersfoot. He was one of the ten children of William Thomas (1782–1855), founder and first minister of Sardis Congregational Church, Saundersfoot. William Thomas married the elder of the two daughters of Clement Phillips of Carn Mill, in the parish of Begelly. David Thomas embarked on a career in business at Tenby, but his abilities as a lay preacher in his father's church so impressed Nun Morgan Harry and Caleb Morris, two London ministers whose roots were in Pembrokeshire, that they persuaded him to devote himself to the nonconformist ministry. Although he was already married and had a son, he became a student at Newport Pagnell Academy in 1839. He was ordained at Chesham Congregational Church in 1841 and moved to Stockwell Green Chapel, London, in 1845. He ministered there until his retirement in 1877.

Thomas's vigorous ministry typifies the intensifying of nonconformist activism in the mid-Victorian period. He founded a working men's club and institute in 1862 and launched an insurance plan for the widows of ministers. He supported such causes as total abstinence and the abolition of the death penalty. He showed his interest in popular journalism as chairman of the National Newspaper League Company and launched *The Dial* newspaper on 7 January 1860. It merged with the *Morning Star* in June 1864. The freshness of his preaching and his personal charm attracted large congregations, especially from among the professional classes. He sought to improve the quality of public worship by publishing *A Biblical Liturgy* in 1855. Each of its twenty services had a theological theme and was composed of a mosaic of biblical quotations. With the same intention he published in 1866 *The Augustine Hymn Book*. Among attenders at his services was Catherine Mumford, at whose marriage to William Booth, founder of the Salvation Army, Thomas officiated. As a child Wilson Carlile, founder of the Church Army, also attended Thomas's church, where his parents were members.

Thomas was a prolific author, publishing during his career some fifty titles. He became a familiar name as the editor of *The Homilist*, which first appeared in March 1852 and ran eventually to fifty volumes. It contained sermons, hundreds of which were composed by the editor, together with items on moral and religious topics and expositions of biblical passages. Thomas explained that it was intended 'not to supply sermons for indolent and incompetent preachers, but stimulus and tonic for the true-hearted, hard-working and genuine teacher' (*Septem in uno*, 1886, foreword). For some time before he retired from the editorship in 1881 he had been helped by his son, Urijah. The journal had a very wide readership in both Britain and America.

Thomas's books were also much appreciated in both countries for presenting a catholic and comprehensive view of religious truth without being disloyal to the evangelical tradition. This appraisal was justified not only by his biblical commentaries but also by such works as *The Crisis of Being* (1849) and *The Progress of Being* (1854). On the other hand *The Practical Philosopher: a Daily Monitor for the*

Business Men of England (1873) exemplifies his constant anxiety to relate his convictions to the contemporary concerns of the secular world. His complete works were published under the title *The Homilistic Library* (9 vols., 1882–9).

On 30 September 1837 Thomas married Elinor, the younger daughter of David Rees JP, a landowner and shipowner, at St Peter's Church, Carmarthen. She died on 9 February 1874, aged sixty-four. They had two sons and four daughters, in order of seniority: Urijah, David, Sissie, Sidney, Ellen, and Angelene. Urijah Rees Thomas (1839–1901) became the minister of Redland Congregational Church, Bristol; David Morgan Thomas JP became a barrister and founded the *Cambrian Daily Leader* (1861–1923), the first daily newspaper in Wales. It was published at Cardiff, as was his other newspaper, the *Cardiff Morning Express*. David Thomas died at 3 Victoria Terrace, Ramsgate, on 30 December 1894, and was buried in Norwood cemetery.

R. TUDUR JONES

Sources *Congregational Year Book* (1896), 237–9 · *The Times* (1 Jan 1895) · *Congregational Year Book* (1856), 234–6 · T. Rees and J. Thomas, *Hanes eglwysi annibynol Cymru*, 3 (1873), 124 · CGPLA Eng. & Wales (1895)
Wealth at death £4033 1s. 11d.: probate, 15 Feb 1895, CGPLA Eng. & Wales

Thomas, David (1880–1967), educationist and socialist, was born on 16 July 1880 at Quarry Cottage, Llanfechain, Montgomeryshire, the son of David Thomas, a mason and farmer, and his wife, Elizabeth Jones. He was educated locally and briefly attended Oswestry grammar school before finding work in a draper's shop. In 1895 he became a pupil teacher in the British School in Llanfyllin. He subsequently worked as a teacher in Anglesey, Glamorgan, and London before moving to the slate district of Caernarvonshire in north-west Wales in 1905, becoming a schoolmaster in Tal-y-sarn in the Nantlle valley in 1909. It was during this period that he established himself as a leading Welsh socialist propagandist. Brought up a Wesleyan, his political principles led him to break with all Christian denominations for a period, although he subsequently returned to the nonconformist fold. His political message and the language he used to express it were both characterized by a strong moral sense informed by the influence of Christian belief.

Thomas joined the Fabian Society and the Independent Labour Party (ILP) in 1907, and in 1908 he was embroiled in a debate on socialism in the columns of a local newspaper, *Yr Herald Gymraeg*. This led him to write his major work, *Y werin a'i theyrnas* ('The people and their kingdom'), which was completed in 1909 and published in 1910. This 248-page volume can be considered the most thorough and eloquent exposition of the socialist analysis of society and the socialist programme for change to be published in Welsh.

By 1911 Thomas was arguing both within the ILP and within the Welsh labour movement more widely that socialists should identify themselves more clearly with Welsh culture and Welsh issues and history. This, he argued, was the only way in which socialism would become acceptable to Welsh-speakers (in 1901 49.8 per cent of the population of Wales spoke Welsh and 15 per cent spoke only Welsh), many of whom were steeped in the values of nonconformity and Liberalism. During 1911 and 1912 he strove to establish a Welsh region of the ILP and for the publication of more socialist material in Welsh. He organized a meeting at the 1911 national eisteddfod of Wales in support of these aims which, although he later denied the allegation, was widely interpreted as an attempt to construct a Welsh labour party. Socialism was often portrayed as being an alien, English intrusion into Wales during this period and his efforts were crucially important in countering these accusations.

In north Wales, Thomas rapidly established himself as the leading socialist activist, establishing branches of the ILP and encouraging trade unionism among quarry workers and agricultural labourers. In 1912 he was instrumental in establishing the Caernarvonshire Labour Council and in 1914 the North Wales Council of Labour, of which he was secretary in 1920–22. During this period he was undoubtedly the most influential socialist working in the Welsh language, and he made an impressive attempt to marry the Welsh radical and nonconformist tradition to socialism and the Labour Party. In his stance as a conscientious objector during the First World War he brought the radical elements of both traditions together in his pacifist arguments. He was sent to work on a farm in Bersham near Wrexham for his opposition to the war. His attempts to fuse socialism with Welsh radical nonconformity have led one historian to conclude that he 'came closest during these years to achieving the required synthesis between Socialism and the Welsh spirit' (Pope, 24).

After the war Thomas married Elizabeth Ann Williams (1881/2–1955) on 26 July 1919, with whom he had two children. He remained a Labour activist, but from 1922 an educational rather than an agitational emphasis can be discerned in his career. He became a teacher at Bangor in 1922, where he remained until 1945. He completed a University of Liverpool MA course in 1928, a study of the maritime and agricultural history of north Wales in the nineteenth century, and became increasingly active in the Workers' Educational Association (WEA) and adult education provision. In 1944 he established *Lleufer* as a journal for the WEA in Wales and he remained as editor until 1965. He published a large number of books in Welsh including a biography (1956) of the influential socialist, poet, and educationist the Revd Silyn Roberts, with whom he had worked closely. He also wrote an autobiography, *Diolch am gael byw* ('Thanks for having lived'), which was published posthumously. He was awarded an honorary MA of the University of Wales in 1960. Thomas died at 2 Pen-y-bryn, Burry Port, Carmarthenshire, his daughter's home, on 27 June 1967, and was cremated three days later at Morriston crematorium, Glamorgan.

R. MERFYN JONES

Sources R. Pope, *Building Jerusalem: nonconformity, labour and the social question in Wales, 1906–1939* (1998) · E. D. Jones and B. F.

Roberts, eds., *Y bywgraffiadur Cymreig, 1951–1970* (1997) • D. Thomas, *Diolch am gael byw* (1968) • C. Parry, *The radical tradition in Welsh politics: a study of liberal and labour politics in Gwynedd, 1900–1920* (1970) • *Lleufer*, 23/2 (summer 1967)
Archives U. Wales, Bangor
Likenesses photograph, repro. in *Lleufer*
Wealth at death £4901: probate, 31 Oct 1967, *CGPLA Eng. & Wales*

Thomas, David Alfred, first Viscount Rhondda (1856–1918), politician and industrialist, was born at Ysguborwen, Aberdâr, on 26 March 1856, the fifteenth of the seventeen children—of whom five survived—born to Samuel Thomas (1800–1879), a Merthyr shopkeeper turned coal entrepreneur, and his second wife, Rachel, daughter of the mining engineer, Morgan Joseph. After attending a private school at Clifton, he studied mathematics at Gonville and Caius College, Cambridge, and was awarded a BA in 1880. Much of his time at college was spent on boxing, sculling, and rowing; but he must have devoted some time to study, for, whereas most businessmen of the time merely practised the precepts of capitalist economics intuitively, Thomas had actually read the texts. In 1882 he married Sybil Margaret (1857–1941) [*see* Thomas, Sybil Margaret], sister of a Cambridge friend and daughter of George Haig of Pen Ithon, Radnorshire. They had one daughter, Margaret Haig *Thomas, Viscountess Rhondda (1883–1958).

After university, his father's death brought Thomas back to south Wales. He was immediately elected to Ystradyfodwg local board of health. If this suggests political patronage, his election as MP for Merthyr in 1888 reflected the Liberal dominance of the area. He continuously represented the constituency from 1888 to 1910, before briefly representing Cardiff in 1910. By then the main focus of his interests had already shifted significantly, from politics to business. After two decades of non-recognition at Westminster, the final straw was the failure in 1905 of Campbell-Bannerman to offer him any preferment. The explanation for this may be that he was said to be a poor speaker and tended to make enemies by arguing too much in the press. Also, the effect of his role in Welsh politics was ambiguous. An initial enthusiast, he was a whip in a loose 'Welsh parliamentary party' in 1888 and 1892, and one of four Welsh rebels who refused the Liberal whip in 1894. In all this he ran alongside Lloyd George; but, when the latter wanted the Welsh Liberal Federation to amalgamate with Cymru Fydd (Young Wales) and give home rule priority over religious equality, the cosmopolitan south rebelled. At a stormy meeting in January 1896 at Newport, Thomas as president of the South Wales Liberal Federation clashed head-on with Lloyd George, who later recollected that his 'fight with Rhondda had been bitter, very bitter … extending over many years' (Rhondda and others, 201).

Initially Thomas's direct involvement in the coal trade was limited to his holding a share in the family's Cambrian collieries at Clydach Vale and running its sales agency (Thomas, Riches & Co.) in Cardiff. His frequent interventions in the industrial affairs of the district were

David Alfred Thomas, first Viscount Rhondda (1856–1918), by Solomon Joseph Solomon, exh. RA 1917

thus mostly made from, and for, his political base. However, by freely offering advice to the workmen he continually provoked the Coalowners' Association (the Cambrian collieries shunned membership until 1908) and particularly antagonized Sir William *Lewis (later Lord Merthyr), the powerful agent for the Bute estates and long-time coalowners' leader.

Two episodes illustrate the difficulties between Thomas and Lewis, the first of which concerned the control of coal output. At the time, wages were governed by a sliding scale related to the price of coal. With no minimum pay, the miners complained that the colliery owners reduced prices too readily in times of bad trade, knowing that much of the cost of this would be borne by the miners; they therefore proposed an alliance between themselves and the owners to prevent price cutting. Thomas sympathized over the problem but rejected the solution. Instead he published a scheme in 1896 to fix a percentage share of total output for each undertaking, with fines for breaches: by avoiding any interference either with prices or with a specified total output this ingeniously kept (almost) intact his belief in his economic principles. The groundswell of support by press, public, and miners obliged Sir William Lewis through gritted teeth to put forward a similar scheme, which he guaranteed would fail by insisting on its acceptance by those representing 95 per cent of all output (including non-associated pits).

The second instance covered the bitter six-month stoppage of 1898. Thomas, whose non-associated collieries continued working throughout, repeatedly lectured the owners (especially the unbending Sir William Lewis) on the folly of enforcing the continuance of the existing scale, and equally often offered advice to the workers over the heads of their leaders. Thus against the owners' insistence he asserted, 'If I were a workman I would most decidedly refuse to give authority to bind me for several years to the present scale' (*Western Mail*, 23 March 1898). If in much of this Thomas was speaking as a politician rather than as a businessman, as a matter of business as well as politics he also defended the right to join unions. For many of his fellow coal owners he compounded these lapses by, in effect, carrying Keir Hardie into parliament on his coat-tails as the junior member for the two-seat constituency of Merthyr. More acceptably, he was intellectually affronted by the export tax on coal in 1901; and his exemplary account of the development of the coal trade in 1903 won the Guy medal of the Royal Statistical Society.

By 1906 Thomas had renounced politics and turned to business. He rejoined the Cambrian collieries board and that, along with his partnership in the sales agency of Thomas and Davey, was his only direct link with the coal trade at that time. Yet a decade later he controlled a dozen colliery undertakings, representing over a fifth of the national coal output (52 million tons), together with their sales agencies; and he abundantly grasped in the Welsh valleys the power that had eluded him in the House of Commons.

During these years Thomas followed two broad strategies: vertical integration of pits through a holding company, and forward integration into marketing and distribution. He also extended his activities across the Atlantic and acquired numerous local directorships and, significantly, newspapers. As creator and controller of the largest coal combine in the region it is perhaps not surprising that Thomas clashed with the South Wales Miners' Federation in its period of new-found militancy. No doubt many ironies could be squeezed out of this. Although the scourge of the owners' association and a sympathetic friend and adviser to the miners in 1898, Thomas himself became embroiled in a year-long conflict, which included the Tonypandy riots. Furthermore, the issue at stake, of payment for work in abnormal places, was intimately related to the tussle over a minimum wage, which had been at the heart of the dispute in 1898. Thomas would, and did, plead in 1910 that 'the machine has been captured by young socialists of immature judgement' (Thomas, *Industrial Struggle*, 19), who caused 'anarchy and red riot', as it was vividly described—not by him but by an English miners' leader (Evans, 157).

Whatever Thomas might have done with his coal empire, the war saw him in 1915 summoned back into the political arena. The source of the call (from Lloyd George) was ironic, and its direction (to leave for the United States to arrange supplies of munitions) seemed threatening, since Thomas and his daughter had only recently survived the sinking of the *Lusitania*. However, in recognition of his success he was created Baron (1916) and then Viscount

Rhondda (1918); and he gained what had eluded him for twenty years of active political engagement—a position in the government, as president of the Local Government Board. He was frustrated in his main aim there of establishing a separate Ministry of Health; but he achieved unexpected popularity when transferred in June 1917 to be minister of food control. In 1917 the problems of food supply and distribution were as threatening to war effectiveness as the paucity of munitions had been in 1915. By grasping the nettle, not only through rationing but also by fixing prices and ensuring government purchase and ownership of supplies, his scheme introduced in early 1918 was very successful. Ironically the scheme was founded on the repudiation of the economic principles which had guided his entire commercial life.

Such concerns did not dominate him completely, however. He was an enthusiastic sportsman and walked the nearby Brecon Beacons. A country lover, Rhondda was also an active freemason. Clean-shaven and spruce, he was unostentatious and generally tolerant—even of his daughter's involvement with the militant suffragettes. He died of heart disease and rheumatic fever on 3 July 1918 at his spacious home at Llan-wern, Monmouthshire, near the River Severn. Maverick to the end he was cremated at Golders Green, but the urn was formally buried in Llanwern churchyard. He was survived by his wife, and his daughter succeeded him as Viscountess Rhondda.

JOHN WILLIAMS

Sources Viscountess Rhondda [M. H. Thomas] and others, *D. A. Thomas, Viscount Rhondda* (1921) · Viscountess Rhondda [M. H. T. Mackworth], *This was my world* (1933) · K. O. Morgan, *Wales in British politics, 1868–1922* (1963) · M. J. Daunton, *Coal metropolis: Cardiff, 1870–1914* (1977) · M. J. Daunton, 'Thomas, David Alfred', *DBB* · D. Evans, *Labour strife in the South Wales coalfield, 1910–1911: a historical and critical record of the Mid-Rhondda, Aberdare Valley and other strikes* (1911) · DWB · K. O. Morgan, 'D. A. Thomas: the industrialist as politician', *Stewart Williams's Glamorgan historian*, ed. S. Williams, 3 (1966), 33–51 · L. J. Williams, 'The strike of 1898', *Morgannwg*, 9 (1965), 61–79 · D. A. Thomas, *The industrial struggle in mid-Rhondda* (1911) · R. P. Arnot, *South Wales miners / Glowyr de Cymru: a history of the South Wales Miners' Federation*, [1] (1967)
Archives NL Wales, corresp. and papers | HLRO, letters to David Lloyd George
Likenesses S. J. Solomon, oils, exh. RA 1917, unknown collection; copyprint, NPG [*see illus.*] · S. J. Solomon, oils, NMG Wales · photograph, repro. in Viscountess Rhondda, *This was my world*, 174
Wealth at death £883,645 7s. 8d.: probate, 6 Feb 1919, CGPLA Eng. & Wales

Thomas, Dylan Marlais (1914–1953), poet, was born on 27 October 1914 at 5 Cwmdonkin Drive, Swansea, the second child and only son of David John (Jack) Thomas (1876–1952), schoolmaster, and his wife, Florence Hannah (1882–1958), daughter of George Williams, railwayman, and his wife, Hannah. Both sides of the family had their roots in rural south Wales. Jack Thomas, the clever son of another railwayman, Evan, and his wife, Ann, came from a bilingual background where English was seen as the language of progress. To his disappointment, a first-class honours degree in English at University College, Aberystwyth, led only to a schoolmaster's career, teaching English at the grammar school in Swansea, a comparatively Anglicized

Dylan Marlais Thomas (1914–1953), by Augustus John, 1937–8

town, where he concealed the fact that he spoke Welsh. His model was the English man of letters.

Early years and early poetry At an early age Dylan was being told about English prosody. A poem from his childhood, preserved by Florence Thomas, rhymed 'real' with 'steel'; on the manuscript the father wrote, 'Real is two syllables and cannot rhyme with steel'. There were Celtic influences as well. Jack Thomas named his son after a minor figure in the Mabinogion, a collection of medieval Welsh tales, more or less inventing Dylan as a forename. The original Welsh pronunciation was 'Dullan', but Thomas as an adult preferred 'Dillan'. His second name acknowledged a paternal great-uncle William, a preacher-poet in the Welsh language whose bardic pseudonym, Gwilym Marles, derived from the local River Marlais.

Dylan Thomas's upbringing in the Uplands, a genteel district on rising ground a mile west of Swansea's town centre, was suburban and orthodox. A garrulous sister, Nancy Marles (1906–1953), outshone him at first. Commonplace scenes and characters from childhood recur in his writing: the park that adjoins Cwmdonkin Drive; the bay and sands that were visible from the windows; a maternal aunt he visited, Ann Jones, a farmer's wife at Fernhill, in Carmarthenshire. His juvenilia was accomplished, as in 'The Mishap', about 'little sonny' who blew himself up by mistake:

Ask of the breeze from foreign shores
Where sonny lingers?
North tells of nose, East speaks of toes,
West whispers fingers.

An undistinguished pupil at the school where his father taught (although he edited the school magazine), Thomas left in the summer of 1931, aged sixteen, to work for the local evening newspaper. There he wrote on literary topics whenever he could, and cultivated a mock-journalistic manner. The autobiographical stories in *Portrait of the Artist as a Young Dog* show a self-conscious transition from shy child to tormented adolescent, a would-be provincial rebel hoping that drunkenness and loud shirts would shock his elders.

Thomas's private life as a poet was already underway. As he wrote each poem he copied it, with the date, into a student's exercise book, an orderliness that contrasted sharply with his louche exterior. Eventually there were four such notebooks, running from 1930 to 1934, containing more than 200 poems. After his brief career as a journalist ended early in 1933 he continued to live at home, ostensibly unemployed, filling the notebooks faster than ever. Half the ninety published poems by which he is known were written, in one form or another, during these early years. His imagery often dwelt on the body—the 'lily bones' of an unborn child, man's 'candle in the thighs', the 'darkness in the weather of the eye'. Echoes of Blake and Donne could be detected, but his voice was his own. It was very personal poetry, indifferent to the social and political concerns of the day. He was painfully aware of sex, time, decay, and death; he also had a powerful sense of his vocation as a poet, easily caricatured by detractors later on.

Gaining fame as a poet and as a personality Thomas's first poem to be seen in London, the bombastic 'And death shall have no dominion', was published by the *New English Weekly* in May 1933. A more characteristic piece, 'The Force that through the Green Fuse Drives the Flower', in which he saw the same energies at work in nature and in the flesh, was published by a newspaper, the *Sunday Referee*, in October the same year, two days after his nineteenth birthday. In March 1934 the BBC's journal, *The Listener*, printed another of his 'organic' poems:

Light breaks where no sun shines;
Where no sea runs, the waters of the heart
Push in their tides.

As a result, T. S. Eliot and Stephen Spender wrote to Thomas, and a selection of his verse, sponsored by the *Referee*, appeared later in the year as *Eighteen Poems*. This was followed in 1936 by *Twenty-Five Poems*, establishing his reputation in literary circles, although elsewhere he remained unknown. A visionary quality was noted, along with his verbal skills; so was intermittent obscurity. Because Thomas was digging deep into the notebooks, many of the poems published in the second volume had been written before those published in the first. He was never again as fecund as in the Swansea years.

An impish, scandalous figure on the London literary scene of the mid-1930s, Thomas lived by tiny fees for poems and stories, occasional book reviewing, and frequent borrowing from friends. Swansea was always available for home comforts. His early friendships there were enduring, notably with Alfred Janes, the painter, Daniel Jones, the composer, and Vernon Watkins, the poet. In appearance Thomas was slight and cherubic, with wavy hair and luminous eyes. A passivity of nature, together with a convenient conviction that the poet's vocation called for charitable treatment, made him unashamedly dependent on others.

Dylan Thomas married Caitlin Macnamara [see Thomas, Caitlin (1913–1994)], a fiery woman with artistic tastes, on 11 July 1937, having met her in a London pub the previous year, and came to rely on her strength of character. Initially Thomas liked to see them as two innocents in a wicked world, a fantasy that soon wore thin. The relationship was passionate, stormy, and ultimately dysfunctional. Married life before the Second World War found them scraping along in poverty, staying with her divorced mother at Blashford in the New Forest or with his parents in Swansea. In Laugharne, a small township on the Carmarthenshire coast not far from his family origins, they lived in rented houses, first Eros and then Sea View (Thomas never owned a property of any kind), with intermittent binges in London: 'city of the restless dead', as he called it in a 1938 letter to Vernon Watkins, adding that 'its intelligentsia is so hurried in the head that nothing stays there; its glamour smells of goat' (Collected Letters, 392–3). His drinking and clowning were indispensable to him, but they were only half the story; 'I am as domestic as a slipper' (Ferris, Dylan Thomas, 155–6) he once observed, with some truth. In this he was the opposite of his wife.

A further sixteen poems, together with seven short stories, made up The Map of Love (1939). 'I make this in a warring absence', originally published as 'Poem (for Caitlin)', expressed forgiveness for her sexual infidelity, of which Thomas was evidently aware. But the lavish imagery of the poem, and of others in the collection, required the skills of a cipher clerk to interpret. There were exceptions, notably the elegiac 'After the Funeral', a reworking of a notebook poem from 1933 that commemorated Ann Jones, the aunt at Fernhill. The seven stories, selected from the twenty or so that magazines had published since 1934, were baroque fantasies, often tiresome. The ten stories in Portrait of the Artist as a Young Dog (1940) have proved more durable: nostalgic, amusing, largely true-life romances about himself in Wales.

Living on 'guile and beer' In the Second World War, Thomas used subterfuge and his recurrent asthma to avoid military service. Work in a munitions factory would have been almost as distasteful. '[D]eary me,' he wrote to a friend, 'I'd rather be a poet anyday and live on guile and beer' (Collected Letters, 540). Even before wartime conditions jeopardized literary earnings, Thomas had begun to develop begging as a form of income. His 'Five Bob Fund' envisaged twelve benefactors (Peggy Guggenheim, Augustus John, and Lord Tredegar were on the list) who would each send him 5s. a week; the resulting £3 promised security. When the scheme failed to mature, he wrote at random to literary figures. Hearing that the author Alec Waugh had suggested Dylan 'write more stories and fewer letters', he suggested tartly that Alec 'write fewer stories and more letters' (ibid., 538).

Salvation came from a film company, where Thomas wrote morale-building scripts for the Ministry of Information. For the first time since his journalist days he had a regular income, and he (and sometimes his wife) were in London for much of the war, staying with friends or renting squalid rooms of their own. The legend of the outrageous poet, which Thomas actively encouraged, has made his life seem even more disorganized than it was. His reputation as a saloon-bar raconteur was well established. But in wartime London he kept appointments, respected deadlines, and, if he was occasionally unfaithful to his wife, quickly crept back to the safety of the marriage.

Throughout his life, few of Thomas's poems were written outside Wales. Towards the end of the war he lived in west Wales for a year—at Llangain, near Carmarthen, then at New Quay, on Cardigan Bay—enjoying a burst of creativity that would not be repeated. The seven poems he wrote included two that came to be enjoyed by many who were deterred by his more complex work. 'Poem in October' celebrated his thirtieth year, and 'Fern Hill', Thomas's best-known poem, dwelt on the Carmarthenshire farm and his childhood. Both pieces were direct and alluring (although 'Fern Hill' is a meditation on time as well as an exercise in nostalgia), and were open to charges of sentimentality. Their themes suggest a turning away from wartime privations, as well as the gathering disquiet of a former enfant terrible.

These seven poems, together with seventeen others, were collected into a tiny pocket-sized volume, Deaths and Entrances, in 1946. Three of the pieces, including 'The Hunchback in the Park'—the Cwmdonkin Park where Thomas had played as a child—originated in the early notebooks, the last of his work to carry these echoes. The collection ranged widely. Another of the late poems, 'A Refusal to Mourn the Death, by Fire, of a Child in London', cunningly verbose, had the ring of a funeral oration with Christian trappings:

> I shall not murder
> The mankind of her going with a grave truth
> Nor blaspheme down the stations of the breath
> With any further
> Elegy of innocence and youth.

A religious poet, or at least a poet making religious gestures, can be detected in Deaths and Entrances. But by 1946 Thomas's progress in any direction had begun to waver. His domestic affairs were increasingly muddled. There were now two small children, a son, Llewelyn, and a daughter, Aeronwy, to accompany their nomadic parents. Caitlin was impatient of her husband's fecklessness. Dylan himself toyed with the idea that the family could escape to America—where his poems, together with some prose, had already appeared in two collections, The World I Breathe (1939) and New Poems (1943)—but nothing came of this idea.

The BBC and writing in the post-war years Work for radio kept Thomas busy. The BBC used him to write scripts for its overseas services during the war, and came to see his more general potential as a broadcaster. A number of separate reminiscences—where he talked about childhood, Christmas, holidays—drew on the same nostalgia as the poems to produce softer-edged memories, affectionate and humorous. His florid style of reading had its critics at the BBC, where an executive spoke of 'that breathless poetic voice' (Maud, *On the Air*, 9). Thomas learned to temper it, but the booming delivery was still there, with its overstressed syllables and elegant enunciation, a Welsh accent lurking within. He was continually in demand to read and discuss verse and to act in the literary plays and features that were then in their heyday at the BBC, which invented its Third Programme in 1946 to cater for such things. Among his many roles was Satan in a serial version of *Paradise Lost*. Thomas's voice became familiar to many who had never read the poetry.

Broadcasting helped keep Thomas afloat after the war. It also gave him frequent excuses to be in London, visiting studios and moving on to convivial pubs around Broadcasting House. His wife, at home with the children in Oxford—where the Thomases temporarily settled—suffered, although not in silence. The composer Elisabeth Lutyens, one of his drinking companions, saw Dylan about to leave for home, carrying a battered briefcase with a gift that was meant to placate Caitlin. Lutyens looked inside. It contained two cans of soup.

For two years after 'Fern Hill' Thomas wrote no poetry. In 1947 Edith Sitwell arranged a travelling scholarship and recommended he seek inspiration in Italy, where he and his family stayed for four months. He spent much of his time groaning at the heat and writing comic letters of complaint to friends. The visit produced one long and rather laboured poem, 'In Country Sleep'. On their returning to England the Thomases were housed at the expense of Margaret Taylor, wife of the Oxford historian A. J. P. Taylor, who (to her husband's dismay) had become Thomas's friend and patron. Previously she had let them live in a summerhouse at the bottom of the Taylors' garden, and when Thomas was in Italy she bought a cottage in the village of South Leigh, 10 miles from Oxford, and let it to him for a token rent, often unpaid.

Despite his permanent air of a man facing financial ruin, Thomas was far from destitute. For a period he wrote feature-film treatments and additional dialogue. A script about the body-snatchers Burke and Hare was taken up by the Rank organization and then abandoned; later it was published as *The Doctor and the Devils*. Altogether his declared earnings in the fiscal year 1947–8 were £2400, a respectable income for a self-employed writer at the time.

By 1948 Thomas had decided that his only hope as a poet was to return to Wales. Mrs Taylor (who was not rich) bought a property for him to occupy in Laugharne, the Boat House, and the Thomases moved there in spring 1949, where he promptly wrote a topographical poem about the town, 'Over Sir John's Hill'. Caitlin's third child, a boy, Colm, was born in July. In Laugharne, Thomas's life fell into disarray. His letters breathe anxiety, and four further poems took another two years to write. Money was swallowed up by private education for the children as well as by taxis, alcohol, and his wife's clothes, and unpaid tax on earlier income had to be found. Meanwhile scripts paid for by the BBC went unwritten.

When John Malcolm Brinnin, newly appointed director of the Poetry Center at the Young Men's and Young Women's Hebrew Association in New York city, invited him to visit America, Thomas accepted at once, and went there in 1950. His readings at the centre, and on campuses across the country, introduced him to young, enthusiastic audiences and gave rise to a legend, exaggerated in the telling, of the wild poet behaving badly. The three-month tour was lucrative, but once again the taxman was waiting. His wife accompanied him on a second visit in 1952, having learned that he had slept with a woman in New York two years earlier. The adulation of student audiences, 'screaming at him as though he was a pop singer' aroused her jealousy (Ferris, *Caitlin*, 126). This time the tour lasted four months, wearying Thomas. Both he and his wife drank heavily, as though competing. At one lecture, at the University of Utah, he described himself as 'a little fat man come to make a fool of himself' (Ferris, *Dylan Thomas*, 287).

Thomas's health was deteriorating. He coughed and wheezed, suffered bouts of gout and gastritis, and had long since ballooned into a caricature of the pretty young poet whom Augustus John had painted. The publication of *Collected Poems, 1934–1952*, just after his thirty-eighth birthday, offered a respite, assembling the contents of his three earlier volumes, together with the five new Laugharne poems. In general the critics approved. Philip Toynbee thought him 'the greatest living poet in the English language' (*Observer*, 11 Nov 1952). The collection won the Foyle's poetry prize.

Among the late poems was an elegy to his dying father, in the rare form of a villanelle, which began, 'Do not go gentle into that good night', a line that became a figure of speech. Jack Thomas died shortly after the book was published. Other work that would give Dylan Thomas a popular currency which transcended literary opinion was in the making. In America he had recorded *A Child's Christmas in Wales*, cobbled together from a radio reminiscence and a magazine article.

Under Milk Wood, final years, and reputation In particular there was a BBC 'play for voices' that Thomas had been trying to finish for years, essentially a series of comic sketches with darker undertones about twenty-four hours in the life of a town called Llareggub—a backwards-reading joke that he resurrected from an early story. The play became *Under Milk Wood*, a poor relation to the poetry, in Thomas's view, but the work by which he is best known. It was completed in spring 1953, during a third visit to America, and first performed there on the stage. (From 1954 it was also broadcast many times on BBC radio in a production with Richard Burton as narrator.) A love affair that Thomas began with Brinnin's assistant, Elizabeth Reitell, was matched by Caitlin's blatant infidelities in Laugharne.

Fears about the future run through letters and manuscript notes of Thomas's last years. After 1951 he failed to complete another poem. Finding himself unable or unwilling to mature as a poet who would meet the exacting, unrealistic standards of what he saw as his vocation, he let despair lead him towards self-destruction. In October he returned to America, Reitell, and exhaustion. Drinking heavily, he became ill and intermittently deranged about the time of his thirty-ninth birthday at the end of the month. On 4 November a doctor unwisely sedated him by injecting half a grain of morphine, which was to prove fatal. He collapsed and went into a coma, and died in St Vincent's Hospital, New York, on 9 November. Pial oedema (swollen brain tissue) was given as the immediate cause of death, with fatty liver and pneumonia as antecedent causes. No mention was made of the morphine. Later suggestions that undiagnosed diabetes was significant can be discounted. His body was returned to Wales and interred at Laugharne on 24 November 1953.

A memorial plaque in Poets' Corner at Westminster Abbey was dedicated in 1982. The Boat House at Laugharne has been restored for visitors, and in Swansea a Dylan Thomas Centre with a permanent exhibition of written and visual material was opened in 1996. The 'Anglo-Welsh' literary tradition, which is Welsh in spirit but not in language, has found an emblem in Thomas. His Welshness, however, owes more to nostalgia for the countryside of his childhood than to any national consciousness, and his work has little to commend it to modern Welsh separatists.

In wider terms Thomas's popular reputation has continued to grow, even if critics have not always been kind. Some had already found his work too florid by the time of his death, and the British Movement poets (Philip Larkin, Donald Davie, and others) began a dismissive tendency that has persisted among those who prefer their poetry served cold.

Paradoxically, it is Thomas's rhetoric and romanticism that appeal so widely to the non-specialist reader, and his more accessible poems are widely anthologized. His position in the English tradition seems secure; Donne, Blake, and Yeats are among the precursors cited, with reservations. His own wry assessment—using a metaphor from cricket, the only game that interested him—that he was 'top of the second eleven' (Fitzgibbon, 49) may be near the truth.   PAUL FERRIS

Sources private information (2004) · P. Ferris, *Dylan Thomas*, rev. edn (1999) · *The collected letters of Dylan Thomas*, ed. P. Ferris, rev. edn (2000) · P. Ferris, *Caitlin: the life of Caitlin Thomas* (1993) · D. M. Thomas, *Portrait of the artist as a young dog* (1940) · C. FitzGibbon, *The life of Dylan Thomas* (1965) · J. M. Brinnin, *Dylan Thomas in America* (1956) · *Dylan Thomas: the notebook poems, 1930–1934*, ed. R. Maud (1989) · *Dylan Thomas: collected poems, 1934–1953*, ed. W. Davies and R. Maud (1989) · D. Thomas, *Under Milk Wood*, ed. W. Davies and R. Maud (1995) · R. Maud, *Dylan Thomas in print: a bibliographical history* (1970) · G. Watkins, *Portrait of a friend* (1983) · D. Jones, *My friend Dylan Thomas* (1977) · *On the air with Dylan Thomas: the broadcasts*, ed. R. Maud (1991) · J. Nashold and G. Tremlett, *The death of Dylan Thomas* (1997) · d. cert., New York department of health, bureau of records and statistics
Archives Harvard U., Houghton L., corresp., poems, and papers · NL Wales, letters · Ransom HRC, papers of and relating to Thomas · University of Toronto, Victoria University, letters | BL, letters to Vernon Watkins, Add. MS 52612 · NL Wales, letters to Desmond Hawkins; letters to Percy Eynon Smart | FILM BFI NFTVA | SOUND NL Wales, Aberystwyth, Colin Edwards Collection, extensive biographical information in the tapes of
Likenesses A. John, portrait, 1937-8, NMG Wales [*see illus.*] · photographs, 1946–52, Hult. Arch. · E. Agar, portrait, Tate collection · M. Ayrton, drawing, NPG · A. Janes, drawing, Glynn Vivian Art Gallery, Swansea · A. Janes, portrait, NMG Wales · A. John, portrait, second version, NMG Wales · M. Levy, drawing, NPG · M. Levy, drawing, Glynn Vivian Art Gallery, Swansea · M. Levy, drawing, NMG Wales · R. Shephard, portrait, NPG · R. Shephard, two drawings, NMG Wales · D. Slivka and I. Lassaw, bronze bust (after death mask), NMG Wales · T. G. Stuart, portrait, NPG
Wealth at death £100: administration, 7 Dec 1953, *CGPLA Eng. & Wales*

Thomas, Edward (1813–1886), scholar of Indian history and numismatics, was born on 31 December 1813, the son of Honoratus Leigh *Thomas (1769–1846), surgeon, and his wife, a daughter of the anatomist William Cumberland *Cruikshank. Thomas was educated at the East India College at Haileybury, and went to India in 1832 as a 'writer' in the Bengal service of the company. Illness interfered with his duties and compelled several absences in England on sick leave. When Lord Dalhousie, impressed by his abilities, offered him in 1852 the post of foreign secretary to the government of India, Thomas was reluctantly obliged to decline it on health grounds. After acting for a short time as judge at Delhi, he was appointed superintending judge of the Saugor and Nerbudda territory. He retired on a pension in 1857, and spent the rest of his life in scholarly pursuits, attending the meetings of learned societies and writing numerous essays and articles on oriental archaeology.

By breaking ground in a dozen hitherto obscure subjects—such as Bactrian, Indo-Scythian, and Sassanian coins, Indian metrology, Persian gems and inscriptions—Thomas rendered important services to science. These were recognized by his election as a fellow of the Royal Society on 8 June 1871, as correspondent of the Institut de France in January 1873, and as honorary member of the Russian Academy, and by his decoration as companion of the Indian Empire. His chief published volumes were his *Chronicles of the Pathan Kings of Delhi* (1847; 2nd enlarged edn, 1871), and his edition of James Prinsep's *Essays on Indian Antiquities* and *Useful Tables* (2 vols., 1858), which he enriched with valuable notes, and rendered indispensable as a work of reference for oriental archaeologists. Other noteworthy publications were *Coins of the Kings of Ghazni* (1847–58), *Initial Coinage of Bengal* (1866, 1873), *Early Sassanian Inscriptions* (1868), *Ancient Indian Weights* (1874, being part 1 of the new *Numismata orientalia* which he edited for the publisher Nicholas Trübner), and *The Revenue of the Mughal Empire* (1871–82). His numerous short papers in the transactions of learned societies, albeit often avowedly premature and containing tentative views which later study caused him to modify or abandon, not only bore the marks of a fine gift for palaeography, numismatics, and a wide command of archaeology, but gave impetus to further studies in these fields. Many of these papers appeared in the *Numismatic Chronicle* between 1847 and 1883, but the greater number were contributed to the *Journal of the Royal Asiatic Society* of which society he was a member for forty

years and treasurer for twenty-five, and in which his influence and advice were deeply felt and valued. A list of his
principal writings is appended to the biographical note in
its annual report (May 1886). His findings in numismatics
are still referred to in standard works of Indian history.
Thomas died at his home, 47 Victoria Road, Kensington,
London, on 10 February 1886.

STANLEY LANE-POOLE, *rev.* J. B. KATZ

Sources personal knowledge (1898) · private information (1898) ·
S. Lane-Poole, *The Athenaeum* (21–8 Feb 1886) · *Journal of the Royal Asiatic Society of Great Britain and Ireland*, new ser., 18 (1886), xxxix–
xliii · *CGPLA Eng. & Wales* (1886)
Wealth at death £4749 0s. 6d.: probate, 1 March 1886, *CGPLA Eng.
& Wales*

Thomas, (Philip) Edward (1878–1917), poet and writer,
was born on 3 March 1878 at 10 Upper Lansdowne Road
North, Lambeth, London, the eldest of the six sons of
Philip Henry Thomas (1854–1920), staff clerk for light railways and tramways at the Board of Trade, and Mary Elizabeth Townsend (*b.* 1855), daughter of William Henry
Townsend, master mariner, of Newport, Monmouthshire.
In *The South Country* (1909) Edward Thomas calls himself
'mainly Welsh', though some family names (including
Eastaway, which he was to use as a pseudonym) have links
with western England. His autobiography, *The Childhood of
Edward Thomas* (1938), evokes holidays in Wales and in
Wiltshire, where he explored the landscape of Richard Jefferies, his first literary hero, and met 'Dad' Uzzell, a model
for the old countrymen who are a touchstone in his work.
Thomas's interest in nature had been fostered by his
family's move to the area in London between Clapham
and Wandsworth commons, but he usually represents the
city as alien, the country as his imaginative ground. His
alienation from Christianity also began in childhood.

Thomas was educated at several schools, including Battersea grammar school and St Paul's, London, where he
disliked the competitive atmosphere. After leaving St
Paul's in 1895, he studied for the civil service examination,
but this expressed his father's ambition rather than his
own. He reacted against the worldly values of his father,
who was locally prominent in Liberal politics. Encouraged
by the critic James Ashcroft Noble and influenced by Jefferies, he was already publishing essays based on his long
country walks and assembling his first book, *The Woodland
Life* (1896). He had also begun a relationship with Noble's
second daughter, Helen Berenice Noble (1877–1967). In her
memoirs *As it was* (1926) and *World without End* (1931) Helen
Thomas records the problems caused by her father's
death in 1896, the lovers' youth, and her mother's hostility to her relationship with Edward Thomas. She describes
Edward as tall and fair: 'His nose was long and straight, his
mouth very sensitive. ... The chin was strong. The eyes
were grey and dreamy and meditative. ... His hands were
large and powerful and he could do anything with them'.
When they married on 20 June 1899 Helen was pregnant
with their son Merfyn, who was born in January 1900. In
March 1898 Thomas, having matriculated at Oxford as a
non-collegiate student (1897), had won a scholarship to
Lincoln College. He graduated with a second-class degree

(Philip) Edward Thomas (1878–1917), *by Frederick Henry Evans,
c.1904*

in history (1900); this disappointed his father, as did
Thomas's decision to become a writer.

In 1901 Thomas and his family moved to Rose Acre Cottage at Bearsted, near Maidstone, Kent. His dependence
on reviewing caused a conflict between necessity and creativity. Despite succeeding Lionel Johnson as a regular
reviewer for the *Daily Chronicle*, he was earning less than £2
a week. He mainly reviewed contemporary poetry,
reprints, criticism, and country books. From 1903, when
their daughter Bronwen was born, to 1913 the Thomases
moved house five times. (Myfanwy Thomas was born in
1910.) Their most significant move was to Petersfield,
Hampshire (1906), and particularly (from August 1913) to
Yew Tree Cottage, Steep, near Petersfield. The countryside
around Steep influenced Thomas's poetic landscapes.

During these years Thomas often saw himself as 'a
doomed hack' (*Letters to Gordon Bottomley*). He had to visit
London to solicit commissions, mostly ill-paid, and to do
research. Besides endless reviews (not only for the *Daily
Chronicle*) and further country books, such as *The Heart of
England* (1906) and *The South Country*, he also produced
essays, anthologies, guidebooks, and folk-tales. His most

important critical and biographical studies are *Richard Jefferies* (1909), *Maurice Maeterlinck* (1911), *Algernon Charles Swinburne* (1912), and *Walter Pater* (1913). It was chiefly the country books which carried Thomas's hopes for 'my silly little deformed unpromising bantling of originality' (ibid.), his quest to find a 'form that suits me' (ibid.). Repressed creativity was a factor in his recurrent physical and psychological breakdowns, and he once nearly committed suicide. All this put great strain on his marriage, as did some platonic friendships with other women. He was loved by the writer Eleanor *Farjeon (1881–1965), who wrote a memoir, *Edward Thomas: the Last Four Years* (1958).

Thomas's country books mix observation, information, stories, portraits, self-portraits, literary criticism, and reflection. He tried various ways of ordering his material, but was slow to modernize his elaborate style. *Childhood* (begun in 1913) achieves this at a stroke, and there are signs of development in his autobiographical novel *The Happy-Go-Lucky Morgans* (1913), *The Icknield Way* (1913), and *In Pursuit of Spring* (1914). In the autumn of 1914 he reported vividly on how people throughout England were reacting to war. In December 1914 he wrote his first real poem, the blank-verse dialogue 'Up in the Wind'. Commentators argue over what turned him into a poet: the First World War, the therapy of autobiography, the theory of speech and literature which fired his critique of Walter Pater, his absorption of contemporary poetry, or the influence of the American poet Robert Frost, whom he met in 1913. He made Frost's reputation in Britain, and hence in the United States where Frost was then unrecognized, with a rave review of *North of Boston* (1914). Frost not only suggested that poetry might be latent in *In Pursuit of Spring* (most of Thomas's poems are concentrations of his prose) and confirmed Thomas's intuitions about speech-rhythms, but he also showed in practice how speech could reanimate verse-forms. Thomas's poem 'The Sun used to Shine' celebrates a friendship, the aesthetic repercussions of which continue.

The war also concentrated Thomas's mind because it focused his vision of England and led him to write 'war poetry' before he actually reached the trenches. His historical sense, cultural definitions, and poetic structures are closely allied. Hostile to imperialism and jingoism, he stresses knowable communities, local microcosms, the complexity of 'home'. His poem 'Lob' presents Englishness as the interpenetration of language and landscape. Yet he found his form at a historical moment which radically challenged the English lyric. Thus, despite his recoveries of tradition and the technical versatility with which he reanimates traditional forms, his poetry is haunted by absence. English rural communities, already victims of economic change, were being devastated once again. In suggesting how the First World War compounded the dislocations of modernity, and in criticizing 'the parochialism of humanity' (*Letters to Gordon Bottomley*), he became an ecological poet. His poetry is psychologically advanced, too, in that it dramatizes the conflicts of which it helped to relieve him.

The wartime collapse of his literary market gave Thomas time to write poetry. He was also deciding whether to enlist or, as Frost urged, to emigrate to New England. In July 1915 he joined the Artists' Rifles, which was, he wrote, 'the natural culmination of a long series of moods & thoughts' (*Letters to Gordon Bottomley*). In November he was sent to Hare Hall Camp at Romford, Essex. He became lance-corporal, then full corporal, and worked as a map-reading instructor, and in September 1916 began training as an officer cadet with the Royal Garrison Artillery. He was commissioned second lieutenant in November and volunteered for service overseas in December. He embarked in January 1917 and served with no. 244 siege battery. On 9 April he was killed by the blast of a shell during the first hour of the battle of Arras and the following day was buried in Agny military cemetery on the outskirts of Arras. He was survived by his wife. Thomas did not live to see *Poems* (1917), published under his pseudonym, Edward Eastaway; *Last Poems* (1918) and *Collected Poems* (1920) appeared under his own name. In two years he had written over 140 poems.

At the end of the twentieth century Edward Thomas's reputation as a poet stood higher than it had ever done before. Earlier, his achievement had been obscured by his prose career, his death, and the vogue of modernism. His significance as a poetry critic has also been underestimated. Besides Frost, he promoted Thomas Hardy, W. B. Yeats, and D. H. Lawrence, and poets such as Walter de la Mare and W. H. Davies who later appeared in Sir Edward Marsh's Georgian anthologies. Thomas never met Wilfred Owen, but Owen possessed a copy of his study *Keats* (1916). His war poetry of the home front complements Owen's; like Owen, he exposed the traditional lyric to forces which some of their English (Georgian) contemporaries excluded. The many poets who have admired his poetry include Hardy, W. H. Auden, Philip Larkin, and Joseph Brodsky. Its centrality is underlined by *Elected Friends: Poems for and about Edward Thomas* (1991), which contains seventy-six items. In a letter to Helen Thomas after Edward's death, Robert Frost asked: 'who was ever so completely himself right up to the verge of destruction, so sure of his thought, so sure of his world?' (*Thomas: Selected Letters*).   E. LONGLEY

Sources R. G. Thomas, *Edward Thomas: a portrait* (1985) · H. Thomas, *'As it was' and 'World without end'* (1956) · E. Thomas, *The childhood of Edward Thomas* (1938) · *Letters from Edward Thomas to Gordon Bottomley*, ed. R. G. Thomas (1968) · E. Farjeon, *Edward Thomas: the last four years* (1958) · H. Coombes, *Edward Thomas* (1956) · W. Cooke, *Edward Thomas: a critical biography* (1970) · A. Motion, *The poetry of Edward Thomas* (1980) · *The collected poems of Edward Thomas*, ed. R. G. Thomas (1978) [incl. war diary] · *Edward Thomas: selected letters*, ed. R. G. Thomas (1995) · *DNB* · b. cert. [Mary Elizabeth Townsend]

Archives Bodl. Oxf., corresp. and papers · NL Wales, literary MSS, diaries, and corresp. · Ransom HRC, corresp. and literary papers · University College Library, Cardiff · University of British Columbia Library, corresp. and literary MSS | Battersea Library, London, Wandsworth Local History Service Library, letters to Eleanor Farjeon · Battersea Library, London, Wandsworth Local History Service Library, letters to John Freeman · Battersea Library, London, Wandsworth Local History Service Library, letters to Ian McAlister · BL, letters to John Freeman, RP 1791 [microfilm] · Bodl. Oxf., letters to Walter de la Mare · NL Wales, letters to Jesse Berridge · NL Wales, letters to Sir Owen M. Edwards · U. Durham L., corresp. with his literary agent

Likenesses photograph, 1899, repro. in Thomas, ed., *Letters from Edward Thomas to Gordon Bottomley*, facing p. 42 · double portrait, photograph, 1900 (with his infant son), repro. in Thomas, *Edward Thomas*, facing p. 118 · F. H. Evans, photograph, c.1904, NPG [*see illus.*] · E. H. Thomas, pencil drawing, 1905, NPG · photograph, 1914, repro. in Thomas, *Edward Thomas*, facing p. 246 · J. Wheatley, pencil drawing, 1915, NPG · M. Thomas, photograph, 1916, repro. in Thomas, *Edward Thomas*, facing p. 279 · J. Wheatley, etching, 1916, NPG

Wealth at death £983 15s. 2d.: probate, 17 May 1917, CGPLA Eng. & Wales

Thomas, Elizabeth (1675–1731), poet, was born on 31 August 1675 and baptized at St Bride's, Fleet Street, on 1 September 1675, the only child of Emmanuel Thomas (d. 1677) of the Inner Temple and Elizabeth (d. 1719), daughter of William Osborne of Sittingbourne, Kent. Both parents came from respectable families, but Thomas and her mother had to contend with financial hardship after her father died when she was not yet two. Little is known about Thomas's childhood, but she received some education at home, was well read, and had a little knowledge of French and Latin. Thomas's earliest 'claim to fame' was receiving her pen-name, Corinna, from Dryden, with whom she shared a brief correspondence in the last year of his life. She had several literary and material friendships with well-known men and women of her day, including the writers Mary, Lady Chudleigh, John Norris of Bemerton, and the painter Sarah Hoadly, Bishop Hoadly's wife, to name a few. As a gentlewoman who could not always afford to live as one, Thomas used her talent as a writer to obtain patronage from friends and family, which often came in the forms of cash gifts, extended visits, and books.

Thomas's longest correspondence was with her fiancé of sixteen years, the Gloucester gentleman, Richard *Gwinnett (1675–1717), which ended upon his death on 16 April 1717. Their letters make up the bulk of correspondence in *Pylades and Corinna* (1731–2) and *The Honourable Lovers* (1732; repr. 1736). Gwinnett was the heir to his father's encumbered estate in Shurdington, Gloucestershire. He studied law at Christ Church, Oxford, and was admitted to the Middle Temple on 22 June 1697. Due to ill health, however, he was unable to practise his profession fully, particularly in London. Their engagement was protracted because neither of them had the means to marry. Denied a union by material circumstances, they continued their engagement through correspondence and annual visits. Both of them gave up lucrative marriage opportunities during the sixteen-year interim because of their mutual devotion. Since she had rejected other suitors in favour of him, Gwinnett partially supported Thomas and her bedridden mother with gifts of money toward the end of his life.

By 1716 Gwinnett pressed for marriage because he felt he could adequately support his bride-to-be and her mother, but Thomas postponed their union so she could nurse her mother, whose death seemed imminent. Ironically, Thomas's mother outlived Gwinnett, who died in the spring of 1717 before he and Thomas could marry. Because of Thomas's long dedication to him, Gwinnett altered his will and bequeathed £600 to her. After Gwinnett's death, however, his younger brother, George, suppressed the will and denied Thomas the money. Hence, in 1718, she initiated what turned out to be a lengthy and costly lawsuit in chancery. Of the £600 Gwinnett bequeathed her, she only received £213 and 6s. for her litigious efforts—not enough to pay off her debts.

The fact that Thomas was active in London and Bath literary circles, particularly between 1696 and 1718, becomes evident from reading her letters and poems. Her reputation as a poet and a wit drew the attention of the *Tatler* editor on several occasions. As a writer Thomas experimented with a wide range of forms and genres and had a sound knowledge of history, natural philosophy, classical literature (mostly from translations), and current issues, to which her letters, lyrics, satires, polemics, panegyrics, pastorals, and religious meditations can attest. Like contemporary women writers such as Mary Astell and Mary, Lady Chudleigh, whom she knew, much of her poetry dealt with women's issues. Although she never argued for complete equality between men and women, Thomas believed in women's inherent right to education as well as fair treatment and respect before and after marriage.

Thomas's first known publication was the anonymous poem 'To the Memory of the Truly Honoured John Dryden, Esq' which appeared in the commemorative compilation, *Luctus Britannici* (1700). Between 1700 and 1722 Thomas followed the long-established tradition of circulating one's poetry among friends and family and apparently did not publish anything. Due to financial problems, which were exacerbated by her disastrous lawsuit, she published *Miscellany Poems on Several Subjects* in 1722 anonymously, which was reprinted under the title of *Poems on Several Occasions* in 1726. During a more fortunate time of her life, she had met Alexander Pope through her acquaintance Henry Cromwell. At her request, Cromwell had given her some letters which had passed between himself and Pope from 1708 to 1711. In her impoverished state in the 1720s, Thomas realized she might profit from the sale of these letters, since Pope's literary reputation had, by that time, greatly increased. Hence in 1726 she sold them for 10 guineas to the notorious bookseller Edmund Curll, who knew their potential value and promptly published them in *Miscellanea in Two Volumes* (1726).

Pope took his revenge in his 1728 satire, *The Dunciad: an Heroic Poem*. In book two, while describing a race between Curll and his rival bookseller, Bernard Lintott, Pope satirizes both Curll and Thomas ('Curll's Corinna'). Her reputation never fully recovered after this scandal, since literary historians were quick to assume the worst about her character. In addition to the Pope–Cromwell letters, Thomas seems to have sold quite a few papers to Curll in 1726 because, from that date forward, her writings and correspondence can be found scattered throughout many of Curll's publications such as *Poetical Works of Philip Late Duke of Wharton* (1726) and *Atterburyana* (1727). The satire attributed to Thomas, called *Codrus, or, 'The Dunciad' Dissected*, was first published in 1728. Thomas's account of Dryden's funeral appeared in the 1729 publication of the *Memoirs of the Life, Writings, and Amours of William Congreve Esq.* This text, however, was thoroughly discredited by Edmond Malone in *The Critical and Miscellaneous Prose Works of John Dryden* (3 vols., 1800, 1.337–419). Curll also printed her *Metamorphosis of the Town* anonymously in 1730 (repr. 1731, 1732). The bulk of her correspondence which had been published previously by Curll was consolidated in *Pylades and Corinna* and *The Honourable Lovers*.

Despite her efforts to settle her debts, especially after her lawsuit in the early 1720s Thomas's financial situation worsened. She attempted to hide from her creditors but she was discovered and thrown into Fleet prison in 1727 for three years. A warrant was issued for her release in June 1729 under an Act of Insolvency, but she was not released until the middle of 1730, presumably because she could not pay her gaoler's fees. She died on 3 February 1731, and was buried two days later in the churchyard of St Bride's, Fleet Street. Margaret, Lady De La Warr, the daughter-in-law of Thomas's former patron, Anne, Lady Dowager De Le Warr, paid for her burial.

After Thomas died Curll continued to publish a scattering of her texts as he had in the late 1720s as well as reissuing both volumes of *Pylades and Corinna* and *The Honourable Lovers* in 1736. In 1743 the fourth and final edition of *Metamorphosis* was printed for J. Wilford, with Thomas's name on the title-page for the first time. The inscription read 'By the late celebrated Mrs. ELIZABETH THOMAS, Who has so often obliged the Town, under the Name of CORINNA'. Thomas's works went out of print thereafter but have had brief appearances in biographical dictionaries and anthologies over the next three centuries.

REBECCA MILLS

Sources Bodl. Oxf., MS Rawl. letters 90 · Glos. RO, D151/F2, PFC31IN1/2:2 [birth; will] · GL, MSS 6540/2, 3408/2, 80 [Thomas's baptism, death, and burial details] · chancery proceedings, PRO, C11, 2372/34, 2372/49 · chancery, decrees and orders, PRO, C33/332-2, fol. 323v; C33/334-1, fols. 185, 244, 250; C33/336-52, fols. 255, 256; C33/338-40 [Thomas's lawsuit] · PRO, PRIS 1/3: 415 #94 [Thomas's prison record] · probate, wills, PRO, PROB 11.561.231 [Gwinnett's will] · I. Grundy, 'Against the dead poets society: non-Augustan, non-Romantic, non-male poets', *Halcyon*, 15 (1993), 181–97 · R. Lonsdale, ed., *Eighteenth-century women poets: an Oxford anthology* (1989), 32–44 · A. McWhir, 'Elizabeth Thomas and the two Corinnas: giving the woman writer a bad name', *ELH: a Journal of English Literary History*, 62 (1995), 105–19 · V. Rumbold, *Women's place in Pope's world* (1989), 162–5 · T. R. Steiner, 'Notes and documents. Richard Gwinnett and his 'virtuous lover', Elizabeth Thomas: a literary romance of eighteenth-century Gloucestershire', *Georgia Historical Quarterly*, 78 (1994), 794–809 · T. R. Steiner, 'The misrepresentation of Elizabeth Thomas, "Curll's Corinna"', *N&Q*, 228 (1983), 506–8 · T. R. Steiner, 'Young Pope in the correspondence of Henry Cromwell and Elizabeth Thomas ("Curll's Corinna")', *N&Q*, 228 (1983), 495–7 · R. Gwinnett and E. Thomas, *Pylades and Corinna*, 2 vols. (1731–2)

Archives Bodl. Oxf., corresp., MS Rawl. letters 90

Likenesses G. King, line engraving (aged thirty), BM, NPG; repro. in Thomas and Gwinnett, *Pylades and Corinna*, vol. 1 · line engraving, BM, NPG

Thomas [*née* Wolferstan], **Elizabeth** (1770/71–1855), novelist and poet, was baptized on 7 October 1771 at Hartland in Devon, the daughter of Mary (d. 1818) and Edward Wolferstan (d. 1788) of Berry House there. Little is known of her early life. She married the Revd Thomas Thomas (d. 1838), vicar of Tidenham, Gloucestershire, about 1795. Elizabeth Thomas wrote religious verse which was variously received, praised on one hand for its 'purity, correctness, and piety' (*Theatrical Inquisitor*, February 1819), but denigrated on the other for its trite or blasphemous versifications of biblical stories (*Monthly Review*, August 1819). Her anonymous collection *The Confession, or, The Novice of St Clare, and other Poems* (1818) was widely reviewed, particularly for the titillating anti-Catholicism of its title poem. Its long preface defends the author's anonymity, arguing: 'her name is so common nothing can be made of it … her character is of the same stamp … she is, in short, quite a creature of ordinary life', disingenuous disclaimers since the title-page advertises the work as penned by the author of *Purity of Heart, or, The Ancient Costume* (1816), a virulent, polemical novel addressed to the anonymous author of *Glenarvon*, the 1816 *succès de scandale*. In her preface to *Purity of Heart*, under the pseudonym 'an old wife of twenty years', Elizabeth Thomas confesses she could not resist ridiculing *Glenarvon* in order to counteract 'its horrible tendency' and 'its dangerous and perverting sophistry'. Estimates of the novel's success in advancing public morals and virtue (the 'ancient costume' of her subtitle) differed, from praise as 'a clever little novel' (*Theatrical Inquisitor*, Dec 1816), to criticism of the 'old wife' for missing her target and digressing into a personally hostile attack on *Glenarvon*'s presumed author in its 'strange extravagant portrait' (*European Magazine*, 1817) of Lady Calintha Limb (Lady Caroline Lamb).

Elizabeth Thomas has also been identified as 'Mrs Bridget Bluemantle', author of nine Minerva Press novels from 1806 to 1818. While this author's conservative disavowal of any identification with learned women, or underdressed 'Bluestockings', may well be in character, bibliographical problems remain in securely fixing Elizabeth Thomas's name to these works. Virginia Blain rightly points to a confusion in attribution with the novelist Maria Elizabeth Budden ('M. E. B.'), and perhaps these Minerva novels should remain where Blakey left them in 1939, as by an unidentified, pseudonymous author. Elizabeth Thomas died, aged eighty-four, of bronchitis on 1 June 1855 at her home, Foxdown, Parkham, near Bideford, Devon.

DEIRDRE COLEMAN

Sources GM, 2nd ser., 44 (1855), 110 · Blain, Clements & Grundy, *Feminist comp.*, 1076 · review, *European Magazine and London Review*, 71 (1817), 333–6, 432–4 · W. S. Ward, *Literary reviews in British periodicals, 1798–1820: a bibliography*, 2 (1972), 536 · W. S. Ward, *Literary reviews in British periodicals, 1821–1826: a bibliography* (1977), 194 [doubtful attribution] · D. Blakey, *The Minerva Press, 1790–1820* (1939) · GM, 2nd ser., 11 (1839), 215 [Revd Thomas Thomas] · *Monthly Review*, new ser., 89 (1819), 432 [review] · review, *Theatrical Inquisitor, and Monthly Mirror*, 9 (1816), 417–18 · review, *Theatrical Inquisitor, and*

Monthly Mirror, 14 (1819), 133–7 · *GM*, 1st ser., 88/1 (1818), 528–9 [review] · review, *New Monthly Magazine*, 10 (1818), 169–70 · D. Bank and others, eds., *British biographical archive* (1984–98) [microfiche; with index, 2nd edn, 1998] · Allibone, *Dict.* · *IGI* · d. cert. · *GM*, 1st ser., 58 (1788), 659 · *GM*, 1st ser., 88/2 (1818), 643

Thomas, Ernest Chester (1850–1892), bibliographer and lawyer, the eldest son of John Withiel Thomas, was born on 28 October 1850 at Birkenhead, Cheshire. He was educated at Manchester grammar school, and matriculated on 17 October 1870 from Trinity College, Oxford, where he graduated BA in June 1875. He became a student at Gray's Inn on 7 May 1874, and, having won the Bacon scholarship of the inn in May 1875, published the following year a volume on *Leading Cases in Constitutional Law Briefly Stated*. In 1875 and 1876 Thomas studied at the universities of Jena and Bonn, and in 1877 he produced the first volume of a translation of Friedrich Lange's *Geschichte des Materialismus*, the second volume of which appeared in 1880, and the third in 1881. In 1878 he published *Leading Statutes Summarised for the Use of Students*, and in the same year became joint honorary secretary of the Library Association with Henry Richard Tedder (1850–1924), with whom he collaborated in writing the article 'Libraries' in the ninth edition of the *Encyclopaedia Britannica* (1882). He held this position for twelve years (1878–1890). He also edited the *Monthly Notes* of the Library Association for 1882 and several other volumes, contributing many articles and papers to the association's proceedings and journals. He published in January 1884 the first number of the *Library Chronicle: a Journal of Librarianship and Bibliography*, which he carried on at his own expense until 1888. Thomas's most significant work was his edition of the *Philobiblon of Richard de Bury, Bishop of Durham, Treasurer and Chancellor of Edward III* (1888), the first really critical text, based upon the early editions and a personal examination of twenty-eight manuscripts of the work; it continues to be used by scholars.

Thomas had at one time a small practice at the bar, but his life was chiefly devoted to literature and librarianship. He was a man of extensive reading, a brilliant talker, a keen debater, and an excellent writer. In the last two or three years of his life he took up business in the City, but his health was undermined by an attack of typhoid fever and he died at Redlands, near Tonbridge, Kent, on 5 February 1892. H. R. TEDDER, rev. NILANJANA BANERJI

Sources J. Minto, *A history of the public library movement* (1932) · H. R. Tedder, 'In memoriam: Ernest Chester Thomas', *The Library*, 4 (1892), 73–80 · Foster, *Alum. Oxon., 1715–1886* · J. Foster, *Men-at-the-bar: a biographical hand-list of the members of the various inns of court*, 2nd edn (1885) · *CGPLA Eng. & Wales* (1892)

Wealth at death £1903 8s. 6d.: probate, 30 April 1892, *CGPLA Eng. & Wales*

Thomas [married name Hyndman], **Ethel Nancy Miles** (1876–1944), botanist, was born on 4 October 1876 at 18 Hartham Road, Islington, London, the daughter of David Miles Thomas, a tutor originally from Carmarthen, and his wife, Mary Emily Davies. She received her early education at home and at Mayo High School, London. In 1897 she became a student at University College, London, where she was prominent as president of the women students' union (and where later she was made a fellow). She also attended botany lectures at Imperial College. She began her research apprenticeship early as assistant (1897–1901) to botanist Ethel Sargant. This experience, and work with Arthur Tansley at University College, awakened her lifelong interest in seedling anatomy and plant evolution. Her first papers appeared in 1900, five years before she received her BSc. She was the first in Britain to publish on the phenomenon of double fertilization in angiosperms (1900). Her hypothesis of the double leaf-trace (*New Phytologist*, 1907), a notable contribution to phylogenetic theory, was founded on investigations of vascular structures in a wide range of seedling types, angiospermous and gymnospermous. She continued to publish intermittently until the mid-1920s, bringing out some twelve reports in scientific periodicals as well as more general articles. Her later work was directed towards a broad interpretation of seedling anatomy, a goal never fully realized.

Assistant lecturer at Bedford College from 1907, Thomas became head of the botany department in 1908 when it was established as a separate unit. She designed the botany garden at the Regent's Park site to which the college moved in 1913 and initiated planning for a plant physiology laboratory. Vigorous and enthusiastic about everything she undertook, she could occasionally arouse considerable antagonism. Hers was a complex personality; although ambitious, courageous, and warm-hearted, she was also impulsively outspoken and sometimes inflexible. As a teacher she set high standards and believed in letting students find their own feet. Growing antipathy between her and Bedford's principal, Margaret Tuke, led to her dismissal in 1916. The move upset the botany department, since she was by then a well-established scientist: a council member of the Linnean Society in 1910–15 (a fellow from 1908), she had taken her DSc in 1915 and had been appointed reader in the University of London in 1912 in recognition of her department development work. She was also an examiner for the University of London.

During the First World War, Thomas carried out research for the War Office and the Medical Research Committee, while also serving as a Women's Land Army inspector. After a year (1918–19) as acting head of the botany department at University College of South Wales and subsequently two years as keeper of the botany department in the National Museum of Wales, she joined the staff of recently established University College, Leicester. There, almost alone, she developed a biological sciences programme; her botany laboratory was the college's first laboratory. She remained head of the biology department until she reluctantly accepted retirement in 1937 at the age of sixty.

Life member of the British Association (vice president, section K (botany) 1933), Thomas attended meetings in Australia (1914), Canada (1924), and southern Africa (1929). She sat on the executive committee of the Imperial Botanical Conference (1924). A strong supporter of the women's movement, she took a particular interest in matters affecting professional status and especially women's research opportunities. For a time she was president of the Leicester branch of the British Federation of University Women.

Handsome and vivacious with dark, lively eyes, Ethel Thomas stood out at social gatherings: a reporter at a British Association meeting, after identifying her as one of the country's leading women botanists, added, clearly impressed, 'she dances like a moonbeam' (*Leicester Evening Mail*, 26 May 1933). In September 1933 she married Hugh Hyndman, a barrister, whose sudden death in 1934 was a severe blow. After retiring she continued professional activities from a research room in Westfield College (London). By 1940 she was in poor health and suffering from severe memory loss, but still lived alone, declining help. She died of heart failure at Brookwood Hospital, Knaphill, Woking, Surrey, on 28 August 1944, and was cremated at Woking four days later.   MARY R. S. CREESE

Sources *Nature*, 154 (1944), 481–2 · E. M. Delf, *Proceedings of the Linnean Society of London*, 157th session (1945), 235–6 · *The Times* (1 Sept 1944) · d. cert. · b. cert. · Royal Holloway College, Egham, Surrey, archives [incl. notes on the history of Bedford College botany department by Dr Sharman] · archives, University of Leicester · E. M. Delf, *Chronica Botanica*, 7 (1942–3), 48 · UCL, records office · *WWW*
Archives RBG Kew, Jodrell laboratory · Royal Holloway College, Egham, Surrey
Likenesses Elliott & Fry, photograph, Royal Holloway College, Egham, Surrey · photograph, repro. in *Leicester Mercury* (7 Feb 1931) · photograph, repro. in *Leicester Evening Mail* (26 May 1933) · two photographs, Royal Holloway College, Egham, Surrey

Thomas, Forest Frederic Edward Yeo- (1902–1964), secret operations officer, was born in London on 17 June 1902, the eldest son of John Yeo-Thomas and his wife, Daisy Ethel Burrows. The Yeo-Thomas family, which had connections with the Welsh coalmining industry, had established itself in Dieppe in the middle of the nineteenth century. 'Tommy' was sent to the Dieppe Naval College where he early learned to defend his British nationality. Later he went to the Lycée Condorcet in Paris until war broke out in 1914. In spite of all his father's efforts to prevent it, he was determined to take part in the war and was accepted as a dispatch rider when the United States joined in. In 1920 he joined the Poles against the Bolsheviks; was captured and sentenced to death; but managed to escape by strangling his guard the night before his execution was due.

Returning to France, Yeo-Thomas eventually settled down to study accountancy. There followed a variety of employments until in 1932 he became secretary to the fashion house of Molyneux. When war broke out in 1939 he at once tried to enlist, but the two years he had added to his age in the first war now told against him. Eventually he managed to join the Royal Air Force with the rank of sergeant. He completed radar training and was in one of the last boats to leave France when that country fell. In October 1941 he was commissioned and sent as intelligence officer to the 308 Polish squadron at Baginton. But he was determined to return to occupied France and eventually,

in February 1942, with the help of a well-known newspaper and a member of parliament, he was taken into Special Operations Executive. Here he became responsible for planning in the RF French section which worked in close association with General De Gaulle's Bureau Central de Renseignements et d'Action (BCRA). It was at this time that he was given the *nom de guerre* the White Rabbit.

After the fall of France small groups of resisters had sprung up all over the country, but they were uncoordinated, ignorant of each other's identities, purposes, or, often, whereabouts. It was essential that these efforts should in some way be knit together to work towards the same end. In February 1943 Yeo-Thomas and André Dewavrin, known as Colonel Passy, the head of BCRA, were parachuted into France to join Pierre Brossolette to investigate the potential of resistance groups in the occupied zone. They succeeded in uniting the various groups in allegiance to De Gaulle, pooling their resources to organize a secret army which would spring into action on D-day. From this mission the three men safely returned in April. But in June the leader and a number of other members of the Conseil National de la Résistance were arrested and its work seriously disrupted. To help restore the situation Yeo-Thomas and Brossolette in September returned to France where movement and meeting together had become much more difficult. In November Yeo-Thomas, concealed inside a hearse, slipped through the controls, and was picked up by Lysander. Brossolette remained behind. In England, Yeo-Thomas's urgent demands for supplies for his organization took him finally to the prime minister, Winston Churchill. This interview produced a considerable increase in aircraft for RF section and consequently in weapons and supplies for the resisters in France.

When in February 1944 Yeo-Thomas heard of Brossolette's capture, he arranged to be parachuted into France yet again in order to replace him and also to try to organize his escape. Another visit by one so well known to the Germans as 'Shelley' was courting disaster, which did indeed befall Yeo-Thomas. He was arrested in Paris and his long period of torture and imprisonment began: in Fresnes, Compiègnes, Buchenwald, and Rehmsdorf. Throughout his appalling tortures he said nothing of any value to the enemy. Despite several bold but unsuccessful attempts, he maintained his resolution to escape. At Buchenwald, in September 1944, when allied agents were being liquidated, he persuaded the head of the typhus experimental station to allow three agents to exchange identities with three Frenchmen who were already dying. Yeo-Thomas, Harry Peulevé, and a Frenchman were selected; Yeo-Thomas, in his new identity, was transferred to Rehmsdorf as a hospital orderly. When the camp was evacuated in April 1945 before the advancing allies he organized an escape from the train when men were engaged in burying those who had died on the journey. Yeo-Thomas was among the ten who succeeded in getting away. Starving, desperately weak from dysentery and other illnesses, he was captured by German troops, posed as an escaping French air force prisoner of war, and was sent to the Grunhainigen Stalag. He again organized an escape with ten others who refused to leave him when he collapsed and finally helped him to reach the advancing American forces.

Yeo-Thomas was among the most outstanding workers behind enemy lines whom Britain produced. He was stocky, well built, athletic (he had boxed in his youth), and his blue eyes had a direct and fearless look. His sense of humour revealed itself in a ready smile which, on occasions, broke into open laughter. His character was exactly suited to his task. He was quick-witted and resourceful, and his endurance under hardship was supreme. He received the George Cross, the Military Cross and bar, the Polish cross of merit, the Croix de Guerre, and was a commander of the Légion d'honneur. Battered and permanently injured in health, he returned to Britain to be cared for devotedly by Barbara Yeo-Thomas, formerly Barbara Joan Dean. A marriage had ended before war broke out, two children remaining in France with their mother.

After helping to bring to trial several Nazi war criminals Yeo-Thomas returned to Molyneux in 1946 but in 1948 ill health forced him to resign. After a period of recuperation he was appointed in 1950 as representative in Paris of the Federation of British Industries. There, in a different way, he still worked for Anglo-French rapprochement. But his sufferings had taken their toll and he died at his home, 3 rue des Eaux, Paris, on 26 February 1964. His wartime exploits formed the basis of a best-selling memoir, *The White Rabbit* (1952), by Bruce Marshall.

JAMES HUTCHISON, *rev.*

Sources B. Marshall, *The White Rabbit* (1952) · M. R. D. Foot, *SOE in France: an account of the work of the British Special Operations Executive in France, 1940–1944* (1966) · private information (1981) · personal knowledge (1981) · *CGPLA Eng. & Wales* (1964) · *The Times* (27 Feb 1964)
Wealth at death £1271: probate, 13 Nov 1964, *CGPLA Eng. & Wales*

Thomas, Francis Sheppard (1793/4–1857), secretary of the Public Record Office, was born at Kington, Herefordshire, where he was baptized on 23 February 1794, the son of Samuel Thomas and his wife, Elizabeth. He entered the State Paper Office as a clerk in 1826, and became a much valued secretary for records business to Lord Langdale, master of the rolls. From 1838 to 1857 he was secretary of the Public Record Office. After Langdale's death in 1851 Thomas's special influence, which had led to friction with the head of the office, diminished when Sir John Romilly, the new master of the rolls, preferred to deal with Treasury communications on records matters directly with the deputy keeper rather than through the secretary.

In 1846 Thomas privately printed a compilation from public records entitled *Notes of Materials for the History of Public Departments*. This was followed in 1848 by a short but more elaborate work on *The ancient exchequer of England, the Treasury, and origin of the present management of the exchequer and treasury of Ireland*, and in 1849 by *A History of the State Paper Office*, which expanded the account given in his earlier *Notes*. In 1852 he wrote an explanatory preface to *Liber munerum publicorum Hiberniae*, by Rowley Lascelles. In 1853 his *Hand-Book to the Public Records* appeared. It was a novel summary and the first of a succession of general guides by later generations of Public Record Office officials. Thomas's *Hand-Book* appears to have been written largely in his own time; its usefulness to the department, and that of his previous *Notes*, helped to secure him an enhancement of salary in 1855. Three volumes of *Historical Notes, 1509–1714* followed in 1856. These are mainly biographical and chronological memoranda, assembled over many years of work on the historical side of the office, set down to assist colleagues then arranging the state papers. They were published under government direction 'rather than at the wish of the compiler'.

Thomas was married to Mary, sister of Charles Lechmere, sometime deputy keeper of state papers. They had a son, Francis Charles, who received a clerical appointment at the Public Record Office but who died aged thirty in 1870. Thomas died at his home, Broad Green, Croydon, on 27 August 1857.   ALAN BELL

Sources J. D. Cantwell, *The Public Record Office, 1838–1958* (1991) · *GM*, 3rd ser., 2 (1857), 469 · Allibone, *Dict.* · Boase, *Mod. Eng. biog.* · *IGI*

Thomas, Frederick Jennings (1786–1855), naval officer, younger son of Sir John Thomas, fifth baronet (1749–1828), of Wenvoe Castle, Glamorgan, and his wife, Mary, daughter of John Parker of Hasfield Court, Gloucestershire, was born in the New Forest, Hampshire, on 19 April 1786. He entered the navy in March 1799 on the *Boston* on the North American station, and afterwards in the West Indies. In autumn 1803 he joined the *Prince of Wales*, flagship of Sir Robert Calder, and was present in the action off Cape Finisterre on 22 July 1805. On 19 September he was appointed acting lieutenant of the *Spartiate* (commission confirmed 14 February 1806) and was at Trafalgar. He continued in the *Spartiate* off Rochefort, and afterwards in the Mediterranean until November 1809, when he was for a few months on the *Antelope*, flagship of Sir John Duckworth, and was then sent to Cadiz, where for the next three years he helped to defend the town against the French flotilla. He was promoted commander on 4 March 1811, and second in command of the British flotilla. Towards the close of 1813 he was acting captain of the *San Juan* (74 guns), flagship of Rear-Admiral Samuel Hood Linzee at Gibraltar. He was posted captain on 8 December 1813 and returned to England with Linzee in the frigate *Eurotas* in 1814. He had no further employment afloat. On 7 August 1816 he married Susannah, only daughter of Arthur Atherley of Southampton. They seem to have settled in that neighbourhood and had three sons and a daughter. In 1818 Thomas invented a lifeboat with three keels, intended to prevent it capsizing, and he proposed a pier at Brighton and a bridge across the River Arun in Sussex. He published *England's Defence*. He accepted the retired rank of rear-admiral on 1 October 1846 and died at Hill, near Southampton, on 19 December 1855. He was buried at Millbrook, near Southampton.

J. K. LAUGHTON, *rev.* ANDREW LAMBERT

Sources D. Syrett and R. L. DiNardo, *The commissioned sea officers of the Royal Navy, 1660–1815*, rev. edn, Occasional Publications of the Navy RS, 1 (1994) · O'Byrne, *Naval biog. dict.* · *GM*, 2nd ser., 45 (1856),

303–4 · W. F. P. Napier, *History of the war in the Peninsula and in the south of France*, 6 vols. (1828–40)

Thomas, Frederick William (1867–1956), orientalist, was born at Wilnecote, Tamworth, Staffordshire, on 21 March 1867, the son of Frederick Thomas, colliery clerk, and his wife, Frances Blainey. He was educated at King Edward VI's High School, Birmingham, whence he gained a scholarship at Trinity College, Cambridge. He was awarded a first class in part one (1887) and part two (with distinction, 1889) of the classical tripos, followed by a first class in the Indian languages tripos (1890). He won medals for Greek epigram (1887), Latin epigram (1888), and Greek ode (1889), the members' prize for Latin essay (1888), and, twice, the Le Bas essay prize (1890–1891). Captain of his school, he took part in many sports at Cambridge and was capped for lacrosse.

In 1892 Thomas was elected to a fellowship at Trinity College, which he held *in absentia* while headmaster's assistant (1891–8) at his old school. In 1898 he was appointed assistant librarian of the India Office under C. H. Tawney, whom he succeeded as librarian in 1903, holding the post until 1927. In 1908 he married Eleanor Grace, daughter of Walter John Hammond, engineer, of The Grange, Knockholt, Kent; they had one son and one daughter. In 1927 he was elected Boden professor of Sanskrit at Oxford. He vacated his chair, and with it his fellowship at Balliol College, in 1937.

As a classical scholar Thomas had specialized in philology, and it was as a philologist that he contributed most to oriental studies. His first publications, the two Le Bas essays, were devoted to the history of British education in India and the mutual influence of Muslims and Hindus. He soon turned to more austere topics and in 1897, in collaboration with his teacher E. B. Cowell, he produced the standard translation of the *Harsa-carita* of Bana. At the India Office he threw himself with enthusiasm into the massive task of arranging and cataloguing the large accumulations of oriental books and manuscripts in many languages. When Sir Aurel Stein discovered the famous 'hidden library' near Tunhuang (Dunhuang) and all the documents in Tibetan passed to the India Office Library, Thomas found a wonderful outlet for his linguistic gifts which occupied him for the rest of his life. Among his many discoveries in this collection was a hitherto unknown language of the Sino-Tibetan borderland which he successfully deciphered and to which he gave the name 'Nam'.

Thomas's specialist interests, however, ranged far beyond pure philology. He made important contributions to Buddhist studies, and was an authority on Jainism. His acute mind found delight in expounding the intricacies of Indian philosophy and logic. He wrote important papers on Tibetan mythology and folklore. In all he published 250 books and articles. True to the exact tradition of Indian scholarship established by men such as Sir William Jones, Sir Charles Wilkins, and H. T. Colebrooke, he also inherited their universality in a time when the frontiers of Indian studies were widely extended to the north and east.

He was a pioneer of the new school of Asian philology and his influence proved to be far-reaching.

In 1937 to mark Thomas's seventieth birthday, ninety-nine colleagues in orientalism of many lands signed a memorial in his honour; two years later he received a volume of studies to which forty-eight scholars contributed and which contained a bibliography of his writings to 1939. A bibliography of his further writings was appended to H. N. Randle's biographical article in the *Proceedings of the British Academy*. He was elected a fellow of the British Academy in 1927; appointed CIE in 1928; received honorary degrees from Munich, Allahabad, and Birmingham; and in 1941 was awarded the triennial gold medal of the Royal Asiatic Society.

To his last years Thomas retained the lean and athletic figure of the strenuous sportsman. His manner was keen and affable, and he enjoyed speaking in learned company. He celebrated his retirement by undertaking a tour of India in 1938 which would have taxed the strength and energies of the most intrepid traveller. He retained the full scope of his great intellectual powers to the end, although deafness at the last diminished his social enjoyment. He died at the Horton General Hospital, Banbury, Oxfordshire, on 6 May 1956.

A. J. Arberry, *rev.* J. B. Katz

Sources H. N. Randle, 'Frederick William Thomas, 1867–1956', *PBA*, 44 (1958), 207–24 · L. D. Barnett, 'F. W. Thomas', *Journal of the Royal Asiatic Society of Great Britain and Ireland* (1957), 142–3 · personal knowledge (1971) · private information (1971) · *CGPLA Eng. & Wales* (1956)
Archives BL OIOC, papers relating to Tibet, MS Eur. F 155 · Bodl. Oxf., papers · U. Birm. L., corresp., diaries, and papers | Bodl. Oxf., corresp. with Sir Aurel Stein
Likenesses Gillman and Soame Ltd, photograph, repro. in Randle, 'Frederick William Thomas', pl. xvii · photograph, BL OIOC
Wealth at death £4466 6*s.* 7*d.*: probate, 10 Sept 1956, *CGPLA Eng. & Wales*

Thomas, Freeman Freeman-, first marquess of Willingdon (1866–1941), governor-general of Canada and viceroy of India, was born at Ratton, Sussex, on 12 September 1866, the only son of Frederick Freeman Thomas (1838–1868), rifle brigade, of Ratton and Yapton, and his wife, Mabel (*d.* 1924), third daughter of Henry Bouverie William *Brand, later first Viscount Hampden. In 1892 he assumed the additional surname of Freeman by deed poll. At Eton College he played in the cricket eleven for three years, the last of them as captain; he was also president of the Eton Society. At Trinity College, Cambridge, he played for four years, 1886–9, in the university eleven, being captain in the last year, and also for Sussex and I Zingari. He never lost his love of sport and was a much admired cricketer. Like his father he was for some years master of the Eastbourne foxhounds. He became a major in the Sussex yeomanry, and for fifteen years was in the Sussex artillery militia. In 1936 he was appointed honorary colonel of the 5th battalion, Royal Sussex regiment.

In 1892 Freeman-Thomas married Marie Adelaide, fourth daughter of Thomas *Brassey, first Baron (later Earl) Brassey (1836–1918), the Liberal politician and naval

Freeman Freeman-Thomas, first marquess of Willingdon (1866–1941), by Walter Stoneman, 1924

authority. They had two sons. A handsome, close-knit pair, her dynamic personality made her a commanding figure in the five government houses in which they lived. His first post abroad was as aide-de-camp to her father, then governor of Victoria. In 1900 Freeman-Thomas was elected Liberal member of parliament for Hastings, and became a junior lord of the Treasury in the Liberal government in 1905. At the general election the next year he lost his seat, but soon won a by-election for the Bodmin division of Cornwall, and thereafter periodically did some secretarial work for Asquith, the prime minister. In 1910 he was created Baron Willingdon of Ratton, and in 1911 became a lord-in-waiting to George V. He was the king's favourite tennis partner.

In April 1913 Willingdon was appointed governor of Bombay. With the outbreak of the First World War he and his wife were much involved with promoting the allied cause, and with the welfare of troops passing through Bombay, particularly the sick and wounded from the Mesopotamian campaign. They were active too in ameliorating some of the current racial social barriers. The Willingdon Sports Club in Bombay and the Willingdon Club in Madras were each created with a view to having Indian as well as British members. Willingdon's quinquennial term as governor of Bombay was extended for eight months to December 1918, and during this time he had his first encounters with Gandhi, both in connection with Gandhi's Kaira satyagraha and with his participation in the government's war council. 'Honest, but a Bolshevik

& for that reason very dangerous', Willingdon called him (Brown, 111).

Willingdon was appointed governor of Madras in April 1919. There, as Gandhi's non-co-operation movement took hold, he sought to exclude him from his province, but was prevented by the government of India from doing so. Willingdon much disliked the prospect of having to institute the Montagu–Chelmsford provincial diarchal reforms in 1921, but arranged that his officials for the 'reserved' and the elected politicians from the Justice Party for the 'transferred' subjects should work as a single governmental team. So successful did these arrangements become that Willingdon soon recommended that Madras should be given full responsible government (though ineffectually).

At the end of his term in 1924 Willingdon was made a viscount. In 1925 he led the Indian delegation to the League of Nations assembly, and in the following year headed an Anglo-Chinese mission in China to review the disbursement to the Chinese of the remaining British share of the Boxer indemnity fund.

In 1926 the governor-generalship of Canada fell vacant in the aftermath of a clash between the previous holder, Lord Byng, and the Canadian prime minister, W. L. Mackenzie King, over the former's refusal to grant a dissolution of parliament which he then granted to Mackenzie King's opponent, Arthur Meighen. It was George V who suggested that Willingdon should be added to the list of those proposed for the position at a critical time and, as a fellow Liberal, he was promptly chosen by Mackenzie King (who was Canadian prime minister once again). Aided by his great personal charm, and as the first holder of his office who, with the appointment of a British high commissioner, was no longer the representative of the British government in Canada but the direct representative of the king, Willingdon soon proceeded to mend imperial fences. In 1927 he became the first governor-general of Canada to make a state visit to the United States—to meet President Coolidge—and, in addition to being assiduous in visiting many parts of Canada, went on an extended tour of the Caribbean in 1929.

In 1931 Willingdon was appointed viceroy of India in succession to Lord Irwin (later the earl of Halifax), raised to an earldom, and sworn of the privy council. Although aged sixty-five he found himself fully stretched over the next five years. He nearly resigned within months of his appointment over the consequences for the Indian economy of the National Government's abandonment of the gold standard. His principal concern, however, was to maintain the authority of the British raj while actively forwarding substantial constitutional change in India. 'We clearly stated', he later recalled, 'that our policy was of a dual nature' (Low, 238, n. 373). While insisting upon 'the due observance of the laws' he was much concerned 'to push forward the Reform scheme' as well (ibid., 238). From August 1931 to August 1933 he became involved in a protracted political dual with Gandhi both before and after he introduced the first India-wide emergency powers ordinance in January 1932 following Gandhi's revival of his civil disobedience campaign, when over 30,000 Congressmen were sent to gaol. 'One of the most astute politically-minded and bargaining little men I ever came across' (ibid., 173) he now called him. At the same time Willingdon became extensively involved—though at a considerable distance—in the protracted constitutional discussions in London which centred upon successive Indian round-table conferences and resulted in the passage of the Government of India Act of 1935. These called for endless negotiations with Muslim and Hindu 'moderate' politicians and with the leaders of the Indian princes. There has been strong criticism of Willingdon's over-optimism in believing the Indian princes would join the long proposed all-India federation, and it has to be said that his general ability did not always match his considerable personal affability.

On returning home in May 1936 Willingdon was made marquess, constable of Dover Castle, and lord warden of the Cinque Ports. He had been appointed GCIE (1913), GBE (1917), GCSI (1918), and GCMG (1926), and now became chancellor of the last order. He was awarded a number of honorary degrees and the freedom (among others) of Canada (1927) and Edinburgh (1934); Lady Willingdon was appointed a lady of the Imperial Order of the Crown of India (1917) and GBE (1924).

In 1937 Willingdon chaired a committee on the supply of army officers. The next year he headed a successful 'goodwill' mission to South America on behalf of the Ibero-American Institute. In 1940 he represented the British government at the centennial celebrations of New Zealand, and later that year he led an important trade mission to the South American republics. He occupied many positions of a non-official character, and was on several boards, including that of the Westminster Bank. To the end of his life he remained an indefatigable traveller by air.

Always a fit man, Willingdon finally succumbed to pneumonia and died at his London home, 5 Lygon Place, on 12 August 1941. His ashes were interred in Westminster Abbey. He was survived by his wife; his elder son had been killed in France in September 1914, and he was succeeded as second marquess by his younger son, Inigo Brassey Freeman-Thomas (1899–1979).   D. A. Low

Sources *The Times* (13 Aug 1941) · personal knowledge (1959) [*DNB*] · private information (1959) · J. Cowan, *Canada's governors-general, 1867–1952* (1952) · R. J. Moore, *The crisis of Indian unity, 1917–1940* (1974) · J. M. Brown, *Gandhi's rise to power: Indian politics, 1915–1922* (1972) · E. F. Irschick, *Political and social conflict in south India: the non-Brahmin movement and Tamil separatism* (1969) · D. A. Low, *Britain and Indian nationalism: the imprint of ambiguity, 1929–1942* (1997) · Burke, *Peerage* (1980) · *CGPLA Eng. & Wales* (1941)
Archives BL OIOC, family corresp. and papers, incl. photographs, MS Eur. F 237 · BL OIOC, corresp. as governor of Bombay and Madras, MS Eur. F 93 · CUL, corresp. · National Archives of India, New Delhi | BL, corresp. with Lord Gladstone, Add. MSS 46059–46063 · BL OIOC, corresp. with Sir John Anderson, MS Eur. F 207 · BL OIOC, letters to Sir Harcourt Butler, MS Eur. F 116 · BL OIOC, corresp. with Lord Erskine, MS Eur. D 596 · BL OIOC, corresp. with Sir G. H. Haig, MS Eur. F 115 · BL OIOC, letters to second earl of Lytton, MS Eur. F 160 · BL OIOC, corresp. with Sir Frederick Sykes, MS Eur. F 150 · Bodl. Oxf., letters to Lord Hanworth · Bodl. Oxf.,

corresp. with Lewis Harcourt · HLRO, letters to Herbert Samuel · NA Scot., corresp. with Lord Lothian · NL Scot., corresp. relating to the liberal league · U. Birm. L., letters to Austen Chamberlain
Likenesses W. Stoneman, photographs, 1924, NPG [*see illus.*] · W. Stoneman, photographs, 1934, NPG · O. Birley, oils, *c.*1936, viceroy's house, New Delhi, India · W. R. Dick, statue, New Delhi, India · P. A. de Laszlo, portrait, Government House, Bombay · M. Nagappa, statue, Madras, India
Wealth at death £120,112 4s. 0d.: probate, 13 Dec 1941, *CGPLA Eng. & Wales*

Thomas, Sir George, baronet (*c.*1695–1774), planter and colonial governor, was born on the island of Antigua, one of six children of Colonel George Thomas (*d.* 1707), planter, and his wife, Sarah Winthrop. His paternal grandfather acquired land on Antigua in the 1660s; his mother was great-granddaughter of the first governor of Massachusetts Bay, John Winthrop. Thomas was educated in Antigua and inherited plantations from his father and his uncle. On 18 April 1717 he married Elizabeth (*c.*1701/2–1763), daughter of Captain John King, planter, at St Philip's Church, Antigua; they had five children.

Both Thomas's father and uncle were prominent officeholders. Consequently Thomas entered the colony's assembly, aged about twenty-one, in 1716; he was re-elected in 1721, 1723, and 1727, and became speaker in 1727. In 1728 he was elevated to the council of Antigua. In the late 1730s he went to England, where the Penn proprietors of Pennsylvania were searching for a successor to their deceased lieutenant-governor. Thomas got this appointment because he agreed to remit £500 to the proprietors and to remain governor for at least four years. He took the post probably to gain credentials in imperial administration.

Thomas's arrival in Philadelphia in June 1738 coincided with the re-emergence in the colony of the vexing question of paper money. The assembly feared the loss of the colony's medium of exchange, were the paper bills of credit not to be re-emitted; the proprietors demanded that they be paid the value of their rents in sterling, not in Pennsylvania paper money. Failing to get the two sides to agree Thomas threatened to resign if the Penns did not compromise. In May 1739 they reached agreement.

When war with Spain began in 1739 the assembly, dominated by pacifist Quakers, refused to establish any defence force, and landowners baulked at letting Thomas enlist servants for the 1740 Cartagena expedition. Thomas considered the assembly's £3000 appropriation for the 1740 expedition inadequate; because he demanded further defence appropriations and the establishment of a militia, and because he would not recover enlisted servants, the house refused to pay his salary for the second half of 1740 and throughout 1741 and 1742. No bills passed during this period. In January 1743 Thomas agreed to accept several assembly bills unamended and the assembly paid him eighteen months' back salary. Disagreement over defence continued when the colonies planned attacks on French Canada in 1745 and 1746. Thomas was successful in getting the assembly to aid the Louisbourg expedition and to provide funds for Pennsylvania volunteers for the 1746 Canada expedition, although he had to agree to re-emit the paper money of the province and to let assembly commissioners supervise expenditures. The assembly continued to refuse to establish a militia for defence. In March 1746 it finally paid Thomas his full salary arrears, having carried most of its points.

In contrast to his relations with the assembly Thomas negotiated successfully with American Indians, particularly the Iroquois confederacy, in treaties signed in 1742 and 1744. In 1747, pleading ill health, he returned to London. His health problems apparently had faded when in July 1753 he arrived in the Leeward Islands as the new governor. He got on better with the four island assemblies, composed of planters like himself, than he had done with the Pennsylvania Quakers. He dissolved the Antigua assembly on only one occasion, but at its request. He even persuaded the assemblies to co-operate on prohibiting exports during the Seven Years' War. He also joined the Antigua assembly in requesting repeal of the Stamp Act. Disputes were minor; he chastised the St Kitts assembly in 1756 for attempting to increase its powers and, over planter objections, he armed slaves for defence and for the 1762 Havana attack.

Thomas returned to London in June 1766 and resigned the governorship in December; he was created baronet on 6 September 1766. He retired to two manors in Sussex, and died in Upper Brook Street, London, on 31 December 1774. He was buried in Willingdon, Sussex.

BENJAMIN H. NEWCOMB

Sources W. R. Shepherd, 'Thomas, George', *DAB* • V. L. Oliver, *The history of the island of Antigua*, 3 vols. (1894–9) • G. Mackinney and C. F. Hoban, eds., *Votes and proceedings of the house of representatives of the province of Pennsylvania*, 8 vols. (1754–76), vols. 3–4 • A. Tully, *William Penn's legacy: politics and social structure in provincial Pennsylvania, 1726–1755* (1977) • J. J. Kelley, *Pennsylvania: the colonial years, 1681–1776* (1980) • J. E. Illick, *Colonial Pennsylvania: a history* (1976) • B. H. Newcomb, *Political partisanship in the American middle colonies, 1700–1776* (1995) • *The papers of Benjamin Franklin*, ed. L. W. Laboree and W. J. Bell, 2–3 (1960–61) • R. Pares, *War and trade in the West Indies, 1739–1763* (1936); repr. (1963) • A. J. O'Shaughnessy, 'The Stamp Act crisis in the British Caribbean', *William and Mary Quarterly*, 51 (1994), 203–26 • *GM*, 1st ser., 44–45 (1774–5)

Archives Hist. Soc. Penn., Thomas Penn papers, official corresp.

Thomas, George (1756–1802), soldier, was born in a farm cottage at Roscrea, co. Tipperary. According to his own account he joined the British navy at Bristol in 1780, where he acquired his knowledge of gunnery. Arriving at Madras in 1781 he deserted ship and went to Kelly's grog shop (the proprietor being a fellow Tipperarian). Advised to offer his services as a mercenary, he travelled south to the Kanara Poligars, a group of armed chieftain-bandits. Thomas subsequently joined the nizam of Hyderabad's army as a private, and there learned his trade as a soldier. He gathered around him a personal bodyguard, nicknamed the Irish Pindaris, after the feared Indian mercenaries who 'issued like wild dogs from between the feet of their nominal masters … to slay, to burn, to plunder, and to disappear' (Smith, 567). Words of command were given by Thomas in Gaelic to maintain secrecy.

Travelling north to Delhi with his troops and a 6-pounder gun, Thomas was recruited by Zeb-un-Nisa, the Begam Samru of Sardhana, widow of Walter Reinhard, a notorious European mercenary. The begam, who had become a Roman Catholic after her husband's death, appointed Thomas an officer in her army, and arranged for his marriage to her god-daughter Maria, which took place on 29 April 1787. The marriage contract, written in Portuguese, was drawn up by the begam's priest, Father Gregorius. Three sons and a daughter were born of the marriage. The begam's confidence in the wild Irishman was justified at the siege of Gokulgarh in March 1788, where the begam was supporting the Mughal emperor Shah Alam II against a rebellious local chief. Thomas gave valuable support and was rewarded with a *jagir* (a temporary grant of land) at Tappal, from which he collected the revenue. By imposing law and order he was shortly able to double the *jagir's* income.

In 1792, during a foray against Sikh bandits north of Sardhana, Thomas was dismissed from the begam's service, most likely for trying to usurp her authority. He took refuge in the British garrison at Anupshahr, on the Ganges, but within the year was employed by the Maratha governor of Meerut, Appa Khande Rao, cousin to Mahadji Sindhia of Gwalior. Here he raised a battalion, whose main purpose was to collect land revenue by using coercion and terrorism. His success was rewarded by gifts and the *jagir* of Jhajjar, 50 miles west of Delhi. This became his base and he built the fort of Georgegarh, the name being corrupted in Hindustani to Jahazgarh. By 1796 Thomas had made peace with the begam, coming to her rescue and helping to suppress a mutiny among her own troops. He left Appa Khande Rao in 1797 to join Bapu Sindhia, governor of Saharanpur, another Maratha chief, and was engaged to harass the Sikhs, then jostling for power in northern India. But in a disgraceful scene the pugnacious Thomas actually attacked his employer in front of a new common enemy, the Afghan invader Zaman Shah. Thomas escaped to the safety of Jhajjar with about 2500 of his own men, but was faced with the problem of paying and feeding them. Unusually for the time, he paid disability allowances to his wounded soldiers, and pensions to the soldiers' widows.

In the fluid situation before the East India Company imposed its rule, and when large areas of land were left virtually ungoverned following the collapse of the Mughal empire, Thomas conceived the extraordinary idea of making himself 'King' of Lahore by conquering the Punjab. He marched his troops into Hariana in 1797 and easily captured the towns of Hissar and Hansi. He found the latter, an ancient fort, inhabited by one fakir and two lions. He stabilized an area of 120 miles by 50 miles in Hariana and repopulated Hansi, later to become the home of Colonel James Skinner (1778–1841), another soldier of fortune. At the height of his fame that year Thomas described himself as 'dictator in all the countries belonging to the Sikhs south of the Sutlej' (Smith, 567), and claimed to hold his land on behalf of the British government.

But the necessity for money led to Thomas's re-employment as a mercenary, by the Maratha Vaman

Rao against the Rajput raja of Jaipur, to collect unpaid taxes, which he succeeded in doing. His ultimate downfall was in a new alliance between the Marathas, commanded by the European mercenaries Colonel Perron, Captain Felix Smith, and Louis Bourquien, and their former enemies the Sikhs, desperate at Thomas's incursions against them. At first Thomas made a spirited resistance, lifting the siege of Georgegarh, but, as more victims of his impartial bloodletting united against him, his own men began to desert. Thomas was forced into a humiliating surrender to Bourquien, although he was honourably treated as a brave soldier, and allowed to leave India for his native Ireland with several lakhs of rupees and property. Many years of constant heavy drinking had weakened Thomas's constitution, and he died from fever at Berhampore, on his way to Calcutta, on 22 August 1802, aged forty-six. He was buried in the cantonment cemetery at Berhampore. His wife and children remained as pensioners at Sardhana until Begam Samru's death in 1836.

ROSIE LLEWELLYN-JONES

Sources S. Bidwell, *Swords for hire: European mercenaries in eighteenth century India* (1971) • N. Shreeve, *Dark legacy* (1996) • M. Hennessy, *The rajah from Tipperary* (1971) • W. Francklin, *Military memoirs of Mr George Thomas* (1803) • V. A. Smith, *The Oxford history of India*, ed. T. G. P. Spear, rev. edn (1970) • T. Wilkinson, *Two monsoons* (1976) • *DNB* • priv. coll. [marriage contract] • private information (2004) [L. B. W. Jones, a descendant]
Archives priv. coll., copy of marriage contract
Likenesses engraving, repro. in Bidwell, *Swords for hire*
Wealth at death Rs.250,000 (2½ lakhs): *DNB*

Thomas, Sir George Alan, seventh baronet (1881–1972), chess and badminton player, was born in the British consulate in Constantinople on 14 June 1881, the son of Sir George Sidney Meade Thomas, sixth baronet (1847–1918), and his wife, Edith Margaret (*d.* 1920), daughter of Morgan Hugh Foster CB, of Brickhill, Bedfordshire. An elder son had died in infancy and there were two younger sisters. Thomas succeeded his father in the baronetcy (created 1766) in 1918. He learned chess at the age of four from his mother, who was one of the best English women players; she won the first women's tournament which was held during the great international tournament at Hastings in 1895, with her son acting as a wall-board demonstration boy. Thomas was briefly (1896) at Wellington College; other details of his education are not known.

Like his father, Thomas had no profession, and lived on his private means. As an amateur, he excelled at a number of sports as well as at chess. He played hockey for Hampshire, was a good enough lawn tennis player to figure in the semi-finals of the men's doubles at Wimbledon in 1911, and became an excellent badminton player. In chess he won some small tournaments before the First World War and played twice with success for England against the USA in the Newnes cup in 1910 and 1911. During the First World War he was a lieutenant in the 6th battalion of the Hampshire regiment and took part in the Mesopotamian campaign, during which he gave up his place in a vehicle to a wounded soldier and walked in the retreat from Kut.

After the war Thomas played fine chess for two decades. He won the British championship in 1923 and 1934 and

Sir George Alan Thomas, seventh baronet (1881–1972), by Bassano, 1925

had a long run of successes in the championship tournaments of the City of London club, the strongest British club of the time. He played for England in the chess Olympiads organized by the Fédération Internationale des Echecs from their start in 1927, when he tied with the Danish player K. Norman Hansen for the best score. He was awarded the first brilliancy prize for his game against Frederick Dewhurst Yates. He played in the subsequent Olympiads of 1930, 1931, 1933, 1935, 1937, and 1939, and achieved the fine score of 12½ points in the Prague team tournament of 1931. His best results in international tournaments were joint first with Sämisch at Spa in 1926, second at Nice in 1930, second again at Sopron in 1934, and, most outstanding of all, joint first with Euwe and Flohr, ahead of Capablanca and Botwinnik, at Hastings in 1934–5.

After the Second World War, Thomas played for a few more years, but gave up competing in tournaments after 1950. He then became a keen spectator who was especially interested in the play of juniors. He excelled at most phases of the game, having a good eye for a combination and a fine grasp of positional play. That he failed to attain supreme heights was due to his lifelong status as an amateur and to a certain lack of originality in his play. He was noted for his fine sportsmanship and was for some time the games editor of the *British Chess Magazine*.

Thomas also excelled at badminton. He first competed in the all-England championships in 1901 and between 1903 and 1928 won twenty-one titles—a record that still stands. He was singles champion four times, men's doubles champion nine times, and mixed doubles champion eight times. He also holds the record as the oldest player (at forty-one years of age) to win the singles title and also the oldest (at forty-seven) to win any title. He played in all but one of the thirty international matches between 1902 and 1929, and won fifty of his games.

Thomas was described as badminton's 'greatest figure' who 'was not only a fine player but also a man of impeccable sportsmanship and modest helpfulness' (*Badminton Gazette*, October 1972). As a player he was noted for his accuracy and deception, and for applying his astute chess-like tactics to the game. He wrote two books on the game—*The Art of Badminton* (1923) and *Badminton* (1936), both seminal works of their time—and was editor of the *Badminton Gazette* for many years. Once his competitive playing days were over he dedicated many hours both to encouraging juniors and to the administration of the game. For twenty years (1930–50) he was vice-president of the Badminton Association of England (BAE), and was president, 1950–52. He played an important part in the development of badminton as a world sport; it was his vision that foresaw the globalization of the sport, and gave up England's control of the game in forming (July 1934) the International Badminton Federation (IBF), which replaced the BAE as the sport's world governing body. He was its founder president, a position he held for twenty years. It is characteristic that he never missed a meeting of the IBF. In 1939 Thomas proposed the establishment of the men's world team badminton championship. Owing to the war, the first championship did not take place until 1948–9. From that date teams from all corners of the world have competed for the much coveted Thomas cup.

Thomas died in a London nursing home on 23 July 1972. As he was unmarried and had no heir the baronetcy became extinct.

HARRY GOLOMBEK, *rev.* MARGARET WHITEHEAD

Sources personal knowledge (1986) · private information (1986) · *The Times* (31 July 1972) · *British Chess Magazine* (1895–1972) · H. Golombek, *The encyclopedia of chess* (1977) · A. Chicco and G. Porreca, *Dizionario enciclopedico degli scacchi* (1971) · D. Hooper and K. Whyld, *The Oxford companion to chess*, 2nd edn (1996) · P. Davis, *The encyclopaedia of badminton* (1987) · *Badminton Gazette* (Oct 1972) · Burke, *Peerage* (1959) · *Wellington College register, 1859–1948* (1951)
Likenesses Bassano, photograph, 1925, NPG [*see illus.*]
Wealth at death £172,103: probate, 1972, *CGPLA Eng. & Wales*

Thomas, George Holt (1870–1929), aviation industrialist, was born on 31 March 1870 at Hampton House, Stockwell Private Road, in south London, the seventh son of William Luson *Thomas (1830–1900), founder of the illustrated weekly *Graphic* and *Daily Graphic* newspapers, and his wife, Annie Carmichael, daughter of marine artist John Wilson *Carmichael (1799–1868). He was educated privately and at King's College School, London, before spending two years (1888–90) at Queen's College, Oxford. He left Oxford without a degree and joined his father's newspaper business. In 1894 he married Gertrude Hesley, the youngest daughter of Thomas Oliver FRIBA, of Newcastle upon

George Holt Thomas (1870–1929), by unknown photographer

Tyne. The marriage was childless. By 1906 Holt Thomas had made a name and fortune as director, then general manager, of his father's newspapers and by founding his own illustrated weekly, *The Bystander*. In these journals, plus his *Empire Illustrated* magazine (1908–14), he vigorously advocated the production of British goods for British people at home and abroad. He was a founder of the Association of British Motor Manufacturers, which sought an import duty on foreign cars.

During 1906, however, Holt Thomas abandoned his active interest in the newspaper business and by 1920 had made a much greater name—and fortune—in the aviation industry. He was quick to recognize that man's early hops into the air would soon become long bounds, with both commercial and military consequences, and that Britain must therefore master the new art. As early as April 1909 he claimed that the sum already spent on military aviation by Germany was about £400,000, by France about £47,000, and by Britain a mere £5000. He was equally quick to recognize in the French pioneers Henry Farman and his brother Maurice allies well able to benefit his own and British interests. In April 1910, as a result of his friendship with the Farmans, Holt Thomas engaged a skilful pilot, Louis Paulhan, to compete for—and win— the tremendous prize of £10,000 put up by his friend Lord Northcliffe, the owner of the *Daily Mail*, for a successful flight from London to Manchester. It was Holt Thomas who inspired Northcliffe's interest in aviation, and the prize was so great because no one had hitherto flown anything like that distance.

Holt Thomas formed the Aircraft Manufacturing Company (often known as Airco) in 1912 to build Farman aeroplanes at Hendon. These aeroplanes would be used as trainers in large numbers by the Royal Flying Corps and were affectionately known as Longhorns and Shorthorns. Although he remained as fervently patriotic as in his newspaper days, urging the government to take a more active interest in developing Britain's infant aviation industry, Holt Thomas was a practical visionary and acknowledged the current superiority of French airframes and engines. He therefore obtained licences to manufacture Gnome and Le Rhone engines, which were widely used in British aircraft during the First World War.

Ever a man with a sharp eye for quality, either in men or material, Holt Thomas invited Geoffrey de Havilland to join Airco in May 1914. One of the most gifted designers in aviation history, de Havilland had recently been unhappily employed as an inspector and occasional test pilot at the royal aircraft factory in Farnborough, and welcomed the opportunity to resume his career as a designer. During the next six years their partnership flourished. De Havilland later recalled how glad he was to work for 'a brilliantly clever as well as a kind and likeable man', a man who was 'far-sighted, extremely able and possessed a knowledge of business only equalled by his ignorance of engineering' (de Havilland, 93–5). Their aircraft, wrote de Havilland, should have been identified as DHTs, the initials of *both* their surnames. About 30 per cent of all fighters, bombers, and trainers used during the First World War by Britain and the United States were de Havilland designs.

By November 1918 Holt Thomas was the largest and most influential aircraft constructor in Britain, operating factories in many places to build not only a line of excellent landplanes, but also flying boats, airships, propellers, and engines in huge numbers. His factories were equipped with the latest metal-working machinery, and at Hendon he had a wind tunnel and a laboratory for material testing.

After the armistice Holt Thomas hoped to keep his massive organization in being and enjoy the same success in civil aviation as he had in military aviation. As early as October 1916 he had formed a company, Aircraft Transport and Travel, to manage this translation. Meanwhile, in March 1916 he founded the Society of British Aircraft Constructors, intended to speak with one voice to government agencies in the hurly-burly of wartime and foster the industry's interests thereafter. One day, he wrote, 'there will be no place on the earth's surface more than four days' journey from London by air' (*Aeronautics*, 17 April 1919).

In May 1917 Holt Thomas told a meeting of the Aeronautical Society that military aviation should have been taken more seriously before 1914 and that the same mistake must not be made over civil aviation after victory was won. He foresaw internal airlines on a trunk route from London to Glasgow via Manchester, with feed-offs to Dublin and Belfast and links to the capitals of every continental country, including Russia, with eventual extensions to the United States and to New Zealand via India and Australia. Mail services and business and tourist flying would all prove profitable. Frederick Handley Page, one of Holt Thomas's keenest rivals, attended the lecture and said later that 'he could not help likening the audience to those who in Columbus' time had listened to that pioneer navigator explaining his project which led to the discovery of America' (*Flight*, 7 June 1917).

Early in 1919 Holt Thomas headhunted men of the highest reputation in aviation—Sefton Brancker, Francis Festing, and Mervyn O'Gorman—and on 25 August he started the world's first scheduled international air service. It operated daily, whether there were passengers or not, between London (Hounslow) and Paris (Le Bourget), using two of de Havilland's wartime designs until April 1920, when the DH 18, a biplane with a roomy cabin seating eight passengers, was brought into service: it was de Havilland's first aircraft designed purely as a civil transport. The service lasted until November 1920.

By then Holt Thomas's hopes for a post-war boom in civil aviation had been dashed. No available aircraft could carry sufficient passengers, freight, and mail over sufficient distances to be profitable, and government support for the research and development needed to produce such aircraft was not forthcoming. In March 1920 Holt Thomas sold Airco to the Birmingham Small Arms Company (BSA), which closed down its aviation activities. De Havilland decided to establish his own company and did so in September 1920, Holt Thomas having made possible the creation of a company that would become world famous by investing £10,000.

Holt Thomas published *Aerial Transport* (1920) and *The Future of British Industry and Trade Unionism* (1925), along with a number of articles and lectures on aviation. He retired to his country home at Hughenden, Buckinghamshire, where he took up the breeding of dairy cattle with something of the same enthusiasm he had formerly shown for newspapers and aeroplanes. His health was poor, and he died at the Queen Victoria Memorial Hospital, Cimiez, near Nice, France, on 1 January 1929 following an operation for throat cancer. A tall man, always smartly dressed, with commanding eyes, a fine Roman nose, and a neatly clipped beard, Holt Thomas was hard but fair, well respected by those who worked for him. Although neither knighted nor decorated for his war services, he was amply consoled in 1925 by a share of the magnificent award of £200,000 from the Royal Commission on Awards to Inventors whose inventions had been utilized during the war: this sum was far more than any other industrialist received. 'Pioneers vary as much as any other individuals,' wrote Hugh Burroughes, his general manager, 'idealists, sheer adventurers, shrewd guessers: Holt Thomas came into the latter category, but it does not make him any less a pioneer' (Penrose, 3.23).

VINCENT ORANGE

Sources *The Aeroplane* (9 Jan 1929) · *Flight* (10 Jan 1929), 25 · *Journal of the Royal Aeronautical Society*, 33 (1929), 1190–1 · WWW · P. Fearon, 'Thomas, George Holt', *DBB* · H. Penrose, *British aviation: the pioneer years, 1903–1914* (1967) · H. Penrose, *British aviation: the Great War and armistice, 1915–1919* (1969) · H. Penrose, *British aviation: the adventuring years, 1920–1929* (1973) · C. M. Sharp, *DH: a history of De Havilland*, rev. edn (1982) · G. de Havilland, *Sky fever: the autobiography of Sir Geoffrey de Havilland* (1961) · J. M. Bruce, *The aeroplanes of the royal flying corps (military wing)* (1982) · W. Raleigh and H. A. Jones, *The war in the air*, 6 vols. (1922–37), vol. 1 · J. T. C. Moore-Brabazon, 'War machines v commercial machines', *War in the air*, ed. J. A. Hammerton (1936), 688–90 · W. J. Reader, *Architect of air power: the life of the first Viscount Weir of Eastwood* (1968) · P. King, *Knights of the air: the life and times of the extraordinary pioneers who first built British aeroplanes* (1989)

Archives NRA, priv. coll.

Likenesses photograph, repro. in *Flight and the Aircraft Engineer* (17 April 1919), 491 · photograph, repro. in Penrose, *British aviation:*

the adventuring years, 607 · photograph, repro. in Penrose, *British aviation: the Great War*, 353 · photograph, Royal Aeronautical Society, London [*see illus.*] · sketch, repro. in *The Aeroplane*

Wealth at death £29,000 10s. 1d.: administration with will, 24 April 1929, *CGPLA Eng. & Wales*

Thomas, George Housman (1824–1868), painter and wood-engraver, was born in London on 17 December 1824, the son of William Thomas, a shipbroker. He was educated at Mr Lord's school in Trowbridge, Wiltshire, and later served an apprenticeship under the wood-engraver George Bonnar. In 1839 the Society of Arts awarded him with a silver palette for *Please to Remember the Grotto*, an illustration of his depicting the commencement of the oyster season. He moved to Paris with his brother-in-law Henry Harrison, a fellow pupil of Bonnar's, to set up an engraving business which employed six or seven assistants. In 1846 he went to New York with Harrison and his brother, William Luson *Thomas (1830–1900), to work on illustrated newspapers, printing one *en route* for the amusement of those on the ship. In the two years he spent in the United States he also sketched the country's slave districts and designed vignettes for American banknotes.

On his brief return to England in 1848, due to ill health, Thomas began a long working association with the *Illustrated London News*. As an illustrator of newspapers he was an innovator: George and Edward Dalziel noted in their *The Brothers Dalziel: Record of Fifty Years' Work* (1901) that he was 'One of the first, if not the first, to draw on wood direct from life' (Dalziel and Dalziel, 41). He travelled to Rome later that year to draw the French siege of the city for the *Illustrated London News*. His ambition to be recognized as an artist of note led him to consider his visit to Italy as a source for future paintings. He returned to England in 1849 to marry Ellen Harrison and to begin painting from his Italian sketches. In 1851 he exhibited *St Anthony's Day in Rome* at the British Institution in London, which was followed by *Garibaldi at Rome, 1849*, shown at the Royal Academy in 1854. He gained the patronage of Queen Victoria, who had seen his work in the *Illustrated London News* and on exhibition at the Royal Academy. The first commission, *The Presentation of Crimean Medals by Queen Victoria, 18 May 1855* (exh. RA, 1858; Royal Collection), was called by the *Art Journal* 'one of the best of the modern ceremonial pictures we have ever seen' (20, 1858, 171). Other important commissions included *Queen Victoria and the Prince Consort at Aldershot* (exh. RA, 1866; Royal Collection) and *The Investiture of the Sultan with the Order of the Garter, 17 July 1867* (exh. RA, 1868; Royal Collection), as well as more intimate portrait drawings of the queen. He also painted many genre scenes such as *The Ghost Story* (exh. RA, 1866).

As an illustrator Thomas was prolific: as well as contributing to *Cassell's Magazine*, *The Quiver*, and *Cornhill Magazine*, he illustrated Harriet Beecher Stowe's *Uncle Tom's Cabin* in 1852 (from his American sketches), Oliver Goldsmith's *The Vicar of Wakefield* in 1857, and Wilkie Collins's *Armadale* in 1866—three of his best-known book illustrations. His influence on his brother William was immense and a very great number of illustrations by George were engraved by

William. After suffering some time from the consequences of a riding accident, he died on 21 July 1868 at Boulogne, France. He left nine children and a widow who was awarded a pension. He was a popular man of energy and humour, though his career was dogged by ill health. The *Illustrated London News* of 22 August 1868 observed his 'keen sense of humour' (177), and his brother William, in an *In Memoriam* volume of 1869 on George, wrote: 'to all who knew him, his character cannot fail to form a model on which to mould' (Thomas, *Drawings*, 15). A retrospective exhibition of his works was held at the German Gallery, Bond Street, London, in 1869.   MARK BILLS

Sources [W. L. Thomas], introduction, *One hundred of the best drawings by George Housman Thomas* (1869) · W. L. Thomas, 'The making of *The Graphic*', *Universal Review*, 2 (1888), 80–93 · 'Pictures and drawings by the late G. H. Thomas', *Art Journal*, 31 (1869), 183 · *Art Journal*, 16 (1854), 46–7, 171 · *Art Journal*, 20 (1858), 171 · *Art Journal*, 30 (1868), 181 · *ILN* (22 Aug 1868), 177–8 · *The Athenaeum* (1 Aug 1868) · *The Times* (30 July 1868), 10 · O. Millar, *The Victorian pictures in the collection of her majesty the queen*, 2 vols. (1992) · [G. Dalziel and E. Dalziel], *The brothers Dalziel: a record of fifty years' work ... 1840–1890* (1901) · G. White, *English illustration, 'the sixties': 1855–70* (1897) · F. Reid, *Illustrators of the sixties* (1928) · R. K. Engen, *Dictionary of Victorian wood engravers* (1985) · *DNB* · Bryan, *Painters* (1903–5) · *CGPLA Eng. & Wales* (1868)

Archives Royal Collection, corresp.

Likenesses wood-engraving, 1868 (after photograph by Cundall & Co.), repro. in *ILN* (22 Aug 1868), 177–8 · M. Jackson, woodcut, BM · wood-engraving (*Our artists, past and present*), BM, NPG; repro. in *ILN* (14 May 1892)

Wealth at death under £4000: administration, 21 Oct 1868, *CGPLA Eng. & Wales*

Thomas, Gerald Cyril (1920–1993), film director, was born on 10 December 1920 at 139 Coltman Street, Hull, the younger son of Samuel Thomas, a petroleum company's inspector, and his wife, Freda Cohen. Educated in Bristol, his subsequent medical studies were interrupted by war service in the Sussex regiment. After the war he went to Denham film studios; his brother, Ralph Thomas (1915–2001), was at that time making film trailers for the Rank Organization. He was soon working as an assistant editor on *The October Man* (1947) and Laurence Olivier's *Hamlet* (1948) and as an associate editor on Carol Reed's *The Third Man* (1949). He became full editor on *Tony Draws a Horse* (1950), and through the early 1950s worked on a number of films directed by his brother and produced by Betty E. Box, including *Appointment with Venus* (1951), *A Day to Remember* (1953), and *Doctor in the House* (1954). He also edited Walt Disney's *The Sword and the Rose* (1953). Thomas married Barbara Tarry, a fashion buyer, on 15 August 1957 at Caxton Hall register office, Chelsea. They had three daughters: Sarah, Deborah, and Samantha.

Box's husband, the writer and producer Peter Rogers, knowing Thomas wanted to direct, asked her to release him. Thereafter, their careers were to be inexorably linked, with Rogers producing all of Thomas's directorial output. His début was *Circus Friends* (1956), a Children's Film Foundation caper, which Rogers also wrote, followed by a good 'whodunnit', *The Vicious Circle*, the excellent suspenseful *Time Lock*, also scripted by Rogers from a television play by Arthur Hailey, and a pacy drama, *Chain of*

Events (all 1957). In 1958 he collaborated for the first time with the writer Norman Hudis, on *The Duke Wore Jeans*, a silly Tommy Steele musical from a story, and with songs, by Lionel Bart and Mike Pratt. In the same year he made *Carry on Sergeant*. Loosely based on R. F. Delderfield's play *The Bull Boys*, it was a farce about a platoon of incompetent national servicemen being knocked into shape by their sergeant (William Hartnell). Received dismissively at the time, chiefly for its cheerful vulgarity, it was quickly apparent that Thomas and Rogers 'had hit a rich seam of lowbrow British humour' (*The Times*, 11 Nov 1993), following a tradition stretching from music-hall, McGill postcards, and Max Miller. It was not intended as the first of a series, but public reaction made sequels inevitable. It had been scripted by Norman Hudis, and he wrote the next five *Carry Ons*—*Nurse*, *Teacher*, *Constable*, *Regardless*, and *Cruising* (1958–62)—which have a more naturalistic style. Writing duties were taken over by Talbot Rothwell for the next twenty, where *double entendres* increasingly ruled, from *Cabby* (1963) to *Dick* (1974). The success of the series centred on the teamwork of so many familiar faces: Kenneth Williams and Sidney James (the team's two most valuable players), Charles Hawtrey, Joan Sims, Kenneth Connor, Hattie Jacques, and others. Apparently never well paid, they were, however, guided by Thomas to become much-loved stars. They rewarded him with unvarying characterizations, which simply emphasized their individual comic styles, and with a respectful affection. Smut and innuendo and jokes about the body's parts and functions became mainstays of the scripts, with the humour becoming bluer and the puns worse as time went on. Within the series the four hospital-based films were particularly popular (brother Ralph was simultaneously responsible for the less broad, but equally successful *Doctor* series of films), but historical send-ups, including *Jack* (1964, covering the Napoleonic wars), *Don't Lose your Head* (1967, about the French Revolution), and *Up the Khyber* (1968, portraying the British empire on the north-west frontier), were also a staple. Better *Carry On* entries included *Cleo* (1964), *Cowboy* (1965), *Screaming!* (1966), and *Doctor* and *Up the Khyber* (both 1968). 'The dinner-party sequence at the end of the last is superbly orchestrated [the band of the 3rd Foot and Mouth regiment plays on as the Governor's residence collapses under bombardment] and the best individual scene in any of them' (Quinlan). By the 1970s, however, following the permissiveness ushered in apace by the 1960s, the formula seemed too mechanical and somewhat dated; some of the entries were simply poor and they 'sputtered out' with *Emmannuelle* (1978). A revival, *Columbus* (1992), was not successful. Rogers considered that 'the title was always the star of the films and then came the script. A director couldn't go wrong!' Thomas perhaps only had to man the helm, but he did 'contribute to one of the most durable and pleasurable mythologies in British cinema' (*The Independent*, 13 Nov 1993). Through the 1960s they had also made a major financial contribution and in mid-decade at last enjoyed a certain critical acclaim.

None of Thomas's other films, all comedies, is of particular note. They include *Please Turn over* (1959), scripted by Hudis, *Watch your Stern* (1960), *Raising the Wind* (1961), *Twice Round the Daffodils* (1962) and *Nurse on Wheels* (1963), both also scripted by Hudis, and *The Big Job* (1965), scripted by Rothwell. In a style not too dissimilar from the *Carry Ons*, they also often starred one or more of the principals from the series. In 1972 he directed the film version of Sid James's popular television series *Bless this House*. In 1990 Thomas and Rogers received lifetime achievement awards for film comedy. Thomas died on 9 November 1993 at his home, 16 Burnham Avenue, Beaconsfield, of coronary thrombosis. His wife and daughters survived him.

ROBERT SHARP

Sources *The Times* (11 Nov 1993), 21 · *The Independent* (13 Nov 1993) · *The Guardian* (11 Nov 1993), 17 · *Daily Telegraph* (11 Nov 1993) · D. Quinlan, *The illustrated guide to film directors* (1983) · www.uk. imdb.com, 25 July 2001 · private information (2004) · b. cert. · d. cert. · *CGPLA Eng. & Wales* (1994)
Likenesses photograph, 1973–7, repro. in Quinlan, *Illustrated guide*, 293
Wealth at death £280,091: probate, 1994, *CGPLA Eng. & Wales*

Thomas, Gwyn (1913–1981), novelist and playwright, was born on 6 July 1913 at 196 High Street, Cymmer, Porth, Rhondda, the last of the eight sons and the youngest of the twelve children of Walter Morgan Thomas (*b.* 1871), colliery ostler, and his wife, Ziphorah Davies (1875–1919), who died when Gwyn was six. The twenty years that followed gave him the material which he worked for the rest of his life into a black comic epic of universal resonance. This early period was one of immense significance in the history of twentieth-century Wales as the populous southern coalfield plunged from relative prosperity to complete economic disaster. He viewed this from the perspective of a small house crammed with highly gifted siblings, all neglected by their sociable father but pulled into a semblance of order by their surrogate mother, their nineteen-year-old sister Hannah (Nana), who put her own life on hold for sixteen years until the family she had inherited went out into the worlds of teaching, medicine, opera, and (in Gwyn's dazzling case) literature.

Long-standing respect for and support of education— and a house full of the books his dreamy father bought before any material necessities—ensured Thomas enjoyed first-rate teaching at the Porth county school, from which in 1931 he proceeded to St Edmund Hall, Oxford, to read modern languages. It was the wrong university, the wrong college, and the wrong time for this young, left-wing Welsh neurotic who found the English upper classes as alien as they were tall. He fared better for six months in 1933 at the University of Madrid on a miners' union grant, but, despite a very good second-class degree in 1934, the Oxford years were unhappy. Now, home again but persistently ill with a thyroid condition which eventually required surgery, he faced unemployment, sporadic classes for the Workers' Educational Association, and bouts of political activism based around the gargantuan anti-means-test marches of 1935 and 1936.

At this time Thomas met his life-partner: Eiluned (Lyn)

Thomas (1911/12–1990), daughter of a collier. She was employed as a typist by the local Unemployment Assistance Board, so an acknowledged marriage would have meant forfeiting her own job; their marriage, on 5 January 1938, was therefore secret. They remained together, childless by choice, until Gwyn's death. On the surface their life was relatively uneventful. After a short period of employment as an educational officer with the National Council of Social Service in the north-west of England, including a year's residence in Manchester in 1939, Thomas was declared unfit for war service and so began a career as a teacher of Spanish and French: at Cardigan grammar school from 1940 to 1942, and then from 1942 until early retirement in 1962 as head of Spanish at the Barry County School for Boys.

Thomas did not publish anything until after the war, when Lyn speculatively sent the work out to publishers. However, in 1937 he had written a naturalistic novel of working-class life for a competition organized by Gollancz. It was rejected as too 'searing' and remained in a drawer until an edited version appeared under its original title, *Sorrow for thy Sons*, in 1986. The Thomas the world first read in the late 1940s had spent the intervening decade discovering and perfecting a style, now oblique and ironic, to fit his main subject. This remained the condition of the working class in south Wales, both as a historical theme and within a contemporary experience, but, crucially, also as a study in human morality. He had become, via a prose style modelled on Dashiell Hammett and Damon Runyon, not so much the chronicler of 'American Wales', of the detail of his country's urban and industrial life, as its distilled vocal essence. His underlying theme was the gap between reasonable individual aspiration and socially enforced, humanly unacceptable settlement.

What disturbed and enthralled Thomas's readers was that the stuff of gritty realism and documentary melodrama was being shifted by hyperbolic wit and cascades of metaphor into a completely different mode: murderously savage in intent and relentlessly conscious that self-aware laughter is the only way the joker ever manages to be the judge. The core of his reputation in the novel will be sustained by *Where did I Put my Pity?* (a collection which contains the superb novella 'Oscar'), *The Dark Philosophers* (1946), *The Alone to the Alone* (1947), and *All Things Betray Thee* (1949)—books which looked back from the stirrings of the welfare state to the conditions and consciousness which had given it birth.

In the 1950s Thomas found a different level of fame as the satirical humorist became more genial in *The World Cannot Hear You* (1951), *Now Lead Us Home* (1952), and *A Frost on my Frolic* (1953). He began to write regularly for *Punch*—three volumes of short stories and one of essays punctuated the years, along with a later autobiography, *A Few Selected Exits*, in 1968—and to appear as a pundit on radio and television, notably on *The Brains Trust*. By this time he had, by dint of an extraordinary comic eloquence in the media, become, to all intents and purposes, a 'personality' both inside and outside Wales. His last novel was his tenth, *The Love Man* (1958), based on the Don Juan story. By

then his literary attention had been diverted fully to the theatre—there had been a number of successful radio plays in the 1950s—and settled there after the critical success of his first and best stage play, *The Keep*, in a London production at the Royal Court in 1962. He left schoolteaching for full-time television work as a scriptwriter and presenter.

Thomas's later literary production—notably five more works for the theatre, two of them ambitious music-plays, from 1962 to 1979—had a mixed reception. His outspoken anti-nationalist views made him a controversial figure in the new Wales that was emerging. Friends, entranced by conversation that deserved a latter-day Boswell, championed his cause but lamented the increasingly severe ill health, the result of a neglected diabetic condition, which led to his death on 13 April 1981 in the University Hospital of Wales, Cardiff.

Since his death there has been a deepening critical interest in Gwyn Thomas's work with the republication and, indeed, first publication of his novels and plays in both Welsh and English. His biography was published in 1992, and in 1993 *Selected Exits*, an award-winning screenplay by Alan Plater, was televised on the BBC, starring Anthony Hopkins as Gwyn Thomas. For anyone in the twenty-first century wishing to feel the pulse of the social powerhouse of twentieth-century Wales, Gwyn Thomas's writing will be the first port of call.   DAI SMITH

Sources M. Parnell, *Laughter from the dark: a life of Gwyn Thomas* (1988) · *The Times* (18 April 1981) · I. Michael, *Gwyn Thomas* (1977) · D. Smith, *Aneurin Bevan and the world of south Wales* (1993) · D. Smith, *Writer's world: Gwyn Thomas* (1986) · D. Smith, *Wales: a question for history* (1999) · private information (2004) · personal knowledge (2004) · CGPLA Eng. & Wales (1981) · d. cert. · b. cert.
Archives NL Wales, literary MSS and papers · NL Wales, notebook · U. Wales, Swansea, South Wales Miners' Library, papers and books
Likenesses R. Thomas, bronze bust, 1983, New Theatre, Cardiff · photographs, repro. in Smith, *Writer's world*
Wealth at death £19,458: probate, 19 May 1981, CGPLA Eng. & Wales

Thomas [*née* Noble], **Helen Berenice** (1877–1967), autobiographer, was born at 13 Moscow Drive, West Derby, Lancashire, on 11 July 1877, the second of three daughters of James Ashcroft Noble (1844–1896), a journalist and literary critic, and his wife, Esther Margaret, *née* Lunt (d. 1907). Helen Noble when growing up felt overshadowed by her two sisters, considering both of them more beautiful and intelligent than herself. Her relationship with her mother was often strained, particularly as Helen began to question the Victorian social and sexual mores that she found restricting, but she had a close and affectionate relationship with her father. At sixteen she left school in Wimbledon to help her mother at home and to nurse her father who had become fatally ill.

She is best-known for her perceptive and honest portrayal of her life with the poet (Philip) Edward *Thomas (1878–1917), in *As it Was* (1926) and *World without End* (1931), reissued with additional material edited by her daughter Myfanwy Thomas as *Under Storm's Wing* (1988). She first met Thomas through his friendship with her father, who acted as mentor to the aspiring young writer. In spite of her mother's dislike of Thomas, and disapproval of their relationship, Helen continued their friendship, soon to become love. After her father's death she left home to work as a nanny and corresponded secretly with Thomas. A mutually passionate response to nature drew them together, and much of their early courtship involved walks through 20 or 30 miles of English countryside. Helen did not consider herself attractive, but photographs show her to have been physically striking, tall with dark hair and strong features, although short-sightedness meant that she had to wear glasses. Her account of this period focuses on her strong sensuous appreciation of nature and of her own body. Influenced by her reading of the Romantic poets, particularly Shelley, as well as contemporaries such as William Morris, she espoused freedom from social and sexual convention, and openness and equality between men and women.

Helen became Thomas's lover, agreeing to marry (on 20 June 1899) only on the advice of friends when she became pregnant with their first child. Her autobiographical reflections on this period of her life are remarkably frank about her relationship with Thomas and about her responses to her sexuality and pregnancy. Her candour is equally evident in the exchanges of letters between them and that allowed her to write movingly, without any hint of sentimentality, of her last hours with him before he left to fight in France in 1917.

Helen's life with Thomas was a continual struggle with poverty and with his bouts of extreme depression when he directed his bitterness and anger towards her. In spite of bleak periods, her writing shows an unfailingly joyful response to her life as wife and mother, revealing her unwavering loyalty to Thomas and her pleasure in caring for a home and giving birth to and raising her three children. 'I have embraced every aspect of my life passionately' she affirmed in the conclusion of *World without End*.

Helen Thomas's autobiographical accounts were written, her daughter asserts, as a form of therapy in the aftermath of her husband's death at Arras on 9 April 1917, which prompted a severe breakdown in the early 1920s. Her writing reflects a finely tuned awareness of her physical environment and a capacity for expressing her acute physical and emotional responses to experience. She can move from the delightfully witty 'the cows going into their stalls like people going into their pews in church' to the sharply poignant memory of Thomas's departure for the front: 'Then with leaden feet which stumbled in a sudden darkness that overwhelmed me I groped my way back to the empty house' (*World without End* in *Under Storm's Wing*, 173). In choosing to end *World without End* there, rather than with Thomas's death, she captures very poignantly how, for the women of her generation, the man's departure to the front evoked the same depth of grief and despair as the death itself. Her account of this experience has brought her to the attention of historians and literary critics writing on women's experiences in the First World War, but Helen Thomas's autobiographies, as well as letters later available in print and on-line, also reveal her exceptional ability to describe the woman's experience as lover, mother, and housewife. It is ironic, but she would have considered it fitting, that her ability as a writer is revealed in her attempt to promote her husband's work, rather than her own. She died at her home—Bridge Cottage, Eastbury, Berkshire—on 12 April 1967.

CAROL ACTON

Sources H. Thomas, *Under storm's wing*, ed. M. Thomas (1988) · R. G. Thomas, *Edward Thomas: a portrait* (1985) · J. Marsh, *Edward Thomas: a poet for his country* (1978) · M. Thomas, *One of these fine days* (1982) · W. R. Evans, 'Robert Frost and Helen Thomas: five revealing letters [2 pts]', www.dartmouth.edu/ · b. cert. · d. cert.
Archives Dartmouth College Library, Hanover, New Hampshire, Robert Frost collection
Likenesses photograph, 1899, University College, Cardiff · group portrait, 1907, University College, Cardiff
Wealth at death £2017: probate, 19 May 1967, *CGPLA Eng. & Wales*

Thomas, Sir Henry (1878–1952), Hispanic scholar and bibliographer, was born at Eynsham, near Oxford, on 21 November 1878, the third child and second son of Alfred Charles Thomas, minister of the local Irvingite congregation, and his wife, Hannah Friday. The Thomas family derived from Coventry, where its members had long been silk-weavers. After his parents moved to Birmingham, Thomas attended a church school. He then entered King Edward VI Grammar School, Aston, where he soon distinguished himself and as head boy matriculated at Mason College, later the University of Birmingham. There he did brilliantly in the classical languages, French, and English philology, becoming research scholar in classics and Constance Naden memorial gold medallist.

In October 1903 Thomas entered the British Museum as assistant in the department of printed books. Soon afterwards he began to learn Spanish in order to work on the extensive collection of Cervantes material, and by 1910 he was already well known as a Spanish scholar. Iberian studies remained his chief interest and brought him many honours; he was an honorary councillor of the Spanish Higher Council for Scientific Research, a member of the Spanish and Luso-Brazilian councils, and president of the Anglo-Spanish Society (1931–47). A monograph, *Spanish and Portuguese Romances of Chivalry* (1920), expanded from his Norman MacColl lectures at Cambridge in 1917, brought Thomas the Bonsoms prize and gold medal of the Institut d'Estudis Catalans in 1921, and in 1922 he delivered the Taylorian lecture at Oxford entitled 'Shakespeare and Spain'. His *Spanish Sixteenth-Century Printing* (1926) was translated into German (1928). For the Bibliographical Society of London, of which he was president (1936–8), he wrote a monograph, *Early Spanish Bookbindings, XI–XV Centuries*, with plates from his own photographs (1939), and a paper, 'Copperplate engravings in early Spanish books' (1940). He produced an edition (1923) and a verse translation (1935) of the anonymous drama *La estrella de Sevilla* (2nd edns, 1930 and 1950) and a verse translation of J. E. Hartzenbusch's *Los amantes de Teruel* (1938; 2nd edn, 1950), doing much of his translation while commuting from his home in Clapham Junction to the museum each day.

Thomas's vacations were usually passed in Spain, where

he had many friends. Retracing on foot the medieval pilgrim way to the shrine of Santiago de Compostela, he corrected certain errors in the accepted itinerary, and he gave a humorous account of a miracle story current among the medieval pilgrims in *Monster and Miracle* (privately printed, 1935); a Catalan translation appeared in 1942, and he himself did a Spanish version in 1946. When after the Spanish Civil War and the Second World War he was able to revisit Spain, Thomas worked hard to improve Anglo-Spanish relations. He broadcast several times in *La voz de Londres*. In 1947 he was the guest of the Spanish government at the Cervantes quatercentenary celebrations.

At the British Museum, Thomas was responsible for the *Short-title catalogue of books printed in Spain and of Spanish books printed elsewhere in Europe before 1601 now in the British Museum* (1921). This volume set out the bibliographical essentials concerning at least 2500 books, and Thomas worked out a very successful scheme for keeping the entries as succinct as was compatible with accuracy. He applied the same method, still within the compass of a single volume, to the museum's 12,000 French books printed before 1601 (1924) and later to the Portuguese (1940) and Spanish-American books (1944). When in 1936 the museum acquired the manuscript of an unknown Portuguese account of the discovery of Abyssinia, Thomas contributed to the officially published edition of this an introduction, an English translation, and notes (1938). Thomas became deputy keeper in the department of printed books in 1924 and principal keeper in 1943, when it fell to him to deal with the problems of post-war reconstruction, and the exertion in this task adversely affected his health. In December 1944 he accompanied the director of the museum to the United States and Canada on a three-month official visit for study of recent library design and organization.

Thomas was knighted in 1946. He was DLitt and honorary LLD of Birmingham University and DLitt of London University, and became a fellow of the British Academy in 1936. Numerous Spanish, Portuguese, and South American learned societies elected him honorary or corresponding member.

Thomas had many subsidiary interests. A skilful photographer, he collected railway photographs, and was long a member of the Oxford and Cambridge Musical Club. He read a paper, 'Musical settings of Horace's lyric poems', before the Musical Association in 1920. A person of unconditional integrity and devotion to duty, his very quiet manner was the cover both for great kindness and generosity and for great determination, and he was the most loyal of friends. Thomas had much dry humour and could on occasion be a great talker. He never married but was devoted to his family at Birmingham. He retired in 1947 and immediately resumed the Spanish studies which other occupations had made him put aside, but his health, which had at all times given him trouble, was now manifestly failing, and in the autumn of 1950 he had a seizure. He also suffered greatly from a skin disease. Thomas died at the Skin Hospital, John Bright Street, Birmingham, on 21 July 1952.   VICTOR SCHOLDERER, *rev.*

Sources V. Scholderer, 'Henry Thomas, 1878–1952', *PBA*, 40 (1954), 241–6 · S. Morison, *PBA*, 40 (1954), 246–51 · *The Times* (23 July 1952) · *WWW* · personal knowledge (1971) · private information (1971) · *CGPLA Eng. & Wales* (1952)
Likenesses J. Russell & Sons, photograph, 1938, repro. in Scholderer, 'Henry Thomas', facing p. 241 · W. Stoneman, two photographs, 1938–48, NPG
Wealth at death £30,010 8s. 0d.: probate, 20 Nov 1952, *CGPLA Eng. & Wales*

Thomas, Herbert Henry (1876–1935), geologist, was born on 13 March 1876 at Exeter, the younger son of Frederick Thomas and his wife, Louisa (*née* Pickford). He began his early education at Exeter School and in 1894 went to Sidney Sussex College, Cambridge, as an exhibitioner, later becoming a scholar. He obtained a first class in both parts of the natural science tripos in 1897–8, and won the Harkness university scholarship in geology.

After graduating Thomas acted as assistant to the professor of geology at Oxford, William Sollas (1849–1936), and joined Balliol College, taking an Oxford BA in 1898 (MA, 1904), and BSc in 1906 (ScD, 1914). He was elected a fellow of the Geological Society in 1898, proposed by Sollas and supported by a pantheon of late-Victorian geologists; he gained the society's Wollaston fund in 1908. A pioneering investigation (1902, 1909) of the detrital minerals of the New Red Sandstone of the west of England revealed the palaeogeography of Triassic times, and it won for Thomas the Sedgwick essay prize of Cambridge University in 1904. Also in that year he married Anna Maria, eldest daughter of Oswald Henry Mosley, rector of Wentworth, Isle of Ely, Cambridgeshire. They later had a son and a daughter.

In 1901 Thomas was appointed geologist to the Geological Survey of Great Britain and found there a career for which he was eminently fitted. He was to make major contributions in three related fields of geology: Welsh petrology, Scottish Tertiary vulcanology, and petrological archaeology (notably as it related to Stonehenge). Thomas worked in the south Wales coalfield and westwards to the Precambrian rocks of Pembrokeshire where he described several new rock types in a classic paper on the volcanic rocks of Skomer Island. With D. A. MacAlister he wrote *The Geology of Ore Deposits* (1909).

Thomas was promoted to petrographer to the survey in 1911 and he took part during the First World War in the preparation of reports on mineral resources, including refractory materials. He also reported on other scientific matters, among them the possible use of the piezo-electric properties of quartz for the detection of submarines, and he verified that the aggregate used in German bunkers near Ypres had been transported through Dutch canals, which violated that country's status as a neutral.

After the war Thomas bore a large share of the investigations of the Tertiary igneous rocks of Mull (published in 1924), Staffa and Iona (1925), and Ardnamurchan (1930), topics to which he devoted his presidential address to the geology section of the British Association in 1927. He took considerable interest in archaeology, being frequently called upon to identify rocks and their provenance. In

1923 he identified the 'bluestones' of Stonehenge as having come from the Preseli Mountains of Pembrokeshire, an area that he knew well. His last purely petrographical paper in 1932 (written jointly) dealt with hybridized granitic rocks in Brittany.

Thomas became much occupied with the move of the Geological Survey and Museum in 1935 from Jermyn Street, central London, to South Kensington. He served the Geological Society as secretary for ten years (1912–22) and as vice-president (1922–4); he received the Murchison medal in 1925.

Thomas was an elegant and charming man who had a genial manner that attracted a large circle of devoted friends. He was an ardent fisherman and had excellent artistic talents that he used for sketches of geology and rock thin-sections in his papers. He was elected a fellow of the Royal Society in 1927 and was a member of its council when, on 12 May 1935, he collapsed alighting from a train at Waterloo Station, London, and died *en route* to hospital. His wife survived him.   PETER A. SABINE

Sources DNB · A. Harker, Obits. FRS, 1 (1932–5), 590–94 · B. Smith, Quarterly Journal of the Geological Society of London, 92 (1936), cxv–cxx · WWW · Nature, 136 (1935), 95 · Mineralogical Magazine, 24 (1935–7), 302–3 · private information (2004)
Archives BGS, corresp.
Likenesses photograph, repro. in Obits. FRS
Wealth at death £3236 18s. 10d.: probate, 3 July 1935, CGPLA Eng. & Wales

Thomas, Herbert John (1892–1947), aircraft and aero-engine manufacturer, was born at Fulham, London, on 20 February 1892, the son of Samuel Herbert Thomas, a commercial traveller, and his wife, Victoria Morgan. His education began in London, but when he was fourteen he entered Clifton College, Bristol, which he left in 1909. He took up flying immediately, in balloons and aeroplanes, obtained the Royal Aero Club pilot's certificate no. 51 in 1910, and for a while tested and raced the new Bristol Boxkite.

As the youngest nephew of the millionaire Bristol tramways entrepreneur, Sir George White, Thomas was soon involved in the business of the Bristol and Colonial Aeroplane Company, one of four founded simultaneously by White. At eighteen Thomas was sent to Paris to examine the designs and methods of the Société Zodiac. He brought back a sample machine from which five copies were made under licence, but as they would not fly the deal was cancelled, with Zodiac paying a penalty of 15,000 Fr. However, all was not lost, as a British empire licence was negotiated for the new 50 hp Gnome engine. Soon French technicians and pilots were crossing the channel to help design Bristol aircraft and to instruct in the company's new school at Larkhill, Salisbury Plain. By 1913, the company's 1910 capital of £50,000 had risen to £250,000 and it would be valued at £553,000 in 1919. By the start of the First World War, Thomas was the works manager at Filton, near Bristol. Like almost all British manufacturers early in the war he had great difficulty in retaining skilled labour, but in August 1916 the company's facilities were declared a 'controlled establishment' concurrently with

the introduction of conscription; by 1918 the workforce numbered five thousand. In 1912 Thomas suffered a near-fatal head injury when the propeller flew off one of the company's new aircraft while the engine was being ground-tested.

By 1916, Thomas was a director of the company. In 1919, when RAF orders for the famous Bristol Fighter (the Brisfit) were cancelled, Thomas used his energy and imagination to keep the works alive with a nucleus of about two hundred workers. On the first day of May, when civil aviation became legal, he flew to Hounslow, near to the modern Heathrow, in a modified Brisfit known as the Tourer to meet with General J. E. B. Seely, the new under-secretary of state for air, to whom he shortly sold the aircraft. Thomas soon had contracts from Armstrong-Siddeley for automobile bodies and from the parent Bristol Tramways for both tram and omnibus bodies.

In 1920 Thomas married Vera Beatrice, daughter of Stephen Codrington, a veterinary surgeon; they had two sons. Also in 1920, the Treasury's demand for the payment of the wartime excess profits duty led to the dissolution of the Bristol and Colonial Aeroplane Company, among many others, and the transfer of its £553,000 of assets to the new Bristol Aeroplane Company, capitalized at £1 million with the same board and employees, but with the addition of Roy Fedden and his Cosmos Engineering Company. Fedden's engines, enormously successful, were licensed in France and other countries. He personally profited immensely from the agreed royalties, but the Bristol board never accepted him as an equal, and for this Thomas must bear some of the responsibility even though he and Fedden were good friends.

During the Second World War, Thomas was the assistant managing director, largely connected with the works management in the production of over 11,000 Blenheims and Beaufighters, as well as Beauforts and well over 100,000 engines. He also saved the second Bulldog fighter demonstrator (1930–35) from the scrapheap and donated it to the Science Museum, London.

A reserved man, like so many British businessmen, Thomas was credited with grace and charm. Not much of a public figure, he was a long-standing member of the Society of British Aircraft Constructors and its chairman in 1933–5. Late in life he became sheriff of Bristol (1946) only to die from cancer on 20 May 1947 following surgery at Frenchay Park Hospital, Bristol. He was survived by his wife. His home was at Old Farm, Sodbury, Gloucestershire.   ROBIN HIGHAM

Sources WWW · R. Higham, 'Thomas, Herbert John', DBB · C. H. Barnes, Bristol aircraft since 1910 (1964) · Western Daily Press (21 May 1947) · Bristol Evening Post (21 May 1947) · d. cert. · Western Daily Press (21 May 1947), 4a · CGPLA Eng. & Wales (1947)
Likenesses group photograph, repro. in Journal of Royal Aeronautical Society (1966), 158 [centenary issue]
Wealth at death £103,368 4s. 10d.: probate, 1 Dec 1947, CGPLA Eng. & Wales

Thomas, Herbert Samuel [Bert] (1883–1966), cartoonist and illustrator, was born in Rodney Wharf, Christchurch,

Herbert Samuel Thomas (1883–1966), by unknown artist, 1913

Newport, Monmouthshire, on 13 October 1883, the youngest of seven surviving children of Job Thomas (1822–1890), a Welsh monumental sculptor and mason who had helped decorate the houses of parliament. His mother was Mary Beeche (otherwise Beechey) Comley (1843–1888), a relative of the portrait painter Sir William *Beechey RA. One of his brothers was the sculptor Ivor Thomas (1873–1913). Soon after Thomas's birth the family moved to Swansea, and, following the death of both his parents by the time he was eight, he was brought up by relatives. After a brief spell at school he was apprenticed in 1897, aged fourteen, to an engraver in Swansea, etching names on brass doorplates and monograms for cutlery and so on.

In his spare time Thomas drew caricatures of personalities at Swansea council sessions and music-halls, and was soon selling these to local papers such as the *Swansea Daily Leader*. In 1900, the famous music-hall comedian, singer, and actor Albert Chevalier (whose songs included 'My Old Dutch') commissioned him to design a poster featuring all his stage characterizations. In the same year a local doctor showed some of his work to Sir George Newnes, MP for Swansea (1900–10) and founder of the *Strand Magazine*, who published some of his drawings. Thomas then moved briefly to London (1900–01), where he met and was encouraged by the cartoonist and illustrator Tom Browne, but failed to make a living and so returned to Wales. In 1903, on Chevalier's recommendation, he got a job working for a London advertising agency and also began freelancing

for *Pick-Me-Up* and *Ally Sloper's Half Holiday*. In 1905 he began an association with *Punch* that lasted until 1948, resulting in more than 1000 cartoons, and in 1909 he became a staff artist on *London Opinion* until it folded in 1954, contributing political and social cartoons. In addition he drew for *The Humorist*, *Men Only*, *The Sketch*, *Passing Show*, *Radio Times*, *The Bystander*, *Fun*, *The Graphic*, and *The World*, and his work was reproduced in the USA in *Life*, *Judge*, and the *New York Times*.

On 7 October 1909 Thomas married Elizabeth Florette Bowen (1887/8–1949) and they had four sons (one of whom, Peter, also drew cartoons for *Punch*) and two daughters. During the First World War he served as a private in the Artists' Rifles (1916–18) and from March 1918 was official artist for the government's war bonds campaign, producing for it Britain's largest poster, a 75 foot long, 30 foot high colour oil painting of Sir Francis Drake facing the Spanish Armada, which covered the front of the National Gallery (1918). He also produced posters for the Royal Exchange, London, and in Cardiff and Manchester. Bert Thomas is perhaps best known for his cartoon 'Arf a mo', Kaiser!' featuring a grinning cockney Tommy lighting a pipe before engaging the enemy. Described as 'the funniest picture of the war' (*Daily Mail*), it was sketched (supposedly in ten minutes) for the *Weekly Dispatch* and published on 11 November 1914, as part of the paper's tobacco-for-troops fund. It raised more than £250,000 for the fund; for this, together with other contributions to the war effort, Thomas was made MBE in June 1918. After the war he also drew regularly for *The Sketch*, illustrated the popular 'Cockney war stories' letters column for the *Evening News* (a collection of which was published in 1930), produced advertisements for Oxo, Player's Navy Cut cigarettes and others, designed postcards, and illustrated a number of books. His own publications included *In Red and Black* (1928), *Fun at the Seaside* (1944), and *Railways by Night* (1947). In the Second World War he also drew regular political cartoons for the *Evening News* and produced a number of memorable posters (such as *Is your Journey Really Necessary?* for the Railway Executive Committee, 1942). In addition he was on the advisory staff of the Press Art School from 1919 and his own supplementary course was later published as *Cartoons and Character Drawing* (1936).

After the death of his first wife in 1949 Thomas married Florence Olive (Fay) Currie (1898/9–1987), the widow of his accountant, on 28 April 1950 and moved from Chelsea to Bayswater. He was a member of the Savage Club, the Chelsea Arts Club, the London Sketch Club, the Pastel Society, and the *Punch* table. Examples of his work are held in the prints and drawings department of the British Museum, the Victoria and Albert Museum, the National Portrait Gallery, the Imperial War Museum, and the University of Kent Cartoon Centre. Thomas disliked using models or on-the-spot sketches and usually worked standing up: his style was spontaneous and his choice of subjects eclectic. An admirer of Henry Ospovat, Phil May, and Steinlen, he was greatly influenced by the German *Simplicissimus* artist

Eduard Thöny and even named his third son Philip (An)thony after him.

In appearance Thomas was about 5 foot 6 inches tall, with brown eyes and short black hair. Described as 'stocky and short, and as friendly as a Toby jug' (*The Times*) he usually wore check trousers. He collected fine antique oak furniture and was a keen golfer, roughshooter, and horseman who rode to hounds regularly (until he broke his collarbone aged fifty) and kept horses at his 300-year-old house in Pinner. Bert Thomas died of a stroke at his home, 33 Inverness Terrace, Bayswater, London, on 6 September 1966. He was buried in Kensal Green cemetery, London.

MARK BRYANT

Sources private information (2004) [family] · M. Bryant, *Dictionary of twentieth-century British cartoonists and caricaturists* (2000) · M. Bryant and S. Heneage, eds., *Dictionary of British cartoonists and caricaturists, 1730–1980* (1994) · D. Hill, *Cartoons and caricatures by Bert Thomas* (1965–74) [exhibition catalogues] · H. Shaw, 'Bert Thomas and his work', *The Strand* (Feb 1929), 130–38 · P. V. Bradshaw, *Bert Thomas and his work* (1918) · *Who's who in art* (1929) · *WW* · b. cert. · m. certs. · d. cert. · *The Times* (7 Sept 1966)

Archives priv. coll. | SOUND BBC Radio, 'Desert island discs', 'In town tonight'

Likenesses oils, 1913, NPG [*see illus.*] · H. Leslie, silhouette, *c.*1928–1930, NPG · H. L. Oakley, silhouette, 1937, NPG · B. Park, photograph, repro. in Bradshaw, *Bert Thomas*, 2 · H. S. Thomas, self-portrait, caricature, repro. in B. Thomas and W. Williams, *One hundred war cartoons* (1919), ii · photograph, repro. in P. V. Bradshaw, 'They make us smile', *London Opinion* (March 1940), 30 · photograph, repro. in *Drawing and Design*, new ser., 4 (1923), 490

Thomas, Honoratus Leigh (1769–1846), surgeon, the son of John Thomas of Hawarden, Flintshire, and his wife, Maria, sister of John Boydell, was born on 26 March 1769. On arriving in London as a young man he presented a letter of introduction to the eminent surgeon John Hunter. Hunter made an appointment with Thomas for 5 a.m. the following morning, at which time Thomas found Hunter busily engaged dissecting insects. Thomas was appointed dresser to Hunter at St George's Hospital and he also became a pupil of the anatomist William Cumberland *Cruikshank (1745–1800). He obtained the diploma of the Company of Surgeons on 16 October 1794, was an original member of the Royal College of Surgeons on its incorporation in 1800, and was elected to the fellowship on its foundation in 1843.

Thomas's early professional work was in the army and navy. He passed as first mate, third rate (navy), on 5 July 1792, and, on the recommendation of Hunter, was appointed assistant surgeon to Lord Macartney's embassy to China in the same year. In 1799 he volunteered for medical service with the duke of York's army in the Netherlands. On the surrender of the forces to the French enemy Thomas wished to remain with the wounded, who could not be moved. He was told that he could only stay as a prisoner, and he decided to remain in that capacity. As soon as his services could be dispensed with, however, he was allowed to return home.

On 10 September 1795 Thomas had married Cruikshank's elder daughter; Edward *Thomas (1813–1886) was their son. In 1800 Thomas succeeded to his father-in-law's practice in Leicester Place, where he afterwards lived for

nearly fifty years. Notwithstanding his position at the Royal College of Surgeons, Thomas seems rather to have avoided surgery and was generally called in for consultation in medical cases. According to J. F. Clarke, Thomas was a poor surgeon but was a shrewd practitioner in medical cases, to which his practice was mainly limited. He also wrote that 'personally he was the beau ideal of a physician' and that 'he had a very extensive practice among licensed victuallers' (Cope, 58).

At the Royal College of Surgeons, Thomas was a member of the court of assistants from 1818 to 1845, examiner from 1818 to 1845, vice-president in 1827, 1828, 1836, and 1837, and president in 1829 and 1838. In 1827 he delivered the Hunterian oration. In this oration there are some interesting personal reminiscences of Hunter. Thomas was elected a fellow of the Royal Society on 16 January 1806. He was also a member of the Imperial Academy of St Petersburg. In addition to his Hunterian oration he published 'Description of an hermaphrodite lamb' (*London Medical and Physical Journal*, 1799), 'Anatomical description of a male rhinoceros' (*PTRS*, 1801), 'Case of artificial dilatation of the female urethra' (*Medico-Chirurgical Transactions*, 1809), and 'Case of obstruction in the large intestines occasioned by a biliary calculus of extraordinary size' (ibid., 1845). Thomas died at Belmont, Torquay, on 26 June 1846.

J. B. BAILEY, rev. MICHAEL BEVAN

Sources *The Lancet* (4 July 1846), 26 · *Abstracts of the Papers Communicated to the Royal Society of London*, 5 (1843–50), 640 · J. F. Clarke, *Autobiographical recollections of the medical profession* (1874), 113 · private information (2004) [Mrs Foss and F. L. Hutchins, grandchildren] · Z. Cope, *The Royal College of Surgeons of England: a history* (1959) · *GM*, 1st ser., 65 (1795), 790

Likenesses J. Green, oils, RCS Eng.

Thomas, Howard (1909–1986), broadcaster and film and television impresario, was born on 5 March 1909 in Cwm, Monmouthshire, the second son and third and youngest child of William George Thomas, stationer and postmaster, and his wife, Alice Maud Stephens. The family left south Wales when Thomas was eleven and moved to Beswick, Manchester. He went to local schools until he was old enough to start work.

Thomas took evening classes in advertising and qualified as a copywriter, which led him to a small but aggressive Manchester advertising agency run by F. John Roe, where he developed the enterprise and showmanship on which he was to draw for the rest of his career. He moved to London in 1934 and in that year married Hilda, daughter of Harrison Fogg, a Manchester journalist; they had two daughters. In 1937 he joined London Press Exchange and obtained his first BBC commission. He set up the commercial radio department of London Press Exchange in 1938, writing and producing most of its programmes himself, and also became one of BBC radio's highest paid freelance scriptwriters.

Rejected for military service in 1940 because of his defective eyesight, Thomas was offered a BBC staff position and in the next three years produced over 500 programmes, among them two of the most notable of the war years. *Sincerely yours* established Vera Lynn as a musical link between servicemen and their partners back home and made her a star to be remembered ever afterwards as the forces' sweetheart. In *The Brains Trust*, a panel of experts answered listeners' questions. This was a simple formula which became an outstanding popular success because of Thomas's selection of the panellists; three regulars—biologist Julian Huxley, philosopher C. E. M. Joad, and retired naval commander A. B. Campbell—became national figures.

In 1944 Thomas resigned from the BBC, where he saw no future for himself, and moved to the film industry as producer-in-chief of Pathé Pictures, the short-film subsidiary of the Associated British Picture Corporation, where he revitalized Pathé News and Pathé Pictorial and extended production into documentaries, such as his colour film of the coronation of Elizabeth II. Thomas was a passionate advocate of commercial television. When the Associated British Picture Corporation was invited by the Independent Television Authority in 1955 to apply for the weekend contract in the north and midlands, his lobbying was finally rewarded. ABC Television was formed as a subsidiary, with Thomas as managing director, and went on the air in February 1956.

ABC was the last and smallest of the original 'big four' contractors, alongside Associated Rediffusion, ATV, and Granada. But Thomas's energy and enthusiasm, and his ability to pick the right like-minded lieutenants, propelled the little company into prominence. *Armchair Theatre*, under Sydney Newman, galvanized the single television play; arts programming was pioneered with *Tempo*, religious programming with *The Sunday Break*, adult education with *Sunday Session*; and London's dominance of popular entertainment at the weekend was successfully challenged with programmes like *Blackpool Night out*, *Candid Camera*, and the stylish thriller series *The Avengers*.

When the structure of independent television was reshaped in 1967, the Independent Broadcasting Authority (IBA) offered the London weekday contract to a new company formed by the merger of Rediffusion and ABC TV, in which majority control was to be exercised by ABC, with Thomas as managing director. In the words of IBA chairman Lord Hill of Luton, 'the combination of these two companies seemed to the Authority to offer the possibility of a programme company of real excellence'. Thames Television began transmission in August 1968 and realized the possibility of excellence in the ensuing years with a programme output high in both quantity and quality, ranging from *This Week* and *The World at War* to *Rumpole of the Bailey* and *Minder*, from *The Naked Civil Servant* and *Edward and Mrs Simpson* to *This is your Life* and *The Benny Hill Show*. In 1974 Thomas succeeded Lord Shawcross as chairman. He retired at the age of seventy in 1979.

Thomas was part of a particularly colourful period in the history of broadcasting in Britain, a bluff, burly showman in both radio and television. Among the founding fathers of independent television, he had the unique distinction of setting up and running two highly successful programme companies. He remained a programme maker throughout his career, brimming with ideas himself and always respectful of the ideas of other programme makers, whose talents he was quick to spot and ready to support. It was remarkable that, apart from his appointment as CBE in 1967, his achievement was never appropriately recognized. He was a governor of the British Film Institute (1974–82) and vice-president of the Royal Television Society (1976–84). He wrote five books, including *How to Write for Broadcasting* (1940). He also served three times as chairman of Independent Television News.

Thomas was above average height, thickset, balding from a quite early age, with a bluff manner and a forceful presence emphasized by his horn-rimmed spectacles. He was capable of great charm and persuasiveness, which served him well in both radio and television. Thomas died in hospital in Henley-on-Thames, Oxfordshire (where his home was Old Ship House, Wharfe Lane), on 6 November 1986.   BRIAN TESLER, *rev.*

Sources H. Thomas, *With an independent air* (1977) · A. Briggs, *The history of broadcasting in the United Kingdom*, 3 (1970) · B. Sendall, *Origin and foundation, 1946–62* (1982), vol. 1 of *Independent television in Britain* (1982–90) · J. Potter, *Companies and programmes, 1968–80* (1990), vol. 4 of *Independent television in Britain* (1982–90) · *Daily Telegraph* (7 Nov 1986) · *The Times* (7 Nov 1986) · personal knowledge (1996) · CGPLA Eng. & Wales (1987)

Likenesses photograph, repro. in *Daily Telegraph*

Wealth at death £50,239: probate, 30 March 1987, CGPLA Eng. & Wales

Thomas, Sir Hugh Evan- (1862–1928), naval officer, was born at Llwynmadog, Brecknockshire, Wales, on 27 October 1862, the fifth son of Charles Evan-Thomas (1817–1902), a JP and deputy lieutenant, of Gnoll, Glamorgan, a member of a prominent Welsh family, and his wife, Cara (d. 1909), eldest daughter of Henry Shepherd Pearson, of the East India Company service. He entered the *Britannia* as a naval cadet in January 1876. In the following year the princes Albert Victor and George (afterwards George V) also joined the ship, and, when they were sent on their three-year cruise in the *Bacchante*, Evan-Thomas was chosen as one of the midshipmen to join them in the gunroom. Before the cruise was over he was promoted sublieutenant, and at the end of 1883 was sent to the *Sultan* on the China station until July 1886, being promoted lieutenant at the end of 1884. He was for a short time flag lieutenant to Admiral Sir Algernon Lyons in the *Bellerophon* on the North America station, then returned to England where he undertook a course on gunnery and torpedo. He served for two years (1890–92) in the *Victoria* in the Mediterranean, after which he was appointed to the royal yacht *Osborne*. In 1894 he married Hilda Florence Awdry, who survived him, daughter of Thomas Barnard, of Cople House, Bedfordshire. They had no children.

From January 1894 Evan-Thomas was for three years flag lieutenant to Admiral Sir Michael Culme-Seymour in the *Ramillies*, Mediterranean, and was promoted commander in 1897. In 1898 he was put in charge of the signal school at Portsmouth for two years. After another two years in command of the *Pioneer* in the Mediterranean, he was promoted captain (1902), and was then employed at the

Admiralty assisting with the development of Lord Fisher's reform proposals for naval personnel. He was flag captain to Lord Charles Beresford in the channel for two years, and in May 1905 he was chosen for the command of the Admiralty yacht *Enchantress*. By this time he had become known as 'one of the most capable and progressive captains in the Navy' (*The Times*, 4 Sept 1928, 17).

In the autumn of 1905 Evan-Thomas was appointed to act as temporary naval secretary to the first lord of the Admiralty, Earl Cawdor. He was confirmed in this post on a continuing basis when the new Liberal administration replaced the Balfour government, and held the office until the end of 1908. He was a more junior officer than was normally appointed to this important post, the holder of which is responsible to the first lord for advice on all naval promotions and appointments to command, but he took the opportunity to become 'acquainted with every side of naval organization and administration' (*The Times*, 4 Sept 1928, 17).

Evan-Thomas then took command of the *Bellerophon* in the Home Fleet until August 1910, when he was appointed captain of the naval college at Dartmouth. He was aide-de-camp to the king from February 1911 until he was promoted to flag rank in July 1912. After a year on half pay he was appointed second in command of the 1st battle squadron with his flag in the *St Vincent*. The outbreak of the First World War in 1914 found him still in this command, which he retained until August 1915, when he was transferred to the command of the 5th battle squadron, flying his flag in the *Barham*.

At the time of the battle of Jutland (31 May 1916), Evan-Thomas's squadron, consisting of the *Barham*, *Valiant*, *Warspite*, and *Malaya* (*Queen Elizabeth* was refitting), sister ships, armed with eight 15-inch guns and capable of 25 knots speed, was acting with the Battle-Cruiser Fleet under the command of Admiral Sir David Beatty. The combined force, which cleared the Forth at 11 p.m. on 30 May, reached the appointed rendezvous off the Danish coast at 2.15 p.m. on the 31st, and turned to the northward to meet Admiral Jellicoe coming with the British battle fleet from Scapa Flow. The 5th battle squadron was stationed 5 miles north-north-west from Beatty's flagship, the *Lion*, and directed to look out for the battle fleet, when at 2.32 Beatty, acting on the *Galatea*'s report of enemy ships in sight, turned to the east, signalling the course to the *Barham*. This signal was not received until 2.37, and at 2.38 the 5th battle squadron turned to the south-south-east and increased to full speed in order to catch Beatty, who was now 8 miles ahead. The distance of the 5th battle squadron from the *Lion* prevented Evan-Thomas from giving the battle cruisers full support during the opening stages of the action, and they suffered severely with the loss of the *Indefatigable* and *Queen Mary*. Evan-Thomas was severely criticized for his part in this tragic incident, for failing to realize more quickly Beatty's intentions. In an episode which hurt Evan-Thomas deeply, Winston Churchill repeated these criticisms a decade later in his work *The World Crisis* (vol. 3, 1927). Arthur Marder considered that perhaps his only real crime was to have been slightly 'slow

on the uptake' (Marder, 3.53). Richard Hough concurred that 'while Evan-Thomas demonstrated a certain lack of imagination, he did not deserve the vilification he suffered from some quarters' and that his actions suggested in fact the 'negative initiative' created by Royal Navy procedures and training at that time (Hough, 293–4). Indeed once Evan-Thomas had joined the battle, in Beatty's words, the 5th battle squadron supported him 'brilliantly and effectively' (*The Times*, 4 Sept 1928, 17). Through skilful manoeuvring and courageous engagement Evan-Thomas's ships inflicted serious damage upon the German fleet and protected much of the rest of the British force. His squadron saw some of the heaviest fighting of the day: his flagship was hit six times and his wireless was wrecked, and the *Warspite* and *Malaya* suffered heavily. Admiral Jellicoe commented later that:

> The magnificent squadron commanded by Rear-Admiral Evan-Thomas formed a support of great value to Sir David Beatty during the afternoon and was brought into action in rear of the battle fleet in the most judicious manner in the evening. (*The Times*, 4 Sept 1928, 17)

At least in regard to this part of the battle, a number of commentators have suggested that 'but for the 5th Battle Squadron, the outcome would have been disastrous' (Marder, 3.66).

For his services in the battle Evan-Thomas was appointed CB (1916) and immediately afterwards promoted KCB, was made a member of the French Légion d'honneur, and was given the first class of the Russian order of St Anne, the second class of the Japanese order of the Rising Sun, and the order of the Crown of Italy.

Evan-Thomas was promoted vice-admiral in September 1917. He retained the command of the 5th battle squadron until October 1918. In 1919 he was created KCMG. He remained without command until March 1921, when, having been promoted admiral in October 1920, he was appointed commander-in-chief at the Nore. In 1924 he retired at his own request. In the same year he was promoted GCB. Despite the controversy over his role at Jutland, he was remembered as 'an efficient officer with a highly deserved reputation as a ship and squadron handler' and as a 'loveable, straightforward and unassuming man' (Marder, 2.441). After his retirement he lived at Charlton House, near Shaftesbury. He died on 30 August 1928 at Cople House, Bedfordshire, and his funeral took place at Cople on 2 September.

V. W. BADDELEY, rev. MARC BRODIE

Sources *The Times* (4 Sept 1928) · *DWB* · Burke, *Gen. GB* · R. Hough, *The great war at sea, 1914–1918* (1986) · A. J. Marder, *From the Dreadnought to Scapa Flow: the Royal Navy in the Fisher era, 1904–1919*, 5 vols. (1961–70) · personal knowledge (1937) · J. S. Corbett, *Naval operations*, 1–3, History of the Great War (1920–23) · *CGPLA Eng. & Wales* (1928)

Archives BL, corresp. and MSS, Add. MSS 52504–52506, 53738 | FILM IWM FVA, actuality footage

Likenesses F. Dodd, charcoal and watercolour drawing, 1917, IWM · W. Stoneman, photograph, 1921, NPG · photograph, repro. in *The Times*, 16

Wealth at death £20,585 4s. 7d.: resworn probate, 1928, *CGPLA Eng. & Wales*

Thomas, Hugh Hamshaw (1885–1962), palaeobotanist, was born on 29 May 1885 in Wrexham, Denbighshire, the second son and third child of William Thomas and his wife, Elizabeth Lloyd, a local farmer's daughter. William Thomas, of Cornish and Leicestershire extraction, was a men's outfitter, a prominent local citizen, JP, Congregationalist, and lifelong Liberal.

After attending school at Grove Park, Wrexham, Thomas entered Cambridge in 1904 as an entrance scholar at Downing College. Through the influence of friends and reading he had become interested in natural history, particularly botany and fossils, and he was fired by the idea of biological evolution. In 1906 he obtained first-class honours in part one of the natural sciences tripos (botany, chemistry, and physics). Intending to enter the civil service, he took part two of the history tripos, obtaining second-class honours in 1907. At the same time he continued research on fossil plants and his first paper (as junior author) was published by the Royal Society in 1908; his first independent paper was published the following year.

In 1908 Thomas did well in the civil service entrance examination but declined an unattractive post to become, instead, an independent scholar in Cambridge, earning a precarious living by coaching students for elementary examinations. The next few years he spent examining specimens provided in museums or by field geologists. He collaborated with A. C. Seward on a study of a collection from Russia. But Thomas, somewhat unusually, chose to study plants preserved as black marks on shale surfaces rather than the three-dimensional petrified specimens, the examination by thin sections of which had been the pride of British palaeobotany.

Thomas began to study the Jurassic plants of Yorkshire, which were preserved compressed on shales, inspired by Alfred Gabriel Nathorst (1850–1921), of Stockholm. Nathorst had shown that, after suitable chemical manipulation, such fossils would yield external cuticles or spore membranes, which could explain complicated reproductive structures, making them potentially as valuable as petrifactions.

Another Stockholm scholar, T. G. Halle, inspired him further and Thomas repeatedly visited his Yorkshire collecting grounds, selecting his specimens carefully, and concentrating on the study of reproductive parts (which were mostly detached and inconspicuous fossils). He wrote a valuable paper on *Williamsoniella*, a flower he named himself, relating it to its previously unrecognized stem and to its leaf, which had long been known but was thought to be of a fern. Thomas also wrote a paper, with Nellie Bancroft, on cycad leaf cuticles; his contribution was to show that fossils belonged to two groups—the living cycads, and a very different category. This paper provided a basis for the classification of fossils by leaf cuticles.

Thomas joined the army early in the First World War and was an officer in the Royal Field Artillery in France in 1915. He was transferred to Egypt, on secondment to the

Hugh Hamshaw Thomas (1885–1962), by unknown photographer

Royal Flying Corps, as officer in charge of aerial photography and his work materially aided the success of the campaign of Sir E. H. H. Allenby. Thomas was twice mentioned in dispatches, was awarded the order of the Nile, and appointed MBE. After the armistice he was sent to India to report on the possibilities of aerial survey and on his return to Cambridge assisted in the direction of research in the aeronautical department. He played an important part in the foundation of the University Air Squadron.

In 1919 Thomas returned to live in Downing College where Seward was master. The following year he was appointed dean and steward and in 1923 became a university lecturer in botany. In 1923 also he married Edith Gertrude, daughter of J. Torrance, from Cape Town; she was a research student in Cambridge. They had a son and a daughter. The South African connection led to Thomas's work on fossils of that region.

In 1925 Thomas published an outstanding paper on the Caytoniales, an entirely new order of angiospermous plants from the Jurassic era. Thomas's *Caytonia* was a group of little berry-like 'fruits' each containing seeds, very like a string of currants. Inventing his own technique, which was possible because he could sacrifice many fruits, he worked out the fruit and seed structure from their cuticles and by sectioning them after long swelling in alkali. Success was rare but he showed that the fruit was indeed closed and had a stigma-like part on which he found pollen grains (and he already knew the fossil which produced this kind of pollen). By examining all associated fossils he discovered that only one (*Sagenopteris*) had a leaf stalk with a cuticle which matched the *Caytonia* fruit stalk. Thus he suggested that the Caytoniales were early angiospermous plants, if not strictly ancestral.

Thomas's paper received a mixed reception, partly because the case he made for identifying the separate parts was not fully convincing. Workers elsewhere confirmed all his main findings, though details were emended. He could have presented a tidier and more convincing case had he been interested in the minute structural points which have no obvious significance but do characterize individual species; but he was never interested in specific characters. He aroused controversy of another kind deliberately, revealing in this paper that his interest was by no means narrowly concentrated on the fossil but rather on the wider issues that arose from it, such as evolutionary changes and the philosophy of the organization of the plant body. He deliberately flouted the convention that plants can, and in general should, be divided into clear categories of organs, root, stem, leaf. Thomas's 1933 paper on pteridospermous fructifications of South African Triassic plants was another great contribution to palaeobotany. The plants concerned were a major element of the southern hemisphere Triassic flora. Again he entered the field of debatable plant morphology but there is no doubt of his contribution to knowledge of a major group of plants.

From 1939 to 1943 Thomas served with the Royal Air Force Volunteer Reserve working on photographic interpretation and rising to the rank of wing commander. In his later years he continued to publish work describing fossils but he preferred to publish papers on general botanical ideas and their history.

Thomas never had or wanted a research school in palaeobotany, preferring to help people to go their own way. He gave unstinting help to many outside palaeobotany, as evidenced by his presidency of the eastern counties branch of the Science Masters Association, the Yorkshire Naturalists, the botany section of the British Association, the Linnean Society, and the British Society for the History of Science. He was active in promoting international co-operation in botany.

Thomas was elected to the Royal Society in 1934 and received the Linnean Society's gold medal in 1960. His most remarkable distinction was to be judged at the Darwin–Wallace centenary in 1958 to be among the twenty biologists who had made the most outstanding contribution to knowledge of evolution, for which he received a commemorative medal. He was a modest man, who left on colleagues an enduring impression of his thoughtful kindness and the breadth of his labours. He died at the Evelyn Nursing Home, Cambridge, on 30 June 1962.

TOM M. HARRIS, *rev.*

Sources T. M. Harris, *Memoirs FRS*, 9 (1963), 287–99 · private information (1981) · personal knowledge (1981) · *Svenskt biografiskt lexikon* · WWW · CGPLA Eng. & Wales (1962)

Likenesses photograph, repro. in Harris, *Memoirs FRS* [*see illus.*]

Wealth at death £57,258 14s. 6d.: probate, 19 Oct 1962, CGPLA Eng. & Wales

Thomas, Hugh Owen (1834–1891), orthopaedic surgeon, was born on 23 August 1834 in Bodedern, Anglesey, the eldest child in the family of five sons and two daughters of Evan Thomas (1804–1884), a bone-setter, of Liverpool, and his wife, Jane, *née* Owen. His father was seventh in a line of bone-setters descended from a farming family in Anglesey, but by the middle of the nineteenth century medical opinion was becoming increasingly hostile to these unqualified practitioners, and Evan Thomas sent all of his five sons to study medicine at Edinburgh University. Hugh Thomas lived with his grandparents in Rhoscolyn, Anglesey, until he was thirteen, attending the local school, and then went to Dr Poggi's school in New Brighton, Cheshire. In 1851 he began four years' apprenticeship with his uncle, Dr Owen Roberts, of St Asaph, doctor at the Liverpool workhouse infirmary, who prepared him for Edinburgh University, where he studied medicine from 1854 until 1857. He then spent time at University College, London, becoming MRCS in 1857. He spent a short time in Paris, studying French surgical methods, and then returned to Liverpool and joined his father's practice in 1858.

After a year Thomas set up his own practice at 24 Hardy Street, in the heart of the Liverpool docklands. In 1864 he married Elizabeth, daughter of Robert Jones, an architect and builder, of Rhyl, Wales. They had no children, and in 1873 they invited Elizabeth's nephew, Robert *Jones, to live with them so that he could study at the Liverpool school of medicine. In 1866 Thomas moved to 11 Nelson Street, Liverpool, where he remained until his death; he later turned 24 Hardy Street into a private nursing home. Although he became critical of the methods of the old bone-setters, and especially of their views on diseases of the joints, he had learned from watching his father's manipulative practices; and in his workshop he followed their practice of making their own splints, constantly experimenting with new designs. He offered to supply his splints to the French army during the Franco-Prussian War in 1870, but this was rejected. His patients were mainly Merseyside dockers and shipyard workers, and seamen injured at sea, and he had to deal with many severe accident cases. His free Sunday clinics at 11 Nelson Street from 1870 onwards became famous, and patients arrived in handcarts, wheelbarrows, and donkey carts. He went on his daily rounds in a scarlet phaeton designed by himself, pulled by two black horses, with his wife beside him.

Because Thomas held neither hospital nor university appointments, his work was slow to gain recognition, but in 1875 he published *Diseases of the Hip, Knee, and Ankle Joints, with their Deformities*, which reached a third edition in 1878. He was elected a member of the Liverpool Medical Institution in 1876, and his splints were praised at the International Medical Congress in 1881. He lectured to the Harveian Society of London in 1887. He published a series of eight Contributions to Surgery and Medicine (1883–90), many of which were polemical, and he made enemies among English surgeons whom he attacked in print, including Sir Frederick Treves. However, he had a wide following in the United States, and several American orthopaedic surgeons visited him, one of whom, John Ridlon, a founder of the American Orthopaedic Association, who first visited him in 1887, became his leading American supporter. In 1890 he received the honorary degree of MD from the University of St Louis.

Thomas was very small, with a brusque, hectoring manner, and his only relaxation was playing his flute, which he had modified in his workshop. He was an agnostic, and a friend of Charles Bradlaugh. Thomas died of pneumonia on 6 January 1891 at his residence at 11 Nelson Street, Liverpool, and was survived by his wife; thousands of Liverpool poor followed the hearse and crowded the church at his funeral.

After his death Thomas's work was largely forgotten, until the First World War, when Robert Jones became director of orthopaedic surgery for the British army. Thanks to his efforts the Army Medical Service introduced the Thomas splint for compound fractures of the lower limbs, and it was in general use from the end of 1915 for the transport of stretcher cases from the front to casualty stations, and in base hospitals, greatly reducing the mortality rate. Thomas made an important contribution to the treatment of fractures. He strongly opposed surgical intervention, especially amputation, and believed in the principle of enforced rest and immobilization of the fractured limb. He felt that the less the surgeon interfered with nature the better.   ANNE PIMLOTT BAKER

Sources D. Le Vay, *The life of Hugh Owen Thomas* (1956) • F. Watson, *Hugh Owen Thomas* (1934) • D. McC. Aitken, *Hugh Owen Thomas: his principles and practice* (1935) • D. Le Vay, *The history of orthopaedics* (1990), 108–23 • G. Thomas, 'From bonesetter to orthopaedic surgeon' (Robert Jones memorial lecture, 1972), *Annals of the Royal College of Surgeons of England*, 55 (1974), 134–42, 190–98 • R. Cooter, *Surgery and society in peace and war: orthopaedics and the organization of modern medicine* (1993), 23–8 • T. McMurray, 'The Life of Hugh Owen Thomas', *Liverpool Medico-Chirurgical Journal*, 43 (1935), 3–41 • A. Keith, *Menders of the maimed* (1919) • E. Bick, *Sourcebook of orthopaedics* (1968), 279–83 • *CGPLA Eng. & Wales* (1891)
Likenesses photograph, c.1885, Wellcome L. • H. Fleury, oils, c.1890, NPG; repro. in Le Vay, *Life of Hugh Owen Thomas*, 64 • double portrait, photograph (with Jones), repro. in McMurray, 'The life of Hugh Owen Thomas', 3 • photograph, repro. in Le Vay, *History of orthopaedics*, 108 • photograph, repro. in Watson, *Hugh Owen Thomas*, frontispiece
Wealth at death £11,148 10s. 2d.: probate, 18 March 1891, *CGPLA Eng. & Wales*

Thomas, Ivor Bulmer- (1905–1993), writer and politician, was born Ivor Thomas on 30 November 1905 at Cwmbrân, Monmouthshire, the third of four children of Alfred Ernest Thomas (1876–1918), brick drawer, and his wife, Zipporah Jones (d. 1954), domestic servant. 'He trailed great clouds of intellectual glory. His academic performance was dazzling': thus in a memorial address Lord Jenkins of Hillhead, a protégé of whose father, Arthur Jenkins MP, Ivor Thomas was. In 1918 he entered Jones's West Monmouth School, Pontypool, and in 1924 he won a scholarship to St John's College, Oxford. He attained a first in

mathematical moderations in 1925 and a first in *literae humaniores* in 1928. While studying divinity, a doctrinal dispute with the college's president led him to move to Magdalen College as a senior demy in theology (1929–30). He represented Oxford against Cambridge at athletics and cross-country running, winning the 3 miles in 1927. In 1926 he was a member of the Welsh international cross-country team. But for an injury he would have been selected for the 800 metres in the 1928 Olympic games.

In 1930 Thomas wrote the first of his thirteen books, *Our Lord Birkenhead*, which resulted from its subject's keen interest in university athletics. It was full of 1920s Oxford wit and was dedicated to 'my creditors'. His biography of Lord Gladstone of Hawarden, the prime minister's son, was published in 1936. It resulted from a year's study at St Deiniol's Library, Hawarden, in 1930. His *Top Sawyer*, a biography of the businessman and politician Lord Davies of Llandinam, followed in 1938. His first book dealing with current affairs, *Coal in the New Era*, appeared in 1930, when the trend was, as he put it, 'definitely away from coal to oil' (*Coal in the New Era*, 213). In that year he joined *The Times* as a sub-editor, contributing occasional leaders, articles on sporting and scientific subjects, and, later on, obituaries. In 1937 he moved to the *News Chronicle* as chief leader writer for two years. Fourteen years later he became for a year acting deputy editor of the *Daily Telegraph*. Over many years he wrote articles for numerous newspapers, and especially reviews for the *Times Literary Supplement*.

On 5 April 1932, at the church of St Mary the Virgin, Pimlico, Thomas married Dilys (1910–1938), daughter of Dr William Llewelyn Jones of Merthyr Tudful; they had one son. Many years after her death he published *Dilysia: a Threnody* (1987), the quality of whose verse was of a very high order. On 26 December 1940, at Hereford Cathedral, he married (Margaret) Joan, daughter of E. F. Bulmer of Adam's Hill, Hereford; they had a son and two daughters. He added Bulmer to his surname by deed poll in 1952.

Having joined the Territorials in 1938, Thomas served during the Second World War as a fusilier in the Royal Fusiliers, and in 1941 was promoted captain in the Royal Norfolk regiment. His command of Italian (one of the six languages he spoke and read fluently) led to a post in Hugh Dalton's Ministry of Economic Warfare, from where he fed propaganda into Mussolini's Italy. In 1942 he published *Warfare by Words*, which *The Times* called 'a direct, if guarded, attack on British propaganda'. This was followed in 1946 by *The Problem of Italy*.

In 1935 Thomas contested Sir John Simon's Spen Valley seat in Yorkshire, as a Labour candidate, losing by only 600 votes. In 1942, under the wartime truce, he was elected unopposed at a by-election at Keighley. This seat he easily retained in the 1945 election. Attlee then appointed him parliamentary under-secretary at the Ministry of Civil Aviation. In 1946 he steered the controversial Civil Aviation Bill through the Commons. Typically, he obtained a pilot's licence so as to appreciate the difficulties facing civil airline pilots. Late in 1946 he was transferred, still as an under-secretary, to the Colonial Office, becoming a delegate to the general assembly of the United Nations and the first British member of the Trusteeship Council, but after a year of much globe-trotting he was summarily dropped from the government in a reshuffle. His disillusionment with socialism had already become apparent. During the debate on the king's speech in 1948 he resigned from the party. In a witty but heartfelt speech from the opposition benches, almost designed to elicit rage from his former colleagues, he excoriated 'the planners, who are trying to make a land fit for zeros' (*Hansard 5C*, 113). His *The Socialist Tragedy* was published in 1949. It is dedicated to 'all Social Democrats', hoping that they would choose democracy and eschew socialism. He joined the Social Democratic Party in 1981. He was soundly defeated as Conservative candidate for Newport, Monmouthshire, in 1950. Thus ended his political career, though in 1965 he published his two-volume *The Growth of the Party System*. Typically, on losing the election he drove with friends across the Sahara Desert in a jeep.

Brought up a strict Baptist, at Oxford he became a devout high-Anglican. He was chairman of the Faith Press and a vice-president of the Church Union. In 1950 he was elected to the house of laity of the church assembly (later the general synod), serving for thirty-five years. The force and pungency of his numerous interventions in debate were much admired but not always agreed with. In the second half of his life his overriding interest lay in the conservation of buildings of historical and architectural quality under threat, especially redundant churches. In 1952 he presented the archbishop of Canterbury with his seminal report, 'The preservation of *our* churches'. This led to the creation of the grant-giving Historic Churches Preservation Trust, which he ran from its inception. In 1955 he piloted through the synod the inspection of churches measure, which made structural surveys compulsory quinquennially, thus largely eliminating 'repairs crises', which hitherto had carried off many fine churches.

In 1956 there occurred Bulmer-Thomas's tempestuous public row with Archbishop Fisher. This led to his resignation from the Historic Churches Preservation Trust. The essence of the quarrel was the trustees' insistence, backed by Fisher, that its funds be withheld from churches that were closed or facing closure, and allocated by diocese irrespective of architectural or historic merit. Bulmer-Thomas is said to have declared that Fisher had 'held a pistol to my face, while the Dean of Gloucester plunged his dagger into my back' (*The Times*, 8 Oct 1993). In time Bulmer-Thomas got his way when the report of the Bridges commission, set up by the two archbishops, appeared in 1960. This led to the 1968 pastoral measure which created the Redundant Churches Fund, of which Bulmer-Thomas was chairman until 1976. The measure established the principle of church and state sharing the cost of keeping redundant churches as monuments in the fund's possession. The Friends of Friendless Churches, which he founded in 1957, maintained those that fell through the net. From 1958 he was for thirty-five years first secretary and then chairman of the Ancient Monuments Society. When he was appointed CBE in 1984 for his

conservationist efforts, he quipped that, in his case, CBE stood for 'Churches Before Evangelism'.

Throughout his varied career Bulmer-Thomas pursued his interest in ancient and medieval mathematics. His two-volume *Selections Illustrating the History of Greek Mathematics* (1939–41) remained in print for many years. His contributions, in various languages, to learned journals were numerous. He conversed with Einstein and knew Planck and Rutherford, but he regarded Newton as 'the supreme genius' (*The Independent*, 13 Oct 1993). In 1979 Warwick University awarded him an honorary DSc degree at the instigation of the mathematics department.

Bulmer-Thomas was a strongly-built, soft-spoken man of exceptional mental and physical stamina, who needed at most five hours' sleep, reading Dante in the original nocturnally. He was a great fighter for what he believed to be right, attacking—no holds barred—big targets, never any that could not return fire. He had virtually total recall, never keeping an engagement diary. Without personal vanity, unpretentious, almost sloppily dressed, he was a workaholic. 'I *like* cold omelettes', he would reply to his wife's despairing call to a meal. He was working a few minutes before he died of a heart attack at his home, 12 Edwardes Square, Kensington, London, on 7 October 1993, having just written a letter to the *Daily Telegraph* (printed on the same day as his obituary) and another to a friend declaring that he was 'refreshing his memory of the theory of relativity'. He was survived by his second wife; his ashes were interred on 22 October.   ANGLESEY

Sources personal knowledge (2004) · private information (2004) [W. Cantelo] · *Debates of the general synod*, esp. 1945 · *Transactions of the Ancient Monuments Society*, new ser., 17 (1970) · G. C. H. V. Paget, marquis of Anglesey, J. H. Harvey, M. Saunders, and J. Bowles, 'Ivor Bulmer-Thomas, 1905–1993: in memoriam', *Transactions of the Ancient Monuments Society*, new ser., 38 (1994), 1–14 · *The Times* (8 Oct 1993) · *Daily Telegraph* (8 Oct 1993) · *The Independent* (8 Oct 1993) · *The Independent* (13 Oct 1993) · *The Guardian* (9 Oct 1993) · *Hansard 5C* (1948), 457.113 · m. cert. · d. cert.
Likenesses Bassano and Vandyk, two photographs, 1946, NPG · M. Ross, portrait, *c*.1950, priv. coll. · photograph, repro. in *The Times*
Wealth at death under £125,000: probate, 3 Dec 1993, *CGPLA Eng. & Wales*

Thomas, James Havard (1853–1921), sculptor and draughtsman, was born at 16 St Michael's Hill, Bristol, on 22 December 1853, the son of John Thomas, a carpenter of Welsh descent, and his wife, Mary, *née* Havard. He studied at the Bristol School of Art and won a national scholarship (1872–5) to the South Kensington Training Schools, London. His earliest-known carving is the relief *The Good Samaritan* (*c*.1873) at the entrance of the Brompton Hospital, London. Thomas established his reputation with a marble bust of Cardinal Manning, exhibited at the Royal Academy in 1876 (bronze cast of 1886, Tate collection). He attended the École des Beaux-Arts in Paris from 1881 to 1884 under Pierre-Jules Cavelier, where he directly carved in marble the life-size figure *The Slave Girl* (*c*.1884, National Museum and Gallery of Wales, Cardiff), a notable example of this technique which received critical acclaim.

From 1884 to 1889 Thomas lived in London, where he

executed public statues. He carved two versions in marble of a statue of Samuel Morley for Bristol and Nottingham. In 1888 he sculpted *A Peasant Girl*, which he offered to his friend the photographer P. H. Emerson. Thomas and Emerson experimented with each other's art and explored the uses of photography for sculpture. Thomas was close friends with Emerson, George Clausen, and Henry Herbert La Thangue, all of whom shared a taste for peasant genre scenes. About 1886 they became founder members of the New English Art Club, and Thomas was its honorary secretary from 1886 until 1889, at which time he destroyed the contents of his studio and moved to Italy.

Thomas studied bronze casting in Naples and subsequently lived on Capri and near Pompeii until his return to London in 1906. In 1891 he married Sofia Milano della Torre, a native of Sorrento; they had three sons (George, Matthew, and Mark) and three daughters (Mary, Sylvia, and Flora). Henry Neville Maugham satirized Thomas's new life in an unpublished short play, 'The Blue Lizard' (BL, MS Cup.407.6.39). Thomas's Italian work depicted scenes drawn from local country life in such finely carved reliefs as *Cow and Calf* (1894, National Museum and Gallery of Wales, Cardiff; 1897, Tate collection), *Agriculture* (1895), and *The Loom* (1896). The small bronze figure *Castagnettes* (1899, National Museum and Gallery of Wales, Cardiff, and elsewhere) and a marble head, *Meditation: Capri* (1891, Cartwright Hall, Bradford), date from the Italian sojourn. However, his master work in Italy was the bronze figure *Lycidas* (1904–5; Tate collection; also Manchester and Aberdeen). This and subsequent figures used a theory, which he developed from the principles of Albrecht Dürer and Greek sculpture, whereby the position of a naturally posed model was established by a series of measurements against horizontal and vertical planes; the figures were modelled in black wax on a wooden support. *Lycidas* was rejected by the Royal Academy but after a public outcry subsequently purchased for the Tate Gallery by Sir Michael Sadler.

Thomas held a one-man show at the Carfax Gallery, London, in 1909. He became assistant lecturer at the Slade School of Fine Art in 1911, and in 1914 the first professor of sculpture. He was appointed assessor for the Cardiff city hall scheme of historical figures and executed for that setting *Boadicea* (1913), a fine group in marble. The subsequent disagreement at the Royal Society of British Sculptors, over the abandonment of open competition by Lord Rhondda, wounded Thomas. However, such was his popularity that a number of eminent sculptors, such as Sir George Frampton, Frederick William Pomeroy, and William Goscombe John, resigned in his support. He went on to make further classical figures, such as *Thyrsis* (wax, exh. RA, 1912; Tate collection; bronzes in the Tate collection, and Melbourne, Johannesburg, and Manchester) and *Cassandra* (1918–21; wax and bronze versions, Tate collection). Thomas executed a portrait medallion of the poet Rupert Brooke for Rugby School (1918; lettering by Eric Gill) and several medals, including a commission from his friend Emerson (British Museum, London). He also continued to carve portrait busts: for example, *Mrs Asher Wertheimer*

(1907, Tate collection). His final commission was the Mountain Ash war memorial (1919–22) in Glamorgan, which was completed by his son George.

Thomas was a 'New Sculpture' pioneer of direct carving long before the work of Jacob Epstein and the modern movement. His work was quickly marginalized as neither following that of Alfred Gilbert nor meeting the contemporary trend for symbolism. His rich correspondence and notes reveal a generosity of spirit and an idealistic love of nature inspired by Greek sculpture. His acute observations from life in draughtsmanship and sculpture sought to capture movement. He was an active member of the Chelsea Arts Club. Under his tutelage at the Slade sprang a new generation of women sculptors such as Maude Wethered and Ursula Edgcumbe. Thomas died at his home at 24 Glebe Place, Chelsea, London, on 6 June 1921. He was survived by his wife. A memorial exhibition was held at the Leicester Galleries in London in 1922 and a further exhibition at the Beaux Arts Gallery in 1936. Principal collections of his work are in the Tate collection, the City of Bristol Museum and Art Gallery, and the National Museum and Gallery of Wales, Cardiff.

FIONA PEARSON

Sources Tate collection, James Havard Thomas MSS · F. Gibson, 'The sculpture of Professor James Havard Thomas', *The Studio*, 76 (1919), 79–85 · F. Pearson, 'The correspondence between P. H. Emerson and J. Havard Thomas', *British photography in the nineteenth century: the fine art tradition*, ed. M. Weaver (1989), 197–204 · M. Chamot, D. Farr, and M. Butlin, *The modern British paintings, drawings and sculpture*, 2 (1964), 714–19 [catalogue, Tate Gallery, London] · F. Pearson, 'Thomas, James Havard', *The dictionary of art*, ed. J. Turner (1996) · H. N. Maugham, 'The blue lizard', BL, MS Cup.407.6.39 · b. cert. · d. cert. · private information (2004) · *CGPLA Eng. & Wales* (1921)
Archives Tate collection, corresp., sketches, drawings, and photographs
Likenesses J. Kerr-Lawson, pencil drawing, 1910, NPG · J. Kerr-Lawson, pencil sketch, 1910, Tate collection · W. Rothenstein, chalk drawing, 1920, Tate collection · photographs, Tate collection
Wealth at death £4229 5s. 7d.: administration, 5 July 1921, *CGPLA Eng. & Wales*

Thomas, James Henry [Jim, Jimmy] (**1874–1949**), trade unionist and politician, was born on 3 October 1874 at Newport, Monmouthshire, the illegitimate son of Elizabeth Thomas, a domestic servant, and was brought up in poverty by his grandmother, Ann Thomas, a widowed washerwoman. He attended St Paul's elementary school, working part-time as a shop errand boy from the age of nine, and, after leaving school at the age of twelve, had various jobs in shops and as a decorator.

Railways, trade unionism, and labour politics In 1889 Thomas joined the Great Western Railway (GWR) as an engine cleaner, and was promoted to fireman five years later. Joining the Amalgamated Society of Railway Servants (ASRS), he quickly proved himself a talented organizer and speaker. By 1897 he was chairman of his local union branch and president of the Newport Trades Council, and in 1898 became a delegate to the ASRS annual conference. That year he married a childhood friend, Agnes

James Henry Thomas (1874–1949), by Walter Stoneman, 1924

Hill; they had three sons and three daughters, one of whom died in infancy. Transferred by the GWR to Swindon, he eventually became an engine driver in the marshalling yards. He again presided over the local trades council, and in the 1901 municipal elections defeated his own GWR superintendent. On Swindon council he was chairman of the finance and law committee from 1904 to 1905, and of the electricity and tramways committee from 1905 to 1906. As a trade unionist, he was among the first to benefit from a career structure leading up through a well-established organization and into labour politics. In 1902 he was elected to the ASRS national executive committee, in 1905 as its youngest ever president, and in 1906 as organizing secretary—a full-time post which brought his resignation from the GWR, and moves to Manchester, Cardiff, and finally London. As Labour MP for Derby from the general election of January 1910 and ASRS assistant secretary from September of that year, he became nationally prominent during the late Edwardian labour unrest.

Character, religious and political views Thomas's rise was the product of exuberant spirits, native shrewdness, broad populist sympathies, and keen assessment of the achievable. He became a remarkable public speaker, inimitably mixing reason, invective, sentimentality, anecdote, and repartee. In negotiation he was a master of bluff and the effective mood, detecting strengths or weaknesses and seizing upon a compromise which would hold. He developed into a fixer *par excellence* within industry, trade unionism, and politics, and especially in the increasingly important borderlands between these. Although his trade unionism brought him into contact with various forms of radicalism and sometimes gave him a radical reputation, the effect and appearance were superficial.

Educated at a church school, for some years Thomas was an active Baptist and taught in a Swindon Sunday school; but his religious commitment evaporated and any nonconformist earnestness was replaced by flamboyant participation in the pleasures and hobbies of the common man—drinking, sports, and gambling. After a 'pro-Boer' phase, he shared conventional imperialist assumptions and enthusiasms. Within the ASRS—the trade union of the Taff Vale and Osborne cases—he advocated independent labour representation, and stood for Labour at Derby in defiance of his 'Lib–Lab' general secretary and the retiring MP, Richard Bell. But he was never a socialist: he was a progressive, and in a manner retaining much from the working-class Conservatism of his childhood home. He wanted working men generally and his union's members in particular to secure a better life and increased power, but by improving their position and opportunities within existing economic, social, and political structures. His collectivism served individualist assumptions, and his economic opinions were mildly redistributionist yet solidly orthodox. In both trade unionism and labour politics he was a constitutionalist, upholding the authority of national leaderships; the limited aims of collective bargaining, with strikes as a weapon only of last resort; the priority of the 'public interest', and the supremacy of the ballot box and parliament.

The strike of 1911 In August 1911 Thomas helped bring together the four main railway unions to take control of a spate of unofficial strikes, and to call the first national railway strike. After two days the railway companies under government pressure agreed to revise existing conciliation boards, advancing the union's principal objective of securing formal recognition from employers. The strike had two wider repercussions. Its success persuaded the ASRS and two smaller railway unions to amalgamate in early 1913 as the National Union of Railwaymen (NUR), of which Thomas was elected assistant secretary; competition with the fourth union, the Associated Society of Locomotive Engineers and Firemen, was to be a major feature of his NUR career. The strike's disruptive effect upon the members and funds of the Miners' Federation and Transport Workers' Federation was a factor in their creation with the NUR of the Triple Industrial Alliance. Though sometimes represented as seeking political objectives, for Thomas this was simply a means to co-ordinate industrial actions and discourage unofficial sympathetic strikes.

The First World War and its aftermath The war made Thomas a major public figure. He supported the war effort, while helping to keep the Labour Party together by defending the freedom of Ramsay MacDonald and other socialists to criticize it. He was impressed equally by wartime class collaboration and the advance in the labour movement's power, and believed the two to be connected.

Government control of the railways brought full recognition of the NUR from the managers, and Thomas's parliamentary position helped secure war bonuses for its members. In July 1916 he became the NUR's general secretary, and thereafter a member of the TUC parliamentary committee (1917–21) and its successor the general council (1921–4, 1925–9). He campaigned against conscription, but only from fear of national divisions and labour unrest, and easily reconciled himself to its eventual peaceful introduction. In May 1915 he opposed the Labour Party's entry into the Asquith coalition government, expecting it to gain more by continued independence, but in December 1916 supported its entry into the Lloyd George coalition. His decision was assisted by hints of a possible war cabinet seat which, once Labour support was assured, Lloyd George gave instead to the party leader, Arthur Henderson. Thomas then declined the post of minister of labour, partly from pique but also from an accurate assessment that his influence as a 'patriotic' leader of a major trade union and impressive non-beneficed Labour MP would be greater than as a second-rank minister. During 1917 he rejected offers of two further ministerial posts, but accepted a privy councillorship and became a member of the government's reconstruction committee and the Balfour mission to the USA and Canada.

The wartime growth of militant trade union movements magnified Thomas's importance as a 'responsible' national leader. Within the NUR he faced prolonged opposition from radicals seeking revisions of war bonuses and attracted by ideas of using trade union power to achieve socialist political purposes, including nationalization. But Thomas prevailed through guile and exploitation of his great popularity with rank-and-file members. In September 1918 he halted unofficial strikes in south Wales by a threat of resignation which caused 840 NUR branches to declare their support for him. When in 1919 the radical-dominated national executive attacked his power by dividing his office, making him parliamentary secretary and the Marxist C. T. Cramp industrial secretary, he persuaded the regional delegates to confirm his overall control. His position was secured by his success in advancing his members' interests during the post-war boom and slump. In March 1919 he obtained a prolongation of wartime bonuses, but government resistance to NUR proposals for a permanent settlement drove Thomas reluctantly into calling a strike in September. Playing upon fears of the triple alliance, the prime minister, Lloyd George, attacked the strike as an 'anarchist conspiracy', but Thomas outmanoeuvred the government by ignoring his executive's instruction to invoke the triple alliance and employing the Labour Research Department to organize the union's appeal to public opinion. Sharing Lloyd George's deviousness of method, he secretly continued negotiations and after nine days persuaded the cabinet that it was better to compromise with him than risk further escalation by militants. This led to the most successful post-war industrial settlement, which cushioned railway wages against the worst effects of the slump. The NUR

expressed its gratitude by a collection which enabled Thomas to buy a new home.

Thomas himself was sufficiently excited by post-war radicalism to publish *When Labour Rules* (1920). But the book's theme was not so much challenge as reassurance: the middle classes had nothing to fear and much to gain, and social amelioration, limited nationalization, and equality of opportunity would be achieved by parliamentary means. Within trade unionism generally—and as TUC chairman from 1919 to 1920 and president of the International Federation of Trade Unions from 1920 to 1924—he was an effective opponent of 'direct action', arguing that political strikes would subvert the Labour Party, and that it was absurd to seek by strikes, alienating many non-trade unionists, what was available peacefully and with consent through elections. In August 1920 he did head TUC participation in the Council of Action which threatened industrial action to resist British intervention in the Russo-Polish war, but he considered this legitimate because the council had Labour Party representation and its purpose—the maintenance of peace—manifestly commanded public support. Similarly, he supported the threat of triple alliance action to assist the NUR's partners in ordinary industrial disputes, but resisted actual strike proposals for what he regarded as unreasonable or politically damaging purposes. His withdrawal of NUR support for the Miners' Federation in April 1921 contributed to the 'black Friday' débâcle which destroyed the triple alliance. Fearing great damage to the labour movement, during early 1926 he worked hard within the TUC and through contacts with ministers, officials, and would-be intermediaries to try to avoid a general strike, and then to bring it to an early end.

A national figure Already a target of the Labour left's enmity for his trade union leadership, during the 1920s Thomas earned their social and moral disapproval. He enjoyed access to the powerful, and embraced the conventions and privileges of high political society. Together with his political 'moderation', an easy familiarity and skills as a raconteur helped him win many friends irrespective of class and political distinctions. He accepted the hospitality of aristocrats and plutocrats, and became a favourite with George V. He was publicly flattered by political opponents and capitalist newspapers; he received honorary doctorates from the universities of Cambridge (1920) and Oxford (1926); he sent his younger sons to public schools. He generated countless humorous stories, turning upon his unrepentant working-class accent, misplaced aspirates, and ribald observations. To a heckler at a fraught mass union meeting who shouted 'You've sold us', for instance, Thomas is reported to have replied: 'I tried to, but nobody would 'ave you.' Complaining to F. E. Smith, Lord Birkenhead, after a hard night's drinking, 'Ooh Fred, I've got an 'ell of an 'eadache', he is said to have prompted Birkenhead to reply: 'Try a couple of aspirates.' With his stocky figure, chubby face, moustache, and round-lensed spectacles, he was a cartoonist's delight.

Thomas openly revelled in a social and popular success which for him symbolized the labour movement's advance. Many of its class-conscious, high-minded, or puritanical members and its later historians were, however, appalled at what they regarded as class betrayal. Yet in epitomizing what many others considered to be the Labour Party's acceptable face, Thomas assisted its advance in the 1920s. He attracted working-class voters who were indifferent or hostile towards socialism, while his constitutionalism helped persuade Conservative and Liberal leaders that a Labour government would not be so dangerous as to require extraordinary obstruction.

Colonial secretary and lord privy seal From 1918 Thomas was a member of the Parliamentary Labour Party's leadership. After the indecisive December 1923 general election, his access to the king and senior officials helped ease the appointment of the first Labour government. He was particularly close to the party leader, MacDonald, and was his first choice for foreign secretary. Opposed by the party's internationalists, he was instead appointed colonial secretary, primarily to handle the Irish boundary problem, and was one of the more successful ministers. Again denied the Foreign Office in the 1929 Labour government, this time by Henderson demanding the post, he became lord privy seal with special responsibility for reducing unemployment. He visited Canada to promote imperial trade and migration, and in early 1930 obtained City of London support for industrial rationalization. But he quickly grasped that Labour's short-term employment policies, notably public works, would make little immediate impact, and as the world depression developed from late 1929 he accepted the conventional view that tax increases should be minimized and business confidence maintained by limiting expenditure on employment schemes. As unemployment rose he became badly demoralized, and ceased to consult his ministerial assistants, George Lansbury, Thomas Johnston, and Sir Oswald Mosley. When they complained to MacDonald in January 1930 and Mosley produced a memorandum proposing a reflationary programme, Thomas offered his resignation. He was persuaded to withdraw it by the appointment of a cabinet committee, whose report in May supported Thomas's cautious approach. But Mosley's consequent resignation finally undermined Thomas's position, and MacDonald moved him to the dominion secretaryship. Converted by the depression and dominion pressure to imperial protectionism, Thomas now met resistance from the chancellor of the exchequer, Philip Snowden. But, as a budget and monetary crisis developed, he shared Snowden's belief in the need for retrenchment. Together with his perception that the depression had destroyed the Labour government's credibility, this persuaded Thomas during the political crisis in August 1931 to follow MacDonald and Snowden in defying the TUC general council's opposition to social service cuts and in joining Conservative and Liberal leaders in the emergency National Government when the Labour cabinet split.

Dominion secretary in the National Government Thomas's decision was consistent with his earlier political and economic opinions, but circumstances had pushed them so far that now most of the labour movement considered him a traitor. He was expelled from the Labour Party along with MacDonald and Snowden, and dismissed from his NUR post and denied his union pension. When the new Labour opposition leaders repudiated much of what they had earlier accepted in office, Thomas turned upon them—ruthlessly exposing their inconsistency, and supporting the Conservative leaders' proposals for a permanent anti-socialist coalition. In the October 1931 general election he held Derby against bitter Labour opposition, and remained dominion secretary in the reconstructed government. During the National Government's internal dispute over trade policy he became an open protectionist, and helped negotiate the trade agreements concluded at the 1932 Imperial Economic Conference in Ottawa. He was also responsible that year for imposing economic sanctions in defence of the Irish treaty against De Valera's unilateral assertions of Irish free state autonomy.

As one symbol of the government's claim to be 'national' rather than merely Conservative, Thomas remained important within the coalition leadership. But after the 1935 election he was demoted to colonial secretary. He had become less credible as a 'Labour' representative, and a less reliable minister as his drinking and gambling tipped into intemperance. During the 1920s he had started speculating in the financial markets, and by the 1930s had acquired dubious obligations and connections. When before the 1936 budget unusual insurance transactions suggested that information on tax increases had been leaked, a judicial inquiry found that Thomas had made unauthorized disclosures to two friends. He had not personally benefited and his denial of intentional leakage was widely believed; but the indiscretion conformed all too well with his known habits. He resigned from the government in May and, after an emotional statement, from the Commons in June.

Retirement and death Although Thomas never returned to public life, he spent some time in business, as chairman of British Amalgamated Transport Ltd. He died in London on 21 January 1949. After cremation at Golders Green crematorium, his ashes were buried in Swindon. He was survived by his wife. His second son, Leslie Thomas (1906–1971) was Conservative MP for Canterbury from 1953 to 1966.   PHILIP WILLIAMSON

Sources J. H. Thomas, *My story* (1937) · J. H. Thomas, *When labour rules* (1920) · G. Blaxland, *J. H. Thomas: a life for unity* (1964) · P. S. Bagwell, *The railwaymen: the history of the National Union of Railwaymen*, [1] (1963) · H. A. Clegg, A. Fox, and A. F. Thompson, *A history of British trade unions since 1889*, 2 (1985) · D. Howell, '"I loved my union and my country": Jimmy Thomas and the politics of railway trade unionism', *Twentieth Century British History*, 6 (1995), 145–73 · T. Adams, 'Leadership and oligarchy: British rail unions, 1914–1922', *Studies in History and Politics*, 5 (1986), 23–45 · M. Cowling, *The impact of labour, 1920–1924: the beginning of modern British politics* (1971) · R. Skidelsky, *Politicians and the slump: the labour government of 1929–1931* (1967) · A. Thorpe, '"I am in the cabinet": J. H. Thomas's decision to join the national government in 1931', *Historical Research*, 64 (1991), 389–402 · P. Williamson, *National crisis and national government: British politics, the economy and empire, 1926–1932* (1992) · D. W. Bebbington, 'Baptist members of parliament in the twentieth century', *Baptist Quarterly*, 31 (1985–6), 252–87 ·

A. Thorpe, 'J. H. Thomas and the rise of labour in Derby, 1880–1945', *Midland History*, 15 (1990), 111–28

Archives CKS, corresp. and papers · Glamorgan RO, Cardiff, letters · HLRO, corresp. · PRO | Bodl. RH, corresp. with Sir Granville Orde Browne and related papers · Bodl. RH, corresp. with Sir Robert Coryndon relating to Kenya · Bodl. RH, papers relating to Tshekedi Khama affair · Bodl. RH, corresp. with Lord Lugard · CAC Cam., corresp. with Sir E. L. Spears · Durham RO, letters to Lady Londonderry · Glamorgan RO, Cardiff, letters to E. C. Gough · HLRO, corresp. with Lord Beaverbrook · PRO, corresp. with Ramsay MacDonald, 1/207/41 · U. Warwick Mod. RC, International Transport Federation MSS · U. Warwick Mod. RC, National Union of Railwaymen MSS · U. Warwick Mod. RC, TUC MSS | FILM BFI NFTVA, documentary footage · BFI NFTVA, news footage

Likenesses photographs, 1911–36, Hult. Arch. · W. Stoneman, photograph, 1924, NPG [*see illus.*] · D. Low, chalk pencil, c.1926, NPG · group photograph, 1932, NPG · W. Stoneman, photograph, 1934, NPG · T. Cottrell, cigarette card, NPG · D. Low, working drawing, NPG · S. Morse-Brown, chalk drawing, NMG Wales · B. Partridge, pen and ink and watercolour caricature, NPG; repro. in *Punch* (1 Nov 1926) · A. P. F. Ritchie, cigarette card, NPG · E. Townsend, two portraits, priv. coll.

Wealth at death £15,032 8s. 8d.: probate, 24 Oct 1949, CGPLA Eng. & Wales

Thomas, James Purdon Lewes, Viscount Cilcennin (1903–1960), politician, was born on 13 October 1903 at Cae-glas, Llandeilo, Carmarthenshire, the only son of John Lewes Thomas (1862–1910), a justice of the peace, and his wife, Anne Louisa (1868–1942), daughter of Commander George Purdon RN, of Tinarana, co. Clare. He was educated at Rugby School (becoming a governor in 1937 and chairman in 1958), and at Oriel College, Oxford, where he obtained an *aegrotat* degree in French in 1926.

From a minor post in the central office of the Conservative Party, Thomas was in 1929 appointed an assistant private secretary to the prime minister, Stanley Baldwin. In the same year he stood unsuccessfully as member of parliament for Llanelli. He was elected in 1931 for Hereford, retaining the seat until created a peer in December 1955.

Preferring the discreet business of political manoeuvre to the open exercise of power, Thomas made an ideal parliamentary private secretary. His first master (1932–6) was his namesake J. H. Thomas, secretary of state for the dominions and later for the colonies. Outwardly they were an ill-assorted pair, the defiant plebeian and the self-possessed patrician. Yet each took a humorous view of life which led many to underestimate their judgement. At no time was the younger man's affection and loyalty more movingly displayed than during his chief's resignation in 1936, the result of a leak of budget secrets. During the war, too, he was to place personal allegiance above cautious conformity by openly visiting Baldwin at the nadir of that statesman's fortunes.

Thomas gave the same unstinted devotion to Anthony Eden, secretary of state for foreign affairs, whose parliamentary private secretary he became in 1937. Less than a fortnight after his appointment, Thomas was approached by emissaries of the prime minister, Neville Chamberlain. Fearing that Eden's open mistrust of Hitler and Mussolini threatened Chamberlain's policy of appeasement, they begged Thomas 'to build a bridge between 10 Downing Street and the Foreign Office'. This he interpreted as an invitation to spy on his chief and he rejected their overtures with indignation. On Eden's resignation in 1938 Thomas unflinchingly followed him into what then seemed the political wilderness, and he abstained from voting in favour of the Munich agreement.

At the outbreak of war in 1939 Thomas volunteered for military service, but was rejected because of a permanently injured knee, and instead joined Eden at the Dominions Office. From 1940 to 1943 he was a tactful and popular government whip in the Commons. Then he became financial secretary to the Admiralty, his first opportunity of showing that attachment to the Royal Navy which was the ruling passion of his life. An irresistible charm and a readiness to admit to ignorance of technical subjects ensured his success in solving labour problems in the dockyards—a necessary prelude to the invasion of Normandy.

After the general election of 1945 Thomas became the opposition spokesman on naval affairs and deputy chairman of the Conservative Party. From Lord Woolton, the chairman, he accepted the task of preparing a list of parliamentary candidates for the guidance of constituencies. His ability to win the confidence of those he interviewed while shrewdly assessing their character enabled him to recruit much youthful talent. This was reflected in the return of his party to power at the general election of 1951.

Thomas had no illusions that he was fitted either by temperament or by reverence for party dogma to occupy the highest offices in the cabinet. Since his wartime years at the Admiralty, however, he had pined to return to this department and his ambition was fulfilled when he became first lord in October 1951. He was sworn of the privy council in November. 'There is only one test of a first lord', he used to remark, 'Will he look well in a yachting cap when visiting the fleet?' Standing over 6 foot, with boldly cut features and a fresh complexion, Thomas was as much at ease on the lower deck as in the ward room. His popularity was immediate and lasting, his progress round any naval establishment a convivial occasion. During his five years at the Admiralty he accepted the controversial recommendation that no officer should be recruited under the age of eighteen, a measure subsequently endorsed by other first lords. He resisted pressure to abolish the Fleet Air Arm, considered by some to be unduly expensive in both men and money. Working with the first sea lord, Lord Mountbatten, he also set up a committee which achieved remarkable economies without substantially reducing naval strength.

In December 1955 Thomas was created Viscount Cilcennin, taking his title from the little river which runs through his family property in Carmarthenshire. Less than a year later, although only fifty-two, he decided with regret to retire from politics to his house at the foot of the Malvern hills. His instinct of hospitality and the splendour of his official residence, Admiralty House, had tempted him to spend more than he could afford. He also suffered increasing pain from arthritis of the hip, which he bore with stoicism. So that his links with the navy should not be snapped too abruptly, he was invited to join the royal yacht *Britannia* for the duke of Edinburgh's tour of the Commonwealth in 1956–7.

Having represented Hereford in the Commons for nearly twenty-five years, Thomas was no less delighted to be appointed lord lieutenant of the county in 1957. His financial burden was eased by invitations to serve on the boards of several companies, and he proved an energetic and lively chairman of Television Wales and Western. In his leisure hours he wrote an attractive little volume on Admiralty House, the profits from which he characteristically decided should be given to a naval charity. He did not live to see its publication, but died in London on 13 July 1960. He was unmarried.

Jim Thomas had a genius for friendship. He was an entertaining talker who radiated gaiety as he sat on into the early hours recounting those personal adventures which owed as much to a sense of poetry as to historical accuracy. He loved gossip but was utterly without malice. The malice of others he dismissed with chuckles and puffs of his pipe. He was quietly well read, a gardener, and a gourmet.   KENNETH ROSE, rev.

Sources personal knowledge (1971) · private information (1971) · Burke, *Peerage* (1959) · *The Times* (14 July 1960) · *CGPLA Eng. & Wales* (1960)

Archives Carmarthenshire RO, corresp. and papers | BL, corresp. with P. V. Emrys-Evans, Add. MS 58242 · U. Birm. L., corresp. with Lord Avon

Likenesses M. Rennell, portrait, priv. coll. · J. Ward, portrait, priv. coll.

Wealth at death £24,649 8s. 7d.: probate, 30 Dec 1960, *CGPLA Eng. & Wales*

Thomas, John (1691–1766), bishop of Salisbury, was born on 23 June 1691, the son of a drayman of Nicholson's brewery in All Hallows parish in the City of London. He attended a parish school, and was admitted, at Nicholson's expense, to Merchant Taylors' School, London, on 11 March 1702, and to St Catharine's College, Cambridge, on 22 January 1709. He graduated BA in 1713, was placed in the *ordo senioritatis*, and proceeded MA in 1717 and DD in 1728, when he was also incorporated at Oxford. He was ordained deacon on 23 May 1714, and priest on 26 February 1716.

About 1720 Thomas accepted the post of chaplain to the English factory, the merchant community, in Hamburg. He was a popular clergyman, and his knowledge of German and publication of a German newspaper attracted the attention of George II during his visits to Hanover. The king preferred Thomas to the living of St Vedast, Foster Lane, London, in 1736, against strong ministerial objections, in order to ensure his attendance as a royal chaplain in 1737, on a similar visit to Hanover. In 1740 George II offered him the vacant deanery of Peterborough, though the duke of Newcastle had offered it to another. At Peterborough he was an active member of both the Peterborough and the Spalding societies. In 1742 he married the niece of Bishop Sherlock of London, the first of four wives about whom little is known. A year later he was nominated to the diocese of St Asaph, but when a vacancy occurred immediately afterwards at Lincoln he asked to be consecrated to that see instead as he hated the prospect of the journey from Wales to London. In 1761 he was appointed to the diocese of Salisbury.

In spite of his easy elevation within the church as a royal favourite Thomas was a conscientious bishop. He took care in examining candidates for holy orders. He was also a celebrated preacher. Thomas's less attractive features included the entertainment he derived from teasing clergymen that he intended to promote them. He also adopted a casual approach to marriage, joking that he had driven his first three wives to their deaths by his refusal to argue with them. The motto, or posy, on the wedding ring at his fourth marriage was: 'if I survive I'll make them five' (Cassan, part 3, 315).

Thomas was an amiable man. His tact may be judged from his ability to dine with the prince of Wales without offending the prince's estranged father, George II. Thomas's deafness and squint did not inhibit his gregariousness. He embodied the latitudinarian regard for compassion above dogma, on one occasion likening a Lutheran minister who would not bury a Calvinist to a woman parishioner of his who had complained that he had buried a man with the pox next to her husband. He is also credited with an emotional charity sermon, imploring his congregation not to let the children perish, and with devoting a tenth of his income to the repair of Lincoln Cathedral.

Bishop Thomas died on 20 July 1766 at the bishop's place, Salisbury, and was buried in Salisbury Cathedral.

John Thomas was also instrumental in the brief revival of support for the Moravian church in Britain in the 1740s. While in Germany he had met Daniel Jablonski, and was convinced that he was the successor to the Bohemian episcopate. In 1746 Thomas attended Count Zinzendorf's sermons in London. During the debate on the bill to give legal recognition to the Moravian church in 1748–9 Thomas argued that their episcopal orders and ordinations were valid. He also acted as an intermediary between Zinzendorf and Bishop Thomas Sherlock of London, whom he converted to a supporter of the Moravian cause. However, within four years of the passage of the Moravian Act of 1749 Thomas had become disaffected to the Morvains, shocked by rumours and allegations that they regarded the Holy Spirit as female and that they blessed genitalia in marriage ceremonies. Bishop Thomas should be carefully distinguished from two of his fellow bishops of the same name, one of whom also occupied the see of Salisbury.

WILLIAM GIBSON

Sources Foster, *Alum. Oxon.* · G. G. Perry and J. H. Overton, *Biographical notices of the bishops of Lincoln: from Remigius to Wordsworth* (1900) · S. H. Cassan, *Lives and memoirs of the bishops of Sherborne and Salisbury, from the year 705 to 1824*, 3 pts (1824) · monumental inscription, Salisbury Cathedral · BL, Add. MS 32702 fol. 13 · G. F. Browne, *St Catharine's College* (1902) · *Memoirs of the life of Gilbert Wakefield*, ed. J. T. Rutt and A. Wainewright, 2 vols. (1804) · *GM*, 1st ser., 54 (1784), 40 · F. Hill, *Georgian Lincoln* (1966) · W. Stubbs, *Registrum sacrum Anglicanum* (1858) · C. J. Podmore, *The Moravian church in England, 1728–1760* (1998) · W. Butler, *Memoirs of Mark Hildesley* (1799) · Venn, *Alum. Cant.*

Archives BL, corresp. with duke of Newcastle, Add. MSS 32710, 32717, 32925, 32958 · Herts. ALS, corresp. with James Wittewronge · Yale U., Farmington, Lewis Walpole Library, corresp. with Edward Weston

Likenesses T. Hudson, portrait, c.1750, Cathedral School, Salisbury

Thomas, John (1696–1781), bishop of Winchester, was born on 17 August 1696 at Westminster, the son of Stremer Thomas, a colonel in the guards, and his wife, Hester. He was educated at Charterhouse School, matriculated from Christ Church, Oxford, on 28 March 1713, and graduated BA in 1716 before proceeding MA in 1719, BD in 1727 and DD in 1731.

In 1720 Thomas was elected fellow of All Souls College; disappointed of church preferment through a friend of his father, he took another route to promotion by establishing a reputation as a London preacher. He began as a curate and became a prebendary of St Paul's in 1731. Two years later he married Susan (d. 1778), daughter of Thomas Mulso of Twywell, Northamptonshire, and they had three daughters. Thomas gave up his All Souls fellowship on marriage, and in the same year was presented by the dean and chapter of St Paul's to the rectory of St Benet Paul's Wharf, a living he retained until 1757; in 1742 he obtained a canonry at St Paul's, which he held until 1748. More importantly he had won the favour of the prince of Wales, and, after the latter was crowned George II, Thomas became one of his chaplains. In 1742 he gave the Boyle lectures, but, as became his wont, did not publish them. He received his reward, however, in the bishopric of Peterborough to which he was consecrated on 4 October 1747.

The peak of Thomas's public career came in 1752 when he was appointed to succeed Thomas Hayter, bishop of Norwich, as preceptor to the young prince of Wales, who was to ascend the throne in 1760. The untimely death of Frederick, the prince's father, from a blow from a tennis ball in 1751, had given a sudden urgency to George's education, and to fears of the influence of his mother. Thomas came in as preceptor under Lord Waldegrave as governor, with George Scott, later a commissioner of excise, as sub-preceptor. The sudden shift in the reversionary interest guaranteed animosity against those in charge of the young prince; but while George III in later life charitably recalled Thomas and Scott 'as men of unexceptionable characters' as distinct from 'Dr Hayter … an intriguing, unworthy man, more fitted to be a Jesuit than an English bishop', Waldegrave set them down as 'men of sense, men of learning, and worthy good men, [who] … had but little weight and influence' and were no match for the dowager princess (*Memoirs and Speeches*, 52). Thomas nevertheless had his reward; in a great reshuffle of the bench contrived by George II in 1757, he succeeded John Gilbert as bishop of Salisbury and clerk of the closet (the duke of Newcastle had intended him for York). From George III, Thomas received the succession to the notorious Benjamin Hoadly as bishop of Winchester in 1761, and remained fulsome in his expressions of gratitude for royal favour.

Thomas left almost as little trace of his activities as bishop as of his pulpit eloquence. Hurd made a snide remark about his patronage. His one visitation of the see of Winchester was the best designed of the eighteenth century, but was treated by many of the clergy with the same casualness as the replies were preserved by the bishop. He did nothing to redress the administrative laxity in his see which went back to the seventeenth century and had become deeply rooted in the time of his predecessor. Thomas died at his home, Winchester House, Chelsea, on 1 May 1781, and was buried in Winchester Cathedral. His wife died on 19 November 1778. W. R. WARD

Sources S. H. Cassan, *The lives of the bishops of Winchester*, 2 vols. (1827) · *The memoirs and speeches of James, 2nd Earl Waldegrave, 1742–1763*, ed. J. C. D. Clark (1988) · W. R. Ward, ed., *Parson and parish in eighteenth-century Surrey*, Surrey RS, 34 (1994) · W. R. Ward, ed., *Parson and parish in eighteenth-century Hampshire*, Hampshire RS, 13 (1995) · F. Kilvert, *Life and writings of Richard Hurd* (1860) · *The correspondence of King George the Third from 1760 to December 1783*, ed. J. Fortescue, 3 (1928) · *The autobiography of Thomas Secker, archbishop of Canterbury*, ed. J. S. Macauley and R. W. Greaves (1988) · IGI · DNB · Foster, *Alum. Oxon.*

Likenesses G. Hayter, oils, c.1771 (after B. Wilson), All Souls Oxf. · R. Houston, mezzotint, c.1771 (after B. Wilson), BM, NPG · N. Dance, oils, 1773, LPL

Thomas, John (*bap.* 1712, *d.* 1793), bishop of Rochester, was born in Abbey Street, St Mary's parish, Carlisle, and baptized in that parish on 7 October 1712, the eldest son of John Thomas (c.1684–1747), minor canon of Carlisle Cathedral and vicar of Brampton, Cumberland, from 1721 to 1747, and his wife, Ann, daughter of Richard Kelsick of Whitehaven, a captain in the merchant navy.

Thomas, like his father, was educated at Carlisle grammar school, where he was admitted for the first time on 5 October 1719, and like his father he attended Queen's College, Oxford, where he matriculated as a commoner on 17 December 1730. He read for the BCL (1742), and the DCL (1742). During the mid-1730s he acted as assistant master at an academy in Soho Square, then became private tutor to William, the younger son of Sir William Clayton, his patron and future brother-in-law.

Thomas was ordained deacon on 27 March 1737, then priest on 25 September 1737. He soon received the valuable rectory of Bletchingley, Surrey, and was instituted on 27 January 1738. Thomas held the benefice until his advancement to a bishopric in 1774, and was a diligent, resident parish priest. He was appointed chaplain-in-ordinary to the king on 17 January 1749, and a canon of Westminster on 19 April 1754. He was a senior member of the abbey chapter for the remainder of his life, being named subdean on 4 July 1758, then dean of Westminster and chancellor of the Order of the Bath in 1768, in succession to his main clerical patron, Bishop Zachary Pearce. It was to Pearce that Thomas in confidence intimated that 'my present business is *to make Hay* while the Sun shines' (WAM 64447, 4 July 1762). There was every sign that he was doing so, for Archbishop Drummond of York had appointed Thomas sub-almoner on 28 December 1761, and he was admitted and instituted to the rectory of St Bride's, Fleet Street, on 7 January 1766. Thomas resigned both these last preferments on taking up the deanery, his preference before any smaller bishopric. He was chosen by Archbishop Cornwallis of Canterbury as his prolocutor to the lower house of convocation in 1768 and 1769. Thomas also followed Pearce in the bishopric of Rochester, in November 1774, holding it like his predecessor *in commendam* with the Westminster deanery. Thomas never lost sight of what he owed to Pearce, telling the Rochester clergy in 1776 he would 'ever account it my greatest merit to follow him, as a son would a father, though with very unequal steps' (*Sermons*, 2.422).

Thomas regularly attended capitular meetings at Westminster and was active in abbey administration while successively canon steward and treasurer between 1754 and 1768. During his deanship, extensive repairs were undertaken to the deanery, the thirteenth century choir of the abbey was replaced with new fittings designed by Henry Keene, and the celebrated Handel memorial festival of 1784 was held with his encouragement. From the late 1780s illness confined him to the episcopal house at Bromley, so chapter documents were sealed without his signature.

While his health held Thomas involved himself fully in the Rochester diocese. He preached frequently at Bromley parish church (he spent £500 on enlarging it), and regularly administered holy communion there. Episcopal visitations were undertaken in 1776 and 1780. He repaired the deanery at Rochester and between 1774 and 1776 spent £3000 on rebuilding the bishop's palace at Bromley, and laid out and adorned the parkscape. A moderate whig and orthodox churchman, he was not involved in politics beyond lending his quiet support in the House of Lords to the administrations of lords North and Pitt. Thomas voted for Roman Catholic relief in 1780 despite a confrontation with the mob in the cloisters of Westminster Abbey.

Thomas married first, on 19 August 1742, at the Chapel Royal, Whitehall, Anne (*c.*1716–1772), sister of Sir William Clayton, and widow of Sir Charles Blackwell, second baronet. She was four years Thomas's junior; she died on 7 July 1772. He married second, on 12 January 1775, by special licence, in Westminster Abbey, Elizabeth, of St George's, Hanover Square, the daughter of Charles Baldwin of Munslow, Shropshire, and widow of Sir Joseph Yates, a judge. There were no children from either marriage. His second wife shared her husband's interest in the fine arts and had copied some of Reynolds's pictures in needlework.

Bishop Thomas died at Bromley on 22 August 1793, after an illness lasting two days, and was buried in the vault at Bletchingley next to his first wife. A man of essentially modest ambition and unblemished life, he had carried out his clerical duties vigorously until ill health overtook him. Thomas was one of the foremost preachers in the reign of George III, and was much appreciated by the king personally. Many of his sermons and charges were published in his lifetime; a collected edition appeared in 1796. He also commanded the respect of his contemporaries on other counts, including his interest in architecture and the fine arts (he left a large collection of rare coins and medals, as well as prints and paintings). As his colleague on the Westminster chapter, Thomas Newton, put it, Thomas had 'a spirit and taste and elegance superior to most men' (Newton, 151). But it was above all for his charity that Bishop Thomas was renowned, as his bequests reveal. During his lifetime, his nephew estimated he had given out about £50,000 in benefactions since about 1743, especially to clergy in financial distress. Thomas was vice-president of the Westminster Infirmary, and a governor of the Middlesex Hospital, and he endowed two scholarships at Westminster School.

NIGEL ASTON

Sources *The sermons and charges of the Right Reverend John Thomas, LL.D. Late Lord bishop of Rochester, and dean of Westminster*, ed. G. A. Thomas (1796) [with an introductory life] · G. B. Routledge, ed., *Carlisle grammar school memorial register, 1264–1924* (1924), 64–5 · Foster, *Alum. Oxon.* · *GM*, 1st ser., 63 (1793), 863, 780, 954 · T. Newton, 'The life of Dr Thomas Newton, late lord bishop of Bristol, written by himself' (1816), 151 · O. Manning and W. Bray, *The history and antiquities of the county of Surrey*, 2 (1809), 315 · U. Lambert, *Blechingley: a parish history*, 2 (1921), 454–5 · *The rectors of Bletchingley, Surrey* (1981), 32–3 · *Fasti Angl.* (Hardy), 3.314, 319 · *Fasti Angl., 1541–1857*, [Ely], 71 · J. C. Sainty and R. Bucholz, eds., *Officials of the royal household, 1660–1837*, 1: *Department of the lord chamberlain and associated offices* (1997), 57 · E. Carpenter, ed., *A house of kings: the history of Westminster Abbey* (1972), 211–12 · J. Perkins, *Westminster Abbey: its worship and ornaments*, 1 (1938), 83–5, 123–4, 131–48 · E. W. Brayley and J. P. Neale, *The history and antiquities of the abbey church of St Peter, Westminster*, 1 (1818), 208–11 · A. P. Stanley, *Historical memorials of Westminster Abbey*, 5th edn (1882), 477–9 · A. J. Pearman, *Diocesan histories: Rochester* (1897) · J. L. Chester and J. Foster, eds., *London marriage licences, 1521–1869* (1887), 1330 · GEC, *Baronetage*, 5.47 · parish register, St Mary's, Carlisle, Cumbria AS, Carlisle · WAM 64447, Thomas to Pearce, 4 July 1762, Westminster Abbey Muniment Room, London

Likenesses J. Bacon, statue, 1793 (after J. Reynolds), Westminster Abbey · J. Swaine, line engraving, pubd 1822 (after B. Vandergucht), BM, NPG · S. W. Reynolds, mezzotint, pubd 1836 (after J. Reynolds), BM, NPG · J. Baker, line engraving (after R. Corbould), BM, NPG; repro. in *The Senetor*, 1 (1791) · G. P. Harding, portrait (after Vandergucht), Carlisle grammar school library · attrib. J. Reynolds (after J. Reynolds), Aston Hall, Birmingham · B. Vandergucht, oils, deanery of Westminster; copy, Carlisle grammar school library

Wealth at death left fortune to relatives; cancelled bonds and promissory notes due to him worth £5000; left £1000 in 3 per cent consols on trust to provide three exhibitions at Queen's College, Oxford, of £10 p.a. for clergymen's sons from the diocese of Carlisle educated at Carlisle grammar school or, failing that, from St Bee's school; £1000 in 3 per cent consols on trust left to Christ Church, Oxford, for the same purpose; £100 bequest to the Middlesex Hospital, London: Queen's College, Oxford; *GM*, 863, 954

Thomas, John [Ioan, John Thomas Rhaeadr Gwy] (*bap.* 1730, *d.* in or before 1806), schoolmaster and Independent minister, was born at Col, a cottage in Myddfai, Carmarthenshire, and was baptized on 25 April 1730, St Mark's day, at Myddfai parish church. He was the illegitimate son of Thomas Evan and an unnamed mother, but was brought up by a foster mother, who died in 1738, and subsequently by an aunt. His childhood was dominated by insecurity, ill health, and severe spiritual anxiety; his only education was three months at a local school. His interest in religion was aroused by reading devotional books and participating in the family devotions at Gellifelen, Myddfai, where, from the age of eleven, he served as a farm labourer. He then came into contact with the Methodist society at Cefn Telych, Myddfai, where he heard of Griffith Jones (1684–1761), of Llanddowror, who later acceded to his request to become his servant. Since Griffith Jones sought to dissuade him from his ambition to prepare for the ministry, he turned to Howel Harris (1714–1773) after hearing him preach at the house of Jethro Dafydd Evan at Llanddeusant. Harris enabled him to attend his school at Trefeca from November 1745 until the autumn of 1746. In 1750 Thomas preached for the first time at Cantref, near Brecon, and, at the Methodist Association at Carmarthen in 1752, he was accepted as an authorized preacher. For the next ten years he travelled widely, conducting circulating schools and preaching.

In 1761 Thomas became convinced that the Independent church view of church government best accorded with scripture and consequently became a dissenter. In that year he entered the nonconformist academy at Abergavenny, under the tuition of David Jardine. While there he was supported by grants from the Independent church fund board from April 1762 until January 1766. On 23 April 1767 he was ordained minister of the three Independent churches at Cae-bach, near Llandrindod, Rhaeadr Gwy, and Garn, all in Radnorshire. This brought him under the generous patronage of an admirer of Howel Harris, the wealthy Thomas Jones (d. 1782), of Trefonnen and Pencerrig, Radnorshire, whose uncle, Thomas Jones (1675–1745), had built Cae-bach chapel in 1715. On 6 June 1768, in the parish church of Llanfynydd, Carmarthenshire, Thomas married Elizabeth, the daughter of John Jones (d. 1778) and his wife Diana (d. 1788), of Dyffryn Isa, Llanfynydd. They had three children: Ioan, born in April 1775, Elizabeth, who was born on 26 September 1781 but died of smallpox in November 1782, and Thomas, of whom nothing is known but that he was a wild character who enlisted in the army in 1795 and no more was heard of him.

During Thomas's visits to Trefeca, Selina, countess of Huntingdon, heard him preach and invited him to take services at the churches of her connexion in Brighton and Sussex, which he did during a two-month visit. He suffered much opposition at Cae-bach after a very flourishing period, and resigned his pastorate in 1778; he continued at his two other churches for a short period. Thereafter he lived an unsettled life and moved house no fewer than eight times between 1775 and 1799 before residing finally at Carmarthen. He supported himself by keeping school and received additional support from the proceeds of his wife's little shop, as well as from occasional gifts from well-wishers and grants from the Societas Evangelica.

In all, Thomas published some twenty-seven titles. The most important of them is his autobiography. Its title, *Rhad ras* ('Free grace'), published in 1810, echoes John Bunyan's *Grace Abounding* upon which it seems to have been modelled, inasmuch as its contents have much to say about his spiritual development. He also published elegies for the countess of Huntingdon and Howel Harris, and collections of hymns in both Welsh and English. He represented the incursion of the methods and spirituality of the

evangelical revival into the older dissent, with his untiring itinerant preaching in every county in Wales and the astonishing charismatic manifestations that accompanied his preaching. John Thomas died before March 1806.

R. TUDUR JONES

Sources I. Thomas, *Rhad ras* (1810) • I. Thomas, *Rhad ras*, ed. J. D. Owen (1949) • J. Thomas, confession of faith, NL Wales, Add. MS 383, D • E. Owen, *Libri Walliae* (1987) • D. B. James, *Myddfai: its lands and peoples* (1991) • T. Beynon, ed., *Howell Harris's visits to Pembrokeshire* (1966), 332 • NL Wales, Griffith E. Owen papers, MS 7794 [abstract of title to half of Dyffryn Isa, March 1806] • R. C. B. Oliver, *The family history of Thomas Jones, the artist, of Pencerrig, Radnorshire* (1970) • D. S. Davies, 'Extract from the diaries and account book of Thomas Jones, Pencerig', *Transactions of the Radnorshire Society*, 12 (1942), 3–40 • A. P. Oppé, ed., 'Memoirs of Thomas Jones, Penkerrig, Radnorshire', *Walpole Society*, 32 (1946–8) [whole issue]

Thomas, John [*pseud.* Ieuan Ddu] (**1795–1871**), composer and schoolmaster, was born at Pibwr Llwyd, a farmhouse near Carmarthen. He was educated at Carmarthen, where he later kept a school for a short time. He moved to Merthyr Tudful, Glamorgan, about 1830 to follow the same occupation. Except for a short period when he was clerk to the Chartist Zephania Williams at Blaenau Gwent, Monmouthshire, his whole life was spent in keeping private schools of his own, first at Merthyr Tudful, and from 1850 at Pontypridd and Trefforest successively. He was twice married; both wives predeceased him. He died at Wood Road, Trefforest, on 30 June 1871, and was buried at Glyntaf cemetery, Pontypridd, where a monument was erected over his grave by his 'friends and pupils'.

Thomas was one of the chief pioneers of choral training in the industrial districts of Glamorgan, and he had many eisteddfod successes with his choirs. For several years he regularly held music classes at Merthyr and Pontypridd. In 1845 he published a collection of Welsh airs entitled *Y caniedydd Cymreig* (*The Cambrian Minstrel*). This contained forty-three pieces of his own composition and 104 old Welsh airs, half of which he obtained through oral research in Carmarthenshire and Glamorgan and which had never been previously published. Almost all these airs were published with both the Welsh and English words. Many were adopted in later collections of Welsh music. In 1849 Thomas published a poem, 'The Vale of Taff', which was followed in 1867 by a volume of poetry entitled *Cambria upon Two Sticks*, in which his disillusionment with eisteddfods is evident. He also contributed many papers to magazines, and a prize essay of his on the Welsh harp was published in the *Cambrian Journal* for 1855.

D. L. THOMAS, rev. TREVOR HERBERT

Sources DWB • J. E. Lloyd, R. T. Jenkins, and W. L. Davies, eds., *Y bywgraffiadur Cymreig hyd 1940* (1953) • M. Stephens, ed., *The Oxford companion to the literature of Wales* (1986) • D. Morgans, *Music and musicians of Merthyr and district* (1922)
Wealth at death under £300: probate, 11 July 1871, CGPLA Eng. & Wales

Thomas, John (**1813–1862**), architectural sculptor, was born at Chalford, Gloucestershire, and rose from modest beginnings to outstanding success. His parents are untraced. Apprenticed in 1825 to a stonemason, he was regarded as a 'prodigy of precocious genius' (*Art Journal*).

In the final year of his apprenticeship, on a visit to his brother Robert, Oxford's architecture fired his ambition as a carver and draughtsman. He settled in Birmingham, where his elder brother William practised as an architect; his carving on monuments impressed Sir Charles Barry, who hired him to carve in wood and stone the coats of arms and other ornamental work for his Gothic-style King Edward VI Grammar School, Birmingham (1833–7; dem.).

Barry, recognizing 'his sureness of hand, celerity of execution and commanding intelligence' (Scott, 79), employed Thomas in 1837 to manage the production of the carving for his new Palace of Westminster. To hone Thomas's knowledge in preparation for this challenge, Barry sent him on a drawing tour of Belgium. The office of woods ratified the arrangement in 1841 and appointed Thomas as superintendent of stone carving in 1846 at a salary of £300 p.a. (£400 from 1847 to 1850). From small drawings supplied by Barry's office, he and his team developed large-scale drawings which formed the basis of the full-size plasters from which the figures and architectural work were carved in stone. Underpinned by 'the complete practical training, with the versatile and inventive ability, displayed by Thomas' (ibid., 80), Barry's vision of a sculpture programme to commemorate British history through heraldry and figures of the kings and queens from Saxon times to Queen Victoria, together with national figures and saints associated with Britain, was carried out triumphantly. Closely overseeing Thomas, Barry estimated that the cost of this work up to 1850 totalled £32,000.

Thomas worked on many other famous building projects of his day. For Robert Stephenson's Britannia Railway Bridge across the Menai Strait to Anglesey (opened in 1850) he carved the monumental lions weighing 80 tons; for Edward Walter's Manchester Free Trade Hall, tympana depicting *The Continents*, *Trade*, *The Arts*, *Industry*, and so on (1853–6); and for Cuthbert Brodrick's Leeds town hall (1858), a tympanum of *Progress, Art and Commerce*. His workshop was equally adept at the Italian Renaissance palazzo style, then especially popular with banks. The sumptuous carving on the former West of England and South Wales District Bank in Bristol by W. B. Gingell and T. K. Lysaght (1854–8) and on the Langside Public Hall in Glasgow (designed as a bank by J. Gibson, 1847) illustrates the high standard that his workshop achieved. Barry went to him for both his Italian Renaissance Bridgewater House, London (1845–54), and for his alterations to Harewood House, Yorkshire (1848–50). The workshop continued to undertake Gothic-style carving, as shown in the series of figures connected with Bristol history for the Guildhall designed by R. S. Pope (1843–6).

The variety of Thomas's output was wide: Italianate garden ornaments and layouts (for example, *The Atlas Fountain*, Castle Howard, and reliefs for the Serpentine, Hyde Park, London); church furnishings (including the font designed by Thomas Willement for Davington Priory, Kent, costing £17 8s. in 1847, and the figure of St Michael for Sowton, Devon, 1845); and designs for the decorative arts such as the *St George Fountain* (des.), manufactured in majolica by Minton & Co., shown at the 1862 Exhibition, London, and glass chandeliers made by Osler of Birmingham for the New Palace, Constantinople.

Through his involvement with the new Palace of Westminster, Thomas met Sir Morton Peto, its building contractor, and his partner, Edward Ladd Betts. For both he worked as an architect. For Betts—a generous buyer of his marble sculpture—he built Preston Hall, Aylesford, Kent (1850), and laid out its garden. Peto commissioned him to rebuild Somerleyton Hall, Suffolk (begun 1844). Here Thomas not only created a vast Italianate/Jacobean pile in red brick with exaggeratedly large stone architectural elements, set in lavish gardens, but rebuilt the church and village too. Peto also had Thomas design the Regent's Park Chapel and carve the memorial to Sir Hugh Myddleton, the originator of the 'new river project' for Islington Green, London (1862).

Thomas presumably met his most illustrious architectural patron, Prince Albert, through his Westminster work. The warm obituary in the *Illustrated London News* recorded, 'The Prince Consort highly esteemed Thomas and appreciated the simplicity of his character; he found in the plain-spoken Gloucestershire artist a man of consummate ability without conceit or arrogance' (*ILN*). Among the no doubt closely supervised commissions for his royal patron were the tiled dairy in the Home Farm, Windsor, reliefs of Peace and War for the interior of Buckingham Palace, and the remodelling of the print room at Windsor.

Thomas also worked as a fine art sculptor, exhibiting frequently at the Royal Academy between 1842 and 1861. His subjects—*Lear* (exh. RA, 1842); *Musidora* (exh. RA, 1849); *Queen Boadicea* (exh. RA, 1856); *Una and the Lion* (exh. RA, 1861); and *Lady Godiva* (plaster, exh. RA, 1861; Maidstone Museum, Kent)—are typical of his time. He undertook some public monuments: for Birmingham, figures of *Thomas Attwood*, the radical (unveiled 1859, cost £900) and *Joseph Surge*, a Quaker philanthropist (unveiled 1862, cost £1000), and, presented to Maidstone, Kent, by Alexander Randal, a drinking fountain incorporating a statue of Queen Victoria under a Gothic canopy (1862).

Thomas died at his home, Florentine Villa, 15 Blomfield Road, Paddington, London, on 9 April 1862 from blood poisoning—or overwork, according to his friends who felt that his life had been shortened by the initially hostile response to the showing of his *National Monument to Shakespeare* in the 1862 Exhibition in London. His obituary in *The Builder* mentioned his wife and daughter.

Contemporaries admired Thomas for his prodigious energy and ambition to work as architect, fine art sculptor, and architectural carver. Barry in a letter summed up the man whose talent had enabled him to build one of the icons of the Victorian age as 'an unassuming self taught genius in his way' (priv. coll.). TIMOTHY STEVENS

Sources *Art Journal* (1849), 340 · *ILN* (Aug 1862), 231 · *The Builder* (1862), 275 · B. Read, *Victorian sculpture* (1982) · W. B. Scott, *The British school of sculpture* (1871) · J. Lever, ed., *Catalogue of the drawings collection of the Royal Institute of British Architects: T–Z* (1984) · B. Read, 'Architectural sculpture', *The Houses of Parliament*, ed. M. H. Port

(1976) · *Art Journal* (1862), 144 · G. T. Noszlopy, *Public sculpture of Birmingham*, ed. J. Beach (1998) · T. Willement, *Historical sketch of the parish of Davington* (1862) · Pevsner · *CGPLA Eng. & Wales* (1862) · Graves, *RA exhibitors* · d. cert.

Likenesses C. Baugniet, lithograph, 1847, BM · C. Baugniet, lithograph, RIBA · engraving (after photograph?), repro. in *ILN* · woodcut (after W. B. Scott), NPG; repro. in Scott, *British school* · woodcut, BM

Wealth at death under £25,000: probate, 1862

Thomas, John (1821–1892), Congregational minister, the son of Owen Thomas (1785–1831), stonecutter, and his wife, Mary, was born in Thomas Street, Holyhead, on 3 February 1821. He had three sisters and four brothers, of whom Owen *Thomas (1812–1891) was one. The family moved to Bangor in 1827. With the death of his father on 8 October 1831 the family suffered extreme poverty and John was put out to work, first as a shop assistant then as a shoemaker. His early education was meagre. In September 1838 he left the Calvinistic Methodist church of his childhood and joined the Congregational church at Bangor under the ministry of Dr Arthur Jones (1776–1860), who encouraged him to start preaching. From February to June 1838 he kept a school at Prestatyn, and from October 1839 to spring 1840 one at Penmorfa, Caernarvonshire. He spent a few weeks as a student at the school of John Jones (1798–1840) at Marton, Shropshire, and six months in 1841 at the academy conducted by Dr William Davies (1805–1859) at Ffrwd-fâl, Carmarthenshire. Thomas in later life bewailed his lack of an effective education.

Thomas was ordained minister of the Congregational church at Bwlchnewydd, Carmarthenshire, on 15 June 1842, but moved to Addoldy, Glyn-nedd, Glamorgan, being inducted there on 18 April 1850. On 14 May 1854 he was inducted minister of the Tabernacle Welsh Congregational Church, Liverpool, and remained there until his death. On 23 January 1843 he married Eliza, the widow of Owen Owens, his predecessor at Bwlchnewydd. She died on 1 August 1888, aged seventy-six. She had five children from her first marriage and four from her second.

Thomas was a man of immense energy. He first attracted public attention as a temperance advocate when no more than eighteen years of age. He soon attained the front rank as a preacher, delivering a vast number of sermons over the years in every part of Wales. As a militant dissenter, he organized the campaign to celebrate the bicentenary of the Ejection of 1662. His plan was to erect a new Congregational college that would absorb the three colleges that served the denomination in Wales. The new building, on the site of the existing Brecon College, was opened in September 1869 as Brecon Memorial College, but the other two colleges refused his 'one college' plan. This brought him into conflict with the formidable principal of Bala College, Michael D. Jones (1822–1898), the pioneer of modern Welsh nationalism. It developed into an intensely acrimonious controversy which convulsed the churches until 1890. One of the points at issue was Thomas's policy (opposed by Jones) of seeking to create a more organized and centralized form of Congregationalism. During the controversy Thomas displayed his abilities as a campaign organizer and as a leader who was

adept at concealing an unbending determination behind a veil of Victorian courtesy. He was the prime mover in the formation of the Union of Welsh Independents in 1871 and was its chairman in 1878. He was chairman of the Congregational Union of England and Wales in 1885.

Thomas was also an able journalist and author. He edited two monthly magazines, *Y Gwerinwr* in 1855 and 1856, and *Yr Anibynnwr* from 1857 to 1861. His most influential literary platform, however, was the weekly newspaper *Y Tyst*, which he edited jointly with William Rees (1802–1883) until 1872, and on his own until his death. After the general election of 1868 he took an enthusiastic interest in Liberal politics, and was one of the leading advocates of disestablishment. He published sermons, biographies, novels, and a massive five-volume history of the Welsh Congregational churches, in co-operation with Thomas Rees (1815–1885).

John Thomas died at Old Colwyn on 14 July 1892 and was buried at Anfield cemetery, Liverpool.

R. TUDUR JONES

Sources O. Thomas and J. M. Rees, *Cofiant y Parchedig John Thomas* (1898) · R. G. Owen, 'Helynt y cyfansoddiadau', MA diss., U. Wales, 1941 · O. M. Edwards, *Gwaith John Thomas* (1905) · D. Griffith, 'Y. Parch. John Thomas, D.D.', *Y Geninen*, 10 (1892), 162–8 · *Cymru* (1892), 177–81 · *Cymru* (1893), 11–20 · *Y Dysgedydd* (1892) [311–12, 315–16, 324–337] · *Y Diwygiwr* (1892), 229–35 · I. C. Peate, 'Helynt y cyfansoddiadau', *Y Llenor*, 12 (1933), 1–10, 231–41; 13 (1934), 163–70; 15 (1936), 209–14 · *Y Dysgedydd* (1881), 77–83 · *DWB* · R. Tudur Jones, *Yr undeb* (1975)

Archives NL Wales, letters to his family · U. Wales, Bangor

Likenesses W. Williams, portrait, College of Welsh Independents, Aberystwyth

Wealth at death £2147 12s.: probate, 10 Aug 1892, *CGPLA Eng. & Wales*

Thomas, John [*pseud.* Pencerdd Gwalia] (1826–1913), harpist, was born on 1 March 1826, in Bridgend, Glamorgan, the eldest of the seven children of John Thomas (1807–1895), a tailor, and his wife, Catherine Jones (1806–1863). In 1838, at the age of twelve, he competed at the Abergavenny eisteddfod, playing in the traditional Welsh manner with his left hand in the treble and his right hand in the bass, and won the major prize of a new triple-strung harp (which is now in the Royal College of Music, London). From 1840 to 1846, sponsored by Ada, Lady Lovelace, he studied at the Royal Academy of Music, where he was obliged not only to reverse his hand position, but to abandon the traditional instrument in favour of the standard double-action pedal harp. He played the pedal harp for the rest of a career which spanned some sixty years, his last concert taking place on 17 June 1905.

In February 1851 Thomas was engaged to play for the summer Italian Opera seasons at Her Majesty's Theatre, London. As he was free to travel during the winter months, the next decade saw him giving concerts in centres such as Leipzig, Vienna, St Petersburg, Paris, and Rome. Berlioz, who heard him play in Paris in 1854, confessed himself 'charmé, fasciné, magnetisé'.

Between 1850 and 1910 Thomas published editions of more than 200 works, including major harp compositions

John Thomas [Pencerdd Gwalia] (1826–1913), by Elliott & Fry, 1870s

by Handel, Spohr, the English harp virtuoso Elias Parish Alvars (1808–1849), and Mozart, whose concerto for flute and harp (K299) he introduced at a Philharmonic Society concert on 14 May 1877, and which he published the following year, 100 years after its composition. In 1857, 1862, 1870, and 1874 he consolidated his Welsh links with the publication of his *Welsh Melodies* for the harp and for the voice, and from 1862 onwards he promoted some forty annual concerts of Welsh music, with large choral forces and multiple harps. He was invested with the title of Pencerdd Gwalia (chief musician of Wales) at the national eisteddfod held at Aberdâr in 1861.

Following the death of his teacher, John Balsir Chatterton, in April 1871, Thomas succeeded him as professor at the Royal Academy of Music and, in 1872, as harpist-in-ordinary to the queen. A further appointment as musician-in-ordinary followed in 1885, and after the death of Queen Victoria he continued as harpist to Edward VII.

Thomas was already fifty-one when, on 21 February 1878, he married Alice Ann Keate (1855–1880), a former pupil. She died on 26 November 1880, six weeks after the birth of their first child, John Llewelyn. On 6 August 1885 he married another pupil, Joan Frances Denny (1849–1926). Their three children were Arthur Charles (*b.* 1886), Ada Myvanwy (*b.* 1889), and Gwilym Ivor (1893–1972), who had a notable career in the army.

Thomas lived at addresses in Great Portland Street, London, from 1852 until 1862, when he moved to 53 Welbeck Street. He lived there for the next forty-nine years, and finally moved to Llanddulas, Station Road, New Barnet, Hertfordshire, where he died, aged eighty-seven, on 19 March 1913. The cause of death was given as 'softening of the brain'. He was buried at Hampstead cemetery on 25 March 1913.   ANN GRIFFITHS

Sources declarations regarding date of birth, NL Wales, Thomas MS 23398F, fols. 8–11 · journals and diaries, 1851–74, NL Wales, Thomas MSS 23389–23397 · scrap album, 1851–85, NL Wales, Thomas MS 23401E · *MT*, 40 (1899), 725–30 · S. Davies, 'John Thomas (Pencerdd Gwalia)', *Y Cerddor* (Oct–Dec 1916) · S. Davies, 'John Thomas (Pencerdd Gwalia)', *Y Cerddor* (Jan–Feb 1917) · A. Morgan, 'Bridgend sixty years ago', *Bridgend Chronicle* (14 Feb–25 April 1890) · correspondence, 1842–1910, NL Wales, Thomas MSS 23389E–23391E · Erard's ledgers, bk 3, Feb 1829–Dec 1917, Royal College of Music, London, Instrument Museum
Archives NL Wales, corresp. · Royal College of Music, London, Instrument Museum · Royal College of Music, London | NL Wales, letters to Johnes family
Likenesses W. Davies, marble bust, 1863, Royal College of Music, London · Elliott & Fry, photograph, 1870–79, NPG [*see illus.*] · Bergamasco, photograph, 1874, National Museum of Folk Life, St Fagan's, Cardiff · S. P. Hall, pencil drawing, NPG · Lavender, photograph, repro. in F. Griffith, ed., *Notable Welsh musicians of today* (1896) · photograph (as young man), NL Wales
Wealth at death £965 12s. 10d.: resworn probate, 1 Aug 1913, CGPLA Eng. & Wales

Thomas, John Evan (1810–1873), sculptor, was born in Brecon, Brecknockshire, on 15 January 1810, the eldest son of John Thomas of Castle Street, Brecon, and his wife, Jane Evans of Aberedw, Radnorshire. His father encouraged his talent in carving and sent him to London to study under Francis Chantrey, and on the continent. Thomas produced the first of numerous church monuments in 1831, and began to practise as a portrait sculptor in London in 1834. He established a studio at 7 Lower Belgrave Place, from which he frequently exhibited marble portrait busts at the Royal Academy until 1862. His brother William Meredyth Thomas (1819–1877), also a student of Chantrey, was his assistant for thirty years. In 1840 Thomas married Mary, daughter of William Gunter.

Despite his move to London, Thomas retained close links with the gentry of his home town, and the principal Welsh landed families. These sitters and patrons included the marquess of Camden (1840), Sir Watkin Williams Bailey Wynn (1840), Sir Charles Morgan (1841), Sir Joseph Bailey (1841, 1853) and Joseph Bailey jun. (1851, 1870), the marquess and marchioness of Bute (1842, 1844, 1848), Walter de Winton (1843) and John Parry de Winton (1850, 1870), vice-chancellor Sir James Lewis Knight-Bruce (1844, 1849), the first Lord Clive (1845, 1857), M. Williams, canon of St David's (1845), Sir William Nott (1848), Colonel Gwynne (1848), Viscount Hereford (1848), Sir Benjamin Hall (1852), William Daniel Conybeare, dean of Llandaff (1853), Alfred Ollivant, bishop of Llandaff (1853), and Rear-Admiral David Price (1855).

In 1834 Thomas received a commission from Queen Victoria to produce a tablet in memory of Madame Louis. In 1844 he exhibited at Westminster Hall his model for the statue of the second marquess of Londonderry, which was executed in marble and erected in Westminster Abbey in 1850. It received a mixed response, being described by the *Literary Gazette* as 'without dignity in the head and without dignity in the attitude', while the *Art Union* considered that it had 'very considerable merit' (both cited in Gunnis, 390). Thomas contributed statues of Henri de Londres, archbishop of Dublin, and William, earl of Pembroke, to Augustus Welby Pugin's rebuilding of the House of Lords in 1848. In the same year, his monumental seated bronze statue of Sir Charles Morgan was 'rapidly progressing' (*ILN*, 3 June 1848, 363); it was erected at Newport in 1851.

Thomas won the prize of 70 guineas at an eisteddfod in Abergavenny in 1848 for *The Death of Tewdrig, King of Gwent and Morganwg*, 'the best model in plaster illustrative of Cambro-British history', designed with the aid of suggestions by Lady Llanover, and modelled by his brother William (Poole, 121). At the Royal Academy in 1849, the *Illustrated London News* found it 'a composition of high merit', 'and we hope to hear of its being executed in marble' (11 Aug 1849). It was cast as an electrotype by Elkington, Mason & Co. and was included in their display at the Great Exhibition of 1851. A cast was presented in 1876 to the antiquary Morris Charles Jones, who gave it to the Powisland Museum in Welshpool. Another, bequeathed to the Birmingham Museum and Art Gallery in 1889, was later transferred to the Brecknock County Museum.

In 1849 Thomas was commissioned to execute a statue of the second marquess of Bute, for a fee of £1900. It was exhibited with its model at the Great Exhibition, in addition to a plaster relief, *Science Unveiling Ignorance*, now at Cardiff city hall. The Bute statue was cast in bronze, and erected by public subscription in Cardiff in 1853. The *Illustrated London News* described the figure as 'standing in a dignified and unaffected attitude, as if addressing a public assembly. The effect is highly agreeable; and the likeness we believe to be undisputable' (19 March 1853). In 1852 Thomas was commissioned by the corporation of Brecon to design a statue in memory of the duke of Wellington, incorporating a relief of the death of General Thomas Picton. The sculptor himself contributed £700 towards the memorial's cost of £1200, and it was set up in 1854. That year he also submitted proposals for the Wellington memorial in the London Guildhall. In 1857 Thomas's bronze statue of John Henry Vivian was erected in the courtyard of the old guildhall in Swansea. According to the *Illustrated Times*, 'The individuality of the original is well and gracefully preserved … the position is easy and dignified, and the relative proportions of the statue and the pedestal are excellent' (20 June 1857). In the same year, the prince of Wales sat to Thomas for the full-length marble statue which the sculptor presented to the Welsh School in Ashford, Middlesex. In 1857–8, following the death of Victoire, duchesse de Nemours, Thomas was commissioned by the duc de Nemours to produce a posthumous bust of his late wife and a portrait of her infant daughter Blanche. In 1865 his marble statue of the prince consort was erected on Castle Heights at Tenby, Pembrokeshire.

Elected a fellow of the Society of Antiquaries of London in 1842, Thomas was one of the original sponsors of the Great Exhibition of 1851. He retired to Penisha'r-Pentre, a mansion at Llansbyddyd, Brecknockshire, in 1857 and served as a JP, deputy lieutenant of Brecknockshire in 1862, and high sheriff in 1868. His nephew recalled that:

> Mr Evan Thomas' social qualities endeared him to a large circle of friends, and his conversational powers and fund of anecdote, as well as his mature judgement of all matters concerning art, made him an honoured guest in all the houses of the great in rank, literature and opulence. (Thomas)

His early style was based upon the classicism of his master, Francis Chantrey, and subsequently loosened into a more diverse Victorian manner. He ran a prolific and successful studio and was the first Welsh sculptor to establish a significant career and reputation largely through Welsh patronage. John Evan Thomas died at his London address, 58 Buckingham Palace Road, on 9 October 1873, his wife having predeceased him; he was buried on 14 October in Brompton cemetery, London.   MARK L. EVANS

Sources H. Elkington, *Catalogue of the art manufactures, bronze sculptures, artistic decorative plate, services &c.* (1851) · E. Poole, *The illustrated history and biography of Brecknockshire* (1886), 121–2 · Graves, *RA exhibitors* · T. M. Rees, *Welsh painters, engravers, sculptors* (1527–1911) (1912), 130–31 · T. Jones, *A history of the county of Brecknock*, 4, rev. J. R. Bailey, first Baron Glanusk (1930), 46, 161–2, 202, 296 · R. Gunnis, *Dictionary of British sculptors, 1660–1851* (1953), 390–91 · *DWB* · *Powys*, Pevsner (1979) · B. Read, *Victorian sculpture* (1982), 50, 120, 190, 208–9 · J. Newman, S. Hughes, and A. Ward, *Glamorgan* (1995) · G. T. H. Thomas, 'Some reminiscences of the Breconshire sculptor by his nephew', typescript, 30 June 1936, NMG Wales · *CGPLA Eng. & Wales* (1873) · *ILN* (3 June 1848), 363 · *ILN* (11 Aug 1849) · *ILN* (19 March 1853) · *Illustrated Times* (20 June 1857)
Archives NMG Wales · V&A NAL, corresp.
Wealth at death under £450: administration, 20 Nov 1873, *CGPLA Eng. & Wales* · further grant: Dec 1877, *CGPLA Eng. & Wales*

Thomas, John Fryer (1797–1877), East India Company servant, was born on 12 November 1797, probably in the parish of St Mary, Newington, Surrey, the son of James Thomas, formerly a commander in the company's service, and his wife, Ann. In 1814 he obtained a writership in the East India Company's service and joined Haileybury College. After the customary two years' study, he landed at Madras in July 1816, which marked the beginning of a long career in the Madras civil service. On 24 October 1820 he married Diana Elizabeth Wheen (1799/1800–1839), with whom he had at least one surviving child, a daughter. Diana died in May 1839 and was buried in the cemetery of St George's Cathedral, Madras.

In 1844, after holding appointments in the *sadr adalat* and officiating in various revenue and judicial appointments, including that of judge of the provincial court of appeal and circuit, Thomas was appointed revenue secretary, and, in the following year, chief secretary, to the government of Madras. In both positions he exercised considerable influence over the governor, George Hay, eighth marquess of Tweeddale, and several of his minutes attracted favourable notice from the court of directors. In 1850 he became a member of the governor's council and chief judge of the *sadr diwani* and *faujdari adalat*. In 1853, prompted in part by the recent Moplah uprisings in Malabar, he published a *Memorandum of Suggestions for the Amelioration of the Madras Ryotwar*. His five-year term on the council expired in 1855, whereupon he resigned from the service and returned to England. The governor, third Baron Harris, was happy to recommend him to Sir Charles Wood as a man of 'considerable sagacity' but warned Wood that he was not without his 'crotchets' (Harris to Wood).

Thomas's minutes were locally renowned for their incisive language. Most notably, he produced a review of T. B. Macaulay's draft of the Indian penal code and a minute on Indian education, the latter written in 1850 shortly after he had joined the council. Thomas's unequivocal views on education were rooted in his conviction that it was Britain's duty to effect the social and moral elevation of India. He disliked the education policy of the anglicists, with its emphasis on Western-style higher education institutions, and argued that the funds available, limited as they were, would be best spent in educating the masses through the medium of the vernacular languages. But, although a champion of vernacular education, he had no desire to uphold or reinforce indigenous values or culture. An evangelical, his hostility to Western-style institutions stemmed solely from his fear that government colleges were educating Indians in a moral vacuum and turning them into lawless atheists. He abhorred both Islam and Hinduism, condemning the scriptures of the latter for their 'puerile absurdities', and threw himself behind the missionaries in their long battle to get the Bible taught in government schools. In retirement he stepped up his attack on secular education and in 1860 published a pamphlet entitled *Bible Education in India*, which argued that diffusion of Christianity in India was the only way to build loyalty and prevent another catastrophe like the uprising of 1857.

Thomas died at his home at 22 Vanbrugh Park, Blackheath, on 7 April 1877. He was survived by his daughter, Louisa Ann, who at the time of his death was unmarried.

KATHERINE PRIOR

Sources J. F. Thomas, *Bible education in India* (1860) · *The Madras almanac for 1855* (1854) · DNB · BL OIOC, Haileybury MSS · ecclesiastical records, BL OIOC · *The Times* (10 April 1877) · Lord Harris to Sir Charles Wood, 14 March 1855, BL OIOC, Wood MSS
Archives NL Scot., Yester MSS of the marquesses of Tweeddale
Wealth at death under £20,000: probate, 16 May 1877, *CGPLA Eng. & Wales*

Thomas, John Godfrey Parry (1884–1927), holder of land speed records, was born at 6 Grove Park, Wrexham, on 6 April 1884, the second son of John William Thomas, a curate, and his wife, Mary Parry. In January 1888 his father became vicar of Bwlchycibau, Montgomeryshire, and the family moved and remained there for the next sixteen years. He attended Oswestry School, and then in 1902 went to pursue a course in electrical engineering at the City and Guilds Engineering College in London, where he met Kenneth Thomson, his later collaborator. At the end of the course he spent some months doing research on induction motors under William Edward Ayrton (1847–

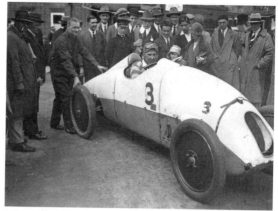

John Godfrey Parry Thomas (1884–1927), by MacGregor, 1925

1908), professor of electrical engineering, at Central Technical College, South Kensington, before becoming an apprentice in 1905 with Siemens Brothers & Co. Ltd, then with Clayton and Shuttleworth Ltd.

In 1907 Thomas set up on his own, with financial help from his mother, and began experimenting on electrical transmission for motor vehicles. Kenneth Thomson's brother Hedley was persuaded to put up money to form two companies, Thomas Transmission Ltd and Thomas Foreign Patents Ltd, and over the next four years he developed the Thomas transmission, which was successfully fitted to various vehicles—buses, trams, railcars—and also began his long association with Leyland Motors Ltd, using their extensive workshop facilities as he outgrew his own. By 1914, however, it became apparent that the Thomas transmission, though efficient, was too expensive to be practical, given the improvement in diesel engines and the size and cost of the parts involved, and the companies were wound up.

During the First World War Thomas advised the government on the design of aero engines. He was a member of a commission on tank design in 1917, the year in which he returned to Leyland, now with the title chief engineer. There he developed aero engines, but Leyland dropped the project after an unfortunate incident: the representatives from the Air Ministry arrived two weeks earlier than anticipated for a demonstration, and the engine seized. Back on auto engines, Thomas enjoyed the freedom of his new project: to design a luxury car without consideration of cost. His best-known model was the Leyland Eight, priced at well over £2500, of which only fourteen were produced (two went, with an engineer to explain them, to the maharaja of Patiala, and one to Michael Collins in Ireland, where it later took a bullet through the windshield). Some of its design features led to torsion springs, anti-roll bars, and vacuum-assisted brakes. One of the reasons, however, for his lack of commercial success was that as a designer he took on too much of the development work himself, rather than leaving it to draughtsmen and assistants, which slowed progress.

In 1921 Thomas asked Leyland if he could race their cars, and after some dispute and on the understanding that it would serve to advertise their product, the directors agreed. His first race—at Brooklands circuit on Easter Monday, 17 April 1922—was a disaster: clutch trouble meant that he stalled on the start line. His Leyland bosses were also less than impressed, as Thomas had stripped the car down from full regalia to racing essentials. By the end of this first season, however, he had gained three first places, eight seconds, and three thirds. The handicap style of motor racing at that time meant that many drivers were also attracted to record-breaking, and Thomas began working to that end; in November 1922 he broke his first record, for the 10 miles flying start, at 115 m.p.h.

Thomas was spending more and more time at Brooklands circuit, and in early 1923, as a result of this and his commercial failings as a designer, Leyland issued an ultimatum, following which the two parted company. He moved into a bungalow inside Brooklands, where he could devote all his time to racing and record-breaking. He achieved some success with the modified Leyland Eight, but the turning point came when he purchased, for £125, a converted Higham special which had belonged to the late Count Zborowski. It consisted of a V12 Liberty aeroplane motor in a chain-driven chassis; Thomas added four Zenith carburettors and his own design of pistons, modified the body and tail, and christened it *Babs*, after a friend's daughter.

When he was ready to attempt the land speed record, Thomas went to Pendine (Pen-tywyn) Sands on the Carmarthenshire coast, where Malcolm Campbell had set a record of nearly 151 m.p.h. in July 1925. Thomas's first record attempt at Pendine, in October 1925, was aborted owing to bad weather, and before he could make another attempt, Major Henry Segrave raised the record to 152 m.p.h. in March 1926. On returning to Pendine in April 1926, Thomas became the first man to break two world land speed records in two consecutive days (27 and 28 April), first to 169 m.p.h., then the next day to 171 m.p.h. Whereas Campbell had spent £9500 on his *Bluebird*, Thomas spent only an additional £800 improving *Babs* to achieve similar success. During the next year he made modifications to *Babs* and to the Leyland-Thomas, which was his rebuilt version of the Leyland Eight. He raced the Leyland-Thomas throughout the season, and won in his last race at Brooklands on 2 October 1926, and the same week broke records for the 500 km, 500 miles, and three-hour run in that car.

On 1 March 1927 Thomas returned to Pendine with *Babs*, determined to beat Campbell's new record of 174 m.p.h., set in February that year, and possibly to reach 200 m.p.h. before Segrave had the chance at the end of March at Daytona. The weather was poor, and Thomas was recovering from flu, but on 3 March 1927, a cold wet day, he decided to go ahead. His first two runs were discounted because the timing device was inaccurate, but he reached almost 180 m.p.h. on his first legitimate run. The record depends on a two-way average, and he was on the second run when the offside driving chain broke, the rear wheel was torn off, and the car overturned, travelling over 300 yards upside down before coming to rest. Thomas was killed almost instantly, the first man to die in a land speed record attempt.

Thomas was buried with his goggles at St Mary's Church, Byfleet, Surrey, on 7 March 1927 after a private service at the Hermitage, Brooklands. *Babs* was buried under Pendine Sands, along with Thomas's leather coat, slit up to discourage souvenir hunters, and his driving helmet. In 1969 *Babs* was excavated and restored by Owen Wyn Owen, a lecturer in engineering at Bangor; it had been thought for many years that Thomas was partially decapitated by the driving chain, but Owen found that it was more likely that Thomas was killed by injuries caused when the car overturned.

Throughout his career Thomas failed to get on with the press, and was considered misogynistic and sullen. He never married. He was a tall, stocky man with a heavy jaw, and had a sharp tongue, but was highly regarded by those who knew him well. At Leyland he was generous to employees and genuinely interested in their welfare. He loved children, organizing races and choosing prizes for them at the staff sports day, and after his death it was discovered that he had made regular donations to Great Ormond Street Hospital and Belgrave Hospital for children. *Autocar* set up a memorial fund, and endowed a *Babs* cot at Great Ormond Street. Although his name is not now the first remembered, he was commemorated on a Royal Mail stamp in 1998 as part of a series celebrating achievement in land speed records. *Babs*, meanwhile, is now on exhibition in winter at the National Museum and Gallery of Wales in Cardiff and returns to Pendine Museum for two months each summer.

JO PAYNE

Sources H. Tours, *Parry Thomas: designer–driver* (1959) · M. Berresford, *Parry Thomas and Pendine* (1985) · W. Boddy, *The world's land speed record* (1964) · P. J. R. Holthusen, *The land speed record* (1980) · C. Posthumus and D. Tremayne, *Land speed record* (1985) · P. Llewellin, 'When John drove *Babs* in the fast lane', *Independent* (26 Sept 1995) · b. cert.
Likenesses MacGregor, photograph, 1925, Hult. Arch. [*see illus.*] · photographs, repro. in Tours, *Parry Thomas* (1961) · photographs, repro. in Berresford, *Parry Thomas and Pendine*
Wealth at death £5951 17s. 4d.: resworn probate, 29 April 1927, CGPLA Eng. & Wales

Thomas, John Wesley (1798–1872), Methodist minister, writer, and translator, was born on 4 August 1798 in Exeter, the son of John Thomas, an Exeter tradesman and preacher, and younger brother of Elijah, who was also to enter the ministry. After a childhood revelation, at nineteen Thomas went to London, hoping to become a missionary, but instead he was selected for the itinerant ministry, and for the next half century passed between one and three years in twenty-six different British locations. Largely self-educated, Thomas acquired several languages, was a respected miniaturist, and wrote authoritatively on a wide variety of topics. His magpie mind acquired enormous general knowledge, exploited in frequent articles, notably for the *Wesleyan Methodist Magazine* and *Notes and Queries*, on subjects as diverse as William the Silent, Wesleyan hymns, and Cornish fairies. His first book was *An Apology for 'Don Juan'*, really a satire against Byron's agnosticism, in a witty parody of his style. His major work, *The Trilogy, or, Dante's Three Visions*, was published by Bohn's from 1859, although extracts appeared as early as 1840. Retaining the original metre, with copious notes and even diagrammatic illustrations by Thomas himself, it is an impressive achievement. One of his aims was to prove that Dante's Christianity more resembled John Wesley's than Pius IX's; *Purgatorio* (1862) is dedicated 'To Garibaldi and the people of Italy'.

Thomas was 'thin, and somewhat of a stooping form … His face, however, would at once fix attention' (Christophers, 345). This was certainly so in 1850 when he filled Dudley town hall to capacity, attacking the papacy. He also turned his satire against Mormonism; and against Bishop Phillpotts of Exeter in a poem, *The War of the Surplice* (2nd edn, 1871). An associate of Lord Brougham, he spent much time at Brougham Castle when minister at Penrith (1858–61). John Wesley Thomas died at Dumfries on 7 February 1872, leaving his widow, Louisa, *née* Drayton, and a daughter and four sons, two of whom followed him into the ministry.   RALPH LLOYD-JONES

Sources S. W. Christophers, *The poets of Methodism* (1875) • *Minutes of conference of Wesleyan Methodists* (1872) • *Methodist Recorder* (23 Feb 1872) • Boase & Courtney, *Bibl. Corn.*, vol. 2 • J. W. Thomas, *Reminiscences of Methodism in Exeter* [n.d., *c*.1870] • *N&Q*, 4th ser., 5 (26 March 1870) • Methodist Church, *Hill's arrangement* (1869) • d. cert.
Archives Duke U., Perkins L., personal and family corresp. • JRL, Methodist Archives and Research Centre, letters | John Murray, London, archives, letters

Thomas, Joshua [Josua Tomos] (*d*. **1759**), author and Church of England clergyman, was born at Penpïod, Llanllywenfel, Brecknockshire, early in the eighteenth century. Virtually nothing is known of his early life though he is reputed to have graduated from the Queen's College, Oxford, a fact not recorded by Foster in *Alumni Oxonienses*. Following curacies at Nantmel, Radnorshire, and thereafter at Tirabad and Llanwrtyd in his home county, and at Llangamarch and Llanllywenfel, also in Brecknockshire, where he served under Theophilus Evans (1693–1767), he was presented with the living of Merthyr Cynog in 1741; he added Llanbister in the neighbouring county of Radnorshire five years later. He also served as a chaplain to the earl of Powys, before returning to his home parish at Llanllywenfel in 1758. His son, also called Joshua, matriculated at Christ Church, Oxford, in May 1758, graduating BA in 1762 and MA two years later.

The elder Joshua Thomas was principally known as a translator into Welsh of pious and didactic works of an Anglican hue. His earliest published work was a translation of Andrew Jones's *The Black Book of Conscience*, which he entitled *Lyfr du y gydwybod* (1723), followed, in 1728, by excerpts from Matthew Henry's *Exposition on the Old and New Testaments*, and, in 1733, by Bishop Edward Synge's *An Essay towards Making the Knowledge of Religion Easy* and Robert Warren's *The Daily Self-Examiner*. Further works were Bishop George Bull's *Discourse Concerning the Spirit of God* (*c*.1740) and a selection from the writings of Dr John Scott of St Giles-in-the-Fields entitled *Yr angenrheidrwydd o gredu gwobrwyon a chosbedigaethau y byd arall tu ag at fod yn wir grefyddol* ('The necessity of believing in rewards and punishments in the next world in order to become truly religious'; 1743). His most celebrated and accomplished work was his translation of Scott's *Christian Life* entitled *Y Fuchedd Grist'nogol, o'i dechreu i'w diwedd mewn gogoniant* (1752), which, stylistically, was of a very high standard.

Although hardly known beyond the borders of Brecknockshire and the diocese of St David's, Thomas typified the orthodox Welsh clergy of his day in his loyalty to a sober Anglicanism which steered well clear of Methodist enthusiasm on the one hand and popish superstition on the other. He died on 23 June 1759 at Llanllywenfel, and was buried there in the parish church.

D. DENSIL MORGAN

Sources O. Thomas, 'Joshua Thomas', *Brycheiniog*, 5 (1959), 51–2 • E. Rees, ed., *Libri Walliae: a catalogue of Welsh books and books printed in Wales, 1546–1820*, 2 vols. (1987) • D. R. Davies, 'Some clergy of the deanery of Melineth in the 18th century', *Transactions of the Radnorshire Society*, 19 (1949), 46–50 • *DNB* • Foster, *Alum. Oxon.*, 1715–1886 [Joshua Thomas, son]

Thomas, Joshua (1719–1797), Particular Baptist minister and historian, was born on 22 February 1719 at Tŷ-hen, Caeo, Carmarthenshire, the eldest son of Thomas Morgan (*c*.1690–1760), carpenter, and his wife, Jane Hughes (*b*. *c*.1689). After a rudimentary education at a school kept by the Independent minister David Williams at Bwlch-y-rhiw, in his home parish, he left for Hereford in 1739 to pursue an apprenticeship, possibly as a mercer. Within months of his departure the family, who had been Independents, transferred their allegiance to the Baptist cause, while Joshua Thomas himself was baptized by immersion at Leominster in May 1740.

On his return from Herefordshire to Caeo in 1743 Thomas became closely involved in the activities of the recently established Bethel branch of the Aberdyar Baptist Church, at which his brother Timothy had been ordained minister. In 1746 he married Elizabeth Jones (*c*.1725–1807) from Cardiganshire before settling, in May of that year, at Hay, Brecknockshire, taking up membership at the Trosgoed (subsequently Maesyberllan) church. It was during this time that he began preaching, confining his labour to Trosgoed's branches at Olchon, on the Hereford side of the Welsh border, and Capel-y-ffin. It was there in 1749 that he was ordained as ministerial assistant. A further move occurred in November 1754, when he accepted a call to the ministry of the Baptist congregation at Leominster, Herefordshire, where he was to remain for the rest of his life.

It was during his Leominster pastorate that Thomas's skills as a researcher were first nurtured and his reputation as a sound historian and accomplished author came to fruition. He had already published a short work, *Ateb i'r ugain rhesymmau* (1751), a reply to an anti-Baptist polemic, during his time at Hay, but a growing fascination with the beginnings of his Leominster congregation during the protectorate served to hone his interest in dissenting history. Using church records and the recollections of his oldest members as his source, in 1764 he began to compose 'A brief history of the Baptist church at Leominster', completing the manuscript five years later. This provided an apprenticeship for subsequent works, including what was to become his most accomplished volume, *Hanes y Bedyddwyr ymhlith y Cymry* ('A history of the Baptists among the Welsh'; 1778), and the one for which he remains best remembered. Although he had been encouraged by his ministerial colleagues as early as 1751 to write a sketch delineating the history of the Welsh Baptists, he did not begin to collate material until 1774. He spent the summer of 1776 travelling throughout south Wales visiting churches and gleaning information, and when the attractive 468-page quarto volume was published it was immediately apparent that a judicious historian and writer of the most elegant Welsh prose had emerged. The *Hanes* would become the principal source for early Welsh Baptist historians for generations to come and a notable contribution to Welsh historiography. His succeeding work, the two-volume manuscript 'Ecclesiastical history of Wales', which described the legends which accompanied the coming of Christianity to Wales and its subsequent history up to the puritan ascendancy, was completed by 1779, while a virtual translation of the *Hanes* entitled 'Materials for a history of the Baptist churches in the principality of Wales from about the year 1630 to 1782' was completed three years later. Although less anecdotal than the original, its factual content had been strengthened by the inclusion of information which Thomas had received from American sources provided by Isaac Backus and Morgan Edwards in Philadelphia. This formed the basis of his meticulous and detailed contributions to John Rippon's *Baptist Annual Register* (1791–), which prompted Rippon's description of him as 'the best informed person on earth concerning the origin and growth of the baptized Churches in Wales'. The bulk of a further manuscript history, 'A history of the Baptist churches in Wales', was completed by 1794, and this became the basis for Benjamin Davies's Welsh translation of 1885, which gave Thomas's historical work a new lease of life and further confirmed his reputation among Victorian nonconformists. His final published work, also based upon his contribution to Rippon's *Register*, was *History of the Baptist Association in Wales from the Year 1659 to the Year 1790* (1795), though less substantial histories of individual churches, including Bewdley, Worcestershire, Hook Norton, Oxfordshire, and Colchester, remain in manuscript form.

Along with his contribution as denominational historian, Thomas was a key figure in eighteenth-century Baptist life in the east midlands as well as in Wales. His long correspondence with his close friend and colleague Benjamin Francis (1734–1799), another expatriate Welshman whose career was spent ministering to Baptist congregations in the west of England, affords a fascinating glimpse of mid-eighteenth-century dissenting life. Though eirenic by temperament he nevertheless argued strongly for doctrinal orthodoxy, as witnessed by his widely used translation of the London Particular Baptists' 1689 confession, *Cyffes ffydd wedi ei gosod allan* (1791) and his 1794 translation

of Robert Hall's essay on the Trinity. His evangelical Calvinism was shared by his brothers Timothy (1720–1768), author of a very able treatise on the doctrine of justification, *Traethiad ar y wisg-wen ddisglair* (1759), and Zacharias (1727–1816), both of whom served as ministers of the Aberdyar church.

The best known of the five of Joshua Thomas's children to survive infancy was **Timothy Thomas** (1753–1821), Particular Baptist minister for forty-seven years at the Devonshire Square church in Bishopsgate, London. Following his marriage to Sarah, daughter of Hugh Evans, president of the Bristol Baptist Academy, he became chairman of the Particular Baptist Fund and a member of the London Education Society, which in turn became the Stepney College and latterly Regent's Park College. He was buried at Bunhill Fields, London.

Joshua Thomas died, aged seventy-eight, on 25 August 1797 at Etnam Street, Leominster, Herefordshire, having served the Baptist community there for forty-three years. He was buried three days later in the Etnam Street churchyard.   D. Densil Morgan

Sources T. L. Jenkins, 'The life, work and contribution of the Rev. Joshua Thomas, 1719–1797', PhD diss., U. Wales, 1993 • 'Memoirs of the late Rev. Joshua Thomas of Leominster', *Evangelical Magazine*, 6 (1798), 89–99 • B. G. Owens, 'Joshua Thomas, hanesydd y Bedyddwyr', *Y Llenor*, 27 (1948), 183–7 • D. D. Morgan, 'Athrawiaeth hanes Joshua Thomas', *Trafodion Cymdeithas Hanes Bedyddwyr Cymru* (1986), 14–23 • D. D. Morgan, 'Cefndir, cymreigiad a chynnwys cyffes ffydd 1689', *Trafodion Cymdeithas Hanes Bedyddwyr Cymru* (1990), 19–34 • G. F. Nuttall, 'Questions and answers: an eighteenth-century correspondence', *Baptist Quarterly*, 27 (1977–8), 83–90 • G. F. Nuttall, 'Joshua Thomas' *History of the Baptist Association in Wales*', *Trafodion Cymdeithas Hanes Bedyddwyr Cymru* (1985), 3–12 • 'Memoir of Timothy Thomas', *New Baptist Miscellany*, 1 (1827), 328–31 • *Baptist Annual Register*, 1 (1791), 2

Archives NL Wales, MSS 612, 613–614, 21160, 21161, 21162–21163, 21164, MS fax 750 • Regent's Park College, Oxford, Angus Library | Hist. Soc. Penn., Irving McKesson collection, Jones section • Regent's Park College, Oxford, Angus Library, John Rippon MSS

Likenesses Ridley, stipple, NPG; repro. in 'Memoirs of the late Rev. Joshua Thomas of Leominster', 89

Thomas [Evans], **Lewis** (1568?–1619?), Church of England clergyman, was probably born in Glamorgan, although he may have been born in Radnor. He matriculated, as Lewis Evans, at Gloucester Hall, Oxford, on 11 December 1584, and graduated BA as Lewis Evans alias Thomas from Brasenose College on 15 February 1587. Shortly afterwards he was ordained and received a benefice 'in his native county of Glamorgan and elsewhere' (Wood, *Ath. Oxon.*).

During his ministry Thomas wrote two volumes of sermons. The first, *Seaven sermons, or, The exercises of seven sabbaoths; together with a short treatise upon the commaundements* (1599), dedicated to Richard Broughton, an assize judge for north Wales, expounded a variety of texts from the Old and New testaments, and proved very popular, appearing in ten further editions up to 1630. In the first two sermons he attacked the vanity and corruption of the period and asserted the need for repentance. Thomas also recalled the 'generall plague' and 'famine' which had devastated the land, in that 'time of sorrow and perplexity' when friends and neighbours kept their distance and 'they who this day carried the dead bodies to their graves, were themselves on the morrow carried by others into their graves' (L. Thomas, *Seven Sermons*, 1599, 21–2). Later sermons attacked transubstantiation as 'a grosse and most absurb opinion, that we should rent with our teeth the very flesh of Christ our Saviour. This is even to crucifie Christ againe like the Jews' (ibid., 33) and claimed that the pope offered 'counterfaite phisicke to purge mens soules and to cleane their sins by his bulls, pardons and indulgences, and such trumpery' (ibid., 69). 'The forming of Eve' spoke of women's duty to help their husbands through hard work, but also presented an ideal of reciprocal responsibility and a mutually supportive, companionate relationship, where 'No bitter wordes must passe betweene them, much less blowes' (ibid., 91–2).

Thomas's *Demegoriai: Certaine Lectures upon Sundry Portions of Scripture* (1600), consisting of eight sermons, again on diverse biblical passages, and dedicated to his first patron, Sir Thomas Egerton, lord keeper of the great seal, expressed conventional Christian values and offered sage advice to magistrates and his parishioners. The former were to 'circumspectly looke into the disorders there' and to avoid corruption which, he noted, was the fashion 'of many magistrats that carry no conscience' (L. Thomas, *Demegoriai*, 1600, 'Christ travailing unto Jerusalem'). He recommended that they ought to examine all crimes, large and small, and punish accordingly. Thus their 'judiciall censures must not be like Spyders webs, which intangle onely the small flies … [they] ought to be Eagle-sighted, the better to looke into abuses … into every corner of corruption, that no sinne may escape without his censure' (ibid.). They were to be like 'Gods' to ensure that 'no weake, or corrupt, or blinde Magistrate be preferred: but the wisest and best approved' (ibid.). In 'The history of the Lord's birth' Lewis observed further that good housekeeping and hospitality were in danger of becoming 'lost through pride and prodigalitie' while in 'The anatomy of tale-bearers' he called on the gentry to remember the poor. All sections of the community were similarly warned about tale-bearing for gossips were 'worse than crowes: for they feed but upon dead carkasses but these carriers of tales feede upon them that are alive'. It is believed that Thomas died in 1619 in Glamorgan, but the exact date and whereabouts of his death and burial are unknown.   D. L. THOMAS, *rev.* RICHARD C. ALLEN

Sources *DWB*, 957 · Foster, *Alum. Oxon.* · R. Williams, *Enwogion Cymru: a biographical dictionary of eminent Welshmen* (1852), 487 · Arber, *Regs. Stationers*, 3.140, 175 · Wood, *Ath. Oxon.*, 1st edn, 2.277 · Wood, *Ath. Oxon.*, 2nd edn, 2.236

Thomas, Lucy (*bap.* **1781**, *d.* **1847**), colliery owner, was baptized at Llansamlet in south Wales on 11 March 1781, the daughter of Job Williams and his wife, Ann James. Much remains obscure about her early life, but she married Robert Thomas (*d.* 1833) at Llansamlet on 13 June 1802. Lucy's husband was a contractor of a coal level at Cyfarthfa ironworks, and in the 1820s he opened his own coal working at Waun Wyllt, near Abercannaid, just south of Merthyr Tudful. Between 1805 and 1825 they had six sons and two daughters.

The relative absence of knowledge about Lucy Thomas's personal details perhaps encouraged the development of her legendary reputation in Welsh industrial history: she was referred to as the 'mother of the Welsh steam-coal trade'. This title derived from the fact that the initial cargoes of steam-coal to London came from the Thomas family's tiny level at Waun Wyllt, and from the belief that these enterprises were negotiated with Robert Thomas's widow, Lucy. Robert Thomas had opened the level in 1828 on a yearly tenancy from Lord Plymouth, and the terms explicitly banned any sale to the four ironworks which dominated the town.

In November 1830 George Insole shipped to London 413 tons of smokeless steam-coal from the (later) celebrated 'Four Feet' seam. In the same year—whether before or shortly afterwards is unclear—James Marychurch and two companions (George Locket and James Duke) also visited Waun Wyllt and are said to have agreed to act as agents in Cardiff and London for the whole output, but Insole continued to pay first Robert and (after his death) Lucy for monthly quantities. Lucy Thomas and her son William later also worked the coal under the neighbouring Graig Farm, for which a lease was signed in 1838. In 1843 William Thomas leased the Llety Siencyn colliery in the neighbouring Aberdâr valley. In his memoirs John Nixon later described how Lucy Thomas conducted business at Graig colliery:

> She sat in her office, a wooden hut near the pit's mouth and traded for cash, placing in a basket over her head the moneys which she received for her coal. Her cleverness, her witty tongue, her pleasant manner were known to all the countryside.   (Smith, 8)

Much of Lucy Thomas's story is taken from the 1888 account given by the Merthyr historian Charles Wilkins, who had a penchant for imaginative touches but was usually sound on essentials. The impression he gives is of an enterprising woman looking for extra markets. However, this is certainly exaggerated: the accounts agree that it was Insole and Marychurch who struggled to seek her out in Abercannaid, and the latter seems to have contracted for a set price, which suggests that Mrs Thomas was not the risk taker. In 1840 John Nixon also claimed that she was reluctant to increase her output to provide him with supplies. Moreover, before her husband died on 19 February 1833, all business references mention only Robert Thomas, who was almost certainly the one to negotiate the initial shipments. Lucy and her eldest son, Robert, were granted probate and thereafter Insole paid to her the sums due for coal dispatched. It was not until 1835 that the account with the Glamorganshire Canal was transferred from Robert to Lucy Thomas. More substantially, although Cardiff later dominated the steam-coal trade, the earliest efforts to open a London market in steam-coal probably came from the ports of Swansea and Llanelli to the west. The Llangennech company, based near Llanelli, sent steam-coal—and not just anthracite—to London as early as 1824, and until the opening of the Aberdâr valley in the 1840s most Welsh coal sent to London came from the west. Indeed, while Lucy Thomas was alive, her Merthyr coal was the only source in the Merthyr area for steam-coal shipments. Nevertheless, such mundane considerations have been unable to withstand the power of a myth based on the singularity of a woman actively engaged in the almost totally male world of the coal industry. The myth was given some sort of material embodiment when her granddaughter's husband, W. T. Lewis, first Baron Merthyr, paid part of the cost of a water fountain built in Merthyr in remembrance of Robert and Lucy Thomas, in 1906.

Lucy Thomas died on 27 September 1847 at Abercannaid, Merthyr Tudful, having suffered from typhoid fever in the two previous weeks. Like other members of the family, she was buried in the cemetery of the Unitarian chapel at Cefncoedycymer, near Merthyr. Her estate, including the Waun Wyllt colliery and her half-interest (with her son William) in the Graig colliery, was valued at £11,448. However adventurous Lucy Thomas may have been as an entrepreneur, she clearly had conventional views about the solidity of real estate: in her will she bequeathed nearly fifty freehold and leasehold houses and cottages to her various children.

JOHN WILLIAMS

Margaret Haig Thomas, *suo jure* Viscountess Rhondda (1883–1958), by Bassano, 1947

Sources J. H. Morris and L. J. Williams, *The south Wales coal industry, 1841–1875* (1958) · C. Wilkins, *The south Wales coal trade and its allied industries* (1888) · E. M. Smith, 'Robert and Lucy Thomas', *Merthyr Historian*, 7 (1994), 1–9 · J. E. Vincent, *John Nixon: pioneer of the steam coal trade in south Wales* (1900) · J. H. Morris and L. J. Williams, 'R. J. Nevill and the early Welsh coal trade', *National Library of Wales Journal*, 10 (1957–8), 59–64 · Merthyr of Senghenydd deeds, NL Wales, docs. 339, 343 · census returns for Merthyr Tydfil, 1841 · 'Select committee on coal duties', *Parl. papers* (1852–3), 22.125, no. 916 · F. Vaughan, 'Women of Merthyr', in Afon Taf History Research Group, *Back into the years: recollections of Merthyr's past* (1979) · M. S. Taylor, 'Notable women of Merthyr Tydfil', *Journal of the Merthyr Tydfil Historical Society*, 1 (1976), 106–12 · R. H. Walters, *The economic and business history of the south Wales steam coal industry, 1840–1914* (1977) · *Merthyr Tydfil: a valley community*, Merthyr Teachers Centre Group (1981)

Wealth at death £11,448 3s. 6d.: Smith 'Robert and Lucy Thomas'

Thomas [married name Mackworth], **Margaret Haig**, *suo jure* **Viscountess Rhondda** (1883–1958), feminist and magazine proprietor, was born at Princes Square, Bayswater, London, on 12 June 1883, and baptized at St Matthew's Church, St Petersburgh Place, the only child of David Alfred *Thomas, first Viscount Rhondda (1856–1918), Liberal politician and industrialist, of Llan-wern, Monmouthshire, and his wife, Sybil Margaret *Thomas (1857–1941), fourth daughter of George Augustus Haig.

Marriage and divorce: the women's suffrage movement Margaret Haig Thomas's formal education got off to a slow start. Until the age of thirteen she was taught by French and German governesses from whom, she said, she learned only 'trifles'. She then attended first Notting Hill High School for Girls, a flagship institution of the Girls' Public Day School Trust, followed by St Leonards School in St Andrews. She received a sound academic education, but there really never was any serious expectation that a girl of her class would work for a living. On leaving school she

took the next logical step in the career progression of an upper-class girl and 'came out'. Chaperoned by her long-suffering mother, she endured three successive London seasons. Paralysed by shyness and incapable of small talk, she found this an agonizing experience and she took herself off to Somerville College, Oxford, primarily to escape the horrors of a fourth London season, but gave that up and returned after less than a year (1904–5) to live in the family home at Llan-wern. Bored by life at home and with no sense of purpose, she drifted into marriage. She married Humphrey Mackworth (1871–1948), son of Colonel Sir Humphrey Mackworth, sixth baronet, from neighbouring Caerleon, on 9 July 1908; he succeeded to his father's baronetcy in 1914. For a while at least she enjoyed being mistress of her own home and genuinely sought to fulfil the role of a country landowner's wife. But they were an ill assorted pair and the marriage ended, quite amicably, in divorce in 1923.

In her youth Margaret was very attractive, with fair curly hair, blue eyes, and a determined jaw and mouth, which was softened by a hint of ready laughter. Short in stature and quite sturdily built, she was, however, not physically a strong woman and frequently wore herself out with her many commitments to a broad range of interests. Her character was marked by determination, persistence, and an intense focus on achieving the goals which she set for herself.

Two events were to change Margaret's life and to save her from the existence of petty futility which she saw stretching before her. The first of these, which occurred within a fortnight of her marriage, was her discovery of the militant women's suffrage movement.

Margaret's introduction to the suffrage movement came through one of her mother's cousins, Florence Haig, who had already been to prison for the cause. Inspired by

Florence, both Margaret and her mother took part in the great suffrage procession to Hyde Park, London, on 21 July 1908. Shortly afterwards she joined the Women's Social and Political Union (WSPU) and set up its Newport branch. Though she was a firm believer in the justice of the cause, it was the promise of activity and excitement which most appealed to her. At last here was something which brought her to life:

> But for me and for many other young women like me, militant suffrage was the very salt of life. The knowledge of it had come like a draught of fresh air into our padded, stifled lives. It gave us release of energy, it gave us that sense of being some use in the scheme of things, without which no human being can live at peace.   (Rhondda, 120)

Between 1908 and the outbreak of the First World War, when the WSPU suspended its operations, Margaret ran the full gamut of suffrage activities. She organized public meetings, inviting down such speakers as Emmeline Pankhurst, and she herself spoke from public platforms on many occasions, often to hostile audiences. Accompanied by Annie Kenney, a star of the WSPU, she addressed the Liberal Club in Merthyr, her father's constituency, where they were both pelted with herrings and tomatoes. During the general election of 1910, following the militant policy of harassing cabinet ministers, she broke through a police cordon and jumped on to the running board of Prime Minister Asquith's car. By 1913 she felt it was her duty, as secretary of the Newport WSPU, to commit arson and thereby give a lead to the others in the branch. She burned the contents of a pillar box on Risca Road, was arrested, tried, and found guilty. Rejecting the offer to pay a fine—to Humphrey's horror—she was sent to Usk gaol, where she proceeded to go on hunger strike but was not forcibly fed; she was released after five days.

Business interests The second event which was to change Margaret Haig Mackworth's life and was to bring her into even greater public prominence was her entry into her father's business. Shortly after her marriage her father declared that he needed someone whom he could trust absolutely to assist him in the running of his business empire, a cross between 'a highly confidential secretary and a right hand man' (Rhondda, 217). It was her mother who suggested Margaret for this role. It was a bold and unorthodox decision on his part to employ her since women, particularly young married women, were almost unheard of in business, but Margaret fitted the bill in terms of trustworthiness and she was familiar with the broad outlines of his enterprises, which he had long been in the habit of discussing with her. At a salary of £1000 a year she took up her position at his offices in the Cambrian Buildings on Cardiff docks. She attended conferences and board meetings, conducted research into special projects, drafted letters and memoranda, and accompanied D. A. (as he was generally known) on overseas business trips. She acquired a knowledge of finance, of the workings of the coal and newspaper industries, and learned the arts of negotiation and bluffing. By mid-1914 D. A. had passed his newspaper interests over to her, and as the First World War progressed and he was brought

once more into the world of politics she took increasing responsibility for the running of all his businesses. By the end of the war she was a director of more than twenty companies. But despite her efforts to fit into this male world—wearing dark business suits and smoking excessively at board meetings—she felt at a disadvantage by the lack of a business-orientated education and by her exclusion from the informal gossip which the men traded daily, along with coal, at the Cardiff exchange. Ironically it was the single most traumatic ordeal of her life which gave her a great boost of confidence. In May 1915, returning with D. A. from a US business trip, she was aboard the *Lusitania*, when it was torpedoed off the Irish coast. Rescued after hours in the freezing water, she later reflected that the shipwreck had altered her opinion of herself. Having gone through that and faced death close up, she no longer feared anything.

The *Lusitania* ordeal made Margaret determined to play her own part in the war effort. She was appointed as commissioner of women's national service in Wales, as controller of women's recruiting and, before the war ended, to the Women's Advisory Council of the Ministry of Reconstruction, which was concerned with issues on which she felt strongly. She was committed to the idea that women should remain an integral part of the postwar workforce, and to that end she set up the Women's Industrial League in 1918 to campaign for the rights of women workers.

When the war ended Margaret was already thirty-five years old but it is only truly from 1918 that she emerged as the fully formed independent woman with a set of ideas that she would hold and try to implement for the rest of her life. Her father died in July 1918, having been promoted to the rank of viscount, with a special remainder to Margaret in the absence of a male heir. For Margaret his death was a devastating blow. He had been her closest friend as well as her father and he was the only man she ever truly loved. Thereafter all her closest relationships were with women, notably the novelist Winifred Holtby, Helen Archdale, the first editor of *Time and Tide*, and Theodora Bosanquet, the secretary of the International Federation of University Women, with whom she lived from 1933 to her death in 1958.

Margaret was left an extremely wealthy woman. Lord Rhondda's estate was valued at £885,645: she inherited his property, his commercial interests, and his title. The *Directory of Directors* for 1919 listed Viscountess Rhondda, as she now was, as the director of thirty-three companies (twenty-eight of them inherited from her father) and chairman or vice-chairman of sixteen of these. Already a famous figure whose activities were widely reported in the London press on account of her business career and of her increasingly leading role as a spokeswoman for feminism, her campaign to take her seat in the House of Lords attracted a great deal more publicity. Women had won a partial victory in the long struggle for the vote in 1918, when some women over thirty were enfranchised in parliamentary elections, but peeresses were not allowed to take their seats in the Lords. Lady Rhondda demanded that she be allowed to take her seat in what she regarded as 'the last feudal assembly in Europe' (*Church Times*, 10 March 1922). But although in 1922 she seemed to have won, when the committee of privileges accepted her plea for admission, the decision was reversed in May 1922 after a remarkable piece of skulduggery by the lord chancellor, F. E. Smith, who referred the matter back to a reconstituted committee and delivered a judgment which rejected the claim that a peeress was entitled to sit and vote in parliament. Women were kept out of the House of Lords, despite her continued efforts, until 1958. Her campaign to enter the Lords was based less on a desire for any personal aggrandizement than on the sense of obligation she felt to the feminist cause to pursue discrimination wherever she encountered it and to promote the cause of equal rights.

Time and Tide   Between the wars Lady Rhondda was arguably Britain's leading feminist. Equal rights were central to her philosophy and she put enormous efforts into promoting her vision. In 1920 she set up the feminist weekly journal *Time and Tide*; in 1921 she launched the Six Point Group, which focused on what she regarded as the six key issues for women (mainly relating to child custody, equal pay, and equal opportunities); and in 1926, along with other feminists, she set up the Open Door Council to campaign against 'protective' legislation for women. A proponent of the equal-rights tradition of feminism, she asked for no favours, only for a level playing field. She was involved in many initiatives both in Britain and internationally, but it was *Time and Tide* which was to play the greatest part in her life from this point.

Time and Tide was for Lady Rhondda the fulfilment of a childhood dream. It was her grand passion, to which she devoted all her energies, at the expense of her business interests and her health. Though it was nominally owned by a limited company (the Time and Tide Publishing Company) and incorporated with £20,000 capital, Lady Rhondda subsidized the journal from the outset. She controlled 90 per cent of the shares, was at first vice-chairman, then chairman of directors, and from 1926 she took over as editor. In that year she attracted a great deal of publicity as the first woman president of the Institute of Directors. She subsidized the magazine throughout its existence, paying between £5000 and £10,000 per year in the early days and more than £250,000 in the course of her lifetime. It was her magazine: the all-female board of directors, for the most part, did her bidding. It reflected her views—liberal, feminist, egalitarian, and individualist.

Time and Tide covered politics, economics, social issues, literature, and the arts. To ensure that the journal was taken seriously Lady Rhondda gathered around her a distinguished group of women writers, who in the 1920s included Virginia Woolf, Vita Sackville-West, E. M. Delafield, Rose MacCauley, Dorothy L. Sayers, and Rebecca West: she was eager to promote young women writers such as Winifred Holtby and Vera Brittain. She could call too on distinguished male literary figures: G. K. Chesterton, Gilbert Murray, and George Bernard Shaw were always supportive. H. G. Wells, T. S. Eliot, Ezra Pound,

Aldous Huxley, E. M. Forster, and George Orwell were contributors and, as she had with the women, she encouraged young male writers: W. H. Auden, Stephen Spender, and Christopher Isherwood published some of their early pieces in *Time and Tide*. The literary contributors, whether established or at the outset of their careers, form an impressive list, but *Time and Tide* also published the work of important scholars such as Harold Laski, G. D. H. Cole, C. V. Wedgwood, and Eileen Power.

Politically the journal, like its proprietor, moved to the right over the years. The feminist element was reduced, especially after 1928 when equal suffrage was secured. But before and during the Second World War it stood firmly against fascism, and when in 1945 the Nazi blacklist (of those to be detained when the Germans invaded) was published, it paid Lady Rhondda the compliment of marking her down for immediate arrest. During the war the circulation of *Time and Tide* had hit a high of some 30,000 copies a week but by the 1950s sales had dropped to some 16,000, and the journal was losing between £400 and £500 every week. Lady Rhondda's personal fortune was almost exhausted and she was forced to appeal to the readers, who rallied to her call: donations to the tune of £25,000 came in.

Lady Rhondda's commitment to *Time and Tide* meant that she spent most of her time in London but she retained her links with Wales. She kept on her mother's old home at Pen Ithon, visiting whenever she could, and served on public bodies in Wales. She was president of the University College of Wales, Cardiff, from 1950 to 1955 and was awarded the honorary degree of doctor of law in 1955. In her seventies she continued to drive herself hard and ignored her own failing health. When she became ill with cancer she refused medication on the grounds that *Time and Tide* demanded a clear mind. She died in the Westminster Hospital, London, on 20 July 1958. Her ashes were buried at Llan-wern.   DEIRDRE BEDDOE

Sources   Viscountess Rhondda [M. H. T. Mackworth], *This was my world* (1933) • S. M. Eoff, *Viscountess Rhondda: equalitarian feminist* (1991) • *The Times* (21 July 1958) • *Western Mail* [Cardiff] (21 July 1958) • *DNB* • GEC, *Peerage* • C. Law, *Suffrage and power: the women's movement, 1918–1928* (1997) • M. Pugh, *Women and the women's movement in Britain, 1914–1959* (1992) • H. L. Smith, ed., *British feminism in the twentieth century* (1990) • *WWW*, 1951–60

Archives   Harvard U., Theodora Bosanquet collection • Hull Central Library, Winifred Holtby collection • IWM, women's war work collection • NL Wales, D. A. Thomas collection | FILM   BFI NFTVA, documentary footage

Likenesses   A. M. Burton, oils, 1932, Trust Houses Forte Ltd, London • Bassano, photograph, 1947, NPG [*see illus.*] • S. J. Solomon, oils, Pen Ithon, Radnorshire • photographs, Mansell Collection, London

Wealth at death   £85,458 1*s*.: probate, 12 Aug 1958, *CGPLA Eng. & Wales*

Thomas, Matthew Evan [Matthew Edward] (1788–1830), architect, became a student of the Royal Academy in 1812, and in 1815 he gained the academy's gold medal for a design for a palace. He went to Italy in the following year, and remained there until 1819. During his stay he was elected a member of the academy at Florence, and of the

Accademia di San Luca at Rome. After his return he exhibited architectural drawings at the Royal Academy between 1820 and 1822. In 1826 he exhibited at the Society (later Royal Society) of British Artists *All Souls College, Oxford* and *L'arco dei Bosari, Verona*. In 1827 and 1828 he exhibited three portraits. Thomas appears in the left foreground of Sir George Hayter's *The Trial of Queen Caroline* (1820–23), holding a pencil, and with a small notebook balanced on the back of the chair behind which he is standing. His name is included in Hayter's Key for the picture and he is described in the National Portrait Gallery's publication of the Key as 'a reporter' (Walker, 1.614). He died at Hackney on 12 July 1830, and was buried in St John's Wood Chapel.

WALTER ARMSTRONG, *rev.* HELENE FURJAŃ

Sources Colvin, *Archs.* · [W. Papworth], ed., *The dictionary of architecture*, 11 vols. (1853–92) · *GM*, 1st ser., 100/2 (1830), 91 · Redgrave, *Artists* · J. Johnson, ed., *Works exhibited at the Royal Society of British Artists, 1824–1893, and the New English Art Club, 1888–1917*, 2 vols. (1975) · B. Stewart and M. Cutten, *The dictionary of portrait painters in Britain up to 1920* (1997) · S. C. Hutchison, 'The Royal Academy Schools, 1768–1830', *Walpole Society*, 38 (1960–62), 123–91 · R. Walker, *National Portrait Gallery: Regency portraits*, 2 vols. (1985)
Likenesses G. Hayter, group portrait, oils (*The trial of Queen Caroline, 1820*), NPG

Thomas, Meirion (1894–1977), plant physiologist, was born at 2 Menai Terrace, Bangor, Caernarvonshire, on 28 December 1894, the only son and youngest of the three children of John Thomas (1834–1901), vice-principal of Bangor Normal College, and his wife, Catherine Anne (*d.* 1937), assistant matron at the same college. She was the daughter of John Roberts, quarryman, of Llandygái, Caernarvonshire. Thomas was educated at the Friars' School, Bangor (1906–12), the University College of North Wales (1912–14), and Trinity Hall, Cambridge (1919–1924). He obtained a second class in part one of the natural sciences tripos in 1921. At Cambridge he was inspired by Frederick Blackman, reader in plant physiology, and F. Gowland Hopkins, head of the school of biochemistry. A lifelong sportsman, Thomas obtained his blue in 1922 in the soccer match against Oxford.

In 1914 Thomas enlisted in the Royal Welch Fusiliers but was soon commissioned into the South Wales Borderers. Transferred to one of the newly formed gas warfare companies in 1915, he was engaged in front line operations in France until his promotion to captain and a staff position in 1917. (From 1939 to 1944 he held a Territorial Army commission for service with the Durham University Officers' Training Corps.)

Thomas began his research at Cambridge on respiratory problems in stored apples, but after a year he declined an offer for the renewal of the grant. In 1924 he was appointed lecturer in botany at Armstrong College, Newcastle upon Tyne (later the University of Newcastle upon Tyne). He was successively lecturer, senior lecturer, and reader in plant physiology, and professor and head of department (1946). He became professor emeritus on his retirement in 1961.

In a department with only four staff he carried a heavy teaching load and throughout his academic career gave many lectures. Even when he no longer ran practical classes in plant physiology he spent time in the teaching laboratories talking to students. The main substance of his teaching, in which plant biochemistry was an essential part of plant physiology, can be seen in his textbook *Plant Physiology* (1935). The outstanding reception of the third edition (1947) led Thomas to observe that 'it was unbelievable that there could be that many plant physiologists in the world'. Subsequently the book was revised and expanded twice with the co-authorship of his colleagues S. L. Ranson and J. A. Richardson (fourth and fifth editions appeared in 1956 and 1973).

Above all Thomas was a true scholar whose probing mind illuminated his subject. One of his greatest achievements was the result of his evaluation of the literature during the preparation of the third edition of his book. On the basis of the discovery, by H. G. Wood and C. H. Werkman, of beta carboxylation in propionic acid bacteria, Thomas explained the previously incomprehensible gaseous exchange data of crassulacean plants by the occurrence of their spectacular accumulation of malic acid in the dark through the fixation of carbon dioxide by beta carboxylation. Novel experiments conducted by his student H. Beevers confirmed the hypothesis which was reported to the Society for Experimental Biology in 1945, first published in the 1947 edition of his book, and for which the definitive papers, which surveyed literature going back to the eighteenth century, were published in the *New Phytologist* in 1949. The comprehensive understanding of crassulacean acid metabolism developed by Thomas in collaboration with S. L. Ranson and several postgraduate students provided the basis for worldwide research on this phenomenon, which is one of the three main strategies for carbon assimilation found in green plants.

Thomas's main research activity was in plant respiration and he was one of a small number of pioneers who established the scientific basis for fruit transport and storage technology. His publications were comparatively few (one book, twelve research papers, and thirteen reviews) but excellent. Among the honours he received were fellowships of the Royal Society of Edinburgh (1946) and the Royal Society (1949), the Charles Reid Barnes life membership of the American Society of Plant Physiologists (1963), and an honorary DSc (Wales, 1964).

Thomas was a bachelor. He was shy and there always seemed to be something of a gap between him and his colleagues and students. Nevertheless, he was well liked and admired. After retirement he returned to Wales where he blended into the small community of Bryn-crug, near Tywyn, but he continued to maintain contact with his family, friends, and subject. He died at the Bay Nursing Home, Pier Road, Bryn-crug, on 5 April 1977.

J. W. BRADBEER, *rev.*

Sources H. K. Porter and S. L. Ranson, *Memoirs FRS*, 24 (1978), 547–68 · personal knowledge (1986) · *WWW, 1971–80* · *CGPLA Eng. & Wales* (1977)
Wealth at death £49,729: probate, 15 June 1977, *CGPLA Eng. & Wales*

Thomas, (William) Miles Webster, Baron Thomas (1897–1980), motor company and airline executive, was born on 2 March 1897 at Garfield Villa, Cefn Mawr, near Ruabon, Denbighshire, north Wales, the son of William Henry Thomas, retired furniture dealer and restorer, and his wife, Mary Elizabeth (Polly), *née* Webster, of farming stock from Derbyshire. William Thomas died of bronchitis shortly after the birth of his only child, leaving his widow to bring up her son on the slender income from the letting of small houses constructed by her late husband in Ruabon, eked out by help from her two brothers. Thomas was educated at Acrefair village school, Ruabon grammar school, and Bromsgrove public school. In 1913 he combined night classes at Birmingham University with a local engineering apprenticeship at Bellis and Morcom Ltd, engineers, of Birmingham.

In August 1914 Thomas enlisted as a private, served in the German East African campaign in armoured cars, transferred to the Royal Flying Corps, learned to fly, was commissioned and, in 1916, became an instructor at the Air Fighting School at Heliopolis. In 1917–18 he saw active service as a pilot with 72 squadron in Mesopotamia, Persia, and southern Russia, and was awarded a DFC. In 1919 he resigned from the RAF to join Temple Press Ltd to become technical editor of *The Motor* and, in 1922, editor of the *Light Car*, at £650 a year.

In January 1924 W. R. Morris (later Lord Nuffield) invited Thomas to join him at Morris Motors, Cowley, as commercial adviser. Six months later, on 2 June 1924, at Littlemore church, Oxford, he married Hylda Church, who had been Morris's secretary. A daughter, Sheila, was born in March 1925 and a son, Michael, in the autumn of 1926.

Working closely with 'the Boss', Thomas advanced rapidly through the Morris Motors hierarchy: sales manager and a director in 1927, general manager and a director of Morris Commercial Cars Ltd, Birmingham, in 1934, and of Wolseley Motors Ltd in 1937, vice-chairman and managing director of Morris Motors and its subsidiary companies in 1940 (he held these posts until 1947), chairman of the Cruiser Tank Production Group, a member of the advisory panel on tank production in 1941, and chairman of the British tank engine mission to the USA in 1942, by which time his income had reached £20,000 a year. He was knighted in 1943.

After the Second World War Sir Miles, while president of the Society of Motor Manufacturers and Traders, joined the board of the Colonial Development Corporation. That precipitated a growing disharmony with Lord Nuffield and a parting, in 1948, on generous terms. Almost at once he was invited by Lord Nathan, minister of civil aviation, to become deputy chairman of the state-owned British Overseas Airways Corporation (BOAC), and to succeed Sir Harold Hartley as chairman from 1 July 1949 at £7500 a year. So began eight years of hard but enjoyable toil and travel. Under Miles Thomas, BOAC became the world's first operator of jet aircraft—the DH Comet—and earned its first profits in 1952, with reduced staff numbers, while doubling its traffic. A natural communicator, Thomas

(William) Miles Webster Thomas, Baron Thomas (1897–1980), by Walter Stoneman, 1943

raised staff morale and public pride in BOAC as one of the world's leading airlines.

In 1954 disasters to two Comets and the grounding of the Comet fleet, together with the loss of a Constellation and a Stratocruiser, brought heavy burdens on chairman and airline alike, further compounded in December 1955 when Sir Miles and the new minister of transport and civil aviation, Harold Watkinson, fell out over management responsibilities. In consequence, Sir Miles resigned from BOAC on 30 April 1956, with an offer of the chairmanship of the UK subsidiary of the large United States Monsanto Chemical Company.

During eight more comfortable years, and a salary back at more than £20,000 a year, Sir Miles was able to add a number of other board appointments, including Sun Life, the *Sunday Times*, and Carbon Electric Holdings Ltd. In 1957 he purchased Remenham Court, Henley-on-Thames, and returned to the air transport industry as the non-executive chairman of Britannia Airways—a substantial charter company. President of the National Savings Committee from 1965 to 1972 and its chairman in 1965–70, Miles Thomas was created a life peer in 1971, as Baron Thomas of Remenham. He died at his home, Remenham Court, Henley-on-Thames, on 8 February 1980 at the age of eighty-two.   PETER G. MASEFIELD

Sources personal knowledge (2004) · private information (2004) · F. H. Ellis, 'The author of Wing C6727: Daniel Coxe, FRS, or

Thomas Coxe, FRS', *Notes and Records of the Royal Society*, 18 (1963), 36–8 • *WWW, 1971–80* • *Directory of British Aviation* (1979) • M. J. Smith, 'British Overseas Airways Corporation', *The Airline bibliography*, 2 (1988), 197–202 • P. Masefield, 'Thomas, William Miles Webster', *DBB* • *The history of B.O.A.C.* (1974)

Likenesses W. Stoneman, photograph, 1943, NPG [*see illus.*]

Thomas, Sir Noah (1720–1792), physician, was born at Neath, Glamorgan, the son of Hophni Thomas, master of a merchant vessel. He was educated at Oakham School, and went to St John's College, Cambridge, in 1738. He graduated BA in 1742, MA in 1746, and MD in 1753. He then settled in London. He was made a fellow of the Royal Society in 1753, was elected a fellow of the College of Physicians in 1757, and delivered the Goulstonian lectures in 1759. In 1761, 1766, 1767, and 1781 he was one of the censors. He became physician-extraordinary to George III in 1763, and physician-in-ordinary in 1775, and was knighted in that year. He was also physician to the Lock Hospital, London. He died at Bath on 17 May 1792. In the College of Physicians he was esteemed for his learning, but he never published any book.

NORMAN MOORE, *rev.* JEAN LOUDON

Sources Munk, *Roll* • Venn, *Alum. Cant.* • *GM*, 1st ser., 62 (1792), 484 • *GM*, 1st ser., 84/1 (1814), 630

Likenesses attrib. J. Romney, oils, 1781, St John Cam. • J. Reynolds, portrait, St John Cam.

Thomas, Oliver (1599/1600–1652), nonconformist minister and author, was the son of a Montgomeryshire gentleman. However, nothing is known of his parents and his early life. He appears to have registered at Shrewsbury School in June 1609, described as 'gen. f. et h.'. At the age of sixteen he matriculated at Hart Hall, Oxford, on 8 November 1616. It was not usual for the sons of gentry to enter Hart Hall at that time; the majority of students were described as 'pleb. filius'. One of his contemporaries there was Richard Parry, son of the bishop of St Asaph. Thomas graduated BA on 28 June 1620. A few months prior to graduation, on 9 February 1620, he married his wife, Mary, in the parish of St Mary's, Shrewsbury. Nothing is known of Mary's family connections.

Oliver Thomas may have held a living or worked as an itinerant preacher before he graduated. However, it appears that he was still at Oxford on 13 March 1622 when Theodore Price's successor, Dr Thomas Iles, was admitted to the principalship of Hart Hall. Thomas was among those called upon to vote on this appointment. He may have been a fellow at Hart Hall. On 8 July 1628 he graduated MA. His whereabouts and activities for the period 1621–8 are unclear. It is possible that he stayed at Hart Hall and delivered lectures there from time to time, as MA candidates were required to be residents at the college for three years after receiving their BA degree. His other activities may have included preaching and lecturing at locations in and around Oxford or the Welsh borderlands. No doubt he was attracted by the powerful Calvinistic influences during his years at Oxford. By 1628 he had set up home for himself and his family in the parish of West Felton, Shropshire. He may have served as unofficial curate to Samuel Hildersham who was appointed to the rectorship in that year.

West Felton parish registers suggest that Thomas and his wife raised a family of eight children: Lazarus (*bap.* 1628), Timothy (*bap.* 1630), Abigail (*bap.* 1632), Elizabeth (*bap.* 1633), Titus (*bap.* 1635), Miriam (*bap.* 1637); the same source records the burials of Ruhamah (1640) and Nathaniel (1642). Thomas's will refers also to two daughters, Mary and Martha, who appear to have been born before 1628.

For the next two decades Thomas was probably part of a network of lecturers who served to spread the gospel in the various market towns on the border. This tallies with the fact that Arise Evans of Llangelynnin heard a sermon by Mr Oliver Thomas at Wrexham in 1629. On 1 September 1639 he preached in the parish of Holt, bishopric of Chester, at the invitation of the churchwardens, having been expelled from St Asaph diocese and his licence taken away for nonconformity. There he was accompanied by Richard Blinman, 'a man who did not ordinarily conforme himself to the discipline of the Churche of England' (consistory court papers, EDC 5, 1639, misc.). His whereabouts during the civil war years are unknown. He may have been a chaplain in the parliamentary armies. In 1647 he was minister at Oswestry and West Felton. He may have held both livings simultaneously. He was also named as a minister 'fit to bee of the Second Classis' (Bodl. Oxf., MS 4D, 62 (12)). In 1649 he was appointed one of the approvers under the Act for the Propagation of the Gospel in Wales, together with others such as Walter Cradock, Morgan Llwyd, Vavasor Powell, and Rowland Nevett. Pluralism was not tolerated by the approvers; in 1649–50 John Williams of Llanrhaeadr was expelled from his living, as part of the campaign to reduce pluralism. But Thomas himself was also guilty of the same sin and was forced to choose between Oswestry and Llanrhaeadr-ym-Mochnant. On 14 May 1650 he 'elected Llanrhaider in the Countyes of Denbigh and Merioneth [*sic*]' (Bodl. Oxf., MS Rawl., c. 261). He went there as successor to Evan Roberts who had died earlier in the same year. It appears that he remained there until his death in 1652.

Thomas was also an author of significance. He published four Welsh books in all: *Car-wr y Cymru* (1630), a catechism for children; *Car-wr y Cymru, yn annog ei genedl* (1631), a treatise exhorting people in Wales to read the Bible; *Sail Crefydd Ghristnogol* (1640), a catechism written in collaboration with Evan Roberts; and *Drych i Dri Math o Bobl* (1647, reprinted 1677), a brief description of various types of Christians. His prose style is essentially plain, as befits a puritan. He also appears to be familiar with the Welsh bardic tradition and strict metres. In 1653 an encomium by Thomas was published in *Testûn Testament Newydd* (Richard Jones). Oliver Thomas was buried at West Felton on 6 April 1652. He bequeathed his property and moneys to his wife and children. On 10 April 1657 his widow received an annuity of £30 towards her maintenance.

MERFYN MORGAN

Sources M. Morgan, ed., *Gweithiau Oliver Thomas ac Evan Roberts* (1981) • parish registers, West Felton, 1628–53 [baptism, burial] •

will, PRO, PROB 11/221 · consistory court papers, misc., 1639, Ches. & Chester ALSS · R. G. Gruffydd, 'Religious prose in Welsh from the beginning of the reign of Elizabeth to the Restoration', DPhil diss., U. Oxf., 1953 · R. G. Gruffydd, ed., *A guide to Welsh literature*, 3: *c.1530–1700* (1997) · *Reg. Oxf.*, vol. 2/2 · E. Calvert, ed., *Shrewsbury School regestum scholarium, 1562–1635: admittances and readmittances* [1892] · T. Richards, *A history of the puritan movement in Wales* (1920) · *Boyd's marriage index for Shropshire*, 2: *1601–1625* (1928) · Shropshire parish registers, Lichfield diocese, vol. 13, St Mary's Shrewsbury · Bodl. Oxf., MS 4D, 62 (12) · W. A. Shaw, *A history of the English church during the civil wars and under the Commonwealth, 1640–1660*, 2 (1900)
Wealth at death approx. £115; plus books and horse: will, PRO, PROB 11/221

Thomas, Owen (1812–1891), Calvinistic Methodist minister, son of Owen (*d*. 1831) and Mary Thomas, was born in Edmund Street, Holyhead, on 16 December 1812. John *Thomas (1821–1892) was a younger brother. His father was a stonemason, and he followed the same occupation from the time of the family's move to Bangor in 1827 until he was twenty-two. In 1834 he began to preach in connection with the Calvinistic Methodists, among whom his father had been a lay officer until his death in 1831, and at once took high rank as a preacher. After keeping school in Bangor for some years, he entered in 1838 the Calvinistic Methodist college at Bala, and thence proceeded in 1841 to the University of Edinburgh.

Poverty forced Thomas to cut short his university course before he could graduate, and in January 1844 he became pastor of Penmount Chapel, Pwllheli. In the following September he was ordained in the North Wales Association meeting at Bangor. Two years later he moved to Newtown, Montgomeryshire, to take charge of the English Calvinistic Methodist church in that town, and at the end of 1851 he accepted the pastorate of the Welsh church meeting in Jewin Crescent, London. On 24 January 1860 he married Ellen (*d*. 1867), youngest daughter of the Revd William Roberts of Amlwch. In 1865 he moved again to Liverpool, where he spent the rest of his days as pastor: first, of the Netherfield Road, and then (from 1871) of the Princes Road Church of the Calvinistic Methodists. He was moderator of the North Wales Association in 1863 and 1882, and of the general assembly of the denomination in 1868 and 1888.

Throughout life Thomas was a close student, and his literary work bears witness to his wide theological reading and talent for exposition. Besides biblical commentaries, Thomas published biographies of the Revds John Jones, Talsarn, and Henry Rees. He was a contributor to the *Traethodydd* from its inception, and for a time one of its two joint editors. Many of the articles in the first edition of the *Gwyddoniadur*, a Welsh encyclopaedia in ten volumes (1857–77), were from his pen. In 1877 the degree of DD was conferred upon him by Princeton College, New Jersey.

It was as a preacher, however, that Thomas won the commanding position he occupied in Wales; his eloquence enabled him to wield in the pulpit an influence which was said to recall that of John Elias, and he never appeared to better advantage than at the great open-air services held in connection with the meetings of the two associations. He died at his home in Catharine Street, Liverpool, on 2 August 1891, and was buried in Anfield cemetery, Liverpool.   J. E. LLOYD, *rev.* MARTIN WELLINGS

Sources DNB · DWB
Archives NL Wales, letters, notes, papers, sermons
Wealth at death £4996 3*s*.: probate, 16 Oct 1891, *CGPLA Eng. & Wales*

Thomas, Sir Percy Edward (1883–1969), architect, was born on 12 September 1883 at 49 Eleanor Street, South Shields, co. Durham, fifth of the seven children of Christmas Thomas (1845–1897), a sea captain from Narberth in Pembrokeshire, and his wife, Cecilia Eliza Thornton, from Wedmore in Somerset. Cardiff's booming coal trade brought his father to south Wales in 1893–4 and the family settled in Penarth. The teenage Thomas spent summers on voyages with his father to ports around Europe, from Balaklava to St Petersburg; his father died abroad in 1897. Thomas attended Hasland House private school in Penarth and then the higher grade school in Cardiff. At the age of fifteen a phrenologist advised that Thomas take up a career in architecture and he was articled to E. H. Bruton FRIBA in Cardiff for five years; in his spare time he entered architectural competitions in the *Building News* under the *nom de plume* Viking. In 1904 he went to work for J. C. Prestwich of Leigh in Lancashire and a year later took up a position with R. A. Brinkworth in Bath, before returning to Prestwich in 1907 as chief assistant. On 14 August 1907 Thomas married Margaret Ethel Turner (1882/3–1953) of Talgarth in Brecknockshire. They had four children: Kathleen (1908–1993), Joy (1911–1996), Norman (1915–1989), and Pamela (*b*. 1925). About 1910 Thomas moved to Manchester to work for Henthorne Stott, where, unenthusiastically, he helped design cotton mills. At this time Thomas began collaborating with Ivor Jones, a friend already in practice in Cardiff.

Jones and Thomas became partners in 1912, after winning the competition for Cardiff Technical College (opened 1916; now Cardiff University's Bute Building in the city's Edwardian civic centre). The Percy Thomas Partnership, as the practice became known, was founded on Thomas's ability to win architectural competitions and it grew into one of the most commercially successful British practices of the twentieth century. Thomas joined the army in 1915, and served most of the war with the Royal Engineers in northern France; he was twice mentioned in dispatches, and became a military OBE. He returned to Cardiff in 1919. Commissions from a local brewer, S. A. Brain, and for private houses, helped him re-establish the practice. His prowess in competitions continued; he was especially successful with fire stations and civic buildings.

The significant period in Thomas's career as a designer was the 1930s. His most accomplished and celebrated work was the civic centre in Swansea, another competition success, completed in 1936. Jones left the practice before work was finished. Thomas's Temple of Peace, also in Cardiff's civic centre, was opened in November 1938. These two buildings are the prime examples of his stripped classical style, based on Beaux-Arts principles, which Professor Charles Reilly described in 1931 as 'a classical approach to modernism, if that were possible' (Reilly, 65). Thomas received the RIBA gold medal for architecture in 1939 and was twice president of the RIBA (1935–7 and 1943–6).

During the Second World War Thomas undertook government work. He became area officer for the Ministry of Supply in Wales in 1940, and chairman of the Wales regional board of the new Ministry of Production in 1942. He was also a lieutenant-colonel in the Home Guard, and later honorary colonel of 109 regiment Royal Engineers (Territorial Army). After the war he was knighted, made deputy lieutenant of the county of Glamorgan in 1946, and high sheriff of Glamorgan in 1949.

Described in his obituary in *The Times* as being 'in outward appearance at least, calm and benign with sparkling white hair and pink unwrinkled cheeks', Thomas moved in influential circles. After the war he enjoyed the role of doyen, acting as consultant to a number of public bodies, and helping adjudicate some prestigious architectural competitions, including that for Coventry Cathedral. He was design consultant for the Ministry of Transport on, among other projects, the Severn Bridge (1961). When he retired in 1960 the practice he founded continued to prosper under the leadership of his son, Norman. Thomas died as the result of a stroke, on 17 August 1969 at his home, Tregenna, Mill Road, Llanishen, Cardiff, and after cremation at Thornhill, Cardiff, his ashes were interred at Llanishen church, Cardiff.   SIMON UNWIN

Sources P. Thomas, *Pupil to president (memoirs of an architect)* (1963) · *The Times* (18 Aug 1969) · C. H. Reilly, 'Some younger architects of today: Percy Thomas', *Building* (Feb 1931), 60–65 · 'Profile: Sir Percy Thomas', *Building* (Jan 1950), 10 · b. cert. · m. cert. · d. cert. · private information (2004) [P. Morgan]
Likenesses J. Gunn, oils, *c*.1946, RIBA · photograph, repro. in Thomas, *Pupil to president* · photograph, repro. in *The Times*
Wealth at death £90,866: probate, 30 Dec 1969, *CGPLA Eng. & Wales*

Thomas, Richard (1837–1916), tin plate manufacturer, was born at Bridgwater, Somerset, on 5 December 1837, the son of Richard Thomas, shipowner and merchant, of Bridgwater. He was educated at Wesleyan (now Queen's) College, Taunton, until the age of eleven. During his early working life he was employed as a clerk, as an assistant to an uncle who ran a draper's business in Oxford (later becoming a partner in the business), and as a coal exporter and commission agent in Cardiff.

While in Cardiff Thomas married, on 18 February 1859, Anne Loveluck (1836/7–1914), daughter of John Loveluck, a farmer, of Ffald, Llangynog; they had five sons and a daughter. His subsequent employment as works manager and accountant of a colliery and firebrick business at Briton Ferry, Glamorgan, in which his father was a partner, was to provide a springboard for his future career. In 1863 his appointment as accountant and sub-manager in charge of overseeing the construction of a new iron plate and tin plate works at Melyn, Neath, Glamorgan, brought him into direct contact for the first time with the industry in which he was to become an important figure. During his four years at Melyn he studied the processes, working methods, and ways of financing the tin plate trade, and he made contacts with important ironmasters and coal owners.

A spell as general manager and secretary at the Ynyspenllwch ironworks was followed by Thomas's most significant development: the formation of Richard Thomas & Co. to acquire and run the idle Lydbrook tin plate works in Gloucestershire in 1871. Expansion through the acquisition of the Lydney works (1875) and the Lydbrook colliery (1877) led, however, to financial difficulties and, in 1883, eventual liquidation, due mainly to problems of flooding at the colliery. Nevertheless, with the backing of the company's major creditor, the Barrow Hematite Steel Company, the business was relaunched in 1884 as Richard Thomas & Co. Ltd, with Thomas as managing director of the new concern and his eldest son, Richard Beaumont Thomas, as general manager.

Gradually the tin plate interests of Thomas and his sons—for he was always concerned to provide jobs for members of his family—were extended. In 1888 he acquired, in conjunction with William Thomas Lewis (later Baron Senghenydd) and others, the Melingriffith tin plate works on the outskirts of Cardiff. This and future expansion was based on Thomas's ability to identify ailing concerns which could be acquired at a low price and turned into profitable businesses. The period following the introduction of the American tariffs on tin plate in the early 1890s provided an impetus for further acquisitions in the late 1890s and enabled the Thomas family to build up control over a significant portion of the British tin plate industry. By 1916 the various companies associated with Richard Thomas & Co. Ltd employed over 11,000 workers and controlled a quarter of the tin plate mills in south Wales. While the problems faced during the inter-war period by the organization he built up may cast some doubts on the strategy he pursued and the organizational structure he established, the growth of the Thomas empire was none the less a considerable feat of entrepreneurship and a testament to his considerable drive and energy.

It has been suggested that the key to Thomas's success lay 'in his concentration of purpose, epitomised perhaps by his insistence on total attention to business' (Wainwright, 55). Indeed, he spared little time for public life, spending only a brief period on the Monmouth board of guardians. A modest and quiet-living man who shunned publicity, he nevertheless gave generously to many a deserving cause, particularly favouring hospital work.

Thomas died on 28 September 1916 at 31 Henrietta Street, Bath, and was buried at Lydbrook churchyard, Gloucestershire, on 30 September. His wife had predeceased him, dying in 1914.   TREVOR BOYNS

Sources D. Wainwright, *Men of steel: a history of Richard Thomas and his family* (1986) · G. M. Holmes, 'Thomas, Richard', *DBB* · *Western Mail* [Cardiff] (29 Sept 1916) · m. cert. · d. cert.
Archives British Steel RO, Shotton, records (especially minute books) of Richard Thomas & Co.
Likenesses photographs, repro. in Wainwright, *Men of steel*

Wealth at death £92,139 10s. 8d.: probate, 28 Dec 1916, *CGPLA Eng. & Wales*

Thomas, Richard Clement Charles [Clem] (1929–1996), rugby player and journalist, was born on 28 January 1929 at 160 Donald Street, Cardiff, the son of a cattle dealer, David John Richard Thomas, and his wife, Edna Madeline Dodd. He was brought up in the mining and hill-farming village of Ammanford, which nestles under the great sweep of the Black Mountains. His father was a great character, notorious at west Wales cattle marts, from whom Thomas inherited his robust independence and entrepreneurial flair. An education at Blundell's School, Tiverton, and St John's College, Cambridge, gave him a refined accent and cosmopolitan tastes, but a tough kulak core remained: this duality was the basis of his charm.

R. C. C. Thomas (as he was invariably listed in match programmes) won four schoolboy rugby caps for Wales in 1946 and 1947 and a Cambridge blue in 1949, having already played in an international: he first wore the red of Wales in Paris at the end of the previous season. His next cap came three years later, by which time this superbly built and handsome athlete had developed into a highly effective wing-forward, at Swansea rugby club, acclaimed for his tight play and his ability to bottle up opposing fly-halves. His career was not without controversy: matches against England were invariably brutal affairs in the 1950s and Thomas was always well to the fore in forward exchanges. The highlight of his career came in 1953, when, according to his own understated account, he had 'hoofed' the ball across the field for Ken Jones to score a try which allowed Wales to beat New Zealand for only the third (and possibly the last) time ever. In 1955 he was selected for the British Lions tour of South Africa. An appendix operation seemed to indicate an early end to his involvement, but he opted to stay on; he recovered and played in the last two tests, including the 9–6 victory in Pretoria. His renowned toughness gave him the lead when the Lions replied to illegal violence on the field. His teammate Cliff Morgan recalled that 'Clem would have kicked his grandmother if she was wearing the wrong shirt, but I loved having the old bugger on my side … he was absolutely fearless' (*Sunday Times*, 6 May 2001). In the company of the Lions Thomas found his natural home, and thereafter his closest friends were players he normally opposed in international fixtures. It was entirely appropriate that later he should write *The History of the British Lions*, published posthumously in 1996 and subsequently updated by his son Greg. He was the obvious man to captain Wales in 1958 and 1959, his last season before retirement.

Thomas was a lifelong businessman, investing in a number of enterprises, initially in the south of France; he later bought a home in the Médoc. His business was wholesale butchery, which prompted one rugby friend, an erstwhile English opponent, to comment that 'Clem was the only player to take his trade on the field with him' (*The Observer*). On 3 April 1954 he married Ann Shirley Barter (*b.* 1932/3), with whom he had a daughter and three sons; all three sons played rugby for Swansea. This marriage ended in divorce and on 18 April 1980 he married Dr Joyce Lilian Rowley, *née* Blakeley.

Following his retirement as a player Thomas took what was, at that time, the relatively unusual step of becoming a rugby correspondent. For almost thirty-five years he was chief rugby writer of *The Observer* and he later wrote for both the *Independent on Sunday* and the *South Wales Evening Post*. He contributed regularly to many rugby magazines and books and in 1980 co-authored *Welsh Rugby* with his friend and *Observer* colleague Geoffrey Nicholson. His journalism was as robust as his forward play. He had always known that rugby union would one day become a professional game and that wider exposure would necessarily involve this most exciting and physically demanding of sports facing new challenges in terms of coaching and administration. In particular, as Welsh rugby declined in the 1980s, he became the scourge of the 'small men' who ran the game and called for root and branch reform. He had become a firm opponent of apartheid and was greatly saddened by the Welsh Rugby Union's determination to preserve South African links in the 1980s. It was his view that 'no leading rugby nation had lost its way more fundamentally than the Welsh' (C. Thomas, 'Wales in turmoil', *Rugby News*, 2 Nov 1989).

Clem Thomas was a political radical: as a Liberal and a dedicated European he contested the parliamentary seat of Carmarthen in 1974 and 1979, and the European constituency of Mid- and West Wales in 1979. He advocated the development of business courses in Wales, he supported devolution, and was a keen collector of Welsh paintings. He died suddenly from a heart attack at his home, 42 De La Beche Road, Sketty, Swansea, on 5 September 1996. His second wife survived him.

PETER STEAD

Sources *The Times* (6 Sept 1996) · *The Observer* (8 Sept 1996) · D. Smith and G. Williams, *Fields of praise* (1980) · P. Stead, 'Clem Thomas', in H. Richards, P. Stead, and G. Williams, 'More heart and soul': the character of Welsh rugby (1999) · C. Thomas and G. Nicholson, *Welsh rugby: the crowning years, 1968–80* (1980) · C. Thomas, *The history of the British Lions* (1996) · H. McIlvanney, 'The roaring fifties', *Sunday Times* (6 May 2001) · b. cert. · m. certs. · d. cert.
Archives FILM BBC, London · BBC, Cardiff | SOUND BBC, London · BBC, Cardiff
Likenesses portrait, repro. in *The Times* · portrait, repro. in Richards, Stead, and Williams, 'More heart and soul'

Thomas, Richard Darton (1777–1857), naval officer, son of Charles Thomas, was born at Saltash, Cornwall. He entered the navy in May 1790 on the *Cumberland* with Captain John Macbride. Afterwards he was in the *Blanche* in the West Indies, and when she was paid off in June 1792 he joined the sloop *Nautilus*, in which he went to the West Indies, and was at the capture of Tobago, Martinique, and St Lucia. At Martinique he commanded a flat-bottomed boat in the brilliant attack upon Fort Royal. He returned to England in the *Boyne*, and he was still with her when she was burnt at Spithead, off Portsmouth, on 1 May 1795. He was afterwards in the *Glory* and *Commerce de Marseille* in the English Channel, and in the *Barfleur* and *Victory* in the Mediterranean, and on 15 January 1797 he was promoted lieutenant of the *Excellent*, in which, on 14 February, he was present in the battle of Cape St Vincent, off the coast of Portugal. He continued in the *Excellent* off Cadiz until June 1798, when he was moved to the *Thalia*. In February 1799 he was transferred to the *Defence*, in December to the *Triumph*, and in October 1801 to the *Barfleur*, Collingwood's flagship in the channel. During the peace he was in the *Leander* on the Halifax station, and was promoted commander on 18 January 1803. The packet *Lady Hobart*, in which he took a passage for England, was wrecked on an iceberg. After seven days in a small boat he and his companions reached Cove Island, north of St John's, Newfoundland. On his arrival in England he was appointed, in December 1803, to the bomb-vessel *Etna*, which he took out to the Mediterranean. On 22 October 1805 he was posted to the *Bellerophon* (74 guns), from which he was moved to the *Queen* (98 guns) as flag captain to Lord Collingwood, with whom, in the *Ocean* (98 guns) and the *Ville de Paris* (110 guns), he continued until Collingwood's death in March 1810. He remained in the *Ville de Paris* until December, and in February 1811 he was appointed to the *Undaunted* (38 guns), in which he assisted the Spanish along the coast of Catalonia. In February 1813, after nine years' continuous service in the Mediterranean, he was obliged by ill health to return to England.

From 1822 until 1825 Thomas was captain of the Ordinary at Portsmouth, and he was in the same capacity at Plymouth from 1834 until 1837. He married, on 2 October 1827, Gratina, daughter of Lieutenant-General Robert Williams of the Royal Marines; they had a son and a daughter. Thomas became rear-admiral on 10 January 1837, and was commander-in-chief in the Pacific from 1841 until 1844, a troubled period. He was involved in obtaining compensation for British residents of San Salvador and Costa Rica, events at Tahiti and the Sandwich Islands, and the detention of a Peruvian squadron until redress was made to British subjects. His conduct was commended by the British government. He was thanked by the American government for helping Americans resident in the Sandwich Islands, and was made an honorary member of the American protestant missionary organization, the Board of Commissioners for Foreign Missions. He was promoted vice-admiral on 8 January 1848 and admiral on 11 September 1854, and he died at Stonehouse, Devonport, Plymouth, on 21 August 1857. That Collingwood kept him as his flag captain for five years is the highest testimony to Thomas's seamanship, professionalism, and personal qualities. J. K. Laughton, *rev.* Andrew Lambert

Sources *Letters and papers of Charles, Lord Barham*, ed. J. K. Laughton, 3, Navy RS, 39 (1911) • D. Syrett and R. L. DiNardo, *The commissioned sea officers of the Royal Navy, 1660–1815*, rev. edn, Occasional Publications of the Navy RS, 1 (1994) • O'Byrne, *Naval biog. dict.* • *GM*, 3rd ser., 3 (1857), 468 • P. Mackesy, *The war in the Mediterranean, 1803–1810* (1957) • Boase, *Mod. Eng. biog.*

Thomas, Rodney Meredith (1902–1996), architect and designer, was born at 11 Hayes Court, Camberwell New Road, London, on 4 May 1902, the only child of Ernest Montague Thomas (1872?–1914), architect, and his wife, Constance Jessica Jones (1875?–1915?), a nurse. Although born in London, Thomas was taken out to India at an early age when his father was appointed consulting architect to the government in Madras. The years in India stocked Thomas's memory with brightly coloured images which resurfaced more than half a century later in hallucinatory landscape paintings.

At the age of eight Thomas was shipped home with his mother to be educated, living in various rented rooms in London before being put to board in Hampshire. His mother returned to India and never saw her son again. Shortly after the outbreak of the First World War Thomas's father died and his mother returned to nursing, dying shortly afterwards. The orphaned boy remained at his Anglo-Indian school until rather dramatically removed from it one night by his eccentric uncle, Sir Alfred Brumwell *Thomas (1868–1948), another architect, who adopted him and sent him to Eton College for a couple of years, afterwards employing him in his own architectural practice. Thomas shared his uncle's rooms in Albany, the exclusive bachelor residences off Piccadilly, and enjoyed his famous salons, to which such luminaries as Noel Coward, Marie Corelli, and Ivor Novello regularly came.

The young Rod Thomas (as he was known) showed a considerable aptitude for drawing—so much so that at school he was much in demand as an expert forger of ten shilling notes and concert tickets—and hoped to pursue a career as an artist. To this end he went to study at the Byam Shaw School of Art, and then at the sculptor Leon Underwood's private school at Brook Green. There he met and became friendly with a group of young artists who were to make names for themselves: Henry Moore, Eileen Agar, Blair Hughes-Stanton, and Gertrude Hermes. His uncle, however, disparaged a future as a painter and persuaded Thomas to study architecture at the Bartlett School, University of London, where he attended lectures by Professor Albert Richardson. However, Thomas preferred to spend time at the nearby Slade School, studying painting with Professor Tonks. Meanwhile he met Violet Mary Guy (1900–1986), a student of painting at the Royal Academy Schools, and was powerfully attracted to her. With some money he had inherited from his parents on his eighteenth birthday, Thomas bought an Amilcar racing car, and eloped in it with Violet Guy. They were married for only a few years and had one son; they were very poor and unhappy and later divorced.

Thomas's schooling had been poor and consequently he had not been able to read until the age of ten and never achieved any academic prowess. None the less, his considerable gifts as an artist and draughtsman made him invaluable as an assistant. He left university and set to work for a number of other architects—first for his uncle, then for Giles Gilbert Scott, Louis De Soissons, and Grey Wornam. It was while working for De Soissons that he met his second wife, Grace Charlotte (1903–1967), a dancer and model, the daughter of George Corderoy Curnock, a journalist. Thomas married Curnock on 9 January 1937, and they had a daughter and a son. The marriage lasted until 1950 and was dissolved.

Thomas was prepared to turn his hand to most things. Other pre-war work included wonderfully curvy interior decor for the surrealist Eileen Agar and her husband (some of it now in the V&A collection), and work for the poster designer Ashley Havinden, and for Crawfords advertising agency. Thomas designed window displays featuring his own paintings for Simpsons, the department store in Piccadilly, worked as an architect for Southern Railways, and designed exhibition displays and showrooms for Ascot Water Heaters.

During the Second World War Thomas joined the Home Guard and manned the anti-aircraft guns in Hyde Park. He also made a number of stabile and mobile sculptures which influenced younger artists. When the hostilities ceased, he co-founded the Arcon group of architects with his old friend Raglan Squire (son of J. C. Squire), Edric Neale, and later Jim Gear. This group worked on developing desperately needed prefabricated houses, and eventually 40,000 of the Mark V prefab were built. The design of a simple structure of double-skin asbestos-concrete under a curved roof proved to be both popular and long-lasting. This was one of Thomas's greatest achievements. He continued to explore the links between architecture and industry, absorbed in long-term research into jointing systems, at an informal atelier in Seymour Walk, Chelsea, attended by a number of young engineers, architects, and artists, including the sculptors Elizabeth Frink and Lynn Chadwick.

In 1949 Thomas was involved in town planning and furniture design for the ill-fated ground nut scheme in Tanganyika. Typically, his designs were beautiful, and his pegged furniture prototypes elegant and practical, but the scheme foundered. In 1951 Thomas built the transport pavilion for the festival of Britain. With an aeroplane suspended from its ceiling behind a wall of glass, this was a spectacular building, though originally conceived in even more dramatic form, before Hugh Casson, overseer of the project, complained 'Rod, your building needs a haircut' (personal knowledge).

Many of Thomas's later ideas went unrealized; in particular schemes for Coventry Cathedral and the Royal College of Art. Increasingly he turned his attention to teaching—at Chelsea School of Art, the London College of Furniture, and Wimbledon School of Art (1963–73), where he taught architectural drawing. On 23 June 1961 he was married for the third and final time, to the critic and poet (Beatrice) Joan Lyon, née Morgan (1925–1999), with whom he organized poetry readings in Moravian Close in Chelsea where they lived. Among those who came to read were Peter Porter, Dannie Abse, and Laurie Lee. The great unfulfilled project of his last years (from, in fact, the 1950s to his death) was a 'sky city'. This organic structure involved building great towers to reach above the clouds, taking piazzas and gardens up with the vertical elements into perpetual sunshine.

Thomas was a creative thinker, a visionary, and dreamer who never received due recognition in his lifetime. A modest man, he never sought success, preferring good company to financial rewards. He was an inspired architect and interior designer, with a subtle feeling for materials, and a painter of extraordinary versatility. He painted abstracts (both organic and geometric), figure studies, poetic landscapes (reminiscent of Paul Nash), tonal drawings about the fall of light, and panoramas of magical realism. As his sight began to fail with increasing age, he devised methods of arranging his colours and making stencils so that he could continue to paint although virtually blind. He dreamed vividly, mostly about birds and angels, and made birds and architectural structures out of clay. His lifelong friend Eileen Agar wrote in her autobiography that he was 'a born non-conformist who became something of a George Orwell character, very tall and lean with a stone-age El Greco look about him' (E. Agar, *A Look at my Life*, 1988, 41). He died in the Avon House Nursing Home, Allen Street, London, on 26 April 1996, and was cremated on 7 May at Putney Vale crematorium.

ANDREW LAMBIRTH

Sources '"A sense of wonder": the autobiography of Rodney Thomas', ed. A. Lambirth • personal knowledge (2004) • *The Independent* (6 May 1996), 16 • *The Guardian* (16 May 1996), 15 • *The Times* (27 April 1996), 21 • b. cert. • m. certs. • d. cert.

Archives priv. coll., family papers

Likenesses E. Agar, ink and watercolour drawing, 1927, repro. in *Eileen Agar, 1899–1991* (1999) [exhibition catalogue, Scottish National Gallery of Modern Art]; priv. coll. • photograph, 1940?–1949, repro. in *The Times* • D. Santini, photograph, *c.*1987, repro. in *The Independent*

Thomas, Ronald Stuart (1913–2000), poet and Church in Wales clergyman, was born at 5 Newfoundland Road, Gabalfa, Llandaff, Cardiff, on 29 March 1913, the only son of Thomas Hubert Thomas (*d.* 1965), merchant seaman, and Margaret, née Davies. From the age of five he lived in Anglesey, and later brilliantly evoked his childhood, during which he acquired his love of the natural world among the cliffs and beaches of Holy Island, in his autobiographical pieces *Y llwybrau gynt* ('Former paths'; 1972) and *Neb* ('No one'; 1985). His mother was the main figure in his early life, guiding him towards the respectable, secure vocation of priesthood. Later he described her as overprotective and sometimes difficult, but he also recalled her tears in the night before he left home for college. His father, working on the ships that crossed the Irish Sea, remains a shadowy figure in Thomas's work. There are glimpses of him as an older man, fishing in the river by the rectory in Manafon, pointing out the constellations, calling birds by the wrong names, but his most striking intervention came from a distance, by letter, when he recognized, in the fine language of his son's correspondence, a nascent poet.

Studying classics at the University College of North Wales, Bangor, Thomas acquired his cognomen RS while in the rugby team, but later depicted himself there as shy: studying quietly in his room, taking long solitary walks through the open country, and failing to find a girl who would accompany him. He met her in his mid-twenties—

Mildred (Elsi) Eldridge (1909–1991), an English painter whose reputation was already established—and their marriage lasted for more than fifty years from 1936. The poetry he addressed to her is among his most intense and moving work.

Moreover, in the development of his own vivid eye, his use of the themes and subject matter of paintings, and perhaps above all in the recognition of the permanent power of transient moments, his poetry became profoundly affected by a life shared with a painter. They had one son, Gwydion, who also features in his poetry. The man so often portrayed as an impersonal figure, and so famously guarded on personal details, brought all four key relationships—father, mother, wife, and son—into the body of his work, sometimes with a searing candour. The heart laid bare in such poems as 'The Way of It' is breathtaking.

By the time of his marriage Thomas was working as a curate in Chirk near the English border, having trained in Llandaff at St Michael's Theological College. He was ordained deacon in 1936 and priest in the following year.

At Chirk, then a mining district, and subsequently Hanmer, from 1940, Thomas took his first practical steps in his new role: sermons, visits to the homes of the sick, evenings at the local branch of Toc H. He felt out of place, however, in the flatlands of Maelor Saesneg, and longed for the deeper landscapes to the west. The opportunity came in 1942 to take up the rectorate of Manafon in Montgomeryshire, a place of isolated hill farmsteads with the church and rectory below in the hollow. Here he came face to face with the stark rural life of mid-Wales and with the men and women who persisted in it. His frank engagement with them—half repelled, half honouring—was the spark of his first published poetry, and of a play for radio, *The Minister*.

Thomas's first collection, *The Stones of the Field*, was privately printed just after the Second World War. Along with selections from two subsequent volumes, this work reached a wider public in 1955 under the title *Song at the Year's Turning*. An introduction by John Betjeman, and the subsequent bestowal of the Heinemann award of the Royal Society of Literature, recognized the arrival of a major new poetic voice (now forty-two years old). The people of the hill farms were embodied in the imagined figure of Iago Prytherch, with whose life and meaning Thomas wrestled over many years and a considerable body of poetry—and in so doing he wrestled with the limitations of his own perspective and character. Like Baudelaire, one of the community of poets named in his work, when he skewered a target—a Welshman, Wales, a God who will not signal—he most revealed his skewered self.

In response to Saunders Lewis and his call for national revival, Thomas emerged as a convinced defender of Welsh culture and language. He felt acutely the sense of exclusion from much of his own culture because of his ignorance of the native tongue, 'all those good words, and I outside them', as he said in the poem 'Welsh'. With difficulty and over some years he became fluent in Welsh, moving from first tentative greetings to passing farm-workers to the day of his first public address in his father's tongue at the hilltop chapel of Penarth. This strong feeling for the national culture and its plight brought a new theme to his poetry, and jolted his verse forward to the fully formed style for which he became best-known, in one of his first great poems, 'Welsh Landscape' (1952). The public image of a severe and righteous poet-prophet, which was to stay with Thomas, owed much to the success with which the blunt lines, and the voice of authority in mourning, were met. Nostalgic for the sea, he moved in 1954 to be vicar of Eglwys-fach, near Aberystwyth, but

Ronald Stuart Thomas (1913–2000), by John Hedgecoe, 1966 [at Eglwys-fach]

again had to recognize a real local community whose ordinary lives were insufficiently preoccupied with striving toward their new vicar's vision.

As well as the appearance every two or three years of another volume of his own, Thomas began to take on a role as a selector and introducer of the verse of others, among them *The Batsford Book of Country Verse*, *The Penguin Book of Religious Verse*, and a selection of the poetry of Edward Thomas, the introduction to which is a typical demonstration of R. S. Thomas's brief, clear prose and his recognition of a man with similar impulses to his own. The growth of his reputation was reflected in the award of the queen's medal for poetry in 1964.

The work and themes of this first twenty years, frequently anthologized over subsequent decades, were those for which Thomas became famous, and they formed the dominant image of him. But by the mid-1960s Thomas had moved on. These changes were greatly fostered by the more congenial environment surrounding him in his next post as vicar of Aberdaron, at the western end of the Llŷn peninsula, from 1967 to 1978. Here the Welsh language was the means of daily intercourse, migrating birds of great variety and fascination to him passed by in spring and autumn, and the ever-changing sea swept against the edges of the churchyard.

Since Manafon days Thomas's life had taken on a regular pattern of study or writing poems in the morning, long walks in the afternoon, and visiting parishioners in the evening. Neither the career ladder nor the literary circuit ever materially distracted him. It was the walks which perhaps gave most to his writing. Astonishing evocations of the natural world began to appear more often—the changing weather, landscape, bird life—in poems of lyricism and wonder which were inseparably entwined with his pursuit of the nature of God.

Thomas was testing his relationship with God in new ways, searching for the signs of his presence, the meaning of his absence, the possibility of his non-existence, trying to see the world through God's eyes. The religious poetry which emerged ranks with the finest written in English. By the time of *Laboratories of the Spirit* (1975) and *Frequencies* (1978) there is an inescapable, exhilarating sense of his having been lifted to new insights, which bloom again in the work of the 1980s and 1990s. God, with whom Thomas establishes what might be called working terms, is approached again with awe and asserted against the gaps in science and the inadequacies of technology and materialism.

The theme of the machine, which had made an early comic entrance in the 1950s with 'Cynddylan on a Tractor', was re-announced with new intent. Thomas rebutted the connection between technology and progress and the modern emphasis on proofs and certainties. He preferred instead the world of poetry, mystery, and faith, and suggested (like Jesus) that wisdom lay in stepping aside from the onward hurry, to live in the illuminated present. 'The Bright Field' (1975) and 'Afon Rhiw' (1992) are among these testaments.

Thomas retired in 1978 to Sarn Rhiw, a cottage in the grounds of Plas yn Rhiw, set high above the great bay of Porth Neigwl with the mountains of Merioneth in the distance. He began to take stock of his life and, perhaps unexpectedly, emerged as a more public figure. His public expression of sympathy with Meibion Glyndwr in setting light to the holiday homes of the English in Wales led to controversy, but it was his lecture in 1976 at the national eisteddfod, 'Abercuawg', which had set out his vision for Wales most cogently. In this he argued that Wales should be a nation moved by a striving for a freedom and an ideal rooted in its own culture, language, and landscape, confident in the truths that they hold, and therefore resistant to internationalizing influences. Internationalizing influences in Wales usually meant the English, who thus remained the target of particular barbs. *Blwyddyn yn Llŷn* ('A year in Llŷn'; 1990), a vivid prose account of the changes in the natural world through the yearly cycle, is interrupted so frequently for this purpose that the reader can feel assailed by Thomas's insistence and anxiety. At his own account too, passing tourists who happened to ask him for directions encountered the apparently baffled response 'No English'. He would relish the moment, returning indoors to his English wife.

Thomas supported the Campaign for Nuclear Disarmament, speaking at rallies and dispatching numerous letters to the press. He had always been a pacifist, seeing no other credible position for a Christian priest to take, but he thought the arrival of nuclear weapons and the associated arms race exemplified man's absurd situation when overreached by his own scientific prowess.

Meeting Thomas in later years, strangers might recall a wild-haired, angular man; parishioners a figure more in communion with the hills than with them—but friends describe a deep thinker and lover of language, lit up by a sense of humour not without mischief, and with a real concern for those in difficulty. When he failed, as he felt, to help a troubled fisherman encountered on the beach, he kept a lobster pot in full view from the pulpit to remind him.

At Sarn Rhiw also Thomas wrote *Neb*, his autobiography, which clarified the coherence of his life and work. He portrayed the physical journey of his life as an oval: from Holyhead to Chirk, returning through Manafon, Eglwysfach, to the Llŷn, within sight of Anglesey. It was a life engaged with enriching the same few themes encountered early, getting to comprehend them truly, not a life of endless search for the new. His work and his life, as a priest in rural parishes, were thus profoundly integrated, sharing the pattern for living which his poetry presented. A telling aspect of its style, and the detached and critical eye with which he regarded himself, was the way he referred to himself in the third person, as the boy, the rector, and so forth, emerging only as RS when he found himself more fully on his return to Welsh landscapes.

Following the death of his wife after very considerable ill health, Thomas produced personal poems of great power, 'A Marriage' and 'No Time' among them. The volume dedicated to her memory, *Mass for Hard Times* (1992), bursts with the energy and gift of a master still growing in his powers, and paved the way for his last restless volume, *No Truce with the Furies* (1995). In 1996, at the age of eighty-three, he was nominated for the Nobel prize for literature. It only remained to complete his circuit back to the haunts of childhood, to live again in the northern corner of Anglesey, with a new Canadian-born wife, Elisabeth Agnes (Betty) Vernon (*b.* 1916), whom he married on 17 August 1996, and who brought him new and unexpected happiness.

R. S. Thomas died at Pentrefelin, on 25 September 2000, acclaimed as one of the greatest writers of poetry in English in the second half of the twentieth century. He was cremated and his ashes were buried in the grounds of St John's, Porthmadog, Caernarvonshire. Thomas—in his themes, imagery, and stature—links back through the Welsh poetic canon to his great fourteenth-century predecessor Dafydd ap Gwilym. In his troubled, elegiac tone he reaches back still further, to Aneirin and the origins of the language. Yet while he translated the Welsh subject matter, he left behind its main poetic form, rejecting a route explored by an earlier Welsh-born poet-priest, George Herbert. His achievement took the one and a half thousand-year Welsh aesthetic tradition, centred as it had always been on the essence of relationships between God, the natural world, and the people, to a greater national and international readership, through the medium of English poetry.

T. J. HUGHES

Sources R. S. Thomas, *Neb* (1985) · R. S. Thomas, *Y llwybrau gynt* (1972) · *The Independent* (27 Sept 2000) · *Daily Telegraph* (27 Sept 2000) · *The Guardian* (27 Sept 2000) · R. S. Thomas, *Autobiographies* (1997) · M. Stephens, ed., *The Oxford companion to the literature of Wales* (1986) · private information (2004) · memorial evenings organized by the Welsh Academy at Bangor and Cardiff, Jan 2001 Archives NL Wales, corresp. and literary papers · U. Wales, Bangor, corresp. and papers | NL Wales, corresp. with Dafydd Elis-Thomas · NL Wales, corresp. with Emyr Humphries Likenesses M. E. Eldridge, pencil and watercolour, 1941, NPG; repro. in W. M. Merchant, *R. S. Thomas* (1979) · J. Hedgecoe, photograph, 1966, NPG [*see illus.*] · M. Roberts, photograph, repro. in R. S. Thomas, *Selected prose*, ed. S. Anstey (1983) · W. Rowlands, oils, priv. coll. · W. Rowlands, sketch, priv. coll. · K. Williams, pencil and wash (with wife), priv. coll. · K. Williams, pencil sketch, NL Wales

Thomas, Samuel (1626/7–1693), nonjuring Church of England clergyman, was born at Ubley in Somerset, the son of William *Thomas (1592/3–1667), the rector there, and his wife, Thomasine (*d.* in or after 1667). A student at both Cambridge and Oxford during the interregnum, Samuel Thomas matriculated pensioner at Peterhouse, Cambridge, in Lent term 1646 and graduated BA in 1649, before moving in 1651 to St John's College, Oxford, where he was made a fellow. Incorporated at Oxford on 20 August 1651, he proceeded MA on 17 December 1651.

Though his father was a presbyterian who was ejected from Ubley in 1662 Samuel Thomas was a devoted episcopalian from early on in his life. In the early 1650s, much to the displeasure of his father, he encouraged George Bull, the future bishop of St David's and at that time William Thomas's student, to read episcopalian writers such as Henry Hammond and Richard Hooker in the hope of winning Bull over to Anglicanism. In October 1658 William

Thomas complained to Richard Baxter how his son was 'in a dangerous condition ... being now 30 year old & yet unsetled in divers more material points of religion, & propending ... in things controverted to the worse side of the controversie' (Keeble and Nuttall, 1.351). Samuel was sent to live with or near Baxter, but the hope that their regular conversation would set Samuel 'in the right way' was disappointed (ibid., 1.405). Baxter sent him back to his father in August 1659. Samuel, he wrote, was unwilling to dispute 'originall sin, & speciall grace & many of the rest in which we differ' either orally or 'expeditiously' in writing. Baxter could 'live comfortably' with Samuel, 'he being of a quiet disposition, & a blamelesse disposition', but as a busy man he simply did not have time 'to follow him any further in his way of copious & long deliberated writings'. That form of debate could as well be done without Samuel's living with him, and indeed the two do seem to have maintained a correspondence for a while (ibid., 1.404). The errors which William Thomas deplored in his son—his 'Exaltation of natural (which is ever corrupt) reason above its due pitch', a preference for 'natural Theology' and 'presumption ... upon natural parts'—all suggest the influence of an important strand developing within Anglican theology (ibid., 1.405). In early 1660 Samuel sought the advice of Henry Hammond on the question of original sin.

At the Restoration Samuel Thomas was deprived of his fellowship at St John's by the royal commissioners, despite his episcopal leanings. However, John Fell, dean of Christ Church, Oxford, appointed him as chaplain or petty canon there. He held this position until his appointment in 1672 as chantour of Christ Church, vicar of St Thomas, Oxford, and curate of Holywell. The people of Oxford frequently visited these two suburban parishes because of 'his edifying way of preaching' (Wood, *Ath. Oxon.*, 2.908). Then, in 1681, he was made vicar of Chard, Somerset, and prebendary of Compton Bishop (3 August 1681) by Peter Mew, bishop of Bath and Wells. His refusal of the oath of allegiance to William and Mary after the revolution of 1688 led to the loss of both ecclesiastical posts on 1 February 1691. Never an active nonjuror Thomas died suddenly on 4 November 1693 at Chard aged sixty-six, and was buried in the chancel of the church on 15 November 1693. There is no evidence that he ever married.

Despite his presbyterian roots Thomas became a strong apologist for the episcopal establishment and an outspoken opponent of Calvinism, leading Anthony Wood to speak of the 'unblameableness of our author's deportment and strictness and regularity of his life' (Wood, *Ath. Oxon.*, 2.908). His books included *The presbyterians unmask'd, or, Animadversions upon a nonconformist book called the 'Interest of England in the matter of religion'* (1676). In 1680 he wrote a preface to the second edition of Thomas Tompkins's *The New Distemper*, republished in 1681 under the title *The dissenter disarmed, or, A melius inquirendum upon a nonconformist book; viz, the 'Interest of England in the matter of religion'*, where he rejected any attempts at conciliation with the dissenters, stating that the 'Presbyterian Party ought not in justice or reason of state to be protected and (much less encouraged), but to be rejected and depressed' (p. 195). His other works included *The charge of schism renewed against the separatists, in an answer to the renewer (John Humphrey) of that pretended peaceable design, which is falsely called, 'An answer to Dr. Stillingfleet's sermon'* (1680); *Remarks on the Preface to the 'Protestant Reconciler', in a Letter to a Friend* (1683); and possibly the anonymous *Animadversions upon a Late Treatise Entit. 'The Protestant Reconciler'* (1683). These works earned him the enmity of his dissenting opponents, not least Richard Baxter, who referred to him as a 'shameless writer' (Allibone, *Dict.*, 3.2389).   ROBERT D. CORNWALL

Sources Wood, *Ath. Oxon.*, 2nd edn, vol. 2 • Venn, *Alum. Cant.* • *The nonconformist's memorial … originally written by … Edmund Calamy*, ed. S. Palmer, [3rd edn], 3 (1803) • *Fasti Angl., 1541–1857,* [Bath and Wells] • Foster, *Alum. Oxon., 1500–1714*, vol. 4 • *Calamy rev.* • R. Nelson, *The life of Dr George Bull* (1713) • E. H. Plumptre, *The life of Thomas Ken*, 2 vols. (1888) • Allibone, *Dict.* • *Calendar of the correspondence of Richard Baxter*, ed. N. H. Keeble and G. F. Nuttall, 2 vols. (1991)

Thomas, Sir (Thomas) Shenton Whitelegge (1879–1962), colonial governor, was born in London on 10 October 1879, eldest of the six children of the Revd Thomas William Thomas, and his wife, Charlotte Susanna Whitelegge. His father's career in the Church of England took him, and his family, to parishes at Norwich and then in Cambridgeshire. Shenton Thomas was educated at St John's School, Leatherhead, from 1890 to 1898 and at Queens' College, Cambridge, from 1898 to 1901, where he held a Sedgwick exhibition and graduated in classics, with second-class honours, in 1901. He became an honorary fellow of the college in 1935. On leaving Cambridge he was a schoolmaster at Aysgarth preparatory school in Yorkshire from 1901 to 1908, with a year off to make a tour round the world in 1904.

Early in 1909 Thomas arrived in the East Africa Protectorate as a recruit to the administrative service. On arrival he was posted to the secretariat in Nairobi, where he showed aptitude for the work, as he thought clearly and expressed himself well on paper. In 1912 he married Lucy Marguerite (Daisy; 1884–1978), daughter of Lieutenant-Colonel James Alexander Laurence Montgomery, of the Indian army and later commissioner of lands in Kenya; they had one daughter. Thomas subsequently went on to similar but more senior posts in Uganda in 1918 and Nigeria in 1921. In 1927 he was appointed colonial secretary of the Gold Coast. His first governorship, in 1929, was in Nyasaland. He returned to the Gold Coast as governor in 1932, but was appointed governor of the Straits Settlements in 1934; he formally retired from that post in 1946.

The rapid rise of a secretariat 'high-flyer'—Thomas never held a district post—might have attracted disparagement from less successful outstation colleagues. However, Thomas was generally popular. He and his wife were an unassuming and approachable couple, with a talent for putting at their ease the people they met. Thomas, who was a strong, thickset man, played tennis and golf, and excelled at cricket (he had played for Cambridgeshire and for the MCC). As governor of Nyasaland he once made a

Sir (Thomas) Shenton Whitelegge Thomas (1879–1962), by Bassano, 1946

century, including three sixes, before breakfast, in a match begun in the early cool of the day. During his time in Singapore he occasionally played for its cricket club, and he was a regular racegoer. Thus he combined social gifts with ability, and in his time in the Gold Coast he showed firmness in dealing with political opposition.

On becoming governor of the Straits Settlements and high commissioner for the Malay states in late 1934, Thomas had responsibility for the decentralized government of four settlements (including Labuan) and ten Malay states (including Brunei), and as British agent he had a vague supervisory role for British North Borneo and Sarawak. More than a decade of attempts to assimilate and integrate the federated and unfederated Malay states into a more rational structure had produced little but acrimony and a resolve by the rulers of the unfederated states to preserve their cherished semi-autonomy. In succeeding a very unpopular predecessor, Thomas had the task of bringing a steadying, emollient influence to a ramshackle regime, without seeking to alter it.

In 1939 Thomas had completed his normal five-year term and, at sixty, was due to retire. However, as during the First World War, the Colonial Office invited the incumbent governor to continue in his post until the war was over. Britain provided the defence forces, each under a service chief who was answerable to superiors far away. As chairman of the local defence committee Thomas was titular head of a bickering trio who held him in little esteem.

The arrival of A. Duff Cooper as UK resident minister in 1941 made the situation worse.

The services required land and local labour for defence works and installations such as camps and airfields. Thomas could only pass on these demands to the state governments, since land was a subject within their exclusive control. In his post-war defence Thomas asserted that service needs were adequately met, but the response was slow and sometimes reluctant. In the later stages there were complaints that civil defence and denial of resources to the enemy by 'scorched earth' measures were inadequate. A younger and more forceful governor might have more easily energized the civilian government. However, Thomas was no Gerald Templer and in 1940–41 Malaya was not ready for leadership of that type. The disastrous defeat of 80,000 British and Commonwealth forces, supported by 30,000 local troops and civil defence workers, was due primarily to failures of strategy, training, and leadership in the armed forces, and to lack of adequate air cover and of armoured units; no civil governor could have altered the result.

On 14 February 1942, with Japanese forces landed on Singapore island and the city besieged, Thomas informed London that further defence was unrealistic. General A. E. Perceval surrendered to the Japanese the next day. A Japanese attempt to humiliate Thomas by marching him through the streets of Singapore to internment was counter-productive. From Changi prison in Singapore Thomas was moved, later in 1942, to imprisonment in Formosa (Taiwan), and in 1944 in Manchuria. When liberated by American forces on 25 August 1945 he weighed 9½ stone (his normal weight was 12 stone). He then proceeded to Calcutta and reunion with his wife, who had been interned in Singapore throughout.

When he saw the drafts of the official dispatches on the campaign by the service commanders, and later of the official history by Kirby (1957), Thomas objected to aspersions on himself and his government. These protests were ignored and his request that a report which he wrote should be published was refused. Yet a modern historian, who has examined it, concludes that 'Shenton Thomas has a case' (Allen, 214). His working papers bear witness to his determination to vindicate himself and the community which he had governed. In addition to this task he found time to be an active chairman of the council of the Royal Overseas League in 1946–9 and then of the British Empire Leprosy Relief Association in 1949–55.

The flood of memoirs and historical writing on the débâcle of 1941–2 generally followed the verdict of Ian Morrison, correspondent of *The Times*, who had interviewed Thomas in 1942, that he was 'a good solid official', who had risen to the top by hard work rather than outstanding ability, that he lacked 'colour or forcefulness', and was not the man to 'rally people in a time of crisis' (Morrison, 157). Thomas was appointed OBE in 1919, CMG in 1929, KCMG in 1931, and GCMG in 1937. He died on 15 January 1962 in London, at his home, 28 Oakwood Court, Melbury Road.

Although maligned by some of his countrymen, the principles which guided Thomas's conduct in 'the greatest disaster in British military history' denied a moral victory to the conquerors. In post-war Singapore a number of highways and buildings were named after him.

J. M. GULLICK

Sources DNB · B. Montgomery, *Shenton of Singapore: governor and prisoner of war* (1984) · I. Morrison, *Malayan postcript* (1942) · L. Allen, *Singapore, 1941–1942* (1977) · P. Elphick, *Singapore, the pregnable fortress: a study in deception, discord and desertion* (1995) · S. W. Kirby and others, *The war against Japan, 1: The loss of Singapore* (1957) · *The Times* (17 Jan 1962) · I. Simson, *Singapore, too little too late: some aspects of the Malayan disaster in 1942* (1970) · *CGPLA Eng. & Wales* (1962)
Archives Bodl. RH, corresp. and papers · CUL, RCS collections, working papers · PRO, corresp. relating to Malaysia, CO 967/74–76
Likenesses Bassano, photograph, 1946, NPG [*see illus.*] · photographs, repro. in Montgomery, *Shenton of Singapore* · portrait, Fort Canning archives, Singapore
Wealth at death £12,938: probate, 5 June 1962, *CGPLA Eng. & Wales*

Thomas, Sidney Gilchrist (1850–1885), metallurgist, was born on 16 April 1850 at Campanile Cottage, Canonbury Villas, Islington, London, the second of the four children of William Thomas (1808–1867), a Welsh clerk in the solicitor's department of the Inland Revenue office, and his wife, Melicent Gilchrist (*b.* 1816), eldest daughter of James Gilchrist, a Scottish nonconformist minister. Educated mainly at Dulwich College, London, where he was a day pupil from 1859 to 1866, Thomas expressed a strong inclination towards applied science, but the death of his father when he was not yet seventeen led him to begin to earn his livelihood immediately after leaving school, at first as an assistant master in a school in Essex. Later in 1867 he obtained a junior clerkship at Marlborough Street police court in London, whence in 1868 he transferred to the Thames court, Arbour Square, Stepney, where he continued until his resignation in May 1879. Meanwhile, after office hours, he studied law and applied chemistry; at the Birkbeck Institution, a sentence used by George Chaloner, teacher of chemistry, seems to have imprinted itself on Thomas's mind: 'The man who eliminated phosphorus by means of the Bessemer converter will make his fortune' (*DNB*). So it was that, about 1870, the solution of this problem became the main purpose of his life.

The age of bulk steel can be said to date from the 1860s, when the two alternative techniques of Bessemer and Siemens both began to be applied extensively. However, neither of these 'steel-making' processes removed phosphorus from the molten metal, and phosphorus rendered the resultant steel brittle and worthless. Consequently, only non-phosphoric ores could be used, so that the larger proportion of British, French, German, and Belgian pig irons remained untreatable by the new processes. As growth of bulk steel took place, so demand increased for a means to deal with the phosphorus; during the 1870s the commercial competition to obtain a solution intensified.

Thomas devoted much of his leisure to the problem posed by phosphorus, attending the laboratories of various chemical teachers, reading up all he could about the

Sidney Gilchrist Thomas (1850–1885), by unknown artist

subject, sitting examinations of the Department of Science and Art and of the Royal School of Mines, and even experimenting in the fireplace at home. Holidays from his police-court duties were largely spent in visiting ironworks in Britain and abroad. In 1873 he was offered the post of analytical chemist to a brewery at Burton upon Trent, but declined it from conscientious scruples about fostering the use of alcohol. During 1874 and several subsequent years he contributed to the technical journal *Iron*.

Towards the end of 1875 Thomas arrived at a theoretical and provisional solution to the problem of dephosphorization. This called for a substance which was chemically basic and physically able to withstand the high temperature involved in the process, because for commercial working the durability of the converter's lining was essential. For the material of the new lining, experiments led him to the selection of lime or its congeners magnesia or magnesian limestone, but the practical realization of such a lining engaged him and his associates until 1879. He foresaw not only that by employing such a lining it would become possible to 'fix' the phosphorus from the pig iron in a separate slag, but also that the phosphorus deposited in the basic slag itself represented a material of great potential value for agricultural purposes.

Demand for the relatively new bulk steel was growing strongly, and makers were desperate for means to enable iron resources containing the element to be used. Thomas, with his single-minded, determined investigation of the subject over several years, produced a solution to the difficulty at exactly the crucial time and in the face of considerable competition. In achieving his goal he was

sufficiently energetic, skilled, and personable to obtain the essential assistance and confidence of several other people and, despite acute shortages of money, he ensured that the key features of his innovation were well protected by patents for his subsequent financial advantage. Besides the invaluable experimental work undertaken from late 1877 by his cousin, Percy C. Gilchrist (later FRS), chemist at Blaenafon iron- and steelworks in south Wales, Thomas received sympathetic help from the manager at Blaenafon, E. P. Martin, and, after September 1878, from the manager of Bolckow Vaughan & Co.'s large works in Cleveland, E. W. Richards, together with his consultant, J. E. Stead.

Thomas took out his first patent in November 1877, and others followed during 1878 and 1879. In the spring of 1878 he first announced, at a meeting of the Iron and Steel Institute in London, that he had successfully dephosphorized iron in the Bessemer converter, but this statement was disregarded by his hearers. On 4 April 1879 successful experiments on a large scale were performed publicly at Bolckow Vaughan's Middlesbrough works. These demonstrations at once secured the practical commercial triumph both of the process and of the inventor. A paper, written earlier by Thomas in conjunction with Gilchrist for the Iron and Steel Institute, on the 'Elimination of phosphorus in the Bessemer converter', was read in May 1879. There, the solution of the problem of how to dephosphorize pig iron cheaply during converting, now experimentally demonstrated by the 'basic' process, was clearly stated to comprise, first, substitution of a durable basic lining for the former siliceous one, and, second, provision of abundant basic material (such as lime) to secure a highly basic slag at an early stage of the blow. The process could also be adapted to the Siemens–Martin system of making steel in open-hearth furnaces. It transpired that the use of lime to separate phosphorus from liquid iron had previously been patented in 1872 by G. J. Snelus, while employment of hot tar as binder for the individual lime fragments in the vessel's lining was covered by a patent filed by E. Riley in November 1878. The interests of the parties were combined and protected by the formation, in 1882, of the Dephosphorizing and Basic Patents Company.

The method was immediately adopted in 1879 and spread rapidly, enabling steel to be produced in much larger quantities. On the continent, the 'Thomas process' (of basic-Bessemer converting) and its product, 'Thomas steel', persisted strongly into the 1950s. In many steelmaking districts open-hearth furnaces using the 'basic' conditions enunciated by Thomas and Gilchrist predominated throughout the first half of the twentieth century. These same conditions continued to be fundamental features of most steel-making techniques during the second half of the century, even though oxygen replaced air as the chief refining reagent. In 1885, the year of Thomas's death, world steel output amounted to some 6 million tons, of which 1 million tons, or nearly 17 per cent, was produced using his principles. A century later, in 1985, world steel output exceeded 700 million tons, with at least 550 million tons, or nearly 80 per cent, being made in the conditions he stipulated. Particularly in the years before 1960, besides the steel product, the basic processing yielded large quantities of slag rich in phosphorus, which, after grinding, was applied as agricultural fertilizer. In this way, by 1937 some 20 million tons of phosphoric acid had been returned to the land to increase its productivity.

Evidently precocious, and brought up in a mentally stimulating home, Thomas was a lively and ready conversationalist and correspondent; he was well informed, with wide interests. His enthusiasm helped him to create a favourable impression upon many. He held pronounced views on the more equable distribution of wealth, wanting to ameliorate the lives of the 'working masses' and arranging to leave the great bulk of his money to 'doing good discriminately'. He believed in life after death. He lived with his mother and sister, and never married. In his youth he was energetic and enjoyed walking and travelling. However, in the pursuit of his objective he drove himself hard and became habitually careless about food and rest. In 1877 he suffered a period of poor health: a few years later serious lung trouble manifested itself, and it became clear that systematic overwork, perhaps coupled with exposure to the ill-ventilated atmosphere of the police courtroom, had resulted in disease.

In early 1881 Thomas paid a triumphal visit to the USA, where he was enthusiastically welcomed by the leading metallurgists and ironmasters. In that year he also founded the North Eastern Steel Company to make products of basic steel in Middlesbrough. In 1882 he was elected a member of council of the Iron and Steel Institute, and in 1883 he was awarded a Bessemer gold medal of the institute, another medal being awarded to G. J. Snelus. Also in 1883 Thomas and Gilchrist received the gold medal from the Society of Arts. Already, however, Thomas was occupied in a vain search for restored health. He made a prolonged voyage round the world in 1883, by way of the Cape of Good Hope, India, Australia, and New Zealand, returning by way of the USA. The winter of 1883 and the first half of 1884 were spent in Algiers, after which he went to Paris with his mother and younger sister Lilian, who had been his close companion and was subsequently his executor. He died of emphysema at 61 avenue Marceau, Paris, on 1 February 1885 and was buried in the cemetery at Passy.   J. K. ALMOND

Sources L. G. Thompson, *Sidney Gilchrist Thomas: an invention and its consequences* (1940) · *Memoir and letters of Sidney Gilchrist Thomas, inventor*, ed. R. W. Burnie (1891) · F. W. Harbord, 'The Thomas–Gilchrist basic process, 1879–1937', *Journal of the Iron and Steel Institute*, 136 (1937), 77–97 · J. Mitchell, 'Sidney Gilchrist Thomas: a commemorative lecture', *Journal of the Iron and Steel Institute*, 165 (1950), 1–8 · J. K. Almond, 'A century of basic steel: Cleveland's place in successful removal of phosphorus from liquid iron in 1879, and development of basic converting in the ensuing 100 years', *Ironmaking and Steelmaking*, 8 (1981), 1–10 · *DNB* · G. W. Maynard, 'Biographical notice of Sidney Gilchrist Thomas', *Transactions of the American Institute of Mining Engineers*, 13 (1884–5), 785–91 · S. G. Denner, 'The pursuit of crotchets: an appreciation of Sidney Gilchrist Thomas on the centenary of the publication of the basic process of steelmaking', *Journal of the Historical Metallurgy Society*, 13/1 (1979), 1–6 · b. cert. · *CGPLA Eng. & Wales* (1885)

Archives Museum of Science and Industry, Cardiff, pump and air receiver probably used in experiments

Likenesses H. von Herkomer, oils, in or after 1885 (after photographs), Institute of Materials, Carlton House Terrace, London · F. Mancini, bronze medallion on memorial, c.1960, Blaenavon, Torfaen · chalk drawing, NPG [*see illus.*] · photograph (aged thirty?), repro. in *Thomas & Gilchrist, 1879–1929, Bolckow & Vaughan* (1929)

Wealth at death £26,801 7s. 7d.: resworn probate, July 1885, *CGPLA Eng. & Wales*

Thomas [*née* Haig], **Sybil Margaret**, Viscountess Rhondda (1857–1941), suffragette, was born at 52 Norfolk Square, Brighton, on 25 February 1857, the fourth daughter in the family of five daughters and five sons of George Augustus Haig (1820–1906), merchant and landowner, and his wife, Anne Eliza Fell (d. 1894) of Pen Ithon, Radnorshire. Her father was descended from the Haigs of Bemersyde, an ancient Scottish border family, to which Field Marshal Sir Douglas Haig also belonged. On 27 June 1882, aged twenty-five, she married, in the billiard room at Pen Ithon, David Alfred *Thomas (later created Viscount Rhondda) of Ysguborwen, Glamorgan (1856–1918), Liberal MP for Merthyr Boroughs (1888–1910), and leading south Wales industrialist. Her husband's political career meant that she spent much time in London but their main home was a large house and estate at Llan-wern, Monmouthshire. The couple had only one child, Margaret Haig *Thomas, who, as Lady Rhondda, became a prominent businesswoman and Britain's leading equal rights feminist in the inter-war years.

The life of Sybil Thomas was overshadowed by the glittering careers of both her husband and her daughter. Usually depicted as quiet and conventional, this small, attractive woman put conscience before propriety, held firm opinions of her own, and was highly regarded by her contemporaries. Her obituary notice in the *Western Mail* (12 March 1941) described her as 'A woman of strong but pleasing personality' and noted her wide contribution to life in South Wales. In fact she made a significant contribution to the Liberal women's organization in Wales, to the women's suffrage movement, and to the First World War effort, as well as playing a key role in shaping her daughter's career.

In the 1890s Sybil Thomas was president of the Welsh Union of Women's Liberal Associations (established 1891) and during her tenure the union pursued a strongly feminist and pro-suffrage agenda. As a Liberal and the wife of a prominent man, she was associated with the moderate wing of the suffrage movement, the National Union of Women's Suffrage Societies, under the leadership of Millicent Fawcett. The other Haig women, including her sisters Janetta and Lotty and cousin Florence, favoured Mrs Pankhurst's militant Women's Social and Political Union (WSPU): both Janetta and Florence had been imprisoned for acts of violence. When her daughter, Margaret, announced her intention of joining the suffrage procession to Hyde Park on 21 July 1908, Sybil decided to accompany her on the grounds '(a) she did not think an unmarried girl should walk unchaperoned through the gutter, (b) because she believed in votes for women' (Mackworth, *My World*, 118). Her mixed motives show a nice balance between her adherence to convention and to principle. Thereafter Sybil became more closely associated with the WSPU, entertaining Mrs Pankhurst and holding fund-raising events at Llan-wern. In 1913 she acted as treasurer to Sylvia Pankhurst's East London Federation of the WSPU. In 1914 she deliberately sought imprisonment by holding a public meeting outside the houses of parliament: on her refusal to pay a fine the magistrate sentenced her to one day's imprisonment.

During the First World War Lady Rhondda, as she became after D. A. Thomas's elevation to the peerage in 1916, chaired the women's advisory committee of the National Savings Committee. She gave over part of the house at Llan-wern as a hospital, and she travelled extensively with her husband in carrying out his duties for the government, notably as food controller (1917–18). Following her husband's promotion to a viscountcy in 1918 she became Viscountess Rhondda. She was appointed a dame commander in the Order of the British Empire in 1920 for her wartime services.

Viscountess Rhondda played a key, but largely unacknowledged, role in shaping her daughter's life. It was she who suggested that her husband should take Margaret into his business, a large conglomerate of coal, shipping, and publishing interests, as his private secretary, and it was she who was most supportive of Margaret's suffrage activities. She survived her husband, who died in July 1918, for twenty-three years, for much of which she continued in public and philanthropic work. She died at her home, Llan-wern Park, Newport, Monmouthshire, on 11 March 1941, and was buried at Llan-wern on 14 March.

DEIRDRE BEDDOE

Sources Viscountess Rhondda [M. H. T. Mackworth], *This was my world* (1933) · A. Mee, ed., *Who's who in Wales* (1921) · *Western Mail* [Cardiff] (12 March 1941) · S. M. Eoff, *Viscountess Rhondda: equalitarian feminist* (1991) · M. H. Mackworth, *D. A. Thomas, Viscount Rhondda* (1921) · E. S. Pankhurst, *The suffragette movement: an intimate account of persons and ideals* (1931); repr. (1984) · Burke, *Gen. GB* (1937) · b. cert. · m. cert. · d. cert.
Archives NL Wales, Aberystwyth, D. A. Thomas MSS
Likenesses H. Cecil, photograph, repro. in Mackworth, *This was my world*, facing p. 270
Wealth at death £39,859 6s. 10d.: probate, 1941, CGPLA Eng. & Wales

Thomas, Terry (1888–1978), headmaster, was born on 19 October 1888 at 40 Sapphire Street, Roath, Cardiff, the son of David Terry Thomas, schoolmaster, and his wife, Mary Ann Walton. He was educated at Howard Gardens School and at University College, Cardiff, graduating in physics in 1909. He was chief science master at Inverurie Academy for two years and, in 1911, he went to St John's College, Cambridge, reading in successive years for the mathematical, natural sciences, and law triposes. From 1914 until December 1922 Thomas served as head of the military and

engineering side at Haileybury College, where he established his reputation as a science teacher and produced a number of books for schools. He gained a London PhD in 1922 for a thesis on the thermoelectric properties of metal wires. On 19 August 1915 Thomas married Mary (b. 1890/91), the daughter of Henry Davies, director of mining education, at the Congregational chapel, Charles Street, Cardiff.

Thomas became headmaster of Leeds grammar school in January 1923. During the time of his predecessor the school had tripled in size to nearly 600 pupils. Like other endowed city grammar schools it had become directly grant-aided by the Board of Education in the first decade of the century and as a condition admitted annually a number of scholarship holders from the elementary schools. The school continued to grow and, by the time of Thomas's retirement thirty years later, there were more than 900 pupils enjoying good facilities for the study of a wide curriculum that included sporting and other non-academic activities. In his early years a playing field was acquired on the outskirts of the city at Lawnswood. New building work was undertaken at the school to provide additional classrooms and a laboratory so that biology might be introduced into the curriculum. By 1939 further building work had been carried out to provide a swimming pool, a gymnasium, a new dining room, accommodation for theatrical performances, a major enhancement of the chapel, and other facilities.

Historically Leeds grammar school was one of the best-endowed in the north of England, and this greatly helped Thomas with his projects. He was very successful in stimulating enthusiastic financial support among 'old boys' and parents for the development fund, which took an institutional shape with the formation in 1937 of the Friends of Leeds Grammar School. He was a man of strong personality who succeeded in evoking a keen sense of loyalty and support, though some saw him as self-willed and possibly too hasty in judgement.

Beyond the school Thomas's reputation grew and he became president of the Incorporated Association of Headmasters in 1936 and then treasurer for 1937–46. He was a very active member of the Headmasters' Conference (HMC) and chaired some of its committees. Along with the heads of Winchester and Charterhouse he served on a group to represent the HMC's views to the Board of Education during the years leading to the enactment and implementation of the Education Act of 1944. He was seen as a firm upholder of the independence enjoyed by direct-grant grammar schools. In 1941 he was appointed by the Board of Education to the Norwood committee to inquire into the curriculum and examinations in secondary schools. He caused some disquiet at the board by his lone refusal, at the committee's very last meeting, to agree to the central recommendations to move nationally from external to internal school-leaving examinations. A few years later, as a member of the Secondary Schools Examinations Council, he had the satisfaction of seeing his own views triumph in the report which led to the creation of the general certificate of education.

Thomas's increasing concern for the prospects of grammar schools such as his own may be seen in his reaction to the order of the Ministry of Education that, after 1944, all direct-grant schools should resubmit applications if they wished to remain on the list. Some were rejected by the ministry. Leeds grammar school submitted its application but withdrew it after the return to office of the Labour Party in 1945, Thomas preferring that it should become an independent school relying upon fully fee-paying clients. This policy continued until reversed by his successor in 1957; in an inflationary climate the absence of grant aid made the financial position of the school more difficult, forcing it to raise fees to a level beyond the reach of able entrants from modest backgrounds, whose exclusion was not helpful in sustaining academic achievement over the longer term.

During the struggles of the 1940s surrounding the future pattern of secondary schooling, Thomas emerged as a vigorous national leader in the headmasters' organizations, fighting to sustain the position of the direct-grant schools. For many years a member of the court of the University of Leeds, his services nationally were recognized when the degree of doctor of laws *honoris causa* was conferred upon him in 1948.

After his retirement in December 1953, Thomas maintained a close interest in the affairs of Leeds grammar school. He also continued to be very active in public service. He had become a magistrate in 1937, served as chairman of the Leeds bench from 1950 to 1963, as chairman of the visiting magistrates for Leeds prison from 1948 to 1963, and as chairman of the West Riding branch of the Magistrates Association from 1956 to 1959. He died at Seacroft Hospital, Leeds, on 22 July 1978. His funeral was held in the school chapel on 27 July, followed by cremation. He was survived by his wife, Mary, and two daughters.

PETER GOSDEN

Sources J. W. D. Marshall, *A history of Leeds grammar school* (1997) · *The Leodensian* (autumn 1978) · *The Leodensian* (1923–54) · T. Thomas, 'Leeds grammar school', *University of Leeds Review*, 3/1 (June 1952), 58–61 · P. H. Kelsey, *Four hundred years, 1552–1952: the story of Leeds grammar school* (1952) · H. M. Christie, *Please, a schoolmarm's reminiscences* (1955) · *The Times* (26 July 1978) · *Yorkshire Evening Post* (25 July 1978) · *Yorkshire Post* (26 July 1978) · private information (2004) · b. cert. · m. cert. · d. cert.
Likenesses portrait, 1952, Leeds grammar school · photographs, Leeds grammar school
Wealth at death £70,102: probate, 5 Sept 1978, *CGPLA Eng. & Wales*

Thomas, Thomas (1553–1588), printer and lexicographer, was born, according to the *Dictionary of National Biography*, in the city of London on 25 December 1553, the son of Thomas Thomas, 'gentleman'. He was educated at Eton College between 1565 and 1571, and on 24 August 1571 entered King's College, Cambridge, as a scholar. Three years later, in accordance with custom, he was elected a fellow. He graduated BA in 1575 and MA in 1579. Probably in 1581 he resigned his fellowship, and it seems that by March 1583 he had married Anne (*d.* 1610), widow of John Sheres (*d.* 1581), a wealthy local bookbinder for whom Thomas had acted as an executor. Their daughter, Joan (*b.*

1583), survived him; a son, John (*b.* 1585), died in infancy. At King's, Thomas's contemporaries had included Richard Day, son of the printer John Day, and it was perhaps through him that Thomas developed an interest in printing.

Thomas was appointed university printer on 3 May 1583. In autumn 1583, in a house in Regent Walk (the street that ran east–west between the west front of the university church and the Schools) he established the first printing house in Cambridge since John Siberch had printed his last work there in the 1520s. Thomas's first book, probably never completed, was a part of Pliny's *Historia naturalis* (1583) intended for the use of university students: only a fragment of this survives, and there is no evidence that it was ever published. His press was established in the teeth of opposition from the London Stationers' Company, who saw him as a rival to their monopolies and who seized his press within a month of his appointment in an effort to prevent him. It was regained only after the intervention of Lord Burghley, chancellor of the university. Thomas's (and the university's) claim to the right to print rested on letters patent granted to the university in 1534 by Henry VIII enabling the university to print *omnimodi libri*; though repeatedly challenged in courts of law these letters patent were upheld in succeeding generations.

Thomas was known for his puritan views, and was referred to in one of the Martin Marprelate tracts as 'that puritan Cambridge printer' (*Oh Read Over D. John Bridges, for it is a Worthy Worke*, 1588, 6). He concentrated his printing and publishing on two principal areas: educational texts primarily for the local market, and protestant theology. One of his first works was an edition of Ramus's *Dialectica* by William Temple (1584); in 1585 he printed a translation of Ramus's Latin grammar; and in 1587 Plato's *Menexenus* in Greek. In theology, his tastes were for the Heidelberg reformers, but his major author and staunch supporter was William Whitaker, regius professor at Cambridge.

Thomas printed his own selection of Ovid for the use of students in 1584, and had presumably been working at this for a while before he resigned his college fellowship. In 1587 he published the first edition of his Latin dictionary, dedicated to Lord Burghley and based on the work of Guillaume Morel and Thomas Cooper. By 1631 Thomas's dictionary had passed through thirteen editions as the standard intermediate dictionary of its time. He continued the binding business inherited through his wife, though there is no evidence that he was himself a binder. Thomas died in Cambridge early in August 1588, and was buried on the 9th in Great St Mary's. His widow inherited the business, and on 6 February 1589 his stepdaughter Alice married John Legate, a printer from London who thus succeeded to his business and equipment. Thomas's will dated 28 July 1588 and proved on 12 October 1588 left his property mostly to his wife and daughter. The post-mortem inventory, with a detailed record of his equipment and stock-in-trade, reveals that he owned a single press, and about 2700 lb of type, with other materials: his estate as a whole was valued at £580.

DAVID MCKITTERICK

Sources will, CUL, department of manuscripts and university archives, wills, 2.108 · will, PRO, PROB 11/72, sig. 56 · G. J. Gray, *Abstracts from the wills and testamentary documents of printers, binders, and stationers of Cambridge from 1504 to 1699* (1915), 64–72 · D. McKitterick, *A history of Cambridge University Press*, 1 (1992) · *STC, 1475–1640* · W. Sterry, ed., *The Eton College register, 1441–1698* (1943) · *DNB* · parish registers, Cambridge, Great St Mary's, Cambs. AS [marriage, burial]
Wealth at death £580: U. Cam. vice-chancellor's court; will, PRO, PROB 11/72, sig. 56

Thomas, Thomas George, Viscount Tonypandy (1909–1997), speaker of the House of Commons, was born on 29 January 1909 in Port Talbot, Glamorgan, the second son and fourth of five children of Zacharia Thomas (1881–1925), coalminer, of Carmarthen, and his wife, Emma Jane (1881–1972), daughter of John Tilbury of Clanfield, Hampshire, who became a building contractor after moving to Tonypandy in 1872. A clever child, whose dissolute father abandoned his family during the First World War, Thomas escaped the familiar options of domestic service or the mines which faced most working-class children in Pen-y-graig and Trealaw, south of Rhondda, where he grew up. Via Tonypandy grammar school (1920–27), he became an uncertified teacher in industrial Dagenham, east of London, then took a two-year teacher training course at University College, Southampton (1929–31). As a young teacher in Lambeth, before his return to south Wales, Thomas took advantage of his proximity to the House of Commons to start attending the strangers' gallery, and thus caught his first glimpse of national politics during the economic crisis of 1931, which consolidated the inter-war depression. Together with his active Methodism at nearby Central Hall, Westminster, it brought together what he would call 'the two threads of my future life' (Thomas, 37).

Already a Methodist lay preacher, Thomas was drawn into politics through the National Union of Teachers. Medically unfit for war service, he was elected to its executive in 1942. By 1945 he was an obvious candidate to fight Cardiff Central, where he was elected to parliament in Clement Attlee's landslide victory of July 1945. At this stage—'an innocent abroad', as he later explained (Thomas, 57)—the future speaker was a left-winger, who opposed the reintroduction of conscription and voted for Aneurin Bevan in Labour's 1955 leadership contest, won by Hugh Gaitskell. As a teetotaller he also opposed reform of the Sunday drinking laws. He also campaigned for leasehold reform, a potent issue in south Wales, where miners' homes were often in danger of reverting to former coal owners, who retained freeholds despite Labour's nationalization of the pits. Success eventually came in 1967 during Harold Wilson's 1964–70 government, by which time Thomas was himself a minister after thirteen years in opposition.

But for Wilson's tiny Commons majority in 1964 Thomas, by now an accomplished chairman, might have been made deputy speaker, with the prospect of succeeding Sir Harry Hylton-Foster. Instead he served as a junior minister in the Home Office (1964–6); next in the newly formed Welsh Office, when he visited Aberfan on the day

Thomas George Thomas, Viscount Tonypandy (1909–1997), by Jane Bown, 1982

the coal tip collapsed, engulfing a school, in October 1966; and then between 1967 and 1968 as minister of state at the Foreign Office, during the Nigerian civil war. Thomas's pacifist instincts made him uneasy over British support for, and arms sales to, the federal government against Biafra, but he did not resign. His ministerial career peaked in 1968–70, when he served as secretary of state for Wales, presiding over the investiture of the prince of Wales at Caernarfon, which temporarily dented the revival of Welsh nationalism, political, cultural, and occasionally violent. To the last of these he was instinctively opposed. As the grandson of an Englishman who had married into a French émigré family, Thomas was a British nationalist, vocally opposed to the end of his life to what he saw as a dual threat: from devolution and from a creeping encroachment of national sovereignty by the emerging European Union. Moreover, his own spoken Welsh was, he conceded, 'faulty' (Thomas, 20).

By the time Labour unexpectedly returned to power during the miners' dispute of 1974, Thomas's virulent attacks on nationalism prompted Harold Wilson to give the Welsh secretaryship to the more emollient John Morris. It came as another severe shock, just two years after the death, at ninety-one, of his formidable mother. Twice engaged, Thomas had never married. 'Mam', who had remarried in 1925 and was herself a well-known figure in south Wales, remained the most important woman in what she would proudly refer to as 'My son George's' life. Her death shook his deeply held faith and prompted thoughts of retirement. But Wilson offered his friend and loyal ally something better. This time he did become deputy speaker, and succeeded his fellow Methodist Selwyn Lloyd to the speakership in February 1976.

Two coincidental events served to make Thomas a national institution and the speaker's ritual cry of 'order; order!' a popular catch-phrase. One was the radio broadcasting of parliament, which he had opposed, though he came to favour the introduction of television cameras. From April 1978 radio made his traditionally aloof office a highly conspicuous one. He enjoyed his fame, and his easy charm allowed him to combine dignity with a new informality. A dry wit, his melodious Welsh baritone, and fine sense of timing quickly turned a middle-ranking former minister into a star. Thomas's wider popularity was further buttressed by his having to preside over an exceptionally unruly House of Commons, where Labour's majority evaporated as its economic problems mounted in the face of industrial unrest and the world oil crisis. The Conservatives had an aggressive new leader in Margaret Thatcher, following Edward Heath's defeat and removal. Within a month of his arrival in the chair the Wilson premiership gave way to James Callaghan's three-year struggle to survive in office with no majority. It was a drama which produced the Liberal–Labour pact of 1977–8, and eventually led to the Social Democratic Party breaking away from Labour in 1981. Thomas presided over it all, and his tenure was turbulent from the start. In May 1976 a disputed one-vote government victory over a contentious bill to nationalize the aircraft and shipbuilding industries led left-wing MPs to sing 'The Red Flag' in the chamber. This prompted Michael Heseltine to seize the mace, symbol of parliamentary authority, and wield it menacingly at the Labour benches. Speaker Thomas kept his nerve amid the uproar, suspending the sitting until the next day, when Heseltine apologized.

Thomas's determination to protect the rights of the Commons, even at the risk of offending old Labour colleagues, put him repeatedly at odds with senior ministers, both in public and private. Callaghan, who had beaten him to the safer Cardiff seat in 1945 and first became a minister in 1950, was a worldlier figure, and their intimate relationship had been strained by rivalry. Now it was strained by the nightly battle over government business. With Michael Foot, Bevan's successor in Ebbw Vale, now leader of the Commons, there were frequent rows over procedural rulings, made public in 1985 when Thomas published his memoirs, *George Thomas, Mr Speaker*. Foot was not alone in protesting that his disclosure of 'confidential conversations' had betrayed the office (*The Scotsman*). Others said the book betrayed malice and spite. Thomas's view was that he resisted unexpectedly shocking pressures from both sides. But the complaint persisted that he was now too much of an establishment man, anxious to show no bias against the Conservatives even after Thatcher, with whom his relations were cordial, swept to

power in May 1979. Bitterness was particularly strong among left-wing critics of the Falklands War in 1982. One such, Tam Dalyell, eventually concluded that Thomas was his 'least favourite' of the six speakers under whom he had sat as an MP (*The Independent*). The critics' suspicions were reinforced by Thomas's evident delight in the company of royalty, and his friendship with the queen mother and with both the prince and princess of Wales, at whose wedding in 1981 he read the lesson. His memoirs confirmed an unabashed pride that a poor miner's son from the valleys should have risen so high. But he took evident comfort from public esteem and the verdict of some MPs that his had not only been a very good speakership but had reasserted the office's authority over the clerks of the house. Robin Maxwell-Hyslop, a political opponent, described him as 'the greatest Speaker in living memory' (*The Guardian*). Speaker Thomas also presided over gentle modernizations of procedure, shorter speeches, and a new system of select committees.

When Thomas retired in 1983 it was to widespread acclaim, which not even his acceptance of Margaret Thatcher's unexpected offer of a hereditary peerage could dim. As Viscount Tonypandy he was an active cross-bencher in the Lords, despite a diagnosis of throat cancer, which later spread. Close to death in 1988, he recovered sufficiently to enjoy another decade in public life. He was chairman of the National Children's Home, active in cancer and heart charities, and preached, lectured, and wrote. He was also widely honoured around the world. Though he never formally broke with the Labour Party, he also made high-profile political interventions which were unhelpful to its cause. In the last year of his life his opposition to a European single currency led him to appear in support of Sir James Goldsmith's Referendum Party. He also opposed Welsh devolution again in the 1997 referendum. In 1979 Thomas had been delighted to see the pro-devolution camp heavily defeated in Wales. This time it narrowly prevailed. He died four days later, on 22 September 1997, in Cardiff. He never married, and on his death the viscountcy of Tonypandy became extinct. He was given honorary degrees by many universities, including Oxford (1983), and was an honorary fellow of Hertford and St Hugh's colleges, Oxford. MICHAEL WHITE

Sources G. Thomas, *George Thomas, Mr Speaker: the memoirs of the Viscount Tonypandy* (1985) · C. M. Swift, *George Thomas, the Rt Hon Viscount Tonypandy* (1990) · J. Callaghan, *Time and chance* (1987) · *The Times* (23 Sept 1997) · *The Independent* (23 Sept 1997) · *Daily Telegraph* (23 Sept 1997) · *The Guardian* (23 Sept 1997) · *The Scotsman* (23 Sept 1997) · WWW · personal knowledge (2004)

Archives Bodl. RH, corresp. on colonial issues · NL Wales, corresp. and papers | NL Wales, corresp. with Leo Abse; corresp. with Huw T. Edwards

Likenesses J. Bown, photograph, 1982, priv. coll. [*see illus.*] · photograph, repro. in *The Times* · photograph, repro. in *The Independent* · photograph, repro. in *Daily Telegraph* · photograph, repro. in *The Guardian* · photograph, repro. in *The Scotsman* · photographs, repro. in Thomas, *George Thomas, Mr Speaker*

Wealth at death £237,134: probate, 3 Feb 1998, *CGPLA Eng. & Wales*

Thomas, Timothy (1753–1821). *See under* Thomas, Joshua (1719–1797).

Thomas, Vaughan (1775–1858), Church of England clergyman and author, was born on 20 September 1775 at Kingston, Surrey, the son of John Thomas, of the same place, and his wife, Frances. Having matriculated from Oriel College, Oxford, on 17 December 1792, he was admitted a scholar of Corpus Christi College on 6 May 1794. He graduated BA in 1796 (MA, 1800; BD, 1809), and in 1803 was elected to a fellowship at Corpus. He was appointed vicar of Yarnton, Oxfordshire, in February 1803; vicar of Stoneleigh, Warwickshire, in June 1804; and rector of Duntisbourne Rouse, Gloucestershire, in March 1811. These three lucrative livings he held in plurality until the end of his life, while continuing to reside in Oxford. From 1814 he also acted as curate of Begbroke, Oxfordshire, on behalf of John Cooke, president of Corpus (1783–1823) and rector of Begbroke and Wood Eaton. In October 1811 he resigned his fellowship on his marriage to Charlotte, daughter of the Revd John Williams, vicar of Catherington, Hampshire. They had no children. She was the sister of George Williams MD, fellow of Corpus, regius professor of botany, and physician to the Radcliffe Infirmary, Oxford.

Thomas was a conservative protestant high-churchman who deployed his formidable powers of management in combating every manifestation of the spirit of the age in the church and the university. In 1821 he opposed the candidacy of Richard Heber for the Oxford parliamentary seat on the grounds of Heber's alleged sympathy with the cause of Catholic emancipation. In 1831 Thomas published a pamphlet on *The Legality of the Present Academical System of the University of Oxford*, challenging the proposals for reform made by Sir William Hamilton in the *Edinburgh Review*. As chaplain of his college from 1832 to 1844 he made it his campaign headquarters during a period of unprecedented controversy. In 1833 he was a co-founder of an association formed to defend orthodox doctrine, and in 1834–5 he masterminded the successful resistance to the admission of dissenters to the university. In February 1836 he was chairman of the 'Corpus committee' which co-ordinated the protest against the appointment of R. D. Hampden as regius professor of divinity. On all these issues he had the support of the Tractarians, but this marriage of convenience broke up after 1838, when Thomas was one of the prime movers behind the proposal to erect a memorial at Oxford to the protestant martyrs. The same year he published an attack on proposals for a general revision of the university statutes. He continued to defend the status quo until his death, and his critique of Sir William Hamilton's proposals was re-issued in 1853 at the height of the debate on university reform.

Thomas was energetic in his promotion of philanthropic and evangelical causes. It was he who prompted his friend Samuel Warneford to endow an asylum at Oxford for the insane which opened in 1826. In 1827 he published *An Account of the Origin, Nature and Objects of the Asylum on Headington Hill*, which sought to educate the public about mental illness. He was a shrewd chairman of the asylum's management committee for twenty-one years, combining broad vision with meticulous attention to detail. Physical exercise and occupational therapy were essential features of the benevolent regime, and restraint was kept to a minimum. Thomas himself designed the layout of the buildings and landscaped grounds. Patients were segregated by class and sex, and he was at pains to prevent 'intercourse by conversation and letter-writing' between males and females (visitors' book, 28 July 1834, 2). In 1828 he instituted a 'fund for poor patients', named after him.

Because of his local reputation for administrative competence, Thomas was appointed chairman of the board of health formed at Oxford in June 1832 upon the outbreak of cholera. His *Memorials of the Malignant Cholera in Oxford* (1835), which took its text from Thucydides' account of the Athenian plague, provides a carefully documented account of the epidemic and the measures taken to combat it, as well as a historical survey of previous epidemics and their causes.

A long-standing visitor and governor of the Radcliffe Infirmary, Thomas was assiduous in his attention to matters of diet, medication, and hygiene, and vigilant in maintaining the moral tone of the establishment. He was insistent that the hospital should promote godliness as well as physical health: the 'disorderly' were excluded, and even the reading matter of the patients did not escape his scrutiny. This pastoral zeal is evident also in his campaign to establish a residential college to provide for the tutelary care of students at the Birmingham Royal School of Medicine, also endowed by Warneford. Both he and Warneford were concerned to 'stamp the [medical] curriculum with the impress and signature of revealed truth' (*Christian Philanthropy Exemplified in a Memoir of the Revd S. W. Warneford*, 1856, 11).

Thomas was active in resisting the secularization of village schools, and maintained that the children of the poor should be taught only what they required for their spiritual welfare and the maintenance of their station in life. Anything that might encourage social mobility was to be discouraged. A watchful custodian of his parish charities, he excluded non-churchgoers and known reprobates from the list of beneficiaries. He served for many years as a justice of the peace, earning a reputation among poachers for the severity of his sentences, and he was equally draconian in his pronouncements on prison administration.

Thomas published nearly fifty works, mostly tracts and pamphlets of a controversial nature. His long association with Stoneleigh bore fruit in a laborious *Italian Biography of Sir Robert Dudley* (1861), and he was the author of some other antiquarian papers. After his wife's death in 1843 he moved from Holywell Street to a house at 83 High Street, overlooking Magdalen Bridge. He died there on 26 October 1858, and was buried on 2 November in his wife's grave in the churchyard of St Peter-in-the-East.

G. MARTIN MURPHY

Sources *Hist. U. Oxf. 6: 19th-cent. Oxf.* • W. R. Ward, *Victorian Oxford* (1965) • D. McClatchey, *Oxfordshire clergy, 1777–1869* (1960) • A. G. Gibson, *History of the Radcliffe Infirmary* (1926) • *The letters and diaries of John Henry Newman*, ed. C. S. Dessain and others, [31 vols.] (1961–), vol. 6 • T. Fowler, *The history of Corpus Christi College*, OHS, 25 (1893) • Mrs B. Stapleton, *Three Oxfordshire parishes: a history of Kidlington, Yarnton and Begbroke*, OHS, 24 (1893) • *GM*, 3rd ser., 5 (1858), 645–6 •

GM, 3rd ser., 6 (1859), 320 • B. Parry-Jones, *The Warneford Hospital, Oxford, 1826–1976* (privately printed, 1976) • visitors' books, Headington Asylum, Warneford Hospital archives, Oxford • *IGI* • parish register (burial), Oxford, St Peter-in-the-East

Archives Bodl. Oxf., corresp. and papers, MSS Top. Oxon. b 15, 18–21, c 2; Add. c 88, 184, 190–191; Add. d 77; Top. Warwicks. b 2, c 9, d 1, e 1; GA Oxon. b 23; Bliss B 210 | U. Birm. L., papers relating to Queen's Hospital, Birmingham • Warneford Hospital, Oxford, papers relating to Warneford Asylum

Likenesses P. Hollins, bust, 1845, Warneford Hospital, Oxford

Wealth at death under £18,000: probate, 9 March 1859, *CGPLA Eng. & Wales*

Thomas, William (d. 1554), scholar, administrator, and alleged traitor, was of unknown parentage but almost certainly of Welsh descent. On 1 February 1552 a William Thomas received a grant of arms in which he was described as a gentleman from Llantomas, the seat of the Thomas family in the parish of Llanigon in Brecknockshire. On the basis of a comment that William Thomas made in 1545, in which he attributed an attempted embezzlement scheme to the 'fragilite and slipperiness of youth', it seems likely that he was in his early twenties at the time and in the service of Sir Anthony Browne, master of the horse (Adair, 133).

Early years and travels, 1540–1550 Nothing is known of his education but Thomas clearly understood Latin and he quickly became fluent in Italian (thanks at least in part to the three years he spent in Italy in the mid-1540s). There are also references to classical texts in his later writing, and all of this speaks to his having received a formal education of some kind. It was once thought that he was the William Thomas who was admitted to the University of Oxford as a bachelor of canon law on 2 December 1529, but this identification has been discredited. Thomas might well have spent time at the university, but there is no definitive record of his having done so. Thomas was married by 19 May 1540, probably to Margaret (d. in or before 1551), sister of David Watkyns of Hereford. William and Margaret Thomas were mentioned in a grant on 13 September 1544. She may have died by the time Thomas fled to Italy in early 1545, as no mention was made of her during the three years he spent abroad or even after he had returned home. He married, by 1553, his second wife, Thomasine (b. c.1512, d. in or after 1579), daughter of Thomas Mildmay of Chelmsford in Essex and his wife, Agnes, and widow of Anthony Bourchier of London (d. 1551). Sir Walter *Mildmay (1520/21–1589) was his brother-in-law. There is no record of children from his first marriage, but his second wife and he had at least one surviving child, Anne.

Thomas's name was common enough to make identifying him firmly in the records between 1540 and 1545 a difficult task. He was probably involved in the dissolution of at least one religious house, the nunnery of Lynebroke, in May 1540 and this might very well have meant that he had come to the attention of Sir Richard Rich, who noted in a letter of 16 February that a William Thomas was living in a Fleet Street tenement formerly belonging to the white friars in London. This property is very likely the messuage called the Blacke Swann. Thomas may also have been the

man who was in May 1540 granted a 21-year lease on Hay-on-Wye rectory, on the Welsh border, and the proximity of the property to Llanigon makes the connection more likely. Similarly, he probably was the person who, on 21 January 1542, was appointed a clerk of the peace and of the crown for the neighbouring counties of Brecknockshire, Radnor, and Montgomeryshire, who, on 23 February 1543, was given the next presentation to the vicarage of Sturminster Newton in Dorset with two other people, and who was living in St Saviour's parish in Southwark, Surrey, by 13 September 1544. This last residence is very likely the property that was reported by Watkyns in February 1554 as having been sequestrated by Mary I.

What kind of duties Thomas carried out for Browne is unclear. What is certain is that he was trusted sufficiently to have access to large sums of Browne's money. Facing gambling debts of some kind Thomas stole some of this and set off for Italy. Along the way he deposited the funds with Acelyne Salvago, an Italian banker, receiving in return bills of exchange that he could cash in once he reached Venice. By 13 February 1545 a servant of Edward Seymour, earl of Hertford, was in hot pursuit, and on 25 March letters were sent to Edmund Harvel, Henry VIII's ambassador in Venice, warning him to be on the look-out for Thomas. By the time he reached Venice on 10 April, coincidentally the same day Harvel received his instructions from London, Thomas had had second thoughts about the whole affair and went immediately to the English ambassador to confess his indiscretions. Payment was stopped on the bills of exchange and Thomas put in prison. Harvel, though, convinced early on of Thomas's contrition, twice wrote to the privy council on his behalf. At a privy council meeting held on 31 May it was decided that Harvel should return the bills to Salvago so that the banker might repay the stolen money to Browne.

Thomas was eventually released from prison though how he supported himself is unclear. He travelled extensively around Italy and was in Bologna, on his way from Florence to Venice, when news of the king's death reached him in February 1547. Once back in Venice he undertook a written defence of Henry, and its purpose may have been to restore Thomas to the good graces of the new government. The tract, which was entitled 'Peregryne', referring to his peregrinations, took the then popular form of a dialogue, in this case between the narrator and several gentlemen of Bologna. Thomas later translated the manuscript into Italian for publication in Italy as *Ill pellegrino Inglese* (1552), but the original English tract did not appear in print until the eighteenth century. A copy of this tract, which may actually be the original itself, is preserved in the British Library (BL, Cotton MS Vespasian D. xviii).

Thomas spent Christmas 1547 in Rome, and from his critical commentary on Paul III's procession into St Peter's, which he made in a later publication, along with his spirited defence of Henry in 'Peregryne', his religious sensibilities can be classified as protestant. Soon afterwards John Tamworth commissioned Thomas to write an

Italian grammar and short dictionary so that he might better learn the language. Thomas had finished this task by 3 February 1548 and he forwarded the work to his patron from Padua. Thomas based his work on Alberto Accarigi's *Vocabulario, grammatica, et orthographia de la lingua volgare* and Francesco Alunno's *Le richezze della lingua volgare*, both of which had first been published in 1543. Tamworth thought the work so important that he eventually sent it to his brother-in-law, Mildmay, so that it might be published. Thomas Berthelet, the king's printer, published it in 1550 as *Principal rules of the Italian grammar, with a dictionarie for the better understandyng of Boccace, Petrarcha, and Dante*. *Principal rules* had the distinction of being the first Italian dictionary and book of grammar published in English, and it was reprinted in 1562 and 1567.

Informal royal tutor and clerk of the privy council, 1550–1553
By the time that *Principal rules* was published Thomas was back in England, having arrived there probably after the death on 28 April 1548 of his former master, Browne. Some time after his return Thomas finished *The historie of Italie, a boke excedyng profitable to be rede: because it intreateth of the astate of many and divers common weales, how thei have ben & now be governed*, begun probably during his final months abroad, since he mentions witnessing the papal procession at Christmas 1547. Berthelet published the work after 20 September 1549, the date of the dedicatory preface. By then, in the aftermath of the western rebellion and Kett's rebellion, Thomas could see which way the political wind was blowing, and he dedicated his work not to Hertford (now duke of Somerset and lord protector), but rather to John Dudley, earl of Warwick. It was a timely work. As Thomas explained at length in the dedicatory preface, *The historie of Italie* provided examples of both good and bad governance, and suggested ways to achieve the one and to avoid the other. He was pragmatic in his approach, and he owed not a little to Niccolè Machiavelli, who was actually mentioned in Thomas's section on Florence. Thomas also seems to have been influenced by the *Memoires* of Philippe de Commynes, a Burgundian and French diplomat. Copies of *The historie of Italie* may have been burnt at the time of Thomas's execution as commentary on his treason, but reissues of the work in 1561 and 1562 testify to its lasting popularity.

The next two years of Thomas's life are obscure. By 23 January 1552 he was returned for Old Sarum in Wiltshire in a by-election through the patronage of William Herbert, first earl of Pembroke. Sitting in Edward VI's first parliament, even though probably late in its session, may have contributed to his being returned to the March 1553 parliament for Downton in Wiltshire. Who his patron on the second occasion was is uncertain, although it was probably Pembroke again. In 1549 Thomas dedicated his book *The Vanitie of this World*, published by Berthelet, to Anne Herbert, William Herbert's wife. Pembroke exercised influence over Downton as a leading Wiltshire landowner, especially after Somerset's execution. Thomas was clerk of the privy council by 1552 and favoured by Warwick (now duke of Northumberland), who may have played some role in getting him returned for Downton. It

is also possible that he knew John Ponet, bishop of Rochester, who was patron of the Downton seat, and approached him directly. Curiously enough the earliest description of a parliamentary division, or rather vote, occurs in Thomas's tract, 'Peregryne'. This seeming first-hand knowledge of parliamentary procedures suggests that he may have sat in an earlier parliament (perhaps one for which there are no surviving returns), or at the very least had good friends who did.

It really is not until Thomas's appointment as clerk of the privy council on 29 April 1550 that he can be more clearly tracked in the records. His duty was to keep a detailed record of decisions made by the privy council. That he was previously engaged in other official affairs is perhaps suggested by the fact that the privy council discharged him from 'all other maner of businesse' so that he might give full attention to his duties as clerk (*APC, 1550–52*, 4). The privy council's trust in him was further demonstrated in their order that the treasurers were not to pay out money unless authorizing warrants carried Thomas's signature, and this was regardless of whoever else might have signed them. For his labours Thomas received a salary of £33 6s. 8d. This was raised to £40 in May 1552. As was customary Thomas also received payments for the basic supplies of his office, such as paper, pens, and ink. The crown further assumed travel expenses related to the performance of his office, as when, for example, he was appointed secretary for the embassy of William Parr, marquess of Northampton, whose mission into France from 24 April to 12 August 1551 was to negotiate a marriage between the king and Henri II's daughter, Elizabeth, as a way of assuring the new amity between the two realms.

In spite of the strict instructions issued by the privy council on his appointment as clerk, Thomas made entries in the conciliar register only to the end of August 1550, at which point other hands appear in the records. Presumably these several hands represented secretaries who worked under Thomas's direction, transcribing notes taken by him during privy council meetings. In addition to the possibility that other official duties took Thomas away from making regular entries in the register the introduction of these new hands may also indicate the point at which he became a mentor, albeit at a distance, to the king.

How it came to pass that Thomas wrote eighty-five questions and several related essays for the benefit of Edward's political education is, as with so much in his life, something of a mystery. Thomas himself cultivated an air of secrecy about the relationship, asking the king to keep to himself the advice which he proffered, and to send whatever questions he might have through Sir Nicholas Throckmorton, a gentleman of the privy chamber. This secrecy, however, may have been more apparent than real, and may reflect a strategy on Northumberland's part to introduce the young king surreptitiously to the art of governing. It seems highly unlikely that, given the alleged attempt by Thomas Seymour, Baron Seymour of Sudeley, to kidnap the king in 1549, Northumberland or anyone else in a position of power would have been ignorant of these kinds of exchanges.

The eighty-five questions, which Thomas called 'Common places of state', addressed issues related primarily to the power and authority of rulers. He produced at least six discourses in response to the king's interest in some of these topics, and several of them were infused with Machiavellian political philosophy, complete with emphasis on practical and pragmatic action. Indeed, Thomas's work on Italian subjects generally probably influenced his thoughts on the issue of governance. However, the discourse that seems most to have caught the king's attention concerned the reform of the coinage. Years of debasement under Henry had seriously undermined the royal finances, and Thomas urged immediate reform, which he estimated would cost 12 pence on the pound. When Edward received different but equally vehement opinions on the subject Thomas stood his ground, arguing that although it was an expensive remedy it was necessary to economic stability. Thomas's letters on the coinage probably coincided with the king's 'Chronicle' entries and the privy council's discussions on the subject in September and October 1551. This would mean that Thomas's 'Common places' and at least his opinions on the coinage were composed during the late summer and early autumn.

Thomas was also at work on other literary projects during the last years of Edward's reign. In 1551 he made a translation of the thirteenth-century text *De sphaera* for Henry Brandon, second duke of Suffolk. Interestingly, he used the preface of this translation to advocate serious study of the English language. The slavish attention to learning Latin in the schoolroom came at the expense of English, and this he greatly lamented. The same year Berthelet published another of Thomas's translations, which appeared as *An argument, wherin the apparaile of women is both reproved and defended*. As a new year's present (probably for 1551 but possibly for 1552 or 1553), Thomas presented the king with a manuscript translation, 'The narration of Josaphat Barbaro, citezein of Venice, in twoo voyages, made th'one into Tana and th'other into Persia' (BL, Royal MS 17 C x), which had originally been printed in 1543.

In addition to prospering politically and socially, Thomas enjoyed an improvement in his finances. Between January 1551 and March 1553 he acquired a considerable amount of property, and the right to exploit other land, in Sussex, Worcestershire, Gloucestershire, the Welsh marches, and especially Herefordshire. One of these purchases was offset by a generous royal grant of £248. By 26 January 1552 Thomas was one of the coroners for Gloucestershire, though how long he held the post is unknown. In August he applied for, and was granted, a commission to try pirates within the Cinque Ports. Thomas's activities, however, were not always successful or unimpeded. On 13 July 1551 the privy council turned down his application for the reversion of the auditorship of Sussex on the grounds that such appointments were a drain on the crown's finances. This rejection was tempered with the promise that he would nevertheless have the first vacancy that became available. About the same time Thomas's pursuit of an ecclesiastical appointment caused friction with Nicholas Ridley, bishop of London. Both men coveted the presentation of the prebend of Cantleurs at St Paul's Cathedral and they used what influence they had to thwart the other: Ridley approached the king's tutor, Sir John Cheke, for help in July 1551, writing on the 23rd that Thomas had 'in times past set the council upon me' in his attempts to obtain the presentation (*Works of Nicholas Ridley*, 331–2). Although the privy council initially favoured Thomas in the dispute, one of Ridley's clients, though not the one he originally intended, was appointed to the living on 24 October.

It would seem as though Thomas also pursued some kind of appointment abroad. In a letter he sent to Sir William Cecil on 14 August 1552 Thomas expressed an interest in returning to Venice for a year or two, so long as he was sent there, presumably, in some official capacity. No action seems to have been taken on his offer. By 31 March 1553 Thomas had surrendered the clerkship, though he continued in the employ of the privy council. In mid-June he carried letters to London from Charles V's court, and he was still connected with the privy council in the opening days of Mary's reign.

Wyatt's rebellion, 1553–1554 Thomas's official connection with the privy council appears to have ended after August 1553, and it may be that he resigned or was relieved of his duties about that time. He was fully aware of what Mary's accession meant to religious reformers, and when his friend Thomas Hancock was omitted from the queen's first general pardon for his outspoken criticism of Catholicism, Thomas advised him to flee the country. Soon disaffection over the queen's proposed marriage to Philip of Spain became widespread and by the end of the year he was involved at the very least in discussions about deposing Mary, and possibly about assassinating her as well. The motives of this group, which included Sir Thomas Wyatt the younger, are difficult to gauge, though they seem to have been mainly political rather than religious, concerned as they were with the queen's marriage to a foreign prince.

Most of what is known about Thomas's involvement in Wyatt's rebellion is from testimony given under duress by those involved. Supposedly on 21 December, Thomas met Sir Nicholas Arnold and broached with him how the queen's marriage might be prevented. He even reputedly suggested assassinating Mary, and nominated John Fitzwilliam for the job. Arnold told Sir James Croft about Thomas's proposal, and Croft repeated it to Wyatt. Both men later confessed to having been appalled at the suggestion, so much so that Wyatt claimed he carried a cudgel around with him for four or five days so that he might beat Thomas with it if he came across him. It is unclear whether or not Thomas knew of these conversations, as on 27 December he reputedly met Sir Peter Carew at Mohun's Ottery in Devon; Carew was supposed to lead an uprising in the south-west concurrent with Wyatt's in

Kent. Carew was ordered to appear before the privy council on 2 January 1554, word of the conspiracy having leaked, and he fled to France on 25 January. Thomas remained in England and travelled to the home of John a Mynde in Bagendon, Gloucestershire, with his former brother-in-law, Watkyns, in tow. While recovering from some illness Thomas sent Watkyns to London on 9 February with a letter for his wife. During his absence Mynde reported that Thomas expressed the hope that his views on the subject of her marriage had not offended the queen. Watkyns returned on 14 February with a letter for Thomas and the news that Mary had sequestrated his house in Southwark. Thomas attributed this action to the rumour that he had fled with Carew, although as he explained to Mynde, his contact with him had been innocent enough, merely the completion of a sale between the two of them. Almost immediately Thomas set out for London with one of his tenants, Thomas Fowler, and Watkyns. Watkyns rode with them part of the way before returning to Mynde and eventually going on to Hereford. Fowler parted company with Thomas at Henley-on-Thames, Oxfordshire. He later noted in his deposition that Thomas had shaved his beard by this point, perhaps by way of a disguise.

By 20 February Thomas had been arrested and sent to the Tower of London. Two days later depositions had been taken from his contacts in Gloucestershire. On the night of 25 February Thomas attempted to kill himself by thrusting a knife into his chest, but he succeeded only in hurting himself and delaying his indictment and trial for treason. As he recovered in the Tower Arnold, Croft, Wyatt, and several others involved in the uprising bandied his name about freely to their interrogators. There is some question about the degree of his guilt in this whole business. Throckmorton, who was also arrested for complicity in Wyatt's rebellion, demanded at his trial to be allowed to call Fitzwilliam in his defence, saying that Arnold was trying to save his own skin by accusing him and Thomas of plotting to murder the queen. It is probably significant that Fitzwilliam was not in the Tower along with everyone else but rather at court, presumably ready to confirm Throckmorton's statements. That the royal officials refused to allow him to testify suggests that they believed Fitzwilliam would indeed clear Throckmorton and Thomas of the charges.

Nevertheless Thomas was formally indicted on 8 May of having encompassed Mary's death. He pleaded not guilty, though his defence in response to the charges has not survived. What does survive, however, in the notes of a contemporary judge, is Thomas's objection to the status of the jurors on his case, who he claimed were not his peers. It was quickly decided, though, that while Thomas was an esquire, merchants and other commoners worth £2 per annum in land or £100 in goods could sit in judgment on cases involving treason. Thomas was convicted, and on 18 May he was drawn on a hurdle from the Tower to Tyburn, where he was hanged, drawn, and quartered. His head was placed on London Bridge while the rest of him was displayed over Cripplegate. For their part, Arnold, Croft, and Carew all escaped punishment. On 13 December some of Thomas's property interests were restored to his widow on compassionate grounds. She was still pursuing some of her husband's forfeited rights a couple of years later, specifically the presentation to the prebend of Nonnington in the diocese of Hereford, which had been granted by the queen to Henry Walshe. Thomasine Thomas wanted to present the living to Mynde, and she and Walshe fought over the issue in court. In 1563 Anne Thomas was restored in blood, and on 18 April 1566 she received yet more property formerly belonging to her father.

By the end of Edward's reign William Thomas had become a moderately wealthy man with property in London but especially in the marches. Further, he had acquired administrative experience locally and in central government. He had already made a significant contribution in popularizing the Italian language and Italy's history and culture in England and might have continued to do so had he lived longer. However, he was an impetuous man, and his rash actions, even though almost immediately regretted, ultimately cost him his life.

DAKOTA L. HAMILTON

Sources 'Six discourses' and 'Peregryne', BL, Cotton MS, Vespasian D. xviii, fols. 2r–46v • BL, Cotton MS, Titus B. ii, 'Common place of state' • 'Travels to Tana and Persia', BL, Royal MS 17 C x • J. Strype, *Ecclesiastical memorials*, 3 vols. (1822), vol. 2/1 (1822) • HoP, *Commons, 1509–58*, 3.439–43 • E. R. Adair, 'William Thomas: a forgotten clerk of the privy council', *Tudor studies presented … to Albert Frederick Pollard*, ed. R. W. Seton-Watson (1924), 133–60 • *LP Henry VIII*, vols. 15–16, 18–20 • *CPR, 1549–55, 1563–6* • *CSP dom., 1547–58, 1601–3, with addenda, 1547–79* • *Deputy keeper's reports. Reports of the deputy keeper of the Public Record Office*, 4 (1843) • *JHL*, 1 (1509–77) • *APC, 1542–7, 1550–54* • *The diary of Henry Machyn, citizen and merchant-taylor of London, from AD 1550 to AD 1563*, ed. J. G. Nichols, CS, 42 (1848) • *Literary remains of King Edward the Sixth*, ed. J. G. Nichols, 2 vols., Roxburghe Club, 75 (1857) • *The chronicle and political papers of King Edward VI*, ed. W. K. Jordan (1966) • P. J. Laven, 'Life and writings of William Thomas', MA diss., U. Lond., 1954 • J. Dyer, *Reports on cases in the reigns of Henry VIII, Edward VI, Queen Mary, and Queen Elizabeth* (1794) • *State trials* • *The works of Nicholas Ridley, sometime bishop of London, martyr, 1555*, ed. H. Christmas, Parker Society (1843) • J. G. Nichols, ed., *The chronicle of Queen Jane, and of two years of Queen Mary*, CS, old ser., 48 (1850) • J. G. Nichols, ed., *Narratives of the days of the Reformation*, CS, old ser., 77 (1859) • D. M. Loades, *Two Tudor conspiracies* (1965) • D. M. Loades, *John Dudley, duke of Northumberland, 1504–1553* (1996) • Emden, *Oxf.*, vol. 4 • *The works of William Thomas, clerk of the privy council in the year 1549*, ed. A. D'Aubant (1774) • *Principal rules of the Italian grammar, with a dictionarie* (1550); facs. edn (1968)
Archives BL, 'Six discourses' and 'Peregryne', Cotton MS, Vespasian D. xviii • BL, 'Common place of state', Cotton MS, Titus B. ii • BL, 'Travels to Tana and Persia', Royal MS 17 C x
Wealth at death executed traitor; probably forfeit; had been moderately wealthy; property in London, Sussex, Worcestershire, Gloucestershire, Welsh marshes, and especially Herefordshire: *LP Henry VIII*, 19/1, 1035 (15); 16, p. 719, May 1540; 19/1, 9.80 (24), (64), early 1544; 19/2, 9.340 (23), Sept 1544; *CPR, 1549–51*, 421–2; *1550–53*, 47, 129, 264–5; *APC*, Jan 1551–Oct 1552, 153; *CPR, 1553*, 4 (31 March 1553) • property restored to widow: *CPR, 1555–7*, 176–7 (13 Dec 1554) • property restored to daughter: *CPR, 1563–6*

Thomas, William (1592/3–1667), clergyman and ejected minister, was probably born at Whitchurch, Shropshire. He was almost certainly educated locally before being admitted as a plebeian scholar to Brasenose College,

Oxford, on 1 December 1609, aged sixteen. He graduated BA on 8 February 1613 and, having proceeded MA on 17 June 1615, was instituted rector of the church at Ubley, Somerset on 4 January 1618. By 1627, when his only surviving child, Samuel *Thomas (1626/7–1693), was born, he had met and married his wife, Thomasine.

Thomas's entire adult life was directed by an uncompromising adherence to godly religion. During the 1620s he became a well-known lecturer in Somerset and he was rewarded in 1633 when he was granted licence to preach throughout the diocese of Bath and Wells. Almost immediately, however, he was in serious trouble with the diocesan authorities. In October 1634 he was suspended for refusing to read the Book of Sports, a sentence confirmed on 23 June 1635. Five days later he was removed from his living and excommunicated for three years. Subsequently he was reinstated by Archbishop William Laud after a petition from colleagues in Somerset. Edward Chetwynd, dean of Bristol and renowned godly preacher, named Thomas in his will of November 1638 as a 'dear friend'. Despite his reinstatement, however, by the outbreak of civil war Thomas was an embittered opponent of the Stuart church.

During the royalist occupation of Somerset between July 1643 and March 1645 Thomas was prevented from preaching. Frustrated, he took the covenant and fled to London, becoming a regular preacher in the parish of St Pancras, Soper Lane. In August 1645 he was named as rector of the parish, and the same year he became a trier for the second classis, a position which he held until early 1646. Encouraged by his success he returned to Somerset and became minister at the church of St Cuthbert, Wells, before April 1646. In 1647 he helped to establish nine 'classes' in the county, and in the following year signed an attestation of ministers wishing to establish presbyterian government in Somerset. Thomas's circle included his neighbour Samuel Crooke of Wrington, at whose funeral on 3 January 1650 he delivered an exhortation, subsequently published by Thomas and John Chetwynd in The Dead Saint Speaking (1653). Thomas may also have been the W. T. who contributed a Latin epitaph to W. G., Anthologia: the Life and Death of Mr Samuel Crooke (1651).

During the interregnum Thomas built a schoolhouse in his birthplace of Whitchurch. He strove to promote moral reformation and to arrest the spread of Independents who claimed to be 'more perfect saints' (Underdown, 146) and in 1654 he assisted the Somerset committee for the ejection of scandalous ministers. During 1656 and 1657 he published three passionate refutations of the work of the Bristol Quaker Thomas Speed, principally over Speed's uses of scripture, preaching, and the question of tithes. Progressively, however, Thomas devoted more of his time to scholarship. He frequently corresponded with the Worcestershire divine Richard Baxter, and reportedly sent his son, Samuel, to Baxter for a disputation over the nature of free will. He was reputed to have assembled volumes of 'Anniversaria', or diaries of comments on events, and more specialized works of 'Aegrotorum visitationes' and 'Meditationes vespertinae' on particular subjects.

After the Restoration Thomas continued to preach at Ubley and considered the establishment of philanthropic projects. His Christian and Conjugal Counsell … Applyed unto the Maried Estate appeared in 1661 and A Preservative of Piety, a manual for the Christian household, the following year. By then, however, he was again in trouble with authority. When asked his view of the prayer book he remarked that 'I bless God, it is so good, but yet it might be better', for which he was ejected on 21 August 1662 (VCH Somerset, 2.52–3). In 1666, he took the Oxford oath, which, by forbidding his coming within 5 miles of any town or city, effectively ended his preaching career, although he has been credited as the author of The Counties Sense of Londons Sufferings (1667), an application of lessons from the Lamentations of Jeremiah to the great fire of 1666. Subsequently his health declined, and his final days were spent at Ubley, where he died on 15 November 1667, probably survived by his wife. Perhaps fittingly, his will of 24 April that year bequeathed 50s. to the parish church which he had served so faithfully and controversially, together with lands in trust for the Whitchurch schoolhouse. He was buried at Ubley, where his son erected a monument in his memory. The future bishop George Bull of St David's, who had lodged in Thomas's household during the 1650s, uncharitably recorded that he had 'received little or no improvement or assistance from him in the study of theology' (DNB). However, Thomas's request to his executors (who included John Chetwynd) to publish some of his writings bore fruit in Practical Piety, or, The Pastor's Last Legacy (1681), which testifies to a lasting reputation among some of the godly.

S. J. GUSCOTT

Sources Calamy rev., 481–2 · M. Stieg, Laud's laboratory: the diocese of Bath and Wells in the early seventeenth century (1982), 34, 337 · D. Underdown, Somerset in the civil war and interregnum (1973), 22, 65, 143, 146 · VCH Somerset, 2.44, 47, 49, 52–9 · Foster, Alum. Oxon. · Tai Liu, Puritan London: a study of religion and society in the City parishes (1986), 117, 124 · T. G. Barnes, Somerset, 1625–1640: a county's government during the personal rule (1961), 15–17 · T. G. Barnes, 'County politics and a puritan cause célèbre: Somerset churchales, 1633', TRHS, 5th ser., 9 (1959), 103–22 · J. Davies, The Caroline captivity of the church: Charles I and the remoulding of Anglicanism, 1625–1641 (1992), 187–9 · DNB · Calendar of the correspondence of Richard Baxter, ed. N. H. Keeble and G. F. Nuttall, 2 vols. (1991)
Likenesses effigy on monument, Ubley parish church, Somerset
Wealth at death some property: Calamy rev., 481–2

Thomas, William (1613–1689), bishop of Worcester, was born on 2 February 1613 at Bristol Bridge, Bristol, the son of John Thomas, a linen draper who had removed there from Carmarthen, and his wife, Elizabeth Blount. William Thomas claimed descent from Henry Fitzherbert, chamberlain to Henry I, and kinship to the lords Ferrers of Groby and Robert Ufford, earl of Suffolk (1238–1269). More immediately, if more parochially, his grandfather, another William Thomas, was prominent in the civic life of Carmarthen, where he was alderman, mayor twice, and recorder by 1603. He is likely to have attended Lincoln's Inn from 1590, and certainly sat in parliament as member for Carmarthen Boroughs in 1614. He subsequently filled various local offices in and around Carmarthen, where his grandson William Thomas was first educated, at the grammar school under the auspices of Morgan Owen, later bishop of Llandaff. After matriculation at St John's College, Oxford, on 13 November 1629, Thomas graduated BA from Jesus College on 12 May 1632, and proceeded MA on 5 February 1635. He became a fellow of Jesus College. He may have received the degree of BCL from St John's on 9 July 1635, was ordained deacon at Oxford on 4 June 1637, and priest the following year. Shortly after this Thomas was presented to the living of Penbryn, Cardiganshire, and apparently became chaplain to Algernon Percy, tenth earl of Northumberland. Through Northumberland's interest he is said to have acquired the livings of Laugharne and Llansadyrnin in Carmarthenshire. The report that his appointment was contested is unsurprising, since the earl is not known to have had significant proprietorial interests in south Wales.

About this time Thomas married Blanch (d. 1677), daughter of Peter Samyne, a London merchant: the couple had four sons and four daughters. In 1644 Thomas was confronted by parliamentarian soldiers in Laugharne church, who threatened to shoot him if he persisted in reading the Book of Common Prayer and in praying for Queen Henrietta Maria, a Roman Catholic. The source of this story, a descendant of Thomas's, may embellish its subject's heroism, just as he himself after 1660 exaggerated his sufferings during the Commonwealth. This same source records that Thomas lost £1500 through his sufferings down to 1660, and kept school at Laugharne as a way of augmenting his reduced income: he had been ejected from the living of Penbryn. Although he is reported as having been ejected also from Laugharne, Thomas was still there in 1657, and was well enough attuned to the regime of the protectorate to deliver an extremely learned sermon to the great sessions at Carmarthen on 16 March 1657, evidently at the invitation of the authorities. This sermon, typical of the genre of assize sermons, was framed as 'a caution for the client, the witness and the counsellor' (Thomas, *The Regulating of Law-Suits*, title-page), and implied an orthodox and uncontroversial view of church–state relations. It was published in London later that year.

In 1660 Thomas was one of many clergy who petitioned on 23 June for a restoration to their livings, citing his ejection from Penbryn. He was quickly successful in securing preferment, first as precentor of the remote and ruinous cathedral of St David's, on 4 August, and was installed there on the 28th of that month. On 2 August he was created DD at Oxford. Thomas was evidently well thought of by Edward Hyde, earl of Clarendon, who was influential in promoting him, on behalf of the crown, to the living of Llanbedr Felffre in Pembrokeshire in 1661. Through Clarendon he came to the attention of his grandest patron, James, duke of York, who selected him as one of his chaplains at a salary of £50 per annum. Thomas is said to have accompanied James during a naval engagement with the Dutch, presumably in 1665. James and Clarendon advanced Thomas to become dean of Worcester, where he was installed on 25 November 1665. Thomas held the deanery *in commendam* with his post at St David's, and still retained the living of Laugharne. With or without the help of his powerful backers Thomas was evidently quickly able to befriend the dominant revanchist cavalier group in Worcestershire, notably Thomas, Lord Windsor, and Sir John Pakington of Westwood. These men formed a nascent tory interest, and Pakington was sufficiently taken with Dean Thomas to appoint him to his living of Hampton Lovett on 12 June 1670, upon which Thomas finally gave up Laugharne.

On 19 November 1677 Thomas was elected bishop of St David's, and was consecrated on 27 January following. With this promotion he was allowed still to hold the Worcester deanery *in commendam*, but he was evidently an active Welsh bishop. His fluency in the Welsh language, and west Wales family roots, provided him with a natural affinity with the gentry and clergy of his see, as did his interest in publishing religious texts in Welsh. Through his encouragement the third part of the works of Rhys Prichard (Vicar Prichard) had been published in 1672, and earned him a place as a dedicatee of the work; in 1671 and 1672 were published a new Welsh language Bible and book of Psalms, and Thomas's influence has been detected in assisting their appearance. The ministers Stephen Hughes and Thomas Gouge were the principal movers in publishing these and the Welsh Bible of 1677, but Thomas doubtless helped foster an environment in which these ventures could prosper. While at St David's he addressed the problems of dilapidation in his see; a start was made in rebuilding the palaces of Abergwili and Brecon. He attempted to move the cathedral services from St David's to the more populous and wealthy town of Carmarthen, but was unable to see through to completion either the rebuilding or the reorganization of the diocese.

On 14 December 1678 Thomas spoke in the House of Lords against the denunciation by Henry Whitaker, recorder of Shaftesbury and an MP in several parliaments, of most of the episcopate as papists. Thomas robustly asserted the protestantism of his colleagues, and was indeed regarded by Richard Baxter as among those bishops most sympathetic to nonconformity, or rather, least likely to persecute protestants excluded from the Church of England. He was in reality a classic defender of the claim by the Church of England to uniqueness. His book, *An Apology for the Church of England in Separation from it*, published in 1679, was, he explained to his archbishop, 'composed, rather huddled … in the eclipse of the Church of England, in a time of discomposure' (Bodl. Oxf., MS Tanner 146, fol. 121) during the 1650s.

Thomas was confirmed in his translation to the bishopric of Worcester on 27 August 1683. Ill health was by then beginning to take its toll on him, and accounted for his reluctance to travel to London. During his time at Worcester as bishop he gained a reputation for liberality towards the poor, who were fed daily at his door and twice weekly if they were in Worcester gaol. He enhanced the stock and accommodation of the cathedral library. In January 1684 he provided Archbishop Sancroft with an account of the Sunday morning service at Worcester Cathedral, where the congregation moved from the choir to the nave to hear the sermon because its numbers were augmented at sermon time by auditors from other churches. He assured Sancroft of his willingness to tackle irregularities among the cathedral clergy: 'I have not a fondness for any popularity' (Bodl. Oxf., MS Tanner 34, fol. 251). Thomas entertained his patron, now James II, at Worcester on 23 August 1687, when James was impressed by the lavish decoration laid on in his honour. But even on this ceremonial occasion tensions were evident between the Catholic king and the Anglican bishop. When Thomas offered to say grace the king substituted his own chaplain, 'upon which the good old man withdrew, not without tears in his eyes' (Nash, 2, appx, clxi). Thomas responded to James's suspension of the penal laws against nonconformists by declining to distribute the declaration of indulgence in his diocese, provoking James's displeasure, but the bishop was in outright opposition to the revolution of 1688. He refused to take the oath of allegiance, and his assertion to the dean of Worcester, George Hickes, that he would suffer at the stake rather than take the oath, provided encouragement to the nonjurors. Had he survived Thomas would surely have been removed from office, but he died at the bishop's palace on 25 June 1689, and was buried in the cloisters of Worcester Cathedral. Little of his estate of £800 remained after debts and small legacies had been settled. 'He was of a stature somewhat tall and slender, of a long visage, his forehead large, his countenance graceful and his aspect venerable' (ibid., clxii). His grandson William *Thomas was a noted antiquary who revised for publication *The Antiquities of Warwickshire* by Sir William Dugdale.   STEPHEN K. ROBERTS

Sources T. Nash, *Collections for the history of Worcestershire*, 2 vols. (1781–2) · Bodl. Oxf., MSS Tanner · Wood, *Ath. Oxon.*, new edn, vol. 4 · *Fasti Angl.* (Hardy) · W. Spurrell, *Carmarthen and its neighbourhood*, 2nd edn (1879) · M. Curtis, *The antiquities of Laugharne, Pendine and their neighbourhoods*, 2nd edn (1880) · W. Thomas, *The regulating of law-suits* (1657) · L. Bowen, 'Thomas, William', HoP, *Commons, 1604–29* [draft] · Foster, *Alum. Oxon.* · *Seventh report*, HMC, 6 (1879), 1–182 [House of Lords] · *Eighth report*, 1, HMC, 7 (1907–9), pt ii [Braybrooke MSS] · W. Rowlands, *Cambrian bibliography / Llyfryddiaeth y Cymry*, ed. D. S. Evans (1869) · *Calendar of the correspondence of Richard Baxter*, ed. N. H. Keeble and G. F. Nuttall, 2 (1991) · G. H. Jenkins, *Literature, religion and society in Wales, 1660–1730* (1978)
Archives Worcester Cathedral Library, corresp. | Bodl. Oxf., Tanner MSS, letters
Likenesses T. Sanders, engraving, repro. in Nash, *Collections*, vol. 2, appx, p. clx · oils, Jesus College, Oxford · oils, Hartlebury Castle, Worcestershire, Hurd Episcopal Library
Wealth at death £800: Nash, *Collections*, vol. 2, appx, p. clxii

Thomas, William (1670–1738), Church of England clergyman and antiquary, was born in Worcester, the only son of John Thomas and Mary, daughter of William Bagnall of Sidbury, Worcestershire. He was educated at Westminster School from 1685 and at Trinity College, Cambridge, from 1688; he graduated BA (1692) and proceeded MA (1695), BD (1723), and DD (1729). A skilful classicist and Anglo-Saxonist, he became fluent in French and Italian on his tour to France and Italy in 1700. Shortly after his return to England he was ordained in the Church of England, and

through the influence of Lord Somers, a distant relative, he was presented to the rectory of Exhall, Warwickshire. Queen Anne was well disposed towards him, for his grandfather William *Thomas (1613–1689), bishop of Worcester, had been her preceptor, but Thomas declined all court preferment.

Thomas married Elizabeth, daughter of George Carter of Brill, Buckinghamshire, from whom he gained 'a considerable fortune' (Nash, clxiii), part of which was a large estate at Atherstone upon Stour, in Warwickshire. He previously had acquired from his uncle William Thomas an estate at Teddington, in Gloucestershire. He and his wife had nine daughters and five sons, and in 1721 the family moved to Worcester for their education. In 1723 he was appointed rector of St Nicholas, in Worcester, through the influence of the bishop, John Hough, to whom he dedicated his published works.

Thomas published three valuable works on the history and antiquities of Worcestershire and Warwickshire. The first was an account of Malvern's antiquities, published in 1725 under the title *Antiquitates prioratus majoris Malverne in agro Wicciensi*. Thomas made considerable use of Thomas Habington's collections and supplemented them with his own transcripts from episcopal, parish, and corporation records, with the intention of publishing a history of Worcestershire. To this end he 'hardly allowed himself time for sleep, meals, or amusement' (Chambers, 338) but the work remained incomplete at his death. In 1730 he produced a fine edition of Sir William Dugdale's *The Antiquities of Warwickshire*, originally published in 1656, which boasted much new material from his own archival research and excellent maps by Henry Beighton. He next published *A survey of the cathedral-church of Worcester, with an account of the bishops thereof … to 1660* (1736).

Thomas died in Worcester on 26 July 1738 and was buried in the cathedral cloisters, close to his grandfather's tomb. Most of his children predeceased him; only one son, George (d. c.1746), survived him and only his daughter Elizabeth, who married George Wingfield of Lipard, near Worcester, was alive in 1782, when Treadway Nash wrote his memoir of Thomas. Thomas's Worcestershire collections were purchased by Charles Lyttelton, who had encouraged him in his history and left the papers to the Society of Antiquaries, where they were used by Nash.   THOMPSON COOPER, *rev.* M. J. MERCER

Sources T. Nash, *Collections for the history of Worcestershire*, 2 (1782), 2, appx, clxii–clxiii · W. Upcott, *A bibliographical account of the principal work relating to English topography*, 3 vols. (1818), vol. 3, pp. 1259–62, 1342–4, 1346–7 · J. Welch, *The list of the queen's scholars of St Peter's College, Westminster*, ed. [C. B. Phillimore], new edn (1852), 203, 210, 212 · Venn, *Alum. Cant.*, 1/4.222 · V. Green, *The history and antiquities of the city and suburbs of Worcester*, 2 (1796), 103–4 · F. L. Colvile, *The worthies of Warwickshire who lived between 1500 and 1800* [1870] · C. R. J. Currie and C. P. Lewis, eds., *English county histories: a guide* (1994) · H. M. Jenkins, *Dr Thomas's edn. of Sir William Dugdales antiquities of Warws.*, Dugdale Society, 3 (1931) · J. Chambers, *Biographical illustrations of Worcestershire* (1820)
Archives Warks. CRO, map and terrier of his estate | BL, letters to Dr C. Lyttelton, Stowe MS 753, fols. 4, 5, 9, 13–16 · S. Antiquaries, Lond., Worcestershire collections and papers

Likenesses V. Green, mezzotint (after unknown portrait), BM, NPG; repro. in Nash, *Collections*, vol. 1

Thomas, William (*d.* 1800), architect, was the son of Elizabeth and William Thomas (1710–1800) of The Green, Pembroke; his father, 'a man of exemplary piety', claimed descent from the Flemish settlers of Pembrokeshire (*GM*, 70, 1800, 87). The date of his birth and details of his early life and training have not been established. By 1780, when he first exhibited an architectural drawing, Thomas was established in Marylebone, where he remained for the next twenty years, maintaining an office at Allsop's Buildings.

Thomas was something of a virtuoso: a surveyor and sophisticated architect, draughtsman, and engraver who enjoyed the company of artists and engineers. He exhibited eight times at the Royal Academy of Arts between 1780 and 1799, and was a member of the Society of Arts and of the Society of Civil Engineers (1781–92). He advertised his competence by publishing *Original Designs in Architecture* (1783), a folio with twenty-seven plates (some his own engravings) of exemplary neo-classical designs for houses, interior features, and garden buildings. The 176 subscribers included nobility and politicians, architects—notably Robert Adam, who influenced Thomas's designs—several patrons, and fellow Pembrokeshire countrymen. His introduction was an interesting statement of the tension between architecture considered as a science and as an art, and also declared Thomas's attachment to a 'favourite science', probably civil engineering. Thomas's engravings included two executed commissions (Brownslade House, Pembrokeshire; the Surrey Chapel, Southwark), but his early work is not well documented. His principal commission was Willersley Castle, Derbyshire, for Sir Richard Arkwright, completed in 1790, an early example of an industrialist's castle–house with Thomas's designs extending to the interior detail.

A portrait depicts Thomas in affluent middle age holding the design for Willersley Castle (RIBA, London). Latterly, Thomas was styled 'architect to HRH the Duke of Clarence' (as was his pupil Thomas Dearn, who probably succeeded Thomas in practice) for his admired geometrical design for a 'grand Naval Obelisk', a monument commemorating the Royal Navy's victories which was to be erected near Portsmouth by public subscription under the duke's patronage (*GM*, 68, 1798, 24–7). The design was exhibited at the Royal Academy in 1799 but Thomas died in October the following year (nine months after his father) and the monument was never erected. Thomas was buried at St Marylebone on 25 October 1800, and his drawings were subsequently auctioned at Covent Garden. He seems never to have married and there is no surviving memorial to him.   RICHARD SUGGETT

Sources Colvin, *Archs.* · *GM*, 1st ser., 58 (1788), 577–9 · *GM*, 1st ser., 68 (1798), 24–7, 100 · *GM*, 1st ser., 70 (1800), 87 · Graves, *RA exhibitors* · R. S. Fitton, *The Arkwrights: spinners of fortune* (1989), 196–9 · E. Harris and N. Savage, *British architectural books and writers, 1556–1785* (1990), 455–6 · G. Watson, *The Smeatonians: the society of civil engineers* (1989) · parish register, London, St Marylebone, 25 Oct 1800 [burial]

Archives AM Oxf., Sutherland collection, sale catalogue, 55 (5) · Bodl. Oxf., plans, Gough maps 41A, fols. 53–81 · Pembrokeshire RO, Haverfordwest, Angle collection, plans, 78, 89, 129–30

Likenesses N. Dance?, oils, *c*.1780, RIBA · M. Brown?, oils, *c*.1790, RIBA

Wealth at death under £1000: administration, 1801, PRO, PROB, 6/177, fol. 447v

Thomas, William [*pseud.* Islwyn] (1832–1878), Welsh-language poet, was born on 3 April 1832 at Tŷ'r Agent, near Ynys-ddu, in the parish of Mynyddislwyn, Monmouthshire, the ninth child and youngest son of Morgan Thomas (1776–1857) and his wife, Mary (1789–1866). His home language was English, and he enjoyed a comfortable upbringing. His father intended that he should become a surveyor, sending him to private schools and, finally, to Dr Evan Davies's College in Swansea. But he was accepted as a preacher in August 1854, and ordained as a Calvinistic Methodist minister in 1859 (he never accepted a pastorate) after experiencing a religious conversion under the ministry of his brother-in-law, Daniel Jenkyns. It was Jenkyns who first recognized his promise and introduced him to local poets and bardic teachers, particularly Gwilym Ilid (William Jones; *fl.* 1835–1853) and Aneurin Fardd (Aneurin Jones; 1822–1904). Thomas adopted his bardic name in the early 1850s, taking it from Mynyddislwyn (Islwyn's Mountain) near his birthplace. Before long Islwyn was well known in the literary life of Gwent, writing in both strict and free metres and competing, with some success, in local eisteddfods. During his time in Swansea he became engaged to Anne Bowen. In October 1853 she collapsed and died, aged twenty, a traumatic experience for the young man which left him with a lifelong psychological scar, although in 1864 he married Martha Davies, the daughter of Anne Bowen's mother's second marriage. Soon after the death of Anne, Islwyn began his major work, a long epic of the soul, 'Y storm' ('The Storm'), written in two parts. The first, a poem of over 6500 lines in blank verse and other metres, was composed between December 1854 and February 1856. In May 1856 he began a second version, finishing in July of that year. Extracts from both parts appeared subsequently in periodicals and in his *Caniadau* (1867), but the poem was not published in its entirety during Islwyn's lifetime. In 1897 a confused text was included in *Gwaith barddonol Islwyn*, edited by Owen M. Edwards. Both parts received more expert editorial treatment from Meurig Walters in 1980 and 1990.

Modern critics, concentrating on one or other of Islwyn's versions, have attempted to elucidate a putative plan for his poem. It is, perhaps, safest to say that 'The Storm' is a discursive, comprehensive meditation, asserting eternal providence and justifying the ways of God to men. The death of Anne Bowen may well have been the initial trigger, but the poem soon broadens its boundaries in ways no Welsh poet had attempted, using the storm image imaginatively to pursue Milton's basic theme. Here and there the Miltonic pattern of paradise lost and regained saves the work from falling apart: a world without spiritual and physical storms (paradise and memories of Eden); the storm (and its metaphorical implications); the restoration of a stormless world (through divine grace and resurrection). 'The Storm' shows that Islwyn was indebted to the popular contemporary Spasmodic school for much of his stance as a poet. Islwyn followed Alexander Smith's *Life-Drama* (1853) in holding that the poet's duty was to go forward 'in his spirit's strength' to wring meaning from 'the questions of all time'. The poet was an intensely imaginative, uniquely sensitive, suffering being, able to pursue these 'king thoughts' in divinely inspired (and often long-winded) poems, finally asserting what another spasmodic, Philip James Baily, described as 'confidence in God and good'. In addition, Islwyn admired Ralph Waldo Emerson and welcomed the American's emphasis on the poet as a prophetic interpreter who should rise above 'stock poetry' and 'the coils of rhythm and number'. This influence helped the Welsh poet to stand apart from the laboured arguments in Wales about the appropriate metre for epic poetry, freeing him to make lively use of a variety of metres (but favouring blank verse), including a pastiche of Longfellow's *Hiawatha* medium and a section in strict metres. He also made consistent and effective use of the Romantic reconciliation of opposites. The grave is a beginning not an end, and is to be welcomed, not feared. The night is full of stars. The storm signifies judgment, death, and destruction, but is followed by peace and happiness. Suffering inspires spiritual victory. The poet of 'The Storm' is Carlyle's hero-soul, seeking to show the ultimate harmony of the apparent opposites and inconsistencies in spiritual life and nature.

Islwyn never again wrote anything to equal this multi-layered poem, which stands unique in nineteenth-century Welsh literature. He went on to busy himself with preaching and editing the poetry columns in several periodicals and newspapers and to reassume the familiar role of a competitive eisteddfod poet and adjudicator, winning prizes but never a major national eisteddfod prize. Always delicate, by 1877 his health was deteriorating, and he died at Y Glyn, Ynys-ddu, on 20 November 1878, saying, according to the testimony of his niece, 'I am going to Anne now'. He was buried at Y Glyn seven days later. The unfortunate legacy of 'Y storm' was the creation of a school of so-called new poets in the last decade of the nineteenth century. Islwyn had sought to make poetry a unique method of understanding man's relation to nature and God, but the attempts of the new poets to imitate him were feeble, lacking his conviction and originality.

E. G. MILLWARD

Sources M. Walters, ed., 'Y storm' gyntaf gan Islwyn (1980) • M. Walters, ed., Yr ail 'Storm' gan Islwyn (1990) • D. G. Jones, Bywyd a gwaith Islwyn (1948) • S. Lewis, 'Thema Storm Islwyn', Meistri'r canrifoedd: ysgrifau ar hanes llenyddiaeth Gymraeg, ed. R. G. Gruffydd (1973), 357–70 • E. G. Millward, Yr arwrgerdd Gymraeg: ei thwf a'i thranc (1998), 235–62 • H. Bevan, Dychymyg Islwyn (1965) • M. Evans, 'Y storm' gyntaf (1988) • W. J. Gruffydd, Islwyn (1942) • G. T. Hughes, 'Islwyn and Y storm', A guide to Welsh literature, ed. H. T. Edwards, 5: c.1800–1900 (2000), 68–96 • D. G. Jones, Y storm: dwy gerdd gan Islwyn (1954) • M. Walters, Islwyn: man of the mountain (1983)

Archives NL Wales, letters, papers, and sermons • U. Wales, Swansea, letters and papers

Likenesses portrait (aged twenty-seven), repro. in O. M. Edwards, ed., Gwaith Barddonol Islwyn (1897), vi

Thomas, Sir William Beach (1868–1957), journalist and author, was born at Godmanchester, Huntingdonshire, on 22 May 1868, the second son of Daniel George Thomas, who became rector of Hamerton, Huntingdonshire, in 1872, and his wife, Rosa Beart. His early years in his father's parish gave him a deep love for the countryside. The idealization of rural Britain later became a central theme of his writing and life: 'The true country seldom lets you down', he wrote (Beach Thomas, 16). He was educated at Shrewsbury School, where he was a member of the football and cricket elevens and distinguished himself as a cross-country runner. In 1887 he went with a Careswell exhibition to Christ Church, Oxford, winning a full college scholarship in 1891 but obtaining only a third class in classical moderations (1889) and *literae humaniores* (1891). Tall and with a huge stride, he was an impressive athlete. For three years in succession he represented the university, first in the mile, then in the hundred yards, and in the quarter-mile which he won in 1890. In 1890–91 he was president of the athletics club. He also played both association and rugby football and cricket for his college.

On leaving Oxford, Beach Thomas—he used his second forename as a surname—taught at Bradfield School (1891–6), then at Dulwich College (1897–8); but he found teaching 'uncongenial' (Beach Thomas, 49) and he turned to journalism as one of the writers of the 'By the way' column in *The Globe*. J. L. Garvin then invited him to write about the countryside for *The Outlook* which he was editing, and Beach Thomas remained there for nearly two years until *The Outlook* changed hands. For some time he was on the staff of the *Saturday Review*, which he did not greatly enjoy, and he contributed both prose and verse to many other papers. On 17 April 1900 he married Helen Dorothea (1876–1969), daughter of Augustus George Vernon *Harcourt FRS, chemist, and tutor of Christ Church, Oxford. They had three sons and one daughter. One son, a lieutenant-commander in the navy, was killed in the Second World War.

Beach Thomas wrote *Athletics*, a work which was published in 1901, but the next milestone in his career was his engagement a few years later as a writer on country life for the *Daily Mail*. Most pleasing of all for Beach Thomas, the paper's owner, Lord Northcliffe, agreed that for his writing to be successful he should live in the country and 'not come to London more than twice a week' (Beach Thomas, 72). Beach Thomas, as *The Times* commented, became a 'partisan' of Northcliffe (14 May 1957, 13), whom he regarded from their first meeting as a 'chief' 'whom it was very pleasant and honourable to serve' (Beach Thomas, 65). He settled in a cottage in the valley of the Mimram in Hertfordshire, and as early as 1908 published a selection of his essays under the title *From a Hertfordshire Cottage*, which displayed well his powers of observation and his unique talent as a writer on natural and rural subjects.

One of Beach Thomas's best works was also one of the earliest—the three volumes of *The English Year* (1913–14), which he wrote in collaboration with A. K. Collett. He spent most of the war as a well regarded correspondent in France for the *Daily Mail*, although his description of the battle of the Somme has been described as fitting the form of 'propagandist prose ... stirring phrases, empty words, palpable lies' desired by Northcliffe (Taylor, 176). Even Beach Thomas's contemporaries felt that his war dispatches, although 'brilliantly written, were always optimistic, and too cheery sometimes for the men who had to do the fighting and the dying'. There was no doubt, however, that 'he agonized over the slaughter' (Gibbs, 15). Beach Thomas said later that he found it 'almost unbearable to watch our troops ... going forward' (Beach Thomas, 116). But he treasured a letter paying tribute to his influence upon civilian morale: 'without your despatches we could never have persuaded the men to work through the bank holiday' (ibid., 112). He subsequently wrote *With the British on the Somme* (1917). In 1918 he was sent on an American tour. After the end of the war he was in Germany until May 1919 (and was back there for the occupation of the Ruhr in 1923). In 1922 he went on a tour of the world for the *Daily Mail* and *The Times*. Most of his later writing on country matters is to be found in *The Observer*, the paper in which, renewing his friendship with its editor J. L. Garvin, he became most at home and for which he wrote regularly until 1956. He also contributed the 'Country life' column to *The Spectator* for many years, and wrote its centenary history, *The Story of the 'Spectator'* (1928).

Beach Thomas showed himself a prolific author in his sixties and seventies. Among other books he produced *A Letter to my Dog* (1931), *The Yeoman's England* (1934), in which he took the reader month by month through the country calendar, *The Squirrel's Granary* (1936), *Hunting England* (1936), *The English Landscape* (1938), *The Poems of a Countryman* (1945), *A Countryman's Creed* (1946), *The Way of a Dog* (1948), and *Hertfordshire* (1950). He also wrote two autobiographies: *A Traveller in News* (1925) and *The Way of a Countryman* (1944). He was a chevalier of the Légion d'honneur (1919) and was appointed KBE (1920) for his work as a war correspondent. Tall and lean, with thin weather-beaten features and a moustache, he was a man of considerable charm and humour. He died at his home, High Trees, Gustard Wood, Wheathampstead, Hertfordshire, on 12 May 1957 and was buried three days later.

DEREK HUDSON, *rev.* MARC BRODIE

Sources *The Spectator* (15 Sept 1950) · *The Times* (14 May 1957) · private information (1971) · P. Gibbs, *The Times* (17 May 1957), 15 · Burke, *Peerage* · Foster, *Alum. Oxon.* · W. Beach Thomas, *The way of a countryman* (1944) · S. J. Taylor, *The great outsiders: Northcliffe, Rothermere and the Daily Mail* (1996)

Archives BL, corresp. with Lord Northcliffe, Add. MS 62219

Likenesses G. C. Beresford, photographs, 1917, NPG · M. Bone, chalk drawing, IWM

Wealth at death £27,069 11s. 6d.: probate, 5 July 1957, *CGPLA Eng. & Wales*

Thomas, William Luson (1830–1900), wood-engraver and newspaper proprietor, the son of William Thomas, a shipbroker, and his wife, Alicia Hayes, was born on 4 December 1830 in London. Little is known of his early life,

though he was educated at Fulham, Middlesex. After leaving school he joined his brother George Housman *Thomas (1824–1868) in Paris, where he had set up an engraving business with his brother-in-law, H. Harrison. He learned engraving from his brother and became the major engraver of his work. In 1846 he travelled to the United States with George and Harrison to work on illustrated newspapers, including *The Republic* and the *Picture Gallery*. After returning to England because of George's ill health, the brothers travelled to Rome, where William studied art at the Académie de France. The large artistic community in which he mixed there gave him a unique insight into artistic life, which proved invaluable for his later career in art journalism.

In 1851 Thomas became an assistant to W. J. Linton in London and established himself as a leading engraver. On 12 July 1855 he married Annie Carmichael, daughter of the marine artist John Wilson *Carmichael (1799–1868); among their children was George Holt *Thomas. Between 1852 and 1855 he worked from an office at 17 Essex Street, the Strand, which he shared with the wood-engraver Horace Harral. In 1856 Thomas and Harral moved to 11 Serjeant's Inn, Fleet Street, and in 1860 to 4 Palgrave Place, the Strand. During this period he engraved and illustrated many books and periodicals, including Edward Macdermott's *The Merrie Days of England* (1859), Hans Christian Andersen's *Eventyr, fortalte for børn* (as *Tales for Children*, 1861), and the *Illustrated London News*. By 1868 his engraving business brought him an annual income of some £800. He continued to paint for leisure and achieved some distinction as a watercolourist, exhibiting regularly at the Suffolk Street Gallery from 1860. He became an associate of the Institute of Painters in Water Colours in 1864, where he exhibited regularly until his death in 1900. He became a full member of the society in 1875 and an RI when it achieved royal status in 1884. In 1868 his brother died: deeply grieved, he planned to produce an *in memoriam* volume of his work for the benefit of his widow and her family. It was published in 1869 as *One Hundred of the Best Drawings by George Housman Thomas* and included many of George's book and small magazine illustrations, but none of his work for the *Illustrated London News*. The periodical had refused to lend the woodblocks of George's drawings for publication, a decision which both angered William and strengthened his resolution to set up an illustrated newspaper in opposition to the weekly, which had hitherto held off any rivals.

'I was ready', Thomas wrote, 'for some big, interesting, far-reaching enterprise' (Thomas, 81)—the founding of an illustrated weekly newspaper characterized by artistic excellence. His good business sense was combined with a rare eye for talent and a deep sympathy and understanding of artists and their working methods, something quite unknown at that time for the director of a pictorial weekly. He later wrote of the unique philosophy which characterized *The Graphic*:

> The originality of the scheme consisted in establishing a weekly illustrated journal open to all artists, whatever their method, instead of confining my staff to draughtsmen on

wood as had been hitherto the general custom. ... it was a bold idea to attempt a new journal at the price of sixpence a copy in the face of the most successful and firmly established paper in the world, costing then only fivepence.   (ibid.)

The Graphic was an immediate success and became known for the excellence of its wood-engravings and the notable artists who worked on the paper, some of whom included Luke Fildes, Hubert von Herkomer, A. B. Houghton, Frederick Walker, and William Small. The format of the paper offered artists an unprecedented opportunity to explore social subjects, and its images of poverty made it a catalyst for the development of social realism in British art. Many of the wood-engravings which it featured were developed into major paintings: Luke Fildes's *Houseless and Hungry*, which appeared in the first edition on 4 December 1869, became the celebrated painting *Applicants for Admission to a Casual Ward* (1874, Royal Holloway and Bedford New College, University of London, Egham), exhibited at the Royal Academy in 1874.

Thomas established the Graphic Gallery to complement the periodical and he commissioned artists of stature to paint images for the paper's summer and winter colour supplements. He also commissioned several notable series, including Shakespeare's Heroines, portrayed by artists such as Leighton and Alma-Tadema, which were exhibited at the gallery and engraved in the paper. *The Graphic* also serialized and illustrated fiction, including Thomas Hardy's *Tess of the D'Urbervilles*, which was illustrated by Herkomer and a select group of his students. With the development of photography and new print techniques the artistic quality of the images declined, but even here Thomas saw a new opportunity: in 1890 he established the *Daily Graphic*, the first daily illustrated paper published in England. He died on 16 October 1900 at Weir Cottage, Chertsey, Surrey, and was cremated at Brookwood cemetery, Woking, Surrey, on 19 October. He was survived by his wife.

Thomas's achievement was impressive. The influence of *The Graphic* within the art world was immense: among its many admirers were Vincent Van Gogh, and Hubert von Herkomer, who wrote that Thomas 'did more ... than improve illustrated journalism, he influenced English art, and that in a wholesome way' (*The Times*, 19 Oct 1900, 9). A precise, good-natured man, Thomas was involved with many charitable works, including the Artists' Benevolent Institution and the Prince of Wales Hospital Fund. His obituarist in *The Sketch* (24 October 1900, 8) described him somewhat unctuously as 'Fair-bearded till time and hard work silvered his hair, ... Mr. Thomas was a true gentleman—one, indeed, of Nature's noblemen.'

MARK BILLS

Sources W. L. Thomas, 'The making of *The Graphic*', *Universal Review* (15 Sept 1888), 80–93 · *ILN* (27 Oct 1900), 597 · *The Times* (18 Oct 1900), 7 · *The Times* (20 Oct 1900), 9 · *The Graphic* (20 Oct 1900), 582–3 · *Daily Graphic* (18 Oct 1900) · *The Sketch* (24 Oct 1900), 8 · *Newspaper Owner & Modern Printer* (24 Oct 1900), 10–11 · J. Hatton, *Journalistic London* (1882) · *ILN* (13 Dec 1890), 743 · H. Herkomer, *The Times* (19 Oct 1900), 9 · M. Jackson, 'Thirty years of pictorial journalism', *ILN* (14 May 1892), 600 · G. White, *English illustration, 'the sixties': 1855–70* (1897) · F. Reid, *Illustrators of the sixties* (1928) · R. K. Engen,

Dictionary of Victorian wood engravers (1985) · *DNB* · J. Treuherz, *Hard times: social realism in Victorian art* (1987) [exhibition catalogue, Man. City Gall., 14 Nov 1987 – 10 Jan 1988] · d. cert. · *CGPLA Eng. & Wales* (1900)

Likenesses M. W. Ridley, portrait, exh. RA 1874 · H. Herkomer, herkomergravure print, BM · Spy [L. Ward], chromolithograph caricature (*The Graphics*), NPG; repro. in *VF* (13 Dec 1894), 399 · photograph, repro. in *ILN* (13 Dec 1890), 743 · wood-engraving (after photograph by Mora), repro. in *The Graphic*, 582 · wood-engraving, repro. in Hatton, *Journalistic London*, 232

Wealth at death £108,416 12*s*.: probate, 28 Dec 1900, *CGPLA Eng. & Wales*

Thomas, William Moy (1828–1910), novelist, journalist, and translator, was born in Hackney, Middlesex, on 3 January 1828, the younger son of Moy Thomas (1787–1844) and Harriet Theresa Thomas. His father was a solicitor and vestry clerk of St Mary Woolnoth. The Moy Thomases were a well-known legal family in the City ward of Walbrook throughout the eighteenth century, William was destined for a legal career, and his uncle, John Henry Thomas, the barrister and legal scholar, took charge of the boy's education. However, J. H. Thomas became mentally ill and mysteriously disappeared in 1834, and from then on Thomas was privately educated. He decided when still a young man to pursue a literary career, and became private secretary to Charles Wentworth Dilke, proprietor of *The Athenaeum*. In 1850 he was introduced by Sir Thomas Noon Talfourd to Charles Dickens, who engaged him the following year as a writer on *Household Words*, to which he contributed until 1858.

During his writing career Thomas wrote on numerous literary and historical subjects for many leading periodicals. His first book was an edition of the *Poetical Works of William Collins* (1858), with notes and a biography. In the same year a series of scholarly papers by him appeared in *Notes and Queries* concerning the vexed issue of the parentage of the poet Richard Savage. In 1861 Thomas published his praised and valuable edition of *The Letters and Works of Lady Mary Wortley Montagu*, and in 1866 he completed the authorized translation of Victor Hugo's *Toilers of the Sea*. From 1866 to 1867 Thomas was London correspondent of the New York *Round Table* under the signature Q, and in 1868 he joined the staff of the *Daily News*, writing the weekly article 'In the recess' and the drama criticism. He also wrote leading articles, reviews, and descriptive sketches for that newspaper until 1901. He was the first editor of *Cassell's Magazine*, in which he published in serial form his novel *A Fight for Life* (3 vols., 1868), which was later dramatized and played in London and the provinces. A volume of his short stories, *Pictures in a Mirror* (2nd edn, 1880), is a useful indication of the range of his fiction. He was honorary secretary of the Authors' Protection Society (1873), and was instrumental in the establishment of the royal commission on copyright which reported in 1878. He was drama critic for *The Academy* from 1875 to 1879, and for *The Graphic* from 1870. A familiar figure at London first nights, his critical evaluations of plays were much followed.

Thomas married Sara Maria Higginson (1828–1918),

daughter of Commander Francis Higginson RN, on 27 September 1846. They had two daughters and five sons. Thomas's eldest son, Frederick Moy Thomas, became a well-known Fleet Street figure, and his younger daughter, Amy Thomas, a French scholar. Thomas's active writing career closed some nine years before his death, which took place after a long illness at the East Sussex County Asylum, Hellingly, Sussex, on 21 July 1910.

MICHAEL ERBEN

Sources *Men and women of the time* (1899) · A. T. C. Pratt, ed., *People of the period: being a collection of the biographies of upwards of six thousand living celebrities*, 2 vols. (1897) · Allibone, *Dict.* · H. S. Clarke, 'Mr Moy Thomas', *The Theatre*, 4th ser., 6 (1885), 13–16 · J. Hannay, 'Lady Mary Wortley Montagu', *Characters and criticisms* (1865) · R. B. Gardiner, ed., *The admission registers of St Paul's School, from 1748 to 1876* (1884) · J. H. Thomas and J. F. Fraser, eds., *The reports of Sir Edward Coke*, new edn, 6 vols. (1826) [Co Rep] · J. Hollingshead, *My lifetime*, 2 vols. (1895) · L. Baillie and P. Sieveking, eds., *British biographical archive* (1984) [microfiche] · parish register (baptism), Hackney, 17 Aug 1828 · m. cert. · d. cert.

Archives University of Rochester, New York, Rush Rhees Library, corresp.

Likenesses N. Barraud, woodburytype photograph, 1885, NPG; repro. in *The Theatre*, 4th ser., 6 (1885), 16

Thomas, (Lewis John) Wynford Vaughan- (1908–1987),

author and broadcaster, was born on 15 August 1908 at 9 Calvert Terrace, Swansea, the second of three sons (there were no daughters) of Dr David Vaughan Thomas, professor of music, and his wife, Morfydd Lewis. He attended Swansea grammar school, where he just overlapped with Dylan Thomas, the poet, of whom he became a close friend. He won a history exhibition to Exeter College, Oxford, and obtained a second class in modern history in 1930.

Having graduated at the depth of the depression Vaughan-Thomas (he had added Vaughan to his name) made a precarious living by lecturing. In 1933 he became keeper of manuscripts and records at the National Library of Wales and in 1934 area officer of the South Wales Council of Social Service. In 1937 he joined the outside broadcasts department of the BBC's office at Cardiff, in order to be close to the girl he was to marry ten years later. Outside broadcasts were then the only BBC programmes where words spoken were not read from a script. The challenging task of an outside broadcast commentator was to convert an event, as it unfolded, into vivid words and structured sentences which immediately conveyed the scene visually to audiences who could only use their ears.

Vaughan-Thomas was a dark-haired, somewhat chubby man of great vitality. His natural effervescence, his Celtic eloquence, his humour, and his well-stocked mind soon brought him to the fore as a commentator on major occasions in both English and Welsh. He gave the Welsh commentary on the coronation of King George VI. On the outbreak of the Second World War he transferred to the London outside broadcasts department as a home front reporter and in 1942, after covering the blitz, he became a war correspondent. He was the first BBC reporter to fly in a Lancaster bomber on a night raid on Berlin (1943). The

(Lewis John) Wynford Vaughan-Thomas (1908–1987), by Haywood Magee, 1949

bomb run which he brilliantly described, as the aircraft was caught by the German searchlights and dodged the flak, gave listeners a vivid picture of the gruelling perils the RAF crews endured.

Later Vaughan-Thomas recorded memorable dispatches on the Anzio beachhead and covered the liberation of Rome. He also 'liberated' the vineyards of Burgundy, remarking typically, 'We had three marvellous days in a cellar and I emerged with the Croix de Guerre' (1945). The closing stages of the war found him in Hamburg, broadcasting from the studio which William Joyce, Lord Haw-Haw, had been using only days before. He visited the Belsen concentration camp shortly after it was opened and was outraged by the assault on human dignity that he found there. In 1946 he married Charlotte, daughter of John Rowlands, a civil servant. There was one son of the marriage, who became a film director.

For the next three decades Vaughan-Thomas was a leading commentator on state occasions, most notably the wedding of Princess Elizabeth to the duke of Edinburgh. He covered the granting of independence to India and many similar celebrations as former colonial territories hauled down the union flag. He went on overseas tours with the royal family. He took the popularity of his broadcasts in his stride. In his television commentary at the memorial service in Westminster Abbey for Richard Dimbleby he said: 'Ours is a transient art, our words and pictures make a powerful immediate impact, and then fade as if they never had been'.

Vaughan-Thomas was happier as a performer on radio than on television, but in 1967 he became a leading member of the group headed by the fifth Baron Harlech, which was unexpectedly awarded the franchise for the commercial television channel serving Wales and the west of England. Vaughan-Thomas became the first director of programmes for Harlech Television (HTV) in Cardiff and three years later was promoted to be executive director of

HTV. His return to Wales brought him into active participation in the affairs of the principality. He was a director of the Welsh National Opera, chairman of the Council for the Preservation of Rural Wales, and an honorary druid (1974). He was also a governor of the British Film Institute (1977–80).

Vaughan-Thomas wrote a number of books, especially about the countryside. He continued to broadcast radio talks about the changing seasons and made regular forays to London where he would regale his friends with scatological limericks involving complicated Welsh place-names, composed by himself. He had an infectious good humour. He was made OBE in 1974, CBE in 1986, and an honorary MA of the Open University in 1982. Vaughan-Thomas died on 4 February 1987 in Fishguard, where his home was Pentower, Tower Mill. He was survived by his wife.   LEONARD MIALL, *rev.*

Sources W. Vaughan-Thomas, *Trust to talk* (1980) · L. Miall, ed., *Richard Dimbleby: broadcaster* (1966) · *The Times* (5 Feb 1987) · *The Independent* (6 Feb 1987) · personal knowledge (1996) · private information (1996) · b. cert. · *CGPLA Eng. & Wales* (1987) · NL Wales, Vaughan-Thomas papers
Archives NL Wales, corresp. and papers incl. war dispatches
Likenesses G. Konig, photograph, 1946, Hult. Arch. · H. Magee, photograph, 1949, Hult. Arch. [*see illus.*] · photograph, repro. in *The Times*
Wealth at death £224,566: probate, 22 May 1987, *CGPLA Eng. & Wales*

Thomason, Charles Simeon (1833–1911), army officer and bagpiper, was born on 25 May 1833 in Azamgarh, Bengal, the third of the seven children of James Thomason (1804–1853), Bengal civil service, and his wife, Maynard Eliza, daughter of William Grant of Wester Elchies and his wife, Margaret (*née* Wilson). His father was English and his mother Scottish; their respective parents, Revd Thomas Thomason and William Grant and their wives, had sailed out to India in the same ship in 1808.

In 1839, when Thomason was six years old, his mother was seriously ill and only just survived the voyage home to England before she died. His father resumed his distinguished career in India and the five surviving children were split up among relations at home. Thomason and his eldest brother, James, were thereafter brought up by their maternal grandparents at Wester Elchies, across the River Spey from Aberlour, near Elgin, and it was here that Thomason acquired his great love of Scottish music, taking lessons on the flute and bagpipe. About 1849 he went to school at Messrs Stoton and Mayor's preparatory military academy in Wimbledon, where began his long friendship with Frederick Roberts (later Field Marshal Earl Roberts of Kandahar and Waterford). At the age of seventeen they both went to the East India Company's Addiscombe College, near Croydon (1850–52).

On 12 June 1852 Thomason was commissioned in the Bengal Engineers, and after engineering courses at Chatham he sailed for India in 1854. This was not only the start of a distinguished military career but also of his lifetime absorption in classical bagpipe music, or piobaireachd (pibroch), for it was at Chatham that he was introduced to this wider aspect of piping by Alex Murray of the 78th highlanders and Sandy MacLennan of the Highland light infantry. When on leave he took lessons from Sandy Cameron in Edinburgh, brother to Donald Cameron, who was regarded as champion piper of Scotland, and set off for India with his grandfather's pipes and a large quantity of music, much of which he had copied out himself.

These precious possessions were, however, all calamitously lost when the Indian mutiny burst upon Delhi on 11 May 1857, and only because Thomason was in hospital outside the walls did he escape the massacre of Europeans in the city. He found a place in a dogcart with the civil surgeon, two ladies, and a baby, and after a fortnight of hardship and fear of imminent death managed to reach the British base at Karnal, 75 miles to the north. Previous engineering work had given him an intimate knowledge of the Ganges and Jumna canals, and this was turned to good use when a British column of only 3000 men outflanked and surprised the enemy at Badli-ki-sarai, retaking the ridge as a base for the siege of Delhi. For the next three months much of his time was taken up with survey, often on foot within snipershot of the walls, to make good the deficiency of maps. When at last the Kashmir Gate was stormed on 14 September 1857 Thomason was one of the few engineer officers to survive, and after the city had been retaken he resumed work on the canals as best he could; but even then he was involved in yet another battle with mutineers at Kankhal in January 1858.

The rest of Thomason's military career followed a typical pattern of strategic works, up to the rank of major-general, in a series of engineer appointments at Agra, Meerut, Allahabad, Madras, Bareilly, and Indore, planning and supervising irrigation, roads, harbour defences, and building projects. These were of importance not only for defence but also for the development of health and communications throughout the subcontinent. However, it is for his collection of piobaireachd music, *Ceol mor*, which stemmed from the loss of his manuscript collection in the mutiny, and not for his soldiering, that he is remembered.

On 20 September 1858 Thomason married Mrs Ellen Fanshawe Dundas Drummond (1832–1899), *née* Boisragon (of Huguenot descent), the widow of Major James Drummond of Balquahandy and Aberuchill, Perthshire. On sick leave from India in 1861 he built for his family home Laggan Lodge, just 2 miles from his Speyside childhood home. At the same time he began to replace his lost collection of piobaireachd music, with much help from Donald Mackay, piper to Sir George Grant of Ballendalloch. Then, back in India, he was further assisted by Pipe-Major A. Paterson and Corporal Piper Keith Cameron of the 2nd battalion Highland light infantry. He was bequeathed the manuscript second volume of Donald MacDonald's collection, and bought copies of the famous Angus Mackay's unpublished manuscripts from the estate of P. E. Dove, barrister, a notable collector. Determined that piobaireachd playing should not die out and old tunes be lost, all his spare time was devoted to getting his new collection into print before he might fall victim to some illness.

In 1888 Thomason moved to Naini Tal in the Kumaon hills on half pay to work on the book, inventing a shorthand notation that would allow 280 tunes to be compressed into one manageable volume. He was helped by two of his younger children, Archibald (1866–1935) and Bessie, later Mrs Clifford Beckett (1870–1947). A 'pilot pamphlet' was produced with the assistance of the survey of India offices in 1893. The task continued when he retired to 103 Warwick Road, Kensington, in 1895, and *Ceol mor* was finally published in three four-shilling parts in 1897, then as one book in 1900, and lastly with a Revised Notation in 1905. Its appearance was greeted with enthusiasm, and Thomason became first president of the newly founded Piobaireachd Society, but the book had its critics on the grounds that his life in India had deprived him of knowledge of some of Angus Mackay's manuscripts, leading him to rely too much on Donald MacDonald's less preferred settings, and because he had dared to correct what were to him obvious mistakes in old respected settings, on 'internal evidence'. Nevertheless, whatever its shortcomings, *Ceol mor* preserved many rarely heard tunes from possible loss, introduced a system of metrical classification which aided memorization and expression, and initiated the principle of abbreviated notation. All these benefits were carried forward, with improvements, in the Piobaireachd Society's publications, but even so the continuing value of *Ceol mor* led to its republication in 1975.

Among his many interests Thomason included watercolour painting and learning Gaelic, and he made a set of bagpipes for his own use. In Scotland he tried to persuade professional makers to standardize the scale of their instruments, though with little success. His tall figure and red Grant tartan were a familiar sight at highland games, and his contribution to piping was recognized by the presentation of an illuminated address on 1 July 1909, signed by almost 800 admiring devotees. A generation later his friend and collaborator Archibald Campbell, in his own *Kilberry Book of Ceol Mor* (1948), said: 'The two great names of the 19th and 20th centuries' history of piping are Angus Mackay and General Thomason' (Campbell, 13). Thomason died at 103 Warwick Road, Kensington, on 12 July 1911 and was buried on 15 July in Inverallan churchyard, Grantown-on-Spey.   B. D. MACKENZIE

Sources C. S. Thomason, *Ceol mor notation: a new and abbreviated system of musical notation for the piobaireachd* (1893); repr. (1975) • B. D. Beckett, 'Mutiny memoirs of Major General Charles Simeon Thomason R.E. (Bengal)', 1907, NL Scot. • C. S. Thomason, 'Piobaireachd: a crack with brother pipers', NL Scot. • B. D. Mackenzie, *The first hundred years: a history of the Royal Scottish Pipers' Society* (privately printed by the Royal Scottish Pipers' Society, Edinburgh, 1983), chap. 5 • B. D. Beckett, personal memoirs, NL Scot., chap. 17 • A. Campbell, *The Kilberry book of ceol mor* (1948) • *Strathspey Herald* (3 Aug 1911) • *The Times* (14 July 1911) • *The Scotsman* (14 July 1911) • V. C. P. Hodson, *List of officers of the Bengal army, 1758–1834*, 4 vols. (1927–47) • H. M. Vibart, *Addiscombe: its heroes and men of note* (1894) **Archives** NL Scot. | NL Scot., Donald MacDonald MSS • NL Scot., Piobaireachd Society MSS **Likenesses** photograph, *c*.1890, repro. in Mackenzie, *The first hundred years* • photograph, *c*.1900, repro. in *Piping Times*, 27/9 (June 1975)

Thomason, Sir Edward (*bap.* **1769**, *d.* **1849**), manufacturer of buttons and jewellery and publisher of medals, was baptized in Birmingham on 14 November 1769, the son of Edward Thomason, a buckle manufacturer, and his wife, Catherine. He served as an apprentice in Matthew Boulton's factory in Soho, Birmingham, from the age of sixteen to twenty-one. In the early 1790s he opened his own factory, in the premises in Church Street, Birmingham, where his father, then retired, had previously had his business. He began by manufacturing gilt and plated buttons, expanding subsequently into the production of jewellery; a medal and token department was added by 1807; three years later he began plating steel cutlery, and the silver- and gold-plating side of the business expanded to include larger objects thereafter. He also did large-scale castings. His experiments with various mechanical devices, recorded in his *Memoirs* (1845), were not always successful, and the automatically folding carriage step, for which he took out patents in 1796 and 1798, was defeated by the fashion from 1799 for curved carriage doors. Nevertheless, in 1800 he was a founder member of the Birmingham Philosophical Society, and, as a result of his entrepreneurial skills and flair for self-promotion, grew to become an eminent citizen of 'the toy shop of Europe', as Birmingham came to be known.

In 1807 Thomason produced the first British electioneering medals, for the candidates in the Yorkshire elections. In 1809 he manufactured a medal of his former employer Matthew Boulton, engraved by Peter Wyon after Peter Rouw, which was one of the largest medals then to have been struck. About this time he also made his first medallic series, of six European sovereigns. In 1811–12 he struck many tokens, produced in response to the scarcity of small change. Notable among these are those produced for his own establishment, for the Douglas Bank Company of the Isle of Man, and for the ironmaster Samuel Fereday, all of 1811. In 1812 he produced gold and silver tokens for Berkeley Monck, and in 1815 he struck penny tokens for Magdalen Island, Canada. In May 1814 Thomason travelled to Paris with his wife, Phillis Bown Glover (*d.* 1861), whom he had married on 26 August 1799, and his son Henry Botfield Thomason (1802–1843).

The Napoleonic wars offered plentiful subjects for medals: one celebrating the peace of Paris (1814) was especially popular. In 1817 Thomason entered into an agreement with James Mudie to strike a series of medals recording British victories over Napoleon; the dies were engraved by English and French artists, and the results were published by Mudie in *An Historical and Critical Account of a Grand Series of National Medals* (1820). Thomason subsequently purchased the dies. In 1819 he began a series of forty-eight medals of the Elgin marbles in the British Museum, which was completed by 1823. In 1828 his workmen finished a series of sixteen medals on scientific subjects, and two years later sixty medals on biblical subjects. Developing his usual practice of presenting medals to important figures, he sent examples of the biblical series to all European monarchs, as well as to the president of the United States and the emperor of China (who returned

Sir Edward Thomason (*bap.* 1769, *d.* 1849), by William Brockedon, 1834

his). In return for these, and also for his work as vice-consul for Birmingham for several countries, he received several orders and decorations.

Thomason was knighted by William IV in 1832. A series of medallets of 'Bible truths' and 'Testamental Truths' was published in 1835. He also continued to strike a series of medals of British monarchs from eighteenth-century dies engraved by the Dassiers. Among the Birmingham engravers to work for Thomason were Thomas Halliday and Thomas Webb, and he was also associated with Charles Jones. Thomason sold his factory to George Richmond Collis, seemingly in 1835, and retired fully in 1844. He subsequently lived in Ludlow, Bath, and Warwick, and died at his home in Jury Street, Warwick, on 29 May 1849. He was buried at St Philip's Church, Birmingham.

PHILIP ATTWOOD

Sources E. Thomason, *Memoirs during half a century* (1845) · L. Forrer, ed., *Biographical dictionary of medallists*, 6 (1916), 73–81 · L. Forrer, ed., *Biographical dictionary of medallists*, 8 (1930), 235 · L. Brown, *A catalogue of British historical medals, 1760–1960*, 1 (1980) · L. Brown, *A catalogue of British historical medals, 1760–1960*, 3 (1995) · W. J. Davis, *The nineteenth century token coinage of Great Britain, Ireland, the Channel Islands, and the Isle of Man* (1904); repr. (1969), 29, 122, 149, 180 · C. Eimer, *Medallic portraits of the duke of Wellington* (1994) · A. Griffiths, 'The end of Napoleon's *histoire métallique'*, *The Medal*, 18 (1991), 41–2, 44 · R. N. P. Hawkins, *A dictionary of makers of British metallic tickets, checks, medalets, tallies, and counters, 1788–1910* (1989), 472–7 · W. K. Cross, *The Charlton standard catalogue of Canadian colonial tokens* (1988), 70 · R. McLean, 'A Matthew Boulton medal: a recent acquisition for Birmingham', *The Medal*, 19 (1991), 43–5 · J. O'D. Mays, *Tokens of those trying times* (1991), 15, 48 · G. Learmonth, *Thomason's 'Warwick vase'*, Birmingham Museum and Art Gallery Department of Local History, Information Sheet, 11 (1981) · d. cert. · E. Thomason, *Copy of a series of scientific and philosophical medals* (1828) · E. Thomason, *Copy of a series of medals illustrative of the holy scriptures* (1830)

Archives Birmingham Museum and Art Gallery · BM | Birm. CA, letters to Boulton family

Likenesses T. Halliday, effigy on penny token, 1811, repro. in Davis, *Nineteenth century token coinage* · W. Brockedon, chalk drawing, 1834, NPG [*see illus.*] · C. Freeman, engraving, repro. in Thomason, *Memoirs*, frontispiece · C. E. Wagstaff, mezzotint, BM, NPG · oils, Birmingham Museum and Art Gallery

Wealth at death approx. £15,000: PRO, death duty registers

Thomason, Edward (1922–1997), local politician, was born on 12 August 1922 at 105A Commercial Street, Lerwick, Shetland, the second of three children of Edward Thomason (1885–1967), merchant seaman, and his wife, Mary Margaret, *née* Anderson (1887–1969). His parents were both Shetlanders; his father was for many years a bosun on the boats plying between Shetland and the Scottish mainland. His grandparents had been crofters, also in Shetland. His older brother, Lowrie, died in 1949. His younger brother, Albert, qualified as a doctor and emigrated to Australia.

Thomason showed early promise at school and from 1934 when he was twelve he attended the Anderson Educational Institute in Lerwick, the only secondary school in the islands which prepared students for university. He developed tuberculosis in 1937 and was bedridden for some years, during which he read avidly and widely and developed a taste for literature which remained with him throughout his life. He also taught himself to play the mandolin in bed, an early sign of later prowess with the fiddle. In other circumstances he would almost certainly have gone to university and quite probably into the armed forces at the onset of war. As it was he left school in 1939, and on his recovery in 1941 took employment with the Pearl Assurance Company, where he remained until his retirement in 1982, having managed the local branch since 1957. Apart from a period between 1949 and 1956 when his duties took him to Orkney and Caithness his entire working life was spent in Shetland.

On 25 April 1949 Thomason married Janet McPherson Patterson Lamont, *née* Hunter (b. 1921), who was known as Dinah. The wedding took place quietly in Edinburgh rather than Shetland because of the recent death of his brother. It was to be the closest of lifelong relationships, to which he attributed his capacity in later years to suffer with stoicism and wry humour the many setbacks and pressures of political life. They had no children.

Thomason returned in 1956 to a Shetland which was both depressed and, in many ways, depressing. The population had been in decline since the war, unemployment was high, and there was little economic activity or employment creation. A substantial proportion of the able-bodied men were in the merchant navy or whaling in Antarctica. There was urgent need of machinery to promote development, but none existed. In this vacuum Thomason first joined in 1957 the newly formed Shetland Development Council; in 1959 it became the Shetland Council of Social Service, and he its first chairman. The council won central government support and funding for development projects as diverse as canning locally made soup called 'Rasmie's choice' and marketing the distinctive Shetland model boat at the International Boat Show. Thus began a life of service and devotion to the well-being of the islands and his training for the years ahead.

The Highlands and Islands Development Board came into existence in 1966. Shetland was well placed to exploit the new machinery and did so through the Shetland Council of Social Service under Thomason's chairmanship; indeed, the board effectively used the council as its local representation. There were several marked successes in the early years, most notably in financing new fishing boats for the northerly islands of Yell and Unst.

In 1961, while remaining chairman of the Shetland Council of Social Service, Thomason had been elected to the North Unst seat of the then Zetland county council. His insurance work took him regularly to that island (and to every part of Shetland), so he easily kept in touch with his constituents. In 1970 he was elected convener of the county council for the first time. Almost immediately the oil boom arrived and with it the prospect of financing his vision of a regenerated Shetland. Controversy soon followed. The council was determined to control the oil companies and took the unprecedented step of promoting an act of parliament, principally to gain powers of compulsory purchase to forestall land speculation. This move was not universally welcomed, not least in Unst, where there was talk of massive development and profit for landowners. Thomason fell foul of the backlash this caused and lost his seat on the county council in 1973. Ironically the act was passed in the following year and proved vitally important for Shetland's future.

Thomason was not long out of county council politics, though he was to say, much later, that he could not have continued his insurance work and done justice to the convenorship. In 1974 he was elected to the newly formed Shetland Islands council as the member for Nesting and Lunnasting. From 1978 until his retirement from politics he was councillor for Lerwick Harbour ward, where he lived. He stood for the convenorship in 1982 when he retired from Pearl Assurance but instead served, somewhat uncomfortably, as deputy to A. I. Tulloch until he succeeded him in 1986. He was then continuously convenor until 1994.

These were turbulent years and Thomason was at or near the centre of every significant act of the council. Sullom Voe was established as the largest oil terminal in Europe, with thirty-two oil companies involved. In 1988 he was responsible for the Busta House agreement (named after the house on mainland Shetland where it was signed) which saw some £150 million flow into the Shetland public purse from these same companies. Infrastructure development throughout the islands was extensive; Shetland developed public services second to none in Britain. The county council had accumulated reserves of about £500 million. More than most, Thomason was conscious that this in itself was a problem. The oil bonanza was bound to decline and he spent his later years in office, and much of his time in retirement, trying to wean the council from its high-spending habits. He judged that

effort a failure, though many would say that he succeeded in some measure. In 1989 he was made OBE in the queen's birthday honours list.

Edward Thomason was a politician through and through, but not in any doctrinaire sense. When asked about his politics, a friend turned to his wife and said, 'Edward was a Liberal, wasn't he?' In fact he sat in council as a member of the Shetland movement. He was by nature a kindly man who valued and sustained lifelong friendships. He was personally modest and incapable of harbouring personal grudges. He served on a host of bodies as diverse as the board of management of the Shetland knitters and the Shetland Islands charitable trust. He took as much pleasure in being a founding member of the Forty Fiddlers as in belonging to any other body or group. In their various ways all of them contributed to realizing his overwhelming passion: the regeneration and revitalizing of his beloved islands. He wrote copiously for local newspapers and for the *New Shetlander*, a quarterly publication. In retirement he wrote his memoirs, *Island Challenge*, published just two months before his death on 16 December 1997 at Aberdeen Royal Infirmary. He was buried in Lerwick new cemetery on 19 December.

IAN HONEYMAN

Sources E. Thomason, *Island challenge* (1997) · Lerwick, Shetland, Shetland Archives · *The Scotsman* (17 Dec 1997) · *Shetland Times* (19 Dec 1997) · personal knowledge (2004) · private information (2004) · b. cert. · d. cert.
Likenesses D. Coutts, photograph, 1982, Lerwick Town Hall · H. Younger, photograph, 1993, repro. in Thomason, *Island challenge*, cover

Thomason, George (*c.*1602–1666), bookseller and collector of civil-war tracts, was the son of George Thomason, husbandman of Sudlow, Cheshire, where Thomason may have been born (some sources suggest he was born at Westham in Sussex). He was apprenticed to Henry Fetherstone, bookseller at The Rose in St Paul's Churchyard, London, on 29 September 1617, and became free of the Stationers' Company on 5 June 1626. Soon afterwards Fetherstone ceased publishing and Thomason took over the management of his business.

Thomason's name appears in the Stationers' register from November 1627, initially in partnership with Octavian Pulleyn, with whom he published six titles. The partnership was dissolved in 1643 and Thomason moved to new premises at the Rose and Crown, St Paul's Churchyard. He was notable as an importer of continental books and as a supplier of the libraries of Oxford and Cambridge universities, regularly attending the Frankfurt book fair; he also visited the Low Countries, Germany, and Switzerland for business purposes. He advertised 2000 works that had been collected during a trip to Italy following his wife's death in 1646, describing them in Latin as 'more Rabbinical and Oriental books and manuscripts than have ever before been collected together' (*Catalogue of Pamphlets*, vi). Parliament authorized purchase on behalf of Cambridge University, where they formed the basis of the oriental collection, but there is no evidence that he received payment.

In 1645 Thomason was implicated in the anonymous publication of David Buchanan's *Truth its Manifest*, which attacked parliament and was burnt by the hangman. After publishing in 1646 Philip Freher's *Treatise Touching the Peace of the Church*, he published nothing until 1659, when Rushworth's *Historical Collections* appeared under Thomason's imprint. He played an active role in the financial administration of the Stationers' Company from 1641. After 1645 he began to press for democratic reforms within the company's elections. In 1651 he was assistant warden, junior warden in 1657, and senior warden in 1661, when he was involved in re-establishing the company's business following the Restoration.

About 1631 Thomason married Catharine Hutton (d. 1646), Henry Fetherstone's niece and ward. The couple had many friends among the presbyterian party, including William Prynne, Henry Parker, John Rushworth, and Edmund Calamy. Other family friends included Edward Reynolds (later bishop of Norwich), Thomas Lockey, (keeper of the Bodleian Library), and the poet John Milton, who wrote his sonnet 14 to the memory of Catharine. Following Catharine's death in 1646, Thomason never remarried; his will spoke of his 'late dear and only wife'. The couple had at least nine children, six of whom were living in 1664. The eldest child, also named George, became a prebendary of Lincoln Cathedral in 1683; the remaining survivors were named Katharine, Edward, Grace, Henry, and Thomas.

In 1642 and 1643 Thomason was a parish collector of subscriptions for the parliamentary army, and in 1646 he was involved in a petition to the lord mayor and common council supporting the presbyterian petition. The following year he became a common councillor for the ward of Farringdon Within. After King Charles's surrender in 1647 Thomason and other members of the council called for a personal treaty with the king; they were thereafter deprived of office following Pride's Purge in December 1648. After the execution of Charles I in 1649 he became involved in the overtures between the presbyterians and Charles II, known as the Love conspiracy. He was implicated in the plot and arrested in April 1651, and he spent several weeks in prison at Whitehall before being bailed for £1000 at the end of May. His estate was seized but later restored to him, and he was not prosecuted. Milton may have interceded on his behalf at this time. Thereafter he suffered bouts of illness, due to his imprisonment, and he ceased political activities. Thomason died at Mickleham, Surrey, and was buried in the church of St Dunstan-in-the-West on 13 February 1666 (although Richard Smyth says he was 'buried out of Stationers' Hall (a poore man) 10 Apr 1666' (*Catalogue of Pamphlets*, xiii). His will, dated 1664, included legacies to his children, grandchildren, servants, the Stationers' and the Haberdashers' companies, St Paul's Cathedral, and St Dunstan-in-the-West. However, by his death he was in reduced circumstances, indicated by later codicils.

Thomason's name is remembered for his remarkable collection of political and religious tracts between 1640 and 1661. In 1641 he 'systematically began his collection, acquiring, either by purchase or occasionally by presentation, every book, pamphlet and newspaper issued in London, and as many as he could obtain from the provinces or abroad' (*Catalogue of Pamphlets*, v). According to Falconer Madan, 'Thomason's achievement is unparalleled in its kind' (Madan, 292), encompassing more than 22,000 items in over 2000 volumes, subsequently catalogued by him in twelve volumes. His practice of adding the dates of publication or acquisition on the works' title-pages has proved invaluable in establishing the chronology of events during this turbulent period, and his marginal notes identify anonymous authors and the clandestine manner in which some works were distributed. The comprehensiveness of this collection, and the historical value of Thomason's two surviving manuscript catalogues, were the subject of detailed analysis and debate in the journal *Albion* in 1988 and 1990.

After Thomason's death his collection was subject to many vicissitudes, but remained intact. The works were acquired from his descendants by the bookbinder Samuel Mearne for Charles II, about 1678. Mearne rebound them, but was never paid and the collection remained in his family. For eighty years members of the Mearne and Sisson families repeatedly tried to sell the collection to the Bodleian Library, Cambridge University, Prince Frederick, and others, without success. Eventually, in 1761, it was sold to George III for £300, and was presented to the British Museum in 1762.   DAVID STOKER

Sources G. K. Fortescue and others, eds., *Catalogue of the pamphlets, books, newspapers, and manuscripts relating to the civil war, the Commonwealth, and Restoration, collected by George Thomason, 1640–1661*, 2 vols. (1908) · L. Spencer, 'The politics of George Thomason', *The Library*, 5th ser., 14 (1959), 11–27 · L. Spencer, 'The professional and literary connexions of George Thomason', *The Library*, 5th ser., 13 (1958), 102–18 · G. C. Thomasson and E. A. E. Thomasson, 'The George and Catherine Thomason family of England', *Thomasson traces: narrative of the Thomasson family, 1677–1995*, 2 (1995), 1–82 · D. Stoker, 'Disposing of George Thomason's intractable legacy, 1664–1762', *The Library*, 6th ser., 14 (1992), 337–56 · F. Madan, 'Notes on the Thomason Collection of civil war tracts', *Bibliographica*, 3 (1897), 291–308 · 'The will of George Thomason', *The Library*, new ser., 10 (1909), 34–43 · J. J. McAleer, 'The king's pamphlets', *University of Pennsylvania Library Chronicle*, 27 (1961), 163–75 · C. Blagden, 'The Stationers' Company in the civil war period', *The Library*, 5th ser., 13 (1958), 1–17 · H. R. Plomer and others, *A dictionary of the booksellers and printers who were at work in England, Scotland, and Ireland from 1641 to 1667* (1907) · D. F. McKenzie, ed., *Stationers' Company apprentices*, [1]: *1605–1640* (1961) · P. W. M. Blayney, *The bookshops in Paul's Cross churchyard* (1990) · S. J. Greenberg, 'Dating civil war pamphlets, 1641–1644', *Albion*, 20 (1988), 387–401 · M. Mendle, 'The Thomason collection: a reply to Stephen J. Greenberg', *Albion*, 22 (1990), 85–93 · S. J. Greenberg, 'The Thomason collection: a rebuttal to Michael Mendle', *Albion*, 22 (1990), 95–8

Wealth at death fortune tied up in collection: 'The will of George Thomason', *The Library*

Thomason, James (1804–1853), administrator in India, was born at Little Shelford, near Cambridge, on 3 May 1804, the son of Thomas Truebody Thomason (1774–1829) and his first wife, Elizabeth, *née* Fawcett (d. *c*.1825). His father, who had been curate to the Cambridge evangelical Charles Simeon, in 1808 accepted a post in Bengal, where he became a student of Indian languages and culture, a promoter of Indian education, a noted churchman, and, for a time, chaplain to Lord Moira. Mrs Thomason founded the European Female Orphanage, Calcutta.

James Thomason was sent back to England from India in 1814 to live with his grandmother Mrs Dornford, and Charles Simeon, both powerful advocates of Christian beliefs, who moulded his firm but unobtrusive adherence to the Church of England. At Aspenden Hall School in Hertfordshire his contemporaries included T. B. Macaulay. In 1818 he moved to a school at Stanstead in Sussex, and then went to the East India College at Haileybury, where he distinguished himself in literary subjects, mathematics, and political economy. He obtained an appointment as a writer with the East India Company, and arrived in Calcutta in September 1822.

Thomason became proficient in vernacular languages at Fort William College, spent his early service in the judicial branch, and was for a while in governor-general Lord William Bentinck's secretariat. About 1825, following his mother's death, illness took him back to England, where he proposed to Maynard Eliza Grant (d. 1839). He returned to India and became registrar to the Bengal *sadr* court, where he developed skills in both Hindu and Muslim law, and spent a period as a district judge. Ill health again sent him to England in 1827. After his return to India, on 19 February 1829 he married Maynard Eliza Grant at Malda, where her father, William Grant, was stationed as a civil servant. They were to have some seven children. In 1832 his career took a decisive turn with his request for appointment as magistrate and collector of Azamgarh in the North-Western Provinces, to gain first-hand knowledge of district administration. Azamgarh came to have special significance for Thomason, who later recorded that 'It was to me a field of victory, where such repute and status as I had in the service was founded' (Temple, *James Thomason*, 54). He spent five years as magistrate, collector, and settlement officer at a time when the reassessment of land revenue by revenue commissioner Robert M. Bird was in train, and produced a well-known work, *Report on the Settlement of Chuklah Azimgurh*, in 1837. This experience influenced Thomason in favour of peasant proprietors, and, more generally, laid the foundations for his later success as lieutenant-governor of the North-Western Provinces. In 1837 he was appointed secretary to the North-Western Provinces government, but had to return to England, this time because of the illness of his wife, who subsequently died in London in 1839. Thomason returned to Agra in 1840, succeeding R. M. Bird as a member of the board of revenue, and in 1842 he became foreign secretary to the government of India.

On 12 December 1843 Thomason was made lieutenant-governor of the North-Western Provinces, at the comparatively early age of thirty-nine. His responsibilities were vast, including aspects of most of the civil and judicial administration of the provinces. His tenure of office was to be formative in the development of a devolved system of government. The administration of land revenue was of special importance. The settlement under regulation IX of 1833 had just been completed, and Thomason brought

an acute mind to the completion of Bird's work. He was determined to set down his interpretation of land revenue principles clearly; he saw a just assessment as crucial to the happiness of the people. The assessment should determine the value of the land and establish the rights that went with it: 'The object of this investigation is not to create new rights but to define those which exist' (Temple, *James Thomason*, 145), he wrote. He was inclined to award responsibility for the revenue, and any profit accruing to cultivation, to the peasant cultivators. Joint responsibility was 'an original and well recognised principle in all village communities … the very bond which had held them together', and it was essential to make the community feel 'the strength of the bond which unites them and the necessity of common exertion for the safety of the whole' (Metcalf, 119–20). Thomason clashed with the board of revenue in support of the village community concept.

Thomason was less doctrinaire than Bird in his interpretation of the 1833 settlement, and recognized that individual cultivators were often unable to stand alone when deprived of the *talukdars* as intermediate revenue holders. He was willing in principle, therefore, to accept *talukdars* being awarded the revenue engagements where peasant and intermediary were of the same kin and mutually anxious to maintain their connection. Thomason was, nevertheless, keen to cut the traditional share of intermediaries by about half, to 10 per cent of the revenue, despite the qualms of the East India Company directors. He was inclined to allow prompt sale of defaulting estates despite the reservations of district collectors, and took the typically early Victorian view that 'the measures of the Government ought to be made to favour the industry of the thrifty rather than to save the unthrifty from the effects of their unthriftyness' (Metcalf, 122).

Thomason's views of land revenue administration in the North-Western Provinces were embodied in his authoritative and influential works *Directions for Settlement Officers* and *Directions for Collectors*, both of 1844, the first complete codes of settlement compiled in India, which continued in use for many years. The place of his land revenue policy in the causes of the Indian mutiny is still debated. While some *talukdars* certainly lost by its working, many other factors have to be taken into account to explain the events of 1857.

Thomason contributed importantly in the area of public works. He was, probably more than any other single individual, the facilitator of two great schemes of northern India—the grand trunk road and the Ganges Canal. The grand trunk road was macadamized and had police posts, resthouses, and caravanserais established. The canal, largely the brainchild of Sir P. T. Cautley, was a vast and unique work, and the first purely British scheme of its kind in India. It stretched 350 miles from Hardwar to Cawnpore, and opened between 1854 and 1857.

Land revenue and public works were connected to Thomason's contributions to education. He thought that a carefully recorded land settlement would be an incentive to basic education. The Roorkee Engineering College, founded in 1848, provided public works training for both

Europeans and Indians, and Thomason was keen to see this principle extended elsewhere in education. His first biographer called him 'the father of primary education by the state in Northern India … no matter lay closer to his heart than this' (Temple, *Men and Events of my Time in India*, 48). Thomason's scheme envisaged a school for each group of villages, government inspection, scholarships, and the establishment of several state-funded schools as models. He wanted to 'stimulate the people to exertions on their own part to remove ignorance', to encourage self-improvement 'in a manner consonant with Native institutions and ideas', rather than 'actually supplying to them the means of instruction at the cost of Government' (ibid., 174–5). He also encouraged training and a more systematic approach within the administration, touring widely among his subordinates, and initiated a statistical department to produce analysis of public policy for wider debate. When the Punjab was annexed in 1849, the governor-general, Lord Dalhousie, turned to Thomason to help provide the officers necessary to administer the new territory. Thomason considered the transfer of nineteen men 'a heavy tax' (Mason, 303), but it was of immense significance to the British administration in India.

Thomason recognized that the British had obligations towards India, noting after the Second Anglo-Sikh War that:

> it is in the quiet operations of peace, which ensue from such a turmoil, that constancy, perseverance, circumspection and diligence are called forth. That is the quiet and unostentatious labour, but also the high and responsible duty, to which we are now called to address ourselves, with regard to this great country, which God has placed in our hands.   (Temple, *James Thomason*, 122)

He hoped that Christianity might spread within India and supported protestant missionaries in his private capacity, but was opposed to any official propagation of the religion; he would not, for example, allow any religious teaching in government schools. He was an unstinting and generous personal supporter of charities and churches, colleges, schools, and dispensaries.

James Thomason became a key figure in the East India Company's government, but at the cost of unremitting effort. In August 1853 he experienced an ill-defined but persistent decline in health; he died at Bareilly, North-Western Provinces, while staying with his married daughter, Mrs Maynie Hay, on 27 September 1853, the day that his appointment as governor of Madras was confirmed in Britain. He was buried at Bareilly church the next day. Dalhousie commented, 'He was a first-rate man, invaluable to India and to me' (Baird, 265). The engineering college at Roorkee was renamed Thomason College (later the University of Roorkee) as a fitting tribute.

DAVID J. HOWLETT

Sources R. Temple, *James Thomason* (1893) · P. Mason [P. Woodruffe], *The men who ruled India* (1954) · T. R. Metcalf, *Land, landlords, and the British raj: northern India in the nineteenth century* (1979) · A. Siddiqi, *Agrarian change in a northern Indian state* (1973) · E. Stokes, *The English utilitarians and India* (1959) · *DNB* · R. Dutt, *The economic history of India under early British rule* (1901) · I. Stone, *Canal irrigation in British India* (1984) · J. A. B. Ramsay, marquess of Dalhousie, *Private letters*, ed. J. G. A. Baird (1910) · R. Temple, *Men and events of my time in India* (1882)

Archives BL OIOC · National Archives of India, New Delhi | BL, corresp. with Captain Cautley, Add. MS 28599 · NA Scot., letters to Lord Dalhousie

Likenesses portrait, repro. in Temple, *James Thomason*, frontispiece

Thomasson, Isabella (*c.*1875–*c.*1952), bookmaker, became a well-known figure in Lancashire, but nothing is known about her origins. Her husband, Stephen (Steve), 'used to hawk kippers, and take sixpenny bets, and when they got enough money, to start big, they took that shop' (interview with Dean, 10). This was a fruit shop at 9 Great Moor Street in the centre of Bolton. The Betting Houses Act of 1853 made it unlawful for people to bet for cash on horse-races in premises away from racecourses. Despite this the Thomassons used their shop as a betting house.

When they were raided by the police in 1905 and prosecuted, Stephen Thomasson faced seven charges and his wife one. At the police court hearings the defence 'asked the Justices to dismiss the woman even if she had been assisting her husband, arguing that she was under his coercion' (*Bolton Journal and Guardian*, 23 June 1905). The bench fined Stephen Thomasson £25 with costs but made no additional penalty on his wife. At the hearing her husband promised that there would be no more betting at any house of his. This promise was unfulfilled and the Thomassons became the best-known betting house proprietors in Bolton.

In the early 1920s the Thomassons installed a ticker tape machine in their back yard. This was a telegraphic device run by the Extel company and it conveyed information from racecourses to subscribers. The facility placed them ahead of all the other local bookies, who relied on the local newspapers for their knowledge. By this time their shop was ostensibly a tobacconist's. In 1938 it was noted as 'a large cigarette shop that doesn't sell any cigarettes; there are dummies in the window, and the counter inside is used only for passing bets over; everybody knows about this, including the police, since anybody can walk in' (Mass-Observation, 265).

During the Second World War racing was suspended but afterwards Bella Thomasson started up in business again. Her husband was ill and although she had a son (called Steve) she took another bookie, Albert Hampson, as a partner. He put the ticker tape in the shop and hired a miner who worked on shifts to read out over a microphone the details given. These included the results and the changes in the betting on each race, and so allowed Thomasson to take race-by-race bets throughout the afternoon. This was an innovation. In much of Britain illegal bookies took their bets on the streets for a couple of hours around midday, with the majority of punters (betters) choosing a number of horses and having multiple bets. Race-by-race facilities encouraged single betting, leading to a higher turnover and bigger profits. In effect, Thomasson and Hampson had a modern betting shop, one punter recalling that it 'was full of men backing horses' (Carl Chinn bookmaking letters, Bootham to Chinn, letter 1, 1–2).

As with other illegal bookies it is likely that Thomasson paid certain police officers to turn a blind eye to her activities. Yet she adhered to a strong code of conduct, believing that the shop was no place for women, and only allowed them to bet before racing started. Thomasson was also well known for her honesty. One punter was in the merchant navy and was called away to sea before he could collect his winnings. Two years later he returned and she paid him his money. He described her as 'always immaculate, always in black' with 'nice bit of jewels on, not too flashy, she was a plump lady, well-built, good mannered. Always spoke like a lady' (interview with Dean, 10). Despite her partner's involvement and her old age, the business was seen as 'Bella's' although 'some also called it Steve Thomasson's' (Carl Chinn bookmaking letters, Green to Chinn, letter 4, 1). Bella Thomasson died in the early 1950s aged seventy-seven.   CARL CHINN

Sources 'The betting raid', *Bolton Journal and Guardian* (23 June 1905) · interviews with Teddy Dean and Albert Hampson, U. Birm. L., special collections department, Carl Chinn bookmaking interviews · *The pub and the people: a worktown study*, Mass-Observation (1987) · John Bootham, letter 1; Ken Green, letter 4, U. Birm. L., special collections department, Carl Chinn bookmaking letters · C. Chinn, *Better betting with a decent feller: bookmakers, betting and the British working class, 1750–1990* (1991) · F. Shawcross, 'The punter's paradise: as the big four go for glamour, real gamblers hark back to Bella', *Today* (6 March 1986)

Thomasson, Thomas (1808–1876), cotton manufacturer, was born on 6 December 1808 at Turton, near Bolton, Lancashire, the second son of John Thomasson (1776–1837), a cotton manufacturer, and his wife, Elizabeth Marsh, the daughter of a farmer at Topping, near Bolton. He attended the Friends' Ackworth School from 1813 to 1816, then joined his father, who having been briefly a partner with his sister's husband, John Ashworth, and later manager of Old Mill, Eagley, had set up on his own account at Mill Hill, Haulgh. Rebuilt in 1829, this was a medium-sized mill, combining steam and water power. Following the death of his father, and after a short-lived partnership with his brother-in-law Richard Pennington, Thomasson built a second mill in 1841, an ambitious project at the trough of an intense commercial depression, but one which paid off in the expanding markets of the later 1840s. After further expansion in the 1850s, the firm employed 650 workers and had gained a considerable hold on the production of warps. Energetic and sagacious, Thomasson had a keen practical command of the market for raw cotton, importing on his own account and for speculation. He later took into partnership his nephew Joseph Mellor and his son John Pennington Thomasson (1841–1904).

Thomasson was distinguished among his fellow cotton masters for his strong radical and democratic beliefs. These perhaps owed much to his Quaker upbringing, but on 17 December 1834 he married, outside the society, Maria, the daughter of John Pennington, a cotton manufacturer and merchant. Thereafter (until the Crimean War) he attended with her Bolton parish church. Unusually among his peers, he was a reader of Spinoza and a freethinker; he earned the admiration of G. J. Holyoake

(who wrote his notice in the *Dictionary of National Biography*) and donated sizeable sums to T. H. Huxley. Thomasson's unconventionality was also seen in his support for universal suffrage in the 1830s—for example, his readiness to second Chartist motions at Kersal Moor in September 1838—and in his opposition (as a poor-law guardian) to the full implementation of the new poor law. However, he differed from the Chartists in wishing first to seek the repeal of the corn laws as the best way in which to reverse 'the black catalogue of the sins of the landed interest against the comforts of the poor'. He therefore became an early supporter of repeal in Bolton: he promoted in 1838 its Anti-Corn Law Association and, to tory anger, urged free-trade motions within the town council. He also became a leading financial supporter of the Anti-Corn Law League and a close friend of its leaders Cobden and Bright. Thereafter he was one of the staunchest followers of the Manchester school, supporting the National Parliamentary and Financial Reform Association, the peace movement, and the campaigns against the 'taxes on knowledge' and for cheap postage. He later became a leading backer (and chairman in 1865) of the National Reform Union and the Reform League. Thomasson was never visibly prominent in these movements but was a ready source of financial support. A fervent admirer of Cobden, he gave generously to the Cobden Testimonial Funds in 1846 and 1860 and later privately donated £20,000 to Cobden's widow. He also acted as one of Cobden's executors, sorting out his tangled business affairs.

Thomasson was intimately involved in the civic life of Bolton. He played a leading part in the movement for its incorporation and served on its council (1838–50, 1853–9). But he was an emphatic advocate of municipal economy, seeking to run public affairs on private business principles. He also defended the Little Bolton Trust (on which he served) and the waterworks (of which he was a director) against the pretensions of the tory-dominated council. An advocate of non-sectarian education and of self-improvement, he served on the committee of the All Saints' British School, and was a patron of the Bolton Mechanics' Institute and of Bolton's industrial school, library, and museum. He was also president of the local Liberal association.

Holyoake's description of Thomasson as 'a political economist' seems awry, but he was undoubtedly among the most radically minded of mid-Victorian entrepreneurs, driven by a strong hostility to aristocratic government and a keen desire for the welfare of the people by voluntary means. But he was also privately kind and strikingly generous in individual cases. He enjoyed salmon fishing and shooting in Scotland, often in the company of John Bright. Thomasson retired in 1871, died at his home, High Bank, Haulgh, Bolton, on 8 March 1876, and was buried on 13 March at Turton church, without any church service. His son John Pennington was MP for Bolton (1880–85) and a millionaire, and his grandson Franklin (1873–1941) was the proprietor of *The Tribune* newspaper and MP for Leicester (1906–10).   A. C. HOWE

Sources Bolton biography, Bolton Public Library, vols. 1, 3, 5 · *Bolton Journal and Guardian* (4 Aug 1933) · *Bolton Free Press* (1830–49) · *The diaries of John Bright*, ed. R. A. J. Walling [1930] · J. Morley, *The life of Richard Cobden*, 2 vols. (1881) · *DNB* · G. J. Holyoake, *Sixty years of an agitator's life*, 3rd edn, 2 (1893) · A. Howe, *The cotton masters, 1830–1860* (1984) · R. Boyson, *The Ashworth cotton enterprise* (1970) · d. cert.

Archives Duke U., Perkins L., corresp. | Bolton Central Library, Bolton metropolitan archives, Heywood MSS · Co-operative Union, Holyoake House, Manchester, letters to G. J. Holyoake · Man. CL, Wilson MSS · Merseyside Archives, Pennington family MSS · NRA, priv. coll., letters to Lord Moncreiff · W. Sussex RO, corresp. with Richard Cobden

Wealth at death under £25,000: probate, 11 April 1876, *CGPLA Eng. & Wales*

Thomlinson, Matthew. *See* Tomlinson, Matthew, appointed Lord Tomlinson under the protectorate (*bap.* 1617, *d.* 1681).

Thomlinson, Robert (*bap.* **1668**, *d.* **1748**), benefactor, was baptized on 10 August 1668 at Wigton, Cumberland, the youngest son of Richard Thomlinson of Akehead, near Wigton, of an old Durham family. He was educated at Queen's College, Oxford, where he matriculated on 22 March 1686, and graduated BA from St Edmund Hall in 1689, proceeding MA in 1692. He was later incorporated at Cambridge, in 1719, and graduated DD from King's College in that year. In 1692 he held for a time the post of vice-principal of St Edmund Hall, and in 1695 he was appointed lecturer of St Nicholas's Church, Newcastle upon Tyne. On 8 April 1702 he married Martha Ray, at East Ardsley, near Leeds, Yorkshire; they do not appear to have had any children. In 1712, after holding minor posts, which he probably owed to a family connection with Dr John Robinson, he became rector of Whickham, co. Durham, on the recommendation of Lord Crewe, bishop of Durham. In 1715 he was appointed master of St Mary's Hospital, Newcastle, and four years later Robinson appointed him to a vacant prebend at St Paul's Cathedral, London.

Between 1720 and 1725, as executor of his brother John, rector of Rothbury, Northumberland, Thomlinson erected at Wigton a hospital (the College of Matrons) for the widows of poor clergymen; he himself contributed part of the expense and provided a schoolmaster's house for the parish. In 1734 he gave liberally to the rebuilding of St Edmund Hall, Oxford, under Thomas Shaw, and shortly afterwards donated some 1600 books to form the nucleus of a public library for Newcastle. A building was provided to accommodate the books, and the library was opened to the public in October 1741. The librarian's salary was funded by an endowment from Sir Walter Blackett, and Thomlinson endowed the library with an annual income of £5 to be spent on the purchase of books. He was also responsible for the rules of the library, which were enforced by the first librarian, Nathaniel Clayton. After Thomlinson's death the library was neglected—a catalogue of 1829 revealed high levels of theft and disrepair—but the collection was later salvaged and housed at the city's central library.

Thomlinson's other benefactions included a chapel of ease at Allenby in Cumberland, the charity school at Whickham, and considerable bequests to Queen's College, Oxford, to the Society for the Propagation of the Gospel (of which he was one of the earliest members), and to the Society for Promoting Christian Knowledge. He died at Whickham on 24 March 1748 and was buried in the north aisle of Whickham church. He was survived by his wife.

THOMAS SECCOMBE, *rev.* PHILIP CARTER

Sources S. Jeffery, *The Thomlinson library* (1981) · *GM*, 1st ser., 18 (1748), 187 · H. Bourne, *The history of Newcastle upon Tyne* (1736) · Foster, *Alum. Oxon.* · *IGI*

Thomond. For this title name *see* O'Brien, Conor, lord of Thomond (*d.* 1539); O'Brien, Murrough, first earl of Thomond (*d.* 1551); O'Brien, Conor, third earl of Thomond (*c.*1535–1581); O'Brien, Donough, fourth earl of Thomond (*d.* 1624); O'Brien, Barnabas, sixth earl of Thomond (1590/91–1657); O'Brien, Charles, styled ninth earl of Thomond (1699–1761); O'Bryen, James, third marquess of Thomond (1769–1855).

Thompson. *See also* Thomson.

Thompson, Alexander Hamilton (1873–1952), historian, the eldest child and elder son of John Thompson, then vicar of St Gabriel's, Bristol, and his wife, Annie Hastings, daughter of Canon David Cooper, was born on 7 November 1873 at Clifton, Gloucestershire. He entered Clifton College as a scholar in 1883, leaving in 1890. He entered St John's College, Cambridge, in 1892, as a minor scholar. He read classics, and graduated BA in 1895 and MA in 1903. Weak health at this time led him to take up tutoring on the Riviera for two years. In 1897 he was appointed extramural teacher by Cambridge University. In that year his first published work appeared, a popular guide, *Cambridge and its Colleges*.

Thompson's professional life can be roughly divided into two parts: the first as an 'extension lecturer' for Cambridge University, 1897–1919, and the second after entering full academic life in 1919. In the first the extensive travelling allowed him to familiarize himself with a wide range of medieval buildings while the teaching caused him to reduce complicated matters to a simple treatment. His slim books *The Ground Plan of the English Parish Church* (1911) and *The Historical Growth of the English Church* (1911) admirably illustrate how he compressed profound knowledge into a small compass, and the books have hardly lost value since they were written. In the field of castles major advances in knowledge required a drawing-together in one coherent work in this field which he did in *Military Architecture in England during the Middle Ages* (1912), which became the standard work on the subject. In the second part of his life transcription of medieval works became his main interest. There is a considerable overlap, of course, between the two. His great skill was to combine in one person an equal facility with medieval written sources and the architectural remains, a very rare gift.

During his extramural years Thompson's interests were partly in literature. His second publication had been a *History of English Literature* (1901) founded on that of T. B. Shaw, and this was quickly followed by school editions of various literary texts, chiefly of the English Romantics. He lived at this time partly at Henbury and partly at Chichester and St Albans. In 1903 he married Amy (d. 1945), daughter of Alfred Gosling of Colchester, and soon after moved to Lincoln. They had two daughters.

By this time Thompson had made the acquaintance of two of the leading medieval archaeologists of the day, William St John Hope and John Bilson, both of whom were to be his closest friends for the rest of their days. The latter was among his sponsors for election to the Society of Antiquaries in 1910. After the First World War he continued to write monographs on particular buildings or localities, including studies of Bolton Priory (1928) and Welbeck Abbey (1938).

In 1919 Thompson was appointed lecturer in English at Armstrong College, Newcastle upon Tyne, where two years later a readership in medieval history and archaeology was instituted for him in recognition of his scholarship. Like his contemporary G. G. Coulton, he thus entered full academic teaching after and not before acquiring a reputation for scholarship. Almost immediately he moved to Leeds, where he became reader in medieval history in 1922, professor in 1924, and head of the department in 1927, a post which he held until his retirement in 1939.

As time went on, Thompson's main interest lay increasingly in the publication of original records of English medieval church history. His first major venture was based on the registers of the medieval bishops of Lincoln and in 1914 appeared the first volume of his *Visitations of Religious Houses in the Diocese of Lincoln*. In 1928 he completed for the Surtees Society part 2 of the *Register of Archbishop Thomas Corbridge*, and followed this up by the publication of the *Register of Archbishop William Greenfield* in five volumes (1931–8). Meanwhile steadily he produced other texts, which included *Northumberland Pleas from the Curia Regis and Assize Rolls* (1922), *Registers of the Archdeaconry of Richmond* (3 vols., 1919–35), *Liber vitae ecclesiae Dunelmensis* (1923), and *A calendar of charters and other documents belonging to the hospital of William Wyggeston at Leicester* (1933). In the year before the latter appeared, he was made Ford's lecturer at Oxford and in 1933 Birkbeck lecturer at Trinity College, Cambridge. For the former he took as his theme the English church at the end of the middle ages, and the fruits of this study finally appeared in 1947 in *The English Clergy and their Organization in the Later Middle Ages*, a comprehensive and masterly consideration of 'ecclesiastical institutions in fifteenth century England'.

As a professor at Leeds Thompson had a unique reputation. He had little interest in the generality of committees, although as chairman of the library committee he put the university not a little in his debt. His innate friendliness led him to entertain great and small in large numbers at his little house at Adel in Yorkshire and this, with his immense memory for detail, gave him a remarkable knowledge of his pupils. He answered indefatigably and thoroughly the host of historical and antiquarian queries which beset him unceasingly, and equally unstintingly gave his services as a lecturer and guide to no small fraction of the local archaeological societies. By his death his output of published works totalled about 420 items of one kind or another, but this did not prevent a considerable social activity or painstaking membership of the various official bodies to which he belonged; he was a member of the cathedrals commission (1925–8), a cathedral commissioner for England (1932–42), a member of the archbishops' commission on canon law (1943–7), of the Royal Commission on Historical Monuments (1933–52), and of the Ancient Monuments Board for England (1935–52). Brought up in a vicarage, he remained steadfastly faithful to the Church of England. So full a life was only made feasible by his remarkable powers of work. Until shortly before his retirement it was usual enough for him to work nightly into the small hours. In later life, although he never took exercise, his health was unbroken until his final illness. He died in St Trinian's Nursing Home, Littleham, Exmouth, Devon, on 4 September 1952. He was buried in the churchyard of St Thomas the Martyr, Oxford, on 8 September and a requiem mass was celebrated on 19 September in London.

Thompson was elected FBA in 1928, honorary ARIBA, an honorary fellow of St John's College, Cambridge (1938), and president of the Royal Archaeological Institute (1939–45). He was a lifelong member of the institute, whose activities closely suited his architectural interests. He was made CBE in 1938 and given honorary doctorates by Durham, Leeds, and Oxford.

J. C. DICKINSON, rev. MICHAEL WELMAN THOMPSON

Sources An address presented to Alexander Hamilton Thompson with a bibliography of his writings (privately printed, 1948) • private information (1971) • personal knowledge (1971) • Archaeological Journal, 109 (1952), 166–8 • C. T. Clay, 'Alexander Hamilton Thompson', Yorkshire Archaeological Journal, 38 (1952–5), 266–9 • E. M. Oakley, ed., Clifton College annals and register, 1860–1897 (1897) • Clifton College register, 1862–1962 (1962) • Venn, Alum. Cant. • The Times (5 Sept 1952) • The Times (9 Sept 1952) • The Times (19 Sept 1952) • CGPLA Eng. & Wales (1952)
Archives Borth. Inst., working notebooks relating to medieval ecclesiastical history • Lincs. Arch., corresp. and notes; extracts and copies of documents from medieval episcopal registers of Lincoln; notes relating to VCH section on religious houses • W. Yorks. AS, Leeds, Yorkshire Archaeological Society, corresp. and papers • W. Yorks. AS, Leeds | S. Antiquaries, Lond., letters to Sir Charles Clay
Likenesses W. Stoneman, photograph, 1945, NPG • photograph, repro. in Clay, 'Alexander Hamilton Thompson' • photograph, repro. in Archaeological Journal • photograph, repro. in An address presented to Alexander Hamilton Thompson
Wealth at death £7573 7s. 4d.: probate, 4 Dec 1952, CGPLA Eng. & Wales

Thompson, Andrew (1824?–1870), land agent and land commissioner, was born at High Ridge Hall, Kelso, Roxburghshire, Scotland, one of twelve children of Andrew Thompson, a successful and substantial farmer at High Ridge Hall. He married Sarah Ann Mullineux (c.1829–1858x61) of Northamptonshire in 1848; they had at least three children.

Thompson was trained in estate management; he received instruction in agricultural matters at home, and obtained financial and accounting experience by working in a Kelso banking house for two years. In 1843 he became bailiff to Charles Arbuthnot's 700 acre estate at Woodford, Northamptonshire, succeeding an elder brother who, having held the position from 1829, left to farm. Arbuthnot was impressed by Thompson, considering him 'more fit to be agent to someone of great landed property', like another brother, John, who was agent to the duke of Beaufort. On learning that Ralph Sneyd required a new agent for his Staffordshire estate Arbuthnot recommended Thompson as 'one of the most intelligent of men in respect to all agricultural concerns ... [understanding] everything relating to the management of a landed estate ... no one [being] so likely to introduce a good system into a badly farmed district' (C. Arbuthnot to R. Sneyd, 23 June and 3 Aug 1848, Keele University, Sneyd MSS, S1467). In 1848 Sneyd appointed Thompson as resident agent at Keele, a position he occupied for the next twenty-one years.

As agent Thompson thoroughly reorganized the agricultural bases of Sneyd's estate through large-scale investment in under-draining and building, encouragement of farming systems favouring livestock, tenant selection orientated to those willing to pursue estate policies, and, with the establishment of the Keele Farmers' Club in 1852, the demonstration of improved farming practices. Thompson's record at Keele was reported in contemporary literature as a model of estate improvement.

Thompson was appointed an assistant, or inspector, to the 'inclosure commissioners' in their administration of the mid-century land-improvement legislation in 1847. The legislation aimed at diffusing agricultural improvement by making loans available to landlords for draining, farm building, and other improvements on their estates. When a landowner applied to borrow funds, the commissioners sought assurance on the appropriateness of the proposed improvements. This information was furnished by inspectors in a series of reports based on field observation during the carrying out of the improvement. Through these reports inspectors occupied a central position in ensuring the adoption of best practice in agricultural improvement. The commissioners made extensive use of Thompson's skills between 1847 and 1869. He supplied reports on at least 180 estates lying mainly in the west midlands. Further, he became one of a select group of 'first-rate' inspectors who, according to inclosure commissioner George Ridley, were used in cases of importance and magnitude—for example, arbitrating between landlords and inspectors or advising landlords on proposed improvements. Thompson made copies of his reports which were entered chronologically in a series of eight volumes. The last five volumes, covering 1857 to 1869, are extant. The only known collection of inspector's reports, they provide a remarkable insight into agricultural improvement and estate management at that time.

Andrew Thompson was recognized as one of the leading land agents in the mid-nineteenth century, whose expertise in the management of agricultural land was employed both locally and nationally. Working largely after the repeal of the corn laws, in 1846, with the loss of agricultural protection, Thompson perceived the need for estate agricultural policies to be revised to accommodate the concepts of 'high farming': for agriculture to flourish, farming systems had to adapt to market demand and farm output had to expand—developments which were obtainable by increased application of fertilizers and feedstuffs, and the provision of under-draining and additional farm buildings. Thompson's judicious implementation of these changes, privately on the estates of Charles Arbuthnot and Ralph Sneyd, and publicly as an assistant inclosure commissioner, contributed to improving the structure and prosperity of English agriculture between 1845 and 1870. After 1867 Thompson suffered from growing ill health, and in 1869 he was forced to resign both his agency at Keele and his inspectorship. He died at Milverton, near Leamington Spa, on 7 June 1870, at the age of forty-six, of a dementing disorder. A. D. M. PHILLIPS

Sources A. D. M. Phillips, *The Staffordshire reports of Andrew Thompson to the inclosure commissioners* (1996), 1–69 · D. Spring, *The English landed estate in the nineteenth century: its administration* (1963), 97–134, 161–5 · A. D. M. Phillips, 'The landlord and the village of Keele', *The history of Keele*, ed. C. Harrison (1986), 103–24 · letters to R. Sneyd, Keele University, Sneyd MSS, S1470 and S1467 · census returns for Keele, 1851, PRO, HO 107/2001, 1861, RG 9/1918 · d. cert. · 'Select committee of the House of Lords on the improvement of land', *Parl. papers* (1873), 16.6, 21, no. 326 [minutes of evidence]
Archives Keele University, Sneyd MSS, reports to the enclosure commissioners · Keele University, corresp. with R. Sneyd

Thompson, Sir Benjamin, Count Rumford in the nobility of the Holy Roman empire (1753–1814), natural philosopher and philanthropist, was born on 26 March 1753 at North Woburn, Massachusetts, the only son of Benjamin Thompson (*d.* 1754) and his wife, Ruth Simonds, daughter of an officer who had fought against the French and the North American Indians in the Seven Years' War. He was descended from James Thompson, who had gone to Massachusetts with John Winthrop in 1630. Thompson's mother married again when he was three, and reared a large family; a small legacy for Benjamin's maintenance came from his grandfather, who died in 1755. He went to school at Woburn, at Byfield, and then at Medford; he is said to have been especially interested in mathematics, and enthusiastic about mechanical contrivances.

Apprenticeships and a brief marriage After leaving school at thirteen Thompson was apprenticed at the seaport of Salem, about 20 miles from home, to John Appleton, a storekeeper selling imported dry goods. However, in 1769 merchants in New England signed a non-importation agreement in protest against taxes levied upon them by the British government and this so damaged Appleton's business that he could no longer support Thompson. Briefly unemployed, the latter wrote memoirs on wind, light, and heat before, on 11 October 1769, Hopestill Capen of Boston wrote to Appleton for a reference, and duly offered Thompson a similar job. Soon, however, Capen was writing to Thompson's mother that 'he oftener found her son *under* the counter with gimlets, knife and saw constructing some little machine or looking over some book of science, than *behind* it arranging the cloths or waiting upon customers' (Brown, *Count Rumford*, 3); the story is told that Thompson lost this job in 1770 after an explosion

Sir Benjamin Thompson, Count Rumford in the nobility of the Holy Roman empire (1753–1814), by Thomas Gainsborough, c.1783

when he was making fireworks to mark the repeal of the Stamp Act.

Less than a year later Thompson was apprenticed to the physician in Woburn, Boston, Dr Hay, with a view to becoming a general practitioner. With a friend, Loammi Baldwin, he constructed an electrical machine—electrotherapy was then becoming fashionable and Benjamin Franklin's dangerous experiment with a kite (which the boys repeated) had made electrical science exciting. Thompson attended some lectures at Harvard, but never matriculated, and wrote out a timetable of medical study for himself. He does not seem to have been a very systematic student and early in 1772 his apprenticeship was terminated.

Thompson had already done some schoolteaching, at Wilmington and at Bradford, Massachusetts, and was now invited to teach in Rumford (now Concord), New Hampshire. The clergyman responsible for the invitation was Timothy Walker, whose recently widowed daughter Sarah (1739–1792) had been married to the local landowner, Colonel Benjamin Rolfe. She soon fell in love with the young schoolmaster, handsome, auburn-haired, and nearly 6 foot tall, and about November 1772 they were married. Their only child, Sarah, was born on 18 October 1774. Thompson settled down as a landowner, at the same time cultivating John Wentworth, the royal governor of New Hampshire, who was interested in natural philosophy and in agricultural improvement. In 1773 the governor made him a major in the second provincial regiment, to the fury of experienced junior officers hoping in vain for promotion. Among Thompson's many talents,

the capacity to recommend himself to the mighty was prominent.

Thompson began experiments on gunpowder which were to be a long-term interest, but in December 1775 he was brought before the local committee of safety and accused of being hostile to American freedom—he had made no secret of his support for the established order. The case was dismissed but faced with threats from a mob Thompson fled to Boston, leaving his wife behind; he never saw her again. In Woburn and in Boston he was involved in covert and then overt support for the royal government, like many other loyalists or tories among the colonists. In March 1776 the British army withdrew from Boston; Thompson sailed for England in the frigate bringing the news from General Thomas Gage to the secretary of state, Lord George Germain.

Military life Once in Britain Thompson presented himself as an expert on America rather than as a refugee and became the main contact between American loyalists in England and the British government, as private secretary to Germain. In 1779 he was appointed secretary for Georgia, a barren honour under the circumstances, and in September 1780 to the more profitable office of undersecretary for the colonies. In 1779 his research on gunpowder led to a cruise with the Royal Navy, when he became interested in signalling and in ship design, and then in 1781 to his first publication in the Royal Society's *Philosophical Transactions* and his subsequent election as a fellow. Amid rumours of embezzlement and treason, and blamed for what he saw as Germain's incompetence, in the summer of 1781 Thompson raised a regiment, the King's American dragoons, sailing with them to Charles Town, and then to New York. In camp at Huntington, Long Island, he became infamous for pulling down a church for fortifications, and building baking-ovens from the gravestones. When peace was made in 1783 he returned to England, retiring from the army on half-pay. On 17 September he went abroad, crossing the channel with his horses on the same packet as Gibbon.

At Strasbourg Thompson attended a review in uniform, and procured an introduction to Duke Maximilian de Deux-Ponts (or Zweibrücken), whose regiment had fought for the Americans; the duke gave him warm letters of introduction to his uncle, the Elector Karl Theodor of Bavaria, who was trying to modernize his country and promptly offered Thompson a position at court. Returning to England Thompson secured permission to enter foreign service, and a knighthood from George III on 23 February 1784. Back in Munich he applied scientific analysis to the problems of clothing and feeding the Bavarian army, in which he was given the rank of colonel. In order to provide cheaper and warmer uniforms he investigated the insulating properties of cloth, and this led him to the discovery of convection currents in gases and liquids: he then realized that fabric where air was trapped would be warmest.

On new year's day 1790 Thompson rounded up the many and troublesome beggars of Munich into workhouses, where they were to manufacture suitable cloth and where nourishing meals were provided and there were school-teachers for the children. Feeding these workers and the soldiers led him into studies of nutrition, and also into the improvement of fireplaces and stoves, with fuel economy and freedom from smoke as the objectives. He introduced potatoes into the Bavarian diet; his recipes for thick soups became famous, and he also promoted the drinking of coffee as an alternative to alcohol. Faced with idle and ill-paid soldiers he set garrisons to work growing vegetables for their own use and for the workhouses, while around them the engineers practised building walls and fortifications. In Munich he constructed the English Garden (out of the elector's former deer park) for the recreation of the inhabitants.

His successes led to Thompson's appointment as minister of war, minister of police, major-general, chamberlain, and councillor of state, and in 1792 he was created Count Rumford. His stoves were the ancestor of the kitchen range, and he also invented a photometer, for comparing light intensities against a 'standard candle', and then an improved lamp for use in his institutions. With all these exertions his health broke down. He went to Italy for sixteen months, returning in 1793 to Munich amid public acclamation.

Improving the stove In the course of his duties as inspector-general of artillery Rumford oversaw experiments on cannon-boring, and found that enormous quantities of heat were generated by friction in the process. Heat, in the newest theory associated with Antoine Lavoisier's chemistry, was a weightless fluid element: Rumford's experiments convinced him of the truth of the older theory, that heat was the motion of the particles composing matter. Taking up his studies on convection he turned to the question of why water freezes from the top downwards. He found in a series of ingenious experiments that instead of contracting steadily as it cools, water reaches maximum density at about 41 °F. Investigating radiant heat he concluded that black is the best colour for stoves, or for clothes in warm climates.

In 1795, anxious to publish his work, Rumford obtained permission to go to London. There his private papers were taken in a daylight robbery which he attributed to political enemies, perhaps in search of information about Bavaria. He spent two happy years in Britain, advising on fireplaces and chimneys. His studies on convection currents enabled him to eliminate downdraughts by installing a narrow throat and a smokeshelf, notably at Lord Palmerston's house in Hanover Square. He was appalled at the waste of fuel indicated by the clouds of smoke which hung over London. In the spring of 1796 he visited Ireland with Lord Pelham, suggested improvements to hospitals and workhouses, and was much acclaimed. In 1796 he gave the Royal Society and the American Academy of Arts and Sciences in Boston £1000 each, the interest to be used for a gold and a silver medal to be presented every second year for research into light and heat and their applications. He was to be awarded the first medals by the Royal Society in 1802, but the American prizes were not awarded

until after his death, and a simplification of the conditions in 1829.

In August 1796 Rumford was urgently recalled to Munich, upon which French and Austrian armies were converging. Accompanied by his unsophisticated daughter, and travelling dangerously from Hamburg, he found himself commanding the Bavarian army. The elector withdrew to Mannheim, leaving Munich in the path of the opposing armies. Rumford persuaded the Austrians, who were first on the scene, to camp outside the city; he then urged the French that, since there were no Austrians within it, they should not attack the city. Confined with a garrison of 12,000 soldiers, and menaced by artillery, he patiently negotiated with the two generals until after two weeks the French withdrew following a defeat elsewhere, at which point the Austrians also retired. In a bloodless victory against the odds he had saved the city and Bavarian neutrality, and in the course of the siege he had invented a portable field stove and set up soup kitchens throughout the city. Rumford's cockiness and enormous prestige made him enemies who detested this foreign royal favourite, and in 1798 the elector sent him as ambassador to London.

London, Paris, and final years To Rumford's chagrin, and to the detriment of relations with Bavaria, George III refused to receive one of his own subjects as the representative of a foreign power. Deprived of diplomatic status, and despite his loyalism in the 1770s, Rumford sought a post in America, giving $2000 for poor children in Rumford. President John Adams contemplated making him superintendent of the military academy being set up at West Point, and eventually did propose that he become inspector-general of artillery—having been assured that Thompson would decline. In London Thompson now found a new opportunity to use his gifts for promoting science and invention; he was the prime mover in setting up the Royal Institution in Albemarle Street. This became a great centre for research and fashionable public lecturing in the sciences, providing the laboratory where Humphry Davy, Michael Faraday, John Tyndall, and others did their fundamental work.

This was not really what Rumford had anticipated, though Davy did preach and practice his gospel of applied science, promoting industrial revolution. Rumford represented to the upper classes 'the essence of scientific philanthropy' (Berman, 11) and the proposals for the institution were approved at a meeting at Sir Joseph Banks's house (where Rumford had improved the chimneys) on 7 March 1799. Its aim was to diffuse knowledge, and introduce useful inventions; Rumford hoped that manufacturers would exhibit new devices (notably stoves), and that there would be lectures, especially concerned with heating and cookery. A steam central-heating system, a handsome lecture theatre to his design (with a separate entrance to the gallery, for artisans), and a basement laboratory were installed in the Albemarle Street premises, and Rumford lived there for a time, and then in leafy

Brompton. He became sufficient of a celebrity to be lampooned by Peter Pindar (John Wolcot):

Now to a Yankey tunes the willing lyre:
Spite of th'ingratitude of COOKS and …
Strikes to COUNT RUMFORD'S *tuneful* name the strings,
Who from his fav'rite little RUMFORD came,
To build on *smoke* his fortune and his fame.
(Pindar, 2)

There are also Gillray cartoons, one of Rumford warming himself in front of his fireplace, and another in which he is administering laughing gas in a lecture. (Occupations in his later years included designing a carriage with wide wheels, and a special coffee-pot.)

Rumford's great success was in appointing Davy, but Rumford's high-handed and dogmatic ways provoked resistance so that when he returned to Bavaria to greet Duke Maximilian, now elector, he left London in September 1801 under something of a cloud. He returned via Paris, where he was fêted, and after packing up in London he left for France in May 1802, never to return. His wife had died on 19 January 1792, and in Paris Rumford had met and fallen in love with Lavoisier's wealthy widow, Marie Anne Paulze (1758–1836). He took her to Bavaria, where he recommended the transformation of the academy into another Royal Institution. They were married in Paris on 24 October 1805, but the marriage was not successful; his wife was far more sociable than Rumford, and they separated on 30 June 1809. Rumford lived thereafter at Auteuil, near Paris, where his daughter joined him from 1811. He died there on 21 August 1814, and was buried in the local cemetery.

Rumford's place in the history of science Rumford bequeathed money for a chair of physics at Harvard University, and £1000 and his apparatus to the Royal Institution. Like Davy's, Faraday's, and Tyndall's, Rumford's is a story of the social mobility which science could bring: the farm boy and shop assistant became the Massachusetts Yankee at the courts of Europe. He spoke well German, French, Spanish, and Italian; he played billiards, against himself, and enjoyed chess; he was a good draughtsman; indifferent to literature, sculpture, and painting he had a great taste for landscape gardening. His daughter, Countess Rumford, returned to America and died in 1852.

In his *éloge* at the Institut de France on 9 January 1815 Georges Cuvier emphasized the revolutions, warfare, and conflicting loyalties which had dominated Rumford's life, and was mildly embarrassed by his pursuit of honours and wealth. He stressed the value of Rumford's practical inventions, with their scientific basis. Later, to Tyndall lecturing at the Royal Institution in 1883, Rumford's researches on the nature of heat put him firmly in the tradition leading to James Joule, conservation of energy, and modern thermodynamics. To the Americans George Ellis, his first editor, and Sanborn Brown, whose edition is now the standard, Rumford's failure to take the right side at independence is perplexing; indeed, with his various loyalties went a certain capacity for opportunism and underhand dealings. Certainly nobody could have risen as he did, in a world of patronage, without great ambition,

charm, and determination; he seems to have preferred humanity in the mass to actual people, and had few friends. Brown places his researches on heat in their context, where the implications Tyndall saw were not perceived by Rumford or his contemporaries, and where the diversity and utility of his discoveries, based on research rather than empiricism, were most impressive. He has an important place in the origins of applied science.

DAVID KNIGHT

Sources *Collected works of Count Rumford*, ed. S. C. Brown, 5 vols. (1968–70) • S. C. Brown, *Count Rumford: physicist extraordinary* (1962) • J. Tyndall, 'Count Rumford, originator of the Royal Institution', *Notices of the Proceedings at the Meetings of the Members of the Royal Institution*, 10 (1882–4), 407–54 • *DSB* • P. Pindar [J. Wolcot], *A poetical epistle to Benjamin Count Rumford, knight of the white eagle* (1801) • G. Cuvier, *Recueil des éloges historiques lus dans les séances publiques de l'Institut Royal de France*, 3 vols. (1819–27) • *DNB* • *DAB* • M. Berman, *Social change and scientific organization: the Royal Institution, 1799–1844* (1978)

Archives American Academy of Arts and Sciences, Cambridge, Massachusetts, corresp. and papers • Harvard U., Houghton L., corresp. and papers • New Hampshire Historical Society, Concord, MSS • PRO, corresp., 30/55 • RIBA BAL, designs • Royal Institution of Great Britain, London, corresp. and papers • RS, papers • U. Birm. L., travel journal [copy] | BL, corresp. with Sir Joseph Banks, Add. MSS 8096–8099 • BL, corresp. with Cadell and Davies, Add. MS 34045 • Dartmouth College, Hanover, New Hampshire, letters to Lady Palmerston • Royal Institution of Great Britain, London, letters to William Savage

Likenesses T. Gainsborough, oils, *c.*1783, Harvard U., Fogg Art Museum [*see illus.*] • plaster medallion, 1796 (after J. Tassie), Scot. NPG • J. Gillray, group portrait, etching, 1802 (*Scientific researches*), NPG • C. Middlemist, stipple, pubd 1815 (after Mademoiselle Roth), NPG • J. Gillray, group portrait, etching (*The comforts of a Rumford stove*), Royal Institution of Great Britain, London • M. Kellerhoven, oils, Royal Institution of Great Britain, London • R. Peale, oils, American Academy of Arts and Sciences, Boston, Massachusetts • J. Rauschmayer, stipple (after G. Dillis), BM, NPG • J. F. Skill, J. Gilbert, W. Walker, and E. Walker, group portrait, pencil and wash (*Men of science living in 1807–08*), NPG • J. R. Smith, oils, RS

Wealth at death estate to daughter; also to fund professorship of physics at Harvard University

Thompson, Benjamin (1775/6–1816), playwright and translator, was the son of Benjamin Blaydes Thompson, a merchant and magistrate of Kingston upon Hull and Eastdale, Yorkshire, and his wife, Deborah Walter. Having 'received a liberal education' ('Some account', 4), he was intended for the law, but, finding it uncongenial, went instead to Hamburg as his father's agent. His leisure hours were spent translating August Kotzebue, whose vogue in England was just beginning and whom he came to know personally. Thompson's translation of *Menschenhass und Reue* ('Misanthropy and repentance') as *The Stranger* was selected for Drury Lane. Revised by R. B. Sheridan—who improved Thompson's stagecraft and contributed the songs—it was performed with John Philip Kemble in the title role on 24 March 1798. The third most successful hit of the season, it became a staple ingredient of the stage throughout London and the provinces for at least the next fifty years. When the play was first printed in 1800, Thompson was obliged to defend it from imputations that translations of *The Stranger* by competitors Schink and Papendick (both published 1798) were the basis of the stage production. After Thompson's death Sheridan, with less than justice, reportedly claimed *The Stranger*, 'as it is acted', as essentially his work, not Thompson's (*Journal of Thomas Moore*, 2.754). It was reprinted, correctly under Thompson's name, in virtually every play series of the century; and its overwhelming success earned him the sobriquet 'Stranger Thompson'. None of Thompson's other translations of Kotzebue was ever performed, but they were printed collectively (3 vols., 1801) and also issued, with unacted translations of Schiller, Babo, Goethe, Iffland, Lessing, Reitzenstein, and Schroeder, as *The German Theatre* (6 vols., 1801 etc.). The melodrama *Rokeby, or, The Buccaneer's Revenge*, based on Scott's poem, was printed in Dublin (1814).

After Thompson's marriage at Chesterfield on 23 May 1799 to Jane (*bap.* 1775), the youngest daughter of the Revd John Bourne, rector of Sutton-cum-Duckworth and South Wingfield, Derbyshire, the couple settled in Arnold, Nottingham. In the summer of 1808 Thompson's theatrical friends Tom Dibdin and Charles Farley visited and spent 'a most delightful week among some of the leading families of the town and neighbourhood' (Dibdin, 1.419). At this time Thompson published his only novel, *The Florentines* (1808). About 1810 Thompson and his family settled in London, where he supplemented his income by editing and theatrical reviewing. At his death he was negotiating to assist Dibdin in his new management venture at the Surrey Theatre.

Outside literature Thompson had a keen interest in agriculture (in which he speculated unwisely), especially sheep-farming. For a short period, until ill health forced his retirement, he was secretary to the Merino Society and translated, from the French of C. P. Lasteyrie, a treatise on the introduction of merinos into Europe and the Cape of Good Hope (1810).

Thompson's two other dramas, performed at Drury Lane, failed badly: an operatic drama, *Godolphin, or, The Lion of the North* (12 October 1812), a historical piece set in Nottingham, and the romance, *Oberon's Oath* (21 May 1816), adapted from Christophe-Martin Wieland. Despite Thompson's high hopes for the latter, it fell victim to an organized claque. According to *The Times*, 'a violent, and, as it appears to us, a most unprovoked and offensive effort, was made by some party, who were scattered through the house, to damn this unpretending production, without the least regard to its actual merits' (23 May). This disappointment, coupled with depression resulting from an earlier illness, is said to have caused Thompson's death from an apoplectic fit at his house in Blackfriars Road, London, on 26 May 1816; he was buried on the 31st. Immediately a public appeal was launched by means of printed bills beseeching 'the benevolence of the public' (Royal Literary Fund archive) towards his distressed widow and six children, the youngest, a girl aged three, being nearly blind. Jane Thompson's application to the Literary Fund, supported by a recommendation from the bookseller–publisher Henry Colburn, produced £25; and a subscription edition of *Oberon's Oath* attracted over 350 subscribers, including Lady Caroline Lamb and old friends like Tom and Charles Dibdin, Grimaldi, and Edmund Kean. In the prefatory memoir Thompson is described as strict in manners but 'an affectionate husband, and a tender father; sincere in his friendship, and scrupulously honourable in all his engagements' ('Some account', 12).

JOHN RUSSELL STEPHENS

Sources 'Some account of the late Mr Benjamin Thompson', B. Thompson, *Oberon's oath* (1816), prefaced to, [3]–14 · 24 June 1816, Royal Literary Fund archive, case 350 · C. Price, 'Sheridan at work on *The stranger*', *Neuphilologische Mitteilungen*, 73 (1972) · J. R. Stephens, 'David Copperfield and *The stranger*: "a Doctors' Commons sort of play"', *The Dickensian* [forthcoming] · C. B. Hogan, ed., *The London stage, 1660–1800*, pt 5: 1776–1800 (1968) · *The journal of Thomas Moore*, ed. W. S. Dowden, 2 (1984) · A. Nicoll, *Early nineteenth century drama, 1800–1850*, 2nd edn (1955), vol. 4 of *A history of English drama, 1660–1900* (1952–9) · T. Dibdin, *The reminiscences of Thomas Dibdin*, 2 vols. (1827) · *The letters of Richard Brinsley Sheridan*, ed. C. Price, 3 vols. (1966) · *The Times* (23 May 1816) · IGI · parish records, St Mary's Hull
Archives Hunt. L., Larpent collection, licensing copies of the staged plays
Likenesses J. R. Smith, mezzotint, pubd 1799, BM

Thompson, Sir Charles, first baronet (*c*.1740–1799), naval officer and politician, is thought to have been the illegitimate son of Norborne Berkeley, later Baron Botetourt (1717?–1770), of Stoke Gifford, Gloucestershire, governor of Virginia. He first went to sea in a merchant ship but in 1755, shortly before the outbreak of the Seven Years' War, he entered the navy on the *Nassau*. Between 1755 and December 1760 he served successively in the *Nassau*, in the *Prince Frederick*, and with Captain Samuel Barrington in the *Achilles*. On 16 January 1761, having passed his lieutenant's examination, he was commissioned fifth lieutenant of the *Arrogant*, in which he served first in the channel and then in the Mediterranean. The *Arrogant* was paid off at the peace, and in August 1763 Thompson joined the sloop *Cygnet*, in which he served on the North American station until July 1768 when the *Cygnet* was sold out of the navy in South Carolina; Thompson, with the other officers, was left to find his own passage to England, for which he was later paid £39 0s. 6d.

In May 1770 Thompson was appointed first lieutenant of the *Salisbury*, again on the North American station, and in February 1771 he was promoted by Commodore James Gambier to command the sloop *Senegal*. Three months later he was appointed acting captain of the *Mermaid*, which he took to England in December 1771. The Admiralty refused to confirm this last commission, but promoted him to captain's rank on 7 March 1772, and appointed him to the *Chatham*, going out to the West Indies with the flag of Vice-Admiral William Parry. From the *Chatham* he was moved into the frigate *Crescent*, before returning to England in 1774. He was appointed to the frigate *Boreas* in 1775, and early in 1776 was sent to Jamaica, where he captured the French ship *Le Compas* (20 guns). He returned to England with a convoy of merchant ships in October 1777, and was again sent out to the West Indies. There in 1780 he began a long-running feud with Sir John Laforey following Laforey's appointment as commissioner of Antigua yard.

Thompson's refusal to recognize this authority led to animosity; this flared up again fifteen years later when Laforey was commander-in-chief at the Leeward Islands. The later confrontation provided Lord Spencer with a reason for sending Laforey home, an act which created alarm in the Admiralty and led to the resignation of Sir Charles Middleton.

Towards the end of 1780 Thompson was moved by Sir George Rodney into the *Alcide* (74 guns). He commanded the *Alcide* in the action off the Chesapeake on 5 September 1781, with Sir Samuel Hood at St Kitts in January 1782, and in the battle of the Saints on 12 April 1782. At the end of the American War of Independence he brought the *Alcide* to England, and later in 1783 he married Jane Selby, daughter and heir of Robert Selby of Bonington, near Edinburgh. They subsequently raised five children. In 1787 he commanded the *Edgar* at Portsmouth, and during the crisis of the Spanish armament in 1790 he was given command of the *Elephant*.

In 1793 on the outbreak of the war with revolutionary France, Thompson was appointed to the *Vengeance* and was attached to the expedition against French possessions in the West Indies led by Sir John Jervis and Lieutenant-General Sir Charles Grey. There, in 1794, as commodore, he took part in the capture of Martinique where he directed the boat attacks against Fort Royal, and Guadeloupe. On 12 April 1794 he was promoted rear-admiral of the blue; he returned to England in 1795 with his flag in the *Vanguard*, and on 1 June he was promoted vice-admiral.

In 1796 Thompson was elected MP for Monmouth and, with his flag in the *London*, he was given command of a detached squadron blockading the French coast off Brest. Towards the close of the year he was sent out to the Mediterranean in the *Britannia*, and was second in command at the battle of Cape St Vincent in February 1797. Thompson's disregard of Jervis's signal to tack to counter a Spanish move to threaten the British nearly lost the battle. Jervis was angered by the failure to act but chose not to make it a public issue. Later in 1797 Thompson was made a baronet for his contribution to the battle. He continued with the fleet for some months, but again came into conflict with Jervis (now Lord St Vincent) when the latter insisted on hanging four mutineers on the Sabbath (Sunday 9 July 1797). St Vincent used the affair as a suitable pretext to write to the Admiralty insisting on Thompson's removal.

Thompson was accordingly recalled, and was appointed to a command in the fleet off Brest. He held this during 1798, but his health had for some time been failing, and early in the following year he was obliged to strike his flag and go on shore. He died at Fareham on 17 March 1799. On 16 April St Vincent wrote of Thompson as a 'gallant man, but the most timid officer', and drew attention to his having 'the manner of a rough seaman' which Thompson cultivated by his habit of dressing casually in a sailor's frock and straw hat (Brenton, 2.7).

J. K. LAUGHTON, rev. TOM WAREHAM

Sources J. Ralfe, *The naval biography of Great Britain*, 2 (1828), 3 · W. James, *The naval history of Great Britain, from the declaration of war by France in 1793 to the accession of George IV*, [8th edn], 6 vols. (1902) · D. Syrett and R. L. DiNardo, *The commissioned sea officers of the Royal Navy, 1660–1815*, rev. edn, Occasional Publications of the Navy RS, 1 (1994) · C. G. Pitcairn Jones, 'List of commissioned sea officers of the Royal Navy, 1660–1815', NMM, NMM 359 (42) (083.81) GRE · A. Aspinall, 'Thompson, Charles', HoP, *Commons, 1790–1820* · *Debrett's Peerage* (1834) · *The dispatches and letters of Vice-Admiral Lord Viscount Nelson*, ed. N. H. Nicolas, 7 vols. (1844–6); repr. (1997–8), vol. 2 · E. P. Brenton, *The naval history of Great Britain, from the year 1783 to 1836*, 2 vols. (1837) · M. A. J. Palmer, 'Sir John's victory: the battle of Cape St Vincent reconsidered', *Mariner's Mirror*, 77 (1991), 31–46 · C. White, *Nelson's year of destiny: Cape St Vincent and Santa Cruz de Tenerife* (1998)

Archives NMM, corresp. and papers

Likenesses T. Gainsborough, oils, 1774, Tate collection · Worthington and Parker, group portrait, line engraving, pubd 1803 (after *Naval Victories* by R. Smirke; *Commemoration of the 14th February 1797*), BM, NPG

Thompson, Charles (1791–1843). *See under* Thompson, John (1785–1866).

Thompson, Charles John Samuel (1862–1943), medical historian and museum curator, was born in Liverpool on 27 August 1862, the second son of John Thompson (1820–1900), pharmaceutical chemist, and his wife, Ann Amelia Miners (b. 1825). His father, a native of Sheffield, had settled in Liverpool in 1840 and was active in local politics and as a local historian. Charles was educated at the Liverpool Institute and, as his elder brother, Epworth, had entered the church, followed his father's wishes and studied pharmacy as an external student at Liverpool University College. He qualified with the Pharmaceutical Society as a chemist and druggist on 17 December 1885 but never practised, embarking instead on a career as a pharmaceutical writer and journalist. His first appearance in print was a privately printed pamphlet *A Chapelet of Verie Presyous Flowers*, produced in 1883. He obtained a PhD degree from an American university.

Apart from articles in the professional press, Thompson produced several practical handbooks, beginning with *Practical Dispensing* (1891); the most successful was *The Chemist's Compendium* (1896), which reached its seventh edition in 1933. In 1893 Thompson married Ethel May Tindall, daughter of the Revd Witt Tindall; they had two sons, one of whom achieved distinction as the film director Paul *Rotha, and two daughters.

Thompson's publications led to his employment on historical research projects for Henry S. Wellcome, proprietor of Burroughs Wellcome & Co., and at the end of 1897 he is first recorded as purchasing books and manuscripts for Wellcome's library, a task which engaged him for the next quarter-century. He became a full-time employee in January 1900, with duties 'difficult to define … inasmuch as they will be very varied in connection with literary and other work' (Burroughs Wellcome & Co., letter-book 12, 18 Dec 1899). After his father's death in 1900 Thompson moved to London; he settled at Harrow about 1906. About 1903, in addition to collecting library materials, he was put in charge of assembling artefacts for what became the Wellcome Historical Medical Museum. He co-ordinated the work of various employees and agents and was himself a collector both in Britain and Europe, travelling as far as Constantinople. Following Henry Wellcome's obsession with secrecy he used the pseudonyms Treve and Epworth.

Thompson continued to write, producing *The Mystery and Romance of Alchemy and Pharmacy* (1897) and *Poison Romances and Poison Mysteries* (1899). For *Zorastro, a Romance* (1899) he adopted the pseudonym Creswick J. Thompson (the artist Thomas Creswick (1801–1869) was a distant relation), and he followed it with *The Love-Letters of a Lady of Quality* (1904) as Rupert Lisle, and with other novels as Treve Roscoe. For Burroughs Wellcome he compiled anonymously more than a dozen illustrated historical booklets for distribution at medical congresses, including *Antient Cymric Medicine* (1903), *Anaesthetics, Antient and Modern* (1907), *Medicine in Antient Erin* (1909), *The Evolution of Urine Analysis* (1911), and *The History of Inoculation and Vaccination* (1913). The Wellcome Museum was established in Wigmore Street, London, in 1911 and was opened on 29 June 1913 as an adjunct to the 17th International Congress of Medicine. Thompson became curator, subordinate to Henry Wellcome as director. He became an active member of the historical section of the Royal Society of Medicine, contributing papers and exhibiting objects from the museum at meetings, and consolidated his reputation as a historian.

During the First World War Thompson organized a Red Cross convalescent home at Harrow on the Hill, eventually styled Holmleigh auxiliary military hospital, acting as commandant, with his wife as matron and quartermaster, assisted by their daughter Caireen. The hospital treated nearly 1000 patients, as described in Thompson's *Story of Holmleigh Auxiliary Military Hospital* (1919). He was appointed MBE in 1920.

After the war the development of the Wellcome Museum continued. Thompson regularly attended the International Congresses of the History of Medicine, the third of which was held in London in 1922, with the Wellcome Museum as its headquarters. In 1922 he was awarded honorary membership of the Accademia di Agricoltura and Accademia di Medicina of Turin. His next book, *Chronologia medica*, written in collaboration with Sir D'Arcy Power, appeared in 1923, and it was pointed out that his acceptance of royalties was in breach of his Wellcome contract. (This had been made clear when the contract was negotiated in 1899.) He agreed to sign his rights over to the museum, but had not done so by November 1925 (perhaps because he had received no payments), at which point Wellcome insisted on his resignation. His salary was continued for six months, after which he formally retired on pension, never to be forgiven by Wellcome. The acrimonious correspondence shows that Thompson had, in various ways, been behaving as a law unto himself more than was wise with a demanding employer. Power and Sir Arthur Keith sympathized with Thompson but were unwilling to provoke a breach with Wellcome.

Thompson now turned his energy again to writing, producing a steady stream of popular books. Most were on medico-historical subjects, such as *The Mystery and Lure of Perfume* (1927), *The Quacks of Old London* (1928), *The Mystery and Art of the Apothecary* (1929), and *The Lure and Romance of Alchemy* (1932), but his interests also encompassed *The Witchery of Jane Shore* (1933) and *Dancing* (1941) for Collins's Peacock Colour Books. Thompson continued to attend international conferences and was appointed an officer of the order of St John in 1926; he was promoted commander in 1936. About 1927 he moved to the country, first to Watford and then to Cuddington near Aylesbury, Buckinghamshire.

In 1927 Sir Arthur Keith arranged Thompson's appointment as honorary curator of the historical collections of the Royal College of Surgeons. This gave Thompson a new focus for his energies, and he produced *A Guide to the Surgical Instruments and Objects* (1929) and a series of articles on surgical instruments in the *British Journal of Surgery* (1937–9). The destruction of much of the collection by bombing in May 1941 led Thompson to publish his articles in book form as *The History and Evolution of Surgical Instruments* (1942). Although many of the instruments were salvaged, Thompson's post was inevitably discontinued in July 1942. He died at Thame, Oxfordshire, on 14 July 1943, and was buried at Hartwell, Buckinghamshire. His wife survived him. His last book, *Magic and Healing*, edited by his children John and Caireen, appeared in 1947.

JOHN SYMONS

Sources L. G. Matthews, 'C. J. S. Thompson memorabilia', *Pharmaceutical Journal*, 223 (1979), 658–9 · *The Lancet* (24 July 1943), 108–9 · *BMJ* (31 July 1943), 153 · *Chemist and Druggist* (7 Aug 1943), 143 · *WWW* · J. Symons, *Wellcome Institute for the History of Medicine: a short history* (1993)
Archives Bucks. RLSS, historical notes relating to Cuddington · Royal Pharmaceutical Society, London, corresp. and MSS · Wellcome L., notes, letters, publications, and MSS · Wellcome L., corresp., personal papers, and reports relating to the Wellcome Historical Medical Museum
Likenesses photograph, Wellcome L. · photograph (late in life), Wellcome L.
Wealth at death £1801 7s. 4d.: probate, 3 Sept 1943, *CGPLA Eng. & Wales*

Thompson, Charles Thurston (1816–1868), photographer, was born on 28 July 1816, the second son of the wood-engraver John *Thompson (1785–1866) and his wife, Harriott Eaton. The outstanding feature of Thompson's career is that it was almost exclusively as an official photographer of works of art within the South Kensington Museum in London, the showcase of the Department of Science and Art. As such his career was inextricably linked with that of his friend Henry Cole, one of the key figures in the Victorian art world: Thompson was, in many respects, an acolyte to Cole's achievements.

Evidence suggests that Thompson initially followed his father's profession, and he is known to have produced engravings, some based on the designs of the artist John Thurston, after whom he may well have been given his second name. By early 1844 Thompson and Cole were working together on the sale of casts of the wooden blocks of the woodcut entitled the *Small Passion*, then attributed to Albrecht Dürer, which was housed in the print room of the British Museum. These casts may subsequently have been marketed by Cole's friend the art historian and publisher Joseph Cundall, who was a prominent figure in the promotion of photography in mid-Victorian England.

Comparatively little is known about Thompson's photographic career, and when it began, though the Great Exhibition of 1851 was the defining moment. In addition to his role as superintendent of class XXVI, furniture, and class XVIII, animal manufactures, he was placed in charge of all the photographic arrangements. Through this position he met the Paris-domiciled English photographer Robert Bingham (1825–1870), who printed many of the photographs which appeared in the photographically illustrated special presentation copies of the *Reports by the Juries*. Bingham subsequently taught Thompson and in 1855 the two worked together to document the Paris Universal Exhibition on behalf of the Department of Science and Art.

Thompson was also intimately involved in the international exhibitions in London in 1862 and Paris in 1867. Commissioned to carry out both official and private photography and to record the construction of the 1862 building, he found himself criticized for having a conflict of interests in that he was not only a juror of class XIV photographs but also an exhibitor. For the Paris 1867 exhibition he helped select photographs for exhibition; his own exhibits, *Reproductions and Views in Spain and Portugal*, won him a silver medal. From 1853, and his first commission to photograph a loan exhibition of furniture at Gore House, London, until his death in 1868, he was the *de facto* official photographer of the Department of Science and Art and the South Kensington Museum. In July 1856 he was appointed superintendent of photography, though his first annual retainer seems to have been agreed only in 1859.

Thompson's photographic career within the Department of Science and Art was closely linked with the military through the Royal Engineers, with whom he had worked at the Great Exhibition of 1851. By 1853 sappers were being used at South Kensington as part of the unofficial yet permanent photographic facilities. This heavily subsidized photographic studio annoyed contemporary commercial photographers. Thompson gave photographic training to a stream of sappers and was paid 10 guineas when each soldier was granted a 'certificate of competency'. As a direct result of this connection with the Royal Engineers, he travelled in 1854 and 1856 to northern France to photograph the military encampments of the French army. He married on 13 January 1857 Charlotte Jane Bond, daughter of William Bond; the couple had one daughter.

On his death it was estimated that Thompson had taken some 10,000 negatives of works of art. His photographs were widely disseminated and appeared in over twenty photographically illustrated publications, including catalogues of the South Kensington Museum. He documented the collections of the museum and temporary exhibitions held there; venturing further afield, he recorded works by

Raphael for the project initiated by Prince Albert to document the artist's entire work. In 1858 he documented the Raphael cartoons at Hampton Court and copies of these photographs, available in five sizes, sold in significant numbers. In 1866 he undertook one of his most ambitious photographic projects when he travelled abroad for the Department of Science and Art and photographed in France, Spain, and Portugal. Selections of his Iberian images were published in 1868, on behalf of the Department of Science and Art, by the Arundel Society in volumes of the photographically illustrated series *Examples of Art Workmanship of Various Ages and Countries*.

Thompson carried out a limited amount of freelance commercial photography, selling photographs directly from a succession of private addresses in the Kensington area. In 1863 he was employed on several occasions by the Belgian art dealer Ernest Gambart to photograph paintings which Gambart was selling. In the following year he briefly collaborated with the amateur photographer Clementina, Viscountess Hawarden, in taking portraits.

Described by contemporaries as having 'a varied art culture [and] possessing a most discriminating taste and judgement' (*Photographic News*, 24 Jan 1868, 38), Thompson was 'modest and unassuming' (*Journal of the Society of Arts*, 7 Feb 1868, 236) and did not actively court fame. He wrote neither books nor manuals on photography, and, although he exhibited photographs regularly in both national and international exhibitions, he was not a founder member of the Photographic Society of London; however, towards the end of his life he was elected a council member. Charles Thurston Thompson died on 20 January 1868 in the Hotel Meyerbeer, Paris, and was buried on 25 January at Kensal Green cemetery, London.

ANTHONY J. HAMBER

Sources A. J. Hamber, 'A higher branch of the art': photographing the fine arts in England, 1839–1880 (1996) · L. Fontanella, *Charles Thurston Thompson* (1996) · M. Haworth-Booth, *Photography: an independent art* (1997) · *Photographic News* (24 Jan 1868), 38 · *Journal of the Society of Arts*, 16 (1867–8), 236 · photograph register, V&A NAL, Cole papers · photograph register, V&A, department of prints and drawings · m. cert.

Archives V&A | V&A, Henry Cole diaries

Likenesses double portrait, photograph (with his wife), V&A

Wealth at death under £600: administration, 11 March 1868, CGPLA Eng. & Wales

Thompson, D'Arcy Wentworth (1829–1902), classical scholar, elder son of John Skelton Thompson, shipmaster, and his wife, Mary Mitchell, both of Maryport, Cumberland, was born at sea on board his father's sailing ship *Georgiana*, off Van Diemen's Land, on 18 April 1829. Nearly all Thompson's male relatives for generations had followed the sea. After twelve years (1835–47) at Christ's Hospital, London, he matriculated from Trinity College, Cambridge, at Michaelmas 1848, afterwards migrating to Pembroke College. At Cambridge he read chiefly with Augustus Arthur Vansittart and with Joseph Barber (afterwards Bishop) Lightfoot, both of Trinity; his closest friends were James Lemprière Hammond of Trinity and Peter Guthrie Tait of Peterhouse. Thompson won the Sir William Browne medal for a Latin ode in 1849, and was

D'Arcy Wentworth Thompson (1829–1902), by unknown engraver (after Lionel Heath)

the ancient languages, a protest against the then narrow education of women, and a passionate defence of the dignity of the schoolmaster's calling. Some skilful translations into Homeric Greek, chiefly of Tennyson, are included. He also produced numerous reviews, translations, and original poems in various newspapers and periodicals. Three sets of short essays were published in 1865 as *Wayside Thoughts of an Asophophilosopher*. For his eldest son in childhood Thompson wrote *Nursery Nonsense, or, Rhymes without Reason* (1863–4) and *Fun and Earnest, or, Rhymes with Reason* (1865). These books, illustrated by Charles H. Bennett, were very popular in their time.

D'A. W. THOMPSON, *rev.* RICHARD SMAIL

Sources *Galway Express* (1 Feb 1902) · G. A. T. Allan, *Christ's Hospital exhibitioners to the universities of Oxford and Cambridge, 1566–1923* (1924) · Venn, *Alum. Cant.* · D. W. Thompson, *Day dreams of a schoolmaster* (1864) · T. P. [T. P. O'Connor], 'Books that have influenced me: the story of my inner life', *T. P.'s Weekly* (17 June 1904), 793–4 · *Mainly About People* (8 Feb 1902) [commonly known as 'M. A. P.']

Likenesses engraving (after L. Heath), repro. in Thompson, *Day dreams* [*see illus.*]

Wealth at death £1032 15s. (in England): Irish probate sealed in England, 6 March 1902, *CGPLA Eng. & Wales*

Thompson, Sir D'Arcy Wentworth (1860–1948), zoologist and classical scholar, was born at 3 Brandon Street, Edinburgh, on 2 May 1860, the only son of D'Arcy Wentworth *Thompson (1829–1902), then a classical master at the Edinburgh Academy, and his first wife, Fanny (1838–1860), daughter of Joseph *Gamgee, veterinary surgeon. His mother died when he was born, and when, in 1863, his father was appointed professor of Greek at Queen's College, Galway, the young D'Arcy was left in charge of an aunt in the home of his maternal grandfather. It was to his grandfather that he was accustomed to attribute the first awakening of his interest in biology. He was educated at Edinburgh Academy (1870–77) and, after three years as a medical student at Edinburgh University where he came under the influence of Sir C. Wyville Thomson, then just returned from the *Challenger* expedition, he went to Trinity College, Cambridge, in 1880. There he joined the talented group of young men gathered round Michael Foster and F. M. Balfour, who were then laying the foundations of the modern Cambridge school of biology. He was awarded firsts in both parts of the natural sciences tripos (1882, 1883), and spent a year as demonstrator in physiology under Foster. In 1884 he was appointed professor of biology (later altered to natural history) in the recently founded University College in Dundee. Several chairs were being filled at that time. He recounted how he applied for three of them—biology, Greek, and mathematics—and was offered his choice. 'So,' he said, 'I chose biology because it was the one I knew least about.' When, in 1897, the college was incorporated in the University of St Andrews he became a member of the senate in the university and in 1917, on the retirement of W. C. M'Intosh, he was translated to the senior chair of natural history in the United College of the university, and thenceforward made his home in St Andrews.

placed sixth in the first class in the classical tripos of 1852, being bracketed with William Jackson Brodribb. After graduating BA in 1852 Thompson became a classics master in the Edinburgh Academy. Among his pupils there, in 1861–2, was R. L. Stevenson, who commemorated the fact in a song entitled 'Their Laureate to an Academy Class Dinner Club' and beginning 'Dear Thampson class'. In 1863, after twelve years' service, Thompson left the school for the chair of Greek in Queen's College, Galway, where T. P. O'Connor was his pupil. In 1867 he delivered the Lowell lectures at Boston. These lectures, which dealt with school and college memories and with the practice and philosophy of education, were published as *Wayside Thoughts* in 1868.

Thompson was twice married: first in Edinburgh in 1859 to Fanny (1838–1860), daughter of Joseph Gamgee and sister of Joseph Sampson *Gamgee, with whom he had one son, D'Arcy Wentworth *Thompson; and second in Dublin in 1866 to Amy, daughter of William B. Drury of Boden Park, co. Dublin, with whom he had two sons and four daughters. He died at his home, 1 The Crescent, Galway, on 25 January 1902, a few hours after lecturing on Thucydides.

Thompson's reputation mainly rested on his *Day Dreams of a Schoolmaster* (1864–5), a record of his schooldays at 'St Edward's', and of his teaching years at the 'Schola Nova' of 'dear Dunedin'. Interwoven with a thread of autobiography, the book is a plea for the sympathetic teaching of

While at Dundee D'Arcy Thompson devoted much attention to building up a teaching museum of zoology which, with the help of the last of the Dundee whalers, became very rich in specimens from the Arctic Seas. In 1896 and again in 1897 he visited the Pribylov Islands as a member of the British–American commission of inquiry on the fur seal fishery in the Bering Sea, and in the latter year he also represented the British government at the international conference on the subject at Washington. For his services on these occasions he was appointed CB in 1898. In that year he was also made a member of the fishery board for Scotland, a position which he held until the supersession of the board in 1939. In 1901 D'Arcy Thompson married Ada Maureen (d. 1949), daughter of William B. Drury, solicitor of Dublin; there were three daughters of the marriage. In 1902 he became one of the British representatives on the newly formed International Council for the Exploration of the Sea. To the official publications of this and many other bodies he contributed reports and papers on fishery statistics, oceanography, and other matters. He also wrote many papers and articles on other subjects. A large number of these were on matters of classical scholarship, especially on the natural history of ancient writers. His major works in this field were *A Glossary of Greek Birds* (1895; 2nd edn, 1936), an annotated translation of Aristotle's *Historia animalium* (1910), and *A Glossary of Greek Fishes* (1945).

The biological work for which D'Arcy Thompson is best-known is his book *On Growth and Form* (1917; rev. 2nd edn, 1942) which brought together classical and modern material. Of this book Sir Peter Medawar wrote that it was

> beyond comparison the finest work of literature in all the annals of science that have been recorded in the English tongue. There is a combination here of elegance of style with perfect, absolutely unfailing clarity, that has never to my knowledge been surpassed. (p. 232)

It dealt with the causes of the shapes of organisms and their structures. In *On Growth and Form* D'Arcy Thompson first developed the notion that biological structures must conform to the laws of physics, expressible in mathematical form; physics must come before function in determining shape. He showed, for example, that, as strengths of bones and muscles depend on their cross-sectional areas, while weight depends on volume, larger animals, to support themselves, must have proportionately thicker legs. The idea that the laws of physics profoundly influence biological structures came to permeate all of biology. However, D'Arcy Thompson realized that physics was not alone responsible for determining biological structure, and in the second edition he wrote, 'the twofold problem of accumulated inheritance, and of perfect structural adaptation, confronts us once again and passes all our understanding'.

D'Arcy Thompson did no experimental work, and made no attempt to test his ideas. This was largely because the mathematical calculations required were too complex to be made with the aids to calculation then available. His work founded no school of followers to extend it, though his ideas were applied in many diverse fields, as was shown by a volume of essays by a group of biologists on

the occasion of his completing sixty years as a professor (W. E. Le Gros Clark and P. B. Medawar, eds., *Essays on Growth and Form*, 1945).

In the later years of his long life D'Arcy Thompson received many honours from universities and other learned bodies ranging from Aberdeen to Johannesburg, and from Boston (USA) to Delhi. He was elected fellow of the Royal Society of Edinburgh in 1885 and was its president in 1934–9. He was elected FRS in 1916, was a vice-president in 1931–3, and received the Darwin medal in 1946. The Linnean Society awarded him the Linnean gold medal in 1938. He was president of the Classical Association in 1929, and of the Scottish Royal Geographical Society from 1942. He was knighted in 1937.

D'Arcy Thompson was a man of very distinguished presence, a ready and polished speaker, whose lectures and addresses displayed a remarkable range of interests and knowledge. He loved teaching, and his lectures were invariably fascinating. He taught to the very last, for even in his final illness he gathered his honours students in his sick-room for memorable discussions. He died at his home, 44 South Street, St Andrews, on 21 June 1948; his widow died the following year.

W. T. CALMAN, rev. D. S. FALCONER

Sources R. D'Arcy Thompson, *D'Arcy Wentworth Thompson: the scholar-naturalist, 1860–1948* (1958) · C. Dobell, *Obits. FRS*, 6 (1948–9), 599–617 · P. B. Medawar, postscript, in R. D'Arcy Thompson, *D'Arcy Wentworth Thompson: the scholar-naturalist, 1860–1948* (1958), 219–33; repr. in *The art of the soluble* (1967), 21–35 · S. J. Gould, 'D'Arcy Thompson and the science of form', *Topics in the philosophy of biology*, ed. M. Greene and E. Mendelsohn (1976), 66–97 · W. E. Le Gros Clark and P. B. Medawar, eds., *Essays on growth and form* (1945) [incl. comprehensive bibliography to 1944] · personal knowledge (2004) · *CGPLA Eng. & Wales* (1948)

Archives Museum of Scotland, Edinburgh, corresp. · U. St Andr. L., corresp. and papers · University of Dundee, corresp. and papers | BL, letters to W. E. Crum, Add. MS 45689 · Elgin Museum, Elgin, letters to Dr George Gordon · Rice University, Houston, Texas, corresp. with Sir Julian Huxley · U. St Andr. L., letters to D. R. R. Burt

Likenesses W. Stoneman, photograph, 1933, NPG · D. S. Ewart, oils, Royal Society of Edinburgh · D. S. Ewart, oils, U. St Andr., zoological department · A. Forrest, bronze head, U. St Andr. L.

Wealth at death £12,965 12s. 10d.: confirmation, 7 Oct 1948, *CCI*

Thompson, Dorothy Evelyn (1888–1961), mountaineer, was born on 29 May 1888 at 17 Colville Mansions, Kensington, London, one of two daughters and a son of Frederick Charles Thompson (d. 1919), a civil servant in the India Office, and his wife, Eleanor Frances, *née* Wilson. With parents who were keen hill walkers, she first climbed in Perthshire during family holidays. On holiday in Wasdale, before the First World War, she met some serious rock climbers, and made friendships that led to her joining the Fell and Rock Climbing Club in 1919. During the war she joined the staff of a relief fund, and afterwards was for many years a secretary at the School of Oriental Studies in Bloomsbury.

Dorothy Thompson was a frequent attender at the Fell and Rock Climbing Club's Easter meets, and went on to tackle climbs in Corsica and the Pyrenees before venturing into the Alps in 1920. There she met Joseph Georges, known as 'Le Skieur', climbed with him for many seasons thereafter, and went ski-mountaineering from 1933. In 1929 she was the first woman to ascend Mont Blanc by Brouillard Ridge and in 1934 she scaled the same peak by the Aiguille de Bionassay, pioneering the return by Peuteret Ridge, the only time it had been descended. She and Georges were an ideal climbing pair and led several parties in the Alps. A small person with a keen sense of humour, she concealed behind a very quiet exterior an indomitable will and purpose. She often led on glaciers, and as she was small and light her friends felt that it would have been easy to retrieve her if she fell into a crevasse.

Thompson never married; during the 1920s she lived with her mother at Porchester Square, Paddington. Subsequently she moved to Sussex, where she could indulge her love of gardening and birds. She had begun working on a book of climbing reminiscences and completed it shortly after the Second World War. This was not a good time to find a publisher, and eventually she decided to have it published privately. By this time she was suffering from heart trouble and its attendant restrictions. She died at her home, Donnithorne, Station Road, Heathfield, Sussex, on 2 December 1961 and was cremated in Eastbourne. Her book *Climbing with Joseph Georges* (1962) was seen into print with the help of the Ladies' Alpine Club and her friends. It captured the spirit of adventure during the inter-war years, when women were first accepted as equal partners with men, willing to share the risks and enjoyment of challenging the highest peaks.   ANITA McCONNELL

Sources D. L. Pilkington, 'In memoriam: Dorothy Thompson, 1915–1961', *Journal, Fell and Rock Climbing Club*, 19 (1960–62), 281–2 · D. E. P. Richards, 'In memoriam: Dorothy E. Thompson, 1888–1961', *Ladies' Alpine Club Journal* (1962), 49 · T. S. Blakeney, 'Review: Climbing with Joseph Georges (1962)', *Alpine Journal*, 68 (1963), 145–6 · *Sussex Express and County Herald* (8 Dec 1961), 7d · b. cert. · d. cert.
Likenesses photograph, repro. in Richards, 'In memoriam', 49
Wealth at death £9962 18s. 6d.: probate, 2 Feb 1962, CGPLA Eng. & Wales

Thompson, Edith [*pseud.* Evelyn Todd] (1848–1929), historian and lexicographer, was born on 16 May 1848 in Greenwich, the eldest of the two surviving daughters (at least one other daughter and one son died young) of Thomas Perronet Edward Thompson (1813–1904), a judge, and his wife, Ellen Mary James (1821–1911), daughter of Edward James of Totnes. Her father was educated at Queens' College, Cambridge, and Lincoln's Inn. Thompson was probably educated at home in Blackheath, London. In 1867 or 1868 she met Edward Augustus Freeman (1823–1892) and they formed a lifelong friendship based on overlapping intellectual interests. His patronage launched her on a publishing career. In 1869 he asked her to review Madame Guizot de Witt's *The Lady of Latham* for the *Saturday Review* and commented on its arrival 'I did not expect anything so good, even from you' (Brynmor Jones Library, MS DX/9/11). In 1870 he asked her to contribute to the Macmillan Historical Course for Schools, and this led to *History of England* (1872), the work for which she is largely remembered.

Thompson moved from London to Gateacre, Liverpool,

in 1872, when her father was made judge of the Liverpool county court. In the next decade she became a major contributor to the *Saturday Review*, writing anonymous articles such as 'The Sicilian Vespers' in 1882 and succeeding Freeman as reviewer of most works of history, including John Richard Green's *A Short History of the English People* in 1874 and Samuel Rawson Gardiner's *A History of England under the Duke of Buckingham and Charles I* in 1875.

About 1880 Thompson began working for James Murray, who found her etymological skills invaluable for the production of the *Oxford English Dictionary*. Ultimately she wrote 15,000 entries for the dictionary, proof-read almost the entire work, and, from 1891, was sub-editor for 'C'. She was aided by her younger sister, Ellen Perronet Thompson (1857–1930), novelist and writer of several historical essays for the *Gentleman's Magazine*. They also collaborated in researching the life of their grandfather Thomas Perronet Thompson (1783–1869). Edith completed a draft biography, but failed to bring it to publication.

Thompson was a prodigious scholar, the full extent of whose literary output is difficult to ascertain because she often sought anonymity. Freeman complained about her obsessive secrecy and use of pseudonyms, such as Evelyn Todd. In 1882 she published 'Carcassonne', a piece of historical travel writing, in *Macmillan's Magazine*, and it was one of the few articles she published in her name.

In 1889 Thomspon's father retired and the family moved, first to Brokes Lodge, Reigate Hill, and then to Beaconfield Lodge, Lansdown, Bath. She was continuously employed on the *Oxford English Dictionary* and on updating *History of England*. The latter went through many editions, including American and Canadian editions, and Freeman told her that the boys of the City of London School called it their 'Edith' (Brynmor Jones Library, MS DX/9/108). Thompson herself called it 'the little history' and it was ultimately revised up to and including the First World War (Macmillan MSS, 69/58, 306). Her smaller projects included abridging and editing Charles Kingsley's *Westward Ho!* for Arnold's English Literature Series (1911), co-writing a historical guide to Bath (1922), and writing a pamphlet, *Sir John Crosby and his Hall* (1928).

Although Thompson sought anonymity for published work, she actively involved herself in professional history networks. She attended conferences of history teachers and was made an honorary member of the Bath branch of the Federation of University Women. She was also a gifted artist and was involved in the Bath and Avon branches of the Shakespeare Society and Poetry Society. Edith Thompson died at Beaconfield Lodge on 26 August 1929, after a bout of influenza, and was buried on 30 August 1929 at Charlcombe in Bath, where her parents and sister are also interred.   AMANDA L. CAPERN

Sources U. Hull, Brynmor Jones L., MSS DX/9 and DTH · U. Leeds, Thompson MSS, 277 [including obituaries at 277/5/28] · U. Reading, Macmillan MSS · *Saturday Review* (1869–92) · *The Times* (30 Aug 1904) · *The Times* (28 Aug 1929) · *The Times* (25 Nov 1930) · CGPLA Eng. & Wales (1929) · register (burial), Charlcombe, Bath, Somerset, 30 Aug 1929 · register (births), Greenwich RO, 16 May 1848 · Venn, *Alum. Cant.* · L. G. Johnson, *General T. Perronet Thompson, 1783–1869*

(1957) • K. M. E. Murray, *Caught in the web of words: James A. H. Murray and the 'Oxford English dictionary'* (1977)
Archives U. Hull, Brynmor Jones L., corresp., research papers, draft MSS, and notes, mainly relating to her biography of T. P. Thompson • U. Leeds, Brotherton L., corresp., mainly letters from her grandfather T. P. Thompson, and papers | U. Reading, Macmillan corresp.
Wealth at death £29,254 2s. 6d.: probate, 6 Nov 1929, CGPLA Eng. & Wales

Thompson [*née* Graydon], **Edith Jessie** (1893–1923), murder trial protagonist, was born on 25 December 1893 at 97 Norfolk Road in Dalston, London, the first of the five children of William Eustace Graydon (1867–1941), a clerk with the Imperial Tobacco Company, and his wife, Ethel Jessie Liles (1872–1938), the daughter of a police constable. When she was five Edith Graydon moved with her family to 231 Shakespeare Crescent in Manor Park, East Ham. After a spell in kindergarten, she started school locally in 1903 at the newly established Kensington Avenue Schools. She was followed there by her sister, Avis (1895–1977), and by her younger brothers Newenham, William, and Harold. She was a prize-winning student and developed into a remarkable dancer.

In the spring of 1909 Edith Graydon left school and by 1911 she was employed by Carlton and Prior, a thriving firm of milliners in the City of London. She became a buyer for the company, and travelled twice to Paris on fashion-inspecting trips. She was by now an attractive, auburn-haired young woman who stood 5 foot 7¼ inches tall, read voraciously, and had a head for figures. Some time in 1909 she first met Percy Thompson (1890–1922), a shipping clerk who also worked in the City of London and with whom she shared a passion for the theatre. In 1914 Edith Graydon and Percy Thompson spent a summer holiday in Ilfracombe. On 15 January 1916 they married in St Barnabas's, Manor Park. Shortly afterwards Percy Thompson enlisted in the London Scottish, but he was honourably discharged a few months later on medical grounds. By his own admission he had duped the army doctor into believing that he suffered from a heart condition. His wife, Edith, seems to have despised him for this act of cowardice, the more so since her brother Newenham was serving in the same regiment, and a 'friend' of her sister Avis was killed at Passchendaele in 1917.

In April of that year Edith and Percy Thompson moved into rented accommodation at 25 Retreat Road, Westcliff. They stayed there until September 1919, when they moved to 65 Mansfield Road in Ilford, which was then a smart north-east London suburb. Finally, in June 1920 Edith and Percy Thompson bought 41 Kensington Gardens, a substantial semi-detached house with a spacious garden.

Six months earlier a former schoolfriend of Edith Thompson's younger brothers had paid a surprise visit to the house in Shakespeare Crescent. He was Frederick Edward Francis (Freddy) Bywaters (1902–1923), a sailor with the Peninsular and Oriental Steamship Company. He had enrolled in the wartime navy by lying about his age, and was a daring, extrovert, and generous character. Although he had grown up in Manor Park, his mother had moved the family to Upper Norwood in south London on being widowed. Bywaters was therefore looking for shore-leave accommodation closer to the London docks. He was welcomed as a boarder at 231 Shakespeare Crescent, and Edith's younger sister, Avis, and he were soon attracted to each other.

In the summer of 1921 Edith and Percy Thompson, Avis Graydon and Freddy Bywaters, and another couple, went on holiday to Shanklin, Isle of Wight. It was here that Edith Thompson and Freddy Bywaters declared their love to each other. An unsuspecting Percy Thompson invited Bywaters to become their lodger, after the holiday, at 41 Kensington Gardens. He accepted, and on his nineteenth birthday, 27 June 1921, he and Edith Thompson committed adultery in her house. On 1 August, a bank holiday, a trivial incident resulted in Percy Thompson striking his wife. Bywaters intervened, and Thompson ordered him to leave the house.

Bywaters's affair with Edith Thompson continued for another twelve months, and she became pregnant at least once from their various sexual encounters. In January 1922 she induced a miscarriage while at home. Throughout the affair Bywaters was away at sea for long spells. During these separations she wrote to him with an incandescent passion. She tried to impress on her lover her readiness to go to any length to break free from her husband, even if it meant killing him. To this end she claimed to be occasionally feeding him bits of glass and poison. That no such attempt on Thompson's life ever took place was proven by the crown's own two eminent pathologists.

In the course of the late summer of 1922 Bywaters tried to end the relationship. But on his return to Britain in late September 1922 their passion flared up again. On 3–4 October 1922, shortly after midnight, Edith and Percy Thompson were returning from a night at a West End theatre when, near their home, Bywaters attacked Thompson with a knife. Thompson collapsed on the pavement and died instantly from multiple stab wounds. His wife was heard screaming 'Oh don't, oh don't' during the assault. Within less than twenty-four hours both lovers were in police custody. On 5 October, by which time the police had discovered her incriminating correspondence, the lovers were jointly charged with the murder of Percy Thompson, she with being a principal in the second degree; hers, it was argued, was the controlling hand behind the murder committed by a much younger, foolish hothead.

The two were tried at the Old Bailey (6–11 December 1922). Edith Thompson was skilfully defended by Sir Henry Curtis-Benett, who presented her as a foolish dreamer who longed for a glamorous man to carry her from suburbia to exotic, far-flung places. But she sealed her own fate when, against his urgent advice, she took the witness box in the hope of saving Bywaters. She and her lover were sentenced to death on 11 December, and their appeal was rejected on 21 December. On 9 January she was hanged at Holloway prison by John *Ellis, while Bywaters perished at the same time at Pentonville.

Rumours about the horror of Edith Thompson's last

moments and a suspected miscarriage on the gallows caused controversy at the time, and again in the 1950s and the 1980s. After initially being buried at Holloway prison after her execution, on 31 March 1971 her body was reinterred at Brookwood cemetery in Surrey. Her innocence has been protested ever since October 1922, and her grave was consecrated in 1993 by the Revd Barry Arscott of St Barnabas's, the church in which she had been married.

RENÉ WEIS

Sources R. Weis, *Criminal justice: the true story of Edith Thompson* (1988) · F. Young, ed., *Trial of Frederick Bywaters and Edith Thompson* (1923) · 'Audrey Russell interviewing Avis Graydon', 1973, priv. coll. · court file, PRO, Crim 1/206 · police file, PRO, Mepo 3/1582 · PRO, HO 144/2685/438338, pts 1–2, P. Com. 8/22/59256, 8/436/59452 · W. Twining, *Rethinking evidence* (1990), 262–331 · L. Broad, *The innocence of Edith Thompson* (1952) · F. T. Jesse, *A pin to see the peepshow* (1934) · *Hansard 5C*, 20–21 Feb 1923; 14 April 1948; 27–9 March 1956 · *CGPLA Eng. & Wales* (1923)
Likenesses photographs, repro. in Weis, *Criminal justice*, 172ff.; priv. coll.
Wealth at death £600: probate, 30 Jan 1923, *CGPLA Eng. & Wales*

Thompson, Edmund Symes- (1837–1906), physician, was born Edmund Thompson at 15 Keppel Street, Bloomsbury, London, on 16 November 1837, the fourth of the five children of Theophilus *Thompson (1807–1860), physician, and his wife, Anna Maria Wathen (1808–1867), daughter of Nathaniel Wathen of Stroud. The name Symes was adopted by his father after an inheritance from the Revd Richard Symes, a descendant of the Sydenham family.

Symes-Thompson was educated at Doctor Grey's School until aged eight, and then at St Paul's School, London, until 1853, before entering King's College, London. Here he gained many awards, winning the Leathes and Warneford prizes and a gold medal for divinity and proficiency. In 1856 he joined King's College Hospital, where he studied medicine and while still a student assisted the physiologist Lionel Smith Beale with his research. He also acted as clinical clerk and dresser to some of the hospital doctors. In 1859 he graduated MB, gaining a medical scholarship and a gold medal and honours in surgery, botany, and midwifery. He obtained his MD degree in 1860 and was appointed honorary assistant physician at King's College Hospital in the same year. In 1863 he obtained a similar post in west London at the Brompton Hospital for Consumption, and in 1865 he resigned the post at King's after deciding to specialize in chest diseases. At the Brompton Hospital he was appointed honorary physician in 1869, full physician in 1870, and honorary consulting physician from 1890. He was also honorary physician to the Royal National Hospital for Consumption and Diseases of the Chest at Ventnor, Isle of Wight, and to the Artists' Benevolent and Annuity Funds and other charitable institutions. He was appointed professor of medicine at Gresham College in 1866, where he became an experienced lecturer. His fine voice held the attention of every audience as he explained his subject in a clear and intelligible manner.

Symes-Thompson was an active and enthusiastic member of numerous societies and organizations. He became a member of the Royal College of Physicians in 1862 and was elected a fellow in 1868. He was also a fellow of the

Royal Medical and Chirurgical Society, and of the Clinical Society of London, serving as secretary of each society for a time. In 1883 he became president of the Harveian Society. As a dedicated Christian and a member of the literature committee of the Society for Promoting Christian Knowledge, he regularly participated in the religious services of the Guild of Saint Luke, which he joined in 1884 and served as provost from 1892 to 1901. He also helped to establish the Medical Missionary College in 1905.

On 25 July 1872 Symes-Thompson married Elizabeth (b. 1848), second daughter of Henry George Watkins, vicar of Potters Bar. They raised four sons (the eldest became a doctor) and two daughters in the family homes in London, 3 Upper George Street followed in 1878 by 33 Cavendish Square. In 1898 Symes-Thompson bought Finmere House in Oxfordshire, where he could relax and pursue his botanical interests.

In addition to his consulting work, Symes-Thompson published several articles on pulmonary consumption and its treatment, and revised two of his father's works: *Clinical Lectures on Pulmonary Consumption* (1863), to which he added some of his own lectures; and *Influenza, or, Epidemic catarrhal fever: an historical survey of past epidemics in Great Britain from 1510–1890* (1890). He took a keen interest in teaching those without hearing or speech, and was chairman for many years of the Training College for Teachers of the Deaf, at Ealing in west London. He also wrote and lectured on the subject.

Symes-Thompson was greatly interested in mountaineering and was a keen traveller, visiting European and more distant lands, including Algeria, South Africa, and Egypt. As a specialist in lung disease he realized the value of climate and spa treatment for patients and had an extensive knowledge of various health resorts. Partly through his influence and his pamphlet *On the Winter Health Resorts of the Alps* (1883), St Moritz and Davos in Switzerland became popular as health resorts. Also through his efforts an invalids' home was established at Davos in 1895, and the Queen Alexandra Sanatorium opened there in 1909 after his death. In 1903 he became president of the British Balneological and Climatological Society, which he helped to found, and he wrote several works concerned with climate. These included *On the Climate of South Africa* (1889); 'South Africa as a health resort' (a paper in a publication of the same title, 2nd edn, 1889, by Arthur Fuller); and *The Climate of Egypt* (1895). In addition he contributed to *The Climate and Baths of Great Britain and Ireland* (2 vols., 1895), produced by the Royal Medical and Chirurgical Society.

Gradually Symes-Thompson spent less time on his consulting practice and concentrated more on insurance work. He became an active member of the Life Assurance Medical Officers' Association and for many years served as physician to the Equity and Law Life Assurance Society. His writings on insurance topics included *Gout in Connection with Life Assurance* (1879), and an article on life assurance which appeared in two editions of Sir Clifford Allbutt's *System of Medicine* (1896 and 1905).

An amiable, hard-working man, Symes-Thompson had

a charming personality and his excellent conversational skills ensured a wide circle of friends. He was always willing to help and advise those who needed aid, and poor patients often benefited from his kind-hearted and generous nature. He was renowned for the rapid examination and diagnosis of patients, a most useful faculty when several insurance applicants were waiting to be vetted.

Shortly before the onset of his final illness, Symes-Thompson had consented to become a justice of the peace for Oxfordshire, but he was unable to take up the position. After a decline in mental and physical activity over the course of a few months, he died on 24 November 1906 at his home at 33 Cavendish Square; he was buried in the churchyard at Finmere, Oxfordshire, and was survived by his wife.   CHRISTOPHER F. LINDSEY

Sources E. Symes-Thompson, *Memories of Edmund Symes-Thompson, M.D., F.R.C.P.: a follower of St. Luke* (1908) • *BMJ* (1 Dec 1906) • *The Lancet* (1 Dec 1906) • *The Times* (26 Nov 1906) • C. D. Marshall, 'The late Dr. Symes-Thompson', *BMJ* (15 Dec 1906), 1751 • *DNB* • d. cert.

Likenesses Byrne, photograph, repro. in Symes-Thompson, *Memories* • crayon drawing, Royal Society of Medicine, London • portrait (after photograph), repro. in *Journal of Balneology and Climatology* (Jan 1907)

Wealth at death £21,889 16s. 6d.: resworn probate, 21 Jan 1907, *CGPLA Eng. & Wales*

Thompson, Edward (1738?–1786), naval officer and author, was the son of a Hull merchant about whom further details are unknown. He was educated at Beverley and Hampstead, and made a voyage to Greenland in 1750. He journeyed to the East Indies in an Indiaman in 1754, and later claimed that he was pressed out of her and into the navy. On his return to England he joined the *Stirling Castle* (64 guns, Captain Samuel Cornish), and was made a midshipman. He was promoted lieutenant on 16 November 1757 and joined the *Jason*, serving in the North Sea and the English Channel. In May 1758 he joined the *Dorsetshire* (70 guns, Captain Peter Denis). The *Dorsetshire* was employed on the Brest blockade and Thompson was present at the battle of Quiberon Bay (20 November 1759). In March 1760 he moved with Captain Denis to the new *Bellona* (74 guns), attached to the western squadron, and was put on half pay at the end of the war in 1763.

After the peace Thompson devoted his time to writing. During the remainder of his life he acquired a wide circle of political and literary acquaintances including John Wilkes, David Garrick, and Richard Brinsley Sheridan whom he apparently detested, describing him as a 'parliamentary impostor and swindler' ('Journal', 632). His satires *The Demi-Rep* (1756) and *The Meretriciad* (1763), published anonymously, proved very popular, the former recounting the attractions of London society and its corrupting moral influence. These and several other pieces were collected in 1770 under the title *The Court of Cupid*. In 1767 *A Sailor's Letters* was published in two volumes. These described Thompson's voyages from 1754 to 1759 along with an account of the battle of Quiberon Bay and a vivid depiction of life in the navy. However, they also tend towards exaggeration and are not wholly reliable as illustrations of naval life (Rodger, 171, 181; Marcus, 183, 185).

Thompson was promoted commander on 10 January 1771 and appointed to the *Kingfisher* in the North Sea and, at the end of the year, to the *Raven* in the Mediterranean. Here he was promoted captain of the *Niger* by Rear-Admiral Sir Peter Denis, and his commission was confirmed by the Admiralty on 2 April 1772. He returned to England and the *Niger* was paid off in July 1772. The following year Thompson produced an adaptation of Charles Shadwell's *The Fair Quaker* at Drury Lane. Typically its naval characters, such as the macaroni Captain Mizen, were 'only fit to seduce their brother officers wives' (Langford, 577). Notwithstanding some popular success, much of Thompson's literary output and particularly his verse 'barely soared up to' mediocrity. He was fond of puns and doggerel and would frequently pen a few lines on the death of someone in the public eye ('Journal', 614, 619). Even so, on an occasion when one of his plays was being staged in Plymouth, fifty of his crew arrived at the door of the theatre and demanded admittance. As well as composing Thompson was engaged in editing the *Westminster Magazine* and later the *London Magazine*. He considered standing for parliament and in 1773 was proposed by John Wilkes as candidate for Westminster in opposition to Charles Fox, but Wilkes found no seconder. He later considered standing for Camelford but despite some encouragement never took up a political career.

In January 1778 Thompson was appointed to the *Hyaena* (24 guns), a new frigate building at Fisher's yard in Liverpool. He commissioned her on 17 April, and early the following year went out to Barbados. The *Hyaena* was attached to John Byron's fleet and present at the inconclusive action with d'Estaing off Grenada on 6 July 1779. In August he was persuaded at the insistence of some merchants at Barbados to leave his station and return to England with a convoy. For this he was court martialled but acquitted. In December the *Hyaena* was attached to the fleet under Sir George Rodney that was sent to the relief of Gibraltar. Thompson was present at the moonlight battle off Cape St Vincent (16–17 January 1780), when Rodney engaged a Spanish fleet. In a letter dated 24 March 1780 George Jackson, second secretary of the Admiralty, informed Rodney of Thompson's 'good Judgement', his reputation as 'an excellent Companion', and of his being 'unfortunate in his Marriage' (PRO, 30/20/26/3, p. 17); further details of Thompson's wife are unknown though his journal also refers to another woman, Emma, with whom he spent much time towards the end of his life.

The *Hyaena* was afterwards sent home with dispatches following the moonlight battle. After refitting she was sent in August to New York with a convoy and then back to Barbados. In 1781, on the surrender of the Dutch territories of Berbice, Demerara, and Essequibo, Thompson was delegated to organize the establishment of the new colonies. By September he was under orders from Rodney to take a convoy to England with the admiral's dispatches but had received no written confirmation. Rodney had already returned to England leaving Hood in command. Thompson took it on his own responsibility to take the convoy to England and in his absence the Guiana colonies were recaptured by the French. On 1 April 1782 he was again court martialled, 'on the letter of Sir Samuel Hood', for deserting his station but was once more acquitted (Popham, 12; PRO, ADM 1/5319, fol. 555).

Professionally Thompson was on very good terms with both admirals Augustus Keppel and Richard Howe; as both were successively at the head of the Admiralty after the American War of Independence, Thompson managed to find employment at sea. Although his scheme for a new signal code received nothing more than 'a polite reply' from Howe, his plans to survey the west coast of Africa obtained support ('Journal', 636). He planned to explore the coast between 20° S and 30° S and proposed a settlement where Indiamen might call to refit. Thompson was appointed to command the *Grampus* (50 guns) and in January 1784 sailed with instructions to survey the trading forts on the Guinea coast. The *Grampus* stopped at Madeira, where Thompson was inspired to write the poem *Belle Monte*. Thompson also kept a painter by the name of Wilson on board to make a number of sketches of the island.

Thompson conducted his surveys off the African coast, and gathered much information on commercial activities and the slave trade as well as settling trading disputes between the Europeans and the local leaders. He also reported on the depredations of pirate vessels, and an attempt by the Danes to build a fort on the River Volta to secure a large part of the British slave trade to themselves. Suffering from fever he returned to England in September 1784, but the following year he sailed again to the African coast. In company with the *Nautilus* (16 guns), the *Grampus* was ordered to survey the south-west coast of Africa. A further object of the voyage was to select a suitable site north of the Cape for a penal colony. Once it was established, Thompson expected to be appointed its governor. Before carrying out these instructions both ships returned to the Guinea coast to complete the work of the previous year. Thompson was again involved in settling disputes but fell ill during the negotiations. On this occasion the fever proved fatal and he died on board the *Grampus* on 17 January 1786. The following day he was buried at sea in the Gulf of Guinea, the ceremony accompanied by minute guns from the *Grampus* and *Nautilus*, and a volley of small arms.

Thompson was very popular with his crew, and took great care in the nautical education of his young officers. Thomas Boulden *Thompson and Home Riggs Popham served on the quarterdeck of the *Grampus* and both became officers of some distinction. In character, he was described as 'an agreeable and gentlemanlike companion', and his reputation as a wit, as well as his writing and literary activities in London society, earned him the nickname Poet Thompson throughout the navy (Stirling, 20).

CLIVE WILKINSON

Sources DNB • 'The manuscript journal of Captain E. Thompson', *Cornhill Magazine*, 17 (1868), 610–40 • H. Popham, *A damned cunning fellow: the eventful life of Rear-Admiral Sir Home Popham* (1991) • E. Thompson, *A sailor's letters*, 2 vols. (1767) • P. Langford, *A polite and commercial people: England, 1727–1783*, new edn (1992) • *Pages and portraits from the past: being the private papers of Sir William Hotham*, ed. A. M. W. Stirling, 2 vols. (1919), vol. 1 • captain's journal, *Hyaena*,

PRO, ADM 51/468 • courts martial, 1781–1782, PRO, ADM 1/5319 • captain's journal, *Grampus*, PRO, ADM 1/382 • N. A. M. Rodger, *The wooden world: an anatomy of the Georgian navy* (1986) • G. J. Marcus, *Quiberon Bay* [1960]

Archives BL, journal, Add. MS 46120 • NMM, journals • PRO, captain's journals, ADM 51/637, 468, 4203, 396, 382 • PRO, captain's letters, ADM 1/2590–2594

Likenesses A. McKenzie, stipple, pubd 1783 (after miniature by T. Hardy), BM • A. McKenzie, engraving (after T. Hardy), NMM • W. Ridley, engraving (after T. Hardy), NMM • oils, Trinity House, Hull

Thompson, Edward Arthur (1914–1994), historian, was born on 22 May 1914 at Bellvue Terrace, Waterford, Ireland, the son of Robert James Thompson, civil servant, and his wife, Margaret, formerly Wallace. His father, who worked in the administration of the national insurance scheme, was of Irish descent, his mother of Scottish descent; both were strict Presbyterians. The family moved to Dublin in 1922. Thompson was educated at Dublin high school and, as a sizar, at Trinity College, Dublin. He graduated with first-class honours in classics in 1936, then remained at Trinity College for a further year to complete a BLitt thesis on the Arcadian league, under the supervision of H. W. Parker. As a postgraduate student in Berlin in 1937–8 he witnessed at first hand Nazi brutality towards Jews and other opponents of the National Socialist regime. Those memories never left him and were formative in impelling him towards Marxism and, later, membership of the Communist Party. He returned to Dublin, and in 1939 was appointed lecturer in classics at Trinity College, for a year. In 1940 he was appointed for a further year, though at a reduced salary.

In 1941, his post at Trinity College having expired, and at a time when university posts in classics were extremely rare, Thompson considered enlistment in the British army. He was diverted by appointment to a lectureship at the University College of Swansea, where he taught until 1945. Here, he came under the influence of Professor Benjamin Farrington, who completed his conversion to Marxism. From 1945 to 1948 Thompson taught at King's College, London, during which time he published two books of great maturity for so young a scholar: *The Historical Work of Ammianus Marcellinus* (1947) and *A History of Attila and the Huns* (1948). Both were later reprinted and retained their significance for over fifty years. While at King's he met and, on 24 November 1945, married Thelma Marjorie Phelps (b. 1921/2), a doctor working at the Essex County Hospital, Wanstead; she was the daughter of William Alfred Phelps, clothing manufacturer. They had a son and a daughter. The marriage was dissolved in 1958, and in 1964 Thompson married Hazel Joyce Casken, with whom he had one daughter.

In 1948 Thompson was appointed professor of classics at the University of Nottingham, a post he held until his retirement in 1979. His academic focus continued to be on the late Roman world and the successor states; in this he was not a conventional professor of classics. But, like his contemporary A. H. M. Jones, he was a pioneer in opening up the long-neglected field of late antiquity, especially in his studies of the Germanic neighbours of the Roman empire and their later settlement within the Roman world. He also gave critical attention to late Roman sources which had hitherto languished in shadow. These included the enigmatic and anonymous *De rebus bellicis* (1951) and the *Vita san Sabae* (1954). He also began his publications on late Roman Britain and St Patrick, to which subjects he returned in later years.

Thompson's major works were devoted to the Germanic peoples and their relations with the Roman world. These appeared in quick succession within six years: *The Early Germans* (1965), *The Visigoths in the Time of Ulfila* (1966), and *The Goths in Spain* (1971). All these rested upon a massive base of research and publication over the previous twenty years. They were followed by four major papers on the end of Roman Spain, later reprinted in a collection of articles, *Romans and Barbarians: the Decline of the Western Empire* (1982), the fruit of a year spent at the University of Wisconsin following his retirement in 1979. Meanwhile he had returned to consideration of the problems surrounding the end of Roman Britain in a major series of papers, crowned by his monograph *Saint Germanus of Auxerre and the End of Roman Britain* (1984). His continuing interest in Ireland was marked by his adventurous *Who was Saint Patrick?* (1985), a carefully crafted book, but one which enjoyed less success than his earlier studies.

Thompson's writing was often terse, always clear, and often shot through with wit. His humour was evident in the briefest of contacts. His turn of phrase was memorable and his ability to entertain in conversation on almost any subject was legendary. He was remarkably tolerant of the foibles of others and supportive of those who needed help, though rigorous in his judgement of second-rate work. He was markedly cool towards university administration and managed to dispense with most of it, without harm to his department. He served a term as dean of arts at Nottingham, of which episode little is recorded except the brevity of the meetings. Research and writing came first, followed by teaching over a very wide range, and last of all administrative paperwork. Curiously, he supervised very few research students and hardly any in his own field of late antiquity. Elected a fellow of the British Academy in 1964, he gave little time to the running of learned societies, though his connections with other scholars on both sides of the Atlantic were wide and fruitful. He was enormously supportive of young scholars in whom he discerned promise, perhaps mindful of the uncertainties that had surrounded his own early career.

Late in life Thompson declared that he was not a Marxist but a Thompsonist. Yet it is true that Marxist ideas influenced his views on relations between the rulers and the ruled in the Roman empire. He left the Communist Party in disgust at the Russian repression in Hungary in 1956; he was equally appalled at events in Czechoslovakia twelve years later. He was critical of British policy in Northern Ireland, but utterly deplored the sectarian violence that broke out there in 1969. Thompson continued to live in Nottingham after his retirement; he died at Nottingham City Hospital on new year's day 1994, of cancer. He was survived by his second wife, Hazel, and his three children.   MALCOLM TODD

Sources R. A. Marks, 'Edward Arthur Thompson, 1914–1994', *PBA*, 111 (2001), 679–93 · *Nottingham Medieval Studies*, 32 (1988) [includes various tributes and articles] · *The Independent* (6 Jan 1994) · *The Guardian* (31 Jan 1994) · *The Times* (2 Feb 1994) · *WWW* · personal knowledge (2004) · private information (2004) [Rt Hon. Sir Andrew Leggatt, great-nephew] · b. cert. · m. cert. · d. cert.
Archives U. Nott., archives
Likenesses C. A. Noble, photograph, repro. in Marks, 'Edward Arthur Thompson', 678

Thompson, Edward John (1886–1946), teacher and writer, was born on 9 April 1886 at Hazel Grove, Stockport, the eldest son of John Moses Thompson (1854–1894), from near Penrith, and his wife, Elizabeth Penney (1851–1928), both Wesleyan missionaries to south India. Mission compounds and Madras beaches were Edward's earliest memories. In 1892 his father's failing health forced them home, with five children and a sixth born at their Colwyn Bay parish. After she was widowed, Elizabeth raised them in near poverty at Stockport. From the Wesleyan school there Edward went to the Methodist Kingswood School, Bath, from 1888 to 1902. His record promised an Oxford or Cambridge scholarship and he early saw poetry as his vocation, but poverty forced him into several years of clerking in a Bethnal Green bank. All his life he bitterly regretted that lost educational opportunity; in many respects he was self-educated, although in 1909 he earned an external London University BA. In 1908 he entered Richmond Theological College; after ordination in 1910, he went to Bankura Wesleyan college, Bengal, to teach English literature, ever his absorbing interest.

Thompson's first period there, to 1916, coincided with Lord Hardinge's term as viceroy and the crucial changes in Bengal's politics after annulment in 1911 of Lord Curzon's 1905 Bengal partition. Thompson viewed those changes in relation to the controversial advance and growing unrest of the educated middle classes. Contrary to government policy, he agreed with his friend Percy Comyn Lyon, Bengal's education secretary, that more education, not more policing, was the solution. He came to share also Lyon's view that dominion status, not independence, was India's best future hope.

Thompson as teacher was a signal success, but Bankura was isolated and its Wesleyan atmosphere oppressive; colleagues looked askance at his poetic aspirations. He found satisfaction in association, from 1913, with the poet Rabindranath Tagore, and in study and translation of Bengali poetry and short fiction, at a time when most Western readers were unaware of the existence of serious, artistic literature in Indian vernaculars. Tagore's friendship and Nobel prize were inspiring but also exemplified early difficulties in East–West literary exchange. Although Thompson saw poetry as his own vocation, friends such as William Canton, the poet and historian of the British and Foreign Bible Society, had to convince him that he excelled also in prose.

Thompson served as chaplain in Mesopotamia from

Edward John Thompson (1886–1946), by Howard Coster, 1940–46

1916 to 1918, with the 2nd Royal Leicestershires. Although he doubted that he had a chaplain's qualifications, he did well in this post, and a Military Cross recognized his conspicuous service to the wounded under fire. His powerful memoir, *The Leicestershires beyond Baghdad* (1919), testifies to his skill as prose writer, his success as battlefield padre, and his everlasting convictions about the wasteful cruelty of war. In 1918 he was posted to Jerusalem, where he met and married, in 1919, Theodosia Jessup (1892–1970), daughter of the American Presbyterian missionary William Jessup. He returned to Bankura College as acting principal, and found changed educational requirements and colleagues who underestimated the power of Gandhi's non-co-operation and of student protests. Under those circumstances Thompson saw little hope for progress and in 1923 moved to Oxford as lecturer in Bengali. He resigned Wesleyan ordination and began a writing career. He became a Leverhulme research fellow (1934–6), and honorary fellow and research fellow in Indian history at Oriel College (1936–40). He preserved Indian contacts, and Congress Party leaders trusted him sufficiently that, in 1939, while there on a cultural mission for the Rhodes trustees, he accompanied Nehru to the secret debate on India's role in the Second World War. As a freelance journalist, he endeavoured to interpret India for the West and the West for India, as in his coverage of the 1930–32 round-table conference.

Thompson followed Indian politics and literature closely. The Amritsar massacre of 1919 so angered him that with other missionaries he joined a minority protest that attracted much animosity. He examined Indian history and culture in works such as *A History of India* (1927), *Suttee* (1928), and *The Life of Charles, Lord Metcalfe* (1937). *The other Side of the Medal* (1925) analyses the Indian perspective on the 1857 mutiny, and *The Reconstruction of India* (1930) pleads for new beginnings in British-Indian relations. From Indian literature, he translated medieval devotional lyrics, and stories from Tagore. *Rabindranath Tagore: his Life and Work* (1921) and *Rabindranath Tagore: Poet and Dramatist* (1926) were the first significant Western assessments of Tagore's work. The latter earned Thompson a PhD from London University, and some sharp criticism in India because it was not exclusively laudatory. Throughout, Thompson wrote poetry, and his later volumes, such as *New Recessional* (1942) and *100 Poems* (1944), were superior to his earlier work in intensity and precision. His novels, *Introducing the Arnisons* (1935) and *John Arnison* (1939), encapsulate his experience of growing up Wesleyan, while six novels with Indian settings use Bankura and other Indian experiences; verisimilitude, striking personalities, and loving descriptions of flora, fauna, and countryside distinguish them.

Thompson attacked mindless prejudice in the strongest terms, but also with wit that could disarm his critics. If he left formal Wesleyanism he kept an evangelistic passion for causes he espoused. High on that list were justice for India and the end of wars.

The Thompsons settled on Boars Hill, Oxford, neighbours of the poet laureate, of whom Edward wrote a biography, *Robert Bridges* (1944). They had two sons: William Frank (1920–1944), who died in Bulgaria in a secret intelligence unit; and the historian Edward Palmer *Thompson (1924–1993). Edward John Thompson died of stomach cancer on 28 April 1946 at his residence at Saunders Close, Bledlow, Buckinghamshire and was buried in Bledlow church.　　　　MARY LAGO

Sources E. P. Thompson, 'Alien homage': Edward Thompson and Rabindranath Tagore (1993) · H. Trivedi, Colonial transactions: English literature and India (1993) · B. Parry, Delusions and discoveries: studies on India in the English imagination, 1880–1930 (1972) · M. Lago, ed., Imperfect encounter: letters of William Rothenstein and Rabindranath Tagore, 1911–1961 (1972) · A. J. Greenberger, The British image of India: a study of the literature of imperialism (1969) · R. Symonds, Oxford and empire: the last lost cause? (1991) · The Times (29 April 1946), 7 · private information (2004)
Archives Bodl. Oxf., corresp. and papers · NRA, corresp. and literary papers | BL, corresp. with Society of Authors, Add. MS 56834 · BL OIOC, letters to Sir W. Foster, MSS Eur. E 242 · Bodl. Oxf., letters to Robert Bridges · Bodl. Oxf., corresp. with Gilbert Murray · CUL, Crewe MSS · CUL, Hardinge MSS · Dartington Hall Trust Archive, Totnes, letters to Leonard Elmhirst · Harvard U., Houghton L., William Rothenstein MSS · JRL, letters to the Manchester Guardian · Kingswood School, Bath, archives · Ministry of Defence records, Whitehall, London · NA Scot., corresp. with Lord Lothian · University of Surrey, Roehampton, London, Methodist Archives
Likenesses H. Coster, photograph, 1940–46, NPG [see illus.] · H. Coster, photographs, NPG · photographs, Oriel College, Oxford
Wealth at death £1875 1s. 2d.: probate, 6 Dec 1946, CGPLA Eng. & Wales

Thompson, Sir Edward Maunde (1840–1929), palaeographer and librarian, was born on 4 May 1840 at Clarendon, Jamaica, the eldest son of Edward Thompson, custos of Clarendon, and Elizabeth Hayhurst, daughter of Samuel Poole, of Clarendon. He was educated at Rugby School (1854–9) and was admitted to University College, Oxford, in 1859, but he had to leave without taking a degree when his father became unable to support him. In 1861 he entered the British Museum as assistant in the office of the principal librarian, Sir Anthony Panizzi. On the latter's advice he transferred to the manuscripts department in 1862, a move not at first welcomed by its keeper, Sir Frederic Madden. Thompson was not sure, however, that he wanted to stay in the museum, and in 1863 he entered the Middle Temple. He married in 1864 Georgina (d. 1917), daughter of George Mackenzie of Frankfield, Jamaica; they had three sons and one daughter. Thompson was called to the bar in 1867, but never practised. When Edward Augustus Bond succeeded Madden as keeper of manuscripts in 1866, Thompson became his principal associate, working mainly on the classed catalogue of manuscripts, which consisted of the printed descriptions of manuscripts cut out of the *Catalogues of Additions*, rearranged by subject and laid down in folio volumes, which eventually exceeded 100 in number. From this infinitely laborious task he gained his profound knowledge of the collections, the solid foundation of his published works on medieval chronicles, palaeography and illuminated manuscripts.

Sir Edward Maunde Thompson (1840–1929), by Bassano, 1899

Thompson's promotion to assistant keeper in succession to William Wright in 1871 brought him increased administrative duties, but he completed the classed catalogue and contributed substantially to the massive *Catalogue of Additions, 1854–75*, which cleared the arrears of cataloguing that had accumulated in the last years of Madden's keepership. He made many important published contributions to scholarship in varied fields. With Bond, in 1873, he founded the Palaeographical Society, which in two pioneering series of publications from 1873 to 1895 made possible the establishment of palaeography as a modern scientific discipline by providing students for the first time with photographic facsimiles of selected classical and medieval manuscripts in various hands. His *Introduction to Greek and Latin Palaeography* (1912), expanded from a shorter work published in 1893, is still among the best initiations into its subject. With Sir G. F. Warner he produced the *Catalogue of Ancient Manuscripts in the British Museum* (1881, 1884). He also supervised and contributed introductions to facsimiles of the Utrecht psalter (1874), the Codex Alexandrinus (1879–1883), and, with Sir R. C. Jebb, the Laurentian manuscript of Sophocles (1885). He edited several medieval chronicles and other works, of which the most important was the *Chronicon Galfridi Le Baker de Swynebroke, 1303–1356* (1889). For the Rolls Series he edited the *Chronicon Angliae, 1328–1388* (the anonymous chronicle of St Albans) (1874) and the *Adae Murimuth continuatio chronicorum, 1303–1347*, with *Robertus de Avesbury, de gestis mirabilibus regis Edwardi tertii* (1889). For the Royal Society of Literature he edited the *Chronicon Adae de Usk*, (1876 and, with its subsequently discovered conclusion, 1904). For the Henry Bradshaw Society he edited the *Customary of the Benedictine monasteries of St. Augustine, Canterbury, and St. Peter, Westminster* (1902). In 1895 he published *English Illuminated Manuscripts*, a series of articles he had written for the periodical *Bibliographica*.

Thompson's interests were by no means exclusively medieval. For the Camden Society he edited *The Letters of Humphrey Pridaux to John Ellis, 1674–1722* (1875), and *The Correspondence of the Family of Hatton, 1601–1704* (1878). For the Hakluyt Society he published *The Diary of Richard Cocks, 1615–1622* (1883). To all his editorial work Thompson brought meticulous accuracy and sound judgement; his readings and datings can rarely be faulted. One of his most interesting propositions, however, was not unanimously accepted. In *Shakespeare's Hand* (1916), he argued that an addition to the 'Book of Sir Thomas More' (BL, Harley MS 7368), included a passage in Shakespeare's autograph, a subject on which he also wrote a chapter in A. W. Pollard, *Shakespeare's Hand in the Play of Sir Thomas More* (1923). Modern expert opinion inclines to agree with him, though the attribution can probably never be established beyond all doubt.

Thompson succeeded Bond first as keeper of manuscripts, in 1878, and then as principal librarian, in 1888; from 1898 he was styled director and principal librarian, the title of all his successors as head of the British Museum until the separation of the library from the museum in 1973. He was a redoubtable and energetic director, insisting on the production of catalogues of the museum's contents as the primary duty of its curators. His objective was to consolidate the museum's reputation as a great scholarly institution, while making its riches more accessible and intelligible to the public by improved exhibition display and labelling, and the publication of inexpensive, well-illustrated popular guidebooks. He had electric lighting installed in the galleries. A new newspaper library was opened at Hendon in 1902. He also encouraged excavations abroad, in order to add to the museum's collections, and was responsible for expeditions to Mesopotamia, Egypt, Cyprus, Ephesus, and Carchemish, and for assistance to Sir Aurel Stein's second expedition to central Asia in 1906–8. In 1898, at Thompson's instigation, the museum's intellectual and scholarly output was investigated by a Treasury committee, which was so impressed by what it found that unprecedented salary increases of 6–11 per cent were approved for senior staff at £250 or more, and 20–25 per cent for staff on lower salaries. Thompson's personal friendship with the prince of Wales (the royal trustee) stood him in good stead in his dealings with government. In 1898 he secured Treasury approval for the purchase, for £200,000, of all the houses to the east, north and west of the museum for expansion. Plans for the King Edward VII building (constructed 1907–13) were laid, in the course of which Thompson rendered what was probably his most important and enduring service to literature and scholarship. As a condition for making building funds available, the Treasury insisted that the museum should reduce its holdings. In 1900 a bill passed the Lords empowering the trustees to disperse the provincial newspaper collection to local authorities, and to dispose of or destroy 'printed matter … which is not of sufficient value to justify its preservation in the museum'. Had this misguided bill become law, the printed collections would have been shaped by the values of contemporary critical opinion, and the historic comprehensiveness of the library would have been destroyed. Although it was introduced into the Commons by one of his own trustees, John Morley MP, Thompson orchestrated a campaign against it, helped by Sir Sidney Lee, and it was eventually withdrawn.

Thompson's colleague Sir George Warner described him as 'a strikingly handsome man, with fine features, dark hair and an erect carriage … full of life, high spirits and geniality' (Kenyon, 490). With a presence that could overawe the boldest, he was undoubtedly one of the most effective heads of the museum in its history, but he was not a man to be crossed; long after ill health forced his retirement in August 1909, stories of his savage temper and autocratic disposition lingered in the folk memory of the museum's staff. He was a stickler for formality in staff relations and dress. He strictly enforced Panizzi's rule that senior staff should wear top hats in the galleries, a practice that certainly kept the warders on their toes; the present writer recalls very elderly warders in the 1960s signalling to distant colleagues by holding up one hand over the other, meaning that a keeper or 'top hat' was coming and

that they should sharpen up. His severe ideas of what constituted indecorous behaviour by his staff were not confined to the museum precincts; he once berated an assistant keeper for riding a bicycle in the street. Sir Frederic Kenyon, another colleague, observed however that his brusque and intimidating manner masked a real kindness of heart, and that he was 'genial, natural and hospitable, with a lively sense of humour' (ibid.). There is certainly evidence of his kindness, and his loyalty to staff who pulled their weight. When R. G. C. Proctor vanished in 1903 on a walking holiday in the Tyrol, his aged mother was unable to pursue any enquiry. Thompson persuaded the trustees to dispatch a colleague to look for him at the museum's expense, despite severe Treasury disapproval.

Thompson was appointed CB in 1893, KCB in 1898, GCB in 1909, and ISO in 1904. He was one of the founding fellows of the British Academy, in 1901, and was president of the British Academy from 1907 to 1909. He was twice Sandars reader in bibliography at Cambridge University (1895–6 and 1905–6), and was a corresponding member of the Institut de France and the Royal Prussian Academy of Sciences. He received honorary degrees from the universities of Oxford, Durham, St Andrews, and Manchester, and was an honorary fellow of University College, Oxford. After his retirement in 1909 he lived successively at Mayfield in Sussex, Wells, Worthing, Tunbridge Wells, and finally at Mayfield again, where he died on 14 September 1929, in his ninetieth year. He is buried at Brookwood cemetery, Woking.

MICHAEL BORRIE

Sources A. Esdaile, The British Museum Library: a short history and survey (1946) · E. Miller, That noble cabinet: a history of the British Museum (1973) · WWW · F. G. Kenyon, 'Sir Edward Maunde Thompson', PBA, 15 (1929), 476–90 · CGPLA Eng. & Wales (1929)
Archives BL, T. S. of Sandars lectures, Add. MS 35088 · BL, draft notes for a history of the British Museum, verses, Add. MSS 52292, 54227 | BL, letters to J. P. Gilson, Add. MSS 47686–47687B · Bodl. Oxf., letters to Lord Acton · CUL, letters to Lord Acton · E. Sussex RO, letters to earl of Ashburnham · NL Scot., corresp. mainly with Lord Rosebery · Pembroke College, Oxford, letters to Sir Peter Renouf · TCD, letters to Thomas French
Likenesses Bassano, photograph, 1899, NPG [see illus.] · E. J. Poynter, oils, 1909, BM · engraving (after E. J. Poynter, 1909), BL
Wealth at death £16,391 5s. 0d.: probate, 28 Nov 1929, CGPLA Eng. & Wales

Thompson, Edward Palmer (1924–1993), historian, writer, and political activist, was born at Boars Hill, Oxford, on 3 February 1924, the second son of Edward John *Thompson (1886–1946), teacher and writer, and his wife, Theodosia Jessup (1892–1970).

Childhood and education to 1948 At the time of E. P. Thompson's birth (he was often known by his initials), his father taught Bengali at Oxford University, having returned to England in the previous year from west Bengal, where he had been a Methodist missionary. Far removed from the stereotype of the proselytizing Christian missionary, Edward John Thompson's life was pervaded by unresolved contradictions and tensions. A Methodist by birth, upbringing, vocation, and education, he was in most respects an instinctive humanist and believer in the possibility of human betterment. Unable completely to shake

Edward Palmer Thompson (1924–1993), by Steve Pyke, 1989

off the legacy of paternalism in British India, E. J. Thompson nevertheless became—as did his wife—a strong critic of imperialism. Leading Indian intellectuals were among his friends. These included the Nobel prize-winning poet Rabindranath Tagore, of whom he was a translator, and the rising politician Jawaharlal Nehru, whom E. P. Thompson remembered as a visitor to the family home. To E. P. Thompson the ambiguities of his father's intellectual positions became of great interest, and at the end of his own life he published *Alien Homage: Edward Thompson and Rabindranath Tagore* (1993). He especially remembered from his youth the general atmosphere and tone which stemmed from his parents' radical-Liberal rejection of imperialism and which passed to him the belief that governments were 'mendacious and imperialist' and that 'one's stance ought to be hostile to government' (Merrill, 11). He persisted in that belief and stance throughout his life.

Edward and his elder brother, (William) Frank *Thompson (1920–1944), attended the highly regarded Dragon preparatory school in Oxford. Frank went on to become a star pupil at Winchester College, but Edward was enrolled at his father's old school, the Methodist-founded Kingswood School, near Bath. He left little comment on experiences there, although the harsh attack on Methodists in his best-known book suggests that Kingswood did nothing to attract him to the church of his father and grandfather. In fact the Kingswood regime in Thompson's time there was remarkably open. Under the headship of A. B. Sackett, wide-ranging debate on political and cultural matters was characteristic. Thompson recalled that as a sixth former in 1940, reading the early work on the English civil war of the Marxist historian Christopher Hill and the seventeenth-century Leveller writings to which it led him, was a 'breakthrough' (*Essential E. P. Thompson*, 491). At eighteen he followed the example of his brother and joined the Communist Party.

At that age too Thompson began his military service with the army in north Africa and Italy, becoming a tank commander and taking part in the battle of Cassino in 1944. Although his own war experiences were significant, a greater impact on Thompson was made by his brother's death. Frank, a brilliant linguist, was recruited by the Special Operations Executive and dropped into Bulgaria to work with the partisans. Captured by the fascist government, he was shot along with the men he was leading. Frank's vision of a united socialist Europe stayed powerfully with Edward. After visiting Bulgaria with his mother, he wrote with her *There is a Spirit in Europe: a Memoir of Major Frank Thompson* (1947). His brother's vision fed into Edward's own later persistent political imagining of European possibilities: in his despising, for example, of the narrowing concept of Europe represented by the European Common Market (*Sunday Times*, 27 August 1975). His last vigorous political commitment was to European Nuclear Disarmament, of which he was a founder, with its aim of bridging the peace movements of eastern and western Europe. The official obstruction and evasion which he encountered when he tried after the war to find out the truth about his brother's mission reinforced his lifelong suspicion of the power of the 'secret state'.

After the war, 1946–1956 Late in 1945 Thompson returned to Corpus Christi College, Cambridge, to complete the history degree he had started in 1942. Wartime regulations allowed him his BA on a two-year part one. His first-class result brought him a scholarship with which he was able to finance a third year of extensive individual study of literature, which was probably then his first love. When he entered on his first teaching post, he taught both literature and history.

At Cambridge Thompson re-joined the Communist Party, his formal membership having lapsed during the war. In the party there he met Dorothy Towers (*b*. 1923), who was completing her history degree after war service in industry. She and Edward began to live together in 1945 and married in 1948. Until ended by Edward's death, it was a remarkable partnership of almost fifty years. The Thompsons then had no inclination to pursue academic careers, and had already decided to move to the north of England, when Edward was offered a teaching post in the extra-mural department at Leeds University. Before taking up this post he and Dorothy had been involved with a volunteer international youth group in building a railway in Yugoslavia, another reinforcement of an internationalism that remained essential in his thinking, and which qualifies overdone attempts to portray him as a quintessentially English radical. The Thompsons moved to Halifax in 1948, shortly before their eldest son, Ben, was born. They lived there for seventeen years, and two more children, Mark and Kate, were born.

Thompson was perhaps fortunate to secure a post when doors were being closed against known communists. He did not see eye to eye on many things with the head of the department, S. G. Raybould, a noted writer on adult education with strong ideas of his own, but from all accounts Thompson was a successful teacher. Departmental records show him to have been committed and thoughtful, expecting a significant input from his students, many of whom were from working-class backgrounds. In later interviews several remembered him as an inspirational teacher. Thompson, in turn, felt that he had much to learn from the life experiences of his working-class students. The whole tone of his most celebrated work, *The Making of the English Working Class* (1963), which made his reputation, testifies to this. It was fittingly dedicated to one of these students, and for all its international success it is impossible not to sense that the audience he felt himself to be addressing was a wider one than that of the academy.

The Thompsons' Halifax household was busy: Dorothy remembered it as a 'shambles'. With three children she restricted herself to part-time work. At the beginning of *The Making of the English Working Class* Edward emphasized his debt to her: 'her collaboration is to be found, not in this or that particular, but in the way the whole problem is seen' (preface, 14–15). They never collaborated in co-writing historical works in the manner of the Hammonds or the Webbs. They wrote separately, but with the same initial interest in working-class history, and as they worked they tended to develop the same approach to writing history, achieving much the same balance between theory and evidence. Although neither had served a formal postgraduate apprenticeship, they later imparted to their research students a sense of the rigour required in the production of written history. Clearly Edward's work took precedence in the Halifax years. Later feminist assertions that this amounted to exploitation gained some credence from the very rapid rise to pre-eminence as a historian of Chartism made by Dorothy once she became a full-time academic from 1968, but she has strongly rejected these allegations (Thompson, *Outsiders*, 9–10).

While teaching at Leeds University, Thompson wrote two books of formidable length. The first, a study of William Morris, *William Morris: Romantic to Revolutionary*, was published in 1955. The date is significant, for in the following year he broke with the Communist Party, later remarking that it was only in his thirty-third year that he had 'commenced to reason' (*The Poverty of Theory*, 1978, i). The study of Morris displayed some signs that its author was still operating within the orthodoxies of official communism. Reviewers certainly read it in that way. Thompson's reclaiming of Morris from woolly-thinking artist to committed and original socialist seemed in places to be implying that the nineteenth-century artist and writer would have approved of Stalin's Soviet Union: 'Visitors return from the Soviet Union with stories of the poet's dream [factory] already fulfilled' (1955 edn, 844). When he revised the work in 1977 Thompson confessed that he had allowed 'a few Stalinist pieties … to intrude upon the text' and that he had then held to 'a somewhat reverent notion of Marxism as a received orthodoxy, and my pages included some passages of polemic'. A different reading is now suggested. Thompson, viewing the book from his post-1956 perspective, suggested that discerning readers might have been able to detect in his stress on Morris's genius as a moralist, 'a submerged argument within the

orthodoxy to which I then belonged'. The truth is that Morris, as Thompson became immersed in his life and works, began to speak to him in the silent spaces of received Marxism. His biography, he suggested, was one of 'muffled revisionism' and when his disagreement with orthodoxy became explicit in 1956, he recalled that he had been much sustained by what he had learnt 'in those years of close company with Morris' (1977 edn, 769–70, 810).

In 1956 Edward and Dorothy Thompson were among 7000 members, including many prominent activists, who left the British Communist Party. The tremors had begun following Khrushchov's secret speech to the twentieth Soviet congress in February. Its revelations of Stalinism's atrocities soon became known outside the Soviet Union. A crisis of belief and of adherence began, which became an outflow by October when Soviet tanks entered Budapest to suppress the Hungarian rising. Explanations of why Thompson and others had remained in the British Communist Party over years when doubts had already been developing are complex. His generation had fought the war against fascism to a victory in which the Red Army had been decisive. They saw no other organization than the party which could provide the support and comradeship for those in whom anti-fascism was combined with a socialist vision. That vision had seemed part of a re-awakening at which many thought they had been present as the war in Europe came towards its end. In the resistance to fascism Thompson's own brother had become a communist martyr. The spirit of that moment was however an interlude of hope which had been crushed with the deadening imposition of the cold war.

Against such a background it is not surprising that Thompson through most of 1956 believed that something positive might still emerge which would allow British communism to develop the moral strength to survive as a legitimate political force, allowing more democratic processes and broader and freer discussion. To this end Thompson and fellow historian John Saville began to produce the critical, but internally directed, journal *The Reasoner*. The party was unwilling to allow even this form of dissidence and ordered publication to cease. Refusal brought the suspension of Thompson and Saville and, with the invasion of Hungary, they resigned.

The events of 1956 were decisive for Thompson and for many others on the left. But what he wrote against Stalinism in the third issue of *The Reasoner* in November hardly reads simply as an immediate response to a present crisis:

> the subordination of the moral and imaginative faculties to political and administrative authority is wrong: the elimination of moral criteria from political judgement is wrong: the fear of independent thought, the deliberate encouragement of anti-intellectual trends among the people is wrong; the mechanical personification of unconscious class forces, the belittling of the conscious process of intellectual and spiritual conflict, all this is wrong.
> ('Through the smoke of Budapest', *The Reasoner*, 3, 1956, 3)

Here, although still in a journal addressing its argument to the morally moribund British Communist Party, is already indicated a challenge to old communist thinking from the mobilizing vision: of the 'socialist humanism', of which Thompson was to be, through his writings, the most prominent proselytizer.

The first new left Socialist humanism would, Thompson hoped, provide the liberating approach around which a new left movement could emerge. In simple terms it would restore to the Marxist tradition (after 1956 Thompson tended to describe himself as a historian working in the Marxist tradition), the dimension which had been partly lost by Marx himself as he moved on from the writings of his youth to the economic certainties of *Capital*. It had certainly been lost from the Soviet version of communism. Later Thompson recalled his sense of a 'real silence' in Marx, lying in the 'area that anthropologists would call value systems'. The 'degeneration of the theoretical vocabulary of mainstream Marxism' had led to a desensitization of human qualities such as imagination and passion. Marx may have replaced the classical economists' economic man with 'revolutionary economic man', but the injury lay in defining man as essentially economic in the first place (D. Thompson, viii–ix).

From 1956 to the ending of its first phase in 1962, the Thompsons strove to further the dream of a new left. Its formative journal *The New Reasoner* was edited and distributed from their Halifax home and in its pages were contained the defining texts of the 'socialist humanist' vision. The first new left, however, amounted to more than a journal: it was a campaign to mobilize manifold voices of protest into a movement. Notably it was strong in its support for the nascent Campaign for Nuclear Disarmament from 1957, something which of itself was a breakaway from the official communist line of the nuclear-armed Soviet Union. Running a national journal was inevitably burdensome, and in 1959 *The New Reasoner* merged with the *Universities and Left Review* to become the *New Left Review*.

The two journals came from different backgrounds. That of the *New Reasoner* was unashamedly provincial, committed to a belief in the revolutionary potential of a medley of protest mobilizations and retaining some hopes of the British labour movement with a belief in the value of the traditions of protest embedded in a long history from peasants in revolt, through Levellers and Luddites to the Chartists and beyond. Based in London and dominated by young Oxbridge socialists, the partner journal, however, was more self-consciously theoretical. It was this approach which came to characterize the *New Left Review*, when, following an editorial coup in 1962, Thompson and his associates were ousted from their various positions on the journal by a group of younger men led by Perry Anderson. This was more than a generational change. It was a fundamental shift in perspective and in the form of socialist vision. As Thompson saw things, it was a displacement of the first new left with a second, which attached no immediacy to mobilizing the diverse protest forces on the left, but rather saw the British working class as hopelessly compromised and supine in its relationship with capitalism. The function of left intellectuals, in its view, was to provide and refine the energizing socialist theory which history had thus far denied it. In short, the first and the second new lefts read British, and especially English, history in fundamentally different ways. That divergence prompted in the mid-1960s a rigorous and at times savage debate, with the lone voice of Thompson embattled against Anderson and his co-editor, Tom Nairn. Ironically in 1963, at the very moment when Thompson was at his most detached from formal association with a socialist organization, his greatest work was published, which brought his writing to a much wider audience.

The making of a historian from 1963 During the early 1960s Thompson had been engaged on what was quickly recognized as a book of monumental importance. The appearance of *The Making of the English Working Class* was a transforming event in twentieth-century historiography. More than 800 pages long and priced accordingly, it did not at first suggest an impact on historical scholarship which has been described as 'truly alchemic' (Eastwood, 637). By 1968 when it appeared in its first British paperback edition, it had already become an established classic. In a work which has come to be seen as the single most influential work of English history of the post-war period, Thompson set out to demonstrate how between 1790 and 1832, under the joint pressures of political oppression and economic exploitation, English working men came to see themselves as a class: a class both made by the changing circumstances in which they laboured and lived, and self-making in terms of the responses they made to this experience. By the time of the crisis over parliamentary reform in 1830–32, a form of working-class consciousness had emerged, drawing on past traditions of resistance and rights as well as on present experiences. Further, Thompson argued, against generations of traditional conservative writing, that consciousness included the possibility of political revolution, which came very close at more than one moment.

At the beginning of the twenty-first century the book remains in print with its main text hardly changed. Its narrative and conclusion are hardly now accepted in all their detail by historians of the period, but the influence of *The Making* has not depended on that. In its preface, which has become a key historiographical text in its own right, Thompson made the defining statement of 'history from below'. He wrote of seeking to rescue groups of dissenting working people, like the Luddites, from 'the enormous condescension of posterity', putting them back into the history which they had made with their own life experiences. Also in that preface is his now classic definition of class and how it eventuates in history. Class, he argued, could not be understood in purely structural terms, be they those of twentieth-century sociology or those of later Marxist orthodoxy: 'class happens when some men, as a result of common experiences ... feel and articulate the identity of their interests as between themselves, and as against other men, whose interests are different from (and usually opposed to) theirs'. The class experience may have been largely determined by the productive relations into which men were born or entered, but class consciousness, the way in which these experiences were handled in cultural terms, in traditions, value systems, and institutions, was not so determined: 'Consciousness of class arises in the same way in different times and places, but never in *just* the same way'. The book is the most significant exposition of socialist humanism in actual historical writing with its insistence that class was defined by men 'as they live their own history' (preface, 9–13). Written with passion and commitment, *The Making* freed the historical imagination, redefined the subject matter of social and labour history, and pushed open more than one door of historical closure.

Thompson's rocketing reputation took him in 1965 to the directorship of the Centre for the Study of Social History at the newly opened University of Warwick and the family moved to Leamington Spa. Then at the beginning of his forties, he was an imposing figure. Tall and sparely built, his craggily handsome features were topped by an unusually thick head of hair, which flopped uncontrollably over his forehead. He had no particular affectation in dress, unless smoking small cigarettes alternately with hardly larger cheroots counts as such. The intensity of his gaze could be at first disconcerting, but it was his habit to listen properly to those who were speaking, for except in moments of anger he was not an interrupter.

Thompson's Warwick experience was mixed. With his postgraduate students his relationship was excellent. They remember with affection a painstaking and inspiring mentor, and most became lifelong friends. With the university itself relations were more strained. Resources for the centre were short of his expectation; undergraduate teaching took up much time, as did boards and meetings, leading him to complain that little time was left for writing. His writing was itself undergoing a shift. *The Making* carried marks of having been written by someone not fully bound by academic conventions. Its invective, for example in its infamously hostile depiction of Methodism as 'ritual psychic masturbation', could be immoderate. He had a blind spot when it came to quantification, and a glimpse of his feelings towards some academic tendencies is exemplified in a passage which summarizes the average worker's share in the benefits of the industrial revolution as: 'more potatoes, a few articles of cotton clothing for his family, soap and candles, some tea and sugar, and a great many articles in the *Economic History Review*' (*The Making*, 1968 edn, 351).

From the mid-1960s Thompson's own historical essays began to appear in leading journals. Two appeared in *Past and Present*, whose editorial board he joined in 1969. 'Time, work-discipline and industrial capitalism' (1967) and 'The moral economy of the English crowd in the eighteenth century' (1971) became classics, and, especially the second, have been internationally influential on how the processes of resistance and adaptation to capitalism have become understood. These articles are part of a body of work centring on the eighteenth century, now most accessible through the collection *Customs in Common* (1991). At Warwick too he developed an interest in the history of crime and the criminal law. *Albion's Fatal Tree: Crime and Society in Eighteenth-Century England* (D. Hay and others, eds., 1975) was a pioneering joint production with several of his research students, while the single-authored *Whigs and Hunters* (1975), a study of the power exercised through the law, is remarkable for a conclusion which recognizes the dichotomous significance of the law as a force which not only empowers but restricts the actions of the empowered. Increasingly Thompson's work showed enriching but cautiously employed inputs from disciplines like anthropology and folklore as he tackled subjects like wife-selling and 'rough music'. In the mid-1960s too he had continued the debate with Anderson and Nairn and *The New Left Review*. Most notably he produced in 'The peculiarities of the English' (*Socialist Register*, 1965, 311–62) a challenging over-arching interpretation of the course of English history rescuing it, as he saw things, from the distortions of the continental Marxisms of the 'lumpen intelligentsia'.

Thompson's final quarrel with the university's authorities was a public one. In 1970 students occupying the registry discovered files revealing a close and secret involvement of the university with prominent industrialists in its region, which included spying upon and informing on the activities of students and academics viewed as political dissidents, unfriendly to industrial capitalism. Thompson became the most conspicuous of those who publicized these revelations. With astonishing speed he edited a volume which situated Warwick as symptomatic of a threatened higher educational system in which values and freedoms were being lost in an increasing subordination to the requirements of industrial capitalism (*Warwick University Limited*, 1970).

Thompson left Warwick in 1971 to become a full-time writer. Dorothy had begun a period as a full-time university teacher at the University of Birmingham in 1968. For almost a decade from the new family home, Wick Episcopi, a splendid Georgian house on the outskirts of Worcester, he furthered his eighteenth-century project and wrote a number of political essays, often concerned with the defence of liberties against the state. In an earlier part of his life most of his essays and reviews had tended to appear in journals little read outside the left, but from the later 1960s they were appearing in periodicals such as *New Society*, the *New Statesman*, the *Times Literary Supplement*, and in the quality newspapers. Many of these essays, alongside some earlier ones, were reprinted in *Writing by Candlelight* (1980) and *The Heavy Dancers* (1985). Much of Thompson's writing, especially within arguments on the left, is bitter and unforgiving, but several of the essays of this period reveal how capable he was of using humour to make his points. He could, as in the essay 'Writing by candlelight', produced at a time when strikes were resulting in power cuts, and parodying the uncomprehending attitude of the upper and middle classes to it, produce very effective satire.

An early critic of the 'betrayal' of socialism by the Labour governments of Harold Wilson, Thompson was, with Raymond Williams and Stuart Hall, an editor of the

Mayday Manifesto in 1967, which explicitly sought to present a socialist alternative (R. Williams, ed., *Mayday Manifesto, 1968*, 1968, 9). Yet he retained a belief that the Labour Party, as the outcome of the history of British workers' struggles, still possessed a potential at least to contribute to a political transformation. As late as 1979 he was stating this view in a defence of the role of Marxists within the party ('The acceptable faces of Marxism', *The Observer*, 5 Feb 1979). The world of contingencies inhabited by party politics was alien to the stances adopted by a man who could not accommodate moral relativism. Something of a sense of isolation, a tendency to see himself as a lone battler on the left, had surfaced in him at various times from at least the collapse of the first new left. It was in such a mood and driven by a sense of its real potential to do harm that in 1978, in *The Poverty of Theory*, he took on the then fashionable French Marxist philosopher Louis Althusser, whose denial of individual agency and dismissal of morality he perceived as a form of neo-Stalinism. In this book Thompson made his most deliberate defence of history as a discipline with a distinguishing epistemology and methodologies. It lost him some friends on the left, who considered his stance arrogant and self-centred, and his language extreme. His apparent refusal to debate the issue of theory in moderate and open terms at an Oxford history workshop session in 1979 has entered the collective memory of the British left, although it has been suggested that he had assumed a sense of irony which his audience seemingly lacked (Rée, 19).

Peace campaigning from 1980 The Thompson angered by the closed thinking of French structuralism was a man becoming increasingly concerned with the threat of nuclear war. At the beginning of the 1980s he put aside his 'trade' as a historian to devote himself to the campaign against nuclear weapons. He believed that in the Reagan–Thatcher era the cold war was entering a phase in which nuclear conflict was becoming probable. In 1980 with Dan Smith he wrote *Protest and Survive*, a pamphlet which did more than any other to revive interest in the peace movement, while his 'Notes on exterminism, the last stage of civilization' (*New Left Review*, 1980) provided a significant analysis of the stage the arms race had by then reached. It had become a self-sustaining system propelled by an internal dynamic and a reciprocal logic. Against this process the Thompsons and their associates pitted their resisting energies for the next several years. Most importantly, in that year he drafted the European Nuclear Disarmament appeal, the mobilizing document which added a new dimension to the peace movement in insisting on the responsibility of both sides for the intensifying arms race and calling for a European movement of protest and resistance. It established the non-alignment of the peace movement as it opened contacts between east and west, associating the campaign for peace with the movement for democracy in Eastern Europe. Thompson was its most prominent public figure, becoming familiar to television audiences and newspaper readers and continuing to write articles and pamphlets, which showed 'how to attack not just a wrong but the official discourse which says that

wrong is inevitable' (N. Ascherson, 'E. P. Thompson: defender of the faithful few', *Independent on Sunday*, 5 Sept 1993).

The contribution made by the peace movement to the ending of the cold war is a matter of continuing debate. Thompson considered it significant. In 1990 he remarked that he had no regrets at having been turned aside from his writing, because he was 'convinced that the peace movement made a major contribution to dispersing the cold war, which had descended like a polluting cloud on every field of political and intellectual life' (*Customs in Common*, ix). A co-founder of European Nuclear Disarmament, Mary Kaldor, predicted that in time Thompson would be viewed, along with Mikhail Gorbachov and Vaclav Havel, as 'one of the key individuals who influenced the course of events in the 1980s' (*The Independent*, 30 Aug 1993). Many would agree, but there is no likelihood of a consensus: students of international relations are reluctant to acknowledge the efficacy of a moral crusade, while conservative historians continue to stress the firmness of the West's leaders in outfacing their cold-war enemy to the point of climb-down and ultimate collapse.

Last years, 1988–1993, and assessment With the ending of the arms race Thompson returned to his 'trade'. The long-delayed *Customs in Common* appeared in 1991 bringing together the essays which had given a new shape to the history of eighteenth-century England. His study of his father's relationship with Tagore came two years later, while progress was made on other projects: notably the completion of his major work on William Blake (*Witness Against the Beast: William Blake and the Moral Law*, 1993). Sadly that book, which meant so much to him, appeared shortly after his death. Thompson's last years were a five-year battle with a series of debilitating illnesses. He was very ill indeed, and what he accomplished in those years was remarkable, but finally on 28 August 1993 he died peacefully with Dorothy at his side in his garden at Wick Episcopi.

E. P. Thompson was one of the most prominent of twentieth-century British intellectuals working within the Marxist tradition. While he was best known for his historical writing and peace campaigning, these did not represent the whole of his intellectual activity. His significance in both roles owed most to his power as a writer, and as a writer his output was prolific and varied. He published poetry from an early age and in 1988 in his mid-sixties he published a satirical novel: *The Sykaos Papers*. His intellectual and writing skills were also displayed in the field of English literature, perhaps most noticeably in his study of William Blake. As a political essayist his was the most distinctive pen from the British left, writing with a passion, polemical verve, and remorseless reasoning which compares with the radical journalists and pamphleteers of the early nineteenth century, whom he much admired.

Had he not been otherwise preoccupied, Thompson would have found himself in the 1980s increasingly responding to critiques of his work. These began even before the collapse of communism influenced all who worked in the Marxist tradition and made 'class' an unfashionable concept around which to organize a historical narrative. The rise of women's history brought comment on what was perceived as a silence about gender in *The Making*; an increasing concern with ethnicity noted that, too, as a silence. The rise of post-modernism and the so-called 'linguistic turn' directed attack on to most existing forms of historical practice. It is a measure of Thompson's stature that his work attracted and continues to attract more critical attention than that of any other historian of his generation. The academic establishment was reluctant to accord him the recognition he merited, the British Academy electing him to a fellowship only in 1992. As the leading British historian Eric Hobsbawm has explained, he was a very special historian:

> He had the capacity to produce something qualitatively different from the rest of us, not to be measured on the same scale. Let us simply call it genius … None of his mature work could have been written by anyone else. (*The Independent*, 30 April 1993)

JOHN RULE

Sources D. Thompson, *Outsiders* (1993) · *The essential E. P. Thompson*, ed. D. Thompson (2001) · B. D. Palmer, *E. P. Thompson: objections and oppositions* (1994) [no bibliography, but its end notes contain the fullest listing of writings on Thompson to 1993] · J. G. Rule and R. W. Malcolmson, eds., *Protest and survival: essays for E. P. Thompson* (1993) [incl. chap. on Thompson as a teacher, and bibliography of writings to 1992] · P. Anderson, *Arguments with English Marxism* (1980) · D. Eastwood, 'History, politics and reputation: E. P. Thompson reconsidered', *History*, 85/280 (2000), 634–54 · M. D. Bess, 'E. P. Thompson: the historian as activist', *American Historical Review*, 98 (1993), 19–38 · M. Merrill, 'Interview with E. P. Thompson', *Visions of history*, ed. H. Abelove (1984), 5–25 · H. J. Kaye and K. L. McClelland, eds., *E. P. Thompson: critical perspectives* (1990) · H. J. Kaye, *The British Marxist historians* (1984) · M. Kenny, *The first new left: British intellectuals after Stalin* (1995) · 'Edward Thompson with Penelope Corfield', *Interviews with historians* (1993) [video, Institute of Historical Research] · D. Hempton and J. Walsh, 'E. P. Thompson and Methodism', *God and mammon: protestants, money and the market, 1790–1860*, ed. M. A. Noll (2002), 99–120 · J. Rée, 'A theatre of arrogance', *Times Higher Education Supplement* (2 June 1995) · E. J. Hobsbawm and M. Kaldor, *The Independent* (30 Aug 1993) · W. L. Webb, 'A thoroughly English dissident', *The Guardian* (30 Aug 1993) · R. Johnson, 'Edward Thompson, Eugene Genovese, and socialist-humanist history', *History Workshop Journal*, 6 (1978), 79–100 · W. Scott, 'Women in *The making of the English working class*', *Gender and the politics of history* (1988), 68–92 · B. D. Palmer, *The making of E. P. Thompson: Marxism, humanism and history* (1981)
Archives Bodl. Oxf., corresp. and papers | UWMRC, corresp. with E. Dodd
Likenesses S. Pyke, bromide print, 1989, NPG [*see illus.*]
Wealth at death £13,937: probate, 20 Oct 1993, CGPLA Eng. & Wales

Thompson, Elizabeth Maria Bowen [*née* Elizabeth Maria Lloyd] (1812/13–1869), missionary in Syria, was the daughter of Hannibal Evans *Lloyd (1771–1847), a philologist and translator, and his wife, Lucy von Schwartzkopff, who was from Hamburg. Her father lived in Hamburg between 1800 and 1813, after which he returned to England on account of the hardships of the French occupation. Elizabeth inherited a spirit of travel and adventure from her paternal grandfather, Henry Humphrey Evans *Lloyd (c.1718–1783), an army officer; her practicality is said to

have come from her mother. She had three sisters who later joined her in her missionary work—Susette, later Mrs Henry Smith, Augusta, later Mrs Mentor Mott, and Sophia, who remained unmarried—and a brother of whom very little is known. Her father's cousin was Henry *Salt, the discoverer of the Rosetta stone and one-time British consul in Alexandria—a family connection with the Middle East. She was religiously inclined from childhood, when she was taunted for being 'a little saint' (Lloyd, 3). She came under revivalist influences in Scotland while visiting friends and relatives there, and also came into contact with Unitarians. She herself notably converted a young sergeant on his way to China, whose fervour was such that he held Bible classes on board the *Himalaya*.

Lloyd identified herself early on with the cause of black education and was a founder, and joint secretary with one of her sisters, of the Ladies Society for the Early Education of Negro Children. She later joined the Syro-Egyptian committee under the presidency of Sir Culling Eardley, in which connection she probably met her future husband, Dr James Bowen Thompson. Thompson had been a medical missionary in Syria and director of the British Syrian Hospital in Damascus, which he had opened and ran from 1843 to 1848. After living in London, where they married on 14 December 1850 at St Botolph, Aldersgate, they went to Constantinople to pursue Thompson's pet project of opening a direct railway communication to India via the Euphrates valley. In December 1852 or January 1853 they moved to Suediah, near Antioch, where Thompson possessed some property, and resided there until June 1855. It was during this time that Elizabeth Bowen Thompson was initiated to the language and manners of the East, and 'her full heart yearned over the darkness and deprivation of the women'. She once began a school in her own house in Suediah. James Bowen Thompson died at Constantinople on 5 August 1855, of a 'malignant fever', reportedly contracted at Balaclava.

Elizabeth Bowen Thompson subsequently returned to London, where she lived with her sister Augusta. She was active with her sisters and other members of her family in several charitable enterprises, such as the committee led by the lady mayoress of London for the Indian mutiny. She also started the Central Association for Soldiers' Wives and became active, in 1860, in the Syrian Temporal Relief Fund. This involvement led to her departure for Beirut after news of the massacres in Mount Lebanon and Damascus reached her. Her voyage was preceded by a prayer meeting at the house of the Revd William Pennefather, the founder of the Mildmay conference hall, the home of much foreign mission work. She arrived in Beirut on 27 October 1860 and took a house called Beyt ʿAyub Bek; her original intention was to stay for six months. However, she was handicapped at the outset by an attack of rheumatic fever, and it was not until December that she began her work, initially with thirty women, mostly widows from the massacres of Hasbaʿiyyah, and sixteen children. Assistance was forthcoming from Lord Dufferin, who was there engaged in a diplomatic mission, and his mother, Helen Selina Blackwood, the dowager duchess.

Bowen Thompson's arrival coincided with a time when the established American missions in Beirut were undergoing a financial crisis caused mainly by the American Civil War, and when the Anglo-American committee was distributing relief without doing any educational or missionary work. She was joined by her sister Augusta Mentor Mott and the latter's husband in January 1861, following the destruction of their house by fire, and was additionally joined by her sister Sophia Lloyd in the summer of 1862. Her third sister, Susette, remained active in the cause from London, until she herself went to work in Beirut in 1875.

Bowen Thompson's friends in England formed a society to support her, the Society for the Social and Religious Improvement of Syrian Females, and there was another association, formed under the leadership of Lord Shaftesbury, for the establishment of English industrial and ragged schools in Syria. The former, which was formally constituted as a mission at the house of the Hon. Arthur Fitzgerald Kinnaird, also enjoyed the patronage of Lord Shaftesbury, who later became its chairman. Mary Jane, Lady Kinnaird, née Hoare, to whom the Lloyds were probably related, was president; the secretary was Elizabeth Bowen Thompson's sister Susette Smith, and her other sister Augusta also sat on the committee. The organization evolved to become the Ladies' Association for the Social and Religious Improvement of the Syrian Females, later the British Syrian Schools and Bible Mission for the Social and Religious Improvement of the Syrian Females (1876), then the British Syrian Schools and Bible Mission (1882), and finally the British Syrian Mission. The successor institution in the late twentieth century was Middle East Christian Outreach.

The schools in Beirut were visited by the prince of Wales during his visit to the Middle East in 1862 and attracted the attention and support of Fuat Pasha, who later became grand vizier. Bowen Thompson also established a good relationship, after an initial clash, with Daoud Pasha, the governor of Mount Lebanon, who gave her an official escort and went personally with her to Ain Zhalta at the opening of the Palm Branch School there on 13 October 1867. Following the establishment of the schools and workrooms and the training of Bible women in Beirut she also established a school in Hasbaʿiyyah on 28 September 1863 and received numerous requests from places like Zahlah, Deir al-Qamar, and, later, Damascus, all cities that had suffered badly in 1860. She was against the provision of free schooling and charged each student 'according to their several ability'. Her aim was to create independent institutions 'unfettered by any official authorization', and she encountered a lot of opposition from Roman Catholic clergy. Furthermore, in 1866 she had to close a small school in Deir al-Qamar because of local opposition, with the native teacher going to prison as a result.

Bowen Thompson's real breakthrough came with the granting of an imperial firman in 1868, giving her full powers to open schools at Zahlah and Deir al-Qamar and

calling for the authorities to give her the fullest aid and protection. This was suggested by the prince of Wales to the sultan during the latter's visit to London in 1867, and supported by the British ambassador to the Porte, and by Fuat Pasha, the grand vizier. In the same year a school for blind children was opened in Beirut. In 1865 and 1866 Bowen Thompson was in England, and took with her some of the products of her schools to sell. She was awarded a prize at the International Reformatory and Schools Exhibition, and also established branch associations in parts of England and Scotland. She was helped by donations from the prince of Wales and Lady Francis Egerton, who established the Ellsmere School in Deir al-Qamar, while funds for the Olive Branch School were contributed by the officers and men of HMS *Mars*. A Mr Tabet gave up his house in Beirut for the establishment of the school there and a notable in Zahlah also donated his house: the mission's motto was *Jehovah jireh* ('God will provide'). Although her initial goal was to work with women left widowed by the civil war, Bowen Thompson also taught children of Druze princes and Muslim notables who came to her. Sitt Naifeh Junblatt gave her support at the initial stages of her setting up in Hasbaʿiyyah. Only one publication by her is known, a simplified version of Edward Greswell's *Harmony of the Gospels* turned into a narrative suited for classes—which was later translated into Arabic by Salim Bustani.

Bowen Thompson, whose family motto was 'Dare and persevere', fell ill after a tough journey from Zahlah to Damascus in snow, and never recovered fully. She later went on business to Constantinople and England, where she died in Charlton, Blackheath, at Morden College, in the house of her sister Susette, on 14 November 1869. Her body was laid to rest by the side of her father and mother at 'God's Acre'—a secluded cemetery at Morden College, which was founded by an ancestor of Susette's husband, Henry William Smith, the treasurer of the college. Her sisters continued the work of the mission after her death.

NADIM SHEHADI

Sources S. H. Lloyd, *The daughters of Syria*, ed. H. B. Tristram (1874) · J. D. Maitland-Kirwan, *Sunrise in Syria* (1930) · A. L. Tibawi, *American interests in Syria* (1966) · *ILN* (3 July 1875) · J. E. Hutcheon, *The pearl of the East* (1920) · J. MacGregor, *The Rob Roy on the Jordan, Nile, Red Sea, and Gennesareth* (1869) · *DNB* · P. Joyce, *A history of Morden College* (1982) · *GM*, 2nd ser., 44 (1855), 441 · d. cert.
Archives U. Durham L., letters to Miss E. M. Copley with related corresp. and papers
Likenesses photograph, repro. in Lloyd, *The daughters of Syria*, frontispiece
Wealth at death under £600: probate, 3 Dec 1869, *CGPLA Eng. & Wales*

Thompson, Sir (John) Eric Sidney (1898–1975), archaeologist and epigrapher, was born on 31 December 1898 at the family home, 80 Harley Street, London, the third child and younger son of George William Thompson FRCS (1865–1947), surgeon, and his wife, Mary Cullen (1858–1933). He was educated at Winchester College (1912–15), but left early to enlist, under age and using the *nom de guerre* Neil Winslow, in the London Scottish to serve in France. He was wounded in 1916, but went back into

Sir (John) Eric Sidney Thompson (1898–1975), by Joya Hairs

action with the Coldstream Guards, ending the war as a second lieutenant. He then went to Argentina, where a branch of the family ranched cattle at Arenaza, west of Buenos Aires, and worked as a gaucho; returning to England in the early 1920s, he published 'A cowboy's experience: cattle branding in the Argentine' in the *Southwark Diocesan Gazette*, his first known work in the popular style which stood him in good stead later on. Photographs of him at this period show a medium build, fairish hair framing a broad, open face, and very direct gaze, together with the black beret and cigarette that were rarely absent from later pictures.

Undecided between medicine at Guy's or politics at the London School of Economics, Thompson eventually plumped for anthropology under A. C. Haddon at Cambridge, and matriculated at Fitzwilliam House (later Fitzwilliam College, where he became an honorary fellow in 1973) in 1924. He obtained the certificate in anthropology in 1925; he had become interested in Maya hieroglyphic writing, at that time virtually undeciphered apart from the complex and highly accurate calendar, and persuaded Sylvanus G. Morley to take him on the Carnegie Institution of Washington's (CIW) ambitious project at the great Maya city of Chichén Itzá in Yucatán. While there, he was sent to investigate the newly reported ruins at Cobá, 60 miles east, and produced decipherments of dates on the stelae there that Morley disbelieved until he saw them for himself.

Later in 1926 Thompson became assistant curator at the Field Museum of Natural History in Chicago, and immediately wrote a popular guide, *The Civilization of the Mayas*, and also the definitive correlation of the Maya and Christian calendars, placing the Classic period of the civilization's greatest florescence between AD 300 and 900. He was seconded to the British Museum's expedition to British Honduras for the 1927 season, working under Thomas A. Joyce at the site of Lubaantun and overturning Joyce's most cherished findings about Maya architectural technique.

Thompson was sent to examine monuments at the newly discovered site of Pusilhà, which became the focus of the British Museum's work from 1928 to 1930, and conversations with Faustino Bol, his Mopan Maya guide, showed him that many pre-Hispanic customs and beliefs survived and that 'archaeological excavations were not the only means of learning about the ancient ways' (Thompson, 117). *Ethnology of the Mayas of Southern and Central British Honduras* (1930) embraced this principle, using also material garnered from Thompson's Maya workers during his first independent archaeological project, published as *Archaeological Investigations in the Southern Cayo District, British Honduras* (1931). In 1930 he married Florence Lucy Keens (d. 1981), daughter of Herbert Edward Keens; they had one son, Donald Enrique Can Thompson, who became a specialist in Inca archaeology. In 1931 Eric Thompson joined Thomas Gann in writing *The History of the Maya from the Earliest Times to the Present Day*, and also began excavations at San Jose, which he hoped would be a more typical Maya 'ceremonial centre' (a term Thompson coined) than the fewer large sites such as Tikal. The San Jose monograph was published in 1939 by the CIW, whose division of historical research Thompson had joined in 1936, and where he remained until his formal retirement at the division's abolition in 1958. For his first two years there, he continued to explore newly reported Maya sites, including El Palmar in Quintana Roo and La Milpa in British Honduras, and also established a ceramic chronology for Benque Viejo (Xunantunich) in the Belize valley.

After 1938 Thompson worked mainly on hieroglyphic decipherment, publishing sixty papers on the topic and almost as many on others; in 1950 the CIW published *Maya Hieroglyphic Writing: Introduction*, still a standard work and complemented by *A Catalog of Maya Hieroglyphs* (1962), *Maya History and Religion* (1970), *A Commentary on the Dresden Codex* (1972), and the popular *Maya Hieroglyphs without Tears* (1972). Thompson argued that Maya inscriptions dealt with esoteric matters of calendrics, cosmology, and ritual, until persuaded otherwise by Tatyana Prokuryakov's 1960 demonstration of historicity. He was also convinced that the hieroglyphic script was not fundamentally phonetic in structure, a point ferociously disputed with the Russian epigrapher Yury Knorosov; Thompson's powers of argument (and Knorosov's numerous initial errors) delayed the general acceptance of phoneticism, and the rapid decipherments that followed, until after his death. His style of writing, sprinkled with literary allusions and quotations, backed by encyclopaedic knowledge, and expressed with a forthrightness that discouraged all but the brave from disputing it, often carried his case in the face of better evidence; his modest, almost shy demeanour surprised many who initially knew him only from his publications.

Thompson's ethnographic and ethnohistoric work

(including an edition of Thomas Gage's *Travels in the New World*, 1958) led to innovative readings of Classic Maya iconography and many other aspects of culture, including the use of tobacco, cacao, and rubber, practices of tattooing and sacrifice, and trade by land and sea, which helped to build the holistic understanding exemplified in his popular *The Rise and Fall of Maya Civilization* (1954), and its many foreign editions.

The interfertile use of archaeological, epigraphic, ethnohistoric, and ethnographic evidence made Thompson's scholarship, and his illumination of ancient Maya civilization, outstanding: he was greatly and rightly honoured for it with fellowship of the British Academy (1959), honorary degrees from the universities of Yucatán, Pennsylvania, Tulane, and Cambridge, the orders of Isabela La Católica (Spain), the Aztec Eagle (Mexico), and the Quetzal (Guatemala), and was made KBE (1975). Of the knighthood he noted, in a letter to his colleague Alberto Ruz Lhuillier:

> Six new Knights of the British Empire were created on New Year's Day: of those, P. G. Wodehouse, the novelist, is 91; Charlie Chaplin is 85 and in a wheelchair; I'm 76—if we are called on to defend the honour of the Empire in a tourney I don't think we'll have much success. (Ruz, 323–4, trans. N. Hammond)

Eric Thompson died at Addenbrooke's Hospital in Cambridge on 9 September 1975, and was buried beside the church at Ashdon in Essex, where he served for many years. NORMAN HAMMOND

Sources DNB · J. E. S. Thompson, *Maya archaeologist* (1963) · N. Hammond, 'Sir Eric Thompson, 1898–1975: a biographical sketch and bibliography', *Social process in Maya prehistory: studies in honour of Sir Eric Thompson*, ed. N. Hammond (1977), 1–17 · N. Hammond, 'Sir Eric Thompson, 1898–1975', *American Antiquity*, 42 (1977), 180–90 · *The Times* (11 Sept 1975) · A. Ruz Lhuillier, 'Semblanza de John Eric Sidney Thompson, 1898–1975', *Estudios de Cultura Maya*, 10 (1978), 317–35 · G. R. Willey, 'John Eric Sidney Thompson, 1898–1975', *PBA*, 65 (1979), 783–98 · personal knowledge (2004)

Archives BM, department of ethnography, personal library · Harvard U., Peabody Museum of Archaeology and Ethnology, card-files | Harvard U., Pusey Library, Carnegie files, field notes

Likenesses J. Hairs, photograph, repro. in Willey, 'John Eric Sidney Thompson' [*see illus.*] · G. Massey, miniature (as a boy), FM Cam. · photographs, repro. in Hammond, 'Sir Eric Thompson'

Wealth at death £61,010: probate, 11 Nov 1975, *CGPLA Eng. & Wales*

Thompson [*née* Timms], **Flora Jane** (1876–1947), author, was born in Juniper Hill, a hamlet in north-east Oxfordshire, on 5 December 1876, the eldest survivor of the ten children of Albert Timms (1854–1918), a stonemason, and his wife, Emma, *née* Dibber or Dipper (1853–1933), a nursemaid. Her favourite brother, Edwin, died in the battle of the Somme in 1916. After elementary education at the village school in Cottisford she became, at the age of fourteen, an unofficial Post Office counter clerk in the Oxfordshire village of Fringford. In 1898 she went to work at the post office in Grayshott, Hampshire, where she served some of the literary figures who lived in the area, including George Bernard Shaw, Arthur Conan Doyle, Grant Allen, and Richard Le Gallienne. Overawed by the talents

Flora Jane Thompson (1876–1947), by unknown photographer

of her literary customers, she almost gave up her own attempts at writing at that time.

On 7 January 1903 Flora Timms married John William Thompson (1874–1948), a Post Office clerk and telegraphist from the Isle of Wight. They moved to Bournemouth, where two of their three children were born. In 1911 Flora Thompson won a magazine essay competition and went on to write short stories and newspaper articles. The family moved to Liphook, in Hampshire, in 1916, and from there Flora contributed two long series of articles for the *Catholic Fireside* magazine; these were nature articles and literary essays written in alternate fortnights. She was a dedicated, self-taught naturalist; her nature articles subsequently appeared in Margaret Lane's *A Country Calendar* (1979) and in Julian Shuckburgh's *The Peverel Papers* (1986). The literary articles were the result of her private study of literature; she made extensive use of the recently established free library system to supplement her elementary school education. Her first published book was a volume of poems, *Bog Myrtle and Peat* (1921). From 1925 until the outbreak of the Second World War, she ran a postal writers' circle called the Peverel Society.

In 1938 Flora Thompson sent a collection of essays on her country childhood to Oxford University Press. They were first published as *Lark Rise* (1939), *Over to Candleford*

(1941), and *Candleford Green* (1943), and subsequently as a trilogy under the title *Lark Rise to Candleford* (1945). The books are the lightly disguised story of Flora Thompson's youth, evoking the life of a hamlet, a village, and a country town in the England of the 1880s. Some historians have cast doubt on their validity as primary sources for the social history of the period, but they have been widely used for that purpose. Few works better or more elegantly capture the decay of Victorian agrarian England. Two musical plays based on the books, *Lark Rise* and *Candleford*, by Keith Dewhurst, were performed at the National Theatre, London, in 1978 and 1979. *Heatherley*, the story of Flora Thompson's time in the post office at Grayshott, was not published in her lifetime; it is included in Lane's *A Country Calendar*. Her last book, *Still Glides the Stream*, was published posthumously in 1948.

Flora Thompson's younger son was lost at sea in the Second World War, when the merchant navy ship on which he was serving was torpedoed in mid-Atlantic. She never recovered from his loss, and died on 21 May 1947 at her home, Lauriston, New Road, Brixham, Devon. She was buried in Longcross cemetery, Dartmouth. Her husband survived her.   GILLIAN LINDSAY

Sources F. Thompson, *A country calendar and other writings*, ed. M. Lane (1979) · G. Lindsay, *Flora Thompson: the story of the Lark Rise writer* (1990) · B. English, 'Lark Rise & Juniper Hill: a Victorian community in literature and in history', *Victorian Studies*, 29 (1985–6) · M. Lane, *Flora Thompson* (1976) · b. cert. · m. cert. · d. cert. · *CGPLA Eng. & Wales* (1947) · Oxon. RO
Archives Ransom HRC, papers · University of Exeter, MSS and corresp. | Oxfordshire Museums Service, Woodstock, photographs
Likenesses photograph, priv. coll. [*see illus.*] · photographs, Oxfordshire Museums Service, Woodstock
Wealth at death £1031 8s. 5d.: probate, 16 Aug 1947, *CGPLA Eng. & Wales*

Thompson, Francis (1808–1895), architect, was born on 25 July 1808 at Woodbridge, Suffolk, the second of the seven children of George Thompson (1777–1862), builder and county surveyor of Suffolk, and his wife, Elizabeth (1786–1856), *née* Miles. The Thompsons had been farmers in nearby Bredfield during the seventeenth and eighteenth centuries, though Francis's grandfather Jacob Thompson (1744–1834), a Quaker, was a builder and his uncle Mark Grayston Thompson (*c.*1785–1852) and his first cousin William Pattison (1805–1878) were local architects.

Thompson was educated at Woodbridge grammar school, and absorbed an early interest in architecture from seeing his uncle's and father's work. A miniature at the age of twenty-one shows him with reddish hair. A full-length photograph of 1859 by William Notman of Montreal shows him of medium height and lean build, with full wavy hair and goatee beard. A photograph of 1871 by J. W. Thomas of Hastings shows receding hair and a groomed beard and moustache.

Thompson was married three times. His first marriage was to Anna Maria Watson (*c.*1810–1832) at Woodbridge

church on 17 May 1830. Ambition and a spirit for adventure took the pair to Montreal in Canada. Their son Francis Jacob was born in 1831. Anna died the following year during the cholera epidemic which claimed 4000 lives in Montreal. With a flair for hard work and a natural ability in design, Thompson received commissions from new settlers and established merchants for houses, commercial buildings, court facilities, a church, and—in partnership with John Wells (1789–1864)—the imposing St Ann's market hall. The building became the Canadian parliament house (1844–9).

Growing civil unrest between the French majority and the increasing number of British settlers prompted Thompson to return to Britain in 1837. The timing was fortuitous. Railway companies, still in their infancy, were eager to employ architects and engineers to meet new and exciting challenges in design and construction. It was into this field of work that Thompson moved. In February 1839 the North Midland Railway, about to construct a 72 mile line from Derby to Leeds, appointed him their architect. Their engineer was Robert Stephenson (1803–1859), and an acclaimed working relationship was established between the pair.

At Derby, Francis designed the world's first comprehensive railway settlement, with a magnificent station and three-bay glazed train-shed, locomotive roundhouse and workshop, workers' houses, and a hotel. Late Georgian in character, the hotel, roundhouse, and houses form part of the Derby Station conservation area. The station was enlarged several times and redevelopment, rather than restoration, was carried out during the 1980s.

Robert Stephenson and Francis Thompson next acted for the Chester and Holyhead Railway (1845–50), and at the Menai Strait produced one of the finest examples of engineering architecture to be found in the nineteenth century. The Britannia Bridge was damaged by fire in 1970, but the elegant masonry escaped damage and now supports steel arches in lieu of wrought-iron tubes. The elegant Italianate station which Thompson built at Chester resembled the one at Derby in layout, but has bay platforms at either end.

Around 1840 Thompson married again, and following the death of his second wife, Elizabeth (1815–1852), he married Mary Ann Groves (1818–1896) of Wareham, Dorset, on 30 June 1853. Retracing steps taken twenty-three years earlier, he sailed with his new wife for Canada. The Grand Trunk Railway of Canada and the Atlantic and St Lawrence railroad, with a 900 mile route planned to link Portland, Maine, with Montreal, Toronto, and Detroit, appointed Francis their architect from 1853 to 1859. He designed the masonry for the Victoria Bridge in Montreal, the terminus at Portland, Maine (claimed to be the largest station in America when opened in 1855), elegant stone and slate standard-plan stations, and workshops.

In April 1859 Thompson returned to London and in 1866 he designed a house at Hastings for retirement. Memories of his childhood, however, induced a move back to Bredfield, where he died on 23 April 1895. He was buried two days later in Woodbridge cemetery. Once a well-paid architect, long retirement drained his resources, and he died intestate and impoverished.

OLIVER F. J. CARTER

Sources O. Carter, 'Francis Thompson, 1808–95: an architectural mystery solved', *Backtrack*, 9/4 (April 1995) · O. Carter, 'Railway Thompson', *ArchR*, 143 (1968) · H. R. Hitchcock, *Early Victorian architecture in Britain*, 2 vols. (1954) · C. Barman, *An introduction to railway architecture* (1950) · *North midland railway guide* (1842); repr. (1973) · N. Bosworth, *Hochelaga depicta* (1839) · C. Legge, *A glance at the Victoria Bridge, and the men who built it* (1860) · Ezra Beal's diary, Maine Historical Society, Augusta, Maine, USA · R. G. Hill, ed., *Biographical dictionary of architects in Canada, 1800–1950* [forthcoming] · *Woodbridge Reporter and Wickham Market Gazette* (25 April 1895) · parish register (baptism) Woodbridge, Suffolk, St Mary, 29 July 1808 · census returns, 1851 · parish register (marriage), 30 June 1853, Bermondsey, Surrey, St James · private information (2004)
Archives Archives Nationales du Québec, drawings of St Ann's market, Montreal · Canadian Inventory of Historical Building, Ottawa, signed drawings of courthouse, Napierville · priv. coll., Thompson/White family archive · RIBA BAL, biography file
Likenesses W. S. Lethbridge, miniature, 1829, Thompson/White family archive, Carmarthen · W. Notman, photograph, 1859, McCord Photographic Archive, Montreal · J. W. Thomas, photograph, 1871, Thompson/White family archive, Carmarthen
Wealth at death impoverished: Thompson/White family archive

Francis Joseph Thompson (1859–1907), by Elliott & Fry, 1880s

Thompson, Francis Joseph (1859–1907), poet and writer, was born on 18 December 1859 at 7 Winckley Street, Preston, Lancashire. He was the second son of Charles Thompson (1819–1896), a physician specializing in homoeopathic medicine, and Mary Turner Morton, (1822–1880), who came from a Manchester business family. An older brother had died at birth the previous year and two sisters, Mary and Margaret, were born in 1861 and 1863, after the family moved to a more spacious home in nearby Winckley Square. In 1864 they settled in Ashton under Lyne on the outskirts of Manchester. Both parents were converts to Roman Catholicism who like hundreds of others had followed Cardinal Newman's lead as a direct result of the Oxford Movement. In addition they were influenced by the solid and unemotional faith of the north-country families who had survived the penal days and developed in consequence a characteristic independence of outlook. They passed these influences on to their son, whose firmly grounded faith was to withstand severe tests. But although two uncles, Edward Healy Thompson and John Costall Thompson, had published minor collections of poetry and prose, there was no precedent in the family background for Francis's poetic career. His love of poetry was clear from the start, while according to his sister Mary he 'wished to be a priest from a little boy' (Boardman, 18). In 1870, at the age of eleven, he was sent to St Cuthbert's College, Ushaw, near Durham, for an education designed to lead to the priesthood.

From there Thompson acquired his knowledge of Catholic liturgy and there too he began to keep the notebooks which became a lifelong habit. Starting with the 'Ushaw College notebook' they number well over a hundred, mostly cheap exercise books, filled with drafts at all stages for his poetry and prose and interspersed with ideas and comments on anything from the issues of the day to memos for nightshirts or trouser buttons. They reveal more clearly than any other source his erratic and unpractical temperament, contrasted with the methodical care that characterizes his method of poetic composition. With a few exceptions the 'Ushaw College notebook' gives little indication of the future poetry, but it shows his schoolboy enthusiasm for the Romantic literature of the time, overriding other interests. Its rich, sensuous imagery and its visual qualities are reminiscent of his early favourite, Dante Gabriel Rossetti, while his preoccupation with medieval themes and ideas are clearly influenced by Tennyson as well as the Pre-Raphaelites. These inclinations were not considered compatible with a priestly vocation and in 1877 he left Ushaw to start a medical training at Owens College, Manchester, soon to become part of the Victoria University of Manchester.

Here Thompson struggled on for the next six years, escaping whenever he could to the city library and art gallery. The training left him with the nightmarish memories of the contemporary operating theatre and dissecting rooms that give his poetry some of its most compelling imagery. But it also left him with his lifelong respect for science and its contributions to the modern world. Shortly before his twenty-first birthday his much loved mother died from a painful disease for which opium was the only relief. Almost certainly it was this which gave rise to his own addiction to the drug. During his creative years he was to learn to keep it in check and, contrary to the view of some critics, such as J. C. Reid or G. Grigson, until his last months it was seldom excessive. But it was undoubtedly so during the three years following the final break with his family soon after it became clear he would never make it to the medical profession.

Thompson went to London in the autumn of 1885 and after a few months' desultory employment he was driven to live on the streets. The few pennies he could earn by calling cabs and selling matches went on the opium that was his only respite. The notebooks surviving from these years, damp-stained and often now barely legible, are the most poignant witnesses to his mental and physical suffering. Yet there was another side, for the notebooks record many small acts of kindness from his fellow outcasts. One such encounter stands out from the rest. In autumn 1887 he came close to suicide, from which he was rescued by a prostitute who took him back to her lodgings and looked after him through that winter. Nothing is known of her or of their relationship except that she encouraged him to write his poetry and it continued until the turning point came for him the following spring.

A year before, in February 1887, Thompson had sent some manuscripts of poems and an essay to Wilfrid Meynell, editor of the Catholic literary journal *Merry England*. But they were mislaid for the intervening months until, on finding them, Meynell recognized their merit and tried unsuccessfully to trace the poet. He therefore printed one of the poems, 'The Passion of Mary', in the Easter issue of his journal: and Thompson, by an almost incredible chance, heard of it. But it took several meetings with Wilfrid Meynell and his wife, Alice, a poet in her own right, before he would agree to leave the streets and accept their hospitality. He did so when the street girl, aware she would be a hindrance now rather than a help, disappeared from her lodgings. Despite his efforts to find her she had gone from his life: but never from his grateful memory, as entries in the notebooks testify as well as poems both published and hitherto unpublished.

A period of recuperation was needed and in February 1888 Thompson went to stay at the Premonstratensian priory in Storrington, Sussex. Here, having overcome the symptoms of opium withdrawal, his poetic gifts appeared at last in two major poems, the 'Ode to the Setting Sun' and 'The Hound of Heaven'. Different as the two are, both poems take the theme of death and rebirth beyond the specific Christian context, relating it to some of humanity's most universal aspirations. In both, these aspirations are expressed through a wealth of cosmic imagery that is unique to Thompson. In 'The Hound of Heaven', his best-known poem, the flight of the soul from God reaches from within 'the labyrinthine ways' of the human mind with its 'Titanic glooms of chasmèd fears' to 'the gold gateways of the stars' (ll. 3, 8, 26). When the flight is over, the self-confrontation that follows takes place in a cosmic setting centred on 'the hid battlements of eternity' (l. 145) and the cry of Everyman against his human limitations:

Whether man's heart or life it be which yields
Thee harvest, must Thy harvest fields
Be dunged with rotten death?
(ll. 152–4)

Though the poem is rooted within Thompson's Catholic

background, his later experiences had widened his vision to embrace, in the final resolution, a restoration that extends beyond any particular creed.

Thompson was back in London early in 1890, spending most of his days at the Meynells' home assisting them with their journalistic work. Here he met the varied circle of their friends and colleagues who, according to the Meynells' daughter Viola, were marked by 'strong independent views, not afraid to be the exception'. In their company his shabby, nondescript appearance went with his diffident manner, recalled by Viola as 'silent, repetitive or irrelevant' (V. Meynell, 65, 86). Yet when roused he could be eloquent on subjects where he felt confident and he shared in many of their more liberal views. His prose writings for the Meynells' journals were often critical of the social and religious attitudes of the time. The most notable was the essay 'In Darkest London', which appeared in *Merry England* (January 1891; the version printed in *The Works of Francis Thompson*, 1913, contains unacknowledged deletions as well as additions from other sources). It drew on his own experiences in showing up the inadequacy of the provisions made for the homeless. With the outstanding exception of the Salvation Army the prevailing response to the population of the streets was too often one of condemnation. You had to deserve mercy, divine or human.

Apart from his poetry and other writings Thompson was developing another interest, begun in the library and art gallery in Manchester and not discarded even during the dark years on the streets. Until turned away on account of his ragged clothing he would spend hours at the Guildhall Library or the National Gallery. Now he was again spending his free time reading widely on all aspects of ancient beliefs and the symbolism by which they were expressed. He kept his studies within the privacy of his notebooks since for Catholics such preoccupations were highly suspect. But his knowledge of these subjects enhances many of his poems, as can now be recognized in the wider context that he had in mind.

During 1892 the demands of journalism, the loneliness of his lodgings, and the need for time to write his poetry began to tell and the Meynells were aware that Thompson was again taking opium. So they arranged, and he had to agree, for a visit to the Franciscan friary at Pantasaph in north Wales, where he was to remain for the next four years. The magnificent scenery of the Welsh mountains combined with the spiritual and intellectual stimulus of the community gave rise to a period of intense creativity. His first volume of poetry, *Poems*, appeared in 1893 and provoked strong reactions for and against. *Sister Songs*, two long poems addressed to two of the Meynell children, was published in 1895 while he was preparing his most extensive collection, *New Poems* (1897), to which the critical responses showed how little the ideas behind his poetry were appreciated. Most of the more notable poems are concerned with one or another aspect of the incarnation of supernatural life within the human and natural order. In 'From the Night of Forebeing' he reinterprets the Easter liturgy of the resurrection in terms of renewal in the natural world and within his own soul. 'Assumpta Maria' celebrates the bodily assumption of the Blessed Virgin into heaven as the ultimate effect of incarnation as he understands it. Furthermore he identifies the role of the Blessed Virgin as queen of heaven with the pagan goddesses who were her precursors. Significantly, after his death the central three stanzas were deleted from all editions published to date. But by now Thompson was full of doubts as to the future of his poetry. Drawing down the supernatural, as it were, within the natural world, might be only a short step from an over-identification with materialistic aims and values that would undermine all he desired his poetry to express. It must wait for an age when harmony between the three orders of existence, supernatural, natural, and human life, would be recognized as essential to the continuing well-being of creation as a whole.

Thompson's friendship with Coventry Patmore contributed to this dilemma. Though it was fruitful in their shared interest in ancient religions and symbolism, Thompson was unable to accept the extent of the older poet's identification between divine and human love—underlined as it was by a mutual infatuation for Alice Meynell which Thompson, unlike Patmore, was able to surmount (Boardman, 232–4). Thompson was aware that his creative life as a poet was waning by this time. But after his return to London, shortly after Patmore's death in 1896, in the prose writings of his later years he was constantly exploring the ideas and aims of the poets of the past and of his own day. His numerous reviews and carefully structured essays have been unfairly neglected, as also the monograph *Health and Holiness*, published in 1905 with a preface by George Tyrrell—already a controversial figure on account of his 'modernist' views. Here Thompson's study of the relations between spiritual and physical health is well ahead of his time. His later odes, although usually commissioned for public occasions, contain passages worthy of his earlier work.

During these years Thompson's friendship with Katharine Douglas King, known as Katie, could have developed further if his circumstances and temperament had been different. They shared their concern for the London poor and her novels of London life, drawn from her own experiences, still await recognition. Her death in 1900 left him with little to lighten his last years apart from his lifelong enthusiasm for cricket and writing the humorous verse that he usually kept to the privacy of his notebooks. Lines from his unfinished poem 'At Lords' have become part of cricket literature but others of his cricket poems remained virtually unknown until the publication of the new edition of his work in 2001.

Towards the end of his life Thompson's opium habit increased, mainly to relieve the symptoms of his declining health. He did not then or at any time suffer from tuberculosis, as has been generally believed. Drawing on his medical knowledge he himself diagnosed the disease as beriberi, originating from his years of deprivation and complicated by the opium and his erratic way of life. This has been professionally confirmed by a medical expert in retrospective diagnosis (Boardman, 314–15, 392, n. 14). The best likeness of Thompson dates from these last months in the pencil sketch by Neville Lytton.

Thompson died on 13 November 1907 at the Hospital of St John and St Elizabeth, London, and was buried on 16 November at Kensal Green Roman Catholic cemetery. The only possessions at his lodgings were some old pipes, the toy theatre he had played with as a child, and a tin trunk full of papers. These were manuscripts and notebooks accumulated over forty years, from which Wilfrid Meynell edited both poetry and prose for publication in journals and in the so-called *Works of Francis Thompson* (3 vols., 1913). The extent of Meynell's alterations and deletions has not been recognized, as all subsequent editions were based on the *Works*. The new edition of the poems restores original texts and adds others hitherto unpublished.

BRIGID M. BOARDMAN

Sources B. M. Boardman, *Between heaven and Charing Cross: the life of Francis Thompson* (1988) · J. E. Walsh, *Strange harp, strange symphony: the life of Francis Thompson* (1968) · *The letters of Francis Thompson*, ed. J. E. Walsh (New York, 1969) · E. Meynell, *The life of Francis Thompson* (1913) · V. Meynell, *Francis Thompson and Wilfrid Meynell* (1952) · O. Chadwick, *The Victorian church*, 2 vols. (1966–70) · K. Chesney, *The Victorian underworld* (1970) · H. Jackson, *The eighteen nineties: a review of art and ideas* (1988) · D. Matthew, *Catholicism in England, 1598–1935*, rev. 2nd edn (1948) · T. M. Parssinen, *Secret passions, secret remedies: narcotic drugs in English society, 1820–1930* (1983) · H. Mayhew, *London labour and the London poor*, 4 vols. (1861–4) · M. Secker, *The eighteen nineties* (1948) · *The poems of Francis Thompson*, ed. B. Boardman (2001) · J. Thomson, *Francis Thompson, the Preston-born poet* (1912) · b. cert.

Archives Boston College, Massachusetts, corresp. and papers · Harris Library, Preston, commonplace book, poetical MSS, letters; notebooks and literary MSS · Indiana University, Bloomington, Lilly Library, corresp. and writings · Lancashire Library, Preston, commonplace book, poetical MSS, letters, notebooks, and literary MSS · State University of New York, Buffalo · Ushaw College, Durham, commonplace book

Likenesses Elliott & Fry, photograph, 1880–89, NPG [*see illus.*] · E. Meynell, oils, 1906, priv. coll. · N. Lytton, chalk drawing, 1907, NPG · N. Lytton, pencil sketch, 1907, Boston College, Chesnut Hill, Massachusetts, J. J. Burns Library · N. Lytton, pastel sketch, 1945, Boston College, Chesnut Hill, Massachusetts, J. J. Burns Library · J. Lavelle, oils (after N. Lytton), Boston College, Chesnut Hill, Massachusetts, J. J. Burns Library · E. Meynell, plaster cast, NPG

Wealth at death no possessions apart from MSS and other papers

Thompson, (William) Frank (1920–1944), poet and secret operations officer, was born at Darjeeling, India, on 17 August 1920, the elder son of Edward John *Thompson (1886–1946), poet, novelist, and historian, and his wife, Theodosia, daughter of Dr William Jessup, a distinguished American missionary.

Thompson's childhood home, at Scar Top, Boars Hill, Oxfordshire, did much to encourage independent thought. As his younger brother, the historian Edward Palmer *Thompson (1924–1993), recalled, the boys' upbringing was 'supportive, liberal, anti-imperialist, quick with ideas and poetry and international visitors' (Thompson, *Beyond the Frontier*, 47). Tagore, Gandhi, and Nehru all came to the house; so too did John Masefield, Gilbert Murray, Sir Arthur Evans, and Robert Graves. Their father's break with the Methodist church only added further stimulus.

After the Dragon School, Oxford, where he gained a solid grounding in classical languages, Frank Thompson won a scholarship to Winchester College. His political consciousness rapidly matured, particularly when a boyhood friend was killed with the International Brigades in Spain, and still more after he went up, again a scholar, to New College, Oxford, in autumn 1938. There, for a year, he read classics, developing a greater taste for philosophy than literature, and indulged his love of poetry and languages. A fine poet, he was a remarkable linguist: by the time he was twenty-three he had added to Latin and ancient Greek a command of modern Greek, German, French, and Italian, as well as Russian, Polish, Serbo-Croat, and Bulgarian, plus a little Arabic. At Oxford he joined the university's Labour Club and, early in 1939, the Communist Party. He formed, too, a close relationship with a young undergraduate at Somerville, Iris Murdoch (1919–1999). It was assumed that they would marry. Once, when she let another man kiss her, Thompson reputedly rushed to Boars Hill and dug up a bed of irises (*The Guardian*, 10 Feb 1999).

Independent, energetic, and passionate, Thompson was fiercely anti-fascist but his communism was more intellectual than social. A strident opponent of appeasement, he was little fazed by the Soviet Union's pact with Nazi Germany or its claim that the conflict was imperialist. On the outbreak of war he enlisted immediately.

Commissioned into the Royal Artillery in March 1940, in July he was posted to the newly created 'Phantom' (general headquarters liaison) regiment. Anxious for action, he volunteered to join a squadron of the regiment at that time fighting in Greece but arrived in the Middle East only after the campaign was over. From May 1941 until April 1943 he served with Phantom's Middle East squadron, first as a patrol officer, then as intelligence officer, and for the last year as second in command. He served throughout the Libyan campaign and the Middle East and, attached to 151 Brigade, took part in the Sicily landings of July 1943. In September 1943 he joined the Special Operations Executive (SOE).

In January 1944, *en route* to lead a mission into Bulgaria, Thompson parachuted into occupied Macedonia with progressive ideals and Byronic expectation. He had written home on Christmas day 1943:

> There is a spirit abroad in Europe which is finer and braver than anything that tired continent has known for centuries, and which cannot be withstood … It is the confident will of whole peoples, who have known the utmost humiliation and suffering and who have triumphed over it, to build their own life once and for all. I like best to think of it as millions—literally millions—of people, young in heart whatever their age, completely masters of themselves, looking only forward, and liking what they see. (Thompson and Thompson, 5)

Late in May he was caught, brutally interrogated, and, following a show trial in which he defended himself in Bulgarian and pronounced himself a communist, executed by firing squad alongside twelve captured partisans on, or shortly before, 10 June 1944 (sources conflict as to the precise date). Together they died giving the clenched fist salute. He was not yet twenty-four.

Thompson's life and loss had an immense impact on the family and friends he left behind. Drawing on diaries, letters, poems, and notes, his mother and brother produced *There is a Spirit in Europe: a Memoir of Frank Thompson* just three years after his death. Indeed, for E. P. Thompson—long influenced by the vision of a democratic, socialist Europe—finding the 'truth' behind his beloved brother's fate became something of an obsession. Unable satisfactorily to piece together the events of 1944, he was furious and suspicious at the British government's reluctance to declassify official documents relating to Frank's SOE mission, and read conspiracy into each obscure turn of the story. Later he portrayed his brother as an unwitting victim of great-power politics and communist double-dealing (Thompson, 1997).

In Bulgaria, Thompson was proclaimed a national hero by the country's post-war communist government, and was awarded two posthumous decorations. In the village of Litakovo the mass grave where he and his partisans were given ceremonious reburial in November 1944 is marked by a national monument. At Prokopnik, where the Bulgarian partisans fought one of their fiercest engagements, a railway station is named after him.

Several of Thompson's poems were published in anthologies. One, 'Polliciti meliora', was read at the broadcast ceremony to commemorate the end of the war, with the following as its concluding verse:

> Write on the stone no words of sadness,
> —Only the gladness due
> That we, who asked the most of the living,
> Knew how to give it too.
> (Thompson, p. i)

The lines also head the roll of honour at Winchester College.

Years later a Byzantine coin, discovered in Thompson's tunic in the moments after his death, was presented to Iris Murdoch. In 1975 she wrote of him:

> He was a poet, a person of exceptional charm and sweetness, always full of jokes and fun, a lover of art and nature, a scholar, a man of the highest principles, delicate, scrupulous and tender … Those who knew him will never cease to mourn the loss of this brilliant, brave and good man. (*The Times*, 27 Aug 1975)

RODERICK BAILEY

Sources T. J. Thompson and E. P. Thompson, *There is a spirit in Europe: a memoir of Frank Thompson* (1947) · E. P. Thompson, *Beyond the frontier: the politics of a failed mission* (1997) · S. Johnson, *Agents extraordinary* (1975) · R. J. T. Hills, *Phantom was there* (1951) · J. D'E. Firth, *Winchester College* (1969) · I. Murdoch, *The Times* (27 Aug 1975) [letter to the editor] · J. Ezard, 'The unseen faces of Iris', *The Guardian* (10 Feb 1999) · private information, 2004 [SOE adviser] · *CGPLA Eng. & Wales* (1947) · P. J. Conradi, *Iris Murdoch: a life* (2001)
Archives Balliol Oxf., Bickham Sweet-Escott papers, records relating to special operations executive service · Bodl. Oxf., E. P. Thompson papers, papers · PRO, SOE archive (HS class), records relating to special operations executive service

Wealth at death £791 7s. 8d.: administration, 20 Jan 1947, *CGPLA Eng. & Wales*

Thompson, George Donisthorpe (1804–1878), slavery abolitionist, born at Liverpool on 18 June 1804, was the third son of Henry Thompson of Leicester. In 1831 he married Anne Erskine, daughter of Richard Spry, a minister in the Methodist Connexion of the countess of Huntingdon. They had six children. He first became widely known as a propagandist for the abolition of slavery in the British colonies. In October 1833 a series of lectures by him led to the formation of 'the Edinburgh Society for the abolition of slavery throughout the world'. He also lectured and took part in public discussions in Liverpool, Manchester, Glasgow, Bath, and elsewhere. In September 1834 he undertook a mission to the United States. He worked with William Lloyd Garrison, Whittier, and the members of the American Anti-Slavery Society in the movement for the abolition of slavery, and was instrumental in forming more than 300 abolitionist branch associations. He is said to have caused by his speeches the failure of Thomas Jefferson Randolph's so-called 'Port Natal' plan for slave emancipation in Virginia and he was denounced by General Jackson in a presidential message.

Thompson's life was frequently in danger, and in December 1835 he was forced to escape from Boston in an open boat to a British vessel bound for New Brunswick, from where he sailed back to Britain. On his return he was enthusiastically received at Glasgow, Edinburgh, Newcastle upon Tyne, and other large towns. He revisited the United States in 1851, and again during the American Civil War, when a public reception was given to him in the house of representatives, in the presence of President Lincoln and the majority of the cabinet.

Thompson was associated with Joseph Hume, Sir Joshua Walmsley, and other prominent Liberal radicals in the National Parliamentary Reform Association. He was also a member of the Anti-Corn Law League, and took part in forming the British India Association, visiting India to study its governance. In 1846 he was presented with the freedom of the city of Edinburgh. On 31 July 1847 he was returned to parliament for the Tower Hamlets constituency, a seat he retained until 1852, and about 1870 a testimonial was raised for him by his friends in Britain and the United States. He settled at Leeds and died there on 7 October 1878.

Thompson was a brilliant speaker, and well regarded socially. John Bright 'always considered him the liberator of the slaves in the English colonies'.

W. A. S. HEWINS, *rev.* MATTHEW LEE

Sources *Howitt's Journal*, 2 (1847), 257–60 · J. G. Wilson and J. Fiske, eds., *Appleton's cyclopaedia of American biography*, 4 (1888), 760; 5 (1888), 173; 6 (1889), 90 · O. Johnson, *William Lloyd Garrison and his times* (1882) · Boase, *Mod. Eng. biog.* · *Annual Register* (1878) · C. C. Burleigh, *Reception of George Thompson in Great Britain* (1836)
Archives Boston PL, corresp. and papers · JRL, corresp., diaries, and papers
Likenesses C. Turner, mezzotint, pubd 1842 (after G. Evans), BM, NPG [*see illus.*] · H. Furniss, caricature, pen-and-ink sketch, NPG · B. R. Haydon, group portrait, oils (*The Anti-Slavery Society convention, 1840*), NPG · portrait, repro. in *Howitt's Journal* · portrait, repro. in

George Donisthorpe Thompson (1804–1878), by Charles Turner, pubd 1842 (after George Evans)

ILN, 14 (1849), 101 · wood-engraving (after photograph by C. Braithwaite of Leeds), NPG; repro. in *ILN*, 73 (19 Oct 1878), 327
Wealth at death under £1000: probate, 3 March 1879, *CGPLA Eng. & Wales*

Thompson, Gertrude Caton- (1888–1985), archaeologist, was born in London on 1 February 1888, the younger child and only daughter of William Caton Thompson, of Lancashire–Yorkshire stock, and his wife, Ethel Gertrude, daughter of William Bousfield Page, surgeon, of Carlisle. Her father, a barrister and head of the legal branch of the London and North Western Railway, died when she was five years old. Her mother remarried in 1900; her new husband was George Moore, a general practitioner of Maidenhead who was a widower with four sons and a daughter. Her father had ensured her financial independence and, after being educated privately and at the Links School, Eastbourne, until the First World War she enjoyed a social life in London and the country, and included one auspicious visit to Egypt among her travels abroad.

In 1917 Caton-Thompson was employed by the Ministry of Shipping and promoted to a senior secretarial post in which she attended the Paris peace conference. She declined a permanent appointment in the civil service, and in 1921, aged thirty-three and with none of the usual qualifications, she began her archaeological studies under the Egyptologist Flinders Petrie at University College, London, joining his excavations at Abydos in Upper Egypt that winter. The next year was spent at Newnham College, Cambridge (with which she remained associated for the rest of her life), and in attending university courses. She returned to Egypt in 1924 and joined Petrie and Guy Brunton at Qau el Kibir. While they concentrated their excavations on predynastic cemeteries she had concluded, well ahead of her time, that settlement sites would be more informative, and in characteristically independent fashion she embarked on her own excavations on the site of a predynastic village at Hamamiyyah. There she made the first discovery of remains, well stratified, of the very early Badarian civilization. With Guy Brunton she wrote *The Badarian Civilization* (1928).

In 1925 Caton-Thompson turned to north-western Egypt and the desert margins of Lake El Faiyûm, accompanied by the Oxford geologist Elinor Gardner, to assist in an attempt to correlate lake levels with archaeological stratification. In three El Faiyûm seasons they discovered two unknown neolithic cultures which proved later to be related to the Khartoum neolithic. They published their findings in *The Desert Fayum* (1934). Her next assignment followed an invitation in 1929 from the British Association for the Advancement of Science to investigate the great monumental ruins at Zimbabwe in southern Africa. She confirmed the conclusion reached by David Randall-MacIver in 1905 that they belonged to an indigenous African culture and were not, as widely believed, of oriental origin. She was also able to date the ruins back to the eighth or ninth century AD and to produce evidence of Zimbabwe's links with Indian Ocean trade.

Having completed her Zimbabwe report with her usual speed (*The Zimbabwe Culture*, 1931) Caton-Thompson embarked in 1930, with Elinor Gardner, on an extended campaign of excavations on prehistoric sites at Kharga oasis. These excavations, the first on Saharan oasis sites, inaugurated a far-ranging programme of research on the palaeolithic of north Africa and led to her book *Kharga Oasis in Pre-History* (1952).

Caton-Thompson's last excavations, in 1937, were the only ones outside Africa apart from some fieldwork in Malta in her student days. These were at al-Huraydah in the Hadhramaut, southern Arabia, where she excavated the Moon Temple and tombs of the fifth and fourth centuries BC. Carried out in a region then rarely visited by Western, let alone female, travellers, they were the first scientific excavations in southern Arabia. Again she was accompanied by Elinor Gardner. A third, less compatible, member of the party was the writer and traveller Freya Stark. *The Tombs and Moon Temple of Hureidha, Hadramaut* appeared in 1944.

Caton-Thompson retired from fieldwork after the Second World War and from her home in Cambridge pursued her research activities and visited excavations in east Africa. She never sought or accepted a professorship. In 1961, already in her seventies, she became a founder member of the British School of History and Archaeology in East Africa (later the British Institute in Eastern Africa), served on its council for ten years, and was later elected an honorary member. An honorary fellowship of Newnham College, Cambridge, and an honorary LittD (1954) of that university were among academic honours bestowed on her. She was elected a fellow of the British Academy in 1944 and not long before her death a fellow of University College, London.

Professionally Gertrude Caton-Thompson was a formidable personality, a trenchant critic, adamant in academic argument, and an indefatigable worker. She was an intrepid traveller and at Abydos, it is said, slept in an emptied tomb with cobras for company and a pistol under her pillow to ward off prowling hyenas. Although by nature quiet and retiring, she was excellent company and her dry humour and laconic, incisive comments on people and events became a rich source of anecdote in Cambridge circles. She was a generous benefactor, especially of the National Trust for the purchase of land near where she lived, Court Farm, Broadway, Worcestershire; a home happily shared with two former Cambridge colleagues, the De Navarros, for thirty years. She died there on 18 April 1985. She was unmarried.   L. P. KIRWAN, *rev.*

Sources G. Caton-Thompson, *Mixed memoirs* (1983) • G. Clark, 'Gertrude Caton Thompson, 1888–1985', *PBA*, 71 (1985), 523–32 • *Newnham College Roll Letter* (1986)
Archives U. Oxf., Griffith Institute, notes, papers, and corresp. on prehistoric Fiyum | BL, corresp. with Sir Sydney Cockerell, Add. MS 52709 • Bodl. Oxf., letters to J. L. Myres
Wealth at death £159,725: probate, 22 July 1985, *CGPLA Eng. & Wales*

Thompson, Gilbert (1728–1803), physician, was born in Lancashire, and for some years kept a well-attended school near Lancaster. He retired from the school and went to Edinburgh, graduating MD in 1753.

Thompson then went to London, but had so little success as a practitioner that he worked first as writing-master in a boarding-school in Tottenham, Middlesex, and then became a dispensing assistant to Timothy Bevan, a druggist. About 1765 his uncle, Gilbert Thompson, of Penketh, Lancashire, died and left him £4000. He was able to set up as a physician in the city, and eventually attained a fair-sized practice. He was admitted a licentiate of the Royal College of Physicians in 1770.

Thompson was a Quaker, and a man of learning. He was described as being of great integrity, mild and unassuming, and professionally skilful. In 1782 he published a memoir of his good friend the physician John Fothergill. On the title-page he is described as secretary to the Medical Society of London, but there is no mention of this in the society's records, although he was a member, being present at the first meeting in May 1773. He also published translations from Homer and Horace, with original poems, in 1801.

Thompson died at his house in Salter's Hall Court, Cannon Street, London, on 2 January 1803; he was seventy-four.   W. W. WEBB, *rev.* JEAN LOUDON

Sources Munk, *Roll* • *GM*, 1st ser., 73 (1803), 89 • London, Medical Society of London Archives • G. Thompson, *Memoirs of the life and a view of the character of the late Dr Fothergill* (1782) • *Nomina eorum, qui gradum medicinae doctoris in academia Jacobi sexti Scotorum regis, quae Edinburgi est, adepti sunt, ab anno 1705 ad annum 1845*, University of Edinburgh (1846)

Thompson, Harold Underwood (1911–1996). *See under* Yeoman, Antonia (1907–1970).

Thompson, Sir Harold Warris (1908–1983), physical chemist, was born in Wombwell, Yorkshire, on 15 February 1908, the only son and younger child of William Thompson (*d.* 1928), chief executive of a colliery, and his wife, Charlotte Emily Warris. He was educated at King Edward VII School in Sheffield and Trinity College, Oxford (of which he became an honorary fellow in 1978), where he derived much inspiration from his tutor, C. N. Hinshelwood. He graduated with first-class honours in chemistry in 1929. The following year he worked in Berlin with Fritz Haber and stayed as a paying guest with Max Planck. He received the degree of PhD from the Humboldt University, and returned to Oxford in 1930 to take up a fellowship at St John's College.

Thompson, who was affectionately known to all his friends as Tommy, was quickly recognized by contemporaries as one of the outstanding teachers of the university and he went on to inspire many pupils during his lifetime. His first research was concerned with chemical reactions in gases, but his interests soon turned to the effect of light on chemical reactions and then to spectroscopy. In 1938 he married Grace Penelope, daughter of William Stradling. The couple had two children, Richard Stradling (*b.* 1941) and Alison Rosemary (*b.* 1943).

During the Second World War Thompson worked in the Ministry of Supply and the Ministry of Aircraft Production with G. B. B. M. Sutherland from Cambridge, J. J. Fox, the government chief chemist, and later W. C. Price from ICI to develop infra-red spectroscopy; this technique was used for the analysis of aviation fuels and many strategic materials. After the war Thompson showed how infra-red spectroscopy could be applied to a large range of chemical problems. From 1964 until retirement in 1975 he was professor of chemistry at Oxford, retaining his fellowship at St John's. He and his colleagues were at the forefront of chemical spectroscopy, making important contributions to the understanding of molecular vibration frequencies, vibration–rotation spectra of gases, intensities of vibrational bands, and the effects of intermolecular forces on vibration frequencies, and latterly on photoelectron spectroscopy. He was elected FRS in 1946. Thompson's scientific work was recognized with many honours, including the Ciamician medal, Bologna (1959), the Davy medal of the Royal Society (1965), and the John Tate gold medal of the American Institute of Physics (1966).

Thompson was remarkable for creative activity in other spheres. In 1928 he had won a blue for soccer at Oxford and he later became treasurer of the university football club. Soon after the war he was the driving force in the establishment of the joint Oxford and Cambridge Pegasus Football Club, which won the amateur cup twice. Throughout the rest of his life he played a major role in national football and was vice-chairman of the Football Association (1967–76), vice-president (1969–80), and chairman (1976–81).

In 1959 Thompson was made a member of the council of the Royal Society, and with only two short gaps of one year each, he remained a member until 1971, giving outstanding service to the society and to international science. He was the society's foreign secretary from 1965 to 1971, during which time he greatly increased the scope of its international activities. He encouraged and expanded scientific exchanges which had already been begun in a modest way with Bulgaria, China, Czechoslovakia, Hungary, Poland, Romania, and the Soviet Union, and initiated a programme of European research conferences and technical exchanges which proved a success. Before his death he saw more than 5000 exchange visits by European scientists.

Thompson's activities for international science were associated with the international scientific unions. From 1963 to 1966 he was president of the International Council of Scientific Unions, followed by a period as president of the International Union of Pure and Applied Chemistry. On the international scene he had a feel for personal and national sensitivities, combined with an unshakeable insistence on the integrity of science. Many people recognized the considerable charisma that was such an asset to him. His fluent German, passable French, inexhaustible fund of amusing stories, and sometimes astounding powers of concentration and hard work all impressed and often won over to his point of view the people he was dealing with, yet this charisma and enthusiasm were counterbalanced by a lifelong air of pessimism and hypochondria, often expressed with the opening gambit, 'Of course you know I'm not at all well'.

Thompson received worldwide honours, which included being made a chevalier of the Légion d'honneur (1971), the grand service cross of Germany (1971), honorary membership of many foreign academies, and honorary degrees at many universities. He was appointed CBE in 1959 and knighted in 1968. Thompson died in Oxford on 31 December 1983, survived by his widow.

REX RICHARDS, *rev.*

Sources R. Richards, *Memoirs FRS*, 31 (1985), 571–610 · *WWW*, 1981–90 · personal knowledge (1990) · private information (1990)
Archives RS, corresp. and papers | Bodl. Oxf., corresp. with C. A. Coulson
Likenesses *The Times*, photograph, c.1960, RS · Associated Press, group portrait, photograph, c.1960 (with members of council), RS · Associated Press, photograph, c.1960, RS · W. Bird, photograph, c.1960, RS · G. Argent, photograph, RS · W. Bird, photograph, RS
Wealth at death £93,245: probate, 12 March 1984, *CGPLA Eng. & Wales*

Thompson, Sir Harry Stephen Meysey, first baronet (1809–1874), agriculturist, was born at Newby Park, Yorkshire, on 11 August 1809, the eldest son of Richard John Thompson (1771–1853), an army officer, of an established aristocratic Yorkshire family, and Elizabeth (*d.* 1840), daughter of John and Mary Turton of Sugnall Hall, Staffordshire. Mary Turton, the daughter and coheir of the Revd Thomas Meysey of Shakenhurst, Worcestershire, claimed descent from the De Meyseys who came to England from Meysey, Brittany, with William the Conqueror.

Thompson was educated by private tutors, initially at home and then in London. He entered Trinity College, Cambridge, in 1829, and graduated in the mathematical tripos in 1832. During this period he studied entomology with Charles Darwin. As part of his grand tour he travelled extensively in Scotland and the south of France, and embarked upon a journey to Constantinople. The sickness of one of his companions, however, prevented him from reaching his destination. Following his return to Britain he intended to pursue a parliamentary or diplomatic career, but in response to pressure from his father, he settled down to the life of a country gentleman. On 26 August 1843 he married Elizabeth Anne (d. 1910), second daughter of Sir John and Lady Croft.

Thompson was very committed to promoting agricultural improvements on both his own estates and nationally. He accompanied John Evelyn Denison (afterwards Lord Ossington), John Lawes, and other leading figures on several practical agricultural tours in various parts of Britain. His views of the agricultural conditions in Ireland were published in *Tait's Magazine* in April 1840. He was a key figure in establishing the Yorkshire Agricultural Society in 1837, becoming president in 1862. He was a co-founder of the Royal Agricultural Society of England in 1838. Following the death of Phillip Pusey, in 1855, Thompson became editor and then chairman of the journal committee. He perceived the society's role, however, as being primarily that of improving standards of crop and stock husbandry, rather than a vehicle for dealing with wider issues such as land tenure. His narrow interpretation tended to undermine the standing of the journal during the period of his editorship. He continued to take an active part in the organization of the society as a member of council until 1858 and then as a trustee until his death.

Thompson's interest in practical agricultural problems led him to carry out a number of experiments in conjunction with Joseph Spence, a chemist of York, relating to the ability of the soil to absorb and retain nitrogen (in, as yet, an undetermined form). In 1848 a summary of their findings was sent to Professor J. Thomas Way, who continued with the research and published his results in the *Journal of the Royal Agricultural Society* in 1850. In the same year Thompson's unfinished 'Investigations on the absorbent power of soils' was also published (vol. 11, 1850, 68–74) in the journal. Collectively their research showed that fertilizers, and nitrogen in particular, were absorbed in the soil by a complex series of chemical reactions. These preliminary investigations foreshadowed the significant discoveries in the 1850s made by John Lawes and J. H. Gilbert at the Rothamsted Experimental Station, which showed that the majority of agricultural crops, especially cereals, required additional nitrogen inputs for high yields. Thompson's research drew attention to the value of covered cattle yards for protecting animals and also for improving the quality of manure. The construction of a covered yard for pigs at Kirby Hall estate attracted widespread interest at the time.

From 1849 Thompson developed a consuming interest in railways. He was instrumental in promoting a meeting of the York, Newcastle, and Berwick shareholders at York, which secured the deposition of George Hudson and the election of a new board of directors. Initially he declined a seat on this reconvened board, but shortly afterwards became chairman of the North Midland Railway Company. In 1854, when the two companies were amalgamated as the North Eastern Railway, he continued as chairman, a position he retained until a few months before his death. He was chairman of the United Railways Company Association from 1867 to 1873. He was an energetic and efficient organizer, whose efforts helped to revitalize the railway companies. In 1853, following his father's death, he inherited the family estates, becoming a justice of the peace, deputy lieutenant, and high sheriff of Yorkshire in 1856. His interest in politics led to his election as Liberal MP for Whitby in 1859. He played a key part in legislation relating to agriculture, the management of railways, and church rating. Following his defeat in 1865 he stood for the eastern division of the West Riding of Yorkshire but was unsuccessful.

Thompson was a dynamic, if somewhat controversial figure. He was, for example, an ardent critic of agricultural colleges and suggested that institutions of this type would be likely to fail. In the late 1840s he claimed that students at Cirencester Agricultural College either idled away their time or waited until they received commissions in the army. He was criticized during his tenureship of the selection committee of the Royal Agricultural Society journal for not wanting an editor but merely a sub-editor who would promote his own views. Nevertheless, he played a significant role in enhancing the professionalism and scientific content of the Royal Agricultural Society's journal, and was a prolific writer in his own right, compiling eighteen articles dealing mainly with agricultural implements. His contributions improved the managerial performance and profitability of the railway companies he chaired.

Thompson was a committed family man, with five sons and five daughters. On 26 March 1874 he was created a baronet, which was accompanied by his assuming the surname of Meysey-Thompson in recognition of his mother's family. He died on 17 May 1874 at Kirby Hall in Yorkshire. He was succeeded in the baronetcy by his eldest son Sir Henry Meysey-Thompson (1845–1929), who in 1905 was created Baron Knaresborough.   JOHN MARTIN

Sources Boase, *Mod. Eng. biog.* · Burke, *Peerage* · N. Goddard, *Harvests of change: the Royal Agricultural Society of England, 1838–1988* (1988) · C. S. Orwin and E. H. Whetham, *History of British agriculture, 1846–1914* (1964) · V. Hall, *A history of the Yorkshire Agricultural History Society, 1837–1987* (1987) · *Journal of the Royal Agricultural Society of England*, 11 (1850) · *Journal of the Royal Agricultural Society of England*, 2nd ser., 10 (1874) · *Annual Register* (1874), 153 · *Agricultural Gazette* (1874), 658, 273, 1435 · *Mark Lane Express* (25 May 1874) · private information (2004) [D. W. Egerton] · T. Nash, *Collections for the history of Worcestershire*, 1 (1781) · S. Shaw, *The history and antiquities of Staffordshire*, 1 (1798), 133
Archives U. Reading, Royal Agricultural Society archives

Likenesses photograph, Royal Agricultural Society · portrait (in captain's uniform), Kirby Hall, Yorkshire
Wealth at death under £180,000: probate, 13 July 1874, *CGPLA Eng. & Wales*

Thompson, Henry (1797–1878), writer, was born in Surrey. He was admitted to St John's College, Cambridge, as a pensioner in 1818, graduating BA in 1822 and proceeding MA in 1825. In 1820 he competed for Sir William Browne's medal, receiving an extra prize for a Latin ode, and in 1824 he obtained the first members' prize for a Latin essay. He married on 30 June 1823 Anne Harrison, daughter of the Revd James Bell, vicar of Lympne, Kent. In December 1823 he was ordained deacon, and priest in December 1827. After being successively curate of St George's, Camberwell, Surrey (1824–7), St Mary's, Salehurst, Sussex (1827–8), and Wrington, Somerset (1828–53), he was appointed by George Henry Law, bishop of Bath and Wells, to the vicarage of Chard, Somerset, on 14 September 1853, where he resided until his death on 29 November 1878. He left two sons—Christopher, and Henry Bell (d. 1887), who had served as his curate at Chard and whom he presented to the vicarage of Tatworth, Somerset.

Thompson was a man of very conservative instincts. In the words of his friend Edward Augustus Freeman, whom he first met at Hannah More's house at Barley Wood, he 'seemed to look at everything in 1878 with exactly the same eyes with which he looked on things in 1839'. At the same time, Freeman adds, 'he showed us that past generation in its best colours'. He was a good classical scholar and knew Hebrew and German.

Thompson was the author of *Davidica: Twelve Practical Sermons on the Life of David* (1827), *Pastoralia: a Manual of Helps for the Parochial Clergy* (1830), which is of interest for its recommendation that the sick should be encouraged to make special confession, *The Life of Hannah More* (1838), which has been found useful by later biographers, and *Concionalia: Outlines of Sermons for the Christian Year* (1853; 2nd ser., 1871). He published editions of Horace (1853) and Virgil (1854; 3rd edn, 1862), and also contributed most of the classical articles to the *Encyclopaedia metropolitana* (1824), several of which he afterwards published separately. In 1845 he translated Schiller's *Maid of Orleans* and *William Tell*, and in 1850 edited a volume of *Original Ballads by Living Authors*, to which E. A. Freeman was a contributor of nine poems. Thompson also contributed to the anthologies of religious verse *Lyra sanctorum* and *Lyra eucharistica*, and to the *Churchman's Companion*.

E. I. CARLYLE, rev. TRIONA ADAMS

Sources *Chard and Ilminster News* (7 Dec 1878) · W. R. W. Stephens, *The life and letters of Edward A. Freeman*, 1 (1895), 23–36 · Venn, *Alum. Cant.* · B. Heeney, *A different kind of gentleman: parish clergy as professional men in early and mid-Victorian England* (1976) · Boase, *Mod. Eng. biog.* · *Men of the time* (1875)
Archives JRL, letters to E. A. Freeman
Wealth at death under £1500: probate, 3 March 1879, *CGPLA Eng. & Wales*

Thompson, Sir Henry, first baronet (1820–1904), surgeon, was born on 6 August 1820 at Framlingham, Suffolk,

Sir Henry Thompson, first baronet (1820–1904), by Sir John Everett Millais, 1881

the first of three children of Henry Thompson (1790–1864), general dealer and tallow chandler, and his wife, Susannah (d. 1872), daughter of Samuel *Medley (1769–1857), artist and one of the founders of University College, London. He was educated by private tutors and entered the family business at sixteen because his parents, who were strict Baptists, were opposed to his long held wish to study medicine. In January 1844 he began a year's apprenticeship with a well-known general practitioner, George Bottomley of Croydon, and entered University College in 1848 as a medical student. He amply made up for lost time by winning gold medals in anatomy, pathology, medicine, and surgery, and qualifying MB (Lond.) in 1851. He became a member of the Royal College of Surgeons in 1850.

On 16 December 1851 he married Kate Fanny *Loder (1825–1904) [see under Loder, George], daughter of George Loder, a flautist, and his wife, Fanny Philpot, a piano teacher. Kate was a pianist and composer and was professor of piano at the Royal Academy of Music; they had three children. Thompson set up practice in Wimpole Street, London, and at the same time began to study urethral stricture (narrowing of the passage by which urine is excreted from the bladder) with the help of a former teacher, James Syme, professor of surgery at Edinburgh. This work was awarded the Jacksonian prize of the Royal College of Surgeons of England in 1853, and was subsequently expanded into Thompson's first book, *The Pathology and Treatment of Stricture of the Urethra* (1854). He became a fellow of the college the same year, and was appointed consulting surgeon to the Marylebone workhouse infirmary, where he acquired considerable surgical experience.

It was apparent that Thompson's interest lay in diseases of the urinary system and he now set out to specialize in the treatment of urethral stricture, enlarged prostate, and bladder stones. He was appointed assistant surgeon at University College Hospital in 1856, published a monograph on *The Enlarged Prostate, its Pathology and Treatment* (1858), and had the unusual distinction of winning a second Jacksonian prize, for an essay on the prostate. Increasingly his attention was drawn to the management of bladder stone, a distressingly common condition at that time. Up until the end of the eighteenth century three different operations had been used in 'cutting for the stone' (lithotomy), all of which involved an incision in the perineum below the anus to get at the stone. Without the benefits of modern anaesthesia and antisepsis, this was extremely painful and dangerous, with a high mortality because of the risk of infection, especially when the stone was large. The Thompson family doctor at Framlingham, William Jeaffreson, was a skilled lithotomist and was associated with what came to be known as the Norwich School of Lithotomy (Shaw). He not only kindled Thompson's interest in medicine, but showed him how instruments could be passed via the urethra directly into the bladder to crush and remove the stones, without cutting (lithotrity), an operation he had first reported in 1834.

In 1858 Thompson visited Jean Civiale, one of the foremost continental masters of the new technique, and because of his dexterity and lightness of touch Thompson soon became a leading proponent of this type of surgery. He was promoted full surgeon at University College Hospital in 1862, and the next year his reputation was considerably enhanced by being called on to treat Leopold I of Belgium, an uncle of Queen Victoria. Repeated attempts to remove the king's stones by continental experts, including Civiale, had failed, and the king was eventually persuaded to consult Thompson. The latter travelled to Brussels with an experienced chloroformist, J. T. Clover, and with a new set of instruments which he had designed himself. The lithotrity, for which he received a fee of £3000, was completed satisfactorily.

In 1866 Thompson was appointed professor of clinical surgery at University College, and he was knighted the following year. He was a superb teacher, and his book, *Clinical Lectures of Diseases of the Urinary Organs* (1868) became a popular text. At the same time he had a large private practice, earning £8000 a year, and had to employ an assistant, whom he paid £1000. In 1873 he performed a lithotrity on Napoleon III, in exile in Chislehurst and already seriously ill with diseased kidneys, but was unable to save the patient. This led him to advocate crushing and removal of fragments of stone in one operation wherever possible, rather than over several sessions as was the usual practice. The next year Thompson resigned his hospital appointments because of the pressures of practice. He was appointed consulting surgeon at University College Hospital in 1877. Thompson maintained his position as the leading British urologist for over twenty years, and his books on urinary diseases 'read as true to-day as they did 150 years ago' (Dunsmuir and Kirby, 187).

In spite of his surgical pre-eminence Thompson had many and varied interests—he was the archetypal Victorian polymath. A tall, thin man with dark brown eyes, bushy eyebrows, and a cavalry moustache, he was endowed with boundless energy, a capacity for hard work, and a passion for delving deeply into anything that interested him. He was a keen observer, an inspired conversationalist, and a lover of music and harmony. But he tended to be serious and dogmatic, was highly strung, and suffered from migraine and insomnia. He was a prolific writer of textbooks, of books on subjects that interested him, and of articles in periodicals; he kept a diary and detailed notes on his patients, and towards the end of his life wrote his (unpublished) reminiscences. He published two best-selling novels on medical themes: *Charley Kingston's Aunt* (1885), under the pseudonym Pen Oliver, and *'All but': a Chronicle of Laxenford Life* (1886).

Thompson was a superb illustrator of his own textbooks, and took up sketching and oil painting as a relief from medical practice. He exhibited landscapes and still-life paintings at the Royal Academy for a number of years. Artists and writers were among his friends: he painted a portrait of Millais and sketched Thackeray. For thirty years Thompson took prolonged holidays on the continent to visit colleagues and to tour art galleries with his daughter Kate; he assisted her in producing a *Handbook to the Public Picture Galleries of Europe* (1877). He was a collector of blue and white Nankin porcelain, and illustrated a catalogue of his collection with James McNeill Whistler; in 1880 Christies sold 377 lots for £4328 7s. 6d.

A lifelong gastronome (his small book *Food and Feeding*, 1880, went through twelve editions), Thompson founded in 1872 the celebrated 'Octaves': dinners of eight simple dishes, beginning at eight o'clock, for eight guests. Renowned for their cuisine and conversation, they were attended by royalty, colleagues, famous men (no women) from the arts, literature, the professions and politics, and foreign visitors. The 301st dinner was held shortly before his death. Thompson bought a property, Hurtside House at East Molesey, in 1880 where he started a market garden and built an observatory; his telescopes, of the latest design, were subsequently given to the Royal Observatory at Greenwich. As a young man he had experimented with photography (and wrote about it) two years after its introduction in 1839 by Louis Daguerre; he took it up again in 1891 as a substitute for painting, and, as with everything he did, soon became an expert. His questing mind was untouched by old age: in 1901 he bought a Daimler car and drove enthusiastically about the country with a young chauffeur; having minutely studied the engine, he wrote a small handbook for users.

The introduction of cremation was one of Thompson's major achievements. His interest was aroused by seeing an incinerator at the Great Exhibition in Vienna in 1873, and he immediately began to experiment with the burning of animals. The next year he published a book, *Cremation: the Treatment of the Body after Death* (1874), and was largely instrumental in founding the Cremation Society, of which he was president. Plans were made to establish a crematorium at Woking, but due to considerable opposition it was not until 20 March 1885 that the first cremation was carried out. In 1902 he played a leading part in the company that built Golders Green crematorium, and his efforts to improve the accuracy of death certification were incorporated in the Cremation Act of the same year.

Thompson was created a baronet in 1899. He died in his sleep on 18 April 1904 at 35 Wimpole Street, where he had lived the whole of his married life, three days after his last motor trip. His body was cremated at Golders Green. His son, Henry Francis Herbert *Thompson, succeeded to the baronetcy. ALEX PATON

Sources Z. Cope, *The versatile Victorian* (1951) • *The Times* (19 April 1904) • *BMJ* (23 April 1904), 991–3 • W. D. Dunsmuir and R. S. Kirby, 'Sir Henry Thompson: the first British urologist (1820–1904)', *Journal of Medical Biography*, 3 (1995), 187–91 • A. B. Shaw, 'The Norwich school of lithotomy', *Medical History*, 14 (1970), 221–59 • *DNB* • *WWW*
Archives Suffolk RO, Ipswich, corresp. | BL, corresp. with Sir A. H. Layard, Add. MSS 38973–38974, 39010, 39097 • RCS Eng.
Likenesses L. Alma-Tadema, oils, 1878, FM Cam. • J. E. Millais, oils, 1881, Tate collection [*see illus.*] • R. Lehmann, crayon drawing, 1902, BM • Ape [C. Pellegrini], chromolithograph caricature, NPG; repro. in *VF* (1 Aug 1874) • Lock & Whitfield, woodburytype photograph, NPG; repro. in T. Cooper, *Men of mark: a gallery of contemporary portraits* (1882) • F. W. Pomeroy, bust, Golders Green, London • Walery, photograph, NPG • woodburytype, carte-de-visite, NPG
Wealth at death £226,298 2*s*. 5*d*.: probate, 11 May 1904, CGPLA Eng. & Wales

Thompson, Henry Langhorne (1829–1856), army officer, was born on 21 September 1829 at the cottage, Clumber Park, in Nottinghamshire, the son of Jonathan Thompson of Sherwood Hall, Nottinghamshire, receiver-general of crown rents for the northern counties, and his wife, Anne, daughter of Ralph Smyth, colonel in the Royal Artillery. After education at Eton College, on 20 December 1845 he was commissioned ensign, and on 20 August 1846 appointed to the 68th Bengal native infantry; on 12 February 1850 he was promoted lieutenant. He served in the Second Anglo-Burmese War (1852–3), receiving a wound which necessitated his return to England. In 1854 he volunteered for the Turkish army, received the rank of major, and reached Kars in March 1855. Under the command of Colonel W. F. Williams, he helped strengthen the fortifications, and he distinguished himself in repelling the Russian assault on 29 September, crushing the Russian columns by his fire from Arab Tabia. His bravery won Russian admiration and, on the surrender of Kars in November, Muravyov, the Russian commander, returned him his sword. On 9 November he was appointed captain unattached in the British army; on 7 February 1856 he received the Mejidiye (third class) and on 10 May was nominated an honorary CB. Shortly after his return from Russia, where he had been a prisoner of war, he died, unmarried, at 70 Gloucester Street, Belgrave Road, London, on 13 June 1856. He was buried in Brompton cemetery. His letters on the siege of Kars were published in H. Atwell Lake's *Kars and our Captivity in Russia* (2nd edn, 1856).

E. I. CARLYLE, *rev.* JAMES LUNT

Sources H. A. Lake, *Kars and our captivity in Russia* (1856) • H. Sandwith, *The siege of Kars* (1856) • *The Times* (14 June 1856) • *GM*, 3rd ser., 1 (1856), 118 • *Annual Register* (1856) • *ILN* (21 June 1856), 255 [chronicle]
Likenesses T. J. Barker, oils, c.1860 (*The capitulation of Kars*), NAM • lithograph, NPG

Thompson, Henry Yates (1838–1928), collector of illuminated manuscripts and newspaper proprietor, was born at Dingle Cottage, near Liverpool, on 15 December 1838, the eldest of five sons of Samuel Henry Thompson, of Thingwall Hall, Lancashire, a partner in the bank of Arthur Heywood, Sons & Co., and Elizabeth Yates, the eldest of the five daughters of Joseph Brooks *Yates, also of Liverpool, a West India merchant and an antiquary. He was educated at Harrow School (where he was head of the school) and at Trinity College, Cambridge, where he won the Porson prize for Greek verse in 1860 and graduated as sixteenth classic in 1861. Yates Thompson was called to the bar by Lincoln's Inn in 1867 but did not practise. He stood unsuccessfully as a Liberal for three Lancashire seats in 1865, 1868, and 1881, and in 1868 to 1873 served as private secretary to the fifth Earl Spencer, then lord lieutenant of Ireland. Between 1862 and 1875 he travelled widely in Europe and in America, where he observed the civil war at close quarters.

In 1878 Yates Thompson married Elizabeth (c.1854–1941), eldest daughter of the publisher George *Smith (1824–1901), founder of the *Dictionary of National Biography*, and his wife, Elizabeth Murray. Two years later Smith made over to his son-in-law the *Pall Mall Gazette*. Yates Thompson turned this previously anti-Gladstonian organ into a Liberal paper, with John Morley, W. T. Stead, and E. T. Cook successively in charge. He had little taste for being a newspaper proprietor, but supported his editors, notably backing Stead in 1885 over his sensational article, 'The maiden tribute of modern Babylon', an exposé of child prostitution. The *Pall Mall Gazette* had required heavy proprietorial investment, but Yates Thompson suffered no loss when he sold the paper to William Waldorf Astor in 1892. He had coveted a baronetcy, but in this he was disappointed.

When he was eighteen, Yates Thompson had been left by his maternal grandfather a group of ten medieval manuscripts, giving him an interest which during the 1880s developed as a serious preoccupation, resulting in his becoming the foremost British manuscript collector of his day. Particularly after the sale of his newspaper, he was able to give much time to efficient and well-informed purchasing from the dealers of Paris and London. It was a good time to be collecting: the library of Sir Thomas Phillipps was being dispersed, manuscripts from the Firmin Didot collection were still available in Paris, the Prussian government sold the Hamilton manuscripts in 1889, and in 1902 John Ruskin's collection was auctioned. Yates Thompson bought discriminatingly from all these

Henry Yates Thompson (1838–1928), by Sir Benjamin Stone, 1906

list of provenances gives any manuscript a special cachet. He was prescient in interesting himself in the then less fashionable area of French Renaissance art, and his memory for detail enabled him to reunite long-dispersed illuminations and separated volumes. He was a generous donor to institutions, and gave the fourteenth-century St Omer psalter to the British Museum and the Metz pontifical to the Fitzwilliam Museum in Cambridge. Recognizing that a defective Josephus manuscript in his collection was the counterpart of one in the Bibliothèque Nationale (MS fr.247) and later locating many of the missing illuminations in the Royal Library, Windsor, he gave his book to King Edward VII so that it could be restored and presented by the king to the French nation; he was made a chevalier of the Légion d'honneur for this imaginative benefaction which reunited two volumes by the great French illuminator Jean Fouquet.

Elsewhere Yates Thompson was a munificent benefactor: he donated a winter garden to Liverpool in 1901, an art school building to Harrow School, and a library building to Newnham College, Cambridge, and funded extensions to the Dulwich College picture gallery. As a director of the London and Yorkshire Railway, he gave hospitals to Crewe and to the Horwich railway works. He had a reputation for being disconcertingly blunt in his opinions, with his directness not wholly offset by a jovial and humorous manner. His wife, who was sixteen years his junior, was a tactful and intelligent hostess with a charm that balanced his forthrightness. They had no children. He died in his ninetieth year at his London house, 19 Portman Square, on 8 July 1928. His wife lived on, mainly at Oving, their Buckinghamshire house, until 1941. She left to the British Museum a group of forty-six illuminated manuscripts, to be known and catalogued as the Yates Thompson collection.

ALAN BELL

Sources DNB · *The Times* (10 July 1928) · H. Y. Thompson, *An Englishman in the American Civil War, 1863*, ed. C. Chancellor (1971) · C. de Hamel, 'Was Henry Yates Thompson a gentleman?', *Property of a gentleman: the formation, organisation and dispersal of the private library, 1620–1920*, ed. R. Myers and M. Harris, St Paul's Bibliographies (1991), 77–89 · J. Q. Bennett, 'Portman Square and New Bond Street', *Book Collector*, 16 (1967), 323–39 · S. E. Koss, *The rise and fall of the political press in Britain*, 1 (1981) · F. Herrmann, *Sotheby's: portrait of an auction house* (1980) · Venn, *Alum. Cant.*
Archives BL, corresp. and papers relating to collection of printed books and MSS, Add. MS 46200 · NL Ire., diary kept as secretary to Lord Spencer | BL, corresp. with Sir Sydney Cockerell, Add. MS 52755 · CAC Cam., letters to W. T. Stead · Indiana University, Bloomington, Lilly Library, corresp. with Sotheby's relating to disposal of his library · NL Wales, letters to A. C. Humphreys-Owen
Likenesses B. Stone, photograph, 1906, NPG [*see illus.*]
Wealth at death £247,778 11s. 1d.: resworn probate, 27 Aug 1928, CGPLA Eng. & Wales

sources, but his largest purchase was of over 200 manuscripts from the collection of the last earl of Ashburnham, acquired for the then high price of £30,000 in 1897. These books, supplementary to the main Ashburnham collection and known as the 'Ashburnham appendix', transformed his library in terms of quantity. He resolved to retain no more than 100 volumes, and sold 177 lesser Ashburnham manuscripts in 1897, thereafter disposing of volumes as he gradually improved the quality of his collection, always with an eye to grand provenance as well as aesthetic quality. He sponsored a descriptive catalogue, with contributions by M. R. James, S. C. Cockerell, G. F. Warner, and others, which was issued in four volumes in 1898–1912, with a complementary set of *Illustrations* in seven volumes, 1907–18.

In the final part of these *Illustrations* Yates Thompson (who was afflicted by cataracts) announced his intention to sell his manuscripts. Despite pleas from his scholarly advisers and substantial offers from other collectors and dealers, the collection—mainly of manuscripts but with some illuminated early printed books—was sent to auction at Sothebys in three sales in 1919, 1920, and 1921. The first two sales, containing sixty-four lots in all, made record prices (£52,360 and £75,265 respectively), but in 1921, in generally unfavourable financial conditions, the result was only £18,000. By then, however, Yates Thompson had recovered his sight, and he was not averse to reviving his collection with some bought-in items.

Yates Thompson had an eye for quality and his name in a

Thompson, Sir (Henry Francis) Herbert, second baronet (1859–1944), Egyptologist, was born on 2 April 1859 at 16 Wimpole Street, London, the second of three children, and only son, of Henry *Thompson (1820–1904), surgeon, and from 1899 first baronet, and his wife, Kate Fanny *Loder (1825–1904) [*see under* Loder, George], concert pianist and composer, daughter of George Loder, a flautist, of Bath. On his mother's side he was related to several notable musicians. He was educated at Marlborough College (1872–5), where he became head of the school at sixteen, although he was not a happy pupil, or a popular one. He then spent a year in Germany in order to study the language. After some months' financial training in the City of London, he matriculated at Trinity College, Cambridge, in 1877. Here, too, he was not altogether happy, partly because of his father's excessively zealous attention. He graduated with a first in history in 1881. At his father's wish he then turned to the law, being called to the bar by the Inner Temple on 26 January 1882. He did not enjoy legal practice but gained valuable experience drafting statutes in the chambers of William Otto Danckwerts and attending at the case of *Crawford* v. *Crawford and Dilke*, in which Danckwerts appeared for the petitioner in 1886.

In 1889 Thompson met T. H. Huxley, who was impressed by his intelligence. But, although past the age of thirty, he had not yet found his vocation in life. Once more at his father's wish, he entered University College, London, in 1896 to study biology. Over-use of the microscope brought on serious trouble with his eyes, and even when work could be resumed use of the microscope was forbidden. At this point the opportunity for a rewarding career, untrammelled by his father's misguided interventions, presented itself. By chance, Sir W. M. Flinders Petrie, then professor of Egyptology at University College, asked Thompson to examine some skeletal remains excavated in Egypt. He became so interested that he began to learn hieroglyphs, at the age of forty, and under the influence of his tutors, F. Ll. Griffith (1862–1934) and W. E. Crum (1865–1944), he began to specialize in the two branches of the subject, demotic and Coptic, in which Griffith and Crum, who came to be among Thompson's greatest friends, were respectively the acknowledged leaders in Britain.

In the following years Thompson collaborated with several scholars in editing ancient texts, most importantly *The Demotic Magical Papyrus of London and Leiden* (3 vols., 1904–9, jointly with Griffith). He also published an account of a number of demotic papyri found by Flinders Petrie at Rifa, in the latter's *Gizeh and Rifeh* (1907). He made his only visit to Egypt in 1907–8, when he helped J. E. Quibell to excavate the monastery of St Epiphanius, and later published the Coptic texts found there (see Quibell's *Excavations at Saqqara*, vols. 3–4, 1909–12). He also contributed the demotic and Coptic sections of *Theban ostraca* (1913; other sections by A. H. Gardiner and J. G. Milne). He developed an especial interest in the Coptic Bible, which led to his publishing *The Coptic (Sahidic) Version of Certain Books of the Old Testament* (1908) and other editions of biblical papyri.

During the First World War Thompson spent his nights at a London terminus on duty as a special constable. After the war he wished to retire to the country and abandon Egyptology in order to devote himself to the classics. He donated most of his Egyptology books, except those on demotic and Coptic, to the Egypt Exploration Society, and moved to Aspley Guise in Bedfordshire, where he shared a house with the biologist and archivist George Herbert Fowler. In 1923, however, a papyrus codex was discovered near Qau el Kibir in Upper Egypt, which proved to contain most of St John's gospel in the earliest known Coptic version. Thompson acceded to Flinders Petrie's request to edit this (*The Gospel of St John According to the Earliest Coptic Manuscript*, 1924). Shortly afterwards he was invited by H. R. Hall, the keeper of Egyptian and Assyrian antiquities in the British Museum, to compile a handlist of the museum's large and important collection of demotic papyri. That in turn led to intensive work on a group of papyri which his own generosity enabled the museum to purchase and which he published as *A Family Archive from Siût* (2 vols., 1934). This is now recognized as a classic of scholarship and a major contribution to demotic studies and to the knowledge of law in ancient Egypt. His expertise was again in demand in 1930, when several papyrus codices from Medinet Madi in the Faiyûm were identified as a rare library of Manichaean religious texts in Coptic translation. Thompson undertook a preliminary study of them.

Meanwhile Thompson had moved to Bath, partly out of fondness for his mother's old home, and partly to be near Crum and help him in the final stages of his monumental *Coptic Dictionary* (1939); Thompson's assistance with this received a special mention in the introduction. At the outbreak of the Second World War he placed his house at the disposal of the Admiralty and moved into smaller quarters at the edge of the city, where it was impossible to house his books. Then at last his intention to cease publication prevailed, although his mind was still active enough for him to start learning Magyar. It was not until his health failed in 1944 that he found it impossible to take his full share of duty as a fire-watcher.

By 1904 Thompson had established himself as a demotic scholar, and on the death of Griffith in 1934 he was left the foremost demotist and among the first few Copticists of his day. Considering his pre-eminence, his output was comparatively small, but this may be explained partly by his readiness to postpone his own work in order to answer the frequent calls for assistance that he received from other scholars and partly by his late entry, at forty, into the field that became his life's work. These factors may also explain why he received relatively few honours: he was awarded the honorary degree of DLitt by the University of Oxford in 1926, became a fellow of University College, London, in 1930, and was elected FBA in 1933. The fact that three years later he resigned in order to make way for a younger man illustrates the modesty and generosity for which he was remembered by his friends. He also gave generous financial support to the Egypt Exploration Society, of which served on the committee from 1901 to 1908.

All Thompson's work was characterized by the breadth of his culture, enriched as it was by legal and scientific training, and by his many other interests. Chief among these were the classics, but they also included classical painting, Italian authors, the theatre, and music, of which he received an early love and knowledge from his mother. He especially liked to recall that he had spoken with three men who had known Beethoven. His acquaintance, indeed, included many distinguished people of the day, for his father had been a great entertainer at his London house. He died at his home, 17 Macaulay Buildings, Bath, on 26 May 1944; he had never married, and the baronetcy became extinct. He left the residue of his estate to Cambridge University to further the study of Egyptology there, and the money was used to endow a new chair named after him.

R. S. SIMPSON

Sources *The Times* (29 May 1944), 6 · *Journal of Egyptian Archaeology*, 30 (1944), 67–8 · S. R. K. Glanville, *The growth and nature of Egyptology* (1947), 12–14 · Burke, *Peerage* (1939) · Venn, *Alum. Cant.* · *Marlborough College register, from 1843 to 1879 inclusive*, Marlborough College (privately printed, London, 1880), 209 · *Cambridge University Calendar* (1882), 262, 268, 745 · *The Times* (20 April 1933), 11–12 · *DNB* · d. cert. · b. cert.
Archives U. Cam., faculty of oriental studies, papers · U. Oxf., Griffith Institute, corresp. relating to publication of Manichaean books | Egypt Exploration Society, London, corresp. with Egypt Exploration Society
Likenesses L. Alma-Tadema, oils, 1877, FM Cam. · photograph (in later years), repro. in *Journal of Egyptian Archaeology*, pl. viii
Wealth at death £78,659 17s. 8d.: probate, 9 Sept 1944, CGPLA Eng. & Wales

Thompson, Jacob (1806–1879), landscape painter, was born in Lanton Street, Penrith, Cumberland, on 28 August 1806, the eldest son of Merrick Thompson (d. 1833), a manufacturer of linen check and a well-known member of the Society of Friends and his wife Mary (d. 1837), daughter of Thomas Roper of Penrith. Thompson attended the free grammar school there and drew from an early age, but grew up in relative poverty after the ruin of his father's business during the trade depression of 1812. His aspirations to become an artist met with little sympathy from his family, and he was apprenticed first to a grocer and then to a house-painter. However, he devoted all his leisure time to his favourite pursuit.

While sketching a bridge crossing the River Lowther one autumn day, Thompson met William Lowther, second earl of Lonsdale, who stopped to comment on his work. The earl invited him to Lowther Castle to sketch and copy as he pleased, and he later sent one of Thompson's paintings to Sir Thomas Lawrence. As a result Thompson was summoned to London in 1829 and admitted as a student at the British Museum and later the Royal Academy Schools. At Lonsdale's instigation he studied at the academy under Robert Smirke. After some time Smirke advised him to 'go to nature' for his studies, arguing that if he stayed at the academy 'all originality of thought and invention would be lost' in him (Jewitt, 15).

Thompson first exhibited in 1824, at the first exhibition of the Society of British Artists, sending a *View in Cumberland*, but he did not exhibit at the Royal Academy until 1832, in which year appeared *The Druids Cutting Down the Mistletoe*. This was followed in 1833 by a picture containing full-length portraits of the daughters of the Hon. Colonel Lowther. On 14 August 1834 he married, at St Saviour's in Southwark, Ann Parker Bidder (d. 1844), sister of George Parker *Bidder, the celebrated engineer; they had one son. She was herself 'a clever painter in water colours' (Jewitt, 23) and they lived briefly at Luton before moving to Hitchin, in Hertfordshire. Thompson's next exhibit was

Harvest Home in the Fourteenth Century, which appeared at the British Institution in 1837, and was presented by the artist to his patron, the earl of Lonsdale.

Ten years elapsed before Thompson next exhibited, during which time he took commissions to paint the mansions of landed proprietors. Having access also to their collections, he spent time copying. In 1841 he settled with his family in a house belonging to his patron in Lowther New Town, Westmorland. There, in January 1844, Ann Parker Thompson died, and the following year Thompson moved into The Hermitage at Hackthorpe, a cottage given to him as a permanent residence by Lord Lonsdale. On 14 March 1850 he married Elizabeth, daughter of Jonathan Varty of Stagstones, near Penrith, a woman 'strongly imbued with artistic feeling' who painted with 'more than average merit' (Jewitt, 23); there were no children.

In 1847 Thompson sent to the Westminster Hall competition *The Highland Ferry-Boat*, which was engraved by James Tibbits Willmore and which proved a success, selling several thousand copies. *The Proposal* appeared at the Royal Academy in 1848; his annual academy exhibits included *The Highland Bride*, likewise engraved by Willmore, in 1851, another success on a large scale, though its composition was later criticized in the *Art Journal*; *The Course of True Love Never did Run Smooth*, in 1854; and *Looking out for the Homeward Bound*, in 1856. He painted in 1858 *Crossing a Highland Loch*, which was engraved by Charles Mottram; but he did not exhibit again until 1860, when he sent to the Royal Academy *The Signal*, which was engraved by Charles Cousen for the *Art Journal* of 1862. In 1864 he had at the academy *The Height of Ambition*, which was also engraved by Cousen for the *Art Journal*. Among his best works are *Rush Bearing* and a view of Rydal Mount.

In his later years Thompson devoted himself chiefly to landscape subjects with figures, the themes of which were for the most part drawn from the mountains and lakes of Cumberland and Westmorland, but occasionally from Scotland. His range, however, was limited, and his work was lacking in poetic sympathy. His attempts at classical and scriptural subjects, such as *Acis and Galatea*, exhibited at the Royal Academy in 1849, and *Proserpine*, were not a success. Thompson also painted two altarpieces for the church of St Andrew's, Penrith, and a number of hunting scenes.

Thompson died at his home, The Hermitage, on 27 December 1879, and was buried in Lowther churchyard on 31 December.

R. E. GRAVES, rev. MARK POTTLE

Sources L. Jewitt, *Life and works of Jacob Thomson* (1882) · J. Dafforne, 'British artists, their style and character: no. LIII, Jacob Thompson', *Art Journal*, 23 (1861), 9–11 · *Art Journal*, 42 (1880), 107 · B. Stewart and M. Cutten, *The dictionary of portrait painters in Britain up to 1920* (1997) · Wood, *Vic. painters*, 2nd edn · L. Jewitt, 'Bundles of rue: lives of artists recently deceased, Jacob Thompson', *Magazine of Art*, 4 (1880–81), 32–5 · *The exhibition of the Royal Academy* (1832–66) [exhibition catalogues] · T. Hall Caine, review of Jewitt, *Life and works*, *The Academy* (1 July 1882), 16 · m. cert. [Elizabeth Varty]
Likenesses W. Ballingall, engraving (after self-portrait on wood), repro. in Jewitt, *Life and works* · photograph, Carlisle City Art Gallery
Wealth at death under £12,000: probate, 10 Jan 1880, CGPLA Eng. & Wales

Thompson, James (1817–1877), county historian and newspaper editor, was born on 6 December 1817 at Leicester, the son of Thomas Thompson (1788–1871), proprietor and editor of the *Leicester Chronicle* from 1813, and his wife, Elizabeth, *née* Garton. He was educated first at W. H. Creaton's Classical and Commercial Academy in Billesdon and afterwards under the Revd Charles Berry, minister of the Great Meeting Unitarian Chapel, Leicester.

Thompson began as an editor on his father's newspaper in 1838, with a brief phase as editor of the radical Owenite paper the *Working Bee* in 1839 and as a sub-editor on O'Connor's *Northern Star* in 1841 to gain experience. He soon became an able leader writer, and for more than thirty years wrote nearly all the leading articles in the *Chronicle*. In the major local dispute over town improvement in the 1840s he took the side of the 'economists' in bitter opposition to William Biggs, urging new sewers before 'Brummagem Town Halls', especially after the 1846 typhus epidemic. His involvement in politics increased after the reformers became divided and the 1852 and 1857 general elections were fought between opposing reform candidates. The *Chronicle* supported the moderate faction, and its rival, the *Leicestershire Mercury*, the radicals. In 1852 Thompson organized the search from the *Chronicle* offices for evidence of corruption for the unsuccessful election petition, and in 1857, with his father, signed the requisition for a rival Liberal candidate. After the Conservative candidate won a crushing by-election victory in 1861 Thompson campaigned effectively for Liberal reunion. He became joint proprietor of the *Chronicle* with his father in 1841 and sole proprietor in 1864, when he bought the *Mercury*, uniting the two rival Liberal papers. He began the *Leicester Daily Mercury* in connection with the 1874 general election. He was briefly elected to the town council in 1867, losing by one vote in 1870.

Thompson was the leading Victorian authority on the history of Leicester. For over thirty years he was responsible for the interpretation and preservation of the town's historic past: lecturing, writing, and recording archaeological discoveries, and opposing the destruction of the town's surviving medieval buildings, most notably the fourteenth-century Guildhall. In 1843 he began to print extracts from the works of local historians in the *Chronicle* as 'Passages from the history of Leicester'. The next year he published his *Handbook of Leicester* (3rd edn, 1860). He was soon led to examine the original records for himself, and his efforts with William Kelly in 1847 to rearrange the borough records, then poorly kept and in considerable disorder, undoubtedly helped to preserve one of the most detailed and complete municipal archives. His major study, *The History of Leicester from the Time of the Romans to the End of the Seventeenth Century* (1849), used this material extensively and revealed his interest in archaeology. The second volume, *The History of Leicester in the Eighteenth Century*, was published in 1871, and a popular account, his *Pocket History*, in 1876 (2nd edn, 1879). His *Essay on English Municipal History* (1867) examined the general history of the origin and development of boroughs. Among his projects was a history of Leicestershire, and shortly before his death he was preparing an account of the kingdom of Mercia. He was one of the founders of the Leicestershire Architectural and Archaeological Society (1855), a fellow of the Royal Historical Society, and a member of the British Archaeological Association and the Society of Antiquaries. He was also one of the founders of the Leicester Mechanics' Institute and honorary curator of the town museum.

A man of singularly independent character in both religion and politics, Thompson was 'conservative in his tastes … [and] Liberal in his convictions' (*Memoir*, 6). He married, on 24 June 1847, Janet Bissett (*c*.1823–1879), daughter of John McAlpin of Leicester. They had no children. He died at Dannett House, Fosse Road, Leicester, on 20 May 1877, and was buried four days later in Welford Road cemetery. His newspaper interests were purchased by Francis Hewitt in July 1877.   DAVID L. WYKES

Sources *Leicester Chronicle and Mercury* (26 May 1877) · *Leicester Chronicle and Mercury* (1 June 1877) · *Leicester Chronicle and Mercury* (21 Jan 1871) · *Leicester Chronicle and Mercury* (1 Nov 1879) · *Memoir of the late Mr James Thompson* (1877) [copy Leicestershire RO, Pamphlet vol. 28, no. 7] · 'Letter from Thomas North to the chairman of the Leicestershire Architectural and Archaeological Society', *Transactions of the Leicestershire Architectural and Archaeological Society*, 5 (1882), 60–61 · 'Select committee on the Leicester borough election petition: minutes of evidence', *Parl. papers* (1852–3), 14.190–3, no. 375 · D. Fraser, 'The press in Leicester, c.1790–1850', *Leicestershire Archaeological and Historical Society Transactions*, 42 (1966–7), 53–75 · R. H. Evans, 'Parliamentary representation since 1835', *VCH Leicestershire*, 4.214–23 · R. A. Rutland, 'Leicestershire Archaeology to 1849: the development of chronological interpretation', *Leicestershire Archaeological and Historical Society Transactions*, 65 (1991), 38–54 · A. K. B. Evans, 'The custody of Leicester's archives from 1273 to 1947', *Leicestershire Archaeological and Historical Society Transactions*, 66 (1992), 105–20 · M. Elliott, 'James Thompson, historian of Leicester', *Leicestershire Archaeological and Historical Society Transactions*, 51 (1975–6), 53–5 · J. Thompson, *The history of Leicester from the time of the Romans to the end of the seventeenth century* (1849), preface · parish register, Leicester, St Martin's, July 1837–1857, Leics. RO, DE 1564/10 [marriage]

Likenesses W. P. Miller, oils, 1843, Leicestershire Museums and Art Galleries

Wealth at death under £6000: probate, 23 June 1877, *CGPLA Eng. & Wales*

Thompson, James Matthew (1878–1956), historian, was born on 27 September 1878 at Iron Acton, Gloucestershire, the eldest son of the rector, the Revd Henry Lewis Thompson (1840–1905), later warden of Radley College and vicar of St Mary's, Oxford, and his wife, Catherine (*d.* 1937), elder daughter of Sir James *Paget, first baronet, the surgeon. After a happy childhood in the country, he was educated at the Dragon School, Oxford, and Winchester College, before going up to Christ Church, Oxford, as an open scholar, in 1897. There he took a second class in classical honours moderations in 1899, a first in *literae humaniores* in 1901, and a second in theology a year later. Ordination as deacon in 1903 (following two terms at Cuddesdon theological college) and a brief curacy at the Christ Church mission at Poplar in the East End of London, were the prelude to his election, on taking priest's orders, as an official fellow and tutor of Magdalen College, Oxford, in July 1904, and his appointment eighteen months later as the dean of divinity. The first post initially ran for seven years, the second for five.

Thompson's early career as an Oxford don was soon mired in controversy. By the summer of 1910 there were signs that the college was dissatisfied with his teaching, concern was raised about his pastoral abilities as dean, and he was warned by (Thomas) Herbert Warren, the president, that he might not be re-elected. In the event, he was retained, but his tenure was immediately imperilled again with the publication in 1911 of his *Miracles in the New Testament*. In the course of the 1900s Thompson, as a result of his reading and travels, had slowly moved from a high Anglican to an ultra-liberal and rationalist conception of Christianity, which at that date was beginning to gain some currency in the church.

In *Miracles* Thompson popularized his new-found position and argued that both the virgin birth and the resurrection were an invention. The bishop of Winchester (the college visitor), the president, several fellows, and a number of parents of prospective Magdalen students were scandalized, and Thompson came under pressure to resign as dean of divinity. Thompson and his college allies fought back under the banner of academic freedom, and a compromise was effected in November 1911 whereby Thompson retained the office until the end of his second five-year term but no longer had any ecclesiastical functions in the college. Over the next few years Thompson moved in liberal church circles and lectured on his beliefs in various places, including St Margaret's, Westminster. On 29 July 1913 he married Mari Meredyth (*d.* 1971?), daughter of the Revd David Jones, vicar of Penmaenmawr, a parish in Caernarvonshire where the Thompson family had their holiday home. They had one son.

For most of the First World War Thompson had leave of absence from his tutorial fellowship, which was due to expire for a second time in 1921. Rejected as an army chaplain, he served instead with the Red Cross in France, then spent some time in the Admiralty before becoming a schoolmaster at Eton College for two years. It was only in the autumn of 1919 that he returned to Magdalen and resumed his duties, this time, on his own suggestion, as a tutor in modern history. It was in this capacity that he remained at the college until he retired in 1938. Thompson's second period at Magdalen was much happier. A well-liked tutor, he gave unstinted service to the college as home bursar between 1920 and 1927, and vice-president from 1935 to 1937. He also turned himself into a respected historian with a good publishing record. His book *Lectures on Foreign History, 1494–1789* (1925) explored what he called the period of Europe's education, from the time it went to school in the Italian Renaissance until it came of age in the French Revolution. He then moved on to the revolution itself, publishing a number of books and collections of documents in subsequent years, notably a series of short biographies of the chief personalities under the title *Leaders of the French Revolution* (1929), and *Robespierre* (1935). In 1931, in recognition of his new expertise, he gained a university lectureship in French history.

On retirement Thompson continued to be an active historian and member of the Oxford intellectual community. His *French Revolution* appeared in 1943, followed by biographies of Napoleon and Napoleon III in 1951 and 1954. At the same time he became a published poet, edited the *Oxford Magazine* (1945–7), and acted as trustee and convener of the Oxford Preservation Trust. In 1944 he was elected to an honorary fellowship at Magdalen, having been suggested as a possible president a few years before, and in 1947 he became a fellow of the British Academy. He died in Oxford on 8 October 1956.

Both as a theologian and as a historian, Thompson believed in the possibility of approaching the truth ever more closely through rational enquiry and in the potential of the human spirit. His verse autobiography, published privately in 1940, is an elegant and often moving account of one man's journey from belief to atheism, but is also infused with a confidence that human beings can create a better world out of the defeat of Nazism. As a historian Thompson was a whig with a social conscience, who believed in the exemplary character and early formation of Britain's representative political institutions, the existence of clear-cut national characteristics, the primacy of the political, and the importance for good or ill of individual political actors. His fascination with the French Revolution lay in the fact that it was an attempt to create a just and free society in a country historically conditioned for absolute monarchy. Although Thompson was not an archival historian, his works on French history were based on close reading of the growing number of printed sources and a good acquaintance with the latest French research. It was thanks to him that the pioneering work of the great French historians of the first half of the twentieth century, Aulard, Mathiez, and Lefebvre, became better known to an English-speaking audience. Thompson also wrote clearly and compellingly: he was the master of the antithesis and the paradox. Not surprisingly, his books were frequently reprinted. In the last thirty years of the century, however, they quickly went out of favour, as Lefebvre's classic histories became available in English and historiographical fashion changed in favour of a bottom-up social and cultural approach to the French Revolution.

          L. W. B. BROCKLISS

Sources J. M. Thompson, *My apologia* (privately printed, 1940) · A. Goodwin, 'Reverend James Matthew Thompson, 1878–1956', *PBA*, 43 (1957), 271–91 · *Magdalen College record* (1909) · *Magdalen College record* (1934) · *Magdalen College record* (1955) · tutorial board minutes, 1904–21, Magd. Oxf., TB M/1/5 · college acta, 1904–11, Magd. Oxf., CMM/1 · letters and documents relating to Thompson's book on miracles, 1910–13, Magd. Oxf., MS 662 · president's notebook, 1904–13, Magd. Oxf., PR/2/17 · vice-president's papers, 1942, Magd. Oxf., VP2/A1/1 · private information (2004) [members, Magd. Oxf.]

Archives Bodl. Oxf., corresp., diaries, and papers · Magd. Oxf., corresp., travel journals, and papers relating to his book on miracles, MS 662 | Bodl. Oxf., letters to Sir Alfred Zimmern · Magd. Oxf., letters to President Warren

Likenesses photograph, 1913, Magd. Oxf. · R. Schwabe, pencil drawing, 1938, Magd. Oxf. · Studio Edmark, photograph, repro. in Goodwin, 'Reverend James Matthew Thompson', pl. XVIII

Wealth at death £12,030 17s. 8d.: probate, 10 Dec 1956, CGPLA Eng. & Wales

Thompson, Jane Henrietta. *See* Poitier, Jane Henrietta (b. 1736, d. in or after 1788).

Thompson, Jean Helen (1926–1992), demographer and civil servant, was born on 2 December 1926 at Inverisla, 22 Kenton Lane, Kenton, Middlesex, the elder of the two daughters of Arthur Thompson (1890–1977), an electrical engineer, of Kenton, and his wife, Jane Davidson, *née* McGill (1895–1987), of Dundee. She received her early education at Priestmead infants' and junior school, Kenton, and Deansfield junior school, Eltham. Her secondary education suffered during the Second World War when she was evacuated after one year at Eltham Hill School and spent three years at Newton Abbot grammar school before returning to Eltham for two years. From there she went to University College, London. Her first interest had been in mathematics but this changed to statistics, in which she took her degree in 1948.

After two years as a demonstrator in the statistical department of University College, Thompson decided that academic life was not for her and entered the civil service as a temporary statistician in the Ministry of National Insurance. In 1951 she became a permanent civil servant, progressing through the Ministry of Fuel and Power and the Board of Trade until she was appointed, in 1967, chief statistician (population statistics), in the General Register Office. There she found her true vocation and dedicated herself to becoming an expert in population analysis and other aspects of demography. She remained in the same post at the General Register Office (subsequently the office of population, censuses, and surveys) until her retirement.

Thompson's expertise in the demographic field coincided with a period when considerable public attention was focused on problems relating to the impact of immigration from new Commonwealth countries. She was much involved with ministers after the furore created by Enoch Powell and others. The high birth rates of the 1960s also caused public concern about the impact of continued population growth. The government set up a population panel in 1971, on which Thompson was influential and active. Its purpose was 'to assess the available evidence about the significance of population growth for both public affairs and private life in this country at the present and in prospect'. It reported at the end of 1972; one of its recommendations was that facilities for academic work outside government should be strengthened. Subsequently the centre for population studies was set up as a department of the University of London. As fertility fell during the 1970s, frequent reappraisals of long-term trends were needed, and again Thompson's views were influential. With hindsight they appear to have been over-cautious, but this was perhaps not surprising after the somewhat over-enthusiastic extrapolation of the upswing of the 1960s.

In 1969 Thompson had crossed swords with R. H. S. Crossman over the interpretation of statistics relating to

Jean Helen Thompson (1926–1992), by unknown photographer

'coloured' immigration, but it was not until after his death, and the publication in the popular press of extracts from volume 3 of *The Crossman Diaries*, in October 1977, that his extremely defamatory opinion of her came to light. In his *Diaries*, Crossman recorded that he had been told by 'Nicky' (Kaldor) that 'There are some fascists' in the registrar-general's office. On 20 February 1970

> I had an important meeting … with the Registrar-General. We have always had a worry with this fellow. For some reason the Registrar-General is never a trained statistician but a sort of squashy humanist from the Ministry of Health, who is perhaps good at Latin verse. The person who really runs the thing is a tough, ruthless lady, whom we must check all the time as these two are hell-bent on providing Powell with the statistics he really wants. We had only just stopped them doing this four months ago.   (Crossman, 828)

Unusually for a civil servant, Thompson was determined to set the record straight. She took Crossman's publishers to court, suing them for libel, and on 16 November 1977 a full public apology was issued, the allegations were withdrawn, and legal costs were paid by the defendants. However, as she did not insist on its being withdrawn, the first edition of volume 3 of *The Crossman Diaries* contained the libel.

By then Thompson had become acknowledged as one of Britain's leading experts on demographic matters both at home and abroad. At home she was a council member of the British Society of Population Studies, and its president from 1983 to 1985. She established strong links between the office of population, censuses, and surveys (OPCS) and academic demographers. Within the OPCS she developed new fields of demographic analysis, including the use of sample surveys for demographic purposes, and played an important role in the development of the OPCS longitudinal study. She contributed many articles to *Population Trends* and other official publications on fertility, marriage, divorce and the family, ethnic minorities, the longitudinal study, and national population projections. Abroad, she represented the United Kingdom on the Population Commission of the United Nations, and so helped to prepare the two world conferences on population which she attended, in Bucharest in 1974 and in Mexico in 1984. She represented the United Kingdom at numerous other meetings of the UN Economic Commission for Europe, the Conference of European Statisticians, and the Council of Europe. She was also a member of the International Union for the Scientific Study of Population.

During the twenty years she spent at the OPCS Thompson refused all offers of promotion. In her notes for her retirement presentation, she made it clear that she had found the post of chief statistician (population statistics) a job of continuing interest and variety. After the Mexican conference on population, in recognition of her work both internationally and at home, her name was submitted for an award. She was appointed CBE in 1986 the new year's honours list.

At the end of 1986 Jean Thompson retired to Steeple Aston, Oxfordshire, and after contributing to the Royal Statistical Society centenary charter conference in April 1987, and organizing a section of the European conference in Finland in June 1987, she dropped out of the demographic world. She became an active participant in village affairs, and led the fight against nuclear weaponry and noise pollution from the US airbase at Upper Heyford, a campaign that contributed in no small measure to its closure shortly before she died, of rhabdomyosarcoma, on 28 December 1992 at Katharine House hospice, Adderbury, Oxfordshire. Her ashes were buried in the eastern cemetery, Dundee, on 31 May 1993. She never married. She was survived by her younger sister Norah.

SARAH KATE LUCAS

Sources R. H. S. Crossman, *The diaries of a cabinet minister*, 3 (1977) • *Daily Express* (21 Oct 1977) • *The Times* (17 Nov 1977) • *The Times* (16 Jan 1993) • Lord Kaldor to Jean Thompson, 27 Feb 1978, priv. coll. • *The Independent* (2 March 1993) • personal knowledge (2004) • private information (2004) [Mrs Norah Frances Shapton, sister] • b. cert. • d. cert.
Likenesses photograph, News International Syndication, London [*see illus.*]

Thompson, John. *See* Tompson, John (*fl.* 1382).

Thompson, John, first Baron Haversham (1648–1710), politician, was born in October 1648 at Worcester House, Mile End Green, London, and baptized at William Greenhill's Independent Church in Stepney on the 31st, the second (but first surviving) son of Maurice *Thomson (1604–1676), merchant, and his second wife, Dorothy (*d.* before 1674), daughter of John Vaux of Pembroke. He was educated by Mr Watkins at Lee, Kent, entered Lincoln's Inn in 1663, and was admitted to Sidney Sussex College, Cambridge, on 2 July 1664, the year his father purchased the Haversham estate in Buckinghamshire. He married, on 14 July 1668 at St James's, Clerkenwell, Lady Frances (*c.*1648–1705), the widow of Sir John Windham of Felbrigg, Norfolk, and daughter of Arthur *Annesley, first earl of Anglesey. They had five sons, only one of whom, Maurice, survived. Of their eight daughters, Mary married her cousin Arthur, fifth earl of Anglesey, and her sister Martha married Sir John Every, baronet. Sheriff of Buckinghamshire in 1669–70, Thompson travelled abroad about this time to further his education. On his father's death in 1676 he inherited Haversham and property in London, Ireland,

the Americas, and the Caribbean. Created a baronet in 1673, he was admitted to the East India Company in 1676.

Thompson was short, stocky, and red-faced, and his actions and speeches were often controversial. He inherited radical whig principles from his father and in the first elections of 1679 may have unsuccessfully stood as MP for Upper Gatton in Surrey, which he had inherited from his Oldfield cousins. He purchased a house at Richmond, and was regarded by Sir Adam Browne MP as a dangerous neighbour during the Rye House Plot of 1683. Although successful at Gatton in the general elections of 1685, Thompson went to the Netherlands in the recess, reportedly carrying jewels worth thousands of pounds. His chaplain, Walter Cross, spoke derogatorily of James II, and Thompson's house in Utrecht was described as 'a private receptacle to the devout brethren' (Greaves, 300) to which he brought those involved in both Monmouth's rebellion and the Argyll expedition. He went to Cleves to see the whig politician Thomas Wharton, his wife liaising with a member of the princess of Orange's entourage. On eighteen committees in the Convention, he made sixteen recorded speeches. He complained that the clergy continued to pray for King James, wanted equality on the Indemnity Bill, voted for the Sacheverell clause, defending the nonconformist clergy against charges of disaffection, and supported the disabling clause in the Corporations' Bill.

Thompson's gift for controversy continued. In 1690 he moved that all those who had advised the king to dissolve the previous parliament should be dismissed. He attacked corruption, defended William III as 'the best of Kings', but lambasted those ministers 'who do not understand their business' (*Parliamentary Diary of Narcissus Luttrell*, 58). He was against increasing the land forces for a French war, seeing it as a mere 'colour' to allow a standing army. Critical of all place-holders and antagonistic to 'junto whigs', he was one of the 'Buff friends' in the country party, who, when new men joined a mixed ministry in 1693, hoped they would not be 'so mollified with place as to betray their country' (Rubini, 49). In 1694 he was listed as a member of the opposition, and re-edited his father-in-law's 1682 political pamphlet. This defended Anglesey against bogus memoirs and also attacked 'the folly or design of false or weak ministers' (*The Earl of Anglesey's State of the Government of the Kingdom*, 1694, 1).

In 1695 Thompson changed sides, his heir, Maurice, having been badly wounded at the siege of Namur. Elected a public accounts commissioner to investigate bribery and corruption, on the other hand he supported the government estimates for the 1696 campaign and, following a royal assassination attempt, he moved that all those MPs who did not subscribe to a loyal association should be expelled and that the captured plotters be examined. Such support for the government probably led to his elevation to the peerage as first Baron Haversham on 2 May 1696. On the reduction of the size of the Admiralty board in 1699 to five, Haversham became a member of the commission of 'his Majesty's own framing'. He then actively promoted measures to prohibit the export of wool, supply the victuallers of ships with sufficient cash, and analyse the state of the fleet. He also, through private bills, defended the interests of his relations when Katherine, countess of Anglesey, sought a separation from her wife-beating husband, the third earl. He was described as 'very eloquent, but very passionate and fiery, a Dissenter by principle, and always turbulent' (S. Macky, *Memoirs of the Secret Services of John Macky Esq.*, 1733, 78).

Haversham's support for the government continued for some time. He strongly opposed the French over the Spanish succession, and during the impeachment in 1701 of lords Somers and Orford, he made reflections on the Commons' conduct to the managers at a free conference. He supported Somers and claimed the Commons acted partially by accusing only some of those involved in the partition treaties. Subsequently his son Maurice moved the impeachment of the earl of Jersey, the lord chamberlain, in the Commons, where an attempt to have Haversham censured created a constitutional precedent over relationships between the houses. He said he had no desire to dishonour the Commons, and he and the impeached lords eventually escaped punishment. He resigned, or was removed, from the Admiralty board and the following year was ridiculed in a cartoon depicting Anglesey's death. He and Thomas Wharton introduced a bill to secure the king against the Pretender, who had recently been recognized as James III by the French. He opposed the Occasional Conformity Bill in 1703, using the occasion to attack the vast expense of the navy and the favouritism involved in appointments.

In 1703–4, as chairman of a committee investigating the naval victualling department, Haversham exposed corruption and criticized the government over its failure to use the navy effectively the previous summer. Moving towards the tories, he stirred them up to attack Godolphin over the Act of Union with Scotland. From 1704 he gave an annual state of the nation speech, which in 1705 called for the Electress Sophia to be invited to England, ostensibly to strengthen the succession, but in fact to embarrass the government. Godolphin, however, was well prepared and defeated 'Lord Haversham's great guns' (*Portland MSS*, 2.191) through delays and the Regency Bill. His change of allegiance created enemies and whig criticism, while his speech-making and alleged whoring were satirized in a poem, *The Dog in the Wheel* (1705). He printed his speech attacking the government for its conduct of the war, but was criticized by Defoe in his *Review*. Hinting that the attack had been inspired by Robert Harley, and justifying his noble status in pompous language, Haversham referred to Defoe as 'a mean and mercenary prostitute' (*Some Memoirs*, xi). In reply Defoe assaulted his recent ennoblement, commenting that some were 'advanced without honour' and others 'raised without merit' (J. Sutherland, *Defoe*, 2nd edn, 1950, 118). Haversham, in vindication, issued a further pamphlet that appeared to attack the king. Defoe then compared Haversham to a dog that bayed at the moon, commenting that he knew no more of William than those who had insulted him knew of his horse. The warfare between Defoe and Haversham,

now identified with the high tories, continued, the former writing to Harley that 'My Lord Haversham's speech is laught at by everybody' (*The Letters of Daniel Defoe*, ed. G. H. Healey, 1955, 247–8). However, Haversham's justification was 'The best way of preserving liberty of speech in parliament is to make use of it' (*Some Memoirs*, 12).

Although seen as a tory, Haversham remained a maverick MP. In the debates on the union with Scotland, he argued against an 'incorporating Union' and for 'a federal union, an union of interests an union of succession' (*Some Memoirs*, 20) and the maintenance of the constitutional balance of power. Opposed to over-powerful politicians, in July 1708 he had an audience with the queen, against whom he suggested the whigs were plotting. In 1709 he stated that 'one of the greatest ends and uses of Parliament, [is] the redressing of grievances and keeping great men in awe' (ibid., 34). An occasional conformist, he resolved from 1707 to regularly attend the Anglican church, though later opposed 'a pretended divine right of the church' (ibid., 50).

Haversham became more controversial with age and remained an inveterate speech-maker. On 10 May 1709 he married his housekeeper, Martha Graham (1647–1724), and was scurrilously identified as the 'old-out-of fashion-lord', father to the incestuous siblings in Mary Manley's *New Atlantis*. When 10,000 refugees arrived from the Palatinate, he proposed the erection of government subsidized workhouses, which would have competed with ordinary industry. During Dr Sacheverell's impeachment in 1710, he argued that the strength of the queen's constitutional position was through her hereditary title rather than the consent of parliament. He often turned a piece of political infighting into a personal confrontation, though the printing of his speeches opened the door to official publication of parliamentary proceedings. By late 1709 he was weary of debate, writing to Harley that he was 'contented after so long being in Parliament to come there very little' (*Portland MSS*, 6.524). However, he promised another speech on the state of the nation in 1710, but Lord Rochester reported he had had a fit of spitting blood. He sent a copy of another proposed speech to Harley in August, but died at Richmond on 1 November and was buried there on the 13th. His wife was buried on 13 March 1724.

ALAN THOMSON

Sources HoP, *Commons, 1660–90*, vol. 3 · R. L. Greaves, *Secrets of the kingdom: British radicals from the Popish Plot to the revolution of 1688–89* (1992) · H. Horwitz, *Parliament, policy and politics in the reign of William III* (1977) · D. Rubini, *Court and country, 1688–1702* (1967) · N. Luttrell, *A brief historical relation of state affairs from September 1678 to April 1714*, 6 vols. (1857) · *The parliamentary diary of Narcissus Luttrell, 1691–1693*, ed. H. Horwitz (1972) · *Some memoirs of the late Right Honourable John Lord Haversham from the year 1640–1710 ... to which are added all his speeches in parliament* (1711) · *A true account of the proceedings relating to the charges of the House of Commons against John Lord Haversham, 13 June 1701* (1701) · *The London diaries of William Nicolson, bishop of Carlisle, 1702–1718*, ed. C. Jones and G. Holmes (1985) · GEC, *Peerage*, new edn · E. Timberland, *The history and proceedings of the House of Lords from the Restoration in 1660 to the present time, 2, 1697–1714* (1742) · Cobbett, *Parl. hist.*, vols. 5–6 · *The life, birth and character of John Lord Haversham* (1710) · *The Marlborough–Godolphin correspondence*, ed. H. L. Snyder, 3 vols. (1975) · G. S. Holmes, *British politics in the* *age of Anne* (1967) • Bucks. RLSS, BAS 327–328/40; BAS 330/40; BAS 814/44; BRS/24/1988 • S. Hilton, *The story of Haversham and Richmond and its historical associations* (1937) • inventory, PRO, PROB 5/1026 • E. B. Sainsbury, ed., *A calendar of the court minutes … of the East India Company*, 11 vols. (1907–38), 1668–70; 1674–6; 1677–8 • K. Lindley, *Popular politics and religion in civil war London* (1977) • parish register, Watton, Herts. ALS, U/P 118.1/1 [baptism of father, Maurice Thompson] • *Report on the manuscripts of the marquis of Downshire*, 6 vols. in 7, HMC, 75 (1924–95), vol. 1, pt 2, pp. 886–7 • J. Thompson to B. Skelton, Utrecht, 1686, BL, Add. MS 41819, fol. 216 • parish register, Haversham, 13 March 1705 [burial: Frances Thompson, first wife] • J. L. Chester and G. J. Armytage, eds., *Allegations for marriage licences issued from the faculty office of the archbishop of Canterbury at London, 1543 to 1869*, Harleian Society, 24 (1886) • PRO, PROB 11/351, sig. 57 • *The manuscripts of his grace the duke of Portland*, 10 vols., HMC, 29 (1891–1931)

Likenesses double portrait, cartoon, 1702 (with his wife)

Wealth at death over £35,000: Bucks. RLSS, BAS 327–328/40; Hilton, *The story*; inventory, PRO, PROB 5/1026; Bucks. RLSS, BRS/24/1988; Sainsbury, ed., *Calendar*

Thompson, John (1775?–1864), naval officer, entered the navy in December 1787 and, having been on the books of various ships on the home station, joined the *Lion* in June 1792 with Captain Erasmus Gower and made the voyage to China. On his return he was promoted, on 18 December 1794, a lieutenant of the *Bombay Castle* in the Mediterranean, which was one of the fleet with Hotham in the action off the Hyères Islands on 13 July 1795; the ship was with Jervis during the blockade of Toulon in 1796 but was wrecked in the Tagus in December 1796. For his exertions then in saving life he was commended by Vice-Admiral Charles Thompson, president of the court martial on the loss of the ship. He was afterwards in the *Acasta* in the West Indies and, having distinguished himself in several boat expeditions, was appointed to his flagship, the *Sans Pareil*, by Lord Hugh Seymour. After Seymour's death he was promoted by his successor, Rear-Admiral Robert Montagu, on 28 April 1802 to command the sloop *Tisiphone*. He returned to England in January 1803 and commanded a division of sea fencibles for a year. He married in 1805 a sister of Dr Pickering of the Royal Military College, Marlow. They had a large family; one son, Thomas Pickering Thompson, died an admiral, aged eighty-one, in 1892.

In January 1806 Thompson was appointed to the sloop *Fly*, in which he was in the West Indies, at the Cape of Good Hope, and in the River Plate, where he commanded the flotilla intended to co-operate in the attack on Buenos Aires and assisted in landing and re-embarking the army. He was then appointed acting captain of the prize-frigate *Fuerte* and went home in charge of convoy; but the Admiralty refused to confirm the promotion and Thompson was sent back to the *Fly*, which he commanded off the French coast during 1808. In 1809 he commanded a division of the flotilla in the Scheldt, and was advanced to post rank on 21 October 1810. He had no further service, but on 1 October 1846 accepted the rank of rear-admiral on the retired list, on which he became vice-admiral on 27 May 1854 and admiral on 9 June 1860. He died at his home at Longparish, Hampshire, on 30 January 1864, aged eighty-eight.

J. K. LAUGHTON, rev. ANDREW LAMBERT

Sources J. D. Grainger, ed., *The Royal Navy in the River Plate, 1806–1807*, Navy RS, 135 (1996) • D. Syrett and R. L. DiNardo, *The commissioned sea officers of the Royal Navy, 1660–1815*, rev. edn, Occasional Publications of the Navy RS, 1 (1994) • O'Byrne, *Naval biog. dict.* • *The Times* (10 March 1892) • *GM*, 3rd ser., 16 (1864), 403, 534 • CGPLA Eng. & Wales (1864)

Wealth at death under £12,000: resworn probate, Dec 1865, CGPLA Eng. & Wales (1864)

Thompson, John (1785–1866), engraver, was born in Manchester on 25 May 1785, the son of Richard Thompson, a London merchant, and his wife, Sarah. He was baptized at the collegiate church, Manchester, on 12 June 1785. Skilled in several media, he ranked at the head of British wood-engravers for fifty years. Wood-engraving was developed into a significant art in Newcastle by Thomas Bewick and in London by Robert Branston, whose pupils Thompson joined at the age of fourteen. These engravers devised a 'white line' technique which achieved effects peculiar to wood-engraving, epitomized in Bewick's *British Birds* (2 vols., 1797–1804). Comparison of these with Thompson's illustrations for W. Yarrell's *British Birds* (1843) shows Thompson's technique to be more exquisitely finished but not more vivid. Thompson's most individual work was in engraving over 900 illustrations by John Thurston, who, having been a wood-engraver, drew to suit the wood-engravers' technique; examples may be found in J. Puckle, *The Club* (1817), Tasso's *Jerusalem Delivered* (1817), and Thomas Dibdin's *London Theatre* (1814–18). The minute skill of Thompson's engravings was sometimes praised as rivalling copper-engraving, for example, the portrait frontispiece to Samuel Butler's *Poetical Remains* (1827), but this was not the way forward for wood-engraving. The new possibilities which it offered included cheap pictorial journalism, but Thompson contributed little here; rather, he worked closely with the fine Chiswick Press, which catered for connoisseurs of illustrated books. Another virtue of wood-engraving was that it permitted exact reproduction of line drawings, though this meant sacrificing the 'white line' technique. Thompson's skill in facsimile engraving was shown in his rendering of the sprightly line of caricaturists such as George Cruikshank (*Mornings at Bow Street*, 1824) and (for French publishers) Grandville and Johannot. Facsimile wood-engraving made possible the celebrated illustrated books of the 1860s, inaugurated by the Moxon edition of Tennyson's *Poems* (1857), to which Thompson contributed. Thompson signed his engravings with his full name in capital letters, and with a monogram of his initials, T superimposed on I (for J), which produced a Latin cross with serifs.

Thompson's address in the 1820s was Barden Place, Peckham; from the 1830s, 3 (later 5) Bedford Place, Kensington, convenient for business with the Chiswick Press and convivial evenings with its owner, Charles Whittingham the younger; and from *c*.1847 to 1859, 1 Campden Hill Terrace, Kensington. In 1819–21 he assisted in Applegath and Cowper's attempts to produce forgery-proof banknotes, and in the 1850s he engraved in relief on steel Maclise's vignette of Britannia, which appeared on English banknotes from 1855 for more than a hundred years. In 1838 he got to know Henry Cole, then writing an article on wood-engraving. When Cole worked on the penny post in 1839–40, he commissioned Thompson to engrave on brass a postage cover design by Mulready. The Cole and Thompson families, neighbours in Kensington, became friendly. Cole's wife's sister married Thompson's son Charles Thurston *Thompson, who, with his brother Richard [see below], worked under Cole at the South Kensington Museum. In 1843–4 Thompson led the wood-engravers of London (with Cole's support) in opposition to the teaching of wood-engraving to women in the Government School of Design, but, when Cole took over the school in 1852, Thompson became director of a revived female wood-engraving class until its abolition in June 1859. He lectured on wood-engraving and formed a collection of historic and modern examples, which he used as teaching aids and donated in 1857 to the new South Kensington Museum, where they were on display during the museum's early years. Thompson's siblings Charles [see below] and Eliza and his daughters Isabel and Augusta were wood-engravers. He married Harriott Eaton in 1807; five of their eight children survived to adulthood. He died a widower at 9 Vicarage Gardens, Kensington, on 20 February 1866, and was buried on 27 February at Kensal Green cemetery.

Charles Thompson (1791–1843), engraver, was born in London, the younger brother of John Thompson, and trained with Robert Branston and his brother John. In 1816 he visited Paris to investigate prospects for wood-engraving, and, encouraged by the printing firm Didot, stayed there, training French engravers and contributing to books illustrated by Grandville, Gigoux, Johannot, and others. He died at his home in Bourg-la-Reine, near Paris, on 19 May 1843.

Richard Anthony Thompson (1819–1908), art administrator, was baptized on 15 September 1819 at St Giles's, Camberwell, London, the son of John Thompson and his wife, Harriott. He was employed at the Great Exhibition of 1851, in the English section of the Paris Universal Exhibition of 1855, and at subsequent international exhibitions. He was one of the first curators at the South Kensington Museum, having joined on 12 January 1857 to set up its educational collection, of which he was keeper until promoted in 1863 to be in charge of the general arrangement of the museum. He was an assistant director from 1866 until his retirement at the end of 1891, and acting director from 1876 to 1878 and in 1886. He died on 25 March 1908.

ANTHONY BURTON

Sources Art Journal, 28 (1866), 153–4 · W. J. Linton, The masters of wood-engraving (1889) · R. K. Engen, Dictionary of Victorian wood engravers (1985) · H. Cole, 'Modern wood engraving', London and Westminster Review, 29 (1838), 265–78 · G. C. Johnson, French and English wood engraving (privately printed, Manchester, 1969) · C. Fox, 'Wood engravers and the city', Victorian artists and the city, ed. I. B. Nadel and F. S. Schwarzbach (1980) · Minutes of the Council of the Government School of Design ... 1836 to ... 1844 (1849) · A. Warren, The Charles Whittinghams: printers (1896) · Henry Cole, MS diaries, 1822–82, V&A NAL · P. Gusman, La gravure sur bois en France au XIXe siècle (Paris, 1929) · A. D. Mackenzie, The Bank of England note: a history of its printing (1953) · R. K. Engen, Dictionary of Victorian engravers, print publishers and their works (1979) · Précis of the board minutes of the science and art department, 1852–1892, 8 vols. (1864–93) · IGI · CGPLA Eng.
& Wales (1866) · Journal of the Royal Society of Arts, 56 (1908), 673–4 · J. Buchanan-Brown, 'British wood-engravers c.1820–c.1860: a checklist', Journal of the Printing Historical Society, 17 (1982–3), 32
Wealth at death under £300: administration, 23 March 1866, CGPLA Eng. & Wales

Thompson, Sir John Sparrow David (1845–1894), lawyer and prime minister of Canada, was born at 5 Argyle Street, Halifax, Nova Scotia, on 10 November 1845, the seventh and last child of John Sparrow Thompson and Charlotte Pottinger. His father was an Irish Methodist who went to Nova Scotia from Waterford in 1827 and became printer to the crown. He taught his shy, quiet son shorthand, and in the 1860s the two became reporters of the assembly debates. The younger Thompson attended the Royal Acadian School and then the Free Church Academy until 1860, and was admitted to the bar in 1865 and began law practice. His father died in 1867 and he became the sole support of his mother and an unmarried sister. On 5 July 1870 he married Annie Emma Affleck (1845–1913), a Roman Catholic; but it was only when she was pregnant with their first child that Thompson was baptized a Roman Catholic. That baptism was the conclusion of his intense search for theological certainties.

In 1871 Thompson was elected alderman in Ward 5, the largest of Halifax's six wards, and remained on the city council until 1877, when he was elected to the provincial assembly for Antigonish, a Roman Catholic county, as a Conservative. With the victory of his party in the general election of 1878 he was made attorney-general. He was premier by 1882, when he resigned to become a judge on the supreme court of Nova Scotia, at thirty-six years of age the youngest on that bench and usually the youngest in the courtroom.

Thompson was a good judge, liking the métier, and his decisions were liberal; in criminal cases he was charitable where evidence was not clear, but firm, even unforgiving, when it was, especially in cases of cruelty to women or children. He loved justice as he hated iniquity; it was a fire that burnt inside him.

In 1885 the federal government of Sir John A. Macdonald desperately needed new strength. Too many ministers were sick or worn out. That ineffectiveness led to the north-west rebellion in March 1885. The Nova Scotia MPs urged Macdonald to appoint Thompson to the cabinet, but Thompson did not want to go; he liked his life as a legal monk. His wife, Annie, however, thought her young and talented husband needed sterner challenges than sitting with the 'sere old crows', as she called them, on the supreme court of Nova Scotia (National Archives of Canada, J. S. D. Thompson MSS, vol. 283, Annie Thompson to Thompson, 5 Nov 1885). She pushed him out of the house on the long way to Ottawa. In 1885 he resigned his judgeship, was sworn in as minister of justice, and was elected, with some difficulty, as MP for Antigonish.

The main burden of the defence of the government after the crisis over the hanging of Louis Riel in November 1885 fell upon the new minister of justice. Thompson had not been involved in that decision, but he took on the responsibility for dealing with its political consequences in parliament. His maiden speech was the first ringing defence of the government that the party had heard in the whole anguished Riel debate. He did not seek to convince by sounding phrases but by force of argument, by sheer good sense, and by his transparent fairness. It was a splendid success. Within two years he had become indispensable to Macdonald. In deciding the difficult questions of Canadian copyright, North American fisheries, and Bering Sea sealing, all of which arose between 1885 and 1894, Thompson could be counted on to produce an elegant, comprehensive, and luminous state paper. Macdonald had never had a minister like him. Thompson's work in the 1887–8 fisheries negotiations with the United States won him a KCMG.

By this time Thompson's family was established in Ottawa, greatly to his relief. He was a passionate family man: an uxorious husband, a solicitous, devoted father of the five of nine children who lived to maturity, he revelled in their company and that of his wife. Macdonald was quite wistful when he saw Thompson with his children.

After Macdonald's death on 6 June 1891 there was a cabinet crisis over his successor. A section of the Conservative Party from Ontario baulked at a Roman Catholic prime minister, and a compromise candidate, Senator J. J. C. Abbott, was selected, with the consequence that Thompson led in the House of Commons, Abbott in the senate.

The biggest problem facing the government in 1891 was the Langevin scandal, alleged corruption in Hector Louis Langevin's department of public works. The government had won the general election of 1891 only narrowly, with a 27-seat majority in a 215-seat house. The scandal was made to order for the Liberal opposition; fourteen defections from the government side would put them into power. With the Langevin scandal hot and ready to serve, the Liberals protested over fifty individual elections, aiming to unseat the government. It was a disaster for the Liberals. The result of Thompson's bringing facts into the open, and forcing the offending minister out, was to defeat that strategy. It gave the government in 1892 a new majority of something like sixty-five seats, a majority it had not enjoyed for a decade.

That big majority ensured passage of Thompson's new Canadian criminal code of 1892. It was based on Sir James Stephen's proposed criminal code of 1879, redrafted to suit Canadian conditions. The rest of Thompson's domestic agenda lay mainly in the difficult Manitoba school question. He counted on the courts to settle it, but the privy council unhinged that; it needed political solutions, and lay on his desk as he became prime minister on Abbott's resignation late in 1892.

In March 1893 Thompson went to Paris as one of two British judges in an international tribunal to settle the Canadian–American dispute over sealing in the Bering Sea. The tribunal decided in favour of Canada. In June 1894 Thompson held in Ottawa the first intercolonial conference convened outside England. That autumn he went to London to be sworn in as member of the privy council, and to see doctors about his health. The doctors were optimistic. On Wednesday 12 December he went down to Windsor to be sworn in; the ceremony was brief, but at lunch he felt faint, then suddenly collapsed. He was dead of a massive heart attack, aged forty-nine. His body was sent back to Canada in HMS *Blenheim*, a mark of the British government's esteem; he was buried in Holy Cross cemetery, Halifax, in a state funeral on 3 January 1895.

Thompson was a considerable lawyer. If not widely read, he had an incisive, rapid, and systematic mind which grasped facts quickly; that was joined to a vast capacity for work. The result was an extraordinary intelligence. He wore it all quietly. His was a mind unclouded by prejudice; Canada lost a prime minister with rare gifts, most of all the 'onward look of that untrammelled mind' (St John, *Daily Sun*, 4 Jan 1895).   P. B. WAITE

Sources P. B. Waite, *The man from Halifax: Sir John Thompson, prime minister* (1985) · *The Canadian journal of Lady Aberdeen, 1893–1898*, ed. J. T. Saywell (1960) · P. B. Waite, 'Thompson, Sir John Sparrow David', *DCB*, vol. 12 · NA Canada, Sir John Thompson collection · J. Castell Hopkins, *The life and work of … Sir John Thompson* (1895) · church records (baptism), 20 May 1847, Brunswick Street Methodist church, Halifax, Provincial Archives of Nova Scotia · church records (baptism), 21 April 1871, St Mary's Cathedral, Halifax, Provincial Archives of Nova Scotia · *St James's Gazette* (13 Dec 1894) · *Morning Herald* [Halifax, Nova Scotia] (4–5 Jan 1895)
Archives NA Canada · Public Archives of Nova Scotia, Halifax | CCC Cam., corresp. with sixteenth earl of Derby · NA Canada, Macdonald MSS · NA Canada, Gowan MSS · NA Canada, Aberdeen MSS · NA Canada, Stanley MSS
Likenesses photographs, 1867–94, NA Canada [PA 12206, C 68645, PA 25799, C 12188] · L.-P. Hebert, bust, 1893, Public Archives of Nova Scotia, Halifax
Wealth at death approx. $10,000 in property, savings, insurance in Ontario: will, Carleton County, Ontario · $11,000 in property in Nova Scotia: will, Halifax, Nova Scotia

Thompson, John Vaughan (1779–1847), surgeon and naturalist, was born on 19 November 1779, in Berwick, the son of John Thompson and his wife, Jane Hall, both of Berwick. That he had an early interest in the natural history of the area is demonstrated by the preparation, before he left Berwick and England, of his *Catalogue of Plants Growing in the Vicinity of Berwick upon Tweed* (1807). His skill as a botanist is revealed in this work, which, according to Britten (1912), exhibited 'a very complete knowledge of the plants of that region and of the literature of the period' and the talent of 'a capable artist'. The *Catalogue* also refers to the botanical guidance given to Thompson by William Percival Pickford of Edinburgh, presumably when he was a medical student in that city in 1797 and 1798. In addition to botany Thompson studied chemistry, anatomy, midwifery, and surgery, presumably with some distinction, as at the age of twenty he was appointed as assistant surgeon to the Prince of Wales's fencibles.

In December 1799 Thompson sailed with the 37th regiment for Gibraltar, and three months later accompanied it to the West Indies and Guiana where British troops were engaged in fierce fighting against the Dutch. Thompson was in the Caribbean for nine years, rising in rank to full surgeon in 1803. While there he continued his interests in natural history, describing a new species of pouched rat from Jamaica, and observing the spawning behaviour of land crabs. Towards the end of 1809 Thompson returned to England and was elected a fellow of the Linnean Society on 6 February 1810. In 1812 he sailed for the Indian Ocean, where he spent four years attached to the garrisons of Madagascar and Mauritius. Given the title of government agent for Madagascar, he undertook important political duties in addition to his medical practice. He also spent considerable time exploring the natural history of the two islands. He discovered in Madagascar a plant for which Robert Brown erected the genus *Thompsonia* (now *Deidamia*) and researched the island's extinct birds, eventually writing an article on the dodo for the *Magazine of Natural History* (1829). Thompson also produced *A Catalogue of the Exotic Plants Cultivated in the Mauritius* (1816), the first list of the island's plants.

Thompson returned to Britain in 1816 and was posted to Cork in southern Ireland as surgeon to the forces. By 1830 he had attained the senior rank of deputy inspector-general of hospitals, an appointment he held at Cork until 1835. In that year he was posted as medical officer in charge of the convict settlements of New South Wales, and never returned to Europe.

Although his publications reveal an early interest in marine bioluminescence (he later wrote vividly about the phenomenon he witnessed first off Gibraltar about 1810) it was on the voyage home from the Mascarene Islands in 1816 that Thompson first used a fine-meshed net to try and capture the organisms that caused it. Writing about the experience he stated

> Individually I feel under great obligations to this beautiful little animal, which by its splendid appearance in the water induced me to commence the use of a muslin hoop-net, which when it failed to procure me a specimen, brought up such a profusion of other marine animals altogether invisible while in the sea, as to induce a continued use of it on every favourable opportunity.

The 'beautiful animal' (J. V. Thompson, *Zoological Researches and Illustrations, 1828–1834*, 1968, 47) was a copepod (Crustacea) that he later named *Sapphirina indicator*. Thompson not only mastered the use of a fine-meshed net from a moving vessel, but also developed the ingenious method of fastening the net over the spout of the ship's sea water pumps—arguably the first use of a continuous plankton sampler.

In terms of his scientific work, Thompson's years at Cork were those of his most productive research, through which he:

> secured a permanent place in zoological literature through his discoveries of the nature and life histories of the feather star …, the polyzoa, the cirripedes (or barnacles) and several divisions of the crustacea. Our present conceptions of the structure of these forms, of their zoological position, and of the metamorphoses which they undergo, date from Thompson's papers. (*DNB*)

Thompson's privately printed series of memoirs on marine biology, his *Zoological researches and illustrations, or, Natural history of nondescript or imperfectly known animals* was conceived either in 1826 or early in 1827. This series of six memoirs (in five numbers) appeared between 1828 and 1834.

Thompson published his *Memoir on the Pentacrinus*

europeaus in 1827 and an erratum slip for this paper issued in May 1827 announced his intention to publish *Zoological Researches*. This paper was more fully developed in the *Edinburgh New Philosophical Transactions* in 1836, and its startling conclusions—that crinoids were echinoderms and that the *Pentacrinus* was a young stage of the feather star *Antedon*—attracted the notice of zoologists throughout Europe. However, the *Zoological Researches* became the principal vehicle for Thompson's discoveries. His skill with the plankton net—developed on the voyage from Mauritius—was used to good effect in the waters off Cork, and the majority of the papers published in the *Researches* relate to the metamorphosis of marine animals (mainly Crustacea) that he found in the plankton. These were remarkable and original discoveries. Thompson's observation of the metamorphosis of the *Zoea* larva of the edible crab (then regarded as a species in its own right) into an adult led to his suggestion that larval stages and metamorphosis were universal in decapod Crustacea. This view was criticized by N. A. Vigors, editor of the *Zoological Journal*, who felt that this was a sweeping conclusion, and Thompson's opinions remained controversial.

Thompson's discoveries of metamorphosis in barnacles enabled him to place the cirripedes within the Crustacea, rather than one of the classes of Mollusca, a major zoological achievement. It was in light of Thompson's major re-evaluation of barnacles as Crustacea—not molluscs as had previously been thought—that Darwin was able definitively to monograph the group in the early 1850s. More controversially, Thompson erected the name Polyzoa at the same time as Ehrenberg proposed the name Bryozoa for the same group of small colonial invertebrates. This caused confusion and controversy for many years, resolved only as late as 1947. However, Thompson's work on this group of animals was as meticulous as all his previous research, and his dissections and figures of them were a major contribution to understanding their structure, classification, and relationships. Thompson died in Sydney on 21 January 1847.

Thompson's studies in marine biology, published in a relatively short period between 1823 and 1836, revolutionized some aspects of zoological thought. His name is unfamiliar however, even to marine zoologists, partly because of the general absorption of his discoveries and the waning of the controversies his research caused. He has not escaped recognition entirely, however, with distinguished naturalists including Charles Darwin, E. R. Lankester, T. R. R. Stebbing, C. M. Yonge, and Sir Sidney Harmer recognizing and paying tribute to his genius. The reproduction of a facsimile of the *Zoological Researches* in 1968 has also enabled his contribution to science to be better appreciated.

PETER DAVIS

Sources A. C. Wheeler, 'An introduction to the *Zoological Researches* of John Vaughan Thompson', in J. V. Thompson, *Zoological researches and illustrations, 1828–1834* (1968), i–vi · *DNB* · J. Britten, 'John Vaughan Thompson (1779–1847)', *Journal of Botany, British and Foreign*, 50 (1912), 169–71 · R. E. Vaughan, 'A forgotten work by John Vaughan Thompson', *Proceedings of the Royal Society of Arts and Science of Mauritius*, vol. 1/pt 3 (1953), 241–8
Archives Linn. Soc., corresp. and papers

Thompson, Josiah (c.1724–1806), Particular Baptist minister and historian, was born at Shrewsbury, the son of the Revd Josiah Thompson (1692–1780), Baptist minister. He was born in the same parish as the Revd Job Orton (1717–1783), with whom he later corresponded for many years. From October 1742 he was educated for the nonconformist ministry at John Eames's academy in Hoxton on the Coward Trust foundation. In June 1744, 'having lately had a considerable legacy left him' (Coward Trust minutes, 74), he refused any further financial help. In November 1744, after he had been called to the ministry by the church at Prescott Street, London, he was dismissed to be minister of the church at Unicorn Yard, Southwark. He was ordained on 23 February 1746. He resigned his charge in August 1761, according to Ivimey, the Baptist historian, because of ill health. Another source states his resignation was 'upon some change of sentiment', having originally been a strict Calvinist (Monthly Repository, 282). Having inherited a considerable estate he was able to live in retirement as a gentleman for the rest of his life and preached only occasionally. Although his property 'gave him weight with his denomination', they did not hold him in very high regard (Wilson, 4.236). He 'does not appear to have done much good as a minister' (Ivimey, 3.427) was Ivimey's view, but Orton had a more favourable opinion. He heard Thompson give the charity sermon at Shrewsbury in June 1778 'with great acceptance', and when a larger collection 'than ever before' was made (Letters to Dissenting Ministers, 1.199). Thompson's considerable property made him increasingly conservative following the French Revolution. Robert Aspland failed to obtain a grant from the Ward Trust in 1797 to study at the Bristol Baptist Academy because Thompson, the senior trustee, considered both Aspland and the institution too radical. Unusually for a dissenting minister, Thompson was said to be a devoted supporter of William Pitt, giving £100 to assist the prosecution of the war against France.

In retirement Thompson undertook to collect materials for a history and account of the contemporary state of dissenting congregations in England and Wales. The work was prompted by the application made to parliament in 1772 for the relief of dissenting ministers and teachers. Through an extensive local correspondence Thompson acquired a mass of historical and contemporary information relating to about half the estimated 600 dissenting congregations in the country, which he arranged on a county basis and copied into a series of volumes. The collections, which he left in his will to Dr William's Library, are of considerable importance, not only for the statistics recording the number of congregations and ministers in 1772–3 but for the histories of many congregations 'taken from their Church Books, the Testimony & Report of old People, private Papers, & other authentic Records' (DWL, MS 38.7, preface), which are no longer available to the historian. Some of the accounts of individual congregations or of churches are of wider significance, notably the account of the rise of the Baptist New Connexion in Leicestershire. Thompson lived for many years in the house of Benjamin Stinton in Bury Street, London, and

after Stinton's death with his widow. He moved with the family to Clapham, where he usually preached once a month, though he also assisted other ministers. He married late in life, but continued to live with his friend Mrs Stinton, to whose relations he was said to have left his substantial fortune, having no family of his own, and 'in whose vault at Bunhill-fields he desired to be buried' (Monthly Repository, 283). He died on 4 June 1806 at Clapham.   DAVID L. WYKES

Sources Monthly Repository, 1 (1806), 282–3 · J. Ivimey, A history of the English Baptists, 4 vols. (1811–30), vol. 3, pp. 429–30 · W. Wilson, The history and antiquities of the dissenting churches and meeting houses in London, Westminster and Southwark, 4 vols. (1808–14), vol. 4, pp. 235–6 · 'Original letter from the late Rev. Josiah Thompson, containing particulars relating to dissenters, in 1775', Christian Reformer, or, Unitarian Magazine and Review, 6 (1839), 137–44 · minute book of the Coward Trust, 16 May 1738–30 Nov 1778, DWL, New College collection, CT1, pp. 48, 51, 67, 74 · Letters to dissenting ministers and to students for the ministry from the Rev. Job Orton, ed. S. Palmer, 2 vols. (1806), vol. 1, p. 199 · R. B. Aspland, Memoir of the life, works and correspondence of the Rev. Robert Aspland (1850), 20
Archives BL, list of dissenting congregations in England and Wales in 1715 and 1772, Add. MS 32057 · Bristol Baptist College, The state of dissenting interest, T.a.7 · DWL, records of nonconformity, Part 1, MS 38.5–6 · DWL, history of protestant dissenting congregations, Part 2, MS 38.7–11xx, 11, 21–22
Wealth at death under £10,000—personal estate: PRO, death duty registers, IR 26/112, p. 211

Thompson, Leslie Anthony Joseph (1901–1987), musician and prison worker, was born on 17 October 1901 at the Lying-in Hospital, Kingston, Jamaica, one of the five children, two sons and three daughters, of Emmanuel Thompson and his wife, Charlotte (d. 1935). When his mother went to work in Panama he was sent to Alpha Cottage School, Kingston, a Catholic orphanage where for five years he was exposed to music training and had access to many instruments. West India regiment bandsmen gave lessons, seeking recruits. In October 1917 Thompson joined that regiment as a bandboy, and went to England in May 1919 to study at Kneller Hall, Twickenham, where his euphonium-playing won the silver medal. He returned to Jamaica at the end of 1920.

He wrote band parts, though this was the officer's role, and went with the band to exhibitions in Toronto (1922) and Wembley (1924). Because of his arranging duties he seldom went on parade and thus had time to develop music for Kingston's cinemas.

Following the disbandment of the West India regiment Thompson played the cello in hotels, performed in cinema bands, and directed the orchestra at Ward's Theatre, Kingston. The introduction of talking films ended much of this work and, remembering his happy experiences there, in July 1929 he migrated to Britain. It was on the ship that he realized that talkies would also have decimated Britain's music profession, a naïvety that he recalled with amusement. In London his skills on trumpet, trombone, and bass and as an arranger were soon recognized. Employment with top-ranking individuals followed. The identification of jazz with black Americans helped (a chapter in Thompson's autobiography was entitled 'My Face is my Fortune'). He recorded with Patrick 'Spike' Hughes, performed in Noël Coward's stage success of 1932, *Cavalcade*, worked with dance bands, toured Europe as first trumpeter with Louis Armstrong (1934–5), appeared in the 'Blackbirds' show (1935), wrote for music magazines, formed an orchestra that became the Ken 'Snake Hips' Johnson West Indian Swing orchestra (several of whose members were born in Britain), and worked for Edmundo Ros, introducing Latin rhythms into dance music. Marriage, in 1933, to a showgirl with whom he had one son, Anthony Christopher (*b*. 1937), and one daughter, did not last.

During the Second World War Thompson served initially as a sergeant in the anti-aircraft defences; then, from 1944, in 'Stars in battledress'. After the war he returned to dance music, and studied at the Guildhall School of Music (1947–8). As the post-war migrants from the Caribbean reached London, Thompson assisted in helping them to settle and adjust. In 1954 he decided to retire from professional music and became the warden of the Alliance Club, a Christian-based hostel for foreign students in London. The evangelical Christian faith that he followed from this time brought him into contact with all manner of people, from the congregations of slum-land churches to bishops, and included visits to eastern Africa and the USA. In 1963 he qualified as a probation officer and started work at Pentonville prison, which continued beyond his retirement in 1971, for he stayed on as a part-time welfare officer, often teaching music. Hundreds of Londoners got to know the quietly spoken Jamaican with a military bearing and a delightfully teasing sense of humour. He spent a month—'a prodigal's return', as he called it—in Jamaica in 1980. He was mugged there, an experience which deeply affected him, as did his return to Alpha Cottage School, where he found that his name was first on their list of achievers.

Thompson's musical associations with jazz brought historians to his door, but he was a trained multi-instrumentalist who gladly played every type of music, not a creator of fresh melodies. He stressed the importance of training and understanding the theory of music, and had deep doubts about performers who lacked such knowledge. Diverse influences helped to shape him, the least likely being the violin lessons that he received from an officer on the German commerce-raider *Emden*, then a prisoner-of-war, in Kingston in 1917. He had great respect for Jamaica's early pioneers in formal music-making, including pianist Henry Nation, choirleader George Goode, and voice coach Louis Drysdale; when working on his autobiography, *Leslie Thompson* (1985), he spent more effort on them than on the jazz players of the 1930s. He died at University College Hospital, Camden, London, of acute myeloid leukaemia, on 20 December 1987.

With the late twentieth-century global association of Jamaica's popular music with Bob Marley and slum-culture language, the earlier contribution made by such people as Thompson was often overlooked. Likewise the jazz-era categorization of his musical activities in Britain was unfair and ill-balanced. He was an eclectic musician, comfortable in a wide range of genres. He contributed greatly to his adopted country and, by emigrating, denied Jamaica the benefits of a broad, mature, and useful citizen. JEFFREY GREEN

Sources L. Thompson, *An autobiography* (1985) · J. Green, 'Conversation with Leslie Thompson', *Black Perspective in Music*, 12/1 (1984), 98–127 · *The Times* (2 Jan 1988) · J. Chilton, *Who's who of British jazz* (1997) · d. cert.
Archives SOUND BL NSA
Likenesses photograph, repro. in *Radio Times* (28 July–3 Aug 1984) · photographs, repro. in Thompson, *Autobiography*

Thompson, Lydia (1836?–1908), dancer and actress, was born in London, probably on 19 February 1836. As her father died during her childhood and her mother remarried, she was compelled at an early age to earn her own living. She had a taste for dancing, which she learned from a Mr Petit, and, with her younger sister Clara, she took to the stage. In 1852 Lydia made her début in the ballet at Her Majesty's Theatre. The following Christmas (1853) she was engaged to play Little Silverhair at the Haymarket in the pantomime *Little Silverhair, or, Harlequin and the Three Bears*. In 1854 she danced for sixty nights at the same theatre in Planché's Easter extravaganza *Mr Buckstone's Voyage Round the Globe*, and caused a sensation on 18 October at the St James's in the burlesque *The Spanish Dancers*, in which she mimicked the celebrated Spanish dancer Señora Perea Nana. At Christmas she returned to the Haymarket, where she was highly praised in the leading character of *Little Bopeep who Lost her Sheep*. At the end of 1856 those who missed her appearances on the London stage were informed that she was dancing her way through Europe, serenaded by torchlight in Germany, Finland, and Russia. She was brought back to England by the death of her mother.

In the winter season of 1859–60 Lydia Thompson was again a hit at the St James's, dancing in a succession of light pieces, including the fairy spectacle *The Swan and Edgar*. In August 1861 she played Norah in the first production of Edmund Falconer's comedy *Woman, or, Love Against the World*. By this period she had begun to make excursions into the provinces, where she was a favourite for many years. On 31 October 1864, at the opening of the new Theatre Royal, Birkenhead, by Alexander Henderson (whose second wife she subsequently became), she took the title role in F. C. Burnand's *Ixion*, the first modern burlesque in more than one act. Afterwards she and Henderson moved to the Prince of Wales's, Liverpool, where she played Mary in Boucicault's *Used up* to the Sir Charles Coldstream of E. A. Sothern and the Ironbrace of Squire Bancroft. Here, also, on Whit Monday 1866 she was seen as the title character in the burlesque *Paris* to the Oenone of Henry Irving. On 15 September 1866 Lydia Thompson made her first appearance at the new Prince of Wales's Theatre, Tottenham Court Road, in the afterpiece *The Pas de fascination*, and on 10 October she played the chief character in H. J. Byron's poor burlesque of *Der Freischütz*, for which he had

Lydia Thompson (1836?–1908), by Lock & Whitfield, 1873

hoped to engage Marie Wilton (later Lady Bancroft). A lawsuit between the two actresses (with a trivial outcome) ensued.

In 1868, after performing at the Strand Theatre in William Brough's extravaganza *The Field of the Cloth of Gold*, Lydia Thompson sailed for America, where she was the pioneer of latter-day English burlesque. She was the first star to take a fully organized company across the Atlantic. The troupe was initially booed and hissed, but rapidly became immensely popular. Lydia Thompson showed herself to be a shrewd businesswoman and a strict taskmistress. Her six years in America began on 28 September 1868 with her New York début at Wood's Museum in *Ixion*, which ran for 102 nights. A tour of the principal American cities followed. In Chicago adverse critical notices led to Thompson and another of her actresses, Pauline Markham, horsewhipping the editor of the *Chicago Times*. They appeared in court, where they were fined 2 cents each. A further trial, however, resulted in fines to a total of $2200, a sum they adjudged to be 'cheap for their satisfaction'. In 1870 the troupe performed successfully at the Californian Theatre in San Francisco. During the winter season of 1870–71, which was passed in New York, Thompson began her long and fruitful professional association with Willie Edouin. When the troupe left America for a successful

tour of Australia and India, Thompson was presented with a silver wreath by the bootblacks of Cincinnati.

Lydia Thompson reappeared in London on 19 September 1874, at the Charing Cross Theatre under the management of W. R. Field. H. B. Farnie's famous burlesque of *Blue Beard*, already performed 470 times in America, was the opening piece. Thanks to the acting of Thompson, Edouin, and Lionel Brough, this poor piece proved a remarkable success both in London and in the provinces. Another short tour of America (1877–8) with her husband and a new burlesque company followed. On her return Thompson was seen at the Gaiety in February 1878 as Morgiana in the famous amateur pantomime *The Forty Thieves*. On 25 January 1879 she played Carmen at the Folly (where her husband was proprietor and manager) in Robert Reece's new burlesque *Carmen, or, Sold for a Song*. After some two years in retirement, she reappeared at the Royalty on 12 November 1881 as Mrs Kingfisher in the farce *Dust*.

Following the death of her husband, on 1 February 1886 at Cannes, Lydia Thompson once more departed for New York, where she was seen in the winter seasons of 1888–9 and 1891. Meanwhile, on 21 September 1886, she opened the Strand Theatre, under her own management, with *The Sultan of Mocha*. Her vivacity showed signs of decay, though she continued to perform, touring England in the autumn of 1896 as Rebecca Forrester in Appleton's farcical comedy *The Co-Respondent*. In May 1899 a testimonial performance of Boucicault's *London Assurance* was given at the Lyceum on her behalf. Her last appearance on the stage was at the Imperial in December 1904, as the duchess of Albuquerque in John Davidson's adaptation of *A Queen's Romance*. She died on 17 November 1908, at 48 Westminster Mansions, London, and was buried in Kensal Green cemetery. Her daughter, Mrs L. D. Woodthorpe, was also an actress, known professionally as Zeffie Tilbury (1862–1950).

W. J. LAWRENCE, *rev.* J. GILLILAND

Sources C. Scott, *The drama of yesterday and today*, 2 vols. (1899) · *Daily Telegraph* (20 Nov 1908) · *The life and reminiscences of E. L. Blanchard, with notes from the diary of Wm. Blanchard*, ed. C. W. Scott and C. Howard, 2 vols. (1891) · F. Hays, *Women of the day: a biographical dictionary of notable contemporaries* (1885) · B. Hunt, ed., *The green room book, or, Who's who on the stage* (1906) · A. T. C. Pratt, ed., *People of the period: being a collection of the biographies of upwards of six thousand living celebrities*, 2 vols. (1897) · H. Morley, *The journal of a London playgoer from 1851 to 1866* (1866) · C. E. Pascoe, ed., *The dramatic list* (1879) · H. B. Baker, *The London stage: its history and traditions from 1576 to 1888*, 2 vols. (1889) · J. Hollingshead, *Gaiety chronicles* (1898) · E. Reid and H. Compton, eds., *The dramatic peerage* [1891]

Archives Theatre Museum, London, letter file

Likenesses Lock & Whitfield, photograph, 1873, NPG [*see illus.*] · Southwell Bros., carte-de-visite, NPG · photograph, repro. in M. Barnham, ed., *The Cambridge guide to world theatre*, new edn (1988) · photographs, BM, NPG · photographs, repro. in Scott, *Drama of yesterday and today* · portrait, repro. in L. Hutton, *Curiosities of the American stage* (1891) · portrait, repro. in *The Theatre* (Jan 1886) · twenty prints, Harvard TC · woodburytype, carte-de-visite, NPG

Thompson, Sir Matthew William, first baronet (1820–1891), railway administrator, born at Manningham in the

West Riding of Yorkshire on 1 February 1820, was the son of Matthew Thompson of Manningham Lodge, Bradford, and his wife, Elizabeth Sarah, daughter of the Revd William Atkinson of Thorparch. He was educated at private schools and in 1840 entered Trinity College, Cambridge, graduating BA in 1843 and MA in 1846. He was called to the bar at the Inner Temple in 1847, and for ten years practised as a conveyancing counsel. Having married on 10 May 1843 Mary Anne, daughter of his uncle, Benjamin Thompson of Park Gate, Guiseley, who possessed the controlling influence in the old brewery, Bradford, he retired from the bar in 1857 and went to Bradford to take a part in the management and development of the brewery. Almost immediately he began to be actively involved in municipal affairs, becoming a town councillor in 1858, an alderman in 1860, and mayor of Bradford in 1862. In 1865 he was elected a director of the Midland Railway, and in 1867 was returned as a Liberal-Conservative borough member for Bradford, with William Edward Forster as his colleague. He was not a committed politician, and did not stand at the general election in 1868; but he did unsuccessfully contest the constituency again in March 1869 after the unseating of the Conservative member, Henry William Ripley. In 1871 and 1872 he was re-elected mayor of Bradford, and in October 1873 he was publicly entertained and a presentation of plate was made to him in recognition of his services.

In 1879 Thompson became chairman of the Midland Railway, and he immediately began to make felt the effects of his rigorous and energetic management. He was also chairman of the Glasgow and South Western Railway, and a director and sometime chairman of the Forth Bridge Railway Company. Parliamentary sanction for the building of the Forth Bridge had been obtained in 1873, but the work was not begun until 1882, when the Midland Railway's policy towards the financing of the bridge was greatly influenced by Thompson. The shareholders of the Forth Bridge Railway Company were guaranteed 4 per cent on their capital by the North British, Midland, Great Northern, and North Eastern railway companies, the Midland Railway under Thompson putting forward the largest single contribution to the bridge's £3 million cost. The bridge was completed in January 1890, and formally opened by the prince of Wales on 4 March 1890. On this occasion a baronetcy was conferred upon Thompson, in recognition of the ability with which he had helped forward the undertaking.

Thompson resigned the chairmanship of the Midland Railway in 1890, because of failing health. He died at Park Gate, Guiseley on 1 December 1891, and was buried on 5 December in the churchyard there. He was survived by his wife, three sons, and two daughters.

WILLIAM CARR, rev. RALPH HARRINGTON

Sources *Annual Register* (1891) · Burke, *Peerage* · R. Williams, *The Midland railway: a new history* (1988)
Likenesses H. von Herkomer, oils, possibly National Railway Museum, York
Wealth at death £76,142 3s. 3d.: probate, 12 Jan 1892, CGPLA Eng. & Wales

Thompson, Muriel Annie (1875–1939), volunteer ambulance driver and member of the FANY, was born on 10 June 1875 at 17 Albyn Place, Aberdeen, the fifth of the eight children of Cornelius Thompson (1843–1894), shipowner and marine architect, and the only daughter of his second marriage, to Agnes Marion Williamson (1846–1926). Her grandfather was George Thompson junior (1804–1895), laird of Pitmeddon, deputy lieutenant of Aberdeenshire, provost of Aberdeen, member of parliament for Aberdeen (1852), and founder of the George Thompson Shipping Company, later the Aberdeen White Star Line. She was educated at Blackheath high school and Hacking College, north London. After the death of her father she lived with her mother at 48 Queensgate, London.

Muriel and her two full brothers, Walter and Oscar, were early and keen motor vehicle drivers. They were involved in the foundation of the Brooklands Automobile Racing Club, and on 4 July 1908 Muriel Thompson won the Ladies Bracelet Handicap at Brooklands, the first race held there for women drivers. She was driving Oscar's Austin racing car, nicknamed Pobble. Her speed over 3 miles was 50 m.p.h.

At the outbreak of the First World War Oscar joined one of the several volunteer ambulance convoys raised to help the French, taking Pobble, splendidly converted into an ambulance, with him. Women were not welcomed so Thompson turned to the First Aid Nursing Yeomanry corps (FANY). This was founded in 1907 by a former cavalry sergeant-major, Edward Baker, as an all-female mounted ambulance unit. By 1914 the FANY had moved to mechanized transport and on 27 October 1914 was the first women's organization to go to France. Their services having been firmly refused by the British authorities, they drove ambulances and ran hospitals and casualty clearing stations for the Belgian and French armies all along the western front. On 1 January 1916 British resistance was finally overcome and the members of FANY Calais convoy became the first women to drive officially for the British army.

Thompson joined the FANY as a driver in January 1915. On 8 February she crossed to Calais to a Belgian military hospital called Lamarck which the corps was running. On 29 March she was personally decorated by King Albert with the chevalier of the order of Leopold II for evacuating wounded Belgian soldiers under fire near Dixmude. She served as second in command to Lilian Franklin on the Calais convoy, and was mentioned in dispatches on 9 April 1917. On 1 January 1918 she was appointed officer commanding of a new joint FANY–VAD (voluntary aid detachment) convoy based at St Omer near the front line. The St Omer convoy became officially part of the Second Army on 4 May, choosing a perky-looking red fish as its official insignia in memory of the surgeon-general's description of the corps in 1915, then in battle with British officialdom, as 'neither fish, flesh nor fowl … but damned good red herrings'.

During the prolonged German spring counter-offensive in 1918 the St Omer convoy worked day and night under heavy bombardment evacuating the dead and wounded.

Muriel Annie Thompson (1875–1939), by unknown photographer, 1915 [wearing the order of Leopold II, Flanders, March 1915]

On 18 May they were called out following a bombing raid on Arques, including one on an ammunition dump. A second raid came over and, with shells exploding all around, they were ordered to take cover. The women worked on regardless, moving the injured to safety. For their coolness and courage under fire they were awarded a total of sixteen military medals and three Croix de Guerre. According to an unpublished memoir by Beryl Hutchinson, all the decorations were questioned, as there were too many for such a small unit; but each one was so strongly supported by the British and French officers on the scene that all were allowed. Muriel Thompson was decorated with her Military Medal in the field by the general officer commanding, Second Army, General Sir Herbert Plumer, and with her Croix de Guerre in the main square of St Omer by General de la Guiche. Her medals were subsequently given to the National Army Museum.

Muriel Thompson was a tall, dark-haired woman as evidenced by the photograph showing her towering over General de la Guiche as she received her medal. Handsome rather than beautiful, other photographs capture her looking out of the many cars she drove over the years, Pobble the Austin racing car, Flossie the Ford ambulance, and Kangaroo, her own Cadillac. Badly affected by the death at Passchendaele in 1917 of her nephew Logie Colin Leggatt, a lieutenant in the Coldstream Guards, and exhausted after nearly four years of continuous service, she returned to England on 2 September 1918. After a

month's recuperation, she joined the Women's Royal Air Force as a recruiting officer. She was demobilized on 1 October 1919. She resigned from the FANY in 1922 in a policy disagreement over the corps' post-war role. Muriel Thompson, who never married, spent the next two decades at her London home, 30 The Grove, Boltons, Kensington, where she died on 3 March 1939 of encephalitis lethargica, an epidemic form of inflammation of the brain, of which there were several outbreaks between the wars. She was buried in Brompton cemetery, London.

LYNETTE BEARDWOOD

Sources *First Aid Nursing Yeomanry Gazette* (1915–18) · M. Thompson, diaries, 1915–18, Duke of York's Headquarters, London, FANY archives · B. Hutchinson, unpublished account, 1920, Duke of York's HQ, London, FANY archives · *ILN* (11 July 1908) · *LondG* (1918) · private information (2004) [The Rt Hon. Sir Andrew Leggatt, great-nephew] · b. cert. · d. cert. · *CGPLA Eng. & Wales*
Archives Women's Transport Service (FANY), Duke of York's Headquarters, London, FANY archives, diaries · Women's Transport Service (FANY), Duke of York's Headquarters, London, FANY archives, scrapbook and other writings
Likenesses photograph, 1915, Duke of York's HQ, London, FANY archives [*see illus.*]
Wealth at death £27,144 12s. 1d.: probate, 20 April 1939, *CGPLA Eng. & Wales*

Thompson, Nathaniel (*d.* 1687), printer, was born in Ireland in the 1640s. At an unknown date he was apprenticed to the leading Dublin bookseller and former lord mayor, William Bladen. The first work to appear bearing Thompson's imprint was Ambrose White's *Almanack and Prognostication for … 1665*, printed by Thompson in Dublin.

By at least 1668, however, Thompson had relocated to London, where he was employed as a workman in the printer's shop of William Godbid. He may have been the Thompson who a year earlier described himself as 'a *Roman Catholique*' and was noted as running a shop in Somerset House selling '*Popish Books* and *Popish Knacks*' when interviewed by a parliamentary committee investigating the causes of the Fire of London (*True and Faithful Account*, 24–5).

Thompson was made a freeman of the Stationers' Company in December 1669. From about 1672 to 1678 he was a partner of Thomas Ratcliffe, a printer who worked from a shop at St Benet Paul's Wharf near Doctors' Commons, and together they printed a few dozen books including music, plays, and dissenting religious works. Thompson married Ratcliffe's daughter, Mary (*d.* 1700), the widow of Thomas Daniel. After the dissolution of their partnership Thompson set up for himself in Fetter Lane, moving to the Old Spring Garden near Charing Cross in 1685, where he expanded from printing for booksellers to publishing books himself. He continued Ratcliffe's printing of dissenting books. Like many printers' wives, Mary assisted her husband in his business, and she ran it when he was in gaol—which was rather often in Thompson's case. They had one daughter, Margaret; Mary also had a daughter from her first marriage, Mary Daniel.

Thompson was brought before the Lords committee of examinations on 29 October 1678 charged with printing thousands of copies of Catholic books. He claimed to be a protestant. This and previous problems he had with the Stationers' Company (in 1677 it had charged him with infringing the company's monopoly in the English stock, and on 1 July 1678 the company had decided to indict him for publishing part of a French mass-book, but nothing came of this) did not prevent him from succeeding to his father-in-law's share of the English stock on the death of the aged Ratcliffe, who had been living in Thompson's household, in late 1678.

Thompson emerged as a public figure in London during the Popish Plot and exclusion crisis. In 1679 he published some whig and pro-Monmouth tracts, but he was best-known as the whigs' leading opponent among London printers. He published a newspaper, the *Domestick Intelligence, or, News both from City and Country*, from 26 August 1679 until 14 May 1680, when it was suspended by the authorities along with other London newspapers. Thompson's *Domestick Intelligence* began as a hoax, as the *Domestick Intelligence* was originally a whig paper printed by Benjamin Harris. Thompson printed a fake version of the sixteenth issue of the paper dated 26 August 1679, and continued to print it with a similar appearance to Harris's paper. Eventually Thompson's paper ran under the title the *True Domestick Intelligence*. It was strongly pro-court and pro-government, but did not deny the reality of the Popish Plot or the murder of Sir Edmund Berry Godfrey. However, on 26 March 1680 the Middlesex justice and zealous Catholic-hunter Sir William Waller had Thompson arrested for treason and sent to the Gatehouse for 'having been privy to a Treasonable Conspiracy of the Apprentices in levying war against His Majesty' (Rostenberg, 'Thompson', 196–7). Thompson escaped trial on that occasion, and the charges seem to have been dropped following Waller's removal from the commission of the peace in April.

From 9 March 1681 Thompson published another paper, the *Loyal Protestant and True Domestick Intelligence, or, News both from City and Country*. This was much more strongly tory than Thompson's previous newspaper, and with it Thompson became London's leading publisher of tory pamphlets and ballads. However, as late as the beginning of 1681 Thompson printed a whig tract, *The Petitioning-Comet*, and in 1684–5 he was noted as 'a mercenary fellow for any side that pays him well' (Knights, 161 n. 59). Thompson was a gifted newspaperman, whose newspapers maintained a steady barrage of attacks on the whig forces and engaged in vicious feuds with the whig newspapermen Harris and Langley Curtiss. Whigs hated Thompson, constantly attacking him in their own writings and nicknaming him Popish Nat. On 17 November 1681, the day of whig celebration for the anniversary of Queen Elizabeth's accession, Thompson was both attacked in the street and burned in effigy in the pope-burning parade; much of his house was torn down during the Gunpowder Plot commemoration of the same year.

More seriously, Thompson was persecuted both by the whigs who controlled the government of London for most of this period and by the Stationers' Company. Thompson's worst legal scrape occurred in 1682, after he had printed pamphlets and newspaper stories that attacked

the official story of the murder of Sir Edmund Berry Godfrey, intimating that Godfrey had killed himself. Thompson was charged with libel. In a trial at the Guildhall presided over by Lord Chief Justice Sir Francis Pemberton on 20 June 1682, Thompson was fined £100 and sentenced to an hour in the pillory. On 5 July he was pilloried alongside the author John Farwell, targets of a hail of dirt, stones, and rotten eggs. Thompson could probably have relied on financial help from tory leaders, but even so he was forced to mortgage his share of Stationers' Company stock to John Leigh on 5 September 1682.

The tory triumph following the exclusion crisis did not end Thompson's woes. In November 1682 he, like other London newspaper publishers, was ordered to shut down his paper; the last issue appeared on 20 February 1683. He was arrested in 1684 for publishing a pro-Catholic tract, *The Prodigal Return'd Home* by E. Lydeott. He also published collections of tory songs, *A Choice Collection of 120 Loyal Songs* (1684), later expanded into *A Choice Collection of 180 Loyal Songs* (1685) and *A Collection of 86 Loyal Poems* (1685). The sources of these collections included ballads printed by Thompson himself, those printed by others, and some previously only circulated in manuscript; one song satirized the Stationers' Company. It is for these collections that he is chiefly known.

After the accession of James II, Thompson emerged as one of London's leading Catholic printers and booksellers. He published, among many other Catholic devotional and controversial works, *The State of Church Affairs in this Island of Great Britain* (1687) by Sir Christopher Milton, brother to the poet John Milton; *The Considerations which Obliged Peter Manby Dean of Derry to Embrace the Catholique Religion* (1687); and for the Stationers' Company *Festum festorum* (1687), a work by Thompson's friend the Catholic astrologer John Gadbury.

Thompson died in London at some point between 22 and 26 November 1687. He was buried on 26 November at St Martin-in-the-Fields leaving a widow, a brother Charles, and three sisters, Margaret Duncombe, Mary Oakley, and Rebecca Thompson. His widow kept the business going, but the last imprint bearing the Thompson name appeared in 1688; the business was taken over by David Edwards, the husband of Thompson's stepdaughter, Mary Daniel.

WILLIAM E. BURNS

Sources G. M. Peerbooms, *Nathaniel Thompson: tory printer, ballad monger, and propagandist* (1983) • J. Sutherland, *The Restoration newspaper and its development* (1986) • L. Rostenberg, *Literary, political, scientific, religious and legal publishing, printing and bookselling in England, 1551–1700: twelve studies*, 2 (1965) • T. Harris, *London crowds in the reign of Charles II* (1987) • M. Knights, *Politics and opinion in crisis, 1678–1681* (1994) • M. Pollard, *A dictionary of members of the Dublin book trade 1550–1800* (2000) • L. Rostenberg, 'Nathaniel Thompson, Catholic printer and publisher of the Restoration', *The Library*, 5th ser., 10 (1955), 186–202 • *A true and faithful account of the several informations exhibited to the honourable committee appointed by the parliament to inquire into the late dreadful burning of the City of London* (1667)

Thompson, Sir Peter (1698–1770), merchant and book collector, was born at Poole, Dorset, on 30 October 1698, the third son of four surviving children of Captain Thomas Thompson and his wife, Amata Edwards. He was put to trade and became a successful and prosperous Hamburg merchant. For some forty years he lived in a house in Mill Street, Bermondsey, London. He became a justice of the peace and in 1745 he was elected high sheriff of Surrey and knighted for presenting a loyal address to the king on the outbreak of the Jacobite rebellion. He was MP for St Albans from 1747 to 1754.

According to John Hutchins, Thompson 'supplied the want of a liberal education by conversation with men and books' (Hutchins, 1.66). He moved in a circle of antiquaries and was a friend of Joseph Ames, to whom he was introduced about 1720 through Poole connections. At the posthumous sale of Ames's library in 1750 Thompson bought Ames's annotated copy of the *Typographical Antiquities* with the copyright and blocks, which he sold to the antiquary William Herbert. Thompson was elected fellow of the Society of Antiquaries on 18 April 1743. He was an active member of the society and for many years attended the meetings as regularly as he could. His friends included Dr Andrew Coltee Ducarel, with whom he corresponded.

In 1745 Thompson built a handsome house in Market Street, Poole, where he installed his widowed sister, Mrs Haseldine. In 1751 he was made a freeman of Poole; and in 1763 he made his will and retired from trade, 'to enjoy the pleasures of studious retirement and reflexion, and the conversation of his friends, in the place of his birth … and at great expence, formed a capital collection of books, manuscripts, fossils, and other literary curiosities' (Nichols, *Lit. anecdotes*, 5.511–14). He collected everything he could find relating to the history and antiquities of Poole, which he made freely available to his friend John Hutchins for his research for his *History of Dorset*. Thompson identified many items relating to Dorset in the public records.

Thompson remained a bachelor and looked after his widowed aunt and his sister, Mrs Haseldine. The latter kept house for him; he left her the house as a life tenant, but she predeceased him by four days, and the house was then let in two tenements. He died on 31 October 1770. Much of his posthumous claim to fame rests on his book collection which included the pioneering topographical works of William Borlase and William Stukeley, and many manuscripts and annotated works of contemporary antiquaries, particularly Joseph Ames and John Lewis. Books bearing his bookplate are to be found in several major libraries. He left his library to his namesake, Captain Peter Thompson of the Dorset militia, who was his godson and relative, and who kept the books packed up in boxes in the house until 1781. However, the collection remained intact until 1815 when it was sold by E. H. Evans.   ROBIN MYERS

Sources Nichols, *Lit. anecdotes*, 5.511–14 · will, PRO, PROB 11/962, sig. 414 · J. Hutchins, *The history and antiquities of the county of Dorset*, 2 vols. (1774) · *A catalogue of the library of Sir Peter Thompson … sold … by R. H. Evans* (1815) · J. Sydenham, *The history of the town and county of Poole* (1839) · M. Noble, *Lives of the fellows of the Society of Antiquaries* (1878) · R. S. Lea, 'Thompson, Sir Peter', HoP, *Commons, 1715–54*

Archives BL, commonplace book, Add. MS 63648 · Dorset RO, corresp., etc.
Wealth at death left two houses (?); library of books and curiosities; cash and annuities: will, PRO, PROB 11/962, sig. 414

Thompson, Pishey (1785–1862), antiquary, was born on 18 June 1785 at Peachy Hall, Freiston, near Boston, Lincolnshire, the eldest child and only son of John Thompson (1756–1792), grazier and butcher of nearby Benington, and his second wife, Mary Evison (*c*.1762–1789). A 'forward' boy, Pishey first attended a dame-school, probably at Benington, the village where he was brought up by his grandmother Bridget Thompson, *née* Pishey (1731–1815), who maintained the family farm after her husband, John, died in 1772. From the age of six Pishey appears to have spent two years at Boston grammar school, where he excelled at Latin and mathematics, then four years at Wragby grammar school, followed by schools at Freiston and Skirbeck, near Boston. At sixteen years of age he returned for some time to the Freiston School as usher, and three years later he became a clerk, firstly in Sheath's Banks and then (in 1814) in Garfit's Bank in Boston; he also ran a bookselling business in the town.

Throughout life Thompson adhered to the Unitarian faith, and in politics was a radical. A keen antiquary, and of literary bent, he collected materials for a history of the town and its neighbouring villages, and his intention to publish such a work was announced in 1807. However, in 1819 he emigrated to Washington, DC, where many relations and friends were already settled. His historical materials were arranged and published in 1820 in Boston by John Noble as *Collections for a topographical and historical account of Boston and the hundred of Skirbeck in the county of Lincoln*.

Granted American citizenship, Thompson set up as a high-class bookseller and publisher in Pennsylvania Avenue, Washington, and became closely acquainted with leading citizens and presidents. He was founder member of All Souls Church Unitarian, and of the National Institute (the later Smithsonian Institution). He was a founder member of the George Washington memorial committee, and president of the first national theatre. He supported George Flower's slave-free settlement at Albion, Illinois, and worked for the national scheme for settling freed slaves in Liberia. These activities, together with a prolonged holiday back in Boston in 1827 at a time of financial crisis in Colombia, rendered him complacent about the interests of his business. Bankrupt and in great debt, he returned to Britain in November 1841 but failed to find adequate employment. In August 1843 he went again to America, having learned of a vacancy on the *New York Herald*. This did not materialize and he returned to Washington, where he reported senate proceedings for *The Globe* and was appointed reporter for the *National Intelligencer*—a position he held almost until his death—and supplemented his income by freelance accountancy. Thompson's most significant activity in America was as initial campaigner for a national bureau of

Pishey Thompson (1785-1862), by Hackford, 1859

statistics. His scheme was presented to congress, and an office was set up. President Tyler practically promised to appoint Thompson to run the bureau, but, apparently because their political views differed, Tyler gave the post to a clerk transferred from another state department.

On 6 November 1807 Thompson married Jane Tonge (1786-1851) of Boston, but there were no children of the marriage. He nevertheless fathered a son born on 23 April 1824; the mother was Mary Wright, the eldest daughter of the Revd Richard Wright of Blakeney, Norfolk, the first missionary of the Unitarian church. The boy, named John Wright, was probably born in Washington (his mother had emigrated there with the Thompsons), but was brought up by his maternal relatives in Kirkstead, Lincolnshire. Despite the circumstances, an affectionate relationship, without rancour, subsisted between all concerned, and the illegitimacy remained a secret for many years to all but the immediate family. In due course John Wright became a leading Unitarian minister in Lancashire, renowned for his introduction of Sunday schools. Thompson returned to Britain in 1846, and settled in Stoke Newington, London. After the death of his wife on 16 July 1851 he finally put together his monumental *History of Boston*, published on 23 October 1856: it remained the only history of the town for 130 years. Thompson's income was meagre and uncertain, but occasionally friends, particularly the Flower family in Stratford upon Avon, found tactful ways of employing his services. Though living thus in considerable poverty, he could say before his death at his lodgings, 44 Church Street, Stoke Newington, London, on 25 September 1862, that he had repaid almost the whole of his debts. He was buried in New Gravel Pit churchyard,

Paradise Place, Hackney. In memory of Thompson, a plaque on the south wall of Boston's parish church was later subscribed to by many of his friends.

ISABEL BAILEY

Sources I. Bailey, *Pishey Thompson: man of two worlds* (1991) · Pishey Thompson's diary, 18 Oct 1841-6 April 1844, Boston Archives · The Shakespeare Centre Archives Dept., Stratford upon Avon, Warwickshire, The Pishey Thompson collection
Archives Boston Borough Archives Department, Municipal Buildings, Boston, Lincolnshire · Boston University, Massachusetts, Mugar Memorial Library · Hackney Archives, London · Harris Man. Oxf. · Historical Society of Washington, Washington, DC · L. Cong. · Lincs. Arch., diary, incl. statistical notes · National Archives and Records Administration, Washington, DC · Shakespeare Birthplace Trust RO, Stratford upon Avon, corresp., diaries, notes, and papers, incl. historical notes relating to Boston · Smithsonian Institution, Washington, DC · Unitarian All Souls Church, Washington, DC · Unitarian Historical Society, Edinburgh · Washington National Theatre Archives, Washington, DC · Wethersfield Historical Society, Wethersfield, Connecticut
Likenesses Hackford, photograph, 1859, Boston Public Library, Lincolnshire [*see illus.*]
Wealth at death under £100: administration, 2 Feb 1867

Thompson, Reginald Campbell (1876-1941), Assyriologist and archaeologist, was born on 21 August 1876 at Cranley Place, South Kensington, London, the eldest of four sons and one daughter of Reginald Edward Thompson (1834-1912), physician, and his wife, Anna Isabella De Morgan (1845-1885), daughter of the mathematician Augustus De Morgan. His childhood predilection towards cuneiform was encouraged by Frederick William Walker, the high master of St Paul's School where Thompson was 'a keen member of the Cadet Corps', becoming 'the best marksman in the school and captain of the Eight' (Driver, 4). Upon a recommendation from Ernest Alfred Wallis Budge to James Smith Reid, Thompson matriculated at Gonville and Caius College, Cambridge, in 1895, with a scholarship in Hebrew. He read for the oriental languages tripos, and took a first class and graduated BA in 1898, passing almost immediately, in 1899, into employment at the British Museum as an assistant of the second class in the department of Egyptian and Assyrian antiquities under its keeper, Wallis Budge, at a salary of £120 plus annual increment of £10. Leonard William King, the rising young cuneiform scholar, was his colleague.

Within a year of his appointment a first example of Thompson's skill as copyist appeared in the prestigious trustees' series *Cuneiform Texts* (pt 11, October 1900), displaying a hand capable of reproducing from tablets minute signs 'as accurate as they were neat' considering his being 'so muscular and almost clumsy a man' (*DNB*; Driver, 12). He prepared nine more parts before 1906 (12, 14, 16-20, 22-23), while privately writing five volumes of studies, some with additional texts. Those in Thompson's handscript remain indispensable; some translations and commentaries require reconsideration. Like King, Thompson possessed the complete concentration necessary to 'search through tiny fragments of clay for bits of text', nourished by the habit 'of repeating aloud in recitative the literary texts' (letter from Sidney Smith to Clyde

Curry Smith, 24 Feb 1964). This ability led to his comprehensive edition, *The Epic of Gilgamish* (1930).

At the British Museum, Thompson and King, together with Harry Reginald Holland Hall and Philip David Scott-Moncrieff, formed a brotherhood within what Thompson called 'the greatest department on earth' (letter to E. A. W. Budge, 13 Jan 1904). Devoted not merely to research, they developed a social comradeship, evinced in frequent letters to one another while individually away from London, illustrated by nicknames and detailed concerns relative to their achievements. On 15 November 1902 the museum trustees sent King to resume excavations at Nineveh, then Thompson, on 19 January 1904, to work jointly with him, before King, after more than a year in the field beset by tropical illnesses, returned home. Thompson arrived at Mosul on 29 February 1904, bringing a tachymeter for the comprehensive mapping of Nineveh, and necessary materials for their venture east into Persia to copy and collate anew the great trilingual rock-inscription of Darius at Behistan (May 1904), of which their joint edition (1907) remains definitive. Upon returning to Nineveh, Thompson continued excavating until their permit to do so expired and the site closed down (22 June 1904 to 11 February 1905). The lure of fieldwork, for which his rugged physical build well suited him, contributed to his dissatisfaction at routine museum duties, and he resigned on 5 December 1905.

Thompson's achievements were recognized by election to the Society of Biblical Archaeology (9 December 1903), to the Royal Geographical Society (26 June 1905), and as fellow of the Society of Antiquaries (1910). He seemed, however, to flounder from one effort to another: surveying for the Sudanese government (1906); assistant professor of Semitic languages at the University of Chicago (1907–9); excavations at Carchemish under David George Hogarth in the company of Charles Leonard Woolley and Thomas Edward Lawrence (1911).

Thompson described himself as being of independent means at the time of his marriage, on 19 September 1911, to Barbara Brodrick (b. 1887), daughter of Sir Richard Atkinson Robinson (1849–1928), chemist, of Whitby. During 1913–1914 he conducted excavations at the Coptic site of Wâdi Sargah in Egypt for the Byzantine Fund. With the outbreak of the First World War he became a commissioned officer in the special service of military intelligence and was posted to the Middle East 'which he reached in time to be present at the battle of Shu'aibah in April 1915' (Driver, 17). After four years of arduous duties with no more than a month's leave in India, he was demobilized early in 1919, having completed survey excavations in April 1918 at Muqayyar (Ur), Tell al-Laham, and Abu Shahrain (Eridu) under the auspices of the British Museum trustees, who were anxious about the conservation of antiquities affected by the war. Once settled into their Oxford home, the Thompsons had one daughter, Yolande, and two sons, Reginald Perronet and John De Morgan.

Thompson's post-war life was devoted to Assyriological studies, but he also wrote two novels under the pseudonym John Guisborough, displaying his propensity to use an Elizabethan vocabulary and an archaic style. He was elected to a stipendiary fellowship by Merton College in 1923 and granted a DLitt by Oxford in 1925. His publications focused upon Assyro-Babylonian natural sciences; he copied medical texts (1923) and produced significant lexical studies of herbals (1924), chemistry (1925), geology (1936), and botany (posthumously, 1949).

In 1927 Thompson successfully proposed to the British Museum trustees that excavations at Nineveh should be renewed. Grants from Merton College and the Percy Sladen Memorial Fund enabled excavations to be undertaken during four winters of 1927–32, with the successive assistance of Richard Wyatt Hutchinson, Robert William Hamilton, and Max Edgar Lucien Mallowan. Mallowan, who completed the deep dig into prehistoric levels, recalled Thompson as 'the most economical man on earth for he contrived to run the dig at Nineveh at a total cost of £1700' (Mallowan, 85). Thereafter Thompson received the Seatonian prize at Cambridge for the poem *Ignatius* [of Baghdad] (1933), was elected fellow of the British Academy (1934), was named editor of the journal *Iraq* (1935), and became Shillito reader in Assyriology, Oxford (1937).

At the beginning of the Second World War, Thompson joined the Home Guard as a major, but as a result of overexertion (and the effect of the loss of his eldest son on return from an RAF bombing raid in April 1941), he died suddenly of coronary thrombosis while coming off duty with the river patrol at Sowberry Court, Moulsford, Wallingford, Berkshire, on 23 May 1941. He was survived by his wife.

CLYDE CURRY SMITH

Sources G. R. Driver, 'Reginald Campbell Thompson, 1876–1941', *PBA*, 30 (1944), 1–39 · *DNB* · T. G. Klein, 'The letters of Reginald Campbell Thompson, from the 1904–05 excavation of Nineveh', MA diss., University of Wisconsin, River Falls, 1992 [inc. comprehensive bibliography] · R. C. Thompson, *A pilgrim's scrip* (1915) · E. A. W. Budge, *The rise and progress of Assyriology* (1925) · R. C. Thompson and R. W. Hutchinson, *A century of exploration at Nineveh* (1929) · *WWW*, 1961–70 · J. E. Mack, *The prince of our disorder: the life of T. E. Lawrence* (1976) · A. Christie, *An autobiography* (1977), 438–51 · M. Mallowan, *Mallowan's memoirs* (1977), 68–85 · private information (2004) · *The Times* (26 May 1941) · *New York Times* (27 May 1941) · *Luzac's Oriental List* (April–June 1941) · *Nature* (28 June 1941), 799 · E. Weidner, *Archiv für Orientforschung* (1918–44), 14, 234–6 · Venn, *Alum. Cant.* · m. cert. · d. cert. · *CGPLA Eng. & Wales* (1941)

Archives University of Chicago, Oriental Institute, Reginald Campbell Thompson collection of cuneiform tablets | BM, department of Western Asiatic antiquities, correspondence files · BM, Trustees' archives, Director's office

Likenesses W. Stoneman, photograph, 1934, NPG · photograph, repro. in Budge, *Rise and progress*, facing p. 179 · photograph, repro. in Driver, 'Reginald Campbell Thompson', facing p. 1

Wealth at death £17,685 9s. 10d.: probate, 1941, *CGPLA Eng. & Wales*

Thompson, Richard Anthony (1819–1908). *See under* Thompson, John (1785–1866).

Thompson, Robert Michael [Bobby] (1911–1988), comedian, was born on 18 November 1911 at 4 The Staiths, Penshaw, near Sunderland, co. Durham, the youngest child of John Thompson, colliery overman, and his wife, Mary

Cain. He had three brothers and three sisters. Having lost both parents before reaching the age of eight, Bobby was brought up by married sisters and moved through a number of schools in the Fatfield and Penshaw area of the county. From the age of fourteen he worked at North Biddick colliery, remaining there until the pit closed in 1931. For ten years he moved between unemployment and casual labouring jobs while entertaining in his spare time as a singer and harmonica player. He was called up for war service in February 1941 and acted as company runner in the Border regiment based at Carlisle, Cumberland. He served until July 1944, returning to the north-east after two years of civilian life in Cumberland.

After a further five years in and out of work Thompson was persuaded to audition for a new regional radio series entitled *Wot Cheor, Geordie*. Success encouraged him to give up a post he had just acquired at the Royal Ordnance Factory, Birtley, to become a professional entertainer. The radio series reached a wide audience in the north-east and brought him work in theatres throughout the region. By Christmas 1958 he was top of the bill in the prestigious Theatre Royal pantomime in Newcastle upon Tyne; this was followed shortly by a television series, *The Bobby Thompson Show*, produced by the newly formed Tyne-Tees company. The series was not a long-term success, perhaps because his material was not extensive enough, or because his act was more suited to the intimacy of a working-men's club or small theatre. As a result, his career began to founder. It was resurrected in the mid-1960s under new management and extensive bookings in working-men's clubs led to a long-playing record of his act in 1978. The record sold out in the region and occasioned his appearance on *Wogan*, a major national television chat show.

Thompson was as popular in the working-men's clubs as he had been in the theatres. This was his secret. Described as a born comedian by his radio producer, Richard Kelly, he performed in a style rooted deep in nineteenth-century north-eastern humour. He worked at times in Yorkshire, but mostly in the area bounded by the Tweed and the Tees, and his ultimate success was limited to his native region. National exposure tended to leave audiences mildly amused, yet baffled by the little man's humour and the impenetrability of his accent. His two acts as the Little Waster and Soldier Bobby—'You didn't laugh at me when I was fighting for yer!'—relied heavily on experiences shared with his audiences: outside toilets, home-made rugs, clothes bought through catalogues, and the intricacies of betting on the horses—these were the very stuff of his act. Small and slight, he brought laughter the minute he appeared on stage as the Little Waster, 'a one-off emaciated figure crowned by a flat cap ... the little man fighting back', as comedian Ken Dodd described him (Nicolson, 8).

Despite a simple act, Bobby Thompson's was a complex character. A lifelong Roman Catholic, he gave much support to charity. He was also famed, in later life in particular, for his unreliability and tendency to double booking. He gambled—in early life on the dogs and later in casinos. Financial problems took him to court on more than one occasion and led to a bankruptcy inquiry in 1986. He was a heavy smoker and drinker. Off-stage he was smart, dapper, and besuited and enjoyed the services of a personal chauffeur at the height of his career. He was married three times: first on 11 April 1936 to Anna Marjoram; they had one daughter and the marriage was dissolved in 1945. In the same year, on 4 October, he married Phyllis Coates (1910–1967); they had two sons. On 31 December 1982 he married Eleanor Cicely (Cissie) Palmer (d. 1995). Between the second and third marriage he was very close to his housekeeper, Lottie Tate. His biography hints at an illegitimate child born elsewhere in the 1950s (Nicolson, 60). In later life he lived at Whitley Bay on the Northumberland coast and continued to perform in the clubs into the 1980s. He died of myocardial infarction and emphysema at Preston Hospital, North Shields, on 16 April 1988. A requiem mass in Cullercoats was followed by cremation at the Whitley Bay crematorium on 20 April 1988. Earlier that year he had featured in a Channel Four television documentary, and he was considered worthy of a *Times* obituary, therein described as a cult figure and folk hero who lost two fortunes.

KEITH GREGSON

Sources D. Nicolson, *Bobby Thompson: a private audience* (1994) · B. Shelley, *The 'Little Waster': the Bobby Thompson biography* (1979) · *Bobby Thompson—the Little Waster*, 1978, Rubber Records, RUB 032 [sleeve note] · K. Gregson, *Corvan: a Victorian entertainer and his songs* (1983) · *The Times* (20 April 1988) · b. cert.
Archives FILM BBC WAC · BFI NFTVA, 'Bobby Thompson—the little waster', Channel 4, 12 Dec 1982 · BFI NFTVA, performance footage · Tyne-Tees Television archives, Newcastle upon Tyne | SOUND BBC WAC · BL NSA, performance recordings
Likenesses cartoon (*The Little Waster*), repro. in *Sunday Sun* (1998) · photograph, repro. in Nicolson, *Bobby Thompson*, cover · photograph, repro. in Shelley, 'Little Waster', cover · photograph, repro. in *Bobby Thompson—the Little Waster*, Rubber Records · photograph, repro. in *The Times*
Wealth at death 'he lost a second fortune': *The Times* (20 April 1988)

Thompson, Samuel (1766–1837), a founder of the Freethinking Christians, born in Aldgate, London, on 7 June 1766, was the son of Samuel King Thompson, victualler, of the Bell, Church Row, Houndsditch, and his wife, Catherine. He was educated at Christ's Hospital (1774–80), after which he was apprenticed to a watchmaker in Whitechapel. Before he was twenty he married, on 27 May 1786, Ann Kilbinton, and set up in business for himself. Their two children died in infancy. He was fond of society and a good singer, and his business did not prosper. He left the watch trade for a wine and spirit business in East Smithfield. His wife's death in 1789 turned him to religion; on 25 December 1793 he married Mary Fletcher (1777–1850), took seriously to business, became eminent as a distiller and dealer in spirits, and regulated his trade by strict measures against drunkenness and loose language. Up to this point he was an Anglican; a casual hearing of Elhanan Winchester, the universalist, led him to become a member of his congregation in Parliament Court, Bishopsgate, in 1794. He was made deacon on 16 August 1795, and 'set apart' with three others for 'public service' on 8 January 1796. He was afternoon preacher, and distinguished himself by arguing against deists at open-air meetings, but soon quarrelled with William Vidler, Winchester's successor, on a point of pastoral authority. With twenty-one others he seceded on 19 November 1798, the schism being primarily a protest against a one-man ministry and the payment of preachers.

On Christmas day 1798 the seceders opened a meeting-room at 38 Old Change, London, and at once announced their rejection of the doctrine of the Trinity, retaining, however, for some time, the doctrine of Christ's pre-existence. They also rejected baptism and the eucharist, as well as public singing and prayer. Their rules of membership and exclusion were strict, and strictly enforced. They took the name of the Church of God, and Thompson was elected an elder in March 1799. In March 1804 large audiences were attracted to their meetings by their public replies to Paine's *Age of Reason*. They were popularly known as the Freethinking Christians.

Thompson left business in April 1806, retiring with about £300 a year to Kingsthorpe, Northamptonshire, for the education of his four sons and eight daughters. Contention in his church brought him back to London; he resumed the spirit business on Holborn Hill at midsummer 1807. In December his followers advertised that they were going to 'inquire' into the existence of 'a being called the Devil'. Beilby Porteus, bishop of London, called the attention of the authorities to these proceedings in an unlicensed conventicle. Thompson and four others were cited (5 February 1808) by the city marshal. They applied for a licence as protestant dissenters, and obtained it with some difficulty. In 1810 they built a meeting-house, on a short lease, in Jewin Crescent, London, soon started a magazine, and made attacks on the Unitarian leaders Thomas Belsham and Robert Aspland. In December 1813 Thompson, regarding marriage as purely a civil act and the Anglican marriage service as 'idolatrous', suggested that, on occasions of marriage, a protest should be delivered to the officiating clergyman and advertised in the newspapers. This policy was carried out (10 June 1814) on the marriage of Thompson's eldest daughter, Mary Ann, herself active among the Freethinking Christians, to William Coates; it was persistently continued, occasionally causing scandalous scenes, as at the marriage of a younger daughter, Julietta, to John Dobell in 1823, until the grievance was remedied by the marriage act of 1836.

In 1821 there was a small secession, led by William Stevens, of members dissatisfied with Thompson's personal rule and dictatorial manner, meeting in Moorfields and claiming to be the true 'church of God'. In 1831 Thompson's friends built a meeting-house on freehold property in St John's Square, Clerkenwell. William Coates was their leader; Thompson, who was now living at Plaistow, Essex, being reduced to inactivity by ill health. He finally retired from business in 1831 (his son-in-law had long been the managing partner), and, at his own request, was released from 'public service' by his church. He was still, however, involved in its disputes. In 1834, having made up his old quarrel with Robert Aspland, he published a series of papers in Aspland's magazine, the *Christian Reformer*, on the 'unity and exclusiveness of the church of God'. This was done 'without the previous consent of the church, as required by their laws'. He asked and obtained indemnity; but the dispute continued, and Thompson, though claiming to be 'the founder of the church, God's agent', was served with notice of expulsion. He was, in fact, expelled in December, but not before he had rallied his immediate following and been elected elder of another, and the only 'real', 'church of God'. The revolt against Thompson had no continuance. The original society became extinct in 1851, having survived its several provincial branches.

Thompson died at Reigate, Surrey, on 20 November 1837, and was buried in the graveyard of the General Baptist chapel at Ditchling, Sussex. An epitaph, his own composition, gives the articles of his creed, and adds 'The good loved him, and the base hated, because they feared'. The most significant of his publications was *Evidences of Revealed Religion* (1812), which reached its fourth edition in 1842.　ALEXANDER GORDON, *rev.* K. D. REYNOLDS

Sources J. D. [J. Dobell], 'Memoir', *Christian Reformer, or, Unitarian Magazine and Review*, 5 (1838), 67ff. · S. Thompson, *Evidences of revealed religion*, 4th edn (1842) · *Freethinking Christians' Quarterly Register*, 1 (1823), 267–318 · I. McCalman, *Radical underworld: prophets, revolutionaries, and pornographers in London, 1795–1840* (1988) · *Life and letters of Sydney Dobell*, ed. E. Jolly, 1 (1878), 64ff. · private information (1898) · tombstone, General Baptist cemetery, Ditchling, Sussex (1898)

Thompson, Silvanus Phillips (1851–1916), physicist and university professor, was born at York on 19 June 1851, the second of seven surviving children of Silvanus Thompson, master at Bootham School, York, and his wife, Bridget Tatham of Settle. From 1858 he underwent a Quaker schooling at Bootham, then famed for its excellent scientific resources. He early showed an aptitude for languages and drawing, and a keen interest in electricity and botany. His study of 'luminous meteors' undertaken in the school's astronomical observatory was published in the British Association's report for 1867. At the age of sixteen Thompson enrolled at the Flounders Institute, Pontefract, to prepare for a career as a Quaker teacher, reading concurrently for the University of London BA which he received in autumn 1869, soon after recovering from severe typhoid fever.

In 1870 Thompson became a junior master at Bootham School, being known as Phillips to avoid confusion with his father, then senior master. Energetically studying chemistry and physics in his spare time, he was appointed science master in 1873—despite the Friends' unease at his indulgence in piano playing and attendance at evensong in York Minster. Finding school teaching rather limiting he left Bootham for London in June 1875 to study at the Science Schools, South Kensington, with Frederick Guthrie and Edward Frankland, passing the University of London BSc with first-class honours in October 1875. Elected a fellow of the Royal Astronomical Society and a member of the Physical Society of London, he continued researches with Guthrie on a novel phenomenon of electric spark induction—a decade prior to Hertz's more famous researches. Thompson frequently attended the Royal Institution lectures of Tyndall and J. H. Gladstone, also attending bible classes at Gladstone's home. Thompson's social and religious life, however, was rooted in the Friends' Westminster meeting, and it was in a literary and artistic sub-circle of this group that he met Jane Smeal Henderson, whom he later married.

In 1876 Thompson was appointed as a lecturer in physics at the newly created University College in Bristol, and quickly established himself as a most effective teacher. In addition to laboratory studies on binaural audition, his developing historical interest in William Gilbert's magnetic researches emerged in his college address 'The methods of physical science' for the new session of 1877. Remarkably he was also able simultaneously to prepare for the University of London DSc examination in spring 1878. His doctorate was followed by a professorship at Bristol. Upholding the Quaker commitment to improving conditions for working people and stimulated by Professor Gladstone's zeal for educational reform, Thompson's wide-ranging interests soon encompassed technical education. The fruits of his study of industrial training on the continent formed his influential lecture to the Society of Arts on 'Apprenticeship, scientific and unscientific' in December 1879.

Thompson's *Elementary Lessons in Electricity and Magnetism* (1881), composed as a resource for his scientific work at Bristol, brought him wide scientific fame. On 30 March that year, Thompson married Jane Henderson at the old Friends' meeting-house at Glasgow. She was to share fully in his social and scientific life. As an authority on the rising electrical lighting industry Thompson served in the British delegation sent to Paris in 1881 to discuss new electrical nomenclature, and lectured at the Universal Exhibition on Electricity in 1882 where he condemned bogus medical applications of electricity. Elected a member of the Society of Telegraph Engineers in the same year, he also participated in the drafting of the Electrical Lighting Act.

Having employed the telephone in his acoustical researches since 1879 Thompson also investigated its history; his biography of Phillip Ries (1883) argued that Ries had pre-empted Alexander Graham Bell by well over a decade. Thompson took out patents of his own as the basis of an alternative to the Bell systems, but the telephone company he started in 1884 soon collapsed in bankruptcy when the United Telephone Company successfully sued for infringement of its own patents. His *Dynamo Electric Machinery* (1884) became a classic of electrical engineering for decades thereafter. With the financial situation at the Bristol college getting ever weaker Thompson applied for the position as principal and professor of electrical engineering at the City and Guilds Finsbury Technical College. Well known as an adviser to the City and Guilds Institute he was duly appointed and the Thompson family moved to London in March 1885. He remained at Finsbury until his death, winning the respect of thousands of students for his dedicated teaching and his well-disciplined administration, while finding time for his own researches. In his optical studies he cultivated a Maxwellian analysis of polarization phenomena and the properties of lenses,

presenting an important paper to the Royal Society in 1891 on the focometry of lenses and lens combinations; in consequence, he was consulted on the formulation of regulations for the licensing of opticians in 1898. In magnetism he concentrated on hysteresis and induced magnetization; Thompson was thus known as Brother Magnetizer when elected to the Sette of Odd Volumes, an idiosyncratic book and dining club, in 1890. Formal recognition brought his election as a fellow of the Royal Society in the following year. While he contributed much to the understanding of X-rays in the late 1890s, probably his most enduringly important research concerned what later became known as photoelasticity. Developed collaboratively in 1909 with E. G. Coker, professor of mechanical engineering at Finsbury, this technique harnessed the properties of polarized light to examine stress patterns in engineering structures.

From 1889 he was often invited to speak in public. His oratorical skills, polymathic expertise, and his fluency in French, German, and Italian served him well not only in the many important speeches he made in connection with Finsbury College and the Guilds, but also as president successively of the Roentgen Society (1897), the Institution of Electrical Engineers (1899), the Physical Society of London (1901–2), the Optical Society (1905), section G of the British Association (1907), and the Illumination Engineering Society (1909). Although a high point in his career, Thompson's presidency of the Institution of Electrical Engineers saw him much vexed by the outbreak of the Second South African War, during which his strict Quaker principles put him at odds with the bellicose institution membership. His outspoken criticisms of British conduct in the Second South African War probably led, despite his standing in the college, to his being passed over for the college's appointment of a new principal officer in 1901.

Thompson's mature years saw him deeply engaged in historical writing. His sophisticated and unpartisan *Life of Faraday* (1898) was illustrated by Thompson himself; twelve years later he published an outstanding two-volume *Life of Kelvin*. In the same year he published what became by far his most famous work, *Calculus Made Easy*. Signed only as 'FRS' in Thompson's lifetime, it bore the characteristically mischievous epigraph 'What one fool can do, another can'. Overtly critical of teaching methods adopted by mathematicians, to whom the book gave enduring irritation, this little masterpiece nevertheless brought invaluable aid to more than three generations of science and engineering students in the twentieth century.

Always an active participant in Friends' meetings, Thompson was an elder at the Westminster meeting from 1892; in 1903 he attained the distinction of being made a minister of the Society of Friends. The complex tensions between his personal and professional life were cogently analysed and resolved in his renowned address to a major conference in Manchester in 1895: 'Can a scientific man be a sincere Friend?'. This address was crucial in achieving the subsequent broad acceptance of modern science by the British Quaker community. The conflagration that broke out in 1914 made his last years his unhappiest. When the age of military conscription was lowered to eighteen he fought hard to win exemptions for some talented Finsbury students whose training as chemists or engineers was incomplete. His failure to achieve this for one of his assistants on 10 June 1916 left him exhausted and dispirited: he suffered a cerebral haemorrhage early the following morning, and died peacefully at his home, Morland, Chislett Road, Hampstead, on 12 June. He was cremated at Golders Green and his ashes were interred at the old Friends' meeting-house at Jordans, Buckinghamshire. A memorial service held on 16 June at the Friends' meeting-house in St Martin's Lane was attended by many eminent scientists and engineers as well as by former students. He was survived by his wife.

Thompson was a devoted husband and father. Strongly committed to women's emancipation he supported one of his four daughters, Helen, in studying physics at the Cavendish Laboratory, Cambridge. He sang as a competent baritone; he sketched and painted with very considerable talent. He was at the heart of the science, engineering, and educational concerns of his day, and was widely admired for his speeches, textbooks, and leadership, as well as for his many innovative laboratory researches.

ARTHUR SMITHELLS, rev. GRAEME J. N. GOODAY

Sources J. S. Thompson and H. G. Thompson, *Silvanus Phillips Thompson: his life and letters* (1920) · J. Greig, *Silvanus Thompson: teacher* (1979) · A. C. Lynch, 'Silvanus Thompson: teacher, researcher, historian', *IEE Proceedings*, A136 (1989), 306–12 · A. A. Campbell Swinton, 'Prof. Silvanus P. Thompson', *Nature*, 97 (1916), 343–4 · J. P. [J. Perry], *PRS*, 94A (1917–18), xvi–xix · election certificate, RS · d. cert. · *Annual Monitor* (1917), 144–58
Archives Bootham School, York · ICL, corresp. and papers · Inst. EE, MS collection and corresp.; corresp. and papers incl. working notes; notes relating to lectures · LUL, corresp. · RS Friends, Lond., corresp. · U. Sussex, corresp. | CUL, corresp. with Lord Kelvin · CUL, letters to Sir George Stokes and J. Larmor · GL, City and Guilds Institute collection · Inst. EE, letters to Oliver Heaviside · RAS, letters to Royal Astronomical Society · UCL, corresp. with Sir Oliver Lodge
Likenesses photograph, 1876, repro. in Thompson and Thompson, *Silvanus Phillips Thompson*, facing p. 34 · J. Hassall, cartoon, 1890–99 (*Brother Magnetizer*), repro. in Thompson and Thompson, *Silvanus Phillips Thompson*, facing p. 252 · portrait, c.1890–1899 (after photograph by Elliott & Fry), repro. in Perry, *PRS* · portrait, c.1890–1899 (after photograph by Elliott & Fry), repro. in Thompson and Thompson, *Silvanus Phillips Thompson*, frontispiece · H. von Herkomer, oils, c.1892, ICL · J. Walker West, oils, 1899, Inst. EE · photograph, 1910, repro. in Thompson and Thompson, *Silvanus Phillips Thompson*, facing p. 338 · group photograph, 1912, RS · Elliott & Fry, photograph, ICL
Wealth at death £8444 5s. 7d.: probate, 31 July 1916, CGPLA Eng. & Wales

Thompson, Theophilus (1807–1860), physician, son of Nathaniel Thompson, was born in Islington, London, on 20 September 1807. His early medical education took place at St Bartholomew's Hospital, London, and at Edinburgh University, where he took his MD in 1830, his inaugural dissertation being 'De effectibus aliquando perniciosis missionis sanguinis'. He also studied in Dublin and then in Paris with Louis, G. Andral, and G. Dupuytren, and he attended the lectures of Geoffroy Saint-Hilaire at the Jardin des Plantes.

Soon after settling down to practise in London, Thompson was appointed physician to the Northern Dispensary, a position he held for fourteen years. He was also one of the lecturers at the Grosvenor Place school of medicine. In 1847 he was elected physician to the Hospital for Consumption, then situated in Marlborough Street; it was here that he began to take an interest in consumption. He gave several lectures on the disease, which were later published in *The Lancet*. He is credited with being the person who introduced cod-liver oil into England, and was the first to give bismuth to arrest the diarrhoea of phthisis, and to treat night sweats with oxide of zinc.

Thompson was elected a fellow of the Royal Society in 1846, and he published two papers in the society's *Proceedings* on the changes produced in the blood by the administration of cod-liver oil and coconut oil. He filled the presidential chairs of the Medical and Harveian societies, and contributed five papers to the *Transactions* of the Royal Medical and Chirurgical Society. He married Elizabeth Anna Maria, the second daughter of Nathaniel Watkin of Stroud, Gloucestershire. They had at least two sons, one of whom, Edmund Symes-*Thompson (1837–1906) was also a physician.

Thompson was the author of: *On the Improvement of Medicine* (1838), an oration; *History of the Epidemics of Influenza in Great Britain from 1510 to 1837* (Sydenham Society, 1852); *Clinical Lectures on Pulmonary Consumption* (1854); and *Lettsomian Lectures on Pulmonary Consumption*. He also contributed the articles 'Chorea', 'Hysteria', 'Neuralgia', and 'Influenza' to Alexander Tweedie's *Library of Medicine* (1840–42).

Thompson died on 11 August 1860 at Vale Lodge, Sutton, Surrey. He was survived by his wife.

T. B. BROWNING, rev. KAYE BAGSHAW

Sources Munk, *Roll* · *The Lancet* (15 Sept 1860), 276 · *London and Provincial Medical Directory* (1861), 1018 · private information (1898) · CGPLA Eng. & Wales (1860)
Likenesses Maull & Polyblank, photograph, 1855, NPG · A. Essex, watercolour · W. Essex, portrait
Wealth at death under £4000: probate, 22 Sept 1860, CGPLA Eng. & Wales

Thompson, Thomas (1708/9–1773), missionary and apologist for the African slave trade, was born at Gilling, Yorkshire, the son of William Thompson, possibly the same William Thompson who was curate and schoolmaster at Kirkby Stephen, Westmorland, from 1697. He was educated at Richmond School and matriculated at Christ's College, Cambridge, on 19 February 1728, aged nineteen. He became a scholar of the college that year, proceeded BA in 1732 and MA in 1735, and was elected a fellow in 1738. Having been appointed to a college curacy at Fen Drayton near Cambridge on 5 May 1744, he resigned after a few months to serve as a missionary for the Society for the Propagation of the Gospel (SPG) and in 1745 was given charge of the churches in Monmouth county, New Jersey. He found them unsettled, many of the members lapsed or become dissenters, and over the next five years worked to revive the scattered congregations, baptizing, and getting derelict churches rebuilt. Sometimes, with the consent of their owners, he baptized household slaves, and admitted them to communion. He also occasionally encountered the indigenous people in their 'native Heathenism' (Thompson, *An Account*, 19).

Feeling that he had fulfilled his mission in America, he asked the SPG to send him as a missionary to west Africa, 'that I might go to make a Trial with the Natives, and see what Hopes there would be of introducing among them the Christian Religion' (Thompson, *An Account*, 23). With the society's approval, granted on 15 February 1751, he crossed the Atlantic to Cape Coast Castle on the Gold Coast, the headquarters of the Royal African Company, as the first Church of England missionary to Africa.

Thompson also officiated as the company's chaplain, lived in the fort, and preached to the surrounding towns-people. But though he found them friendly, and at first attentive to his message, which had to be conveyed through uninstructed interpreters, they soon lost inter-est. None were ever converted. So instead he chose three boys to be sent to England for education, one of whom, Philip Quaque, was eventually to return as a missionary. In 1756 he resigned on health grounds and returned to parish work. He became vicar of Reculver in Kent in 1757, of Darenth in 1758, of Hoo St Werburgh in 1759, and moved to the living of Eleham, also in Kent, in 1761.

Thompson published in 1758 *An Account of Two Missionary Voyages*, a lively narrative of his experiences. Then, when the abolition campaign began, he seems to have been asked by his former employers to write in their defence. As he had been for five years the employee of a company which was principally concerned with trading in slaves, and had associated in an always perfectly amicable way with their African suppliers and customers, it need be no surprise that he was ready to publish, in 1772, a thirty-one page pamphlet, *The African trade for negro slaves shown to be consistent with principles of humanity and with the laws of revealed religion*. He drew on the Bible to justify slavery, and also on African practice, remarking that: 'The customs of the blacks are many of them good rules of policy, such as would not disgrace a more regular constitution' (Thomp-son, *The African Trade*, 25). His pamphlet elicited a few pages of angry retort from Granville Sharp, beginning: 'For shame, Mr Thompson!' (Sharp, 29), incorporated in his *The Just Limitation of Slavery* (1776).

Thompson, who had been elected a member of the SPG in 1770, died at Eleham, Kent, on 5 June 1773.

CHRISTOPHER FYFE

Sources T. Thompson, *An account of two missionary voyages* (1758); facs. edn (1937) [facs. repr., 1937] · T. Thompson, *The African trade for negro slaves shown to be consistent with the principles of humanity and with the laws of revealed religion* (1772) · *DNB* · G. Sharp, *The just limitation of slavery* (1776) · Venn, *Alum. Cant.*

Thompson, Sir Thomas Boulden, first baronet (1766–1828), naval officer, was born at Barham, Kent on 28 Febru-ary 1766. His parentage is uncertain. He was the heir of Captain Edward Thompson RN (*d.* 17 Jan 1786) of Epsom, his patron in his early naval career. According to one

account Edward Thompson was his father, and his mother was Sarah, *née* Boulden, of Kent; by another he was the son of an impecunious man named Boulden and his wife, Sarah, daughter of Richard Thompson and sister of Edward Thompson. Known in his youth as Boulden, in Edward Thompson's will he was referred to as Boulden alias Thompson. He assumed the name Thompson pre-sumably as a compliment to his uncle and patron, or because Edward Thompson was his father. Borne on the books of different ships, he first went to sea in 1778 in the *Hyaena* with Captain Edward Thompson, who was princi-pally responsible for his early education. He was pro-moted to lieutenant on 14 January 1782 and in 1783 appointed to the *Grampus*, in which Edward Thompson was commodore, on the west coast of Africa. On Edward Thompson's death in January 1786 he was promoted to command the sloop *Nautilus*, a promotion confirmed on 27 March 1786. He brought the *Nautilus* home in 1787 when he went on half-pay and, though advanced to post rank on 22 November 1790, had no employment until autumn 1796. He was then appointed to the 50-gun ship *Leander*, in which during spring 1797 he joined Lord St Vincent off Cadiz, to be shortly afterwards detached with the squad-ron under Nelson, against Tenerife, where he was wounded in the attack on Santa Cruz. The following sum-mer, he was again detached with the squadron sent into the Mediterranean to reinforce Nelson, and eventually to fight the battle of the Nile on 1–2 August 1798. Although not a ship of the line, by taking up a position between two of the French ships, the *Leander* was able to rake these French ships and the ships beyond them with terrible effect, while remaining herself in comparative safety. Thompson was afterwards ordered by Nelson to carry home Captain Edward Berry with his dispatches; but encountering the French 74-gun ship *Généreux*, near the west end of Crete on 18 August the *Leander*, after a defence of six-and-a-half hours, was captured and taken to Corfu. Both Thompson and Berry were severely wounded and were allowed to return overland to England. Thompson was tried by court martial for the loss of his ship but acquitted and praised for the length and determination of *Leander's* resistance to so superior a force. He was knighted in 1799 and awarded a pension of £200 per annum.

On 25 February 1799 Thompson married Anne (*d.* 9 Sept 1846), eldest daughter of Robert Raikes of Gloucester; they had three sons and three daughters. In spring 1799 he was appointed to the 74-gun ship *Bellona*, one of the fleet off Brest under Lord Bridport. In March 1801 the *Bellona* was one of the ships attached to the fleet for the Baltic under Sir Hyde Parker, and was selected for the attack on the Danish fleet and the defences of Copenhagen, but in entering the channel on the morning of 2 April she stuck fast on the edge of the shoal within long range of the Dan-ish guns. She had eleven killed and sixty-three wounded, among whom was Thompson, who lost a leg. His pension was raised to £500 (£700 from 27 November 1815), and he was appointed to the command of the yacht *Mary*. On 20 June 1806 he was appointed comptroller of the navy, an office which he held until 24 February 1816, when he was appointed treasurer of Greenwich Hospital and director of the Chatham Chest. He was created a baronet on 11 November 1806, became a rear-admiral on 25 October 1809, vice-admiral on 4 June 1814, KCB on 2 January 1815, and GCB on 14 September 1822. From May 1807 to June 1816 he was a tory MP for the freeman-franchise borough of Rochester, Kent, on the Admiralty interest. He supported the government, voted against criminal-law and parliamentary reform, and Roman Catholic relief, and supported Christian missions to India. He died at his residence, Hartsbourne Manor Place, Hertfordshire, on 3 March 1828. He was succeeded by his son Thomas Raikes Trigge Thompson (1804–1865).

J. K. LAUGHTON, rev. ROGER MORRISS

Sources GM, 1st ser., 98/1 (1828), 563 · Navy List · J. Marshall, Royal naval biography, 4 vols. (1823–35) [with 4 suppls.] · Burke, Peerage (1999) · J. Ralfe, The naval biography of Great Britain, 4 vols. (1828) · HoP, Commons, 1790–1820
Archives BL, papers, Add. MS 46119
Likenesses F. Engleheart, stipple, pubd 1799 (after G. Engleheart), BM · W. Bromley, J. Landseer, and Leney, group portrait, line engraving, pubd 1803 (after Victors of the Nile by R. Smirke), BM, NPG · G. Engleheart, miniature, exh. RA before 1835

Thompson, Thomas Perronet (1783–1869), army officer and politician, was born on 15 March 1783 at 17 Lowgate, Hull, eldest of the four children of Thomas Thompson (1754–1828) and his wife, Philothea Perronet Thompson, née Briggs (1753–1823). His father was a banker and merchant, MP for Midhurst 1807–18, and a prominent Wesleyan preacher and friend of William Wilberforce. His mother was the granddaughter of Vincent Perronet, vicar of Shoreham and associate of John Wesley. Thompson was educated at Hull grammar school, then under the headmastership of Joseph Milner, the church historian. In 1798 he went up to Queens' College, Cambridge, and began a long friendship with its president, Isaac Milner, brother of Joseph and later dean of Carlisle. Thompson gained the BA degree as seventh wrangler in 1802, and was elected to a fellowship of his college in 1804. In 1803 he joined the navy as midshipman on HMS Isis, flagship of Vice-Admiral (later Lord) Gambier, but transferred to the army three years later. He was commissioned as second lieutenant in 1806, lieutenant in 1808, captain in 1814, major in 1825, and lieutenant-colonel (unattached) in 1829, at which time he retired from military service. His subsequent promotions were made by brevet: to colonel (1846), major-general (1854), lieutenant-general (1860), and general (1868). Thompson was involved in several important battles. He was captured by the Spaniards after General John Whitelock's ill-fated expedition against Buenos Aires in July 1807. In 1813–14 he saw action against the French at Nivelles, Nive, Orthez, and Toulouse, and was later awarded the Peninsula medal with four clasps. By this time he was a husband and father. In 1811 he had married Anne Elizabeth Barker (1793–1871) of York. They had three sons and three daughters.

In 1808, after returning from captivity in South America, Thompson became the first crown-appointed governor of Sierra Leone. Wilberforce and the Saints had

Thomas Perronet Thompson (1783–1869), by Herbert Watkins, 1856

established the colony in 1787 as a place where free black people would cultivate the land, carry on profitable trade, and demonstrate to the world that they were not peculiarly suited to slavery, despite the claims of slave traders. But the Sierra Leone Company had never provided effective administration. There were civil disorders and food shortages, and relations with surrounding native peoples were far from cordial. Firmly opposed to slavery, and enjoying Wilberforce's patronage, Thompson was keenly interested in the fate of the colony and, when the Saints transferred Sierra Leone to the crown, the British government accepted their suggestion that he would be a suitable governor. When he discovered undisguised slavery in Sierra Leone, however, and realized that the Saints and the British government had been misled about the colony's social and economic conditions, Thompson introduced an extensive range of reforms and made serious allegations against the colony's former administrators. Embarrassed by his revelations, the Saints advised the government to recall him and he returned to Britain in 1810. Thompson was convinced that the Saints sacrificed him in order to save face. They feared that Thompson's claims about Sierra Leone would threaten their reputations and achievements, particularly the 1807 abolition act. Thompson was deprived of opportunities publicly to vindicate his policies in Africa, and deeply disappointed by removal from the governorship. He also blamed the British government for failing to respond to his call for an inquiry.

In 1815 Thompson went to Bombay as interpreter and

political adviser attached to the 17th light dragoons. After several military engagements in India, where he served under Francis Rawdon Hastings and Sir John Malcolm, he inserted an anti-slave-trade clause in a treaty concluded between the British crown and peoples of the Persian Gulf. But this success was followed by a serious disappointment for Thompson. In November 1820 he led an ill-conceived expedition against Arab pirates, which led to a court martial. Though acquitted, he was also reprimanded for undertaking an important mission with inadequate forces. Thompson blamed his Sepoy troops for failing to stand and face an enemy charge. The Bombay authorities could not risk trouble with their Sepoys, however, and forced Thompson to take the blame. He often referred to this disappointment, and to the Sierra Leone controversy, in later years. These were significant opinion-shaping experiences.

Thompson engaged in political and literary activities after returning from the east in 1822. With much of Europe in turmoil, he joined London committees for the support of political refugees and interested himself in the cause of Greek and Spanish liberals. He became a close friend of John Bowring, who introduced Thompson to Jeremy Bentham and his circle of philosophical radicals. Thompson later accepted an invitation to translate part of Bentham's *Constitutional Code* into Arabic. Developing an ever keener interest in political economy, Thompson contributed an article 'On the instruments of exchange' to the first issue of the *Westminster Review* (January 1824). In 1826 he published his *True Theory of Rent*. This supported Adam Smith's idea that rent levels were determined by demand for agricultural products, and rejected the principle advanced by David Ricardo and James Mill that rent was dependent on production costs. Thompson's arguments were favourably received by Jean-Baptiste Say, and also influenced later commentators such as J. M. Keynes and J. A. Schumpeter. Thompson believed that the Ricardian idea of rent was a weak link in the case against the corn laws, and followed the *True Theory of Rent* with his most famous pamphlet, the *Catechism on the Corn Laws* (1827). This persuasive argument for repeal proved extremely influential, went into eighteen editions by 1834, and prompted Thompson's election as fellow of the Royal Society in 1828. As well as his political and economic writing in subsequent years, he published works on enharmonic principles, just intonation, geometry, and the theory of parallels. His enharmonic organ was displayed at the Great Exhibition in 1851, and one of his mathematical pamphlets was extremely popular in France after its translation by Professor M. van Tenac of the royal establishment at Rochefort. During the 1830s Thompson joined the Foreign Learned Society and the Société Française de la Statistique Universelle, and was a corresponding member of several other such bodies.

But it was mainly as a politician that Thompson now made his mark. The death of his father in 1828 brought him a modest fortune, and he began to devote himself to radical causes. The financial difficulties of the *Westminster Review* prompted him to become its part owner and co-editor from 1829 until he sold up to Sir William Molesworth in 1836. He was a prolific contributor to the review, and his articles on parliamentary reform, Catholic emancipation, and free trade were particularly influential (40,000 copies of the piece on Catholic emancipation were issued as *The Catholic State Waggon* in 1829). He also wrote the articles of 1829–30 which defended utilitarianism against the assault published by T. B. Macaulay in the *Edinburgh Review*. An unsuccessful parliamentary candidate at Preston in January 1835, Thompson narrowly won in Hull the following June, but the tories petitioned against his return. Though this petition was dismissed after an inquiry, Thompson lost £4000 in costs, which he considered an outrage. He did not contest Hull at the 1837 general election, but stood instead at Maidstone, where he came bottom of the poll. He was then an unsuccessful candidate in Marylebone (1838), Manchester (1839), Hull, and Cheltenham (both 1841), and Sunderland (1845), before his victory in Bradford at the 1847 general election. He lost this seat in 1852, but served again as MP for Bradford from 1857 to 1859. In the Commons, Thompson was a consistent supporter of radical reform and free trade, but his political alliances could and did change because he placed principle above party. He was not reluctant to vote against usual allies when he thought they were in the wrong. One such occasion came in 1851, when Thompson supported the Ecclesiastical Titles Bill. As an MP, he wrote reports about political affairs to his constituents, and these were regularly published in the Liberal press. He continued to send letters and articles to London and provincial newspapers throughout his career. Contributions on military affairs in the Crimea appeared in the *Daily News* in 1854. Much of his work was published in two collections, *Exercises, Political and Others* (6 vols., 1842) and *Audi alteram partem* (3 vols., 1858–61). The latter collection included Thompson's criticism of the policies pursued in India at the time of the mutiny. He always retained his early fascination with the customs and religions of the east.

Thompson knew and co-operated to varying degrees with most of the leading radicals of his era. His most active period outside parliament came in the late 1830s and early 1840s, when he was a tireless spokesman and fund-raiser for the Anti-Corn Law League (which republished some of his writings), a promoter of 'sensible' Chartism, and the advocate of broad liberal alliances in towns where co-operative effort drawing in whigs, moderate reformers, and radicals seemed to be most viable. Among his later writings were the *Catechism on the Currency* (1848), which stressed the advantages of a paper currency, unconvertible but limited, and an exposure of *Fallacies Against the Ballot* (1855), later reissued as *A Catechism* (1859). He also involved himself in the agitation of the National Parliamentary Reform Association (1848–52).

Thompson was a short man, stout and physically strong, with a large nose and high forehead. His hair turned grey relatively early, and he lost teeth as a result of illness in Sierra Leone. Known for simple and abstemious habits, he never seemed concerned about physical comforts and preferred to devote money and attention to politics. For much of his adult life he was vegetarian and teetotal, which suited his austere disposition and, he believed, prolonged good health. Thompson spoke with a slight northern accent and habitual solecisms. He enjoyed relating stories for the amusement of himself and others, but was also prone to bouts of depression, particularly when disappointed in his public career. In particular, the delay in brevet promotions to which he was entitled was a source of much anguish in the 1840s and 1850s. He was slow to forgive a slight, and in his public activity proved not to be effective as part of a team. Headstrong and independent, he was sometimes too abrasive and blunt even for close associates. With advancing years he was dismissive of those he regarded as his juniors in terms of intellectual accomplishments and public service.

Though born in the Church of England and reared a Methodist, Thompson rejected the faith of his parents. He described himself as a Sabellian, though he later drifted back towards orthodoxy. He had no narrow denominational ties and remained firmly committed to religious toleration, but was staunchly protestant and in his final years expressed deep respect for the church, regarding it as an indispensable institution in spite of its shortcomings.

Thompson was never fond of Cottingham Castle, the country house to which the Thompsons moved from nearby Hull in 1797, and when his father died it was let to tenants. After retiring from the army in 1829 he settled with his own family in London. During the 1830s they resided at 13 Hanover Terrace, Regent's Park, and in 1841 moved to Eliot Vale, Blackheath. Thompson died there on 6 September 1869. He was buried in Kensal Green cemetery.

MICHAEL J. TURNER

Sources U. Hull, Brynmor Jones L., Thompson MSS · U. Leeds, Brotherton L., Thompson MS 277, 823 · L. G. Johnson, *General T. Perronet Thompson* (1957) · J. R. Morrison, 'Thomas Perronet Thompson: a middle-class radical', DPhil diss., University of York, 1993 · A. R. B. Robinson, *The counting house: Thomas Thompson of Hull (1754–1828) and his family* (1992) · Wellesley index
Archives U. Edin. L., corresp. · U. Hull, Brynmor Jones L., corresp. and papers · U. Leeds, Brotherton L., mainly corresp. and papers | BL, letters to Richard Cobden, Add. MS 43663 · BL, corresp. with Francis Place, Add. MSS 35145–35151, 37949 · JRL, letters to H. B. Peacock · Man. CL, Manchester Archives and Local Studies, letters to George Wilson
Likenesses J. R. Herbert, portrait, 1847 (*Anti-Corn Law League*) · S. Bellin, group portrait, mixed media, pubd 1850 (after *Anti-Corn Law League* by J. R. Herbert), BM, NPG · H. Watkins, photograph, 1856, NPG [see illus.] · W. H. Mote, stipple (after B. Duppa), BM, NPG; repro. in J. Saunders, *Portraits and memoirs of eminent living political reformers* (1840) · portrait, repro. in Johnson, *General T. Perronet Thompson*, frontispiece
Wealth at death under £12,000: administration with will, 4 Oct 1869, *CGPLA Eng. & Wales*

Thompson, Sir William. *See* Thomson, Sir William (1678–1739).

Thompson, William (*bap.* 1712, *d. c.*1766), poet, baptized at Brough in Westmorland on 1 January 1712, was the second son of Francis Thompson (1665–1735), vicar of Brough, and his wife, Isabel (*d.* 1737), the widow of Joseph Fisher, archdeacon of Carlisle. William was educated at Appleby and then matriculated from Queen's College, Oxford, on 26 March 1731, graduating BA in 1735 and MA on 26 February 1739. He was elected a fellow of his college, and succeeded to the rectory of Hampton Poyle with South Weston in Oxfordshire.

While still an undergraduate, in 1734, Thompson wrote 'Stella, sive, Amores, tres libri' and two years later 'Six Pastorals', but considered neither production worthy of publication. In 1745, while at Hampton Poyle, he published *Sickness, a Poem*, in which he paid a tribute to the memory of Pope and Swift, both recently dead.

In 1751 Thompson was an unsuccessful candidate for the Oxford professorship of poetry against William Hawkins (1722–1801), and in the same year published *Gondibert and Bertha*, a tragedy, the subject of which was taken from Davenant's poem *Gondibert*. On the presentation to the University of the Pomfret statues, in 1756, he wrote *Gratitude*, a poem in honour of the donor, Henrietta Louisa Fermor, countess dowager of Pomfret.

In 1758 Thompson published *Poems on Several Occasions* in which he demonstrated his enthusiasm for the 'ancient English poets, in whose history and writings he was critically skilled' (Chalmers, 5). A noted imitator of Spenser, his poems 'Hymn to May', 'Nativity', and *Sickness* were once highly esteemed. He died about 1766, probably at South Weston, and his library was sold by Thomas Davies (1712?–1785) in 1768.

Thompson also superintended an edition of Joseph Hall's *Virgidemiarum* (1753), and at his death he left manuscript notes and observations on William Browne's *Works*, which were revised and published by Thomas Davies in his edition of Browne's *Works* (1772). Earlier biographical studies have confused William Thompson with Anthony Thompson, dean of Raphoe, who died on 9 October 1756 (H. Cotton, *Fasti ecclesiae Hibernicae*, 1860, 5.265).

E. I. CARLYLE, *rev.* JEFFREY HERRLE

Sources Foster, *Alum. Oxon.* · A. Chalmers, 'The life of William Thompson', *The works of the English poets from Chaucer to Cowper*, ed. A. Chalmers, 15 (1810), 3–6 [see also poems, pp. 7–57] · R. Inglis, 'Rev. Wm. Thompson', *N&Q*, 3rd ser., 1 (1862), 220 · J. Pickford, 'The Rev. William Thompson', *N&Q*, 8th ser., 3 (1893), 306 · W. Oldys, 'Choice notes: Spenser', *N&Q*, 2nd ser., 11 (1861), 182–3 · 'Rev. William Thompson', *N&Q*, 2nd ser., 11 (1861), 49 · Nichols, *Lit. anecdotes*, 3.636 · *Monthly Review*, 18 (1758), 319–25 · IGI
Likenesses line engraving (aged forty-seven), BM
Wealth at death library sold 1768: Nichols, *Lit. anecdotes*

Thompson, William (*c.*1730–1800), portrait painter, sometimes referred to as Blarney Thompson, was born in Dublin. He received his artistic education in London, and does not seem to have exhibited his works elsewhere. He lived for several years at Warwick Court, Holborn, and subsequently at Half Moon Street, Piccadilly. Between 1760 and 1782 he exhibited forty-three pictures at the Society of Artists, of which he was for some time secretary, and one at the Free Society of Artists. The majority of these were portraits, but he also showed pictures of historical and classical subject matter, for example, *A Wounded Officer Supported from the Field of Battle at Minden* (exh. Society of Artists, 1762) and *Jupiter and Leda* (exh. Society of Artists, 1764). Though acknowledged as good likenesses, his portraits, now known chiefly in print form, were generally considered to have been of limited artistic merit. Thompson's portraits include *Cadwallader, 9th Baron Blayney, Lord Lieutenant of Co. Monaghan and Grand Master of the Masons*; *Anna Swan*; *Sir Edward Hamilton, 1st Bart. of Trebinshun*, and *Henry Baker*, a portrait of the naturalist and author. All of these were engraved in mezzotint, stipple, or lithograph. His marriage to a wealthy woman allowed him temporarily to relinquish his profession, but he fell into debt and was incarcerated in the king's bench prison. His noisy protests against his imprisonment earned for him considerable notoriety; Thompson produced a portrait of James Stephen, author of *Considerations on Imprisonment for Debt*, who had been a fellow prisoner in the king's bench. After the death of his first wife Thompson married Mary, another rich woman in whose boarding-school he had taught drawing, which enabled him to retire for good from active work. He joined the notorious circle associated with Mrs Theresa Cornely's house in Soho Square, where he founded and ran a school of oratory. He died suddenly in London early in 1800, his will being proved on 4 February; his wife survived him.

Thompson published *An Enquiry into the Elementary Principles of Beauty in the Works of Nature and Art*, and also, anonymously, in 1771, *The Conduct of the Royal Academicians while Members of the Society of Arts, from 1760 to their Expulsion in 1769*. He was, according to Strickland, given the nickname Blarney because of his 'specious address and love of talking' (Strickland, 447).   BRENDAN ROONEY

Sources W. G. Strickland, *A dictionary of Irish artists*, 2 (1913) · E. Edwards, *Anecdotes of painters* (1808); facs. edn (1970) · Redgrave, *Artists* · Bryan, *Painters* (1865); (1921) · Thieme & Becker, *Allgemeines Lexikon* · Bénézit, *Dict.* · Graves, *Soc. Artists* · *Engraved Brit. ports.*, vols. 1, 4, 6 · Graves, *Artists* · will, PRO, PROB 11/1338, fols. 51v–52r
Wealth at death left leasehold property in St Mary-le-Bow and elsewhere to his wife

Thompson, William (1733–1799), Methodist minister, was born at Newtonbutler, co. Fermanagh; little is known about his parentage or early life. It is reported how, as a young man undertaking a business journey to Dublin, Thompson heard a Methodist preach and experienced an evangelical conversion. On becoming a Methodist preacher in 1757 he crossed to Britain, where he laboured at various locations, including Newcastle upon Tyne, Leeds, Edinburgh, and Glasgow. About 1758 he was pressed as a sailor but was released through the intervention of the countess of Huntingdon. In 1764, while preaching in Lancashire, Thompson 'caught a violent cold by sleeping in a damp bed', an illness which apparently 'laid the foundation, and was the principal cause of those dreadful spasms in his stomach, which he laboured under for many years, and which, in the judgement of some of his friends, occasioned his death' (Atmore, 226). In 1769 he married in Edinburgh, though details of his wife are unknown.

Thompson was one of the hundred preachers appointed by John Wesley in his Deed of Declaration in 1784, which provided for the government of the Methodist Connexion after his own death. While serving as assistant minister of the Halifax circuit Thompson met with a group of preachers at Halifax, Yorkshire, in 1791 and produced a circular which suggested, among other things, that Wesley, having recently died, should be succeeded by a president and secretary who would be elected annually. This Halifax circular was sent out to the 'preachers in general and the assistants in particular' and described the dangers which then faced the nascent Methodist church. Owing mainly to 'Thompson's peculiar genius for ecclesiastical polity' (Atmore, 225) and his reputation as a moderate, the Methodist conference meeting at Manchester in July 1791 elected him its first president after John Wesley.

Thompson was the main figure behind the 'plan of pacification' (1795), which tried to resolve the sacramental question. This, together with his Halifax circular, constituted him one of the main architects of Methodism as it evolved following Wesley's death. Thompson's influence was also felt in his contribution as president. He was, according to Atmore, a 'man of remarkably strong sense, a fertile genius, a clear understanding, a quick discernment, a retentive memory, and a sound judgement—one of the closest reasoners and most able speakers that ever sat in the Methodist Conference' (Atmore, 225).

In April 1799 ill health caused Thompson to leave Manchester and retire to Birmingham, where his eldest daughter had married a man of considerable wealth. It is reported that he 'suffered extreme pain in his last illness, which he bore with great patience, and with entire resignation to the Divine will' (*Minutes of the Methodist Conference*, 511). He died at Birmingham on 1 May 1799 and his body was interred in a vault in St Mary's Chapel, Birmingham.   SIMON ROSS VALENTINE

Sources *Minutes of the Methodist conferences, from the first, held in London by the late Rev. John Wesley ...*, 3 vols. (1812–13) [1799 conference] · C. Atmore, *The Methodist memorial*, new edn (1871) · W. Myles, *A chronological history of the Methodists* (1814) · C. H. Crookshank, *History of Methodism in Ireland*, 3 vols. (1885–8) · W. J. Townsend, H. B. Workman, and G. Eayrs, *A new history of Methodism*, 2 vols. (1909) · A. Stevens, *The illustrated history of Methodism*, 2 vols. [n.d.] · R. E. Davies, A. R. George, and G. Rupp, eds., *A history of the Methodist church in Great Britain*, 4 (1988)
Archives JRL, Methodist Archives and Research Centre, letters
Likenesses portrait, JRL, Methodist Archives and Research Centre · portrait, repro. in Townsend, Workman, and Eayrs, *New history of Methodism*, vol. 1

Thompson, William (1775–1833), socialist and economist, was born into an ascendancy family at Cork. His grandfather was a protestant clergyman and his father, John Thompson, a wealthy Cork merchant who became speaker and mayor of the municipality and later high sheriff of the county. Thompson displayed an early interest in ideas of social improvement. He read the works of Godwin and Bentham and was exposed to the influence of continental writers such as Sismondi and St Simon during a period spent in France and the Low Countries. It was, no doubt, the articulation of the views of these writers in milieux such as the Cork Philosophical and Literary Society, of which Thompson was a prominent member, that led to his being branded locally as a 'red republican', and brought about an estrangement from his family. This radical reputation was further enhanced by his support for Christopher Hely Hutchinson, a candidate favouring Catholic emancipation, in the Cork elections of 1812 and 1826 and his championing of popular education in a pamphlet entitled *Practical Education for the South of Ireland*, which was published in 1818.

Thompson's concern with the iniquities of existing economic and social arrangements was also made apparent, although in a more practical manner, when, after the death of his father in 1814, he took over the management of the family's mercantile interests and in addition inherited an estate of some 1400 acres near Glandore in co. Cork. In Ireland these arrangements were characterized by absentee landlords, rapacious rack-renting agents, evictions, and, as a result, a poverty-stricken and disaffected peasantry. In contrast to contemporary practice, Thompson took an interest in his estate, giving his tenants long leases on favourable terms, encouraging the introduction of improved agricultural techniques, and establishing a model farm to illustrate best practice. Such actions established among the Catholic population of the area a long-lived reputation for kindness and fair dealing which persisted despite his professed atheism.

In 1819 Thompson was invited by Bentham, with whom he had corresponded on educational questions, to visit him at his home in Queen Square Place, Westminster, an invitation which he accepted in 1822, staying from 10 October until 22 February 1823. Here he met some of the leading utilitarians and political economists of the period, such as Robert Torrens, James Mill, John Black (editor of the *Morning Chronicle*), and John Bowring (editor of the *Westminster Review*). Such figures undoubtedly had a profound impact on a mind which, on educational theory, had already proved susceptible to Benthamite ideas. Indeed Thompson wrote of Bentham in 1824 that he 'had done more for moral science than Bacon did for physical science' (*Inquiry into the Principles of the Distribution of Wealth*, 1824, x).

Yet at this time the socialist ideas of Robert Owen were also leaving their mark upon Thompson's thought. They led him to consider in a different light the material evils inflicted by the existing economic and social order and, specifically, the reasons for the inequitable distribution of wealth which it produced. Such thoughts were to be expressed at some length in a work which was to establish Thompson as the leading thinker of the early nineteenth-century co-operative movement, *An Inquiry into the Principles of the Distribution of Wealth* (1824).

In this, the *magnum opus* of nineteenth-century co-operative political economy, Thompson considered the distribution of wealth which resulted first under existing arrangements, secondly where there existed 'truly free' competition, and thirdly where a system of mutual co-operation prevailed. The existing order was characterized by 'absolute violence, fraud … [and] the operation of unequal laws interfering with the freedom of labour … and the perfect freedom of voluntary exchange' (*Inquiry*,

160). What resulted was the appropriation of rent, profits, and taxes from the product of labour by 'a class of capitalists, a class of rent or landowners, sometimes a class of farmers … sometimes a class of fundholders and an always imperious class of idlers' (ibid., 581). A system of truly free competition would, however, tend to raise the remuneration and eliminate extremes of wealth and poverty producing 'blessings of equality comparable to those enjoyed under Mr. Owen's system of mutual co-operation by common labour' (ibid., 150).

Yet such an economic regime would still be characterized by the deleterious social, moral, and psychological consequences which necessarily resulted from the conflict of interests intrinsic to competition. For that reason Thompson advocated the creation of a system of mutual co-operation with the establishment of communities whose product would be distributed on the basis of need rather than individual exertion. Such a move in the direction of equality would, Thompson accepted, contravene the notion of the labourer's right to his/her whole product and thence the Benthamite notion that, when in conflict, the principle of security must prevail over any move to greater equality. However, Thompson believed that such a conflict could be rendered nugatory where, *pari passu* with the formation of communities, communitarians voluntarily relinquished their property rights. They would then enjoy greater equality and also increased security against the vicissitudes of contemporary economic life. Further, the absence of competition would eliminate those existing pressures which made for morally repugnant and socially corrosive behaviour. The nuts and bolts of establishing these communities were elucidated in *Practical Directions for the Speedy and Economical Establishment of Communities* (1830).

Some of these ideas were to be developed in a subsequent work, *Labour Rewarded: the Claims of Labour and Capital Conciliated* (1827), written to rebut Thomas Hodgskin's view (*Labour Defended Against the Claims of Capital*, 1825) that a truly effective competitive economic system would bestow upon labour its full product. In *Labour Rewarded* Thompson was now clear that 'free competition' was a chimera requiring at the outset of the competitive struggle that all should be in possession of equal means of knowledge and skill, equal freedom of action, equal materials for production and accumulation, equal rights and duties, and equal fortunes. The impossibility of this meant that competition must, in reality, involve coercion and exploitation by the favoured few of the disadvantaged many.

In both the *Inquiry* and *Labour Rewarded* Thompson also attacked the subjugation of women which the existing system of private property entailed. This theme was to be developed more fully in *An Appeal of one Half the Human Race* (1830), one of the classics of early nineteenth-century feminist literature; described by one commentator as 'the most significant work in the seventy odd years between the publication of Mary Wollstonecraft's *Vindication of the Rights of Woman* (1792) and John Stuart Mill's *Subjection of Women* (1869)' (Pankhurst, 67). The work was the fruit of his collaboration with Anna Doyle Wheeler, whom he probably met at Bentham's gatherings in Queen Square Place. She penned part of the finished work, which was written to refute James Mill's article 'On government' (published in the 1824 supplement to the *Encyclopaedia Britannica*), which had argued that as women's interests were subsumed in those of men there was no need to extend the franchise to the female of the species.

Thompson's works made him the foremost theoretician of the co-operative movement. At a practical level too he was deeply involved, helping to establish the *Co-Operative Magazine*, participating in the co-operative congresses of the 1830s, and taking part in the formation of labour exchanges in Birmingham and London, where goods were exchanged according to the labour time which they embodied.

Thompson, who remained unmarried, lived frugally and became a non-smoker, a vegetarian, and a teetotaller. He habitually lunched on potatoes and turnips, but had a weakness for honey, which was produced in abundance on his estate. At the height of his involvement in the co-operative movement he died of inflammation of the chest, on 28 March 1833, at Clounksen, Ross Carbery, co. Cork. He was, despite his atheism, and against his wishes, buried according to Anglican rites in the churchyard of Dromberg, near Glandore. However, when the reading of his will (dated 27 October 1830) made his wishes clear, his body was exhumed and dissected in the cause of medical science.

The will itself precipitated a lengthy legal battle. After bestowing an annuity of £100 on Anna Doyle Wheeler and setting aside £4000 to cover any claims which might be advanced by the trustees of his father's estate, the rest of Thompson's property (valued at between £15,000 and £16,000) was left to the co-operative movement. But relatives contested the will in the Irish court of chancery and, after a prolonged legal battle of some twenty-five years, judgment was given in their favour, a pyrrhic victory for by that time the greater part of the estate had been absorbed in legal costs.

The influence of Thompsonian political economy within co-operative ranks was considerable. In addition his critical ideas came to form part of the ideological baggage of some of the political radicals of the National Union of the Working-Classes in the early 1830s; many of whom were to provide leadership for the Chartist movement in the 1840s. The nature and extent of his influence on Marx is problematic, but a continuing interest in his work in its own right has assured Thompson an honoured place in the pantheon of socialist political economy.

NOEL THOMPSON

Sources R. Pankhurst, *William Thompson (1775–1833): pioneer socialist* (1954); repr. (1991) • N. Thompson, *The market and its critics: socialist political economy in nineteenth century Britain* (1988) • H. S. Foxwell, 'Introduction', in A. Menger, *The right to the whole produce of labour* (1899) • G. Claeys, *Machinery, money and the millennium: from moral economy to socialism, 1815–60* (1987) • G. D. H. Cole, *Socialist thought: the forerunners, 1789–1850* (1959) • E. K. Hunt, 'Utilitarianism and the labour theory of value: a critique of the ideas of William Thompson', *History of Political Economy*, 11 (1979), 545–71 • E. Lowenthal, *The Ricardian socialists* (1911) • J. F. C. Harrison, *Robert Owen and the Owenites in Britain and America: the quest for the new moral world* (1969) • R. G. Garnett, *Co-operation and Owenite socialist communities in Britain, 1825–45* (1872) • H. L. Beaks, *The early English socialists* (1933) • M. Beer, *A history of British socialism*, 2 vols. (1940) • D. Dooley, *Equality in community: sexual equality in the writings of William Thompson and Anna Doyle Wheeler* (1996)

Archives Co-operative Union, Holyoake House, Manchester, Robert Owen corresp.

Wealth at death £100 p.a. legacy; £4000 to cover claims advanced on father's estate • £16,000: Pankhurst, *William Thompson*

Thompson, William (1793–1854), ironmaster and financier, was born at Grayrigg Head, near Kendal, Westmorland, the second son of James Thompson. He was educated at Charterhouse before joining the business of his uncle William Thompson, who had been a partner with Richard Crawshay (1744–1799) in the leading firm of iron merchants in the City of London. After Crawshay's death Thompson's uncle formed a new merchant house with Samuel *Homfray (1762–1822) [see under Homfray family (*per.* 1702–1833)] and William Henry Forman (d. 1869) of the Penydarren ironworks at Merthyr Tudful in Wales.

The elder William Thompson, like the Crawshay family, had major interests in south Wales iron furnaces. In 1799 he leased the Tintern ironworks, and in 1806 he purchased three-tenth shares of the Redbrook and Lydbrook ironworks. Most important was his involvement with Homfray, one of the leading south Wales ironmasters at the end of the eighteenth century and the beginning of the nineteenth. In 1800 Homfray leased coal and iron ore from the Tredegar estate and formed a partnership with Thompson and others to establish the Tredegar ironworks with a capital of £30,000. Homfray was also involved in establishing the Aberdâr works in 1801 and was a partner in the Penydarren company at Merthyr Tudful where Thompson acquired an interest. The younger William inherited his uncle's fortune, and in 1817 he married Amelia (d. 1861), the second daughter of Homfray and niece of Sir Charles Morgan of Tredegar. By the early 1820s he was the sole owner of Penydarren; he seems to have left day-to-day operations to managers at Merthyr Tudful and he concentrated on more general issues such as leases and, possibly, marketing.

Lady Charlotte Guest, the wife of Sir Josiah John Guest of the Dowlais works, commented in 1836 that Thompson 'is the *Alderman* in every sense, and has not the uprightness which I should have been inclined to give most City merchants credit for' (Guest: *Extracts*, 41). Her comment probably reflects the simmering boundary dispute between the two works, but in 1846 Sir Josiah Guest and Thompson were willing to submerge their differences in hostility to a greater foe, namely, John Crichton-Stuart, the second marquess of Bute, who was demanding more realistic terms for the renewal of leases. They proposed to form a single joint-stock company in order to negotiate with Bute, but this was declared inadmissible under the lease. In 1848 the Bute estate attempted to make terms with Thompson to take over the Dowlais works. By this stage the south Wales works were past their peak, and

William Thompson (1793–1854), by Charles Edward Wagstaff (after Henry William Pickersgill, 1840)

Penydarren was in decline. On his death in 1854, Thompson's interests in the south Wales iron industry and related canals and tramways went, in trust, to the younger sons of his brother James as tenants-in-common. The trustees were to manage the works with full rights as owners, including the power to sell; Penydarren was sold to the Dowlais Iron Company for £59,875 in 1859.

Although the iron industry formed the basis of Thompson's fortune, his interests were diverse. The centre of his business career was in London. Through his interests in marine insurance, he was most actively and publicly involved in shipping. In 1720 the Royal Exchange Assurance and London Assurance were granted a monopoly of marine insurance by corporations, and the act also prohibited underwriting by partnerships. The result was to stimulate individual underwriting, which was organized at Lloyd's Coffee House. An attack on the monopoly of the Royal Exchange and London assurance companies was, therefore, an indirect attack on Lloyd's. In 1806 and 1810 assaults on the monopoly failed; in 1824 the outlook was less auspicious when Nathan Mayer Rothschild (1777–1836) and other City figures, including Alexander Baring, Samuel Gurney, and Moses Montefiore, launched the Alliance British and Foreign Fire and Life Insurance Company. The Alliance was, in the opinion of one critic, 'the whole united money interest of the empire' (*Hansard 2*, 11, 1824,

928), and it had the support of the government. William Huskisson, for example, was prepared to see Lloyd's destroyed. 'Unquestionably, the public would go wherever they could get their business done in the best and cheapest manner. And why, he begged to ask, ought they not to be permitted to do so?' (*Hansard 2*, 11, 1824, 772). Such a view was firmly opposed by Thompson, who had entered parliament in 1820 as member for Callington in Cornwall:

> So far from creating competition, the present bill, when passed, will only give rise to a new monopoly in the establishment of a huge, all-absorbing joint-stock undertaking. Everybody knows that it is impossible to have more and sharper competition in marine insurance than exists at present. There are more than a thousand underwriters at Lloyd's, and competition is as open to the insurer who goes to the Royal Exchange as Mark Lane is open to the corn merchants and Mincing Lane to the sugar dealers. (Martin, 295)

In the event, most marine insurance continued to be effected at Lloyd's, and Thompson served as chairman of its committee from 1825 until he was obliged to resign as a result of criticism of his joining the Sunderland Shipowners' Mutual Assurance Association. Unfortunately, it is not possible to establish how active he was in underwriting and how far this contributed to his considerable fortune.

Thompson's subsequent parliamentary career was marked by his staunch defence of the navigation laws. He followed the line of London shipowners such as Joseph Somes and G. F. Young that shipping had been in decline since Huskisson's reforms in the 1820s. Although the navigation laws might be modified, Thompson was opposed to their repeal which could destroy British shipping and the security of the country. The question of repeal, he informed the Commons, was 'one of the greatest national questions which had been discussed in modern times' (*Hansard 3*, 99, 1848, 35–43). He may also have invested in shipping, as was common for many merchants in the first half of the nineteenth century.

Thompson was a leading figure in the City and public life from the 1820s. In 1821 he became an alderman of the City; he retained the position to his death, and was lord mayor in 1828–9. He was active in his livery company, the Ironmongers' Company, of which he was master in 1829 and 1841. He was also president of Christ's Hospital from 1829 until his death; treasurer of King's College; and colonel of the Royal London militia from 1851 to 1854. He became a director of the Bank of England in 1829, and remained on the court until his death. His standing in the City was confirmed by his election, at the head of the poll, as one of its MPs in 1826. He was, nominally, a whig and moderate reformer, but he received tory support as a result of his opposition to Catholic emancipation. He was re-elected in 1830 and 1831, but in 1832 he stood for Sunderland as a moderate whig and advocate of the repeal of the corn laws. He came bottom of the poll, but was elected in 1833 and was again returned in 1837.

By this time, Thompson was associated with the tories and by 1841 had shifted to support agricultural protection.

Although re-elected for Sunderland in 1841, he resigned his seat in order to stand for Westmorland, which he represented from that year until his death. He opposed the Bank Charter Act, and he voted against repeal of the corn laws which he considered a concession to the unconstitutional power of the Anti-Corn Law League. He was a leader of City Conservatism, and part of the world of protection which was overturned in the 1840s as the City was remade in an open, competitive form with which he had little sympathy. At the same time, the south Wales iron industry was passing its peak of prosperity.

Thompson, one of the wealthiest and most important figures in the City, owned a fortune considered to be on a par with James Morrison (1790–1857) and Nathan Mayer Rothschild. The comparison with Morrison is more apt than that with Rothschild, for Thompson did not create a continuing presence in the City. In association with Isaac Lyon Goldsmid (1778–1859) Thompson was involved in managing remittances for the payment of the dividends on the Brazilian debt to Portugal, which was taken over by the Rothschilds on his death. He was almost certainly involved in various other City ventures, as a director or investor: there is, for example, a passing reference to his involvement in the Santiago Mining Company. However, Thompson, like James Morrison and Morrison's son Charles, increasingly concentrated on accumulating railway stocks (he acted as chairman of the Cambrian and the Gloucester and London railways) and, above all, land. The explanation was, in part, that his only child was a daughter, Amelia (d. 1864). In 1842 she married the earl of Bective (1822–1894), who became third marquess of Headfort; his family held considerable landed estates in Ireland.

It was claimed by the *Gentleman's Magazine* after Thompson's death in 1854 that Thompson lived well below his means, and he certainly invested heavily in both land and railway shares. A few months before his death he purchased the Barnacre estate from the duke of Hamilton for £98,000, and he also owned the Underley estate at Kirkby Lonsdale. In the new Domesday survey of 1883 the estates were recorded as being held by his son-in-law and amounted to 12,851 acres in Westmorland with a gross annual value of £13,686; 4534 acres in Yorkshire with a gross annual value of £2305; 3393 acres in Lancashire with a gross annual value of £4198; and 178 acres in Glamorgan with a gross annual value of £42 (Bateman, 214). The Headfort estates in Ireland had by this time a gross annual value of £19,372 and the land accumulated by Thompson in England and Wales £20,234.

Thompson died on 10 March 1854 at Bedwellty House, Monmouthshire. His estate was sworn at under £900,000 in Canterbury, £60,000 in York, and £16,000 in Ireland, which excluded the investment in land. He had been one of the greatest figures in the City of London in the 1830s, and a significant ironmaster in south Wales. His wife died in 1861 and his daughter in 1864, and his considerable fortune disappeared—in common with the Crawshays and his partner William Henry Forman—into the landed élite without leaving any apparent dynastic trace.

MARTIN DAUNTON

Sources GM, 2nd ser., 41 (1854), 650–51 · Boase, *Mod. Eng. biog.* · R. S. Ferguson, *Cumberland and Westmorland MPs: from the Restoration to the Reform Bill of 1867* (1871), 443 · B. E. Supple, *The Royal Exchange Assurance: a history of British insurance, 1720–1970* (1970) · S. Palmer, *Politics, shipping and the repeal of navigation laws* (1990) · A. C. Howe, 'Free trade and the City of London, *c.*1820–1870', *History*, new ser., 77 (1992), 391–410 · *Lady Charlotte Guest: extracts from her journal, 1833–1852*, ed. earl of Bessborough (1950) · F. W. Martin, *The history of Lloyd's and of marine insurance in Great Britain* (1876) · A. B. Beaven, ed., *The aldermen of the City of London, temp. Henry III–[1912]*, 2 (1913) · *The letter books of Richard Crawshay, 1788–1792*, ed. C. Evans (1990) · A. H. John, *The industrial development of south Wales, 1750–1850: an essay* (1950) · M. Elsas, ed., *Iron in the making: Dowlais Iron Company letters, 1782–1860* (1960) · J. Bateman, *The great landowners of Great Britain and Ireland*, 4th edn (1883) · Hansard 2 (1824), 11.772, 928 · Hansard 3 (1848), 99.35–43 · W. M. Acres, 'Directors of the Bank of England', *N&Q*, 179 (1940), 167–70, esp. 168
Archives GL, diary of mayoralty
Likenesses T. L. Busby, line engraving, pubd 1826, BM · H. W. Pickersgill, oils, 1840, Christ's Hospital, Sussex · C. E. Wagstaff, mezzotint (after H. W. Pickersgill, 1840), BM, NPG [*see illus.*]
Wealth at death under £900,000 Canterbury; £60,000 York; £16,000 Ireland: PRO, death duty registers, IR 26/2012, fols. 521–9

Thompson, William (1805–1852), naturalist, was born on 2 November 1805 at a house in Wellington Place, Belfast, the eldest son and third child of William Thompson (*d. c.*1830), linen merchant, and his wife, Elizabeth Calwell (or Callwell; *d.* 1853). He received a commercial education in Belfast, intended to enable him to follow his father in the linen trade (an occupation which held little interest for him). After his father's death, Thompson devoted his time to his interests in natural history. A quiet person of gentle and fastidious demeanour, he was never comfortable with the details required to dissect animals and prepare them for study. Instead he concentrated on the observation of birds, plants, algae, and Cirripedia (barnacles).

Thompson travelled to the eastern Mediterranean (with the naturalist Edward Forbes) as a guest on the surveying ship *Beacon*. He also travelled to many locations in Ireland and Scotland to observe and make detailed notes of the appearance and behaviour of birds, both rare and common. Except when travelling for scientific purposes, he lived at his house in Donegall Square, Belfast, from which he conducted an extensive scientific correspondence. Active in the Belfast Natural History Society from the age of twenty-one, Thompson was elected president in 1843; he retained the office until his death. He was also a corresponding member of the Natural History Society of Boston and of the Academy of Natural Sciences in Philadelphia, USA.

Thompson's major work is *The Natural History of Ireland*. The first three volumes appeared between 1849 and 1851; the fourth was published posthumously in 1856, under the combined editorship of Robert Patterson, George Dickie, and Robert Ball. The work is a detailed account of Thompson's observations of birds in Ireland and Scotland, many of which later became rare. It was the first comprehensive and detailed book on Irish birds and was planned to be part of a complete Irish natural history. Thompson also published about seventy-five minor papers on subjects of natural history.

Thompson was highly regarded by his contemporaries,

William Thompson (1805–1852), by Thomas Herbert Maguire, 1849

including Forbes and Charles Darwin (who wrote of him as a 'most accurate observer'), and he has been described as the foremost Irish zoologist of his day. Darwin's copy of *The Natural History of Ireland* survives with hundreds of handwritten annotations; when read together, these show that Darwin paid close attention to Thompson's meticulous observations of wild and domesticated birds and the changes in their habitat or behaviour that may have contributed to their survival or extinction. Darwin cites Thompson in his works as a source of information, and the two men corresponded. Thompson was aware of several of Darwin's works, including his narrative of the *Beagle* voyage.

Little of Thompson's own scientific correspondence survives but, in a letter to him from Darwin (1 March 1849), Darwin praises Thompson for having provided much of interest in his natural history, and comments that Thompson's extensive collection of British and North American barnacles and other Cirripedia 'will be *invaluably* useful to me' (*Correspondence*, vol. 4).

Thompson died on 17 February 1852 at his lodgings in Jermyn Street, London, apparently after a heart attack while on a visit to give a scientific lecture. He was buried soon after in the Clifton Street graveyard, Belfast. He never married.   GEOFFREY V. MORSON

Sources W. Thompson, *The natural history of Ireland*, ed. R. Patterson, 4 vols. (1849–56) • W. Sinclaire, 'Memoir of the late William Thompson', in W. Thompson, *The natural history of Ireland*, ed. R. Patterson, 4 (1856), x–xxx • *DNB* • J. W. Foster, ed., *Nature in Ireland: a scientific and cultural history* (1997), 266–7, 291–2, 421–2 • *The correspondence of Charles Darwin*, ed. F. Burkhardt and S. Smith, 3–6 (1987–90) • Belfast Municipal Art Gallery and Museum, 'William Thompson, of Belfast, naturalist', *Quarterly Notes*, 31 (1915), 13–14 •

Desmond, *Botanists*, rev. edn, 680–81 • R. Burgess, *Portraits of doctors and scientists in the Wellcome Institute of the History of Medicine* (1973) • *Centenary volume, 1821–1921*, Belfast Natural History and Philosophical Society, ed. A. Deane (1924) • R. L. Praeger, *Some Irish naturalists: a biographical note-book* (1949), 166–7 • *Charles Darwin's marginalia*, ed. M. A. Di Gregorio and N. W. Gill (1990), 804–6 • 'The late William Thompson esq. of Belfast', *Dublin University Magazine*, 39 (1852), 531–2 • *Bulletin of the Irish Biogeographical Society* (1984) • C. Darwin, *Living Cirripedia* (1854), 272

Archives NL Ire., notes and papers • possibly Ulster Museum, Belfast, collection of algae • possibly Ulster Museum, Belfast, corresp. and MSS | Harvard U., Arnold Arboretum, letters to Asa Grey • NHM, letters to Joshua Alder and Alfred Merle • Royal Literary and Scientific Institution, Bath, letters to Leonard Blomefield

Likenesses T. H. Maguire, lithograph, 1849, BM, NPG, Wellcome L. [*see illus.*]

Thompson, William [*known as* Bendigo] (1811–1880), pugilist, was born at Nottingham on 11 October 1811, the youngest of the twenty-one children (according to some accounts) of Benjamin Thompson (*d. c.*1826), a mechanic in the lace industry, and his wife, Mary (1769–1851). He later said that he was born one of three sons at a birth and that these boys became popularly known as Shadrach, Meshach, and Abednego. The record of his baptism at St Mary's, Nottingham, on 16 October 1811, however, records him as the younger of twins. He learned the trade of iron turning from an elder brother, but as a youth became a formidable pugilist. In 1832 he beat Bill Faulker, a Nottingham notoriety, and in the following year defeated Charles Martin. In his first challenge reported in *Bell's Life in London* in 1835 he styled himself Abednego of Nottingham, and from that date he was spoken of in the sporting press as Bendigo. Rather improbably, Dowling ascribed the nickname instead to his evasive tactics in the ring (Dowling, *Fights*, 140).

Bendigo's first important fight was on 21 July 1835, near Appleby House, about 30 miles from Nottingham, when he met Benjamin Caunt. In the twenty-third round Caunt, wearied with Bendigo's shifty conduct in continually hitting him and then dropping to render retaliation 'foul', struck him a blow while he was on his second's knee; by this foul blow he lost the fight. On 24 May 1836, 9 miles from Sheffield, he defeated John Leechman, known as Brassey, in fifty-two rounds after a severe contest.

Again facing Caunt on 3 April 1838, Bendigo was this time unsuccessful; his 'dropping without a blow' was deemed foul. In the presence of 15,000 people, including many aristocratic spectators, he fought Deaf Burke at Heather, Leicestershire, on 12 February 1839 (the first fight under the new London rules), when in the tenth round Burke butted him twice, and the referee gave a decision that the blows were 'foul'. During the same year James Ward presented 'a champion's belt' to Bendigo at the Queen's Theatre, Liverpool.

On 23 March 1840, while throwing a somersault at Nottingham, Bendigo so hurt his kneecap that he was laid up for two years. He was taken into custody by the police on 28 June 1842 and bound over to keep the peace to prevent his fighting Hazard Parker. A fight for £200 a side and the belt came off with his old opponent Caunt on 9 September 1845, when a decision was given in his favour—rather an

William Thompson [Bendigo] (1811–1880), by Thomas Earl, 1850

arbitrary one after a fight in which 'both men committed every known foul and invented a good deal more' (Johnson, 98). Bendigo's backing by the so-called 'Nottingham lambs', armed with bludgeons, may have influenced the referee. His last appearance in the ring took place on 15 June 1850 at Mildenhall, Suffolk, when, for £200 a side, he fought Tom Paddock. His 82-year-old mother, who had always encouraged his pugnacity, is said to have threatened to fight Paddock herself if he did not answer the challenge. He would probably have been defeated, as his age told against him, had he not incited Paddock to a foul blow.

Bendigo was 5 feet 9¾ inches tall, and his fighting weight was 11 stone 12 lb. Fighting men such as Caunt, at least 3 stone heavier, encouraged him to 'shiftiness', but his unprecedented leading with the right was also a factor in his success. After his retirement from the ring, Bendigo took to drink, and was incarcerated in the Nottingham house of correction on twenty-eight occasions. But after attending a revivalist meeting in 1872, addressed by Richard Weaver (1827–1892), the collier evangelist, he 'saw the light': 'Jesus came to me and had a bout with me, and I can tell you He licked me in the first round' (Cieszkowski, 29). He took the teetotal pledge, joined the Good Templars, and became an evangelist preacher in Nottingham and elsewhere. His new career still entailed some bouts with hecklers. When he told Lord Longford that now he fought Beelzebub, that gentleman is said to have replied, 'I hope you fight him more fairly than you did Ben Caunt, or my sympathies will be all with the devil' (Johnson, 98). While on a visit to London he was a preacher and a leader of revivalist services at the Cabmen's Mission Hall, King's Cross Circus, and also a preacher in the Holborn Circus.

Bendigo died at Beeston, near Nottingham, on 23 August 1880, broken ribs having punctured a lung after a fall downstairs. He was buried in St Mary's cemetery, St Ann's Well Road, Nottingham. The goldfield and city in Australia took the name Bendigo from him, horse races were named after him, and he was the subject of numerous popular ballads.　　　G. C. BOASE, *rev.* JULIAN LOCK

Sources H. D. Miles, *Pugilistica: being one hundred and forty-four years of the history of British boxing*, 3 vols. (1880–81), vol. 3, pp. 1–46 · K. Z. Cieszkowski, 'Bendigo the boxer', *History Today*, 34/2 (1984), 25–30 · J. Greenwood, *Low-life deeps: an account of the strange fish to be found there* (1876), 86–94 · D. Johnson, *Bare fist fighters of the 18th and 19th century: 1704–1861* (1987) · B. Lynch, *Knuckle and glove* (1922) · H. Cleveland, *Fisticuffs and personalities of the prize ring* (c.1923) · Boase, *Mod. Eng. biog.* · [F. Dowling], *Fights for the championship; and celebrated prize battles* (1855) · [F. Dowling], *Fistiana* (1868) · C. M. Davies, *Unorthodox London, or, Phases of religious life in the metropolis*, 2nd ser. (1875), 156–64 · d. cert. · parish register, Nottingham, St Mary's, 16 Oct 1811 [baptism]

Likenesses T. Earl, oils, 1850, NPG [*see illus.*] · drawing (*Bendigo's conversion*), repro. in Greenwood, *Low-life deeps*, facing p. 86 · portrait, repro. in Miles, *Pugilistica*, vol. 3, facing p. 1

Thompson, William Hepworth

Thompson, William Hepworth (1810–1886), college head, was born at York on 27 March 1810, the eldest of eleven children of William Thompson, a solicitor. He was educated first at a school in York kept by a Mr Richardson, and thereafter by a succession of private tutors, the last of whom was the Revd Thomas Scott, perpetual curate of Gawcott, Buckinghamshire, and father of Sir George Gilbert Scott. Thompson entered Trinity College, Cambridge, as a pensioner in 1828, with the Revd George Peacock as his tutor. He developed a lifelong friendship with Peacock whom he described as 'the best and wisest of tutors'. Julius Charles Hare was one of the assistant tutors and Connop Thirlwall junior dean. Thompson derived great benefit from Thirlwall's lectures, and in 1830 was elected a scholar of his college. In 1831 he obtained one of the members' prizes for a Latin essay. He proceeded to the BA degree in 1832, being placed tenth senior optime in the mathematical tripos. He was subsequently fourth in the first class of the classical tripos, and obtained the second chancellor's medal for classical learning. In 1834 he was elected fellow of his college, and in the following year proceeded to the MA degree.

Thompson's classical attainments marked him out for work in college, but, as there was no immediate prospect of a vacancy among the assistant tutors, in 1836 he accepted the headmastership of an experimental school at Leicester, called the collegiate school. In 1837, on the appointment of E. L. Lushington to the Greek chair at Glasgow, he was recalled to Trinity College and became one of the assistant tutors. He was ordained deacon on 4 June 1837 and priest on 27 May the following year. In 1844 he was appointed a tutor. In his approach to this office Thompson followed the lead of his predecessor, George Peacock. At a time when undergraduates were kept at a distance by their seniors, he made his pupils feel that he really stood to them *in loco parentis*. He could be severe when discipline required it, but he was always inflexibly

William Hepworth Thompson (1810–1886), by Sir Hubert von Herkomer, 1881

just and untrammelled by pedantic adherence to tradition.

Thompson remained tutor of Trinity until 1853, when he was elected regius professor of Greek, and was appointed to a canonry at Ely, at that time annexed to the professorship. After his election as Greek professor, he was nominated one of the eight senior fellows of his college, under the belief that the statutes, as revised in 1844, permitted the Greek professor to remain a fellow. A chancery suit was instituted against him, however, by the Revd Joseph Edleston, the fellow next below him on the list, and, judgment having been given against Thompson by the lord chancellor on 4 March 1854, he became a nominal fellow only, retaining his rooms in college and residing there when not at Ely. In the spring of 1856, in company with William George Clark, he visited Greece, and spent some months in studying Athens and the Peloponnese.

Thompson's lectures were modelled upon those of his early teachers, Hare and Thirlwall, while containing characteristics of his own. He was particularly remembered for his own translations of the books he was teaching, which were delivered without notes during his lectures. J. E. Sandys commented that 'By his published writings and by his personal influence he did much towards widening the range of classical studies in Cambridge, and preventing their being unduly limited to verbal scholarship' (Sandys, 3.401). Most of Thompson's published work was on Plato, although he never produced the complete edition or translation he is said to have contemplated. He published editions of the *Phaedrus* (1868) and the *Gorgias*

(1871), and a paper on the *Sophist* (*Transactions of the Cambridge Philological Society*, 10.146), in which he supported the genuineness of the dialogue and discussed the influence of the Eleatics on later Greek philosophy.

In March 1866, on the death of Dr William Whewell, Thompson was appointed master of Trinity College. Soon afterwards he married Frances Elizabeth, *née* Selwyn, the widow of George Peacock. He resigned the professorship of Greek in December of the same year. In 1867–8 he was vice-chancellor of the university. The twenty years of his mastership were years of activity and progress. Although he disliked the routine of ordinary business, he had a strong sense of the responsibilities of his office, and shrank from no effort where the good of his college was concerned. He was alert to the necessity for reform, and the statutes framed in 1872, as well as those which received the royal assent in 1882, owed much to his criticism and support. He died at the master's lodge at Trinity on 1 October 1886.

Thompson was tall, and bore himself with a stately dignity which was enhanced by singularly handsome features and, during the last years of his life, by silvery hair. His portrait by Sir Hubert von Herkomer (1881) gives a lifelike idea of him at that time, though the deep lines on the face and the sarcastic expression of the mouth are slightly exaggerated. When Thompson first saw the picture he is said to have exclaimed, 'Is it possible that I regard all mankind with such contempt?' Those who knew him superficially thought him cold, haughty, and sarcastic. In reality he was shy, diffident, and slightly nervous in society. But he had a quick appreciation of the weak points in an argument or a conversation, together with a keen literary faculty, so that he would rapidly gather up the results of a discussion into a sentence which fell, as though of itself, into an epigram. One of Thompson's sayings, 'We are none of us infallible, not even the youngest among us', has become proverbial. It was a reply made incidentally at one of the college meetings held for the alteration of statutes in 1877 or 1878, to a junior fellow who had proposed to throw upon the senior members of the society a new and somewhat onerous responsibility. Thompson had a wide knowledge of English and foreign literature; he travelled a good deal, and spoke French and German fluently; he was fond of art, and a good judge of pictures and sculpture.   J. W. CLARK, *rev.* RICHARD SMAIL

Sources *The Times* (2 Oct 1886) · H. Jackson, *The Athenaeum* (9 Oct 1886), 466 · J. E. Sandys, *A history of classical scholarship*, 3 (1908) · J. W. Clark, *Old friends at Cambridge and elsewhere* (1900) · D. A. Winstanley, *Later Victorian Cambridge* (1947) · J. J. Thomson, *Recollections and reflections* (1936) · M. L. Clarke, *Classical education in Britain, 1500–1900* (1959) · Venn, *Alum. Cant.* · *CGPLA Eng. & Wales* (1886) · Boase, *Mod. Eng. biog.*

Archives Trinity Cam., corresp. and papers | Bodl. Oxf., letters to Sir William Harcourt · Durham Cath. CL, letters to J. B. Lightfoot · Trinity Cam., corresp. with J. W. Blakesley · Trinity Cam., letters to William Whewell and others · Trinity Cam., letters to Henry Sidgwick · U. Leeds, Brotherton L., letters to Edmund Gosse

Likenesses S. Laurence, chalk drawing, 1841, NPG · S. Laurence, oils, 1869, Trinity Cam. · H. von Herkomer, oils, 1881, Trinity Cam. [*see illus.*] · J. Spedding, pencil drawing, Trinity Cam.

Wealth at death £22,548 13s. 10d.: resworn probate, July 1887, CGPLA Eng. & Wales (1886)

Thompson, William Marcus (1857–1907), journalist and barrister, born at Londonderry, northern Ireland, on 24 April 1857, was the second son in a family of four sons and four daughters of Moses Thompson, a customs official, and his wife, Elizabeth Smith. His family was of intensely Orange and anti-nationalist sympathies. After education at a private school, Thompson was for a time clerk in the office of James Hayden, solicitor. At the age of sixteen he contributed verses to the *Derry Journal* and developed an aptitude for journalism. He found employment on the *Belfast Morning News*, and then in 1877, at the age of twenty, and through the influence of Londonderry MP Sir Charles Lewis, bt, he joined the staff of the Conservative newspaper *The Standard* in London, writing chiefly on non-political themes. In 1884 he became a parliamentary reporter on the paper, which he served until 1890. He married on 3 April 1888 Mary, only daughter of Thomas Crosbie, editor and later proprietor of the *Cork Examiner*.

Despite his political background, Thompson developed a strong radicalism and an aggressive sympathy with the Irish nationalists. Having entered as a student at the Middle Temple in 1877, he was called to the bar in 1880, and formed a practice as the leading professional advocate of trade societies and those of radical views charged with political offences. As a member of the democratic club in Chancery Lane from 1886, he became closely associated with leading democrats, including John Burns, Robert Bontine Cunninghame Graham, and Bennet Burleigh. On 3 March 1886 he successfully defended Burns at the Old Bailey against the charge of inciting a crowd to violence at Trafalgar Square in February of that year. In January 1888 he again defended Burns, on a similar charge dating from November 1887, this time unsuccessfully as Burns was sentenced to six weeks' imprisonment. Thompson also appeared for the defence in the Walsall conspiracy case (March–April 1892). He represented many trade unions in the arbitration over the prolonged Grimsby fishing dispute (November 1901). During this period he contributed to *The Radical* newspaper (started in 1880), and on its demise to the weekly Sunday *Reynolds's Newspaper*, for which he wrote most of the leading articles as well as general contributions under the pseudonym of Dodo. He succeeded Edward Reynolds as editor of the paper in February 1894, and held the post until his death. The uncompromising critiques of privilege and status which had always characterized *Reynolds* were maintained during Thompson's editorship.

Thompson, who was a powerful platform speaker, was elected to the London county council as radical member for West Newington in 1895, but was defeated in his attempt to enter parliament for the Limehouse division of Tower Hamlets in July of that year. He was largely responsible for the establishment in 1900 of the National Democratic League, of which he was the first president. He was a founder member and promoter of the National Liberal Club (1882).

Thompson died of bronchitis and pneumonia on 28 December 1907 at his residence, 14 Tavistock Square, London, and was buried at Kensal Green cemetery. He was survived by his wife and one daughter.

W. B. OWEN, rev. MATTHEW LEE

Sources *The Times* (29 Dec 1907) • *Reynolds's Newspaper* (30 Dec 1907) • *Derry Journal* (30 Dec 1907) • J. Foster, *Men-at-the-bar: a biographical hand-list of the members of the various inns of court*, 2nd edn (1885) • J. Burgess, *Life of John Burns* (1911) • H. M. Hyndman, *Record of an adventurous life* (1911) • private information (1912) • CGPLA Eng. & Wales (1908)
Likenesses J. B. Yeats, oils, National Liberal Club, London • J. B. Yeats, portrait, priv. coll.
Wealth at death £1247 1s. 8d.: administration, 8 Feb 1908, CGPLA Eng. & Wales

Thoms, William John (1803–1885), antiquary, was born in Westminster, London, on 16 November 1803, the son of Nathaniel Thoms, a clerk in the Treasury and acting secretary of the first commission of revenue inquiry, and his wife, Ruth Ann. Thoms began his working life as a clerk in the secretary's office at Chelsea Hospital, a position he held until 1845. His principal interests, early conceived, were in literature and bibliography, especially the latter. In bibliography he received much help from Thomas Amyot, the antiquary, through whom he became acquainted with Francis Douce. Douce encouraged Thoms in his studies, lent him books and manuscripts from his great library in Gower Street, and gave him much assistance in editing his first publication, *Early Prose Romances*. This was composed of eleven tales, divided into three volumes published in 1827 and 1828. Henry Morley edited the collection in 1907, adding three tales. In 1828 Thoms married Laura (b. 1807/8), the youngest daughter of John Bernard *Sale [see under Sale, John], singer and composer; they had three sons and six daughters. Thoms's next publications were *Lays and Legends of France, Spain, Tartary, and Ireland* and *Lays and Legends of Germany*, in which he was assisted by Douce; both appeared in 1834. In 1832 he had tried his hand at periodical literature as the editor of *The Original*, a 'miscellany of humour, literature, and the fine arts'. It lasted a little over four months, running to twenty-two numbers.

In 1838 Thoms was elected a fellow of the Society of Antiquaries, and in the same year was appointed the first secretary of the Camden Society, a post he held until 1873. His *Book of the Court* (1838; 2nd edn 1844) gave an account of the nature, origin, duties, and privileges of the several ranks of the nobility, of the great offices of state, and the members of the royal household. He illustrated this treatise with anecdotes and quotations drawn from sources often inaccessible to the ordinary student. In 1839 he compiled for the Camden Society *Anecdotes and traditions illustrative of English history and literature from manuscript sources*, made up largely of Sir Nicholas L'Estrange's *Merry Passages and Jests*. In 1842 his edition of John Stow's *Survey of London* was published (it was reissued in 1876 without his sanction). In 1844 he prepared for the Early English Poetry series of the Percy Society an edition of *The history of Reynard the fox, with notes and an introductory sketch of the literary history of the romance* from the edition by William Caxton in 1481. There were twenty-five pages of appended notes,

William John Thoms (1803–1885), by Poulton, 1861

largely of a philological nature, and the dedication reads to 'Thomas Amyot by his Faithful and Attached Friend'.

Thoms was appointed a clerk of the House of Lords in 1845. Soon his reputation as an antiquary, coupled with his conversational charm, drew to his room a number of the more literate members of the house, and among those who came to enjoy learned conversations were Brougham, Lyndhurst, Macaulay, and Stanhope. The duties of his new position enabled Thoms to continue his literary endeavours, so that in 1846, under the pseudonym Ambrose Merton, he published two volumes of tales and ballads (reprinted in 1969). He went on to publish *Primeval Antiquities of Denmark* (1849), a translation of the work by Jens Jacob Asmussen Worsaae.

Shortly after this, Thoms turned his attention to another form of literary enterprise. As early as 1841 he had strongly felt the need for a periodical which would give antiquaries and bibliographers some avenue for making known to one another points on which they needed information. Hence, in that year, with the co-operation of his friend John Bruce (1802–1869), he projected such a periodical. It was entitled 'The Medium', and some specimen pages were actually set up in type. But Bruce was compelled for domestic reasons to move to the country, and the project was abandoned. In 1846, however, Thoms persuaded Charles Wentworth Dilke, proprietor of *The Athenaeum*, to open its columns 'to notices of old-world manners, customs, and popular superstitions'. He introduced the subject on 26 August in an article titled 'Folk lore', a term which he introduced into the English language. In the article he wrote that what in English would be designated 'Popular Antiquities, or Popular Literature' would be 'most aptly described by a good Saxon compound, Folk-Lore—the Lore of the People' (*The Athenaeum*).

The items submitted to *The Athenaeum* soon became so numerous, however, that they began to demand more space than was available, and so Thoms established a separate periodical: *Notes and Queries: a Medium of Inter-Communication for Literary Men, Artists, Antiquaries, Genealogists, etc.*, priced at 3*d.* with a stamped edition for four pence. The first number bore the date 10 November 1849 and included, among other notes, J. P. Collier on Shakespeare and deer stealing, and contributions by other members of the Camden Society, notably Thoms's friend John Bruce. Thoms's own contribution was entitled '"Pray remember the grotto!" on St James's Day'. The periodical proved popular, with a circulation of 600 copies after a few weeks. Thoms resigned as editor in September 1872, and was succeeded by John Doran. The periodical continued into the twenty-first century, and in establishing it Thoms had provided a valuable service to literary and historical scholarship, 'joining the efforts of amateur collectors with the disciplined researches of the anthropologists' (Spurgeon, 282). *Notes and Queries* played an important role in the founding of the English Dialect Society, and in the preparation of the *English Dialect Dictionary*, the *Dictionary of National Biography*, and the *Oxford English Dictionary*.

Charles Dickens admitted to being a 'diligent reader of … N and Q' (*Letters of Charles Dickens*, 10.461), and also told Thoms at the periodical's inception that 'It has given me, I assure you, great pleasure to see my good friend Captain Cuttle's name (and sentiment) appended to your very curious and interesting publication', referring to the motto of *Notes and Queries*, taken from *Dombey and Son*: 'When found, make a note of' (*Letters of Charles Dickens*, 6.108). Dickens was at this time answering Thoms's request for a donation towards the repair of Chaucer's tomb in Westminster Abbey (Thoms was secretary of the committee formed for this project, and among its other members were John Payne Collier, Peter Cunningham, and Sir Frederick Madden). The two men went on to become better acquainted, with Dickens visiting Thoms for a holiday in the summer of 1862 (*Letters of Charles Dickens*, 9.551, n. 4), and later thanking Thoms for a pre-publication copy of his *Three Notelets on Shakespeare* (1865).

This latter work was produced during Thoms's tenure as deputy librarian of the House of Lords—he had been appointed in 1863, and held the post until three years before his death. The *Three Notelets* consisted of 'Shakespeare in Germany', 'Folk-lore of Shakespeare', and 'Was Shakespeare ever a soldier?', copiously annotated essays originally published in 1840, 1847, and 1859. Thoms dedicated the *Three Notelets* to his wife, 'Who in Herself Realizes Many of Shakespeare's Types of Womanly Excellence'. He reprinted in 1867 in book form four articles from *Notes and Queries* with some additions, followed in

1872 by a reprint from *Notes and Queries* of 'The death warrant of Charles I, another historic doubt', demonstrating the difficulty in obtaining the necessary signatures for Charles I's death warrant, and the irregularity of the expedients to which army leaders were reduced. His iconoclastic treatise entitled *Human Longevity, its Facts and its Fictions* (1873) raised a storm of protest by its contention that the authentic cases in which human life had been prolonged to a hundred years and upwards were extremely rare.

William John Thoms died in London at his house at 40 St George's Square, Belgrave Road, on 15 August 1885, and was buried in Brompton cemetery.   ARTHUR SHERBO

Sources *DNB* · *The Athenaeum* (26 Aug 1846) · D. A. Spurgeon, 'Notes and Queries', *British literary magazines*, ed. A. Sullivan, [3]: *The Victorian and Edwardian age, 1837–1913* (1984), 281–5 · F. Algar, 'W. J. Thoms: our first editor', *N&Q*, 198 (1953), 125 · W. H. Holden, 'W. J. Thoms: our first editor', *N&Q*, 198 (1953), 223 · W. J. Thoms, 'The story of *Notes and Queries*', *N&Q*, 5th ser., 6 (1876), 1, 41, 101, 221; 5th ser., 7 (1877), 1, 222, 303 · *The letters of Charles Dickens*, ed. M. House, G. Storey, and others, 6, 9–10 (1988–98)

Archives BL, letter to Sir Frederic Madden, Egerton MSS 2840–2848, *passim* · Hunt. L., corresp. · U. Edin. L., corresp. with J. O. Halliwell-Phillipps

Likenesses Poulton, carte-de-visite, 1861, NPG [*see illus.*]

Wealth at death £6946 4*s.* 11*d.*: probate, 29 Aug 1885, *CGPLA Eng. & Wales*

Thomson. *See also* Thompson.

Thomson, Sir Adam (1926–2000), airline executive, was born on 7 July 1926 at 206 Clarkston Road, Cathcart, Glasgow, the only son and younger child of Francis Thomson, a railway shunter on the London, Midland and Scottish Railway, and his wife, Jemima (*b.* 1888), *née* Rodger, a shopkeeper. He was educated at Rutherglen Academy and Coatbridge Technical College. After being turned down for age reasons by the RAF in 1943 he joined the Royal Navy as a pilot recruit, and entered the Royal Technical College in Glasgow (later Strathclyde University), where he studied engineering until he was called up for the Fleet Air Arm pilots' course in 1944. By the time he had qualified, in 1945, after flying training in Canada, he was too late to see active service. After demobilization in 1947 he qualified as a civilian pilot and started his own airline, Amphibian Air Charter, with one biplane, taking holidaymakers on short excursions. This enterprise was short-lived, and from 1947 to 1950 he worked as a pilot on the Isle of Wight, taking summer visitors on joyrides and stunt flights; from 1949 he worked for Newman Airways flying between the Isle of Wight and the Channel Islands. On 17 July 1948 he married Dawn Elizabeth (*b.* 1926/7), a nursery nurse, daughter of George Burt of Surbiton, Surrey, a contractor's clerk; they had two sons.

For the next decade Thomson was employed as a pilot, including a period with British European Airways (BEA) in Glasgow from 1951 to 1953, and with the West African Airways Corporation from 1953 to 1954 in Lagos, Nigeria. As an employee of British Aviation Services he flew for Silver City Airways on its cross-channel service, and from 1954 for Britavia, flying troops to east Africa and Singapore. But

Sir Adam Thomson (1926–2000), by John Wonnacott, 1985–6

he still aimed to start his own business, and in 1961, with John de la Haye, a former BEA steward, as managing director, he founded Caledonian Airways (Prestwick) Ltd, with one aircraft, a DC-7, leased from Sabena, and himself as the only pilot. He decided that the airline should have a strong Scottish identity: the company was registered in Scotland, and the planes carried the symbol of the lion rampant of Scotland. The cabin crew wore tartan uniforms, and in 1970 he formed a pipe band, the Pipes and Drums of Caledonian, which turned out on special occasions. A pioneer of charter flights, he focused on the transatlantic market, as well as European package holidays. He targeted ethnic organizations, clubs for Americans and Canadians of British origin who wanted to go home cheaply to visit their families. His first transatlantic flight was on 21 December 1961, advertised as the first ever flight to the United States by Scotland's own international airline; it carried members of the St Margaret's Guild of Scotland to visit their relations in New York, returning with a group from the Lennox Clan Albion in New York on their way to spend hogmanay with their families in Scotland.

By 1969, when the report of the Edwards committee of inquiry into civil aviation, *British Air Transport in the Seventies*, was published, Caledonian Airways had built up a flourishing charter business, operating mainly from Gatwick airport, south of London, and had taken delivery of its first jet aircraft, in 1967. Edwards recommended that a 'second force' airline should be created through amalgamating two or more existing carriers, to compete on scheduled routes with the new state airline, British Airways (BA), which was to be formed in 1972 through amalgamating British Overseas Airways Corporation (BOAC) and BEA. Thomson's bid succeeded, and in October 1970 Caledonian Airways bought British United Airways, taking the name British Caledonian (BCAL) the following year. He became chairman and managing director of the new company, and won the first businessman of the year award in December 1970. As part of the deal BOAC had to surrender some of its scheduled routes to BCAL, and the Ghana and Nigeria routes were transferred in 1971, as well as the Libya route, while BCAL also took over the BEA services to Paris (Le Bourget). BCAL was awarded licences to operate services to New York and Los Angeles in 1972, and the airline was allowed further expansion in 1973 when it was given the route to Houston via Boston and Atlanta, the route to Singapore via Bahrain, and the London–Toronto route.

Despite set-backs in the 1970s—including the effects of the oil crisis and the recession of 1973 to 1974, and the loss of all the north American routes (except Houston) in 1975 when the government ended the practice of allowing two British airlines to operate on the same route—British Caledonian managed to survive. As directed by the secretary of state for trade, it concentrated on its west African and south American services, inaugurating new routes to Caracas, Bogota, and Lima in 1976, and it took delivery of four new DC-10 wide-bodied jets for long-haul services. It won the Hong Kong route in 1980, and in 1981 opened Caledonian House, its new headquarters near Gatwick airport. Most of its business was now on scheduled routes, with very little charter work. But when in 1979 the new Conservative government announced plans to privatize British Airways, Thomson could see that the future of British Caledonian was threatened. Sir John (later Lord) King became chairman of BA in 1981, with responsibility for preparing the airline for privatization, and he managed to write off the £545 million deficit for 1981–2. It became British Airways plc in 1984, and was floated in 1987. Meanwhile, British Caledonian suffered a series of set-backs as a result of the international situation: it lost the Buenos Aires route in 1982 because of the Falklands War, flights to Tripoli were suspended in 1986 when the USA began bombing raids on Libya, and the Chernobyl nuclear disaster in 1986 as well as the fear of terrorism cut the number of Americans flying across the Atlantic. In addition, the collapse in oil prices affected flights to Lagos and Houston. As a final blow Airlink, the very profitable BCAL helicopter service between Gatwick and Heathrow airports, which started in 1978, was closed down in 1987 on environmental grounds. But Thomson believed that the turning point came in 1984, when the government turned down the recommendation of the Civil Aviation Authority to allocate a significant number of BA routes to BCAL, and to allow BCAL to fly from Heathrow. BA was the only UK airline allowed to operate flights from Heathrow, the biggest international hub in the world, and it was hard for BCAL to compete on equal terms. Thomson always believed that if BCAL had been allowed a wider route network and given access to Heathrow, it might not have faced such difficulties.

British Airways made a take-over bid for British Caledonian in 1987, and when the Department of Trade and Industry referred this to the Monopolies and Mergers Commission, Thomson entered into negotiations with Scandinavian Airlines (SAS) for it to become a major shareholder in BCAL, in order to keep the company going. But after the merger was approved BA made a higher offer, and Thomson and the board had no alternative but to recommend that the shareholders accept the £250 million offer. Although British Caledonian had been voted airline of the year five times by travel writers, in the end it was unable to survive in competition with British Airways, backed as it was by the government. Thomson resigned in 1988 when British Caledonian was absorbed into British Airways.

Thomson was appointed CBE in 1976 and knighted in 1983. He served on the council of the Institute of Directors from 1972 and was its chairman from 1988 to 1991, and he was a director of the Bank of Scotland from 1982 to 1991. He was awarded honorary degrees by the universities of Glasgow, Sussex, and Strathclyde. In 1990 he published his autobiography, *High Risk: the Politics of the Air*. He died on 23 May 2000 in Downs Christian Nursing Home, Laburnum Avenue, Hove, Sussex. ANNE PIMLOTT BAKER

Sources A. Thomson, *High risk: the politics of the air* (1990) · *British Airways plc and British Caledonian Group plc: a report on the proposed merger*, Monopolies and Mergers Commission (1987) · *The Times* (25 May 2000) · *The Scotsman* (27 May 2000) · *Daily Telegraph* (31 May 2000) · *The Guardian* (1 June 2000) · *WW* · b. cert. · m. cert. · d. cert.
Likenesses J. Wonnacott, oils, 1985–6, Scot. NPG [*see illus.*] · J. Wonnacott, pencil drawing, Scot. NPG · photograph, repro. in *Daily Telegraph*
Wealth at death £247,098—gross; £241,478—net: probate, 5 March 2001, *CGPLA Eng. & Wales*

Thomson, Sir Alexander (1744?–1817), judge, was born and educated in Wolverhampton. His parentage is unknown. He entered Lincoln's Inn on 6 November 1764 and was called on 6 November 1769. Practising in chancery, mostly as an equity draftsman for he had no pretensions to oratory and was rather diffident, he came to the notice of John Russell, fourth duke of Bedford, through his efficient conduct of several suits for him and became auditor of the Bedford estates, a position he did not relinquish until he became a judge.

Thomson probably owed his advancement to the patronage of Lord Chancellor Thurlow, an intimate friend who had a high opinion of his talents. He reached the bench by way of the court of chancery, becoming first a master (11 May 1782) and then accountant-general (4 January 1786). From 14 December 1782 he was also a bencher of his inn. He was made a baron of the exchequer on 9 February 1787, having been knighted on 7 February, and became a serjeant in the same month. The barrister Nicholas Ridley commented that Thomson and his colleague Nash Grose were 'both men of abilities: and it ought to be mentioned to the Chancellor's credit that they are neither of them indebted to Parliamentary influence for their promotion' (D. Lemmings, *Professors of the Law*, 2000, 279).

Thomson remained in the court of exchequer for thirty years and came to be well regarded for his knowledge of the law and the quality of his judgments, so that when he eventually succeeded Sir Vicary Gibbs as chief baron on 23

February 1814 his promotion was considered well merited. Thomson and the three puisne barons were seldom in disagreement, except for Sir George Wood's occasional dissents, usually in tithe cases. He was generally cautious about changing the practice of the court, was scrupulous in holding the balance between crown and subject in revenue cases (*A.-G. v. Norstedt*, 1816, for example), and in *R. v. Wilton* (1816) took a strong line against the abuse of extents by crown debtors to recover their own debts, a practice soon afterwards curbed by statute. Other notable decisions were *A.-G. v. Holford* (1815) on the equitable doctrine of conversion, *Compton v. Stephens* (1814) on easements, and *Dawson v. Duke of Norfolk* (1815) on prescriptive rights. Increasing business on the common-law side caused delays in equity cases and a short act, passed just before Thomson died, with the aim of speeding up the equity side unfortunately proved misconceived and led suitors to desert the court.

Thomson was reputed to be learned in scholastic literature and was amiable, sociable, and jocular. Owen's portrait of 1812 shows a full, rather fleshy face beneath bushy eyebrows, redolent of the 'table gratifications' (Farington, *Diary*, 14.4963) whose enjoyment was said to have contributed to his demise. He missed the whole of the Hilary term of 1817 endeavouring vainly to recover his health in Bath, where he died at his lodgings in South Parade on 15 April. He did not marry and by failing to update the will he had long before made in favour of his sister Mary, who predeceased him, he is said by Hayes and Jarman to have precipitated a lawsuit in chancery.   PATRICK POLDEN

Sources Foss, *Judges*, vol. 8 · *Strictures on the lives and characters of the most eminent lawyers of the present day* (1790) · G. Price, *Reports of cases argued and determined in the court of exchequer (and the exchequer chamber) from Easter term 1814*, 13 vols. (1816–32) · *Annual Biography and Obituary*, 2 (1818) · Farington, *Diary*, vol. 14 · *Hayes and Jarman's concise forms of wills*, ed. C. E. Shebbeare, 17th edn (1947) · A. Polson, *Law and lawyers, or, Sketches and illustrations of legal history and biography*, 2 vols. (1840) · Sainty, *Judges* · *Law List* (1775) · *Staffordshire Advertiser* (19 April 1817) · W. P. Baildon, ed., *The records of the Honorable Society of Lincoln's Inn: the black books*, 4 (1902) · will, PRO, PROB 11/1592, fol. 275
Likenesses H. H. Meyer, mezzotint, 1812 (after portrait by W. Owen), BM, NPG · J. Opie, oils, 1814, Lincoln's Inn, London · T. Rowlandson, caricature, Laing Art Gallery, Newcastle upon Tyne
Wealth at death £21,399 13s. 6d. residue of personalty: PRO, death duty registers, IR 26/723, fol. 386; will, PRO, PROB 11/1592, fol. 275

Thomson, Alexander (1763–1803), poet, was born on 7 August 1763. He resided in Edinburgh and was a close friend of Robert Anderson (1750–1830). Thomson wrote *The Choice* (1788), and (his two best-known works) *Whist* (1791) and *An Essay on Novels* (1793). His other publications included *The Paradise of Taste* (1796) and *The British Parnassus at the Close of the Eighteenth Century* (1801). He also published *The German Miscellany* (1796), consisting of translations from Kotzebue and Meissner, and translated Kotzebue's comedy, *The East Indian* (1799). Anderson was with Thomson at his house in Buccleuch Street, Edinburgh, when he suffered a stroke from which he died on 7 November 1803,

leaving a widow and six daughters. At the time of his death he had been working on a history of Scottish poetry which remained unpublished.

E. I. CARLYLE, *rev.* SARAH COUPER

Sources GM, 1st ser., 73 (1803), 1096 · Nichols, *Illustrations*, 7.78, 122–3, 8.343–4 · D. E. Baker, *Biographia dramatica, or, A companion to the playhouse*, rev. I. Reed, new edn, rev. S. Jones, 1/2 (1812), 710 · [D. Rivers], *Literary memoirs of living authors of Great Britain*, 2 (1798), 307

Thomson, Alexander [called Greek Thomson] (1817–1875), architect, was born on 9 April 1817 at Endrick Cottage, Balfron, Stirlingshire, the seventeenth of the twenty children of John Thomson (1757/8–1824), bookkeeper at Kirkman and Findlay's cotton spinning mill at Balfron, and the ninth of his second wife, Elizabeth Cooper (d. 1830), whose father, George Cooper, was a schoolmaster in Aberdeen and whose brother became the Burgher minister in Balfron. John Thomson's widow moved to Glasgow with her younger children in 1825 and Alexander eventually began work in a writer's office before his talent as a draughtsman was noticed by the Glasgow architect Robert Foote, who took him as an apprentice. Thomson then worked in the office of the architect John Baird I (1798–1859), with whom he stayed for about ten years, becoming his chief draughtsman. In 1847, in a joint ceremony, Thomson and the unrelated John Baird II (1816–1893) married Jane Nicholson (1825–1899) and Jessie Nicholson (1827–1866), daughters of the London architect Michael Angelo *Nicholson (1794–1841) [see under Nicholson, Peter (1765–1844)].

Thomson set up in independent practice in Glasgow in 1848, when he entered into partnership with his brother-in-law John Baird II. This partnership was amicably terminated in 1857, when Thomson was joined by his younger brother George (1819–1878), who was an architect who had also worked in the office of John Baird I. In 1871 George left Glasgow to work as a missionary in the Cameroons, and in 1873 Thomson took Robert Turnbull (1839–1905) as a partner; the firm became known as A. and G. Thomson and Turnbull.

Baird and Thomson began by building villas in the new suburbs of Glasgow and along the Clyde estuary; these were designed in a variety of styles, including the Gothic and Romanesque. However, by the mid-1850s Thomson had developed the refined and abstracted Grecian manner with which he would become associated. This was employed for his unique double villa in Langside, Glasgow (1856–7), in which two identical semi-detached houses faced in opposite directions, and in Holmwood House in Cathcart, near Glasgow (1857–8), his finest villa, built for the paper manufacturer James Couper. Thomson's first biographer, the Glasgow architect Thomas Gildard, wrote of Holmwood that, 'If architecture be poetry in stone-and-lime—a great temple an epic—this exquisite little gem, at once classic and picturesque, is as complete, self-contained, and polished as a sonnet', recognizing that he had done something unprecedented (Gildard). Although he was influenced by the neo-classical work of the Prussian state architect Karl Friedrich Schinkel, Thomson

Alexander Thomson [Greek Thomson] (1817–1875), by unknown photographer, 1850s?

beginning, in the councils of eternity, the laws which regulate this art were framed. ('Presidential address to the Glasgow Institute of Architects', *The Architect*, 15 April 1871, 198; repr. in Stamp, *Lectures*, 101)

In this insistence upon eternal laws Thomson's approach to architecture verged on the mystical, and, as a devout Presbyterian, he was strongly influenced by the paintings and engravings of John Martin, which depicted the exotic architecture of the cities of the Old Testament with a remorseless horizontality receding towards infinity. Yet, from such images, he evolved a successful modern commercial architecture for Glasgow. More than any other architect, Thomson gave a distinct character to the second city of the British empire in his designs for warehouses and commercial buildings, and for terraces of houses and tenements. In all these he arrived at novel treatments for urban façades, in which depth and variety were achieved by the unusual arrangements of trabeated masonry combined with large windows of plate glass. The tragedy, however, is that for all his admiration of the 'imperishable thought' of the Egyptians, Thomson's achievement was constructed of weak and friable Giffnock sandstone.

Thomson's commercial designs included Grecian Buildings in Sauchiehall Street (1867–8), the Cairney Building in Bath Street (1860–61; dem.), the block in Gordon Street which he owned with his brother (1859; altered), and Egyptian Halls in Union Street (1870–72), which the London-based *Architect* noted was 'in Mr Thomson's well-known "Egyptian-Greek" style—a style which he has made his own, and in which he has no rival' (*The Architect*, 13 July 1872). Thomson's domestic work included Moray Place in Strathbungo (1859–61), where the architect himself lived from 1861 until his death, Eton Terrace in Oakfield Avenue (1862–4), and Great Western Terrace (1867–77), arguably the finest in the city in its grandeur and austerity. Gildard said of it that 'the windows have no dressings, but Greek goddesses could afford to appear undressed' (Gildard). Queen's Park Terrace in Eglinton Street (1856–60; dem.) was highly influential on the design of Glasgow's many tenements.

In addition, Thomson designed monumental urban churches for United Presbyterian congregations, which the American historian Henry Russell Hitchcock considered were 'three of the finest Romantic Classical churches in the world' (Hitchcock, 63). Of these, the only intact survivor is the St Vincent Street Church (1857–9), with its tall and exotic steeple. In this building, stone construction was combined with cast-iron columns and large sheets of glazing were applied directly to the masonry. Thomson's first church, the Caledonia Road Church (1855–7), was gutted by fire in 1965. His most extraordinary and innovative ecclesiastical building, the Queen's Park Church (1868–9), was Scotland's worst architectural loss of the Second World War; its richly decorated interior moved the painter Ford Madox Brown to exclaim 'Well done Glasgow!' and to put it 'above everything I have seen in modern Europe' (*Glasgow Evening Times*, 9 Oct 1893).

Owing to the loss of most of his drawings (a few remain

would seem to have been the first to apply picturesque principles of composition to the Greek style in his villas. Holmwood was also remarkable for its scheme of interior painted decoration, all designed by the architect along with furniture, carpets, and other furnishings.

Thomson came to reject the use of the arch, whether pointed or round, and held that the trabeated language of the Greeks could be the basis of a modern architecture which incorporated iron construction, arguing that 'Stonehenge is really more scientifically constructed than York Minster' ('An inquiry as to the appropriateness of the Gothic style for the proposed buildings for the University of Glasgow', *Proceedings of the Glasgow Architectural Society*, 6–7, 1865–7, 47; repr. in Stamp, *Lectures*, 67). He was never, however, a conventional Greek revivalist, and his work was conspicuous for the originality with which he adapted and combined precedents from Greece, Egypt, and elsewhere. For all his admiration of such buildings as Thomas Hamilton's Royal High School in Edinburgh, he argued that the promoters of the Greek revival had failed, 'because they could not see through the material into the laws upon which that architecture rested. They failed to master their style, and so became its slaves' (*Art and Architecture*, 1874, 8; repr. in Stamp, *Lectures*, 147). He was insistent that

architecture in its highest forms does not bear the least resemblance to anything in nature, that it is peculiarly and exclusively a human work; and yet, long before man came to need it, long before the foundation of the world, at the very in the Mitchell Library in Glasgow) and all of his professional papers, it is not possible to catalogue the whole range of Thomson's artistic activity. What is clear is that his career was to some extent paradoxical as, for all his intense idealism, Thomson was a successful commercial architect willing, on occasion, to employ the styles of which he theoretically disapproved. It also must be admitted that his insistence on such features as low-pitched roofs was not always wholly practical in the climate of the west of Scotland. It is clear, however, that contemporaries regretted that he was never awarded a commission for a public building commensurate with his talents. Thomson's designs for the Albert Memorial in London and for the South Kensington Museum must have seemed unfashionable in England to the point of perversity in the 1860s and only Glasgow, perhaps, could allow his idiosyncratic approach to flourish. Yet he was denied the opportunity of submitting a design for the new buildings on Gilmorehill for the University of Glasgow when the commission was awarded, without competition, to the London architect George Gilbert Scott. Thomson ridiculed the universalist claims of the Gothic revival in general and Scott's design in particular in his published lecture of 1866.

Thomson was much involved in the affairs of the Glasgow Architectural Society and the Glasgow Institute of Architects, and served as president of both. In 1874 he delivered four lectures on art and architecture to the Glasgow School of Art and Haldane Academy; these covered the creations of the Egyptians, Greeks, and Romans and essentially constituted his architectural testament. Further lectures on medieval architecture were planned but never delivered owing to Thomson's death, from asthma and heart failure, at his home at 1 Moray Place, Strathbungo, on 22 March 1875. He had been ill for some years and increasingly delegated his professional practice to Turnbull. Had he survived the severe winter of 1874–5, Thomson planned to make his first ever trip abroad, to Italy, to recover his health.

Thomson's achievement was widely recognized at the time of his death and a memorial fund was established. This was used to present a marble bust of the architect, carved by his friend the sculptor John Mossman, to the Glasgow corporation galleries in 1877, and to endow a travelling studentship, awarded first in 1887, to the architect and historian William J. Anderson, and second, three years later, to Charles Rennie Mackintosh.

His pupil (William?) Clunas later recorded that

Alexander Thomson was, in appearance, a distinguished-looking man, of a good average height, stout, well and proportionally made, a fine manly countenance with a profuse head of hair … for the strictly professional side of his business he had but little capacity—punctual, he was not, neither was he persevering. You could not say he was indolent, but there was a dreamy unrest about him even when engaged on important work which caused matter-of-fact people who were waiting for further details some annoyance. But when he did plunge into a piece of work his attitude was that of a real devotee—patient, forceful, and painstaking. (Clunas, 'My impressions')

Despite this, his estate was valued for Scottish inventory duty at £15,395 5s. 3d. He was buried in the Southern Necropolis in Glasgow; the plot is now unmarked. Of the twelve children he had with Jane Nicholson, seven survived infancy.

GAVIN STAMP

Sources private information (2004) [Mrs W. L. Stewart] • J. Stark, 'Memoir', Glasgow Institute of Architects • R. McFadzean, *The life and work of Alexander Thomson* (1979) • T. Gildard, '"Greek" Thomson', *Proceedings of the Philosophical Society of Glasgow*, 19 (1888), 1–27; repr. in *Alexander Thomson Society Newsletter*, 20 (Jan 1998), 2–15 • G. Law, 'Greek Thomson', *ArchR*, 115 (1954), 307–16 • G. Stamp and S. McKinstry, eds., *'Greek' Thomson* (1994) • A. Gomme and D. Walker, *Architecture of Glasgow*, rev. edn (1987) • H. R. Hitchcock, *Architecture: nineteenth and twentieth centuries*, 2nd edn (1963), 63 • G. Stamp, *Alexander 'Greek' Thomson* (1999) • G. Stamp, ed., 'The light of truth and beauty': the lectures of Alexander 'Greek' Thomson, architect, 1817–1875 (1999) • W. (?) Clunas, 'My impressions and recollections of Greek Thomson', NL Scot., Ross MS 694

Archives NRA, priv. coll., letters

Likenesses J. Mossman, bust, c.1840, National Trust for Scotland • photograph, 1850–1859?, repro. in McFadzean, *Life and work* [see illus.] • photograph, c.1860, priv. coll. • J. Mossman, marble bust, 1877, Kelvingrove Art Gallery, Glasgow; plaster cast copy, Royal Incorporated Institute of Architects, Scotland

Wealth at death £15,395 5s. 3d.: confirmation, 16 April 1877, *CCI*

Thomson, Allen (1809–1884), anatomist and embryologist, was born on 2 April 1809 in Edinburgh, the only surviving son of John *Thomson (1765–1846), surgeon, and his second wife, Margaret, daughter of John *Millar (1735–1801), professor of jurisprudence at Glasgow University. William *Thomson (1802–1852) was his half-brother.

Allen Thomson's schooling took place at the high school of Edinburgh, after which, at his father's behest, he attended Edinburgh University from 1824 to study medicine. He also attended classes at the Edinburgh extramural medical school. He graduated MD from Edinburgh University in 1830. His graduation thesis was entitled 'De evolutione cordis in animalibus vertebratis', revealing his early interest in what was to become his life's work. As an undergraduate he was president of the Royal Medical Society. His father had a profound influence in Thomson's choice of career, and as it was Thomson senior's 'great desire that he should become a teacher of anatomy, and devote himself to anatomical and physiological pursuits' (Aitken, xiii), Thomson travelled to Europe to undertake further anatomical and physiological study, visiting anatomical and pathological collections in Amsterdam, Strasbourg, and Berlin.

Thomson returned to Edinburgh in 1831 and immediately took up teaching. He entered into partnership with William Sharpey, the two offering a course in anatomy and physiology. Sharpey taught the anatomical portion of the course, Thomson the physiological. Thomson became a fellow of the Royal College of Surgeons of Edinburgh in 1832. His partnership with Sharpey lasted until 1836, being interrupted in 1833 by a trip Thomson undertook with his father to London and Europe for further anatomical study. In London, some indication of the direction Allen Thomson was expected to take surfaced when he was introduced to Lord Melbourne by Lady Holland with

Allen Thomson (1809–1884), by Sir Daniel Macnee, 1878

the words 'Melbourne, allow me to introduce to you the future Professor of Anatomy in the University of Glasgow' (Aitken, xvi).

In 1836 the Sharpey–Thomson partnership was dissolved because Sharpey had been appointed professor of anatomy at University College, London. Thomson gave up teaching temporarily at this time because of ill health. He entered the service of the duke of Bedford as physician to his family in that year, and remained in post until 1837, travelling with the family to the highlands in 1836 and 1837, and accompanying the duke on his European tour. Correspondence between Thomson and Sharpey during this period shows that Thomson had no intention of making ducal service his long-term career, and that he wished to resume teaching when he was able.

In session 1837–8 Thomson began to teach again in Edinburgh, and was elected a fellow of the Royal Society of that city in 1838. In 1839 he was appointed professor of anatomy at Marischal College in Aberdeen. He remained at Marischal College until 1841, when he returned to Edinburgh as extramural lecturer in anatomy. His reasons for leaving Aberdeen are unclear, but he may not have been earning enough from his anatomy classes, which were small, and there has also been conjecture that he wished to return to Edinburgh to await the post of professor of the institutes of medicine (physiology) at the university becoming vacant. This it did in 1842, with the resignation of William Pulteney Alison, and Thomson was appointed to the post. One of the innovations he introduced on his return was to use the microscope in the teaching of anatomy. He commenced a course of weekly lectures on microscopic anatomy in the summer of 1842.

Throughout his career Thomson was regarded as a great teacher, who utilized fully contemporary scientific advances in his lectures. Professor John Struthers of Aberdeen remarked that, 'his abilities as a teacher and observer were fully recognised by the medical profession of Edinburgh' (Struthers, 1154). Thomson was also possessed of great artistic talent, and his lectures were well illustrated by chalk drawings. His approach to lecturing was systematic and methodical, with perhaps his main fault being that he gave no clear lead to the students as to his own views when lecturing on areas which were the subject of much scientific debate. He was, however, very highly regarded by his students, in whom he had a great interest.

Thomson remained at Edinburgh until 1848, in which year he was elected a fellow of the Royal Society. In that same year, after much intense politicking, he was appointed regius professor of anatomy at the University of Glasgow in succession to Professor James Jeffray, who had held that chair since 1790. Under Jeffray the teaching of anatomy in the University of Glasgow had fallen into disrepute, but the arrival of Thomson reinvigorated the subject, and he introduced a more up-to-date view of anatomy, and of its teaching. Thomson's appointment did not meet with the complete approval of his fellow professors, who have been described as a 'notoriously conservative, self-perpetuating clique' (Jacyna, xxiv). Indeed Thomson was antipathetic to any suggestion of nepotism or favouritism in the appointment of chairs in Glasgow University and fought strongly against such means being used to fill the chair of chemistry, in 1852, and the regius chair of surgery, in 1859.

Thomson, as well as teaching, was much involved in the administration of Glasgow University during his time there. His greatest contribution to the university's welfare was made during its move from the High Street in the 1860s to Gilmorehill. In 1864 he was appointed convenor of the removal committee, charged with overseeing the move. On 6 June 1866 he cut the first sod at the new site in Gilmorehill. He was also one of the main planners in the construction of the Western Infirmary in Glasgow, opened in 1874. He represented Glasgow University on the General Medical Council from 1859 until 1877. In 1871 the University of Edinburgh conferred upon him the degree of LLD, as did Glasgow University in 1877. He was awarded the degree of DCL by Oxford University in 1882.

Anatomical and embryological research featured heavily in Thomson's life, and he made a number of original contributions to the scientific literature, although he made no one great eponymous discovery. He edited a number of textbooks, including the seventh, eighth, and ninth editions of Quain's *System of Human Anatomy*. In 1859 he also published a second edition of his father's *Life of William Cullen*. In the late 1840s Thomson married Nina Jane, daughter of Ninian Hill, writer to the signet, Edinburgh, and the sister of his half-brother William's wife, Eliza. They had one son.

Having held his professorship for twenty-nine years Thomson retired from Glasgow University in 1877 with the reputation 'throughout the scientific world as one of the most careful, judicious, accurate, and learned of investigators and teachers of his favourite subjects' (Aitken, xxii). He and his wife went to London to live with their son, John Millar Thomson. He remained in London until his death. Late in 1883 he suffered a short episode of glaucoma in his left eye for which an iridectomy was performed. Shortly after this, however, he lost the sight in his right eye. He began to suffer from local paralyses, which became more generalized. His breathing finally became obstructed, and he died on 21 March 1884 at his address, 66 Palace Terrace Gardens, Kensington, London, leaving a widow.

JAMES BEATON

Sources W. A. [W. Aitken], *PRS*, 42 (1887), xi–xxviii · L. S. Jacyna, ed., *A tale of three cities: the correspondence of William Sharpey and Allen Thomson* (1989) · J. Struthers, *Edinburgh Medical Journal*, 29 (1883–4), 1151–62 · D. Murray, *Memories of the old college of Glasgow: some chapters in the history of the university* (1927) · J. Coutts, *A history of the University of Glasgow* (1909) · *BMJ* (5 April 1884), 699 · *The Lancet* (12 April 1884), 685–7 · *Glasgow Medical Journal*, new ser., 21 (1884), 388–90 · *DNB* · bap. reg. Scot. · *CGPLA Eng. & Wales* (1884)

Archives NL Scot., corresp. and papers · RCS Eng., journal, corresp., MSS · U. Glas., corresp. and papers · U. Glas., papers and lists of anatomical preparations · U. Glas. L., corresp. and papers | Wellcome L., corresp. with W. Sharpey and E. A. Sharpey-Schafer

Likenesses D. Macnee, oils, 1877, U. Glas. · D. Macnee, oils, 1878, Royal College of Surgeons, Edinburgh [*see illus.*] · W. H. Townsend, lithograph, Wellcome L. · photograph (after mezzotint), Wellcome L.

Wealth at death £3771 12s. 8d.: probate, 22 May 1884, *CGPLA Eng. & Wales*

Thomson, Andrew Mitchell (1779–1831), Church of Scotland minister and journalist, was born on 11 July 1779 in the manse at Sanquhar, Dumfriesshire, the third of four children of John Thomson (1741–1822), Church of Scotland minister, and his first wife, Helen Forrest (d. 1801). His father, a devout evangelical, was translated to Markinch, Fife, in 1785 and to New Greyfriars, Edinburgh, in 1800. Thomson was educated at the Markinch parish school (from 1785), and at the University of Edinburgh (1796–9, and later, 1810–11, to complete the MA). He was licensed to preach in the Church of Scotland by the presbytery of Kelso on 7 October 1800, served briefly as a private tutor and school teacher, and was ordained to the ministry of the rural parish of Sprouston, in Roxburghshire, on 11 March 1802. In that year, on 26 April, he married Jane Carmichael (d. 1840), of Greenock; they had ten children (seven of whom survived Thomson). Their eldest son was the composer John *Thomson. In 1808, Thomson was translated to the East Church, Perth; two years later, he was presented by the magistrates and town council to succeed his father as minister of the Edinburgh parish of New Greyfriars.

From the beginning of his ministry, Thomson was active in ecclesiastical politics, and joined with the evangelical, or popular, party in the church courts, in opposition to the ascendant moderate party. He combined his evangelicalism with whig political commitments. In 1805, he championed John Leslie, the whig natural philosopher, in a successful contest against the moderate party candidate, Thomas MacKnight, for the Edinburgh chair of mathematics. Two years later, Thomson joined with David Brewster and several young whig evangelicals in commencing the multi-volume *Edinburgh Encyclopedia*, for which Thomson eventually wrote forty-three articles. In 1810, together with several whig evangelicals, Thomson founded the *Edinburgh Christian Instructor*, a monthly magazine intended to do in the religious world what the whig *Edinburgh Review* was doing in the political world—that is, offer a lively critique of the established order in church and state, and press for the reform of abuses and an increased recognition of the popular voice. Thomson edited the *Christian Instructor* for twenty years, making it an organ for the rising evangelical party.

In 1814 Thomson was translated by the Edinburgh magistrates and town council to the splendid St George's Church, recently completed in the prosperous New Town. It was a controversial appointment, as many of the wealthy parishioners were cool toward evangelicalism, which they associated with enthusiasm. In the event, Thomson soon attracted a large and influential congregation. He delivered carefully composed sermons, employing a refined language and emphasizing practical Christian virtues, which appealed to the Edinburgh élite. He also won favour through his regular pastoral visiting. Thomson was a cultivated man, with a particular love and talent for music, and he insisted on a high quality of singing in worship. In 1820 he published a collection of psalm tunes, *Sacred Harmony*, which contained thirteen original compositions of his own, including the popular 'Redemption' and 'St George's, Edinburgh'. His keen interest in furthering popular education led him in 1823 to establish a parish day school, St George's Institution: he taught occasionally in the school and prepared school textbooks. He also became a zealous campaigner for the extension of parish schools in Scotland. In 1823, he was granted the degree of DD by Marischal College of Aberdeen.

A man of strong evangelical and reforming convictions, Thomson did not shrink from controversy. A zealous backer of the British and Foreign Bible Society, he became indignant in the early 1820s over the society's decision to include the Apocrypha in some of the Bibles it distributed. Thomson's uncompromising condemnations of the Apocrypha contributed to a violent controversy. In 1825 he and his supporters broke with the parent Bible Society, and established an independent Edinburgh Bible Society. Thousands in Scotland and England followed their lead. A champion of popular rights in the Church of Scotland, Thomson helped to found in 1825 the Society for the Improvement of Church Patronage, which worked to restore the right of parishioners to select their own ministers. Following the death of Sir Henry Moncrieff-Wellwood in 1827, Thomson was generally acknowledged as the leader of the evangelical party in the Church of Scotland. A long-time advocate of Catholic emancipation, he took a leading part in the final campaign in 1829. He also threw himself into the campaign for the abolition of slavery, insisting upon the immediate liberation of the slaves and opposing those who argued for a gradualist programme. At a great public meeting in October 1830 his stand divided the Edinburgh abolitionists, but Thomson refused to modify his demand for an immediate end to what he viewed as an unspeakable evil.

Thomson died suddenly, of heart failure, in the street outside his Edinburgh home, 29 Melville Street, on 9 February 1831. He was buried, after a great public funeral, in St Cuthbert's churchyard. A man of considerable gifts, his early death was a blow to the evangelical party, which was then gaining an ascendancy within the Church of Scotland. In religion, Thomson was a strict Calvinist and Presbyterian, with his roots in Scotland's covenanting past. In politics, he was a liberal whig, committed to reforms aimed at increasing liberty and popular rights. A genial and generous man in his private life, he was in public life a man of intense convictions and stormy moods, who could direct fierce invective and cutting sarcasm at his opponents. 'No man', wrote his lifelong friend Thomas McCrie, 'ever loved or hated him moderately' (T. McCrie, 137).

STEWART J. BROWN

Sources C. Watson, 'Memoir of the Rev. Andrew Thomson, D.D.', in A. Thomson, *Sermons and sacramental exhortations* (1831), xi–lxii · J. L. Watson, *Life of Andrew Thomson* (1882) · J. W. Craven, 'Andrew Thomson (1779–1831): leader of the evangelical revival in Scotland', PhD diss., U. Edin., 1955 · T. McCrie, 'Character of Dr Thomson', *Edinburgh Christian Instructor*, 30 (Feb 1831), 135–8 · *Fasti Scot.* · Chambers, *Scots.* (1835) · W. Hanna, *Memoirs of the life and writings of Thomas Chalmers*, 4 vols. (1849–52) · T. Chalmers, *Sermon preached in St. George's Church, Edinburgh, ... on occasion of the death of the Rev. Dr. Andrew Thomson* (1831)
Archives NL Scot., letters to Robert Lundie · NL Scot., corresp., mainly with Robert Lundie · U. Edin., New Coll. L., letters to Thomas Chalmers
Likenesses W. Walker, stipple, pubd 1827 (after H. Raeburn), BM, Scot. NPG · B. W. Crombie, caricature, pencil sketch, c.1830, repro. in B. W. Crombie, *Modern Athenians: a series of original portraits of memorable citizens of Edinburgh* (1882) · A. Edouart, silhouette, 1831, U. Edin., New Coll. L. · T. Hodgetts, mezzotint, pubd 1834 (after G. Watson), BM · A. H. Ritchie, bust, 1837, Presbyterian Hall, Edinburgh · C. Hull, engraving (after portrait by G. Watson), repro. in A. Thomson, *Sermons and sacramental exhortations* (1831)
Wealth at death £964 15s. 6d.: 1831, inventories, NA Scot., SC 70/1/45, 918 (1831); SC 70/1/60, 771 (1841)

Thomson, Anthony Todd (1778–1849), physician, was born on 7 January 1778 in Edinburgh, where his parents were temporarily resident, the younger son of Alexander Thomson (d. c.1800), a Scot who held British government appointments in America as postmaster-general for Georgia and as collector of customs for the town of Savannah, and his wife (d. 1779?), the daughter of an American called Spencer. He was named after Anthony Todd, the postmaster of Edinburgh, who was his godfather. Thomson accompanied his parents when they returned to America. When he was about one year of age his mother died, and he was brought up by a relative, Mrs Rennie (or Rainie), whom his father later married. When the American republic was established Alexander Thomson refused to swear allegiance to the new government, and he returned to settle in Edinburgh, where he lived on a pension 'in humble circumstances' (Parkes, xii–xiii).

During his childhood Anthony Thomson acquired an

Anthony Todd Thomson (1778–1849), by Thomas Bridgford (after unknown artist, c.1820s)

enduring love of nature and the countryside while roaming the hills and fields around Edinburgh. He was educated at Edinburgh high school and, from 1795 to 1797, at Edinburgh University, where his circle of friends included Henry Brougham, Henry Cockburn, and Francis Jeffrey. At the university he helped to finance his studies by working as a Post Office clerk; contrary to most accounts of his life he never graduated. He joined the Speculative Society in 1798 and the Royal Medical Society in 1799.

Thomson considered joining the East India Company but, following the death of his father, he decided upon a medical career. He moved to London, where he became a member of the Royal College of Surgeons in 1800, and, with the help of money loaned by his two sisters, he set up a general practice in Sloane Street, Chelsea. His resuscitation of a man dragged from a river seemingly drowned, for which he was awarded a medal by the Humane Society, helped him to transform his struggling practice into a successful one. He also gained a reputation for the care and attention he bestowed on patients. When he retired as a general practitioner in 1826, his practice was worth around £3000 per annum; soon after his death *The Lancet* described it as having been 'one of the largest and most profitable in London' (*Lancet*, 14 July 1849, 46).

Thomson was tall and slim, yet powerful; 'even at 70 his figure was as erect and as agile as that of a healthy man at 30'. He had great conversational powers and was 'full of information and of racy anecdote'. He eschewed dissemblance and 'always expressed his sentiments in strong and vigorous language' (Clarke, 307). Thomson was twice married. His first marriage, in 1801, was to Christiana née Maxwell (d. 1815), from Dumfriesshire; they had one son,

Alexander (d. 1838), who entered the medical profession, and two daughters. His second marriage, in 1820, was to Katherine, the seventh daughter of Thomas Byerley of Etruria, Staffordshire, who was related by marriage to the Wedgwood family [see Thomson, Katherine (1797–1862)]. She drew some of the illustrations for Thomson's books. At his prompting she herself took up writing and achieved success as a biographer and historical novelist; in later life she worked in collaboration with two of her three sons, Henry William Byerley *Thomson (1822–1867), the jurist, and John, who took holy orders. Their father had advised all three against following medical careers. The marriage also produced five daughters.

While in general practice Thomson helped found the Chelsea, Brompton, and Belgrave Dispensary (in 1812), and an infant school in Chelsea. He lobbied for the passing of the Apothecaries Act of 1815 and was active in several professional and learned societies. These included the Association of Apothecaries and Surgeon-Apothecaries, the Linnean and Ethnological societies, in both of which he held fellowships, the Medico-Chirurgical Society, the Westminster Medical Society, and the Harveian Medical Society; he also helped to found the Pathological Society of London. Thomson lectured extensively on botanical and medical subjects, at the Pharmaceutical Society, where he held the title of professor of botany, and elsewhere.

Thomson was a prolific author from an early age. He published an essay on philosophy and chemistry in 1800, and 'Ode to the Memory of Sir Ralph Abercrombie' in the following year. Between 1814 and 1817 he was joint editor, with George Burrows and William Royston, of the London Medical Repository, to which he contributed many articles. He also published papers in the Cyclopaedia of Medicine, Medico-Chirurgical Transactions, The Lancet, which published his 'Lectures on medical jurisprudence' (1836–7), and other professional journals. His main books were A Conspectus of Pharmacopoeias (1810), the London Dispensatory (1811), both of which went into many editions and were translated into foreign languages, Medical Statement of the Case of the Princess Charlotte of Wales (1817), Lectures on the Elements of Botany (1822), Elements of Materia medica and Therapeutics (1832), which James Fernandez Clarke deemed to be the 'best work' on the subject (Clarke, 305–10), and The Domestic Management of the Sick-Room (1841). At the time of his death he was writing A Practical Treatise on Diseases Affecting the Skin, which was completed and edited by E. A. Parkes and published in 1850. Thomson's edited works included the seventh edition of Thomas Bateman's Practical Synopsis of Cutaneous Diseases (1829), an edition of James Thomson's The Seasons (1847), and a translation of A. J. Salvarte, The Philosophy of Magic, Prodigies, and Apparent Miracles (1846).

On 1 May 1824 Thomson was admitted doctor of physic at St Andrews University. In London he moved from Chelsea to 3 Hinde Street, Manchester Square, in 1826; he later resided at 30 Welbeck Street, Cavendish Square, and at a rented cottage in Kingston upon Thames in Surrey. In 1828 he was appointed the first professor of materia medica and therapeutics at the newly founded London University. In the same year he was awarded the licentiate of the Royal College of Physicians. Around this time he became involved in Lord Brougham's Society for the Diffusion of Useful Knowledge. In 1832 he was appointed joint professor of medical jurisprudence, a position he had to himself from 1837 to 1849, following the resignation of his fellow postholder, Andrew Amos.

Thomson was also physician to the North London (later University College) Hospital. His time at the hospital was a period of much quarrelling among the medical staff. Thomson, closely allied with Robert Liston, had a particularly poor relationship with John Elliotson. His achievements as a professor included experimental work on the properties of alkaloids and iodides, and he may have invented an important device which became known as the 'Gibson spoon', for administering medicines to unco-operative patients. In 1835 Thomson's health broke down as a result of overwork. It was further impaired by his inhaling chlorine gas while giving a demonstration in the course of a lecture. Up to this point his 'industry and energy were truly marvellous' (Clarke, 307), but for several years afterwards he was obliged greatly to reduce his workload, though he continued to lecture, write, and practise medicine, giving great attention to skin diseases, in which he became a specialist. In 1842, 'rather late in life' (Clarke, 307), he became a fellow of the Royal College of Physicians.

James Fernandez Clarke had a grudging respect for Thomson's erudition and his ability to lecture on materia medica. However, he was scathing about his clinical and pedagogical capabilities. Clarke recalled him as having been 'deficient in the faculty of perception', as well as indecisive in the diagnosis and treatment of cases in his care. An unoriginal lecturer on medical jurisprudence, Thomson's clinical lectures were 'heavy and elaborate'. Clarke also maintained that Thomson's 'knowledge of physiology and pathology was scarcely up to the level which should have been possessed by a physician in an important hospital' (Clarke, 305–10).

From autumn 1848 Thomson's health began to decline, and in early 1849 he suffered an attack of bronchitis from which he never fully recovered; he died at Ealing, Middlesex, on 3 July 1849. He had expressed a wish to be buried in a rural location and was interred in the nearby Perivale churchyard on 10 July. The government purchased his materia medica collection for Queen's College, Cork.

P. W. J. BARTRIP

Sources E. A. Parkes, 'Memoir of Anthony Todd Thomson', in A. T. Thomson, A practical treatise on diseases affecting the skin, ed. E. A. Parkes (1850) · The Lancet (14 July 1849), 46–7 · Pharmaceutical Journal and Transactions, 9 (1849–50), 90–95 · J. F. Clarke, Autobiographical recollections of the medical profession (1874), 305–10 · R. Radford, 'Anthony Todd Thomson', University College Hospital Magazine, 38 (1953–4), 160–64 · Munk, Roll · Allibone, Dict. · GM, 2nd ser., 32 (1849), 426–7 · C. Knight, ed., The English cyclopaedia: biography, 3 (1856) · C. Symons, 'Gibson's spoon', Journal of the Royal College of Physicians of London, 18 (1984), 20 · DNB

Archives UCL, letters | UCL, letters to the Society for the Diffusion of Useful Knowledge
Likenesses T. Bridgford, engraving (after unknown artist, *c.*1820–1829), Wellcome L. [*see illus.*] · portrait, repro. in Radford, 'Anthony Todd Thomson'

Thomson, Arthur (1858–1935), anatomist, was born in Edinburgh on 21 March 1858, the youngest son of John Thomson RN, fleet surgeon, and his wife, Mary Arthur. He was educated at Edinburgh collegiate school and studied medicine at Edinburgh University, graduating MB in 1880; he subsequently served as demonstrator of anatomy to William Turner.

In 1885 Thomson was appointed to the new post of university lecturer in human anatomy at Oxford, where hitherto anatomical teaching had been undertaken by the professor of comparative anatomy. The medical school at Oxford, the creation of Sir Henry Acland, was then in its infancy; Thomson's first class, consisting of seven students, worked in a tin shed. The new anatomical department, largely of his design, was opened eight years later. In 1888 he married Mary Walker, daughter of Norman *Macbeth RSA (1821–1888); they had two daughters. From 1893 Thomson held the title of extraordinary professor of human anatomy, and in 1919 became the first Dr Lee's professor, a post which carried with it a studentship at Christ Church. This process was part of the development of the whole medical school, in which Thomson came to take a leading share, in the face of considerable opposition. The work of organization was eminently congenial to him, and to it he devoted much of his energies for the greater part of his life. He brought to the task a slow and cautious mind, remarkable tenacity, and a fine sense of loyalty. He took keen personal interest in his pupils, and the advice and help which he was always ready to give were especially valuable in the early days of the school, when there

was no dean and few of the colleges had medical tutors. However, after the First World War when women students entered his department he insisted that they had to dissect in a room separate from the men, 'and that they were to be taught surface anatomy only, down to the level of the umbilicus' (Bett, 269). Thomson eventually resigned his chair in 1933.

In pure research, mainly in the early development of the human embryo, Thomson was indefatigable, but he opened up no new field of inquiry, although he made several fresh observations; his work on 'squatting facets' on the knee and ankle bone became well known. Outside his own subject of anatomy he was greatly interested in ophthalmology, being the author of *Anatomy of the Human Eye* (1912), and anthropology, being co-author, with David Randall-MacIver, of *The Ancient Races of the Thebaid* (1905); the establishment of a diploma in each of these subjects, at his instigation, gave him great satisfaction. As a lecturer he was conscientious and competent rather than brilliant, his lectures being principally memorable for their magnificent ambidextrous blackboard illustrations. For Thomson was a born artist and lover of painting; sketching in watercolour was his chief recreation. Some of his works were exhibited at the Royal Academy, to which body he was, in 1900, appointed professor. He held the position until 1934, and delighted in the opportunities thus afforded for meeting other artists. In 1896 he published *A Handbook of Anatomy for Art Students*. He was president of the Oxford Art Society in 1922.

Thomson received honorary degrees from the universities of Edinburgh (1915), Durham (1919), and Oxford (1933). He was elected FRCS in 1907, and was a representative of Oxford University on the General Medical Council from 1904 to 1929. He was also a Ruskin trustee in the University of Oxford. He died at his home, 163 Woodstock Road,

Arthur Thomson (1858–1935), by unknown photographer, 1885–93 [centre, in a dissection room at the department of anatomy, University of Oxford]

Oxford, on 7 February 1935, and was buried in Wolvercote cemetery after a funeral service in Christ Church Cathedral, Oxford. He was survived by his wife.

T. B. HEATON, rev. MICHAEL BEVAN

Sources BMJ (16 Feb 1935), 334 · The Lancet (16 Feb 1935) · W. R. Bett, 'Arthur Thomson (1858–1935): an Oxford worthy', The Medical Press (19 March 1958), 268–9 · The Times (8 Feb 1935) · Nature, 135 (1935), 295 · private information (1949) · personal knowledge (1949) · WWW · D'A. Power and W. R. Le Fanu, Lives of the fellows of the Royal College of Surgeons of England, 1930–1951 (1953) · CGPLA Eng. & Wales (1935)
Likenesses photograph, 1885–93, Wellcome L. [see illus.] · photograph, repro. in The Lancet · portrait, repro. in Annals of Science, 1 (1936), facing p. 444 · portrait, repro. in Journal of Anatomy, 69 (1935), 292–302
Wealth at death £5561 3s. 7d.: resworn probate, 9 March 1935, CGPLA Eng. & Wales

Thomson, Sir Basil Home (1861–1939), intelligence officer and colonial administrator, was born on 21 April 1861 at Oxford, the third son of William *Thomson (1819–1890), provost of the Queen's College and later archbishop of York, and his wife, Zoë, daughter of James Henry Skene, sometime British consul at Aleppo. He was educated at Worsley's School, Hendon (1866–74), and at Eton College (1874–9). He went up to New College, Oxford, in 1879. In early life he was subject to bouts of profound depression, one of which led him, after only two terms at Oxford, to abandon university studies in 1882, and to emigrate to the USA to train as a farmer in Le Mans, Iowa, with the agricultural firm Close, Benson & Co. Before leaving England he had formed an attachment to Grace Indja Webber, daughter of Felix Stanley Webber RN. In 1883 he learned that Grace was contemplating marriage to another, which led to a relapse of his nervous condition and a precipitate return to England. He was able to reach an understanding with the Webbers that if he could establish himself financially a marriage proposal might be entertained, and with that end in mind, and through the good offices of his father, he obtained a place as a cadet in the colonial service attached to Sir William Des Voeux, governor of Fiji.

Thomson arrived in Fiji early in 1884 and began assiduously learning the Fijian language. He was appointed stipendiary magistrate, first at Nadroga, then in the Lau Islands, and later at Colo West in the central highlands of Viti Levu. He spent a three-month furlough in Tonga in 1886, where he gained a smattering of the Tongan language and made important contacts among the Tongan chiefs. When William Macgregor was appointed administrator of British New Guinea in 1887 Thomson volunteered to join his staff. In New Guinea he contracted malaria and was invalided home.

In England, Thomson renewed his suit to Grace Webber and they were married in October 1889. They were to have two sons and a daughter. The couple returned to Fiji in January 1890, when Thomson was appointed commissioner of native lands. However, in July 1890 the governor, Sir John Thurston, who was also high commissioner for the Western Pacific, visited Tonga and deported its premier, the Revd Shirley Baker, as being 'prejudicial to the peace and good order of the Pacific'. A pro-British chief,

Tuku'aho, was appointed premier, and Basil Thomson was dispatched from Fiji to be his adviser and assistant premier. During his tenure of eleven months Thomson reformed taxation, thus restoring solvency to the government, and introduced penal reforms based on the Indian penal code.

From 1891 Thomson worked in Suva in the native lands office and as assistant commissioner for native affairs. However, in 1893, owing to the deteriorating health of his wife, Thomson quit the colonial service and returned to England, where he accepted a position acting in loco parentis to two Siamese princes who were in England for their education. During this period he embarked on a career as a writer. While in Fiji he had published South Sea Yarns (1894). In London he wrote The Diversions of a Prime Minister (1894), his most enduring work, based on his experiences in Tonga, and The Indiscretions of Lady Asenath (1898), an amusing explanation of population decline in Fiji. These works led to his becoming a reviewer for the Pall Mall magazine and to a friendship with Lord Northcliffe.

At the same time Thomson entered the Inner Temple and read for the bar examinations. He was admitted in 1896 but accepted an appointment as deputy governor of Liverpool prison. From 1896 to 1908 he was successively governor of Northampton, Cardiff, Dartmoor, and Wormwood Scrubs prisons and from 1908 until 1913 he served as secretary to the Prison Commission. As a prison governor Thomson had to attend all executions carried out in his prison. This seems to have affected him little and he remained a firm advocate of capital punishment. As secretary of the Prison Commission he had to deal with those opposed to it and gave them short shrift. He was equally dismissive of suffragettes, especially when they responded to imprisonment by engaging in hunger strikes.

It was Tonga, however, which catapulted Thomson to eminence. In 1899 an Anglo-German agreement was signed exchanging rights and claims over Tonga and Samoa respectively. Thomson, as someone with special knowledge of Tongan affairs, was charged with gaining Tongan acceptance of a British protectorate over the islands. Despite considerable resistance in Tonga the protectorate was established in May 1900.

In 1913 Thomson was appointed assistant commissioner of the Metropolitan Police and head of the CID at New Scotland Yard. When war broke out in 1914 the CID became the enforcement arm of the War Office and Admiralty in intelligence matters. The Admiralty and the War Office had existing intelligence arms dealing with tactical matters, but it was not until 1910 that a secret service bureau was established (later the Secret Intelligence Service). The secret service bureau collected information on a lot of suspected spies, but on the outbreak of war had no machinery for arresting them. It therefore fell to the Metropolitan Police, and especially the head of the CID, Thomson, to carry out the arrests of these suspects. Thomson had something of a flair for self-advertisement, and made much of his role as 'spycatcher'. In fact, of the twenty-one German suspects arrested only one was brought to trial. The reality was that although a small German secret service agency did exist before the war its espionage efforts were directed almost exclusively towards France and Russia. After the commencement of hostilities, however, real spies did begin to infiltrate Britain, and Thomson had a role in arresting and interrogating them. Twelve of these were executed between 1914 and 1918, the best-known being Carl Hans Lody, a lieutenant in the German navy, who was executed in November 1914. Thomson also interrogated Margareta Zelle, better known as Mata Hari, and concluded that there was no evidence that she was a spy. She was, however, arrested by the French, tried by court martial, and executed in November 1917. The evidence against her remains very suspect.

Another famous case in which Thomson was involved was that of Sir Roger Casement, captured while attempting to run guns to Irish rebels in 1916. Casement's diaries were retrieved from his luggage, and they revealed in graphic detail his secret homosexual life. Thomson had the most incriminating pages photographed and gave them to the American ambassador, who circulated them widely. They were a significant, if unmentioned, ingredient in the trial and subsequent execution of Casement. After the Easter rising in Ireland, Thomson was again involved in Irish affairs. He was called in to advise the viceroy, Sir John French, on the best way of dealing with the emergency. His advice, he claimed, fell on deaf ears.

Thomson's most controversial activities concerned his surveillance of labour organizations. In 1916 the Ministry of Munitions asked him to organize an intelligence operation to report to it on industrial unrest. Thomson culled some of the best men from the CID for this service, and on the basis of their assessments issued regular reports to the ministry and later to the Home Office. In May 1917 a major strike occurred among engineering and munitions workers in response to a 'comb-out' to draft unskilled workers from these protected industries into the army. The war cabinet sought Thomson's advice on the matter. He advised prosecuting the ringleaders. Seven were arrested and the strike was called off in return for a pledge that no further arrests would be made and that no men with trade cards would be called up. In 1916 Thomson received a CB and in 1919 he was knighted.

After the war the army dismantled its surveillance of industrial matters, and the CID was left as the sole source of information on the mood of labour. The growth of left-wing activism, that took its lead from the Bolshevik Revolution in Russia, had increased the importance of surveillance of labour activities. It was a reflection of the new priorities that the Home Office directorate of intelligence was created in 1919, with Thomson as its director. He was thus the supremo with overall control of naval, military, foreign, and domestic intelligence. In 1921, however, for reasons that remain obscure, Thomson lost the confidence of Lloyd George and was asked to resign. In 1925, in circumstances which cannot be explained, Thomson was convicted of an act of indecency with a Miss Thelma de Lava. He was let off with a fine.

Thomson was a prolific writer, both during his working life and after his retirement, his writings covering aspects of his very varied experience. His autobiography, *The Scene Changes*, was published shortly before his death on 26 March 1939 in Teddington. NOEL RUTHERFORD

Sources NL Aus., Basil Thomson papers · B. Thomson, *The scene changes* (1939) · B. Thomson, *The diversions of a prime minister* (1894) · *DNB* · N. Rutherford, ed., *Friendly Islands: a history of Tonga* (1977) · C. Andrew, *Secret service: the making of the British intelligence community* (1985) · J. Morgan, *Conflict and order: the police and labour disputes in England and Wales, 1900–1939* (1987) · P. Knightley, *The second oldest profession: spies and spying in the twentieth century* (1988) · N West, *MI6: British secret intelligence operations, 1909–45* (1983) · H. Kirk-Smith, *William Thomson, archbishop of York* (1958) · *CGPLA Eng. & Wales* (1939) · *The Times* (27 March 1939)

Archives NL Aus. | HLRO, letters to Lloyd George

Likenesses photograph, *c.*1910–1920, NPG · W. Stoneman, photograph, 1920, NPG · photograph, *c.*1920, Hult. Arch.; repro. in Andrew, *Secret service*

Wealth at death £66 16s. 2d.: probate, 19 July 1939, *CGPLA Eng. & Wales*

Thomson, Charles (1729–1824), revolutionary politician in America, was born in November 1729 in the townland of Gorteade, Maghera, co. Londonderry, the third of the six children of John Thomson (d. 1739), probably a flax grower, and his wife (d. 1739), both probably of Scottish birth. Following his mother's death he left for America in 1739 with his father and two or three brothers, but his father died at sea. The impoverished sons were dispersed at New Castle, Delaware. About four years later Thomson commenced several years of classical education at Francis Alison's academy at New London, Pennsylvania, and in 1750 he became a Latin tutor at the Philadelphia Academy.

Thomson's appointment in 1755 as head of Latin at the Friends' public school in Philadelphia brought him to the attention of the Quaker Friendly Association, which was actively opposing the Indian policy of Pennsylvania's proprietors. Thomson was secretary to the Delaware Native Americans in meetings with colonial officials in 1757 and 1758. His *Enquiry into the causes of the alienation of the Delaware and Shawanese Indians from the British interest* (1759) fitted well the political policy of Benjamin Franklin, with whom Thomson had struck up a close relationship. He remained in broad sympathy with Franklin's objectives until the Stamp Act crisis of 1765, when Thomson emerged a conspicuous leader of Philadelphia's Sons of Liberty. After marrying in 1758 Ruth Mather (*bap.* 1732, *d.* 1770) he had, in 1760, ceased teaching; first he established an unsuccessful dry goods business in Philadelphia and then he invested in land. His hectic political and business activities apparently caused Thomson and his wife to separate in 1769. She became mentally deranged following the deaths of their infant twin children and soon died, probably by her own hand.

Upon the breakdown of his marriage Thomson had briefly turned to rum distilling; following his wife's death he moved, in 1770, to New Jersey as business manager of an iron works of which he was part owner. By autumn 1772 he had returned to Philadelphia, and the following year he resumed his role as political agitator; he wrote inflammatory handbills in support of resistance to the landing of East India Company tea. During the decade preceding the outbreak of the War of Independence, Thomson was a member of more extra-legal committees than any other Pennsylvanian. John Adams called him the 'Sam. Adams of Phyladelphia' (Schlenther, *Charles Thomson*, 119). However, when on 1 September 1774 Thomson married a wealthy Quaker, Hannah (1731–1807), the daughter of Richard Harrison, and days later became secretary to the Continental Congress, he attempted to shake off his noted reputation as a 'rash man', freely boasting of having been elevated to a 'station in the higher ranks of life' (ibid., 104, 150).

Thomson served as secretary to the first, second and confederation congresses for fifteen years. During the War of Independence he took a direct role in the conduct of foreign and domestic affairs, in the process gaining a depressing array of enemies who thwarted his desperate desire for office under the new national government. This was particularly galling for one who passionately pursued status. However, he was also concerned for the rights of Native Americans and Quakers and was firmly opposed to slavery. Thomson boasted a distinctively prominent nose, once being described in print as 'old nosey Thomson' (Schlenther, *Charles Thomson*, 214). He struck many as haughty.

Thomson retired, financially comfortable, to his wife's estate, Harriton, near Philadelphia, in 1789. In 1787 he had published *Notes on Farming*, and he took a keen interest in agriculture. However, retirement was marked by his translation of the Greek Old Testament (the Septuagint) and the New Testament, published in four volumes as *The Holy Bible, Containing the Old and New Covenant, Commonly called the Old and New Testament* (1808–9). This was followed by *A Synopsis of the Four Evangelists* (1815). Thomson was a Presbyterian of the non-revivalist school who managed to combine a high regard for biblical authority with a generally rationalistic approach to religion. The last decade of his life was a slide into senility; he died at Harriton on 16 August 1824, where he was buried two days later.

BOYD STANLEY SCHLENTHER

Sources B. Schlenther, *Charles Thomson: a patriot's pursuit* (1990) · K. Bowling, 'Good-by "Charle": the Lee–Adams interest and the political demise of Charles Thomson', *Pennsylvania Magazine of History and Biography*, 100 (1976), 314–35 · B. Schlenther, 'Training for resistance: Charles Thomson and Indian affairs in Pennsylvania', *Pennsylvania History*, 50 (1983), 185–217 · P. Smith, 'Charles Thomson on unity in the American Revolution', *Quarterly Journal of the Library of Congress*, 28 (1971), 158–72 · 'The papers of Charles Thomson, secretary of the continental congress', *Collections of the New York Historical Society* (1878), 3–286 · *The papers of Benjamin Franklin*, ed. L. W. Labaree and others, [35 vols.] (1959–) · P. H. Smith and others, eds., *Letters of delegates to congress, 1774–1789*, 26 vols. (1976–2000)
Archives Dietrich American Foundation, Philadelphia, day-book · Harvard U., papers · Hist. Soc. Penn., papers · L. Cong., papers · New York Historical Society, papers · NYPL, papers · Princeton University, New Jersey, letters | Hist. Soc. Penn., Gratz collection; society collection · National Archives and Records Administration, Washington, DC, Continental Congress MSS
Likenesses P. E. Du Simitière, engraving, c.1780, Hist. Soc. Penn. · C. W. Peale, oils, c.1781, Independence National Historical Park, Philadelphia · M. Pratt, oils, c.1794, Frick Art Reference Library, New York · C. W. Peale, oils, 1819, Independence National Historical Park, Philadelphia

Thomson, Charles Poulett, Baron Sydenham (1799–1841), politician and governor-in-chief of British North America, was born on 13 September 1799 at Waverley Abbey, Wimbledon, Surrey, the third son and youngest of the nine children of John Thomson (after 1820 John Poulett Thomson), a London merchant engaged in trade with Russia and the Baltic, and his wife, Charlotte, the daughter of John Jacob, a Salisbury physician. Educated privately, at the age of sixteen Thomson entered the family firm in St Petersburg. In 1817 he left Russia because of poor health, but embarked on several lengthy continental tours before joining the firm's London office. He returned to Russia from 1821 until 1824, when he settled permanently in London. Thomson was not particularly interested in business, travelled frequently on the continent, and was an early advocate of free trade, despite his family's support for protection. As an advocate of parliamentary reform and the ballot, he was a member of the Political Economy Club.

With the support of Jeremy Bentham and Joseph Hume, and at great financial cost, Thomson was elected as MP for Dover in May 1826. In the whig administration formed in November 1830 he became vice-president of the Board of Trade and treasurer of the navy. Since his superior, Lord Auckland, was a nonentity, Thomson conducted the real business of the board and helped to draft the abortive free-trade budget of 1831, thus incurring the undying enmity of the protectionists and completely alienating his family. He was re-elected for Dover in 1830 and 1831. In 1832 he was elected for both Dover and Manchester but chose to sit for the important industrial centre of Manchester, where he was re-elected in 1834 and 1837. From June until November 1834 and again after April 1835 he served as president of the Board of Trade, filling the department with free-traders, making numerous minor reductions in customs regulations, and negotiating free-trade agreements with several European countries. He dramatically expanded the responsibilities of the board by exercising more effective control over railway bills and bank charters and attempting to extend greater superintendence over colonial legislation. But Thomson, whom Charles Greville described as 'the greatest coxcomb I ever saw, and the vainest dog' (*Greville Memoirs*, 3.230), was not particularly effective in the Commons or popular with his aristocratic whig colleagues. Early in 1839 he was passed over for the post of chancellor of the exchequer, and he was increasingly disillusioned by the cabinet's failure to adopt a major change in economic policy and embrace free trade. Suffering from declining health and aware of the growing unpopularity of the whig government, he declined the post of chancellor in the summer of 1839; on 6 September, however, he became governor-in-chief of British North America, and received an unusually high salary and the pledge of a peerage.

Thomson had played only a minor part in formulating the cabinet's response to the rebellions of 1837 in Upper

Charles Poulett Thomson, Baron Sydenham (1799–1841), by T. C. Wilson

and Lower Canada, but he supported the recommendation made in the 1839 Durham report for an immediate union of the two Canadas, and before departing he met with Durham, once his friend, and received the latter's blessing. He arrived at Quebec city and assumed control of the administration of Lower Canada on 19 October 1839. His priority was to secure legislative support for union. In Lower Canada he faced few difficulties, since the assembly had been replaced by an appointed council dominated by the British minority. Although Thomson admired French culture (and French cuisine, which he introduced into the colony) and spoke French fluently, like Durham he believed it was undesirable—and ultimately impossible— for French Canadians to preserve their separate nationality on the North American continent. He saw the gradual assimilation of the French Canadians as essential to maintain imperial control, and he pushed through the council after two days' debate a union on terms which were clearly unfair to Lower Canada. He was castigated by the French-Canadian press, which satirically referred to him as 'notre poulet' (Monet, 37).

Thomson then travelled to Toronto, and assumed control of the government of Upper Canada on 23 November 1839 in order to persuade the Upper Canadian legislature to vote itself out of existence. Although he rejected the more extreme demands of the conservative-dominated assembly, he promised an imperial loan to pay the huge public debt of the colony and equal representation for both Canadas within the union. He managed to win the support of the Upper Canadian reformers by appointing

Robert Baldwin as solicitor-general. After securing the support of the Upper Canadian legislature early in 1840, he sent home the draft of a union bill. He also sent home a bill which, although modified in London, resolved the controversial issue of the clergy reserves. Having prorogued the Upper Canadian legislature he returned to Lower Canada, where he shoved through the special council a series of ordinances designed to pave the way for union. Particularly important were those incorporating the cities of Quebec and Montreal, reorganizing the system of justice, and establishing an efficient police force. Although he failed to persuade any prominent French-Canadian politician to join his administration, he refused to accede to the more extreme demands of the British minority, and his actions helped convince French-Canadian reformers such as Louis-Hippolyte LaFontaine to moderate their opposition to the union. To Thomson's disappointment the whig government, in order to get the consent of Sir Robert Peel and the Conservatives, dropped his arrangements for the creation of municipal institutions and inflated the number of constituencies dominated by the British minority in Lower Canada. None the less, the Union Act of 1840 was largely Thomson's work, and he arranged for the union to come into effect on 10 February 1841. On 19 August 1840 he was raised to the peerage as Baron Sydenham and on 19 August 1841 was further rewarded with a GCB (civil division).

At the request of the secretary of state for the colonies, Lord John Russell, Thomson, although suffering from gout, travelled to Nova Scotia in July 1840 to try to resolve the dispute between Lieutenant-Governor Sir Colin Campbell and the Nova Scotian assembly. On his return he persuaded Russell to dismiss Campbell and appoint a more conciliatory governor. During the trip he also visited Prince Edward Island and New Brunswick, where he was particularly impressed by Lieutenant-Governor Sir John Harvey's success in working with the New Brunswick assembly. Ironically, when Harvey failed to take aggressive measures to prevent American encroachments in the disputed territory between Maine and New Brunswick in 1840, Thomson complained to Russell, who dismissed Harvey.

The first elections to the assembly of the united province of Canada were held in March and early April 1841. Lord Sydenham, in effect acting as his own prime minister, interfered flagrantly in the elections and managed to get the support of a majority in the assembly, but the moderate Upper Canadian reformers led by Robert Baldwin had become disenchanted and they constructed an alliance with the French-Canadian reformers led by LaFontaine. On 12 June, when Baldwin demanded that Sydenham reorganize his executive council and give all the seats to the Baldwin–LaFontaine reform alliance, Sydenham dismissed him as solicitor-general. Although Sydenham was able to push a number of important measures through the first session of the legislature, which he convened on 15 June, his majority was increasingly precarious. On 3 September the reformers sought to embarrass him by demanding that he accept that the executive council would be reconstructed if it lost the confidence of the assembly, thus in effect conceding the principle of responsible government. Sydenham refused to make an absolute commitment. He continued to act as his own prime minister and to dictate the policies of the government, but his ministers increasingly functioned like a cabinet and indicated they would resign if they lost the confidence of the assembly. In fact, Sydenham's ability to command the support of the assembly was already breaking down when he had a riding accident and contracted lockjaw. On 19 September 1841 he died, in agony, in Kingston, Canada West. He was buried in St George's Church, Kingston, on 24 September. Although he was known as a 'sensualist' whose affairs with married women caused a scandal in Canada (Richardson, 186), he had never married and left no heirs.

From an imperial perspective Thomson was probably the most successful governor ever sent to Canada. He made union possible and established a workable form of responsible government, although in line with imperial policy he did not concede the principle itself. French Canadians did not view his regime sympathetically, and the measures he introduced to promote assimilation were quickly abandoned after his death. The union of the Canadas, however, endured until 1867 and laid the foundation for confederation. Irving Abella has described Thomson as 'a ruthless Machiavellian, unprincipled and cunning, selfish and egotistic, autocratic, narrow-minded, and unbelievably vain' (Abella, 326–7). All of this is true, if overstated, but no governor had greater influence on the future development of British North America—not even Lord Durham.   PHILLIP BUCKNER

Sources P. A. Buckner, 'Thomson, Charles Edward Poulett', *DCB*, vol. 7 · G. P. Scrope, *Memoir of the life of the Right Honourable Charles Lord Sydenham, GCB*, 2nd edn (1844) · *The Greville memoirs*, ed. H. Reeve, 8 vols. in 3 pts (1874–87) · J. Richardson, *Eight years in Canada* (1847) · L. Brown, *The board of trade and the free-trade movement, 1830–42* (1958) · P. Knaplund, ed., *Letters from Lord Sydenham, governor-general of Canada, 1839–1841, to Lord John Russell* (1931) · J. Monet, *The last cannon shot* (1969) · P. A. Buckner, *The transition to responsible government: British policy in British North America, 1815–1850* (1985) · I. M. Abella, 'The "Sydenham election" of 1841', *Canadian Historical Review*, 47 (1966), 326–43 · J. M. S. Careless, *The union of the Canadas: the growth of Canadian institutions, 1841–1857* (1967) · A. Shortt, *Lord Sydenham* (1909) · PRO, CO 42, vols. 296–300
Archives BL, corresp. and papers relating to Somerset House, Add. MS 31218 · NA Canada | BL, corresp. with Lord Holland, Add. MS 51570 · NL Scot., Ellice MSS · PRO, corresp. with Lord John Russell, 30/22 · U. Durham L., letters to third Earl Grey · U. Southampton L., corresp. with Lord Palmerston
Likenesses S. Reynolds junior, mezzotint, pubd 1833, BM, NPG · G. Hayter, group portrait, oils (*The House of Commons, 1833*), NPG · W. H. Mote, stipple (after G. Hayter), BM, NPG; repro. in J. Saunders, *Portraits and memoirs of eminent living political reformers* (1840) · T. C. Wilson, lithograph, NPG [*see illus.*]

Thomson, Sir Charles Wyville (1830–1882), naturalist, was born on 5 March 1830 at Bonsyde, near Linlithgow, the son of Andrew Thomson, surgeon in the East India Company, and his wife, Sarah Ann Drummond Smith, daughter of Dr Wyville Smith, inspector of military hospitals. He was christened Wyville Thomas Charles, but appears to have used the forenames Charles Wyville throughout his adult life, adopting this form formally when he was knighted in 1876. His early education was at Merchiston Castle School and then at the University of Edinburgh where he became a medical student in 1845. However, he was more interested in biology and geology and, after three years of formal medical study, he devoted his efforts entirely to natural history, mainly under Robert Jameson.

In 1850, despite his lack of formal qualification, Thomson was appointed to a lectureship in botany at King's College, Aberdeen. In 1853 he became professor of natural history at Queen's College, Cork, and the same year married Jane Ramage Dawson, elder daughter of Adam Dawson, deputy lieutenant of the county of Linlithgow; their only son, Frank Wyville Thomson, was born about 1860. In 1854 Thomson was transferred to Queen's College, Belfast, as professor of mineralogy and geology, being appointed professor of natural history in 1862. To this post was added that of professor of botany at the Royal College of Science, Dublin, in 1868. Finally, having been elected to the fellowship of the Royal Society in 1869, he obtained the chair of natural history at the University of Edinburgh in 1870 and held this post until his death.

Thomson had broad interests and knowledge, not only in natural history but also in other sciences and in art and literature. His zoological interests were mainly with the invertebrates, initially the coelenterates and polyzoans, and subsequently the sponges and particularly the echinoderms. By the mid-1860s he was collaborating with the physiologist William Benjamin Carpenter on the structure and development of the sea lilies or crinoids, an echinoderm group well represented in the fossil record. Both men were also intrigued by the recent results counteracting Edward Forbes's azoic theory, according to which the deep ocean was totally devoid of life. The two interests came together when Thomson visited Michael Sars in Norway in 1867 and saw a variety of organisms dredged from deep water off the Lofoten islands, including a crinoid which resembled a form otherwise known only as a fossil. A request to the Royal Society, and thence to the Admiralty, for support for deep-ocean research resulted in a series of short cruises around the British Isles and into the Mediterranean, in the small paddle gun vessels HMS *Lightning* in 1868 and HMS *Porcupine* in 1869 and 1870. Thomson took part in most of these cruises and wrote a general account of the results in *The Depths of the Sea* (1873), a classic summary of oceanographic knowledge at the time.

These cruises finally dispelled the azoic theory, obtaining a variety of bottom-living animals in dredge hauls at depths down to 4289 metres in the Bay of Biscay, far deeper than any previous hauls. They also produced interesting physical results, particularly in the region to the south of the Faeroes where very different deep temperature measurements were obtained only a few miles apart. The 'warm' and 'cold' regions proved subsequently to be separated by a submarine ridge, named the Wyville Thomson Ridge in Thomson's honour.

The *Lightning* and *Porcupine* results were so impressive

that Carpenter proposed a much larger undertaking, a properly equipped and staffed circumnavigation to investigate the physics, chemistry, geology, and biology of all the world's oceans. This time the Admiralty provided the 226 foot long steam-assisted screw corvette HMS *Challenger* under the command of Captain (later Sir) George Strong Nares. Since Carpenter was too old to take part in the voyage, the 41-year-old Thomson was appointed scientific director with a civilian staff of five including the naturalists John Murray and Henry Nottidge Moseley and the chemist John Young Buchanan.

The *Challenger* sailed from Portsmouth on 21 December 1872, returning to Spithead on 24 May 1876. In the meantime she had spent 713 days at sea and had covered 68,890 nautical miles through all the major oceans except the Indian. A total of 362 official 'stations' had been occupied, more or less equally spaced along her track, obtaining soundings and samples of the bottom sediment, and taking serial measurements of the temperature and collecting water samples between the surface and the bottom. But above all the expedition collected biological specimens; mid-water nets were used to about 3000m deep, and bottom dredges and trawls were fished successfully twenty-five times at depths greater than about 4.5 km, the deepest from 5.7 km on the edge of the Japan trench in the western Pacific.

In recognition of the expedition's achievements, acknowledged as marking the beginning of the modern science of oceanography, Thomson was knighted and received a royal medal on the ship's return. He was also given responsibility for overseeing the working up of the specimens and the publication of the results in the official expedition *Reports*. In the face of considerable opposition, particularly from the authorities of the British Museum in London, he set up a Challenger office in Edinburgh where he resumed his university duties and in 1877 published an excellent account of the expedition's work as *The Voyage of the Challenger: the Atlantic* (2 vols.).

Thomson represented the University of Edinburgh at the tercentenary of the University of Uppsala in 1877 and was created a knight of the order of the Polar Star (Sweden). As president of the geography section of the British Association at its 1878 meeting in Dublin he was awarded an honorary LLD degree by Trinity College (having already received an honorary LLD in 1853 from Aberdeen, an LLD in 1860 and DSc in 1871 from Queen's University, Belfast, and a PhD from Jena).

In the meantime, the *Challenger*'s biological specimens had been sent out to an international galaxy of specialists to prepare the official *Reports*. Thomson published the introduction to the zoological series in 1880, and expected to see the remaining ten or twelve volumes through the press within five to ten years. In fact, the *Reports* ran to fifty volumes, the last not appearing until 1895. Although they all carry Thomson's name, they were edited mainly by his successor John Murray. For the strain of the *Challenger* expedition, the administration of the Challenger office, and Thomson's professorial duties, had taken their toll

and he suffered recurring bouts of increasingly serious illness, particularly from the summer of 1879. He died at Bonsyde on 10 March 1882 and was survived by his wife.

A. L. RICE

Sources D. Merriman, 'Challengers of Neptune: the philosophers', *Proceedings of the Royal Society of Edinburgh*, 72B (1972), 15–45 · W. A. Herdman, *Founders of oceanography and their work* (1923) · D. Merriman and M. Merriman, 'Sir Charles Wyville Thomson and letters to Staff Commander Thomas H. Tizard, 1877–1881', *Journal of Marine Research*, 17 (1958), 347–74
Archives Harvard U., Museum of Comparative Zoology, corresp. · NHM · RS, corresp. with RS · U. Edin. L., lecture notes; papers · Ulster Museum, Belfast, papers on zoophytes | BL, corresp. with Macmillans, Add. MS 55218 · ICL, corresp. with Thomas Huxley
Likenesses W. Hole, etching, NPG; repro. in W. Hole, *Quasi cursores* (1884) · C. H. Jeens, stipple (after photograph), BM, NPG; repro. in C. W. Thomson, *Voyage of the 'Challenger'* (c.1877) · bust, U. Edin., Talbot Rice Gallery, Old College · wood-engraving, NPG; repro. in *ILN* (8 June 1976)

Thomson, Christopher Birdwood, Baron Thomson (1875–1930), army officer and politician, was born at Nasik, India, on 13 April 1875, the third son in the family of five sons and five daughters of David Thomson (1833–1911), a major-general in the Royal Engineers, and his wife, Emily Lydia, the daughter of General Christopher Birdwood and the sister of Sir George Birdwood and H. M. Birdwood. He was educated at Cheltenham College, where he distinguished himself in modern languages, and at the Royal Military Academy, Woolwich, whence he entered the Royal Engineers in 1894. After spending some time studying submarine mining at Plymouth, Thomson took part in the operations in Mashonaland under Sir Frederick Carrington in 1896 and received the medal. Thence he went to Mauritius, where he spent three years, and from 1899 to 1902 he served through the Second South African War. He took part in the advance on Kimberley and was commended by Lord Kitchener for the manner in which he cleared a block on the railway (February 1900); he was present in the Transvaal at the actions of Elands River (4–16 August 1900) and Lydenberg (6 September 1900), and in the Orange Free State at the actions of Lindley (1 June 1900) and Rhenoster River (29 November 1900). He distinguished himself in command of a field company section and received a brevet majority with his captaincy and the two war medals, and he was mentioned in dispatches.

After the war Thomson served first as an instructor at the School of Military Engineering at Chatham and then at Sierra Leone. He became a captain and brevet major in 1904, and in 1909 joined the Army Staff College, Camberley, where Sir Henry Hughes Wilson was then commandant. After leaving the college in 1911 he went to the War Office, where he served under Wilson, who had become director of military operations. In 1912 Thomson was appointed military attaché with the Serbian army and served throughout the Turkish and subsequent Bulgarian campaigns; he returned to the War Office in 1913.

On the outbreak of war in 1914 Thomson served first as liaison officer with the Belgian army and with the British 1st corps, then proceeded in February 1915 as military attaché to Bucharest, where he spent two years. He regarded the entry of Romania into the war as ill-timed, and he protested that her value was greater as a neutral than as one of the allies, since the Romanian supplies of corn and oil would thenceforth be at Germany's mercy. After being present at the inter-allied conference at Petrograd in 1917, Thomson joined the 60th division in Palestine as commanding royal engineer. He took part in the advance on Jerusalem and temporarily commanded a brigade at the capture of Jericho, receiving the DSO in 1918. He was promoted brigadier-general on the staff of the supreme war council at Versailles, whence he was sent to Mudros as bearer of the terms of the British armistice with the Turks. He was appointed CBE at the end of the war in 1919.

After serving on the British delegation to the peace conference in Paris, Thomson left the army in 1919 with the rank of honorary brigadier-general in order to enter politics and joined the Labour Party. He stood for parliament as Labour candidate for Bristol (central) in 1922 but was defeated. He was also unsuccessful at St Albans in 1923, so that he never sat in the House of Commons. In 1920 he went to Ireland as a member of the Labour Party committee of investigation into the rebellion then in progress and the measures taken to combat it. In 1921 he served on an International Red Cross committee which inquired into the condition of refugees in Russia and the Near East, and in 1923 he took part in the socialist deputation to the Ruhr. At this time he also devoted himself to writing, and published *Old Europe's Suicide* (1919), an account of events from 1912 to 1919, and *Victors and Vanquished* (1924).

In January 1924 Thomson was appointed secretary of state for air in the first Labour government; he was also sworn of the privy council and raised to the peerage (11 February 1924) as Baron Thomson of Cardington, taking his title from the place in Bedfordshire where the government airship works were situated. He set to work to master the technicalities of the air service and visited Egypt and Palestine on an air inspection tour. Thomson was largely responsible for the government's mistaken decision on a three years' scheme of airship development, which involved the construction of two airships (R100 and R101) and experiments with them in flight overseas. He also encouraged the study of the problem of the replacement of petrol by heavy diesel oil, for he had a great belief in the future of lighter-than-air craft.

After the fall of the Labour government in November 1924 Thomson was one of the most indefatigable of the small number of Labour peers in opposition. He was a clear and vigorous speaker, and his cheerfulness and good temper gained him many friends in the house; indeed, he seemed marked out as the future leader of the Labour Party in the House of Lords. Meanwhile he became one of the closest political friends of the Labour leader, Ramsay MacDonald. In opposition he still maintained his interest in the air, and he associated himself with the Royal Aero Club, of which he was chairman, and with the Royal Aeronautical Society and the Air League. He undertook a lecturing tour in the United States in 1926, and in 1928 represented the government at an international air conference in New York. He also contributed to the press, and in 1927 published a collection of articles and lectures on aviation entitled *Air Facts and Problems*, in which he emphasized his belief in the future of airships.

In June 1929, on the formation of the second Labour government, under MacDonald, Thomson returned to the Air Ministry more than ever convinced that the Royal Air Force had become the first line of home defence. In the House of Lords the defence of the government in important debates was entrusted largely to him, and he spoke on many leading questions of the day, such as the resumption of relations with Russia (4 December 1929), British policy in Egypt (9 December 1929), and the Singapore Dock question (18 December 1929); and he conducted the Coal Miners' Bill through committee in 1930. He was also actively concerned in representing the government at the naval conference in London in 1930 and defended the naval treaty, which was its outcome, in parliament.

When Thomson came to the Air Ministry for the second time he found that the development of lighter-than-air craft had progressed, and on 28 July 1930 the petrol-engined 'capitalist' airship, R100, built by Vickers, left Cardington for Canada, reaching Montreal in seventy-nine hours. She returned on 16 August after a flight of fifty-seven hours. When a flight was contemplated to India the task necessarily fell upon the 'socialist' airship, R101, constructed at the government airship works. This used heavy oil, a fuel which could be safely carried and burnt in the tropics. The flight was at first designed to coincide with the Imperial Conference, and there seems no doubt that the later decision to start as early as 4 October was influenced by considerations of public policy and by the strong desire of the secretary of state that a start should be made in time to enable him to take the flight himself and return triumphant for the Imperial Conference. The R101 left Cardington on 4 October 1930 at 6.36 p.m. Sir Sefton Brancker, director of civil aviation, and ten other passengers and officials accompanied Thomson, and the crew numbered forty-two.

The 'socialist' ship was inherently unstable because the fins and rudders, or elevators, were too small—even more so when extra gas bags were installed in summer 1930—and her novel bag netting allowed the cells to slosh and vent hydrogen. Nor had she been sufficiently test-flown at her new 777 foot length. There is no doubt that the secretary of state exerted subtle pressure for departure. When R101 crashed near Beauvais, France, at 2 a.m. on Sunday 5 October 1930 she was flying much too low and was brought down by the down-draft in the lee of the notorious hills. The ship crashed nose first to the ground, and immediately burst into flames. There were only six survivors of the fifty-four people on board. Thomson was among those killed, and he was buried with the other members of the expedition at Cardington.

Although the subsequent inquiry into the disaster under Lord Simon expressly exonerated Thomson and his advisers from deciding to take an unjustifiable risk in making the flight, the writer Nevil Shute, an engineer on the competitor R100 project, left a sharply critical account of Thomson's conduct. He identified Thomson as having primary responsibility for the organization that produced the disaster and described 'the unhappy ship' R101, as 'the plaything of a politician', whose belief in the inherent efficiency of state-run enterprise blinded him to the ship's technical shortcomings. The fatal journey to India was, Shute alleged, embarked upon in an experimental ship which had never been flown at full power (Shute, 130–39). Whatever interpretation is placed on the R101 disaster, the developmental curve of the aeroplane had, since 1924, been rising above that of the airship, and Thomson's death marked the end of the development of the airship in Britain.

Thomson was a man of varied tastes. He was widely, if not deeply, read in several languages, and was accustomed to memorize his favourite passages, so that he had an abundant fund of quotations, and he enjoyed public speaking. He was devoted to music and interested in painting and sculpture. Besides the works mentioned above, he was the author of *Smaranda* (1926), a book of war memories and tales of the Near East, in which he manifested his love of Romania. He enjoyed a longstanding friendship with the Romanian princess and writer Marthe Bibesco, whom he introduced to Ramsay MacDonald. He was fond of sport and rode well to hounds. Thomson was unmarried, and the barony became extinct on his death.

ONSLOW, *rev.* ROBIN HIGHAM

Sources War Office records, PRO · *Hansard 5C* (1929–30) · E. N. M., 'Lord Thomson of Cardington', *Royal Engineers Journal*, new ser., 45 (1931), 128–34 · 'Report of the R.101 inquiry', *Parl. papers* (1930–31), 10.125, Cmd 3825 · private information (1937) · personal knowledge (1937) · *The Times* (6 Oct 1930) · M. Bibesco, *Lord Thomson of Cardington: a memoir with some letters* (1932) · R. D. S. Higham, *The British rigid airship, 1908–1931: a study in weapons policy* (1961), esp. 247ff. and 304ff. · N. Shute, *Slide rule: the autobiography of an engineer* (1954) · *The Aeroplane* (8 Oct 1930), 794–804B · *The Aeroplane* (15 Oct 1930), 865–72 · *The Centenary Journal of the Royal Aeronautical Society, 1866–1966* (1966), 48, 50, 144, 209, 309, 340 · Burke, *Peerage* (1925) · GEC, *Peerage* · *The Labour who's who* (1927) · D. Marquand, *Ramsay MacDonald* (1977) · D. H. Robinson, *Giants in the sky: a history of the rigid airship* (1973)

Archives IWM, diary · NAM, family corresp. · PRO, journals and private office MSS, AIR 19 | King's Lond., Liddell Hart C., corresp. with Sir B. H. Liddell Hart · PRO, corresp. with Ramsay MacDonald, 30/69/1/208 | FILM BFI NFTVA, 'R101 disaster', Gaumont Graphic, 5 Oct 1930 · BFI NFTVA, news footage · IWM FVA

Likenesses W. C. Dongworth, miniature, *c.*1920–1930, NPG · W. Stoneman, photograph, 1924, NPG

Wealth at death £1822 2s. 3d.: resworn administration, 6 Nov 1930, CGPLA Eng. & Wales

Thomson, David (d. 1815). *See under* Thomson, George (1757–1851).

Thomson, David (1817–1880), university teacher and administrator, was born on 17 November 1817 in the Italian city state of Leghorn, the eldest son of David Thomson, a Scottish merchant based in that city. Thomson received a multilingual education and attended a M. Godin's boarding-school at Lausanne, Switzerland, from the age of eleven. At the age of fifteen he entered the University of Glasgow, where he was a student of James Thomson (1786–1849), the professor of mathematics, and after

four years there he continued his mathematical studies at Trinity College, Cambridge. He was considered a promising mathematician but, according to his biographer, his health prevented him from becoming a candidate for wrangler status. In the context of the strenuous preparation required for the higher divisions of the tripos, this was not an unusual decision even for promising students, and it does not imply that he was in particularly bad health. After graduating Cambridge in the *ordo senioritatis* he became private tutor to a family of the Irish aristocracy for a brief period. In 1840 he returned to Glasgow University as assistant to the professor of natural philosophy, William Meikleham; one of his students there was William Thomson, later Lord Kelvin, the son of his former professor.

On 14 September 1843 Thomson married Helen Stuart; they had nine children. His career took off in earnest in 1845, when he was appointed professor of natural philosophy at King's College, Aberdeen, where he also occupied a series of senior administrative positions. A rigorous teacher, tenacious and aggressive administrator, and strict disciplinarian, his activities were central to the reform and restructuring of the University of Aberdeen in the middle years of the nineteenth century. His manner was revealed early in his tenure. In dispute with his class over the conduct of examinations after his first session as professor, he suspended their April bursaries until the following October. His teaching was largely mathematical, experiments generally being used for illustration only. Much given to the public humiliation of students who attended lectures without adequate preparation, his oral examinations were known as 'the pillory'. There is no evidence that he engaged in research or encouraged it in others. His only publication in his field is the article on acoustics in the ninth edition of the *Encyclopaedia Britannica* (1875). This article is strongly pedagogical in tone, combining a graduated introduction to the relevant mathematics with many interesting practical examples. It is, however, weak on physical theory.

Thomson's administrative energies were directed to establishing the superiority of King's, a pre-Reformation foundation situated in the Old Town, over Marischal's College (founded 1593), which was situated in the New Town. The latter had gained the lead in the sciences and in professional education in the course of the eighteenth century, and was strongly identified with the values of the Scottish Enlightenment. It also had the affections of the local citizenry. Thomson's particular involvement in the cause of King's came during the debates over the union of the colleges into one university. It was common ground that the faculties of law and medicine would remain at Marischal's, and the faculty of divinity at King's, but the fate of the faculty of arts, the centre of the traditional university, was in dispute. Thomson was instrumental in maintaining and pushing through the proposition that there could only be one faculty of arts, and that it would be situated at King's. His leading opponent in academic circles was the psychologist Alexander Bain, a Benthamite active in *Westminster Review* circles; and he also faced vigorous opposition from local people. Lay government of universities was well established in Scottish academic culture, and Thomson gained considerable notoriety when he questioned the credentials of his auditors at a public meeting set up by the town council. He was, however, successful and the union of the colleges was passed by parliament along the lines of his plan in 1860. As a result of this success, his opposite number at Marischal's, James Clerk Maxwell, left Aberdeen to take up a position in London.

Thomson continued as the leading teacher of physical sciences at the unified University of Aberdeen until the Michaelmas term of 1879, with only occasional absences due to illness. He died at the university in the Old Town on 31 January 1880, shortly after suffering a stroke. His wife survived him.   JOSEPH GROSS

Sources W. L. Low, *David Thomson* (1894) · Venn, *Alum. Cant.* · Boase, *Mod. Eng. biog.* · *DNB*
Likenesses photograph, *c.*1860, repro. in Low, *David Thomson*, facing p. 50 · F. W. Wilson, photograph, *c.*1875, repro. in Low, *David Thomson*, frontispiece · J. Hutcheson, bust, U. Aberdeen
Wealth at death £4202 6s. 11d.: confirmation, 23 March 1880, *CCI*

Thomson, David (1912–1970), historian, was born in Edinburgh on 13 January 1912, the only son and elder child of Robert Thomson, printer, and his wife, Isabella Barr. Educated at Sir George Monoux Grammar School, Walthamstow, and Sidney Sussex College, Cambridge, he remained in the college for the rest of his life. He was research fellow (1938–45), teaching fellow (1945–57), and master (1957–70).

Having obtained first-class honours with distinction in both parts of the historical tripos in 1933 and 1934, Thomson did research under Sir Ernest Barker on attitudes to political parties in eighteenth-century Britain, winning the Gladstone memorial prize in 1937 and receiving his PhD in 1938. By then he was already working on recent French history; he had begun his lifelong association with the Workers' Educational Association as lecturer and committee man; and he could write in 1942 (in a letter to Kingsley Martin, Thomson papers), that he had 'several years of free-lance journalism' behind him. During the Second World War he was much in demand from the BBC and the Ministry of Information for lectures and pamphlets, some of them explicitly countering Nazi propaganda. He became involved in organizations such as the London Institute of World Affairs which were promoting serious debate about the war, the future peace, and reconstruction. As an expert on France he had some awkward dealings with the Free French in London. From this time date his small book *The Democratic Ideal in France and England* (1944) and *Patterns of Peacemaking* (1945), written with E. Meyer and Asa Briggs.

After the war Thomson became a much appreciated lecturer in Cambridge (university lecturer, 1948–68; reader in modern French history, 1968–70). It was no doubt mainly because the focus of his interests had shifted that he did not pursue earlier plans to publish his important PhD thesis. But he was conscious that its subject matter

and argument were deeply suspect to the school of eighteenth-century historians who followed Sir Lewis Namier and were believed to exercise a virtual veto on academic publication in their period. The broader standpoint of his own teaching and lecturing on modern British history had a significant impact on his pupils and was conveyed to a wider audience in his two volumes in the Pelican History of England, *England in the Nineteenth Century* (1950) and *England in the Twentieth Century* (1965). But his most notable influence as a teacher in Cambridge was exercised through his lectures on French history and especially those on theories of the modern state, in which he not only gave an account of the work of major thinkers but also brought out the interaction between ideology and political developments in nineteenth- and twentieth-century history.

Thomson's writing on France was crowned by his seminal *Democracy in France* (1946), which emphasized the underlying continuity and stability of the Third Republic despite its frequent changes of ministry. He was fascinated by the character and political career of de Gaulle, about whom he wrote in many newspaper articles and (with Laval) in *Two Frenchmen* (1951); and in the early sixties the Foreign Office commissioned from him a report on Gaullism. Of his other writings his substantial *Europe since Napoleon* (1957) has held its place for half a century as one of the best general surveys of its field. He also wrote a *World History from 1914 to 1968* (1969; 1st edn to 1950, 1964) and edited the controversial volume 12 of the *New Cambridge Modern History*. He held that the study of history is 'the best liberal education a student can have in the modern world' and defended the writing of contemporary history against those who maintained that the historian could form worthwhile judgements only about distant periods. He believed that dons should seek to enlighten the public and the government, and that governments should draw on the knowledge and wisdom of dons. In his last book, *The Aims of History* (1969), he described himself when he wrote of the historical 'general practitioner' who is 'a craftsman of synthesis rather than of analysis, a weaver of other men's threads (and some of his own) into patterns which they had not foreseen or even expected'.

Thomson was active in Cambridge University affairs: member of the council of the senate from 1950 to 1958, chairman of the faculty board of history from 1958 to 1960, from 1962 to his death chairman of the governors of the Institute of Education; and then the first chairman of the colleges' committee set up after the report in 1962 on the relationship between the colleges and the university, chaired by Lord Bridges. Meanwhile, he was one of the first history dons to become a regular visitor to the United States: he was visiting professor of public law and government at Columbia University, New York, in 1950 and 1953. In his Hoernlé memorial lecture at the University of the Witwatersrand in 1958, 'The government of divided communities', he tackled a dangerously topical issue. He continued to write for the national press, especially *The Times*, to which he contributed some anonymous leaders, many signed articles on France, and numerous letters.

Deeply attached to his college, Thomson was a dedicated and much loved teacher and (from 1946 to 1953) a benevolent and conscientious senior tutor. He worked to maintain academic standards and took pride in the fact that Sidney Sussex admitted relatively more students from grammar schools than most colleges did at that period: among those for whose admission his intervention was directly responsible was Royston Lambert. As master his contribution was distinctive. Neither of his two predecessors had been productive scholars or in the public eye, and the lodge had seen little hospitality. It now became a family place where he and his wife, Margaret Gordon, daughter of James Dallas, schoolmaster, whom he had married in 1943, lived with their two schoolboy sons, entertaining with great warmth and without the least sign of pomposity. He brimmed over with amusing anecdotes and his large frame frequently shook with laughter. In his day the lodge was visited by such notables as Adlai Stevenson, Pierre Mendès-France, and Hubert Humphrey; research seminars took place in it; and yet the master was always accessible to undergraduates and old members of the college, particularly his ex-pupils. During his mastership the number of fellows almost doubled and the first post-war block of undergraduate accommodation was built.

Thomson's historical breadth and the range of his other activities were made possible only by exceptional energy and application, a calm and cheerful temperament, and extraordinary powers of concentration. Visitors noticed that, after a chat in which he had seemed to have all the time in the world, he would be back at his typewriter before they were out of earshot.

Amid all his other activities Thomson was first and foremost a don and an educationist. He was a strong believer in the species of grammar school which he himself had attended. He thoroughly enjoyed his duties as chairman of the governors of the Perse School, which included planning its move from central Cambridge. He was in many ways an innovator, helping to pioneer educational films and the BBC's schools history programmes and joining in an unsuccessful campaign in Cambridge to establish a centre of advanced study. But he was suspicious of the proposals for large-scale university expansion made in the report of the committee on higher education (1961–4) chaired by Lord Robbins. By the end of the sixties he was seen by radicals as a reactionary, and undergraduate militancy was making residence in the middle of a college less agreeable—a particularly unkind reward to this most approachable of dons.

In 1968 Thomson was found to have lung cancer, from which he died, in Cambridge, on 24 February 1970. He was cremated at Cambridge crematorium.

DEREK BEALES

Sources Sidney Sussex College, Cambridge, muniment room, Thomson papers · *Sidney Sussex College Annual* · *Annual register of the University of Cambridge* · personal knowledge (2004) · private information (2004) [Margaret Thomson] · *DNB*
Archives Sidney Sussex College, Cambridge, muniment room, papers

Likenesses W. Hutchinson, portrait, Sidney Sussex College, Cambridge
Wealth at death £54,528: probate, 22 June 1970, *CGPLA Eng. & Wales*

Thomson, David Couper (1861–1954), newspaper proprietor, was born on 5 August 1861 in Dundee, the elder of the two sons of William Thomson (*d.* before 1912), shipowner, and his wife, Margaret Couper. He grew up in Newport, Fife, and was educated at Dundee high school, before leaving in 1877 to join his father, who had acquired his first steamship in 1871, and traded in fruit and wine between France, the Mediterranean, and Canada. After finishing an apprenticeship to a marine engineer in Glasgow, Thomson was taken into partnership by his father in 1884. He married Margaret (*d.* 1952), daughter of John McCulloch of Ballantrae, Ayrshire, in 1894: they had three daughters.

In 1886 Thomson left the shipping business to manage the new company of W. and D. C. Thomson, set up by his father to run the newspapers he had been acquiring: the *Dundee Courier*, *The Argus*, and the *Weekly News*. After being joined by his younger brother Frederick in 1888, Thomson bought another paper, *My Weekly*, which he turned into a weekly magazine for working girls, and which became very popular among workers in the jute mills in Dundee. William Thomson increasingly left the running of the newspaper side of his businesses to his sons, and in 1905 a private limited company, D. C. Thomson & Co. Ltd, was set up, with all but four of the 6000 shares divided equally between William Thomson and his sons. The business expanded rapidly, and moved to larger premises in Meadowside, Dundee, in 1906, and in 1913 the Thomsons opened an office in Manchester, followed by a Glasgow office in 1915. In 1915 Thomson started a new paper, the *Sunday Post*, in Glasgow, and his first boys' paper, *The Adventure*, in 1920. Frederick Thomson died in 1917, leaving David in sole control.

Increasingly conservative in his political views, Thomson waged a two-year campaign in the Dundee newspapers against Winston Churchill, Liberal MP for Dundee from 1908 and a supporter of Lloyd George, which culminated in Churchill's overwhelming defeat in the general election of 1922. In his speech at Broughty Ferry the day before the poll Churchill attacked Thomson for 'two years of ceaseless detraction, spiteful, malicious detraction', depicting him as 'narrow, bitter, unreasonable, eaten up with his own conceit, consumed with his own petty arrogance' (Gilbert, 885–6). In 1926 Thomson took over John Leng & Co., a newspaper business based in Dundee, built up by Sir John Leng MP (1828–1906), including the rival local newspaper the *Dundee Advertiser* (which Thomson merged with the *Courier* into one paper, the *Dundee Advertiser and Courier*), the *People's Friend* (a weekly paper), and the *Evening Telegraph and Post* (a daily paper). Later in 1926—after the general strike, during which a number of his workers came out in sympathy—Thomson became adamantly opposed to trade unions, and thereafter his employees had to sign a document to say that they were not members of a union, and to undertake not to join one. Although some of his former employees set up a rival paper, the *Dundee Free Press*, which campaigned against Thomson's anti-union position, it did not survive the depression, and closed in 1933. The Thomson organization continued to oppose unionization, despite a major dispute and court of inquiry following the dismissal of a union member in 1952.

Aloof and reclusive, Thomson remained chairman and managing director of D. C. Thomson & Co. Ltd until his death, but it was his nephew Harold Thomson who took over the running of the business in the 1930s. He started *The Hotspur*, a boys' paper, in 1933, followed by the popular children's comics *The Dandy* in 1937, and *The Beano* in 1938, with famous cartoon characters such as Desperate Dan, Dennis the Menace, and the Bash Street Kids, drawn by Dudley D. Watkins. Watkins also illustrated the strip cartoons in the 'Fun' section of the *Sunday Post*, introduced in 1936, featuring Oor Willie and the Broons. Harold Thomson started new women's magazines, too, including *Secrets* (1932). Meanwhile the *Sunday Post* began to attract a mass readership, becoming a leading Scottish Sunday paper, and by the early 1950s the Thomson organization owned over twenty newspapers, women's magazines, and children's comics, all of which catered for the mass popular market.

Thomson was deeply concerned with local affairs. He was a deputy lieutenant for the city of Dundee for fifty-four years, and a governor of the university college of Dundee for sixty-two years. He died on 12 October 1954 at 2 Ellieslea Road, Broughty Ferry, Dundee.

ANNE PIMLOTT BAKER

Sources DSBB · *The Times* (13 Oct 1954) · WWW · D. Phillips and R. Thompson, *Dundee: people and places to remember* (1992) · M. Gilbert, *Winston S. Churchill*, 4: 1916–1922 (1975), 885–6 · F. C. Bowen, *A century of Atlantic travel* (1932) · H. Fry, *The history of north Atlantic steam navigation* (1896), 261–2 · d. cert.
Wealth at death £225,433 10s. 10d.: DSBB

Thomson, David Patrick (1896–1974), Church of Scotland minister, was born on 17 May 1896 in Dundee, the second son of the five children of James Thomson, lawyer, and his wife, Helen Pringle. He became known throughout his adult life as D. P. He was educated at Dundee high school and Madras College, St Andrews. In 1912 he entered the jute industry in Dundee.

On the outbreak of the First World War, Thomson volunteered for service, was commissioned in the Army Service Corps, and in 1915 posted to Salonika. A committed Christian since childhood, Thomson organized various facilities for his men, including religious services. A turning point in his life came when, following a service held in the open air, a Red Cross worker challenged him with the words 'Lieutenant Thomson, God wants you to be an evangelist'. His own sense of vocation confirmed, he sought throughout his life to be 'an evangelist'. Invalided home in 1916 with heart and stomach troubles which were always to be with him, Thomson was discharged from the army in 1917.

For some time Thomson was involved with independent missionary organizations, but in October 1919 he began studies for the ministry of the United Free Church of Scotland at Glasgow University, graduating MA in 1922. During his student years he led various evangelistic campaigns throughout Scotland. To encourage team support in this work he founded the Glasgow Students Evangelistic Union. In 1923 Thomson recruited Eric Liddell, famous for his athletic powers, as a member of his team. On 1 February 1928 he was inducted minister of Gillespie Church, Dunfermline, Fife, persuaded that service in the parish would be invaluable preparation for wider evangelistic work.

In 1934 Thomson was appointed evangelist of the Church of Scotland with a special remit to organize seaside mission work among holidaymakers at Scottish resorts. In 1939, while conducting an evangelistic campaign in Jamaica, he met and in September married, Mary Callander (1903–1974), daughter of the Revd Dr Rothnie of Lucea, Jamaica. Mary's quiet personality, her generous hospitality, her capacity for hard work, and her loyalty to her husband and his calling made her a wonderful helpmeet to him. Wartime circumstances necessitated his return to parish ministry in Trinity Church, Cambuslang, but in 1945 he resumed full-time evangelistic service.

Two important developments marked the following years. Thomson began to enlist the laity of the church in evangelistic work, and this necessitated training. In preparation for campaigns, training classes became a regular feature. In 1958 he was enabled to transform a redundant church into St Ninian's Lay Training Centre at Crieff, Perthshire. This work has developed steadily across the years.

In the post-war years Thomson had realized the value of parish missions, encouraging congregations throughout Scotland to see themselves as agents of mission to their own parishes. This approach was a main contributory factor to the establishment of the 'Tell Scotland' movement which, involving all the major protestant denominations and led by Thomson's younger colleague the Revd Tom Allan, made a great impact throughout Scotland in the 1950s. This concept of 'parish mission' is still the basic missionary strategy of the Church of Scotland. In 1962 Thomson was awarded an honorary doctorate of divinity by Glasgow University. He retired in 1966, and died of cancer on 16 March 1974, at his home, Barnoak, Crieff, predeceased ten days before by his wife. He was cremated in Perth on 19 March.

D. P. Thomson was a big man physically, with a commanding presence, a stentorian voice, and a forefinger that subdued audiences. He was completely dedicated to his missionary calling in a way that made him seem almost too forceful and demanding, but he had a great capacity for affection and evoked a wonderful loyalty from the many who were called to share his work. He wrote many booklets and pamphlets, some biographical, some devotional, many related to his work in evangelism. His teaching, his writing, and his work in evangelism for more than fifty years made Thomson a unique figure in Scottish church history.

IAN B. DOYLE

Sources J. A. Lamb, ed., *The fasti of the United Free Church of Scotland, 1900–1929* (1956) • D. P. Thomson, *The road to Dunfermline* (1951) • D. P. Thomson, *Personal encounters* (1967)

Thomson, Sir Edward Deas (1800–1879), administrator and politician in Australia, the third son and fourth child to survive infancy of Sir John Deas Thomson (*c*.1764–1839), commissioner for the navy, and his wife, Rebecca (*d*. 1825), the daughter of John Freer, a South Carolina planter, was born at Edinburgh on 1 June 1800. He was educated at Edinburgh high school and at Harrow School, before spending two years in private tuition at Caen. On his return to London he prepared for a mercantile career, and in the meantime assisted his father with the public accounts in a semi-official capacity.

In 1826 Thomson made a journey to the United States to wind up his father's affairs, and afterwards travelled through the eastern states and Canada, recording his impressions in letters to his father. These helped win him the patronage of William Huskisson, who appointed him clerk of the council of New South Wales. Thomson arrived in Sydney in December 1828 and soon won the favour of the tory governor, Ralph Darling, and his whig successor, Sir Richard Bourke, whose second daughter, Anne Maria, Thomson married in 1833. In 1837 Bourke appointed him to be colonial secretary and registrar of deeds and a member of the executive and legislative councils. The appointment was denounced then and later as a job, but Thomson proved himself a capable administrator.

With the introduction of an experimental, partially representative form of government in 1843, Thomson was thrust into the centre of a conflict between the energetic but sometimes impetuous governor Sir George Gipps and talented colonists, including William Charles Wentworth and John Dunmore Lang, who were eager to assert their power. As leader and senior member of the government in the legislative council, Thomson won respect for his tact and political acumen. Under Gipps's successor, the more languid Sir Charles FitzRoy, he was widely regarded as the most powerful man in the colony. He was instrumental in introducing uniform postage arrangements, a fiscal system based on the principles of free trade, and electoral legislation based on town, rural, and pastoral interests. When the gold rushes began in 1851, he was responsible for a licence system that allowed ready access to the diggings and helped maintain social order during a period of tumultuous change.

Early in 1854 Thomson was granted two years' leave on the grounds of ill health, and he travelled with his family to London, where he was often consulted by members of the Colonial Office. In 1855 he acted as commissioner for New South Wales at the Paris Universal Exhibition.

After returning to Sydney in 1856, Thomson found it hard to come to terms with the new political order that followed the introduction of responsible government. Invited to form a ministry, he made political miscalculations and failed to win sufficient support. He did, however, remain briefly as caretaker colonial secretary and helped determine administrative arrangements under the new system. From 1856 until his death he was a member of the upper house, except for a short interruption in 1861, when he and his conservative colleagues resigned in protest against the intended swamping of the chamber. He served in the ministry of Henry Watson Parker in 1856–7 as vice-president of the legislative council. An early advocate of intercolonial union, he proposed in the council in 1857 a motion for the federation of the Australian colonies. This made him one of the first federationists, though his support for the cause owed more to his desire for administrative efficiency than to national sentiment.

In his later years Thomson devoted his attention chiefly to educational questions; he was vice-chancellor of Sydney University from 1862 to 1865, and was elected chancellor annually from 1865 to 1878. He was president of various institutions, including the Australian Jockey Club and the Sydney Infirmary. In the late 1860s he corresponded with Florence Nightingale about hospital improvements and the introduction of Nightingale nurses to New South Wales.

Throughout his long career Thomson remained committed to administrative efficiency, social order, and the welfare and improvement of the colony. Although radicals criticized his conservative politics, he won and retained the respect of most colonists as well as successive governors. He died at his home, Barham, Darlinghurst, Sydney, on 16 July 1879, leaving his wife, two sons, and five daughters. He was buried at St Jude's Church, Randwick, New South Wales. He had been made CB in 1856 and KCMG in 1874.   S. G. FOSTER

Sources S. G. Foster, *Colonial improver: Edward Deas Thomson, 1800–1879* (1978) • Mitchell L., NSW, Deas-Thomson MSS • Deas Thomson MSS, priv. coll. • colonial secretary's records, State Archives of New South Wales, Sydney
Archives Mitchell L., NSW • priv. coll. | BL, corresp. with Florence Nightingale, Add. MS 47757 • State Archives of New South Wales, Sydney, colonial secretary's records
Likenesses A. Capalti, oils, 1855, Mitchell L., NSW • A. Capalti, oils, 1855, University of Sydney • photographs, 1860–79, Mitchell L., NSW • Fantacchiotti, marble bust, University of Sydney
Wealth at death £14,000 effects in Australia: Deas Thomson MSS, priv. coll. • under £4000: resworn administration with will, *CGPLA Eng. & Wales*

Thomson, George (*bap.* 1607, *d.* 1691), merchant and politician, was baptized on 12 April 1607 at Watton-at-Stone, Hertfordshire, the second son of Robert Thomson (1570–*c*.1638), and his wife, Elizabeth Halfhead (or Harsnett; *bap.* 1579, *d.* after 1622), and younger brother of Maurice *Thomson, colonial merchant. He emigrated to Virginia in 1623, was elected to the Virginia house of burgesses for Elizabeth county, and became a lieutenant and JP. He returned to London and traded with St Kitts, Montserrat, and New England, and with Virginia, where he sent emigrants and accumulated land. In the 1640s he helped intrude the radical John Simpson as lecturer in St Dunstan's parish, and was appointed a lay trier and a member of the tenth London classis, for St Olave's parish, Southwark. A captain of horse under the earl of Bedford during the first civil war, he rose to command a London regiment of horse. He served under Waller at Basing House and lost a leg at the battle of Cheriton (29 March 1644), replacing it with a wooden one. In October 1644 he supported a petition in favour of Colonel Sam Jones retaining his command at Farnham, an act subsequently voted a breach of privilege. Recruited MP for Southwark in 1645, the following year he was accused of outspoken words against Lord Mayor Adams for the latter's reception of a letter from the king.

Thomson was a witness to the battle of Maidstone in 1648, and sat on the militia and assessment committees for a number of south-eastern counties. As an MP in the Rump Parliament he dealt with the planter petitions from the Caribbean. He served as chairman of the Rump's navy committee and as such was to the fore in reporting to parliament on the financial reorganization of the navy, and reported the act for imposing customs duties on tobacco imported through New England. Appointed to the council of state in 1651, he was one of the six-strong commission to reorganize the navy during the First Anglo-Dutch War and travelled to the Downs to supervise the fleet. He protested at the dissolution of the Rump Parliament and was later imprisoned for conspiracy against Cromwell. In 1659 he returned to the council of state, his local committee roles, and his position as a naval commissioner, in which role he put pressure on the East India Company for a loan to the restored republic.

Thomson lived at Lee in Kent, purchased 4000 acres of Irish land, and married thrice, with Elizabeth Brickland of Thorncliffe, Cheshire, Elizabeth Humphries of Surrey, and Abigail Barnes of Barking, Essex. He was the father of George, Elizabeth, and Mary. In 1661 he was under suspicion of involvement with the Fifth Monarchists and of supporting seditious sermons at Lee, and was briefly arrested. In 1667 he was nominated to the 1668–9 committee named by parliament to investigate the commissioners of the navy for failure in the Second Anglo-Dutch War, and in January 1670 accused Pepys of insufficient eagerness in the purchase of English plank. He died in Clerkenwell in January 1691 and was buried at St Olave's, Southwark.

George Thomson's youngest brother, **Robert Thomson** (1622–1694), merchant, had emigrated to Massachusetts in the 1630s, where he purchased the old Boston meetinghouse. He returned to England and became a major in a London regiment, serving as rear-admiral in the 1642 'sea adventure' expedition to Ireland. Apparently a presbyterian, he was purged from the London militia committee in 1648 though 'a valiant and faithful commander' (Liu, 60). In 1649 he was appointed a commissioner to regulate the navy and the customs, and to the commission for propagating the gospel in New England. In the 1640s he was engaged in the East Indies trade and was active in his brother Maurice's Assada adventure. He acted as a commissioner in disputes between patentees for Connecticut and Rhode Island and was reputed to have offered £13,000 for New York. In 1663 Pepys said he talked 'very highly of liberty of conscience, which now he hopes for by the King's declaration' (Pepys, 4, 5). He represented the East

India Company at the 1667 peace of Breda and in negotiations for the purchase of Bombay. Elected deputy governor, he was involved in secret discussions with the crown over trade to Japan and the East, and was a supporter of Increase Mather's plans for New England. With his wife, Frances, he had six children, and he died at Stoke Newington in 1694.

ALAN THOMSON

Sources Greaves & Zaller, BDBR · DNB · R. Brenner, *Merchants and revolution: commercial change, political conflict, and London's overseas traders, 1550–1653* (1993) · H. F. Waters, *Genealogical gleanings in England*, 2 vols (1901) · Pepys, *Diary*, vols. 4–5, 10 · Tai Liu, *Puritan London: a study of religion and society in the City parishes* (1986) · R. K. G. Temple, 'Discovery of a manuscript eye-witness account of the battle of Maidstone', *Archaeologia Cantiana*, 97 (1981), 209–20 · JHC, 4–8 (1644–67) · CSP col., vol. 5 · N. C. Briggs, *English adventurers and Virginian settlers*, 2 vols. (1969) · S. R. Gardiner and C. T. Atkinson, eds., *Letters and papers relating to the First Dutch War, 1652–1654*, 6 vols., Navy RS, 13, 17, 30, 37, 41, 66 (1898–1930) · K. Roberts, '"Citizen soldiers": the military power of the City of London', *London and the civil war*, ed. S. Porter (1996), 89–116 · parish register, Watton-at-Stone, Herts. ALS, D/P.118/1/1, Cheshunt D/P.29/1/1 · *The visitation of London, anno Domini 1633, 1634, and 1635, made by Sir Henry St George*, 2, ed. J. J. Howard, Harleian Society, 17 (1883), 282
Archives BL, Add. MSS 22546, 46500, 46373 | Herts. ALS, 4228–30 manorial records of Watton-at-Stone Court Baron, 1634

Thomson, George (1619–1677), physician, of whose early life little is known, received some medical education as a young man from an apothecary (possibly Job Weale), who instructed him in both Galenic and chemical medicine. The death of his father prevented Thomson from enrolling at Oxford or Cambridge universities. He travelled to France and returned in 1644 to Weymouth. He joined the royalist army, served under Prince Maurice, and took part in the royalist victories in Cornwall. In October 1644 Thomson was taken prisoner at Newbury in Berkshire and was kept in the Fleet prison for several months. He continued his medical studies and on 19 June 1647 obtained an MA from Edinburgh. He then applied to the College of Physicians, London, for a licence to practise in London. He was first examined on 3 December 1647, and later on 7 January 1648, by a committee consisting of the president and censors. Although the committee acknowledged his medical skill, Thomson was not awarded the licence, as he was not able to pay the fee required by the college. Thomson, apparently on the suggestion of one senior member of the committee (possibly Baldwin Hamey), decided to go to Leiden. He matriculated at Leiden in June 1648 and on 14 July 1648 submitted his dissertation, entitled 'De apoplexia'. It was dedicated to his uncle Colonel Thomas Serle, mayor of Bandon Bridge, Ireland, to the Revd Walter Collins, the Revd Thomas Hazelwood, and the Revd John Cacket, ministers in Kent, to the Revd Robert French, to Baldwin Hamey, and to Job Weale, of Kingston.

After taking his medical qualification Thomson practised at Rochford, Essex, where in 1651 he performed an experimental splenectomy. The excision of the spleen was performed on a dog, which survived for two years and three months. Thomson's experiment attracted the attention of William Harvey, Charles Scarburgh, Robert Boyle, and Henry Pierpont, marquess of Dorchester. It appears that Thomson, who brought the dog to London, did not get the recognition he expected for being the first to perform a splenectomy. He subsequently accused an anonymous Galenist (later identified as Charles Scarburgh) of plagiarism. Thomson defended his claim to be the first to perform a splenectomy in two of his works: *Misochymias* (1671) and *Splenotomia*, which was published posthumously by his disciple Richard Hope as part of *Tria peireteria anekousta, sive, Experimenta admiranda* (1680).

It is apparent that already in the 1650s Thomson had regular recourse to chemically prepared medicines. These remedies he used both in the cure of the dog he had operated on in 1651, and in his successful treatment of Ann Taylor, of Romford, Essex, who was afflicted by stones. Thomson's adherence to J.-B. van Helmont's medicine dated back to the mid-1650s and was reinforced by George Starkey, who became his friend and mentor.

In 1659 Thomson settled in London, where he prepared chemical remedies and practised medicine—though without a licence. During the plague of 1665 Thomson, along with other Helmontians, stayed in London, where he studied the disease minutely, cured several people who had been infected, sold his medicaments, and dissected the body of a plague victim. He wrote two works on the plague: *Loimologia: a Consolatory Advice, and some Brief Observations Concerning the Present Pest* (1665), which contains a letter from Starkey, and *Loimotomia* (1666), dedicated to William Craven; the latter contains a narrative of Starkey's death from the plague. In the confrontation that took place in 1665 between the Helmontian iatrochemists and the members of the College of Physicians, Thomson's attacks on the college were particularly virulent. He severely criticized the members of the college for leaving the city during the plague epidemic. In the same year he was among the Helmontians who projected a college of chemical physicians to challenge the college's monopoly. In *Galeno-Pale, or, A Chymical Trial to the Galenists* (1665), dedicated to Gilbert Sheldon, archbishop of Canterbury, Thomson supported the Helmontian view that the physician is made by God. Though he recognized the importance of anatomy and extolled Harvey's discovery of circulation, he claimed they were of little or no help in medical therapy, which needed to act on the spiritual, invisible principles ruling the human body. Like other Helmontians, Thomson rejected bloodletting and the use of purgatives, ruled out humoral medicine, and maintained that the main functions of the human body were directed by a spiritual entity, that is, the Helmontian *archeus*, or vital spirit. Thomson also embraced the Helmontian theory of water and seminal principles as the beginnings of all natural bodies. In *Aimatiasis, or, The True Way of Preserving Bloud* (1670) and in *Orthometodos iatrochymike, or, The Direct Method of Curing Chymically* (1675) he criticized Thomas Willis's version of the Paracelsian theory of chemical principles (spirit, water, earth, sulphur, and salt) by claiming that they were not the ultimate constituents of bodies, but the product of fire. He supported Tachenius's theory of acid and alkali and engaged in the preparation of van Helmont's universal solvent, the alkahest, which, he maintained, was made of pure mercury and which could be prepared by liberating mercury from its sulphur.

Thomson was attacked by William Johnson, chemist to the College of Physicians, in his *Agurto-Matrix, or, Some Brief Animadversiones upon Two Late Treatises* (1665); by John Heydon in his *Psonthonphankia, or, A Quintuple Rosicrucian Scourge* (1665); and in *The Lord Bacons Relation of the Sweating-Sickness* (1671) by Henry Stubbe, with whom he engaged in a pamphlet war. While Johnson linked Thomson to empirics, such as Thomas O'Dowde and Lionel Lockyer—an association which Thomson firmly rejected—Stubbe attacked Thomson and the Royal Society.

From 1659 to his death Thomson lived in London: at Duke's Place, Aldgate, until 1671 and from 1672 at Soper Lane, near Cheapside, in Well Court, where he had a laboratory. He died in London (having never married) on 11 March 1677 and was buried at St Mary-le-Bow. Richard Hope, whom he had taught chemical medicine, received some of Thomson's manuscripts from the executor of his will and published them in 1680.

ANTONIO CLERICUZIO

Sources C. Webster, 'The Helmontian George Thomson and William Harvey: the revival and application of splenectomy to physiological research', *Medical History*, 15 (1971), 154–67 • P. M. Rattansi, 'The Helmontian–Galenist controversy in Restoration England', *Ambix*, 12 (1964), 1–23 • R. W. Innes Smith, *English-speaking students of medicine at the University of Leyden* (1932) • J. Ferguson, ed., *Bibliotheca chemica*, 2 vols. (1906)

Likenesses engraving, 1666, Wellcome L. • W. Sherwin, engraving, 1670, Wellcome L.

Thomson, George (1757–1851), music collector and publisher, was born on 4 March 1757 at Limekilns, Dunfermline, Fife, the son of Robert Thomson, schoolmaster, and his first wife, Anne Stirling. Little is known of his parents, though Robert remarried following Anne Stirling's death in the late 1760s or early 1770s. By this time the family had moved north to Banff, where Robert taught English language in the council school. George received his early education there (1762–72) before moving to Edinburgh in 1774.

After working in a legal office, in 1780 Thomson was appointed junior clerk to the board of trustees for manufactures in Scotland. He states in an autobiographical letter that this was made possible only by the 'influence of Mr John Home, author of *Douglas*, with one of the members of the honourable Board of Trustees' (Wilson, 38–42). Soon afterwards he became senior clerk to the board, and he retained this post until his retirement in 1839. On 11 December 1781 he married Katharine Miller (1764–1841); they had two sons and six daughters. One daughter, Georgina, married the music critic George Hogarth, and their daughter Catherine became the wife of Charles Dickens.

Thomson was an amateur violinist and singer, and through connections with the board he gained access to the select concerts of the Edinburgh Musical Society. There he heard the best of contemporary European composers and performers. The castrato Ferdinando Tenducci made a particularly strong impact with his renditions of traditional Scots songs. Thomson was so inspired that he decided to collect, commission, and publish 'all our best melodies and songs' with 'accompaniments to them worthy of their merit' (Hadden, 20). With the financial help of Robert Arbuthnot, secretary to the board of trustees, Thomson launched the first of his publications, *A Select Collection of Original Scotish Airs* (1793). The title-page and preface explained his intentions: he provided 'Introductory & Concluding Symphonies & Accompanyments for the Piano Forte & Violin' (often performed with cello and later with flute too); he also presented 'Select & Characteristic Verses by the most admired Scottish Poets adapted to Each Air', some of which were 'entirely new', and provided 'Suitable English verses in addition to such of the songs that are written in the Scottish Dialect'. Over the next fifty years he commissioned Pleyel, Kozeluch, Haydn, Beethoven, Hummel, and Weber to provide musical arrangements, as well as British musicians George Farquhar Graham, Henry Bishop, and Thomson's son-in-law Hogarth. Thomson was an early champion of Beethoven's works in Britain, in his capacity as one of the first directors of the Edinburgh musical festival (from 1815). In addition to his selection of lyrics from other publications, he commissioned and corresponded with around forty writers, including Robert Burns, Walter Scott, Alexander Boswell (brother of the more famous James), James Hogg, Joanna Baillie, Amelia Opie, Anne Grant, William Smyth, and Lord Byron.

Thomson conducted his publishing business from home, and used banking and diplomatic channels to transport his correspondence and manuscripts to and from Europe. He appeared on the title-pages as the proprietor, never as the publisher. His volumes were all issued by John and Thomas Preston of London. They included drawings by R. T. Stothard, David Wilkie, David Allan, Alexander Nasmyth, and Thomson's brother David [*see below*]. Thomson continued publishing and reissuing volumes until just a few years before his death. They finally numbered six volumes of Scottish airs (1793–1846), three of Welsh airs (1809–17), and two of Irish airs (1814–16). He also issued a six-volume royal octavo edition between 1822 and 1825, which was later reissued. The bibliography of his collections is complex in the extreme, and the survey by Cecil Hopkinson and C. B. Oldman (1940) is invaluable.

Portraits reveal a serious and studious man, with spectacles and rounded features. Thomson masterminded many of the trustees' events and was well liked, and a testimonial dinner was given in his honour in Edinburgh in 1846. He remains best known as the Scottish music publisher associated with famous composers and with Robert Burns. He is unpopular with Burns readers and scholars, primarily for his adaptation and alteration of many of Burns's songs, and for his pompous obituary of the poet (*London Chronicle*, July 1796). Cedric Thorpe Davie's opinion that Thomson's 'huge pretentious volumes' were a 'sad memorial to misplaced enthusiasm and ignorant amateurishness' (Davie, 16) is typical of twentieth-century musicologists. Thomson died at his home, 1 Vanbrugh Place, Leith, Edinburgh, on 18 February 1851, and was buried beside his wife at Kensal Green cemetery, Middlesex.

Thomson's brother, **David Thomson** (*d.* 1815), landscape painter and musician, provided illustrations and some songs for George's collections of national airs. With Muzio Clementi of London he published his own collection, 'The melodies of different nations', and a collection of Mozart songs with his own lyrics. In 1806 he made a tour to Wales to create some illustrations for George's collection of Welsh airs, and by 1813 he was based in London. Joanna Baillie wrote fondly of him in a letter to George Thomson of 17 June 1815 (BL, Add. MS 35264, fols. 218–20), the year of David's death.   KIRSTEEN C. McCUE

Sources J. Wilson, *The land of Burns: a series of landscapes and portraits illustrative of the life and writings of the Scottish poet* (1840) · J. C. Hadden, *George Thomson, the friend of Burns: his life and correspondence* (1898) · K. C. McCue, 'George Thomson, 1757–1851: his collections of national airs in their Scottish cultural context', DPhil diss., U. Oxf., 1994 · C. Hopkinson and C. B. Oldman, 'Thomson's collections of national song', *Edinburgh Bibliographical Society Transactions*, 2 (1938–45), 3–64; 3 (1948–55), 123–4 · *The letters of Robert Burns*, ed. J. de Lancey Ferguson, 2nd edn, ed. G. Ross Roy, 2 vols. (1985) · R. Chambers, *Traditions of Edinburgh*, new edn (1868) · L. F. Harris, *Saint Cecilia's Hall in the Niddry Wynd* (1899) · G. Hogarth, review of G. Thomson, *The select melodies of Scotland interspersed with those of Ireland and Wales, EdinR*, 39 (1823–4), 67–84 · G. F. Graham, *An account of the first Edinburgh musical festival* (1816) · C. T. Davie, *Scotland's music* (1980)

Archives BL, corresp. and letter-books, Add. MSS 35263–35279 · NL Scot., papers; letters to his wife | BL, corresp. with J. Flaxman, Add. MSS 39781–39791 · Mitchell L., Glas., Cowie MSS · NA Scot., record books of the board of trustees for fisheries, manufacturers, and improvements in Scotland · NL Scot., corresp. with R. Chambers · NL Scot., letters to K. Miller · NL Scot., letters to Thomas Stothard · NL Scot., Watson MSS · U. Edin. L., corresp. with Anne Grant

Likenesses J. Edgar, group portrait, wash drawing, *c.*1854 (*Robert Burns at an evening party of Lord Monboddo's 1786*), Scot. NPG · B. W. Crombie, pen caricature, 1882, Edinburgh · W. Nicholson, watercolour, Scot. NPG · H. Raeburn, oils, Courtauld Inst. · W. S. Watson, oils, Scot. NPG · oils (after H. Raeburn), Scot. NPG

Thomson, George (1792–1838), tutor and chaplain in the household of Sir Walter Scott, was the eldest son of George Thomson (1758–1835), and his wife, Margaret, daughter of Robert Gillon of Lessudden, Roxburghshire. He was born at Melrose, Roxburghshire, on 7 May 1792, his father having been licensed by the presbytery of Dunblane on 4 July 1786, and called to Melrose about two years later. He caused the church to be moved from the abbey and a new building erected near at hand in 1810.

From a young age George did his utmost to relieve the necessities of his family, as his father's stipend was very small. He not only educated himself with the aid of a bursary, but took upon himself the education of two brothers out of his small income. In 1812 Scott wrote that his son was being tutored by Thomson, who walked between Melrose and Abbotsford 'with one leg of wood, and another of oak' (Lockhart, 3.8). As well as a respect for Thomson's learning, Scott had a special kindness for him, which was strengthened by Thomson's mishap—he had lost a leg in some rough play during childhood and had refused to give the name of the boy involved. Thomson was tall and vigorous, an expert fencer and a dashing horseman, despite his infirmity, and Scott remarked of him that accident had spoiled 'as bold and fine looking a grenadier as ever charged bayonet against a Frenchman's throat' (Lockhart, 4.248). Thomson's personality was characterized, like that of his father, by independence and simplicity. To Scott, there was 'an eccentricity about him that defies description' (*Journal*, 1.67), although it seems that he may have intended to capture some of it in his depiction of Dominie Sampson in *Guy Mannering*; Thomson himself did not discourage the belief that he was the original of that character. On one occasion, after a day's hunting at Abbotsford, Thomson kept the company waiting while he extemporized an exceptionally lengthy form of grace.

Scott frequently tried, though without success, to get Thomson a permanent post. Writing in 1819 to the duke of Buccleuch, he says, 'He is nearer Parson Adams than any living creature I ever saw—very learned, very religious, very simple, and extremely absent' (Lockhart, 3.247). He added that he was a very fair preacher and a staunch anti-Gallican. In 1820 Thomson left Abbotsford to coach the sons of Mrs Dennistoun of Colgrain, but Scott still hoped to procure him a 'harbour on his lee' (ibid., 5.33). He went to see Scott at Christmas 1825, when his kind heart and eccentricities were again noted in the *Journal*. In 1830 Scott was still petitioning the duke of Buccleuch on Thomson's behalf. Thomson died at Edinburgh on 8 January 1838. His only literary production seems to have been an 'Account of the parish of Melrose' contributed to Sir John Sinclair's *Statistical Account of Scotland* (1791–9).

THOMAS SECCOMBE, rev. SARAH COUPER

Sources J. G. Lockhart, *Memoirs of the life of Sir Walter Scott*, 7 vols. (1837–8) · *The journal of Sir Walter Scott*, 2 vols. (1890–91) · IGI · GM, 2nd ser., 9 (1838), 328 · *Familiar letters of Sir Walter Scott*, ed. D. Douglas, 2 vols. (1894) · *Fasti Scot.*

Thomson, George (1799–1886), army officer in the East India Company, second of six sons of George Thomson of Fairley, Aberdeenshire, formerly purser, East India Company service, and his wife, Agnes, daughter of Bailie John Dingwall of Rannieston, Aberdeenshire, was born at Fairley on 19 September 1799. He was educated by a private tutor and at Addiscombe College (1814–16), and passed out in October 1816 as an engineer cadet for the Bengal service. He arrived at Calcutta on 18 September 1818, and went to Cawnpore. In 1820 he joined the recently formed Corps of Bengal Sappers and Miners, commanded by Major Thomas Anburey, at Allahabad. On 28 January 1821 he took command of the detachment of sappers at Asirgarh. In 1822 he was constructing a road between Asirgarh and Nagpur, and later between Nagpur and Chapra. From March to June 1823 he was dismantling and blowing up the fort of Mandla. He was appointed adjutant of the Bengal Sappers and Miners on 29 May, and on 5 September he was promoted lieutenant.

In March 1824 war was declared with Burma, and in September Thomson went to Calcutta to join the pioneer department, for active service under Captain Schalch. On 14 December he left Calcutta for Chittagong, where a force of 11,000 men, under Brigadier-General Morrison of the 44th foot, had been assembled to penetrate to Ava through Arakan. Thomson was appointed field engineer to the force and placed in command of the pontoon train. On 10 January 1825 he started with Morrison's force by a route along the sea-coast, and, after crossing the Mayu estuary, a little to the west of the modern port of Akyab, advanced north-east through difficult country, and crossed the Kaladan or Great Arakan River. Thomson was almost always in front on reconnaissance, and, the forests being too thick and the rivers too deep to allow any other way of travelling, he went on foot and suffered greatly from fatigue. The approach to Arakan lay across a narrow valley, bounded by a range of hills crowned with stockades and garrisoned by 9000 Burmese. An attack on 29 March failed, but on 1 April Thomson assisted in the assault and capture of the stockades, and Arakan was taken. He was mentioned in dispatches.

On 7 May 1825 Thomson was appointed executive engineer, south-eastern division, of the public works department, and he was busy with the erection of cantonments in Arakan at the close of the rainy season. The division suffered very heavily from the unhealthy climate. Thomson was sent to survey and report upon the best situation in the islands near the mouth of the Beatong River for cantoning the division. He returned to Bengal in September 1826.

On 7 October 1826 Thomson was appointed executive engineer in the public works department at Neemuch, and was employed in building a fort there. He was promoted captain in the Bengal Engineers on 28 September 1827. On 6 December he was appointed to the Bengal Sappers and Miners, and on 21 February 1828 he returned to the public works department as executive engineer of the Rohilkhand division. In February 1829 he took furlough to Europe. He married in Aberdeen on 4 February 1830 Anna (1812/13–1900), daughter of Alexander Dingwall of Rannieston, Aberdeenshire, postmaster of Aberdeen, and they had several children.

Thomson returned to India in November 1831. On 9 December 1831 he was appointed to survey the country between Bankura and Shirghatti, and to estimate the cost of constructing a road from Jemor to the Karamnasa River. He was next placed in charge of the construction of the grand trunk road between Burdwan and Benares. In 1834 he had the additional task of constructing barracks at Hazaribagh for a European regiment; in this work, despite occasional conflict with the authorities, he adopted successful methods of his own for using convict labour.

In March 1837 Thomson was appointed to command the Bengal Sappers and Miners at Delhi, and to be at the same time executive engineer of the Delhi division of the public works department, a combination which he did not think was for the good of the service. On 13 September 1838 he was selected to be chief engineer of the army of the Indus assembling at Karnal for the invasion of Afghanistan. He marched from Delhi with two companies of sappers and miners on 20 October to Karnal, thence on 9 November to Ferozepore, and on to Bahawalpur (230 miles), where he arrived on 29 December. Rohri, on the left bank of the Indus, was reached on 24 January 1839, and the fort of Bukkur, on a rocky island between Rohri and Sukkur, on the right bank, was seized without opposition on 29 January, and preparations made by Thomson to bridge the river. The channel between Rohri and Bukkur was some 360 yards wide, and that between Bukkur and Sukkur about 130 yards, and in both the water ran very fast. Thomson had asked the political officer to assemble at Rohri materials for bridging, but when he arrived none were there. By great exertion he procured boats, cut down and split palm trees, made grass cables, constructed anchors of small trees joined together and loaded with stone, made nails on the spot, and in eleven days completed an effective pontoon bridge: a notable achievement for which he was rightly praised.

Thomson's services were of value in the long march through the Bolan Pass to Kandahar, which was reached at the end of April. On 27 June the march was resumed. Reports by the political officers of the weakness of Ghazni had induced the commander of the expedition, Sir John Keane, to leave his small battering train at Kandahar, but on arriving at Ghazni on 21 July he found it to be a formidable fortress which could be besieged only with a regular battering train. Thomson proposed to storm it, dash to the Kabul gate, blow it in, and admit the storming party. This was successfully done by Lieutenant H. M. Durand and others on 23 July. In the assault Thomson had a narrow escape. Keane, in his dispatch, ascribed to Thomson 'much of the credit of the success of this brilliant *coup de main*' (*LondG*, 30 Oct 1839). For this Thomson was promoted brevet major, dated from the capture of Ghazni. His account, 'Storming of Ghazni', and a description of his Indus Bridge by Lieutenant H. M. Durand, were published in the *Professional Papers of the Corps of the Royal Engineers* (1840).

The march to Kabul was resumed on 30 July, and it was occupied on 7 August. Thomson made an expedition over the mountains to Bamian to reconnoitre the route. In November he returned to India with some of the troops. For his services in the war Thomson received the thanks of the government and was made a CB, military division (December 1839), and from Shah Shuja received the order of the Durani empire (second class).

Thomson resumed the duties of the command of the Bengal Sappers and Miners, and of those of the public works department at Delhi; but, as he found them incompatible, a warm correspondence ensued with the military board, which resulted in Thomson's retiring from the service on 25 January 1841, despite Lord Auckland's efforts to dissuade him. He believed he had been unjustly treated by the board, and resigned disgusted at this. His health had suffered and he had lost several children; also his brother John (1801–1840), captain, Bengal Engineers, had died on 12 August 1840 and left him a considerable bequest. Before leaving India he submitted to the government suggestions for the improvement of the Bengal Sappers and Miners.

Thomson joined a brother in business in Liverpool; but this did not prosper, he lost money, and on 24 July 1844 he was glad to accept from the East India Company the appointment of recruiting officer and paymaster of soldiers' pensions in the Cork district, with the local rank of major. The former post he held until the company ended in 1861, and the latter until 1877, when he resigned and settled in Dublin. He was promoted brevet lieutenant-colonel on 28 November 1854. He became a director of the Great Southern and Western Railway Company of Ireland in 1846, and was practically the inspecting director, superintending the completion of the southern portion of the line and of the tunnel into Cork. He was tall, wiry, and 'a favourite in society' (Vibart, 333). He died at his residence, 33 Leeson Park, Dublin, on 11 February 1886. His eldest son, Hugh Gordon, born on 21 November 1830, became major-general of the Indian staff corps, and died on 23 May 1910.   R. H. VETCH, *rev.* ROGER T. STEARN

Sources *The Times* (15 Feb 1886) · *Royal Engineers Journal* (1886) · H. M. Vibart, *Addiscombe: its heroes and men of note* (1894) · BL OIOC · V. C. P. Hodson, *List of officers of the Bengal army, 1758–1834*, 4 (1947) · dispatches, *LondG* · W. F. B. Laurie, *Our Burmese wars and relations with Burma: being an abstract of military and political operations*, 2nd edn (1885) · Major Snodgrass [J. J. Snodgrass], *Narrative of the Burmese war* (1827) · J. W. Kaye, *History of the war in Afghanistan*, rev. edn, 3 vols. (1857–8) · H. M. Durand, *The First Afghan War and its causes* (1879) · E. W. C. Sandes, *The military engineer in India*, 1 (1933) · E. W. C. Sandes, *The military engineer in India*, 2 (1935) · J. A. Norris, *The First Afghan War, 1838–1842* (1967) · P. Macrory, *Signal catastrophe: the story of a disastrous retreat from Kabul, 1842* (1966); repr. as *Kabul catastrophe* (1986) · *Professional Papers of the Corps of Royal Engineers*, 4th ser., 4 (1840) · *Occasional papers of the Corps of Royal Engineers*, 3 (1879) · Boase, *Mod. Eng. biog.* · *WWW, 1897–1915* · *CGPLA Eng. & Wales* (1886)

Wealth at death £16,162 1s.—effects in England; £27,319 18s. 6d.: probate, 7 April 1886, *CGPLA Ire.*

Thomson, George Derwent (1903–1987), classical scholar, was born at 2 Allison Grove, Dulwich Common, London, on 19 August 1903, the eldest of five children of William Henry Thomson, chartered accountant, and his wife, Minnie Clements. He was educated at Dulwich preparatory school, Dulwich College (1916–22), and King's College, Cambridge, where he took firsts in both parts of the classical tripos (1924, 1926), and was elected to a fellowship in 1927. Thomson's father was an Ulsterman who had espoused nationalism, and his mother too championed Irish independence. While still at school, Thomson took lessons in the Irish language run by the Gaelic League. In 1923 he made the first of several visits to the Blasket Islands off the south-west coast of Ireland. There his experience of the vibrant, pre-capitalist culture of the people, and especially of the everyday poetry of their language, which he mastered thoroughly, made on him a profound impression that affected his conception of ancient Greece. He edited and translated *Twenty Years a-Growing* (1933), a memoir of growing up in the Blaskets by his close friend Muiris O'Sullivan that became a best-seller. His debt to Irish peasant poetry is acknowledged in his first book, *Greek Lyric Metre* (1929). Other early publications by him are translations into Irish of Plato, Euripides, Aeschylus, and the Book of Common Prayer. His last book, *Island Home* (1988), is his own memoir of the Blaskets.

In 1931 Thomson became lecturer in classics at University College, Galway. In 1934 he returned to his fellowship at Cambridge, and on 4 October married Katharine Stewart, a distinguished musician, the daughter of Hugh Fraser Stewart, fellow of Trinity College. Of their two daughters Elisabeth became a teacher in Birmingham and Margaret professor of modern Greek at Harvard. In 1933 he had joined the Communist Party, and from 1937 to 1970 was professor of Greek at Birmingham, where the vice-chancellor greeted him with the remark that the classics were to be admired as the best defence against communism.

Thomson's early work on Aeschylus produced editions with commentaries of the *Prometheus Bound* (1932) and the *Oresteia* (1938). *Aeschylus and Athens* (1941) studies Aeschylus in the context of the social process that had produced drama out of ritual, combining the approach to ritual inherited from the Cambridge school with Marxist attention to economy and society. *The Prehistoric Aegean* (1954) is an ambitious synthesis of archaeology, linguistics, the historical relationship of poetry to music, the anthropology of kinship, and much else. *The First Philosophers* (1955) studies the relationship between early Greek philosophy and the economy, but with characteristic breadth begins with the origins of language. His extraordinary range is evident also in the steady stream of articles, on kinship, poetry, land tenure, textual criticism, word order, linguistics, religion, Marxism, Thomas Hardy, communist political strategy, and much else. He combined communism with an imaginative feel for religion, absorption in the distant past with an intense and active interest in the present, mastery of 'high culture' with admiration for the language and culture of peasants and workers.

The Greek Language (1960) was based on the recognition, incorporated into Thomson's teaching at Birmingham, that to study ancient Greek without knowing modern Greek is like studying Chaucer without knowing modern English. In Greece in the 1960s he lectured to huge audiences. He translated Palamas into English (1969), and produced an excellent *Manual of Modern Greek* (1967).

Politically active throughout, Thomson was a popular lecturer in factory branches in Birmingham and a member of the national executive committee of the Communist Party. With the Sino-Soviet split he transferred his political allegiance to China. In 1955 he had spent six months at Peking University, studying Chinese and the relationship between early Greek and Chinese philosophy. For the China Policy Study Group he wrote three introductions to Marxism, *From Marx to Mao* (1972), *Capitalism and After* (1973), and *The Human Essence* (1974).

Thomson was, largely as a result of his Marxism, undervalued by the British classics establishment, all of whom he surpassed in breadth of vision and understanding, and to none of whom he was inferior in mastery of scholarly detail. He was much better known and appreciated outside the UK, especially in Ireland, Czechoslovakia, and Greece, and many of his books were (unusually for books on ancient Greece) translated into many languages.

Thomson's personality was one of great charm, with a musical quality of speech that is evident also in his entrancing and lucid style of writing. He inspired great devotion in students, colleagues, friends, and those who knew him only from his writings. He died at his home, 58 Billesley Lane, Moseley, Birmingham, on 3 February 1987. His wife survived him.   R. A. S. SEAFORD

Sources T. Enright, 'George Thomson, 1903–1987', in G. Thomson, *Island home: the Blasket heritage* (1988), 119–52 · *WWW* · R. H. Bulmer and L. P. Wilkinson, *A register of admissions to King's College, Cambridge, 1919–1958* (1963) · T. L. Ormiston, *Dulwich College register, 1619 to 1926* (1926) · b. cert. · m. cert. · d. cert.
Wealth at death £144,018: probate, 27 March 1987, *CGPLA Eng. & Wales*

Thomson, George Julius. See Scrope, George Poulett (1797–1876).

Thomson, Sir George Paget (1892–1975), physicist and Nobel prizewinner, was born in Cambridge on 3 May 1892, the elder child and only son of Sir Joseph John *Thomson FRS (1856–1940), later Cavendish professor of experimental physics and master of Trinity College, Cambridge, and his wife, Rose Elizabeth, daughter of Sir George Edward Paget, regius professor of physic at Cambridge. As his sister was some eleven years younger, he had virtually a full-time teacher in his mother and great encouragement, particularly in practical things, from his father. His early hobbies were model soldiery, ships, and armament, largely home made; these led to a lifelong love of sailing and a highly professional interest in aircraft.

From the Perse School, Cambridge, Thomson entered Trinity College, Cambridge, in 1910 as a scholar. He gained first-class honours in both parts of the mathematical tripos (1911 and 1912) and in part two of the natural sciences tripos (physics) in 1913, and was elected fellow and lecturer of Corpus Christi College, Cambridge, in 1914.

Thomson was on war service from late 1914 until 1919, first with the Queen's regiment in France, then on secondment to the Royal Flying Corps and based at what later became the Royal Aircraft Establishment at Farnborough. He worked, in the air as at the desk, on navigational problems and on general aerodynamics, with particular attention to stability and performance of aircraft. His first book, *Applied Aerodynamics* (1919), remains a valuable record of the contemporary state of that science.

In 1922, after three years of college and university teaching and of research into the physics of electrical discharges in gases, including the discovery (simultaneously with F. W. Aston) that lithium has two isotopes, Thomson left Cambridge for Aberdeen. In 1924 he married Kathleen Buchanan (d. 1941), daughter of the Very Revd Sir George Adam Smith, principal of the University of Aberdeen. They had two sons and two daughters; one son, John Adam, became British ambassador to the UN.

As professor of natural philosophy, Thomson was now in full charge of a small department in which his gas discharge research included equipment for applying comparatively high voltages (around 50 kilovolts) to positive ions. The ideas put forward by de Broglie on the wave theory of matter, first published in 1923, were being tested by C. J. Davisson of Bell Laboratories in New York, who was experimenting on the scattering of low energy electrons, looking for evidence of their wave nature. This concept was widely discussed at the British Association meeting in Oxford in 1926, where Thomson and Davisson were both present, though they did not then meet. Both men returned from Oxford determined to explore the subject further, but they proceeded in entirely different directions. Thomson found that he had apparatus in his department that could be easily modified; he used a solid target, first celluloid, later thin films of gold, silver, and platinum, as scatterer, and as beam, the high energy electrons that could be produced in the tube used for experiments on positive rays. The emerging beams were captured on photographic plates as bright centres surrounded by haloes, clearly demonstrating the wave nature of the electrons, and in December 1927 Thomson was able to report his findings to the journal *Nature*. He had arrived at these results at the same time as Davisson, who had been engaged on more sophisticated researches for a longer period, backed by the resources of the vast Bell Laboratories. At the British Association meeting of 1928, held in Glasgow, de Broglie, Davisson, and Thomson were able to meet, and to continue their discussions as house guests of Thomson. The importance of direct experimental tests of wave theory was understood only after they were performed, but the discovery of electron diffraction was accepted by the scientific community without opposition. Thomson and Davisson shared the 1937 Nobel prize for physics.

Appointed in 1930 as professor of physics at Imperial College, London, Thomson used the more extensive resources to exploit electron diffraction as a tool for the study of metal surfaces, as well as for investigating details of the diffraction process itself. He also introduced nuclear physics on a small scale, which became significant when the discovery that neutrons could cause nuclear fission in uranium raised the possibility of a chain reaction. Members of his laboratory had shown that neutrons losing speed by passage through matter could reach equilibrium with the thermal motions of the molecules of the material, and he had rapidly organized equipment for directly measuring their velocities. In 1938, with war imminent, he obtained a ton of uranium oxide, used paraffin wax and water as slowing down materials, and by the end of 1939 had satisfied himself that no simple assembly of these materials would work. (The first successful reactor, in the USA in 1942, used graphite.)

Having already organized a semi-official 'uranium committee', Thomson was well placed when in March 1940 O. R. Frisch and R. E. Peierls realized that a chain reaction using *fast* neutrons was feasible if uranium-235 could be separated from the much more abundant isotope uranium-238, to produce not merely heat but an explosion of unprecedented power. Their memorandum was quickly passed to the highest government circles, and led to the formation of the MAUD committee, generally known as Maud, a name intended to obscure its purpose. Under Thomson's chairmanship its duties were to supervise investigation into the possibilities of uranium's contributing to the war effort. Research, assigned to various universities, was pushed forward in several directions. It started work on 10 April 1940, and at first centred on isotope separation, with a group at the Cavendish Laboratory aiming to produce a chain reaction with normal uranium and heavy water. Before many months elapsed it was realized on both sides of the Atlantic that any chain reaction offered possibilities for making a bomb, and tests in the USA supported this. The Maud committee delivered two reports in July 1941, the first stated definitively that it would be possible to make a uranium bomb which would be both destructive and release large quantities of radioactive substances; the second dealt with the use of uranium as a source of power. These reports led to complete reorganization of work on both bomb and boiler. In its short life it had been one of the most effective committees ever set in motion. Thomson left for America in August; his wife had become very ill, and she died there later that year. He became British liaison officer in Ottawa until 1942 when he returned to England as scientific adviser to the Air Ministry. He was knighted in 1943, and was already resuming some contact with Imperial College.

In 1945–6 Thomson conceived and partly developed the idea that an electrodeless ring discharge in deuterium might release energy by nuclear fusion; experiments, first started at Imperial College, were moved by several stages and on an increasing scale to the government's laboratory at Aldermaston where their descendant became part of a major European project.

In 1952 Thomson returned to Cambridge as master of Corpus. His decisive approach to practical matters had full scope here, for there was much college development in the ten years of his mastership. He combined great charm as a host with a certain pugnacity in conversation. His voice was powerful, his philosophy generally conservative but occasionally iconoclastic, and his sizing up of a conversational situation very rapid. So formidable an equipment naturally tended to overwhelm; but, as one of his sons wrote, he did not press for unconditional surrender but left open a line of retreat. He read widely and critically, with more attention to content than to craftsmanship; his pleasure in pictures was concentrated on nautical subjects, while of music he said, 'I judge it by its mean square amplitude'. He was essentially a practical man, and his distinction both in physics and in service to the nation rested much upon catching the tide of events. Of medium build, with an oddly springy step, he remained physically active even after his retirement, which began in 1962 and which was spent quietly in Cambridge.

In the University of Cambridge, Thomson was Smith's prizeman for 1916; five other universities conferred honorary degrees upon him and in later years he was an honorary fellow of Trinity and Corpus Christi colleges, Cambridge, and Imperial College, London. Elected FRS in 1930 he received the Royal Society's Hughes medal in 1939 and royal medal in 1949; he was also a medallist of the Institution of Electrical Engineers and of the Franklin Institute of Philadelphia, USA. He was an active member of the Voluntary Euthanasia Society, and its vice-president from 1970.

Thomson died at his home, Little Howe, Mount Pleasant, Cambridge, on 10 September 1975. He was commemorated by the George Thomson building in Leckhampton.

P. B. MOON, *rev.* ANITA MCCONNELL

Sources P. B. Moon, *Memoirs FRS*, 23 (1977), 529–56 · G. Thomson, *Nuclear energy in Britain during the last war: the Cherwell-Simon lecture delivered in Oxford on 18 October 1960* (1962) · *The Times* (12 Sept 1975), 17g · *The Times* (17 Sept 1975), 18g · *Physics Today* (Dec 1975), 77 · Contemporary Scientific Archives Centre, 75/5/80 · A. Russo, 'Fundamental research at Bell Laboratories: the discovery of electron diffraction', *Historical Studies in the Physical Sciences*, 12 (1981–2), 117–60 · M. Gowing, *Britain and atomic energy, 1939–1945* (1964) · private information (1986) · personal knowledge (1986) · d. cert.
Archives Trinity Cam., corresp. and papers; papers mainly relating to the life of his father Sir J. J. Thomson | CAC Cam., corresp. with Sir James Chadwick · CAC Cam., papers relating to Maud committee · ICL, corresp. with Herbert Dingle · IWM, corresp. with Sir Henry Tizard · Nuffield Oxf., corresp. with Lord Cherwell · U. Glas., corresp. with William Cochrane · University of Copenhagen, Niels Bohr Institute for Astronomy, Physics and Geophysics, corresp. with Niels Bohr
Likenesses W. Stoneman, photograph, 1946, NPG · E. Nelson, oils, *c.*1953, CCC Cam. · M. Ayrton, pencil drawing, *c.*1961–1962, CCC Cam. · G. Argent, photograph, 1970, NPG
Wealth at death £66,642: probate, 1976

Thomson, Sir George Pirie (1887–1965), naval officer and press censor, was born on 30 January 1887 at Jubbulpore in India, the son of Robert Brown Thomson, a civil engineer in the public works department, and his wife, May Forbes, daughter of William R. Pirie, moderator of the general assembly of the Church of Scotland and principal of Aberdeen University. His uncle, the Revd George Pirie, was professor of mathematics at Aberdeen University from 1878. Thomson was taken by his parents to Switzerland and until he was six years old was unable to speak anything but French. He began his education in English at George Watson's College, Edinburgh, and joined the Royal Navy at the age of fifteen, claiming that the main reason for this choice was that naval uniform might make him look slimmer. He passed for lieutenant with five firsts and specialized in submarines, which were then (1908) in the very early stages of their development. He married in 1909 and had two daughters.

Thomson spent twenty-five years in the navy, reaching the rank of rear-admiral in 1939. His final appointment before retirement was as second member of the Australian naval board (1937–9). However, when Hitler invaded Poland, Thomson, who had retired from the navy in February 1939, was on holiday in the south of France. Returning to London he presented himself to Churchill, then the first lord of the Admiralty, and received his orders: 'Go at once to the Ministry of Information and give Admiral Usborne a hand with the Press Censorship. He appears to be hard pressed' (Thomson, 1).

Before war began, a machinery for press censorship had been set up, staffed by retired officers from the three services. On 3 September, a few hours after Britain declared war on Germany, the whole machine collapsed when the British liner *Athenia*, carrying civilians (including many women and children), was torpedoed and sunk without warning by a German submarine, with a loss of 112 lives. Overseas correspondents jammed the censors' office with long cables containing all available details and outward cable traffic came to a halt.

Nine days later another breakdown, of a different kind, occurred. On 4 September, in great secrecy, the British expeditionary force had begun its move to France. Silence was broken on 13 September by French radio. Having received permission, the British press issued news items and pictures which had been prepared in advance. Two and a half hours later the War Office cancelled the permission which it had given. By now whole editions had been printed, packaged, and placed in trains and vans for dispatch all over the country and to neutral Ireland. The War Office ordered that all copies of all papers carrying the news should be seized. Police occupied newspaper offices, removed the papers from trains, and stopped private cars, confiscating single copies. Fleet Street reacted with vigour, proprietors intervened forcefully in Whitehall, and three hours later, at 2.30 a.m., the cancellation of the permission was itself cancelled.

This was the situation in which Thomson found himself within ten days of the outbreak of the war, previously having had, as he wrote in his book, *Blue Pencil Admiral* (1947), 'an experience of the Press which was limited to reading my newspaper at the breakfast table' (Thomson, 1). He showed the frame of mind in which he attacked his new job when he said to a reporter in the very earliest days: 'I should be awfully grateful if you wouldn't address me as "sir"' (ibid.).

The original body of censors, retired officers, had always been used to giving orders or carrying them out, while the journalists were used to challenging authority and arguing with it. Now, however, confidence between press and censorship soon developed; the press learned that Thomson was on their side and would go to the limit to help them. He himself came to trust the press and to know that he could count on them not to let him down.

This relationship was essential to the working of the British censorship system, which was voluntary, with a series of D (for Defence) notices warning of particular topics to be avoided. Items were not submitted for censorship unless there was doubt about whether they conflicted with the D notices. A single set of figures quoted by Thomson in *Blue Pencil Admiral* shows how the system operated and the amount of work involved: 'there were over 400,000 separate issues of newspapers during the war … [from which] only 650,000 news items were submitted [to censorship]—that is, only one and a half items from each separate newspaper' (Thomson, 216).

Admiral C. V. Usborne remained at the ministry of information until January 1940. After a short interregnum, in December 1940 Thomson became chief press censor, a post he held until the end of the war amid a swirl of changes in the senior appointments at the ministry.

It was then decided that the essentials of the system which Thomson had been operating should be continued in peacetime under the title of the services, press, and broadcasting committee, with Thomson as secretary. He was also appointed public relations officer of the Latin American Centre.

Thomson was appointed OBE in 1919, CBE in 1939, and CB in 1946; he was knighted in 1963. He died at Queen Mary's Hospital, Roehampton, on 24 January 1965.

DAVID R. WOODWARD, rev.

Sources G. P. Thomson, *Blue pencil admiral: the inside story of press censorship* (1947) · *The Times* (26 Jan 1965) · *WWW* · Kelly, *Handbk*
Archives SOUND BL NSA, current affairs recordings
Likenesses photograph, repro. in *The Times*, 14

Thomson, George Reid (1893–1962), judge, was born in Glasgow on 11 June 1893, the eldest of the four children of William Rankin Thomson, a minister of the United Presbyterian Church of Scotland, and his wife, Agnes Macfee. His father spent much of his life as a clergyman in South Africa, and Thomson received his early education at the South African College School, Cape Town. He went up to Corpus Christi College, Oxford, as a Rhodes scholar in October 1911 and obtained a second class in classical honour moderations in 1913. Like many of his contemporaries, he abandoned Oxford at the outbreak of war in 1914. He joined the Royal Fusiliers as a private soldier, was commissioned in the 5th Argyll and Sutherland Highlanders in 1915, and served in Egypt, Palestine, and France. He was wounded in action, promoted captain, and mentioned in dispatches. On demobilization he did not return to Oxford but took his degree in 1920 under the decree which exempted those who had served in the armed forces from further examination. He was elected an honorary fellow of Corpus Christi in 1957. In 1925 he married Grace (*d.* 1980), daughter of the Revd Daniel Georgeson of Bowling. They had no children.

Thomson entered the law faculty of Edinburgh University in 1919, and graduated bachelor of laws with distinction in March 1922, after having been awarded the Muirhead prize, the Dalgety prize, the Thow scholarship, and the Vans Dunlop scholarship, which he shared with John Cameron. He was given the degree of honorary doctor of laws by Edinburgh University in 1957. He was admitted advocate in 1922. He had no legal connections and was an unspectacular pleader and it was some time before solicitors appreciated the virtue of his firm grasp of legal principles, his thorough preparation of even the most trivial case, and his sound common sense. He gradually built up a substantial practice in cases under the Workmen's Compensation Acts and similar fields, but it was not until 1936, when he took silk, that his talent for synthesis and his ability to reduce a complex argument to a few and concisely stated propositions emerged. It was quickly recognized and he acquired a large and broadly based practice. He was an advocate depute from 1940 to 1945.

On the formation of the Labour government in 1945 Thomson was appointed lord advocate and sworn of the privy council. The government had a large legislative programme and the prime minister, Attlee, wished to have his assistance in the Commons. Against his better judgement, Thomson was persuaded to stand for East Edinburgh, where a vacancy was created for him by the elevation of F. W. Pethick-Lawrence, the sitting member, to the peerage. Thomson was elected by a substantial majority. His commitment to the Labour Party resulted from his sympathy with the underprivileged, and his approach to political problems was pragmatic and not ideological. This approach, his dislike of rhetoric, and, above all, his contempt for what he called 'the ya-boo' of party strife, and the heated atmosphere of a House of Commons largely concerned with bitterly fought nationalization legislation, made this an unhappy period in an otherwise happy life.

In March 1947 the office of lord justice-clerk fell vacant. Thomson wished for the appointment, but the prime minister felt unable to do without him in the Commons, and Alexander Moncrieff was appointed. This was clearly a stopgap appointment and, when Lord Moncrieff resigned in October 1947, Thomson was appointed lord justice-clerk. He presided over the second division of the Court of Session and the court of criminal appeal and, from time to time, sat as a judge of first instance. He was a patient and attentive judge, courteous to all; he rarely interrupted a witness or counsel, and then only in a search for clarification. He desired the truth, but he was very conscious of the limitations of the legal process and, as he put it in an often quoted judgment, 'A litigation is in essence a trial of skill between opposing parties conducted under recognized rules, and the prize is the judge's decision' (private information). His judgments were based on the application of broad legal principles to the ascertained facts, and were couched in simple and sometimes racy language, which reflected his knowledge of human affairs and wide reading. He is said to have quoted Homer in the original Greek in the course of a hearing before him.

Thomson's real genius lay in his sincerity, simplicity, and friendliness. He and his wife had a most happy marriage and created in their home a centre of hospitality for a wide circle of friends. Every young advocate—and his bride, when acquired—was bidden to, and made most welcome at, their home, not as a duty imposed by his office, but because they both liked young people and lively minds. He was a discerning collector of modern Scottish paintings, a fisher, and an enthusiastic and skilful golfer, who delighted to select, organize, and captain the Scottish team in the annual match against the English bench and bar. He was taken ill while on holiday in Spain and died on 15 April 1962 at Gibraltar.

DOUGLAS JOHNSTON, rev.

Sources private information (1981) · personal knowledge (1981) · *WWW* · *CGPLA Eng. & Wales* (1962)
Likenesses double portrait, photograph, 1970 (with Olof Palme), Hult. Arch.
Wealth at death £39,554 18s. 11d.: confirmation, 1962, Scotland

Thomson, Sir Godfrey Hilton (1881–1955), educational psychologist and psychometrician, was born at 19 Corporation Road, Carlisle, Cumberland, on 27 March 1881, the son of Charles Thomson, a domestic machinery agent, and his wife, Jane Hilton. Shortly after the birth his mother left the marital home, taking the infant Godfrey with her, and settled with her mother and sisters in Felling, Northumberland. Godfrey attended the local board elementary school and then, aged thirteen, he won a scholarship for a free place for secondary education at Rutherford College in Newcastle upon Tyne. A full-time pupil there from 1894 to 1897, he then attended evening classes in science while employed as a pupil teacher at his old school at High Felling, passing the London University intermediate BSc examinations in 1899.

In 1900, having won a queen's scholarship, Thomson embarked on a full-time science course, while training as a teacher at the normal department, at the Durham College of Science (soon renamed Armstrong College) in Newcastle, then part of the University of Durham. He achieved a BSc with distinction in mathematics and physics in 1903, having obtained his teaching certificate the previous year. He was appointed Pemberton fellow of the University of Durham in 1903, which enabled him to travel to the University of Strasbourg to study under Professor Ferdinand Braun, the foremost German expert in wireless telegraphy. After obtaining his PhD in 1906 for research on Hertzian waves, Thomson returned to Armstrong College as assistant lecturer in education, fulfilling a condition of the queen's scholarship that he should teach for a certain period 'in an elementary school, the army, the navy, or the workhouse'. As his duties included lecturing on educational psychology, Thomson threw himself into learning about psychology and, as he put it in his autobiographical sketch of 1952, 'felt the change pleasant from studying only dead matter' (Thomson).

A turning point came in the summer vacation of 1911, which Thomson spent at C. S. Myers's laboratory in Cambridge. He was introduced to William Brown's book *The Essentials of Mental Measurement* (1911), a work whose subsequent editions (1921, 1925, 1940) Thomson co-authored with Brown. At first, the psychophysical aspects caught his interest, leading to publications in the *British Journal of Psychology* and a DSc in 1913. But it was Brown's criticisms of Spearman's two-factor theory of intelligence, and especially his insistence on a single underlying general factor, that really caught Thomson's mathematical eye. With the aid of dice and a house slipper, Thomson generated at his fireside artificial test scores whose correlational structure still satisfied Spearman's theory even without any general factor. The eventual publication of this finding in the *British Journal of Psychology* in 1916 sparked off a long-running, sometimes vituperative, but essentially unresolved, dispute with Spearman. None the less, it marked the start of Thomson's many significant contributions to the debates on intelligence and the newly emerging method of factor analysis. Thomson's own theory of intelligence evolved into his 'sampling hypothesis', which supposed that the mind consisted of numerous 'bonds' and that, inevitably, overlapping samples of these connections would be invoked by tests of different mental abilities. Hence, in Thomson's view, the resulting correlational structure indicated a statistical rather than a mental phenomenon. His most important work on factor analysis, *The Factorial Analysis of Human Behaviour*, ran to five editions between 1939 and 1951.

Thomson married, on 16 July 1912 at the Primitive Methodist Chapel, Kingsley Terrace, Newcastle, Jane Hutchinson (*b.* 1882/3), a graduate of Armstrong College and an assistant lecturer in the department of education; she was the daughter of Thomas Hutchinson, a builder and contractor. They had one son. Before his marriage Thomson was a volunteer with the Northumberland Fusiliers; he re-joined Armstrong College's Officers' Training Corps in 1915 and was engaged in military duties until 1919. In 1920, newly promoted to the chair of education at Newcastle, he began devising 'mental' tests for Northumberland county council designed to identify children in more underprivileged schools who might benefit from secondary education.

Thomson's growing reputation brought an invitation to visit E. L. Thorndike at Columbia University, and the family spent the academic year 1923–4 in the USA. The lectures he gave there were published in 1924 as *Instinct, Intelligence and Character*. Soon after returning to Newcastle, Thomson was offered a chair of education at Edinburgh University which carried with it the directorship of Moray House teacher training college. The tests that Thomson developed after moving to Edinburgh in 1925, known as the Moray House tests, became widely employed throughout the UK and elsewhere. Selection for secondary education was not the only use to which the tests were put. Thomson and his many collaborators also carried out large-scale investigations on Northumbrian and Scottish schoolchildren, relating the test results to social factors such as family size and father's occupation.

Among Thomson's many honours in his later years were a knighthood in 1949, vice-presidency of the Royal Society of Edinburgh, and presidency of section J of the British Association for 1949, as well as membership of several foreign academies and learned societies. He was an honorary fellow of the British Psychological Society and its president for 1945–6. Even after retirement from his Edinburgh chair in 1951 Thomson was still busy with the Scottish survey material and his writing. His last book, *The Geometry of Mental Measurement*, appeared just a year before his death, and not until 1953 did he relinquish the editorship of what became the *British Journal of Mathematical and Statistical Psychology*, a journal he had edited jointly with Cyril Burt from its founding in 1947.

Colleagues and former students described Thomson as forthright in his speech and opinions, a brilliant teacher, and a man of integrity, though to students, who nicknamed him 'God Thom', his manner could seem rather haughty and remote. He died from cancer in Edinburgh Royal Infirmary on 9 February 1955, survived by his wife.

P. LOVIE and A. D. LOVIE

Sources G. Thomson, 'Godfrey Thomson', *A history of psychology in autobiography*, ed. E. G. Boring and others, 4 (1952), 279–94 · G. Thomson, *The education of an Englishman: an autobiography* (1969) · S. Sharp, '"Much more at home with 3.999 pupils than with four": the contributions to psychometrics of Sir Godfrey Thomson', *British Journal of Mathematical and Statistical Psychology*, 50 (1997), 163–74 · J. J. Robertson, 'Godfrey Thomson', *Seventh Godfrey Thomson lecture* (1964) · P. E. Vernon, 'The contributions to education of Sir Godfrey Thomson', *British Journal of Educational Studies*, 10 (1962), 123–37 · *American Journal of Psychology*, 68 (1955) · *British Journal of Educational Psychology* (1955) · *British Journal of Psychology*, 46 (1955) · *British Journal of Statistical Psychology*, 8 (1955) · *Psychometrika*, 20 (1955) · *The Times* (29 May 1964) · private information (2004) · J. C. Tyson and J. P. Tuck, *The origins and development of the training of teachers in the University of Newcastle upon Tyne* (1971) · b. cert. · m. cert. · d. cert.
Archives U. Edin., Moray House test collection
Likenesses Swaine, photograph, repro. in Thomson, *Education of an Englishman*, frontispiece · photograph, repro. in *British Journal of Statistical Psychology*, facing p. 1 · portrait, U. Edin., Moray House Institute of Education
Wealth at death £8193 9s. 3d.: confirmation, 16 April 1955, *CCI*

Thomson, Greek. *See* Thomson, Alexander (1817–1875).

Thomson, Henry (1773–1843), painter and illustrator, the son of a purser in the navy, was born at St George's Square, Portsea, Hampshire, on 31 July 1773. He was at school for nearly nine years at Bishop's Waltham, Hampshire. In 1787 he went with his father to Paris, and returned to London on the outbreak of the revolution in 1789. He entered the Royal Academy Schools in 1790, and became a pupil of John Opie at about the same time; remaining Opie's friend, he finished his former master's portrait of the duke of Gloucester in 1807, when Opie was on his deathbed. In 1793 he returned to the continent with his father, to complete his studies, and travelled in Italy until 1798—visiting Parma, Bologna, Florence, Rome, Naples, and Venice. He returned by Vienna, Dresden, Berlin, and Hamburg in 1799.

Back in London, Thomson became a contributor to Boydell's Shakspeare Gallery notably *Perdita* and some subjects from *The Tempest*. As early as 1792 he had exhibited a portrait at the Royal Academy, but he did not become a regular contributor until 1800. In 1801 he was elected an associate member of the Royal Academy and in 1804 Royal Academician, *Prospero and Miranda* being his diploma work. From this time until 1825 he continued to exhibit many mythological and domestic subjects, as well as portraits, at the academy. Major works included *Love Sheltered* and *The Red Cross Knight* (both painted in 1806 and engraved in mezzotint by William Say), *The Infancy of Jupiter* (1812; engraved by Henry Meyer), *Eurydice* (1814; engraved by William Ward), and *Christ Raising Jairus's Daughter* (exh. RA, 1820; Tate collection). During the same period he contributed a large number of small illustrations to *The British Classics* (1803–10), edited by John Sharpe, and other works and portraits to *The Theatrical Recorder* (1805). He also translated A. C. Quatremère de Quincy's *The Destination of Works of Art* (1821).

In 1825 Thomson was appointed keeper of the Royal Academy, in succession to Henry Fuseli, but resigned the office after two years owing to a severe illness from which he never recovered sufficiently to work again at full strength. In 1828 he retired to Portsea, where he amused himself with boating, and with making sketches of marine objects in oil on rough paper, which he presented to his friends. However, he contributed some illustrations to *The Ladies' Pocket Magazine* (1830), and continued to exhibit paintings until 1834. He died at his home, 18 Union Street, Portsea, apparently unmarried, on 6 April 1843, and was buried in Portsmouth churchyard near his mother's grave. 'From his secluded habits very little was known of him, except that his charity was extensive considering his means' (*GM*, 100). In his will Thomson made several bequests, totalling about £4000, to his friends and servants. Examples of his work are in Stourhead, Wiltshire; the Tate collection, London; and Norwich Castle Museum.

Though Thomson's pictures were extremely popular in his own day, they were subsequently known chiefly by the good mezzotint engravings in which they were reproduced.

CAMPBELL DODGSON, *rev.* DAVID WOOTTON

Sources Redgrave, *Artists* · Bryan, *Painters* (1903–5) · A. Earland, *John Opie and his circle* (1911) · S. Houfe, *The dictionary of 19th century British book illustrators and caricaturists*, rev. edn (1996) · Graves, *Artists* · J. Turner, ed., *The dictionary of art*, 34 vols. (1996) · will, PRO, PROB 11/1980, sig. 368 · *GM*, 2nd ser., 20 (1843), 100–01 · B. Stewart and M. Cutten, *The dictionary of portrait painters in Britain up to 1920* (1997)
Archives BL, corresp., Add. MS 50066 | RA, corresp. with Thomas Lawrence · Yale U., Beinecke L., Osborne collection
Likenesses J. Jackson, watercolour, 1810, NPG · R. Cooper, engraving, 1817 (after J. Jackson) · M. A. Shee, oils, RA
Wealth at death several bequests totalling £3000–£4000; plus other property incl. named works of art: will, PRO, PROB 11/1980, sig. 368

Thomson, Henry William [*later* Henry Byerley] (1822–1867), judge in Ceylon, was born in Chelsea, London, in May 1822, the son of Anthony Todd *Thomson (1778–1849), physician, and his second wife, Katherine Byerley (1797–1862) [*see* Thomson, Katherine], novelist and biographer, of an old Durham family (in 1846 he changed his second forename to Byerley). He was educated at University College, London, and at Jesus College, Cambridge, where he matriculated in 1841, was a scholar in 1844, and graduated BA as senior optime in 1846. He was admitted at the Inner Temple on 25 April 1846, called to the bar on 14 May 1849, and practised on the northern circuit.

Thomson specialized in military and international law, and published *Laws of War Affecting Commerce and Shipping* (1854), *The military forces and institutions of Great Britain and Ireland: their constitution, administration, and government, military and civil* (1855), based on much unused material from parliamentary blue books and similar sources, and *The choice of a profession: a concise account and comparative review of the English professions* (1857).

Thomson was then living at 8 Serjeant's Inn, Temple, and professional success seemed distant when, in May 1858, he was appointed queen's advocate in Ceylon by the colonial secretary, Lord Stanley [*see* Stanley, Edward Henry, fifteenth earl of Derby]. The same year Thomson married Mlle Sarita Beaumont; they had two sons, Henry Byerley, who took orders in 1888, and Arthur Byerley. In 1861 Thomson was promoted puisne judge of the supreme court of Colombo. He soon started work on a digest of the law as administered in Ceylon, and in 1866 he was in London superintending the publication of his most permanent memorial, *Institutes of the Laws of Ceylon* (2 vols., 1866), which ranked as an authority together with the judgments of Sir Charles Marshall, and which, as the chief justice of Ceylon Sir Edward Creasy said at Thomson's death, 'will long be cited with admiration and gratitude'. Thomson died at Colombo, as the result of an apoplectic seizure, on 5 January 1867. He was buried that month, probably in Colombo, and was survived by his wife.

The judge's younger brother **John Cockburn Thomson** (1834–1860), Sanskritist, was born in London, and after studying at Bonn matriculated from Trinity College, Oxford, on 7 June 1852 and graduated BA from St Mary Hall (later incorporated into Oriel College) in 1857. At Oxford he worked at Sanskrit (continuing studies begun at Munich) under Horace Hayman Wilson, and before he graduated, when only twenty-one, he published *The Bhagavadgita, or, A discourse between Krishna and Arjuna on divine matters: a Sanskrit philosophical poem, translated [into English prose] with copious notes, an introduction on Sanskrit philosophy, and other matter* (2 vols., 1855). This was praised by Wilson and by foreign scholars and was used in the East India College, Haileybury. In 1857 Thomson won the Boden Sanskrit scholarship at Oxford, and was awarded a gold medal by Maximilian of Bavaria. He was a member of the Asiatic Society of Paris and the Antiquarian Society of Normandy. Under the pseudonym Philip Wharton he was joint author with his mother of *Queens of Society* (1860) and *Wits and Beaux of Society* (1860), two anecdotal volumes well received by the public. Following Wilson's death in 1860 Thomson became a candidate for the India Office librarianship but he was accidentally drowned when swimming at Tenby, Pembrokeshire, on 26 May 1860. He was unmarried.

THOMAS SECCOMBE, rev. ROGER T. STEARN

Sources GM, 4th ser., 3 (1867), 392 · Colonial Office List (1867), 252 · Ceylon Bi-Monthly Examiner (15 Jan 1867) · North American Review, 86.435 · Foster, Alum. Oxon. · Allibone, Dict. · Venn, Alum. Cant. · Boase, Mod. Eng. biog. · L. A. Mills, Ceylon under British rule, 1795–1932 (1933) · CGPLA Eng. & Wales (1860) [John Cockburn Thomson]
Wealth at death under £5000: administration, 1867, CGPLA Eng. & Wales · under £1500—John Cockburn Thomson: administration, 1860, CGPLA Eng. & Wales

Thomson, Hugh (1860–1920), illustrator, was born in Kingsgate Street, Coleraine, co. Londonderry, on 1 June 1860, the eldest of the three surviving children of John Thomson (1822–1894), a tea merchant in the town, and his wife, Catherine, née Andrews (d. 1871), a shopkeeper. Thomson was destined for a business career when he left the model school in Coleraine at the age of fourteen to work in a local linen factory. Instead, his talent for drawing took him to Belfast in 1877 to work for Marcus Ward & Co., a large and technically advanced firm of colour printers and publishers. Here he came under the guidance of John Vinycomb, head of the art department, who cultivated his talent for illustration and encouraged him to move to London in 1883. He married Jessie Naismith Miller in Belfast on 29 December 1884 and they returned to London.

From February of that year Thomson had been working with Macmillan & Co. on the recently founded *English Illustrated Magazine*, edited by Joseph Comyns Carr with a stable of the most distinguished writers and illustrators of the day. Carr was another influential mentor for whom Thomson provided scenes of Covent Garden and Regency Bath and the illustrations for the Addison and Steele *Spectator* papers *Days with Sir Roger de Coverley* (1886–7). For the second instalment Thomson's drawings were reproduced by photomechanically produced line-block, the first to be printed this way. The speed and low cost of reproduction of the process opened a new era in book illustration in which Thomson played an important part, but although he shared the pages of the *English Illustrated Magazine* with his most distinguished contemporaries, exhibited with Kate Greenaway, and had studied the work of Caldecott in particular—both of whose work was produced by his Belfast employer, Marcus Ward—he remained remarkably free of the influence of the artists and the art movements of his time. His style seems to have emerged fully formed and to have corresponded perfectly with popular taste, and, while he refined his technical skills during his career, he rarely departed from it. A contemporary of the Brock brothers, he shared their feeling for line, detail, and period atmosphere but remained untouched by the aesthetic movement and the work of other contemporaries such as Arthur Rackham or Edmund Dulac. Through Sir Roger de Coverley's mild adventures he could exploit his interests in eighteenth-century settings and costumes and develop a limited range of figures in idealized settings. Reflecting successfully the nostalgia of the time, his fine line drawing of rural characters and gentle countrified society appealed to the imagination of the public; most of Thomson's best-known work is in this idiom. This style sat lightly on the page and reproduced well in smaller formats. Macmillans recognized its popular contemporary appeal, and Thomson's next commission was for a series on historic coaching roads, *Coaching Days and Coaching Ways*, by W. Outram Tristram in 1887–8, published in book form in the latter year. The illustrations were so popular that a series of Staffordshire pottery, 'Coaching Days Ware', was produced with Thomson scenes.

Although Thomson had little formal education or art training, as a boy he had read widely and drawn and copied horses and dogs and the vigorous hunting scenes which first established his reputation. His other precocious interest was in the eighteenth-century furniture in his family home, an interest he pursued in museums in London all his life and which gave a precision and exactitude to his period settings.

Mrs Gaskell's *Cranford*, illustrated for Macmillan (1891), belongs to the world which Thomson had made his own in the *English Illustrated Magazine* and *The Vicar of Wakefield* (1890). *Cranford* was widely imitated by other publishers and gave its name to a series of gift books in the same format—crown octavo with three edges gilt, bound in dark green cloth, front and spine heavily stamped in gold. Thomson illustrated eleven of the twenty-four books which came to be called the Cranford series. At this period he also worked on the first two books for his lifelong friend the poet Austin Dobson, *The Ballad of Beau Brocade* (1892) and *The Story of Rosina* (1896). In 1894 Thomson illustrated *Pride and Prejudice* for George Allen. He returned to Macmillan for five more of Jane Austen's novels—*Emma* (1896), *Sense and Sensibility* (1896), *Mansfield Park* (1897), and *Northanger Abbey* and *Persuasion* (1898). The depth of Austen's characters is missing, although the books are attractive and the artist's light touch and feeling for period manners provide a charming and accessible gloss to the author's work.

Thomson derived considerable satisfaction from his books on Ireland written by Stephen Gwynne (1864–1950). *Highways and Byways of Donegal and Antrim* (1899) was much reprinted and contains some notable pen-and-ink character sketches. In all Thomson was involved with twelve volumes of the Highways and Byways series, which stretched from *Donegal and Antrim* to *Devon and Cornwall*.

From the early 1890s Thomson's drawings were exhibited on several occasions, beginning with a joint exhibition with Kate Greenaway at the Fine Art Society in 1891. For these he tinted many of his drawings which had been prepared and printed in black and white, but from 1910 the Leicester Galleries were showing illustrations which had been prepared for printing in colour. The last two volumes in the Cranford series, both illustrated by Thomson, *Scenes from Clerical Life* (1906) and *Silas Marner* (1907), included colour, as did many of his later commissions in larger formats and rather grandiose style for Heinemann and Hodder and Stoughton. These included works by Shakespeare, Sheridan, Goldsmith, and Hawthorne, and the popular plays of J. M. Barrie, all appearing in the years 1910 to 1915. During this time Thomson moved from simple country scenes and characters to the more elaborate world of crinolines and powdered wigs of the Queen Anne school.

The war years brought ill health and, with few publications and, in particular, less demand for the lavish and sentimental volumes illustrated by Thomson, financial hardship. In 1915 for the first time in many years there was no Thomson book or magazine illustration for the Christmas market. With very little work apart from some commissions from friends and an American edition of Thomas Hughes's *Tom Brown's Schooldays* (1918), by 1917 Thomson was obliged to take a job with the Board of Trade, where he worked until 1919. He was granted a civil-list pension of £75 in 1918. After the major technical advances in printing in the late nineteenth century there was little change in production or demand before 1920, when the introduction of the net book agreement and interest in private presses began to influence the quality of commercial publishing. There was still some demand for Thomson's work, and in spite of his deteriorating health he accepted a commission from Macmillan in 1919 to do a Highways and Byways volume on Gloucestershire, for which he prepared the sketches in the summer of 1919. There were offers of work from other publishers, but before he could benefit from the post-war recovery in publishing he died of heart disease at his home, 8 Patten Road, Wandsworth Common, on 7 May 1920. He was survived by his wife and only son, John Thomson, born in 1886.

Mild-mannered and retiring, with a gift for friendship, Thomson was both popular and influential in his time. Although he was never a confident draughtsman, his grasp of design and his 'unerring sense of period and literary sympathy' (Jamison) gave his best work a lasting charm. The Ulster Museum in Belfast holds a number of his watercolours and drawings as well as a complete set of his illustrated books.   OLIVIA FITZPATRICK

Sources M. H. Spielmann and W. C. Jerrold, *Hugh Thomson: his art, his letters, his humour and his charm* (1931) · P. Muir, *Victorian illustrated books* (1971), 197–200 · G. N. Ray, *The illustrator and the book in England from 1790 to 1914* (1976) · M. Felmingham, *The illustrated gift book, 1880–1930* (1988) · I. Rogerson, *The Cranford series* (1987) · T. Balston, 'Illustrated series of the "Nineties"', *Book Collector's Quarterly*, 11 (1933), 33–56 · S. Houfe, 'Colouring the past', *Country Life* (5 Jan 1989), 48–50 · O. Fitzpatrick and D. Shorley, *Illustrated by Hugh Thomson, 1860–1920* (1989) · M. Lennox, *The fairy thorn: gleanings and glimpses of old Kilrea* (1984), 37–41 · S. O'Sáothraí, 'The Bann near Kilrea: Hugh Thomson's misplaced illustration', *Irish Booklore*, 2 (1972), 177–80 · *Irish Booklover*, 4 (1918), 193 · 'Personal and incidental', *Belfast News-Letter* (2 June 1915) · F. F. Moore, 'Modest beginnings: the art of Hugh Thomson, his debt to John Vinycomb', *Belfast Telegraph* (3 April 1924) · E. Jones, 'Centenary of Coleraine artist', *Belfast Telegraph* (17 May 1960), 8 · H. Jamison, 'Thomson centenary', *Belfast Telegraph* (24 May 1960), 8 · *Coleraine Chronicle* (15 May 1920) · *Belfast News-Letter* (10 May 1920) · m. cert.

Archives BL, corresp. with Macmillans, Add. MS 55231 · LUL, letters to Austin Dobson

Likenesses Hoppé, photograph, 1912, repro. in Speilmann and Jerrold, *Hugh Thomson*

Wealth at death £2362 4s. 9d.: probate, 14 June 1920, CGPLA Eng. & Wales

Thomson, James (1700–1748), poet, was born on 11 September 1700 (and baptized on 15 September) in the village of Ednam, 2 miles north of Kelso, Roxburghshire, the son of Thomas Thomson (c.1666–1716), a Presbyterian minister, and Beatrix Trotter (d. 1725) of Fogo, Berwickshire, who was distantly related to the noble house of Hume. Thomas Thomson, son of Andrew Thomson, gardener, was educated at the College of Edinburgh, ordained as a Presbyterian minister, and in 1692 appointed to his native parish.

In Scotland, 1700–1725 James was the fourth child of Thomas and Beatrix, in a family of four boys and five girls. Eight weeks after his birth his father was admitted minister of Southdean, close to the English–Scottish border. This hamlet was on the upper reaches of Jed Water in the wide bare foothills of Cheviot where snow would lie until April; it was mostly a harsh landscape, but the scenery was more gentle northwards towards Jedburgh and the dales of Teviot and Tweed. Here the future poet of *The Seasons* received his first impressions of nature.

Thomson perhaps attended the parish school in Southdean before being sent, about 1712, to the ancient grammar school that was housed in a transept of the abbey

James Thomson (1700–1748), by Stephen Slaughter, 1736

church at Jedburgh. He was a mediocre scholar, but began to write poetry under the encouragement of two men—the scholar, poet, farmer, and (from 1717) Presbyterian minister Robert Riccaltoun (1691–1769), and Sir William Bennet (d. 1729), a whig laird who was also a patron of Allan Ramsay (1686–1758). In autumn 1715 Thomson entered the College of Edinburgh. On 9 February 1716 his father died, probably of an apoplectic stroke, though local legend said he was struck by a ball of fire while carrying out an exorcism. Thomson completed his arts course at Edinburgh (Latin, Greek, logic, metaphysics, ethics, and natural science) by 1719, but did not choose to graduate. He entered Divinity Hall, Edinburgh, as a candidate for the Presbyterian ministry, supported by bursaries from the Jedburgh presbytery from 1720 to 1724. He studied divinity for over five years and performed the homilies, lectures, and other public exercises needed to qualify him for the pulpit, but also joined fellow collegians in secular literary clubs devoted to discussion and imitation of modern English authors. Among the lifelong friends he made at Edinburgh were the writers David Malloch, later Mallet (d. 1765), Patrick Murdoch (d. 1774), and William Paterson (d. in or after 1760).

Thomson's first published poems appeared in the *Edinburgh Miscellany* (January 1720); one of them, 'Of a Country Life', a short georgic distantly modelled on John Gay's *Rural Sports*, anticipates in little *The Seasons*. Another poem, 'Psalm 104 paraphrazed', was seen in manuscript by the critic William Benson (1682–1754), who said that if its author were in London he would meet with encouragement equal to his merit. David Malloch migrated to London in 1723 and had verse published there the following

year. Encouraged by his example, Thomson sailed from Leith in February 1725.

To London: *Winter*, *Summer*, and *Newton*, 1725–1727 Thomson went to London almost certainly with literary ambitions, thinking of English ordination only as a last resort, but his first employment was as tutor to the four-year-old son of the poet Charles Hamilton, Lord Binning (1697–1732), a post probably obtained through Hamilton's mother-in-law, Lady Grisell Baillie, a distant cousin of Thomson's mother. Through Malloch, who had now Anglicized his name to Mallet, and through introductions provided by well-wishers in Scotland, he soon made the acquaintance of English poets, including Richard Savage, Aaron Hill, John Dyer, and Alexander Pope, and influential expatriate Scots such as Duncan Forbes, the artist William Aikman, and the duke of Montrose, Mallet's patron. Aikman painted Thomson's portrait in 1725 or 1726. Thomson's mother died on 12 May 1725 in Edinburgh. He wrote an elegy upon her, but the most notable works from his first year in England were early versions of a 'Hymn on Solitude' (influenced by Milton's *Il Penseroso*) and *Winter*, a blank-verse poem of nature description with devotional overtones, prompted by one of Riccaltoun's poems, perhaps 'A Winter's Day' (first printed in *GM*, 1st ser., 10, 1740, 256).

Winter was published in April 1726 by John Millan, who, it was said, paid 3 guineas for the copy; it was dedicated to Sir Spencer Compton, speaker of the House of Commons, who tardily gave the author a present of 20 guineas. In June a second, revised and enlarged edition appeared, with a preface in which Thomson disparages satire and advocates sublime verse on lofty themes. By then he was writing *Summer* and had left Lord Binning's household in order to act as tutor to a young gentleman at Watts's academy in Little Tower Street. *Summer* was published in February 1727 and was dedicated to George Bubb Dodington—like Compton, a prominent whig politician, but a far more generous and enduring patron. *Summer* is descriptive and devotional, but it is also the first poem in which Thomson gives prominence to the Newtonian scientific ideas he had encountered in his fourth year at Edinburgh and had grasped more surely at Watts's academy, where one of his colleagues was the mathematician James Stirling (1692–1770). There is more Newtonian science in Thomson's next publication, a *Poem to the Memory of Sir Isaac Newton* (May 1727), dedicated to Sir Robert Walpole, who responded with a gift of £50. Thomson's poem is an apotheosis rather than an elegy: it is a hymn on the works and wonders of almighty power in which the imagination follows Newton's soul on a great celestial voyage.

Shortly afterwards Thomson left Watts's academy, hoping to live by his pen. He acquired more patrons, notably Frances Seymour, countess of Hertford, and Thomas Rundle, future bishop of Derry, who introduced him to Charles Talbot (1685–1737), solicitor-general. From 1727 Thomson was a regular summer guest at the country seats of Dodington, Talbot, and Lord and Lady Hertford. On his first visit to Eastbury, Dodington's mansion in Dorset, he met Voltaire, who later wrote of Thomson, 'I discovered in him a great genius and a great Simplicity, I liked in him the poet and the true philosopher, I mean the Lover of Mankind' (McKillop, 212). Johnson's assertion that Lady Hertford discontinued her invitations after Thomson's first visit to Marlborough Castle, Wiltshire, because he 'took more delight in carousing with lord Hertford and his friends than assisting her ladyship's poetical operations' is not true (Johnson, *Poets*, 3.287): Thomson's visits continued for more than ten years, during which he and the countess wrote a number of pleasing songs for one another. That said, Thomson was a keen and practised drinker.

Spring, *Britannia*, *Sophonisba*, and *The Seasons*, 1728–1730

In January 1728 Thomson issued proposals to publish *The Seasons* by subscription. This did not prevent him from publishing *Spring*, dedicated to Lady Hertford, on his own account in June 1728, apparently with little success, because in January 1729 the bookseller Andrew Millar bought up remainder copies and reissued them over his own imprint. January 1729 also saw publication of Thomson's first politically controversial poem, *Britannia*, which called for greater belligerence from the British government towards Spain. Four short poems of his, including the 'Hymn on Solitude' and 'The Happy Man', a eulogy of Dodington, were printed in *Ralph's Miscellany* (April 1729) and he began to write his first play.

By writing for the stage Thomson associated himself with his friend Aaron Hill's project to revive high-classical tragedy. Thomson's *Sophonisba*, set in ancient Carthage and based on a story from the Second Punic War, opened at Drury Lane on 28 February 1730, and, though Johnson observed that in its splendid audience 'nobody was much affected, and that the company rose as from a moral lecture' (Johnson, *Poets*, 3.288), it had a moderately successful run of ten nights, giving the author three benefit performances. One line, 'Oh Sophonisba! Sophonisba Oh!' (III.ii.19), was promptly parodied as 'Oh Jemmy Thompson! Jemmy Thompson Oh!' in an anonymous *Criticism on the New 'Sophonisba'*, and, a year later, as 'Oh! Huncamunca, Huncamunca, oh!' (II.v.1), in Henry Fielding's *Tragedy of Tragedies* (1731), but Thomson was so little moved that he allowed the line to stand in all new editions of the printed play in his lifetime. The prologue to *Sophonisba* was written by Pope and Mallet and the play was dedicated to Queen Caroline, probably through the agency of Lady Hertford, who was a lady of the queen's bedchamber.

The queen also headed a glittering list of subscribers to *The Seasons* in June 1730. The subscription quarto edition, which was also sold to the public through the trade, was printed by Thomson's friend Samuel Richardson and illustrated by engravings after William Kent. The poem now included 'Autumn', dedicated to Arthur Onslow, Compton's successor as speaker, and a concluding 'Hymn', as well as revised, enlarged texts of the three previously published 'Seasons'. The general tendency of the revisions, despite the addition of a pantheistic 'Hymn', is to make the poem more secular; it is more excursive, patriotic, and overtly whiggish than the earlier texts.

By the middle of 1730, five years after leaving Scotland,

Thomson had achieved a measure of fame and fortune. He had received royal notice as playwright and poet, he enjoyed the friendship and respect of men of wit, and the support of some discriminating patrons; his *Seasons* had attracted 457 subscriptions at 1 guinea or more each, and he had profited from three author's benefit nights in the theatre and the sale of copyrights to booksellers: *Spring* and *Sophonisba* for £137 10s. to Millar in January 1730 and all the other long blank-verse poems for £105 to Millan in July 1729.

Grand tour and *Liberty*, 1730–1736

From November 1730 to early 1733 Thomson was in France and Italy, with an allowance of £200 p.a., as travelling companion of Charles Richard Talbot, eldest son of the solicitor-general. There are tantalizingly few surviving records of their travels, so the only places it is now certain they visited are Paris, Lyons, Rome, Florence, Naples, and Petrarch's Fontaine de Vaucluse, near Avignon. The only people it is now certain they met were English or Scots: Joseph Spence, John Forbes (son of Duncan), Lord Binning, and Lady Grisell Baillie. From this period there are only three surviving letters by Thomson and none to him, though Johnson testifies that Pope wrote to him:

> he had much regard for Thomson, and once expressed it in a poetical Epistle sent to Italy, of which, however, he abated the value by transplanting some of the lines into his *Epistle to Arbuthnot*. (Johnson, *Poets*, 3.291)

Travel for the most part confirmed Thomson's patriotic insularity. Seeing Voltaire's *Brutus* acted in Paris made him wonder what ideas a French audience might take from an old Roman republican declaiming on liberty; nevertheless he was impressed by French public work and cultural achievements. In Italy he thought the statues and paintings were fine enough, but he was more struck by poverty and misery brought about by bad government, civil and religious, and a potentially beautiful landscape made barren. His next long poem, *Liberty*, was prompted by those impressions of Italy, but the only poem he is known to have written abroad is a moving elegy in heroic couplets on his friend William Aikman, the painter, who died in June 1731. On 27 September 1733 Charles Richard Talbot died, but his tutor was not forgotten by his father, who, on becoming lord chancellor a month later, appointed Thomson secretary of the briefs in the court of chancery. The income from this sinecure (after payment to a deputy to carry out the duties of the post) was said to be £300 p.a., later reduced to a nominal £100, of which Thomson received nothing.

Though Talbot was Walpole's lord chancellor, his relations with Walpole became strained in 1734; also his son William opposed Walpole in the Commons. Another of Thomson's patrons, Dodington, had gravitated to the opposition court of Frederick, prince of Wales. Government corruption at home had grown worse in the years when Thomson was abroad. Such factors drew him into the orbit of the prince, who, unlike his father, was an appreciative patron of literature. Thomson's new long blank-verse poem, *Liberty*, was therefore dedicated to Frederick. This whiggish historical narrative traces the rise and fall of liberty in ancient Greece and Rome and in modern Europe until its perfection in England at the revolution of 1688. The poem ends, however, as it had begun, among the ruins of Rome, with an implicit warning that luxury and political corruption might ruin even Britain. Thomson set great store by *Liberty*; so did Andrew Millar, who paid £250 for the copyright in December 1734. The poem was published in five parts, three in early 1735, the remaining two a year later, and its ill-success is measured by a print order that diminished from 3250 copies of the first part to 1250 of the last two parts. Even so, Thomson wished to be known as the author of this poem, for his portrait by Stephen Slaughter shows him holding a drawing of personified Liberty. Verses by G. W. (probably Gilbert West, (1703–1756)) on this portrait appeared in the *Gentleman's Magazine* (1st ser., 6, 1736).

Retreat to Richmond: *Poem to Talbot***, 1736–1737** After returning from the continent in 1733 Thomson lived in or near the Strand, close to where he had lodged on his first arrival in London eight years earlier. By April 1736, though, he had moved to a cottage in Kew Foot Lane, in the fashionable village of Richmond, from which (being no horseman) he regularly walked to visit friends in London, 9 or 10 miles away, with The Doves inn at Hammersmith as his customary watering hole. Other friends were closer to hand, such as Pope at Twickenham and Mallet at Strand on the Green. Thomson was often visited by Pope, dressed in a light-coloured greatcoat which he commonly kept on in the house, and Thomson was always admitted to Pope, whether he had company or was alone.

Most of Thomson's relatives were in Scotland, but were not forgotten. He gave his younger unmarried sisters, Jean and Elizabeth, capital to enable them to set up a milliner's shop in Edinburgh and he funded medical treatment for his youngest brother, John, who died in September 1735. A death with more effect on Thomson's pocket was that of his patron Charles Talbot on 14 February 1737. Talbot's successor as lord chancellor was Philip Yorke, earl of Hardwicke, a closer ally of Walpole than Talbot had been. Thomson had moved with Talbot's son William into opposition. Consequently his secretaryship was not renewed by the incoming lord chancellor, though some early biographers claimed that he could have kept the post had he not been too indolent to reapply for it. Whether or not that was so, he lost no time in writing a long blank-verse, *Poem to the Memory of Lord Talbot*, dedicated to William, now Lord Talbot, and published by Millar in June 1737. In September of that year Thomson's congratulatory 'Ode' to the prince of Wales, published in several newspapers less than a week after the prince was expelled from his father's court, stridently proclaimed Thomson's political position.

Thomson was habitually careless in money matters. There is a story that after he lost his secretaryship he was imprisoned for debt of nearly £70 and released through the generosity of the actor James Quin. Certainly, the epicurean, witty Quin was a close friend of Thomson and a congenial spirit. So was the poet Richard Savage, whose notoriously irregular habits made him an impossible house guest for normal families. Their presence in Kew Foot Lane, or coming home drunk from The Castle inn, Richmond, at four in the morning, was a trial to Thomson's housekeeper, Mrs Hobart, but not to her bachelor master, who disliked regular hours and loved food, drink, and wit. Savage was master of ceremonies when Thomson was admitted freemason on 9 September 1737, along with two Scots bachelor poet friends, John Armstrong and William Paterson. It was about this time that Thomson was befriended by George Lyttelton, who would become his chief patron in the last decade of his life. Lyttelton, the prince of Wales's secretary, introduced Thomson to the prince, who interrogated him about his affairs and, receiving the reply that 'they were in a more poetical posture than formerly', allowed him a pension of £100 per annum (Johnson, *Poets*, 3.291).

Opposition playwright: *Agamemnon, Edward and Eleonora, and Alfred***, 1738–1740** April 1738 saw the performance at Drury Lane of Thomson's second heroic tragedy, *Agamemnon*. The name part was taken by Quin, but he was not the leading character. As in Thomson's *Sophonisba*, the emotional and dramatic centre of the play is a woman: in this case Clytemnestra, played by Mary Porter. *Agamemnon* ran for nine nights (three author's benefit performances), but was never revived. It was heavily cut during the run in order to make it more acceptable to audiences who had no taste for the long declamations so typical of Thomson's plays. Two performances were by command of the prince and princess of Wales, and the printed play, published by Andrew Millar, was dedicated to the princess. Pope, who had written letters of recommendation to the theatre managers, appeared in a box on the first night and was recognized with a round of applause. He rarely attended the theatre: his presence on this occasion displayed his friendship for Thomson and his own politics. The evil counsellor in *Agamemnon* is all too clearly intended to represent Sir Robert Walpole, as Pope himself underlined a month later in his *Dialogue I*, line 51, when he cited Aegisthus as a name for Walpole.

Two slighter pieces of opposition polemic in 1738 were a reprint of *Britannia* and Thomson's preface to a cheap edition of Milton's *Areopagitica*, both published by Andrew Millar, who became Thomson's sole publisher when, in June 1738, he bought all of Millan's Thomson copyrights. Thomson dined with the arch-tory Bolingbroke at Pope's house in July 1738, but he was more often in the company of the opposition whig George Lyttelton, and he readily lent himself to the political literary campaign orchestrated by Lyttelton on behalf of the prince of Wales. Thomson was one of three opposition playwrights who, early in 1739, had tragedies ready for the stage: the plays were Mallet's *Mustapha*, Henry Brooke's *Gustavus Vasa*, and Thomson's *Edward and Eleonora*, all of which parade highminded patriotic sentiments and denounce evil ministers.

Thomson wrote the prologue to *Mustapha*. He alludes to the play's political theme of the monarch, 'To the false herd of flattering slaves confin'd' (line 18), but his remarks on the psychological effect of tragedy more interestingly throw light upon the aim of his own work. His tragic muse is a 'Queen of soft sorrows, and of useful fears' (line 6); tragedy should make the good man better and the bad man repentant. Pope, who read *Edward and Eleonora* at this time, declared that Thomson excelled in the pathetic. Certainly this play is Thomson's most sentimental. It is based on the story of Prince Edward being stabbed by a poisoned dagger during the last crusade and his wife sucking the poison from his wound: so a woman is again at the drama's emotional centre.

On 16 March 1739 the acting of *Gustavus Vasa* was forbidden by the lord chamberlain: it was thus the first play to fall foul of the 1737 Licensing Act. Eleven days later, and two days before it was due to open at Covent Garden, *Edward and Eleonora* was banned too. This play was on the whole far less politically contentious than *Agamemnon*, but a few speeches in which, for instance, Prince Edward is begged to save his father and his country from evil ministers were undoubtedly provocative. As the stage licenser received the text of *Edward and Eleonora* as early as 23 February, his last-minute prohibition, after actors and theatre management had invested much time and money, was admonitory and vindictive. Thomson lost his benefit nights, but profited when he published subscription and trade editions of the play in May 1739. It was dedicated to the princess of Wales and carried a note about its prohibition, printed in Gothic lettering to remind readers of ancient liberties now at risk through the Licensing Act. *Edward and Eleonora* was first acted in 1775 and revived successfully several times in the last quarter of the century. John Wesley (*Journal*, 14 Oct 1772) thought it was Thomson's masterpiece.

The profit from *Edward and Eleonora* enabled Thomson to move to a larger cottage (with seven rooms and a kitchen), further down Kew Foot Lane and next to Richmond Gardens. His first production after this move was *Alfred: a Masque*, which glorifies the idea of a patriot king, implicitly embodied in Frederick, prince of Wales. This work was written in collaboration with Mallet and was first performed on 1 August 1740, by command of the prince, in the garden at Cliveden House, his country retreat on the Thames, near Maidenhead. The performers were professional actors, singers, and dancers from the London theatres; the music was composed by Thomas Augustine Arne. Earliest newspaper reports attribute the words solely to Thomson, but the advertisement to a revised version published over Mallet's sole name in 1751, after Thomson's death, suggests that he wrote the larger share of the 1740 text also. This is probably true, though Mallet on other occasions was not above claiming other men's work as his own. What is beyond dispute is that Thomson wrote the words of the best-known song in *Alfred*: 'Rule Britannia' [see also Britannia].

Courtship and revised *Seasons*, 1741–1744 Thomson now enjoyed an uncertain but not inconsiderable income from his writings and pension, though he was notoriously careless about money: he lived on long credit, settling his accounts erratically but generously. His indolence was well known. It was said that, at Eastbury, he ate the ripe side of peaches hanging on the tree, without taking his hands from his pockets. Also that, at home in Richmond, he was found in bed one day at 2 p.m. by Charles Burney, the musicologist, who asked him why he was in bed at that hour and received the reply: 'I had no motive to rise' (*Public Advertiser*, 16 April 1790). In his forties Thomson was apparently settled into a confirmed, easy-going, self-indulgent bachelor's life of late hours, over-eating, and hard drinking with witty and sociable male friends. However, it seems that late in 1742 he fell in love with a Richmond neighbour. She was Elizabeth Young, sister-in-law of a Scots physician at Kew with whom Thomson was friendly. He declared his love in a vehement letter of 10 March 1743 and in a series of agitated letters and love lyrics through the following two and a half years.

Little is known about Elizabeth Young. It seems that she was red-haired, and that, like Thomson, she spoke with a broad Scots brogue. Further testimony is contradictory: she is described on the one hand as a quick-tempered, harsh-tongued tomboy, on the other as a gentle-mannered, elegant-minded woman. There is general agreement, though, that her mother (the widow of a naval captain) was a coarse, vulgar woman, and that she opposed the match because Thomson's financial prospects were uncertain. Reportedly, she said to her daughter, 'What! would you marry Thomson? He will make ballads and you will sing them' (*Universal Magazine*, 67, 1780, 368). Her daughter may have seen other objections too. For all his poetic sensibility, Thomson gormandized and drank heavily; he carried himself awkwardly, had run to fat, was negligent in his dress, and sweated copiously; his love letters are eloquent but perhaps too self-pitying to please a woman of spirit. There is no evidence that Elizabeth Young ever encouraged Thomson's advances, and the man she married—a gallant, talented, tall, handsome, wealthy naval officer (a future admiral)—was as unlike Thomson as can be imagined. Nevertheless she carefully preserved Thomson's letters: they are now in the Pierpont Morgan Library, New York.

Thomson's letters repeatedly assure Miss Young that his love for her will inspire him to overcome his indolent habits, and perhaps this was so (up to a point) because in the eighteen months following his proposal of marriage he wrote *Tancred and Sigismunda* and parts of *The Castle of Indolence* and *Coriolanus*; he also planned a tragedy on Socrates and revised *The Seasons*. This last project may have arisen from the reversion of copyright to Thomson fourteen years after the contracts of 1729–30. It was a very thorough revision, some of which was done at Hagley Hall, Worcestershire, where Thomson was the guest of George Lyttelton in August and September 1743. The manuscript of these revisions shows many by Lyttelton, generally in the interests of decorum or metrical regularity. Thomson's compliance was remembered twenty years later by James Grainger (d. 1766), when he sent a poetical manuscript to friends and wrote: 'let Mr Shenstone know, that I can bear to have my verses butchered, as Thomson used to call it' (Nichols, *Illustrations*, 7, 1848, 279).

The revised edition of *The Seasons*, published in June

1744, was enlarged to include more georgic material, such as fishing in 'Spring' and sheep-shearing in 'Summer', more tropical excursions (on fruits, beasts, sandstorms, hurricanes, plagues), and more compliments to opposition politicians. Additionally, hundreds of small revisions improved the precision, harmony, or vividness of the poem. Each 'season' retained the verse dedication to its original patron—Lady Hertford, Dodington, Onslow, and Compton—but the whole work was now dedicated to Frederick, prince of Wales. With further minor revisions in 1745 and 1746, this was the text by which *The Seasons* became best known. It was influentially translated into German by Brockes (1745) and imitated in French by Saint-Lambert (1769).

Tancred and Sigismunda, Coriolanus, and a sinecure, 1745–1746 Before the end of 1744 Thomson had completed *Tancred and Sigismunda*, a tragedy set in twelfth-century Sicily, with a complicated love-and-honour plot from Le Sage's *Gil Blas*. It was acted for nine nights (three author's benefit performances) at Drury Lane in March and April 1745, with David Garrick in the lead. Thomson wrote both prologue and epilogue: the latter was an unusual protest against customary flippant epilogues to serious plays. His new play marked the end of a development from *Sophonisba*, through *Agamemnon* and *Edward and Eleonora*, which drew Thomson away from the historical and heroic towards the melodramatic, sentimental, and domestic. After 'Rule Britannia', it proved to be his most popular work for the theatre: it was revived on the London stage in most seasons to the 1790s, was still being acted as late as 1819, and was translated into German in part by Lessing and by Schlegel.

Pitt and Lyttelton interested themselves in the first production by attending rehearsals and giving instruction to the players. As the play's political theme, insofar as it has one, is reconciliation rather than conflict, those quondam opposition patriots were making a political signal by their attendance: a point noted by satirists. Walpole had fallen in 1742; Lyttelton joined the new ministry under Pelham in December 1744 and Pitt lent his support to that ministry; both men withdrew from the prince of Wales's service. Thomson was still the prince's man to the extent that he dedicated the printed text of *Tancred and Sigismunda* (considerably longer than the successfully acted version) to Frederick. However, the eventual result of Lyttelton's defection from the prince's court was that Thomson lost his pension. It is not clear whether this occurred before or after May 1746 when, thanks to Lyttelton's influence in government, Thomson was appointed, jointly with his old college friend William Paterson, to the office of surveyor-general of customs for the Leeward Islands. Paterson went to Barbados and carried out the duties of the post for £400 per annum while Thomson remained in Richmond and received, it was said, £300 per annum as a sinecure.

With his added wealth Thomson doubled the size of his garden at Richmond, built a hothouse and greenhouse, and employed two nephews as gardeners. Here he continued to entertain old friends and new literary acquaintances, including William Collins and Joseph Warton.

Aged forty-six Thomson had his portrait painted by John Patoun: it was an unprepossessing likeness, said by William Pitt to be 'beastly like'. A new edition of *The Seasons*, with the author's last revisions, was published in May 1746: 4000 copies were printed—more than any earlier edition of that poem (though Thomson's plays each sold 4500 copies).

Thomson completed *Coriolanus* before the end of 1746. This play's theme is the invasion of a country by one of its natives and it was written during and just after the Jacobite rising of 1745, but it contains no obvious reference to contemporary politics. Rather it is a series of cerebral debates upon the just war, the legitimacy of revenge, the individual person's duty to the community, and other such general politico-moral questions. Its lack of dramatic action may have deterred theatre managers, though Thomson and his friends blamed rivalry between Garrick and Quin as to who should take the role of Coriolanus for the fact that the play was not staged during the remaining eighteen months of Thomson's life.

Last years: *The Castle of Indolence*, 1746–1749 Thomson's *The Castle of Indolence*, published in May 1748, was conceived about 1733 as detached Spenserian stanzas satirizing himself and friends. By 1742, when Thomas Morell (1703–1784), curate at Kew Chapel, wrote his Spenserian stanzas about Thomson's poem, its non-completion because of its author's indolence was a joke among those friends, some of whom are identifiable among the castle-dwellers in the completed poem. One of them, the physician John Armstrong (1708/9–1779), contributed four stanzas on diseases resulting from indolence. Thomson himself is in the poem as a bard 'more fat than bard beseems' (canto 1, line 604). The castle is described seductively as an earthly paradise, presided over by a smooth-tongued epicurean wizard, but in the second canto of the poem it is overthrown by a stern and energetic 'Knight of Industry'. Thomson's conventional message is that the penalty of Adam is hard, but idleness is worse. However, the poem also implicitly dramatizes a conflict between the didactic public poet and the romantic dreamer. Canto 1, stanza 40, has perhaps the earliest published reference in English to the Aeolian harp. This device is the subject of an ode by Thomson in the second edition of Dodsley's *Collection of Poems* (June 1748); Thomson's 'Hymn on Solitude' and 'The Happy Man' had appeared in the first edition (January 1748).

These were the last publications of Thomson's lifetime. Having overheated himself walking one summer evening from central London to Hammersmith, he took a boat for the rest of the journey to Kew and caught a chill, from which he had not fully recovered before he exposed himself once more to the evening dews. This brought on a tertian fever and then a malignant nervous fever, from which he died on 27 August 1748, at his house in Kew Foot Lane. His physician friends John Armstrong and William Robertson (brother-in-law of Elizabeth Young) were with him at the end. Thomson's remains were buried under a plain stone in the north-west corner of St Mary's Church, Richmond, on 29 August. It seems that the wake was as drunken as Thomson could have wished (see his *Seasons*,

'Autumn', 565–9), for it is said that an unidentified clergyman 'boasted, that at a supper after Thomson's funeral, he left Quin drunk under the table, whilst he was able to walk home' (R. O. Cambridge, *Works*, 1803, 50n.).

Thomson died intestate and, it was said, hundreds of pounds in debt through ill economy. Letters of administration were granted to Lyttelton and to the diplomat Andrew Mitchell (1708–1771) in the interest of Thomson's sisters Mary Craig and Jean Thomson, both still living in Scotland. *Coriolanus* was staged at Covent Garden; it ran for ten nights in January 1749, providing three benefit nights. Quin took the lead and unaffectedly wept as he spoke an emotional prologue written by Lyttelton. In May, William Collins's noble *Ode on the Death of Thomson* was published. Thomson's effects, including his library, were sold in May 1749, after which his house was bought by his friend George Ross, who enlarged it. Later, in the ownership of Admiral Boscawen's widow, the house was a shrine of literary pilgrimage; in the 1860s it was incorporated into the buildings of Richmond Royal Hospital. In February 1750 Millar issued a new edition of Thomson's *Works*, with many unauthorized revisions and cuts made by Lyttelton to the great confusion of later editors, but no doubt to the profit of Thomson's estate. Thus Thomson's debts were cleared and 'a handsome sum' was remitted to Mary and Jean; this included £200 paid by Millar in February 1751 for Thomson's latest copyrights. Seemingly, the generous Millar bought *Alfred* (which he regarded as Thomson's) and *Coriolanus* twice over.

Reputation *Tancred and Sigismunda* held the stage for over half a century, as did the last three acts of *Coriolanus*, conflated with two acts of Shakespeare in versions of *Coriolanus* by Thomas Sheridan (1752) and John Philip Kemble (1789). All six plays were often reprinted, almost invariably in Lyttelton's greatly impaired versions (the last example as recently as 1979), but one suspects that, like *Liberty*, they were little regarded. *The Castle of Indolence* contributed notably to the romantic vogue for Spenserian imitation and never lacked appreciative readers, but for most of the time since his death Thomson has been regarded primarily as the poet of *The Seasons*. Over four hundred editions of this poem, including translations, were published before the flood of reprints began to slacken in the 1870s. Coleridge found a little worn-out copy of *The Seasons* in the parlour of an obscure country ale-house and exclaimed '*That* is true fame!' (W. Hazlitt, 'My First Acquaintance with Poets', *The Liberal*, April 1823).

The Seasons provided subjects for Haydn's oratorio and for artists as various as William Kent, Richard Wilson, Thomas Gainsborough, J. M. W. Turner, Henry Fuseli, William Etty, and Richard Westall. It did much to establish natural description as a proper subject and blank verse as a normal medium for long serious poems. Though not strictly a didactic or topographical poem itself, it gave impetus to a stream of blank-verse georgics and loco-descriptive poems in the second half of the eighteenth century. More significantly it was Thomson who, with Young and Cowper, showed how the sublimity of *Paradise Lost* might be reshaped and internalized to suit the intellectual and spiritual concerns of their own age, and thereby prepared the way for Wordsworth. After Wordsworth's death Thomson still had a large popular readership, but was no longer a significant influence upon other poets. At the beginning of the twenty-first century most general readers know Thomson only through short passages of *The Seasons* in anthologies. The chorus of 'Rule Britannia' remains a kind of national anthem, but very few of its singers could say who wrote the words.

The earliest lives of Thomson were written by compatriot friends: Robert Shiels (d. 1753) in Cibber's *Lives of the Poets* (1753), and Patrick Murdoch in a subscription edition of Thomson's *Works* published by Millar (1762). Shiels, unusually among early critics, found in Thomson's *Castle of Indolence* 'more genius and poetical judgment than all his other works put together' (Cibber, 205). Subscriptions to Murdoch's 1762 edition and profits donated by Millar paid for the monument to Thomson, designed by Robert Adam and carved by Michael Spang, that stands between Shakespeare and Rowe in Westminster Abbey. Nearly fifty years later, thanks to the enthusiasm of David Steuart Erskine, earl of Buchan, a commemorative obelisk was raised on Ednam Hill, near Thomson's birthplace. Buchan was one of many eighteenth- and nineteenth-century writers who contributed to biographical information on Thomson, down to Léon Morel's thorough critical biography in 1895. Twentieth-century Thomson scholarship benefited most from McKillop's edition of the letters and his background studies. The fullest critical biographies to date are by Douglas Grant (1951) and James Sambrook (1991).   JAMES SAMBROOK

Sources *James Thomson (1700–1748): letters and documents*, ed. A. D. McKillop (1958) • P. Murdoch, 'Account of the life and writings of Thomson', in *The works of James Thomson*, ed. P. Murdoch, 1 (1762) • J. Sambrook, *James Thomson, 1700–1748: a life* (1991) • D. Grant, *James Thomson, poet of 'The seasons'* (1951) • R. Shiels, *The lives of the poets of Great Britain and Ireland*, ed. T. Cibber, 5 (1753), 5.190–218 • S. Johnson, *Lives of the English poets*, ed. G. B. Hill, [new edn], 3 (1905), 281–301 • D. S. Erskine, *Essays on the lives and writings of Fletcher of Saltoun and the poet Thomson* (1792) • L. Morel, *James Thomson: sa vie et ses œuvres* (Paris, 1895) • A. H. Scouten, ed., *The London stage, 1660–1800*, pt 3: *1729–1747* (1961) • D. F. Foxon, ed., *English verse, 1701–1750: a catalogue of separately printed poems with notes on contemporary collected editions*, 2 vols. (1975) • Boswell, *Life*, vols. 1–4 • J. Spence, *Observations, anecdotes, and characters, of books and men*, ed. J. M. Osborn, 2 vols. (1966) • H. H. Campbell, *James Thomson (1700–1748): an annotated bibliography of selected editions and the important criticism* (1976) • R. Wodrow, *Analecta, or, Materials for a history of remarkable providences, mostly relating to Scotch ministers and Christians*, ed. [M. Leishman], 4 vols., Maitland Club, 60 (1842–3), vols. 3–4 • A. S. Bell, 'Three new letters of James Thomson', *N&Q*, 217 (1972), 367–9 • A. N. L. Munby, ed., *Sale catalogues of libraries of eminent persons*, 1 (1971) • *Fasti Scot.*, new edn, 2.139 • A. Bissett, *Memoirs and papers of Sir Andrew Mitchell* (1850) • *Autobiography of the Rev. Dr. Alexander Carlyle ... containing memorials of the men and events of his time*, ed. J. H. Burton (1860); repr. as *Anecdotes and characters of the times*, ed. J. Kinsley (1973) • [H. R. Duff], ed., *Culloden papers* (1815) • *The life of Mr James Quin, comedian* (1766) • *The tell-tale* (1756) • M. J. W. Scott, *James Thomson, Anglo-Scot* (1988) • C. Atto, 'The Society for the Encouragement of Learning', *The Library*, 4th ser., 19 (1938–9), 263–88

Archives John Murray, London, corresp. and poems • Morgan L., corresp. and poems, MS MA 1575 • Morgan L., love letters • NL

Scot., letters [copies] · U. Edin. L., corresp. and papers | BL, department of printed books, James Thomson, *Works* (1738), vol. 1: interleaved copy with MS revisions by Thomson and Lyttelton, C.28 e 17 · NL Scot., Culloden MSS, corresp. · NL Scot., letters to Miss Young · V&A NAL, juvenile poems and letters to Dr Cranston **Likenesses** oils, 18th cent. (after J. Basire), Hunt. L.; repro. in Sambrook, *James Thomson*, pl. 3 · stipple, 18th cent., BM · W. Aikman, oils, 1720, Scot. NPG · J. Vanderbank, oils, 1726, Scot. NPG; repro. in Sambrook, *James Thomson*, pl. 4 · S. Slaughter, oils, 1736, Yale U. CBA [*see illus.*] · oils, *c.*1746 (after J. Patoun), NPG · M. H. Spang, monument, *c.*1760, Westminster Abbey · J. Basire, engraving (after J. Patoun), repro. in J. Thomson, *Works*, quarto (1762), vol. 2, frontispiece · J. Basire, line engraving (after W. Aikman), BM; repro. in J. Thomson, *Works*, quarto (1762), vol. 1, frontispiece · J. Medina the younger, oils (after J. Patoun), U. Edin. · J. Patoun, oils, repro. in J. Kerslake, *Early Georgian portraits* (1977), pl. 796 · S. Slaughter?, oils, Leicester City Art Gallery; repro. in Sambrook, *James Thomson*, pl. 6 · marble bas-relief, NPG · marble medallion (posthumous), NPG · oils (after J. Patoun), Scot. NPG; repro. in Sambrook, *James Thomson*, pl. 12 · oils (after J. Basire), Scot. NPG **Wealth at death** many hundreds of pounds in debt: Thomas Birch to Lord Hardwicke, 17 Sept 1748, McKillop, ed., *James Thomson*, 208 · debts cleared by sale of effects and copyrights, and proceeds from posthumous performances of his *Coriolanus*, after which 'a handsome sum' remitted to surviving sisters: Murdoch, 'Life'

Thomson, James (1768–1855), editor of the *Encyclopaedia Britannica*, born in May 1768 at Crieff, Perthshire, was the second son of John Thomson and his wife, Elizabeth Ewan. Thomas *Thomson (1773–1852) was his younger brother. He was educated at the parish school in Crieff and then at Edinburgh University. He was licensed to preach by the presbytery of Haddington on 6 August 1793, and frequently assisted his uncle, John Ewan, minister of Whittingehame, East Lothian. In 1795 he became associated with George Gleig, bishop of Brechin, as co-editor of the third edition of the *Encyclopaedia Britannica*. He wrote several articles himself, including 'Scripture', 'Septuagint', and 'Superstition'. That on scripture was retained in several later editions. During the same period he prepared an edition of *The Spectator*, with short biographies of the contributors (8 vols., 1799). Also in 1799, he published *Rise, Progress, and Consequences of the New Opinions ... Lately Introduced into France*. In 1796 he became tutor to the sons of John Stirling of Kippendavie, and resigned his post on the *Encyclopaedia Britannica* to his younger brother, Thomas. Both brothers were frequent contributors to the *Literary Journal* founded in 1803 by James Mill, James Thomson contributing the philosophic articles. On 26 August 1805 Thomson was ordained minister of Eccles, Berwickshire. In his country life he wrote a sketch of Berwickshire agriculture published in his brother's *Annals of Philosophy*. He also devoted himself to the study of the Bible in the original tongues, and to the careful editing of his discourses on St Luke and the Acts of the Apostles published in 1845–51 and 1854 respectively. In 1842 he received the honorary degree of DD from the University of St Andrews, and in 1847 he resigned his charge and retired to Edinburgh. In 1854 he moved to London, where he died on 28 November 1855.

On 10 October 1805 Thomson had married Elizabeth, eldest daughter of James Skene of Aberdeen, second son of George Skene of Skene, Aberdeenshire. She died in 1851, leaving three sons: Robert Dundas *Thomson; James Thomson, chairman of the government bank of Madras, and Andrew Skene Thomson. There was also a daughter, Eliza.   E. I. CARLYLE, *rev.* H. C. G. MATTHEW

Sources *Literary Gazette* (26 Jan 1856), 58 · *Fasti Scot.*, 2.413 · *GM*, 2nd ser., 45 (1856), 309–10 · Boase, *Mod. Eng. biog.*

Thomson, James (1779–1850), calico printer, was born on 6 February 1779 at Blackburn, Lancashire, the second of the five children of John Thomson, an iron-liquor merchant (iron-liquor, acetate of iron, was a mordant for the calico dyeing industry), and his wife, Elizabeth (*d.* 1824). Thomson wrote of his 'closeness' to the Peel family, and it has been suggested that his mother was a sister of the first Sir Robert *Peel.

Thomson, whose skill as an industrial chemist and whose success in improving the quality of design led to his being called the 'Duke of Wellington of calico printing' (Turnbull, 80), grew up in Lancashire before beginning in 1793 a year's study at Glasgow University. There he began lifelong friendships with Gregory Watt, the son of James Watt, and the poet Thomas Campbell. At the age of sixteen he began work for Joseph Peel & Co., the London house of the extensive calico printing business. He remained there for six years, furthering his education by private study and through friendships with Sir Humphrey Davey and other scientists. Thomson's knowledge of chemistry impressed his employers, who sent him to manage their works at Church, near Accrington, where he remained until 1810. In that year he and John Chippendale, a Blackburn cotton merchant, became calico printers at Clitheroe, briefly at Up Brooks, and in 1811 at Primrose, where they established an industrial colony renowned both for the superiority of its products and for its paternalism.

Thomson travelled widely on the continent between 1814 and 1817, and was elected a fellow of the Royal Society in 1821. Though he combined 'in an eminent degree scientific with practical knowledge' (Baines, 277), he combed Europe for outstanding chemists and artists. And as a means of enhancing standards in the trade, he supported schools of design and successfully campaigned for the act of 1842, which extended the copyright on dress patterns to nine months and on those for furnishings to three years. It was said of him, however, that 'His love of art, taste and progress carried him in many cases beyond the taste of his consumers, and he often reaped the reward of genius in advance of the age—disappointment' (Potter, 17–18).

Primrose, 'a large village, in which square and lofty mills ... stand in lieu of cottages and ordinary dwellings', employed 'twelve hundred people in ... stamping millions of yards of cotton' with indelible colours and designs (Granville, 363). During the 1840s the firm registered on average more than 500 dress designs each year, and 'there was no house did better work than Primrose in its halcyon days' (Hargreaves, 80).

Thomson married, on 18 March 1806, Cecilia, the eldest daughter of the Revd Thomas Starkie, vicar of Blackburn. They had four sons and two daughters. Thomson, a Liberal in politics, was the second mayor of Clitheroe, in 1836–7, and he became a JP in 1840. As well as a number of trenchantly argued pamphlets on the copyright question, he wrote the article on 'Manufacture of cotton' in Rees's *Cyclopaedia* (1812).

One of Thomson's favourite sayings was that men who became calico printers had only two choices—'the Gazette or the grave'—something he himself bore out. On 17 September 1850, he was at home preparing for the Great Exhibition of the following year when he died from an attack of paralysis, aged seventy-one. He was buried at St Mary's Church, Clitheroe, on 23 September.

CHRISTOPHER ASPIN

Sources G. Turnbull, *A history of the calico printing industry of Great Britain* (1951) · E. Potter, *Calico printing as an art manufacture* (1852) · A. B. Granville, *The spas of England and principal sea-bathing places: northern spas* (1841) · B. Hargreaves, *Messrs Hargreaves' calico print works at Accrington and recollections of Broad Oak* (1882) · E. Baines, *History of the cotton manufacture in Great Britain* (1835) · J. Thomson, *A letter to the vice president of the board of trade on protection to register designs and patterns printed upon woven fabrics* (1840) · W. I. Addison, ed., *The matriculation albums of the University of Glasgow from 1728 to 1858* (1913) · R. H. Kargon, *Science in Victorian Manchester* (1977) · D. Greysmith, 'The printed textiles industry in England, 1830–70', MPhil diss., Middlesex Polytechnic, 1985 · 'Recollections of Clitheroe by an old east-Lancashire man', newspaper cuttings, probably from *Preston Guardian*, c.1876, Clitheroe Library · *Manchester Guardian* (21 Sept 1850) · *Blackburn Standard* (25 Sept 1850) · d. cert.
Likenesses oils, c.1820, Clitheroe Public Library · oils, c.1820, Lancashire County Museums Service, Preston · J. Lonsdale, portrait, c.1830, priv. coll. · Obici of Rome, marble effigy, 1852, St Mary's Church, Clitheroe · S. W. Reynolds, engraving (after J. Lonsdale)
Wealth at death £40,000: administration bond, Lancs. RO, Ref. WCW, 1850

Thomson, James (1786–1849), mathematician, was born on 13 November 1786 at Annaghmore, near Ballynahinch, co. Down, the third son of James Thomson, farmer, and his wife, Agnes Nesbitt. The Thomsons had settled in presbyterian Ulster, having migrated in the 1640s from Ayrshire to escape religious persecution from episcopacy. Beyond the rudiments of education from his father James was largely self-taught. He made for himself a sundial and a night-dial (by which to tell the time by one of the stars of Ursa Major) and at the age of eleven or twelve he worked out, with the aid of slate and stone, how to make dials for any latitude. At the same age he witnessed the battle of Ballynahinch when the presbyterian United Irishmen's vision of an independent united republic was vanquished. Seeing the wanton destruction of the town by the king's forces, and the futility of the armed rebellion, moulded the young Thomson, whose lifelong radicalism would lead him to challenge all manner of establishments.

About 1800 Thomson attended the school opened by a secessionist presbyterian minister, Samuel Edgar, to prepare intelligent young men for the ministry. There he

James Thomson (1786–1849), by Agnes Gardner King and Elizabeth King, 1847

studied mathematics and classics, and by the age of twenty-one he:

> was teaching eight hours a day at Dr Edgar's, and during the extra hours—often fagged and comparatively listless—I was reading Greek and Latin to prepare me for entering College, which I did not do till nearly two years after. (Smith and Wise, 8)

In 1810 he entered Glasgow University, supporting himself through the six-month winter sessions by teaching at Dr Edgar's during the summer. In 1812 he graduated MA, then took medical and theological courses, intending to become a minister. However, the launch of a radical educational enterprise in Belfast redirected his ambitions. Appointed in 1814 to teach arithmetic, geography, and bookkeeping in the school department, and in 1815 as professor of mathematics in the college department, of the Belfast Academical Institution, Thomson found himself among like-minded liberal and radical presbyterians eager for religious and economic reform.

Within that circle Thomson met Margaret Gardner (c.1790–1830), daughter of William Gardner, a well-to-do merchant from Glasgow; they married in 1817. The Thomsons settled in a town house in College Square East, facing the institution, where their seven children were born. Throughout these Belfast years Thomson published a series of school textbooks: *A Treatise on Arithmetic in Theory and Practice* (1819); *Trigonometry, Plane and Spherical* (1820); *Introduction to Modern Geography* (1827); and *The Differential and Integral Calculus* (1831). His textbooks avoided everything of a metaphysical or disputed character, and aimed to be useful to the growing mercantile classes. Thomson was free to adopt and teach the methods of the continental analysts which he eagerly procured and studied.

Thomson was awarded the honorary degree of LLD from Glasgow in 1829. Following the death of his wife in 1830, he accepted the offer of the chair of mathematics in Glasgow College. Moving with his young family to Glasgow just after the city's first major cholera epidemic in 1832, he discovered that his predecessor had not only failed to maintain authority over a declining class but also continued to be entitled to the salary attached to the mathematics chair, the new professor receiving only income from student fees. Moreover, the college was dominated by a tory oligarchy, led by the redoubtable principal, Duncan Macfarlan, opposed to all reform of the university to meet the needs of a rapidly industrializing city. Alone at first, but increasingly building a powerful radical and whig network of reform-minded allies among the newer generation of professors, Thomson championed the causes of the disenfranchised regius professors (who were denied equality with college professors) and of the abolition of university tests (by which anyone appointed to a Scottish university chair had to sign allegiance to the presbyterian Westminster confession of faith). Thomson's reform campaigns began fundamentally to change the character of Glasgow University from that of an ancient, inward-looking corporation whose primary function was the training of ministers of the established kirk to that of a knowledge-producing institution whose aims harmonized with the industrial, progressive goals of the second city of the empire. Thomson successfully promoted the election of his second son, William *Thomson, later Lord Kelvin (1824–1907), to the moribund chair of natural philosophy in 1846. He did not live to see his first son, James *Thomson (1822–1892), occupy the chair of engineering from 1872.

During his Glasgow years Thomson rebuilt the mathematics classes, and educated his children. By 1842 he had 160 students, his best year so far. Textbook publication also prospered. He edited a version of Euclid's *Elements of Geometry* (1834) while *An Elementary Treatise on Algebra Theoretical and Practical* (1844) went through three editions in less than two years. Earlier texts went through successive editions, *Arithmetic* reaching its seventy-second edition by 1880. In 1845 his net profits on all his texts amounted to a substantial £378. The recently established national schools in Ireland accounted in part for the huge demand and conformed to Thomson's conviction that practical, useful knowledge was the means by which to destroy sectarianism of all kinds within his native land. About 1845 he seemed likely to be appointed principal of the new Queen's College in Belfast, but was passed over in favour of an ordained clergyman. Less than four years later the second major cholera epidemic struck Glasgow and he died of the disease, on 12 January 1849.

Crosbie Smith

Sources C. Smith and M. N. Wise, *Energy and empire: a biographical study of Lord Kelvin* (1989) · E. King, *Lord Kelvin's early home* (1909) · S. P. Thompson, *The life of William Thomson, Baron Kelvin of Largs*, 2 vols. (1910) · A. Gray, *Lord Kelvin: an account of his scientific life and work* (1908) · [J. Thomson], 'Recollections of the battle of Ballynahinch', *Belfast Magazine*, 1 (1825), 56–64 · DNB

Archives CUL, Kelvin collection · CUL, corresp. with his son William and others · U. Edin., New Coll. L., letters to Thomas Chalmers

Likenesses A. G. King and E. King, drawing, 1847, NPG [*see illus.*] · G. Gilbert, portrait, Hunterian Museum and Art Gallery, Glasgow · E. Thomson, pencil drawing, NPG · portrait, Royal Belfast Academical Institution

Wealth at death £13,299 9d.: confirmation, 1849, Scotland

Thomson, James (*bap.* **1788**, *d.* **1850**), engraver, was baptized on 5 May 1788 at Mitford, Northumberland, the fourth son of James Thomson, curate then rector of Ormesby, Yorkshire, and his wife, Ann. His name is often misspellt 'Thompson', both on his work and in art dictionaries. Because he showed an interest in art, he was sent to London to be articled to an engraver named Mackenzie in Margaret Street, and was given up for lost by his family when he took nine weeks to reach London by boat from South Shields. After completing a gruelling apprenticeship with Mackenzie (*c.*1803–*c.*1810) he worked for two years under Anthony Cardon and then established himself independently. He married a Miss Lloyd of Rhayader and had two daughters, Eliza and Ann, who married Frederick Goodall RA. He joined the Artists' Annuity Fund in 1825 and signed the 1837 petition.

Thomson became an accomplished engraver, employing both stipple and a mixed style of etching and line or stipple. He produced figure and portrait engravings. Much of his earliest work was after reliefs and sculpture, including plates for the annuals after Francis Chantrey, John Flaxman, Richard Westmacott, Edward Baily, and William Wyon. However, he is best known for his portraits, of which he completed a large number for important illustrated works such as E. Lodge's *Portraits of Illustrious Personages of Great Britain* (4 vols., 1821–34), Horace Walpole's *Anecdotes of Painting*, ed. J. Dallaway (5 vols., 1826–8), C. Heath's *Book of Beauty* (1833–49), *The Keepsake*, and *A Description of the Collection of Ancient Marbles in the British Museum* (1812–61). A stipple portrait, *John Britton*, after R. W. Satchwell and T. Uwins, was the frontispiece to Britton's *Autobiography* (1850). Further portraits appeared in *The Imperial Dictionary of Universal Biography* (1861). Thomson's principal single plates include portraits of Lydia Storey, after Sir Thomas Lawrence (1826), John Wesley, after John Jackson (1828), Queen Victoria riding with Lord Melbourne, after Sir Francis Grant, Prince Albert, after Sir William Charles Ross, and Louis-Philippe and his queen, a pair, after E. Dubufe (1850). He also executed a number of figure subjects, including works by David Wilkie and Rembrandt, and *Royal Recreation*, after his own work. R. A. Artlett was his pupil. He died at his house at 97 Albany Street, Regent's Park, London, on 27 September 1850.

F. M. O'Donoghue, *rev.* Greg Smith

Sources B. Hunnisett, *A dictionary of British steel engravers* (1980), 130 · R. K. Engen, *Dictionary of Victorian engravers, print publishers and their works* (1979) · *Engraved Brit. ports.* · B. Hunnisett, *An illustrated dictionary of British steel engravers*, new edn (1989) · IGI

Archives BM, department of prints and drawings · V&A, department of prints and drawings

Thomson, James (1800–1883), architect, son of David Thomson of Melrose, was born on 22 April 1800. His boyhood was spent in Lambeth, London. From 1814 to 1821 he was a pupil and later assistant to John Buonarotti Papworth before practising independently from c.1825. He married twice, on the second occasion, in 1838, to Anne Hudson. Their son John James was apprenticed to his father in 1854.

In 1826–7 Thomson acted as executant architect for Cumberland Terrace and Cumberland Place, Regent's Park. In 1838 he designed the Royal Polytechnic Institute, Regent Street, and in 1848 the theatre adjoining it. He also designed the new buildings at Clement's Inn, and the Polygraphic Hall, King William Street. In 1842 Thomson was involved in the planning of the Ladbroke estate development, Notting Hill. His designs were later superseded, although some of his terraces in Ladbroke Grove were constructed and his concentric road plan largely remained. In 1850 Thomson worked on the Derbyshire Bank, Derby. He built the Russian Chapel, Welbeck Street, London, for the Russian embassy in 1865 and in the 1870s he made alterations and additions to Charing Cross Hospital. Between c.1827 and 1853 Thomson worked for Joseph Neeld, a lawyer and later MP, and collector of Victorian sculpture, who had inherited a fortune and bought an estate on the Wiltshire–Somerset border. Construction, centring particularly on the villages of Alderton, Grittleton, Leigh Delamere, and Sevington, included schools, farmhouses, lodges, and cottages. Thomson's most notable works for Neeld were: an Italianate castle-villa at Kelston (1835); the rebuilding of Alderton church (1845) and Leigh Delamere church (1846); a new town hall for Chippenham (1833 and 1850); and the transformation of Grittleton House into a mansion mixing Jacobean and Romanesque forms (before 1843 and then 1851–3, when Thomson's involvement ceased before completion).

Thomson was one of the earliest members of the Institute of British Architects, elected 1835, and as a fellow he read the following papers to the institute: 'Composition in architecture: Sir J. Vanbrugh' (15 June 1840); 'National advantages of fresco painting' (6 March 1843); 'Hagioscope at Alderton church' (28 April 1845); and 'Leigh Delamere church' (15 May 1848). He published *Retreats: Designs for Cottages, Villas, and Ornamental Buildings* (1827) and *School Houses* (1842). Thomson exhibited at the Royal Academy twenty-eight times between 1822 and 1853. He was a liveryman of the Loriners' Company. He died at home at 57 Devonshire Street, Portland Place, London, on 16 May 1883 and was buried at Finchley.

CAMPBELL DODGSON, *rev.* M. SLOCOMBE

Sources *The Builder*, 44 (1883), 705 · *Dir. Brit. archs.* · F. H. W. Sheppard, ed., *Northern Kensington*, Survey of London, 37 (1973), 203–4, 207–10 · 'Grittleton House', *The Builder*, 11 (1853), 279–81 · Graves, *RA exhibitors* · *ILN* (29 April 1865) · *Building News*, 12 (1865), 181 · *Wiltshire*, Pevsner (1963) · *London: north-west*, Pevsner (1991) · *Derbyshire*, Pevsner (1953) · J. Orbach, 'Notes on James Thomson', c.1980, Wiltshire Buildings Record · T. Mowl, 'Towers of the Williamane', 1986, Wilts. & Swindon RO, Wiltshire Buildings Record · English Heritage (Historians' section), files on Regent Street, Charing Cross, Notting Hill

Archives RIBA, drawings collection · RIBA BAL, RIBA nomination papers

Wealth at death £789 4s. 1d.: probate, 2 July 1883, CGPLA Eng. & Wales

Thomson, James (1822–1892), mechanical engineer, was born on 16 February 1822 in College Square, Belfast, the third among the seven children of James *Thomson (1786–1849), professor of mathematics, and his wife, Margaret (d. 1830), daughter of William Gardner, a merchant in Glasgow. His father was an Ulsterman and his mother a Scot. His younger brother William *Thomson (1824–1907) later became Baron Kelvin of Largs. After his wife's death in 1830, James Thomson senior chose to educate his family largely at home even after being appointed to the mathematics chair at Glasgow College in 1832. Having informally attended the junior mathematical class for two years, James matriculated in 1834, took his BA in 1839, and at the close of the 1840 session graduated MA with honours in mathematics and natural philosophy.

From the age of fourteen James displayed a passionate interest in practical engineering. Even his earliest inventions shared a concern to minimize waste of useful work and to maximize economy of operation. Noting how the paddles of Clyde steamers 'wasted' power in lifting water prompted him in 1836 to devise a self-adjusting paddle blade which would minimize such losses of useful work. The efficient production of motive power from fluid flow was a central theme of his engineering career.

Following an educational tour of Germany in 1840, Thomson entered the Dublin office of the engineer John MacNeill, but a knee injury sustained while walking in the Black Forest forced him home after only three weeks. During the early months of 1841 he spent some hours each day studying practical engineering at the Lancefield Spinning Mills in Glasgow, then acquired further practical experience before entering the Horsely Iron Works, Tipton, Staffordshire, early in 1843 as a pupil in the drawing office. By August he had become a premium apprentice (his father having paid £100 as his fee) at the Millwall shipbuilding and marine engineering works of William Fairbairn, then in the forefront of the new ocean-going iron steamship technology.

At Millwall, Thomson studied the theoretical and practical problems of economy in relation to long-distance steam navigation. By August 1844 he had encountered the relatively unfamiliar theory of the motive power of heat (due to Sadi Carnot and Émile Clapeyron) which set theoretical limits to the perfection of heat engines. Working closely with his brother William, he used Carnot's theory to predict the effect of pressure in lowering the freezing point of water, a prediction for which William soon claimed experimental confirmation. The results were presented to the Royal Society of Edinburgh in January 1849. Over the next few years Carnot's theory was transformed into the new sciences of thermodynamics and energy. In 1857 Thomson used the principle of liquefaction by pressure as the basis for an explanation of the 'plasticity of ice', observed by Professor J. D. Forbes during extensive investigations of glacier motion.

Upon his transfer to Fairbairn's Manchester works in October 1844, Thomson's health, never robust, broke down and he returned to Glasgow. For the next five years he based himself in the college, moving in Glasgow Philosophical Society circles and benefiting from the friendship of Lewis Gordon, first professor of engineering in the university. Gordon's familiarity with French horizontal water-wheels or water turbines encouraged Thomson to construct his own model, first tested in the spring of 1847 and finally patented on 3 July 1850 (no. 13156). Messrs Williamson Bros. of Kendal became the principal manufacturers. One such turbine, installed in a mill at Gayle in Upper Wensleydale about 1878, apparently ran for ninety-six years without requiring repair (*The Independent*).

Thomson's patent involved the injection of high-pressure water at the same speed as, and in a spiral motion towards the outside of, the horizontal wheel. The water gradually transferred its energy to the wheel as it moved along vanes curving from radial to tangential and finally passed down a central drain. The guiding principle was to keep any given portion of the water as close as possible to a state of equilibrium while it moved from high to low pressure and so to minimize waste in the extraction of useful work. In contrast, French designs tended either (in the case of Fourneyron) to introduce water from the centre or (in the case of Poncelet) to transfer the kinetic energy of fast-flowing water to the wheel by redirecting it from tangential to radial along curved vanes. Thomson claimed efficiencies of 75 per cent, equal to the best conventional overshot water-wheels and superior to French water turbines.

After his father's death in 1849 Thomson worked with Gordon in London, then returned in 1851 to Belfast, where he opened an office for civil engineering practice. On 28 December 1853 he married Elizabeth (*d.* 1892), daughter of the Irish poor-law commissioner William John Hancock and sister of Neilson Hancock, professor of jurisprudence and political economy in Queen's College, Belfast. The Thomsons had two daughters and one son. By 1854 Thomson had become acting professor of engineering in Queen's. Three years later he was appointed to the chair that he retained until he succeeded Rankine as professor of engineering at Glasgow in 1873.

In Belfast, Thomson's new concern was with centrifugal pumps. Conventional designs lost as much as half of the driving power in expelling water from their circumference with a rotational velocity which was then wasted as friction in the discharge pipe. Thomson added a second 'whirlpool' chamber which permitted conversion of the tangential velocity into increased water pressure capable of raising the water to a greater height at discharge. Efficiencies rose from below 50 per cent to about 70 per cent. As with his turbine, the guiding principle was to maintain approximate equilibrium between neighbouring portions of the vortex, which he subsequently named the 'whirlpool or vortex of equal energies' or 'vortex of free mobility'. In his own words,

a duck could swim from place to place without expenditure of energy in like manner as in still water: Also that a fish in the interior of any whirlpool, except one of Free Mobility, would require a real finite quantity of energy in order to move from place to place. (Smith and Wise, 417)

Thomson also devised a 'jet pump' whereby a jet of water created a suction capable of raising water. A subsequent project, requiring a series of jet pumps, aimed to transform waste swamps into productive land. Related projects of public utility included service as engineer to the Belfast water commissioners (when pumping steam engines supplying water to the expanding town were erected under his charge), a scheme for the promotion of public parks in large towns, and superintending the construction of a flood sluice weir on the River Lagan navigation system between Belfast and Lough Neagh.

Departing from his family's liberal Presbyterianism, but consistent with his devotion to causes of 'practical improvement' and 'rational reform', Thomson became a Unitarian. Professing belief in 'one God the Creator, the Preserver, and Governor of all other beings', he denied revelation other than through the works of nature and in the ideas implanted by God in the human mind. In politics James and William Thomson shared a powerful devotion to liberal causes but parted from the Liberals over Gladstone's espousal of Irish home rule. James's character, and his relationship with his more famous younger brother, was summed up by Hermann Helmholtz in 1863:

> [James] is a level-headed fellow, full of good ideas, but cares for nothing except engineering, and talks about it ceaselessly all day and all night, so that nothing else can be got in when he is present. It is really comic to see how the two brothers talk at one another, and neither listens, and each holds forth about quite different matters. But the engineer is the most stubborn, and generally gets through with his subject. (Smith and Wise, 283)

Thomson received an honorary degree of DSc from Queen's University in 1875 and that of LLD from Glasgow University in 1870 and from Dublin in 1878. He was elected fellow of the Royal Society in 1877. He was president of the Belfast Literary Society in 1864–5, president of the mechanical section of the British Association in 1874, and president of the Institution of Engineers and Shipbuilders in Scotland in 1884 and 1885. Serious eyesight problems led him to resign the Glasgow chair in 1889. He died at his home, 2 Florentine Gardens, Hillhead Street, Glasgow, on 8 May 1892, followed within a week by his wife and younger daughter.   CROSBIE SMITH

Sources J. Thomson, *Collected papers in physics and engineering*, ed. J. Thomson and J. Larmor (1912) · C. Smith and M. N. Wise, *Energy and empire: a biographical study of Lord Kelvin* (1989) · E. King, *Lord Kelvin's early home* (1909) · *The Independent* (17 Nov 1987)

Archives Queen's University, Belfast, papers | CUL, corresp. with Lord Kelvin · U. Glas., corresp. mainly with Lord Kelvin

Likenesses pencil drawing, repro. in E. King, *Lord Kelvin's early home*, facing p. 141 · photograph, repro. in Thomson and Larmor, *Collected papers*, frontispiece

Thomson [*formerly* Thompson]**, James** [*pseud.* B. V.] (1834–1882), poet and satirist, was born at Church Street, Port Glasgow, on 23 November 1834, the eldest of three children of James Thompson (1806–1853), a merchant seaman,

James Thomson (1834–1882), by unknown engraver, pubd 1889 (after unknown photographer, 1869)

and his wife, Sarah Kennedy (1798–1843), a court dressmaker. Both parents were Scottish, and his mother was a devout follower of the preacher Edward Irving. In 1840 James's father suffered a disabling stroke while at sea, and about then the family moved to east London. In 1842 his mother, struggling to support the family, secured him a place at the Royal Caledonian Asylum (which decided he should be known as Thomson, his father's name at baptism). She died a few months later.

Having done well at school, where he remained until 1848, Thomson trained in 1850–51 and 1853–4 as an army schoolmaster at the Royal Military Asylum, Chelsea. In 1851 he went as a student teacher to Ballincollig, near Cork, where he first met the future political activist Charles Bradlaugh. He also developed a tender relationship with a pupil, Matilda Weller, then only thirteen years old. Her death in 1853 was long thought to have had a profound effect on his pessimistic outlook, though later biographers have cast doubt on this.

From 1854 Thomson spent eight nomadic years as an army schoolmaster in England, Ireland, and Jersey. Unexpectedly, on 30 October 1862, he was discharged in disgrace for an apparently minor breach of discipline. Intellectually these years were not wasted, however: he had studied languages, read widely, and discovered a special enthusiasm for Shelley and the German Novalis. He had also written much poetry, some of it published in *Tait's Edinburgh Magazine*.

Thomson now settled in London, and with Bradlaugh's help found work as a clerk and journalist. As B. V. or Bysshe Vanolis (to commemorate Shelley and Novalis) he published much of his poetry and literary reviews in Bradlaugh's *National Reformer*. He participated actively in the propaganda of free thought and secularism, but never fully subscribed to the beliefs of his more militant colleagues. Lacking a wide audience he none the less came to the attention of discerning critics such as W. M. Rossetti. Attacks of alcoholism, however, aggravated by his poverty, loneliness, insomnia, and deeply pessimistic temperament, seriously affected his work. In 1866 he left the Bradlaughs' family home, and until his death, except for a few months in Colorado in 1872–3 as agent of a mining company, and a visit to Spain as war correspondent in 1873, lived in a succession of one-room lodgings, in Pimlico and Bloomsbury. Under these circumstances he contributed to the *National Reformer* in 1874 his great visionary poem 'The City of Dreadful Night', which brought him the appreciation of George Eliot and George Meredith.

After 1875, having quarrelled with Bradlaugh, Thomson transferred his services to *The Secularist*, and the monthly *Cope's Tobacco Plant*. Through his friend Bertram Dobell he eventually achieved publication in book form of some of his poetry in a collection entitled *The City of Dreadful Night and other Poems* (1880), followed by *Vane's Story, Weddah and Om-el-Bonain and other Poems*, and a prose collection, *Essays and Phantasies*, in 1881. During 1881–2 he spent some happy weeks with secularist friends, the Barrs, at their home near Leicester, spoiled by recurrent bouts of drinking. After setting fire to his landlord's kitchen, a fortnight in prison for the offence, and a final drunken binge when he seemed beyond rescue by his devoted friends, he took refuge in the home of the blind poet Philip Bourke Marston, where another friend found him in a state of collapse from an internal haemorrhage. He died on 3 June 1882 in University College Hospital, London, and on 8 June was buried in the grave of the secularist Austin Holyoake, in Highgate cemetery.

Temperamentally 'B. V.' was capable of flashes of brilliant joyousness but the predominant mood of his verse was uncompromisingly sombre. His beliefs moved from pantheism to an atheism which causes less of a frisson now than it did in his own day, and his apocalyptic vision of the megalopolis in 'The City of Dreadful Night' continues to have resonance. The poet wanders in a vast city of endless night. Faith, Love, and Hope have died. A ranting preacher tells of visions of cosmic fire. Even the gate of hell is closed to one who has no hope left to abandon. There is no God and death is final—'The unsexed skeleton mocks shroud and pall' (VII, l. 14). Another preacher finds in the universe only 'Necessity Supreme' (XIV, l. 75), and finally the dreamer sees a great image of Melancholy, drawn from an engraving by Dürer. The poem ceases in a blaze of moonlight with 'confirmation of the old despair' (XXI, l. 84). His poem 'In the Room', in which articles of furniture in a lodging-house room converse about its tenant, can still send a shiver down the reader's spine: only the bed is aware that its silent occupant is a corpse.

H. S. Salt in the *Dictionary of National Biography* described his 'courageous, genial spirit, coupled with an intolerable melancholia; spiritual aspiration with realistic grasp of fact; ardent zeal for democracy and free thought with stubborn disbelief in human progress'—qualities reflected in his prose as much as in his verse. The obscurity of the journals in which he published made it difficult in his lifetime to evaluate the merits of his prose, but the judicious selection made by W. D. Schaefer, *The Speedy Extinction of Evil and Misery* (1967), has done much to reveal its vitality, pungency, and remorseless wit. If Shelley was the presiding genius of Thomson's poetry, along with Dante, Heine, Leopardi, and Blake, the shade of Swift looms over his *Satires and Profanities*, among which may be highlighted his 'Proposals for the speedy extinction of evil and misery' and 'The Story of a Famous Old Jewish Firm' (a satire on the Trinity).

Posthumously, in 1884 Bertram Dobell edited *A Voice from the Nile and other Poems*, while G. W. Foote edited *Satires and Profanities*. Salt's ground-breaking biography appeared in 1889. Even then Thomson's reputation was dogged by misfortune, as a warehouse fire in 1890 destroyed most of his publisher's stock, making the earliest editions exceptionally scarce. Thomson's *Poems, Essays and Fragments*, edited by J. M. Robertson, followed in 1892, but it was Dobell's two-volume edition of the *Poetical Works* (1895) which ensured his survival.   ANN MARGARET RIDLER

Sources T. Leonard, *Places of the mind, the life and work of James Thomson ('B. V.')* (1993) • *Poems and some letters of James Thomson*, ed. A. Ridler (1963) • J. Thomson, *The speedy extinction of evil and misery: selected prose*, ed. W. D. Schaefer (1967) • H. S. Salt, *The life of James Thomson … with a selection from his letters and a study of his writings* (1889); rev. edn (1898) • I. B. Walker, *James Thomson (B. V.), a critical study* (1950) • J. Thomson, *The poetical works*, ed. B. Dobell, 2 vols. (1895) • J. Thomson, *A voice from the Nile and other poems*, ed. B. Dobell (1884) • J. Thomson, *Poems, essays and fragments*, ed. J. M. Robertson (1892) • J. Thomson, *Satires and profanities* (1884) [incl. a preface by G. W. Foote]
Archives Bodl. Oxf., journals, corresp., literary MSS, and papers | Bishopsgate Institute, London, Bradlaugh papers • Bodl. Oxf., corresp. with Bertram Dobell • Bodl. Oxf., Salt MSS • U. Lpool L., corresp. with John Fraser and others
Likenesses photograph, 1860, repro. in J. M. Robertson, ed., *Poems, essays and fragments* (1892) • photograph, 1869, Bishopsgate Institute, London, Bradlaugh collection • photograph, c.1881 • engraving (after photograph, 1869), repro. in Salt, *Life* [see illus.] • photographs, repro. in Leonard, *Places of the mind*
Wealth at death £58 10s. 7d.: administration, 12 Jan 1883, CGPLA Eng. & Wales

Thomson, James Bruce (1810–1873), medical criminologist, was born in January 1810 at Fenwick in Ayrshire, the son of James Thomson and Helen Bruce. The parents appear to have died while their children were young. Left in destitute circumstances, James was raised and educated by a family friend. He studied at Glasgow University, and began medical practice in Tillicoultry, near Stirling, some years before taking his diploma as a licentiate of the Royal College of Surgeons of Edinburgh in 1845. He married Agnes Laing about 1845, but the marriage was not a success and resulted in a separation.

In the woollen mills around Tillicoultry, Thomson acted as a factory surgeon, and in his first publication he extolled the healthiness of mill labour, especially for children. This gained him the attention of Sir John Kincaid, inspector of factories and prisons for Scotland, who subsequently drew the attention of the general board of prisons to Thomson's abilities. Consequently, he was appointed first resident surgeon to Perth general prison in 1858.

Thus placed in medical charge of a large number of prisoners, Thomson was able to lend statistical weight to the developing medical literature on crime and criminality. Immediately prior to his appointment he had written on the hereditary predisposition to dipsomania, regarding severe cases of it as a form of moral insanity. Thomson's writings on criminals similarly emphasized hereditary factors and alleged a close connection between insanity and crime, or between 'madness and badness'. In his two most widely regarded papers, 'The hereditary nature of crime' and 'The psychology of the criminal', both published in the *Journal of Mental Science* in 1870, he maintained that 12 per cent of prisoners were mentally weak, and that one in forty-seven was insane. Thomson's inclination to interpret crime in biological and psychological terms led him to search for physiognomical and other physical stigmata of criminality. From prison statistics, he established that tuberculosis was the most common ailment of criminals, and that diseases of the nervous system were next in frequency. Although in 1865, when he and Sir Robert Christison prepared a special report on the prison dietaries of Scotland, Thomson was hopeful that criminals might be reformed by improvements in their diet and environment, by 1870 he had become convinced that they were incorrigible.

Thomson's work was contemporaneous with that of the medical statistician William Guy and the prison medical officers George Wilson and David Nicolson. In general, these men's writings amplified the progressive degeneration theory of the French criminal anthropologists B. A. Morel and P. Despine, and anticipated the work of the Italian C. Lombroso (1835–1909). Thomson regarded his work as more empirically based and practically orientated than that of the European theorists, and, indeed, it was these features which rendered it attractive both to penal reformers in Britain (especially those interested in refining the classification and segregation of criminals), and to professionalizing practitioners in the treatment of mental disorders. Chief among the latter was Henry Maudsley who celebrated Thomson's writings for the support they gave to his belief that mental illness was largely inherited and that a tendency to insanity could not be controlled by the will of the individual. Maudsley's appreciation mainly accounts for the attention Thomson's work has continued to receive from historians.

Thomson maintained medical interests beyond those relating to criminality. In the *Edinburgh Medical Journal* and the *Journal of Mental Science*, where most of his publications appeared between 1858 and 1870, he also wrote on the diseases of coalminers, epilepsy, the external use of medicines, poisoning, and the dietary of Scottish agricultural labourers. He was also the originator, in 1861, of the Perthshire Medical Association and was an active member of other local and regional professional bodies. In 1872 his health broke down. He suffered from gangrene of the leg for many months, and died at High Fenwick, Ayrshire, on 19 January 1873.   ROGER COOTER

Sources *DNB* · *Perth Advertiser* (23 Jan 1873) · C. H. S. Jayewardene, 'The English precursors of Lombroso', *British Journal of Criminology*, 4 (1963–4), 164–70 · J. Saunders, 'Quarantining the weak-minded: psychiatric definitions of degeneracy and the late-Victorian asylum', *The anatomy of madness: essays in the history of psychiatry*, ed. W. F. Bynum, R. Porter, and M. Shepherd, 3 (1988), 273–96 · J. B. Thomson, 'The influence of the woollen manufactures on health', *London Medical Gazette*, new ser., 2 (1839–40), 462 · J. B. Thomson, 'Hereditary predisposition to dipsomania', *Edinburgh Medical Journal*, 3 (1857–8), 890–92 · J. B. Thomson, 'Statistics of prisoners: their death-rate and their diseases [6 pts]', *Edinburgh Medical Journal*, 6 (1860–61), 135–44, 336–44, 972–81; 7 (1861–2), 136–44, 524–31, 1109–20 · J. B. Thomson and [R. Christison], 'Notes on the prison dietaries in Scotland [pt 1]', *Edinburgh Medical Journal*, 11 (1865–6), 987–97 · *London and Provincial Medical Directory* (1858) · d. cert.

Thomson, Jocelyn Home

Thomson, Jocelyn Home (1859–1908), chief inspector of explosives, was born at Oxford on 31 August 1859, the second of four sons of William *Thomson (1819–1890), archbishop of York, and his wife, Zoë (*d.* 1913), *née* Skene. After education at Eton College, where he won the Tomline prize for mathematics, and the Royal Military Academy, Woolwich, he entered the Royal Artillery in December 1878, took part in the Anglo-Zulu War of 1879, and then served as captain with the Royal Horse Artillery in India and Egypt.

An interest in science and especially in astronomy led Thomson to tour the European observatories in 1881, after which the Royal Society obtained leave for him to observe the transit of Venus from Barbados in 1882. Thomson then held various scientific appointments at Woolwich; from 1887 to 1892 he served on the staff of the department of artillery and stores, afterwards becoming an assistant to the director-general of ordnance factories. In 1886 he married Mabel Sophia, daughter of Thomas Bradley Paget, of Chipping Norton; there were no children. During 1888 he was secretary under Sir Frederick Abel to the War Office explosives committee, for whom he carried out the first experiments on a new smokeless explosive. Thomson named this new substance cordite because it was extruded by the production machinery in the form of cords. This explosive was recommended to the government in 1890 and adopted for military use in 1893. Thomson spent the winter of 1891 in Canada testing the performance of cordite under cold weather conditions. In 1893 he was appointed inspector of explosives, succeeding Sir Vivian Majendie as chief inspector in August 1899.

For five years from 1900 Thomson took leave to act as consulting engineer in India to the project to carry electrical power from the Cauvery Falls to the Mysore goldfields, for which he visited Mysore, and then advised on a similar transmission and railway project in the Jhelum valley. Thomson was a versatile mechanic; among the devices that he invented or improved were instruments for electrical telegraphy and petroleum testing apparatus. He also devised a position finder, for which the government war department awarded him £500. He wrote a number of reports and guides, both technical and popular, dealing with explosives and with the petroleum lamp. In 1901 the Belgian government conferred upon him the order of Leopold. He was made a CB in 1907.

In August 1907 Thomson suffered a nervous breakdown, which left him with occasional loss of speech and marked slowness of thought, infirmities that caused him considerable distress. On 13 February 1908 he shot himself at his residence at 18 Draycott Place, Chelsea. He was buried at Brompton cemetery.   ANITA McCONNELL

Sources *The Times* (15 Feb 1908), 10e · *The Times* (18 Feb 1908), 10b · E. C. Rickards, *Zoë Thomson of Bishopthorpe … * (1916) · *DNB*

Wealth at death £4573 10s.: probate, 25 March 1908, *CGPLA Eng. & Wales*

Thomson, John

Thomson, John (1765–1846), physician and surgeon, was born at Paisley, Renfrewshire, on 15 March 1765, the son of Joseph Thomson, a silk weaver, and his wife, Mary, formerly Millar. At the age of eleven Thomson was bound apprentice to his father for seven years. His father destined him for the ministry; the boy, however, wished to study medicine, and persuaded his father to apprentice him in 1785 to Dr White of Paisley, with whom he remained for three years. He entered the University of Glasgow in the winter session of 1788–9, and in the following year migrated to Edinburgh. He was appointed assistant apothecary at the Royal Infirmary, Edinburgh, in September 1790, and a year later he became house surgeon to the institution under the designation of surgeon's clerk, having already from the previous June filled the office of an assistant physician's clerk. He became a member of the Medical Society at the beginning of the winter session in 1790–91, and in the following year he was elected one of its presidents. On 31 July 1792 Thomson resigned his appointment at the infirmary on account of ill health, and went to London, where he studied at John Hunter's school of medicine in Leicester Square.

In London, Thomson made many valuable friendships, and on his return to Edinburgh early in 1793 he became a fellow of the College of Surgeons of Edinburgh and attended the Royal Infirmary as a surgeon. He married, in 1793, Margaret Crawford, second daughter of John Gordon of Caroll, Sutherland. She died early in 1804; of their three children only William *Thomson (1802–1852), physician, survived him.

During this period Thomson was occupied with the study of chemistry. He conducted a chemical class during the winter of 1799–1800 which met at his house, under the auspices of the earl of Lauderdale, and consisted chiefly of gentlemen connected with the parliament house. In 1800, nominated one of the six surgeons to the Royal Infirmary, he began teaching surgery. He also lectured on the nature and treatment of those injuries and diseases familiar to military surgeons, and he visited London in the autumn of 1803 to be appointed a hospital mate in the army in order to qualify himself, should it be found necessary to establish a military hospital in Edinburgh in the event of an invasion.

The College of Surgeons of Edinburgh established a professorship of surgery in 1804, and, in spite of objections from the university, Thomson was appointed to the post. In 1806 he was appointed regius professor of military surgery in the University of Edinburgh, but he continued to hold the college professorship until 1821. Also in 1806 Thomson married Margaret, third daughter of John Millar being given in conjunction with his son, William Thomson. In 1831 he addressed Lord Melbourne on the advantages likely to flow from the establishment of a separate chair of general pathology. He was appointed professor of general pathology in the university, commencing in 1832.

Thomson was a prolific writer and translator; among his major works *Elements of Chemistry and Natural History*, prefaced by 'Philosophy of chemistry', a translation of the work by Fourcroy (3 vols., 1798–1800), reached a fifth edition; *Observations on Lithotomy, with a New Manner of Cutting for the Stone* (1808; with appendix, 1810) was translated into French; and *Lectures on Inflammation: a View of the General Doctrines of Medical Surgery* (1813) was issued in America in 1813 and 1817, and was translated into German in 1820 and into French in 1827. The lectures were founded on the Hunterian theory of inflammation which was later modified.

Repeated attacks of illness compelled Thomson to discontinue his visits to patients after the summer of 1835, but he continued to see those who came to his house. He resigned his professorship in 1841. The duties had long been performed by a deputy. He died at his home, Morland Cottage, near the foot of Blackford Hill, on the south side of Edinburgh, on 11 October 1846.

Thomson died with the reputation of being in his time the most learned physician in Scotland. 'To almost the last week of his life he was a hard student', says Henry Cockburn in his journal,

> and not even fourscore years could quench his ardour in discoursing upon science, morals, or politics. … He never knew apathy, and, medicine being his first field, he was for forty years the most exciting of all our practitioners and of all our teachers. (*Journal of Henry Cockburn*, 163–4)

D'A. POWER, *rev.* ANITA MCCONNELL

Sources A. Miles, *The Edinburgh school of surgery before Lister* (1918) • C. H. Cresswell, 'The Royal College of Surgeons of Edinburgh: their professors of surgery', *Edinburgh Medical Journal*, 3rd ser., 12 (1914), 533–51 • *GM*, 2nd ser., 26 (1846), 670 • H. L. Gordon, *Sir James Young Simpson and chloroform* (1897), 73–4 • *The Lancet* (9 Jan 1847), 52 • [W. Thomson and D. Craigie], *Edinburgh Medical and Surgical Journal*, 67 (1847), 131–93 • *Journal of Henry Cockburn: being a continuation of the 'Memorials of his time', 1831–1854*, 2 (1874), 163–4 • bap. reg. Scot.

Archives NL Scot., corresp. and travel journal • Royal College of Physicians of Edinburgh, lecture notes • U. Edin. L., lecture notes | Glos. RO, letters to Daniel Ellis, D 1501, 2227

Likenesses A. Geddes, oils, exh. RA 1818, Royal College of Surgeons, Edinburgh [*see illus.*]

Wealth at death £185 3s. 11d.: confirmation, 1849, Scotland

John Thomson (1765–1846), by Andrew Geddes, exh. RA 1818

(1735–1801), professor of jurisprudence at Glasgow University. Of their children, only a daughter and a son, later Professor Allen *Thomson (1809–1884), biologist, reached adulthood.

On 11 January 1808 Thomson obtained the degree of MD from the University and King's College of Aberdeen. In 1810 he resigned his post at the Royal Infirmary following criticism of his surgery by the surgeon John Bell. He continued to lecture, however, and in the summer of 1814 he visited the various medical schools in Europe to examine the different methods followed in the hospitals of France, Italy, Austria, Saxony, Prussia, Hanover, and the Netherlands. He was admitted a licentiate of the Royal College of Physicians of Edinburgh on 7 February 1815, since he was by then acting as a consulting physician as well as a consulting surgeon. In the following summer Thomson again returned to the continent to watch the treatment of the men wounded at Waterloo, and in September 1815 he was mainly instrumental in founding the Edinburgh New Town Dispensary.

The smallpox epidemic of 1817–18 showed that vaccination conferred less protection than had been supposed, and Thomson published his views upon the subject in two pamphlets of 1820 and 1822. He delivered a course of lectures on diseases of the eye in the summer of 1819, paving the way for the establishment of the first eye infirmary in Edinburgh in 1824. During 1822–6 he was involved in the study of general pathology, and in 1821 he was an unsuccessful candidate for the chair of the practice of physic in the university, rendered vacant by the death of James Gregory. In 1828–9 and again in 1829–30 he delivered a course of lectures on the practice of physic, both courses

Thomson, John (1778–1840), landscape painter, was the fourth son of Thomas Thomson (d. 1799), minister of Dailly, Ayrshire, and his second wife, Mary (1746–1822), daughter of Francis Hay. Born in his father's manse on 1 September 1778, he was educated at the parish school. He attended Glasgow University in 1791–2, studying for the ministry, the chosen profession of his grandfather and great-grandfather as well as his own father. In November 1793 Thomson moved to Edinburgh University, following his elder brothers, Thomas (1768–1852), who was training in the city for the bar, and Adam (*b.* 1776), who was working at the banking house of Sir William Forbes. John and Thomas in particular were supported through the patronage of Lady Hailes, a former parishioner of their father's, and spent much time at New Hailes, near Musselburgh. There, the young men were introduced to such rising stars of Edinburgh life as Francis Jeffrey and Walter Scott (then young advocates). During the vacations from his studies at Edinburgh University, Thomson sketched from nature in the wooded countryside around his native Dailly. During his last session at Edinburgh (1798–9), he enrolled for the landscape drawing classes offered by Alexander Nasmyth.

Thomson was licensed by the presbytery at Ayr on 17 July 1799. His father had died a few months earlier, on 19 February 1799, and the son was presented by George III with the parish of Dailly. He was ordained, still aged only twenty-one, on 24 April 1800. On 7 July 1801 he married Isabella, daughter of John Ramsay, minister of Kirkmichael in Ayrshire. She died on 18 April 1809, leaving two sons—Thomas and John—and two daughters; the younger, Isabella, married the painter Robert Scott Lauder. During the next five years Thomson, while fulfilling his obligations as a minister, was increasingly preoccupied with painting, sending a group of drawings for sale in Glasgow in 1803. In autumn 1805 Thomson was translated from his Ayrshire parish to the living at Duddingston on the outskirts of Edinburgh. The parish was in the gift of the marquess of Abercorn, whose factor was Thomas Scott, the brother of Sir Walter Scott. Scott and Thomson's brother Thomas had remained close friends. It was very shortly after this that Thomson sold his first landscape painting, for 15 guineas.

At Duddingston Thomson was close to the intellectual and cultural life of Edinburgh. His friendship with Scott in particular had a powerful influence on the subjects of his pictures as well as on his patrons, who included Scott's near neighbour and kinsman, the duke of Buccleuch. It was through his acquaintance with Scott that Thomson met Turner, entertaining the English painter as his guest in 1822 while both men were working on illustrations for Scott's *Provincial Antiquities of Scotland*. Thomson started exhibiting in Edinburgh at the 1808 Associated Society of Artists exhibitions, continuing until the year of his death (1840). He declined ordinary membership of the Scottish Academy because of his clerical office but was elected (1830) an honorary one. Despite this determination to maintain his amateur status, his commercial success was considerable; he apparently earned £1800 a year from his painting during the 1820s.

Thomson married, second, on 6 December 1813, Frances Ingram Spence (*d.* 1845), widow of Martin Dalrymple of Fordell, Fife. With her he had three sons—Francis, Charles, and Henry—and a daughter, Mary Helen. Thomson's love for art was not confined to painting; he was also passionately fond of music, and played the violin and the flute. He was a member of a number of Edinburgh clubs and he contributed several articles on scientific subjects to the *Edinburgh Review*, then recently started.

Thomson died at his home, Duddingston manse, near Edinburgh on 28 October 1840 and was buried in Duddingston kirkyard. His wife Frances died on 11 October 1845. Thomson had little or no formal training as a painter and this undoubtedly hampered his development considerably. He remained, however, the greatest Scottish painter of his generation, and the first to echo fully on canvas the scenery so extraordinarily and influentially conjured up by Sir Walter Scott in both poetry and prose; Thomson produced at least eleven views of Fast Castle, the probable model for Wolf's Crag in Scott's *The Bride of Lammermoor*, at least one for Scott himself (Abbotsford House, Roxburghshire).

Unfortunately, many of Thomson's pictures are now in poor condition owing to his habit of painting upon an insufficiently hardened ground of flour boiled with vinegar, which he described as 'parritch', and a considerable use of bitumen. His slighter and more directly painted pictures are, however, in a much sounder state, freshly and elegantly painted and showing a considerable sensitivity and charm of handling which one would hardly expect from his more elaborate work where exaggeration of topography and of expression appears at times over-rhetorical and self-indulgent.

Thomson does not appear to have travelled on the continent and most (though not all) of his subjects were found in the lowlands of Scotland. His vision of his native country and its scenery had a profound influence on the next generation of Scottish landscape painters, particularly Horatio McCulloch, whom Thomson befriended when the young man first arrived from the west of Scotland in the 1820s.

Thomson is represented in the National Gallery of Scotland by some fourteen works which span every period of his career; there are five examples at Kelvingrove Art Gallery, Glasgow, and one in the Tate collection.

There are portrait drawings of Thomson by William Bewick and Sir Thomas Dick Lauder, and two painted portraits by William Wallace in the Scottish National Portrait Gallery, Edinburgh. The present location of a bust-length portrait by Raeburn is unknown.

J. L. CAW, *rev.* MUNGO CAMPBELL

Sources W. Baird, *John Thomson of Duddingston* (1895) · D. Irwin and F. Irwin, *Scottish painters at home and abroad, 1700–1900* (1975) · J. Holloway and L. Errington, *The discovery of Scotland* (1978) · H. Smailes, *The concise catalogue of the Scottish National Portrait Gallery* (1990) · *Catalogue of paintings and sculpture*, National Gallery of Scotland, 51st edn (1957) · C. Thompson and H. Brigstocke, *Shorter catalogue: National Gallery of Scotland*, 2nd edn (1978) · W. D. McKay and F. Rinder, *The Royal Scottish Academy, 1826–1916* (1917); repr. (1975) · Graves, *Artists* · file notes, NG Scot. · K. Thomson, *Turner and Sir Walter Scott: the provincial antiquities and picturesque scenery of Scotland* (1999) [exhibition catalogue, NG Scot., 17 Dec 1999 – 19 March 2000]

Archives NL Scot., corresp. and accounts

Likenesses W. Bewick, chalk drawing, 1824, Scot. NPG · T. D. Lauder, pencil drawing, 1831, Scot. NPG · H. Raeburn, oils · W. Wallace, two portraits, oils, Scot. NPG

Thomson, John (1805–1841), composer, eldest son of Revd Andrew Mitchell *Thomson (1779–1831) and his wife, Jane Carmichael (*d.* 1840), was born at Sprouston, near Kelso in the Scottish borders on 28 October 1805. Although initially trained for the law, he was brought up in a household which valued music highly. His father, who was minister of St George's, Edinburgh, contributed a number of vocal works to R. A. Smith's *Sacred Harmony* (he also secured Smith's choral expertise for St George's). The family lived at 29 Melville Street, Edinburgh, where Thomson started composing at the age of fourteen. By his mid-twenties he had projected an Arabian opera to a text by C. B. Sillery (from which one or more numbers survive), composed music for *The House of Aspen* at the Edinburgh Royal and a *Benedictus and hosanna* for voices and orchestra, and had to his credit two piano trios, as well as a piano quartet, a fine rondo for solo piano, and a number of songs. It was probably the sunny C major trio of 1825, rather than the dark obsessive G minor trio of 1826, that impressed Mendelssohn as 'pretty'. Following their meeting in Edinburgh in July 1829, and with Mendelssohn's warm recommendation, Thomson went to Berlin and Leipzig, where he met Schumann and Ignaz Moscheles. The trip also took in Paris, but he was back in Edinburgh by July 1830. In Leipzig he became a student of Schnyder von Wartensee, but Thomson's autograph scores (held in the Reid Music Library in Edinburgh) show only that he submitted some of his works to Moscheles for comment; and it was to Moscheles that he dedicated the impressive sonata for pianoforte and violin, completed in 1835.

Perhaps Thomson's most imposing large-scale work is the opera *Hermann, or, The Broken Spear*, first produced in London at the Lyceum in 1834. The simple and melodramatic plot is set in the southern Alps and features bandits, a fine drinking song, abduction, and repentance. Some of the numbers were popular for a time, and the powerfully dramatic overture has remained in the repertory. His other opera, *The Shadow on the Wall*, dates from 1835, in which year it was produced, again at the London Lyceum.

Other works include a five-part glee, 'When whispering winds', composed in 1836 for the association in aid of the Edinburgh Professional Society of Musicians. The piece is, in essence, an ode to music, of great beauty and skilfully scored for the voices. A flute quartet and an allegro maestoso for flute and orchestra are sufficiently showy to suggest that Thomson was a flautist. His only works available on sound recordings are the overture to *Hermann*; a flute concerto; a touching *Bagatelle* for solo piano; and the *Drei Lieder*, the first of which is a ravishing setting of Byron (in German) followed by striking settings of poems by Schiller and Uhland. The work was published in Frankfurt in 1838, and Thomson (apparently in Leipzig at the time) dedicated a copy to Mendelssohn which the latter retained in his library until his death. A choral work composed in 1829 to honour the memory of R. A. Smith remains to be discovered. Although his music betrays no Scottish influences, Thomson made many arrangements of Scottish songs for *The Vocal Melodies of Scotland*, a joint publication with Finlay Dun in 1836. In October 1839, with recommendations from Mendelssohn and M. W. Balfe, Thomson was elected first Reid professor of music at Edinburgh University, and therefore the first such professor in Scotland. He set about preparing lectures on the history of music and, at the inception of the annual Reid concerts, introduced programme notes (probably the earliest instance of such a practice); but he did not live long enough to establish the chair or, indeed, fully to realize his considerable compositional gifts.

Thomson married Jane Helen Lee, the daughter of the principal of Edinburgh University, on 8 December 1840. His portrait is in the Reid School of Music; from a letter to Catherine Jameson it would appear that he was short in height. He was remembered as a man of sweet disposition, and this is borne out by his surviving correspondence. At the time of his death (from dropsy), on 6 May 1841, he was living with his wife at 16 Howe Street, Edinburgh. His burial place is not known.   JOHN PURSER

Sources J. Purser, *Scotland's music: a history of the traditional and classical music of Scotland from earliest times to the present day* (1992), 212–17 • H. G. Farmer, *A history of music in Scotland* (1947), 495–8 • *The Harmonicon* • *DNB* • S. Hensel, *The Mendelssohn family* (1882), 197–8 • S. Hensel, ed., *Die Familie Mendelssohn, 1729–1847: nach Briefen und Tagebüchern*, 1 (1879), 224 • N. Temperley and M. Greenbaum, eds., *The overture in England, 1800–1840* (1984), xv–xvi, 87–131 • A. Grant, *The story of the University of Edinburgh during its first three hundred years*, 2 (1884), 458–9 • m. cert. • J. Lee, correspondence with his daughter, Jane, NL Scot., MS 3443, fol. 212 • P. Aris and S. Hough, eds., *Piano works from the autograph box of Mary Alexander* (2002) • R. B. Gotch, ed., *Mendelssohn and his friends in Kensington* (1938)
Archives U. Edin., Reid Library • U. Edin. | SOUND Scottish Music Information Centre, Glasgow, recordings of the overture to *Hermann*, the flute concerto, the G minor piano trio and vocal and piano pieces
Likenesses W. Hensel, drawing, 1829, repro. in [W. Hensel] and C. Lowenthal-Hensel, *19th century society portraits: drawings by Wilhelm Hensel* (1986) [exhibition catalogue, Ashmolean Museum, Oxford] • oils, U. Edin., Reid School of Music

Thomson, John (1837–1921), photographer and travel writer, was born on 14 June 1837 at Portland Place, Edinburgh, the third of the four children to survive infancy of William Thomson (1794–*c*.1870), tobacconist, and his wife, Isabella Newlands (1801–1863). His early education is unknown, but by 1851 he had become an apprenticed optician in Edinburgh, probably with the firm run by James Mackay Bryson on Princes Street. While an apprentice, he attended the Watt Institution and School of Arts during the sessions 1856–7 and 1857–8, gaining the attestation of proficiency in natural philosophy, and in junior mathematics and chemistry. He was awarded the life diploma in 1858, and also gained a Watt Club prize for English. Bryson proposed him for election to the Royal Scottish Society of Arts, although he became a member only for 1861–2.

For reasons that are not entirely clear Thomson left Edinburgh on 29 April 1862 to join his elder brother William in Singapore. Soon after his arrival he began advertising his services as a photographer, although the following year he and his brother joined forces as makers and repairers of optical and nautical instruments. While in Singapore he began to take serious photographs, mainly cartes-de-visites, although some landscapes have survived. He also used the opportunity to travel widely around the neighbouring territories, especially Penang, and Province Wellesley. In 1865 he decided to travel to Angkor in Cambodia, accounts of which had recently been published by Henri Mouhot. He sailed first to Bangkok, arriving there on 28 September 1865, and with the assistance of H. G. Kennedy, an official at the British consulate, he gained audience with the Siamese royal family, many of whom, including King Mongkut, were the subjects of important portrait photographs. Mongkut granted permission for Thomson and Kennedy to travel to Angkor, for which they set out on 27 January 1866, and where he became the first photographer to document the site. They travelled on to Phnom Penh, returning to Bangkok to leave a set of photographs with King Mongkut. In May 1867 several of Thomson's images were reproduced in the *Illustrated London News*. By the middle of 1866 he had returned to Britain, where he set about publicizing his travels and photographs, writing articles for the *British Journal of Photography*, and exhibiting and lecturing in Edinburgh, Glasgow, and London. His first major work, *The Antiquities of Cambodia*, was published in Edinburgh in 1867.

Late in 1867 Thomson returned to the Far East, visiting Vietnam at first, then moving his studio from Singapore to Hong Kong in 1868. He wrote a number of articles, illustrated with his own photographs, for the *China Magazine*, became the official photographer for the duke of Edinburgh's visit in 1869, and published a second book of photographs, *Views on the North River*. After marrying Isabel Petrie in Hong Kong on 19 November 1868, he began an intensive period of travelling around mainland China, taking a large series of wet-collodion photographs with the intention of returning to Britain and publishing them in book form. Between 1870 and 1872 he undertook four distinct journeys, up the north branch of the Pearl River, up the River Min to the area around Foochow (Fuzhou), to Peking (Beijing), and finally up the great Yangtze (Yangzi) River. The photographs taken on these journeys form one of the most extensive photographic surveys of any region taken in the nineteenth century. The range and depth of his photographic vision mark Thomson out as one of the most important travel photographers. During the early part of this period he was based in Hong Kong, but in 1870 he sold his business as a going concern, leaving part of his stock of collodion negatives behind but taking the best material with him. In Foochow he worked closely with Justus Doolittle, an important American missionary in the area, and in 1871 he travelled to Formosa (Taiwan), visiting a Scottish medical missionary, the Revd James Laidlaw Maxwell, in whose company he took the earliest extant photographs. In Peking, Thomson again sought out westerners, especially through the British legation, and for a time acted as the correspondent of the *Illustrated London News*. The British minister, Sir Thomas Wade, gave him the important task of photographing senior Chinese officials including Li Hongzhang, Shen Kew Fen, and Prince Gong himself. Thomson's photographs of China form what he himself intended to be a 'visual encyclopaedia' of the land, its people, customs, industry, and architecture. The surviving body of work embraces most of the principal genres of photography with equal skill. Although Thomson's intention for his photographs was for them to be an impassive documentary record—truthful in a way that he felt only photography could be—they none the less betray a viewpoint coloured by his background as a product of Britain's imperial ascendancy.

In the autumn of 1872 Thomson returned to Britain, reunited himself with his family, who had returned in 1870, and settled in London. He immediately began the task of promoting and disseminating his photography. He contributed a series of illustrated articles on life in China to *The Graphic* in 1872–3, published privately a magnificent portfolio of carbon prints, *Foochow and the River Min* (1873), and more importantly a large-scale work, *Illustrations of China and its People* (1873–4), which was responsible for firmly establishing his reputation as a photographer, traveller, and leading authority on China. A series of well-received books and articles followed, most importantly *The Straits of Malacca, Indo-China, and China* (1875), a condensed version of his Far Eastern travels, and his edition and translation of Gaston Tissandier's work as *History and Handbook of Photography* (1876) which, in its second edition (1877), included the last writings of William Henry Fox Talbot. In 1876 he joined forces with the journalist Adolphe Smith on an important monthly publication entitled *Street Life in London*, which pioneered the genre of photojournalism, combining hard-hitting, albeit posed, street photography, with documentary-style prose. His final overseas travelling took place in 1878 to Cyprus, a journey that resulted in the de luxe two-volume publication *Through Cyprus with the Camera in the Autumn of 1878*.

Throughout the 1880s Thomson concentrated on building up his commercial portrait studio, which he moved from Buckingham Palace Road to settle eventually in New Bond Street, and which gradually acquired a clientele of the fashionable rich, which increased after he gained the royal warrant on 11 May 1881. Throughout the 1880s and 1890s Thomson was employed on a number of commissions to take portraits of the royal family, both in Scotland and London. He also gained commissions through his associations with the Royal Geographical Society, of which he was made a fellow in 1867, and for whom he became instructor in photography in 1886, tutoring prospective travellers in photography, writing instructive articles in the society's publications, and organizing exhibitions, such as the Sixth International Geographical Congress, for which he acted as secretary. As his reputation grew, lucrative commissions followed, including those to document the art collection of Alfred de Rothschild, and to act as one of the official photographers at the Devonshire House fancy dress ball in 1897. In later life he continued to allow his photographs to be reproduced in a wide variety of publications, most notably children's encyclopaedias, and a number of awards followed, including a gold medal at the Paris International Geographical Exhibition in 1889. In 1890 the explorer Sir Halford Mackinder named a peak of Mount Kilimanjaro Point Thomson in honour of his services to the Royal Geographical Society. Thomson died on 29 September 1921 in London, and was buried on 4 October in Streatham Vale cemetery. His latter years were spent in relative comfort and wealth, divided between the Royal Geographical Society and the Royal Societies Club. He was survived by his wife and six children. Some of Thomson's negatives are held by the library of the Wellcome Institute for the History of Medicine, London; his photographs appear in the Lacock Abbey collection and the Stephen White collection in the Tokyo-Fuji Art Museum, Tokyo.   RICHARD OVENDEN

Sources R. Ovenden, *John Thomson (1837–1921): photographer* (1997) · S. White, *John Thomson: life and photographs* (1985) · C. S. Lee, 'John Thomson: a photographic vision of the Far East, 1860–1872', MLitt diss., U. Oxf., 1985 · J. Thomson, *The Straits of Malacca, Indo-China, and China* (1875) · I. Gibson-Cowan, 'John Thomson on Cyprus', *Photographic Collector*, 3 (1985), 309–19 · I. Gibson-Cowan, 'Thomson's street life in context', *Creative Camera*, 251 (1985), 10–15
Archives NRA, priv. coll. | Lacock Abbey, Wiltshire · NL Scot., Blackwood's MSS
Likenesses photograph, *c.*1867, priv. coll.
Wealth at death £4174 11*s.* 3*d.*: administration with will, 23 Dec 1921, *CGPLA Eng. & Wales*

Thomson, John (1856–1926), paediatrician, was born at 18 Walker Street, Edinburgh, on 23 November 1856, the second of three children and only son of Thomas Thomson (*d.* 1876), writer to the signet, and his wife, Elizabeth (*d.* 1871), daughter of Alexander Cleghorn. A shy and solitary boy, he was educated from 1867 to 1874 at the Edinburgh Academy. At Edinburgh University he was able and diligent, winning six medals, other prizes, and graduating in medicine in 1881. After holding coveted resident posts at the Royal Infirmary, he spent seven months in Vienna and Berlin. In Berlin he came under the influence of E. H. Henoch, the famous German paediatrist, and in 1888 published a translation of his *Vorlesungen über Kinderkrankheiten*. On returning to England in 1884 Thomson was appointed resident medical officer at the Hospital for Sick Children, Great Ormond Street, London, where he worked under Walter Butler Cheadle and Thomas Barlow. Great Ormond Street was the only hospital in which systematic teaching was carried on; he saw and treated an enormous number of cases of every kind. In August 1886 Thomson became physician to the New Town Dispensary, Edinburgh, where he established a clinic for diseases of children. Gifted with an excellent memory and systematic mind, Thomson accumulated more valuable experience. In 1887 Thomson obtained by examination membership of the Royal College of Physicians, Edinburgh. In the same year he married Isobel Finlayson McPhail, daughter of the Revd John S. McPhail, of the United Free Church, Kilmuir, Isle of Skye; they had four sons and two daughters.

In 1889 Thomson was appointed extra physician to the Royal Hospital for Sick Children, Edinburgh, the hospital with which he was actively associated for the rest of his life. From this time onwards he contributed to journals and textbooks articles on diseases of childhood, which were characterized by accurate and detailed observation. His most important contributions to medical knowledge included his account of congenital pyloric stenosis, an obscure and formidable affection of the alimentary canal.

He was the first to make known acute pyelitis in infants, and its effective treatment. He also drew attention to Down's syndrome. In 1898 appeared Thomson's *Guide to the Clinical Study and Treatment of Sick Children*. It was soon considered invaluable. By the fourth edition (1925), a comprehensive manual, it had been translated into Spanish and French.

When, on the expiry of his period of office as physician at the Children's Hospital in 1918, he was appointed consulting physician, Thomson retained a clinic for mentally deficient children, in whom he took great interest. For the parents of these he wrote a booklet, *Opening Doors* (1923), in the simplest language, giving valuable hints for training. His work resulted in the foundation of the Edinburgh Crippled Children's Aid Society.

Thomson's writings were widely appreciated. In the United States and Canada he was made an honorary member of many paediatric societies; his own university in 1922 conferred on him the honorary degree of LLD, and the Royal College of Physicians, London, in recognition of his valuable work, elected him a fellow in 1926.

Thomson had a lovable nature. Kind and wise, he never lost a friend. He was a good angler, and a student of French poetry. Credited as being the father of Scottish paediatrics, and an excellent teacher, he died at his home, 14 Coates Crescent, Edinburgh, on 2 July 1926, and was buried on 5 July in the Dean cemetery there. He was survived by his wife, two sons, and his daughters.

G. F. STILL, *rev.* ROGER HUTCHINS

Sources W. S. Craig, *John Thomson, pioneer and father of Scottish paediatrics, 1856–1926* (1968) · *BMJ* (10 July 1926), 95–7 · *The Lancet* (10 July 1926), 99 · Munk, *Roll* · personal knowledge (1937) · private information (1937)
Likenesses C. D'O. P. Jackson, bronze medal, 1929, Scot. NPG · photograph, repro. in *The Lancet*, 99
Wealth at death £22,345 5*s.* 4*d.*: confirmation, 10 Sept 1926, *CCI*

Thomson, John Cockburn (1834–1860). *See under* Thomson, Henry William (1822–1867).

Thomson, John Murie Galloway McCallum (1909–1931), footballer, was born at 74 Balfour Street, Kirkcaldy, Fife, on 28 January 1909, son of John Shepherd Thomson, a miner, and his wife, Jane Boyd, *née* McCallum. He showed an early aptitude for sports (football in particular), and by 1924 he was playing in goal for Bowhill West. He moved on to Bowhill Rovers, then in 1925, to Wellesley Juniors. In October 1926 Steve Callaghan, a Celtic scout, attended Wellesley's match with Denbeath Star to watch Star's goalkeeper and centre forward. However, it was Thomson's performance, which included a penalty save, that caught Callaghan's eye, and Thomson signed for the Glasgow club on 1 November 1926. Celtic had sprung from, and drew their support from, Glasgow's Irish Catholic community, but the club had formally decided in 1893 not to exclude potential staff on the basis of religion, so Thomson's membership of a presbyterian sect, the Church of Christ, was no bar to his joining them.

Since Celtic had dispensed with their reserve side Thomson was loaned to Ayr United to gain experience, but by early 1927 he was back with Celtic, making his début at

Dens Park on 12 February 1927 in a 2–1 victory against Dundee. Thomson was at fault with Dundee's goal, but when Tom Colgan, a Celtic director, made to console the eighteen year old he was taken aback at the youngster's assurance in vowing never to repeat the error. Thomson's self-confidence was justified, and he regained his place in the side which ended the season with a Scottish cup final win over second-division East Fife. The lack of a reserve team severely hampered Celtic the next season, and though Thomson's own reputation grew—his performance was largely responsible for an undeserved Scottish cup semi-final win over Queens Park—he could do nothing to prevent disappointment in the league and a 4–0 loss to Rangers in the Scottish cup final.

Thomson's international career began with appearances for the Scottish league side against their counterparts from Ireland and England. In the match against the English league side Thomson helped to keep the English margin of victory down to 2–1. In a repeat of this fixture, in November 1930, Thomson emerged with great credit despite a 7–3 loss. One newspaper reported that 'his handling was sure … and his daring was thrilling to watch. Thomson defended his charge with courage, skill, and bulldog tenacity, even when it was obvious that every man in the Scotland team was outplayed, outclassed and leg-weary' (*Glasgow Herald*, 6 Nov 1930). His full international début was delayed by a broken jaw and collarbone sustained against Airdrie in February 1930, but on 18 May he played in a 2–0 victory over France in Paris.

These injuries resulted directly from one element in Thomson's style of goalkeeping: in an age when most goalkeepers confined themselves to their 6 yard box, he made any ball in the penalty box his. He frequently came beyond the penalty spot to catch or punch crosses, and was pioneering in rushing out to meet advancing forwards, either to narrow the angle for the forward's shot, or to dive at his feet to claim the ball. A newspaper report describes him as 'diving riskily and spectacularly' to save from Elliot, a Partick Thistle forward. The same report, though, sardonically notes an error by the 'Prince of Keepers' (*Sunday Mail*, 8 March 1931) in attempting to punch away a cross leading to a Thistle goal. His bravery was all the more remarkable considering that he was small for a goalkeeper—5 feet 9 inches tall, weighing around 11 stone. His agility and sharp reflexes compensated for his lack of height. Jimmy McGrory, Celtic centre forward from 1923 to 1938, likened Thomson's ability to get extra thrust in mid-air to the hitch-kick employed by American athlete Jesse Owens (*Lifetime in Paradise*, 40). Robert Kelly, Celtic's chairman from 1945 to 1971, said Thomson had 'the clutching hands of a world class fielder' (Kelly, 91), while McGrory compared them to 'an artist's hands, a surgeon's … fine but powerful' (*Lifetime in Paradise*, 40).

In May 1931 Thomson was part of the side which beat Motherwell in a Scottish cup final replay, gained after a last-minute own goal by Motherwell's Alan Craig. The next season started well for both Celtic and Rangers, but their meeting on 5 September 1931 was tense and dour.

Five minutes after half-time Sam English, the Rangers centre forward, was put through on goal. 'English sped past the backs,' wrote 'Clutha' in the *Evening Times* (7 September 1931), 'John Thomson advanced, hesitated, then threw himself at the forward's feet as the latter shot'. As the ball trundled past the post, English's knee caught Thomson's head. Seeing Thomson lie still, English immediately signalled for medical attention. Jimmy McGrory recalled seeing a small fountain of blood spurting from Thomson's temple. Thomson died in the Victoria Infirmary, Glasgow, at 9.25 p.m. that evening of a depressed fracture of the skull, never having regained consciousness, with his family and fiancée, Margaret Finlay, at his side.

The public had taken John Thomson to heart, and reaction to his death was powerful and emotional. His appeal lay not only in his great talent, but also in his youth, and his 'touch of glamour' (Campbell and Woods, 139). His goalkeeping combined style and courage, and he was dapper in appearance, with a distinctive high-quiffed hairstyle. At a memorial service at Trinity Congregational Church in Glasgow on 8 September 1931 police had to control a crowd of over 3000 people who were trying to get in. Thousands more gathered to see a special train service off from Glasgow Queen Street to his funeral in Cardenden, Fife. A goods carriage in this train was given over to wreaths and tributes. The *Daily Express* of 10 September 1931, the day after the funeral, reported that 30,000 people had made their way to Cardenden, some of these on foot from Glasgow. He was buried in Bowhill cemetery, Fife. Many songs and poems have been written in his memory, and Celtic Park houses a memorial plaque and statue.

Contemporaries recognized that Thomson's was a remarkable, ground-breaking talent. Some of the strongest tributes to his ability come from opponents such as J. B. McAlpine, a Queens Park forward of the 1920s and 30s (Campbell and Woods, 142n.). Jimmy McGrory thought that Thomson would have found fitting the finding of the fatal accident inquiry into his death, that he died 'engaged in his employment … in an attempt to save a goal' (*Lifetime in Paradise*, 47).

JOHN MCMANUS

Sources John Thomson Memorial Committee, *A tribute to John Thomson* (privately published, 2001) · *A lifetime in paradise: the Jimmy McGrory story*, ed. G. McNee (1975) · T. Campbell and A. Woods, *The glory and the dream: the history of Celtic F.C., 1887–1986* (1986) · B. Wilson, *Celtic: a century with honour* (1988) · R. Kelly, *Celtic* (1971) · *Sunday Mail* (8 March 1931) · *Evening Times* (6 Nov 1930)

Likenesses bronze statue, Celtic Park, Glasgow · memorial plaque, Celtic Park, Glasgow

Thomson, Joseph (1858–1895), explorer in Africa, the fifth and final son of William Thomson and Agnes Brown, was born on 14 February 1858 in the village of Penpont, Dumfriesshire, in a house which his father, a stonemason and master builder, had built for himself and his family. In 1868 the household moved 4 miles away to Gatelawbridge, where William Thomson leased an underdeveloped freestone quarry.

The budding explorer Thomson began his education in the village school in Penpont, but owed his growing interest

Joseph Thomson (1858–1895), by J. Thomson, pubd 1895

in the wider world to the stimulation of a new school and new acquaintances in the nearby small town of Thornhill. It was in the classes of the Morton School, and particularly from the lectures and cane of its stern Presbyterian principal, that Thomson obtained the bulk of his formal education. He read avidly: Shakespeare and Scott, the adventure stories of Robert Michael Ballantyne, and, some time after his eleventh birthday, a volume of travel literature that prominently featured the explorations of Mungo Park, James Bruce, Robert Moffat, and David Livingstone. The young Scot determined to follow in Livingstone's footsteps.

From age fourteen Thomson also became a budding geologist. Stimulated by Dr Thomas Boyle Grierson, a warm-hearted eccentric and self-appointed popularizer of science and scientific thinking who had established a flourishing medical practice in Thornhill, Thomson began to collect botanical and geological specimens, and to discuss his findings with the members of Grierson's local Society of Inquiry. With hammer in hand he roamed the hills of Nithsdale looking for unusual outcrops or formations of rock. He discovered a few fossil forms that were new to the Lower Carboniferous limestone of Scotland. It was during a solitary outing in the narrow ravine of Crichope Linn that Thomson met Professor Archibald Geikie of the University of Edinburgh, who was then examining Nithsdale for the Geological Survey. Geikie apparently persuaded Thomson to take geology seriously, and to leave his apprenticeship in his father's stone quarry (he had left school at fifteen) for Edinburgh. There Thomson matriculated in 1875, studied with Geikie, Alexander Crum Brown (chemistry), John Hutton Balfour (botany), and Thomas Henry Huxley (natural history), and ultimately achieved medals in natural history and geology in the examinations of 1878.

Leading the Tanganyika expedition In that year Thomson, aged twenty, was appointed geologist and naturalist to an expedition under Alexander Keith Johnston the younger, which was sent by the Royal Geographical Society to open up a road from Dar es Salaam to lakes Nyasa and Tanganyika. After a practice trek from Pangani into the Usambara Mountains, Johnston, Thomson, James Chuma (a Presbyterian-trained Yao, who had worked with Livingstone and was a professional caravan leader), five assistant headmen, and 125 porters set out from Dar es Salaam for the interior on 19 May. Johnston died on 28 June 1879 from dysentery and malaria near what is now Kwa Mhinda along the northern banks of the Rufiji River. Thomson found himself in charge. 'I felt I must go forward,' he wrote, 'whatever might be my destiny' (Thomson, *To the Central African Lakes and Back*, 1881, 1.150). Thomson and Chuma led their expedition via Kilengwe and Mgunda across the Rufiji to Ifakara and on through the countries of the Hehe and the Bena into the Kipengere Mountains. Finally, his body racked with fever, Thomson plunged into the northern waters of Lake Nyasa on 22 September 1879.

Thomson next examined the unexplored plateau separating lakes Nyasa and Tanganyika, becoming the first European to traverse its 250 miles of mountain and valley. He met chiefs of the Nyakyusa, Namwanga, Mambwe, and Lungu peoples, and on 3 November camped on the southern shores of Lake Tanganyika, which had first been sighted by Livingstone and Chuma in 1867 from a village nearby. He could have returned home with honour. Instead, taking just thirty-eight of his men (he wanted to trek briskly), he continued northward along the western shores of Lake Tanganyika. He reached the stockaded village of Pamlilo, where Verney Lovett Cameron had stopped in 1874, and went through the hostile country of the Tumbwe, to the village of M'pala, which Livingstone had visited in 1869. On Christmas day 1879 Thomson finally reached the Lukuga River and found it unmistakably flowing swiftly west, and thus emptying, not filling, Lake Tanganyika. His epic journey continued across the lake to Ujiji, then back to the Lukuga River, and then westward towards the headwaters of the Zaïre River. After almost reaching that point, he went back to the lake, and then by sailing vessel south along its eastern shores to rejoin the remainder of the caravan on 5 April 1880. Thomson and the whole caravan proceeded via Lake Rukwa, which he was the first European to see, and what is now Tabora to Bagamoyo on the coast, where he arrived on 10 July.

Thomson had trekked 3000 miles in the unusually short period of fourteen months. There had been no major fights, no defections, and no unnecessary loss of life. He had collected nearly 200 new species of flora (including a tree fern named after him) and 15 new species of lacustrine conchology (one named after him), and had made some general observations on geology, terrain, and cartography.

Thomson's next enterprise was undertaken for the sultan of Zanzibar, who believed that the coal which Livingstone had reported in 1862 to exist in the Rovuma valley might be turned to profitable account. The sultan invited Thomson to make an expert examination. This he did for eight weeks in 1881, covering some 700 miles only to bring the sultan the disappointing news that the 'coal' was only useless shale.

Exploring Lake Victoria and the Niger A very different task was that to which Thomson, under the auspices of the Royal Geographical Society, next braced himself—the opening up of a route between the seaboard of eastern Africa and the northern shores of Lake Victoria. The society wanted Thomson to explore the 'snowy mountains' of eastern equatorial Africa, to find a route through or around the country of the fearsome Maasai, and to discover new trading opportunities in the face of threatened German competition.

On 15 March 1883, Thomson, a Maltese named James Martin, and five experienced African headmen, led a caravan of 110 porters up country from Mombasa. They were a few months behind Dr Gustav A. Fischer, a German naturalist, and his entourage. Thomson's expedition traversed the hills of Tahta and reached Taveta on 5 April. Two weeks later, while enjoying the hospitality of the Chagga, he tried to climb Kilimanjaro in a day, but failed to reach beyond 8700 feet. In July Thomson finally attempted to lead his party across dreaded Masai. In order to do so peacefully, he had to persuade various groups of Maasai warriors that he had magical powers. This task he accomplished by popping two false teeth in and out of his mouth and, whenever danger approached, brewing up a fizzy froth of Eno's fruit salts. The expedition reached Ngong, near what is now Nairobi, in September, entered hilly Kikuyu country, then descended to the floor of the Great Rift valley. Thomson climbed the 9000 foot Mount Longonot, stopped along the shores of Lake Naivasha (where Maasai tormented him), climbed steamy Mount Eburru, and walked to Lake Elmenteita.

With thirty of his porters, Thomson impulsively decided to investigate Mount Kenya. On 28 October he viewed its 'chaste beauty' from the banks of the Uaso Nyiro River. He could have been the first European to climb it but instead, always in haste, he and his men trekked to rejoin the rest of their party at Lake Baringo. Then he continued onward, through Nandi country, reached the vicinity of modern Eldoret, glimpsed and named Mount Elgon, and easily crossed northern Kavirondo reaching the shores of Lake Victoria near the modern border of Kenya and Uganda on 10 December. On the return journey, Thomson was gored by a wounded buffalo and, weak from that injury and from malaria, and subsequently from acute dysentery, was carried much of the distance to the coast, which he reached early in June 1884.

Once again Thomson had travelled nearly 3000 dangerous miles without firing a shot in anger. He had demonstrated the accessibility of Lake Victoria, described many lakes new to Europeans, verified and provided information about Kilimanjaro and Mount Kenya, added considerably to the world's ethnographic knowledge of the Maasai and other indigenous peoples, shot and named a gazelle, and collected five new species of flora as well as 135 other important specimens.

By the end of 1884 Thomson was fit to undertake new explorations, and when, in 1885, the Royal Geographical Society bestowed on him the founder's gold medal, he was already in Nigeria. On this occasion he was employed by the National African Company. His mission was to forestall the efforts of Germany by obtaining territorial concessions from the sardauna of Sokoto and the emir of Gwandu. By mid-March 1885 Thomson was in Akassa, at the mouth of the Niger River. He proceeded up river to Lokoja, at the confluence of the Benue River, and thence to Raba. He assembled a caravan of 130 porters and then went overland to Kontagora, and into Hausaland. Traders and people were everywhere; nothing reminded him of east Africa. In May he was welcomed into the palace of the sardauna, the ninth Sarkin Musulmi, ruler of nearly all of what was to become Northern Nigeria. At the end of the month, after exchanges of presents and promises of more, the Sarkin Musulmi signed a treaty giving the company territorial and trading privileges. The emir of Gwandu did likewise two weeks later, and Thomson returned to Britain where, however, his treaties were never confirmed by the Foreign Office.

Thomson was twenty-seven, and, for some months, seriously ill. 'There seems to be very little chance of any more exploring on the big scale,' he wrote. 'Africa is played out …' (Thomson, 174). During 1886 he lectured in Britain, and travelled on the continent as far as Italy. He campaigned for a friend and home-rule parliamentary candidate in Thornhill, and one summer's day walked the 70 miles from Thornhill to Edinburgh in sixteen hours. He was asked to lead an expedition to rescue Emin Pasha (Eduard Carl Oscar Theodor Schnitzer), then supposedly cut off in the southern Sudan; but Henry Morton Stanley was chosen instead. In 1888 Thomson published *Ulu: an African Romance*, a two-volume novel about Africa, to take his mind off not being chosen to relieve Emin. The setting was Chagga, and Africans and whites were involved in a contrived but delightful love triangle, a kidnapping, and a battle against a marauding Maasai war-party.

'I am thoroughly tired and disgusted with life in England,' Thomson confided in early 1888 (Thomson, 199). A few months later he decided to explore the Atlas Mountains of Morocco, and by May he was in Marrakesh. Despite troubles with his porters, a street brawl, and difficulties with local sheikhs, he climbed two high peaks, the 11,000 foot Jebel Ogdemt and the 12,870 foot Jebel Likoumt. He also surveyed other promontories in the mountains and visited many of the mountain towns before passing along the north-western flanks of the Atlas range to Agadir, on the Atlantic coast. By October he was in Casablanca, *en route* for home.

Thomson's last journey Thomson's final foray into Africa was at the behest of Cecil Rhodes. In 1890, after spending the intervening year writing several articles on Africa as well as a commissioned biography of Mungo Park, Thomson was asked to go on a treaty-making expedition to copper-rich Katanga (Shaba). He first sailed to Cape Town, and then went by rail to meet Rhodes in Kimberley. There Rhodes gave him orders to fill out the British South Africa

Company's claims to trans-Zambezia by making treaties with local chiefs and, if possible, to persuade Msiri, believed to be the leading chief in Katanga, to do so as well.

Thomson and James Grant sailed up the Zambezi and Shire rivers from Quelimane, on the Mozambique coast. From Chiromo, at the southern end of modern Malawi, they and their porters tramped overland to Blantyre, where Charles Wilson joined the expedition. Soon the party reached Nkhota Kota, on the western shores of Lake Nyasa, from where they began their westward trek in August. Thomson began making treaties with Bisa chiefs in the Luangwa River valley of what became eastern Zambia. Across the Muchinga Mountains, somewhere east of Serenje, he discovered that several of his porters had come down with smallpox. Despite a growing contamination, he pushed his party westward to the Luapula River, about 200 miles from Msiri's town. At Kavoi, near the modern Ndola, it became difficult to obtain local guides and Thomson himself was in terrible pain from cystitis.

There, in the middle of central Africa, 50 miles from the great copper deposits of modern Zambia and Zaïre, Thomson lost much of his appetite for exploration and discovery. Yet he crossed the Zaïre–Zambezi watershed, headed south-west toward the Kafue River, made treaties near the modern Kapiri Mposhi and Kabwe, crossed the Mkushi, Lukusashi, and Luangwa rivers going eastward, and returned to Lake Nyasa in early January 1891. He had traversed 1200 miles, made thirteen treaties of dubious authenticity with chiefs across central and eastern areas of modern Zambia, and was himself very sick. He suffered from very painful stricture of the urethra, incontinence, and other complaints that were probably caused by schistosomiasis and pyelo-nephritis.

Thomson was never again free from pain. Nevertheless, he managed to write several articles for geographical and literary journals before contracting serious pneumonia in 1892. In 1893, seeking relief for his damaged lungs, he sailed for Cape Town and spent three months in the tiny Karoo rail town of Matjiesfontein. Subsequently, Rhodes sent him to Kimberley for more recuperation. He went back to Scotland, still weak and wasted, in mid-1894. In the hope of easing what was probably rampant pulmonary tuberculosis, Thomson travelled to Italy and southern France in early 1895, but on 2 August of that year, at 3 York Gate, London, he died, aged thirty-seven.

Thomson travelled more than 15,000 miles in Africa without causing more than occasional hard feelings. He bothered and disturbed Africans little. His motto was 'He who goes gently, goes safely; he who goes safely goes far' (Rotberg, 300). As a traveller, Thomson was swift and economical; but he was also hasty, missing many opportunities to claim a significant place in the annals of African discovery. His scientific methods were too often impressionistic, though now and then based on flashes of insight. He was a man of action, not a student of the little known.

It was as a man of action that Thomson provided valuable information about Kilimanjaro and Mount Kenya,

about the flow of the Lukuga River, and about the absence of coal along the Rovuma. He 'discovered' the Rift valley. He demonstrated the accessibility of lakes Nyasa and Tanganyika overland, and then of Lake Victoria. Active during the twilight of exploration in Africa, he filled in details and corrected earlier impressions.

Thomson's important books were *To the Central African Lakes and Back* (2 vols., 1881) and *Through Masailand* (1883). He also wrote *Ulu* with E. Harris Smith (2 vols., 1888); *Travels in the Atlas and Southern Morocco* (1889); and *Mungo Park and the Niger* (1890). In addition there were some thirty-five articles, thirty of which were about Africa.

ROBERT I. ROTBERG

Sources R. I. Rotberg, *Joseph Thomson and the exploration of Africa* (1971) · J. B. Thomson, *Joseph Thomson: African explorer* (1896) · **Archives** BL, letters to John Bolton, Add. MS 46152 · Bodl. RH, Cawston MSS · NL Scot., corresp. with J. G. Bartholomew · NL Scot., letters to J. A. Grant · RGS, corresp. with the Royal Geographical Society and African scientific notes · U. Edin. L., letters to Sir Archibald Geikie · **Likenesses** J. Thomson, photograph, 1895, NPG [*see illus.*] · C. McBride, marble bust, 1896, RGS · C. McBride, bronze bust, Thornhill, Dumfriesshire · R. T., wood-engraving, NPG; repro. in *ILN* (30 Dec 1884) · photographs, repro. in Rotberg, *Joseph Thomson and the exploration of Africa*, 192–3, 224–5w · photographs, RGS

Thomson, Sir Joseph John (1856–1940), physicist, was born on 18 December 1856 at Cheetham Hill, near Manchester, the elder son of Joseph James Thomson (d. 1873), antiquarian bookseller, and his wife, Emma Swindells (d. 1901), of the local Vernon family. The Thomsons had been established in Manchester for three generations but held to a family tradition that originally they came from lowland Scotland. The family was a very close and united one, largely occupied with parochial church work. After his father's death his mother and his brother, Frederick Vernon Thomson, made considerable sacrifices to see Thomson through college, moving to 11 Egerton Terrace, Fallowfield, near Owens College, Manchester, about 1874. Both sons remained devoted to their mother, spending their summer holidays with her until her death in 1901. In 1914 when Frederick was seriously ill, he moved to Cambridge to be near Thomson, and lived there the remaining three years of his life.

Education Thomson's parents sympathized with his scientific interests, encouraged his enthusiasm for botany, and intended him to become an engineer. After his initial education at small private schools Thomson, aged fourteen, was sent to Owens College, Manchester, to fill in time until he could begin an apprenticeship. This, Thomson considered, was the turning point of his career. At Owens he came under the influence of three men who set his intellectual outlook for the rest of his life: Thomas Barker (professor of mathematics), Balfour Stewart (professor of natural philosophy), and Osborne Reynolds (professor of engineering). They instilled in him a great enthusiasm for original research, a willingness to speculate freely about fundamental questions, and a grounding in the prevalent Victorian methods of reasoning by physical analogy and ether physics. The ether, Thomson believed, was a subtle fluid in terms of which all other phenomena

Sir Joseph John Thomson (1856–1940), by Arthur Hacker, 1903

could be explained; experimental physics he learned by helping Stewart in the laboratory. He was given free rein to explore his own ideas and published his own first paper, elucidating a detail of Maxwell's electromagnetic theory, in 1876.

Thomson's father died in 1873. The family could no longer afford an engineering apprenticeship and Thomson had to rely on scholarships, compelling him to concentrate on mathematics and physics, the subjects in which he excelled. With Barker's encouragement Thomson tried for a mathematical scholarship at Trinity College, Cambridge, and was successful at his second attempt. Shortly before he left Owens, Thomson met Arthur Schuster and John Henry Poynting with whom he later co-authored a well-known series of textbooks and whose friendship he counted 'one of the greatest joys of my life' (J. J. Thomson, 22).

In 1876 Thomson went up to Trinity to study mathematics, living as an undergraduate at 16 Malcolm Street. He essentially remained in Cambridge for the rest of his life, priding himself on having 'kept' every term. He claimed that the climate of Cambridge suited him and he felt well and vigorous when there.

Like most aspiring wranglers (first-class degree men), Thomson went to a private coach, in this case Edward Routh. From him Thomson received a thorough grounding in analytical dynamics (the use of Lagrange's equations and Hamilton's principle of varying action to coordinate phenomena). Thomson also attended university lectures by Arthur Cayley, John Couch Adams, and George Gabriel Stokes. College lectures were given by William

Niven, who fostered Thomson's existing enthusiasm for Maxwell's electromagnetic theory and became a lifelong friend, and by James Glaisher, the only mathematician to encourage Thomson's interest in research during his undergraduate days. Thomson graduated in 1880 as second wrangler, Joseph Larmor being first.

Early work Like many graduates Thomson remained in Cambridge, hoping to win a college fellowship, and it was now that he began work at the Cavendish, the university physics laboratory, participating in the electrical standards programme instituted there by Lord Rayleigh. However, as he was manually clumsy and had insufficient regard for the limitations of his apparatus, he did not shine at this type of work.

At the same time Thomson pursued an independent line of research which established him as a theoretical physicist of outstanding ability. This early work was dominated by his commitment to analytical dynamics and Maxwell's electrodynamics. He resurrected an idea, which first occurred to him during Stewart's lectures at Owens, that all forms of energy were manifestations of the motion of unseen structures in the ether. Using a form of Lagrangian equation devised by Routh, he showed that potential energy was mathematically equivalent to kinetic energy provided the right coordinates were chosen to represent the system. In this case the system had the essential property that its mechanism remained hidden. In addition Thomson demonstrated that it was impossible to discover the mechanism. He found this idea theoretically liberating, for it enabled him to speculate freely about diverse underlying mechanisms without the constraint of having to seek the 'truth'. His vigorous imagination and theoretical virtuosity became much admired by his contemporaries. As he often repeated, 'a theory of matter is a policy rather than a creed; its object is to connect or co-ordinate phenomena, and above all to suggest, stimulate and direct experiment' (*Corpuscular Theory of Matter*, 1907, 1).

Thomson began to develop these ideas in his fellowship thesis for Trinity College and later published them in two long papers and a book, *Applications of Dynamics to Physics and Chemistry* (1888). In 1881 Thomson showed, for the first time, that the mass of a charged particle increases as it moves. This idea was extensively developed in the early twentieth century as a possible fundamental explanation of matter. Thomson thought that the increase in mass was due to the particle's dragging some of the ether with it.

In 1882 Thomson won the Adams prize with an essay later published as *Treatise on the Motion of Vortex Rings* (1883), which investigated the stability of interlocked vortex rings, developing the then popular idea that atoms were vortex rings in the ether by suggesting a systematic arrangement of the rings which would account for the periodic table. Thomson was elected to a fellowship at Trinity College in 1881, moving to rooms in college, and subsequently to a college assistant lectureship in 1882, and a university lectureship in 1883. He was elected as a fellow of the Royal Society in 1884.

Cavendish professorship In December 1884 Lord Rayleigh resigned the Cavendish professorship of experimental physics and Thomson, despite being a theoretician, was elected to succeed him at the age of twenty-eight. He probably owed his election not only to his promise as a theoretical physicist, but to his identification with Cambridge values and college interests. He was unlikely to upset the delicate balance then existing between the rich colleges, which tried to preserve a gentlemanly way of life, and the increasingly powerful but impoverished university which was promoting research as its rationale.

Thomson now had an established position and a salary of £500 per annum. Soon after his election he met Rose Elizabeth Paget (1860–1951), the elder of twin daughters of Sir George *Paget, regius professor of physic at Cambridge. Rose had 'an adoration of science, especially physics', and attended some classes at the Cavendish Laboratory (G. P. Thomson, 'Autobiography', A2, fol. 2). In 1888 Thomson admitted her to do some research which, however, she abandoned a year later when the couple became engaged. They were married on 2 January 1890 at Little St Mary's Church and set up home, first at 15 Brookside and then at 6 Scroope Terrace, where they remained for nine years. By his marriage Thomson entered the heart of Cambridge society, and their home became the social focus for a wide circle of friends and particularly for Cavendish workers. They had a son, George Paget *Thomson (1892–1975), and a daughter, Joan (b. 1903), an intermediate child having been still born. In 1899 the family moved to Holmleigh, on West Road, where the garden was the main attraction for Thomson, and where Rose's at-homes on Saturdays for laboratory workers were a feature.

On his election as Cavendish professor Thomson became, overnight, a leader of science. He wrote review articles, beginning with 'Report on electrical theories' for the British Association in 1885, and held an increasing number of positions in scientific administration, as editor of journals, on education committees, and as one of the four members of the Board for Invention and Research during the First World War. He was president of the Royal Society in 1915–20 and presided over the government commission of 1916 to inquire into the position of science in education. His work was recognized by a knighthood in 1908, the Order of Merit in 1912, and his election in 1918 as master of Trinity, a crown appointment.

With a secure position for life as Cavendish professor of experimental physics, Thomson had free choice of scientific direction and a duty to perform experiments. He chose the academically unpopular subject of discharge of electricity through gases, a topic ideally suited to his talents and which unified his theoretical and experimental research programmes for the first time. Discharge phenomena had fundamental implications, were visually beautiful, stimulated his imagination, and did not lend themselves to refined measurements.

This choice was to change totally the nature of the Cavendish Laboratory. Gaseous discharge did not fit in with the prevalent concern of Cambridge physicists to reach definite answers to definite questions. The subject was too poorly understood for formulation of such questions and, as such, was considered fit only for 'cranks and visionaries' (A. Schuster, *The Progress of Physics during 33 Years*, 1911, 52). Following the approach suggested by analytical dynamics, Thomson resorted to comparing trends and co-ordinating phenomena by analogy, seeking accuracy only to the extent of obtaining 'results whose magnitude admit of being compared roughly with theory' (J. J. Thomson, dissertation, c.1881, CUL, MS Add. 7654 UD3).

Thomson benefited from collaborating, in his first discharge experiments, with his friend Richard Threlfall, a highly skilled experimentalist—a fortunate choice since there was little technical expertise in discharge in the laboratory and it was difficult to find competent assistants. In the first few years his work was often held up, especially for lack of a glass blower. In 1887, in frustration, he poached from the chemistry laboratory Ebeneezer Everett, a self-taught glass blower whom Thomson paid out of his salary as his own personal assistant. Everett rapidly became central to the discharge research programme and worked for Thomson until 1930, when he retired due to ill health.

Thomson's techniques and approaches took a long time to percolate through the laboratory as a whole. Being young and inexperienced when he took over, Thomson was unwilling, or unable, to exercise the sort of benevolent despotism over the Cavendish that the aristocratic, landowning Rayleigh had done. He left practical teaching in the hands of Richard Glazebrook and William Napier Shaw who continued to promote existing Cambridge methods and approaches. Researchers were encouraged to choose their own topics, which they generally did along well-established lines, and Thomson made little attempt to draft them into his discharge programme.

Only after 1895, when Cambridge changed its statutes and admitted research students from other universities, did Thomson acquire a strong following within the Cavendish. Most of these new research students chose to go specifically to work with Thomson in his new and exciting field, Ernest Rutherford and John Sealy Townsend being the first. With Thomson's help they overcame the considerable opposition from established Cambridge-educated researchers and set the tone for a vigorous and exciting research school with an 'atmosphere of a stimulating quality which I have never seen equalled in any other place' (T. Lyman, 'Letter of congratulation on Thomson's 70th birthday', *Nature*, 118, 1926, 884).

Thomson instilled in his students tremendous enthusiasm by 'his vital personality, his obvious conviction that what he and we were all doing was something important, and his camaraderie' (Richardson, 355). Known affectionately as 'J. J.', he encouraged the research students to centre their social lives on the Cavendish. Laboratory tea became a daily institution and the annual dinner the highlight of the year. Thomson's students went on to fill most of the important physics positions in the UK and many abroad and became the leaders of the next generation of physicists. Eight of them subsequently won Nobel prizes—E. Rutherford, W. L. Bragg, C. G. Barkla, F. W.

Aston, C. T. R. Wilson, O. W. Richardson, G. P. Thomson, and E. V. Appleton.

At the same time the atmosphere in the Cavendish was one of considerable financial stringency. Thomson was unwilling to compromise the financial independence to which the laboratory owed much of its vitality and which enabled it to be the first in Cambridge to stress professional training and research. Hence he ran the Cavendish largely from student fees, from which he managed to accumulate £2000 in 1896 and again in 1908 for badly needed extensions. His students found that 'The smallest expenditure had to be argued with him, and he was fertile in suggesting expedients by which it could be avoided—expedients which were more economical of money than of students' time' (Rayleigh, *Life*, 47). Rutherford described Thomson during this period as looking:

> quite young, small rather straggling moustache, short, wears his hair (black) rather long, but has a very clever looking face and a very fine forehead and a radiating smile, or grin as some call it when he is scoring off anyone.   (ibid., 49)

Scientific work from 1885 Thomson first realized the fundamental theoretical possibilities of gaseous discharge during his work on the vortex atom in 1882. According to this theory the chemical bonds holding atoms in molecules were mediated by the ether. During discharge the electric field disturbed the ether and disrupted the molecule. Thus an investigation of gaseous discharge was an investigation of the relation between the disruption of molecules (matter), the electric field, and the ether. For the next six years Thomson sought experimental evidence of chemical dissociation in discharge, published in seven papers including his Bakerian lecture to the Royal Society in 1887 ('On the dissociation of some gases by the electric discharge', *PRS*, 42, 1887, 343–5).

About 1890, in response to evidence from electrolysis and Heinrich Hertz's new high frequency electrical techniques, Thomson ceased using ethereal vortices to explain atoms and instead used them to model the electric field. His concepts were outlined in *Notes on Recent Researches in Electricity and Magnetism* (1883). The vortices, which he called 'Faraday tubes', were either closed rings which carried an electrical disturbance, or filaments ending on atoms and giving rise to a discrete, unitary charge. His experiments consequently began to examine the nature and velocity of charge transfer in a discharge tube.

In 1895 the discovery of X-rays stimulated a breakthrough in Thomson's research. X-rays dissociated the gas molecules into charged atoms (ions) in a controllable manner and clearly distinguished the effects of ionization and secondary radiation. Working with Rutherford, Thomson formulated the equations describing the equilibrium between production and removal of ions, reaching for the first time a general and readily testable form of his theory of discharge by ionization. They described their work to the British Association in September 1896 (Rutherford and Thomson, 'On the passage of electricity through gases exposed to rontgen-rays', *Philosophical Magazine*, 42, 1896, 392–407).

The discovery of X-rays revived interest in the nature of the cathode rays which caused them and which were seen in discharge tubes at very low pressures. Whether these rays were charged atomic particles or ethereal waves became a subject of considerable controversy. Thomson started investigating cathode rays in the winter of 1896/7. Guided by evidence of the rays' uniform magnetic deflection and the comparatively long distances they travelled before being absorbed by a gas, and prompted by his previous speculations about discrete charges and structured atoms, Thomson proposed, at the Royal Institution on 30 April 1897, that cathode rays were subatomic, negatively charged particles from which all atoms were built up ('Cathode rays', *The Electrician*, 104–9). He called the particles 'corpuscles' but they soon became known as electrons. He supported his hypothesis by calculating the charge-to-mass ratio of the corpuscles by combining magnetic deflection measurements with the heating effect when they hit a target. This suggested that the corpuscles were about 1000 times smaller than the hydrogen atom. In this series of experiments Thomson provided the first direct methods of investigating subatomic particles.

In June 1897 Thomson considered the hitherto puzzling absence of electric deflection of cathode rays, demonstrating for the first time that at sufficiently low pressures such a deflection was indeed observed. This led him to the 'classic' method of measuring the charge-to-mass ratio of the rays by combining electric and magnetic deflection measurements. The results reinforced his previous conclusions.

Eventually, in 1899 Thomson measured the charge of corpuscles independently of their mass and showed that the mass was indeed very small. He envisaged corpuscles as located at the end of an ethereal vortex, prompting a convergence of the particle and ether views of cathode rays which saw a rapid end to the controversy. His suggestion of small, negatively charged particles fitted in very well with the emerging electron theories of H. A. Lorentz and Joseph Larmor and as evidence for electrons his work was rapidly adopted. The novel idea that corpuscles were constituents of a divisible atom was less popular and was not widely accepted for another ten years or so, until evidence from radioactivity suggested that atoms could indeed split up.

Over the next few years Thomson unified his previous work, bringing most discharge phenomena within the scope of one all-embracing theory. His book *Conduction of Electricity through Gases* (1903) became the standard text. His work was recognized by the award of the Nobel prize in 1906.

Thomson next investigated whether the electromagnetic mass of corpuscles might explain matter entirely. He suggested an atom containing thousands of corpuscles orbiting in well-defined rings within a sphere of positive electrification. The arrangement of the rings explained the periodic properties of the elements, and their eventual instability provided a natural mechanism for radioactivity. The theory looked promising until 1906 when

Thomson himself undermined it, suggesting experiments which showed that the number of corpuscles in the atom was comparatively small. This raised problems with the origin of the atom's mass, and of its stability. He began experiments on positive ions in a discharge tube, hoping to find a fundamental particle, corresponding to the corpuscle, which would account for the mass of the atom and the nature of positive electricity. A series of some twenty papers chronicled his failure to do this and his development, with Francis Aston, of the positive-ray experiments into a method of chemical analysis, the basis of the mass spectrograph. In 1913 the two men discovered the first non-radioactive isotopes, those of neon, described in 'Some further applications of the method of positive rays' (*Notices of Proceedings of the Royal Institution*, 20, 1913, 591–600).

Concurrently with his work on positive rays, the problems of accounting for details of X-ray ionization and the photoelectric effect led Thomson to theorize about the structure of light and radiation. He suggested that radiation, although an ethereal phenomenon, was confined in vortices in the ether, leading to a 'speckled wavefront' for light, while X-rays were localized as a kink in the vortices and thus behaved much like particles. About 1913 he united these ideas with his experimental findings about the nature of positive ions, into a new atomic theory in which a positive atomic core was surrounded by valence electrons bound within vortex tubes. He put this to the Solvay Conference of 1913.

By such methods Thomson tried, and continued to try through the 1920s and 1930s, to retain the ether which most physicists had now abandoned in their adoption of relativity and quantum theory. Thomson considered that these provided merely a mathematical description, devoid of any physical understanding. As early as 1893 he had argued for the benefits of 'physical', visualizable theories, such as that of Faraday tubes for 'obtaining rapidly the main features of any problem' before subsequent analysis (*Recent Researches in Electricity and Magnetism*, 1893, vi). He now pointed out that the results explained by quantum mechanics:

> if they were dependent, as they probably were, on universal constants like the velocity of light, the charge and mass of the electron, and Planck's constant, were bound by the theory of dimensions to come out much the same, and that the numerical agreements, such as they were, did not count for much. (G. P. Thomson, *Thomson and the Cavendish*, 156)

As indicated to Thomson years before by analytical dynamics, a large number of theoretical models might produce the same experimental correlations. It behoved the physicist, then, to choose the model he found the most productive. In Thomson's case this model was of ethereal vortices.

Master of Trinity In 1918 Thomson was elected master of Trinity College, an office which he retained until his death. He resigned the Cavendish professorship the following year and was succeeded by Rutherford. Thomson and his family moved into Trinity master's lodge, where official entertaining became a large part of his role, and he devoted himself to the welfare of the college. He promoted research strongly as of economic benefit to the university and to the colleges. He was outstanding for his accessibility, welcoming informal contact and discussion with all members of the college from senior officers to undergraduates. He took a keen interest in student sporting events and enjoyed watching football, cricket, and rowing.

Thomson continued as a spokesman for science, being a member of the University Grants Committee in 1919–23, and instrumental in setting up the Department of Scientific and Industrial Research in 1919; he remained on its advisory council until 1927. His views on science education were much sought and he argued strongly against too much formalism, and for the positive benefits of research experience.

Thomson pursued experimental work at the Cavendish, as an honorary professor, until a few years before his death. He developed his positive-ray experiments further and resumed work on electrodeless discharge, begun in 1890, which contributed to early plasma physics. He published more than fifty papers after 1918 and, with his son, George, undertook a major revision of *Conduction of Electricity through Gases* in 1933.

Thomson remained a committed Anglican throughout his life, praying privately every day, although he did not generally parade his convictions in public or scientific life. Financially he showed considerable skill in managing his personal investments. When his will was proved at more than £83,000 even his family were surprised, for he had started life with no capital and had always been generous in entertainment and to those in need.

Honours were showered upon Thomson. He received three Royal Society medals—the royal (1894), Hughes (1902), and Copley (1914)—as well as medals from numerous other societies. He delivered the Bakerian lecture twice (1887, 1913), was invited to give lecture tours of the United States, and was appointed professor of physics at the Royal Institution in 1905, president of the British Association in 1909, of the Physical Society in 1914, and of the newly created Institute of Physics in 1921. He was an honorary member of all the leading foreign scientific academies and received twenty-three honorary degrees. During his life he published more than 230 papers and eleven books, including his autobiography, *Recollections and Reflections* (1936).

Thomson died at home on 30 August 1940, having been suffering from senile decay for the previous few years. He was cremated and his ashes were buried in the nave of Westminster Abbey.

Thomson's greatest achievement is generally held to be his demonstration that cathode rays were electrons, work which opened up the whole field of subatomic physics to experimental investigation. However, his influence was far wider. He was a pivotal figure in the transition from nineteenth-century physics and set the stage for British physics in the twentieth century, outlining both its interests and *modus operandi* in a 'broad brush' approach and a concern for microphysics.   ISOBEL FALCONER

Sources Lord Rayleigh [R. J. Strutt], *The life of Sir J. J. Thomson* (1942) · J. J. Thomson, *Recollections and reflections* (1936) · G. P. Thomson, *J. J. Thomson and the Cavendish Laboratory in his day* (1964) · I. Falconer, 'Theory and experiment in J. J. Thomson's work on gaseous discharge', PhD diss., University of Bath, 1985 [contains full list of archive sources and bibliography] · Lord Rayleigh [R. J. Strutt], *Obits. FRS*, 3 (1939–41), 586–609 · O. Richardson and others, *Nature*, 146 (1940), 351–7 · *The Times* (31 Aug 1940) · *The Times* (4 Sept 1940) · G. P. Thomson and J. Thomson, 'J. J. Thomson as we remember him', *Notes and Records of the Royal Society*, 12 (1956–7), 201–10 · G. P. Thomson, 'Autobiography', Trinity Cam., G. P. Thomson MSS, A2–A14 · I. Falconer, 'Corpuscles, electrons and cathode rays: J. J. Thomson and the "discovery of the electron"', *British Journal for the History of Science*, 20 (1987), 241–76 · I. Falconer, 'J. J. Thomson's work on positive rays, 1906–1914', *Historical Studies in the Physical and Biological Sciences*, 18 (1987–8), 265–310 · I. Falconer, 'J. J. Thomson and "Cavendish" physics', *The development of the laboratory*, ed. F. A. J. L. James (1989), 104–17 · d. cert.
Archives CUL, corresp., notebooks, and papers · RS, referee reports and corresp. · Trinity Cam., corresp. and papers · U. Cam., Cavendish Laboratory | California Institute of Technology, Pasadena, corresp. with G. E. Hale · CUL, corresp. with Lord Kelvin · CUL, corresp. with Lord Rutherford · CUL, letters to Sir George Stokes · Ransom HRC, corresp. with Sir Owen Richardson · RS, letters to Sir Arthur Schuster · U. Birm. L., O. Lodge MSS | FILM Inst. EE
Likenesses photographs, 1880–1936, U. Cam., Cavendish Laboratory · A. Hacker, oils, 1903, U. Cam., Cavendish Laboratory [*see illus.*] · W. Strang, chalk drawing, 1909, Royal Collection · photograph, *c.*1910, repro. in Rayleigh, *Obits. FRS* · F. Derwent Wood, marble bust, 1920, Trinity Cam. · F. Dodd, charcoal drawing, 1920, FM Cam. · G. Fiddes Watt, oils, 1922, RS · R. de l'Hôpital, oils, 1923, Royal Institution of Great Britain, London · W. Nicholson, oils, 1924, Trinity Cam. · H. Lund, drawing, 1932, Oslo · W. Monnington, pencil drawing, 1932, NPG · W. Stoneman, photograph, 1933, NPG · F. Dodd, etching, NPG
Wealth at death £83,069 11s. 7d.: resworn probate, 22 Nov 1940, CGPLA Eng. & Wales

Thomson [née Byerley], **Katherine** [*pseud.* Grace Wharton] **(1797–1862)**, historian and novelist, was the seventh daughter among the thirteen children of Thomas Byerley (1748–1810) of Etruria, Staffordshire, and his wife, Frances Bruckfield (1761/2–1838). Her father was a nephew by marriage and sometime partner and manager of the pottery works of Josiah Wedgwood. She was well-educated, attending the Misses Jacksons' school in Brighton. During her youth, she met distinguished figures like Samuel Parr (1747–1825) and Samuel Taylor Coleridge. In 1810, her elder sisters opened a prestigious girls' school in Warwick, and a year later Katherine became an assistant teacher there. In 1817, the school moved to Barford, outside Stratford upon Avon. On 1 February 1820, she became the second wife of Anthony Todd *Thomson (1778–1849), a Scottish physician; they had three sons, including Henry William *Thomson (1822–1867), the jurist, and five daughters. A. T. Thomson's younger sister became the second wife of William Stevenson, the father of Elizabeth Gaskell; as a result of the family connection, the future novelist was sent to the Byerley sisters' school. The school

moved in 1824 to Avonbank, which was the setting for Gaskell's *My Lady Ludlow*.

Katherine Thomson's marriage was a very happy one. She and her husband spent most of their married life in London, living first in Sloane Square, then in Hinde Street, and later in Welbeck Street. They were part of a literary and artistic circle, which included Francis Jeffrey and Lord Cockburn. Thackeray and Browning also visited them, and Edward Bulwer Lytton and Letitia Landon were close friends. In 1843, Katherine's sister Anne—then married to Samuel Coltman—recorded that she 'never saw any person so full of life, animation, and enjoyment as Mrs Thomson—the people are all in love with her' (Hicks, 117).

Apparently encouraged by her husband, in 1824 Katherine Thomson wrote a brief biography for the Society for the Diffusion of Useful Knowledge, *The Life of Wolsey*, which was commended by Henry Brougham. This was followed two years later by *Memoirs of the Court of Henry VIII* (1826), which is one of her best works. Although, inevitably, most of her sources were standard printed ones, such as Holinshed's *Chronicle*, Cavendish's *Life of Wolsey*, and Strutt's antiquarian works, her material is well-organized and her judgement frequently intelligent. The *Memoirs* showed close reading of the recently published work of John Lingard, and was deservedly commended by the *Edinburgh Review* as a work of 'much good sense, impartiality, and research'. It was followed in 1830 by *Memoirs of the Life of Sir Walter Raleigh*.

In 1833 Mrs Thomson published the semi-autobiographical *Constance, a Novel* (3 vols.), which she described in the preface as 'a natural picture of the affairs of life'. It is a well-written and interesting domestic novel, containing many amusing if rather superfluous cameos of minor characters, including Dr Clayton, a portrait of the Johnsonian Samuel Parr. Favourably mentioned in *The Athenaeum*, which described it as 'an animated picture of country life some forty years ago', *Constance* was more successful than its successors, *Rosabel* (1835) and *Lady Annabetta* (1837). In the 1840s Katherine Thomson wrote several historical novels, including *Anne Boleyn* (3 vols., 1842), a monotonous and melodramatic work in the style of W. H. Ainsworth and G. P. R. James.

In her more serious work she abandoned the sixteenth century in favour of more recent history. In 1839 she published the *Memoirs of Sarah, Duchess of Marlborough, and of the Court of Queen Anne* (2 vols.). This work is caustically described in the *Dictionary of National Biography* as 'diffuse, indexless … and inexact', but is nevertheless a readable and informative biography, which remained the standard work on its subject until the 1930s. It was based mainly on the correspondence of the duchess, which had been printed in 1838, but Mrs Thomson had also consulted the Marlborough papers, then in the British Library. In 1847 she published the *Memoirs of Viscountess Sundon* (2 vols.), a far less reputable work, which was deservedly criticized in the *Quarterly Review*; the reviewer, J. W. Croker, described the work as 'one of the most flagrant specimens of book making that even this manufacturing age has produced', and criticized it as unnecessarily inflated with irrelevant material and grossly inaccurate. The last failing was evident even on the title-page, where the subject of the biography, Charlotte Clayton, Baroness Sundon (d. 1742), was incorrectly described as viscountess and mistress of the queen's robes, when she could pretend to neither the rank nor the office. In the 1840s Mrs Thomson also wrote the first of her collections of biographical sketches, *Memoirs of the Jacobites of 1715 and 1745* (3 vols., 1845–6).

After 1849, when her husband died, Katherine Thomson spent some time abroad, before returning to London. Her later publications were works of light literature. In 1854 she published *Recollections of Literary Characters and Celebrated Places* (2 vols.), a collection of essays of 'anecdotal topography' (*DNB*), which had originally appeared in *Fraser's Magazine*. Her *Celebrated Friendships* (2 vols., 1861) was, in her opinion, merely 'the details of private affairs'; it is an agreeable but generally unoriginal account of the relationships of diverse characters, including Sir Philip Sidney and Sir Fulke Greville, Marie Antoinette and the princesse de Lamballe, and Elizabeth Carter and Catherine Talbot. Other works of the same ilk were *The Queens of Society* (2 vols., 1860), *The Wits and Beaux of Society* (2 vols., 1860), and *The Literature of Society* (2 vols., 1862). These three works were written jointly with her son, John Cockburn *Thomson (1834–1860) [see under Thomson, Henry William], the Sanskrit scholar, under the pseudonyms of Grace and Philip Wharton. She also published more novels, including the rather sensationalist *Court Secrets* (1857), a contemporary tale based on the life of Kaspar Hauser. In 1860 John Cockburn Thomson was drowned while swimming at Tenby. Katherine Thomson is believed never fully to have recovered from his death; she died on 17 December 1862 at Dover, of gastric fever according to one of her obituaries.

Katherine Thomson's work soon fell into obscurity, though her obituary in *The Athenaeum* claimed that her *Memoirs of the Court of Henry VIII* and her biography of Sarah Churchill had won her 'a good place in literature'. Her output, consisting largely of biographical works concentrating on social and cultural history, and of historical novels which were inspired by her research, was typical of the early Victorian woman historian. With the increasing professionalization of history after 1850, her work became by comparison more marginal and lightweight in character. It has been rightly said that she carried 'anecdotal biography' to 'the furthest limits of which this genre is susceptible' (*DNB*).   ROSEMARY MITCHELL

Sources P. D. Hicks, *A quest of ladies: the story of a Warwickshire school* (1949) · *GM*, 3rd ser., 14 (1863), 245 · *The Athenaeum* (3 Jan 1863), 21 · *DNB* · [J. W. Croker], review, *QR*, 82 (1847–8), 94–108 · *EdinR*, 45 (1827), 321 · *Wellesley index*
Archives BL, letter to, and business transactions with, Richard Bentley, Add. MSS 46612, 46614, 46651 · BL, letters to Royal Literary Fund, Loan 96 · UCL, letters to Lord Brougham · UCL, letters to Society for the Diffusion of Useful Knowledge
Wealth at death under £450: administration, 31 March 1863, CGPLA Eng. & Wales

Thomson, Sir (Arthur) Landsborough (1890–1977), ornithologist and medical administrator, was born on 8 October 1890 at 30 Royal Circus, Edinburgh, the oldest of the three sons and a daughter born to (John) Arthur Thomson (1861–1933) and his wife, Margaret Robertson Stewart. His father, later regius professor of natural history at Aberdeen University (1899–1930), played a leading role in promulgating the new biological thinking engendered by Darwin's concept of evolution and in promoting ornithology as a science rather than a hobby.

Landsborough, the great-grandparental name by which he became known, was educated at Edinburgh's Royal High School, Aberdeen grammar school, and Aberdeen University. Doubtless inspired by parental example, his first publication was a note in *British Birds* when he was only seventeen. He later cited as an 'undergraduate indiscretion' his publication of *British Birds and their Nests* (1910), but his bird-ringing scheme was Britain's first, inspired by a fortnight spent studying pioneer work in East Prussia, at Rossitten on the Baltic. After the war it merged with H. F. Witherby's system to become the nationally accepted scheme. Still aged only twenty, Thomson was elected to the British Ornithologists' Union (BOU).

Graduating MA in 1911, but keen to broaden his scientific experience, Thomson studied in Heidelberg and Vienna, returning in August 1914 to serve the entire war in France with the Argyll and Sutherland Highlanders. His administrative flair was evident, and in the final stages of war he was transferred to staff duties, ending his service as assistant quartermaster-general at general headquarters, with the rank of lieutenant-colonel. He was appointed military OBE in 1919 and completed his DSc thesis—which had been interrupted by the hostilities—in 1920. In the same year, on 13 July, he married Mary Moir Trail (b. 1890/91), daughter of James Trail, a former professor of botany at Aberdeen. Thomson's wife assisted his work in many ways before she died in 1969. They had no children.

Briefly appointed to the Treasury on demobilization in 1919, Thomson was soon transferred, effectively as second in command, to the new Medical Research Council (MRC), in London, where he remained until retirement in 1957. In that time staff numbers grew from five to 130, with sixty research units in British universities and teaching hospitals. At the outbreak of the Second World War, the MRC established public health laboratories in case of bacteriological warfare, but they became so vital in the fight against everyday infections that they were subsequently transferred, as efficient working units, to the National Health Service, overseen by an advisory board chaired by Thomson. Appointed CB in 1933, he was knighted in 1953 for his services to the MRC. In retirement he wrote a record of its work in his two-volume *Half a Century of Medical Research* (1973–5) which, typically of Thomson, considered not only the development of scientific knowledge, but also its integration into the machinery of government.

Thomson was equally influential in ornithology and nature conservation, building on his father's work by setting new standards of attainment in both the status and the performance of ornithology, and the administrative skills of its practitioners. He published *Problems of Bird Migration* (1926), *Birds: an Introduction to Ornithology* (1927), and *Bird Migration: a Short Account* (1936), as well as many papers, and the article on migration in the fourteenth edition of the *Encyclopaedia Britannica* (1929). At the age of sixty-six, greatly assisted by his wife, he began work on the monumental and important *A New Dictionary of Birds* (1964), for which he was editor and major contributor of forty sections.

Thomson's practical involvement in bird and conservation bodies was prodigious: chairman of the British Ornithologists' Club (1938–43) and the British Trust for Ornithology (1941–6); president of the BOU (1948–55), of the eleventh International Ornithological Congress at Basel (1954) and of the Zoological Society of London (1954–60); chairman of the Wildfowl Trust's scientific advisory committee (1953–66), of the Home Office advisory committee on the protection of birds (1954–69), of the Council for Nature (1964–9), and of the trustees of the Natural History Museum (1967–9). He served many more spells with many more organizations as council or committee member, held honorary membership of ornithological bodies in France, Germany, and North America, and was on the committee of inquiry into the Serengeti National Park (1957–61). He received the Bernard Tucker medal of the British Trust for Ornithology (1957), the BOU's Godman-Salvin medal (1959), the Royal Society's Buchanan medal (1962), and honorary LLDs from the universities of Aberdeen (1956) and Birmingham (1974).

Thomson found time and inclination for yet more interests, including travel—his work with the MRC took him to the Gambia and confirmed his preference for the tropics—and mountaineering, which he called hill climbing. In recognition of his sixty years of passion for hills, he was elected to the Alpine Club in 1961.

Thanks to Thomson's immense capacity for work, every office was conscientiously discharged. His vast experience in interrelated fields provided a wealth of knowledge, which he sought to share further by encouraging closer ties among different organizations. His influence certainly brought about greater mutual understanding. He did not complicate administrative procedures by mistaking means for ends; every case was tackled on its own merits, not on the basis of precedent. For many his engaging charm, wise counsel, and readiness with practical help, supported by his quiet humour, integrity, and generous nature, made him 'a guide, philosopher and friend of unfailing reliability' (Elliott, 68). He had the ability to translate scientific policy into administrative practice and thereby played a vital role both in medical research and in the work of numerous environmental bodies. Both the MRC and the worlds of ornithology and nature conservation will bear the mark of his influence for many years to come. He died on 9 June 1977 in Queen Mary's Hospital, Roehampton, leaving his autobiography in manuscript form.   DAVID E. EVANS

Sources DNB • H. Elliott, *The Ibis*, 120 (1978), 68–72 • E. M. Nicholson, 'Sir Arthur Landsborough Thomson', *British Birds*, 70 (1977), 384–7 • H. Himsworth, 'Sir Landsborough Thomson', *Nature*, 268 (1977), 471–2 • K. Williamson, 'Sir Arthur Landsborough Thomson', *Bird Study*, 24 (1977), 202–3 • S. Zuckerman, 'Sir Landsborough Thomson', *Journal of Zoology*, 188 (1979), 1–4 • WWW • b. cert. • m. cert.

Archives PRO, personal administrative corresp. • Scottish Ornithologists Club, Edinburgh, autobiography, papers | CUL, corresp. with Sir Peter Markham Scott • Rice University, Houston, Texas, Woodson Research Center, corresp. with Sir Julian Huxley • Wellcome L., letters to Sir Edward Mellanby • Wellcome L., corresp. with Sir Graham Selby Wilson

Likenesses D. C. Seel, photograph, 1970, repro. in Zuckerman, 'Sir Landsborough Thomson', facing p. 1 • studio of Bassano, photograph, repro. in Nicholson, 'Sir Arthur Landsborough Thomson', 385 • Wallace Heaton Ltd, photograph, repro. in Elliott, 'Sir Arthur Landsborough Thomson', 72 • photograph, repro. in Williamson, 'Sir Arthur Landsborough Thomson', facing p. 202

Wealth at death £78,839: probate, 6 Sept 1977, *CGPLA Eng. & Wales*

Thomson, Louis Melville Milne- (1891–1974), applied mathematician, was born on 1 May 1891 at 4 The Avenue, Ealing, London, the eldest son of Colonel Alexander Milne-Thomson, physician and surgeon (d. 1944), and Eva Mary, daughter of the Revd J. Milne. He was educated at Clifton College, Bristol (1906–9), and won a scholarship to Corpus Christi College, Cambridge, to study mathematics; he gained first-class honours in the mathematical tripos part one in 1911, and graduated as a wrangler with distinction in 1913. On 12 September 1914 he married (Johanne) Gertrude, eldest daughter of Dr Karl Frommknecht. They had three daughters. In the same year he took up the post of assistant mathematics master at Winchester College, leaving in 1921 to go to the Royal Naval College, Greenwich, where he later became professor of mathematics. During this time he was made a fellow of the Royal Society of Edinburgh, the Royal Astronomical Society, the Cambridge Philosophical Society, and, later, the Institute of Aerospace Sciences. He was made CBE in 1952.

Milne-Thomson's career was based on teaching, table making, and research into applied mathematics. In 1929 he published a table of square roots. He then began a joint project with L. J. Comrie, an already established table maker, and together they published *Standard Four Figure Tables* (1931), a book designed to be accessible to the non-specialist. His other great table-making project of the early 1930s was the calculation of *Jacobian Elliptic Function Tables*, published first in German (1931) and later in English (1950). Many of his publications of the 1930s (for example in the *Journal of the London Mathematical Society*, the *Proceedings of the Cambridge Philosophical Society*, and the *Proceedings of the Royal Society of Edinburgh*) reflect his involvement with table making. In 1939–48 he served on the British Association for the Advancement of Science mathematical tables committee; he actively contributed to the work of this body and that of its successor at the Royal Society.

In 1933 Milne-Thomson published the first of several textbooks. *The Calculus of Finite Differences* (1933) was based on his own experience of making tables and, in its preface, he states that one motivation for writing it was the lack of other texts suitable for his students at Greenwich. The book went on to become one of the classic texts of student mathematics. However, by the mid-1930s his interests were moving away from tables and into other areas of mathematics related to his work at Greenwich teaching the Royal Corps of Naval Constructors. His books *Theoretical Hydrodynamics* (1938) and *Theoretical Aerodynamics* (1948) went through several editions right up until the mid-1960s.

After retiring from Greenwich in 1956 Milne-Thomson travelled widely, taking up visiting professorships at: Brown University, Rhode Island; the US Army Mathematics Research Center, University of Wisconsin (1958–60); University of Arizona (1961–70); University of Rome (1968); University of Queensland (1969); University of Calgary (1970); and University of Otago (1971). At Wisconsin he carried out research into the application of the complex variable to plane and antiplane elastic problems. The results of this work were published as technical reports for the US army and as two textbooks, *Plane Elastic Systems* (1960) and *Anti-Plane Elastic Systems* (1962). During his time at Wisconsin he also edited a Russian–English mathematical dictionary (1962); he had learned to read Russian in order to keep abreast of Russian developments in applied mathematics, and prepared this dictionary as a result—which reinforces the view that all his books were written with the intention of making mathematics accessible to the beginner or non-specialist. At Arizona, Milne-Thomson's leadership of a very active group of research students working on hydrodynamics resulted in the naming of a general type of integral equation after him.

In 1971 Milne-Thomson finally retired, to 2 Bullfinch Lane, Sevenoaks, Kent. He died at Sevenoaks Hospital on 21 August 1974.   MARY CROARKEN

Sources WWW · private information (2004) · R. E. Wilson and H. A. Jackson, eds., *Winchester College: a register for the years 1901 to 1946* (1956) · *Sevenoakes News* (28 Aug 1974) · *The Times* (24 Aug 1974) · 'The BAASMTC now RSMTC', *Mathematical Tables and Other Aids to Computation*, 3 (1949), 333–40 · b. cert. · d. cert.
Likenesses photograph, 1956, Royal Naval College, Greenwich
Wealth at death £41,200: administration with will, 9 April 1975, *CGPLA Eng. & Wales*

Thomson [*née* Hunter], **Margaret Henderson** (1902–1982), physician and prisoner of war, was born on 20 August 1902 at 30 Lomond Road, Trinity, Leith, Scotland, one of the six children and the third of the four daughters of George Alexander Hunter (1861–1939), a bank secretary and solicitor of Edinburgh, and his wife, Margaret Hutchison, *née* Robertson (1864–1931). She was educated, like her sisters, at Edinburgh Ladies' College and at Edinburgh University, where she qualified MB ChB in 1926. Her younger sister also qualified in medicine.

On 8 June 1929, after practising in Lanarkshire, Margaret Hunter married Daniel Stewart Thomson (1899/1900–1971), son of Alexander Thomson, a rubber planter, and his wife, Christina, with whom she then went to Carey Island, Malaya. They later moved to the place of her husband's work with the Rubber Research Institute (RRI) experimental station—a rubber plantation—at Sungi Bulo, near Kuala Lumpur, while Margaret was attached to the Malaya medical service, organizing first aid classes and lectures on medicine when war broke out.

After the fall of Singapore to the Japanese in February 1942 Thomson left on the last ship to escape, the SS *Kuala*, where she tended the injured and kept up morale among the mothers and children. The ship was then systematically dive-bombed and machine-gunned until it was pounded to pieces. Survivors took to the lifeboats though Thomson swam for several hours and floated on a mattress near the wreckage before she was picked up by one. She had been wounded in the upper thigh during the attack on the docks on 13 February, and, though the wound had been stitched on board the *Kuala*, it had reopened and was bleeding. She said that there were others among the thirty-nine in the lifeboat who needed attention more urgently and she insisted on helping to pull the front oar as they rowed for hours, narrowly missing a rocky reef, but being taken by the current further and further from land. 'The sun was very hot, and there was little room in the boat to move, and the bilge was full of a mixture of blood and salt water which the women were trying to bale with their shoes' (Brooke, 38). They managed to land on Kebat Island, after four enemy fighters had actually held their fire. Thomson immediately took charge of the wounded: 'We had no dressings of any kind and the only lotion was salt water. Splints were cut from driftwood with [a] sheath knife under her directions, and all wounds … cleaned in the sea' (Brooke, 39). The little party of survivors was moved by Dutch rescuers to Senajang Island where they joined more sick and wounded. Thomson took charge of over fifty cases and even performed emergency operations with the crudest of instruments. Knowing that on neighbouring Sinkep Island there was a hospital, she helped to organize a shuttle service of small boats to evacuate the injured. One of these boats was the cargo steamer *Tanjong Penang* with 300 women and child refugees plus sick and wounded aboard: 'The lady doctor had her work cut out' (Dame Margot Turner, quoted in Smyth, 81). Thomson's own wound having by now turned septic, she was taken to Sinkep by stretcher, recovering in time to make the sea voyage to Sumatra and begin the long land trek, still trying to help and encourage the women survivors before the advancing Japanese. She was captured and imprisoned for the rest of the war, first in Djambi gaol, where she was very badly treated (Smyth, 172), and later in the same Sumatran jungle prisoner of war camp as Dame Margot Turner. Thomson was one of the camp doctors, having to watch her patients die because the Red Cross supplies of bandages, quinine, vitamin tablets, powdered milk, and mosquito nets had all been hoarded by the Japanese guards instead of being distributed to the prison hospital. She was later consulted by the BBC for their series *Tenko*, but she herself could not bear to watch that re-enactment of the women's suffering; she would talk about the camp in after years only with former fellow prisoners. In August 1943, when it was not known whether Thomson was free or captured or indeed alive at all, the *London Gazette* announced that she had been appointed MBE 'for her resolution and disregard of self, her sacrifice and admirable courage' (*Daily Herald*).

Having survived the prisoner of war camps, though

greatly emaciated, both Thomson and her husband (who had been a slave worker on the Burma Railway) returned to Edinburgh in 1945 to recover. They then returned to the RRI experimental rubber station in Kuala Lumpur for a five-year tour of duty which coincided with and was cut short by the 'emergency'. The Thomsons' bungalow was never attacked by the communist insurgents, probably because Margaret conducted a health clinic for the estate workers, but they had to live within a barbed wire compound and Margaret slept with a handgun under her pillow. She was not happy about the attitude of some of the colonial service wives towards the Malays and Chinese, and she and her husband left Malaya permanently around 1950.

In 1952 the Thomsons bought Little Daugh, a 600 acre mixed farm in Ruthven, Huntly, Aberdeenshire. They spent the rest of their working lives there as innovative farmers. Margaret Thomson died of bronchopneumonia in Jubilee Hospital, Huntly, on 16 June 1982, and was privately cremated in Huntly. Her husband had died in 1971. There were no children. SYBIL OLDFIELD

Sources Daily Herald (3 July 1943) · G. Brooke, Singapore's Dunkirk (1989) · J. Smyth, The will to live: the story of Dame Margot Turner (1970) · private information (2004) [family] · b. cert. · d. cert.
Likenesses photograph, c.1960, priv. coll.

Thomson [Thompson], **Maurice** (1604–1676), merchant, was born in Watton, Hertfordshire, the eldest son and third child in the minor gentry family of five sons and four daughters of Robert Thompson of Cheshunt and his wife, Elizabeth, daughter of John Halfehead. One of his brothers was George *Thomson, parliamentarian. He arrived in Virginia at the age of twelve or thirteen, perhaps as one learning seamanship. He quickly established himself near the settlement of William *Tucker, who had married his sister Mary and brought over three of their younger brothers. Thomson was married twice, first to Ellen Owen on 12 August 1628, and second to Dorothy Vaux. Their children were John *Thompson (later first Baron Haversham), Maurice, who died in infancy, and four daughters, Mary, Katherine, Martha, and Elizabeth. Thomson and his partners (probably his three brothers) enjoyed a short-lived monopoly to market the entire tobacco crop, supplied provisions amid protests by the planters about engrossing (1632–3), participated in a huge land grant (1636), and came to dominate the tobacco trade, Thomson paying the largest duties on imports into England in 1642.

With other partners Thomson developed wider markets. He brought slaves to their 1000 acre plantation on St Kitts (1626), entered the North American–Canadian fur and provisioning trades (1631), re-exported tobacco to Europe with an agent in Amsterdam (1638–9), and interloped against the Levant and Guinea companies. Other triangular trade centred on the East Indies, where he had been associated with the interloping of Sir William Courteen against the East India Company from the late 1630s. Leading dissident merchants, he was elected a director of the company in 1647, gaining a majority for a 'free well-regulated trade' and an expansive policy including colonization, voyages to the Far East, incorporation of the west African trade, and compensation from the Dutch for the interlopers (1649–50). The council of state ordered a settlement, but Thomson's group won only a partial victory. The East India Company was re-capitalized and he was elected governor, but the joint-stock system was retained (1657).

Thomson had been prominent in trade, colonization, and legalized piracy in the Caribbean, and in enterprises such as Providence Island, favoured by Sir Philip Warwick, John Pym, and opposition leaders (1639–42). He presented to the king in York a huge petition from Londoners for a parliament, and signed Pym's petition against Spain (1640) and another critical of the Lords after the Irish rising (1641). He was much involved in Irish land investment and naval actions and led a mission to the Netherlands for relief of Irish protestants (1643). He was an early recruit to the Honourable Artillery Company (1628), to the London militia committee (1642), and to his local Tower Hamlets militia (1647–60). Among the three richest men in Billingsgate ward in 1640, he was a commissioner for contributions in London, Middlesex, and Westminster (1642), and for customs (1643–7), a plum of parliamentary finance.

A stream of offices followed, showing both Thomson's high standing with the parliamentary leadership and his commercial prominence: he joined in the pacification of Kent; recovered mutinous ships in the Netherlands; and held appointments to trade committees, the high court of justice, and the excise (1645–54). Thomson and other merchants were consulted by the government when some of the colonies sought independent policies. Trade with them was forbidden, and Thomson himself sailed with the fleet in an expedition which forced the colonies to submit (1650–55). He was a major war contractor whose interests extended to nascent industrial enterprises, such as the growing sugar capitalism of the West Indies, the mines, works, and specialist timbers of the East, and saltpetre imports and gunpowder production at home. He influenced the first Navigation Act (1650), when foreign ships were banned from the colonies, but in the second act (1651) the trade was opened. The new merchants lacked the political power to prevail. When Thomson and other radicals signed a petition against the dismissal of the Rump (1653), Oliver Cromwell dismissed them from their offices and contracts. But Thomson was soon back in favour again, receiving instructions on the management of the impending war with Spain in the Caribbean from the protector, who told him to liaise with the fleet commanders (1654), and joining an enlarged trade committee (1655).

Thomson's religious outlook was consistently that of an Independent puritan: he was a petitioner in St Dunstan-in-the-East for a radical lecturer (1642), a regularly elected vestryman and parish leader, a trier (1645–8), and a Middlesex commissioner judging scandalous ministers (1654). He was left undisturbed at the Restoration, though he lost his place as a Trinity brother. An informer's report (1666) accusing him of treason with the Dutch and always opposing 'kingly government' was ignored. He even sailed with the fleet to Barbados (1667). Almost to the last he kept his director's seat in the East India Company, attending over half the courts in a year (1672–3).

Thomson died in 1676 and was buried at Haversham church. In his will he left £1 each to '100 poor silenced ministers', and properties in England, Ireland, Virginia, and throughout the Caribbean.   VALERIE PEARL, *rev.*

Sources V. Pearl, *London and the outbreak of the puritan revolution: city government and national politics, 1625–1643* (1961) · R. P. Brenner, 'Commercial change and political conflict', PhD diss., Princeton University, 1970 · *CSP dom.*, 1627–66 · *CSP col.*, vols. 1, 5 · calendars, East India Company · R. Brenner, *Merchants and revolution: commercial change, political conflict, and London's overseas traders, 1550–1653* (1993) · will, PRO, PROB 11/351, sig. 57
Wealth at death 'died possessed of great wealth with properties in England & W. Indies etc': *DNB* archive

Thomson, Richard (*d.* 1613), philologist and Church of England clergyman, was born in the Netherlands of one English parent, the other, and most likely his mother, probably being a native of Brabant. Popularly known, therefore, as Dutch Thomson upon migrating to England, he matriculated as sizar at Clare College, Cambridge, on 26 June 1583, and proceeded BA in 1587 and MA in 1591. He was subsequently made a fellow of the same college, and in 1612 became senior proctor, in addition to being incorporated into Oxford University on 1 July 1596.

It appears that Thomson never married, but he had at least one brother, Emmanuel. In 1612 Thomson was presented by Lancelot Andrewes, bishop of Winchester, to the rectory of Snailwell, Cambridgeshire. He relied on the patronage of Sir Robert Killigrew and Sir Henry Savile during the early part of his career. About 1610 Thomson, along with Augustine Lindsell, helped Richard Montague with his edition of Gregory of Nazianzus. His continued reputation in England as a philologist was enough for him to be selected as one of the translators of the King James Bible, working with Andrewes and John Overall on the first Westminster committee responsible for translating Genesis to 2 Kings. However, according to Mountague, he was 'better knowne in Italy, France, and Germany, than at home' (Montagu, 126). Thomson's wide circle of friends and his international reputation are reflected in the surviving correspondence of William Camden, Janus Gruterus, the librarian to Heidelberg University, Isaac Casaubon, Joseph Scaliger, Hugo Grotius, and Dominicus Baudius of Leiden University.

Yet as the 'diligent Auditor, and familiar' of Overall (Plaifere, 22), Thomson also made a number of enemies due to his strongly held Arminian convictions. It appears that he was in the habit of making frequent visits to the Netherlands (for example, he visited Leiden in 1594) and in 1605 he was one of the few Englishmen who could speak of a personal acquaintance with Jacobus Arminius. In January 1611 Casaubon spent a day with Thomson in Killigrew's country house, where he read Petrus Bertius's recently published *De sanctorum apostasia problemata duo* (1610). The copy of this notorious Dutch Arminian work was furnished by Thomson, who also showed Casaubon the manuscript of his own *Diatriba de amissione et intercisione gratiae, et justificationis*, which maintained the same basic position as Bertius. Thomson's treatise was refused an English licence in the late 1590s, and Overall arranged for it to be published posthumously at Leiden in 1616 and 1618. In this book Thomson argued that a man who was truly justified by faith may not always remain justified but could fall from grace entirely. The reprobate could be in Christ and justified, but then be cut off. As for the elect, although they finally persevered, this did not mean to say that they could not temporarily lose their faith and hence lose their justification also. To receive saving or justifying grace was not necessarily, therefore, to receive salvation. The refutation of this book, by Robert Abbot, bishop of Salisbury, published in 1618 and 1619 in both London and Frankfurt, *De gratia, et perseverantia sanctorum*, dismissed it as a mixture of Roman Catholic, Arminian, and philosophical error.

Although Thomson laid himself open to the charge of Romanizing, he still held the pope to be Antichrist, as the only book he published during his own lifetime, *Elenchus refutationis torturae torti pro reverendissimo in Christo patre domino episcopo eliense, adversus Martinum Becanum Jesuitam* (1611), makes plain. The entire book, dedicated to Sir Thomas Jermyn, was written against Jesuits in defence of Andrewes's case for the oath of allegiance. It was the charge of Arminianism, however, that was to stick the most. George Carleton, bishop of Chichester, associated Thomson with the Anti-Calvinists William Barret and Peter Baro in disturbing the prevailing 'uniformity in doctrine' and being justly 'refuted and rejected' by the Church of England (Carleton, 8–10). According to Thomas Hill, these men were 'a new brood of such as did assert Arminianisme' (Fenner, sig. A4v). Peter Heylyn also associated Thomson with the doctrines of Arminius, the remonstrants, William Laud, John Howson, and John Richardson. Thomson's presbyterian opponents tended to reject him on moral grounds as well as doctrinal ones. William Prynne described him as a 'dissolute, ebrious, prophane, luxurious' and 'deboist drunken English-Dutchman, who seldome went one night to bed sober' (Prynne, 268, fol. *4r). William Barlee wrote of him as 'Drunken dick Thomson, a man bewitched with the Conceit of his own parts as much as any Babylonian intoxicated by the Cup of the Whore' (Barlee, 26). Following in the same vein Henry Hickman also described Thomson's Arminianism. Allegedly, 'when men reproved him for his prophaness he would say, "My will is free, I am a Child of the Devil to day; to morrow I will make my self a Child of God"' (Hickman, 227). Thomson died in 1613 and was buried at St Edward's Church, Cambridge, on 8 January.

JONATHAN D. MOORE

Sources PRO, PROB 6/8 fol. 85v · Venn, *Alum. Cant.*, 1/4.226 · I. Casaubon, *Ephemerides*, ed. J. Russell, 2 vols. (1850), vol. 2, pp. 811–12 · R. Montagu, *Diatribae upon the first part of the late history of tithes* (1621), 126 · C. Carleton, *An examination* (1626), 8–10 · W. Prynne, *Anti-Arminianisme* (1630), 268, fol. *4r · J. Plaifere, *Appello evangelium* (1651), 22–3 · W. Fenner, *The works* (1651), A4 · W. Barlee, *A necessary vindication of the doctrine of predestination* (1658), 26 · H. Hickman, *Historia quinq-articularis exarticulata* (1674), 91, 227 · N. Tyacke, *Anti-*

Calvinists: the rise of English Arminianism, c.1590–1640 (1987) • P. White, *Predestination, policy and polemic: conflict and consensus in the English church from the Reformation to the civil war* (1992), 166, 168–74, 216 • C. Anderson, *The annals of the English Bible*, ed. H. Anderson (1862), 478 • BL, Add. MS 5882 fol. 19r • *DNB* • CUL, MS UA.V.C.Ct.III.18, fol. 83

Thomson, Richard (1794–1865), antiquary and librarian, was born at 25 Fenchurch Street, London, the second son of a Scotsman. Little else is known of his family; he may have been the person of that name who was baptized at St Botolph without Bishopsgate on 29 June, the son of Joseph and Susan Thomson, but this cannot be confirmed. His father travelled for and became a partner in a firm of seed merchants called Gordon, Thomson, Keen & Co., and variant names (London directories). A brother, James, was to continue in the family business in Fenchurch Street and also became honorary secretary to the Royal Highland School Society. It must be assumed that Richard was educated privately, and he never attended university. He appears to have enjoyed private means; there is no evidence that he entered any profession before he reached the age of forty. Instead he developed an interest in exploring the antiquities of London, and published a number of valuable historical studies. Heraldry was one of his hobbies, and he assisted enquirers in investigating their pedigrees.

In 1820 Thomson published *Account of processions and ceremonies observed in the coronation of the kings and queens of England, exemplified in that of George III and Queen Charlotte* and also *The Book of Life: a Bibliographical Melody*, presented to the members of the Roxburghe Club (though he was not, as became customary, a member), followed by a particularly finely printed edition of Izaak Walton's *The Compleat Angler* (1823) and *Chronicles of London Bridge*, 'by an Antiquary' (1827; 2nd edn, 1839), a useful, if not entirely accurate (cf. Gordon Home, *Old London Bridge*, 1931) compilation of historical sources (a special enlarged edition, with manuscript continuation, is in the Guildhall Library). He published *Illustrations of the History of Great Britain* (1828) in volumes 20 and 21 of *Constable's Miscellany* and the anecdotal *Tales of an Antiquary* (1828; 2nd edn, 1832), published anonymously in three volumes and dedicated (and sent) to the author of *Waverley*, in the apparent hope of a review in *Blackwood's Magazine*. Sir Walter Scott described the book as 'one of the chime of bells which I have some hand in setting a ringing', and believed that its author 'really is entitled to the name of an antiquary. But he has too much description in proportion to the action. There is a capital wardrope of properties but the performers do not add up to their character' (*Journal*, 448). 'The Legend of Killcrop the Changeling' was printed in *Nimmo's Popular Tales* of 1866 (pp. 238–53). *Historical Essay on Magna Charta* appeared in 1829.

Thomson was a frequenter of the London Institution in Finsbury Circus, where he met and became a lifelong friend of the architect William Tite, its honorary secretary from 1824 until 1869. It was undoubtedly through the latter's influence that on 14 August 1834 Thomson and Edward William Brayley were elected joint librarians of the London Institution, following the retirement of William Maltby and the resignation of William Upcott. The catalogue of that library (then containing about 27,000 volumes), issued in four volumes between 1835 and 1852 and considered a model for its period, was largely compiled by Thomson, who published little else during these years. He did arrange, classify, and illustrate the antiquities found during the excavations for Tite's new building of the Royal Exchange; they were deposited in the museum of the corporation (W. Tite, *Descriptive Catalogue of the Antiquities Found in the Excavations at the Royal Exchange*, 1848, xlv). Thomson contributed poems imitating the great authors to *A Garland for the New Royal Exchange* (1845), edited by Tite. He produced, anonymously, *Historical notes for a bibliographical description of mediaeval illuminated manuscripts of hours, offices, &c.* (1858), *Lectures on Illuminated Manuscripts and the Materials and Practice of Illuminators* (1858), and *An Account of Cranmer's Catechism*, printed as a memorial book for his friends and Tite's (1862).

Thomson died at the institution on 2 January 1865, aged seventy and unmarried. During his lifetime he had given the institution anonymously many valuable works and bequeathed it the sum of £500. He was buried at Kensal Green cemetery in the same grave as his brother James, who had predeceased him in 1858.   K. A. MANLEY

Sources R. Thomson, *An account of Cranmer's catechism* (1862) • *London Directory* • London Institution minute books (MS), GL • R. W. Frazer, *Notes on the history of the London Institution* (1905) • *The journal of Sir Walter Scott*, ed. W. E. K. Anderson (1972) • G. Home, *Old London Bridge* (1931) • *DNB* • Kensal Green cemetery register
Archives GL, London Institution archives
Wealth at death under £12,000: probate, 26 Jan 1865, *CGPLA Eng. & Wales*

Thomson, Robert (1622–1694). *See under* Thomson, George (bap. 1607, d. 1691).

Thomson, Robert Dundas (1810–1864), medical officer of health, one of the four children of James *Thomson (1768–1855), minister of Eccles, Berwickshire, and editor of the *Encyclopaedia Britannica*, and his wife, Elizabeth (d. 1851), daughter of James Skene of Aberdeen, was born at Eccles manse on 21 September 1810. He was educated for the medical profession in Edinburgh and Glasgow. In Glasgow he studied chemistry under his uncle, Thomas *Thomson (1773–1852), then professor there, and in 1840 he studied at Giessen under J. Von Liebig. He graduated MD and CM at Glasgow University in 1831, and became a member of the Royal College of Physicians, in London, in 1859. After making a voyage to India and China as assistant surgeon in the service of the East India Company, he settled as a physician in London about 1835, and took an active part in the establishment of the Blenheim Street school of medicine. About this time he married his first cousin, Margaret Agnes, the daughter of Thomas Thomson.

Early in his career Thomson investigated a variety of physiological questions—including the composition of the blood, especially in cholera—and he soon made himself a reputation as an acute observer. He was employed by the government to make a series of experiments on cattle food and to analyse the water supplied by the different London companies. His researches on the constituents of food in relation to the systems of animals was published as *Experimental Researches on the Food of Animals* (1846); this work became a standard source of reference for physiologists pursuing similar inquiries, and it was influential in later nineteenth-century dietary debates.

In 1841 Thomson went to Glasgow as deputy professor and assistant to his uncle, the professor of chemistry, who was ill. Thomson's lectures were heavy and hesitating, his experiments slow, and his matter too profound for the students. He was unsuccessful as a candidate for the chair at his uncle's death in 1852, but after returning to London he was appointed lecturer on chemistry at St Thomas's Hospital, on the retirement of Dr Leeson. This post he held for some years. In 1856, when medical officers of health were appointed under the Metropolitan Local Management Act, he was the successful candidate for Marylebone. Thomson enthusiastically set about organizing a system of inspection in Marylebone, and upon the formation of the Metropolitan Association of Medical Officers of Health he became the association's first president. He became widely known as an authority on sanitary matters, and he was employed by the registrar-general to make a monthly report of the amount of impurity in the waters of the different London companies.

Thomson was elected a fellow of the Royal Society on 1 June 1854 and was also a president of the British Meteorological Society. He lived in London at 41 York Terrace, Regent's Park, and died at his brother's residence, Dunstable House, Richmond, Surrey, on 17 August 1864; his wife survived him.

Thomson contributed numerous papers to the British and foreign medical and scientific journals. He also published nine books on subjects as diverse as school chemistry, diet, the effects of alcohol on health, and cholera.

W. W. WEBB, rev. RICHARD HANKINS

Sources *The Lancet* (20 Aug 1864) · *BMJ* (27 Aug 1864) · *Medical Times and Gazette* (27 Aug 1864), 225–6 · *GM*, 3rd ser., 17 (1864), 523–4
Wealth at death under £6000: probate, 24 Nov 1864, *CGPLA Eng. & Wales*

Thomson, Robert William (1822–1873), engineer, son of John Thomson, a merchant, and his wife, Elspeth (*née* Lyon), was born at Stonehaven, Kincardineshire, on 29 June 1822. He was destined for the pulpit, but, showing little aptitude for academic study, was sent in 1836 to Charleston, United States of America, to be taught the trade of a merchant. In a short time he returned home and began his self-education, aided by a weaver who was a mathematician. After a brief practical apprenticeship in workshops at Aberdeen and Dundee he was employed by a cousin, Mr Lyon, on the demolition of Dunbar Castle. The work was accomplished by blasting, and Thomson conceived the idea of electrically ignited controlled explosions. When Thomson went to London in 1841, Faraday gave him encouragement, and Sir William Cubitt engaged him in connection with the blasting operations on the Dover cliffs. For some time after this he was with a civil engineer in Glasgow, and then worked for Robert Stephenson. In 1844 he began business on his own account as a railway engineer, making plans and surveys for a line in the eastern counties of England.

The collapse of the railway boom in the mid-1840s left Thomson with no employment so he began experimenting with new inventions. He proposed the use of rubber for tyres, taking out a patent on 10 December 1845; but rubber was then too expensive for such general use. He took out a patent on 4 July 1849 for a fountain pen, and contributed his design to the Great Exhibition of 1851. In 1852 he went to Java as agent for an engineering firm, and while there he designed new machinery for refining sugar. This machinery was so superior to anything previously in use that levels of production were greatly increased, and up to the time of his death he continued to supply the best sugar-refining machinery used in Java. Thomson also designed the first portable steam crane for use in the docks of Java. He did not patent the idea, but Messrs Chaplin, who made the first small steam crane for him, had begun mass production of the devices by the time he returned to Britain. The success of Thomson's invention consisted mainly in using the weight of the boiler as a counterpoise to the weight of the jib. In 1860 he visited Europe to oversee the design and construction of a hydraulic dock, based on a series of standardized, interchangeable components. A dock for the French government at Saigon and another for a company at Callao in Peru were successfully constructed on this plan.

In 1862 Thomson retired from business in Java and settled in Edinburgh. He went on to take out patents for improvements in control mechanisms for steam engines, for alterations in the construction of steam boilers, and for 'improvements in steam-gauges'. His next invention, the 'road-steamer', was the result of the need for some form of traction engine for the transport of sugar cane in Java, capable of moving over rough, hard surfaces and soft, treacherous ones alike. Thomson returned to his old idea of rubber tyres, and produced what was essentially an early design for a continuous 'caterpillar'-tracked vehicle. He took out various patents connected with this invention between 1867 and 1873. The vehicle was very successful, proving the viability of continuous tracks; its chief disadvantage was the use of the very expensive rubber.

Thomson died at his home, 3 Moray Place, Edinburgh, on 8 March 1873. He left a widow, Clara (*née* Hertz); the date and place of their marriage is not known.

G. C. BOASE, rev. RALPH HARRINGTON

Sources A. Boyle and F. Bennet, eds., *The Royal Society of Edinburgh: scientific and engineering fellows elected, 1784–1876* (1984), vol. 5 of *Scotland's cultural heritage* (1981–4) · *Annual Register* (1873) · *ILN* (29 March 1873) · *CGPLA Eng. & Wales* (1873) · d. cert. · b. cert.
Likenesses R. & E. Taylor, woodcut (after photograph by Peterson of Copenhagen), NPG; repro. in Boyle and Bennet, *Royal Society of Edinburgh*

Wealth at death £8764 7s. 1d.: confirmation, 22 April 1873, NA Scot., SC 70/1/162, p. 118 · £58,841 2s. 11d.—estate held abroad: confirmation, 22 April 1873, NA Scot., SC 70/1/162, p. 118

Thomson, Roy Herbert, first Baron Thomson of Fleet (1894–1976), newspaper proprietor, was born on 5 June 1894 in Toronto, Ontario, Canada, the elder son and elder child of Herbert Thomson (*b.* 1867), a barber, and his wife, Alice Maud, a hotel maid, the daughter of William Coombs, of Dunkerton, Somerset. His great-great-grandfather, who came from Dumfriesshire, had emigrated to Canada in 1773. He was educated at Jarvis Collegiate School, Toronto, which he left at the age of fourteen. After learning bookkeeping for a year he was a clerk and salesman for ten years. In 1920 he failed as a farmer in Saskatchewan; in 1925 as a dealer in motor supplies in Toronto; in 1928 as a salesman of radio sets in Ottawa. He then moved to the northern part of Ontario; and there, in 1931, at the depth of the depression, he founded a radio station at North Bay. In 1933 he founded a second station yet further north at Timmins, and bought an ailing weekly paper on the floor below.

All these transactions were made largely on credit. It was not until 1944 that his little empire was financially secure. By then he owned eight radio stations, and in that year he bought four more newspapers. He was guided, then and later, by a simple but powerful philosophy which made legitimate profit-making into an ideal. As a multiple newspaper owner he now added to this his great discovery: that, on grounds of both practicality and principle, editors were best left alone to do their job.

His acquisitions continued; but it was when he was in his sixtieth year that his life changed—indeed, he titled his autobiography *After I was Sixty* (1975). He had married, on 22 February 1916, Edna Alice, daughter of John Irvine, of Drayton, Ontario; they had two daughters (the younger of whom died in 1966) and a son. Edna Thomson died in 1951 and at about the same time Jack Kent Cooke, one of Thomson's colleagues, left him to run a rival company. Thomson simultaneously failed in an attempt to enter Canadian federal politics. As a result of these three blows he decided to embark on a new career in Britain. By then wealthy, he bought from the reluctant Findlay family a majority interest in the Edinburgh daily paper *The Scotsman*. Thus, with one trusted colleague, James Coltart, he ousted the family interests, horrified the entrenched Edinburgh establishment, and gained the foothold he needed for other and larger conquests. The editor left and he appointed in his place Alastair Dunnett. From then on Thomson became a remarkably consistent and successful newspaper proprietor.

Although Thomson moved for a while to Edinburgh, he continued to regard Canada as his home country and its culture as the basis of his outlook. In 1954 he took a stake in two Canadian television stations. Thus stimulated, and against the advice of his fellow Canadian Lord Beaverbrook, he saw an opportunity to enter the new world of commercial television in Britain. Against the odds, and with very modest backing, he was awarded the franchise for Scotland (which, with his characteristic frankness,

Roy Herbert Thomson, first Baron Thomson of Fleet (1894–1976), by Sir William Coldstream, 1964–6

and in a phrase which became famous, he later described as 'a licence to print money').

He had been twice rebuffed in his attempt to buy an Aberdeen paper belonging to J. G. Berry, Viscount Kemsley. But in July 1959 it was to Thomson that Kemsley turned when he decided to sell his whole newspaper group, which was the largest in Britain; and Thomson's television holding was important in the convoluted deal which enabled him to take it over. The jewel of the group was the *Sunday Times*, but in addition there were two other national Sunday papers, two provincial Sundays, thirteen provincial dailies, and several weeklies. Thomson closed some, exchanged others, and introduced new budgetary disciplines into all. At the *Sunday Times* he put in new presses and in 1962 launched—in face of scepticism—the first newspaper colour magazine in the country. Its success caused other Sunday papers to follow suit.

In 1964 Thomson became first Baron Thomson of Fleet. In January 1967, after long negotiation, he acquired *The Times*, which was making heavy losses. Part of Thomson's promise to the owners (the Astor family) and the Monopolies Commission was that he and his son would be prepared to put all their large personal fortune in the United Kingdom at the disposal of the paper in order to keep it going. This pledge, honoured when necessary, gave *The*

Times fifteen years of financial stability. Thomson was a model newspaper proprietor. 'The attitude of Lord Thomson to *The Times*', wrote that paper in its first leader on the morning after his death:

> was utterly generous and utterly reassuring ... He never complained to us about the very heavy losses that he was bearing in the worst years of the 1960s, or the smaller losses of the 1970s. He made us know that he loved and respected *The Times*, and his attitude towards the newspaper was totally unselfish. He was determined that the standards and authority of the paper should be maintained. (*The Times*, 5 Aug 1976)

In addition to newspapers and periodicals—he was still buying in America, and ventured briefly into Africa—he acquired several publishing houses, including Nelson, Hamish Hamilton, and Michael Joseph. He rationalized his extensive holdings in provincial newspapers into Thomson Regional Newspapers, expanded into publishing Yellow Pages directories, and saw the successful launch of Thomson Travel. A last coup was financially the most rewarding of all—with Armand Hammer, J. Paul Getty, and others he invested in drilling for oil in the North Sea, acquiring a 20 per cent interest in the Piper and Claymore fields.

Thomson was a thickset figure with pebble glasses and a flat, North American style; a good mixer, he moved immediately to first names and enjoyed bantering conversations, appraising new people for intelligence and acumen, with a shrewd eye on future business dealings. He was in many ways a simple man. He had a Victorian belief in the virtues of work and thrift, and a New World faith in technical progress. If he lacked elegance, he also lacked megalomania. He was notable for common sense and candour; and he ruled his staffs through encouragement not fear. He was a self-taught genius with a balance sheet, who could discern trends, strengths, and potential weaknesses within seconds. In the good years of the 1960s and early 1970s his touch was golden. First he imposed financial order on the newspaper industry, inculcating the importance of revenue, chiefly from advertising (and especially classified advertising). Second, and even more vital, he was scrupulously non-interventionist. His editors were genuinely independent. Lobbyists were told that they must communicate with the editors themselves, since he would not. More than any newspaper owner of the century, he justified the principle of a privately owned press.

Thomson was commemorated in a plaque in the crypt of St Paul's Cathedral in London, unveiled in 1979 by the former prime minister Harold Macmillan, reading: 'He gave a new direction to the British newspaper industry. A strange and adventurous man from nowhere, ennobled by the great virtues of courage and integrity and faithfulness.'

Thomson was appointed GBE in 1970. He died on 4 August 1976 in the Wellington Hospital, St John's Wood, London, and was succeeded in the barony by his son Kenneth Roy (*b.* 1923).

ROBIN DENNISTON and DENIS HAMILTON, *rev.*

Sources R. Braddon, *Roy Thomson of Fleet Street* (1965) · R. H. Thomson, *After I was sixty: a chapter of autobiography* (1975) · *The Times* (5–6 Aug 1976) · *The Times* (11 Aug 1976) · *The Times* (13 Aug 1976) · *The Times* (27 Oct 1976) · *The Times* (11 Dec 1979) · personal knowledge (1986) · Burke, *Peerage* (1999) · A. Dunnett, 'Press baron who set the editors free', *The Scotsman* (12 Aug 1997)

Archives HLRO, corresp. with Lord Beaverbrook | SOUND BL NSA, documentary recording · BL NSA, performance recording

Likenesses W. Bird, photograph, 1964, NPG · W. Coldstream, oils, 1964–6, Thomson Works of Art Ltd, Toronto [*see illus.*] · D. Low, caricature, pencil sketches, NPG

Thomson, Sir St Clair (1859–1943), laryngologist, was born on 28 July 1859 at Fahan, Londonderry, the seventh child of the five sons and three daughters of John Gibson Thomson, a civil engineer (and past pupil of Thomas Telford) of Ardrishaig by Loch Gilp, Argyll, and his wife, Catherine (*b.* 1818), a daughter of John Sinclair of Lochaline House, Lochaline, Morven, Sound of Mull. He always considered that the time spent at the village school at Ardrishaig, where he mixed with the sons and daughters of Loch Fyne fishermen, was the most important part of all his education, second only to that which he learned from his Gaelic speaking highland mother. Sent to King's School, Peterborough, at the age of ten he excelled but left early to become apprenticed to his eldest brother, William, who was in practice locally. During his pupillage he matriculated and passed the University of London first MB from private study. William Sinclair-Thomson, who had been a pupil of Lister in Scotland, recommended that his brother join Lister, who was moving to King's College Hospital, London, on 1 October 1877. Arriving there on the same day Thomson found that his experience in general practice helped him to win prizes and scholarships, and after qualifying MRCS LSA (1881) and graduating MB (1883) he became Lister's house surgeon.

After working at Queen Charlotte's, where he used the strictest Listerian methods and managed during his tenure not to lose a single child or mother, Thomson made several voyages to the Cape of Good Hope as a surgeon on the Union Castle Line. Next he travelled in Europe as a personal physician to a rich invalid who gave him not only a chance to master several languages but also to appreciate many works of art. This experience led Thomson to practise for seven years in Florence in the winter and in St Moritz in the summer (for which purpose he took the Lausanne MD by examination in 1891). Not satisfied with the challenge of general practice he took the opportunity to visit the famous laryngologists of Vienna (von Schrotter, Stoerk, von Kristelli, and Hajek) and the otologist Politzer. In Freiburg he learned submucous resection of the nasal septum from Killian.

After returning to London in 1893 Thomson gained his FRCS and set up as a consultant laryngologist. (He had already gained the London MD in 1888.) Thomson would regularly remember his time in Vienna and in particular the long summer of 1893 when the Redehöf, commemorated in the operetta *Lilac Time*, was crowded with students. During these rather lean years leading to the end of the century Thomson sub-edited *The Practitioner* and later became foreign editor on *The Laryngoscope*. He lectured at the London Medical Graduates' College and Polyclinic, and researched into the bacterial and bacteriostatic function of the nose with Richard Tanner Hewlett at the Lister Institute (1895) and into cerebrospinal fluid in 1899 with W. D. Halliburton. He also helped to found the National Association for the Prevention of Tuberculosis. Thomson married, on 20 December 1901, Isabella (Isobel), *née* Huxham (d. 1905), widow of Henry Vignoles.

Election as surgeon to the Royal Ear Hospital and physician to the Throat Hospital in Golden Square provided Thomson with clinical experience. In 1901 he was appointed assistant physician to the throat department at King's College and the Seamen's hospitals. Elected FRCP in 1903 he became physician in charge at King's in 1905 on the retirement of Greville Macdonald, whose deafness prevented him from continuing to teach, and in 1908 became professor of laryngology. This rapid advancement was soon halted by his development of pulmonary and laryngeal tuberculosis. Aided by Patrick Watson-Williams he practised what he preached, namely strict voice rest for six months. This time was not wasted as he read the works of Shakespeare and noted all references to medicine. Hardly had he overcome this disease when, in 1905, he lost his wife, less than five years after their marriage. Thomson never remarried but instead devoted himself wholeheartedly to his chosen speciality.

Private practice soon prospered, especially when he became throat physician to Edward VII, and his standing in the profession was confirmed by the publication of his *Diseases of the Nose and Throat* (1911) which ran to four editions in his lifetime. In the same year he joined the visiting staff of King Edward VII Sanatorium, Midhurst. A collection of papers of his experience there was published in 1924 by the Medical Research Council.

Thomson was knighted in 1912, and in 1913 he was president of the section of laryngology at the International Medical Congress held in London. His command of languages enabled him to welcome each national group of delegates in their own tongue. He was president of the Medical Society of London in 1917 (having given the oration 'Shakespeare and medicine' in 1916), president of the section of laryngology of the British Medical Association three times between 1909 and 1932, president of the Tuberculosis Association, and president of the Royal Society of Medicine (1925–7). Through his generosity and drive the society was granted an achievement of arms and received from him a presidential badge and chain. During his presidency 175 laryngologists subscribed to give him a loving cup in recognition of his professional standing.

Thomson made safe and successful the operation of laryngofissure for malignant disease of the larynx, previously pioneered by Sir Henry Butlin and Sir Felix Semon. With Lionel Colledge he published *Cancer of the Larynx* in 1930. Laryngology, by the time Thomson retired from King's in 1924, was gradually beginning to pass from medicine to surgery. At the Royal College of Physicians he served as an examiner (1924–6) and on council (1925–7). He gave the Mitchell lecture 'Tuberculosis of the larynx, and its significance to the physician' in 1924, and in 1936 was awarded the Weber Parkes medal prize for his research into tuberculosis. He was a corresponding honorary member of most of the laryngological societies of Europe and of the American Laryngological Association.

Though he could appear to strangers as pompous and affectedly formal Thomson had an extraordinary sense of gentleness, not only in his professional touch, but in his approach. Sympathetic and understanding, he inspired hope and confidence. Although his air of worldly self-assurance did not fail to provoke jealousy he was an accomplished peacemaker. An excellent speaker, he was a fund of wit and bubbled with gaiety and *joie de vivre*. He mixed with the famous actors and singers of the time, many of whom had been his patients. His favourite recreation was dancing, but he still rode in his early eighties and at weekends sculled on the Thames at Long Wittenham, near Abingdon. He kept himself in condition, he said, 'by temperance in all things except sound sleep'. His elegant home at 64 Wimpole Street housed a collection of Shakespearian prints (bequeathed to Stratford upon Avon), miniatures and pharmacy jars (many of which were given to the Royal College of Surgeons of England). His elder sister, Matilda (Maud) Louisa Thomson (1854–1944), kept house for him. Friends and colleagues were welcomed for dinners, dancing, or concerts. Thomson usually travelled in a 40/50 hp yellow Rolls Royce which drew much attention, particularly on the continent.

Damage to his London home during an air raid caused Thomson to return to Scotland where initially he settled in his native Argyll, but, missing the pace of city life, he moved to Edinburgh, where, on 29 January 1943, he was killed in a street accident. One of his last public acts was to visit a medical person suffering from tuberculosis of the larynx. 'Not that I can do much for him', he remarked, 'but I can at least tell him of my own experience and that always cheers a patient up'. NEIL WEIR

Sources D'A. Power and W. R. Le Fanu, *Lives of the fellows of the Royal College of Surgeons of England, 1930–1951* (1953), 767–70 • *The Lancet* (13 Feb 1943), 221–2 • *BMJ* (6 Feb 1943), 173–4 • *Journal of Laryngology and Otology*, 58 (1943), 75–6 • *Annals of Otology, Rhinology and Laryngology* (1943), 272–5 • *Laryngoscope*, 53 (1943), 139–46 • V. E. Negus, 'Great teachers of surgery in the past: Sir St. Clair Thomson (1859–1943)', *British Journal of Surgery*, 53 (1966), 653–7 • *Medical Directory* (1920) • C. E. Newman, *The Medical Society of London: 1773–1973* (1972), 84 • *Oban Times* (27 March 1909) • WWW, 1941–50 • m. cert.
Archives King's Lond., lecture and case notes
Likenesses J. S. Sargent, drawing, 1924, Royal Society of Medicine, London • bust, Royal Society of Medicine, London • photograph, Royal Society of Medicine, London, section of laryngology, album presented to Sir Felix Semon on occasion of his retirement • photographs, Royal Society of Medicine, London

Thomson, Thomas (1768–1852), record scholar and advocate, was born on 10 November 1768 at the manse in Dailly, Ayrshire, the eldest son of the Revd Thomas Thomson, the parish minister, and his second wife, Mary Hay, daughter of Francis Hay in Lochside, Ayrshire. He was educated in the parish school until 1782, when he matriculated at Glasgow University, aged fourteen. During three sessions he distinguished himself in the Greek and other classes.

Thomas Thomson (1768–1852), by Robert Scott Lauder

Through his father's patron, Sir Adam Fergusson of Kilkerran, he gained a Dundonald bursary in 1785, and graduated MA on 27 April 1789. While sometimes assisting with the education of his younger brothers at Dailly, he spent two more years attending theology and philosophy classes, as well as law and political science under John Millar, who influenced his decision to enter the law rather than the church. He moved to Edinburgh, where he passed his first civil law trial in November 1792 and was admitted as advocate on 10 December 1793. In 1797 he set up house in Castle Street with his brothers Adam and John, who later became well known as a landscape painter.

Thomson built a solid practice at the bar, including important cases such as the Craigingillan case (1807), appeals to the House of Lords such as the Bargany case (1797), and peerage cases. His strength lay in written pleadings, for his easy and conversational delivery in court lacked oratorical force. Freehold and entail cases particularly attracted him because of his study of feudal law, inspired perhaps by his early acquaintance with Lord Hailes. Although he abandoned a commission from Hailes's family to write a memoir and edit his works and letters, Thomson was drawn to the study of original records and charters, of which Hailes had been a pioneer. His profound acquaintance with the complexities of feudal tenure was best shown in his memorial 'on old extent' of 1816, written for the case of *Cranstoun v. Gibson* over a disputed vote in the Midlothian election of 1812, which minutely interpreted historical forms of land taxation.

During his studies and early practice Thomson formed lifelong friendships with his contemporaries at the bar

Walter Scott, Francis Jeffrey, George Cranstoun, Thomas Kennedy, Francis Horner, Henry Cockburn, and other Edinburgh luminaries. They accepted him as their equal, admired his legal and historical learning, and cherished the genial hospitality of his supper parties. He was interested in politics, but his own activities were mainly confined to faculty affairs. As one of the whig literati who planned the *Edinburgh Review*, he contributed three articles in 1803–4, and edited the spring 1804 number. His painstaking writing method decided him against contributing again, but he obliged Jeffrey by editing three issues in 1813–15.

A growing reputation for legal antiquities led Thomson to be consulted in 1804 by the lord clerk register, Lord Frederick Campbell, about the unpublished edition of the records of the Scottish parliaments in Register House prepared by William Robertson in terms of the record commission of 1800. The commissioners accepted Thomson's recommendation for the suppression of the whole work because it used flawed texts and omitted authentic ones, and in December 1804 they appointed him their Scottish subcommissioner. During 1805 he persuaded the commissioners to adopt his own larger publication scheme. At the same period they became convinced of the need to place Thomson in charge of Scotland's public records, particularly to stop irregularities in the framing of registers. Following Treasury approval for a post in March 1806, the king granted a warrant on 19 June, and on 30 June Thomson was appointed the first deputy clerk register, at an annual salary of £500. In July he was recommended to be a confidential adviser to Grenville's government, on account of his moderate whig politics, but nothing came of it, and he began his commission at General Register House to draft regulations for the formation, custody, and transmission of all the public records under the clerk register's authority.

Reforms in Thomson's report to the commissioners on the state of the records were recommended to the Scottish law officers and keepers of registers and records in July 1807, and most of them were enacted by the court of session in 1808–11, and by parliament in 1809 (49 Geo. III.c. 42). They included improvements in the methods of compiling the registers of the great seal, deeds, sasines, and diligence. Thenceforward the register volumes issued by himself were a standard size and more uniformly filled, and by degrees Thomson established regular transmissions of registers from their keepers. Most of the reforms had been proposed by his predecessor, Robertson, but Thomson's achievement was to execute a series of well-planned measures which overcame the vested interests of the keepers and clerks.

Beside these changes, Thomson initiated an overdue conservation programme, personally inspecting the bindings and condition of volumes, and bringing a specialist paper repairer from London, Mrs Weir, to work and to train assistants. Between 1807 and 1816 repairs were carried out on many of the almost 12,000 volumes in Register House, including the rebinding of 6500 and the inlaying of 30,000 leaves in 180 of them. His other innovations included repertories of the records in Register House, and, more importantly, abridgements and indexes sanctioned and financed by the record commissioners, to facilitate searching of the records. The first series covered were the retours up to 1700, the records of chancery dealing with heirs inheriting property, which Thomson abridged and indexed in three volumes under the title *Inquisitionum ad capellam domini regis retornatarum ... abbreviatio* (1811–16). Although he continued the abridgements from 1701, they lacked the intended indexes, and were not published in his lifetime. In order to ease searching and reduce fees, he compiled and printed abridgements and indexes to the registers of sasines, inhibitions, and adjudications for 1781–1830.

Another project was an abstract of royal charters in the great seal and elsewhere in the public records, authorized by the commissioners in May 1806, and resulting in *Registrum magni sigilli* (1814), which covered the period 1306–1424. It set a high standard of accuracy, but was only published after pressure by the commissioners, who were alarmed at the slow progress of Thomson's multiplying editorial schemes. Since 1806 he had also been transcribing crown charters in burgh and private muniments which were not among the public records. After being suspended between 1812 and 1824, transcribing resumed, and by 1831 over 1500 charters from before Mary's reign had been copied. Thomson's abridgements and transcriptions laid the foundations of later editions of charters.

Of all Thomson's editing projects and achievements, the greatest was the *Acts of the Parliaments of Scotland*, starting with the second volume, published in 1814, and concluding with volume 11 in 1824. Thomson drew on the official records of parliament and supplemented them with other sources to compile what he held to be authoritative texts. However, there were gaps in the record which caused him considerable problems. Fresh discoveries of manuscripts in 1826 rendered volumes 5 and 6 obsolete, but he was unable to produce new editions. For the years before 1424 the lack of official records posed special difficulties. In trying to overcome them Thomson delayed publication of volume 1 year after year, acutely aware of the need to surpass the standards of Robertson's text, which he had condemned in 1804. His labour was immense and his scholarship exacting, but he failed to make a definitive selection of texts or to write an introduction, owing to what his friend Cosmo Innes described as his 'grand defect ..., a morbid reluctance to commit his opinions to paper' (Innes, 184). The work was taken from him in 1841, printed but still unpublished. Innes edited and amplified it for publication in 1844, acknowledging his mentor's immense achievement. Thomson's edition has remained the standard one, but its main weakness, unlike Robertson's work, lies in the failure to identify the sources blended and presented as definitive versions. Further criticisms have attached to his decision, based on mistaken interpretations of their nature, to publish records of parliament's judicial proceedings separately as the *Acts of the Lords Auditors* and *Acts of the Lords of Council in Civil Causes*. The official pressure to publish them in 1839 prevented Thomson from writing a substantial introduction.

Besides official works, Thomson edited prolifically for the Bannatyne Club, formed in 1823 to publish historical texts, of which he issued fourteen, including *The History and Life of James the Sext* (1825). Having been the club's vice-president from 1823, he succeeded Scott as its president in 1832 and became 'our master and our guide', in Henry Cockburn's words (Laing, 7). He made up for not writing a historical work by generously imparting his knowledge to many other scholars. At his own expense he edited and published privately several other texts, ranging from medieval accounts to eighteenth-century memoirs. He also subscribed to the Maitland and Spalding clubs, and with Scott, Cockburn, Jeffrey, and others, belonged to convivial clubs such as the Friday Club and the Blair Adam Club. He was elected a fellow of the Royal Society of Edinburgh in 1807, and of the Society of Antiquaries of Scotland in 1817, and he was the latter's vice-president from 1828 to 1836. Probably through his friendship with the mathematician John Playfair, he was a founding director of the Edinburgh Astronomical Institution in 1812, and he also served as a curator of the Advocates' Library.

In 1822–3 Thomson acted in appeal cases in London while lobbying for funds to complete the Register House work, but he was practising law less than formerly. He considered a place on the Scottish bench in 1827 but in January 1828, largely in order to continue his record work, he chose instead to be appointed a principal clerk of session, at a salary of £1000. Like Walter Scott, Thomson was able to fulfil his court duties with time to spare for his main interests, including the Bannatyne Club. Scott shared a passion for books with his close friend 'Mr Register Thomson', and sought his advice on legal as well as historical matters. Thomson served on the committees for Scott's monument from 1832, as he had for his friend Dugald Stewart's from 1828.

Thomson married Ann Reed, daughter of Thomas Reed, a former army contractor of Dublin, at St Pancras parish church in London on 25 October 1836. They had no children. At this period financial problems beset him as a result of his admitted dilatoriness regarding money, his zeal for the public records, and generosity to a needy relation. After the record commissioners suspended payments for the sasine abridgements in June 1831, he had continued to employ twelve clerks at his own expense rather than lose their experienced skill. He obtained loans of £4000 on the security of his own and of his deputy's salaries in 1834–5. By 1836 the irregularity of payments to Thomson's assistants became known through the complaints of Robert Pitcairn, writer to the signet, hired to work on the great seal, but not until 1839 did the exchequer repeatedly demand the production of the Register House annual accounts from 1824. Thomson was reluctant to face his growing predicament, arising from the entanglement of his private and official finances, but eventually responded.

The conclusion in November 1840 was that £8570 was owing to the crown, but Thomson avoided prosecution by convincing the government that the money had been applied to record work and not for his private use. A secret attempt by Jeffrey and other friends, who were to subscribe £1000 each to help repay the crown first, failed when Thomson's private creditor sought to recover the loans and the matter became public. The lord clerk register, being personally responsible for his deputy's mismanagement, dismissed and replaced Thomson on 19 April 1841. However, Thomson retained his clerkship and, like Scott, insisted on paying all his debts, applying most of his salary to them until he resigned in February 1852. The sale of his fine library in 3339 lots over twelve days in 1841 liquidated somewhat under half of the readjusted debt to the crown of £7000.

After 1839 Thomson did no substantial editing work and largely withdrew from view, although he continued to preside over the Bannatyne Club and to enjoy the friendship of Cockburn and others who believed he had acted unwisely but not corruptly. In 1841 he left his house at 127 George Street, Edinburgh, for a series of smaller ones, and made several trips to London; in 1847 he even visited the continent. Following bronchial trouble he died at Shrubhill, Edinburgh, on 2 October 1852, and was buried in the Dean cemetery on 8 October.   TRISTRAM CLARKE

Sources C. Innes, *Memoir of Thomas Thomson, advocate* (1854) · M. Ash, 'Thomas Thomson and the "Foundations of history"', in M. Ash, *The strange death of Scottish history* (1980), 41–58 · M. D. Young, 'The age of the deputy clerk register, 1806–1928', *SHR*, 53 (1974), 157–93, esp. 157–66 · P. Gouldesbrough, 'The record commissions and Scotland', *Prisca munimenta*, ed. F. Ranger (1973), 19–26 · J. Fergusson, 'Thomas Thomson, deputy clerk register', *The man behind 'Macbeth', and other studies* (1969), 142–9 · A. L. Murray, introduction, *Acts of the lords of council, 1501–1503*, ed. A. B. Calderwood, 3 (1993), viii–xxxvi · *Annual Report of the Deputy Clerk Register of Scotland* (1807–21) · [C. P. Cooper], ed., *The case of Robert Pitcairn* (1835) · *Catalogue of the valuable and extensive library of Thomas Thomson, esq., advocate: consisting of a rare assemblage of works on history, antiquities, general literature, and law* (1841) [sale catalogue, 28 June – 10 July 1841] · J. D. Mackie, ed., *Thomas Thomson's memorial on old extent* (1946) · D. Laing, *Thomas Thomson* (1853) · F. McCunn, *Sir Walter Scott's friends* (1909), 40–47 · *GM*, 2nd ser., 6 (1836), 651 · *Edinburgh Evening Courant* (9 Oct 1852)
Archives NL Scot., corresp. and papers | Falkirk Museums History Research Centre, Falkirk, letters to William Forbes · NA Scot., deputy clerk register and exchequer papers, E801, E884 · NL Scot., Bannatyne Club MSS · NL Scot., letters to Archibald Constable · NL Scot., Elliot-Murray-Kynynmound MSS · NL Scot., letters to John Lee · NL Scot., letters to second earl of Minto · NL Scot., corresp. with Lord Rutherford and others · NL Scot., letters to Sir Walter Scott · U. Edin., letters to David Laing
Likenesses T. Faed, group portrait, oils, 1849 (*Sir Walter Scott & friends at Abbotsford*), Scot. NPG · R. C. Bell, engraving (after K. C. Schmidt), repro. in Innes, *Memoir of Thomas Thomson* · W. Berrick, chalk drawing, Scot. NPG · R. S. Lauder, oils, Scot. NPG [*see illus.*] · K. C. Schmidt, oils, NA Scot. · G. B. Shaw, engraving (after R. S. Lauder), Scot. NPG · J. Steell, marble bust, Parliament House, Edinburgh · J. Steell, plaster bust, Scot. NPG · J. Steell, relief bust on monument, Dean cemetery, Edinburgh · engraving (after W. Berrick), Scot. NPG · engraving (*Parliament House Group*), repro. in McCunn, *Sir Walter Scott's friends* · photograph (after oil painting by H. Raeburn, exh. 1876), Scot. NPG
Wealth at death £424 18s. 3d.: inventory, NA Scot., SC 70/1/78, 669–75

Thomson, Thomas (1773–1852), chemist, was born on 12 April 1773 at Crieff, Perthshire, the seventh child and youngest son of John Thomson, a retired woolman, and his wife, Elizabeth Ewan. He was educated at home by his mother and his brother James, at Crieff parish school, and from 1786 to 1788 at the borough school of Stirling. In 1788 he won a bursary to the University of St Andrews where he studied classics, mathematics, and natural philosophy. From 1791 to 1795 he was a private tutor at Blackshields, near Edinburgh, which enabled him to attend a variety of classes at the university there from 1791. In 1794 he began to study medicine, graduating MD in 1799, but he was inspired by Joseph Black's lectures of 1795–6 to devote his life principally to chemistry. From 1796 to 1800 he replaced his brother James as assistant editor of the *Supplement to the Third Edition of the Encyclopaedia Britannica*, to which he contributed the articles 'Chemistry', 'Mineralogy', and 'Vegetable, animal and dyeing substances'; these formed the basis of his *System of Chemistry* (1802; 6th edn, 1820).

From 1800 to 1811 Thomson was a private teacher of chemistry in Edinburgh where by 1807 he had instituted a pioneering practical laboratory class. In 1802 and 1803 he collaborated with his brother James and his friend James Mill, the editor, in planning, and for a short time in contributing to, a postal periodical, the *Literary Journal*. In 1805 he acted as a well paid consultant to the Scottish excise board, invented the instrument known as Allan's 'saccharometer', and was elected fellow of the Royal Society of Edinburgh. He was a pugnacious opponent of Hutton's geology and helped to found the Wernerian Natural History Society of Edinburgh in 1808. He became FRS in 1811 and launched himself as a historian with his unofficial *History of the Royal Society* (1812). That year he visited Sweden, and in the next published an account of his travels, paying special attention to mineralogy and geology. From 1811 he resided in London, where he and James Mill lived rent-free in Jeremy Bentham's town house. In 1813 Thomson founded his own scientific journal, *Annals of Philosophy*, which he edited until 1821. With attractive features such as annual reports on the progress of science, it rapidly overtook its proprietary competitors. In 1816 Thomson married Agnes (d. 1834), daughter of R. Colquhoun, a distiller near Stirling. They had three children, the elder son, Thomas *Thomson (1817–1878), becoming well known as an Indian botanist and explorer and the daughter, Margaret Agnes, marrying Thomson's nephew, Robert Dundas *Thomson.

The last phase of the entrepreneurial career of this Scottish man of parts began in 1817 when Thomson was unanimously appointed lecturer in chemistry at the University of Glasgow. Within seven months he was made regius professor through the influence of James Graham, third duke of Montrose and chancellor of the university. As professor, Thomson worked hard to re-establish Glasgow's distinguished chemical tradition and to improve its growing medical school. Particularly during the 1830s he led the unsuccessful political attempts made by the regius professors to elevate their status and increase their rights

Thomas Thomson (1773–1852), by James Faed, pubd 1853 (after John Graham Gilbert, c.1830) [detail]

multiple proportions some months before the appearance of the latter's *New System of Chemical Philosophy* (1808). After 1808 Thomson used the successive editions of his *System* and his own *Annals* to promote chemical atomism and to countervail the scepticism with which Wollaston and Humphry Davy received it. In 1815 he espoused a second and related chemical cause when he published in his journal William Prout's anonymous paper on the specific gravities of gases. From this time Thomson's research had three connected aims: to put Dalton's atomic theory on a wider and firmer experimental basis; to provide incontestable experimental evidence for Prout's hypothesis that the atomic weights of all elements were multiples of that of hydrogen; and to extend his own work on the composition and formulae of salts to include those of all known minerals.

During his early years at Glasgow, Thomson and his laboratory students devoted themselves to the first two projects. Their results were eventually revealed in 1825 in his *An Attempt to Establish the First Principles of Chemistry by Experiment*. The analyses recorded had not been carried out with sufficient care to justify the claim of high accuracy made for them by Thomson, and the work was very severely criticized, especially by the Swedish chemist Berzelius, himself an analyst of extraordinary skill, who went so far as to accuse the author of having done 'much of the experimental part at the writing table' (J. Berzelius, *Jahresbericht*, 6, 1827, 77). Even so, Thomson's atomic weights were widely accepted in Britain and the USA for ten years from 1825. In 1836 he completed his research programme with his uncontroversial *Outlines of Mineralogy, Geology, and Mineral Analysis*, in which minerals were arranged on the basis of experimentally determined chemical composition and not of physical properties.

The outstanding pedagogic feature of Thomson's professorship was his emphasis on the laboratory teaching of practical chemistry. In autumn 1818 he extracted from the university a laboratory, and thus became the first teacher of practical chemistry in a British university. Some of his pupils subsequently worked in the Glasgow chemical industry, others formed a small research school. His pupils were prominent in the chemistry section of the British Association in the 1830s and in the founding of the Chemical Society of London in 1841. By the mid-1830s his new laboratory, opened in 1831 at a cost of about £5000, had become a nursery from which ambitious chemists migrated to complete their training elsewhere.

Thomson became the patriarch of Glasgow science. His *History of Chemistry* (2 vols., 1830, 1831), unique and authoritative for the period after 1760, presented chemistry as a noble, rational, autonomous, and useful science. From 1834 until his death he was the president and chief ornament of the Philosophical Society of Glasgow, which he changed from a moribund affair dominated by artisans into a nationally important society led by Glasgow's learned professionals. Though he was sometimes arrogant and perpetually sardonic, the short and muscular Thomson, well known though not unassailed as teacher, researcher, writer, editor, and historian, was happy to end

in the university. Tired by unremitting effort, in 1841 he relinquished the supervision of his laboratory and part of his teaching to his nephew, R. D. Thomson, whom he had groomed as his successor and assisted as editor of *Records of General Science*, 1835–6. From 1846 to 1852 all Thomson's duties were discharged by his nephew who, however, failed to succeed his uncle.

A self-taught practical chemist, Thomson secured his reputation through his *System*, which went through six editions in eighteen years and appeared in French, German, and American versions. As the first systematic textbook of a non-elementary kind to break the French monopoly of such works, it stressed the contributions made by British chemists to the so-called new chemistry created in the late eighteenth century. Unusually for British treatises of the time, Thomson's digest was based on a wide range of original and recent papers as well as on standard compilations. Thomson's style was usually clear, often succinct, and occasionally trenchant. He was well known for the warm and effective support which he accorded to the chemical atomic theory of John Dalton, whom he first met in Manchester in 1804. In the third edition of his *System* (1807) he began a thirty-year stint as Dalton's bulldog when he made the first detailed public announcement of the theory and extended it from gases to include acids, bases, and salts. Early in 1808 Thomson was the first to publish an experimental illustration of Dalton's law of his career as Glasgow's senior scientific host and figure. A widower since 1834, he died on 2 July 1852 at Kilmun, near Dunoon, and was buried in Glasgow later that month.

JACK MORRELL

Sources 'Biographical notice of the late Thomas Thomson', *Glasgow Medical Journal*, 5 (1857), 69–80, 121–53 • W. Crum, 'Sketch of the life and labours of Dr Thomas Thomson', *Proceedings of the Philosophical Society of Glasgow*, 3 (1855), 250–64 • R. D. Thomson, 'Memoir of the late Dr Thomas Thomson', *Edinburgh New Philosophical Journal*, 54 (1852–3), 86–98 • J. B. Morrell, 'The chemist breeders: the research schools of Liebig and Thomas Thomson', *Ambix*, 19 (1972), 1–46 • J. B. Morrell, 'Thomas Thomson: professor of chemistry and university reformer', *British Journal for the History of Science*, 4 (1968–9), 245–65 • A. Kent, ed., *An eighteenth century lectureship in chemistry: essays and bicentenary addresses relating to the chemistry department, 1747, of Glasgow University* (1950) • J. R. Partington, 'Thomas Thomson, 1773–1852', *Annals of Science*, 6 (1948–50), 115–26 • W. H. Brock, ed., *The atomic debates: Brodie and the rejection of the atomic theory* (1967) • W. H. Brock, *From protyle to proton: William Prout and the nature of matter, 1785–1985* (1985) • S. H. Mauskopf, 'Thomson before Dalton: Thomas Thomson's considerations of the issue of combining weight proportions prior to his acceptance of Dalton's chemical atomic theory', *Annals of Science*, 25 (1969), 229–42 • R. F. Bud and G. K. Roberts, *Science versus practice: chemistry in Victorian Britain* (1984) • C. A. Russell, '"Rude and disgraceful beginnings": a view of the history of chemistry from the nineteenth century', *British Journal for the History of Science*, 21 (1988), 273–94
Archives BL • NL Scot. • RBG Kew Library • U. Edin. L. • UCL | BL, letters to M. Napier, Add. MSS 34611–34617, *passim*
Likenesses J. Faed, mezzotint, pubd 1853 (after J. G. Gilbert, c.1830), Wellcome L., Hunterian Museum and Art Gallery, Glasgow [*see illus.*] • F. J. Skill, J. G. Gilbert, W. Walker, and E. Walker, group portrait, pencil and wash, c.1857–1862 (*Men of science living in 1807–8*), NPG • Cook, engraving (after J. G. Gilbert), repro. in 'Biographical notice of the late Thomas Thomson' • W. Holl, engraving (after medallion by Mrs Robinson), Royal College of Physicians of Edinburgh • engraving, RS • oils, Scot. NPG

Thomson, Thomas (1817–1878), botanist and geologist, was born in Glasgow on 4 December 1817, the eldest son of Thomas *Thomson (1773–1852), professor of chemistry at Glasgow University, and his wife, Agnes Colquhoun (d. 1834), daughter of a distiller near Stirling. Thomas was educated at Glasgow high school and Glasgow University. When only seventeen he published a well-regarded paper on his discovery of fossil marine mollusca on the Firth of Clyde. Intending initially to adopt chemistry as a profession, Thomson studied inorganic chemistry in the university laboratory under his father, and spent the summer of 1837 at Giessen under J. von Liebig, when he discovered pectic acid in carrots. However, on entering medical classes at Glasgow University, he concentrated his attention on botany, under Sir William Jackson Hooker.

On 21 December 1839, having graduated MD, Thomson entered the service of the East India Company as an assistant surgeon. Subsequent promotions were to surgeon (1 December 1853) and surgeon-major (21 December 1859). On his arrival in Calcutta early in 1840 he was appointed curator of the Asiatic Society's museum, but in August he was sent to Afghanistan in charge of a party of European recruits. He reached Kabul in June 1841, and proceeded to Ghazni, where he was attached to the 27th native infantry.

There he began a botanical and geological study of the area, but was besieged during the winter of 1841–2 and was taken prisoner when the town fell in March 1842. He was destined to be sold into slavery in Bukhara, but, together with some fellow prisoners, bribed his captor to convey him to the British army of relief.

Thomson returned to India having lost all his specimen collections and personal effects, and from 19 June 1843 until 1845 was stationed at Moradabad where he acted as civil surgeon. Following service through the Sutlej campaign of the first Anglo-Sikh War he was stationed at Moradabad, Lahore, and Ferozepore. During this period he investigated the botany of the plains and outer Himalayas. In June 1847 he was appointed one of the British commissioners for defining the boundary between Kashmir and Chinese Tibet. Having reached Leh in October the commissioners split up, Thomson subsequently making extensive explorations in the Kashmir territories, going as far north as the Karakoram Pass, and obtaining important geographical information and specimen collections. On his return to Ferozepore he suffered repeated attacks of malaria and took furlough at Simla, where he made further botanical researches. He published an account of his explorations in his *Western Himalaya and Tibet* (1852), a well-received though prosaic work.

In early 1850 Thomson joined his friend Joseph Dalton Hooker in Darjeeling, and from May 1850 undertook fieldwork with him in the Sikkim forests, Assam, and Chittagong, finally returning to England in bad health in March 1851. The next few years were spent at Kew, laboriously working on the extensive collections made during these travels. In the mistaken belief that financial assistance would be given by the East India Company, he and Hooker brought out the first volume of their *Flora Indica* (1855), the publication of which was subsidized by a legacy from Thomson's father. However, the sole support obtained from the company was an offer to purchase 100 copies. No more volumes appeared, Thomson withdrawing from a plan to resume publication in 1870, following an argument with Hooker.

At Bath, in early 1855, Thomson married Catharine, daughter of R. C. Sconce of Malta. Thomson then proceeded immediately to Calcutta where he was installed as superintendent of the botanical garden in April. He was also appointed professor of botany at the Calcutta medical college, and held the two posts until 1861, when he retired and returned to England in ill health. He lived first at Kew and then at Maidstone and retired officially from the medical service in September 1863. In October 1871 he returned to India as treasurer and translator to the expedition under Sir Norman Lockyer sent out to observe the solar eclipse on 12 December 1871. He died at his home, 16 Horbury Crescent, Notting Hill, London, from 'malignant disease' on 18 April 1878. He was survived by his wife; they had no children.

Thomson was elected a fellow of the Linnean Society in 1852, of the Royal Geographical Society in 1854, and of the Royal Society in 1855. He was for twelve years an examiner in natural science for the medical services of the army and navy, and on several occasions examiner in botany for the University of London and the Royal School of Mines.

B. B. WOODWARD, rev. ANDREW GROUT

Sources R. Alcock, *Proceedings* [Royal Geographical Society], 22 (1877–8), 309–15 · R. Desmond, *The European discovery of the Indian flora* (1992) · Desmond, *Botanists*, rev. edn · F. A. Stafleu and R. S. Cowan, *Taxonomic literature: a selective guide*, 2nd edn, 7 vols., Regnum Vegetabile, 94, 98, 105, 110, 112, 115, 116 (1976–88) · D. G. Crawford, ed., *Roll of the Indian Medical Service, 1615–1930* (1930) · *Bengal Directory and Annual Register* (1842) · *Bengal Directory and Annual Register* (1845) · *Bengal Directory and Annual Register* (1847) · W. I. Addison, ed., *The matriculation albums of the University of Glasgow from 1728 to 1858* (1913) · *The correspondence of Charles Darwin*, ed. F. Burkhardt and S. Smith, 4–8 (1988–94) · W. H. Brock, 'Liebig's laboratory accounts', *Ambix*, 19 (1972), 47–58 · J. B. Morrell, 'The chemist breeders: the research schools of Liebig and Thomas Thomson', *Ambix*, 19 (1972), 1–46 · [N. Lockyer], 'The eclipse expedition in India', *ILN* (20 Jan 1872), 63 · assistant surgeon certificate, BL OIOC, L/MIL/9/387, 168–9 · *CGPLA Eng. & Wales* (1878)
Archives Botanic Gardens, Oxford, plant specimens · Conservatoire et Jardins Botaniques, Geneva · NHI, London, plant specimens · RBG Kew, plant specimens · RBG Kew Library, corresp. with Sir Joseph Hooker
Likenesses crayon drawing, 1854 (after G. Richmond, 1852), RBG Kew · Maull & Polyblank, photograph, 1855, NPG · photograph (after oil painting), RBG Kew; repro. in Desmond, *European discovery* · portrait, Hunt Botanical Library, Pittsburgh
Wealth at death under £450: probate, 14 May 1878, *CGPLA Eng. & Wales*

Thomson, Thomas Napier (1798–1869), historian and biographer, was born at Glasgow on 25 February 1798, and was the fifth son of Hugh Thomson, West India merchant, and his wife, Agnes, *née* Davidson. About 1812 the family moved to London, and Thomson was placed at a boarding-school near Barnet in Hertfordshire. Having contracted a bronchial affection, he was sent to his uncle's house in Ayrshire, and in October 1813 he entered the University of Glasgow as Thomas Thomson, having dropped the 'Napier' owing to a disagreement with the Napier family. Thomson was a distinguished student. In 1818 he published *The Immortality of the Soul, and other Poems*, his only publication in verse. After entering the Divinity Hall as a student for the ministry, he was reduced to poverty by his father's misfortunes, but managed to support himself at college as a private tutor, and in 1823 he obtained the two highest prizes in the University of Glasgow. Having received a licence as a preacher, he officiated in many parts of Scotland, as well as in Newcastle and Birmingham, besides writing for the *Christian Instructor*. In Glasgow he delivered a series of lectures to women on the philosophy of history.

In 1827 Thomson was appointed assistant to Laurence Adamson, minister of Cupar, Fife; but, owing to a return of his throat affection, he had to resign. He was then ordained to the charge of the Scottish church in Maitland, New South Wales, Australia, for which he sailed on 11 May 1831 with a brother and sister. On arriving at Maitland, he found there was neither church, manse, nor congregation, so he initiated a charge at Bathurst on 13 July 1832. About this time he married Lucy Agnes Hall. Shortly after the birth of their second child he resigned his charge and

returned to Britain, where he arrived in 1835, to devote himself to literature. Charles Knight (1791–1873) engaged him to edit and remodel Robert Henry's *History of Great Britain*. This was afterwards abandoned in favour of a new work, *The Pictorial History of England* (1838), to which Thomson was one of the principal contributors. He also wrote extensively for the periodical press, and contributed biographical and critical notices for *The Book of the Poets: Chaucer to Beattie* (1842).

In 1840 Thomson was commissioned by the Wodrow Society to edit David Calderwood's *Historie of the Kirk of Scotland*. As he had to transcribe the original manuscript in the British Museum, the task took him nearly five years. In July 1844 he left London for Edinburgh, where he had been appointed by the Free Church to edit a series of works it was about to publish. After the appearance of several volumes, comprising the *Select Works* of John Knox and other Scottish ministers, the scheme collapsed, and Thomson again turned his attention to the periodical and newspaper press. In 1851 he became connected with Messrs Blackie & Son, the publishers, for whom he afterwards turned out an immense amount of work, notably (along with Charles Macfarlane) *The Comprehensive History of England* (4 vols., 1858–61). In 1851 he had written a supplemental volume of R. Chambers's *Biographical Dictionary of Eminent Scotsmen*, and immediately before his death he prepared a new edition in three volumes, revised throughout and continued with a supplement, which was published between 1869 and 1871. His own biography is contained in the supplement. Having suffered for some years from chronic bronchitis, Thomson died at his house, Summer Lodge, Trinity, Leith, on 1 February 1869.

Thomson was the author of small works written in his college days, entitled *Richard Gordon*, *The Christian Martyr*, *A Visit to Dalgarnock*, and *The City of the Sun*. He also published naval biographies (1839), army biographies (from Alfred to Wellington, 1840), and a history of Scotland for schools (1849). He edited Robert Fleming's *Discourse on the Rise and Fall of the Papacy* (1846), Milton's *Poetical Works* (1853), and the works of James Hogg, the Ettrick Shepherd (2 vols., 1865).

GEORGE STRONACH, rev. H. C. G. MATTHEW

Sources Chambers, *Scots.* (1835) · Boase, *Mod. Eng. biog.* · d. cert. · *CGPLA Eng. & Wales* (1869)
Wealth at death £634 6s. 8d.: inventory, 20 April 1869, NA Scot., SC 70/1/143/297

Thomson, Sir William (1678–1739), judge, born in London, was the second son of Sir William Thompson (*d.* 1695), king's serjeant-at-law, and his wife, Mary Stephens. He received his early education at Brentwood grammar school before matriculating at Trinity College, Cambridge, in 1691, where he took a BA in 1695. Both William and his elder brother, Stephen (later attorney-general of Virginia), had already been entered at the Middle Temple in 1688, and he was called to the bar there in 1698. On 16 February 1701 he was married to Joyce Brent, a widow, of St Clement Danes, Middlesex. He became recorder of Ipswich in 1707, and was returned to parliament for Orford, another Suffolk borough, on 29 January 1709.

Although a relative newcomer to parliament, in March

Sir William Thomson (1678–1739), by Enoch Seeman, in or before 1739

1710 Thomson took a prominent part in the whig-inspired impeachment of Dr Henry Sacheverell, being principally responsible for the Commons' case on the third article (that Sacheverell had declared the Church of England was in danger under the present administration). He clearly gave satisfaction, because immediately afterwards he was also retained as junior counsel in the proceedings against some ringleaders of the riots inspired by Sacheverell's cause. While such a high profile resulted in the loss of his parliamentary seat at the general election which followed, Thomson capped the year by marrying on 4 November an heiress—Julia, daughter of Sir Christopher Conyers, baronet, of Horden Durham, and widow of Sir William Blackett, baronet, of Newcastle upon Tyne, and said to have a fortune 'upwards of £20,000' (Luttrell, 6.651). He was returned again for Ipswich in September 1713, and although unseated on petition, 1 April 1714, regained the seat at the first election after the accession of George I, and continued to hold it until he became a judge.

As a reliable whig lawyer and parliamentarian Thomson was useful to the new Hanoverian regime, and in March 1716 he acted as one of the Commons' managers at the trial of the Jacobite earl of Wintoun. In the preceding year (3 March 1715) he had succeeded Sir Peter King as recorder of London, a position of considerable political and professional importance, which involved regular attendance on the Old Bailey bench and reports to the king in cabinet about the eligibility of condemned criminals for pardons. Shortly afterwards he was knighted, and in February 1717

he also became solicitor-general. By his unique combination of these offices he appears to have had a major impact on the administration of criminal law in the capital, for he introduced into parliament the Transportation Act of 1718 (4 Geo. I c. 11), a measure which created an effective form of secondary punishment by providing for the transportation of non-capital and pardoned convicts to the colonies, and also included provisions against the kind of trade in organized property crime which was then being carried on by Jonathan Wild. Two years later he promoted another statute (6 Geo.I c. 23), which established arrangements for financing the carriage of the convicts across the Atlantic.

Despite these successes, in 1720 Thomson overreached himself in the House of Commons by accusing the attorney-general, Nicholas Lechmere, who was a privy councillor, of benefiting corruptly from fees for matters referred to the attorney by the council. After some witnesses had been heard the charges were voted 'malicious, false, and scandalous' (Cobbett, *Parl. hist.*, 7.644), and on the following day Thomson's patent as solicitor-general was revoked. In fact the main reason for his dismissal seems to have been his association with the ousted Walpole–Townshend group of whigs, which he had signalled in 1719 by voting against the ministry's Peerage Bill in the House of Commons. He continued as recorder of London, however, and in 1724, after the return of Walpole and Townshend to office, he received a patent giving him precedence in court after the law officers of the crown, with a pension of £1200 a year. This may have been reward for services rendered at the Old Bailey, where he remained an important member of the bench, playing a significant role in the final conviction of Wild in 1725. Further promotion followed, first in the shape of the administrative place of cursitor baron of the exchequer (1726), and finally in November 1729, when he became one of the judicial barons of the exchequer. Remarkably he continued to hold the recordership at the Old Bailey, and died in possession of both offices on 27 October 1739, at Bath. Both his marriages were childless.   DAVID LEMMINGS

Sources Foss, *Judges* · HoP, *Commons, 1715–54* · *DNB* · *State trials*, 15.157–63, 550, 616–17, 847–50, 869–72, 887–8 · Sainty, *Judges* · Sainty, *King's counsel* · N. Luttrell, *A brief historical relation of state affairs from September 1678 to April 1714*, 3 (1857), 430; 6 (1857), 555, 573, 651 · *GM*, 1st ser., 9 (1739) · J. M. Beattie, 'The cabinet and the management of death at Tyburn after the revolution of 1688–1689', *The revolution of 1688–1689: changing perspectives*, ed. L. G. Schwoerer (1992), 218–33 · G. Howson, *Thief-taker general: the rise and fall of Jonathan Wild* (1970) · Cobbett, *Parl. hist.*, 7.643–4 · Venn, *Alum. Cant.* · private information [J. M. Beattie, University of Toronto]

Archives PRO, MSS, SP 44

Likenesses E. Seeman, oils, in or before 1739, Guildhall Art Gallery, London [see illus.] · J. Faber junior, mezzotint (after E. Seeman the younger), BM, NPG · E. Seeman, oils, copy, Wallington Hall, Northumberland · print (after E. Seeman the younger); at Lincoln's Inn, London, in 1898

Thomson, William (1746–1817), writer, was born at Burnside in the parish of Forteviot, Perthshire, the son of Matthew Thomson, carpenter and farmer, and his wife, the daughter of Mr Miller, the schoolmaster of Avintully, near

Dunkeld. He was educated at the parish school, at Perth grammar school, and at St Andrews University, which he entered at the age of fifteen, despite his family's very limited means. There he was made private librarian to the university chancellor, Thomas Hay, earl of Kinnoull, who encouraged him to study for the church and promised him a parish in his patronage. Having completed his theological studies at St Andrews and, later, at Edinburgh University, Thomson was ordained on 20 March 1776 as assistant to James Porteous, minister of Monivaird, Perthshire, but he soon displayed tastes and affinities discordant with his office. He did not always confine himself within the bounds of ascetic puritanism, and the parishioners made urgent complaints about his irascible temper and his taste for sensual and social pleasures. He eventually resigned his post, on 1 October 1778, and settled in London as a man of letters.

At first unsuccessful, for several years Thomson depended mainly on an annual income of £50 granted by the earl of Kinnoull. At length he won notice and regard by his successful continuation of Robert Watson's *History of Philip III of Spain* (1783), for which he wrote the fifth and sixth books. On 31 October of the same year he received the honorary degree of LLD from Glasgow University, and he soon had his hands full of work. For the next thirty-five years he wrote on a great variety of subjects, producing pamphlets, memoirs, elaborate biographies, voyages, travels (in Europe, Asia, and Africa under the names of Thomas Newte, Sergeant Donald Macleod, or Andrew Swinton), commentaries on the Bible scripture (under the name of Harrison), and treatises on national history, such as the *History of Great Britain from the Revolution of 1688 to the Accession of George* (1787), or on military tactics (*Memoirs Relative to Military Tactics* [1805]). He seems to have avoided verse but he essayed into novels and dramas. Most of these had a decidedly philosophical bent, such as *The Man in the Moon* (1783), a satirical novel in the manner of Swift, where a lunar sovereign visits the earth, comments on man's intellectual and artistic achievements, and meets Charles Fox, or *Mammuth, or, Human nature displayed on a grand scale, in a tour with the tinkers into the central parts of Africa* (1789), a travel book intended to demonstrate the adaptability and universality of man's intellectual and social faculties. Besides writing under his own name Thomson collaborated with others and he appears to have used many different pseudonyms. From 1790 to 1800 he prepared the historical part of *Dodsley's Annual Register*. From 1794 to December 1796 he owned the *English Review* and largely furnished its contents with political and literary articles. In a letter to Dr Parr (1 March 1792), much reprinted and circulated, he defended the principles of the French Revolution, but not its methods, and advocated progressive changes. The *English Review* was later incorporated into the *Analytical Review*. Thomson also wrote for the *European Magazine*, the *Political Herald* (where, in articles signed Ignotus, he supported Fox's policies and party), *The Oracle*, and the *Whitehall Evening Post*, for which he wrote a weekly report of parliamentary debates. Thomson was twice married: his first wife was Diana Miltone, a Scot; his second

was a minor novelist, of whom no other details are known. There were children of both marriages, two sons and two daughters in all. A man of great and varied ability and very wide attainments, Thomson could always produce respectable and sometimes even excellent results, but he had no extraordinary literary ambition or perseverance. Thomson died at his home at Kensington Gravel Pits, London, on 16 February 1817.

T. W. BAYNE, *rev.* S. R. J. BAUDRY

Sources Chambers, *Scots.* (1835) · Anderson, *Scot. nat.* · *GM*, 1st ser., 87/1 (1817), 279, 647 · private information (1898) [J. M. Anderson] · *Fasti Scot.* · *Annual Biography and Obituary*, 2 (1818), 74–117
Archives NL Scot., corresp. with James Stuart

Thomson, William (*bap.* 1760, *d.* 1806), mineralogist and physician, was baptized on 13 September 1760 in Worcester, the eldest son of William Thomson (*c.*1722–1802), physician at the Worcester Infirmary from 1757 to 1793, and his wife, Ann (*c.*1730–1773). Thomson attended King's School, Worcester, and matriculated at Queen's College, Oxford, in 1776. In 1779 he was awarded a studentship at Christ Church, and graduated BA in 1780.

Thomson's first interests were archaeological and in 1781 he helped Richard Gough with his edition of Camden's *Britannia*. In 1781–2 Thomson studied medicine at Edinburgh University, attending chemistry classes under Joseph Black. At Edinburgh he was elected to the Royal Medical Society in 1781 and, in the following year, was a founder member of the Natural History Society (he was only the fifth to attend John Walker's new university course in that subject). In the summer of 1782 he went on tour to the highlands, collected minerals on Staffa, and presented resulting archaeological material to the Society of Antiquaries of Scotland.

On return to Oxford, Thomson graduated MA in 1783 and joined the Medical Society of Oxford. In 1784 he joined the London Society for Promoting Natural History and recommended that his friend James Macie (later Smithson) should join the tour which then took B. Faujas de St Fond to Scotland. The following year Thomson graduated BM, was elected Dr Lee's lecturer in anatomy at Oxford at a salary of £150 a year in April, and in November became public reader in anatomy. He spent the rest of 1785 in London preparing lectures and in the winter of 1785–6 attended John Hunter's lecture course on surgery (of which his notes survive). He graduated DM in 1786, the year in which he was elected physician to the Radcliffe Infirmary and a fellow of the Royal Society. In 1787 he gave what was probably the first Oxford lecture course on mineralogy, and these lectures, together with those he gave on anatomy, were among those later described as having 'produced [there] a taste for scientific researches which bordered on enthusiasm' (J. E. Stock, *Memoirs of the Life of Thomas Beddoes*, 1811, 24). In 1788 Thomson was a founder member of the Linnean Society; he was also trying to find fossils for his Scottish geologist friend James Hutton. In 1789 Thomson purchased many of William Gilpin's drawings and helped with metallurgical experiments on the agency of heat on geology, experiments which impressed on Thomas Beddoes the 'very strong conviction of the truth of Hutton's Theory of the Earth', since 'Dr Thomson admits the facts … and thinks my specimens justify the inferences' (Beddoes to Black, 21 April 1789, Black MSS).

In September 1790, having lectured publicly on anatomy in the spring using two executed murderers' bodies, Thomson suddenly left Oxford and resigned from the Royal Society. He had suffered 'a most scandalous imputation from an Experiment performed on a man 4 years ago' (Thomson to George Paton, 25 Sept 1790, Paton MSS). However, in Oxford some members of convocation wanted him 'most publically censured on a charge of suspicion' that Thomson had been guilty of 'sodomy and other unnatural and detestable practices with a servant boy' (*Minutes and Register of Convocation*, Oxford University Archives) and, although John Hunter and other medical experimentalists rallied to Thomson's defence, he was stripped first of his studentship and his degrees and banished from the university in November 1790. Although H. R. V. Fox, third Lord Holland, recorded that 'the memory of his ready eloquence and extraordinary perspicuity survived the ruin of his moral character' (Fox, 340), Thomson now left England never to return.

Thomson passed first via Paris, on his way to Marchese Ippolito Durazzo in Genoa. He then travelled on to Siena (November 1791), Florence (February), Rome (March), and arrived in Naples by April 1792, having met a wide range of European savants on his travels. In Naples, William became Guglielmo and he started again to practise medicine. Lord Holland, his patient, noted that 'here his medical attainments so far expiated his religious and other heresies that the Pope condescended to consult him and appoint him physician-in-ordinary' (Fox, 340).

Thomson became a prominent member of the British community in Naples (which by 1793 numbered almost sixty). He was soon helping Sir William Hamilton edit publication of volume two of J. H. W. Tischbein's *Collection of engravings from ancient vases discovered in the kingdom of the two Sicilies between 1789–90*. However, Thomson's main interests were scientific. Living in one of the most volcanic areas of Europe he built up fine collections of volcanic specimens, published classifications of volcanic productions and named several new minerals. Thomson wrote many articles for the *Giornale Litterario di Napoli* and other German, French, Swiss, and Italian journals, only a few of which were translated (in the *Monthly Magazine*). He was of great assistance to the Italian pioneer of vulcanology, Scipione Breislak. The Scot, T. C. Hope, noted how these 'hints of Beddoes and the more correct views of Dr Thomson [had] preceded Sir James Hall's decisive paper, [and] they are the emanations of Huttonism, since both Beddoes and Thomson were in Edinburgh when Dr Hutton's theory was brought into view' (Hope to Gregory Watt, 24 April 1804, Watt MSS).

Throughout this period Thomson was in a city terrified by fears of Napoleonic war. In 1797 he had contemplated publishing his own *Theory of the Earth*, clearly inspired by the appearance of Hutton's in 1795, but this never appeared, since in mid-1798 Thomson fled to Palermo for three years, fearful of the political situation in Naples. By

September 1801 Thomson was back in Naples where he published on his newly discovered Sicilian fossils, later called rudists. His financial situation was helped by the £4000 left him on his father's death in March 1802.

Thomson had long been busy as a student of meteorites, having been heavily involved in the analysis of the Siena chondrite fall of 16 June 1794. In 1804 he published, in the *Bibliothèque Britannique*, another important paper on the Krasnojarsk pallasite. This recorded the three-component structure of such meteoritic iron for the first time. It is clear that what were later called Widmanstätten structures should rightly be named after Thomson.

The fame of Thomson's fine collections and the depth of his knowledge were widely known and he was visited in Naples by Gregory Watt with the American William Maclure in May 1802, and by Alexander von Humboldt in August 1805. But in 1803 Thomson, noting that a previous letter had miscarried when its carrier was murdered in Piedmont, warned that 'if another illness is supplanted by the apprehensions of warfare, you shall hear no more of me and my studies' (Thomson to Watt, 6 Sept 1803, Watt MSS). In January 1806 the French threatened to enter Naples and Thomson again fled to Palermo. He died there in November 1806. He had been an important contact between continental and British scientists, but the circumstances of his peregrinations and publications across Europe long obscured his contributions. His main collections and library arrived at Edinburgh University in 1808 (having been refused by Christ Church), supported by an endowment of half his estate. Another collection he willed to Lady Elizabeth Anne Hippesley (c.1761–1843), wife of a former diplomat in Italy; a little of this went to the Natural History Museum, London.   H. S. TORRENS

Sources G. Waterston, 'William Thomson (1761–1806): a forgotten benefactor', *University of Edinburgh Journal*, 22 (1965), 122–34 • R. T. Gunther, 'William Thomson FRS: a forgotten English mineralogist', *Nature*, 143 (1939), 667–8 • H. R. V. Fox, third Lord Holland, *Further memoirs of the whig party, 1807–1821*, ed. Lord Stavordale (1905) • *The journal of Elizabeth, Lady Holland, 1791–1811*, ed. earl of Ilchester [G. S. Holland Fox-Strangways], 2 vols. (1908) • K. Bruhns, *Life of Alexander von Humboldt*, 2 vols. (1873) • R. S. Clarke jun. and J. I. Goldstein, 'Schreibersite growth and its influence', *Smithsonian Contributions to the Earth Sciences*, 21 (1978), 1–80 • A. V. Carozzi, 'Histoire des sciences de la terre entre 1790 et 1815', *Mémoires de la Société de Physique et d'Histoire Naturelle de Genève*, 45/2 (1990), 1–411 • E. G. W. Bill, *Education at Christ Church, Oxford, 1660–1800* (1988) • W. H. McMenemey, *A history of the Worcester Royal Infirmary* (1947) • J. Chambers, *Biographical illustrations of Worcestershire* (1820) • Nichols, *Illustrations*, vol. 4 • J. G. Burke, *Cosmic debris* (1986) • parish register, Worcester, St Nicholas, 13 Sept 1760 [baptism] • NL Scot., Paton MSS • Birm. CL, Watt MSS • U. Edin. L., Black MSS • *Taschenbuch für die gesammte Mineralogie*, 2 (1808), 321
Archives U. Edin. | Birm. CL, J. and G. Watt MSS • Cornwall RO, J. Hawkins MSS • NL Scot., G. Paton MSS, letters • U. Edin., J. Black MSS
Wealth at death £3000: will, Edinburgh City Archives; Waterston, 'William Thomson', p. 134

Thomson, William (1802–1852), physician, was born on 3 July 1802 in Edinburgh, the second son of John *Thomson (1765–1846), surgeon (subsequently professor of surgery at the College of Surgeons of Edinburgh, professor of military surgery at Edinburgh University, and professor of pathology at Edinburgh University), and his first wife, Margaret Crawford Gordon (d. 1804). From the high school in Edinburgh, Thomson matriculated as a medical student at Edinburgh University in the session 1818–19 and studied medicine there and at the Edinburgh extramural school until 1821. He spent the session 1821–2 at Glasgow University studying medicine and philosophy.

By the beginning of the 1820s the pathological discoveries being made in France had attracted the attention of British medical men. Thomson's father, who resigned his post as professor of military surgery at Edinburgh in 1822, had become interested in the study of pathological anatomy. At his father's behest Thomson and another Edinburgh medical practitioner, Robert Carswell, spent the best part of the years 1822 to 1824 in France, initially in Paris and subsequently in Lyons, studying French methods in pathology and surgery. The information gleaned from this was used by John Thomson in his subsequent lectures on pathology.

After returning from Paris, Thomson became a fellow of the College of Surgeons of Edinburgh in 1825. In 1826 he was elected one of the surgeons of the New Town Dispensary in Edinburgh. From 1826 to 1828 he gave lectures on the institutes of medicine. In December 1827 he married Eliza, daughter of Ninian Hill, a solicitor. They had six children. From 1828 to 1841 Thomson worked closely with his father, lecturing initially on the practice of medicine, and in 1830 taking over his father's course on the practice of physic.

In 1831 Thomson was awarded the MD of Marischal College, Aberdeen, by examination, and two years later, in 1833, was elected a fellow of the Royal College of Physicians of Edinburgh. In that same year he acted as a delegate from the College of Surgeons of Edinburgh to parliament during its consideration of amendments to the 1815 Apothecaries Act. In 1834 he was again a delegate to parliament, this time as part of a deputation from the Edinburgh colleges of physicians and surgeons and Edinburgh University, which was monitoring and giving evidence to a select committee on medical education and privileges. He was also involved in professional and public affairs in Edinburgh outside the colleges, being for a time secretary of the Medico-Chirurgical Society of Edinburgh, as well as holding the office of secretary to the Edinburgh School of Art. Thomson was appointed physician to the Edinburgh Royal Infirmary in 1841, but held this office for only a short time. Later that year he was appointed professor of the practice of medicine at Glasgow University.

As well as his medical duties Thomson undertook a heavy administrative workload during his time as professor, although he had no private practice. He again accepted appointment as physician to the Royal Infirmary from 1843 to 1846, and from 1848 to 1851, since the tenure of high medical office within the university was no guarantee of the right to have beds at the Royal Infirmary. He was by virtue of his professorship a director of the Royal Infirmary. In the university he was also clerk to the faculty (a general administrative body, not to be confused with the faculty of medicine) for a number of years in the 1840s. In this capacity he was closely involved with the selection of records for the *Munimenta alme universitatis Glasguensis*, edited by Cosmo Innes and published in 1854. Thomson was also a director of the lunatic asylum at Gartnavel, where he acted as physician during the winter of 1848–9, while there was a vacancy in the post of physician superintendent. During that period there was an outbreak of cholera in the asylum which resulted in the deaths of more than forty patients.

Thomson made a number of contributions to the medical literature, and was particularly well regarded by his contemporaries for his ability to cut to the heart of the matter in his writing. His only book was *A Practical Treatise on Diseases of the Liver*, published in Edinburgh in 1841. Thomson was cultured in his manners, which were described as being 'dignified and polished' (Cowan, 204). He was not considered a great success as a teacher because of his inability to organize the material on which he was lecturing, although he was very warmly disposed to his students and interested in their careers and well-being.

Towards the end of the 1840s Thomson's health, which had never been good, began to fail. At the beginning of the 1850s he began to have symptoms of heart disease. This gradually worsened, and during the first week of May 1852 he suffered shortness of breath and chest pains. On 10 May he travelled to Edinburgh to consult medical colleagues on his symptoms, but he died suddenly on the morning of 12 May 1852. He was survived by his wife.

JAMES BEATON

Sources J. Thomson, 'Biographical notice of Dr William Thomson', in J. Thomson, W. Thomson, and D. Cragie, *An account of the life, lectures and writings of William Cullen*, ed. A. Thomson, 2 (1859) • S. Jacyna, 'Robert Carswell and William Thomson at the Hôtel-Dieu of Lyons: Scottish views of French medicine', *British medicine in an age of reform* [London 1987], ed. R. French and A. Wear (1991), 110–35 • D. Murray, *Memories of the old college of Glasgow: some chapters in the history of the university* (1927) • J. B. Cowan, 'Glasgow Royal Infirmary, 1847–51', *Glasgow Medical Journal*, new ser., 42 (1894), 203–6 • J. Coutts, *A history of the University of Glasgow* (1909)
Archives NL Scot., corresp. • Wellcome L., lecture notes | NL Scot., corresp. with Lord Rutherford and Rutherford family • U. Edin., Carswell MSS, MS Gen 590–591 • U. Glas., MS Gen and MS Cullen

Thomson, William (1819–1890), archbishop of York, born at Whitehaven on 11 February 1819, was the eldest son of John Thompson of Kelswick House, near that town. Both his parents were of Scottish extraction. His mother, Isabella, was maternally descended from Patrick Home of Polwarth, and was related to the earls of Marchmont. His father migrated to Whitehaven in 1813 to join the business of his uncle, Walter Thompson. John Thompson became director of the local bank and chairman of the Cleator Moor Hematite Iron Company, the first hematite company formed in the north of England. He died at Bishopthorpe Palace on 18 April 1878, aged eighty-seven (*West Cumberland and Whitehaven Herald*, 25 April and 2 May 1878).

William Thomson (1819–1890), by Bassano

Education and early career William was educated at Shrewsbury School, entering at the age of eleven. During his schooldays he preferred science to classics, although at Shrewsbury he had no opportunity of following his bent. On 2 June 1836 he matriculated from Queen's College, Oxford. He was elected a scholar in the following year and a fellow in 1840. He graduated BA in that year and MA in 1844.

While an undergraduate, Thompson devoted himself chiefly to the study of logic, somewhat to the detriment of his work for the schools, and before he graduated he had practically completed a treatise entitled 'Outlines of the laws of thought'. This was published in 1842, and brought him his earliest reputation. The germ of his work, he states, he derived from Christian von Wolff's *Philosophia rationalis* and Daniel Albert Wyttenbach's *Praecepta philosophiae logicae*. Thompson's treatment of his topic was remarkably clear, and he arranged his matter with great skill. The merits of the treatise brought him into communication with many authorities on the subject, including Sir William Hamilton, Professor De Morgan, James McCosh, Philip Henry, Lord Mahon (later fifth Earl Stanhope), and William Whewell. From these, and especially from Sir William Hamilton, Thompson received many suggestions which induced him to make considerable alterations in the later editions of his work. Thompson's 'Outlines' in some respects anticipated John Stuart Mill's *System of Logic*, and was long used extensively as a textbook.

Soon after the publication of his treatise in 1842, Thompson was ordained deacon, and left Oxford to devote himself to clerical work. He took priest's orders in 1843,

and in the next four years served curacies, first at St Nicholas, Guildford, Surrey (1844–6), and afterwards at Cuddesdon, near Oxford, under the nominal vicar, Samuel Wilberforce, bishop of Oxford. About this time he dropped the 'p' from his name, thinking 'Thomson' less plebian; he was mocked for this for the rest of his life, especially at Queen's.

Thomson's growing reputation as a logician led Queen's College in 1847 to recall him to Oxford to act as college tutor. In this capacity he did much to retrieve the standing of the college. Indefatigable in his attention to its affairs, he filled the office not merely of tutor, but also of chaplain and dean. In 1852 he became junior bursar, and in 1854 bursar. At the same time he was recognized in the university as a preacher of power. In 1848 he was appointed select preacher, and in 1853 he was chosen Bampton lecturer. Taking as his subject the atoning work of Christ, he dwelt on the expiatory character of the atonement, and his sermons constitute a very complete exposition of that theory of the purpose of Christ's incarnation. They attracted great attention, and St Mary's was more crowded than it had been since the time of Newman (*The Times*, 7 June 1853).

University and college reform In the matter of academic organization Thomson was strongly in favour of reform. He disapproved of the principles on which college fellowships were filled. At that period they were nearly all confined to persons born in particular districts, and at Queen's College, contrary to the statutes, elections were restricted to natives of Cumberland and Westmorland. In conjunction with another fellow, George Henry Sacheverell Johnson, Thomson endeavoured to remedy this state of things. In 1849 the fellows rejected the candidature of Goldwin Smith, afterwards regius professor of modern history, and elected instead a native of Cumberland whom they had previously removed from the list of expectants on account of his insufficient attainments. Thomson appealed against this action to Lord John Russell, the prime minister; as a result of this and other representations a royal commission was appointed in 1850 to inquire into the constitution and revenues of the university, and in 1854 a second commission was empowered to revise the statutes of the university and of the colleges and halls. The proposed innovations alarmed the more conservative members of the university, and several attacks on the commissions appeared. In reply to one of these, entitled *The Case of Queen's College* (1854), by the Revd John Barrow, Thomson penned *An Open College Best for All* (1854). This pamphlet was generally considered the ablest contribution to the reformers' side of the controversy, and was much quoted in the parliamentary debates.

Marriage and provost of Queen's In 1855 Thomson married Zoë, daughter of James Henry Skene, British consul at Aleppo, and his wife, Rhalon Rizo-Rangabe, a Greek beauty of aristocratic descent. With her he had five daughters and four sons, including the 'spycatcher' Sir Basil Home *Thomson and Jocelyn Home *Thomson. As a result of his marriage, Thomson lost his fellowship; he was presented by the crown to the rectory of All Souls, Marylebone. Within a few months, however, on the death of the Revd John Fox, on 11 August, he was elected provost of Queen's College and resigned his living. As provost he steadily pursued his liberalizing policy. He advocated the enlargement of the curriculum of university studies, and, with a view to aiding scientific study, was one of the projectors of the university museum, which was afterwards erected in the university parks. Outside Oxford he accepted preferment, whereby he extended his reputation as a preacher who appealed to the intellect rather than to the emotions of his audience. In 1858 he was elected to the preachership of Lincoln's Inn, and in 1859 he was appointed chaplain-in-ordinary to the queen.

Thomson's theological position was conspicuously defined during the controversy that followed the publication in 1860 of *Essays and Reviews*. In his ardour for reform at Oxford he had associated himself with Benjamin Jowett and the newer school of broad-churchmen, and in 1855 he had contributed a paper, 'Crime and its excuses', to *Oxford Essays*. He was to have been one of the contributors to *Essays and Reviews*, but failed to get his paper to the printer in time (happily for him, in view of the events of the next two years). However, when *Essays and Reviews* was published, in 1860, Thomson led the orthodox campaign against it, editing in reply *Aids to Faith* (1861). This volume included contributions from Edward Harold Browne, Frederick Charles Cook, Charles John Ellicott, and Henry Longueville Mansel, besides an article of his own, 'The death of Christ', which was substantially a restatement of his Bampton lectures in more popular form. *Aids to Faith* was the most substantial general answer to *Essays and Reviews*, and possesses historical value as a clear statement of the orthodox position at that period. Almost at the same time Thomson was engaged, as one of a committee of ten, in preparing the Speaker's Commentary, to which he contributed an 'Introduction to the synoptical gospels', probably the best treatise on the subject then extant.

Archbishop of York In the same year (1861), on the translation of C. T. Baring to the see of Durham, Thomson, whose established fame as a preacher marked him out for promotion, was appointed Baring's successor in the see of Gloucester and Bristol. Within ten months of his consecration, however, Charles Thomas Longley, the archbishop of York, was translated to Canterbury, and, though so junior a bishop, Thomson was appointed Longley's successor, A. C. Tait having declined. This rapid advancement, coupled with public knowledge of his ambivalent role in the *Essays and Reviews* affair, excited envy and distrust among his clerical colleagues. He was enthroned at York Minster on 26 March 1862, and entered on an archiepiscopate which extended over twenty-eight years. The new archbishop was a very tall man (and wore a size eight hat). He was imposing in full episcopal dress, with long, bushy hair and side-whiskers. He and his wife were known as a handsome couple. He was vain about his appearance and had a reputation for vulgarity. He signed a hotel register: 'His Grace, the Lord Archbishop of York'. None the less Thomson performed the various duties of his office with

success. From the commencement of his archiepiscopate he realized that, to keep its place in English life, the English church must show itself able to meet modern needs. He was active in his support of diocesan conferences and church congresses, and showed a keen interest in social, economic, and political questions, together with a just discernment of their relation to ecclesiastical matters. He made his first public appearance as archbishop at a meeting of the Castle Howard Reformatory in 1863, and from that time onwards he was present at every large public meeting in the diocese, whether its object was the amendment of the criminal law, the amelioration of the state of the poor, the encouragement of education, or the cultivation of art or science.

In 1862 the increase of population in the north of England had surpassed the resources of the church, and in the large towns the numbers of the clergy were quite inadequate for the needs of the people. Sheffield, for example, had only one church for 8000 inhabitants, and that town, like all its neighbours, was a centre of anti-clerical feeling. Thomson from the first set himself to meet these difficulties. In 1865, at the church congress at York, he suggested the addition of a working men's meeting to the ordinary programme. In 1869 he gained the attention of the workers of Sheffield, who had hitherto treated the clergy with scorn, by a speech defending the English church from the charge that it was a useless institution maintained at an undue cost to the nation. This speech was followed by others of like tenor. The population of Sheffield at once acknowledged the force of his argument, and their attitude of hostility or indifference to all that concerned the church was converted into one of devoted esteem for himself and his aims. His artisan admirers subscribed to give him a present of cutlery in 1883 (*Yorkshire Post*, 13 June 1883). His success in Sheffield was only typical of what he achieved throughout the labour centres of northern England. During the latter part of his life no man equalled him in the affections of the working classes, and it is difficult to overestimate the effect of his influence in strengthening the position of the English church in the northern province. He was one of the first English clergymen who, while not himself a socialist, recognized the good elements that went to the making of socialism. When he dissented from opinions which to most people of the time seemed revolutionary, he did so without bitterness and with full allowance for differences in the point of view from which the question was approached.

A church disciplinarian From the time of his elevation to the bench of bishops Thomson took an important part in ecclesiastical legislation. One of the first problems that engaged his attention was the reconstitution of the final ecclesiastical court of appeal. He was thus involved in a prolonged controversy with Samuel Wilberforce, bishop of Oxford, who was ultimately victorious. At the outset in 1871 Thomson successfully opposed Wilberforce's proposal to reduce the bishops to the position of assessors in the judicial committee of the privy council. But in 1873 a clause was introduced into the Supreme Court of Judicature Act removing the episcopal members from the judicial committee altogether, and, though two years later they reappeared as assessors, they did not regain their judicial functions. In 1871, with John Jackson (1811–1885), bishop of London, Thomson introduced the Dilapidations Act, intended to compel the clergy to keep their residences and church buildings in repair. It was not, however, very happily framed, and some years later was condemned by a committee of the House of Commons. In 1874 he joined his friend Tait, by then archbishop of Canterbury, another disciplinarian of liberal origin, in introducing the Public Worship Regulation Bill. The measure was intended in part to check the growth of ritualistic practices, and in its original form largely increased the authority of the bishops; the extensive modifications it received in its passage through parliament, however, partially destroyed the effect that its framers had in view. Gladstone and the Tractarians vigorously opposed the bill, and the act led to a number of notorious imprisonments. In 1883 Thomson supported Tait's motion for the appointment of a commission on ecclesiastical courts. But, though he signed the general report of the commission, he joined with a minority in issuing a dissentient report, and was the author of a severe criticism on the work of the commission which appeared in the *Edinburgh Review* for January 1884.

A strict disciplinarian, Thomson came conspicuously forward in 1887 as the champion of ecclesiastical order. He had refused to admit Canon Tristram's election as a proctor in convocation, on the ground that he was not duly qualified. In consequence he was required to show cause in the court of queen's bench why Tristram's election should not be accepted. Thomson conducted his case in person, and, appearing before the court on 28 November 1887, took exception to the court's jurisdiction. His pleading was successful, and the ability he displayed led Lord Coleridge, who tried the case, to remark that, had Thomson been a lawyer, he would have been the second person in the kingdom instead of the third.

In 1888 the Clergy Discipline (Immorality) Bill was introduced into parliament. It was materially altered in committee, and Thomson, disapproving of it in its amended form, hastened to London to oppose it on the third reading in the House of Lords. He pointed out that it tended to increase the cost of prosecution, and at the same time prevented an appeal to a higher court on matters of fact; the bill, after passing the third reading, was allowed to drop. In the conduct of the ecclesiastical affairs of his province Thomson displayed both strength and tact. Though he had been accused of narrowness and intolerance, he earned the gratitude of people of opinions widely different from his own, and from each other's, by interposing his authority to shield them from petty annoyance. The only clerical prosecution for doctrine or ritual which he promoted took place in 1869, when he instituted proceedings for heresy against the Revd Charles Voysey, rector of Healaugh in Yorkshire, author of *The Sling and the Stone*, who, among other things, had published a sermon entitled *Is every Statement in the Bible about our Heavenly Father Strictly True?* The case was finally decided against Voysey on 11 February 1870. The result did not, however, affect the personal friendship which had existed for many years between Voysey and the archbishop. In the judicial committee of the privy council Thomson's voice was frequently raised for toleration, and when, on 16 December 1863, Robert Gray (1809–1872), the bishop of Cape Town, pronounced sentence of deposition against John William Colenso, Thomson warned him of the illegality of his proceedings. On another occasion, in the case of William James Early Bennett, he laid down the maxim that the question to consider in cases of difference is not whether a person's views are in strict accord with the teaching of their church, but whether their views are so discordant as to render toleration impossible.

Final years Prior to the appointment of Archdeacon Crossthwaite in 1880 as bishop of Beverley, Thomson had no suffragan. He always dispatched the business of the see with punctuality, but the labour and anxiety gradually undermined his health and compounded the diabetes which affected him from about 1880. He was taken ill while boating at Keswick in September 1890 and died on Christmas day 1890 in Bishopthorpe Palace. He was buried in the churchyard of Bishopthorpe, near York. The pall was borne by working men of Sheffield. His wife, Zoë, died on 30 December 1913 and was buried with her husband.

E. I. CARLYLE, *rev.* H. C. G. MATTHEW

Sources H. Kirk Smith, *William Thomson, archbishop of York* (1958) • *The Guardian* (31 Dec 1890) • *Sheffield and Rotherham Independent* (26 Dec 1890) • I. Ellis, *Seven against Christ: a study of 'Essays and reviews'* (1980) • CGPLA Eng. & Wales (1891)

Archives Borth. Inst., official corresp. and papers; papers relating to him and his family • York Minster Library, corresp. and papers | BL, corresp. with W. E. Gladstone, Add. MSS 44377–44390, *passim* • Borth. Inst., corresp. with second Viscount Halifax • Durham Cath. CL, letters to J. B. Lightfoot • LPL, corresp. with E. W. Benson • LPL, corresp. with Baroness Burdett-Coutts • LPL, corresp. with A. C. Tait • NL Wales, letters to George Stovin Venables • U. Nott. L., corresp. mainly with J. E. Denison

Likenesses Onslow Ford, bust, 1886 • W. W. Ouless, oils, exh. RA 1886, Bishopthorpe Palace, York • Ape [C. Pellegrini], chromolithograph caricature, NPG; repro. in *VF* (24 June 1871) • Bassano, photograph, NPG [*see illus.*] • Dalziel, woodcut, BM • W. Holl, stipple and line engraving (after photograph), NPG • C. Johnson, portrait (after W. W. Ouless), Queen's College, Oxford • W. D. Keyworth, marble bust, Sheffield parish church • Lock & Whitfield, woodburytype photograph, NPG; repro. in T. Cooper, *Men of mark: a gallery of contemporary portraits* (1878) • Mason & Co., carte-de-visite, NPG • Moira & Haigh, carte-de-visite, NPG • D. J. Pound, stipple and line engraving (after photograph by Mayall), repro. in *Illustrated News of the World* • J. Watkins, carte-de-visite, NPG

Wealth at death £55,929 2s. 4d.: probate, 23 Jan 1891, CGPLA Eng. & Wales

Thomson, William, Baron Kelvin (1824–1907), mathematician and physicist, was born on 26 June 1824 at College Square, Belfast, second son among seven children of James *Thomson (1786–1849), professor of mathematics in the collegiate department of the Belfast Academical Institution, and his wife, Margaret Gardner (*c.*1790–1830), whose mother was Elizabeth Patison of Kelvin Grove to the west of Glasgow. After Margaret's death in 1830 James

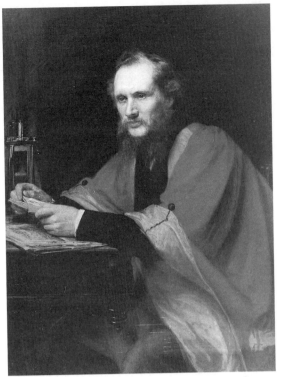

William Thomson, Baron Kelvin (1824–1907), by Lowes Cato Dickinson, 1869

Thomson assumed full responsibility for the education of his children, and two years later took up his appointment to the Glasgow College chair of mathematics. The family lived in the old college off the High Street during the six-month winter sessions but in the summer they moved to rented accommodation at various localities on the Firth of Clyde, most notably Arran. Although William and his elder brother James *Thomson had attended some school classes at the Academical Institution (and won first and second prizes respectively in 1831), they had received almost no formal schooling. Having attended as listeners their father's junior class in Glasgow, the brothers matriculated in 1834 when William was just ten.

Making a Cambridge wrangler For the next six years the brothers were constantly together, James increasingly committed to engineering problems and William to mathematics and natural philosophy. Early in 1835 their older sister Anna reported that 'James and William are quite delighted just now, having been making an electrical machine. It gives strong shocks' (E. King, 135n.). The following year William told his eldest sister, Elizabeth, that 'We have not begun the steam-engine, for papa was not wanting us to do it' (E. King, 138). By the end of the year the brothers had each built an electrical machine, James's machine apparently larger and more carefully finished than his younger brother's but the latter was well satisfied with the utility of his production, its power demonstrated by subjecting other members of the family to frequent shocks. In due course the brothers were allocated a room

in the college house where they pursued their mechanical and philosophical researches. In college classes William took first prize, his physically less robust elder brother often coming second.

By May 1839 the brothers were eligible for the degree of BA, but Thomson did not take the degree because he planned to enter Cambridge University as an undergraduate. A further session (1839–40) saw the brothers attending the senior natural philosophy class which, initially under the ailing William Meikleham, passed to the control of John Pringle Nichol, radical professor of astronomy. At the end of the session William won a university medal for an 85-page essay on 'The figure of the earth' which drew on advanced texts by Laplace, Poisson, and Airy. In that summer the Thomsons and the Nichols travelled together to the Rhine. Fired by Nichol's enthusiasm for Joseph Fourier, Thomson took with him a library copy of Fourier's *Théorie analytique de la chaleur* (1822), and secretly read right through the treatise when he was supposed to be giving his undivided attention to the German language. He nevertheless quickly announced to his incredulous father that the Edinburgh professor of mathematics, Philip Kelland, was mistaken in recent criticisms of Fourier's mathematics. The outcome was the publication of William Thomson's first paper, under the pseudonym 'P. Q. R.', in the *Cambridge Mathematical Journal*. He had only just turned sixteen.

Thomson was formally entered at Peterhouse on 6 April 1841 but did not come into residence as an undergraduate until the following October. The connections of the mathematical coach, William Hopkins, with Peterhouse probably influenced the choice of college. In any case, Cambridge offered the best mathematical training available anywhere in Britain, training which could open careers in the church and in the legal profession as well as in the universities. Hopkins himself recognized deficiencies in undergraduates who came to Cambridge by way of the Scottish universities with their emphasis on a broad philosophical education rather than on rigorous mathematical practice: 'men from Glasgow and Edinburgh require a great deal of drilling' (Smith and Wise, 55). Only days after arriving in Cambridge, Thomson was singled out as the likely senior wrangler of his year.

Thomson's Cambridge years were lived with characteristic intensity. He quickly made the acquaintance of distinguished Trinity College Scots such as D. F. Gregory (editor of the *Cambridge Mathematical Journal*) and Archibald Smith (senior wrangler in 1836). With one eye on his father's financial imperatives to avoid dissipation and the other on Cambridge's moral strictures designed to shape its wranglers, he attempted to adhere to highly disciplined routines of reading and exercising. His private diary (1843) suggests a different story. Rising at six or seven on February mornings, his days were filled by passionate rather than disciplined involvement in walking, skating, swimming, reading, and, above all, wide-ranging discussions with a large circle of friends extending well into the night. Against the wishes of his father he became increasingly enthusiastic about rowing. By the end of his second year he had joined the college eight and towards the close of 1843 won the Colquhoun silver sculls for single-seater boats. The family too had been won over. As his sister Anna perceptively observed:

> I got your letter today containing all your reasons for having joined the boat races, which has one good effect at least— that of convincing us all that you are a most excellent logician, and that … you possess the excellent talent of being able to defend yourself most eloquently when anything you do is in the least blamed.   (Smith and Wise, 78)

As an enthusiastic musician and player of the cornet, William also became a founder member of the Cambridge University Music Society in the spring of 1844.

From his second undergraduate year Thomson's coaching took the form of constant rehearsals according to Hopkins's training methods. In the summer of 1844 he joined Hopkins's reading party, which included his friends Hugh Blackburn (later professor of mathematics at Glasgow) and W. F. L. Fischer (later professor of natural philosophy at St Andrews), at Cromer in the months leading up to the Senate House examinations. In January 1845, twelve mathematical examination papers later, Thomson emerged as second wrangler, after Stephen Parkinson of St John's College. One of the examiners, R. L. Ellis, remarked to a fellow examiner that 'You and I are just about fit to mend his [Thomson's] pens' (Thompson, 97–8) while William Whewell noted to J. D. Forbes that 'Thomson of Glasgow is much the greatest mathematical genius: the Senior Wrangler was better drilled' (ibid., 103). The fault lay not with Hopkins, however, but with Thomson's irrepressible zeal for physical problems that interested him. In the subsequent Smith's prize examination the order was reversed. By June 1845 he had been appointed a fellow of Peterhouse and in the same year took over as editor of the *Cambridge Mathematical Journal* which he soon expanded into the *Cambridge and Dublin Mathematical Journal*.

The mathematical theory of electricity During his undergraduate years Thomson had published eleven papers in the *Journal* which, under the editorship of first Gregory and latterly Ellis, represented the young and reforming generation of Cambridge mathematicians. Whigs both in mathematics and politics, as Thomson noted approvingly, the three successive editors regarded Fourier as their inspiration (Smith and Wise, 174). On the basis of Fourier's treatment of heat conduction, Thomson's 'On the uniform motion of heat in homogeneous solid bodies, and its connexion with the mathematical theory of electricity' (1841–2) constructed a mathematical analogy between electrostatic induction and heat conduction. Instead of forces acting at a distance over empty space, he viewed electrical action mathematically as represented by a series of geometrical lines or 'surfaces of equilibrium' intersecting at right angles with the lines of force. These surfaces would later be called equipotential lines or surfaces. At each stage he correlated the mathematical forms in thermal and electrical cases, but avoided any physical inferences about the nature of electricity as an actual contiguous action like fluid flow.

Thomson soon deployed the analogy to reformulate the action-at-a-distance mathematical theory of electricity (developed by Poisson and employed in Robert Murphy's Cambridge textbook on electricity) into Faraday's theory of contiguous action, though without Faraday's quantity–intensity distinction. In the analogy, force at a point was analogous to temperature gradient while specific inductive capacity of a dielectric was analogous to conductivity. Over the next decade or so Thomson would search for the mechanism of propagation, perhaps in terms of an elastic-solid model such as that used to explain the wave nature of light, or in terms of a hydrodynamical model which would show not only electricity, magnetism, and heat, but ponderable matter itself, to result from the motions of an all-pervading fluid medium or ether. This quest for a unified field theory acquired special urgency once he adopted a dynamical theory of heat about 1850. However, Thomson also pursued other analogies as problem-solving geometrical techniques, including the method of images (1847) which deployed a simple analogy from geometrical optics to solve complex problems in electrostatics.

By 1850 Thomson had contributed more than thirty papers to the *Cambridge Mathematical Journal*; two years later he relinquished its editorship, his strenuous efforts to expand it into a national journal for mathematical sciences having been hampered by what he saw as the stubborn preponderance of contributions from pure mathematicians and correspondingly few papers on physical subjects. With few converts to his own style of electrical science, he especially welcomed in 1854 the enthusiasm of a recent Cambridge graduate and second wrangler, James Clerk Maxwell, for following through Thomson's insights into the mathematical theories of electricity and magnetism.

The Glasgow chair and the motive power of heat As early as 1843 Thomson's father had begun to prepare him as a potential successor to the Glasgow professor of natural philosophy, Meikleham, who had been unable to conduct the class since 1839. In alliance with Nichol and the new professor of medicine, another William Thomson, James Thomson agreed that a mere mathematician, unskilled in lecture demonstrations, could not command the class. In order to fill this lacuna in his training, Thomson was dispatched to Paris after graduation from Cambridge. His brief was to observe, and if possible to participate in, a full range of experimental practice, from lecture demonstrations by the finest of the French experimentalists to the physical laboratory of Victor Regnault at the Collège de France. Thomson later acknowledged his principal debt to the French *physicien* as 'a faultless technique, a love of precision in all things, and the highest virtue of the experimenter—patience' (Thompson, 1154).

Regnault's accurate measurements on the properties of steam and other gases were being funded by the French government with a view to improving the efficiency of heat engines. A year earlier James had written from William Fairbairn's Thames shipbuilding works to his younger brother asking if he knew who it was that had offered an account of the motive power of heat in terms of the mechanical effect (or work done) by the 'fall' of a quantity of heat from a state of intensity (high temperature as in a steam-engine boiler) to a state of diffusion (low temperature as in the condenser), analogous to the fall of a quantity of water from a high to a low level in the case of water-wheels. While in Paris, Thomson located Emile Clapeyron's memoir (1834) on the subject but failed to locate a copy of Sadi Carnot's original treatise (1824). At the same time he began to consider solutions to problems in the mathematical theory of electricity (notably that of two electrified spherical conductors, the complexity of which had defied Poisson's attempts to obtain a general mathematical solution) in terms of mechanical effect given out or taken in, analogous to the work done or absorbed by a water-wheel or heat engine. He therefore recognized that measurements of electrical phenomena and of steam were both to be treated in absolute, mechanical and, above all, engineering terms. The contrast to the action-at-a-distance approach of Laplace and Poisson, as well as to Michael Faraday's non-mechanical perspective, was striking.

After returning to Cambridge, Thomson bided his time by coaching four or five pupils during the long vacation and then taking on the duties of college lecturer in mathematics from October 1845. The death of Professor Meikleham the following May publicly opened the campaign for the succession, a competition which ended with the unanimous election of Thomson to the Glasgow chair on 11 September 1846. Six years later, in September 1852, he married his second cousin, Margaret Crum, daughter of the prosperous cotton manufacturer and calico-printer Walter Crum FRS, of Thornliebank, who had a strong interest in industrial chemistry. The Crums had always been closely associated with the Thomsons and the couple had known each other since childhood. Soon after the marriage, however, Margaret's health broke down and she remained, despite all attempts at finding a cure, an invalid until her death in 1870.

The focal point of Thomson's academic life was the natural philosophy classroom. Filling a chair which had been largely neglected for the seven years since he himself had attended the class as an undergraduate, the 22-year-old professor's most immediate challenge was to fashion his authority over a class of more than 100 students and to establish his credibility within a college still largely ruled by a 75-year-old principal, Duncan Macfarlan, who deployed all his power to oppose academic and political reform. Yet the election had actually tipped the numerical balance of reforming over tory professors within the college, and the reformers therefore gave the young professor a practical vote of confidence when they won financial backing from the college for the rapid replacement of the existing stock of physical apparatus. Thomson immediately embarked on an investment programme which, over the first few years, saw the classroom equipped with the latest and finest electrical, acoustical, and optical apparatus and instruments from prestigious instrument makers such as Watkins and Hill in London and Pixii in Paris. Travelling to London and Paris in the summer following his first session with the class, he told his brother James that he aimed to see for himself the kind of apparatus, 'on the best possible scale for a lecture room', deployed by celebrated natural philosophers such as Faraday (Thompson, 202).

Early in 1847 Thomson rediscovered a model air engine, presented to the college classroom in the late 1820s by its designer, Robert Stirling, but long since clogged with dust and oil. Having joined his elder brother as a member of the Glasgow Philosophical Society in December 1846, Thomson addressed the society the following April on issues raised by the engine when considered as a material embodiment of the Carnot–Clapeyron account of the motive power of heat. If, he suggested, the upper part of the engine were maintained at the freezing point of water by a stream of water and if the lower part were held in a basin of water also at the freezing point, the engine could be cranked forward without the expenditure of mechanical effect (other than to overcome friction) because there existed no temperature difference. The result, however, would be the transference of heat from the basin to the stream and the gradual conversion of all the water in the basin into ice. Such considerations raised two fundamental puzzles: on the one hand, the production of seemingly unlimited quantities of ice without work, and on the other hand the seeming 'loss' of work which might have been produced from heat generated at high temperature if that heat were instead used to melt ice. As he explained the second puzzle to J. D. Forbes:

> It seems very mysterious how power can be lost in such a way [by the conduction of heat from hot to cold], but perhaps not more so than that power should be lost in the friction of fluids (a plumb line with the weight in water for instance) by which there does not seem to be any heat generated, nor any physical change effected. (Smith and Wise, 294)

At the close of his first Glasgow College session Thomson attended the Oxford meeting of the British Association for the Advancement of Science. He had long been acquainted with these annual spectacles—as long before as 1840 he and James had played supporting roles during the association's Glasgow meeting. However, 1847 marked his first appearance as a professor of natural philosophy and author of a string of avant-garde articles on electricity. It also marked his first encounter with James Prescott Joule who had been arguing since 1843 for the mutual convertability of work and heat according to an exact mechanical equivalence. Thomson immediately recognized in Joule's claim for the conversion of work into heat an answer to the puzzle of what happened to the seeming 'loss' of that useful work which might have been done but which was instead 'wasted' in conduction and fluid friction. Unconvinced by Joule's complementary claim that such heat could in principle be converted into work, Thomson remained deeply perplexed by what seemed to him the irrecoverable nature of that heat. Furthermore, he could not accept Joule's rejection of the Carnot–Clapeyron theory, with its 'fall' of heat from high to low temperature, in favour of mutual convertibility.

With regard to the first puzzle raised by the Stirling engine, however, James Thomson quickly pointed out the implication that, since ice expands on freezing, it could be made to do useful work: in other words, the arrangement would function as a perpetual source of power, long held to be impossible by almost all orthodox engineers and natural philosophers. He therefore concluded that avoidance of this implication would require that the freezing point be lowered with increase of pressure. His prediction, and its subsequent experimental confirmation in William Thomson's laboratory, did much to persuade the brothers of the value of the Carnot–Clapeyron theory.

Within a year Thomson had added another feature to the Carnot–Clapeyron construction, namely, an absolute scale of temperature. In presentations to the Glasgow and Cambridge philosophical societies in 1848 he explained that an air-thermometer scale provided 'an arbitrary series of numbered points of reference sufficiently close for the requirements of practical thermometry'. In an absolute thermometric scale 'a unit of heat descending from a body A at the temperature $T°$ of this scale, to a body B at the temperature $(T-1)°$, would give out the same mechanical effect [motive power or work], whatever be the number T'. Its absolute character derived from its being 'quite independent of the physical properties of any specific substance' (Thomson, 1.104). In other words, unlike the air-thermometer which depended on a particular gas, he deployed the waterfall analogy to establish a scale of temperature independent of the working substance.

The Glasgow College natural philosophy classroom had long been complemented by an adjacent professor's room and apparatus room for the storage of instruments and the preparation of lecture demonstration apparatus. Having worked with his brother James since childhood on mechanical and philosophical apparatus in the college, and having participated himself in the Parisian physical laboratory of Regnault, Thomson also used these spaces for the production of new scientific knowledge, aided by his classroom assistant Robert Mansell and, increasingly, by enthusiastic students. The location of the college near the heart of a growing industrial city also provided Thomson with many material resources for experimental work. Indeed, he later declined the offer of the new Cambridge chair of experimental physics on the grounds that 'the convenience of Glasgow for getting mechanical work done' gave him 'means of action which I could not have in any other place' (Thompson, 563).

Thomson's lectures to the experimental natural philosophy class became increasingly linked to the experimental practices of the 'apparatus room'. Thus in the 1849/50 session he instructed his class on the skills required for thermometry, insisting that, for instruments of the highest precision, accurate testing of the suitability of the glass tube in the laboratory was necessary before the thermometer was made by the instrument maker. Indeed,

such testing, calibration, and standardization soon became another characteristic function of the Glasgow research and teaching programme. The professor and his assistant deployed one such highly sensitive thermometer to investigate the depression of the freezing point of ice under pressure. The results, confirming his brother's prediction of the lowering of the freezing point in accordance with Carnot's theory, were announced to the class and to his opposite number in Edinburgh, J. D. Forbes, prior to being made public at a meeting of the Royal Society of Edinburgh.

When Thomson acquired from his colleague Lewis Gordon (professor of civil engineering and mechanics) a copy of the very rare Carnot treatise, he presented an exposition, especially in the light of the issues raised by Joule, to the Royal Society of Edinburgh. In particular, Thomson read Carnot as claiming that any work obtained from a cyclical process can only derive from transfer of heat from high to low temperature. From this claim, together with a denial of perpetual motion, it followed that no engine could be more efficient than a perfectly reversible engine (Carnot's criterion for a perfect engine). It further followed that the maximum efficiency obtainable from any engine operating between heat reservoirs at different temperatures would be a function of those temperatures (Carnot's function).

The science of energy Prompted by the competing investigations of Macquorn Rankine and Rudolf Clausius, Thomson finally laid down two propositions in 1851, the first a statement of Joule's mutual equivalence of work and heat and the second a statement of Carnot's criterion for a perfect engine. His long-delayed acceptance of Joule's proposition rested on a resolution of the problem of the irrecoverability of mechanical effect lost as heat. He now believed that work 'is *lost to man* irrecoverably though *not lost in the material world*'. Thus although:

> no destruction of energy can take place in the material world without an act of power possessed only by the supreme ruler, yet transformations take place which remove irrecoverably from the control of man sources of power which … might have been rendered available. (Smith and Wise, 329)

In other words, God alone could create or destroy energy (i.e., energy was conserved in total quantity) but human beings could make use of transformations of energy, for example in water-wheels or heat-engines.

In a private draft Thomson referred these transformations to a universal statement that 'Everything in the material world is progressive' (Smith and Wise, 330). On the one hand, this statement expressed the geological directionalism of Cambridge dons such as Hopkins and Adam Sedgwick in opposition to the steady-state uniformitarianism of Charles Lyell, but on the other it could be read as agreeing with the radical evolutionary doctrines of the subversive *Vestiges of Creation* (1844). In his published statement, Thomson opted instead for universal dissipation of energy, a doctrine which reflected the presbyterian (Calvinist) views of a transitory visible creation rather than a universe of ever-upwards progression.

Work dissipated as heat would be irrecoverable to human beings, for to deny this principle would be to imply that they could produce mechanical effect by cooling the material world with no limit except the total loss of heat from the world.

This reasoning crystallized in what later became the canonical 'Kelvin' statement of the second law of thermodynamics, first enunciated by Thomson in 1851: 'it is impossible, by means of inanimate material agency, to derive mechanical effect from any portion of matter by cooling it below the temperature of the coldest of the surrounding objects' (Thomson, 1.179). This statement provided Thomson with a new demonstration of Carnot's criterion of a perfect engine. Having resolved the recoverability issue, he also quickly adopted a dynamical theory of heat, making it the basis of Joule's proposition of mutual equivalence and abandoning the Carnot–Clapeyron notion of heat as a state function (with the corollary that in any cyclic process the change in heat content is zero).

Thomson's 'On a universal tendency in nature to the dissipation of mechanical energy' took the new 'energy' perspective to a wide audience. In this short paper for the *Philosophical Magazine* the term 'energy' achieved public prominence for the first time and the dual principles of conservation and dissipation of energy were made explicit: 'As it is most certain that Creative Power alone can either call into existence or annihilate mechanical energy, the "waste" referred to cannot be annihilation, but must be some transformation of energy' (Thomson, 1.511). Now the dynamical theory of heat, and with it a whole programme of dynamical (matter-in-motion) explanation, went unquestioned; and now, too, the universal primacy of the energy laws opened up fresh questions about the origins, progress, and destiny of the solar system and its inhabitants. Two years later Thomson told the Liverpool meeting of the British Association that Joule's discovery of the conversion of work into heat by fluid friction, the experimental foundation of the new energy physics, had 'led to the greatest reform that physical science has experienced since the days of Newton' (Thomson, 1.34).

From the early 1850s the Glasgow professor and his new ally in engineering science, Macquorn Rankine, began replacing an older language of mechanics with terms such as 'actual' ('kinetic' from 1862) and 'potential energy'. Within a few years they had been joined by like-minded scientific reformers, most notably the Scottish natural philosophers James Clerk Maxwell and Peter Guthrie Tait and the engineer Fleeming Jenkin. With strong links to the British Association, this informal grouping of 'North British' physicists and engineers was primarily responsible for the construction and promotion of the 'science of energy', inclusive of nothing less than the whole of physical science. Natural philosophy or physics was thus redefined as the study of energy and its transformations. It was a programme which served a wide range of functions. At the level of the Glasgow classroom, consisting largely of students destined for the ministry of

the Scottish kirk, Thomson could represent the new physics as a counter to the seductions of enthusiast biblical revivals on the one hand and of evolutionary materialism on the other at a time of considerable instability in Scottish society. At a national level Thomson and his friends could offer through the British Association a powerful rival reform programme to that of the metropolitan scientific naturalists (including T. H. Huxley and John Tyndall) who aimed at a professionalized science free from the perceived shackles of Anglican theology.

To these ends Thomson examined the principal source of all the mechanical effect on earth. Arguing that the sun's energy was too great to be supplied by chemical means or by a mere molten mass cooling, he at first suggested that the sun's heat was provided by vast quantities of meteors orbiting round the sun but inside the earth's orbit. Retarded in their orbits by an etherial medium, the meteors would progressively spiral towards the sun's surface in a cosmic vortex analogous to James's vortex turbines (horizontal water-wheels). As the meteors vaporized by friction, they would generate immense quantities of heat. In the early 1860s, however, he adopted Hermann Helmholtz's version of the sun's heat whereby contraction of the body of the sun released heat over long periods. Either way, the sun's energy was finite and calculable, making possible order-of-magnitude estimates of the limited past and future duration of the sun. In response to Charles Darwin's demand for a much longer time for evolution by natural selection and in opposition to Charles Lyell's uniformitarian geology upon which Darwin's claims were grounded, Thomson deployed Fourier's conduction law to make similar estimates for the earth's age. The limited time-scale of about 100 million years (later reduced) approximated to estimates for the sun's age, but the new cosmogeny was itself evolutionary, offering little or no comfort to strict biblical literalists within the Scottish kirk, especially the recently founded Free Church of Scotland.

The most celebrated textual embodiment of the 'science of energy' was Thomson and Tait's *Treatise on Natural Philosophy* (1867). Originally intending to treat all branches of natural philosophy, Thomson and Tait in fact produced only the first volume of the *Treatise*. Taking statics to be derivative from dynamics, they reinterpreted Newton's third law (action–reaction) as conservation of energy, with action viewed as rate of working. Fundamental to the new energy physics was the move here to make extremum conditions, rather than point forces, the theoretical foundation of dynamics. The tendency of an entire system to move from one place to another in the most economical way would determine the forces and motions of the various parts of the system. Variational principles (especially least action) thus played a central role in the new dynamics.

Although never published in treatise form, Thomson's subsequent attempts to produce a unified theory of matter and ether at first centred on the 'vortex atom' which also had a powerful practical foundation in James Thomson's vortex turbines and pumps. From 1867 Thomson drew extensively on Hermann Helmholtz's mathematical work on vortex motion and on Tait's experimental demonstrations of smoke rings. The theory supposed matter to consist of rotating portions of a perfect (that is, frictionless) fluid which continuously filled space. Without internal friction the fluid and everything therein would require a creative act for the production or destruction of rotation and hence of matter. Although the model seemed ideal for simple thermodynamic systems, stability remained a serious problem.

In the wake of Maxwell's electromagnetic theory of light, Thomson defended an elastic-solid model for light waves and remained for the most part highly sceptical of the work of Maxwell's scientific heirs. Grounding his criticism upon the practical success of his own telegraph theory, he continually argued against any methodology which dealt in theoretical entities without a basis in direct sensory perception. These views were forcefully expressed in his Baltimore Lectures, delivered to a distinguished academic audience at Johns Hopkins University in 1884, when he famously asserted: 'I can never satisfy myself until I can make a mechanical model of a thing … and that is why I cannot get the electro-magnetic theory'. For him, Maxwell's 'beautiful theory of electro displacements' had no foundation in such sensory reality (Smith and Wise, 470).

Towards a system of electrical standards Thomson's energy physics had its focal point in the physical laboratory. Ever since his participation in Regnault's laboratory practice in 1845 he had resolved to make physical measurements in absolute or mechanical measures. This commitment derived from a realization that electricity could be measured simply in terms of the work done by the fall of a quantity of electricity through a potential just in the way that work was done by the fall of a mass of water through a height. His absolute scale of temperature utilized the same notion of absolute measurement in the case of heat. His first public commitment to a system of absolute units for electrical measurement coincided both with his reading of Wilhelm Weber's contribution 'On the measurement of electric resistance according to an absolute standard' to Poggendorff's *Annalen* (1851) and with his own 'Dynamical theory of heat' series. In contrast to Weber's system founded on absolute measures of electromotive forces and intensities, Thomson's approach continued to be grounded on measurements of mechanical effect or work. His 1851 paper on the subject deployed Joule's mechanical equivalent to calculate the heat produced by the work done in an electrical circuit. Further applying Joule's earlier relationship of heat to current and resistance squared yielded an expression for resistance in absolute measure.

Production of knowledge in this manner, and the establishment of new functions for laboratory work, led to an increasing number of student volunteer assistants whose labour was divided into a range of skills from basic measurement techniques to involvement in the most advanced experimental practice. By the winter session of 1860 the number of such volunteers had risen to about twenty, a large proportion of whom were deployed on telegraphic work which from the mid-1850s formed an integral part of the laboratory. By 1857, after resistance to further territorial expansion had been overcome, Thomson gained official recognition for the 'physical laboratory' which was now centred in a converted ground-floor space beneath the classroom but which was expanded by the early 1860s by annexation of the redundant Blackstone examination room, also on the ground floor and beneath the apparatus room. Even the college tower, however, was secured for experiments where a long perpendicular drop was required. Constituting the first university physical laboratory in Britain, Thomson's college spaces were replaced by a new, purpose-built laboratory when the whole University of Glasgow transferred to its Gilmorehill site in 1870.

Laboratory concerns with measurement of physical properties of matter soon connected directly with a matter of national importance. Unforeseen retardation effects upon signalling in long submarine telegraph cables threatened the viability of several ambitious projects aimed at giving rapid communication, and hence physical unity, to the scattered British empire. Faraday's qualitative diagnosis of the problem as one of treating underwater cables as Leyden jars of vast capacity for electric charge inspired Thomson's mathematical analysis, using Fourier's techniques, in 1854. His resulting law of the squares showed the dependence of the retardation effect on resistance and inductive capacity and suggested optimum dimensions for the planned Atlantic telegraph. His approach facilitated a new demand for accurate measurement of electrical quantities and his physical laboratory became a major source for the supply of such data. Employing his 1851 method of determining resistances in absolute measure, for example, he drew attention to the great variation in the resistance of different specimens of supposedly pure copper wire manufactured by different firms for use in telegraph cables. The effects on the commercial transmission of signals over long distances would be to reduce profitability and perhaps even render the project unworkable. Accurate measurement of resistances during manufacture would introduce quality control, and hence greater commercial stability, into the highly volatile telegraph business.

Submarine telegraphy By 1856 Thomson had been made a director of the newly formed Atlantic Telegraph Company. He accompanied the first expedition in 1857 but the parting of the cable after only a few hundred miles had been laid halted the project. The following year he again joined the cable-laying ships, taking with him a new instrument, the marine mirror galvanometer, which he had recently invented and developed in Glasgow. The company's electrician, W. O. W. Whitehouse, remained ashore and Thomson took charge of the electrical testroom aboard HMS *Agamemnon*, monitoring the condition of the cable. Soon after completion, however, signals became more and more unreliable, culminating in the total failure of communication. Other long-distance cables of the period suffered similar fates. A joint Board of

Trade/Atlantic Telegraph Company inquiry published its findings in 1861. Given the scientific representation on the committee, it was not surprising that Whitehouse was portrayed as representing a discredited 'trial-and-error' approach and thus the principal scapegoat for telegraphic failures. The inquiry came down strongly in favour of Thomson's laboratory-centred methods, characterized by accurate measurement and absolute units.

Unable to attend the 1861 Manchester meeting of the British Association on account of a broken thigh sustained while curling on ice at Largs, Thomson had nevertheless been working vigorously behind the scenes to secure the appointment of a committee on standards of electrical resistance. Fleeming Jenkin, only recently introduced to Thomson, handled on his behalf the delicate negotiations among practical electricians and natural philosophers. The outcome was a committee, already heavily weighted towards scientific men, which eventually included most members of the North British energy group: Thomson, Jenkin, Joule, Balfour Stewart, and Maxwell. Throughout the 1860s Thomson played a leading role both in shaping the design of measuring apparatus and in promoting the adoption of an absolute system of physical measurement such that all the units (including resistance) of the system should bear a definite relation to the unit of work, 'the great connecting link between all physical measurements' (Smith and Wise, 687).

In 1865 the largest ship in the world, Isambard Kingdom Brunel's *Great Eastern*, had been converted for the laying of a new Atlantic cable. Although the cable parted in midocean, the *Great Eastern* laid another new cable the following season before recovering and completing the severed original. Thomson's direct involvement in the two expeditions brought him a knighthood. Meanwhile, he had secured his first joint telegraphic patent with Jenkin. By 1865 the partnership included the telegraph engineer Cromwell Varley. This pooling of patent property enabled the partners, after protracted legal negotiations, to win favourable financial terms from the Atlantic telegraph companies—£7000 initially to the partners, with a guaranteed £2500 per annum for ten years thereafter. Many other patents followed, including in 1867 that for Thomson's 'siphon recorder' which, by the automatic recording of telegraph signals on moving paper tape, served to minimize waste of time and improve economy of working. Thomson's involvement with ocean telegraphy continued: in 1869, for example, he and Varley were consulting electricians for the French Atlantic cable project. Thomson indeed later claimed that between 1866 and 1883 all signalling on ocean telegraphs was carried out with his instruments.

The instruments of navigation With the wealth generated by telegraph patents Thomson purchased the 126 ton schooner-rigged yacht *Lalla Rookh* in 1870, a few months after the death of his wife, Margaret. Laid up during the six-month Glasgow session, the *Lalla Rookh* served as Thomson's floating laboratory and home throughout the summer as she voyaged among the Western Isles or made much longer cruises to Lisbon (1871), Gibraltar (1872), and Madeira (1874 and 1877). His absences from more familiar workplaces prompted his friend G. G. Stokes to remark that it was 'not easy to say where to find a man who owns a yacht' (Smith and Wise, 736). However, Thomson was never idle. By the early 1870s he was testing both a new sounding apparatus (using pianoforte wire) and a new design of dry-card magnetic compass. The original sounding apparatus aided the cable ship *Hooper* in the laying of the Brazilian cable in 1873. As the *Hooper* lay at Madeira for sixteen days, Thomson made the acquaintance of the Blandy family, who lived on the island; he returned aboard the *Lalla Rookh* a year later and proposed to Frances Anna Blandy (c.1838–1916), who became his second wife in June 1874. There were no children from either of his marriages. During a voyage to North America in 1876 aboard the Cunard liner *Russia*, Thomson carried out extensive trials with both sounding machine and compass for navigational purposes. Patents quickly followed and soon he was marketing sounder and compass to the prestigious mail-liner companies of the empire, including Cunard, White Star, P. & O., and British India. Thanks to the vigorous support of Jacky Fisher (later first sea lord) the Admiralty in 1889 adopted as its standard compass Thomson's design which retained its naval pre-eminence until the Admiralty began switching to liquid compasses in the 1900s.

Although the laboratory and the *Lalla Rookh* remained the principal sites for invention, the expansion into manufacturing of telegraphic and navigational instruments required the construction of a separate factory. Thomson's association with the Glasgow instrument maker James White dated from about 1854 and had developed especially during the peak of telegraphic work in the 1860s. By the 1880s the business had been transformed into a large-scale instrument factory, effectively under Thomson's control and devoted to the production of his instruments. By 1900 the firm took the formal title of Kelvin and James White Ltd, with a rigorous division of labour among its 400-strong labour force from drawing office to polishing shop. The firm typically produced some 400 compasses per annum in the 1890s. With the growth of electric lighting and power in the 1880s, the firm added electrical measuring instruments to its production. Thomson, meanwhile, became directly involved in numerous electrical projects which ranged from electric traction for trams and trains to the production of hydroelectric power from Niagara and in the Scottish highlands (especially for the large-scale smelting of aluminium at Foyers by Loch Ness). By the end of his life he had a total of some seventy patents to his credit, either separately or jointly with his business partners.

Politics and peerage A lifelong Liberal in politics, Thomson split with the Liberal Party at the time of Gladstone's first Home Rule Bill (1886). As president of the West of Scotland Liberal Unionist Association between 1886 and 1892, he therefore took an active role in opposing the moves for an Irish parliament. He firmly believed that liberal values of free trade, equality before the law, and freedom of religion were best preserved within a United Kingdom of Great Britain and Ireland and that local rule was a sure guarantee of sectarian strife, fruitless factionalism among parties, and the stifling of free commerce under protectionist legislation. Through his friendship with Liberal Unionist aristocrats such as Lord Hartington (eighth duke of Devonshire from 1891) and the duke of Argyll, Thomson was well placed for elevation to the peerage in 1892, the first scientist to be thus honoured. With maternal connections to Kelvin Grove and with the university's location adjacent to the River Kelvin since 1870, it was appropriate that William Thomson should have become Baron Kelvin of Largs. Begun in the 1870s, his country seat, Netherhall, near Largs, provided the new peer with a permanent residence, although in his later years he and his wife would frequently travel to their London home at 15 Eaton Place.

The very high level of national and international credibility which Lord Kelvin had built up through his 53-year reign as Glasgow professor meant that he wielded immense scientific authority, but for the new generation, his views looked increasingly anachronistic. As younger groups of physicists grew more enthusiastic about Maxwell's electromagnetic theory of light, for instance, so Kelvin's resistance to Maxwellian approaches and his own commitment to elastic-solid models made him appear increasingly conservative. Likewise, his reluctance to abandon his age-of-the-earth estimates (based on secular cooling of an originally molten earth) presented advocates of radioactivity (based on the generation of heat by radioactive elements distributed in the earth's crust) with a serious obstacle to easy acceptance of the new views. Even his representation of his dry-card compass as a major Admiralty reform came to be seen as a barrier to the introduction of liquid compasses in the 1900s.

During his life, Lord Kelvin received some twenty-one honorary doctorates from universities around the world (including Princeton, Yale, Toronto, and Heidelberg). He was a member or honorary member of nearly ninety learned societies and academies. Elected fellow of the Royal Society in 1851, he was awarded its Copley medal in 1883 and served as its president from 1890 until 1895. He was also president of the British Association in 1871 and president of the Society of Telegraph Engineers in 1874. In 1881 he was made commander of the French Légion d'honneur, and he became a grand officer eight years later. He was made knight of the Prussian order of merit in 1884. He served on Admiralty committees in 1871 (for designs of ships of war) and in 1904–5 (for designs of the new dreadnought battleships and battle cruisers). He was appointed to the Order of Merit and was sworn of the privy council in 1902. Lord Kelvin retired from the Glasgow chair in 1899, but became chancellor of the university in 1904 and continued working right up to his death, from a severe chill, at Netherhall on 17 December 1907. His funeral and burial took place in Westminster Abbey two days before Christmas. CROSBIE SMITH

Sources C. Smith and M. N. Wise, *Energy and empire: a biographical study of Lord Kelvin* (1989) · E. King, *Lord Kelvin's early home* (1909) · S. P. Thompson, *The life of William Thomson, Baron Kelvin of Largs*, 2 vols. (1910) · J. L. [J. Larmor], *PRS*, 81A (1908), iii–lxxvi · A. Grey, *Lord Kelvin: an account of his scientific life and work* (1909) · A. G. King, *Kelvin the man* (1925) · C. Smith, '"Nowhere but in a great town": William Thomson's spiral of classroom credibility', *Making space for science*, ed. C. Smith and J. Agar (1998), 118–46 · W. Thomson, *Mathematical and physical papers*, 6 vols. (1882–1911) · *DNB*

Archives CUL, corresp. and papers · Mitchell L., Glas., Glasgow City Archives, letters relating to Atlantic telegraph cable; testamentary papers · NL Scot., corresp. with instrument makers; letters and notes to scientific-instrument makers · NMM, letters and reports · NRA Scotland, priv. coll., corresp. relating to laboratory supplies · Royal Institution of Great Britain, London, letters to Royal Institution · U. Glas., Archives and Business Records Centre, business papers relating to patent compass · U. Glas. L., corresp. and papers; lecture notes | Balliol Oxf., letters to Sir John Conroy · CUL, letters to his sister, Elizabeth King · CUL, corresp. with James Clerk Maxwell · ICL, letters to Silvanus Thompson · Inst. EE, letter to Oliver Heaviside · Inst. EE, letter to Sir William Henry Preece · MHS Oxf., corresp. with Frederick J. J. Smith · Mitchell L., Glas., Glasgow City Archives, corresp with Walter Crum and the Crum family · NL Scot., letters to Bottomley and Barlow families · PRO, corresp. with Balfour Stewart, BJ1 · RS, letters to Sir Arthur Schuster · Trinity Cam., scientific corresp. with Sir Joseph John Thomson · U. Aberdeen L., letters to David Thompson · U. Glas., Archives and Business Records Centre, corresp. with David Reid · U. St Andr. L., letters to James David Forbes · UCL, letters to Sir Oliver Lodge | SOUND Sci. Mus.

Likenesses E. King, pencil drawing, 1840, NPG · L. C. Dickinson, oils, 1869, Peterhouse, Cambridge [see illus.] · E. T. King, oils, 1886–7, NPG · H. von Herkomer, oils, 1891, U. Glas. · A. M. Shannan, bronze bust, 1896, Scot. NPG · W. Q. Orchardson, oils, exh. RA 1899, RS · Elliott & Fry, photograph, 1900, NPG · W. W. Ouless, oils, exh. RA 1902, Clockmakers' Company, London · W. Rothestein, pastel drawing, 1904, Scot. NPG · statue, 1910, Botanical Gardens, Belfast · Annan & Sons, photogravure photograph (after photograph by Elliott & Fry), NPG · Berlin Photographic Co., photogravure photograph, NPG · Dickinson, photogravure photograph, NPG · W. & D. Downey, woodburytype photograph, NPG; repro. in W. Downey and D. Downey, *The cabinet portrait gallery*, 3 (1892) · H. Furniss, pen-and-ink sketch for a caricature, NPG · M. M. Giles, wax medallion, NPG · E. T. King, oils, Scot. NPG · E. King & A. G. King, sketch, NPG · E. G. Lewis, oils, Inst. EE · London Stereoscopic Co., photographs, NPG · W. Q. Richardson, charcoal drawing, Scot. NPG · Spy [L. Ward], watercolour study for a caricature, NPG; repro. in *VF* (29 April 1897) · medallion on decorative frieze, School of Science and Art, Stroud · statue, Kelvingrove Park, Glasgow · woodburytype photograph, NPG

Wealth at death £128,925 0s. 7d.: confirmation, 10 April 1908, *CCI*

Thomson, Sir William (1843–1909), surgeon, born at Downpatrick, co. Down, Ireland, on 29 June 1843, was the youngest son (in a family of three sons and two daughters) of William Thomson, civil servant, of Lanark, Scotland, and his wife, Margaret, daughter of Thomas Patterson of Monklands, Lanarkshire. His father died in Thomson's infancy, and his mother married Mr McDougal, proprietor of the *Galway Express*. As a youth Thomson worked in the newspaper's editorial office, and in 1864, without giving up his journalistic work, he entered Queen's College, Galway, a constituent college of the Queen's University. He graduated BA in 1867 and obtained a post on the *Daily Express*, in Dublin, where he also attended the Carmichael school of medicine. He graduated MD and MCh (they were primary degrees) in the Queen's University in 1872 and became house surgeon in the Richmond Hospital, where in the following year he was appointed to the staff. He lectured in anatomy in the Carmichael school, and in 1874 he passed the examination for FRCSI. A year later he was appointed examiner in anatomy and surgery and in due course he became secretary to the court of examiners in the Royal College of Surgeons in Ireland. On 27 June 1878 Thomson married Margaret Dalrymple, younger daughter of Abraham Stoker, chief clerk in the office of the chief secretary at Dublin Castle, and sister of Sir William Thornley Stoker, first baronet (1845–1912), surgeon, and of Bram Stoker, author of *Dracula*. They had a son and a daughter; the former served as a captain in the Royal Army Medical Corps.

Thomson accepted an examinership in surgery in the Queen's University in 1879 and was granted an MA *honoris causa* in 1881. The Queen's successor, the Royal University of Ireland, appointed him to its senate and for some years he represented the university in the General Medical Council. From 1896 to 1906 he was the Irish medical profession's direct representative on the GMC. A contemporary described Thomson as a courteous gentleman, much esteemed by his friends and patients. He was a skilled surgeon and in 1882 he ligatured the innominate artery, an operative feat which he described in the *British Medical Journal*. He was the first in Ireland to remove the prostate gland by the technique of enucleation.

Thomson was at his best as an organizer. He played an important part in the reorganization of the school of the Royal College of Surgeons in Ireland during the 1880s and in the organization of the Royal Academy of Medicine in Ireland, formed in 1882 by the amalgamation of several old societies. He became the new body's general secretary and put his journalistic experience to good advantage when appointed editor of its *Transactions*. He edited, too, Christopher Fleming's *Clinical Record of Injuries and Diseases of the Genito-Urinary Organs* (1877), and John Hatch Power's *Surgical Anatomy of the Arteries* (1881). He was the *British Medical Journal's* Dublin correspondent. His own publications included clinical reports and articles on abdominal surgery. His paper, 'Some surprises and mistakes', appeared in the *Transactions of the Royal Academy of Medicine in Ireland* in 1896–7. His most notable publication was an exhaustive and judicious report on the poor-law medical service of Ireland, undertaken in 1891 at the request of Ernest Hart, editor of the *British Medical Journal*.

From 1896 to 1898 Thomson was president of the Royal College of Surgeons in Ireland, and in 1897 he was knighted. In December 1899 he was invited by Lord Iveagh to organize a field hospital for service in South Africa. In February 1900 he accompanied Lord Roberts on his march to Pretoria. He proved his powers of rapid organization by establishing, immediately on entering the city, a hospital of 600 beds in the Palace of Justice, and it was largely due to Thomson and his colleagues that Pretoria escaped a disastrous outbreak of enteric fever. While in South Africa, Thomson was appointed surgeon-in-ordinary to Queen

Victoria in Ireland, and in 1901 he became honorary surgeon to Edward VII. For his services in the Second South African War he was mentioned in dispatches and received the queen's medal with three clasps. He was also made CB in 1900. From 1895 to 1902 he was surgeon to the lord lieutenant, Earl Cadogan. He was from 1906 to his death inspector of anatomy for Ireland.

Thomson was a polished speaker and ready debater. In 1901 he delivered the address in surgery at the annual meeting of the British Medical Association held at Cheltenham, choosing as his subject 'Some surgical lessons from the campaign in South Africa' (*BMJ*, 3 Aug 1901, 265–70).

Thomson died after a period of ill health owing to chronic nephritis with cardiac complications, at his residence, 54 St Stephen's Green, Dublin, on 13 November 1909, and was buried in Mount Jerome cemetery. He left his possessions to Lady Thomson, trusting her to dispose of them between their children according to his wishes.

R. J. ROWLETTE, rev. J. B. LYONS

Sources C. A. Cameron, *History of the Royal College of Surgeons in Ireland*, 2nd edn (1916) · *Daily Express* [Dublin] (15 Nov 1909) · *The Lancet* (20 Nov 1909) · *BMJ* (20 Nov 1909), 1502–3 · *Dublin Journal of Medical Science*, 129 (1910), 78–80 · WWW
Likenesses J. S. M. Carré, commemorative bas-relief, Beaumont Hospital, Dublin
Wealth at death £3291 5s. 3d.: probate, 7 Jan 1910, *CGPLA Ire.*

Thomson, William George (1865–1942), tapestry historian, was born on 7 February 1865 at Roman Camp Gatehouse, Fochabers, Moray, Scotland, youngest of four children of James Thomson (*d.* 1875/6), head gamekeeper to the duke of Richmond at Gordon Castle, and Ellen (*b.* 1829/30), daughter of Alexander Burnett, millwright, and his wife, Margaret. Crippled by poliomyelitis at the age of three, Thomson thereafter walked with a crutch. He later told his son that his disability had led to his being mistaken in Paris for Toulouse-Lautrec, although there was no facial resemblance between the two men, judging from Thomson's portrait painted in 1886 by James Hector, a fellow student at Gray's Art School, part of Robert Gordon's College, Aberdeen. Thomson trained as an artist, becoming a national scholar (1891–3) in South Kensington, London, at the National Art Training School (later named the Royal College of Art); he also studied briefly in France and Spain. He obtained work as examiner in art for the Board of Education (1894–1912), with occasional commissions from the South Kensington Museum for paintings of textiles (1893–1918). Fascinated by the tapestries he saw in the course of his work, Thomson began to study them, writing articles in the *Art Workers' Quarterly* from 1902, illustrated from his watercolours. In 1906 his monumental *History of Tapestry* was published.

W. G. Thomson was a pioneer both as a writer in English about tapestry and as an archival researcher on tapestry woven in England. When the 1930 revised edition of his book appeared, a reviewer in the *New York Times* commented: 'most of the pages are sewn, thick as a porcupine's darts, with documentation' (15 Nov 1931). This standard work was prepared for a third edition in 1973 by

Thomson's son. The seminal section on English tapestry was reworked by Thomson into six articles which were published in the *Art Journal* in 1911–12, and again for his second ground-breaking book, *Tapestry Weaving in England* (1914). In his *History of Tapestry* Thomson acknowledged the assistance of Elizabeth Hannah Tann (1872–1942), teacher of needlework, whom he was later to marry. The *Art Workers' Quarterly* of April 1906 noted a further collaboration, describing 'A very successful Exhibition of Art Work by Miss Elizabeth H. Tann, Miss Edith M. Tann, and their pupils', with 'panels of stained cloth and woven tapestry … lent by W. G. Thomson' (p. 95). Elizabeth Tann and Thomson also co-operated with Louise Chart, daughter of the superintendent of works at Hampton Court Palace, in setting up, about 1910, a tapestry repair workshop in her father's house in Palace Yard, a business which later moved to Surbiton.

In 1911 the marquess of Bute appointed Thomson to establish and direct a tapestry workshop at Corstorphine near Edinburgh, later the famous Dovecot Studios. Financially secure at last, William and Elizabeth married at Corstorphine on 20 April 1912; their only surviving child, Francis, was born in 1914. But the First World War led to the closure of the workshop in 1916, half-way through *The Lord of the Hunt*, the sole tapestry to bear the mark of W. G. Thomson. Although weaving recommenced in 1919 Thomson did not rejoin. He was disheartened by disagreements with the Dovecot's artist Skeoch Cumming and by the deaths in the war of the two most experienced weavers. Moreover, he had expectations of employment from Sir George Frampton's War Memorial Tapestry Guild, which sought to establish a workshop for disabled servicemen at Knole in Kent. This project, however, was abandoned in the early 1920s.

Rejecting proposals for emigration from his brother James, a banker in Chicago, Thomson remained in England, living in or near London on consultancies engendered by his publications. In the 1920s he contributed extensively to *Country Life*, his pieces including saleroom articles under the pseudonym D. Van de Goote. He also wrote on tapestry and carpets for *Apollo* and for Macquoid's *Dictionary of English Furniture*. Revision of his first book involved much labour for little profit. From 1927, in failing health, Thomson became dependent on charity from the Royal Literary Fund and the Royal Academy's Cooke Fund, with a civil-list pension granted in 1933. He died of heart failure at his home, 23 Ardingley Drive, Goring by Sea, Sussex, on 13 February 1942, and was buried on 19 February in Durrington cemetery, Worthing, followed five weeks later by his wife, who died on 23 March 1942.   WENDY HEFFORD

Sources F. P. Thomson, *Tapestry: mirror of history* (1980), 159–70 · civil-list pension applications, recommendations and reports, 1931–3, PRO, Premier 5/75 · V&A NAL, Thomson papers · M. Hodge, 'A history of the Dovecot Studios', *Master weavers: tapestry from the Dovecot Studios, 1912–1980* (1980), 39 [exhibition catalogue, Edinburgh International Festival, 15 Aug – 14 Sept 1980] · W. G. Thomson, preface, *A history of tapestry from the earliest times until the present day* (1906); rev. edn (1930) [prefaces to both edns and see also p. 500 of 1930 edn] · 'An exhibition of art work', *Art Workers' Quarterly*

(April 1906), 95 · E. A. Jewell, review, *New York Times Book Review* (15 Nov 1931) · Robert Gordon's College in Aberdeen, minutes and proceedings of the board of governors, Aberdeen, 1886–92 · b. cert. · d. cert.

Archives NRA, priv. coll., Bute archive on the establishment of Dovecot studios · PRO, civil list papers, Premier 5/75 · V&A, Francis P. Thomson MSS · Edinburgh, daybooks of Dovecot Studios

Likenesses J. Hector, watercolour?, 1886, Aberdeen Art Gallery · photograph, repro. in Thomson, *Tapestry*, 159

Wealth at death only regular income from 1927 was from charities

Thorburn, Grant [*pseud.* Lawrie Todd] (1773–1863), entrepreneur and author, was born at West Houses, near Dalkeith, Edinburghshire, on 18 February 1773, the son of Elizabeth Fairley (*d.* 1776) and James Thorburn, a nailmaker. His mother died when he was three years old and his subsequent neglect left him physically undersized. In 1792 he joined the Friends of the People, a group committed to reforming parliament by more equal representation, and in the winter of 1793, along with seventeen others, was held in Edinburgh as 'a suspicious person', but dismissed. In 1794 he emigrated to New York, where at first he worked at the nailmaking trade. In 1796 he and his brother started a hardware business, which presently became Thorburn's sole concern. In June 1797 he married Rebecca Sickles, with whom he had a son. Rebecca died in 1800, and in 1801 Thorburn married Hannah Wortemby (*d.* 1852). By this year the introduction of cut-nails forced him to abandon his trade and he opened a grocery store which he stocked with flowering plants. From this he developed a seed business and in 1812 issued the first seed catalogue in America, *The Gentleman and Gardener's Kalender for the Middle States of North America*. Although faced with such setbacks as fire, crop failure and imprisonment for debt, he re-established his business in 1816, and thereafter it prospered.

From his youth Thorburn believed that he was under the care of a special providence, and his 'self-help' autobiography, *Forty years' residence in America, or, The doctrine of a particular providence exemplified in the life of Grant Thorburn* (1834), while it is meant to justify this theory, reveals that he was an extraordinarily resilient character whose unflagging optimistic outlook turned many of his failures into successes.

Thorburn first became widely known as the model for the hero of John Galt's *Lawrie Todd, or, The Settlers in the Woods* (1830). Now financially independent, Thorburn wrote articles and sketches for newspapers and magazines. Noted for his energy, originality, candour, and wide interests, many of these are humorous and 'folksy' pieces on current affairs. Some give accounts of his meetings with famous radicals such as Thomas Muir (with whom he was imprisoned in Edinburgh) and Thomas Paine, while others recount his experiences in the wake of the yellow fever outbreak in New York in 1798. Among the most interesting works of this dedicated republican is his *Men and manners in Britain, or, A bone to gnaw for the trollopes, fiddlers, & c., being notes from a journal on sea and land, 1833–4* (1835), a caustic response to Frances Trollope's *Domestic Manners of*

Grant Thorburn (1773–1863), by G. Freeman, c.1846 (after Joseph Napoleon Gimbrede)

the Americans (1832), in which he pronounces on the savagery of English history, the servility of English shopkeepers, and the profound ignorance of the British about America, but the work is also invaluable for Thorburn's more serious observations of British culture in that period, in particular his sense of social and cultural change in his native Scotland. His other works include *Fifty Years' Reminiscences of New York* (1845), *Sketches from the Note-Book of Lawrie Todd* (1847), *Lawrie Todd's Hints to Merchants, Married Men, and Bachelors* (1847), *Notes on Virginia, with a Chapter on Puritans, Witches and Friends* (1848), and *Lawrie Todd, Life and Writings of Grant Thorburn* (1852). His second wife died in 1852, and in 1853 he married Maria, with whom he moved from New York to Winsted, Connecticut, and then to New Haven, where he died on 21 January 1863. He was buried in New Haven. CATHERINE KERRIGAN

Sources DAB · G. Thorburn, *Forty years' residence in America* (1834) · G. Thorburn, *Men and manners in Britain* (1835) · *New York Herald* (25 Jan 1863) · W. Barrett [J. A. Scoville], *Old merchants of New York city*, 5 vols. (1863–70) · *Fraser's Magazine*, 7 (1833), 668–81 · review, *The Athenaeum* (14 Dec 1833), 847–8 · Irving, *Scots.* · Allibone, *Dict.* · *Literary Gazette* (14 Dec 1833), 787
Likenesses photograph, 1833, repro. in *Fraser's Magazine* · G. Freeman, engraving, c.1846 (after J. N. Gimbrede), NPG [*see illus.*] · line print, NPG · photograph (aged seventy-three), repro. in Thorburn, *Forty years' residence*
Wealth at death substantial: *DAB*; Thorburn, *Forty years' residence*

Thorburn, Robert (1818–1885), miniature painter, was born at Dumfries on 10 March 1818, the son of a tradesman. He received his early education at Dumfries high school, where he developed a love of art. At fifteen he was sent to Edinburgh to study under Sir William Allan at the drawing academy of the Royal Institute of Scotland; he made rapid progress and won two first prizes. He exhibited at the Royal Scottish Academy between 1835 and 1856, and was made an honorary member in 1857; a self-portrait, now very badly bituminized, is in the academy's collection. As a native of Dumfries he enjoyed the special patronage of the duke of Buccleuch. About 1836 he went to London and entered the Royal Academy Schools. He exhibited at the Royal Academy between 1837 and 1884, and was elected an associate in 1848. On 16 October 1846, in Edinburgh, he married Elizabeth Robertson.

On 23 February 1844 Queen Victoria wrote of Thorburn in her journal: 'He is a young Scotchman, of great talent, who studied 2 winters in Italy, & has painted some splendid miniatures, with such depth of colouring & such power, as I have never before seen in a miniature' (D. Millar, 886). In that year he painted several important miniatures for the queen and Prince Albert; she described one of herself, given to her by the prince, as 'so like & so beautiful' (ibid.). Also in 1844 Thorburn was paid £123 15s. for five watercolour sketches, including portraits of Albert Edward, prince of Wales; Ernest II, duke of Saxe-Coburg and Gotha; and Duke Ernest of Württemberg (Royal Collection). Ernest II was drawn during a visit between 20 November and 17 December 1844, when his wife also sat to Thorburn for a miniature. The sketch of the duke of Württemberg formed the basis for the life-sized half-length portrait painted for the 1844 room at Buckingham Palace. A miniature of Prince Albert in full armour, painted by Thorburn in 1843 (Royal Collection), was said to be the queen's favourite. In the Royal Academy exhibition of 1848 Thorburn exhibited a portrait of her with Princess Helena and Prince Alfred that had been painted 'by command of the Queen' (Graves, *RA exhibitors*, 378).

Thorburn's success as a miniature painter was soon secured, and for many years he shared the patronage of fashionable society with Sir William Charles Ross. Foster's *British Miniature Painters* contains a reproduction of a self-portrait miniature and a list of Thorburn's principal sitters, comprising most of the beautiful women of the time (pp. 95–7); one of his most widely known portraits is that of Louise, duchess of Manchester (c.1853; priv. coll.). His carefully finished miniatures were larger than is usual, showing more of the figure and often accompanied by a landscape background. They were painted on large pieces of ivory, sometimes on pieces joined together, and are now subject to cracking. They were very much admired at the time of their production, and at the Paris Exposition Universelle in 1855 Thorburn was awarded a gold medal. When photography began to supersede miniature painting he took to painting in oils more frequently; in later years he exhibited portraits, including crayon drawings, and subject pictures, often of a religious nature, at the Royal Academy, with moderate success. Examples of his work are in the Royal Collection, the Scottish National

Portrait Gallery, Edinburgh, and the National Gallery of Scotland, Edinburgh.

Thorburn died at Tunbridge Wells, Kent, on 2 November 1885, having outlived the great reputation of his earlier years, and was survived by his wife. For probate his address was given as Winkston, Peeblesshire, sometime of Forest Field, Kelso; he gave the latter address when he exhibited at the Royal Academy in 1879. In 1884, the last year in which he exhibited at the academy, his address was 17 Cumberland Walk, Tunbridge Wells, where his son Archibald was living when he was nominated executor of his will; another son, John, was living in London. Archibald Thorburn (1860–1935) was a wildlife artist, well known for his paintings of birds.

L. H. CUST, *rev.* ARIANNE BURNETTE

Sources D. Millar, *The Victorian watercolours and drawings in the collection of her majesty the queen*, 2 (1995) · Graves, *RA exhibitors*, vol. 7 · C. B. de Laperriere, ed., *The Royal Scottish Academy exhibitors, 1826–1990*, 4 vols. (1991), vol. 2 · J. J. Foster, *British miniature painters and their works* (1898) · O. Millar, *The Victorian pictures in the collection of her majesty the queen*, 2 vols. (1992) · P. J. M. McEwan, *Dictionary of Scottish art and architecture* (1994) · J. Halsby and P. Harris, *The dictionary of Scottish painters, 1600–1960* (1990) · D. Foskett, *Miniatures: dictionary and guide* (1987) · artist's boxes, Courtauld Inst., Witt Library · artists' boxes, NPG, Heinz Archive and Library · private information (2004) [D. Thomson] · *DNB* · *CGPLA Eng. & Wales* (1886) · *IGI*
Likenesses Elliott & Fry, photograph, carte-de-visite, NPG · R. Thorburn, self-portrait, Royal Scot. Acad. · engraving (after R. Thorburn), repro. in Foster, *British miniature painters*
Wealth at death no value given: confirmation, 18 Feb 1886, *CGPLA Eng. & Wales*

Thorburn, Robert Forrester (1821–1898), merchant, the only son of George Thorburn (*c.*1795–1871), a tea merchant, and Anne, *née* Forrester, was born at 5 Fyfe Place, Leith, on 13 April 1821. Nothing is known of his education but in February 1847 he was listed as a clerk in Canton (Guangzhou), employed by Maclean, Dearie & Co., and he spent the best part of the next fifty years on the China coast. From 1850 he worked in Shanghai for Turner & Co., but left them at the end of December 1860. On 11 April 1861, probably on his return from a trip to Britain, he began, with the Revd W. R. Beach, the Revd Samuel W. Bonney, and Dr W. Dickson, what was then a singular and possibly dangerous overland trip from Canton to Hankou. The travellers intended to take advantage of the new treaty, which afforded the right to travel in the Chinese interior, and were keen to explore the possibilities of the route as a possible conduit for the tea trade. Canton itself was still under British occupation, and more than once the travellers were met by crowds shouting *Sha* ('kill'), but on the whole the 41-day journey was smooth and the crowds just intensely curious. Bonney rhapsodized about the potential for railway development along the route, but Thorburn left no record of his impressions, and instead of going on with the missionaries to Nanking (Nanjing), then controlled by the Taiping insurgents, he stayed briefly in the newly opened treaty port of Hankou.

In 1878, after several years as an independent merchant in Shanghai, Thorburn was appointed secretary of the Shanghai municipal council (SMC). The climax of his quiet but firm custodianship of the council was the jubilee celebration in November 1893, which marked the fiftieth anniversary of the settlement. From its shaky start in 1843 the British-dominated settlement had grown to encompass the heart of the growing metropolis of Shanghai. 'In what region of the earth is not Shanghai known?' asked the banners strung across the settlement's streets during the celebration and, more menacingly, 'Shanghai guards its own' (*Jubilee of Shanghai*, 44). The secretary headed the administration that did this guarding for the smug settler oligarchy, which in turn provided the elected councillors and which made immense fortunes from land speculation in and around the international settlement. Thorburn was unusual among long-term residents in not profiting so well out of land, and the secretaryship might well have been an act of charity for the owner of an ailing merchant house.

In 1897 Thorburn resigned owing to ill health, on a generous pension of £500 per annum. He returned to his native Leith, where he died of chronic diarrhoea at his home, 12 Hermitage Place, on 17 September 1898, leaving his estate to his four unmarried sisters. He was buried in South Leith parish churchyard on 22 September. A memorial stained-glass window was ordered from Britain by the SMC and placed in the south aisle of Holy Trinity Cathedral, Shanghai.

Thorburn's successor, J. O. P. Bland, was a more bellicose and self-conscious agent of British imperialism in China, but such forward policies were either unsuccessful—China coast lobbyists (the 'China hands') failed to secure a Yangtze (Yangzi) protectorate—or else they provoked violent responses from the Chinese population of Shanghai, such as the 1905 'Mixed Court riot'. Shanghai's rise to international prominence was rooted in the previous decades of basic stability after the turmoil of the Taiping uprising (1850–65). Under the quiet handling of Alex Thorburn, as he was familiarly known, the SMC, the principal agency of British settler power in China, had grown greatly year by year in strength, capability, and ambition.

ROBERT BICKERS

Sources *Annual Report* [Shanghai municipal council] (1878–99) · C. V. R. Bonney, ed., *A legacy of historical gleanings*, 2nd edn, 2 (1875) · 'X', 'Account of an overland trip from Canton to Hankow', *North China Herald* (15 June 1861), 95 · 'X', 'Account of an overland trip from Canton to Hankow', *North China Herald* (22 June 1861), 98–9 · W. Dickson, 'Narrative of an overland trip, through Hunan, from Canton to Hankow', *Journal of the North China Branch of the Royal Asiatic Society*, new ser., 1 (1864), 159–73 · *The jubilee of Shanghai, 1843–1893: Shanghai, past and present, and a full account of the proceedings on the 17th and 18th November 1893, with photograph* (1893) · R. F. Thorburn, will, NA Scot., SC70/4/312, 136–41 · *Post Office annual directory of Edinburgh and Leith* (1822–56) · probate file, PRO, FO 917/8112 · *An Anglo-Chinese calendar for the year 1847* (1847) · *Shanghai almanac and miscellany* (1854) · *Shanghai almanac and miscellany* (1856) · *The chronicle and directory for China, Japan, and the Philippines for the year 1877* (1877) · d. certs [George Thorburn; Robert Forrester Thorburn] · H. Mui and L. H. Mui, eds., *William Melrose in China 1845–1855: the letters of a Scottish tea merchant* (1973) · Toronto University, Rare Books Library, Bland MSS · parish register (birth and baptisms), South Leith, 13 April 1821 · parish register (birth and baptisms), South Leith, 1 May 1821

Thoresby, John (*d.* 1373), archbishop of York, came of a family that took its name from the Lincolnshire village of North Thoresby, in Lindsey. Styled *magister* by 1326, he had graduated as bachelor of canon law at Oxford by 1341, having served between 1326 and 1334 as chaplain and attorney to William Melton, archbishop of York (*d.* 1340), who secured for him a position in chancery. During the 1330s and early 1340s Thoresby was frequently employed as a diplomat, on missions to France and the papal curia. Keeper of the privy seal between July 1345 and September 1347, he accompanied Edward III on his French campaigns of those years; and on 16 June 1349 he was promoted to the chancellorship. His civil service income was supplemented by the revenue from a total of twenty-one benefices, all no more than profitable sinecures. Crown service prevented him from making much impact on his first two dioceses, St David's (1347–9) and Worcester (1350–52); and when Edward III advanced Thoresby to the see of York in 1352 he ensured that his two most trusted ministers were in control of the English church—Simon Islip (*d.* 1366), keeper of the regency government's seal in 1346 and keeper of the privy seal after Thoresby, had been appointed archbishop of Canterbury in 1349. The bull licensing Thoresby's translation to York was issued by the pope on 17 November 1352, and the temporalities were restored on 8 February 1353, though he was not enthroned until 8 September 1354. As archbishop Thoresby continued to further crown interests, for instance, ordering prayers of thanksgiving throughout his diocese in 1356 for the victory of Poitiers, and zealously enforcing collections of clerical tenths which helped to finance Edward III's wars.

On 27 November 1356 Thoresby resigned as chancellor. The energy he subsequently devoted to the administration of his diocese, in which he would be continually in residence, suggests that he welcomed the opportunity to give exclusive priority for the first time in his life to diocesan administration. Thoresby's friendship with Islip and the diplomatic skills he had acquired in government service were applied to the ending of the long-standing dispute between the archbishops of Canterbury and York over the right to bear the primatial cross in each other's province. In 1353 it was agreed that each archbishop could bear his cross in the province of the other. Thoresby also devoted the wealth he had amassed as a crown servant and ecclesiastical careerist to building projects in his cathedral. He laid the foundations of the new choir in York Minster in 1360, making an immediate donation of 100 marks and contributing £200 a year until his death, and he also built the lady chapel in the east end of the cathedral.

Thoresby's qualities as an experienced government official and administrator made him realistic in his attempts to discipline layfolk and to cater for their social and moral welfare. His first pastoral initiative was to restore the morale of the clergy in a diocese suffering from the after-effects of the black death of 1348–9. Morale was low among the religious communities where mortality rates were high; not only did he undertake visitations of monasteries in the diocese in 1352–3, but he also issued commissions of inquiry into the condition of certain houses. Mortality rates were also high among parish priests; the consequent shortage of parochial incumbents was exacerbated by the way in which many parish priests deserted their parishes to profit from the increasing demand for chantry priests to celebrate for the souls of victims of plague. Thoresby responded by ordaining more priests, usually officiating at ordination services himself. In 1361 and 1362 he issued pastoral mandates enforcing residence in the chapter at York and in the archdeaconries in the diocese. Among the constitutions he issued in September 1367, and had approved before the northern convocation, was legislation echoing the Statute of Labourers of 1350, which fixed wages of stipendiary chaplains at 6 marks and forbade clergy to leave their parishes to work in chantries. He also issued instructions forbidding clergy to depute the administration of any sacraments to laymen, something that had occurred during plague years when laymen had felt obliged to hear confession and celebrate mass for want of a priest.

Thoresby's most important pastoral reform was his plan to improve the religious instruction of the laity, embodied in a Latin injunction recorded in the archbishop's register on 25 November 1357. After prefatory remarks on the ignorance of the laity and the need for instruction in the vernacular, Thoresby suggests the items on which teaching is needed: the articles of faith, the commandments, the works of mercy, the cardinal virtues, the sacraments, and the deadly sins. So that the clergy have no doubt as to what information should be given on these matters, a brief exposition of each in turn is given. The injunction concludes with an exhortation to the clergy to convey this information and to examine their parishioners on their knowledge of it during confession, and with a promise to the laity of forty days' indulgence for those whose knowledge and practice of the material is adequate. This programme of instruction (in which there is envisaged a significant extension of the scope of the sacrament of penance by thus including an examination of penitents' religious knowledge) was modelled on that published in 1281 by Archbishop John Pecham of Canterbury (*d.* 1292), which was itself issued in response to the demands of the Lateran Council of 1215, which made annual confession to the parish priest compulsory.

Thoresby's injunction, and the instructions accompanying it, are preceded in his register by an expanded vernacular version of the teaching, which refers to Thoresby's ordinance and to his indulgence. The author of this English text, which was made at Thoresby's behest, was John Gaytryge, a Benedictine monk of St Mary's Abbey, York, who stayed in Thoresby's household in December 1356. Presented in rough, alliterative verse to facilitate memorization, this so-called *Lay Folk's Catechism* is a penitential handbook whose originality lies in its simplicity and conciseness. Its appeal is shown by its wide circulation. There are twenty-six surviving manuscripts, many reworked with interpolated texts; and it gained considerable currency outside the diocese. Archbishop Islip seems to have followed Thoresby's example, for in 1361 he provided a *Brevis libellus* (which does not survive) on the seven deadly sins and ten commandments for the use of the clergy of his province.

In such legislation as the 1357 injunction, and in *The Lay Folk's Catechism*, Thoresby tried to instil in parishioners a sense of community, with the parish church as the focus for order and stability of life. His legislation expresses concern over the high levels of violence among clergy and laity in a society where vendettas were pursued. He envisaged that during annual confession priests would discover if parishioners harboured hostile attitudes towards their neighbours, and then impose penances whose performance would reconcile them to their communities. Thoresby may also have been behind such other vernacular pastoral initiatives as the religious plays. The York Corpus Christi cycle of forty-eight biblical plays was first performed by the York craft guilds on the feast of Corpus Christi around the time of the publication of *The Lay Folk's Catechism*. These plays, written by clergy of the diocese and probably supervised by the York Minster clergy, were an important means of transmission of biblical education.

Thoresby had considerable influence on the careers of his kinsmen. Yorkshire clerks had been prominent in secular government since the reign of Edward I, and Thoresby perpetuated this tradition, ensuring that members of his family held important positions in chancery until the reign of Richard II. Thus he may be presumed to have introduced into government circles his brother Ralph Thoresby, who was keeper of the hanaper from 1345 to 1357, and his relations by marriage Richard and John Ravenser, both of whom also became keeper of the hanaper. Richard Ravenser, moreover, was archdeacon of Lincoln between 1368 and 1386. And the archbishop's great-nephews John and William Waltham were later to be keeper of the privy seal, and later treasurer, and keeper of the hanaper, respectively. Two other nephews, a younger John Waltham, a fellow of Balliol College, Oxford, who became an official in the court of York in 1367, and another John Thoresby, who incepted as doctor of civil law at Oxford in 1356, lectured there on canon and civil law, and became provost of Beverley in 1373, also had their paths made easier by their uncle's patronage. The great theologian John Wyclif (*d.* 1384), who was probably ordained priest in York Minster in 1351, may have been introduced to his patron, Archbishop Islip, by Thoresby. Wyclif was a contemporary at Merton and Balliol of Thoresby's nephews Dr John Thoresby and John Waltham. His later emphasis on the performance of pastoral duty, condemnation of non-residence, and belief in the importance of the vernacular dissemination of religious knowledge may well owe much to early exposure to the reforming ambitions of Thoresby and his followers.

In his surviving letters Thoresby emerges as an urbane, courtly man, with a sense of humour and a high regard for good wine and friendship, especially among his old chancery colleagues. He died at Bishopthorpe on 6 November 1373 and is buried in his lady chapel in York Minster. A good illustration of the truth that civil servants and lawyers, when they had the opportunity, could make good pastors, by raising standards of religious knowledge and moral awareness in his diocese, Thoresby, with his clerks, laid the foundations for a perceptible growth of lay piety and dissemination of devotional literature there towards the end of the fourteenth century. They also established principles of pastoral care that enabled the next generation of York clergy to adapt the pastoral office from the provision of basic religious instruction to controlling and moderating the religious enthusiasm that had been aroused among the laity by Yorkshire mystical writers.

JONATHAN HUGHES

Sources Emden, *Oxf.* · J. Hughes, *Pastors and visionaries: religion and secular life in late medieval Yorkshire* (1988) · A. Hudson, 'A new look at the *Lay folk's catechism*', *Viator*, 16 (1985), 243–58 · S. Powell, 'The transmission and circulation of the lay folk's catechism', *Late medieval religious texts*, ed. A. J. Minnis (1991), 67–85 · W. H. Dixon, *Fasti Eboracenses: lives of the archbishops of York*, ed. J. Raine (1863) · Tout, *Admin. hist.* · J. L. Grassi, 'Clerical dynasties from Howdenshire, Nottinghamshire and Lindsey in the royal administration, 1280–1340', DPhil diss., U. Oxf., 1960 · reg. 11, Thoresby, Borth. Inst. · reg. 12, Neville, Borth. Inst. · BL, Cotton MS Galba E.x · acta capitularia (chapter act book), 1352–1426, York Minster, dean and chapter library

Archives Borth. Inst., reg. 11

Wealth at death £833—cash bequeathed: J. Raine, ed., *Testamenta Eboracensia*, 1, SurtS, 4 (1836), 88–91

Thoresby, Ralph (1658–1725), antiquary and topographer, was born on 16 August 1658 at Kirkgate, Leeds, the son of John Thoresby (1626–1679), a wool merchant of that city who had served in the parliamentarian army under Fairfax, and his wife, Ruth (*d.* 1669), the daughter of Ralph Idle of Bulmer, near York. The Thoresby lineage could allegedly be traced back to the time of King Canute and at the time of the Norman conquest was seated at Thoresby in Yorkshire. Ralph Thoresby did extensive research on his pedigree and was especially proud of the connection with John Thoresby, the archbishop of York.

Learning the wool trade Thoresby was educated at a private grammar school under the Revd Robert Garnet and then at Leeds grammar school. Destined by his father for the wool trade, in 1677 Thoresby was placed with John Dickenson, a cloth merchant of London related to his father, in order to learn the profession. While in London, Thoresby spent much of his time visiting the remarkable places about the city, copying inscriptions, and attending nonconformist meetings. On the advice of his father, while in London, Thoresby began his diary on 2 September 1677, a habit which he kept throughout his adult life. The diary was published in 1830.

Having returned to Leeds in February 1678, in July of that year Thoresby was sent by his father to Rotterdam, to learn Dutch and French, and to further his knowledge of the wool trade. He spent much of the summer travelling through the principal towns of Holland, including a visit to collections in the physick garden and anatomy theatre

Ralph Thoresby (1658–1725), by George Vertue, 1712

in Leiden. His time abroad was cut short when he developed a serious ague, and he returned home in December.

Thoresby spent many months recuperating during which time he made several small excursions in the Yorkshire countryside, taking advantage of these trips to improve his knowledge of local antiquities. His travels continued over the next decade, visiting London and Scotland, visiting men of learning, and viewing collections, including the Ashmolean Museum in 1684, Mr Charlton's museum, and the repository at Gresham College in 1695. He also scoured the local countryside making observations and recording inscriptions. About 1690 he resolved to write a county history.

John Thoresby died in October 1679, having been predeceased by his wife and his eldest son. Thoresby, who had been much influenced by his father, felt the loss deeply but determined to continue his father's business as a wool merchant and also assumed responsibility for the care of his younger brother and sister. The foreign wool trade to Leeds had fallen off in the years before and Thoresby diversified his interests to include linens. For this he bought his freedom in the incorporated Society of Merchant Adventurers trading to Hamburg, and in the Eastland Company in 1685. By his own admission, however, Thoresby 'never made a merchant worth a farthing' (Atkinson, 1.222). He retired from the cloth trade in 1704.

Adopting conformity On 25 February 1685 Thoresby married Anna (d. 1740), the third daughter and coheir of Richard Sykes of Leeds. They had ten children, three of whom survived: a daughter and two sons, both of whom were bred to the church. The marriage was happy, Thoresby describing his wife after thirty-five years of marriage as 'the greatest blessing' (Atkinson, 1.245). It was, however, marred by differences of opinion on religion and the proper education of their children after Thoresby changed his views on conformity.

Thoresby was raised a presbyterian but had always occasionally conformed. In December 1683 he was indicted at quarter sessions under the Conventicle Act. He was acquitted but after this attended conformist services weekly. About 1699 he committed to the established church, 'judging it to be the strongest bulwark against popery and a union of protestants absolutely necessary'. Religion remained important to him throughout his life. When a charity school was founded at Leeds, he was instrumental in raising money in support of it. Likewise, he was a corresponding member of the Society for Promoting Christian Knowledge and took pains in distributing pious books among the poor. His correspondence includes many letters devoted to questions of religion.

Thoresby was elected a common councillor for Leeds in 1697 and took the oaths of allegiance and supremacy in June of that year. The following year he was much occupied with difficulties stemming from an oil-mill speculation in Sheepscar in which he had embarked a decade earlier. It involved him in a lawsuit, caused the loss of his capital, and for a short time he was imprisoned for debt.

Antiquarian pursuits After his retirement from trade, Thoresby's interests turned increasingly to antiquarian pursuits and the study of antiquities. His father had founded the Musaeum Thoresbyanum by purchasing the cabinet of coins and library of Lord Fairfax from his heir for £185. Thoresby now continued his father's antiquarian interests and expanded the collection.

The museum expanded rapidly under Thoresby's care and by the time the catalogue was published in 1715 included a great variety of material. The largest part was given over to coins and medals, numbering over two thousand. These formed the heart of the collection, as well as the primary focus of Thoresby's researches. As early as 1682 he lent a number of the Saxon coins to Obadiah Walker to be engraved in his edition of Spelman's *Life of King Alfred*. Edmund Gibson and Sir Andrew Fountaine benefited from a similar loan for illustrations in Camden's *Britannia* and the *Numismata*.

In addition to the coins and medals, the museum contained a substantial collections of plants, shells, minerals, and fossils. Thoresby also kept remains of animals, including feet, horns, and skin, many of which were of exotic species. He had numerous funerary urns with human remains, as well as parts of human bodies testifying to unusual medical or accidental occurrences. By his own estimation his most notable of the human curiosities was the arm of the marquess of Montrose, whose quarters had been disposed of to several cities in Scotland, whence his specimen had come. Thoresby also kept instruments of war and of mathematics, and a variety of statues and amulets collected not only in Yorkshire but from around the world.

Thoresby's museum attracted virtuosi and the curious to visit his home in Leeds. His diary frequently reports him showing his collection to visitors whose numbers included members of both houses of parliament and visitors from abroad. In addition to this, the collection, and especially his study of and observations on its contents, brought him into discussion with many of the eminent men of his time. Two volumes of their letters to him were published in 1832, another volume in 1912.

The Musaeum Thoresbyanum was remarkable not only for the variety of material which it contained but also as a highly developed manifestation of what was largely a metropolitan pastime in a provincial setting. While many of the fellows of the Royal Society collected, few had collections as large or esteemed as Thoresby's. Richard Gough considered him to have inherited Tradescant's mantle as the foremost private collector in Britain, though he found the curiosities demonstrated a 'credulity and want of judgement' (Gough, 2.436). In its mixture of natural specimens and cultural artefacts, the collection is typical of its day and the narratives which Thoresby constructed around them were welcomed into the most sophisticated intellectual circles in England.

From early adulthood Thoresby cultivated and expanded his father's antiquarian circle in Leeds, including Mr Thornton, the recorder of Leeds, Bishop William Nicholson, Bishop Edmund Gibson, Thomas Gale, the dean of York, and his son Roger Gale, Sir Andrew Fountaine, Thomas Hearne, William Richardson, John Ray, and Bishop White Kennet. His interest in and skill at heraldry brought him into correspondence with John Anstis, garter principal king at arms, and Peter Le Neve, Norroy king at arms, while his study of medals brought him into contact with other virtuosi, including the earl of Pembroke.

In 1697 Thoresby was elected a fellow of the Royal Society on the strength of an account of some Roman antiquities he had discovered in Yorkshire, communicated to the society by his correspondents Martin Lister and Dr Gale. Following his election, at least thirty of his communications to the society were published in the *Philosophical Transactions*. These deal with Roman and Saxon monuments in the north of England, with inscriptions on coins, or with accounts of uncommon accidents. Thoresby expanded his correspondence to include the prominent antiquarians and collectors within the Royal Society of the day, including Sir Hans Sloane.

The Ducatus Leodiensis Thoresby's great work was the *Ducatus Leodiensis, or, The Topography of Leedes* (1715). From the time he settled on the project in the early 1690s, Thoresby worked industriously towards its completion.

This was not the first topographical publication of importance about a provincial town but it was the first work of importance by a Yorkshire antiquary. Attached to the main body of the text was a catalogue of the Musaeum Thoresbyanum and the volume included a very fine map of the area. *Ducatus* was published by subscription and was dedicated to Peregrine Osborne, marquess of Carmarthen and heir apparent to the duke of Leeds, and to the mayor of Leeds and aldermen of Leeds. About 2000 copies were printed and sold for £3. A second edition appeared in 1816, with notes and additions by Thomas Dunham Whitaker.

Encouraged by the success of *Ducatus*, Thoresby planned to complete the work with a historical account of the area. In 1724 *Vicaria Leodiensis, or, The History of the Church of Leedes* was published. On his death he left the completed manuscript for the history, beginning with the Britons, through the Romans, Danes, and Normans to the sixth century. This was published, along with a biography by his eldest son, in *Biographia Britannica*.

Thoresby remained active until almost the end of his life. He was esteemed by others an ingenious and sober gentleman, and an industrious antiquary. He was skilled in the Saxon language. He was kind to his friends and never more happy than when he could share with them some piece of antiquity or a valuable manuscript.

In October 1724 Thoresby had a major stroke, losing his speech and the ability to walk. Though he recovered over the coming months, one year later he had a second stroke and, after languishing for six days, he died on 16 October 1725. He was buried among his ancestors in the chancel of St Peter's Church, Leeds, on 19 October.

Thoresby's elder son inherited his collection. After the son's death it was sold at auction in London in 1764 over three days. The sale included coins and medals, manuscripts, curiosities, and ancient deeds. The sale was attended by many of the prominent antiquarians and collectors of the second half of the eighteenth century, including Horace Walpole, but it realized only £450. The printed books were sold separately. Many of the curiosities languished in a garret in Leeds after Ralph Thoresby's death; they were sold eventually to Jonathan Swale and some by him to Dr Burton. Much of the once-celebrated collection was left to rot and was eventually simply thrown out.

P. E. KELL

Sources *The diary of Ralph Thoresby*, ed. J. Hunter, 2 vols. (1830) · A. Kippis and others, eds., *Biographia Britannica, or, The lives of the most eminent persons who have flourished in Great Britain and Ireland*, 2nd edn, 5 vols. (1778–93) · D. H. Atkinson, *Ralph Thoresby, the topographer* (1885) · R. Thoresby, *Ducatus Leodiensis, or, The topography of … Leedes* (1715) · *Musaeum Thoresbyanum* (1764) · R. G. [R. Gough], *British topography*, [new edn], 2 (1780), 435–6 · Nichols, *Lit. anecdotes*, 9.707 **Archives** BL, collections, Add. MSS 4212, 4274–4277, 4460, 4926–4933, 26732 · Cornwall RO, collection of MSS · Cornwall RO, seventeenth-century collected MSS · FM Cam., corresp. and annotated copy of *Vicaria Leodiensis* · W. Yorks. AS, Leeds, Yorkshire Archaeological Society, antiquarian MSS · W. Yorks. AS, Leeds, Yorkshire Archaeological Society, collections, diaries, corresp. and papers · York Minster Library, diary and annotated copy of *Ducatus Leodiensis* | BL, Sloane MSS, letters to Sir Hans Sloane, etc. · BL, letters to John Strype, Add. MS 5853 · Bodl. Oxf., letters to Thomas Hearne · CUL, letters to John Strype · RS, letters to Royal Society

Likenesses Parmentier, portrait, 1703, S. Antiquaries, Lond. ·
G. Vertue, line engraving, 1712 (after oil painting), BM, NPG [*see illus.*] · R. Rapkin, engraving (after Parmentier), repro. in Atkinson,
Ralph Thoresby · oils, S. Antiquaries, Lond.

Thorfinn (II) Sigurdson [Þorfinnr Sigurðarson, Þorfinnr
inn Ríki] (*c.*1009–*c.*1065), earl of Orkney, was called inn
Ríki ('the Mighty') in later sources and remembered as
being the most powerful of all the earls of Orkney; he was
also the first to be recorded as having been granted the
earldom of Caithness in the kingdom of Scotland. He was
the son of *Sigurd (II), earl of Orkney, and of a daughter of
'Malcolm, king of Scots', most probably *Malcolm II (*r.*
1005–1034). He was born *c.*1009, as he is said to have been
'only five years old' in *Orkneyinga Saga* when his father was
killed at the battle of Clontarf in 1014: he was then living
with his grandfather, Malcolm, king of Scots, who gave
him Caithness and Sutherland, with the title of earl, 'and
appointed counsellors to govern with him' (*Orkneyinga
Saga*, chap. 13).

Despite his Scottish upbringing Thorfinn became thoroughly immersed in the late viking world of the Norse
settlements around the northern and western coasts of
Scotland, which had been raided and conquered by his
ancestors. He built on the successes of his father and
maintained a maritime 'empire' stretching from Shetland
and Orkney to the southern Hebrides, even including Man
(and 'a large realm in Ireland' if the saga is to be believed).
This was the result of his successful career as a warrior and
leader of a war-band (*hirð*) whose generosity is lauded by
his court skald Arnórr Earls' Poet (Arnórr Jarlaskáld).
Administrative and tax-raising structures (as seen in the
territorial units of ouncelands) in the northern isles and
the Hebrides were probably developed by him, and the
saga writer provides the significant information that after
his pilgrimage to Rome Thorfinn gave up piracy and
'devoted all his time to the government of his people and
country and to the making of new laws' (*Orkneyinga Saga*,
chap. 31). He certainly made Birsay in Orkney his chief
residence and established the seat of the first bishop
there, building Christchurch, 'a fine minster'. It is to this
period of time that the full ecclesiastical establishment of
churches and priests in Orkney, Shetland, and Caithness
can be attributed. Thorfinn's own piety is beyond doubt,
as is evident from his pilgrimage to Rome. Neither liaisons
nor offspring of any union is mentioned other than with
his wife, Ingebjorg (Earls' Mother; *d. c.*1070), daughter of
Finn Árnason of Norway, and one of their sons is named,
significantly, *Paul (the first Christian name in the earldom family).

The preliminary phase of Thorfinn's rise to eminence
concerned his struggle with his half-brothers, Sumarlidi,
Brúsi, and Einarr, to gain a share of the earldom of Orkney
which they had divided between them on the death of
their father in 1014. After Sumarlidi's death Thorfinn
claimed his third of Orkney, although it was argued by
Einarr that Caithness and Sutherland—which Thorfinn
held—constituted over a third of their father's earldom.
With the support of Thorkel Amundson, an Orkney
farmer who fostered Thorfinn when young, he succeeded

in acquiring one-third of the islands. The rivalry with Earl
Einarr came to a head at a feast at Thorkel's farm at Sand-
wick, when the earl was murdered by Thorkel (recorded
in the Icelandic annals in the early fourteenth century as
having taken place in 1020). These events gave the king of
Norway, Óláf Haraldsson, an opportunity to intervene in
the affairs of the earldom to his own advantage, and there
are some highly imaginative scenes, described in the section of *Orkneyinga Saga* devoted to Thorfinn, of the occasion when the king announced the terms of the agreement made with Brúsi and Thorfinn over Earl Einarr's
third of the earldom. The Icelandic annals describe this as
Thorfinn and Brúsi giving the Orkneys into the power of
King Óláf. Later, when Óláf was exiled from Norway (1028–
30), Thorfinn managed to reverse the balance of power
and secure two-thirds of the islands, and Brúsi kept one.

During the negotiations with Óláf, Brúsi had to leave
behind as a hostage his son, **Rögnvald (II) Brúsason**
(*d.* 1046), earl of Orkney, an outstanding member of the
earldom family, who also played a foremost role in the
stirring events that took place in Norway in the following
decade. He participated in the battle of Stiklestad, and
went into exile with Harald Hardrada to Novgorod,
returning with Magnús Óláfsson the Good to Norway in
1035. The following year he was given the title of earl,
three fully equipped long ships, and one-third of the
islands by Magnús, although when he arrived in Orkney
he claimed his father's third also, which Thorfinn
allowed, 'because his hands were full with the Hebrideans
and the Irish' (*Orkneyinga Saga*, chap. 22). The two campaigned together in the Hebrides, Ireland, and a wide area
of western Scotland, and this successful partnership continued for several years, culminating in raids on England
during Harthacnut's reign (1040–42). They must have
made a dramatic contrast: Rögnvald, 'one of the hand-
somest of men, with a fine head of golden hair, smooth as
silk', who had 'a great reputation for his shrewdness and
courtesy' (ibid., chap. 19), and Thorfinn, 'unusually tall
and strong, an ugly-looking man with a black head of hair,
sharp features, a big nose and bushy eyebrows' but 'a
forceful man, greedy for fame and fortune' (ibid., chap.
20).

At some point during this period (the chronology of the
saga account does not permit any specific date to be haz-
arded), Thorfinn faced attack from a powerful ruler of
Scotland, called in the saga Karl Hundason, who claimed
Caithness and expected tribute to be paid for it by the earl.
The claim on Caithness, and the location of the movement of the armies of both Earl Thorfinn and King Karl
around the Moray Firth make it very likely that the
Scottish rival was a ruler of the province of Moray, rather
than of the southern mac Alpin dynasty: that he may have
been Macbeth has often been suggested, though never
entirely proven. He was clearly a famous warrior and the
battles fought with Thorfinn—one in Orcadian waters, off
Deerness, and the other near Karl's own home base at
'Torfness' (possibly Tarbat Ness in Easter Ross)—were
close-won victories for Thorfinn. The descriptions of
them and of Thorfinn, accoutred with 'a golden helmet on

his head, a sword at his waist, wielding a great spear in both hands' are highlights of the saga narrative and among the best in Icelandic literature. 'People agree that he went ahead of all his troops', and Arnórr Earls' Poet sang of the encounter:

> Well the red weapons
> fed wolves at Tarbat Ness,
> young the commander who created that Monday-combat.
> Slim blades sang there
> south on Oykel's bank.
> (*Orkneyinga Saga*, chap. 20)

After this encounter Karl disappears from the saga narrative, which (if he can be identified with Macbeth) could be accounted for by his movement south on the take-over of Duncan's kingdom. Such a unique turn of events created an unprecedented situation and might explain the succeeding description of Thorfinn's conquering raids as far south as Fife.

The next dramatic scenario centres on the falling-out of the two earls, Thorfinn and Rognvald, over the third of the earldom that had belonged to Earl Einarr. Thorfinn's resources were stretched by the arrival of a relative by marriage, Kalf Arnason, who was fleeing from King Magnús, with 'a large following'. The earls came to blows at the naval battle of Roberry, off south Ronaldsay, which was decided when Kalf decided to put his 'six large ships' into Thorfinn's force. Rögnvald was finally hunted down and killed on Papa Stronsay just before Christmas 1046, betrayed by the barking of his lap-dog as he hid among the rocks; he was buried on Papa Westray. This was after he had set Thorfinn's house (on the mainland of Orkney) on fire when the earl had made a dramatic escape, unnoticed by the attackers, through a wooden partition wall with Ingebjorg in his arms. The saga tells us that Rögnvald's death 'was mourned by many' and that 'everyone agrees that of all the Earls of Orkney he was the most popular and gifted' (chap. 30).

Thorfinn thereafter ruled the Orkneys unopposed; but presumably in expiation for his murder of Rögnvald and at least thirty of his supporters he went on pilgrimage to Rome, where he had an audience with the pope 'and received absolution from him for all his sins' (*Orkneyinga Saga*, chap. 31). This famous journey included a visit to Swein Estrithson in Denmark and the emperor Heinrich III in Germany 'who gave him a warm welcome and many fine gifts' (ibid.). Thorfinn died 'towards the end of the reign of Harald Sigurdarson' (Harald Hardrada), that is c.1065, and was buried at Christchurch, Birsay, Orkney, in 'the very church he had built' (*Orkneyinga Saga*, chap. 32). A foremost ruler of the Scandinavian world, Thorfinn's 'empire' fell apart at his death and his earldoms were divided between his two sons, Paul and *Erlend [see under Paul]. His widow, Ingebjorg, is said in *Orkneyinga Saga* to have married Malcolm III Canmore, king of Scots: a liaison recorded in no other source, but which may have produced Malcolm's two eldest sons.

BARBARA E. CRAWFORD

Sources H. Pálsson and P. Edwards, eds. and trans., *The Orkneyinga saga: the history of the earls of Orkney* (1978) • B. E. Crawford, *Scandinavian Scotland* (1987) • G. Storm, ed., *Islandske Annaler indtil 1578*

(Oslo, 1888) • J. Jesch, 'England and *Orkneyinga saga*', *The viking age in Caithness, Orkney and the North Atlantic*, ed. C. E. Batey, J. Jesch, and C. D. Morris (1993), 222–39 • B. E. Crawford, 'Birsay and the early earls and bishops of Orkney', *Birsay: a centre of political and ecclesiastical power* (1983), vol. 2 of *Orkney heritage*, 97–118 • B. Fijestøl, 'Arnórr þórðarson: skald of the Orkney jarls', *The Northern and Western Isles in the viking world*, ed. A. Fenton and H. Palsson (1984), 239–57

Thorius [Thorie], **John** (b. 1568), writer and translator, son of John Thorius MD, of Bailleul, Flanders, was born in London. He matriculated from Christ Church, Oxford, on 1 October 1586, having supplicated for the degree of BA on the 15th day of the previous April. John Thorius is noteworthy not so much because of his own accomplishments as because of the minor part which he played in the tragicomedy acted out by Gabriel Harvey and Thomas Nashe.

Thorius became involved in this literary quarrel between Harvey and Nashe when he wrote two letters and several poems which Harvey attached to *Pierce's Supererogation* (1593), a reply to Nashe's attack on him in *Strange News* (1592). Harvey dedicated *Pierce's Supererogation* to John Thorius, Barnabe Barnes, and Anthony Chewt, describing Thorius as 'the many-tonged Linguist' and urging him not to 'forget thy Netherlandish traine under Him, that taught the Prince of Navarre, now the valorous king of Fraunce'. Thorius apparently regretted the position in which Harvey's publication had placed him, even though his contributions are distinctly more restrained than their companions. In *Have with You to Saffron Walden* (1596) Nashe writes, 'Of this John Thorius more sparingly I wil speake, because hee hath made his peace with mee, & there be in him sundrie good parts of the Tungs and otherwise' (*Works of Thomas Nashe*, 3.105). Nashe includes in his text a letter from Thorius in which Thorius claims that he did not see the entire text of Harvey's work, denies that one of the sonnets is his, and claims that Harvey has altered his work (ibid., 3.135).

Thorius translated from the Spanish Bartolome Felippe's *The Counseller* (1589), Antonio de Corro's *Spanish Grammer* (1590), and Francisco de Valdes's *The Sergeant-Major* (1590); from the Dutch he translated *A Spiritual Wedding* (1597). Thorius also contributed verses to Florio's *Queen Anna's New World of Words* (1611).

HOWARD JONES

Sources *Reg. Oxf.*, 2/2.154, 2/3.138 • G. Harvey, *Pierce's supererogation* (1593) • *The works of Thomas Nashe*, ed. R. B. McKerrow, 5 vols. (1904–10) • Wood, *Ath. Oxon.*, 1st edn

Thorius, Raphael (d. 1625), physician and poet, was born at Belle, Flanders, the son of Francis Thorius, a well-known French physician and poet, who befriended the protestant poet Daniel Rogers during the latter's visit to Paris in 1565. In May 1570 Rogers wrote a poem for and about Francis, *Ad Franciscum Thorium medicum et poetam*, which indicates that by then Francis had fled France as a protestant, to settle in Belle. Raphael Thorius studied medicine at Oxford, but graduated MD from Leiden, where he matriculated in medicine on 31 December 1590 and received his MD only twelve days later, with a thesis on dropsy. He then began to practise in London, but without a licence from the College of Physicians. In 1593 he was threatened with imprisonment after one of his English patients died, and three years later found himself in trouble again with the College of Physicians for practising without a licence. This time, however, on 23 December 1596, he was admitted to the college as a licentiate. On his return from Leiden, Thorius first resided in the parish of St Gabriel Fenchurch in London, where he developed a successful practice. Later he moved to the parish of St Benet Finck.

Like his father, Thorius was a learned humanist and a distinguished Latin poet. He published only a couple of works during his lifetime. His *In orbitum Jo. Barclaii elegia* (1621) includes a poem entitled 'Venator', which defends the then embattled Archbishop George Abbot. The following year one of his poems was included in the commemorative volume *Epicedia in orbitum*, for Simon Ruytinck, the minister to the Dutch Reformed community in London. Among those who contributed to this volume were some of his colleagues and fellow Reformed refugees from the College of Physicians, Johannes Brovaert and Baldwin Hamey, not to mention two of his friends, the Anglo-Dutch merchant Jacob Cool and the Dutch diplomat and humanist Sir Constantijn Huygens. Thorius was closely associated with the foreign Reformed communities in London. In 1604 he and Jacob Cool were chosen to write the poetry needed in connection with the triumphal arch erected by the Dutch community in London to celebrate James I's coronation entry into the city.

Thorius's most famous work, *Hymnus tabaci*, written in 1610, but later revised and augmented in 1625, was published posthumously in London in 1626. It proved popular and went through several editions. The poem, which is divided into two books, is an elegant composition in hexameters and deserves a place among the metrical works of physicians beside the *Syphilis* of Hieronymus Fracastorius, which may well have inspired it. Thorius also completed, in 1625, another long poem, *Hyems*, which he dedicated to Constantijn Huygens, whom he had befriended during the latter's visit to England in 1618–19. A manuscript volume of his and his father's poems is preserved in the British Library (Sloane MS 1768). It contains mainly Latin poems, some of which, like those praising the Huguenot prince Henri of Navarre, later King Henri IV of France, show their protestantism. The volume also incorporates a number of smaller poems by Raphael Thorius to friends, such as Theodore de Mayerne, William Camden, Meric Casaubon, and Matthias Lobel, plus the poems written for King James's coronation entry, and what is probably the original copy of book 1 of his poem on tobacco.

Thorius had a wife, Mary, and seven children: Jean, Elizabeth, John, Paul, Francis, Matthew, and James. John became a physician and received his MD from Leiden in 1626. Thorius died of the plague in his house in St Benet Finck in July or August 1625.   OLE PETER GRELL

Sources Wood, *Ath. Oxon.* · R. W. Innes Smith, *English-speaking students of medicine at the University of Leyden* (1932) · Munk, *Roll* · J. Van Dorsten, *Poets, patrons and professors* (1962) · O. P. Grell, *Calvinist exiles in Tudor and Stuart England* (1996) · P. R. Sellin, *Daniel Heinsius* (1968) · G. Clark and A. M. Cooke, *A history of the Royal College of Physicians of London*, 1 (1964) · R. E. G. Kirk and E. F. Kirk, eds., *Returns of aliens dwelling in the city and suburbs of London, from the reign of Henry VIII to that of James I*, 4 vols., Huguenot Society of London, 10 (1900–08) · I. Scouloudi, *Returns of strangers in the metropolis, 1593, 1627, 1635, 1639: a study of an active minority*, Huguenot Society of London, 57 (1985) · will, PRO, PROB 11/146, sig. 91

Thorkell the Tall [þorkill inn Hávi], **earl of East Anglia** (*fl.* 1009–1023), viking leader, magnate, and regent, was, according to saga tradition, the son of Strút Harald, earl of Sjælland, and the brother of Sigvaldi, the supposed leader of the Jómsvikings. He may have been married to a daughter of Æthelred II the Unready, whom sources variously name as Edith or Wulfhild. In August 1009, after an adventurous early career in Scandinavia, Thorkell arrived off the coast of Sandwich with a large fleet intent upon pillage. He immediately joined forces with other viking chieftains then operating in England, including his brother Hemingr, and for the next three years plundered towns and villages in Kent, Essex, East Anglia, Wessex, and the eastern midlands. The English response to the threat, which included a programme of public prayer and penance, proved ineffectual and in 1011 King Æthelred II agreed to pay £48,000 to the raiders as tribute (*gafol*), in return for peace. In September 1011, however, while the money was being raised, Thorkell's forces seized Canterbury and took its archbishop, Ælfheah, captive. The archbishop's refusal to pay ransom led to his martyrdom on 19 April 1012 at the hands of his enraged, drunken captors, despite Thorkell's strenuous efforts to protect him. When the tribute was finally paid and oaths of peace were sworn, the viking fleet dispersed, but Thorkell chose to remain in England and, in a remarkable turnabout, entered the service of Æthelred II with forty-five ships, promising to defend his country in return for food and clothes.

Thorkell fought for Æthelred II against Swein Forkbeard, king of Denmark, when the latter, inspired and perhaps goaded by Thorkell's success, invaded England in 1013 and he was with the English king in London during Swein's unsuccessful first siege of the town. But Thorkell proved almost as costly an ally as enemy: despite demanding and receiving payment and provisioning, his forces still 'ravaged as often as they pleased' (*ASC*, s.a. 1013, text C). When London finally submitted late in 1014, Thorkell abetted King Æthelred's flight to Normandy to join his wife and children in exile at the court of his brother-in-law Duke Richard (II). From 1014 to 1016 Thorkell disappears from the pages of the Anglo-Saxon Chronicle. For these critical years historians are forced to rely upon cryptic skaldic poetry and the dubious authority of the *Encomium Emmae Reginae* and the later Norse sagas, which present conflicting traditions about his relations with King Æthelred, Edmund Ironside, and their great opponent, Cnut. Thorkell apparently helped restore Æthelred to his throne in the spring of 1014, a month or two after Swein's sudden death, but how long he remained loyal to the English king is questionable. The favour that Cnut showed Thorkell in 1017 suggests that he had switched his support to the Danish victor at a most opportune moment. According to the *Encomium Emmae*, this occurred even before Cnut's invasion. The encomiast reports that Thorkell, regretting that he had remained in England without Cnut's permission after the death of King Swein, sailed to Denmark with nine ships to make amends. There he renewed his fealty to Cnut and pledged him the aid of thirty-nine ships for his planned conquest of England. A later Scandinavian tradition asserts that Thorkell defected in response to the death of his brother Heming, who was supposedly treacherously killed in a massacre of Swein's 'thingmen' engineered by Ulfcytel and Edmund Ironside. But it is more likely that Thorkell remained loyal to Æthelred for some months following Cnut's arrival in England. He may have commanded the fleet of forty ships which, according to the Anglo-Saxon Chronicle, Eadric Streona 'seduced' and brought over to Cnut in late 1015. Thorkell distinguished himself fighting for Cnut in the battle of Sherston in the summer of 1016 and, according to the 'Supplement to *Jómsvíkinga saga*', preserved in the late fourteenth-century *Flateyjarbók*, avenged his brother by slaying Ulfcytel (here called Snilling) during the battle of 'Assandun' on 18 October 1016. This same source also claims that he married Ulfcytel's widow, Wulfhild, the daughter of King Æthelred, and was instrumental in arranging Cnut's marriage to Æthelred's widowed queen, Emma.

King Cnut rewarded Thorkell's services handsomely, bestowing upon him the earldom of East Anglia, one of the four great provinces into which England was now divided. Between 1017 and 1021 Thorkell was the most powerful secular magnate in England, his name invariably appearing first among the earls in the witness lists of Cnut's surviving charters. He probably served as regent during Cnut's sojourn in Denmark in 1019–20, since he is the only earl Cnut addresses by name in his letter to the English people (*English Historical Documents*, 1, no. 48) and is explicitly charged in that text with enforcing royal authority and law. In 1020 he was present with Cnut at the dedication of a minster at 'Assandun' and in that same year supported Bishop Ælfwine of Elmham's replacement of clerics with monks at Bury St Edmunds.

In November 1021 Thorkell, for reasons not explained in the sources, fell out with Cnut and was outlawed. He returned to Denmark and may have resumed his old profession of marauder. Just as mysteriously, two years later he and Cnut met together in Denmark and were reconciled. Cnut entrusted Denmark and the care of his son to Thorkell and Thorkell gave Cnut his own son to take back with him to England. How Thorkell achieved this stunning reversal of fortune is unclear, but his activities in Scandinavia after his exile may have persuaded Cnut that it was more dangerous to have him as an enemy than a friend. After 1023 Thorkell disappears from the historical record. When and how he died is unknown.

RICHARD ABELS

Sources S. Keynes, 'Cnut's earls', *The reign of Cnut*, ed. A. R. Rumble (1994), 43–88, esp. 54–7, 82–4 · ASC, s.a. 1009, 1013, 1017, 1020 [texts C, D, E]; s.a. 1021, 1023 [text C] · R. G. Poole, *Viking poems on war and peace: a study in skaldic narrative* (1991), 86–115 · M. K. Lawson, *Cnut: the Danes in England in the early eleventh century* (1993), 15–19, 83, 92–6, 101, 142n., 174–6 · A. Campbell, ed. and trans., *Encomium Emmae reginae*, CS, 3rd ser., 72 (1949) · M. Ashdown, *English and Norse documents relating to the reign of Ethelred the Unready* (1930), 293–4 · F. M. Stenton, *Anglo-Saxon England*, 3rd edn (1971), 382–401 · John of Worcester, *Chron.* · S. Keynes, *The diplomas of King Æthelred 'The Unready' (978–1016): a study in their use as historical evidence*, Cambridge Studies in Medieval Life and Thought, 3rd ser., 13 (1980), 216–28 · E. John, 'The return of the vikings', *The Anglo-Saxons*, ed. J. Campbell (1982), 194, 199, 208 · *English historical documents*, 1, ed. D. Whitelock (1955), no. 48

Thorn, Sir Jules (1899–1980), businessman, was born in Vienna, Austria, on 6 February 1899 to Jewish parents: his father was Leon Thorn, an insurance company director, and he was the youngest of three brothers, one of whom moved to Britain, the other to the USA. On leaving school he was conscripted into the Austrian army to fight in the First World War; he saw action on the Russian front, where he was taken prisoner. After the war he studied business and management at the Handelshochschule—the commerce school in Vienna. On graduation he obtained a position as representative of an Austrian electric lamp manufacturer, and first arrived in Britain in that capacity. When that company went bankrupt in 1926 Thorn found himself responsible for a number of its debts, but, such was his business reputation already, he was able to raise sufficient capital to pay them off and start up in business for himself, as an importer of Hungarian lamps, selling them through his own Electric Lamp Service Company Ltd, which he incorporated in March 1928. In 1928, however, following government restrictions on lamp importations, imposed under pressure from a cartel of the British lamp manufacturers (which he was later to break), Thorn went into manufacturing under the Atlas brand. In the same year he married Dorothy Olive Tanner; they had two children, Cedric and Ann. In 1936, having diversified into the manufacturing and selling of radio equipment, his company, named Thorn Electrical Industries, went public, its shares being oversubscribed by a factor of 35. It was at this time that Thorn was joined by radio engineer and fellow Austrian, Alfred (Freddy) Deutsch, in a partnership that lasted forty years.

Thorn's aggressive move into the new area of manufacturing in the face of opposition from established firms was typical of him. He possessed an entrepreneurial attitude then unusual in the British industrial establishment, and was motivated by the challenge of success itself rather than personal gain. Time and again he committed his own and his family fortune to high-risk ventures, entering new markets, buying companies, or investing in new ideas. Concomitant with this calculated high risk-taking, Thorn concentrated control of the company entirely in his own hands. Short in stature and unflinchingly courteous, he was nevertheless ruthless and renowned for his tireless energy and ebullient flair. Throughout a period of increased corporate bureaucratization, Thorn retained a high degree of independence and maintained his self-made image as a rebel.

Thorn was interested in psychology and used it in his sales and management method, instilling in all his staff a belief in Thorn Electrical Industries, urging them to identify as much as possible with the company's interests. Equally, he strove to convince retailers how Thorn products could improve their businesses. In the 1930s he knew the majority of his staff by name, and tried to help them both personally and professionally. By 1976, 15,000 staff (of a total workforce of 75,000) had more than ten years service, and 30,000 had more than five years.

In 1946 Thorn secured a crucial coup, signing an agreement with an American company, Sylvania Electric Products, for co-operation in the development and manufacture of fluorescent tubes. With this deal he established the basis for the company's post-war success in lighting equipment. In the same year Thorn Electrical Industries produced their first television receiver, under the Ferguson brand, continuing their trademark expansion and diversification, which by 1950 had encompassed Ekco-Ensign Electric. In the immediate post-war years Thorn acquired more British lamp factories, and plants in Australia and South Africa. With the acquisition of Tricity Cookers in 1951 he moved into a new and booming field in domestic electrical appliances. In the same decade he took over the manufacture of the HMV and Marconiphone range of consumer products from Electric and Musical Industries Ltd and purchased Ultra Radio and Television—moves that consolidated his position as a leading manufacturer of consumer appliances.

In 1961 Thorn entered the retail market, merging his manufacturing interests with Radio Rentals, then the country's leading domestic appliance rental organization. Further expansion in this side of the business occurred in 1975 when he purchased J. and F. Stores. In 1968 he bought Kenwood, manufacturers of food mixers, and the Parkinson Cowan range of gas cookers and meters. To ensure supplies of sheet metal, essential to the production of cookers, he purchased Metal Industries, and as a result diversified into engineering; Clarkson International Tools was bought in 1974 and Cleveland Twist Drill in 1976. Thorn also invested £1,250,000 in lighting laboratories at Enfield.

The extent of Thorn's control over the company was demonstrated by his unwillingness to retire and to relinquish control to a successor, and in the last years of his career there were open quibbles over his leadership. However, in 1976, the year he retired as chairman, the company showed pre-tax profits of £74.4 million on a turnover of £956 million.

A naturalized British citizen, Thorn was knighted in 1964. Of his private life, little is known. His family were sent to America on the outbreak of the Second World War. His marriage never recovered from this separation and the couple parted in 1950. In 1971 his first marriage was dissolved, and on 23 June 1971 he married a divorcée, Jane Norfolk, the daughter of Arthur Mayle, a farmer. Late in life he became a successful racehorse owner and bought an important collection of Impressionist paintings. Thorn gave generously to charity, particularly to Jewish charities, and specifically to the Haifa Technion, which married his Jewish sentiment to an abiding interest in scientific development. Throughout his career he combined great accuracy of judgement over business and take-over issues with determined ruthlessness and an institutional drive, which motivated both him and his employees and made him and the company important factors in the post-war British economy. He died at his home, 21 York Terrace East, Westminster, London, on 12 December 1980, survived by his second wife.   PETER MARTLAND

Sources EMI Music Archive, London, Sir Jules Thorn · EMI Music Archive, London, Thorn Electrical Ind Ltd · EMI Music Archive, London, Thorn EMI Ltd · *The Times* (15 Dec 1980) · *Jewish Chronicle* (19 Dec 1980) · S. M. Bowden, 'Thorn, Sir Jules', *DBB* · d. cert. · m. cert. · S. A. Pandit, *From machinery to music: the history of Thorn EMI* (1996) **Archives** Central Research Laboratories, Hayes, Middlesex, EMI Music Archives **Likenesses** portrait, EMI Music Archive, London **Wealth at death** £8,547,108: probate, 25 June 1981, *CGPLA Eng. & Wales*

Thorn, Sir Nathaniel (*d.* 1857), army officer, was commissioned ensign in the 3rd (Buffs) on 15 October 1802, and became lieutenant on 25 June 1803. He went with his regiment to Madeira in December 1807, and from there to Portugal in August 1808. The Buffs did not take part in the advance into Spain under Moore, but they formed part of Wellesley's army in 1809. They were the first troops to cross the Douro, and at Talavera they were hotly engaged as part of Hill's division, Thorn being in command of the light company.

Thorn was promoted captain on 4 January 1810, and in March he was appointed deputy assistant quartermaster-general to the 2nd division. He held this post until the end of the war. He was present at Busaco, the first siege of Badajoz, Albuera, Arroyo Molinos de Montanches, Almaraz, Vitoria, the battles of the Pyrenees, the Nivelle and the Nive, Garris, Orthez, Aire, and Toulouse. He was wounded at the battle of St Pierre (13 December 1813), and General W. Stewart strongly recommended him for promotion, as it was the fourth time he had brought his services to notice during that campaign. He received a brevet majority on 3 March 1814, and ultimately the silver medal with ten clasps.

In July 1814 Thorn was appointed assistant quartermaster-general to one of the brigades sent from Bordeaux to Canada, and he was present at the action at Plattsburg in September. He was made brevet lieutenant-colonel on 21 June 1817. On 14 August 1823 he was placed on half pay, but on 29 June 1826 he was appointed to the permanent staff of the quartermaster-general's department, on which he served for twenty years. He was promoted colonel on 10 January 1837, major-general on 9 November 1846, and lieutenant-general on 20 June 1854. On 25 July 1854 he was given the colonelcy of the Buffs. He was made CB in 1831, KH in 1832, and KCB in 1857. He went to Windsor for the installation on 24 January 1857, caught cold, and on his return home died suddenly at Upcott House, Bishop's Hull, near Taunton, Somerset, on the

28th. He was buried at Halse, Somerset, where a fine window was installed to his memory. He was married, and his wife survived him.   E. M. Lloyd, *rev.* James Lunt

Sources *GM*, 3rd ser., 2 (1857), 363 · *Supplementary despatches (correspondence) and memoranda of Field Marshal Arthur, duke of Wellington*, ed. A. R. Wellesley, second duke of Wellington, 15 vols. (1858–72), vol. 9 · *Somerset County Herald* (31 Jan 1857) · *Somerset County Herald* (4 Feb 1857) · J. Paget, *Wellington's Peninsular War* (1990) · J. Weller, *Wellington in the Peninsula, 1808–1814*, new edn (1992) · Boase, *Mod. Eng. biog.*

Thorn, Sir William [*formerly* Wilhelm] (**1780–1843**), army officer and cartographer, was born on 22 May 1780 in Neuwied, near Koblenz, Germany, the youngest of five sons and one daughter born to master tailor Johann Philipp Thorn (1733–1798), whose second wife, Anna Catharina Singmeister, of Heddesdorf, was William Thorn's mother. After attending local schools he came about 1796 under the patronage of Major George Gordon, deputy inspector-general of foreign corps serving with HM forces on the continent, and it was this connection which determined his subsequent career. He began his military education in England, purchasing a cornetcy in 1799 in the 29th light dragoons, to which Gordon had transferred, and joined the regiment in India. Promoted lieutenant in 1801, he saw much action in the Second Anglo-Maratha War (1803–6) and distinguished himself in 1803 at the battle of Laswari in which he was also wounded. He was promoted captain in 1807 and was brigade major to the cantonment of Bangalore, Mysore, until in November 1810 he accompanied the expedition against French-held Mauritius, where he saw action before returning to India in 1811.

That year Thorn took part in the expedition to Java. Despite being wounded while attacking the French at Weltevreden (Gambir, central Jakarta), he took part in the main assault on Fort Cornelis. He was thanked in public orders by Sir Samuel Auchmuty, the leader of the expedition, and, after the conquest of Java was complete, he was appointed deputy quartermaster-general of the British forces in Java and promoted brevet major.

In 1812 Thorn served with distinction and was commended for his part in actions in Sumatra and Java. He stayed in Java, making a geographical study tour of the island, but ill health obliged him to resign his staff appointment in 1814 and he returned to Europe where he spent six months writing his *Memoir of the Conquest of Java* (1815). Thorn left England to fight at Waterloo and after peace was declared returned to Germany. He is believed to have married Johanna Maria Giese in Wiesbaden in September 1815. They settled in Neuwied where he immersed himself in local affairs, becoming an active member of the local Lutheran church, helping its school and founding a society which succeeding in erecting a bridge over the Rhine at Neuwied which opened in 1817 and which was of great use to the local inhabitants. He continued to write, publishing *A Memoir of Major-General Sir R. R. Gillespie*, anonymously in 1816 and *A Memoir of the War in India* in 1818, of which French and German editions were published in 1818 and 1819 respectively. He was put on half pay in 1818, breveted lieutenant-colonel in 1819, and

resigned in 1825. For his services he was made a knight of the Royal Guelphic Order in 1832.

At various stages of his army career Thorn had had responsibility for surveying and map making, and his three books all contained maps and plans. He continued to make maps in retirement, notably for the house of Wied, since he counted Prince Maximilian of Wied a personal friend. He published a map of the possessions of the princely house in 1824 and contributed a map and geographical notes to Prince Maximilian's *Reise in das innere Nord-America* (3 vols., 1839–41), which is best known for the engravings of Native American life by Karl Bodmer, the prince's travelling companion, and which went through numerous editions in German, French, and particularly English. After a brief illness Thorn died of apoplexy on 29 November 1843, leaving a widow and six children. He was buried in the cemetery in Neuwied, later renamed the Julius Remy Friedhof.

R. H. Vetch, *rev.* Francis Herbert

Sources F. Herbert, 'Wheat revised and Thorn recognized: Maximilian of Wied's cartographer', *Terra Incognita* [in press] · P. Wirtgen, *Neuwied und seine Umgebung* (1872) · *Wöchentliche Neuwiedsche Nachrichtung* (5 Dec 1843) · *GM*, 2nd ser., 21 (1844), 430–31 · War Office records, War Office · *Annual Register* (1844) · church records, Evangelischer Kirchengemeinde, Neuwied · *Der Alte Friedhof in Neuwied* (1987)
Archives RGS
Likenesses Prinz Carl zu Wied, portrait, Fürstlich-Wiedisches Archiv, Neuwied, Germany; repro. in verso of Thorn's map of 1824 'Charte des Fürstlich-Wiedischen Besitzungen'; repro. with notes by Konrad Schneider (1990?)

Thornborough, John (1551?–1641), bishop of Worcester, was probably the son of Giles Thornborough of Salisbury, Wiltshire. In 1569, aged seventeen, he was admitted a demy of Magdalen College, Oxford, as of Wiltshire. He led a raffish undergraduate life, employing as his servant the young Simon Forman, who recorded that among other dubious activities Thornborough jilted a daughter of Giles Lawrence, archdeacon of Wiltshire. He graduated BA on 1 April 1573, and proceeded MA on 27 June 1575.

Having become chaplain to Henry Herbert, second earl of Pembroke, Thornborough accumulated a series of west country rectories: Ockford Fitzpaine, Dorset, and Orcheston St Mary, Wiltshire, in 1575; Marnhull, Dorset, in 1577; and Chilmark, Wiltshire, in 1578. On 16 June 1576 he was installed prebendary of Netherbury in Salisbury Cathedral on the presentation of a local brewer. Probably by 1582 he had become chaplain-in-ordinary to Queen Elizabeth, and on 22 March that year proceeded BTh at Oxford. In January 1586 he received letters patent for the mastership of the Savoy Hospital, London. On 14 July following he exchanged Netherbury for the Salisbury prebend of Bedminster and Ratcliffe. On 12 June 1587 letters patent for the archdeaconry of Norfolk proved ineffective.

According to his own account Thornborough was in 1588 responsible for bringing 'that concealed land of the Dacres to her majesty's receipts of exchequer' (BL, Lansdowne MS 75, fol. 32*r*). This financial coup, and perhaps

John Thornborough (1551?–1641), by unknown artist, 1630

petitioned Elizabeth herself, offering to resign the deanery and live on an *ex gratia* pension. Elizabeth was predictably sympathetic and in September 1593 he was duly granted Limerick and allowed to hold his deanery *in commendam*.

For the next five years Thornborough shuttled between Ireland, London, and York, successfully petitioning for the regularization of Limerick's revenues, preaching there when in residence, and championing the cause of a government agent, William Udall, who had supplied information about the activities of Spanish spies and of the earl of Tyrone. In 1597 he was again a candidate for the bishopric of Salisbury.

Thornborough is last mentioned in the Irish state papers in December 1598 and in March 1599 he returned to York as a member of the council in the north. In 1601 and 1602 he obtained the Yorkshire rectories of Kirby Misperton and Brandesburton.

All this despite a scandal that would have destroyed a man who did not have the queen's entire backing. About 1582 Thornborough had married Elizabeth Bold. In 1594 or 1595, having reared several children, they were divorced, probably on the grounds of Elizabeth's adultery. Thornborough immediately remarried, even though as the law then stood divorce was no more than judicial separation and remarriage an impossibility. His new wife, Elizabeth Baynes, was moreover suspected to be pregnant at the time. Yet the queen seems to have condoned his actions: the second Mrs Thornborough was specifically mentioned in a deed of indenture which Elizabeth ordered to be drawn up to provide maintenance for Thornborough's former wife, and when he returned to York in 1599 it was with her 'special directions' that the council in the north 'yield him such countenance as may be seeming for one of his sort' (PRO, SP 15/34/3).

Thornborough certainly required such countenance. As Archbishop Matthew Hutton observed to Robert Cecil, his remarriage was 'flat contrary' to English law and 'much misliked by most of the clergy of this realm' (PRO, SP 12/270/75). Yet Hutton himself thought him the innocent party in the divorce case and, assured by Thornborough that he had not had sexual relations with his second wife before marriage, was prepared to consider it lawful.

Hutton may have come to regret his acquiescence. In 1601 the former Mrs Thornborough brought an action at common law, claiming that the bishop had defaulted on his alimony payments and invoking a penalty clause by which she was entitled to a lump-sum payment of £250. He countered with a plea in the court of requests, accusing her of deliberate fraud: that having secretly remarried she then remained in hiding, circulating a rumour that she was dead in order to cause his default and liability to the penalty clause. The outcome of the case is unknown but on 17 November 1602 Thornborough preached what proved to be Elizabeth's last accession day sermon. John Chamberlain pronounced it dull but perhaps it was Elizabeth's way of demonstrating her continuing belief in him.

On resigning Limerick, but again retaining his deanery

other secret services, evidently rendered him *persona grata* at court and secured him Elizabeth's unwavering support. When in May 1589 she demanded his further preferment Sir Francis Walsingham suggested the bishopric of Salisbury. Archbishops John Whitgift and John Piers pronounced him too young and insufficiently learned for so senior a post, proposing a junior deanery (Peterborough or Rochester) instead. Elizabeth therefore ordered Walsingham to 'bring him to accept one of these … for a beginning to further advancing of him' (PRO, SP 12/224/39). Thornborough managed to drive a better bargain and in October was elected dean of York. On 17 March 1590 Archbishop Piers collated him to the prebend of Tockrington in York Minster.

Although the deanery yielded over £300 per annum Thornborough quickly fell into debt. In July 1592 he applied in abject terms to the lord treasurer, Lord Burghley, for the bishopric of Limerick, to be held *in commendam* with his deanery. He was prepared to resign the Savoy and live in Ireland, solely on Limerick's revenues, until his debts were discharged. By July 1593 he and his sureties (his father and brother) had become liable to imprisonment for defaulting on payment of his first fruits. Desperate, he *in commendam*, Thornborough was enthroned bishop of Bristol on 23 August 1603. He perhaps owed his new sinecure to his wholehearted espousal of James I's plans for political union, for in 1604 he published *A discourse plainly proving the evident utilitie and urgent necessitie of the union of England and Scotland*. The House of Commons took immediate offence. Having emasculated James's proposals on the subject in April, they launched an attack on the book as violating the parliamentary privilege of secret debate. Their attempts to suppress it did not deter Thornborough, who returned to his theme in *The Joiefull and Blessed Reuniting the Two Kingdomes, England & Scotland* (1605).

Never resident in Bristol, Thornborough remained an active dean of York. It was complained that his visits were usually infrequent and that he refused to allow important business to go forward in his absence but he was certainly preoccupied with the question of recusancy. Although his relations with archbishops Hutton and Toby Matthew are obscure he antagonized Edmund, third Lord Sheffield, president of the council in the north from 1603. In 1607, describing him as 'the unholy bishop of Bristol', Sheffield accused Thornborough of neglecting his preaching duties for his own gain and in order to curry favour with the government, 'for what time he could spare from bowling and carding' he spent in hounding recusants (*Salisbury MSS*, 19.274). In fact Thornborough's efforts were more statesmanlike than Sheffield was prepared to admit. He was as concerned with recusant conformity as with extracting recusancy fines and after 1611 had the backing of the new primate, George Abbot.

Yet scandal was never far from Thornborough's door. In February 1612 an (unnamed) son committed suicide, apparently terrified of admitting to his stepmother that he had lost money at tennis. In 1615 Thornborough fell foul of the privy council for failing to provide a preaching minister in Pickering, capitulating only when summoned to London to answer charges. During the winter of 1615–16 Mrs Thornborough was obscurely implicated in the *cause célèbre* of James's reign, the poisoning of Sir Thomas Overbury.

Still Thornborough prospered. After more than thirty years of government service and despite the candidature of Henry Beaumont, the duke of Buckingham's kinsman, he was elected bishop of Worcester on 25 January 1617 at the suit of William, third earl of Pembroke. Still vigorous, he immediately conducted a primary visitation, thereafter visiting triennially until 1636, proved an energetic Worcestershire magistrate, and seldom delegated episcopal functions to subordinates.

In 1621 Thornborough celebrated his lifelong interest in chemistry and alchemy by publishing, in Latin, *Lithotheorikos*. Parading his wide knowledge of ancient, medieval, and Renaissance authorities on the subject, it argues a deep, dark strain in his psyche. In 1627 he prepared for himself a grandiose tomb, decorated with obscure mottoes and astrological symbols rather than scriptural texts.

That year Thornborough secured the presentation of the next vacant prebend in the cathedral for his son Giles and in 1629 collated his son Edward to the archdeaconry of Worcester. In February 1630 Giles Thornborough recorded the sudden death of his stepmother. The bishop subsequently took a third wife, Anne (*née* Beswick), widow of Sir Henry Bromley of Holt Castle, Worcestershire.

Always at heart an Elizabethan Calvinist, Thornborough won the good opinion of Richard Baxter, who noted with approval that he never used the sign of the cross in baptism. Yet his one work of theology, *The last will and testament of Jesus Christ touching the blessed sacrament of his body and blood* (1630), was perhaps, like his later visitation articles, an attempt to move with the times. His last years were nevertheless overshadowed by an increasingly acrimonious relationship with his chapter and its Laudian dean, Christopher Potter, installed in 1636, as well as by further family scandals. He evidently recognized that Charles I's church was doomed and told the king not long before his death that, while he had outlived several men who had expected to succeed him, he was now afraid that he would outlive the bishopric itself. Among his manuscripts was a plea for unity and peace in the church, *Pax vobis*. He returned to an abiding theme in his last published work, *A Discourse … Advocating the Union of England and Scotland* 'into one Great Britain' (1641).

Thornborough died at Hartlebury, Worcestershire, on 9 July 1641 and was duly buried in his tomb in Worcester Cathedral. His third wife predeceased him. In his will he provided for the children of his eldest son, Sir John, and his second, Sir Benjamin, who had both predeceased him. He made bequests to Edward and his family, and to the families of his daughters Jane Finch, Anne Smith, and Lady Elizabeth Willoughby. His son Giles, prebendary of Worcester (*d.* 1663), goes unmentioned. His son from his second marriage, Sir Thomas, already in receipt of a yearly annuity, received only a token bequest. One son-in-law, Francis Finch, was made overseer; another, Emmanuel Smith, his chaplain, witnessed the will.

BRETT USHER

Sources Foster, *Alum. Oxon.* · J. R. Bloxam, *A register of the presidents, fellows … of Saint Mary Magdalen College*, 8 vols. (1853–85) · *Calendar of the manuscripts of the most hon. the marquis of Salisbury*, 7, HMC, 9 (1899); 10–11 (1904–6); 13 (1915); 15–23 (1930–73) · *Fasti Angl., 1541–1857*, [Salisbury; Ely; York] · R. Somerville, *The Savoy* (1960) · *CSP dom.*, 1595–1633 · *CSP Ire.*, 1592–8 · BL, Lansdowne MSS 72, 75 · court of requests, proceedings, PRO, REQ 2/51/45 · K. Fincham, ed., *Visitation articles and injunctions of the early Stuart church*, 1 (1994) · K. Fincham, ed., *Visitation articles and injunctions of the early Stuart church*, 2 (1998) · M. Questier, 'Sir Henry Spiller, recusancy and the efficiency of the Jacobean exchequer', *Historical Research*, 66 (1993), 251–66 · *The letters of John Chamberlain*, ed. N. E. McClure, 2 vols. (1939) · A. L. Rowse, 'Bishop Thornborough: a clerical careerist', *For Veronica Wedgwood These*, ed. R. Ollard and P. Tudor-Craig (1986), 89–108 · E. H. Pearce, *Hartlebury Castle* (1926) · I. G. Smith and P. Onslow, *Diocesan histories: Worcester* (1883) · J. Hawkins and B. Usher, *John Thornborough, bishop of Worcester: a life* [forthcoming] · PRO, state papers domestic, Elizabeth I, SP 12/224/39; SP 12/270/75 · PRO, state papers domestic, addenda Edward VI–James I, SP 15/34/3 · C. Cross, 'From the Reformation to the Restoration', *A history of York Minster*, ed. G. E. Aylmer and R. Cant (1977), 193–232 · PRO, SP 16/156/44

Archives BL, Lansdowne MSS · Glos. RO, Bristol diocesan records · Hatfield House, Hertfordshire, Hatfield MSS · PRO, state papers domestic • PRO, state papers Ireland • Worcs. RO, Worcester diocesan records • York Minster, dean and chapter records **Likenesses** oils, 1630, NPG [*see illus.*] • school of R. Lockey, portrait, NPG • portraits, Hartlebury Castle, Worcestershire **Wealth at death** unquantifiable; £400–£500 in cash legacies to family: will

Thornbrough, Sir Edward (1754–1834), naval officer, was born at Plymouth Dock on 27 July 1754, the only son of Commander Edward Thornbrough (*d.* 1784) and his wife, Mary. He had two younger sisters. In June 1761 he went to sea as servant to his father, first lieutenant of *Arrogant* (74 guns), and spent two years in the Mediterranean. For the next five years he was on the books of the *Firm* (60 guns), guardship at Plymouth, and was presumably at school.

In March 1768 Thornbrough rejoined his father in *Temeraire* (74 guns), also guardship at Plymouth, commanded by Captain Edward Le Cras (*d.* 1793), two of whose daughters he was later to marry; the tedium of guardship life was broken by a short trooping visit to Gibraltar. After four months in *Albion* (74 guns) at Spithead he again joined his father, now first lieutenant of *Captain* (64 guns), flagship of Rear-Admiral John Montagu, and sailed for North America in June 1771. After nearly two years berthed in Boston harbour he was promoted lieutenant on 16 April 1773 and joined the sloop *Cruizer*, but he rejoined the *Captain* and his father in September, and returned home in August 1774. In October he joined the sloop *Falcon* as second in command and returned to North America; she was soon supporting the army at Bunker Hill on 17 June 1775. On 8 August Thornbrough led a gallant but unsuccessful attempt by the ship's boats to capture a well-armed American schooner which *Falcon* had chased into Cape Ann harbour. Twenty-four of his men were taken prisoner, and several were wounded, including Thornbrough. He was invalided home but in April 1776 joined the frigate *Richmond*, and served in her for three years mostly off North America. After seven months in the frigate *Garland* escorting a convoy to Newfoundland and back, he joined the frigate *Flora* (Captain William Peere Williams) and distinguished himself in a sanguinary action when the French frigate *Nymphe* was captured off Ushant on 10 August 1780.

For this Thornbrough was immediately promoted commander and given command of *Britannia*, a hired ship protecting trade in the North Sea and escorting a convoy to New York. On arrival he was promoted captain (24 September 1781) and appointed to command the frigate *Blonde*. In May 1782 she captured an American ship laden with naval stores; when towing her to Halifax *Blonde* ran aground in thick fog off Nantucket. While the prize continued to Halifax, *Blonde*'s crew and her American prisoners landed on an uninhabited islet, and were rescued two days later by two American ships. In return for Thornbrough's humane treatment of his prisoners, he and his ship's company were released by the Americans at New York, which was in British hands. At the subsequent court martial Thornbrough was commended for his conduct and acquitted. On his return home he was appointed

to the *Egmont* (74 guns), intended for the East Indies, but she paid off at the peace in 1783.

However, in October Thornbrough assumed command of the frigate *Hebe*. By now his reputation was such that *Hebe* was selected by Lord Howe to take the nineteen-year-old Prince William Henry (later William IV) on his promotion to lieutenant in June 1785. William served as her third lieutenant for nine months, including on a cruise round Great Britain, and told his brother that he was 'upon the best terms with Captain Thornbrough, who is a very worthy man and does everything to make me happy' (25 Nov 1785, *Correspondence of George, Prince of Wales*, 1.150). On 16 March 1784 Thornbrough had married Ann (*d.* 1801), elder daughter of Edward Le Cras, then a commissioner of the navy. Their elder son, born while the prince was serving in *Hebe*, was baptized William Henry at the prince's request; he died aged fourteen, already a lieutenant in the navy. The younger son became a rear-admiral, and there were four daughters who died young. After six years in command of *Hebe* in home waters, 'a period unexampled in time of peace' (Marshall, 165) and in which he was particularly active against smugglers, Thornbrough commissioned *Scipio* (64 guns) in July 1790 for six months during the Spanish armament.

On 21 December 1792, in anticipation of war with France, Thornbrough commissioned the frigate *Latona*, in the Channel Fleet under Howe. For the courageous way in which, on 18 November 1793, he approached a French squadron under heavy fire and endeavoured to delay it until the British line of battleships could get up, he was publicly commended in a letter from the Admiralty to be read to all the ships' companies. At the battle of 1 June 1794 *Latona* was stationed abreast the centre of the British line to repeat Howe's signals, but entered the thick of the fight to assist the hard-pressed *Bellerophon* under attack from two French 74s. *Latona* answered the fire of the 74s 'with as smart a return as a frigate's battery could give' (James, 1.155).

In July Thornbrough was rewarded with command of *Robust* (74 guns), and served in her in the Channel Fleet for nearly five years. She took part in the ill-fated royalist expedition to Quiberon in 1795, giving passage to 'two French Dukes, five Field-Marshals, four Admirals and 10 ADCs etc.etc.etc., in all upwards of 50' (26 Jan 1796, PRO, ADM 1/2597). On 12 October 1798 Thornbrough led Sir John Borlase Warren's squadron into action, suffering severe damage when a French squadron was defeated near Tory Island off Donegal, thus thwarting an invasion of Ireland. All participants received the thanks of parliament. On 14 February 1799 Thornbrough was appointed colonel of marines and in the same month transferred to *Formidable* (90 guns), 'which ship Captain Thornbrough has had the merit of making the crack ship of the fleet' (St Vincent to Lord Spencer, 14 Sept 1800, *Private Papers of George, Second Earl Spencer*, 4.17). *Formidable* sailed to the Mediterranean under Sir Charles Cotton and took part in the unsuccessful search for Bruix's fleet. Promoted rear-admiral on 1 January 1801, Thornbrough hoisted his flag in

Mars (74 guns) and for six months held the arduous command of the inshore squadron off Brest. His first wife died on 20 November 1801 and on 14 December 1802 he married Elizabeth (1775–1813), daughter of Sir Edwin Jeynes (1750–1810), mercer and banker of Bristol.

With the renewal of war in 1803 Thornbrough commanded a squadron in the North Sea and off the Texel under Viscount Keith for two years, and was then captain of the fleet to Lord Gardner in the Channel Fleet for four months. In October 1805 he hoisted his flag in *Kent* (74 guns) and was about to sail to join Nelson off Cadiz when news of Trafalgar was received. He was promoted vice-admiral on 9 November and in *Prince of Wales* (90 guns) commanded a detached squadron off Rochefort and subsequently in the channel until October 1806, when ill-health obliged him to go ashore. By February, however, he was again afloat, in the *Royal Sovereign* (100 guns), and he joined Lord Collingwood in the Mediterranean as his second in command. He spent most of the next three years guarding Sicily or blockading Toulon until his health obliged him to return home in December 1809. He was an admirable second in command but, as St Vincent wrote of him, though he was 'as brave as a lion in the presence of the enemy' (16 Nov 1806, *Naval Miscellany*, 4.482), he lacked the nerve to take the weight of great responsibility. Collingwood perhaps felt the same when he wrote to his wife in October 1809: 'I do not like to part with so firm a man. He would be a host to me in battle' (*Public and Private Correspondence*, 2.408).

From August 1810 to November 1813 Thornbrough was commander-in-chief of the Irish station; on 4 December 1813 he was promoted admiral of the blue and on 2 January 1815 he was created KCB. His second wife died in November 1813 and on 23 August 1814 he married Frances Le Cras (1764/5–1851), younger sister of his first wife. He was commander-in-chief, Portsmouth, for three years from April 1815 with his son as his flag lieutenant. Advanced to GCB on 11 January 1825, on 30 January 1833 he was appointed vice-admiral of the United Kingdom and lieutenant of the Admiralty. He died, an admiral of the red, in Bishopsteignton Lodge, Devon, on 3 April 1834, aged seventy-nine, and was buried in Bishopsteignton on 11 April. There is a memorial to him in Exeter Cathedral.

Thornbrough's career is remarkable for the exceptional length of his sea service—forty-nine and a half years between 1761 and 1818 by his own reckoning (PRO, ADM 9/1/21). 'As a practical seaman', wrote Sir William Hotham, who served under him,

he had very few rivals and certainly no superior ... This knowledge of the minutiae of a seaman's duty extended to the managing of a fleet ... He was very good-natured and ... it was not easy to leave Sir Edward's society and conversation without acquiring some increase in professional knowledge. (*DNB*; Hotham, 1.198–203)

C. H. H. Owen

Sources DNB · PRO, ADM 1/2597; ADM 9/1/21; ADM 1; ADM 1/99; ADM 1/485; ADM 1/5320; ADM 36; ADM 51 · J. Ralfe, *The naval biography of Great Britain*, 2 (1828), 357–66 · J. Marshall, *Royal naval biography*, 1/1 (1823), 165–72 · Burke, *Gen. GB* (1838), 4.300–02 · *United Service Journal*, 2 (1834), 204–10 · W. James, *The naval history of Great Britain, from the declaration of war by France in 1793, to the accession of George IV*, [3rd edn], 6 vols. (1837), vol. 1 · *Private papers of George, second Earl Spencer*, ed. J. S. Corbett and H. W. Richmond, 4 vols., Navy RS, 46, 48, 58–9 (1913–24) · *A selection from the public and private correspondence of Vice-Admiral Lord Collingwood, interspersed with memoirs of his life*, ed. G. L. Newnham-Collingwood, 5th edn, 2 vols. (1837) · *Pages and portraits from the past: being the private papers of Sir William Hotham*, ed. A. M. W. Stirling, 2 vols. (1919) · *The correspondence of George, prince of Wales, 1770–1812*, ed. A. Aspinall, 1: 1770–1789 (1963) · J. K. Laughton, ed., *The naval miscellany*, 1, Navy RS, 20 (1902) · parish register (baptism), 19 Aug 1754, Stoke Damerel · parish register (burial), 11 April 1834, Bishopsteignton · *LondG*

Archives BL, corresp. with Col. H. Lane, Add. MSS 20107–20108, 20163, 20166, 20189–20190 · Hunt. L., letters to Greville family · NA Scot., corresp. with Lord Melville · NMM, letters to Lord Keith

Likenesses S. Lane, oils, *c*.1825, NMM · W. T. Fry, stipple (after A. Huey, *c*.1815), NMM, NPG

Wealth at death £60,000: PRO, death duty registers, IR 26/1367, no. 216

Thornbury, (George) Walter (1828–1876), author, was born in London on 13 November 1828, the son of George Thornbury (1795–1873), solicitor, of 16 Chancery Lane, and his wife, Jennet Ann. He was educated at Cheam, Surrey, by the rector, Barton Bouchier, who was the husband of his father's sister, Mary. His parents had hoped that he would enter the church, but Thornbury wanted to be an artist, and spent some time at the academy of James Mathews Leigh. By the age of seventeen he had published topographical and antiquarian papers in Felix Farley's *Bristol Journal*, and ultimately decided to be a writer.

Thornbury was living in London by 1851, and became a regular contributor to many other periodicals, including *Bentley's Miscellany, Ainsworth's, Welcome Guest, Once a Week*, and *Chambers's Journal*. He was a prolific writer, but not meticulous in his habits; one friend spoke fondly of his 'disastrously bad hand. The prevailing impression in your mind was that not ink, but a succession of small bombshells had been discharged from poor Walter's pen, and that these petards had exploded on the paper' (Sala, 1.276–7). Thornbury was also a frequent contributor to the later volumes of Dickens's *Household Words*, and became one of a group of journalists—including G. A. Sala, Percy Fitzgerald, and Edmund Yates—commonly referred to at the time as Dickens's 'young men' (Sala, 1.77, 94). Many of Thornbury's articles dealt with geographical and topographical themes, and he travelled widely in search of material for the journal—to the United States and Palestine, the Iberian peninsula and Turkey. His articles on Spain printed in *Household Words* were later collected and reprinted as *Life in Spain: Past and Present* (2 vols., 1859). His contributions to Dickens's second periodical, *All the Year Round*, consisted of two more extended series. 'Old stories retold', fifty-three articles running from 20 October 1866 to 18 July 1868, recounted events in recent history, and often dealt with crimes and criminal proceedings. The content and tone of some of these articles worried Dickens, as he began to feel that Thornbury was 'rather given to horrors' (*Letters of Charles Dickens*, 11.371). He rejected one article, feeling that its detailing of criminal acts was 'not wholesome for a large audience' and 'scarcely justifiable ... as claiming to be a piece of literature' (ibid., 11.346–7). But Dickens valued Thornbury as a contributor, and interested himself in his reprinted collections as well, cautioning him away from 'too many murders' (ibid., 11.394). Thornbury's later series of thirty-one articles on the safer topic of travel around Britain was instigated at Dickens's suggestion and was printed in *All the Year Round* between 12 December 1868 and 27 November 1869 under the title 'As the crow flies'. When Thornbury reprinted the series in two volumes in 1870 as *A Tour Round England*, he dedicated it with permission to Dickens. Throughout their association Dickens demonstrated regard for Thornbury and his writing, remarking in a letter in 1866 that 'For some years I have had so much pleasure in reading you, that I can honestly warrant myself "a good audience"' (ibid., 11.245–6).

All the while Thornbury was engaged in art criticism; he was a regular contributor to *The Athenaeum* and the *Art Journal*. His first contributions in this vein to *The Athenaeum* were reprinted as *The Courts of the Crystal Palace in Hyde Park* (1851). But his most important publication was his *Life of J. M. W. Turner* (2 vols., 1861), based on original letters and papers. It was written under the supervision of John Ruskin, a situation which Thornbury likened to 'very much like working bareheaded under a tropical sun!' (*DNB*). In the same year he also produced *British Artists, from Hogarth to Turner: a Series of Biographical Sketches* (1861). His other writings were varied in style and subject matter, including translations such as *Pierre Dupont's Legend of the Wandering Jew* (1857) and *The Fables of La Fontaine* (1867), and historical works such as *Shakespeare's England* (1856). His *Haunted London* (1865) was 'a huge book, full of most curious matter' (*The Athenaeum*, 829), where his slightly macabre interests seemed more acceptable than in his purely historical writing. His collections of poetry were generally undistinguished, although one poem from *Songs of the Cavaliers and Roundheads* (1857), 'The jester's sermon', is occasionally still anthologized, and sections of its catalogue of follies remain quotable, such as: 'The fool that eats till he is sick must fast till he is well'. Thornbury was also a novelist, although his fiction was less highly regarded than his other work. *True as Steel* (1863) was based on Goethe's *Götz von Berlichingen*, and *Wildfire* (1864) was an expansion of a sketch by Diderot, and dealt with the French Revolution. His best-known novel at the time was probably *Greatheart* (1866), the eponymous hero of which was modelled on John Douglas Cook, the temperamental editor of the *Saturday Review*, an identification which 'got its author into some trouble' (Escott, 233).

On 7 October 1873 Thornbury married Harriett, the daughter of William Furmedge. They had known each other for some time—Dickens had teased him about their relationship in a letter in 1868 referring to 'the specially gentle and beautiful face' (*Letters of Charles Dickens*, 12.210). Thornbury was afflicted with mental illness during his last years, and he died on 11 June 1876 at the Camberwell House Lunatic Asylum, Peckham Road, London from, as his death certificate records, 'exhaustion from acute mania'. He was buried on 13 June at Nunhead cemetery, London, survived by his wife and three young sons. The second volume of his popular descriptive history of London, entitled *Old and New London*, had appeared just before his death. The series was completed in four additional volumes by Edward Walford.

M. CLARE LOUGHLIN-CHOW

Sources *DNB* · m. cert. · d. cert. · *The Athenaeum*, 61 (17 June 1876), 828–9 · *The letters of Charles Dickens*, ed. M. House, G. Storey, and others, 12 vols. (1965–2002) · G. A. Sala, *Things I have seen and people I have known*, 2 vols. (1894) · A. Lohrli, '*Household Words*', a weekly journal, 1850–1859, conducted by Charles Dickens: table of contents, list of contributors and their contributions (1973) · Boase, *Mod. Eng. biog.* · *ILN* (24 June 1876) · T. H. S. Escott, *Masters of English journalism* (1911)
Archives NL Scot., letters to Blackwoods · Wellcome L., letters to Henry Lee · Yale U., Beinecke L., letters to Frederick Locker-Lampson
Likenesses wood-engraving (after photograph by C. Watkins), NPG; repro. in *ILN*
Wealth at death £200: administration, 16 June 1876, *CGPLA Eng. & Wales*

Thornden, Richard (*c*.1490–1558), Benedictine monk and bishop-suffragan of Dover, was probably born about 1490. He is first recorded on 1 September 1511, when he was tonsured as a novice monk of Canterbury Cathedral priory; he made his monastic profession in the following year. He was ordained subdeacon in 1513, deacon in 1514, and had become a priest by 12 April 1517, when he celebrated his first mass. In the meantime, possibly as early as 1511, he had gone as a student to Canterbury College, Oxford, becoming a fellow by 1514. On 21 June 1522 he was admitted BTh, supplicating DTh five years later, but not incepting until 1532. On 8 March 1524 he was appointed warden of Canterbury College, and held this office for ten years, during which he was at various times acting chancellor and pro-vice-chancellor of the university. In 1534 he resigned his college wardenship and became warden of the priory manors, an office he obtained with the support of Thomas Cromwell, to whom he sent papers concerning Elizabeth Barton, the Nun of Kent.

Thornden's religious views in the early 1530s were flexible, not to say doubtful. He maintained links with the conservative prior of Christ Church priory, Thomas Goldwell, yet obtained the good will of Cromwell and Archbishop Thomas Cranmer, as a man 'as ready to set forward his Prince's causes as no man more of his coat' (*LP Henry VIII*, 13/1, no. 527). At the dissolution in 1540 he was given a £10 pension, and in 1541 was appointed to the first prebendal stall in the new secular chapter of Canterbury Cathedral. His relationship with Cranmer is difficult to fathom. Never part of Cranmer's circle of committed reforming preachers and household officials, he was nevertheless not regarded as an opponent of the Reformation. Besides his canonry he accumulated additional benefices during the 1540s, several directly from the archbishop. However, although he remained outwardly loyal when conservative gentry and cathedral clergy combined to embarrass Cranmer with evidence of alleged heretical activity in the diocese, investigations held in the wake of the exposure of the prebendaries' plot of 1543 revealed that Thornden had in fact been party to it. According to the anonymous biography of Cranmer printed by John

Foxe (probably by Stephen Nevinson), when confronted with the evidence of his duplicity Thornden offered a grovelling apology and pleaded for Cranmer's pardon. Foxe reports that Cranmer forgave him and within a year of the incident Thornden was created bishop-suffragan of Dover. Other parochial preferments followed.

Very little is known of Thornden's activities between 1547 and 1553. His private religious attitudes are unclear, but his ambition was central. He conformed to the protestant reforms of the period and retained his many livings. In 1554 one of Cardinal Pole's staff (in a letter recorded by Foxe) reminded Thornden, who was publicly demonstrating his Catholic credentials, that he had supported all aspects of the crown's protestant programme since the break with Rome. On the death of Edward VI Thornden very quickly showed his new commitment to Catholicism by restoring the mass in Canterbury Cathedral before it was legally permitted, and while Cranmer was under duress in London, for which Cranmer called him 'a false, flattering, lying and dissembling monk' (Strype, 435). He collected two additional livings in 1554, but gave one up about this time. Sustained by the incomes of a canonry and five parochial benefices, Thornden was second in importance only to Archdeacon Nicholas Harpsfield in administering Canterbury diocese in 1554–7. Active in ordaining new priests, he was commissioned to hear heresy cases by Pole in December 1554, was appointed a Kent county JP in 1555, and was also one of the quorum of the Canterbury diocese heresy commission of April 1556. During these years he and Harpsfield were the leading inquisitors in heresy cases brought against protestants in Kent, and Thornden figures prominently in the pages of Foxe's *Acts and Monuments* as 'Dick of Dover'. According to Foxe, while in apparently good health and watching a game of bowls Thornden 'fell suddenly in a palsy and so being had to bed was willed to remember God: "Yea, so I do," said he, "and my lord Cardinal too"'. He had died at Bishopsbourne, Kent, by March 1558, when new appointments were made to his benefices.   MICHAEL ZELL

Sources registers of Thomas Cranmer and Reginald Pole, LPL · BL, Lansdowne MS 980, fol. 236 · state papers, Mary and Philip and Mary, PRO, SP 11/5, fols. 36–70 · Emden, *Oxf.*, vol. 4 · W. A. Pantin, *Canterbury College, Oxford*, 3, OHS, new ser., 8 (1950), 152 · E. Hasted, *The history and topographical survey of the county of Kent*, 2nd edn, 2 (1797), 605; 4 (1798), 335 · *The acts and monuments of John Foxe*, ed. J. Pratt, [new edn], 8 vols. in 16 (1853–70), vol. 7, pp. 297–8; vol. 8, pp. 29–30, 253, 321, 629, 667 · J. G. Nichols, ed., *Narratives of the days of the Reformation*, CS, old ser., 77 (1859) · *Writings and disputations of Thomas Cranmer*, ed. J. E. Cox, Parker Society, [17] (1844) · J. Strype, *Memorials of the most reverend father in God Thomas Cranmer*, 3 vols. in 4 (1848–54) · S. Robertson, *Richard Thornden, the second bishop of Dover* [in Canterbury Dean and Chapter Library] · D. Loades, *The Oxford martyrs* (1970) · M. L. Zell, 'The prebendaries' plot of 1543: a reconsideration', *Journal of Ecclesiastical History*, 27 (1976), 241–53 · D. MacCulloch, *Thomas Cranmer: a life* (1996) · *CPR, 1555–7*, 24–5 · J. Greatrex, *Biographical register of the English cathedral priories of the province of Canterbury* (1997), 303–4 · *LP Henry VIII*, 13/1, no. 527

Thorndike, Herbert (*bap.* 1597?, *d.* 1672), biblical scholar and theologian, was probably baptized on 16 April 1597 at Cumberworth, Lincolnshire, the third of four sons of Francis Thorndike (*d.* 1645) of Scamblesby in the same county, and of his wife, Alice (*d.* 1623), daughter of Edward Coleman of Waldingfield, Suffolk. Like his father he was admitted to Trinity College, Cambridge, from where he matriculated as a pensioner in Michaelmas term 1613. He became a scholar in 1614, graduated BA in 1617, and proceeded MA in 1620, when he was incorporated at Oxford. In the 1620s he acted as deputy to his friend and colleague George Herbert, public orator in the university until 1627. He was a university preacher in 1631 and served as proctor in 1638–9. His interest in Near and Middle Eastern languages was evidenced in his *Epitome lexici Hebraici, Syriaci, rabinici et Arabici* (1635), and in 1640 he was Hebrew lecturer at Trinity. Ordained priest, he was a prebendary of Lincoln Cathedral from 1636 to 1640 and vicar of Claybrooke, Leicestershire, from 1639 to 1642, but he continued to reside in Cambridge.

When traditional episcopal government was under attack in the Long Parliament in 1641, Thorndike published *Of the Government of Churches: a Discourse Pointing at the Primitive Form*. Like Archbishop James Ussher's *Judgement of Doctor Rainolds Touching the Originall of Episcopacy* of the same year, it presented a historical case that the apostles had appointed presbyters to serve the churches they had founded and that they were then succeeded by bishops, who presided over groups of presbyters in the major cities of the ancient Mediterranean world. Current circumstances, Thorndike contended, demanded not the abolition of the episcopate but the restoration of presbyters (priests, in the language of the church's ordinal) to their role of assisting bishops, perhaps by associating the latter more closely with their cathedral chapters. His *Of Religious Assemblies and the Public Service of God* (1642), which drew extensively on Hebrew and Greek sources, defended the Book of Common Prayer as providing services that were consistent with biblical and ancient models. He rejected the Roman Catholic doctrines of the sacrifice of the mass and of transubstantiation, while he cited approvingly Calvin's teaching that the Lord's supper should be celebrated frequently.

Following the outbreak of civil war in 1642, Thorndike, who that year became senior bursar of his college as well as rector of Barley, Hertfordshire, was among a number of Cambridge scholars considered dangerous by parliamentary leaders. In September 1643 he was the leading candidate for master in a closely contested election at Sidney Sussex College, but parliamentary soldiers seized and carried off John Pawson, a fellow who supported Thorndike, thus throwing the election to Richard Minshull. Subsequently Thorndike lost not only his fellowship at Trinity but also, some time before 31 May 1645, his living at Barley. By 1648 Thorndike was associated with Sir Justinian Isham of Lamport, Northamptonshire, a royalist whom he assisted with advice about book purchases; in the late 1650s he was a guest at Isham's country house. He was also among 'distressed clergy' assisted by John Scudamore, Viscount Scudamore. According to his biographer Arthur Haddan, despite his expulsion, Trinity College gave him money in 1649, 1650, 1651, 1654, and 1659.

These years of dislocation were a time of remarkable

achievement for Thorndike as a scholar and writer. In the wake of parliament's abolition of episcopacy and ban on the public use of the prayer book, he published *A Discourse of the Right of the Church in a Christian State* (1649). Departing from the tradition of Richard Hooker and other conformist writers, he attempted to distinguish the appropriate spheres of responsibility of the church and the civil government. Referring several times to Thomas Hobbes's *De cive* (1642), he described the church as a society with its own organization and activities, chiefly assembling for worship, which it was bound to continue against, if necessary, all the civil law in the world. In a Christian state, he argued, it was appropriate for the civil authorities to regulate the church's external affairs, but they could not by right alter the church's polity or curtail its spiritual functions; bishops were those who exercised the highest ecclesiastical power in the church and must be left in place. In 1650, Thorndike's earlier treatises on the government of the church and on Christian worship were reissued in Cambridge with a 'review', answering objections that had been raised, under the title *Two Discourses*. His *Letter Concerning the Present State of Religion* (1656) advised his correspondent to have nothing to do with any pastor intruded in his parish church under the terms of the ordinance setting up 'triers' for ejecting scandalous ministers and those who adhered to 'Popery and Prelacy' (p. 1). To Thorndike, the ordinance contradicted the idea of 'one holy Catholic and apostolic church' in its rejection of those clergy committed to the historic episcopate, especially since they fulfilled its other criterion of profession of faith in Jesus Christ according to the scriptures. Indeed, he concluded that it also violated presbyterian and congregational polity. However, he reassured his correspondent that he could find clergy of the pre-war church who were willing to catechize children and administer the sacraments, and that, in any case, he had the prayer book, homilies, and scriptures authorized by that church and could use them in private.

From the early 1650s Thorndike had been working as one of the chief compilers of the edition of the Bible in its original languages, prepared under the direction of Brian Walton and published as *Biblia sacra polyglotta* (1657); he had special responsibility for the Syriac portion. Soon after its appearance, in 1657–8, he considered an invitation from William Sancroft, a former fellow of Emmanuel College, Cambridge, to migrate to the Netherlands, but did not immediately accept, probably because he wanted to stay in London, where he was busy with his scholarly projects. Thorndike did go abroad in late November 1659 to visit Isaac Vosius, the Dutch classicist and patristics scholar, and to search for manuscripts, particularly of the writings of the ancient Greek Christian theologian Origen. He obtained from Vosius the *Codex Holmiensis*, containing the only complete Greek text of Origen's treatise 'On prayer' (Trinity College Library, Cambridge), but he was suffering from a serious stomach illness and he cut his trip short, returning to London by the end of the year.

Thorndike's own major publication of the interregnum, *An Epilogue to the Tragedy of the Church of England*, used what he called 'the Present Calamity of the Church of England' as the basis for discussing a wide range of theological issues: scripture and tradition, the Trinity, justification, predestination, the sacraments, and relations between church and state. His intention was evidently to lay a foundation not only for the restoration of the Church of England but also for the bringing together of the major Western churches. Reason was the means of resolving differences, but it was to be guided by the scriptures as understood by the 'whole Church, from the beginning' (bk 1, pp. 1–3, 35). In the section entitled 'The covenant of grace' he combined a doctrine of justification by grace through faith with a doctrine of the church as the body of the baptized who sought to be obedient to God's commands and were nurtured by the word and sacraments. The 'Epilogue' expressed both a protestant soteriology and a largely Catholic ecclesiology. Thorndike regarded the Roman Catholic church as 'a true Church' which 'continueth the same visible body, by the succession of Pastors and Lawes' from the apostles' days, but considered that it was corrupt in many ways and had made unwarranted additions to the historic Christian faith. He saw a mean between the extremes of Roman Catholicism and the radical protestant sects as the surest way to salvation. The work was not universally well received by Anglican loyalists: Edward Hyde reacted sharply in May 1659 to news of the book's publication, expressing dismay that Thorndike had cast doubt on the English church's prospects for survival and had thus aided its enemies.

With the Restoration and the reinstatement of bishops in the established church, Thorndike received back posts he had lost fifteen years before, taking up residence as a fellow of Trinity College, Cambridge, and regaining the rectory of Barley, although he resigned from the latter in 1662. He set out his plans for a reunited English church in *The Due Way of Composing the Differences on Foot Preserving the Church* (1660), where he argued that like the ancient church, it should be episcopally governed and its life centred on the celebration of the eucharist. He saw the reconstitution of the English church as an opportunity for Christians of all kinds, including protestant sectarians and recusant Roman Catholics, to form a single body which would reflect the greater unity that Christians sought. In practical terms, however, he was less eirenic, opposing, for example, the recognition of non-episcopal ordinations of the period of the civil wars and interregnum. Comprehension of the kind he had encouraged was not the result of the Savoy conference of 1661, of which he was a member, and he assisted in the preparation of the more narrowly drawn revised Book of Common Prayer, imposed by the Act of Uniformity of May 1662. A hardening attitude can be detected in his *Just Weights and Measures* (1662), which attempted to describe, using reason and the evidence of the practice of the church through the ages, the essential characteristics of the universal church. The sacraments of baptism and the eucharist were placed at the heart of the life of the church while the other traditional sacraments—confirmation, ordination, marriage, penance, and unction—were closely linked to the latter.

In 1663 Thorndike was nominated as a Cambridge DD by royal mandate, but he did not proceed to the degree. After resigning his fellowship at Trinity College, Cambridge, in 1667, Thorndike retired to Westminster Abbey, where he had been a prebendary since 5 September 1661, and lived in a residence in the cloisters. From 1668 he was joined by his nieces Alice and Martha, daughters of his late brother, John, recently returned from America. He had not retired from ecclesiological controversy. In *A Due Discourse of the Forbearance, or, The Penalties which a Due Reformation Requires* (1670), he argued against a proposed comprehension of ministers who had been ordained by presbyters only, on the grounds that episcopal ordination was now available to them. He acknowledged that foreign reformed divines who had been ordained by presbyters only had been recognized by the English church, but he asserted that their ordinations had been carried out by necessity, since bishops had not been available. He was, however, sympathetic to the presbyterian stress on the need for greater spiritual discipline in English parishes, which for Thorndike would include the use of private confession, and he proposed a conference on this subject. The same year he published a work he had evidently worked on for some time, *De ratione ac jure finiendi controversias ecclesiae disputatio*, a restatement in Latin of his fundamental theological principles, reflecting his continuing interest in reconciliation among the churches. This was the first volume of a projected longer work, and was reissued in 1674 as *Origines ecclesiasticae, sive, De jure et potestate ecclesiae Christianae exercitationes*.

Thorndike died on 11 July 1672 in Chiswick, where he had moved to a facility maintained by Westminster Abbey for those in failing health. He was buried in the abbey on 13 July. In his will he left funds for the augmentation of Trinity College livings, especially the vicarage of Trumpington, and benefactions for his nieces Alice and Martha and his great-niece Alice Alington (granddaughter of his brother Francis). Thorndike left unpublished Latin writings to Peter Gunning, bishop of Chichester. Several works, unpublished in Thorndike's lifetime, were first printed in his *Works*, edited by Arthur W. Haddan, from manuscripts in the chapter library at Westminster Abbey.

Thorndike was a controversial writer in his time, as Edward Hyde's response to the 'Epilogue' suggests. Henry More, the Cambridge Platonist, in his *Brief Reply to a Late Answer* (1672) took issue with what he saw as Thorndike's too favourable view of the Roman Catholic mass. Meanwhile, George Whitehead, in *The Popish Informer Reprehended for his False Information Against the Quakers Meetings* (1670), had attacked Thorndike for his assertion that the Quakers' reliance on the guidance of the Holy Spirit was greater than their reliance on the scriptures. Edward Stillingfleet took the side of More against Thorndike on the question of the Roman Catholic church's alleged idolatry in the use of images, in *A Defence of the Discourse Concerning the Idolatry Practised in the Church of Rome* (1676). On the other hand, the Roman Catholic writer Thomas Godden cited Thorndike's views approvingly in his *Catholicks No Idolators* (1672). A few years later, in an effort to vindicate

Thorndike from suspicion of popery, Stillingfleet published a manuscript by Thorndike, written 'a little before his death', which he included as part of *Several Conferences between a Romish Priest, a Fanatic Chaplain, and a Divine of the Church of England* (1679). Here the Church of England spokesman cited Thorndike's opinions on several doctrines of the Church of Rome, including transubstantiation, the papal deposing power, and the efficacy of indulgences, showing that he was soundly protestant. Nevertheless, Thorndike continued to be viewed in some quarters as pro-papal. Isaac Barrow, in *A Treatise of the Pope's Supremacy* (1680), found Thorndike's stress on the unity of the visible church as too close to the Roman Catholic claim that all churches should be under one government. Richard Baxter, in his treatise *Against the Revolt to a Foreign Jurisdiction* (1691), charged that Thorndike advocated a universal church with legislative powers, governed by general councils, in which the papacy would play a key part, both in the councils and in the regular life of the church.

In the nineteenth century Thorndike was rediscovered and his ideas championed by adherents of the Oxford Movement. In *Tracts for the Times* (6 vols. in 5, 1834–41), J. H. Newman, J. Keble, W. Palmer, and others quoted excerpts from Thorndike's writings on baptism, on the authority of doctrine, and on the eucharist. J. S. Brewer edited a new edition of Thorndike's *A Discourse of the Right of the Church in a Christian State* in 1841, and John David Chambers edited passages from Thorndike's writings for his *The Doctrine of the Holy Eucharist* in 1855. Edward B. Pusey wrote to H. E. Manning on 12 August 1845 that it was Thorndike's writings that first caused him to question 'our hereditary maxim that a particular church had a right to reform itself', and had thus led him to a broader view of the church (Nockles, 179). Of the greatest importance for this revival of interest in Thorndike was the edition of his *Theological Works* in the Library of Anglo-Catholic Theology (1844–56), with a detailed life of the theologian by Arthur W. Haddan. Haddan included several hitherto unpublished works as well as letters and papers relating to Thorndike.

Yet Thorndike's standing as a theologian has never been altogether secure. In the early twentieth century T. A. Lacey wrote that Thorndike, while learned, 'lacked the gift of a noble and lucid style which was shared by most of his compeers' (Lacey, 5). More recently it has been questioned why Thorndike was 'given such massive attention' in the Library of Anglo-Catholic Theology, 'when his contorted writings were regarded with deep suspicion by contemporaries' (Spurr, 395). The most recent full-length study, by Ernest Charles Miller, shows Thorndike, in his emphasis on reason, to be more closely connected to the latitudinarian tradition of rational theology in the seventeenth century than has been acknowledged. Miller sees Thorndike's ecclesiology as a creative integration of Anglican themes into a cohesive system that remained largely unappreciated before the Tractarians rediscovered his thought. From the evidence cited here, Thorndike emerges as an original, critical, and scholarly theologian and biblical commentator who began his career as a moderate Calvinist and ended it—impelled by his experience of religious and political radicalism during the civil wars and interregnum—as a forerunner of the Tractarians. His stress on the church's autonomy, on the importance of episcopacy, on the centrality of the sacraments, and on the eventual goal of a reunited, universal, visible church all mark him as an Anglican who anticipated many of the values and ideas expressed in his church in later centuries.   W. B. PATTERSON

Sources A. W. Haddan, 'Life of Herbert Thorndike', in H. Thorndike, *Theological works*, ed. A. Haddan, 6 vols. in 7 (1844–56), 6.153–266 · T. A. Lacey, *Herbert Thorndike, 1598–1672* (1929) · E. C. Miller, 'The doctrine of the church in the thought of Herbert Thorndike (1598–1672)', DPhil diss., U. Oxf., 1990 · J. Walker, *An attempt towards recovering an account of the numbers and sufferings of the clergy of the Church of England*, pt 2 (1714), 160 · *Walker rev.* · Venn, *Alum. Cant.* · H. M. Innes, *Fellows of Trinity College, Cambridge* (1941) · W. W. Rouse Ball and J. A. Venn, eds., *Admissions to Trinity College, Cambridge*, 5 vols. (1911–16) · Wood, *Ath. Oxon.*, new edn · Wood, *Ath. Oxon.: Fasti* (1815) · Foster, *Alum. Oxon.* · W. Kennett, *A register and chronicle ecclesiastical and civil* (1728) · *The correspondence of Bishop Brian Duppa and Sir Justinian Isham, 1650–1660*, ed. G. Isham, Northamptonshire RS, 17 (1951) · L. Twells, 'Life of Dr. Edward Pocock', in E. Pocock, *Theological writings*, 2 vols. (1740), 1.1–84 · I. Walton, *The life of George Herbert* (1670) · E. Calamy, ed., *An abridgement of Mr. Baxter's history of his life and times, with an account of the ministers, &c., who were ejected after the Restauration of King Charles II*, 2nd edn, 2 vols. (1713), vol. 2 · *Calamy rev.* · J. Nichols, *The history and antiquities of the county of Leicester*, 4 vols. (1795–1815) · M. Gibson, *A view of the ancient and present state of the churches of Door, Home-Lacy, and Hempsted, endow'd by the right honourable John, Lord Viscount Scudamore, with some memoirs of that ancient family* (1727) · J. H. Newman and others, *Tracts for the times. By members of the University Oxford*, 6 vols. in 5 (1834–41) · J. Twigg, *The University of Cambridge and the English Revolution, 1625–1688* (1990) · W. K. Jordan, *The development of religious toleration in England*, 4 vols. (1932–40), vol. 4 · P. B. Nockles, *The Oxford Movement in context: Anglican high churchmanship, 1760–1857* (1994) · J. Spurr, *The Restoration Church of England, 1646–1689* (1991) · E. G. Jay, ed., *Origen's treatise on prayer* (1954) · *IGI* [parish register of Cumberworth]

Archives Westminster Abbey, treatises and sermons | Bodl. Oxf., d'Orville MSS, corresp. with I. Voss · Northants. RO, Isham MSS, corresp. with Sir J. Isham

Wealth at death see will, repr. in Haddan, 'Life of Herbert Thorndike', 6.143–52

Thorndike, (Arthur) Russell (1885–1972), actor and writer, was born on 6 February 1885 in the cathedral precincts, Rochester, one of two sons and two daughters of the Revd Arthur John Webster Thorndike (1853–1917), a minor canon, and his wife, Agnes Macdonald Bowers. The actress Dame Sybil *Thorndike (1882–1976) was his sister. He was educated at St George's School, Windsor, and became a chorister of the Chapel Royal: he later proudly recalled singing in that choir at Queen Victoria's funeral. Thorndike then went on to the King's School in Rochester.

In 1903 Thorndike joined Ben Greet's dramatic academy, and he made his first stage appearance as John Rugby in *The Merry Wives of Windsor* at the Theatre Royal, Cambridge, in 1904. His first London appearance was at the Marlborough Theatre, Holloway, in 1905. After performing with Ben Greet's company for three years Thorndike and his sister toured in the company across America. He

acted in the Shakespeare season at the Court Theatre, London (1909), and he subsequently toured South Africa, India, and the Far East with Matheson Lang (1911–13). On his return he joined Miss Horniman's repertory company at the Gaiety Theatre, Manchester.

During the First War Thorndike served with the Westminster dragoons in Egypt and Gallipoli, where he was severely wounded. In 1916, on being invalided home, he joined one of the very first Old Vic companies, directed by Lilian Baylis, as leading man and sometimes producer–director. On 17 August 1918 Thorndike married Rosemary Benvenuta Dowson (1894/5–1970), daughter of a well-known actress, Rosina Filippi, and Henry Martin Dowson, a brewer.

Though never as starry or mesmeric as Sybil, Russell was always a useful member of a classical stage company. In two wartime seasons he played many major Shakespearian parts, such as King John, Richard II, and King Lear. In the latter Sybil was Fool to his Lear, and on the first night the storm scene was performed while an air raid was taking place. During the 1919–20 season he was leading man and joint director of plays. Subsequently he joined his sister and her husband, Lewis Casson, at the Little Theatre in John Adam Street, London, 'in their attempt to establish an English Grand Guignol' (*The Times*). Thorndike wrote two of the plays himself, and had notable success as an actor in Reginald Berkeley's play about a condemned prisoner, *Eight O'Clock*, and also as Peer Gynt in Henrik Ibsen's play.

In 1927 Thorndike came into his own, and escaped his sister's long shadow, when he wrote and starred at the Lyceum in *Dr Syn*, a smuggling melodrama, which drew on his considerable experience of Grand Guignol. He was to play this role at home and abroad, in addition to a variety of Shakespearian parts, for much of the rest of his long career. In 1929–30 he led the Ben Greet Company on another Shakespearian tour of America.

Thorndike published a dozen books, many of which were based on his fascination with Shakespeare, or with smugglers. His works included several novels, as well as a first, rather slender, biography of his sister (1929): this contained fascinating insights into their childhood in the Rochester Cathedral close. In 1938 he wrote a memoir of Lilian Baylis. *Children of the Garter* (1937) was a memoir of his early life in Windsor and as a boy soloist in the Chapel Royal. In later years Thorndike became a favourite with generations of children for his annual appearances in J. M. Barrie's *Peter Pan* as Smee, yet another pirate; and he also frequently led the summer companies at the Open Air Theatre in Regent's Park.

During the last three years of his life, Thorndike was too fragile to work in the theatre, though he continued to lecture on a long theatrical life which had started when, as a Windsor choirboy, he had been deputed to guide Sir Henry Irving around the castle. Despite professional success, he had financial problems in later life and was declared bankrupt in 1952. A proud and long-standing member of a theatrical clan, Russell Thorndike remained devoted to his wife, sister, and overacting, in approximately that order, across more than half a century of greasepaint touring. It was his proud belief that, were all of Shakespeare's texts to be lost in a fire, he could rewrite almost all from memory. He died at his home, King's Head House, Foulsham, near Norwich, on 7 November 1972.

SHERIDAN MORLEY

Sources *The Times* (9 Nov 1972) · WWW · R. Thorndike, *Children of the Garter* (1937) · R. Thorndike, *Sybil Thorndike* [1929] · J. C. Trewin, *Sybil Thorndike* (1955) · S. Morley, *Sybil Thorndike* (1977) · 'Thorndike, Dame (Agnes) Sybil', *DNB* · b. cert. · m. cert. · d. cert. · F. Gaye, ed., *Who's who in the theatre*, 14th edn (1967)
Archives FILM BFI NFTVA, performance footage
Likenesses Sasha, double portrait, photograph, 1925 (with Alma Taylor), Hult. Arch. · Sasha, photograph, 1925, Hult. Arch. · Sasha, double portraits, photographs, 1929 (with Jane Wood), Hult. Arch.

Thorndike [*married name* Casson], **Dame** (**Agnes**) **Sybil** (**1882–1976**), actress, was born on 24 October 1882 at Gainsborough in Lincolnshire, the eldest of the four children of the Revd Arthur John Webster Thorndike (1853–1917) and his wife, Agnes Macdonald, daughter of John Bowers, shipping merchant. The other children—Russell *Thorndike, Eileen, and Frank—all went into the theatre for some time as, later, did all four of Sybil Thorndike's own children and many of her grandchildren. When she was two her father was appointed a minor canon of Rochester Cathedral and the family moved to Kent, where they stayed throughout the rest of her childhood.

Dame (Agnes) Sybil Thorndike (1882–1976), by Bertram Park, 1920s? [in the title role of *Saint Joan* by George Bernard Shaw]

Sybil Thorndike made her parlour début at the age of four and within three years was regularly performing, for family and cathedral friends in Rochester, a melodrama called *The Dentist's Cure* and subtitled 'Saw Their Silly Heads Off' (after *Sweeney Todd*), which she and Russell had written and produced—the beginnings, perhaps, of a fascination with Grand Guignol which was to lead to her celebrated seasons at the Little Theatre in the 1920s.

About the time of her tenth birthday, Sybil Thorndike's father was offered the living of the nearby St Margaret's parish and the family moved from Minor Canon Row (immortalized by Charles Dickens in *Edwin Drood*) to more spacious vicarage quarters. By now there was little doubt that Sybil Thorndike would be going into public performance of one kind or another, although it might well have been musical rather than dramatic since her mother was an excellent pianist. Educated at Rochester high school, she also made weekly visits to London for lessons at the Guildhall School of Music, which were coupled with occasional visits to Her Majesty's Theatre when Herbert Beerbohm Tree was performing Mark Antony.

On 13 May 1899 Sybil Thorndike gave a recital of Bach, Schumann, and Chopin at the Corn Exchange in Rochester. Very soon afterwards however, she began to feel pain in her right wrist which made it impossible to span an octave; piano cramp was diagnosed, and although she persevered for a while with the dogged tenacity which was already a hallmark of her personality, it was soon clear that she would be in need of another career.

Sybil Thorndike auditioned for Ben Greet, who agreed that she should join his company on 24 August 1904 as they set off to tour America; in the preceding weeks she was to walk on with the company during a summer season at Cambridge, where she made her professional début in the grounds of Downing College on 14 June, as Palmis in *The Palace of Truth*.

The following two years were spent largely with Greet in America, touring the length and breadth of the country in often rough conditions, playing a clutch of lesser roles (including Lucianus, nephew to the king, in the play scene of *Hamlet* and Ceres in the masque in *The Tempest*) as well as frequently stepping into the breach for more important actresses afflicted by the rigours of primitive touring schedules and appalling transport. Thus by 1907 Sybil Thorndike had played 112 parts in all for Greet on the road, ranging from Viola, Helena, Gertrude, and Rosalind to Ophelia, Nerissa, 'Noises Off', and (in Kansas City, 1905) Everyman. It was a baptism of fire, but on those American tours Sybil Thorndike, still in her twenties, learned the elements of her trade, of which the most important remained sheer survival.

On her final return to London in 1907 Sybil Thorndike landed a Sunday-night job with the Play Actors' Society as an American girl in a farce called *The Marquis*; George Bernard Shaw was present for the play's sole performance and next morning asked her if she would be willing to understudy Ellen O'Malley in a revival of *Candida* for Annie Horniman's company. They were to play a split week in Belfast, the first three evenings being taken up with Shaw's *Widowers' Houses*, in which Sybil Thorndike noticed, playing Trench, 'a young man called Lewis Casson'. Lewis Thomas *Casson (1875–1969), who was knighted in 1945, was the son of Major Thomas Casson, of Ffestiniog and Port Madoc.

That one Belfast week in the spring of 1908 was to condition the remaining seventy years of Sybil Thorndike's public and private life; it established an alliance with Shaw (who in 1923 was to write *Saint Joan* for her) and with Casson, whom she married the Christmas (22 December 1908) after that first meeting. They had two daughters and two sons, including John *Casson, and celebrated their diamond wedding anniversary in 1968, by which time she was over eighty and he over ninety. He died the following year.

At the time of her wedding Sybil Thorndike was a permanent member of Miss Horniman's pioneering repertory company at the Gaiety, Manchester; the following year she joined the Charles Frohman company at the Duke of York's in London, before returning briefly to America to tour and appear on Broadway as Emily Chapman in *Smith* by W. Somerset Maugham. Then, in June 1912, she returned to the Gaiety, Manchester, to play Beatrice in *Hindle Wakes* by W. Stanley Houghton, a major play of the 'northern' school of semi-documentary dramas. Until the outbreak of the First World War she remained a leading player for Miss Horniman's company in Manchester and on their occasional London visits with productions of which Lewis Casson was, increasingly, the director.

Three children were born to Sybil Thorndike during short breaks from repertory work at the Gaiety. When war was declared Lewis Casson at once joined the army and his wife moved the rest of the family down to London, where she had been offered a season at the Old Vic by Lilian Baylis. In the event she was to stay at the Vic for four years playing Rosalind, Lady Macbeth, Portia, Beatrice, Imogen, Ophelia, the Fool in *King Lear* (male actors being hard to come by in wartime), Kate Hardcastle, Lydia Languish, and Lady Teazle among a vast range of other and sometimes lesser roles: 'Miss Thorndike will be a great actress', wrote a *Sunday Times* critic, 'so long as she learns to keep her hands beneath her shoulders'. But those wartime seasons at the Vic, some of them played during the earliest air raids, forged, fired, and confirmed for London audiences the talent that was soon to hallmark her St Joan.

But first came the Greek plays: Sybil Thorndike played Hecuba in the translation by Gilbert Murray of Euripides' *The Trojan Women* for a series of special matinées at the Vic in October 1919; by March 1920 she was at the Holborn Empire (though again for matinées only) as Hecuba and Medea, performances to which she would also add Candida for good measure. Then came a two-year run at the Little Theatre in a series of Grand Guignol melodramas which was something of a family concern: Sybil Thorndike and her brother Russell co-starred with Casson (who also directed) in plays such as *The Hand of Death*, *The Kill*, and *Fear*, in which they were gainfully employed terrifying theatregoers, never more so than in *The Old Women*, where Sybil Thorndike had her eyes gouged out by the knitting needles of the crazed fellow inmates of an asylum.

But as the vogue for horror drew to a close, the Cassons themselves set up in management of the New Theatre, with Bronson Albery and Lady Wyndham; they opened with *The Cenci* in 1922, and at one of its matinées Sybil Thorndike was seen again by Bernard Shaw. *Saint Joan*, which he then wrote for her, opened at the New Theatre in March 1924, and marked the early but unchallenged climax of her career. It ran initially for 244 performances, and was to be revived at regular intervals at home and abroad until Sybil Thorndike's final performance of the role in March 1941. Throughout the late 1920s and 1930s she also did a great deal of other classical and modern work, often under her husband's direction, ranging from Jane Clegg in the play of that name to Emilia in *Othello* in 1930, playing with Paul Robeson, to Miss Moffat in *The Corn is Green* (1938) by Emlyn Williams. In 1931 she was appointed DBE, the sixth actress to be so honoured.

As the Second World War started the Cassons toured the Welsh mining villages and towns, bringing *Macbeth*, *Medea*, and *Candida* to audiences who had often never seen plays before. In 1944 Sybil Thorndike joined the legendary Laurence Olivier–Ralph Richardson Old Vic season at the New, playing, among many other roles, Margaret to Olivier's Richard III and Aase to Richardson's Peer Gynt as well as the Nurse in *Uncle Vanya* and, in 1946, Jocasta in *Oedipus Rex*.

Then began a gentle post-war decline; the great years of Shaw and the Greeks and Miss Horniman all belonged to a lost pre-war world. Sybil Thorndike was already in her early sixties and, though still indefatigable, having now to spend her time in minor West End comedies or guest-starring in films. The 1950s brought her considerable successes (*Waters of the Moon*, *A Day by the Sea*) in London but it was on long and gruelling tours of Australia and South Africa that the Cassons were now to be seen in their more classical work.

But in 1962, when Olivier was forming at Chichester the company he would take with him to open the National Theatre at the Old Vic, both Cassons were in his *Uncle Vanya* again, Sybil Thorndike now playing the old nurse Marina. From that, as if to prove her now septuagenarian versatility and vitality, she went into a short-lived musical of *Vanity Fair* (1962). The stage roles now were fewer and further between, and in 1966 the Cassons made their farewell appearance in London with a revival of *Arsenic and Old Lace*. Then came the opening of the Thorndike Theatre in Leatherhead, where she was to make her final appearance, in October 1969, six months after the death of her husband. In 1970 she was made a Companion of Honour; she also had several honorary degrees, including an Oxford DLitt (1966). After two heart attacks within four days, Sybil Thorndike died at her flat at 98 Swan Court, Chelsea, on 9 June 1976. SHERIDAN MORLEY, *rev.*

Sources J. C. Trewin, *Sybil Thorndike* (1955) · R. Thorndike, *Sybil Thorndike*, 2nd edn (1950) · S. Morley, *Sybil Thorndike* (1977) · E. Sprigge, *Sybil Thorndike Casson* (1971) · J. Casson, *Lewis and Sybil* (1972) · personal knowledge (1986) · WW · I. Herbert, ed., *Who's who in the theatre*, 16th edn (1977) · m. cert.

Archives Theatre Museum, London, corresp. and papers | BL, letters to George Bernard Shaw, Add. MS 50531 · Bodl. Oxf., letters to the Bickersteth family · Bodl. Oxf., corresp. with Gilbert Murray · King's Cam., letters to G. H. W. Rylands · King's Lond., Liddell Hart C., corresp. with Sir B. H. Liddell Hart | FILM BFI NFTVA, *This is your life*, BBC, 10 Oct 1960 · BFI NFTVA, performance footage | SOUND BL NSA, Bow dialogues, 17 Sept 1998, C 812/26 C11 · BL NSA, 'Lewis and Sybil', NP2322W BD1 · BL NSA, documentary recordings · BL NSA, oral history interviews · BL NSA, performance recordings

Likenesses B. Park, bromide print, 1920–29, NPG [*see illus.*] · J. Epstein, bronze bust, 1925, NPG · E. Kapp, drawing, 1926, Barber Institute of Fine Arts, Birmingham · P. Tanqueray, photograph, 1926, NPG · B. Park, bromide print, 1928, NPG · F. Man, photograph, 1943, NPG · W. Stoneman, photograph, 1958, NPG · K. Green, oils, 1961, Sybil Thorndike Theatre, Leatherhead · J. S. Lewinski, photograph, 1967, NPG · N. Vogel, two photographs, *c.*1968, NPG · G. Argent, double portrait, photograph (with Lewis Casson), NPG · C. Beaton, photograph, NPG · J. Epstein, bronze bust, Doncaster Museum and Art Gallery · K. Pollak, photograph, NPG · photograph, NPG

Wealth at death £13,277: probate, 14 Oct 1976, *CGPLA Eng. & Wales*

Thorne, Sir (Augustus Francis) Andrew Nicol (1885–1970), army officer, was born on 20 September 1885 at Dornhurst, Sevenoaks, Kent, son of Augustus Thorne (1825–1901), businessman and farmer, and his second wife, Mary Nicol (1857–1924). Having been educated at Mulgrave Castle School, Whitby (1894–9), Eton College (1899–1902), and the Royal Military College, Sandhurst (1903–4), he was commissioned in the Grenadier Guards in 1904. He married Margaret Douglas-Pennant (1886–1967), tenth daughter of the second Baron Penrhyn, on 29 July 1909. It was a strong and happy marriage and they had five children.

Thorne, a staff captain with 1st guards brigade, who was nicknamed Bulgy, landed in France in August 1914. The brigade was heavily involved in the first battle of Ypres in October–November 1914, particularly around the village of Gheluvelt where Thorne had his horse shot from under him. After twelve months on the staff he was appointed second in command of the 1st battalion Grenadier Guards in March 1916. He commanded the 3rd battalion from September 1916 through the Somme, Passchendaele, Cambrai, and the retreat in the wake of Ludendorff's offensive of 1918. A leader with great energy and courage, he inspired his men with confidence which may in part have been due to his apparent invulnerability. Thorne's most serious injury of the war was sustained while playing football. He was made DSO three times and was mentioned in dispatches on seven occasions. In October 1918 Thorne assumed command of 184th infantry brigade with the temporary rank of brigadier-general.

Thorne was unsure whether he wanted to remain in the post-war army and chose to become a CMG in 1919 rather than accept a brevet. He went to Washington as assistant military attaché, where he decided to stay in the service. He attended Staff College, Camberley, from 1921 to 1922, and after returning a year later became an instructor there (1923–5). Following a brief period as military assistant to the chief of the Imperial General Staff (CIGS), Lord Cavan, he returned with some relief to regimental soldiering to command the 3rd battalion Grenadier Guards. He attended the Imperial Defence College in 1931. As military

attaché in Berlin from 1932 to 1935 Thorne, on several occasions, met Hitler, who always discussed the fighting around Gheluvelt in 1914 where Hitler too had served. Indeed a translation of Thorne's 1932 article in the *Household Brigade Magazine* about Gheluvelt was found in the wreckage of Hitler's bunker in 1945. Thorne returned to Britain to command the 1st guards brigade in 1935 and saw active service in Palestine in 1936. He was made major-general and general officer commanding London district, in 1938.

On the outbreak of the Second World War Thorne received command of the 48th (South Midland) territorial division, which arrived in France in January 1940. The standard of equipment and training of the British expeditionary force's (BEF) territorial divisions was low. Thorne's efforts to rectify the situation before the Germans attacked in May 1940 were rewarded as his division performed creditably in the retreat from the Dyle and their desperate defence of the western perimeter of Dunkirk was vital to the safe withdrawal of the BEF. Back in England, Thorne took command of 12th corps in June 1940 with responsibility for the defence of the vital Sussex–Kent coastline, the likely site of a German invasion attempt. Thorne put his customary energy into his preparations and the training of his men. On 7 May 1941 Thorne was promoted lieutenant-general and made general officer commanding-in-chief, Scottish command. This was the turning point of Thorne's career. Scotland, though an army command, was peripheral to the war, whereas 12th corps had been in the front line. The decision to move Thorne was made by General Alan Brooke, then commander-in-chief, home forces, who appears to have regarded it as an advancement. Yet it left Thorne sidelined, ensuring he was never again seriously considered for active command. He was made KCB in 1942.

None the less Thorne approached Scottish command's work with his usual vigour. Scotland was the obvious springboard for any operations launched against German-occupied Norway. While no such operations were undertaken, Thorne was responsible for the large scale deception scheme, Fortitude North, which ensured that the twelve German divisions in Norway stayed there throughout the Normandy landings. He was promoted full general in February 1945. Following careful planning for the liberation it says much for his abilities that as commander-in-chief, allied land forces, Norway, Thorne was able to take the surrender of 400,000 Germans in May 1945 and smoothly hand power back to the Norwegian authorities.

Thorne retired in May 1946. In 1950 the Norwegian government asked the War Office to help restructure the Norwegian army. Thorne accepted this task with alacrity. The Norwegians implemented the majority of his recommendations. With justice Thorne can be considered the father of the modern Norwegian army. In his retirement Sir Andrew Thorne enjoyed family life, maintained close links with Norway, and worked on his golf. He died in Spynie Hospital, Elgin, on 25 September 1970, following a heart attack. He was buried in Sonning-on-Thames, Berkshire, on 1 October.

CHRISTOPHER MANN

Sources D. Lindsay, *Forgotten general* (1987) · O. Riste, ed., *Fredsgeneralen* (1995) · P. Thorne, 'Andrew Thorne and the liberation of Norway', *Britain and Norway in the Second World War*, ed. P. Salmon (1995), 206–20 · PRO · Riksarkivet, Oslo · P. Thorne, 'Hitler and the Gheluvelt article', *Guards Magazine* (autumn 1987) · L. F. Ellis, *The war in France and Flanders, 1939–1940* (1953) · R. H. Whitworth, *The grenadier guards* (1974) · Burke, *Peerage* (1939) · *CGPLA Eng. & Wales* (1970)
Archives IWM, papers relating to battle of Gheluvelt · NAM, corresp. and papers | IWM, letters to his wife · King's Lond., Liddell Hart C., corresp. with Sir Basil H. Liddell Hart
Likenesses photograph, 1945, Norges Hjemmefrontmuseum, Oslo
Wealth at death £34,572: probate, 15 Jan 1971, *CGPLA Eng. & Wales*

Thorne, Isabel Jane (1833/4–1910). *See under* Edinburgh Seven (*act.* 1869–1873).

Thorne, James (1795–1872), a founder of the Bible Christians, was born on 21 September 1795 at North Furze Farm, Shebbear, Devon, the third child of John Thorne (1762–1842), farmer, and his wife, Mary (1760–1843), daughter of Samuel and Mary Ley of Rightadown Farm in the neighbouring parish of Bradford. Educated at Langtree School, Thorne was a serious-minded child of evangelical disposition; confirmed in 1812, he even entertained thoughts of becoming an Anglican clergyman. However, on 17 August 1815 he heard the Methodist preacher William O'Bryan (1778–1868) preach at Cookbury, and was sufficiently impressed to invite him to come to Lake Farm (to which the Thornes had moved). In the kitchen of the farm, on 9 October, the first Bible Christian society was formed; among its first members were John and Mary Thorne and their five children.

James Thorne quickly became immersed in the Bible Christian movement. He preached his first sermon on Christmas day 1815, and became a local preacher on 1 January and a full-time itinerant minister on 15 March 1816. He evangelized Devon and Cornwall for four years, mostly on foot, suffering privation and opposition, frequently preaching five times every Sunday and twelve times each week, and securing conversions at nearly every service. On 21 February 1820 he set out to evangelize Kent, spending much of the next six years there or in London. His exertions at this period are described in his diary for 1816–27, extracts from which appeared in his son's memoir. It was in London that he married, on 15 September 1823, Catherine Reed (1797–1874), the third daughter of William and Catherine Reed of Holwell Farm, Buckland Brewer, Devon, and herself a Bible Christian itinerant. They had six children between 1824 and 1838, three of whom predeceased Thorne.

As secretary of conference, Thorne worked alongside O'Bryan in devising the connexional polity, preparing the hymnbook, establishing the book room, and founding chapels. After O'Bryan's separation from the Bible Christians in 1829, it was largely due to Thorne's leadership skills that the whole movement did not collapse, spiritually and financially, an achievement which, from his base

around Shebbear, left him in virtually undisputed authority over the connexion for the next forty years. Throughout this period he constantly held high office, including the presidency of conference on five occasions, and was particularly active in publishing, chapel building, and educational and foreign missionary work. Until 1844 he also travelled extensively in southern England, visiting the societies. In 1870 failing health caused him to retire to Plymouth, where he died on 28 January 1872, after a fortnight's illness and within hours of conducting his last service. He was buried in the graveyard of Ebenezer Chapel, Shebbear.

It was rightly said by Frederick William Bourne (1830–1905), the connexion's third leader, of Thorne's contribution to the Bible Christians that 'he either originated nearly every forward movement or his executive ability was speedily requisitioned to carry it to a successful issue' (Bourne, *Bible Christians*, 31). When he became a preacher in 1816 the connexion had 237 members and no chapels; on his death it had 18,438 and 560 respectively. However, Thorne's efforts were not confined to one denomination, nor his skills to the pulpit or office. He was a noted platform orator, denouncing slavery, tithes, and religious discrimination; supporting temperance, Sunday schools, Methodist union, the Anti-State Church Association, the Evangelical Alliance, and the Bible Society; and campaigning for the Liberals. Such vitality owed much to his physical strength (he was a large-limbed man of above average height), cheerful disposition, and personal habits verging on the puritanical.   CLIVE D. FIELD

Sources J. Thorne and others, *A jubilee memorial of incidents in the rise and progress of the Bible Christian connexion* (1865), 1–174 · J. Thorne, *James Thorne of Shebbear: a memoir, compiled from his diary and letters, by his son* (1873) · F. W. Bourne, *The centenary life of James Thorne, of Shebbear* (1895) · G. J. Stevenson, *Methodist worthies: characteristic sketches of Methodist preachers of the several denominations*, 6 (1886), 868–75 · M. J. L. Wickes, *The westcountry preachers: a new history of the Bible Christian church (1815–1907)* (1987) · T. Shaw, *The Bible Christians, 1815–1907* [1965] · F. W. Bourne, *The Bible Christians: their origin and history (1815–1900)* (1905) · *Bible Christian Magazine*, 51 (1872), 134–7, 183–6 · E. Lott, *James Thorne of Shebbear, 1795–1872, remembered in 1995* (1995)
Likenesses T. W. Dean, engraving, 1830–39, repro. in Thorne, *James Thorne of Shebbear* · D. J. Pound, engraving, 1867, repro. in *Bible Christian Magazine*, 46 (1867)
Wealth at death under £1000: probate, 8 March 1872, *CGPLA Eng. & Wales*

Thorne, James (1815–1881), topographical writer and antiquary, was born in London in September 1815. He was probably the James Thorne baptized on 8 October at St Mary's, Whitechapel, the son of James and Rebecca Thorne. He was educated at a private school, and for several years afterwards worked as an artist. As a young man he supplied short articles on antiquarian subjects to *The Mirror*, the *Gentleman's Magazine*, and other publications, the result of research in libraries and of frequent rambles through many districts of England. In 1843 he became connected with the author and publisher Charles Knight, and they collaborated for more than twenty-five years. The reissue, in 1873, of Knight's *Passages of a Working Life* contained an introductory note by Thorne.

Under Knight's direction Thorne contributed many topographical articles to the second series of the *Penny Magazine*, and wrote large portions, besides supplying many illustrations, of the four volumes, entitled *The Land we Live in* (1847–50). His *Rambles by Rivers*, published under Knight's aegis between 1844 and 1849, covered mainly rivers in the south of England; a contemporary critic found them 'delightful volumes' (Allibone, *Dict.*). Thorne was also working editor of the two volumes on geography in *The Imperial Cyclopaedia* (2 vols., 1830–53) and of the *English Cyclopaedia* (1854–70) with its supplements, and for twenty-five years he wrote for the *Companion to the British Almanac*. He was elected a fellow of the Society of Antiquaries on 21 March 1872.

Thorne's energies were for several years devoted to the compilation of the two volumes of his *Handbook to the Environs of London* (1876), a painstakingly detailed survey of the topography, buildings, and historic remains for 20 miles around London. His great knowledge and immense industry are shown throughout its pages, and it remains his lasting achievement; an overview of London histories published in 1968 called it 'a useful and well documented reference book' (Rubinstein, 138), and its enduring value has been further attested by its reissue in facsimile (1970 and 1983). At the time of his death he was engaged in preparing a new edition of Peter Cunningham's *Handbook of London*, which he thoroughly revised, adding 'much fresh information and many illustrative quotations' (preface, v). The revision was completed by Henry B. Wheatley, who published it as *London Past and Present* in 1891 and paid generous tribute to Thorne in his preface. Thorne died of cancer of the colon at his home, 52 Fortess Road, Kentish Town, London, on 3 September 1881, leaving his widow and their children in straitened circumstances. An obituarist noted that he 'was not a prolific writer, but he did his work most carefully and conscientiously, and in a manner which commanded the respect of those in whose service his pen was employed' (*The Times*, 7 Sept 1881).

W. P. COURTNEY, rev. H. J. SPENCER

Sources *The Times* (6–7 Sept 1881) • C. Tomlinson, *The Athenaeum* (10 Sept 1881), 336 • *The Academy* (10 Sept 1881), 199 • *N&Q*, 6th ser., 4 (1881), 260 • S. Rubinstein, *Historians of London* (1968) • Allibone, *Dict.* • d. cert. • census returns, 1881

Thorne, John (d. 1573), composer and poet, is of obscure origins; nothing is known about his parents or the place and date of his birth. From 1550 he resided in the York parish of St Michael-le-Belfry; he was wealthy and had lands at Clifton and leases of the tithes of two parsonages. He is probably to be identified with John Thorne, singing-man of the choir of the parish church of St Mary-at-Hill, London, in 1539–40.

Thorne was appointed organist at York Minster on 24 July 1542, having received payment the previous year as 'organist within the choir'. When the minster organs were temporarily silenced in 1552, Thorne, as master of the choristers, was ordered to 'helpe to sing Divyne Service within the quere of the churche' (Raine, *Statutes*, 77), though his stipend as organist continued without interruption until 1573. He also served as keeper of the fabric

from 1567; his account for the year 1567–8 reflects the zeal with which the Marian decorations were swept away under orders from the new dean, Matthew Hutton, and includes the entry 'for making playne and washyng over with whyte the places where the altar stood' (Raine, *Fabric Rolls*, 113–14).

Thomas Morley cited Thorne, with Redford, Tallis, and others, as a composer particularly skilled in writing upon plainsong. In view of this high opinion of his abilities it is unfortunate that so little of Thorne's music has survived. In the Bodleian Library, Oxford, there is a four-part In nomine (MSS mus. sch. D.212–216), and a manuscript in the British Library (Add. MS 29996) contains the organ score of a motet, *Exultabant sancti*. Both works are in the imitative polyphonic style of the mid-century, as is the three-part Marian motet *Stella coeli*, included by Baldwin in his commonplace book of c.1600 (BL, Royal Music MS 24.d.2, fols. 161v–163r) and later printed by Hawkins. The text of this motet pleads for deliverance from pestilence, making it probable that the work was composed in one of the years in which York suffered a particularly severe plague. The setting is hardly comparable to the best work of Redford or Tallis, but the counterpoint is technically assured and there is considerable rhythmic subtlety. Thorne's willingness to adapt to changing circumstances is evident from his setting of the Te Deum (English words), of which only the tenor part is extant. The underlay is predominantly syllabic, no doubt to fulfil Archbishop Holgate's requirement in 1552 that music sung at York should be 'withoute any reportes or repetinges which may induce any obscurenes to the herers' (Raine, *Statutes*, 74).

Three poems by Thorne are in a manuscript once thought to be in John Redford's hand (BL, Add. MS 15233). One, 'The Hunt ys up' (fols. 33r–34v), is a religious parody of Gray's popular ballad; the others were subsequently printed in Richard Edwards's *Paradyse of Daynty Devises* (1576). Another poem in this collection (no. 21) is signed 'M. T.' and is probably also by Thorne.

Thorne died in York on 7 December 1573 and was buried in York Minster. His epitaph, recorded by Drake, celebrated his skill in logic as well as in music. He was succeeded as organist and master of the choristers by his son Henry Thorne, who continued in office until his death in 1597.

PETER ASTON

Sources T. Morley, *A plaine and easie introduction to practicall musicke* (1597) • J. Hawkins, *A general history of the science and practice of music*, 5 vols. (1776) • R. Edwards, *Paradyse of daynty devises* (1576) • F. Drake, *Eboracum, or, The history and antiquities of the city of York* (1736) • J. Raine, ed., *The fabric rolls of York Minster*, SurtS, 35 (1859) • J. Raine, ed., *The statutes etc. of the cathedral church of York*, 2nd edn (1900) • P. Le Huray, *Music and the Reformation in England, 1549–1660* (1967) • J. C. H. Aveling, *Catholic recusancy in the city of York, 1558–1791*, Catholic RS, monograph ser., 2 (1970) • P. Aston, *The music of York Minster* (1972) • G. E. Aylmer and R. Cant, eds., *A history of York Minster* (1977) • J. Baldwin, commonplace book, c.1600, BL, Royal Music MS 24.d.2 • BL, Add. MS 15233 • Bodl. Oxf., MSS Mus. Sch. d.212–216 • York Minster chamberlain's roll, 1541, York Minster Library, York, MS E1/79 • register of leases, etc., York Minster Library, York, MSS Wa (1508–43) and Wb (1543–87) • York chapter acts, 1565–1634, York Minster Library, York, MS AC 17 • St Peter's accounts, York Minster Library, York, MS E2 (21) • BL, Add. MS 29996 •

H. Littlehales, ed., *The medieval records of a London city church (St Mary at Hill), AD 1420–1599*, 2, EETS, 128 (1905), 384
Wealth at death see Aveling, *Catholic recusancy*, 312

Thorne [*née* O'Bryan], **Mary** (1807–1883), Bible Christian preacher, was born on 3 April 1807 at Gunwen, Luxulyan, Cornwall, daughter of William *O'Bryan (1778–1868), founder in 1815 of the Bible Christian Connexion, and his wife, Catherine (*née* Cowlin). Mary and her two brothers and five sisters were brought up in a Wesleyan Methodist household until 1815, when they became Bible Christians. She received a good private education, first at home, then as a day scholar before being sent to a boarding-school in Penzance. She became proficient in French, which stood her in good stead during her ministry in the Channel Islands and in teaching in her husband's school.

Urged by friends to pray and speak in public, Mary O'Bryan eventually began to preach, becoming known as 'the Maiden Preacher'. The Bible Christian Connexion readily allowed women to become itinerant and local preachers. In April 1823 she went with her father, William, to London, where she addressed meetings both indoors and in the open air. Eloquent and attractive, she seemed older than her years and caused a considerable stir. She remained in London, working there and in Kent when William returned home. Mary was sent to the Guernsey mission, which included Jersey, in August 1823. After attending the Bible Christian conference and visiting home Mary set sail to her new appointment in the Isle of Wight mission on 6 August 1824. This mission also included the Portsmouth and Southsea areas, so Mary crossed and recrossed the Solent on preaching tours during the following months. Her father and Samuel Thorne (1798–1873) joined her in September 1825 at Portsmouth. All three went to the Isle of Wight for several days. Then William and Samuel departed, leaving Mary in the Portsmouth area. However, in October Samuel booked a ticket for Mary and himself to sail to Plymouth, and so she came back to her mother's house in Cawsand. At 8 o'clock on Monday 28 November 1825 Mary and Samuel, youngest son of John and Mary Thorne, farmers at Lake in Devon, were married at Stoke church, Plymouth.

In January 1826 Mary and Samuel Thorne were living at Mill Pleasant, Stoke, Plymouth, where they printed hymn books, magazines, and plans for the Bible Christian Connexion, while both continued to preach whenever they could. Their first son, John, was born on 15 October 1826 and a daughter, Mary, in 1828. The family moved to Shebbear, north Devon, on 20 March 1829, where they lived for several months with Samuel's parents at Lake. They moved into Prospect House, Shebbear, which served as home, printing press, and school, in January 1830, and the Bible Christian Conference was held there that year. Mary's parents and other members of her family emigrated to America in early 1831. Lady day 1832 saw the opening of the school, the forerunner of the connexional college, at Prospect House with about twenty pupils. Soon Mary found that in addition to being a housewife, printer's assistant, and teacher she was matron to several boarders. The school flourished. Mary continued to preach into old age. She and Samuel had thirteen children. Samuel died in 1873 and Mary died at Stonehouse, Plymouth, on 12 November 1883. Both were buried at Lake, Shebbear.
E. DOROTHY GRAHAM

Sources S. L. Thorne, *The maiden preacher, wife and mother* (1889) · F. W. Bourne, *The Bible Christians: their origin and history (1815–1900)* (1905) · J. Woolcock, *A history of the Bible Christian churches on the Isle of Wight* (1897) · *Arminian Magazine* (1822–1927); *Bible Christian Magazine* (1829–1907) · T. Shaw, *The Bible Christians, 1815–1907* [1965] · Z. Taft, *Biographical sketches of the lives … of various holy women*, 1 (1825) · *Minutes of the Bible Christian Conference* (1823–4)
Archives JRL, Methodist Archives and Research Centre, Lewis Court Bible Christian MSS
Likenesses photograph, JRL, Methodist Archives and Research Centre, Lewis Court Bible Christian collection

Thorne, Nicholas (1496–1546). *See under* Thorne, Robert, the elder (c.1460–1519).

Thorne, Sir Richard Thorne (1841–1899), physician and public health officer, was the second son of Thomas Henry Thorne, banker, and his wife, Joanna Hughes, of Bath Street, Leamington Spa, Warwickshire, where he was born on 13 October 1841. He was sent to school first at Nieuwied in Rhenish Prussia and then moved to France at the age of fourteen, to attend, after a year's schooling there, the *cours de troisième* at the Lycée St Louis, Paris, where he gained two first prizes. He then returned to England and became a pupil at Mill Hill School, from which he matriculated at London University. He began his medical studies as an apprentice to a medical practitioner in Leamington Spa, and afterwards entered as a student at St Bartholomew's Hospital, London. In 1863 he was admitted a member of the Royal College of Surgeons, London, and served as a midwifery assistant at St Bartholomew's Hospital. In 1865 he became a licentiate of the Royal College of Physicians of London, and in the following year he graduated MB at London University, with first-class honours in medicine and obstetric medicine. He married on 5 April 1866 Martha, daughter of Joseph Rylands, a merchant of Sutton Grange, Hull; they were to have three sons and a daughter.

From 1864 to 1866 Thorne worked as junior resident medical officer at the Sussex House Asylum, Hammersmith, London, and in 1867 he was elected assistant physician to the general dispensary in Bartholomew Close in the City, a post he resigned in the following year, when he was appointed physician to the Hospital for Diseases of the Chest in the City Road. From 1869 to 1871 he was assistant physician to the London Fever Hospital. He was chosen to be demonstrator of microscopic anatomy in the medical school of St Bartholomew's Hospital in 1869, and from April 1870 he was casualty physician to the hospital.

Thorne entered the field in which he was to become known best, on being employed as a supernumerary inspector in the medical department of the privy council in 1868. In this capacity he conducted several investigations into outbreaks of typhoid fever, helping to establish that the fever could be spread by an infected water supply, and demonstrating the value of isolation hospitals. Thorne showed such marked ability that in February 1871 he was appointed a permanent inspector. After the privy council department was merged with the London government board, he rose gradually from this position until in 1892 he succeeded to the post of principal medical officer to the Local Government Board on the retirement of Sir George Buchanan. As medical officer Thorne persuaded the board to institute a national cholera survey in 1892, which awakened local authorities to the threat of the disease and which became a valuable index of the sanitary state of the country. He continually emphasized the need for higher standards of cleanliness and secured some important sanitary measures. Under his direction the board was highly successful in preventing a cholera outbreak in Britain during the continental epidemic of 1894–5. Thorne was a major influence in the decision to abandon quarantine in Britain, and to replace it with port inspections.

Thorne's knowledge of French and German, no less than his polished manners and courtly address, and his experience in collating information from foreign sources, soon made him especially acceptable to his political chiefs. He was repeatedly selected to represent Britain in matters of international hygiene. He was the British delegate at the International Conference on Cholera Prevention held at Rome in 1885, at Venice (Paris sitting) in 1892, at Dresden in 1893, at Paris in 1894, and at Venice in 1897; and he signed the conventions of Dresden in 1893, Paris in 1894, and Venice in 1897, the last being largely drawn up under his guidance. He had a difficult role in persuading other countries of the effectiveness of the British system of inspection, which replaced the quarantines imposed in other countries. His services were recognized by the government, which increased his salary on the recommendation of a special committee in 1898.

At the Royal College of Physicians of London Thorne was admitted a member in 1867, and was elected a fellow in 1875; he acted as an examiner from 1885 to 1889, and was a member of council from 1894 to 1896. In 1891 he delivered the Milroy lectures, 'Diphtheria: its natural history and prevention'. These lectures, later published, utilized board data to show that diphtheria mortality was unaffected by sanitary improvements. Thorne began to lecture on hygiene at the medical school of St Bartholomew's Hospital in 1879, and he was formally appointed there as the first permanent lecturer on public health in 1891. He was elected FRS on 5 June 1890 and was awarded the Stewart prize of the British Medical Association in 1893. In 1895 he succeeded Sir John Simon as crown nominee at the General Medical Council, and in 1898 honorary degrees were conferred upon him by the University of Edinburgh, the Royal University of Ireland, and the Royal College of Physicians of Ireland. His services to public health were recognized by his selection as an honorary member of the Royal Academy of Medicine at Rome, a corresponding member of the Royal Italian Society of Hygiene, and a foreign associate of the Society of Hygiene of France. He was president of the Epidemiological Society from 1887 to 1889, and in 1898 he delivered the Harben lectures, 'On the administrative control

of tuberculosis'. He was a member of the royal commissions on tuberculosis in 1896, and on sewage disposal in 1898. He was made CB in 1892, and KCB in 1897. He died at his home at 45 Inverness Terrace, Hyde Park, London, on 18 December 1899, and was buried at St John's, Woking.

Thorne ranked as one of the foremost exponents of the science of public health, both in Britain and elsewhere, and he worthily filled the position occupied in succession by Sir Edwin Chadwick, Sir John Simon, and Sir George Buchanan. He became well known for his research on sanitary issues, particularly concerning diphtheria and typhoid fever. He showed a remarkable ability in integrating such knowledge into practical sanitary administration, as seen in the board's 'model' by-laws. Throughout Europe his name became inseparably connected with attempts to abolish the expensive and tedious methods of quarantine in favour of a higher standard of cleanliness combined with the early and efficient notification of individual cases of epidemic disease. Almost the whole of Thorne's work is recorded in the form of reports in the blue books of the medical department of the privy council and the Local Government Board. Munk considered that 'He represented the ideal type of official—painstaking, firm, progressive, and open-minded' (Munk, *Roll*).

D'A. POWER, *rev.* PATRICK WALLIS

Sources Munk, *Roll* · J. L. Brand, *Doctors and the state: the British medical profession and government action in public health, 1870–1912* (1965) · W. M. Frazer, *A history of English public health, 1834–1939* (1950) · *PRS*, 75 (1905), 110–12 · *BMJ* (23 Dec 1899), 1771–3 · *The Lancet* (23 Dec 1899) · V. C. Medvei and J. L. Thornton, eds., *The royal hospital of Saint Bartholomew, 1123–1973* (1974) · personal knowledge (1901) · private information (1901) · b. cert. · m. cert. · *CGPLA Eng. & Wales* (1900)

Likenesses lithograph, Wellcome L.

Wealth at death £8379 5s. 8d.: resworn probate, July 1900, *CGPLA Eng. & Wales*

Thorne, Robert, the elder (*c.*1460–1519), merchant, was the fourth of five sons of Thomas Thorne (*d.* 1471) of St Albans and his wife, Rose. The family's long-established position in the wine trade of Bristol, Cyprus, Rhodes, and Seville, gave Robert scope for speculative engagement in the sugar trade of the Canaries and the Azores and in stockfish with Iceland from 1479.

Trading intelligence he gained in 1493 in Seville may well have encouraged Thorne to anticipate John Cabot's discovery of Newfoundland in 1497. On the back of a map drawn up in 1577–80 John Dee posited this formal claim to North America by writing 'Circa 1494 Mr Robert Thorn his father, and Mr Eliot of Bristow, discovered Newfound Land' (BL, Cotton Augustus 1.I.i). In 1527 his eldest son, Robert [*see below*], described them as 'the discoverers of the Newfound Lands' but in another passage implies they were frustrated by their pilot's behaviour (BL, Cotton MS Vitellius C. vii, fols. 329–45). In 1501 both men received a bounty for ship construction from Henry VII. On 7 January 1503, with his brother William Thorne and Hugh Elliott, the elder Robert bought shares in a ship built at Dieppe for the wine trade, securing another £20 bounty from Bristol's customs on renaming her the *Gabriel*. As mayor of Bristol, Robert Thorne received a commission from the lord admiral of England to form Bristol's court of admiralty to act with thirteen others as from 13 May 1510. In 1515–16 he devised city ordinances on metering and aulnage of woollen cloth and linen.

The 'great orphan book' of Bristol (Bristol RO, 04421/1, fols. 141–2) says Robert Thorne 'finished his days in London' and transcribes his will, made on 20 January 1518. His wish to be buried in St Nicholas, Bristol, was not met; he was interred in Temple Church, London, where the memorial stone was noted by Richard Hakluyt in *Divers Voyages* (1582, p. 258). His will, proved on 6 July 1519, made many ecclesiastical and charitable bequests for Bristol including a cellar of salt (83 tons worth) for the almshouses of the Three Kings, Greyfriars, and others in Long Row and Newgate, again suggesting a trading interest in salted fish from the Azores, Newfoundland, and Iceland. His widow, Jone or Johane Wytheypolle, in her will of 10 April 1523 left large legacies to their children, Robert, Nicholas [*see below*], and Alice (*d.* 1548), but little to Ellen, left in the abbess's care at Lacock.

Robert Thorne the younger (1492–1532), merchant, followed his father into the international trade of Seville and Bristol, investing heavily in the woad trade from the Azores and the Canary Islands as well as in pearls, which he bought at Venice and stored in two trunks until his death. In 1523 Thorne the younger became MP for Bristol. On his father's death he inherited £60, much plate, and a home in Seville. His Sevillian business invested 1400 ducats in Sebastian Cabot's ill-fated voyage to the River Plate in 1526–30, also sending two Englishmen, Roger Barlow (*d.* 1554) and Henry Latimer, as skilled pilots. Although Barlow returned from La Plata with an unfavourable account and the syndicate refused further funds, Robert Thorne kept faith with Roger Barlow.

Thorne's notions of a near polar passage to Cathay were first advanced in royal and diplomatic circles in 1526 to Dr Ley, then Henry VIII's ambassador to the court of the emperor Charles V. Transcribing Thorne's texts as 'An information of the lands discovered and of the way to the Moluccas by the north' and 'A declaration of the Indies and lands which Robert Thorne discovered' in his *Divers Voyages* (London, 1582, sigs. B1r–D4v), Hakluyt added an engraved version of Thorne's map of 1527 (opposite sig. B4v), while elsewhere (sig. B3) he cites Thorne's claim that the north-western route would be 'nearer by almost two thousand leagues than the southern ones'. This text also speaks of an astrolabe and a chart in use well before 1519 by his father, who 'with an[o]ther merchant of Bristol, named Hugh Elliot [were] the discoverers of the Newfounde Lande; for all is one coast as by the carde appeareth'. Robert Thorne's apprentice Emmanuel Lucar (1494–1574) is reported in his old age, while living with his son, Cyprian (1544–1611?) in Botolph's Lane near Aldgate, London, as having a copy of Robert Thorne's text and perhaps the map lent to John Dee at Mortlake in 1577. Dee certainly had the letter from Robert Thorne to Ley copied as the 'Declaration of the Indies' (now BL, Cotton MS Vitellius CVII, fols. 329–43, but without the map).

Strype's revision of *The Survey of London* (1720, bk 2, p. 1213), transcribes Thorne's memorial stone in the south choir of St Christopher-le-Stocks, providing his vital dates. That memorial was surpassed by one in the south aisle of Walthamstow church completed in 1535 with £1000 used at the discretion of his executor, Paul Withypoll. Thorne's other executor, his brother Nicholas, dealt with his Bristol estate and his trading partner's commitments, making a detailed inventory and disbursing £16,935 under the terms of the will. This left a residue of £4286 for Nicholas. However, charged to that inheritance there were trading debts in Spain, England, Flanders, and Italy, including debts of adventure in Ancona and for pearls bought at Venice; and the major debts owed in trade with his brother (£4091) plus £94 for a house and slaves in Seville. Robert allocated £3000 to Vincent Thorne—'my sonne being in Spayne'—to be banked in St George of Genoa in the whaling port of St Jean-de-Luz, where Anagaria, mother of this illegitimate son, Vincent, was awarded £50 on condition that she renounce any claim to his inheritance should Vincent die before coming of age.

Thorne gave some very large awards to his home city of Bristol, including £100 to five Bristol almshouses, £100 to repair the highways of Bristol, and £100 for the road from Commermarsh to Bristol, plus similar sums to those imprisoned in London and Bristol and other sums to be spent in various parishes in London and Bristol. He gave at least £700 to Thomas and Emmanuel Lucar to spend on worthwhile civic causes, as well as £100 for 'the making a place for the merchants of Bristol'. He also gave £300 to relief of the poor of Bristol and 'toward the making up of the free scole of Saincte Bartilmews in Brystowe, £300' as well as £25 to Thomas Moffett, first master of that grammar school, and £25 to Moffat's son, Robert. The creation of Bristol's grammar school was an interest he shared with his brother Nicholas from adolescence, as they both tried to establish navigational instruction and foreign language tuition in the city of Bristol. The derelict hospital of St Bartholomew in Christmas Street was converted to a 'conveyent Schole house to be for a fre[e] grammar schole to taught and kept within the towne of Bristowe' (Bristol RO, 04026 (1), fols. 141–2). The idea developed further through a trading partnership with Sebastian Cabot's erstwhile associate, Roger Barlow, and saw more significant steps taken in 1526 and 1530. On 6 October 1532 Robert Thorne added a bequest of £400 towards its rebuilding. Robert's will was entered in the great orphan book and book of wills of Bristol (Bristol RO, 04026 (1), fols. 139–42) because his civic bequests and initiative in maritime education were thought significant.

Nicholas Thorne (1496–1546), merchant and a founder of Bristol's grammar school, was the younger son of Robert Thorne the elder and Jone (Johane) Wytheypolle. He lived in Aller Court off Small Street, Bristol. Richard Hakluyt records that Nicholas Thorne traded with Thomas Spatcheford to the Canary Islands in 1526 using a ship laden with coarse and fine cloth, both broad and narrow, and also with pack thread and soap (Hakluyt, *Principal Navigations*, 2.2). These cargoes were exchanged for 'a good store of Orchell' (woad) as well as sugar, and hundreds of kid skins.

By 1526 Robert Thorne the younger and Nicholas Thorne became co-partners in a Sevillian soap factory. Shortly before 1533 Nicholas joined his factor William Ballard to import wine from the eastern Mediterranean. Actions in the court of exchequer in 1535 (PRO, E 159/312) allege he exported coloured English cloth without paying export duties.

When Henry VIII visited the manor of Thornbury, near Bristol, for ten days from 18 August 1534, he was escorted by Nicholas Thorne, Thomas White, and the chamberlain of Bristol, and gifts were presented to the king and his queen, Anne Boleyn. Although he was once characterized as a 'nigard' (BL, Cotton MS Cleopatra E. v.361), Nicholas had many children to support—a problem vividly represented on his memorial brass, which records that he died on 19 August 1546 aged fifty, having been lord mayor and having been married twice, with four sons and four daughters (two of whom survived him) through his first marriage, to Mary Wigston, and one son and one daughter, John and Bridget, from his second marriage, to Bridget Miles.

Of Nicholas's sons with his first wife, Robert had children but no obvious wife; Nicholas (d. 1591) had three legitimate children: Edward married Sir William Harper's widow, Margaret; and the youngest, John, was left £100 to invest in Thomas Shipman's shipbuilding business through John Millis of Southampton. To Robert, Nicholas, and Edward, children of his second marriage, Nicholas left his share in another shipbuilding business conducted with Thomas Shipman, then building a ship called the *Saviour*.

In his will of 4 August 1546, proved on 15 October 1546, Nicholas made provision for his second wife's earlier daughters by her first husband, Alice, Barbara, and Katheryn. He apprenticed his illegitimate Spanish children, Robert and Nicholas Thorne, to William Ostrich of London, haberdasher, paying him '£66 13s 4d, which is to be the keeping of the master to whom Nicholas is prentis for seven years'. That family bond was significant, for it was Henry Ostrich who brought Sebastian Cabot back to Bristol in 1548 at the privy council's charge to inform a strategy of exploiting near polar passages.

Nicholas Thorne's complex will allocated his school 'all such books as I have meat for the said library, more my astrolabia, which is the keeping of John Sprynt, [a]poticary, numbers of cardes etc., maps and all such instruments belonging to the science of astronomye or cosmography' (Bristol RO, 04421, fol. 276). It also provided for coloured glazing of the school's windows. His executor, Robert Barlow (d. 1554), wrote for this college *A Brief Summe of Geographie*—a further copy of which he presented to Henry VIII in 1541 (BL, Royal MS 18 B. xxviii). Nicholas provided £20 for a lawyer to vest his school (and 250 tons of salt) in the mayor and commonality, expecting litigation from his illegitimate son, Nicholas Thorne, and John Goodrich over the family wills. Unexpectedly Francis Galliardet of Messina also took action against the heirs of Nicholas Thorne for recovery of his freight on shipping wine from Sicily and Candia (Crete) in the high court of admiralty in 1546 (PRO, HCA, 24/7 24/17 and 18; HCA 14/3 and 4). None the less the school survived, finally moving to Tyndall's Park, Bristol.   R. C. D. BALDWIN

Sources G. C. Moore Smith and P. H. Reaney, 'The family of Withypoll', *Walthamstow Antiquarian Society*, 34 (1936), 13–14, 24–6 · J. A. Williamson, ed., *The Cabot voyages and Bristol discovery under Henry VII*, Hakluyt Society, 2nd ser., 120 (1961) · D. B. Quinn, 'Thorne, Robert the elder', *DCB*, vol. 1 · E. Ralph, ed., *The Great White Book of Bristol*, Bristol RS, 32 (1979) · G. Connell-Smith, 'English merchant trading to the New World in the early 16th century', *BIHR*, 23 (1950), 53–67 · R. Hakluyt, *Divers voyages touching the discovery of America* (1582) · R. Hakluyt, *The principal navigations, voyages, traffiques and discoveries of the English nation*, 2nd edn, 3 vols. (1598–1600), vol. 2 · C. P. Hill, *The history of Bristol grammar school* (1951) · J. Vanes, *Education and apprenticeship in sixteenth-century Bristol* (1982), 7–9 · J. A. Vanes, *Documents illustrating the overseas trade of Bristol in the sixteenth century*, Bristol Records Society, 120 (1979) · PRO, E 122/19/1; E 122 19/LO; C 1/911, 27–9; C 1/1579, 12–14, C 1/2845, 2–5 · will, PRO, PROB 11/19, fols. 146–7 · will, PRO, PROB 11/24, fol. 137 [will of Robert Thorne the younger] · will, PRO, PROB 11/31, fols. 138–40 [will of Nicholas Thorne] · will, PRO, PROB 11/21, fols. 156–7 [will of John Wytheypolle]

Thorne, Robert, the younger (1492–1532). *See under* Thorne, Robert, the elder (c.1460–1519).

Thorne, Sarah (1836–1899), actress and theatre manager, was born in London on 10 May 1836, the eldest of the ten children of Richard Samuel Thorne (d. 1875), an actor and theatre manager, and his wife, Sarah, née Rogers (c.1813–1896). A member of a family connected extensively for several generations with the stage, Sarah Thorne was to become a talented and versatile actress and an able theatre manager. Her stage début was on 26 December 1848 in a pantomime put on by her father at the Pavilion Theatre, Whitechapel. After further appearances there, as Little Pickles in *The Spoiled Child* and in E. G. Burton's blank-verse play *The Warrior Boy*, for which she practised broad-sword combat, she played in minor roles at the Surrey Theatre in the spring of 1854 under Richard Shepherd and William Creswick. In the next years she performed in stock companies at Ryde, Sunderland, Newcastle upon Tyne, Sheffield, Hanley, and the Britannia Theatre, Hoxton. She also joined her father for the summer seasons at Margate (which he had taken in 1855); playing opposite some of the leading actors of the day, she contributed to the growing status of that theatre. She first appeared there on 6 August 1855, shortly after Thorne's opening on 28 July. In time, most of her seven brothers and three sisters also performed at Margate.

For three seasons in the late 1850s Sarah Thorne was the leading lady at the Theatre Royal, Dublin, where, *inter alia*, she played Desdemona to Charles Kean's Othello and Lady Macbeth opposite Gustavus Vaughan Brooke. There followed starring tours in Ireland and Scotland. Some time between 1856 and 1859 she was married in Ireland to Thomas *Macknight (1829–1899), already the author of an anonymous book attacking Disraeli, who later became editor of the *Northern Whig*. The couple had two children, Edmund (b. 1860) and Elizabeth (b. 1862), who married the actor–manager Henry Dundas (Arthur Harrison) in 1883.

However, Sarah Thorne's commitment to the stage and Macknight's interests in politics and philosophy proved incompatible, and after only a short period they lived separately. In August 1863 she starred at Brighton and in 1865 she appeared, again in leading roles, including that of the eponymous Leah, at Paisley Theatre Royal, the Prince of Wales's Opera House, Edinburgh, and the New Theatre Royal, Jersey. Between October 1865 and March 1866 she played at the National Standard Theatre, Shoreditch, taking principal parts in a lengthy season of Shakespeare's plays.

Sarah Thorne's first experience of management came in 1867, when she succeeded her father as lessee of the Theatre Royal, Margate; she opened on 29 July with H. T. Craven's *Meg's Diversions* and *The Child of the Regiment*. Her declared policy was to offer the 'newest pieces approved in the metropolis as occasion permits' but never to neglect 'old and legitimate productions' (*Era*, 4 Aug 1867). Her lease ended when the theatre was sold at auction in August 1873 to Robert Fort, and for the 1874 stock season she held a lesser management role. She returned briefly to Margate at Christmas 1874 during the tour of her now established annual pantomime.

Thorne's second period of management was at the recently rebuilt Theatre Royal, Worcester, where she opened on 27 March 1876. There she engaged touring productions and provided, as at Margate, a stock company with a repertory of both classical and contemporary drama. Her association with Worcester came to an abrupt end when the theatre burnt down on 24 November 1877. She then formed a touring company to support the ageing Charles James Mathews.

The withdrawal of Fort's latest tenant enabled Thorne to resume a lease at Margate in January 1879. Committed to the rapidly disappearing stock-company system, she maintained an annual summer season. For the remainder of the year she opened the theatre to some of the burgeoning touring companies, among them that of her brother Tom Thorne (1841–1918), who brought productions he had first put on at the Vaudeville Theatre, London (where he was manager from 1870). For a brief period in the autumn of 1879 she also leased Astley's Amphitheatre, London, where she appeared with her youngest brother, George Tyrrell Thorne (1856–1922), who had been apprenticed to her, in Boucicault's *The Flying Scud*. George was later a leading member of the D'Oyly Carte Opera Company.

Sarah Thorne gained a substantial reputation for training young players. In 1885 she opened her School of Acting, advertising for 'Ladies and Gentlemen' wishing to enter the theatrical profession and charging £20 for three months' or £30 for six months' training. The regime, in which she was assisted on occasions by her sister Emily (Mrs Frank Parker Gillmore, *d.* 1907), included classes in 'voice production, gesture and mime, dialects and accents, make-up, the portrayal of characters, the value of pace and the value of pauses' (Morley, 110). Among her pupils were Harley Granville Barker, Helen Brinckman, Sarah Brooke, Louis Calvert, Gertrude Kingston, Beatrice Lamb, Evelyn Millard, her niece Nellie Thorne, Irene and Violet Vanbrugh, and Florence Ward. While it was customary for actor–managers to take apprentices, this school is regarded as the country's first formal drama school. In 1894 she leased the Chatham Lecture Hall, which she renamed the Opera House and used as a second venue for her stock company.

Although she was acclaimed in a wide range of parts and genres, Sarah Thorne's preferences were for Shakespeare's Beatrice, Desdemona, Juliet, and Lady Macbeth, Kate Hardcastle in *She Stoops to Conquer*, Lady Teazle in *The School for Scandal*, and Leah. She insisted on good taste in her choice of plays and in their production, avowedly rejecting 'anything vulgar in costume or language' (*Chatham, Rochester and Brompton Observer*). She is said to have had a 'somewhat imperious manner' (*Thanet Times*, 3 March 1899), but a Margate contemporary spoke of her generosity, especially to the poor and elderly, whose rent she would sometimes pay herself (*Chatham Observer*).

Thorne's last performance was in September 1898, at her benefit at Margate, when she took the part of Parthenia in Maria Lovell's *Ingomar*. Her last appearance on the Chatham stage had been in May 1896, as Lady Gay Spanker in *London Assurance*. She died at 3 New Road Avenue, Chatham, on 27 February 1899, just as what was to have been a celebration of her theatrical jubilee was being arranged by George Alexander and Gertrude Kingston at St James's Theatre, London, for 16 March. She was buried at Brompton cemetery on 3 March 1899. After her death her son, who had been her business manager since the early 1880s, took over the leases of the Chatham and Margate theatres.

C. M. P. TAYLOR

Sources M. Morley, *Margate and its theatres, 1730–1965* (1966) • C. E. Pascoe, ed., *The dramatic list*, 2nd edn (1880) • *The Era* (4 March 1899) • *The Stage* (2 March 1899) • *Thanet Times* (3 March 1899) • *Chatham, Rochester and Brompton Observer* (4 March 1899) • *Thanet Times* (10 March 1899) • *Chatham Observer* (11 March 1899) • *Worcester Herald* (25 March 1876–1 Dec 1877) • d. cert. • b. cert. [Edmund Macknight] • b. cert. [Elizabeth Macknight] • review, *Theatre Notebook*, 21 (1966–7), 191–2 • files, Astley's Theatre, 1879, Theatre Museum • files, National Standard Theatre, Shoreditch, 1865–6, Theatre Museum • files, Surrey Theatre, London, 1854, Theatre Museum • P. Hartnoll, ed., *The Oxford companion to the theatre*, 2nd edn (1957) • W. M. Pope, *St James: theatre of distinction* (1958) • *The Era* (1885) • *The Era* (4 Aug 1867) • photocopies of playbills, Theatre Royal, Margate, Margate Library • *CGPLA Eng. & Wales* (1899)

Archives Margate Library

Likenesses Goodman & Schmidt, photograph, repro. in *Thanet Times* (3 March 1899)

Wealth at death £8556 8s. 6d.: probate, 8 April 1899, *CGPLA Eng. & Wales*

Thorne, William (*fl. c.*1397), Benedictine monk and chronicler, of St Augustine's Abbey, Canterbury, wrote a history of that house from its foundation in 598. This survives in two manuscripts: Cambridge, Corpus Christi College, MS 189, which ends in 1375 and dates from about the late fourteenth century; and BL, Add. MS 53710, which comes down to 1397 and dates from no more than a few years later. The latter also forms a revision as well as an expansion of the former, adding or altering material in a good many places.

Thorne's work is disappointing for Anglo-Saxonists

because down to the 1220s he relies heavily on the late thirteenth-century chronicle of Thomas Sprott, while right through his work he is careless in his copying of charters and other texts, omitting such details as the names of witnesses and sometimes the date as well. He wrote in a spirit of zeal for his abbey's prosperity, and was interested neither in the minutiae of its documentary history nor in events of national significance; archbishops of Canterbury are portrayed only in terms of their actions or intentions *vis-à-vis* the abbey, and the black death is ignored totally.

Thorne's method was to quote or paraphrase documents (doubtless all drawn from the abbey's archives or such works as Sprott's chronicle), making a paragraph or two out of each such text, and setting them into a chronological sequence. These texts were mostly concerned with the estates, rights, and legal proceedings of the abbey; he gives detailed information about such matters as appropriations of churches and ordinations of vicarages, dealings with the royal justices, and similar financial and administrative affairs. He has relatively little to say about the internal history of his house and virtually nothing about its spiritual life, though he does find space for a copy of the papal grant by which St Augustine's feast day was made a double office.

Thorne's account of events in his own century is increasingly lively, and he knew how to tell a good story. A short tale is that of Solomon Ripple, a monk of St Augustine's who acted on the abbot's behalf as a tax collector in 1335 and extorted so much money that royal justices fined the abbot £80; Thorne concludes with an account of Ripple's improvements to the abbey's estates. Much longer is the narrative of the time that he himself spent following the papal court around Italy in 1387–90, as he struggled in vain to obtain confirmation from Pope Urban VI (*r.* 1378–89) of the election of William Welde as abbot of St Augustine's. The tale of his dealings with Cardinal Brancaccio, 'a grasping and avaricious man, most notably tainted with the sin of simony' (*William Thorne's Chronicle*, 656), who with his auditor had to be given 100 florins before he would act, is an essay in restrained irony.

Almost nothing is known about Thorne beyond the little that is revealed in his chronicle. He was a candidate for the abbacy of St Augustine's in 1375, but was unsuccessful despite initially having the prior and sacrist on his side. His loyalty to his house was unaltered and he worked hard for both the abbot who had defeated him, Michael Peckham, and for his successor, William Welde.

Thorne's chronicle was edited by Sir Roger Twysden, in his *Historiae Anglicanae scriptores X* (1652), and it was translated by A. H. Davis as *William Thorne's Chronicle of St Augustine's Abbey, Canterbury* (1934).   NIGEL RAMSAY

Sources CCC Cam., MS 189 · BL, Add. MS 53710 · 'Chronica Guillielmi Thorne', *Historiae Anglicanae scriptores X*, ed. R. Twysden (1652), cols. 1757–2202 · *William Thorne's chronicle of St Augustine's Abbey, Canterbury*, trans. A. H. Davis (1934) · S. E. Kelly, ed., *Charters of St Augustine's Abbey, Canterbury, and Minster-in-Thanet*, Anglo-Saxon Charters, 4 (1995), esp. lv–lvi, xcviii

Archives BL, Add. MS 53710 · CCC Cam., MS 189

Thorne, William (1568?–1630), classical and Hebrew scholar and Church of England clergyman, was born in Semley, Wiltshire. His father, according to Oxford University records, was *plebeius*: neither a gentleman nor a clergyman. There is no record of any marriage. Thorne entered Winchester College in 1582 and New College, Oxford, in 1586, and graduated BA on 12 April 1589. He proceeded MA in 1592, and later the same year published *Ducente Deo Willelmi Thorni Tullius seu Rētōr, in tria stromata diuisus*, a commonplace book reorganizing Cicero's ideas on rhetoric into logical categories, with extensive references to a wide range of other sources, especially Aristotle and the Hellenistic rhetoricians. *Ducente Deo* was the first work to be dedicated to William Herbert, future earl of Pembroke, who was then twelve years old. There was apparently a pre-existing link between Thorne's family and the Pembrokes, since William acknowledged their generosity towards his family in the dedication. The work also included a dedicatory verse by John Case, the well-known Aristotelian, and Thorne himself wrote a verse for Case's posthumous work *Lapis philosophicus* (1600). About the same year Thorne assembled a manuscript anthology of verse in praise of Thomas Sackville, baron of Buckhurst, then newly appointed chancellor of Oxford University.

Thorne and his collaborators exhibited their linguistic skills, including poems in both Latin and Greek, and he peppered his prose dedication with Hebrew expressions. Licensed to preach in 1597, he qualified BD in 1600, and DD in 1602. At his vespers or doctoral disputation, he defended the positions of the Church of England on the canonicity of the Bible, and made enough of an impression to be cited as an authority in Thomas Pye's *Epistola ad Iohannem Honsonum* ('Epistle to John Honson', 1603). He was regius professor of Hebrew from 1598 to 1604. There is good evidence of Thorne's ability in Hebrew, since there are extant letters and poems written to him in Hebrew; he is known to have written at least one poem in Hebrew, and he was a frequent correspondent of the famous Dutch Hebraist Johan Drusius. The latter dedicated a work to him, *Opuscula quae ad grammaticam spectant* (1609) in gratitude for Thorne's generosity in taking in Drusius's son for two years in Oxford. In that work, there is a quotation in Syriac and a remark implying that Thorne also knew that language. There is, in addition, ambiguous evidence that he knew Arabic.

With the accession of James I, Thorne published his second book, an English sermon addressed to the king: *Esoptron basilikon, or, A Kenning-Glass for a Christian King* (1603), an extended interpretation of Pontius Pilate's words, 'behold the man'. A document signed by fifteen bishops in 1605 or 1606 recommends Thorne for promotion, referring to him as the king's chaplain and as one of the Oxford translators of the Authorized Version of the Bible. He received much preferment: he was installed dean of Chichester on 30 December 1601 and in the same year was presented to the rectory of Tollard Royal, Wiltshire. He resigned his fellowship in 1602, and was collated to the prebend of Bussall in 1603, which he also resigned the following year. In 1606 he became vicar of Amport,

Hampshire, and in 1607 he was presented to the rectory of Birdham, Sussex. In 1613 he was collated to the prebend of Hova Villa. In 1616 he became rector of North Marden, Sussex, and in 1619 of Warblington, Hampshire. He died on 13 February 1630 and was buried in Chichester Cathedral.

MATHEW DECOURSEY

Sources J. W. Binns, *Intellectual culture in Elizabethan and Jacobean England: the Latin writings of the age* (1990) · *Reg. Oxf.*, vol. 2 · Foster, *Alum. Oxon.* · L. Fuks, 'Het Hebreeuwse brievenboek van Johannes Drusius jr. Hebreeuws en Hebraïsten in Nederland rondom 1600', *Studia Rosenthaliana*, 3/1 (1969), 1–52 · A. Hamilton, *William Bedwell the Arabist, 1563–1632* (Leiden, 1985) · *Fasti Angl., 1541–1857*, [Chichester] · T. F. Kirby, *Winchester scholars: a list of the wardens, fellows, and scholars of … Winchester College* (1888) · *Hist. U. Oxf. 3: Colleg. univ.* · F. Madan, *Oxford books: a bibliography of printed works*, 3 vols. (1895–1931); repr. (1964) · *VCH Sussex*, vol. 2 · G. S. Paine, *The learned men* (New York, 1959) · C. B. Schmitt, *John Case and Aristotelianism in Renaissance England* (Kingston and Montreal, 1983) · F. W. Steer, ed., *The archives of New College, Oxford* (1974) · *Hist. U. Oxf. 4: 17th-cent. Oxf.*, 454 · Wood, *Ath. Oxon.* · A. Wood, *The history and antiquities of the colleges and halls in the University of Oxford*, ed. J. Gutch (1786) · A. Wood, *The history and antiquities of the University of Oxford*, ed. J. Gutch, 2 vols. in 3 pts (1792–6) · private information (2004) [E. A. Malone] · *DNB*

Thorne, William James [Will] (1857–1946), trade unionist and politician, known as Will Thorne, was born in Farm Street, Hockley, Birmingham, on 8 October 1857, the son of Thomas Thorn (the 'e' was added later) and his second wife, Emma Everiss. Both his parents worked in the brickyards, as their parents had done before them. Thomas Thorn also worked as a gas-stoker at Saltley gasworks during the winter months. He had a family from his first marriage and four children from his second—Will, the eldest, and three girls. He was a heavy drinker, and was often involved in drunken brawls. He died when Will was seven years old, as the result of a blow from a horse dealer who was sent to prison for nine months for manslaughter. After his death the family was very poor. Emma Thorn supported her children with home sewing work, and an allowance of 4s. a week and four loaves of bread from the Birmingham guardians.

Thorne had his first job at the age of six, helping in his uncle's barber-shop at weekends. At seven he was also employed turning a wheel for a rope maker nine hours a day for half a crown a week. He next worked 'carrying off' bricks at a brick and tile works. After this he held a succession of labouring jobs as plumber's mate, metal roller's assistant in an ammunition factory, nut and bolt tapper in a wagon works, builder's labourer, and brickmaker's assistant.

In 1875 Thorne's mother married again—her second husband, a carpenter and joiner named George Thompson, more violent in temper and an even heavier drinker than her first. Consequently Will went 'on the tramp' and worked for a time as a navvy on the construction of the Burton and Derby Railway. On his return to Birmingham he was again employed in the brickfields and then went to the Saltley gasworks which belonged to the Birmingham corporation. On 9 February 1879 he married Harriet, daughter of John Hallam, a fellow worker at Saltley and an active radical.

William James Thorne (1857–1946), by James Jarché, 1933

Thorne led a successful campaign for the abolition of Sunday work at Saltley, but dissatisfied with the conditions at the works he left and in November 1881 tramped to London with two friends to seek work at the Old Kent Road gasworks of the South Metropolitan Gas Company. By this time his wife had had twins—a boy and a girl; the boy died at six months. Thorne's family joined him in south London, but soon after he was dismissed because work was slack, and returned with his family to Birmingham, going back to work at Saltley. He again left owing to a dispute about conditions and, tramping once more to London, got a job at the Beckton gasworks, lodging in Canning Town and soon bringing his wife, now with three children, to join him.

Thorne joined the Social Democratic Federation of H. M. Hyndman about 1884, for which he became an active propagandist. He had already tried to lead several strikes at his places of employment, although no trade unions existed for the less skilled workers. At Beckton, attempts had been made in 1884 and 1885 to form a union; but these had failed. In March 1889, with the assistance of Ben Tillett, Thorne established the National Union of Gasworkers and General Labourers, initially around the demand for a reduction in shift hours at gasworks from twelve to eight. A petition was drawn up and sent to the London gas companies; the Gas Light and Coke Company, which owned the Beckton and other works, was the first to concede the eight-hour day, without the need for a strike. Other companies followed suit, and the movement, and with it the union, spread rapidly to other parts of the country. By late 1889 the union had 20,000 members, with forty-four branches in London and twenty outside the capital. Its success in London helped to prepare the ground for the great dock strike of 1889 and the rapid growth of unionism among labourers on the docks and wharves.

In June 1889 Thorne was elected general secretary of his union—the first of the 'new unions'—and occupied the position until he retired in 1934. Having received no formal education—at the time of his first marriage he could not sign his own name—he had a difficult time in adapting himself to the unfamiliar tasks of office and financial administration. As the union grew, however, he employed skilled office assistants and was able to spend most of his time in organizing and negotiating work. After the concession of the eight-hour day, the union put forward a demand for double pay for Sunday work. While the negotiations were in progress Sir George Livesey launched a profit-sharing scheme at the South Metropolitan Gas Company's works in the hope of breaking the union. This led to a strike which lasted more than two months, cost the union £20,000, and was not successful.

In 1890 Thorne was a delegate to the Trades Union Congress at Liverpool, where he helped to carry a resolution in favour of the legal eight-hour day. From 1894 to 1933 he was a member of the parliamentary committee (from 1921 the general council) of the congress. He was its chairman in 1896–7 and 1911–12, presiding over the annual congress of 1912. In 1891 he was elected as a socialist to the West Ham town council on which he remained, as an alderman from 1910, for the rest of his life. He was mayor in 1917–18 and was later made a freeman of the borough. In 1898 he went as a fraternal delegate to the American Federation of Labor convention at Kansas City, and in 1913 as first fraternal delegate from Great Britain to the Canadian Trades and Labour Congress at Saint John, New Brunswick. He stood as parliamentary candidate for West Ham (South) in 1900 but was defeated. In 1906 he won the seat (renamed Plaistow in 1918) and held it until he retired in 1945.

On the outbreak of war in 1914 Thorne took a similar stance to Hyndman in supporting it; he joined the 1st volunteer battalion of the Essex regiment and was made lieutenant-colonel. In 1917, as a Labour delegate, with James O'Grady and William Stephen Sanders, he went to Russia during the period between the two revolutions to support attempts to keep Russia in the war against Germany. Thorne came into growing conflict with others in the socialist movement and the Labour Party over his support for the war. After the war he was seen to be moving to the right in his politics. After previously refusing honours, he accepted a CBE in 1930. He became a privy councillor in 1945.

Thorne was a big man, very strongly built, and capable in his younger days of great feats of physical endurance. He gained education mainly in adulthood, through his friendship with fellow socialists, especially Ben Tillett, Edward Aveling, and Eleanor Marx Aveling, who greatly assisted him in building up his union. Thorne was not a good speaker in parliament. His straightforward and unsubtle approach was more suited to open-air meetings and he attracted great loyalty from the unskilled workers in his union. He was respected for his honesty and devotion to the union's cause and for his immense capacity for hard work. Politically he remained faithful to the Social Democratic Federation, of which he was chairman in 1930, but he did not play an active part in it after the early years. The union was always his priority and he did not aspire to political leadership. His only book, an autobiography, *My Life's Battles*, appeared in 1925.

In 1895, not long after his first wife's death, Thorne married Emily, daughter of his friend William Byford, treasurer of the Gasworkers' Union. In 1925, after Emily's death, he married Rebecca Cecilia, daughter of Thomas Sinclair, chief marine draughtsman. She died in the following year and on 26 April 1930 he married Beatrice Nellie, daughter of George Collins. With his first wife he had four sons and three daughters, and with his second, three sons and three daughters. Thorne died of a heart attack at his home, 1 Lawrence Road, Plaistow, West Ham, on 2 January 1946, and was buried in the East London cemetery on 10 January. He was survived by his fourth wife.

G. D. H. COLE, *rev.* MARC BRODIE

Sources W. Thorne, *My life's battles*, new edn (1989) [with introduction by John Saville] · *The Times* (3 Jan 1946) · *The Times* (11 Jan 1946) · *Stratford Express* (4 Jan 1946) · *Stratford Express* (11 Jan 1946) · *DLB* · *WWBMP*

Archives Labour History Archive and Study Centre, Manchester, papers; corresp. | BL, corresp. with John Burns, Add. MSS 46289–46298 · BLPES, corresp. with independent labour party · People's History Museum, Manchester, Labour Representation Committee archive · People's History Museum, Manchester, labour party trade union file

Likenesses W. Stoneman, two photographs, 1921–38, NPG · J. Jarché, photograph, 1933, NPG [*see illus.*] · F. Slater, oils, 1934, Woodstock College, Surrey · C. Harris, photograph, NPG · M. Hicks, oils, National Union of General and Municipal Workers archives · oils, Woodstock College, Surrey · pencil drawing, Woodstock College, Surrey · photograph, NPG · six photographs, repro. in Thorne, *My life's battles*, following p. 114 · three photographs, repro. in E. A. Radice and G. H. Radice, *Will Thorne: constructive militant* (1974), frontispiece and following p. 64

Wealth at death £7187 0s. 11d.: probate, 15 March 1946, *CGPLA Eng. & Wales*

Thorneycroft, (George Edward) Peter, Baron Thorneycroft (1909–1994), politician, was born on 26 July 1909 at Dunston Hall, Staffordshire, the only son and one of two children of Major George Edward Mervyn Thorneycroft (1883–1943), soldier and landowner, and Dorothy Hope Franklyn (1883–1929), only daughter of Lieutenant-General Sir William Edmund Franklyn. The Thorneycrofts had originally been Staffordshire ironmasters. He was educated at Eton College (1922–7), where he showed little academic ability. He had to attend a crammer before gaining admission to the Royal Military Academy at Woolwich, which he entered in 1928. He was commissioned into the Royal Artillery in 1930, though he quickly formed the ambition to become a barrister. This was perhaps because of the influence of his twin sister, Elizabeth (1909–1984), who was then reading jurisprudence at Lady Margaret Hall, Oxford, and who communicated her

(George Edward) Peter Thorneycroft, Baron Thorneycroft
(1909–1994), by unknown photographer

enthusiasm for the law to him. Developing late intellectually he started to study law while still a serving officer. He found a pupil master in Theobald Matthew at 4 Paper Buildings, a fellow pupil being Quintin Hogg, later Lord Hailsham and a cabinet colleague. In 1933 Thorneycroft resigned his commission to study law full time. He was called to the bar of the Inner Temple in 1935, and thereafter practised in Birmingham on the Oxford circuit.

Into parliament Thorneycroft was elected Conservative MP for Stafford—his reputation in the county, especially in field sports, having helped him to the candidacy—at a by-election on 9 June 1938. He took a practical view of his calling—'the most that a man can ever really do in politics is to edge the world just a tiny bit more in the direction he wants' (*Guardian*, 28 Oct 1985)—but his was a career that would, paradoxically, be marked by stands on principle. He had a robust personality, self-confident without being arrogant. He was blessed with a fine oratorical style and a loud, sonorous voice, though he spoke in the mock upper-class cockney accent favoured by fashionable people in the 1920s and 1930s.

At the outbreak of war in 1939 Thorneycroft rejoined the Royal Artillery, serving on the south coast, and then as a captain on the joint planning committee of the general staff, doing preliminary work on the Normandy landings. Frustrated by not having been offered either a combatant or overseas posting he realized by late 1942 that he could contribute better to the war by returning to the House of Commons, and resigned his commission. Seconding the

Gracious Speech in November 1942 he was deemed by Chips Channon to have held the house in an 'admirable performance' (*Chips*, ed. James, 341). He was an active, and not always loyal, back-bencher. With other radical minded Conservative MPs, like Hogg and Lord Hinchingbrooke, he formed the Tory Reform Committee. It met regularly at a restaurant in the Charing Cross Road and co-ordinated the members' activities in parliament. At a time when the party leadership seemed uninterested in Conservative policy, this group, of which Thorneycroft was elected joint secretary and soon became the leading personality, tried to formulate one that broke with the pre-war past. They supported, in particular, an enthusiastic approach to the Beveridge report on welfare, published in 1942. Despite having made some trouble—not least in defying R. A. Butler over equal pay for women teachers—Thorneycroft was appointed parliamentary secretary to the Ministry of War Transport in the caretaker government on 26 May 1945. In the Labour landslide that summer he lost Stafford.

However, an early by-election at Monmouth took Thorneycroft back to the Commons in October 1945. He was invited to sit on the front bench by Churchill. However, within a few weeks he realized he was too junior to have the opportunity to speak as often as he would have liked, so decided to return to the back benches and have the freedom to speak more widely. He quickly made his mark: a speech on the Coal Bill in February 1946 was commended to Churchill by the chief whip, James Stuart, who said that Thorneycroft 'seems to be a man who cannot be ignored' (Gilbert, 190).

Thorneycroft further developed his creed in the 1946 pamphlet *Design for Freedom*, produced by a committee of like-minded radicals and signed by 111 Conservative and Liberal candidates and MPs. The pamphlet advocated 'a degree of planning and state activity which would have been wholly unacceptable to the Conservative Party in the years between the wars' (*Independent*, 6 June 1994). He further honed his debating style, so that by the end of the 1945 parliament he had become one of his party's most effective performers.

On 3 May 1938 Thorneycroft had married Sheila Wells Page (1914–1999), daughter of Edgar Page of Tettenhall, Wolverhampton; they had one son. She obtained a divorce in 1949, and Thorneycroft married Countess Carla Roberti (b. 1914), fashion editor of *Vogue* and daughter of Count Malagola Cappi of Ravenna, Italy, on 2 April 1949; they had a daughter.

Into the cabinet When the Conservatives regained power Thorneycroft was, to general surprise, made president of the Board of Trade, on 30 October 1951. He was the youngest member of Churchill's cabinet, popular with colleagues and opponents, with a reputation for kindness, courtesy, and geniality. He was temperamentally well suited to his post, and happy in it. He was a free trader and supporter of the General Agreement on Tariffs and Trade. Also, he was an early advocate of closer ties with Europe, having been a member of the United Europe Movement since its inception in 1947. During 1956 he and Harold

Macmillan, the chancellor of the exchequer, laid the foundations of the European Free Trade Association. Thorneycroft was a persuasive negotiator, and enjoyed the overseas missions on which he strove to remove the barriers to international trade. He was equally happy at home, dismantling socialist controls on industry. It was during his time at trade that the Conservatives dropped any residual commitment to imperial preference and became a party of free trade.

On Macmillan's becoming prime minister Thorneycroft's work at trade was rewarded with a promotion. He became chancellor of the exchequer on 13 January 1957, when sterling was under pressure after Suez, and the public finances less than sound. As Thorneycroft himself later noted in his resignation speech in January 1958, Britain was trying to be a nuclear power and a welfare state when it lacked the funds to do either properly. The new chancellor would be ably assisted in seeking to restore confidence by the financial secretary, J. Enoch Powell, and the economic secretary, Nigel Birch, both of whom were 'sound money' men. His relationship with Macmillan, however, would not be happy. Macmillan had, in 1956, recorded of Thorneycroft's manner that 'he shouts at one (with a cockney accent) as if we were a public meeting' (Horne, 72). In later life Macmillan would, in conversation, affect to forget Thorneycroft's name, and refer to him as 'that man who looked like an English butler, with the nice Italian wife' (ibid.).

The flight from sterling continued throughout early 1957. By the summer it was clear that strong corrective measures would be needed if the economy were to be put on a sure footing. On becoming chancellor Thorneycroft insisted on carrying through cuts of £200 million in defence spending and between £80 and £100 million on social security that had been ordered by Macmillan. However, when it became clear that even stricter economies were needed Thorneycroft found that his officials at the Treasury—notably the chief economic adviser, Sir Robert Hall, and the joint permanent secretary, Sir Roger Makins, both of whom were Keynesians—could barely conceal their distaste. Initially Thorneycroft had been happy to consider other methods of controlling inflation, agreeing to establish the Council on Prices, Productivity and Incomes. Within a few months, however, he came to believe that only control of the money supply could work. His earlier belief in Keynesianism had worn thin.

Thorneycroft delivered his only budget on 9 April 1957. Despite the need for stringency he found £98 million for tax cuts, though he courted controversy by directing these at surtax payers and at British firms operating abroad. He continued to resist pressures from the governor of the Bank of England, Cameron Cobbold, for rises in interest rates. Cobbold became ever more insistent, and Powell and Birch believed that tough monetary measures could not be long delayed. Thorneycroft agreed. He accepted Powell's monetarist logic that the government could control inflation by holding the rate of growth in the money supply to a level demanded by economic growth plus inflation. This was Thatcherism twenty years before

Thatcher, and it pre-empted Milton Friedman, the supposed father of monetarist economics, too. In July 1957, therefore, Thorneycroft asked his officials 'to consider possibilities of checking inflation by taking firmer control of the money supply' (Heffer, 218). On 17 July he told cabinet colleagues that, unless reduced, present spending plans would 'far outstrip the rise in revenue' (ibid.). On 16 July he warned Macmillan that 1958's civil estimates would have to be at 1957 levels. On 7 August he requested a study on how a measure of deflation could be brought to the economy.

By early September there was open hostility between Thorneycroft and his senior officials, who felt, in Hall's words, that he had taken against all of them (Heffer, 220). The impression was fostered by Thorneycroft's decision to call upon Lionel Robbins, the arch anti-Keynesian academic, for advice. Meanwhile, reserves had fallen by $200 million during July and August. Thorneycroft had been told on 22 August by Cobbold that a drastic rise in the bank rate was the only option, since Makins (behind Thorneycroft's back) had told Cobbold that there was no question of spending cuts. Macmillan had grave doubts about deflation. However, the cabinet realized it had run out of options. On 19 September 1957 the bank rate rose from 5 to 7 per cent, its highest level in peacetime. It was a great success of Thorneycroft's that he had convinced the cabinet to support the rate rise. However, he achieved this at the price of entrenching the hostility of his officials, and exhausting the capacity for boldness of his colleagues. For his part, he was landed with the nickname 'Mr Seven Per Cent'.

Macmillan was being advised by Roy Harrod, Keynes's friend and biographer, who railed against him for the practice of the 'antiquated doctrine' of limiting the supply of money (Heffer, 222). By November it was apparent that the interest rate rise would not in itself be enough, and stringent economies were required. A wrangle between the Treasury and departmental heads began, earlier than would normally have been the case. Macmillan would be away on a Commonwealth tour for much of the winter, and matters needed to be settled before his departure on 7 January 1958.

There has been much speculation about whether Thorneycroft was put up to his monetarist stand by Powell and Birch, or whether he came to the conclusion himself. He was no fool, and could see the logic of the position and the honesty of proceeding with it. He did, though, go into meetings armed with detailed arguments supplied by Powell, whose great intellect complemented Thorneycroft's advanced political and personal skills.

Resignation By early December 1957 Thorneycroft had become confrontational with Makins, telling him that the financial situation was 'grave' and could not 'be defended in terms either of economics or politics'. He added, 'I do not believe that it is impossible to save £200 million out of a proposed spending of £2926 million. I do not believe there is a single department which could not within 18 months be in a healthier condition as a result of such a policy' (Heffer, 227). On 8 December he sent Macmillan a warning of the 'grim picture' of the existing estimates. Macmillan invited the Treasury to submit a paper on how to make the necessary savings. Thorneycroft had Powell write it. It suggested cuts, which Thorneycroft supported, to welfare services, the introduction of board and lodging fees for hospitals, and an increase in the price of school milk. On 27 December he told Macmillan that it was crucially important such cuts be agreed. Macmillan had already discerned that Thorneycroft was in a 'resigning mood' (Horne, 71). When the cabinet discussed the cuts in a series of meetings at the turn of the year, £153 million had to be saved. Macmillan had decided this was impossible, for he feared provoking organized labour. He urged his colleagues to find ways of meeting the chancellor's concerns, but never intended to force the issue. When £100 million of cuts were agreed Macmillan chose not to push for the rest. His personal relations with Thorneycroft had deteriorated sharply, to the point where he noted the 'rude and *cassant*' way in which the chancellor had allegedly behaved (Heffer, 231).

Thorneycroft did not prevail. When it became clear that the cabinet would not match its own anti-inflationary rhetoric—Macmillan, while refusing to implement the cuts, had protested that 'the Chancellor of the Exchequer could feel assured of the wholehearted determination of his colleagues to support him in his disinflationary policy' (Heffer, 231)—Thorneycroft, Powell, and Birch resigned. The chancellor's letter of resignation was regarded by Macmillan as 'a formal and somewhat contemptuous document' (Heffer, 234) because it outlined why he and his two colleagues had gone: that, for all the protestations to the contrary, the cabinet was not serious about cutting spending to control inflation. Macmillan was offended that Thorneycroft had sent no covering note with his letter expressing personal regret. The prime minister, as he departed for his Commonwealth tour, referred to the resignations as a 'little local difficulty', which his party chairman, Lord Hailsham, described as showing 'more panache than accuracy' (Hailsham, 163).

In his resignation speech to the House of Commons, on 23 January 1958, Thorneycroft spelt out the problem he had been trying to treat: 'For twelve years we have been attempting to do more than our resources could manage, and in the process we have been gravely weakening ourselves'. He said, pointedly,

> any hon. Member in this House would say he was against inflation, as men say they are against sin. The question is where and when we choose to stand and fight it ... I believe that there is an England which would prefer to face these facts and make the necessary decisions now. I believe that living within our resources is neither unfair nor unjust, nor, perhaps, in the long run even unpopular. There are millions of men and women in this country, in the Commonwealth, and in many other countries of the world who depend for the whole of their future on sustaining the value of our money. Self-interest and honour alike demand that we should take the necessary steps to hold it. (*Hansard 5C*, 580, 23 Jan 1958, 1294–7)

He claimed that the policy was 'not the path to greatness. It is the road to ruin' (ibid.).

The two years after his resignation Thorneycroft devoted to extensive overseas travel, including a world tour, and to his increasingly compelling hobby of painting watercolours, which he had embarked upon during a rainy family holiday in 1951. He was not prepared to carp from the backbenches, however justifiable such behaviour might have been as inflation crept upwards. He was keen to work his passage back, and on 27 July 1960 he returned to the cabinet, albeit in the lowly post of minister of aviation. By this time any serious attempt to control public spending had been discarded; within a decade the results would be obvious. Thorneycroft's one doubt about his resignation, voiced in 1980, was that he and his colleagues 'probably made our stand too early' (*Daily Telegraph*, 6 June 1994). It had, however, been a highly principled and courageous act that would resonate for decades.

At aviation, Thorneycroft's main achievement was to convince a sceptical cabinet of the importance of backing the Concorde project. On 14 July 1962, after the so-called 'night of the long knives', when Macmillan sacked a third of the cabinet, Thorneycroft was promoted to minister of defence. Soon after taking up his post he had to handle both the Vassal spy case, concerning an employee at the Admiralty, and the Cuban missile crisis. Thorneycroft was part of the inner cabinet formulating the British response to the situation. He also had to handle Kennedy's threat to end the Skybolt nuclear missile project, which risked leaving Britain without any independent nuclear deterrent.

Much of Thorneycroft's time at defence was spent planning a reorganization of the services in collaboration with the chief of the defence staff, Earl Mountbatten of Burma. This important reform, first considered in 1958 but postponed because of hostility from service chiefs, was intended to improve co-ordination between the three service departments and the Ministry of Defence. It meant that the war department, the Admiralty, and the Ministry of Aviation were amalgamated under a secretary of state for defence. Thorneycroft became the first holder of that office in April 1964. He served for just six months, until his party's election defeat in October that year. He shadowed the defence brief in opposition after the election.

When Heath became party leader in July 1965 he made Thorneycroft shadow home affairs spokesman. That role was cut short by Thorneycroft's defeat at Monmouth, after boundary changes, at the March 1966 election. He tried to return to the Commons, but after failing to find a suitable candidacy took a life peerage in 1967, becoming Baron Thorneycroft of Dunston in the county of Stafford.

Business and the chairmanship From then on, with one significant exception, business dominated Thorneycroft's life. When out of office in 1958–60 he had been invited to become a director of Pirelli, having been well known to Dr Alberto Pirelli during his years at the Board of Trade. He rejoined the firm in 1967, becoming chairman of Pirelli General Cable Works Ltd (later Pirelli General plc) from 1967 to 1987, and president from 1987 until his death; and also chairman of Pirelli plc from 1969 to 1987, and president from 1987. Additionally, he was chairman of Pirelli

UK plc from 1987 to 1989, and president from 1989 to his death. He also chaired Trusthouse Forte Ltd (later Forte plc) from 1969 to 1981, serving as president from 1982 to 1992. Other chairmanships were of Pye of Cambridge Ltd, from 1967 to 1979, of British Reserve Insurance Co. Ltd from 1980 to 1987, of Gil, Carvajal, & Partners Ltd from 1981 to 1989, and of Banca Nazionale del Lavoro from 1984 until his death. In all his business activities he was never content to be a figurehead, but rather an active chairman. From 1968 to 1975 he chaired SITPRO (Simplification of International Trade Procedures), and the British Overseas Trade Board from 1972 to 1975.

The exception to this portfolio of business interests was the six-year period, from 1975 to 1981, when Thorneycroft chaired the Conservative Party. When Heath had been pressed to resign the leadership in 1974 Thorneycroft urged him to fight his corner. It was a surprise to him, and many others, that this 66-year-old businessman should return to politics at Margaret Thatcher's behest. Thorneycroft's 1958 resignation was not, however, lost on her, who saw it as an early prophecy of the inflationary indiscipline that brought Heath down. Also, she sensed that Thorneycroft would help neutralize the hostility some Conservatives of his generation felt about her regime. In fact, those loyal to Heath had reason to thank Thorneycroft for his willingness to stand up to Mrs Thatcher, notably over manifesto commitments that might prove impossible to deliver. He was persuaded to take the job by William Whitelaw, the deputy leader and a cousin. His business connections were also useful to the party.

A back operation in mid-1975 meant that it was the autumn before Thorneycroft could get to work streamlining the party machine. He did so with a vengeance, courting criticism but restoring a level of professionalism to central office not seen since the days of Lord Woolton, a quarter of a century earlier. He was soon stumping the country making speeches, engendering great popularity for the leadership at a time of unease, after two election defeats. During the 1979 election there were tensions between central office and Mrs Thatcher over how the campaign should be conducted. Thorneycroft wanted to avoid controversy, especially over the party's plans to limit the power of the trades unions. Mrs Thatcher saw things differently, and had her way. It did not affect the result. She praised Thorneycroft as having been 'shrewd and authoritative' in the way he handled the tactical side of the campaign (Thatcher, 442). He was also responsible for forging a team of highly gifted policy staff, speechwriters, fund-raisers, and advertising men, who ensured the maximum impact for the party's message. Crucially, it was he who hired Saatchi and Saatchi to mastermind the party's publicity.

Thorneycroft was rewarded for these achievements by being made a Companion of Honour in 1980. Although now past seventy he wished to carry on as chairman, though to maintain his business interests he declined a place in the cabinet. This put him at a disadvantage, for he lost touch with the detail of what the government was doing. In the summer of 1981, during a serious financial downturn, he sharply discounted the claim by the chancellor, Sir Geoffrey Howe, that the recession was at an end. In a reference to the division between wets and dries in the government Thorneycroft claimed he had 'rising damp' and could see 'no sign of the economy picking up at the moment, not anywhere where I am'. He left politics for the last time in a reshuffle that autumn, though headlines claiming he had been sacked were at odds with the truth: he had never wanted to fight another election.

It was a mark of Thorneycroft's lack of vanity, and his healthy perspective on life, that the only book he published was on painting. Modestly entitled *The Amateur: a Companion to Watercolour* (1985), it was about how to enjoy painting rather than how to paint, and displayed a comprehensive knowledge of and expertise upon the subject. Though an amateur in the truest sense, there was nothing mediocre about Thorneycroft's abilities as a painter. He was a member of the Royal Academy and of the Royal Society of British Artists, and held nine exhibitions: at the Trafford Gallery in 1961 and 1970, at Chichester in 1963, at the Café Royal in 1976, 1981, and 1989, at the Mall Galleries in 1984, at the Cadogan Gallery in 1987, and at Lichfield in 1989. When meeting his civil servants at the Ministry of Aviation in 1960 he told them that his one indulgence was that he wished to be left free to draw in the life class of the Chelsea School of Art on Tuesdays and Thursdays from 6 p.m. to 9 p.m. Lord Clark once observed of Thorneycroft: 'There are plenty of VIPs who happen to paint; Peter is a painter who happens to be a VIP' (*Independent*, 6 June 1994). He painted until shortly before his death, making long annual trips to Venice with his wife—a founder member of the Venice in Peril fund—where he indulged his hobby.

On his book's publication Thorneycroft gave his last interview, at the age of seventy-six. He said

> I am one of the most contented men you can imagine. I happened to be the right age just at the moment my party was going to be in power for about 13 years. I held one high office after another. I met men like Lloyd George and Winston [Churchill], and Margaret [Thatcher]. And Chairman of my party. No doubt I was spoken of as a prime minister in earlier days, as a future prime minister. I never attained the highest office, but you don't go round the world disappointed if you're a vicar and haven't been made Archbishop of Canterbury. It would be absolutely bloody ridiculous (*Guardian*, 28 Oct 1985)

Although a very senior politician, he was never earnest, and had what one of his obituarists termed 'a prodigious gift for enjoying life' (*Independent*, 6 June 1994). He was a first-class cook and a keen fisherman, and loved family life. He died at his home, 42 Eaton Square, London, on 4 June 1994 after a long period of poor health, and was buried near his family's home at St Leonard's, Dunston, Staffordshire, on 9 June. He was survived by his wife and two children.

Thorneycroft's political achievement consisted mainly in four things. First, he was instrumental in divorcing his party from protectionism in trade. Second, his stand on monetarism identified an economic principle that would be adopted by both Conservative and Labour governments from 1979 onwards. Third, he greatly improved the administration of defence. And fourth, as chairman of the Conservative Party he instigated vital reforms and provided important advice to Margaret Thatcher which undoubtedly helped the party win the 1979 general election. SIMON HEFFER

Sources private information (2004) · personal knowledge (2004) · The Independent (6 June 1994) · Daily Telegraph (6 June 1994) · The Times (6 June 1994) · WWW, 1991–5 · The Guardian (28 Oct 1985) · S. Heffer, Like the Roman: the life of Enoch Powell (1998) · Hansard 5C (1958), 580.1294–7 · Dod's Parliamentary Companion (1994) · M. Gilbert, Winston S. Churchill, 8: Never despair, 1945–1965 (1988) · Lord Hailsham [Q. Hogg], The door wherein I went (1975) · A. Horne, Macmillan, 2: 1957–1986 (1989) · M. Thatcher, The path to power (1995) · 'Chips': the diaries of Sir Henry Channon, ed. R. R. James (1967)
Archives U. Southampton L., papers incl. files relating to work as president of the board of trade, chancellor of the exchequer, and secretary of state for defence | Bodl. Oxf., conservative party archive · PRO, cabinet and government MSS | FILM HLRO | SOUND BL NSA, documentary recording · BL NSA, performance recording
Likenesses R. Bouché, oils, 1953, priv. coll. · J. Ward, portrait, 1979, priv. coll. · B. Organ, oils, 1985, priv. coll. · J. Orr, oils, 1985, priv. coll. · B. Organ, oils, 1989, priv. coll. · T. Ramos, oils, 1989, NPG · photograph, repro. in The Times · photograph, repro. in The Independent · photograph, repro. in Daily Telegraph · photograph, NPG [see illus.]
Wealth at death £533,232: probate, 9 Nov 1994, CGPLA Eng. & Wales

Thornham [Turnham], **Robert of** (d. 1211), soldier and administrator, was a son of Robert of Thornham, a Kentish landowner. Like his elder brother Stephen of *Thornham (d. 1213/14), the younger Robert made his career in royal service. He first came to prominence on crusade, when Richard I gave him command of half the fleet that secured Cyprus in 1191, and left him in charge of the island with Richard de Camville when the main body of crusaders departed for Palestine. After Camville, too, departed, it was Thornham who suppressed a Cypriot rebellion and hanged its leader. Having joined the king in the Holy Land, Thornham made his own way back to England with Richard's gear, being now described as the king's *familiaris*. He then went to Germany, to be one of the pledges for the payment of Richard's ransom, but had joined the king at Poitiers by July 1194. At about that time he was appointed seneschal of Anjou, and, though also appointed sheriff of Surrey, for the rest of the reign he served Richard in France. His services were rewarded by 1197 with the hand of Joan, the daughter and heir of the Yorkshire baron William Fossard (d. 1194?), a marriage that raised Thornham to the ranks of the baronage. It was through this Yorkshire connection that he subsequently became a valuable source of information for the chronicler Roger of Howden. Though usually resident in Anjou, Thornham was often with the king in Normandy in 1198–9, but did not accompany Richard on his fatal expedition to Châlus.

On Richard's death Thornham's decision to admit John, count of Mortain, to Chinon, and to the treasure stored there, was the first step to set the late king's brother on the path to the throne. He accompanied John during his stay in Normandy (1199–1200), and in March 1200 went back to England with him, staying there for over a year. As well as attending the king, he looked after his own interests, especially in Yorkshire, litigating against several monasteries, and against the bishop of Durham, for lands and churches claimed as part of his wife's inheritance. He returned to France in the summer of 1201, as seneschal of Gascony and Anjou, but as French pressure on the Angevin lands grew he relinquished his southern commands, to concentrate on defending the Loire and subduing the rebellious barons of Poitou. Early in 1203 he led a raid on Angers, captured by the French in the previous November, which sacked and partly burnt the city. But in spite of his efforts the English defences fell, and late in 1204 or early in 1205 Thornham was himself captured. He had been released by July 1205, perhaps helped by a gift of 400 marks from the king, though he was still paying off his ransom in the following February, and returned to England. Several times recorded in attendance on John—whom he also accompanied on his abortive campaign in Anjou in 1206—Thornham attended to his own affairs in Yorkshire, and acted as sheriff of Surrey again from 1205 to 1207. But late in 1207 he went back to France, to be once more seneschal of Poitou. Returning to England in May 1209, he clearly remained in the king's favour. Matthew Paris names him as one of the king's counsellors who in 1210 advised John to extort money from religious houses, and who all came to bad ends.

Although Thornham had custody of the lands of Canterbury Cathedral priory when he died, he was in fact a significant benefactor to monasteries. The founder of the Premonstratensian abbey of Bayham in Kent, and of a hospital at Doncaster, he also confirmed and added to the endowment of his wife's foundation of Grosmont in Yorkshire—the first Grandmontine house in England. A dispute with Meaux Abbey over Wharram-le-Street ended with Thornham's surrendering to the monks the grange he had recovered from them. His own resources he owed primarily to his services to successive kings, who rewarded him with a valuable marriage and profitable wardships. In the year after his death his estates were estimated to have yielded £411 9s. 2d., with additional receipts, mainly from his wardships, worth £200 more. In 1214 Peter de Mauley proffered 7000 marks for the marriage of Thornham's only surviving child and heir, his daughter Isabel. Robert of Thornham died in 1211, perhaps on 26 April. In his charter confirming his wife's grant to Grosmont (probably made on his deathbed, since its witnesses included the doctors of the king and the bishop of Winchester), he begged King John to safeguard and confirm his charter, 'for the service which I have faithfully and devotedly done to him' (Dugdale, Monasticon, pt 2, 1025–6). HENRY SUMMERSON

Sources Chronica magistri Rogeri de Hovedene, ed. W. Stubbs, 4 vols., Rolls Series, 51 (1868–71), vols. 3–4 · W. Stubbs, ed., Gesta regis Henrici secundi Benedicti abbatis: the chronicle of the reigns of Henry II and Richard I, AD 1169–1192, 2 vols., Rolls Series, 49 (1867), vol. 2 · Paris, Chron., vol. 2 · Radulphi de Coggeshall chronicon Anglicanum, ed. J. Stevenson, Rolls Series, 66 (1875) · Chronica monasterii de Melsa, a fundatione usque ad annum 1396, auctore Thoma de Burton, ed. E. A. Bond, 1,

Rolls Series, 43/1 (1866) · *Chancery records* (RC) · *Pipe rolls* · *Curia regis rolls preserved in the Public Record Office* (1922–), vols. 1–5, 8 · W. Farrer and others, eds., *Early Yorkshire charters*, 12 vols. (1914–65), vol. 2 · Dugdale, *Monasticon*, new edn, vol. 6/2 · P. M. Barnes and W. R. Powell, eds., *Interdict documents*, PRSoc., new ser., 34 (1960) · D. M. Stenton, ed., *Pleas before the king or his justices, 1198–1202*, 1, SeldS, 67 (1953) · D. M. Stenton, ed., *Pleas before the king or his justices, 1198–1202*, 2, SeldS, 68 (1952) · D. M. Stenton, ed., *Pleas before the king or his justices, 1198–1212*, 3, SeldS, 83 (1967)

Likenesses seal, repro. in Farrer and others, eds., *Early Yorkshire charters*, vol. 2, p. 144

Wealth at death £411 9s. 2d. value of lands; £200 additional revenues: *Pipe rolls* 14 John, 5–6

Thornham [Turnham], **Stephen of** (*d.* 1213/14), justice and administrator, was the son of Robert of Thornham, a Kentish landowner. First recorded in the 1170s in association with his father as a benefactor to Combwell Priory in Kent, he entered the service of Henry II, and was several times recorded in attendance on the king in France, while in February 1188 he was one of the royal agents sent to Canterbury to see that divine services were resumed there, during the dispute between the archbishop and the monks of Christ Church over the former's proposals for a collegiate church at Hackington. He was rewarded with lands at Artington in Surrey, where he quickly acquired considerable local authority. In attendance on Richard I in June 1190 Thornham accompanied the new king on crusade. In April 1192 he visited Jerusalem, and in the following year he escorted Queen Berengaria and Joan of Sicily on their journey from Palestine to Rome. His loyalty to Richard is shown by the grant of land that he made to Combwell Priory in May 1194, shortly after the king's release from captivity, for the soul of Henry II 'and for the body and soul of my lord King Richard of England' ('Charters of Cumbwell Priory', 204–5). Thereafter he continued his career primarily in England, above all in the field of finance, where he served as a manager of royal demesnes, escheats, wardships, and vacant bishoprics in many counties. He would appear to have preserved a better reputation than most royal servants engaged in such activities— Adam of Eynsham described him as 'a faithful and godly man and devoted to our holy bishop'—even when engaged in seizing the possessions of the see of Lincoln in 1198 (*Life of St Hugh of Lincoln*, 114–15). Thornham was also in the late 1190s sheriff of Berkshire, Wiltshire, and (briefly) Lancashire, while in addition to these administrative duties he acted as a justice between 1197 and 1199, both at Westminster and on eyre in south-east England.

Thornham witnessed royal charters at the beginning of John's reign, but then not between 9 May 1200 and 5 May 1204, and his career may have faltered somewhat, while his accounts were scrutinized and his debts summoned, though the fact that in 1203 he had the custody of the king's niece, Eleanor of Brittany, shows that he was not entirely out of favour. But in 1204 he was allowed to make fine for all his outstanding arrears for 1000 marks—a generous settlement in itself, and ultimately pardoned in its entirety. Between May 1204 and June 1207 he attested a number of royal charters, while in 1206 he was able to secure confirmation of his wife's inheritance. He was still

on occasion engaged in financial administration, above all in the king's chamber, where he was sometimes involved in the payment and receipt of considerable sums of money—on 11 December 1207, for instance, the king notified the treasurer that he had lately received 5100 marks in the presence of Thornham and two others. But his trustworthiness in John's eyes is perhaps more strikingly shown by his responsibility for the custody not only of some of the king's wards but also of members of the royal family—Queen Isabella and the king's eldest son, the future Henry III, as well as Eleanor of Brittany, were at various times in Thornham's keeping at Winchester. Stephen of Thornham was dead by 6 March 1214. Some time before 1206 he had married Edelina, one of the three daughters and coheirs of Ranulf de Broc. His marriage brought him lands in several counties, especially in Surrey, Kent, and Hampshire, and royal serjeanties attached to the king's chamber and to the Marshalsea. Although the latter appears originally to have been a subordinate marshal's office, it was confirmed by John in 1205 as 'the superior and chief marshalsea of our household and court' (*Rotuli chartarum in Turri Londinensi asservati*, ed. T. D. Hardy, RC, 1837, 160). The king may have been trying to advance Thornham at the expense of William (I) Marshal, who was then out of favour. If so, his efforts had no effect. William Marshal and John were reconciled in 1208, while Thornham died without a male heir, his estates being subsequently divided among his five daughters and their husbands. HENRY SUMMERSON

Sources *Chancery records* (RC) · *Pipe rolls* · *Curia regis rolls preserved in the Public Record Office* (1922–), vols. 8, 10 · H. C. M. Lyte and others, eds., *Liber feodorum: the book of fees*, 3 vols. (1920–31) · L. Delisle and others, eds., *Recueil des actes de Henri II, roi d'Angleterre et duc de Normandie, concernant les provinces françaises et les affaires de France*, 3 (Paris, 1920) · 'Charters of Cumbwell Priory', *Archaeologia Cantiana*, 5 (1863), 194–222 · C. R. Cheney and B. E. A. Jones, eds., *Canterbury, 1162–1190*, English Episcopal Acta, 2 (1986) · C. R. Cheney and E. John, eds., *Canterbury, 1193–1205*, English Episcopal Acta, 3 (1986) · W. Stubbs, ed., *Chronicles and memorials of the reign of Richard I*, 2: *Epistolae Cantuarienses*, Rolls Series, 38 (1865) · Adam of Eynsham, *Magna vita sancti Hugonis / The life of Saint Hugh of Lincoln*, ed. D. L. Douie and D. H. Farmer, 2 vols., OMT (1961–2) · D. Crook, *Records of the general eyre*, Public Record Office Handbooks, 20 (1982) · J. E. A. Jolliffe, *Angevin kingship*, 2nd edn (1963) · T. D. Hardy, ed., *Rotuli de oblatis et finibus*, RC (1835), 339 · T. D. Hardy, ed., *Rotuli litterarum clausarum*, RC, 1 (1833), 141

Thornhill [Thornhull], **Sir James** (1675/6–1734), decorative painter, came from a family which had owned the lordship of the manor of Thornhill, Dorset, from at least 1227. His father, Walter Thornhull (*b.* 1637), was the eighth son and the youngest of the sixteen children of George Thornhull of Thornhill and Woolland; the latter, acquired in 1540, became the principal family home. His mother was Mary, the daughter of Colonel William *Sydenham, governor of Weymouth, and later of the Isle of Wight during the protectorate.

Early years James Thornhill was born in 1675 or 1676. The register of baptisms at St Mary's, Melcombe Regis, records his baptism there on 7 September 1675, but the entry is a later pencil addition, squeezed between the lines, and some doubt is cast on the reliability of the date by the

Sir James Thornhill (1675/6–1734), attrib. Dietrich Ernst
Andreae, c.1724–6

inscription 'J. Thornhill Etat.57/ on this July ye 25th', on
Jonathan Richardson's portrait sketch of Thornhill (BM).
Little is known of Thornhill's childhood. His father
appears to have been largely an absentee, first operating
as a grocer or merchant in Dorchester, contracting a debt
to a Sydenham sister-in-law and evading it by absconding
to New England and later to Ireland. The young Thornhill
may have joined the London household of his great-uncle
Dr Thomas *Sydenham (d. 1689), the eminent physician;
in his will, made the previous year, Dr Sydenham left
Thornhill £30 for apprenticeship to some trade or profession. On 9 May 1689 Thornhill was apprenticed for seven
years to a relative, Thomas Highmore, later sergeant-
painter to William III.

The earliest evidence of Thornhill's practice as a decorative artist is the date 1699 inscribed on the frontispiece to
a sketchbook (BM) used intermittently until 1718. On 1
March 1703 he was made free of the Painter–Stainers'
Company. Thornhill possibly provided the design (sketch-
book, fol. 15v, BM) for the ceiling of the great cabin of the
Royal Sovereign (now in the admiral superintendent's
house, Chatham Dockyard, Kent), executed by another
artist and completed in 1701. Thornhill's style was greatly
influenced by the work of Antonio Verrio and, more particularly, Louis Laguerre. He may have been one of
Verrio's assistants in the decoration of the queen's
drawing-room at Hampton Court Palace (c.1702–4):
sketches for the feigned tapestries (sketchbook, fols. 113v
and 114r, BM) appear to be alternative designs for, not
after, those executed, and passages of the ceiling itself
indicate Thornhill's hand, although Giovanni Battista
Catenaro and Nicholas Scheffers are the only assistants
recorded by Vertue.

In 1705 Thornhill designed the scenery for Thomas
Clayton's opera Arsinoe, Queen of Cyprus (designs V&A), performed at the Theatre Royal, Drury Lane. In the same year
he completed his first large-scale independent commission, from Thomas Foley MP, for the decoration of the
hall, staircase, and overmantels at Stoke Edith, Herefordshire; only the overmantels survived destruction by fire in
1927 (now at Marble Hill, Twickenham, Surrey, English
Heritage). More important was his activity at Chatsworth;
his principal work there, in the Sabine Room (c.1706), is
his most substantial early surviving œuvre. Executed in
what Croft-Murray describes as his distinctive 'happy palette' of clear blues, pinks, crimsons, and warm browns
(Croft-Murray, 1.170), the scheme shows Thornhill at ease
with classical sources. A drawing of the Peak Castle and
the Devil's Arse at Castleton, Derbyshire (Bodl. Oxf),
signed and dated 22 July 1707, suggests that Thornhill was
then still working at Chatsworth.

Major commissions   In 1707, though still relatively
unknown, Thornhill won his greatest secular commission
for decorating the painted hall at the Royal Naval Hospital, Greenwich, a work which was to occupy him
throughout the greater part of his career and to earn him
£6685. Arguably the most impressive baroque interior in
England, it is Thornhill's masterpiece and established
him as the leading native decorative history painter in a
field hitherto dominated by foreigners. Thornhill concentrated on the lower hall first, painted between 1708 and
1712 or 1714. Details of the commission, progress of work,
and payments to Thornhill are recorded in the Admiralty
papers; on 17 July 1707 the governors of the hospital
ordered that:

as soon as the Scaffolding in the Hall is ready Mr James
Thornhill do proceed upon the painting thereof, by primeing
it himself, or servants, and that he make such Alterations in
his designe, in inserting what more he can relating to
maritime affairs.   (PRO, ADM 67–8)

It is thus clear that Thornhill had submitted designs prior
to this date. The evolution of the scheme can be traced
through numerous sketches and oil modellos. Through an
elaborate iconographical programme the lower hall glorifies the constitutional monarchy of William III and Queen
Mary, sustained through maritime strength and mercantile prosperity, notably demonstrated by a great ship's
stern at the ceiling's west end. Thornhill's 'great and
Noble design, an Honour to our Nation' (Bold, 148) was
publicly applauded by Richard Steele in The Lover (1715).

In 1715 the scaffolding was removed from the lower hall
to the upper. By 1717 Thornhill had received only £635
and, before commencing work on the upper hall, submitted a memorandum to the governors requesting further
payment; but, as was to become a recurring theme
throughout his career, his bill was queried. Nicholas
Hawksmoor and John James, clerks of works at Greenwich, were requested to compare payments made to other
artists for similar schemes, and leading artists were
invited to inspect Thornhill's work. After favourable
reports, the governors awarded Thornhill £3 per yard for

the ceiling and £1 per yard for the walls, less than Thornhill had requested but, as they argued, 'this was the first great work he ever undertook in England, and served as an introduction to bring him into reputation' (Croft-Murray, 1.75–6).

In 1710 Thornhill was employed by the lawyer Thomas Vernon at Hanbury Hall, Worcestershire, and at nearby Hewell Grange, near Bromsgrove, owned by the earl of Plymouth (oil sketch, Tate collection); and, as a foray into portraiture which he continued intermittently throughout his career, he painted *Sir Isaac Newton* and *Ezechiel Spanheim* (Trinity College, Cambridge). The following year, 1711, he completed work in the chapel royal and royal closet, Hampton Court.

On 21 May 1711 Thornhill set out on a trip to the Low Countries with the mason-contractor Edward Strong (1676–1741) and Joseph Roberts (1679–1742), sergeant plumber, known to him through their employment by the office of works at Greenwich and St Paul's (Edward Strong, or his father of the same name, provided Thornhill's scaffolding at Greenwich). Thornhill's sketchbook journal (V&A NAL, L.1380–11.IV.1961) documents their progress through East Anglia to Harwich, the voyage to Hellevoetsluis, and thence to Delft, Rijswijk, The Hague, Honselaarsdijk, and other towns to Tournai. Abroad for the first time and at leisure, Thornhill sketched and noted things of personal interest such as the decoration in Huis ter Nieuburch, Rijswijk; the dramatic mix of architecture, ceremonial, and music in the churches of Ghent; and details of the interior of Tournai Cathedral. After he left Tournai on 22 June 1711, Thornhill's text stops. On 15 August, however, he painted a set of twelve Delft plates with the signs of the zodiac (BM).

By 1713 Thornhill had probably completed the staircase of Easton Neston, Northamptonshire, for Thomas Fermor, first earl of Pomfret. In 1714 he won the commission to paint the bedchamber of the prince of Wales (later George II) at Hampton Court Palace, through the influence of the prominent whig Charles Montagu, Lord Halifax, first lord of the Treasury, who overruled Lord Chamberlain Shrewsbury's preference for Sebastiano Ricci, telling Shrewsbury (according to Vertue) that 'if Richi was imploy'd he would not pay him for it' (Vertue, *Note books*, 1.45). Halifax added that:

> Mr Thornhill our Country man has strove against all oppositions & difficultys & now had got near the very Top of the Mountain & his grace would thro' him down & crush all his endeavours. wich would prevent & discourage all countrymen everafter to attempt the like again. (ibid.)

Thornhill himself keenly advocated the need to foster home-grown talent. In October 1711 he had been elected one of the twelve directors of the new Great Queen Street Academy; with Sir Godfrey Kneller as its governor, it offered through its life class a degree of informal instruction as well as professional alliance. Several of its members, for example, Richard Steele and Jonathan Richardson, as well as members of the Rose and Crown Club to which Thornhill also belonged, publicly argued for the establishment of a Royal Academy to train a British school

of painters able to compete with the best in Europe. In 1714 Thornhill sought official sponsorship through Lord Halifax, submitting to him architectural plans 'for to Build an Accademy for Painting at the upper end of the Meuse [Mews]', the cost estimated at £3139 (Vertue, *Note books*, 3.74).

The dome of St Paul's Cathedral A competition to decorate the dome of Sir Christopher Wren's St Paul's Cathedral had been announced in March 1709. The most coveted contemporary commission, it attracted Thornhill, Antonio Pellegrini, Pierre Berchet, Louis Chéron, and Catenaro. The subject matter, determined by the commissioners of the fabric, was to be 'confined to the Scripturall History taken from the Acts of the Apostles' (St Paul's Cathedral, 'Minute Book of H. M. Commission for rebuilding St Paul's Cathedral', *Wren Society*, 16, 1939). At what stage Thornhill elected to concentrate on the life of St Paul, dividing the dome into eight scenes, is not clear. By 1710 the field was narrowed to two candidates, Thornhill and Pellegrini, each being required to execute their proposed designs on a model of the cupola. Political contention between successive building committees delayed decision—'mighty contests and parties were made about it' (Vertue, *Note books*, 2.125)—but recent examination of events by Carol Gibson-Wood (1993) exonerates Thornhill himself from old charges of intrigue. On 28 June 1715 Thornhill was awarded the commission by a whig, low-church dominated committee inspired by a moral Anglican nationalism. Archbishop Tenison's supposed pronouncement 'I am no judge of painting, but on two articles I think I may insist: first that the painter employed be a Protestant; and secondly that he be an Englishman' has no known contemporary source, but echoes the patriotic sentiment published in June 1715 in the *Weekly Packet*, that the committee's decision will 'put to silence all the loud applauses hitherto given to foreign artists' (Meyer, 71 n. 212).

The commissioners of the fabric stipulated in 1715 that the decoration was to be 'in Basso-Relievo' (grisaille). On 1 May 1716 Thornhill hosted an entertainment in the cupola to celebrate the start of painting, and on 29 August Dudley Ryder, a student at the Middle Temple on a visit to St Paul's, noted that the architectural painting was complete but the 'history part' not yet begun. Thornhill worked with at least two or three assistants, one of whom, Robert *Browne, reputedly saved his master from falling to his death from the scaffolding platform—although some sources identify this individual as Bentley French, Thornhill's 'attentive footman' (Croft-Murray, 2.322). The committee's minute books record progress and regular payments to Thornhill. In 1718 he persuaded the committee to have the lantern painted, and in 1719 he was asked to paint the Whispering Gallery with further incidents in the life of St Paul (no longer extant). In May 1720 he presented to George I a set of engravings of his St Paul's cycle, executed by professional engravers chosen by himself, such as Charles Simmoneau, Bernard Baron, and Gerard Vandergucht. By September 1721, when his outstanding bill was paid, Thornhill had received over £6500. A large number of pencil, ink, and oil sketches survive which trace the evolution of the scheme from inception to completion, and which reveal Thornhill's considerable skill as a baroque draughtsman. The painted hall at Greenwich and the decoration of the dome of St Paul's combined to establish Thornhill's contemporary standing beyond doubt.

Further commissions and honours While engaged on the St Paul's project, Thornhill completed various decorative commissions in Oxford. At the east end of the chapel of All Souls College he completed (by Easter 1716) a painting of the apotheosis of Archbishop Chichele, founder of the college, in a full-blooded baroque style appropriate to high-church Oxford, and in direct contrast to the style required for St Paul's. For Queen's College, he painted the ascension on the chapel's chancel ceiling, and produced designs of Queen Anne as Britannia to be executed in sculptural relief on the pediment of front quad; he also designed lead figures (positioned in 1717) for the roof of Hawksmoor's Clarendon Building. In June 1716 Thornhill was at work at Blenheim Palace, Oxfordshire, painting the hall. In 1714 he had estimated the cost of decorating the hall, saloon, and gallery, with scenes glorifying the military triumphs of John Churchill, first duke of Marlborough, at £1800; but, in the first major setback of his career, his spiralling costs so alarmed the duchess that he was dismissed, having completed only the hall. Laguerre painted the saloon for half Thornhill's estimate.

On Kneller's resignation as governor of the Great Queen Street Academy, Thornhill accepted the governorship, in a letter of 29 October 1716. In February 1717 he set out on a three months' trip to Paris and its environs, sketching and making notes on buildings at Fontainebleau, Marly, and Versailles, as well as buildings and art collections in Paris, in a pocket book (V&A NAL, L.1455-18.IV.1961). In Paris he purchased Annibale Carracci's *Virgin and Child Surrounded by Angels* (Christ Church, Oxford) and, more famously, Poussin's *Tancred and Erminia* (Barber Institute of Fine Arts, Birmingham). The Poussin was particularly acclaimed on his return. Thornhill's friend and associate Jonathan Richardson devoted extensive analysis to it in *Two Discourses* (1719). A conversation piece attributed to Gawen Hamilton depicts *Sir James Thornhill Showing his Poussin to his Friends* (Beaverbrook Art Gallery, Fredericton, New Brunswick).

In June 1718 Thornhill was officially recognized as the foremost decorative painter in England by his appointment as history painter-in-ordinary to the king. In October, at his house on the north side of the Piazza, Covent Garden, where he had lived since at least 1716, he hosted the annual dinner of the Virtuosi of St Luke, the oldest and most prestigious art club, to which he had been admitted on 18 December 1716 (his design for the invitation card is in the Tate collection). In many ways the period 1718–21 was the apex of Thornhill's career. Other court appointments followed in quick succession. In March 1720 he became the king's sergeant-painter, in place of his old master, Highmore, and on 2 May he was knighted, the first British-born artist to be so honoured. Vertue claims that these positions were gained through the patronage of

Lord Sunderland, first lord of the Treasury, as a favour to John Huggins, a solicitor and warden of the Fleet prison, and an intimate of Thornhill's, to whom Sunderland was indebted. On 19 October Thornhill was appointed master of the Painter–Stainers' Company. His mounting fortune and the sale of £2000 worth of South Sea stock in 1720 enabled him that year to purchase the old family manor of Thornhill in Dorset, sold by Robert Thornhull in 1686. Thornhill later transformed it into a handsome summer residence, the drawing-room ceiling decorated by himself 'with his head in the centre' (Hutchins, 3.675). The desire to possess a country estate no doubt followed his knighthood, but from at least 1718 Thornhill had been spending time in his native county, carrying out three commissions there: from General Thomas Erle in 1718 for the staircase of Charborough Park, interestingly signing it 'Thornhull', the local version of his name which he had abandoned on moving to London; he was employed by Henry Seymour Portman, a patron of his work at All Souls, Oxford, for Sherborne House (*c*.1718–20), and by George Bubb Dodington, first Lord Melcombe, his neighbour in Covent Garden, at Eastbury House.

In 1721 Thornhill was granted the freedom of the city of Weymouth, Dorset, and presented an altarpiece of *The Last Supper* to the parish church of St Mary's, Melcombe Regis (perhaps his own place of baptism, and certainly that of his two elder brothers). In 1721, sponsored by Bubb Dodington, Sir James Thornhill was elected MP for the constituency of Weymouth and Melcombe Regis, a seat he retained until his death.

Other projects continued to engage him. In December 1717 Thornhill submitted fresh designs for the upper hall, Greenwich, and began work on them in 1718, completing the ceiling by 1722. At some point between 1719 and 1724 he painted the saloon at Cannons, Middlesex, a palatial house built for John Brydges, first duke of Chandos, where many decorative painters were employed. He designed scenery for the temporary theatre in the great hall, Hampton Court (1718); and he designed book illustrations, for the Oxford Bible (1717) and for Jacob Tonson's editions of Milton (1720) and Addison (1721). In 1720–21, in the role of architect to which he aspired, he submitted designs for the church of St Martin-in-the-Fields (RIBA), and in 1721 he designed, for stained glass, the figures of Christ and eleven apostles for the great rose window, Westminster Abbey. By March 1721 Thornhill had been commissioned by the patriotic tory patron Edward Harley, second earl of Oxford, to paint the chapel at Wimpole Hall, Cambridgeshire. On 16 March Charles Bridgeman, James Gibbs (architect of the chapel), John Wootton, and Thornhill, a coterie of native talent, travelled to Wimpole together, the coach journey being the subject of a humorous ballad by Thornhill, 'A Hue and Cry', composed on 18 March. He refers to himself as 'Monte Spinosa' (*Wren Society*, 17, 1940, 12–13). The colourful *Adoration of the Magi* at the east end of the chapel is evidence of Thornhill's embracement of new stylistic tastes, being a successful blend of traditional baroque movement with classical restraint and Raphaelesque gesture.

In March 1722 Thornhill lost the commission to decorate the king's new apartments at Kensington Palace, a project which should have been his as the king's history painter, but which was given to the cheaper William Kent (Thornhill had asked £800 for one room; Kent underbid him at £300). It was a 'mighty mortification' that marked him for the rest of his life. Thornhill's personal influence diminished after 1718, when whig dominance of the board of works removed Wren and Hawksmoor, with whose buildings he had been closely associated. His own bid in 1719 for the surveyorship of the king's works antagonized many; and he had increasingly to contend with the third earl of Burlington's patronage and active promotion of William Kent. In 1730, still bitter, he described himself as 'disgraced and supplanted in his Royall Masters favour', attributing the decline in his career to 'the overbearing power of the late Vice Chamberlain Coke & the present Earle of Burlington' (Paulson, 1991, 1.85).

In 1723 Thornhill was elected a fellow of the Royal Society, and in 1724 he opened a free drawing academy in a room at the back of his house in Covent Garden. In the same year he 'took a draught' (ink sketch, Museum of London) of the convicted criminal Jack Sheppard in Newgate prison, as reported in the *Daily Journal* (10 November 1718). He became master of the freemasons' Greenwich lodge in 1725 and senior grand warden of London's grand lodge in 1728. In 1725-8 Thornhill executed what appears to have been his last great commission, Moor Park, Hertfordshire, for the City financier Benjamin Styles. Thornhill acted both as architect and decorative painter, but Styles challenged his bill and brought two lawsuits against him, in 1728 and 1730. The courts found in Thornhill's favour. Vertue surmises that the difficulty arose, once again, through 'Mr Kents friends & interest' who 'no doubt endeavourd to foment this difference & slurr the reputation of Sr James' (Vertue, *Note books*, 3.35). In 1730–32, 'intended as a mortification' to Thornhill (ibid., 3.63), Styles had Thornhill's paintings replaced by the Italian Jacopo Amigoni (in an important adaptation to changing tastes, Thornhill's paintings had been on canvas framed by high-relief plasterwork. The latter, also designed by Thornhill, was retained). Meanwhile, in 1726 Thornhill had completed work at Greenwich. The walls of the upper hall, which celebrated the protestant succession and the new Hanoverian dynasty, had been carried out largely by an assistant, Dietrich Ernst André, a 'Polander' recently arrived from Brunswick (Croft-Murray, 1.263). It was completed in 1725, and was followed by the vestibule in 1726. The painted hall had been a paying tourist attraction since 1720; to aid visitors in an understanding of the complicated iconography, 1000 copies of Thornhill's *An Explanation of the Painting in the Royal-Hospital, Greenwich* were printed in 1726-7, in English and French.

In 1729 Thornhill was granted a royal warrant to make copies of Raphael's *Acts of the Apostles* cartoons, then at Hampton Court Palace. The cartoons were revered as ideal exemplars of artistic excellence, central to current aesthetic and religious discourse; Thornhill hoped to make them the focus of academic instruction. He set out to surpass previous artists' attempts at copying them (for example, the engraved sets by Simon Gribelin, 1707, and Nicolas Dorigny, 1720). He made three sets of copies, one full-size, later displayed in the Royal Academy's lecture theatre, Somerset House (RA); one quarter-size (Columbia University, New York), and one small set (one-sixteenth), incorporating what had been lost at the hands of restorers, thus presenting what he believed to be the true Raphael. He also made separate studies of heads, hands, and feet, intended to be engraved as a manual for students. An album of more than 200 such tracings, made directly from the originals, survives (St Paul's Cathedral), as well as an album of more than 160 smaller-scale drawings (V&A), several of which were published in John Boydell's *School of Raphael* (1759).

Later years, death, and reputation After completing his copies in 1731, Thornhill seems to have lived much in retirement. In 1732 he was appointed a commissioner for the rebuilding of Blandford Forum, Dorset, and resigned his office of sergeant-painter in favour of his son John. In April 1734, according to Vertue, a 'violent Illness' took away Thornhill's voice. Slightly recovered, on 29 April he set out for Dorset, 'were being arrivd. but fatigued with his journey he did not survive many dayes' (Vertue, *Note books*, 3.70). Thornhill died, intestate, on 4 May 1734. The following February his important collection of pictures was sold (Cock's sale catalogue, 24–5 February 1734, V&A), followed on 26–8 February by his 'Prints, Drawings, Models, Plasters etc.' (sale catalogue, copy BM). His wife, Judith, whose maiden name, date of birth, and date of marriage are unknown, died on 12 November 1757, two months after their son John.

Thornhill's obituarist in the *Gentleman's Magazine* proclaimed him 'the greatest History painter this Kingdom ever produced' (GM, 1st ser., 4, 1734, 274). In his day he was an eminent public figure who positioned himself as the figurehead of the emerging British school of painting. Today, however, his importance in the history of British art curiously neglected, he is known chiefly as the father-in-law of William *Hogarth, who eloped with his daughter Jane in 1729. They are said to have remained estranged from Thornhill until about 1731, by which time they had joined Thornhill's household in Covent Garden. Thornhill was the chief influence on Hogarth's life: in his early years, Hogarth recalled, it was 'the Painting of St Paul's and greenwich hospital which were ... running in my head' (Paulson, 1991, 1.95). His deep patriotism, championship of British artists, antipathy towards Burlington and all things Italian, and aspirations towards grand-manner history painting were inspired in him by his father-in-law. Hogarth's defence of Thornhill in the *St James' Evening Post* (7-9 June 1737), signed 'Britophil', is a measure of his loyalty and respect.

Thornhill's earliest biographer, A. J. Dezallier, admitted weaknesses in the artist's draughtsmanship, the result of a lack of sound training. To contemporaries such as Vertue, however, who considered him 'the most Excellent Native history painter' (Vertue, *Note books*, 3.38), neither

Thornhill's skill nor his prominent position in the artistic community was ever in question. Thornhill's arrogant self-confidence was noticed by the duchess of Marlborough, who 'never saw any great man more imposing than hee is in all that concerns his trade' (Marlborough to James Craggs, BL, Stowe MS 751, fol. 205). By the early nineteenth century, however, Thornhill's reputation had already suffered a decline: in 1813, on a visit to the painted hall, Greenwich, Joseph Farington and a group of connoisseurs, including Benjamin West, PRA, greatly admired the decoration of the hall but attributed the work to Thornhill's assistant, André. West made the pertinent observation, however, that the work had undergone 'ill advised' restoration, which had 'blackened the surface & very much injured the purity of the Colour' (Farington, Diary, 20 Aug 1813, 12.4413). Twentieth-century critical assessments of Thornhill's ability usually commend his talent as a draughtsman but are less complimentary about his ability on a large scale, comparing him unfavourably with the great Venetian decorators then active in England. It should be borne in mind, however, that the painted surface of the majority of his surviving schemes is in fact the handiwork of a succession of restorers, not Thornhill himself. Croft-Murray (1962) did much to re-establish Thornhill's reputation, although he perceived him as working in an idiom already established by Verrio and Laguerre. His death, nevertheless, closed the epoch of grand baroque decorative painting in Britain. It is only in recent years that Thornhill's importance in other areas, such as architecture, collecting, connoisseurship, and the formulation of art theory, has been and continues to be explored. Though he holds a central place in the growing consciousness of a British school of painting, Thornhill remains the least studied of the great names in British art history.   TABITHA BARBER

Sources E. Croft-Murray, Decorative painting in England, 1537–1837, 2 vols. (1962–70), vol. 1, pp. 69–78, 265–74; vol. 2, pp. 286, 322–4 • J. Simon, English baroque sketches: the painted interior in the age of Thornhill (1974) [exhibition catalogue, Marble Hill House, Twickenham, 1974] • R. Paulson, Hogarth: his life and times, 2 vols. (1971), vol. 1, pp. 85–109 • R. Paulson, Hogarth, 2 vols. (1991) • Vertue, Note books • J. Brocklebank, 'The childhood of Sir James Thornhill', Somerset Notes & Queries, 30 (March 1975), 73–82 • J. Brocklebank, Sir James Thornhill of Dorset, 1675–1734: tercentenary exhibition [exhibition catalogue, Dorset County Museum, Dorchester, 1975] • Sir James Thornhill's sketch-book travel journal of 1711: a visit to East Anglia and the Low Countries, ed. K. Fremantle, 2 vols. (Utrecht, 1975) • A. Meyer, Apostles in England: Sir James Thornhill & the legacy of Raphael's tapestry cartoons (1996) [exhibition catalogue, Miriam and Ira D. Wallach Art Gallery, Columbia University, New York, 1996] • C. Gibson-Wood, 'The political background to Thornhill's paintings in St Paul's Cathedral', Journal of the Warburg and Courtauld Institutes, 56 (1993), 229–37 • C. Gibson-Wood, Jonathan Richardson: art theorist of the English enlightenment (2000) • A. J. Dezallier d'Argenville, Abrégé de la vie des plus fameux peintres (Paris, 1745), vol. 2, pp. 227–30 • J. Hutchins, The history & antiquities of the county of Dorset, 1st edn (1774), vol. 1, p. 410; 2nd edn (1796–1815), vol. 2, pp. 93–5; 3rd edn (1861–73) • E. de Noailles Mayhew, Sketches by Thornhill in the Victoria and Albert Museum (1967) • J. L. Howgego, An exhibition of paintings and drawings by Sir James Thornhill (1958) [exhibition catalogue, Guildhall Art Gallery, 1958] • I. Bignamini, 'George Vertue, art historian, and art institutions in London, 1689–1768', Walpole Society, 54

(1988), 1–148 • L. Stainton and C. White, Drawing in England from Hilliard to Hogarth (1987) [exhibition catalogue, British Museum, 1987, 232–42] • W. Osmun, 'A study of the work of Sir James Thornhill', PhD diss., U. Lond., 1950 • W. T. Whitley, Artists and their friends in England, 1700–1799, 2 vols. (1928); repr. (1968) • H. M. Colvin and others, eds., The history of the king's works, 5 (1976), 57ff • Colvin, Archs. • 'Sir James Thornhill's Collection', Burlington Magazine, 82 (June 1943), 133–6 • I. Williams, 'Sir James Thornhill's petition', Bookman, 86 (April 1934) • J. Bold, Greenwich: an architectural history of the Royal Hospital for Seamen and the Queen's House (2000), 145 • B. Allen, 'Thornhill at Wimpole', Apollo, 122 (1985), 204–11 • T. P. Hudson, 'Moor Park, Leoni and Sir James Thornhill', Burlington Magazine, 113 (1971), 657–60 • K. Garas, 'Two unknown works by Sir James Thornhill', Burlington Magazine, 129 (1987), 722–3 • J. Cray, 'Paintings by Thornhill at Chinnor', Burlington Magazine, 132 (1990), 789–93 • The diary of Dudley Ryder, 1715–1716, ed. W. Matthews (1939), 306–8 • C. H. Collins Baker, 'Sir James Thornhill as Bible illustrator', Huntington Library Quarterly, 10 (1946–7), 323–7 • J. Burgess, The lives of the most eminent modern painters, who have lived since, or were omitted by, Mons. De Piles (1754) [suppl. to R. de Piles, The art of painting, 3rd edn (1754), 136–9]

Archives BL, diary, Add. MS 34788 • NRA, typographical MSS • S. Antiquaries, Lond., sketchbook • V&A NAL, diary and notebook
Likenesses J. Thornhill, self-portrait, c.1707, NPG • J. Highmore, etching, 1723, NPG • attrib. D. E. Andreae, oils, c.1724–1726, NPG [see illus.] • J. Richardson, oils, c.1730–1734, NPG • J. Faber junior, mezzotint, 1732 (after J. Highmore), BM, NPG • J. Richardson, pencil drawing, 1733, BM • attrib. W. Hogarth, oils, Uffizi Gallery, Florence • S. Ireland, etching (after W. Hogarth), BM, NPG • J. Thornhill, self-portrait, mural, Painted Hall, Greenwich

Thornhill, William (1702?–1755?), surgeon, was a member of one of the younger branches of the Dorset family of Thornhull of Woolland, and a nephew of the artist Sir James Thornhill, whose mother was a niece of Thomas Sydenham's. Thornhill was educated in Bristol under John Rosewell, a noted barber–surgeon of the city. He married, in 1730, Catherine (d. 1782), daughter of Richard Thompson, a wine merchant of York; they had a daughter, Anne (d. 1800), who married, in 1749, Nathaniel Wraxall (1725–1781) of Mayse Hill, near Bristol. Their son, Sir Nathaniel William Wraxall, wrote the Historical Memoirs of my Own Time (1815). Thornhill was elected on 20 May 1737 at the surgeons' hall in the market place to be the first surgeon to the Bristol Infirmary, founded in 1735.

Thornhill's attendance at the infirmary was so remiss that he more than once fell under the censure of the house visitors, and in 1754 he was called upon to resign his office. He refused to do so, and it was not until June 1755 that he retired. His services were, however, recognized by a unanimous vote of the committee. He left Bristol and practised for a short time at Oxford, but without much success, and he finally retired to Yorkshire, where he died.

Thornhill was one of the earliest English surgeons to adopt and improve the operation of suprapubic lithotomy. The records of his work, published by his colleague John Middleton, prove that his experience in the operation and his success were greater than any contemporary English surgeon could show. He performed his first suprapubic operation on a boy privately on 3 February 1723. In 1727, when his cases were recorded by Middleton, he had performed like operations thirteen times. He did not confine his attention to this part of his profession, for he was also celebrated as a man-midwife. He was a handsome man, of polished manners, and habitually wore an entire suit of black velvet with an elegant steel handled rapier. D'A. POWER, *rev.* MICHAEL BEVAN

Sources J. Hutchins, *The history and antiquities of the county of Dorset*, 2 (1774) · J. Foster, ed., *Pedigrees of the county families of Yorkshire*, 3 vols. (1874) · private information (1898) · P. J. Wallis and R. V. Wallis, *Eighteenth century medics*, 2nd edn (1988) · J. Middleton, *Essay on the operation of lithotomy* (1727)

Thornton, Abraham (*c.*1793–1860), bricklayer and accused murderer, was the son of a builder of Castle Bromwich. He was accused of rape and murder after attending a dance where he became intimate with a gardener's daughter named Mary Ashford. They left the dance together and her body was found the next morning in a deep pool of water near a local footpath. Thornton was tried at the Warwick assizes on 8 August 1817. Since the marks on Mary's body were not necessarily inconsistent with Thornton's claim that she had consented to sexual intercourse, and since the times on the morning in question when Thornton was seen walking home to Bromwich suggested he could not have been with her when she met her death, the jury found him not guilty.

The case aroused much interest and reminded people of the similar murder of a local woman a year earlier. Many were convinced of Thornton's guilt and he was assailed in local and London newspapers. A group collecting around the Birmingham solicitor William Bedford invoked the old legal process of 'appeal of murder', by which a person acquitted of murder could be tried again for the same offence. This process was generally regarded as obsolete, though there had been several instances in the eighteenth century. More controversy arose when Thornton came before the court of the king's bench in November 1817 and demanded ordeal by battle, which was open to the subject of an appeal of murder but had not been claimed since Charles I's reign. After several hearings between November 1817 and April 1818 the court decided that the appellee did have this right. The appeal of murder was dropped. Appeals of murder were abolished in 1819 partly because of this case.

Thornton was corpulent, about 5 feet 7 inches tall, of 'forbidding' and 'very lusty' appearance, with powerful limbs, a short, thick neck, and a swollen, shining face. He had a local reputation as a sportsman and a strong man, and also as a womanizer. In all his court appearances he was noted for his calmness and composure. Opinion remained hostile towards Thornton; he had to be protected from the London crowds during the hearings there, and back in Bromwich he was hated. Unable to live a normal life, he emigrated to the USA in September 1818. He prospered, married, and died in Baltimore in 1860.

MICHAEL J. TURNER, *rev.*

Sources J. Hall, *Trial of Abraham Thornton* (1926) · *The Times* (11 Aug 1817) · *The Times* (25 Aug 1817) · *The Times* (7 Nov 1817) · *The Times* (18 Nov 1817) · *The Times* (24 Nov 1817) · *The Times* (28 Jan 1818) · *The Times* (30 Jan 1818) · *The Times* (7 Feb 1818) · *The Times* (9 Feb 1818) · *The Times* (17 April 1818) · *The Times* (21 April 1818) · E. A. Kendall, *An argument for construing largely the right of an appellee of murder* (1817) · L. Booker, *A moral review of the conduct and case of Mary Ashford*

(1817?) · E. Holroyd, *Observations upon the case of Abraham Thornton* (1819)

Thornton, Alfred Henry Robinson (1863–1939), painter, was born on 25 August 1863 at Delhi, India, the only child of Thomas Henry Thornton (*b.* 1832), chief secretary to the government of the Punjab from 1864 to 1876, and his wife, Alfreda, daughter of J. C. Spender of Bath and Englishcombe, Somerset. Sent home from India at the age of seven, he was educated at Harrow School and at Trinity College, Cambridge, from where he graduated in 1886.

Travel in Germany and France aroused in Thornton a lively interest in painting. It was intended that he should take up a career in the Foreign Office, and he worked there from 1888 to 1890, but at the same time he was studying at the Slade School of Fine Art in London; and in 1890 he went to Le Pouldu, in Brittany, to paint. He spent three summers at this village (where Paul Gauguin was then at work), studying each autumn and winter under Frederick Brown at the Westminster School of Art and at the Slade School. His *Diary of an Art Student of the Nineties* (1938) remains a valuable source of information on the issues and factions of the period.

In 1893 Thornton was launched as a practising artist in London and for one session he was teaching assistant to Walter Richard Sickert. He became a contributor to the *Yellow Book*, founded in 1894, and in 1895 a member of the New English Art Club. He made a wide acquaintance among prominent artists of the day, including Whistler, Charles Conder, and Philip Wilson Steer. The art critic Roger Fry gave him a great deal of technical information about the methods of the old masters. In 1900 he married Hilda Eliza, daughter of Thomas Walker of Seaton Carew, co. Durham; the couple had no children.

Thornton was primarily a landscape painter who was in some degree influenced by the French Impressionists, but he never dissolved form in light as some of them did, instead remaining true to an English tradition. He was a man of wide culture and alert intellect who, as he worked, became more and more keenly interested in the philosophical implications of painting and in the underlying motives that produce art. In 1911 he first learned of the psychological theories of Sigmund Freud and proceeded to relate them to aesthetics. With the psychologist Dr Ronald Gordon of Bath he collaborated in three articles on this subject which were published in the *Burlington Magazine*: 'The influence of certain psychological reactions in painting' (May 1920) and 'Art in relation to life' (July and August 1921). At about this time he settled in the Cotswold village of Painswick, near Stroud, Gloucestershire.

Always alive to innovation, though not himself an innovator, Thornton joined the London Group in 1924, having been a non-member exhibitor since 1920. His association with the New English Art Club continued throughout his working life, and he was honorary secretary of the club from 1928 until his death. In 1932 he acted as examiner and moderator in drawing to the training colleges' delegacy of the University of London, continuing as moderator from 1933 to 1935. He died at his home, The Poultry Court, Painswick, on 20 February 1939.

Thornton had a quiet, naturalistic style and he believed in a high degree of simplification, but he stopped short of the Post-Impressionists' formal experiments. He had a subtle appreciation of tone values, which is especially apparent in the strong monochromes that are among his best works. He was adept in the difficult art of rendering the character of trees. His work is represented in the Tate collection and the British Museum, London, Leeds City Art Gallery, and Manchester City Galleries.

H. B. GRIMSDITCH, *rev.* BEN WHITWORTH

Sources WW (1938) · B. Dolman, ed., *A dictionary of contemporary British artists, 1929*, 2nd edn (1981) · S. Houfe, *The dictionary of British book illustrators and caricaturists, 1800–1914* (1978) · D. J. Wilcox, *The London Group, 1913–1939: the artists and their works* (1995) · F. Spalding, *20th century painters and sculptors* (1990), vol. 6 of *Dictionary of British art* · J. Johnson and A. Greutzner, *The dictionary of British artists, 1880–1940* (1976), vol. 5 of *Dictionary of British art* · G. M. Waters, *Dictionary of British artists, working 1900–1950* (1975) · Venn, *Alum. Cant.* · J. H. Stogdon, ed., *The Venn school register, 1845–1925*, 2 (1925) · *CGPLA Eng. & Wales* (1939) · *The Times* (21 Feb 1939) · personal knowledge (1949) · private information (1949)
Likenesses C. Hey, pen and ink, priv. coll.
Wealth at death £3818 1s. 5d.: probate, 5 April 1939, *CGPLA Eng. & Wales*

Thornton [*née* Wandesford], **Alice** (1626–1707), autobiographer, was born on 13 February 1626 in Kirklington, North Riding of Yorkshire, and baptized there the following day. She was the fifth child and youngest daughter in the family of four sons and three daughters of Christopher *Wandesford (1592–1640) of Kirklington, lord deputy of Ireland, and his wife, Alice (1592–1659), daughter of Sir Hewett Osborne of Kiveton, Yorkshire. Christopher *Wandesford, second Viscount Castlecomer (d. 1719) [*see under* Wandesford, Christopher (1592–1640)] was her brother. Her father was the kinsman, friend, and protégé of Thomas Wentworth (later first earl of Strafford), and she spent her childhood as the pampered daughter of a prospering family: 'I enjoyed great easiness and comfort during my honoured father's life, having the fortunate opportunity … of the best education that kingdom could afford.' She was educated with Wentworth's daughters in the traditional female pursuits of French, music, dancing, embroidery, and 'other suitable housewifery', besides receiving 'pious, holy and religious instructions' from her parents (*Autobiography*, 8).

The death of Christopher Wandesford in December 1640 was 'the beginning of troubles in our family' (*Autobiography*, 26), followed as it was by the public catastrophes of the Irish rising of 1641 and the English civil war. The family escaped to Chester and then settled, much impoverished, on their mother's jointure estates in Yorkshire. On 15 December 1651 Alice married William Thornton (*b.* 1624), of East Newton, Yorkshire, son and heir of the late Robert, whose parliamentarian connections were seen as useful to her royalist family. William's health was poor, while his improvidence and family quarrels weakened their estate, but on Alice's own account the marriage was an affectionate one and she mourned him sincerely on his early death in 1668. Between 1652 and 1667 Alice gave birth to nine children, five daughters and

four sons, only three of whom survived to adulthood. Little is known of Alice's long widowhood: she lived in retirement in East Newton, noted for her charitable and religious activities, and supervised the education and marriages of her children. Her son Robert (1662–1692), an Anglican clergyman, predeceased her.

Alice Thornton's life made little public impact but her 800-odd pages of autobiographical writings, preserved by the Comber family and published, in part, in the nineteenth century, provide a fascinating account of her personality, and more generally, of the family life of a gentlewoman in later seventeenth-century England. It was perhaps the poignant contrast between her privileged youth and the straitened circumstances of her later life that stimulated Alice to write 'my own book of my life, the collections of God's dealings and mercies to me and all mine till my widowed condition' (*Autobiography*, 259). More immediately the autobiography, several times reworked, was circulated among friends and relatives to vindicate her conduct in a series of family quarrels with her husband's kin, her own niece, and especially with her younger brother Christopher, the eventual heir to the Wandesford estates.

Within a providential framework, Alice Thornton's writings reveal staunch royalist views and a distinctly Anglican Restoration piety expressed through the set forms of the Book of Common Prayer and the regular orderly celebration of the sacraments. They commemorate her father and mother, 'such a holy and sanctified a couple' (*Autobiography*, 102); and describe, in great detail, her relationships with her siblings, her husband, and her children. They are an invaluable source for women's health problems in this period, especially the 'dangerous perils' of childbirth (ibid., 145), and movingly discuss the traumas of the early deaths of children, which she met with resigned submission to the will of God.

Above all, Alice Thornton's autobiography suggests the tensions between her strong-minded, independent personality and the allotted role of a seventeenth-century woman. While overtly and inevitably she accepts women's subordinate position, there are strong undercurrents of resentment at the restrictions of marriage and at her lost prosperity. She was reluctant, given her 'more than competent fortune', to give up 'that happy and free condition' of a single life and suffered a collapse on her wedding day (*Autobiography*, 75). When her younger brother tried to challenge her inheritance from her mother:

> I told him that though he was now the heir, as being son, yet I was two years the elder by my birth, and though he had got the birthright, yet I ought to have a share of her blessing. (ibid., 120)

A sense of her own importance, which survived despite the sadnesses of her adult life and prompted her to tell her own story at such length, is summed up in her quotation of a relative's comment on her autobiography, 'it was not writ as if a weak woman might have done it, but might have become a divine' (ibid., 260).

Alice Thornton died in 1707 in East Newton and was buried on 1 February in the parish church at Stonegrave. Her will indicates a modest estate, although the bulk of her household goods had been settled earlier on her daughters Alice (b. 1654), the widow of Dr Thomas Comber, dean of Durham, and Katherine (b. 1656), wife of Robert Danby of Northallerton, gentleman.   ANN HUGHES

Sources The autobiography of Mrs Alice Thornton, ed. [C. Jackson], SurtS, 62 (1875) · parish registers, N. Yorks. CRO
Archives East Riding of Yorkshire Archives Service, Beverley, autobiography, DDHV/75/1 [copy in BL, RP 2346]
Wealth at death modest estate: Autobiography of Mrs Alice Thornton

Thornton [Meynell], **Alicia** (fl. 1804), horsewoman, is of uncertain lineage (her name is sometimes given as Alicia Meynell), the daughter possibly of a Norwich watchmaker or an Essex landowner. Her fame rests very largely on a race she rode, side-saddle over 4 miles, at Knavesmire at the 1804 York races. It was proclaimed in The Times of 14 August as 'unprecedented in the annals of the turf', and was run before what was probably the century's biggest crowd attracted by a sportswoman. Her opponent was her brother-in-law Captain T. Flint, and the match appears to have arisen after she had beaten him in an informal gallop. The stake was 500 guineas a side, but there was said also to be a large side-bet made by the wealthy landowner Colonel Thomas *Thornton, described as her husband, whose horse Vinigrillo she was riding. The Times of 28 August claimed that there was well over £2 million depending on the match.

On the race day Alicia was a striking sight in her close-fitting leopard-coloured jacket with blue sleeves and cap, and with a buff skirt enveloping her side-saddle. Although Flint had demanded that she should ride always on his left side, so inhibiting her use of the whip, she led for most of the race: 'her close-seated riding astonished the beholders, and inspired a general confidence in her success' (Sporting Magazine, August 1804, 227). After 3 miles, however, her saddle girth slipped, she could not keep up the pace, and then her horse went lame, to the disappointment of most of the crowd. Some days later, on 1 September, a letter appeared above her name in The Times, complaining of Flint's discourtesy and challenging him to a rematch. This never took place as Thornton refused to pay the 1000 guineas side-bet, maintaining that the wager was purely nominal, to heighten interest: York was then trying desperately to draw back the crowds it had lost with the recent ending of public hangings on the course on the morning of the races.

Subsequently, at the next year's meeting, in August 1805, the captain horsewhipped the colonel, who later took him to court—and won. This incident took place immediately after Alicia had ridden again, this time beating the best-known jockey of the day, Frank *Buckle, albeit with a considerable weight advantage. Again her riding amazed spectators, and stage imitations of her feats followed. Her performances also raised considerable interest in the sporting press on the problems of riding

Alicia Thornton (fl. 1804), by Mackenzie, pubd 1805

side-saddle, with one eminent breeches maker intriguingly claiming that 'by means of a simple contrivance, he could remove all objections to a lady's sitting astride' (Sporting Magazine, September 1804, 281). As for Alicia, she seems to have disappeared from public view. Although she was referred to in court and elsewhere as Mrs Thornton there are strong doubts about her true marital status. She was said to have eloped with a soldier in 1806. Colonel Thornton was reported to be a widower when he married, in July 1806, Eliza Cawston of Mundon, Essex, described, more soberly than Alicia ever was, as 'an accomplished lady of some fortune' (Egan, 133).

       DENNIS BRAILSFORD

Sources Sporting Magazine (Aug 1804) · Sporting Magazine (Nov 1805) · Sporting Magazine (March 1806) · P. Egan, Book of sports (1832) · Racing Calendar (1800–05) · J. Tyrrel, Racecourses on the flat (1989) · The Times (14 Aug 1804) · The Times (1 Sept 1804) · The Times (24 Aug 1805) · GM, 1st ser., 76 (1806), 676 · Annual Register (1805), 46–7
Likenesses Mackenzie, engraving, pubd 1805, NPG [see illus.] · print, repro. in Egan, Book of sports, 129

Thornton, Anne Jane (b. 1817), sailor and cross-dresser, was born in Gloucestershire, the daughter of a prosperous merchant. After her mother's death in 1823 her father moved to Donegal, Ireland, where he opened another highly successful shop. At age fifteen she met an American, Captain Alexander Burke, with whom she fell in love. But when Captain Burke left Donegal to return to his father's home in New York in 1832, Thornton decided

Anne Jane Thornton (b. 1817), by unknown engraver, pubd 1835

to follow him. She left Donegal with a maid-servant and a boy who helped her to find a suit of male clothes and to obtain a passage to England. There she engaged as a sailor aboard the *Rover* while the maid-servant carried a message about Anne Jane's plans back to Mr Thornton in Donegal.

Thornton, in her sailor's disguise, docked at East Port, Maine, and then walked 70 miles to the home of Captain Burke in St Andrew's, New York state, where she learned that her lover had recently married. Forced to support herself financially, she maintained her male disguise and obtained a situation as cook and steward aboard the *Adelaide* for $9 per month. The ship set sail for the Mediterranean and Anne Jane's 'swarthy complexion favoured her deception' for the next two years (*Interesting Life*, 5). While the ship was docked in Lisbon, Portugal, she engaged on the *Sarah*, but it was aboard that ship that her female identity was discovered. 'One day as she was washing in her berth, with her jacket loose in the front, one of the crew caught an accidental view of her bosom' (ibid.).

The sailor threatened that unless Anne Jane agreed to have sex with him, he would reveal her to the ship's Captain M'Intre. She refused her shipmate's advances, and he then went to the captain who, according to one account, 'turned her out to work amongst the men, by whom she upon all occasions was most grossly insulted' (*Interesting Life*, 5). The captain later described his astonishment upon learning that his young sailor was female: 'I could scarcely credit the mate when he told me of it. I can bear testimony to the extraordinary propriety of her conduct and I ask again whether I have not acted properly towards her' (*The Times*). However, her work was exemplary; until she arrived in London in February 1835, 'she did the duty of a seaman without a murmur and had infinitely a better use of her hands than her tongue' (ibid.).

Before the *Sarah* docked at London, several other crew members had already begun to have suspicions about Thornton's true identity. An interview in *The Times* with Captain M'Intre confirmed both that she had been abused by the other sailors and that she had worked hard aboard the ship. 'She performed [the duties of a seaman] to admiration. She would run up the top gallant-sail in any sort of weather and we had a severe passage. Poor girl, she had a hard time of it, she suffered greatly from the wet but she bore it all excellently and was a capital seaman', he said.

Anne Jane Thornton was interviewed by the lord mayor of London after he had read newspaper reports about her adventures and sent a city police inspector to investigate her story. The mayor scolded Anne Jane for abandoning her father while praising her courage and propriety aboard ship. He offered her financial support until she could be reunited with her father and return home to Ireland. Her story was popularized in an autobiographical chapbook and inspired the ballad 'The Female Sailor'.

JULIE WHEELWRIGHT

Sources *Weekly Dispatch* (8–15 Feb 1835) · 'A female sailor', *The Times* (11 Feb 1835), 6 · *Interesting life and wonderful adventures of that extraordinary woman Anne Jane Thornton, the female sailor, disclosing important secrets, unknown to the public, written by herself* (1835) **Likenesses** engraving, pubd 1835, NPG [*see illus.*]

Thornton, Bonnell (1725–1768), writer, was born in February 1725, probably in Maiden Lane, Westminster, but not baptized until 28 September, the son of Rebecca and John Thornton. His father was a successful apothecary who later styled himself 'Gent.' and moved to the somewhat grander Chandos Street. In 1736 Thornton was admitted to Westminster School; he became a king's scholar in 1739. Here he met Charles Churchill and William Cowper; his later friends Robert Lloyd and George Colman the elder were also at Westminster. He was elected to Christ Church, Oxford, and matriculated there on 1 June 1743. He took his BA in 1747, his MA in 1750, and the MB in 1754. His father wished him to practise as a doctor. Thornton had however already commenced a literary career while at Oxford. He produced an *Ode on Saint Caecilia's Day, Adapted to the Ancient British Musick* (1749), a parody of the odes produced each 22 November, comically designed for hurdy-gurdy, Jew's harp, saltbox, and marrow bone and cleaver. He assisted Christopher Smart on *The Midwife, or, The Old Woman's Magazine* (October 1750) and *The Student, or, Oxford and Cambridge Miscellany* (1750–51).

In 1751 Thornton was one of the early governors of St Luke's Hospital for Lunatics. In 1752 he was hired to write a paper countering Fielding's the *Covent Garden Journal*. Thornton's *Have At You All, or, The Drury-Lane Journal* ran for twelve numbers from 16 January to 9 April 1752 and consisted of a close parody of Fielding's style, though it included other targets such as Johnson's *Rambler*. On 16 November 1752 he began the *Spring-Garden Journal*, another Fielding parody, which ran for four issues. On 14 November he began contributing to John Hawkesworth's *Adventurer*, an association which lasted until 3 April 1753; he appears to have written those papers marked 'A'.

On Thursday 31 January 1754 Thornton and Colman

began *The Connoisseur*. It ran for 140 numbers to 30 September 1756, and was jointly written, though there were contributions from Cowper and Lloyd. Colman's son (not a disinterested witness) suggests that Thornton was lazy, or drunk, and occasionally left the efficient Colman to repair his omissions. Johnson thought the periodical's essays on contemporary life 'wanted matter', but Boswell defended its 'just views of the surface of life, and ... very sprightly manner' (Boswell, *Life*, 1.420) and the periodical was much reprinted. In 1755 Thornton and Colman produced the two-volume *Poems by Eminent Ladies*, a broad-minded anthology of poetry by women from the Restoration onwards, with biographical notes. About this time the Nonsense Club began to meet every Thursday to plan burlesques and practical jokes; the main members were Thornton, Colman, Lloyd and Cowper.

Thornton wrote *Idler* no. 15 (22 July 1758), a Hogarthian exploration of henpecked tradesmen. In 1760 he published *City Latin*, demolishing with assurance John Patterson's published Latin inscriptions for the new bridge at Blackfriars. He and Colman became closely associated with Garrick, whose side they took during the theatre controversies of the period. Robert Lloyd's *The Actor: a Poetical Epistle to Bonnell Thornton* (1760) includes much praise of Garrick's style. On 14 March 1761 Thornton, with Colman, Garrick, and other investors, founded the *St James's Chronicle*, a thrice-weekly literary newspaper born from the theatre war and partly designed to manipulate public opinion. Thornton was a substantial contributor and adviser. The paper was successful and prestigious, but a *Yearly Chronicle* of pieces from the paper lost money and was discontinued.

On 22 April 1762 a 'Grand exhibition of the Society of Sign-Painters' opened at Thornton's rooms in Bow Street. The project of mocking the exhibitions of the Society of Arts and its rival the Society of Artists with a collection of 'street art' appears to have been his, though Hogarth retouched some of the signs, which were extracted from various sites in town and country. The exhibition, which ran until 8 June (thus matching the 'serious' exhibitions), was much described and catalogued, especially in the *St James's Chronicle*. The joke was reviewed warmly as a sample of Thornton's humour in the *London Register* (April 1762, 345–52).

On 24 May 1763 Boswell called on Thornton and found him 'a well-bred, agreable man, lively and odd'. He ascertained that Thornton's father had left him about £15,000. Wilkes, Churchill, and Lloyd arrived and Boswell found himself 'just got into the middle of the London Geniuses' (*Boswell's London Journal*, 286). Thornton's rooms were a sort of political office during the Wilkes crisis. Thornton tried to help Wilkes through his influence in the *Public Advertiser*, the other paper with which he was closely associated, and offered to indemnify its printer, Henry Sampson Woodfall, against legal expenses. He was kept under surveillance for his association with Wilkes and Churchill, with whom he travelled in the summer of 1763. He revived his burlesque St Cecilia *Ode*, using letters, essays, and accounts of rehearsals in the newspapers to publicize

it. Wilkes was at the performance at Ranelagh House (10 June 1763), giving a political edge to the robust 'Englishness' of the ode. The music was apparently by Thomas Arne, though Charles Burney also claimed to have produced a setting. Johnson 'praised its humour and seemed much diverted with it' (Boswell, *Life*, 1.420).

On 3 February 1764 Thornton married Sylvia, the daughter of Colonel John Braithwaite, governor of Cape Coast Castle in Africa. This seems to have cut his political links.

Lloyd, arrested for debt and thrown into the Fleet, was furious that Thornton failed to bail him out (he died in gaol on 15 December 1764). Wilkes found parts of a satire on Thornton among Churchill's papers but suppressed it at Colman's request. Thornton's son Bonnell George was born on 6 January 1765 (Christopher Smart dedicated his *The Parables of our Lord and Saviour Jesus Christ* to the child in 1768); his daughter Sylvia was born in July 1766 and another son, Robert John *Thornton, was born in 1768 after his father's death.

Thornton had announced his intention to translate Plautus into English verse as early as December 1762, publishing specimens in Lloyd's *St James's Magazine*. Colman's successful completion of a similar translation of Terence in 1765 finally spurred him to publish and in 1767 two volumes, containing seven plays, were published. Colman, to whom the translation was affectionately dedicated, contributed the translation of *Mercator* while Richard Warner translated *Captivi* and supplied some of the critical matter. After Thornton's death Warner completed the project in three further volumes (1772 and 1774), using Thornton's partial translations of two further plays. The translation was highly regarded for its purity and elegance, and its ability to replicate the wit of the original.

Thornton's last publication, *The Battle of the Wigs*, a Scriblerian satire on a subject similar to that of Samuel Garth's *Dispensary*, appeared early in 1768. Colman's son records that as he lay on his deathbed (at his home in Orchard Street, Westminster) Thornton was still full of mischief (G. Colman, *Random Records*, 1830, 1.142–3). He died on 9 May 1768. The *St James's Chronicle* (7–10 May 1768) published a warm tribute to his sensibility and benevolence. He was buried in the east cloister of Westminster Abbey, under a Latin epitaph by Joseph Warton celebrating his sincerity and liveliness as a writer and as a companion.

Thornton made no formal will. On 9 February 1764 he had written two memoranda leaving all his goods to his wife. Small bequests for mourning were made to Colman, Lloyd, and Cowper, alongside bequests to his wife's family and his servants. He asked for such papers as were not business documents to be burnt. The court granted probate to the widow and the Revd Thomas Winstanley (PRO, PROB 11/940, sig. 260, 1768). A picture of Thornton in the British Museum shows him wearing his own hair, a peculiarity for which he was noted.   PAUL BAINES

Sources L. Bertelsen, *The Nonsense Club: literature and popular culture, 1749–1764* (1986) • W. C. Brown, 'A belated Augustan: Bonnell Thornton, Esq', *Philological Quarterly*, 34 (1955), 335–48 • E. R. Page, *George Colman the elder: essayist, dramatist, and theatrical manager, 1732–1794* (1935) • C. Ryskamp, *William Cowper of the Inner Temple,* *esq.: a study of his life and works to the year 1768* (1959) • A. Chalmers, ed., *The British essayists*, 25 (1823) • *The works of William Cowper*, ed. R. Southey, 15 vols. (1836–7), vol. 1 • *Boswell's London journal, 1762–1763*, ed. F. A. Pottle (1951), vol. 1 of *The Yale editions of the private papers of James Boswell*, trade edn; repr. (1982) • *The annotated letters of Christopher Smart*, ed. B. Rizzo and R. Mahoney (1991) • H. Fielding, *The Covent-Garden Journal and a plan of the universal register-office*, ed. B. A. Goldgar (1988) • Boswell, *Life* • *Old Westminsters* • Foster, *Alum. Oxon.*, *1715–1886* • will, PRO, PROB 11/940, sig. 260

Archives BL, letters, Add. MSS 27780, fols. 1, 2; 36593, fol. 70; 30868, fol. 42; 30869, fol. 34 • Yale U., letters

Likenesses Rivers, line engraving, pubd 1802, NPG • Rogers, stipple, pubd 1826, BM, NPG • engraving, BM; repro. in Bertelsen, *The Nonsense Club*

Wealth at death £450; furniture, books, china, silver, and plate; received £15,000 from father before 1763: will, PRO, PROB 11/940, sig. 260

Thornton, Sir Edward, count of Cassilhas in the Portuguese nobility (1766–1852), diplomatist, was born on 22 October 1766. He was the third son of William Thornton, a Yorkshireman settled in London as an innkeeper, and brother of Thomas *Thornton (d. 1814). Early left an orphan, he was educated at Christ's Hospital, before being admitted sizar of Pembroke College, Cambridge, on 19 June 1785; he graduated BA as third wrangler in 1789. He took the members' prize in 1791, being elected a fellow and proceeding MA in 1798.

In 1789 Thornton became tutor to the sons of James Bland Burges, under-secretary of state for foreign affairs. Burges took a great liking to him, and recommended him to George Hammond, who, when he became the first minister accredited to the United States in 1791, appointed Thornton as his secretary. In June 1793 Thornton became British vice-consul in Maryland, and in March 1796 secretary of legation at Washington; he acted as chargé d'affaires from 1800, when the then minister returned to England, until 1804. In November 1804 Thornton accepted an appointment in Egypt, which he did not take up; in May 1805 he became minister-plenipotentiary to the circle of Lower Saxony and resident with the Hanse towns, his headquarters being at Hamburg. From there he had to retire to Kiel on the approach of the French troops, and in August 1807 he returned to England.

On 10 December 1807 Thornton was sent to Sweden as envoy-extraordinary and minister-plenipotentiary, with a view to obtaining an offensive and defensive alliance against Napoleon. In November 1808 he returned to England unsuccessful, and for a time was prevented by the hostile attitude of Sweden from returning to his post. In October 1811 he again went to Sweden on a special mission in HMS *Victory*, negotiated treaties of alliance with both Sweden and Russia, and thus assisted in the first step towards the union of the northern powers against Napoleon. On 5 August 1812 he was again appointed envoy-extraordinary. In 1813 he negotiated the treaty with Denmark by which Heligoland was ceded to Great Britain. From 1813 to 1815 he accompanied the prince royal of Sweden (Bernadotte) in the field, and was present at the entrance of the allies into Paris. In 1816 he was sworn of the privy council.

On 29 July 1817 Thornton was appointed minister to Portugal, and in this capacity went to the Portuguese court in Brazil. On 12 April 1819 he was temporarily granted the rank of ambassador, and held it until March 1821, when he returned to England. In August 1823 he went to Portugal as envoy-extraordinary and minister-plenipotentiary, but was only there a year, during which he invested the king with the Order of the Garter, and sheltered him during the insurrection. For this he was created count of Cassilhas by the king of Portugal, the title to run for two further lives. He became a GCB in 1822. He retired from the service on a pension in August 1824.

Thornton married, in 1812, Wilhelmina Kohp, a Hanoverian, with whom he had one daughter and six sons, one of whom, Sir Edward *Thornton, GCB (1817–1906), followed him in the diplomatic service. After his retirement Thornton purchased Wembury House, Plymouth, where he died on 3 July 1852. He was an unusual example of a self-made diplomatist.

C. A. HARRIS, *rev.* H. C. G. MATTHEW

Sources *GM*, 2nd ser., 38 (1852), 307–8 • *Annual Register* (1852) • personal knowledge (1898)

Archives L. Cong., memoirs • PRO, corresp. and papers, FO 933 | BL, corresp. with Sir Hudson Lowe, Add. MSS 20111, 20131–20133, 20149–20150, 20191, 20233 • BL, letters to Sir John Moore, Add. MS 57543 • Harrowby Manuscript Trust, Sandon Hall, Staffordshire, letters to Lord Harrowby • NL Scot., corresp. with Robert Liston • NL Scot., corresp. with Lord Melville • PRO, corresp. with Francis Jackson, FO 353 • PRO, corresp. with H. M. Pierrepont, FO 334 • PRO NIre., corresp. with Lord Castlereagh • U. Durham L., corresp. with Earl Grey

Thornton, Edward (1799–1875). *See under* Thornton, Edward Parry (1811–1893).

Thornton, Sir Edward (1817–1906), diplomatist, born in London on 13 July 1817, was only surviving son of the diplomatist Sir Edward *Thornton (1766–1852) and his wife Wilhelmina Kohp. He was educated at King's College, London, and at Pembroke College, Cambridge, where he graduated BA among the senior optimes in 1840, proceeding MA in 1877. He was appointed attaché at Turin in April 1842, paid attaché at Mexico in February 1845, and secretary of legation there in December 1853. He witnessed the occupation of Mexico by the United States forces in 1847, and rendered some secretarial assistance in the subsequent peace negotiations. He served as secretary to Sir Charles Hotham's special mission to the River Plate (1852–3), which resulted in the conclusion of a convention for the free navigation of the Parana and Uruguay rivers.

On 15 August 1854 Thornton married Mary, daughter of John Maitland and widow of Andrew Melville. They had a son and two daughters. Also in 1854 he was appointed chargé d'affaires and consul-general at Montevideo, and in 1859 he was appointed minister-plenipotentiary at Buenos Aires. He was made CB in 1863 and was accredited to the republic of Paraguay in the same year. In July 1865 he was sent on a special mission to Brazil for the renewal of diplomatic relations (which had been broken off by the Brazilian government in 1863), and shortly afterwards he received the definitive appointment of British envoy at Rio de Janeiro.

In September 1867 Thornton was nominated British envoy at Lisbon, but within a few days he was selected for the difficult post of minister at Washington, on the death of Sir Frederick W. A. Bruce. Thornton remained at Washington for over thirteen years. During the earlier period a state of tension existed between the two countries which at times almost threatened an open rupture. The American public resented the recognition by Great Britain of the southern states as belligerents. British sympathy for the south and the depredations of the *Alabama* and other Confederate cruisers which had escaped from or been received in British ports increased the soreness of feeling. Other causes of dispute included questions of boundary between the United States and Canada, especially in the Strait of San Juan de Fuca to the south of Vancouver Island, and the exclusion of United States citizens from fishing privileges in the coastal waters of Canada, which had been secured to them by the reciprocity treaty of 1814 but had been withdrawn in consequence of the denunciation of that treaty by the United States in 1865.

Thornton brought to his work much patience and a spirit of calm, fair-minded moderation. But although some of the difficulties were settled, others persisted, and the irritation in the United States tended rather to augment than to diminish. Thornton handled the negotiations of the early 1870s competently. He was a member of the consequent joint commission which met in Washington in February 1871. The result was the conclusion of the celebrated treaty of Washington of 8 May 1871, by which the various outstanding questions and claims were referred to arbitration under specified conditions. Thornton, who was made KCB in 1870, was sworn of the privy council in August 1871. Further serious misunderstandings threatened during the progress of the arbitrations, but these were removed, and the eventual settlement did much to lead to more cordial feelings on the part of the United States towards Great Britain. The United States government fully recognized that Thornton had effectively contributed to this result, and paid a tribute to his impartiality and judgement by selecting him in 1870 to act as arbiter on the claim made on the Brazilian government for compensation on account of the loss of the American merchant vessel *Canada* on the coast of Brazil, and again from 1873 to 1876 on claims of United States and Mexican citizens. He was warmly thanked for these services, but declined offers of remuneration.

On 26 May 1881 Thornton succeeded Lord Dufferin as British ambassador at St Petersburg. Here he again found himself faced by a situation of increasing gravity as Russia advanced east of the Caspian Sea. When Merv was annexed in 1884, Thornton, in accordance with his instructions, arranged for the delimitation of the northern frontier of Afghanistan by a joint commission. Before the boundary commissioners got to work a Russian and an Afghan force found themselves face to face at Panjdeh, a debatable point on the frontier, and on 30 March 1885, despite the assurances of the Russian foreign minister, General Komarov drove the Afghan troops off with considerable loss. A period of extreme tension followed. But in the end an agreement was arrived at by the two governments, and a protocol as to the general line of the frontier was signed by Lord Salisbury (who had succeeded Lord Granville as foreign secretary) and by the Russian ambassador, de Staal, on 10 September 1885. Thornton had been appointed on 1 December 1884 to succeed Lord Dufferin at Constantinople, but he remained at St Petersburg during the whole of this episode, and his place at Constantinople was temporarily filled by Sir William White.

Thornton's arrival at Constantinople was delayed until February 1886, in order to leave in White's hands the negotiations consequent on the revolution in eastern Roumelia, which broke out in September 1885, and the subsequent war between Serbia and Bulgaria. A settlement was arrived at, but a fresh serious crisis was created by the abduction and abdication of Prince Alexander in August and September 1886. The cabinet wanted White, who had a unique knowledge of Balkan questions, to resume charge of the embassy. Thornton, despite some feeling of mortification, procured the sultan's acceptance of White's appointment, placed his own resignation in the hands of the government and returned to Britain. As no embassy was vacant to which he could be appointed, he retired on pension in January 1887, a disappointing end to a career marked by competent handling of important negotiations where a wrong step could have quickly led to a major crisis.

On his return to Britain, Thornton took a considerable part in various commercial undertakings, and was also a member of the Council of Foreign Bondholders, where his experience of South America was of much service. He declined the government's offer of a baronetcy. He had been promoted in 1883 to be GCB. He received honorary degrees of DCL and LLD respectively from the universities of Oxford and Harvard, and was made an honorary fellow of Pembroke College. He had inherited on the death of his father in 1852 the title of conde de Cassilhas, which had been conferred on his father by King John VI of Portugal for three generations. Thornton died at his house, 5 Tedworth Square, London, on 26 January 1906. His widow died on 6 January 1907. Their son, Edward Thornton (1856–1904), a young diplomatist of great promise, graduated BA from Trinity College, Cambridge, in 1878, and after serving in eastern Europe rose to be British minister in Central America where he succumbed to the climate.

T. H. Sanderson, *rev.* H. C. G. Matthew

Sources *The Times* (27 Jan 1906) · *The Times* (6 Feb 1906) · *FO List* (1906) · Gladstone, *Diaries* · A. Cook, *The Alabama claims: American politics and Anglo-American relations, 1865–1872* (1975) · *The political correspondence of Mr Gladstone and Lord Granville, 1868–1876*, ed. A. Ramm, 2 vols., CS, 3rd ser., 81–2 (1952) · *The political correspondence of Mr Gladstone and Lord Granville, 1876–1886*, ed. A. Ramm, 2 vols. (1962)

Archives Bodl. Oxf., letter-book · PRO, corresp. and papers, FO 933 | BL, corresp. with Lord Ripon, Add. MSS 43622–43625 · Bodl. Oxf., letters to earl of Clarendon · Bodl. Oxf., corresp. with Lord Kimberley · Lpool RO, corresp. with earl of Derby · priv. coll., letters to Lord Monck · PRO, corresp. with Lord Hammond, FO 391 ·

PRO, corresp. with Lord Odo Russell, FO 918 · PRO, letters to Sir William White, FO 364/1–11 · PRO NIre., corresp. with Lord Dufferin
Likenesses Ape [C. Pellegrini], caricature, watercolour study, NPG; repro. in *VF* (27 March 1886)
Wealth at death £30,822 10s. 3d.: probate, 22 Feb 1906, *CGPLA Eng. & Wales*

Thornton, Edward Parry (1811–1893), administrator in India, born on 7 October 1811 at Clapham Common, was second son of John *Thornton (1783–1861) [*see under* Thornton, Samuel] of Clapham, commissioner of Inland Revenue, and his wife, Eliza, daughter of Edward Parry. He was educated at Charterhouse School and Haileybury College, where he was ranked second in his class. In 1830 he obtained a writership in Bengal. He was appointed assistant to Robert Merttins Bird, the commissioner of revenue in the Gorakhpur division in 1831. Here his first important task was to complete the Gorakhpur district settlement. He subsequently became the chief settlement officer of Saharanpur and Muzaffarnagar, and in 1840 and 1841 published the settlement reports for each district. He enjoyed the unwavering support of Bird against those commissioners who retained reservations about the terms of the settlement regulations.

On 14 January 1840 he married Louisa Chicheliana (1816–1883), daughter of Richard Chicheley Plowden of the Bengal civil service and his wife, Sophia Fleming. They had six sons and two daughters.

Thornton returned to England on furlough early in 1842, and when he returned to India in 1845 was appointed joint magistrate and deputy collector at Meerut, and later in the same year chief magistrate and collector. In 1848 he was transferred in the same capacity to Saharanpur. In 1849, when Dalhousie was choosing the ablest officials for the task of organizing the Punjab, Thornton was appointed a commissioner and placed at Rawalpindi, in the Jhelum division. In 1852 he distinguished himself by his arrest of Nadir Khan, a discontented son of the raja of Mandla, who was endeavouring to promote a rising of the hill tribes. He received a bullet wound in the throat while executing his mission, but succeeded in preventing the rising. In May 1857, at the time of the mutiny, John, Lord Lawrence, made Rawalpindi his headquarters. Thornton was constantly with him, and he afterwards gave interesting details of Lawrence's conduct at that time, which have been preserved in Smith's *Life of Lord Lawrence* (1885). After Lawrence had taken the troops from the Punjab to assist in the operations against Delhi, Thornton was called on to exercise more independent authority. In the beginning of September 1857 the intelligence reached Lady Lawrence that the tribes in the lower Hazara country contemplated revolt. She communicated the report to Thornton, who succeeded in arresting the leaders within a few hours, and by this prompt action prevented any attempt at rebellion. On the conclusion of the mutiny Thornton was appointed judicial commissioner for the Punjab, and on 18 May 1860 he was made a companion of the Bath in recognition of his services. He retired from the Indian service in 1862,

having been on extended leave on full salary since 1860. In retirement he joined the banking firm of H. S. Thornton.

Thornton died in London at his home, 61 Warwick Square, on 10 December 1893.

Several works on India commonly attributed to Thornton are by other writers of the same name, principally **Edward Thornton** (1799–1875), who was at East India House from 1814 to 1857, and was head of the maritime department from 1847. Among his publications were gazetteers of the territories held by the East India Company and the 'countries adjacent to India on the North-West', and a six-volume *History of the British Empire in India* (1841–5). He was also responsible for entries in the eighth edition of the *Encyclopaedia Britannica* on Indian subjects, which have also been attributed to Edward Parry Thornton. This Edward Thornton died at 1 Montpelier Street, Brighton, on 24 December 1875.

E. I. CARLYLE, rev. PETER PENNER

Sources E. Stokes, *The peasant and the raj: studies in agrarian society and peasant rebellion in colonial India* (1978) · P. Penner, *The patronage bureaucracy in north India* (1986) · P. M. Thornton, *Some things we have remembered* (1912) · F. C. Danvers and others, *Memorials of old Haileybury College* (1894) · P. Penner, *Robert Needham Cust* (1987) · R. B. Smith, *Life of Lord Lawrence*, 6th edn, 2 vols. (1885) · B. Montgomery, *Monty's grandfather* (1984) · Burke, *Gen. GB* (1914)
Archives BL OIOC, corresp. and papers | Uttar Pradesh State Archives, near Lucknow, Gorakhpur and Meerut division records
Wealth at death £96,960 11s. 4d.: resworn probate, March 1894, *CGPLA Eng. & Wales* (1893)

Thornton, Gilbert of [Gilbert de Bussy, Gilbert Buscy] (*b.* in or before **1245**, *d.* **1295**), justice, was the son of Robert de Bussy, of Thornton-le-Moor in Lincolnshire, which lies about 6 miles north-east of Market Rasen. Gilbert is himself commonly called Gilbert de Bussy of Thornton in local property deeds before the late 1280s. His appointment as the attorney of the abbot of the Lincolnshire abbey of Thornton (a different Thornton, about 15 miles to the north of Thornton-le-Moor) in 1266 indicates that he cannot have been born after 1245 and may well have been born several years earlier. One of the earliest surviving law reports shows him acting as a serjeant in the eyre of 1271–2 held in his home county of Lincolnshire, and other evidence suggests that he also acted as a serjeant in the same group of eyre justices in Warwickshire in 1272. The earliest surviving report of an identifiable case heard in the common bench in which he appears as a serjeant comes from 1275, but it seems clear that he was by then already well established as one of the serjeants of the court, and reports show him appearing there on a regular basis thereafter. Late in 1280 Thornton succeeded Alan of Walkingham as the king's serjeant on the northern eyre circuit, challenging claims to franchises on behalf of the king and attempting to recover lands in the same cause. He managed to combine this with what was clearly an extensive private practice, not just in the same eyres but also (in between eyre sessions) in the common bench.

In the autumn of 1284 Thornton was dispatched by the king to Ireland to act in *quo warranto* proceedings brought in the Dublin bench against Thomas Fitzmaurice relating to the shrievalties of the counties of Waterford, Cork, and

Kerry, and in other proceedings in which the king was asserting his claim to the Decies and Desmond. He remained in Ireland until the summer of 1285. While in Dublin he also acted for the earl of Norfolk in litigation in the Dublin bench, and was well rewarded by the earl for his forensic success. The autumn of 1285 saw him resume his previous position as king's serjeant on the northern eyre circuit and also his extensive private practice, both on eyre and at Westminster. During the course of the Gloucestershire eyre of 1287 he was superseded as king's serjeant by the younger William Inge. Puzzlingly he also disappears from the reports of litigation heard in the common bench during 1288 and 1289, though he reappears acting for the king in a case heard there towards the end of Hilary term 1290. This can have been only just before his appointment as a justice of the court of king's bench, which had occurred before the end of that same term. When Ralph Hengham was disgraced, probably in late February 1290, Thornton succeeded him as chief justice of the court, and remained chief justice until his death, which took place in London on 28 August 1295.

The name of Thornton's wife is unknown and it seems likely that she had predeceased him. He may also have had an elder son who predeceased him, for his heir was his son Alan, who was in clerical orders and who in 1286 received permission from the archbishop of York to absent himself from his living of Rowley to study theology or canon law. The Gilbert of Thornton who succeeded Hengham in 1294 as rector of the Yorkshire living of Middleton in Pickeringlithe may have been another son. Thornton also had at least two daughters: Richilda, who was still alive in 1313 and claimed to be Alan's coheir, and another whose name is unknown but whose son, William Cateby, claimed to be Alan's other coheir.

Gilbert of Thornton may have been involved in the teaching of law. A *summa de casibus* which contains mainly brief notes on various points of law, and which apparently belongs to the period 1272–5, survives in two Cambridge University Library manuscripts (Dd.7.14 and Ee.6.18) and in a manuscript now in the Carson collection of the Free Library of Philadelphia (LC 14.13). It probably derives from teaching, and its use of the names Gilbert of Thornton and Gilbert Buscy by way of example may well indicate that Gilbert was the teacher. It may also have been for didactic purposes that Gilbert prepared the epitome and partial updating of *De legibus et consuetudinibus Angliae*, formerly attributed to Henry of Bratton or Bracton (d. 1268), which is known to have been owned by his son Alan (Lincoln's Inn, Hale MS 135); he also prepared a revised (and still further abbreviated) version of the same epitome, one copy of which is now in Harvard law school and a second (but mutilated) copy of which was once owned by John Selden. This revised version must have been finished while he was chief justice of the king's bench, as it incorporates references to two of the legislative enactments of 1290 (*Quia emptores* and the Statute of *Quo warranto*).

PAUL BRAND

Sources P. A. Brand, ed., *The earliest English law reports*, 2, SeldS, 112 (1996) · A. L. Spitzer, 'The legal careers of Thomas of Weyland and Gilbert of Thornton', *Journal of Legal History*, 6 (1985), 62–83 · S. E. Thorne, 'Gilbert de Thornton's summa de legibus', *University of Toronto Law Journal*, 7 (1947), 1–23
Archives Harvard U., law school, MS 77 · Lincoln's Inn, London, Harte MS 135 · Northumbd RO, Newcastle upon Tyne, Belsay MSS, property deeds

Thornton [*formerly* Ford], **Henry** (*bap.* 1750, *d.* 1818), theatre manager, was born in Clare, Suffolk, the fifth son of Daniel Ford and his wife, Elizabeth, and baptized there on 6 March 1750. He attended Clare School and later claimed to have resided as a law student at the Inner Temple. However, no formal enrolment was made. At the age of twenty-three, having changed his surname to Thornton, he was leading a band of itinerant players in the west country. John Bernard was among them, and described their life in *Retrospections of the Stage* (1830). About 1780 Thornton married Elizabeth Pritchard, the daughter of a provincial theatre manager. They had at least two sons, who died young, and three daughters. After conducting other strolling groups, in the early 1780s Thornton became prompter, a job akin to stage manager, at the Portsmouth theatre.

By 1785 Thornton was the established manager of the theatre at Newbury. Shortly afterwards he added Henley and Andover to his circuit, and in 1788 at Reading he set up his first purpose-built theatre. Early in his career he appears to have had a clear idea of the disposition of his circuit. He leased or bought a number of buildings along the London to Bath road in towns used as overnight rests by the coaching companies. A similar pattern of theatres was acquired along the Chichester road and the Portsmouth road, with the circuit terminating on the Isle of Wight at East Cowes and Ryde.

In 1791 the Windsor theatre, then no more than a shed in a muddy field at the lower end of Peascod Street, was bought from the writer, bookseller, and actor Francis Waldron. Thornton rebuilt it at the foot of the castle ramparts. With its sumptuous furnishings, the playhouse proved to be popular with George III and his family, and a description of their visits is given by Charles Knight in *A Volume of Varieties* (1844).

Throughout his management Thornton attracted eminent performers to his theatres. Various members of the Kemble family played in them. Comedians such as John Quick and Richard Suett, both favourites of George III, made regular forays. Dorothy Jordan appeared throughout his management, starring in the first season of the Reading theatre and making her last appearance for Thornton at Ryde in 1813. The circuit was one of the first to stage hippodramas in the provinces, and employed Andrew Ducrow and his horsemen for this purpose.

Thornton was a man with flair but with no eye for detail. Highly forgetful, he is said to have put on all six shirts his wife packed for his tour and removed each as it became too dirty to wear. He had little patience with learning lines, a habit which spread to members of his company. Nevertheless, when staging epics such as Sheridan's *Pizarro* he did so with tremendous verve. With such presentations he was helped by one of his sons-in-law, William Hatton, whose own interest lay in the spectacular.

Another son-in-law, Edward Barnett, after Thornton's retirement in 1817, took up the reins of management, and cared for the theatres at Newbury, Chelmsford, Guildford, Oxford, and Reading. The last of these Barnett relinquished in 1853 at the age of eighty-three. Thornton died in High Street, Chelmsford, Essex, on 21 April 1818 and was buried on 26 April in the churchyard of St Mary's (later the cathedral). His wife had predeceased him on 11 March 1816.   PAUL RANGER

Sources P. V. Ranger, *Under two managers: the everyday life of the Thornton–Barnett theatre company, 1785–1853* (2001) • P. V. Ranger, 'Henry Thornton, 1750–1818', MLitt diss., University of Bristol, 1978 • E. C. Everard, *Memoirs of an unfortunate son of Thespis* (1818) • J. Winston, *The theatric tourist* (1805) • H. Angelo, *Reminiscences*, 1 (1828) • J. Bernard, *Retrospections of the stage*, ed. W. B. Bernard, 2 vols. (1830) • P. V. Ranger, 'The Thornton circuit, 1784–1817', *Theatre Notebook*, 32 (1978), 130–36 • *Monthly Mirror*, 1–22 (1795–1806) • *Monthly Mirror*, new ser., 1–9 (1807–11) • parish register (baptism) parish of Clare, Suffolk, Suffolk RO, Bury St Edmunds, FL 501/3 • *Reading Mercury* (4 March 1805) • *Chelmsford Chronicle* (24 April 1818) • parish register (burial), Chelmsford Cathedral, bk 16, p. 67

Archives Birm. CL, Winston collection • Theatre Museum, London, provincial files

Thornton, Henry (1760–1815), banker and political economist, was born on 10 March 1760, the youngest son of John *Thornton (1720–1790), of Clapham, Surrey, merchant and philanthropist, and his wife, Lucy (1722–1785), daughter of Samuel Watson of Hull. John Thornton was one of the leading lay patrons of the early evangelical movement. Henry's brother Samuel *Thornton achieved prominence as a merchant and governor of the Russia Company. At five Henry was sent to school with a Mr Davis on Wandsworth Common, and at thirteen he was moved to a Mr Roberts at Point Pleasant, Wandsworth. In his 'Recollections', written for his children, Thornton described his schooldays as unprofitable. He learned more than the usual amount of Latin and Greek from Davis, but suspected him of having been an 'unbeliever' who rushed over prayers. Roberts offered a curriculum, taught entirely by himself, of 'latin, greek, french, rhetoric, drawing, arithmetic, reading, writing, speaking, geography, bowing, walking, fencing' (Thornton, 'Recollections'), besides Hebrew and mathematics. Thornton acquired only 'habits of idleness' (ibid.) and many of his fellow pupils there were 'vicious' (ibid.). Henry spent 1778–80 in the counting-house of his cousin Godfrey Thornton, in 1780 entering his father's house, where he subsequently became a partner. He left in 1784 (against his parents' advice) to join the banking firm of Down and Free which soon became Down, Thornton, and Free, of which he remained an active partner until his death. Under his management, and with the help of a legacy of about £40,000 inherited from his father, Thornton's bank grew from a smallish concern into one of the largest in London, with an extensive network of country connections.

In 1782, at his mother's prompting, Thornton set out to contest Hull for parliament, but withdrew on finding that he was expected to make each voter a present of 2 guineas.

Henry Thornton (1760–1815), by James Ward (after John Hoppner, c.1802)

In September that year he was elected for the London seat Southwark, which he held for the rest of his life. Although he refused to follow the custom of treating the Southwark voters to a guinea each, and lacked popular appeal, Thornton was respected for his integrity and independence. His share of the vote dropped in later years, partly, he felt, because he had neglected his constituents for occupations 'which I have thought more useful and becoming' (Thornton, 'Recollections').

Thornton regarded his father as 'on the whole a great character' (Thornton, 'Recollections'). But he was a more cultivated and fastidious evangelical than his parents, whom he criticized for their 'peculiarities' (ibid.), ignorance of the world, and over-reliance on the doctrine of predestination which led them to be unsystematic about his education (ibid.). His cousin William Wilberforce had been given house room by John Thornton after his conversion, and it was Wilberforce who became Henry's model in religion and one of his closest friends. In 1792 Thornton bought Battersea Rise, a villa on Clapham Common which he shared with Wilberforce until his marriage. The library at Battersea Rise (reputedly designed by William Pitt) became a meeting-place for the so-called Clapham Sect, a group that gathered informally around Wilberforce and became a powerful instrument of evangelical enterprise.

Like other Clapham evangelicals, Thornton felt called to public life by God. In politics he distrusted party spirit and insisted on 'the inconsistency of private vice with public virtue' (*Christian Observer*, February 1807, 139). He came to regard the French Revolution as 'an experiment made upon human nature by men insensible of our natural corruption' (ibid., 140), and Napoleon as an extraordinary figure 'whom the Almighty has ordained to execute his righteous judgements on the earth' (ibid., September 1807, 628). Thornton was a diffident orator and spoke infrequently in parliament. His most valuable work there was done in committee. As an MP his first vote was in favour of peace with America, which immediately connected him with the friends of Pitt. Thornton generally supported Pitt, Henry Addington, and the Grenville–Fox administration. He considered the war with France 'more just than almost any other in the British history' (Thornton, 'Recollections'), yet favoured most initiatives for the restoration of peace. He approved of the peace of Amiens and was averse to the subsequent renewal of hostilities. Thornton voted for Catholic emancipation earlier than Wilberforce, and disagreed with his Clapham friends in opposing Spencer Perceval's orders in council (1807), fearing rightly for their effect on relations with America. He supported Earl Grey's 1797 motion for parliamentary reform and backed measures against sinecures and the sale of seats, while having no sympathy for the ideas of radicals and 'democrats'.

Thornton served on parliamentary committees to examine the public debt (1798), the Irish exchange (1804), and public expenditure (1807 onwards). In 1810 he was appointed to the bullion committee, which investigated the high price of gold, the state of the currency, and foreign exchange. The committee's report, written by Thornton, Francis Horner, and William Huskisson, pressed unsuccessfully for the resumption of cash payments (suspended by the Bank of England in 1797) after two years. He published two speeches on the report in 1811.

Thornton lived at a time of change and turbulence in the banking system, and it was the crisis of 1797 that produced his most enduring legacy as an economist, *An Enquiry into the Nature and Effects of the Paper Credit of Great Britain* (1802). Intended to expose some popular errors, such as the notion that an increase in paper was itself responsible for current economic ills, the book grew into a general treatise, described by J. S. Mill as 'the clearest exposition that I am acquainted with, in the English language, of the modes in which credit is given and taken in a mercantile community' (Mill, 3.11.4). The work provided a complete account of the English monetary system: not only the circulation of money, but also a detailed discussion of how the Bank of England should act to prevent instability, and also how to deal with instability whenever it occurred. According to the *New Palgrave* 'Thornton's exposition of the issues involved represents an important contribution to monetary economics' (Laidler, 'Thornton, Henry').

An article by Horner in the first number of the *Edinburgh Review* helped to spread Thornton's ideas; the book appeared in French and German translations (Geneva, 1803; Halle, 1803), in America (Philadelphia, 1807), and was reprinted in 1857 by J. R. McCulloch. Marx owes something to Thornton and quotes him in the *Grundrisse*. Among his contemporaries Thornton was generally eclipsed by David Ricardo. His twentieth-century reputation, initially the result of transatlantic interest, rates highly his originality and powers of analysis, and places him in the front rank of monetary economists.

Thornton played a leading role in the Clapham Sect's opposition to slavery, support for Christian missions, and concern to reform public manners. In 1791 he became chairman of the court of directors of the newly constituted Sierra Leone Company, which took over Granville Sharp's failed 'Province of Freedom' settlement dedicated to establishing a colony of freed slaves in Africa. The company aimed to confer on Africa the blessings of European religion and civilization through a trading operation that would be both profitable and free from the taint of slavery. Thornton was the company's most influential director and remained chairman throughout its life, writing virtually all its published reports and administering Sierra Leone from offices alongside his bank in Birchin Lane. He formed a lasting friendship with Zachary Macaulay, governor of the colony from 1794 to 1799 and then secretary to the company. Sierra Leone was transferred to the crown in 1808. The company had not prospered. It was undermined by the continuing slave trade, disasters suffered in the French war, disputes between groups of settlers, and also (as Thornton acknowledged in his 'Recollections') inexperience and over-optimism on the part of himself and his fellow directors. Notwithstanding the commercial failure, Thornton blessed the project for teaching him 'to feel for the african race' (Thornton, 'Recollections'), and hoped that providence would still make it an instrument of good. Thornton became treasurer of the African Institution, founded in the wake of slave trade abolition with similar aims to the Sierra Leone Company.

Thornton is said to have contributed over eighty articles to the Clapham Sect's journal, the *Christian Observer*, which he helped to launch in 1802. He enjoyed a warm friendship with Hannah More, to whom Wilberforce introduced him in 1789. He gave money to her schools, and wrote and revised tracts for her Cheap Repository series, visiting hawkers on her behalf to learn the secrets of the distribution trade. He was first president of the Sunday School Society, founded in 1785. Other evangelical societies predictably chose Thornton as treasurer, including the British and Foreign Bible Society (1804) and the Society for Missions to Africa and the East (1799, later the Church Missionary Society). Thornton shared in the efforts of Wilberforce, Charles Grant, and other friends to change the East India Company charter in favour of evangelizing the Indians. Like his father, he bought church livings to present to suitable clergymen.

On 1 March 1796 Thornton married Marianne Sykes (1765–1815), only daughter of Joseph Sykes, a Hull merchant and an evangelical. They had nine children. The eldest son, Henry Sykes Thornton (1800–1881), succeeded his father in banking; the youngest, the Revd Charles Thornton (1810–1839), became a friend of John Henry

Newman and the Tractarians. The marriage was affectionate; in his family Thornton was warmer and more spontaneous than he usually appeared to the outside world. He took great care over the education and religious upbringing of his children, insisting on their being useful and aware of public affairs from an early age. His eldest daughter's 'Recollections', quoted extensively by Thornton's great-grandson E. M. Forster in *Marianne Thornton, 1797–1887: a Domestic Biography* (1956), show the Thornton household as a model of evangelical family life, that great influence on the Victorians. The children's guardian, Sir Robert Inglis, published a number of Thornton's writings after his death, all concerned with domestic worship and education: *Family Prayers* (1834), family commentaries on the sermon on the mount and the Pentateuch (1835, 1837), *Lectures on the Ten Commandments* (1843), and *Female Characters* (1846). *Family Prayers* was widely used, and went through more than thirty editions in twenty years.

According to Sir James Stephen's essay on the Clapham Sect, Thornton 'never laid aside the Ermine' (Stephen, 295). He was grave, dispassionate, and rational, inspired by Wilberforce but utterly unlike him. Yet Wilberforce himself recognized 'the generous heart that glowed within' (Wilberforce and Wilberforce, 4.231); as the story of the Sierra Leone Company shows, Thornton could be moved by vision and enthusiasm as much as by prudence and business sense. Brougham called Thornton 'the most eminent in every respect' of Wilberforce's associates (Brougham, 1.273). His charity, mostly to evangelical causes, was considerable: Stephen says that he gave away between £2000 and £9000 a year, six-sevenths of his income before his marriage and one-third after it. When income tax was introduced he paid more than required, believing that the tax, though just, was not fairly distributed. As a banker he would stand by insolvent clients who had, for example, obtained credit from a third party because of their association with him: a moral obligation which once cost him more than £20,000. He valued a good income, but declined to build up a great fortune for his children, urging them in his 'Recollections' to follow his own and his father's example of limited expenses and large liberality. Thornton's health was never good. His headaches, sleeplessness, and digestive troubles were exacerbated by overwork; from 1799 he took opium. He became ill in the autumn of 1814 and died of consumption on 16 January 1815 at Wilberforce's house in Kensington Gore, London. He was buried in the Thornton vault at the Old Church, Clapham, Surrey, on 24 January.

CHRISTOPHER TOLLEY

Sources H. Thornton, 'Recollections', CUL, Thornton family MSS, Add. MS 7674/1/N · S. Meacham, *Henry Thornton of Clapham* (1964) [incl. list of Thornton's known contributions to the *Christian Observer*] · H. Thornton, *An enquiry into the nature and effects of the paper credit of Great Britain*, ed. F. von Hayek, new edn (1939) · E. M. Forster, *Marianne Thornton, 1797–1887: a domestic biography* (1956) · J. Stephen, 'The Clapham sect', *Essays in ecclesiastical biography*, 3rd edn, 2 (1853), 289–385 · *DNB* · C. Fyfe, *A history of Sierra Leone*, rev. edn (1968); repr. (1993) · R. I. Wilberforce and S. Wilberforce, *Life of William Wilberforce*, 5 vols. (1838) · M. J. Trevelyan, *Life and letters of Zachary Macaulay* (1900) · J. S. Mill, *Principles of political economy* (1848) · H. Brougham, *Historical sketches of statesmen who flourished in the time of George III*, 3rd ser. (1843) · *Christian Observer*, 14 (1815), 127–36 [text of a sermon delivered 'by a clerical friend' on the Sunday following Thornton's funeral] · C. Tolley, *Domestic biography: the legacy of evangelicalism in four nineteenth-century families* (1997) · D. Laidler, 'Thornton, Henry, 1760–1815', *The new Palgrave: a dictionary of economics*, ed. J. Eatwell, M. Milgate, and P. Newman, 4 vols. (1987)

Archives CUL, personal and family corresp. and papers · Derbys. RO, letter-book and diary | BL, letters to Thomas Clarkson, Add. MSS 41262–41263 · Bodl. Oxf., corresp. with William Wilberforce

Likenesses J. Hall, engraving, 1774 (*The Marine Society*; after E. Edwards) · T. Gainsborough, oils, *c.*1782, Marine Society, London · S. Jennings, oils, 1792 (*Liberty displaying the arts and sciences*), Winterthur Museum, Delaware · J. Ward, mezzotint, *c.*1802 (after J. Hoppner, *c.*1802), BM, NPG [*see illus.*] · J. Hoppner, portrait, *c.*1814, repro. in Forster, *Marianne Thornton*, facing p. 22

Thornton, James (1787–1854), cook, was born on 15 March 1787, the sixth of the seven children of William Thornton (1747–1814) and Ann Morris, at 17 Bryanston Street, Portman Square, London. After attending a local school he was apprenticed to a Mr Farrance, a prosperous cook at Charing Cross, at the age of thirteen, and then to John Escudier, a hotel-keeper in Oxford Street. James's employers were probably French émigrés from the revolution. The pay was good and so were the prospects (male cooks were then employed by some four hundred wealthy families, the duke of York paying the highest salary, £500). On 6 January 1809 Thornton married Sarah Oakley at St James's, Westminster. They had two children, James and Sarah, both cooks, as were four of the fourteen grandchildren.

Adventurous and restless, Thornton was engaged by Major Colin Campbell (1776–1847) on 20 August 1811 to be the duke of Wellington's cook in the Peninsula, where the war was in its second year. Thornton's service to the commander-in-chief was his road to success, though his skills were not fully exploited by Wellington, a notoriously moderate eater. On 5 September Thornton sailed for Lisbon, joining Wellington in his winter quarters on the borders of Portugal and Spain. Few cooked luncheons were required, since Wellington preferred to carry a hard-boiled egg in his pocket. He breakfasted alone, but dinner was convivial, despite the monotonous 'cold meat' after a specially long march (Thornton, 27). Normally Thornton, assisted by the son of Lord Enniskillen's cook and a scullery-man, would serve two courses to Wellington and his staff, heaping their plates with food all mixed together, roasts with dessert. He would not have been encouraged to serve up to eight elegant, separate courses, as was the practice of leading French cooks. Thornton himself procured vegetables and fruit, paying the peasants for everything, whereas Napoleon's armies requisitioned their supplies, often provoking fierce retaliation. Thornton's later account provides many insights into Wellington's campaigning: descriptions of balls, earth ovens, and of Wellington's famous boots being kissed by admiring crowds. By 1814 victory was won and Thornton was sent home. He took a winter job with Sir Patrick Murray in Scotland and in 1815, after Napoleon's escape from Elba, Campbell again engaged him to cook for Wellington, in Brussels.

At 4 a.m. on 18 June 1815 Thornton was woken by the butler, did his marketing, rode to Waterloo and cooked Wellington's 'hot dinner' after the battle. Soon after the duke's death in 1852, a French cook claimed the honour, but Thornton refuted him in a letter to *The Times*:

> Having seen in your widely circulated paper that the late and ever-to-be-honoured Duke of Wellington had a French cook at Waterloo who is reported to have said, 'He knew that the Duke would return to his dinner'. I beg most respectfully to inform you that I cooked his dinner on the day … his Grace rode up after the battle, and on getting off his horse Copenhagen he saw me and said, 'Is that you? Get dinner.' (Thornton, 49)

In 1818 the duke returned to England after being ambassador in Paris, where he 'kept French Cooks' (Thornton, 95). Thornton had rejoined his service, becoming steward at Apsley House in 1820, a prestigious post. However, he resigned on 29 December after a disagreement with the duchess, herself an embarrassingly inefficient housekeeper, over his alleged extravagance: 298 pounds of meat, excluding lamb, calves' feet, and sweetbreads, had been ordered for thirteen people for three days. He subsequently served as cook in a number of great households.

Documentary evidence of Thornton's later career is scarce, but he wrote from Lowther Castle, Westmorland, to his daughter on 21 October 1841, enclosing a recipe for white fish. He had been too busy to write sooner, having twenty for dinner most days and 'an Enormous Quantity of Servants to feed every Day'. Recipes followed for curry and strawberries, with news of a wedding breakfast and a supper in Regent's Park on the same day. Thornton spent about five years as cook to Lord Frederick Fitzclarence, lieutenant-governor of Portsmouth in succession to Wellington's brother-in-law Sir Hercules Pakenham, and in 1852, during that time, he answered questions about his wartime experiences. When Thornton moved on, Fitzclarence recommended him highly in a character reference: 'I can not give him *too* good a character' (Thornton, 51).

Thornton's recollections of his time in Wellington's service were published in 1985, but much of his life remains obscure. His wife is presumed to have predeceased him. Thornton died on 12 August 1854, at 8 Caroline Street, Belgravia, London, thirty hours after contracting cholera.

ELIZABETH LONGFORD

Sources J. Thornton, *Your most obedient servant, cook to the duke of Wellington*, ed. E. Longford (1985) · E. Longford [E. H. Pakenham, countess of Longford], *Wellington*, 1: *The years of the sword* (1969) · E. Longford [E. H. Pakenham, countess of Longford], *Wellington*, 2: *Pillar of state* (1972) · A. Brett-James, *Wellington at war, 1794–1815: a selection of his wartime letters* (1961) · private information (2004) · baptismal fee book, St Marylebone parish church, London, 28 March 1787 · m. cert. · d. cert.
Archives Stratford Saye House, Hampshire, Wellington MSS

Thornton, John (*fl.* 1405–1433), glass painter, is first recorded in 1405, when he contracted with the dean and chapter to glaze the great east window of York Minster. He is described as of Coventry and, although he became a freeman of York in 1410, he retained a residence in his native city. He is last recorded in York in 1433.

Thornton's only documented work is the minster east window, which ranks among the major achievements of English late medieval glazing. This vast translucent wall comprises a rich mixture of biblical, historical, and apocalyptic images, of which the scenes from Revelation are the most numerous. The enterprise was carried out on a grand scale; not only did it involve cutting, painting, and leading the glass itself, but it also required the preparation of numerous different cartoons to guide the work. This, together with the brief time-span of three years in which the project had to be completed, would explain why Thornton's employment of other craftsmen was envisaged. His principal role was to design the scheme and presumably he was provided with the iconographical models by the patrons. The way in which he adjusted the pictorial narrative to the demands of the architectural framework, together with the clarity of the scenes, bears witness to his talent as a monumental painter.

Although Thornton must have been involved in numerous commissions in and around York during his career, he is unlikely to have monopolized production. It seems that his style and design traits were adopted wholesale by other glaziers in the city; collectively the York craftsmen seem to have secured some of the most important glazing programmes in the north. However, Thornton's style was not exclusive to York. It is a variant of the so-called (and problematic) international Gothic style, which dominated English monumental painting and illumination during the first third of the fifteenth century. There is also much glass in the midlands which is indistinguishable from York work of the period, and Thornton's origins in, and lasting connections with, Coventry, suggest that he was operating workshops concurrently in both cities. Quite apart from the intrinsic merits of his work, Thornton's career demonstrates that in the early fifteenth century London did not enjoy a monopoly of the best glass painters.

RICHARD MARKS

Sources T. French, *York Minster: the great east window*, Corpus Vitrearum Medii Aevi: Great Britain summary catalogue, 2 (1995) · J. Lancaster, 'John Thornton of Coventry, glazier', *Transactions of the Birmingham Archaeological Society*, 74 (1956), 56–8 · R. Marks, *Stained glass in England during the middle ages* (1993), 180–83
Archives BL, glazing contract, Harley MS 6971, fol. 141v [transcript] · York Minster Library, glazing contract, YML L1/2, pt 2, 34; L1/7, 7 [transcripts]

Thornton, John (*bap.* 1641, *d.* 1708), hydrographer, was baptized at St Botolph, Aldgate, London, on 8 October 1641, the second of seven children of John Thornton, cutler and razor maker, and his wife, Ann Gomer. The family lived on Tower Hill and later East Smithfield, the road to Ratcliff which had long been a centre of chart making. In 1656 Thornton was apprenticed to John Burston of Ratcliff Highway, a leading chart maker and freeman of the Drapers' Company. There he learned the skills of manuscript chart making developed in England over the previous hundred years and passed down from master to pupil by members of the Drapers' Company.

Having married Ann Boult on 23 June 1664, Thornton completed his apprenticeship and became a freeman of the company on 11 January 1665. His earliest surviving signed chart, dated 1667, shows the east coast of England and is a typical 'platt' of the time, drawn on vellum and mounted on two hinged wooden panels for protection. Thornton was by now working on his own account from premises in East Smithfield and the following year took on two apprentices. Soon after this he moved to the Minories, where he remained for the rest of his career, working principally 'at the Sign of England, Scotland, and Ireland'.

Some forty manuscript charts with Thornton's name are known, dated between 1667 and 1701, showing European, American, Mediterranean, and eastern waters. They include large oceanic charts on four panels but the majority are pilot charts of smaller areas drawn in his later years. Most of these larger scale charts are for navigation in eastern seas and were at first drawn from traditional Dutch sources, but they gradually incorporated material from East India Company voyages and reflected English interests in the area. By 1673 Thornton had extended his activities into printed map and chart publishing, and may well have mastered engraver's skills himself. Charts of the Strait of Magellan by Sir John Narborough and Hudson's Strait were followed by numerous other printed works, including the first map of Philadelphia.

Thornton's contemporary John Seller conceived the idea of the first English printed maritime atlas and published the first two volumes of *The English Pilot* in 1671 and 1672. In 1677 Thornton joined a partnership which took over the project from Seller and played an important part in the subsequent history of the work and its companion volume, the *Atlas maritimus*. Thornton contributed charts to the Mediterranean volume published by the partnership in 1677 and in 1689 was responsible, with a partner, William Fisher, for *The English Pilot: the Fourth Book*, covering the Atlantic coasts of North America and the Caribbean. In 1703 he was the sole compiler and publisher of *The Third Book*, the first English seaman's guide for the route to the East. Many of its thirty-five charts were engraved versions of charts he had previously been producing in manuscript form. The volume was dedicated to the directors of the East India Company and produced with their encouragement. Thornton described himself as 'Hydrographer to the Company' and also to the Hudson's Bay Company, although there is no evidence of official appointment to either office.

Thornton's charts, both manuscript and engraved, were distinguished by a bold clear style, and attention to improvement by frequent correction, unusual for the time. His working life straddled the transition of the fast-expanding English chart trade from manuscript to printed charts and he was unique in playing a leading role in both fields. His major contributions to three of the five volumes of *The English Pilot* were used by English seamen almost unaltered for over half a century after his death.

Thornton died early in 1708 and was buried on 23 January at St Botolph, Aldgate. His wife had predeceased him, as had their daughter Sarah and possibly a second wife, Ann Greenleafe, whom he may have married at St Katharine by the Tower on 31 March 1694. By his will, drawn up on 12 March 1707, Thornton left substantial bequests to his daughter Ann, Sarah's six children, and his sons, Macabees and Samuel. **Samuel Thornton** (*c*.1665–1715) also inherited his father's business with his stock of charts, copper plates, and instruments. He had not been formally apprenticed to his father but had worked with him and learnt his trade. Only one manuscript chart with Samuel Thornton's name is known, of the entrance to Canton (Guangzhou), 1707, but he almost certainly drew at least one chart which bears his father's name and made an important contribution to his father's later work. On John Thornton's death Samuel became a freeman of the Drapers' Company by patrimony and continued to publish many of his father's printed charts, including a revised edition of *The English Pilot, Third Book* in 1711. Samuel Thornton died in September or October 1715 and most of the Thornton chart plates passed to the firm of Mount and Page. SUSANNA FISHER

Sources C. Verner, 'John Thornton: hydrographer, 1641–1708', *Information Bulletin Western Association of Map Libraries*, 7/1 (1975), 3–9 · A. Campbell, 'The Drapers' Company and its school of seventeenth-century chart-makers', *My head is a map: essays and memoirs in honour of R. V. Tooley*, ed. H. Wallis and S. Tyacke (1973), 81–99 · M. de la Roncière, 'Manuscript charts by John Thornton, hydrographer of the East India Company', *Imago Mundi*, 19 (1965), 46–50 · T. R. Smith, 'Manuscript and printed sea charts in seventeenth century London: the case of the Thames school', *The compleat plattmaker: essays on chart, map, and globe making in England*, ed. N. J. W. Thrower (1978) · A. S. Cook, 'More manuscript charts by John Thornton for the oriental navigation', *Imago et mensura mundi* (1985) · C. Verner, 'Bibliographical note', in J. Seller and C. Price, *The English pilot: the fifth book*, facs. edn (1973) · C. Verner, 'Bibliographical note', in J. Thornton, *The English pilot: the third book*, facs. edn (1970) · C. Verner, 'Bibliographical note', in W. Fisher and J. Thornton, *The English pilot: the fourth book*, facs. edn (1967) · C. Verner, *A carto-bibliographical study of 'The English pilot': the fourth book* (1960) · S. Tyacke, *London map-sellers, 1660–1720* (1978) · parish register, St Botolph, Aldgate, London · 'Register of apprentices and freemen of the Drapers' Company of the city of London', Drapers' Company, Drapers' Hall, Throgmorton Avenue, London EC2 [transcript of Drapers' Company binding book by P. Boyd]
Archives BL · Bodl. Oxf. · NMM | Bibliothèque Nationale, Paris, collection of Service Hydrographique de la Marine · Cambs. AS, Cotton family papers
Wealth at death business stock of maps, charts, instruments, copper plates, etc., left to son; annuities of £20 and £30 p.a. respectively to son Samuel and daughter; also legacies of £600 to his son Macabees and £20 each to his deceased daughter's six children: will, PRO, PROB 11/499/184

Thornton, John (1720–1790), merchant and philanthropist, was born on 1 April 1720, the only son of Robert Thornton of Clapham, Surrey, and his first wife, Hannah Swynocke. His father was a merchant, and became a director of the Bank of England. After his death Thornton inherited the Clapham estate and about £100,000, which he increased greatly in the Russian trade. A large part of Thornton's income was devoted to the encouragement of a gospel ministry in various parts of the world. Much of this money was donated anonymously through third parties so that he would not have excessive demands on his charity, and it is impossible to discover the extent of his charitable gifts. In 1772, for example, he got a Mr Bentley to purchase 1000 copies of a hymnbook published by the Revd Dyer of St George's, Southwark, which had failed to sell. These were to be sent to Lady Huntingdon for distribution. Similarly he employed the Revd Thomas Scott of the Lock Hospital in London to distribute bibles in England and Wales.

Although Thornton was a devout evangelical Anglican and disliked Wesleyans and Baptists, his support extended to most protestant denominations. The Revd William Bull who trained Independent ministers at Newport Pagnell was a close friend; the Revd Mr Winter also took some of his students. His allowance for a student was 25 guineas a year, and in 1783 he supported three. For these and other evangelical curates he endeavoured to find livings, with only limited success. When he was unable to persuade the lord chancellor to appoint them to crown livings he resorted to buying advowsons which he eventually placed in a trust, with Henry Venn and two other clergy as trustees. In 1783 he responded to a request from Lady Huntingdon on behalf of an Essex curate with the statement that he was considered 'a speckled Bird' with no influence (Thornton to Lady Huntingdon, 7 Oct 1783, Cheshunt archives, F1/554). Even his contribution to building new churches at Clapham and elsewhere did not give him the power to appoint a minister.

Thornton travelled widely in later life and used every opportunity to advance the evangelical cause. During a long stay at Swansea in 1783 he rented a room in the town for occasional preaching as there was no gospel ministry. He also visited Scotland, St Edmund Hall in Oxford (the home of Calvinistic Methodist students), and Lady Huntingdon's training college for ministers at Trefeca, near Brecon. Although he made no donation to the college he did assist Lady Huntingdon with a loan at no interest. In 1761 he and George Whitefield handled the negotiations by which she bought the advowson of Aldwincle All Saints, Northamptonshire, to save the patron, John Kimpton, from bankruptcy. Better known was his gift of £200 a year to John Newton while curate of Olney, Buckinghamshire, which he increased when Newton took charge of the affairs of the poet William Cowper. Thornton's closest association was with his brother-in-law, the Revd Richard Conyers, rector of Helmsley, Yorkshire, whom he described as his chaplain. He related how on one occasion he persuaded Conyers to enter a Quaker meeting.

On 28 November 1753 Thornton married Lucy (1722–1785), the heir of Samuel Watson of Hull. They had four children: Samuel *Thornton (1754–1838), who went into business and became a director of the Bank of England; Robert, who went into parliament; Jane, who married the earl of Leven; and Henry *Thornton (1760–1815), who continued his father's religious and charitable work. Thornton died on 7 November 1790 as the result of an accident at Bath and was buried at Clapham. Notwithstanding his many benefactions he died a very wealthy man, able to leave £40,000 to the youngest of his sons (his other bequests are not known). Henry described his father as 'rough, vehement and eager' (Forster, 11), and disapproved of his behaviour, but was greatly influenced by his example.   EDWIN WELCH

Sources J. Bull, *The life of John Newton* (1868) · J. Clapham, *The Bank of England: a history*, 1 (1944) · E. M. Forster, *Marianne Thornton, 1797–1887: a domestic biography* (1956) · D. E. Jenkins, *The life of Thomas Charles* (1910) · H. Venn, *The life and letters of Rev. Henry Venn* (1836) · correspondence of Lady Huntingdon, Westminster College, Cambridge, Cheshunt archives · CUL, Add. MSS 7674/1/A–D · LPL, MSS 2935, 3096, 3097 · C. Tolley, *Domestic biography: the legacy of evangelicalism in four nineteenth-century families* (1997) · D. M. Lewis, ed., *The Blackwell dictionary of evangelical biography, 1730–1860*, 2 vols. (1995)
Archives Bodl. Oxf., corresp., MS Eng. lett. b 5 · CUL, family corresp. and papers · Dartmouth College, Hanover, New Hampshire, corresp. · LMA, journals · LPL, corresp. · NL Wales, letters | NA Scot., corresp. with Lord Leven · Westminster College, Cambridge, Cheshunt Foundation, Lady Huntingdon's corresp.
Likenesses J. Hall, group portrait, line engraving, pubd 1774 (*The Marine Society*; after E. Edwards), BM · T. Gainsborough, oils, c.1782, Marine Society, London · engraving, repro. in Jenkins, *Life of Thomas Charles*, vol. 2, facing p. 36
Wealth at death very wealthy; bequeathed youngest son £40,000

Thornton, John (1783–1861). *See under* Thornton, Samuel (1754–1838).

Thornton, Norman (1896–1984), confectionery manufacturer, was born on 6 November 1896 in Sheffield, the eldest son in the family of four sons and one daughter of Joseph William Thornton (1870–1919), commercial traveller, and his wife, Kate Elizabeth, née Hinsby (b. 1873). He left Sheffield grammar school in 1911 when his father opened a sweet shop at 159 Norfolk Street, Sheffield, leaving Norman, then aged fourteen, to run it, while he continued to work as a travelling salesman for the Don Confectionery Company. This shop brought in £20 a week, enabling him to open a second shop in 1913, on The Moor, and the family moved to live over the shop, hand-rolling sweets, boiling mint rock over a gas fire in the basement, and hand-dipping violet creams, although most of the confectionery sold in the early days was bought in. Norman took over the business on his father's death in 1919, opened two more sweet shops—Chocolate Kabins—and took over a fruit business. In 1921 he was joined by his brother Stanley [*see below*], forming a private limited company, J. W. Thornton Ltd, with Norman as chairman. He married Muriel, daughter of Joseph Illingworth, engraver of silver and Sheffield plate, in 1928: they had three sons and one daughter.

Norman concentrated on the retailing side of the business, opening the first Thorntons shop outside Sheffield, in Rotherham, in 1928, and increasing the number of shops to thirty-five by 1939. As the business grew, it was no longer possible to make all the confectionery, including the hand-made luxury chocolates, on the premises, and in 1927 the brothers moved production to a small factory in the Hillsborough area of Sheffield. It was at this time that Norman Thornton had the idea of icing customers' names on to Easter eggs, an idea which proved very successful. They moved to a bigger plant in 1931, and again in 1935, to a purpose-built factory in the Millhouses area of Sheffield, which was to be their headquarters until the 1980s.

Expansion stopped with the outbreak of the Second World War, and although the Thorntons factory was not bombed, toffee production was transferred to a small factory in Bury, and continued throughout the war. Refused permission to extend the factory after the war, because of the shortage of building materials, Thorntons bought Castle Factory, near Belper, in Derbyshire, an old mill which had been used by Rolls Royce to store aircraft engines during the war, and before that had been a music-hall, and in 1947 began to manufacture boiled sweets there. With the end of sweet rationing in 1952, the firm began to expand again: in 1954 the Swiss confiseur Walter Willen joined the company to develop Swiss chocolates known as the Continental range, and the sons of Norman and Stanley Thornton joined the business during the 1950s. Following rapid expansion in the 1960s, with Thorntons winning many international awards, Norman Thornton retired in 1971. He died on 3 November 1984 at his home in Sheffield. His funeral was held on 9 November at Eccleshall church.

(Joseph) Stanley Thornton (1903–1992), the second son of Joseph William Thornton, was born on 5 September 1903 in Sheffield, and educated at Sheffield grammar school. He won a scholarship to Sheffield University, but decided to work in the family business during the day, and study food technology, in particular confectionery making, in the evenings. While Norman Thornton ran the shops, Stanley concentrated on the production side of the business. In 1925, after a year of experimenting on his kitchen stove with different combinations of butter, milk, and sugar, he created the recipe for Thorntons' Special Toffee, which for a long time was their most famous and successful product. He married Jeanetta (d. 1982), daughter of George Jamieson, boot and shoe retailer, in 1932: they had six children, including one son, Michael, who joined the company in 1956 and later became deputy chairman.

After working closely with Norman Thornton from the beginning, Stanley Thornton became chairman of the company in 1971, and company president in 1982. Despite problems in the chocolate confectionery industry in the 1970s, with wild swings in the price of cocoa beans, Thorntons continued to open new shops, including two in Scotland, and to develop new lines—ice cream was introduced in 1983. A large new plant, Thornton Park, on a 65 acre site at Swanwick, near Alfreton, in Derbyshire, was opened in 1985, to enable the business, for so long concentrated in the north, to expand into the south of England. An attempt to open a chain of shops in the United States in the 1980s, starting in 1982 with two shops in Chicago, was unsuccessful, but in France the company owned over fifty shops, and there was a large international mail order service. By 1988 Thorntons had over 1500 employees in the United Kingdom, over 200 shops, and 92 franchises, and increasing sales to corporate customers: 8½ per cent of sales in 1988 were to Marks and Spencer. The annual turnover in 1988 was £46 million. They no longer made the raw chocolate themselves—this was made to Thorntons' specifications by Cadburys in Birmingham, and by a Belgian supplier.

In 1988, when the company was floated on the stock exchange, valued at £78.6 million, the shares were eight times oversubscribed. 73 per cent of the shares were retained by members of the family, to avoid take-over, as had happened to Rowntree Mackintosh, taken over by Nestlé in 1988. Stanley Thornton became life president of the new company, Thorntons plc. After seventy-seven years, the link with Sheffield was broken, when the Millhouses factory was closed, concentrating chocolate production at Thornton Park, and toffee and ice cream at Belper. Thorntons remained a family business. Its share of the chocolate and confectionery markets was tiny compared with that of firms such as Cadburys and Frys—even in the Christmas chocolate sector Thorntons had only 6 per cent of the market in 1988—but it had built up a reputation for high-quality, luxury chocolates, sweets, and toffee, made to traditional recipes. Thorntons was unusual in operating as both manufacturer and retailer, selling as well as making its own confectionery. By the time of Stanley Thornton's death, on 27 February 1992, at the Derbyshire Royal Infirmary, Derby, the company was embarking on a new expansion drive. Stanley Thornton's ashes were interred at Winster church, Derbyshire, on 5 March, after a funeral in Derby Cathedral.

ANNE PIMLOTT BAKER

Sources J. W. Thornton Ltd, *Thorntons, 1911–1981: the history of a family firm* (1981) · T. Potter, *The British confectionery industry* (1980) · D. Edwards, *Confectionery in the UK* (1989) · D. Whyatt, 'Derbyshire enterprises: Thorntons', *Derbyshire Life and Countryside* (1982) · S. Allen, 'Sweet success', *The Spectator* [Sheffield] (Feb 1980) · *Sheffield Star* (5 Oct 1982) · *Sheffield Star* (4 Nov 1982) · *Sheffield Star* (9 Nov 1982) · *Sheffield Star* (5 Nov 1984) · *Sheffield Star* (9 May 1988) · *Sheffield Star* (10 May 1988) · *Sheffield Star* (27 May 1988) · *Sheffield Star* (28 May 1988) · *Sheffield Star* (6 June 1990) · *Morning Telegraph* [Sheffield] (16 Sept 1983) · *Morning Telegraph* [Sheffield] (10 March 1982) · *Morning Telegraph* [Sheffield] (6 Oct 1982) · *Morning Telegraph* [Sheffield] (10 Nov 1982) · *The Times* (6 May 1988) · 'The sweet taste of success', *Derbyshire County Magazine* (Nov 1980) · *The Times* (10 Nov 1984) · *The Times* (2 March 1992) [Stanley Thornton] · *Ashbourne News Telegraph* (5 March 1992) [Stanley Thornton] · private information (2004) [John Thornton and Michael Thornton]

Likenesses photograph (Joseph Stanley Thornton), repro. in *The Times* (2 March 1992) · portrait, Thorntons plc, Thornton Park, Somercotes, Derby · portrait (Joseph Stanley Thornton), Thorntons plc, Thornton Park, Somercotes, Derby

Wealth at death £593,764: *Sheffield Star* 8 Feb 1985

Thornton, Richard (1776–1865), merchant, underwriter, and financier, was born on 20 September 1776 in Burton in Lonsdale, Yorkshire, the third son in the family of four sons and five daughters of Robert Thornton, an impecunious yeoman farmer, and his wife, Ellen. He entered Christ's Hospital school, London, in 1785, leaving in 1791 to become an apprentice to his uncle, Richard Thornton, a hop merchant in Southwark. By 1798 he had moved into the business of insurance as a member of Lloyd's. He also established himself in the Russian trade, which during the French wars offered exceptional opportunities for profit.

The government's need for naval stores, above all hemp, during the Napoleonic blockade, tempted Thornton into daring ventures through the Baltic in his own armed ships, especially in 1810, when this illicit trade was described as the most lucrative in the world. Two years later, apprised by his elder brother and partner, Laurence, of the defeat of Napoleon at Moscow before this was publicly known, he secured large contracts for the forward delivery of Russian imports from the Baltic at their peak wartime prices. He was said to have made over £100,000 from this masterly stroke. Not surprisingly, he earned the lasting sobriquet, 'the Duke of Danzig' (Hoskins, 575). In 1815 the Thornton brothers moved their base from Southwark to the City side of the river, and carried on their business from Old Swan Wharf, near London Bridge, for the next fifty years.

The return of peace saw a redirection of Thornton's interests towards the recently opened markets in the East Indies. In partnership with the West family, Thornton exploited the rich pickings of the Dutch East Indies. Thornton, West & Co. were one of the leading British merchant houses in the eastern seas. The firm was based in Rotterdam, though it was reorganized in London in 1837. The East Indies remained a primary destination for Thornton's British-registered ships—for example, in 1857 six ships traded between London, Java, and Singapore. His fleet also carried French troops to the Crimea.

Thornton became a leading financier of struggling constitutional regimes in Iberia. In 1834, for example, he headed a subscription for the Spanish politician and financier Mendizabal. But these foreign debts were only intermittently repaid and, as a result, in the 1830s and 1840s Thornton headed the committee of Spanish bondholders urging British governments to intervene on their behalf. Thornton was also an important lender to the British government, and at one point reputedly the largest holder of consols.

By the 1840s Thornton was in the forefront of the City of London, not only as merchant and financier but as shipowner and leading marine insurance broker. He now receded from the City, rarely appearing at the exchanges, even the Baltic, the scene of his most memorable deals in Russian tallow. He left a reputation for cockney oratory, for daring gambling of all types, but also for geniality and charitableness. He built and endowed almshouses in Barnet for the Leathersellers' Company when he was its master in 1836–7. In his will he left sizeable sums for schools he had built in his home parishes, as well as for Christ's Hospital, of which he had been a donation governor in 1833. In all, his public bequests amounted to the order of £100,000, an impressive sum, yet only a small proportion of his total wealth, the probate value of which—nearly £2,800,000—represented the largest fortune left in Britain before 1870.

Thornton was a strong, if irregular, family man. The bulk of his fortune was left to Thomas Thornton and Richard Thornton West, his nephews and partners. He never married, but he lived with his housekeeper Lee, and his four illegitimate children were major beneficiaries: his son Richard Napoleon Lee inheriting £400,000, and his three daughters sufficient to maintain them in gentility. Thornton died at his suburban mansion, Cannon Hill, in Merton, Surrey, on 20 June 1865, and was buried in Norwood cemetery.   A. C. HOWE, rev.

Sources GM, 3rd ser., 19 (1865), 386 · D. M. Evans, 'Within and without', GM, 5th ser., 6 (1871), 307–10 · W. G. Hoskins, 'Richard Thornton, 1776–1865: a Victorian millionaire', History Today, 12 (1962), 574–9 · LMA, Christ's Hospital papers · H. A. Roberts, The records of the Amicable Society of Blues (1924) · 'Correspondence between Great Britain and foreign powers ... relative to loans made by British subjects', Parl. papers (1847), 69.453, no. 839 · PRO, RG 9/453 · The Times (18 Feb 1854) · The Times (21 June 1865) · The Times (28 June 1865) · Boase, Mod. Eng. biog. · CGPLA Eng. & Wales (1865)
Likenesses R. Dighton, cartoon sketch, 1818, GL; repro. in Hoskins, 'Richard Thornton' · R. Dighton, line engraving, 1823 (after his portrait), BM, NPG · oils, Leathersellers' Company, London; repro. in Hoskins, 'Richard Thornton'
Wealth at death under £2,800,000: probate, 27 July 1865, CGPLA Eng. & Wales

Thornton, Robert (b. in or before **1397**, d. in or before **1465**?), compiler of miscellanies and copyist, son of Robert Thornton and perhaps of Isabel Gray, and brother of Richard, became lord of the manor of East Newton in the parish of Stonegrave, wapentake of Ryedale, North Riding of Yorkshire, on his father's death in 1418. His grandfather, also Robert, died in 1402. Thornton was alive in 1456 and appears, it seems, as a witness to a charter dated 1468, though this evidence conflicts with a family pedigree, originally compiled by a family relative, Thomas Comber, dean of Durham (d. 1699), which suggests that he must have died by 1465, when his second wife, Isabel, is recorded as marrying John Mekylfield. Thornton's first wife was Agnes.

Robert Thornton is believed to be the gentleman amateur compiler and generally careful copyist of two manuscript miscellanies in which he occasionally signs his name: Lincoln Cathedral, MS 91 (A.5.2), known as the 'Thornton manuscript', and BL, Add. MS 31042 (the 'London Thornton manuscript').

Thornton was probably educated at home; he did not attend either university. Local landholdings afforded him a respectable degree of prosperity and influence. In 1441 he was named as an executor of the will of Sir Richard Pikeryng of nearby Oswaldkirk; he appears as witness in land transactions in 1442 and 1448–9; and he was commissioned as a tax collector for the North Riding, in 1453. He may have been a distant relative of Robert Stillington, bishop of Bath and Wells and chancellor of England, and have held some official post such as steward to the abbot of Rievaulx. With his second wife he had three sons, William, Thomas, and Richard. In the Lincoln manuscript William apparently records the birth of a grandchild, Robert, in 1453–4 (Lincoln Cathedral MS 91, fol. 49v).

This paper manuscript of 314 folios, written c.1430–50 (rebound in 1974), is divided into three main sections: secular, religious, and medical (Liber de diversis medicinis). It is a major source for Middle English romances, both tail-rhyme and alliterative, including the northern version of *Octavian*, *Sir Isumbras*, *Diocletian*, *Sir Degrevant*, *Sir Eglamour*, *Lyarde*, *Thomas of Erceldoune*, and *The Awntyrs off Arthure at the Terne Wathelyne*. It preserves unique copies of the *Prose Life of Alexander*, the alliterative *Morte Arthure*, and *Sir Percival of Galles*. The religious section contains a variety of prayers, meditations, and instructional material in English and Latin, including works by the Yorkshire hermit Richard Rolle, three short items from Walter Hilton, *John Gaytryge's Sermon*, *The Mirror of St Edmund*, *The Abbey of the Holy Ghost*, *A Revelation of Purgatory* (1422), and the unique alliterative *St John the Evangelist*. Textual variants suggest that Thornton may have had access to exemplars from a house for female religious, such as the Benedictine priory of St Mary at Nun Monkton. A prayer to St Leonard may connect with the Thornton family's reverence for this saint by whose altar their tomb lay in Stonegrave church. The volume comprises a variety of material for the entertainment and spiritual and bodily health of the compiler and his family, who seem to have read it, and resewn leaves, and jotted their names down in it, until their fortunes waned and it passed into the possession of Lincoln Cathedral, probably via Comber's association with Daniel Brevint, dean of Lincoln (1682–95), and possibly in 1692 when East Newton and its furnishings were sold.

Watermarks suggest that BL, Add. MS 31042 was being compiled contemporaneously with the Lincoln manuscript. Its 179 folios contain English verse romances and religious works less distinctly separated, including two long excerpts from *Cursor mundi*, *The Quatrefoil of Love*, *Richard the Lionheart*, 'the Romance of the childhode of Ihesu Criste' (BL, Add. MS 31042, fol. 163v), *The Parliament of the Three Ages*, short religious and didactic pieces by Lydgate, and unique copies of *The Siege of Jerusalem*, *The Siege of Milan*, *Roland and Otuel*, and *Winner and Waster*. There is no Chaucer, Gower, or Langland in either volume.

ROBERT EASTING

Sources G. R. Keiser, 'Lincoln Cathedral Library MS 91: life and milieu of the scribe', *Studies in Bibliography*, 32 (1979), 158–79 · G. R. Keiser, 'More light on the life and milieu of Robert Thornton', *Studies in Bibliography*, 36 (1983), 111–19 · M. S. Ogden, ed., *The Liber de diversis medicinis in the Thornton manuscript*, EETS, old ser., 207 (1938); repr. (1969) · *The autobiography of Mrs Alice Thornton*, ed. [C. Jackson], SurtS, 62 (1875) [incl. pedigree of the family of Thornton of East Newton] · D. S. Brewer and A. E. B. Owen, introductions, *The Thornton manuscript (Lincoln Cathedral MS 91)* (1975); 2nd edn (1977) · J. J. Thompson, *Robert Thornton and the London Thornton manuscript* (1987) · J. J. Thompson, 'Another look at the religious texts in Lincoln, Cathedral Library, MS 91', *Late-medieval religious texts and their transmission*, ed. A. J. Minnis (1994) · A. McIntosh, 'The textual transmission of the alliterative *Morte Arthure*', *English and medieval studies presented to J. R. R. Tolkien*, ed. N. Davis and C. L. Wrenn (1962), 231–40 · K. Stern, 'The London "Thornton" miscellany', *Scriptorium*, 30 (1976), 26–37, 201–18 · R. Hanna, 'The growth of Robert Thornton's books', *Studies in Bibliography*, 40 (1987), 51–61 · J. J. Thompson, 'The compiler in action: Robert Thornton and the "Thornton romances" in Lincoln Cathedral MS 91', *Manuscripts and readers in fifteenth-century England*, ed. D. Pearsall (1983), 113–24 · M. Hamel, 'Scribal self-corrections in the Thornton *Morte Arthure*', *Studies in Bibliography*, 36 (1983), 119–37 · G. R. Keiser, '"To knawe God Almyghtyn": Robert Thornton's devotional book', *Spätmittelalterliche geistliche Literatur in der Nationalsprache*, 2, ed. J. Hogg (Salzburg, 1984), 103–29

Thornton, Robert John (1768–1837), physician and writer on botany, was probably born in London, youngest of the two sons and a daughter of the writer Bonnell *Thornton (1725–1768), who died before his son's birth, and his wife, Sylvia, daughter of Colonel John Braithwaite. After early private education, and intended for the church, Thornton entered Trinity College, Cambridge, in 1786 aged eighteen, but was drawn into medicine. He was strongly influenced by the botanical lectures of Professor Thomas Martyn, who introduced him to Linnaeus's sexual system for plants. Subsequently he attended lectures by Henry Cline and William Babbington at Guy's Hospital medical school, and graduated as MB at Cambridge in 1793. His thesis on 'oxygen air imbibed by the blood' signals the interests in life forces in terms of the new chemical theories of Lavoisier and others that were to characterize much of his subsequent writings.

After travels in Scotland, Ireland, France, the Netherlands, and Germany, Thornton set up as a physician in London in 1797, using techniques advocated by Thomas Beddoes (founder of the Pneumatic Institute and follower of the Brunonian system), which involved the inhalation of 'factitious airs', including laughing gas. He had already begun the publication of *The Politician's Creed* (8 vols., 1795–9) and *The Philosophy of Medicine, being Medical Extracts* (4 vols., 1796, and subsequent editions). Apart from an uncertain income from popular writing, Thornton appears to have depended upon practising medicine for his living, since he additionally became an MD of the University of St Andrews (1805), and a licentiate of the Royal College of Physicians (1812). However, in 1796 he was appointed lecturer on medical botany at Guy's and St Thomas's hospitals, and was devoted to the latter science. Already he was working on a gigantic literary speculation which was to ruin him. This work, the *New Illustration of the Sexual System of Linnaeus* (better known under its 1804 title of *The Temple of Flora*), was first advertised in 1797 and began to appear in parts from 1799, published by T. Bensley and priced at 1 guinea (later 25s). The complete text with illustrations was advertised as available in 1799 for 20 guineas. Its bibliographic history was complicated, the three main parts being issued at a variety of times and in different formats. Thornton's subsequent publications, including *Botanical Extracts* (2–4 vols., 1810) and *The British Flora* (5 vols., 1812), annexed material from the *New Illustration* in a characteristically opportunistic and bibliographically confusing manner. The huge costs of illustration and printing seriously eroded Thornton's personal fortune. As a promotional exercise in 1804 he exhibited the originals of his plates at 49 New Bond Street, and in 1811 an act of parliament (51 George III, cap. 103) authorized his 'Royal Botanical Lottery', for which he issued 20,000 tickets at 2 guineas each. The top prize was the set of original paintings, with other prizes of his printed illustrations and texts. In spite of his efforts to market his publications, his finances never recovered.

At the heart of the *New Illustration* was Thornton's

Robert John Thornton (1768–1837), by John Russell, 1799

scheme to produce a specifically British botanical publication of a magnificence to surpass all previous examples. Teams of master engravers and colourists, including Francesco Bartolozzi, Richard Earlom, and John Landseer, used the full range of modern printing techniques to produce coloured illustrations after paintings by such prominent artists as Sir William Beechey, James Opie, Henry Raeburn, John Russell, Abraham Pether, and his two favoured illustrators, Peter Henderson and Philip Reinagle. The illustrations were not restricted to the 'choicest flowers' in the world, but included portraits of eminent botanists—including the famous portrait of Linnaeus in Lapp (Sami) dress—elaborate allegories, such as 'Cupid Inspiring the Plants to Love', and a bust of Linnaeus being honoured by Aesculapius, Flora, Ceres, and Cupid. The text, which includes a translation of Linnaeus's 'Prize dissertation' on the sexuality of plants (1759), is similarly not bound to accounts and texts of scientific botany, but deals with a wide range of religious, political, spiritual, social, and emotional issues, not only in prose but also through extensive use of poems by modern and ancient authors. It is easy to regard much of this material as irrelevant to the publication's botanical aims, but this is to miss the universal human and religious purposes of botanical learning in Thornton's system of thought.

The tenor of Thornton's enterprise shares much in common with Erasmus Darwin's poem *The Botanic Garden*, especially the second part, *The Loves of Plants* (1789), but Thornton's fervent religious beliefs, moral conservatism,

royalist passion, and disgust for the French Revolution stand in marked contrast to Darwin's radicalism and libertarianism. For Thornton the study of botanical science in the wake of Linnaeus's system of classification inculcated, particularly in the young, a love of order and proper feelings of awe for divine providence. The power of love expressed by plants through their sexual activities, conducted with instruments of such beauty and wonder, provided exemplary expressions of the highest sentiments which human beings could attain in the context of conjugal fidelity. His dedicatee, Queen Charlotte, who had given her family name to *Strelitzia* (the 'queen plant', imported by Sir Joseph Banks), provided the supreme model. Her chastising letter to the king of Prussia, lamenting the miseries of European wars, was quoted by Thornton among the supporting material for his plate of roses (drawn by himself) to reinforce his advocacy of universal peace. The botanical diversity of the world, the result of the wide variety of geographical habitats, gave unequivocal support for the notion of free trade rather than military conquest and perpetual strife: Thornton's model of peaceful civilization for the world was that provided by Britain under its monarchy.

The twenty-eight illustrations in the *Temple of Flora* in its large format (about 24 x 18 in.) are the most overtly dramatic in the history of botany. Each plant is characterized assertively against an evocative background. The 'Night blowing cereus' from Jamaica, as drawn by Reinagle, is shown in a moonlit landscape of church and 'dimpled' river by Pether; the 'American cowslip' appears in front of a sea view with sailing ships, evoking travel; the 'Egyptian bean' assumes a geometrical air before the pyramids; while the 'Dragon arum' displays the 'confusion dire' of its phallic sexual equipment against a stormy mountainscape, appropriate for such a 'foetid' plant. The settings are not consistently ecological; rather they play in various ways to the plants' aesthetic potential, their exotic origins, the seasons and times of their flowering, their personalities and emotional associations, their socio-political connotations, and, above all, to their significance within the spiritual system of meaning in God's creation. The plates may be seen as complementary to the other systems of illustration used by Thornton, ranging from diagrammatic tabulations of the sexual organs according to the Linnaean system and illustrations of experiments, to pictorial representations of the 'anatomy' and 'dissection' of particular flowers.

Viewed as a whole, Thornton's publications embrace, in a single if loosely organized system, many of the varied motivations in British science at the turn of the century: a respect for experiment; a search for systems of mathematical rigour; an awe at the power of life forces, particularly those of chemical and electrical nature; a rhapsodic delight in the magic of nature in all its dramatic manifestations; a strong sense of national pride in the political and scientific achievements of Britain; a love of freedom in nature and society, as opposed to continental mores; an enthusiasm for the role of lavish, large-scale illustrations for the portrayal of truths of man and nature; and, above all, a keen awareness of the supreme power of the provident creator, designer of the 'great chain of being', at the top of which stand God's Englishmen.

The date of Thornton's marriage to his wife, Susannah, is not known; two children, Robert John and Septima Elizabeth, were baptized in 1817. He continued to write popular or elementary books on his favoured botanical, educational, and religious themes, including *A New Family Herbal* in 1810 with illustrations by Thomas Bewick, and *Illustrations of the School Virgil* (1814), the second edition of which contained woodcuts by William Blake (1824). His final publication was *The Lord's Prayer, Newly Translated with Notes* in 1827. Thornton had failed to recover his losses from *The Temple of Flora* when he died at Howland Street, Fitzroy Square, on 21 January 1837, leaving his children on the edge of poverty. *The Temple* has been characterized as a visually magnificent failure, with 'little botanical value' (Blunt and Stearn, 236), but this is to misunderstand its place in Thornton's writings and within a particular phase of British science in the era of Romanticism.

MARTIN KEMP

Sources W. B. Hemsley, 'Robert John Thornton', *Gardeners' Chronicle*, 3rd ser., 16 (1894), 89–90 · W. F. Perkins, 'Dr Thornton's works', *Gardeners' Chronicle*, 3rd ser., 16 (1894), 276–8 · W. Blunt and W. T. Stearn, *The art of botanical illustration*, new edn (1994) · G. Grigson, *Thornton's 'Temple of Flora'* (1972) · L. T. Tomasi, *An oak spring flora* (1997), 354–8 · J. Browne, 'Botany for gentlemen: Erasmus Darwin and *The loves of the plants*', *Isis*, 80 (1989), 593–621 · N. Jardine, J. A. Secord, and E. C. Spary, eds., *Cultures of natural history* (1996) · M. Kemp, *Natura-cultura*, ed. L. T. Tomasi (1999), 11–22 · *GM*, 2nd ser., 7 (1837), 93 · Munk, *Roll* · Venn, *Alum. Cant.* · *DNB*

Likenesses J. Russell, pastels, 1799; Sotheby's, 13 Nov 1997, lot 54 [*see illus.*] · B. Smith, stipple, pubd 1808 (after G. H. Harlow), BM · F. Bartolozzi, engraving (after J. Russell), repro. in R. J. Thornton, *New illustration of the sexual system of Carolus von Linnaeus* [1799–1807] · B. Thompson, engraving (after Harlow), repro. in R. J. Thornton, *Outline of botany* (1812) · print (after J. Russell), repro. in *European Magazine* (July 1803) · print (after J. Russell), repro. in R. J. Thornton, *A new family herbal* (1810)

Thornton, Samuel (*c*.1665–1715). *See under* Thornton, John (*bap.* 1641, *d.* 1708).

Thornton, Samuel (1754–1838), merchant and bank governor, was born on 6 November 1754, the eldest son in the family of three sons and one daughter of John *Thornton (1720–1790), a merchant, of Hull and Clapham, and his wife, Lucy, the daughter of Samuel Watson, a Russia merchant of Hull. Henry *Thornton (1760–1815), philanthropist and economist, was his younger brother. Samuel married on 12 December 1780 Elizabeth, the only daughter of Robert Milnes, of Fryston Hall, in Yorkshire; they had four sons and six daughters.

When his father died in 1790, worth about £600,000, Samuel Thornton succeeded him as head of the family business in Hull, which was engaged in trade with the Baltic countries. He was appointed a director of the Bank of England in 1780, a post he held for fifty-three years, serving as deputy governor between 1797 and 1799 and governor from 1799 until 1801. He became an assistant of the Russia Company in 1778 and governor from 1810 until his

Samuel Thornton (1754–1838), by Charles Turner, pubd 1827 (after Thomas Phillips, 1815)

death. He was also an assistant of the Eastland Company from 1795 and deputy governor from 1810 until his death.

In March 1784 Thornton was returned as a tory member of parliament for Hull, together with his cousin William Wilberforce. He held this seat until 1806. In May 1807 he was returned for Surrey, where he had bought an estate at Albury in 1800, defeating Lord William Russell, who had held the constituency in five parliaments. Thornton himself was defeated at the general election in 1812, but was returned at a by-election in the following year. He was defeated in 1818, and then decided to retire from public life.

In the House of Commons Thornton was an informed, and often influential, speaker on commercial and business affairs, especially when they related to the Bank of England. He took, for example, a leading part in the debates on the Bank Restriction Bill of 1797, a bill which, when eventually passed, authorized the suspension of cash payments. He usually, although not always, supported William Pitt, and privately approved of Pitt's proposed income tax as beneficial to the state. He defended the policy of the bank when it issued exchequer bills during the commercial crisis of April 1793.

As governor, Thornton moved the renewal of the bank's charter in 1800, some twelve years before it expired—part of measures adopted to prevent the founding of a rival institution—saying that the banknotes issued by the bank were both valid and adequate. He opposed the resumption of cash payments in 1811, but insisted in 1815 that the bank was anxious to resume cash payments as soon as possible. As late as 1818, however, in his last important speech before his retirement, Thornton said that such a step would be dangerous, in view of the number of foreign loans and a recent run of bad harvests. He defended on numerous occasions the steps taken by the bank to prevent the forgery of its notes.

Although widely regarded as a member of the Clapham Sect, Thornton did not wholeheartedly maintain all of its views. He supported Wilberforce's campaign against the slave trade, was in favour of the repeal of the Test Act, and opposed public lotteries. He voted in favour of Catholic relief in 1816 and again in 1817. In 1796 he supported plans for a wet dock in London, citing the example of the new schemes at Hull, which at first were unpopular, but in 1802 he came top of the poll at Hull, where the dock schemes were proving successful. He was both surprised and offended to lose his seat there in 1806.

By about 1810 Thornton was experiencing financial difficulties. The failure of the business firm of Watson of Preston cost his own firm £50,000, and the depressed state of the trade with the Baltic brought the London branch of his firm to a temporary halt in 1810. He sold his Albury estate in 1811 for £72,000.

Thornton was a governor of the Royal Naval Hospital, Greenwich, and president of Guy's Hospital, and in 1798 became lieutenant-colonel of the Clapham Volunteers. He died at his house in Brighton on 3 July 1838.

His eldest son, **John Thornton** (1783–1861), was born on 31 October 1783. He graduated BA at Trinity College, Cambridge, in 1804 and MA in 1809. In 1780 he married Eliza, the daughter of Edward Parry; they had six sons and four daughters. She published Lady Alice: a Ballad Romance, in 1842, The Marchioness, a Tale, in the same year, and a third novel, Truth and Falsehood, a Romance, in 1847. John Thornton became successively commissioner of the boards of audit, stamps, and inland revenue, as well as treasurer of the Church Missionary Society and of the Bible Society. He died at Clapham on 29 October 1861.

MICHAEL REED

Sources L. Taylor and R. G. Thorne, 'Thornton, Samuel', HoP, Commons · DNB · GM, 3rd ser., 11 (1861), 694 · B. Hilton, The age of atonement: the influence of evangelicalism on social and economic thought, 1795–1865 (1988) · F. K. Brown, Fathers of the Victorians: the age of Wilberforce (1961) · D. Kynaston, The City of London, 1 (1994) · J. Clapham, The Bank of England: a history, 2 vols. (1944) · CGPLA Eng. & Wales (1861) [John Thornton]
Archives Bodl. Oxf., letters to J. C. Brooke · NA Scot., letters to Lord Melville · U. Birm. L., letters to J. Venn
Likenesses A. Hickel, oils, 1794, Bank of England, London · C. Turner, mezzotint, pubd 1827 (after T. Phillips, 1815), AM Oxf., BM [see illus.]
Wealth at death under £45,000—John Thornton: will, 1861

Thornton, (Joseph) Stanley (1903–1992). See under Thornton, Norman (1896–1984).

Thornton, Thomas (1751/2–1823), sportsman, was born in London, the only son, with one daughter, of William Thornton (1713–1769) of Thornville, Cattal, Yorkshire, and his second wife, Mary (d. 1800), daughter of John Myster of Epsom. His father was MP for York (1747–54 and 1758–1761) and in 1745 he financed and commanded the West Riding militia, serving in Scotland and later Hanover. Thomas

Thomas Thornton (1751/2–1823), by Philip Reinagle and Sawrey Gilpin, 1790

Thornton was educated at Charterhouse School before entering Glasgow University in 1766; he continued his education there until 1771 when he left aged nineteen. After he inherited his father's estates on his coming of age he pursued his sporting interests, achieving fame with his several packs of hounds, with which he provided free hunting of foxes, stags, and hares for the Yorkshire gentry. From 1772 to 1781 he managed the Falconers' Club near Cambridge, which he had inaugurated as an upper-class society for hawking and falconry. Fishing and competitive shooting also interested him and he was a member of a notorious savoir-vivre club, but he had little interest in gambling on games of chance, preferring to bet upon his own prowess, and that of his hounds and horses. He rode his own horse to win a match at York in 1778, and acted as steward at Boroughbridge races in 1783, but it was his gambling on the rider Alicia Meynell [see Thornton, Alicia] that made him publicly infamous. In 1804 at York races she rode his horse for a bet of £1000 in an unprecedented match. She lost the race and Thornton reneged on the bet, so the dispute went to court but the case was thrown out. Alicia made another match at York in 1805 for more than 2000 guineas, which she won, but Thornton was publicly horsewhipped there by the previous opponent, all of which was reported in the press. The precise nature of Thornton's relationship with Alicia remains unclear. Alicia, though frequently referred to as Mrs

Thornton, was thought by the diarist Charles Fothergill to be Thornton's mistress. She eloped with a soldier in 1806, and in July of that year, at Lambeth, Thornton married Eliza Cawston of Mundon, Essex. Their son, William Thomas, was born at Kenyon House, London, the following year. Thornton also had a daughter, Thornvillia-Rockingham Thornton, who was born to a mistress, Priscilla Duins, in 1801.

Thornton made two expeditions to the Scottish highlands about 1786, which were described as one journey in his book *A sporting tour through the northern parts of England and great parts of the highlands of Scotland* (1804), which was probably ghost-written by a Revd Martyn. A sloop was chartered for Thornton, his guests, servants, dogs, hawks, and guns; other supplies were sent by road so that the party lived in luxurious conditions in floored tents with doors and stoves, and they entertained visitors to lavish dinners. A tour of France during which Thornton met Napoleon was described in *A Sporting Tour through Various Parts of France* (1806). Thornton was a substantial patron of the artists George Garrard, Philip Reinagle, and Sawrey Gilpin, whom he took with him on his travels to record his exploits. Thornton had been appointed colonel of the West Yorkshire militia but was forced to resign after a court martial in 1795 for allowing his soldiers to draw him into camp in a triumphal carriage, although he retained his rank.

Thornton entertained lavishly, with unbounded hospitality, providing field sports for large groups of gentlemen, but contemporaries wrote that he became greatly unpopular and lost people's respect by his shabby tricks and deceitful behaviour. He led an ostentatious life with two London houses and his family seat of Thornville. The latter was sold and he bought the duke of York's large mansion at nearby Allerton Mauleverer in 1789, and in 1791 he built a hunting lodge, Falconer's Hall, at Boythorpe. These Yorkshire properties were sold in 1805 to pay his debts and he quitted Yorkshire with great panache, moving to Spye Park, Wiltshire, which he rented. Reports in the *Hull Advertiser* for November 1808 refer to his final departure followed by a cavalcade consisting of a 'boat waggon covered with skins of stags … otter spears, fishing rods and guns … a dog cart with milk white terriers [and] … a hundred staghounds'. The procession was made up of horses, a falconer in livery, and nine more wagons. His considerable art collection, including pictures by Rubens and Van Dyck, was auctioned to pay his debts in London in 1819. After several visits to France, Thornton went to live there some time after 1817. He bought a derelict château at Pont-sur-Seine, south-east of Paris, and rented the Château de Chambourd there, from which he styled himself marquis de Pont and prince de Chambourd. He died in lodgings in Paris on 10 March 1823, leaving his estate to his illegitimate daughter. The will was successfully contested in London and France by his wife, on behalf of their son.   IRIS M. MIDDLETON

Sources *Annals of Sporting and Fancy Gazette*, 3 (1823), 291–8, 362–6 · *Annals of Sporting and Fancy Gazette*, 4 (1823), 293–6 · *GM*, 1st ser., 39 (1769), 367 · *GM*, 1st ser., 93/1 (1823), 567–8 · *GM*, 1st ser., 76 (1806), 676 · *GM*, 1st ser., 77 (1807), 374 · *DNB* · W. W. Bean, *The parliamentary representation of the six northern counties of England* (1890), 1133–4 · HoP, *Commons, 1754–90*, 3.526 · *The diary of Charles Fothergill*, ed. P. Romney, Yorkshire Archaeological Society, 142 (1982) · *The memoirs of George Elers, 1777–1842*, ed. Lord Monson and G. L. Gower (1903), 191–2, 233–9, 218–20 · T. Thornton, *A sporting tour through the northern parts of England and great parts of the highlands of Scotland*, ed. H. Maxwell (1896) · private information (2004) [Glasgow University] · *York Courant* (9 Nov 1773) · *Hull Advertiser* (31 Aug 1805) · *Hull Advertiser* (5 Oct 1805) · *Hull Advertiser* (8 Feb 1806) · *Hull Advertiser* (5 April 1806) · *Hull Advertiser* (Nov 1808) · H. Cox and G. Lascelles, *Coursing and falconry* (1896), 298, 330–35 · J. Charlesworth, ed., *The register of the parish of Thornhill*, 3 vols. (1907–15), 10 Feb 1713 · J. G. Alger, *Napoleon's British visitors and captives, 1801–1815* (1904), 109

Likenesses P. Reinagle and S. Gilpin, oils, 1790; Sotheby's, New York, 20 Jan 1983, lot 8 [*see illus.*] · Mackenzie, stipple and line engraving, pubd 1805 (after R. Reinagle), BM, NPG · W. N. Bate, stipple, pubd 1810 (after Capon and R. Reinagle), BM · stipple, pubd 1823, BM

Thornton, Thomas (*bap.* 1767?, *d.* 1814), writer on Turkey, was the son of William Thornton, a Yorkshireman settled in London and working as an innkeeper. He was probably the Thomas Thornton who was baptized on 29 December 1767 at St Peter Cornhill, London, the son of William and Dorothy Thornton. That couple also had a son Edward baptized on 16 November 1766; the latter may be identified as Sir Edward *Thornton (1766–1852), who is known to have been Thomas's brother. Thomas was the uncle of Sir Edward Thornton (1817–1906).

Thornton was left orphaned when young and engaged in commerce from an early age. About 1793 he was sent to the British factory at Constantinople, where he lived for fourteen years; he also stayed for fifteen months in Odessa and paid occasional visits to Asia Minor and the islands of the archipelago. While at Constantinople and before 14 July 1799 he married Sophie Zohrab, the daughter of a Greek merchant and a member of a powerful family well connected in the Middle East, with whom he had a large family. His youngest son was William Thomas *Thornton (1813–1880).

After his return to England Thornton published in *The Present State of Turkey* (1807) a brief summary of Ottoman history and a detailed and comprehensive account of the political and social institutions of the Turkish empire; a second edition, revised and improved, was published in two volumes in 1809. Thornton had gleaned his information from living so long at Constantinople, from his friendship with the European ambassadors, from his extensive reading of previous works, and from his facility in languages. His account was hailed as 'by far the best book ever published on that country' (*GM*, 1st ser., 84/1, 1814, 418). Thornton was sympathetic towards Turks, who he felt had been unjustly disparaged by previous authors. He severely criticized William Eton's *Survey of the Turkish Empire* (1798), and drew from Eton in reply *A letter to the earl of D… on the political relations of Russia in regard to Turkey, Greece, and France* (1807).

About the end of 1813 Thornton was appointed consul to the Levant Company, but on 28 March 1814, on the eve of setting out for Alexandria, he died, 'of a pulmonary complaint' (*GM*, 1st ser., 84/1, 1814, 418), at Burnham, Buckinghamshire.   ELIZABETH BAIGENT

Sources *GM*, 1st ser., 84/1 (1814), 418–19 · T. Thornton, *The present state of Turkey* (1807); 2nd edn (1809) · *GM*, 2nd ser., 38 (1852), 307–8 · IGI

Thornton, Thomas (1786–1866), journalist and writer, born in London on 12 July 1786, was the son of Thomas Thornton, East India agent, and his wife, Sarah, *née* Kitchener. In early life he was employed in the custom house, and published several works dealing with East Indian trade. The first of these, *A Compendium of the Laws Recently Passed for Regulating the Trade with the East Indies*, appeared in 1814. It was followed by *The duties of customs and excise on goods … imported, and the duties, drawbacks, &c., on goods exported, brought down to August 1818* (1818) and by a supplementary edition published in the succeeding year. In 1825 he published *Oriental Commerce, or, The East Indian Trader's Complete Guide*, a geographical and statistical work originally compiled by William Milburn, an employee of the East India Company. Thornton greatly reduced the historical part of this work, but added supplementary matter.

In 1823 Thornton married Elizabeth, daughter of Habbakuk Robinson of Bagshot, Surrey, with whom he had three sons and three daughters. In 1825 their eldest son, Robinson Thornton, was born, and in this same year Thornton became connected with *The Times*, and remained a member of its staff until the year before his death. For forty years he supplied highly regarded summaries of parliamentary debates, characterized by their unfailing terseness and grasp. Between 1841 and 1850 he was engaged in recording the proceedings of the ecclesiastical and maritime courts. His *Notes of Cases*, published monthly and collected in seven volumes in 1850, came to be regarded as authoritative.

Thornton also published *A History of China … to the Treaty with Great Britain in 1842* (2 vols., 1844) and, in 1846, a *History of the Punjab and the Sikhs* (3 vols.). In 1813 he edited the *Complete Works of Thomas Otway* (3 vols.) and prefixed a short life of the dramatist.

Thornton died on 25 March 1866 at 29 Gloucester Street, Belgrave Road, London, survived by his wife and several children. His son Robinson Thornton was warden of Trinity College, Glenalmond, from 1870 to 1873, Boyle lecturer in 1881–3, and became archdeacon of Middlesex in 1893. His second son, Thomas Henry (*b.* 1832), was judge of the chief court of the Punjab and member of the legislative council of India in 1878–81. His third son, Samuel (1835–1917), was first bishop of Ballarat (1875–1900) and was vicar of Blackburn from 1901 to 1910.

G. LE G. NORGATE, rev. VICTORIA MILLAR

Sources *The Times* (27 March 1866), 1 · *The Times* (29 March 1866), 7 · *GM*, 4th ser., 1 (1866), 759–60 · Walford, *County families* · catalogue [BM] · Allibone, *Dict.* · Boase, *Mod. Eng. biog.*
Wealth at death under £8000: probate, 4 May 1866, CGPLA Eng. & Wales

Thornton [*married name* Chase], **Valerie Musgrave** (1931–1991), etcher and printmaker, was born on 13 April 1931 at 34 Eaton Square, London, the only daughter and oldest of four children of Nigel Heber Thornton (1895–1942), businessman, and his wife, Margaret Marion Gwendolen, *née* Gault (1905–1997). After serving with the Royal Engineers on the western front, where he was awarded the Croix de Guerre, her father became general manager of Shell in west Africa. Her mother was descended from Huguenots who emigrated from France to Scotland and then Ulster, and thence to Canada in 1838. These antecedents may have helped Thornton to take a non-parochial view of the world, for while all her buildings spoke eloquently of their particular place in it, they also spoke of her understanding of the great sweep of the Romanesque through medieval Europe. From a little Suffolk church to Vézelay, from Ely to Estella, she saw it plain in all its powerful variants. Having to come close to her subjects, often for days on end, made her a constant traveller. 'Their essential stillness and order', she said, was what really attracted her (private information); she also said that the drawings of them on the spot were the most creative part of her work. In contrast, back at the studio the etching was done with a happy violence.

> I feel challenged by shiny metal plates and have the feeling of wanting to destroy them in order to create something new out of them. The plates are violently and deeply etched and then scraped and burnished, this all being repeated several times for each one. In handling of the actual plate I like to use subtle and transparent colours in the printing, aiming at unity of strength and delicacy. (Thornton, unpublished autobiographical notes)

Thornton was four when a school report found her painting and modelling 'full of meaning' (private information). She was still a child when she discovered that the Winifred Nicholson paintings which her parents owned were pointing her to her own future. The broad outlook which would become such an important part of it was given an early start when she and her brothers Vernon and Adrian were evacuated to Montreal, from 1940 to 1943. In 1949 she studied in London at the Byam Shaw School of Drawing and Painting before registering at the Regent Street Polytechnic. But her real education began when she watched William Hayter's film on etching. It overwhelmed her. She would later speak of this cinematic revelation as a kind of epiphany. In 1954 she went to Paris to be taught etching by Hayter in his Atelier 17, then returned to buy her first press and to begin making a long sequence of prints, some 240 in all, of stones fashioned into walls, whether of farmyards or cathedrals it was no matter. What Thornton achieved was a picture of the handling of stone and an interpretation of the thinking and impulse which went into its practical use and into its endless possibilities as decoration. Medieval building-stone was a marriage between what could be picked up or quarried locally and what was brought to the site, often from another land. Thornton's etchings were a contemplation of what this looks like after many centuries. Abstract rubble, classic carving, the saved odds and ends from a previous house or shrine built into a later structure, and especially the life which architecture, humble or mighty, gives to stone, these were her subjects, as were all building materials. Throughout her life she travelled to where they were best set together, whether in North America or Spain, East Anglia or Wales, first to meditate on them and then to return to get them down, these exquisite or jumbled images, onto paper via the tortured metal plate. She would talk of her ideas 'stacking like aeroplanes until I can bring them down to earth to work upon' (*Essex County Standard*, 5 April 1974).

Thornton's first one-woman exhibition was at the Philadelphia Print Club, at the invitation of Bertha van Moschziska, in 1960. She later lived in New York for a few months and worked at the Pratt Graphic Art Center. In 1965 (Oliver) Michael Chase (1915–2001) gave her an exhibition at the Zwemmer Gallery, London. On 29 October the following year (the year in which he was appointed curator of the Minories, Colchester), they were married. It was an ideal partnership. He was an artist as well as a distinguished figure in the galleries world who knew her worth. They toured the Romanesque world together and he, with her agent Anthony Dawson, was able to provide all she needed for her talent to be recognized both in Britain and abroad. She was made a fellow of the Royal Society of Painter-Etchers and Engravers in 1970 and appointed to the engraving faculty of the British School at Rome in 1974. She and her husband were both Christian Scientists. Their beliefs fashioned their lives. With her they created a noticeable serenity and calm which made a balance to her restlessness as an artist. She appeared robust and strong, and liked to talk about the physical battles she had with the big printing press, but her quiet voice betrayed the religious artist who was able not only to draw but to draw out the intention behind the sacred use of stone, and to show in a unique way the hues and characteristics of the material itself. She died suddenly of an aneurysm at her home, Lower Common Farmhouse, Chelsworth, Suffolk, on 13 March 1991. She was survived by her husband. (There were no children of the marriage.) A memorial service and exhibition were held in Lichfield Cathedral on 4 July 1991. RONALD BLYTHE

Sources V. Thornton, 'Bill Hayter', *Art Monthly* (June 1988) · interview by Graham Hughes, *Arts Review* (26 March 1982) · interview by Vivienne Loomes, *Essex County Standard* (5 April 1974) · M. Chase, 'Valerie Thornton', *Printmaking Today* (1991) · V. Thornton, autobiographical notes, priv. coll. · *The Independent* (28 March 1991) · personal knowledge (2004) · private information (2004) [Michael Chase, husband; Adrian Thornton, brother]

Archives priv. coll. | SOUND BL NSA

Likenesses V. M. Thornton, self-portrait, priv. coll. · photographs, priv. coll.

Thornton, Sir William (1779?–1840), army officer, was the elder son of William Thornton of Muff, near Londonderry, and his wife, Anne, daughter of Perrott James of Magilligan. He obtained a commission as ensign in the 89th foot on 31 March 1796, and served with it in Ireland. He was promoted lieutenant in the 46th foot on 1 March 1797, and captain on 25 June 1803. Early in 1803 he had been appointed aide-de-camp to Lieutenant-General Sir James Henry Craig, then inspector-general of infantry. On Craig's appointment as commander-in-chief in the Mediterranean, Thornton accompanied him as aide-de-camp in April 1805, arriving at Malta on 18 July. On 3 November he left Malta with Craig in the expedition to Naples, to co-operate with the Russians under General Maurice Lacy; after disembarking at Castellamare, in the Bay of Naples, on 20 November, Thornton took part in the operations for the defence of the Neapolitan frontier. On 14 January 1806, the Russian troops having withdrawn to Corfu, Thornton embarked at Castellamare with the British army for Messina; after disembarkation, which did not take place until 17 February, he was busy with his general in organizing the defence of the fortress. In April Thornton returned to England with Craig, who had resigned because of ill health.

Thornton next served as aide-de-camp to Lieutenant-General Earl Ludlow, commanding the Kent military district, and on 13 November 1806 he was promoted major in the Royal York rangers. He was in temporary command of the regiment in Guernsey until August 1807; he then went to Canada as military secretary and first aide-de-camp to Craig, who had been appointed governor-in-chief and captain-general in British North America. On 28 January 1808 Thornton was promoted brevet lieutenant-colonel, and appointed inspecting field-officer of militia in Canada, in addition to his other duties. He returned to England with Craig in 1811, and on 1 August of that year was brought into the 34th foot as a lieutenant-colonel. On 23 January 1812 he was transferred from the 34th and became lieutenant-colonel commanding the Greek light infantry corps, and assistant military secretary to the commander-in-chief, the duke of York. On 25 January 1813 he was given the command of the 85th light infantry.

In July 1813 Thornton went to the Peninsula in command of the 85th, and took part in the siege of San Sebastián. He commanded the regiment at the passages of the Bidassoa, Nivelle, Nive, and Adour rivers, and in all the operations of the left wing of Wellington's army, including the siege of Bayonne.

In May 1814 Thornton embarked with the 85th at Bordeaux, and sailed in the expedition under Major-General Robert Ross for North America. He was promoted brevet colonel on 4 June 1814 for his services in the Peninsula. He landed with the expedition on 19 August at St Benedict's on the Patuxent, and was given the command of a brigade consisting of the 85th foot, the light infantry companies of the 4th, 21st, and 44th regiments, and a company of marines. The army marched on Washington by way of Nottingham and Marlborough, Thornton leading with his light brigade. On 24 August the enemy were met at Bladensburg, where they were posted in a most advantageous position on rising ground on the other side of and above the river. Thornton pushed quickly through the town, and although suffering much from the fire of the enemy's guns when crossing the bridge, he was no sooner over than, spreading out his front, he advanced to attack. He was severely wounded, and, the enemy being completely defeated, he was left at Bladensburg when the British army advanced to and entered Washington.

In reprisal for American burning of the public buildings at York (later Toronto) in April 1813, the British force on the night of 24 August burned the Washington public buildings, including the Capitol and the president's house, then withdrew on 25 August and returned to their ships. They left their wounded at Bladensburg under Commodore Burney, US Navy, who had been wounded and taken prisoner at the battle of Bladensburg, and who was given parole. It was arranged with Burney that Thornton and the other wounded should be considered prisoners of war of the Americans, and exchanged as soon as they were fit to travel. Early in October Burney himself escorted Thornton and the other prisoners in a schooner to join the British fleet in the James River, where the British army, after the failure at Baltimore and the death of Ross, had embarked.

Thornton sailed with the army on board the fleet to Jamaica, where Major-General Keane, having arrived from England with reinforcements, took command. The expedition sailed on 26 November for New Orleans, which was reached on 10 December; but it was 21 December before all the troops were landed on Pine Island in Lake Borgne. An advance guard, consisting of the 4th, 85th, and 95th regiments, was formed under Thornton's command, and, embarking in boats, proceeded up the creek Bayo de Catiline by night to within a few miles of New Orleans on its northern side, where they landed and established themselves. After repulsing a night attack with considerable loss, the advance guard was reinforced gradually by the arrival in detachments of the main body, and the whole army was in position by 25 December, when Sir Edward Michael Pakenham arrived from England and took command. After an ineffectual attack on 27 December Thornton was busy cutting a canal across the neck of land between Bayo de Catiline and the river. This was completed on 6 January 1815, when he embarked the 85th and other details, amounting to under 400 men, crossed the river on the night of 7 January and took a gallant part in the attack of 8 January, gaining on his side of the river a complete success. Storming the entrenchments, he put the enemy to flight, capturing eighteen guns and the camp of that position. In this attack he was severely wounded, and learning in the moment of his victory of the death of Pakenham and the disastrous failure of the main attack, he retired to his boats, recrossed the river, and joined the main body. The reunited army retreated to the fleet and re-embarked. Thornton was sent to England, where he arrived in March 1815. He was made a CB, military division.

On 12 August 1819 Thornton was appointed deputy adjutant-general in Ireland. He was promoted major-general on 27 May 1825, and appointed colonel of the 96th foot on 10 October 1834. He was made a KCB in September 1836, and lieutenant-general on 28 June 1838. On the death of Sir Herbert Taylor he was transferred to the colonelcy of his old regiment, the 85th light infantry, on 9 April 1839. For the last few years of his life he resided in the village of Greenford, near Hanwell, Middlesex. He became subject to delusions—that he had been accused of smuggling, and that he possessed forged banknotes—and shot himself at about seven o'clock in the morning on 6 April 1840 at his residence, Stanhope Lodge, Greenford. He was buried on the same day in Greenford churchyard. He was unmarried. The order announcing his death to the 85th stated it was 'to his unremitted zeal and noble example the regiment is principally indebted for that high character which it has ever since maintained' (*GM*, 649).

R. H. VETCH, rev. ROGER T. STEARN

Sources Burke, *Gen. GB* · War Office records, PRO · J. Philippart, ed., *The royal military calendar*, 3rd edn, 5 vols. (1820) · H. Bunbury, *Narratives of some passages in the great war with France, from 1799 to 1810* (1854) · *United Service Journal* (1840) · W. F. P. Napier, *History of the war in the Peninsula and in the south of France*, new edn, 6 vols. (1886) · *A narrative of the campaigns of the British army at Washington and New Orleans* (1826) · A. J. Guy, ed., *The road to Waterloo: the British army and the struggle against revolutionary and Napoleonic France, 1793–1815* (1990) · R. Muir, *Britain and the defeat of Napoleon, 1807–1815* (1996) · *GM*, 2nd ser., 13 (1840) · R. Horsman, *The war of 1812* (1969) · W. A. Ganoe, *The history of the United States army* (1924)
Archives NL Scot., corresp. with Sir George Brown

Thornton, William Thomas (1813–1880), economist and civil servant, born at Burnham, Buckinghamshire, on 14 February 1813, was the youngest son of the merchant Thomas *Thornton (*bap.* 1767?, *d.* 1814) and his wife, Sophie Zohrab, daughter of a Greek merchant. Having been educated at the Moravian settlement at Ockbrook in Derbyshire, he spent three years in Malta with his cousin Sir William Henry Thornton, the auditor-general. From 1830 to 1835 he was in Constantinople with consul-general Cartwright, and in August 1836 he obtained a clerkship in the East India House. Twenty years later he was put in charge of the public works department, and in 1858 became first secretary for public works to the India Office. In 1873 he was created CB on the recommendation of the duke of Argyll. In spite of weak health, he devoted the greater part of his leisure to literary work, and more especially to the study of economic issues. He was a close friend of John Stuart Mill, and one of the most able adherents of Mill's school of political economy. But he differed widely from Mill on other subjects, and the friendship was based largely on a fondness for discussion (A. Bain, *J. S. Mill*, 1882, 174). Thornton contributed to the *Examiner* of 17 May 1873 an account of Mill's work at the India House.

Thornton's first work on economics, which appeared in 1845, was *Over-Population and its Remedy*. His argument for the colonization of Irish wastes by Irish peasants was referred to in laudatory terms by Mill in his *Principles of Political Economy* (1st edn, 392). Thornton attached little value to emigration, but argued strongly in favour of the subdivision of the land and against state intervention. The work did much to confute the views of John Ramsay McCulloch as to the effect of a wider distribution of landed property on the increase of population, and challenged then current notions as to the comparative prosperity of the labouring population in medieval and Victorian times. On the latter point Thornton's work was adversely criticized (probably by Herman Merivale) in the *Edinburgh Review* of January 1847.

Thornton developed his views in more detail in *A Plea for Peasant Proprietors, with the Outlines of a Plan for their Establishment in Ireland*, published in 1848. Mill read the proofs, and the book appeared a few weeks before his *Political Economy*, on which it had an important influence (A. Bain, *J. S. Mill*, 86 n.). Thornton's book, which had gone out of print, came into request again during the discussion which attended the passing of the Irish Land Act of 1870. It was republished in 1874 with two additional chapters, one dealing with the 'Social and moral effects of peasant proprietorship' (chap. 4), and the other with 'Ireland: a forecast from 1873' (chap. 7). Thornton looked to the nationalization of the land as his ultimate ideal, but argued that the minimization of the evils of private ownership was all that was practical in the short term (chap. 7).

In 1869 Thornton published his most influential work on economics. The book, entitled *On Labour, its Wrongful Claims and Rightful Dues: its Actual Present and Possible Future*, presented critiques of both the classical approach to supply and demand theory and the wages-fund doctrine. In a review of the book in the *Fortnightly Review* in the same year, John Stuart Mill argued against most of the criticisms levelled at supply and demand theory but accepted Thornton's argument against the predetermined nature of the wages-fund doctrine. Building on this, Mill went on to criticize and recant from the wages-fund doctrine. Mill's recantation, prompted by Thornton, has come to be regarded as a significant event in the decline of classical economics and has provoked numerous interpretations. In a second edition of *On Labour*, published in 1870, Thornton attempted to rebut Mill's criticisms of his analysis of supply and demand but incorporated some of Mill's recantation arguments concerning the wages-fund doctrine into his own discussion. A German translation by Heinrich Schramm was published in 1870.

Besides his works on economics, Thornton was the author of *Old-Fashioned Ethics and Common-Sense Metaphysics*, a volume of essays published in 1873, in which the ethical and teleological views of Hume, Huxley, and the utilitarians were adversely criticized; and of *Indian Public Works and Cognate Indian Topics* (1875). In 1854 he published a poem, 'The siege of Silistria', and in 1857 a volume of verse entitled *Modern Manichaeism, Labour's Utopia, and other Poems*. In 1878 he produced *Word for Word from Horace*, a literal verse translation of the Odes. The version showed a lack of metrical grasp, but was praised by Professor Robinson Ellis for seventeenth-century quaintness.

Thornton's last publication was, perhaps fittingly, a delayed review in the *Nineteenth Century* (August 1879) of J. E. Cairnes's *Some Leading Principles of Political Economy Newly Expounded* (1874). In his volume Cairnes attempted an unsuccessful rehabilitation of the wages-fund doctrine. Once again Thornton's main point was that the wages fund was not predetermined. Thornton died at his home, 7 Cadogan Place, Sloane Street, London, on 17 June 1880. He left a son, Edward Zohrab Thornton.

G. LE G. NORGATE, rev. JOHN VINT

Sources *Men of the time* (1875), 950 • R. Ellis, 'Thornton's Word for word from Horace', *The Academy* (29 June 1878), 572 • *ILN* (26 June 1880) • *The Athenaeum* (26 June 1880), 822–3 • Allibone, *Dict.* • Boase, *Mod. Eng. biog.* • W. D. Adams, *Dictionary of English literature*, rev. edn [1879–80], 634 • R. H. I. Palgrave, ed., *Dictionary of political economy*, 3 vols. (1894–9), vol. 3, pp. 537–8 • J. Eatwell, M. Milgate, and P. Newman, eds., *The new Palgrave: a dictionary of economics*, 4 vols. (1987), vol. 4, p. 636 • T. Negishi, 'Thornton's criticism of equilibrium theory and Mill', *History of Political Economy*, 18 (1986), 567–77 • R. B. Ekelund and S. Thommesen, 'Disequilibrium theory and Thornton's assault on the laws of supply and demand', *History of Political Economy*, 21 (1989), 567–92 • J. Vint, *Capital and wages: a Lakatosian history of the wages fund doctrine* (1994)

Likenesses lithograph, NPG

Wealth at death under £8000: probate, 12 July 1880, *CGPLA Eng. & Wales*

Thornycroft, Sir (William) Hamo (1850–1925), sculptor, was born on 9 March 1850 at 39 Stanhope Street, Regent's Park, London, the sixth of the seven children of Thomas *Thornycroft (1815–1885), sculptor, and his wife, Mary *Thornycroft (1809–1895), sculptor, daughter of the sculptor John *Francis. Although Thornycroft's parents were prominent figures in mid-nineteenth-century sculpture, they were not prosperous and they sent their son at the age of four to live with Thomas's brother William, a farmer, of Gawsworth, Cheshire, where he spent the next nine years. Thornycroft was educated at Macclesfield grammar school and, after rejoining his parents, at University College School, London (1863–7). Despite his father's initial opposition, Thornycroft resolved to become a sculptor himself, and was trained in the family studio. In 1869 he enrolled at the Royal Academy Schools, London, where he was inspired by the teaching of Frederic Leighton.

In 1871 Thornycroft visited Paris, where he admired the work of François Rude and Paul Dubois, and then went to Italy, where works by Donatello and Michelangelo greatly impressed him. His sculptural career received an early boost with a commission for a bronze equestrian monument to the sixth earl of Mayo (1872–4; Old Flagstaff House, Barrackpore, India). In 1875 Thornycroft won a Royal Academy gold medal for *A Warrior Bearing a Wounded Youth from the Field of Battle* (Leighton House, London). It beat a work by his greatest contemporary, Alfred Gilbert, into second place and was praised at the 1876 Royal Academy. The Art Union commissioned a limited edition bronze statuette based on the sculpture.

Over the next ten years Thornycroft became established as Britain's leading sculptor. His work evolved from cautious Victorian classicism towards a powerful realism, the latter a key component of the emerging New Sculpture movement. The life-sized marble *Lot's Wife* (1878; Leighton House, London) convincingly portrays her transformation and reflects G. F. Watts's symbolism as well as Leighton's emphasis on careful rendering of drapery. *Artemis and her Hound* (plaster, 1880; Macclesfield town hall) combines untamed nature with visual grace. It was described by M. H. Spielmann as 'epoch-making … from every point of view the group is beautiful' (Spielmann, 39). The *Teucer*, which portrays the *Iliad* archer (bronze, 1881; Tate collection), is more stylized and archaistic. Its critical success coincided with Thornycroft's election to associate membership of the Royal Academy.

The *Mower* (1884; bronze, 1894, Walker Art Gallery, Liverpool) is widely regarded as Thornycroft's masterpiece. This life-sized portrayal of a man in working clothes is a pioneering example of modern life realism in sculpture. It

Sir (William) Hamo Thornycroft (1850–1925), by J. P. Mayall

Between 1889 and 1892 Thornycroft designed the frieze sculptures of the Institute of Chartered Accountants' (ICA) building in Moorgate Place, City of London. From the outset of the project, Thornycroft worked closely with the ICA architect, John *Belcher. Both were members of the Art Workers' Guild and in their collaboration they attempted to realize the ideals of the arts and crafts movement. The 43 metre long frieze incorporates seventy-two figures carved in high relief, representing 'all the varied interests which look to the Chartered Accountants for financial guidance and order' (Friedman and others, 7). Classicized personifications are combined with figures in modern working dress, related to the *Mower*. Among Thornycroft's assistants on the project were C. J. Allen and John Tweed, both of whom later became significant sculptors. While Thornycroft is not at his best in the frieze, the end result proved highly influential and was described by Reginald Blomfield as 'the most remarkable and successful instance of the combination of architecture and sculpture carried out in England in this century' (ibid., 1).

Related to his arts and crafts interests was Thornycroft's desire to bring sculpture within the reach of ordinary people and in this, too, he was a pioneer. He supervised the production of bronze reductions of his sculptures, including the *Teucer*, the *Mower*, and the *Gordon*, as well as works specifically intended to be statuettes, such as *Joy of Life* (1895) and *Bather* (1910). Edmund Gosse gave valuable publicity to the venture in his *Magazine of Art* article 'Sculpture in the house' (1895). This attempt to broaden public taste enjoyed limited success. Thornycroft found himself frustrated by production costs and refused to compromise on quality. The so-called *Wee Gordon* (1888), cast by A. L. Collie, did however sell well initially and led to Leighton issuing a statuette version of *The Sluggard* (1890).

Between 1899 and 1914 commissions for public monuments dominated Thornycroft's activities. These sculptures showed his qualities of realism, emotional sympathy with subject matter, and prowess in modelling. Examples include *Oliver Cromwell* (1899; houses of parliament, London), which won a grand prix for its plaster model at the 1900 Paris Exhibition; *Alfred the Great* (1900–01; The Broadway, Winchester); *John Colet* (1900–02; St Paul's School, Hammersmith); and *W. E. Gladstone* (1900–05; Strand, London). The last work was praised by Gosse for showing 'alertness and vigour and determination carried *just* over the verge of the normal' (Manning, *Marble and Bronze*, 140). The surrounding sculptures, *Courage*, *Brotherhood*, *Aspiration*, and *Education*, convincingly convey Gladstone's perceived virtues. The *Gladstone*'s success led to Thornycroft's final major commission in this genre, the memorial commemorating the first Marquess Curzon as viceroy of India (1908–13; The Maidan, Calcutta; Curzon statue now at Old Flagstaff House, Barrackpore). Surviving documentation reveals Thornycroft's 'monumental' patience in coping with—and eventually winning over—his imperious and critical sitter.

By the 1890s the imaginative fantasies and precious materials of Alfred Gilbert and George Frampton were regarded as more characteristic of the New Sculpture

originated in Thornycroft's observation of a mower resting on the Thames riverbank and was subsequently refined through drawings and sketch models into a statue shown at the 1884 Royal Academy. When exhibited, it was accompanied by lines from Matthew Arnold's elegiac poem 'Thyrsis'. Thornycroft's childhood experiences of rural Cheshire informed the work, as did his new-found political beliefs, sympathetic to the dignity of labour and socialism. Art-historical precedents influencing the *Mower* included Donatello's *David* (1434; Bargello, Florence) and the paintings of Jean-François Millet and Frederick Walker. Thornycroft followed this success with the *Sower* (1886; bronze, Kew Gardens, London), which has obvious affinities with Millet.

Thornycroft's memorials to Major-General Charles George Gordon (1885–8; Waterloo Place, London; 1887–9; Fountain Reserve, Melbourne) established him at the forefront of late Victorian portrait statuary. He followed the advice of Gordon's brother, Sir Henry Gordon, to make the statue 'as little "military" as possible' and instead stressed 'strength of mind, love, kindness, affection' (White, *Martyr General*, 15). Gordon's meditative gaze makes him the *Mower*'s kindred spirit. The pedestal reliefs in the London version (*Charity and Justice* and *Fortitude and Faith*) are deliberately blurred in their modelling, contrasting with the crisper realism of the statue itself. Following the unveiling, the *Illustrated London News* commented that the Gordon memorial should 'redeem British sculpture from the contempt which has not been altogether undeserved' (p. 7).

than the work of Thornycroft. To some extent he suffered for his restraint, Spielmann observing in 1901, 'One rarely looks at the work of Mr Thornycroft without feeling that he belongs to the classic school more nearly than perhaps any other sculptor of the day' (Spielmann, 44). He remained prolific and productive until the outbreak of the First World War. Although his late work, such as the life-sized marble *The Kiss* (Tate collection), is described by Susan Beattie as 'bland and trivialised', it was perceived very differently at the 1916 Royal Academy (Beattie, 251). In the carving, Thornycroft reveals awareness of Auguste Rodin's *The Kiss* (1898; example, Musée Rodin, Paris). Thornycroft distinguished Rodin's 'genius' in modelling from his fragmented sculptures which 'appealed to our primeval and animal passions' (Manning, *Marble and Bronze*, 181). He loathed the self-conscious modernism of Jacob Epstein, and in one of his last letters he upbraided Gosse for being 'noncommittal' and 'not altogether against' the monument to W. H. Hudson (1925; Hyde Park, London) (Stocker, 297).

Thornycroft was elected to full membership of the Royal Academy in 1888, he was knighted in 1917, and in 1924 he was the first recipient of the Royal Society of British Sculptors' gold medal. According to Gosse, Thornycroft was 'very fine looking, extremely powerful in frame, curly, golden-red haired' (Thwaite, 192). The friendship between the two men was intimate and productive. Not only did Gosse influence Thornycroft's sculptures of the early 1880s, but Thornycroft in turn stimulated Gosse's critical writings on the New Sculpture, which long remained the definitive statement on the subject. Thornycroft's marriage in 1884 to Agatha Cox (1864–1958) was a happy one. He died at the Acland Home in St Giles', Oxford, on 18 December 1925, and was buried in Wolvercote church, Oxfordshire. He was survived by his widow and their four children.

Thornycroft's archive, in the Henry Moore Institute, Leeds, comprises an extensive collection of his correspondence, diaries, drawings, and sketchbooks. It provided the basis for Elfrida Manning's biography of her father, *Marble and Bronze: the Art and Life of Hamo Thornycroft* (1982), which coincided with a retrospective exhibition at Leeds City Art Gallery. Sensible, sensitive, liberal, and loyal in character, Thornycroft was befriended by many notable figures in the arts, including Watts, Leighton, Alfred Waterhouse, John Addington Symonds, Thomas Hardy, and his nephew Siegfried Sassoon. Thornycroft's studio assistants included Allen, Tweed, Henry Pegram, Charles Hartwell, and Allan Gairdner Wyon; many more artists were taught by him at the Royal Academy between 1882 and 1914. The assertion by Spielmann that 'he must be recognised as in the very forefront with the finest sculptors England has produced' is too easily forgotten (Spielmann, 45). Thornycroft's contribution to the New Sculpture was certainly far more consistent and sustained than that of the brilliant but erratic Gilbert.

MARK STOCKER

Sources E. Manning, *Marble and bronze: the art and life of Hamo Thornycroft* (1982) · A. White, *Hamo Thornycroft and the martyr general* (1991) · T. Friedman and others, eds., *The alliance of sculpture and architecture: Hamo Thornycroft, John Belcher, and the Institute of Chartered Accountants building* (1993) [exhibition catalogue, Heinz Gallery, RIBA, London, 14 Jan – 20 Feb 1993] · T. Friedman, '"Demi-gods in corduroy": Hamo Thornycroft's statue of *The Mower*', *Sculpture Journal*, 3 (1999), 74–86 · A. White, *Hamo Thornycroft: the sculptor at work* (1983) · M. H. Spielmann, *British sculpture and sculptors of to-day* (1901) · M. Stocker, 'Edmund Gosse on sculpture', *University of Leeds Review*, 28 (1985–6), 283–310 · S. Beattie, *The New Sculpture* (1983) · E. Gosse, 'The new sculpture, 1879–1894 [pts 1–3]', *Art Journal*, new ser., 14 (1894), 138–42, 200–03, 277–82 · B. Read, *Victorian sculpture* (1982) · A. Thwaite, *Edmund Gosse: a literary landscape, 1849–1928* (1984) · E. Manning, 'Thornycroft, Sir (William) Hamo', *The dictionary of art*, ed. J. Turner (1996) · CGPLA Eng. & Wales (1926)

Archives Centre for the Study of Sculpture, Leeds, Henry Moore Institute, corresp., journals, papers, and sketchbooks · PRO, papers, Work 20/100, 20/115 | BL, corresp. with Lord Gladstone, Add. MSS 46055–46056 · CUL, letters to Siegfried Sassoon · CUL, letters to Sir George Stokes and J. Larmor · JRL, letters to M. H. Spielmann · NL Scot., corresp. with Lord Rosebery · PRO, papers relating to Gordon memorial, Work 20/50 · RA, letters to the Royal Academy · State Library of Victoria, Melbourne, Gordon Memorial Fund minute book · U. Leeds, letters to Sir Edmund Gosse

Likenesses T. B. Wirgman, pen-and-ink drawing, 1880 (*Hanging Committee, Royal Academy, 1892*), NPG · T. B. Wirgman, oils, 1884, Aberdeen Art Gallery · H. Thornycroft, portrait, 1892, Institute of Chartered Accountants, London · photograph, *c.*1914, NPG · W. Stoneman, photograph, 1917, NPG · R. Cleaver, pen-and-ink caricature, NPG · Done & Ball, cabinet photographs, NPG · F. W. Edwards, cabinet photographs, NPG · attrib. F. W. Edwards, photograph, repro. in White, *Hamo Thornycroft and the martyr general* · Maull & Fox, cabinet photographs, NPG · J. P. Mayall, photogravure, NPG [*see illus.*] · R. W. Robinson, photograph, NPG; repro. in R. W. Robinson, *Members and Associates of the Royal Academy of Arts, 1891* (1892) · Spy [L. Ward], caricature, watercolour study, NPG; repro. in *VF* (20 Feb 1892)

Wealth at death £24,903 2s.: probate, 24 Feb 1926, CGPLA Eng. & Wales

Thornycroft, Sir John Isaac (1843–1928), naval architect, was born in Rome, Italy, on 1 February 1843, the elder son of Thomas *Thornycroft (1815–1885) and his wife, Mary *Thornycroft (1809–1895), daughter of John *Francis (1780–1861). His father, his mother, and her father were all sculptors, as was his younger brother, Sir William Hamo *Thornycroft (1850–1925). His father was also an amateur engineer, and it was in his studio, a workshop furnished with model engines and railways, that John's career began.

After making smaller craft Thornycroft constructed the *Nautilus*, a steam launch which was the first that was able to keep pace with the crews in the university boat race of 1862. Shortly after this success his father sent him to work as a draughtsman with Palmer's Shipbuilding Company at Jarrow and thence to Glasgow University, where he studied natural philosophy and engineering under Sir William Thomson (afterwards Lord Kelvin) and Professor MacQuorn Rankine and obtained a certificate in engineering science. He then worked for some time in the drawing office of Randolph, Elder & Co. at Fairfield, Govan, near Glasgow.

In 1866 his father assisted Thornycroft to establish at Chiswick the shipyard which later became noted for the production of high-speed launches and torpedo craft. Between 1866 and 1870 he also studied at the Royal School

Sir John Isaac Thornycroft (1843–1928), by Sir William Hamo Thornycroft, 1918

vessels navigating shallow rivers—devices which were successfully employed in 1875 in a twin-screw launch built for Sir John Fowler to navigate the Nile, and in five river gunboats which he was commissioned to build in 1885 for the Gordon relief expedition.

Thornycroft also improved the type of boiler employed in torpedo craft. He soon recognized that the locomotive type would not stand the high rate of forcing to which it was subjected in these vessels, and turned his attention to boilers of the water-tube type. The *Ariete*, a torpedo boat which he built for Spain in 1887, held the record for speed at the time, developing over 26 knots. Ultimately he evolved a light, fast-running reciprocating engine of the triple expansion type, which was adopted in a large number of torpedo craft, but eventually was superseded by the Parsons turbine. Thornycroft was one of the civilian members of the famous Admiralty committee of design, appointed at the instance of Admiral Fisher in December 1904, which recommended the adoption of the Parsons turbine for the dreadnought class of battleship and for new destroyers.

During the 1890s Thornycroft had taken an interest in motor vehicles, developing steam-powered vans which were first built at the Homefield works near the Chiswick shipyard and later at Basingstoke. After 1902 the company turned away from steam and adopted the internal combustion engine. 'Pleasure cars' were produced between 1903 and 1912, but then the company decided to concentrate on commercial vehicles alone.

Thornycroft's partner, John Donaldson, died in 1899, and his executors pressed Thornycroft to fulfil his obligation to buy Donaldson's share of the business. He did not have the money, and it became necessary to convert the private firm into a public company and bring in outside capital. This was chiefly provided by the Scottish industrialist William *Beardmore (1856–1936), and the new public company, John I. Thornycroft & Co. Ltd, was registered in 1901. Beardmore had hoped to make the shipbuilding firm a tied customer for the products of his iron and steel works and to benefit from the firm's commercial vehicle experience so as to expand the infant Scottish motor industry. In both hopes he was to be largely disappointed. By 1904 Beardmore had lost interest in Thornycroft's company and from then onwards the firm was largely run by Thornycroft's eldest son, John Edward, who oversaw the removal of the shipyard from Chiswick to Woolston in Southampton, a move made necessary by the increasing size of torpedo boats and destroyers.

Thornycroft's health was not good, and he now retired to Bembridge on the Isle of Wight. He continued to design and experiment, and his last major contribution to naval architecture was during the First World War. Thornycroft had taken out patents for surface-skimming craft back in the 1870s, but the engines of the time had been too heavy to make his designs a reality. However, with the development of the light internal combustion engine, he revived his ideas and worked on surface-skimming designs in his test tank at Bembridge. He was assisted by his eldest

of Naval Architecture and Marine Engineering at South Kensington, where he was a contemporary of Philip Watts. Thornycroft married Blanche, daughter of Frederick Coules of Gloucester, in 1870; they had two sons and five daughters.

In 1872 John Donaldson, who had been an engineer in the public works department of India, became Thornycroft's partner in the shipyard, and also married his sister, Frances Sarah. Thornycroft subsequently devoted most of his attention to design, and his partner to administration. In 1870 the torpedo invented by Robert Whitehead was adopted in the Royal Navy, and it was realized that to make it effective a fast launch was needed to carry it. In 1873 Thornycroft built the *Gitana*, constructed for the Norwegian government, which was said to have reached 20.8 knots with engines of 458 hp. This boat, being fitted with a spar torpedo, was in fact the first torpedo boat. She had also a closed stokehold system of forced draught, and served as a model for the first torpedo boat of the British navy, the *Lightning*, built by Thornycroft in 1877, which, however, was furnished with a revolving torpedo tube. In the succeeding years he turned out large numbers of torpedo boats, and when in 1892 torpedo-boat destroyers were introduced he was commissioned to build the *Daring* and the *Decoy*, two of the first four vessels of this class.

During this period Thornycroft's vessels showed rapid improvement, owing to his continual experiments with hull form and propeller design. He introduced the flat, wide form of stern at the waterline to prevent 'squatting', with the propeller shaft at downward inclination, and wing-rudders on each side of the stern. He was the first to carry out experiments with screw propellers, measuring simultaneously the thrust, power transmitted, and speed. He took out patents for improvements in turbine screw propellers and for the tunnel form of stern for high-speed daughter, Blanche, who was one of the first women to become a member of the Institution of Naval Architects. Thornycroft developed the 'single-step' hull form for surface-skimming, later adapted for fast naval craft, racing boats, and seaplanes.

In 1916 the Admiralty wanted a design for a fast launch that could skim safely over minefields and carry a torpedo. Using his design, Thornycroft's firm built such craft, known as coastal motor boats (CMBs), in great secrecy at Hampton on the Thames. Although never used to attack the German fleet in its anchorages, the CMBs did take part in the raids on Zeebrugge and Ostend in 1918, and scored notable successes against the Bolshevik fleet in the Gulf of Finland in 1919.

Thornycroft was elected a fellow of the Royal Society in 1893, and received the honorary degree of LLD from Glasgow University in 1901. He was knighted in 1902. He served on the council of the Institution of Naval Architects from 1881 and on the council of the Institution of Civil Engineers from 1899 to 1908. Thornycroft died of myocardial degeneration at Steyne, near Bembridge, Isle of Wight, on 28 June 1928; he was buried at Bembridge. His elder son, John Edward Thornycroft, succeeded as head of the firm.

E. I. CARLYLE, rev. ALAN G. JAMIESON

Mary Thornycroft (1809–1895), by Roger Fenton, c.1855 [with her statue of Princess Helena]

Sources K. C. Barnaby, *100 years of specialized shipbuilding and engineering* (1964) · P. Banbury, *Shipbuilders of the Thames and Medway* (1971) · S. Pollard and P. Robertson, *The British shipbuilding industry, 1870–1914* (1979) · J. R. Hume and M. S. Moss, *Beardmore: the history of a Scottish industrial giant* (1979) · A. G. Jamieson, 'Thornycroft, Sir John Isaac', *DBB* · *The Times* (29 June 1928) · *Transactions of the Institution of Naval Architects*, 70 (1928) · E. H. T. d'E. [E. H. Tennyson d'Eyncourt], *PRS*, 121A (1928), xxv–xxxvii · *PICE*, 140 (1899–1900) · *PICE*, 227 (1928–9), 275–9 · E. Manning, *Bronze and steel: the life of Thomas Thornycroft, sculptor and engineer* (1932) · P. Watts, *Encyclopaedia Britannica*, 11th edn (1910–11), vol. 24, pp. 915–16 · d. cert. · *CGPLA Eng. & Wales* (1928)

Archives NMM · Southampton City RO

Likenesses A. J. Nowell, oils, exh. RA 1905, Institution of Mechanical Engineers, London · W. H. Thornycroft, marble bust, 1918, NPG [*see illus.*] · Spy [L. Ward], caricature, chromolithograph, NPG; repro. in *VF* (19 Jan 1905) · portrait, repro. in *Royal Academy Pictures* (1919) · portrait, repro. in *Transactions of the Institution of Naval Architects*

Wealth at death £151,029 17s. 10d.: probate, 28 Aug 1928, *CGPLA Eng. & Wales*

Thornycroft [née Francis], **Mary** (1809–1895), sculptor, born at Thornham, Norfolk, and baptized on 24 December 1809 at Redruth, Cornwall, was the third daughter of the four children of John *Francis (1780–1861), sculptor, and his wife, Mary (née Nelson?), though she told her husband and children that she was born in 1814. In 1823 the Francis family settled at 56 Albany Street in London, where John Francis ran a sculpture studio with assistants and pupils, among them his daughter, Mary. In 1835 Mary Francis made her début at the Royal Academy with her *Bust of a Gentleman*. In the same year Thomas *Thornycroft (1815–1885) of Chiswick, Middlesex, came to the Albany Street household and studio to be apprenticed to John Francis. Five years later, on 29 February 1840, he married Mary. Of their six surviving children, four studied at the Royal

Academy Schools: Sir (William) Hamo *Thornycroft (1850–1925) became a sculptor and member of the Royal Academy, (Mary) Alyce Thornycroft (1844–1906) was a sculptor and painter, and Helen Thornycroft (1848–1937) and Theresa Thornycroft (1853–1947) were both painters. The first-born son, Sir John Isaac *Thornycroft (1843–1928), became a naval architect, and Frances (Fanny) Thornycroft (1846–1929) married John Donaldson of her brother's engineering firm. Both Fanny and Hamo had children and grandchildren who became artists as well.

Ideal works of children and portraits in a neo-classically inspired, Romantic style predominate in Mary Thornycroft's œuvre. She exhibited regularly at both the Royal Academy (1835–77) and the British Institution (1845–64) but is best-known for her work for the royal family. Her works in the Royal Collection exemplify the salient features of her style: a highly naturalistic rendering of human form and movement with crisp and detailed carving of surfaces. Her works are by no means radical or unusual for her period, but they manifest a virtuosity in modelling, proportion, and design which is strikingly successful in reconciling the sometimes conflicting nineteenth-century allegiances to classicism and naturalism. Although consistent with the idealizing tendencies of sculpture in the period, her portraits retain a high degree of likeness, as seen, for example, in her bust of *Mary, Duchess of Gloucester* (1852, Royal Collection, Frogmore House, Windsor). Her allegorical statues of the royal children are similarly closely observed and modelled in an unobtrusive style which manages to be both realistic and ideal.

Some accounts credit the sculptor John Gibson with launching Mary Thornycroft's career as a court sculptor by recommending her to produce portrait statues of the royal children. However, Mary's father had established a connection with Queen Victoria when he was commissioned to sculpt a bust of her about 1838, and Mary herself had already achieved critical acclaim in 1838–40 for her ideal marble *Orphan Flower Girl*, exhibited at the Royal Academy and the British Institution (called *Orphan Girl* when exhibited in plaster initially at the RA in 1838). Thus, she may have been known to the queen and Prince Albert as a sculptor of children before she and her husband became friendly with Gibson during their sojourn in Rome from 2 December 1842 to 26 April 1843. While in Rome, having left their first-born child, Ann (1841–1858), in the care of Thomas's mother in England, Mary Thornycroft not only gave birth to her second child, John, on 1 February 1843, but also sculpted a marble statue of a sleeping child watched over by a spaniel (priv. coll.)—another work which could have recommended her ability to portraying children to Gibson.

Mary Thornycroft's first work for the royal family was a statue of Princess Alice in 1845, which the sculptor soon adapted for an allegorical series, produced between 1846 and 1848, representing the eldest royal children as the four seasons. Various versions of these figures were produced in marble, bronze, and statuary porcelain for the royal collections at Osborne House and Buckingham Palace (exh. RA, 1850; British Institution, 1851; Great Exhibition, London, 1851). Further marble statues for Osborne House of Princess Helena as *Peace* (1856), Princess Louise as *Plenty* (1856), *Princess Beatrice in a Nautilus Shell* (1858), the prince of Wales as a hunter (1860), and Prince Leopold as a fisher (1860) followed, as well as numerous busts and statues of four generations of the royal family. Many of these were reviewed in the *Art Journal*, accompanied by engraved reproductions. Reduced-scale Parian versions of her bust of Alexandra, princess of Wales, were Art Union of London prizes in 1863–4. From this same period came her *Skipping Girl*, shown at the Paris Exhibition in 1855 (exh. RA, 1856 and 1867; British Institution, 1857; Parian version exh. Universal International Exhibition, London, 1862; Osborne House, Isle of Wight), and reportedly praised by the Danish sculptor J. A. Jerichau as 'one of six of the finest statues in the world' for its precisely balanced, light, and energetic rendering of the child in mid-skip (*The Queen*, 16 Feb 1895). Tragedy followed shortly thereafter, however, when in 1858 her daughter Ann died of tuberculosis; *Jephthah's Daughter* (exh. British Institution, 1858), sculpted in that year, was perhaps the artist's response to her loss.

Mary Thornycroft's steady income from portrait and royal commissions was the mainstay of the Thornycroft family, as Thomas did not enjoy such regular demand for his sculpture. Professional insecurity seems to have incited Thomas in letters to his patron, W. B. Dickinson, to promote his role in the production of Mary's works to the point of implying his own authorship of them. Their granddaughter, Mary Donaldson, recounts that Thomas Thornycroft had been known to cut the heads off Mary's clay models, ostensibly to position them better, but provoking exasperated cries of 'Only *tell* me! Thorny, only *tell* me!' from his wife as she tried to protect her works (Manning, *Bronze and Steel*, 51–2). The Thornycrofts did, however, collaborate on large sculptural projects. Thomas Thornycroft did much of the carving of the numerous works and replicas ordered from Mary's royal commissions; he wrote in 1861 that: 'We have executed in Bronze or Marble for the Queen not less than thirty original works not counting minor commissions of copies in plaster' (Thomas Thornycroft MSS, letter TTC161). Together the couple produced the funerary portrait of the child John Hamilton-Martin (d. 1851), completed in 1857 for Ledbury church in Herefordshire, and there is some suggestion that they collaborated on the statues of James I and Charles I for the houses of parliament (now in the central criminal court of the Old Bailey). Later the entire Thornycroft coterie participated in realizing two of Thomas's major works: *The Poet's Fountain* (1871–5, formerly Park Lane, London; destroyed) and the *Boadicea* group (begun 1856; erected 1902, Westminster Bridge, London).

Mary Thornycroft's letters to her children are replete with words of encouragement for their artistic careers. In addition to teaching her children, she was engaged by Queen Victoria to instruct the royal princesses in modelling; of them, Princess Louise went on to work as a sculptor in her own right. After a short illness, Mary Thornycroft died on 1 February 1895 and was buried in Chiswick churchyard at her husband's side as she requested, 'within sound of the hammers' (Manning, *Bronze and Steel*, 70). NANCY PROCTOR

Sources E. Manning, *Bronze and steel: the life of Thomas Thornycroft, sculptor and engineer* (1932) · P. McCracken, 'Sculptor Mary Thornycroft and her artist children', *Women's Art Journal* (1996–7), 3–8 · E. Manning, *Marble and bronze: the art and life of Hamo Thornycroft* (1982) · F. G. Stephens, 'The late Mrs Mary Thornycroft', *Magazine of Art*, 18 (1894–5), 305–7 · R. Gunnis, *Dictionary of British sculptors, 1660–1851*, new edn (1968) · 'The late Mrs Mary Thornycroft', *The Queen* (16 Feb 1895) · E. I. Barrington, *The Spectator* (23 Feb 1895) · 'The work of the Thornycrofts', *The Sculptor*, 1/2 (April 1898), 29–30 · *Art Journal*, 11–42; new ser., 1–15 (1849–95) · *The Athenaeum* (27 May 1848), 536 · C. E. Clement and L. Hutton, *Artists of the nineteenth century and their works: a handbook containing two thousand and fifty biographical sketches*, 2 vols. in 1 (Boston, MA, 1893) · C. E. Clement, *Women in the fine arts* (1904); repr. (1974) · P. Dunford, *A biographical dictionary of women artists in Europe and America since 1850* (1990) · Graves, *RA exhibitors* · Graves, *Artists* · *The illustrated exhibitor of the Great Exhibition of the industry of all nations, 1851* (c.1851) · C. H. Gibbs-Smith, *The Great Exhibition of 1851* (1981) · 'Mothers of celebrated men', *The Lady's Realm* (Oct 1897) · N. Penny, *Church monuments in Romantic England* (1977) · *Herefordshire*, Pevsner (1963) · P. G. Nunn, *Victorian women artists* (1987) · Henry Moore Institute, Leeds, Centre for Sculpture Studies, Thomas Thornycroft MSS · Bénézit, *Dict.* · Thieme & Becker, *Allgemeines Lexikon* · IGI

Archives Courtauld Inst., Conway Library · Henry Moore Institute, Leeds, Centre for the Study of Sculpture

Likenesses R. Fenton, photograph, c.1855, Henry Moore Institute, Leeds, Centre for Sculpture Studies, Thornycroft archives [*see illus.*] · M. A. Thornycroft, bronze bust, c.1892, NPG · H. Thornycroft, bust, repro. in Stephens, 'The late Mrs Mary Thornycroft', 305 · photograph, repro. in McCracken, 'Sculptor Mary Thornycroft and her artist children', 5 · photograph, repro. in Stephens,

'The late Mrs Mary Thornycroft', 305 · photographs, repro. in Manning and Read, *Marble and bronze*, 31, 50

Thornycroft, Thomas (1815–1885), sculptor, was born in Great Tidnock, near Gawsworth, Cheshire, on 19 May 1815 and baptized on 16 June 1816 in Gawsworth church, the eldest of three sons of John Thornycroft (1791–1822), a farmer, and his wife, Ann Cheetham (1795–1875), who also came from a farming background. Thornycroft was educated at Congleton grammar school. After a brief apprenticeship to a surgeon, in 1835 he went to London, where he spent four years as a studio assistant to the sculptor John *Francis. On 29 February 1840 Thornycroft married at the Old Church, St Pancras, Francis's daughter, Mary (1809–1895) [*see* Thornycroft, Mary], a fellow sculptor. Following a visit to Italy (1842–3), the Thornycrofts returned to London, where they established a studio near Regent's Park.

Through the recommendation of John Gibson, Mary Thornycroft received commissions for portrait busts and statuettes of the children of Queen Victoria and Prince Albert. The royal couple admired Thomas Thornycroft's over-life-sized plaster equestrian statue of Queen Victoria, shown at the Great Exhibition in 1851. Thornycroft portrayed the queen wearing a close-fitting riding habit and gave her horse a jaunty gait. While the statue's informal realism drew mixed critical reactions, it contrasted refreshingly with the more dignified, iconic images usually accorded to monarchs. Thornycroft was subsequently commissioned by the Art Union to produce fifty bronze statuettes, several of which he cast in his studio, and in 1868 he executed a full-sized version for Liverpool town council (St George's Hall, Liverpool). Thornycroft's accompanying memorial statue of Prince Albert, commissioned in 1862, stands near by; there are similar versions in Halifax (1864) and Wolverhampton (1866).

Although Thornycroft was now established as a leading English sculptor, few major commissions were forthcoming. In 1857 he was placed joint fifth in the competition for the Wellington memorial at St Paul's Cathedral. Ten years later he was commissioned to carve the marble group representing *Commerce* for the Royal Albert Memorial (Kensington Gardens, London), a competent, if mundane, Victorian allegory. From the mid-1850s onwards Thornycroft's sculptural ambitions focused on the monumental equestrian group *Boadicea and her Daughters* (Westminster Bridge, London). Although Prince Albert warmly supported the idea, the monument was not cast in bronze until 1902, seventeen years after Thornycroft's death. Its erection was made possible by the donation of the plaster model and £1500 by his son, the marine engineer Sir John *Thornycroft.

In his later years Thornycroft devoted little attention to sculpture and more towards assisting his son John with designs for steam launches. One of his last works, the *Poets' Fountain*, near Hyde Park Corner, London (1875, destr. 1947), was jointly executed with Mary and another son, (William) Hamo *Thornycroft. Photographs of it indicate an incongruous amalgam of high Victorian realism and the elegance of Hamo Thornycroft's New Sculpture. More successful is the charming, if sentimental, memorial to

Thomas Thornycroft (1815–1885), by Roger Fenton, c.1855 [with his statuette of Queen Victoria, c.1853]

John Hamilton-Martin (1857; St Michael's, Ledbury, Herefordshire). It is signed by both Thomas and Mary Thornycroft; the latter carved the effigy which, following the tradition of Thomas Banks and Francis Chantrey, portrays the child not dead, but sleeping.

Although the Thornycrofts' marriage was a happy one, Mary's more sustained and distinctive talent aroused her husband's periodic jealousy. Thomas Thornycroft died at Brenchley, Kent, on 30 August 1885, survived by his wife and six of their seven children. He was buried in Chiswick Old Church, Middlesex. His correspondence (Henry Moore Institute, Leeds) indicates a man of lively intelligence and inventiveness who practised sculpture during a creatively bleak era, caught between the neo-classicism of Gibson and the 'renaissance' of the New Sculpture. Further examples of his work are in the Old Bailey and Westminster Abbey, London. MARK STOCKER

Sources E. Manning, *Marble and bronze: the art and life of Hamo Thornycroft* (1982) · B. Read, *Victorian sculpture* (1982) · R. Gunnis, *Dictionary of British sculptors, 1660–1851* (1953); new edn (1968) · *DNB* · J. Blackwood, *London's immortals: the complete outdoor commemorative statues* (1989) · J. Physick, *The Wellington monument* (1970) · P. Curtis, ed., *Patronage and practice: sculpture on Merseyside* (1989) · J. Darke, *The monument guide to England and Wales* (1991) · S. Bayley, *The Albert Memorial: the monument in its social and architectural context* (1981) · E. Darby and N. Smith, *The cult of the prince consort* (1983) · *The Times* (4 Sept 1885) · N. Penny, *Church monuments in Romantic England* (1977) · Graves, *RA exhibitors* · E. Manning, *Bronze and steel: the life of Thomas Thornycroft, sculptor and engineer* (1932) · *CGPLA Eng. & Wales* (1885)

Archives Henry Moore Institute, Leeds, papers

Likenesses M. Thornycroft, marble bust, c.1840, repro. in Manning, *Marble and bronze* · R. Fenton, photograph, c.1855, Henry Moore Institute, Leeds [see illus.] · photograph, c.1855, repro. in Manning, *Marble and bronze* · photograph, c.1870–1875, repro. in Manning, *Marble and bronze* · E. Edwards, photograph, NPG; repro.

in L. Reeve, ed., *Portraits of men of eminence*, 2 (1864) · engraving, repro. in Blackwood, *London's immortals* [for *The Graphic*, c.1885–6] **Wealth at death** £11,046 3s. 3d.: probate, 23 Dec 1885, *CGPLA Eng. & Wales*

Thorold [Turold] (*fl. c.*1100), supposed author of the *Chanson de Roland*, bore a common Norman name which appears as Turoldus in the concluding line (*explicit*) of the oldest copy of the *Chanson de Roland* (Bodl. Oxf., MS Digby 23; 1125–40, or 1150–70) and as Turold in the Bayeux tapestry. Every word of the line 'Ci falt la geste que Turoldus declinet' bears multiple meanings and the ambiguity of the line is irreducible. 'Turoldus' may indicate the author of the *Chanson de Roland* (at an indeterminate stage in its evolution), a redactor, the scribe of the Digby copy, or the performer of the work. *Declinet* may mean 'recites', 'composes', 'copies', and 'grows weak'. *Ci falt* suggests 'here [spatial or temporal] ends', with or without the sense of completion. The *geste* might refer to subject matter of the poem, the poet's written source, or possibly the performance. Even the simple word *que* is equivocal, functioning either as a relative pronoun object or as a causal conjunction ('for'). Any attempt to identify Turoldus is therefore arbitrary, whether consideration is given to Thorold, abbot of Peterborough (*d.* 1098), or Thorold of Envermeu, bishop of Bayeux (1097–1104) and subsequently a monk at Bec. In the case of the Bayeux tapestry the critical issue is whether the name Turold refers to a messenger (one of two speaking with Gui de Ponthieu) or the small-scale figure of the *jongleur* who, to the right, holds the bridle of one of the messengers' horses. The latter hypothesis has found recent support.   TONY HUNT

Sources T. A. Jenkins, *La chanson de Roland: Oxford version* (1924), xlvi–lxv · P. Aebischer, *Préhistoire et protohistoire du 'Roland' d'Oxford* (1972), 203–34 · M. de Riquer, *Les chansons de geste françaises* (1957), 105–16 · P. E. Bennett, 'Encore Turold dans la tapisserie de Bayeux', *Annales de Normandie*, 30 (1980), 3–13
Likenesses embroidery (Bayeux Tapestry), Bayeux, France [*see illus.*]

Thorold family (*per. c.*1492–1717), gentry, is recorded from 1368 onwards as holding property in Marston and nearby villages north of Grantham, Lincolnshire, near the county's boundaries with Nottinghamshire.

Rise to prominence The first member of the family to achieve standing outside as well as within Lincolnshire was **William Thorold** (*b.* in or before 1492, *d.* 1569) of Marston and Hougham, who purchased the manor of Blankney. He may have been the first member of the family to have London connections, for he became a merchant of the staple, and his name appears, for the years 1559 and 1560, on a long list of merchants who received pardons for contravening a statute of Edward VI when shipping wool to Bruges. But he used his wealth to accumulate property in his home county. Like many others he acquired former monastic lands, notably in 1544, when he secured confirmation to himself and his second wife of his purchase of half of the site of the former Gilbertine priory of Haverholme, and of two of its manors, from a vendor who undertook to convey the other half to the Thorolds as well. A JP for Kesteven in 1543, he was a commissioner of

Thorold (*fl. c.*1100), embroidery (Bayeux Tapestry) [standing, right, at the horse's head]

sewers there a year later, while in 1558–9 he was sheriff of Lincolnshire. When he died, on 20 November 1569, William Thorold was possessed of ten full manors and of properties and rents in some twenty-five other villages: he also held the full advowsons of three parish churches and fractions of two more. He was buried in Marston church, where his memorial survives.

William Thorold married twice. With his first wife, Dorothy, daughter of Thomas Leke of Halloughton, Nottinghamshire, he had four sons and a daughter, and with his second, Margaret Sutton (*née* Hussey), he had two sons. The younger sons of both marriages founded successful gentry families, while the Marston line continued with the eldest son by the first marriage, **Sir Anthony Thorold** (*b.* in or before 1520, *d.* 1594), who was the first member of his family to play a part in national as well as local affairs. In large measure this was due to his also being the first Thorold to have trained in the law: he was admitted in 1537 to Gray's Inn, where he was an ancient in 1547 and a reader in 1555. By the 1550s he was acting on government commissions, while soon after 1550 he became recorder of Grantham, an office he probably held until his death. His upward progress was much helped by his close links with another rising family: the Manners, earls of Rutland. The second earl supported Thorold's candidacy for Grantham in the parliament of 1558. He was duly elected. A year later conflict erupted over both the election of an MP and the appointment of a recorder for the city of Lincoln. When the writ for the parliamentary election reached Lincoln, George St Paul, the former MP who was also recorder, was dying, and before the election could take place he had died. The corporation decided to return Rutland's nominee Robert Ferrers, and with him Robert Monson, whom they probably intended to make their new recorder, as the other member. Then Rutland intervened to impose on the corporation his protégé Anthony Thorold. There was no instant submission, however, and Monson was chosen as recorder at 40s. a year for life. But Thorold, doubtless backed by the earl, promptly counter-attacked and on 16 January 1559 obtained the recordership for life at £4 per annum. He was described as 'learned in the law', although there is no evidence that he was ever called to the bar. In 1570 he resigned the recordership in favour of Monson, whom the city had retained in the meantime.

Having thus gained the recordership, Thorold was then elected MP for Lincoln in the 1559 parliament, in which, however, he played no active part. Indeed, that was the end of his parliamentary career, but he remained active not only in the county but also as the attorney to the council of the north. No doubt it helped him that he was considered reliable in religion, being described as 'earnest' in 1564 in a report to the council by Bishop Bullingham of Lincoln; his father, by contrast, was named as a 'hinderer'. In 1566 both Sir William Cecil and Archbishop Thomas Young of York urged him to become a full member of the council, but he pleaded that he was 'unworthy' and 'unfit'. In 1570 he said he was too sick to continue as attorney, but perhaps this was a diplomatic illness, as in the previous year he had inherited his father's estates and so could live quietly as a country gentleman. In fact he continued to receive appointments and commissions. He was made a commissioner for ecclesiastical causes in the dioceses of Lincoln and Peterborough in 1571, and for Lincoln alone in 1575. He was sheriff of Lincolnshire in 1571–2 and a deputy lieutenant by 1584, when he helped to organize the city's muster. He was knighted in 1585.

Occupations and offices Although Sir Anthony Thorold rebuilt Marston Hall, as a large H-shaped structure (it was substantially remodelled in the early eighteenth century), his main source of delight was not building but coursing. He wrote to the third earl of Rutland on 28 October 1575 that his dogs were unexercised as he had been unable to leave his house for a fortnight, but that he would come to Belvoir the following day; however, he also expressed the wish that the meeting might be deferred until a week or two later, when 'the hares would be better and the dogs would be set in breath so we might see some trial of our dogs'. He remained in good health and spirits well into his sixties. In 1582 he fell out with his neighbour Arthur Hall over the election of a new alderman for Grantham. Thorold, who was still the town's recorder, was now too old for Hall to make 'any convenient challenge to him', but this

did not stop him assembling a large number of his servants at the hiring fair at Billington, near Marston, claiming that Hall intended to 'pluck him out of his house perforce or fire it on his head'. The privy council demanded an investigation, which was eventually made by the third earl of Rutland. The earl's uncle Roger Manners commented drily on 29 November 1582 that 'I am glad to hear that Mr Thorold in his old age is becoming so lively that he is charged with making a riot or unlawful assembly' (HoP, *Commons, 1558–1603*, 3.488–9).

Sir Anthony Thorold made his will on 11 April 1594, making arrangements for the running of his farms and leaving bequests to his daughters. His servants were to receive a year's wages, and he left small sums to the poor of fifteen parishes near Marston. On 17 May he made a codicil giving his 'singular good lord' Lord Burghley £40 in old angels 'for the dutiful remembrance of the manifold benefits and favours by his lordship to me in my lifetime showed' (HoP, *Commons, 1558–1603*, 3.488–9). He died on 26 June and was buried in Marston church, where his monument shows him in full armour. He had married twice. His first wife was Margaret, daughter of Henry Sutton of Wellingore, with whom he had four sons and two daughters; after her death he married Anne, widow of George Babington and daughter and coheir of Sir John Constable of Kinoulton, Nottinghamshire, with whom he had a daughter, Winifred.

Sir Anthony's eldest son, Thomas, died in 1574, and he was also predeceased by his second, **William Thorold** (*d.* in or before 1594), but not before the latter played some part in public life. Like his father he was educated at Gray's Inn, where he may have been admitted in 1577. He was a JP for the Kesteven division from about 1583, while in 1584 he represented Grantham in parliament. The fourth earl of Rutland had asked to nominate one member while the earl of Lincoln requested the other, but was informed that Arthur Hall and William Thorold had already been elected. The fact that William had been in Rutland's entourage, possibly as a gentleman usher, doubtless made the apparent rebuff less offensive to the earl. But given the antagonism between Hall and William's father only two years earlier, the relationship between the two MPs must have been a very uneasy one. William married Frances, daughter of Sir Robert Tyrwhitt of Kettleby, and they had two sons and six daughters; after his death she married George Hatcliffe of Grimsby.

The civil war and its aftermath William's elder son, Sir Anthony Thorold, who was sheriff of Lincolnshire in 1617, left only one daughter, and the Thorold inheritance therefore descended to William's second son, **Sir William Thorold**, first baronet (*c.*1591–1678). He was knighted in 1607, aged only sixteen, and subsequently followed his father and grandfather by going to Gray's Inn, which he entered in 1610. He served as high sheriff of Lincolnshire in 1632–3 and was a JP for Kesteven 1634–46 and again from 1660 until his death. As the break in his service on the bench suggests, Sir William was a staunch royalist: he rallied to the king when he raised his standard at Nottingham on 22 August 1642 and was created a baronet two days later. His niece Mary had in 1630 married the royalist commander William, Baron Widdrington, who died in the battle of Wigan in 1651. The Thorold family had to pay for its loyalty to the crown: damage was done to Marston church and to the hall by Cromwellian forces in 1643. Sir William's composition was set at a third of £4160, and he also had to pay £320. In 1659 Gervase Holles listed him as prominent among the Lincolnshire royalists who would be 'serviceable to his majesty in his present affairs'. After the Restoration he was appointed to a number of commissions—for sewers, loyal indigent officers, and recusants. Recovering well from the trials of the 1640s and 1650s, he prospered, having an income of £2500 a year in the mid-1660s, when the Thorolds were described as 'a very spreading family of the county'. He was returned as MP for Grantham to the Cavalier Parliament and was again elected in 1678, the year of his death.

Sir William Thorold was not very active in parliament, though his name was added to the committee to consider the regulation of printing in 1666. In 1676 he was described by Sir Richard Wiseman as 'very ancient and attends not', but he was never named as a defaulter at a call of the house, and in 1677 Shaftesbury classed him as 'doubly worthy' (HoP, *Commons, 1660–90*, 3.558). He died a year later, aged eighty-six, and once again the inheritance went to a grandson, Sir William's two eldest sons, William and Anthony, having predeceased him.

The baronetcy of the Thorolds of Marston (several other lines of the family also held baronetcies during the seventeenth century) passed in rapid succession to three brothers, Sir William, second baronet, who died without heirs in 1685, Sir Anthony, third baronet, who died in France that same year, and **Sir John Thorold**, fourth baronet (1664–1717). However, Sir John was still a minor, and so the third and only surviving son of Sir William, the first baronet, another **John Thorold** (*d.* 1700), became the effective head of the family. He was twice married, first to Elizabeth Tredway, who died by 1674, and then to Elizabeth Sanderson (*née* Whincop), and had a son from each marriage; it was to his descendants that the baronetcy eventually passed. Having played no part in public life before the death of his octogenarian father, John Thorold had become a JP by 1680, an alderman of Grantham in 1685, and a commissioner for assessment in Lincolnshire 1689. A staunch supporter of the court, he was able to remain on the commission of the peace during the exclusion crisis of 1680–81, while on James II's accession he presented a loyal address from Grantham and was returned as MP for the borough a few weeks later. But he took no part in parliamentary proceedings and apparently did not stand again. He accepted the revolution of 1688 and probably remained a magistrate until his death in January 1700, when he owned property in and around Grantham as well as the manor of Grayingham.

Collaterals and descendants John Thorold's nephew John, the fourth baronet, briefly attended St John's College, Cambridge, where he matriculated in 1680, aged sixteen, before going on to Lincoln's Inn, London, two years later. In 1697 a by-election enabled him to follow his kinsman into parliament as MP for Grantham, and he continued to represent either that borough or the county in seven further parliaments between 1697 and 1714. He was a high tory at first, one whose return in 1697 owed much to ecclesiastical support. In 1705 the duke of Newcastle wrote to the secretary of state Robert Harley that Colonel Whichcote, the other MP for the county, would not be sorry for the defeat of 'lofty Sir John' (Hill, 195). Later, however, he was referred to as a whig who sometimes voted with the tories. He was active in parliament, both in national politics and in attending to local interests, notably bills for draining Lincolnshire fens. In 1701 he married Margaret Coventry (*née* Waterer); they had no children. Consequently when Sir John died, on 14 January 1717, the line yet again passed through collaterals. He was succeeded as baronet by Sir William Thorold, the son of John Thorold (*d.* 1700) from his first marriage, then by Sir William's son Sir Anthony, who died under age and unmarried in 1721, and finally by another Sir John Thorold (*d.* 1748), the son of John Thorold and his second wife, in whose descendants the lineage continued.

Thereafter the Thorold family achieved distinction in several fields, both lay and ecclesiastical, but perhaps most notably as bibliophiles. The ninth baronet, Sir John *Thorold (1734–1815), and his son Sir John Hayford *Thorold (1773–1831) [see under Thorold, Sir John, ninth baronet (1734–1815)] formed a large and notable collection, and built a splendid library at their principal residence at Syston Park to accommodate it. They certainly had the means wherewith to indulge their passion. By the eighteenth century the Thorold estates were extensive enough to warrant a peerage, and indeed, such an offer is reported to have been made to the ninth baronet, but to have been turned down by Sir John with the remark that he preferred an ancient baronetcy to a new barony.

GERALD A. J. HODGETT

Sources *Debrett's Peerage* (2000) · Burke, *Peerage* (1999) · HoP, *Commons, 1509–58* · HoP, *Commons, 1558–1603* · HoP, *Commons, 1660–90* · P. Watson and P. L. Gauci, 'Thorold, Sir John', HoP, *Commons, 1690–1715* [and draft], 5.632–3 · Lincolnshire, Pevsner (1989) · E. Trollope, *Descent of the various branches of the ancient family of Thorold* (1874) · A. Oswald, 'Marston Hall Lincolnshire', *Country Life*, 138 (1965), 612–15, 688–92 · G. A. J. Hodgett, *Tudor Lincolnshire* (1975) · C. Holmes, *Seventeenth-century Lincolnshire* (1980) · private information (2004) · F. Hill, *Tudor and Stuart Lincoln* (1956) · A. R. Maddison, ed., *Lincolnshire pedigrees*, 3, Harleian Society, 52 (1904) · J. H. Baker, *Readers and readings in the inns of court and chancery*, SeldS, suppl. ser., 13 (2000) · *LP Henry VIII*, 19/2.420

Archives Lincs. Arch., title deeds, estate papers, family papers, documents, 2 THOR HAR · Lincs. Arch.

Thorold, Sir Anthony (*b.* in or before **1520**, *d.* **1594**). *See under* Thorold family (*per. c.*1492–1717).

Thorold, Anthony Wilson (1825–1895), bishop of Winchester, was born at Hougham, Lincolnshire, on 13 June 1825. His father, Edward Thorold, was the fourth son of Sir John Thorold, ninth baronet, and held the family living of Hougham-cum-Marston, Lincolnshire. His mother was Mary, daughter of Thomas Wilson of Grantham, Lincolnshire. Thorold was educated privately, and matriculated from Queen's College, Oxford, in 1843. Having obtained an honorary fourth class in mathematics he graduated BA in 1847 and MA in 1850, receiving the degree of DD by diploma on 29 May 1877. Thorold was ordained deacon in 1849 and priest in 1850. He married in 1850 Henrietta, daughter of Thomas Greene MP. In opinion he belonged to the evangelical school. His first curacy was the parish of Whittington, Lancashire, where he worked from 1849 until 1854. Three years at Holy Trinity, Marylebone, followed, and then, in 1857, the exertions of his friends procured for him the lord chancellor's living of St Giles-in-the-Fields, London, where he became well known as a preacher and organizer. He also began to write, and was one of the early contributors to *Good Words*. His first wife died in October 1859 and he married, in 1865, Emily, daughter of John Labouchere.

Ill health led Thorold to resign St Giles's in 1867. But after a little rest and a short incumbency at Curzon Chapel, Mayfair (1868–9), he resumed parish work in 1869 as vicar of St Pancras, London. Here, as at St Giles's, he showed organizing power. He improved the schools of the parish, was one of the first to adopt parochial missions, and was returned in 1870 as a member for Marylebone to the first school board for London. In 1874 Archbishop Thomson, formerly a tutor at Queen's College and for whom he had long worked as examining chaplain, gave Thorold a residentiary canonry in York Cathedral. Higher promotion soon came. In 1877 Disraeli offered him the see of Rochester, one of several appointments of low-churchmen by Disraeli. He was consecrated in Westminster Abbey on 25 July.

The great work of Thorold's episcopate was his extensive reorganization of the diocese, and he has been considered an example of a devoted parish priest who made an admirable bishop (Carpenter, 283). He consolidated the existing diocesan organizations; carried to a successful issue a Ten Churches Fund; encouraged the settlement of public school and college missions in south London; promoted diocesan organizations for deaconesses, lay workers, higher education, and temperance; and began the restoration of St Saviour's, Southwark, projecting its elevation to the rank of a quasi-cathedral. For recreation he travelled much, going as far afield as America and Australia. He spoke occasionally and with effect in the House of Lords, and he was one of the assessors in the trial of the bishop of Lincoln at Lambeth in 1889. In 1890 he succeeded Harold Browne in the see of Winchester. But his health was not equal to the business of the diocese. He died, worn out, at Farnham Castle, Farnham, Surrey, on 25 July 1895, the eighteenth anniversary of his consecration. His second wife had predeceased him in December 1877.

Although without striking characteristics or powerful mind, Thorold had a grasp of detail, and inspired others as much by his own industry as by his words. Strong mannerisms repelled many, but threw into relief his real sincerity and goodness. He read widely, and, although given to tricks of style, he both spoke and wrote well. His published works were exclusively devotional or diocesan.

A. R. BUCKLAND, *rev.* TRIONA ADAMS

Sources C. H. Simkinson, *Life and work of Bishop Thorold* (1896) · *Record* (1895), 721, 725 · S. C. Carpenter, *Church and people, 1789–1889* (1933) · Boase, *Mod. Eng. biog.* · G. R. Balleine, *A history of the evangelical party in the Church of England* (1908)
Archives LPL, notebook relating to trial of King Edward | LPL, corresp. with E. W. Benson · LPL, corresp. with A. C. Tait
Likenesses attrib. E. U. Eddis, oils, St Giles-in-the-Fields, London · Lock & Whitfield, woodburytype photograph, NPG; repro. in T. Cooper, *Men of mark: a gallery of contemporary portraits* (1881) · Spy [L. Ward], caricature, watercolour study, NPG; repro. in *VF* (10 Jan 1885) · portrait, repro. in *Church Portrait Journal*, 4 (1883), 33 · portrait, repro. in *St James's Budget* (2 Aug 1895), 11
Wealth at death £31,331: probate, 14 Oct 1895, *CGPLA Eng. & Wales*

Thorold, John (*d.* 1700). *See under* Thorold family (*per. c.*1492–1717).

Thorold, Sir John, fourth baronet (1664–1717). *See under* Thorold family (*per. c.*1492–1717).

Thorold, Sir John, ninth baronet (1734–1815), landowner and book collector, was born on 18 December 1734, the eldest son of Sir John Thorold, eighth baronet (1703–1775), landowner and Methodist preacher, and his wife, Elizabeth (*d.* 1779), daughter and coheir of Samuel Ayton of West Herrington, co. Durham. His father was a former fellow of Lincoln College, Oxford, and in 1751 served as high sheriff of Lincolnshire, an office also held by his father, Sir John Thorold, seventh baronet, in 1723. The Thorolds were a long-established Lincolnshire family who had been resident in the county since the middle years of the sixteenth century. Sir William Thorold (*c.*1591–1678) was created a baronet by Charles I on 24 August 1642.

Thorold matriculated from Hertford College, Oxford, on 24 November 1752, aged eighteen, but did not graduate. On 18 March 1771, at St Marylebone, Middlesex, he married Jane (*d.* 1807), daughter and heir of Millington Hayford, of Oxton Hall, Nottinghamshire, and Millington, Cheshire. They had three sons and one daughter. He served as MP for Lincolnshire from 1776 to 1796, and succeeded his father as baronet and owner of the family seat Syston Park, near Grantham, in 1775.

Thorold is chiefly known as a book collector, and as one of the leading figures of the 'bibliomania' of the late eighteenth and early nineteenth centuries, when bibliophiles such as William Beckford, the third duke of Roxburghe, and the second Earl Spencer vied to outbid one another in the sale rooms. He began collecting about 1775; the pace of acquisitions is believed to have slacked somewhat round about 1800. He died on 25 February 1815.

Thorold was succeeded by his eldest son, **Sir John Hayford Thorold**, tenth baronet (1773–1831), who was born on 30 March 1773. He was married twice, first to Mary (*d.* 1829), eldest daughter of Sir Charles Kent, first baronet, and Mary Wordsworth; they had at least one son, John Charles (*b.* 1816). His second wife, whom he married on 12 July 1830, was Mary Anne (*d.* 1842), widow of John Dalton of Turnham Hall, Lancashire, and daughter of George Cary and his second wife, Frances Stonor, of Tor Abbey, Devon. He continued in his father's collecting habits, and commissioned the architect Lewis Vulliamy to build a new library for him at Syston between 1822 and 1824. This was visited by T. F. Dibdin and described by him as 'perhaps one of the most splendid and taking book repositories in Europe'. Thorold died on 7 July 1831 and was survived by his second wife, who later married a Mr Ogle.

The interior of the Syston Park library is known from an engraving by A. W. and R. G. Reeve after a view by Thomas Kearnan, c.1824. No complete catalogue is extant, but much can be gleaned from a sale catalogue produced when the dispersal of the collection began in 1884. The library was rich in early printing, including classical *editiones principes*, many printed on vellum or on large paper, and books of famous provenance. It included a copy of the 1459 psalter on vellum, bought from Sir Mark Masterman Sykes's sale in 1824 for £4950, at that time the most expensive volume ever sold. There were many incunables, numerous editions by the Leiden publishing house Elzevier—a particular enthusiasm of the ninth baronet— and many volumes with famous associations, including books from the libraries of Lorenzo de' Medici and Diane de Poitiers, and no fewer than five from the collection of the French Renaissance bibliophile Jean Grolier.

The sales in 1884 raised £28,000. There were further sales of books and furniture in 1923; the gutted shell of the library and the rest of Syston Park were demolished soon afterwards.   MARK PURCELL

Sources B. Quaritch, ed., *Contributions towards a dictionary of English book-collectors* (1892), 285–7 · Burke, *Peerage* (1999) · GEC, *Baronetage* · T. Knox, 'Sir John Thorold's library at Syston Park, Lincolnshire', *Apollo*, 146 (Sept 1997), 24–9 · T. F. Dibdin, *Bibliographical, antiquarian and picturesque tour in the northern counties of England and Scotland* (1838) · W. Y. Fletcher, *English book collectors* (1902) · S. de Ricci, *English collectors of books and manuscripts* (1930) · L. B. Namier, 'Thorold, Sir John', HoP, *Commons, 1754–90* · R. G. Thorne, 'Thorold, Sir John', HoP, *Commons, 1790–1820*

Thorold, Sir John Hayford, tenth baronet (1773–1831). *See under* Thorold, Sir John, ninth baronet (1734–1815).

Thorold, Sir Nathaniel, baronet (d. 1764), entrepreneur and adventurer, was the son of John Thorold and his wife Anne (née Alcock), of the Grantham branch of the family. He inherited Harmston Hall, Lincolnshire, quite unexpectedly in January 1738 following the death of his distant cousin Sir Samuel Thorold, second baronet. He was created a baronet on 24 March 1741. Overwhelmed by this sudden change in circumstance, he ran through his new fortune and, deeply in debt, was obliged to go abroad in 1745. He left in a hurry, for it was discovered that breakfast was still on the table, the chairs hastily pushed aside. But Sir Nathaniel emerged triumphant. In the Netherlands he befriended a Jewish merchant, and together they devised a method of salting cod so that the fish would last long enough to be transported to southern Europe. Thereafter he moved to Italy, and settled first in Leghorn. There he lived with a beautiful young woman from Capri, Anna della Noce, the wife of a Signor Antonio Canale, who accepted his wife's affair. However, the scandal of the *ménage à trois* drove Thorold and his lover from Leghorn to Naples, where he re-established his salted cod business. Further scandal forced the couple to move to the island of Capri. There Sir Nathaniel built a large and beautiful

home, the Palazzo Inglese, and his business flourished. He and Anna had several children, who took the name Canale. In 1754 the bishop of Capri wrote in his report to the pope, *Ad limina apostolorum*, that 'a scandal had been caused by the co-habitation, for almost ten years, of a certain married woman with an heretical English nobleman'. However, the pope refused to be drawn on the issue. Thorold lived with Anna on Capri until his death at the Palazzo Inglese on 28 August 1764. He is said to have been buried near the springs of Marucella, where tradition has it that he introduced the growing of cress, sent out to him from Lincolnshire. His son Samuel, to whom his father had left his English property, came to Harmston to inherit, assumed the name Thorold, and was made high sheriff of Lincolnshire at the age of twenty-five.

HENRY THOROLD

Sources [Rosco, bishop of Capri], *Ad limina apostolorum* (1754) · G. S. Clark, 'Memorandum' [n.d.] · Viscount Halifax [C. L. Wood], *Lord Halifax's ghost book*, 2 (1939) · E. Cerio, *Il miracolo del baccala* (1938) · E. Cerio, *The masque of Capri* (1957) · J. Money, *Capri, island of pleasure* (1986) · H. Thorold, *Lincolnshire* (1996) · GM, 1st ser., 34 (1764), 545
Likenesses Battone, oils, 1740, Marston Hall, Lincolnshire · oils, 1750–60, priv. coll.

Thorold [alias Carwell], **Thomas** (c.1600–1664), Jesuit, belonged to the Lincolnshire family of Thorold and is sometimes described as brother of Sir Robert Thorold, bt. He appears to have converted to Catholicism about 1622 and, after studying at St Omer, entered the English College, Rome, on 1 November 1629. He was ordained priest in Rome on 2 February 1633 and was admitted to the Society of Jesus at St Andrew's noviciate, Rome, on 7 September 1633, having formally completed his theological studies. He undertook a period of teaching in the society's college at Liège, where he became a professed father on 13 December 1643. From 1646 he served on the English mission, acting as rector of the London district by 1654; later he served as vice-provincial of England. He published one controversial work, *Labyrinthus Cantuariensis*, bulky, but addressing the somewhat moribund controversy between Archbishop Laud and John Fisher SJ, both long since dead. Dated 1658, it may not have appeared until 1664; certainly he claimed he had delayed his answer, not wishing to attack the Church of England at a time of 'publique distraction' (Clancy, 135). He may have been the Thomas Thurrall appointed chaplain to Queen Catherine of Braganza by warrant of 13 May 1663. He died in London in 1664, probably on 9 August.

THOMPSON COOPER, rev. R. M. ARMSTRONG

Sources H. Foley, ed., *Records of the English province of the Society of Jesus*, 7 vols. in 8 (1875–83) · T. M. McCoog, *English and Welsh Jesuits, 1555–1650*, 2 vols., Catholic RS, 74–5 (1994–5) · T. H. Clancy, *A literary history of the English Jesuits: a century of books, 1615–1714* (1996) · G. Anstruther, *The seminary priests*, 2 (1975), 139 · A. Kenny, ed., *The responsa scholarum of the English College, Rome*, 2, Catholic RS, 55 (1963)

Thorold, William (b. in or before 1492, d. 1569). *See under* Thorold family (per. c.1492–1717).

Thorold, William (*d.* in or before **1594**). *See under* Thorold family (*per. c.*1492–1717).

Thorold, Sir William, first baronet (*c.***1591–1678**). *See under* Thorold family (*per. c.*1492–1717).

Thoroton, Robert (**1623–1678**), antiquary, was born on 4 October 1623 at Morin Hall, Car Colston, Nottinghamshire, the eldest son of Robert Thoroton (1601–1673) and his wife, Anne Chambers of Stapleford (married in St Mary's, Nottingham). His ancestors had long been small landowners in Nottinghamshire and the family owed its name to the hamlet and chapelry of Thoroton, formerly Thurveton, near Newark. Thoroton entered Christ's College, Cambridge, as a sizar, in 1639, graduating BA in 1642–3 and MA in 1646. He married on 27 October 1645, probably at Nottingham, Anne, daughter of Gilbert Boun, serjeant-at-law, recorder of Newark, and MP, raising three daughters. In 1646 he was licensed by the university to practise medicine.

Thoroton settled at Car Colston where he combined medical practice with the occupations of a country gentleman, and although, on his own authority, he met with competent success as a physician, he acknowledged that he was unable 'to keep people alive for any length of time'. Consequently, he:

> charitably attempted, notwithstanding the Difficulty and almost contrariety of the Study, to practice upon the dead, intending thereby to keep all which is or can be left of them, to wit the Shadow of their Names, (better than precious Ointment for the Body,) to preserve their memory, as long as may be in the World. (Thoroton, *Antiquities of Nottinghamshire*, preface)

Although a staunch royalist, Thoroton apparently took little part in the civil war. He seems to have been among those 'gentry of the county' of whom Clarendon said the garrison of Newark, besides its inhabitants, mainly consisted. In writing later of that town, Thoroton referred to the second siege, where in 1644 he saw troops under Prince Rupert relieve the town.

After the Restoration Thoroton became a justice of the peace for his county, and a commissioner of royal aid and subsidy. In the former office, together with his fellow justice and friend Penistone Whalley, he rendered himself notorious by stringent enforcement of the laws concerning conventicles against the Quakers. This retaliation for the imprisonments and confiscations suffered by his relatives and friends during the Commonwealth called forth some abusive pamphlets. He also rebuilt Morin Hall, Car Colston, now the Old Hall, illustrated by the Leicester topographer John Throsby (1740–1803).

Thoroton commenced his *Antiquities of Nottinghamshire* in 1667. He first worked on some transcript notes which his father-in-law Gilbert Boun had made from Domesday Book. He assisted Sir William Dugdale in his *Visitation of Nottinghamshire, 1662–1664*. For his researches he employed paid assistants at considerable expense to himself, delving into family archives, registers (some now lost), estate papers, church monuments, and epitaphs. Like a number of county antiquaries he was little concerned with his own times, or indeed with his own century, but tried to trace the manorial history of each parish back to Domesday. He showed little interest in Roman remains, while protesting at enclosure and destruction of woods. His notes, made on the back of letters from his patients in Nottinghamshire, Leicestershire, and Derbyshire, are now in Nottingham Public Library.

The folio volume of Thoroton's *Antiquities* was printed in London in 1677, illustrated with engravings by Hollar after Richard Hall and dedicated to Gilbert Sheldon, archbishop of Canterbury, and Dugdale, both personal friends. Dugdale wrote to the antiquary Sir Daniel Fleming, 'Dr Thoroton's book cost me 16s to 18s. I do esteem the book well worth your buying, though had he gone to the fountain of records it might have been better done' (1 Sept 1677, *Le Fleming MSS*, 139–40). John Throsby published a reprint of *Antiquities* with additions, in three volumes (published 1790–96 but dated 1797).

Thoroton erected in 1664 a memorial outside the south aisle of Car Colston church recording the names of his ancestors, which survives at the time of writing, and in 1672 he designed for himself an imposing coffin of carved Mansfield stone. In 1673 Thoroton presented an alms dish to the church, while his wife, Anne, presented a silver flagon engraved with her arms. Thoroton died at Car Colston on 21 November 1678 and on 23 November was buried in the coffin, where his remains rested until 1842. The level of the churchyard by the church door was then lowered, and after re-burial of its contents, the coffin was brought into the church. Thoroton's wife survived him. He left his property to his daughter Anne Sherard, having earlier helped his younger brother to buy Screveton Hall estate, which remained in the family. The Thoroton Society, Nottinghamshire's local history society, is named after him. Sir Frank Stenton said of him:

> It is perhaps the greatest merit of Thoroton's work that he fully grasped the essential fact that the key to all manorial history lies in the distribution of land recorded in Domesday, and … as far as the work of identification is concerned, independent investigation can often do little more than confirm his minuteness and accuracy. (*VCH Nottinghamshire*, 1.246)

MYLES THOROTON HILDYARD

Sources M. T. Hildyard, 'Dr Robert Thoroton', *Transactions of the Thoroton Society*, 61 (1957), 8–20 · R. Thoroton, 'Dr Thoroton's notebook', Flintham Hall, Newark · R. Thoroton, *The antiquities of Nottinghamshire*, rev. J. Throsby, 2nd edn, 3 vols. (1790–96); repr. with introduction by M. W. Barley and K. S. S. Train (1972) · R. Thoroton, letters, Nottingham Public Library · M. T. Hildyard, *The Thorotons* (privately printed, 1990) · admissions, U. Cam. · *The manuscripts of S. H. Le Fleming*, HMC, 25 (1890)

Archives BL, papers and extracts from 'History of Notts', Add. MSS 5522, 11757, 38141; Add. MS Ch. 5846 · CUL, extracts from his *Antiquities of Nottinghamshire* · Flintham Hall, Newark, notebook, horoscope, etc. · Nottingham Central Library, letters · Notts. Arch., Nottingham collections

Likenesses I. Whood, oils, 1736, Flintham Hall, Newark · W. G. Walker, line engraving, NPG; repro. in J. Throsby, *History of Nottinghamshire* (1791)

Wealth at death Dr Thoroton and father sold 80 acres in 1660 for £1700; left 152 acres in Car Colston freehold and 127 acres leasehold from dean and chapter of Lincoln; tithes of Thoroton value

£60 p.a.; 34 acres and tithes of Screveton; land in Hawkesworth and Aslockton (Nottinghamshire): More-Molyneux papers, Guildford Museum

Thoroton, Thomas (1723?–1794), politician, was the eldest son of Robert Thoroton, of Screveton, Nottinghamshire, a landowner, and his wife, Mary, the daughter of Sir Richard Levett, lord mayor of London, and widow of Abraham Blackborne, a London mercer. He was educated at Westminster School (1736–42) and Trinity Hall, Cambridge (1742–5), and entered Lincoln's Inn in 1745. A descendant of Thomas, the younger brother of the antiquary Robert Thoroton, he was also distantly related to John Manners, third duke of Rutland, and he lived at Belvoir Castle and Rutland House. Thoroton acted as agent to the duke in all his political and private business, and became the Rutland group's parliamentary whip or 'man of business'. On 6 October 1751, at Knipton, Leicestershire, he married Roosita Drake (b. 1735), the illegitimate daughter of the duke of Rutland. They had eight sons and five daughters.

In gratitude for the assistance rendered by the Rutland connection, the first duke of Newcastle returned Thoroton to parliament on 15 January 1757 for the borough of Boroughbridge, and on 27 March 1761 for the town of Newark. On the appointment of the duke's son, John Manners, marquess of Granby, as master-general of the ordnance on 1 July 1763, Thoroton became secretary to the board, a post which he held until 1770. Although he was regarded as one of Newcastle's Nottinghamshire friends, his loyalty was to the Rutland family, and he voted consistently with Granby. He supported the Grenville ministry, opposed the repeal of the Stamp Act, and supported the Chatham ministry. After a period of strained relations with Newcastle, Thoroton withdrew from Newark, and on 14 February 1769 he was returned for Bramber, Sussex, as Granby's nominee. He retained his seat until 1782. In January 1770 he followed Granby into opposition, but after Granby's death his conduct was less predictable. Although he voted against the government on the Middlesex motion on 26 April 1773, he was classified by John Robinson at the end of this parliament as a government supporter.

After retiring from parliament Thoroton continued to look after the interests of the Rutland family, and between 1784 and 1787, while Charles Manners, fourth duke of Rutland, was lord lieutenant of Ireland, he looked after the latter's English business. He died at his home, Screveton Hall, on 9 May 1794 and was buried in the neighbouring church of St Wilfrid's. Of his thirteen children, John became rector of Bottesford and chaplain of Belvoir Castle, and was knighted in 1814; Robert was appointed private secretary to the fourth duke of Rutland during his viceroyalty of Ireland, and clerk to the Irish parliament; and Mary in 1778 married Charles Manners-Sutton (1755–1828), who became in 1805 archbishop of Canterbury.

W. E. MANNERS, rev. MARTYN J. POWELL

Sources L. Namier, 'Thoroton, Thomas', HoP, *Commons* · L. B. Namier, *The structure of politics at the accession of George III*, 2nd edn (1957) · W. E. Manners, *Some account of the military, political and social*

life of the Right Hon. John Manners, marquis of Granby (1899) · R. Browning, *The duke of Newcastle* (1975) · *The manuscripts of his grace the duke of Rutland*, 4 vols., HMC, 24 (1888–1905), vol. 2
Archives Belvoir Castle, Leicestershire, Rutland MSS · BL, corresp. with duke of Newcastle, Add. MSS 32911–32974, *passim* · U. Nott. L., corresp. with duke of Newcastle

Thoroughgood, Sir John (*bap.* 1594?, *d.* 1675), government official, was the second son in the family of seven sons and a daughter of William Thorowgood (*d.* 1625) of Grimston, Norfolk, and Anne, his first wife, the daughter of Henry Edwards of Norwich, gentleman. He was probably the son of that name whom they baptized on 4 May 1594. His father, who belonged to an armigerous family in Felsted, Essex, had served as commissary to Edmund Scambler, bishop of Norwich, and continued his career as ecclesiastical administrator until his death. It seems reasonable to suppose that John was born and spent his early years in Grimston, Norfolk, where his family was recorded as having an estate in 1664, but there is no record of his educational background.

By 1633 Thoroughgood was already moving in court circles. He went to Scotland as a gentleman pensioner to King Charles I in that year and was knighted by the king. In the civil war he sided with parliament, though the strength of his commitment is unclear. By now resident in fashionable Kensington, he was appointed to the Middlesex militia committee in 1644 and to both the Middlesex and the Norfolk militia committees in 1648. He was an assessment commissioner for Westminster and Middlesex in 1649, and in the 1650s he held a number of minor central and local offices and was a commissioner of oyer and terminer.

Thoroughgood's most important position was as one of the trustees for the maintenance of ministers, appointed in 1649 to supplement the work of the parliamentary plundered ministers' committee by augmenting the stipends of clergy and teachers out of funds at their disposal. He was active, usually as senior trustee, until 1660. Nevertheless no measures were taken against him at the Restoration, suggesting perhaps that he had not been a republican by choice and may have worked towards the return of Charles II. He was even appointed honorary gentleman of the privy chamber to Charles II. His moralizing work, *The King of Terrors Silenced, by Meditations and Examples of Holy Living and Holy Dying* (1664), reveals an orthodox Calvinism, but neither this nor his will gives any hint of Puritan enthusiasm, despite their author's central role in the administration of the interregnum church.

Thoroughgood married Frances, daughter of Thomas Meautys (1590–1649) of West Ham, Essex, clerk to the privy council and MP. She died childless when still a minor in 1651 and he never remarried. He died at some point between 12 November 1675, when he signed his will, and 5 December 1675 when the will was proved; he asked to be buried next to his wife in the church of High Ongar, Essex. With no direct heirs he made elaborate provisions in his will to prevent legal disputes between his nephews; the bulk of his estate, including a manor in Bagthorp, Essex, which he was in the process of buying at the time of writing his will, was left to Robert Thoroughgood, the son of his brother Robert.   ROSEMARY O'DAY, *rev.*

Sources G. E. Aylmer, *The state's servants: the civil service of the English republic, 1649–1660* (1973) • R. O'Day and F. Heal, eds., *Princes and paupers in the English church, 1500–1800* (1979) • W. C. Metcalfe, ed., *The visitations of Essex*, 2 vols., Harleian Society, 13–14 (1878–9), vol. 1, p. 247; vol. 2, pp. 607–8 • A. W. Hughes Clarke and A. Campling, eds., *The visitation of Norfolk … 1664, made by Sir Edward Bysshe*, 2, Harleian Society, 86 (1934), 219–20 • will, PRO, PROB 11/349, sig. 132

Thorp, Charles (1783–1862), university principal, born at Gateshead rectory in co. Durham on 13 October 1783, was the fifth but second surviving son of Robert Thorp and his wife, Grace (1745–1814), daughter of Thomas Alder of Horncliffe, on the Tweed.

Robert Thorp (1736–1812), Church of England clergyman, was born at Chillingham in Northumberland, where his father was vicar, on 18 December 1736, the second and only surviving son of Thomas Thorp (1698–1767) and his wife, Mary Robson (*d.* 1786) from Egglescliffe, near Stockton-on-Tees. He was educated at Durham School and Peterhouse, Cambridge, graduating BA in 1758 as senior wrangler, MA in 1761, and DD in 1792, and was elected fellow in 1761. He was ordained deacon in 1759, succeeded his father at Chillingham in 1768, and became perpetual curate of Doddington in 1775 before moving to be rector of Gateshead in 1781. In 1792 he was appointed archdeacon of Northumberland, and in 1795 he was presented to the rectory of Ryton, co. Durham, which he resigned in favour of his son in 1807. Besides several sermons and charges, Thorp published excerpts from (1765), and a translation of, Newton's *Principia* (1777; 2nd edn, 1802). He died at Durham on 20 April 1812 and was buried in Ryton church.

His son Charles Thorp, who spoke with a distinct Northumbrian burr, was educated at the Royal Grammar School, Newcastle upon Tyne, and then at Durham School. Having originally been intended for Cambridge, where he was admitted pensioner at Peterhouse on 29 June 1799, he matriculated from University College, Oxford, on 10 December the same year, graduating BA in 1803, MA in 1806, BD in 1822, and DD in 1835. In 1803 he was elected a fellow and tutor of his college and was ordained in that year. In 1807 he was presented by Shute Barrington, bishop of Durham, to the rectory of Ryton, in succession to his father. He retained the living until his death. Thorp refused several valuable preferments, including the lucrative living of Stanhope, on account of his attachment to his parish. He built at his sole expense a church at Greenside in commemoration of his parents and later arranged the separation of Winlaton and Blaydon, diminishing his own income to provide the endowment of the former. For many years he was chaplain to Earl Grey. He married twice: first, at Alnwick on 7 July 1810, Frances Wilkie, only child of Henry Collingwood Selby of Swansfield, Northumberland. She died childless in 1811, and on 7 October 1817 Thorp married, at Little Ouseburn, Yorkshire, Mary, daughter of Edmund Robinson of Thorp Green, with whom he had a son, Charles Thorp (*d.* 1880), later vicar of Ellingham, and five surviving

daughters. Four of the daughters married clergymen, two of whom were Durham graduates.

At Ryton, Thorp helped establish the first savings bank in the north of England, and in 1818 he delivered a sermon to a Gateshead friendly society which led to the formation of a successful savings bank at Newcastle. The sermon, which contained statistical information, was published as *Economy, a Duty of Natural and Revealed Religion* (1818). In 1829 he was presented to the second prebendal stall in Durham Cathedral, and in December 1831 he was appointed archdeacon of Durham, declining the living of Easington which was thereupon detached from the archdeaconry. He served on the royal commission to inquire into ecclesiastical revenues and patronage in 1832–5, as a representative of capitular interests. As prolocutor of York convocation Thorp led a long and acrimonious struggle to secure the restoration to that body of the right to debate church affairs, finally succeeding in 1861. He was the author of many published sermons and charges; some, dealing with the duties of parochial clergy, were printed and circulated at his own expense and enjoyed wide popularity. Thorp was elected FRS in 1839. He was interested in natural history, being active in protecting the birds of the Farne Islands from egg collectors, whom he abhorred. He was a keen bibliophile and patron of the arts with a valuable gallery of ancient and modern masters, including copies by Verrio, commissioned by William III, of Raphael's cartoons at Hampton Court, of which he was particularly proud.

The great achievement of Thorp's life, for which he has never received full credit, was the founding of Durham University in 1832. If not the sole projector he was, with Bishop Van Mildert, the prime mover in its establishment. Both feared the Church of England to be in imminent danger of attack once the Reform Bill of 1832 was passed and they sought to retain its extraordinary wealth in Durham. A university there would pre-empt a mooted 'infidel' college in Newcastle upon Tyne and benefit the Anglican cause. Bishop and chapter made considerable financial sacrifices, and the first students were admitted in October 1833 with Thorp as warden and master of University College. Thorp had ambitions to become dean of Durham, and when the deanery fell vacant in 1840 some of his colleagues unsuccessfully petitioned Melbourne to that effect on the grounds that if future deans were to be wardens of the university when Thorp vacated the post then he as incumbent warden ought to be made dean.

Modelled to some extent on Christ Church, Oxford, with dean and chapter as governors, and pioneering the external examining system to maintain Oxford standards for its degrees, the university initially flourished, providing under Henry Jenkyns a better theological training than was available elsewhere. Teaching expanded to include civil engineering in 1837 and the medical school in Newcastle became affiliated in 1852. At its peak the university had one college and two halls of residence in Durham and another in Newcastle. However, its Anglican ethos, while ensuring that 90 per cent of Durham students became clergymen, deterred members of other denominations. As the city of Durham, bypassed by the railway, became ringed by coal pits and coke ovens the university entered a period of decline. Thorp, who could not endure criticism of his beloved university, failed to perceive the need for reform, and despite advancing years and ill health was unwilling to delegate responsibility to colleagues. The consequence was a statutory commission of inquiry, set up in 1862, which found severe faults in management. Too ill to give evidence, Thorp finally offered to retire on a pension and was in the process of resigning his wardenship when he died at Ryton rectory on 10 October 1862. He was buried in the family vault at Ryton church on the 15th. His wife died in 1879.

C. D. WATKINSON

Sources *A short sketch of the life of the Venerable Charles Thorp, archdeacon of Durham* (1862) · U. Durham L., archives and special collections, Thorp correspondence · Balliol Oxf., Jenkyns MSS · A. Heesom, *The founding of the University of Durham: Durham Cathedral lecture, 1982* (1982) · A. Heesom, 'Who thought of the idea of the University of Durham', *Durham County Local History Society Bulletin*, 29 (1982), 10–20 · E. A. Varley, *The last of the prince bishops: William Van Mildert and the high church movement of the early nineteenth century* (1992) · C. E. Whiting, *The University of Durham, 1832–1932* (1932) · D. A. Jennings, *The revival of the Convocation of York, 1837–1861*, Borthwick Papers, 47 (1975) · transcripts of Belford, Berwick and Ryton parish registers, Newcastle City Libraries, Local Studies Library · J. C. Hogdson, 'Northumberland pedigrees', Newcastle City Libraries, Local Studies Library [unpubd MS vols.] · IGI · H. O. Horne, *A history of savings banks* (1947) · CGPLA Eng. & Wales (1863) · Venn, *Alum. Cant.* [Robert Thorp] · GM, 1st ser., 82/1 (1812), 595 [Robert Thorp] · 'Thorp, Robert', DNB · *Durham Advertiser* · *Durham Chronicle* · *Newcastle Courant*
Archives U. Durham L., corresp. and papers relating to Durham University | Balliol Oxf., letters to Henry Jenkyns · BL, corresp. with Sir Robert Peel · U. Durham L., Auckland Castle episcopal records · U. Durham L., letters to second Earl Grey
Likenesses G. R. Ward, mezzotint, pubd 1846 (after J. R. Swinton), U. Durham L. · T. Heaviside, photograph, c.1860, U. Durham L. · photograph, c.1860, Durham Cath. CL · J. R. Swinton, oils, Great Hall, Durham Castle · oils, Durham Cath. CL · oils, possibly U. Durham
Wealth at death under £45,000: probate, 4 March 1863, CGPLA Eng. & Wales · real estate in Durham, Ryton and Bamburgh: probate registry

Thorp, Robert (1736–1812). *See under* Thorp, Charles (1783–1862).

Thorp, Thomas (1797–1877), Church of England clergyman, was born at Pontefract, Yorkshire, on 4 March 1797, the eldest son in the family of three sons and two daughters of Robert William Disney Thorp (1766–1849), medical practitioner and sometime mayor of Leeds, and his wife, Ann Katharine, daughter of Gregory Grant MD. He was educated at Richmond School, Yorkshire, and was admitted a pensioner at Trinity College, Cambridge, in April 1814. He was elected a scholar in 1817 and graduated BA in 1819 as eighth wrangler. In 1818 he was president of the Cambridge Union. He won the chancellor's classical medal in 1819 and was elected a fellow of Trinity in the following year. He graduated MA in 1822 and held a number of college offices, including a tutorship (1833–44) and the vice-mastership (1843–4). He graduated BD in 1824. Thorp

had been admitted to the Middle Temple in 1824, but in 1829 was ordained deacon and priest.

Thorp's name is closely associated with the Cambridge Camden Society, of which he was president for twenty years. Many future members of the society matriculated at Trinity between 1833 and 1841 while he was a tutor. The society, formed by two Trinity men, J. M. Neale and Edward Jacob Boyce, began as a group of friends paying visits to churches. Thorp, recently appointed archdeacon and chancellor of Bristol (1836), was elected president in 1839. Many who joined the society, especially those in senior positions in the church or the university, 'thought that they were merely encouraging an antiquarian and artistic society with a practical interest in church building' (White, 28). Thorp himself was strongly influenced by Romanticism and Wordsworth's appropriation of whatever was 'pure and imaginative, whatever was not merely utilitarian, to the service of both Church and State' (ibid.).

Thorp himself was a high-churchman, and together with H. J. Rose and W. H. Mill was regarded as a leading preserver of high-church tradition in Cambridge. Influenced by the Oxford Movement, he once said that Wordsworth might be considered among the founders of the society. However, he recognized that allying the society too closely with Tractarianism could be counter-productive. Theological debates were actively discouraged during his time as president. For him, the society's only theological position was 'the recognition and extension of sound principles of Church membership'. He was a moderating influence on the radical voices in the society.

Thorp published *A Few Words to Churchwardens on Churches and Church Ornaments* in 1841. J. M. Neale was, in fact, the original author and Thorp toned down his text. He made recommendations about the care and reordering of churches. His arguments against box pews, galleries, and three-decker pulpits, and his support for singing and practices such as the use of candles, were taken up by A. W. N. Pugin, who recommended them to Roman Catholics. It being the year of Newman's Tract 90, Thorp was very sensitive to a charge of romanizing and felt that he should have censored the work more heavily before publication.

In 1841 the Camden Society took over restoration of the Round Church, a medieval church in central Cambridge. Thorp was chair of the restoration committee. In 1843 a row broke out because a stone altar had been erected there, though this was declared legal by a consistory court. Thorp was very concerned by a pamphlet published in 1845 under the society's auspices by S. N. Stokes, who was shortly to convert to Rome, which recommended auricular confession. Bishop Phillpotts of Exeter resigned from the society in disapproval. The committee, under Thorp's leadership, gave serious consideration to dissolving itself. In later years Thorp was less active in the society's affairs, but did not resign as president until 1859, when he claimed pressure of work.

Thorp's attempts to rebuild his parish church at Kemerton, Gloucestershire, were also controversial. Thorp had been appointed rector in October 1839 by J. H. Monk, bishop of Gloucester, and began to hold daily services in 1844, when he came into residence there. There were more frequent celebrations of holy communion and he introduced a surpliced choir. He engaged Anthony Salvin, who had been the architect on the Round Church project, to advise about the church. Salvin believed that the church needed complete rebuilding, but in the meantime he opened up the chancel, removed the box pews and replaced them with low seats, and lowered the pulpit. Thorp's attempt to pay for rebuilding the church by levying a rate was contested. Objections focused more on the cost than the substance of the proposed changes. After lengthy legal wrangles, the rebuilding was completed in 1849.

Thorp, who resigned as archdeacon and chancellor of Bristol in 1873, died at Kemerton rectory, Gloucestershire, on 24 February 1877. He was unmarried.

J. R. GARRARD

Sources Venn, *Alum. Cant.* · J. F. White, *The Cambridge movement: the ecclesiologists and the Gothic revival* (1962) · N. M. Herbert, 'Archdeacon Thorp and the rebuilding of Kemerton church', *Trans. Gloucs and Bristol Archaeol. Soc.*, 90 (1971), 192–215
Archives BL, corresp. with Lord Aberdeen, Add. MSS 43248–43250 · Trinity Cam., letters to William Whewell, etc.
Likenesses portrait, repro. in *Church of England Photographic Portrait Gallery*, pt 55 (1859)
Wealth at death under £16,000: probate, 30 July 1877, *CGPLA Eng. & Wales*

Thorp, Sir William (d. 1361), justice, was of obscure origins. He first appears as a clerk of the king's bench in 1315, and in that status was assaulted in 1318 by enemies who caught him on the way to court, trampled upon him, and contemptuously urinated on him. He is quoted in two cases during the eyres of 1329–31. At this time an apprentice, he was created a serjeant-at-law in Michaelmas term 1339, while on 20 January 1341 he became a king's serjeant, an office he held until 1344. He was elevated to justice of the king's bench on 20 May 1345, and was knighted at the same time. Promotion to chief justice of the king's bench came soon after, on 16 November 1346.

Venality may have been a constant companion to Thorp's judicial skill, and helps to explain how he came to hold a considerable collection of estates in several counties, particularly in Lincolnshire. An ordinance of 1346 prohibited justices from taking fees and robes from anyone but the king, and from giving advice in any matters relating to the king's affairs. Thorp took this oath in an impressive gathering attended by the king, prelates, and magnates; the king pointedly and personally warned him about the penalties for breaking the oath, namely, death by hanging and confiscation of all goods. The stringencies of the new oath were balanced, however inadequately, by an additional annual fee of 50 marks provided for each justice. However, Thorp persisted in his older and more profitable ways, maintaining close relationships with the town of Cambridge, the abbot of Glastonbury, and especially the abbot of Ramsey, from whom he accepted a retaining fee within a year of the ordinance, and by whom he was feed in 1347–50, 1354–5, and 1361–2. As he later admitted, he took bribes amounting to £100 (probably at Lincoln sessions, Easter term 1349) for respiting the exigent against five men who appeared before him.

Thorp was arrested on 25 October 1350 and imprisoned in the Tower of London. He was tried on 4 November by an imposing panel (the earls of Warwick, Arundel, and Huntingdon, the steward of the royal household, and the king's chamberlain). After he confessed his receipt of bribes, the judges ordered confiscation and sought the king's will. An angry Edward III, apparently seeing Thorp's misdeeds as a rebellious breaking of the personal bond between justice and sovereign, told his judges to proceed; they decreed hanging and confiscation of Thorp's considerable wealth—his moveables were deposited in no fewer than eight monastic houses. Yet by a privy seal letter issued the same day the king pardoned Thorp his life. The imprisonment continued, however, as did the seizures of land and goods. On 24 November the records of the case were sent into chancery, and a new investigation into all aspects of Thorp's judicial proceedings was also ordered. Thorp was released before Christmas, for he and his household spent that holiday as guests of his old friend, the abbot of Ramsey. In the parliament of February 1351 the entire proceedings in the case were laid before the magnates, who approved the sentence.

On 10 March 1351 Edward (citing compassion and appreciation for Thorp's previous good service) provided him with a full pardon and restoration of goods and lands. On 24 May 1352 Thorp was appointed second baron of the exchequer, and he soon was named to a variety of judicial commissions, although he was never returned to the king's bench. Along with other royal justices he was formally excommunicated in 1357 for his failure to appear at the papal court in Avignon in the case of Thomas Lisle, bishop of Ely (d. 1361). His last judicial service seems to have been an oyer and terminer commission for several counties in 1359. He remained on the books of Ramsey Abbey as recipient of a fee until his death, which occurred on 27 May 1361. He appears to have had a son, William, who was pardoned in May 1356 for killing a servant in the New Temple, London.

RICHARD W. KAEUPER

Sources J. Maddicott, *Law and lordship: royal justices as retainers in thirteenth- and fourteenth-century England*, Past and Present, Supplement 4 (1978) · G. O. Sayles, ed., *Select cases in the court of king's bench*, 7 vols., SeldS, 55, 57–8, 74, 76, 82, 88 (1936–71), vols. 4–7 · *Chancery records* · M. C. B. Dawes, ed., *Register of Edward, the Black Prince*, 4 vols., PRO (1930–33) · *RotP* · Baker, *Serjeants* · *CIPM*, vol. 12

Thorpe, Benjamin (1781/2–1870), Old English scholar, is of obscure origins. Nothing is recorded of his parentage, birth, early life, or education. Contemporaries refer only to his works, which are self-effacing. Having decided to study early English antiquities, then much neglected in Great Britain, Thorpe set out about 1826 to Copenhagen, attracted there chiefly by the fame of the great philologist Rasmus Christian Rask, who had recently returned from the East and been appointed professor of literary history at the Danish University. While he was living in Copenhagen he made the acquaintance of Mary Anne Otté, whom he married. In 1830 Thorpe published at Copenhagen an English translation of the second edition of

Rask's *Anglo-Saxon Grammar* (a second edition of this translation appeared at London in 1865). He took his wife and her daughter, Elise Charlotte *Otté (1818–1903), back to England in this same year. Thorpe taught Elise several languages, perhaps launching her lifelong interest in linguistics, but apparently their pedagogic relationship grew more taxing as time went on, and the increasing strain is certainly cited by Edmund Gosse as one of the reasons for Otté's departure for the United States in 1840, though E. S. Day denies the severity of Gosse's interpretation (Gosse, 15; Day, 83).

In 1832 Thorpe published *Cædmon's metrical paraphrase of parts of the holy scriptures in Anglo-Saxon; with an English translation, notes, and a verbal index*. This was hailed at the time as one of the best Old English texts yet issued. It was followed in 1834 by *The Anglo-Saxon version of the story of Apollonius of Tyre, upon which is founded the play of 'Pericles'* and by *Analecta Anglo-Saxonica*, a useful anthology of Old English texts, which was promptly adopted by the Rawlinsonian professor of Old English at Oxford (Robert Meadows White). In this Thorpe sought to promote 'the study of the old vernacular tongue of England, so much neglected at home, and so successfully cultivated by foreign philologists' (Preface, iv). The *Analecta* was praised with discrimination by his peer John Mitchell Kemble, and up to 1876, when Henry Sweet's *Anglo-Saxon Reader* appeared, though beginning to be dated, it remained, with Vernon's *Anglo-Saxon Guide*, the chief book in use.

In 1835 appeared *Libri psalmorum versio antiqua Latina; cum paraphrasi Anglo-Saxonica … descripsit et edidit B. Thorpe* and then in 1840 Thorpe's well-known *Ancient Laws and Institutes of England*, which formed two volumes of 'supreme value to the student of early English history' (Adams, 474; cf. *QR*, 281). Two more volumes were published by Thorpe in 1842, *The Holy Gospels in Anglo-Saxon* and *Codex Exoniensis: a Collection of Anglo-Saxon Poetry, with English Translation and Notes*. Next came, for the Ælfric Society, *The Homilies of the Anglo-Saxon Church*, with an English translation, published in ten parts between 1843 and 1846). In recognition of the importance of all this unremunerative work, in 1835 Thorpe was granted a civil-list pension of £160, which increased on 17 June 1841 to £200 per annum.

As early as 1834 Thorpe had begun a translation of J. M. Lappenberg's works on old English history, but had paused, feeling the inadequacy of his own knowledge. By 1842 better informed, he began another version, with numerous alterations, corrections, and notes of his own. This was published in two volumes in 1845 as *A History of England under the Anglo-Saxon Kings*. It was followed in 1857 by a translation and revision of the same writer's *History of England under the Norman kings … from the battle of Hastings to the accession of the house of Plantagenet*. The literary introduction to both these works, though valuable, was largely superseded by the works of Kemble, and other later Anglo-Saxon scholars. Of more lasting importance was Thorpe's two-volume edition of Florence of Worcester, issued in 1848–9 as *Florentii Wigorniensis monachi Chronicon ex chronicis ab adventu Hengesti*, collated and edited with English notes. In 1851, after a long negotiation with

Edward Lumley, Thorpe sold to him for £150 his valuable *Northern Mythology … from Original and other Sources* (3 vols.), a work containing meticulous notes and illustrations. Continuing in the same vein of research, he produced in 1853 his *Yule Tide Stories: a Collection of Scandinavian and North German Popular Tales and Traditions*, which appeared in Bohn's Antiquarian Library. For the same library he produced in 1854 *The Life of Alfred the Great*, a translation from the work by R. Pauli. In 1855 appeared Thorpe's *Anglo-Saxon Poems of Beowulf*, with translation, notes, glossary, and indexes. Kemble's literal prose translation had appeared in 1837, and Wackerbarth's metrical version in 1849, but Thorpe's text was collated with the Cottonian manuscript before Kemble's; and as the scorched edges of that manuscript, already 'as friable as touchwood', suffered further detriment very shortly after his collation, a particular value attaches to Thorpe's readings, which vary in many respects from those of his predecessor. In 1861 Thorpe gained the lasting gratitude of historical students by his 'excellent edition' for the Rolls Series of *The Anglo-Saxon Chronicle, According to the Several Authorities*. Volume 1 prints synoptically the Corpus Christi, Cambridge, the Bodleian, and the various Cottonian texts, with facsimiles and notes; volume 2 provides a translation (cf. *The Athenaeum*, 1861, 1. 653). Four years later, through the liberality of the antiquary and collector Joseph Mayer of Liverpool, Thorpe was enabled to publish his invaluable supplement to Kemble's *Codex diplomaticus aevi Saxonici*, entitled *Diplomatarium Anglicum aevi Saxonici: a Collection of English Charters, 605–1066*. His last work, done for Trübner in 1866, was *Edda Sæmundar hinns frôða: the Edda of Sæmund the Learned, from the Old Norse or Icelandic*, with a mythological index and an index of persons and places, issued in two parts.

Thorpe, who was an FSA and a member of the Royal Academy of Sciences at Munich and of the Society of Netherlandish Literature at Leiden, spent the last twenty years of his life at Chiswick. He died at The Mall, Chiswick, aged eighty-eight, on 19 July 1870. Of his own generation he was the great exception to Kemble's charge against English scholars of apathy in relation to Anglo-Saxon literature and philology. His widow was granted a civil-list pension of £80 in 1872.

THOMAS SECCOMBE, *rev.* JOHN D. HAIGH

Sources *GM*, 1st ser., 103/1 (1833), 329–31 · *GM*, 2nd ser., 2 (1834), 483–6 · *GM*, 2nd ser., 43 (1855), 611 · review, *QR*, 74 (1844), 281–325 · C. R. Smith, *Retrospections, social and archaeological*, 1 (1883), 70–72 · F. Metcalfe, *The Englishman and the Scandinavian* (1880), 18 · *The Athenaeum* (1861), 653 · *The Athenaeum* (23 July 1870), 117 · E. Gosse, *The Athenaeum* (2 Jan 1904), 15 · E. S. Day, letter, *The Athenaeum* (16 Jan 1904), 82–3 · W. M. Colles, *Literature and the pension list* (1889), 15, 62 · C. K. Adams, *A manual of historical literature* (1882), 428, 474 · *CGPLA Eng. & Wales* (1870)

Archives BL, corresp. with John Allen, Add. MSS 52185–52186 · BL, letters to Philip Bliss, Add. MSS 34571–34580, *passim* · JRL, letters to E. A. Freeman · Wellcome L., corresp. with Thomas Hodgkin

Wealth at death under £200: probate, 10 Aug 1870, *CGPLA Eng. & Wales*

Thorpe, Francis (*bap.* 1594, *d.* 1665), judge, was baptized on 1 October 1594 at Leconfield, Yorkshire, the eldest son of Roger Thorpe (d. c.1626), of Birdsall, Yorkshire, and his wife, Elizabeth, daughter of William Danyell of Beswick. He was born into a cadet branch of a long-established East Riding family, the Thorpes of Thorpe. His father, a Gray's Inn lawyer, was one of James I's gentleman ushers and quarter waiters, and he served as a JP and as sewers commissioner for the East Riding. Thorpe was admitted to Gray's Inn on 12 February 1611 and to St John's College, Cambridge, on 8 November following (graduating BA in 1614). He was called to the bar at Gray's Inn on 11 May 1621. By the mid-1590s Thorpe's family had moved to Leconfield, and in 1624 Thorpe was elected recorder of the nearby borough of Beverley, where he took up residence. He married Elizabeth (d. 1666), daughter of William Oglethorpe of Rawdon, and widow successively of Thomas Wise and Francis Denton. Thorpe was appointed an ancient of Gray's Inn in 1632, a bencher in 1640, and an autumn reader in 1641.

During the course of his legal practice Thorpe fell foul of Thomas, Viscount Wentworth (the future earl of Strafford), president of the council of the north. About 1630 Wentworth had Thorpe removed from the East Riding bench, and then detained in London for failing to pay 'knighthood money', although the real reason, according to Thorpe, was his use of writs of prohibition, which Wentworth saw as a slight to conciliar authority (Rushworth, 8.142). With the help of George, Lord Goring, Thorpe obtained Wentworth's permission to leave London, but back in Yorkshire he was made to kneel in submission before the council. Thorpe was a witness at Strafford's trial in 1641, giving evidence on the first article, that Strafford had exercised an arbitrary power in the north. Strafford's hostility towards Thorpe was not shared by his friend Algernon Percy, tenth earl of Northumberland, who retained Thorpe as one of his counsellors-at-law. Northumberland owned considerable property in Leconfield, and Thorpe's father had served as an estate officer to the Percies. It was possibly on Northumberland's recommendation that Thorpe had been appointed recorder of Hull in 1639.

Thorpe seems to have remained in London for much of the civil war, and in 1643 he served as a legal assistant to the Lords. On 20 October 1645 he was elected as a 'recruiter' MP for the North Riding borough of Richmond, although he was apparently more assiduous in serving Hull's interests at Westminster than those of his constituents. He was probably returned on the recommendation of northern peer and ally of Northumberland, Philip, Lord Wharton, who enjoyed considerable influence in the borough. Thorpe was closely aligned at Westminster with the independent faction, of which Northumberland and Wharton were leading members. He was named to several committees for drawing up the Newcastle peace propositions (which struck at the Scots' confederalist terms for settlement), and was instrumental in introducing legislation over the winter of 1646–7 to recompense Viscount Saye and Sele for losing the mastership of the recently abolished court of wards. Saye was a leading independent, and the leveller John Wildman claimed that the scheme to

recompense the court's officers was part of a design by Oliver Cromwell and Henry Ireton to enrich their political allies. Thorpe's letters to Hull corporation during the mid-1640s reveal that he shared the Independents' distrust of the king, and their desire to impose a stringent settlement upon him. He also emerges as a friend of the Hull preacher John Shawe—a moderate Independent divine who probably favoured an Erastian presbyterian church with limited toleration.

During the second civil war Thorpe played a leading role in organizing parliament's forces in the north, and was rewarded with the stewardship of the duke of Buckingham's sequestered estates in Yorkshire. In October 1648 parliament appointed Thorpe a serjeant-at-law, Lord Wharton acting as one of his sponsors. Thorpe retained his seat at Pride's Purge, and was seen by William Prynne and others as a firm adherent of the pro-army 'junto' (W. Prynne, *A Brief Memento to the Present Unparliamentary Junto*, 1649, 10; *Remonstrance and Declaration of Severall Counties, Cities and Burroughs*, 1648, 4–8). Nevertheless, although named as a commissioner to try the king, Thorpe took no part in the trial proceedings, and he did not make his dissent to the vote on 5 December until after the king's execution. Evidently trusted by the Rump Parliament, he was appointed in February 1649 to ride the northern circuit. In his charge to the grand jury at York in March he justified the establishment of the Commonwealth, arguing that although the people, under God, were 'the original of all just power', the only proper agency of such authority was the Rump (*Harleian Miscellany*, 2.2–3). In April he was thanked by the house for his 'great services done to the Commonwealth in the last circuit' (*JHC*, 6.187). On 1 June he was made one of the barons of the exchequer, an office reputedly worth £1000 per annum, but he was obliged to resign his recorderships. On 1 April 1650 he was named one of the commissioners in the act for establishing a new high court of justice.

Although Thorpe was active under the Rump Parliament, particularly in a legal capacity, several commentators alleged that he became disaffected to the republican interest. A royalist agent described him in 1650 as mistrustful of the army and willing to comply with its supporters only to avoid exciting their suspicion. However, Thorpe's commitment to the Rump Parliament was sufficient to make him exchange 'a gown for a sword' (*Mercurius Politicus*, 14–21 Aug 1651, 1001) in 1651 to help resist the invading Scots. In the elections to the first protectorate parliament in 1654 Thorpe was returned for Beverley. In November 1654 he was appointed one of the judges on the western circuit and the following March he became a commissioner for trying the insurgents in Penruddock's rising. After proceeding against the western rebels he was ordered by Cromwell to sit in judgement on their Yorkshire counterparts. He and Sir Richard Newdigate, however, protested against dispensing with the usual lapse of fifteen days before acting upon a newly issued commission, and objected to trying men without evidence of treasonable intent. The two judges's delay in proceeding was rightly interpreted as a refusal to serve, and they were removed from office on 3 May. In the elections to the second protectorate parliament in 1656 Thorpe was returned for Beverley again, but was prevented from sitting—probably as an opponent of the major-generals—and he signed the remonstrance of the excluded members. In November 1657, in a petition to Cromwell for his arrears of salary, he acknowledged that he had incurred the protector's displeasure, but hoped that since he had now returned to private practice his petition would be allowed. A warrant was issued for payment of his arrears on 8 February 1658. At the start of the second session in January 1658 Thorpe was allowed to take his seat in the Commons. He spoke against the Cromwellian upper house, arguing that although the 'old constitution, by Lords and Commons' was best, it was dangerous to give the peers or their replacements a negative voice (*Diary of Thomas Burton*, 2.447).

Thorpe resumed his seat when the Rump Parliament was restored in May 1659, and in the summer of that year rode the northern circuit with John Parker. He was reinstated as one of the barons of the exchequer by the Rump on 19 January 1660 and ordered to ride the northern circuit for the Lent assizes. He was one of only three judges whose patent of office was not renewed at the Restoration. In May 1660 he petitioned the king for a special pardon, avowing that he had opposed the regicide, had never purchased crown lands, and had refused to try the Yorkshire royalists in 1655. He was among those named in the Commons on 13 June for exclusion from the Act of Indemnity and, having been accused of detaining £25,000 as receiver of public money in Yorkshire, William Prynne desired that Thorpe might suffer death, like the Judge Thorpe who had been executed in 1350 for taking bribes. However, several members spoke in Thorpe's defence and he was given the benefit of the act. Thorpe died intestate (leaving a personal estate of about £9000) and without surviving children at his country seat of Bardsey Grange, near Leeds, and he was buried at Bardsey church on 7 June 1665. His widow died on 1 August 1666 and was buried with him.   DAVID SCOTT

Sources D. Scott, 'Thorpe, Francis', HoP, *Commons* [draft] · *JHC*, 4–8 (1644–67) · T. T. Wildridge, ed., *The Hull letters* (1886) · *CSP dom.*, 1649–51 · C. H. Firth and R. S. Rait, eds., *Acts and ordinances of the interregnum, 1642–1660*, 3 vols. (1911) · *Diary of Thomas Burton*, ed. J. T. Rutt, 4 vols. (1828), vol. 2 · T. D. Whitaker, *Loidis and Elmete* (1816) · W. R. Douthwaite, *Gray's Inn, its history and associations* (1886) · *The writings and speeches of Oliver Cromwell*, ed. W. C. Abbott and C. D. Crane, 3 (1945) · W. Oldys and T. Park, eds., *The Harleian miscellany*, 10 vols. (1808–13), vol. 2 · J. Rushworth, *Historical collections*, new edn, 8 (1721) · Thomason tracts: *A fourth word to the wise, or, A plaine discovery of Englands misery* [1647] [E 391(9)]; *A remonstrance and declaration of severall counties, cities, and burroughs* (1648) [E 536(23)]; W. Prynne, *A breife memento to the present unparliamentary junto* (1648/9) [E 537(7)]; *The countrey committees laid open* (1649) [E 558(11)]; [W. Prynne], *A full declaration of the true state of the secluded members case* (1660) [E 1013(22)]; [see also E 640(14)]

Archives East Riding of Yorkshire Archives Service, Beverley, BCII/7/4/1, fol. 94; BCII/5/1/1, fol. 11 · East Riding of Yorkshire Archives Service, Beverley, PE 116/1 · PRO, C 10/108/144; C 181/3–6; C 192/1; C 231/4–6; E 115/391/117; E 179/205/465; REQ 2/413; SP 14/33, fol. 20 | Hull Archives, Hull letters, L321–509

Wealth at death personal estate valued at £8000–£10,000: PRO C 10/108/144

Thorpe, John, **first Lord Thorpe** (*c.*1270–1324), baron and administrator, was the son of Robert of Thorpe or Ashwellthorpe, a village south-west of Norwich, and his wife Matilda. His father, who had died by 1304, was a landowner in Norfolk and Suffolk; his mother's parents are unknown, but she was the niece of Richard of Eye, parson of Fundenhall, Norfolk, making it likely that John was of East Anglian descent on both sides. He had a sister Alice and brothers Philip and George. A tenant of the Bigod earls of Norfolk, John Thorpe is first recorded in 1291 as serving the king in Scotland. Some time before 1304 he served in Gascony, and he was regularly summoned to fight in Scotland between 1309 and 1323. He possessed legal and administrative skills as well as military ones. A knight of the shire for Norfolk in 1305, in that year and in 1307 he was a trailbaston justice there and in Suffolk, while from 1299 he was regularly an oyer and terminer commissioner in both shires. He was also employed in assessing and collecting taxes and in organizing food supplies for the king's armies. Moreover he was *persona grata* at court, becoming on 23 May 1307 steward of the king's household, a position he held until the death of Edward I on 7 July following.

Thorpe had no similar employment under Edward II, but he was among the justices summoned to the latter's first parliament, while on 4 March 1309 he received an individual summons and is regarded as having thereby become Lord Thorpe. In 1310 he received custody of the lands of Roger (IV) Bigod, now in the possession of the crown, to administer them on behalf of two of the king's half-brothers. He went overseas in the king's service at least twice, and also acted as a justice of assize and gaol delivery, as well as continuing to receive numerous commissions, almost always in East Anglia. In December 1311, for instance, he was appointed to enforce the Statute of Winchester; a year later to assess a tallage; in 1317 to investigate a dispute between the count of Hainault and the men of Yarmouth; and in 1320 to deal with official malpractices in four counties. Regularly a keeper of the peace in Norfolk, he was appointed sheriff of Norfolk and Suffolk on 7 June 1320, but was replaced on 12 July. Possibly Thorpe's loyalty to Edward II's regime was becoming suspect. On 30 November 1321 he was ordered to levy the men of East Anglia against rebels, but earlier in the month he had been forbidden to attend the earl of Lancaster's assembly at Doncaster, and in the following June he was briefly arrested as an associate of the rebel Sir William Trussell. But it seems unlikely that he was seriously disaffected, for he continued to be summoned to councils and parliaments, and to Scottish campaigns, probably until his health failed. His last commission was issued on 15 November 1323, and he died on 15 or 16 May 1324. His wife survived him, dying some time before 1346.

John Thorpe married twice. His first wife, named Agnes, who was the mother of his children, died in 1300 or 1301, and by 28 July 1301 he had remarried; his second wife was Alice, widow of William Mortimer of Attleborough, who brought him a number of manors and portions of manors in East Anglia. Thorpe acted alone in 1311 when he endowed a modest chantry at Ashwellthorpe, but in 1322 he and Alice together gave lands to Pentney Priory. However, Thorpe is more often recorded acquiring property than giving it away. The family cartulary records numerous purchases from 1290 onwards. Some represent significant additions to his estates, as when he paid £40 in 1290 for lands, rents, and serfs in three vills in Norfolk and Suffolk, and 220 marks in 1299 for everything two vendors owned in Wreningham. But many were on a very small scale, 30d. for a yearly rent of 3d. from lands in Tittleshall, for instance, and properties of just an acre or two, suggesting that Thorpe was as concerned to consolidate his possessions as to extend them. At his death he was recorded as the lord of sixteen manors or half-manors in East Anglia, with outlying estates in Northamptonshire and Yorkshire.

John Thorpe's heir was his eldest son, **Robert Thorpe**, second Lord Thorpe (1293/4–1330), who was aged thirty when his father died, and had been married since at least 1316 to Beatrice, daughter of Thomas Hengrave. He was several times employed as a diplomat. On 18 January 1323 he was granted protection to go to the papal court at Avignon, while in March 1324 he was about to go to Gascony with the earl of Kent. Possibly delayed by his father's death, he had arrived by 1 September, and was briefly mayor of Bordeaux following the death of Sir Robert Shirlaund. Following a number of peace-making missions within the duchy he went to Aragon, under a commission of 16 February 1325, to treat for the marriage of Prince Edward to the Infanta Iolanta. The mission failed, and as he returned Thorpe was captured by the Seigneur d'Albret on 11 May, and not released until 16 February 1326. He was back in England by 23 June following, when he was sent on embassy to Scotland. But his captivity may have ruined his health, for he was not employed again, and he died on 8 April 1330. His heir was his fourteen-year-old son, John, whose wardship was granted to the Suffolk magnate Sir Oliver Ingham. Robert was long outlived by his wife, who died on 4 July 1361.   HENRY SUMMERSON

Sources GEC, *Peerage*, new edn, 12/1.718–21 · Chancery records · Thorpe cartulary, CUL, MS Mm. 5.35 · A. Musson, *Public order and law enforcement: the local administration of criminal justice, 1294–1350* (1996) · Rymer, *Foedera*, new edn · F. Blomefield and C. Parkin, *An essay towards a topographical history of the county of Norfolk*, [2nd edn], 11 vols. (1805–10), vol. 5 · *Members of parliament: return to two orders of the honorable the House of Commons*, House of Commons, 1 (1878) · *Reports … touching the dignity of a peer of the realm*, House of Lords, 3 (1829) · F. Palgrave, ed., *The parliamentary writs and writs of military summons*, 2/3 (1834) · *CIPM*, vols. 4, 6 · P. Chaplais, ed., *The War of Saint-Sardos (1323–1325): Gascon correspondence and diplomatic documents*, CS, 3rd ser., 87 (1954) · *Itineraries [of] William Worcestre*, ed. J. H. Harvey, OMT (1969) · *RotP*, vol. 1 · Tout, *Admin. hist.*, vol. 6

Thorpe, John (1564/5–1655), surveyor and architect, was born into a family of masons in the quarrying village of Kingscliffe, Northamptonshire. He was the second son of Thomas Thorpe (d. 1596), who worked as master mason on the building of Kirby Hall, Northamptonshire, for Sir Humphrey Stafford, where the infant John symbolically laid the first stone in 1570. His grandfather, also Thomas, was a mason and his younger brother, another Thomas,

had a successful career as a mason and a stone supplier on various royal works from 1603 onwards and as one of the principal contractors for Blickling Hall, Norfolk, between 1619 and 1624. The family was armigerous and descended from the Thorpes of Ashwellthorp, near Wymondham, Norfolk.

John Thorpe does not appear to have been trained in the family craft and he first entered the building world at about eighteen years of age in an administrative capacity. From 1583 to 1601 he worked as a clerk in the office of works at Richmond, Greenwich, Whitehall, and various other royal houses. During this lengthy period of public service he exhibited a notable talent as a draughtsman and developed a circle of useful connections both with patrons and with influential officers of the works, many of whom lived in an area around St Martin-in-the-Fields, where Thorpe had a house in Little Church Lane next to Thomas Fowler, the comptroller of the works. On 15 September 1592 he married Rebecca Greene (b. 1575), the daughter of a woodmonger originally from Brampton in Huntingdonshire, some 20 miles from Kingscliffe; this union produced a family of five sons and seven daughters. Thorpe played an active role in parish affairs, serving as a vestryman for more than thirty-five years and providing his professional expertise whenever it was required. In common with other members of the central works team he was able to carry out private commissions in addition to his official employment. Thus in 1600 his unsuccessful suit for the reversion of one of the senior posts in the organization was supported by Sir Henry Neville, ambassador in Paris, for whom he had prepared plans for extending his country seat at Billingbear in Berkshire. In the following year, possibly as a result of this setback to his ambitions, he left the office of works and set up on his own in the emerging profession of surveyor, offering a service that covered both land and buildings.

It was an opportune moment and Thorpe rapidly built up a successful practice in response to the increasing demand for accurate estate surveys stimulated by the land transactions of the new king and his court. He took a major share of this new business and his commissions included Holdenby, Hatfield, and Theobalds for the crown, as well as many surveys for the duchy of Cornwall, the prince of Wales, and other private clients. As a land surveyor he must be counted among the two or three most eminent practitioners of the period. It brought him sufficient income to invest in land and property and in 1611 he was awarded an annuity of £20 for life when he re-entered government service as one of the two assistants to Robert Treswell, the surveyor-general of woods south of Trent.

The surveying side of his practice must have kept Thorpe exceedingly busy around the Jacobean court, but at the same time he was forging a reputation as a designer of buildings, the enigmatic legacy of which is contained in his manuscript volume of house plans and elevations, rediscovered by Horace Walpole in 1780 and now preserved in Sir John Soane's Museum. It contains a collection of more than 150 plans, mainly of country houses but also including some architectural details and exercises in perspective. Sir John Summerson's careful analysis, published for the Walpole Society in 1966, has demonstrated that the genesis of the collection was a group of thirteen plans inherited from Thorpe's father at his death in 1596. The rest of the book is made up of surveys of existing houses, copies of designs made by others, and projects for new houses, not all of which were executed. Together with the roughly contemporary collection of drawings made by the Smythson family, it is a key text for an understanding of the processes of design, the circles of patronage, and the architectural influences which shaped the distinctive domestic architecture of the late Elizabethan and Jacobean élite.

The collection continues to present problems in distinguishing those plans which are original designs by Thorpe himself from the many commissioned surveys of extant buildings which he also carried out but for which he had no design responsibility. Late twentieth-century research extended the attributions made by Summerson to include Thornton College, Lincolnshire (*c*.1607–1610), for Sir Vincent Skinner, possibly Dowsby Hall in the same county (*c*.1610) for Richard Burrell, the outer court of the earl of Suffolk's magnificent mansion at Audley End, Essex (*c*.1615), and Aston Hall, Warwickshire (1618–35), for Sir Thomas Holte. It is probable that a number of other buildings could be added to the corpus of his original work if only the documentation could be found. His designs are not as innovative as those by Robert Smythson, but they show a similar delight in the manipulation of geometrical forms and patterns of fenestration and a growing interest in the development of the house plan away from its medieval outline towards the more compact silhouette which was to dominate the remainder of the seventeenth century.

Thorpe was an accomplished linguist and it is clear from his drawings that he was conversant with a number of continental publications, including those of Palladio, Vredeman de Vries, Giacomo Vignola, and Jacques Perret. A particularly powerful influence was the Frenchman Jacques Androuet du Cerceau: Thorpe copied a number of illustrations directly from du Cerceau's *Le premier volume des plus excellents bastiments de France* (1576), as well as incorporating elements from the same book in his own designs. The curious design for a house based on his own initials is presented in perspective using a method derived from du Cerceau's *Leçons de perspective positive* (1576), and Thorpe's own copy is in the Bodleian Library interleaved with a manuscript translation partly in his own hand. The evidence suggests that he was preparing the book for publication, and had the project gone ahead it would have been the first book in English on the subject of perspective.

The manuscript translation is not dated but it is probable that John Thorpe was the IT who translated Hans Blum's Latin treatise on the orders (1550) on its English publication as *The Booke of Five Collumnes of Architecture* in 1601. If this assumption is correct, he enjoyed moderate success as a translator, with a second edition coming out in 1608. Evidence of his knowledge of Latin is provided by the epigram that he contributed to the 1612 edition of Henry Peacham's *The Gentleman's Exercise*, where he was described as an 'excellent Geometrician and Surveiour … not onley learned and ingenuous himselfe, but a furtherer and favorer of all excellency whatsoever, of whom our age findeth too few' (p. 172).

The latest architectural drawings in Thorpe's book date from the 1620s. In 1625–7 he was supervising building works at Belvoir Castle, Leicestershire, for the earl of Rutland, and he seems to have retired shortly afterwards. He continued to live in his London house until about 1651, when he moved to Egham, Surrey, where he owned some land. He died in 1655 at nearly ninety years of age and was buried in the churchyard of St Paul's, Covent Garden, on 14 February of that year. His name is inscribed on the Thorpe family monument which was erected in 1623, long before his death, in the parish church of Kingscliffe. In the absence of his will, Peacham's character study can stand as his obituary. He was one of a group of men who expanded the vocabulary of English architecture in the late sixteenth and early seventeenth centuries and helped to establish the nascent professions of surveyor and architect. In the metropolitan world, where he spent most of his long life, he was a respected professional who helped to disseminate continental learning and a conscientious public servant both to his adopted parish and to the state. His collection of drawings remains as a graphic testimony to his achievements as both a recorder and a creator of some of the most important buildings of the age.

MALCOLM AIRS

Sources J. Summerson, 'The book of architecture of John Thorpe in Sir John Soane's Museum', *Walpole Society*, 40 (1964–6) [whole issue] · J. Bridges, *The history and antiquities of Northamptonshire*, ed. P. Whalley, 2 (1791), 432 · Colvin, *Archs.* · K. J. Höltgen, 'An unknown manuscript translation by John Thorpe of du Cerceau's *Perspective*', *England and the continental renaissance*, ed. E. Chaney and P. Mack (1990), 215–28 · P. J. Drury, 'No other palace in the kingdom will compare with it: the evolution of Audley End, 1605–1745', *Architectural History*, 23 (1980), 1–39 · O. Fairclough, 'John Thorpe and Aston Hall', *Architectural History*, 32 (1989), 30–51 · D. L. Roberts, 'John Thorpe's designs for Dowslay Hall and the Red Hall, Bourne', *Lincolnshire History and Archaeology*, 8 (1973), 13–34 · D. L. Roberts, 'John Thorpe's drawings for Thornton College, the house of Sir Vincent Skinner', *Lincolnshire History and Archaeology*, 19 (1984), 57–63 · A. Wells-Cole, *Art and decoration in Elizabethan and Jacobean England* (1997) · H. M. Colvin and others, eds., *The history of the king's works*, 3 (1975), 88, 101–2

Archives Bodl. Oxf., LL23* Art. Seld. · Sir John Soane's Museum, London | Belvoir Castle, Leicestershire, Belvoir MSS · PRO, close rolls · PRO, Exchequer · PRO, state papers · PRO, patent rolls · Rockingham Castle, Culme-Seymour MSS

Wealth at death property in London, Kingscliffe, Egham: Summerson, 'Book of architecture', 12

Thorpe, John (1682–1750), physician and antiquary, eldest son of John Thorpe, landowner, and his wife, Ann, sister and coheir of Oliver Combridge, of Newhouse, Penshurst, Kent, was born at his father's house, Newhouse, on 12 March 1682. His father owned a good estate in the Kentish

John Thorpe (1682–1750), by J. Bayly, pubd 1769 (after John Wollaston)

parishes of Penshurst, Lamberhurst, Tonbridge, and Chiddingstone. He attended the grammar school at Westerham, where the master was Thomas Manningham, afterwards bishop of Chichester. On 14 April 1698 he matriculated from University College, Oxford, whence he graduated BA at Michaelmas 1701, MA on 27 June 1704, MB on 16 May 1707, and MD in July 1710. Elected a fellow of the Royal Society on 30 November 1705, he was then living in Ormond Street, London, near his friend Richard Mead, the physician. For some years he assisted another friend, Sir Hans Sloane, in publishing the Royal Society's *Philosophical Transactions*, which included on 24 July 1704 a letter to Sloane on worms in the heads of sheep.

On 5 May 1715 Thorpe married Elizabeth, daughter of John Woodhouse of Shobdon, Herefordshire, at St Benet Paul's Wharf, London. In the same year he settled as a physician in Rochester, where he and his wife lived within the precincts of the cathedral. He developed a considerable practice and gave free medical aid to the poor in his district. He was noted in the 1740 medical diary of Dr Jeremiah Cliff of Tenterden. In 1734 he became a freeman of the city of Rochester. Devoting himself to the study of the architecture, antiquities, and the history of the county of Kent, he made numerous manuscript extracts relating to Kent from central archives; his papers eventually made their way to the Society of Antiquaries. The Scotgrove chantry, part of the long defunct manor of Scotgrove, in the parish of Hartley, was rescued from oblivion by Thorpe's enquiring mind in 1728. His collections were published posthumously in 1769 by his son, John *Thorpe,

in folio, under the title of *Registrum Roffense*. The book contains numerous charters (all given in full), monumental inscriptions, and other historical materials.

Thorpe was generous in his historical assistance to Thomas Hearne, Browne Willis, and other scholars, and he edited the 'Itinera Alpina Tria' of Scheuchzer. He improved the management and finances of Rochester Bridge in his role as a warden and assistant of the bridge from 1731 until his death, serving as senior warden in 1733 and 1742 and as junior warden in 1746. In 1731 he published *A List of the Lands Contributory to Rochester Bridge*. He compiled the earliest surviving record of its archives, had the accounts bound in leather, and presented to the Bridge Chamber a splendid set of chairs and staves suitable for the senior and junior wardens. In a useful report he examined in detail repairs to the bridge undertaken during the previous three centuries. A mass of material about the bridge occupies four volumes in the Thorpe MSS in the library of the Society of Antiquaries. In 1733 he published a collection of statutes of Richard II, Henry V, Elizabeth, and Anne, concerning the bridge. Thorpe died on 30 November 1750 at Rochester and was buried in the church of Stockbury, Kent, in which parish he had purchased a house and land called Nettlested, once owned by the family of the antiquary Robert Plot.

NORMAN MOORE, rev. JOHN WHYMAN

Sources A. Winnifrith, *Men of Kent and Kentish Men: biographical notices of 680 worthies of Kent* (1913), 464 · N. Yates and J. M. Gibson, eds., *Traffic and politics: the construction and management of Rochester bridge, AD 43–1993* (1994), 18, 26, 175–6, 179, 192–3, 298, pl. 9 · F. F. Smith, *A history of Rochester* (1928); repr. (1976), 243, 417 · W. B. Rye, 'Tombs of Sir William Arundel and others in Rochester Cathedral', *Archaeologia Cantiana*, 13 (1880), 141–5, esp. 142 · A. A. Arnold, 'Quarry House, on Frindsbury Hill', *Archaeologia Cantiana*, 17 (1887), 169–80, esp. 178 · A. A. Arnold, 'Rochester bridge in AD 1561', *Archaeologia Cantiana*, 17 (1887), 212–40, esp. 212–13 · S. W. Wheatley, 'Heraldic decoration of the drawbridge of the medieval bridge of Rochester', *Archaeologia Cantiana*, 63 (1950), 140–43, esp. 140 · F. Hull, '*Memento mori* or Dr Cliff's diary, an unusual demographic document', *Archaeologia Cantiana*, 89 (1974), 11–23, esp. 22 · W. H. Proudfoot, 'The manor and chantry of Scotgrove', *Archaeologia Cantiana*, 94 (1978), 7–26, esp. 19–20 · J. Boyle, 'Hasted in perspective', *Archaeologia Cantiana*, 100 (1984), 295–304, esp. 298 · J. Thorpe, ed., *Registrum Roffense, or, A collection of antient records, charters and instruments … illustrating the ecclesiastical history and antiquities of the diocese and cathedral church of Rochester* (1769) · Nichols, *Lit. anecdotes*, 3.509–14 · T. Thomson, *History of the Royal Society from its institution to the end of the eighteenth century* (1812) · IGI

Archives S. Antiquaries, Lond., corresp. and Kent collections | BL, Sloane MSS, corresp. with Sir Hans Sloane and J. Petiver · Bodl. Oxf., letters to Thomas Hearne

Likenesses J. Bayly, line print, pubd 1769 (after J. Wollaston), BM, NPG [see illus.]

Thorpe, John (1715/16–1792), antiquary, was probably born in Rochester, Kent, the only son of John *Thorpe (1682–1750), physician and antiquary, and Elizabeth Woodhouse. He was educated nearby at Luddesdown under the Revd Samuel Thornton, and at the age of sixteen matriculated from University College, Oxford, on 22 March 1732, graduating BA in 1735 and MA in 1738. In 1746 he married Catharina (d. 1789), daughter of Laurence

Holker, physician, of Gravesend, and Katharine Allen; they had two daughters, Catharine and Ethelinda.

Thorpe commenced the study of medicine but abandoned it, and, like his father, devoted himself to antiquarian research. In 1755 he was elected a fellow of the Society of Antiquaries. In 1769 he published, with the assistance of John Baynard of the Navy Office, his father's *Registrum Roffense*, a collection of materials relating to Rochester. In 1788 he supplemented the work by publishing the *Custumale Roffense* from the original manuscript, adding other memorials from the cathedral. For this purpose he used his father's papers and, like other antiquaries, undertook visits to Darenth church (1768), Scotgrove chantry (1769), Higham Priory (1776), the lost village of Merston (1776), Horsted (1777), Manor Farm, Ruxley, and Shorne. He wrote the *Custumale Roffense* while residing at High-street House, Bexley, from where, after the death of his first wife on 10 January 1789, he moved to Richmond Green, Surrey, and then to Chippenham, Wiltshire. Catharina's grave is in the churchyard adjoining High-street House. On 6 July 1790 he married his second wife, Mrs Holland, his housekeeper and 'the widow of an old collegiate acquaintance'. Thorpe also contributed 'Illustrations of several antiquities in Kent which have hitherto remained undescribed' to the first volume of the *Bibliotheca Topographica Britannica*. A letter from him to Andrew Coltée Ducarel in which he argued, contrary to Daines Barrington, that the cherry is indigenous to England, was published in the *Philosophical Transactions* of the Royal Society (1771, 152). He frequently made contributions on antiquarian subjects to the *Gentleman's Magazine*. He was a friend of the great Kent historian Edward Hasted, with whom he corresponded and to whom he lent family manuscripts, as Hasted recorded in 'The following Notes, Coats of Arms, Drawings of Monuments and churches were copied by me from a curious MS in the possession of John Thorp [*sic*] of Bexley, Esqr. in the year 1768' (BL, Hasted MSS, Add. MS 5479 D.IV). As a great Kent antiquary Thorpe followed in the footsteps of his father, being prominent among many who rendered advice and assistance to Hasted. Thorpe died at Chippenham on 2 August 1792 and was buried in the churchyard of the neighbouring village of Hardenhuish.

E. I. Carlyle, *rev.* John Whyman

Sources A. Winnifrith, *Men of Kent and Kentish Men: biographical notices of 680 worthies of Kent* (1913), 464–5 · J. Boyle, *In quest of Hasted* (1984), 49, 50, 57–61, 65, 133 · *GM*, 1st ser., 62 (1792), 769–70, 1101 · *GM*, 1st ser., 63 (1793), 129 · Nichols, *Lit. anecdotes*, 3.515; 6.386 · Nichols, *Illustrations*, 4.646, 673 · A. Chalmers, ed., *The general biographical dictionary*, new edn, 32 vols. (1812–17) · Foster, *Alum. Oxon.* · J. H. Evans, 'The tomb of Horsa', *Archaeologia Cantiana*, 65 (1952), 101–13, esp. 107–8 · A. F. Allen, 'The lost village of Merston', *Archaeologia Cantiana*, 71 (1957), 198–205, esp. 204 · 'Annual report, 1959', *Archaeologia Cantiana*, 73 (1959), xlii–lvi, esp. liii · J. E. L. Caiger, 'The Crepehege Brass at Darenth', *Archaeologia Cantiana*, 77 (1962), 153–5 · P. J. Tester, 'Excavations on the site of Higham Priory', *Archaeologia Cantiana*, 82 (1967), 143–61, esp. 143, 153, 155 · 'Investigations and excavations during the year', *Archaeologia Cantiana*, 93 (1977), 219–27, esp. 226–7 · W. H. Proudfoot, 'The manor and chantry of Scotgrove', *Archaeologia Cantiana*, 94 (1978), 7–26, esp. 19–20 · A. Cronk, 'Oasts in Kent and east Sussex, part 1', *Archaeologia Cantiana*, 94 (1978), 99–110, esp. 107 · J. Boyle, 'Some discoveries about Edward Hasted and his *History of Kent*', *Archaeologia Cantiana*, 97 (1981), 235–59, esp. 257 · J. Boyle, 'Hasted in perspective', *Archaeologia Cantiana*, 100 (1984), 295–304, esp. 298, 300, 302

Archives S. Antiquaries, Lond., historical corresp., notes, and papers

Likenesses T. Cook, engraving (after W. Hardy), repro. in J. Thorpe, *Custumale Roffense* (1788) · T. Cook, line engraving (after W. Hardy), BM; repro. in Nichols, *Illustrations* (1827) · W. Radcliffe, portrait (after W. Hardy), NPG

Thorpe, Robert of (*d.* 1291/2), justice, was probably born some years before 1250. His surname was derived from Thorpe Acre near Garendon in Leicestershire; the names of his parents are unknown. He studied at Oxford University and by 1271 had already gained a degree; in 1274 he was a party to the peace treaty between the scholars of the north and the scholars of the south which put an end to several months of violent disturbances between the two groups and their allies. By 1281 he had probably entered the service of Master Jordan of Wimborne, the archdeacon of Chester, as he was appointed one of his general attorneys when he went abroad. In the Oxfordshire eyre of 1285 he was among those presented as having been involved in the killing of an Irish tailor, probably during the course of the student disturbances of 1273–4, but when he surrendered to gaol after the eyre was over a jury cleared him of any part in the killing. At the end of 1286 Thorpe was summoned into the king's service in Gascony, and for most of 1287 acted as leader of a group of *inquisitores*, probably those inquiring into the misconduct of the late seneschal, Jean de Grailly. When most of the justices of the common bench were dismissed in early January 1290, Thorpe was pressed into service as a junior justice, though there is no evidence of his having any previous expertise in the common law. His final term as a justice of the court was Michaelmas term 1291, and it is likely that he died during the following vacation. His heir was his brother Serlo; he was probably also survived by a second brother, John.

Paul Brand

Sources PRO, court of common pleas, writ files, CP 52(1) · exchequer of pleas, plea rolls, PRO, E 13 · eyre and assize rolls, PRO, JUST 1 · B. F. Byerly and C. R. Byerly, eds., *Records of the wardrobe and household, 1286–1289* (1986), nos. 633, 684 · H. E. Salter, ed., *Mediaeval archives of the University of Oxford*, 1, OHS, 70 (1920), 23 ff.

Thorpe, Robert, second Lord Thorpe (1293/4–1330). *See under* Thorpe, John, first Lord Thorpe (*c.*1270–1324).

Thorpe, Sir Robert (*d.* 1372), justice, was the son of Sir Robert Thorpe of Orton Waterville, Huntingdonshire, steward of the liberties of Peterborough Abbey, and his wife, Margaret. He has often been confused with a contemporary who was the second master of Pembroke College, Cambridge. The Thorpe family produced a number of prominent lawyers, and Robert's relative, Sir William Thorpe, chief justice of the king's bench, may have been influential in guiding him towards a legal career. Robert was created a serjeant-at-law in 1339 and was king's serjeant between 1345 and 1356. He served regularly on commissions of assize, gaol delivery, and oyer and terminer, and as justice of the peace, in Cambridgeshire, Huntingdonshire, Norfolk, Suffolk, Bedfordshire, and

Buckinghamshire. His local connections are illustrated by the generous pensions and fees paid to him from 1352–3 onwards by Ramsey Abbey. He also built up his landed base in the region, gaining life interests in estates in Northamptonshire, Cambridgeshire, and Hertfordshire.

On 27 June 1356 Thorpe was appointed chief justice of the court of common pleas and assumed knighthood, and on 1 October he was awarded a grant of £40 a year from the exchequer to support his new rank. His influence in the courts was recognized by both the Black Prince and John of Gaunt, who appointed him to their councils. In 1365 he was involved in an important debate on the relative status of ordinances and statutes. Appointed a trier of petitions in every parliament between 1362 and 1371, he took part in the parliamentary trial of Sir John de la Lee, steward of the king's household, in 1368, and in 1371 he was a member of the committee of royal judges appointed to inquire into the embezzlement of ransoms collected for the king by Sir William Latimer.

In the parliament of 1371 an anti-clerical movement forced the crown to dismiss the chancellor, treasurer, and keeper of the privy seal and replace them with laymen. Thorpe was appointed to succeed William Wykeham as chancellor on 26 March, though he did not formally vacate his judicial post until 14 April. The circumstances of his appointment suggest that he was in good political standing with the Commons. His tenure of office was, however, brief. On 29 June 1372, at the house of Robert Wyville, bishop of Salisbury, in Fleet Street, London, being very ill, he put the great seal out of commission by having it enclosed in a bag sealed with his own seal and the seals of Sir John Knyvet, the chief justice of the king's bench, and others. At the same time he made a will by which his executors, who included Knyvet, were empowered to sell all his moveable property and use the proceeds for the benefit of his soul. He died the same night.

In 1367 Thorpe had acquired a licence to alienate property in mortmain for the provision of prayers for himself, his parents, and benefactors in the chapel of St Mary, Maxey, in Northamptonshire. On 24 March 1373 his executors received a similar licence to found a chantry in Helpston church (also in Northamptonshire), served by three chaplains, to celebrate divine service for the king, the souls of queens Isabella and Philippa, and those of Thorpe and his parents. Thorpe, who evidently never married, was buried with other members of his family in Peterborough Abbey; a commemorative brass depicting him in his judge's robes was destroyed during the civil war.

W. M. ORMROD

Sources Baker, *Serjeants* · *Henry of Pytchley's book of fees*, ed. W. T. Mellows, Northamptonshire RS, 2 (1927) · Emden, *Cam.* · Tout, *Admin. hist.* · Sainty, *King's counsel* · Sainty, *Judges* · *Chancery records* · G. Holmes, *The Good Parliament* (1975) · S. Walker, *The Lancastrian affinity, 1361–1399* (1990) · J. R. Maddicott, *Law and lordship: royal justices as retainers in thirteenth- and fourteenth-century England* (1978) · *CIPM*, 13, no. 211 · N. H. Nicolas, ed., *Testamenta vetusta: being illustrations from wills*, 1 (1826), 88 · R. R. Sharpe, ed., *Calendar of wills proved and enrolled in the court of husting, London, AD 1258 – AD 1688*, 2 (1890), 149–50

Thorpe, Thomas (*d.* 1461), administrator and speaker of the House of Commons, was of unknown parentage, but was almost certainly a native of Northamptonshire, where he later acquired the manor of Barnwell All Saints. He obtained employment in the exchequer, where by about 20 July 1437 he was a summoner. He probably owed his subsequent advancement to the patronage of the Beauforts, perhaps mediated through John Somerset, physician to the king and also chancellor of the exchequer, with whom Thorpe was associated in the grant of a wardship in 1443. On 4 February 1444 he became lord treasurer's remembrancer, at first during good behaviour, but on 16 September for life. On 8 January 1446 he was granted an annuity of 50 marks for life. Promotion brought riches, and Thorpe was able to buy estates at Great Ilford in Essex, and a house in the parish of St John Zachary in London. In 1448 he became a JP in Essex and Northamptonshire, and was appointed to an important commission to inquire into concealments of royal revenues in Middlesex. In October 1449 he was elected a knight of the shire for Northamptonshire, and a year later was MP for Ludgershall, Wiltshire.

His associations with government did not bring Thorpe popularity and good repute. In 1450 he was denounced by Kentish rebels as a supporter of the duke of Suffolk, and was nearly dislodged from his post in the exchequer by the new treasurer, Lord Tiptoft. But he held on, and on 2 December 1452 was made third baron. He was returned for Essex to the parliament that met at Reading on 6 March 1453, and on 8 March was elected speaker of the Commons. The first two sessions were easily managed on the government's behalf; a grant of taxation was made for the recovery of Gascony, and Thorpe was rewarded by the king with a gift of £200. He also became a royal councillor during the summer, no doubt on the strength of his understanding of finance and his parliamentary experience.

In November 1453, however, Thorpe's career was threatened in a way that had lasting repercussions for him. Reportedly acting on the king's orders, he attached chattels belonging to the duke of York, who promptly sued Thorpe in the exchequer, securing damages of £1000 and the defendant's imprisonment in the Fleet. When parliament reassembled for a second session in February 1454, the Commons petitioned for their speaker's release. But notwithstanding their claim of privilege, the Lords ruled against them, and a new speaker was chosen. Thorpe himself came to terms with York in July, but was hardly reconciled with him, and was thereafter consistently associated with the duke's enemies. Resuming his administrative career, on 24 March 1455 he became chancellor of the exchequer, but shortly afterwards was again embroiled in politics. In attendance on the king when the court confronted York at St Albans on 22 May, he was later charged, along with the duke of Somerset and one William Joseph, with having twice intercepted messages from York to King Henry which might have prevented the battle. Somerset was killed there, and Thorpe was among those subsequently accused of having fled 'and left her harneys behynde hem cowardly' (*Paston Letters*, 1.331).

York, who was now clearly set upon ruining him, proceeded to blame Thorpe in parliament for causing the battle, and secured his dismissal from all his offices. An attempt to have him imprisoned was thwarted by the king, but York was able to secure payment of all the damages awarded against Thorpe in 1454. However, as the court recovered control of government from 1456, Thorpe returned to favour. On 16 November 1457 he was made keeper of the privy wardrobe in the Tower of London for life, and on 12 September 1458 he was appointed second baron of the exchequer. At the Coventry parliament of November–December 1459 he secured revenge upon York, by helping to draw up the bill of attainder declaring York and his leading followers to be traitors.

On 9 April 1460 Thorpe secured a life grant of £40 per annum, charged upon the estates of the duke of York and the earl of Salisbury. But he did not enjoy it for long. In July he was captured after the battle of Northampton, and brought back to London a prisoner. Once more deprived of his offices, he escaped from prison, but was recaptured and sent to the Tower. Yet again he escaped, and on 17 February 1461 tried to make his way out of London, presumably to join the Lancastrian army which had just won the second battle of St Albans. But he was caught at Harringay by a party of Londoners, and beheaded forthwith. His estates were subsequently forfeited. Not until 1485 did Roger Thorpe, the son of Thomas's marriage to a woman named Joan (who had died in 1453), achieve a partial restitution.
HENRY SUMMERSON

Sources J. S. Roskell, 'Thomas Thorpe, speaker in the parliament of 1453–4', *Nottingham Medieval Studies*, 7 (1963), 79–105 · R. A. Griffiths, *The reign of King Henry VI: the exercise of royal authority, 1422–1461* (1981) · *The Paston letters, 1422–1509 AD*, ed. J. Gairdner, new edn, 3 vols. (1872–5); repr. in 4 vols. (1910), vol. 1 · C. A. J. Armstrong, 'Politics and the battle of St Albans, 1455', *BIHR*, 33 (1960), 1–72 · Sainty, *Judges*, 118 · J. C. Sainty, ed., *Officers of the exchequer: a list* (1983)

Thorpe [Thorp], **Thomas** (1571/2–1625?), bookseller, was born in Barnet, Middlesex, the son of Thomas Thorpe, innkeeper. On 24 June 1584 he was apprenticed as a stationer for nine years to Richard Watkins, co-holder of the patent on almanacs and prognostications, and he was admitted as a freeman of the Stationers' Company on 4 February 1594. On 19 March 1597, giving his address as St Faith's parish and his age as twenty-five, Thorpe testified that the previous autumn he had been in Madrid as a guest of the fugitive Jesuit Father Robert Persons, and had stayed in the house of the recently deceased Catholic fugitive Sir Francis Englefield.

In 1600 Thorpe surfaces as the author of a dedication addressed to his 'kind and true friend', the publisher Edward Blount, attached to Christopher Marlowe's translation of the first book of Lucan's *Pharsalia*. The rights to this translation had previously passed through four other stationers, including Blount, but Thorpe's is the earliest known edition. In the dedication Thorpe depicts Marlowe

as a ghost haunting St Paul's Churchyard through his posthumous publications, and also humorously instructs Blount how to be a literary patron, telling his friend to 'sweat with the invention of some dry jest or two', but in the end, 'give nothing' (Marlowe, 261–2).

The first three publications with Thorpe's name on the title-page, all dated 1603, include two pamphlets about the East India Company (reflecting his long-standing interest in exploration) and a speech by Richard Martin. Two of these were originally entered in the Stationers' register to William Aspley, and all were sold in Aspley's shop, in which Thorpe may have worked. Aspley had previously published several plays (including two by Shakespeare), and in partnership with Thorpe he published two which became best-sellers: John Marston's *The Malcontent* (1604), and *Eastward Ho!* (1605), by Marston, Ben Jonson, and George Chapman. On his own, Thorpe subsequently published many important dramatic texts by Marston, Jonson, and Chapman. These included Marston's *What you Will* (1607) and *Histriomastix* (1610); Jonson's *Sejanus* (1605, with Blount), *Hymenaei* (1606), *Volpone* (1607), and *The Character of Two Royal Masques* (1608); and Chapman's *All Fools* (1605), *The Gentleman Usher* (1606), and *Charles, Duke of Biron* (1608). For the most part these are excellent texts, almost certainly authorized by the playwrights. The survival of two presentation copies of *Sejanus*, plus the fact that the notoriously demanding Jonson used the quarto text virtually unchanged in his 1616 folio *Works*, show how satisfied he was with Thorpe's work.

In 1609 Thorpe published the work for which he is known to posterity: *Shake-speares Sonnets*. Despite the claims of commentators uncomfortable with the sequence's homoeroticism, there is no indication that the volume was surreptitious or unauthorized. It was entered normally in the Stationers' register on 20 May, and it fits well with the authorized volumes Thorpe published for other theatre people. It was published during a plague outbreak which closed the theatres, as Shakespeare's narrative poems had been, and is structurally similar to earlier published sonnet sequences by Sidney, Spenser, Daniel, and Lodge, as Duncan-Jones demonstrates. Like earlier sonnet sequences by Barnabe Barnes, Henry Constable, and others, it also contains a dedication written by the stationer (Thorpe) rather than by the poet. This epigraph, addressed by Thorpe to 'the onlie begetter of these insuing sonnets Mr. W. H.' (sig. A2r) has occasioned volumes of speculation on the identity of W. H., but no consensus. Some critics have taken 'begetter' to mean the 'procurer' who brought the manuscript to Thorpe, but none of the various candidates has attracted widespread support. Others have taken 'begetter' to mean 'inspirer', or the young man addressed in the sonnets; here the two main candidates have been Henry Wriothesley, earl of Southampton, and William Herbert, earl of Pembroke, the latter notably championed by Duncan-Jones. Others have found none of these solutions satisfactory. Foster points out that 'begetter' always meant 'author' in dedications of the time, and suggests that Thorpe was addressing Shakespeare, with 'our ever-living poet' being God.

On 18 January 1609 Thorpe entered in the Stationers' register *A Discovery of a New World*, John Healey's translation of Joseph Hall's *Mundus alter et idem*, but he later transferred the rights to Edward Blount and William Barret, who published it with the earl of Pembroke's financial assistance. The following year, Thorpe, Blount, and Barret jointly published Healey's translation of *Epictetus his Manuall and Cebes his Table*. For this volume Thorpe wrote a dedication to John Florio in which he praises Pembroke's earlier generosity to Healey, and asks for Florio's help in securing Pembroke's support for 'a greater body of Saint Augustines', to which the present volume is merely a 'hand-maide' (sig. A3v–A4r).

The 'greater body' was Healey's translation of St Augustine's *City of God*, which Thorpe published later in 1610 in an elaborate folio edition. Thorpe dedicated the volume to Pembroke in his characteristic witty and punning style, telling him that before departing for Virginia 'your late imaginery, but now actuall Travailer' (Healey) had asked Thorpe to deliver the book 'to your Honours humbly thrise-kissed hands' (sig. A3–A3v). In 1616, after Healey had died in Virginia, Thorpe published a second edition of *Epictetus his Manuall* with Healey's translation of Theophrastus' *Characters* added, and with an apologetic and self-deprecating dedication to Pembroke replacing the earlier dedication to Florio.

Between 1610 and 1615 Thorpe published several more religious works, alongside lighter fare such as the collection *Odcombian Banquet* (1611) and works by Thomas Nashe, John Taylor, and Humphrey King. In 1612 he published *A Funerall Elegy for Master William Peter* by W. S., a poem which Foster argued was written by Shakespeare but which is now generally accepted as the work of John Forde. Over the last decade of his career Thorpe's publications were mostly of a religious nature. Three of these contain unsigned prefaces almost certainly written by Thorpe: Arthur Dent's *Hand-Maid of Repentance* (1614), John van Oldenbarneveld's *Apology* (1618), and Theophilus Field's *A Christian's Preparation* (1622). In late 1623 Thorpe began receiving a pension from the Stationers' Company poor fund, indicating that he had fallen on hard times. His last publication was in 1625, and at the end of that year he stopped receiving his pension, presumably because he had died.

Thorpe may be the Thomas Thorpe who married Susan Hack on 12 July 1609 at St James Clerkenwell, London, and who had a son Robert baptized there on 17 August 1616. He may also be the Thomas Thorpe who had a son Thomas baptized at St Stephen, Coleman Street on 11 May 1610. However, he is probably the Thomas Thorpe of St Olave, Southwark, London, whose wife Dorcas was granted administration of his estate on 30 July 1625.

DAVID KATHMAN

Sources K. Duncan-Jones, 'Was the 1609 Shake-speares Sonnets really unauthorized?', *Review of English Studies*, 34 (1983), 151–71 · L. Rostenberg, 'Thomas Thorpe, publisher of "Shake-speares Sonnets"', *Papers of the Bibliographical Society of America*, 54 (1960), 16–37 · Arber, *Regs. Stationers* · *STC, 1475–1640* · K. Duncan-Jones, introduction, in *Shakespeare's sonnets*, ed. K. Duncan-Jones (1997), 1–105 · D. Foster, 'Master W. H., R. I. P.', *Publications of the Modern Language Association*, 102 (1987), 42–54 · D. Foster, 'A funeral elegy: W[illiam] S[hakespeare]'s "best-speaking witnesses"', *Publications of the Modern Language Association*, 111 (1996), 1080–1105 · W. C. Ferguson, 'The Stationers' Company poor book, 1608–1700', *The Library*, 31 (1976), 37–51 · C. Marlowe, *Poems*, ed. L. C. Martin (1931) · H. Morris, *Richard Barnfield, Colin's child* (1963) · P. H. Martin and J. Finnis, 'Thomas Thorpe, "W. S.", and the Catholic intelligencers', *English Literary Renaissance*, 33 (2003), 3–43 · *IGI* · private information (2004) [P. W. M. Blayney]

Thorpe, Sir Thomas Edward (1845–1925), chemist, was born in Goodier Street, Harpurhey, near Manchester, on 8 December 1845, the eldest of the eight children of George Thorpe, cloth and yarn agent, later of Trafford Bank, near Manchester, and his wife, Mary Wild. He was educated at Manchester diocesan school (Hulme grammar school). He initially worked as a clerk in a commission agent's (possibly with his father) but in 1863 entered the chemistry department of Owens College, Manchester, where he worked as a junior assistant (and later as demonstrator) to Henry Roscoe, then professor of chemistry.

With Roscoe, Thorpe carried out some notable scientific work, including a series of experiments on the chemical action of light. For this work he travelled to Brazil and Lisbon in 1866 and 1867 and was awarded the Dalton senior chemical scholarship in Owens College in 1867. With a letter of introduction to the famous chemist Robert Bunsen, Thorpe then travelled to the University of Heidelberg, where two years later he graduated PhD. Subsequently he worked for a short time in the laboratory of Friedrich Kekulé at the University of Bonn. Soon after his return to England in 1870 he was appointed to the chair of chemistry at Anderson's University, Glasgow. On 24 September 1870 he married Caroline Emma, daughter of Dr John Watts, a prominent Manchester educationist. There were no children.

In 1874 Thorpe was appointed professor of chemistry at the Yorkshire College of Science at Leeds, where, besides spending much time and energy in the development of this new college (he designed its laboratories among other duties), he maintained a steady output of scientific work. With other results this led to important conclusions concerning the relation of the molecular weights of substances to their specific gravities in the liquid state. For this work he was elected a fellow of the Royal Society in 1876. He also received the first Longstaff medal of the Chemical Society in 1881.

In 1885 Thorpe was appointed to the chair of chemistry at the Normal School of Science, South Kensington (later the Royal College of Science), where, among much other research, he continued his work on the compounds of phosphorus, begun at Leeds. This work led, *inter alia*, to the isolation of phosphorus trioxide, and was particularly important in that it made possible the elimination of the terrible necrosis of the jaw caused by this oxide which afflicted workers in the match industry. As well as his work on chemical investigations, he also took part in four eclipse expeditions (1890–93), and in collaboration with

Sir Arthur Rücker he made, in 1884–8, an extensive magnetic survey of the British Isles, the earlier results of which formed the subject of a joint Bakerian lecture before the Royal Society in 1889.

Thorpe left the academic world in 1894 when he was appointed principal chemist of the Inland Revenue laboratory which, later that year, became the government laboratory. He supervised its removal in 1897 to a new purpose-built laboratory building, largely designed by himself. With his staff he conducted investigations in the fields of industrial and public welfare. These included the detection of arsenic in beer and the elimination of lead from pottery glazes and of white phosphorus from matches, as well as work on the original gravity of beers and alcoholic strength tables. Both of these latter were important for their bearing on the public revenue. With colleagues he also continued his work on the accurate determination of the atomic weights of metals (begun at Leeds and South Kensington, and for which he had received the Royal Society royal medal in 1889), including the confirmation of the atomic weight of radium, first determined by Madame Curie. He was an active member of the international committee of atomic weights for many years.

On his retirement from the government laboratory in 1909 Thorpe was knighted (having been appointed CB in 1900), and was then reappointed to his post as professor of general chemistry at the Royal College of Science, which was by then the Imperial College of Science and Technology. He finally retired in 1912, with the title of professor emeritus. As well as being an original scientific thinker, Thorpe was also a talented writer. His many important scientific articles range widely in scope and importance, mostly published in the *Journal of the Chemical Society*, but he also wrote valuable textbooks, such as his *Inorganic Chemistry* (1873), and his well-known *Dictionary of Applied Chemistry*. This first appeared in three volumes in 1890 and Thorpe was correcting the proofs of the seven-volume third edition when he died. He also wrote a *History of Chemistry*, which was reprinted many times, and lives of a number of other chemists, including his first mentor, Sir Henry Roscoe, (1916).

Thorpe's other great interest, yachting, is shown in his two books *A Yachtsman's Guide to the Dutch Waterways* (1905) and *The Seine from Havre to Paris* (1913). While he was mainly a chemist he was also a man of very wide scientific interests, and immense energy, physical and mental. He took an active part in the activities of British scientific bodies. Among other posts he acted as foreign secretary of the Royal Society from 1899 to 1903, was president of the Chemical Society (1899–1901) and of the Society of Chemical Industry in 1895, and in 1921 was president of the British Association. In addition he served on many royal commissions and departmental committees. He was a keen sportsman, particularly in his younger days, and had a large circle of friends; he had a strong sense of humour and was an excellent story teller, but notwithstanding this was a hard taskmaster to assistants and staff. He was short, with a resonant voice, an able speaker and an excellent teacher. He died of a heart attack at his home, at Whinfield, Salcombe, Devon, on 23 February 1925 and was buried in Salcombe. His wife survived him.

P. W. HAMMOND

Sources P. P. B. [P. P. Bedson], *JCS* (1926), 1031–50 · G. Stubbs, *The Analyst*, 50 (1925), 210–13 · A. E. H. T. [A. E. H. Tutton], *PRS*, 109A (1925), xviii–xxiv · P. W. Hammond and H. Egan, *Weighed in the balance: a history of the laboratory of the government chemist* (1992) · A. E. H. Tutton, *Nature*, 115 (1925), 343–5 · *The Times* (24 Feb 1925) · 'Recent chemical appointments', *Chemical News* (2 Sept 1870), 117 · 'Proceedings of societies', *Chemical News* (31 July 1874), 49 · b. cert. · d. cert. · m. cert.
Archives ICL, corresp. · PRO, DSIR 26 · RS, letters and papers · U. Leeds, Brotherton L., data tables and corresp.
Likenesses photograph, *c*.1890, repro. in Hammond and Egan, *Weighed in the balance* · photographs, *c*.1890, laboratory of the government chemist, Queen's Road, Teddington, Middlesex, file 'Senior staff'
Wealth at death £18,593 11s. 1d.: resworn probate, 18 April 1925, CGPLA Eng. & Wales

Thorpe, Sir William de. *See* Thorp, Sir William (*d*. 1361).

Thorpe, William (*fl.* 1381–1407), Lollard preacher, seems to have been a Yorkshireman. Documentary evidence concerning his life is scant, but in a letter of the north-country heretic Richard Wyche, written *c*.1402 but surviving only in a Bohemian copy, there is mentioned a sister 'domini Wilhelmi Corpp' resident at that time in Topcliffe in the North Riding of Yorkshire; 'Corpp' may reasonably be identified with Thorpe, whose origins were probably in the same area. In March 1395 a William Thorpe was instituted to the vicarage of Marske in Cleveland, a living in the gift of the Augustinian canons of Guisborough, by Thomas Arundel (*d*. 1414), then archbishop of York. The identification is not entirely certain, but a more secure link is provided by the six charges of erroneous preaching in London brought against a William Thorpe by three priests before Bishop Robert Braybrooke some time between January 1382 and June 1386. The outcome is unclear, though Thorpe's reply to the charges survives; a later note states that he was excommunicated because of his failure to recant. Later evidence for Thorpe is provided by a recently discovered writ, dated 16 June 1407, requiring the bailiffs of Shrewsbury to produce him before the chancellor, Archbishop Thomas Arundel, at Westminster; Thorpe, together with an associate, John Pollyrbache, had been imprisoned following his preaching of three conclusions (listed on the schedule attached to the document, and covering images, pilgrimages, and the withholding of tithes) at St Chad's Church in Shrewsbury on 17 April.

Beyond these documentary details, the chief source for Thorpe's life (though its bias is clear, and its reliability can only be ascertained in part) is the account, claimed to be autobiographical, of an informal examination of Thorpe by Arundel on 7 August 1407. No record of this, or of any case against Thorpe, appears in Arundel's register, though the date is compatible with the evidence for Thorpe's arrest. According to Thorpe, after forceful persuasion by family and friends to continue his education for the priesthood, he went, apparently before mid-1381, to Oxford to join John Wyclif (*d.* 1384) and his adherents; there he enthusiastically embraced their radical views. When he left Oxford is not made clear. Allusion is made to a period of preaching in the north; this could indicate that the incumbent of Marske was indeed the same man. Arundel, in Thorpe's story, reminds him that he had been arrested by Bishop Braybrooke, and that he had been set free on Arundel's own exile in 1397; Thorpe maintains that he had been released because no valid charge against him had been found. The date of Braybrooke's arrest of Thorpe is unspecified; difficulties arise over the chronological relation of this episode to the Marske institution.

Thorpe's conversation with the archbishop, in his account, dealt with five errors alleged against him by the Shrewsbury officials: the three mentioned in the legal document, together with the error of maintaining that bread exists after the consecration in the eucharist and that oaths are unlawful. The encounter, according to Thorpe, ended with his own implacable resolution to stand by his views, without judgment from Arundel, though with Thorpe's relegation to the archbishop's prison. How Thorpe's account was put into circulation is entirely obscure: one early fifteenth-century English copy survives, together with two Bohemian copies of a Latin version. The English text was known to Lollard suspects from the 1490s to the 1520s, before it was put into print *c.*1530 (probably from the Antwerp press of Hans Luft, *STC* 1475–1640, no. 24045). At the end of this appears 'The testamente of William Thorpe', dated 20 September 1460; there are obvious chronological difficulties in accepting this, and the otherwise impersonal document may originally have had no connection with Thorpe. The other works later ascribed to him by John Bale reflect Bale's deductions from references within Thorpe's autobiography, and not direct evidence.

The views that Thorpe was accused of holding in the 1380s, and that he defended then and in 1407, are typical of early Lollardy and for the most part derive directly from Wyclif's own teaching. They cover the eucharist, images, pilgrimages, oaths, tithes, scripture, preaching, oral confession and sacerdotal absolution, and the right of the laity to correct erring clerics. In the autobiography Thorpe's admiration for Wyclif's learning and for his upright life is undiminished, and is accompanied by strong deprecation for the turncoat activities of Philip Repingdon and Nicholas Hereford. The picture given of Archbishop Arundel—often angry, frequently obtuse himself, and outwitted by the ever reasonable and ingenious Thorpe—makes the account of their conversation an unusually lively and attractive piece of Lollard propaganda.   ANNE HUDSON

Sources *The testimony of William Thorpe, Two Wycliffite texts*, ed. A. Hudson, EETS, 301 (1993) • *John Lydford's book*, ed. D. M. Owen, Devon and Cornwall RS, new ser., 20 (1974), nos. 206, 209 • Bale, *Cat.*, 1.538 • F. D. Matthew, 'The trial of Richard Wyche', *EngHR*, 5 (1890), 530–44 • Borth. Inst., MS reg. Arundel, fol. 49 • PRO, C250/4 no. 23 • M. Jurkowski, 'The arrest of William Thorpe in Shrewsbury and the anti-Lollard statute of 1406', *Historical Research*, 75 (2002), 273–95

Archives Österreichische Nationalbibliothek, Vienna, Thorpe's autobiography (Latin), MS 3936 • Bodl. Oxf., Thorpe's autobiography (English), MS Rawlinson C.208 • Metropolitan Chapter Library, Prague, Thorpe's autobiography (Latin), MS D.49

Thorpe, William Homan (1902–1986), ethologist, was born on 1 April 1902 at Hastings, Sussex, the third child of Francis Homan Thorpe (*d.* 1918), an accountant, and his wife, Mary Amelia (*née* Slade). Thorpe's parents were actively involved in the Congregational church and he spent his childhood at home in Hastings and then in Weston-super-Mare before being sent to Mill Hill School at the age of fourteen. He was a delicate and solitary child, and in later life remained somewhat remote.

Academically, Thorpe was a late starter. He entered Jesus College, Cambridge, in 1921 and obtained a second-class degree in agriculture in 1924, but went on to complete the diploma in agricultural science (plant pathology) in 1925, and a PhD in entomology in 1929. After working as a research entomologist at Farnham Royal Parasite Laboratory (1929–32), he returned to Cambridge as university lecturer in entomology and tutor and fellow of Jesus College. On 16 November 1936 he married Winifred Mary Vincent (1897/8–1978), a zoologist, daughter of George Herbert Vincent, a clergyman; their only child, Margaret Frances, was born in 1938. During the Second World War Thorpe registered as a conscientious objector on religious grounds, and devoted himself to the cause of self-sufficient food production and the eradication of invertebrate pests. He was deeply religious, and in 1945, after several years of reflection, he became a member of the Society of Friends. Thorpe was promoted to reader in entomology in 1959 and to a personal chair in 1966, and served as senior tutor of Jesus College from 1945 to 1947; he was its president from 1969 to 1972. He was elected a fellow of the Royal Society in 1951, and was president concurrently of the Association for the Study of Animal Behaviour and the British Entomological Society (1951–3). He held a Rockefeller fellowship at the University of California (1927–9) and a Leverhulme fellowship in east Africa (1939), and was Prather lecturer in biology at Harvard (1951–2) and Gifford lecturer, St Andrews University (1969–71). Thorpe was an accomplished pianist, although he seldom performed for others, not even friends. He had a large collection of classical 78 r.p.m. records which he used to play on an old-fashioned horn gramophone. He donated his collection to Cambridge University Library in 1978.

Although an amateur naturalist since childhood, Thorpe's research interest in animal behaviour developed in the 1930s out of his own studies of host selection in parasitic insects and his enthusiastic discovery of Konrad Lorenz's papers on instinct. Towards the close of the Second World War he came actively to promote the cause of ethology, and along with Nikolaas Tinbergen (who moved from Holland to Oxford in 1949) established the subject within Britain. In 1943, Thorpe became a member of the Institute for the Study of Animal Behaviour (later the Association for the Study of Animal Behaviour) and quickly took the intellectual lead, championing the work of the continental ethologists. From 1948 to 1951, Thorpe made several attempts to bring Lorenz to England so that he could resume his research after the war. However, by the time a post became available (which, according to the Lorenz family, was at Bristol), the German authorities had finally granted Lorenz a salaried position.

In 1950, Thorpe founded the ornithological field station at Madingley, later the university sub-department of animal behaviour, beginning with a small but distinguished group of researchers, including Robert Hinde, its first curator, G. V. T. Matthews, and Peter Marler. Thorpe's classic research on birdsong investigated the integration of inborn and learned sound patterns in normal development. His publications include *Learning and Instinct in Animals* (1956), *Bird Song: the Biology of Vocal Communication and Expression in Birds* (1961), *Science, Man and Morals* (1965), *Animal Nature and Human Nature* (1974), and *Purpose in a World of Chance* (1978).

Profoundly concerned by the tensions between science and religion, Thorpe had a deeper purpose in promoting ethology. He was opposed to the mechanistic prejudices of traditional science, a view he shared with such figures as Alister Hardy, Arthur Koestler, David Lack, E. S. Russell, and C. H. Waddington. Animals, he insisted, are not mere puppets in the hand of circumstances; as his own research on host selection demonstrated, behaviour can shape the very context of natural selection. Nevertheless, by the time his last book, *The Origins and Rise of Ethology*, appeared in 1979, the new discipline seemed ripe for reductionist take-over by sociobiology or neurophysiology. Its central concepts, such as instinct, were in question, and its distinctive method, naturalistic observation, was being supplanted by standard experimental techniques. Indeed, the Cambridge research, in part because of an informal division of labour with Tinbergen's team at Oxford, was primarily based not on field study but the investigation of captive animals subject to independently imposed conditions. Thorpe's holistic, even intentionalist, vision continued to find a place within biology, but remained marginal to the traditional causal–analytical methods of science. Thorpe died on 7 April 1986 in a nursing home near Woodwalton Fen, one of the many nature conservation sites for which he so actively campaigned.

ALAN COSTALL

Sources R. A. Hinde, *Memoirs FRS*, 33 (1987), 620–39 · J. R. Durant, 'The making of ethology: the Association for the Study of Animal Behaviour, 1936–1986', *Animal Behaviour*, 34 (1986), 1601–16 · N. C. Gillespie, 'The interface of natural theology and science in the ethology of W. H. Thorpe', *Journal of the History of Biology*, 23 (1990), 1–38 · A. Costall, 'The "meme" meme', *Cultural Dynamics*, 4 (1991), 321–5 · J. Hall-Craggs, *The Ibis*, 129 (1987), 564–9 · m. cert. · WWW
Archives CUL | CUL, corresp. with Sir Peter Markham Scott · Rice University, Houston, Texas, Woodson Research Center, corresp. with Sir Julian Huxley · U. Oxf., Edward Grey Institute of Field Ornithology, corresp. with David Lack
Likenesses E. Leigh, photograph, c.1951, repro. in Hinde, *Memoirs FRS*, facing p. 621 · L. Garden, photograph, c.1980, repro. in Hall-Craggs, *The Ibis*, 568
Wealth at death £215,310: probate, 23 May 1986, *CGPLA Eng. & Wales*

Thouless, Robert Henry (1894–1984), psychologist, the son of Henry James Thouless, an iron-founder's clerk, and his wife, Bell Maud Bird (*née* Harper) was born at 48 Grove Avenue, Lakenham, Norwich, on 15 July 1894. He attended the City of Norwich School before moving to Corpus Christi College, Cambridge in 1912, gaining a BA in natural sciences in 1915. After war service as brigade signal officer in the British Salonica forces he obtained an MA in 1921, was elected to a fellowship of Corpus Christi the same year, and obtained his PhD (Cambridge) under C. S. Myers in 1922. As lecturer in psychology, he subsequently helped to establish psychology at the universities of Manchester (1921–6) and Glasgow (1926–38), before joining the education department, Cambridge, as reader in educational psychology (emeritus reader after his retirement in 1961), becoming a much loved Cambridge figure. In 1923 he married Priscilla Gorton (author of *Modern Poetic Drama*, 1934); they had a son and a daughter. He was re-elected fellow (non-resident) of Corpus Christi College in 1945 (his earlier fellowship had lapsed in 1924). Actively involved in the British Psychological Society (serving as president in 1949) and in intra-disciplinary affairs throughout his long career, Thouless played an invaluable role in establishing psychology as an academic discipline and a profession in Britain.

Thouless's most long-standing interest was in the relationship between psychology and religion; he turned his PhD thesis into the first British textbook on the topic, *Introduction to the Psychology of Religion* (1923, 3rd edn 1961). A monograph on the medieval mystic Julian of Norwich (*The Lady Julian*, 1924), academic papers (including the 1954 Hulsean lectures, published as *Authority and Freedom: some Psychological Problems of Religious Belief*, 1954), and several popular works followed. Devoutly Christian, he strove to allay fears of psychology among fellow believers and to identify links between the new psychotherapies and Christian approaches to the cure of souls. Associated with this was an intense involvement in psychical research, on which he published *Experimental Psychical Research* (1963), and over ninety articles, as well as being president of the Society for Psychical Research (1942–5). He left two, as yet uncracked, ciphered messages for posthumous decoding via a medium.

Thouless's reputation within the discipline rested on more orthodox work, notably his highly successful textbook *Social Psychology* (1925), the first such British work to address social psychology. On occasion he linked the religious and social psychological strands (for example, in his Riddell memorial lectures, 1940). Thouless was one of the few British psychologists of his generation to specialize in social psychology (then expanding rapidly in the USA). His approach was initially largely non-experimental, ignoring the quantitative research on attitudes and their measurement which, by 1937, was dominating the sub-discipline in the United States, but later editions of *Social Psychology* laid increasing stress on statistical procedures, on which he also published specialist articles. His experimental research concentrated on psycho-galvanic skin response changes in relation to emotion, and perception, including the discovery in 1931 of 'phenomenal regression to the real object' in which, for example, obliquely viewed discs appear less elliptical than they should. A claim by Thouless made in 1933 for a racial difference in the extent of this was subsequently rejected. Thouless's major educational work was *A Map of Educational Research* (1969). Lay readers knew him best for his popular *Straight and Crooked Thinking* (1930) and its sequel, *Straight and Crooked Thinking in War Time* (1942).

The range of Thouless's work, his contribution to the discipline's institutional development in Britain, and popularization of its findings render him a major figure, while his efforts towards reconciling psychology and religion countered the image of psychology as intrinsically anti-Christian. He was, however, an eclectic rather than an original theorist. Thouless died at his home, 2 Leys Road, Cambridge, on 25 September 1984.

GRAHAM RICHARDS

Sources M. Argyle, 'Robert Henry Thouless', memorial address, 17 Nov 1984 [St Benet's Church, Cambridge] · *The Times* (28 Sept 1984) · *Bulletin of the British Psychological Society*, 37 (1984), 431 · *Journal of Psychical Research*, 799 (1985), 56–60 · b. cert. · d. cert. · WWW
Wealth at death £136,098: probate, 21 March 1985, *CGPLA Eng. & Wales*

Thrale, Henry (1728–1781), brewer and politician, was the only son of Ralph Thrale (d. 1758), a wealthy brewer of Southwark who was master of the Brewers' Company, high sheriff of Surrey, and MP for Southwark in 1741–7. Thrale's grandfather was a 'yeoman' of Offley, Hertfordshire. Thrale's father was head clerk of the Anchor Brewery in Southwark, a leading London brewery founded in 1616. He doubtless secured the appointment through family connections: he was a cousin of Anne Halsey, sister of the then owner of the Anchor, Edmund Halsey, and subsequently his heir, who married Richard Temple, first Baron Cobham, uncle to the Grenvilles and the Lytteltons. After a number of years Ralph Thrale was able to buy the brewery for £30,000 from Anne Halsey's executors, paying for it out of the profits over eleven years.

Ralph Thrale's lavish social spending caused some attrition to the business, which was increased under his son, who, unlike other prominent brewers such as Samuel Whitbread and Benjamin Truman, was born and brought up to affluence in the trade. Henry Thrale was sent to University College, Oxford, in 1744 (at the age of fifteen) with the princely allowance of £1000 p.a., and thereafter on a grand tour in the company of W. H. Lyttelton (Lord Westcote), who had family links with the Thrales. Henry nevertheless developed an ambition to become the greatest brewer in London.

When Ralph Thrale died in 1758 the assets of the firm were valued at £56,200 (a considerable decline over recent years) and annual output was 32,600 barrels, the Anchor Brewery lying about sixth in the league table of London porterhouses. Great expansion then ensued to a temporary peak of 87,000 barrels in 1778, when only Samuel Whitbread and John Calvert remained ahead of Thrale. Expansion, however, was far from smooth. Extravagant spending caused a series of crises within the family, particularly when coinciding with business depressions (1772), boom conditions (1778), and a personal crisis compounding Thrale's own health, and the death and bankruptcy in June 1779 of his brother-in-law, Arnold Nesbitt, to whom Thrale was said to be committed financially for over £200,000. On these occasions both Thrale's family and his wife's relations helped out with loans.

Thrale married Hester Lynch Salisbury (1741–1821) [*see* Piozzi, Hester Lynch], a fashionable, literary lady with good family connections, on 11 October 1763 (supposedly at the urging of her uncle, Sir Thomas Salisbury, as the condition of his making a settlement on her). Henry and Hester Thrale had two sons, the elder dying in 1776 aged nine and the younger in 1775 aged two, and ten daughters. Only five daughters survived to benefit from Thrale's will, each receiving £20,000. The eldest daughter, Hester Maria [*see* Elphinstone, Hester Maria], became Viscountess Keith.

The Thrales lived in style with a house at the brewery (which Mrs Thrale hated), a country house at Streatham Place, a hunting box (with a pack of hounds) near Croydon, and a further property at Brighton. Thrale was elected MP for the borough of Southwark in December 1765 having failed previously as a candidate for Abingdon and Camelford. He kept his seat at Southwark, almost a fief of the brewery, until defeated in 1780, when he was already prostrate and dying. As an MP he voted regularly with the administration but spoke mainly on brewing matters.

The Thrales were 'an ill-assorted couple: she, highly intelligent, with literary ambitions, hard and masculine, yet sentimental; he, matter-of-fact and unemotional, though kindly, sensual and a glutton … he could not be her hero, and she felt wasted on him' (HoP, *Commons*, 529). Although Thrale may have elicited such a harsh judgement from his wife, Samuel Johnson described his manners as those 'of a plain independent English squire' (ibid., 529). Thrale's friendship with Johnson began in 1764 through Hester Thrale, who made Southwark and Streatham Place lively literary salons. Johnson lived with the Thrales for periods at a time and accompanied them on various tours in England and to France. At times of crisis, and then as executor following Thrale's death, Johnson was drawn into the affairs of the brewery, assisting Mrs Thrale, who perforce had to cope with the business in alliance with the salaried manager, John Perkins.

Thrale had an apoplectic nature, from over-indulgence, which meant that he was threatened with seizures at times of stress in the brewery. He suffered a severe attack in June and again in the autumn of 1779, with a further stroke on 21 February 1780 from which he never fully recovered. The economic effects of the Anglo-American War were damaging the trade but a more immediate crisis arrived in June, when Thrale was in Brighton. At one point during the Gordon riots a mob attacked the brewery, but John Perkins placated them with porter until the troops arrived.

The lack of a male heir at Thrale's death on 4 April 1781

forced the sale of the brewery. As Johnson commented, 'what can misses do with a brewhouse. Lands are fitter for daughters than trade' (Boswell, 2, 69). Johnson presided over the sale as an executor ('we are not here to sell a parcel of boilers and vats but the potentiality of becoming rich beyond the dreams of avarice' (ibid., 397), and the brewery was bought for £135,000 by John Perkins and the rich Quaker relatives of his wife—Robert Barclay, David Barclay, and Sylvanus Bevan.

The Anchor Brewery prospered mightily under this new family dispensation. It took the lead in the London porter trade after 1800, Quaker dynasties like the Hanburys and the Buxtons at the Black Eagle Brewery in Spitalfields providing greater direct family continuity than either Thrale or Truman.   PETER MATHIAS

Sources P. Mathias, *The brewing industry in England, 1700–1830* (1959), 258–60, 265–74, 551 · L. Namier, 'Thrale, Henry', HoP, *Commons* · will, JRL, English MS no. 600. fol. 33 · *Thraliana: the diary of Mrs. Hester Lynch Thrale (later Mrs. Piozzi), 1776–1809*, ed. K. C. Balderston, 2nd edn, 2 vols. (1951) · J. L. Clifford, *H. L. Piozzi* (1941) · *Autobiography, letters and literary remains of Mrs Piozzi*, ed. A. Hayward, 2 vols. (1861) · *The letters of Samuel Johnson*, ed. R. W. Chapman, 3 vols. (1952) · J. Boswell, *The life of Samuel Johnson*, 2 vols. (1791) · *GM*, 1st ser., 52 (1782), 194
Archives LMA, business records of Barclay Perkins brewery
Likenesses E. Scriven, stipple (after J. Reynolds), BM, NPG
Wealth at death brewery sold for £135,000; private property at Streatham Place and elsewhere: will, JRL, English MS no. 600, fol. 33

Thrale, Hester Lynch. *See* Piozzi, Hester Lynch (1741–1821).

Threlfall, Sir Richard (1861–1932), physicist and chemical engineer, was born at Hollowforth, Woodplumpton, near Preston, Lancashire, on 14 August 1861, the eldest son of Richard Threlfall (1804–1870), of Hollowforth, wine merchant and sometime mayor of Preston, and his second wife, Sarah Jane Mason (d. 1898). He was educated at Clifton College and at Gonville and Caius College, Cambridge, where he obtained first-class honours in the natural sciences tripos in 1884. He also studied mathematics privately with W. J. Ibbetson. While still an undergraduate he made a major contribution to biology by designing and building the first automatic microtome for cutting thin uniform sections of specimens for microscopical examination. Midway through his course he worked for nearly a year at Strasbourg under August Kundt and Rudolph Fittig; his course completed, he became a demonstrator in the Cavendish Laboratory under his friend J. J. Thomson, recently appointed director.

In 1886 Threlfall was appointed professor of physics at the University of Sydney, which looked to him to revitalize the teaching of his subject. However, the directness of his methods came as a shock. Threlfall introduced to Australia the new vision of physics that emerged in those years, a body of knowledge expressed in the language of mathematics and grounded upon ever-increasing precision of measurement. He arrived with a large quantity of workshop and laboratory equipment, purchased without authorization; a first-rate technician accompanied him, likewise without authorization, to operate this; and he

Sir Richard Threlfall (1861–1932), by Walter Stoneman, 1920

immediately demanded a new building to house his department. This was completed by mid-1888 and was, in Thomson's judgement, 'at least as good as any in the world' (*Nature*, 130 1932) at that time.

As well as initiating laboratory-based teaching in his discipline, Threlfall embarked at once on an active programme of research, at the heart of which lay his passion for precision measurement. His mastery of technique was legendary (despite his having lost two fingers as a boy while experimenting with explosives) and was later strikingly displayed in his book, *On Laboratory Arts* (1898), which remained a standard work for many years. He pursued three lines of enquiry. One, a continuation of his youthful interest in explosives, led to his becoming a consultant to the local military authorities. A wide-ranging study of the electrical properties of dielectric materials such as sulphur and selenium was intended to shed light on the nature of electricity itself. Finally, he and his student J. A. Pollock built a quartz-thread torsion balance for use as a portable gravity meter and made observations with this over 6000 miles of eastern Australia. Additionally, in the early 1890s, Threlfall established a lucrative business as a consultant on the installation of the first electrical distribution systems in many Australian cities and towns.

Threlfall was president of the Royal Society of New South Wales in 1895, and chairman of a royal commission on the spontaneous heating of coal cargoes in 1896. His 'wild prophecy' that Hertz's newly discovered electromagnetic radiation might be useful in communication affected the wording of section 51 (v) of the Australian constitution, under which control over 'postal, telegraphic, telephonic, and other like services' was vested in the newly created federal government.

Short, with a powerful physique and vigorous personality, and a tremendous zest for life, Threlfall was a born leader. At Cambridge he was a formidable rugby blue and later claimed that 'only an aversion from treading on a man's face had prevented him from playing for England' (Threlfall, 'Memories', 237); in Sydney he turned out with the university team. He loved shooting, fishing and the outdoors, and also good food, wine and cigars, being, according to Thomson, 'one of the most sociable and "clubbable" of men' (Thomson, *Obits. FRS*, 52) and an excellent host. On 18 January 1890, at St John's Anglican Church, Hobart, Threlfall married Evelyn Agnes Baird (1866–1929) of Bowmont Hill, Northumberland. She was a talented artist and also published two books of poetry. They had four sons and three daughters.

In 1898 Threlfall resigned his professorship and returned to England, where soon afterwards he was appointed director of research with the chemical manufacturing firm Albright and Wilson of Oldbury, Birmingham. Here he remained for the rest of his life, becoming in 1901 a director of the firm. By systematically applying physical chemistry considerations he brought about major improvements in the firm's manufacturing processes, especially in relation to the production of phosphorus and the electrolytic manufacture of sodium and potassium chlorate. He also installed a gas engine plant for the production of electric power, in the course of this work devising new and accurate methods for determining the efficiency of electric generators, and for measuring the rate of flow of gases in tubes and ducts.

Following the outbreak of hostilities in 1914, Threlfall was completely occupied in important war-related work, especially on the use of phosphorus in smoke screens and in tracer ammunition. On his own initiative, he arranged for the exploration of sources of helium in gas wells in America, and worked out a scheme for the production of helium in quantity, and its use in balloons and airships. As a result he was invited by the Admiralty to serve on the board of invention and research, which was formed in 1915. The following year he became one of the original members of the government Advisory Council on Scientific and Industrial Research; he served for ten years on the council, and remained closely associated with its work until his death. He was chairman of the Fuel Research Board and of the Chemical Research Board, and acted as the first (part-time) director of the Chemical Research Laboratory at Teddington, Middlesex, for the establishment of which he was largely responsible. In 1919 he was offered but refused the directorship of the National Physical Laboratory.

Threlfall was appointed KBE in 1917 and GBE in 1927. He was elected FRS in 1899 and an honorary fellow of Gonville and Caius College in 1905; he received the honorary degree of DSc from Manchester University in 1919 and the gold medal of the Society of Chemical Industry in 1929. He remained active on government committees after the war, but from about 1925 his health began to fail. His wife died in 1929; earlier in the same year he had suffered a stroke and thereafter was in poor health until his death at his home, Oakhurst, Church Road, Edgbaston, Birmingham, on 10 July 1932. He was buried at Woodplumpton, near Preston.   R. W. HOME

Sources J. J. Thomson, *Obits. FRS*, 1 (1932–5), 45–52 · H. T. Tizard, *JCS* (1937), 186–95 · R. W. Home, 'First physicist of Australia: Richard Threlfall at the University of Sydney, 1886–1898', *Historical Records of Australian Science*, 6 (1984–7), 333–58 · R. E. Threlfall, *The story of 100 years of phosphorus making, 1851–1951* (1951) · R. E. Threlfall, 'Sir Richard Threlfall … some personal memories', *Notes and Records of the Royal Society*, 16 (1961), 234–42 · J. J. Thomson and H. T. Tizard, *Nature*, 130 (1932), 228–32 · J. J. Thomson, *Recollections and reflections* (1936) · J. A. La Nauze, '"Other like services": physics and the Australian constitution', *Records of the Australian Academy of Science*, 1/3 (1968), 36–44 · *DNB* · private information (2004)
Archives Birm. CA, corresp. and papers · University of Sydney, corresp. and papers | CUL, corresp. with Sir Joseph Thomson · Trinity Cam., corresp. with Sir Joseph John Thomson
Likenesses photograph, 1890, University of Sydney · W. Stoneman, photograph, 1920, NPG [*see illus.*] · W. Stoneman, photograph, 1931, NPG · Lady Robertson, silicon ester on asbestos board, repro. in Threlfall, *Story*
Wealth at death £57,133 2s. 2d.: probate, 26 Oct 1932 · £5460: administration with will, 30 Aug 1933

Threlkeld, Caleb (1676–1728), physician and botanist, the third son of Thomas Threlkeld (1646–1712) and Bridget Brown (*c.*1654–1712), was born on 31 May 1676 at Keibergh, Kirkoswald, Cumberland. By 1696 he was enrolled as a student in the University of Glasgow; he matriculated into the third class (logic) that year, but did not graduate. He married, on 7 March 1698, Elizabeth Dalrymple, whose father was described as the feudatory laird of Auchin Houry, near Glasgow. He was home in Cumberland by 1699, where John, first of their six children born in England, was baptized on 1 May 1699 in Kirkoswald parish church. Between 1699 and 1712 Threlkeld apparently lived as a 'preacher of the word' (Pulteney, 63); there is confusion about his faith, one source stating that he was curate in Kirkoswald, and therefore an Anglican, whereas others suggest that during his time in Glasgow Threlkeld converted from the established church, returning to Cumberland 'in the character of a dissenting minister' (ibid.). Meanwhile he also studied botany and medicine, collecting and observing plants in Cumberland and elsewhere—for example, during 1707 he botanized around Newcastle upon Tyne.

In 1712 Threlkeld applied to the University of Edinburgh for the degree of doctor of medicine. Having been examined by the Royal College of Physicians of Edinburgh, he was admitted to the degree, the third awarded by the university, and graduated on 20 January 1713. On 26 March 1713 he left Cumberland for Dublin; it is uncertain when his wife and family joined him, but a daughter, Mary, was born in Dublin and died there in February 1715, aged three. In Dublin he practised as a physician and was greatly respected by poorer members of the community. He also preached on Sundays in a conventicle.

Threlkeld botanized about Dublin, collecting specimens and compiling what its title-page defined as the 'first essay' on the native flora of Ireland, published in Dublin on 27 October 1726; two subsequent issues are known (Dublin, 1727; London, 1727). *Synopsis stirpium Hibernicarum* contained records of over 500 flowering plants, gymnosperms, ferns, and various other cryptogams; 119 plants were recorded from specified localities and over 400 vernacular Irish names were noted.

Threlkeld was accused of plagiarism by Johann Jacob Dillenius (1684–1747), editor of John Ray's *Synopsis methodica stirpium Britannicarum* (3rd edn, 1724). This accusation is difficult to maintain. A botanical author frequently relies on the works of his predecessors and Threlkeld acknowledged at least four separate sources for *Synopsis*: his own collections, a manuscript attributed to the Revd Richard Heaton (*fl.* 1633–1666), notes supplied by Dr Thomas Molyneux (1661–1733), and previously published works. Only seventy-five records of Irish native species could have been gleaned from works published before 1726, and most of the alleged lavish, unacknowledged borrowing from John Ray was translated textual material such as accounts of medicinal properties.

Synopsis stirpium Hibernicarum, which, *inter alia*, contained the earliest printed account of the myth of St Patrick's sermon on the Holy Trinity illustrated by a shamrock, has provoked many contrary opinions. William Sherard (1658–1728) called it 'a wretched piece' (Nichols). Nathanial Colgan (1851–1919), author of *Flora of the County Dublin* (1904), described the same book as a 'piquant medley of herbal and homily in which this medical missionary from Cumberland delivers himself of his opinions on botany, medicine, morals, theology, witchcraft and the Irish question' (Colgan, xx). The publication of *Synopsis stirpium Hibernicarum* provoked a letter from 'Hibernicus' (Francis Hutcheson), printed in the *Dublin Weekly Journal*, lambasting Threlkeld's remarks on the political implication of the introduction of the potato into Ireland.

Threlkeld died on 28 April 1728, probably in his home at Mark's Alley, Francis Street, The Coombe, Dublin, and is reported to have been buried in the Cabbage Garden cemetery, near Kevin Street, Dublin. His herbarium—'From twelve Years Observation I collected Specimens for an *Hortus Siccus*' (*Synopsis stirpium Hibernicarum*, preface)—has not survived intact, although possible fragments are in Trinity College, Dublin.

Threlkeldia, a genus of shrubs in the beet family, endemic in Australia, was named by Robert Brown after Threlkeld.

E. CHARLES NELSON

Sources *The first Irish flora: Caleb Threlkeld's Synopsis stirpium Hibernicarum*, ed. E. C. Nelson and D. M. Synnott (1988) • E. C. Nelson, 'The publication date of the first Irish flora, Caleb Threlkeld's *Synopsis stirpium Hibernicarum* 1726', *Glasra*, 2 (1978), 37–42 • E. C. Nelson, '"In the contemplation of vegetables": Caleb Threlkeld (1676–1728), his life, background and contribution to Irish botany', *Journal of the Society of the Bibliography of Natural History*, 9 (1978–80), 257–73 • E. C. Nelson, 'Records of the Irish flora published before 1726', *Bulletin of the Irish Biogeographical Society*, 3 (1979), 51–74 • E. C. Nelson and M. Raven, 'Caleb Threlkeld's family', *Glasra*, 3 (1998), 161–6 • M. E. Mitchell, 'The sources of Threlkeld's *Synopsis stirpium Hibernicarum*', *Proceedings of the Royal Irish Academy*, 74B (1974), 1–6 • Nichols, *Illustrations* • R. Pulteney, 'Memoir relating to Dr Threlkeld', *GM*, 1st ser., 47 (1777), 63–4 • parish register (baptism), Kirkoswald, Cumberland [John Threlkeld], 1 May 1699 • Mitchell L., NSW, Lancelot Threlkeld MSS
Archives Mitchell L., NSW, Lancelot Threlkeld MSS

Thring, Edward (1821–1887), headmaster, born at Alford, near Castle Cary, Somerset, on 29 November 1821, was the third son and fifth child of John Gale Dalton Thring (1784–1874) and his wife, Sarah (1790–1891), daughter of John Jenkyns, vicar of Evercreech, near Alford. His father was squire and rector of Alford; his mother was sister to Richard Jenkyns (1782–1854), master of Balliol College, Oxford. Edward's four brothers included Henry *Thring and Godfrey *Thring.

Thring attended a private classical school, Ilminster grammar, before going on to the Eton College of Dr Keate and Dr Hawtrey, where he eventually became captain of the collegers. His early experience in Long Chamber, the collegers' dormitory, and his previous harsh experience at Ilminster influenced his later thinking on educational reform. As captain of Eton collegers he was one of the last to benefit from the ancient custom of Montem, a day given over by the school for the pecuniary benefit of the college captain before he departed for university. Thring went to Cambridge in 1841 as a scholar of King's College, winning the Porson prize for Greek iambics in 1844 and graduating BA in 1845 and MA in 1848. He was a fellow of King's from 1844 to 1853.

In 1846 Thring was ordained and appointed to the curacy of St James's parish in Gloucester, the city where Robert Raikes developed the Sunday school movement in the 1780s. During a year's teaching in a national school in Gloucester, Thring encountered an educational problem and also devised a solution: the use of different teaching techniques in the education of less able or culturally deprived children. Throughout his pedagogic career Thring was convinced that a school needed the most skilful teachers for the less able or elementary classes, a principle he tried to apply later at Uppingham. He was in Gloucester for only a year, having suffered a breakdown in health. He became a private tutor in Marlow, Buckinghamshire, for two years and then spent the following two years as curate at Cookham Dean, Berkshire, during which time he was an examiner at Rugby and Eton and for the classical tripos at Cambridge. He had already developed a strong belief in the analytical teaching of English grammar as the best foundation for language teaching, publishing *The Elements of Grammar Taught in English* (1851; 3rd edn, 1860) and *The Child's Grammar* (1852). On 10 September 1853, at the age of thirty-one, Thring was elected headmaster of Uppingham School, which was to be his life's work. Shortly afterwards, on Christmas day 1853, he married Marie Louise (*d.* 1907), daughter of Carl Johann Koch of Bonn, commissioner of customs for the Prussian government. He had been sent abroad by his father to stop the marriage of his younger brother to Marie Koch and, a

Edward Thring (1821–1887), by Sir Emery Walker

dutiful son, achieved this by marrying her himself. Subsequently Thring's methods showed the mild influence of German educational theories.

During thirty-four years as head Thring refounded this small midland grammar school, founded originally by Archdeacon Robert Johnson in 1584, and turned it into a leading mid-Victorian public school. Thring always claimed that when he arrived at the school there were only twenty-five boys; within ten years he had raised the numbers to over 300. He could have recruited even more boys but preferred, much to the chagrin of his housemasters, to keep the school relatively small: one of his guiding principles for the conduct of Uppingham was that a headmaster should know all his boys. A major event in Thring's career at Uppingham was 'the flight to Borth' in 1875/6 when the school was temporarily closed because of typhoid fever arising from the town's poor drainage. In this hour of crisis Thring showed great leadership and arranged for the school to stay largely in a hotel and a few other houses at Borth, on the Welsh coast, near Aberystwyth. He saw the year's exile as a rejuvenating process, restoring some of the school's original ideals. Moreover the school's return to Uppingham in 1876 caused him to be regarded as a returning hero by the townsfolk, with whom Thring did much to foster good relations.

As well as knowing all his pupils, Thring applied at least

five other principles in his conduct of Uppingham School. His egalitarian nature led him to acknowledge secondly that 'every boy was good for something' and it was the task of the teacher to discover what that 'something' was. In order to do this a wide curriculum and a range of extra-curricular subjects were required. He expanded the Uppingham curriculum to enable boys not only to engage in academic subjects other than the classics, such as English composition, French, German, and chemistry, but also to experience subjects which were normally considered outside the average school curriculum: drawing, woodwork, art, and music. He was particularly concerned that music be well established in the school under the master of music, Paul David. About a third of the boys learnt to play a musical instrument and several well-known Victorian musicians, including Sir William Sterndale Bennett, Sir Charles Villiers Stanford, and Herr Joseph Joachim, visited the school. The 'Almighty Wall' was a third principle of Thring. Like Vittorino da Feltre, the Renaissance educator, Thring believed in the educative value of fine surroundings to encourage learning. During his headship he converted his modest provincial grammar school into a fine architectural example of a handsome English public school. 'Machinery, machinery, machinery' was a fourth principle in which he took pride. He felt that Uppingham, which he sometimes likened to a ship, was so well organized that, if needs be, it could run well without his presence.

'Manliness', a common enough Victorian value, was fully taken on board by Thring. As an ordained clergyman and a good games (cricket and fives) player, Thring was himself an outstanding example of a muscular Christian. As such he was totally dedicated to the concept of manliness and was supportive of the games ethic within the school. But an even more overarching notion governed his thinking: a fifth, visionary, principle of 'True Life'. The phrase 'True Life' was constantly on his lips and was the principle to which he appealed daily in the governance of his school. Manliness (*thymos*) was part of this principle of True Life, but only a part. Thring's True Life was similar to the old Greek aristocratic notion of *aretē* or virtue, a notion shared by the Greeks, Romans, and men of the Renaissance. For Thring, education was training for True Life. It was because his ultimate loyalty lay with True Life, which held connotations of the Platonic concept of balance and harmony, that in his later years at Uppingham he began to take a restrictive view of organized games and athleticism, believing their undue prominence gave an imbalance to school life. In short, they militated against his master principle, which in the long term made the boys responsible for their own behaviour.

During his headship of Uppingham, Thring pioneered a number of educational innovations: the school was, in 1859, the first public school to possess a gymnasium. In 1869 it was the first public school also to set up an educational mission in the East End of London (north Woolwich). Further, Thring is the acknowledged founder, in 1869, of the powerful Headmasters' Conference in collaboration with his close colleagues John Mitchinson of

King's School, Canterbury, and H. D. Harper of Sherborne School. Among his fellow public school headmasters Thring stood out as a champion of girls' secondary education and invited the leaders of the girls' public school movement in 1887 to hold their annual conference at Uppingham.

Thring's influence was greatest in the wider pedagogical world, where his writings on education were highly regarded. His *Theory and Practice of Teaching* (1883) was a popular textbook in training colleges in Britain and was read widely in America. Between 1883 and 1912 it was reprinted sixteen times, being the vade-mecum of many a training college student. Thring regarded teachers as his co-workers or 'skilled workmen' in a very important field of human endeavour, and they were attracted by his suspicion of bureaucratic control of education. He differentiated, as many have done before him and since, between teaching and 'pumping' or cramming. Thring's *Theory and Practice of Teaching* is written in his very idiosyncratic style, with colourful imagery, pithy aphorisms, and egalitarian earnestness, especially where he expounds his 'Legs not wings' theory. Thring wrote several other books in the context of education, including *Education and School* (1864), a much less successful book than *Theory and Practice*, though significant since it contains a major exposition of Thring's concept of True Life, which could be equated with moral education.

Thring died at Uppingham on 22 October 1887 and was buried in the nearby churchyard under a large Celtic cross which lies beyond the school walls. His wife, three daughters, and a son survived him. Sometimes compared with Thomas Arnold in his educational achievement, Thring was the greatest public school headmaster during the second half of the nineteenth century.

DONALD P. LEINSTER-MACKAY

Sources D. Leinster-Mackay, *The educational world of Edward Thring* (1987) · G. R. Parkin, *Life, diary and letters of Edward Thring*, 2 vols. (1898) · C. Rigby, 'The life and influence of Edward Thring', DPhil diss., U. Oxf., 1968 · E. Thring, manuscript diary, Uppingham School, Leicestershire · A. Percival, *Very superior men* (1973), 177–246 · M. Tozer, *Physical education at Thring's Uppingham* (1976) · J. H. Skrine, *A memory of Edward Thring* (1889) · W. F. Rawnsley, *Edward Thring, maker of Uppingham School* (1926) · G. Hoyland, *The man who made a school* (1946) · J. H. Skrine, *Uppingham by the Sea* (1878) · J. H. Skrine, manuscript diary, Uppingham School, Leicestershire · J. Roach, *Secondary education in England, 1870–1902* (1991) · *DNB*

Archives Uppingham School, Leicestershire, corresp., diaries, and papers | BL, corresp. with Macmillans, Add. MS 55171 · Headmaster's Conference MSS

Likenesses C. Johnson, oils, exh. RA 1880, Uppingham School, Leicestershire · T. Brock, marble statue, exh. RA 1892, Uppingham School, Leicestershire · E. Walker, photograph, NPG [*see illus.*] · portrait, repro. in E. Thring, *Addresses* (1887) · portrait, repro. in *Educational Review* (June 1892), 85 · portrait, repro. in *The Graphic* (11 Oct 1891), 414 · portraits, Uppingham School, Leicestershire

Wealth at death £5096 5s. 4d.: probate, 30 Dec 1887, CGPLA Eng. & Wales

Thring, Godfrey (1823–1903), hymn writer, born at Alford, Somerset, on 25 March 1823, was the fourth son of the seven children of John Gale Dalton Thring (1784–1874), rector and squire of Alford, and his wife, Sarah (1790–1891), daughter of John Jenkyns, vicar of Evercreech, Somerset, and sister of Richard Jenkyns (1782–1854), master of Balliol College, Oxford. Henry Thring, Baron *Thring (1818–1907), parliamentary counsel, and Edward *Thring (1821–1887), headmaster of Uppingham School, were elder brothers.

Educated at Shrewsbury School, Godfrey Thring matriculated at Balliol College in 1841, graduating BA in 1845. After his ordination as deacon in 1846 he held successively the curacies of Stratfield Turgis (1846–50), and Stratfield Saye (1850–53), both in Hampshire, Euston, Suffolk (1856), and Arborfield, Berkshire (1857), and in 1858 succeeded his father as rector of Alford, becoming in 1876 prebendary of Wells in Somerset. On 18 January 1870 he married Mary Jane, only daughter of Charles *Pinney (1793–1867), former mayor of Bristol; they had one son, Leonard Godfrey Pinney Thring.

Thring published *Hymns and other Verses* (1866), *Hymns, Congregational and Others* (1866), and *Hymns and Sacred Lyrics* (1874). In 1880 he edited *A Church of England Hymn Book, Adapted to the Daily Services of the Church throughout the Year* (rev. edn, 1882; 3rd edn, 1891). The literary standard of this collection was very high, but its practical use was limited. He wrote many hymns which have attained popularity, including 'The radiant morn hath passed away', 'Fierce raged the tempest', 'Saviour, blessed Saviour', and 'Thou, to whom the sick and dying'. He produced one of the best translations of Martin Luther's 'Ein' feste Burg', 'A fortress sure is God our king', which was included in the *Church of England Hymn Book* (1882). Thring resigned his living in 1893 and died at Plonk's Hill, Shamley Green, near Guildford, Surrey, on 13 September 1903.

J. C. HADDEN, rev. SAYONI BASU

Sources *The Times* (15 Sept 1903) · G. Parkin, *Life, diary and letters of Edward Thring* (1900) · A. J. Hayden and R. Newton, *British hymn writers and composers*, rev. edn (1979) · Burke, *Gen. GB* · CGPLA Eng. & Wales (1903)

Wealth at death £5687 15s. 6d.: probate, 11 Nov 1903, CGPLA Eng. & Wales

Thring, Henry, Baron Thring (1818–1907), parliamentary draftsman, born at Alford, Somerset, on 3 November 1818, was the second son of the Revd John Gale Dalton Thring (1784–1874) and his wife, Sarah (1790–1891), daughter of John Jenkyns, vicar of Evercreech, Somerset. His father was both squire and rector of Alford; his mother was a sister of Richard Jenkyns, master of Balliol College, Oxford. Thring came of a long-lived stock. His father died at the age of ninety, his mother lived to be 101. Of his younger brothers, Edward *Thring was headmaster of Uppingham School and Godfrey *Thring was a well-known hymnist.

Education and early legal career Henry Thring was educated at Shrewsbury School under Benjamin Hall Kennedy, to whose teaching, and that of his brother George, Thring used in after years to attribute that nice sense of the exact meaning of words which he rightly considered essential to the work of a good draftsman. From Shrewsbury Thring went in 1837 to Magdalene College, Cambridge, was in 1841 third classic in the classical tripos, and was that year elected to a fellowship at his college. He

Henry Thring, Baron Thring (1818–1907), by C. W. Carey

occasionally examined for the classical tripos, but does not seem to have taken any other part in university or college work. He went to London, studied law, and on 31 January 1845 was called to the bar as a member of the Inner Temple. He worked at conveyancing, 'the driest of all earthly studies', as he describes it in the autobiographical introduction to his little book *Practical Legislation* (2nd edn, 1902). Finding that the task of a conveyancer was neither profitable nor attractive, he passed to the study of the statute law, and there found the work of his future life. He read the English statute book critically from its earliest pages downwards, extolled Stephen Langton as 'the prince of all draftsmen', and contrasted the draftsman of Magna Carta favourably with his wordy successors. He convinced himself that a radical departure ought to be made from the conveyancing models then followed by the draftsmen of acts of parliament. He sought for better principles and a better type of drafting in Coode's book on legal expression (1845) and in the American codes, especially those of David Dudley Field, which then enjoyed a high reputation. In 1850 he tried his hand as an amateur in framing for Sir William Molesworth a colonial bill in which he endeavoured to simplify and shorten the expression of legal enactments. In 1851 he published portions of this bill as an appendix to a pamphlet which he entitled *The Supremacy of Great Britain not Inconsistent with Self-Government of the Colonies*. In this pamphlet he carefully enumerated and analysed the powers exercisable by the home government and the colonial government respectively, and distributed them on lines which foreshadowed the lines of the Irish Home Rule Bill drawn at the end of his official life.

Early years as a draftsman, and marriage Sir William Molesworth's bill did not become law, but drew attention to its draftsman, who soon obtained employment from the government on the lines in which he had specialized. Thring's start as a draftsman coincided with a great complexity of public law and a need for a more professional approach to its statement. Thring drew the Succession Act of 1853 which formed part of Gladstone's great budget of that year and thus began a partnership with Gladstone by which Thring drew most of Gladstone's legislative initiatives. At the same time he was engaged on a more comprehensive piece of legislative work. Edward *Cardwell was then president of the Board of Trade, and wished to recast the body of merchant shipping law administered by his department. Accordingly, under Cardwell's instructions, and in co-operation with Thomas Henry Farrer, Thring drew the great Merchant Shipping Act of 1854 which for forty years was the code of British merchant shipping law. In the preparation of this measure he found an opportunity for putting into practice those principles of draftsmanship which he afterwards expounded in his 'Instructions to draftsmen'. He divided the bill into parts, divided the parts under separate titles, arranged the clauses in a logical order, and constructed each clause in accordance with fixed rules based on an analysis of sentences. From working with Cardwell on the measure, Thring married, on 14 August 1856, the politician's sister, Elizabeth (d. 1897), daughter of John Cardwell of Liverpool and his wife, Elizabeth, *née* Birley. They had one daughter, Katherine Anne.

From merchant shipping law Thring passed to another branch of law with which the Board of Trade was intimately concerned, that relating to joint-stock companies, and drew the series of bills which culminated in the Companies Act of 1862. His treatise on this act went through three editions. Thring's work on these measures began when he was still in private practice at the bar, but in 1860 he was appointed to the important office of Home Office counsel. This office had been created in 1837, when, as a consequence of the Reform Act of 1832, the responsibility of the government for current legislation had been largely increased, and had devolved mainly on the home secretary. John Elliot Drinkwater Bethune was the first holder of the post, and, on his appointment in 1845 to the governor-general's council at Calcutta, his successor, Walter Coulson, was entrusted with the wider duties of preparing under the direction of the home secretary bills originating from any department of the government, and of revising and reporting on any other bills referred to him by the Home Office. These were the duties taken over by Thring, and in his performance of them he appears to have drawn all the most important cabinet measures of the time. In his introduction to *Practical Legislation* he described how he drew for Lord Derby's government the famous 'ten minutes' bill, the bill which, after radical alterations in parliament, became law as the Representation of the People Act, 1867. The rapid and often rather offhand way in which cabinet ministers sometimes acted required a draftsman who was well versed in the technicalities of the issues of the day and at Disraeli's request

Thring completely redrafted the 1867 bill with two short-hand writers on 16 March ready for the cabinet on the 17th.

Parliamentary counsel to the Treasury At the end of 1868 Disraeli was succeeded as prime minister by Gladstone, with Lowe as chancellor of the exchequer. One of Lowe's first steps was to improve the machinery for the preparation of government bills. The most important of them were, at that time, prepared by the Home Office counsel, but some departments continued to employ independent counsel to draw their bills, and other bills were drawn by departmental officers without legal aid. The result of this system, or absence of system, was unsatisfactory. The cost was great, for counsel charged fees on the parliamentary scale. There was no security for uniformity of language, style, or arrangement in laws which were intended to find their places in a common statute book. There was no security for uniformity of principle in measures for which the government was collectively responsible. And, lastly, there was no check on the financial consequences of legislation, nothing to prevent a minister from introducing a bill which would impose a heavy charge on the exchequer and upset the budget calculations for the year. The remedy which Lowe devised was the establishment of an office which should be responsible for the preparation of all government bills, and which should be subordinate to the Treasury, and thus brought into immediate relation not only with the chancellor of the exchequer but with the first lord of the Treasury, who was usually prime minister. The office was constituted by a Treasury minute dated 8 February 1869. The head of the office was to be styled parliamentary counsel to the Treasury, and was given a permanent assistant and a Treasury allowance for office expenses and for such outside legal assistance as he might require. The whole of the time of the parliamentary counsel and his assistant was to be given to the public, and they were not to engage in private practice. The parliamentary counsel was to settle all such departmental bills and draw all such other government bills (except Scottish and Irish bills) as he might be required by the Treasury to settle and draw. The instructions for the preparation of every bill were to be in writing or sent by the head of the department concerned to the parliamentary counsel through the Treasury, to which latter department he was to be considered responsible. On the requisition of the Treasury he was to advise on all cases arising on bills or acts drawn by him and to report in special cases referred to him by the Treasury on bills brought by private members. Thring was appointed head of the office and was given as his assistant Henry Jenkyns, who succeeded to the office on Thring's retirement.

Thring held the office of parliamentary counsel during Gladstone's first ministry of 1868 to 1874, during Disraeli's ministry of 1874 to 1880, and until the close of Gladstone's brief third ministry of 1886. This period was one of great legislative activity. The first important measure prepared by Thring as parliamentary counsel was the Irish Church Act of 1869; the last was Gladstone's Irish Home Rule Bill of 1886. In the interval, among a host of other bills which

did or did not find their way to the statute book, but which absorbed the time of the parliamentary counsel and his office, were the Irish Land Act of 1871 and the Army Act of 1871, which was based on instructions given to Thring by Cardwell in 1867, and the labours on which, as its draftsman remarked, lasted longer than the siege of Troy. The preparation of many bills relating to Ireland, which strictly lay outside the scope of his office, is accounted for by the circumstance that Irish bills always involved finance, and in practice the work of preparing them was apt to fall mainly on the office which worked immediately under the Treasury. Thring's experience of Irish legislation made him a convinced home-ruler, and in 1886 Gladstone turned to him at an early stage in the development of the plans for the first Home Rule Bill. Thring contributed to James Bryce's *Handbook of Home Rule* (1887).

Thring was a great parliamentary draftsman. He broke away from the old conveyancing traditions and introduced a new style, expounded and illustrated in the 'Instructions to draftsmen', which was used for many years by those working for and under him and eventually embodied in *Practical Legislation*. His drafting was criticized by the bench and elsewhere, often without regard for the difficulties inherent in parliamentary legislation, but the value of the improvements which he introduced into the style of drafting was emphatically recognized by the select committee on acts of parliament which sat in 1875.

Thring was not merely a skilful draftsman. He was also

a great legislator, so far as his duties and functions allowed, in the constructive sense. The quickness of his mind and the force of his imagination, controlled and restrained as they were by his rare technical skill, his vast knowledge of administrative law, and his instinctive insight into the nature, ways, and habits of both houses of parliament, enabled him at once to give effect to the views and wishes of the ministers who instructed him in a form best adapted to find the line of least parliamentary resistance. (*The Times*, 6 Feb 1907)

He thought in bills and clauses, and knew by instinct whether suggestions presented to him were capable of legislative expression, and if so how they should be expressed and arranged.

Legal reformer, retirement, and final years Improvement of the statute law was the object to which Thring persistently devoted the energies of his long and active life. He endeavoured to effect this object not merely by introducing a better style of drafting new laws but by throwing light upon the contents, diminishing the bulk, and reducing to more orderly arrangement the vast and chaotic mass of existing statute law. He was an original member of the statute law committee which was first appointed by Lord Cairns in 1868; he was for many years, and until his death, chairman of that committee and the last survivor of its original members. The work done by this committee fell under four heads: indexing; expurgation; republication; and consolidation. The chronological table of the statutes and the index to them were prepared in accordance with a plan and in pursuance of detailed instructions carefully framed by Thring. The contents of the statute book having been thus ascertained, the next step was to purge it of dead matter. This was done by a long succession of statute law revision bills, most of which were framed under the directions of the statute law committee at a time when Thring was its most active member. Then came the republication of the living matter under the title of the statutes revised. The first edition of these statutes substituted eighteen volumes for 118 volumes of the statutes at large; the second comprised in five volumes the pre-Victorian statutes which had formerly occupied seventy-seven volumes. In the process of consolidation much was done in Thring's time and under his guidance, and his name takes the first place in the history of this important task.

It was to Thring's initiative that was due the valuable publication of state trials from 1820, when Howell's series ended, to 1858. Its preparation arose out of a memorandum which he wrote in 1885, while he was parliamentary counsel, and he was an unfailing attendant at the meetings of the committee which supervised the publication.

Thring was made a KCB in 1873 and was created a peer in 1886, on his retirement. In 1893 he seconded the address to the crown, but he was not a frequent speaker in the House of Lords, though, when he did speak, he could express himself clearly, cogently, and incisively. His quick mind and constructive intellect made him a valuable member of many public bodies, especially after his retirement from office in 1886. He had a country house, Alderhurst, at Englefield Green, in Surrey, and was an active member of the Surrey county council and of the governing body of Holloway College. He also took a large part in the work of the council of the Imperial Institute and of the Athenaeum, where he was a well-known and popular figure.

Thring was a keen, vivacious little man with a sharp tongue, which was often outspoken in its criticism of those whom he efficiently and loyally served. Robert Lowe seems to be responsible for the story that Cardwell said one day, at the outset of a cabinet committee, 'Now, Thring, let us begin by assuming that we are all d—d fools, and then get to business.'

Thring's published writings arose out of his professional or official work. Besides those mentioned he contributed an article to the *Quarterly Review* (January 1874), republished in 1875 as *Simplification of the Law*. He superintended the compilation of the first edition of the War Office *Manual of Military Law* and contributed to it four chapters, one of which, on the laws and customs of war on land, was made by Sir Henry Maine the text of some lectures on international law.

Thring died at his London house, 5 Queen's Gate Gardens, on 4 February 1907, and was buried next to his wife at Virginia Water, Surrey. The peerage became extinct on his death. C. P. ILBERT, rev. H. C. G. MATTHEW

Sources *The Times* (6 Feb 1907) · Gladstone, *Diaries* · 'Autobiographical introduction', H. Thring, *Practical legislation*, 2nd edn (1902) · GEC, *Peerage* · CGPLA Eng. & Wales (1907)

Archives NA Canada, papers relating to Newfoundland fisheries | Bishopsgate Institute, London, letters to George Howell · BL, corresp. with W. E. Gladstone, Add. MS 44332 · LPL, corresp. with Archbishop Benson · NA Canada, corresp. with Sir George Parkin

Likenesses C. W. Carey, photograph, NPG [*see illus.*] · Spy [L. Ward], caricature, chromolithograph, NPG; repro. in *VF* (29 June 1893)

Wealth at death £35,437 0s. 11d.: probate, 27 April 1907, CGPLA Eng. & Wales

Throckmorton family (*per. c.*1500–1682), gentry, was descended from a younger son of the Throckmortons or Throgmortons [see Throgmorton family] of Fladbury, Worcestershire, who acquired an estate in Gloucestershire through marriage in the early fifteenth century. **William Throckmorton** (d. 1537) was the son of Christopher Throckmorton (d. 1513) and Mary, daughter of Sir John Harley of Herefordshire. His father had been sheriff of Gloucestershire in 1489–90 and William inherited from him the manor of Apperley, along with Underhills Court in Hasfield and Corse Court in Tirley. He also held the manor and advowson of Pendock and other land in the south of Worcestershire. He was himself pricked as sheriff in 1529. The Throckmortons established themselves in the south of the county through William's marriage to Margaret, coheir of David Mathews of Rayder and his wife, Alice, who was herself the heir of Robert Veel of Tortworth. William supplemented his wife's interest in Tortworth by leasing the other half of the manor from her sister Anne, the wife of John Baynham of Westbury. By 1532 the family was living in the manor house at Tortworth, described by Leland as next to the parish church. William and Margaret had four sons and four daughters. Through the daughters' marriages the family established ties with significant neighbouring gentry families, for instance the Daunts, Huntleys, and Thorpes. Towards the end of his life William acquired the lease of the manor of Cromhall Abbots from the bishop of Bristol. He died in 1537. William's younger brother George Throckmorton (d. 1548) had also established himself among the Gloucestershire gentry, adding to the family's property in the north of the county by leasing the site and manor of Deerhurst Priory in 1540 and acquiring the manor of Woolstone in 1543. He was a JP in 1547.

George died without an heir and his lands descended to his nephew, William's son **Sir Thomas Throckmorton** (d. 1568). Thomas married Margaret (d. 1578), one of the six coheirs of Thomas Whittington of Pauntley, Gloucestershire. His inheritance of additional property close to the Worcestershire border from his uncle, along with his marriage, appears to have prompted Thomas to establish his main residence at Corse Court. Thomas was a JP by 1547, and by then had also done military service in France and Scotland. He came to be associated with the earl of Somerset and with John Thynne, the latter's principal henchman, leading to his being elected MP for Heytesbury in 1547. He was knighted on 2 October 1553. In 1555 he sat for Westbury, like Heytesbury a Wiltshire seat. He remained a justice during Mary's reign, although his younger brother John was implicated in Wyatt's rebellion and was executed for treason in 1556. Thomas served as sheriff in the first year of Elizabeth I's reign and was subsequently appointed to the council of the marches. His association with Thynne led to his receiving a substantial grant of ex-chantry lands in the 1540s, much of which he later sold. He also sold parts of his patrimony, but purchased the remainder of Tortworth and at his death left an estate of two compact groups of manors worth a little over £120 per annum. Thomas and Margaret had two sons and three daughters. Their younger son, Anthony (d. 1616), established himself in business in Gloucester, while their daughter Anne made an advantageous marriage to Sir John Tracy of Toddington. Thomas died on 1 March 1568 and was buried at Tortworth.

Thomas's eldest son, **Sir Thomas Throckmorton** (1539–1607), inherited a prominent position in the county from his father, and like him was active in county affairs. His first wife, whom he married before 1567, was Elizabeth, daughter of Elizabeth I's comptroller, Sir Edward *Rogers (c.1498–1568) of Cannington, Somerset. She had died by 1572. They had no children. He subsequently married Ellen, daughter of Sir Richard Berkeley, with whom he had two sons and four daughters. He was a JP, served twice as sheriff (1560–61 and 1587–8), represented Gloucestershire in the parliament of 1589, and acted as a member of the council in the marches of Wales. In 1587 he was knighted. However, he had an overbearing and bellicose nature and exploited his official positions in his personal feuds, being described by John Smyth of Nibley as 'that powerful and plottinge gent' (Smyth, *Description*, 312). He was bound over to keep the peace towards Sir Thomas Proctor in 1580, accused of provoking a riot against Nicholas Poyntz in 1589, and in the following year was summoned before the privy council to explain various misdemeanours and outrages. He seems to have used his position as subsidy commissioner to falsify the lists, and as captain of the trained bands pressed his enemies and their servants for campaigns in Ireland. In 1602 he and Sir Henry Winston denounced one another in Star Chamber. Both were convicted; Sir Thomas was fined 2000 marks and disabled from bearing office. His marriage to the recusant Ellen was also turbulent. He extended the family's landholdings in Gloucestershire by the purchase of the manor and advowson of Cromhall Ligon in 1596, but sold the site of Deerhurst Priory in 1604. He died on 31 January 1607 and was buried at Tortworth.

Sir Thomas had been predeceased by his elder son, John (b. 1572), who died without children, and his heir was his younger son, **Sir William Throckmorton**, first baronet (1579–1628), who matriculated at University College, Oxford, in 1594. Sir William inherited his father's combative nature, which led to his fighting a duel with Walter Walsh of Little Sodbury. Smyth describes him as devouring his patrimony 'by riot & improvidence' (Smyth, *Description*, 307–8), and within months of inheriting his estate he employed Smyth to value his manors of Tortworth, Charfield, and Cromhall Ligon with a view to disposing of them. They were calculated to be worth about £630, excluding the profits from the coppiced woods. In the military survey of Gloucestershire in 1608 he was described as lord of the manors of Woolstone, Tirley, Apperly, Whitley (jointly), Tyrley, Cromhall, Huntingford, Charfield, Tortworth, and Shenhampton. Tortworth was

sold that year and the family moved to Clearwell in the parish of Newland in the Forest of Dean, which William had acquired through his marriage to Cicely (b. 1586), coheir of Thomas Baynham. Huntingford was alienated to Thomas Tracy in 1608–9 and sold in 1615–16. Apperly was sold in 1613 and the advowson of Woolstone in 1616. Despite his financial difficulties William was knighted and created a baronet on 29 June 1611. He leased 550 acres in the Forest of Dean for the growing of rape to the entrepreneurial clothier Benedict Webb, with whom he subsequently had an acrimonious relationship. In 1618 he was granted wood and ironworks in the forest, where he acted as deputy constable. He was also both a JP and master of Corse Lawn Chase, but had sold the latter office to Sir Richard Tracy by 1628. In 1619 he joined with Smyth, Richard Berkeley of Rendcomb, and George Thorpe of Wanswell in undertaking to send a ship of settlers to Virginia, but withdrew from the partnership the following year. With Cicely he had four sons and two daughters. Following Cicely's death Sir William married successively Alice Morgan and Sarah Hale (d. 1636), described by Smyth as his maids. He died in 1628 and was buried at Newland on 20 July. His monument mentions only his first wife and their children.

Sir William was succeeded by his eldest son, **Sir Baynham Throckmorton**, second baronet (1606–1664), who was born in June 1606. He entered the Inner Temple in 1623. He developed the family's interests in the Forest of Dean while disposing of its property in the north of the county. Woolstone was sold to Lord Coventry in 1630, followed by Corse Court in 1632. By 1634 he was chief forester in the Forest of Dean and in 1636, with Sir Sackville Crowe and others, he was granted a twenty-one-year lease of the ironworks there. In the following year he conveyed his estate to trustees for the payment of his debts. About 1628 he married Margaret (d. 1635), daughter of Robert Hopton of Witham, Somerset, and sister of Ralph, Lord Hopton. Sir Baynham succeeded his father as a JP and was sheriff in 1643.

As the king's sheriff at the time of the siege of Gloucester Sir Baynham played an important part in raising men. Frustrated by the reluctance of the miners of the Forest of Dean to serve Charles I, he was forced to recruit in south Wales. Thereafter he acted as a royalist colonel until surrendering at Gloucester in December 1645. In 1647 he was assessed for a composition fine at a sixth or £1515, subsequently reduced to a tenth or £1000. Following the Restoration Sir Baynham re-established himself as a royal officer in the forest, which had become militarily important as a source of timber and iron. He also sat in parliament as one of the county members between 1661 and his death in 1664. His committee work suggests that he was a strong Anglican—he was among those appointed to bring in a bill against the growth of popery and to provide remedies against meetings of nonconformists, and he also served on the committee for the bill against seditious conventicles. He died on 24 May 1664 and was buried at St Margaret's, Westminster.

Sir Baynham and Margaret had five sons, but only the

eldest survived to marry and have children. This dynastic accident and the death of Lord Hopton without an heir helped to restore the family's finances. The heir, **Sir Baynham Throckmorton**, third baronet (1629–1681), was born on 11 December 1629 and entered Lincoln's Inn in 1647. He became a Gloucestershire JP in 1657, and having represented Gloucestershire in parliament in 1656–8, sat for Wootton Basset, Wiltshire, in 1660. At the Restoration he was knighted and became a gentleman of the privy chamber and deputy warden of the Forest of Dean. The following year he was appointed a JP in Herefordshire and Monmouthshire. On his father's death he followed him in representing Gloucestershire in parliament until 1679. He was apparently popular among those who earned their living in the Forest of Dean, being elected a free miner in 1668. Unlike his ancestors Sir Baynham was regarded as being concerned with the maintenance of the forest and its population rather than simply its commercial exploitation for his own ends. His support for the king was rewarded by a grant of Kingswood Forest and £200 per annum. On 11 December 1652 he married Mary (d. 1666), the heir of Giles Garton of Billinghurst, Sussex, with whom he had three daughters. In 1669 he married Katherine, the daughter of Piers Edgcumbe of Mount Edgcumbe, Devon, with whom he had another daughter. By his will he authorized the sale of his estate in order to pay an outstanding obligation of £4240, provide a £5000 settlement for his wife, and to divide the residue among his three daughters from his first marriage. His heir male is not mentioned in the will, which was written in July 1680. He was buried on 31 July 1681 in Clerkenwell, London. Two of his daughters from his first marriage died shortly after their father, while the survivor, Carolina, married Captain Scrimshaw, the second son of Sir Charles Scrimshaw. Katherine, Sir Baynham's daughter from his second marriage, married Thomas Wild, esquire, of Worcester in 1690.

Sir Baynham was succeeded by his first cousin **Sir William Throckmorton**, fourth baronet (1658–1682), the son of the first baronet's younger son Nicholas Throckmorton of Hewelsfield (d. 1664) and Alice Gough (d. 1670). Sir William matriculated at Christ Church, Oxford, in 1677 and was admitted to the Inner Temple in 1681. He apparently inherited his grandfather's aggressive nature, for he was killed in a duel in 1682. He was unmarried, and as his only brother had died in 1667 the baronetcy became extinct.

JAN BROADWAY

Sources J. Burke and J. B. Burke, *A genealogical and heraldic history of the extinct and dormant baronetcies of England, Ireland, and Scotland* (1838), 526–7 · J. Smyth, *The description of the hundred of Berkeley*, ed. J. Maclean (1885) · HoP, *Commons, 1509–58*, 3.461–2 · HoP, *Commons, 1558–1603*, 3.501–2 · HoP, *Commons, 1660–90*, 3.558–60 · R. Atkins, *The ancient and present state of Gloucestershire*, 2 vols. (1712) · C. Hart, *Royal forest* (1966) · J. Smyth, *Men and armour for Gloucestershire* (1980) · VCH *Gloucestershire*, vol. 8 · 'Gloucestershire justices of the peace', *Gloucestershire N&Q*, 5 (1894), 142–6 · will, PRO, PROB 11/27 [William Throckmorton, d. 1537], fols. 51v–53r · will, PRO, PROB 11/50 [Sir Thomas Throckmorton, d. 1568], fols. 53r–53v · will, PRO, PROB 11/111 [Sir Thomas Throckmorton, d. 1607], fols. 216r–216v · will, PRO, PROB 11/191v–193r [Sir Baynham Throckmorton, d. 1681] · will, Glos. RO, 1636/103 [Sarah Throckmorton]

Archives Bristol RO, letters to Thomas Smyth [Sir Baynham Throckmorton] · Glos. RO, letters to Lord Berkeley [Sir Thomas Throckmorton]
Wealth at death evaluation of part of estate in 1608 was £630; civil war composition puts family estates at £625 p.a.: Gloucester Public Library, Smyth papers, vol. 5, fol. 64; HoP, *Commons*

Throckmorton, Sir Baynham, second baronet (1606–1664). *See under* Throckmorton family (*per. c.*1500–1682).

Throckmorton, Sir Baynham, third baronet (1629–1681). *See under* Throckmorton family (*per. c.*1500–1682).

Throckmorton [Throgmorton], **Francis** (1554–1584), Roman Catholic conspirator, was the son of Sir John Throckmorton (*c.*1518–1580) of Feckenham in Worcestershire and his wife, Margaret (d. 1591), daughter of Robert Puttenham. The Throckmorton or Throgmorton family first emerged from relative obscurity in the early part of the fifteenth century, when the lawyer John Throgmorton (d. 1445) rose to the office of chamberlain of the exchequer, or under-treasurer of England. This John married an heiress who brought Coughton in Warwickshire into the family, and his great-grandson Sir George *Throckmorton took them further up the social ladder by becoming an esquire of the body to Henry VIII, flourishing in spite of his outspoken disapproval of the king's divorce from Katherine of Aragon. He married the daughter of Lord Vaux of Harrowden and produced a numerous family. Sir John, father of Francis, was the fifth of seven sons and, like his forebear and namesake, was trained to the law. Following the break with Rome several of the Throckmorton brothers adopted the new reformed religion, but John, possibly influenced by his wife, remained a staunch Catholic and consequently did well under Queen Mary, who rewarded his loyal service with the office of puisne justice of Chester. By 1565 he had risen to become vice-president of the council of the Welsh marches and was knighted by Queen Elizabeth, which means that he must have conformed, outwardly at least, to the established church, but his sons Francis and Thomas were certainly brought up as Catholics.

Little seems to be known about Francis Throckmorton's early life, although he was described by William Camden as 'a gentleman well-educated and of good wit' (Camden, 846). He matriculated from Hart Hall, Oxford, in 1572. In 1576 he married Anne or Agnes and was entered as a student of the Inner Temple. Two years after this the family's Catholic sympathies began to get them into trouble, when the headmaster of Shrewsbury School affirmed before Justice George Bromley that Lady Throckmorton and others had heard mass in the house of her brother-in-law; 'that one Hughes was the chief sayer and came from beyond the sea'; that he taught the son of Sir John Throckmorton; and that these priests distributed 'certain Beads called Pardon Beads and another monument called Agnus Dei' (Strype, *Whitgift*, 2.83). As a result Francis was committed to the custody of the dean of St Paul's to be examined on suspicion of 'being present at exercises of religion contrary to present practices' (APC, February 1578). But his protestant cousins interceded for him and he was freed after a month.

In 1579 John Throckmorton, now chief justice of Chester, was accused of having shown undue partiality in a case before him. Suspended from office, fined and disgraced, he died a year later a broken man. By this time Francis was already dabbling in treason. He and his brother Thomas had gone abroad at some time prior to their father's death and Francis had become involved with the English Catholic expatriates gathered at Spa in the Low Countries, discussing with them 'the altering of the state of the realme here; and how the same might be attempted by forraine invasion' ('A discovery', 191). He had had 'sundrie conferences' on this dangerous topic with Sir Francis Englefield, once a member of Queen Mary's privy council, and had been put in touch with Thomas Morgan in Paris. His brother stayed on in France, but Francis Throckmorton was back in England by the early 1580s to join the small but growing band of idealistic young Catholic laymen eager to serve the cause of Rome and the captive queen of Scots.

In April 1583 Francis Walsingham received a report from Henry Fagot, his agent inside the French embassy, that Francis Throckmorton had dined with the ambassador, having recently sent the Scottish queen the sum of 1500 crowns, 'which is on the ambassador's account' (*CSP Scot.*, 1581–3, 432). A month later Fagot wrote again with the information that 'the chief agents for the Queen of Scots are M. Throckmorton and Lord Henry Howard. They never come to bring things from her except at night' (Bossy, 200). This, together with further reports of 'what secret resorts he had to the French ambassador, what long and private conferences at seasons suspicious' (ibid., 203), was enough for Walsingham to set a watch on Throckmorton and in November he was arrested at his London house. He just had time to destroy a letter he was in the act of writing to the queen of Scots and send a maidservant with a casket of incriminating documents to the Spanish ambassador, Bernardino Mendoza, but among his seized papers was a list of the names of 'certain Catholic noblemen and gentlemen' and also details of harbours 'suitable for landing forraine forces' ('A discovery', 192). Confronted with these Throckmorton at first 'impudently' denied they were his, saying they must have been planted by the government searchers, but later admitted they had been left in his chamber by a man named Nutby who had since fled the realm. When he refused to say any more he was put on the rack and 'somewhat pinched', but 'continued in his former obstinacy and denial of the truth' (ibid., 191). He managed to smuggle a message out to Mendoza, written in cipher on the back of a playing card, saying he would die a thousand deaths before he betrayed his friends, but, racked a second time, he broke down and 'yielded to confess anything he knew' (ibid.).

Walsingham had long suspected the existence of some 'great hidden treason' involving Mary, queen of Scots, her friends in Scotland, the Jesuits, and either France or Spain—perhaps both. Now Throckmorton revealed that it was Mary's formidable kinsman, the duke of Guise, who

had been preparing to lead an invasion of England with the declared objective of releasing the queen of Scots and forcing Elizabeth to grant the Catholics a measure of toleration. The real intention, however, was to remove Elizabeth from her crown and state. The foreign forces were ready, the king of Spain would bear half the cost, while Francis Throckmorton and his brother (who had returned secretly to England during the summer), together with the Spanish ambassador, were to organize a welcoming committee of Catholic gentlemen at the port of Arundel in Sussex, which had been chosen by Guise for his landing. Throckmorton's confession did not tell the whole story—his had always been a subordinate role—but Walsingham now knew that it was the Spanish rather than the French ambassador who had been abusing his diplomatic privileges. He was also now able to make some further arrests, although most of those in the plot, including Thomas Throckmorton, had had time to make their escape and in the end it was only Francis who suffered the death penalty.

Francis Throckmorton remains a somewhat shadowy figure, but an anonymous correspondent was to write of 'the good partes wherewith he was indued, and of the pleasant humour that for the most part did possess him when hee came in companie of friendes' ('A discovery', 191). He was undoubtedly sincere in his convictions. After first making his confession he had exclaimed in obvious distress: 'Nowe I have disclosed the secrets of her who was the deerest thing to me in the worlde (meaning the Scottish Queene) … and sith I have failed of my faith towards her, I care not if I were hanged' (ibid., 195). At his trial he attempted to retract the matters he had confessed because the rack had forced him to say something to ease the torment. He was executed at Tyburn on 10 July 1584 and was reported to have died 'very stubbornly', refusing to ask for the queen's forgiveness. He was survived by his wife, who later remarried and became Mrs Wilks.

ALISON PLOWDEN

Sources 'A discovery of Francis Throckmorton's treasons', *The Harleian miscellany*, ed. W. Oldys and T. Park, 3 (1809) · A. L. Browne, 'Sir John Throckmorton of Feckenham', *Transactions of the Birmingham Archaeological Society*, 59 (1938), 123–42 · A. L. Rowse, *Ralegh and the Throckmortons* (1962) · C. Read, *Mr Secretary Walsingham and the policy of Queen Elizabeth*, 3 vols. (1925) · J. Bossy, *Giordano Bruno and the embassy affair* (1991) · *CSP Scot.*, 1581–3 · *CSP Spain*, 1580–86 · *LP Henry VIII*, 12/2.332ff. · J. Strype, *The life and acts of John Whitgift*, new edn, 3 vols. (1822) · *CPR*, 1557–8 · *APC*, 1578–80 · G. Camdeno [W. Camden], *Annales rerum Anglicarum et Hibernicarum regnante Elizabetha* (1615)

Throckmorton [Throgmorton], **Sir George** (c.1489–1552), member of parliament, was the eldest son of Sir Robert *Throgmorton or Throckmorton (c.1451–1518), a landowner of Coughton, Warwickshire, and his wife, Katherine, daughter of William Marrow or Marrowe of London. He had at least two other brothers, one of whom was Michael *Throckmorton, agent for Cardinal Reginald Pole, and at least one sister, Ursula. He was admitted to the Middle Temple on 1 May 1505, and by 1512 had married Katherine, daughter of Nicholas Vaux, first Baron Vaux of

Harrowden, a soldier, councillor, and courtier, whose family connection to the Parrs was of subsequent advantage to his children. In 1518 Throckmorton's father, one of Henry VII's courtiers, died on his way to the Holy Land, and George succeeded to a considerable estate, which he further enlarged during his lifetime.

Throckmorton first attracted attention at court in the 1520s when he was in conflict with Cardinal Thomas Wolsey over land. The cardinal, engaged at the time in a campaign against enclosures, in July 1524 ordered Throckmorton to be bound in £100 to appear before the council to be fined, probably for ignoring Wolsey's policy. Nothing further ensued, however, and the next year the two men traded lands, perhaps to facilitate Wolsey's plans for dissolving several small monasteries. An apparent connection developed which allowed Throckmorton to ask Wolsey for favours and for the cardinal to use Throckmorton to resolve local disputes on behalf of the crown. Although he was active in the local government of Warwickshire, Worcestershire, and, more briefly, Buckinghamshire, Throckmorton's chief claim to fame is as an active member of the conservative political faction in the 1530s. Sitting in the Reformation Parliament as knight of the shire for Warwickshire, Throckmorton, a staunch Catholic, constantly fought against Henry VIII's divorce from Katherine of Aragon, the royal supremacy, and all efforts to reform the church. During the critical year, 1532, Throckmorton visited and plotted with men from all the conservative constituencies. After one speech in the House of Commons, he was summoned before the king himself. There he warned Henry that his conscience would be greatly troubled if he married Anne Boleyn, 'for that it is thought that ye have meddled with both the mother and the sister'. Taken aback, Henry replied weakly that he had not had carnal relations with Anne's mother, and Thomas Cromwell, who was present, firmly interposed that the King had not had relations with the sister either.

Committed to the papal supremacy and dedicated to fighting against legislation directed against clerical liberties, Throckmorton enmeshed himself in factional politics. He met several other conservative country gentlemen in the Queen's Head tavern in Fleet Street to discuss parliamentary affairs. Cromwell regarded them with some anxiety, and in 1533 he made Throckmorton promise that he would 'stay at home and meddle little with politics' (HoP, Commons, 1509–58, 453).

Late in 1536, however, Throckmorton was arrested for showing an unwise interest in the grievances of the northern rebels. He was questioned about his earlier activities, and told his interrogators that he had been encouraged in his attack on royal policies by several leading members of the conservative faction. William Peto from the house of Franciscan Observants in Greenwich encouraged Throckmorton to oppose the Act for the Submission of the Clergy, and he had several meetings with John Fisher, bishop of Rochester, who gave him a pamphlet on papal primacy and recommended him to Nicholas Wilson, formerly the king's confessor but lately a bulwark of Katherine of Aragon's cause. Finally, Throckmorton travelled to

Syon and absorbed the counsel of Richard Reynolds, who insisted that he continue to speak in parliament against reform legislation even if it did no good. Throckmorton also claimed that Sir Thomas More had once sent for him and promised that if he continued 'in the same way' and was not afraid, he would 'deserve great reward from God'. Soon released, Throckmorton was in trouble again in 1537 because his younger brother, Michael, who had been sent to spy on Cardinal Pole, instead became his loyal servant. Sir George was taken into custody and held for several weeks. He confessed that he had been blinded by the 'sayings and counsels of men who had led him astray', and begged for forgiveness. By the end of the year his release was assured.

The fall of Thomas Cromwell in 1540 improved Throckmorton's position, though there is no evidence that he played a significant role in these events. The change in the religious climate did prove beneficial to Throckmorton and his conservative associates. He apparently returned his full attention to acquiring additional lands and consolidating his holdings, and in 1542 he married for a second time. He was able to see his family of eight sons and eleven daughters well established. His sons shared their father's resolute frame of mind, but not necessarily his commitment to conservative doctrine. Some, including the eldest, Robert (c.1513–1581), were famous for recusancy, while others, like Clement (c.1515–1573), his third son, were convinced puritans. His fourth son, Sir Nicholas *Throckmorton (1515/16–1571), a diplomat and MP, was indicted and acquitted of treason in 1554. George (fl. 1523–1573) was a courtier; Kenelm (c.1514–1583x7) an MP; John (c.1524–1580), Throckmorton's seventh son, was an administrator; and his eighth son, Anthony (d. 1592/3), was also an MP. Clement's son was Job *Throckmorton (1545–1601), a politician and religious pamphleteer. Throckmorton and his father were enthusiastic builders, who erected an impressive stone gatehouse at Coughton, with polygonal turrets, large windows, and a battlemented skyline. However, Sir George's plan of making the remainder of the timber-framed house 'suitable' to the gatehouse was not fulfilled. He died on 6 August 1552 and was buried in the impressive marble tomb he had had erected for himself in the church at Coughton.

JENNIFER LOACH, rev. JOSEPH S. BLOCK

Sources MSS, Coughton Court, Warwickshire · LP Henry VIII · W. Dugdale, The antiquities of Warwickshire illustrated (1656) · S. M. Thorpe, 'Throckmorton, Sir George', HoP, Commons, 1509–58, 3.450–55

Throckmorton, Job (1545–1601), politician and religious pamphleteer, was the eldest of the seven sons (and brother of seven daughters) of Clement Throckmorton (c.1515–1573) of Haseley, Warwickshire, third son of Sir George Throckmorton of Coughton, Warwickshire, and of his wife, Katherine, daughter of Lord Nicholas Vaux of Harrowden and aunt of Queen Katherine Parr, whom Clement Throckmorton served as cup-bearer. Haseley was acquired after the attainder of John Dudley, duke of Northumberland, when Michael Throckmorton, Clement's uncle and secretary to Cardinal Pole, secured the property from the crown and sold it to his nephew. The numerous Throckmortons were divided in religion. Sir George was a conservative opponent of Henry VIII, and his eldest son, Sir Robert, followed in that tradition, as did a younger brother John, father of Francis Throckmorton, the traitor executed in 1584. But the fourth of Sir George's sons, Sir Nicholas Throckmorton, the diplomat, was a protestant, while the commitment of Job's father, Clement, to the evangelical cause was more pronounced. He was close to his Warwickshire cousin, the hot protestant courtier Edward Underhill, and a friend of the Essex gentleman, courtier, and Marian martyr Thomas Haukes. In 1567 Clement was one of the midland gentry who administered funds to maintain 'preachers of the Gospel' in Warwickshire under the terms of a patent procured by the earl of Leicester. It was this tradition that Job Throckmorton inherited, and it must have been reinforced by Oxford, where he graduated BA in February 1566. His college is unknown, but two of his sons and two grandsons were at Queen's. Throckmorton may have proceeded to the inns of court, but of this there is no record, although two brothers and two sons were at the Middle Temple.

When Clement Throckmorton died on 13 December 1573, Job inherited a debt-burdened estate. He was never a county magnate, and but for the cause of religion would be a historical nonentity. He was returned to parliament for East Retford in 1572 (the earl of Rutland, a relative, would have seen to that), but there is no evidence that he spoke or sat on committees. January 1584 witnessed his only recorded intervention in local politics which concerned, significantly, Catholicism. Under an order from the privy council Throckmorton investigated the activities of William Skynner, a recusant supporter of Mary, queen of Scots, and 'a deadly enemye to the gospell'. Throckmorton expressed his frustration at the reluctance of witnesses to testify: 'Our papistes heere are woondrous cunning' (PRO, SP 12/167/21). Yet, as is revealed by the diary kept by his cousin, Sir Nicholas's son Arthur Throckmorton, blood was thicker than religious bile when it came to social civilities within the confessionally divided Throckmorton clan.

In October 1586 parliament met at a moment of extraordinary interest to all earnest protestants. Its primary purpose was to decide the fate of Mary Stewart in the aftermath of the Babington plot. But England was now effectively at war with Spain in the Netherlands, which for hot protestants was a war of religion. And the organized puritan movement saw an opportunity to renew its agitation on behalf of the godly preaching ministry, and even to bring about a presbyterian revolution in the church. Job Throckmorton prepared speeches on all three topics. But first he had to find a parliamentary seat. The way in which this was contrived makes the most remarkable story in Elizabethan electoral history, for Throckmorton was returned for Warwick by means of what can only be called a conspiracy. Backed by powerful outside interests (which must have included the earl of Leicester, who had made Thomas Cartwright master of his hospital in the town), and threatening to exploit the popular franchise, which

he treated at a 'solemn dinner' for as many as eighty voters, this blatant carpet-bagger enforced his adoption as a burgess, even while it was well known that his motive in seeking election was not to serve the interests of the borough 'but for the parliament, where peradventure some friends of yours … may have some causes in handling' (Kemp, 390, 394).

Copies of Throckmorton's extraordinary parliamentary speeches are preserved in the Pierpont Morgan Library in New York. On 4 November 1586 he denounced Mary Stewart as 'the daughter of sedition, the mother of rebellion, the nurce of impietie'. On 27 February he spoke on the presbyterian bill and book and echoed Peter Wentworth's speech of 1576 in a call for the widest possible definition of parliamentary free speech, offering a vigorous defence of what was called puritanism. 'I feare me we shall shortly to this, that to doe God and her Majestie good service shalbe coumpted puritanisme'. But his greatest offence was offered four days earlier, when Throckmorton launched a gratuitous attack on England's 'popish' neighbours, including the obnoxious 'litter' and 'brood' of Queen Catherine de' Medici, the 'idolatrous' and 'lycentious' king of Spain, and even 'the younge impe of Scotlande', his mother's son. 'No hope of Spayne, no trust in Fraunce, colde comforte in Scotlande' (Hartley, 229, 314, 280, 285). Lord Burghley had to apologize for this speech to James VI's London agent, and promised to clap Throckmorton in the Tower. But the offender made himself scarce, lying low in his sister's house in Hillingdon, whence he wrote a letter of grovelling submission to the lord treasurer.

In the autumn of 1588 the radical puritan cause found a new voice in the rollicking, seditious satire of the Marprelate tracts. There is copious evidence that Throckmorton was up to his neck in this literary conspiracy. Most of the tracts were printed in Warwickshire, and Throckmorton was involved at every stage in their production. Comparison of the Marprelate tracts with his parliamentary speeches and with the only printed pamphlet to which he put his name (*The Defence of Job Throkmorton Against the Slaunders of Maister Sutcliffe*, 1594) has persuaded modern critical opinion that if these satires had a single author, that author was Throckmorton. The case is almost clinched by the attribution to Throckmorton of a tract called *Master Some Laid Open in his Coulers*, for whoever wrote that was surely Martin. Leland H. Carlson overstated the case by using somewhat shaky stylistic evidence to link Throckmorton with the authorship of as many as thirty anonymous puritan pamphlets, from 1572 onwards, which would make him almost a monopolist of radical puritan print. But Throckmorton may well have been responsible for a Martinesque 'Survey of the state of the ministry in Warwickshire', linked to the parliamentary campaign of 1586, with its characterization of the curate of Grafton, who may have married Shakespeare: 'His chiefest trade is to cure hawks that are hurt or diseased' (Peel, 2.167).

Although he stood trial in 1590 for his role in the Marprelate affair, and was widely suspected to be Martin, Throckmorton's social position and legal technicalities saved him from punishment, which for his co-conspirator, the Welsh pamphleteer John Penry, meant the gallows. Throckmorton's protestations 'I am not Martin, I knewe not Martin' (J. Throckmorton, *The Defence*, sig. Eii) were equivocations, for Martin did not exist.

Throckmorton's polemical pen remained active for a few more years, but he eventually reverted to an obscure and private life. The story that Throckmorton ended his days at Canons Ashby, Northamptonshire, undergoing treatment from the spiritual therapist John Dod, and that thirty-seven years of doubting his salvation culminated in an edifying deathbed performance, is apocryphal and arises from a confusion of identity. Throckmorton died suddenly, intestate, at Haseley in February 1601, survived by his wife, Dorothy, daughter of Thomas Vernon of Howell, Staffordshire. He was buried at Haseley on 23 February. His son Clement and grandson Clement were both in their times MP for Warwickshire.

PATRICK COLLINSON

Sources L. H. Carlson, *Martin Marprelate, gentleman: Master Job Throkmorton laid open in his colors* (1981) · T. Kemp, ed., *The Black Book of Warwick* [1898] · T. E. Hartley, ed., *Proceedings in the parliaments of Elizabeth I*, 2 (1995) · state papers domestic, Elizabeth I, PRO, SP 12/167/21 · J. E. Neale, *The Elizabethan House of Commons* (1949) · HoP, *Commons, 1558–1603*, 3.492–4 · A. L. Rowse, *Ralegh and the Throckmortons* (1962) · *The Marprelate tracts, 1588, 1589*, facs. edn (1967) [Scolar Press Facsimile] · A. Peel, ed., *The seconde parte of a register*, 2 (1915) · administration of the estate of Job Throckmorton, 18 May 1601, PRO, PROB 6/6, fol. 83v · *DNB*

Throckmorton, Sir John. *See* Throgmorton, John (d. 1445).

Throckmorton, Sir John Courtenay, fifth baronet (1753–1819), Roman Catholic leader, was born and baptized on 27 July 1753 at Weston Underwood, Buckinghamshire, the second son of George Throckmorton (d. 1767) and his wife, Anna Maria, *née* Paston, of Horton in Gloucestershire. He was educated at the English Benedictine priory of St Gregory, Douai, in the late 1760s. During the 1770s he was in Italy with his brother George, under the tutorship of his uncle James Paston and the English Benedictine Dom Augustine Walker.

> The two young Mr Trockmortons [*sic*] reside with the Monk Walker in a wretched situation in Trastevere. They frequent low English company, because there is the favourite card table of their tutor [Walker], unless when he chooses to exhibit with Cups & Balls, or declaim against the Jesuits in the vile hole of an English Coffee House. The two young gentlemen appear to be very capable of improvement, & the elder of them [Mr Courtenay] to be of a most agreeable character. (Ingamells, 942)

In Rome Throckmorton became closely acquainted with the artistic and antiquarian circle attached to James Byres, through whom he was encouraged to collect works of art. By January 1778 he had returned to the family estate at Weston Underwood, Buckinghamshire, and on 19 August 1782 married Maria Catherine (1762–1821), daughter of Thomas Giffard of Chillington, Staffordshire, but they had no children.

On 3 June 1782 Throckmorton was elected as a member of the revived Catholic Committee. The committee

Sir John Courtenay Throckmorton, fifth baronet (1753–1819), by Thomas Phillips

sought to further the achievements of the 1778 Catholic Relief Act through encouraging the independence of English Catholics from papal control. They demanded that, instead of vicars apostolic being appointed by the pope, the laity and clergy should elect their own bishops. On 15 January 1786 Throckmorton urged the adoption of the Anglo-Gallican *Roman Catholic Principles*, republished by Joseph Berington. With other members of the committee in 1787 he supported the establishment of a lay Catholic school which would teach a modern curriculum, and in July 1788 was one of the trustees appointed to raise subscriptions for the Bavarian Chapel in Warwick Street, London. It is possible that he influenced the 'protestation' made by Charles, third Earl Stanhope, in November 1788 in support of Catholic emancipation.

By this time the committee was locked in conflict with the vicars apostolic over the acceptable measure of compromise with the government in return for a measure of relief. Throckmorton was now recognized politically as a whig, and in ecclesiastical affairs continued to support a radical Anglo-Gallicanism. His *A letter addressed to the Catholic clergy of England, on the appointment of bishops. By a layman* (1790), which was sent free of charge to all interested parties, demonstrated primitive and Gallican precedents for episcopal election. He succeeded to the baronetcy on the death of his grandfather Sir Robert Throckmorton in December 1791, the year of the second Catholic Relief Act. This act introduced an oath of allegiance for Catholics based on that introduced in Ireland in 1774, removing the phrase 'protesting Catholic dissenter' preferred by the committee. On 12 April 1792 the committee, including

Throckmorton, decided to perpetuate their principles by forming themselves into the Cisalpine Club. A second edition of his work on episcopal election was answered by a pastoral letter, dated 26 December 1792, drawn up anonymously by John Milner. It condemned twelve statements, cited from Throckmorton's book, as

> false, erroneous, scandalous, injurious to the Head of the Church, and to a general Council, subversive of ecclesiastical discipline, tending to schism, favouring heresy, inducing to schism and heresy, schismatical, contrary to a formal definition of a general council, and to the faith of the Church. (Ward, *Dawn of the Catholic Revival*, 2.4041)

The following winter was spent by Throckmorton and his wife in Italy. In Naples they stayed with Sir William and Lady Forbes, and in Rome were shown around by Patrick Moir, and lavishly entertained English Catholics at a ball in the English College. Throckmorton refused to visit the pope, despite the latter wishing to meet the person who had described him as a 'foreign prelate'. In Rome he met Monsignor Charles Erskine, the papal envoy to England, and probably influenced him in favour of the Cisalpines.

On his return from Italy Throckmorton continued his attachment to the whigs by becoming chairman of the Society of Friends of the People, and moved closer to the prince of Wales and to Fox, who believed that 'he did not know a person from whom it was more unsafe to differ, than Sir John Throckmorton' (Butler, 4.180). He also maintained his Cisalpinism by accepting Joseph Berington as chaplain on his estate of Buckland, Berkshire, in May 1793 despite the censures of Bishop John Douglass of the London district. On 15 June 1796 he was created DCL by the University of Oxford. In 1797, the year he joined the Society of Dilettanti, the Cisalpine lawyer Charles Butler dedicated his *Horae biblicae* to Throckmorton; and in 1806 Throckmorton extended his Catholic liberal sympathies to Ireland by publishing his *Considerations Arising from the Debates in Parliament on the Petition of the Irish Catholics*, in which he encouraged Catholics to recognize the king as head of the church and subscribe to the oath of supremacy. He became a member of the Catholic Board, established 23 May 1808 to press for Catholic emancipation, and in 1811 made his peace with Bishop Douglass by chairing a meeting to establish a fund for relieving the bishop's financial embarrassment.

Earlier, at Weston, Throckmorton and his wife had become great friends of their neighbour, the poet William Cowper, who wrote affectionate verses for his wife. After he had begun to reside at Coughton, Throckmorton celebrated the 1791 Catholic Relief Act by building a capacious new chapel. At his third house, Buckland, he laid a bet in 1811 for 1000 guineas that a team of his workers could make a coat by sunset from the wool on two sheep at sunrise. The wager was won, and the coat, 'illustrative of manufacturing celerity', according to the contemporary poster, is displayed at Coughton. Throckmorton died at Coughton Court on 3 January 1819 and was, following his wishes, buried in the tomb of Robert the Pilgrim in the centre of Coughton parish church, his Latin epitaph being composed by Joseph Berington. He was succeeded in the

baronetcy by his brother, George Throckmorton-Courtenay. His widow died on 7 January 1821, 'in her 59th year' (GEC, *Baronetage*, 2.198), at Hengrave Hall, Suffolk.

GEOFFREY SCOTT

Sources B. Ward, *The dawn of the Catholic revival in England, 1781–1803*, 2 vols. (1909) · B. N. Ward, *The eve of Catholic emancipation*, 3 vols. (1911–12) · J. Ingamells, ed., *A dictionary of British and Irish travellers in Italy, 1701–1800* (1997) · C. Butler, *Historical memoirs of the English, Irish, and Scottish Catholics since the Reformation*, 3rd edn, 4 (1822) · Gillow, *Lit. biog. hist.* · J. Kirk, *Biographies of English Catholics in the eighteenth century*, ed. J. H. Pollen and E. Burton (1909) · M. Carmichael, 'Cowper and the Throckmortons', *Dublin Review*, 190 (1932), 195–210 · E. Duffy, 'Ecclesiastical democracy detected [pt 1]', *Recusant History*, 10 (1969–70), 193–209 · G. Scott, 'Dom Joseph Cuthbert Wilks (1748–1829) and English Benedictine involvement in the Cisalpine stirs', *Recusant History*, 23 (1996–7), 318–40 · J. P. Chinnici, *The English Catholic Enlightenment: John Lingard and the Cisalpine movement, 1780–1850* (1980) · Burke, *Peerage* (1967) · GEC, *Baronetage*

Archives Warks. CRO, corresp. and papers | Archives du Nord, Lille, France, Throckmorton to Walker, 18H · Berks. RO, Wellesley MSS, D-EWE · Warks. CRO, Coughton MSS, CR 1998

Likenesses C. Hewetson, bust, 1800, Coughton Hall, Warwickshire · T. Phillips, portrait, Coughton Hall, Warwickshire [see illus.] · oils, Coughton Hall, Warwickshire; repro. in Ward, *The dawn of the Catholic revival*, vol. 2

Throckmorton [Throgmorton], **Michael** (*d.* 1558), agent for Cardinal Reginald Pole, was a son (perhaps the youngest) of Sir Robert *Throgmorton or Throckmorton (*c.*1451–1518) of Coughton, Warwickshire, and Katherine, daughter of William Marrow or Marrowe of London. The family was well connected and Michael's elder brother Sir George *Throckmorton (*c.*1489–1552) often sat in parliament. Michael Throckmorton was a cousin of William Peto and of Queen Katherine Parr. Although he may have enjoyed Cardinal Wolsey's patronage along with John Helyar, nothing certain is known of him before he appears in Padua in 1533 as a student of law; he was in Venice two years later, perhaps already in Reginald Pole's service. He may have carried Pole's *Pro ecclesiasticae unitatis defensione* to Henry in 1536 and was certainly in service with Pole in 1537. Thomas Cromwell tried to capitalize on his position and use him as a spy on Pole. Throckmorton, however, either deliberately manipulated Cromwell, or came to believe that Pole was right in his controversy with Henry; and when Cromwell discovered this in mid-1537, the minister threatened Throckmorton's family with ruin. Meanwhile, Throckmorton had played a key role in Pole's legation of 1537 intended to aid the Pilgrimage of Grace; his special remit seems to have been Pole's personal safety.

At the reorganization of the English Hospice in Rome in 1538 Michael Throckmorton was among its members, the following year serving as auditor when he was identified as Pole's secretary. On 19 May 1539 he was attainted, second on a list beginning with Pole. He appears regularly in the hospice's records as auditor until 1551, but only once as *camerarius* ('chamberlain'). He accompanied Pole to Viterbo, and during at least some of the 1540s probably also served as his agent in Rome. At the end of the decade

Throckmorton along with Richard Hilliard acted as intermediaries between Protector Somerset and Pole, and they may actually have gone to England in 1549; at least a passport for them was issued on 15 February 1549. In 1551 Peter Vannes described Throckmorton as Pole's principal servant. To Throckmorton fell the honour of carrying to Queen Mary in 1553 Pole's bull of appointment as legate to England. He left Maguzzano on 28 August. There were difficulties over his admission to the country, but he seems finally to have secured entry and thereafter to have shuttled back and forth to Pole throughout the first nine months of 1554. In return for services rendered, Mary I granted him a pardon and restored the family manor of Coughton (which was then conveyed to a cousin). Throckmorton apparently did not accompany Pole to England, instead going to Mantua where he seems to have remained for the rest of his life. This move may have been planned by Pole, who relied heavily on Mantuan agents in his diplomatic manoeuvres and on the support of the regent Cardinal Gonzaga. The fact that Throckmorton continued to identify Pole as his master supports this supposition. Then again, Throckmorton had married Agnes Hyde in Mantua, probably in 1553 when the papal licence for the ceremony identified him as living in the Roman curia. After his death he was described as having lived in Mantua 'for many years' (Archivio di Stato, Mantua, 'Registrationi notarili anno 1558', fols. 94v–97v). Once Throckmorton reached Mantua (before June 1555), he assisted the voluntary exile to Italy Edward Courtenay, lending him money and inviting him to visit. They certainly met in Verona. In 1557 Luigi Schiffanoia forwarded an English report of the victory of St Quentin, suggesting that the duke's secretary have 'our' Throckmorton translate it (Archivio di stato, Mantua, Archivio Gonzaga, b. 578, Inviati Inghilterra/Scozia, fols. 169r–170v).

Throckmorton has been incorrectly identified as the author of or translator responsible for *A copye of a very fyne and wytty letter sent from the ryght reverende Lewes Lippomanus byshop of Verona in Italy*, apparently identical copies of which were published in Emden and London in 1556. The book is really a protestant satire as Throckmorton's identification on the title page as 'Curtigiane of Rome' indicates, together with the dedication to Pole accusing him of 'propping up prelacy' and trying to seduce the English nobility. Throckmorton is supposed to have died on 1 November 1558, leaving in Mantua a son, Francis, from a previous, undocumented, marriage. A herald's visitation of 1619 incorrectly recorded Michael Throckmorton and a brother killed at Pavia in 1525.   T. F. MAYER

Sources CSP Spain, 1553, 316, 323 • HoP, Commons, 1509–58, 3.450–55 • LP Henry VIII, 8, no. 536; 11, nos. 4, 1250, 1297,1363, 1379, 1387; 12, nos. 86, 552, 619, 635, 725, 795, 1293; 13/2, nos. 117, 507, 797, 804, 818 (p. 327), 960 • CSP Venice, 1534–54, nos. 766, 776 • CPR, 1548–9, 225; 1553–4, 401, 467; 1554–5, no. 209 • Cooper, Ath. Cantab., 1.182 • The Venerabile, 21 (May 1962), 186, 203, 269 [sexcentenary issue: The English hospice in Rome] • CSP dom., 1601–3; addenda, 1547–65, 11; 1547–80, 67, 75–6 • J. Woolfson, Padua and the Tudors: English students in Italy, 1485–1603 (1998) • W. Camden, The visitation of the county of Warwick in the year 1619, ed. J. Fetherston, Harleian Society, 12 (1877), 87 • Friedenslegation des Reginald Pole zu Kaiser Karl V. und König Heinrich II (1553–1556), ed. H. Lutz (Tübingen, 1981), no. 6 • M. Firpo and D. Marcatto, eds., I processi inquisitoriali Pietro Carnesecchi (1557–1567), 2: Il processo sotti Pio V (Vatican City, 2000), p. 407 • T. F. Mayer, 'A diet for Henry VIII: the failure of Reginald Pole's 1537 legation', Journal of British Studies, 26 (1987), 305–31 • T. F. Mayer, Reginald Pole: prince and prophet (2000) • CSP for., 1547–53, 110 • Archivio segreto vaticano, MS Bolognetti 94, fol. 46v; Bolognetti 95, fol. 201v; Segreteria di stato, Inghilterra, 3, fol. 141v–141r [sic] • Bodl. Oxf., MS Bodley Ital. C. 25, fols. 260r–261r • BL, Cotton MS Nero B.VII, fol. 112r–112v • PRO, SP 1/124 fols. 76r–79v, 144r; SP 1/125, fols. 87r–89v • DNB • original acts, HLRO, 31 Henry VIII c. 15 • Archivio segreto vaticano, Misc. arm 41:67, fol. 48R • J. Pits, Relationum historicarum de rebus Anglicis, ed. [W. Bishop] (Paris, 1619), 706

Throckmorton, Sir Nicholas (1515/16–1571), diplomat and member of parliament, was the fourth of the seven sons of Sir George *Throckmorton (c.1489–1552) of Coughton, Warwickshire, and his wife, Katherine, daughter of Nicholas, first Baron Vaux of Harrowden, and his wife, Elizabeth Parr. Nicholas always regarded Katherine Parr as his first cousin. His birth date is based on John Foxe's statement that Throckmorton was thirty-five at the time of the trial of Stephen Gardiner, bishop of Winchester, in January 1551.

Early career under Henry and Edward When Sir George Throckmorton died in 1552 Coughton passed to his eldest son Robert. As a younger son, Nicholas could expect little in the way of patrimony. A biographical poem, written some years later by his nephew Thomas, provides some details of his youth; the poem is demonstrably unreliable at some points, but is at least plausible here. It relates that as 'a brother fourth' he was 'far from hope of land', so 'by parents' hest [he] served as a page to Richmond's Duke' (Rowse, 9). This was Henry Fitzroy, duke of Richmond and illegitimate son of Henry VIII. Sir William Parr was Richmond's steward, and it is likely that Throckmorton's parents secured this post for him. In 1532 he accompanied the young duke to France, for Henry VIII's meeting with François I at Boulogne. He stayed abroad for nearly a year, 'and learned the tongue, though nothing readily' (ibid.). After Richmond's death in 1536 Throckmorton entered the service of the Parrs. He served on the Scottish borders in 1543. Then, when the king married Katherine Parr later that year, he joined her household at court, along with his brother Clement. He returned to France in 1544 as a captain in the army that captured Boulogne. He began to acquire lands in Hertfordshire, and was granted an annuity from revenues that had formerly belonged to Pipewell Abbey. Other members of his family remained staunch Catholics, but he and his brothers Clement, Kellam (or Kenelm), and George began to move in the evangelical circles favoured by Queen Katherine. He visited the protestant martyr Anne Askew in prison and was present at her execution on 16 July 1546.

The influence of Queen Katherine was probably also behind Throckmorton's entering parliament. With few intervals he was an MP during four reigns, being first returned in 1545 for the Essex borough of Maldon, where the queen was a major landowner. His connections and his religious stance helped him to continue to gain favour

Sir Nicholas Throckmorton (1515/16–1571), by unknown artist, *c.*1562

during Edward VI's reign. In 1547 he served under Protector Somerset in the Scottish campaign which culminated in the battle of Pinkie, and brought news of the English victory to the young king afterwards; for this he was granted an annuity of £100 and knighted in what the poem describes as an irregular ceremony performed by Edward in high spirits. No official record of this knighthood survives. The same source describes Throckmorton becoming a personal favourite of Edward's:

> The King fancied me more and more,
> For as his years so did my favour grow.
> (Rowse, 15)

About 1549 Throckmorton married Anne, daughter of Sir Nicholas Carew of Beddington. The Carews, like the Throckmortons, had long-standing court connections.

After the fall of the duke of Somerset in autumn 1549 Throckmorton was appointed a gentleman of Edward's privy chamber and given the lucrative office of treasurer of the mint. His promotion suggests that he was already *persona grata* with John Dudley, earl of Warwick. In April 1551 he was a member of the retinue which accompanied the marquess of Northampton on embassy to France, while after his return Throckmorton, according to Edward's *Chronicle*, was one of the gentlemen who escorted the dowager queen of Scots to Hampton Court in October, after a storm had forced her fleet to land at Portsmouth. He was involved in the king's progressive introduction to government business, and is said to have suggested that William Thomas, a humanist scholar who was also one of the clerks of the council, should prepare

papers discussing political issues for Edward's consideration. As part of the government's peace-keeping policy he was licensed in 1552 to retain a small force of twenty-five men. In the previous year he had exchanged his annuity for the Northamptonshire manor of Paulerspury and additional lands in several counties. He had remained an MP, representing Devizes in the parliament that sat from 1547 to 1552 and Northamptonshire in that of March 1553; it was a measure of his continuing favour with Dudley, now duke of Northumberland, that his return for the latter seat should have been supported by the council.

Queen Jane and Queen Mary Throckmorton apparently supported the attempt to crown Lady Jane Grey after Edward VI's death. He was one of the signatories of the letters patent of mid-June 1553 designating her the rightful successor, and his wife, Anne, deputized for Jane when the latter agreed to be godmother to Edward Underhill's son. According to contemporary reports Throckmorton tried to prevent Sir Thomas Tresham from proclaiming Mary Tudor as queen at Northampton, and barely escaped with his life. It is possible, however, that his objection was to Tresham's usurping his own role as sheriff, rather than to Mary's accession, for there are signs that he tried to hedge his bets; he is said to have been one of those who sent word to Mary of Edward's death, warning her not to fall into Northumberland's hands, and he was certainly among those appointed to escort her to London.

Throckmorton remained a member of the Commons, sitting in Mary's first parliament (October 1553) for the borough of Old Sarum rather than for Northamptonshire. His fellow burgess was his brother John, and it is likely that they secured their seats through the patronage of their kinsman William Herbert, earl of Pembroke. Nicholas Throckmorton appears to have opposed the queen's restoration of Catholicism—his name is on a list of those who 'stood for the true religion' during this session. But although he recalled hearing Sir Richard Southwell speak against Mary's Spanish marriage—'I did see the whole realm against it', he wrote (HoP, *Commons, 1509–58*, 3.460)—there is no record of his having spoken against it himself.

Whether or not it was because of his behaviour in parliament, Throckmorton soon came under suspicion, and on 1 January 1554 he was bound over in £2000 to be of good behaviour. Despite this, on 20 February, nearly three weeks after the surrender of Sir Thomas Wyatt, Throckmorton was committed to the Tower and charged with treason for supporting Wyatt's attempt to prevent the queen's marriage to Philip of Spain. The indictment at his trial, on 17 April 1554, went so far as to say that he was 'a principal, deviser, procurer and contriver of the late Rebellion; and that Wyatt was but his minister' (*State trials*, 892). The judges, as always, favoured the crown, but Throckmorton gave a bravura display of eloquence and learning to run rings round his accusers, quite possibly with the assistance, in spite of official prohibitions, of a sympathetic legal adviser. He poured ridicule on the prosecutors' attempts to find him guilty by association, and repeatedly caught them out on points of law, to the extent that Serjeant Stanford observed ruefully that 'If I had thought you had been so well furnished with Book Cases I would have been better provided for you' (ibid.). He was helped in this by the fact that the Henrician treason statutes had been repealed, and that his own alleged activities were arguably not treasonous under the statute of 26 Edward III. Addressing himself at least as often to the jury as to the judges, Throckmorton also played the patriotic card for all it was worth, making no effort to conceal his distaste for the queen's marriage, only denying that there was anything treasonable about this: 'It was no treason, nor no procurement of treason, to talk against the coming hither of the Spaniards' (ibid., 893). His strategy worked, and the jury acquitted him.

The London populace rejoiced, and Wyatt's head was stolen that night, but the jurors were taken into custody, most of them having to pay heavily to be released. Throckmorton himself was kept in gaol until January 1555, in the expectation that further charges would be brought against him. After his release on a bond of £2000 he retired to his home in Northamptonshire, but in June 1556 he fled to France, fearing that he would be suspected of complicity in Henry Dudley's conspiracy. He protested his innocence, however, and Mary came to believe him, allowing his wife to send him money and then pardoning him and allowing him to return to England in May 1557. She also restored property confiscated at the time of his flight. Shortly before Mary's death Throckmorton served in the army fighting in France under the earl of Pembroke, and he also began a correspondence with Princess Elizabeth.

Elizabeth's ambassador At the time of Elizabeth's accession Throckmorton sent her a list of suggested political appointments. Although his choice for secretary, Sir William Cecil, was indeed appointed, Throckmorton's advice was probably of little consequence; his other recommendations were ignored. He had suggested that Nicholas Heath, the Catholic archbishop of York, should remain lord chancellor and that some further members of Mary's council might also be retained. Sir Richard Morison had characterized Throckmorton as a 'Machiavellist', and some of his advice to the queen validated the description. 'It shall not be meet', he wrote, 'that either the old [councillors] or the new should wholly understand what you mean, but to use them as instruments to serve yourself with' (HoP, Commons, 1509–58, 3.497).

Throckmorton had not sat in Mary's latter parliaments, but he was returned for Lyme Regis in 1559 and for Tavistock in 1563. The journals do not record any speeches by him in the Commons, but in the 1566 session he was a member of committees dealing with law reform and the succession, and on 5 November he was one of thirty members summoned to court to hear the queen's message regarding the succession.

Throckmorton's chief employment under Elizabeth was as a diplomat. He was well served by his intimate knowledge of public affairs and his flair for gathering intelligence. Like many of Elizabeth's advisers, he was preoccupied by fear of a continental Catholic conspiracy to unseat the queen and restore the old faith. He was eager to support the Huguenots in France, a policy to which Elizabeth was not yet converted. In May 1559 he was sent to France on his first embassy. He was given a magnificent allowance of plate with which to impress the French but had to borrow £1000 to meet his living expenses. His goals were to terminate French influence in Scotland and to regain English control of Calais, which the French had seized just before Mary's death. His correspondence with Cecil reveals the religious difficulties he had to face: when he refused to kneel at the elevation of the host he was ordered either to conform or to absent himself from services. In 1560 the Guises accused him of being involved in the conspiracy of Amboise. He overestimated the strength of the Huguenots, urged the queen to accept their offer of Le Havre in exchange for military aid, and berated Cecil for indecision. When Cecil negotiated the treaty of Edinburgh guaranteeing that Scotland would ally with England, not France, Throckmorton was given the task of securing its ratification by Mary, queen of Scots, and her husband, the French king, François II. He also had to bear the scandalous reports of Elizabeth's romance with Sir Robert Dudley (later earl of Leicester); there were nasty speeches which, he said, 'my ears glow to hear' (CSP for., 1560–61, 348).

When Queen Mary decided to return to Scotland following her husband's death in 1561, she sought permission to travel through England. Throckmorton was not able to obtain it, so in the end she sailed directly from France to Scotland, not without some resentment at her treatment. In 1561 Throckmorton asked to be allowed to return to England himself, but the queen, troubled by a lack of competent diplomats, ignored his pleas. Lady Throckmorton did go home in 1562, and on her urging Elizabeth told Sir Thomas Smith to prepare to succeed Throckmorton as ambassador. But although Smith went to France, Catherine de' Medici, the French dowager queen, refused to grant Throckmorton permission to leave and, after the English accepted Le Havre from the Huguenots, imprisoned him. Moreover Smith and Throckmorton quarrelled, it having become clear that Smith was Cecil's man, whereas Dudley was Throckmorton's patron. In France Throckmorton came to be hated by both the Catholic Guises and the Huguenots. Finally in 1563 he succeeded in negotiating the treaty of Troyes, which settled little and spelt the end of English hopes of regaining Calais.

In 1564 Throckmorton was at last allowed to return to England. Compensation for some of the expenses of his embassy came in the form of appointment to two lucrative offices, those of chamberlain of the exchequer and chief butler of England. He was soon sent to Scotland, with instructions to prevent Mary Stuart's marriage to Lord Darnley and if possible encourage her to marry Dudley, who had been created earl of Leicester. Success was hardly to be hoped for, and Throckmorton came home empty-handed. In 1567, after Darnley's murder and Mary's abdication and imprisonment, he returned to Scotland seeking Mary's release from captivity and a concord between her and the rebel Scottish lords. This too was unachievable. On Elizabeth's orders he declined to attend the coronation of James VI; having once again alienated both sides, he was recalled in September 1567.

His unsuccessful diplomatic career now ended, Throckmorton attempted to avoid public life. But in 1569 he was charged with advocating the marriage of Queen Mary to the fourth duke of Norfolk. After a brief imprisonment at Windsor he remained under house arrest until the spring of 1570. He died in London of what was called 'a peripneumonia' on 12 February 1571. Leicester wrote to Walsingham:

> We have lost on Monday our good friend Sir Nicholas Throckmorton, who died in my house, being there taken suddenly in great extremity on Tuesday before; his lungs were perished, but a sudden cold he had taken was the cause of his sudden death. God hath his soul, and we his friends great loss of his body. (HoP, *Commons, 1558–1603*, 3.499)

The rumour that he had eaten a poisoned salad is unlikely to be true.

Burial, family, and achievements Sir Nicholas Throckmorton was buried in the chancel of the parish church of St Katharine Cree in Aldgate, near his London residence, a mansion that had belonged to the abbey of Evesham. He had never been able to build a country house on his land at Paulerspury; instead he and his wife, who survived him, used her family home at Beddington, Surrey, when they found it possible to enjoy country life. In his will, dated 8 February 1571, Throckmorton confirmed an earlier deed in which he left a life interest in his properties in Northamptonshire, Buckinghamshire, and Oxfordshire to his wife, who was named his executor, with reversion to their eldest son William, then aged about eighteen. Lands in Worcestershire were to go to their second son Arthur, with reversions to his younger brothers Robert, Thomas, Nicholas, and Henry. (In the event William, who was a lunatic, did not inherit the eldest son's share, which went to Arthur.) Thomas was to have the London house, and Throckmorton's daughter Elizabeth, together with her brothers Nicholas and Henry, were to receive £500 each. Further bequests were made to Throckmorton's brothers Kellam and Clement, his cousin Margaret Butler, his niece Katherine Throckmorton, and several of his servants. The earl of Leicester, Sir Walter Mildmay (chancellor of the exchequer), Sir John Throckmorton, and Francis Carew were among those named to supervise the execution of the will and were left such mementoes as standing gilt cups and bowls adorned with rosemary branches. Throckmorton showed his protestant convictions in his stated desire that his funeral sermon should be preached by either Thomas Sampson or Thomas Lever, both leading puritan divines, as well as in his gift of 40s. to the Dutch church in London. His relative Job Throckmorton, the likeliest author of the Martin Marprelate tracts, was left a coat, a cloak, and a sword. Throckmorton's daughter Elizabeth, who was only eight when he died, later married Sir Walter Ralegh.

Throckmorton's large Renaissance tomb may still be seen at St Katharine Cree, where his head lies on his helmet, tilted towards the viewer. A fine anonymous portrait of him is preserved in the National Portrait Gallery, London. Most of his personal papers came into the possession of Sir Henry Wotton, who gave them to Charles I; they are now in the Public Record Office, London. Despite his involvement in many of the crucial episodes of the mid-Tudor period, Throckmorton never established himself as a diplomat or politician of the first rank. In intellect he was no match for Cecil, Walsingham, or Mildmay, and he lacked Leicester's charisma and connections. His Machiavellian qualities enabled him to ingratiate himself, if only temporarily, with both Mary and Elizabeth, but all too often served only to complicate his conduct of business. He seems, indeed, to have been an obsessive conspirator, who always did things in a roundabout way, when a straightforward approach might in fact have served him better. Consequently his greatest interest for posterity is arguably as a representative of the protestant side of the prolific Throckmorton family, perhaps less well known than their Catholic kinsmen but abler and more interesting.   STANFORD LEHMBERG

Sources A. L. Rowse, *Ralegh and the Throckmortons* (1962) · HoP, *Commons, 1558–1603*, 3.497–9 · HoP, *Commons, 1509–58*, 3.458–60 · W. T. MacCaffrey, *The shaping of the Elizabethan regime: Elizabethan politics, 1558–1572* (1968) · D. Loades, *The reign of Mary Tudor: politics, government and religion in England, 1553–58*, 2nd edn (1991) · D. M. Loades, *Two Tudor conspiracies* (1965) · *The chronicle and political papers of King Edward VI*, ed. W. K. Jordan (1966) · will, PRO, PROB 11/54/8, fols. 64r–65r · *CSP for.*, 1560–61 · D. M. Loades, *John Dudley, duke of Northumberland, 1504–1553* (1996) · *State trials*, vol. 1

Archives BL, corresp., Add. MSS 35830–35831 · Warks. CRO, papers | BL, biographical poem, 'Legend of Sir Nicholas Throckmorton', Add. MS 5841 and Harley MS 6353

Likenesses oils, c.1562, NPG [*see illus.*] · Vertue, engraving, 1747; portrait; formerly at *Coughton Court, Warwickshire*, in 1898 · tomb effigy, St Katharine Cree, Aldgate, London

Wealth at death not very rich: will, PRO, PROB 11/54, sig.8

Throckmorton [*née* Lok; *other married name* Hickman], **Rose** (1526–1613), businesswoman and protestant exile, was born on 26 December 1526 in London, the third of eleven children of Sir William *Lok (1480–1550), great-great-great-grandfather of the philosopher John Locke (1632–1704), London mercer, sheriff, and alderman, and gentleman usher of the chamber to Henry VIII, and his second wife, Katherine (d. 1537), daughter of Sir Thomas Cook of Wiltshire. Her parents were early English protestants and supporters of the royal divorce between Henry VIII and Katherine of Aragon, and her father and several brothers sometimes served as agents of the king in Flanders and France in the 1540s. In 1536 the Lok family lived in Cheapside 'at the sign of the Padlock'. Rose's father served as sheriff of London in 1548 and was knighted by Edward VI the following year.

Rose's first husband, Anthony Hickman (d. 1573), whom she married on 28 November 1543, was the son of Walter Hickman of Woodford, and was also a London merchant. They had at least two children. Her second husband, Simon Throckmorton (1526?–1585), of Brampton, was the third son of Richard Throckmorton of Higham Ferrers, and Joan Beaufort of Whilton, the nephew of Sir George

Throckmorton of Coughton Court, and MP for Huntingdon in 1554 and 1559.

In 1610, aged eighty-four, Rose wrote an account of her life that began with her father's removal of the pope's bull against the king posted in Dunkirk in 1534. Rose claimed her father brought back religious books from overseas for the new queen, Anne Boleyn. Rose became a strong protestant through her mother's reading evangelical books to her and her sisters in secret at about this time. Her mother died after giving birth while in the country during a bout of the plague. Rose's husband, Anthony, was a merchant adventurer in partnership with her brother, Thomas Locke. They owned a number of ships and Richard Hakluyt wrote about several of their voyages 'to the south and southern parts of the world'. One of these ships, the *Mary Rose*, was named after their wives. The Hickmans entertained eminent clergymen such as John Hooper, John Foxe, and John Knox, the last of whom made mention of them several times in his letters to his friend and Rose's sister-in-law, Anne Locke, between 1556 and 1561.

During the reign of Mary I Anthony and Thomas were charged with giving assistance to imprisoned protestants and for maintaining their heresy. They were committed to the Fleet prison and continued to be examined. After being remitted to confinement at the home of the lord treasurer, the marquess of Winchester, the two men were set free. Anthony thereafter travelled to Antwerp while Rose went to a remote area of Oxfordshire to give birth. In her account Rose talked to the bishops in prison in Oxford (Cranmer, Latimer, and Ridley), who agreed that she might have her child baptized according to the Catholic rite.

Out of conscience, Rose then left her homes in London and Rumford to join her husband in Antwerp. Rose chastised her sister-in-law Mary for her love of luxury and for not letting her husband, Thomas Locke, leave England. Rose preferred Antwerp because few attempts were made there to monitor attendance at Catholic services. While there she gave birth again and, this time, being part of a secret protestant congregation, had her child baptized by a protestant minister. She left Antwerp to return to England after Queen Mary's death (1558). Her account ends at this point so little is known about the later years of her life. She died on 21 November 1613 at the age of eighty-six, and an epitaph was written for her in 1637. While her recollections reflect a devoted protestant of evangelical theology and piety, she was also very caught up with business and material concerns, and with the impact of religious changes on her standard of living. Her interactions with many people of known repute testify to the high profile her family enjoyed in mid-Tudor politics and society.

BEN LOWE

Sources R. Throckmorton, 'Certaine old stories recorded by an aged gentlewoman … about the yeer our lord 1610', BL, Add. MS 43827, fols. 1–18v · J. Shakespeare and M. Dowling, 'Religion and politics in mid-Tudor England through the eyes of an English protestant woman: the recollections of Rose Hickman', *BIHR*, 55 (1982), 94–102 · J. L. Chester, 'The descent of Margaret Locke, third wife of deputy governor Francis Willoughby', *New England Historical and Genealogical Register*, 35 (1881), 59–65 · J. G. Locke, *Book of the Lockes: a genealogical and historical record of the descendants of William Locke, of Woburn, with an appendix, containing a history of the Lockes in England, also of the family of John Locke, of Hampton, N.H., and kindred families and individuals* (1853) · HoP, *Commons, 1509–58*
Archives BL, Add. MS 43827, fols. 1–18v

Throckmorton, Sir Thomas (*d.* 1568). See under Throckmorton family (*per. c.*1500–1682).

Throckmorton, Sir Thomas (1539–1607). See under Throckmorton family (*per. c.*1500–1682).

Throckmorton, William (*d.* 1537). See under Throckmorton family (*per. c.*1500–1682).

Throckmorton, Sir William, first baronet (1579–1628). See under Throckmorton family (*per. c.*1500–1682).

Throckmorton, Sir William, fourth baronet (1658–1682). See under Throckmorton family (*per. c.*1500–1682).

Throgmorton family (*per.* 1409–1518), gentry, held land at Fladbury in Throckmorton, Worcestershire, from the late twelfth century. They remained, however, no more than farmers from the bishopric of Worcester until the marriage in 1409 of John *Throgmorton (*d.* 1445) to the coheir of Guy Spine of Coughton, west Warwickshire, greatly enhanced the family's standing. By this match the Throgmortons acquired the manor of Coughton, their first fee simple estate and their first Warwickshire property, and further land in Worcestershire. For much of the fifteenth century the family's history was bound up with that of the earls of Warwick, whose estate, like the Throgmortons', was centred on Warwickshire and Worcestershire. John's father, **Thomas (I) Throgmorton** (*d.* 1411), and Thomas's father-in-law, Alexander Besford of Besford, Worcestershire, had both served Thomas Beauchamp, the appellant earl of Warwick, as had John's father-in-law, Guy Spine, and it may well have been the Warwick connection that secured the Spine match for John. But none of the family was ever to be as close or important to the earls as John was to Richard Beauchamp from 1416 to the earl's death in 1439. John's son and heir, **Thomas (II) Throgmorton** (*d.* 1472), was a life annuitant and officer of Richard Neville, the eventual heir to the Warwick earldom, but he retained the connections with lords Sudeley and Beauchamp of Powick that his father had forged during the period of Beauchamp minorities from 1439 to 1449, while Thomas (II)'s son and heir, **Sir Robert Throgmorton** (*c.*1451–1518), never formalized ties with George, duke of Clarence, the last effective earl of Warwick. While none of John's successors seems to have had the professional legal training that enabled John to found the family's fortunes, both Thomas (II) and Robert apparently knew enough law to be valued as agents by their noble, clerical, and gentry neighbours. In particular, like other associates of the earls of Warwick from the west midlands, members of the family acted as officials to the bishops of Worcester for much of the century.

Whether close or not to the earls of Warwick, the Throgmortons played a central role in the networks of west-midland gentry which, although they had their own internal dynamics, tended to look to the earls for leadership and then to the earls' successors, the crown. Throgmortons often intermarried with other midland families, like Russell, Gifford, Knightley, and Peyto. Thomas (II) married Margaret, daughter and heir of Robert Onley of Birdingbury, Warwickshire, and Weston Underwood, Buckinghamshire, and, although Robert married Katherine, daughter of William Marrowe, alderman of London, it is significant that Katherine's brother had already married the heiress of another Warwickshire family.

The family was buying land all through the fifteenth century. John's several purchases included the Warwickshire manor of Spernall in 1441–3, and he was able to secure recognition of the title to Throckmorton as a hereditary fee-farm by the bishop in 1418. Thomas (II)'s most notable purchase was the other half of Coughton from the coheirs, the Tracys, in 1449. By Thomas's death the family owned property in a large number of places in Warwickshire, Worcestershire, Gloucestershire, and Buckinghamshire. Although Robert Onley outlived Thomas (II), Robert Throgmorton was eventually to inherit the Onley estates. Despite the importance of Coughton in the family's rise, the greater part of the estate lay in Worcestershire and so, although Throgmortons held all the significant local offices, they tended to serve more often in Worcestershire than Warwickshire until the time of Robert. In 1474 Robert effected a rearrangement with his widowed mother of the lands willed to her for life by his father. By this, he transferred the weight of his interests to Warwickshire and it is no accident that he was the first of the family to serve the king predominantly in Warwickshire nor that he reputedly undertook the substantial rebuilding of Coughton which occurred in the late fifteenth and early sixteenth centuries.

Despite the Throgmortons' high profile in local office and local politics, they contrived to remain largely unscathed by the traumas of fifteenth-century local and national politics. Chiefly this was because they were adept at keeping sufficiently broad connections with the local nobility to be able to find a bolt-hole in times of national trouble and because they were usually remarkably good at keeping out of local disputes in the periods of local disorder caused by weak kingship, ineffective noble leadership, or both. In the late 1450s, when the connection with the earl of Warwick was becoming dangerous, Thomas (II) managed to exploit his link to Sudeley and Beauchamp of Powick to keep in with those around Henry VI and was even made attorney to the prince of Wales in 1457. He was then able to use the Warwick connection to escape any vengeance from the triumphant Yorkists; by 1464 he had been restored to the Worcestershire commission of the peace and in 1465 became a JP in Warwickshire. He evaded official duty during the readeption, while his son managed to serve Edward IV, Richard III, and Henry VII as local officer in quick succession—and was indeed Henry's first sheriff in Warwickshire. Characteristically avoiding more than a passing implication in the disputes which increasingly convulsed Warwickshire in the first ten years of Henry VII [see Mountford family], Robert eventually became closer to the inner circles of Henry's court than almost any of his west midland neighbours. He was made KB at the creation of the duke of York in 1494 (the first of the family to be knighted), turned out for the king to resist Perkin Warbeck at Blackheath in 1497, and was the recipient of a certain amount of royal favour in the last decade of the reign. The obverse was that, from 1502, he was also caught up in Henry's notorious system of bonds and recognizances. Both the greater proximity to the king and the recognizances are partly attributable to the match made in 1501 for Robert's son and heir, George *Throckmorton or Throgmorton, with Katherine, the heir apparent of Sir Nicholas Vaux, one of Henry's closer associates. It was a cadet branch, the Throgmortons of Haresfield, Gloucestershire, that lacked the political acumen of the main line: John (i), Thomas (II)'s younger brother, was executed after fighting for the Lancastrians at Mortimer's Cross in 1461, while John (i)'s son and heir, John (ii), fought for the Lancastrians at Tewkesbury but was later pardoned.

The Throgmortons' religious dispositions followed the pattern of their political and official activities: concentration on Worcestershire until Robert and thereafter on Coughton. The family burials and chantry at Fladbury [see Throgmorton, John] were complemented by the annuities for chantry priests that Thomas (II) and his widowed mother gave to Evesham and Pershore abbeys in 1448. Robert was probably the first of the family to wish to be buried at Coughton. The chancel of Coughton parish church was under reconstruction when he died and in his will he left precise instructions for the glazing of the east windows. The centrepiece of this detailed and fairly lavish will was a chantry in the church, which was to double as a school to teach the children of Robert's tenants. An elaborate tomb had been prepared for him in Coughton but he died in Rome on his way to the Holy Land.

The Throgmortons have left little evidence of their estate management but enough to see that they were probably as careful in this as in their other enterprises. Although Thomas (I) bought a salt pit in Worcestershire in 1402 and Thomas (II) enclosed some pasture, the family seems to have operated a mainly rentier economy for most of the century. It helped that, as valued officials of the bishops of Worcester, they were able to build up £240 of rent arrears to the bishopric between 1440 and 1470, nearly all of which was eventually cancelled. It was Robert who was apparently the first to exploit the growing market for wool in the later fifteenth and early sixteenth centuries. The exchange with his mother gave him a compact estate, suitable for sheep farming; he added to it by further purchases and exchanges and enclosed pastures as well as woods and parkland.

Throughout the century the Throgmortons evinced a combination of enterprise and circumspection more readily associated at this time with gentry families in the process of establishing themselves than with those that were already among the leaders of local society, as the family certainly was by the time of John's death. This explains why, unusually, they were able to continue their rise without set-back through three generations in a period that was politically dangerous and, until the late fifteenth century, economically unpromising. It was in the sixteenth century that they lost their ability to keep on the winning side: two sons of Robert, who had been with him in Rome at his death, died at the battle of Pavia in 1525; the family remained steadfastly Catholic after the Reformation and their seat of Coughton was sacked twice during the upheavals of the seventeenth century. Nevertheless, they continued owners of Coughton until the National Trust acquired the house in 1948. The Throgmorton arms were gules, a chevron argent, with three gimel bars sable thereon.   CHRISTINE CARPENTER

Sources C. Carpenter, *Locality and polity* (1992) · *CClR* · *CPR, 1399–1509* · *Calendar of the fine rolls*, PRO, 12–22 (1931–62) · Throckmorton papers, Shakespeare Birthplace Trust RO, Stratford upon Avon · W. Dugdale, *The antiquities of Warwickshire illustrated*, rev. W. Thomas, 2nd edn, 2 vols. (1730) · PRO, PROB 11 · *VCH Warwickshire*, vol. 3 · *CIPM, Henry VII* · king's bench records, PRO, KB 9, KB 27 · HoP, *Commons, 1386–1421* · C. Dyer, *Lords and peasants in a changing society: the estates of the bishopric of Worcester, 680–1540* (1980)
Archives Shakespeare Birthplace Trust RO, Stratford upon Avon, Throckmorton papers
Wealth at death impossible to say but, by Robert's death, likely to be in £250 p.a. plus range

Throgmorton, John (*d.* 1445), landowner and administrator, was the eldest son of Thomas *Throgmorton (*d.* 1411) [*see under* Throgmorton family] of Fladbury, Worcestershire, and Agnes (*d.* after 1428), daughter and coheir of Alexander Besford of Besford, Worcestershire. His father had served Thomas Beauchamp, earl of Warwick (*d.* 1401), as had his Besford grandfather, and it is probable that it was through this connection that in 1409 John was married to Eleanor, daughter and coheir of Guy Spine of Coughton, west Warwickshire, a marriage that considerably enhanced his landed position and brought him lands in Warwickshire. However, after a training in the law, Throgmorton's first employer was Sir John Phelip of Kidderminster. Phelip having died at Harfleur in 1415, Throgmorton was serving Richard Beauchamp, earl of Warwick (*d.* 1439), by late 1416. The tie with Warwick was close: Throgmorton was a life retainer and councillor, especially important to Warwick when the earl was overseas, was often in his household, and travelled extensively on his behalf, at least twice to France. He was a key member of the Warwick-dominated gentry network in west Warwickshire and Worcestershire, acting on numerous occasions as feoffee and witness, often with other followers of the earl. As a lawyer connected to the most powerful local nobleman he was a frequent local officer, notably in Worcestershire. His offices there included JP from 1414 until his death, MP in 1414, 1420, 1422, 1432, 1433, and 1439, escheator in 1418–19, and under-sheriff—an office held under the Beauchamps, hereditary sheriffs—in 1416–18,

1419–20, and 1430–31. He played little role in Warwickshire local government until the 1430s, when he was JP from 1433 until 1439, and Worcestershire remained the family's principal sphere of interest until the 1470s.

It was through the earl of Warwick that Throgmorton entered the king's service; he held the Beauchamp chamberlainship of the exchequer from 1418 to his death, and was under-treasurer from 1433 to 1443. Various royal grants followed, including custody of the temporalities of the see of Worcester in 1433, which he shared with some of his Worcestershire friends. The office of under-treasurer brought him into close association with Ralph, Lord Cromwell (*d.* 1456), the treasurer, and, from at least the early 1420s, he was associated with the lords Ferrers of Chartley, a family of growing importance to Warwick in midlands politics at that time. His various employments brought him the wealth and connections to acquire extensive further property in Warwickshire and Worcestershire, as well as a better title from the bishops of Worcester to the family estate in Fladbury.

Throgmorton was named as an executor of Warwick's will and, after Warwick's death in 1439, was made keeper of the lands of Henry Beauchamp (*d.* 1446), the earl's under-age heir, and feoffee to Isabel, Warwick's widow. Among his fellow feoffees was Ralph Boteler, Lord Sudeley (*d.* 1473), a rising power at court, who became Throgmorton's last patron and, with his close associate, John, Lord Beauchamp of Powick, the patron of several other men formerly associated with the earls of Warwick. In Throgmorton's will Sudeley was named as overseer, 'for grete affians and trust þt I haue hadde in his Lordeship' (PRO, PROB 11/3, fol. 248v).

Throgmorton died on 12 April 1445, asking that restitution be made to all those he had harmed in his career. At his death he had two sons and six married daughters, his sons-in-law nearly all from prominent midland gentry families, some from within the Warwick connection. He was buried at Fladbury, where he requested a marble stone to dignify the graves of his parents, as well as those of himself and his wife. In 1448 his widow was licensed to found a chantry there, which was eventually established in 1460. In reflection of the family's connection with the crown at both dates, it commemorates Throgmorton's service to Lancaster rather than to Warwick. Throgmorton's widow died some time after May 1449.

CHRISTINE CARPENTER

Sources Chancery records · Shakespeare Birthplace Trust RO, Stratford upon Avon, Throckmorton MS · PRO · HoP, *Commons* · C. Carpenter, *Locality and polity: a study of Warwickshire landed society, 1401–1499* (1992) · W. Dugdale, *The antiquities of Warwickshire illustrated*, rev. W. Thomas, 2nd edn, 2 vols. (1730) · *VCH Warwickshire* · *VCH Worcestershire* · *Members of parliament: return to two orders of the honorable the House of Commons*, House of Commons, 2 vols. (1878) · F. J. Thacker, 'The monumental brasses of Worcestershire, part 2', *Transactions of the Worcs. Archaeological Soc.*, new ser., 4 (1926–7), 129–56 · prerogative court of Canterbury wills, PRO, PROB 11/3, fol. 248v
Archives Shakespeare Birthplace Trust RO, Stratford upon Avon, Throckmorton MS

Likenesses double portrait, brass (with his wife), Fladbury church, Worcestershire

Throgmorton, Sir Robert (c.1451–1518). *See under* Throgmorton family (*per.* 1409–1518).

Throgmorton, Thomas (I) (d. 1411). *See under* Throgmorton family (*per.* 1409–1518).

Throgmorton, Thomas (II) (d. 1472). *See under* Throgmorton family (*per.* 1409–1518).

Throsby, John (1740–1803), antiquary and artist, was born in the parish of St Martin's, Leicester, on 21 December 1740, the eldest son of Nicholas Throsby (*bap.* 1700, *d.* 1782), a tailor and alderman of Leicester who was the younger son of Robert and Ann Throsby of Anstey, Leicestershire. His mother was his father's second wife, Martha Mason (*bap.* 1701, *d.* 1797), daughter of Anthony Mason of St Nicholas's, Leicester. He was baptized at St Martin's, Leicester, on 13 January 1741 and remained in Leicester all his life, for a large part resident in the High Street.

Educated at the free grammar school, Throsby was apprenticed as a woolcomber on 29 September 1754 and admitted as a freeman of Leicester on 29 September 1760, during his father's mayoralty. He was married by licence at St Martin's, Leicester, on 29 October 1761 to Ann Godfrey (*bap.* 1743, *d.* 1813), daughter of Richard and Ann Godfrey of that parish. They had seventeen children, although at least six of these died in infancy. The struggle to maintain such a large family was to be a constant preoccupation. When on 24 September 1770 he was appointed parish clerk of St Martin's, a post he was to hold until his death, Throsby was first able to indulge his taste for writing.

Throsby's first work, *The Memoirs of the Town and County of Leicester*, appeared in six volumes between 1777 and 1778, and contained a historical account from pre-Roman times onwards, drawn from previous antiquarian writings and his own research. In 1789 he raised sufficient subscriptions to commence issuing in twelve parts *Select views in Leicestershire from original drawings containing the seats of the nobility and gentry, town views and ruins*, in which he published his own drawings with an accompanying historical account and description. One part of the series appeared every two months but delays in printing the plates meant that the last part was not issued until 1792. His supplementary volume, entitled *A Series of Excursions in the Year 1790 to the Villages and Places of Note in the County*, also appeared in 1792.

There followed, again in parts, Throsby's *The History and Antiquities of the Ancient Town of Leicester*, which he intended to be completed in 1791, as the title-page suggests, but which was actually finished in 1793. A portrait of the author aged fifty appeared as a frontispiece. Also between 1790 and 1797 he worked upon a new edition of Robert Thoroton's *Antiquities of Nottinghamshire* (1677). The portion dealing with Nottingham, containing also 'all that is valuable in Deering', appeared first in 1795. In 1797 this volume was reprinted as part of a three-volume series entitled *Thoroton's History of Nottinghamshire Republished with Large Additions*, illustrated again with Throsby's drawings.

As a collector and antiquarian, Throsby followed with interest the unearthing of archaeological remains. In 1793 he published an open letter to the president of the Society of Antiquaries entitled *Letter to the earl of Leicester on the recent discovery of the Roman cloaca or sewer at Leicester with some thoughts on the jewry wall*. Reporting in detail on the discovery of Roman remains, he urged a closer investigation. Among other pamphlets, in 1795 he published *Thoughts on the provincial corps raised and now raising in support of the British constitution at this awful period, by a private in the Leicestershire regiment*, drawing on his own experience of service with the Loyal Leicestershire volunteer cavalry.

In later life Throsby suffered a lingering illness and impoverished circumstances, and was supported by the efforts of friends who raised money by subscription. He died on 5 February 1803 and was buried on 8 February at St Martin's, where a tablet in his memory was erected over the old vestry door.

A man of humility and integrity, Throsby enjoyed great respect locally, although he suffered from the prejudice of other scholars owing to his relative poverty and lack of education. John Nichols incorporated much of his work in his own history of the county, particularly relating to Leicester, and purchased the copperplates for Throsby's Leicester volume after his death. Although he recalled Throsby as 'a man of natural genius' (Nichols, *History and Antiquities*, 1.602), Nichols, in emphasizing the difficulties suffered by Throsby in later life, effectively belittled his achievements. Throsby deserves fuller credit both for his own research and for his drawings. JESS JENKINS

Sources J. Throsby, *The history and antiquities of the ancient town of Leicester* (1791) [annotated copy with insertions incl. biographical details, Leics. RO, DE5344, 268] · H. Hartopp, ed., *Register of the freemen of Leicester*, 1 (1927) · parish register, Leicester, St Martin, 1740–1813, Leics. RO, DE1564/1, 5, 14–16 · H. Hartopp, ed., *Roll of the mayors of the borough of Leicester, 1209–1935* (1935) · J. Nichols, *The history and antiquities of the county of Leicester*, 1 (1795–1815), 602; facs. edn (1971) · marriage bond and licence, 28 Oct 1761, Leics. RO, ID41/38 · A. Broadfield, 'John Nichols: historian and friend', unpublished MS, 295–315 · J. Nichols, *The history and antiquities of the county of Leicester*, 4 vols. in 8 (1795–1815) [Nichols' annotated copy, Leics. RO, 7D62] · F. S. Throsby, 'File of notes on J. Throsby', c.1978, Leics. RO, DE3497/21 · subscription book, archdeaconry of Leicester, 1770, Leics. RO, ID41/34/4, fol. 81 · *Records of the borough of Leicester*, 6: *The chamberlain's accounts, 1688–1835*, ed. G. A. Chinnery (1967), 264 [esp. 1792 accounts] · C. J. Billson, *Leicester memoirs* (1924)

Archives Bodl. Oxf., corresp. · Leics. RO, authorial copy of *The history … of Leicester* with annotations and insertions, incl. biographical detail · Leics. RO, parish book compiled by him listing christening and burial fees | S. Antiquaries, Lond., letters to Hayman Rooke

Likenesses W. & J. Walker, line engraving (aged fifty; after J. Walker), BM, NPG; repro. in Throsby, *The history and antiquities of Leicester* (1791)

Wealth at death impoverished: Nichols, *The history and antiquities*, 1.602

Thrower, Percy John (1913–1988), broadcaster and writer on gardening, was born on 30 January 1913 in Little Horwood, Buckinghamshire, the second child and second son

Percy John
Thrower (1913–
1988), by Jon Blau,
1979

in the family of three sons and two daughters of Harry
Thrower and his wife, Beatrice Dunnett. Just before Percy's birth his father had been appointed head gardener at
Horwood House, near Winslow, where a new garden was
to be made on an old site. An intelligent child but not a
bookish one, Percy grew up with the new garden, becoming attuned to the daily rituals of garden nurture. With his
ambition—'to be a head gardener, like my father'—
already named, he was withdrawn from Little Horwood
Church of England school shortly after his fourteenth
birthday, in order to join his father's staff as pot-and-crock
boy.

In 1931 Thrower was offered a job as an improver in the
royal gardens at Windsor. There he met and courted his
future wife, Constance, daughter of Charles Cook, the
head gardener of Windsor. In 1935 he moved to Leeds to
sample municipal gardening as a journeyman, taking
with him a sense of hierarchy and an adherence to the frugal and disciplined methods of Windsor. From 1937 he
was able to put some of these into practice at Derby, as
deputy parks superintendent; the job included maintaining the country's first public arboretum. Opened in 1840
that now mature amenity was, a century on, unregarded
by the citizens, whose preferences, if any, inclined
towards the formal bedding schemes that were the staple
of municipal gardening. Thrower found a role in that style
for fuchsias, whose seemingly exotic but generally very
tolerant qualities he was to help popularize. In the summer of 1939 the focus of his work shifted to organizing the
local 'dig for victory' effort, and he spent the next five
years instructing often motley groups of non-gardeners in
the cultivation of roots and basic brassicas, supporting
the wartime aim of self-sufficiency in food. Thus he discovered his distinguishing gift—as a natural teacher. On 9
September 1939, he married Constance Cook. They subsequently had three daughters.

From 1946 until his retirement in 1974 Thrower was
parks superintendent at Shrewsbury. His responsibilities
included helping to revive the annual flower show after
the war and maintaining its place near the top of the gardener's calendar. From its resumption in 1947 the show
was covered by the BBC, which was keen to develop its
treatment of all leisure interests. In the course of
co-operating with BBC producers it became apparent that
Thrower had the qualities of a natural broadcaster. The
corporation's principal gardening voice—C. H. Middleton, 'the best-known gardener since Adam'—had died
prematurely in 1945 and an unofficial vacancy existed.
Thrower's services were soon much in demand.

Most remarkably on the radio, and later on television,
Thrower believed in letting his material speak for itself.
Without a script, and with scarcely any comment or elab-
oration, he would describe a plant and its capabilities, its
strengths and foibles, likes and dislikes, and how to draw
out its best. The same technique was later brought to
larger themes: how to discover the genius of a site, however small, by observation and experiment; how to create
a microclimate by the judicious planting of trees and
shrubs; how to reconcile the desire for immediate effect
with long-term aims.

No attempt was made to change Thrower's not particularly appealing south-midland accent, nor to soften a
mode of utterance reminiscent of a mild-mannered
sergeant-major. The tone of voice could be heard too in his
journalism, principally for the *Daily Mail* and *Amateur Gardening*, and in the sixteen books, among them the often
reprinted *In your Garden Week by Week* (1959), commissioned as his reputation grew. When he proceeded from
wireless to television it was not a surprise to behold a
rather formal, somewhat top-heavy figure, who might put
aside his pipe and often his jacket to demonstrate some
arduous task, but seldom his tie. The image thus inno-
cently created was that of the nation's head gardener.

Through simple education and encouragement Thrower helped to restore gardening as Britain's favourite leisure activity, bringing it back as a source of often productive pleasure after the unduly protracted season of the war
and the allotment. As one who had known a little too
much hands-and-knees drudgery during his early years in
the garden, Thrower became a fervent advocate of all
labour-saving machines and gadgets. His unrestrained use
of chemicals and fungicides tended to isolate him from
the new generation of gardeners who rose to prominence
as his own career drew to a close. This was the indirect
cause of the BBC's decision in 1976 to end his thirteen
years as principal presenter of their leading garden programme, *Gardeners' World*. But Thrower had already
started a new television career describing gardening on
children's programmes, particularly *Blue Peter*, and with
that audience he was soon an even bigger cult figure than
he had been with adults. His last broadcast was made a
week before his death from his hospital bed in Wolverhampton, where he was being treated for Hodgkin's disease and where he died on 18 March 1988. His home latterly was The Magnolias, Merrington, Bomere Heath,
Shropshire.

Recognition from his peers had come for Thrower when
the Royal Horticultural Society made him an associate of

honour in 1963. He took particular pleasure from the society's Victoria medal of honour, awarded in 1974. He was appointed MBE in 1984.   TIMOTHY O'SULLIVAN, *rev.*

Sources *The Times* (19 March 1988) · P. Thrower, *My lifetime of gardening* (1977) · T. O'Sullivan, *Percy Thrower* (1989) · *The Independent* (19 March 1988)
Archives FILM *This is your life* (March 1976)
Likenesses two photographs, 1973–5, Hult. Arch. · J. Blau, photograph, 1979, Camera Press, London [*see illus.*] · photograph, repro. in *The Independent* · photograph, repro. in *The Times*
Wealth at death £807,358: probate, 19 Oct 1988, *CGPLA Eng. & Wales*

Thrupp, Dorothea Ann (1779–1847). *See under* Thrupp, Frederick (1812–1895).

Thrupp, Frederick (1812–1895), sculptor, was born on 20 June 1812 at Paddington Green, Middlesex, the youngest son of Joseph Thrupp (*d.* 1821), a coachmaker, and his second wife, Mary Pillow (*d.* 1845). The family had been settled for many years near Worcester, but Joseph Thrupp moved to London about 1765, and from 1774 managed a coach factory in George Street, near Grosvenor Square. Frederick went to the Revd W. Greenlaw's school at Blackheath, Kent, and then attended Henry Sass's academy in Bloomsbury. In 1829 he won a silver medal from the Society of Arts for a chalk drawing from a bust, and on 14 June 1830 he was admitted to the Royal Academy Schools. Thrupp first exhibited at the Royal Academy in 1832, when he showed *The Prodigal Returned*, and thereafter he exhibited there regularly until 1880. He also showed at the British Institution between 1837 and 1862.

On 15 February 1837 Thrupp started for Rome, accompanied by James Uwins, nephew of the painter Thomas Uwins, and arrived there on 17 March. He soon involved himself in the international community of artists in the city: he made the acquaintance of the Danish sculptor Bertel Thorvaldsen and formed lasting friendships with the British sculptors William Theed (1804–1891) and R. J. Wyatt and the painters Joseph Severn, Penry Williams, and Edward Lear. He also received advice and encouragement from the sculptor John Gibson, who is said to have admired his statue *Ferdinand* (1837) and who obtained several commissions for him.

Thrupp returned to London in October 1842 and bought a house at 232 New Road, where he built a large gallery and studio. He remained at the family home, 15 Paddington Green, until his mother's death in 1845, after which he moved with two of his sisters to New Road. In 1844 he showed two works at the exhibition held in Westminster Hall to choose sculptors to design statuary for the new houses of parliament: three years later he received commissions for two figures of Robert, earl of Oxford, and Robert Fitzwalter for the chamber of the House of Lords, which he executed in electroplated zinc. In 1846 he had been commissioned to produce the marble statue of Sir Fowell Buxton in Westminster Abbey. Thrupp's success, however, was marred by rumours of favouritism following the competition held for the monument, as one of the judges was the sculptor's close friend, the painter George Richmond. His most prestigious public commission was

the Wordsworth memorial (marble; 1854), also for Westminster Abbey. His design was chosen from a field of forty-two competing entries, though this decision too courted controversy, for according to the *Art Journal* his model was removed from the competition 'as soon as the decision was declared, without the other competitors having had an opportunity of seeing it' (*Art Journal*, 13, 1851, 222). In 1855 he executed a marble figure, *Timon of Athens*, one of a series of statues illustrating national history and literature installed in Mansion House, London. His church monuments included those to Jane, Lady Coleridge (marble; 1879), at St Mary's Church, Ottery St Mary, Devon, and the effigy of Canon Hugh Pearson (marble; 1883) at Sonning church, Berkshire.

Thrupp made a speciality of sculpture in relief, the subjects of which he often conceived in series or cycles following Renaissance models. His pair of bronze doors with ten panels illustrating *The Pilgrim's Progress* (exh. RA, 1868) was purchased by the ninth duke of Bedford and in 1876 presented to the Bunyan Chapel in Bedford. Another pair of doors with bronze panels illustrating George Herbert's poems (exh. RA, 1878) is in the Divinity School in Cambridge.

Many of Thrupp's ideal works reflect his deeply held Christian beliefs, including *A Magdalene* (exh. RA, 1841), *The Good Shepherd* (marble, 1861, Torre Abbey, Devon), and *St John Blessing Little Children* (exh. RA, 1875). Others treat themes from classical mythology, for example, *Arethusa* and *Hebe and the Eagle*, and English literature, as in *Ariel*. Although many of these were never made in permanent form (marble or bronze), their appearance is known from the large collection of the sculptor's plaster models, terracotta maquettes, and drawings which are now preserved at Torre Abbey, Torquay, Devon. These preliminary designs are a rare survival, and they show that Thrupp was a skilful draughtsman and modeller of form with an eclectic and often highly original approach to his subject matter. His drawings and clay sketches from life and his studies of animals are particularly sensitive and well observed.

Late in life, on 11 July 1885, Thrupp married Sarah Harriet Ann Frances (1845–1916), the eldest daughter of John Thurgar of Norwich and Algiers. He spent the winter of 1885–6 in Algiers and in the following year stayed at San Remo, Italy, and visited the Pyrenees. In 1889 he visited Antwerp, Brussels, and Cologne. In 1887 he had left London and moved to Torquay. He had a house in Upton, Devon, and frequented the art school at the Vivian Institute. The years 1892–4 were spent in negotiations for the ultimate disposal of the works from his studio. He loaned a large part of his studio collection to the corporation of Winchester in 1894 and on 8 November a Thrupp gallery was opened in the eighteenth-century Abbey House.

Failing eyesight, followed by paralysis agitans in 1893, compelled Thrupp to abandon active work. He died of influenza and pneumonia at Thurlow, Torquay, on 21 March 1895 and was buried on 26 March in Torquay cemetery. He bequeathed to his wife all his property, including his remaining works, which, in accordance with his wishes, were presented to the city of Winchester. In 1911, however, the works were returned to the sculptor's widow, who presented the collection, in two instalments in 1911 and 1916, to Torquay corporation. The collection was subsequently stored and parts of it displayed in various locations in the town (including the Free Library and the Marine Spa) until it was transferred to Torre Abbey in 1930–32.

In addition to his work as a sculptor, Thrupp designed and engraved an edition (1879) of Milton's *Paradise Lost* and illustrated in lithography Coleridge's *The Ancient Mariner* and Byron's *The Prisoner of Chillon*. He was the author of *The Angelic Nature* (1879) and *The Antient Mariner and the Modern Sportsman* (1881), two essays in which he discussed his Christian beliefs in relation to art, poetry, and cruel sports.

Frederick Thrupp's half-sister **Dorothea Ann Thrupp** (1779–1847), writer, was born on 20 June 1779 in London, the eldest daughter of Joseph Thrupp and his first wife, Mary Burgon (*d.* 1795). She contributed under the signature Iota to juvenile magazines edited by Caroline Fry. She wrote several hymns; one, 'A Little Ship on the Sea', was a great favourite with children. She also published some manuals, including *Songs by the Way* and *Thoughts for the Day* (1836–7), and translations from Pascal and Fénelon. She died at Hamilton Place, St John's Wood, London, in November 1847. MARTIN GREENWOOD

Sources DNB · M. Greenwood, *Frederick Thrupp (1812–1895): survivals from a sculptor's studio* (1999) [exhibition catalogue, Henry Moore Institute, Leeds, 21 Jan – 28 Feb 1999] · R. Gunnis, *Dictionary of British sculptors, 1660–1851* (1953); new edn (1968), 394–5 · Graves, *RA exhibitors*, 7 (1906), 388–9 · Graves, *Brit. Inst.*, 537 · *The Athenaeum* (30 March 1895), 415 · B. E. Reade, 'Anecdotes of Torbay in transition', *The Brian Edmund Reade collection on display at Torre Abbey* (c.1977), 48 · *Torquay Directory and South Devon Journal* (27 March 1895), 3 · *Torquay Times and South Devon Advertiser* (29 March 1895), 6 · B. Read, *Victorian sculpture* (1982) · G. Waterfield and others, *Art treasures of England: the regional collections* (1998), 216 [Royal Academy exhibition catalogue] · S. C. Hutchison, 'The Royal Academy Schools, 1768–1830', *Walpole Society*, 38 (1960–62), 123–91

Archives Hants. RO, papers relating to the Thrupp Gallery in the Abbey House, Winchester, W/C1/5/353 · Torbay Borough Council, Torquay, Devon, minutes books, 1930–32

Likenesses J. C. Dinham, portrait (after cabinet photograph, NPG), NPG; repro. in Greenwood, *Frederick Thrupp*, fig. 1 · photograph (in old age), BM

Wealth at death £8102 14s. 6d.: probate, 8 May 1895, CGPLA Eng. & Wales

Thrupp, George Athelstane

Thrupp, George Athelstane (1822–1905), coach-builder, was born on 16 July 1822 in Somerset Street, Portman Square, London, the second son of Charles Joseph Thrupp (*d.* 1866), coach-builder, and his wife, Harriet Styan. A younger brother was Admiral Arthur Thomas Thrupp (1828–1889).

Educated privately at Clapham, Thrupp subsequently joined the family coach-building firm in Oxford Street, London, that had been founded by his great-grandfather in 1740. On the death of his father in 1866 he brought into partnership George Henry Maberly, who had joined the firm in 1858. The business was thereafter known as Thrupp and Maberly. In August 1858 Thrupp married

Elizabeth Massey; they had one son, George Herbert Thrupp.

George Thrupp became a leading British coach-builder, and known to his fellow craftsmen throughout the world. In 1856 he was a founder of the Coach-makers' Benevolent Institution, and in 1881 played an important role in the formation of the Institute of British Carriage Manufacturers. He took a leading part in establishing technical schools for coach artisans, which, in 1884, were taken over by the Regent Street Polytechnic. In addition Thrupp was a liveryman of the Coachmakers' and Coach Harness Makers' Company serving as master in 1883. He did much to promote the general welfare of the trade, and Thrupp and Maberly held royal appointment as coach-makers to Queen Victoria.

In 1876 Thrupp delivered a series of lectures on coach-building to the Society of Arts. Published in 1877 as *A History of the Art of Coachbuilding*, the volume became a standard work. He also published with William Farr a volume on *Coach Trimming* (1888), and edited in the same year William Simpson's *Hand Book for Coach Painters*. Thrupp retired from business about 1889, and residing at Maida Vale divided his interests between local affairs and foreign travel. He died at his London home, 111 Maida Vale, on 24 August 1905, and was buried in Paddington old cemetery, Willesden Lane. Thrupp's son in turn joined Thrupp and Maberly, which in 1926 became part of the Rootes group. BRYAN K. GOODMAN

Sources *Coach Builder and Wheelwright's Art Journal*, 26 (1905), 278 · *Coach Builder and Wheelwright's Art Journal*, 47 (1926), 96 · *Autocar* (1905) · *Autocar* (1926) · private information (1912) · *City Press* (9 Sept 1905) · *Journal of the Society of Arts*, 53 (1904–5), 1038, 1144 · DNB · CGPLA Eng. & Wales (1905)

Wealth at death £14,429 12s. 4d.: probate, 19 Oct 1905, CGPLA Eng. & Wales

Thrupp, John

Thrupp, John (1817–1870), historian, was born on 5 February 1817 at Spanish Place, Manchester Square, London, the eldest son of John Augustus Thrupp (1785–1844) and his wife, Caroline Esther. His father was the eldest son of Joseph Thrupp of Paddington Green and his first wife, Mary Burgon. The sculptor Frederick *Thrupp was his uncle, and Joseph Francis *Thrupp, religious writer, was a cousin. Thrupp was baptized on 2 January 1818 at St Marylebone, and was educated at Dr Laing's school at Clapham. He was articled in 1834 and admitted a solicitor in 1838; he practised afterwards at Bell Yard, Doctors' Commons. His first book, *Historical Law Tracts* (1843), demonstrates his early fascination with both history and the origin and evolution of laws, particularly those relating to marriage and parental authority, but also to slavery, property, and criminal jurisprudence. 'The history of a nation', he contended, 'is in its laws' (p. 5). His book was well received and, after the death in 1844 of his father who left him a competency, he became a regular correspondent on a wide range of historical, judicial, and cultural themes in *Notes and Queries*. He was a fellow of the Royal Geographical Society and the Ethnological Society, and wrote for the journal of the latter. Through his interests in chess and the history of civilization he became an associate of the better-known Henry Thomas Buckle. Thrupp's second book was *The Anglo-Saxon home: a history of the domestic institutions and customs of England from the fifth to the eleventh century* (1862), in which he credited the assistance of his friend and fellow historian Thomas *Wright. Concerned to 'give a true picture of the domestic life of our Anglo-Saxon forefathers', and 'to trace the gradual development among them of the domestic affections and of the morals and manners of private life' (p. 1), Thrupp reviewed a vast quantity of 'laws and legal documents', which he regarded as 'by far the most trustworthy and valuable evidence' (p. iii), though he also used archaeological sources to underline his conclusion that 'the social history of the Anglo-Saxons exhibits a state of moral and domestic improvement, and that this advance may be mainly traced to the influence of the Christian religion, and of Roman laws and literature, and to the adventurous self-reliant spirit of the Anglo-Saxon race' (p. 407). The work is of its time, and is seldom now consulted.

Apparently Thrupp was thrice married, but had no children (*DNB*); the only details that have been uncovered are of his second marriage which was to Sarah Maria, the younger daughter of Edward Crowley of Lavender Hill, Wandsworth, which took place on 21 September 1854. He evidently suffered from illness, possibly of a neurological kind; he gave up chess in 1856 on the advice of his doctor, and ceased professional practice in 1867. He died of 'paralysis' (d. cert.) at his home, Sunnyside, Falkland Road, Dorking, on 20 January 1870. All his personal effects passed to his third wife, Susan.

KATHARINA ULMSCHNEIDER

Sources *DNB* · *Law Times* (19 Feb 1870) · *GM*, 2nd ser., 42 (1854), 619 · *The Post Office directory* (1850) · *The Post Office directory* (1873) · *Law List* (1841) · *Law List* (1851) · *Law List* (1861) · *Law List* (1865) · m. cert. · d. cert.
Wealth at death under £4000: administration with will, 15 March 1870, *CGPLA Eng. & Wales*

Thrupp, Joseph Francis (1827–1867), Church of England clergyman, was the only son of Joseph William Thrupp, solicitor, and Ruth Louisa, daughter of Thomas John Burgoyne. He was born in Guildford on 20 May 1827. Frederick Thrupp was his uncle. He was educated at Winchester College from 1840 to 1845 (where he was head prefect) and also at Trinity College, Cambridge, where he graduated BA in 1849 as seventh wrangler and eleventh classic, proceeding to an MA in 1852. He was a fellow at Trinity College from 1850 to 1853 and also travelled in Palestine. He was ordained a deacon at Ely and then a priest in 1852, and in the same year accepted the small college living of Barrington, Cambridgeshire. On 12 April 1853 he married Elizabeth Bligh, fourth daughter of the Revd John David Glennie of St Mary's, Park Street.

While at Royston, Thrupp wrote *Ancient Jerusalem* (1855) and an *Introduction to the Psalms* (2 vols., 1860), which was well regarded at the time, but which did not become a classic. He also wrote a translation of the Song of Solomon (1862). He was a member of the board of theological studies at Cambridge for a time, and in 1865 was select preacher. He was also a contributor to the Speaker's Commentary and to Smith's *Dictionary of the Bible*. He died at Ewell Road, Kingston, Surrey, on 24 September 1867, and was buried at Merrow, also in Surrey. His wife, who survived him, paid for commemorative windows to be placed in Trinity College chapel and in Barrington church.

E. C. MARCHANT, *rev.* GERALD LAW

Sources *GM*, 4th ser., 4 (1867), 550 · Venn, *Alum. Cant.* · *Clergy List* (1866) · d. cert. · m. cert.
Wealth at death under £3000: administration, 31 Oct 1867, *CGPLA Eng. & Wales*

Thubron, Henry James [Harry] (1915–1985), artist and art teacher, was born on 24 November 1915 at 7 Victoria Avenue, Bishop Auckland, co. Durham, the son of Percy Thubron, journeyman joiner (and later a newsagent and tobacconist), and his wife, Martha Ada, *née* Thompson (*d.* 1929/30). His mother, who died when he was fourteen, would shut him away in a room to paint from the age of seven. Having attended Henry Smith Grammar School, Hartlepool, he went on to Sunderland School of Art (1933–8) and to the Royal College of Art, London (1938–40). On 6 March 1940 he married, in Battersea, London, Joan Sawdon (*b.* 1917/18), a schoolteacher, daughter of Frank Sawdon, hairdresser.

Thubron's wartime experience of teaching soldiers via the text of the Army Council of Current Affairs *Newsletter* gave him a vision of a 'new post-war world' and the rhetoric to achieve it. On demobilization he realized that in art also a new start was required. While teaching at Sunderland School of Art from 1946, he began to elaborate new courses (from 1948 onward), contributing (from 1954) to those directed by John Wood of North Riding county council, which allowed for greater innovation. On his move north in 1956, Victor Pasmore also worked with Wood. Pasmore had worked at the Central School of Arts and Crafts, London, on the basic design course, instigated in 1949 with William Johnstone and Arthur Halliwell. These developments owed much to the *Vorkurs* of the German Bauhaus, but Thubron was always careful to dissociate his own methods from those of others and in his own teaching insisted on freedom, openness, development, and research. These chosen phrases gave expression to his perception of rapid contemporary changes in technology and society, and he rejected the label 'basic design' which he thought was given too freely to radical modernist teaching.

John Wood became further education officer for Leeds, enabling Thubron to apply his ideas to full-time education as head of painting and research at Leeds College of Art (1955–64) under the principal, Eric Taylor. This was at the time when old housing in the city was being pulled down and replaced by high-rise buildings. Helped at first by Tom Hudson, and Leeds University Gregory fellows (in particular, Terry Frost), Thubron deeply influenced Frank Lisle's Leeds Art College foundation course, taken by all students. His successful attempt to weld painting, ceramics, sculpture, serigraphy, art history, and general lecture programmes into a vision of modernist unity inevitably met with objections from some of the staff.

With Thubron, students first engaged in communal exercises making marks or collages on inexpensive paper laid on the floor in an atmosphere of invention. They experimented, for example, with families of forms whereby a square could by repeated modification become an oval; or, given a blob of red paint, a student would be directed to mix and place next to it on the paper what he or she perceived to be the most enhancing green. The traditional study of natural form as structure remained central to his students' development as did that of the human figure, but drawn in movement.

Thubron's strength of character could overdetermine student responses, and his enthusiasms yawed abruptly from philosophy to mathematical sculpture or to expressive painting. Young followers whom he appointed to the staff found themselves with much reading. With their preconceptions under assault by his methods and their ideas at the mercy of his forceful personality, some students, perhaps particularly women students, foundered.

The spoken, not the written, word was Thubron's natural medium. With tousled hair and animated eyes he would hold forth in the main painting studio, his delivery disjointed, aphoristic, even incoherent. His audience would feel that nevertheless here was an expression of that 'next step' in the current prevailing culture of single-issue, innovative modernism.

Thubron ran many summer schools between 1954 and 1968, notably at Scarborough (Yorkshire) and Barry (Wales), enjoying contact with students, some of whom—for example, John Walker, Bridget Riley, and John Hoyland—became internationally famous. Restless even in the face of success, he moved from one distinguished position to another. He left Leeds for Lancaster College of Art in 1964, then to Illinois University as visiting professor (1965), and to Leicester College of Art (1966–8). 'Basic research', held at the Artists' International Association Gallery, London, in the late 1950s, and 'The developing process', at the Institute of Contemporary Arts, London, in 1959, were important exhibitions of work from Thubron's classes. Following his divorce in 1962, he married, on 4 August 1965 in Lancaster, Elma Askham (b. 1924/5), an artist and lecturer, daughter of William Marsh Askham.

Out of the turbulence of these years Thubron produced comparatively few works of art, but these, based on a dialogue between old and new materials, and painting and collage, were treasured by friends and colleagues who rightly judged them to be sensitive and beautiful. With Dennis Harland as technical adviser he produced a fine relief in plastics for the exterior of the Branch College, Leeds (1963–4; removed), which fulfilled his ambition to make art for public, architectural settings. He showed work in Leeds at the Queen Square Gallery in 1967, and again that year with Elma Thubron. Later, in 1976, he showed paintings and collages at the Serpentine Gallery, London. He was also included in major surveys, among them 'British Art' at the Hayward Gallery, London, in 1974, and 'British Painting, 1952–77' at the Royal Academy, London, in 1977. After 1969 he concentrated more on his own painting, and funded by an Arts Council grant spent the following year in Spain. He spent part of 1971 in Jamaica before beginning an association with Goldsmiths' College, New Cross, London, as part-time teacher. In 1978 he was made an OBE. He continued making paintings and collages during the last eight years of his life, though experiencing ever deteriorating health. Thubron died at his home, 41B Granville Park, Lewisham, London, on 30 March 1985 and was survived by his widow, four children from his first marriage, and one child from his second.

Thubron's specific innovations in art education are still controversial. While he is remembered for his warm personality and vivid use of the spoken word, an extensive documentary record of his work as a teacher is held in the National Art Archive, Bretton Hall, Yorkshire. Examples of his work are in the Tate collection; Leeds City Art Gallery; Leeds University Gallery; and the Museum of Hartlepool, co. Durham. STEPHEN CHAPLIN

Sources *Harry Thubron* [1976] [exhibition catalogue, Serpentine Gallery, London, 23 Oct – 21 Nov 1976; incl. biography, bibliography, commissions, and collections] · *Harry Thubron retrospective, 1915–1985* (1987) [exhibition catalogue, Museum of Hartlepool, 1987] · C. Parry-Crooke, ed., *Contemporary British artists* (1979) · *The developing process: work in progress towards a new foundation of art teaching* (1959) [exhibition catalogue, Institute of Contemporary Arts, London, 1959] · *Basic research* [n.d., c.1957] [exhibition catalogue, Artists' International Association Gallery, London] · *Leeds College of Art* [Prospectus] (1964) · personal knowledge (2004) · private information (2004) · I. T. Jenkin, *William Johnstone* (1979) [exhibition catalogue, Hayward Gallery, London] · *British art in the twentieth century* (1987) [Royal Academy of Arts, London, exhibition catalogue] · b. cert. · m. cert. · d. cert.

Archives NRA, priv. coll., papers · U. Leeds, Lawrence Batley Centre | FILM Lawrence Batley Centre for the National Education Archive, Bretton Hall, West Bretton, Wakefield, West Yorkshire, *Drawing with the figure*, film, 1962 [by John Jones] · Lawrence Batley Centre for the National Education Archive, Bretton Hall, West Bretton, Wakefield, West Yorkshire, *All sherry trifle and no bread*, film, 1965/6

Thudichum, John Louis William [*formerly* Ludwig Johann Wilhelm] (1829–1901), physician and chemist, was born on 27 August 1829 at Büdingen, Hesse, Germany, the eldest son of Georg Thudichum (1794–1873), Lutheran minister, Greek scholar, and founder and principal of Büdingen Gymnasium, and his wife, Friederike, *née* Baist (1805–1879), daughter of a wealthy local justice of the peace. The Thudichum family was distantly related to the German poet Schiller.

Thudichum was educated at Büdingen, and matriculated at the University of Giessen in 1847. He studied under Justus Liebig and T. L. W. von Bischoff at Giessen, before going on to the University of Heidelberg. There, in May 1850, he won a prize for an original paper on urea in amniotic fluid in which he disagreed with Friedrich Wöhler's view that urea was a constant component of that fluid. Thudichum was also a talented singer and musician with a love of literature and poetry.

During the winter of 1850–51 Thudichum served as a volunteer surgeon at Kiel under Friedrich von Esmarch during the conflict between Denmark and Germany over control of the province of Schleswig-Holstein. In August

1851 he graduated MD at Giessen with a thesis on fractures of the upper end of the humerus. He practised medicine at Giessen for a short time, but having supported the republicans in the 1848 revolution he was banned from the University of Giessen and from many other German universities. Unable to obtain a university post in Germany he went to London in 1853. On 15 May 1854 he married his third cousin Charlotte Dupré (1828–1915), whom he had met in Frankfurt six years earlier. She was the daughter of J. F. Dupré, a merchant who, like Thudichum, had moved to London with his family. There were six daughters and two sons of the marriage.

In 1855 Thudichum became a member of the Royal College of Surgeons. Under Liebig's influence, physiological chemistry became his main interest and he lectured on natural philosophy and chemistry at the Grosvenor Place School of Medicine until it closed in 1863. In 1858 he published his first important book, *A Treatise on the Pathology of the Urine, Including a Complete Guide to its Analysis*. In 1859 he wrote a paper on the pathology and treatment of gallstones in which he proposed an original two-stage operation for their removal. In the same year he became a naturalized British subject and in 1860 he became a member of the Royal College of Physicians. In 1863 he published *A Treatise on Gall Stones: their Chemistry, Pathology and Treatment* which was reviewed very favourably. In the following year he won the first Hastings gold medal of the British Medical Association for his original work on urochrome, the normal pigment of the urine. Also in 1864 he was honorary Lettsomian professor at the Medical Society of London.

From 1864 to 1883 Thudichum was chemist to the Local Government Board under John Simon (1816–1904) and it was during this period that an annual government grant allowed him to pursue his most creative researches. Under Simon's auspices he undertook a series of 'chemical researches to promote and improve the identification of disease', the results of which were published in Simon's annual report of the medical officer of health, 1868–72. Thudichum's conclusions were not well received, although he made some important discoveries and valuable suggestions. In 1866 he won a silver medal of the Society of Arts for a paper entitled 'Diseases of meat as affecting the health of the people'. In 1865 he was appointed lecturer and first director of a new laboratory of chemistry and pathology at St Thomas's Hospital medical school, but by 1871 financial considerations persuaded him that he must devote more of his time and energy to his medical practice and he therefore resigned from his teaching post. His private practice became very large and as a physician he was highly regarded by his patients.

Thudichum was a pioneer in applying spectrum analysis to biological materials; in 1867 he accurately described the absorption spectrum of 'cruentine' (later rediscovered and renamed haematoporphyrin by Felix Hoppe-Seyler) and in 1869 by the same means, he discovered the 'luteines' (now known as carotenoids), precursors of vitamin A. About this time too he began his original work on the chemistry of the brain. He also studied diseases of the nose, the uses of electricity in the treatment of disease, and the composition of wine. In 1870 he spent a second period as a volunteer surgeon, again under Esmarch, at the base hospital at Johannesburg in the Franco-Prussian War. Then, in 1872, with his brother-in-law, August Dupré, lecturer in chemistry at Westminster Hospital, he wrote a treatise on wines and viticulture.

In 1874 Thudichum first published his systematic studies on the chemistry of the brain. Three years later Arthur Gamgee published an unsigned, violent criticism of this work. Hoppe-Seyler, who had already criticized Thudichum's work on cruentine, and Maly, both leading biochemical editors, joined the attack which discredited Thudichum's researches and eventually resulted in the loss of his government subsidy. An original explorer in the field of physiological chemistry, he continued his expensive work, impoverishing himself in the process. He made some important discoveries, but his scientific achievements rarely fulfilled the initial promise of his researches.

In 1878 Thudichum was elected a fellow of the Royal College of Physicians. He was also a leading member of the West London Medico-Chirurgical Society and in 1883–4 was its president. His important book *A Treatise on the Chemical Constitution of the Brain*, based on his original researches, was published in 1884; a second, enlarged and revised, edition was published in 1901, the year in which he was awarded an honorary degree by the University of Giessen. Thudichum died on 7 September 1901 of a cerebral haemorrhage at his home, 11 Pembroke Gardens, Kensington, London. He was cremated at Woking.

N. G. COLEY

Sources D. L. Drabkin, *Thudichum, chemist of the brain* (1959) · J. L. W. Thudichum, *A treatise on the chemical constitution of the brain* (1884); facs. edn with introduction by D. L. Drabkin (1962) · *BMJ* (14 Sept 1901), 726 · *The Times* (10 Sept 1901) · Munk, *Roll* · *Nature*, 64 (1901), 527 · *Medical Press and Circular* (18 Sept 1901), 322 · *Journal of the American Medical Association*, 37 (1901), 844 · *Biographisches Jahrbuch und Deutscher Nekrolog*, 6 (1901–2), 107 · H. McIlwain, 'Thudichum and the medical chemistry of the 1860s to 1880s', *Proceedings of the Royal Society of Medicine*, 51 (1958), 127–32 · C. Chatagnon and P. Chatagnon, 'L'étude chimique des constituants du tissu cerebral au cours du XIXe siècle: un pionnier en Grande-Bretagne, J. L. W. Thudichum (1828–1901)', *Annales Médico Psychologiques*, 116 (1958), 1.267–82 · R. S. Sparkman, 'The early development of gall-bladder surgery: centennial of the proposed cholecystostomy of J. L. W. Thudichum', *BMJ* (17 Oct 1959), 753–4 · H. Debuch and R. M. C. Dawson, 'Prof. J. L. W. Thudichum, 1829–1901', *Nature*, 207 (1965), 814 · J. D. Spillane, 'A memorable decade in the history of neurology: 1874–84', *BMJ* (28 Dec 1974), 757–9
Archives Medical Research Council, London, notebooks · RS, papers
Likenesses photograph, repro. in Drabkin, *Thudichum* · photograph, Pennsylvania School of Medicine; repro. in Drabkin, *Thudichum*
Wealth at death £1353 6s. 4d.: administration with will, 30 Oct 1901, *CGPLA Eng. & Wales*

Thuillier, Sir Henry Edward Landor (1813–1906), army officer and surveyor, born at Bath on 10 July 1813, was the youngest of eleven children (five sons and six daughters) of John Pierre Thuillier, merchant, of Cadiz and Bath, and his wife, Julia, daughter of James Burrow of Exeter. His elder sister, Julia, married Walter Savage Landor in 1811. The family descended from Huguenots who, on the revocation of the edict of Nantes in 1685, first settled in Geneva. Thuillier was educated at the East India Company's military academy, Addiscombe, in 1831–2, was gazetted to the Bengal artillery on 14 December 1832, and was stationed at the headquarters, Dum-Dum. In 1836 he married Susanne Elizabeth (d. 1844), daughter of the Revd Haydon Cardew of Curry Malet, Somerset, with whom he had a son (Colonel Sir Henry Ravenshaw Thuillier, KCIE, who, like his father, became Indian surveyor-general, 1887–95), and a daughter. He transferred to the survey department in December 1836, served first with parties in Ganjam and Orissa, and later was in charge of the revenue surveys in the Bengal districts of Cachar, Sylhet, Cuttack, and Patna. In January 1847, ten months before receiving his captaincy, he was appointed deputy surveyor-general and superintendent of revenue surveys, a post he held for seventeen years. His first wife died in 1844 and in 1847 he married Annie Charlotte, daughter of George Gordon Macpherson, Bengal medical service, with whom he had six sons (three of whom became officers in the Indian army) and two daughters.

Thuillier's revenue surveyors followed in the track of the different trigonometrical surveys, and thus had the advantage of fixed stations on which to base their detailed surveys. They produced large-scale cadastral maps intended initially for taxation purposes, but also to remove the need for partial surveys for irrigation, canals, railways, roads, and other purposes. Thuillier considered this provision of a uniform, complete, and trigonometrically accurate cadastral survey the model of economy and efficiency. His office in Calcutta was the mapping centre of the Indian survey (as opposed to Dehra Dun, the scientific centre) and thus had modern printing equipment. It was here that in 1854 he prepared the postage stamps first used in India, receiving the special thanks of government. He was joint author with Captain R. Smythe of *The Manual of Surveying in India* (1851), in which he discussed the difficult question of Indian orthography, officially standardized while he had charge of the department.

Thuillier succeeded Sir Andrew Scott Waugh as surveyor-general on 13 March 1861, and was promoted lieutenant-colonel in the same year, colonel on 20 September 1865, and major-general on 26 March 1870. The survey of the more settled parts of India had been completed, and many of the surveys successfully carried out under Thuillier were over mountainous and forested regions or sandy deserts, and frequently in parts never before visited by Europeans. About 1861 he transferred most of the survey activities to large new premises in Calcutta, finding the seat of government a better location for his headquarters than Dehra Dun. In 1868 he transferred the preparation of the atlas of India from England to Calcutta, selecting a staff of engravers in India for the purpose, and encouraging John Baboneau Nickterlien Hennessey to introduce the photozincographic process to add to the improvements in lithography which Thuillier had previously overseen.

Under Thuillier's superintendence of the Indian survey, 796,928 square miles, or more than half the dependency, were dealt with. He was elected a fellow of the Royal Society in 1869, made a CSI in May 1870, and KCSI in May 1879. In July 1876 he was awarded a good-service pension and he retired on 1 January 1878, with congratulations on the achievements of his forty-one years' service. He was gazetted lieutenant-general on 10 July 1879, general on 1 July 1881, and (a rare distinction for an officer with little actual military service) colonel commandant of the Royal Artillery on 1 January 1883. He settled at Richmond, Surrey, and was long a useful member of the Royal Geographical Society's council. He died on 6 May 1906 at his home, Tudor House, Richmond Green, Richmond, Surrey, and was buried at Richmond.

F. H. BROWN, *rev.* ELIZABETH BAIGENT

Sources *The Times* (8 May 1906) · *Army and Navy Gazette* (12 May 1906) · C. R. Markham, *A memoir on the Indian surveys* (1871) · E. W. C. Sandes, *The military engineer in India*, 2 vols. (1933–5) · R. J. P. Kain and E. Baigent, *The cadastral map in the service of the state: a history of property mapping* (1992) · M. Edney, 'Mapping and empire', PhD diss., University of Wisconsin, Madison, 1990 · *India List, and India Office List* (1906) · H. M. Vibart, *Addiscombe: its heroes and men of note* (1894) · private information (1912) · d. cert. · *CGPLA Eng. & Wales* (1906)
Likenesses Beetham, oils, 1846; known to be in family possession, in 1912 · E. G. Palmer, oils, 1885; known to be in the surveyor-general's office, Calcutta, in 1912 · Mrs Rowley, oils, 1896; known to be in family possession, in 1912
Wealth at death £11,208 10s. 7d.: probate, 14 June 1906, *CGPLA Eng. & Wales*

Thuku, Harry (1895–1970), Kenyan nationalist politician and farmer, was born near Kambui, Kiambu district, Kenya, to Wanjiku (d. 1934), the fourth wife of Kairianja (d. 1899), an elder of the powerful Gathirimu clan of southern Kikuyu. In the same year Britain declared a protectorate over Kenya. Having lost his father, a farmer, at an early age Thuku abandoned his family's goats to herd for the Gospel Missionary Society mission station at Kambui, founded in 1902. At thirteen, entering a new world while stealing a march on his old one, he was both baptized and circumcised, having got the mission to perform the surgery that entitled him to adolescent privileges before his non-Christian peers were eligible. Such ingenious energy marked the rest of his career. Three years later, by that time literate in Swahili and English, the diminutive Thuku sought work in Nairobi, a tin-roofed railway town notorious for its insanitary slums no less than for its excitable white-settler politics. Having started as a bank messenger he was gaoled for two years for forgery. Next he became a compositor for a settler newspaper, and then telephonist at the treasury. At the centre of multi-ethnic black urban life, yet with a privileged view of white politics, Thuku took a lead in articulating African protests after the First World War against the pro-settler policies of the governor, Major-General Sir Edward Northey: women's forced coffee-picking labour; a new pass (kipande) system; higher taxes; and threatened wage cuts. In June 1921, influenced by Baganda in Nairobi, Thuku formed the Young Kikuyu Association—in imitation of the Young

Baganda Association—which he soon renamed the East African Association and which became multi-tribal, if largely Kikuyu. He travelled around Kenya by car to contact members of other tribes. His association scandalized chiefs by its youthful impudence, offended missionaries with its messianism, and antagonized officials and settlers by enlisting the aid of local Indian politicians. Thuku himself advocated civil disobedience as a political weapon. His arrest on 14 March 1922, for threatening peace and good order, caused popular disturbances in Nairobi. A crowd attacked the police station where he was detained, and police and settlers shot dead 25 African demonstrators. Africans subsequently believed (with some exaggeration) that this excess of oppression shamed the British government into issuing, in 1923, the Devonshire declaration [see Cavendish, Victor Christian William, ninth duke of Devonshire (1868–1938)]—that Kenya was an African, not settler, territory, in which native interests were paramount. In his nine-year detention Thuku ran a private school and, befriended by a horticulturally expert official, Major H. B. Sharpe, became a successful farmer and trader. Colonial oppression had its compensations.

Having returned to Kambui in 1930 Thuku wrote the history of his clan, sued his brother, and expelled his tenants—all in order to secure an indefeasible right to the 25 acres on which he built his porticoed, whitewashed home, Paradise. In 1935, after clashing with his political heirs—radicals in the Kikuyu Central Association of which he was elected president in August 1932—he founded a new party, the Kikuyu Provincial Association. He favoured gradual constitutional advance, and his association became dedicated to agricultural improvement in alliance with the colonial administration. When war broke out in 1939 he supported the government. In 1944 he helped to found, and was first chairman of, the multi-tribal Kenya African Study Union (KASU), in 1946 renamed the Kenya African Union (KAU). This acted as a constituency association for the first black member of Kenya's legislative council, Eliud Mathu, who had been nominated by the governor after consulting élite African opinion.

Not until 1948 did Thuku consolidate his respectability with a Christian marriage to his long-standing 'customary' wife, Tabitha. By then Kikuyu politics was sharply divided between the moderate constitutionalism of landed elders and the secret, potentially violent impatience of the young and landless that erupted, in the early 1950s, in the Mau Mau emergency. Thuku, protected by the police and allied with Dr Louis Seymour Bazett Leakey (1903–1972), palaeontologist and self-proclaimed 'white Kikuyu', committed himself to the British—and propertied Kikuyu—cause. To support its military campaign of counter-insurgency the colonial government embarked on a second prong of agrarian reform that stripped white farming of many of its former protections. Thuku was one of the first Kikuyu to be permitted to plant coffee, and in 1959 became the first African board member of the Kenya Planters Coffee Union. He celebrated the day of Kenya's independence, 12 December 1963, by planting out coffee seedlings, in defiance of quota controls, while every official back was turned. A few years later, in his seventies, he supported Kenya's claim for a larger coffee quota by setting fire to his coffee nursery in front of television cameras. Following a short illness he died in Nairobi on 14 June 1970. A man whose early audacity had helped to temper colonial exactions, Thuku ended his life as a beneficiary of colonial reform, representative of those who did well out of independence. JOHN LONSDALE

Sources H. Thuku and K. King, *Harry Thuku: an autobiography* (Nairobi, 1970) · K. Kyle, *The politics of the independence of Kenya* (1999) · B. A. Ogot, *Historical dictionary of Kenya* (1981)

Thurcytel (d. 975?), abbot of Crowland, is known almost entirely from a life attributed to his kinsman and successor but one, Abbot Egelric the younger, but preserved only as part of the history of Crowland fabricated in the late middle ages. Parts of it may represent authentic early tradition and were also reported by Orderic Vitalis in the early twelfth century. Stripped of its worst anachronisms, the Crowland tradition was that Thurcytel was a wealthy kinsman and leading adviser of kings Edward the Elder and Æthelstan, fought at 'Brunanburh' in 937, and led embassies abroad. A friend of the leaders of the Benedictine reform movement, he refounded Crowland in 948 with the support of King Eadred, whose service he left to become abbot. He gave Crowland six of his manors, recovered others by purchase from Eadred's ealdormen, and had King Edgar confirm them in 966. Crowland tradition also held that he had rebuilt the ruined abbey church, given gold and silver plate, drawn up a monastic rule supplementary to the rule of St Benedict, and had the abbey's earlier history written down. According to the history he died on 28 June 975.

Perhaps the same Thurcytel was in 971 abbot of Bedford, where he buried his kinsman Archbishop Oscytel of York. According to Ely tradition he was later expelled from Bedford and bargained for a fraternity with the canons of St Paul's in London, where he had first been a priest, by leaving them a manor after his death. Historians since Orderic have identified the two Thurcytels, but the case is not clear-cut. C. P. LEWIS

Sources Ingulf, 'Historia Ingulphi', *Rerum Anglicarum scriptorum veterum*, ed. [W. Fulman], 1 (1684), 1–107, esp. 29–53 · Ordericus Vitalis, *Eccl. hist.*, 2.340–43 · E. O. Blake, ed., *Liber Eliensis*, CS, 3rd ser., 92 (1962), 78, 96, 105 · J. Earle, ed., *Two of the Saxon chronicles parallel: with supplementary extracts from the others*, rev. C. Plummer, 1 (1892), 119 · D. Whitelock, 'The conversion of the eastern Danelaw', *Saga-Book of the Viking Society for Northern Research*, 12 (1937–45), 159–76 · W. G. Searle, *Ingulf and the Historia Croylandensis: an investigation*, Cambridge Antiquarian RS, 27 (1894)
Likenesses manuscript illumination, line drawing, 1160–99, BL, Harley Roll Y6

Thurgood, Walter Leonard (1903–1973), transport entrepreneur, was born in Church Lane, Cheshunt, Hertfordshire, on 24 January 1903, the son of Charles Thurgood, labourer in a gun factory, and his wife, Lily Amelia, *née* Durton. He was educated in Enfield and at the Regent Street Polytechnic, London, and apprenticed to a coachbuilder in 1918.

Thurgood became a foreman at the Phoenix coach works in Ware, Hertfordshire, and this small home counties town, a centre of the malting industry, was to become the fixed base of most of his varied business activities, and to benefit from them in terms of employment opportunities. In 1925 he founded his own coachworks, W. L. Thurgood (Coachbuilders) Ltd, which built up a widening clientele of smaller stage carriage and private hire operators, spreading through the home counties into East Anglia and further afield. The coach-building side of his entrepreneurial activities remained a constant factor (apart from wartime production) throughout the diversification of his business interests, and the works, in its final physical form, was sold to a rival as a going concern at the end of Thurgood's active business life.

In 1928 Thurgood diversified into bus operation, running mainly vehicles bodied at his own works on a network of routes radiating from the nearby county town of Hertford. The People's Motor Services network prefigured part of the subsequent operating pattern of London Transport from its Hertford garage. Nineteen single-deck buses and a van were acquired from People's by the London Passenger Transport Board in November 1933, Thurgood having previously sold two thirds of his interest to Messrs Overington and Randall.

Thurgood then turned to civil aviation, which was growing in both popularity and reliability. With Louis T. H. Greig as fellow director, Thurgood formed Jersey Airways Ltd and acquired its first 'airliner', a twin-engine De Havilland Dragon of 6/8 seats, which flew from St Helier beach to Portsmouth on 18 November 1933, three days after delivery. A fleet of eight such aircraft carried nearly 25,000 passengers in 1934 and six four-engined DH 86s were ordered. In November 1934 Thurgood, with Whitehall Securities, formed Guernsey Airways, but in December a holding company was established, Channel Island Airways, in which Railway Air Services and Whitehall Securities held part interests with Thurgood, who retained his shareholding until 1939. His links with Channel Islands transport lasted longer, with a large order being placed for Thurgood bodies by Guernsey Motors after the war.

Thurgood's pattern of reinvestment repeated itself after his close involvement in aviation came to an end, when he established a factory for the production of decorative, laminated plastic sheet with the punning trade name of Wareite. This was sold to the Bakelite group in 1940, Thurgood obtaining shares in the controlling company.

Wartime production in the coachworks appears to have concentrated on aircraft equipment, including jettison tanks, rather than vehicles. The works was destroyed by enemy action in October 1940, but rebuilt within a few months. At the end of the war coachwork production recommenced in late 1945 and the next few years, marked by a shortage of both private cars and new buses and coaches, were probably the heyday of the firm. New vehicle building was combined with a flourishing second-hand and refurbishing trade. The business moved to new, purpose-built premises on the edge of the town in 1953,

which could handle double-deck buses. The BBC acquired the vacant works as a property store and also occupied additional buildings which Thurgood erected on his new coachworks site. In 1967 the coachworks was sold as a going concern to Plaxtons (Scarborough) Ltd, whose southern service centre it became.

Thurgood was active in local civic life, serving on Ware urban district council for nine years and meeting the cost of a coat of arms for the town (with the punning motto 'Cave'). Thurgood can be epitomized, in John Hibbs's description of one of Thurgood's contemporaries, Edward Hillman, as a 'flying busman'. His coach-building led to bus operation, which in turn financed civil flying. Further diversification took in plastics manufacture and eventually property development. Throughout this varied career, the town of Ware and coach-building were constant factors. Thurgood died of heart failure at the Queen Elizabeth II Hospital, Welwyn Garden City, on 23 May 1973. He was survived by his wife, Maud, *née* Wilkinson, and six children. He was cremated at Enfield crematorium following a funeral service at St Mary's Church in Ware.   RICHARD A. STOREY

Sources G. R. Mills, 'Thurgood of Ware', *Buses*, 206 (May 1972) · G. R. Mills, 'Thurgood of Ware', *Buses*, 216 (March 1973) · *Hertfordshire Mercury* (25 May 1973) · R. E. G. Davies, *A history of the world's airlines* (1964) · T. U. Fielding, *History of Bakelite Limited* (c.1948) · W. J. Carman, *100 years of public transport: a short history of the Guernsey Railway Co. Ltd* (1979) · personal knowledge (2004) · d. cert. · b. cert.

Archives Southampton RO, Southampton corporation airport files

Wealth at death £48,588: probate, 24 Oct 1973, *CGPLA Eng. & Wales*

Thurkilbi, Roger of. *See* Thirkleby, Roger of (d. 1260).

Thurkill. *See* Turges (d. 845).

Thurland, Sir Edward (1607–1683), lawyer and politician, was born at Reigate, Surrey, on 22 February 1607, the eldest son of Edward Thurland (d. in or before 1644) of Reigate and his wife, Elizabeth (d. 1642), daughter and coheir of Richard Ellyott, also of Reigate. Although his family originally came from Nottinghamshire, both his grandfather and father were London merchants. Thurland matriculated as a pensioner from Clare College, Cambridge, at Easter 1624, but then entered the Inner Temple on 20 October 1625, being called to the bar on 15 October 1634. He was elected to the Short Parliament for Reigate on 20 April 1640, but played no discernible part in its affairs or in the ensuing civil wars. Following the decease of his father, in August 1644 he was assessed at £2000 by the committee for the advance of money. By 1647 he had married Elizabeth (d. 1676), daughter of Lionel Wright of Buckland, Surrey. They had one son, Edward, who was fifteen in 1663.

During the 1640s and 1650s Thurland appears to have kept a low profile, quietly going about his legal practice. He returned to public affairs in 1659, being returned to parliament for Reigate and accepting local office as a Surrey JP. He was re-elected to the Convention of 1660, and following the Restoration, which saw the duke of York granted the manor of Reigate, he was named on 17 June as solicitor-general to the duke. Thurland was named to several parliamentary committees on ecclesiastical issues, and Lord Wharton felt that he might be friendly towards a church settlement embodying a form of modified episcopacy. In the event Thurland opposed the incorporation of the Worcester House declaration into law. Re-elected to the House of Commons again in 1661, he proved to be a supporter of the court and of the interests of the duke of York. In 1661 he became recorder of the Surrey boroughs of Reigate, Kingston, and Guildford, and was named a commissioner for corporations in that county in 1662. On 14 April 1665 he was appointed a king's counsel, saving for his office of solicitor to the duke, and on 22 April he was knighted. Thurland made strenuous efforts to delay the attack on the earl of Clarendon in 1667, and that same year Andrew Marvell characterized him as a one of 'the lawyers mercenary band' of court supporters (*Poems and Letters*, 1.145). On 12 May 1670 Thurland became attorney-general to the duke of York. He was still considered a member of the court party in 1671.

In December 1672, following the furore over the declaration of indulgence, a decision was taken in the committee for foreign affairs of the privy council that Thurland would be made a judge. In January 1673 Thurland became a serjeant-at-law, his sponsors being the dukes of York and Monmouth. On 24 January he was made a baron of the exchequer. Thurland retained his judgeship until 29 April 1679, when it was revoked, officially on the grounds of ill health, but the times were then unpropitious for an adherent of the duke of York. Thurland died on 14 January 1683 and was buried at Reigate. His will exhibited some distrust of his son and heir, Edward, making legacies specifically for the use of his daughter-in-law and her children, but instructing that his chambers be sold to pay his son's debts and that his law books be kept for the use of his grandson, also Edward, who eventually served as MP for Reigate.　　　STUART HANDLEY

Sources HoP, *Commons, 1660–90* · Venn, *Alum. Cant.* · Sainty, *Judges* · Sainty, *King's counsel* · Baker, *Serjeants* · will, PRO, PROB 11/372, sig. 28 · O. Manning and W. Bray, *The history and antiquities of the county of Surrey*, 1 (1804), 40, 295, 317–18, 342 · W. Hooper, *Reigate: its story through the ages* (1945), 31, 118, 162 · *Eighth report*, 1, HMC, 7 (1907–9), 279–80 · *The poems and letters of Andrew Marvell*, ed. H. M. Margoliouth, 2nd edn, 1 (1952), 145 · A. F. Havighurst, 'The judiciary and politics in the reign of Charles II [pt 1]', *Law Quarterly Review*, 66 (1950), 62–78, esp. 73
Likenesses M. Wright?, portrait; at Guildhall, London, in 1898 · portrait; in possession of Lord de Saumarez, 43 Grosvenor Place, London, 1898

Thurlby, Thomas (d. **1486**), mathematician and teacher, came from the diocese of Durham. Educated at Oxford, he took rather a long time over his junior arts career and did not receive his MA until 1462; but in 1453 he (together with the MA John Weston) was already renting from Osney Abbey the lecture hall known as the school of metaphysics, in a block recently built by Abbot Hooknorton. In 1459 he is found as Bible clerk at Merton College, and from 1460 to 1462 he was chaplain there. From 1463 he was a fellow and bursar of University College, and still had rooms

there in 1474. From 1475 he was for a relatively short time rector of Brinkley in Cambridgeshire, and, presumably thereafter, was accommodated at Osney Abbey until his death in 1486, possibly, like his successor in the apartment, as grammar master and chaplain.

In 1464–5, in conjunction with one William Taylor, Thurlby rented the school of arithmetic (in the same block as the school of metaphysics) from Osney Abbey. It is tempting to see him actually teaching arithmetic there, for it is sometimes said that there is a tract on the subject by him, in BL, Egerton MS 2622, fols. 80v–83r), but this is misleading. It is true that the folios do contain mathematical material inserted on blank pages, but it falls into two parts written in different hands. The first part (fols. 80v–82r) contains a fragmentary treatment of the well-known rule of 'casting out nines' for checking arithmetical calculations; there is no reason to associate it with Thurlby. The remaining two (facing) pages give diagrams representing a counting board or abacus (or possibly two such). On the left-hand page there is a configuration of squares, each capable of holding nine or more counters, and the labels make it clear that they are meant to represent monetary denominations. And on the right-hand page there is what appears to be a very incomplete diagram of the common late-medieval method of 'reckoning on the lines'. There is no rubric beyond the heading 'Novus modus computandi secundum inventionem Thome Thurlby' ('New method of computation according to the discovery of Thomas Thurlby'). Without an explanatory canon it is hard to see what is new about it, but perhaps serendipity or thorough searching will one day bring more complete evidence of Thurlby's achievement to light.　　　GEORGE MOLLAND

Sources Emden, *Oxf.*, 3.1872 · H. E. Salter, ed., *Cartulary of Oseney Abbey*, 3, OHS, 91 (1931) · BL, Egerton MS 2622, fols. 80v–83r · W. A. Pantin, 'The halls and schools of medieval Oxford: an attempt at reconstruction', *Oxford studies presented to Daniel Callus*, OHS, new ser., 16 (1964), 31–100 · *Snappe's formulary and other records*, ed. H. E. Salter, OHS, 80 (1924) · R. Steele, *The earliest arithmetics in English*, EETS, extra ser., 118 (1922) · L. Thorndike and P. Kibre, *A catalogue of incipits of mediaeval scientific writings in Latin*, rev. edn (1963) · K. W. Menninger, *Number words and number symbols: a cultural history of numbers*, trans. P. Broneer (1969)
Archives BL, Egerton MS 2622, fols. 80v–83r

Thurloe, John (*bap.* **1616**, *d.* **1668**), government official, was baptized on 12 June 1616, the only son of Thomas Thurloe (*bap.* 1578, *d.* 1633), rector of Abbess Roding, Essex, and his wife, Sarah (*d.* 1637), widow of a Mr Ewer, with whom she had three sons, including the regicide Isaac *Ewer (*d.* 1650/51).

Early life Thurloe's father, who was probably from Landbeach, Cambridgeshire, matriculated from Corpus Christi College, Cambridge, about 1593, and graduated BA in 1598 and MA in 1610. He was presented to Abbess Roding in 1612 but died in November 1633. Administration of the estate was secured to Sarah Thurloe in January 1634 by their son. John Thurloe's first marriage, in or before 1636, was to a member of the Peyton family, possibly related to Sir Robert Peyton of Wisbech. She died soon afterwards

John Thurloe (*bap.* 1616, *d.* 1668), by unknown artist, 18th cent.? [after original, 1650s]

and their two sons died in infancy. His second marriage was to Ann Lytcott or Lycott (*b.* 1620, *d.* after 1674), daughter of Sir John Lytcott and nephew of Sir Thomas Overbury; they had four sons and two daughters.

Thurloe's first patron, the lawyer and politician Oliver St John, claimed that he was 'bred from a youth' in his service. He was sponsored through Furnival's Inn by St John, who employed him as 'a sort of personal assistant' (Aubrey, 9). He appears as a witness in St John's legal business from 1637. In the 1630s he was a trustee for Oliver Cromwell's aunt, Lady Joan Barrington, as well as legal agent for St John, the husband of a favourite cousin of Cromwell, so his relationship with the latter probably dates from this period. In January 1645 he acted as secretary to St John and the other parliamentarian commissioners at the abortive peace negotiations at Uxbridge. He was admitted to Lincoln's Inn on 6 July 1646 for a fee of £3 10s., and acted for St John as a legatee of the earl of Essex. In June 1647 he was one of Richard Cromwell's sureties at Lincoln's Inn. In March 1648 he became clerk or receiver of the cursitors' fines (fees), a post under the commissioners of the great seal. He later claimed, with regard to the king's death, that 'he was altogether a stranger to that fact, and to all the counsels about it, having not had the least communication with any person whatsoever therein' (Thurloe, *State papers*, 7.914). In February 1650 he was made one of the treasurers of the company set up to drain the fens, in which capacity he assisted in draining the south level near Ely, one of the smaller drainage channels being named after him. He was allotted 500 acres of drainage land and

became deputy governor of the company in 1656. In October 1650 he appeared on Cromwell's behalf before the admiralty court and in January 1651 delivered a petition to the committee for compounding to recover Monmouthshire rents for him. In 1652 his association with St John led to his acting as a trustee of the Buckinghamshire estates of Cromwell's late son-in-law, Henry Ireton.

St John and Walter Strickland were sent to the United Provinces in early 1651 to negotiate an alliance and possibly a federal union on behalf of the English republic, and Thurloe accompanied them as secretary. In April he was sent back to London to secure an extension of the time allowed the ambassadors for their negotiations and immediately on his return wrote to the states general informing them the ambassadors would stay but warning of the need to redress assorted affronts the English believed themselves to have suffered. Cynical about Dutch goodwill, he informed Walter Frost, secretary of state, that the Dutch seemed to have learned from the Scots and the French to profess much but perform nothing, except as to their own advantage. Though the mission returned empty-handed, his career prospered.

Secretary of state, 1652–1658 Thurloe's reliability in the Netherlands was probably the main reason for his appointment as secretary to the council of state on 29 March 1652 in succession to the late Walter Frost, with a salary of £600 p.a. and 'convenient lodgings' in Whitehall. On 1 December 1652 he took over as clerk to the committee for foreign affairs and on 8 July 1653 (after the fall of the Rump Parliament) was given direction of the intelligence service, replacing Thomas Scot, with his salary now set at £800 p.a. On 22 December 1653 he 'took his place at the [council] board, being thereunto called by the Council', in effect, 'a full Councillor in all but name' (Aubrey, 37), though not appointed to the council of state in his own right until July 1657. He held the crucial co-ordinating role connected to the central organ of government from March 1652 to May 1659. Though he retained chambers at Lincoln's Inn (where he became a bencher in February 1654), was elected MP for Ely for 1654–5 and 1656–8, and was named a governor of the Charterhouse (November 1657) and chancellor of Glasgow University (February 1658), his time was devoted to his Whitehall affairs. From November 1655 he also had total control over the dissemination of news, with the banning of all printed newsbooks except the government controlled *Mercurius Politicus* and *Public Intelligencer*. His agents had the right to open all letters, providing him with a mass of information to assess. From 3 May 1655 he was postmaster-general, and from 1657 farmed the Post Office revenues for £1000 p.a. He recruited a number of assistants including William Jessop for foreign affairs and Philip Meadowes to assist Milton with Latin translation. Samuel Moreland and the younger Isaac Dorislaus assisted with deciphering royalist codes.

Thurloe's intelligence work was crucial to the regime, given the extent of disaffection and the royalist threat, coupled with the possibilities of invasion, particularly from France. He took over and extended a large network of government informers and occasional correspondents, keeping watch on domestic disaffection, the movements of exiled royalists, and the intentions of foreign governments. His task was made easier not merely by his command of the state's resources, but by the amateurishness of the royalist plotters, while each of his cumulative successes dissuaded potential plotters as they added to the myth of the 'all seeing little secretary' (Marshall, 24). But his vigilance, ability to assess gossip and confessions, and repeated round-ups of suspects hamstrung most serious plots. Thus in January 1655 he broke up the midland arms network of the royalist 'action party', pursuing the investigation of their planned series of risings and thereby unravelling the series of planned conspiracies which in the end produced only Penruddock's revolt. He correctly reckoned that the royalist failure in spring 1655 would limit active resistance in future and discourage foreign meddling. Thereafter a number of double agents on the continent like Sir John Henderson and Henry Manning enabled him to keep watch on the court of Charles II and pre-empt further risings. Most notably, by November 1656 he had suborned Sir Richard Willys, or Willis, one of the leaders of the 'sealed knot'. Henderson and Willys even visited London to meet Thurloe in secret, though Manning was detected by the royalists and shot in 1655. His information allowed him to arrest royalist plotters in southern England in the spring of 1658, plans for a London rising being 'allowed … to mature until its leaders had been given rope enough to hang themselves' (Underdown, 227). But small groups of dedicated men had always remained undetected and, most notably, he failed to stop Miles Sindercombe, who managed to plant incendiary materials in the chapel at Whitehall on 8 January 1657 before capture, having disregarded Jean-Baptiste Stouppe's warnings. The regime's formulation of foreign policy also depended on the accuracy and loyalty of his informants. Pepys later reported statements that Cromwell had allowed him £70,000 p.a. 'and thereby carried all the secret of all the princes of Europe at his girdle' (Pepys, Diary, 9.70–71). Official payments to him for intelligence work rarely met his expenditures, and by May 1659 he was owed £1665 3s. 2d. But his expenditure was nowhere near some post-Restoration estimates, and his successor, Morrice, put his resources at £1200–£2000 p.a.

Thurloe played a central role in foreign affairs in his time as secretary. He corresponded not only with unofficial agents across Europe but also with English ambassadors abroad, beginning with Bulstrode Whitelocke, in Sweden, early in 1654, and drafted instructions for the various missions. He developed a lucid and relaxed style of correspondence, but insisted on being comprehensively informed of useful news. He also received and dealt with the ambassadors of lesser powers, though one such, the Venetian envoy, Paulucci, reckoned him 'most difficult of access and with scant knowledge of foreign affairs'. Numerous committees on matters of foreign policy had 'Mr Secretary to assist' (Venning, 31). He took part in negotiations with the Dutch ambassadors in autumn 1653 and thereafter was the council's conduit to the resident ambassador, Nieupoort, and part of the negotiating team for the maritime treaty. He claimed, to Henry Cromwell, that the Dutch intended 'no goodwill to this nation or indeed to the Protestant cause, however they profess the contrary'. From April 1654 he assisted the councillors delegated to negotiate simultaneously with rival French and Spanish ambassadors. According to Ellis Leighton he headed the council faction which was not fixedly pro-France or pro-Spain but sought to keep England free of formal treaty commitments to promote domestic stability and to keep France and Spain at war, though the French ambassadors' reports indicate that they believed him to be hostile. In negotiations with the Swedish ambassador, Count Bonde, in spring 1656 he was the tough talker who insisted that Sweden cease supplying pitch, tar, hemp, and flax to Spain, as they were of use in war. Bonde said that they were principal exports, and he retorted that in that case they could easily find new outlets. Thurloe formally joined the council of trade only in autumn 1656, and the Jamaica committee in October 1657. His brother-in-law Martin Noell, for example, was the government's principal supplier for the Caribbean expedition.

As with the council Thurloe's real influence was behind the scenes. His access to information and the range of his duties allowed him to develop a broader and more informed view than most of his colleagues. As to his views, he believed that Cromwell should become the *caput et dux feoderis protestantis*. But in his summary of protectoral foreign policy, written for Clarendon about 1660, he understandably chose to downplay the importance of protestant links as against strategic considerations. English policy, he claimed, was based on a fear of royalist invasion and of France as its principal promoter. Accordingly, Spain, the weaker power, was a less dangerous enemy. Thus England sought to contain France by aiding rebels in 1654–6, and thereafter to tie it into alliance, but only when convenient to England. The acquisition of Dunkirk in 1658 was designed both to aid European protestants and to threaten France and the Dutch.

Thurloe took a greater role in Cromwell's second parliament than in its predecessor, being called upon to set forth government policy on various issues. On 25 December 1656 he spoke in favour of continuing the decimation tax on royalists, and may also have delivered a speech in January 1657 denouncing pre-1642 royal arbitrariness and religious oppression. On 7 March 1657 he announced the levying of more troops. He orchestrated the government's efforts in the spring to get all legislation passed since 1642 ratified and on 28 June he and other councillors recommended that Cromwell create a union of foreign protestants. But he is reckoned to have 'performed poorly in parliament and was out of his depth in the rough and tumble of the Commons' (Marshall, 66). With a commitment to conservative, constitutionalist politics and a lack of sympathy for the military, he took a leading role in encouraging Cromwell to take the crown, a debate which dominated his time in the spring of 1657, later complaining that Cromwell did not follow his instincts enough.

Thurloe's effectiveness was limited by bouts of serious

ill health, one of which, in early 1658, indisposed him for weeks. Business was paralysed in his absence. As the Venetian ambassador, Giavarina, reported, 'all must pass through the hands of this Secretary, who alone attends to and superintends all the most important interests of State' (*CSP Venice*, 1655–6, 188). Cromwell placed complete trust in him: according to George Downing only Thurloe also knew the 'scheme of things' (Thurloe, *State papers*, 6.856) while in 1657 Bulstrode Whitelocke named him as one of the few intimates with whom Cromwell would 'lay aside his greatness' and both discuss policy and relax to smoke a pipe and make verses (*Diary of Bulstrode Whitelocke*, 464). Successive chief governors of Ireland, Charles Fleetwood and Henry Cromwell, relied on him for information and assistance. Outside commentators held a similar view: the 1656 satire *A Game of Picquet* depicted him watching Cromwell's advisers and proposing to 'stand behind a chair and make and shuffle the cards with which you are to play the next game'.

Fall of the protectorate and the Restoration, 1658–1660 Thurloe had not abandoned hopes of reviving the kingship proposals as late as July 1658. When Cromwell lay dying he took the lead in persuading him to nominate his elder surviving son, Richard, as heir and subsequently acted as Richard's principal adviser. A serious rift arose between civilians such as Thurloe and senior army officers and another illness afflicted him that autumn. He was returned to Richard Cromwell's parliament in January 1659 for Huntingdon, Wisbech, and Cambridge University and chose to sit for the university. He probably drafted Richard's opening speech and on 1 February tackled disaffection head on by proposing a bill of recognition to legalize Richard's position and stop any reassertion of the Commons' powers, which he called tyranny. The government's principal business manager in parliament, he also gave a masterly analysis of their Baltic policy on 19 February, explaining the need for even-handedness between Sweden and Denmark to keep the sound open and castigating Dutch machinations. He somewhat desperately maintained that with God's help the protectorate could survive the hostility of the senior officers and the Commonwealthsmen in parliament. He alone advised Richard not to dissolve parliament as the army leader Desborough insisted.

Following the Rump's recall on 6 May, Thurloe was dismissed by the new council of state and Thomas Scot recalled. He refused to communicate his ciphers to Scot, calling him a 'noisy windbag'. Turned out of his Whitehall lodgings to bystanders' jeers, he retired to John Upton's house at Hammersmith. He was approached in the summer of 1659 to assist the Restoration but refused. He also had to face a civil lawsuit claiming £10,000 for wrongful imprisonment, and on 11 October 1659 parliament annulled his Post Office contract. He still kept up some correspondence abroad, and had leave to travel in and out of London without hindrance, taking new lodgings at Dial Court, Lincoln's Inn. He may have received support from his wife's relative, Colonel John Clarke, a member of the committee of safety from October 1659.

Thurloe's position improved with Monck's arrival in London, and on 2 February 1660 he began an attempt to reclaim about £3000 for disbursements on intelligence and other matters. Monck secured his reappointment as joint secretary of state on 27 February and his Whitehall lodgings were restored. Monck also recommended him, unsuccessfully, as MP for Bridgnorth in the Convention. Unfortunately since the summer of 1659 his assistant, Moreland, had been secretly passing on his intelligence to the royalists. According to Moreland, Willys approached him on the king's behalf, but he replied 'I prefer to go the nation's pace, no faster' (Aubrey, 159). Preferring a limited protectorate, in May 1660 he was still working with St John and Pierrepoint to obtain Richard Cromwell's restoration, putting principle before safety. On 14 May the Convention House of Commons resolved that 'Mr Secretary Thurloe, being accused of high treason, be secured' and that a committee examine him (*JHC*, 8.26). According to rumour he had boasted that he had 'a black book which should hang half them that went for Cavaliers' if he was prosecuted (*Fifth Report*, HMC, 208). Whether or not he managed to blackmail the new government, on 27 June he was released and on 29 June the Commons resolved that he should have liberty to attend the secretaries of state, presumably to pass on his expertise. He was supposed to have met Clarendon, and his memoranda on foreign policy may be a result. On 8 August the Lords committee considering the Bill of Indemnity struck out the clause referring to him.

Thurloe retired into obscurity, living partly at Lincoln's Inn and partly at Great Milton in Oxfordshire. Apart from testifying to St John's innocence of regicide he kept out of politics, though in January 1661 some of his property was seized when Upton's house was searched. He was removed as governor of the Charterhouse in January 1661, along with Whitelocke, whose house at Anvills, Hungerford, he considered buying in 1667. On 22 May 1667 Whitelocke met him and his fellow ex-councillor Sir Charles Wolseley at a Greenwich conventicle where John Owen preached. His health declined quickly thereafter and in January 1668 he had a severe attack of the stone at Lincoln's Inn. On 21 February he had dinner at his chambers in Dial Court with his fellow ex-councillor Philip Jones, requested him to withdraw while he took some medicine, and as he returned collapsed into his arms 'but never spake word and immediately died', probably of a heart attack (Aubrey, 210). He was buried in Lincoln's Inn chapel. He was survived by his second wife, who lived until at least 1674. John, the eldest of his three sons, was admitted to Lincoln's Inn in 1672, acquired the manor of Astwood, Buckinghamshire, in 1674, and died in 1682.

Assessment Giavarina wrote spitefully that from a 'mere lawyer's notary' Thurloe had 'amassed a heap of gold' and had shown 'utter absence of gratitude' (*CSP Venice*, 1659–61, 17). He does not appear to have been notably corrupt, but he did make financial gains, and could afford to build a grandiose new house—possibly designed by John Webb—at the confiscated Wisbech Castle. He had obtained the manors of Wisbech Barton, Elm, and Tydd St Giles during the 1650s, all previously episcopal property and all, like Wisbech Castle, repossessed by the bishop of Ely at the Restoration. In Richard Cromwell's parliament he was accused of receiving £1000 p.a. from the farmers of the London ale and beer excise to keep them from lawsuits by the brewers. He did propose a giant fee farm for all duties except ale and beer, and a separate one for them, in 1657 but it was dropped. He was also accused of making excessive profits as postmaster-general and confidently prepared his accounts, but this was not pursued either. The only visible evidence is of two unsuccessful attempts to corrupt him—Richard Wylde offered him £500 p.a., a share in pearl fisheries, and a diamond for his wife if he secured the Surat consulship in the new East India Company—he did not—and the intelligencer Joseph Bampfield offered to divide the pre-emption of tin from Cornwall. Thurloe occasionally tried to exert influence on behalf of his relations, and Broghill in Scotland rebuked him concerning his intervention on behalf of his relative by marriage Colonel Lydcott in 1655, but not to an excessive extent, and Thurloe was more often the recipient of such requests for favours.

The importance of the 'little secretary' to the protectoral regime cannot be exaggerated, both through his indispensability as central co-ordinator of government activity and his roles as chief of intelligence and resident expert on European affairs and royalist machinations. Like many intelligencers, his success owed much to luck and guesswork, and was mingled with failures, but he has been considered 'one of the forefathers of espionage and intelligence gathering in England' (Marshall, 304). He has been described as 'no radical, let alone revolutionary, but … a highly efficient and … honest public servant', but one 'out of his depth as a political and parliamentary leader' (Aylmer, 258–9). Government policy coincided with his known views, but his dominance in input, under Richard Cromwell, was brief. His appetite for work, ability at assimilating information, shrewd judgement, and commitment to the protectorate are as evident as his quiet ruthlessness. His fate in 1659–60 testifies both to his limited hold on power and his loyalty to his principles. Thurloe's papers, of major value for the history of the protectorate, were hidden behind a false ceiling in the garret of his chambers, discovered there in the reign of William III, sold to lord chancellor Somers and eventually presented to the Bodleian Library, Oxford.

TIMOTHY VENNING

Sources Thurloe, *State papers* · council books, PRO, SP 18, SP 25, SP 55–6, SP 77–8 · French ambassadors' MSS, PRO, SP 31/3/93–101 · BL, Add. MSS 3404–3415, 4156–4159, 4200, 5804, 6194, 22546, 28094, 32093 · BL, Lansdowne MSS 755, 821–823 · BL, Egerton MSS 2357, 2542, 2616, 2645 · BL, Sloane MS 4365 · BL, Stowe MSS 185, 497 · Essex RO, MSS D23/356, 472/14 · *CSP dom., 1651–61* · Bodl. Oxf., MSS Carte 63, 73–74, 80, 103, 131, 223, 228 · Bodl. Oxf., MSS Rawl. A. 37, A. 39, A. 41–3, A. 45, A. 48–50 · Bodl. Oxf., MSS Tanner 51–52, 54 · 'Extract of a letter … the death of Mr Thurloe', *N&Q*, 8th ser., 11 (1897) · P. Aubrey, *Mr Secretary Thurloe: Cromwell's secretary of state, 1652–1660* (1990) · E. Baker, 'John Thurloe, secretary of state, 1652–1660', *History Today*, 8 (1958), 548–55 · *JHC*, 7–8 (1651–67) · *VCH Cambridgeshire and the Isle of Ely*, vol. 4 · *Diary of Thomas Burton*, ed. J. T. Rutt, 4 vols. (1828) · *The Clarke papers*, ed. C. H. Firth, 4 vols., CS, new ser., 49, 54, 61–2 (1891–1901) · *The diary of Bulstrode Whitelocke, 1605–1675*, ed. R. Spalding, British Academy, Records of Social and Economic History, new ser., 13 (1990) · G. E. Aylmer, *The state's servants: the civil service of the English republic, 1649–1660* (1973) · A. Marshall, *Intelligence and espionage in the reign of Charles II, 1660–1685* (1994) · T. Venning, *Cromwellian foreign policy* (1995) · D. Underdown, *Royalist conspiracy in England, 1649–1660* (1960) · R. Spalding, *Contemporaries of Bulstrode Whitelocke, 1605–1675*, British Academy, Records of Social and Economic History, new ser., 14 (1990) · B. Whitelocke, *Memorials of English affairs*, new edn, 4 vols. (1853) · R. Vaughan, ed., *The protectorate of Oliver Cromwell and the state of Europe*, 2 vols. (1839) · private information (2004) [S. Sadler] · Pepys, *Diary* · memorial, Lincoln's Inn chapel, London · *Fifth report*, HMC, 4 (1876)

Archives BL, corresp. and papers, Add. MSS 4155–4159, 4166–4167, 4364–4365 · Bodl. Oxf., corresp. and papers; state MSS · PRO, council order books, SP 25/45, 75, 77–8 | BL, Add. MSS; Egerton MSS; Sloane MSS; Stowe MSS; Lansdowne MSS · Bodl. Oxf., MSS Carte; MSS Rawl. A; MSS Tanner · PRO, Cromwell's council of state papers, SP 18, 25, 77, 84, 99, 103

Likenesses A. & T. Simon, caricature, medallion, *c.*1653, BM · oils, 18th cent. (after original, 1650–59), NPG [*see illus.*] · R. Dunkarton, mezzotint, pubd 1813 (after W. Dobson), BM, NPG · J. Bullfinch, watercolour drawing, NPG · S. Cooper, miniature, Buccleuch estates, Selkirk · G. Vertue, engraving (after medal), repro. in Thurloe, *State papers*

Wealth at death substantial house at Great Milton, Oxfordshire; wealthy enough to contemplate purchasing estate from Bulstrode Whitelocke, Dec 1667; chambers at Lincoln's Inn, London; major residence Wisbech Castle, Cambridgeshire, confiscated 1660: *Diary of Bulstrode Whitelocke*, 725

Thurlow, Edward, first Baron Thurlow (1731–1806), lord chancellor, was born at Bracon Ash, Norfolk, on 9 December 1731, the eldest son of Thomas Thurlow (*bap.* 1695, *d.* 1762), a Church of England clergyman who held a series of small livings in Suffolk and Norfolk, and his wife, Elizabeth (*d. c.*1736), the daughter of Robert Smith of Ashfield, Suffolk. The roots of his father's family at Burnham Overy, Norfolk, went back at least to the sixteenth century. It was characteristic of Thurlow's inverted snobbery that, in later life, he claimed descent not from Oliver Cromwell's secretary John Thurloe, but from a (possibly invented) humbler ancestor, 'Thurloe the carrier'. He had two sisters and three brothers, of whom Thomas *Thurlow (1737–1791) became successively bishop of Lincoln and of Durham and John Thurlow (*d.* 1782) became an alderman of Norwich.

Education and early career Thurlow was for his first few years educated at home, but at the age of nine he was sent to Tacolneston, Norfolk, for two years under the tutorship of one Mr Browne. Then he studied under a Mr Brett at a small school at Seckars, Scarning, from approximately 1742 until 1747. He quickly acquired, and never lost, a reputation for recalcitrance and rudeness which was probably as well deserved as the recognition of his intellectual abilities. Later in his life, when attorney-general, Thurlow is said to have rebuffed a greeting from his former schoolmaster Brett with the words 'Am I bound to recollect every scoundrel who recollects me?' (Gore-Browne, 4). Thurlow's last school was King's, Canterbury, where he spent a year under the tuition of the formidable

Edward Thurlow, first Baron Thurlow (1731–1806), by Sir
Thomas Lawrence, 1803

headmaster Robert Talbot. Here he showed more amen-
ability, and he subsequently spoke of Talbot with appreciation. On 5 October 1748 he was admitted as a pensioner to
Gonville and Caius College, Cambridge, where he was a
Perse scholar from 1748 to 1751. His conduct at university
was, by all accounts, ill-mannered and rebellious in the
extreme, and his idleness and sardonic wit brought him
into constant conflict with authority. Only John Smith, his
tutor, earned his approval. In 1751 Thurlow withdrew
from Cambridge without a degree; according to the tactful obituary notice in the *Gentleman's Magazine* 'the vivacity
of his conduct obliged him to leave' (*GM*, 1st ser., 76, 1806,
882). Thurlow had determined to study for the legal profession, and on 9 January 1752 he was admitted a member
of the Inner Temple. He worked as a pupil in the offices of
Chapman, a solicitor in Holborn, where he formed a lifelong friendship with a fellow pupil, the poet William Cowper. Although Cowper recorded that he and Thurlow
spent their time 'giggling and making giggle instead of
studying the law' (Gore-Browne, 7), it is clear that Thurlow
worked diligently, albeit irregularly, at his studies; he also
spent much of his time in witty conversation at Nando's
Coffee House in Fleet Street, which was to play an important part in his private as well as his professional life.

Thurlow was called to the bar on 22 November 1754,
took chambers in Fig-Tree Court, and began to practise on
the western circuit. Although he established firm professional friendships with Lloyd Kenyon and John Dunning,
his early years at the bar were not marked by success. His
earnings were meagre, he was severely chastised by Lord

Mansfield when defeated in a suit over a marriage settlement, and in 1762 he appears to have contemplated quitting the legal profession. But there were achievements as
well. In 1758 he made a powerful impression when he
resisted, and repaid with interest, the aggressive tactics of
Sir Fletcher Norton in the case of Luke Robinson versus
the earl of Winchilsea. He also received favourable attention when appearing for the defence of the publisher
Jacob Tonson in a copyright suit in 1761. His forensic techniques depended on massive if rather unsystematic
knowledge, the ability to master a brief very quickly, and a
courtroom manner which could switch rapidly from the
ferocious to the sardonic. He cultivated an image of
rough, undeferential integrity. His success, though
delayed, was substantial. He was elected a bencher of the
Inner Temple in 1762 and took silk later in the same year.

By this time Thurlow's oratorical abilities had come to
the attention of politicians, and he became friendly with
Lord Weymouth, a leading figure among the followers in
parliament of the duke of Bedford. In June 1765 Weymouth was briefly appointed to the lord lieutenancy of
Ireland and proposed to make Thurlow his chief secretary. Although in August Weymouth had to yield the lord
lieutenancy to a Rockinghamite successor, he admired
Thurlow sufficiently to bring him into parliament as
member for the Staffordshire borough of Tamworth in
December 1765. In the House of Commons Thurlow
quickly established himself as the legal authority, and
prominent speaker, of the Bedford group. He associated
himself fully with that group's strong advocacy of British
authority over the North American colonies and with its
opposition to the domestic radicals, whose current champion was John Wilkes. Further honours now came
Thurlow's way; in 1769 he became reader at the Inner
Temple, and in the same year was elected recorder of Tamworth.

Private life It seems that Thurlow never married, but in
1759 or 1760 he became acquainted with Catherine (Kitty)
Lynch (d. c.1760), the daughter of John Lynch, the dean of
Canterbury, and his wife, Mary Wake. A romantic affair
quickly developed, but it is not clear whether they were
married, or, if they were, when and where the ceremony
took place. There is evidence, however, that Kitty Lynch
gave birth to a son in 1760, that she died in childbirth in so
doing, and that the paternity of Thurlow was widely
acknowledged. In 1769 the *Town and Country Magazine*
referred to Kitty Lynch's brother William Lynch (c.1730–
1785), MP for Canterbury, as Thurlow's brother-in-law,
while the entry of Charles Thurlow at Corpus Christi College, Cambridge, in 1785 is recorded by Venn. In 1788 the
European Magazine noted the death at Canterbury of 'Mr
Thurlow of Bennett College, Cambridge, son of the Lord
Chancellor' (*European Magazine*, 13, 1788, 463), and the
Gentleman's Magazine of that year made a similar comment.
The claim that 'Kitty Lynch and Edward Thurlow, however
impetuous their courting, were married before her
untimely death' (Gore-Browne, 22) is plausible but cannot
be confirmed. Later Thurlow formed a public but non-
marital relationship with Polly Humphries, the daughter

of the keeper of Nando's Coffee House. He purchased a comfortable, although not ostentatious, residence at Knight's Hill, near Dulwich, and lived with Polly Humphries in domestic tranquillity for the rest of his life. Their first child was stillborn in 1771; later they had three daughters.

Legal and political advancement Thurlow's legal career was considerably advanced by his role in the celebrated Douglas case. There is no reason to reject the tradition that he became involved in the lawsuit concerning the disputed succession to the duke of Douglas's estates through a chance meeting in Nando's Coffee House with lawyers representing the Douglas claimant, Archibald James Edward Douglas. The court of session in Edinburgh had in 1767 decided by a narrow majority in favour of the rival Hamilton claimant. Thurlow, in animated conversation with a friend, is reported to have denounced the verdict and, in vehement terms, to have upheld the Douglas claim. He was promptly engaged by the Douglas party to represent them in the appeal before the House of Lords. On 16 January 1769, immediately before the case was heard, Thurlow was involved in a duel at Kensington Gravel Pits with the leading agent on the Hamilton side, Andrew Stuart. According to one account, 'One ball went through Mr T.'s wig, and T's ball went through S.'s coat, whereupon the seconds interfering, both parties were reconciled' (*Town and Country Magazine*, 1, 1769, 53). It was characteristic of Thurlow that his sardonic attacks upon Stuart, which had provoked the duel, were followed by a warm friendship between them. The Douglas case was heard before the House of Lords in February 1769, and, although speaking on the opposite side from his fellow Bedfordites, Thurlow helped to persuade the Lords to reverse the judgment of the court of session and to uphold the claim of the Douglas candidate. The case did not make Thurlow famous overnight—he had already attained a reputation for competence in court and in parliament—but it greatly enhanced his prestige. Lord John Campbell's verdict, that 'by his admirable pleading he showed what excellence he might have reached, and what solid fame he might have acquired, if his industry had been equal to his talent' (Campbell, 5.494), was somewhat ungenerous.

At the time of Thurlow's entry to the House of Commons the principal issue was the Rockingham administration's move to repeal the Stamp Act that had been passed by the Grenville ministry in 1765. Some of Thurlow's earliest interventions in debate and parliamentary votes were directed against the repeal. Later he attributed the rebellion of the colonies to 'a want of connection and dependance in the form of their government upon the mother country' (Ditchfield, 'Lord Thurlow', 66) and to a lack of ministerial firmness in 1766. With the entry of the Bedford group into the Chatham ministry in 1767–8, Thurlow's career advanced further. He assisted in the prosecution cases against John Wilkes and, in June 1770, against John Almon, the publisher of Junius's 'Letter to the king' of 19 December 1769. When the Bedfordites extended their support into the administration of Lord North, Thurlow achieved major office for the first time. He became solicitor-general in March 1770 and attorney-general in January 1771. As a leading law officer he was frequently called upon to pronounce in the Commons on the legality of the government's position, and in that capacity he became one of the most powerful spokesmen in favour of coercing the colonies. He reacted strongly to the colonial seizure of the revenue ship the *Gaspee* in 1772; according to John Pownall, under-secretary to the Board of Trade, Thurlow considered the incident to be of 'five times the magnitude of the Stamp Act' (*Dartmouth MSS*, 2.91). He warmly advocated the punitive legislation of 1774. His direct and bluff manner won him the respect, if not the affection, of the Commons, a large majority of whom supported North's American policy, while Thurlow's impatient disdain for dry pedantry distinguished him from many MPs who were lawyers. Grafton acknowledged Thurlow's status as 'a speaker of the first rate, as well in Parliament as at the Bar', but complained that 'his principles leaned to high Prerogative' (*The Autobiographical and Political Correspondence of the Duke of Grafton*, ed. W. R. Anson, 1898, 229). Thurlow himself argued that he was the advocate of a ministerial policy which sought to uphold the authority of parliament and thus to defend, not to subvert, the letter and spirit of the settlement of 1688–9.

By the later 1770s Thurlow's opinions and political effectiveness commended him to George III. It is noteworthy that what the king might have been expected to perceive as moral failings did not prevent the growth of a personal friendship between them. After the surrender at Saratoga in 1777 and the French entry into the war the following year, the ministry of Lord North required a measure of stiffening, both internally and to fend off its increasingly numerous parliamentary critics. The need for intellectual reinforcement in the House of Lords led George III personally to arrange for Thurlow's promotion: 'I want an able Chancellor and therefore have pitched on Mr Thurlow', he wrote on 3 April 1778; five days later he added, 'I cannot begin to form any plan untill Mr Thurlow is in possession of the Great Seal' (*Correspondence*, ed. Fortescue, 4, nos. 2272 and 2284). On 3 June Thurlow was created Baron Thurlow of Ashfield, Suffolk, and became lord chancellor. At the same time he was sworn of the privy council. He took his seat in the House of Lords on 14 July 1778, in time to preside over its prorogation at the end of the session.

Lord chancellor As lord chancellor Thurlow was meticulous in attending the House of Lords. In his first full session (1778–9) he was present on each of the 121 days of its duration; for the rest of his two terms in that office his level of attendance rarely fell below 90 per cent. His aggressive domination of debate caused the opposition peer Lord Pembroke to write in 1781: 'Mon Chancelier is a clever fellow, but his wings must be clipped, or La Chambre Haute had better be shut up' (G. M. Ditchfield, 'The House of Lords in the age of the American revolution', in *A Pillar of the Constitution: the House of Lords in British Politics, 1640–1784*, ed. C. Jones, 1989, 216–17). An early manifestation of his ascendancy was his contemptuous dismissal in March 1779 of the duke of Grafton's sneer at his undistinguished social origins; asserting that 'the peerage solicited me, not I the peerage', he retorted by describing the duke as 'the accident of an accident' (Ditchfield, 'Lord Thurlow', 66). Thurlow's nicknames in the court of chancery—Tiger, or sometimes Lion—indicate a similar fierceness, although he was recognized to be above any hint of corruption. For all his skill in equity cases, Lord John Campbell, an admittedly hostile whiggish commentator, was exaggerating only slightly when he ascribed delays in chancery to Thurlow's 'want of industry and exertion' and observed 'he was not patient or pains-taking … he did little in settling controverted questions or establishing general principles' (Campbell, 5.521–2, 528). What Campbell called his 'awe-inspiring manners' contributed more to his authority than any depth of learning.

Thurlow saw himself primarily as the king's servant rather than as a party man. He remained in office when the remainder of the Bedfordite group, including Gower and Weymouth, resigned from North's ministry in 1779, and he took part in the confidential negotiations to reconstruct the ministry that autumn. He grew increasingly impatient with the indecisiveness of North's ministry in its latter years and irritated some of his colleagues by his reluctance to conceal his impatience. For his part, North complained of Thurlow's indecision: 'in the Cabinet he opposed everything—proposed nothing—and decided nothing' (Farington, *Diary*, 1.175). It is true that Thurlow at times spoke out in the Lords against measures which had government approval. Lord Sandwich in 1781 lamented that 'The Chancellor has made a Point of opposing most Bills that have lately been brought up to the House of Lords, and has usually been backed by the whole Opposition' (Ditchfield, 'Lord Thurlow', 70). On the other hand, allegations that he was secretly planning a coup whereby a Bedfordite would gain control of the ministry were wide of the mark, and on key items, such as the attacks on Sandwich's conduct of the naval war (1779) and Shelburne's attempt to censure the ministry over Ireland and over public expenditure (1780), he was prominent in his loyalty. While he was no pro-Catholic, he accepted the Catholic Relief Bill introduced by Sir George Savile, with ministerial support, in 1778, and strongly resisted the efforts of the Gordon rioters to secure its repeal two years later. His brother Thomas, by then bishop of Lincoln, narrowly escaped death at the hands of the rioters.

After the defeat at Yorktown, North's ministry lost its majority in the House of Commons (although not in the House of Lords) and Thurlow was one of the king's most trusted advisers as he tried desperately, and unsuccessfully, to avoid the Rockinghamite alternative. When Rockingham formed his second ministry, in coalition with Shelburne, in March 1782, he was reluctantly obliged to retain Thurlow as lord chancellor. It was an uneasy arrangement. Thurlow opposed the ministry's economical reform proposals, notably the Contractors' Bill, and after Rockingham's death, on 1 July 1782, Thurlow grew rather more at ease in the new ministry headed by Lord Shelburne and purged of most of its Rockinghamites.

Although not on close personal terms with Shelburne, and without any illusions that the ministry would last, he gave it loyal support. When in February 1783 Shelburne's ministry was defeated in the House of Commons over the peace preliminaries with America, Thurlow's speeches helped to ensure that Shelburne was not defeated in the Lords. Shelburne none the less resigned, and the king again turned to Thurlow as confidential adviser. On the accession to office six weeks later of the Fox–North coalition, George III contemplated abdication and Thurlow was deprived of the great seal, which was placed in commission. His chagrin was increased by the appointment of his great rival, Alexander Wedderburn, Lord Loughborough, as one of the commissioners.

Return to office Thurlow stiffened George III's resolve to resist, and, if possible, to overthrow the Fox–North coalition. He alone of the king's leading servants—unlike Grafton, North, and Shelburne—had not deserted him in his hour of need. He was involved in the arrangement whereby the king, via Lord Temple, encouraged members of the House of Lords to vote against the coalition's India Bill in December 1783 and whereby the younger Pitt would form a ministry following its consequent dismissal. In the debates Thurlow spoke powerfully against the India Bill, denouncing in particular the proposed transfer of the East India Company's patronage to commissioners nominated by the coalition government. Should the king give the royal assent to the bill, Thurlow declared, he would 'take the diadem from his own head, and place it on the head of Mr Fox' (Cobbett, *Parl. hist.*, 24.125). On 23 December 1783, four days after Pitt's appointment as prime minister, Thurlow became lord chancellor for the second time. His return to the woolsack gave the insecure new ministry essential leadership in the House of Lords—especially important after Temple's enforced resignation on 22 December. Pitt's ministry, surviving early setbacks in the House of Commons, was secure in the Lords, and in March 1784 Pitt felt sufficiently confident to dissolve parliament. At that moment the great seal was mysteriously stolen from Thurlow's house in Great Ormond Street, an event which, though the subject of much amusement to caricaturists and satirists, had no political consequences. At the ensuing general election Pitt secured a Commons majority of well over one hundred, and Thurlow embarked upon his most harmonious period of high office.

Before Pitt fully established his ministry and became less dependent on the king, Thurlow provided vital ballast. He used all his eloquence to promote ministerial proposals, including those which were unpopular. Of his support for Pitt's Irish trade proposals in 1785 Charles Jenkinson wrote: 'In carrying the business through the House of Lords, the chancellor is the most firm and able person that government has, and I can assure you he is very zealous and steady' (*Buckinghamshire MSS*, 187). In 1788 the archbishop of Canterbury, John Moore, believed that all Thurlow's ill humour must be tolerated, since 'without him the House of Lords would be a wretched, insupportable place' (Ditchfield, 'Lord Thurlow', 72). The elevation of Thomas Thurlow to the see of Durham in 1787 cemented Thurlow's relationship with his cabinet colleagues. Even his opposition to mild measures of parliamentary reform in the House of Lords and his private criticism of the possibility of military intervention in the Netherlands in 1787 caused no serious friction. Bearing in mind that the ministry was divided over the abolition of the slave trade and never sponsored abolition officially, Thurlow's vehement denunciations of abolition were not inconsistent with cabinet membership.

Declining fortunes The causes of Thurlow's political decline lie in the Regency crisis of 1788–9 and in the impeachment of Warren Hastings. In the former, there is little doubt but that Thurlow was willing to compromise with the opposition, in the event of the king's permanent incapacity or death, in order to retain the great seal (and to deny it to Loughborough). He had a genuine sympathy with the prince of Wales's claim to an immediate regency; later on in his life he became a trusted confidant and adviser to the prince over the latter's debts and unhappy marriage to Princess Caroline. But in 1788–9 the verdict of Sir Gilbert Elliot that 'The Chancellor has been the whole of this time playing a shabby trimming game, keeping himself open to both parties till one should be completely victorious' (*Life and Letters*, 1.249–50) was uncomfortably accurate. By nominating Lord Grenville to the House of Lords in 1790 Pitt showed that he no longer had confidence in the lord chancellor's reliability. Although Grenville took care to consult Thurlow over important matters of policy, it was not long before the latter began to complain vigorously of neglect by the prime minister. His choleric outbursts and open criticisms of ministerial policy caused his relations with Pitt and Grenville to become increasingly strained. When he strongly (and abusively) attacked the Sinking Fund Bill in May 1792, Pitt and Grenville presented George III with an ultimatum: either Thurlow was to be dismissed, or Pitt would resign. If this was bluff, George III could not afford to call it, and, after vainly seeking a compromise through the mediation of Henry Dundas, he reluctantly consented to Thurlow's dismissal. This took place at the end of the session, in June 1792, and was sweetened by the grant of the barony of Thurlow of Thurlow, Suffolk, with a special remainder to his nephews; his pension was increased and he retained the tellership of the exchequer, which he had held since 1786. The news was greeted with disbelief, and at least one London newspaper, *The Oracle*, predicted his rapid return to office. He remained on friendly, if more distant, terms with George III, who commended his advice to the royal princes.

As lord chancellor Thurlow had presided over the opening years of Warren Hastings's impeachment in Westminster Hall, which began in February 1788. He formed a close personal friendship with Hastings, asserted his innocence, sought to nominate him for a peerage, and worked diligently on his behalf. Following his dismissal from office Thurlow continued to attend the Lords regularly, and he was among the majority of peers who voted for the acquittal of Hastings on 23 April 1795. Although he told his friend Lord Kenyon that he did not wish to waste his breath in a 'vain opposition' (Ditchfield, 'Lord Thurlow', 76), Thurlow did not hesitate to criticize the policies of his former cabinet colleagues, notably over the restrictive measures of 1794–5. As late as the session of 1801–2 he was present on more than half of the days when the Lords were in session, and he attacked the treaty of Amiens. Though his latter years were soured by the elopement of his daughter Caroline, he lacked neither means nor convivial company, encouraging younger lawyers he admired, including the future lord chancellor John Scott, Lord Eldon. He spent much time in spas and seaside resorts. He died at Brighton on 12 September 1806, one day before Charles James Fox, and was buried on 25 September in the Temple Church, London.

Assessment Thurlow's physical appearance was impressive. His features were dark and stern, and the ferocity of his demeanour could inspire respect, and sometimes fear. It occasionally gave rise to allegations that he was acting: Fox observed, 'It proved him dishonest, since no man could *be* so wise as Thurlow *looked*' (Campbell, 5.661). Many anecdotes surround his profanity of language and his unconcealed neglect of religious observance. As lord chancellor, however, he controlled considerable ecclesiastical patronage; according to *Drewry's Derby Mercury* of 2–9 December 1784 he disposed of church livings worth a total of £80,000 per annum. His preference was consistently exercised in favour of clergymen whose theological orthodoxy was not in doubt, and one of his ecclesiastical protégés was the ultra-orthodox Samuel Horsley, who became bishop of St David's in 1788. He could be a very loyal friend, personally kind (as to the ageing Samuel Johnson in 1784) and ready to forgive old enmities; one of his close friends in later life was the radical John Horne Tooke, with whom he shared classical and literary interests. Although he was caricatured as an inveterate reactionary in the age of the French Revolution, his opinions were far from predictable. He regarded military intervention in Europe with caution, and his public support for Pitt's bellicose stance towards Russia over Ochakov in 1791 was accompanied by private warnings.

Thurlow exploited his role as an outsider and preferred to stress aggressively, rather than to conceal, his relatively humble origins. Many observers emphasized the intimidatory power, as opposed to the intellectual depth, of his forensic and parliamentary skills. Charles Butler described him as 'a kind of guarda costa vessel, which cannot meet every turning and winding of a frigate that assails her, but, when the opportunity offers, pours a broad-side which seldom fails of sinking the assailant' (Butler, 201). He left no written legacy of legal wisdom; 'his way was to decide, not to reason', opined Lord Brougham (Brougham, 88). Holdsworth noted his 'imperfect mastery of principle' (Holdsworth, *Eng. law*, 12.323) but allowed that he made some contributions to the administration of equity law, notably in the protection of married women from undue pressure from husbands and other interested parties to use their powers of disposition unwisely. Campbell, who heard him speak on a divorce bill in the House of Lords on 20 May 1801, described him as 'this great imitator of GARAGANTUA' (Campbell, 5.476). He was one of the most eminent legal practitioners, if not theorists, of his age, and was the last of the great eighteenth-century lord chancellors.   G. M. DITCHFIELD

Sources R. Gore-Browne, *Chancellor Thurlow: the life and times of an XVIIIth century lawyer* (1953) · J. Campbell, *Lives of the lord chancellors*, 8 vols. (1845–69), vol. 5 · G. M. Ditchfield, 'Lord Thurlow', *Lords of parliament: studies, 1714–1914*, ed. R. W. Davis (1995), 64–78, 201–7 · *The correspondence of King George the Third from 1760 to December 1783*, ed. J. Fortescue, 6 vols. (1927–8) · *The later correspondence of George III*, ed. A. Aspinall, 5 vols. (1962–70) · *GM*, 1st ser., 76 (1806), 882–3 · *European Magazine and London Review*, 13 (1788) · *The manuscripts of the earl of Dartmouth*, 3 vols., HMC, 20 (1887–96) · *The manuscripts of the earl of Buckinghamshire, the earl of Lindsey … and James Round*, HMC, 38 (1895) · *The manuscripts of J. B. Fortescue*, 10 vols., HMC, 30 (1892–1927) · Cobbett, *Parl. hist.*, vols. 18, 24 · Farington, *Diary* · J. Cannon, *The Fox–North coalition: crisis of the constitution, 1782–4* (1969) · *Life and letters of Sir Gilbert Elliot, first earl of Minto, from 1751 to 1806*, ed. countess of Minto [E. E. E. Elliot-Murray-Kynynmound], 3 vols. (1874) · C. Butler, *Reminiscences*, 3rd edn, 1 (1822) · H. Brougham, *Historical sketches of statesmen who flourished in the time of George III*, 2nd edn, 6 vols. (1845) · E. Foss, *Biographia juridica: a biographical dictionary of the judges of England … 1066–1870* (1870) · Venn, *Alum. Cant.* · J. Venn and others, eds., *Biographical history of Gonville and Caius College*, 1: *1349–1713* (1897) · P. Langford, *Public life and the propertied Englishman, 1689–1798* (1991) · F. C. Mather, *High church prophet: Bishop Samuel Horsley (1733–1806) and the Caroline tradition in the later Georgian church* (1992) · J. A. Cannon, 'Thurlow, Edward', HoP, *Commons, 1754–90* · DNB

Archives BL, corresp. and MSS, Egerton MSS 2232, 3598 · CKS, family corresp. · NRA, corresp. and papers | Beds. & Luton ARS, corresp. with Lord Grantham · BL, corresp. with Lord Grenville, Add. MS 58938 · BL, corresp. with fifth duke of Leeds, Add. MSS 27916, 28061–28067 · BL, corresp. with first earl of Liverpool, Add. MSS 38192, 38307–38310 · Bodl. Oxf., corresp. with William Beckford · CKS, Camden MSS · CKS, Hibgame MSS · Hunt. L., HA 12836–12838 · Hunt. L., MO5148 · NMM, letters to Lord Sandwich · NRA, priv. coll., corresp. with Lord Kenyon · NRA, priv. coll., letters to Lord Shelburne · PRO, Chatham MSS 30/8 · PRO, letters to Lord Stafford and Lady Stafford, PRO 30/29 · Royal Arch., corresp. with George III · Sheff. Arch., corresp. with Edmund Burke; corresp. with second marquess of Rockingham

Likenesses G. Romney, oils, c.1780–1784, Inner Temple, London · attrib. G. Romney, oils, c.1780–1784, Inner Temple, London · J. Reynolds, oils, c.1781, Longleat, Wiltshire · J. Gillray, caricature, coloured etching, pubd 1791, NPG · S. Collings, engravings, 1792, repro. in S. W. Fores (Piccadilly) · J. C. F. Rossi, marble bust, 1801, Royal Collection; plaster replica, Inner Temple, London · T. Lawrence, oils, 1803, Royal Collection [*see illus.*] · T. Phillips, oils, 1806, NPG; on loan to law courts · T. Phillips, oils, 1806, NPG · T. Phillips, oils, 1807, Houses of Parliament · T. Phillips, engraving, pubd 1809 (after unknown portrait, 1807) · J. C. F. Rossi, bust, 1809, Royal Collection · J. C. F. Rossi, bust, 1809, NPG · attrib. R. Evans, oils, NPG · J. Reynolds, oils, Courtauld Inst. · G. Romney, oils, NPG; repro. in Gore-Browne, *Chancellor Thurlow, passim* · J. Sayers, caricatures, NPG · marble bust, priv. coll. · plaster medallion (after C. Andras), Scot. NPG · wax, priv. coll.

Wealth at death under £20,000—excl. landed property; property at Dulwich left to mistress: will, PRO, PROB 11/1449/758, fols. 389–95; Gore-Browne, *Chancellor Thurlow*, 351

Thurlow, Edward Hovell-, second Baron Thurlow (1781–1829), poet, was born on 10 June 1781 in the Temple, London, the first son of Thomas *Thurlow (1737–1791), bishop of Durham, and his wife, Anne (d. 1791), daughter of William Bere of Lymington, Hampshire. He was educated at Charterhouse School and at Magdalen College, Oxford,

matriculating in 1798, and graduating MA in 1801. He succeeded his uncle, Lord Chancellor Edward *Thurlow (1731–1806), to the barony of Thurlow in 1806, but did not take his seat in the House of Lords until 1810. In tribute to his grandmother, he took the additional name Hovell by royal licence on 8 July 1814.

In accordance with a custom frequent at this time, on 30 December 1785, then aged four, Thurlow was made one of the principal registrars of the diocese of Lincoln, and in 1788 he was made clerk of the custodies of idiots and lunatics. Later, he was appointed clerk of the presentations in the petty bag office (1796), patentee of commissions in bankruptcy (1803), and clerk of the Hanaper (1821). He retained all of these positions until his death.

On 13 November 1813 Thurlow married an actress, Mary Catherine (d. 1830), eldest daughter of James Richard Bolton, attorney; they had three sons, of whom Edward Thomas (1814–1857) succeeded his father in the title.

Hovell-Thurlow was a great admirer of Sidney, and his first publication was a private edition of the *Defence of Poesy*. His original poetry was published in several collections, along with some classical translations (1814) and an attempt to continue Shakespeare's *Tempest* in *Angelica, or, The Rape of Proteus* (1822). The reception of his work tended to be lukewarm or hostile. The *Edinburgh Review* (1814) lamented: 'his Lordship … loves the Muse with a warmth which makes us regret that the passion is not mutual', and Byron parodied him cruelly. On the other hand, Lamb praised his sonnet 'To a Bird, that Haunted the Waters of Lochen, in the Winter', which ends:

> Nature is always wise in every part.

Hovell-Thurlow died on 4 June 1829 in Regency Square, Brighton.   JESSICA HININGS

Sources E. H. Thurlow, *Poems on several occasions* (1813); repr. (1978) · *GM*, 1st ser., 83/1 (1813), 41 · *GM*, 1st ser., 99/2 (1829), 174–5 · Burke, *Peerage* · *EdinR*, 23 (1814), 411–24 · E. H. Thurlow, *Poems on several occasions* (1813); repr. (1978) · *Royal Kalendar* (1788–1829) · J. Martin, *A bibliographical catalogue of books privately printed* (1834) · *The life of Lord Byron, with his letters and journals*, ed. T. Moore, new edn (1847) · [J. Watkins and F. Shoberl], *A biographical dictionary of the living authors of Great Britain and Ireland* (1816) · *London Kalendar* (1797), 186 · P. W. Clayden, *Rogers and his contemporaries*, 2 vols. (1889), vol. 1, pp. 128–30 · DNB

Archives Bodl. Oxf., corresp. with John Nichols

Thurlow, Thomas (1737–1791), bishop of Durham, was born at Ashfield, Suffolk, the second son of Thomas Thurlow (bap. 1695, d. 1762), rector of Little Ashfield, and his wife, Elizabeth Smith (d. c.1736). Edward *Thurlow, first Baron Thurlow, was his elder brother. Thomas matriculated from Queen's College, Oxford, on 13 July 1754, and was a demy of Magdalen College from 1755 to 1759, when he was elected a fellow. He graduated BA on 11 April 1758, and proceeded MA on 9 March 1761, BD on 13 April 1769, and DD on 23 June 1772. In 1771 he became rector of Stanhope in Durham, and in the following year was appointed master of the Temple, a post held until 1787. On 2 November 1775 he was nominated dean of Rochester, and on 30 March 1779 he was consecrated bishop of Lincoln. On 13

March 1782 he became dean of St Paul's, but he resigned the office in 1787 on being translated to the see of Durham. He died in Portland Place, London, on 27 May 1791, and was buried in the Temple Church. He and his wife, Anne, daughter of William Bere of Lymington, Hampshire, who died in August the same year, left three daughters and two sons, Edward Hovell-*Thurlow (1781–1829), who in 1806 succeeded his uncle as second Baron Thurlow, and Thomas (b. 1788).

In 1780 Thurlow was in London during the Gordon riots and was among those attacked. He was rescued in a fainting state by a young law student who obtained refuge in a neighbouring house, from which he escaped over the roof wearing women's clothes. Thomas published a few sermons, but like many of his contemporaries was an indifferent preacher, although his elocution was excellent. He owed his advancement in the church to the advocacy of his brother, who overshadowed him, rather than to his own ability. He had business acumen in matters such as tithe, but diocesan affairs were left mostly in the hands of officials, of whom his second son, Thomas, became one in the Durham court of chancery. His income from the Durham palatinate and bishopric estates was considerable. He was, however, said to be a zealous patron of literary merit but there is no firm evidence of this. He was a persistent seeker of recipients for benefactions in his Lincoln diocese. Although retiring in manner in public, he was well liked in his private encounters and was a devoted and affectionate husband. No original portrait of him has been traced, and none exists either at the Temple or in the gallery of Durham bishops at Auckland Castle; but an anonymous engraving was done when he was bishop of Lincoln.   E. I. CARLYLE, rev. MARGOT JOHNSON

Sources Foster, *Alum. Oxon.* · J. R. Bloxam, *A register of the presidents, fellows … of Saint Mary Magdalen College*, 8 vols. (1853–85), vol. 6, pp. 296–9 · *Fasti Angl., 1541–1857*, [Canterbury] · Nichols, *Lit. anecdotes* · T. Campbell, 'Notes of seven visits to England', *EdinR*, 110 (1859), 322–42, esp. 322–9 · *N&Q*, 2nd ser., 9 (1860), 392 · H. D. Beste, *Personal and literary memorials* (1829), 225 · J. H. Jesse, *Memoirs of the life and reign of King George the Third*, 2nd edn, 3 vols. (1867), vol. 2, p. 265 · *Town and Country Magazine*, 18 (1787), 333–4 · *GM*, 1st ser., 61 (1791), 494 · *GM*, 1st ser., 61 (1791), 782 · U. Durham L., archives and special collections, CCB, 34457A · U. Durham L., archives and special collections, AUC 1/64, item 145 [Stanhope clergy visitation return, 774] · J. Ingamells, *The English episcopal portrait, 1559–1835: a catalogue* (privately printed, London, 1981) · J. Foster, *The peerage, baronetage, and knightage of the British empire for 1882*, 2 vols. [1882]

Archives U. Durham L., CCB, 34457A; AUC 1/64, item 145, Stanhope clergy visitation return, 774

Likenesses engraving, 1779–87, Auckland Castle, Co. Durham · line engraving, BM

Thurmond [*née* Lewis], **Sarah** (d. 1762), actress, was born at Epsom, Surrey. Her first recorded appearance on stage was in 1711, with Pinkethman's troupe at Greenwich, where John Thurmond (d. 1754) was a dancer and choreographer. The couple are said to have married in 1713; the baptism of Lewis, the son of John and Sarah Thurmond, on 28 October 1712 at St Martin-in-the-Fields may refer to a

different family, but their two daughters, Mary and Catherine, were baptized in London in 1727 and 1732 respectively. Between 1712 and 1715 Mrs Thurmond was in Dublin, where her husband's parents, John and Winifred Thurmond, were also on the stage. Confusion between the two John Thurmonds and the two Mrs Thurmonds is inevitable, but it seems likely that Sarah Thurmond acted at the Smock Alley Theatre. In 1715 all the Thurmonds returned to London, where Sarah's husband was announced to be dancing at Lincoln's Inn Fields on 2 June 1715. On 23 June Sarah, 'who never acted on this stage', appeared there for the first time, as Cosmelia, in Newburgh Hamilton's *The Doting Lovers, or, The Libertine Tamed*; she also spoke the epilogue. She played major roles in a variety of works that season, among them Portia in Lord Lansdowne's *The Jew of Venice* and Julia in Aphra Behn's *The False Count*. She remained at Lincoln's Inn Fields for four years, where her parts included the title role in Thomas Shadwell's *The Woman Captain*, Belinda in John Vanbrugh's *The Provoked Wife*, and Calista in Nicholas Rowe's *The Fair Penitent*.

In 1718 the Thurmonds moved to Drury Lane, where John became the dancing-master and, on 8 September, Sarah gave her first performance, as Aspasia in Beaumont and Fletcher's *The Maid's Tragedy*. She remained at that theatre until 1732. Among her later roles were Desdemona, Lady Macduff, Isabella in Richard Steele's *The Conscious Lovers*, and the title role in Rowe's *Jane Shore*. Her salary for the 1729 season was £166 plus benefit money. The range of her roles made her a 'lady utility' (Doran, 2.60). At the beginning of the 1732–3 season, she moved to Goodman's Fields Theatre, and made her début there on 18 October 1732 as Almeria in Congreve's *The Mourning Bride*, a role she had played previously at Drury Lane. She took with her some of her Drury Lane roles, and added others, including Polly in John Gay's *The Beggar's Opera*. Mrs Thurmond was joined at this theatre by her husband in December; they appear to have left Drury Lane because of a disagreement with the management there, and the following season many of the company moved elsewhere, returning only when the conflict was settled early in 1734. Here she extended her repertory to include Marcia in Joseph Addison's *Cato*, Lady Brute in *The Provoked Wife*, and the Queen in Dryden's *The Spanish Fryar*. Her last appearance was on 5 May 1737, as Lady Wronghead in Vanbrugh's *The Provoked Husband*.

John Thurmond died in 1754, leaving half of his estate to Sarah and one-quarter each to their two daughters, Mary and Catherine. Sarah Thurmond died in London in 1762, and was buried on 18 May at the church of St Paul, Covent Garden. Her will, dated 13 July 1761, left everything to Catherine, with instructions to look after her sister, Mary Jackson, and her children. Catherine married John Addy in May 1762 and had died by 6 June 1764, when her husband took over the administration of Sarah's estate.

Contemporary comments on Sarah Thurmond's performances are scarce. In 1729 several oblique references were made to her appearing drunk on stage. Aaron Hill described her as having an affected style of delivering poetry, '*whining* out good Verses, in a *Drawl* so unpleasantly extended' (*The Prompter*, 27 Dec 1734), but W. C.

Chetwood thought she had 'an amiable person and a good voice', and commended her retirement from the stage: 'in her full and ripe performance, and, at that time, left behind her but few that excelled her' (*DNB*).

JANE GIRDHAM

Sources Highfill, Burnim & Langhans, *BDA* · E. L. Avery, ed., *The London stage, 1660–1800*, pt 2: *1700–1729* (1960) · A. H. Scouten, ed., *The London stage, 1660–1800*, pt 3: *1729–1747* (1961) · *DNB* · J. Doran and R. W. Lowe, *'Their majesties' servants': annals of the English stage*, rev. edn, 2 (1888), 60 · J. Milhous and R. D. Hume, eds., *A register of English theatrical documents, 1660–1737*, 2 (1991), 736 · W. R. Chetwood, *A general history of the stage, from its origin in Greece to the present time* (1749) · *IGI*

Thurnam, John (1810–1873), psychiatrist and ethnologist, was born on 28 December 1810 at Lingcroft, near York, the son of William Thurnam, manufacturer, and his wife, Sarah Clark. He belonged to a Quaker family. After a private education, which included study in London at Dermott's school of anatomy, Soho, and the Westminster Hospital, Thurnam became a member of the Royal College of Surgeons in 1834. He also became a licentiate of the Royal College of Physicians in 1843, a fellow in 1859, and graduated MD at King's College, Aberdeen, in 1846.

Having served as resident medical officer at the Westminster Hospital from 1834 to 1838, Thurnam was appointed medical superintendent of the Friends' Retreat in York, of which his father had been a director. He held this post until 1849. At that time the Wiltshire County Asylum was being built and Thurnam was appointed superintendent. It opened in 1851 and he remained in active charge until his death. On 18 June 1851 he married Frances Elizabeth, daughter of Matthew Wyatt, a barrister, and sister of Sir Matthew Digby Wyatt (1820–1877). They had three sons.

In 1843 Thurnam published *Observations and Essays on the Statistics of Insanity, and on Establishments for the Insane*, the work for which he is best-known. This monograph contained a reprint of the *Statistics of the York Retreat*, first issued in 1841, together with a historical sketch of that institution. Thurnam's appointment as resident medical officer was instrumental in breaking the tradition of lay therapists started by William Tuke, and mirrored a wider national trend of medical practitioners' taking over control of the care of the insane.

Thurnam was a founder member of the Medico-Psychological Association in 1841, and remained a committed member of the association, twice serving as president. Unusually for an asylum superintendent, Thurnam found time to research and publish. While at Westminster Hospital he had gained some reputation for his observations on aneurysm of the heart, and at the York Retreat he developed an interest in phrenology. He gave a paper entitled 'Scientific cranioscopy of Professor Carus' at the British Association for the Advancement of Science in September 1844, and began to apply phrenological assumptions to his care of patients. As with James Cowles Prichard, another psychiatrist from a Quaker background, this area of study appears to have kindled an interest in ethnology and comparative craniology.

After moving to Wiltshire, Thurnam developed this enthusiasm, and with Joseph Barnard Davis published in 1865 a work in two volumes called *Crania Britannica*. In the same year he wrote an important paper, 'Two principal forms of ancient British and Gaulish skulls', which was reprinted from the *Memoirs* of the Anthropological Society of London (1, 1865). Thurnam was indefatigable in exploring ancient British barrows, and reported his findings to the Society of Antiquaries (of which he was a member) in 1869. During the later years of his life he collected a large number of skulls and objects of antiquity. The former were transferred to the University of Cambridge, the latter are in the British Museum. Although much of the craniometric and anthropometric data generated by men like Thurnam, and later in the nineteenth century by the Italian psychiatrist and sociologist Cesare Lombroso is now discredited as attempting to support theories associating biological race with levels of cultural and intellectual development, Thurnam made a significant contribution to racial typings.

Contemporaries considered one of Thurnam's papers to be particularly important, 'Synostoses of the cranial bones regarded as a race character' (*Natural History Review*, 1865). Thurnam believed he had recognized the obliteration of the sutures of the skull, which he had observed in the long-headed crania of the Stone Age, but not in the short-headed crania of the Bronze Age, believing this to be a racial characteristic. Thurnam was noted to be an efficient and zealous man beloved of his patients, who was described as dapper and professional by colleagues. He died at the Chapelry of St James, Bishop's Cannings, near Devizes, Wiltshire, on 24 September 1873. His wife survived him.

A. R. URQUHART, rev. NICK HERVEY

Sources *Journal of Mental Science*, 19 (1873), 644–5 · *Medical Times and Gazette* (11 Oct 1873), 424 · *Medical Times and Gazette* (25 Oct 1873), 479 · A. Digby, *Madness, morality and medicine: a study of the York Retreat, 1796–1914* (1985) · m. cert. · d. cert. · *IGI* · private information (1898) · personal knowledge (1898) · *London and Provincial Medical Directory* (1860) · B. M. Marsden, *The early barrow diggers*, [new edn] (1999)
Archives Bodl. Oxf., corresp. with Sir J. G. Wilkinson
Wealth at death under £5000: resworn probate, June 1875, *CGPLA Eng. & Wales* (1873)

Thursfield, Sir James Richard (1840–1923), naval historian and journalist, was born at Kidderminster on 16 November 1840, the younger son of Thomas Thursfield MRCS, and his wife, Sarah, daughter of Thomas Pardoe. On his father's death in 1855, the family moved to London. He was educated at Merchant Taylors' School (1855–9), and at Corpus Christi College, Oxford, gaining firsts in classical moderations (1861) and *literae humaniores* (1863). He was elected to a fellowship at Jesus College, Oxford, in 1864, and held a series of college and university posts until obliged to resign in 1881 after his marriage, in 1880, to Emily Elizabeth Hannah, eldest daughter of the Revd Samuel Asher Herbert, rector of St James's, Gateshead; they had a son and a daughter. On returning to London, Thursfield was appointed by the editor, Thomas Chenery, to the staff of *The Times* as a leader writer. Thursfield demonstrated in his writing his wide knowledge of public

Sir James Richard Thursfield (1840–1923), by unknown photographer

affairs, and though his demeanour was quiet and retiring he boldly maintained views that were not always consonant with the policy of the paper. This was accepted, if sometimes reluctantly, even by Chenery's successor, G. E. Buckle, who valued and encouraged a collegiate editorial spirit among his leader writers. Thursfield never wrote in support of a policy of which he disapproved: in 1908, for example, he refused to write a critical editorial, at Buckle's dictation, on the correspondence between Lord Tweedmouth and the Kaiser over the naval estimates.

In 1887 Thursfield was asked to cover the annual naval manoeuvres. An early, enthusiastic disciple and promoter of Captain A. T. Mahan, the American naval historian, he very soon established himself as both an outstanding correspondent and a naval authority. Apart from his regular columns in The Times, Thursfield published a collection of essays, written jointly with Sir George Sydenham Clarke (later Lord Sydenham of Combe), entitled The Navy and the Nation (1897). He also wrote Nelson and other Naval Studies (1909), and Naval Warfare (1913). He was invited to lecture on naval reform and strategy to the Staff College, Camberley, and the Royal United Service Institution. He enjoyed the confidence of successive first lords of the Admiralty, Unionist and Liberal, from Lord George Hamilton to Tweedmouth. Most importantly and significantly, Thursfield was for a time Admiral John Fisher's most valued and valuable press coadjutor in a wide-ranging campaign for naval reforms. Fisher respected Thursfield as 'a great student of naval affairs', and valued his articles, always 'close and precisely reasoned, unadulterated by vituperation' (Marder, 1.137–9; 2.64, 394). Thursfield was invariably cautious and discreet in what he wrote, unlike so many other and more colourful press allies of Fisher. Prince Louis of Battenberg, when director of naval intelligence, recognized that Thursfield's great strength was 'never being afraid to state a contrary view'. When his opinions no longer coincided with those of Fisher, the admiral accused the naval correspondent of 'not smiting as he should', and

more unfairly of being 'senile' and 'under Northcliffe's thumb' (ibid.).

In his political judgements, although careful and judicious, Thursfield was never pusillanimous. He did not welcome but did not fear the censures of editors, proprietors or friends. During the darkest days of the First World War, his independent, fair-minded comments tempered the prejudices of friends. He wrote to Theresa, Lady Londonderry: 'Until this war is at an end I shall have no party politics' (Londonderry MSS, NIPRO). He criticized 'Mr Garvin's blatantly partisan bombastics', in The Observer. To radical tory friends he was prepared to defend the universally execrated Winston Churchill: 'He has his faults, but has great qualities too … To genius much should be forgiven for what should we do without it' (ibid.).

Although specializing in naval affairs, Thursfield wrote on general political topics as well. From 1891 he was in charge of The Times's 'Books of the week', which in 1902 became The Times Literary Supplement; he became its first editor and a frequent contributor. He was chosen by Northcliffe as much the best candidate to write a history of The Times, but after three years he abandoned the project. His short biography, Peel (1891), had earlier earned critical acclaim. He was made an honorary fellow of Jesus College in 1908, and was knighted in 1920. He died at his house, 57 Rotherswick Road, Golders Green, on 22 November 1923. Thursfield's son, Rear-Admiral Henry George Thursfield (1882–1963), who after his retirement from the navy in 1932 wrote extensively on naval matters, was editor of Brassey's Annual (1936–63), and, like his father before him, was a naval correspondent of The Times (1936–52).

A. J. A. MORRIS

Sources The Times (23 Nov 1923) · [S. Morison and others], The history of The Times, 3 (1947); 4/1 (1952) · Fear God and dread nought: the correspondence of Admiral of the Fleet Lord Fisher of Kilverstone, ed. A. J. Marder, 3 vols. (1952–9) · A. J. A. Morris, The scaremongers: the advocacy of war and rearmament, 1896–1914 (1984) · The Times (27 Nov 1923) · WW · PRO NIre., Londonderry MSS
Archives NMM, corresp. and papers | CAC Cam., letters from first Baron Fisher · News Int. RO, papers related to The Times · NL Scot., corresp. with Lord Haldane · NMM, letters to Sir Julian Corbett · PRO NIre., Londonderry MSS
Likenesses photograph, repro. in History of The Times, 3, part 1, facing p. 604 [see illus.] · portrait, repro. in The Times (24 Nov 1923)
Wealth at death £1084 14s. 1d.: probate, 3 Jan 1924, CGPLA Eng. & Wales

Thurso. For this title name see Sinclair, Archibald Henry Macdonald, first Viscount Thurso (1890–1970); Sinclair, Robin Macdonald, second Viscount Thurso (1922–1995) [see under Sinclair, Archibald Henry Macdonald, first Viscount Thurso (1890–1970)].

Thurstan (c.1070–1140), archbishop of York, was the son of a married priest from the Bessin named Anskar (Anger), and his wife, Popelina, and was born in the Bessin area of Normandy.

Youth and career to 1114 Thurstan may have received his education at Caen, or in the Bayeux of Bishop Odo, from where a number of aspiring clerics crossed the channel. His own family moved to England during the time of Bishop Maurice of London (1086–1107) from whom Anskar obtained the prebend of Kentish Town in the cathedral church of St Paul, while his sons came to hold prebends in the same church: Audoin (later bishop of Évreux) succeeded to his father's prebend of Kentish Town when he died some time after 1104, and Thurstan acquired that of Consumpta-per-Mare. The brothers also held positions as chaplains of Henry I, Thurstan being first mentioned in this capacity in 1103. For his service to the king he held the churches and chapels of Tickhill Castle, Stoneleigh, Shorne, and Cobham. Apart from his occasional attestation of royal charters, and the possibility (suggested by John of Hexham) that he was associated with Archbishop Thomas (II) in the foundation of the Augustinian priory of Hexham in 1113, the only recorded event of Thurstan's life before 1114 was his visit (date unknown) to Cluny, where he made a vow that he would at some time in his life take the habit of a Cluniac monk. It was a pledge that he was to fulfil in his final days.

Archbishop of York: relations with Canterbury, 1114–1118
Thurstan was still in subdeacon's orders when, at Winchester on 15 August 1114, six months after the death of Thomas (II) in February 1114, Henry I appointed him archbishop of York. This was done without reference to the chapter of the cathedral, but no opposition was forthcoming. Thurstan was ordained deacon by William Giffard, bishop of Winchester (d. 1129), some time between September and December 1114 and in December was enthroned archbishop at York by the bishop of Coventry. In the weeks that followed he began to learn something of his new diocese. According to Hugh the Chanter he visited Durham, where he met Turgot, bishop of St Andrews, during his final illness, although as Turgot died in August 1115 Hugh may have conflated the events of two summers. He also visited Hexham, and on his return to York conferred with the chapter about the matter of the profession of obedience to Canterbury. He declined an invitation from Ralph d'Escures, archbishop of Canterbury (d. 1122), to journey to Canterbury to be ordained priest and consecrated archbishop, and instead crossed to Normandy on Christmas day, intending to ask permission of the king to go to Rome to put his case before the pope. Thurstan had no intention of accepting ordination from the archbishop of Canterbury or any of his suffragans lest this should prejudice his case when the question of the primacy of Canterbury was raised, as he anticipated it would be. Therefore, with the king's permission, he accepted ordination as priest from his own suffragan, Ranulf Flambard, bishop of Durham (d. 1128), at Bayeux on 6 June 1115, although his request to go to Rome was denied. In September that year Thurstan was present at the king's council in Westminster, and complained to the king of the delay in receiving consecration. Henry ordered Archbishop Ralph to consecrate Thurstan, and in the presence of witnesses who included the archbishop of Rouen and the bishops of Lisieux and Durham, Thurstan made his request. Ralph agreed to consecrate him, provided that he make profession of obedience. This Thurstan refused to do.

The opposition of Thurstan to the claims of Canterbury to primacy over York dominates Hugh the Chanter's highly favourable account of Thurstan, as indeed it dominated the first five years of Thurstan's pontificate. Thurstan had made his opinion quite clear to the king: it was unheard of elsewhere for one metropolitan to profess obedience to another, and this he was not prepared to do. Thurstan asked the king's leave to appeal to Rome, but Henry refused. Moreover, Henry was incensed when the chapter of York sought and obtained a papal letter confirming their election of Thurstan, forbidding him to make profession, and permitting him to accept consecration from his own suffragans. The king now lent his backing to the archbishop of Canterbury, and, seeing that he lacked royal support, Thurstan resigned during a council held at Salisbury in March 1116. However, despite Henry's support for Canterbury's case the king did not wish to see Thurstan resign, and for the next eighteen months Thurstan accompanied the royal court and continued to be addressed as archbishop. The king continued to refuse to allow Thurstan to go to Rome, fearing that he would be consecrated by the pope. Both the archbishop of Canterbury and the chapter of York appealed to papal authority, and in response to a letter from Paschal II, Henry took the decision to restore Thurstan to the see of York.

Consecration and return to York, 1118–1126 In January 1118 on the death of Paschal II, who had supported the York cause, Thurstan returned to Normandy to ask the king's permission to seek the advice of the new pope, Gelasius II, but Henry again refused. The letters dispatched by Gelasius show him too to have been sympathetic to York's cause, but he died on 28 or 29 January 1119, and it was his successor, Calixtus II (r. 1119–24), who took steps to end the uncertainty. He summoned Thurstan to his council at Tours on 22 September 1119, which Thurstan attended with the king's permission, and on 19 October he consecrated him archbishop at Rheims, two days before the opening of his council there. The English and Norman bishops who arrived the following day too late to object to the consecration refused to communicate with Thurstan. Pope Calixtus bestowed the pallium on Thurstan on 1 November. Henry's anger at Thurstan's disobedience—according to Eadmer he had forbidden him to accept consecration should the pope offer it—led him to forbid Thurstan to return to York. Henry and the pope met at Gisors in November 1119 but Henry refused to pardon Thurstan, and on his return to England confiscated his estates.

Thurstan remained in the entourage of the pope from his consecration until March 1120, during which time he assisted Calixtus, and secured papal bulls of confirmation for religious houses in his diocese. He also attempted to placate Henry I by arranging a treaty of peace between him and the king of France. Thurstan parted from the pope at Gap on 6 March, and spent the remainder of the year in France. He was present when Adela, countess of Blois, the mother of the future King Stephen, made her profession as a nun at Marcigny in April. Henry I, now finding Thurstan useful in negotiating with the king of France, was softening towards him, and in May he agreed to allow Thurstan to enter Normandy provided he did not return to England before the king made his final judgment. Thurstan's presence is recorded at the Council of Beauvais held by the papal legate in October 1120. Early in 1121, in response to a papal threat to place England under an interdict should Thurstan's exile be prolonged further, Henry took the decision to recall Thurstan, and in February 1121, seven years after his appointment as archbishop, he was able to enter York as a consecrated archbishop. He marked his return by celebrating the feast of St Peter's Chair (22 February) and by remitting chrism payments from the diocese, and in the following month with Bishop Ranulf Flambard of Durham he heard the claims of the monks of Durham to Tynemouth church.

This was not, however, the end of the primacy question. A new archbishop of Canterbury, William de Corbeil (d. 1136), was elected, on the advice of Thurstan, in February 1123. But Thurstan refused to consecrate him when he insisted on being recognized as primate of all Britain, and William was consecrated on 18 February 1123 by his suffragans. Both William and Thurstan journeyed to Rome to put their case before the pope. It was on this occasion, according to Hugh the Chanter, that the Canterbury party resorted to producing forged charters in an attempt to prove their case. Thurstan made a second journey to Rome, in October 1125, and eventually Canterbury's claim to primacy was overruled, and its archbishop compensated with a papal legation. This marked the end of the most bitter phase of the Canterbury–York dispute, although at the Christmas court of 1126 in London the archbishops quarrelled again over Thurstan's right to have his cross borne aloft before him in the southern province.

Relations with the northern bishoprics It was not just in relation to Canterbury but also in Scotland that Thurstan had to define his authority. In 1119 and again in 1121 he obtained papal bulls addressed to all the Scottish bishops enjoining them to profess obedience to him, orders the pope repeated in 1122. John, bishop of Glasgow (d. 1147), consecrated by the pope at Thurstan's request, refused to profess obedience to York, something about which Thurstan complained during his visit to the papal curia in October 1125. Robert (d. 1159), prior of the Augustinian house of Scone, was named by Alexander I (r. 1107–24) as bishop of St Andrews in late 1123 or 1124, but his consecration was delayed by the dispute over the demand for York's profession to Canterbury. At the instance of Pope Honorius II (r. 1124–30) the question of Robert's consecration was discussed at a meeting between Alexander's successor, David I (r. 1124–53), and the papal legate Giovanni da Crema at Roxburgh in late 1125, and John of Glasgow was sent as David's envoy to the papal curia to seek metropolitan status for St Andrews. The matter seems to have been settled by compromise, and Thurstan consecrated Bishop Robert at York in the spring or early summer of 1127 without obtaining a profession of obedience, but without prejudice to the church of York. In July of that year Thurstan was at Roxburgh with King David when Bishop Robert, in their presence, released the priory of Coldingham from the payment of certain dues. Thurstan revived the ancient

Scottish see of Galloway (Whithorn), whose bishop, Gilla-Aldan, he consecrated in York in 1125.

It was perhaps the difficulties he encountered in Scotland that encouraged Thurstan to develop a further diocese in the north of England. In 1133 he received papal permission for the creation of a see at Carlisle. Plans had evidently been long in the making. An Augustinian priory was planted in the city in 1122, and it may have been that the idea for a new bishopric in an area where Scottish bishops had from time to time exercised authority was discussed in 1126, when Henry I and King David of Scotland met to ask Thurstan to request the pope to adjourn the hearing of the case of the Scottish bishops. It is from 1126 that Thurstan appears to have dropped his claims to metropolitan authority over Scotland. As first bishop of Carlisle, Thurstan appointed Athelwold (Athelwulf; d. 1156/7), prior of the prestigious Yorkshire Augustinian house of Nostell. It was a shrewd choice: Athelwold was a former royal chaplain, and it was the patronage of Henry I that had raised Nostell to its position of pre-eminence in the diocese. Athelwold continued to hold the priorate of Nostell in plurality with the bishopric, thus enabling the revenues of his priory to shore up the financial position of the new see. The creation of the bishopric of Carlisle was a real success for Thurstan, even though it was not until the early thirteenth century that the see became firmly established.

The patron of the Cistercians As archbishop of York, Thurstan was an energetic churchman. He continued the consolidation of the chapter of York by creating two prebends: that of Bramham comprised three churches granted by Robert Fossard, and was assigned to the priory of Nostell; that of Salton was held by the canons of Hexham. Thurstan issued decrees confirming the status of the lands of deceased canons of York, and granted the cathedral school 100s. a year, 40s. to be drawn from the archdeaconry of the East Riding and 30s. from the Romescot, or Rome penny, of the archdeaconry of Nottingham. He did not neglect the collegiate churches of the diocese, and restored lands to the church of Ripon, assigning them for a prebend there, and created a further prebend at Southwell.

However, it is for his encouragement of the monastic orders within his diocese that Thurstan is perhaps best known. He was himself the founder of two religious houses, and of a small hospital, that of St Mary Magdalen, Ripon. At a date between c.1125 and 1133 he established the first post-conquest nunnery in the north, that of St Clement's, situated just outside the walls of York. He attempted, unsuccessfully, to persuade Christina of Markyate to become its first prioress. The foundation of St Clement's appears to have acted as a catalyst, for the establishment of further houses for religious women followed in quick succession. Thurstan's second monastic foundation was less carefully planned, and came about as a result of Thurstan's intervention, in his capacity as ordinary of the diocese, in affairs at St Mary's Abbey, York. The arrival of the Cistercian monks in the city of York, on their way from the king's court to the site of their first northern plantation at Rievaulx, in March 1132, exercised a profound effect on some of the black monks of St Mary's. They began to demand reform in their own house, on the lines of Cistercian austerity. The abbot refused to listen, and the reforming party within the abbey turned to Archbishop Thurstan for advice. Thurstan was familiar with Cistercian reform, having been associated with Henry I and Walter Espec (d. 1158) in the foundation of Rievaulx. In October 1132 Thurstan conducted a visitation of the abbey, evidently intending to act as mediator. However, Abbot Geoffrey had summoned to his side the abbots and priors of other Benedictine houses, and far from bringing reconciliation the archbishop's visit ended with the ejection from the abbey of a party of thirteen monks, including the prior.

Thurstan took the monks into his household, and after spending Christmas on the archiepiscopal manor of Ripon, he provided them with land on which to settle. This was the site in the valley of the River Skell of what was to become the Cistercian abbey of Fountains. Thurstan was clearly sympathetic to the aspirations of the new orders. Not only did he encourage the foundation of Rievaulx, and some years earlier that of the Savigniac house of Furness, but he wrote personally to Roger de Mowbray asking him to afford protection to the monks of Furness who were to found Byland Abbey on Roger's estates. Historians have debated the likelihood that Thurstan was the author of the fierce, anti-Cluniac, invective enshrined in the so-called 'Letter of Thurstan'. This exists in several copies, including two dating from the late twelfth century and deriving from Cistercian houses—Fountains itself and its daughter house of Sawley—and was incorporated into the fifteenth-century manuscript of the *Narratio de fundatione* of Fountains Abbey. The letter is a polemic, designed to explain and justify the actions of the St Mary's monks in demanding reform. Many features, including its address to the archbishop of Canterbury and the criticism of the Cluniac monks whom Thurstan would choose to join in his final days, have led some historians to judge the letter a fabrication. The matter is not easily resolved, but the critical role played by Thurstan in the foundation of Fountains and the dispersal of the Cistercians in the north cannot be doubted.

The supporter of the Augustinians; the leader of the north Thurstan's major contribution to the monastic settlement of the diocese was less spectacular than the events of late 1132. From his early years in the north he encouraged the barons of the region to found and endow monastic houses, and priories of Augustinian canons found special favour with him. Charters of foundation bear witness to Thurstan's endeavours in this respect. He and Henry I were closely involved in the transformation of the hermitage of Nostell into an Augustinian house, and under his guidance barons established Augustinian canons at Guisborough, Kirkham, Bolton, Drax, and Worksop. The regular canons were then in fashion, and particularly favoured

by bishops, since as monk–priests they might serve in parish churches. Thurstan's hand may have also been behind the type of endowment that the Yorkshire Augustinians received, for their founders and patrons conveyed to them the patronage of a large number of parish churches. Thurstan doubtless looked on the foundation of religious houses by the laity as something to be encouraged for its own sake; but in promoting the cause of the canons he was also securing for himself a way of bringing order and discipline, as well as pastoral care, to a large and unwieldy diocese. It was this that led him to associate the Augustinian priories of Nostell and Hexham with prebends in York Minster, and to appoint the Augustinian prior of Nostell as first bishop of Carlisle. He clearly took a personal interest in Hexham, making gifts of relics, books, vestments, candlesticks, and ornaments. His *acta* bear witness to his concern to strengthen the possessions and privileges of the northern religious houses by issuing charters of confirmation, and in addition he took the opportunity, when he was in Rome, to secure papal confirmation and privileges for them.

Thurstan's activities were not confined to his own diocese, for he was a figure of European standing. He acted as a papal judge-delegate, hearing the case between the bishops of St David's and Llandaff (1132). In 1138 he wrote to the pope to advise against the election of Abbot Anselm of Bury St Edmunds (d. 1148) as bishop of London, and indeed urged his deposition as abbot; and in 1139 after the death of his brother, Audoin, bishop of Évreux, he wrote to the canons of Évreux requesting them to allow Gilbert the Chamberlain to continue to reside in the house that Thurstan had purchased for the canons.

Thurstan came to be regarded as the leader of the north. His negotiations with David I in 1137 helped to prevent a Scottish invasion of Northumbria, and when in 1138 the truce disintegrated and the men of Scotland turned south to invade, it was Thurstan who assembled the northern barons at York to plan their defence of the shire. Although too weak to appear on the field of battle—by this time illness compelled him to be carried in a litter—he handed over the banner of St Peter to the English army, and placed by their side against the Scots his suffragan Ralph Nowell, bishop of Orkney. The army inspired by Thurstan defeated the Scots at the battle of the Standard, on Cowton Moor near Northallerton, in August 1138.

Resignation and death By 1138 Thurstan was approaching seventy years of age, and ill health prevented his attending the peace conference in Carlisle in November and the legatine council in December. Just over a year later, on 25 January 1140, before the altar of St Andrew in his cathedral church, he resigned his office. If Richard of Hexham is to be believed, he had been trying to secure the succession to York of his brother Audoin, using as an intermediary at Rome Richard, abbot of Fountains. However, Audoin died first, having become an Augustinian canon at Merton in July 1139. Thurstan retired to the Cluniac priory of Pontefract, and in accordance with his youthful vow he took the habit of a Cluniac monk. He died on 6 February and was buried in the priory church of St John the Evangelist, Pontefract, before the high altar.

Historical significance Thurstan was in one sense a member of the 'old order', the son of a married priest, and member of an ecclesiastical dynasty. He secured the appointment of his nephew, Osbert de Bayeux, to the archdeaconry of Richmond, and may have sought to pass on the diocese of York to his brother. He was appointed archbishop by the king with no reference to the chapter of York. And, in the tradition of Thomas (I) of York (*d.* 1100), he was a vigorous champion of the cause of York against Canterbury. But Thurstan also stepped over into the new world of the twelfth century. He was not afraid to appeal to papal authority over that of the king. His long period of office saw the consolidation of the chapter of York, and those of the collegiate churches of his diocese, and the remarkable spread and growth of the monastic orders in which Thurstan himself was a prime force. John of Hexham praised his steadfastness, his sense of principle, his devotion to the cause of religious women, his frugal life, his generosity in alms-giving, and pastoral care. Thurstan achieved and retained the affection and respect of the king whom he opposed, the barons of the north whom he inspired in battle, and the church of York which he served.   JANET BURTON

Sources *Hugh the Chanter: the history of the church of York, 1066–1127*, ed. and trans. C. Johnson (1961) · *Eadmeri Historia novorum in Anglia*, ed. M. Rule, Rolls Series, 81 (1884) · *Willelmi Malmesbiriensis monachi de gestis pontificum Anglorum libri quinque*, ed. N. E. S. A. Hamilton, Rolls Series, 52 (1870) · J. E. Burton, ed., *York, 1070–1154*, English Episcopal Acta, 5 (1988) · 'Historia regum', Symeon of Durham, *Opera*, vol. 2 · John of Hexham, 'Historia regum continuata', Symeon of Durham, *Opera*, vol. 2 · *Florentii Wigorniensis monachi chronicon ex chronicis*, ed. B. Thorpe, 2 vols., EHS, 10 (1848–9) · J. Raine, ed., *The priory of Hexham*, 1, SurtS, 44 (1864) · J. R. Walbran, ed., *Memorials of the abbey of St Mary of Fountains*, 1, SurtS, 42 (1863) · J. Raine, ed., *The historians of the church of York and its archbishops*, 3 vols., Rolls Series, 71 (1879–94) · Ordericus Vitalis, *Eccl. hist.* · R. Howlett, ed., *Chronicles of the reigns of Stephen, Henry II, and Richard I*, 1, Rolls Series, 82 (1884) · *The letters of Sr Bernard*, trans. B. S. James (1953) · St Aelred [abbot of Rievaulx], 'Relatio de standardo', *Chronicles of the reigns of Stephen, Henry II, and Richard I*, ed. R. Howlett, 3, Rolls Series, 82 (1886) · R. Hexham, 'De gestis regis Stephani et de bello standardi', *Chronicles of the reigns of Stephen, Henry II, and Richard I*, ed. R. Howlett, 3, Rolls Series, 82 (1886) · D. de Sainte-Marthe and others, eds., *Gallia Christiana in provincias ecclesiasticas distributa*, 16 vols. (1715–1865) · D. Nicholl, *Thurstan: archbishop of York, 1114–1140* (1964) · F. Barlow, *The English church, 1066–1154: a history of the Anglo-Norman church* (1979) · C. N. L. Brooke, 'The composition of the chapter of St Paul's, 1086–1163', *Cambridge Historical Journal*, 10 (1950–52), 111–32; repr. in *Medieval church and society* (1971) · M. Brett, *The English church under Henry I* (1975)

Thurston, Frederick John (1901–1953), clarinettist, was born on 21 September 1901 at the barracks in Lichfield Road, Whittington, Staffordshire, the younger of the two children (he had an elder sister) of Sergeant Frederick Thurston, military bandsman, of the 3rd South Staffordshire regiment, and his wife, Emma Goodman (*b.* 1866x9). He spent his childhood in Oxford, where he attended St Mary and St John School, and his father, when not away on band engagements, taught him the clarinet. At the age of

ten he was noticed by Adrian Boult, then an undergraduate at Christ Church, and it was thanks to Boult's encouragement that in 1920, by now a member of the Cheltenham Municipal Orchestra, Thurston entered for, and won, an open scholarship to study with Charles Draper at the Royal College of Music, where Boult was teaching. After hearing Thurston play his clarinet concerto with the college orchestra in March 1922, Sir Charles Stanford wrote a letter of congratulation on his excellent performance. During his time at the college, and for some time afterwards, Thurston was able to survive financially through the generosity of Oscar Street, an amateur clarinettist. On 30 July 1927 he married Eileen (1901/2–1947), a violinist, daughter of Dr A. C. King-Turner of Fairford, Gloucestershire; they had one daughter.

In December 1922 Thurston joined the first BBC music ensemble, which went on the air on 23 December with eight players, broadcasting from the 2LO studio in Marconi House. After the BBC's move to Savoy Hill the studio orchestra grew, becoming known as the 2LO Wireless Orchestra in 1924. Thurston, the principal clarinettist, signed a contract in August 1924 agreeing to play in at least six performances a week. Although this was not a full-time contract, and he appeared with other London orchestras in the years that followed, it was his main employment. When the BBC Symphony Orchestra was founded in 1930, Thurston was one of those asked to join, as principal clarinettist. The BBC Symphony Orchestra became the leading British orchestra, with Boult as chief conductor from 1931, but was directed also by conductors such as Bruno Walter and Arturo Toscanini; the latter, who first visited in 1935, became Thurston's idol. Although members of the orchestra were not allowed to accept outside engagements without permission from the BBC, making it difficult to pursue a solo career, Thurston began to attract the attention of contemporary British composers, who were inspired by his playing to write for the clarinet. He was largely responsible for the acceptance of the clarinet as a solo instrument by British composers, as British audiences had rarely heard anything written for the clarinet other than Victorian salon pieces until he began performing such early twentieth-century masterpieces as Debussy's *Rhapsody*, Berg's *Four Pieces*, and Stravinsky's *Three Pieces*. On 17 February 1933 he made his Wigmore Hall début in the first performance of Arthur Bliss's quintet for clarinet and strings, with the Kutcher Quartet, and he went on to give the first performances of Arnold Bax's sonata with Harriet Cohen in 1935, Gordon Jacob's quintet for clarinet and strings with the Griller Quartet in 1943, and John Ireland's *Fantasy-Sonata* with Kendall Taylor in 1944: these last two works were dedicated to him.

Thurston left the BBC Symphony Orchestra in 1946, and in the next seven years gave the first performances of works by most of the leading British composers, many of them dedicated to him: these included Phyllis Tate's sonata for clarinet and cello (1947), Alan Rawsthorne's quartet for clarinet and strings (1948), Herbert Howells's clarinet sonata (1948), and the clarinet concertos by Malcolm Arnold (1949) and Gerald Finzi (1949). He also introduced

British audiences to the clarinet concertos by Darius Milhaud (in 1947), Aaron Copland and Paul Hindemith (both in 1951), and Carl Nielsen (in 1952), and to the *Pastorale variée* by the Israeli composer Paul Ben-Haim in 1952. With the bassoonist Archie Camden he gave the first London performance of Richard Strauss's *Duet concertino* in July 1949 in a Promenade Concert conducted by Sir Malcolm Sargent at the Royal Albert Hall. Although most of the music he performed was modern, he played the Mozart clarinet concerto many times, including an annual performance of the work at the Proms. He became principal clarinettist of the Philharmonia Orchestra in 1949, but this did not prevent him from touring abroad: in 1949 he went on a British Council tour of Yugoslavia and Bulgaria, and in 1950 toured Germany as soloist with the Jacques Orchestra.

An inspiring and much loved teacher, Thurston taught at the Royal College of Music from 1934 until his death, this period including the war years when the BBC Symphony Orchestra was evacuated first to Bristol and then to Bedford; when Ruth Railton founded the National Youth Orchestra of Great Britain in 1948 she invited him to coach the woodwind section. The only recording with which he was satisfied was one of the Bliss quintet which he recorded with the Griller Quartet in 1935; he preferred the excitement and spontaneity of live performances. His clarinet playing was distinguished by his firm, clear tone, without vibrato, a style very different from that of the other leading clarinettist of his generation, Reginald Kell. After Toscanini had conducted his first rehearsal with the Philharmonia Orchestra in September 1952 he told Walter Legge, its founder, 'That first clarinet—*that* is a great artist! He plays with the accents of a human voice' (Pettitt, 66). With his former pupil Alan Frank, Thurston published a clarinet tutor in 1939, and he brought out three books of passage studies (1947); his book *Clarinet Technique* was completed after his death by Thea King and John Warrack and published in 1956.

Thurston was made a CBE in 1952. On 22 January 1953 he remarried: his second wife was a former pupil, the clarinettist Thea King (*b.* 1925), later Dame Thea King, daughter of Henry Walter Mayer King, manufacturer of agricultural machinery, of Hitchin, Hertfordshire. A keen golfer, a member of the Savage Club, and a *bon viveur*, Thurston was also a heavy smoker, and developed lung cancer. Although he returned to the concert platform after having one lung removed in 1952, he died of cancer on 12 December 1953 in the London Hospital, Whitechapel, London.

ANNE PIMLOTT BAKER

Sources P. Weston, *Clarinet virtuosi of the past* (1971), 271–4 · C. Bradbury and T. King, eds., *Frederick Thurston, 1901–1953: a centenary celebration* (2001) · S. Pettitt, *Philharmonia Orchestra* (1985) · N. Kenyon, *The BBC Symphony Orchestra: the first fifty years, 1930–1980* (1981) · *The Times* (14 Dec 1953) · *New Grove*, 2nd edn · WW · private information (2004) [Dame Thea King, widow] · b. cert. · m. certs. · d. cert. · CGPLA Eng. & Wales (1954)
Archives SOUND BBC Sound Archives
Likenesses photograph, repro. in P. Weston, *Clarinet virtuosi*, pl. 32, facing p. 145

Wealth at death £8,448 16s. 1d.: probate, 1954, CGPLA Eng. & Wales

Thurston, Herbert Henry Charles (1856–1939), Jesuit, liturgical scholar, and spiritualist investigator, was born at 6 Ratcliffe Terrace, London, on 15 November 1856, the only child of George Henry Thurston, MRCS, and his wife, Theresa Ellen (*née* Tuck). He was baptized a Catholic at the church of Sts Peter and Paul, Clerkenwell, on 9 December of the same year. Thurston was educated at the seminary of St Malo (1868–9), at Mount St Mary's Jesuit school in Derbyshire (1869–71), and at Stonyhurst College in Lancashire (1871–4), where he completed his schooling. A precocious and introspective child, he described himself at thirteen as 'a solitary man thrown upon the world without friends or resources' (Crehan, 4). His lifelong interest in liturgical matters seems to have been as well developed by the age of eleven as was his love of cricket.

Having resolved to join the Society of Jesus, Thurston underwent the usual noviciate at Manresa House, Roehampton, from 1874 until 1876, when he took his first vows. He then spent a further year at Manresa, studying classics. He matriculated at the University of London in 1874, won a Latin exhibition in 1877, and was awarded his BA, along with a university prize, in 1878, by which time he had moved to St Mary's Hall, Stonyhurst. From 1877 to 1880 he studied scholastic philosophy, and in 1878 brought out the first of many articles which he was to publish over the course of a long and prolific life. He taught at Beaumont College (1880–87), studied theology at St Beuno's College (1887–91), and spent a year as a staff writer for *The Month* at Farm Street, the Jesuit House, in Mayfair, before returning to Roehampton for his third year's noviceship. He was ordained priest on 21 September 1890 and was made prefect of studies of the Jesuit school at Wimbledon before returning, in 1894, to Farm Street, which was to be his permanent home for the next forty-five years.

Thurston's scholarly articles on literary, historical, and controversial matters number nearly 800, and were published over a period of sixty-one years, mainly in *The Month*, *The Tablet*, and the *Dublin Review*, but also in *Studies*, the *Universe*, the *Catholic Times*, *Light*, and elsewhere. Among his contributions to *The Month* were an enquiry into familiar prayers and a series of investigations into popular devotions; the latter included findings on the origins of the rosary which aroused controversy, especially in Dominican circles. Thurston contributed more than 150 articles to the *Catholic Encyclopedia*, including such sensitive entries as 'England before the Reformation', 'Mary Tudor', 'Popular devotions', 'Roman Catholic', 'Shakespeare', 'Thomas Becket', 'Virgin Mary', and 'Witchcraft', while his contributions to the *Dictionary of Ethics and Religion*, edited by James Hasting, included 'Jesuits' and 'Inquisition'. He edited the folio edition of T. E. Bridgett's *History of the Holy Eucharist in Great Britain*, co-edited the Westminster Library, and re-edited Alban Butler's *Lives of the Saints* (1926–38). He also wrote various pamphlets for the Catholic Truth Society and published more than a dozen books, including *The Church and Spiritualism* (1933), *No*

Popery (1930), and *Beauraing and other Apparitions* (1934). *The Physical Phenomena of Mysticism* (1952), *Surprising Mystics* (1955), and *Ghosts and Poltergeists* (1953) were published posthumously by his biographer and fellow Jesuit, Joseph Crehan.

Thurston's writings were marked by painstaking research and a refusal to allow pious sentiment, tact, or his own pride in the English Catholic tradition to cloud his scholarly judgements. His reputation for exposing popular legends of the saints and pious myths led to the apocryphal story that he had been begged by a dying Jesuit to 'spare the blessed Trinity' (Crehan, 66). His equally impartial scrutiny of the claims of spiritualists and psychics led some orthodox Catholics to fear that his treatment of the paranormal was too sympathetic to be compatible with his priesthood. But this same quality made him, as was tacitly recognized by many of his Catholic contemporaries, a strong apologist for Catholicism, and has given his work enduring value.

Despite his legendary scepticism, Thurston's faith appears to have been untroubled: his entry into the Society of Jesus proceeded without drama, and he practised devotions of the sort which he was popularly believed to have debunked, being particularly attached to the rosary and to St Theresa of Lisieux. He was said to have been a popular confessor, and he instructed and received into the Catholic church approximately ninety converts. A man of robust health, a fact which he attributed to his avoidance of doctors, Thurston spent most of his life in study, but was also a great walker: he regularly walked 5 miles to Hampstead to say mass at The Nook nursing home, and even in his seventies he was said to have walked the 20 miles to Lord Russell of Killowen's house at Tadworth. Those who knew him attested to his gentleness and old-world courtesy, and one remembered how 'when he was sad or gay, the soft brown eyes and the nervous hand with the long fingers ever betrayed his feelings' (Crehan, 75).

At the age of eighty-two Thurston fell and developed heart trouble. He was sent to The Nook nursing home, where he remained for six months, continuing to work when able. He died on the evening of 3 November 1939. His requiem mass was celebrated at Farm Street on 6 November and he was buried at Kensal Green Roman Catholic cemetery.   MARY HEIMANN

Sources J. Crehan, *Father Thurston: a memoir with a bibliography of his writings* (1951) • J. Murray, 'Father Herbert Thurston, S. J.', *The Month*, 174 (Dec 1939), 492–502 • J. Murray, *The Tablet* (11 Nov 1939), 565–7 • *Dictionary of Catholic Biography* (1961), 1122–3 • F. C. Burnard, ed., *The Catholic who's who and yearbook* (1934), 480 • b. cert.

Archives Archives of the British Province of the Society of Jesus, London, corresp. and papers | Archives of the British Province of the Society of Jesus, London, Crehan MSS • Auckland Institute and Museum, letters to F. J. Moss

Likenesses photograph, 1920?–1939, Archives of the British Province of the Society of Jesus, London

Thurston, John (1774–1822), draughtsman, was born at Scarborough and educated at the Hornsey Academy. He commenced his career as a copperplate-engraver working under James Heath, whom he assisted on two of his chief plates, *The Death of Major Peirson*, after J. S. Copley, and *The Dead Soldier*, after Joseph Wright of Derby. Later he took up wood-engraving, and eventually he devoted himself exclusively to designing book illustrations. In this he was highly successful, and most of the editions of the poets and novelists published during the first twenty years of the nineteenth century, especially those issued by the Chiswick Press, were embellished by his pencil. Many of Thurston's drawings were engraved on copper for Sharpe's and Cooke's classics and similar works, but the bulk of them, drawn on the block, were cut by Luke Clennell, Robert Branston, Charlton Nesbit, John Thompson, and other able wood-engravers. Among his designs of this class are the illustrations to James Thomson's *Seasons* (1805); James Beattie's *Minstrel* (1807); J. Thomas's *Religious Emblems* (1809), a much admired work which was reissued in 1816 and published in Germany in 1818; Shakespeare's works (1814); Somerville's *Rural Sports* (1814); James Puckle's *The Club* (1817); and William Falconer's *The Shipwreck* (1817).

Thurston's drawings, outlined in pen or pencil and tinted with India ink, were pleasing though somewhat stiff affairs. They were admirably adapted to the wood-engraver's art, which was carried to its greatest perfection under his influence. Thurston was for a time 'the principal artist in London who had any repute as a designer on the wood' (Redgrave, *Artists*, 431), and he made a significant contribution to the formation of a modern school of wood-engraving. He was elected an associate of the Society of Painters in Water Colours in December 1805 but contributed only to the exhibition of 1806, sending five Shakespearian groups; he was also an occasional exhibitor at the Royal Academy from 1794 to 1812. Being of a delicate constitution and retiring nature, Thurston was personally little known; he died at his house at Holloway, London, in 1822, his life being shortened by overwork in pursuit of his art. He had two sons, G. and J. C. Thurston, who practised as artists and occasionally exhibited at the Royal Academy.

F. M. O'DONOGHUE, *rev.* MARK POTTLE

Sources W. Chatto and J. Jackson, *A treatise on wood engraving* (1839) • W. J. Linton, *The masters of wood-engraving* (1889) • R. K. Engen, *Dictionary of Victorian wood engravers* (1985) • S. H. Pavière, *A dictionary of British sporting painters* (1965) • Redgrave, *Artists*, 2nd edn • Mallalieu, *Watercolour artists*, vol. 1 • B. Stewart and M. Cutten, *The dictionary of portrait painters in Britain up to 1920* (1997) • Bryan, *Painters* (1903–5)

Thurston, Sir John Bates (1836–1897), colonial governor, was born in London on 31 January 1836. He was the eldest son of John Noel Thurston (1802–1847) and Eliza, *née* West (1807–1873), both from Bath, the short-lived father sprung from a family long established at Thornbury, the mother a painter; and he was brought up latterly in Jersey until on 20 April 1849, fatherless and poor, he went to sea as an apprentice for Liverpool shipowners. 'I began life at sea', he once warned a Melbourne luncheon gathering of investors in Fiji who were disappointed by his refusal to allow alienation of Fijian land or open access to Fijian labour, 'and I preferred stormy to fine weather' (Scarr, *I, the Very Bayonet*, 5).

Thurston had made voyages to India and Australia. An unsuccessful foray in 1853–4 to the goldfields was followed by return to the sea, first as mate in a Sydney schooner trading to the Pacific islands, next in a brig to Mauritius. Then a botanical voyage to Rotuma in 1864–5 ended in shipwreck. Rescued and, bound south for Sydney, arriving *en route* in Fiji again in June 1865, he found the British consul there in need first of a clerk and then of a successor, who would be faced with much more than mere consular duties. Coincidentally, Thurston acquired in Fiji, on 20 July 1867, a wife much older than himself, the formidable, twice-married, Mauritius-born Marie Valette Olsson, *née* Prince (d. 1881), with whom he had no children. His second marriage, on 14 January 1883, was to Amelia Murray, *née* Berry, with whom he had two daughters and three sons; when it took place he had long justified the nickname, given him by the high chief Ratu Seru Cakobau, of *Na Kena Vai*—the Spearhead, the Very Bayonet. Fiji's hierarchical socio-political structures rendered the archipelago very capable of creating an independent political identity in the eyes of the world, but already the islands were on the verge of becoming a crypto-European colony through the influx of cotton planters, mostly without much capital or knowledge of cotton culture either, whose general attitude by 1871 was profoundly racist.

Thurston's opposition to the settlers' argument that all power passed from Fijian chiefs along with the land they were selling to Europeans appeared in the *Fiji Times* when he was establishing a new plantation himself; and he was actually recruiting labour for it in the New Hebrides, when settlers formed the Cakobau government under the, in their intention, nominal kingship of the *vunivalu* of Bau, Ratu Seru Cakobau. Thurston first mocked but then, at the *vunivalu's* request, joined this government, as a means of averting racial war. He turned government's focus toward securing Fijian sovereignty and equality before the law, tried to bring a vacillating but interfering Britain to decide between annexation and *de jure* recognition by sending London a question that was misinterpreted there as an offer of cession such as Fijians by now were unwilling to make, and then protected Fiji's *de facto* independence against the resulting British commissioners. One of them, Commodore J. G. Goodenough RN, had a bankrupt brother-in-law among the pro-annexation planters' leaders.

Thurston succeeded in making the first offer of cession in early 1874 a conditional one, with safeguards for Fijians. He made it plain the clause ruling Fijian landownership in the final document of 10 October 1874 would have to be interpreted liberally; and then, by force of character, knowledge, and initially through support of the first governor, Sir Arthur Hamilton Gordon, he startled the local white and adjacent Australasian colonial world by surviving and ruling.

Since from about 1871 Thurston never changed, his administration as colonial secretary and then as governor was conducted on the principle that Fiji was not a 'white man's country', and neither was the rest of the western Pacific. The necessity of finding more labour than the health of Fijian society would permit for the nascent sugar industry in Fiji made the colony, from 1879, increasingly an Indian country, however, at Gordon's instance; but the main influx of Indian indentured labour took place after Thurston's premature death and, given his view of Fijians' own interests, would never have been countenanced by him. If, through successive international commissions and conferences during the 1880s, he could have made high commission policy binding on France, Germany, and America, too, white settlement and the extension of colonial power in the western Pacific would have stopped with the annexation of Fiji. In a system there which looked seriously oppressive only to interested Europeans and uninformed theoreticians of a later age, Fijian self-rule was conducted, with threats of Fijian revolt when it was done otherwise, through a tier of local councils ascending to the *boselevuvakaturaga* or great chiefly council, which itself always had room for able commoners and in Thurston's day actively encouraged them. In the high commission territories of the western Pacific, sale of alcohol, arms, and dynamite by British subjects to islanders was forbidden, much as labour recruiting for plantations there under no colonial government was restricted; and by the early 1890s, as high commissioner, Thurston would have forbidden all labour recruiting, in islanders' interests, if the French, Germans, and Queenslanders could have been brought to agree.

A man short in stature, surrounded by commonly tall Fijians, Thurston was sometimes opprobriously represented by Europeans as an especially great friend to the chiefs, one of whom was his foster son; and he would respond by drawing attention to frequent and savage lectures he read chiefs in government office on their liking for other men's wives or personal attachment to public moneys. His understanding of Fijian societies was not to be lightly challenged; he stood between the indigenous community and exploitation, and without his continued precedence through the 1870s, 1880s, and 1890s Fijians might very well have ended up as subdued as the Maori, whose subordination to white settlers' rule he denounced as an object lesson in bad imperial policy. The well-educated and soldierly twentieth-century Fijian leader Ratu Sir Lala Sukuna, who as a child knew Thurston, looked back to his time as something of a golden age. Men of most races knew there was a power in the western Pacific then—principled, tenacious, uncommonly well informed, and inimitably sardonic. Thurston, who was made a KCMG in 1887, died in harness, at sea, of some form of muscular collapse beyond the diagnostic science of his day, while leaving Fiji for treatment, on 7 February 1897. He was buried on 11 February in the Melbourne general cemetery in what was intended by his foster son Ratu Josefa Lalabalavu to be a temporary grave preparatory to a return to Fiji, which was never to be made.

DERYCK SCARR

Sources D. Scarr, *I, the Very Bayonet* (1973), vol. 1 of D. Scarr, *The majesty of colour: a life of Sir John Bates Thurston* · D. Scarr, *Viceroy of the Pacific* (1980), vol. 2 of D. Scarr, *The majesty of colour: a life of Sir John Bates Thurston* · b. cert.

Archives National Archives of Fiji, journal · NL Aus., journals, diaries, and notebooks · RBG Kew | BL, letters to Lord Stanmore, Add. MS 49204 · Bodl. RH, Anti-Slavery Society MSS
Likenesses Ball, wood-engraving (after photograph), NPG · photograph, priv. coll.
Wealth at death approx. £1325: private MSS, Fiji

Thurston, Joseph (1704–1732),

Thurston, Joseph (1704–1732), poet, was born on 16 June 1704 and baptized on 18 June in Colchester, the son of Joseph Thurston (1672/3–1714), lawyer, of Little Wenham, Suffolk, and Mary (*bap.* 1677, *d.* 1736), eldest daughter of Sir Isaac Rebow MP (*d.* 1726). His father was descended from a line of wealthy Colchester woollen drapers, and was recorder of Colchester; his maternal grandfather, a wealthy clothier descended from Dutch immigrants, was the leading whig in Colchester, a town of which he was, on different occasions, high steward and mayor. Joseph was the eldest son and fifth child (two girls had died in infancy). He was educated at Westminster School (admitted February 1716), before being admitted on 13 April 1720 as a fellow commoner to Gonville and Caius College, Cambridge. There is no record of his graduating. He was admitted to the Inner Temple on 25 July 1719 but not called to the bar. He was friendly with William Broome, Pope's co-translator, and was perhaps known to Pope, though he was unrelated to the Mr Thurston, master in chancery— that is, Mark Thurston (1700–1749)—who handled the affairs of Pope's half-sister.

Joseph Thurston's verse derives for the most part from Pope. His first volume, *Poems on Several Occasions* (1729), contains love poems and light verse on subjects such as chess and the tea-table. *The Toilette* (1730, two editions) and a more substantial mock-heroic poem, *The Fall* (1732), owe much to *The Rape of the Lock* but have merits of their own. However, Thurston's progressively more ambitious career as a minor poet was soon cut short. He died, unmarried, on 22 December 1732 and was buried on 29 December at Little Wenham. He was survived by his mother, two sisters, and a younger brother, Thomas, who was his residuary legatee and who sold the family seat at Little Wenham in 1765. All the verse mentioned above was reprinted in *Poems on Several Occasions* (1737). JAMES SAMBROOK

Sources VCH Essex, vol. 9 · C. Partridge, 'The Thurstons of Colchester', *Essex Review*, 60 (1951), 216 · monumental inscriptions in All Saints' Church, Little Wenham, Suffolk · J. Venn and others, eds., *Biographical history of Gonville and Caius College*, 2: 1713–1897 (1898) [annotated copy, Gonville and Caius College, Cambridge] · *Old Westminsters*, 2.919 · *The correspondence of Alexander Pope*, ed. G. Sherburn, 3 (1956), 7, 24 · GM, 1st ser., 2 (1732), 1126 · W. C. Metcalfe, ed., *The visitations of Essex*, 2, Harleian Society, 14 (1879), 698 · R. P. Bond, *English burlesque poetry, 1700–1750* (1932); repr. (New York, 1964)
Wealth at death considerable; incl. much property in Suffolk and Essex: will, 28 Nov 1732

Thurston [née Madden], Katherine Cecil (1875–1911),

Thurston [*née* Madden], **Katherine Cecil** (1875–1911), novelist, was born at Wood's Gift, co. Cork, on 18 April 1875, the only child of Paul Madden, banker, and his wife, Catherine Barry, both of Wood's Gift. Madden was chairman and director of the Ulster and Leinster Bank and a close friend of Charles Stewart Parnell. He was elected mayor of Cork and took a leading part in local politics on the nationalist side. Katherine Madden was privately educated at home. In 1901 she married the novelist Ernest Charles Temple Thurston.

Thurston's career as a writer began with *The Circle* (1903), which was less sensational than her subsequent novels. It was the publication of *John Chilcote, M. P.* (1904; published simultaneously in the United States as *The Masquerader*) which made her famous. Originally serialized in *Harper's Bazaar*, the story was set against a political backdrop and was a novel of impersonation and mistaken identity which she handled with much skill and force. It was dramatized by her husband with considerable success and two cinematic versions were later produced. None of her subsequent works attained the same degree of popularity. *The Gambler* (1906), a brightly written study of Irish life and scenery, was followed by *The Mystics* (1907) and *The Fly on the Wheel* (1908), novels with more conventional plots but of great psychological power. In *Max* (1910) Katherine Thurston repeated with less success the theme of impersonation, this time involving a change in gender. In all her work a genuine gift for story-telling is combined with a fluent style and intellectual insight.

Thurston was vivacious and lively and much in demand as a speaker. She divorced her husband on 7 April 1910. She suffered periodic bouts of epilepsy and died from asphyxia at 13 Morrison Island, co. Cork, on 5 September 1911. Contrary to the coroner's findings, however, the circumstances of the death suggested the possibility of suicide. She had been due to remarry later in the month. Thurston was buried in the family grave at Cork.

G. S. WOODS, rev. SAYONI BASU

Sources 'Introduction', in K. Thurston, *The fly* (1987) · *The Times* (7 Sept 1911) · R. Welch, ed., *The Oxford companion to Irish literature* (1996) · *The Athenaeum* (9 Sept 1911), 297 · private information (1912) · CGPLA Eng. & Wales (1911)
Archives NL Scot., papers incl. corresp. and manuscripts
Wealth at death £14,659 15s. 3d.: probate, 22 Dec 1911, CGPLA Eng. & Wales

Thurtell, John (1794–1824),

Thurtell, John (1794–1824), murderer, born on 21 December 1794, was the eldest son in the large family of Thomas Thurtell (1765–1846), merchant (and in 1828 mayor of Norwich), and his wife, Susanna. The family home was at Lakenham, Norwich, and Thurtell may have received the rudiments of education at Norwich grammar school. After five years as a second lieutenant in the Royal Marines he became in 1814 a bombazine manufacturer, but went bankrupt in 1821 and moved to London. His venture of running a public house in Long Acre soon failed. He then acted intermittently as a trainer and backer of pugilists. Robustly built and muscular, he was an amateur boxer and had already been prominent in prize-fighting circles in his Norwich days. George Borrow's *Lavengro* (1851) gives a memorable account of him at one such fight. His downward progress continued as he lost heavily at gambling. In June 1823 he and his brother Thomas, in the teeth of the evidence indicating arson, were awarded £1900 in their action against the County Fire Office over a warehouse fire. Payment was, however, withheld pending an indictment for conspiracy to defraud. Thurtell's desperate financial situation was aggravated by continued gambling, in which he was no match for crooked adversaries. Among these was William Weare of Lyon's Inn, a former waiter and professional gamester against whom Thurtell bore a grudge for cheating him of £300 at cards. He persuaded Weare to accompany him out of London on 24 October 1823. He may have been seeking revenge for the lost £300; he may have been hoping that Weare would be carrying a sizeable sum of money. For whatever reason, he was determined on murder.

Thurtell had two accomplices, William Probert and Joseph Hunt. It was to Probert's cottage in Gill's Hill Lane, near Radlett, Hertfordshire, that the gig carrying Thurtell and Weare headed. Probert and Hunt followed on behind. Once in the lane Thurtell shot Weare at point-blank range with a pistol, but the bullet glanced off the victim's cheekbone. He then cut Weare's throat and jammed the pistol into his skull. Probert and Hunt arrived shortly afterwards and helped to dump the body in a pond in Probert's garden, but later it was transferred to a more distant pond. Thurtell had mislaid the pistol and knife, which were discovered by two labourers. An investigation soon led to the arrest of the three suspects, and Hunt, against a promise of his life, lost no time in disclosing where the corpse was. The magistrates' examination touched off an outburst of sensation-mongering, making the case the first trial by newspaper and the most notorious of the decade. Liberal use of engravings secured the future of illustrated crime journalism; broadsheets, chapbooks, and ballads flooded the streets. The case was also taken up on stage, even before the trial, with a play called *The Gamblers*, in which appeared the very horse and gig used by Thurtell.

Probert turned king's evidence. In accordance with the custom of the time the accused men had to defend themselves. No confession of guilt entered Thurtell's measured speech. The best passages were of his own composition; the judge described them as 'eminently manly, energetic, and powerful'. Hunt could utter no more than one sentence before having his plea read for him. Both were found guilty and sentenced to death. Thurtell showed remarkable sang-froid throughout. One full day elapsed between sentencing and hanging. During it, Thurtell was anxious to learn the result of the big prize-fight of the day before, and repeatedly assured Hunt that he was forgiven. He appeared just as self-possessed on the scaffold outside Hertford gaol on 9 January 1824. The inglorious Hunt had his sentence commuted to transportation to Botany Bay.

The Gill's Hill murder took powerful hold of the popular imagination, despite its bungling brutality. The fever aroused by press and pamphlets was heightened by Thurtell's studied composure during his final week and his perceived fall from respectability through evil acquaintance. Relics were much sought after. Bits of Thurtell's corpse disappeared when it was dissected in front of a throng at St Bartholomew's Hospital. Memorabilia were preserved in several museums. The skeleton eventually passed to the Royal College of Surgeons of England, where the skull was displayed. The case was manna from heaven for the moralists of post-Regency England, who inveighed against the twin evils of gambling and pugilism. Magistrates cracked down on the ring. The card-playing, prize-fighting, horse-racing, and cock-fighting set known as the Fancy faded away. The affair was treated by a remarkable array of authors: De Quincey, Borrow, Bulwer-Lytton, Carlyle, and Dickens all made use of it; Lamb, Thackeray, FitzGerald, and Browning were intrigued by it. Walter Scott made a detour on the way from London to Scotland in 1828 to visit the scene of the crime, and revelled in the lines ascribed to William Webb (which Browning also admired):

> His throat they cut from ear to ear,
> His brains they battered in,
> His name was Mr William Weare,
> Wot lived in Lyon's Inn.

ANGUS FRASER

Sources A. Borowitz, *The Thurtell–Hunt murder case* (1988) · E. R. Watson, ed., *Trial of Thurtell and Hunt* (1920) · A. Fraser, 'Two blockheads … and a dark lane', *Antiquarian Book Monthly Review*, 19 (1992), 112–17
Archives Aldenham School, Elstree · BL, s/m 6497 d.1
Likenesses T. Medland, stipple, pubd 1823, BM · W. Mulready, pencil sketch, 1823, V&A · death mask, 1824, Castle Museum, Norwich · H. White, group portrait, woodcut, BM · group portrait, etching, BM, NPG

Thwaites, Edward (*bap.* 1671, *d.* 1711), Anglo-Saxon and Greek scholar, was born at Crosby Ravensworth, Westmorland, and baptized there on 15 November 1671, the son of William Thwaites, a resident there. He attended a school in Kendal, before being admitted a batteler at Queen's College, Oxford, where he matriculated on 22 October 1689, aged eighteen; he graduated BA in 1694 and MA in 1697. At Queen's he quickly came under the influence of the enthusiasm for Anglo-Saxon studies promoted by George Hickes, who came to live at Gloucester Green, in Oxford, in 1696 and encouraged Thwaites to undertake the publication of texts in Old English. Hickes suggested that he prepare an edition of the Alfredian Orosius (a project in fact undertaken by William Elstob), while Humfrey Wanley had earlier proposed for him an edition of parts of the Bible in Old English, which Thwaites realized with his edition of the Heptateuch in 1698.

In the same year, 1698, that he was ordained priest (2 January) Thwaites was admitted fellow of Queen's (31 October) and designated Anglo-Saxon preceptor. His letters to Hickes and Wanley during the years 1697–1703 reveal how quickly he learned Old English, how busy he was with his own work and his teaching, and how, with his efficient and brisk approach, he acted as project manager for a major co-operative enterprise in Anglo-Saxon studies that was to eventuate in 1703–5, under Hickes's name, as the *Thesaurus linguarum septentrionalium*. It was Thwaites—as one learns from his businesslike and sometimes brusque letters urging Wanley to hurry up with his copy, and his sending material to Hickes as the latter moved between safe houses—who kept the *Thesaurus* on track and ensured its publication. He also took his teaching duties very seriously, recognizing that the necessary textbooks, dictionaries, and grammars of Old English were lacking or unsuitable for beginners, and setting out, with the help of others, to supply that want himself. In 1699 he was appointed dean of Queen's, and attempted to improve college discipline. By all accounts he was a good-humoured, energetic man and rather handsome. Elizabeth Elstob represented him as St Gregory within the initial G that begins the Old English text of her *English-Saxon Homily on the Birthday of St. Gregory* (1709, p. 1) with her own portrait in the initial of the first word of the adjacent column.

In addition to his work on the *Thesaurus* and his dedicated and inspirational teaching of Old English, Thwaites's most important contribution to Anglo-Saxon studies was his 1698 edition of hitherto unedited parts of the Old Testament in Old English, including Genesis, Exodus, Leviticus, Numbers, Deuteronomy, Joshua, Judges, and the book of Job, together with the apocryphal Judith and the Gospel of Nicodemus. Several colleagues, among them Hickes, Wanley, Gibson, and Nicolson, showed an active interest in the project during its preparation. Although some of his contemporaries criticized Thwaites's edition—partly because it included apocryphal material, partly for its lack of a Latin translation and notes—it was for its time a ground-breaking enterprise and one that was not repeated until 1922, when S. J. Crawford edited the Heptateuch afresh, using a different base manuscript. Thwaites's edition had been based on Bodleian MS Laud misc. 509, and his text was reprinted, with some emendations, by C. W. M. Grein in 1872. Thwaites dedicated his edition to George Hickes, at that time still proscribed as a nonjuror, and this caused some political embarrassment to the vice-chancellor, who threatened to suppress the edition unless Thwaites cut out the dedication. He bluntly refused—and prevailed.

Thwaites published two other works in the Old English field, *Notae in Anglo-Saxonum nummos* (1708) and *Grammatica-Anglo-Saxonica ex Hickesiano Linguarum septentrionalium thesauro excerpta* (1711). The second of these, as its name suggests, was an abridged and simplified version of the Old English grammar in Hickes's *Thesaurus*, for student use. In addition Thwaites was probably the main contributor to the Anglo-Saxon dictionary printed in 1701 that bears the name of Thomas Benson. This was a revised but abbreviated version of Somner's dictionary, and Thwaites's copy of Somner, with his additions and annotations revealing his wide reading in Old English texts, is extant as Bodleian MS Ballard 51. Two projects that Thwaites began but never finished were an edition of the Old English *Pastoral Care* and a gospel harmony.

Besides his work in Old English, Thwaites evidently had considerable expertise in Greek. His first published work was an edition of *Dionysii orbis descriptio* (Oxford, 1697). In 1704 he was appointed university lecturer in moral philosophy, in 1707 regius professor of Greek, and in 1708

Whyte's professor of moral philosophy. In 1709 he published another Greek text, the works of St Ephraim the Syrian: *Ephraem Syrus, Graece e codicibus manuscriptis Bodleianis*—an edition that has not been superseded. Although some, like Thomas Hearne, had a rather poor opinion of Thwaites's performance in these offices his alleged neglect of them is likely to have been influenced by the worsening state of health that afflicted him from at least 1705 until his death. He suffered from tuberculosis, which first affected his right leg at the knee, causing him such pain that he was moved to have his leg amputated above the knee by Queen Anne's surgeon, Charles Bernard. There are several graphic descriptions by contemporaries of Thwaites's courage and determination during this operation, which he survived. Queen Anne is said to have been so impressed by Bernard's account of Thwaites's behaviour that she granted him £200 and probably influenced his appointment to the chair of Greek. The disease later spread to his lungs and reduced him to 'a meer Sceleton' (*Remarks*, 3.287). In the last year of his life he retired to Littlemore, near Oxford, where he died on 12 December 1711. He was buried, at about 5 pm on the day of his death, in Iffley church, 'where a small black slab upon the altar-floor marks the spot of his interment' (Nichols, *Lit. anecdotes*, 4.147) and gives his age at death, erroneously, as forty-four. He died intestate—survived by his mother, his father having predeceased him—and, as Hearne confirms, his college laid claim to his possessions, his books being sold at Oxford in May 1712.

MARGARET CLUNIES ROSS and AMANDA J. COLLINS

Sources 'Memoranda of Thwaites the Saxonist', *GM*, 2nd ser., 2 (1834), 260–63 · H. Wanley and E. Thwaites, letters, Bodl. Oxf., MS Eng. hist. c. 6, fols. 45–119 · E. Thwaites, letter to William Brome, 6 Jan 1698, Bodl. Oxf., MS Rawl. letters 108, fol. 245 · W. Brome, letters to Thomas Rawlins, Bodl. Oxf., MS Ballard 19 · Nichols, *Lit. anecdotes*, 4.141–9 · *Remarks and collections of Thomas Hearne*, ed. C. E. Doble and others, 11 vols., OHS, 2, 7, 13, 34, 42–3, 48, 50, 65, 67, 72 (1885–1921), vol. 2, p. 127; vol. 3, pp. 278–9, 287, 376 · Foster, *Alum. Oxon.* · *A chorus of grammars: the correspondence of George Hickes and his collaborators on the 'Thesaurus linguarum septentrionalium'*, ed. R. L. Harris (1992) · *Letters of Humfrey Wanley: palaeographer, Anglo-Saxonist, librarian, 1672–1726*, ed. P. L. Heyworth (1989) · J. A. W. Bennett, 'The history of Old English and Old Norse studies in England from the time of Francis Junius till the end of the eighteenth century', DPhil diss., U. Oxf., 1938, Bodl. Oxf., MS D. Phil. d. 287, 68–82 · *The Old English version of the Heptateuch: Ælfric's treatise on the Old and New Testament, and his preface to Genesis*, ed. S. J. Crawford, EETS, orig. ser., 160 (1922); repr. with two additional manuscripts (1969) · M. Murphy, 'Edward Thwaites: pioneer teacher of Old English', *Durham University Journal*, 73 (1980–81), 153–9 · D. C. Douglas, *English scholars, 1660–1730*, 2nd edn (1951), 66–8 · *DNB* · admon. bond, and inventory, 4 March 1712, U. Oxf., chancellor's court, archives

Archives BL, letters to John Bagford and Humfrey Wanley, Harley MS 4966 · BL, letters to Nicolson, Add. MS 4276, fol. 149r · BL, corresp. of H. Wanley, Harley MS 3781, fols. 188–232 · Bodl. Oxf., letters of H. Wanley and E. Thwaites, MS Eng. hist. c. 6, fols. 45–119 · University of Kansas, Kenneth Spencer Research Library, certification by Edward Thwaites of the cost of Hickes's *Thesaurus* and an advertisement of the same, MS Clubb/E/1704.1

Likenesses Gribelin?, engraving (as St Gregory; after E. Elstob?), repro. in E. Elstob, *An English-Saxon homily on the birthday of St. Gregory* (1709), (inside an initial capital G at the beginning of the Old English text)

Thwaites, George Henry Kendrick (1812–1882), botanist and entomologist, was born at Bristol on 9 July 1812. Nothing is known of his childhood. He worked as an accountant, but devoted his leisure to entomology and the microscopical botany of cryptogams (flowerless plants). In 1839 he became Bristol secretary of the Botanical Society of London, and was soon appointed by Dr William Benjamin Carpenter to revise the second edition of his *General Physiology* (1841). An acute observer and expert microscopist, his most important observations at this period were those on the mode of propagation and the algal nature of diatoms, which organisms had been previously regarded as animals. This discovery led J. François Camille Montagne in 1845 to dedicate to him the algal genus *Thwaitesia*. Thwaites was so isolated in England in his expertise in microscopical botany that many of his discoveries were overlooked and subsequently attributed to later continental workers.

Thwaites was not solely interested in cryptogams. He contributed to Hewett Watson's *Topographical Botany*, listing the flowering plants within a 10 mile radius of Bristol, and was an early contributor to the *Gardeners' Chronicle*. One of the first of his discoveries having a direct bearing on horticulture was the raising of two distinct varieties of fuchsia from the two embryos in a single seed. In 1846 he was lecturer on botany at the Bristol School of Pharmacy and afterwards at the medical school, and in 1847 he applied unsuccessfully for a chair of natural history at the Queen's colleges in Ireland.

In March 1849, on the death of George Gardner, Thwaites was appointed superintendent of the botanical gardens at Peradeniya, Ceylon, where he adopted a programme of progressive clearance and supported both economic and informal ornamental planting. His duties were at first mainly scientific, and, turning his attention to the flowering plants, between 1852 and 1856 he contributed numerous descriptions of Sinhalese plants to Hooker's *Journal of Botany*, including twenty-five new genera. However, from 1857, when the title of his post was changed from superintendent to director, he became more and more engrossed by the duties of investigating the application of botany to tropical agriculture. In 1858 he began the printing of his only major work, the *Enumeratio plantarum Zeylaniae*, which was published in five fascicles (1858–64). In this he was assisted by J. D. Hooker and William Ferguson. In the preface he announced his adherence to the Darwinian view of the nature of species. On the completion of this work he was elected a fellow of the Royal Society, on 1 June 1865, and received the degree of doctor of philosophy from the Imperial Leopoldo-Carolinian Academy, and in 1867 Hooker dedicated to him the beautiful genus of Sinhalese climbing plants *Kendrickia*.

However, Thwaites himself never considered his work as other than a prologue to a complete flora and a catalogue of the extensive sets of dried plants which he communicated to the chief herbaria. In 1860 he established the cinchona nurseries at Hakgala, the success of the cultivation of these plants in Ceylon being largely due to his efforts. His successive official reports deal also with the cultivation of vanilla, tea, cardamoms, cacao, and Liberian coffee. In 1869 he sent the Revd Miles Joseph Berkeley the first specimens of *Hemileia vastatrix*, the coffee-leaf fungus, and his reports from 1871 to 1880 deal with it and the suggested preventives. After the completion of the *Enumeratio* he returned to the study of cryptogams, sending home more than 1200 fungi, which were described by Berkeley and C. E. Broome (*Journal of the Linnean Society*, 11, 1871, 494–572), besides mosses, which were published by William Mitten in 1872, and lichens, some of which were described by the Revd William Allport Leighton in 1870. Thwaites's health began to fail in 1867; Dr Henry Trimen arrived in 1879 to take his place, and Thwaites resigned in February 1880 and retired on a pension, purchasing a pretty bungalow named Fairieland above Kandy.

Thwaites became a fellow of the Linnean Society in 1854, and was made a companion in the Order of St Michael and St George in 1878. He died following a few weeks' illness, unmarried, in Kandy, on 11 September 1882; his funeral took place at the Mahaiyawa cemetery, Kandy, on the following day. In addition to official reports, Thwaites contributed some thirty papers to scientific journals, among others to the *Transactions of the Entomological Society*, to the *Phytologist*, and to the *Annals and Magazine of Natural History*. He also contributed to Frederick Moore's *Lepidoptera of Ceylon* (3 vols., 1880–89). According to his successor, Henry Trimen, Thwaites 'suffered all his life under the enormous drawback of a delicate and excitable organisation and constantly feeble health; and continually found it necessary to spare himself fatigue and worry' (Trimen and others, 79).

G. S. BOULGER, rev. ANDREW GROUT

Sources H. Trimen and others, *Tropical Agriculturalist*, 14 (1894), 75–9 • R. Desmond, *The European discovery of the Indian flora* (1992), 164–6 • F. A. Stafleu and R. S. Cowan, *Taxonomic literature: a selective guide*, 2nd edn, 6, Regnum Vegetabile, 115 (1986), 341–3 • *Journal of Botany, British and Foreign*, 20 (1882), 351–2 • *Proceedings of the Linnean Society of London* (1882–3), 43–7 • *Gardeners' Chronicle*, new ser., 1 (1874), 438 • G. H. K. Thwaites, *Testimonials in favour of George Henry Kendrick Thwaites* (1847) • E. Nelmes and W. Cuthbertson, eds., *Curtis's Botanical Magazine: dedications, 1827–1927* [1931], 131–2

Archives NHM, letters • RBG Kew, corresp. | New York Botanical Garden Library, letters to William Wilson • Oxf. U. Mus. NH, letters to J. O. Westwood • RBG Kew, letters to Sir William Hooker

Likenesses engraving, c.1872, repro. in Desmond, *European discovery*, 164 • portrait, Hunt Institute for Botanical Documentation, Pittsburgh

Thwaites, Sir John (1815–1870), public servant, was born on 24 May 1815 at Maulds Meaburn, Westmorland, the third son of Christopher Thwaites (1785–1864), yeoman farmer of Toddy Gill Hall, Warcop, and his wife, Hannah Smith (1789–1841). Educated at Reagill School, Thwaites moved to London in 1832 and found employment at Henry Bardwell's woollen draper's on Holborn Hill. He became a partner in the business shortly after his marriage, on 15 September 1835 at Holy Trinity, Cloudesley Square, Islington, to Harriott (1814/15–1860), the daughter of William Bardwell of Uggleshall, Suffolk. In 1842 Thwaites set up his own woollen drapery in Southwark, initially at 18 Blackman Street, and later at 61–2 Borough High Street.

Thwaites was a Strict and Particular Baptist, preaching at the Surrey Tabernacle where he was deacon for sixteen years. He also undertook parochial duties at St Mary's, Newington Butts; St Paul's, Deptford; and St Saviour. These offered him scope for involvement in public affairs as overseer, guardian of the poor, churchwarden, and chairman of the board of guardians. He sought wider responsibilities by participating in the early closing movement, campaigning for Apsley Pellatt (the Liberal MP for Southwark), and representing Southwark on the metropolitan commission of sewers. He also helped (in 1849) to set up the Surrey Gas Consumers' Company, which aimed to secure cheaper gas by breaking local monopolies.

When the Metropolitan Board of Works was established in 1855 Thwaites was elected to represent both St Saviour's and Greenwich. He wrote *A Sketch on the History and Prospects of the Metropolitan Drainage Question* in the same year, and was elected chairman of the board. His salary of £1500 allowed him to work full time. Between 1855 and 1870 the board carried through the main drainage schemes for London (for which he was knighted on 18 May 1865) and the construction of the Thames Embankment which opened on 13 July 1870. In 1861 he was appointed a member of the royal commission on plans for embanking the Thames and he gave evidence to various select committees about London's gas supply, local government and taxation, and sewage. His concern that the gas monopoly worked against the consumers' interest elicited a *Letter from Sir John Thwaites to Sir Stafford Northcote as to the proposals of the board for the future control of the gas companies of the metropolis* (1867) suggesting the board should buy out the gas companies. He was a member of the royal commission on water supply which reported in 1869.

Thwaites's first wife died in 1860, and on 13 August 1861 he married Eliza Carrington, née Woodruffe (1815/16–1883), the widow of Benjamin Carrington (d. 1851), resident medical officer of the Holloway and North Islington Dispensary. Thwaites was a magistrate for Surrey and both magistrate and deputy lieutenant for Middlesex. Ill through overwork, he succumbed to diabetes and English cholera on 8 August 1870 at his home, Meaburn House, Upper Richmond Road, Wandsworth. He was buried five days later near his first wife at Nunhead cemetery, Linden Grove. His second wife, three sons, and a daughter survived him. A self-made man, impassive in manner, Liberal in politics, and dissenting in religion, he had achieved a position of much influence across greater London.

BRIAN LANCASTER

Sources *The Elector* (13 June 1857) · *South London Press* (13 Aug 1870) · *South London News* (24 Oct 1857) · *ILN* (24 July 1858) [incl. drawing] · *The Builder*, 28 (1870), 639 · *The Earthen Vessel* (1 Sept 1870) · parish register, Crosby Ravensworth, Cumbria AS, WPR 7/6 · D. Owen and others, *The government of Victorian London, 1855–1889*, ed. R. MacLeod (1982) · *South London Press* (20 Aug 1870) · m. cert. · d. cert. · private information (2004) · census returns for London, 1851 · parish register (marriage), 15/9/1835, Islington, Holy Trinity [Metropolitan Archives] · parish registers (births), 1832–42, Marylebone, Titchfield Chapel [PRO R6 4/4355]

Likenesses A. Melville, portrait, priv. coll.; repro. in *The Builder* (18 March 1865) · drawing (after photograph by Cox), repro. in *ILN* (24 July 1858), 33 · photograph, priv. coll.

Wealth at death under £7000: administration with will, 17 Oct 1870, *CGPLA Eng. & Wales*

Thwing [Thweng] **family** (*per.* 1166–*c*.1234), gentry, held land in Yorkshire, Lincolnshire, and Northumberland, from at least 1166. The family is first represented in the historical record by **Robert (I) of Thwing** (*d.* in or before 1166). He was succeeded by his son **Robert (II) of Thwing** (*d.* 1172×99), referred to as Robert son of Robert of Tegneg in a charter of Henry II's reign. In 1166 he was recorded as holding a knight's fee in Legsby, Holtham, and Ludford, Lincolnshire, from William de Percy, and, it is assumed, Thwing in the East Riding of Yorkshire from Adam de Brus. Through Robert (II)'s marriage to Emma, one of the sisters and coheirs of Duncan Darel, the Thwings received part of the east Yorkshire estate of Lund, which in 1203 comprised a third share in four carucates in the village. The Thwings held their Lund estate from the bishop of Durham and this together with heraldic similarities to the arms of the fitz Marmadukes, barons of Hordern in Durham, have led to suggestions that the family originated from that county. Robert was a patron of the Lincolnshire priory of Sixhills, to which he gave the town and church of Legsby. He was living in 1172, when he witnessed a charter to Rievaulx Abbey, but had presumably died and been succeeded by his son **Marmaduke (I) of Thwing** (*d.* in or after 1234) by 1199 when Marmaduke was acting as a surety for Richard de Malebisse.

Marmaduke was imprisoned for homicide in 1204, although the exact details of the crime are unclear. In the same year Marmaduke paid 100*s.* to be placed in the custody of twelve lawful men and his sureties, including Peter de Brus, paid a fine of 40 marks and pledged themselves to prevent him from causing further disorder. Marmaduke was evidently released shortly afterwards and he served as a juror in 1208. He joined the baronial opposition to the crown during the civil war after 1215, but in 1217 he made peace with the minority government of Henry III and thereafter he appears to have been active as a royal official in northern England. In 1218 he was part of a commission that investigated the bishop of Durham's complaint concerning obstructions across the River Tyne; in 1226 he was involved in inspecting the condition of Scarborough and Pickering castles; and in 1230 he was ordered with other officials to take oaths from anyone who had been sworn to arms at the end of King John's reign. In addition to these specific functions he served as an assize justice during the years 1221–9 and as a coroner until August 1230, when he was replaced on account of his infirmity. The influence of the Thwings in the East Riding at this time was indicated by the marriage before 1227 of Marmaduke's daughter Cecily to William the Constable, the son of Robert the Constable of Holderness. In 1227 he came to an agreement with William concerning a bovate of land in demesne and the service of six carucates in Kilham in the East Riding, which Marmaduke had given to William as marriage settlement with his daughter. The date of

Marmaduke's death is not known but the last reference to him is in November 1234 when he was party to a final concord. He was succeeded by his son Robert (III) of *Thwing (d. 1245x57), who was an opponent of papal provisions in England, then by Robert's son Marmaduke (II) Thwing (d. 1282x4). The arms of the Thwing family, first recorded in 1227, are given as argent, a fesse gules between three popinjays vert. JOHN WALKER

Sources GEC, *Peerage*, new edn, 12/1 · W. Brown, ed., *Cartularium prioratus de Gyseburne*, 2, SurtS, 89 (1894) · W. M. I'Anson, 'Kilton Castle', *Yorkshire Archaeological Journal*, 22 (1913) · W. Farrer and others, eds., *Early Yorkshire charters*, 12 vols. (1914–65), vol. 2

Thwing, Marmaduke (I) of (d. in or after **1234**). *See under* Thwing family (*per.* 1166–c.1234).

Thwing, Marmaduke (III) of, **first Baron Thwing** (d. **1323**). *See under* Thwing, Sir Robert (III) of (d. 1245x57).

Thwing, Robert (I) of (d. in or before **1166**). *See under* Thwing family (*per.* 1166–c.1234).

Thwing, Robert (II) of (d. **1172x99**). *See under* Thwing family (*per.* 1166–c.1234).

Thwing [Thweng], **Sir Robert (III) of** [*alias* William Wither] (d. **1245x57**), knight, was the son of Marmaduke (I) of *Thwing (d. in or after 1234) [*see under* Thwing family]. Robert makes his first appearance in 1229, suing Richard de Percy (*fl.* 1181–1244) for customs and services in Kilton and Kirkleatham, land that he had acquired by his marriage to Mathilda, widow of Richard de Autrey and niece and heir of William of Kilton. In 1231 he became conspicuous for his opposition to the Roman and Italian clergy who had received papal provision to churches in England. With the assistance of the archbishop of York, an Italian had been intruded to the church of Kirkleatham, the advowson of which Robert and his wife had recovered in 1230 following litigation against the prior of Guisborough. Robert adopted the alias William Wither, literally 'William the Angry'; he placed himself at the head of an armed agitation against the foreigners and about Easter 1232 pillaged their corn and barns and distributed the spoils among the poor. In response to complaints from the pope Henry III ordered the arrest of various leading courtiers who were implicated in these disturbances, including Hubert de Burgh (d. 1243), the chief justiciar, who is said to have lent tacit support to the 'Withermen' out of anger at a papal inquiry into the legality of his marriage. Thwing is later to be found witnessing a charter of Hubert's son, John de Burgh, but in 1232 there is nothing to suggest that Hubert and Thwing were in any way close associates. Thwing himself was sent by the king for absolution in Rome. In 1239 he made a second visit to Rome, carrying with him a general letter of complaint from the English barons. Perhaps through the influence of Richard, earl of Cornwall, to whose household Thwing had attached himself, he obtained letters from Pope Gregory IX (r. 1227–41) protecting the rights of lay patrons against papal provision. Early in the following year Thwing set out with Earl Richard on

crusade. In September 1240, from Marseilles, he was sent as an envoy to the emperor, Frederick II (r. 1212–50), with information about the pope's attempts to delay the crusade. As a result, he may never have reached the Holy Land. In 1244 he was accused of making a violent attack upon a clerk of the archbishop of York in the king's hall at Windsor. His lands were seized, but restored the following year. The date of his death is unknown, but he was probably dead by 1257 when his eldest son and heir, Marmaduke (II) of Thwing, had control of the chief family estates.

Confusion arises between Sir Robert of Thwing and at least two other namesakes: his grandson, also named Robert, who was still a minor in 1266, and another Robert, perhaps an illegitimate son of Sir Robert, who married a woman named Hugolina, participated in negotiations with the Scots, and from 1262 was employed as a knight of the royal household. Marmaduke (II) of Thwing (d. 1282x4), son and heir of Sir Robert, had by 1242 married Lucy, sister of Peter de Brus and heir to part of the barony of Skelton, with whom he had several sons. Robert, the eldest of these, died without male children before 1283 and was succeeded in the Thwing estates by his brother Marmaduke, who was prominent in the Scottish wars of the reign of Edward I. **Marmaduke (III) of Thwing** [Thweng], first Baron Thwing (d. **1323**), played a leading role at the battle of Stirling in 1297, but in 1299 was taken prisoner and ransomed by the Scots. By writ of summons issued in 1307 he is considered to have become the first Baron Thwing or Thweng. In 1312 he joined Thomas, earl of Lancaster, in the attack upon Piers Gaveston, and in 1321, at the time of Lancaster's great rebellion, his loyalties were the subject of suspicion by the crown. He died in 1323 and was succeeded in the barony by his three sons—William, Robert, and Thomas—all of whom died childless. On the death of Thomas in 1374 the barony fell into abeyance, and the Thwing estates were partitioned among various of Thomas's sisters and nieces. St *John of Bridlington (c.1320–1379), sometimes called John Twenge or Thwing, author of caustic, prophetic verses against the government of Edward III, may have sprung from the same family. NICHOLAS VINCENT

Sources Chancery records · Paris, *Chron.* · N. Vincent, *Peter des Roches: an alien in English politics, 1205–38*, Cambridge Studies in Medieval Life and Thought, 4th ser., 31 (1996) · GEC, *Peerage* · W. Farrer and others, eds., *Early Yorkshire charters*, 12 vols. (1914–65), vols. 2, 9 · W. Brown, ed., *Cartularium prioratus de Gyseburne*, 2 vols., SurtS, 86, 89 (1889–94) · A. H. Thompson, ed., *Northumberland pleas from the curia regis and assize rolls, 1198–1272*, Newcastle upon Tyne Records Committee Publications, 2 (1922) · I. J. Sanders, *English baronies: a study of their origin and descent, 1086–1327* (1960) · Warter cartulary, Bodl. Oxf., MS Fairfax 9, fols. 42r–43v

Thyer, Robert (*bap.* **1709**, *d.* **1781**), librarian and literary editor, was born in Manchester and baptized at Manchester collegiate church on 20 February 1709, the son of Robert Thyer (*bap.* 1672), a silk weaver or barber, and Elizabeth Brabant, who married on 25 August 1703. Educated at Manchester grammar school, he won an exhibition in

1727 to Brasenose College, Oxford, whence he graduated BA on 12 October 1730. On returning to his native town he was elected librarian of Chetham's Library in February 1732, and continued in that office until 3 October 1763.

Thyer, the first man not in holy orders to be elected to the librarianship, brought about a modernization of the library. He abandoned the practice of chaining books, increased the storage capacity, introduced a new classification system derived from that set up by Conyers Middleton at Cambridge University Library, and commenced work on a new catalogue based on subject access. His diligence was certified by the library's trustees on his retirement, and by his successor, in the Latin preface to the Chetham's Library catalogue of 1791. During his librarianship the library became a focus for religious and philosophical debate, centred on a series of informal seminars held by Thyer and a group of friends.

On 9 December 1741 Thyer married Silence Leigh (1714–1753), daughter of John Wagstaffe of Glossop and Manchester, and widow of John Leigh of Middle Hulton in Deane, Lancashire. Through his marriage he became close friends of the Egertons of Tatton, Cheshire; Samuel Egerton MP left him an annuity of £200 on his death in 1780. Thyer was also an intimate friend of his fellow townsman, the poet John Byrom, and many of his letters, as well as a specimen of his verse, are printed in Byrom's *Literary Remains*.

Thyer was a keen literary scholar and he supplied notes to Thomas Newton, later bishop of Bristol, for his edition of Milton's *Paradise Lost*. In 1755 he published a proposal for a new annotated edition of Samuel Butler's *Hudibras* and in 1759 he published his edition of *The Genuine Remains in Verse and Prose of Samuel Butler, with Notes*, in two volumes, which was praised by Dr Johnson, but condemned by Bishop Warburton. Warburton's criticisms are at best uncharitable. Thyer was a diligent if pedantic scholar, more suited to editorial work than original thought, but his edition of Butler was both accurate and scholarly and Johnson's view is a fairer assessment of his work.

Thyer died on 27 October 1781 in Long Millgate, Manchester, and was buried with his ancestors in Manchester collegiate church. His wife and all their children had predeceased him.   C. W. SUTTON, rev. MICHAEL POWELL

Sources E. Ogden, 'Robert Thyer: Chetham's librarian, 1732–1763', *Transactions of the Lancashire and Cheshire Antiquarian Society*, 41 (1924), 90–136 • E. Ogden, 'Robert Thyer: family letters and some speeches written for public recitation', *Transactions of the Lancashire and Cheshire Antiquarian Society*, 47 (1930–31), 58–83 • J. F. Smith, ed., *The admission register of the Manchester School, with some notices of the more distinguished scholars*, 1, Chetham Society, 69 (1866), 39 • *The private journal and literary remains of John Byrom*, ed. R. Parkinson, vol. 1, pt 2, Chetham Society, 34 (1855), 509–13 • *The poems of John Byrom*, ed. A. W. Ward, 1–4, Chetham Society, new ser., 29–30, 34–5 (1894–5) • [J. E. Bailey], 'Byrom–Thyer correspondence, 1755?, 1773', *Palatine Note-Book*, 3 (1883), 203–6 • Foster, *Alum. Oxon.* • *IGI*
Archives Chetham's Library, Manchester, commonplace book, incl. theological extracts • JRL, corresp. and papers | JRL, Bellot papers
Likenesses G. Romney, oils, Chetham's Library, Manchester • W. H. Worthington, line engraving (after G. Romney), BM, NPG • miniature, repro. in Ogden, 'Robert Thyer: family letters and some speeches'
Wealth at death see will, repr. in Ogden, 'Robert Thyer: Chetham's librarian', pp. 135–6

Thynne, Francis (1545?–1608), herald and antiquary, came of a family which also sometimes used the name Boteville, claiming descent in the early seventeenth century from a Ralph Botevile of Church Stretton, Shropshire. The only son of William *Thynne, the editor of Chaucer, and his wife, Anne Bond, Francis was probably born at Erith, Kent, in 1545, the year before his father's death. He spent some of his early years at Longleat House, Wiltshire, built by his cousin Sir John *Thynne. Francis studied at Tonbridge School under John Procter. He was admitted a member of Lincoln's Inn on 23 June 1561, but there is no evidence of his staying there very long. He did, however, form lasting friendships with William Lambarde, with whom he collaborated in collecting Anglo-Saxon chronicles, and Thomas Egerton, afterwards lord keeper and lord chancellor. He may have become an attorney, but there is no record of his legal practice. In 1564 he married Elizabeth (d. 1596), daughter and coheir of Thomas de la River of Brandsby, Yorkshire. There were no children of the marriage.

From his earliest years Thynne was devoted to the collection and study of alchemy, heraldry, medieval history, and antiquities. These activities centred on the transcription and translation of Latin and English Anglo-Saxon chronicles and homilies, lives of the saints, and monumental inscriptions from Kent churches. His earliest work, however, was on alchemy, whose poetical side he pursued as a 'lover of wisdom' (Carlson, 205), aiming to collect rare knowledge in the natural sphere that would complement his antiquarian researches into history. His occult emblems and poems were impractical, however, in the sense that they pursued rare knowledge rather than wealth through the transmutation of metals, and in any case did not reach the level of John Dee's. Thynne's longest alchemical verse, 'A Discours upon the Philosopheres Armes' (1573), was allegorical, referring to biblical and mythological alchemists with numerous coloured illustrations. Since alchemy was an expensive pursuit, it contributed to his early financial problems. Although he maintained his interest in the occult, his last alchemical collection dates from April 1578.

Thynne lived for a time in Poplar, Middlesex, and by 1573 was in Bermondsey Street, Surrey. Now facing severe financial difficulties, he sold off some of the twenty-five Chaucer manuscripts that he had inherited from his father. In January 1574 he also tried to obtain money from his mother's estate. None the less he was imprisoned in the White Lion, Southwark, shortly afterwards for a debt of £100. On 13 March 1576 he wrote an impassioned letter from there to Lord Burghley, requesting help in his distress. His adversaries were his own kinsmen, who under the colour of providing for the assurance of his wife's jointure had withheld from him 200 marks a year over four years. He wrote another long letter to Burghley on the

19th, stating that he was famished and destitute of clothing and means of subsistence. Eventually released, he returned to Longleat to live with Sir John Thynne, having missed the chance to accompany his fellow Kentishman William Brooke, tenth Lord Cobham, as ambassador to Flanders in summer 1578. Following Cobham's return Thynne presented him with a discourse respecting ambassadors dated 8 January 1579. In the meantime he had written again to Burghley in October 1578, begging for employment, and was later evicted from Longleat when his cousin died in 1580. By 1588 he was living on Clerkenwell Green, Middlesex, where he appears to have remained for the rest of his life.

After the death of Raphael Holinshed in 1580, Thynne, together with Abraham Fleming and John Stow, was employed by John Hooker, who acted as editor, to continue Holinshed's *Chronicles*. His contributions to this massive undertaking of revision and original work were begun in the period 1579–81. Thynne was responsible for the sections on Scotland, and his most original work consisted of large lists of office-holders. His thirteen substantial articles included 'The annales of Scotland, 1571–1586', 'A collection concerning the high constables of England', 'The protectors of England collected out of ancient and modern chronicles', 'The cardinals of England', 'The discourse and catalog of all the dukes of England', 'A treatise of the treasurers of England', and 'The chancellors of England'. Sections of four other contributions—'A discourse of the earles of Leicester', 'The lives of the archbishops of Canturburie', 'A treatise of the Lord Cobhams', and 'The catalog of the lord wardens of the Cinque Ports'—were excised by order of the privy council, owing perhaps to their political sensitivity but more likely because of their tedious length. They were included in the 1728 and later editions. The value of Thynne's work, however, was recognized by the council when it ordered the publication of his critique of Holinshed and of his 'Annales of Scotland' (1587).

Thynne became a member of the Elizabethan Society of Antiquaries in 1591. He read seven papers at its meetings, including discourses on heralds, the antiquity of shires, and the offices of high steward and earl marshal that were published in Hearne's *Collection* (2nd edn, 1771). Thynne was a central figure in the society, though he often relied on his fellow members for access to the materials he copied. These included William Camden, Sir Robert Cotton, Joseph Holland, Charles Howard, earl of Nottingham, Lord William Howard, William Lambarde, and John Stow. During this period Thynne, whose father had published an edition of Chaucer in 1532, prepared notes for a commentary on the poet's works. He abandoned it in 1598 when Thomas Speght published an edition. He did, however, criticize Speght's production in a letter of 'Animadversions' (1599), and afterwards assisted Speght in producing a revised edition (1602), himself contributing a short poem 'Upon the Picture of Chaucer'.

The patronage of Burghley, Egerton, Lord Cobham, and Gilbert Talbot, seventh earl of Shrewsbury, together with the strength of his scholarly reputation, led to Thynne's being appointed Lancaster herald upon Egerton's nomination by the privy council on 22 April 1602. The support of the council may have owed something to the de luxe, illustrated manuscript editions of Thynne's revised Holinshed contributions that were presented to some of its members—'England's treasurers' to Burghley in 1594, 'England's chancellors' to Egerton in 1596, and 'Lords Cobham and lords warden of the Cinque Ports' to Cobham in 1598. His work on Anglo-Saxon and medieval chronicles was solid and factual, based on his firm belief in the accuracy of the original manuscripts. The council must have been impressed with the strong protestant bias in his writings, and after 1603 by his criticisms of the disgraced Sir Walter Ralegh's histories as 'conjectures' (Smith Fussner, 97). He demonstrated his loyalty to the crown when on 2 April 1605 he dedicated his 'Plea betwene the advocat and the ant-advocat' on the antiquity of royal creations of knighthoods to James I. When Augustine Vincent began his work on England's baronage, he considered Thynne's collections indispensable.

Thynne became a herald at a critical time in the history of the College of Arms, when rife corruption among its members contributed to a flood of fraudulent claims for grants of arms in a period of rapid social mobility. His most widely circulated discourse, and also his last, was a 'Discourse of the dutye and office of an heraulde of arms' written in March 1606 for Henry Howard, earl of Northampton, to help him reform the college's practices. He produced a table of its faults along with remedies to resolve them, urging an extension of the legal powers of the earl marshal.

While honours only came to Thynne near the end of his life, they never provided material relief. He spent his life in libraries and his study, and relations with his wife were not good. He wrote later that 'thy wife allwaies is but a needefull ill, and best is bad', and observed that marriage is best when the husband is deaf and the wife blind (*Emblemes and Epigrames*, 59, 78–9). No less personally, in his discourse on heralds he refers to 'That cruell Tyrante the unmercyfull Gowte [which] paynefully imprisoned me in my bedd, mannacled my hands, fettered my feete to the sheetes' for nearly three months ('Discourse', 230). In June 1606 he wrote to his cousin's grandson Thomas Thynne asking for money to ease his financial difficulties. He died at Clerkenwell Green in November 1608.

Thynne left some 52 works in manuscript, of which 28 were eventually published, and more than 100 copies of medieval texts. His transcript of a valuable account of the peasants' revolt was printed in the *English Historical Review* in 1898. His 'Catalogue of the lord chancellors of England' came into the possession of Robert Glover, Somerset herald, and Thomas Talbot, clerk of the records in the Tower, and was used by John Philipot, Somerset herald, for his *Catalogue of the Chancellors of England* (1636). It had been dedicated to Thynne's friend Sir Thomas Egerton, as were several other manuscript works from the 1580s and 1590s. Most of Egerton's history of Britain in his famous judgment of 1607 on *Colvin's Case*, concerning the status in England of persons born in Scotland after the accession of

James I, was taken from Thynne's 'Comentaries of Britayne' (1587). Both men converted from Catholicism to protestantism in the 1570s.

Thynne's significance lies in the manuscripts he collected, transcribed, and translated. His massive collections, full of lists and catalogues, were later dispersed, to find their way into the Cottonian, Lansdowne, and Stowe collections in the British Library, the Ashmolean in the Bodleian Library, and the Ellesmere in the Huntington Library. His method was one that made his intellectual pursuits of alchemy and antiquarianism complementary. The acquisitive, archaeological approach to recover and understand 'the arcana of nature and the arcana of the past' enabled future alchemists and antiquaries to construct new interpretations (Carlson, 215–16). It was no less so for forward-thinking contemporaries like Sir Francis Bacon. LOUIS A. KNAFLA

Sources BL, Ayscough MS 3836 [epitaph] · Bodl. Oxf., MSS Ashmole 383, 520, 559, 625 · B. Botfield, *Stemmata Botevilliana: memorials of the families of de Boteville, Thynne, and Botfield* (1858), 21, 51–3, 56, 59, 66, cxxxvi, clxxvi, cccxliii · *Francis Thynne's Animadversions upon Speght's first (1598 AD) edition of Chaucer's works*, ed. F. J. Furnivall and G. H. Kingsley, EETS, original ser., no. 9 (1865), vii–xix, xlvii–cxxvi [20 Dec 1599] · Wood, *Ath. Oxon.*, new edn, 2.107–11 · C. H. Cooper and T. Cooper, 'Francis Thynne, Lancaster herald', *GM*, 3rd ser., 19 (1865), 85–90 · J. Morris, 'Historical account of the family of Thynne', *The Topographer and Genealogist*, 3 (1855), 471–3, 485 · BL, Stowe MS 1047 [commonplace book, 1585–1604: extracts from chronicles, monastic registers, marriage documents, aristocratic creations, precedence, and funerals; inscribed 14 Feb 1563] · BL, Lansdowne MS 27, fols. 70–75v, 117–19 [letters to Lord Burghley, 1573–9] · *Holinshed's chronicles of England, Scotland and Ireland*, ed. H. Ellis, 6 vols. (1807–8) [many of Thynne's tracts] · F. Thynne, *Emblemes and epigrames from my howse in Clerkenwell Greene the 20th of December 1600*, ed. F. J. Furnivall, EETS, original ser., 64 (1876) · D. Carlson, 'The writings and manuscript collections of the Elizabethan alchemist, antiquary, and herald Francis Thynne', *Huntington Library Quarterly*, 52/2 (1989), 203–72 · *Two Elizabethan women: correspondence of Joan and Maria Thynne, 1575–1611*, ed. A. D. Wall, Wilts RS, 38 (1983) · P. Ruggiers, ed., *Editing Chaucer: the great tradition* (1984), 3–5, 38–40, 72, 80–86 · L. A. Knafla, *Law and politics in Jacobean England* (1977), 48–9, 52–3, 69, 231 · M. McKisack, *Medieval history in the Tudor age* (1971), 67–8, 78, 116–17 · C. J. Wright, 'The Elizabethan Society of Antiquaries and the formation of the Cottonian Library', *The English library before 1700: studies in its history*, ed. F. Wormald and C. E. Wright (1958), 183, 187–8, 197 · F. Smith Fussner, *The historical revolution: English historical writing and thought, 1580–1640* (1962), 97 · L. A. Knafla, 'The "country" chancellor: the patronage of Sir Thomas Egerton, Baron Ellesmere', *Patronage in late Renaissance England*, ed. F. R. Knogle and L. A. Knafla (1983), 61–2, 114–15 · H. Ross Steeves, *Learned societies and English literary scholarship* (1913), 16–18 · W. P. Baildon, ed., *The records of the Honorable Society of Lincoln's Inn: admissions*, 1 (1896), 68 · M. Noble, *A history of the College of Arms* (1804), 184, 188, 213 · *N&Q*, 1 (1849–50), 60; 3rd ser., 1 (1862), 242; 4 (1863), 505 · *The Herald and Genealogist*, 1 (1863), 74–5 · F. Thynne, 'A discourse of the dutye and office of an heraulde of arms', *Collection of curious discourses*, ed. Hearne (1720), 230–68 [3 March 1606; copies BL, Add. MS 25247, fols. 252–71; Stowe MS 569a, fols. 237–66, dedication to earl of Northampton]
Archives BL, antiquarian, genealogical, and heraldic collections and papers, Add. MSS 11388, 12514, 12530, 25247, 37666, 39184 · BL, historical and antiquarian collections, MS of *Lives of the treasures of England*, commonplace book, Stowe MSS 573, 1047 · BL, Lincolnshire church notes, Add. MS 36295 · BL, monumental notes, Sloane MS 3836 · Harvard U., Houghton L., notes on Speght's *Chaucer* · S. Antiquaries, Lond., genealogical account of Griffith family of Burton Agnes · W. Yorks. AS, Leeds, discourse of arms

Thynne, Henry Frederick. *See* Carteret, Henry Frederick, first Baron Carteret of Hawnes (1735–1826).

Thynne, Henry Frederick, sixth marquess of Bath (1905–1992), landowner and businessman, was born in the great Elizabethan house of Longleat, Wiltshire, on 26 January 1905, the second son and youngest of five children of Thomas Henry Thynne, fifth marquess of Bath (1862–1946), and his wife, Violet Caroline (1869–1928), putative daughter of Sir Charles Mordaunt, tenth baronet, and his first wife, Harriet Sarah, *née* Moncreiffe. His childhood was spent principally at Longleat, where the fifth marquess lived in high pomp even after the First World War, keeping twenty indoor servants, the footmen kitted out in silk stockings and cocked hats. On the death of his elder brother on the western front on 13 February 1916, Henry Thynne became Viscount Weymouth and heir to the massive Longleat estate. 'How can I look after you?', he asked the great south front of the house upon hearing the news of his inheritance, 'I'll never be able to do it' (*The Independent*, 1 July 1992).

As Viscount Weymouth, Thynne was given a traditional upper-class education at Harrow School and at Christ Church, Oxford, where he studied agriculture. At Oxford he formed part of an odd intersection between the horsey and the arty sets, joining the 'bright young people' and befriending extreme aesthetes such as Brian Howard, the model for Anthony Blanche in Evelyn Waugh's *Brideshead Revisited*. As a result of their friendship Howard uncharacteristically took up riding and designed colours for Weymouth: four yellow hearts on a black background. Through Howard, Weymouth met Daphne Winifred Louise Vivian [*see* Fielding, Daphne (1904–1997)], only daughter of George Crespigny Brabazon Vivian, fourth Baron Vivian, and his first wife, Barbara, daughter of William Atonar Fanning. Facing parental opposition, they married privately at St Paul's, Knightsbridge, under the names of Frederick Thynne and Winifred Vivian, on 8 October 1926. Weymouth then left for America with his friend and future brother-in-law Lord Nunburnholme. After an eventful period working on a Texas ranch and exploring Latin America, Weymouth returned to announce his engagement to Daphne Vivian in May 1927; the couple were married publicly at St Martin-in-the-Fields on 27 October 1927.

Weymouth buckled down to the responsibilities of Longleat, the management of which he took over in 1928. After some further training with the agent of Lockinge Park (owned by relatives of Daphne's), he set about vigorously modernizing and professionalizing the estate. Unnecessary staff were laid off and commercial forestry was undertaken. Weymouth also had the foresighted idea of developing the tourist potential of the caves at Cheddar Gorge, for which he had an unusually modernistic restaurant and museum designed by the landscape architects

Henry Frederick Thynne, sixth marquess of Bath (1905–1992), by Eve Arnold, 1961

Geoffrey Jellicoe and Russell Page. He left alone for the time being the big house, where his father continued to reside. Instead he and Daphne lived in more modest houses on the estate, where they could keep up a bohemian lifestyle and friendships with the likes of Cecil Beaton and Robert Byron. They had five children: (Thomas) Timothy (1929–1930), Alexander George (b. 1932), Christopher John (b. 1934), Valentine Charles (1937–1979), and Caroline Jane (1928–1995). At his father's insistence Weymouth also took on the Conservative candidacy for Frome in 1931 and he served reluctantly as its MP until 1935, but his heart was in land management and the good life, not in politics.

The Second World War disrupted this idyllic existence. Weymouth joined the Royal Wiltshire yeomanry. He was wounded at the battle of El Alamein, taking a piece of shrapnel in the throat, 'when I was walking about the battlefield on my own … I was bored—I had lost my tank and I had nothing to do' (Longleat MSS). It was not, as one obituary had it, while leading the Moonrakers tank charge at Tel-el-Aquaquoir, which he missed entirely. Weymouth was invalided home and an old shooting friend, General Pete Corlett, invented a position for him as British liaison officer to the American 19th corps, posted near Longleat. Weymouth's exploits with the 19th corps after D-day earned him bronze and silver stars from the Americans.

Shortly after the war's end, on 9 June 1946, the fifth marquess of Bath died. Although he had long before handed over to Weymouth the Longleat estate, hoping to escape death duties, he had retained too much capital for too long and the sixth marquess was faced with a bill of £700,000. To pay this he sold 5400 of his 16,000 acres. Almost as daunting as death duties was the great house, then occupied by an evacuated girls' school. To cover its running costs, estimated at £30,000 per annum, Bath thought first of converting it into a luxury hotel, but then decided to open it to the public on a commercial basis, inspired by his success at Cheddar. Apart from Warwick Castle, there was no precedent for mounting a commercial tourist operation at a stately home and in conditions of post-war austerity the venture was a considerable risk. The Baths approached the project with their customary flair, paving estate roads for what they hoped would be a flood of traffic, opening a café in the basement, and courting all the publicity they could get. They opened for business on 1 April 1949. To the world's amazement Longleat drew 135,000 visitors in that first year and a new tourist industry took off on its example. Bath soon had the whole estate on a sound economic footing; he also continued in commercial forestry and again called in Russell Page, this time to develop the gardens around the house.

The Baths' marriage had suffered badly from their wartime separation and their joint venture with the house did not serve to repair the damage. The marriage was dissolved in May 1953 and both parties remarried almost immediately. Daphne married the writer Xan Fielding, Henry (on 15 July 1953) married Virginia Penelope Tennant (b. 1917), daughter of Alan Leonard Romaine Parsons and his wife, Viola, née Tree, and formerly the wife of the Hon. David Tennant. Soon after their remarriages the publication of Daphne's memoir *Mercury Presides* (1954) revealed the secret of the private wedding, which had not been annulled; it took an appeal to the High Court to get the annulment extended, in 1955. 'Darling', remarked Osbert Lancaster's cartoon character Maudie Littlehampton, 'do you remember betting me a fiver that it was going to prove a lot easier to unite the Germans than to separate the Baths?' Safely unbigamized, the marquess and his new marchioness then had a daughter, Silvy Cerne (b. 1958).

As the stately home business expanded, Bath remained constantly alive to the need to keep his own pioneering operation competitive. He had put pedalos on the lake as early as 1953, opened a garden centre in 1960, and employed a public relations officer, simply to keep numbers at their initial high levels. He was determined to maintain Longleat as a commercial business independent of government subsidy, scorning grants to historic buildings as 'iniquitous' (though he took them eventually to staunch an infestation of death-watch beetle). In 1964 he leapt at a proposal, advanced by the circus impresario Jimmy Chipperfield, for an open-air safari park on the estate. When it was announced that the park would feature a drive-through lion enclosure, the local and national press attacked the 'mad Marquess', *The Times* growling that 'cattle, sheep and deer ought to be good enough for a

Wiltshireman' (*The Times*, 2 Sept 1965). But the opening of the joint venture in April 1966 was a popular triumph, and, boosted further by a new exhibition of Churchilliana in the house, tourist numbers jumped to 300,000 for the house and 100,000 for the safari park. Other gimmicks followed: kitchens with waxwork servants, television tie-ins, and teddy bear rallies.

Somewhat grudgingly, Bath had already handed over management of the bulk of the estate to his heir, Alexander, Viscount Weymouth, having taken care to convey legal ownership as early as 1958, with death duties keenly in mind. As he aged, edging out of the limelight that he had so much enjoyed, Bath devoted himself more to building up his personal collections, which included children's books and items associated with Churchill, Edward VIII, Margaret Thatcher, and, controversially, Hitler. Much criticism had attached to him for his purchase of two Hitler watercolours at auction in 1960. More came when he confessed to admiring the man. Ultimately he built up the world's largest collection of Hitler paintings, garnished with other ghoulish Nazi memorabilia. A huge sale of books netting over £300,000 in 1979 cleared remaining debts, and under his son's management, and with land values soaring, the estate was riding high. He died at Crockerton, Wiltshire, on 30 June 1992, and his ashes were buried in the family vault at Longbridge Deverill church. By the time of his death the sixth marquess had answered triumphantly his youthful question to the great house, 'How can I look after you?'   PETER MANDLER

Sources D. Burnett, *Longleat: the story of an English country house* (1978) · D. Fielding, *Mercury presides* (1954) · private information (2004) · *The Independent* (1 July 1992) · *The Times* (1 July 1992) · Lord Montagu of Beaulieu, *The gilt and the gingerbread* (1967) · R. Page, *The education of a gardener* (1962) · Longleat House, Wiltshire, Longleat MSS · *WWW*, 1991–5 · m. cert.

Archives Longleat House, Wiltshire | FILM Longleat House, Wiltshire | SOUND Longleat House, Wiltshire

Likenesses S. Sorine, oils, 1935, Longleat House, Wiltshire · S. O'Sullivan, oils, 1947, Longleat House, Wiltshire · A. Sutherland, oils, 1960, Longleat House, Wiltshire · E. Arnold, bromide print, 1961, NPG [*see illus.*] · G. Sutherland, oils, 1970, Longleat House, Wiltshire · photograph, 1974, Hult. Arch. · F. Topolski, ink and pencil, Longleat House, Wiltshire · A. Waysard, pencil and watercolour drawing, NPG · photograph, repro. in *The Times* · photograph, repro. in *The Independent*

Wealth at death £44,395,085: probate, 8 April 1993, *CGPLA Eng. & Wales*

Thynne [*née* Hayward], **Joan**, Lady Thynne (*bap.* 1558, *d.* 1612), gentlewoman, was baptized on 28 August 1558 in London, the third daughter of Sir Rowland *Hayward (*c.*1520–1593), alderman and lord mayor of London, and his first wife, Joan Tillesworth (*d.* 1580). The details of her education are unknown. Her arranged marriage with John Thynne (*c.*1551–1604), heir to Sir John *Thynne (1512/13–1580) of Longleat, was probably solemnized on 26 February 1576, and Hayward settled Caus Castle in Shropshire on them. However, the previous owner, Edward, Lord Stafford, clung on until the Thynnes forcibly took Caus in 1591. Thereafter Joan managed and defended it,

Joan Thynne, Lady Thynne (*bap.* 1558, *d.* 1612), by unknown artist

while her husband stayed mostly at Longleat or Westminster.

As suggested by her portrait, Joan was a strong, capable woman, and she established a following in Shropshire in addition to her Wiltshire and London alliances. From the age of seventeen she instructed her husband on family relationships, estate business, and tactics, including their unsuccessful attempts to secure annulment of their elder son Thomas's secret marriage in 1594 to Maria, daughter of their political enemy Lord Audley. Joan worked on the legal disputes against Stafford, dealing with sheriffs and other officials, and intrigued to secure favourable juries. She kept muskets in her bedroom, and requested supplies of gunpowder. She hunted, and supervised the farming of both cattle and crops. She arranged for tradesmen to repair the castle, and dealt with gentlemen retainers, stewards, and servants, as well as the accounts, reporting to Thynne; early letters end 'your obedient wife', but later she signed 'your everloving wife'. He wrote to his 'Good Pug'.

After Thynne, recently knighted, died on 21 November 1604, Joan continued to manage Caus and commenced a lead mine in Somerset. Her widowed brother-in-law, Sir Henry Townshend, lived at the castle, persuading her not to treat tenants harshly. Thomas was not forgiven, and in 1605 she conducted a chancery lawsuit against him on behalf of her three other children. However, her life was not all hard manoeuvring: she carried on the usual family, medical, sewing, and household cares. She always kept up with gentry fashion for herself and her two daughters: gowns, farthingale, petticoat, silver, and spangles came from London; there were silk curtains, pictures, lutes, and virginals. She arranged tutors for her children, employing John Maynard for music; he fulsomely dedicated his satirical songs *The XII Wonders of the World* (1611) to Joan. She negotiated extensively for her daughter Dorothy's marriage, and tried to protect her allies by long leases before she died suddenly in London on 3 March 1612. She nominated her two daughters to execute her will, but left insufficient funds for the legacies.   ALISON WALL

Sources *Two Elizabethan women: correspondence of Joan and Maria Thynne, 1575–1611*, ed. A. D. Wall, Wilts RS, 38 (1983) · W. Jay, 'Sir Rowland Hayward', *Transactions of the London and Middlesex Archaeological Society*, new ser., 6 (1933), 509–27 · B. Botfield, *Stemmata Botevilliana: memorials of the families of de Boteville, Thynne, and Botfield* (1843) · G. B. Hall, ed., *Records of St Alphage, London Wall* (1882), 59–60 · A. D. Wall, 'Elizabethan precept and feminine practice: the Thynne family of Longleat', *History*, new ser., 75 (1990), 23–38 · Longleat House, Wiltshire, Marquess of Bath MSS, Thynne MSS, esp. vols. 4–8, and MSS 3848, 3952 [with permission of the marquess] · will of Joan Thynne, 28 Feb 1612, proved 4 March 1612, PRO, PROB 11/119, fols. 179–80 · W. A. Leighton, ed., 'Early chronicles of Shrewsbury, 1372–1603', *Transactions of the Shropshire Archaeological and Natural History Society*, 3 (1880), 239–352, esp. 320 · VCH *Shropshire*, 1.399–400; 8.308–11, 313 · J. Maynard, *The XII wonders of the world* (1611) · A. Collins, *The peerage of England: containing a genealogical and historical account of all the peers of England*, 2.500–02
Archives Longleat House, Wiltshire
Likenesses oils, Longleat House, Wiltshire; repro. in Wall, ed., *Two Elizabethan women* [*see illus.*]
Wealth at death will, PRO, PROB 11/119, fols. 179–80 · left debts: 3 March 1612 letter to son Thomas, Longleat House, Wiltshire, Thynne MSS, vol. 8, fol. 82

Thynne, Sir John (1512/13–1580), estate manager and builder of Longleat, was born in Church Stretton, Shropshire, the eldest son of Thomas Thynne of Church Stretton, and Margaret, daughter of Thomas Eynns, also of Church Stretton. He was a nephew of William *Thynne, and was probably encouraged to move to London by his uncle's well-established position in the royal household of Henry VIII; there is no evidence, however, that he was ever in the king's service himself, and he first appears in 1535 as one of the household of Lord Vaux of Harrowden. In 1536 he entered the service of Edward Seymour, Viscount Beauchamp. He served as Seymour's steward from 1536 to 1552, and his fortunes rose with those of his master. He accompanied Seymour on his northern and Scottish expeditions in 1542 and 1544, and was knighted after the battle of Pinkie in 1547. His main activities, however, were in London and the west, where Seymour built up enormous estates following his rise to power as lord protector and his elevation to the dukedom of Somerset in 1547. In London Thynne became a freeman of the City, a member of the Mercers' Company, and Packer of Stranger's Goods, all in 1547, and in 1549 he allied himself to the most powerful of City and Mercer families by his marriage to Christian, daughter of Sir Richard Gresham and sister of Sir Thomas Gresham.

In 1549 Sir William Paget expostulated that 'there is no one thing whereof his Grace hath need to take such heed as that man's proceedings' (Paget to William Petre, 22 July

Sir John Thynne (1512/13–1580), by unknown artist, 1566

1549, Tytler, 190), but in fact little has come to light to suggest that Thynne was anything except a hard-working servant of his master, though far from averse to feathering his own nest in the process. On the basis of his stewardship, and his commercial interests in the City, he commenced the building up of large estates, mainly in the west and centring on the former Carthusian priory at Longleat, which he bought from Sir John Horsey in 1540.

The fall of Somerset in 1549 brought Thynne two sessions in the Tower of London, confiscation of a substantial portion of his estates, and the imposition of a large fine. He survived, however, retired to Longleat, and kept a low profile under Mary. The accession of Elizabeth, the return to office of his old friends and colleagues William Cecil, Thomas Smith, and others, and the continuing importance of Thomas Gresham assured him position and prosperity. He consolidated and expanded his estates, not without arousing resentment among longer-established neighbours. When he made his will in 1580, the year of his death, he possessed property in Wiltshire, Somerset, Gloucestershire, Oxfordshire, London, Bristol, and Westminster. In 1566 or 1567 he had married, as his second wife, Dorothy (d. 1616), daughter of Sir William Wroughton, of Broad Hinton, Wiltshire, with whom he had five sons. With his first wife, Christian Gresham, he had three sons and three daughters. His descendants by his first wife were successively elevated to a baronetcy in 1641, to a viscountcy, as Viscounts Weymouth, in 1682, and to a marquessate, as marquesses of Bath, in 1789.

Thynne was elected member of parliament for Marlborough (probably in 1539 and 1542 as well as 1545), Salisbury

(1547), Wiltshire (1559, 1571), Great Bedwyn (1563), and Heytesbury (1572). He was a conscientious member, who sat on various committees, but he never played an important role at Westminster or in national politics. His hostile neighbour William Darrell satirized Thynne as 'infecting his master's head with plots and forms and many a subtle thing', and made the house of Longleat complain:

> but now see hym that by these thirty years almost with such turmoil of mind hath been thinking of me, framing and erecting me, raising many a time with great care and now and then pulling down this or that part of me to enlarge sometimes a foot or some few inches, upon a conceit, or this or that man's speech, and by and by beat down windows, for this or that fault here or there. (*Records of the Building of Longleat*, 3.213, Thynne Archives, Longleat)

This, though written in no friendly spirit, in fact expresses fairly enough Thynne's main claim to fame: less as the servant of the Protector Somerset and the founder of a dynasty than as a patron of architecture whose obsessive and restless perfectionism produced the great house at Longleat, deservedly acclaimed by John Summerson as representing 'as no other building does, the momentary High Renaissance of Tudor architecture' (Summerson, 62).

There is documentary evidence for Thynne's supervision of Somerset's huge house at Bedwyn Brail in Wiltshire, which never got beyond its early stages, and he was almost certainly closely involved with the design and building of Somerset House in the Strand. The design of Somerset House related closely to contemporary classical architecture in France, and was stylistically in advance of anything else being built in England at the time. But in his own house at Longleat, Thynne, at the end of a thirty-seven-year process involving constant rebuilding, rethinking, and enlargement, and interrupted by a serious fire in 1567, developed the forms to be found at Somerset House into a far more integrated classical whole, a compact unity, in which a consistent design based on superimposed Doric, Ionic, and Corinthian pilasters was carried round all four external façades, and given modelling, strength, and rhythm by the constant repetition of rectangular bay windows.

Although Thynne was capable of making drawings to show what he wanted, his buildings resulted from a combination of his own search for perfection and his employment of a succession of often gifted craftsmen. In its final form the design and detailing of Longleat owed much to a French mason, Alan Maynard, who arrived in 1563, and an English mason, Robert Smythson, who arrived in 1568. Because of the many craftsmen who worked there during its long gestation and moved on elsewhere, Longleat became the seat of a school of building which had repercussions all over the west country and, to a lesser extent, all over England. Thynne died on 21 May 1580 and was buried in the church at Monkton Deverill, Wiltshire.

MARK GIROUARD

Sources HoP, *Commons, 1509–58*, 3.463–7 · HoP, *Commons, 1558–1603*, 3.506–7 · J. Summerson, *Architecture in Britain, 1530–1830*, 7th edn (1983) · M. Girouard, 'The development of Longleat House between 1546 and 1572', *Archaeological Journal*, 116 (1959), 200–22 · M. Girouard, *Robert Smythson and the Elizabethan country house*, [new edn] (1983) · P. F. Tytler, *England under the reigns of Edward VI and Mary*, 1 (1839) · will, PRO, PROB 11/62
Likenesses portrait, 1566, Longleat House, Wiltshire [*see illus.*]

Thynne, John Alexander, **fourth marquess of Bath** (1831–1896), diplomatist and politician, born in Westminster on 1 March 1831, was the eldest son of Henry Frederick Thynne, third marquess of Bath (*d.* 1837), and Harriet, daughter of Alexander *Baring. He succeeded his father on 24 June 1837. Bath was educated at Eton College and matriculated from Christ Church, Oxford, on 31 May 1849. He soon began to take an active part in county business, being appointed a deputy lieutenant of Somerset in 1853, and of Wiltshire in 1860. He was also active in the volunteers and yeomanry. In 1889 he was appointed lord lieutenant of Wiltshire and chairman of the county council.

In May 1858 Bath was sent to Lisbon as ambassador-extraordinary and plenipotentiary, when he received from Pedro V the order of the Tower and Sword. Nine years later, in July 1867, when ambassador-extraordinary on a special mission at Vienna, he received from the emperor Franz Josef the grand cross of the order of Leopold of Austria. A keen Anglo-Catholic and a violent enemy of the Public Worship Regulation Act of 1874, Bath, though in general conservative in politics, played an active role in 1876–8 in the campaign against the 'Bulgarian atrocities' and Disraeli's handling of them. Longleat, Bath's house, became a centre for meetings and consultations attended by Gladstone and others. In 1880 he published *Observations on Bulgarian Affairs*. He was appointed trustee of the National Portrait Gallery in 1874, and of the British Museum in 1883. He was a member of the Academy of Belgrade in 1884. He also served on the Historical Manuscripts Commission.

Bath married, in August 1861, Frances Isabella Catherine Vesey (*d.* 31 Oct 1915), eldest daughter of Thomas Vesey, third Viscount de Vesci. They had three sons and three daughters. He died on 20 April 1896 at Venice and was buried at Longbridge Deverill, Wiltshire. His first son, Thomas Henry, succeeded to the title.

G. LE G. NORGATE, rev. H. C. G. MATTHEW

Sources GEC, *Peerage* · *The Times* (21 April 1896) · Gladstone, *Diaries* · R. T. Shannon, *Gladstone and the Bulgarian agitation, 1876* (1963) · Burke, *Peerage*
Archives BL, corresp. with Lord Carnarvon, Add. MSS 60771–60772 · BL, corresp. with W. E. Gladstone, Add. MSS 44453–44485, *passim* · Bodl. Oxf., letters to Benjamin Disraeli · JRL, letters to E. A. Freeman · NL Ire., letters to J. E. Vernon
Wealth at death £272,049 6s. 8d.: probate, 24 July 1896, CGPLA Eng. & Wales

Thynne [*née* Touchet], **Maria**, **Lady Thynne** (*c.*1578–1611), gentlewoman, was the second daughter of George Touchet or Tuchet, Lord Audley, later earl of Castlehaven (*d.* 1617), and his first wife, Lucy (*d. c.*1611), daughter of Sir James Marvin or Mervyn (*d.* 1611). She was known in the family as Mall. She attended Queen Elizabeth at the court briefly in 1594. In May 1594 Maria married Thomas Thynne (1578–1639), an Oxford undergraduate and son and heir to John Thynne and Joan *Thynne of Longleat,

Wiltshire, clandestinely, at an inn at Beaconsfield. They kept the marriage secret from the Thynnes, bitter enemies of Maria's family. After discovering the marriage Thomas's parents struggled for annulment, but a long lawsuit ended in 1601 with confirmation of its legality.

Such a marriage brought no dowry, which further angered the Thynnes. Maria attempted to conciliate her mother-in-law, Joan Thynne, and, when she failed, wrote a vituperative letter to her. Maria's letters to Thomas, although few, are also exceptionally vividly expressed and revealing. She fretted over his health, sending medical recipes. She wrote of her attitude to their combative and emotional marital relationship, and playfully reprimanded him for making her pregnant; she referred to their companionship in hard times.

In November 1604 Thomas Thynne, who had been knighted in August, inherited Longleat and Maria became mistress of a great house. During Thomas's absences at Westminster, Maria took responsibility for managing the estates, and her letters show her detailed knowledge. She recommended a supervisor for the stables, and dealt with gentlemen retainers and tenant farmers, giving Thomas advice on unsatisfactory leases. She collected rents from substantial landholders, and compiled accounts in her own hand. She arranged the movement of cattle, and instructed Thomas about cutting woods and selling the timber. In 1609 and 1610 she arranged the financial details of major purchases, including the manor of Warminster from her brother Mervin Touchet or Audley, later earl of Castlehaven.

Maria and Thomas had three sons: the first, John, born in 1604, died young. Maria feared she would die in childbirth, and had her portrait painted during her last pregnancy in 1611. Her fears were realized, but the infant son Thomas survived, cared for initially by Joan Thynne, in a final gesture of reconciliation.   ALISON WALL

Sources GEC, *Peerage*, new edn · B. Botfield, *Stemmata Botevilliana: memorials of the families of de Boteville, Thynne, and Botfield* (1843) · *Two Elizabethan women: correspondence of Joan and Maria Thynne, 1575–1611*, ed. A. D. Wall, Wilts RS, 38 (1983) · A. D. Wall, 'For love, money or politics? A clandestine marriage and the Elizabethan court of arches', *HJ*, 38 (1995), 511–33 · Longleat House, Wiltshire, Marquess of Bath MSS, Thynne MSS, vols. 6–8, boxes XLIII, XXXVII, and bk 191 [with permission of the marquess of Bath] · J. A. Thynne and M. L. Boyle, *Biographical catalogue of the portraits at Longleat in the county of Wilts, the seat of the marquis of Bath* (1881) [details of Maria's children incorrect] · W. Drake, *Notes of the family of Mervyn of Pertwood* (1873)
Archives Longleat House, Wiltshire
Likenesses Mytens, oils, 1611, Longleat House, Wiltshire; repro. in *Two Elizabethan women*; photograph, Courtauld Inst.

Thynne, Thomas, first Viscount Weymouth (*bap.* 1640, *d.* 1714), politician, was baptized on 8 September 1640, the first son of Sir Henry Frederick Thynne, first baronet (1615–1680), landowner of Kempsford, Gloucestershire, and his wife, Mary (*bap.* 1619), daughter of Thomas Coventry, first Baron Coventry of Aylesborough. Thynne was educated at Kingston grammar school. From a staunchly Anglican and royalist family, in the 1650s he was taught by

ejected Anglican clergymen such as Thomas Triplett, corresponded regularly with Henry Hammond, and was 'one of the prize pupils' tutored privately by ejected Anglican dons at Oxford (Seaward, 65). He did, however, eventually go to Christ Church, Oxford, matriculating on 21 April 1657, but was not awarded a degree. While at Oxford he befriended his Christ Church tutor Thomas Ken, later bishop of Bath and Wells, and acquired the extensive manuscript collection of William Burton, his former teacher. Thynne's lifelong interest in manuscripts and coins earned him recognition from the Royal Society, which elected him a fellow in 1664.

In 1664 Thynne was supported by the duke of York in a by-election at Salisbury, but he had little prospect of success against the other candidate, Edward Hyde, who had been put up by his father Lord Chancellor Clarendon, the city's high steward, and Thynne probably withdrew before the poll. In 1666 he was appointed a groom of the duke's bedchamber, a post he held until 1672, and was sent as an envoy to Sweden from 1666 to 1669. In or before 1673 he married Lady Frances (*bap.* 1650, *d.* 1712), daughter of Heneage *Finch, third earl of Winchilsea. They had three sons, who all predeceased their father, and one daughter. Thynne's new connections enabled him to enter parliament in 1674, when he was returned for Oxford University after a by-election caused by the promotion of the incumbent MP, Heneage Finch, later first earl of Nottingham, to the lord keepership. Thynne's success may be attributed as much to his connection with Finch as to the large sums expended upon entertaining the electorate, for the constituency normally returned only former members of the university. Thynne had no degree, his contribution to the work of the house during this parliament was slight, and he notably made no attempt to have the clergy exempted from the hearth tax, an issue of some concern to the colleges, and consequently there was little scope for his re-election for the university in 1679. His recent marriage had, however, brought him a substantial estate at Drayton Bassett, Staffordshire, and a strong interest in nearby Tamworth, which borough elected him to both parliaments of 1679. He shortly afterwards became high steward of the town, a post he held until his death. In parliament Thynne supported the Comprehension Bill and a measure to remove Roman Catholics from the capital, but acted against attempts to exclude the duke of York from the succession, telling against committing the first Exclusion Bill on 21 May 1679. His personal ambition was checked by his failure to secure nomination from the Levant Company as ambassador to Turkey. On 6 March 1680 Thynne succeeded his father as second baronet, and two years later, following the sensational assassination of his cousin, Thomas Thynne, he came into the extensive Somerset and Wiltshire estates centred upon Longleat. His 32-year tenure at Longleat was spent redesigning much of the house's interior, rebuilding a number of rooms, and completing the chapel, while the gardens were laid out with fashionable contemporary formality. On 11 December 1682 Thynne's steadfast opposition to exclusion was rewarded with a peerage, when he was created Baron Thynne and Viscount Weymouth. He deferred taking his seat in the Lords, however, until 1685. Although he was not sounded on the repeal of the Test Act and penal laws against dissenters, he was known as an opponent of James II's religious measures. In December 1688 he was named as one of four emissaries sent to ask William of Orange to summon a free parliament. In the Lords he voted for a regency, and though he took the oaths to the new monarchs he supported the nonjurors, and offered his old friend Bishop Ken private apartments at Longleat as well as the family chaplaincy. Weymouth's membership of the new missionary Society for the Propagation of the Gospel from 1701 may be a testament to his religious devotion.

Weymouth was a vocal opponent of the government, and legislative measures which he sought to undermine included the Triennial Act and the 1697 bill for regulating elections. He refused to sign the 1696 association for the defence of William III after the discovery of an assassination plot. Certainly a high tory, he was soon suspected of also being a Jacobite, but is not known to have intrigued actively with the exiled James II. In June 1702, soon after the accession of Queen Anne, Weymouth was appointed a privy councillor, keeper of the Forest of Dean, and the first lord commissioner of trade and plantations. In 1711 he was reappointed *custos rotulorum* of Wiltshire, a post which he had held almost continuously since 1683 before being displaced by the whigs in 1706.

Weymouth's wife died on 17 April 1712 and was buried on 3 May at Longbridge Deverill, Wiltshire. Two years later, on or shortly before 28 July 1714, Weymouth himself died, probably at Longleat; he too was buried in the family vault at Longbridge Deverill. In his will, made in November 1709, he confirmed an annuity to Bishop Ken and bequeathed £40,000 to four granddaughters and £1000 to build a church in East Woodlands, Frome. Paintings by Van Dyck and Antonio di Cortena were bequeathed to the earls of Rochester and Nottingham. Thynne's titles and the bulk of the estate were devolved on his great-nephew Thomas Thynne, second Viscount Weymouth and father of the first marquess of Bath, on the condition that he confirmed his Anglicanism.   HENRY LANCASTER

Sources A. M. Burke, ed., *Memorials of St Margaret's Church, Westminster* (1914) · *Collins peerage of England: genealogical, biographical and historical*, ed. E. Brydges, 9 vols. (1812), vol. 2, pp. 502–7 · R. C. Hoare, *The history of modern Wiltshire*, 1/2: *Hundred of Heytesbury* (1822) · N. Luttrell, *A brief historical relation of state affairs from September 1678 to April 1714*, 6 (1857), 386, 574 · will, PRO, PROB 11/541, fol. 306v · W. D. Christie, ed., *Letters addressed from London to Sir Joseph Williamson*, 2 vols., CS, new ser., 8–9 (1874) · T. B. Macaulay, *The history of England from the accession of James II*, new edn, 4, ed. C. H. Firth (1914), 2006 · GEC, *Peerage*, new edn · L. Naylor, 'Thynne, Thomas I', HoP, *Commons, 1660–90* · L. Naylor, 'Oxford University', HoP, *Commons, 1660–90*, 1.360–62 · P. Seaward, *The Cavalier Parliament and the reconstruction of the old regime, 1661–1667* (1989) · IGI
Archives BL, letters to first and second marquesses of Halifax, C 10 · TCD, corresp. with William King
Likenesses W. Wissing, oils, c.1862, Longleat, Wiltshire · attrib. N. Dixon, miniature (after P. Lely), NPG · P. Lely, oils, Longleat, Wiltshire · P. Lely, oils, Courtauld Inst. · school of J. Riley, oils, Longleat, Wiltshire
Wealth at death over £50,000 capital; vast real estate; among wealthiest peers; at least £50,000 in cash bequests; land in Wiltshire, Somerset, Middlesex, and Staffordshire: will, PRO, PROB 11/541, fol. 306v

Thynne, Thomas [*nicknamed* Tom of Ten Thousand] (1647/8–1682), landowner and murder victim, was the only surviving son of Sir Thomas Thynne (1609/10–1669?) of Richmond, Surrey, and his wife, Stuart or Stuarta, daughter of Walter *Balcanquhall (c.1586–1645). He matriculated from Christ Church, Oxford, on 14 December 1666, aged eighteen, and was admitted to the Middle Temple in 1668. Following the death in 1670 of his uncle, Sir James Thynne, he succeeded to the estate of Longleat in Wiltshire. His nickname, popular at the time, derived solely from his wealth and his love of extravagance. Thynne was an active parliamentarian, being a member for Wiltshire from 1670 to 1682. At first he appeared to favour the court in his politics and was fairly intimate with the duke of York and his friends; only later did he express those country and whig views that led him into opposition. By 1674 he had become an opposition leader in Wiltshire, as well as a deputy lieutenant and a colonel in the local militia. Depicted as 'Issachar, his wealthy western friend' in John Dryden's notorious satire *Absalom and Achitophel* (line 738), Thynne was a close associate of the duke of Monmouth. Sir John Reresby too claimed that Thynne was one that had opposed the court's interest and 'engaged himselfe in that of the Duke of Monmouth' (Geiter and Speck, 243).

Thynne would not have been averse to holding government office, but he was not noted for his intellectual abilities. In the event he became an exclusionist in the early 1680s. Indeed on 22 January 1680 Thynne, Sir Walter St John, and Sir Edward Hungerford presented a petition from Wiltshire to the king for the sitting of parliament, to which Charles II replied that Thynne was an 'Impertinent foole to meddle with what did not concerne him' (Knights, 235). Undeterred, Thynne also entertained Monmouth during his western tour of 1680, but in the latter stages of the exclusion crisis he appeared to begin to shift his political position. He was associated with Ralph Montagu and tried, in vain, to obtain the office of the secretary of state.

It was in his personal life that Thynne gained most notoriety. Thynne was noted as one always 'very civill [to the ladies] and allways courteuse & debonnaire' (BL, Add. MS 37047, fol. 244). Like most of his companions he was a man of loose character and notoriously seduced Miss Trevor, one of the queen's maids of honour, with promises of marriage. As a consequence he was involved in a duel in the spring of 1678. In July 1681 he married Elizabeth, countess of Ogle (1667–1722), daughter and heir of Josceline Percy, eleventh earl of Northumberland (1644–1670) and widow of Henry Cavendish, earl of Ogle, having paid a goodly sum of money to her guardians, since she was only fourteen years old. The marriage was never consummated, for Elizabeth, who continued to be known as Lady Ogle, having first taken the advice of Lady Temple,

Thomas Thynne (1647/8–1682), by Sir Peter Lely, c.1673

fled to the Netherlands. Thynne took legal action to ensure that he held onto her estate and that she be returned to Longleat. But his actions in marrying Elizabeth had also raised the jealousy of Count Karl Johann *Königsmark, one of her more unsuccessful suitors. It was later claimed that Thynne had merely ignored the many challenges sent by the count and even sought to rid himself of the count and his 'ancient', Captain Christopher Vratz, by hiring some men to kill them. An attack apparently took place, but failed and left Vratz wounded and burning for revenge against Thynne. Vratz subsequently recruited Lieutenant John Stern, another professional soldier, into his plans. There is little doubt that Vratz was also in communication with Königsmark over the affair. The latter was lying low in London, ostensibly recovering from a venereal disease. It was Königsmark who ultimately supplied the man who would kill Thynne: Charles George Borosky, alias the Polonian.

On Sunday 12 February 1682 Vratz informed Borosky that he had a quarrel with an English gentleman, had sent him two challenges, and had been ignored; and that as Thynne had attempted to have both himself and Königsmark murdered he was bent on revenge. He gave Borosky a musquetoon and reassured him that, as in Poland, servants were never held responsible for carrying out the orders of their masters. The pair soon joined Stern, who informed them that Thynne was out in his coach, and all three rode off in pursuit. They caught up with Thynne just after he had dropped off his passenger, the duke of Monmouth, at Hedge Lane and was proceeding up St James Street towards the countess of Northumberland's house.

While Stern moved in front of the coach, Vratz and Borosky came up alongside. Vratz called on the coach to stop and as it came to a halt Borosky fired his weapon into it. Five or six shots hit Thynne in the stomach and hip, mortally wounding him. The trio then rode off in some haste. Thynne was taken home, where after 'languishing all night … between five & six in the morning' of 13 February he 'expired' (BL, Add. MS 37047, fol. 244). His body was subsequently embalmed, and buried in Westminster Abbey on 9 March. It was placed under a large and rather pompous tombstone that depicted his murder, but whose original inscription, firmly placing the blame for his death on Count Königsmark, was suppressed by the dean of the abbey. Thynne's cousin Sir Thomas *Thynne, later first Viscount Weymouth, went on to 'possess all his estates … [but] not his good nature' according to one contemporary (ibid.).

In the aftermath of the killing Charles II was fearful that the whigs would attempt to make some political capital out of it; given the presence of Monmouth in Thynne's coach only moments before the murder this was highly likely. However, Vratz, Stern, and Borosky were soon arrested. Königsmark attempted to flee the country, but was captured while trying to escape on a vessel bound for Sweden. Brought back to London he denied any complicity in the murder and claimed to have only left London because he feared the rage of the mob. He was committed to Newgate, but Charles II was not keen to see the young man suffer too much for his crime. Indeed at the subsequent trial, having bribed some of the jury, Königsmark escaped punishment, while Vratz, Stern, and Borosky were all found guilty and went to the gallows on 10 March 1682.

Thynne's death, and his wealth, were ultimately the most remarkable things about the man. As a whig plutocrat of some note on the Wiltshire scene he at least believed himself worthy of higher office. Yet, although his association with Monmouth was central to his later career, there are hints that problems in his personal life, particularly those with his wife, led not only to heavy drinking but also to a potential political change of heart. At length, while whig propagandists sought to use Thynne's murder for political ends, and so tried to revive the heady days of the Popish Plot, this, like Tom of Ten Thousand's final reputation, was soon dissipated.

ALAN MARSHALL

Sources *Memoirs of Sir John Reresby*, ed. A. Browning, 2nd edn, ed. M. K. Geiter and W. A. Speck (1991) • BL, Add. MSS 37047, fol. 244, and 38855, fol. 114 • M. Knights, *Politics and opinion in the exclusion crisis, 1678–1681* (1994) • H. Vizetelly, *Count Königsmark and 'Tom of Ten Thousand'* (1890) • Foster, *Alum. Oxon.* • HoP, *Commons, 1660–90*, 3.564–8 • *Domestic Intelligence* (15 Feb 1682) • *The tryal and condemnation of George Borosky, alias Boratzi, Christopher Vratz and John Stern, for the barbarous murder of Thomas Thynne Esq.* (1682) • J. L. Chester, ed., *The marriage, baptismal and burial register of the collegiate church and abbey of St Peter Westminster* (1876) • N. Luttrell, *A brief historical relation of state affairs from September 1678 to April 1714*, 6 vols. (1857) • *A hue and cry after blood and murder* (1682) • *N&Q*, 5 (1852), 183, 269–70 • E. Godley, *The trial of Count Königsmark* (1929) • *State trials*
Likenesses P. Lely, portrait, c.1673, Longleat House, Wiltshire [see illus.] • oils, c.1680 (after P. Lely), Longleat House, Wiltshire • oils,

c.1680 (after G. Kneller), Longleat House, Wiltshire • A. Quellin, effigy on monument, c.1682–1684, Westminster Abbey, London • A. Browne, mezzotint (after P. Lely), BM, NPG • R. White, line engraving, BM, NPG

Wealth at death see will, PRO, PROB 11/369/25

Thynne, Thomas, third Viscount Weymouth and first marquess of Bath (1734–1796), courtier and politician, was born on 13 September 1734, the eldest son and heir of Thomas Thynne, second Viscount Weymouth (1710–1751), landowner, and his second wife, Louisa (d. 1736), the second daughter of John *Carteret, Earl Granville. He seems to have been educated by his family and then at a school in Market Street, Hertfordshire, before matriculating from St John's College, Cambridge, in Lent 1752. He received his MA in 1753 and subsequently undertook a grand tour on the continent. In January 1751 he had succeeded his father, becoming the third Viscount Weymouth. The young aristocrat devoted considerable time and money to improving the family seat at Longleat in Wiltshire, employing Capability Brown, who from 1757 onwards and at considerable cost created the modern gardens and park which surround the house. But Weymouth's principal activities, then and in the future, were the common aristocratic pursuits of gambling and dissipation. In 1757, when his gambling losses were the talk of the court, George II expressed concern that Weymouth 'could not be a good kind of man, as he never kept company with any woman, and loved nothing but play and strong beer' (*Correspondence of John, Fourth Duke of Bedford*, 2.231). Two years later, on 22 May 1759, Weymouth married Elizabeth Cavendish (1735–1825), the eldest daughter of William Bentinck, second duke of Portland, and his wife, Margaret Cavendish Harley.

Royal favour and entry into politics This aristocratic marriage was central to Weymouth's rise. When George III became king the following year, Weymouth was appointed a lord of the bedchamber (1760–63), while his wife became first a lady of the bedchamber to Queen Charlotte (1761–93) and subsequently mistress of the robes (1793–1818). These positions at court, and the support of the ruler to which they led, were important during two decades when George III played an active role in government and ministerial politics. Weymouth attached himself to the duke of Bedford and was named master of the horse when the duke's followers joined George Grenville's ministry in spring 1763. The family finances, however, were unable to bear the costs of the third viscount's lifestyle, and by 1765 he was on the point of fleeing his creditors and travelling to France. Court and ministerial favour provided temporary salvation with the appointment (April–July 1765) as lord lieutenant of Ireland; at the end of May Weymouth was sworn of the privy council. This appointment was accompanied by the usual grant of £3000 for equipage, though Weymouth never crossed the Irish Sea to take up his post and resigned within three months.

Aristocratic birth, political connections, and royal favour were still sufficient to secure entrance to the highest level of government. Weymouth possessed all three and, with a rising reputation as a speaker in the House of

Thomas Thynne, third Viscount Weymouth and first marquess of Bath (1734–1796), by Sir Thomas Lawrence, c.1795

Lords, by the mid-1760s he was on the brink of a public career. In January 1768, when the duke of Bedford's followers finally joined the ailing Chatham–Grafton administration, he became secretary of state for the northern department at the unusually early age of thirty-three, though he wholly lacked experience of either diplomacy or government office. At this period formal control of British foreign policy was divided on a geographical basis. In the following October, Weymouth requested and received the senior southern secretaryship. He remained at that post until December 1770. Five years later, in November 1775, he returned to the southern department, acting as secretary of state until November 1779, when he resigned. The seven years during which he was involved in the running of Britain's foreign policy made him one of the longest-serving secretaries of state in the age of the American War of Independence, in spite of his notorious personal failings which troubled his contemporaries and flawed his career.

Secretary of state Weymouth was notoriously lazy, devoted to the gaming table, and given to dissipation and drunkenness: shortly after he entered office Junius sneered about the northern secretary and 'the bewitching smiles of Burgundy' (Francis, 31). He was not without ability, and his correspondence contains periodic flashes of high intelligence and real political insight, while on occasions he was a spirited and effective government spokesman in the House of Lords. This was aided by his tall and handsome appearance and patrician demeanour. In private he could charm and enchant by his conversation and lively mind. He was capable of occasional bouts of activity, not always with beneficial consequences, and these interspersed his habitual indolence. This was a crucial failing: the secretaries of state were the key executive agents of British government, responsible for turning cabinet decisions into precise orders to government agents at home and abroad. The smooth running of foreign policy depended upon the maintenance of regular communications with diplomats, and this Weymouth consistently failed to do. Instead he depended heavily, during his first period in office, on his loyal under-secretary, Robert Wood, to transact official business. While this did something to disguise Weymouth's chronic laziness, it carried an additional price, since Wood himself was widely suspected by contemporaries of abusing his position, and the inside information which it provided, to speculate in the financial markets.

Weymouth's two periods as secretary of state provoked a series of thinly disguised complaints and even overt protests by members of Britain's diplomatic corps that they had found themselves without specific instructions or even general guidance from London at crucial moments. In nine months during 1779, at a critical period for Anglo-Russian relations, James Harris in St Petersburg received only one letter, which was both belated and very general. Early in his ministerial career Weymouth expressed a very odd sentiment for a secretary of state, that British ministers 'should *hear* as much and *say* as little as possible' (*SIRIO*, 12.369), and he himself reinforced precept by example. His taciturnity and evasiveness towards the foreign diplomatic corps were notorious and widely and correctly interpreted as an attempt to cover up his ignorance of European issues, on which he remained badly informed even towards the end of his spell in office. His relations with his ministerial colleagues were equally frosty: the neglect of his duties, together with the limited impact which he had on wider government policy, was accompanied by evident ambition and periodic ruthlessness in pursuit of personal advancement. The shrewdest assessment was that offered by Sir Nathaniel Wraxall, who remarked that Weymouth's 'application to business by no means kept pace with his abilities, nor was he ever a popular Minister' (Wraxall, 2.198).

Foreign relations British foreign policy during Weymouth's months at the northern department in 1768 was dominated by an Anglo-French confrontation over the Mediterranean island of Corsica. France's leading minister, the duc de Choiseul, secretly concluded a treaty with the declining Italian republic of Genoa to purchase the island, at a bargain price. Its acquisition would strengthen France's position in the western Mediterranean and provide protection for her important southern naval base at Toulon; it would also boost her flagging prestige after the severe defeats in the Seven Years' War (1756–63). When a Franco-Genoese agreement was suspected in spring 1768, the southern secretary, the earl of Shelburne, together with the effective leader of the ministry, the duke of Grafton, Lord Camden (lord chancellor), and Sir Edward Hawke (first lord of the Admiralty), argued within cabinet

for a vigorous response and were prepared to fight if necessary. They were opposed by Weymouth, along with Lord Gower (lord president of the council), Lord North (chancellor of the exchequer), and the earl of Hillsborough (American secretary). Weymouth had long been a follower of the duke of Bedford, the leading Francophile in British public life, and seems to have been taking his cue from him. The divisions within the cabinet were known to the French government and undermined Britain's position over Corsica. It was further weakened by Weymouth's calculated indiscretions to members of the foreign diplomatic corps, to the effect that the Grafton ministry would never fight over the French annexation of the island. Shelburne's policy had been wrecked by his brother secretary—with whom he was already on bad terms—and in the summer of 1768 France's take-over went ahead, Britain doing nothing to resist it.

In the autumn Shelburne resigned and was replaced by a career diplomatist, the earl of Rochford. But the latter, despite his relevant experience as an ambassador to Spain and France, was consigned to the northern department. This was because Weymouth requested and received the southern secretaryship, still recognized to be the senior province: had he not switched departments, Rochford's appointment would have appeared to slight him. As far as Weymouth was concerned, it was a matter of political prestige, not any new-found zeal for the business of government. From autumn 1768, for almost two years, he exhibited little interest in British diplomacy, being content to allow the hard-working Rochford to shape policy. Weymouth exerted real influence only on two areas of government activity during this spell in office. He acted vigorously to restore order in the capital during the riots in London in spring 1768 and the unrest associated with the Middlesex election. His actions were prompted by George III and strengthened his links with the king. Weymouth long remained an advocate of firm measures against John Wilkes. In 1769 he intervened decisively but without immediate consequences in the affairs of the East India Company, setting a precedent for taking unilateral action behind the back of his cabinet colleagues, which was to be so important in 1770 over the Falkland Islands.

The context to this confusing episode was the expansion of the company's territorial power and economic influence in the subcontinent during and after the Seven Years' War. At times it could act independently of the government in London over important issues of strategy in India, which had implications for Britain's wider policy. In 1768–9 disquiet had arisen over the East India Company's annexation of Balambangan without apparent approval from the Grafton ministry. On this occasion Weymouth, again prompted by George III, expressed disquiet to the governors of the company. When in 1769 the company's military problems with Haidar Ali led it to seek government support, Weymouth seized the opportunity to raise the question of ministerial control. His efforts, including an unprecedented appeal to the general court, were unsuccessful, at which point he calmly issued secret instructions—which contradicted his public orders—to

Sir John Lindsay, who was dealing with problems on the spot in India. Nothing came of this attempt to weaken the East India Company's independence, and the episode is interesting primarily for the light it sheds on Weymouth's personality and character.

The Falkland Islands crisis In the second half of 1770 Weymouth's influence upon British foreign policy returned, and during these months his involvement was at its peak. The occasion was a revival of an earlier Anglo-Bourbon confrontation over the Falkland Islands in the distant south Atlantic. In 1766–7 there had been a sharp dispute over a British settlement at Port Egmont on West Falkland, which Madrid claimed as Spanish territory. On that occasion a compromise had been patched up, with both sides wanting to avoid war. But the issue had been shelved rather than solved, and it re-emerged three years later when Spain adopted a much firmer stance. In June 1770 a Spanish force evicted the tiny British garrison from Port Egmont.

In September word of the expedition against Port Egmont reached London. Britain's response was the responsibility of Weymouth, who now demonstrated greater vigour than at any point in his career. The southern secretary, being one of the principal executors of government policy, possessed considerable freedom of action under the prevailing constitutional conventions. This, together with the absence from London of North (now leader of the ministry) and his brother secretary, Rochford, enabled him to determine Britain's initial response. From the first Weymouth was determined to force Spain to fight or to surrender, believing that British naval superiority could achieve this. Without consulting his cabinet colleagues he set in motion a substantial naval mobilization and adopted an intransigent and bellicose attitude in the diplomatic exchanges with Madrid. By the closing months of 1770 a war over the Falklands appeared very likely, as it was assumed in both London and Madrid that France would support her Spanish ally.

Weymouth's motive for seeking hostilities with Spain was to achieve political supremacy for himself. North, slowly consolidating his own government, was the main obstacle to his dominance. He calculated—perhaps acting at Wood's instigation—that war would bring down the ministry and restore to power the legendary architect of British victories in the Seven Years' War—William Pitt, now earl of Chatham. But Chatham would only be a figurehead in any new ministry, given the extent of his physical and mental collapse, and so Weymouth might expect to wield effective authority. This naked bid for power proved stillborn. George III, whose oversight of the official correspondence enabled him to monitor the southern secretary's actions, realized that the scale of naval preparations would bring about hostilities and acted to preserve peace: in company with most members of the ministry, he wanted a firm stance towards Spain, but he did not wish to force her to fight. Together with North, the king orchestrated cabinet opposition to Weymouth's actions and reassured Bourbon diplomats in London that Britain did not wish a war. During late November and early December

the southern secretary's policy was overturned, to his unconcealed fury. After a stormy cabinet meeting on 7 December, Weymouth resigned. North, Rochford, and George III supervised a settlement with Madrid, finally concluded in late January 1771.

One mysterious dimension of Weymouth's resignation in late 1770 is that at some point he received an assurance from the king that he would one day be restored to the southern department. Barely six months after he left office Weymouth, who had not joined the opponents of North's ministry, was mentioned as a possible lord privy seal, should Grafton not accept the post. In the following year he was offered a secretaryship of state, but haughtily declined. His phoenix-like resurgence came during the first half of the War of American Independence (1775–83). In November 1775 he was restored to the southern department, where he remained until his final departure from office in October 1779. The passage of time had done little to remove the shortcomings apparent throughout his whole career. He remained indolent, aloof, and isolated within cabinet, though he acted as a government spokesman in the House of Lords and intermittently intrigued very actively against his colleagues. His earlier hard line towards the Bourbon powers did not immediately resurface after autumn 1775, when it would have been difficult to reconcile with the official policy of maintaining good relations with Versailles and Madrid. When his return to office was being considered, George III had discreetly noted—with one eye firmly on the Falklands episode— that 'Lord Weymouth and the Court of Spain cannot pleasantly transact business' (*Correspondence of George III*, 3.283). In fact he accommodated himself for a time to the official strategy of conciliating the Bourbon powers in order to facilitate the suppression of the American colonial rebellion.

The drift towards war Before long, however, the hostility towards France and Spain re-emerged. Weymouth aligned himself with the earl of Sandwich, who had also followed Bedford during his earlier career. Sandwich, who was first lord of the Admiralty, feared Bourbon intervention in the American struggle and favoured a firm diplomatic and naval response to this threat. The two men were isolated within a cabinet which advocated conciliation of France and Spain. In 1776–7, when Weymouth's attitude was diametrically opposed to the ministry's policy, he was simply bypassed by his own colleagues and by French and Spanish diplomats: the southern secretary ceased to transact relations with the two principal countries within his department, which the complacent viscount happily accepted. His influence on Britain's foreign policy during the American war was slight. Indeed, he found an ingenious way to circumvent his indolence by circulating extracts from the dispatches of the influential ambassador in Paris, Viscount Stormont, as instructions to other British diplomats. This was a unique episode in the history of Britain's eighteenth-century foreign relations and had a coda which was entirely apposite: Stormont succeeded him as southern secretary.

By mid-1777 war with France was believed to be inevitable, and Weymouth's earlier hostility towards the Bourbons now fitted with Britain's overall policy. He could therefore return to a day-to-day role in the conduct of London's diplomacy, which he did from that summer. Yet his impact upon British diplomacy or the wider conduct of the war was minimal, and his commitment to his office no greater than hitherto. This became particularly evident in 1779. The final illness and death of the northern secretary, the earl of Suffolk, made Weymouth for the first nine months of the year *de facto* foreign secretary, responsible for relations with countries in both departments. Edmund Burke was quick to sneer, noting sarcastically that 'The whole of the laborious and arduous correspondence of this Empire rested solely upon the activity and energy of Lord Weymouth' (Mackesy, 246). Throughout these months Britain's diplomacy was allowed to drift towards the rocks by its inattentive pilot. His principal initiative was a volcanic outburst during an interview with the Spanish ambassador in May 1779. Blending anger and menaces in equal proportions, he censured Madrid's duplicity throughout the colonial rebellion and reversed in one ill-considered outburst a year's careful diplomacy aimed at conciliating Spain. The impact was slight: Madrid's decision to intervene openly on the American side, announced in the summer, had already been made and proceeded from far more fundamental causes. But the episode once more highlighted Weymouth's shortcomings as a foreign minister, apparent throughout his final months in power. One well-placed contemporary, John Robinson, believed that this final phase of neglect proceeded from the viscount already having decided to resign, which he duly did in November when he left office for the last time.

Final years Weymouth and his wife were established figures at court. The extent of this royal favour was apparent in June 1778, when he was created a knight of the Garter, though he was never to be installed. In August 1789 he was created marquess of Bath. He had served as groom of the stole between March and November 1775, and was reappointed in 1782. Weymouth held the office and the substantial income of £2000 per annum which it conferred until his death, in Arlington Street, London, on 19 November 1796. He was buried at Longbridge Deverill. His eldest son, Thomas Thynne (1765–1837), succeeded to the title; two other sons and five daughters of his marriage survived him. His life was a salutary reminder that a flawed personality and manifold failings as a minister were no obstacle to a career at the highest level of government during the second half of the eighteenth century, provided they were accompanied by sufficient aristocratic pedigree and reinforced by connections at court.

H. M. SCOTT

Sources H. M. Scott, *British foreign policy in the age of the American revolution* (1990) · H. V. Bowen, *Revenue and reform: the Indian problem in British politics, 1757–1773* (1991) · J. Brooke, *The Chatham administration, 1766–1768* (1956) · P. D. G. Thomas, *John Wilkes* (1996) · P. G. Mackesy, *The war for America, 1775–1783* (1964) · I. de Madariaga, *Britain, Russia and the armed neutrality of 1780* (1962) · *Correspondence of John,*

fourth duke of Bedford, ed. J. Russell, 3 vols. (1842–6) · *Sbornik imperatorskogo russkogo istoricheskogo obshchestva*, 148 vols. (St Petersburg, 1867–1916) [SIRIO] · *DNB* · GEC, *Peerage* · *GM*, 1st ser., 66 (1796), 972 · [P. Francis], *The letters of Junius*, ed. J. Cannon (1978) · N. W. Wraxall, *Historical memoirs of my own time*, 2nd edn, 2 vols. (1815) · *The correspondence of King George the Third from 1760 to December 1783*, ed. J. Fortescue, 6 vols. (1927–8) · Venn, *Alum. Cant.*
Archives BL, corresp. relating to India, home misc. series · Longleat House, Wiltshire, corresp. and papers | BL, letters to Lord Grantham, corresp. with F. Robinson, Add. MSS 24161–24179 · BL, corresp. with Sir William Hamilton, Add. MSS 41197–41198 · BL, letters to Lord Hardwicke and Sir R. M. Keith, Add. MSS 35500–35594, *passim* · NA Scot., corresp. with Harry Dundas · NRA Scotland, priv. coll., corresp. with Lord Stormont · priv. coll., letters to Lord Cathcart · Suffolk RO, corresp. with earl of Albemarle
Likenesses T. Lawrence, oils, *c.*1795, Longleat House, Wiltshire [*see illus.*] · Heath, engraving (after T. Lawrence)

Thynne, William (*d.* 1546), literary editor, is of obscure origins. His family bore the alternative surname of Botfield or Boteville and he is also cited as 'Thynne alias Boteville'. The claim that he was the younger son of John de la Inne, with his wife, Jane Bowdler, seems to lack evidence (Round, 193–5). Wood asserts that he was from Shropshire and educated at Oxford. He may be the William Thynne who is described in 1518 as 'chief clerk' (*LP Henry VIII*, 2, pt 2, app. 58). He is first certainly recorded in February 1524 when he is described as second clerk of the kitchen in Henry VIII's household. By October 1526 he was chief clerk of the kitchen and the recipient of an annuity of £10. In July 1528 he became bailiff and keeper of the park of Beaudley, and in July of the following year he was appointed customer of wools, hides, and fleeces in the port of London. In October that year he was made receiver-general of the earldom of March and keeper of Gateley Park.

Further indications of royal favour followed. In March 1532 Thynne received, with others, an annuity of 100 marks, and in May 1533 he was almoner and surveyor of the dressers at the wedding of Anne Boleyn. By April 1537 he was Henry's clerk controller. By 1543 he was one of the two masters of the household for the king, and in the year of his death he appears to have been the sole master. In 1544 he had also become one of the officers of the counting house.

Thynne's career as a courtier was conducted simultaneously with his literary activities, particularly his interest in Chaucer, which led to the publication by Thomas Godfray of his first collected edition of *The Workes of Geffray Chaucer* in 1532. This edition was clearly the outcome of sustained research and editing. Thynne's son, Francis *Thynne, reports that his father had owned a number of manuscripts of Chaucer's works 'of whiche written copies there came to me after my fathers deathe some fyve and twentye, whereof some had moore and some fewer tales' (Thynne, 11–12). Several manuscripts survive that Thynne used in the preparation of his edition. These include a manuscript of the Middle English *Romaunt of the Rose* (Glasgow University, MS Hunterian V. 3.7), and Longleat MS 258 which provided the source for six other poems. In addition, a copy of Caxton's edition of Chaucer's *Boece*, also at Longleat, the Thynne family seat, again contains printer's marks, which indicates that, like the manuscripts, it was used as setting copy for the 1532 edition. For other works Thynne seems to have used Pynson's 1526 editions of Chaucer as his copy-texts. It seems that in some instances he undertook careful comparison of different versions of texts to establish his own editions of Chaucer's works.

In his 1532 edition Thynne provides the first printed editions of a number of Chaucer's major works in verse and prose, including *The Book of the Duchess*, *The Legend of Good Women*, *Boece*, *The Treatise on the Astrolabe*. He also printed a large number of works not by Chaucer, including poems by John Lydgate, Thomas Hoccleve, Richard Roos, and Robert Henryson. The introductory materials to the edition, which include the first life of Chaucer and a genealogy, are prefaced by an unsigned dedication to Henry VIII by Bryan Tuke, the king's secretary. (Tuke's authorship is established by a note in his hand in the copy of Thynne's edition in Clare College, Cambridge.)

Thynne evidently had more extensive literary interests. His son, Francis, reports that the poet John Skelton wrote most of his poem 'Colin Clout' at Thynne's house in Erith, Kent (Thynne, 10). Francis also records that his father had wished to include the anti-Catholic *Plowman's Tale* (which Francis appears to confuse with a mid-sixteenth-century poem, 'The Pilgrim's Tale') in the 1532 Chaucer but was thwarted by Wolsey (ibid.). A separate edition was issued by Godfray (c.1533). (There is no direct evidence that Thynne himself was involved in this printing, but its publication by a printer with whom he had other associations at this time is suggestive.) The *Plowman's Tale* was added to the 1542 reprinting of Thynne's edition of Chaucer and appeared in subsequent sixteenth-century editions of his works.

Thynne died on 10 August 1546, and was buried in the church of All Hallows Barking by the Tower, where there is a brass to his memory. His will, dated 16 November 1540, was proved on 7 September 1546. His wife, Anne, daughter of William Bond, clerk of the green cloth, was sole executrix and chief legatee.

SIDNEY LEE, *rev.* A. S. G. EDWARDS

Sources LP Henry VIII · F. Thynne, *Animadversions upon the annotacions and corrections of some imperfections of impressions of Chaucers workes*, ed. F. J. Furnivall and G. H. Kingsley, EETS, 9 (1865); repr. (1876) · J. E. Blodgett, 'Some printers' copy for William Thynne's 1532 edition of Chaucer', *The Library*, 6th ser., 1 (1979), 97–113 · J. E. Blodgett, 'William Thynne', *Editing Chaucer: the great tradition*, ed. P. Ruggiers (1984), 35–52, 255–9 · A. S. G. Edwards, 'The text of Chaucer's *House of Fame*: editing and authority', *Poetica*, 29–30 (1989), 80–92 · J. H. Round, 'The origin of the Thynnes', *The Genealogist*, new ser., 11 (1894–5), 193–5 · Wood, *Ath. Oxon.*, new edn

Tiarks, Frank Cyril (1874–1952), merchant banker, was born on 9 July 1874 in Balham, London, the fourth of the eleven children of Henry Frederic Tiarks (1832–1911), merchant banker, and his wife, Agnes Morris. His grandfather, the Revd Johann Gerhard Tiarks (1794–1858), from Jever in the duchy of Oldenburg, was the pastor of the Reformed Lutheran church in east London from 1827 until his death;

he was also chaplain to the duchess of Kent and a prominent figure in Anglo-German circles. In 1847 Henry Tiarks joined the merchant bank J. Henry Schroder & Co., sponsored by a parishioner of his father who was a partner in the firm. In 1862 he married Agnes Morris, the adopted daughter of Alexander Schlüsser, another partner and a distant relation of the Schröder family; in the same year he was promoted to office manager. In 1871, upon Schlüsser's retirement, Henry Tiarks was made a partner.

The 1870s were prosperous years for Schroders and in 1877 Henry Tiarks and his family moved to Foxbury, a forty-room house with 170 acres at Chislehurst, Kent. Henry Tiarks retired at the end of 1905 and died in 1911. His legacy was not only an estate worth £0.5 million, but the establishment of a dynastic partnership with the Schröder family that continued for two more generations and lasted altogether for more than a century.

Frank Tiarks's education began at a private school in Greenwich and continued, from 1887, at HMS *Britannia*, the naval training college. Commissioned as a lieutenant he joined HMS *Warspite*, but he left the navy in 1894 following the death of his elder brother, who had been intended for the Schroder partnership. Now it fell to Frank to become the banker.

Tiarks's career as a merchant banker began in the traditional manner. After becoming acquainted with the procedures of the London office, he worked as an unpaid 'volunteer' in several firms with which Schroders had close connections, in Le Havre, New York, and Hamburg. While in Hamburg he fell in love with Emmy Broedermann (d. 1943), the daughter of a Hamburg banker, and they were married in 1899. In 1902, aged twenty-eight, Tiarks was made a partner, joining his father and Baron Sir John Henry Schröder, the senior partner, who were both in their sixties, and the senior partner's nephew, Bruno Schröder, aged thirty-five. Within a few years the two younger partners had taken over the running of the firm.

Tiarks quickly established a formidable reputation in the City. He was appointed to the court of the Bank of England in 1912, having been obliged to decline an earlier invitation because Baron Sir John Henry Schröder objected to his 'wasting time on outside business' (DBB). Ironically, just two years later, in August 1914, it was Tiarks's influence at the Bank of England that saved Schroders from seizure as enemy property, by arranging the hurried naturalization of Baron Bruno Schröder, by then the firm's principal proprietor, three days after the outbreak of war. In recognition of this service, the new partnership agreement drawn up in 1919 gave Tiarks a one-third interest in the firm's profits, which was considerably greater than his contribution to capital.

In the early part of the war Tiarks actively assisted the governor of the Bank of England in handling the disruptions to the City caused by the conflict, particularly the non-repayment of credits by German clients to British banks. In May 1917 he rejoined the navy, working in naval intelligence. In 1919 he served as financial adviser to the British army of occupation in Germany.

In the 1920s Tiarks played a leading role in the development of Schroders' business, along with Baron Bruno Schröder and Major Albert Pam. Tiarks was particularly active in the development of the corporate finance side of the business. Notable among his achievements in these years were the establishment of the Pressed Steel Company of Great Britain Ltd at Cowley, Oxford, which pioneered the cold steel pressing process for car bodies in Britain, and the formation of Schroders' New York investment banking business, the J. Henry Schroder Banking Corporation. In 1926 his son Henry [see below], the eldest of his five children, joined him in the partnership.

Schroders' business in the finance of international trade expanded greatly in the 1920s, by serving the desperate credit needs of banks and businesses in Germany and central Europe. By the early 1930s approximately four-fifths of Schroders' acceptance business was with such clients. Thus the German suspension of international payments in July 1931 was potentially disastrous. Tiarks's knowledge and experience made him ideally qualified to act as chairman of the body established to make terms for the recovery of British credits. These negotiations produced the first 'standstill agreement' of September 1931, and Tiarks played a leading part in the discussions which led to its annual renewals over the decade. From 1934 he was also chairman of the International Committee of Creditors.

Like many prominent British nationals with strong German ties, Tiarks hoped for a reconciliation between Britain and Germany. Thus in 1935 he participated in the foundation of the Anglo-German Fellowship to promote mutual trust and understanding. A visit to Cologne in March 1939 to address the fellowship was attacked by critics of appeasement, though his words were unobjectionable.

Aged sixty-five in 1939, Tiarks's retirement from active involvement in Schroders' affairs coincided with the lull in business brought about by the Second World War. Tiarks stepped down from the court of the Bank of England in 1945 and from the Schroders partnership in 1948. The latter year also saw his retirement from the board of the Anglo-Iranian Oil Company, upon which he had served from 1917 and on whose behalf he paid two visits to Iran in the 1940s. His distinguished career and his public services were recognized by appointment as OBE, as a lieutenant of the City of London from 1911, and as high sheriff of Kent in 1927.

Energy, common sense, decisiveness, and humour were the qualities commonly ascribed to Frank Tiarks. Henry Andrews, a manager at Schroders in the 1920s, recalled:

[Tiarks] had a strong personality and no doubt those who did not regularly come into contact with him may have thought he was rather frightening because he was also very quick. The strongest impression was one of vitality and gaiety. He laughed for sheer enjoyment and his laugh had a gay ring and you could watch the images and ideas forming themselves on his face and those thoughts always led to a conclusion. (DBB)

Prentiss Gray, an American colleague, esteemed him the best 'closer' of a deal he had ever met. 'Toughness tempered by human graces', wrote his obituarist in The Times, 'made him a first-rate banker, a resourceful negotiator, and at all times the best of company.'

Tiarks spent most of the last decade of his life in Somerset, having sold Foxbury in 1936. He enjoyed country pursuits and with his brother founded the Mendip foxhounds, of which he was joint master for forty years. In his youth he was a keen polo player, and he was responsible for the introduction of the game to Germany in 1898; he had maintained two polo grounds and a riding school at Foxbury. In later life he took an enthusiastic interest in the Webbington cricket club. His wife predeceased him, dying in 1943. Tiarks died on 7 April 1952, at his home, North Lodge, Loxton, Somerset.

Tiarks's eldest son, **Henry Frederic Tiarks** (1900–1995), merchant banker, was born on 8 September 1900 at Foxbury and educated at Eton College (1913–18), where he acquired his lifelong interest in astronomy. He served briefly as a midshipman in the Royal Naval Volunteer Reserve in 1918, then gained banking experience overseas, represented Schroders in Chile and Bolivia, and in 1926 joined the partnership. On 28 April 1930 he married Lady Millicent Olivia Mary (d. 1975), only daughter of Geoffrey Thomas Taylour, fourth marquess of Headfort; they had one son. The marriage was dissolved in 1936, and on 3 October 1936 Tiarks married Joan (1903–1989), daughter of Francis Marshman-Bell and, until her marriage, a popular West End and film actress under the name Joan Barry; they had one son and one daughter. In the Second World War, Tiarks served as an RAF officer and had charge of London barrage balloons, but was invalided out by tuberculosis and returned to Schroders as a senior partner. Used to a different lifestyle, he disliked the modern professional City and adopted an ambassadorial role, cultivating new clients and government contacts. He was a director of companies linked with Schroders (including Pressed Steel and Joseph Lucas) and led overseas delegations for the board of trade. He resigned as an executive of Schroders a few months after it merged with Helbert Wagg in 1962, but remained on the board until 1965. Tiarks was tall, dark, and slim, and among his interests (besides astronomy) were nature conservation, polo, and golf. He retired for health and tax reasons to Marbella, Spain, and died there on 2 July 1995. He was survived by his daughter, Henrietta, who in 1961 married the marquess of Tavistock; his two sons predeceased him.   RICHARD ROBERTS

Sources R. Roberts, *Schroders: merchants and bankers* (1992) · *WWW* · R. Roberts, 'Tiarks, Frank Cyril', *DBB* · *The Times* (9 April 1952) · private information (2004) · *CGPLA Eng. & Wales* (1952) · *The Independent* (6 July 1995) · *The Times* (11 July 1995) · *Daily Telegraph* (25 July 1995)
Archives Schroders plc, London, archive
Likenesses portrait, Woburn Abbey, Bedfordshire
Wealth at death £222,830 6s. 1d.: administration with will, 8 July 1952, *CGPLA Eng. & Wales*

Tiarks, Henry Frederic (1900–1995). *See under* Tiarks, Frank Cyril (1874–1952).

Tichborne claimant (*d.* **1898**), claimant of baronetcy, was the person who identified himself, in a series of dramatic legal cases, to be the long-lost Sir Roger Tichborne. The Claimant, as he was commonly known, is usually assumed not to have been Sir Roger Tichborne, but Arthur Orton [*see below*], although doubt remains as to his identity. **Roger Charles Doughty-Tichborne** (1829–1854?) was born in Paris on 5 January 1829, the elder of the two sons of Sir James Tichborne, tenth baronet (1784–1862), and his wife, Harriette-Felicité (*d.* 1868), the daughter of Henry Seymour of Knoyle and his French mistress, Felicité Dailly-Brimont, daughter of Louis François, duc de Bourbon Conti. He was educated privately and at Stonyhurst College, after which he joined the 6th dragoon guards. A romance with his cousin Katherine Doughty was marred by her family's resistance to a possible marriage because of Roger's drunkenness. In 1852, after the engagement was delayed, Roger abandoned the army and sailed for South America. Before leaving he entrusted a 'sealed packet' to Vincent Gosford, the steward of the Tichborne estate, a document which was later destroyed but was to assume considerable significance. He toured Chile, crossed the Andes, and was last sighted alive on a ship called the *Bella*, which left Rio de Janeiro on 20 April 1854, bound for Kingston, Jamaica. It was never seen again.

In 1862 Sir James Tichborne died; were Roger still alive, he would have inherited the title and the property. In his absence, Sir James's second son, Alfred, succeeded to his title and estates, to be succeeded in his turn in 1866 by his own infant son, Henry. However, Roger's mother refused to believe that her son was dead, and in 1863 she placed advertisements in the world's press, asking for his whereabouts. Then, in 1865, a butcher calling himself Tomas Castro from Wagga Wagga, Australia, came forward, claiming to be Sir Roger. He reported that the *Bella* had been overturned during a storm but that he had survived in a lifeboat and had been rescued by a ship, the *Osprey*, bound for Melbourne. In Australia he had worked as a cattle rancher before marrying an illiterate woman, Mary Ann Bryant, in 1865 and settling down to life as a butcher. The name Castro was adopted from a man he had met in Melipilla, Chile. The Claimant was identified as Sir Roger by a lawyer, William Gibbes, who was dealing with Castro's bankruptcy case. Gibbes's wife had noticed Lady Tichborne's advertisement and remembered that Castro had mentioned that he was entitled to some property in England. When challenged, Castro claimed that he was Sir Roger and contacted Lady Tichborne, who asked him to return home.

After reaching London at the end of 1866, the Claimant discovered that Lady Tichborne had left for Paris. However, he took the opportunity to go to Wapping, where he asked after the Orton family (an incident that later helped bring about his downfall). In Paris, Lady Tichborne recognized him as her son on 10 January 1867. Most of the Tichborne family insisted that the new arrival was an impostor who was a threat to the inheritance of the infant baronet, Henry Tichborne. The Claimant (weighing about 27

stone) looked nothing like Roger, who had been extremely slim. He was also unable to speak French, in which Roger had been fluent, and had scant knowledge of Roger's past. However, there was little that the family could do as long as the dowager was still alive. An examination in chancery led to the revelation by the Claimant that, before leaving for South America, he had seduced Katherine Doughty (now Lady Radcliffe) and had been told she was pregnant. He had left instructions with Vincent Gosford about what to do in this eventuality (the contents of the 'sealed packet'). Enquiries in Australia and South America then began to connect the Claimant with Arthur Orton. A photograph of the Claimant was identified as Orton by the wife of a former employer of the Claimant in Melbourne. Furthermore, when enquiries were made with the family of Tomas Castro in Chile, no memories were forthcoming about Roger Tichborne, but they did remember a young sailor called Arthur Orton.

Arthur Orton (*b.* 1834) was born on 20 March 1834 in Wapping, the youngest son of George Orton, a shipping butcher. As a sailor he had visited Chile in 1849–51 and then in 1852 had embarked for Australia, where he mysteriously disappeared. The Claimant always said he knew Orton and that they had worked as cattle ranchers together. He also hinted that they had been outlaws, frequently exchanging names, and had even been involved in a murder, which explained why Orton could no longer be found and why the Claimant did not want to talk about his past. The trail then led back to Wapping, where the Claimant's visit to the Ortons in 1866 was discovered. A former sweetheart of Orton's identified the Claimant as Orton, although most of the Orton family denied that he was their relative.

In March 1868 Lady Tichborne died from heart failure, clearing the way to further legal action. A civil action was brought in the court of common pleas in the form of an action of ejectment against Colonel Lushington, the current lessee of Tichborne Park. Although he was nominally the plaintiff, it was clear that the Claimant was really the defendant. *Tichborne v. Lushington* lasted from 10 May 1871 to 6 March 1872. The Claimant found more than 100 witnesses to support him in court, and the other side had 250. The case was particularly notorious for its revelation about the contents of the 'sealed packet', and the newspaper reports of the trial were eagerly read throughout the nation. The case finally ended in a non-suit after Lord Bellew testified that, during his schooldays at Stonyhurst, he had tattooed Sir Roger, marks that the Claimant did not possess.

Criminal charges for perjury were then brought against the Claimant. Having no money to defend himself, he launched an appeal for funds and stumped the country in 1872–3, assisted by the Liberal MP Guildford Onslow, who had known Sir Roger and believed the Claimant to be genuine. An enormous popular campaign developed, drawing most support from working-class people, who believed in the Claimant and felt that his case represented the problems the poor faced in obtaining justice in a court of law. Subscriptions to the Claimant's defence fund came in from all over the country, and several Tichborne newspapers were published to promote his cause. In the criminal trial the Claimant was defended by a maverick Irish lawyer, Edward *Kenealy, whose erratic behaviour in the courtroom contributed to the Claimant's defeat. *R.* v. *Castro* lasted from 23 April 1873 to 28 February 1874, then one of the longest trials in English legal history. After a month-long summing up by the lord chief justice, Alexander Cockburn, the jury found against the Claimant, who was given two sentences of seven years, to run sequentially.

Kenealy was disbarred from the legal profession for his hostile comments towards the judge during the case. He then took over the Tichborne movement, creating an organization called the Magna Charta Association, edited a Tichborne newspaper, *The Englishman* (1874–86), and was elected to parliament as a 'people's candidate' in the Stoke by-election of February 1875, largely on the strength of the Tichborne cause. He failed in his attempt to obtain a royal commission on the Tichborne case. The Claimant was perceived by many as a martyr and his cause became one of the largest popular agitations between the end of Chartism and the coming of socialism. The movement began to decline in the later 1870s but retained pockets of strength well into the 1880s. Under Kenealy it became a focus for many radical causes, including demands for triennial parliaments, opposition to the income tax, and (half-heartedly) votes for women. The religion of the Tichborne family also introduced an anti-Catholic dimension into the agitation.

A model prisoner, the Claimant was released on a ticket-of-leave on 11 October 1884, still insisting that he was Sir Roger Tichborne. He immediately signed with a theatrical agent and took no interest in the political dimensions of the Magna Charta Association, which shortly afterwards collapsed. Kenealy had died in 1880, having lost his seat in the general election. The Claimant began to appear in music-halls and circuses around the country. In 1886 he went to America to give lectures but was not a great success and ended up becoming a bartender; he returned home without any money. His wife had deserted him for another man while he was in prison and he subsequently married a singer called Lily Enever. He failed to make a living by showing himself off in pubs and the two were reduced to poverty. This may explain why in 1895 he signed a confession in *The People* admitting he was Orton. After its publication he immediately retracted the confession and used the money to set up as a tobacconist. The business collapsed, and he was destitute when he died of heart failure on 1 April 1898 at 21 Shouldham Street, Marylebone. The Tichborne family graciously gave permission for Sir Roger Tichborne's name to be placed on his coffin when he was buried in an unmarked grave in Paddington cemetery. The Claimant had two sons and two daughters from his marriage to Mary Ann Bryant. His four children with Lily Enever all died in infancy. One daughter, Teresa, continued her father's crusade and, in 1912, attempted to shoot Joseph Tichborne on his wedding day after demanding financial assistance. Sir Joseph eventually married in 1913, in which year Teresa Tichborne, or Alexander, was

imprisoned for six months for sending him and his mother threatening letters.

The Claimant's identity remains elusive. While most commentators have assumed him to be Orton, Douglas Woodruff in the most substantial study of the case, *The Tichborne Claimant* (1957), has raised the possibility that he might have been Sir Roger after all. Whoever he was, the Claimant provided the Victorian working class with a flamboyant hero.   ROHAN MCWILLIAM

Sources J. D. Woodruff, *The Tichborne claimant: a Victorian mystery* (1957) · R. McWilliam, 'The Tichborne claimant and the people', DPhil diss., U. Sussex, 1990 · M. Roe, *Kenealy and the Tichborne case* (1974) · Burke, *Peerage* (1939) · B. Falk, *The naughty Seymours* (1940) **Archives** Hants. RO, Seymour MSS · W. Yorks. AS, Radcliffe MSS · Warks. CRO, Dormer MSS | FILM *The Tichborne claimant*, film directed by D. Yates, 1998 **Likenesses** Sampson Smith of Longton, Staffordshire figurine, 1873, Stoke City Museum and Art Gallery · W. Sickert, portrait, c.1930, Southampton City Art Gallery

Tichborne, Chidiock (c.1558–1586). *See under* Babington, Anthony (1561–1586).

Tichborne, Sir Henry (1581?–1667), army officer and politician, was the fourth son of Sir Benjamin Tichborne, first baronet (c.1540–1629), of Tichborne, Hampshire, gentleman of the privy chamber to James I, and Amphillis (d. in or after 1629), daughter of Richard Weston, justice of the common pleas. Appointed a captain of foot in Ireland in 1620, he was made governor of Lifford soon afterwards and was knighted on 23 August 1623. He was appointed to commissions to investigate the plantations in Ulster, and built up Irish estates, particularly in co. Tyrone, but also in counties Leitrim, Donegal, and Fermanagh. In 1634 he represented County Tyrone in the Irish parliament. He married Jane (d. 1664), daughter of Sir Robert Newcomen, with whom he had five sons and three daughters: Benjamin, William, Richard, Henry, Samuel, Dorcas, Amphillis, and Elizabeth.

Following the outbreak of the rising of 1641, Tichborne was appointed governor of Drogheda and reached there on 4 November. Ormond thought him 'a very honest and gallant gentleman … and one that I beleeve will render a good accoumpt of it or leave his bones there' (*Irish Confederation*, ed. Gilbert, 1.233). The town came under siege from the insurgents, Tichborne's successful resistance winning him lasting acclaim. The siege was abandoned in early March 1643, and he undertook a series of sorties in the vicinity, capturing Dundalk on 26 March.

Tichborne was named to the Irish privy council on 11 May 1642 and appointed governor of co. Meath on 27 March 1643. On 31 March 1643 Charles I named him one of two lords justices, and he took up office, alongside Sir John Borlase, on 1 May, resigning power to Ormond as lord lieutenant on 21 January 1644. He later claimed that the post was 'unsuitable to my Parts or Fortune … there being a Necessity of my Obedience', and that he opposed the royal plan for a cessation with the confederate forces, which 'was … as much hindered by me, as was in my

Power' (*Letter of Sir Henry Tichborne*, 31), signing the cease-fire order as a military necessity. In 1644 he was summoned to the royal headquarters at Oxford to advise Charles I on the royal plans for a peace with the confederate Catholics. Again, he later claimed to have voiced his dissent, arguing that the confederate terms were 'destructive to the Protestant Religion, exceeding hurtful to his Majesty's present Service, and to the utter ruin of the *English* Interest in this Kingdom' (ibid., 34). Returning with instructions for Ormond, he was captured at sea by the English parliamentarians on 31 December 1644, and from February 1645 was imprisoned in the Tower. He was held until September when he was exchanged for prisoners held by Ormond, and returned to his post at Drogheda. Regardless of any possible doubts, on 30 July 1646 he was one of the privy councillors who signed the proclamation of the short-lived peace between Ormond and the confederates.

Tichborne retained his command—'with Chearfulness' (*Letter of Sir Henry Tichborne*, 34)—after Ormond handed his garrisons to the English parliamentarians in 1647, and served in parliament's victory at Dungan's Hill on 8 August 1647 and in further expeditions into south Ulster and north Leinster. But by April 1648 London was entertaining doubts about his reliability, as a former associate of Ormond. Aware that others with his background were being arrested he obtained permission to travel to London in the autumn of 1648. By April 1649 he had been awarded funds for past services and it was ordered that the 'test is also to be subscribed by him, and he dispatched away to his command' (*CSP dom.*, 1648–9, 72). Even so there remained a 'prejudicate Opinion' of him in some quarters, and he 'therefore freely reposed my Arms, and forsook my Employment' (*Letter of Sir Henry Tichborne*, 39). His wife fled from Ireland to the royalist stronghold of the Isle of Man about August 1649.

Tichborne composed an account of his exploits, dated 1651, intended for his wife to use to secure some recompense for his past services, and which argued his reluctant acquiescence in royalist peace plans in the 1640s. He undertook a long-running campaign for payment of what he considered to be his remaining arrears and for which he sought satisfaction in the form of a grant of lands at Beaulieu, co. Louth, of which he had been awarded possession, as tenant to the state, by Cromwell. Repeated journeys to England won him the lord protector's approval but the Dublin administration stalled the award, on the grounds that land in the county had been earmarked for other uses. In the meantime he appears to have bought up rights to lands awarded to 'adventurers' (investors in the war effort) in Leinster and Ulster.

With the restoration of Charles II, Tichborne was appointed marshal of the army for Ireland on 31 July 1660, and was elected to the Irish parliament of 1661 for Sligo borough. He continued to petition for his arrears, while one of his sons eventually secured ownership of Beaulieu. He died there in 1667 and was buried the same year in St Mary's Church, Drogheda. The confederate Richard Bellings later spoke of Tichborne as 'a man trusty to the King,

valiant and moderate' (*Irish Confederation*, ed. Gilbert, 1.162). Of his courage there seems little doubt, but Bellings may have overestimated Tichborne's support for the royal policy of accommodation, evidence for his stance being rendered murky by his later self-justification. The regicide John Moore spoke of him as 'so great an enemy to the rebels in Ireland, killing many hundreds of them at his own hand or standing by to see them executed' and Tichborne later admitted that there was 'little mercy shown in those times' (O'Sullivan, 65). It was for military, rather than politic or humane, virtues and abilities that Tichborne won his contemporary renown and reward.

Tichborne was succeeded by his son Sir William (d. 1694), who married Judith Bysse. Their son, **Henry Tichborne**, first Baron Ferrard of Beaulieu (1662–1731), politician, was born in Dublin and educated there at Trinity College. He was MP for Ardee (1692–3) and for co. Louth (1695–9 and 1710–13). Knighted on 28 March 1694, he was created a baronet on 12 July 1697 and Baron Ferrard of Beaulieu on 9 October 1715. He married in July 1683 Arabella, daughter of Sir Robert Cotton, baronet, of Combermere, Cheshire, but his titles became extinct on his death from apoplexy on 3 November 1731.   R. M. ARMSTRONG

Sources A letter of Sir Henry Tichborne to his lady (1772) • *CSP Ire.*, 1615–70 • *History of the Irish confederation and the war in Ireland … by Richard Bellings*, ed. J. T. Gilbert, 7 vols. (1882–91) • H. O'Sullivan, 'The Tichborne acquisition of the Plunkett estate of Beaulieu', *Journal of the Old Drogheda Society*, 7 (1990), 57–68 • *CSP dom.*, 1648–50 • *DNB* • GEC, *Peerage* • GEC, *Baronetage* • R. Lascelles, ed., *Liber munerum publicorum Hiberniae … or, The establishments of Ireland*, later edn, 2 vols. in 7 pts (1852) • J. Morrin, ed., *Calendar of the patent and close rolls of chancery in Ireland, of the reign of Charles I* (1863) • A. Clarke, *Prelude to Restoration in Ireland* (1999) • J. T. Gilbert, ed., *A contemporary history of affairs in Ireland from 1641 to 1652*, 3 vols. (1879–80)

Likenesses T. Athow, wash drawing, AM Oxf.

Tichborne, Sir Henry, third baronet (*bap.* 1624, *d.* 1689), landowner, was baptized on 24 May 1624 at Winchester Cathedral, the son of Sir Richard Tichborne, second baronet (*d.* 1657), and Helen, the daughter and coheir of Robert White of Aldershot. The Tichbornes had been landowners in Hampshire and lords of the manor of Tichborne since the twelfth century, and they were one of the leading Catholic families in the county. Sir Henry married Mary (*d.* 1698), the daughter of Charles Arundell, second brother to Thomas, Lord Arundell of Wardour, with whom he had four sons and five daughters, four of whom died in infancy.

Tichborne came to maturity at the point when civil war broke out, and wrote later of his son's 'more refined education than so bustling a time as mine could afford' (Morris, 419). As a Catholic and committed supporter of the Stuart monarchy, he lived his life against the political and religious tensions of the second half of the seventeenth century. He fought for the king in the civil war, family tradition identifying the Tichborne oak in which he is supposed to have hidden after the battle of Cheriton (1644). He was said to have been captured at sea in 1645, after fighting in Ireland. Sent to the Tower, he was released in an exchange of prisoners. On inheriting the baronetcy on the death of his father in 1657 Tichborne had to unravel the financial affairs of the family. In 1650 his father had claimed to be £15,000 in debt, and in a letter written to his son Sir Henry himself described having found a broken and almost ruined estate which he had then repaired. By the Restoration, when Sir Henry's name was included as a possible recipient of the proposed knighthood of the Royal Oak, he was said to be worth £1000 a year.

After the Restoration, Tichborne's loyalty was rewarded by appointment as lieutenant of the ordnance and of the New Forest. With the political tensions aroused by the Popish Plot in 1678 Sir Henry and his household became the focus of popular suspicions. The family were devout Catholics, and household and chapel had been served by a succession of priests. Some sense of their commitment is perhaps reflected in Tichborne's acknowledgement that some blamed his wife 'for too much tediousness in prayer' (Morris, 417). In 1678 his house was besieged by a crowd and, after his arrest, rumours of strange happenings in the Tichborne family chapel led to an order from the privy council for the chapel to be searched for hidden arms. Sir Henry was one of those named by the informer Titus Oates as having accepted a commission in the supposed Catholic army being assembled by the pope's authority. He was arrested and held in Winchester Castle with the family's priest, before being transferred for a second spell of imprisonment in the Tower. At some point he had travelled to Rome, and his friends, anxious that this might be held against him, burned his papers, including his history of the family. But as the crisis eased, he was released on bail in 1680. In 1688 he was included on the commission of peace for Hampshire, as James II's attempt to secure compliant local magistracies who would agree to toleration for Catholics led to a wholesale purge of the county bench. Sir Henry was probably already ill, and his death in 1689 allowed him to escape any further political recrimination. A letter of 1690, referring to his recent death, says 'he was a great while lingering, and doubtless made a happy end … knowing now so long that he was to dye' (Finch MSS, 2.401). He was succeeded by his son Henry Joseph.

More recently Tichborne has attracted greater historical notice for the painting of him and his family by the Flemish painter Gillis van Tilborch, following the wider notice given to the painting by its inclusion in the 1985 'Treasure Houses of Britain' exhibition. Painted in 1670, The Tichborne Dole shows Sir Henry and his family, attended by family retinue and priest, presiding over the ritual distribution of loaves to the poor of the neighbourhood. This custom, to which Sir Henry makes reference in his memoir to his son, is said to have originated in the thirteenth-century deathbed request of Lady Mabel Titchborne. Her husband promised to give her as much land as she could encompass while holding a burning torch. Lady Mabel is said to have managed to navigate, mostly crawling on all fours, some 23 acres, still known as 'the crawls'. The staging of the portrait, dominated by Sir Henry and his family standing in front of Tichborne House emblazoned with the family's arms, can be seen to celebrate both Sir Henry's restoration of the family's fortunes and those values of nobility, virtue, continuity, and charity that run through his memoir, which fancifully traced the family's lineage back to Roman times. It has been said, 'that as a document of social history this has no peer' (Harris, 43).

Sir Henry Tichborne, third baronet (bap. 1624, d. 1689), by Gillis van Tilborch, 1670 [centre left, in The Tichborne Dole]

But given knowledge of the troubles Sir Henry's confession of the Catholic faith brought him and his family, it is perhaps more appropriate to see it less as a 'document of stark realism' (ibid., 40) than as a deliberate invocation of the deferential social hierarchy that the landed classes, and particularly the Catholic landed classes, wished to see maintained after the turmoil of the civil war.

JOHN WALTER

Sources G. D. Squibb, ed., *The visitation of Hampshire and the Isle of Wight, 1686*, Harleian Society, new ser., 10 (1991) · J. Morris, ed., *The troubles of our Catholic forefathers related by themselves*, 1 (1872), 413–23 · J. Harris, *The artist and the country house: a history of country house and garden view painting in Britain, 1540–1870* (1979) · G. N. Godwin, *The civil war in Hampshire, 1642–45, and the story of Basing House*, new edn (1904) · *VCH Hampshire and the Isle of Wight*, vol. 3 · W. Dugdale and T. C. Banks, *Antient usage in bearing of … arms* (1811), 170–72 · A. M. Coleby, *Central government and the localities: Hampshire, 1649–1689* (1987) · J. Kenyon, *The Popish Plot* (1972) · M. A. E. Green, ed., *Calendar of the proceedings of the committee for compounding … 1643–1660*, 5 vols., PRO (1889–92) · 'The Titchborne dole', *Hampshire Family Historian*, 18/2 (Aug 1991), 112–13 · H. Foley, ed., *Records of the English province of the Society of Jesus*, 5–6 (1879–80) · *Report on the manuscripts of Allan George Finch*, 5 vols., HMC, 71 (1913–2003), vol. 2, p. 401 · Burke, *Peerage* (1907)

Archives Archives of the British Province of the Society of Jesus, London, department of historiography and archives, memoir in form of letter to son

Likenesses G. van Tilborch, oils, 1670, priv. coll. [*see illus.*]

Tichborne, Henry, first Baron Ferrard of Beaulieu (1662–1731). *See under* Tichborne, Sir Henry (1581?–1667).

Tichborne, Robert, appointed Lord Tichburne under the protectorate (1610/11–1682), politician and regicide, was born in London, the eldest son of Robert Tichborne (d. 1644/5) of St Michael-le-Querne, London, and Cowden, Kent, a gentleman free of the Skinners' Company, and his wife, Joan, daughter of Thomas Banks, gentleman, a London merchant. He was married twice: first by licence dated 27 April 1638, when aged twenty-seven, to Mary Priest (b. 1614); they had two sons. His second wife was Anne, eldest daughter of William Johnson of Ingham, Norfolk, gentleman; they had two more children.

Tichborne followed his father into the Skinners' Company, from apprentice in 1631 to his freedom in 1637, and on to common council in 1643, as a member for Farringdon Within. Having joined the Honourable Artillery Company in 1636, by 1642 he was also serving as a captain in the Yellow regiment of the London trained bands. Already well established as a wealthy Cheapside linen draper, he benefited substantially from his father's will. On the outbreak of civil war he was quick to display a militant parliamentarianism in opposition to peace campaigners in the capital and in 1643 he became lieutenant-colonel of a regiment of London auxiliaries. His militancy earned him notoriety in royalist circles as one of seven rebellious citizens believed to be chiefly responsible for London's disaffection from the king. In the spring of 1643 he joined other City militants on a London subcommittee established at Salters' Hall to raise a volunteer citizens' army. This brought him into close contact with other emerging leaders of political Independency in the City as well as a future Leveller leader, William Walwyn. When the City

decided to reassert its control over the subcommittee Tichborne was one of seven Salters' Hall nominees added to the London militia committee in July 1643 as a conciliatory gesture. In the following September he saw service with his militia regiment at the first battle of Newbury.

By the closing stages of the war Tichborne was busy establishing himself as a leader of political Independency in the City. He spoke out in common council against presbyterian attacks on the anticlericalism of the October 1645 ordinance appointing lay triers; led protest against the political presbyterian City remonstrance of May 1646; and, the next month, was a principal supporter of the London Independent petition to the Commons. City presbyterians retaliated during the attempted counter-revolution of 1647, when Tichborne and other leading Independents were purged from the militia committee, only to be subsequently restored to it after the army's intervention. When the latter occupied London in August, Fairfax paid tribute to Tichborne's political reliability by appointing him lieutenant of the Tower and colonel of a new regiment to guard it. He subsequently participated in both the Putney and Whitehall debates of 1647–8 within the council of officers, adopting a relatively radical stance on the question of the power of the king and Lords to veto legislation and that of the civil magistrate over religion, but stopping short of an endorsement of the Leveller's platform. After the second civil war, however, he took part in the Nag's Head tavern discussions held between leading City Independents and Levellers and was a member of the committee of sixteen which drew up the second *Agreement of the People*.

Tichborne was an active supporter of the king's trial and execution, attending all but three of the high court's seventeen meetings and signing the death warrant. He also helped organize a common council petition in mid-January 1649, calling for the execution of justice upon Charles and others responsible for the recent bloodshed [*see also* Regicides]. The ensuing political transformation in London saw Tichborne elected alderman for Farringdon Within in July 1649 and a London sheriff and master of the Skinners' Company in 1650. His religious Independency had already brought him into close acquaintance with other prominent radicals who similarly gained commanding positions in the City after 1649. A member of George Cockayn's influential Independent congregation at St Pancras, Soper Lane, he was also on friendly terms with members of John Goodwin's church in Coleman Street. He wrote two lengthy works of spiritual devotion in early 1649, *A Cluster of Canaan's Grapes* and *The Rest of Faith* (dedicated to Fairfax and Cromwell respectively), and established a lectureship in St Olave, Silver Street.

Appointments to major positions of responsibility followed from 1649 onwards, including membership of the indemnity committee, probate judge, and commissioner of customs, a post he was removed from in 1656 amid suspicions of fraud. In addition Tichborne was named a commissioner to the high courts of justice of 1650 and 1654 and, in 1651–2, was one of eight commissioners sent to Scotland to prepare for its union with England. In 1653 he was appointed to the nominated assembly, becoming one of its most active MPs, and was a member of the two councils of state elected by it. His politics now moved in a more moderate direction: he clashed with radicals over proposals for the abolition of tithes and lay patronage and was accused of having helped bring the assembly to its early end. He enjoyed further favour under the protectorate and in 1656 was elected lord mayor of London and knighted by Cromwell. A contemporary print of Tichborne on horseback wearing his full mayoral regalia is to be found in the Guildhall Library. He was made a member of the new upper house in 1657, taking his seat as Lord Tichburne; other distinctions included a directorship of the East India Company and, in 1658, appointment to the presidency of the Honourable Artillery Company. The restoration of the Rump in 1659 did not bring immediate political eclipse; this was to happen finally as a result of his brief service on the committee of safety set up by the army when it again interrupted parliament in October.

At the Restoration he surrendered in obedience to the proclamation of 16 June and was tried for regicide in October 1660. Despite pleas of ignorance and repentance, he was formally sentenced to death, yet his life was spared as a result of the combined benefits of the Act of Indemnity and reports that he had previously saved some royalists from execution. He spent the rest of his days in prison, although his wife and children were permitted to live with him during his imprisonment in Dover Castle in 1664–74. He died in the Tower on 6 July 1682 and was subsequently buried with the utmost privacy in Mercers' Chapel; he was survived by his second wife, Anne. Administration of the little that was left of his estate was granted to his eldest son, John, in September 1682.

KEITH LINDLEY

Sources 'Boyd's Inhabitants of London', Society of Genealogists, London, nos. 10298, 15594, 35377 · A. B. Beaven, ed., *The aldermen of the City of London, temp. Henry III–[1912]*, 2 (1913), 72 · *The visitation of London, anno Domini 1633, 1634, and 1635, made by Sir Henry St George*, 2, ed. J. J. Howard, Harleian Society, 17 (1883), 289 · 'Robert Tichborne', HoP, *Commons* [draft] · K. Lindley, *Popular politics and religion in civil war London* (1997) · Greaves & Zaller, *BDBR*, pp. 239–40 · *DNB* · *History of the Worshipful Company of Skinners of London* (1837), 173–9 · C. H. Firth and R. S. Rait, eds., *Acts and ordinances of the interregnum, 1642–1660*, 1 (1911), 990, 1007–8, 1057, 1254, 1261; 2 (1911), 75, 82, 149, 365 · journals, CLRO, court of common council, vol. 40, fol. 67 · PRO, PROB 11/192/24 [will of Robert Tichborne sen.] · London marriage allegations, 27 April 1638, GL, MS 10091/19 · H. W. Woolrych, *Lives of eminent serjeants-at-law of the English bar*, 2 vols. (1869)

Likenesses print, 1656, GL; repro. in *History of the Worshipful Company of Skinners*, 174 · line engraving, 1657, BM, NPG

Wealth at death most of property forfeited as a regicide: PRO, PROB 8/75/123

Tichburne. For this title name *see* Tichborne, Robert, appointed Lord Tichburne under the protectorate (1610/11–1682).

Tickell, Richard (1751–1793), playwright and satirist, was a grandson of the poet Thomas *Tickell (1685–1740), Addison's friend, and the second son of the three sons and two daughters of John Tickell (1729–1782) and his wife, Esther, daughter of Thomas Pierson. John Tickell was born at Dublin Castle, and was given the lease of house and demesne lands of Glasnevin by his mother on 24 October 1754. He held these until 1765, and during this time he was six clerk in chancery and a magistrate in Dublin, until he moved his family to New Windsor, Berkshire, as a result of the disturbances in Dublin. Richard is said to have been born at Bath, where he later built Beaulieu House, Newbridge Hill. In Samuel Parr's *Works* (8.129) the editor, John Johnstone, states that Tickell was 'acquainted with Parr at Harrow', but there is no other record of this. Also unsubstantiated is Horace Walpole's assertion that Tickell had been an assistant at Eton College: his name has not been found in the archives of that school. A twentieth-century genealogical researcher, however, maintains that Tickell entered Winchester College on 19 June 1764 and Eton College on 29 May 1765 (Tickell, 62). Whatever the conflicting reports of his early education, it is certain that he was entered at the Middle Temple on 8 November 1768. He has been confused with William Tickell, a surgeon and chemist of Bath, who invented the Aethereal Anodyne Spirit elixir.

After being called to the bar, Tickell was appointed one of the sixty commissioners of bankruptcy who were divided into twelve 'lists' of five, Tickell being in the third. Owing, as he contended, to an unjust complaint of the other gentlemen of his list, he was deprived of his place in 1778; but David Garrick, whose acquaintance he had made, successfully interceded for him with Lord Chancellor Bathurst. He told Garrick at the time that he was 'wholly dependent on his grandmother's assistance' (*Private Correspondence*, 2.305). His friend William Brummell, private secretary to Lord North, thereupon obtained for him a pension of £200 for writing in support of the ministry, and the further reward of a commissionership in the stamp office, his appointment being dated 24 August 1781, and his salary £500 a year.

On 15 October 1778 a musical entertainment by Tickell, called *The Camp*, was represented at Drury Lane 'with great success' according to Genest (4.75). Three weeks later Tickell declined to write a prologue for Garrick on the ground that he was employed in a work that would make or mar his fortune (*Private Correspondence*, 2.317). This may have been the satirical *Anticipation: containing the substance of his Majesty's most gracious speech to both h-s of p-t on the opening of the approaching session* of which the preface is dated 23 November 1778. It attracted general attention. Tickell was worried about its reception until he learned that the house had roared with laughter when Isaac Barré, who had not seen the pamphlet, used words and phrases which were attributed to him in it. Nothing, however, in the imaginary speech closely resembles the one which, according to *The Parliamentary History of England* (1814), was spoken by Barré. Gibbon, writing to Holroyd on Tuesday night (24 November 1778), expressed the view that: 'In town we think it an excellent piece of humour … but serious patriots groan that such things should be turned to farce.' The prince of Wales, as reported by Croker, praised Tickell's talents very highly. A second pamphlet (also anonymous), with the same title, of far inferior interest, probably by another hand, appeared five days before the meeting of parliament in 1779. *Anticipation* was reprinted in New York in 1942, edited by L. H. Butterfield, with a biographical introduction, notes, and a bibliography.

On 25 July 1780 Tickell married Mary *Linley (1758–1787), a vocalist [*see under* Linley, Thomas (1733–1795)]. Her elder sister, Elizabeth Ann, was married to Richard Brinsley Sheridan. Tickell is said, however, already to have had a family with a mistress, Miss B., with whom he had lived (Baker, 1.714). After his marriage he had a grant of rooms in Hampton Court Palace. His opera in three acts, called *The Carnival of Venice*, was successfully produced at Drury Lane on 13 December 1781, Linley's music and some of the songs by his wife's sister contributing to the favourable impression. An adaptation of *The Gentle Shepherd*, performed on 27 May 1789, was the last of Tickell's theatrical works.

Intimacy with his brother-in-law, Sheridan, led to Tickell's transferring his party pen to the support of Charles James Fox. After several rejections he was elected a member of Brooks's Club in 1785. Tickell was zealously engaged at the time in influencing public opinion, and wrote to Parr for 'a list of the inns in Warwickshire where farmers resort to, and of such coffee-houses or hotels as are in your county' (*Works of Samuel Parr*, 8.130). He was active with his pen in denouncing the commercial treaty made with France in 1787, and he told Parr that he had written the *Woollen-Draper's Letter on the French Treaty* and answered the *Political Review*, 'I mean the pamphlet which traduced the Prince of Wales and every one else except Hastings' (ibid., 131). He was also a contributor to the *Rolliad*. Sheridan's sister Elizabeth, writing on 20 December 1788 from her brother's house in Bruton Street, says, 'Yesterday … Tickell and Joseph Richardson were here all day preparing an address to come from different parts of the country to counteract Mr. Pitt' (*Betsy Sheridan's Journal*, ed. W. Lefanu, 1986, 136).

Thomas James Mathias in the *Pursuits of Literature* paid Tickell the compliment of styling him 'the happiest of any occasional writer in his day'. According to Adair, he had in private conversation a good deal of wit and was an admirable mimic. Some of his other plays and his pamphlets include: *The Wreath of Fashion* (1778); *The Green Box of Monsieur de Sartine*, an adaptation from the French (1779); and *Epistle from Charles Fox to John Townshend* (1779).

Tickell was experiencing some financial difficulties in 1793; he had borrowed £1000 from Thomas Hammersley of Pall Mall by a bond dated 8 January 1793, with a promise to pay £500 within two years. The bond was called in suddenly, however, and he is recorded as having asked for a loan of £500 from Warren Hastings. On 19 May he wrote again, professing respect and gratitude for Hastings's 'spirited and noble manner in acceding to my request' (*Warren Hastings MSS*, BM). On 4 November 1793, however, Tickell committed suicide. In a fit of depression, he jumped from the parapet outside the window of his rooms at Hampton Court, but owing to the efforts of Sheridan, the inquest's verdict was that of accidental death. Sheridan also took the children of Tickell's first

marriage into his care, obtaining admission into the navy for Richard (1782–1805), and a writership in India for Samuel (1785–1817). R. E. Tickell maintains that the third child of this marriage was a daughter, Elizabeth Anne (1781–1860), who was unmarried when she died at her Bedford Square London home. It is certain, however, that Tickell had another daughter, Zipporah, who later married Ebenezer Roebuck, an employee of the East India Company, and became the mother of John Arthur Roebuck (1802–1879).

Tickell's second wife, whom he had married in 1789, was Sarah, daughter of Captain Ley HEICS of the *Berrington* East Indiaman. A beautiful girl of eighteen at the time of her marriage, she survived her husband, but her behaviour after his death gained her the censure of Tickell's contemporaries, as she was said to have had a small dowry and expensive tastes, and to have kept a coach and four while her husband's debts remained unpaid. In 1796 she remarried; her new husband was John Cotton Worthington, a major in the Sussex fencible cavalry.

W. F. RAE, *rev.* REBECCA MILLS

Sources R. E. Tickell, *The Tickell and connected families, Fairfax, Eustace, &c …* (1948) · D. E. Baker, *Biographia dramatica, or, A companion to the playhouse*, rev. I. Reed, new edn, rev. S. Jones, 1/2 (1812), 713–14 · W. Smyth, *Memoir of Mr Sheridan* (1840), 53–5 · *The works of Samuel Parr … with memoirs of his life and writings*, ed. J. Johnstone, 8 vols. (1828), vol. 8, pp. 129–32 · J. Murch, *Biographical sketches of Bath celebrities, ancient and modern* (1893), 317 · *The private correspondence of David Garrick*, ed. J. Boaden, 2 (1832), 304–5, 317 · R. E. M. Peach, *Historic houses of Bath and their associations*, 1 (1883), 119–20 · *GM*, 1st ser., 48 (1778), 594–5 · *N&Q*, 2 (1850), 38 · *N&Q*, 3 (1851), 129–31 · J. Hutchinson, ed., *A catalogue of notable Middle Templars: with brief biographical notices* (1902), 242–3 · H. A. C. Sturgess, ed., *Register of admissions to the Honourable Society of the Middle Temple, from the fifteenth century to the year 1944*, 1 (1949), 368 · Genest, *Eng. stage*, vol. 4 · W. F. Rae, *Sheridan: a biography* (1896), vol. 1 · Watt, *Bibl. Brit.*, vol. 2 · will, PRO, PROB 6/169, fol. 180

Wealth at death widow reportedly had trouble paying his debts

Tickell, Thomas (*bap.* 1623, *d.* 1692), estate steward, was baptized at Crosthwaite church, Cumberland, on 6 May 1623, eldest son of Richard Tickell (*d.* 1667) of Ullock, a small landowner of marginal gentility, and Katherine (*d.* 1666), daughter of Thomas Fairfax, rector of Caldbeck and prebendary of Carlisle. Little is known of his early career. He was surveyor of the customs at Newcastle before the civil war, served as a royalist officer, and by 1647 was assisting in his father's partnership in a lead mine in the Vale of Newlands. By 1662 he had settled at the embryonic port town of Whitehaven, Cumberland, as collector of excise, lessee of salt pans, and partner in trading ventures.

Whitehaven lay within the manor of St Bees, whose absentee landlord Sir John Lowther in June 1666 appointed Tickell as his steward. Tickell was the archetype of the steward of an estate which is predominantly urban, and which includes commercial, and even industrial, enterprises. Besides his regular duties of holding courts, collecting rents, negotiating leases of land, coal steaths (waterside depots), and stone quarries, and remitting the estate income to London, he assumed increasing responsibility for managing the Whitehaven collieries, which in his time developed from primitive 'bear mouths' into a network of races, served by deep shafts and drained by expensive levels, their output dominating the trade to Dublin. Even after Lowther appointed a specialist colliery agent in 1682 he expected Tickell to provide independent reports on the mining operations and to conduct delicate negotiations to purchase more collieries.

Tickell also gathered evidence and marshalled witnesses for the various lawsuits Lowther had with numbers of his tenants and nearby landowners, advised on the layout and physical character of the town, including the rebuilding of Flatt Hall as Lowther's Whitehaven residence, and in 1679 and 1680 oversaw major harbour works which deepened the basin and strengthened and extended the pier to accommodate growing numbers of larger ships. He reported on the character and suitability of possible ministers for the new church, and was appointed a governor of St Bees grammar school in September 1685. After 1689 he reported on Irish news and on French and Jacobite privateers in the Irish Sea.

Tickell's salary was at first only £20 per annum, raised to £40 in 1679, and in the interim augmented by stages with the farm of the rectorial tithes, a beneficial lease of Flatt tenement and lodging in Flatt Hall, and successive contracts for pumping water out of the collieries, which others, if not he himself, believed to be lucrative. He had at various times colliery leases, ship shares and a partnership in a ropery selling to both ships and collieries. In 1671 Lowther obtained him appointment as surveyor of customs for Whitehaven and Carlisle, and was repaid with a stream of inside information. Lowther's strenuous exertions also secured two church livings for Richard Tickell, son of Tickell and his wife, Elizabeth (d. 1694), who graduated from Trinity College, Dublin, and a third for a son-in-law. Landlord and steward corresponded at least once a week except during the former's rare visits to Whitehaven. 'I see with others' eyes', Lowther wrote on 27 December 1681 (Cumbria AS, Carlisle, D/Lons/W2/1/16), but Tickell's alert and observant eyes relayed much more than was strictly necessary to determine estate policy.

Adept and confident in business, whether his own or his employer's, Tickell lacked self-assurance in social encounters. Choleric and whimsical expressions punctuate his letters as he interprets the conflicts and factions within the town, where 'such ungrateful people as these no persons can oblige, for condescensions whet their litigious appetites, never to be satisfied or quieted until they fall into their primitive dust' (Cumbria AS, Carlisle, D/Lons/W2/1, 22 Feb 1677). During his quarter-century service the village of Whitehaven developed into a significant port. However, he was usually regarded with suspicion by the town's inhabitants, who, correctly, perceived him as the landlord's surrogate, not as a fellow citizen. Tickell died at Whitehaven in December 1692 and was buried in the chapel burial-ground there; his wife, Elizabeth, died in October 1694. Their grandson was Thomas Tickell (1685–1740), the poet. CHRISTINE CHURCHES

Sources J. Lowther, letters to Thomas Tickell, with Tickell's draft replies, 1666–92, Cumbria AS, Carlisle, Lonsdale papers, D/Lons/W2/1/1–28 • C. M. Churches, 'Sir John Lowther and Whitehaven, 1642–1706', PhD diss., University of Adelaide, 1990 [copy in Cumbria AS] • R. E. Tickell, *Thomas Tickell and the eighteenth-century poets* (1931) • 'Newlands lead', Cumbria AS, Carlisle, Leconfield papers, D/Lec/81 • W. A. Shaw, ed., *Calendar of treasury books*, 7, PRO (1916), 449, 714, 877

Archives Cumbria AS, Carlisle, Lonsdale MSS • Cumbria AS, Carlisle, Leconfield MSS

Tickell, Thomas (1685–1740), poet and government official, was the son of the Revd Richard Tickell (c.1648–1692), rector of Distington, Cumberland, and his wife, Margaret, *née* Gale (d. 1729). Thomas, who was sixth child and fourth son in a family of eight, was born on 17 December 1685 and baptized on 19 January 1686 at Bridekirk, his father's former parish. After his father died on 22 June 1692 at Distington the family moved to Whitehaven and Thomas was sent in 1695 to school at St Bees, under his uncle the Revd Richard Jackson. He matriculated at Queen's College, Oxford, aged fifteen, on 16 May 1701, entering the college as a 'taberer' or scholar on the foundation; he graduated BA on 7 July 1705 and MA on 22 February 1709, and was elected fellow on 9 November 1710. As he did not comply with the college statute by taking orders, he belatedly obtained a dispensation from the crown (25 October 1717) and held his fellowship until he married in 1726.

Tickell's first publication was *Oxford* (November 1706), a long topographical poem inscribed to his friend and fellow collegian, Richard, Viscount Lonsdale (d. 1713). Next he contributed eight short amatory or complimentary poems to Tonson's *Poetical Miscellanies* (1709), including an elegant address to Joseph Addison on his opera *Rosamond*. In 1711 he lectured in place of Joseph Trapp, professor of poetry: his one surviving lecture, 'De poesi didactica', expresses the hope that poets of Britain will gird themselves up for the grandeur of writing didactic poetry. Meanwhile his own poetry and scholarship were disparaged by the peevish Thomas Hearne, who called him 'a vain, conceited Coxcomb' (*Remarks*, 3.218) and claimed that he was the true author of an untraced short-lived weekly Oxford paper called *The Surprise* (1711). Tickell's next traced work, a long poem, *The Prospect of Peace*, dedicated to the bishop of Bristol, a plenipotentiary in negotiations for the treaty of Utrecht, was published in October 1712; it rapidly ran into six editions, and was praised by Addison in *The Spectator* (no. 523).

Tickell repaid the compliment with interest in verses 'To the supposed author of the *Spectator*' (calling Addison the 'British Virgil') in *The Spectator*, no. 532, and in 'Verses to the Author' in the seventh edition of *Cato* and a prologue for a performance of *Cato* at Oxford (both 1713). In April 1713 he wrote five anonymous papers on pastoral poetry for Richard Steele's *The Guardian*. Tickell favoured a pastoral naturalized to English rustic life; he praised Ambrose Philips as the English descendant of Theocritus, but did not mention Pope, who, like Philips, had recently published pastorals. Pope resentfully responded with his ironic *Guardian* no. 40, which occasioned his quarrel with Philips. Tickell's uncontroversial *Guardian* no. 125 (August 1713) included a fragment of a georgic, 'Hunting'. By 1714

Thomas Tickell (1685–1740), attrib. Sir Godfrey Kneller

he had joined the group of Addison's disciples who met regularly at Button's Coffee House in Russell Street.

Tickell welcomed the arrival of George I in verse with 'The Royal Progress' (*The Spectator*, no. 620), and four more poems by him appeared in Steele's *Miscellanies* (1714), including a specimen of his projected translation of Lucan's *Pharsalia*, begun in 1713. A subscription list for an edition of Lucan was opened but the work was never completed, perhaps because it was overtaken by Rowe's translation (1718). Tickell also never completed a translation of the *Iliad*, for which he was contracted by Jacob Tonson on 31 May 1714, two months after Bernard Lintot agreed with Pope for a translation of the same work. It seems that Tonson wanted to spoil Lintot's market by employing a better classical scholar than Pope; it is certain that Addison and fellow whigs backed Tickell, and Pope convinced himself that Addison, not Tickell, was the actual translator. The rival translations of book 1 were published in the same week of June 1715, when Tickell announced that he would not proceed with the *Iliad* because it had fallen into an abler hand, but he hoped the public would encourage him to translate the *Odyssey*. Each translator privately made hostile notes on the other's work, but they did not enter into direct public controversy beyond a few remarks in Pope's *Peri Bathous* (1728, chap. 12). Pope adopted some of Tickell's lines in preference to his own in the second edition of his *Iliad*; he was eventually reconciled to Tickell (Addison's cat's-paw as Pope believed), but was unable to forgive Addison himself for what he thought was underhand dealing. Hence his satirical character sketch, later called 'Atticus' (first published 1722), to which Tickell

wrote a neat riposte which fell into the hands of Edmund Curll, who printed it without authorization in *Cythereia* (1723), attributing it to Jeremiah Markland.

The change of dynasty brought Addison back into government: first, in September 1714, as secretary to the lord lieutenant of Ireland, then, from April 1717, secretary of state for the southern department (responsible for relations with France, southern Europe, Ireland, and the plantations, as well as a huge variety of domestic affairs). In both offices he employed Tickell as under-secretary, against the advice of Sir Richard Steele, who observed that Tickell 'was of a temper too enterprising to be governed', which 'produced a great animosity between Sir Richard and Mr. Tickell, which subsisted during their lives' (Cibber, 5.18). Addison, his health failing, resigned the secretaryship in March 1718. Tickell's reputation and record were such that he was retained as under-secretary by Addison's successor, James Craggs, and by Craggs's successor, Lord John Carteret, who became secretary in March 1721. One of Tickell's many duties was the collection of news for the *Gazette*, but his own literary work at this time was scanty: no more than a few complimentary poems, a long topographical poem, *Kensington Garden* (1722), and a clever anti-Jacobite epistle, *From a Lady in England to a Gentleman at Avignon* (1717), which, according to Johnson, 'stands high among party poems; it expresses contempt without coarseness and superiority without insolence' (Johnson, 2.310).

Addison died on 17 June 1719, bequeathing the task of editing his works to Tickell rather than his quondam closest literary associate, Steele. The edition in four quarto volumes was published in October 1721; it was thought to have earned £1350 for Tickell and certainly provoked a dispute with Tonson over copyright. Steele, too, was dissatisfied. Thinking himself belittled in Tickell's preface, he published in 1722 a new edition of Addison's *The Drummer* (omitted from Tickell's edition) with a prefatory epistle which repeated the charge that Addison wrote the Homer translation published over Tickell's name, and complained of Tickell's 'cold, unaffectionate, dry, and barren' account of Addison. Whatever the tone of Tickell's preface, his noble elegy on Addison is anything but cold, unaffectionate, dry, and barren: Johnson, Goldsmith, and others thought it one of the finest in the language. Pope's lines to Addison, 'On Medals', also printed in this edition, signalled that poet's reconciliation with Tickell and Addison's shade.

When Carteret was appointed lord lieutenant of Ireland in April 1724 he retained Tickell in his service as chief secretary to the lords justices, who deputized in the absence of the lord lieutenant. Tickell moved to Dublin and devoted himself to official business, not literature, though he cultivated a friendship with Swift. In the sixteen remaining years of his life he published only three short poems: his popular ballad *Lucy and Colin* (1725), much admired by Thomas Gray and Oliver Goldsmith, 'The Horn-Book', 'written under a fit of the gout' (Lewis's *Miscellany*, 1726), and, in 1733, lines celebrating the classical rebuilding of medieval Queen's College, Oxford (to which Tickell had contributed £50).

On 23 April 1726, in Dublin, Tickell married Clotilda Eustace (1700/01–1792), heir to a fortune of £10,000; Clotilda and her mother were old friends of Swift. By marriage Tickell became a considerable landowner in co. Kildare, but his principal residence was at Glasnevin, Dublin (later the home of the National Botanic Gardens). Tickell retained his post under Carteret's two successors as lord lieutenant, the duke of Dorset (1730–37) and the duke of Devonshire. Between 1729 and 1738 he and Clotilda had three daughters and two sons, one of whom was the father of the author Richard *Tickell (1751–1793). Thomas Tickell did not live long to enjoy his family: he died at Bath on 21 April 1740, aged fifty-four, and was buried at Glasnevin. The inscription on his monument in the church there enumerates his public offices, but adds 'his highest honour was that of having been the friend of Addison'. Clotilda died in 1792, in her ninety-second year, after which her late husband's library was sold.

Tickell's poems had a place of honour at the beginning of the first volume of Dodsley's *Collection* (1748) and, with the occasional addition of verse unpublished in his lifetime, were included in most standard collections of English poetry down to the early nineteenth century. Some were not printed until 1931 (in the biography by R. E. Tickell). Johnson assigned Tickell 'a high place among minor poets', adding 'he is said to have been a man of gay conversation, at least a temperate lover of wine and company, and in his domestick relations without censure' (Johnson, 2.311). Tickell's nephew, the Revd Daniel Watson (1718–1804), said his uncle 'had a placid look, and yet was as waspish a cur as you would wish to meet with' (Nichols, *Illustrations*, 1.436). JAMES SAMBROOK

Sources R. E. Tickell, *Thomas Tickell and the eighteenth-century poets* (1931) • S. Johnson, *Lives of the English poets*, ed. G. B. Hill, [new edn], 2 (1905), 304–11 • R. Shiels, *The lives of the poets of Great Britain and Ireland*, ed. T. Cibber, 5 (1753), 17–23 • P. Smithers, *The life of Joseph Addison* (1954) • Burke, *Gen. Ire.* (1958) • Foster, *Alum. Oxon.* • *Remarks and collections of Thomas Hearne*, ed. C. E. Doble and others, 11 vols., OHS, 2, 7, 13, 34, 42–3, 48, 50, 65, 67, 72 (1885–1921), vol. 1, p. 309; vol. 2, p. 341; vol. 3, pp. 77, 111, 218; vol. 4, pp. 29, 270, 289, 422; vol. 5, p. 315; vol. 6, pp. 51, 105 • J. C. Sainty, ed., *Officials of the secretaries of state, 1660–1782* (1973) • *The correspondence of Edward Young, 1683–1765*, ed. H. Pettit (1971) • *The correspondence of Jonathan Swift*, ed. H. Williams, 5 vols. (1963–5) • *The correspondence of Alexander Pope*, ed. G. Sherburn, 5 vols. (1956) • *Letters of Joseph Addison*, ed. W. Graham (1941) • J. Spence, *Observations, anecdotes, and characters, of books and men*, ed. J. M. Osborn, new edn, 2 vols. (1966) • Nichols, *Illustrations*, 2.436 • J. R. Magrath, *The Queen's College*, 2 (1921), 66 • *Dublin Weekly Journal* (30 April 1726) • *GM*, 1st ser., 10 (1740), 261 • J. E. Butt, 'Notes for a bibliography of Thomas Tickell', *Bodleian Quarterly Record*, 5 (1926–8), 299–302

Archives Derbys. RO, corresp. relating to Ireland • HLRO, corresp. and papers [copies] • HLRO, papers relating to work as secretary to the lords justices in Ireland • PRO, corresp., SP 35/1, 9–10, 17, 20 • PRO NIre., corresp. relating to work as secretary to the lord lieutenant, D 2707/A1/7, D 3078/3/6/1–45 | BL, letters to Humfrey Wanley, Harley MS 3781, fols. 169–75

Likenesses Clamp, stipple, 1796 (after oil painting by G. Kneller (attrib.)), NPG; repro. in S. Harding, *Biographical mirrour* (1796) • E. Finden, engraving (after oil painting by G. Kneller (attrib.)), Bodl. Oxf., Montagu d.1, fol. 136 • attrib. G. Kneller, oils, Queen's College,

Oxford [*see illus.*] • Vanderbank, oils; in possession of his family, 1931

Wealth at death landed property in Cumberland and Ireland; money in the funds, jewels, plate, coach and horses, pictures; £250 p.a.: will

---

Tickhill, Agnes (*fl.* 1410–1417). *See under* Women traders and artisans in London (*act. c.*1200–*c.*1500).

Tidcomb [Tidcombe], **John** (1642–1713), army officer, was the son of Peter Tidcomb of Calne, Wiltshire. He matriculated as a servitor at Oriel College, Oxford, on 22 March 1661. During the reign of Charles II he was appointed gentleman pensioner and officiated at the coronation of James II. Gazetted captain in the earl of Huntingdon's foot on 20 June 1685, he was absent without leave in part of 1688, probably helping to co-ordinate the army conspiracy against James II. Between 14 and 16 November 1688, in company with Ensign Samuel Bonfoy, a known conspirator, Tidcomb left his post in Plymouth garrison and deserted to William's camp at Exeter. Promoted colonel of the 14th foot on 14 November 1692, he accompanied William III to Oxford in 1695 and was created DCL on 9 November. His regiment was transferred to the Irish establishment during the great disbandment following the peace of Rijswijk in 1697. In August 1701, on receipt of notice to embark for the West Indies, one company deserted from Limerick and fled into the mountains. A protégé of the second duke of Ormond, he was created brigadier-general on 17 August 1702, major-general on 1 January 1704, and lieutenant-general on 1 January 1707. Tidcomb,

> while he continued a subaltern officer, was every day complaining against the pride, oppression, and hard treatment of colonels towards their officers; yet in a very few minutes after he had received his commission for a regiment, walking with the friend on the Mall, he confessed that the spirit of colonelship was fast coming upon him, which spirit is said to have daily increased to the hour of his death. (*Prose Works of Jonathan Swift*, 192)

A member of the Kit-Cat Club, Tidcomb was a society figure and wit. When Mrs Manley (Mary de la Rivière) was dismissed by the duchess of Cleveland, he 'offered her asylum at his country house', but she declined his overtures (Noble, 2.199). Tidcomb is the Sir Charles Lovemore who, in Mrs Manley's memoirs, relates her story to his friend, the Chevalier d'Aumont, in the gardens of Somerset House. In the introduction he is characterized as a 'person of admirable good sense and knowledge' (*Rivella*, 1). Tidcomb died at Bath in June 1713. JOHN CHILDS

Sources DNB • C. Dalton, ed., *English army lists and commission registers, 1661–1714*, 6 vols. (1892–1904) • J. Childs, *The army, James II, and the Glorious Revolution* (1980) • *Calendar of the manuscripts of the marquess of Ormonde*, new ser., 8 vols., HMC, 36 (1902–20) • *The letters and dispatches of John Churchill, first duke of Marlborough, from 1702 to 1712*, ed. G. Murray, 5 vols. (1845) • N. Luttrell, *A brief historical relation of state affairs from September 1678 to April 1714*, 6 vols. (1857) • [M. D. Manley], *The adventures of Rivella, or, The history of the author of 'Atalantis'* (1714) • *A biographical history of England, from the revolution to the end of George I's reign: being a continuation of the Rev. J. Granger's work*, ed. M. Noble, 3 vols. (1806) • *The prose works of Jonathan Swift, 12: Irish tracts, 1728–1733*, ed. H. Davis (1955)

Likenesses G. Kneller, oils, c.1710, NPG • J. Faber junior, mezzotint, 1735 (after G. Kneller), BM, NPG; repro. in H. Bromley, *A catalogue of engraved British portraits* (1793)

Tidd, Richard (*bap.* 1773, *d.* 1820). *See under* Cato Street conspirators (*act.* 1820).

Tidd, William (1760–1847), legal writer, was the second son of Julius Tidd, a merchant of the parish of St Andrew, Holborn. He was admitted to the society of the Inner Temple on 6 June 1782, and was called to the bar on 26 November 1813, after having practised as a special pleader for upwards of thirty years. Among his pupils were three who became lord chancellors—John Singleton Copley, Baron Lyndhurst, Charles Pepys, Earl Cottenham, and John Campbell, Baron Campbell—and one who became lord chief justice, Thomas Denham.

Tidd is best known for his *Practice of the Court of King's Bench*, the first part of which appeared in 1790 and the second in 1794. For a long period it was almost the sole authority for common-law practice, going through nine editions by 1828. Several supplements were also issued, which in 1837 were consolidated into one volume. The work was also extensively used in America, where one edition with notes by Asa I. Fish appeared as late as 1856. Tidd was favoured by the approval of Uriah Heep: "'I am improving my legal knowledge, Master Copperfield", said Uriah. "I am going through Tidd's "Practice". Oh, what a writer Mr Tidd is, Master Copperfield!"' (Charles Dickens, *David Copperfield*, chap. 12).

Tidd died on 14 February 1847 in Walcot Place, Lambeth. His wife, Elizabeth, survived him a few months, dying on 21 October 1847. Tidd bequeathed the copyright of the *Practice* to Edward Hobson Vitruvius Lawes, serjeant-at-law.

Along with the *Practice*, Tidd wrote three works on forms and procedure which were intended to supplement it. He also published an account of law costs in civil actions (1792).   E. I. CARLYLE, *rev.* JONATHAN HARRIS

Sources *GM*, 2nd ser., 27 (1847), 553–4 • *GM*, 2nd ser., 28 (1847), 665 • Allibone, *Dict.* • F. A. Inderwick and R. A. Roberts, eds., *A calendar of the Inner Temple records*, 5 (1936), 427 • W. Story, ed., *Life and letters of Joseph Story* (1851), 434 • PRO, PROB 11/2053/275
Wealth at death £60,000: will, PRO, PROB 11/2053/275

Tiddy, Reginald John Elliott (1880–1916), collector of folk plays, was born at Berlin House, 43 Godwin Road, Margate, on 9 March 1880, the elder son of William Elliott Tiddy (1850–1933), schoolmaster, and his wife, Ellen (1853?–1896), *née* Willett, daughter of a farmer from Ramsden, Oxfordshire. Tiddy attended his father's school, Albion House School, Margate, until 1893, when he entered Tonbridge School. In his final year at Tonbridge he was head boy, and left in 1898 with a scholarship to University College, Oxford. Here he achieved firsts in both classical moderations and Greats. After a spell as junior prize fellow at University College, he became lecturer in classics and a fellow of Trinity College; but his real interest now was English literature, and he worked to qualify as a tutor in the new honour school of English, being appointed university lecturer in English literature in 1910.

Reginald John Elliott Tiddy (1880–1916), by unknown photographer, c.1910

Tiddy knew the Wychwood area from childhood, when he had spent many holidays with his mother's family, and about 1909 he took up residence in Ascott under Wychwood, living first at the Corner House and later at Priory Cottage with his father. He felt an affinity with the working classes, actively supporting Ruskin College, campaigning to reduce working hours in bookshops, and arranging Workers' Educational Association courses in Ascott. The reading-room he built in the village in 1912 (posthumously named Tiddy Hall) was intended partly for the association's activities, but incorporated a sprung floor to cater for the folk-dance revival in which he was by then playing a prominent role.

Folk dances had been demonstrated in Oxford in 1911, and Tiddy was one of several university men who took up the pastime. Three months after the foundation of the English Folk Dance Society in December 1911, its first provincial branch was inaugurated in Oxford, with Tiddy as the moving spirit and chairman. The society's men's morris dance side consisted of the requisite six men only, but Tiddy was first reserve. He accepted the invitation from the Oxford University Dramatic Society to supply morris dancers for the February 1913 production of Thomas Dekker's *Shoemaker's Holiday*; the dramatic society advertised the Dancing Dons in bold letters in its announcements, and the performances were immensely successful, being encored each night and attracting widespread attention.

Combining his recreational and scholarly interests, Tiddy now began to collect folk plays. Some came from correspondents and acquaintances, others from personal collecting: he would walk or cycle to a village, strike up a conversation with those he met on reaching it, and rapidly find someone who acted in a mummers' or other folk play, and who could recite it. He continued this activity even after he was commissioned 2nd lieutenant in the 2/4 battalion, Oxford and Bucks light infantry, on 16 February 1915. The total of his collection which has survived is thirty-three plays, but he undoubtedly had information on many more, both from his own fieldwork and from his contacts with other interested scholars, notably Thomas Fairman Ordish and Cecil Sharp.

Even in army camp, Tiddy's letters record, he taught morris dances to the men, and performed them with his batman, Ralph Honeybone, who had been one of his Ascott dancers and with whom, Tiddy confessed, it was hard to observe the formalities of rank. He found it difficult to impose strict discipline in general, moreover, and the stress of army life made him an unsmiling person. He survived one push for which his company had been an expendable decoy, but on the night of 10 August 1916 he was killed by the blast of a shell bursting behind him while he was searching a trench under fire, alone, for wounded men. He was buried at the military cemetery at Laventie, France.

Before the war Tiddy had produced only a couple of articles on English literature, and his projected book on mummers' plays was to be his first major publication. In the event his papers were prepared for publication by friends and appeared in 1923. Though Tiddy's scholarly contribution was eclipsed by E. K. Chambers a decade later, and hundreds more plays are now known to scholars, Tiddy's collection remained the best published, and hence most accessible, assemblage of texts of folk plays throughout the twentieth century.

MICHAEL HEANEY

Sources R. J. E. Tiddy, *The mummers' play ... with a memoir* (1923) · *Oxford Magazine* (10 Nov 1916), 29–30 [extra number] · private information (2004) · b. cert. · *CGPLA Eng. & Wales* (1917)
Archives Folklore Society, London, Ordish collection
Likenesses photograph, c.1910, NPG [*see illus.*] · G. Segar, line drawing, 1913, repro. in *The Varsity* (Feb 1913) · portrait, Tiddy Hall, Asott under Wychwood, Oxfordshire
Wealth at death £3274 14s. 3d.: resworn probate, 9 Jan 1917, *CGPLA Eng. & Wales*

Tidey, Alfred (1808–1892), miniature painter, was born at Worthing, Sussex, on 20 April 1808, the second son of John Tidey (1773–1849), schoolmaster, and his wife, Elizabeth Fryer (1778–1858) of Worthing. Henry Ferey *Tidey (1814–1872), painter in watercolours, was his younger brother. Alfred Tidey was taught to paint by his father; there is no record of Tidey's receiving any formal training as a miniaturist. However, he received support from John Constable, whose sister Maria rejected a proposal of marriage from Tidey, and from the principal miniaturist of the period, Sir William Ross, who may have helped Tidey to gain some of his earliest commissions. Through the patronage of Henry Neville, second earl of Abergavenny, Tidey was introduced to Sir John Conroy, comptroller of the household to Victoria, duchess of Kent, and in 1836 he painted her miniature (NPG). Tidey thus became known to the duchess's daughter, Victoria, who, when queen, commissioned him in 1841 to paint a miniature of the Hon. Julia Henrietta Anson, one of her maids of honour (Royal Collection), and two copies of a miniature by Ross of Victoria, princess royal. He later painted the princess royal, when she was Empress Frederick of Germany, as well as a watercolour portrait of her daughter Princess Victoria of Schleswig-Holstein (1873). Tidey exhibited miniatures at the Royal Academy from 1831 to 1857, and watercolours occasionally from 1857 until 1887.

In 1855 Tidey married Justina Gertrude Campbell (d. 1907), one of the five daughters of Alexander Campbell of the West Indies, with whom he had three sons. After his marriage Tidey turned from miniature painting to oil portraiture and lived and worked in Jersey (1863–9), then in France, Switzerland, Italy, and Germany (1869–73). He produced only occasional portraits after his return to London in 1873 and died on 2 April 1892 at his home, Glenelg, Springfield Park, Acton, Middlesex. Examples of his work are in the Victoria and Albert Museum and the National Portrait Gallery, London, as well as in the Royal Collection.

V. REMINGTON

Sources S. Tidey, draft biography of Alfred Tidey, 1808–92, V&A NAL, MS 86.X.35 · S. Tidey, list of miniatures by Alfred Tidey, 1808–92, 1924, V&A NAL, MS 86.X.34 [typescript] · *The Times* (7 April 1892) · M. Tidey, *The Tideys of Washington, Sussex* (1973), 31–58 · B. Stewart and M. Cutten, *The dictionary of portrait painters in Britain up to 1920* (1997) · D. Foskett, *Miniatures: dictionary and guide* (1987), 444, 664 · B. S. Long, *British miniaturists* (1929), 438 · L. R. Schidlof, *The miniature in Europe in the 16th, 17th, 18th, and 19th centuries*, 2 (1964), 820 · Graves, *RA exhibitors* · *CGPLA Eng. & Wales* (1892) · *DNB*
Wealth at death £345 14s. 4d.: probate, 30 Sept 1892, *CGPLA Eng. & Wales*

Tidey, Henry Ferey (1814–1872), portrait painter, was born on 7 January 1814 at Worthing House, Worthing, Sussex, one of at least three sons of John Tidey (1773–1849), schoolmaster at Worthing House, and his wife, Elizabeth Fryer (1778–1858). He was the younger brother of Alfred *Tidey (1808–1892), a miniature painter. He learned to draw at his father's school, and as a child he painted several pictures for Princess Augusta, who was staying at Worthing. He practised there for some years as a portrait painter before moving to London. Between 1839 and 1869 he exhibited sixty-seven paintings at the Royal Academy, mainly portraits, including many of children. At first he usually painted miniatures, but after the success of his watercolour portrait of Lieutenant-Colonel Pakenham of the Grenadier Guards in action at the battle of Alma (exh. RA, 1855) he turned to watercolours of historical and poetic subjects.

In 1859 Tidey was elected a member of the New Society of Painters in Water Colours, and his *The Feast of Roses*, a scene from Thomas Moore's *Lalla Rookh*, was bought by Queen Victoria from the 1859 exhibition of the society as a birthday present for Prince Albert. In the 1860s Tidey continued to exhibit at the New Watercolour Society. In 1860 he was awarded two medals for *Queen Mab*, and other pictures included *The Last of the Abencerages*, a scene in the garden of the Alhambra in medieval Spain (exh. 1862); *The Night of the Betrayal*, a triptych (exh. 1864); and a series of paintings of children, *Sensitive Plants*, with names such as *Sweet William and Mary Gold* (exh. 1866–7). Tidey died suddenly on 21 July 1872 at his home, 30 Percy Street, Bedford Square, London.

ANNE PIMLOTT BAKER

Sources J. Dafforne, 'Henry Tidey', *Art Journal*, 31 (1869), 109–11 · B. Stewart and M. Cutten, *The dictionary of portrait painters in Britain up to 1920* (1997) · Graves, *RA exhibitors* · A. G. Temple, *Guildhall memories* (1918), 163–4 · Mallalieu, *Watercolour artists*, vols. 1–2 · Boase, *Mod. Eng. biog.* · exhibition catalogues (1858–72) [New Society of Painters in Water Colours] · Redgrave, *Artists* · *DNB* · *CGPLA Eng. & Wales* (1872)
Wealth at death under £2000: probate, 13 Aug 1872, *CGPLA Eng. & Wales*

Tidferth [Tidfrith] (*d.* 816×24), bishop of Dunwich, succeeded Alfhun in 798 as ninth bishop of that see. His profession of obedience to Æthelheard, archbishop of Canterbury, made either on his consecration or on his reconciliation after the abolition of the archbishopric of Lichfield, is extant. From 798 to 816 he attested at least seven genuine charters. In 798 he was present at a synod at 'Clofesho' and in 801 at another held at Chelsea. He attended the important council at 'Clofesho' in 803 and about the same time received a letter of advice from Alcuin, who said that he had heard of Tidferth's exemplary life from an East Anglian abbot named Lull. Tidferth was also present at the Council of Chelsea in August 816. After 816 there is no trace of a bishop of Dunwich until 824, by which time Tidferth was dead. He must be distinguished from a contemporary Tidfrith or Tilferd, the last bishop of Hexham, who held that see at the beginning of the ninth century.

A. F. POLLARD, rev. MARIOS COSTAMBEYS

Sources *ASC*, s.a. 798 [text F] · *AS chart.*, S 40, 41, 153, 173, 180, 1260, 1431 · A. W. Haddan and W. Stubbs, eds., *Councils and ecclesiastical documents relating to Great Britain and Ireland*, 3 (1871) · E. Dümmler, ed., *Epistolae Karolini aevi*, MGH Epistolae [quarto], 4 (Berlin, 1895), no. 301

Archives BL, Cotton MS Cleopatra E.i

Tidswell, Charlotte (1759/60–1846), actress, may have been the daughter of an improvident army officer, with whom she spent an unsettled childhood and whose death left her destitute, but there is much about her early life that is known only from gossipy rumour. She was acting in Bristol in 1776, and perhaps as a child at the Crow Street Theatre in Dublin as early as 1768, but the first London playbill to carry her name dates from 24 January 1783, when she played the small part of Scentwell in Susannah Centlivre's *The Busy Body* at Drury Lane, the theatre with which she remained primarily associated for the next thirty-nine years. The whisper was that she owed her Drury Lane engagement to the dissolute Charles *Howard, eleventh duke of Norfolk (1746–1815), whose mistress she had been. No one, at that time, would have predicted that she would become such a stalwart company member: her early specialism in chambermaid roles later transmuted into the mixed blessing of type-casting as wicked or wanton women on the fringes of the main plot. But it is less to her acting than to a tangle of youthful relationships that Tidswell owes her place in theatre history. At some time in the 1780s she became associated with a solo entertainer called Moses Kean, the middle one of three brothers. It was more likely the unstable younger brother than Moses himself who fathered the future star Edmund Kean, but there were many who suspected Tidswell of being the mother. She and Moses, until his early death in 1792, certainly did more to care for young Edmund (*b.* 1787) than either of his putative parents. It was she who guided his early career as an infant prodigy, though how willingly is not clear. She had a career of her own to sustain, and the care of a boy not her own was a burden. Kean's appreciation of the woman he knew as Aunt Tid

was tempered, but there were many periods in his wayward life when he was dependent on her alone.

Despite her long Drury Lane career, Tidswell never graduated to major roles. Her few Shakespearian appearances, for example, were as the Player Queen in *Hamlet*, the Duchess of York in *Richard III*, Margaret in *Much Ado about Nothing*, and Lady Capulet in *Romeo and Juliet*. A weekly wage which seems never to have risen above £3 was supplemented, after 1792, by annual shared benefits. As is implied by her frequent changes of address, penury was never far away. When Drury Lane closed for the summer she found work where she could: at the little theatre in the Haymarket, in Brighton, and, most frequently, in Liverpool. She seems to have lived down the memory of a scandalous past and to have garnered a reputation for respectability. When she took her farewell benefit at Drury Lane on 21 May 1822 she was summoned for her curtain address by Edmund Kean, and stumbled tearfully through the words written for her. In retirement she continued to respond to calls from the ailing Kean, keeping house for him in Richmond, and nursing him there in his last days. She outlived him by nearly thirteen years, and died on 3 September 1846, at the age of eighty-six, at her home, 4 Camera Street, Chelsea.   PETER THOMSON

Sources Highfill, Burnim & Langhans, *BDA* · G. Playfair, *Kean* (1950) · H. N. Hillebrand, *Edmund Kean* (1933) · F. W. Hawkins, *The life of Edmund Kean*, 2 vols. (1869) · R. FitzSimons, *Edmund Kean* (1976) · J. F. Molloy, *The life and adventures of Edmund Kean*, 2 vols. (1888) · [J. Haslewood], *The secret history of the green rooms: containing authentic and entertaining memoirs of the actors and actresses in the three theatres royal*, 2 vols. (1790) · C. B. Hogan, ed., *The London stage, 1660–1800*, pt 5: *1776–1800* (1968)

Tidy, Charles Meymott (1843–1892), sanitary and analytical chemist, was born on 2 February 1843 at Cambridge Heath, Hackney, Middlesex, the third son of William Callender Tidy, surgeon, and his wife, Charlotte Meymott. After attending Hackney Church of England school, he entered the London Hospital as a student under Henry Letheby, taking his LSA and MRCS in 1864. In 1865 he entered the University of Aberdeen, graduating CM and MB with the highest honours in 1866.

After returning to London, Tidy took up his father's medical practice in Hackney for about ten years. During this time he was joint lecturer in chemistry with Henry Letheby at the London Hospital medical college. Under Letheby's influence Tidy gradually became interested in questions of sanitary reform and public health, and became one of the first public analysts appointed under the Adulteration of Food Act of 1872, being responsible for Hertfordshire, Essex, and the boroughs of Islington and Whitechapel. When Letheby died in 1876 Tidy took over as professor of chemistry, medical jurisprudence, and public health, and also succeeded him as medical officer of health for the City of London. Tidy married Violet Fordham Dobell, daughter of Horace Dobell, physician, on 5 October 1875; they had a son and a daughter. Their son, Sir Henry Letheby Tidy (1877–1960), was one-time dean of St Thomas's Hospital and an extra-physician to George VI and Elizabeth II.

The London Hospital had a tradition of championing defendants in poisoning trials, stemming from a rivalry between Henry Letheby and Alfred Swaine Taylor, of Guy's, which dated back to the Tawell case, in Slough, in 1845. In 1881 Tidy advised the defence counsel for Dr George Lamson, accused of poisoning his nineteen-year-old brother-in-law with aconite. Tidy asked to be present at the prosecution's toxicological analysis of the victim's remains, but his request was refused. A week after the trial, in 1882, the home secretary was asked in the House of Commons whether it would not be more satisfactory for defendants to be represented professionally at such analyses. In response, the home secretary asked the royal colleges of physicians and surgeons to appoint two independent experienced men of science who could be consulted in cases of this kind. The Royal College of Surgeons appointed Tidy to be one of the first two Home Office analysts. His fees were paid by the Home Office and his independence would seem to stem from the fact that he could appear either for the defence or the prosecution. In 1889 Tidy appeared for the defence in the trial of Florence Maybrick for the murder of her husband. Cautious, modest, and precise in court, Tidy genuinely believed that James Maybrick did not die from arsenic poisoning and that only a medicinal quantity of the substance was present in the body. Tidy wrote two books on medical jurisprudence. The first, *A Handy-Book of Forensic Medicine and Toxicology*, with W. B. Woodman, appeared in 1877. The second, *Legal Medicine*, prepared from lecture notes, appeared under his sole authorship in 1882.

Tidy was also keen to improve the health of the metropolis with a pure water supply. He published *The London Water Supply* in 1878, closely followed by a paper on 'The process for determining the organic purity of potable waters' in the *Journal of the Chemical Society* (1879, 46–106). This was a scholarly and painstaking analysis of monthly samples supplied by the metropolitan water companies over the previous nine years. It was followed by an equally exacting undertaking in his paper 'River water' (*Journal of the Chemical Society*, 1880, 268–327). In 1881 he, together with Professor Odling and William Crookes, was appointed by the London water companies to examine the quality of the city's water.

Tidy's position as professor of medical jurisprudence and his frequent experience in courts of law convinced him that a counsel thoroughly acquainted with medicine and chemistry was an urgent requirement. He therefore took up the study of law and was called to the bar at Lincoln's Inn in 1885; he was later appointed reader in medical jurisprudence to the inns of court. Tidy received the Royal College of Physicians' Swiney prize for legal medicine in 1889. He was on the examining boards of the royal colleges of physicians and surgeons, and was a fellow of the Chemical Society, being at one time vice-president of the Institute of Chemistry. In 1888 he gave the Christmas lectures to young people at the London Institution and took as his theme 'The story of a tinder-box: the romance of science', in which he described the history of matches and firelighting methods. These lectures were published

as a book under the same title in 1889. Besides the works mentioned Tidy wrote *A Handbook of Modern Chemistry* (1878, 1887) and contributed many journal papers on chemistry, medicine, and toxicology. He died at his home at 3 Mandeville Place, London, on 15 March 1892, having suffered from cancer for the previous five years.

JENNY WARD

Sources *The Lancet* (19 March 1892), 651 · *The Times* (17 March 1892), 10b · *JCS*, 63 (1893), 766–9 · *Medical Directory* (1892) · *Hansard 3* (1882), 267.1141 · *BMJ* (24 April 1882), 747 · H. B. Irving, ed., *Trial of Mrs Maybrick*, Notable British Trials (1927) · W. P. Baildon, ed., *The records of the Honorable Society of Lincoln's Inn: admissions*, 2 (1896) · C. M. Tidy and R. Macnamara, *The Maybrick trial: a toxicological study* (1890) · b. cert. · m. cert. · d. cert. · *CGPLA Eng. & Wales* (1892) · personal knowledge (1898) [*DNB*] · *DNB*
Wealth at death £42,914 3s. 7d.: resworn probate, July 1893, *CGPLA Eng. & Wales* (1892)

Tiedeman, May Louise Seaton- (1864?–1948), campaigner for divorce law reform, was born in Boston, Massachusetts, the daughter of Alfred Herbert Seaton, an export merchant and lay preacher. She claimed descent from Scottish Presbyterians on one side of her family and from English Anglicans on the other. The Seaton family moved from America to England when she was in her teens. On 5 January 1886 she married Frederick Henry Lewis Tiedeman (1847–1915), a Dutch journalist and editor of the *Nieuwe Rotterdamsche Courant*; they had one son, Henry Seaton Tiedeman. Although the couple were based in London they travelled around the world and had a wide circle of friends, including many writers, politicians, and social reformers. May Tiedeman's happy marriage of thirty years ended with her husband's death in 1915: within the year, on 31 July 1916, she married Edward Woolf Abrams (1865–1945), a metal mining agent and a long-time family friend. This marriage also lasted nearly thirty years, ending only with Abrams's death in 1945.

May Seaton-Tiedeman's role in the divorce law reform campaign of the inter-war years has been overlooked because the organization of which she was honorary secretary, the Divorce Law Reform Union, left few traces in the history books. This is partly owing to the fact that most of its records were destroyed during the Second World War. A more significant reason is that, despite the union's best efforts, its primary contribution to divorce reform was as a resource centre, drafting and promoting bills for parliamentary allies, rather than as a high-profile mass-membership pressure group: accordingly, the union did not receive any public recognition when its central object, the enactment of reform based on the recommendations of the 1909–12 royal commission on divorce and matrimonial causes, was achieved with the passage of A. P. Herbert's Matrimonial Causes Bill in 1937.

As a courageous and indefatigable campaigner Seaton-Tiedeman was the driving force behind the Divorce Law Reform Union, rather than its famous figureheads such as Sir Arthur Conan Doyle and Lord Birkenhead. Herbert described her as a 'brave fighter [who] had been at it for I know not how many years, speaking in Hyde Park on Sundays, lobbying the House of Commons and all the time keeping her little Union alive with hardly any resources'

(Herbert, 73). As the union's primary propagandist she was the editor of its quarterly paper, *The Journal*, which was published from 1919 to 1931. She was not motivated by personal experience of an unhappy marriage, but rather by her belief that immorality, injustice, and unnecessary human suffering were not to be tolerated. A member of the Ethical Union, her secular humanism found its fullest expression in the divorce reform movement not least because the primary ideology of opponents of reform was Christianity; for her the extension of matrimonial juris-diction was as important as the extension of the divorce grounds themselves. She therefore advocated the estab-lishment of courts of domestic relations, and in 1925 sub-mitted evidence to a lord chancellor's committee set up to investigate the working of the poor persons' rules, devised to assist litigants with low incomes to pursue divorce petitions in the High Court.

Despite her membership of the World League for Sexual Reform on a Scientific Basis, May Seaton-Tiedeman was not a libertarian; indeed, in many ways she was a conser-vative reformer. She did not believe that sexual relations were solely a private concern, and she wished to see legal marriage become coterminous with a loving relationship, thereby ending society's tolerance of promiscuity and non-marital unions. This led her to campaign for the aboli-tion of permanent legal separation and the extension of fault-based divorce grounds: although she believed that divorce should be permissible on the ground of incom-patibility of temperament, she remained hostile to divorce being granted on the ground of mutual consent.

May Seaton-Tiedeman campaigned for further divorce law reforms after 1937, but retired during the Second World War. She moved first to Hove and then to London to be with her son, before dying at Friern Hospital, New Southgate, Middlesex, on 22 October 1948. She was cre-mated privately on 26 October.   CORDELIA MOYSE

Sources An appreciation: Mrs May Louise Seaton-Tiedeman (c.1948) · *The Journal* (1919–31) · C. A. Moyse, 'Marriage and divorce law reform in England and Wales, 1909–37', PhD diss., U. Cam., 1996 · A. P. Herbert, *The ayes have it: the story of the Marriage Bill* (1937) · D. Stetson, *A woman's issue: the politics of family law reform in England* (1982) · m. certs. · d. cert. · *Daily Telegraph* (28 Oct 1948) · *Morning Post* (28 Oct 1948)
Archives PRO, PREM 1/38 · Wellcome L., Marie Stopes collec-tion · Women's Library, London, universal decimal classified pamphlets [Divorce Law Reform Union]
Wealth at death £1771 10s. 4d.: probate, 1 Feb 1949, CGPLA Eng. & Wales

Tierney, George (1761–1830), politician, was born at Gib-raltar on 20 March 1761, the third son of Thomas Tierney, a native of Limerick, sometime London merchant and prize agent at Gibraltar, and his wife, Sabina (d. 23 July 1806). Thomas Tierney, a man of some affluence, spent his later years in Paris, but his wife lived in England, where their children were educated. George attended Boteler's School, Warrington; Eton College; and Peterhouse, Cam-bridge. He was entered at Lincoln's Inn in 1780 and called to the bar in 1784, but did not practise. On 9 July 1789 he married Anna Maria (d. 1844), the daughter of Michael

George Tierney (1761–1830), by William Behnes, 1822

Miller of Bristol, with whom he had one son and three daughters.

At the general election of 1784 Tierney unsuccessfully contested Wootton Bassett as a supporter of Pitt; but when he stood for Colchester on a vacancy in December 1788 it was as an adherent of the whig opposition. After a double return (both candidates polled the same number of votes) he was seated by an election committee in April 1789. At the general election the following year he was defeated at Colchester, against the return for which he lodged an abortive petition, and at Wootton Bassett. These electoral adventures, though partially subsidized from opposition funds, took a heavy toll of his finances. As co-treasurer of the Association of the Friends of the People, he gained the friendship of Charles (later Earl) Grey and a reputation as an enthusiast for French repub-lican principles. At the general election of 1796 'Citizen' Tierney, financed by public subscription, contested South-wark as a supporter of peace and reform. He was defeated by his niece's wealthy husband, George Woodford Thel-lusson, but had the election declared void on petition. Although he was beaten by the same opponent at the con-sequent by-election, his petition secured him the seat in December 1796.

Tierney, who had joined the Whig Club in 1791, went into active opposition to Pitt. He refused to countenance the Foxite secession from parliament and established himself during it as the ministry's most potent opponent in the Commons, where he excelled on financial questions, which suited his essentially practical mind. Ever the pragmatist, he retreated from his advanced position on parliamentary reform, though he remained convinced of the need for moderate change. A clash in the house with Pitt on 25 May 1798 led to their fighting a bloodless duel at Putney two days later. By flouting the secession, Tierney seriously damaged himself in the eyes of many Foxite whigs. Fox himself never had much time for him; and while Grey and Lord Holland stayed friendly, they felt that he had been misguided. Having forfeited much of the popular support on which his seat depended and alienated most of the influential whigs, he was in urgent need of political and personal security. In early 1801 he renounced all allegiance to Fox and gravitated to the Carlton House group. He responded eagerly to the advances of Pitt's successor Addington in the autumn, tempted by the prospect of becoming paymaster with £3000 a year and a house. Thwarted by the refusal of Grey and Lord Moira to join the ministry, he kept the negotiations alive for four months, but finally lost his nerve in January 1802. He was given an uncomfortable time at Southwark at the general election in July, when he was returned second in the poll.

Convinced by a visit to France that Bonaparte was determined on renewed war, Tierney backed Addington's belligerent response in May 1803 and soon afterwards took office as treasurer of the navy. He was pleased with his bargain, but it did him little good: Pittites as well as many Foxites now held him in contempt, and his patent unease in the house gratified his enemies. Pitt would have retained him in office in May 1804, but he resigned with Addington. He acted as a go-between in Pitt's subsequent attempts to effect a reconciliation between the prince of Wales and George III, but the postponement of the royal reunion in August prompted him to decline for the moment the proffered reward of the Irish secretaryship. By working thereafter to try to separate the prince from opposition and attach him to Pitt, Tierney further angered the Foxites and Grenvillites. Aware that it would be politically suicidal to commit himself to Pitt at this stage, he turned down the secretaryship (which it was later alleged that he had wished to hold without a seat in the Commons) in November 1804. By going into desultory opposition to Pitt the following session he restored some of his credibility with the Foxites, but no place was found for him on the formation of the Grenville ministry in February 1806. He rejected offers of the governorship of the Cape and a special mission to Lisbon later in the year. The death of Fox removed a major obstacle to his advancement, and in October he was taken in as president of the Board of Control, where he proved to be highly efficient. At the general election that month he was defeated at Southwark, but he was hastily accommodated at Athlone through a government bargain with the patron. This marked the end of his career as a political freelance.

Tierney, who had established himself as an unofficial whip and party factotum, resigned with his colleagues in April 1807. He was largely responsible for organizing the opposition effort at the ensuing general election, but was himself left without a seat, and it was not until August that the duke of Devonshire provided him with one at Bandon Bridge. He was anxious to promote the creation of an active, efficient opposition, to be remodelled from the Grenvillite right if the more unruly elements on the far left proved unmanageable. He soon grew disillusioned with the feeble Commons leadership of George Ponsonby, Grey's successor, and with Grey's laziness and reluctance to assert his overall authority. His attempts to mediate between Grey and his brother-in-law Samuel Whitbread, whose personal pique and espousal of advanced views threatened to split the party, were generally unsuccessful, though through no fault of his own. At times during the 1807 parliament, when opposition was often in a state of chaos, Tierney lapsed into hopeless despondency, and talked of giving up politics or of letting the insurgents destroy the party so that it could be reconstructed on a sounder basis. Thomas Creevey, Whitbread's mischievous henchman, gave him the nickname of 'Mrs Cole', after a brothel keeper in Samuel Foote's farce *The Minor* who was forever proclaiming her own respectability. Yet his nervousness, pessimism, and irresolution in council were in marked contrast to his forcefulness and skill in debate, where his mastery of sarcasm and forensic argument made him a formidable parliamentarian.

At the general election of 1812 Tierney again failed to find a seat, but at the end of the year Holland secured his return for Appleby on Lord Thanet's interest. Although he initially discounted the chances of mounting effective opposition in the new parliament, he took a bold personal line against the renewal of war in 1815, when he belatedly joined Brooks's Club. That summer his most pressing debts were paid off by a discreet party subscription, to which most of the whig grandees contributed. He obtained further relief in 1816 through legacies from a brother-in-law. He encouraged whig involvement in the popular campaign against the property tax that year, and in 1817 came out strongly in favour of moderate but significant parliamentary reform. Ponsonby's death seemed to clear the way for Tierney to replace him as leader in the Commons; but it was not until after the general election of 1818, when he was returned by the duke of Devonshire for Knaresborough (where he sat for the rest of his life) that he was installed. With many misgivings, he accepted a requisition got up by lords Duncannon and Sefton, signed by 113 members and half-heartedly endorsed by Grey. He was chosen in part *faute de mieux*; but in the opinion of all those who mattered in the mainstream of the party, his merits marginally outweighed his defects. The left had little faith in him.

Although Grey refused to clarify the problem of the overall leadership, which Tierney considered essential if the party was to be presented as a credible alternative government, the opposition made an impressive start to the 1819 session under his direction. On 18 May, however, he blundered by moving for inquiry into the state of the nation. His speech for once was not impressive, and, as usual on questions of confidence, disgruntled tories and waverers rallied to the ministry; the motion was humiliatingly crushed by 358 votes to 178. Tierney favoured a vigorous response to the Peterloo massacre and the subsequent repressive legislation; but during a speech in the house on 22 December 1819 he was taken ill. His health had been deteriorating for some years and, although he recovered and soldiered on as leader into the new reign, he made it clear to Grey and others that his future exertions must be on a restricted scale. He took a lead in trying to promote petitions in support of Queen Caroline at the end of 1820 and did well personally in the debates of early 1821. The failure of the whig campaign, the continued intransigence of the party's more extreme elements, over whom his authority was largely gone, his exasperation with Grey's selfish idleness, and his own unreliable health brought him formally to resign the leadership in March. Though far from being an unqualified success, he had generally performed with credit in a difficult, perhaps an impossible situation.

Old Tierney, as he was now habitually called, though he was only sixty, was intermittently active in the Commons for the remainder of the 1820 parliament. His correspondence with Grey appears to have ceased in 1825. They fell out politically in April 1827 when, after complex negotiations, Tierney joined Lord Lansdowne and Devonshire in taking office in Canning's ministry, as master of the Royal Mint with a seat in the cabinet. On Canning's death in August he stayed on with Lansdowne under Lord Goderich, but vehemently objected to the proposed appointment of the anti-Catholic Herries as chancellor of the exchequer. After suffering agonies of indecision in the ensuing crisis, he capitulated with Lansdowne in order to save the government. His subsequent efforts to secure the neutrality of Lord Althorp and the young whigs were frustrated, but in November 1827 he persuaded Goderich to appoint Althorp chairman of the finance committee. The impasse caused by Herries's belatedly revealed hostility to this broke Goderich's nerve and destroyed the ministry. Tierney was dismissed by the duke of Wellington when he formed his administration in January 1828, but received assurances, which were honoured, that something would be done for his son George (d. 1883), a minor diplomat in delicate health. His political career was effectively over, though he voted silently for Catholic emancipation in 1829. He died suddenly, of heart failure, at his London house at 11 Savile Row on 25 January 1830. He died intestate and relatively impoverished, and the government granted his widow a civil-list pension of £400 a year.

Tierney was a man of great personal charm. Holland wrote that 'his pleasantry and easy manners shed a charm over all intercourse with him' (Holland, 266). A master of debate, he would probably have made a fortune had he opted for a career at the bar. As a working politician he could be combative and effective, but he was often indecisive and prone to enervating pessimism. A pragmatist above all, he was perhaps too much given to intrigue, though he served the whig party faithfully after expiating his earlier sins, for which some, however, never forgave him. Sir James Mackintosh recalled him as 'so shrewd and droll—the words seemed made for him' (Memoirs of … Mackintosh, 475).   D. R. FISHER

Sources D. R. Fisher, 'Tierney, George', HoP, Commons, 1790–1820 · HoP, Commons, 1820–32 [draft] · J. A. Cannon, 'Tierney, George', HoP, Commons, 1754–90 · H. K. Olphin, George Tierney (1934) · H. R. V. Fox, third Lord Holland, Further memoirs of the whig party, 1807–1821, ed. Lord Stavordale (1905), 265–7 · Memoirs of the life of the Right Honourable Sir James Mackintosh, ed. R. J. Mackintosh, 2nd edn, 2 vols. (1836), vol. 2, p. 475 · H. Brougham, Historical sketches of statesmen who flourished in the time of George III, 2nd ser. (1839), 143–55 · GM, 2nd ser., 21 (1844), 552 [death notice of Anna Maria Tierney] · The Times (28 Jan 1830) · The Times (29 Jan 1830)
Archives Hants. RO, corresp. and papers | All Souls Oxf., letters to Charles Richard Vaughan · Beds. & Luton ARS, corresp. with Samuel Whitbread · BL, corresp. with Lord Grenville, Add. MS 58964 · BL, corresp. with Lord and Lady Holland, Add. MSS 51584–51586 · U. Durham L., letters to second Earl Grey
Likenesses W. Nutter, stipple, pubd 1798 (after L. Abbott), BM, NPG · W. Behnes, marble bust, 1822, NPG [see illus.] · G. Hayter, oils, 1823, NG Ire. · R. J. Lane, lithograph, 1830 (after W. Hunt), NPG · R. Westmacott jun., bust, 1830, Westminster Abbey · G. Hayter, group portrait, oils (The trial of Queen Caroline, 1820), NPG
Wealth at death under £2000: administration, PRO, PROB 6/206

Tierney, Mark Aloysius (1795–1862), historian, born at Brighton in September 1795, was sent at an early age to the school directed by the Franciscan fathers at Baddesley Green, Warwickshire, from which he was transferred in 1810 to St Edmund's College at Old Hall Green, near Ware. He completed a programme in classical studies with distinction, and in 1815, while still a student, became professor of mathematics and plainchant. In 1818 he was ordained to the priesthood, though he remained at the college as professor and procurator until 1819, when he was appointed assistant priest at Warwick Street, London. He was later transferred to Lincoln's Inn Fields.

Because of ill health, from which he suffered throughout his life, Tierney was moved to the country mission of Slindon, Sussex, the estate of the Newburgh family, where he remained until 1824, when he became chaplain to Bernard Edward Howard, twelfth duke of Norfolk. For the rest of his life he lived at Arundel, where he had ample leisure to pursue his historical and antiquarian studies. On 7 February 1833 he was elected a fellow of the Society of Antiquaries of London, and on 25 July 1841 a fellow of the Royal Society. He was also a corresponding member of the Society of Antiquaries of Scotland. On the formation of the Sussex Archaeological Society in 1846 he became its local secretary, and in 1850 he also joined the committee. He supervised many papers for the society, and contributed in 1849 to volume 3 of its Proceedings 'Notices of recent excavations in the collegiate church of Arundel', and in 1860 to volume 12 'An account of the discovery of the remains of John, seventeenth earl of Arundel'.

For many years Tierney was a member of the old chapter of England, established in 1623, and when the diocese of Southwark was created by Pope Pius IX in 1852 he became the first canon penitentiary of the cathedral chapter. Throughout much of his life Tierney was identified with a group of Catholics who were opposed to the policies of Nicholas Wiseman, first archbishop of Westminster. The antagonism between the two men seems to have dated from at least 1837 when Wiseman, one of the founders of the *Dublin Review*, appointed his friend Henry Bagshawe as editor of the journal in spite of the fact that Tierney had served briefly in the position. Considered to represent a Gallican, or anti-Roman, position, Tierney, along with other English Catholics including the historian John Lingard, disapproved of what they judged to be undue Roman influence and practice, as well as a tendency to favour the regular over the secular clergy. In 1858 Tierney entered into public controversy with Wiseman, who denied that Lingard had been created a cardinal *in petto* (never announced) by Pope Leo XII. Tierney expressed himself intemperately in an article entitled 'Was Dr Lingard actually a cardinal?', which was published in *The Rambler* in 1858. When Wiseman responded in a printed but unpublished letter to his chapter, Tierney responded in kind in 'A reply to Cardinal Wiseman's letter to his chapter' (1858), also printed but not published.

Tierney's chief work was a new edition of Charles Dodd's *Church History of England* (5 vols., 1839–43). Because it was considered inopportune to reopen the seventeenth-century controversies between the secular and regular clergy, especially the Jesuits, Tierney was directed to discontinue his edition, which is therefore incomplete, ending with the year 1625. Most of the documents printed in the valuable notes to this edition were collected by John Kirk of Lichfield. Tierney contributed a 'Life of Dr. John Lingard' to the *Metropolitan and Provincial Catholic Almanac* in 1854; this memoir was afterwards prefixed to volume 10 of the sixth edition of Lingard's *History of England*, published in 1855. He also assisted James Dallaway with his *History of the Western Division of Sussex*.

Tierney died at Arundel on 19 February 1862, and was buried in the Fitzalan chapel in Arundel Castle. He left all his manuscripts to Thomas Grant, bishop of Southwark, and they are now housed in the Southwark Diocesan Archives. His printed books were sold by Sotheby & Co. on 1–4 December 1862.

THOMPSON COOPER, rev. RICHARD J. SCHIEFEN

Sources R. J. Schiefen, *Nicholas Wiseman and the transformation of English Catholicism* (1984) · R. J. Schiefen, '"Anglo-Gallicanism" in nineteenth-century England', *Catholic Historical Review*, 63 (1977), 14–44 · B. Ward, *History of St Edmund's College* (1933) · B. Ward, *The sequel to Catholic emancipation*, 2 vols. (1915) · W. Ward, *The life and times of Cardinal Wiseman*, 2 vols. (1897) · *The correspondence of Lord Acton and Richard Simpson*, ed. J. L. Altholz, D. McElrath, and J. C. Holland, 3 vols. (1971–5) · J. L. Altholz, *The liberal Catholic movement in England: the 'Rambler' and its contributors, 1848–1864* [1962] · W. G. Roe, *Lamennais and England* (1966) · M. Clifton, 'Young Mark Tierney', *The Edmundian* [St Edmund's College, Hertfordshire], 33 (1993–4), 117–22 [centenary issue, 1893–1993] · *The Times* (24 Feb 1862)

Archives Arundel Castle, corresp. and papers · Brompton Oratory, London, catalogue of books and papers · CUL, corresp. and papers · St George's Roman Catholic Cathedral, Southwark, London, corresp. and papers | Archives of the British Province of the Society of Jesus, letter-book, corresp., and papers · Ushaw College, Durham, letters to C. Newsham · Westminster Archdiocesan Archive

Wealth at death under £4000: probate, 27 March 1862, *CGPLA Eng. & Wales*

Tierney, Sir Matthew John, first baronet (1776–1845), physician, was born on 24 November 1776 at Ballyscandland, co. Limerick, the eldest son of John Tierney and his wife, Mary, daughter of James Gleeson of Rathkinnon, co. Limerick. Tierney's early education is unknown, but he received his medical training at Guy's and St Thomas's hospitals in London. He then briefly practised as a surgeon to the South Gloucester regiment of militia. In 1799 he matriculated at the Edinburgh University medical school, but graduated MD from Glasgow University in 1802 with a thesis on vaccination. Tierney set up in practice again, this time in Brighton. In 1806 he became a licentiate of the Royal College of Physicians. Two years later, on 8 October 1808, he married Harriet Mary, daughter of Henry Jones of Bloomsbury Square. The couple had no children.

From this rather lowly beginning Tierney rose through patronage to become a royal physician. Early in his career he became acquainted with the earl of Berkeley, to whom he owed his appointment to the militia. Either through the influence of the earl, his own skill, or by chance (all are suggested by his biographers) Tierney was introduced to the prince of Wales's household at Brighton, and he steadily climbed up the hierarchy of royal appointments. In 1809 he was appointed physician-extraordinary to the prince of Wales, in 1816 he became physician-in-ordinary to the prince regent, and he continued to hold the post on the prince's accession to the throne. He held the same appointment under William IV. Tierney was valued for his medical skills. When the prince regent was struck down with a fever before his father's funeral, Tierney famously contradicted the advice of all the other royal practitioners and recommended bleeding—a therapy which proved successful. In recognition of his royal service Tierney was created a baronet on 3 October 1818 and a knight commander of the Royal Guelphic Order of Hanover on 7 May 1831. On 5 June 1834 he was awarded a second patent of baronetcy with the remainder passing to his younger brother, Edward Tierney. In keeping with his new standing Tierney became a fellow of the Royal College of Physicians in July 1836.

Tierney was an early and lifelong supporter of vaccination. Through his connections with the earl of Berkeley he met Edward Jenner in 1798—the year in which Jenner published his discovery of vaccination—and became a convert to the new practice. While at Edinburgh University he persuaded James Gregory, one of his lecturers, of the merits of the procedure and was subsequently invited to vaccinate his son. Tierney drew up plans for the Royal Sussex Jennerian Institution, a charity to offer free vaccination to the poor in the principal towns of the county, and he wrote a pamphlet celebrating its launch. This was reprinted in *Observations on Variola vaccina or Cow-Pock* (1845), a brief account of his early experience of vaccination. Tierney died at his home on the Pavilion Parade, Brighton, on 28 October 1845, of an attack of gout.

DEBORAH BRUNTON

Sources *GM*, 2nd ser., 25 (1846), 206–7 · *Medical Times*, 13 (1845), 468–9 · *The Lancet* (1846), 291–2 · *DNB* · Munk, *Roll*, 3.44 · matriculation records, U. Edin. L., special collections division, university archives
Archives RCP Lond., letters
Likenesses F. Chantrey, plaster bust, AM Oxf. · watercolour drawing, NPG
Wealth at death £30,000: *GM*, 207

Tietjens [Titiens], **Therese Carolina Johanna** (1831–1877), singer, was born of Hungarian–German parents on 17 July 1831 at Hamburg, where she received a private musical education. Her voice was a soprano of singular sweetness and power; after a début in Auber's *Le Maçon* she made a mark (1849) as Donizetti's Lucrezia Borgia. Until 1856 she sang principally at Frankfurt, Brno, and Vienna. She was engaged for the 1858 season at Her Majesty's by Benjamin Lumley, who simplified her name to Titiens, and her London début as Valentine in *Les Huguenots* was a great success. From that date, though she occasionally appeared on the continent (Turin, 1861; Paris, 1863; Naples, 1863, 1864) and in North America (1874, 1876), she made her home in London, and in 1868 became a naturalized British subject. She was known for opera mainly in London and in Dublin and for oratorio in the chief British cities. Her power and grandeur, her irreproachably maiden condition, her kindness, and her geniality met the expectations of mid-Victorian Britain; even her ultimate fatness and her weakness for travelling with unnecessary luggage became incorporated into a stereotype of the prima donna. As Lucrezia, Semiramide, and Countess Almaviva, she had competitors, but she had none as Cherubini's Medea or Beethoven's Leonore: here she was reckoned a 'consummate tragedian' (Davison). She gave the first London performances of several Verdi and Gounod parts, and sang Ortrud in *Lohengrin*. Though the *Musical Times* called her 'one of the greatest artists the world has yet seen', Shaw was to write of her 'essential obsolescence'.

In 1875 cancer was diagnosed; after several operations and considerable pain Tietjens made on 19 May 1877 her last appearance (as Lucrezia), but collapsed at the end. She died on 3 October 1877 at her home, 51 New Finchley Road, St John's Wood, and was buried at Kensal Green cemetery on the 8th. Her funeral was attended by a large crowd, and marred by the presence of a 'rough element', who damaged trees, stole flowers, and pressed around the grave.

R. H. LEGGE, *rev.* JOHN ROSSELLI

Sources *From Mendelssohn to Wagner: being the memoirs of J. W. Davison, forty years the music critic of The Times*, ed. H. Davison (1912) · L. Arditi, *My reminiscences*, ed. Baroness von Zedlitz, 2nd edn (1896) · *The Times* (4 Oct 1877) · *The Times* (6 Oct 1877) · *The Times* (8 Oct 1877) · *The Times* (9 Oct 1877) · *The Times* (11 Oct 1877) · *The Times* (13 Oct 1877) · *The Times* (15 Oct 1877) · *MT*, 18 (1877), 530 · G. B. Shaw, *London music as heard in 1888–89 by Corno di Bassetto* (1937) · G. B. Shaw, *Music in London, 1890–94*, 3 vols. (1932) · H. Klein, *Thirty years of musical life in London* (1903) · F. Regli, ed., *Dizionario biografico dei più celebri poeti ed artisti … che fiorirono in Italia dal 1800 al 1860* (Turin, 1860) · H. Rosenthal, *Two centuries of opera at Covent Garden* (1958) · P. Forster, 'Titiens: the earnest prima donna', *Opera*, 31 (1980), 224–31 · d. cert.

Likenesses drawing, 1862, repro. in Davison, *From Mendelssohn to Wagner*, 480 · Elliott & Fry, photograph, NPG · London Stereoscopic Co., cartes-de-visite, NPG · London Stereoscopic Co., photograph, NPG · Window & Bridge, carte-de-visite, NPG · photograph, repro. in H. Rosenthal, ed., *The Mapleson memoirs* (1966), 62 · photograph, repro. in Arditi, *My reminiscences* · photograph, repro. in Klein, *Thirty years*, 16 · photographs, repro. in Forster, 'Titiens', following p. 224 · portrait, repro. in *Drawing Room Portrait Gallery*, 2nd ser. (1859) · prints, BM, NPG · prints, Harvard TC
Wealth at death under £16,000: probate, 25 Oct 1877, *CGPLA Eng. & Wales*

Tiffin, William (1695/6–1754), phonetician and stenographer, was born at Crimplesham, near Downham Market, Norfolk, the son of Roger Tiffin, gentleman, of a family long settled in that area. He was educated at Downham Market under Mr Robinson, and at Norwich under Mr Pate, before matriculating aged seventeen at Gonville and Caius College, Cambridge, on 11 February 1713, under surety of Mr Macro. Tiffin was a scholar at Cambridge from 1713 to 1718 and graduated BA in 1716/17. On 21 September 1718 he was ordained deacon at Norwich and became curate of the parishes of Wereham and Wretten, near Downham Market. His unwillingness to subscribe to the Thirty-Nine Articles limited his opportunities for preferment, but in 1735 Tiffin was recommended by the Revd Thomas Pyle of King's Lynn to the Revd John Jackson, master of Wigston's Hospital, Leicester, who advanced him for the position of confrater. The place was congenial to Tiffin, a 'very worthy, modest clergyman' (Nichols, 1, pt 2, 503), for it did not require subscription. Tiffin assisted Jackson with his collations of the New Testament. A son William, born to him and his wife, Margaret, was baptized at St Martin's, Leicester, on 29 April 1739. Another child, a daughter Ann, was mentioned in his will.

In 1751 Tiffin published by subscription a shorthand textbook entitled *A New Help and Improvement of the Art of Swift Writing*. An abject failure as a practical shorthand system—John Nichols remarked that 'it never got on' (Nichols, 1, pt 2, 503)—Tiffin's *New Help* is now generally viewed as the first system constructed on a phonetic basis, a discovery made by Sir Isaac Pitman only after he had published his seminal *Stenographic Sound-Hand* (1837). 'Tiffin was much more interested in phonetics than in shorthand, and one might claim with some justice that he was the best English phonetician before the 19th century' (Matthews, 'English pronunciation', 138).

Acutely aware of the defects of English orthography and the lack of a 'sufficient Alphabet' (Tiffin, 32), Tiffin stated that it was his 'peculiar Intention … to suit the Alphabet to the Utterances of the Language' (ibid., 5), taking care 'to give every Character one Power of its own, in which no other Character is allow'd to interfere' (ibid., 7).

In the lengthy appendix, Tiffin discusses vowels (recognizing nine distinct sounds) and diphthongs, articulation, and early eighteenth-century dialects. Tiffin's is perhaps the earliest study of English dialects, of which he was a keen observer, remarking on county and sometimes local pronunciations in Norfolk, Lancashire, Yorkshire, Nottinghamshire, and North Britain (Scotland). His interest in dialect for its own sake, coupled with his powers of scientific detachment and observation, suggest that he was 'unique in his age' (Matthews, 'William Tiffin', 105). Unlike many contemporary orthoepists, he was not prescriptive:

> But be pleas'd to understand, that when the Pronunciation of particular Counties, of Rustics, of the Polite, or illiterate is mention'd, it is not with Intention either to recommend or censure; but in Compliance with the Opinion of the Public; the Purpose and End of every Remark being to give the Reader Opportunity to discern the Description of his own Pronunciation. (Tiffin, 37)

Tiffin's own style is lively and colloquial but (unfortunately for prospective students of his system) diffuse and disorganized. Notably absent is the fulsome dedication to patrons that characterized shorthand textbooks of the day.

On 15 September 1754 Tiffin made his will, bequeathing to his wife and daughter the books in which he had written their names, and disposing of properties in Norfolk for the future benefit of his wife and children. He died before 3 December when the will was proved, and was buried in the cross aisle of St Martin's Church, Leicester, under the steeple. The brass plate on his tomb containing a Latin inscription written by John Jackson was removed by the next incumbent. PAGE LIFE

Sources J. Nichols, *The history and antiquities of the county of Leicester*, 1/2 (1815), 503, 509, 600 · J. Venn and others, eds., *Biographical history of Gonville and Caius College*, 1: 1349–1713 (1897) · W. Matthews, 'William Tiffin: an 18th century phonetician', *English Studies*, 18 (1936), 97–114 · W. Matthews, 'English pronunciation and shorthand in the early modern period', *University of California Publications in English*, 9 (1940–43), 135–213 · H. Kökeritz, 'English pronunciation as described in shorthand systems of the 17th and 18th centuries', *Studia Neophilologica*, 7 (1934–5), 73–146 · I. Pitman, *A history of shorthand*, 3rd edn (1891) · A. Paterson, 'Some early shorthand systems, VI: William Tiffin's "New help to the art of swift writing"', *Phonetic Journal*, 46 (1887), 14–16 · will, 1754, PRO, PROB 11/812, sig. 343 · *Monthly Review*, 5 (1751), 159 · E. H. Butler, *The story of British shorthand* (1951) · *IGI* · W. Tiffin, *A new help and improvement of the art of swift writing* (1751)

Wealth at death property at Tilney, Norfolk, to daughter Ann Tiffin; account to settlement made on his marriage, freehold estates at Cripplesham and Stradsett, Norfolk, to John Elgar for five hundred years; at decease of survivor of himself or wife in trust to raise up to £300 for any younger child: will, PRO, PROB 11/812, sig. 343

Tigernach mac Coirpri (d. 549). *See under* Ulster, saints of (act. c.400–c.650).

Tighe [*née* Blachford], **Mary** (1772–1810), poet, was born on 9 October 1772 in Dublin, the daughter of William Blachford (d. 1773?), a Church of Ireland clergyman and librarian, and his wife, Theodosia Tighe (b. c.1740, d. in or after 1810), a granddaughter of the first earl of Darnley. Theodosia Blachford, an acquaintance of John Wesley, was active in the Methodist movement in Ireland, and she gave her daughter a strict religious upbringing. On 6 October 1793 Mary Blachford married Henry Tighe (1768–1836), who was her first cousin and a member of the Irish parliament

for Inistioge, co. Kilkenny, until the union of the parliaments. Relatively little is known about the Tighes' marriage, which remained childless, but it is said to have been unhappy.

In the early years of the nineteenth century, the couple spent time in London, where Mary Tighe had some literary friends, most notably Thomas Moore, who was an early admirer of her writing. Although she began writing poetry before her marriage, Tighe published nothing until 1805, when her major work, *Psyche* (probably begun in 1801 and completed by 1803), was privately printed. A long allegorical poem in Spenserian stanzas, *Psyche* was admired by a number of Tighe's literary contemporaries, including Moore, who praised it in one of his own poems. Keats, even while claiming in 1818 to have outgrown his earlier admiration for Tighe's work, was influenced by *Psyche*.

In 1805 Tighe endured a dangerous attack of the consumption from which she had already been suffering for at least a year. According to Thomas Moore, she had 'a very serious struggle for life' in February 1805 and was still so ill in August that she was 'ordered to the Madeiras'. Moore himself was convinced that 'another *winter* will inevitably be her death' (*Memoirs*, 1.86, 90), but in fact Tighe lived for another five years, spending the last few months of her life as an invalid at her brother-in-law's estate at Woodstock, co. Wicklow, Ireland, where she died on 24 March 1810. She was buried in Inistioge church, co. Kilkenny.

Following Tighe's death, *Psyche* was republished in 1811 in an edition which included some previously unpublished poems, many of them laments for pleasures irretrievably lost because of illness, or poems expressing religious anxieties and fears of death. In her final poem, dated December 1809, Tighe writes that her

> soul … with agonizing grasp
> Of terror and regret,
> To all in life its love would clasp
> Clings close and closer yet.
> (*Psyche, with other Poems*, 308)

(An editorial note in the 1811 volume reassures readers that Tighe's 'fears of death were perfectly removed before she quit this scene of trial and suffering' (ibid., 311)). It was this edition, which was probably the one read by Keats, which established Tighe's literary reputation. While Tighe's work had, according to the 1811 preface, already circulated fairly widely and won her the admiration of readers beyond her immediate friends, the first public response to *Psyche* appeared in the *Quarterly Review's* article on the 1811 edition. The review combined some high literary praise (it would not 'be difficult to extract from the poem many passages as flowing and as musical as the finest in the Fairy Queen') with tributes to the poet's feminine delicacy and sentimental reflections on her premature death (*QR*, 5, 1811, 478). Despite the bleakness of many of the short poems in the 1811 volume, in much of the nineteenth-century writing on Tighe there is a tendency to turn her into an exemplar of patiently (and picturesquely) long-suffering femininity, a tendency exemplified most famously in Felicia Hemans's tribute to her, 'The

Grave of a Poetess': Hemans concludes her meditation on her Inistioge church monument by wondering

> Where couldst thou fix on mortal ground
> Thy tender thoughts and high?

Besides this poem, Hemans wrote at least two other tributes to Tighe, 'Lines for the Album at Rosanna' and 'Written after Visiting a Tomb'. Another nineteenth-century admirer wrote that admiration for *Psyche* was increased by sympathetic identification with 'the young and beautiful poetess' whose poem 'was not more tenderly beautiful to the imagination than herself' (Howitt, 282). Mary Tighe also wrote a novel, *Selena*, which is unpublished, and some other poems are included in the privately printed volume *Mary: a Series of Reflections during 20 Years* (1811), edited by William Tighe, the author's cousin and brother-in-law. *Psyche* went into numerous nineteenth-century editions, but like many other women poets of her generation, Tighe was almost entirely overlooked in literary criticism and histories for much of the twentieth century, until her work was republished and started to be anthologized again in the 1990s.   PAM PERKINS

Sources M. Tighe, *Psyche, with other poems* (1811) · review of *Psyche*, *QR*, 5 (1811), 471–85 · W. Howitt, *Homes and haunts of the most eminent British poets* (1903) · *Memoirs, journal and correspondence of Thomas Moore*, ed. J. Russell, 8 vols. (1853–6) · Burke, *Gen. GB* · Blain, Clements & Grundy, *Feminist comp.* · E. V. Weller, *Keats and Mary Tighe* (1928) · *The letters of the Rev. John Wesley*, ed. J. Telford, 8 vols. (1931) · *DNB* · *The works of Mary Tighe, published and unpublished*, ed. P. Henchy, 6, no. 6 (1957)
Archives NL Wales | TCD, letters to J. C. Walker
Likenesses E. Scriven, stipple, 1812 (after G. Romney), BM; repro. in M. Tighe, *Psyche* (1812) · J. Hopwood jun., stipple (after E. Drummond), BM, NPG · A. Robertson, miniature (after Romney), NPG · portrait, repro. in Tighe, *Psyche*

Tilak, Bal Gangadhar (1856–1920), Indian nationalist and journalist, was born on 23 July 1856 in Ratnagiri district, the last of the four children and only son of (Pandit) Gangadharpant Ramchandra Tilak (1820–1872), deputy inspector of primary schools, author, and small landowner, and his wife, Parvitabai. The family had been administrators under the peshwas in the Maratha confederation but had, like other Chitpavan Brahmans, retired to their ancestral village when Britain established its rule over the region in 1818. Although given the name Keshav at birth, Tilak was known throughout his life by his family petname of Bal or Balwant. While studying at the English School in Poona in 1871 he married ten-year-old Tapibai, renamed at marriage Satyabhamabai, of the Bal family of Dapoli district in Bombay presidency. They had three sons and three daughters.

Tilak studied at the Deccan College in Poona from 1873, graduating with a BA in mathematics and Sanskrit in 1876 and an LLB in 1879. With other intellectuals concerned with promoting Western education among the city's élites, he established the New English School in Poona in 1880, the Deccan Education Society in 1884, and Fergusson College in 1885. The group set up two newspapers, the English-language *Mahratta* and the Marathi-language *Kesari* in 1881. The tone of the papers soon led the two editors, G. G. Agarkar and Tilak, into a defamation case, for

Bal Gangadhar Tilak (1856–1920), by unknown engraver, pubd 1897

which they were jailed for four months in 1882. During the late 1880s serious differences emerged among the founding members over the issues of religious conservatism, orthodoxy, and reform. Tilak left the society in 1890, but took the two newspapers with him. As he chose not to practise law, he lived on a minute income from landed property inherited from his father and from the newspapers when they finally began to make a profit after 1899. Throughout much of his life, court litigation placed a heavy drain on his financial—and indeed emotional—resources.

Tilak was courageous, strong-willed, and determined, and his life was full of controversy and conflict. In the early 1890s he engaged in a heated debate against the raising of the age of consent at marriage by attacking government legislation on the grounds that change should not be imposed by a foreign government outside Hindu society. Tilak's stand won him Brahman support, which was enhanced by his pro-Hindu position following serious Hindu–Muslim riots in Poona in 1894. Concurrently he built up his base in the leading regional political association, the Poona Sarvajanik Sabha, and finally captured it in 1896. In 1895 he had successfully campaigned against M. G. Ranade and other moderate politicians hitherto dominant in Poona politics by preventing them from holding the National Social Conference at the same time as the Indian National Congress, the major nationalist organization, founded in 1885, which met in session at the end of each year. In 1894, he inaugurated public celebration of the regional festival of the elephant-headed god, Ganapati, using it to spread patriotic sentiment. In fiery editorials and speeches he opposed British rule, and, through the use of the metaphor of Maratha resistance to the Mughals in the seventeenth and eighteenth centuries, seemed to imply ways of resisting the British. In 1897 he instituted the celebration of the birth of Shivaji, the seventeenth-century Maratha leader who had founded the Maratha state against the might of Aurangzeb's Mughal empire. During the 1896 famine in Maharashtra he organized relief works and cheap grain shops, and when plague broke out he set up hospitals for the relief of victims. The British imposition of sanitary measures against plague evoked widespread antagonism, speeded the establishment of revolutionary and terrorist groups, and led to the assassination of W. C. Rand, the official charged with plague operations in Poona. Tilak was suspected of complicity in the Rand assassination and in 1897 was jailed for eighteen months for sedition. He had been elected to the Bombay legislative council in 1895, and re-elected in 1897, but resigned when he was tried.

In 1898, released early as a result of lobbying from European Sanskrit scholars, Tilak became embroiled in a complicated and extended controversy over the posthumous adoption of a male heir to his recently deceased friend, Baba Maharaj. Involved as an executor, Tilak faced criminal charges in what became known as the Tai Maharaj adoption case. It dragged on from 1901 to 1904, when he was cleared of the charges, but was not finally settled, after references to the privy council in 1915 and the Bombay high court, until just before his death in 1920. Tilak moved to the forefront of all-India politics between 1903 and 1908, when he opposed the partition of Bengal and advocated the boycott of British goods, the use of swadeshi goods ('of one's own country'), national education, and Hindi as a national language. With Bipin Chandra Pal and Lala Lajpat Rai he became a central figure in a new, extremist party which opposed the more moderate and constitutional tactics of nationalists like G. K. Gokhale and P. M. Mehta. The triumvirate were behind the split of the Indian National Congress at Surat in 1907. The rise of extremist and radical politics brought a reaction from the government, and in 1908 Tilak was tried for inciting disaffection and transported to Mandalay, where he remained until 1914.

On his release, Tilak set up a network of home-rule leagues in Maharashtra, working in alliance with similar leagues organized by Annie Besant. He and his followers were readmitted to Congress in 1916. After the war he urged that Indians meet the new constitutional offers under the Montagu–Chelmsford declaration with responsive co-operation, intending that they should enter the new councils and continue opposition from within. In 1919 he was in London, bringing a libel case against the writer Valentine Chirol, who had called him the 'father of Indian unrest', but he lost and returned to India in November of the same year. In April 1920 he established the Congress Democratic Party, but it was barely active before he died in Bombay of pneumonia related to malarial complications on 1 August 1920, the day on which M. K. Gandhi inaugurated his first non-co-operation campaign. Tilak's funeral procession of over a mile and a half was the longest in Bombay's history, a testament to his political popularity and the charisma which he enjoyed.

Tilak coined the potent slogan 'Swaraj [self- or home rule] is my birthright and I will have it', and earned the title of Lokamanya ('the beloved of the people') for his passionate defence of Indian interests. In achieving mass popularity in and outside the presidency he had pointed out the tactical direction of nationalist politics thereafter;

with his strong and forceful nationalist rhetoric he pointed the way for future nationalist objectives and ideology. In the process he restructured Marathi as a modern language of polemic and protest, and rethought classic Sanskrit texts in terms of the current situation, seeing in the *Bhagavad Gita* (published as the *Gita rahasya* in 1915) an exemplar of political action. Earlier, writing in the 1890s, he had sought to establish the antiquity of Vedic scriptures by combining textual analysis with astronomical calculations, and had won repute as a Sanskrit scholar. He was a formidable political figure who rewrote nationalist ideology and voiced it with unmistakable éclat, but his ideas were complex and subtle in handling traditional notions at a time of stress. Tilak used traditional elements as rallying points for modern political interventions and created a contemporary political polemic by utilizing rather than destroying past traditions. Although his style and approach were superseded by the different strategies and ideas championed by M. K. Gandhi in the following decades of nationalist agitation, he remains an icon of modern India.   JIM MASSELOS

Sources N. C. Kelkar, *Life and times of Lokamanya Tilak*, trans. D. V. Divekar (1928) · R. I. Cashman, *The myth of the Lokamanya: Tilak and mass politics in Maharashtra* (1975) · *Bal Gangadhar Tilak: his writings and speeches* (1918) · S. A. Wolpert, *Tilak and Gokhale: revolution and reform in the making of modern India* (1962) · N. G. Jog, *Lokamanya Bal Gangadhar Tilak* (1962) · D. Keer, *Lokamanya Tilak: father of the Indian freedom struggle* (1969) · D. V. Tahmankar, *Lokamanya Tilak: father of Indian unrest and maker of modern India* (1956)
Archives Kesari-Mahratta Library, Poona
Likenesses R. K. Phadke and Kolhatkar, bronze statue, Chowpatty Beach, Bombay · engraving, NPG; repro. in *The Graphic* (11 Sept 1897) [*see illus.*] · portraits, Kesari-Mahratta Library, Poona

Tilbury, Gervase of (*b.* 1150s, *d.* in or after 1222), author, presumably came from Tilbury in Essex. Nothing is known of his family except that he was related to Patrick *Salisbury, earl of Salisbury, with whose son Philip he enjoyed a close friendship. Gervase was probably born in the 1150s; he was at any rate a boy in the time of Pope Alexander III (*r.* 1159–81). He studied and taught canon law at Bologna; this probably accounts for his presence in Venice in 1177, where he witnessed the reconciliation between Alexander and Frederick Barbarossa. In his *Chronicon Anglicanum*, Ralph of Coggeshall relates a story that he heard from Gervase himself: in the time of Louis VII (*d.* 1180), Gervase was a clerk in the service of Guillaume de Champagne, archbishop of Rheims (1176–1202); one day he met a pretty girl who, in refusing his advances, gave herself away as a member of the sect of Publicani (Catharist heretics who held that procreation was evil); the archbishop arrived on the scene, and the incident ended with the girl's being burnt at the stake (*Chronicon Anglicanum*, 121–4). Gervase also spent some time in the service of Henry II, and of his son, Henry, the Young King. For the latter he composed a *Liber facetiarum* ('Book of entertainment'), now lost; he was preparing a longer work for him (later to form the basis of the *Otia imperialia*), when Henry died in 1183, to Gervase's evident distress. Some time after this he entered the service of William II, king of Sicily (*r.* 1166–89), and a son-in-law of Henry II. Having received from William the gift of a villa at Nola, he was there in the June of 1189 or 1190. By 1201 at the latest Gervase had settled in Arles, where he married a relative of Imbert d'Aiguières, archbishop of Arles (1190–1202); her name and date of death are alike unknown. His marriage brought Gervase a palace, and established him in the highest echelons of Provençal society. Master Gervase is mentioned in documents dating from 1201 to 1222. In some he is designated 'judge of the count of Provence', in others 'marshal of Arles'. He received the latter title from the Guelph emperor Otto IV, a grandson of Henry II; the appointment, which was essentially honorific, may have been made at the time of Otto's coronation in 1209.

It was for Otto that Gervase brought together the materials he had begun to collect thirty years earlier, producing the *Otia imperialia* ('Recreation for an emperor'). He was engaged on the work at least from 1211 to 1214, and probably sent it to Otto in 1215; by then Otto's cause had been irreparably lost at the battle of Bouvines (1214). Gervase's status in Arles seems to have been unaffected by Otto's reverses and eventual demise in 1218. The theory that Gervase ended his life as provost of Ebstorf in Lower Saxony has received wide support, but all that can be stated with certitude is that his work was known to the authors of the famous Ebstorf world map. On the other hand, Ralph of Coggeshall records that Gervase became a canon in later life; furthermore, his only other known extant work is a short commentary on the Lord's prayer (preserved in Hereford Cathedral Library, MS P.i.13), written for the *collegium Massiliense* (probably the Premonstratensians of l'Huveaune), from which it appears that he may by then have been a member of the order himself. Gervase was also the author of a *Vita abbreviata et miracula beatissimi Antonii* ('Short account of the life and miracles of the Blessed Antony') and a *Liber de transitu beate virginis et gestis discipulorum* ('Book on the death of the Blessed Virgin and the deeds of the disciples').

The *Otia imperialia* enjoyed a wide currency in the later middle ages, and was twice translated into French. Thirty manuscripts have survived; one of these, Vatican City, Biblioteca Apostolica Vaticana, MS Vat. lat. 933, is an idiograph, with corrections and additions in the hand of the author; others contain a body of addenda, showing that Gervase continued to add to the work after its dedication to Otto. His avowed purpose was to provide instruction and entertainment for the emperor in his leisure moments. The work is divided into three *decisiones*. The first describes the creation and early history of the world, for the most part taking the popular medieval form of a commentary on Genesis. The second constitutes an *imago mundi*, combining a description of the world (*mappa mundi*) with chronicles of its peoples. Information on miscellaneous subjects is inserted into this general plan, including accounts of various marvels; the third *decisio* is entirely devoted to a collection of the world's marvels. Some of these are taken from written sources, but many were collected by Gervase himself on his travels; they range from brief descriptions of rocks or springs to longer tales of magicians, werewolves, fairies, and the 'other world'. While a few serve as the basis for moral or religious instruction, most are recorded for their own sake. This section of the work earned Gervase severe censure from some of his early critics, but its importance as a collection of folklore is now recognized. The *Otia imperialia* also occupies a significant place in the history of geography, providing the most comprehensive and detailed Latin chorography up to that time. Further, it contains serious reflection on the relationship between empire and papacy, supported by the author's training in canon law; and it affords many insights into the ideas, beliefs, and attitudes of the time. Gervase was a competent Latinist, and drew on a wide range of literary sources. The first two *decisiones* are in fact largely derivative; but the material is generally well organized, and the work as a whole bears the stamp of its author's personality to a marked degree. Possessed of a lively curiosity, an eye for detail, and a remarkable breadth of interest and experience, Gervase was able to create a colourful and fascinating mosaic of the world he knew.   S. E. BANKS

Sources Gervase of Tilbury, *Otia imperialia: recreation for an emperor*, ed. and trans. S. E. Banks and J. W. Binns, OMT (2002) · *Radulphi de Coggeshall chronicon Anglicanum*, ed. J. Stevenson, Rolls Series, 66 (1875) · J. R. Caldwell, 'The autograph manuscript of Gervase of Tilbury', *Scriptorium*, 11 (1957), 87–98 · J. R. Caldwell, 'Gervase of Tilbury's addenda to his *Otia imperialia*', *Mediaeval Studies*, 24 (1962), 95–126 · Gervais de Tilbury, *Le livre des merveilles*, ed. and trans. A. Duchesne (Paris, 1992) · H. G. Richardson, 'Gervase of Tilbury', *History*, new ser., 46 (1961), 102–14 · R. Busquet, 'Gervais de Tilbury inconnu', *Revue Historique*, 191 (1941), 1–20 · F. Liebrecht, *Des Gervasius von Tilbury Otia imperialia* (Hanover, 1856) · H. J. Schulze, 'Ist Gervasius von Tilbury Propst von Ebstorf gewesen?', *Niedersächsisches Jahrbuch für Landesgeschichte*, 33 (1961), 239–44 · H Kugler, 'Die Ebstorfer Weltkarte', *Zeitschrift für Deutsches Altertum und Deutsche Literatur*, 116 (1987), 1–29

Archives Biblioteca Apostolica Vaticana, Vatican City, MS Vat. lat. 933

Tilden, Sir William Augustus (1842–1926), chemist, was born on 15 August 1842 at 163 Arlington Street, Regent's Park, London, the elder son (there were no daughters) of Augustus Tilden, a clerk of the Bank of England, and his wife, Anne, daughter of Henry Balls of Cambridge. He was educated at schools in Kidderminster, Bedford, and East Dereham. When Tilden was fifteen, he was apprenticed for five years to Alfred Allchin, a London pharmacist, and attended lectures at the Royal College of Chemistry and the Pharmaceutical Society. Between 1863 and 1872 he worked as a demonstrator at the Pharmaceutical Society under Professor John Attfield; he also obtained a BSc in chemistry (1868) and a DSc (1871) from the University of London. Tilden became senior science master at Clifton College, Bristol, in 1872 and was elected to the chair of chemistry at the newly founded Mason College in Birmingham (later the University of Birmingham) eight years later. In 1894 he replaced T. E. Thorpe as professor of chemistry at the Royal College of Science, which became part of the Imperial College of Science and Technology in 1907, two years before Tilden retired in 1909.

In 1875 Tilden found that nitrosyl chloride could be used to characterize terpenes, compounds which are found in turpentine and other essential oils. Thereafter, the terpenes and related compounds were Tilden's major interest. One important consequence of this research was his discovery in 1884 that isoprene (the building block of natural rubber) could be prepared by passing turpentine oil vapour through a red-hot iron tube. Much later, in 1892, a sealed bottle of this isoprene was found to contain yellowish lumps which appeared to be similar to natural rubber. Tilden even vulcanized this forerunner of synthetic rubber with sulphur, but did not pursue this line of research in the absence of any pressing need for rubber. In his later years Tilden also studied the specific heat of metals over a wide range of temperatures, and the history of chemistry. He published seven textbooks, the most enduring being his *Introduction to the Study of Chemical Philosophy* (1876), and four historical works, including a biography of the chemist Sir William Ramsay (1918).

Tilden was president of the Institute of Chemistry (1891–4) and of the Chemical Society (1903–5). He was elected FRS in 1880, and was awarded the Davy medal in 1908. Honorary degrees were bestowed by the universities of Dublin and Birmingham, and the Victoria University of Manchester, and Tilden was knighted in 1909. In 1869 he married Charlotte Pither, daughter of Robert Bush of St Helier, Jersey. They had one son. She died in 1905 and in 1907 he married Julia Mary, daughter of C. W. Ramié of St Helier, who survived him. Tilden died at his home, The Oaks, 57 Murray Road, Northwood, Middlesex, on 11 December 1926. PETER J. T. MORRIS, *rev.*

Sources M. O. F., *JCS* (1927), 3190–202 · J. C. P., *PRS*, 117A (1928), i–v · b. cert. · *CGPLA Eng. & Wales* (1927) · d. cert.

Wealth at death £6461 9s. 2d.: probate, 8 Feb 1927, *CGPLA Eng. & Wales*

Tildesley, Miriam Louise (1883–1979), anthropologist, was born on 1 July 1883 in Walsall Street, Willenhall, Staffordshire, the second daughter of William Henry Tildesley, curry-comb maker, and his wife, Rebecca, *née* Fisher. She was educated at King Edward's Grammar School for Girls, Aston, Birmingham (1894–9) and at King Edward's High School for Girls, Birmingham (1899–1902).

Tildesley's parents were reluctant to send her on to higher education, having done so for two of her sisters who went to Girton and to Newnham. From 1912 to 1914 she was trained as a teacher in north London, obtaining a National Froebel Union certificate. She spent three years teaching. Afterwards she was involved in wartime statistical work, under the aegis of Professor Karl Pearson, head of the department of applied statistics at University College, London. She took a six-month course in elementary statistical theory and practice. In 1918 she was appointed Crewdson Benington research student in craniometry, again under Pearson, who was also Galton professor of eugenics and head of the biometric laboratory at University College, London. A summary of her research work was published as 'A first study of a Burmese skull' in *Biometrika* (12, 1921).

In 1920 Tildesley was appointed by the Council for Scientific and Industrial Research to work on the human osteological collections at the Hunterian Museum at the Royal College of Surgeons under Arthur Keith. In 1923 she was made a research assistant there in charge of the human osteological collection. Also in 1923 she produced her best-known work, 'Sir Thomas Browne: his skull, portraits and ancestry' (originally in *Biometrika*, 15, 1–76); it was also published separately with thirty-four plates and a pedigree. From this study of the disinterred skull of a seventeenth-century physician, she raised the possibility, already hinted at by similar work on the skull of Bentham, that there might be no connection between craniometric data and intelligence. Later she was appointed a curator of human osteology at the museum, and was chairman of the Comité de Standardisation de la Technique Anthropologique during the 1930s. She wrote several articles about the anthropological and archaeological use of teeth, including 'Dentition as a measure of maturity' (*British Dental Journal*, 1928, 1–8). In 1939 she was elected a fellow of the Royal Anthropological Institute.

In 1921 Tildesley had obtained three months' leave from her anthropological work to make the first of several visits to Albania, her interest in which had been aroused by an American friend, Charles Telford Erickson, who had established a school of agriculture there. Later she took a leading role in the Friends of Albania Committee, established in August 1942 with the support of the deposed King Zog I. Latterly her interest in Albania was reflected in her academic work; for example 'The Albanian of the north and south' (*Biometrika*, 25, 1930, 21–9). She was appointed MBE for her services to anthropology.

Miriam Tildesley died, unmarried, on 31 January 1979 at Henley-on-Thames, Oxfordshire. She was cremated in Wolverhampton. BEJTULLAH D. DESTANI

Sources personal knowledge (2004) · private information (2004) · *Flamuri* (Sept 1979) · b. cert.

Archives Royal Anthropological Institute, London, corresp., notes, and papers | RCS Eng., papers of Sir Arthur Keith, corresp.

Tilghman, Matthew (1718–1790), planter and colonial politician, was born on 17 February 1718 at The Hermitage, Queen Anne's county, Maryland, the youngest of the nine children of Richard Tilghman (1673–1739), also a planter and politician, and Anna Maria (1677–1748), daughter of Philemon Lloyd of Talbot county, Maryland, and his wife, Henrietta Maria Neale Bennett. A third-generation Marylander, Tilghman belonged to one of the most powerful families on the eastern shore. His early education was possibly under the direction of the Revd Hugh Jones, the rector of St Stephen's parish, Cecil county, and he remained a member of the Anglican and, from 1776, the Protestant Episcopal church for the rest of his life. At the age of fifteen he was adopted by his cousin Matthew Ward Tilghman (*c.*1676–1741), who groomed him for public service and granted him a sizeable estate in Talbot county. On 6 April 1741 Tilghman married his first cousin Anne (*c.*1723–1794), daughter of James Lloyd (1680–1723) and Anne Grundy (1690–1732). They had three sons and two daughters. Their younger daughter, Anna Maria (1755–1843), married Lieutenant-Colonel Tench Tilghman, George Washington's aide-de-camp, in 1783.

Tilghman's entry into public life also took place in 1741. He served as captain of a troop organized to protect the eastern shore against American Indian attack, and shortly afterwards began a long career as justice for Talbot county. Tilghman ascended the provincial stage in 1751 when he was elected to the Maryland assembly as a representative from the same county. He served in that capacity until 1758, then sat for Queen Anne's county in 1760–61. He was again returned by Talbot county in 1768, and served until the assembly's demise in 1774. During 1773 and 1774 he was its speaker. While an assemblyman Tilghman was one of the leaders of the anti-proprietary or 'country' party, and resisted all efforts to lure him into the camp of the rival 'court' party; he even refused an appointment to the governor's council in 1768.

Having been elected as a delegate to the Stamp Act Congress in 1765, he played a prominent role in the colony's mounting opposition to British imperial policy. In June 1768 he was on the assembly committee that drafted a remonstrance to the king against the Townshend Acts, and he also signed the non-importation agreement of 22 June 1769. As the crisis deepened, his political and organizational skills were in demand. Perceived as knowledgeable, capable, and level-headed, he consistently held executive positions throughout the revolutionary period. Tilghman presided over seven of the nine Maryland provincial conventions held in the years 1774–6. He was also chairman of the committee of correspondence for Talbot county, president of the eastern shore council of safety in 1775, and head of every Maryland delegation to the continental congress from June 1774 until November 1776. Although wary of independence, Tilghman recognized its inevitability. However, he sought to ensure that the revolution did not threaten social order and the propertied interest. His opportunity came when he was chosen president of the convention that met on 14 August 1776 to draft the first Maryland state constitution. He also served as chairman of the committee elected by that body to prepare the new framework of government. What emerged under his aegis was one of the most conservative state constitutions in revolutionary America.

In December 1776 Tilghman was elected to the state senate, and, after being chosen for a second term in 1781, became its president on 24 December 1782. While senator, he opposed the confiscation of British property and, as president of a special council, helped to restore order and security to the troubled eastern shore. Having resigned from the upper chamber on 22 November 1783 owing to ill health, Tilghman retired to his home plantation of Rich Neck in Talbot county. He resided there until his death from a paralytic stroke on 4 May 1790, and was buried there in the family cemetery. The size of his personal estate is unknown, but he probably held about 7900 acres in Talbot and Queen Anne's counties.   KEITH MASON

Sources E. C. Papenfuse and others, eds., *A biographical dictionary of the Maryland legislature, 1635–1789*, 2 vols. (1979–85) · N. D. Mereness, 'Tilghman, Matthew', *DAB* · J. W. McWilliams, 'Tilghman, Matthew', *ANB* · R. Hoffman, *A spirit of dissension: economics, politics, and the revolution in Maryland* (1973) · D. C. Skaggs, *Roots of Maryland democracy, 1753–1776* (1973) · C. A. Barker, *The background of the revolution in Maryland* (1940) · P. A. Crowl, *Maryland during and after the revolution: a political and economic study* (1943) · O. Tilghman, *History of Talbot county*, 2 vols. (1915) · K. Mason, 'A region in revolt: the eastern shore of Maryland, 1740–90', PhD diss., Johns Hopkins University, 1984 · W. H. Browne and others, eds., *Archives of Maryland* (1883–) · P. H. Smith and others, eds., *Letters of delegates to congress, 1774–1789*, 26 vols. (1976–2000) · A. Pedley, *The manuscript collections of the Maryland Historical Society* (1968)

Archives Maryland Hall of Records, Annapolis, provincial and state records: executive MSS; red books · Maryland Hall of Records, Annapolis, Talbot county court records · Maryland Hall of Records, Annapolis, St Michael's parish minutes

Likenesses R. Peale, drawing

Wealth at death perhaps 7900 acres in Talbot and Queen Anne's counties, Maryland: Papenfuse and others, eds., *Biographical dictionary*, 2.827

Tillam, Thomas (*fl.* 1638–1668), Seventh Day Baptist minister, was by his own testimony born a Roman Catholic, and in his youth travelled on the continent. Like many other Englishmen during the political and economic hardships of the 1620s and 1630s, Tillam had looked towards the New World and arrived in America on 29 June 1638. He commemorated his freedom with a poem, 'Uppon the First Sight of New-England', which still appears in anthologies of early American verse. Tillam returned to England during the revolutionary 1640s and eventually became a member of the Baptist church in London led by Hanserd Knollys. Tillam seems to have distinguished himself in this community, for by the end of 1651 he was selected to be their 'messenger' to the town of Hexham, about 12 miles up the River Tyne from Newcastle. He was also appointed to one of the puritan lectureships in the gift of the parliamentary commission for propagation of the gospel in the northern counties. Despite this promising start, by March 1653 Tillam was already under attack from the slightly older and neighbouring Baptist congregation at Newcastle, whose leaders prevailed upon the parent assembly in Coleman Street, London, to deny him the status of full pastor.

It was the scandal of the so-called False Jew of Hexham, however, that brought Tillam down and propelled him on his extravagant adventures. A man calling himself Joseph ben Israel had arrived in Hexham from Newcastle on 4 June 1653, claiming to be a Jew of the tribe of Judah, born in Mantua, conversant in eight languages, and educated in philosophy as well as the religion of his ancestors. Curiously, he also spoke English with a local accent, but Tillam did not think this linguistic talent significant at the time. Joseph told of his conversion to Christ and his wanderings through Europe, until he arrived one day in Hamburg and heard of the English Baptists. He made his way to Newcastle, he said, and lived for about a month at the home of Paul Hobson, the deputy governor of the town and one of the founders of the new Baptist congregation there. Hobson told Joseph that if he really wanted to become a Baptist, he might like to try the brethren at nearby Hexham. Tillam baptized Joseph only a few days after his arrival, in the wake of declarations and public confessions by this 'Jew' who had 'seen the light'. However, Joseph had arrived in Hexham with a letter of introduction from Hobson himself which also warned Tillam not to believe everything he was told by his latest spiritual conquest, and as soon as the report of Tillam's hasty baptism reached Newcastle it was announced that this supposed Italian Jew might actually be a certain Thomas *Ramsay (alias Horsley), who had just recently passed through the city. Tillam and Joseph were called to Newcastle to answer charges there at meetings held from 21 June 1653. Joseph's story soon began to unravel, its falsehood clinched by a misdirected letter from his mother, the wife of a Dr Alexander Ramsay of Scotland. Joseph-Horsley-Ramsay broke down and confessed to being a former student at various Scottish and continental universities, sent to England by the Jesuits to stir up trouble. Ramsay was imprisoned without trial in London for about six years, and two months before the Restoration was allowed to leave the country.

It was quite apparent that Tillam's mission to the north, while not quite a failure, had succeeded in bringing shame and disgrace to the Baptist movement as a whole. Yet he was allowed to remain in his post for another two and a half years, until doctrinal differences with the central congregation at Coleman Street led the Baptists in the first fortnight of November 1655 to replace Tillam with George Ritschel, the Bohemian divine then serving as chief master at the free school in Newcastle. Tillam's movements that winter are unknown, but the revelation in December 1655 of a genuine secret Jewish community in London must have brought back bitter memories. Notwithstanding, by May 1656 Tillam was baptizing dozens of converts in Colchester, and a number of local aldermen successfully petitioned Cromwell himself that something more permanent be found for him in the town. Some time before the following January, however, Tillam underwent his final metamorphosis, and began proclaiming in the pulpit and in print that Saturday was the sabbath, and that at least on that score the Jews were correct. It was also at about this time that Tillam met Christopher Pooley, the Cambridge-educated Baptist and Fifth Monarchist, whose millenarian views Tillam enthusiastically shared. The two men travelled together in the last few years before the king's return, as Tillam preached the Saturday sabbath and flirted with Quakerism. Between 1651 and 1660, Tillam published six works, the most notable being his account of the 'False Jew' episode which was printed in Newcastle in 1653.

Tillam was arrested along with many other old radicals at the Restoration, but he and Pooley managed to escape to the Netherlands. They returned to England in August 1661 in the company of a mysterious Dr Love. This was none other than Paul Hobson, the original magnet for the False Jew of Hexham, freshly ejected from his post as chaplain at Eton College and driven now to forget old quarrels and plot more dramatic action. The plan was to establish an émigré sabbatarian colony in the Palatinate, and whereas Hobson was soon occupied with his own seditious affairs, Tillam and Pooley led an underground life in 1662 and 1663 and may have returned to the continent to promote their settlement. They were certainly back in England by the end of 1664 before they fled abroad again, and Pooley at least spent the second half of 1666 travelling in the north, trying to convince believers to join the continental colony and to subscribe to its sabbatarian covenant. A vessel with eight or nine passengers set sail in March 1668, bound for Tillam's little colony. According to English intelligence reports it had actually been established, at a monastery granted by the duke of Brandenburg, the tolerant 'great elector', and was thriving. The subsequent fate of Tillam and his band of Saturday sabbatarians remains unknown.   DAVID S. KATZ

Sources D. S. Katz, *Sabbath and sectarianism in seventeenth-century England* (1987), chap. 2 • E. B. Underhill, ed., *Records of the Churches of Christ, gathered at Fenstanton, Warboys, and Hexham, 1644–1720*, Hanserd Knollys Society (1854) • T. Tillam, *Banners of love* (1653) • T. Weld and others, *A false Jew, or, A wonderfull discovery of a Scot* (1653) • W. T. Whitley, 'The Rev. Colonel Paul Hobson', *Baptist Quarterly*, 9 (1938–9), 307–10

Tillemans, Peter (*c.*1684–1734), painter and draughtsman, was born in Antwerp, the Netherlands, the son of a diamond cutter. He was brother-in-law to the painter Pieter *Casteels (it is assumed he married before leaving Antwerp) and studied painting under various masters before being brought to England in 1708 by a picture dealer named Turner.

Establishing an exact chronology is difficult as Tillemans worked in many different styles, rarely dating his works. However, after initially working as a copyist, he seems to have rapidly made a name for himself, gaining in 1709 two prestigious commissions, *Queen Anne in the House of Lords* (*c.*1709; Royal Collection) and *The House of Commons* (*c.*1709; Gov. Art Coll.). He became a founder member of the Great Queen Street Academy in 1711, describing his speciality as 'landskip', and by 1715 was painting battle scenes for the Revd Dr Cox Macro. 1717 saw a further expansion of Tillemans's repertoire, his picture of the royal family making music being exhibited at Bartholomew fair. This theatrical vein in Tillemans's work continued in the 1720s, including a collaboration with Joseph Goupy, in 1724, on scenery for the Haymarket opera house.

Between 1719 and 1721 Tillemans worked as a topographical artist for the antiquarian John Bridges, completing about 500 drawings for Bridges' proposed history of Northamptonshire; a number of these were later published in Peter Whalley's *History and Antiquities of the County of Northamptonshire* (2 vols., 1791). The early 1720s also saw Tillemans moving successfully into the field of horse painting and racing scenes. He produced several versions of such works, including his *Newmarket: the Long Course* (1723; Gov. Art Coll.). It was also during this period that Tillemans painted some of his best Thames-side views. His grand panorama *The Thames from Richmond Hill* (*c.*1723; Gov. Art Coll.) was one of three pieces done for Lord Radnor.

A member of the Rose and Crown Club, Tillemans was recorded by Vertue as steward, for 1725, to the Society of the Virtuosi of St Luke. Vertue also noted that he was in a position of 'acquaintance amongst … people of fashion & persons of Quality' (Vertue, 3.14), much in demand as a painter of country-house and estate views. *Chatsworth House* (1720s; Holker Hall, Cumbria) and *Chirk Castle* (1725; Chirk Castle, Denbighshire) stand out among his best essays—the houses situated firmly within finely painted landscapes enlivened by animals and hunting scenes.

However, Tillemans's work at Little Haugh Hall, Suffolk, for Dr Cox Macro remains the best documented. In addition to battle scenes, landscapes, hunting pieces, and renovation work, he also painted one of his finest portraits, *Master Edward and Miss Mary Macro* (*c*.1733; Norwich Castle Museum). Such versatility must have been a major factor in Tillemans's success and is tacitly acknowledged in *The Artist's Studio* (*c*.1716; Norwich Castle Museum)—a self-portrait, with Cox Macro and pupils, surrounded in the studio by a variety of works, complete and incomplete, after different masters.

In 1733 Tillemans retired to Richmond, Surrey, and died on 5 December 1734 while staying at Little Haugh Hall. He was buried on 7 December at Stowlangtoft church, Suffolk. The auction of his picture collection, conducted by Cox on 19 and 20 April 1733, included paintings by James Tillemans—likely to have been a son or close relative—and Arthur Devis, who, like Joseph Francis Nollekins, was almost certainly a pupil.   EDWARD BOTTOMS

Sources R. Raines, 'Peter Tillemans, life and work: with a list of representative paintings', *Walpole Society*, 47 (1978–80), 21–59 · Vertue, *Note books*, 3.1–162 · A. Moore, *Dutch and Flemish painting in Norfolk: a history of taste and influence, fashion and collecting* (1988) [exhibition catalogue, William and Mary tercentenary exhibition, Norfolk] · B. A. Bailey, ed., *Northamptonshire in the early eighteenth century: the drawings of Peter Tillemans and others*, Northamptonshire RS, 39 (1996) · J. Harris, *The artist and the country house: a history of country house and garden view painting in Britain, 1540–1870* (1979) · J. Egerton, ed., *British sporting and animal paintings, 1655–1867* (1978) · parish register, Stowlangtoft church, 7 Dec 1734 [burial]

Archives BL, Macro C, MS catalogue of Cox Macro's collections, Add. MS 25473 · Bodl. Oxf., Macro D, Cox Macro's 'Diary of purchases', English miscellany e. 346 · Norwich Castle Museum, Macro A, Macro B, Macro E, MS catalogue of Cox Macro's paintings

Likenesses P. Tillemans, oils, *c*.1716, Norwich Castle Museum [*see illus.*] · H. Hysing, oils, before 1723; now missing · J. M. Rysbrack, terracotta bust, 1727, Yale U. CBA · J. Goupy, crayon drawing, before 1734; now missing · T. Chambars, line print (after H. Hysing), BM, NPG; repro. in H. Walpole, *Anecdotes* (1762)

Tiller, Terence Rogers (1916–1987), poet and radio producer, was born in Comprigney Cottage, Truro, Cornwall, on 19 September 1916, the son of George Henry Rogers Tiller, a clerk working for the Territorial Army, and his wife, Catherine Mary, *née* Stoot. He was educated at the Latymer Upper School, Hammersmith, London, and in 1934 went to Jesus College, Cambridge, where he read history and in 1936 won the chancellor's medal for English verse. He acted as director of studies at Jesus until 1939, when he went to Cairo to teach English literature and history at Fuad I University. During the Second World War he became closely associated with the group surrounding *Personal Landscape*, a review in the Middle East that had been founded and was edited by Lawrence Durrell, Robin Fedden, and Bernard Spencer. In 1945 he married Doreen Hugh, *née* Watson, and they had two children.

Tiller published six volumes of poetry, beginning with *Poems* (1941), in which Virginia Woolf, who had read it in manuscript, found 'music and imagination … rare for a first book'. This was followed by *The Inward Animal* (1943),

Peter Tillemans (*c*.1684–1734), self-portrait, *c*.1716 [*The Artist's Studio* with Dr Cox Macro]

and *Unarm, Eros* (1947). Much of the verse found in these volumes deals with the condition of a poet-in-exile, and charts Tiller's slow coming to terms 'with the seediness of the Egyptian scene'. In this alien land, his 'customary self', by which he meant that of the aloof intellectual, was put under siege, and his final reaction to the Sphinx in a poem bearing that name was: 'we cannot gaze him down.' Occasionally, a surrealist image would appear in his early work—'a camel in a bath', for instance.

After Tiller's third book had come out there were no further references in his poetry to oases, Coptic churches, or giving lectures to the troops in Tripoli. Nevertheless, it was these poems, with their Middle Eastern setting, which proved his most popular; they were frequently reprinted in anthologies about the Second World War. In his three subsequent books—*Reading a Medal* (1957), *Notes for a Myth* (1968), and *That Singing Mesh* (1979)—he indulged in speculations about Adam and the fall of man, Shakespeare's tragic heroes, and the influence of the planets upon mankind. There was a strong metaphysical strain throughout his work (he also translated and edited John Gower's *Confessio amantis*, 1963), and, as he acknowledged, he was indebted to his reading of Dante and Rilke. However, despite the fact that Tiller declared these later poems to be love poems, readers found them difficult and sometimes obscure; for instance, the opening title poem of *Reading a Medal* breaks off with the word 'because' in midline.

If Tiller's readership shrank, as a successful radio producer he gained a wide audience of enthusiastic listeners. He had joined the BBC features department in 1946, and consequently belonged to the golden period of the Third Programme. His acclaimed radio programmes included adaptations of Chaucer's *Parlement of Foules* in 1958, of Dante's *Inferno* in 1966, and of *The Vision of Piers Ploughman* (broadcast 1980, published 1981). He also produced several features on modern poets, including Durrell and Spencer.

In manner Tiller was precise and punctilious, and did not always carry his learning lightly. He was a formidable chess player, and an authority on astronomy and astrology. He kept regular drinking hours, went daily at twelve sharp to the BBC club bar, and sat in the same chair. He was shy and secretive but, like many shy men, could be bold when the occasion called for it. His two daughters held him somewhat in awe, but generally speaking theirs was a loving family.

Tiller retired from the BBC in 1975, and died at Queen Mary's University Hospital, Roehampton, London, on 24 December 1987, the eve of a feast day which he had at several times celebrated with nativity poems. His earliest, called 'The Birth of Christ', closed with this line: 'And over his thin cry, the noise of angels.' His wife survived him.

NEVILLE BRAYBROOKE

Sources *The Times* (5 Jan 1988) · *The Independent* (11 Jan 1988) · A. Cooper, *Cairo in the war* (1989) · R. Bowen, 'Many histories deep': the 'Personal Landscape' poets in Egypt, 1940–1945 (1995) · private information (2004) [R. D. Smith, O. Manning] · b. cert. · d. cert. · J. Stringer, ed., *The Oxford companion to twentieth-century literature in English* (1996)

Archives Temple University, Philadelphia, literary MSS and papers · U. Reading L., corresp. and literary MSS
Wealth at death £10: probate, 1988, *CGPLA Eng. & Wales*

Tillesley, Richard (1582–1624), Church of England clergyman, was born at Coventry, the son of Thomas Tillesley of Eccleshall, Staffordshire, and his wife, Katherine, daughter of Richard Barker of Shropshire. Having matriculated from Balliol College, Oxford, on 20 January 1598, he was a scholar of St John's College by 1599. He graduated MA on 26 June 1607, BD on 22 November 1613, and DD on 7 July 1617. On 25 November 1613 he was licensed to preach, and was collated by John Buckeridge, bishop of Rochester, and late president of St John's College, to the rectories of Cuxton (26 March 1614) and Stone (1 December 1615). On 9 April 1614 he was installed as archdeacon of Rochester, and on 13 June 1615 admitted to a canonry on the presentation of James I. Wood alleges that Tillesley owed his rapid preferment to his marriage with Elizabeth Buckeridge, daughter of the bishop's brother George.

In 1619 Tillesley published *Animadversions upon M. Seldens History of Tithes and his Review Thereof*. He was one of a number of authors who undertook to answer Selden's book: Tillesley and Richard Mountague dealt with the legal part, while Stephen Nettles and Sir James Sempill discussed the rabbinical or Judaical. Like Mountague in his *Diatribae upon the First Part of the Late History of Tithes*, Tillesley discussed the historical aspect of the controversy. Although he professed admiration for his predecessor Sempill's earlier critique of Selden (which was based on a weak grasp of the issues involved), the archdeacon wrote a much more aggressive attack on the *History of Tithes*. Tillesley even reported, erroneously, that Selden had been compelled by the high commission to recant his views on the historical development of tithing practices; in fact, Selden had merely apologized for publishing the book. Selden's book had asserted that the clerical right to tithes, so far from having been asserted *jure divino* since the advent of the church in England, had in fact been based on custom and precedent. Tithing practices, and indeed the very parochial organization of the church on which they were now based, had varied considerably over time. Selden had based his arguments on a rigorous philological examination of ecclesiastical documents, and in particular of medieval cartularies. Tillesley attacked this method on several fronts. First, he decried Selden's use of French philological methods to study the changing meaning of words such as *decimae*, arguing that this Latin word essentially denoted tithes, provided *jure divino*, in their current sense. Second he accused Selden of intellectual dishonesty, claiming that the latter had refused to grant him access to the same cartularies, and charging Selden with misquoting and manipulating his sources to prove a case. (He was in fact correct in that many of Selden's quotations were either inaccurate or careless). Finally, rather than denying the great weight of Selden's evidence concerning changing tithing customs, he instead asserted that such evidence was insignificant, since divine law ought to take precedence over human custom. In 1621 Tillesley published a second edition of his attack, including some additional material. Selden wrote angry replies to Tillesley and his other critics but was restrained by James I and the duke of Buckingham from publishing them; they appear in the 1726 edition of Selden's *Opera omnia* edited by David Wilkins.

In 1622 Tillesley became rector of Llandogo, in the diocese of St David's. Shortly after having drawn up a nuncupative will on 30 November 1624, while 'sicke in body', he died at Rochester. The main beneficiary of his will, proved on 14 December, was his widow Elizabeth; a son, John, also survived him. He was buried in the choir of Rochester Cathedral.   E. I. CARLYLE, *rev.* D. R. WOOLF

Sources Wood, *Ath. Oxon.*, new edn, 2.303 · *Joannis Seldeni juris consulti opera omnia*, ed. D. Wilkins (1726) · *Fasti Angl., 1541–1857,* [Canterbury], 58, 67 · D. R. Woolf, *The idea of history in early Stuart England* (1990) · R. Hovenden, ed., *The visitation of Kent, taken in the years 1619–1621*, Harleian Society, 42 (1898), 25 · PRO, E331/Rochester/21–2 · PRO, E334, fol. 112*r* · will, CKS, DRb/Pwr/21, fol. 122 · private information (2004) [St John's College, Oxford]
Wealth at death exact sum unknown: CKS, DRb/Pwr/21, fol. 122

Tillett, Benjamin [Ben] (1860–1943), trade unionist and politician, was born in Lower Easton, Bristol, on 11 September 1860, the son of Benjamin Tillett, a hard-drinking labourer, and his first wife, Elizabeth, *née* Lane, who died when he was a baby. Ben Tillett grew up in poverty and, according to his unreliable *Memories and Reflections* (1931), his childhood was characterized by repeated attempts to run away from home, intermittent unskilled employment, and neglected education. At thirteen he joined the Royal Navy, and at sixteen became a merchant seaman. After serving a few years on the north Atlantic, Baltic, and coastal routes, he settled in Bethnal Green, London, where he married Jane Tomkins in 1882. They had several children, but only two daughters survived infancy.

As a young man in east London, Tillett developed many of the hallmarks of the respectable artisan. He embarked on an eclectic programme of self-education, and became a teetotaller and an active chapel-goer. Nevertheless, his economic position was insecure: unlike many former sailors, he was refused admission to the Stevedores' Union (one of the few specialized and organized groups among the London waterside workers), and had to find casual employment as a shoemaker and as a dock labourer in a tea warehouse.

In 1887, Tillett and some fellow workers formed a Tea Operatives and General Labourers Association in an attempt to prevent a wage reduction, but it remained small and ineffective until the sudden outburst of mass discontent among the waterfront workers of London in August 1889 made it the focus for organization among the unskilled. The great dock strike not only achieved the 'docker's tanner' and the regularization of many working practices, it also turned Ben Tillett overnight into a household name, and brought him into contact with leading London socialists and trade unionists such as John Burns and Tom Mann and also with prominent public sympathizers such as Cardinal Manning. In the euphoria which

Benjamin Tillett (1860–1943), by London Stereoscopic Co.

followed the end of the strike, Tillett relaunched his union as the Dock, Wharf, Riverside, and General Labourers' Union and proceeded to recruit thousands of unskilled workers from a variety of occupations in different parts of the country. Contemporaries recognized it as a new phenomenon in the trade union world, and as its general secretary Tillett quickly made his mark in the wider union and socialist movements. In the course of 1892, he was elected to the parliamentary committee of the Trades Union Congress (TUC), and supporters secured his co-option as an alderman to the London county council. In the general election of the same year he fought an impressive campaign as independent labour candidate at Bradford West, and in 1893 he was present at the Bradford conference which resulted in the establishment of the Independent Labour Party (ILP).

However, as the economic recession of the early 1890s showed, Tillett's union was in reality very weak. It was riven by internal dissension, partly because of Tillett's autocratic behaviour and inefficiency as an administrator, but it was also the target of a deliberate counter-attack by port employers and shipowners, who refused to countenance the closed shop. A disastrous dock strike in Hull in 1893 destroyed the union's main regional stronghold, and, except in the Bristol Channel ports, its waterfront membership elsewhere dwindled. By 1900, it was essentially a small provincial union, and many of its 10,000 members were not dockers. Meanwhile, Tillett lost his place on the TUC parliamentary committee as a result of the revision of the standing orders which conservative union leaders engineered in 1895, and he ceased to be active in the ILP after unsuccessfully contesting Bradford West a second time in the same year. He also suffered pecuniary loss following an unsuccessful libel action against *The Morning* newspaper, which accused him of enriching himself at his union's expense—the first of several hints of financial impropriety which were to dog Tillett throughout his career. Emotionally depressed and physically debilitated, he spent most of 1897 and 1898 on an improvised lecture tour of Australia and New Zealand in an attempt to recover his health and his finances. While in Australia he began a liaison with a Sydney-born actress, Eva Newton (*c.*1877–1955), which appears to have lasted, intermittently, until at least the outbreak of the First World War. Tillett returned a convinced supporter of the systems of compulsory arbitration in industrial disputes which had recently been set up in several of the colonies, and from 1899 he brought forward an annual motion at the TUC in favour of their introduction in Britain. However, the leaders of older and stronger unions, who enjoyed types of collective bargaining from which the state was rigorously excluded, consistently secured its defeat.

Although Tillett's trade union career continued to languish during the first decade of the twentieth century, his long-standing commitment to independent labour representation in parliament and his popularity as a public expounder of a quasi-religious form of socialism ensured that he took an active but idiosyncratic role in the early development of the Labour Party. He was present at the famous meeting on 27 February 1900 which set up the Labour Representation Committee, served for a time on its executive, and stood unsuccessfully as its candidate at Eccles in the 1906 general election, although ill health prevented him from campaigning in person. His relations with Keir Hardie and Ramsay MacDonald were never easy, however, and a second tour of Australasia in 1907–8 convinced him that parliamentary labourism was inadequate. His increasingly sybaritic lifestyle had in any case left him with little personal sympathy for many of the party's more sober and strait-laced leaders. Although his socialism remained nebulous and unscientific, Tillett worked closely with the Social Democratic Party of H. M. Hyndman in the years before 1914; during his last unsuccessful pre-war election campaign—at Swansea in January 1910—the Labour leadership actually recommended support for his Liberal opponent.

Tillett's second experience of Australia and New Zealand also left him less enthusiastic about compulsory arbitration, and converted him to the syndicalist arguments in favour of a single union and direct action as the best means of improving the workers' lot in a world increasingly dominated by corporate capitalism. Renewed contact with his old ally Tom Mann was particularly influential in pushing Tillett in this new direction. The short-run consequences were dramatic. In 1910, Tillett persuaded the leaders of several other transport unions to form the National Transport Workers Federation (NTWF), and 1911–12 saw a virtual rerun of the events of 1889–90 in most of Britain's major seaports. A national wave of labour unrest at a time of economic recovery helped to revive both the Dockers' Union and Tillett's reputation as a firebrand, particularly in London. However, the gains made there in 1911 were quickly lost, and the weakness of the NTWF was clearly demonstrated when its provincial leaders refused to support the London dockers against an employers' counter-attack in the following year. Tillett remained committed to the ideal of creating a strong amalgamation of transport unions, but nothing had been achieved by the outbreak of war in 1914.

The First World War transformed Tillett from a dangerous demagogue into a minor, but well-loved, national institution—a role in which he revelled for the rest of his life. After some initial hesitation, he identified himself with the patriotic wing of the labour movement, demanded the whole-hearted prosecution of the war effort, and pressed the claims of soldiers and war workers for decent treatment. His recruiting speeches at home and his morale-boosting visits to the front earned him the praise of lords Kitchener and French and helped to secure his belated entry to parliament as Labour MP for North Salford at a by-election in 1917. He held the seat until the fall of the first Labour government in 1924, and regained it in 1929. However, his enhanced public role during the war meant a corresponding neglect of his union work, and by 1920 effective leadership of the Dockers' Union had passed to Ernest Bevin. It was Bevin who in 1922 finally created the amalgamation of transport unions which Tillett had long dreamed about, and in the new Transport and General Workers' Union Tillett had to be content with the largely sinecure office of international and political secretary. He held the post until his enforced retirement—on a pension which proved inadequate to his free-spending habits—at the age of seventy.

Throughout the 1920s, Tillett filled the role of elder statesman to the labour movement. He sat on the general council of the TUC from 1921 to 1931, and served on numerous trade union committees, deputations, and delegations at home and abroad. In 1929, on the fortieth anniversary of the great dock strike, he presided over the annual congress, and delivered a statesmanlike address advocating co-operation between unions, employers, and government. But his influence on the real work of the union movement had vanished, and in politics he remained on the back benches during the first and second Labour governments. After losing his seat in Labour's crushing electoral defeat in 1931, he entered unwillingly and unhappily into permanent retirement. His first wife—who played a loyal but unobtrusive part in women's labour organizations—died in 1936, and in 1939 he married Lilian Morgan, his junior by more than thirty years. The coming of the Second World War depressed him profoundly, but in his last years he found consolation in the Moral Re-Armament movement. Tillett died in hospital in Golders Green, Middlesex, on 27 January 1943 and he was cremated at Golders Green crematorium four days later, following an address by Ernest Bevin. He was survived by his second wife.

Tillett's career defies easy categorization, and simple images—a meteor, a chameleon, or a weathercock—fail to capture its complexity. His long-term impact was more limited than that of most of his leading contemporaries in the labour movement, and his personality was less attractive than, for example, that of his lifelong associate, Tom Mann. He was not helped by recurrent ill health, and his extravagance in language and lifestyle made him an unpredictable, infuriating, and embarrassing colleague. To his admirers, Tillett was a tireless fighter against injustice and an irrepressible champion of the rights and dignity of the working man. To his opponents (inside as well as outside the movement) he was the ultimate agitator: an irresponsible trouble-maker, vain, mercenary, and unprincipled, who was violent in speech but timid in action. Yet despite the many twists and turns of his career, his reputation as one of the most eloquent and inspiring orators of Labour's pioneer generation remained untarnished. At a time when political awareness was still most often awakened by the impact of the spoken word on the large crowd, Tillett's skills as a 'platform man' won thousands of converts to the basic tenets of socialism and trade unionism. The medium may have been flawed, but the message it conveyed was crucially important in the great realignment of British politics between the 1880s and the 1920s. DUNCAN BYTHELL

Cecil Edgar Tilley (1894–1973), by Lafayette, 1927

Sources B. Tillett, *Memories and reflections* (1931) · J. Schneer, *Ben Tillett: portrait of a labour leader* (1982) · *DLB*, vol. 4 · *Annual Report* [Trades Union Congress] (1890–1929) · H. A. Clegg, A. Fox, and A. F. Thompson, *A history of British trade unions since 1889*, 1–2 (1964–85) · J. C. Lovell, *Stevedores and dockers* (1969) · A. Bullock, *The life and times of Ernest Bevin*, 1 (1960) · K. Coates and T. Topham, *The making of the Transport and General Workers Union: the emergence of the labour movement, 1870–1922*, 1 (1991) · D. Howell, *British workers and the independent labour party, 1888–1906* (1983) · B. C. Roberts, *The Trades Union Congress, 1868–1921* (1958) · 'Royal commission on labour: group b: docks, wharves, and shipping', *Parl. papers* (1892), 34.111, C. 6708-II; vol. 35, C. 6708-V · *The Times* (28 Jan 1943) · C. Joseph, 'Revealed: the secret philandering ways of a labour party icon', *The Independent* (24 Feb 2000), 8

Archives Labour History Archive and Study Centre, Manchester, papers · Labour History Archive and Study Centre, Manchester, scrapbook · U. Warwick Mod. RC, working papers for proposed biography · U. Warwick Mod. RC, corresp. and papers | BL, corresp. with John Burns, Add. MS 46285 · HLRO, corresp. with Lord Beaverbrook · HLRO, letters to David Lloyd George · HLRO, letters to Herbert Samuel · NL Wales, corresp. relating to Barry docks strike · U. Warwick Mod. RC, corresp. with the International Transport Workers Federation | FILM BFI NFTVA, current affairs footage

Likenesses I. Opffer, sanguine, 1930–39, NPG · J. A. Stevenson, bust, c.1959, Bristol City Museum and Art Gallery · London Stereoscopic Co., photograph, NPG [*see illus.*] · Spy [L. Ward], caricature, chromolithograph, NPG · photograph, repro. in *The Independent* (24 Feb 2000), 8

Tilley, Cecil Edgar (1894–1973), mineralogist and petrologist, was born on 14 May 1894 at Adelaide, South Australia, the son of John Thomas Edward Tilley, civil engineer, and his wife, Catherine Jane Nicholas. After attending schools in the city he proceeded to the University of Adelaide and in 1914 graduated with first-class honours in geology. The following year he completed the final year BSc course at the University of Sydney, and was awarded medals in chemistry and geology. Both departments offered him the post of junior demonstrator. He chose geology but in late 1916 went to the UK to an appointment as chemist in the department of explosives supply at Queensferry, Edinburgh. At the end of the First World War he returned to Australia to resume his demonstratorship at Adelaide. An award of an 1851 Exhibition scholarship enabled him to go in 1920 to Cambridge to work under Alfred Harker, university reader in petrology. In 1923 Tilley was appointed to a university demonstratorship in geology and in 1928 to a lectureship in petrology in the Sedgwick Museum of Geology. Tilley had been slow to settle in Cambridge but in 1928, in addition to gaining his lectureship, he married Irene Doris Marshall. The couple had one daughter.

Rapid changes in mineralogy and petrology, consequent on the application of X-ray diffraction techniques to mineral structure determination and the increasing use of analytical and physical chemistry in the investigation of igneous and metamorphic rocks, occurred during the 1920s but during this period mineralogy and petrology were still taught in different departments. The simultaneous retirements of Harker and Arthur Hutchinson, professor of mineralogy, enabled a department of mineralogy and petrology to be established. Tilley was appointed its first head, and a new building, largely designed by him, was ready for occupation in 1933. Tilley's reputation for hard work was by then legendary and he made it clear by his example that nothing less than an outstanding teaching and research laboratory would be acceptable.

Tilley's work ranged very widely across the span of his science and may be divided roughly into two periods. The first, covering the field of metamorphism, ran from 1920 (investigation of the Precambrian dolomites in South Australia) to 1950. During this period he published a succession of outstanding papers which included the classic account of the contact metamorphism in the Comrie area of Perthshire (1924), and the major innovative investigation of the dolerite–chalk contact of Scawt Hill, Larne, co. Antrim (1931). No less important were his studies of the anthophyllite–cordierite hornfelses of the Kenidjack and Lizard areas of Cornwall, the green schists of the Start area in Devon, and the eulysites of Loch Duich, Ross-shire. This period was also marked by the discovery of the new minerals larnite, scawtite, portlandite, hydro-calumite, rankinite, and harkerite, demonstrating Tilley's skill with the petrological microscope. In addition to these specialized studies Tilley published a number of papers dealing with more general aspects of metamorphism.

Tilley was now internationally recognized as the outstanding figure in metamorphic petrology, and his change to a second field of research, into problems of the igneous rocks, marked by his presidential address to the Geological Society of London in 1950, evoked surprise. However, Tilley had published a much earlier paper (1933) on the phase relations in the system $Na_2O-Al_2O_3-SiO_2$, and this was the stimulus for his interest in the genesis of alkaline rocks, which was expressed in eleven papers between 1952 and 1961. His study of the nepheline–feldspar association of the nepheline syenites and their relation to the $NaAlSiO_4$-$KAlSiO_4$-SiO_2 system was instrumental in stimulating the experimental studies that provided the basis of the understanding of the crystallization processes of the undersaturated rocks. Prior to these studies Tilley's interests had concentrated on the diversity of basalt magma types, on which subject his presidential address provided an authoritative and comprehensive survey. Tilley and the American petrologist H. S. Yoder published a classic paper on the origin of basalt magma in 1962. Problems of the genesis of primary and derived basic and intermediate magmas continued as Tilley's main interest and, with Yoder, I. D. Muir, and others, he wrote a succession of papers that ended only shortly before his death.

Tilley's contributions to mineralogy and petrology were widely recognized. The Geological Society of London awarded him the Bigsby medal in 1937 and the Wollaston medal, its highest award, in 1960. He was president of the society in 1949 and its William Smith lecturer in 1957. That he had two spells, 1948–51 and 1957–60, as president of the Mineralogical Society is unique in the annals of the society, as was its publication of a special volume of the *Mineralogical Magazine* on the occasion of his seventieth birthday. Tilley was elected a fellow of the Royal Society in 1938 and awarded its royal medal in 1967. Abroad his reputation was acknowledged by his presidency, in 1964–70, of the International Mineralogical Association, an honorary DSc of Sydney University, honorary fellowships of many foreign academies and societies, and in 1954 by the award of the Roebling medal of the Mineralogical Society of America. He also received an honorary DSc from Manchester University. Tilley died at his home, 30 Tenison Avenue, Cambridge, on 24 January 1973. He was survived by his wife. W. A. DEER, *rev.*

Sources W. A. Deer and S. A. Nockolds, *Memoirs FRS*, 20 (1974), 381–400 · personal knowledge (1974)
Likenesses Lafayette, photograph, 1927, NPG [*see illus.*] · Ramsey & Muspratt, photograph, RS
Wealth at death £28,427: probate, 6 April 1973, *CGPLA Eng. & Wales*

Tilley, Sir John (1813–1898), Post Office administrator, was born on 20 January 1813 in Peckham, Surrey, the son of John Tilley, merchant, and his wife, Elizabeth, daughter of Thomas Fraser. After being educated at a private school in Bromley, Kent, Tilley in 1829 was appointed a clerk in the General Post Office in London, partly on the basis of family connections with Sir Francis Freeling, its secretary. For the next five decades the bureaucracy which Tilley had entered was to provide the central focus of his life, both personal and professional. There he became a confidant of Anthony Trollope, who joined the Post Office in 1834. The relationship was further strengthened by Tilley's marriage to Trollope's sister Cecilia in 1839; she died of consumption in 1849. Tilley's subsequent marriages also ended sadly. Both Mary Anne Partington, a first cousin of Trollope's, whom Tilley married in 1850, and Susan Montgomerie (*d.* 1880), whom he married in 1861, predeceased him. These marriages produced two sons and one daughter.

Tilley's professional life was to lead to happier outcomes. Indeed, he was the fastest rising man of his generation at St Martin's-le-Grand. In 1838 he was appointed surveyor for a district in northern England, thus gaining the field experience regarded by many as a prerequisite for promotion. In 1848 he returned to London as assistant secretary. In 1864, on the retirement of Sir Rowland Hill, he became secretary and, in effect, director of the largest business in the United Kingdom.

When Tilley joined the Post Office in 1829, it had the reputation of being a somewhat sleepy organization, its City headquarters removed from other government departments and its management often more interested in its revenue-collecting function than in public service. Yet Tilley was to see and to oversee major transformations in how the department conceived its purpose and how it conducted its business. From the 1830s on railways and steamships quickly emerged as the chief means of mail conveyance, raising difficult contractual questions. In 1840 the agitation of Hill and Robert Wallace bore fruit in the penny post. The mid-century decades were to experience the first waves of labour agitation inside the department, civil service reform, and the coming of new services: Post Office Savings Banks in 1861, the sale of life insurance in 1864, and postcards and a nationalized telegraph system under departmental control in 1870. Another way of gauging this growth is to note that between 1864 and 1880—Tilley's years as secretary—the number of letters conveyed increased from 650 million to 1000 million, gross revenue from £3.8 million to £7.8 million, and net revenue (profit) from £0.9 million to £2.6 million.

Tilley should by no means be given all the credit for this record of expansion and change: in part it was the natural outcome of a growing economy. It also was the result of policies of reformers such as Hill, whom Tilley disliked; and he was often opposed to such progressive schemes. A traditionalist, Tilley consistently held that civil service examinations would allow candidates with academic training—but without the necessary personal qualities—to enter government service. Further, he initially objected to the idea of a state-managed telegraph system, and, when the department assumed control, he allowed Frank Ives Scudamore, the second secretary, who had led the campaign for take-over, a free hand in its management.

Displaying a tough-minded pragmatism, Tilley brought a real concern for the needs of the nation to his direction of departmental affairs. Whether negotiating with shipping companies or dealing with staff unrest, his goal remained to ensure the best possible outcome for the public and the Post Office. The two were virtually identical in his mind, and it was not simply a question of winning ideological battles. Without question, his approach contributed to a broad, if temporary, consensus that the Post Office was the best-administered government department.

In 1880 Tilley became KCB and retired on full pay. He remained active in public and charitable activities, including service as a JP and as chairman of the Eastern Hospital, London. He died from old age on 18 March 1898 at his home, 73 St George's Square, London.   C. R. PERRY

Sources C. R. Perry, *The Victorian Post Office: the growth of a bureaucracy*, Royal Historical Society Studies in History, 64 (1992) · M. J. Daunton, *Royal Mail: the Post Office since 1840* (1985) · R. H. Super, *Trollope in the Post Office* (1981) · R. Mullen, *Anthony Trollope* (1990) · N. J. Hall, *Trollope* (1991) · C. R. Perry, 'Tilley, Frank Cyril', *DBB* · *WWW* · Boase, *Mod. Eng. biog.* · d. cert. · *The Times* (19 March 1898)
Archives Royal Mail Heritage, London, letter-books | Chatsworth House, Derbyshire, letters to Lord Hartington
Wealth at death £11,390 10s. 8d.: probate, 12 May 1898, CGPLA Eng. & Wales

Tilley, Sir Samuel Leonard (1818–1896), politician in Canada, was born at Gagetown, New Brunswick, on 8 May 1818, the eldest son of Thomas Morgan Tilley, a storekeeper, and his wife, Susan, the daughter of William Peters, a farmer. Descended from loyalists on both sides, he was educated at the local Church of England school and grammar school, but at the age of thirteen he moved to Saint John and became apprenticed to a druggist. In 1838 he qualified as a pharmacist, and later established one of the largest drug stores in the province. A highly respected Saint John businessman, Tilley was an enthusiastic supporter of the evangelical wing of the Church of England, taught in Sunday school, and served as the most worthy patriarch of the Sons of Temperance. After the British government ended imperial preferences in the 1840s, he became a founder member of the Railway League and of the New Brunswick Colonial Association, which supported the protection of colonial industries. He was an early advocate of a federal union of British North America. On 6 May 1843 he married Julia Ann Hanford (d. 1862); they had eight children.

In 1850 Tilley was elected to the assembly for Saint John and joined the Reformers in opposition. In 1851, however, the unity of the Reform movement temporarily disintegrated, and he resigned from the assembly and devoted his energies to campaigning for prohibition. In 1852 he was re-elected for Saint John. When the Reformers took office he became provincial secretary, and revamped the province's financial system. He also introduced a stringent prohibition bill banning the sale of alcohol, which became law on 1 January 1856. The law aroused so much opposition that Lieutenant-Governor John Henry Manners-Sutton dissolved the assembly in May. Tilley's party—dubbed the Smashers by their opponents—suffered an overwhelming defeat, Tilley lost his seat, and the prohibition bill was repealed. A chastened Reform Party abandoned prohibition and won re-election in 1857. Tilley returned as provincial secretary, raised the provincial tariffs to the highest in British North America, and borrowed money in London to finance an ambitious programme of railway building. In 1860 he presided over the completion of the railway, optimistically called the European and North American, from Saint John to Shediac, but the construction costs raised the debt to unprecedented levels. In March 1861 Tilley became head of the Reform government, which was re-elected later that year.

Tilley's relations with the new lieutenant-governor, the arrogant Arthur Hamilton Gordon, were frequently uncomfortable. Although Tilley was prepared to discuss a legislative union of the three maritime colonies, to Gordon's dismay he preferred a larger confederation of all of British North America. Partly Tilley saw confederation as a means of funding an intercolonial railway to run across New Brunswick and link Nova Scotia and the united province of Canada. In 1861 and again in 1862 he went to London to try to persuade W. E. Gladstone, the chancellor of the exchequer, to give an imperial guarantee for a loan to finance the railway, but when Gladstone insisted on a sinking fund, the Canadian government withdrew from the arrangement and Tilley returned empty-handed. In 1863 he travelled to Quebec City for further negotiations, again to no avail. Although he pushed enabling legislation through the New Brunswick assembly, he faced considerable opposition from within his own party, and so in 1864 he committed the government to generous subsidies for regional railways within New Brunswick, stretching the colony's credit to its limits.

Tilley undoubtedly saw confederation as the means to build the Intercolonial Railway and free New Brunswick from its substantial debt, but he was motivated by more than mere financial considerations. Like most pro-confederates, he viewed with alarm the growing power of the United States. In 1861 he rushed home from England to assist in the arrangements for colonial defence during the *Trent* affair, and he was genuinely alarmed by the Fenian raids in 1866. He sincerely believed that the imperial connection could not be preserved unless the British North American colonies formed a new (but not independent) nation under the British crown. When the 'Great Coalition' in Canada in 1864 embraced confederation, Tilley abandoned his lukewarm support for maritime union and strongly endorsed confederation at the Charlottetown conference in September 1864. At the Quebec conference in October he headed the New Brunswick delegation and helped to shape the constitutional arrangements for a federal union. But when he returned to New Brunswick he found the tide running against the proposed terms of union. In February 1865 the pro-confederates were overwhelmed at the polls and Tilley was defeated. Within a year the anti-confederate administration, internally divided between those seeking better terms and those adamantly opposed to confederation, fell apart, and a second election in May 1865 brought the confederates back to power. In 1866 Tilley passed the necessary enabling legislation and sailed for England to participate in the London conference, where a measure was prepared for the British parliament. Tilley was able to persuade the delegates to improve the financial terms on which New Brunswick entered confederation, and he vetoed an attempt to entrench denominational schools in the Maritimes. He is also believed to have suggested calling the new country the dominion of Canada, a title he took from Psalm 72. For his efforts he was made a CB on 1 July 1867 and was created a KCMG in 1879. He married Alice Starr Chipman on 22 October 1867; they had two children.

In the new federal administration Tilley initially held the comparatively lowly post of minister of customs. In February 1873 he was promoted to minister of finance, but only briefly held office before the government was forced to resign. In November he was appointed lieutenant-governor of New Brunswick, and so did not stand in the election of 1874, which saw the Conservatives decimated. Even though he held a theoretically non-partisan office, he helped to organize Conservative clubs across the province and to formulate the party's platform for the election of 1878, in which the Conservatives campaigned for a 'national policy' of tariff protection. As minister of finance he introduced the new policy, raising the Canadian tariff in 1879 to encourage investment in Canadian industry. The tariff structure he created remained essentially unaltered until the end of his life. As minister of finance he was less happy with the government's almost open-ended commitment to the Canadian Pacific Railway, and he became increasingly isolated in the cabinet. In 1885 he fell ill and retired as minister of finance, but was reappointed lieutenant-governor of New Brunswick in November and held the post until autumn 1893. A member of the Imperial Federation League, he opposed unrestricted reciprocity in 1891, and in 1896 he bravely published a letter defending the right of Manitoba Catholics to denominational schools. On 25 June 1896 he died of blood poisoning in Saint John, where he was then buried.

A man with deep religious convictions but also a pragmatist prepared to abandon prohibition when its unpopularity became obvious, and to work with Roman Catholics even though he abhorred their religious values, Tilley was easily the most important New Brunswick politician of his generation. An early advocate of protection and a railway enthusiast, he laid the basis of a modern industrial economy in New Brunswick. A firm supporter of confederation, he led his province into the federal union, and without New Brunswick confederation could not have taken place. Tilley was the real architect of the 'national policy', a policy not entirely abandoned until 1988. Although less colourful than many of his contemporaries, he was one of the most important fathers of confederation.   PHILLIP BUCKNER

Sources C. M. Wallace, 'Tilley, Sir Samuel Leonard', *DCB*, vol. 12 · C. M. Wallace, 'Sir Leonard Tilley, a political biography', PhD diss., University of Alberta, 1972 · P. A. Buckner and J. G. Reid, eds., *The Atlantic region to confederation: a history* (1994) · E. R. Forbes and D. A. Muise, eds., *The Atlantic provinces in confederation* (1993) · T. W. Acheson, *Saint John: the making of a colonial urban community* (1985) · P. B. Waite, *The life and times of confederation, 1864–1867* (1962) · J. Hannay, *Sir Leonard Tilley* (1897) · J. K. Chapman, *The career of Arthur Hamilton Gordon, first Lord Stanmore, 1829–1912* (Toronto, 1964)
Archives NA Canada · New Brunswick Museum, Saint John, New Brunswick | NA Canada, John A. Macdonald MSS

Tilley, Vesta [*real name* Matilda Alice Powles; *married name* Matilda Alice de Frece, Lady de Frece] (**1864–1952**), music-hall entertainer, was born in Commandery Street, Worcester, on 13 May 1864, the second of the thirteen children of Henry Powles (*c.*1842–1889), a china painter with theatrical ambitions, and his wife, Matilda, *née* Broughton.

In the mid-1860s music-hall enjoyed an enormous expansion, and on the strength of this Harry Ball (as Powles called himself)—an enterprising extrovert and considerable musician—gave up his trade in 1867 and took a job as chairman (master of ceremonies) first of the new Theatre Royal in Gloucester, and then in 1868 of the St George's in Nottingham. The family moved there and the city became Matilda Powles's home base until her marriage. Not that she was there very often—in 1869, after some local success, she turned professional at the age of five, and began a gruelling life as a touring artiste which would continue with one break until 1920. In 1872 she added cross-dressing elements to her act, and that year her father resigned his chairmanship to become her personal manager. She thus became the sole financial support of the still-increasing family.

The explosive growth in provincial music-hall had led to an infinite appetite for new touring artistes and the eight-year-old, appearing as the Great Little Tilley in a singing and dancing solo act, began to achieve a considerable reputation. In 1874 she had her first London season—then an exhausting routine since all successful performers had to put on 'turns' at three or four halls a night in order to earn a reasonable wage. During this season Edward Villiers, then manager of the Canterbury, became aware that his audience was uncomfortable with an uncertainty as to the child's natural gender and he suggested a name change. Harry Ball chose Vesta (after the popular matches,

Vesta Tilley (1864–1952), by Brown, Barnes & Bell

advertised as 'a bright spark') Tilley: this became more than a stage name—she was always called Vesta by her family and friends.

By the 1870s London's West End music-halls were detaching themselves from their working-class roots and, with the introduction of effective public transport, a new suburban audience developed. This audience for the first time included women, who seem to have enjoyed both the childish precocity and the mocking of masculinity which Vesta Tilley offered. Unlike the fans of other major women stars such as Marie Lloyd, Tilley's were predominantly female. From the outset of her career Tilley was always committed to the elevation of music-hall to respectable family entertainment; her act was famously 'clean'.

Although she proved enormously popular and worked steadily, at ever higher wages, throughout the 1880s, it was not until the death of her father in 1889 that Vesta Tilley fully developed the act which was to earn her the unique status and lasting fame that she came to enjoy. On 16 August 1890 she married (Abraham) Walter de *Frece (1870–1935), eldest son of Henry de Frece, a theatrical entrepreneur. Henry de Frece had considerable social ambition and, excluded from the British public-school system as much because he was Jewish as because of his working-class origins, had had his son educated in Brussels and apprenticed to an architect. Walter de Frece, however, broke free of such paternal control, married Vesta

Tilley and followed his father, very successfully, into music-hall management.

It appears to have been an ideally happy, if childless, marriage. Following it Vesta Tilley developed not just in fame, but as a performer. She started to introduce a sophisticated level of characterization into her drag act, and created a particular dissonance between the immaculately observed and represented male visual characters, and her own mocking female voice:

> Instead of merging her own personality into that of the character, she brought her wits to bear on him critically … we had to see them, ourselves, not as we could see them in real life, but as they were when viewed through a clever woman's eyes.   (Disher, 78)

She was noted for her extraordinary attention to detail, especially in matters of male sartorial effects, her powers of observation (during the war she insisted on having a full-weight soldier's knapsack since a straw-stuffed one would not swing properly), and her personal charm, as well as a series of perfectly chosen songs—'Following in Father's Footsteps', 'Burlington Bertie', 'Algy, the Piccadilly Johnny with the Little Glass Eye', and, later, 'Jolly good luck to the girl who loves a soldier', which proved a massive recruiting success during the First World War when her championship of the soldier was particularly welcome since most music-hall songs favoured sailors.

On the strength of these roles Vesta Tilley became the highest-earning woman in Britain in the 1890s. She became a great hit in American vaudeville, which did not usually take to visiting British performers. She made six triumphant visits to the United States, including touring her own company in 1897–8. She also had enormous success as a principal boy in pantomime: here she personally introduced a lasting innovation—the serious emotional and sentimental scene (now usually played by the heroine). Disher was of the opinion that 'she might have changed our ideas of the principal Boy entirely … but she was too good a trouper to upset its frolics' (Disher, 77).

Tilley, together with entrepreneurs such as her husband, Oswald Stoll, and Edward Moss, had raised the tone of music-hall so much that in 1912 there was a royal command performance. Although this marked an important moment for music-hall the event was not a great success and Vesta Tilley herself had to endure the humiliation of seeing the queen and her ladies-in-waiting covering their faces with their programmes rather than watch a woman's legs. Thereafter, although Tilley continued her performing schedule, the couple began to look beyond the theatrical world for a social base and de Frece developed an interest in Conservative Party politics.

The outbreak of the First World War gave them both a new public role; apart from her recruiting drives, Tilley performed frequently for charities, especially those on behalf of wounded soldiers. James Barrie wrote a special part for her into *The Admirable Crichton* for a fund-raising performance which starred such luminaries of the 'straight' stage as Gerald Du Maurier and Ellen Terry. In 1919 de Frece was knighted for his work in rehabilitating wounded soldiers and decided to run for parliament. This necessitated Vesta Tilley's quitting the stage. She had a stupendously successful farewell tour in 1919–20, during the course of which de Frece was elected to Ashton under Lyne. Her final performance was at the Coliseum on 5 June 1920. Her last song received a forty-minute standing ovation, and Ellen Terry presented her with 'The people's tribute', which nearly two million individuals had signed. The *Daily Telegraph* reported:

> There are many reasons for the pre-eminence Miss Tilley enjoys … she has stood with the clean and wholesome song … when her rivals have gained applause and kudos by the suggestive and vulgar … The demonstration which followed her performance was without precedence in music hall history. It mingled warm admiration of an artistic genius with warm appreciation of a personality. (*Daily Telegraph*, 7 June 1920)

In 1923 Vesta Tilley, now known as Lady de Frece, was presented at court, and in 1924 her husband became MP for Blackpool and deputy lieutenant of Lancashire. In 1932, on his retirement, the couple moved to Monte Carlo, where he died in 1935. Vesta Tilley lived in Monaco, but died at 13 Arlington House, Arlington Street, on a rare visit to London, on 16 September 1952.   SARA MAITLAND

Sources S. Maitland, *Vesta Tilley* (1986) · Lady de Frece, *Recollections of Vesta Tilley* [1934] · M. W. Disher, *Winkles and champagne: comedies and tragedies of the music hall* (1938) · *The Times* (17 Sept 1952) · *DNB*
Archives Manders and Mitcheson Theatre Museum, London · Theatre Museum, London · V&A | FILM BFI NFTVA, actuality footage · BFI NFTVA, news footage · BFI NFTVA, performance footage | SOUND BL NSA, performance recordings
Likenesses Brown, Barnes & Bell, photograph, Theatre Museum, London [*see illus.*] · H. van Dusen & Hassall, lithograph, NPG · Rotary Photo, postcard, NPG · photographs, Theatre Museum, London
Wealth at death £84,945 2s.: probate, 9 Dec 1952, CGPLA Eng. & Wales

Tilling, Thomas (1825–1893), horse bus operator, was born at Gutter Edge Farm, Hendon, London, and was baptized on 22 February 1825 in St Marylebone, Middlesex. He was the son of James Tilling and his wife, Sarah Elizabeth. His father was a Gloucestershire farmer who had moved to London earlier in the century; and by the time of Thomas's birth, James Tilling had already acquired West End shops, from where the farm's milk was delivered to customers by women dressed in traditional Welsh costume, who carried the milk in pails suspended from yokes across their shoulders.

Thomas Tilling's interest, however, was in horses and in 1847 he bought a carriage, which, driven by himself and drawn by his grey mare, Kitty, he hired out for weddings and other functions. He later added other greys to his stud and in 1850, with W. Stevens, bought a horse omnibus to take advantage, in the following year, of the great influx into London of visitors to the Great Exhibition. The business did not collapse, as did so many others, without these additional passengers. On 28 January 1847 Tilling married Cornelia Sevile, and they had a number of children, including Richard Stephen Tilling (1851–1929) and Edward (*b*. 1858).

From his base in Peckham, Tilling ran his single bus, called The Times, to and from central London. A man of strict habits and with a great gift for organization, he ran his bus four times daily to a strict timetable, whether or not it was carrying many passengers. Those using it, knowing they could rely on its punctuality, increased in number and, by increasing the number of vehicles, he was eventually able to provide a quarter-hour service and to offer monthly fares to a regular clientele.

When, in the mid-1850s, an attempt was made to buy up all the horse buses in London, as had already occurred in Paris, Tilling refused to sell but ran in collaboration with the new combine, and his business continued to grow. In due course, when the combine, the name of which had been Anglicized as the London General Omnibus Company, had become slack and inefficient, Tilling was among the independents who also ran in opposition to it. In 1892, on the eve of his death, Tilling was running eight vehicles in association with the London General and eighteen in opposition to it.

Tilling also continued to act as a job master, hiring out horses and vehicles to a vast number of customers in various parts of London and then elsewhere in the country. From the outset his buses advertised 'T. Tilling, job masters, wedding carriages'. In 1864 he began to horse the Peckham fire engine and in due course other London brigades. That year he started to operate four cabs, and was soon hiring out others. He also supplied a special service for London's doctors, many of whom did not want the trouble of looking after the horse and vehicle they needed to make their rounds. Every week he provided forage and a visit from his veterinary surgeon, who attended to all aspects of the horse's welfare, including instructions for shoeing when required. John Tilling, in *Kings of the Highway*, has recalled that his great-grandfather claimed that he 'would replace a lame horse, a broken carriage or a drunken coachman within the hour' (Tilling, 45).

With such facilities available, many other Londoners soon sought Tilling's services, especially after his sons Richard and Edward joined the business in 1867 and 1872 respectively. His many well-known clients, such as Blondin, the high-wire artist, were soon joined by others. On 12 February 1873 he married a widow, Emma Sophia Buck, *née* Rawlinson. In all, he had eleven children. In 1874 Tillings got the contract to supply 113 horses to the Metropolitan Board of Works. The firm built the snow ploughs which cleared its own bus routes and other streets after a particularly heavy snowfall in 1881 had brought London to a virtual standstill. It supplied many horses and carriages for the lord mayor's show and, in 1887, twenty-six landaus, each drawn by a pair of greys, for Queen Victoria's jubilee. Tillings was later able to display the royal warrant after supplying all the horses and carriages for the royal family. By this time Thomas Tilling had built up the leading private hire business in the capital.

Tilling soon cast his eyes further afield. When a woman requested a coach and four to take a month's holiday touring round Wales, they were provided. He became involved in the finance and organizing of hiring from Durham to Cornwall. The great effort involved in this further expansion, when he was no longer young and vigorous, was said by the family to have hastened his death. He died at Swanley Cottage, Perry Hill Farm, Perry Hill, Catford, London, on 8 January 1893, aged sixty-seven. He was buried at Nunhead cemetery on 13 February. *The Times* did not consider him worthy of an obituary, though another London paper, quoted by his great-grandson, referred to his 'marvellous energy, unfailing pluck and business aptitude … [He was] the prince of organizers' (Tilling, 58).

Thomas Tilling would not, however, be so well remembered without the public company which his sons, Richard and Edward, and his son-in-law, Walter Wolsey, formed in 1897. Thomas Tilling Ltd, with an issued capital of £400,000, took over 4000 horses. The company negotiated the difficult transition from horse to motor vehicle and was, in 1907, involved in the creation of the Tilling-Stevens petrol-electric bus. It operated a number of regional bus concerns jointly with British Automobile Traction, in which Thomas Tilling Ltd acquired a considerable holding.   THEO BARKER

Sources J. Tilling, *Kings of the highway* (1957) · T. C. Barker and M. Robbins, *A history of London Transport*, 2 vols. (1963–74) · J. Hibbs, *The history of British bus services*, 2nd edn (1989) · J. Hibbs, ed., *The omnibus* (1971) · 'The London omnibus business of Thomas Tilling Ltd', *Tramway and Railway World* (7 Dec 1911) · *The Times* (7 June 1929) [obit. of Richard Stephen Tilling] · parish register (baptisms), St Marylebone, London, 22/2/1825 · m. certs. · d. cert. · *CGPLA Eng. & Wales* (1893) · b. cert. [Richard Stephen Tilling]
Likenesses photograph (after painting by L. J. Fuller), repro. in Tilling, *Kings of the highway*, facing p. 33
Wealth at death £91,026 15s. 11d.: probate, 29 March 1893, *CGPLA Eng. & Wales*

Tillinghast, John (bap. 1604, d. 1655), Fifth Monarchist, was baptized on 25 September 1604 at Streat, Sussex, the son of John Tyllinghast (d. 1624), rector of Streat. After attending grammar school at Newport, Essex, Tillinghast entered Caius College, Cambridge, as a pensioner on 24 March 1621. He graduated BA in 1625, and was ordained deacon and priest at Bristol on 2 April of the same year. He became rector of Tarring Neville, Sussex, on 30 July 1636, and then of Streat on 29 September 1637. In the sermon *Demetrius his Opposition to Reformation* (1642), dedicated to the countess of Holland, Lady Beaudesert, and his uncle, the future regicide Robert *Tichborne, Tillinghast stressed the need to continue the work of reformation and denounced illegal taxation, the subversion of the kingdom's fundamental laws, innovations in church and state, and Anabaptists, Familists, and other sectaries for endangering the Reformation. He also warned that dissension in the church normally led to divisions in the state. By late 1650 Tillinghast had become an Independent and joined the congregational church at Syleham, Suffolk. Called on 22 January 1651 by the Independent church at Great Yarmouth, Norfolk, to assist William Bridge, he accepted on 4 February. The Independent churches at Fressingfield and Walpole, Suffolk, also sought his services. Tillinghast left Great Yarmouth in early 1652 to accept the rectorship of Trunch, Norfolk. Shortly thereafter, he began writing the first part of *Generation Work*, which he addressed to parliament on 8 July 1653, and also to the saints, urging them to unify in order not to obstruct the work of reformation. If parliament ignored its reforming duties, he warned, God would overthrow it.

In *Knowledge of the Times* (1654) and the second and third parts of *Generation Work* (both 1654) Tillinghast distinguished himself as the only Fifth Monarchist capable of systematically expounding the prophetic texts on which the group's millenarian tenets were based. He was influenced by John Owen, whose sermon to parliament on 24 October 1651, *The Advantage of the Kingdome of Christ in the Shaking of the Kingdoms of the World* (1652), he had read. In *Knowledge of the Times* Tillinghast laid out the chronology of the end times, averring that the papacy would collapse in 1656 and that the millennium would commence in 1701. In the second part of *Generation Work* he interpreted the seven vials of Revelation 16 in a historical context, identifying the first with Luther's reforms; the second with the Long Parliament's repudiation of episcopacy; the third with the execution of Charles, the overthrow of the Long Parliament, the Fronde, and the mid-century conflict in the Netherlands; and the fourth with the Holy Roman empire's collapse. The fifth vial would bring the fall of the Catholic church, the sixth the demise of the Ottoman empire, and the seventh the battle of Armageddon preparatory to the Jews' conversion and Christ's return. At this point, he contended, the millennium would commence, the conclusion of which would bring the last judgment.

In a late sermon published posthumously, Tillinghast stressed that the second coming was imminent, for a key sign of the end times was 'the Defection and Apostasy of Eminent leading men in the Churches, from their first light and Principles' (J. Tillinghast, *Mr. Tillinghasts Eight Last Sermons*, 1655, 95). God's present work, he asserted, was the overthrow of 'lofty men' as well as Antichrist (ibid., 219). The attack on the government in these sermons marked a major change in Tillinghast's position, for he had dedicated the third part of *Generation Work*, with its explication of the two witnesses' prophecies in Revelation 11, to Cromwell, but by June 1655 he had turned sharply against the lord protector. He was probably influenced by the leading London Fifth Monarchist Christopher Feake, who was then imprisoned at Windsor, where Tillinghast visited him. Feake likened Tillinghast to Apollo because of his interest in prophecy. Thereafter Tillinghast went to London, where the Independent minister Nathaniel Brewster took him to see Cromwell. Tillinghast reproached Cromwell for his reputed abominations, prompting cries of 'shame' from onlookers offended by his language. Cromwell reported the incident to Charles Fleetwood. Tillinghast had intended to visit other incarcerated saints, but he died in London by the end of June. Bridge's son-in-law, Richard Lawrence, succeeded Tillinghast at Trunch.

Tillinghast's wife, Mary Flight, had died before him. In his will, dated 6 June 1655 and proved on 27 November 1655, Tillinghast left his only surviving daughter, Mary, £136 and his household goods. The will had been witnessed by his kinsman Benjamin Tillinghast and the radical bookseller Livewell Chapman, and the executors were the Suffolk Independents John Manning, rector of Sibton-cum-Peasenhall, and his brother Samuel Manning, rector of Cookley-cum-Walpole.

Feake moved quickly to publish *Mr. Tillinghasts Eight Last Sermons*, the epistle to which he dated 2 August 1655. Among the sermons were two on signs of the times, one on the fifth monarchy, and another on the period's evils. Reflecting the appeal of Tillinghast's works beyond the Fifth Monarchists, in December 1656 the Independent ministers Samuel Petto and John Manning finished editing Tillinghast's *Six Severall Treatises* (1657), a collection of sermons on such themes as Christ's promises, the life of faith, and Jesus' commandment to love one another. In 1658 Petto and the Congregationalist minister Samuel Habergham, a Fifth Monarchist, issued Tillinghast's *Elijah's Mantle*. Although Tillinghast's life was marked by his mid-career embrace of Independent polity and Fifth Monarchist tenets, two key threads provided unifying themes throughout his ministry: a strong commitment to further reform and an international perspective. Sensitive in *Demetrius* to the persecution of protestants throughout much of Europe, in his later works he urged missionary work as far afield as Turkey and India, and prophesied protestant military victories over the Catholic states, the papacy, and the Turks.

RICHARD L. GREAVES

Sources Venn, *Alum. Cant.*, 1/4.242 · *The writings and speeches of Oliver Cromwell*, ed. W. C. Abbott and C. D. Crane, 3 (1945), 756–7 · B. S. Capp, *The Fifth Monarchy Men: a study in seventeenth-century English millenarianism* (1972) · G. F. Nuttall, *Visible saints: the congregational way, 1640–1660* (1957) · C. Feake, *A beam of light* (1659) · B. S. Capp, 'Extreme millenarianism', *Puritans, the millennium and the future of Israel: puritan eschatology, 1600–1660*, ed. P. Toon (1970), 66–90 · *DNB* · J. Browne, *A history of Congregationalism and memorials of the churches in Norfolk and Suffolk* (1877) · PRO, PROB 11/251, fols. 346v–347r
Archives BL, Add. MS 15226, fol. 84
Wealth at death over £136: will, PRO, PROB 11/251, fols. 346v–347r

Tilloch, Alexander (1759–1825), journalist and inventor, was born at Glasgow on 28 February 1759, the sixth of eleven children of John Tilloch or Tulloch, tobacco merchant and member of Glasgow town council, and Elizabeth Stivenson or Stevenson. He matriculated at Glasgow University in 1771, but did not graduate. He subsequently entered a tobacco warehouse.

Tilloch became interested in practical science and reinvented stereotyping in 1781–2, in ignorance of the work done in the Netherlands at the beginning of the century and later by the Scot William Ged. In partnership with the stationer and printer Andrew Foulis the younger in 1783–6, he published a number of stereotyped books in Glasgow, deliberately choosing cheap editions so that they did not attract the attention of other printers. Together they took out a British patent, no. 1431 of 1784, for 'Printing books by plates instead of moveable types, by which a greater degree of accuracy, correctness and elegance, will be obtained'. Seventeen years later Tilloch was to summarize their process in the *Philosophical Magazine*. Foulis went to Chevening in Kent for eight months to show the process to Charles, third earl of Stanhope, and to the

printer he employed, Andrew Wilson, for which he was said to have been paid £800. Wilson developed the process and it was widely used by the time of Tilloch's death. While still in Glasgow, Tilloch married Elizabeth Simson (d. 1783) on 29 July 1780. They had one daughter, Elizabeth, who lived with her father until she married the novelist John Galt in 1812. Tilloch moved to London in 1787.

In 1789, with a number of others, Tilloch purchased a newspaper, *The Star*, which he edited until 1821. His obituary in the *Gentleman's Magazine* said: 'In this respectable paper his political opinions were mild and temperate, equally remote from the violence of party, the clamours of faction, and the unmanly servility of temporizing baseness' (*GM*, 277). Tilloch was deeply religious, and like Michael Faraday was a member of the Sandemanian church in Goswell Street. As Biblicus, he published in *The Star* papers on the book of Revelation, which were collected as *Dissertation on the Opening of the Sealed Book*, published at Arbroath in 1819. He also wrote *Dissertations introductory to the study and right understanding of the language, structure and contents of the Apocalypse* (1823).

Much of the motivation for Tilloch's activities contained a philanthropic element which was of a part with his religious views. Struck by the number of executions for forgery, he invented a method for printing banknotes which he believed would make forgery impossible. Tilloch offered it to the British government about 1790, to the Bank of England in 1797, and to a royal commission in 1818: all rejected it. The French showed interest but were unable to make it work before the Napoleonic wars interrupted communication. Tilloch's process was similar to that of Augustus Applegath, which was adopted by the bank, and Tilloch unsuccessfully petitioned parliament in 1820 for some reward. He took out patents on mill machinery and a compound steam engine, but not on his method of printing banknotes.

In 1798 Tilloch began the *Philosophical Magazine*:

> the grand Object of it is to diffuse Philosophical knowledge among every Class of Society, and to give the Public as early an Account as possible of every thing new or curious in the scientific World, both at Home and on the Continent.
> ('Preface', *Philosophical Magazine*, 1, 1798)

At first the magazine competed with William Nicholson's *Journal of Natural Philosophy, Chemistry and the Arts*, founded a few months earlier, before taking it over at the end of 1813. The plan of the *Philosophical Magazine* owed much to the widely circulated *Observations sur la physique* which Abbé François Rozier had begun in Paris in 1771: both appeared monthly and covered physics, chemistry, natural history, and the practical arts. They printed translations of important papers from foreign journals and their frequency enabled them to announce discoveries far more quickly than the transactions of learned academies, the main pre-existing means of communication. In 1822 Tilloch took on Richard Taylor as joint editor. In Tilloch's lifetime the *Philosophical Magazine* was vital for the expansion of science at a time when new fields were being opened up rapidly. As the number of scientific journals grew the status of the magazine rose until by the middle of the century it was in Britain second in prestige only to the *Philosophical Transactions* of the Royal Society. Tilloch remained interested in technical education throughout his life and with the rise of the mechanics' institutes he started the monthly *Mechanic's Oracle* in 1824.

Tilloch was proposed as a fellow of the Royal Society but he withdrew his name because he believed that as the proprietor of two periodicals, one of them scientific, he would be blackballed. He was, however, a member of the Royal Irish Academy, the Geological Society, the Society of Antiquaries, and the Society of Antiquaries of Scotland.

After several months' illness Tilloch died on 26 January 1825 at the house he shared with one of his sisters in Barnsbury Street, Islington, London. 'In private life he was amiable; in conversation, acute, intelligent and communicative; few persons possessed a clearer understanding, or a warmer heart' (*GM*, 281). The British Library has a catalogue of the sale of his collection of paintings, prints, coins, medals, and scientific instruments.

JOHN BURNETT

Sources *GM*, 1st ser., 95/1 (1825), 276–81 · A. T. [A. Tilloch], 'A brief account of the origin and progress of letter-press-plate or stereotype printing', *Philosophical Magazine*, 10 (1801), 267–77 · P. Gaskell, *The Foulis Press*, 2nd edn (1986), 364–73, 450–53 · W. I. Addison, ed., *The matriculation albums of the University of Glasgow from 1728 to 1858* (1913), 96 · T. C. Hansard, *Typographia: an historical sketch of the origin and progress of the art of printing* (1825), 820–25 · P. Gaskell, *A new introduction to bibliography* (1972), 201–5
Likenesses pencil drawing, 1815, Scot. NPG · J. Thomson, stipple, pubd 1821 (after Frazer, *c.*1820), NPG; repro. in A. Tilloch, *Mechanic's Oracle* (1825), facing p. 220

Tillotson, John (1630–1694), archbishop of Canterbury, was born at the end of September or beginning of October 1630 at Haugh End, Sowerby, Halifax, Yorkshire, the eldest of the three sons of Robert Tillotson (*d.* 1683), clothier, and his wife, Mary (*d.* 1667), daughter of Thomas Dobson of Sowerby. He was baptized on 10 October 1630 at the church of St John the Baptist, Halifax; his godfather was Joshua Witton (*d.* 1674), one of the ministers ejected in 1662. His brothers were named Joshua and Israel. Robert Tillotson later was a member of the congregational church in Sowerby gathered by Henry Root, and a friend of the presbyterian Oliver Heywood. In his prayers before his consecration in 1691 the archbishop thanked God that he was 'born of honest and religious parents, tho' of a low and obscure condition', that he was born in a time and place where 'true religion was preached and professed', and that out of his small estate his father had given him a liberal education. He was also grateful that he had not inherited the loss of understanding from which his mother had suffered for so many years (*Works*, 12.5510–12).

Cambridge, 1647–1656 Tillotson's reaction to his puritan upbringing was of enormous importance in shaping his subsequent views of theology and church discipline. Although he abandoned his father's beliefs he kept to the end of his life a deep sympathy with nonconformists for which his high-church enemies never forgave him. He belonged, crucially, to the generation of young men who

John Tillotson (1630–1694), by Sir Godfrey Kneller, 1691

were educated at Cambridge in the civil war and Commonwealth period and who turned against Calvinist theology, a generation so memorably described by Gilbert Burnet in his *History of my Own Time* (*Bishop Burnet's History*, 1.186–9). After a grammar school education Tillotson was admitted a pensioner at Clare College, Cambridge, on 23 April 1647 and matriculated on 1 July. His tutor was David Clarkson, subsequently ejected in 1662 from the living of Mortlake, Surrey, and described by Richard Baxter as 'a Divine of extraordinary worth' (*Reliquiae Baxterianae*, 3.97); his fellow students Francis Holcroft, John Denton, and James Calvert themselves became nonconformist ministers, though Denton later conformed. Clarkson's fellowship had previously been held by the royalist Peter Gunning. Tillotson supported the Independents; he wrote to Root that he felt no scruple about taking the engagement (the 1650 declaration of loyalty to the Commonwealth) and referred to the college's receding hopes of obtaining as master the Independent Thomas Goodwin (who went to Magdalen College, Oxford, in 1650; Ralph Cudworth, the somewhat reluctant master of Clare since 1645, moved to Christ's in 1654). Tillotson graduated BA in 1650, proceeded MA in 1654, and was admitted to a probationary fellowship on 14 November 1650; his first pupil, John Beardmore, was put under him on 7 April 1651. About 27 November 1651 he was elected fellow in succession to Clarkson. Tillotson's conduct in college during the interregnum was much criticized for some years after his death by the nonjurors George Hickes, Charles Leslie, Bevil Higgons, and George Smith; this should not be entirely discounted, despite the indignation of Burnet, Tillotson's biographer Thomas Birch, and other supporters. Apart from unverifiable accusations, for example that Tillotson had introduced thanks for the victory over Charles Stuart at Worcester into the college grace, the principal charge was that he had illegally held the fellowship of which Gunning had been deprived, even though his immediate predecessor was Clarkson, a charge borne out by the fact that the college on Gunning's request ejected him from the fellowship after the Restoration. Tillotson thought himself unfairly treated. In answer to Hickes's accusation in *Some Discourses upon Dr. Burnet and Dr. Tillotson* (1695) that during the interregnum the fellows had not dared oppose him because of his interest with his great masters, Denton wrote that Tillotson 'was much respected by the senior fellows'; this was confirmed by the sole surviving senior fellow from that time, James Mountain, who had himself fought for Charles I (Whiston, 1.26; Birch, *Life*, 12–14). Beardmore is explicit about the feud between the old and new fellows, but says that he 'never heard … any particular reflections upon [Tillotson] from the other party' (Beardmore, 385).

According to Beardmore's sketch of Tillotson's methods as a tutor and his religious leanings he was 'an acute logician and philosopher [and] a quick disputant' (Beardmore, 382–5). He taught in Latin, which he spoke very well; on Sundays he examined his students in English on the sermons they had heard. He had a great faculty for '*conceived* [extempore] *prayers*' (ibid.) and was 'a very attentive hearer of sermons' (ibid.), attending four every Sunday and the Wednesday lecture at Trinity Church, given in rotation by the best preachers in the university. Beardmore observes that most of the preachers were contra-remonstrants, that is, Calvinists, and that Tillotson regularly heard Thomas Hill, master of Trinity, who preached at St Michael's Church on Sunday mornings and at Trinity Church in the afternoons. Among young preachers 'of a freer temper and genius' (ibid.) Beardmore notes Simon Patrick, with whom Tillotson was later closely associated. It is very likely that he also heard the most influential of the anti-Calvinists, Benjamin Whichcote, then provost of King's College: in his funeral sermon for Whichcote (24 May 1683), Tillotson pointed out that Whichcote preached in Trinity Church every Sunday afternoon for almost twenty years (until his ejection at the Restoration), and 'contributed more to the forming of [Cambridge] students … to a sober sense of religion than any man in that age' (*Works*, 2.154).

Early career, 1657–1663 It is not clear at what date Tillotson gave up his sympathy for the Calvinist doctrine and congregational discipline of his youth. Beardmore said he 'got out of the prejudices of his education, when but a very young man in *Cambridge*, divers years before the restoration in 1660, or any prospect of it' (Beardmore, 398). According to Burnet 'he happily fell on' William Chillingworth's *Religion of Protestants*, 'which gave his mind the ply it held ever after, and put him on a true scent' (Burnet, *Sermon*, 11), but the timing is unknown. In 1656 or 1657 (though still a fellow of Clare) he left Cambridge for London in order to act as chaplain to Edmund Prideaux, Oliver Cromwell's attorney-general, and as tutor to his son.

There is no evidence that Tillotson was ordained at this stage. Through Prideaux he ensured that the college was financially compensated for materials seized by parliament during the civil war. He was present at the fast held in Whitehall a week after the protector's death on 3 September 1658, and in later years told Burnet of his revulsion at the blasphemous language used on that occasion by Thomas Goodwin and Peter Sterry, 'enough', Burnet said, 'to disgust a man for ever of that enthusiastick boldness' (*Bishop Burnet's History*, 1.82–3).

From the last years of the interregnum to the Act of Uniformity of 1662 Tillotson maintained close links with the groups who were to become nonconformists, but moved towards the episcopal church. In London he met Ralph Brownrigg, the deprived bishop of Exeter, who was preacher at the Temple in 1659, and John Hacket, later bishop of Lichfield. After the Restoration he was present for part of the abortive Savoy conference (April to July 1661) between episcopalians and so-called presbyterians on the reform of the liturgy; Baxter, principal spokesman for the latter, describes him as one of 'two or three Scholars and Lay-men, that as Auditors came in with us' (*Reliquiae Baxterianae*, 2.337). About this time he was ordained. The exact date is unknown: Beardmore and Birch suggest 1660 or early 1661, but if Baxter's description is accurate it must have been after the Savoy conference. However, Tillotson is said to have been recommended for a prebend at Ripon in 1660, where John Wilkins was the new dean. This implies an ordination date in 1660, and is difficult to square with Baxter's statement. (Neither Beardmore nor Birch refers to this episode.) Tillotson obtained episcopal ordination from Thomas Sydserf, bishop of Galloway, the only surviving Scottish bishop, who, according to *Bishop Burnet's History*, did not require oaths or subscriptions. The nonjuror George Smith suggested that Tillotson chose him for that reason. Charles II was initially keen to promote prominent puritan divines to high office in the church: Tillotson told Beardmore in 1661 that if Edmund Calamy had accepted the king's offer of the bishopric of Lichfield, William Bates would have been made dean and he would have been a canon. Tillotson preached his first sermon (date unknown) for his Cambridge friend Denton, at Oswaldkirk, Yorkshire. His first published sermon was a lecture delivered at short notice at St Giles Cripplegate in September 1661 on behalf of Bates, vicar of St Dunstan-in-the-West, which was subsequently included in *The Morning-Exercise at Cripple-Gate* (1661), edited by Samuel Annesley, rector of St Giles. Denton, Bates, and Annesley were soon ejected from their livings; Tillotson, however, chose to conform to the established church. His first office, in 1661–2, was as curate to Thomas Hacket, vicar of Cheshunt, Hertfordshire. After Calamy was ejected from St Mary Aldermanbury, Tillotson was elected to fill his place by the parishioners in December 1662, but refused their offer. He did, however, accept the presentation of the rectory of Ketton, or Kedington, Suffolk, worth £200 a year, from Sir Thomas Barnardiston in June 1663, after the ejection of Samuel Fairclough. According to the historian Edmund

Calamy, grandson of the ejected Calamy, 'it was no small Ease to Mr. *Fairclough*, that a man of that Worth did succeed him' (Calamy, 2.638). Hickes regarded this as another example of Tillotson taking another man's property to which he was not entitled. Fairclough's former parishioners were displeased for a different reason: they 'universally complain'd, that Jesus Christ had not been preach'd amongst them, since Mr. TILLOTSON had been settled in the parish' (Birch, *Life*, 18). Tillotson soon abandoned this unfortunate if lucrative rural experiment for far more prominent urban pulpits.

Mid-career, 1663–1688 After the ejection of the nonconformist ministers (24 August 1662) Tillotson became a popular and extremely influential preacher in London. He was an occasional Tuesday lecturer at St Lawrence Jewry (a sermon he published in 1694, *Of the Advantages of an Early Piety*, was preached at St Lawrence in 1662); on one such occasion when he was acting as a replacement preacher he was heard by Edward Atkyns, later baron of the exchequer, who used his influence to have Tillotson elected preacher to the Society of Lincoln's Inn (26 November 1663). The salary was £100 a year, paid at the end of each term, together with a chamber, commons (meals) for himself and his servant, and £24 for commons during the vacations. He thereupon resigned his Suffolk living. The post at Lincoln's Inn provided him with an audience both intellectually receptive and socially and politically important. In the following year he was elected to the Tuesday lectureship at St Lawrence. His sermons in these pulpits attracted 'crouds of auditors', including lawyers, city merchants, and especially members of the clergy: 'many, that heard him on *Sunday* at *Lincoln's-Inn*, went joyfully to St. *Laurence* on *Tuesday*, hoping they might hear the same sermon again' (Beardmore, 408). Tillotson steadily accumulated other pulpits and preferments which he held together with these two (St Lawrence was burnt down in the great fire of 1666 and rebuilt by Christopher Wren, 1670–86). He was invited to preach at St Paul's before the lord mayor in March 1664, and expanded the sermon the same year into his first major publication, *The Wisdom of being Religious*. He proceeded DD in 1666. His talents were recognized by the court as well as the city: he was appointed one of Charles II's chaplains, and preached from time to time before the king at Whitehall (his first such sermon seems to have been preached on 30 June 1667) and to the House of Commons. The king gave him a prebend at Canterbury (14 March 1670; his predecessor, somewhat ironically, was Gunning, now made bishop of Chichester), and promoted him dean of Canterbury (October 1672), the latter on the separate recommendations of Archbishop Gilbert Sheldon, the duke of Buckingham, and Lord Berkeley. The king also made him a prebendary and residentiary canon of St Paul's (18 December 1675, 14 February 1678), the second of these on the recommendation of John Sharp (later archbishop of York) through the influence of Heneage Finch (later earl of Nottingham). Tillotson held the preferments at Canterbury and St Paul's jointly 'in compliance with the times, and because he

would not decline what was so frankly offered him' by the king (ibid., 395).

The vicar of St Lawrence from 1662 to 1668 was John Wilkins, the most important single influence on Tillotson's intellectual development: 'that which gave him his last finishing', said Burnet, 'was his close and long Friendship with Bishop Wilkins' (Burnet, *Sermon*, 12). Tillotson said in his edition of Wilkins's *Sermons* (1682, sig. A3) that he did not know Wilkins before the Restoration (Wilkins moved from Oxford to Cambridge as master of Trinity in 1659, when Tillotson was in London), but they had a great deal in common. Both were firmly convinced of the rational basis of Christianity; both were conformists whose links with nonconformists were close; both regarded ecclesiastical organization and ceremonies as 'things indifferent'—things not prescribed in scripture, that the state had the right to determine; both opposed persecution as the way to bring nonconformists into the established church, but neither really understood the reasons for nonconformity; both thought that the pulpit, in the 1640s and 1650s the principal medium of puritan thought with all the doctrinal and political conflict that implied, should be made instead the means of propagating a moderate, reasonable, reconciling religion with a stronger emphasis on morality than on doctrine (but without devaluing the latter). Their nonconformist and high-church critics derisively labelled them and their associates 'latitude men' or 'latitudinarians'. Tillotson preached at Wilkins's consecration as bishop of Chester at Ely House on 15 November 1668 (John Evelyn was in the congregation) and subsequently spent some time helping him in his diocese in 1671 and 1672. Wilkins was succeeded at St Lawrence by another of Tillotson's formative influences, Whichcote. Tillotson helped Wilkins with his *Essay towards a Real Character, and a Philosophical Language* (publication was delayed until 1668 because of the great fire). On the nomination of Wilkins's friend Seth Ward, bishop of Salisbury and Wilkins's predecessor at St Lawrence, Tillotson was elected on 25 January 1672 a fellow of the Royal Society, of which Wilkins was the guiding spirit. Wilkins died at Tillotson's house in Chancery Lane on 19 November 1672. He made Tillotson executor of his will—on 9 October 1673 the Royal Society decided it was time to call on Tillotson for Wilkins's legacy—and left him his papers to publish at his discretion. Tillotson thus became the guardian of Wilkins's posthumous reputation.

The two men also had a familial relationship. On 23 February 1664 Wilkins officiated in St Lawrence at the marriage between Tillotson and Wilkins's stepdaughter Elizabeth French (d. 1702). (Wilkins was the second husband of Robina French, widow of Peter French and sister of Oliver Cromwell.) The Tillotsons had two daughters, who predeceased them: Elizabeth, the younger, died in 1681; Mary, the elder, married James Chadwick and left two sons and a daughter at her death in November 1687. The fact that Tillotson was related by marriage to the Cromwell family was not lost on his nonjuring critics.

Tillotson's relations with nonconformists in the reigns

of Charles II and James II remained cordial and encouraging but also cautious. He advised Beardmore in 1661 not to be sharp on them in sermons, but to win them to the church by good preaching and good living. (In this respect Tillotson was much closer to Wilkins than to his colleagues Simon Patrick and Edward Stillingfleet, who offended the nonconformists by attacking them in print and pulpit.) Beardmore was sure that Tillotson brought in great numbers of nonconformists and was the chief agent for preserving the majority of the citizens of London 'from running into extravagancies' against the government of the church (Beardmore, 400). With the apparent encouragement of Ward and George Morley, bishop of Winchester, and through the medium of Bates, in 1674 Tillotson and Stillingfleet met Baxter and drew up a draft proposal for the comprehension of nonconformists within the established church (a similar attempt made in 1668 by Wilkins and Baxter had come to nothing). But the bishops backtracked, just as Baxter had expected. Tillotson wrote to Baxter on 11 April 1675, 'I am unwilling my Name should be used in this Matter; not but that I do most heartily desire an Accommodation, and shall always endeavour it', explaining that the Comprehension Bill would not pass either house without the agreement of the king and a considerable part of the bishops (*Reliquiae Baxterianae*, 3.157). Tillotson tried in other ways to break down the barrier between conformity and nonconformity. In 1674 he became a member of the trust (which included Whichcote, Stillingfleet, and the unitarian Thomas Firmin) formed to oversee the scheme for distributing Welsh bibles set up by the ejected minister and philanthropist Thomas Gouge; in his funeral sermon for Gouge (4 November 1681) he emphasized the contributions Gouge obtained from bishops and clergy. In his sermon preached at the Yorkshire feast in London on 3 December 1678 he urged that there should be no differences between adherents of the protestant reformed religion. Only an established national religion could be a sufficient bulwark against popery; 'little sects and separate congregations' could never do it. At the same time as arguing that the continuance of nonconformity weakened the protestant cause, he gave great offence to high-churchmen by suggesting that the governors of the church in order to achieve union would give up some 'little things … to the infirmity or importunity, or, perhaps in some very few things, to the plausible exceptions' of the nonconformists (*Works*, 2.24–5).

Tillotson's Erastian view of the established church involved him in some difficulty from both the high-church and nonconformist perspectives when he preached before the king at Whitehall on 2 April 1680. The sermon was subsequently entitled 'The protestant religion vindicated from the charge of singularity and novelty'. Hickes seized with glee on this episode. At one point Tillotson claimed that conscience did not warrant any man without an extraordinary commission confirmed by miracles, such as the apostles had, to affront the established religion of a nation, even if it were false, and to draw men off from it, in contempt of the law. All that persons of a different religion could do was enjoy the private liberty and exercise of their own conscience and religion (*Works*, 2.253). This was regarded as Hobbism by a lord who heard it and told the dozing king, who immediately commanded its publication. When the nonconformist John Howe read it he expostulated with Tillotson that he had used a sermon against popery to plead the popish cause, and he reduced him to tears. Tillotson's old antagonist Gunning made the same complaint in the Lords. Evelyn thought the whole discourse incomparable.

Despite his many London commitments Tillotson was active throughout these years in the archdiocese of Canterbury. As prebendary (1670–72) and dean (1672–89) of Canterbury he was required by statute to spend at least ninety days a year in residence, twenty-one of them continuous; according to Burnet he more than fulfilled this requirement. In 1683 he was responsible for introducing the weekly celebration of the eucharist in the cathedral. However, in some quarters it was felt that London drew him away: George Thorp, another prebendary and chaplain to William Sancroft, archbishop of Canterbury, suggested unsuccessfully to Sancroft in 1684 that Tillotson be given a living in the diocese so that he could leave Lincoln's Inn.

Tillotson's advice to Lord Russell before his execution in 1683 for his part in the Rye House plot was to be thrown in his face after the revolution. He and Burnet, who both attended Russell in the Tower and on the scaffold, took pains 'to persuade him of the unlawfulness of taking arms against the king in any case' (*Supplement to Burnet's History*, 130), even if, as Russell put it, 'our religion and rights should be invaded'. Russell was unconvinced, so Tillotson wrote a letter to the condemned man (on 20 July 1683), soon published against the writer's wishes. Here he argued that the Christian religion forbade resistance to authority; that the same law which established the Church of England also declared that it was unlawful to take up arms against authority on any pretence; and that Russell's opinion was contrary to the doctrine of all the protestant churches. Burnet tried to defend Tillotson against Hickes's accusation that at the revolution of 1688 he had apostatized from the doctrine of non-resistance with the argument that he 'was restrained by some particular considerations from mentioning … the case of a total subversion of the constitution, which he thought would justify resistance' (Birch, *Life*, 114–15).

There was no restraint in Tillotson's repeatedly expressed hostility to Catholicism in this period. Beardmore commented 'that he scarcely ever preach'd a sermon, without some very home-blow against' popery (Beardmore, 393). He believed that Catholics had burnt the city on purpose in 1666. When Charles II complained to Sheldon in 1672 about the orchestrated preaching of the London clergy against Catholicism Tillotson suggested as an answer that 'it would be a thing without a precedent, that he should forbid his Clergy to preach in defence of a religion which they believed, while he himself said he was of it' (*Bishop Burnet's History*, 1.308–9). The

Catholic duke of York was so offended by his sermon 'The hazard of being saved in the church of Rome' (April 1672; privately printed, 1673) that he ceased attending the Chapel Royal. When the duke became King James II, Tillotson was one of several clergy, including Stillingfleet, Patrick, and Thomas Tenison, his successor as archbishop, who directed a 'controversial war' against Catholicism in 1686 (ibid., 1.674), and the king complained to Sancroft specifically about Tillotson, Patrick, and Stillingfleet for preaching so much on the subject. When in the following year James II forced Laurence Hyde, earl of Rochester, to have a conference about his religion in his presence with two Catholic priests and two Church of England clergy, with the object of converting Rochester to Rome, Burnet considered that 'The king did in this matter great honour to my two friends Tillotson and Stillingfleet, for he excepted against them', so Rochester chose William Jane and Patrick instead (*Supplement to Burnet's History*, 224). Tillotson was a member of the conference held at Lambeth by Sancroft on 18 May 1688, which led to the decision to disobey James's order that his declaration of indulgence, aimed at Catholics as much as nonconformists, should be read in all churches.

Tillotson had lost the favour of Charles II towards the end of his reign, and never won that of James II. He bought a house at Edmonton, Middlesex, where he could retire during this difficult period. Nevertheless he continued preaching at Lincoln's Inn and St Lawrence 'with his usual freedom, or rather with greater zeal and fervency' against Catholicism (Beardmore, 394). He had many visitors, and his conversation was much valued. Despite the loss of his remaining daughter he had the consolation of friendships kept up by letters with Robert Nelson, soon to be a nonjuror, and Lady Rachel Russell, widow of the executed whig, many of which are included in Thomas Birch's *Life*. In the final, most public stage of his life he was to be far more isolated.

Writer, controversialist, and editor Tillotson published six collections of his writings: four designed as a sequence, his *Sermons Preach'd upon Several Occasions* (1671), *Sermons Preach'd upon Several Occasions … the Second Volume* (1678), *Sermons and Discourses … the Third Volume* (1686), and *Sermons Preach'd upon Several Occasions … the Fourth Volume* (1694); and two other important collections, *Sermons Concerning the Divinity and Incarnation of our Blessed Saviour* (1693) and *Six Sermons* (1694). He also published a large number of sermons separately, and his first three volumes in revised editions. He always wrote out his sermons before delivery in the pulpit (some autograph shorthand examples survive at the Bodleian as MS Rawlinson E. 125), and he revised them meticulously for publication and between editions. His object was evidently through artful rewriting to give the reader the illusion of fluent speech. Joseph Spence noted that 'Some of the sermons of Archbishop Tillotson which seem easiest to be wrote and the least laboured, were found several of them wrote over the eighth or ninth time in his study' (Spence, 1.323, no. 794). He deliberately avoided pedantry, in the form of Latin quotations and references to authorities, and rhetorical tropes and ornaments; he set out to differentiate his practice from that of witty high-church preachers of the earlier part of the century and more recent enthusiastic puritans and nonconformists who worked on their readers' emotions. He strongly supported the theories of Wilkins and the Royal Society on the reform of prose style, which included a pronounced distrust of metaphor. Like Wilkins he thought the misuse of metaphor responsible for doctrinal error. According to Burnet he prepared himself by studying the scriptures, 'all the antient Philosophers and Books of Morality', and the works of Basil and Chrysostom. His work with Wilkins on the *Essay towards a Real Character* 'led him to consider exactly the Truth of Language and Stile, in which no Man was happier, and knew better the Art of preserving the Majesty of things under a Simplicity of Words' (Burnet, *Sermon*, 13). Beardmore said 'his endeavour was to make all things clear, to bring truth into open light; and his arguments of persuasion were strong and nervous, and tended to gain the affections by the understanding' (Beardmore, 409). He defined his religious position in relation to four main groups: the two intellectual targets to whom he was unremittingly hostile, atheists and Catholics, and the two groups from whom he carefully dissociated himself but with whom he retained ties of friendship, the nonconformists and the Socinians or unitarians. To atheists and Catholics he stressed the rational grounds of faith and the close connection between natural and revealed religion; to nonconformists that justification included obedience and faith included works; and to Socinians that Christianity required the acceptance of mysteries incomprehensible to reason. His collections were carefully structured to lead the reader through arguments for natural religion and the advantages, both worldly and otherworldly, of practising the precepts of revealed religion, culminating in a carefully restrained exposition of its mysteries. He gave the greatest weight to Christian practice. Burnet summed up his position very fairly as follows:

> He indeed judged that the great design of Christianity was the reforming Mens Natures, and governing their Actions, the restraining their Appetites, and Passions, the softning their Tempers, and sweetning their Humours, the composing their Affections, and the raising their minds above the Interests and Follies of this present World, to the hope and pursuit of endless Blessedness: And he considered the whole Christian Doctrine as a System of Principles, all tending to this.   (Burnet, *Sermon*, 31–2)

In the course of the 1660s Tillotson shifted his attack from atheism and infidelity (his target in *The Wisdom of being Religious*) to Catholicism. According to Burnet he did this because 'he saw that Popery was at the root of this, and that the Design seemed to be laid, to make us first Atheists, that we might be the more easily made Papists' (Burnet, *Sermon*, 15). In 1666 he published *The Rule of Faith*, an attack on *Sure-Footing in Christianity, or, Rational Discourses on the Rule of Faith* (1665) by the Catholic apologist John Sergeant, who had attacked Stillingfleet's *Rational Account of* the *Grounds of the Protestant Religion* (1664) in his third appendix. Tillotson dedicated his book to Stillingfleet, and included as an appendix a reply by Stillingfleet to Sergeant; he went on to make a lengthy attack on Sergeant's ironically titled *Letter of Thanks* (1666) in the preface to his first collection of sermons (1671). *The Rule of Faith* was a contribution to a long-running debate going back to the anti-Catholic writing of William Laud and William Chillingworth in the 1630s; its philosophical importance lies in its attempt to define the basis of certainty, the relation between reason and faith, and the grounds of assent to Christian doctrine. Tillotson further developed part of his argument in *A Discourse Against Transubstantiation* (1684, included in the third volume of 1686).

Later in his career Tillotson turned his attention to a completely different target, Socinianism or unitarianism (which denied the doctrine of the Trinity on scriptural grounds), but his tone here was much more accommodating. He had long been a friend of the Socinian philanthropist Firmin, who, according to Stephen Nye, knew all the London divines and had provided preachers for St Lawrence when Tillotson was busy as dean at Canterbury. In 1679–80 Tillotson preached a group of four sermons on the divinity of Christ; he published these in 1693 partly to counter the malicious accusations of nonjuring critics that he was himself a Socinian, and partly for Firmin's benefit. He thought the Socinians (unlike the Catholics, whom he held in contempt) 'a pattern of the fair way of disputing', but they had one great defect: truth was not on their side (*Works*, 3.244–5). The unpersuaded Firmin engaged Nye to write an answer, *Considerations on the … Doctrine of the Trinity* (1694); after reading it Tillotson told Firmin, 'My Lord of Sarum [Burnet] *shall humble your Writers*', but he continued their friendship unaltered (Nye, 17).

Tillotson served an extremely valuable function as an editor, scrutinizer, and promoter of other men's writings. In 1675 he published what proved the most influential and popular of Wilkins's works, *Of the Principles and Duties of Natural Religion*, with a preface explaining his contribution (Wilkins had left twelve chapters prepared for the press, and Tillotson edited fourteen more) and summarizing the book's argument. In 1682 he brought out the second collection of Wilkins's sermons; his prefatory essay, 'The publisher to the reader', contains an interesting account of their author, whom he defended energetically from the attack in Anthony Wood's *Historia et antiquitates universitatis Oxoniensis* (1674). He also acted as literary executor to Isaac Barrow. In 1680 he published Barrow's anti-Catholic *Treatise of the Pope's Supremacy*, for which Barrow gave him permission on his deathbed. He worked for ten years on Barrow's sermons, only one of which had appeared in print in his lifetime: he published a number of separate collections, and the *Works* in a three-volume folio edition (1683–7). (The accusation by Barrow's nineteenth-century editor Alexander Napier that Tillotson extensively altered the sermons has been conclusively refuted by Irène Simon.) He also edited Hezekiah Burton's posthumous *Discourses* (1684–5).

In addition to acting as literary executor Tillotson read and commented on his friends' work in progress and gave them valuable advice. He was probably the 'judicious and learned Friend, a Man indefatigably zealous in the service of the Church and State' referred to by John Dryden in the preface to *Religio laici* (1682), the friend who advised the poet to omit his bold criticism of Athanasius (Brown, 'Dryden's *Religio laici*'). He helped the nonconformist Samuel Cradock with writing his *Harmony of the Four Evangelists* (1668), and another nonconformist, Matthew Poole, with the subscriptions for his *Synopsis criticorum* (1669–76). The person to whom he gave most help of this kind was Burnet. Tillotson, William Lloyd (later bishop of Worcester), and Stillingfleet were asked by Burnet to read the manuscript of his *History of the Reformation of the Church of England*, a work that proved central to anti-Catholic polemic in the 1680s; Burnet thanked them effusively in his preface to the first volume (1679). Tillotson may have had a hand in Burnet's life of John Wilmot, earl of Rochester (1680). When he became archbishop he enlisted Burnet in his and Mary II's campaign for church reform. Burnet's *Discourse of the Pastoral Care* (1692) was written at the suggestion of Tillotson and the queen; Tillotson read it in manuscript and told Burnet, 'The work is as perfect in its kind, as I hope to see any thing' (Birch, *Life*, 266). Burnet's *Exposition of the Thirty-Nine Articles* (1699) was written as a result of a similar request; Tillotson read it in manuscript, made some alterations, and congratulated Burnet on his treatment of some very difficult theological questions. He also asked Burnet to contribute to his proposed new book of homilies, a scheme which came to nothing; Burnet, however, was to publish his contribution in 1713. A work with which Tillotson became associated in a rather different way is the *Historia Inquisitionis* (1692) by the Dutch remonstrant theologian Philip van Limborch. Limborch wrote to their mutual friend John Locke on 17 June 1692, saying that he wanted to dedicate the *Historia* to Tillotson. Tillotson agreed, subject to checking the text of the dedication, and a copy of the book duly reached him in November. In the dedication approved by Tillotson, Limborch praised him as chosen by providence so that under his influence the reformed churches might lay aside their disputes and unite in support of the gospel against the cruelty of Rome; it illustrates both his growing international reputation and the way in which he wanted his career to be understood.

The final stage, 1689–1694 Tillotson felt unqualified admiration for the new monarchs, William III and Mary II. He believed that God 'in great mercy to a most sinful and perverse people' had set them on the throne of the three kingdoms 'to be our deliverers and benefactors for many generations yet to come' (prayers before his consecration, *Works*, 12.5510). They embodied his two main aims: William was to unite his protestant subjects and deliver them from popery, and Mary was to effect their religious and moral reformation by her example. He saw these hopes only partly fulfilled. Among other London clergy Tillotson was recommended for preferment to the prince of Orange by Burnet in December 1688 (he may have met the prince and princess at Canterbury in 1677, but he was not involved in the invitation extended to William). He preached before the prince at St James's on 6 January 1689, and gave 'A thanksgiving sermon for our deliverance' at Lincoln's Inn on 31 January, the official thanksgiving day. When Patrick published his own sermon delivered on the same occasion he met with such obloquy that Tillotson published his, so Patrick said, 'that I might not stand single, but they might have somebody else to rail at as well as me' (*Auto-biography*, 142–3). Tillotson was soon promoted: the new king on his accession made him one of his chaplains, and on 27 April his clerk of the closet. At this time Tillotson let it be known that he did not wish to be a bishop. However, in August the chapter of Canterbury Cathedral gave him archiepiscopal jurisdiction, following Archbishop Sancroft's suspension for refusing to recognize the new monarchs, and in September William agreed to move him from the deanery of Canterbury to that of St Paul's (he was installed on 21 November), following Stillingfleet's promotion as bishop of Worcester. This was the limit of Tillotson's ambition, but William indicated that he intended in due course to make him archbishop of Canterbury. The dismayed Tillotson blamed Burnet for this arrangement (letter to Lady Russell, 19 Sept 1689; Birch, *Life*, 205–6).

The year 1689 saw the lasting failure of Tillotson's hope for the comprehension of the nonconformists within the established church. In 1688 Sancroft had made conciliatory moves towards them as a way of making them allies against James II's attempt to tolerate Catholics, and had formed a committee, of which Tillotson was a member, with the intention of making alterations to the liturgy in order to bring the nonconformists in. According to Patrick, on 14 January 1689 Tillotson, Patrick, and others met at Stillingfleet's house to discuss the preparation of a comprehension bill, apparently with Sancroft's permission. But under William comprehension was less important to nonconformists than toleration, and it was deeply unappealing to most churchmen. After the withdrawal of the Comprehension Bill and the passing of the Toleration Act (24 May), William agreed that the question of comprehension should be considered by convocation (the assembly of the clergy) before it went to parliament again, and on 13 September he set up an ecclesiastical commission to prepare matters. This procedure, which Tillotson recommended to the king, proved disastrous, but Tillotson optimistically sent a list of 'Concessions, which will probably be made by the church of *England* for the union of Protestants' to Lord Portland on the same day. The members of the commission, initially consisting of ten bishops and twenty other divines, including Tillotson, were to make recommendations concerning the liturgy and canons, the ecclesiastical courts, and clerical conduct to convocation, parliament, and king. They met regularly in October and November (Tillotson attended fourteen sessions), but many high-church members either failed to appear or dropped out. The hard core, who included Tillotson, Stillingfleet, Patrick, Burnet, Tenison, Richard Kidder, and John Williams (later bishop of Chichester), produced a revised liturgy in the form of an interleaved folio prayer book (Lambeth MS 2173, text in Fawcett), in which there were many concessions to nonconformist sensibilities. But this liturgy was never discussed by convocation, which met first in late November, and never reached parliament. Tillotson was the comprehenders' nominee for prolocutor of the lower house of convocation, but the high-church candidate, William Jane, easily defeated him. After fruitless exchanges between the two houses of bishops and clergy convocation was prorogued and dissolved (January 1690). Comprehension was now a lost cause.

William pressured Tillotson into accepting the archbishopric partly by telling him that if he refused he would not fill any of the bishoprics held by nonjurors. Tillotson capitulated in October 1690, but succeeded in delaying his appointment until the following year. The nonjuror Henry Dodwell wrote to warn him on 12 May 1691 that by accepting he would 'make it impossible for the Catholick [which is to say, universal] Church to subsist, as distinct & independent on the State; which will fundamentally overthrow the very Being of a Church as a Society' (G. Every, *The High Church Party, 1688–1718*, 1956, 66). Tillotson was nominated on 23 April 1691 and consecrated on 31 May at St Mary-le-Bow by, among others, bishops Burnet and Stillingfleet; the sermon was preached by Ralph Barker, later his chaplain and editor. Sancroft was still living at Lambeth Palace until his ejection on 23 June. Tillotson was granted the emoluments of the see, backdated to the previous autumn; he moved into Lambeth on 26 November, having made many repairs and improvements, including the building of a new apartment for his wife. Evelyn, who was shown the house, furniture, and garden by Tillotson's successor Tenison, described them as 'all very fine, & far beyond the usual ABshops' (6 July 1695; Evelyn, 5.213).

Tillotson told Lady Russell on 23 June 1691 that 'The Queen's extraordinary favour to me, to a degree much beyond my expectation, is no small support to me' (Birch, *Life*, 249). In his three and a half years as archbishop, with Burnet's assistance he worked closely with Mary on a programme to reform the manners of the people in general and the clergy in particular. His position gave him more privacy than before, and the opportunity to revise his sermons: though he thought 'the reformation of this corrupt and degenerate age in which we live is almost utterly to be despaired of', he published his *Six Sermons* (1694) on family religion and education in order to help 'recover the decayed piety and virtue of the present age' (*Works*, 3.395–6). Mary and he organized an elaborate series of national fasts and thanksgivings in connection with William's military campaigns. Large numbers of sermons preached at court were published, at least nine of them by Tillotson. In 1692, after meeting his bishops at Lambeth, he instructed them by letter to exercise control of clerical ordinations and residence and remove scandalous clergy, and to enforce the moral discipline of their congregations, a programme that had already been set out in a letter from the king to the bishop of London, Henry Compton, in 1690, and that was embodied in the clerical handbook Tillotson admired so much, Burnet's *Discourse of the Pastoral Care*. In August 1694, after another such meeting with his bishops, he decided to follow Burnet's suggestion that the injunctions he had drafted should be issued by the king and queen, partly 'that their Majesties care and concernment for our religion might more manifestly appear to the general satisfaction of the nation' (Birch, *Life*, 310). The injunctions required the bishops among other things to ensure that the clergy led exemplary lives, regularly held public prayers and celebrated communion frequently, and fulfilled their pastoral duties. This scheme had the queen's approval. However, the deaths of both archbishop and queen later that year meant that the injunctions were not issued by King William until the following February.

Tillotson presided over a divided church. Though dearly loved by his latitudinarian colleagues and many nonconformists, he was hated by some of the nonjurors (a bundle of their libels was found among his papers after his death), and distrusted by many of the clergy. Burnet was convinced that he 'was persecuted by Malice to his grave' (G. Burnet, *Discourse of the Pastoral Care*, preface to 3rd edn, 1713, sig. A9). One of Tillotson's last letters to Burnet (23 October 1694), on the latter's *Exposition of the Thirty-Nine Articles*, indicates why he was so controversial: he wrote dismissively of the Athanasian creed (which required acceptance of the doctrine of the Trinity and anathematized anti-Trinitarians), 'I wish we were well rid of it' (Birch, *Life*, 315). Yet the manner of his death shows his capacity for transcending party rancour. A few days after suffering a stroke in the chapel at Whitehall he died on 22 November 1694 in the arms of his nonjuring friend Nelson. He was buried on 30 November in St Lawrence Jewry, the church with which he had been associated for thirty years, as recorded in the monument erected by his wife. Burnet's laudatory funeral sermon was judged by Calamy not to exceed the truth (Calamy, 1.537). The king told Tillotson's son-in-law James Chadwick, 'He was the best man, that I ever knew, and the best Friend, that I ever had' (Birch, *Life*, 424).

Tillotson spent all his income on charity and the expenses of his position. According to *The Tatler*, no. 101 (1 December 1709), after her husband's death Elizabeth Tillotson would have been left 'in a narrow Condition' (Bond, *Tatler*, 2.122) had not the copyright of his sermons brought in £2500 (Birch gives the figure in guineas). Probably no thought had been given to providing for the first widow of an archbishop of Canterbury since the Reformation. The king granted her an annuity of £400 on 2 May 1695, increased by £200 on 18 August 1698, following her son-in-law's death and representations made on her behalf by William Sherlock and Nelson. She was responsible for educating Tillotson's nephew Robert—his brother Joshua's son, who, like his uncle, became a fellow of Clare College—and her three Chadwick grandchildren. Birch obtained some information from Tillotson's great-nephew Joshua, his brother Israel's grandson, surmaster of St Paul's School; Sir Philip Nichols, author of the article on Tillotson in the *Biographia Britannica*, knew Robert Tillotson in Cambridge between 1722 and 1728.

Reputation and influence At the time of his death Tillotson seemed to his supporters to have saved the church, and to his detractors to have reduced it to an instrument of the state. His two elegists, Nahum Tate and Samuel Wesley, celebrated his triumphs over 'Gigantick *Atheism*', '*Rome's Dragon*', and 'the *Polish Monster*' Socinianism (N. Tate, *An Elegy on … John, Late Lord Archbishop of Canterbury*, 1695, 6; S. Wesley, *Elegies on the Queen and Archbishop*, 1695, 20–22). George Hickes, repudiating Burnet's saintly portrait, called him 'a Person of great and dangerous Example, both to present Times and Posterity' and 'a Man of all Times, and all Governments, Right or Wrong' (Hickes, sig. bv, 52). In the century following his death Tillotson was widely read and admired, and sometimes berated, misused, and argued with; he exercised a continuing influence in many fields, the pulpit, literature, lexicography, education, philosophy, and theology.

Burnet's account of Tillotson as preacher remained true for many years: 'His Sermons were so well heard and liked, and so much read, that all the Nation proposed him as a Pattern, and studied to copy after him' (*Bishop Burnet's History*, 2.135). By the time of his death fifty-four sermons and *The Rule of Faith* had appeared, but he left 200 unpublished; these were edited by Ralph Barker in fourteen volumes from 1695 to 1704, with a dedication to the king by Elizabeth Tillotson. According to Birch a sermon attacking the nonjurors was suppressed at this time and probably lost. Up to 1735 there were ten collected editions of the fifty-four sermons and *The Rule of Faith*; between 1712 and 1735 there were five editions of Barker's posthumous collection of the 200 sermons; in 1728 the two collections were brought together, totalling 254 sermons and *The Rule of Faith*. In 1752 Birch in his new edition increased the number to 255 by including Tillotson's sermon in Annesley's *Morning-Exercise at Cripple-Gate*. Tillotson's contribution to this last collection was flagged in the second edition of *Athenae Oxonienses* by Anthony Wood, with the ironic description of Tillotson as 'then a Nonconformist, since gainer of considerable Preferments' (Wood, *Ath. Oxon.*, 2nd edn, 2 vols., 1721, 2.968). Twenty years after Birch's edition of 1752 a collection of the works was published in Edinburgh. There was no nineteenth-century collected edition.

Country clerics found these readily available editions invaluable. In *The Spectator*, no. 106 (2 July 1711), Sir Roger de Coverley informs Mr Spectator that together with the living he presented the village parson with 'all the good Sermons which have been printed in *English*, and only begged of him that every *Sunday* he would pronounce one of them in the Pulpit' (Steele and Addison, 1.441). The list for the year is headed by Tillotson. Other users were more subtle. The mid-century sermons of Laurence Sterne and

James Woodforde, like those of so many of their colleagues, are full of echoes and borrowings from Tillotson.

Reliance on Tillotson's works was by no means limited to the clergy. Congreve's telling comment on Dryden, first published in his dedication of Dryden's *Dramatick Works* (1717), was regularly repeated in the biographical dictionaries: 'I have heard him frequently own with pleasure, that if he had any talent for English Prose, it was owing to his having often read the writings of the great Archbishop *Tillotson*' (Bayle and others, 4.685, n. EE). Locke championed Tillotson as a model for clearness and propriety of language in 'Some thoughts concerning reading and study for a gentleman', first published in 1720. Nelson advised his godson George Hanger, who was going to Smyrna as a merchant, to study his works not only to learn 'true notions of religion, but also the way and manner of writing English correctly and purely; his style I take to be the best standard of the English language' (C. F. Secretan, *Memoirs of … Robert Nelson*, 1860, 199–200). This view was shared by eighteenth-century lexicographers: Joseph Addison marked phrases in the sermons Tillotson published in his lifetime for a projected dictionary, Alexander Pope included Tillotson in a list for a similar venture (Spence, 1.170 [no. 389]), and Samuel Johnson cited him over 1000 times in his *Dictionary* (1755), far more often than Stillingfleet, Burnet, or Wilkins.

Tillotson's presence can also be traced in guides for students published right through the century. In a letter to Richard King of 25 August 1703 (first published in 1714) Locke wrote in answer to a request for advice:

> if you desire a larger View of the Parts of Morality, I know not where you will find them so well and distinctly explain'd, and so strongly inforc'd, as in the Practical Divines of the Church of England. The Sermons of Dr. Barrow, Archbishop Tillotson, and Dr. Whitchcot, are Masterpieces in this kind. (*Correspondence of John Locke*, 8.57)

Wilkins's handbook *Ecclesiastes*, as revised by John Williams on Tillotson's instructions for the seventh edition of 1693 and dedicated to him, and further revised in the eighth edition of 1704, adds the names of the major latitudinarian authors of the previous thirty years to Wilkins's reading lists, including of course Tillotson himself. The Cambridge Calvinist John Edwards objected strongly to this procedure in his own handbook *The Preacher* (1705): complaining of the great degeneracy from Reformation doctrines in some churchmen in late times he emphasized that Wilkins's original lists consisted of orthodox Calvinist writers, and that the recent editors of *Ecclesiastes* had 'filled it with a great deal of Trash' (J. Edwards, *The Preacher*, 2nd edn, 1705, xxii). Tillotson's name is pointedly omitted from Edwards's own 'Catalogue of some authors who may be beneficial to young preachers and students in divinity'. A much more positive view of Tillotson was taken by the high-churchman Daniel Waterland in his *Advice to a Young Student* (first published in 1730 but written twenty-five years earlier for the use of his students at Magdalene College, Cambridge, and reissued in a revised edition in 1755). The four-year course for the divinity student is divided into three categories, philosophical, classical, and religious. In the table of religious books for the second year, only one author is recommended: Tillotson. Waterland does, however, warn the student, 'There is one or two Points of Doctrine, particularly that of Hell-Torments, justly exceptionable' (1730, 22, 24). (The reference here is to Tillotson's sermon of 7 March 1690, which caused great offence through the suggestion that hell torments might not be eternal. There is a long note on this topic in Birch's article on Tillotson in *A General Dictionary*, 9.575–6, n. N.) As a young man the dissenting educationist Philip Doddridge was unsympathetic to the mid-seventeenth-century Calvinist tradition; in a letter of 1722 he wrote, 'In practical divinity, Tillotson is my principal favourite' (*Calendar of the Correspondence of Philip Doddridge*, ed. G. F. Nuttall, 1979, 2, no. 8). In his *Lectures on Preaching* (containing lectures delivered in the 1730s and 1740s, but not published until 1804), Doddridge included an account of the writers of the established church and explained his admiration for Tillotson:

> There is such an easiness in his style, and beautiful simplicity of expression, as seems easy to be imitated; yet nothing more difficult … in controversy no man found such lucky arguments, nor represented the sentiments of his adversaries more fully, artfully, and advantageously for confutation. (1821 edn, lecture 4, 25)

A late example of the educational use of Tillotson is to be found in *A Collection of Theological Tracts* (1785) by Richard Watson, regius professor of divinity at Cambridge. Although no work by Tillotson is included among the tracts, in the lengthy 'Catalogue of books in divinity' (appended to volume 6) Tillotson's works are recommended several times, together with Birch's *Life*, and Watson's admiration for Tillotson and his latitudinarian contemporaries is frequently stressed.

Throughout the century many writers of different persuasions made use of or responded to specific aspects of Tillotson's arguments. Early eighteenth-century freethinkers often associated themselves with Tillotson and drew on his assumed sympathy for their views about the role of reason to bolster their positions. The third earl of Shaftesbury quotes at length from *The Rule of Faith* in the final chapter of *Characteristicks* in support of freethinking, nominating Tillotson together with Jeremy Taylor 'Free-*thinking Divines*' (2nd edn, 1714, 3.329–34, 297). Anthony Collins in *A Discourse of Free-Thinking* (1713) notoriously praised Tillotson as one 'whom all *English Free-Thinkers* own as their Head, and whom even the Enemys of *Free-Thinking* will allow to be a proper Instance to my purpose' (p. 171). Jonathan Swift's parody, *Mr. C—ns's Discourse of Free-Thinking* (1713), has been wrongly interpreted by some modern readers as supporting the same view. '[N]one better understood Human Nature' than Tillotson, claimed Matthew Tindal in *Christianity as Old as the Creation* (1730, 64). David Hume developed the argument that Tillotson had used against transubstantiation and in defence of miracles (in 'The hazard of being saved in the church of Rome' and elsewhere) as the basis for his attack on miracles in his *Philosophical Essays* (1748). Edmund Gibson, bishop of London, who defended Tillotson and his colleagues in his *Second Pastoral Letter* (1730), was anxious to prevent them being misread as rationalists; Gibson emphasized in reply to Tindal that the arguments of Wilkins and Tillotson about reason and morality should be understood historically, as responses to the tradition of puritan preaching.

Just as Tillotson's name was invoked on both sides in the debate about freethinking and the sufficiency of natural religion without revealed, so it figured in the Methodist debate about formal or nominal versus inward Christianity. In *Three Letters from the Reverend Mr. G. Whitefield* (1740), published in Philadelphia, Whitefield defended an earlier statement 'That Archbishop Tillotson *knew no more about* true *Christianity than* Mahomet' on the grounds that Tillotson 'knew of no other than a bare historical Faith: And as to … our Justification by Faith alone (which is the doctrine of Scripture and of the Church of England), he certainly was as ignorant thereof as Mahomet himself'. He claimed that he had heard this view first from John Wesley (pp. 2–3). In an early unpreached sermon, 'Hypocrisy in Oxford' (written in 1741, published in 1797), Wesley did attack Tillotson for teaching that good works were necessary to justification. However, Wesley came to take a more lenient view: in volume 45 of *A Christian Library* (1755) he extracted two of Tillotson's sermons with the comment that he had done it for those who were unreasonably prejudiced for and those unreasonably prejudiced against Tillotson. Readers would be able to judge impartially 'that the Archbishop was as far from being the *worst*, as from being the *best* of the English writers' (*A Christian Library*, 2nd edn, ed. T. Jackson, 30 vols., 1819–27, 27.3).

Tillotson as rationalist and moralist had his eighteenth-century supporters and detractors, and so did Tillotson the Socinian sympathizer. Locke lamented to Limborch after Tillotson's death that there was now scarcely anyone whom he could consult freely about theological uncertainties (11 Dec 1694; *Correspondence of John Locke*, 5.238). The Huguenot Jean Le Clerc published a lengthy adulatory account in volume 7, article 8, of his *Bibliothèque choisie* (1705), with a long analysis of the hell torments sermon, and a general defence of Tillotson against the charge of Socinianism that was to be much quoted: 'accusation qu'on n'a presque jamais manqué de faire contre ceux qui ont mieux raisonné, que le Vulgaire, & qui ont préféré les expressions de l'Ecriture Sainte au langage des Scholastiques' (p. 290): 'an accusation almost always made against those who have used their reason better than the vulgar, and who have preferred the expressions of Holy Scripture to the language of the scholastics'. In the later eighteenth century a prominent unitarian came forward to claim Tillotson as a forebear. In *Vindiciae Priestleianae* (1788), a defence of Joseph Priestley against the high-churchman George Horne, the Anglican turned unitarian Theophilus Lindsey provided a particular reading of the latitudinarian tradition of Whichcote, Tillotson, and Burnet through Locke, Samuel Clarke, and Benjamin Hoadly to Francis Blackburne, Edmund Law, and William Paley, which saw it as leading inevitably to unitarianism. On the

evidence partly of Tillotson's funeral sermon for Whichcote, Lindsey singled out Tillotson as a theologian like Priestley who believed that Christianity was a perpetual enquiry after truth and that the creed of a Christian could not be fixed.

The modern reader who goes through Tillotson's works sympathetically in the light of the contemporary controversies in which he was engaged—about the function of reason in religion, the relation between faith and works, the comprehension and/or toleration of nonconformists, the reform of the liturgy, the role of Jesus as sacrifice and example—becomes aware that he was performing with considerable success a delicate balancing act. That this balance worked for most eighteenth-century Anglicans (and for some dissenters) is clear from Tillotson's stature as measured by the editions of his works and his literary and educational roles. To others who did not appreciate it Tillotson provided an example, depending on the interpreter's point of view, of the rationalist who did not dare to see where his rationalism led, or the moralist who had contributed to the undoing of Reformation protestantism.

ISABEL RIVERS

Sources T. Birch, *The life of the most reverend Dr. John Tillotson, lord archbishop of Canterbury, compiled chiefly from his original papers and letters*, 2nd edn (1753) · J. Beardmore, 'Some memorials of the most reverend Dr. John Tillotson, late lord archbishop of Canterbury', in T. Birch, *The life of the most reverend Dr. John Tillotson, lord archbishop of Canterbury, compiled chiefly from his original papers and letters*, 2nd edn (1753), appx 1, 381–415 · *The works of the most reverend Dr. John Tillotson, lord archbishop of Canterbury*, ed. R. Barker, 12 vols. (1742–4) · G. Burnet, *A sermon preached at the funeral of the most reverend father in God John* [*Tillotson*] … *lord archbishop of Canterbury* (1694) · I. Simon, *Three Restoration divines: Barrow, South, Tillotson*, 2 vols. (1967–76) · I. Rivers, *Reason, grace, and sentiment: a study of the language of religion and ethics in England, 1660–1780*, 1 (1991), chap. 2 · B. J. Shapiro, *John Wilkins, 1614–1672: an intellectual biography* (1969) · [P. Nichols], 'Tillotson (John)', *Biographia Britannica, or, The lives of the most eminent persons who have flourished in Great Britain and Ireland*, vol. 6, pt 1 (1763), pp. 3944–54 · [T. Birch], 'Tillotson (John)', in P. Bayle and others, *A general dictionary, historical and critical*, 9 (1739), 565–76 · [G. Hickes], *Some discourses upon Dr. Burnet and Dr. Tillotson* (1695) · *Reliquiae Baxterianae, or, Mr Richard Baxter's narrative of the most memorable passages of his life and times*, ed. M. Sylvester, 1 vol. in 3 pts (1696) · *Bishop Burnet's History* · E. Calamy, ed., *An abridgement of Mr. Baxter's history of his life and times, with an account of the ministers, &c., who were ejected after the Restauration of King Charles II*, 2nd edn, 2 vols. (1713) · *The auto-biography of Symon Patrick, bishop of Ely* (1839) · T. J. Fawcett, *The liturgy of comprehension, 1689* (1973) · G. Reedy, 'Interpreting Tillotson', *Harvard Theological Review*, 86 (1993), 81–103 · D. D. Brown, 'The text of John Tillotson's sermons', *The Library*, 5th ser., 13 (1958), 18–36 · D. D. Brown, 'John Tillotson's revisions and Dryden's "talent for English prose"', *Review of English Studies*, new ser., 12 (1961), 24–39 · T. Claydon, *William III and the godly revolution* (1996) · C. Rose, *England in the 1690s* (1999), chap. 5 · P. Harth, *Contexts of Dryden's thought* (1968) · H. G. Van Leeuwen, *The problem of certainty in English thought, 1630–1690* (1963) · J. Gregory, *Restoration, Reformation and reform, 1660–1828: archbishops of Canterbury and their diocese* (2000) · L. G. Locke, *Tillotson: a study in seventeenth-century literature* (1954) · I. Simon, 'Tillotson's Barrow', *English Studies*, 45 (1964), 193–211, 273–88 · N. Sykes, *From Sheldon to Secker: aspects of English church history, 1660–1768* (1959) · W. M. Spellman, *The latitudinarians and the Church of England, 1660–1700* (1993) · B. Higgons, *Historical and critical remarks on Bishop Burnet's history of his own time* (1727) · F. H. [F. Hutchinson], *The life of the most reverend father in God John Tillotson … compiled from the minutes of the Reverend*

Mr. Young (1717) • G. Smith, *Remarks upon the life of the most reverend Dr. John Tillotson compiled by Thomas Birch, D.D.* (1753) • D. D. Brown, 'Dryden's *Religio laici* and the "judicious and learned Friend"', *Modern Language Notes*, 56 (1961), 66–9 • monumental inscription, St Lawrence Jewry, London • *The Rev. Oliver Heywood … his autobiography, diaries, anecdote and event books*, ed. J. H. Turner, 2 (1883), 31–2, 146 • 'Original letter from Archbishop Tillotson' [to Henry Root], *Universal Magazine of Knowledge and Pleasure*, 57 (1775), 8–9 • W. Whiston, *Memoirs of the life and writings of William Whiston*, 2nd edn, 2 vols. (1753), 1.26–7 • [J. T. Fowler], ed., *Memorials of the church of SS Peter and Wilfrid, Ripon*, 2, SurtS, 78 (1886), 288 • *A supplement to Burnet's History of my own time*, ed. H. C. Foxcroft (1902) • Evelyn, *Diary* • T. Birch, *The history of the Royal Society of London*, 4 vols. (1756–7), vol. 3 • [S. Nye], *The life of Mr Thomas Firmin … with a sermon on Luke X. 36, 37, preached on the occasion of his death* (1698) • *The correspondence of John Locke*, ed. E. S. de Beer, 8 vols. (1976–89), 4.463, 5.238, 8.57 • T. Lindsey, *Vindiciae Priestleianae* (1788), 77–8 • J. Locke, *Some thoughts concerning education*, ed. J. W. Yolton and J. S. Yolton (1989), 320 • M. New, ed., *Notes to sermons* (1996), vol. 5 of *The Florida edition of the works of Laurence Sterne*, ed. M. New and M. New (1978–96), 24 • *The works of John Wesley*, ed. A. C. Outler, 4 (1987), 396 • D. F. Bond, ed., *The Tatler*, 2 (1987), 122 • R. Steele and J. Addison, *The Spectator*, ed. D. Bond, 5 vols. (1965), vol. 1, p. 441 • J. Spence, *Observations, anecdotes, and characters, of books and men*, ed. J. M. Osborn, new edn, 2 vols. (1966)

Archives Bodl. Oxf., corresp. • LPL, letters in cypher • W. Yorks. AS, Calderdale, papers | BL, letters to Robert Nelson, Gilbert Burnet, and Edward Stillingfleet, Add. MS 4236 • NRA, priv. coll., letters to Sir Robert Atkyns

Likenesses M. Beale, oils, *c*.1672, Canterbury Cathedral, deanery • G. Kneller, oils, 1691, LPL [*see illus.*] • oils, *c*.1691–1694 (after G. Kneller), NPG; version, LPL • R. White, engraving, *c*.1692 (after M. Beale), NPG • R. White, line engraving, pubd 1717 (after his earlier work), BM, NPG • J. Faber junior, mezzotint, pubd 1780 (after G. Kneller), BM, NPG • A. Blooteling, line engraving (after P. Lely), BM, NPG • P. Vanderbank, line engraving (after M. Beale), BM, NPG • R. White, line engraving, BM, NPG; repro. in *Sermons* (1668) • engraving, repro. in J. Tillotson, *Six sermons* (1694) • line engraving (after medallion on monument at St Lawrence Jewry, London), BM; repro. in Hutchinson, *Life*

Wealth at death nothing except for copyright of sermons, worth £2500: *The Tatler*, 101 (1 Dec 1709); T. Birch, *The life of the most reverend Dr. John Tillotson, lord archbishop of Canterbury, compiled chiefly from his original papers and letters*, 2nd edn (1753), 345

Tillotson, William Frederic (1844–1889), newspaper proprietor and publisher, was born on 19 March 1844 in Bolton, Lancashire, the grandson of the Revd Samuel Tillotson, superintendent of the Bolton circuit of Primitive Methodists from 1830 to 1836, and the son of John Tillotson (1821–1906), printer, and his wife, Mary Ann Holden (*d*. 1871). William Frederic received a commercial education before being apprenticed as a young man to his father. On 20 April 1870 he married Mary Lever, daughter of James Lever, and sister of William Lever, later to become the first Viscount Leverhulme; they had four sons, John, James, Frederic, and William, and two daughters, Mary and Eliza. After serving his apprenticeship, Tillotson began his career in newspaper publishing in 1867, when he founded the *Bolton Evening News*, the United Kingdom's first daily evening halfpenny paper published outside London. He founded the *Bolton Journal*, in 1871, and in the early 1870s created the Lancashire Journal series, a small chain of weekly newspapers in the south of the

county, with the *Farnworth Journal and Observer*, *Leigh Journal*, *Tyldesley Journal*, *Eccles and Patricroft Journal*, and the *Swinton and Pendlebury Journal*.

Tillotson was more than simply a prominent Lancashire newspaper publisher. His most significant contribution to newspaper history is the Tillotson's Newspaper Literature Syndicate, the first of its kind in the world. In an effort to increase the circulation of his weekly Lancashire newspapers, and bring higher quality fiction to the provincial masses, in 1873 he commissioned the author Mary Elizabeth Braddon (Mrs John Maxwell) to write a novel, *Taken at the Flood*, which he published simultaneously in serial instalments in his and other newspapers. He greatly expanded this business in the late 1870s, selling stereotype plates of serial novels, along with a 'London letter' and a 'Woman's page', to numerous provincial daily and weekly newspapers throughout the UK. In the 1880s Bolton, a small town, became the hub of a vast international network of fiction distribution as the Tillotson syndicate began selling galley proof copies of primarily British fiction to newspapers in the United States, Australia, and other colonies; many works were also translated and sold for publication in French and German newspapers. The contributors to this syndicate included Thomas Hardy, Wilkie Collins, Ouida (Marie Louise de la Ramée), Sir Walter Besant, Arnold Bennett, Sir Arthur Conan Doyle, H. G. Wells, and Hall Caine. Although Tillotson is best remembered for having turned down one serial novel he commissioned—Thomas Hardy's *Too Late Beloved* (later known as *Tess of the D'Urbervilles*)—for its supposed immorality, the syndicate purchased and distributed Hardy's later novel, *The Pursuit of the Well-Beloved* (1892; rev. in 1 vol., 1897), as well as a number of his short stories. Tillotson also syndicated such works as Besant's *Herr Paulus*, Conan Doyle's 'The Crime of the Brigadier', Caine's *The Prophet*, and Collins's *The Evil Genius*. Tillotson's syndicate had a great impact on the course of newspaper history for its success inspired others, especially in the United States and Australia, to found their own syndicates.

Unfortunately, Tillotson did not live to see his newspaper syndicate flourish in the 1890s and early 1900s (it declined after the First World War and was sold to Newspaper Features Ltd of London in 1935); after a brief illness he died at Westfield, his home on Chorley New Road, Bolton, on 19 February 1889 at the age of forty-four. Described by John Nayler, one of his employees, as being 'a shade below average height' and possessing 'really brilliant blue eyes' (Singleton, 14), he was remembered as a compassionate employer who took an active interest in civic affairs, serving as borough magistrate from June 1885 until his death, as treasurer of the local Liberal council, and as one of the chief advocates of a Bolton infirmary. He was buried in St Peter's churchyard, Halliwell, Bolton.

CHARLES JOHANNINGSMEIER

Sources F. Singleton, *Tillotsons, 1850–1950: centenary of a family business* (1950) • *Bolton Weekly Journal and District News* (23 Feb 1889) • W. Westall, 'Newspaper fiction', *Lippincott's*, 40 (1890), 77–88 • M. Turner, 'Reading for the masses: aspects of the syndication of fiction in Great Britain', *Book selling and book buying: aspects of the nineteenth-century British and North American book trade*, ed. R. G. Landon (1978) • R. L. Purdy, 'MS adventures of Tess', *TLS* (6 March 1943), 120

Archives Bolton Central Library, *Bolton Evening News* archive
Wealth at death £30,644 2s. 6d.: probate, 16 March 1889, *CGPLA Eng. & Wales*

Tilman, Harold William (1898–1977x9), mountaineer and sailor, was born in Wallasey, Cheshire, on 14 February 1898, the youngest of three children and younger son of John Hinkes Tilman (1861–1936), a Liverpool sugar broker residing in Wallasey, and his wife, Adeline Rees (d. 1937), who came from a long line of Cumberland hill farmers. He went to Berkhamsted School in 1909, and then to the Royal Military Academy, Woolwich, in 1915. He was commissioned on 28 July 1915 into the Royal Field Artillery, and began active service on the western front in January 1916; he subsequently took part in the battles of the Somme, Nieuport, Ypres, and Passchendaele. He was twice wounded, and was awarded the MC and bar. He was promoted lieutenant in 1917 and transferred to the Royal Horse Artillery, before leaving the army in 1919. Bill Tilman, as he was always known, moved out to Kenya that same year to become a coffee planter, at Kericho and Sotik. For the next twelve years he concentrated on building up the farm he had cleared from the bush, but in 1930 he met Eric Shipton, another young planter, and they started their long and successful climbing partnership with ascents of the two peaks of Kilimanjaro (Kibo and Mawenzi) and of Mount Kenya and the Ruwenzori range (the Mountains of the Moon).

In 1932 Tilman returned to Britain and damaged his back in a serious fall while climbing on Dow crag in the Lake District; he was told he would never climb again. As soon as he was out of hospital he went to the Alps to prove the doctors wrong. In 1933 he prospected for gold in Kenya and bicycled across Africa from Uganda to the west coast. He visited the Himalayas for the first time in 1934, when he made a reconnaissance of Nanda Devi with Eric Shipton. They found their way through the formidable gorge blocking the route to the foot of the mountain. In 1935 he took part in the reconnaissance expedition to Mount Everest and then in 1936 climbed Nanda Devi, which at 25,646 feet was the highest peak hitherto climbed. This record, which established Tilman as one of the most distinguished mountaineers in the world and earned him the leadership of the 1938 Mount Everest expedition, was to remain unbroken until 1950. In 1937 Tilman explored and mapped a little-known area of the Karakoram. The small and lightly equipped Mount Everest expedition which he led the following year reached a height of 27,198 feet before being driven back by bad weather.

Tilman's mountaineering activities were halted by the outbreak of the Second World War. He immediately returned to Britain to rejoin the Royal Artillery with his former rank of lieutenant. He served in France in 1940, was mentioned in dispatches, and took part in the evacuation at Dunkirk. After a short spell in India and Iraq he joined the Eighth Army in the western desert in 1942. In

Harold William Tilman (1898–1977x9), by unknown photographer, 1938

1943 he volunteered for parachute training and special service behind the lines in the Special Operations Executive, fighting with the partisans in Albania in 1943 and in Italy during 1944 and 1945, when he was appointed to the DSO and awarded the freedom of Belluno. He reached the rank of major. After the war he returned to mountaineering, and attempted Rakaposhi (25,550 feet) in the Karakoram and Muztagh Ata (24,757 feet) in the Chinese Pamirs in 1947. In 1948 he travelled across China to the Chitral, attempting with Eric Shipton ascents of Bogdo Ola (17,864 feet) in the Tien Shan (Tianshan) range of mountains and also Chakar Aghil (22,070 feet) in the Chinese Pamirs. In 1949 he explored in Nepal, which had just opened its frontiers to foreigners, and in 1950 he undertook his last Himalayan expedition to Annapurna IV in Nepal and accompanied Charles Houston on the first ever approach to Everest from the south up the Khumbu glacier.

Tilman now felt that he was getting too old for high-altitude mountaineering, and so, after a spell in 1952 as British consul at Maymyo in Burma, he returned to Britain, and made his home at Bodowen, near Barmouth, north Wales, with his sister, Adeline. He took up sailing and commenced a series of unique voyages in *Mischief*, an old Bristol Channel pilot cutter. He was particularly interested in sailing in the far north and south, and made his first voyage to Patagonia from 1955 to 1956, crossing the

Patagonian ice-cap, and circumnavigating South America. From 1957 to 1958 he circumnavigated Africa and in 1959–60 sailed to the Crozet Islands and Kerguelen Island in the southern Indian Ocean.

From 1961 to 1964 Tilman made a series of voyages to east Greenland, and in 1964–5 he navigated the schooner *Patanela* for Warwick Deacock's Heard Island expedition. From 1966 to 1967 he sailed *Mischief* to the South Shetlands and South Georgia in the south Atlantic but in 1968 the boat foundered off Jan Mayen Island off the east coast of Greenland. Though deeply distressed by its loss, he was not deterred from sailing and purchased another cutter, *Sea Breeze*, in which he made four further voyages to Greenland before it was shipwrecked off east Greenland in 1972. He then bought the cutter *Baroque*, in which he made three further voyages to Greenland and in 1974 circumnavigated Svalbard. In 1977 he set sail in the converted tugboat *En Avant* with an expedition led by Simon Richardson to Smith Island in the South Shetlands. On 1 November *En Avant* left Rio bound for the Falklands and was never seen again. Tilman was presumed dead in April 1979.

Tilman was one of Britain's most distinguished mountain explorers and long-distance voyagers. He was renowned for his modesty, his sharp wit, and his austerity while in the mountains or at sea. He always avoided all forms of publicity and was more interested in mountain exploration than the attainment of height records or ascents of extreme technical difficulty. He was ascetic in his ways and a staunch believer in small expeditions that lived off the land and made the minimum impact on the local environment. He was unmarried. He was awarded the founder's medal of the Royal Geographical Society in 1952 and made an honorary LLD by the University of St Andrews in 1954. In 1973 he was appointed CBE. He wrote fifteen books describing his various expeditions and voyages.   CHRIS BONINGTON, *rev.*

Sources J. R. L. Anderson, *High mountains and cold seas: a biography of H. W. Tilman* (1980) · T. Madge, *The last hero, Bill Tilman: a biography of the explorer* (1995)
Archives Gwynedd Archives, Dolgellau, papers and photographs · RGS, corresp., papers, photographs, incl. letters, logbooks, diaries, maps, and slides · University of Wyoming, Laramie, diaries and logs | FILM BFI NFTVA, 'No pay, no prospects, not much pleasure!: the story of H. W. Tilman', HTV Wales, 25 March 1986
Likenesses photograph, 1938, RGS [*see illus.*] · W. G. Lee, photograph, repro. in Madge, *The last hero*, facing p. 161

Tilney, Agnes. *See* Howard, Agnes, duchess of Norfolk (*b.* in or before 1477, *d.* 1545).

Tilney, Charles (1561–1586). *See under* Babington, Anthony (1561–1586).

Tilney, Edmund (1535/6–1610), courtier, was born in 1535 or 1536 (in a chancery suit in 1599 he gave his age as sixty-three), the only son of Phillip Tilney (*d.* 1541), an usher of the privy chamber to Henry VIII, and his wife, Malyn Chambre, a chamberwoman to Queen Katherine Howard. His paternal grandfather, Sir Philip Tilney, was closely attached to Thomas Howard, second duke of Norfolk, who

married first his cousin Elizabeth and later his sister Agnes. These marriages allied the Tilneys to virtually every important family in the country, including the royal family. Malyn Tilney, however, was implicated in the scandal of Katherine Howard's adultery. She was sentenced to life imprisonment and loss of goods in 1543, but was pardoned after the principals were executed. Phillip Tilney died in debt in 1541 and was buried in St Leonard's Church, Streatham.

Malyn and the young Edmund were perhaps taken into the household of Agnes Howard, the dowager duchess of Norfolk, since their Howard connections remained strong. There is no record of Tilney's having received formal education, but he was trained for a career at court. His later writing shows knowledge of Latin, Spanish, French, and Italian as well as history, topography, law, geography, genealogy, and government. No evidence survives of travel on the continent, but it is not unlikely. In 1568 Tilney published *A Brief and Pleasant Discourse on the Duties of Marriage, called the Flower of Friendshippe*, which he dedicated to his distant cousin the queen. An accomplished exercise in courtly taste and rhetorical skill, it adroitly advertised his suitability for employment, and went through at least five editions in his lifetime.

In April 1569 Tilney was chief mourner at the funeral of Edward, the third son of Lord William Howard, and in 1572 he joined his cousin Charles Howard (later lord admiral) in the House of Commons as burgess for Gatton in Surrey. It was Charles who secured Tilney the post of master of the revels, first under a yearly commission from February 1578, and formally under patent from 24 July 1579. The revels office arranged entertainment at court, and there had been dissatisfaction with its costs and poor service. A 'man of credit' was sought to reform it, and Tilney was that man. His success owed much to greater reliance on professional actors, flourishing in London's new theatres. Their plays were cheaper to stage than the court's own masques and more polished than other entertainments. On 24 November 1581 Tilney received a special commission, giving him powers to impress workmen and materials at fair prices, to require actors to rehearse their plays before him (from 1586 to 1607 in his spacious quarters in St John's, Clerkenwell), and to revise them for court performance. Rivalry between nobles at court was another problem, as each wanted his own actors to perform. In 1583, and instructed by Sir Francis Walsingham, Tilney created the Queen's Men, an élite company picked from the finest performers available, who then dominated court theatricals for several years.

On 4 May 1583 Tilney applied for a licence to marry Mary Bray (*d.* 1604), the daughter of Sir Thomas Cotton and the widow of Sir Edward Bray, whose lands in Surrey she inherited for the term of her life. Tilney had to go to law over these, as also over the will of John Digges, of which he was executor with his cousin Phillip. Digges was employed in the revels office from 1579 to his death in 1585 and was described by those opposing the Tilneys as a thief and shifter, 'named and reputed to be one Tyllney's bastard' who died in 'Mr. Tyllney's house in St John's'.

Wrangling continued into the 1590s, but Tilney eventually acquired property in Middlesex under the will. Income from Mary's inheritance bought their principal property, the largest house in Leatherhead, Surrey, where the Tilneys entertained the queen on progress in August 1593. By 1594 Tilney was the greatest landholder of the parish and a county justice, and was thereafter much involved in local affairs.

From Tilney's arrangements with the actors at court there grew a general system of licensing plays, companies, and theatres in the London area, as reflected in Philip Henslowe's *Diary*. The relationship had a profound effect on the development of Elizabethan drama. Progressively fewer companies were allowed in the capital, but Tilney was their protector as much as their overseer. His licences protected them from civic officials and gave their plays a kind of performance copyright. In 1592 the lord mayor of London identified him as an obstacle to eradicating the actors from the city altogether. Tilney's censorship (evident in the extant manuscript of *Sir Thomas More*) ensured that plays would not offend important people or friendly foreign powers, and that they did not openly address matters of state or religious doctrine, but he left actors creative scope to be 'the abstracts and brief chronicles of the time' (*Hamlet*, II.ii). In 1598 the privy council expressly placed Tilney in control of the only companies then allowed to perform around London, the Chamberlain's Men and the Admiral's Men. In 1604 Queen Anne appointed Samuel Daniel licenser of the children of the queen's revels, but that arrangement did not last, and by his death Tilney securely controlled the London stage as well as licensing actors and other entertainers on tour in the provinces.

Tilney was never knighted but was entitled to be marshalled with bachelor knights. Between fees for attendance at court, his salary (£100 in 1595), and his income from theatrical licensing (estimated at £50 per annum), he perhaps earned £200 per annum beside rents from his estates, making him a wealthy man. Even so, by 1601 he was in financial difficulty, and his cousin Thomas agreed to pay 50 marks per annum against the expectation of inheriting his property. Mary Tilney died childless on 20 February 1604, and her Surrey lands reverted to her first husband's grandson. In 1607 Tilney was sued by Elizabeth Cartwright, seller of the Leatherhead house, for the annuity which the deal included. Perhaps in response to financial difficulties, Tilney had for some years sought further advancement at court. In the late 1590s, to advertise his claims, he set about a confidential work of diplomatic intelligence, 'Topographical descriptions, regiments, and policies' of the eight major countries of Europe; running to a quarter of a million words, it was meant to be an aid to foreign policy. He planned to present it to the queen in a scheme backed by Lord Admiral Howard, whereby Tilney would become master of ceremonies, while the revels would go to Sir George Buc. The queen died, but Tilney revised his 'Descriptions' and added a dedication to James I. Sir Lewis Lewkenor, however, was made master of ceremonies in 1603. Tilney remained in post, and Buc received

only the reversion to his office. Tilney abandoned his manuscript, which survives in two states (Folger Shakespeare Library, MS V.b. 182; University of Illinois Library MS, uncatalogued, *c*.1603).

Buc was a distant relative of Tilney, but there is no substance to suggestions that he was involved in the revels office before Tilney's death. Indeed there may have been tension between them: after Phillip Tilney died in 1602 the family lost land in Lincolnshire, when Buc sued as the nearest relative of Phillip's mother. From 1606 Buc began to license plays for the press, an authority not previously associated with the revels office. Tilney licensed for the press only Edward Sharpham's *Cupid's Whirligig* in June 1607. The accounts reveal his constant attendance at court throughout his final revels season of 1609–10. On 1 July 1610 he made out his will in 'his own hand and form' and with Christian piety, settling debts, making liberal provision for the poor and bequests to friends and relatives, and leaving the promised proceeds of his house to Thomas Tilney. He died on 20 August, and was buried on 6 October at St Leonard's Church, near his father's monument.

Edmund was related to Charles Tilney, one of the Babington conspirators, and the son of Edmund's cousin Phillip. Phillip and Edmund Tilney were bitter about the treatment Charles received; in a Star Chamber suit Rafe Bott testified that they 'thyrsted and longyd to be revengd on him', believing he had had custody of Charles in the Tower. A copy of *Locrine* (in the Bibliotheca Bodmeriana, Cologny-Genève) contains a note by Sir George Buc, claiming the play was written by Charles Tilney under the title 'Elstrid', and that Buc himself had written dumb-shows for it. Tilney's grandmother Margaret was Buc's aunt, so the claim is plausible, though the play as printed was probably revised by a later hand. RICHARD DUTTON

Sources W. R. Streitberger, 'On Edmond Tyllney's biography', *Review of English Studies*, new ser., 29 (1978), 11–35 · W. R. Streitberger, *Edmond Tyllney, master of the revels and censor of plays: a descriptive index to his diplomatic manual on Europe* (1986) · E. Tilney, *The flower of friendship*, ed. V. Wayne (1992) · A. Feuillerat, ed., *Documents relating to the office of the revels in the time of Queen Elizabeth* (1908) · F. S. Boas, 'Queen Elizabeth, the revels office and Edmund Tilney', *Queen Elizabeth in drama and related studies* (1950) · P. Berek, 'Locrine and Selimus', *Elizabethan dramatists*, ed. F. Bowers, DLitB, 62 (1987) · R. Dutton, *Mastering the revels: the regulation and censorship of English Renaissance drama* (1991) · *DNB* · W. R. Streitberger, 'The Armada victory procession and Tudor precedence', *N&Q*, 225 (1980), 310–12 · PRO, C24/272/44 · parish register, Streatham, 1541, P45-LEN · parish register, Streatham, 1610, P95-LEN · *The control and censorship of Caroline drama: the records of Sir Henry Herbert, master of the revels, 1623–73*, ed. N. W. Bawcutt (1996)

Archives Folger, MSS · University of Illinois, Urbana-Champaign, MSS

Tilney, John (*d*. after 1455), prior of Yarmouth and theologian, joined the Carmelite order in Yarmouth, Norfolk. He undertook his studies at Cambridge and incepted as a doctor of theology *c*.1430. He returned to Yarmouth, where his name occurs as prior in 1435 and 1437, and he was still in office in 1455. It was probably during his time lecturing in Cambridge that Tilney wrote a commentary on the Apocalypse which Bale saw and for which he recorded the incipit. Bale describes how Tilney taught that the remission of sins is due to the free grace of Christ and that his death brings reconciliation with God the Father. However, this is simply an expansion of the second half of the incipit which Bale had copied in one of his early notebooks. Bale also notes a compendium on *The Sentences* with incipit and a collection of forty-four sermons. Later he added the usual 'Scholastic lectures'. None of these works survives, and although an exposition on St John's gospel, found in Cambridge, Gonville and Caius College, MS 357, has been attributed to Tilney, it also survives in an anonymous thirteenth-century copy (Bodl. Oxf., MS Bodley 20, fols. 113–153*v*), and so cannot be by him.

RICHARD COPSEY

Sources J. Bale, Bodl. Oxf., MS Bodley 73 (SC 27635), fols. 119, 200 · J. Bale, 'Anglorum Heliades', BL, MS Harley 3838, fols. 96, 205 · Emden, *Cam.* · Bale, *Cat.*, 1.573–4 · J. Bale, Bodl. Oxf., MS Selden supra 41, fol. 178*v* · *Commentarii de scriptoribus Britannicis, auctore Joanne Lelando*, ed. A. Hall, 2 (1709), 446–7 · J. Pits, *Relationum historicarum de rebus Anglicis*, ed. [W. Bishop] (Paris, 1619), 621 · Tanner, *Bibl. Brit.-Hib.*, 713–14

Tilsley, John (*c*.1614–1684), clergyman and ejected minister, was born in Lancashire, possibly near Bolton; nothing is known of his parents. He was educated at Edinburgh University, where he graduated MA on 22 July 1637. He became curate to Alexander Horrocks, vicar of Deane, Lancashire, and signed the protestation there on 23 February 1642. On 4 January 1643 Tilsley married Margaret Chetham (1621–1663) at the collegiate church in Manchester. She was the daughter of Ralph Chetham and a niece of Humphrey Chetham, the founder of Chetham's Hospital. Margaret died on 28 April 1663, two weeks after the miscarriage of her ninth child. Of their children, only four survived infancy.

Tilsley was with Sir John Seaton's parliamentary forces when they took Preston on 9 February 1643, and he wrote an account of the affair. The benefice of Deane was given to him by a draft order of the House of Lords on 10 August 1643, his predecessor, Horrocks, being retained at Deane as assistant minister until 1648. Tilsley was appointed by parliament on 13 December 1644 as one of the ordaining ministers in Lancashire. He took the covenant and became one of the leading presbyterians in the county. In 1646 he joined with Richard Heyrick, Richard Hollinworth, and others in petitioning parliament to set up an ecclesiastical government in Lancashire as according to the advice of the Westminster assembly. Adam Martindale described Tilsley and other Manchester presbyterians as 'zealous (usually called Rigid) Presbyterians, that were for the setting up of the governance of the Church of Scotland amongst us' (*Life of Adam Martindale*, 62–3). In the same year Tilsley wrote a vindication of the petition and its promoters (*A True Copy of the Petition of the Twelve Thousand, Two Hundred*). This was in answer to a pamphlet in the Independent interest entitled *A New Birth of the City Remonstrance*. Parliament answered the petition by establishing presbyterianism in Lancashire by an ordinance dated 2 October 1646, and Tilsley became a principal member of the Bolton or second classis. In 1648 he signed the 'harmonious consent' of the ministers of Lancashire with those of London, which upheld the solemn league and covenant and fiercely condemned the toleration of sectaries, as did his assistant Alexander Horrocks.

Tilsley refused the engagement in 1650. Humphrey Chetham, who died in 1653, made Tilsley one of the feoffees of his hospital and library, and one of the purchasers of books for the five church libraries that he founded: responsibilities which Tilsley conscientiously fulfilled. In 1655 Tilsley seemed inclined to accept an invitation to Newcastle, but pressure was brought upon him to stay at Deane church. On 13 July 1659 he subscribed to the accommodation between the presbyterian and Independent ministers of Lancashire. After ejection following the Act of Uniformity in 1662, Tilsley continued to live in Rumworth in Deane parish, where he acted as trustee of a fund for the relief of the poor of Rumworth and also as a trustee of Deane School.

In 1665 Tilsley attracted the attention of the authorities for holding conventicles, and the episcopal returns of 1669 record two or three meetings a week of 'ministers and others' in Deane parish (Turner, 1.335). In 1670 Tilsley was threatened under the Five Mile Act of 1665. However, in the same year he conformed and was licensed as a lecturer at Deane. In late July 1670 John Rawlet passed on the news to Richard Baxter that Tilsley was one of three or four nonconformists, and the only one 'of Note', who had been persuaded to conform by the 'candour' and 'arguments' of Bishop John Wilkins (Keeble and Nuttall, 2.96). Thereafter Tilsley preached not only at Deane but also at Bolton and nearby Cocky chapel. However, he was prosecuted under the Oxford Act in 1675 and after protracted legal proceedings (which included his opponents providing graphic accounts to the central government of his evasions of the requirements of due conformity and his local power) he was ejected from the lectureship.

The diaries of Henry Newcome and Oliver Heywood and the autobiography of Adam Martindale show Tilsley to have been on intimate terms with those divines. According to Edmund Calamy, Tilsley 'had prodigious parts, a retentive memory which made whatsoever he read his own, a solid judgment, a quick invention, and a ready utterance' (Calamy, *Abridgement*, 2.402). Tilsley died at Manchester on 12 December 1684. Oliver Heywood accorded him the epitaph 'an admirable man', and recorded his age as seventy (Heywood and Dickenson, 70). Although Newcome and Tilsley had sometimes had differences of opinion, Newcome nevertheless sincerely mourned the loss of his friend and attended the funeral and burial at Deane church on 16 December. Afterwards he preached to Tilsley's surviving children as the dead man had requested. By his will, proved at Chester on 13 June 1685, Tilsley left bequests to a number of nonconformist ministers, including Newcome and Martindale. He provided for his grandchildren, and named his daughter Margaret Partington and son-in-law Richard Partington as executors.

C. W. SUTTON, *rev.* CATHERINE NUNN

Sources *Catalogue of graduates of the University of Edinburgh*, 2 vols. (1863) • J. E. Bailey, 'The Reverend John Tilsley, M.A., vicar of Deane, near Bolton', *Lancashire and Cheshire antiquarian notes*, ed. W. D. Pink (1885) [also pubd separately as J. E. Bailey, *A memoir of the Reverend John Tilsley* (1884)] • *The Rev. Oliver Heywood … his autobiography, diaries, anecdote and event books*, ed. J. H. Turner, 4 vols. (1881–5) • *The autobiography of Henry Newcome*, ed. R. Parkinson, 2 vols., Chetham Society, 26–7 (1852) • *The diary of the Rev. Henry Newcome, from September 30, 1661, to September 29, 1663*, ed. T. Heywood, Chetham Society, 18 (1849) • *The life of Adam Martindale*, ed. R. Parkinson, Chetham Society, 4 (1845) • J. H. Turner, T. Dickenson, and O. Heywood, eds., *The nonconformist register of baptisms, marriages, and deaths* (1881) • R. C. Christie, ed., *The old school libraries of Lancashire*, new ser., Chetham Society, 7 (1885) • G. Ormerod, ed., *Tracts relating to military proceedings in Lancashire during the great civil war*, Chetham Society, 2 (1844) • W. A. Shaw, ed., *Minutes of the Manchester presbyterian classis*, 3 vols., Chetham Society, new ser., 20, 22, 24 (1890–91) • W. A. Shaw, ed., *Minutes of the Bury presbyterian classis, 1647–1657*, 2 vols., Chetham Society, new ser., 36, 41 (1896–8) • W. A. Shaw, *A history of the English church during the civil wars and under the Commonwealth, 1640–1660*, 2 vols. (1900) • J. P. Earwaker, ed., *Lancashire and Cheshire wills at Chester*, new ser., Chetham Society, 3 (1884) • A. Sparke, ed., *Registers of the parish of Deane*, 1–2, Lancashire Parish Register Society, 53–4 (1916–17) • E. Baines and W. R. Whatton, *The history of the county palatine and duchy of Lancaster*, new edn, ed. J. Croston and others, 5 vols. (1888–93) • *Calamy rev.* • E. Calamy, ed., *An abridgement of Mr. Baxter's history of his life and times, with an account of the ministers, &c., who were ejected after the Restauration of King Charles II*, 2nd edn, 2 vols. (1713) • B. Nightingale, *Early stages of the Quaker movement in Lancashire* (1921) • G. L. Turner, ed., *Original records of early nonconformity under persecution and indulgence*, 3 vols. (1911–14) • *CSP dom.*, 1670; addenda, 1660–70, 1675 • *Calendar of the correspondence of Richard Baxter*, ed. N. H. Keeble and G. F. Nuttall, 2 (1991), 96 • registers, collegiate church, Manchester, 1643
Archives Chetham's Library, Manchester, manuscript autobiography of Henry Newcome, A3-123 • Man. CL, deeds of Deane School, L85/6/3/1–4
Wealth at death approx. £800

Tilson, Henry (1659–1695), portrait painter, was born into a respectable Lancashire family, the son of Nathaniel Tilson, and grandson of Henry Tilson (1576–1655), the bishop of Elphin, formerly chaplain to the earl of Strafford in Ireland. He entered the studio of Sir Peter Lely with whom he also resided, and worked as his pupil and assistant until the master's death in 1680. Vertue records that before he went to Italy, Tilson painted a group portrait of his own family 'representing His Father setting leaning on his hand. his mother with her younger son [Christopher] by her. his sister standing behind & himself with his pallet in his hand. … in a masterly manner well disposed, firmly drawn & freely pencild' (Vertue, *Note books*, 2.68). In 1685 he travelled to Rome via Paris and Venice in the company of his friend the Swedish painter Michael Dahl, who painted his portrait, and made a name for himself there by doing crayon copies of the old masters. Tilson also painted a self-portrait, 'a head with a pencil in his hand. leaning on a bust very well behind it written "H. Tilsona Roma. 1687"' (ibid.). Both this and the family portrait were formerly in the possession of Tilson's descendant Henry Tilson Shaen Carter of Watlington House, Oxfordshire, and were exhibited at the National Portrait Exhibition, South Kensington Museum, in 1867. He had returned to England by 1689, and appears to have earned enough respect as a portraitist to build up a sound practice, painting in a style somewhere between Kneller, Riley, and Dahl. He was considered one of the most able of the lesser native portrait painters of his time. Despite this growing reputation, however, Tilson suffered from both unrequited love for his patroness, a Mrs Green, and depression, and 'retir'd into his Closett. & with a pistol shot [himself] thro' the heart. aged about 36' (ibid., 1.68). He was buried on 25 November 1695 at St Dunstan-in-the-West, London. Examples of his work are in the Guildhall, London; National Galleries of Scotland, Edinburgh; and Belton House, Lincolnshire, and Dyrham Park, Hertfordshire.

SUSAN COOPER MORGAN

Sources Vertue, *Note books*, 1.48, 68, 72, 143; 2.5, 68, 78, 141–2; 5.20 • E. Waterhouse, *Painting in Britain, 1530–1790*, 4th edn (1978) • E. K. Waterhouse, *The dictionary of British 16th and 17th century painters* (1988) • M. Whinney and O. Millar, *English art, 1625–1714* (1957) • *Redgrave, Artists* • H. Walpole, *Anecdotes of painting in England: with some account of the principal artists*, ed. R. N. Wornum, new edn, 2 (1849); repr. (1862) • *Bénézit, Dict.*, 4th edn • *Bryan, Painters* (1886–9) • C. H. C. Baker, *Lely and the Stuart portrait painters: a study of English portraiture before and after van Dyck*, 2 (1912) • A. Davies, *Dictionary of British portraiture*, 1 (1979), 137 • J. Granger, *A biographical history of England, from Egbert the Great to the revolution*, 4th edn, 4 vols. (1804)
Likenesses T. Chambars, line engraving (after H. Tilson), NPG; repro. in H. Walpole, *Anecdotes of painting in England* (1762) • H. Meyer, engraving (after H. Tilson), Courtauld Inst., Witt Library

Tilt, Charles (1797–1861), bookseller and publisher, was born in June 1797, the son of William Tilt, a confectioner of St Paul's Churchyard, London, and his wife, Mary. It is thought that the Tilt family originated in Worcestershire and had a connection with the family of Oliver Cromwell. Charles Tilt attended boarding-schools outside London, but after his father's death was apprenticed by his mother at fourteen to Mr Whitehead, a bookseller and stationer at Portsea, Hampshire. He returned to London in January 1817 and worked intermittently at Hatchards and other bookselling businesses, and from 1818 to 1819 at Longman & Co., where his brother Henry (d. 1829) was also probably, by that time, an employee. He returned to Hatchards in April 1820 and continued there until September 1826.

On 9 October of that year Tilt started his own extremely lucrative publishing and bookselling business at 86 Fleet Street, at the corner of St Bride's Passage or Avenue, where he remained until 1840. He shrewdly marketed richly illustrated books in a variety of formats appropriate for all classes. He frequently used the extensive side windows of his shop to display his offerings, which were often so popularly received that railings were required to hold back the crowds who came to view them, and their availability was reported in newspapers such as *The Times*. Besides gift books, annuals, travel books, and children's literature, Tilt published novelty items such as an almanac which would fit neatly into the top of a man's hat, and a series, Tilt's Miniature Classics, which was sold with a satin or rosewood cabinet and a glass door and lock. On 16 December 1828 Tilt married Jane May (d. 1858) of Reading; they had one daughter, also named Jane May, who married the physical chemist John Hall *Gladstone (1827–1902).

Like many in his trade, Tilt was regularly involved in copyright and remuneration disputes with authors, artists, editors, and his fellow publishers. Thomas Hood, George Cruikshank, William Makepeace Thackeray, J. M. W. Turner, and Mary Eliza Lamb were among those who were unhappy with Tilt's treatment of them at one time or another, but these disagreements were nearly always resolved to Tilt's benefit, while he maintained the persona of a genial commonsensical tradesman. His wealth from the 1830s onwards is often mentioned by contemporaries. The greater part of his success derived from his virtual monopoly of the early lithography market, which he achieved by importing at low cost sheets of elaborate designs from the continent. He was also well known for purchasing the rights to previously published prints by famous artists after copyright had lapsed, having them re-engraved on steel plates on a smaller scale by other less well-known artists, and selling the newer versions at comparatively inexpensive rates while retaining the original and usually much more famous artists' names on the new plates. J. M. W. Turner complained before the lord mayor of London about such treatment in regard to some illustrations that he completed for some of Walter Scott's works. But the account of the hearing in *The Times* of 16 October 1833 gives Tilt the last word: 'Oh, Mr. Turner, you ought to let your brother artists have a little slice. (Laughter).'

Tilt's collaborations with George Cruikshank and Thomas Hood were the most significant over the course of his career. Hood knew Tilt by at least 1827, when the author's mother-in-law Charlotte Reynolds published through Tilt *Mrs. Leslie and her Grandchildren* under the *nom de plume* Mrs. Hamerton. Tilt published the second volume of *Hood's Whims and Oddities* (November 1827), Hood's *The Epping Hunt* with illustrations by Cruikshank (September 1829), and an edition of his *Dream of Eugene Aram* (November 1831). Tilt also published four volumes of Hood's popular *Comic Annual*, but after an intense quarrel—probably over Tilt's unwillingness to publish Hood's novel *Tylney Hall*—the relationship ended with the publication in November 1833 of the 1834 *Comic Annual*. Hood died twelve years later, after feuding with several other publishers and persisting in his ill will towards Tilt.

The association with Cruikshank also began as early as 1827, but took on a more significant character with the publication of Cruikshank's nine-part *My Sketch Book* (1833-6) and his *Comic Almanack* (1834-52), which was edited for its first four years by James Henry Vizetelly (Rigdum Funnidos). Along with a fictional co-publisher (Mustapha Syried [must-have-as-a-read] of Constantinople) Tilt issued *The Loving Ballad of Lord Bateman* (1839) with famous illustrations by Cruikshank, and text almost certainly by Charles Dickens but long associated with Thackeray, who may have contributed the bogus scholarly apparatus to the book. Until Tilt's death he and his successors were Cruikshank's primary publishers, especially when the artist wanted complete control of projects such as *My Sketch Book* and the later *Omnibus* (May 1841–January

1842), edited by Laman Blanchard with contributions by Frederick Marryat, Horace Mayhew, and Thackeray.

In 1840 Tilt chose from his employees a junior partner, David *Bogue (1807/8-1856), who in 1843 assumed, according to Tilt's plan, sole ownership of the firm. The firm's imprint from late 1840 until 1843 was Tilt and Bogue, but then became simply David Bogue or D. Bogue. Tilt retired from publishing to his house at Clapham Rise and then travelled extensively on the continent and in the Middle East, writing for children a popular account of one trip: *The Boat and the Caravan: a Family Tour through Egypt and Syria* (1847).

After 1848 there were fewer trips abroad and Tilt now divided his time between Brighton, London, and Bath, where he was residing at the time of his wife's death in Southsea, Hampshire, on 27 September 1858. At the untimely death of his successor Bogue in November 1856, Tilt served as executor of his estate. Tilt was a short man, 'with dark curly hair, bright eyes and a square jaw' (Gladstone). He remained active in various philanthropic activities in Bath until his death from heart disease at his home, 28 Pembridge Gardens, Bayswater, London, on 28 September 1861, leaving Bogue's estate still not entirely settled.   LOGAN DELANO BROWNING

Sources 'Civil actions—vice-chancellor's court—Baldwin v. Tilt', *The Times* (12 Aug 1836) • T. Hepworth, letter, *The Times* (13 Aug 1836) • J. Clubbe, *Victorian forerunner: the later career of Thomas Hood* (1968) • *GM*, 3rd ser., 5 (1858), 539; 11 (1861), 691-2 • *The letters of Charles Dickens*, ed. M. House, G. Storey, and others, 1-2 (1965-9) • *The letters of Thomas Hood*, ed. P. F. Morgan (1973) • M. Macleod, 'Tilt family', *N&Q*, 3rd ser., 1 (1862), 4-5 • 'Master Tilt publishes a sketch of the three ruffians, May, Williams, and Bishop', *The Times* (12 Dec 1831) • R. L. Patten, *George Cruikshank's life, times, and art*, 2 vols. (1992-6) • *The Times* (16 Oct 1833); (1 Oct 1861) • *IGI* • *The letters and private papers of William Makepeace Thackeray*, ed. G. N. Ray, 1 (1945) • H. Vizetelly, *Glances back through seventy years: autobiographical and other references*, 2 vols. (1893) • M. Thomas Hester, ed., *Seventeenth-century British nondramatic poets: second series*, DLitB, 126 (1993) • F. Gladstone, 'Charles Tilt, publisher, 1826-1842', *Publishers' Circular and Booksellers' Record* (23 April 1927) • d. cert. • *CGPLA Eng. & Wales* (1861)

Likenesses portrait, repro. in G. Cruikshank, *A comic alphabet* (1836), back cover (letter 'T') • portrait, repro. in G. Cruikshank, *Comic Almanack* (1835), pl. for 'March'

Wealth at death under £180,000: probate, with a codicil, 25 Oct 1861, *CGPLA Eng. & Wales*

Tilt, John Edward (1815–1893), physician, was born at Brighton on 30 January 1815, and received his medical education first at St George's Hospital, London, and then at Paris, where he graduated MD on 15 May 1839. He does not appear to have held any English qualification until he became a member of the Royal College of Physicians in 1859. During his time in Paris, Tilt learned from Récamier about the use of the speculum as an aid to diagnosis and he later encouraged its use in Britain. He acted as travelling physician in the family of Count Shuvalov during 1848–50, before settling in London about 1850, specializing in midwifery and the diseases of women. He was then appointed physician-accoucheur to the Farringdon General Dispensary and Lying-in Charity. He was one of the original fellows of the Obstetrical Society of London, which was formed in 1859, where, after filling various offices, he was elected president for 1874–5. The title of cavaliere of the Crown of Italy was conferred upon him in 1875, and at the time of his death he was a corresponding fellow of the academies of medicine of Turin, Athens, and New York. He died at Hastings on 17 December 1893.

Tilt's works include *On Diseases of Menstruation and Ovarian Inflammation* (1850), *On the Elements of Health and Principles of Female Hygiene* (1852, German translation published in 1854), and *A Handbook of Uterine Therapeutics and of Diseases of Women* (1863), translated into German (1864) and into Flemish (1866).   D'A. POWER, *rev.* SUSAN SNOXALL

Sources *Transactions of the Obstetrical Society of London*, 36 (1894), 107 · *Medico-Chirurgical Transactions*, 77 (1894), 36–7

Tiltman, John Hessell (1894–1982), cryptanalyst, was born at 70 Torrington Square, Bloomsbury, London, on 25 May 1894, the youngest in the family of one daughter and two sons of Alfred Hessell Tiltman, architect, and his wife, Sarah Ann Jane Kerr. Tiltman was educated at Charterhouse School, where at the age of thirteen he was offered a place at Oxford University which the family was unable to take up. On leaving school, between 1912 and 1914 he taught at three schools, the last of them Northcliffe House School, Bognor. At the outbreak of the First World War he enlisted and was commissioned in the King's Own Scottish Borderers, and from 1915 to 1917 he served in France, where he won the MC and was severely wounded on the Somme.

In August 1920, almost by chance, Tiltman was attached for a year to the small peacetime signal intelligence organization in London; he was then posted to Simla in India, where for eight years he performed cipher-breaking duties with remarkable success. On 7 April 1926 he married Tempe Monica (*b.* 1898), daughter of Major-General Oliver Robinson of the Army Medical Service. They had one daughter. Having become a War Office civilian in 1925, he was recalled to the colours as a lieutenant-colonel in September 1939 to command no. iv intelligence school. Before that he had helped to earmark dons and outstanding undergraduates for signal intelligence work in the event of war. Many wartime recruits came under his influence through the Bedford training courses, which he organized and supervised. During the 1930s he led the team which successfully decrypted all Comintern radio traffic with England. The texts of this traffic, released in 1997 to the Public Record Office, revealed the dependence of the Communist Party of Great Britain on secret Soviet monetary support; the names and activities of British individuals engaged in this clandestine liaison; and similar dealings between the USSR and the communist parties of several other countries. By 1939 Tiltman was head of the military section at the Government Code and Cypher School. During the course of the war he was promoted colonel and brigadier, and was made chief cryptographer at the Government Code and Cypher School at Bletchley Park.

The unrivalled versatility of 'the Brig' was shown by the contributions he made to the solution of a number of

John Hessell Tiltman (1894–1982), by unknown photographer

machine ciphers during the Second World War. For example, he broke the German railway enigma in February 1941, which revealed in detail German preparations to attack Greece and the USSR. His work was crucial to the initial break into the German enciphered teleprinter systems used for the highest level of German services communications. As a solver of non-machine systems he was pre-eminent, through intuition, experience, and dogged persistence producing answers to problems of the most difficult and complex kind and constantly improving the speed and elegance of the methods used. When faced with a new target country he was able quickly to learn enough of the language to enable him to work on its ciphers. For example, in addition to his varied work on German ciphers during the Second World War, he learned sufficient Japanese to enable him to be the key figure in the decipherment of the main Japanese naval code known as JN–25 soon after its introduction in 1939 and of the Japanese military attaché code in the summer of 1942. His work on the JN–25 was of value to the Americans after collaboration with them in cryptanalysis began in February 1941. He continued as a civilian in GCHQ after the war and retired at assistant secretary level in 1954.

Tiltman was every inch a soldier but of unassuming modesty. He believed that the success of his work depended upon personal anonymity and public nondisclosure. From his work against Soviet agent and Comintern systems before the war he knew how governmental revelations could nullify success. His wide-ranging contribution to allied security during the Second World War was recognized by the USA with the award of the US

Legion of merit in 1946. He was appointed OBE (1930), CBE (1944), and CMG (1954). Tiltman moved to Washington, DC, after his retirement, and was employed as a consultant by the national security agency, where, in 1980, the director, Admiral Bobbie Inman, and deputy director, Ann Caracristi, presented him with a scroll to celebrate 60 years 'of distinguished cryptologic service'. He died on 10 August 1982 in Hawaii.   D. R. NICOLL

Sources *The Times* (24 Sept 1982) · personal knowledge (2004) · private information · C. Andrew, *Secret service: the making of the British intelligence community* (1985) · F. H. Hinsley and others, *British intelligence in the Second World War*, 3/1 (1984) · F. H. Hinsley and A. Stripp, eds., *Codebreakers: the inside story of Bletchley Park* (1993) · b. cert. · m. cert. · *CGPLA Eng. & Wales* (1983)
Archives JRL, letters to the *Manchester Guardian*
Likenesses photograph, priv. coll. [*see illus.*]
Wealth at death £552—in England and Wales: probate, 30 Nov 1983, *CGPLA Eng. & Wales*

Timberlake, Henry (*d.* 1625/6), merchant and traveller, came from the parish of Titchfield, near Portsmouth. Although nothing is known of his parents or his early life, in 1597 Timberlake is noted as owning shares, with Francis Cherry and Edward Dartnall, in the ship *Edward Bonaventure*, which traded with Russia and the Levant.

On 9 March 1601 Timberlake, having crossed the Mediterranean in the *Troyan*, embarked on a pilgrimage to Jerusalem accompanied by John Burrell, a merchant from Middlesbrough. When they reached the holy city on 25 March, Burrell advised Timberlake to explain to the Turkish authorities there that he was Greek, in order to be permitted entry; when he reached the west gate, though, Timberlake loudly proclaimed that he was English and was promptly gaoled. When he was visited by the Roman Catholic defender of pilgrims of the city a short while later, he refused his help stating that he would rather place his trust in the Turk than the pope. Eventually, though, he was released through the intercession of a Muslim he had previously assisted in Algiers. He was reunited with Burrell and the two men were guided through the city by a party of friars before travelling to Alexandria and returning to England. In 1603 Timberlake wrote a short account of his pilgrimage, entitled *A True and Strange Discourse of the Travailes of Two English Pilgrimes*, which was reprinted eight times in the seventeenth century. In this tract he related the topography of the Holy Land to that of London in an attempt to impress upon his readers the relative location of all the significant sites in the life of Christ. As a result, Timberlake described Bethlehem as standing in the same relation to Jerusalem as Wandsworth to London.

Timberlake was a member of the Company of Merchant Adventurers, formed in 1612 to discover a north-west passage, and he also held stock in the East India Company until 1617. In 1615 he was one of the original adventurers for the plantation of Somers Island (Bermuda) and owned two shares in each of Smith and Southampton tribes; his holdings in the latter now comprise part of the Port Royal golf course. In his will, dated 10 July 1625, he left his lands in Bermuda and Essex to his elder son, Thomas; his younger son, Henry, received his holdings in London.

After more than £1100 in legacies and gifts had been dispersed, especially to his daughter Hester Williams, formerly Mitchell, and her children, Timberlake's wife, Margaret, received the balance of his estate. The exact date of his death is unknown; his will was proved on 13 May 1626.   RICHARD RAISWELL

Sources H. Timberlake, *A true and strange discourse of the travailes of two English pilgrimes* (1603) · J. H. Lefroy, *Memorials of the discovery and early settlement of the Bermudas or Somers Islands, 1515–1685*, another edn, 2 vols. (1932) · V. A. Ives, ed., *The Rich papers: letters from Bermuda, 1615–1646* (1984) · *APC, 1597–98* · T. S. Willan, *The early history of the Russia Company, 1553–1603* (1956), 264 · *CSP col.*, 2.238–40 · will, PRO, PROB 11/149, fols. 52–3
Wealth at death land in Bermuda and Essex; £1100 in legacies; balance of estate to wife: will, PRO, PROB 11/149, fols. 52–3

Timberlake, Henry (1730–1765), army officer in America and writer, was born in Hanover county, Virginia, the son of Francis Timberlake and Sarah Austin. He received 'almost as good an education as Virginia could bestow' on him (Timberlake, 5). His father died when he was young and, finding that his inheritance could not support him, he turned first to commerce and then to soldiering. Henry Timberlake joined the 'patriot blues' for their campaign of 1756 against the French and their Indian allies but saw no action. In 1758 he was appointed ensign and simultaneously cornet of light horse in the regiment of William Byrd III, with which he saw action against the French at Fort Duquesne. In the following year he served under John Stanwix who put him in command of Ford Burd, also called Fort Necessity, near Pittsburgh, Pennsylvania. In spring 1761 he joined Byrd's regiment, which was to relieve the Cherokee siege of Fort Loudon on the Little Tennessee River. When peace had been made the Cherokee asked that an officer visit them: Timberlake volunteered and was sent in the company of Sergeant Thomas Sumter.

They made their way by canoe down the Holston and up the Little Tennessee rivers, a difficult journey of twenty-two days through uncharted waters in territory where hostile Indians were known to move. After arriving at their goal they spent three months with the Overhill Cherokee; Timberlake was the personal guest of *Ostenaca, who saw Timberlake's visit as a chance to recover some of the ground he had lost among the Cherokee to the rival leader Attakullakula. Timberlake formed an attachment to Ostenaca's daughter Sakinney, who later gave birth to their son, Richard Timberlake.

Ostenaca demanded to go to London to meet the king, as Attakullakulla had done some thirty years earlier. It was agreed that Timberlake and Sumter would accompany Ostenaca and two other Cherokee (Pouting Pigeon and Stalking Turkey) with their interpreter, and the party left in the summer of 1762. The party, less the interpreter who died *en route*, were fêted in London and had audience with the king, after which the Indians returned immediately to Virginia, leaving behind Timberlake who, now married against his bride's father's wishes, was prevented from returning by lack of funds. Eventually the couple reached

America, where Timberlake was promoted lieutenant in the 42nd regiment but put on half pay. This added to his financial woes and he was obliged to sell the land and slaves he had inherited. In 1764 Timberlake accompanied to England a second group of Cherokee who hoped to secure the king's protection against English settlers who were encroaching on their lands. This time the king refused them an audience since they were not chiefs and their mission was unofficial; in March 1765 the party returned home.

In London in 1765 Henry Timberlake published his *Memoirs*. His end seems to have been to raise money, but he pursued it very maladroitly. His tone is querulous and peevish as he constantly seeks to justify his actions and particularly to rebut suggestions that he profited from the visits of the Indians. This was not the way to secure sales, and the book was not reprinted in Britain, though a German and a French translation appeared in 1769 and 1796 respectively (the London edition was reissued on microcard by the perhaps appropriately named Lost Cause Press of Louisville, Kentucky, n.d.). Later authors, however, have valued his memoirs highly for his fine map of the river system of the Overhill country and his often perceptive descriptions of the Cherokee. He says, for example, of the Cherokee custom of burying the dead with their possessions: 'This custom was probably introduced to prevent avarice and, by preventing hereditary acquisitions, make merit the sole means of acquiring power, honour and riches.' He then describes how the custom was bolstered and made acceptable by being given a spiritual or, as he had it, a superstitious significance (*Memoirs*, 68). He does not casually assume European superiority, writing rather enviously for example, that 'The sole occupations of an Indian life, are hunting, and warring abroad and lazying at home. Want is said to be the mother of industry, but their wants are supplied by an easier rate' (ibid., 76). Robert Southey used the memoirs in compiling his epic *Madoc* (1805), which tells of the twelfth-century Welshman supposed to have reached America and encountered the Cherokee.

Timberlake died in London on 30 September 1765, before his *Memoirs* appeared. His wife survived him and in recognition of his service was in December 1765 granted a full pension despite his having been on half pay at the time of his death. They are not thought to have had children. In 1819 Henry's illegitimate son Richard Timberlake accepted a reserve in Hamilton county, Tennessee, under a treaty with the Cherokee. This treaty enabled individual Cherokee to remain on land which the nation had earlier ceded to Americans. Richard Timberlake and others who accepted the reserves became the core of the eastern band of the Cherokee.   ELIZABETH BAIGENT

Sources H. Timberlake, *Memoirs* (1765) · *GM*, 1st ser., 35 (1765), 491 · S. C. W., 'Timberlake, Henry', *DAB* · J. Oliphant, 'The Cherokee embassy to London, 1762', *Journal of Imperial and Commonwealth History*, 27/1 (1999), 1–26 · J. Oliphant, *Peace and war on the Anglo-Cherokee frontier, 1756–1763* (2001) · W. L. Anderson, 'Ostenaco', *ANB* · www.geocities.com/Heartland/Plains/7906 [Timberlake Family Association], 10 Jan 2003 · www.roserockmuseum.com [Timberlake Rose Rock Museum, Noble, Oklahoma], 10 Jan 2003

Timbrell, Benjamin (*c*.1683–1754), carpenter and builder, was one of the most noted master builders working in London in the first half of the eighteenth century. He may have been the son of Benjamin and Elizabeth Timbrell, who were living in Westminster in the mid-1680s, but his date and place of birth have not been traced. On 21 December 1707, when he was about twenty-four years old and living in the parish of St James, Piccadilly, he married Mary Salter at St James's Church. They had several children, a number of whom died in infancy.

Timbrell took part in most of the major developments which led to a vast expansion of west London in the early Georgian period. What tended to set his work apart from that of the generality of speculative builders was the size and splendour of the houses he erected in the vicinity of Hanover Square, on the Grosvenor estate (where he built at least ten very substantial houses including two in Grosvenor Square), in Sackville Street, and on the Burlington estate near Piccadilly, and in St James's Square.

As a carpenter he worked (with Thomas Phillips) on the construction of St Peter's Church, Vere Street (1721–4) and St Martin-in-the-Fields (1722–6). He was one of the initial vestrymen of the parish of St George, Hanover Square, and helped to erect several buildings for the parish. Like many another master builder, he was perfectly capable of designing a building, as at nos. 1–3 Crown Office Row, Inner Temple (dem.), which he built in 1737–8 and, of the four developers who undertook the construction of the charming Grosvenor Chapel in South Audley Street in 1730–31, he is the most likely to have provided the design. He was also responsible in 1743 for the fitting up of Leicester House, Leicester Square, for the prince of Wales, and in 1750 for alterations to Charterhouse School in Clerkenwell. Although the vast bulk of his work was in London, he is known to have undertaken some work elsewhere, as at Huntingdon, where he built the town hall, possibly to his own designs, in 1745.

Timbrell lived from 1729 to 1751 at 12 Upper Grosvenor Street, Mayfair, a house built, naturally, by himself. He died on 6 January 1754, and was buried on 25 January, probably at St George's, Hanover Square. His wife had shortly predeceased him, and he had six surviving children. His eldest son, William, followed his father's trade of carpenter and builder. One of his daughters, Martha, who had also married a builder, claimed in a lawsuit that at his death Benjamin Timbrell had owned freehold land and houses to the value of £1000 per annum, and leasehold property (including 'several large and magnificent dwelling houses') and personal effects worth £20,000, but that his executors were defrauding her by pretending that he died in mean and low circumstances (PRO, C12/356/33). It is likely that he did own a considerable amount of property, but that, as was often the case even with successful builders, it was heavily mortgaged.   VICTOR BELCHER

Sources *The parish of St James, Westminster*, 1, Survey of London, 29–30 (1960) · *The parish of St James, Westminster*, 2, Survey of London, 31–2 (1963) · *The parish of St Anne, Soho*, 2 vols. (1966) · F. H. W.

Sheppard, ed., *The Grosvenor estate in Mayfair*, 1: *General history*, Survey of London, 39 (1977) · F. H. W. Sheppard, ed., *The Grosvenor estate in Mayfair*, 2: *The buildings*, Survey of London, 40 (1980) · V. Belcher, 'An old-fashioned place of worship', *Godly Mayfair*, ed. A. Callender (1980), 9–12 · Colvin, *Archs.*, 980 · vicar general marriage allegations, LPL, 1707(2), fol. 693 · will of Benjamin Timbrell, PRO, PROB 11/806, fol. 222 · Barlow v. Timbrell, PRO, C 12/356/33 · parish register (burial) London, St George's, Hanover Square, 25 Jan 1754 · parish register (marriage) London, St James's, Piccadilly, 21 Dec 1707 **Wealth at death** owned considerable property

Timbrell, Henry (1806–1849), sculptor, was born in Dublin, the son of James Timbrell, clerk of the ordnance, and his wife, Susanna, *née* Shelling. He began his studies about 1823 under the Irish sculptor John Smyth (Smith) and in 1825 entered the schools of the Royal Dublin Society, where he was awarded several prizes. Between 1827 and 1829 he also exhibited six works and won various prizes at the Royal Hibernian Academy in Dublin, showing in 1827 a figure of a Grecian warrior and in 1828 a bust of his master, John Smyth. In 1830 he went to London and worked in the studio of William Behnes, and as a pupil of Edward Hodges Baily, who continued to employ him occasionally for several years. He was at the same time a student at the Royal Academy Schools. In 1833 he exhibited *Phaeton*, in 1834 the bas-relief *Satan in Search of the Earth* (both of which he also exhibited at the Society of British Artists in 1834 and 1835), and in 1835 *Sorrow*, a monumental group. On 10 December 1835 he gained the gold medal for his group, *Mezentius Tying the Living to the Dead*, which was exhibited in 1836. On 3 February 1838 he married Susan Flather in St Pancras's, London.

Among Timbrell's other works shown at the Royal Academy were several busts: *Grief*, a bas-relief (1839); *Psyche* (1842); *Hercules Throwing Lycas into the Sea* (1843). With the *Hercules* group he won the travelling scholarship of the Royal Academy, and went to Rome in the same year. While there he completed a bas-relief for the temple at Buckingham Palace, London, and in 1845 a life-sized group, *Instruction*, which was ruined in the wreck of the ship bringing it to England. At the time of his death he was working on statues of Richard, earl of Clare, and William, earl of Aumale, for the chamber of the House of Lords in the new houses of parliament, and another in marble of *The Lamp of the Ganges* for Queen Victoria, an engraving of which by W. Roffe appeared in the *Art Journal* in 1855. Henry Timbrell died of pleurisy in Rome on 10 April 1849. Buried in Rome, his funeral was attended by fellow sculptors John Gibson, John Hogan, and Richard James Wyatt. A later historian noted that 'Timbrell's early death terminated a career of much promise' (Strickland, 2.448).

Timbrell's younger brother, **James Christopher Timbrell** (1810–1850), painter and sculptor, was born in Dublin. In 1825 he entered the Royal Dublin Society's Schools, and in 1827 sent a landscape to the Royal Hibernian Academy exhibition. In 1829 he presented one of his lithographs, *The Scotch Fisher*, to the Dublin Society. He went to London in 1830 and exhibited three paintings of figurative subjects at the Royal Academy and five at the British Institution between 1830 and 1848, including *Summer* and *The*

Fisherman's Return. He contributed eight illustrations to *Ireland: its Scenery and Character* (3 vols., 1841–3) by Mr and Mrs Samuel Carter Hall. He died in Portsmouth on 5 January 1850.

CAMPBELL DODGSON, rev. CHRISTOPHER WHITEHEAD

Sources R. Gunnis, *Dictionary of British sculptors, 1660–1851* (1953), 395 · *Art Journal*, 11 (1849), 198 · M. H. Grant, *A dictionary of British sculptors from the XIIIth century to the XXth century* (1953), 245 · Graves, *RA exhibitors*, 7 (1906), 396 · B. Read, *Victorian sculpture* (1982) · Redgrave, *Artists*, 2nd edn, 432 · Bénézit, *Dict.*, 3rd edn · W. G. Strickland, *A dictionary of Irish artists*, 2 (1913); repr. with introduction by T. J. Snoddy (1989)

Timbrell, James Christopher (1810–1850). *See under* Timbrell, Henry (1806–1849).

Timbs, John (1801–1875), author, was born on 17 August 1801 at Clerkenwell, London, and was educated at a private school at Hemel Hempstead. He was apprenticed to a printer and druggist at Dorking, and while there began to write, his first contributions appearing in the *Monthly Magazine* in 1820. About that year he came to London, and was for some time amanuensis to Sir Richard Phillips, publisher of the magazine. From that time he contributed to a large number of London publications, but chiefly to the *Mirror of Literature*, which he edited from 1827 to 1838; *The Harlequin*, which appeared between 11 May and 16 July 1829, and which was stopped by the commissioners of stamps insisting that it should be stamped as a newspaper; the *Literary World*, which he edited during 1839 and 1840; and the *Illustrated London News*, of which he was subeditor under Dr Charles Mackay from 1842 to 1858. He was also the originator and editor of the *Year Book of Science and Art*, begun in 1839 after he left the *Mirror*.

Timbs's works, which run to more than 150 volumes, are compilations of interesting facts gathered from every conceivable quarter, and relating to the most varied subjects. They include, on subjects of domestic interest, *Family Manual* (1831), *Domestic Life in England* (1835), and *Pleasant Half-Hours for the Family Circle* (1872), and, on scientific subjects, *Popular Zoology* (1834), *Stories of Inventors and Discoverers* (1859), *Curiosities of Science* (1860), and *Wonderful Inventions: from the Mariner's Compass to the Electric Telegraph Cable* (1867). He also wrote on artistic and cultural matters works such as *Companion to the Theatres* (1829), *Painting Popularly Explained* (jointly with Thomas John Gulick) (1859), and *Manual for Art Students and Visitors to the Exhibitions* (1862). On contemporary city life his works included *Curiosities of London* (1855), *Club Life of London with Anecdotes* (1865), *Romance of London: Strange Stories, Scenes, and Persons* (1865), and *London and Westminster, City and Suburb* (1867). He also published on subjects of biographical and historical interest, including *Schooldays of Eminent Men* (1858), *Columbus* (1863), *Curiosities of History* (1859), *Anecdote Biography* (1859–60), *Anecdote Lives of Wits and Humourists* (1862), *Ancestral Stories and Traditions of Great Families* (1869), and *Abbeys, Castles and Ancient Halls of England and Wales* (1869). He also edited *Manuals of Utility* (1847), the *Percy Anecdotes* (1869–

70), and *Pepys's Memoirs* (1871). In recognition of his antiquarian labours he was elected a fellow of the Society of Antiquaries in 1854. He died in considerable poverty in London on 6 March 1875.

J. R. MacDonald, rev. Nilanjana Banerji

Sources Allibone, *Dict.* · *Men of the time* (1862) · Ward, *Men of the reign* · H. R. Fox Bourne, *English newspapers: chapters in the history of journalism*, 2 (1887), 120 · *Annual Register* (1875), 138 · E. H. Yates, *Edmund Yates: his recollections and experiences*, 4th edn (1885), 207 · *N&Q*, 5th ser., 3 (1875), 220
Archives BL, corresp. with Charles Babbage, Add. MSS 37196–37197
Likenesses T. J. Gullick, miniature, *c*.1855, NPG
Wealth at death died in considerable poverty: *DNB*

Timperley, Charles H. (1794–1861), printer and writer, was born at Manchester; nothing is known of his parents. After education at Manchester grammar school, he was apprenticed to an engraver and copperplate printer. In March 1810 he enlisted in the 33rd regiment of foot, was wounded at Waterloo, and received his discharge on 28 November 1815. He resumed his apprenticeship and in 1821 became a letterpress printer by indenture to Messrs Dicey and Smithson, proprietors of the *Northampton Mercury*. In April 1828 he gave two lectures on the art of printing before the Warwick and Leamington Literary Institution and began collecting information about printers and printing. Timperley clearly moved from job to job, as was the practice with journeymen printers, and eventually became foreman to T. Kirk of Nottingham, printer of the *Nottingham Mercury*. While working for Kirk, Timperley began editing a monthly magazine, the *Nottingham Wreath*. He married a widow and soon after left Nottingham.

In 1833 Timperley produced *Songs of the press and other poems relating to the art of printing, original and selected; also epitaphs, epigrams, anecdotes, notices of early printing and printers*, of which an enlarged edition of the poetry section appeared in 1845. It is still the only collection of printers' songs in English and some of the verse is by Timperley himself. In 1838 he published *The printers' manual, containing instructions to learners, with scales of impositions and numerous calculations, recipes, and scales of prices in the principal towns of Great Britain, together with practical directions for conducting every department of a printing office*. This was followed by *A dictionary of printers and printing, with the progress of literature, ancient and modern, bibliographical illustrations* (1839).

Timperley had charge of a bookseller's shop owned by Bancks & Co. of Manchester, printer of his *Printers' Manual*. The managing partner of the firm, named Hayward, made his staff accept bank bills for the firm under their own names, which were discounted on the Manchester Bank, and when the firm's crash came the concern had debts of £120,000 to the bank and a further £100,000 to the London booksellers. To pay his debt Timperley sold the stock of his publications, but the auctioneer ran off with the proceeds. The stock of these works was purchased by H. G. Bohn, who issued the two together, with twelve pages of additions, under the title of *Encyclopaedia of literary and typographical anecdote, being a chronological digest of the most*

interesting facts illustrative of the history of literature and printing from the earliest period to the present time* (1842). Timperley also wrote *Annals of Manchester, biographical, historical, ecclesiastical, and commercial, from the earliest period* (1839).

Timperley accepted a literary engagement with Fisher and Jackson, publishers, of London, where he worked as a general editor for a handsome salary, and in his later years seems to have had a life of modest prosperity. 'Timperley was neither tall, stout, nor handsome: but there was something about him that could not but win for him respect and confidence … His dress, his address, and tone altogether bespoke the gentleman and scholar' (S. Hall, *The Lithographer*, 4, p. 221). He died in London in January 1861.

A. P. Woolrich

Sources C. H. Timperley, *Dictionary of printers* (1839), preface · E. C. Bigmore and C. W. H. Wyman, *Bibliography of printing*, 3 (1880) · *The Lithographer*, 4 (April 1874) · *Printers' Register* (6 Dec 1873) · H. Curwen, *A history of booksellers, the old and the new* (1873) · Boase, *Mod. Eng. biog.* · A. E. Musson, *The typographical association* (1954) · *DNB*

Tinbergen, Nikolaas (1907–1988), authority on animal behaviour, was born on 15 April 1907 at The Hague in the Netherlands, the third of five children and second of four sons of Dirk Cornelis Tinbergen, schoolteacher, who taught Dutch language and history and was a scholar of medieval Dutch, and his wife, Jeannette van Eek, primary school teacher. Niko Tinbergen, as he was familiarly known, went to school in The Hague. At Leiden University his career was at first undistinguished, and much of his time was spent on hockey or natural history. He was, however, very influenced by a number of amateur and professional ornithologists and, rebelling against the arid nature of the laboratory curriculum, he preferred to study wasps in the field. Perhaps affected by the rising influence of physiology, he resisted the subjectivism of A. F. J. Portielje and Bierens de Haan, and sought for more objective explanations of behaviour. As a result he was able to defend his behavioural work against the scepticism of the biological establishment and he became PhD in 1932 with a thesis only thirty-two pages long, the shortest on record in Leiden University.

In 1932 Tinbergen married a chemistry student, Elisabeth (Lies) Amélie, daughter of Louis Martien Rutter, geologist. They set off on a fourteen-month 'honeymoon' with a meteorological expedition to Greenland, where they lived with an unwesternized group of Inuit, learned their language, and acquired an interest in the hunter-gatherer's way of life. Tinbergen concentrated his research efforts on the snow bunting (*Plectrophenax nivalis*), a small bird that arrived as the snows melted, expended much energy in territorial battles with rivals, and bred in the brief summer. He also studied a variety of other Arctic animals.

After he returned Tinbergen became an instructor at Leiden in 1936, with the task of organizing laboratory practicals. For this he chose the three-spined stickleback (*Gasterosteus aculeatus*) and other animals that could easily be kept in the laboratory. The three-spined stickleback

Nikolaas Tinbergen (1907–1988), by Walter Bird

was a happy choice, for its natural environment could easily be imitated in an aquarium, and simple experiments were possible. Tinbergen mapped the reproductive cycle, analysed the stimuli eliciting attack and courtship, and showed that the complex zigzag courtship dance might be seen as a compromise between incompatible response systems. It is said that at this time Tinbergen wrote above the departmental library door 'Study Nature and not Books'. The stickleback became the classical animal of ethology, the work being subsequently continued by Jan van Iersel, Piet Sevenster, and many others. Around the same time Tinbergen started to study the herring gull (*Larus argentatus*), working on the reproductive cycle and setting up experiments on egg recognition and the stimuli releasing begging. This also became one of the classics of ethology, giving rise to a comparative study of gull behaviour in which many students participated and to a programme of experimental work, which continued under the leadership of Gerard Baerends.

In 1936 Tinbergen met Konrad Lorenz at Leiden, and he spent some of 1937 working with him near Vienna. Together they refined the methods of early ethology, Lorenz making observations of hand-reared greylag geese and Tinbergen inserting experimental probes. At this time Tinbergen and Lorenz had much in common. Both loved being in the open, observing wildlife and 'walking and wondering'. They were similarly unconventional and shared a common sense of humour. They associated easily with their students. But they also differed in critical ways. Whereas 'wondering' led Lorenz to an intuitive solution,

with Tinbergen it led to patient experiments. Such differences were of great importance in the subsequent development of ethology.

Tinbergen became a senior lecturer in 1940. However, later in the Second World War he spent two years in a German hostage camp for refusing to co-operate with the occupation authorities in their attempts to 'Nazify' Leiden University and for protesting against the removal of Jewish professors from the university. After the war he returned to Leiden, and he became a full professor in 1947.

At the suggestion of W. H. Thorpe, the Society for Experimental Biology organized a conference on physiological mechanisms of animal behaviour in 1949 in Cambridge. As a result, there was renewed contact between Tinbergen and Lorenz, and the conference provided a forum for open controversy between Lorenz, who defended the view that motor patterns were co-ordinated centrally, and James Gray and Hans Lissmann, of the Cambridge zoology department, who believed that peripheral reflexes were important. This led to the establishment of a biennial series of ethological conferences in which Tinbergen played a major role, and which became of enormous importance in the growth of ethology.

Tinbergen had paid a brief visit to the United States before the war and saw that the generalizations made by comparative psychologists there were based on laboratory studies of a few species, mostly rodents. He thus conceived a desire to teach ethology in the English-speaking world, and in 1949 he resigned his professorship at Leiden and accepted a less well-paid and less prestigious lectureship at Oxford and a fellowship at Merton College (from 1950). Although the facilities that he had looked for at Oxford never fully materialized, he built up a research group that had a profound influence on the development of ethology. He was reader from 1960 to 1966 and professor in animal behaviour from 1966 to 1974, holding a fellowship at Wolfson College at the same time as his chair. However, he was never attracted to college life.

One of Tinbergen's major contributions was to emphasize clearly the distinction between the four basic questions about behaviour—its immediate causation, development, function, and evolution—while at the same time showing how the factors are interrelated. *The Study of Instinct*, his first and perhaps most important book, appeared in 1951. It contained 127 pages on causation, but only 24 on development, 34 on function, and 26 on evolution. From then on, however, Tinbergen changed the emphasis to questions of function ('What is this behaviour for?') and evolution ('How did it evolve?'). In tackling these problems he worked primarily with gulls, and his work was especially noteworthy for his use of field experiments and detailed observation.

By the 1960s two ethologies had developed, one stemming from Lorenz, and more influential in Germany and the USA, and the other from Tinbergen, more prevalent in Britain and the Netherlands. Among the differences were Lorenz's adherence to an energy model of motivation which Tinbergen abandoned, Lorenz's more traditional approach to the nature/nurture controversy, and Tinbergen's clearer recognition of the importance of an individual selection approach to evolutionary questions. Tinbergen was an inspiring teacher. Unlike Lorenz he was never paternalistic, but created an atmosphere, with his charm and simplicity of manner, in which his students felt that he was working with them. He was a man of boundless energy and enthusiasm and an inspiring leader, who also wrote various semi-popular books (such as *The Herring Gull's World*, 1953, and *Curious Naturalists*, 1958) and books for children, and was an expert photographer.

Tinbergen gave more and more of his time to establishing the science of ethology, writing freely in natural history journals. He took films of gull behaviour which won international prizes. He also played a part in establishing the Serengeti Research Institute in Tanzania in the mid-1960s. Later he put a lot of energy into the implications of ethology for human behaviour, and helped to establish the human biology course at Oxford. He wrote on the effects of human activities on the environment, and drew lessons from animal behaviour about the incidence of human aggression. Throughout his career his wife was a constant support and colleague. During the last years of his life they collaborated in a study of human autism, drawing lessons from animal behaviour for its treatment. They had two sons and three daughters. Small, energetic, and white-haired for the last thirty years of his life, Tinbergen always dressed in field clothes unless under strong pressure. He was an inveterate smoker until fifteen years before his death.

Tinbergen was awarded the Nobel prize in medicine (together with Lorenz and Karl von Frisch), the Swammerdam medal, and the Wilhelm Boelsche medal (all in 1973). He received many other distinctions, including honorary DSc degrees from Edinburgh (1973) and Leicester (1974). He was elected a fellow of the Royal Society in 1962. He became a British subject in 1954 and died on 21 December 1988 at his home, 88 Lonsdale Road, Oxford. Exhibitions in his honour were held at the University Museum, Oxford, and the National Zoological Park, Washington, DC, in 1993.   R. A. HINDE, rev.

Sources R. A. Hinde, *Memoirs FRS*, 36 (1990), 547–65 · personal knowledge (1996) · *The Times* (24 Dec 1988) · *The Independent* (24 Dec 1988) · *Oxford Today* (1993), 25 [Trinity Term] · M. Dawkins, T. R. Halliday, and R. Dawkins, *The Tinbergen legacy* (1991)
Archives Bodl. Oxf., corresp. and papers · U. Oxf., department of zoology | CUL, corresp. with Sir Peter Markham Scott · Rice University, Houston, Texas, Woodson Research Center, corresp. with Sir Julian Huxley · U. Oxf., Edward Grey Institute of Field Ornithology, corresp. with David Lack · Wolfson College, Oxford, corresp. with H. B. D. Kettlewell | FILM BBC Natural History Unit · Oxford Zoology Department
Likenesses W. Bird, photograph, RS [*see illus.*] · photograph, repro. in Hinde, *Memoirs FRS* · photograph, repro. in *Oxford Today* (1993), 25 [Trinity Term]
Wealth at death £303,733: probate, 21 April 1989, *CGPLA Eng. & Wales*

Tincommius (*fl. c.*25 BC–AD 5). *See under* Roman Britain, British leaders in (*act.* 55 BC–AD 84).

Tindal [*née* Harrison], **Henrietta Euphemia** (*bap.* 1817, *d.* 1879), poet and novelist, was baptized on 19 July 1817 at Duffield, Derby, the only surviving child and heir of John Harrison of Ramsey, Essex, vicar of Dinton, Buckinghamshire, and Elizabeth Henrietta, *née* Wollaston. A limited education still afforded her some command of French and Italian and familiarity with a wide range of English poetry. On 30 July 1846 she married Acton Tindal (1811–1880), a well-connected clerk of the peace for the county of Buckingham, and resident of the Manor House, Aylesbury; they had three sons, Nicolas, Acton Gifford, and Charles Harrison, and twin daughters, Margaret Sabina and Henrietta Diana, the latter of whom died at the age of nine. She published poems and articles in periodicals, including book reviews which demonstrated her knowledge of art and foreign languages. Her poems and stories, like 'The Infant Bride', which was promoted and praised by her friend and correspondent Mary Russell Mitford, often drew on historical incidents or themes, deriving from her own antiquarian and genealogical interests. 'The Strange Story of Kitty Hancomb', an article first published in 1862 under her pseudonym Diana Butler, combined her interests in art, history, and legend in the romantic tale of an ancestral adulteress; it was posthumously reprinted in *Temple Bar*, this time as the story of 'Kitty Canham' by Mrs Acton Tindal, with an elaborate editor's note detailing the author's link to her subject. She published her first volume of poems, *Lines and Leaves*, in 1850. Her second, *Rhymes and Legends*, published posthumously in 1879, and dedicated to her children, includes an anonymous memoir. As Diana Butler, she published one novel, *The Heirs of Blackridge Manor* (1856). Mitford found a 'sparkling vividness in her style, which has the life and colour of painting' (Mitford, *Recollections*, 277) and claimed that 'her poems have force and finish of no common order, resembling the best and most picturesque of Mrs. Hemans's, without imitation' (*Mary Russell Mitford: Correspondence*, 80). Twentieth-century assessments, however, have found her narrative poems to be her most effective. Henrietta Tindal died on 6 May 1879 at her home, the Manor House in Aylesbury.
                                                        ALICIA GRIBBEN

Sources Blain, Clements & Grundy, *Feminist comp.*, 1082 · *The Times* (29 Oct 1880) · *Mary Russell Mitford: correspondence with Charles Boner and John Ruskin*, ed. E. Lee (1915), 80, 241 · M. R. Mitford, *Recollections of a literary life* (1852), 276–9 · H. E. Tindal, *Rhymes and legends* (1879), preface · *IGI* · d. cert.

Tindal, Matthew (*bap.* 1657, *d.* 1733), freethinker and religious controversialist, was baptized on 12 May 1657 at Bere Ferrers, Devon, the son of John Tindal, who was the minister there, and his wife, Anne Halse. He was taught by his father before entering Lincoln College, Oxford, in 1672, and there he was a pupil of George Hickes, the future nonjuror; he migrated to Exeter College, and graduated BA on 17 October 1676. He was elected to a law fellowship at All Souls College, Oxford, in 1678, taking the degrees of BCL in 1679 and DCL in 1685, after which he became a member of Doctors' Commons. He had become a Roman Catholic at Oxford, and attended mass frequently during James II's reign; he worked in his service during Monmouth's rebellion. Tindal, a great frequenter of London coffee houses, 'fell into the acquaintance of some persons, whose conversation led him into a dislike of Popery' (Lloyd, 3960), and he returned to the Church of England, taking communion from the warden of All Souls on Easter day 1688.

A warm defender of the revolution in 1688, Tindal became an increasingly strong critic of the powers claimed by Church of England clergy, turning from Christianity to freethinking within a decade. Many of his contemporaries saw him as an opportunist in religion, having converted to Catholicism allegedly in the hope of securing the wardenship of All Souls under James II and returning to the Church of England just before the king's defeat by William of Orange. He was notoriously immoral, and was publicly reprimanded at All Souls as 'an *Egregious Fornicator*' (Lloyd, 3960). The poet Abel Evans combined both of his principal vices when denouncing Tindal in *The Apparation* (1710):

> In Vice and Error from his *Cradle* Nurs'd:
> He studies hard, and takes extreme Delight,
> In Whores, or Heresies to spend the Night.
> (p. 6)

In the course of this satire, Evans has Tindal surprised by Satan in the form of a female bedmaker with whom he has previously had an affair; Satan then reverts to his true form and plots, with his 'Vassal sworn', the destruction of the Church of England in favour of atheism, Spinozism, and dissent, before obligingly disappearing up a chimney. Thomas Hearne, the Oxford antiquary, thought Evans's work ingenious, and reported that Tindal was 'dejected at it'; Hearne always kept a close eye on Tindal the 'Libertine', 'that notorious Atheist', 'that Rascal', a promoter of other 'vile, republican Rascals' (*Remarks*, 2.332, 72; 3.255, 381, 439).

Whatever his personal reputation, Tindal had made a name for himself as a lawyer in the early years of William III's reign, first in the case of an Italian count who had sought protection as a foreign subject from prosecution for murder, and second for arguing, in a controversial judgment in 1693, that followers of James II who had taken to the seas ought to be prosecuted as pirates, on the grounds that a deposed monarch had no authority to issue a commission for the high sea. He developed his case, citing Cicero and Grotius and other legal precedents, in a blatantly anti-Jacobite tract, *An Essay Concerning the Laws of Nations, and the Rights of Soveraigns* (1694), which denounced all James's followers as either robbers or pirates. Such loyalty to the Williamite regime gained him a considerable public reputation, and, it was claimed, an annual salary of £200 from the crown. This was the high point of his legal career, and he devoted his remaining years to pamphleteering on political and religious matters, continuing to practise law at Gray's Inn and retreating regularly to All Souls, where he gathered around him a group of whig secularist lawyers opposed to the religious requirements made of fellows by the college's statutes. He enjoyed baiting college fellows on religious matters; Herbert Croft reported a characteristic remark he made about a younger

fellow, Edward Young, which found its way into Johnson's life of the poet: '"The other boys," said the atheist, "I can always answer, because I always know whence they have their arguments, which I have read an hundred times; but that fellow Young is continually pestering me with something of his own"' ('Young' in S. Johnson, *Lives of the English Poets*, ed. G. B. Hill, 1905, 3.364).

As his friend Edmund Curll observed, Tindal's life was to prove 'a continual Warfare in the Republic of Letters, for the Space of above forty Years' (Curll, 1). The general direction of Tindal's future thoughts on politics and religion can be traced in the first pamphlet which he devoted to these matters, *An essay concerning the power of the magistrate, and the rights of mankind, in matters of religion* (1697). The tract was written to further Locke's arguments in his 'three incomparable Letters concerning Toleration', as Tindal emphasized that 'impartial Liberty and mutual Toleration' were the 'only way to preserve both Church and State' (p. 2). Tindal argued that the rights of the magistrate were secured from the people, not from God, so that he had no powers over religion. To enforce conformity against the pleas of individual conscience was to destroy each individual's chance of eternal happiness, and to act against God's honour: it was 'consequently the greatest and most comprehensive of all Sins whatever' (p. 67). He went on to argue for the rights of dissenters to worship as they pleased, and in favour of a nationalization act for religious refugees, which would have had, he contended, a markedly beneficial impact on trade and commerce. The chief part of religion was, he insisted, 'promoting the Publick Good' (pp. 173–4), and his defence of toleration was designed to do just that. The tone of this pamphlet was even-handed and decorous; his writings quickly became altogether more sarcastic and contentious when his battles with high-churchmanship become much more explicit in the early 1700s.

By far the most contentious of Tindal's writings at mid-career appeared in 1706: *The rights of the Christian church asserted, against the Romish, and all other priests who claim an independent power over it*. The enemy he identified was at least as much high-churchmanship as it was Roman Catholicism, and he adopted the apparently moderate tones of a supporter of an Anglican *via media* in a defence of the Reformation which actually had profound implications for all styles of churchmanship. He opposed the claims for two independent powers subsisting in the same society, the one ecclesiastical, the other magisterial, condemning 'the Spiritual Babylon' promoted by high-church contenders for such a separation (p. 33). He argued that it was in the interests of the clergy to complicate religion, thereby making themselves indispensable in the religious lives of the people: their powers made the protestant call for further reformation impossible, and the interests of their church were declared to be incompatible with those of true religion. 'From this Conduct of the High-flown Clergy', he concluded, 'some have taken the Liberty to compare a High-Church Priest in Politicks to a Monkey in a Glass-shop, where as he can do no good, so he never fails of doing Mischief enough' (p. 270). He saw in this attitude of clerics a means to defend himself, noting of it that 'nothing sooner [gives] a Man the Character of an Atheist than being an Enemy to Priestcraft' (p. 415).

Hickes, Tindal's former tutor, wrote one of the most effective replies to the work, having discovered that his former pupil had told 'a Gentleman, who found him at it with Pen in Hand, *That he was Writing a Book which would make the Clergy Mad*'. *The Rights of the Christian Church* was denounced by Hickes as 'the Commonplace-Book of *Atheists and Deists*', as he found, 'In one word, That it is Atheistical all over' (*Spinoza Reviv'd*, 1709, [1], [50], 3). William Wotton delivered an equally pugnacious reply, declaring of Tindal's book that it was written with 'Petulancy and Indecency of Stile' (*The Rights of the Clergy in the Christian Church Asserted*, 1706, 3). An anonymous reply quickly appeared, denouncing both Wotton and Hickes and pointing out that Le Clerc had made admiring noises about the book in his *Bibliotheque choisie*. Entitled *A Defence of the Rights of the Christian Church* (1709), this reply aroused almost as much anger as had Tindal's book, and it was burnt on the orders of the House of Commons, along with its high-church analogue, Sacheverell's *Sermons*, on 25 March 1710. Dozens of replies had been made to *The Rights of the Christian Church*, and a campaign was launched against it at Oxford, where Tindal was denounced as a Lockean and an extreme whig. Hearne lamented the impact of *The Rights of the Christian Church*, 'a most Violent, poysonous Book, and levell'd against ye Church of England' (*Remarks*, 2.72). Jonathan Swift was less certain of the book's impact on Christian commitment, asking ironically, 'What other Subject through all Art or Nature could have produced Tindal for an Author, or furnished him with Readers?' (*An Argument Against Abolishing Christianity*, in *The Prose Works of Jonathan Swift*, ed. H. Davis, 1939, 2.36).

Aside from sporadic contributions to the anti-clerical cause, notably *New High-Church Turn'd Old Presbyterian* (1709), *Merciful Judgements of the High Church Triumphant* (1710), and *A New Catechism with Dr. Hicke's Thirty Nine Articles* (1710), Tindal reverted to politics as his main focus in the early years of the reign of George I. He censured Robert Walpole for splitting the whig party—he had looked to him for a reform of the universities, and had particularly hoped to laicise the fellowship at All Souls—in two tracts, *Defection Considered* (1717) and the consequent *Account of a Manuscript, Entitul'd, 'Destruction the Certain Consequences of Division'* (1718). This soon became a more positive relationship, as can be seen in two further tracts, *A Defence of our Present Happy Establishment, and the Administration Vindicated* (1722) and his *Enquiry into the Causes of our Present Disaffection* (1722). Tindal was something of a court whig, and was quick to denounce opposition whiggery, as in his critique of the polemicists John Trenchard and Thomas Gordon in *The judgement of Dr. Prideaux concerning the murder of Julius Caesar, by the conspirators, as a most villanous act, maintain'd* (1721), where he praised England's political system as 'the best, and easiest of all Governments; where the utmost Liberty and Safety are joined together' (p. 94).

Religious issues dominated the closing years of Tindal's life, and he was one of the principal propagandists during the anti-clerical warfare that dominated the 1730s. His first contribution to this debate was in the form of two replies to Bishop Edmund Gibson's immensely influential pastoral letters to his London clergy on the increase in freethinking and infidelity. In *An Address to the Inhabitants of the Two Great Cities of London and Westminster* (1729; 2nd edn, 1730) Tindal voiced his shock at Gibson's defence of revelation as being, in Tindal's reading, above reason. Citing on his side a long line of rational divines, Tindal found in Gibson and his clerical allies such as Daniel Waterland an abrogation of reason which could only compromise religion; in *A Second Address* (1730) he also pointedly adverted to West Indian slavery and bad behaviour in India as indicating the hypocrisies attendant on a merely external adherence to Christianity. Much of Tindal's language was consciously modulated in the style of latitudinarian divines, hence something of the anger of clerical respondents to his writings. This register was distilled most effectively in his final work, *Christianity as Old as the Creation* (1731). This takes the form of a dialogue, and is essentially a detailed argument for the supremacy of natural over revealed religion. For Tindal, reason was to be employed first to discover, and then to put into practice, the obligations of morality which flow from discovering the existence of a beneficent creator. While he pays lip-service to Christianity as being what his subtitle proclaims a 'republication of the religion of nature', it is abundantly clear to the reader that natural religion effectively makes revealed religions—Judaism, Islam, Christianity—redundant and, as polemical distortions of natural religion, potentially dangerous. It was a notably contentious book; Tindal claimed that natural religion would bring out the 'same sentiment' in 'Men of good Sense', so that 'a Shaftesbury will say the same as a Tillotson' (*Christianity as Old as the Creation*, 78), thereby eliding a freethinker with the most revered of latitudinarian divines. He blamed priestcraft as the cause of religious controversy, for the imposers of creeds had proved themselves 'the common Plagues of Mankind' (ibid., 163–4). When a Christian divine attempted to prove the superiority of revealed over natural religion, as in the writings of Samuel Clarke, Tindal saw only that 'on Pretence of promoting the Honour of Revelation, [he] is introducing universal scepticism' (ibid., 381). Though in many ways a grand summation of freethinking at mid-century, *Christianity as Old as the Creation* is, as one authoritative commentator has observed, 'a disappointing book which deserved some at least of the scorn of its contemporary critics' (Rivers, 2.15). Scorn there was in plenty, and answers to the book encompassed a wide arc of clerical (and lay) opinion, from the nonjuror William Law to the dissenter Nathanial Lardner. In all, something like thirty replies, from pamphlets to quartos, appeared to repudiate its message. Even John 'Orator' Henley added his contribution in *Deism Defeated, and Christianity Defended* (1731), and an anonymous poem appeared in 1730, *Blasphemy as Old as the Creation*, in which Tindal's Epicureanism was turned against him:

This Tindal knew; and pious vow'd to quit
Doctrines, that very seldom turn'd his Spit:

Tir'd with a Church, whose Canons did define
That to believe, was sweeter than to Dine.
(p. 8)

Tindal's reputation for sensual indulgence, both sexual and at the table, was often used against him. An anonymous fellow of All Souls pitched on his 'Canine Appetite' as a recurring metaphor for his venal character in *The Religious, Rational, and Moral Conduct of Matthew Tindal, L.L.D.* of 1735 (p. 10). Debauchery was his other great sin, and the writer referred to the 'Doctor's Amours and natural Children' (p. 22), before retelling older tales of his attempts on young women's honour, concluding of his subject that he was 'a notorious and bare-faced Factor for the Devil, a Debauchee, a Renegade, an Atheist' (p. 62). A fault of which the author made little was Tindal's abstemiousness when it came to drink. After the furore over *Christianity as Old as the Creation*, Tindal fell into a decline. Only the first thirty-two pages of the second part of *Christianity as Old as the Creation* were subsequently printed.

Tindal died, following complications from a gallstone, in his rooms at Gray's Inn on 16 August 1733. He was buried, as he had wished, next to the latitudinarian bishop Gilbert Burnet in the cemetery attached to Clerkenwell church, London, on 23 August. Even in death he was subject to controversy. The writer Eustace Budgell insisted that he and Mrs Price, the widow of a judge (who seems to have been Tindal's last mistress), were his only legatees, but the will so promoted was disputed by his nephew, the historian Nicholas Tindal, in whose favour the matter was resolved. Budgell claimed to have been entrusted with a copy of the second part of *Christianity as Old as the Creation*; if so, it was never recovered, and the story that Bishop Gibson acquired it before destroying it is spurious.

B. W. Young

Sources *Remarks and collections of Thomas Hearne*, ed. C. E. Doble and others, 11 vols., OHS, 2, 7, 13, 34, 42–3, 48, 50, 65, 67, 72 (1885–1921) • E. Curll, *Memoirs of the life and writings of Matthew Tindall* (1733) • N. Lloyd, 'Tindall, Matthew', *Biographia Britannica, or, The lives of the most eminent persons who have flourished in Great Britain and Ireland*, ed. A. Kippis and others, 6 (1763), 3960–65 • Foster, *Alum. Oxon.* • *GM*, 1st ser., 3 (1733), 439 • *Hist. U. Oxf.*, 4.424–5; 5.78–82, 391 • [C. Coote], *Sketches of the lives and characters of eminent English civilians, with an historical introduction relative to the College of Advocates* (1804) • I. Rivers, *Reason, grace and sentiment: a study of the language of religion and ethics in England, 1660–1780*, 2 vols. (1991–2000) • J. A. I. Champion, *The pillars of orthodoxy shaken* (1992) • J. Redwood, *Reason, ridicule and religion* (1975) • Nichols, *Lit. anecdotes*, 4.303 • D. Berman and S. Lawlor, 'The suppression of *Christianity as old as the creation*, volume II', *N&Q*, 229 (1984), 3–6 • *DNB*
Likenesses J. Faber junior, mezzotint, 1733 (after B. Dandridge), BM, NPG • copper and silver medal, BM

Tindal, Nicholas (1687–1774), historical writer and translator, was born on 25 November 1687 at Plymouth, the only son of John Tindal, vicar of Cornwood, Devon, and his wife, Elizabeth Prideaux. His uncle was the deist Matthew Tindal (1657–1733), and his aunt Elizabeth was the mother of Nathaniel Forster (1718–1757). He matriculated from Exeter College, Oxford, on 6 March 1707, graduated BA in 1710, and proceeded MA in 1713. On 29 January 1710 he married Anne Keate (*bap.* 1681) of Hagbourne, Berkshire; they had three sons, John, George, and James. In

1716 Tindal was presented to the rectory of Hatford, Berkshire, and in 1722 to the vicarage of Great Waltham, Essex.

Tindal's first published work was a translation of Augustin Calmet's *Antiquities Sacred and Profane* (1724). Soon afterwards the booksellers James and John Knapton began to publish Tindal's translation of Paul de Rapin Thoyras's *History of England* (originally published in French, 1723–5). His translation, with notes, appeared in fifteen octavo volumes from 1725 to 1731. Tindal began the work at Great Waltham but continued his translation while serving as a chaplain in the navy. The second volume was dedicated on 12 July 1726 to Sir Charles Wager, to whom Tindal was then acting as chaplain in the Baltic, and the fourth was dated 'on board the *Torbay* in Gibraltar Bay, Sep. 4, 1727'. A second edition was brought out in 1732–3, and a third in 1743.

Tindal then wrote a *Continuation* of Rapin's *History of England* from the revolution of 1688 to the accession of George II in 1727. The first volume was published in 1744, and the second in 1745 (numbered as the third and fourth volume of Rapin's *History*). The work subsequently appeared in numerous forms, including an *Abridgement* (1747) and a *Summary* (1751). Through copious footnotes and politicized prefaces Tindal was an important contributor to the remarkable success of Rapin's *History*. His footnotes added extra topical detail and recounted well-known legends about English history. They also incorporated political criticisms of church history and revealed religion. Tindal's dedications to Frederick, prince of Wales (1732), and to the duke of Cumberland (1745), both attempted to show how Rapin's *History* could inform understanding of contemporary politics.

Tindal's *Continuation* incorporated Rapin's conceptual framework of the ancient Saxon constitution and the necessity of limiting royal power, and applied it to English history since the revolution of 1688. Tindal lacks some of Rapin's narrative flair, and relies on lengthy quotation, but one nineteenth-century commentator found Tindal's work 'a temperate and candid narrative of carefully ascertained facts' (Gardiner and Mullinger, 375). It also, according to Burton, became the authoritative work for the history of Queen Anne's reign. The work's detractors, however, doubted Tindal's authorship or suggested political interference, while William Duncombe published an anonymous attack on Tindal's style, *Remarks on Mr. Tindal's Translation* (1728).

While vicar of Waltham, Tindal also wrote a scrappy *History of Essex* (*c.*1732) based upon the manuscripts of William Holman, which was nevertheless an important precursor to the work by his close friend and correspondent, Philip Morant. In 1731 he was appointed master of the Royal Free School at Chelmsford, and in 1732 chaplain-in-ordinary at Chatham. Following the death of his uncle, Matthew Tindal, in 1733, he became embroiled in a very public dispute with Eustace Budgell over the will, which Tindal believed had been forged by Budgell and had robbed him of his inheritance. Tindal published his case in *A Copy of the Will of Matthew Tindal* ... (1733), but he failed to obtain restitution from Budgell.

In 1738 Tindal was appointed chaplain to Greenwich Hospital, and in 1740 he was presented to the rectories of Calbourne, Isle of Wight, and Alverstoke, Hampshire. In 1764 he published *A Guide to Classical Learning, or, Polymetis Abridged*, which proved a very popular handbook, and subsequent editions appeared in 1765, 1777, 1786, and 1802, all in duodecimo. Tindal was married again, on 11 August 1753 at the chapel of Greenwich Hospital; his second wife was Elizabeth Judith Gugelman. He died at Greenwich Hospital on 27 June 1774, in his eighty-seventh year, and was buried on 2 July 1774 in the second burial-ground of the hospital, known as Goddard's Garden.

A. F. POLLARD, rev. M. G. SULLIVAN

Sources *Essex Review*, 2 (1893), 168–79 · A. Chalmers, ed., *The general biographical dictionary*, new edn, 29 (1816), 398–400 · J. H. Burton, *A history of the reign of Queen Anne*, 2.324–5 · S. R. Gardiner and J. B. Mullinger, *Introduction to the study of English history* (1881), 375 · M. G. Sullivan, 'Historiography and visual culture in Britain, 1660–1783', PhD diss., U. Leeds, 1998 · A. Shell, 'Antiquarians, local politics and the book trade: the publication of Philip Morant's *History of Colchester* (1748)', *The Library*, 6th ser., 21 (1999), 223–46 · *GM*, 1st ser., 44 (1774), 333 · *Hasted's history of Kent: corrected, enlarged, and continued to the present time*, ed. H. H. Drake (1886) · Q. J. Raoul de Cazenove, *Rapin-Thoyras, sa famille, sa vie et ses oeuvres* (1866) · Foster, *Alum. Oxon.* · W. T. Lowndes, *The bibliographer's manual of English literature*, ed. H. G. Bohn, [new edn], 6 vols. (1864) · N. Tindall, *A copy of the will of Dr Matthew Tindal with an account of what passed concerning the same between Mrs Lucy Price, Eustace Budgell esq; and Mr Nicholas Tindal* (1733)
Archives BL, letters to T. Birch, Add. MS 4319, fols. 157–59 · BL, corresp. with P. Morant, Add. MS 37222, fols. 1, 9, 22, 23, 87
Likenesses B. Picart, line engraving (after G. Knapton), BM, NPG; repro. in P. de Rapin, *The history of England*, 2nd edn, 2 vols. (1732–3) · G. Vertue, engraving (after B. Picart), repro. in Fitch and Dalton, eds., *Essex review*

Tindal, Sir Nicholas Conyngham (1776–1846), judge, was born at Coval Hall, near Chelmsford, on 12 December 1776, the son of Robert Tindal, a solicitor of Chelmsford, and his wife, Sarah, only daughter of John Pocock of Greenwich. He was related to the celebrated deist Matthew Tindal and was the great-grandson of the historian Nicholas Tindal. He was educated at Chelmsford grammar school, where Thomas Naylor was master, before going at the age of nineteen to Trinity College, Cambridge, where he graduated BA in 1799 as eighth wrangler, winning the chancellor's gold medal. He was elected fellow of Trinity in 1801, and in 1802 graduated MA; he was awarded an honorary DCL degree from the University of Oxford in 1834. In 1802 he entered as a student at Lincoln's Inn in London. Seven years later, on 2 September 1809, he married Merelina (d. 1818), the youngest daughter of Thomas Symonds, a captain in the Royal Navy. They had one daughter and four sons; their eldest son, Nicholas Tindal (d. 1842), became vicar of Sandhurst in Gloucestershire, and the youngest, Charles John (d. 1853), a barrister of Lincoln's Inn.

On 20 June 1809 Tindal was called to the bar, having previously read with Sir John Richardson and practised as a special pleader. He joined the northern circuit, and

earned a considerable practice on the strength of his wide and accurate learning (he was never a good advocate). His learning, even in obsolete law, was shown to advantage in the case *Ashford* v. *Thornton*, in which he successfully claimed for his client the right of wager of battle, later abolished by statute. Henry Brougham and Parke (afterwards Lord Wensleydale) were among his pupils. He was subsequently with Brougham as counsel for Queen Caroline in her trial in 1820 (H. P. Brougham, *The Life and Times of Henry Lord Brougham*, 1871, 2.381).

Tindal entered parliament in 1824 as a tory member for the Wigtown burghs, and became solicitor-general on 20 September 1826 at a time of change caused by Copley's appointment as master of the rolls, and was knighted. Also in 1826, he was returned to parliament for Harwich; but in 1827, Copley's becoming lord chancellor created a vacancy at the University of Cambridge, and Tindal was elected by 479 votes against 378 for William John Bankes. With characteristic modesty he declined to assert his claim to become attorney-general, either against James Scarlett (afterwards first Baron Abinger) in 1827 or against Sir Charles Wetherell in 1828 (Arnould, *Life of Lord Denman*, 1873, 1.206). On 9 June 1829 he was appointed chief justice of the common pleas in succession to William Draper Best, first Baron Wynford, a position which he kept until his death. Among the cases which he tried were Norton's action against Lord Melbourne for criminal conversation and the murder trials of Courvoisier and MacNaghten. He worked up to ten days before his death from a stroke at Folkestone on 6 July 1846. He was buried at Kensal Green cemetery, Middlesex, on 14 July.

Tindal was esteemed by contemporary lawyers for his grasp of principle, accuracy of statement, skill in analysis, and store of case law. He became somewhat procrastinating and eccentric as a judge at the end of his life, but retained the respect and affection of those who practised before him. He had a considerable, highly legal wit, of which some examples are given in Benjamin Robinson's *Bench and Bar* (1889, 153–8).

J. A. HAMILTON, rev. HUGH MOONEY

Sources E. Foss, *Biographia juridica: a biographical dictionary of the judges of England ... 1066–1870* (1870) · *Law Magazine*, 36 (1846), 105–11 · *GM*, 2nd ser., 26 (1846), 199
Archives BL, letters, legal opinions · Harvard U., law school, memoranda and notes of public business as solicitor-general | BL, letters to Theresa Whitby, Add. MS 63091
Likenesses T. Wright, stipple, pubd 1821 (after A. Wivell), BM, NPG · W. J. Ward, mezzotint, pubd 1834 (after W. J. Newton), BM · J. Lucas, mezzotint, pubd 1835, BM · T. Phillips, oils, 1840, NPG · J. Doyle, pencil drawing, BM

Tindal, William (1756–1804), antiquary, was born at Chelmsford on 14 May 1756, the son of James Tindal (d. 1760), captain in the 4th regiment of dragoons, who was the youngest son of the historian Nicholas *Tindal (1687–1774). His mother was Lucy Shenton, who, after James Tindal's death in 1760, married Dr Smith, a physician at Cheltenham and Oxford. At four years of age William Tindal and his mother went to live with her brother, a minor canon of Chichester, and six years later they moved to

Richmond. On 19 May 1772 Tindal matriculated from Trinity College, Oxford, and he was elected a scholar in the same year. He graduated BA in 1776 and proceeded MA in 1778. In 1778 he was ordained deacon and obtained a fellowship, which he held until his marriage.

After serving as curate at Fladbury, Worcestershire, Tindal became rector of Wallingford in Norfolk in 1789. In 1792 he also became rector of Kington, Worcestershire. In 1799 he exchanged the living at Wallingford for the chaplainship of the Tower of London. In the same year he was elected a fellow of the Society of Antiquaries.

Besides writing several political pamphlets, Tindal published a work on Dr Johnson's life and the works of Gray (1782). In 1794 he published *The History and Antiquities of the Abbey and Borough of Evesham*. This was well reviewed by the *Gentleman's Magazine*, which commented, 'this history is executed just as such works should be, and in an agreeable and correct style' (*GM*, 1st ser., 64/2, 1794, 836). It was also said to have won high praise from Horace Walpole.

Tindal committed suicide by shooting himself with a musket in his residence at the Tower on 16 September 1804 while suffering from mental depression. He was to have joined his wife on the day of his suicide, when she was staying with an aunt in Exeter. A verdict of lunacy was returned by the coroner's court, amid scurrilous rumours regarding his wife's conduct, which were vehemently denied by Tindal's friends.

E. I. CARLYLE, *rev.* J. A. MARCHAND

Sources *GM*, 1st ser., 74 (1804), 889–90, 975 · *GM*, 1st ser., 64 (1794), 836 · D. C. Cox, 'Worcestershire', *English county histories: a guide*, ed. C. R. J. Currie and C. P. Lewis (1994), 423–32, esp. 430 · Nichols, *Illustrations*, 6.772 · J. Chambers, *Biographical illustrations of Worcestershire* (1820), 567–72 · Foster, *Alum. Oxon.* · IGI

Tingewick, Nicholas (*d.* in or before **1339**), ecclesiastic and physician, was an intermittently active university official and churchman, with a medical practice which has left more records than that of most physicians of his time. As Master Nicholas, clerk, he was presented to the rectory of Broughton in Craven, in Yorkshire, on 21 November 1291 and was admitted to the living as subdeacon a year later. In 1294 he was granted leave to study in England or abroad for three years; and in 1296 he received letters of protection to accompany the bishop of Winchester abroad. Having been presented to an additional rectory, that of Coleshill, in Berkshire, when he had still not returned to Broughton in Craven, he was ultimately deprived of the revenues from his first benefice. But Edward I seems to have acquired another living for Tingewick, who by 1310 was parson of Reculver, Kent, after his royal patron had interceded with the pope on his behalf, on the grounds that he was the 'best doctor for the king's health' (Emden, *Oxf.*, 3.1877).

If Tingewick's career as a churchman excited the usual objections of pluralism directed against medical practitioners, his career as physician seems to have been unusually uncontroversial. Edward I praised his doctor enthusiastically. During the king's residence at Lanercost Priory near Carlisle at the end of his life (1306–7), Tingewick ordered for his master rich ointments and medicines to the value of nearly £135. The list of medicinal substances includes material for embalming the king's remains, and demonstrates the intimate involvement of the king's physician in the care of the royal body, and the trust he must have enjoyed. Another patient, Henry Eastry, prior of Christ Church, Canterbury, was equally enthusiastic about Tingewick's medical skills, thanking his doctor in 1324 for the swift relief of his fever. Tingewick may have served as physician to Henry de Lacy, earl of Lincoln (*d.* 1311), who was present at the king's death in 1307, since Henry gave him an annuity of 16 marks. And he also served Edward II, but probably not as a physician.

Tingewick's fame as a physician outlived him. John Mirfield, a London priest who wrote a medical compendium at about the end of the fourteenth century, mentions him twice. In one instance, he reports with admiration that the doctor gave a certain widow a sum of money to teach him her jaundice cure (sheep's lice crushed with honey and water), having ridden 40 miles to visit her.

From the early 1320s until the end of his life, Tingewick seems to have resided in Oxford. In 1302 he bought a substantial property on the east side of Cat Street, known as Tingewick's Inn or Corbet Hall, which he granted to the university in 1322, together with another property in St Ebbe's, with the provision that he could live there as principal for life. The revenue from his benefaction was to pay for two regent masters who would supervise the grammar schools. Tingewick had taken the degree of doctor of medicine by 1325, and, as was not unusual with university-educated physicians of his time, he was bachelor of theology also by 1325. He became active in university affairs and in 1325 was appointed one of two external masters who enforced the wishes of the founder that only arts be taught at Balliol College. Since Balliol had a medical fellow as late as 1321 and none afterwards, perhaps Tingewick was attempting to limit medical study there. He was dead by 1339.

FAYE GETZ

Sources C. H. Talbot and E. A. Hammond, *The medical practitioners in medieval England: a biographical register* (1965) · F. M. Getz, 'The faculty of medicine before 1500', *Hist. U. Oxf. 2: Late med. Oxf.*, 373–405 · J. R. H. Moorman, 'Edward I at Lanercost Priory, 1306–7', *EngHR*, 67 (1952), 161–74 · Pembroke College, Oxford, MS 2, fol. 32 · Emden, *Oxf.*, 3.1877

Tinker, Hugh Russell (1921–2000), historian, was born on 20 July 1921 at 105 St Helen's Road, Southend-on-Sea, Essex, the only child of Clement Hugh Tinker, marine insurance broker, and his wife, Gertrude Marian Russell, a schoolmistress. He attended Holly School, Sheringham (1930–34), and then Taunton School (1934–8), where he was awarded the T. S. Penny history prize. On leaving school he trained as a librarian, but soon tried to join first the RAF and then the army, before enlisting in the Royal Armoured Corps on 3 October 1939. He served in Burma and on the north-west frontier, and was commissioned on 1 October 1941, eventually becoming a captain. He was seconded to India's civil administration in 1945–6 and then acted as a first class magistrate in Uttar Pradesh.

On demobilization Tinker went to Sidney Sussex College, Cambridge, to read history. He obtained a 2:1 in his first tripos in 1947, and a first in his second tripos in 1948. He was awarded the college essay prize for an essay on 'The British achievement in India, illustrated by a study of the Punjab administration, 1840–1870'. His tutor, David Thomson, author of a number of standard texts on modern European history, wrote of Tinker on 24 May 1948:

> Personally he is a man of great energy and industry, of real intellectual and practical ability, and of attractive personality. He is mature and sound in judgement, and … can be relied upon to complete any task he undertakes with good sense and efficiency. (*Independent*, 4 May 2000)

He considered graduate work in Cambridge but in 1948 he was appointed lecturer in the modern history of southeast Asia at the School of Oriental and African Studies (SOAS) in the University of London. In the same year he obtained a mark of distinction in the diploma in public administration of London University. On 23 August 1947 he had married Elisabeth McKenzie Willis, a ballet dancer. They had three sons, all born in the 1950s.

Tinker's first book, *The Foundations of Local Self-Government in India, Pakistan and Burma* (1954), sprang from his SOAS doctorate (supervised by D. G. E. ('George') Hall, then the doyen of British historians of Burma and of south-east Asia). It was dedicated to his first two sons, Jonathan and Mark, 'tireless protagonists of self-government', and came with an unusually long commendatory preface by that eminently proconsular figure Lord Hailey. Wide-ranging and lucid, this first book took up several themes which he worked out in subsequent articles, chapters in scholarly symposia, and his many subsequent books.

Burma had featured in his wartime experiences, his PhD, and thus his first book. And he became Britain's foremost historian of modern Burma. A spell as visiting professor in the University of Rangoon (1954–5) led to his authoritative study *The Union of Burma: a Study of the First Years of Independence* (1957), which appeared in three more editions. In his preface dated February 1956 Tinker affirmed that his wife Elisabeth's training in 'Burmese classical dancing penetrated more deeply into the life of Burma than I did'—an early and often repeated tribute to his wife's help. He recounted Burmese efforts to 'create a parliamentary democracy in the face of heavy pressure, known and unknown, internal and external' only two years before the relapse into military rule, thus giving particular piquancy to his assertion, also in his preface, that 'strenuous unemotional thinking is earnestly needed in Burma in the years immediately ahead'.

In the late 1950s and throughout the 1960s at SOAS, Tinker sought to confirm and demonstrate Abraham Lincoln's conviction that 'the ballot is stronger than the bullet' and he coined and popularized the phrase 'broken-backed state', a phrase reminiscent of Otega's *Invertebrate Spain* but actually derived, so Tinker avowed, from the notion of broken-back warfare after nuclear exchanges, as adumbrated in Duncan Sandys's notorious defence white paper of 1957. He was a fecund essayist, especially in the 1960s. One collection of his essays, *Re-Orientations* (1965), conveyed a strong sense of what he had learned about politics from being a parliamentary candidate at the hustings: he stood unsuccessfully as a Liberal Party candidate three times, in Barnet (1964, 1966) and Morecambe and Lonsdale (1979). In the early 1980s Tinker edited with magisterial style and skill two volumes of British papers, based on India Office Library records, on the demission and transfer of power entitled *Burma: the Struggle for Independence, 1944–48*, 1983 and 1984, which became a standard authoritative source on this subject. The Burmese opposition leader and Nobel laureate, Aung San Suu Kyi, was one of his students.

In 1970 Tinker became director of the Institute of Race Relations, succeeding Philip Mason, its founding director. This was an acrimonious penny-pinching time for the institute and for race relations generally. Class and generational conflict between the council and some of Tinker's youngest radical staff disrupted his own lifestyle, and his writing plans suffered. But he was convinced that the institute should be no ivory tower, but frank and open about policies and their implications.

In 1972 with some sense of relief Tinker found a new but familiar base at the Institute of Commonwealth Studies in the University of London and embarked on a remarkably productive five-year period even by his own high standards of lucid and eminently readable scholarship. Funded by a generous grant from the Ford Foundation to write a trilogy on the Indian diaspora, he wrote at least four books on this theme (including a sympathetic biography of Charlie Andrews, the Indophile British missionary) and also entered fully into the life of the small research institute which was his base, helping and encouraging young members of staff as was his wont. But whether at the Institute of Commonwealth Studies, the India Office, at home in Mill Hill, or at his cottage in Buckinghamshire he kept on writing.

He was professor of politics at Lancaster University from 1977 to 1982; on his retirement he was made professor emeritus. With the move to Lancashire, Hugh and Elisabeth bought a house in Hornby, and both soon became active in local village and church affairs. His youngest son, David, was killed in HMS *Glamorgan* in the Falklands War of 1982. Swiftly, and in part to assuage his grief, Tinker produced *A Message from the Falklands: the Life and Gallant Death of David Tinker* (1982), a lovingly edited version of family correspondence, especially between father and son. This book was rendered into a play, *Falkland sound/ Voces de Malvinas*, which ran for several months in 1983 at the Royal Court Theatre, London.

Tinker was a lifelong Liberal and liberal, giving consistent meaning to these notoriously elastic party political and intellectual labels. Equally at ease whether occupying chairs of history or of politics, he did not take naturally to the routines of academic administration, but his congeniality and interest in the intellectual development of his younger colleagues were always evident.

Hugh Tinker carried his learning lightly, and often with a wry, modest self-deprecation. He was no solemn methodologist, but one who loved writing. He much enjoyed a visiting professorship at Cornell University in upstate

New York in 1959, but he often poked gentle fun at some of the pretentiousness of American academia. In *Who's Who* he described his recreations as 'pottering'. In his last years, crippled with arthritis and by encroaching Parkinson's disease, he could not even hold a pen, but he kept on writing (his output including two articles for the *Oxford Dictionary of National Biography*) by dictating to his wife and drawing on his remarkable, unimpaired memory.

His family, faith, and friendships were central values in Hugh Tinker's life. The epigraph for one of his many books was from Isaiah 32: 8—'But the liberal deviseth liberal things; and by liberal things shall he stand'—sentiments which could well serve as an epitaph on his life. He died in the Royal Infirmary, Lancaster, on 15 April 2000, and was buried four days later in St Margaret's churchyard, Hornby, Lancaster.   PETER LYON

Sources H. Tinker, *Reorientations: studies on Asia in transition* (1965) · college records, Sidney Sussex College, Cambridge · *The Independent* (4 May 2000) · *The Guardian* (8 May 2000) · *The Times* (20 April 2000) · b. cert. · m. cert. · d. cert. · private information (2004)
Archives U. Lond., Institute of Commonwealth Studies, corresp. and papers rel. to various publications

Tinling, Cuthbert Collingwood [Teddy] (1910–1990), fashion designer, was born on 23 June 1910 in Eastbourne, Sussex, the youngest of the three sons of James Alexander Tinling, chartered accountant, and his wife, Florence Mary Elizabeth Buckland. He was christened Cuthbert after his great-grandfather Admiral Cuthbert (first Baron) *Collingwood, but his parents changed his name to Teddy during the First World War because Cuthbert was the name given to conscientious objectors in cartoons in the *Evening News*. Much later he shortened this to Ted, on the advice of his agent, when he became a popular guest on television chat shows in the United States. Because of his chronic asthma the family moved to the French riviera after the war, and he spent the rest of his childhood in Nice, on his own with his mother after his father had to return to England. He attended a Roman Catholic day school.

As a schoolboy Tinling joined the Nice tennis club; he umpired a match for Suzanne Lenglen at the age of thirteen, and became a devoted member of her entourage. He mixed with high society on the French riviera while still in his teens, umpiring and refereeing matches and organizing tournaments. Suzanne Lenglen, with her flowing pure silk dresses and silk bandeau around her head, became his idol and inspiration. His first tennis dress was designed for her, in 1937, for her last world tour.

In 1927 Tinling was sent to London to study dress designing, and when he set up his own business there in 1931 many of his clients were friends he had made in the south of France. Within a year he had expanded into premises in Mayfair and shown his first collection. He soon had a reputation in haute couture to rival that of Hardy Amies and Norman Hartnell, and in 1938 he made fourteen wedding dresses for society weddings at St Margaret's, Westminster.

At the same time Tinling remained involved in the world of tennis, especially at Wimbledon, where he worked from 1927 to 1949 during the two weeks of the championships as the 'call boy', responsible for escorting players from their dressing-rooms to the centre court and court no. 1 for their matches. In 1928 he was also asked to act as a liaison between the Wimbledon committee and the players, and he did this until 1949. A keen amateur player himself, Tinling played on the amateur circuit from 1935 until 1950, captaining Sussex for many years, and he first played at Wimbledon in 1948.

During the Second World War, Tinling served in the intelligence corps in Algiers and Germany, and he remained in the army until 1947. He reached the rank of lieutenant-colonel.

Having resumed his career as a couturier in 1947, Tinling became known as a designer of tennis dresses. He believed that women tennis players should wear clothes that stressed their femininity. He designed his first Wimbledon tennis dress for Joy Gannon in 1947, and became famous in 1949 when 'Gorgeous Gussy' Moran asked him to design her tennis dresses for Wimbledon, and the underwear to go with them. The lace-trimmed panties he made for her caused a sensation, and, told he had put vulgarity and sin into tennis, he was barred from working at Wimbledon for many years. However, he continued to design tennis dresses for the leading women players. For ten successive years, from 1952 to 1961, he dressed the winner of the Wimbledon women's singles title, and in 1973 the five major championships in the world were won by players wearing his dresses. In 1970 he was appointed official designer to the Virginia Slims women's professional circuit, and in eight years he created more than 1000 different dresses, embroidered with sequins, woven with silver threads, and covered with frills and bows. However, in the late 1970s the top players were attracted by large sponsorship contracts to wear sportswear separates designed by large manufacturers, and Tinling gave up designing tennis dresses. He settled in Philadelphia in the USA in 1976.

Tinling made fourteen wedding dresses for tennis stars, including a dress for 'Little Mo' Connolly for her wedding in California in 1955, and ones for Christine Truman and Chris Evert. In June 1986, as part of the celebration of the centenary of the Wimbledon championships, an exhibition of Tinling's tennis creations was mounted at the Victoria and Albert Museum. The exhibits included some of the coloured dresses he had designed during the war, when the all-white rule was suspended, such as Kay Stammers's pink dress of 1941. Also on display were Maria Bueno's dress with its 'Cleopatra' embroidery, Rosie Casals's black-sequinned dress, and Billie Jean King's rhinestone-studded dress of 1973. In the 1980s he admired the ice dancer Jayne Torville, and always said that the movements of a good tennis player were as beautiful and graceful as those of an ice skater or ballerina. In 1982 Tinling became assistant to the president of the International Tennis Federation in Paris, and shortly afterwards he was invited to become head of the Wimbledon liaison committee once again, a job he continued to do until his death.

Very tall (6 feet 6 inches), with a shining bald head, shaved on the advice of Vidal Sassoon, Tinling wore a large diamond in one ear and several bracelets on his wrists. He was witty and outrageous, and was often compared with Oscar Wilde and Sir Noël Coward. Apart from tennis and fashion, his other enthusiasms included the music of Richard Wagner and tenpin bowling. Tinling died on 23 May 1990 in Cambridge. He was unmarried. Many tennis stars attended his memorial service at St James's, Piccadilly, London, on 24 June 1990, the eve of Wimbledon. ANNE PIMLOTT BAKER, *rev.*

Sources *The Independent* (24 May 1990) · *The Independent* (2 June 1990) · *The Independent* (25 June 1990) · *The Times* (24 May 1990) · *The Times* (25 May 1990) · C. C. Tinling, *White ladies* (1963) · C. C. Tinling, *Tinling: sixty years in tennis* (1983) · M. Robertson, ed., *The encyclopedia of tennis* (1974) · *CGPLA Eng. & Wales* (1990)
Likenesses photograph, repro. in Tinling, *White ladies*
Wealth at death £17,364: probate, 24 June 1991, *CGPLA Eng. & Wales*

Tinmouth, John de. See Tynemouth, John (*fl. c.*1350).

Tinney, John (*c.*1706–1761), engraver and printseller, the son of John Tinney (*b. c.*1673), of the Merchant Taylors' Company, was probably born in London. He was apprenticed for seven years to the engraver John Sturt on 3 August 1721 and made free of the Goldsmiths' Company on 8 April 1730. He was trading in Great Eastcheap, Cannon Street, in 1734 but is said to have spent some time in France. He took livery in the Goldsmiths' Company in May 1737 and set up at the sign of the Carved Golden Lion in Fleet Street, between Peterborough Court and the Globe tavern. In 1745 the contents of his shop were insured for £300. There, according to his trade label, he sold 'great variety of French prints and several fine prints done from his own new copper plates, in neat frames and glasses or without, and all sorts of maps; also several new drawing books, copy books and great variety of royal sheets, lotteries &c' and 'performs engraving in all its branches in the neatest manner'. He engraved competently in line and in mezzotint and trained a number of apprentices, of whom Anthony Walker, William Woollett, and John Browne became distinguished engravers. Advertisements in newspapers further reveal that Tinney published a wide variety of topical, satirical, and decorative prints. His *Compendium anatomicum* (1743) was an important early guide to human anatomy intended for artists. He was an important publisher of maps, the most remarkable being John Rocque's twenty-four-sheet *Plan of the Cities of London and Westminster* (1746), one of the greatest of all London maps.

About 1752 Tinney acquired from John Hinton the plates for Emanuel Bowen and Thomas Kitchen's *Large English Atlas* (1749–60) which remained the most important English county atlas until the appearance of John Cary's in 1787. Robert Sayer and the Bowles brothers shared the cost of this enterprise from about 1755 and they also acquired shares in several of the sets of prints of country houses, villas, and gardens that Tinney published. He

probably engraved the earliest of these himself, but later views were drawn and engraved by his pupils, notably by William Woollett. These views for tourists included sets depicting Chiswick House (1738, 1754), Hampton Court and Kensington Palace (1744), the Oxford colleges (1754), and Whitton and West Wycombe (1757). Tinney died a widower at Fulham, administration of his goods being granted to his sister Elizabeth Mackrabie on 14 April 1761. TIMOTHY CLAYTON

Sources K. F. Russell, 'John Tinney's *Compendium anatomicum* and its publishers', *Medical History*, 18 (1974), 174–85 · D. Hodson, *County atlases of the British Isles published after 1703: a bibliography*, 2 (1989), 97–147 · T. Clayton, *The English print, 1688–1802* (1997) · T. Chubb, *The printed maps in the atlases of Great Britain and Ireland: a bibliography, 1579–1870* (1927), 456 · grant of administration, PRO, PROB 6/137, fol. 255v · J. Howgego, *Printed maps of London, circa 1553–1850*, 2nd edn (1978) · R. M. Wiles, *Serial publication in England before 1750* (1957), 312 · private information (2004) [Laurence Worms] · insurance policy, GL, MS 11936, vol. 73, no. 102383

Tinsley [*née* Turner], **Annie** (1808–1885), novelist and poet, was born at Preston, Lancashire, into the large family of Thomas Milner Turner and his Scottish wife (*née* Carruthers) on 11 January 1808. Her mother, a zealous Roman Catholic convert (*d.* 1852), was much older than her father, who was her chief teacher, although she also attended school from an early age. Described as 'studious, poetical, and sombre, but practical' (Peet, 7), she later claimed to have read the 'British classics' by the age of nine, and to have begun writing much earlier.

Annie's first publication, at the end of 1826 (dated 1827), *The Children of the Mist and other Poems*, failed to cover its costs and as its author she was arrested (illegally, at her age) for debt. She met her future husband, Charles Tinsley (1805/6–1899), a solicitor, in the sponging house, and was saved at the last moment from the Fleet prison. They married on 1 August 1833, but Tinsley seemed incapable of making a success of his profession, and Annie was soon publishing novels to feed their growing family of six children. She was forced to abandon her ambition to be a poet: 'my books were written and sent to press hurriedly, for the simple reason that money was needed. I … never revised one, —I had no time' (Peet, 22). Several of her novels were published serially in the *Family Herald* and never reprinted, and many short stories were published anonymously in the *Monthly Chronicle*, *Metropolitan Magazine*, *People's Journal*, *Literary Gazette*, and other periodicals.

The improvidence of her father, who had decided to become a strolling player when she was eight, and then of her husband, who also moved his family from town to town in search of suitable employment, caused Annie Tinsley to lament that women did not rely more on their own strengths rather than those of men, a view that she developed in her autobiographical novel *Women as they are. By one of them* (1854). Her previous novel, *Margaret* (1853), had been likened to Charlotte Brontë's *Villette*; Tinsley's preface denies plagiarism, claiming that hers had been written earlier, and alludes to her own 'joyless and hardly tasked youth' as her inspiration. Her best work lies in her second published volume of poems, *Lays for the Thoughtful and Solitary* (1848), which shows a fine gift for verse as well as a mature awareness of the injustice of woman's lot. In December 1872 Charles Tinsley inherited his brother William's wealth, but their son George Herbert Tinsley, his mother's favourite, who had been prospering in North America, died of typhoid in August 1873 and she never really recovered from this. Apart from a brief sneer in *Margaret*, which she later regretted (Peet, 23), she retained her mother's Catholic faith to the last, despite the objections of her husband, and after her death at 83 Windmill Street, Milton, Gravesend, Kent, on 20 January 1885, she was buried in the Roman Catholic portion of Gravesend cemetery.   VIRGINIA H. BLAIN

Sources H. Peet, 'Mrs Charles Tinsley, novelist and poet: a little-known Lancashire authoress', *Transactions of the Historic Society of Lancashire and Cheshire*, 81 (1929); pubd separately (1930)

Tinsley, William (1831–1902), publisher, was born on 13 July 1831 at South Mimms, Hertfordshire, the second son of the ten children of William Tinsley (*b.* 1800), gamekeeper, and Sarah Dover, who married in 1827. By the age of nine he worked in the fields, later remembering long days scaring birds from crops and a terror of roaming poachers after dark. His father had no interest in education; his kindly mother read and wrote letters for neighbours. An uncle who kept the village toll-gate lent him books, and he widened his interests by reading newspapers and conversing with coachmen and travellers in the toll-house. At the age of twenty he walked to London, and found lodgings and employment in Notting Hill. He dealt in secondhand books, spending evenings and earnings in Oxford Street bookshops.

Tinsley's younger brother Edward had walked to London some months earlier, and was found work by another uncle, a South-Western Railway manager. Edward met Lionel Brough and his elder brother Robert, who stimulated his interest in the stage and literature. He soon left the railway, worked for small publishers, writing book reviews and other pieces, and was employed on a periodical, *Diogenes*. By then the three-decker novel and the circulating libraries of Mudie and W. H. Smith dominated the fiction market, and in that system the Tinsley brothers learned their trade, having jointly agreed on a career in publishing. In 1854, two years after William had left home, they started in business near the Strand.

The Tinsleys were encouraged by the Brough family, in particular by Lionel, equally successful as a stage comedian and as assistant publisher of the *Daily Telegraph*. On 29 April 1860 William Tinsley married Louisa (*b.* 1830), daughter of William Rowley, and they went on to have six daughters. Two years after his marriage the first three-volume novel published by Tinsley Brothers, now in Catherine Street, Strand, was George Augustus Sala's *The Seven Sons of Mammon* (1862), but in that year their newly appointed reader Lionel Brough helped them acquire what became one of the best-selling novels of the nineteenth century, *Lady Audley's Secret*, by Mary Elizabeth Braddon. The book's outstanding success (eight three-volume impressions from October to December 1862, and many cheaper editions in subsequent years) made reputations

and fortunes for both author and publisher. William Tinsley's brother Edward built a villa in Barnes, and named it Audley Lodge. Soon the brothers had also built a substantial list, and Chapman and Hall acknowledged they were their chief rivals in the fiction market. In 1865 Edward Tinsley made an unsuccessful offer for the entire Chapman and Hall business. In the following year he died of a stroke.

William Tinsley continued under the name of Tinsley Brothers, sadly missing Edward's partnership and skills, although not his excitable nature and the occasional tiresome disagreements. In the 1870s he successfully produced six three-deckers for Harrison Ainsworth, and in 1871 he acquired Thomas Hardy's first novel, *Desperate Remedies*, followed by *Under the Greenwood Tree* and *A Pair of Blue Eyes*. From the first he had an instinctive feeling for Hardy's work, rejected by more established publishers; but his loyal perseverance, including a series of cheap editions and serialization in his magazine of the third novel, failed to spark public interest. Tinsley has been accused of unfair treatment of Hardy, but John Sutherland has established his honest dealings there beyond doubt (Sutherland, 218–22). In 1868 Tinsley had published *The Moonstone*, but afterwards Wilkie Collins perhaps had greater justification than Hardy for uncertainty about his publisher's courage and conviction, and he found more satisfying agreements elsewhere. Other Tinsley authors included Walter Besant, William Black, Rhoda Broughton, G. M. Fenn, G. A. Henty, Mrs Cashel Hoey, Thomas Hood, Jean Ingelow, Richard Jefferies, Justin McCarthy, George MacDonald, George Meredith, Mrs Molesworth, John Morley, Ouida, Mayne Reid, and Anthony Trollope.

An eccentric businessman, Tinsley preferred contracts made with handshakes rather than documents and was, he said, bored by accounts. Sadleir refers to Tinsley Brothers as a 'speculative' firm (*DNB*) that 'did not command the real confidence of the trade' (Sadleir, *Trollope*, 254), but many treated William with respect: even Hardy admitted his shrewdness with young authors, and relations with Mudie were clearly satisfactory. Among his loyal assistants was Edmund Downey, whose *Twenty Years Ago* (1905) reveals much of life at Catherine Street. *Tinsleys' Magazine* was published from 1868, edited at first by Edmund Yates, then by Tinsley himself, and from 1879 to 1884 by Edmund Downey.

Tinsley had many literary and theatrical friends in the Savage Club. He generously gave, and later in life received, the kind of support considered normal in his bohemian world. Business meetings were sometimes held next door, in the old Gaiety restaurant, where he privately dispensed charitable help to the unsuccessful, when he was not entertaining his valuable authors. The latter included George Moore, who wrote affectionate lampoons of the 'h-less' Tinsley and the Irishman Downey. But quixotic business methods caused several failures, and the office finally closed in 1887. Tinsley had always depended on a natural flair for finding authors, and on inspired but sometimes wavering common sense. He quickly and fiercely warned against the notorious Library Company, an intended rival to Mudies: 'I never could get them to see, until it was too late, that their venture spelt ruin from the first hour they began business' (Tinsley, 1.66). But he was prone to naïve mistakes caused by his persistent, if touching, need to like other people, and equally to be liked by them.

William Tinsley died of chronic Bright's disease at his home, 36 High Road, Wood Green, London, on 1 May 1902.   PETER NEWBOLT

Sources W. Tinsley, *Random recollections of an old publisher*, 2 vols. (1900) • E. Downey, *Twenty years ago* (1905) • G. Moore, *Confessions of a young man* (1888) • J. A. Sutherland, *Victorian novelists and publishers* (1976) • A. Waugh, *A hundred years of publishing: the story of Chapman & Hall* (1930) • P. Newbolt, *G. A. Henty (1832–1902): a bibliographical study* (1996), appx 2, pt 1 • M. Sadleir, *Trollope: a bibliography* (1928) • M. Sadleir, *XIX century fiction: a bibliographical record based on his own collection*, 1 (1951) • 'Maxwell, Mary Elizabeth', *DNB* • 'Brough, Lionel', *DNB* • P. Newbolt, *William Tinsley (1831–1902), 'speculative publisher': a commentary* [forthcoming] • m. cert. • d. cert.
Likenesses A. Bryan, pen-and-ink caricature, repro. in Downey, *Twenty years ago*, following p. 3 • H. Furniss, pen-and-ink caricature, NPG; repro. in Newbolt, *William Tinsley* • F. Waddy, pen-and-ink caricature, repro. in F. Swinnerton, *The bookman's London* (1951), following p. 40 • photograph, repro. in Newbolt, *G. A. Henty*
Wealth at death £147: administration, 23 June 1902, CGPLA Eng. & Wales

Tinwald. For this title name see Erskine, Charles, Lord Tinwald (*bap.* 1680, *d.* 1763).

Tinworth, George (1843–1913), sculptor and potter, the fourth son of Joshua Tinworth, wheelwright, and his wife, Jane Daniel, was born at 6 Milk Street, Walworth, London, on 5 November 1843. The family was extremely poor and, as a child, he suffered considerable hardship. The strict, dissenting, religious beliefs of his parents restricted his education to biblical texts; throughout his life he remained semi-literate. His talent for wood-carving and modelling was developed first at the Government School of Design, Lambeth (1861), and later the Royal Academy Schools (1864). In 1867 he joined the pottery works of Messrs Doulton of Lambeth, and he remained with the firm until his death. Throughout his career Tinworth worked as a pottery decorator as well as a sculptor. He was accorded special status within the firm, with his own studio and assistants, and had time to initiate his own work programme, including commissions for public monuments. Distinguished visitors coming to Tinworth's studio as early as the mid-1870s included Sir Henry Cole and George Eliot, and his work drew praise from critics including Edmund Gosse and John Ruskin, whose notice of Tinworth's small reliefs in his *Notes on some of the Principal Pictures Exhibited in the Rooms of the Royal Academy* (vol. 6, 1875) led to the artist's collaboration with the architect George Edmund Street in the large crucifixion panel for the reredos at York Minster in 1876 and the twenty-eight panels (now mostly destroyed) for the guards' chapel, Wellington barracks, in St James's Park, London, in 1878. This work led to many other similar commissions, including panels in the pulpit and reredos of the English church, Copenhagen, at Truro Cathedral, Cornwall, and the church of St John the Baptist, Erith, Kent; a statue in St

Augustine's, Stepney; and a relief in the church of the Mediator, New York. The prince and princess of Wales were enthusiasts of Tinworth's work and subsequently opened his exhibition in Conduit Street in 1883.

Tinworth exhibited at the Royal Academy from 1866 until 1885, showing in 1880 *Going to Calvary* (Truro Cathedral, Cornwall), and in 1881 the *Triumphant Entry of Christ in to Jerusalem* (V&A). He ceased to show there after the rejection, for lack of space, of his *Preparation for the Crucifixion* (366 × 157 cm) now in South London Art Gallery. Tinworth also carried out a considerable body of decorative work which, apart from many hundreds of decorated pots, comprised small humorous figural subjects including children and animals, mainly mice and frogs. Since his death these have become the most widely admired and sought-after aspect of his work. Examples of these are in the Victoria and Albert Museum, London, and the Royal Doulton Collectors' Centre, Burslem. Tinworth married on 8 February 1881 Alice (*b.* 1856), third daughter of William Digweed; they had no children.

Tinworth's work was exhibited abroad, both in Europe, notably at the Paris Universal Exhibition in 1878, when he was made an officer of the French Academy, and in America. In 1876 he exhibited at the Philadelphia Centennial Exhibition, and in 1893 at the Chicago World Fair where he showed his *History of England* vase; standing 130 cm high, this was one of the largest and most complex pots ever conceived. His work is full of vigorous realism showing much technical skill, but he belonged to no current sculptural tradition or artistic coterie, apart from his fellow artists and decorators at Doulton. His style failed to develop, and he resisted Ruskin's attempts to introduce him to a more sophisticated low-relief technique. He continued to undertake public commissions throughout his life, though in later years these became less frequent. Tinworth died at Putney railway station on his way from his home at 8 Maze Road, Kew, Surrey, to his studio at Lambeth on 10 September 1913, and was buried in Norwood cemetery. During his lifetime he was awarded many foreign medals and prizes.

R. P. BEDFORD, rev. PETER ROSE

Sources E. Gosse, *A critical essay on the life and works of George Tinworth* (1883) • P. Rose, *George Tinworth* (1982) • C. Handley-Read, 'Tinworth's work for Doulton', *Country Life* (Sept 1960), 430–31, 560–61 • CGPLA Eng. & Wales (1913) • B. Read, *Victorian sculpture* (1982), 311–13 • MS autobiography, Southwark Local Studies Library, London
Archives Southwark Local Studies Library, London, MS autobiography and letters
Likenesses Done & Ball, cabinet photograph, NPG • photographs, Royal Doulton Tableware, London; repro. in Rose, *George Tinworth*
Wealth at death £549 9s. 6d.: probate, 8 Oct 1913, CGPLA Eng. & Wales

Tipper [*née* Elam], **Constance Fligg** (1894–1995), metallurgist and crystallographer, was born on 16 February 1894 in Station Road, New Barnet, Hertfordshire, the daughter of William Henry Elam, surgeon, and his wife, Lydia, *née* Coombes. She was educated at St Felix School, Southwold, followed by Newnham College, Cambridge, from where

Constance Fligg Tipper (1894–1995), by unknown photographer

she gained a third in part one of the natural sciences tripos in 1915. After working briefly at the National Physical Laboratory, metallurgical department, in Teddington, she joined the Royal School of Mines, South Kensington, in 1916, and was appointed research assistant to Professor Harold Carpenter in 1917. Later she won two successive fellowships, the Frecheville (1921–3) and the Royal Society Armourers and Brasiers (1924–9). During this time she carried out significant research into the strength of single crystal aluminium. Though still employed by the Royal School of Mines she began working in Cambridge. Her research there, in collaboration with Geoffrey Taylor, led to the modern understanding of crystal plasticity and inspired Taylor's theory of dislocations (1934). In recognition of this and earlier work London University awarded her the DSc degree (1926).

In 1928 Elam married George Howlett Tipper (d. 1947), a Clare College graduate and superintendent of the geological survey in India; there were no children. Officially leaving the Royal School of Mines in 1929 she settled in Cambridge where Newnham College awarded her a research fellowship (1930–31). This association would last over thirty years. The university gave her testing facilities in the engineering department, but no official status, although the Leverhulme Trust awarded her a two-year research fellowship in 1936. Naturally shy, and always happier in research than in teaching, she nevertheless undertook considerable lecturing. In 1947 Newnham elected her an associate fellow for three years; and in 1949 Cambridge University made her a reader in mechanical engineering. Thenceforth until her retirement in 1960 she was a full member of the faculty of engineering.

Tipper's most significant contributions to metallurgy from 1943 onwards were in relation to the deformation and fracture of iron and steel. When the new Admiralty ship welding committee asked Professor John Fleetwood Baker, head of the engineering department, to investigate fractures in all welded ships, he assigned the metallurgical investigations to Tipper. Brittle fracture in large steel structures had become an urgent naval problem: several Liberty ships built in the accelerated wartime shipbuilding programme to bring vital supplies across the Atlantic had broken up in heavy seas as a crack ran instantaneously right around the ship. One split in half while still in harbour. The ships, built in both Britain and

America, brought vital supplies across the Atlantic to Britain during the war years. These ships were the first to be all welded, rather than riveted. Tipper found that the cause lay not in the fabrication and welding, as first thought, but was intrinsic in the material used, which became dangerously brittle under certain circumstances. Her work in this area led to the development of the Tipper test for determining the brittleness of steel. This edge notched tensile test can predict whether steel will behave in a brittle or ductile manner at service temperature. As a result of her research manufacturers began improving both the quality of the steel and annealed welds. The results were published in the scientific literature and in her book *The Brittle Fracture Story* (1962), which Baker, who had given her so much encouragement and advice over the years, persuaded her to write.

Colleagues held Tipper in high esteem and found her a pleasure to work with, although independent and outspoken. Her work was always meticulous and remains one of the principal contributions to the development of metallurgical science. There can be no doubt that she was a brilliant metallurgist who should have had a great deal more recognition in her lifetime. Although she officially retired in 1960, she continued working well into her seventies, taking on consultancy work at the Barrow shipyards and on metal bridge construction. As her husband had died earlier, she went to live with her brother at Bank House, Langwathby, Penrith, Cumberland, where she could enjoy the family hobby of fly-fishing. She also enjoyed gardening, watercolour painting, and playing the piano and organ. To mark the occasion of her 100th birthday, in 1994, Newnham College planted a variegated sweet chestnut in the gardens, now known as the Tipper tree. She died at Penrith on 14 December 1995.

ANNA LEENDERTZ FORD

Sources C. F. Tipper, *The brittle fracture story* (1962) · J. Charles and G. Smith, 'Constance Tipper: her life and work', *Materials World*, 4/6 (1996), 336–7 · *The Times* (30 Dec 1995) · *The Independent* (20 Dec 1995) · private information (2004) [Newnham College, Cambridge] · b. cert.
Archives Newnham College, Cambridge
Likenesses photograph, News International Syndicate, London [see illus.]
Wealth at death £200,978: probate, 1 March 1996, CGPLA Eng. & Wales

Tipper, John (b. before 1680, d. 1713), mathematician and almanac maker, was born at Coventry. In 1699 he was elected master of Bablake Hospital school there at a salary of £20, which he supplemented by teaching mathematics, surveying, dialling, accounting, and music to private pupils. Some boarded with him; others living within 10 miles of Coventry he visited on a weekly basis. By 1705 he was able to hire an assistant master. In 1704 Tipper launched the *Ladies' Diary*, a hybrid almanac and pioneering women's magazine. Early editions covered elementary astronomy, with data on the universe and notes on Halley's work on comets. There were also features on cooking and diet, medical recipes (from the writings of Robert Boyle), and advice on the care of small children. In lighter vein he wrote on the virtues of the female sex, mused on love (drawing on Rochester, Dryden, and Otway), and ran a serialized burlesque romance. His friend Humfrey Wanley the antiquary, a Coventry man by origin, acted as his London intermediary, giving advice on material, liaising with Halley, and procuring specialist books.

The *Ladies' Diary*, dedicated to Queen Anne and carrying her portrait each year, proved a success from the start. In 1706 Tipper introduced verse 'enigmas' sent in by readers, which quickly became its most popular feature. He printed the names of those who set or solved them (some of them men) and offered small prizes. Though most of the early riddles were verbal, others were mathematical and these gradually became more challenging. An early prize was won by Henry Beighton, a future fellow of the Royal Society. There were soon so many correspondents that in 1711 Tipper launched a monthly journal of the same kind, *Delights for the Ingenious*, price 3*d*., though this soon fell victim to the new stamp tax.

Tipper's *Diary* printed meteorological data, but no prophecies; he had no interest in astrology. In 1710 he founded another annual title, *Great Britain's Diary*, which supplied useful notes for tradesmen. In addition he published *The Art of Reading* (1705), a manual (now lost) designed for parents and teachers, and planned an ambitious history of Coventry to be published by subscription, for which he issued a detailed prospectus in 1711. He did not live to complete it, but some of his work was incorporated in the 1730 edition of Sir William Dugdale's *Antiquities of Warwickshire*. Tipper died in 1713. After his death the *Ladies' Diary* was continued by a succession of able mathematicians and played a significant part in promoting the subject for over a century until it merged with the *Gentleman's Diary* in 1840. BERNARD CAPP

Sources B. S. Capp, *Astrology and the popular press: English almanacs, 1500–1800* (1979) · W. Dugdale, *The antiquities of Warwickshire illustrated*, rev. W. Thomas, 2nd edn, 2 vols. (1730) · H. Ellis, ed., *Original letters of eminent literary men of the sixteenth, seventeenth, and eighteenth centuries*, CS, 23 (1843) · E. G. R. Taylor, *The mathematical practitioners of Tudor and Stuart England* (1954) · F. L. Colvile, *The worthies of Warwickshire who lived between 1500 and 1800* [1870], 755–6 · R. V. Wallis and P. J. Wallis, eds., *Biobibliography of British mathematics and its applications*, 2 (1986) · F. W. Steer and others, *Dictionary of land surveyors and local cartographers of Great Britain and Ireland, 1550–1850*, ed. P. Eden, [4 vols.] (1975–9)

Tippett, Sir Michael Kemp (1905–1998), composer, was born on 2 January 1905 in a London nursing home at 51 Belgrave Road, the second son and younger child of Henry William Tippett (1858–1944), a retired lawyer, and Isabel Clementina Binny Kemp (1880–1969), a novelist and suffragette. His father was of Cornish stock and his mother from Kent. Later in 1905 the family moved from Eastcote, Middlesex, to the village of Wetherden in Suffolk, where they remained until 1919.

Formative years Tippett's happy childhood in the depths of the English countryside did not include any form of musical training, though he enjoyed singing as a treble in

Sir Michael Kemp Tippett (1905–1998), by Michael Ward, 1972

the local church choir. He later recalled that hearing the soldiers singing popular songs as they marched off to the First World War had affected him deeply: at the age of nine or ten he knew intuitively that he wanted to be a composer, even though he had no idea of what this meant in reality. His education from 1914 to 1922 was ironically to delay his formal musical development even though he flourished intellectually. At Brookfield preparatory school, Swanage, Dorset, he distinguished himself with an essay denying the existence of God. He went on to Fettes College, Edinburgh, but found it almost intolerable. Having at least broken the traditional cycle of bullying, he was removed by his parents on admitting to a homosexual involvement with a fellow pupil. He then went as a boarder to Stamford grammar school, Lincolnshire, where he was much happier, though still a notorious character largely on account of his now fully developed atheism. By 1919 the family home and unit had been broken up in the aftermath of the First World War, when financial problems had forced Tippett's parents to move to the hotel they owned near Cannes and thereafter to sell the hotel and live in hotel suites in the south of France and Italy until 1932. Tippett felt orphaned and abandoned as a result, and despite the broadening cultural outlook engendered by these years of foreign holidays and adventurous travelling the emotional scars were deep and longlasting. Musical matters, however, improved at Stamford, where alongside piano lessons he began to teach himself composition, persuading his parents at length to pay for his studies at the Royal College of Music, London, which he entered in 1923 with few, if any, of the necessary qualifications other than determination and vision.

Apprentice composer At the Royal College of Music from 1923 to 1928 Tippett studied composition with Charles Wood and C. H. Kitson, conducting with Malcolm Sargent and Adrian Boult, and the piano with Aubin Raymar. The chief value of these years for Tippett was his delayed encounter—often by means of the Henry Wood Promenade Concerts—with the great tradition of Western music, most of which was unfamiliar to him. Beethoven immediately became the most profound and lasting influence, and his structural procedures were fortuitously central to Charles Wood's teaching of composition. Wood's long illness and eventual death in 1926 proved a severe blow to Tippett in that C. H. Kitson, to whom he then went, was pedantically unrewarding as a teacher and personally unsympathetic, even scornful, of his compositional aspirations. Sargent was similarly rather patronizing, but Tippett was particularly fortunate in Adrian Boult, who took him under his wing by installing him at his side for weekly orchestral rehearsals, thus enabling him to learn about the orchestra from the inside (he was nicknamed Boult's Darling in the process). An unconventional student, he perhaps not unsurprisingly failed his finals at the first attempt but eventually graduated BMus in 1928.

As a self-confessed late developer Tippett was not deterred in pursuing his compositional destiny by the dazzling brilliance of such already successful contemporaries as Walton, Lambert, Rawsthorne, and—a little later—the precocious Benjamin Britten. He stubbornly ploughed a lonely furrow and never wavered in his self-belief, even when this meant living at virtually subsistence level. In 1929 he settled in Oxted, Surrey, where he conducted a madrigal group, supervised the activities of the amateur Oxted and Limpsfield Players, and became a part-time French teacher at Hazelwood School, Limpsfield. A concert at Oxted in 1930 of his compositional output to date, though notionally successful (and sympathetically reviewed in *The Times*), prompted him to withdraw the lot and return to study counterpoint at the Royal College of Music with R. O. Morris for eighteen months. He then became increasingly drawn to quasi-political, socially inclined musical activities and gave up teaching to undertake posts as conductor with two amateur choirs in London sponsored by the Royal Arsenal Co-operative Society and with the South London Orchestra (based at Morley College, with Tippett employed under the aegis of the London county council), drawn from newly unemployed professional musicians. He also helped at work camps for unemployed ironstone miners at Boosbeck, Yorkshire, where in 1933 he composed a folk-song opera *Robin Hood* (material from which was re-channelled into the suite in D of 1948). Thus strengthened, his left-wing sympathies now drew him towards Trotsky, and in 1935 he briefly joined the Communist Party, abandoning his branch after three months when he failed to convert the members to his own brand of Trotskyism. More significantly, he realized that direct political involvement would distract him from the single-minded pursuit of composition. This now

moved into a higher gear with the first performances in 1935 of the first movement of a completed symphony in B♭ (immediately withdrawn) and the string quartet in A. Here at last—in the passionately lyrical slow (third) movement and rhythmically exuberant fugal finale—he detected the sound of his own personal voice for the first time. Following revision in 1943 (replacing the first two movements with a single opening movement) this quartet no. 1 became the first work in Tippett's official canon of compositions and marked the end of his long-drawn-out apprenticeship.

Turmoil and maturity Tippett's next two works—a piano sonata completed in 1937 and the concerto for double string orchestra of 1938-9—consolidated his early maturity by drawing the fruitful but divergent influences of Beethoven, Elizabethan madrigals, folk-song, and jazz into a compelling individual fusion. Crucial to this emerging creative maturity were two pivotal personal relationships—one, intense and sexual, with the painter Wilfred Franks (later identified by Tippett as 'a major factor underlying the discovery of my own individual musical "voice"'), and the other, passionate but non-sexual, with the musician Francesca Allinson, who shared his love of folk-music in particular. The relationship with Franks came to a troubled end in 1938 when Franks announced that he was to marry, thus precipitating for Tippett a personal crisis which became entangled with a heightened awareness of the political turmoil then drawing Europe inexorably towards a second world war. After an encounter with the Jungian analyst John Layard, Tippett undertook a nine-month period of self-analysis in which he transcribed and analysed his own dreams (transcriptions of which are included in his autobiography *Those Twentieth Century Blues* of 1994). The outcome was technically the process of 'individuation' or rebirth, confirming for Tippett the nature of his homosexuality while simultaneously strengthening his destiny as a creative artist at the possible expense of personal relationships.

A Child of our Time This turbulent period coincided with the drafting of a libretto for an oratorio triggered by an incident in Paris—the shooting of a German diplomat (vom Rath) by a Polish Jew (Herschel Grynsban)—which led to the Nazi pogrom of the Jews chillingly immortalized as *Kristallnacht*, 9 November 1938. Tippett at first approached his artistic mentor T. S. Eliot with a view to his writing the text. Eliot's advice on reading the detailed draft he had requested, however, was that Tippett should go on to complete it himself, in that the words were already appropriate for musical setting: adding 'poetry' to them would only get in the way of the music. The Second World War finally broke out on 3 September 1939 (three days after Tippett completed his Jungian analysis), and within days he began to compose the music of *A Child of our Time*. It was completed two years later in 1941, but was put aside with no immediate hope of a performance. This was the first work in which Tippett felt that he was writing from the depths of what Jung called the 'collective unconscious', and it crystallized all his current political, moral, and psychological concerns within a universal framework. It was consciously a modern counterpart of Bach's passions and Handel's *Messiah*; Tippett discovered in the negro spiritual a living substitute for Bach's Lutheran chorales. The collective emotion thus released gives the score a depth of compassion unique in twentieth-century music. When eventually performed at the Adelphi Theatre, London, in 1944, *A Child of our Time* belatedly established Tippett at the forefront of the composers of his generation. It became his most frequently performed work internationally.

War and prison In practical terms the outbreak of war caused Tippett immediate difficulties. His conducting posts in London came to an end and he briefly returned to Hazelwood School to teach classics. A significant chapter opened, however, with his appointment in 1940 as director of music at Morley College, where his concerto for double string orchestra had just been premiered in April. On 15 October 1940 the college was virtually destroyed by a bomb, and Tippett later recalled salvaging from the rubble several expensive volumes of Purcell's music, previously beyond his reach, which he now kept for his own use (Tippett, interview, 1986). (The immediate impact on his music is discernible in the flexible structure and fluid word-setting of the cantata *Boyhood's End* composed for Peter Pears and Benjamin Britten in 1943 and first performed at Morley College.) Tippett's daunting task now was the rebuilding of Morley College's musical activities. This he achieved by strengthening the choir (composing his *Two Madrigals* for the singers in 1942) and in creating a haven for musical refugees from Europe. These included Mátyás Seiber, Walter Goehr, and Walter Bergmann and three members of what later became the famous Amadeus Quartet. The college was soon established as the innovative hub of London's musical life, promoting concerts notable for their adventurous programmes. At this time Tippett was also at the forefront of the pacifist movement. Back in 1935 he had responded to the Revd Dick Sheppard's postal crusade for peace, and in 1940 he formally joined the Peace Pledge Union. Knowing that his deeply held convictions were likely to bring him into conflict with the authorities, he applied in 1940 for provisional registration as a conscientious objector. When Tippett's case was eventually heard in 1942 he was given non-combatant military duties. He appealed against this decision and was then given conditional registration. On refusing to comply with the conditions Tippett was finally sentenced on 21 June 1943 to three months' imprisonment in Wormwood Scrubs (and released for good behaviour a month early). The experience was a watershed in Tippett's public and personal life: for his mother (herself imprisoned a generation earlier for her suffragette beliefs) it was his finest hour. Tippett himself later described the experience as one of 'coming home' and claimed that though he was sufficiently well connected to have escaped imprisonment had he wished, it had been a moral responsibility to take the punishment as a gesture of solidarity with the cause.

Taking stock On his release from prison Tippett took up the reins at Morley College with renewed vigour. His compositional profile too was now in the ascendant as performers of stature began to champion his works. Phyllis Sellick made the first commercial recording of his music in 1941 when she recorded the piano sonata no. 1, and this attracted considerable critical acclaim. In 1943 the Zorian String Quartet premiered the revised quartet no. 1 as well as the quartet no. 2, written in 1941–2. With its synthesis of freely flowing madrigalian sprung rhythm and Beethovenian sonata dialectic, the second quartet is imbued with a sense of spiritual ecstasy and sheer compositional mastery that was new to Tippett's music. Commissions for short choral works now came from Canterbury Cathedral and the BBC, and Benjamin Britten was instrumental in the commission of a fanfare for the fiftieth anniversary of the consecration of St Matthew's Church, Northampton. Tippett's friendship with Britten and his partner, the tenor Peter Pears, was very significant. They had much in common, as pacifists and homosexuals and as passionate advocates of Purcell's music, but in other respects the two composers were complementary characters. Britten had prodigious early ability and evinced a compositional fluency which Tippett naturally envied. Eight years younger than Tippett, Britten was already established as a leading figure in British musical life, and he happily used his influence to help Tippett where he could. On seeing the score of *A Child of our Time* in 1943 he immediately assisted Tippett with arrangements for its belated première, in which Pears took part. Pears also commissioned the song cycle *The Heart's Assurance*, the first performance of which he eventually gave with Britten in 1951. This was a long-considered, deeply felt tribute to Francesca Allinson, whose suicide just before the end of the Second World War affected Tippett profoundly. In taking professional stock at the end of the war, however, Tippett was buoyed by the critical success of *A Child of our Time*, had just completed his symphony no. 1— premiered later in 1945 by the Liverpool Philharmonic Orchestra under his former teacher Malcolm Sargent— and was embarked on the string quartet no. 3 for the Zorian Quartet, which he completed in 1946. Both works are richly complex in detail and were his most ambitious instrumental structures to date.

The Midsummer Marriage Tippett now began to contemplate the most ambitious and risky project of his whole career—a first opera. With no commission in hand for it, let alone any prospect of a performance, it was an enormous gamble to devote some six years to its composition. This was no ordinary opera, for having followed T. S. Eliot's advice in relation to the text of *A Child of our Time* Tippett decided now to write his own libretto. Eliot's guidance was again pertinent: 'For you who are so very slow, don't go to poets, because you may be given something too quick. You've got to know what your music is first' (Tippett, interview, 1986). A Jungian dream-vision of 'a warm and soft young man … rebuffed by a cold and hard young woman' set in train an archetypal scenario which sought to present in theatrical terms the vision of whole-ness prefigured at the end of *A Child of our Time*:

> I would know my shadow and my light
> so shall I at last be whole.

Tippett later declared that this was 'the only truth I shall ever say'. In musical terms the opera presents a summation of everything in Tippett's output to date combined with an irresistible sense of dramatic momentum and unprecedented lyrical warmth. The harmonic richness of the score is the perfect mirror of the drama's philosophical quest for spiritual and psychic union. The specific dramatic genre is a blend of Mozart's *The Magic Flute* and Shakespeare's *A Midsummer Night's Dream*—a sublime comedy of manners with Jungian resonances drawn from a wide variety of mythic backgrounds. The interaction of its extended cast of characters with a large chorus and—most innovatively—a group of dancers broke new ground in English operatic history. The extended gestation and prolonged composition took a heavy toll on Tippett's health and stamina, and when completed in 1952 the opera had to wait until January 1955 before it was first produced at the Royal Opera House, Covent Garden. The première was something of a scandal in that most critics declared themselves completely baffled by the scenario, and as a result the glories of the music tended to pass unnoticed. For Tippett, however, it represented the culmination of virtually a decade's work, and it remains the critical watershed of his career. He described its composition as 'an act of faith' possible only once in a lifetime.

Consolidation and operatic aftermath Between 1946 and 1952 Tippett allowed very little to distract him from work on *The Midsummer Marriage*. In 1946 Morley College presented the first complete performance in modern times of Monteverdi's celebrated Vespers of 1610, and Tippett composed a *Preludio al vespro di Monteverdi* (his only organ work as it turned out) to precede this notable event. In 1948 the BBC commissioned a work to be broadcast in celebration of the birth of Princess Elizabeth's first child. The rather anonymously entitled suite in D then became known more characterfully as the *Suite for the Birthday of Prince Charles*. Incorporating as it did some material from the early ballad opera *Robin Hood* of 1933, it also provided a preview of the delicious march for the ancients from act I of *The Midsummer Marriage*. Indeed, at the suggestion of the Swiss conductor Paul Sacher, Tippett constructed in 1952 a concert suite in which the three 'ritual dances' embedded at the heart of the opera's second act are joined to the climactic fourth dance from act III and framed by the music which opens and closes act II. In this form the music was heard in Basel two years before the opera's actual première and went on to become firmly established in the general orchestral repertory. As work on *The Midsummer Marriage* progressed Tippett began to curtail his commitments at Morley College so that he could concentrate on creative work. With the gradual development of regular radio broadcasting for the BBC he felt able to resign from the college in 1951. In the same year he moved from Oxted, which had been his base since 1929, to live

with his mother, who—following the death of Tippett's father in 1944—had just bought Tidebrook Manor in Wadhurst, Sussex. With him went his partner at the time, the painter Karl Hawker (*d*. 1984).

The sound-world of *The Midsummer Marriage* proved so potent that Tippett extended it very naturally in a series of works for the concert hall. The antiphonal choral writing of the madrigal 'Dance, clarion air', written as part of a collective tribute to mark the coronation of Elizabeth II in 1953, is full of the opera's evocative echo effects. Perhaps most quintessentially of all, the *Fantasia concertante on a theme of Corelli* (an Edinburgh Festival commission to mark the tercentenary of Corelli's birth in 1953) seems saturated in the harmonic effulgence and lyrical outpouring of *The Midsummer Marriage*. The same is true of parts of the piano concerto of 1953–5 and the symphony no. 2, completed in 1957. In these works Tippett also broke new ground and began to introduce a harder edge in both linguistic and structural terms. Given in the years immediately following the first performance of *The Midsummer Marriage*, the premières of both works were fraught with difficulties—the symphony even breaking down within a few minutes—and contributed to a perception that Tippett's music was either exceptionally difficult to perform or, worse still, impractical and clumsily written. It took a decade or more to eradicate these prejudices and the impressions stuck. But by 1957, having pondered very carefully the impact of *The Midsummer Marriage*, Tippett was already contemplating a second opera which would break open his musical and dramatic language irrevocably.

King Priam and The Knot Garden Taking a scenario from the *Iliad* of Homer, the tragedy of *King Priam* is presented with a Brechtian clarity of dramatic image and adopts from the start a hard-hitting musical rhetoric which effectively jettisons much that was hitherto fundamental to Tippett's language. Such a shift was partly dictated by the war-coloured subject matter, but it also points towards a widening of tonal horizons and a radical approach to structure and instrumental texture. The impact of the opera's première in a production by the Royal Opera House, first seen in Coventry as part of the Coventry Cathedral Festival of 1962, was enormous, and critical acceptance of this new departure for Tippett was immediate. As with his previous opera, the abstract works which followed immediately—the piano sonata no. 2 and the concerto for orchestra—extend the expressive world of *King Priam*, thus establishing a pattern which Tippett followed for the rest of his compositional career. His position as a leading composer was now recognized: having been appointed CBE in 1959, he was knighted in 1966. During the composition of *King Priam* in 1960 Tippett moved to live in Parkside, a beautiful Georgian house in Corsham, Wiltshire, where he remained until 1970. These years saw the composition of the visionary choral masterpiece *The Vision of Saint Augustine* in 1963–5 and the vivid psychodrama of the *Tempest*-inspired third opera *The Knot Garden*, which was completed in 1969 and premiered at Covent Garden in 1970. In 1970 it was announced that the onset of macular dystrophy had drastically curtailed Tippett's sight, but he overcame this problem with remarkable courage and determination. He was now artistic director of the Bath Festival (in succession to Yehudi Menuhin), which he ran from 1969 until 1974, and in 1970 (following the death of his mother the previous year) he moved to a secluded house called Nocketts, near Calne in Wiltshire, where he lived in peaceful seclusion for the rest of his creative life. Following the irretrievable breakdown of his relationship with Karl Hawker, Tippett enjoyed from the mid-1960s until the end of his life a rewarding relationship with Meirion (Bill) Bowen, who also acted as his manager, amanuensis, and musical confidant.

America and beyond In 1965 Tippett visited America for the first time and fell in love with the wide-ranging culture he encountered there. The influence was immediately apparent in the jazz and blues inflections of *The Knot Garden* and the vocal 'blues' finale of the symphony no. 3 (1970–72). The symphony also shows the powerful influence of the maverick American composer Charles Ives, whose work increasingly fascinated Tippett. The fabric of American life also had a profound bearing on the scenario for the fourth opera, *The Ice Break*, which was premiered at Covent Garden in 1977. Its enaction of a fatal race riot and a drug-induced 'trip' caused some controversy at the time, and its often splintered language arguably failed to realize Tippett's intentions fully. But in his own terms he had 'come out of the garden into the street' (Tippett, interview, 1986) and soon confessed that he was 'turning his back with some pleasure on the cruel world of *The Ice Break*' (Tippett, interview, 1977). A trilogy of instrumental works written between 1976 and 1979—the symphony no. 4, string quartet no. 4, and triple concerto—became conscious works of stylistic synthesis in preparation for *The Mask of Time*, an evening-long choral work for the concert hall commissioned by the Boston Symphony Orchestra and first performed in Boston in 1982. Partly inspired by Jacob Bronowski's television series *The Ascent of Man*, this hugely ambitious work evolves from myths of creation to the presentation of man's place in history with a breathtaking sweep of invention. The climax is a moving elegy for the victims of war and specifically of Hiroshima out of which Tippett presents an exhilarating concluding vision of hope in the future, thus setting a seal on a vivid and idiosyncratic summation of the concerns of a lifetime. After his appointment as CH in 1977, the queen appointed Tippett to the Order of Merit in 1983.

Grand old man Having declared in 1977 that *The Ice Break* would be his final opera, Tippett entered his eighties in 1985 with the announcement of a fifth opera—*New Year*. Premiered by Houston Grand Opera in 1989, this hybrid of musical and masque, television play and pantomime presents another summation of Tippett's abiding preoccupations. The inclusion in the scenario of a spaceship and time travel, alongside the sounds of rap, reggae, and electronics from the pit, provided further evidence of Tippett's seemingly inexhaustible capacity for self-renewal. This Indian summer of his career continued with a setting

of Yeats's *Byzantium* for soprano and orchestra for the Chicago Symphony Orchestra (1988–90), the string quartet no. 5 (1990–91), and *The Rose Lake*—'a song without words for orchestra' (1991–3) which Tippett designated his swansong. Even then he came out of retirement briefly in his ninetieth year with a moving setting of Caliban's song from *The Tempest* as a tribute to Purcell on the tercentenary of his death in 1995. By 1996 Tippett's frailty necessitated his moving from Nocketts to a house in Isleworth, west London. A mild stroke in the same year curtailed his ability to travel, but even in November 1997 he was determined to visit Stockholm for an extensive festival of his music. Having just arrived he fell ill with pneumonia, and although he recovered sufficiently to return to Britain he died peacefully at his home, 13 Herons Place, Isleworth, on 8 January 1998, having just passed his ninety-third birthday. He was cremated on 15 January at Hanworth crematorium, at an explicitly non-religious service.

At his death a general consensus emerged that Tippett would take his place alongside the greatest English composers of the twentieth century—Elgar, Vaughan Williams, Britten, and arguably Walton. His reputation had grown steadily during the 1970s and 1980s, thus reversing the earlier decades of neglect. But while the value of his works up to but not necessarily including the second opera *King Priam* is uncontroversial, it is perhaps ironic that no consensus yet exists in respect of the works composed from the 1960s onwards. There is a school of thought—articulated by the composer Robin Holloway and the musicologist Derrick Puffett among others—which sees the last three decades as a 'tragic decline'. It could equally be argued, however, that this point of view reveals a failure to understand the very nature of Tippett's undoubted genius. Terms of reference in such matters are notoriously difficult to pinpoint, and the debate will continue. What cannot be gainsaid is that Tippett will emerge as one of the most original and powerful musical voices of twentieth-century Britain when countless others are forgotten—and this partly because he so vividly reflected the century through which he lived.   GERAINT LEWIS

Sources I. Kemp, *The composer and his work* (1984) · M. Bowen, *Michael Tippett* (1983); rev. edn (1997) · *A man of our time* (1977) [exhibition catalogue] · I. Kemp, ed., *Michael Tippett: a symposium on his 60th birthday* (1965) · G. Lewis, ed., *Michael Tippett O.M.: an 80th birthday celebration* (1985) · M. Tippett, *Moving into Aquarius* (1959); rev. edn (1974) · M. Tippett, *Those twentieth century blues* (1991); repr. (1994) · M. Tippett, interview, *The Guardian* (7 July 1977) · M. Tippett, interview, *The Guardian* (6 Oct 1986) · *The Times* (10 Jan 1998) · *The Guardian* (10–11 Jan 1998) · *The Independent* (10 Jan 1998) · b. cert. · d. cert.

Archives Barber Institute of Fine Arts, Birmingham, MSS · BL, music collections, corresp., music MSS, and papers, Add. MSS 53771, 61748–61804, 63820–63840, 69422 · Britten–Pears Library, The Red House, Aldeburgh, Suffolk, MSS · FM Cam., MSS · L. Cong., MSS · Paul Sacher Stiftung, Basel, MSS · St John Cam., MSS | BL, music collections, letters to Brian Douglas Newton, deposit 1996/10, Tippett letters · W. Sussex RO, letters to Walter Hussey

Likenesses O. Kokoschka, pencil drawing, c.1960 · G. Hermes, bronze cast of head, 1966, NPG · M. Ward, bromide print, 1972, NPG [*see illus.*] · photograph, 1974, repro. in *The Independent* · A. Newman, bromide print, 1978, NPG · photograph, c.1979, repro. in *The Times* · M. Rose, acrylic on canvas, 1989, NPG · D. Glass, bromide print, NPG · H. Leslie, silhouette drawing, NPG · N. Libbert, photograph, repro. in *The Guardian* (10 Jan 1998)

Wealth at death £156,718: probate, 15 July 1998, *CGPLA Eng. & Wales*

Tippetts, Sir John (*d.* 1692), shipbuilder, probably served his shipwright apprenticeship at Portsmouth naval dockyard, though little is recorded of his early years. In 1645 he became assistant master shipwright at Portsmouth before promotion to the post of master shipwright in August 1656. As master shipwright he was responsible not only for all shipbuilding and ship repair work at Portsmouth, but for the design of ships. He was in charge of the drafts of the 54 gun *Bristol* (launched at Portsmouth in 1653), 52 gun *Lyme* (1654), and 60 gun *Monck* (1659). As well as ship design, the master shipwright was also responsible for new buildings and works associated with ship construction. At Portsmouth he successfully oversaw construction of a double dock, capable of holding two third rates, and completed in 1658 by Nicholas Poirson under contract. Paralleling Tippetts's achievements within the dockyard at Portsmouth was his increasing recognition in the local community. Invited to become an alderman of the borough, he held mayoral office in 1659–60 and was a justice of the peace in 1659–61. This rise in local influence was brought to an abrupt end as a result of his support for Sir Arthur Hesilrige's abortive attempt to re-establish the power of parliament immediately prior to the Restoration, with Tippetts disfranchised in 1662 as a person not to be trusted. Nevertheless, his undoubted skills led to a reconfirmation in the office of master shipwright with his position further secured by the intervention of James, duke of York, who wrote to the secretary of state indicating his desire for Tippetts to have his patent. It was during the reign of Charles II that Tippetts built his largest ship, the 90 gun *St Michael*, which was launched at Portsmouth in 1669. In recognition of his services to the restored monarchy, he was promoted to the Navy Board in 1668, becoming resident commissioner at Portsmouth before his later appointment, in 1672, to the post of surveyor. This latter post was procured for him by Samuel Pepys, who praised Tippetts for his 'vigour and method' (Pepys, 10.446). As surveyor, Tippetts oversaw a large new programme of warship construction, which added thirty new ships to the fleet. Aware that not all ship constructors had sufficient technical ability to produce suitable designs, he introduced the first establishment of dimensions for English warships, laying down precise design specifications for each warship according to the number of guns carried, and so creating a uniformity in the fleet that had not previously existed. In July 1675 he received a knighthood in recognition of his contribution to shipbuilding. A subsequent decline in the state of the English navy, following the removal of James from the office of lord high admiral, resulted in the need for a commission in 1686–8 empowered to build and repair naval warships. Tippetts, a member of the commission, might well have chaired this body had it not been for increasing ill health, to which Pepys drew attention, noting Tippetts to be suffering from gout, this 'keeping him generally within doors or at least

incapable of any great action abroad' (Johns, 190). Although the commission was held to have performed a generally successful task, Tippetts proved critical, observing that many of the ships repaired had been forced to make an early return from sea. He was reappointed surveyor in 1688 and remained in office until his death, which took place between 25 June and 18 July 1692. His will named a daughter and several grandchildren.

PHILIP MacDOUGALL

Sources J. M. Collinge, *Navy Board officials, 1660–1832* (1978) · D. Dymond, *Portsmouth and the fall of the puritan revolution* (1971) · A. W. Johns, 'Sir Anthony Deane', *Mariner's Mirror*, 11 (1925), 164–93 · Pepys, *Diary*, vol. 10 · A. J. Marsh, 'The navy and Portsmouth under the Commonwealth', *Hampshire Studies* [ed. J. Webb, N. Yates, and S. Peacock] (1981), 115–40 · M. Oppenheim, *A history of the administration of the Royal Navy* (1896) · BL, Add. MSS 9305–9306 · Bodl. Oxf., MS Rawl. A. 119 · *CSP dom., 1660–61* · PRO, C/66/3136 · PRO, ADM 2/1725, fols. 15–16 · BL, Harl. MS 7476, fol. 58 · PRO, PROB 11/410, fols. 312v–313v

Wealth at death property in Hampshire, London and New England: will, PRO, PROB 11/410, fols. 312v–313v

Tipping [Typing], **William** (1598–1649), author, was the second son of Sir George Tipping (1560/61–1627), of Whitfield and Draycott, Oxfordshire, and his wife, Dorothy (1564–1637), daughter of John Burlace of Little Marlow, Buckinghamshire. With his younger brother Samuel he matriculated on 23 June 1615, aged sixteen, from Queen's College, Oxford, where his tutor was John Langhorne and from where he graduated BA on 23 October 1617. The brothers were admitted together on 29 January 1618 to Lincoln's Inn, but while Samuel pursued his legal studies and became a barrister in 1625, William returned to Oxfordshire. On the death of his father in 1627 he inherited land at Draycott and Attington. Anthony Wood, who says that he 'lived a single life many years in Canditch', Oxford, 'for the sake of scholastical company and of books' (Wood, *Ath. Oxon.*, 3rd edn, 3.243–4), also asserts that he never married, but by 5 October 1628, when his daughter Dorothea or Dorothy was baptized, Tipping had married Ursula, daughter of Sir John Brett of Edmonton, Middlesex. Their other children were George (their elder son), William (*bap.* 1631), and Margaret.

In 1633 Tipping published in Oxford *A Discourse of Eternitie*, thereby earning himself the nickname Eternity Tipping in the university. Relying on Latin rather than vernacular biblical quotation, it contends that both the ancients and 'newly discovered nations' (p. 10) possess a knowledge of God and eternity, and exhorts the reader to holiness and to reliance on the mercy of God. Tipping had become a justice of the peace for Oxfordshire, but in 1635 and 1636 he appeared several times before the court of high commission, having been charged with puritan practices. In 1639 he sold part of Draycott Manor.

In 1640 recovery from serious illness prompted Tipping to publish *A Return of Thankfulness*. Several sources claim that in the same year he was made vicar of Shabbington, Buckinghamshire, a family living, but it was his cousin John (*b.* 1601/2), a graduate of Magdalen Hall, Oxford, who was inducted. It is not clear whether Wood's statement that Tipping also took the covenant is correct, but his subsequent publications place him firmly among the godly. *The Father's Counsell* (1643) aimed to give 'usefull directions, for all young persons, especially elder brothers, whose portion it is … to be left in a fatherlesse or friendlesse condition'. Addressed to 'my son' it is a robust affirmation of the Calvinist doctrine of calling, castigating the 'pernicious sin' and 'destructive vice' of idleness: 'let no elder brother shelter himself under his fair estate, or plead the inheritance of his father, for his sloth'; 'better thy son were a basket maker, than an idle drone' (p. 196). Regular, twice-daily religious exercises and catechizing of children and servants was to be accompanied by frugality, charity, and hospitality. In *The Preachers Plea* (1646), Tipping (named Typing on the title-page) deplored the lack of progress 'in debate on church-government' (p. 4) and the 'many drunken, ignorant, superstitious, Prophane Ministers [who] are crept into every corner of the land' (pp. 17–18), criticized those who worried that prelatical power would be replaced by presbyterial power, and called for appropriate maintenance for pastors and for a parliamentary directory for catechizing the kingdom. His *The Remarkable Life and Death of the Lady Apollina Hall* (1647) was a conventional puritan 'pattern of imitation' (p. 3).

Tipping died at Waterstock, Oxfordshire, on 2 February 1649, and was buried in the chancel of the church there six days later. By his will, dated 2 October 1648, he left an annuity for an annual Good Friday sermon at All Saints' Church, Oxford, £200 for other charitable uses in the city, and smaller sums for the poor and for maimed soldiers elsewhere. In keeping with his writings, his children were exhorted to industry and godliness. The will was proved by his widow and executor on 23 March 1649.

VIVIENNE LARMINIE

Sources Foster, *Alum. Oxon.* · W. P. Baildon, ed., *The records of the Honorable Society of Lincoln's Inn: admissions*, 1 (1896), 179 · *VCH Oxfordshire*, 7.175 · W. H. Turner, ed., *The visitations of the county of Oxford … 1566 … 1574 … and in 1634*, Harleian Society, 5 (1871), 275 · G. Lipscomb, *The history and antiquities of the county of Buckingham*, 4 vols. (1831–47), vol. 1, pp. 310, 450–53 · PRO, PROB 11/207, 267–268v · Wood, *Ath. Oxon.*, new edn, 3.243–4 · *CSP dom.*, 1635–6, 108, 116, 121, 128 · *Walker rev.*, 76–7 · *STC, 1475–1640* · Wing, *STC*

Tiptoft, John, third Baron Tiptoft (c.1378–1443), administrator and speaker of the House of Commons, was son and heir of Sir Payn Tiptoft (c.1351–c.1413) of Burwell, Cambridgeshire, and Agnes, sister of Sir John Wroth (d. 1407) of Enfield, Middlesex, whose estates he inherited in 1413. Sir Payn, as the youngest son of John, second Lord Tiptoft or Tibetot (1313–1367), held substantial estates in Cambridgeshire. Although Sir Payn was a prominent retainer of Richard (III) Fitzalan, earl of Arundel (d. 1397), his son joined the household of Henry, earl of Derby, serving in 1397 at a wage of 7½d. a day, and probably shared his exile during the next two years, for he was among those knighted on 11 October 1399, on the eve of Derby's coronation as Henry IV, and was formally retained for life with an annuity of 100 marks. By 1402 both he and his father were receiving livery as knights of the chamber. His prowess on campaign in Wales and the north won him considerable

rewards, so that by 1406 his income from fees and annuities came to £91 p.a. and land placed in his keeping provided £34 p.a. more. He was elected for Huntingdonshire to the parliaments of January 1404, October 1404, and 1406, and in the last, notwithstanding his request for exoneration 'because of his youth and lack of sense and discretion' (*RotP*, 3.568), the Commons chose him as their speaker. Although he was the conduit of vociferous criticism of the administration, expressed in the three sessions of an unprecedentedly long parliament, which culminated in the nomination of the council in parliament and its subjection to articles drawn up by both houses, it is most unlikely that Tiptoft himself was opposed to the government (as historians have generally assumed). Rather, working for the crown, he first successfully contained a hostile house and then helped persuade it to accept a compromise package of reform. With considerable skill he offended neither his fellow MPs nor the king. On 8 December the council entrusted him with the proposed reform of the royal household by appointing him its treasurer. For eight months in 1407 he also held the office of chief butler, and he was removed from the treasurership of the household, in July 1408, only to be promoted to that of the exchequer. There he enjoyed considerable control over royal patronage, directly benefiting by further acquisitions of property for himself.

In 1406 or 1407, and before May 1407, Tiptoft made the first of two lucrative marriages. His first wife was Philippa (c.1367–1417), sister and coheir of John Talbot (d. 1388) of Richards Castle, Herefordshire, and widow of Edward III's last chamberlain, Sir Robert Ashton (d. 1384), and of the distinguished soldier Sir Matthew Gournay (d. 1406). She brought him estates in ten shires, notably the Gournay holdings which he sold in reversion to Henry V for £4000, enabling him to become a major landowner in the south and west, and particularly in Somerset. Tenure of the Gournay lordships in the Bordelais resulted in his appointment as seneschal of the Landes and constable of Dax, and in his involvement in the defence of that region. In 1408 he dispatched a ship to Bordeaux containing goods worth £3000, but despite the truce it was taken by a vessel from Bilbao. Henry IV wrote to his nephew Juan II, king of Castile, to seek redress for him.

Dismissed from the treasurership in December 1409, during Prince Henry's ascendancy, Tiptoft remained in comparative obscurity for the next five years, and although he sat in parliament again in April 1414, for Somerset, he was not re-elected speaker. Henry V initially restricted his royal fees to £120 a year, but he soon won the king's confidence, and in April 1415 was appointed seneschal of Aquitaine. His force of 480 soldiers was mustered at Plymouth on 19 June and disembarked at Bordeaux before 20 August. In 1416 he was empowered to treat for an extension of the truce between England and Castile, and following his return home he became closely involved in the diplomatic preparations for the invasion of Normandy, being the person most frequently entrusted with secret negotiations. In September he was attached to the retinue of Emperor Sigismund, with whom he travelled to

Dordrecht and Luxembourg, discussing the ways Sigismund might support Henry V's campaign; and diplomatic work at the Council of Constance, lasting until May 1417, earned him a daily wage of £2. On 25 January, Henry wrote instructing him to disclose secretly to Sigismund the duke of Bourbon's promise to recognize Henry as king of France. He again visited Constance in August. Having undertaken to provide a force of 120 men for service in Normandy, he joined the king there before November, and was appointed president of the duchy exchequer. In 1418 he received an entailed grant of a manor house in Caen for his residence. He occupied the presidency until January 1419, all the while continuing diplomatic work. Largely due to his initiative, Valois-inspired attacks on Gascony were suspended, but following renewed threats to the region he sailed there again in 1420, with a retinue 900 strong. He took Budos, and his viceregal authority was further enhanced by the royal grant of the lordship of Lesparre.

Before 8 July 1421 Tiptoft had contracted to marry again, and in February 1422 he secured Henry V's permission for the marriage to proceed because of his good services overseas. Joyce (c.1403–1446), younger daughter and coheir of Edward, Baron Charlton of Powys (d. 1421), brought him not only considerable additions to his landed estate, but also social advancement, for her mother, Eleanor, was a daughter of Thomas Holland, fifth earl of Kent (d. 1397), and the widow of Roger Mortimer, fourth earl of March (d. 1398). Joyce was a coheir of her uncle Edmund, earl of Kent (d. 1408), and successive partitions of the Holland estates, notably in 1425 when her half-brother Edmund, earl of March, died, resulted in Tiptoft's further enrichment. He also added to his estates in Cambridgeshire, where his landed interests, centred on Burwell, had always been greatest. His annual income from land trebled, from £360 in 1412 to £1098 in 1436.

Henry V's death in 1422 led to Tiptoft's resignation of the seneschalcy of Aquitaine, and reinstated him in a position of authority at home. During the first parliament of Henry VI's reign he was appointed a member of the newly constituted council, with a salary of £100 a year, and until 1432 he was conspicuous among the councillors for the regularity of his attendance at meetings. Well placed to enjoy the fruits of royal patronage, he secured the wardships and marriages of Sir Edmund Ingoldisthorpe (grandson and heir to both Sir John Ingoldisthorpe and Sir Walter de la Pole), to whom he married his daughter Joan, and of the heir of Thomas, Lord Ros of Helmsley, who married his eldest daughter, Philippa. A third daughter, Joyce, was matched with the eldest son of a fellow councillor, John, Lord Dudley. In 1425 his colleagues appointed him chief steward of the Welsh possessions late of the earl of March. Preferential treatment at the exchequer helped him recover large debts owing for past services. Numerous diplomatic assignments led to further travels abroad, and he visited France in December 1424 for talks with the regent, John, duke of Bedford (d. 1435). His summons (as Lord Tiptoft) to the parliament at Leicester in February 1426, and his appointment shortly afterwards as steward of the

household, indicate that he supported Bedford's policies. From May to July 1427 he was absent on an embassy to the dukes of Bedford and Burgundy, and in 1430 he accompanied the king to France for his coronation. During the next two years he made several journeys home on governmental business, on one such spending Christmas with Cardinal Henry Beaufort (d. 1447) at Canterbury. At the parliament of 1431 he successfully presented petitions regarding his wife's inheritance and the sale of the Gournay estates. Following the coronation in Paris on 16 December he returned home with the king in February 1432, only to be displaced from the stewardship of the household in a coup staged by Humphrey, duke of Gloucester (d. 1447). His appearances at council meetings became sporadic, although he was among the councillors who in November 1434 protested to the king about his susceptibility to the advice of others.

Probably because of the threat to Marck Castle, of which he had been made governor five years earlier, in June 1436 Tiptoft led a troop of eighty-five men on Gloucester's expedition to relieve Calais. His negotiations with delegates from the Hanseatic League later that year resulted in a commercial treaty. Following Henry VI's formal assumption of control over the government in 1437 he joined the 'prive counseill', and although his salary was reduced to 100 marks this was guaranteed for life, even if he was absent through ill health. Further diplomatic assignments attest that his faculties remained unimpaired for some years more. Yet in Cambridgeshire, where he had long been dominant, his rule was successfully challenged at the elections to the parliament of 1439 by Sir James Butler (d. 1461), the heir to the earldom of Ormond, who asserted that Tiptoft had done countless wrongs to the local people.

Tiptoft's last recorded attendances on the council fell in August 1442, and he died about the end of January 1443, having left instructions for the foundation of a chantry in Ely Cathedral, his likely burial place. He apparently composed the commonplace book of English history known as Tiptoft's chronicle, showing scholarly interests that he evidently transmitted to his son, the humanist John *Tiptoft (1427–1470), who was created earl of Worcester in 1449.　　　　　　　　　　　　　　　　　　　LINDA CLARK

Sources J. S. Roskell, *Parliament and politics in late medieval England*, 3 vols. (1981–3), vol. 3, pp. 107–50 • HoP, *Commons* • J. S. Roskell, *The Commons and their speakers in English parliaments, 1376–1523* (1965) • A. J. Pollard, 'The Lancastrian constitutional experiment revisited: Henry IV, Sir John Tiptoft and the parliament of 1406', *Parliamentary History*, 14 (1995), 103–19 • R. Virgoe, 'The Cambridgeshire election of 1439', *BIHR*, 46 (1973), 95–101 • R. J. Mitchell, *John Tiptoft, 1427–70* (1938) • *RotP*, 3.568 • H. L. Gray, 'Incomes from land in England in 1436', *EngHR*, 49 (1934), 607–39, esp. 615
Wealth at death over £1098 p.a. excl. possessions in Wales and France: Gray, 'Incomes from land'

Tiptoft [Tibetot], **John, first earl of Worcester** (1427–1470), administrator and humanist, was the only son of John *Tiptoft, third Baron Tiptoft (c.1378–1443), and his second wife, Joyce (c.1403–1446), younger daughter of Edward Charlton, fifth Baron Charlton of Powys (d. 1421). Born at Great Eversden, Cambridgeshire, on 8 May 1427, he was educated in arts at University College, Oxford, where he had rooms as a *commensalis* ('lodger') for three terms in 1440–41, 1441–2, and 1442–3 with his tutor John Hurley, and for one term in 1443. Upon his father's death, about the end of January 1443, he succeeded to his honours and estates in East Anglia as Lord Tiptoft, and also to Nether Wallop and Brockenhurst, Hampshire, Enfield, Middlesex, and to the Wroth estates at Wimbish in north-west Essex. At his mother's death, on 22 September 1446, he divided the Powys estates in Gloucestershire on the Welsh border with his cousin Henry, son of Sir John Grey and Joanna Charlton. In April 1449 he married Cecily, widow of Henry Beauchamp, duke of Warwick (*d.* 1446), and daughter of Richard Neville, earl of Salisbury (*d.* 1460); his wife's aunt *Cecily was wife of *Richard, duke of York (*d.* 1460), and sister of George *Neville, the future archbishop of York (*d.* 1476), and Richard *Neville, earl of Salisbury and Warwick, the Kingmaker (*d.* 1471). On 16 July 1449 Tiptoft was created earl of Worcester by patent. Following Cecily's death, on 28 July 1450, he married another widow, Elizabeth Baynham, daughter of Robert Greyndour, with whom he had a son who died in infancy. Elizabeth died before 4 April 1452, when in a letter to Henry Cranebroke, monk of Christ Church, Canterbury, Tiptoft asked for prayers, 'with special remembraunce of her soule whom I loved best' (Pantin, 3.103). Elizabeth had been an only child, and her death brought him the Greyndour estates in Gloucestershire. Remaining close to the Yorkist members of his first wife's family, Tiptoft was appointed treasurer of England on 15 April 1452 (an office he held until 7 October 1454), and was already a member of the king's council when on 24 October 1453 he signed a minute calling for the attendance of York at a great council summoned for the settlement of the regency during Henry VI's insanity. On 3 April 1454 he was appointed joint keeper of the sea for three years. On 5 August 1457 he was appointed, with Robert Flemming (*d.* 1483) and Philip Wentworth, to offer the king's obedience to Pope Calixtus III (*r.* 1455–8).

Although this mission was not in fact carried out, early in 1458 Tiptoft left England, which was then on the brink of civil war, to visit Italy and make a pilgrimage to the Holy Land. Letters of attorney to go abroad were issued to him on 28 January 1458, and he and his party arrived in Venice in time to attend the ceremonial 'wedding of the sea' on Ascension day (11 May). With the Milanese soldier Roberto da Sanseverino, and the Paduan noble Gabriele Capodilista, he sailed for Jaffa on 17 May. His ship reached Durazzo on 2 June, Cyprus on the 15th, and Jaffa on the 19th. He arrived in Jerusalem on the 25th and bathed in the Jordan on the 29th, departing from Jaffa on 5 July and arriving back in Venice on 6 September 1458. In the autumn of 1458 he resided briefly on the Capodilista estates in the Euganean hills, south of Padua, and began his studies at the university, almost certainly in civil law, which he continued with some interruptions until the summer of 1461. There he made the acquaintance of Ognibene da Lonigo and Galeotto Marzio, and also met two English scholars, Peter Courtenay (*d.* 1492) and John Free

(*d.* 1465), probably engaging the latter as his secretary. Tiptoft probably spent the autumn of 1459 in Ferrara at the school of Guarino da Verona, where he met Lodovico Carbone, whom he later tried to persuade to return with him to England.

Tiptoft returned to Padua, from where he addressed a letter to the University of Oxford, offering to present a collection of choice Latin works, on which students would be encouraged to model their Latin style. The proposal was met with immediate acceptance in a letter of 1 April 1460, averring that this largesse made Tiptoft the successor to the late Humphrey, duke of Gloucester (*d.* 1447) in the university's affections. Although the donation did not take place as planned, several of his books were eventually given to Oxford. In the summer of 1460 Tiptoft travelled to Florence, where he heard at least one lecture by John Argyropoulos, and commissioned books from Vespasiano da Bisticci. Appointed an envoy on 16 May 1459 to convey the obedience of Henry VI to the new pope, Pius II (*r.* 1458–64), Tiptoft probably travelled from Florence to Rome, where he made a Latin oration which, according to John Free, moved the pope to tears of joy for the beauty of his Latinity. Following another visit to Venice in the autumn of 1460, Tiptoft returned to Padua for a final year of study and book collecting, and commissioned John Free to make a Latin translation of Synesius's *Laus Calvitii*, and Francesco Griffolini a Latin version of Lucian's *De calumnia*, which he received just as he left Italy.

The accession of Edward IV in the summer of 1461 opened the way to high office. An elegy by Carbone, rejecting Tiptoft's offer of employment in England, asserts that John '"Gunthorp told me that the king has called you home"' (Weiss, 'Tiptoft and Carbone', 212). Tiptoft landed in England on 1 September 1461, and two months later he was appointed to the king's council. On 25 November he was made chief justice of north Wales, which office he resigned on 28 August 1467 in favour of William Herbert, earl of Pembroke, in return for a life pension of £200 a year. On 2 December 1461 he was appointed constable of the Tower of London for life, and on 7 February 1462 as constable of England was commissioned to try all cases of treason on simple inspection of fact (that is, without a jury). An earlier generation of historians regarded Tiptoft's judicial activities as entailing a substantial extension of the powers of his office. But this is unlikely. Basing its jurisdiction upon civil- rather than common-law principles, the constable's court had long been empowered to proceed to judgment upon the king's record alone, without either indictment or jury trial. It would have been at Edward IV's bidding that later in February, Tiptoft tried and sentenced to death for high treason John de Vere, earl of Oxford, and his son Aubrey, Sir Thomas Tuddenham, and others. He was created knight of the Garter on 21 March 1462 and appointed treasurer on 14 April, an office he held for fourteen months. He accompanied Edward IV north in the autumn of 1462 and took part in the siege that led to the surrender of Dunstanburgh Castle. Next year he was appointed lord steward of the household, and in July 1463 was given command of a fleet that failed to prevent the escape of Queen Margaret from Northumberland to Flanders. On 31 January 1464 he was appointed chancellor of Ireland for life. But he was with Edward IV that spring and summer in the north, where he tried and condemned to death a number of prisoners after the battle of Hexham on 15 May, and Sir Ralph Grey on 10 July, after the surrender of Bamburgh. On 12 August 1464 he was commissioned to arrange a truce with envoys of the duke of Brittany; in June 1466 he was responsible for organizing the famous tournament held outside London at West Smithfield between Antoine, the Bastard of Burgundy, and Anthony Woodville, Lord Scales (d. 1483). That autumn Tiptoft was sent to Wales to capture rebels loyal to Henry VI holed up in Harlech Castle but he could not force them to surrender. In 1467, during the lieutenancy of the duke of Clarence, Tiptoft was appointed deputy governor of Ireland to replace the suspect Thomas Fitzgerald, seventh earl of Desmond. Soon after reaching Ireland he summoned a parliament to Drogheda at which he attainted Desmond and his brother-in-law, Thomas Fitzgerald, the seventh earl of Kildare. There he had Desmond executed, and tortured his two young sons, eventually having them put to death. In revenge for these executions the Fitzgeralds of Munster rebelled and ravaged Meath and Kildare. At a second parliament Kildare was pardoned, and he was later installed as deputy governor, Tiptoft having been recalled to England early in 1470.

Tiptoft remained loyal to the king when Warwick and Clarence rebelled in 1469. Campaigning in the north with Edward, on 14 March 1470 he was reappointed constable of England. On 23 March he received the lieutenancy of Ireland, from which the duke of Clarence had been dismissed, and on 10 July he was reappointed treasurer of England. He accompanied the king south to Southampton, where he had twenty of the earl of Warwick's men who had been captured at sea handed over to him for trial, and condemned them to execution for high treason, adding impalement to the sentence of hanging, drawing, and quartering. This cruelty outraged public opinion and earned him the reputation, reported in a contemporary chronicle, as 'that fierce executioner and horrible beheader of men' (Gairdner, 183). In October 1470, after the flight of Edward IV to Flanders, and the consequent readeption of Henry VI, Tiptoft left London and took refuge in the Forest of Weybridge, Huntingdonshire, disguised as a shepherd. When a man sent to buy food for him aroused suspicion by presenting an unexpectedly valuable coin in payment, soldiers were sent to search for him and found him concealed in a tree. Taken prisoner and brought back to London, on 15 October 1470 Tiptoft was arraigned and condemned for high treason before the newly appointed constable of England, John de Vere, earl of Oxford (d. 1513), whose father and brother he had sentenced to death. His execution was fixed for the 17th, but the crowd pressing to see him so interrupted his passage by foot that the sheriffs were obliged to lodge him in the Fleet prison for the night. At his execution on Tower Hill on the afternoon of 18 October, he bore himself with quiet dignity, requesting the executioner to strike off his head

with three blows in honour of the Trinity. He was buried, head and body together, in the church of the Blackfriars at Ludgate, where his sister Joan Ingoldisthorpe later put up a tablet to his memory. Hated for his cruelty, he was called (by later Tudor propagandists) the Butcher of England. For his swift and ruthless justice Tiptoft earned the reputation that he 'juged by lawe padowe' (Warkworth, 5), that is, he followed summary legal procedures, learned from his study of Roman law. This same charge is repeated by his Italian biographer, Vespasiano da Bisticci, writing in 1490 (Bisticci, 1.419).

On his way to Ireland in the autumn of 1467 Tiptoft had met and promptly married (without the king's licence) his third wife, Elizabeth, daughter of Thomas Hopton and widow of Sir Roger Corbet of Morton Corbet, Shropshire. Elizabeth gave birth, on 14 July 1469, to the earl's only surviving child, a son named Edward in honour of the king. Since Tiptoft was not attainted, Edward succeeded de jure to the earldom of Worcester at his father's death. When he died, childless, on 12 August 1485, this earldom became extinct. Edward's heirs were his three aunts, his father's sisters, who probably commissioned Tiptoft's effigy (with two of his wives) on the cenotaph erected in the south aisle of Ely Cathedral in the 1470s.

Infamous for his cruelty, Tiptoft was also renowned for his learning and his love of books, especially the Latin classics, humanist works, and fresh Latin translations of ancient Greek texts. Of his own writings only some survive. These include his English translations of Cicero's *De amicitia*, and Buonaccorso's *De vera nobilitate*, both printed by Caxton in 1481; the latter was reprinted as *The Declamacion of Noblesse* (Mitchell, *John Tiptoft*, appx 1, 215–41). Several of his ordinances, issued as lord constable or as treasurer, survive: *For Jousts and Triumphes* (J. Harington, *Nugae antiquae*, 1804, 1.1–11); 'For Placing the Nobility' (BL, Cotton MS Tiberius E.viii, and Bodl. Oxf., MS Ashmole 763); and various ordinances published in *Excerpta historica* (ed. S. Bentley, 1833). His letter to Oxford University is published by J. Tait (Tait, 571–2), and those of 1452 to and from Henry Cranebroke are edited by W. A. Pantin (Pantin, 3.103–4). A supposed work is the compendium of English history compiled under the title *Cronice regum Anglie de diversis historiografis per dominum Iohannem Wigornensem Comitem sparsim collecte* (Hunt. L., HM 19960). Lost works include an oration to the people of Padua and the speech given before Pope Pius II and cardinals at Rome in 1460. A great loss is the *Liber epistolarum Johannis Tiptofti*, which Thomas Tanner reports (*Bibl. Brit.-hib.*, 1748, 716–17) was once housed in the library of Lincoln Cathedral.

Tiptoft's real passion was book collecting: as Carbone observed in his funeral oration for Guarino da Verona, Tiptoft 'despoiled the libraries of Italy so he might adorn England with handsome monuments of books' (Carbone, 398, 400). At least a dozen books from his library survive, including classical texts: Lucretius, *De rerum natura*, Tacitus, *De oratoribus claris*, Suetonius, *De claris grammaticis rhetoribusque*, and Sallust, *Bellum Catilinarium* and *Bellum Jurgurthinium*, which he commissioned from Vespasiano as a gift for Peter Courtenay. Humanist works include

Ognibene da Lonigo's commentary on Juvenal, Basinio da Parma's *Astronomicon*, and Free's Latin version of Synesius's *Laus Calvitii*, and Griffolini's version of Lucian's *De calumnia*, mentioned above. Even after taking into account various scholastic collections, John Lydgate's *Fall of Princes*, and books of hours, inherited from family members or perhaps confiscated from political enemies, the collection remains heavily classical, reflecting the critical importance of the years in Italy. Tiptoft may thus be justly called the first Italianate Englishman in two different respects. He brought the texts of the 'new learning' of the University of Padua, Guarino's school in Ferrara, and Medicean Florence back to English libraries, and he applied the harsh lessons of Italian politics to the service of his sovereign, Edward IV, in ways that in the end were to cost him his life. BENJAMIN G. KOHL

Sources R. J. Mitchell, *John Tiptoft (1427–1470)* (1938) · R. Weiss, *Humanism in England during the fifteenth century*, 3rd edn (1967), 112–22, 195 · C. L. Scofield, *The life and reign of Edward the Fourth*, 1 (1923) · Emden, *Oxf.*, 3.1877–9 · J. Gairdner, ed., *Three fifteenth-century chronicles*, CS, new ser., 28 (1880), 157, 159, 177, 182–3 · V. da Bisticci, *Le vite*, ed. A. Greco (1970), 1.417–20 · J. Warkworth, *A chronicle of the first thirteen years of the reign of King Edward the Fourth*, ed. J. O. Halliwell, CS, old ser., 10 (1839), 5, 13, 38, 63 · R. J. Mitchell, *The spring voyage: the Jerusalem pilgrimage in 1458* (1964) · L. Carbone, 'Oratio habita in funere … Guarini Veronensis', *Prosatori latini del Quattrocento*, ed. E. Garin (1952), 382–417, 398–400 · R. Weiss, 'The library of John Tiptoft, earl of Worcester', *Bodleian Quarterly Record*, 8 (1935–7), 157–64 · R. Weiss, 'John Tiptoft, earl of Worcester, and Ludovico Carbone', *Rinascimento*, 8 (1957), 209–12 · R. Weiss, 'A letter-preface of John Phreas to John Tiptoft, earl of Worcester', *Bodleian Quarterly Record*, 8 (1935–7), 101–3 · [A. C. de la Mare and R. W. Hunt], eds., *Duke Humfrey and English humanism in the fifteenth century* (1970), 41–51 [exhibition catalogue, Bodl. Oxf.] · J. Tait, ed., 'The letters of John Tiptoft, earl of Worcester and Archbishop Neville to the University of Oxford', *EngHR*, 35 (1920), 570–74 · H. Anstey, ed., *Epistolae academicae Oxon.*, 2, OHS, 36 (1898), 354–5, 389–91 · W. A. Pantin, *Canterbury College, Oxford*, 3, OHS, new ser., 8 (1950), 103–4 [two letters by Tiptoft to Henry Cranebroke (9 Jan 1452, 4 April 1452)] · GEC, *Peerage*, new edn, 12/2.842–6
Archives BL, Cotton MS Tiberius E.viii · Hunt. L., MS HM 19960 | Bodl. Oxf., MS Ashmole 763
Likenesses group portrait, sculptured effigy, c.1470–1479 (with two of his wives), Ely Cathedral
Wealth at death lands in East Anglia, Enfield, Middlesex, Great Eversden, Cambridgeshire, Nether Wallop, Brockenhurst, Hampshire, and Wimbish, Essex; Powys estates in Gloucestershire: Mitchell, *John Tiptoft*, 11, 20

Tiptoft [Tibetot], **Robert**, **Lord Tiptoft** (1228?–1298), soldier and administrator, succeeded to the lands of his father, Henry, in January 1250. He was a staunch supporter of Henry III and the Lord Edward during the troubles of the 1260s. In November 1265 he was made constable of Portchester Castle. He accompanied the Lord Edward to the Holy Land in 1270, and in January 1275 was made constable of Nottingham Castle. He took a leading part in the negotiations with, and campaigns in, Wales in 1277 and 1282–3 and after the conquest become one of Edward I's key officers in Wales. He was appointed justice of south Wales on 8 June 1281 and held the post until his death; he was also constable of the royal castles of Carmarthen and Cardigan. He sat in parliament in 1290, but there is no record of the writs of summons.

Tiptoft took a leading part in the suppression of the revolt of Rhys ap Maredudd in 1287–8. Rhys's pretext for revolt was the compulsory introduction of 'English customs' by Tiptoft. Tiptoft took Rhys's chief castles, but he did not effect his capture until 1292. In 1294 Tiptoft was appointed a counsellor and lieutenant of John of Brittany, earl of Richmond, in the expedition sent to recover Gascony. John of Brittany sent him to negotiate an alliance with Sancho IV of Castile. He was also left in command of Rions on the retreat of the English army before Charles of Valois, but had to surrender on 7 April 1295. He was summoned to take part in Edward I's Scottish expedition of 1297, and died at his manor of Nettlestead (Suffolk) on 22 May 1298.

With his wife, Eve (perhaps a member of the Chaworth family of Kidwelly), Tiptoft had a surviving son, Pain (1279–1314), who is commonly reckoned first Lord Tibetot or Tiptoft. His son, John (1313–1367), second lord, was grandfather of John Tiptoft (c.1378–1443).

W. E. RHODES, *rev.* R. R. DAVIES

Sources GEC, *Peerage* · H. C. Maxwell-Lyte, ed., 'Calendar of Welsh rolls', *Calendar of various chancery rolls … 1277–1326*, PRO (1912) · J. G. Edwards, *Calendar of ancient correspondence concerning Wales* (1935) · J. G. Edwards, ed., *Littere Wallie* (1940) · R. A. Griffiths, 'The revolt of Rhys ap Maredudd, 1287–88', *Welsh History Review / Cylchgrawn Hanes Cymru*, 3 (1966–7), 121–45 · J. B. Smith, 'The origins of the revolt of Rhys ap Maredudd', *BBCS*, 21 (1964–6), 151–63 · *CIPM*, 3, no. 475

Tírechán [St Tírechán] (*fl. c.*690), bishop and writer, was the author of the so-called *Collectanea* about St Patrick that forms part of the Book of Armagh. His feast day is 3 July, but his sainthood may have been acquired late: he is not in the Genealogies of the Saints, nor in any martyrology before the twelfth century. Reportedly a native of Tirawley, co. Sligo, he became a bishop, though no see is named. The *Collectanea* implies that he belonged to the Uí Amolngada (in the north-west of the present-day co. Mayo), and to a branch (descended from Conall, son of Éndae, son of Amolngaid) who were servants of Patrick. His kinship may thus explain why Tírechán became, with Muirchú maccu Machtheni, one of two major Patrician hagiographers of the late seventh century. He was a disciple of Ultán, bishop of Ardbraccan in Brega (in what is now co. Meath), who died in 657, from whom he claims to have derived information, both by word of mouth and from his book, the exact nature of which is unknown. On the other hand, the *Collectanea* was probably written c.690: before 696, the beginning of the reign of Loingsech mac Óengusso (of Cenél Conaill), since he takes for granted the supremacy of the southern Uí Néill dynasties; also probably before 693, since he seems to assume that the king of Leinster belongs to the Uí Dúnlainge. The reign of the Uí Dúnlainge king of Leinster, Bran mac Conaill maic Fáeláin, from 680 to 693, was preceded and followed by kings of a rival dynasty. The date is probably after 688 since he refers to 'the recent plagues' in the plural (*Collectanea*, chap. 25). Adomnán, writing c.700, speaks of two major plagues in his lifetime, presumably those of 664–6 and the one he dates himself, 686–8.

The *Collectanea*—first given this title by Archbishop James Ussher (1581–1656)—is not a life such as that written at much the same date by Muirchú. It purports to recount a journey taking Patrick round the northern half of Ireland, beginning in Brega (on the coast north of Dublin), going west across the midlands through the kingdoms of the southern Uí Néill, across the Shannon into the lands of the Connachta, round the northern coast as far as what is now co. Antrim, then south-west to Armagh, and finally back to Brega. At the end Tírechán briefly takes Patrick via Leinster to Cashel, seat of the kings of Munster. The journey is a convenient framework: he himself admits that Patrick crossed the Shannon not once, but three times. The purpose was to assert that Patrick was the founder of numerous churches as well as the arbiter of the fates of some local dynasties. Tírechán's loyalty, however, was to Patrick and his *familia* in general rather than to Armagh in particular, which he mentions only once, and then only in passing. The churches to which he gave his greatest attention were Donaghpatrick (Domnach Pátraic), in co. Meath, and a church by 'the Wood of Fochluth' (chap. 42), which may well have been Tírechán's own local church. Donaghpatrick was adjacent to two other sites mentioned by Tírechán. The first was Tailtiu, the site of the annual assembly and fair, the greatest such event in Ireland, and by Tírechán's time an essential element in the high-kingship, monopolized since 637 by the Uí Néill. The other site, Ráith Airthir, was the royal seat of the kings of Brega; the current ruler, Finsnechtae mac Dúnchada, was also king of Tara (as the high-kings were called). Tírechán's text expressed the hope that an alliance between the Uí Néill of Brega and the heirs of Patrick might dominate Ireland; he may also have envisaged Donaghpatrick being the chief Patrician church rather than Armagh.

Tírechán apparently did not know Muirchú's work, and the reverse may also be true. In any case their intentions, both literary and political, were quite different: while Muirchú was the champion of Armagh, Tírechán wished to uphold the claims of the heirs of Patrick, without any special reference to Armagh, by attaching the saint on the one hand to many small, often ancient, churches and, on the other, by harnessing the power of the leading Uí Néill dynasty of the time behind the *familia* of Patrick. Tírechán's text offers the first detailed picture of the ecclesiastical and political geography of Ireland. Later lives of Patrick, notably the tripartite life, were principally based on a combination of Muirchú's life and Tírechán's *Collectanea*. Some of the personalities he records as disciples of Patrick may well be early figures, but it is difficult to see how this can be demonstrated.

DAVID E. THORNTON

Sources L. Bieler, ed. and trans., *The Patrician texts in the Book of Armagh*, Scriptores Latini Hiberniae, 10 (1979) • *Félire húi Gormáin / The martyrology of Gorman*, ed. and trans. W. Stokes, HBS, 9 (1895) • R. Sharpe, 'St Patrick and the see of Armagh', *Cambridge Medieval Celtic Studies*, 4 (winter 1982), 33–59 • C. Doherty, 'The cult of St Patrick and the politics of Armagh in the seventh century', *Ireland and northern France, AD 600–850*, ed. J.-M. Picard (1991), 53–94

Tirel, Walter (*d.* in or before 1130), courtier and landowner, was the son and heir of another Walter Tirel and was lord of Poix in Picardy, some 17 miles south-west of Amiens, and Domesday lord of Langham, Essex. He was a vassal of the count of Pontoise and Amiens and held his English estate of his father-in-law, Richard de *Clare. Walter Tirel is described by some contemporary authorities as having fired the arrow that killed King William Rufus. But Suger of St Denis and John of Salisbury both report that in later years Walter denied the allegation, at a time when (as Suger observes) 'he had nothing to fear or gain'. Walter declared repeatedly that he had not so much as seen Rufus in the New Forest on the day of his death and had not set foot in the part of the forest where Rufus was hunting. Theories of an assassination conspiracy involving Walter Tirel, Henry I, and the Clare family are not supported by contemporary evidence and are no longer taken seriously.

Walter Tirel was a friend of Anselm, abbot of Bec, who, on a visit to Poix of uncertain date, correctly prophesied the unexpected arrival of a large sturgeon for their dinner. Anselm's visit is one of several indications of Walter's association with the abbey of Bec. The connection probably resulted from the close relationship between the abbey and the family of Walter's wife, Adeliza de Clare, who spent her widowhood at Conflans, a daughter house of Bec, and whose brother Richard had been a monk of Bec before becoming abbot of Ely. The Clares were benefactors of Bec itself and also founded the Bec priories of St Neot's, Huntingdonshire, and Stoke by Clare, Suffolk.

Walter Tirel was active in both France and England. William of Malmesbury reports that he was on the friendliest of terms with William Rufus, who brought him from France to his court in England. He was clearly at Rufus's court at the time of the king's death on 2 August 1100 and was doubtless in Rufus's company at other times as well, although he attests no surviving royal charters. But he is also known to have entered into an agreement with the count of Pontoise and Amiens in 1087 and he was in attendance at the French royal court in 1091. His two major monastic foundations were both French: the abbey of St Pierre de Selincourt, and the priory of St Denis de Poix to which he granted two marks annually from the tithes of Langham in Essex.

Walter had presumably died by 1130: the pipe roll of that year records Langham, Essex, as being held by his wife (or widow) Adeliza. Their lands at Poix and Langham passed to their son and heir, Hugh, who subsequently sold Langham to Henry of Cornhill on joining the second crusade in 1147.

C. WARREN HOLLISTER

Sources J. H. Round, 'Walter Tirel and his wife', *Feudal England: historical studies on the eleventh and twelfth centuries* (1895), 468–79 • Eadmer, *The life of St Anselm, archbishop of Canterbury*, ed. and trans. R. W. Southern, 2nd edn, OMT (1972) • Suger, abbot of St Denis, *Vie de Louis VI le Gros*, ed. and trans. H. Waquet (Paris, 1929) • Joannes Saresberiensis, 'Vita S. Anselmi', *Patrologia Latina*, 199 (1855), col. 1031 • D. C. Douglas, ed., *The Domesday Monachorum of Christ Church, Canterbury* (1944) • Ordericus Vitalis, *Eccl. hist.*, 5.292–4 • *Willelmi Malmesbiriensis monachi de gestis regum Anglorum*, ed. W. Stubbs, 2 vols., Rolls Series (1887–9), vol. 2, p. 378 · F. Barlow, *William Rufus* (1983), 419–26

Tisdal, Philip (*bap.* **1703**, *d.* **1777**), lawyer and politician, was baptized on 1 March 1703 at St Mary's Church, Dublin, the son of Richard Tisdal (*d.* 1742), registrar of the Irish court of chancery, and MP for Dundalk (1707–13) and Louth (1713–27), and his wife, Marian, daughter of Richard Boyle, MP for Leighlin. He was educated at Thomas Sheridan's school in Capel Street, Dublin, and from 1718 at Trinity College, Dublin, where he was tutored by Swift's friend Patrick Delany. He graduated in 1722 and entered the Middle Temple in 1728. In 1733 he was called to the Irish bar, where he achieved rapid success. His marriage in 1736 to Mary, daughter of the Revd Rowland Singleton, and niece and coheir of Henry Singleton, chief justice of the common pleas and master of the rolls, aided his political career. Not only was she a distinguished beauty, but she was also extremely wealthy. His influential connections enabled him to stand as a parliamentary candidate for Dublin University in 1739, and although initially defeated by Alexander McAuley, who was backed by Swift, Tisdal's petition was successful and he represented the university in the Irish parliament until 1776.

On 21 January 1742 Tisdal was appointed third serjeant-at-law, and became a bencher of the King's Inns, and on the death of his father in October he succeeded him as registrar of the court of chancery. In 1743 he was one of the leading counsel for the plaintiff in the celebrated Anglesey peerage case. In 1751 he was appointed solicitor-general, and on 31 July 1760 attorney-general, appointments which he owed in part to the influence of his new patron, the primate, George Stone. The first of these appointments sparked resentment among the speaker Henry Boyle's party and it was a contributory factor in the increase of tension that led to the money bill dispute of 1753.

Tisdal's parliamentary talents raised him to great eminence as a politician and he was invaluable as a parliamentary speaker to a succession of viceroys. However, his bitter rivalry with John Hely-Hutchinson, MP for Cork City, occasionally persuaded him to obstruct government measures, as did the influence of Primate Stone. During the duke of Bedford's administration he refused to support a money bill until resolutions against the burden of pensions on the Irish establishment were transmitted to London. After the government's defeat Tisdal persuaded the patriot clubs of Dublin to organize a celebration. Although he quickly returned to the government fold once Bedford had made his peace with Stone, he threatened to go into opposition when Richard Rigby, chief secretary, appeared likely to be appointed as master of the rolls. He was eventually assuaged by the offer of the reversion of the post of secretary of state.

At the general election of 1761 Tisdal was again returned, by a large majority, for Dublin University, and in the same year received the freedom of the city of Cork. In the Irish Commons his pre-eminence was challenged by an alliance between Hely-Hutchinson and the new chief secretary, William Gerard Hamilton. But with the assistance of Stone and Lord Shannon, Hamilton's personal ambitions were scuppered and Tisdal returned as leader in the Commons. His political comeback, however, was short-lived as the new viceroy, Lord Hertford, opted for Hely-Hutchinson as his chief parliamentary manager. Tisdal's position had been undermined by the death of Stone and inconsistent government majorities during the previous viceroyalty.

On the death of the lord chancellor, John Bowes, in 1767, Tisdal made a strenuous effort to gain the seals. But despite support from Lord Townshend, the ministry was unwilling to appoint an Irishman to this post, and it went to James Hewitt, Viscount Lifford. Smarting at his treatment Tisdal did not proffer his support for Townshend's planned augmentation of the army. Nevertheless he was able to retain a great degree of influence in the Townshend administration, and that of his successor, Lord Harcourt; his luxurious living and social habits added, in the eyes of both Townshend and Harcourt, to his merits as an adviser. Tisdal, his wife, and their two daughters divided their time between their town mansion in Leinster Street, Dublin, and Stillorgan Park, co. Dublin. The artist Angelica Kauffman, who was patronized by Mary Tisdal, was a frequent visitor to their homes during her stay in Ireland in 1771. As a leading member of the Dublin Castle government Tisdal was satirized in *Baratariana*, a compilation of anti-Townshend propaganda pamphlets written by prominent opposition MPs. In this work Tisdal was Don Philip the Moor, but he was more commonly known as Black Phil due to his dark complexion, grave demeanour, and sardonic temper.

Tisdal's support for government was always conditional on his personal advancement, but he was not devoid of patriot sympathies. He voted for the absentee tax despite Harcourt's withdrawal of support, and was reluctant to offer support for parliamentary approval of the American war—although this was partly motivated by pique following the appointment of Henry Flood to the post of Irish vice-treasurer, which Tisdal wanted for himself. In 1776 Tisdal's election for the university seat was opposed by Richard Hely-Hutchinson, the son of his rival. Tisdal was defeated, but was returned at the same general election for Armagh. A petition was lodged against Hutchinson's return, which was subsequently declared void. Tisdal's death at Spa in the Netherlands on 11 September 1777 was a severe blow to government, which struggled against a rejuvenated opposition during the Buckinghamshire viceroyalty. Tisdal was buried at Finglas, near Dublin.

C. L. FALKINER, *rev.* MARTYN J. POWELL

Sources M. J. Powell, 'An early imperial problem: Britain and Ireland, 1750–1783', PhD diss., U. Wales, 1997 · R. E. Burns, *Irish parliamentary politics in the eighteenth century*, 2 vols. (1989–90) · *The manuscripts of the duke of Beaufort … the earl of Donoughmore*, HMC, 27 (1891) · F. Hardy, *Memoirs of the political and private life of James Caulfeild, earl of Charlemont* (1810) · PRO NIre., Macartney MSS, D 572 · H. Walpole, *Memoirs of the reign of King George the Third*, ed. G. F. R. Barker, 3 (1894) · *Baratariana: a selection of political pieces published during the administration of Lord Townshend in Ireland* (1772) · E. Magennis, *The Irish political system, 1740–1765* (Dublin, 2000)

Archives PRO NIre., Macartney MSS · TCD, Donoughmore MSS
Likenesses A. Kauffman, oils · J. Latham, oils, TCD

Tisdale, John (*b.* **1530/31**, *d.* in or after **1563**), printer, freed in 1555, aged twenty-four, began to print in partnership with John Charlewood in 1557 or 1558 at the Saracen's Head, near Holborn conduit. His next book, in 1558 or 1559, he apparently printed alone at the sign of the Mitre in Smithfield. In 1560–61 he was in Knightrider Street, south of St Paul's Cathedral, and in 1561–3 at the sign of the Eagle's Foot in All Hallows churchyard, Lombard Street. He was an original member of the Stationers' Company, and is mentioned in its first charter, on 4 May 1557. The first entry to him in the register is in 1558 for a licence 'to prynte an A B C in laten for Rycharde Jugge, John Judson, and Anthony Smythe', which is the 'first instance recorded in the "Register" of one printer printing for another' (Arber, *Regs. Stationers*, 1.95). He is also known to have printed for Rafe Newbery and Francis Coldocke.

Tisdale married, on 5 November 1559, Katherine Master. He began to take apprentices in the same year, on 25 December. One of his devices was an angel driving Adam and Eve out of paradise; another was Abraham's sacrifice. He printed several of Bishop Bale's treatises. His last production is dated 1563, and the latest entry referring to him is one for taking an apprentice on 25 June of the same year (Arber, *Regs. Stationers*, 1.227).

H. R. TEDDER, rev. ANITA MCCONNELL

Sources J. Ames, T. F. Dibdin, and W. Herbert, eds., *Typographical antiquities, or, The history of printing in England, Scotland and Ireland*, 4 vols. (1810–19), vol. 4, pp. 345–53 · *STC, 1475–1640*, 3.169 · marriage register, London, St Gregory by St Paul, 5 Nov 1559, GL, MS 10,231, fol. 74*r* · Arber, *Regs. Stationers*, 1.xxviii–xxix, 95, 119, 227 · Grocers' Company, wardens' accounts, 1555–78, GL, MS 11,571, fol. 121*v*

Tisdall, Edmund Charles (1824–1892), milk retailer, was born on 19 December 1824 in Kensington, the son of Edmund Tisdall, dyer, of Church Street, Kensington, and his wife, Martha. Although born into a nonconformist family, he was baptized on 18 December 1825 at his parish church of St Mary Abbott. He attended the City of London School, and on 3 July 1847 married Emma (*b.* 1822), the daughter of George Tunks, cowkeeper, and his wife, Mary Ann. He went into partnership with Emma's elder sister Elizabeth, and as Tunks and Tisdall they took a lease on 63 acres of pasture in Holland Park. In 1851 the company employed eight men, and at its peak Tunks and Tisdall supplied milk to 1200 families.

With a herd of Jerseys, Alderneys, and dairy shorthorns, the quality of Tunks and Tisdall's milk was renowned in the middle-class residential neighbourhood of Kensington, not just for its richness of butterfat but also because Tisdall abhorred the common practice of adulterating milk with added water. He also maintained what were then advanced standards of cleanliness in the dairy. The improvements in milk production and retailing which were later enforced by legislation and inspection were partly the result of his influence and energy.

Tisdall was an enthusiast for dairy science. He regularly monitored the daily yield of all his animals and attempted to convince other farmers that this was the route to herd improvement by organizing milking competitions at dairy shows and by publishing papers on breeding and milk-recording in the *Journal of the British Dairy Farmers' Association*. He was also ahead of his time in his vision of the production of sterile milk for consumption on the long voyages of the Royal Navy. Unfortunately the experimental sterilization process was imperfect and his sample bottles are reported to have burst at the naval board of inquiry.

The idea of producing milk in a built-up area has become increasingly alien in the highly regulated modern world but it was common in the mid-nineteenth century. Inevitably there were additional costs in maintaining a herd in the heart of London, but Tunks and Tisdall was able to survive both these and the competition from country milk imported by rail. Gradually, however, their pastures were eroded by building land and eventually they became merely agents for the receipt and distribution of country milk.

Tisdall selflessly devoted much of his time to trade organizations. He was a founder member of the Metropolitan Dairymen's Society (1873), the Metropolitan Dairymen's Benevolent Institution (1875) (of which he was in turn president and treasurer), and the British Dairy Farmers' Association (1877). An elected member for thirty-five years, he became father of the Kensington vestry and was an active member of its works and sanitary committee. He chaired the special purposes committee and for many years was on the commission of baths and workhouses. He was a clear and emphatic debater, a cool-headed man of business, and thoroughly respected. In politics he was a Liberal but, like many others, was unhappy with Gladstone's Irish policy.

Tisdall's father had been a founder member of the London Temperance League, and Edmund himself before the age of twenty was president of the Kensington and Hammersmith Youths' Temperance Society. Later he was a manager of the London Temperance Hospital and a founder member (1853), director (1854–78), chairman (1874–8), vice-president (1878–90), and president (1890–92) of the Temperance Building Society.

About 1890, while out shooting, Tisdall was accidentally wounded in the eye and partially blinded, which considerably handicapped him in both business and private life. He underwent an operation for a stomach tumour but died three months later at his residence, Holland Park Farm, 3 Holland Park Road, Kensington, on 14 July 1892. Family and trade friends joined representatives of temperance organizations and Kensington gentry at his funeral on 16 July at Brompton cemetery.

P. J. ATKINS

Sources P. J. Atkins, 'Tisdall, Edmund Charles', *DBB* · *Cowkeeper and Dairyman's Journal*, 13 (1892), 589–90 · *Journal of the British Dairy Farmers' Association*, 7 (1892), 96–9 · *The Dairy*, 4 (1892), 128 · *The Dairyman*, 17 (1892), 210 · S. J. Price, *From queen to queen: the centenary story of the Temperance Permanent Building Society, 1854–1954* [1954] · F. H. W. Sheppard, ed., *Northern Kensington*, Survey of London, 37 (1973) · P. J. Atkins, 'The milk trade of London, *c.*1790–1914', PhD diss., U. Cam., 1977 · E. C. Tisdall, 'The improvement of dairy cattle', *Journal of the British Dairy Farmers' Association*, 1/2 (1878), 1–8 ·

'Departmental committee to inquire into pleuro-pneumonia and tuberculosis', *Parl. papers* (1888), 32.267, C. 5461 • 'Select committee on the Adulteration of Food Act', *Parl. papers* (1874), 6.243, no. 262 • 'Select committee on the causes of the outbreak of cattle plague', *Parl. papers* (1877), vol. 9, no. 362 • *Kensington News* (23 July 1892), 6 • *Kensington News* (16 July 1892), 5 • census returns, 1851

Archives LMA, MSS of the Holland Park estate, Acc 1316/56–60
Likenesses portrait, repro. in *Journal of the British Dairy Farmers' Association*, 97
Wealth at death £16,171 9s. 8d.: probate, 7 Oct 1892, CGPLA Eng. & Wales

Tisdall, William (1669–1735), Church of Ireland clergyman, was born in Dublin, the son of William Tisdall, sheriff of Carrickfergus, and his wife, Anna. He entered Trinity College, Dublin, on 16 August 1688, where his tutor was Edward Smith, later bishop of Down and Connor. He became scholar in 1692, fellow in 1696, and obtained the degree of DD in 1707. Tisdall seems to have made the acquaintance of Jonathan Swift as early as 1695–6, while the latter was at Kilroot, co. Antrim, during one of his estrangements from Sir William Temple. Swift sympathized with Tisdall's arrogant churchmanship and hatred of Presbyterians, and thought a good deal of his capacity as a preacher. He and Tisdall corresponded too on political questions, and were in agreement as to the desirability of passing a bill against occasional conformity by dissenters. These relations were abruptly changed in 1704, when Tisdall announced to his friend that he had designs upon the hand of Swift's companion, Esther Johnson (Stella). Swift replied in a letter dated 20 April 1704, in which rage and irony are apparent enough beneath the studied calmness which he affected. The episode was very soon over but Swift never got over his grudge against the 'interloper'. When he wanted a contemptuous epithet for Richard Steele he called him a 'Tisdall fellow'. Tisdall consoled himself by marrying, on 16 May 1706, Eleanor (d. 1736), daughter of Hugh Morgan of Cottlestown, co. Sligo.

In 1706 Tisdall became vicar of Kerry and Ruavan, co. Antrim. He was appointed rector of Drumcree, co. Armagh, on 29 November 1711, and was admitted vicar of Belfast in the following year. His reputation as a controversialist was already considerable in the north of Ireland. His ironical *A Sample of True-Blew Presbyterian Loyalty, in All Changes and Turns of Government* appeared in 1709; this was followed, in 1712, by his vigorous *Conduct of the Dissenters in Ireland*. Tisdall declared in jest (though the joke was not relished by Swift) that he had saved Ireland by this work, as Swift had saved England by his *Conduct of the Allies*. John McBride retorted in *A Sample of Jet-Black Prelatic Calumny*. Tisdall published two other small tracts before the dominion of the whigs was definitely established in 1715. After this he was silent. His relations with Swift became closer again after Stella's death, and he was a witness to Swift's will. Tisdall died on 8 June 1735 and was survived for just a year and a day by his wife. A son, William, became vicar of St James's, Dublin. He married Lady Mary, daughter of Chambre Brabazon, fifth earl of Meath.

THOMAS SECCOMBE, rev. J. FALVEY

Sources I. Ehrenpreis, *Swift: the man, his works and the age*, 3 vols. (1962–83), vol. 2 • E. Hardy, *The conjured spirit* (1949) • *Jonathan Swift: the complete poems*, ed. P. Rogers (1983) • Burtchaell & Sadleir, *Alum. Dubl.* • *The correspondence of Jonathan Swift*, ed. H. Williams, 5 vols. (1963–5)

Tisquantum (d. 1622), interpreter in America, was born of unknown parentage, a member of the Patuxet tribe, which resided in present-day eastern Massachusetts. Little is certain about his life before he encountered the pilgrim colonists at Plymouth. William Bradford, second governor of the colony, notes in his chronicles of the colony's history that Squanto, as he was known to the pilgrims, had been captured by Thomas Hunt, captain of one of the ships in John Smith's expedition to New England in 1614, and taken to Malaga, Spain, to be sold as a slave. There he and several other American Indians were taken by the friars for conversion and instruction. Somehow Tisquantum made his way to England by 1617, where he resided in the London home of John Slany, treasurer of the Newfoundland Company. In 1618 he travelled to the English settlement of Conception Bay in Newfoundland, where he met Thomas Dermer, a member of Smith's 1614 voyage, who worked for Sir Fernando Gorges, army officer and promoter of colonization in New England. Tisquantum returned to his Patuxet homeland in the following year but found only devastation. Presumably European in origin because of white immunity, a disease claimed the lives of between 75 and 90 per cent of the region's American Indian population, wiping out some tribes such as the Patuxet. When the pilgrims arrived shortly afterwards, Bradford described the scene as 'a spectackle to behould' where 'skulls and bones were found in many places lying still above ground' (*History of Plymouth Plantation*, 118). Tisquantum was taken captive by American Indians fearing his English connections and handed over to the Wampanoag. A once powerful tribe destroyed by the recent epidemic, the Wampanoag at Pokanoket were forced to pay tribute to the Narragansett, who had escaped much of the disease's devastation. Through Tisquantum the Wampanoag leader, Massasoit, hoped to regain prominence with the English settlers at Plymouth, who had arrived in December 1620. After a terrible first winter in which they lost half their number, the pilgrims were anxious to secure sufficient sources of food and supplies.

The appearance of Samoset, an English-speaking Mohegan, on 16 March 1621 caused great joy among the dwindling colonists. He told them of Tisquantum, 'a native of this place, who had been in England and could speak better English than himselfe' (Garraty). A few days later Tisquantum appeared with Massasoit, who concluded a treaty of mutual protection with the colonists. Thereafter Tisquantum stayed in Plymouth, acting as a guide and diplomat for the pilgrims. To the ill-prepared colonists this English-speaking Indian appeared to be 'a special instrument sent of God' (ibid.). He showed them how to plant corn successfully, and negotiated a series of treaties that gave the Plymouth American Indians tributaries who could provide added protection and food.

Tisquantum also worked to secure his own importance as an intermediary between the English and American

Indians. He undermined rival interpreters and threatened neighbouring tribes with English military force. As Bradford described,

> Squanto sought his owne ends, and plaid his owne game, by putting the Indeans in fear, and drawing gifts from them to enrich him selfe; making them beleeve he could stur up warr against whom he would, and make peece for whom he would. Yea, he made them beleeve they kept the plague buried in the gourmd, and could send it amongs whome they would, which did much terrifie the Indeans.   (*History of Plymouth Plantation*, 128)

Ultimately, the American Indians turned against him, capturing and holding him prisoner before a heavily armed English force rescued him. Massasoit turned against him, demanding he be handed over, but the English refused. From then on, Bradford noted, Tisquantum stayed close by the English until he succumbed to fever and died in November 1622.

Most widely remembered as 'Squanto the friendly Indian', Tisquantum was a far more complex character than the children's classic *Squanto: Indian Adventurer* suggests. He was a shrewd negotiator who persevered in a world that disease and European colonization were rapidly transforming. He helped to secure both the continued prominence of the Wampanoag and the survival of the English at Plymouth, whose initial friendship is mythologized in the celebration of Thanksgiving in the United States.   TROY O. BICKHAM

Sources Bradford's History of Plymouth Plantation, 1606–1646, ed. W. T. Davis (1908) · N. Salisbury, 'Squanto: last of the Patuxets', *Struggle and survival in colonial America*, ed. D. G. Sweet and G. B. Nash (1981) · J. A. Garraty, 'Tisquantum', *ANB* · K. Kupperman, *Indians and English: facing off in early America* (2000) · P. Gay, *A loss of mastery: puritan historians in colonial America* (1966) · G. D. Langdon, *Pilgrim colony: a history of Plymouth, 1620–1691* (1966) · S. Graff, *Squanto: Indian adventurer* (1965)

Titchener, Edward Bradford (1867–1927), experimental psychologist, was born on 11 January 1867 in Little London, Chichester, Sussex, the son of John Bradford Titchener, railway clerk, and his wife, Alice Field Habin. Titchener obtained successive scholarships to Malvern College (1881) and Brasenose College, Oxford (1885), where he took a first in classical moderations (1887) and a first in classics (1889) before taking a further year's research studentship in physiology. During this period he discovered Wilhelm Wundt, the Leipzig-based German founder of experimental psychology, some of whose work he translated (though did not publish). Oxford being unsupportive of such interests he went to Leipzig in 1890 where he gained his PhD in 1892. Here he met such fellow doctoral students, and subsequently eminent psychologists, as the Americans E. W. Scripture, F. Angell, L. Witmer, and H. C. Warren, and the Germans O. Külpe and E. Meumann. Titchener's doctoral research concerned reaction times and perception. In 1892, after a term spent teaching biology at Oxford, he emigrated to Cornell University in the United States, initially as director of the psychology laboratory; he was then Sage professor of psychology from 1895 to 1910. There he remained, returning to Europe only for the 1896 Munich International Congress of Psychology. In

1894 he married Sophie Kellogg Bedlow, of Portland, Maine, who assisted his work in various ways thereafter; they had three daughters and a son. Titchener was professor in charge of music at Cornell (1896–8) and Sage professor of psychology in the graduate school from 1910.

While Wundt's numerous American students usually abandoned both his methods and his concept of psychology, Titchener professed to remain loyal, casting himself as Wundt's leading apostle in the United States. It is, however, now generally agreed that Titchener's position actually diverged profoundly from the German pioneer's, his elementism, empiricism and positivism markedly differing from Wundt's neo-idealism. He did, though, successfully emulate Wundt's academic style. Titchener saw his task as being threefold. The first was to translate key German works, most importantly Wundt's *Lectures on Human and Animal Psychology* (1894, with J. E. Creighton) and *Physiological Psychology* (1902, the first six chapters of the fifth edition), and Külpe's *Outlines of Psychology* (1895). Second he produced a laboratory teaching manual, *Experimental Psychology: a Manual of Laboratory Practice*, which appeared in 1901–5 (two volumes each on qualitative and quantitative methods, the pairs comprising students' and instructors' manuals). Widely used even among those otherwise unsympathetic to Titchener, these were important in consolidating the scientific character of psychology courses. *A Primer of Psychology* (1898), *A Text-Book of Psychology* (1910), and *A Beginner's Psychology* (1915) were also primarily pedagogic. Third he needed to state his theoretical position, which he termed 'structuralism', expounding this in *An Outline of Psychology* (1896), *Lectures on the Elementary Psychology of Feeling and Attention* (1908), and *Systematic Psychology: Prolegomena* (posthumously published in 1929). Especially influential were two *Philosophical Review* papers, 'The postulates of structural psychology' (1896) and 'Structural and functional psychology' (1899), which were responses to John Dewey's 'The reflex arc concept in psychology' (*Psychological Review*, 1896). A *Text-Book of Psychology* is, however, the only thorough single volume account of his position. Titchener's journal publications, both experimental and theoretical, exceeded 200. An insightful critique of the psychological research of the 1898 Cambridge anthropological expedition to the Torres Strait identified many problems in conducting research beyond the laboratory (*Proceedings of the American Philosophical Society*, 1916). He was the American editor of *Mind* between 1894 and 1920 and from 1921 to 1925 he edited the *American Journal of Psychology* but his productivity, which had been declining since 1909, almost ceased after 1920. He was awarded a DSc Oxford (1906), LLD Wisconsin (1904), DLitt Clark (1909), and DSc Harvard (1909). Always a collector of curious artefacts, he turned in later years to numismatics (in which he became quite expert).

For Titchener, psychology was the science of mind (as opposed to behaviour), the nature of conscious states being its immediate subject matter. Its initial task was to analyse consciousness into constituent elements, rather than study how it operates or how the elements interact.

These latter must wait until the elements themselves have been identified. This analysis was a pure scientific endeavour with no immediate practical consequences. It could be undertaken only by rigorously trained introspection, avoiding stimulus error (confusing the properties of the conscious experience with those of the stimulus object itself). Doing this properly was an acquired professional skill. By 1915 German Gestalt psychologists were effectively challenging the clarity of this distinction.

A fine lecturer, and combining independent mindedness with personal charm, Titchener occupied a respected place in American psychology, but his intellectual isolation became acute and relations with the American Psychological Association were chequered. First functionalism, then behaviourism and psychoanalysis overshadowed structuralism. Moreover, the very rationality, even possibility, of scientific introspection was called into doubt. The notion of pure private sensations unmodified by the introspector's concepts and expectations, *and* capable of being unambiguously verbally reported, grew ever more dubious on numerous philosophical, theoretical, and methodological grounds. Additionally, Titchener's self-conscious combination of traditional English demeanour and autocratic German academic style did not help his cause, however much they reinforced his personal charisma. Perhaps a further factor was that such experiments were, as William James observed in *Principles of Psychology* (1890), extremely dull.

Titchener's former student E. G. Boring became psychology's leading historian in the United States. This requires additional comment. His highly influential *History of Experimental Psychology* (1929, revised 1950) cast Wundt and Titchener in central heroic roles, and Titchener's canonical eminence is in part due to Boring's advocacy. From the late 1960s historians also argued that Boring's version of Wundt's original position reflected distortions of it made by Titchener. A major figure among those who created scientific academic psychology in the United States during the 1890s and early 1900s, Titchener's own version was always anomalous there, despite his indefatigable and sophisticated expositions and defences of it. In Britain his textbooks initially enjoyed a certain popularity, some early British psychologists not entirely lacking sympathy, but such influence rapidly waned after about 1920. Titchener's home was at Ithaca, New York state; he died suddenly on 3 August 1927.

GRAHAM RICHARDS

Sources E. G. Boring, *American Journal of Psychology*, 38 (1927), 489–506 · E. G. Boring, *History of experimental psychology* (1929); 2nd edn (1950); repr. (1957) · L. Zusne, *Biographical dictionary of psychology* (1984), 429–30 · C. S. Myers, *British Journal of Psychology*, 18 (1927–8), 460–63 · b. cert. · *The historical register of the University of Oxford … to the end of Trinity term 1900* (1900) · *Who was who in America*
Archives Cornell University, Ithaca, New York, Carl A. Kroch Library | UCL, letters to Sir Francis Galton
Likenesses photograph, repro. in Boring, *American Journal of Psychology*, 489

Titchmarsh, Edward Charles (1899–1963), mathematician, was born at Newbury on 1 June 1899, the son of Edward Harper Titchmarsh and his wife, Caroline Farmar.

Edward Charles Titchmarsh (1899–1963), by Walter Stoneman, 1932

He had an elder sister and a younger sister and brother. His father was minister of the Congregational church at Newbury from shortly before 1899 until 1907, when he moved to Nether Chapel in Sheffield. There was a strict religious tradition on both sides of his family, and Titchmarsh endured a restricted childhood. From 1908 to 1917 he was educated at King Edward VII School, Sheffield. He first specialized in classics, but failed in Greek in the higher certificate, and turned to mathematics and physics.

Titchmarsh arrived at Balliol College, Oxford, on an open scholarship in 1917. He was subsequently on war service for two years (1918–19) as a second lieutenant, Royal Engineers (signals), and was in France and Belgium from August 1918. He never talked about his experiences and wrote deprecatingly of his abilities as an officer, but he acquired a useful ability to deal with domestic electrical appliances.

After Titchmarsh returned to Oxford in 1919 his tutors were J. W. Russell and, later, J. W. Nicholson; Russell's methods of teaching were grossly over-organized, while Nicholson seldom saw his pupils. G. H. Hardy went to Oxford as Savilian professor of geometry in 1920 and was mainly responsible for Titchmarsh's determination to devote his life to research in pure mathematics. Titchmarsh won the junior mathematical exhibition in 1920 and the junior mathematical scholarship, jointly with H. O. Newboult, in 1921. He was placed in the first class in honour moderations in 1920 and in the final honours school of 1922, taking his BA degree in 1922 and his MA in 1924. In addition, in 1924 he won the senior mathematical scholarship. He spent a year at Oxford working for a DPhil under Hardy's supervision, but never completed the requirements for the degree. He also acted as secretary to Hardy.

In the summer of 1923 Titchmarsh was appointed a senior lecturer at University College, London, and in 1925 reader. In 1923 he obtained by examination a prize fellowship at Magdalen College, Oxford, and remained a fellow from 1924 to 1930, although he resided only occasionally.

In 1925 Titchmarsh married Kathleen, daughter of Alfred Blomfield JP, who was a farmer and secretary and senior deacon of Titchmarsh's father's church, by then at Halstead, Essex. They had three daughters who all married, and he was always much concerned with family and domestic matters.

In 1929 Titchmarsh became professor of pure mathematics at Liverpool, and in 1931 he was elected Savilian professor of geometry at Oxford to succeed Hardy. This chair carried with it a fellowship at New College, which he held until his death. Hardy had regularly given lectures on geometry as well as subjects connected with his own research, but Titchmarsh said in his application that he could not lecture on geometry and the statute was altered for him. He was a dominant figure in Oxford mathematics for many years and had many research students. As senior mathematical professor he became curator of the Mathematical Institute when it was established, delegating much to his staff. His habits were extremely regular and his mathematical output prodigious. Titchmarsh's textbook, *The Theory of Functions* (1932), made easily available much of the theory of functions of a complex and of a real variable which had previously been inaccessible in English. A short tract, *The Zeta-Function of Riemann* (1930), later revised and enlarged (1952), gave a connected account of his work on the subject. *Introduction to the Theory of the Fourier Integrals* (1937) synthesized his earlier papers on Fourier transforms and was translated into several foreign languages. All the subjects on which he worked were linked and his work led to results of importance in other fields. He studied a certain type of integral function with a view to applying the methods to the zeta function, and obtained thereby his 'convolution theorem' which is important in functional analysis because it shows that a certain algebra has no zero divisors. In middle life he began to consider the applications of Fourier integrals in quantum mechanics, but only 'as exercises in analysis'. This led to his work on eigenfunction expansions, summed up in the two-part *Eigenfunction Expansions Associated with Second-Order Differential Equations* (1946–58). These studies represent an outstanding contribution to functional analysis by completely classical methods. He also wrote *Mathematics for the General Reader* (1948).

Both in term and vacations, except for short holidays, Titchmarsh worked in the mornings and after tea, never later than 8 p.m. He had no telephone in his room at the institute. He seldom discussed mathematics, preferring to write everything down, and submitted work for publication in clear manuscripts unless compelled to have it typed. On committees he spoke late and little, but clearly and effectively. He found lecturing difficult and, although he was very clear, he showed little enthusiasm. He was tall and broad-shouldered and a little inclined to stoop. He had dark brown eyes with strongly marked eyebrows and was rather diffident and shy. He served on various committees at New College and was a courteous and benevolent sub-warden. Like Hardy he enjoyed watching cricket, and he played in the annual match at New College for the senior common room against the choir school.

Titchmarsh joined the London Mathematical Society in 1922 and was on its council (1925–9, 1932–6, and 1945–8), vice-president (1928–9), and president (1945–7). He received the De Morgan medal in 1953 and the Berwick prize in 1956. He was elected a fellow of the Royal Society in 1931 and received its Sylvester medal in 1955. An honorary DSc was conferred upon him by Sheffield University. He seldom went to mathematical colloquia, but gave an invited address at the International Congress of Mathematicians at Amsterdam in 1954 and attended the congresses at Edinburgh in 1958 and at Stockholm in 1962. At the time of his death he was expecting to go to the USSR for a fortnight. Titchmarsh died at his home, 4 Capel Close, Summertown, Oxford, on 18 January 1963. He was survived by his wife.   M. L. CARTWRIGHT, *rev.*

Sources M. L. Cartwright, *Memoirs FRS*, 10 (1964), 305–24 · *Journal of the London Mathematical Society*, 39 (1964) · *The Times* (19 Jan 1963) · *The Times* (23 Jan 1963) · personal knowledge (1981) · private information (1981) · *CGPLA Eng. & Wales* (1963)
Archives New College, Oxford, papers
Likenesses W. Stoneman, photograph, 1932, NPG [*see illus.*]
Wealth at death £17,679 14s. 1d.: probate, 7 March 1963, *CGPLA Eng. & Wales*

Titcomb, Jonathan Holt (1819–1887), first bishop of Rangoon, was born, with a twin sister, in Kensington, London, on 29 July 1819, the son of Jonathan Holt Titcomb (*d.* 1851) of Fulham. He was educated in London at Clapham and at King's College School and, after a lacklustre university career, graduated BA (junior optime) from Peterhouse, Cambridge, in 1841. In the spring of 1842 he was engaged by Lady Harriet Forde of Hollymount, near Downpatrick in co. Down, as tutor to her nephew, and in the following September was ordained deacon and appointed curate on the estate. Initially he was a high-churchman, but his ministry among the estate workers converted him to evangelicalism and awakened an interest in missionary endeavour. In September 1843 he was ordained priest and in April 1845, after several months as curate at St Mark's, Kennington, London, he accepted the living of St Andrew-the-Less at Barnwell near Cambridge. He took to it his new wife, Sarah (1824–1876), eldest daughter of John Wood of Southport, Lancashire, whom he married on 24 May 1845 and with whom he was to have eight daughters and two sons.

Barnwell offered considerable scope for an evangelical preacher. Contemporaries described it as a sinkhole of moral impurity brought about by a massive population increase—from 400 in 1820 to 7000 in 1841. Titcomb initially concentrated on drawing new people into the church with lecture programmes and Sunday schools; but in 1850, fretting about the thousands of people beyond the church's reach, he braved unfavourable comparison with nonconformists by plunging into open-air preaching. He defended the practice in letters to the *Christian Guardian* and with growing confidence had made for himself a folding iron pulpit so that he could preach outdoors in style. While at Barnwell he also published the first of several works designed to minimize the effects of doctrinal controversy on churchgoers and broaden evangelicalism's outlook, including *Heads of Prayer for Daily Private Devotion* (2nd edn, 1850), and *Bible Studies, or, An Inquiry into the Progressive Development of Divine Revelation* (1851). Later publications included *Baptism: its Institution, its Privileges, and its Responsibilities* (1866); *Cautions for Doubters* (1873); and *Before the Cross: a Book of Devout Meditation* (1878).

In June 1859 Titcomb became secretary of the Christian Vernacular Education Society, but he missed direct pastoral work and in April 1861 he accepted the living of the new church of St Stephen's, South Lambeth, London—then in the Winchester diocese. He successfully built up a new congregation while maintaining a busy schedule of London speaking engagements and commitments to the Religious Tract Society and the *True Catholic*, which he edited for two years. From 1870 to 1876 he was additionally rural dean of Clapham, London, and in 1874 was made an honorary canon of Winchester Cathedral. The years at South Lambeth were marked by personal sadness: the deaths of two daughters; of his beloved twin sister; and finally, in January 1876, of Sarah, 'one of the wisest and best of wives' (Edwards, 16).

Titcomb struggled to see the wisdom of God in his losses and in March 1876 he was grateful to move on to the living of Woking, Surrey, offered to him by the earl of Onslow. The challenge of a new parish revitalized him and in 1877 he accepted the bishopric of Rangoon, in Burma, a new post funded largely by the Winchester diocese. He arrived in Rangoon with three of his daughters in February 1878 and embarked enthusiastically on strengthening the Burmese church and raising funds to remedy its deficiencies in chaplains and buildings. Among other activities, he held a confirmation in the Andaman Islands, consecrated a missionary church at Toungoo, ordained as deacons several Tamil and Karen Christians, and baptized numerous converts from among Rangoon's indigenous, Indian, and Chinese populations. In July 1879, however, illness again struck his family with the death of his eldest daughter, and another fell so seriously ill that Titcomb had to return with her to England to await her death. During this unhappy vigil he wrote a slim volume entitled *Personal Recollections of British Burma and its Church Mission Work* (1880). He returned to Burma in late 1880 but in February 1881 fell over a cliff in the Karen hills and was eventually forced back to England, where he resigned the bishopric in March 1882.

Titcomb did not expect to work heavily again but in

January 1884 the bishop of London appointed him his coadjutor for supervising the English church in northern and central Europe, a job hardly less physically challenging than his previous one and which committed him to extensive visitation tours to France, Germany, Scandinavia, Poland, Russia, and numerous countries in between. In 1886, very nearly worn out, he took up the perpetual curacy of St Peter's, Brockley, in Kent. He died at 28 Marina Street, St Leonards, Sussex, on 2 April 1887 and was buried in Brompton cemetery, London, on 7 April. His two sons and four of his daughters survived him.

G. C. BOASE, rev. KATHERINE PRIOR

Sources A. T. Edwards, *A consecrated life: memoir of Bishop Titcomb* (1887) · *Church Portrait Journal*, new ser., 1 (Aug 1880) · Venn, *Alum. Cant.* · *Conference on missions held in 1860 at Liverpool*, ed. Secretaries of the conference [1860] · *Forty years in Burma, by Doctor Marks* (1917) · *ILN* (16 April 1887), 443 · *The Times* (27 Jan 1876), 1 · *CGPLA Eng. & Wales* (1887)

Likenesses A. E. Fradelle, photograph, c.1880, repro. in *Church Portrait Journal* · Elliott & Fry, photograph, repro. in Edwards, *A consecrated life* · R. T., wood-engraving, NPG; repro. in *ILN* (16 April 1887)

Wealth at death £39,869 6s. 6d.: probate, 14 May 1887, *CGPLA Eng. & Wales*

Tite, Sir William (1798–1873), architect, was born on 7 February 1798 in the parish of St Bartholomew-the-Great, London, the son of Arthur Tite, a Russia merchant, and his wife, Anne, daughter of John Elgie. Educated at a day school in Tower Street in the City of London and afterwards at a school in Hackney, at the age of fourteen he was articled to the architect David Laing (1774–1856), a pupil of Sir John Soane chiefly remembered as the designer of the London custom house of 1813–17. During his pupillage he assisted Laing in rebuilding the nave of Wren's church of St Dunstan-in-the-East (1817–20) and published in 1818 a history of the building (of which only Wren's tower remained after extensive bomb damage in 1940). He also appears to have visited Italy at this time (Briggs, 39).

In July 1818 Tite was admitted to the Royal Academy Schools, where he attended Soane's lectures on architecture. However, his first commission was executed in a medieval Gothic idiom far removed from Soane's cool neo-classicism. Having failed to win a number of architectural competitions of the early 1820s, in 1824 he was appointed by the Revd Edward Irving to design a new church in Sidmouth Street, off Regent Square, for the Church of Scotland—a commission which enabled him to set up his own office in Jewry Street in the City of London that year. The church, completed in 1827 (and demolished in 1950 following serious war damage), was couched in a Decorated Gothic style, and its west front modelled rather incongruously on York Minster. However, his second major commission—Mill Hill School, Middlesex, of 1825–6—signalled the exuberant eclecticism that was to characterize his career, being executed in a severely neo-classical style.

In 1832 Tite designed the austerely classical Golden Cross Hotel in London's Strand (dem. 1936 to make way for South Africa House), and the following year began work on the King's Weigh-House Church in Fish Street Hill (dem. 1890s). By the time he was elected a fellow of the Royal Society, in 1835, his growing practice, and a financially advantageous marriage in 1832 to Emily, daughter of John Curtis of Herne Hill, Surrey, had enabled him to move out of the City to the prestigious Bloomsbury address of 25 Upper Bedford Place. In 1838 he was elected president of the Architectural Society (merged with the new Royal Institute of British Architects in 1842). The same year he designed the Anglican and nonconformist chapels (dem. late 1950s) and other buildings at Norwood cemetery in south London in an attractive Perpendicular Gothic. He also began work, in partnership with C. R. Cockerell, on the headquarters of the London and Westminster Bank in Lothbury (dem. 1928 to make way for the Mewès and Davis building now known as NatWest Hall). In 1839 he was elected a fellow of the Society of Antiquaries, whose vice-president he was from 1860 until his death in 1873. Two years later he was working in Scotland, on the Gothic parish church at Dollar, Clackmannan (1841; altered 1921).

The building which made Tite's name was the new Royal Exchange at the heart of the City of London. Having failed to enter the first open (and ultimately fruitless) competition of 1839, in February 1840 Tite was chosen as one of the judges for the subsequent closed competition, for which five leading national architects—among them Sir Charles Barry, Sir Robert Smirke, and Cockerell—were invited to submit designs. In the event only Cockerell entered a scheme, which then lost by thirteen votes to seven to a treatment entered, somewhat unprofessionally, by Tite himself. (A watercolour perspective of Cockerell's splendid design survives in the RIBA drawings collection.) Work on Tite's design began in 1841, and the exchange was opened by Queen Victoria on 28 October 1844. Tite's massive Corinthian portico still dominates this part of the City, but the building itself was converted in 1988 to mixed retail and office use, for which an additional attic storey was added.

During the 1840s Tite was increasingly employed by the new railway companies in valuing and buying land and, most importantly, in designing their new stations. His first major station, built in 1838, was the first London terminus of the London and Southampton Railway (after 1848 the London and South-Western Railway or LSWR) at Nine Elms, a handsome though reticent Italianate building whose most prominent feature was its five-bay arcade. By 1848 Nine Elms had been superseded by a new LSWR terminus further east, at Waterloo (where Tite merely advised the architect Joseph Cocke). However, Tite's Nine Elms survived as a goods depot until demolished in the early 1970s, to make way for the New Covent Garden market. At the other end of the line Tite built stuccoed Italianate termini at Southampton (1838–40) and Gosport (1842). The latter flanked the line, and was dominated by a splendid Tuscan colonnade (the ruin of which was, following closure and fire, safeguarded by English Heritage and the local authority after 1990). Most of the LSWR's intermediate stations were also designed by Tite; of these, Eastleigh and Winchester still survive, but are much altered, and

only the small building at Micheldever appears in anything like its original guise.

Following his work for the London and Southampton, Tite was employed as a station architect by a large number of other railway companies. In 1846–51 he completely rebuilt the Liverpool and Manchester Railway's terminus at Liverpool Lime Street, its new stuccoed Renaissance façade (since altered) being dominated by a nineteen-bay Tuscan colonnade. At his Carlisle Citadel Station of 1847–8, for the Caledonian and Scottish Central Railway, Tite abandoned the refined Italianate classicism of his London and Southampton stations for an asymmetrical, collegiate late Gothic style, even incorporating a crenellated clock tower. Carlisle was followed by two similarly styled Caledonian and Scottish stations: Perth and Edinburgh Caledonian, both of 1848. In his presidential address to the RIBA in 1862 Tite declared that 'At Carlisle and Perth I have done my best to mould the forms and modes of thinking of medieval architects to the unusual requirements of railways', though six years later he did admit that his Carlisle design was 'troublesome, and did not go very well with the platforms and sheds' (Briggs, 95). For the LSWR's terminus at Windsor (now Windsor and Eton Riverside) of 1851, he employed a Tudor Gothic idiom, lighting the booking hall with a vast, cross-framed Tudorbethan window. His surviving Chiswick Station of 1849 for the same company was, however, a complete contrast: a demure, three-bay Georgian cottage in brick and stucco. During the 1840s Tite also designed the small terminus at Blackwall, east London, of 1840 (dem.), the stations on the Exeter and Yeovil Railway (later incorporated into the LSWR), and the intermediate stations from Le Havre to Paris via Rouen for the Compagnie des Chemins de Fer du Nord. (His station at Le Havre, much rebuilt, was immortalized in Émile Zola's darkly pessimistic La bête humaine of 1890, and finally demolished in 1930.)

After a serious illness, followed by a trip to Italy in 1851–2, Tite gradually wound down his once-thriving practice. He designed only four buildings between 1853 and 1859, three with the help of assistants, and nothing during the remaining fourteen years of his life. The buildings at the London metropolis cemetery at Brookwood, Surrey, of 1854–6 were devised in partnership with Sidney Smirke; his Gresham House in London's Old Broad Street, also of 1854–6 (and demolished after the First World War), was built with the assistance of E. N. Clifton; while St James's, Gerrards Cross, of 1858–9 was built in partnership with his former office assistant Ebenezer Trotman. (Tite's brick church was in an uncompromisingly strident Byzantine style, complete with octagonal dome and tall campanile, since labelled 'aggressively un-English' and 'exotic' (Briggs, 96).) His other last work, the carpet warehouse for Tapling & Co. in Gresham Street of 1857, was destroyed in an air raid of 1940.

After 1859, however, Tite was far from idle. He was president of the RIBA in 1861–3 and again in 1867–70, and after an unsuccessful attempt to win the seat of Barnstaple for the Liberals in 1854 was elected as MP for Bath in 1855; he served as the city's MP until his death. In parliament he strenuously opposed the scheme of Sir George Gilbert Scott to clothe his new Foreign Office in a Gothic style, decrying the proposal as 'inconvenient and expensive' (Hansard 3, 152, 11 Feb 1859, cols. 260–63). He subsequently helped to persuade the prime minister, Palmerston, to force Scott to alter his design to 'a light and correct Italian style, consistent with the general character of the buildings in the neighbourhood' (Hansard 3, 152, 18 Feb 1859, col. 522). Ironically, Tite later warmly welcomed Scott's unapologetically Gothic design for the Albert Memorial as 'appropriate', 'elegant', and 'satisfactory to the nation' (Hansard 3, 170, 23 May 1863, col. 605).

Tite was also a member of London's Metropolitan Board of Works, in which capacity he advised on the construction of the Victoria Embankment; a director of the London and Westminster Bank; a magistrate for the counties of Middlesex and Somerset; a governor of Dulwich College and St Thomas's Hospital; and, in 1862, master of the Spectaclemakers' Company. Although not a Royal Academician, he exhibited 'a composition from the works of Inigo Jones' at the academy in 1854. Winner of the royal gold medal for architecture in 1856, he was knighted in 1869, and made a companion of the Bath the following year.

Tite was also active as an antiquary. He was elected a fellow of the Society of Antiquaries in 1839 (in 1848 he published a descriptive catalogue of the finds from the excavations conducted during the rebuilding of the Royal Exchange), honorary secretary of the London Institution between 1824 and 1869, and president of the Cambridge Camden Society in 1866. Eminent as an architect, Tite was also a renowned book collector of omnifarious taste. The sale of his library at Sothebys in May and June 1874 occupied sixteen days and produced the sum of £19,943 6s. As it was one of the greatest collections of the time (including many rare books and historical autographs), and the auction was almost the first of a series of events of the kind, a large selection of his books is included in *Contributions towards a Dictionary of English Book Collectors* (ed. B. Quaritch, 1969, 288–92).

Tite died during a trip to Torquay on 20 April 1873 (by which time he was living at the fashionable Belgravia address of 42 Lowndes Square) and was, appropriately, buried in Norwood cemetery. His wife survived him, but they had no children. His personal property was valued after his death at nearly £400,000. (Tite had reportedly boasted 'that he had inherited one fortune from his father, had married another, and had earned a third by his own exertions' (Briggs, 96).) Of this he left £1000 to the RIBA to establish an annual Tite prize, having already founded a Tite scholarship at the City of London School before his death. The architectural pupils who survived him included his assistants Ebenezer Trotman and C. F. Porden, and E. N. Clifton. S. P. PARISSIEN

Sources M. S. Briggs, 'Sir William Tite', *The Builder*, 178 (1950), 39–42, 95–8 • Colvin, *Archs.* • *Dir. Brit. archs.* • *The Builder*, 7 (1849), 78–9 • *The Builder*, 17 (1859), 588, 616–17 • *The Builder*, 31 (1873), 337–9 • A. Stratton, 'The Royal Exchange, London', *ArchR*, 42 (1917), 44–50 • *Journal of Proceedings of the Royal Institute of British Architects*, 14 (1863), 24 • *Transactions of the Royal Institute of British Architects* (1873–4), 209–12 • *Proceedings connected with the rebuilding of the Royal Exchange, 1838–1844* (1845) • M. Binney and D. Pearce, eds., *Railway architecture* (1983) • J. Hair, *Regent-Square* (1898) • E. Kay, *The King's Weigh-House Church* (1968) • CGPLA Eng. & Wales (1873)

Archives RIBA • RIBA BAL, drawings collection | U. Edin. L., corresp. with James Halliwell-Phillipps

Likenesses W. Theed junior, marble bust, 1869, Guildhall, Bath • J. Prescott Knight, oils, RIBA • J. Renton, portrait, RIBA

Wealth at death under £400,000 in UK: probate, 7 June 1873, CGPLA Eng. & Wales

Titford, William Jowett (1784–1823), accountant and botanist, was born on 13 May 1784 at Kingston, Jamaica, the eldest of four children of Isaac Titford (1760–1834), army surgeon in the 60th Royal American regiment and apothecary, and his first wife, Mary Greenaway (c.1765–1789), daughter of John Jowett of Jamaica. His mother, younger brother, and two sisters died of yellow fever, but in 1787 William was taken to London by his maternal grandfather, where he was brought up by his father's elder brother William (1752–1824) and his wife, Susannah, and received his early education at the academy of the Revd Stephen Freeman at Enfield, Middlesex. He was a member of the congregation of the General Baptist Chapel, Worship Street, Bishopsgate, and later became a member of the Unitarian congregation at South Place Chapel, Finsbury. In 1802 he received adult baptism from Revd John Evans before returning to his birthplace to take over his father's plantation of coffee and pimento at Mount Moreland, in the hills near Spanish Town. In Jamaica, Titford collected seeds and plants, sending samples to the Society for the Encouragement of the Arts, Manufactures and Commerce (later the Royal Society of Arts) in London. He was later elected a corresponding member of the society. In 1805 the island's governor, General Nugent, appointed Titford master extraordinary in the court of chancery while he was engaged in the chambers of Mr James Taylor at Kingston. In addition to his professions of law and accountancy, Titford played the harpsichord and flageolet and assisted the organist at the parish church of St Catherine. In 1807 Titford sailed to North America, visiting Boston, New Jersey, and Philadelphia, collecting more botanical specimens, which he sent to the Society of Arts with over fifty drawings and a description of each type, classified under the system of Linnaeus, which he intended to publish in a book. In New York he stayed with his father's second wife, Alice Margaret Dunscomb, and his three surviving half-sisters, Elsey, Ann, and Susannah. He enrolled at Columbia University to study botany with Dr David Hosack, but left before being granted a degree.

In 1810 Titford's stepmother and half-sisters Elsey and Ann died and, after settling the family's affairs, he returned to England early the following year and began preparations for the publication of his *Sketches towards a Hortus Botanicus Americanus*. It was issued in six parts in 1811 and 1812 in London by George Stower; the list of subscribers included the prince regent, Louis XVIII of France, the Royal Institution, the Royal Society of Arts, and many eminent botanists in England, Jamaica, and North America. The *Critical Review* of November 1811 described the first parts of the *Hortus* as 'a most excellent work for persons learning botany and all things pertaining to natural history and associated sciences' (*Critical Review*, 333). In London directories of the period, Titford was listed as accountant, agent, and referee, at his uncle's address at 1–2 Union Street, Bishopsgate, where he was working in the family business of Titford & Son, silk manufacturers. On 14 March 1812 he married Nancy (1793–1819), daughter of George Walters, silk weaver, and his wife, Mary (*née* Vandome), of Spitalfields, London. Their first child, Richard Vandome, was born in 1813; Titford returned to Jamaica shortly afterwards, stayed only about eighteen months, and was back in London in early 1815. A second child, Mary Alice, was born in 1816 and in 1819 another daughter, Nancy Walters, but Titford's wife died giving birth to her, aged twenty-five. Titford took his three children to live with his brother-in-law William Wilkinson, law stationer, and his wife, Mary Ann, at 49 Coleman Street, London.

During his several voyages to and from Jamaica, Titford took star observations while on board ship, to be used in support of his proposed method for the calculation of longitude at sea. He continued to send them to the board of longitude for ten years, until his death, although the board rejected all his proposed methods. His last known letter to the secretary to the board, sent from Kingston on 1 January 1823, said 'I am going to New York for my Health.' He sailed in the brigantine *Hope* in mid-January, but died on the voyage the following month and was buried at sea, somewhere off the coast of North America, leaving three orphan children living with their grandfather in Cranbrook, Kent. ANTHONY RICHARD TITFORD

Sources A. R. Titford, 'A biographical study of William Jowett Titford (1784–1823/7)', *Journal of the Society of the Bibliography of Natural History*, 8 (1976–8), 120–42 · *Critical Review*, 3rd ser., 24 (1811), 332–3 · *Royal Gazette* [Kingston, Jamaica] (June 1823), 24 · board of longitude, CUL, RGO 14/7, 14/8 · b. cert.
Archives CUL, Royal Greenwich Observatory board of longitude, letters · priv. coll. · RSA, letters

Titiens, Teresa Caroline Johanna. *See* Tietjens, Therese Carolina Johanna (1831–1877).

Titley, Walter (*bap.* **1698**, *d.* **1768**), diplomatist, baptized on 6 December 1698 at Ingestre, Staffordshire, was the son of Abraham Titley of Hopton, Staffordshire. He was admitted a king's scholar at Westminster School in 1714. While there he acted as 'help' to Osborn Atterbury, the son of Francis Atterbury, bishop of Rochester, and was afterwards his tutor. On 28 May 1719 he was admitted to Trinity College, Cambridge, where he matriculated in 1720; he graduated BA in 1722, was elected a fellow of Trinity in 1725, and proceeded MA in 1726. He then entered the diplomatic service, wishing for 'some sort of employment abroad, in which I might have an opportunity of acquainting myself with business and seeing the world' (Black, *British Diplomats*, 101), and became secretary of the British embassy at Turin. On 3 January 1729 he was selected to act as chargé d'affaires at Copenhagen in the absence of John Campbell, Lord Glenorchy (later third earl of Breadalbane), and on 3 November 1730 he was named minister-resident. Titley's diplomatic career was henceforward devoted to Britain's ongoing efforts to exclude Denmark from any alliance led by France. The policy was pursued throughout the century, usually with success.

In 1733 Richard Bentley (1662–1742), master of Trinity, appointed Titley to the physic fellowship at that college. Titley resigned his diplomatic position to accept it, but had become so attached to his life at Copenhagen that he was unable to leave it. He accordingly resumed his post. In 1736 Horatio Walpole proposed that Titley be made envoy-extraordinary to the Danish court; his nomination was initially unsuccessful, but Titley received the promotion in 1739. He became the century's longest-serving British diplomatist, exceeded in his time overseas only by Sir Horace Mann. The emphasis he placed on socializing was well known: Walpole thought him 'amused and deceived by little outward personal civilities' (Black, *British Diplomats*, 100), and in 1746 Titley complained that, with his pay in arrears, he was unable to give dinners and so alienated prospective friends at court. His efforts to ensure that successive Danish kings were friendly to Britain included not only outbidding proffered subsidies from France, but also a role in the arrangement of two royal marriages: that of Princess Louisa of Great Britain to Prince Frederick, later King Frederick V of Denmark, in 1743, and of the Princess Caroline Matilda of Great Britain to King Christian VII of Denmark in 1766. Another particular achievement was an agreement in 1761 whereby the king of Denmark agreed to order the seizure and extradition of deserters from the British army and navy, on condition that the British government reciprocated with Danish absentees. Two years later, in 1763, Titley reported his exhaustion to London—his 'gouty legs' would no longer support him 'in paying court or pursuing the noble pastime of levée-hunting' (ibid., 99)—and he was granted an assistant. He died, greatly respected and lamented by his contemporaries, at his estate at Lyngby, near Copenhagen, on 27 February 1768. In his will he bequeathed £1000 each to Westminster School, Trinity College, and the University of Cambridge. Part of the last bequest was to be devoted to buildings.

In addition to a number of original Latin verses, Titley wrote an 'Imitation' in English of the second ode of the third book of Horace; this was much admired by Bentley, who parodied it.

G. LE G. NORGATE, *rev.* MATTHEW KILBURN

Sources J. Black, *British diplomats and diplomacy, 1688–1800* (2001) · D. B. Horn, *The British diplomatic service, 1689–1789* (1961) · J. Welch, *The list of the queen's scholars of St Peter's College, Westminster*, ed. [C. B. Phillimore], new edn (1852) · J. W. Wilkes, *A whig in power: the political career of Henry Pelham* (1964) · J. Black, *Natural and necessary enemies: Anglo-French relations in the eighteenth century* (1986) · *London Chronicle* (19 March 1768) · Venn, *Alum. Cant.*
Archives BL, corresp. and papers, Egerton MSS 2680–2695 | BL, corresp. with Lord Carteret, Add. MS 22534 · BL, corresp. with Lord Holdernesse, Egerton MSS 1755, 3419, 3464 · BL, corresp. with duke of Newcastle, Add. MSS 32766–32935, *passim* · BL, letters to Thomas Robinson, Add. MSS 23780–23823, *passim* · BL, corresp. with Lord Sandwich and Richard Phelps, Stowe MSS 258–261 · U. Cal., Berkeley, Bancroft Library, letters to Lord Chesterfield ·

W. Yorks. AS, Leeds, Vyner collection, corresp. • Yale U., Farmington, Lewis Walpole Library, letters to Edward Weston

Wealth at death owned/had use of estate in Denmark; left £1000 bequests to Westminster School, London, Trinity College, Cambridge, and University of Cambridge: Horn, *British diplomatic service*

Titmuss, Richard Morris (1907–1973), historian and teacher of social administration, was born on 16 October 1907 at Lane Farm, Stopsley, near Luton in Bedfordshire, the second child of an unsuccessful small farmer, Morris Titmuss, whose wife, Maud Louise Farr, of rather less modest farming origins, bore him four children. The family lived an isolated and impecunious life in Bedfordshire and, from the early 1920s, in Hendon where, as a haulage contractor, Morris was no more successful than as a farmer. He died in 1926, leaving Richard to support the family, and particularly to accommodate his mother's emotional and financial needs until her death in 1972.

Titmuss's education was not untypical of the son of a petty proprietor in his day. He began at St Gregory's, a small preparatory school at Luton, and was 'finished' at Clark's Commercial College to which he went at the age of fourteen for a six-month course in bookkeeping. He was then employed as an office boy in Standard Telephones until aged eighteen when he was engaged as a clerk by the county fire insurance office, and there he served for sixteen years.

Titmuss never sat an examination or secured a formal credential. Nor did he regret his uncertified career, preferring instead to applaud the public library as among the most precious of British social services, and to hold the PhD in sceptical suspicion. Yet in 1950 he was elected to the chair of social administration at the London School of Economics (LSE). In the years between, and indeed as a child often absent from school with poor health, he had been an indefatigable and imaginative autodidact. Afterwards, when fellowship of the British Academy (1972) and honorary degrees from the University of Wales (1959), Edinburgh (1962), Toronto (1964), Chicago (1970), and Brunel (1971) were conferred on him, he remained a devotee of the spirit rather than the conventions of academic institutions. He was also appointed CBE in 1966, having refused a peerage offered by Harold Wilson.

The first step out of obscurity was made in 1934 in a Welsh youth hostel where Titmuss met Kathleen Caston (Kay) Miller, who became his wife in 1937, and his supportive companion for the rest of his life. Their daughter, Ann, has written a sensitively penetrating book, *Man and Wife* (1996), which reveals much of the private relationship between Richard and Kay that underlay his public emergence in their years together. His first unpublished writing in 1936 was under his wife's middle name. Her father, Thomas Miller, was a sales representative for a cutlery firm. They set up house at St George's Drive near Victoria Station, London, Titmuss still working for the county fire insurance office, his wife supporting his efforts to write in the evenings and stimulating his social and political interests.

Richard Morris Titmuss (1907–1973), by Elliott & Fry, 1953

Titmuss's first book, *Poverty and Population* (1938), reflected both his wife's influence in its social concern, and his insurance work in its mastery of vital statistics and statistical technique. It was noticed enthusiastically by Lord Horder, the physician, Eleanor Rathbone, Harold Macmillan, and the liberal intellectuals of the day, including the Laytons, the Rowntrees, and the Cadburys. It established his place in the distinctive English tradition of political arithmetic which runs from Sir Thomas More to R. H. Tawney, and bears a literature down the centuries of responsible social criticism based on private numerical enquiry into public issues. Titmuss became the main inheritor and exponent of this tradition of humanistic social accounting.

The second step towards distinction eventually yielded a book which made Titmuss nationally and internationally well known, the official history *Problems of Social Policy* (1950). Titmuss had been invited by W. Keith Hancock to join the group of historians commissioned to write the official civil histories of the Second World War and to cover the work of the Ministry of Health. So Titmuss entered Whitehall, became industriously familiar with the social services, and was recognized by Hancock as possessed of 'really creative insight into human problems' and 'the most unusual gift for asking the right questions'.

The answers led Titmuss from his pre-war allegiance to the Liberal Party, through active interest in the short-lived Common Wealth Party, to the Fabian wing of the Labour Party. Not that his passions for social justice and equality ever made him a strident politician, for he was always essentially a private citizen and scholar, a teacher and adviser, rather than a political leader, though he was strenuously dutiful in public service, whether as a member of the fire-watching squad at St Paul's during the war, or as deputy chairman of the Supplementary Benefits Commission from 1968. His socialism was as English as his patriotism—ethical and non-Marxist, insisting that capitalism was not only economically but socially wasteful, in failing to harness individual altruism to the common good. The most startling and impassioned statement of his conviction was in his book *The Gift Relationship: from Human Blood to Social Policy* (1970), in which, on the basis of characteristically meticulous statistical enquiry, he expounded the theory of a Gresham's law of selfishness such that commercialized blood markets undermine social integration.

This book and many others were the product of over twenty years as incumbent of the LSE chair. From that position Titmuss established the academic respectability of social administration both outside and inside the LSE, where it involved him in a protracted conflict with Irene Younghusband, whom Ralph Dahrendorf described as 'the unusual, flamboyant and yet deeply committed social work teacher' (Dahrendorf, 383). He taught and inspired a generation of university teachers, social policy researchers, administrators, and social workers from New York and Toronto to Mauritius and Tanganyika, until he died in the Central Middlesex Hospital, London, on 6 April 1973.

Titmuss was indeed a remarkable figure. Indefatigable in his obligation to his colleagues and students, unsparing in his loyalty to his college and his country, a bench-mark of integrity and virtue for the vast majority of those who knew him—whether at work in Houghton Street or at his modest house in Acton with his wife and their daughter, who was born in 1944. In another age he might have been an ascetic divine, painted by El Greco, with his long, thin body and large, round compelling eyes. In fact, he was no saint, but a secular agnostic—in Sir Edmund Leach's phrase, 'the high priest of the welfare state'.

A. H. HALSEY, rev.

Sources *The Times* (9 April 1973) · *The Times* (12 April 1973) · *The Times* (15 April 1973) · *The Times* (16 April 1973) · M. Gowing, *PBA*, 61 (1975), 401–28 · personal knowledge (1986) · A. Oakley, *Man and wife: Richard and Kay Titmuss* (1996) · R. Dahrendorf, *LSE: a history of the London School of Economics and Political Science, 1895–1995* (1995) · b. cert.

Archives BLPES, papers · Wellcome L., papers | U. Warwick Mod. RC, corresp. with Lady Allen

Likenesses Elliott & Fry, photograph, 1953, NPG [*see illus.*] · Bassano and Vandyk studios, photograph, repro. in Gowing, *PBA*

Wealth at death £37,949: probate, 12 Sept 1973, *CGPLA Eng. & Wales*

Tituba (*fl.* **1692**). *See under* Salem witches and their accusers (*act.* 1692).

Titus, Silius (1622/3–1704), royalist conspirator and politician, was born at Bushey, Hertfordshire, the first son of Silas Tyto (*d.* 1637) and his second wife, Constancia Colley (*d.* 1667). His father was of Italian ancestry and was a soap manufacturer and salter of some wealth who lived at Bushey and Holborn, London. Titus matriculated from Christ Church, Oxford, in March 1638, aged fifteen. In the following year he entered the Middle Temple, where he remained until the outbreak of civil war in 1642 (he was to hold on to his rooms there until 1652). He joined the forces of parliament in Hertfordshire, where he was granted a commission in the county militia and also served as a captain under Colonel Ayloffe; he was present at the siege of Donnington Castle in October 1644. Titus was of presbyterian persuasion and chose to resign his commissions rather than serve in the New Model Army. Appointed to attend the king when the latter was at Holdenby House in 1647, he brought news of the king's seizure by Cornet George Joyce and was granted an annuity of £50 by parliament. Later he served in the king's household while the latter was held in the Isle of Wight, and was won over to the royalist side. As part of his new service to Charles I, Titus attempted to engineer the king's escape from the island and was expelled from Carisbrooke Castle. He remained on the Isle of Wight, however, and in September 1648 was once more in attendance on the king until Charles was taken into final custody by the army. The presbyterian faction in parliament, desiring a messenger to Jersey, used Titus, but the discovery of this action meant that he was forced to become an exile in December 1649.

After the regicide Titus sought service with the new king and accompanied Charles II into Scotland. There his presbyterianism led to his appointment as one of the grooms of the bedchamber to the king. Thereafter Titus was frequently used as a confidential messenger, especially in 1651 when he carried the idea of Charles II's marriage to the marquess of Argyll's daughter to the queen mother. Exile and the royal court in the 1650s also brought Titus into the world of intrigue, where he often used the alias of John Jennings. He was daring in his exploits as he went back and forth carrying messages to the king's allies in England; some thought him 'negligent of his own safety' in such business (Routledge, 4.226). In June 1659 he was observed prowling undisguised in a bookbinder's shop in London when he had already been closely involved in Booth's royalist rising of that year and would have been severely dealt with if caught. Titus had, however, previously made overtures to secretary of state John Thurloe for permission to return to England in 1654, even offering to swear fidelity to Cromwell. These overtures were rejected and the exiled Charles II and Sir Edward Hyde continued to trust Titus. Hyde noted 'unless he is the greatest dissembler in the world ... he sets the least value on himself and gives the greatest testimony to others' (Routledge, 4.460).

In the 1650s Titus was associated with the exiled George Villiers, second duke of Buckingham, and through Buckingham he became acquainted with the plotters John Wildman and Edward Sexby. It was Titus who encouraged the former Leveller Sexby in his plans to assassinate Cromwell and from March to April 1657 the pair lurked in the Netherlands. It was at this time that Sexby composed his pseudonymous pamphlet *Killing Noe Murder*. In 1697 Titus claimed sole authorship of this notorious publication, but it is likely that Sexby, who was no fool, and a very capable author in his own right, had the main part in its creation. It may be that Titus, who later became known for his quips in parliament, added some of the wit that sparkles throughout the work. But after Sexby's arrest in July 1657 it was he, not Titus, who publicly acknowledged the pamphlet as his own.

With the restoration of the monarchy in 1660 Titus returned home. He was rewarded for his former service with £3000 from the Convention Parliament and the keepership of Deal Castle. He sat in the Convention as a member for Ludgershall in Wiltshire and went on to serve in the parliaments of three reigns: for Lostwithiel in 1670, Hertfordshire in 1679, Huntingdonshire in 1679 and 1681, and Ludlow in 1691. While managing to remain in the Commons during a large part of this period he was noted as a speaker willing to use wit even in the dullest debates. Although he was never sufficiently significant to gain major office, there were rumours of his receiving a secretary of state's post in the 1680s. He was often seen as a court supporter, but he also remained very much the back-bench agitator, preferring to play to the gallery and relish his own jokes. Nevertheless, Titus was serious enough in seeking revenge against the regicides and was one of those who moved for the exhumation of the bodies of Cromwell, Ireton, and Bradshaw in 1661. He lost his seat at the election that same year and remained out of the Commons for some time, but he retained his post as groom of the bedchamber. In 1663 he married Katherine (*d.* in or after 1705), daughter of James Winstanley, counsellor at law of Gray's Inn and Braunstone, Leicestershire; they had three daughters. In 1666 during the Dutch war Titus was made a captain of a company and colonel of the Kent militia. During the 1670s he became a propertied gentleman, resigning his post as groom of the bedchamber and buying Ramsey Abbey in Huntingdonshire.

During the years of the Popish Plot, Titus was an active leader of the anti-Popish faction in the Commons, where among other matters he served as one of the examiners of Edward Coleman, the duke of York's secretary, and attacked a French version of the *London Gazette* (and by implication its translator) for its papist interpretations. He was often a melodramatic speaker during the period of the plot. Although he sometimes missed the humour of the house because of this, he also tended to be one of those who dominated its debates. Titus had both personal and financial reasons to hate Thomas Osborne, earl of Danby, the king's chief minister, who became a target during the plot on grounds of his dealings with the French on Charles II's behalf. Titus cited non-payment of £4000 owed for his offices on the council of plantations and as groom of the bedchamber; he was also against popery and arbitrary government in any form. He was thus one of the first to attack Danby in the Commons in 1679 and was also very active in the second Exclusion Parliament of 1680–81, especially against the earl of Halifax. He was one of the managers of Viscount Stafford's trial and undertook any

number of interventions on the matter of exclusion itself, although he may well have been trying to get the government to buy him off with office and was never that popular with other exclusionists. He made his most famous speech in January 1681 on the matter of limitations on a Catholic sovereign with his usual wit.

Titus was out of politics for some years after the dissolution of 1681, but was suspected of complicity in the Rye House plot of 1683 and in Monmouth's rebellion of 1685. He attracted attention once again in 1687 when he spoke in favour of the repeal of the penal laws and was thus brought into the privy council by James II, who sought both a presbyterian counterweight to the Church of England men and aid in the remodelling of parliament. Titus was rapidly disillusioned with James, claiming he would have nothing to do with the regime by February 1688, and he attempted to switch sides to William of Orange later that year. However, Titus seems to have overplayed his hand by accepting the patronage of a Catholic monarch and although he came back into parliament in 1691 he gained only limited success. He died in December 1704 at Bushey and was buried there the same month in St James's Church. He was survived by his wife and at least two of their daughters, Susan and Catherine.

ALAN MARSHALL

Sources W. A. [E. Sexby], *Killing noe murder* (1689) • S. Titus, *A seasonable speech: made by a worthy member of parliament in the House of Commons, concerning the other house, March 1659* (1659) • G. Hillier, *A narrative of the attempted escape of Charles the First from Carisbrooke Castle … including letters of the king to Colonel Titus* (1852) • *Calendar of the Clarendon state papers preserved in the Bodleian Library*, 4: 1657–1660, ed. F. J. Routledge (1932) • D. Underdown, *Royalist conspiracy in England, 1649–1660* (1960) • D. T. Witcombe, *Charles II and the cavalier House of Commons, 1663–1678* (1960) • *The Nicholas papers*, ed. G. F. Warner, 1, CS, new ser., 40 (1886) • C. H. Firth, 'Killing no murder', *EngHR*, 17 (1902), 308–11 • J. E. Cussans, *History of Hertfordshire: hundred of Daeorum* (1879) • *VCH Hertfordshire* • *The autobiography of Sir John Bramston*, ed. [Lord Braybrooke], CS, 32 (1845) • *The life and letters of Sir George Savile … first marquis of Halifax*, ed. H. C. Foxcroft, 2 (1898) • will, PRO, PROB 11/480, sig. 18 • M. Knights, *Politics and opinion in crisis, 1678–1681* (1994) • M. W. Helms and E. R. Edwards, 'Titus, Silius', HoP, *Commons, 1660–90*, 3.570–74
Archives BL, corresp. and papers, Add. MS 33573 • BL, corresp. and papers, Add. MS 61682 • BL, corresp. and papers, Egerton MS 1533 • BL, corresp. and papers, Sloane MS 2332
Wealth at death Ramsey manor and estates (farms, land, tenancies); land, farms, tenancies at Bushey; all property left to wife and daughters (Ramsey Abbey property to be sold to settle debts); remainder in thirds to wife and two daughters; wife to have Bushey lands and properties for life; they would then fall to eldest daughter Susan: will, PRO, PROB 11/480, sig. 18

Tiwana, Sir Khizr Hayat (1900–1975), prime minister of the Punjab, was born on 7 August 1900 in Chak Muzaffarabad, Sargodha, in the Shahpur district, Punjab, India. He was the son of Umar Hayat Khan *Tiwana (1874–1944)—an honorary major-general in the Tiwana lancers (later the 19th (King George's own) lancers) who saw active service both in France with the Indian expeditionary force and in Mesopotamia during the First World War—and his wife, Fateh Khatun. The General, as his father was commonly called, was the family patriarch and exerted a profound influence on Khizr's life. The Tiwanas were Rajputs who had entered the Shahpur region nearly seven centuries earlier from Rajputana. Khizr was descended from the cadet Mitha Tiwana branch. It rose to prominence after the Second Anglo-Sikh War (1848–9) and the 1857 Indian mutiny. The family's prosperous Kalra estate was carved out of crown wasteland awarded to Khizr's grandfather Malik Sahib Khan. It was greatly developed during Umar's minority, when it was administered by the court of wards.

Khizr entered Aitchison Chiefs' College, Lahore, in 1908, and later attended Government College, Lahore. He volunteered for military service at the time of the 1919 Punjab disturbances and was attached to the 17th lancers, which guarded Government House and other public buildings in Lahore. He accompanied the regiment to the front at the time of the Third Afghan War. Although still only a teenager, he earned a mention in dispatches and was appointed OBE in 1921. For the next fifteen years he devoted himself to the running of the Kalra estate. He married his first wife, Sultan Bibi, daughter of a kinsman, Malik Muzaffar Khan, and took Fateh Bibi, the wife of one of his tenants, as a mistress. Khizr eventually married her, although this was kept a secret from Umar for many years. With his father Khizr attended the 1935 silver jubilee celebrations in London of George V and Queen Mary.

Khizr stood for the Khushab constituency in the 1937 Punjab provincial elections after the devolution of provincial power to Indian hands after the 1935 Government of India Act. Despite his lack of experience he became minister of public works and local self-government in Sir Sikander Hayat's Unionist cabinet. In 1939 he also took charge of the manpower committee of the Punjab war board and the civil defence departments. Sikander and the prominent Hindu Jat leader Sir Chhotu Ram chalked out a programme of agrarian reform which curbed the power of the moneylenders and cemented the Unionist Party's rural intercommunal appeal. Its support from the Punjab's three major communities, Muslim, Hindu, and Sikh, had been a unique feature of the region's politics since the party's foundation in 1923. The Unionists' subsequent channelling of political divisions in the countryside along rural–urban rather than communal lines severely handicapped the Muslim League's development.

Sikander's celebrated pact with M. A. Jinnah in 1937, in which a Muslim assembly member could be simultaneously recognized as a Unionist and a Muslim Leaguer, in fact ensured a close Unionist supervision of the Muslim League organization in the province. The ambiguities surrounding the pact were, however, to be later exploited by Jinnah in his tussle with Khizr in April 1944. Khizr became prime minister after Sikander's sudden death in December 1942. Growing economic dislocation had already undermined the Unionists' popularity. The Muslim League increasingly sought power in the geographical 'cornerstone' of Pakistan. Behind the 1944 tussle over the interpretation of the Sikander–Jinnah pact there existed two conflicting accommodationist and communalist visions of Punjab politics.

Jinnah journeyed to Lahore in March 1944 for negotiations which were temporarily suspended after Umar's death on 24 March. Despite this family tragedy Khizr resumed the discussions on 20 April. When they finally collapsed he was unprecedentedly expelled from the All-India Muslim League.

Khizr refused to compromise because of loyalty to his non-Muslim colleagues. He had also been encouraged to resist Jinnah by the governor, Sir Bertrand Glancy, who feared that a Muslim League ministry would disrupt the war effort. Khizr relied increasingly on Glancy's advice, after the severe blow of Chhotu Ram's death in January 1945, but he later felt that the British had let him down in their dealings with Jinnah, particularly at the time of the July 1945 Simla conference. From then on Khizr was accused of betraying the Pakistan cause. After the 1946 elections the Unionist Party was reduced to a rump of eighteen members in the assembly of 175. The Muslim League was the single largest party, but could not form a government in an increasingly polarized situation. Despite the protests of the League, Sir Bertrand Glancy invited Khizr to form a coalition Unionist, Akali, and Congress ministry on 7 March 1946.

Khizr attended the Paris peace conference between 29 July and 15 October 1946. He was, however, an increasingly isolated figure in Punjab politics: the Muslim League launched a direct action campaign on 25 January 1947 in response to the banning of the Muslim League national guards, and the agitation revealed the unpopularity of the coalition government. Khizr only finally resigned, however, after Attlee's announcement of 20 February that the British would quit India by June 1948. The Unionist departure precipitated an outbreak of serious communal disturbances; the Sikh desire to avenge these attacks contributed to the later communal holocaust of August 1947. Khizr's warnings that partition would unleash widespread violence were chillingly vindicated.

Khizr feared for his safety and only entered Pakistan in October 1949, after a period of self-imposed exile in London. Unlike other Muslim Unionists, he never again resumed public life. His remaining years were spent at Kalra and in travel to Britain and the United States. He was knighted in 1946. As his economic fortunes declined he entered into two further unsuccessful marriages. Khizr died near Chico, Glen County, California, on 20 January 1975. His body was flown home for burial four days later in the family graveyard at Kalra.

Khizr's legacy lies in his style of statecraft. His natural tolerance and flexibility enabled him to practise intuitively a consociational system of power-sharing based on decentralization in political representation and government appointments, and cross-communal coalition building. Significantly, the abandonment of such traditions of political accommodation has been accompanied in contemporary south Asia by a recrudescence of communal and ethnic violence. Khizr's attachment to the politics of accommodation is likely to be of increasing interest in a critical reappraisal of the partition era.   Ian Talbot

Sources I. A. Talbot, *Khizr Tiwana, the Punjab unionist party and the partition of India* (1996) · D. Gilmartin, *Empire and Islam: Punjab and the making of Pakistan* (1988) · I. Ali, *The Punjab under imperialism, 1885–1947* (1988) · I. Talbot, *Punjab and the raj, 1849–1947* (1988) · I. A. Malik, *The history of the Punjab, 1799–1947* (Delhi, 1983) · S. N. Ahmad, *From martial law to martial law: politics in the Punjab, 1919–1958*, ed. C. Baxter, trans. M. Ali (1985) · I. H. Malik, *Sikandar Hayat Khan (1892–1942): a political biography* (1985) · P. Chowdhry, *Punjab politics: the role of Sir Chhotu Ram* (1984) · S. M. Rai, *Legislative politics and freedom struggle in Punjab, 1847–1947* (1984) · A. Jalal, *The sole spokesman: Jinnah, the Muslim League and the demand for Pakistan* (1985) · K. Singh, ed., *The partition of the Punjab* (1972) · G. R. Mehr, ed., *General Sir Umar Hayat Khan Tiwana Sawaneh Hayat awr unki Khandani Tarekh Ka Pas-e-Manzar* (1965) · private information (2004)

Archives U. Southampton L., corresp. and papers | BL OIOC, Mian Fazli-Husain MSS · BL OIOC, Linlithgow MSS · Karachi, Pakistan, Syed Shamsul Hasan collection · National Library of Pakistan, Islamabad, Quaid-i-Azam MSS

Tiwana, Sir (Muhammad) Umar Hayat, nawab (1874–1944), landowner and army officer, was born at Kalra, Punjab, on 1 October 1874. He was a member of the class of conservative Muslim landowners whose loyal co-operation was a crucial element in the reconstruction of British rule after the events of 1857–8. His father, Sahib Khan Tiwana (*d.* 1878), had seen the East India Company's destruction of the Sikh kingdom as the liberation of Muslims from oppression, and was henceforth a loyal supporter of the British, a fealty recognized by his appointment as a CSI. He, in turn, sent his only son to Aitchison Chiefs' College in Lahore, an institution designed to fit the sons of Indian landowners firmly into the imperial framework. Umar Hayat Tiwana received an honorary commission as a lieutenant in the 18th (Tiwana) lancers in 1901 and thereafter it was in connection with Indian military organization that he would play his most important role. He served abroad both on a classic pre-1914 punitive expedition in Somalia (1903) and in the last important 'great game' sortie, Francis Younghusband's march to Lhasa (1904). He went to France with a staff appointment as part of the Indian expeditionary corps (one of whose divisions was based at Lahore) in 1914 and, when the Indian forces were shifted to the Mesopotamian theatre of war, served there as well. In 1916 his contribution to soldiers' welfare and intelligence work was recognized by appointment as KCSI. Britain's use of Indian Muslim troops against the Ottoman sultan–caliph, necessary if active campaigning in the Middle East was to be carried on without a major diversion of resources from the western front, made the support of Muslim landowners like the Tiwanas in prime recruiting areas crucial, and heightened the need for their continuing assistance in sustaining soldiers' morale in the field.

Tiwana's wartime role was judged to be so important—and his views so reliable—that when both the wartime performance and appropriate post-war structure of the Indian army were brought under review in 1919 by the army in India committee, he was named a member of it. This committee confronted a complex situation—Indian expectations and Britain's post-war situation alike created great pressure for change, in the army as in India generally. On the other hand, as the committee noted, the army was expected to remain 'a vital attribute of government in the hands of the dominant authority'. To men like Tiwana this meant the preservation of the Indian army as it had been in 1914, with a special position for the 'martial races' of the Punjab, whose representative he was. (The martial races were a post-1857 British concept, indicating groups whose past reliability and combat records made their members, supposedly, ideal military recruits.) He argued that change and reform could not be allowed to undermine military tradition; that in 'Indianizing' the officer corps, young men from the traditional sources should still receive the coveted king's commissions. His experience of the Third Anglo-Afghan War in 1919, and traditional 'great game' fears, led him to argue that foreign attack and domestic upheaval might combine to assail the raj. His conclusion was that British troops would remain necessary to guarantee sepoy loyalty—an interesting indication that post-1857 fears were not confined solely to Europeans in India. He also argued vigorously, if somewhat self-interestedly, that wartime experience had proven the soundness of the 'martial races' concept (he noted the failure of Bengali units, but not the 1915 Singapore mutiny by troops drawn from the 'martial races'). His views must have reinforced the generally conservative approach that marked the last great Indian army reorganization of the British era—one which left the favoured position of the Punjab intact.

Tiwana remained a pillar of the raj (and a vigorous opponent of the Congress Party) for the remainder of his active life, as a member of the council of state (1921–8) and the Council of India (1929–34). He was appointed GBE in 1934, and, in the following year, became an honorary major-general, as well as honorary colonel, of a British cavalry regiment, the 19th (King George's own) lancers. Thereafter he largely retired from public life. When he died at Kalra on 24 March 1944 his son, Sir Khizr Hayat *Tiwana (1900–1975), was prime minister of the Punjab, leading a party that attempted to transcend communal politics, and the Indian army was winning the raj's last great victory in Burma. RAYMOND CALLAHAN

Sources I. Copeland, *The Indian princes in the endgame of empire, 1917–1947* (1997) · P. Mason, *A matter of honour: an account of the Indian army, its officers and men* (1974) · private information (2004) [A. Deshpawde] · *DNB* · Burke, *Peerage* (1939)

Archives priv. coll., family MSS | BL OIOC

Tizard, Sir Henry Thomas (1885–1959), physical chemist and science administrator, was born on 23 August 1885 at Gillingham, Kent, the only son and third of five children of Thomas Henry *Tizard (1839–1924), naval officer and hydrographer, and his wife, Mary Elizabeth (*d.* 1931), daughter of William Henry Churchward, a civil engineer. In 1891 the family moved to Surbiton to be closer to Thomas Tizard's work for the Admiralty.

Education and first research Tizard first attended Enfield House, a small private school in Surbiton, where he received a good grounding in mathematics. Unable to enter the navy because of a blind spot in his right eye (which later cleared), he went first as an exhibitioner (1899), later as a queen's scholar (1900) to Westminster

Sir Henry Thomas Tizard (1885–1959), by Howard Coster, 1942

School, where he studied science and mathematics and learned to write good English. He took up an open demyship at Magdalen College, Oxford, in 1904 and graduated first class in mathematical moderations (1905) and chemistry (1908). His chemistry tutor was Nevil Sidgwick, with whom he formed a lifelong friendship. It was at Sidgwick's suggestion that he spent the winter semester of 1908 with Walther Nernst in Berlin, where he met and formed a close friendship with Frederick A. Lindemann.

As the research proposed by Nernst proved unproductive Tizard returned to Oxford in 1909 but, after spending a month or so working with Sidgwick on the colour and ionization of copper solutions, he went to live with his family in London. In the autumn of 1909, following a temporary science mastership at Eton College, he became a freelance researcher in the Davy–Faraday Laboratory of the Royal Institution, where he established his reputation as an investigator with two eloquent papers on the colour changes of indicators. He also translated the sixth edition of Nernst's *Theoretical Chemistry* (1911).

In 1911 Tizard returned to Oxford as a tutorial fellow at Oriel College and to work as a demonstrator in the electrical laboratory, which led to several co-authored papers on the motion of ions in gases. In July 1914 he sailed for Australia to attend the annual meeting of the British Association. News of the outbreak of the First World War reached the ship as it approached Australia, and although the meeting went ahead, Tizard sailed back at its conclusion to enlist. In October 1914 he began war service in the

Royal Garrison Artillery at Portsmouth, his method of training recruits being based more on his mathematical skill than on regular army procedures.

Wartime work and fuel investigations In June 1915 R. B. Bourdillon, who had started experimental work on bombsights with G. M. B. Dobson at the Central Flying School at Upavon, Wiltshire, secured Tizard's transfer to the Royal Flying Corps as an experimental equipment officer. Tizard, whose eyesight had improved, soon learned to fly, an indispensable qualification for understanding the pilot's problems. From bombsights Tizard turned his attention to testing new aircraft; aviation was becoming increasingly important to the military and there was an urgent need to speed technical advancement.

In 1917 Bertram Hopkinson, who was responsible for research and development in aeronautics, appointed Tizard as scientific officer in charge of aircraft testing at the newly established experimental station at Martlesham, Suffolk. Before the end of 1917 Tizard had set up methods of accurately measuring aircraft performance in various weather and service conditions and had developed a range of new flying techniques. He flew as one of his own test pilots, showing skill and courage, and developed his expertise in organizing operational personnel to work closely with scientists. When Hopkinson went to the headquarters of the Ministry of Munitions at the end of 1917 Tizard went with him as his deputy. His results were so successful that when the Royal Air Force was established in 1918 Tizard was appointed assistant controller of research and experiments at the newly created Air Ministry, and became the acting controller in the last few months of the war following Hopkinson's death in an air crash.

On 24 April 1915 Tizard married Kathleen Eleanor (d. 1968), daughter of Arthur Prangley Wilson, a mining engineer. There were three sons: (John) Peter Mills *Tizard, who became a professor of paediatrics at London University; Richard (b. 1917), an engineer and senior tutor at Churchill College, Cambridge; and David (b. 1922), a general practitioner in London. The family knew little of Tizard's work other than where he was based; he was a safe recipient of secrets.

In the spring of 1919 Tizard returned to Oxford and early in 1920 was made a reader in chemical thermodynamics. By then he had started developing work which originated from his wartime experiences when supplies of aviation fuel from Pennsylvania were in short supply. He proposed the augmentation of supplies by the addition of gasworks benzol (impure benzene) and found it gave good results, apart from freezing at low temperatures; the problem was resolved by the substitution of toluene. This brought Tizard into contact with Harry Ricardo, who was then investigating the performance of petrol engines. Ricardo invited Tizard and David Pye to join him at his Shoreham laboratory. Tizard accepted on the condition that the results of research were published, to which Robert Waley Cohen of Shell, which was financing the project, agreed.

By the summer of 1919 Tizard and Pye had prepared an analysis of the physical and chemical properties of the range of fuels which were to be examined and Ricardo had built a new variable compression engine. Tizard's contribution was particularly valuable in devising ingenious tests and in his astuteness in analysing results. As they expected, the incidence of detonations (pinking and knocking) was found to be the most important factor limiting performance of the petrol engine. Tizard suggested the term 'toluene number' to express the detonation characteristics of each fuel. Toluene was the least prone to detonate of all the fuels they examined, and the toluene number was the proportion of toluene that was added to heptane, the most prone to detonate, in order to match the performance of each fuel. Several years later the Americans substituted the use of iso-octane for toluene and the expression 'octane number' became universal. The results of this investigation, published in a series of papers, were Tizard's major contribution to scientific literature and marked a new era in the understanding of the internal combustion engine. Tizard realized that he was unlikely ever to do outstanding work in pure science and instead recognized the great opportunities offered in the application of science to practical problems. Hereafter, his career was to be focused primarily on government scientific administration.

Government science and the move to Imperial College In 1920 Tizard accepted an invitation from Sir Frank Heath, permanent secretary of the Department of Scientific and Industrial Research, to become assistant secretary. His first task was to implement a government decision to co-ordinate the scientific work of the defence and civil departments. His administrative abilities quickly led him to the most senior positions in the department and in 1927 he succeeded Heath as permanent secretary. During these years he exercised an increasing influence on departmental policy and was largely responsible for establishing the Chemical Research Laboratory at Teddington, soon renamed the National Chemical Laboratory.

Tizard left the Department of Scientific and Industrial Research in 1929 to become rector of Imperial College, London, an office he held until 1942. His decision was influenced by his conviction of Britain's need for more scientists and engineers, as well as a salary of £800 per annum more than he was receiving as a civil servant. His great service to the college was his imaginative grasp of site planning for its future growth: his foresight in securing the whole area north of Imperial Institute Road for education, and all museums south of it, made the college's later expansion possible. It also benefited by his creative approach to educational policies, such as the introduction of an undergraduate course in chemical engineering, and a scheme for entrance scholarships for boys who had not specialized in science at school.

Having been one of the most influential scientists in full-time government employment, Tizard remained occupied with problems of defence. He had been a member of the Aeronautical Research Committee since 1919 and he became its chairman in 1933; he was also chairman of its engine sub-committee. It was a time of revolutionary advances in aircraft engines, a subject in which Tizard had good background experience. While he did not have many original ideas he was a stimulating chairman and an able communicator at all levels, always able to bridge gaps in language and understanding when he discussed complex technical questions. He was described as a master of the searching question. Such clear thinking and honesty inspired loyalty from those who worked with him and he gave great encouragement to those, such as Frank Whittle with his jet engine, who were endeavouring to break new ground. However, his inability to understand those who did not meet his high standards did not always endear him to others.

Air defence and Biggin Hill trials Tizard's strong personality and administrative talents made him an ideal choice to chair the sub-committee on aerial defence, proposed in 1934 by H. E. Wimperis, the first director of scientific research in the Air Ministry, in response to the growing German air force and the increasing speed of bomber aircraft compared with defending fighter aircraft. Lindemann wrote a letter to *The Times* in August 1934 calling for action, and in November he told Tizard of his plan for a sub-committee of the committee of imperial defence (CID). A few days earlier Wimperis had recommended a committee, with Tizard as chairman, to consider how far recent advances in scientific and technical knowledge could be used to strengthen defence against hostile aircraft. Early detection and interception of intruding aircraft was made a high priority. Other members of the committee included A. V. Hill and P. M. S. (later Lord) Blackett.

In December 1934 Lindemann, unaware of these proceedings, wrote to the Air Ministry pressing for just such a committee, and when told of the existence of the Tizard committee regarded it as a plot by the Air Ministry and Tizard to circumvent his own proposal. This was the start of the unfortunate quarrel between the two men that was to loom large over the next five years. Both were convinced of the importance of science in future warfare and each was anxious to play his part. With this common objective they might have worked together, but the trouble lay largely in their different avenues of approach. Tizard relied on his influence with the air staff and civil servants with whom he had worked and whose confidence he had won; Lindemann relied on politicians, which, in Tizard's mind, implied intrigue and was anathema to him.

The Tizard committee met first on 28 January 1935, when Wimperis reported that it was the view of Robert Watson-Watt, then superintendent of the radio research laboratory at Slough, that it might be possible to detect the presence of aircraft by a radio beam. At the next meeting on 21 February they had a memorandum from Watson-Watt and, after a successful experiment to detect an aircraft in flight at Daventry on 26 February, Sir Hugh Dowding, air force member for research and development, agreed to spend £10,000 on experiments at Orford Ness, Suffolk. By June planes were detected at 15 miles. The Tizard committee was only advisory but Tizard kept air staff in close touch with its proceedings so that they were actively concerned with its deliberations from the start.

Meanwhile Lindemann and Winston Churchill combined to press for a CID group to deal with the political and financial problems of air defence and in April such a committee held its first meeting under the chairmanship of Sir Philip Cunliffe-Lister (later earl of Swinton), soon to become air minister. The Tizard committee became its sub-committee, responsible for research. In June 1935 Churchill joined the CID committee, of which Tizard was a member, and Lindemann became a member of Tizard's sub-committee.

From his first meeting Lindemann was at odds with his colleagues over both projects and priorities, and crisis came in June 1936 when Lindemann went behind their backs by arranging a meeting between Churchill and Watson-Watt, who said that he was dissatisfied with the rate of progress under the normal ministry machinery. This led to a stormy meeting of the Swinton committee when Churchill attacked Tizard. Shortly afterwards Lindemann announced his intention of standing for parliament where he could raise the question of the country's air defences. Four days later A. V. Hill sent his resignation to Swinton; this was followed by Blackett's and Tizard's. In October, Swinton reconstituted the committee, substituting Edward Appleton for Lindemann, and in 1939 T. R. Merton was added as a member.

In spite of these controversies the development of radar went on and when Tizard reported progress to the Swinton committee the large sums needed for the work were always forthcoming. In September 1935 Watson-Watt moved to Bawdsey and in December 1935 sanction was given to build the first five radar stations. In the summer of 1936 Tizard told the air staff that the time had come for the Royal Air Force to learn how to use radio direction-finding, RDF as it was called, in combat and to find out the ground organization which would be needed. On 4 August 1936 Tizard met officers of the bombers and fighters who had been detailed to Biggin Hill, Kent, for such trials and explained to them that they were to investigate the best way of intercepting a formation of enemy bombers, if they were given fifteen minutes' warning of its approach and its position and altitude at minute intervals. Hitherto the normal procedure was to put fighters up on patrol at suitable points in anticipation of attacks. The Biggin Hill trials were a classic instance of operational research. Methods were gradually evolved for tracking the bombers which gave their position by radio, thus enabling fighters to take off and make an interception. Tizard took an active part in the trials.

The trials having proved the practicability of this new method of interception, Fighter Command then took over introduction of the technique into the defence organization. This was a complex task and it had its difficulties, but Tizard kept in close touch with developments, ever ready with help and advice. He was largely responsible for the introduction of the 'filter room' by means of which the corrected courses of enemy aircraft were clearly presented to the controller in the operations room.

When the Second World War broke out in 1939 both the radar chain and the means of using the information it obtained were ready, thus providing a new system of air defence by day.

Night-time radar and scientific intelligence The Biggin Hill trials (for which Tizard was knighted in 1937) were only one of the practical steps which Tizard took to ensure the effective use of radar. In 1938 he persuaded Mark Oliphant, then at Birmingham, to drop some of his nuclear research and concentrate on development of an improved source of short-wave radiation. This led to the invention by John Randall and H. A. H. Boot of the cavity magnetron, a major advance in radar technology that produced very short wavelengths. The original ground radar stations used long waves and were not effective by night. Tizard realized that the solution to the problem of night defence lay in the development of short-wave airborne radar and, with his encouragement, the research team led by E. G. Bowen produced in 1939 an airborne radar set, AI, which needed considerable development before it was suitable for operational use. Tizard gave it his full support in its early stages when doubt was cast on its operational value. Success depended on intimate co-operation between radar observer and pilot and gradually the difficult art of interception was learned. The air-crews' confidence in AI owed much to Tizard's advice on visits to the squadron. He was also responsible for the night interception committee and the fighter interception unit for carrying out scientific trials of AI in combat, which paid a dividend in its later stages. Tizard's advocacy won the day and airborne radar played a decisive part in the air war by land and sea.

Intelligence was another field in which Tizard's initiative was to prove decisive, for it was through his recommendation that R. V. Jones was appointed to the Air Ministry to deal with scientific intelligence. During the first ten months of the war Tizard advised the chief of air staff on scientific matters in addition to continuing chairmanship of the defence and offence committees which in October 1939 amalgamated as the committee for the scientific survey of air warfare. Its most important decision was to form the Maud committee under George Thomson in March 1940 to investigate the feasibility of an atomic bomb after Oliphant had given Tizard the remarkable memorandum by O. R. Frisch and R. E. Peierls.

When Churchill went to the Admiralty in 1939 with Lindemann as his scientific adviser, and in 1940 became prime minister, Tizard's position gradually became more difficult, and when Sir Archibald Sinclair (later Viscount Thurso) became air minister he also sought Lindemann's advice. This uncertainty as to his responsibility led to Tizard's resignation in June 1940 from all his Air Ministry commitments except the Aeronautical Research Committee. Nevertheless, despite the unedifying quarrels between Lindemann and Tizard, Churchill proposed in August 1940 that Tizard should lead a scientific mission to Canada and the United States to win sympathy and technical support in fighting the war. Tizard's outstanding leadership of this mission was one of his greatest services to Britain. It gave Canada her first start in war research and lent the Americans' independent work on radar a new stimulus. After his return in the autumn of 1940 Tizard became a semi-official adviser to successive ministers of aircraft production, sitting on the aircraft supply committee and representing the ministry on the Air Council from 1941. He was particularly active in securing the flow of up-to-date information to Washington. The development of Barnes Wallis's dam-busting bomb owed much to Tizard's support. His influence was also felt in greater use of scientific evaluation of Britain's military operations, such as the expansion of operational research.

In 1942 Tizard was briefly chairman of a policy committee that dealt with the growth in the use of radar and radio jamming techniques, but internal battles between Tizard and Lindemann, now Lord Cherwell, and the need to reconstitute it with greater powers as a committee of the war cabinet, led Tizard to threaten resignation. However, Churchill persuaded him to remain a member of the new Radio Board, as the policy committee became.

Magdalen College, post-war work, and final years In 1942 Tizard left Imperial College for the presidency of Magdalen College, Oxford, where in the years which followed his advice was sought by visiting scientists, service chiefs, and politicians; this impressed him and caused him to have doubts on the wisdom of the step he had taken, but he quickly acquired a grasp of complicated college statutes and did much to improve its finances. He recognized the problems which would arise at the end of the war when demobilization would produce an increased number of students, and adapted the administration towards the expansion of university education which he foresaw. While he gave good leadership in directing the affairs of the college, he preferred the small committees to the large college meetings when he had to pilot controversial issues through a very varied and independent-minded body of fellows.

Tizard was invited by the Australian government in 1943 to spend three months visiting defence establishments and advising on scientific developments in relation to the Pacific war. Churchill advised him to accept and his visit was a great success. In 1944 Tizard was chairman of a committee set up by the chiefs of staff to assess probable effects of new weapons on defence policy, and soon after its report in 1945 the Labour government turned to him for advice on the place of science in post-war development. In September that year, at a meeting of the chiefs of staff, Tizard pressed for the formation of a scientific organization under the defence ministry to keep scientific development under continuous review, an idea which he developed the next month in an internal paper, 'The central direction of the scientific effort'; this advocated the appointment of a scientific adviser who would act as chairman of a deputy chiefs of staff committee and would also serve on a new body to consider science in relation to civilian needs. These recommendations were approved but a year elapsed before action was taken. In

the spring of 1946 Tizard acted as chairman of a Commonwealth conference on defence science at which he advocated the dispersal of scientific effort and the encouragement in the dominions of great centres of scientific education and research. (In 1945 he had already made suggestions which led directly to the Woomera rocket range in Australia.) In August 1946 he was invited to undertake the chairmanship of the two committees he had suggested, which would necessitate his resignation from Magdalen. He asked the advice of his colleagues, who suggested combining one chairmanship with the presidency; a large majority wished him to remain at Magdalen, but since the feeling was not unanimous he resigned.

In January 1947 Tizard found himself again in Whitehall. His new positions, as chairman of the defence research policy committee and the Advisory Council on Scientific Policy, were fraught with difficulties, and the fact that the defence committee was debarred from discussing nuclear weapons did not help. It was an uphill fight and some of Tizard's most effective work was done during visits to Canada and Australia. He achieved three important civil successes: agreement that a long-term plan was required for the training of scientists, particularly technologists; persuasive and effective influence in ensuring that scientific views were fed in at the policy-forming stage; and success in securing the appointment of a chief scientist, who had the necessary powers and appropriate access in ministries which lacked such senior scientific officers and needed them most.

The long strain told on Tizard's health and by 1949 he wished to retire; he finally left Whitehall for the last time in 1952. The rest of his life was directed partly to his educational interests as pro-chancellor of Southampton University and chairman of the Goldsmiths' education committee, and partly to his services on the board of the National Research Development Corporation and of several chemical concerns. He took an active interest in their affairs, frequently visiting their plants and research laboratories where his presence gave encouragement to younger chemists and engineers. Tizard died of a cerebral haemorrhage at his home, Keston, Hill Head, near Fareham, Hampshire, on 9 October 1959. His ashes were buried in the floor of the ante-chapel of Oriel College.

Together with Tizard's quick wit, well-stored mind, and great moral and physical courage, went a high sense of integrity that proved a handicap in political infighting. Although he occupied prestigious academic positions, his dynamic work was within the armed service ministries of government where he excelled at the management of the committee structure and the machinery of government. His outstanding contributions were the Tizard mission, which was one of the key events in forging the Anglo-American alliance in the Second World War, and, although he did not invent radar, with his knowledge of what it could do he used all his influence to see that it was put to practical use in the air defence of Britain.

Tizard received many honours including an Air Force Cross (1918) and American medal for merit (1947), and was appointed CB (1927), KCB (1937), and GCB (1949). He was elected FRS in 1926 and was the society's foreign secretary (1940–45), and its vice-president (1940–41 and 1944–5). He held honorary doctoral degrees from ten British and Commonwealth universities, and was an honorary fellow of Oriel and Magdalen colleges, Oxford, and of Imperial College and University College, London. He was awarded the gold medals of the Royal Society of Arts and of the Franklin Institute (Philadelphia), and the Messel medal of the Society of Chemical Industry. In 1948 he was president of the British Association, and from 1937 until 1959 he served as a trustee of the British Museum. His hobbies were tennis, golf, and fishing. Possessed of an abundance of wit and humour, he used to make it known to the bishops he met at the Athenaeum that he was a non-believer which, it is said, resulted in a second-rate funeral.　　G. J. PILLER

Sources W. S. Farren and R. V. Jones, *Memoirs FRS*, 7 (1961), 313–48 • R. W. Clark, *Tizard* (1965) • R. V. Jones, 'Air defence clash in the Thirties', *The Times* (6 April 1961), 13 • R. V. Jones, 'Fruitless attempts to patch quarrel', *The Times* (7 April 1961), 15 • R. V. Jones, 'Complete change in bombing methods', *The Times* (8 April 1961), 9 • R. V. Jones, 'Lord Cherwell's judgement in WWII', *Oxford Magazine* (9 May 1963), 279–86 • C. P. Snow, *Science and government* (1961) • C. Webster and N. Frankland, *The strategic air offensive against Germany, 1939–1945*, 4 vols. (1961), vol. 1 • H. Hartley, *JCS* (1964), 153–60 • P. M. S. Blackett, 'Tizard and the science of war', *Nature*, 185 (1960), 647–53 • A. R. Collar, 'Tizard and the Aeronautical Research Committee', *Journal of the Royal Aeronautical Society*, 71 (1967), 529–38 • D. Zimmerman, *Top secret exchange: the Tizard mission and the scientific war* (1996) • private information (2004) • *CGPLA Eng. & Wales* (1960)
Archives ICL, corresp. • IWM, diaries, corresp., and papers • PRO, papers relating to defence research policy committee, DEFE 9 | CAC Cam., corresp. with A. V. Hill • Nuffield Oxf., corresp. with Lord Cherwell • RS, corresp. with Lord Blackett • Trinity Cam., corresp. with Sir Joseph John Thomson • U. Birm. L., letters to C. T. Onions
Likenesses H. Coster, photograph, 1942, NPG [*see illus.*] • W. Dring, pastel drawing, 1956, Magd. Oxf. • H. Coster, photographs, NPG • B. Hailstone, oils, IWM • C. Orde, oils, ICL
Wealth at death £31,610 19s. 8d.: probate, 21 Jan 1960, *CGPLA Eng. & Wales*

Tizard, Jack (1919–1979), psychologist, was born in Stratford, New Zealand, on 25 February 1919, the only son and eldest of three children of John Marsh Tizard, a policeman, and his wife, Leonelle Washington Ward. He was educated at Timaru Boys' High School and after 1936 at Canterbury University College, Christchurch. He graduated from the University of New Zealand in psychology in 1940 with first-class honours. Between 1940 and 1945 he served with the New Zealand expeditionary force in the Middle East as a member of the medical corps.

In 1945 Tizard was made assistant lecturer in educational psychology at the University of New Zealand and in 1946 accepted an ex-servicemen's study grant to go to Oxford where he studied history under G. D. H. Cole and was awarded a BLitt (1948). In 1947 Tizard married Barbara Patricia, daughter of Herbert Parker, journalist. She was a psychologist. There were three children, two boys (one of whom died in 1983) and a girl, and two adopted children, one boy, who died in 1975, and one girl. Also in 1947 Tizard

became a lecturer in psychology at the University of St Andrews but resigned in 1948 to join the newly established Medical Research Council unit for research in occupational adaptation, later the social psychiatry unit, headed by Sir Aubrey Lewis. He began work on 1 April 1948 and stayed in this post until 1964.

The work initiated at this time was concerned with the suitability of people with mild mental handicaps for industrial employment and social independence. Social aspects of this investigation were developed subsequently by Tizard to include surveys of prevalence (with N. Goodman, 1962), demonstrations of 'model' improvements in services (1964), and critical evaluation of existing services. By using social psychological techniques Tizard attempted to influence social policy. There is little doubt that work carried out in this way by him and by others at this time had considerable effects on the deliberations of the royal commission on the law relating to mental illness and mental deficiency (1954–7) and on the Mental Health Act (1959).

Tizard was awarded a London PhD in 1951. In 1964 he became professor of child development at London University Institute of Education, a post he held until 1971. Among other distinctions awarded him during this period and subsequently was a Kennedy international scientific award, 1968. He was president of the British Psychological Society, 1975–6. A member of the Social Science Research Council, he was chairman of its educational research board in 1969–71. He was consultant adviser in mental subnormality to the Department of Health and Social Security (1965–75), and a member of its chief scientists' research committee (1973–7); consultant to the Home Office research unit (1975–8); member of the secretary of state's advisory committee on handicapped children (1970–3); and consultant on mental subnormality to the World Health Organization. He was an honorary member of the British Paediatric Association, a fellow of the British Psychological Society, a fellow of the Royal Society of Medicine, and the recipient of a research award from the American Association on Mental Deficiency. In 1973 he was appointed CBE and also the Thomas Coram Research Unit was set up under his direction.

Tizard's research philosophy was set out in detail in his presidential address to the BPS of 1976. There he cautioned against the preoccupation of academic psychology with causes and recommended instead the exploration of the effects of remedial intervention and favourable environmental conditions in minimizing handicap. He advised at one point: 'Devote less time to the study of supposedly general laws governing the behaviour of a species and more to the rules governing the behaviours of individuals in different environments.' His approach to psychology was not that of the experimental method which he consciously rejected, but an attempt to provide demonstrations of the feasibility of fulfilling patently desirable human needs. Always an egalitarian, Tizard was in many senses a crusader for the underprivileged and used social psychology in the service of the handicapped. After 1964 his studies were concerned with general childhood disorders such as malnutrition and its consequences and with services for the under-fives.

Tizard's personality was characterized by attractive qualities of humour, sympathy, and generosity of spirit which inspired both loyalty and regard in many friends and colleagues. His interests outside his profession and his family were predominantly political, but whether in his work or outside it, his sharp wit and healthy iconoclasm made him both an amusing and agreeable colleague. Tizard died in the Royal Free Hospital in London on 2 August 1979. He was survived by his wife.

NEIL O'CONNOR, rev.

Sources private information (1986) · personal knowledge (1986) · *WWW* · *The Guardian* (3 Aug 1979) · *CGPLA Eng. & Wales* (1980) **Wealth at death** £49,504: probate, 14 April 1980, *CGPLA Eng. & Wales*

Tizard, Sir (John) Peter Mills (1916–1993), paediatrician, was born on 1 April 1916 at 12 Lancaster Place, Hampstead, London, the eldest son of the scientist Sir Henry Thomas *Tizard (1885–1959) and his wife, Kathleen Eleanor Wilson (1891–1968). Peter, as he was generally known, was educated at Rugby School (1929–34) and at Oriel College, Oxford, before progressing as a scholar to Middlesex Hospital medical school, where he qualified in medicine in 1941. After war service in the Royal Army Medical Corps, he married, on 29 June 1945, Elisabeth Joy (*b.* 1920), a physiotherapist and the younger daughter of Clifford John Taylor, a physician and surgeon. They had two sons and one daughter, and lived for thirty years at Ickenham Manor, Uxbridge, a house that the family had owned for 200 years.

His paediatric training in London led to Tizard's first consultant appointment at the Paddington Green Children's Hospital in 1949. A Nuffield research fellowship in 1951 at the Harvard Medical School children's centre strengthened his interest in the neurology of the developing brain and his enthusiasm for effective care for very premature infants and the sick newborn. He became reader in child health at the Hammersmith Hospital in 1954, was elected FRCP in 1958, and proceeded to a personal chair in paediatrics at the Royal Postgraduate Medical School, London University, in 1964. There he developed and was head of the Nuffield neonatal research unit, a clinical and research base which set new standards for neonatal care in the UK. Ambitious paediatricians saw his unit as the place to work in order to learn intensive care of the newborn. Tizard ensured that they emerged not only clinically competent in neonatal intensive care, but also as participants in scientific studies from his unit and with a desire to pursue future clinical and scientific excellence. He trained a generation of paediatricians who were to head academic departments in Britain and abroad. His skill was in leadership, and in selecting and developing talented young doctors. The intense work ethic and scientific rigour of the unit was feared as well as admired; yet those who worked there considered, at least in retrospect, that it had been a fulfilling and happy experience. Tizard's

publications were relatively few, but included the important *Medical Care of Newborn Babies* (1972), written in collaboration with four senior members of his Hammersmith department.

In 1972 Tizard was appointed to the inaugural chair of paediatrics at Oxford University and a fellowship of Jesus College. He thrived on the opportunity to develop another new academic department of paediatrics, and once again attracted the most able trainees to his unit, of which he remained head until his retirement in 1983.

Tizard enjoyed institutions, particularly if ancient, and understood how to use their influence. He was a determined and efficient leader. In 1982, the year of his knighthood, he became the first president of the British Paediatric Association to be elected by a ballot of all its members. During his three-year term of office he tackled, with clarity of thought and wisdom, the difficult issue of integrating hospital-based paediatricians with community child health specialists. He was influential in developing the British Paediatric Surveillance Unit, to monitor the incidence of rare childhood disorders, and was chairman of its scientific committee. Before his presidency there had been increasing clamour by paediatricians for secession from the royal colleges of physicians and the development of an independent college of paediatrics. Tizard firmly opposed such a development, and during his presidency took steps to reduce its likelihood. Despite his strong convictions on that and other contentious issues, and although he appeared a somewhat forbidding and acerbic man, he had a great sense of fun and considerable generosity of spirit. After an impassioned speech by a younger colleague about the need to form an independent college of paediatrics, Tizard leant across to whisper in the ear of the man, whom he did not know, 'I disagree with every point you make. You are wrong. That was an outstanding speech; well done.'

Probably the best-known in other countries among British paediatricians of his time, Tizard enjoyed international contacts and meetings. He received many fellowships and awards from other countries and was president of the European Society for Paediatric Research. Within the UK he was president of the Neonatal Society, master of the Worshipful Society of Apothecaries, and the recipient of many awards, including the James Spence medal of the British Paediatric Association in 1986. He died, survived by his wife, at Hillingdon Hospital on 27 October 1993; after cremation at Breakspear crematorium, Ruislip, Middlesex, his ashes were buried in the memorial gardens, Stoke Poges.

ROY MEADOW

Sources *The Independent* (5 Nov 1993) · *The Times* (30 Oct 1993), 17 · J. Forfar, A. Jackson, and B. Laurance, *The British Paediatric Association, 1928–1988* · J. Osborne, ed., *The Royal College of Paediatrics and Child Health at the millennium* (2000) · *WW* · private information (2004) [family] · J. A. Davis, *The Lancet*, 342/2 (1993), 1168 · R. Robinson, *BMJ* (6 Nov 1993), 1207 · D. Winnicott, 'The president's view of a past president', *Journal of the Royal Society of Medicine*, 74 (1981), 267–74 [presidential address to section of paediatrics, 24 Oct 1981] · b. cert. · m. cert. · d. cert. · *DNB* · A. H. Maude and A. Archer, eds., *Rugby School register, 1911–1946*, rev. edn (1957) **Archives** Wellcome L., corresp. and papers

Tizard, Thomas Henry (1839–1924), naval officer and hydrographer, was born at Weymouth on 13 March 1839, the third son of Joseph Tizard, shipowner and coal merchant, and his wife, Sarah Parsons. He was educated at the Royal Hospital school, Greenwich—then noted for its mathematical training—and entered the Royal Navy by competitive examination as master's assistant in 1854. At the age of fifteen he saw active service in the *Dragon* with the Baltic fleet during the Crimean War. Tizard next served in the *Indus* on the West Indian station, and gained his first experience of surveying on the Newfoundland coast. He was promoted second master in 1860 and appointed to the surveying vessel *Rifleman* on the China station. During his seven years' service there he laid the foundation of his subsequent reputation as a surveyor. For a survey of reefs and shoals in the South China Sea the schooner *Saracen* was attached as tender to the *Rifleman*. Tizard was in command of the *Saracen* for three years after his promotion to the rank of master in 1864.

From 1868 to 1871 Tizard served as navigating lieutenant and senior assistant surveyor of the *Newport* in the Mediterranean and the Red Sea under Captain George Strong Nares, and he was present at the official opening of the Suez Canal in 1869, when the *Newport* led the procession of ships. During this period he brought out the *Table of Chords*, a most useful publication for surveyors. In 1871 the officers and crew of the *Newport* were transferred to the *Shearwater*; on the way out from England in the latter ship to continue the survey of the Gulf of Suez, Tizard was largely responsible for an important series of observations on the surface currents and undercurrents in the Strait of Gibraltar.

Towards the end of 1872 Captain Nares was appointed to the command of the famous *Challenger* expedition, on which he was joined by Tizard. The latter was by this time a man of strong personality and resourcefulness, an experienced navigator, and a master at handling a ship. The appointment gave him a great opportunity in bringing him into contact with the leaders of the science of oceanography. The *Challenger* expedition resulted in a vast increase of knowledge of all aspects of oceanography, and great improvements in apparatus and methods of research. As navigating officer, Tizard's duties involved close collaboration with the leader of the expedition and the scientific staff. When Captain Nares left the ship in order to take command of the Arctic expedition of 1875, Tizard remained with the *Challenger* until she was paid off in 1876, and spent the next three years at the Admiralty, writing the narrative of the voyage in association with the naturalist John Murray.

In 1879 Tizard, who had been promoted staff commander in 1874, resumed surveying duties afloat, and in the following year took command of the new paddle surveying vessel *Triton* for surveys in home waters. During the nine years that he held this command he published scientific papers on marine surveying and related subjects in the *Proceedings of the Royal Society*, *Professional Papers of the Corps of Royal Engineers*, *Nature*, and elsewhere. He was promoted staff captain in 1889, and in 1891 was appointed assistant hydrographer, and was elected a fellow of the Royal Society. He was placed on the retired list with the rank of captain in 1896, but continued to serve at the Admiralty until the autumn of 1907. In 1899 he was made a civil CB.

Tizard's last public service was to assist the committee appointed by the Admiralty in 1912 to examine Nelson's tactics at the battle of Trafalgar. An exhaustive examination of ships' logs and journals enabled him to prepare the first plans of any phase of the battle drawn exactly to scale.

In 1881 Tizard married Mary Elizabeth (*d.* 1931), daughter of William Henry Churchward, civil engineer; they had one son, Sir Henry Thomas *Tizard, the noted scientific administrator, and four daughters. He died on 17 February 1924 at his home, 23 Geneva Road, Kingston upon Thames, and was buried four days later at St John's Church, Kingston.   A. M. FIELD, rev. R. O. MORRIS

Sources *The Times* (25 Feb 1924) · A. Day, *The admiralty hydrographic service, 1795–1919* (1967) · *GJ*, 63 (1924), 460–62 · *CGPLA Eng. & Wales* (1924)
Archives NMM, journals · NMM, logs · NMM, papers
Wealth at death £931 7s. 10d.: probate, 5 May 1924, *CGPLA Eng. & Wales*

Tobias (*d.* 726), bishop of Rochester, was probably a native of Kent. Bede gives most of what is known about him, stating that he had been a pupil of Theodore and Hadrian at Canterbury and had become familiar with Latin and Greek as well as English. He was consecrated ninth bishop of Rochester by Archbishop Berhtwald, in succession to Gefmund, who died between 699 and 716. His name appears as a witness to a charter of dubious authenticity, dated 706. He died in 726 and was buried in the chapel of St Paul which he had built in St Andrew's Cathedral at Rochester.   A. F. POLLARD, rev. MARIOS COSTAMBEYS

Sources Bede, *Hist. eccl.*, 5.8, 23 · *ASC*, s.a. 693, 727 [text A] · *AS chart.*, S 54

Tobin, George (1768–1838), naval officer and artist, born in Salisbury on 13 December 1768, was the second of eight children of James *Tobin (1736/7–1817), a sugar planter and merchant of Nevis in the West Indies and Bristol, and his wife, Elizabeth, daughter of another Nevis planter, George Webbe; he was an elder brother of John *Tobin and James Webbe *Tobin. After attending King Edward VI School, Southampton, in May 1780 he entered the navy as a captain's servant on the *Namur*, in which he took part in the battle of the Saintes in April 1782, before transferring to the *Bombay Castle*. In February 1785 Tobin joined the *Thisbe* which sailed for Halifax, Nova Scotia, where he completed his time as midshipman in the *Assistance* and *Leander*. Being unemployed on his return to Britain in 1787, he sailed as sixth mate on board the East Indiaman *Sulivan* to Madras and Whampoa (Huangpu) between the autumn of 1788 and June 1790. After rejoining the navy, in the *Tremendous*, he was made a lieutenant on 22 November 1790.

In April 1791 Tobin was chosen as third lieutenant of the *Providence* for William Bligh's second breadfruit voyage. When the expedition's official artist withdrew, Tobin became the principal illustrator for the journey to Otaheite (Tahiti) and the West Indies. His journal of that voyage, now in the Mitchell Library, Sydney, shows he was an interested, witty, and tolerant observer of Tahitian life and the accompanying sketches show a scientific interest in natural history and a romantic vision of landscape. Those from his fifteen days on Australian soil at Adventure Bay are among the first European records of Tasmania. Tobin was always generous about Bligh in later years.

On his return to Britain in August 1793 Tobin was happy to learn that Nelson, related through his wife to Tobin's mother, was no longer able to keep open for him a vacancy as third lieutenant of the *Agamemnon*. It seemed to Tobin, as a protégé of Marjory, duchess of Atholl, better to be appointed, in November 1793, second lieutenant of the frigate *Thetis* under the command of Captain Alexander Cochrane. In general Tobin recorded the more eventful moments of his career in his sketches and watercolours and this is true of his service in the *Thetis*, and in Rear-Admiral George Murray's flagship *Resolution*, in the Halifax squadron between May 1794 and 1798.

In July 1798 Tobin was appointed commander of the cedar sloop *Dasher*, in which, having returned home and changed his mind about Nelson's fortune, he tried to get himself posted to the Mediterranean with Nelson. However, Tobin spent the next two years harrying French coastal trade off Brittany before being paid off in October 1801. He was promoted captain on 29 April 1802. On 13 June 1804, still on half pay, he married Dorothy (1767/8–1840), daughter of Captain Gordon Skelly RN, and widow of Major William Duff; they had a daughter, (Eliza) Lucy Hope, and a son, George Webbe. In September 1804, at the request of Rear-Admiral Alexander Cochrane, Tobin was appointed captain of the flagship *Northumberland*, blockading Ferrol and, later, chasing a French fleet to the West Indies where, in September 1805, he was moved into a 38 gun frigate, the *Princess Charlotte*. On 5 October 1805, by disguising his ship as a merchantman, Tobin captured the French corvette *Cyane* off Tobago.

Between 1806 and 1810 the *Princess Charlotte* operated with the Irish squadron, based in Cork, mainly protecting trade to the West. From April 1811 Tobin acted on occasions as senior officer of the squadron harassing French forces off the north coast of Spain in co-operation with guerrillas before his ship, renamed *Andromache*, joined the Channel Fleet off Ushant in June. The *Andromache* was present at the fall of San Sebastian in September 1813 and on 23 October captured the Franco-Batavian frigate *La Trave* off the Saintes. Having previously acted as senior officer off the Gironde, Tobin returned there in December 1813 and successfully led Rear-Admiral Penrose's squadron in the difficult task, requested by Wellington, of forcing an entry into the Gironde.

When the *Andromache* was paid off in July 1814, Tobin retired to Teignmouth. On 8 December 1815 he was made a CB. Still contributing to the *Naval Chronicle*, he continued to sketch and paint naval and local scenes with his fellow painters Thomas Luny and Commander Rowland Mainwaring, the latter of whom had married Tobin's stepdaughter Sophia Henrietta Duff. From July 1830 he commanded the royal yacht *Prince Regent* until it was sold in August 1836. Having been promoted rear-admiral of the White on 10 January 1837, Tobin died in Teignmouth on 10 April 1838 and was buried there in St Michael's Church ten days later.   DAVID SMALL

Sources *United Service Journal*, 2 (1838), 240–44 · J. Marshall, *Royal naval biography*, 2/2 (1825), 629–35 · D. Oliver, *Return to Tahiti: Bligh's second breadfruit voyage* (1988) · survey, PRO, ADM 9/2 (1817), 238 · G. Tobin, 'Journal on H.M.S. Providence, 1791–93', Mitchell L., NSW, ML MSS A562 and ML ZPX A563 · captain's logs of HMS *Dasher*, 1798–1801, PRO, ADM 51 · captain's logs of HMS *Princess Charlotte/Andromache*, 1805–14, PRO, ADM 51 · Admiralty index and digest, 1793–1814, PRO, ADM 12 · NL Scot., Cochrane MSS 2264–2570 · *Nelson's letters to his wife and other documents, 1785–1831*, ed. G. P. B. Naish, Navy RS, 100 (1958) · V. L. Oliver, ed., *Caribbeana*, 5 (1917–18), 1–5 · *Naval Chronicle*, 1–40 (1799–1818) · C. F. Russell, *A history of King Edward VI School, Southampton* (privately printed, Cambridge, 1940), 277–85 · J. G. Cavenagh-Mainwaring, 'The Mainwarings of Whitmore and Biddulph in the county of Stafford', Collections for a history of Staffordshire, William Salt Archaeological Society, 3rd ser. (1933), 92–119 · *Trewman's Exeter Flying Post* (19 April 1838) · parish register, Teignmouth, St Michael, Devon RO [burial] · parish register, St Edmund's, Salisbury, Wiltshire [baptism]

Archives Mitchell L., NSW, 'Journal of HMS *Providence*', ML MSS A562 · Mystic Seaport Museum, Connecticut, VFM 965 · NL Aus., Rex Van Kivell collection · NMM · PRO, 'Logs of HMS *Providence*', ADM 55, 94–5 · PRO, 'Captain's logs of HMS *Princess Charlotte*', ADM 51 · PRO, 'Captain's logs of HMS *Andromache*', ADM 51 | Blair Castle, Perthshire, Atholl MS 59, 1 and 2 · NL Scot., Cochrane MSS 2264–2570 · PRO, Admiralty index and digest, ADM 12 · PRO, Admirals' journals, ADM 50 · PRO, captains' letters, ADM 1 · Whitmore Hall, Whitmore, Staffordshire, diaries of Rowland Mainwaring

Likenesses oils, *c*.1820–1830, priv. coll.

Wealth at death substantial; proceeds from naval prize money, sale of slave plantation in Nevis, West Indies, and sugar factor business in Bristol; included 3 per cent government consolidated bank annuities and other parliamentary stocks and securities: will, PRO, PROB 11/1901

Tobin, James (1736/7–1817), sugar planter and pro-slavery campaigner, born in London, was probably the son of a sea captain, James Tobin (1698–1770); his mother may have been a Miss Hope. He was educated at Westminster School and took articles as a solicitor. However, in 1758 he went to Nevis in the West Indies to help manage the family plantations. In 1766 he returned to England and immediately, on 30 June, married Elizabeth (1744/5–1824), the daughter of a wealthy Nevis planter, George Webbe. The couple settled in Salisbury, where their eight children were born. Leaving behind the three eldest sons, Tobin departed again for Nevis in 1777 with the rest of his family to take control of his plantation, Stoney Grove. As a member of the island council, with his friend John Pinney he negotiated good terms for surrender of the island to the French in 1782.

After returning to England in 1784 Tobin settled in Bristol, and together with Pinney established a successful firm of sugar factors and became an active organizer of the West Indies interest. He engaged in an extremely acrimonious and personal exchange of pamphlets on the issue of slavery with the leading abolitionist James Ramsay, who had published an essay on the subject. Tobin's *Cursory Remarks upon the Reverend Mr Ramsay's Essay* (1785) was one of a number of replies published anonymously. Although not a very successful planter, Tobin was probably not brutal himself, and he tried in the pamphlet to discredit the evidence of cruelty produced by Ramsay (who had lived in the West Indies and had personal knowledge of the institution of slavery). Personally sensitive on the issue of race, Tobin emulated the racial purity arguments of Edward Long and bemoaned 'the rapid increase of a dark, contaminated breed' in England (Tobin, 118n.). Further exchanges of pamphlets followed, and at one stage Ramsay accused Tobin of twice challenging him to a duel. The debate was reviewed in the press, and *Cursory Remarks* clearly stirred the abolitionists; Tobin was immediately attacked by Thomas Clarkson, who deplored the attempt to discredit Ramsay personally, and by the former slave Olaudah Equiano, who accused him of telling lies 'faster than Old Nick can hear them' (Shyllon, 99).

As a planter and active member of the Bristol West India Association, Tobin was called in February 1790 to give evidence to the House of Commons inquiry into the slave trade. He argued that slavery was necessary to the plantation economy because free black men would not work on the estates, that slave numbers could not be supported by breeding and that therefore the slave trade was essential. While conceding, in theory, that freedom was preferable to slavery, he maintained that slaves were in a better position than the labouring poor in England, that they were treated mildly and protected by the law. Twenty years later his own son James Webbe *Tobin, an abolitionist, showed that there was no effective legal protection when he publicized the brutalities of the Nevis planter Edward Huggins. In 1792, Tobin's final pamphlet defended the high price of sugar and called for garrisons in the West Indies to protect planters against the possibility of slave rebellion.

A cultured man with a liking for Pope and Dryden, Tobin was a fellow of the Linnean Society and knew Sir Joseph Banks and Sir Joshua Reynolds. He seems to have painted, for he exhibited at the Royal Academy in 1776, and was probably the etcher and engraver mentioned in Joseph Strutt's contemporary *Biographical Dictionary of Engravers* (1785). As was noted by Fanny Nelson, to whom he was related by marriage, he was keen to promote the naval career of his son George *Tobin through the distribution of expensive presents, but he seems to have been unaware of the largely unsuccessful efforts of his son John *Tobin, a playwright.

As well as having to cope with the early death of four of his sons, Tobin fell out with the Pinneys, to whom his plantation was mortgaged, over his actions as their agent

on Nevis. He died in Bristol on 6 October 1817 and was buried on 13 October in the lower churchyard of St Andrew's, Clifton.   DAVID SMALL

Sources R. Pares, *A West India fortune* (1950) · F. Shyllon, *James Ramsay, the unknown abolitionist* (1977) · S. Lambert, ed., *House of Commons sessional papers of the eighteenth century* (1975), vol. 71, pp. 260–87 · J. Tobin, *Cursory remarks upon the Reverend Mr Ramsay's essay on the treatment and conversion of the African slaves in the sugar colonies, by a friend to the West-India colonies and their inhabitants* (1785) · University of Bristol Library, Pinney MSS, DM 1705 · V. L. Oliver, ed., *Caribbeana*, 5 (1917–18), 1–5 · J. Tobin, *A short rejoinder to the Reverend Mr Ramsay's reply: with a word or two on some other publications of the same tendency* (1787) · J. Tobin, *A farewel address to the Reverend Mr James Ramsay* (1788) · P. Fryer, *Staying power: the history of black people in Britain* (1992) · E. O. Benger, *Memoirs of John Tobin, author of the Honey Moon* (1820) · J. Strutt, *A biographical dictionary, containing an historical account of all the engravers, from the earliest period of the art of engraving to the present time*, 2 vols. (1785–6) · M. Lewis, *A social history of the navy, 1793–1815* (1960) · private information (2004) · IGI · *GM*, 1st ser., 94/2 (1824), 94 · M. V. Campbell, *The registers of the church of St Andrew, Clifton, 1813–1837*, 2 (1994)
Archives BL, MSS · Bodl. RH, MSS · Linn. Soc., MSS · Society of Merchant Venturers, Bristol, MSS | NL Scot., Alexander Houston & Co. MSS · University of Bristol Library, Pinney MSS
Likenesses J. Reynolds?, oils?, probably priv. coll. · miniature, oils?, priv. coll.
Wealth at death left at least one mortgaged plantation to eldest son; annuity to wife: will, 1811, PRO, PROB 11/1597, fol. 549

Tobin, James Webbe (1767–1814), slavery abolitionist, was born at Stratford-sub-Castle, outside Salisbury, on 19 October 1767. He was the first of eight children of James *Tobin (1736/7–1817), a sugar planter and merchant of Nevis and Bristol, and his wife, Elizabeth Webbe (1744/5–1824). When his parents left Salisbury in 1777 to manage the family plantations on Nevis he and his brothers George *Tobin and John *Tobin were brought up by their maternal grandfather and sent to King Edward VI School in Southampton until their parents returned from Nevis in 1784 and settled in Bristol, where Tobin may have attended the grammar school. Immediately after graduating BA from Wadham College, Oxford, in 1791 he visited revolutionary France. However, he may have come to share his brother John's growing disillusionment with both the violence in France and the increasing repression in England.

It seems probable that Tobin was involved in radical politics in England at this time, perhaps as a member of the London Constitutional Society, for it was suggested later that his father's partner, John Pinney, had been required to help him escape arrest by smuggling him out of the country to Philadelphia in February 1793. During this visit and before his return from Nevis in September 1794 his eyesight began to fail, a condition which plagued him for the rest of his life, ended his interest in the church as a profession, and led to the epithet 'Blind Tobin'. From at least April 1796 he shared chambers with his playwright brother, John, at the Temple in London. About this time he re-entered radical circles becoming a devout follower of William Godwin, though later he grew disillusioned with Godwinian rationalism. It was probably through Basil Montagu, or perhaps through the sons of John Pinney, that Tobin became friendly with William Wordsworth,

Samuel Taylor Coleridge, and Robert Southey. Tobin may have visited the Wordsworths at Alfoxden in 1797 with Tom Wedgwood; he was certainly included by Coleridge in the original first line of 'We are Seven' as the 'little child, dear brother Jem' (Moorman, 383–5) although Tobin pleaded unsuccessfully with Wordsworth to drop the poem. About 1798 he began a lifelong friendship with Humphry Davy, who wrote an amusing account of Tobin's part in the experiments with nitrous oxide. Coleridge, meanwhile, was eager for Tobin and Davy to join him, along with Wordsworth and Southey, in a utopian colony abroad. Tobin contributed at least five poems to the second volume of Southey's *Annual Anthology* and urged Southey to produce a third. He also corresponded regularly with Coleridge, who stayed with Tobin at Barnard's Inn, London, in early 1804. However, later that year Coleridge began to believe that Tobin was an inveterate and mischievous gossip, and they fell out on the eve of Coleridge's departure for Malta over Tobin's constant advice on the subjects of health and debts. Shortly after this Tobin suffered a terrible blow with the death of his constant companion, his brother, John, in December 1804.

Tobin recovered some of his cheerfulness when he married Jane Mallet (d. 1837) on 8 September 1807 at St Botolph without Bishopsgate, London. They had at least four children. In 1809 the family moved to his father's plantation, Stoney Grove, on Nevis. Unlike his father Tobin was a fervent critic of slavery and became an advocate for its abolition. His correspondence with the abolitionist African Institution and others was responsible for the widespread publicity given to the flogging of thirty-two slaves by the notorious Edward Huggins in the public market in Charlestown, Nevis, on 23 January 1810, and to the subsequent acquittal of Huggins by a rigged jury of planters. In his correspondence Tobin advocated the right of free black people to vote and attacked the standard of justice in the islands as well as other practices. This stance led both to threats from planters and to the publicly expressed gratitude of the African Institution.

Tobin died on his father's plantation of a fever on 30 October 1814 and was buried a day later at St John Figtree, Nevis. His wife continued to play a role in the abolition cause since, when she left the island, she took with her to Bristol a free black man, Charles Hamilton, who had been enslaved illegally on the islands of St Barts and St Kitts and who had been freed by the courts.   DAVID SMALL

Sources D. Small and C. Eickelmann, 'Pinney and slavery', University of Bristol Library, Pinney MS DM 1867 · E. O. Benger, *Memoirs of John Tobin* (1820) · *J. W. Tobin's reply to Mr Cottle's pamphlet* (1812) · PRO, CO 152/96, 98, 100, 105, 106 · *Report of the African Institution*, 5, 9, 10 (1811–16) · *Collected letters of Samuel Taylor Coleridge*, ed. E. L. Griggs, 6 vols. (1956–71) [repr. (1966)] · M. Moorman, *William Wordsworth, a biography*, 1: *The early years, 1770–1803* (1957) · B. Evans and H. Pinney, 'Racedown and the Wordsworths', *Review of English Studies*, 8 (1932), 1–18 · J. A. Paris, *The life of Sir Humphry Davy* (1831) · V. L. Oliver, ed., *Caribbeana*, 5 (1917–18), 1–5 · letterbooks 10, 11, 13, University of Bristol Library, Pinney MSS · IGI · *The letters of Charles and Mary Lamb*, ed. E. W. Marrs, 3 vols. (1975–8) · F. K. Brown, *The life of Godwin* (1926) · *New letters of Robert Southey*, ed. K. Curry, 2 vols. (1965) · C. F. Russell, *A history of King Edward VI School, Southampton* (privately printed, Cambridge, 1940) · parish register, Nevis, St John Figtree, Nevis Archive, 31 Oct 1814 [burial] · parish register, Stratford-sub-Castle, Wilts. & Swindon RO, 25 Oct 1767 [baptism] · *GM*, 1st ser., 85/1 (1815), 178

Archives Keele University, Mosely collection · Keele University, Wedgwood MSS main collection · NL Scot., Minto MSS, MS 13058 · PRO, CO 152/96, 98, 100, 105, 106 · University of Bristol Library, Pinney MSS

Wealth at death subsequent to death, provision made for wife and children in will of father

Tobin, Sir John (1763–1851), merchant, was born on the Isle of Man, the eldest son of Patrick Tobin (1735–1794), merchant. His family came originally from Dublin, but had lived on the Isle of Man since 1728. He began his career as a merchant seaman sailing from Liverpool, and by the 1790s was a master, operating in the slave trade between Africa and the Caribbean. During the early years of the war with France he was a highly successful privateer, capturing several French slaving ships.

In 1798 Tobin married Sarah Aspinall (1770–1853), daughter of James Aspinall (1729–1787), a prominent Liverpool slave trader. They had eight children—five daughters and three sons, of whom three daughters and one son survived Tobin. This marriage may have brought him capital, for by 1799 he was trading on his own account, as John Tobin & Co., and by 1803 he had left the sea and settled in Liverpool. The abolition of the British slave trade in 1807 proved to be the making of his business for he was to be one of the pioneers of the trade in 'legitimate' products between west Africa and Britain, particularly in palm oil for industrial and railway lubrication and for the manufacture of soap and candles. His success lay in his development of the trade from Calabar, the centre of the palm-oil trade in these years, and his close ties with the ruling élite in that state. The rapid increase in the trade in the 1810s and 1820s made his fortune as well as that of his brother Thomas; by the early 1830s he was probably the largest African trader in Britain.

His success in the African trade allowed Tobin to pursue an active political career. He was one of the leading tories in Liverpool, a friend of George Canning and William Huskisson, and closely connected to the Gladstone family. With John Gladstone MP he was a prominent member of a local committee set up to defend the crown and constitution in the troubled climate of 1819. In the same year he stood for election as mayor of Liverpool and was elected in what his political opponents described as one of 'the most barefaced acts of bribery that ever disgraced even the electioneering annals of this venal rotten borough' (*Liverpool Mercury*, 22 Oct 1819). He received a knighthood in May 1820 on the accession of George IV. He remained a member of Liverpool common council for many years and was at the centre of a network of tory and African trading interests on it.

Tobin's business interests covered a variety of spheres. During the early 1820s he was involved in promoting a railway between Liverpool and Manchester and in 1838 was one of the directors that formed the Transatlantic Steam Company, operating between Liverpool and New York. In 1837 he built the *Liverpool* (1150 tons), at that time the largest steamship launched on Merseyside, for the transatlantic run. His ships were also to be found trading to India for cloth and to the West Indies for sugar, tobacco, and rum, all items needed for the African trade. By the 1830s he had moved into insurance broking. He also became involved in land speculation on Merseyside in the late 1820s, purchasing land in Wallasey with William Laird, which shortly afterwards was bought by the Liverpool council, netting him a substantial profit.

In 1819 Tobin purchased Oak Hill House, Old Swan, Liverpool, and lived there until 1835, when he built Liscard Hall on land he had bought in Wallasey. He retired from the African trade shortly after 1840 and died, at Liscard Hall, on 27 February 1851. He was buried at St John's Church, Egremont, Wallasey. MARTIN LYNN

Sources R. C. Reid, 'Annals of the Tobin family of Liverpool and the Isle of Man', 1940, Lpool RO, Hq 920 TOB · *GM*, 2nd ser., 35 (1851), 434 · *Liverpool Mercury* (4 March 1851) · *Liverpool Mercury* (15 Oct 1819) · *Liverpool Mercury* (22 Oct 1819) · B. G. Orchard, *Liverpool's legion of honour* (1893) · G. Williams, *History of the Liverpool privateers and letters of marque* (1897) · *Gore's Directory of Liverpool* (1819–51) · B. D. White, *A history of the corporation of Liverpool, 1835–1914* (1951) · G. S. Veitch, *The struggle for the Liverpool and Manchester railway* (1930) · A. J. H. Latham, 'A trading alliance: Sir John Tobin and Duke Ephraim', *History Today*, 24 (1974), 862–7 · M. Lynn, 'Trade and politics in 19th-century Liverpool: the Tobin and Horsfall families and Liverpool's African trade', *Transactions of the Historic Society of Lancashire and Cheshire*, 142 (1992), 99–120 · B. K. Drake, 'Liverpool's African commerce before and after abolition of the slave trade', MA diss., U. Lpool, 1974

Likenesses bust, 1800–40, Walker Art Gallery, Liverpool

Tobin, John (1770–1804), playwright, was born in Endless Street, Salisbury, on 26 January 1770, the third of eight children of James *Tobin (1736/7–1817), a sugar planter and merchant of Nevis and Bristol, and his wife, Elizabeth (1744/5–1824), daughter of another Nevis planter, George Webbe.

Tobin's father, a partner of the Bristol West India merchant John Pinney, campaigned against the abolition of slavery. An older brother, Rear-Admiral George *Tobin (1768–1838), sailed on Bligh's second voyage to Tahiti and was an amateur marine painter. James Webbe Tobin (1767–1814), the eldest of the children with whom he was very close, moved in radical and dissenting circles and was a friend of Coleridge, Southey, Lamb, the philosopher William Godwin, and Sir Humphry Davy. Unlike his father, James Webbe campaigned for the abolition of slavery and was instrumental in bringing to the attention of the British public the cruelties of the Nevis planter Edward Huggins.

In 1777 James Tobin set out with his wife for Nevis in the West Indies, leaving his three eldest sons in the care of their grandfather who sent them to King Edward VI School in Southampton. When his father returned to settle in Bristol in 1784 John Tobin was sent to Bristol grammar school. In 1787 he left Bristol to be articled to a solicitor in Lincoln's Inn, taking over the partnership with three others in the office some ten years later. Disagreements arose and Tobin left to join a new firm with a Mr Ange.

A quiet, contemplative, but disorganized man, Tobin

was bored with legal work. Always interested in poetry and the theatre as a child, he devoted all of his spare time and energy to writing, trying his hand at opera and tragedy, but feeling most at ease with comedies and stage lyrics. These tended to be imitative and his explanation was that he had 'great difficulty in getting good plots, or in making them' (Benger, 38–9). One such comedy about gambling, *The Faro Table*, was provisionally accepted by Sheridan who then rejected it on the grounds that it bore too close a resemblance to *School for Scandal* and it might have libelled a well-known dowager who gambled.

In 1796 Tobin's brother James, whose eyesight was failing, came to live with him at the Temple. His brother played an important role in sustaining Tobin when thirteen of his plays (including *The Curfew* and *School for Authors*) were rejected by theatre managers. Tobin suffered again when he was persuaded to put his name to Godwin's dull play *Antonio* and attend the rehearsals to keep up the deception. Godwin was afraid that his play would be suppressed because of his radical reputation. It is not clear how far Tobin shared Godwin's political views, as in 1792 he had complained about 'the present growing system of mental tyranny' in England, but was becoming disillusioned with the outcome of the French Revolution (Benger, 28–30). Desperate to have some of his own work performed, Tobin was encouraged to get the popular actor John Shepherd Munden to stage a piece as a benefit. This early and insignificant farce, *All's Fair in Love*, was put on successfully in April 1803 but was speedily forgotten.

Tobin's final effort, *The Honey Moon*, was inspired by a discussion one day in his chambers as to how far it would be possible to revive old English comedy as it existed in the days of Shakespeare and Fletcher. Tobin set out to write a play imitative of this style. It was rejected in 1804 by Covent Garden and submitted to Drury Lane. Without knowing the result Tobin left London with some resignation to recover his failing health in Cornwall. While there he concluded that producing a new edition of Shakespeare's work would be less arduous than combating the obduracy of managers, and he began collecting materials. He was almost delirious with joy on hearing that *The Honey Moon* had been accepted; but in the meantime alarming symptoms of tuberculosis had become evident. He was told that to save his life he must winter in the West Indies. He left Cornwall to see his family in Bristol where he learned that the play was in rehearsal and his father heard of his writing activities for the first time. Tobin left for the Caribbean, possibly on board the *Pilgrim* from Bristol, in late November 1804. His ship sailed out of Cork on the afternoon of 7 December but he died that night. The ship was driven back by a contrary wind and this allowed Tobin to be buried, unmarried, in what is now known as the Lusitania graveyard near Cobh, where his father, visiting some years later, erected a plaque in his memory.

The Honey Moon, a romantic comedy written in blank verse interspersed with prose, was staged at Drury Lane on 31 January 1805, with Elliston as Duke Aranza and Bannister as Orlando, and proved a great success. Much of it was imitative as Tobin had planned and his success at this is demonstrated by the reactions to it. Hazlitt thought the plot owed much to the *Taming of the Shrew*; Genest detected reminiscences of Massinger and other Elizabethans; others saw Beaumont and Fletcher. A favourite on the English stage for twenty years and still being put on in 1869 at Sadler's Wells, it was translated into French and performed in North America. After this initial posthumous success, Tobin's rejected pieces were eagerly sought after.

The Curfew, a tragi-comedy set in feudal times alternating prose with blank verse, was produced at Drury Lane on 19 February 1807 and would have run longer than twenty nights but for Sheridan's anxiety to avoid providing a benefit for Tobin's relatives as had been agreed. Two further pieces, *The Fisherman*, an opera, and *Attraction*, were accepted by Drury Lane and Covent Garden respectively but the music was lost in a fire at these sister theatres.

The School for Authors, a prose comedy, was the next success. Based on *The Connoisseur*, one of Jean-François Marmontel's tales, this amusing and well-constructed little play owes something to Samuel Foote's *The Patron*. The part of Diaper, the sensitive author, provided a triumph for J. S. Munden when he played the role at Covent Garden on 5 December 1808. Tobin's brother, who had been an energetic literary executor, then had to set out himself for Nevis for the sake of his own failing health and no new work was staged until he began to renew pressure on theatre managers from the Caribbean.

In 1813, a year before he died, James Webbe Tobin wrote a letter from Nevis in which he noted the earlier withdrawal by Sheridan of *The Faro Table*. He noted also that on the death of the dowager it had been brought forward again and put into rehearsal. However two days before its presentation he was told that it could be considered as a satire on another lady and it was withdrawn. He continued 'Now Sir, should there be no more peeresses or ladies of quality standing in the way, I may justly require that this piece ... may be brought forward' (Benger, 157–8). This was done eventually at Drury Lane on 5 November 1816, nearly twenty years after it had been written, when the manners it satirizes were already passing away. It was not a success nor was *The Fisherman* which was staged unexpectedly in 1819.   DAVID SMALL

Sources E. O. Benger, *Memoirs of John Tobin* (1820) · C. F. Russell, *A history of King Edward VI School, Southampton* (privately printed, Cambridge, 1940), 272–94 · Genest, *Eng. stage*, 7.646–7, 8.35–8, 128–9, 586–7 · V. L. Oliver, *The history of the island of Antigua*, 3 (1899), 138 · V. L. Oliver, ed., *Caribbeana*, 5 (1917–18), 1–5 · O. Elton, *A survey of English literature, 1780–1830*, 2 (1924), 304–9 · *The letters of Charles and Mary Lamb*, ed. E. W. Marrs, 3 vols. (1975–8) · A. Nicoll, *Early nineteenth century drama, 1800–1850*, 2nd edn (1955), vol. 4 of *A history of English drama, 1660–1900* (1952–9), 412–13 · D. Mullin, ed., *Victorian plays: a record of significant productions on the London stage, 1837–1901* (1987) · D. E. Baker, *Biographia dramatica, or, A companion to the playhouse*, rev. I. Reed, new edn, rev. S. Jones, 3 vols. in 4 (1812) · P. Fitzgerald, *A new history of the English stage*, 2 (1882), 354–5 · C. A. Prance, *Companion to Charles Lamb: a guide to people and places, 1760–1847* (1983) · *Collected letters of Samuel Taylor Coleridge*, ed. E. L. Griggs, 6 vols. (1956–71) [repr. (1966)] · letterbook 19, University of Bristol Library, Pinney MSS, fols. 52, 68 · parish register (baptism), 28 March 1770, Salisbury, St Edmund's

Likenesses silhouette miniature, priv. coll.

Tod, Isabella Maria Susan (1836–1896), campaigner for women's rights, was born on 18 May 1836 in Edinburgh. Her father, James Banks Tod, was a Scottish merchant, and her mother, Maria Isabella Waddell, was a native of co. Monaghan. Tod was always proud of her Scottish blood and frequently alluded to the fact that one of her ancestors signed the copy of the solemn league and covenant at Holywood, co. Down, in 1646. Little else is known of her family background or circumstances, though she had at least one brother, Henry, a merchant who lived in London. She was educated at home, apparently by her mother, who had a profound influence on her life. By the 1860s she was living in Belfast with her mother, who remained with her until her death in 1877. For a period Tod earned her living by writing leaders for the Belfast newspaper the *Northern Whig*.

Tod first entered public life in 1867, when her paper 'On advanced education for girls of the upper and middle classes' was read for her at a meeting of the National Association for the Promotion of Social Science. The immediate result of this meeting was Tod's organization of a committee to promote alterations in the married women's property laws. In 1867 she was instrumental in establishing in Belfast the Ladies' Institute, whose original function was to provide classes for young women interested in improving their education and hence their employment prospects. The institute organized lectures on such subjects as modern languages, history, and astronomy, and it also petitioned the Queen's College, Belfast, eventually successfully, to allow women to take their examinations. Tod played a leading role in ensuring the inclusion of girls in the Intermediate Education Act (1878), which proved an important step toward making university education available to women. She was also instrumental in setting up the Ulster Schoolmistresses' Association to look after the interests of girls' education.

The difficulties involved in securing educational rights for women led Tod to believe that the acquisition of the franchise was the clearest way to secure change for women in society. In 1871 she organized the first suffrage society in the country, the North of Ireland Women's Suffrage Committee. Her speeches were widely reported in the suffrage journals and daily newspapers of both Ireland and England. She shared platforms with, and was a friend of, many of the leading English suffragists, such as Helen Blackburn, Josephine Butler, and Lydia Becker. She campaigned to ensure that women were granted the municipal franchise and was rewarded for her efforts by the granting of this franchise to Belfast women in 1887, eleven years before women in other Irish towns were bestowed with the same privilege.

From the beginning of her career Tod was a strong temperance advocate, and in 1874, with Margaret Byers, she formed the Belfast Women's Temperance Association. She established a Belfast branch of the Ladies National Association (LNA) to campaign for the repeal of the Contagious Diseases Acts and served on the executive committee of the London-based LNA until 1889. 1886 saw the introduction of Gladstone's first Home Rule Bill for Ireland. The bill was seen by Tod as the instrument that would destroy all her work. In later years she was to write:

> I can scarcely write of the sickening shock of the Home Rule proposals of 1886. Knowing Ireland thoroughly, I knew that all the social work in which I had taken so prominent a part for twenty years was in danger, and that most of it could not exist for a day under a petty legislature of the character which would be inevitable. … I shrank in horror from the revival of the religious and racial difference which was certain to ensue. (*The Queen*)

As always, Tod threw herself into a campaign to ensure that the bill would not pass. The resulting crusade, which found her canvassing in Devon, Cornwall, and London, not only lost her a number of friends in the suffrage movement but also seriously damaged her health. The last ten years of her life were devoted primarily to ensuring that home rule would not become a reality.

Isabella Tod died at her home at 71 Botanic Avenue, Belfast, on 8 December 1896. The cause of her death was given as pulmonary illness, an illness, it was claimed, that was brought on and exacerbated by the stress of her campaigns against home rule. She was buried in Balmoral cemetery, Belfast. MARIA LUDDY

Sources *Northern Whig* (10 Dec 1896) • *Englishwoman's Review*, 28 (1897), 58–63 • *Women's Penny Paper* (12 Oct 1889) • *Wings* (July 1893), 217–19 • *The Queen* (10 Sept 1892), 447 • J. Dewar, ed., *A history of Elmwood Church* (1900) • *Northern Whig* (1860–97) • *The Witness* (11 Dec 1896) • PRO NIre., MIC 15c/2/41 • parish register (births and baptisms) Edinburgh, St Cuthbert, 8 Aug 1836 • M. Luddy, 'Isabella M. S. Tod, 1836–1896', *Women, power, and consciousness in nineteenth-century Ireland*, ed. M. Cullen and M. Luddy (1995), 197–230
Likenesses group photograph, Mary Evans Picture Library • photograph, repro. in Dewar, ed., *History of Elmwood Church* • portrait, Victoria College, Belfast
Wealth at death £1463 7s. 4d.: PRO NIre., MIC 15c/2/41

Tod, James (1782–1835), army and political officer in India, born at Islington on 19 March 1782 and baptized there on 5 May, was the son of James Tod (b. 1745), and his wife, Mary, the daughter of Andrew Heatly, a Scot who settled at Rhode Island. He was educated in Scotland. In 1798 his uncle, Patrick Heatly, procured him an East Indian cadetship, and, after training at the Royal Military Academy, Woolwich, he went (March 1799) to Bengal, arriving on 26 August; he was posted to the 2nd European regiment (ensign's commission dated 9 January 1800). After volunteering for service with Lord Wellesley's projected expedition to the Moluccas, he served for a short time with the marines on board the *Mornington*. Appointed on 29 May 1800 lieutenant in the 14th Bengal infantry, he went up country; in 1801, when stationed at Delhi, he was ordered to survey an old canal in the neighbourhood. In 1805 he was attached to the escort sent with his friend Graeme Mercer, envoy and resident at Sindhia's court. While travelling with the maharaja's camp, and afterwards from 1812 to 1817 when it remained at Gwalior, he was constantly surveying or collecting topographical information. In 1815 he submitted a map to the governor-general (Lord Hastings), in which for the first time the term 'central India' was applied to the Indian states later under the central India agency. Rajputana was also included in the area of his researches. He wrote:

> Though I never penetrated personally further into the heart of the Indian desert than Mundore … my parties of discovery have traversed it in every direction, adding to their journals of routes living testimonies of their accuracy, and bringing to me natives of every *t'hul* from Bhutnair to Omurkote and from Aboo to Arore. The journals of all these routes, with others from Central and Western India, form eleven moderate-sized folio volumes. (Tod, *Annals of Rajasthan*, 2, 1832, 289)

Most of Tod's extra salary was spent in paying his Indian explorers. In October 1813 he was promoted captain, with command of the resident's escort; and in October 1815 the resident, Richard Strachey, nominated him second assistant.

When Lord Hastings, in 1817, began operations against the Pindaris, Tod's local knowledge became invaluable. He had already sent in reports on the Pindaris and plans of a campaign, and on volunteering for service was sent to Rowtah in Haraoti, where he organized and superintended an intelligence department, which in the governor-general's opinion contributed significantly to the success of the campaign. He also induced the regent of Kotah to capture and surrender to the British officers the wives and children of the leading Pindari chiefs.

In 1818, after the chiefs of Rajputana had accepted the protective alliance offered to them, Tod was appointed by the governor-general political agent in the western Rajput states, and was so successful in his efforts to restore peace and confidence that within less than a year some 300 deserted towns and villages were repeopled, trade revived, and, in spite of the abolition of transit duties and the reduction of frontier customs, the state revenue had reached an unprecedented amount. During the next five years Tod earned the respect of the chiefs and people, and was able to rescue more than one princely family, including that of the ranas of Udaipur, from the destitution to which they had been reduced by Maratha raiders. Bishop Heber, who travelled through Rajputana in February 1825, was told that the country had never known prosperity until Tod came, and that everyone, rich or poor, except thieves or Pindaris, loved him. According to Heber, because Tod so favoured Indian princes, the Calcutta government suspected him of corruption, and consequently limited his powers and associated other officers with him until he was disgusted and resigned; but the government later came to believe its suspicions were groundless. However, ill health was the reason given for Tod's retirement in June 1822, though it did not prevent his journeying to Bombay by the circuitous route described in *Travels in Western India*, published after his death.

Tod left Bombay for England in February 1823, and never returned. The rest of his life was mostly spent in arranging and publishing the immense mass of materials accumulated during his Indian career. He also acted for a time as librarian to the Royal Asiatic Society, before which he read several papers on his favourite subjects. According to the *Gentleman's Magazine*, 'to him also belongs the praise of having initiated the study of Indo-Grecian antiquities'

(204). On 1 May 1824 he was promoted major, on 2 June 1826 lieutenant-colonel, being retransferred to the 2nd European infantry, and on 28 June 1825 he retired from the service. On 16 November 1826 he married Julia (1808/9–1850), third daughter of Henry *Clutterbuck MD, a London physician, and they had two sons and a daughter.

Thenceforth Tod lived much on the continent, and in 1827 visited Comte de Boigne, Sindhia's old general, at Chambéry. Tod published archaeological papers in the Royal Asiatic Society's *Transactions*; a paper on the politics of western India, appended to the report of the House of Commons committee on Indian affairs, 1833; *Annals and Antiquities of Rajasthan* (1829–32); and *Travels in Western India* (1839), with an anonymous memoir of Tod.

In September 1835 Tod bought a house in Regent's Park, London, and on 16 November, his wedding anniversary, while transacting business at his banker's, Robarts & Co., in Lombard Street, had an apoplectic stroke from which he never recovered. He died at Regent's Park on 18 November 1835, aged fifty-three.

STEPHEN WHEELER, rev. ROGER T. STEARN

Sources J. Tod, *Annals and antiquities of Rajasthan*, 2 vols. (1829–32) • J. Tod, *Travels in western India* (1839) • *Journal of the Royal Asiatic Society of Great Britain and Ireland*, 3 (1836), lxi • *Asiatic Journal*, new ser., 21/1 (1836), 165 • V. C. P. Hodson, *List of officers of the Bengal army, 1758–1834*, 4 (1947) • *GM*, 2nd ser., 5 (1836) • P. Moon, *The British conquest and dominion of India* (1989) • T. A. Heathcote, *The military in British India: the development of British land forces in south Asia, 1600–1947* (1995)

Likenesses drawing, *c*.1820, V&A • gouache drawing, *c*.1820, V&A

Tod, Marcus Niebuhr (1878–1974), ancient historian and epigraphist, was born at The Park, Highgate, Middlesex, on 24 November 1878, the second son of John Tod, a tea merchant originally from Leith in Scotland, and his wife, Gertrude von Niebuhr. His maternal grandfather was Marcus von Niebuhr, the son of the historian B. G. Niebuhr. Brought up in a strongly Presbyterian family, he was educated at Merchant Taylors' School, London (1892–7), where he concentrated on Greek and Latin, and went up to St John's College, Oxford, with a scholarship in 1897. He emerges in his long correspondence with his elder brother, James, as intensely competitive, both at school in a manner typical of the way public school boys were expected to behave, and at Oxford. Firsts in classical moderations (1899) and Greats (1901)—the latter, he was told, the best first of his year—were followed by the award of a senior studentship at the British School of Archaeology at Athens, where he spent the next four years (1901–5), together with a senior scholarship at St John's, and the university's Craven travelling scholarship. It is not known whether he applied for the studentship at Athens as the result of any particular influence in his undergraduate teaching, but he would have heard lectures by H. F. Pelham, who had played a major part in the foundation of the British School at Athens and was during Tod's undergraduate career engaged in promoting the foundation of the British School at Rome.

Tod was elected to a fellowship at Oriel College, Oxford,

in 1903 but was granted leave to remain in Greece. After returning to England in 1905 he became tutor in ancient history at the college. Among his pupils was his younger sister, Constance, who was reading Greats at Somerville College, and through her he met Mabel Bowker Byrom (1887–1973), daughter of George F. Byrom, a cotton mill owner of Manchester. They were married on 8 September 1909 and had a son and a daughter.

Tod's early research was mostly on the inscriptions of Sparta, an interest retained throughout his career. In 1907 he was appointed university lecturer in Greek epigraphy at Oxford (becoming reader in 1927), his wider interest in Greek epigraphy emerging in his *Greek International Arbitration* (1913), the chapter on clubs and societies in his *Sidelights on Greek History* (1932), and in his lectures at Oxford on Greek dramatic performances.

On the outbreak of the First World War, Tod worked initially for the Ministry of Labour in Oxford. In the autumn of 1915 he worked with the YMCA on the western front, where he found that the troops did not share his own strong religious commitment. It was characteristic of his eirenic and generous nature that he collected published material to be given to German and Austrian scholars after the war was over. From November 1915 to January 1918 and from March 1918 to February 1919 he was in Salonika, first as an interpreter and then as a captain in the intelligence corps decoding ciphers, for which his training in epigraphy equipped him well. He was mentioned in dispatches three times, was awarded the Croix de Guerre, and was appointed OBE.

On his return to Oxford, Tod settled into the standard mix of lecturing, tutorials, and administrative duties for university and college, serving as secretary to the royal commission, and as vice-principal of Oriel from 1934 to 1945. At least one of his pupils remembered his tutorials as rarely responding to the essay which had been read, but as consisting of a lecture on the topic set, which was the same for everyone.

Tod was best known for the two volumes of *Greek Historical Inscriptions*, which superseded the *Manual of Greek Historical Inscriptions* edited by E. L. Hicks. The first volume, extending to the end of the fifth century BC, was published in 1933, the second, covering the fourth century, appearing in 1948. They were dedicated to Adolf Wilhelm, whose lectures on Greek epigraphy Tod had attended while a student in Athens, the lectures being conducted in the Epigraphical Museum, in front of the stones. In 1903 he had expressed a desire to participate in R. C. Bosanquet's scheme for excavation in Laconia; digging was to take place only as an adjunct to 'exploration'—what would later be called archaeological survey. Despite the advanced nature of these ideas, in his later work Tod treated 'historical' inscriptions as those illuminating the great cruces of Greek history defined by the literary tradition. His annotations in his own copy of Dittenberger's *Sylloge inscriptionum Graecarum* are bibliographical, without noting either corrections to the text or material relevant to its interpretation; many of his publications were indeed bibliographical in nature. He was elected a fellow of the British Academy in 1929; it is hard to think that a record such as his up to that date would have led to election in later periods. His meticulousness and eye for detail underlay his work on Greek numerical systems and coin denominations, as it did the generosity with which he read, commented on, and contributed to the work of others.

When Tod retired in 1947 honorary fellowships were conferred on him by Oriel and St John's colleges. He settled in Birmingham, and died on 21 February 1974 in Sheldon Hospital, Rubery, his wife having predeceased him in the previous year.   MICHAEL H. CRAWFORD

Sources R. Meiggs, *PBA*, 60 (1974), 485–95 · Oriel College, Oxford, M. N. Tod MSS · *An address presented to Marcus Niebuhr Tod on his seventieth birthday with a bibliography of his writings* (1948) · books, articles, and other materials annotated by M. N. Tod, priv. coll. · P. A. Brunt, autobiographical memoir, British Academy · b. cert. · m. cert. · d. cert.
Archives Oriel College, Oxford, MSS | Bodl. Oxf., corresp. with J. L. Myres, 39, 29–37; 49, 145–54; 77, 143–5, 163, 166; 80, 65
Likenesses Lafayette, photograph, repro. in Meiggs, *PBA*
Wealth at death £33,732: probate, 26 April 1974, *CGPLA Eng. & Wales*

Tod, William (*c*.1718–1799), linen manufacturer and financial agent, was born into an Edinburgh mercantile family. He started his business career in the late 1730s, in partnership with Ebenezer MacCulloch, as a retailer of linen in the Luckenbooths area of the city. Shortly thereafter they set up a linen 'factory' at Leith which brought them to the notice of the board of trustees for fisheries and manufactures, and won them important patronage. Lord Milton, with whom Tod was to maintain contact until Milton's death in 1763, secured for them in 1743 the running of the board's colony of French fine-linen weavers at Picardy Place in Edinburgh. From this was to grow a much bigger scheme for the manufacture of linen in Scotland. The Edinburgh Linen Company was established in 1744 with a capital of £20,000, but the need for more finance could be satisfied only by securing a royal charter, which conferred limited liability on the shareholders. Tod was closely involved in protracted negotiations at London, which finally succeeded in July 1746.

This early experience of lobbying was to stand Tod in good stead over the following decades, when he acted as the board of trustees' agent at London, gathering intelligence about any proposed changes in legislation affecting the linen industry. This appointment, however, was abruptly terminated in 1766 when he supported a proposal to allow French linen into Britain on payment of a moderate duty. The board strongly disapproved, wishing to retain the existing prohibition, a policy which, Tod argued, merely promoted smuggling. Tod also undertook specific missions on behalf of the trustees. He went to Germany in 1745 to find out how linen was manufactured there, leaving MacCulloch to manage the company's affairs during the Jacobite occupation of Edinburgh. Ten years later he and another experienced manufacturer undertook a tour of the highlands in order to advise the board on how best to use the funding that parliament had

just provided to promote the development of linen manufacturing in that region.

Central to all Tod's activities during this period was his role, with MacCulloch, as joint manager of the British Linen Company, established in 1746. While MacCulloch looked after the company's manufacturing operations, Tod focused on the marketing and found himself increasingly at London, where a series of agents had proved unsatisfactory. In 1756 he moved there permanently, to act as the company's factor. Tension grew with MacCulloch over the quality and cost of the company's linen, and in 1759 Tod resigned as manager to set up as a linen factor in London; his business there traded as Tod & Co. Within a few years the British Linen Company under MacCulloch's management was—as Tod had predicted—in severe financial straits. MacCulloch departed, but the survival of the company was in doubt for a considerable time, and no dividend was paid for ten years. Tod took advantage of the depressed price to become, by 1780, the company's largest shareholder. This gave him considerable leverage, and he was a favoured borrower from the company, using his stockholding as security. His firm, which had its office in Milk Street, was used to handle all the company's purchases of government stock. Other services that Tod performed included lobbying for a renewal of the company's charter in 1774. Recognition came in the form of his election as deputy governor of the British Linen Company in 1795, when he had begun to withdraw from day-to-day involvement in his own business. As correspondence confirms, he died in August 1799 at home in Percy Street, Soho, London. Company stock with a face value of nearly £30,000 was subsequently transferred to his three sons, who had already benefited from his gifts of stock. During the next decade they divested themselves of these holdings to considerable advantage; shares which Tod had bought in the early 1770s at less than half of par had quadrupled in value by 1812.   ALASTAIR J. DURIE

Sources A. J. Durie, 'Contrasting careers: the first managers of the British Linen Company, 1745–1800', *Enterprise and Management*, ed. D. H. Aldcroft and A. Slaven (1995), 229–50 · A. J. Durie, *The Scottish linen industry in the eighteenth century* (1979) · C. A. Malcolm, *The history of the British Linen Bank* (privately printed, Edinburgh, 1950)
Archives Bank of Scotland, Edinburgh, British Linen Company MSS · NL Scot., Saltoun MSS
Wealth at death £29,638 in company stock: British Linen Company stock transfer ledger, Bank of Scotland, Edinburgh, archives department

Todd, Alexander Robertus, Baron Todd (1907–1997), organic chemist, was born on 2 October 1907 in Newlands Crescent, Cathcart, Glasgow, the elder son and second of the three children of Alexander Todd (1877–1952), a clerk in the Glasgow Subway Railway Company, who later became managing director of the Drapery and Furnishing Co-operative Society, Glasgow, and his wife, Jean Ramsay, *née* Lowrie (*d*. 1945), third daughter of Robert Lowrie, a foreman engineer from Polmadie. His parents were both from unprivileged Scottish families who had bettered themselves by hard work and respect for education. His younger brother, Robert (*b*. 1912), and older sister, Jean (*b*.

Alexander Robertus Todd, Baron Todd (1907–1997), by Kristinn Ingvarsson, 1989

1903), showed no inclination towards the sciences. Todd was educated first at Holmlea public school, Cathcart, and from 1918 at Allan Glen's School in Glasgow, a high school which emphasized the teaching of mathematics, physics, and chemistry. He shone in all subjects except drawing, which led his art master to comment on the sense of humour of his parents in giving him the initials A. R. T.

Early research In 1924 Todd entered Glasgow University as a pensioner to read chemistry, a subject he had pursued practically at home since receiving a chemistry set at the age of eight. At Glasgow he attracted the attention of the professor of organic chemistry, T. S. Patterson, who offered him a problem connected with the Walden inversion as a final-year project. This led to Todd's first publication—a paper entitled 'The action of phosphorus pentachloride on ethyl tartrate', co-authored with Patterson, and published in the *Journal of the Chemical Society* in 1929, a year after he had graduated BSc with first-class honours. With the financial support of a Carnegie scholarship, Todd then worked with Patterson on the optical rotatory dispersion of mannitol, but he found the subject dull and uncongenial.

Since the 1860s organic chemistry had become defined as the chemistry of carbon compounds; but Todd wanted to return to the early nineteenth-century tradition of Berzelius, in which the term organic chemistry referred to the chemistry of substances in living organisms. Accordingly, in October 1929 he began doctoral research under Walther Borsche at the University of Frankfurt am Main. Todd had a flair for languages (later he taught himself Russian, Mandarin, and Hebrew) and he became fluent in German. The only other English students at Frankfurt were A. L. Morrison and Bertie K. Blount, who became lifelong friends. The Frankfurt laboratories were expensively equipped compared with the primitive conditions Todd

had experienced in Glasgow, and he rapidly became proficient in microanalysis—a necessary technique in biochemical research. At Borsche's suggestion he seized the opportunity of working on the structure of a constituent of bile, cholic acid, and specifically its degradation product, apocholic acid. Work on his seven-membered ring structure for cholic acid was published in German in 1931 and challenged the structural interpretations that had gained H. O. Wieland and A. Windaus the Nobel prize, but soon proved erroneous. Todd never worked on steroid chemistry again. An attempt to work in Moscow with the Russian chemist N. D. Zelinsky on natural products fortunately proved abortive. Instead, having completed his DrPhilNat at Frankfurt in 1931, Todd was invited by Robert Robinson, Britain's leading organic chemist, to the University of Oxford on an 1851 Exhibition senior scholarship.

Robinson was fascinated by the chemistry of plant pigments and shared Todd's addiction to solving *The Times* daily crossword puzzle. Between 1931 and 1934 Todd successfully completed an investigation in the Dyson–Perrins Laboratories (which, like Glasgow's, were poor compared to those at Frankfurt) on the synthesis of red and blue 3,5-diglucosidic anthrocyanins of the rose, pelargonium, wild mallow, and peony (hirsutin, pelargonin, malvin, and cyanin), gaining his second doctorate as DPhil in 1933. Todd's period in Oxford, during which he lived in Oriel College, proved stimulating and productive and led to an outstanding friendship with Robinson, who sponsored Todd's election to the Royal Society in March 1942. Together at Oxford they also worked out the constitution of the coloured metabolic products of species of pathogenic moulds of *Helminthosporium*.

In 1934 Todd was awarded a Medical Research Council grant to work under George Barger in the medical school of the University of Edinburgh on the structure of thiamin (vitamin B_1), with a view to its commercial synthesis by the Swiss pharmaceutical company Hoffmann-La Roche. In 1935 Todd, as well as Windaus in Germany, showed that thiamin was composed of a thiazole (a 5 atom ring containing sulphur and nitrogen) linked to a pyrimidine. Although the first complete synthesis of vitamin B_1 was made by the American biochemist R. R. Williams in 1935, Todd (with the help of Franz Bergel) independently developed an industrial synthetic route in 1937 that enabled Hoffmann-La Roche to become a major player in the vitamin manufacturing market. The grateful company supported much of Todd's later research.

In Edinburgh, Todd met the Cambridge-educated physiologist Alison Sarah Dale (1905–1987), the eldest daughter of the physiologist Sir Henry Hallett *Dale. She was then doing post-doctoral research in pharmacology. They were married on 30 January 1937 and had a son, Alexander Henry (Sandy; *b*. 1939), who became a chemist, and two daughters, Helen Jean (*b*. 1941) and Hilary Alison (*b*. 1946).

The contact with Dale was of great significance in furthering Todd's career in biomedical science and as a scientific statesman. In 1936, on the recommendation of Dale, Barger, and Robinson, Todd joined the Lister Institute of

Preventive Medicine in Chelsea Bridge Road, London, as a lecturer (and later, reader) in biochemistry. Years later, when he came to examine Robinson's private papers to write an obituary, Todd discovered that Robinson's reference had stated that while Todd would be good for the Lister Institute, he doubted whether the institute was good enough for Todd. At the institute Todd began preliminary studies of the structure of vitamin B_{12}, completed at Cambridge with A. W. Johnson and Dorothy Hodgkin in 1955, as well as vitamin E (from which he isolated the active principle, α-tocopherol). He also began the investigation of cannabinol, an inactive constituent of cannabis, showing it to be derived from dibenzopyran. The latter research brought him into brief conflict with the Home Office, which accused him of illegal possession of the drug. The matter ended amicably, with generous acknowledgements being made to the Home Office official in all of the published papers on the subject.

Manchester and Cambridge By 1937 Todd had established himself as the most innovative and productive of younger British organic chemists. In that year he was invited to teach bio-organic chemistry in the USA at the California Institute of Technology at Pasadena; he and his wife visited in the following year, making friends with important American scientific figures in their travels. While on the point of accepting the position in 1938 Todd was invited to succeed I. M. Heilbron as the Sir Samuel Hall professor of chemistry at the University of Manchester. Because this was the second most prestigious chair of organic chemistry in Britain, Todd decided to accept and to remain in Britain.

Todd bonded immediately with Michael Polanyi, his opposite number in physical chemistry, with whose anti-socialist views on the freedom of science from state interference he agreed. Mancunian chemistry, deriving from the German tradition, had always flourished when two professors worked in harmony (as with Roscoe and Schorlemmer, Perkin and Dixon, and Robinson and Lapworth), and Todd and Polanyi proved no exception. The experience of being head of the well-equipped Manchester laboratories proved invaluable. Todd learned how to administer a large department, and to organize, sustain, and co-ordinate a complex research programme. Todd completed a synthesis of α-tocopherol in 1938 and began his most important work on the structure of nucleic acids. He did not neglect his old interest in colouring matters, publishing on the chemical structure of blood coagulants and the colouring matters of the haemoglymph of aphids.

The Second World War temporarily disrupted Todd's plans for deeper involvement in natural products chemistry of cellular metabolites. During the war he engaged in research for the Ministry of Supply on chemical warfare agents that were never used; for the chemical defence research department on the hatching factor in the parasitic potato eelworm, and blood coagulants; and he worked as a member of the Anglo-American penicillin research programme. Although he succeeded in showing that penicillin possessed a lactam (cyclic amide) structure, no successful synthesis was discovered.

The nucleic acid research programme was continued at the University of Cambridge where, having refused an invitation to succeed Sir Gowland Hopkins in the chair of biochemistry in 1943, Todd was appointed, in 1944, professor of organic chemistry in succession to William Pope and fellow of Christ's College. Unlike Manchester, the Cambridge laboratories in Pembroke Street, which had been erected in 1886, had been poorly maintained during the inter-war years and were overcrowded and technically unsuited to modern conditions. Todd therefore took the post only on the condition that major improvements, such as the replacement of gas by electric light, were made immediately. After the war he superintended the design and erection of new laboratories in Lensfield Road which were opened in 1958. He later deplored the physicists' decision to rebuild the Cavendish Laboratory in west Cambridge, fearing damage to Cambridge science by such split-site development.

Nucleic acid research Living organisms are the most complex of chemical systems. Since the 1870s organic chemists interested in natural products had largely confined their attention to the analysis and synthesis of chemical substances extracted from living materials. Biochemists, on the other hand, had begun to examine the dynamic interactions of such compounds within living systems, using new insights generated by physical chemistry. Although much of Todd's early work was concerned with the chemistry of natural products, using synthesis as a way of elucidating and confirming structures, he moved closer to biochemistry when, as a consequence of his work on vitamins, he saw that the determination of their structures could be used as a guide to the functions of these biologically important compounds. Research on vitamin B_1 raised the issue of its specificity in breaking down the pyruvic acid formed in carbohydrate metabolism. This led Todd to the realization that it, as well as other vitamins, acted as co-enzymes (in this case co-carboxylase, or diphosphothiamine) in metabolic processes. By the mid-1930s work by the Russian-born American biochemist P. A. Levene on the degradation of the nucleic acids by hydrolysis, had revealed them to be composed of a small number of nucleotides that contained sugars and organic bases that were related to well-known purines and pyridines, such as adenine, guanine, uracil (or thymine), and cytosine. Nucleotides themselves could be hydrolysed into nucleosides and phosphoric acid.

Given this existing chemical knowledge it was Todd's key insight that many of these fragments were related to the B-group vitamins and other intermediate molecules such as adenosine diphosphate and triphosphate (ADP and ATP) that played fundamental roles in metabolism and energy exchanges, and which were themselves clearly products of nucleic acid degradation. To this end, and over a twenty-year period, he and his co-workers developed new methods of synthesizing purines and pyrimidines, as well as their sugar derivatives, the glycosides (nucleosides). This enabled deductions to be drawn concerning the structure of nucleosides, and the processes of phosphorylation whereby nucleosides could be built into nucleotides. Such studies demanded deeper understanding of organic phosphate chemistry and of phosphorylation using dibenzyl phosphorochloridate or diesters of phosphorous acid. Todd's ambitious research programme at Cambridge embraced, among many other successes, the synthesis of the energy-providing coenzyme ATP (adenosine triphosphate, 1948), and FAD (flavin–adenine dinucleotide, 1954). The development of pathways for polynucleotide synthesis also had a great bearing on the elucidation of the structures of ribonucleic and deoxyribonucleic acids (RNA and DNA). Todd's synthesis of nucleotides with Don Brown in 1952 established unequivocally that the sugars in both RNA and DNA were linked to specific nitrogen atoms of a purine or pyrimidine ring by a β-glycosidic bond. Further syntheses of nucleotides by phosphorylation of nucleosides confirmed such linkages, as did enzymatic degradation of the nucleic acids, which gave identical nucleotides. Todd's work, using chromatography and ion-exchange methods, therefore confirmed that both RNA and DNA contained 3′, 5′ linked polynucleotides, the links being made by phosphoric acid residues.

Once Todd had made a preliminary announcement concerning the structures of nucleic acids at the seventy-fifth anniversary meeting of the American Chemical Society in 1951, he became an inevitable candidate for the Nobel prize for chemistry, which duly arrived in 1957. His nominators were not unmindful of the fact that Todd's work on the structures and syntheses of nucleosides, nucleotides, and their coenzymes, as well as the related problems of their phosphorylation, had proved to be a necessary preliminary to the elucidation of the double-helix structure of DNA by James Watson and Francis Crick in 1952. It had also inspired the interest of Linus Pauling. Francis Crick later stated that 'on the chemical side it would not have been possible to build correct models without the general formula for DNA, established largely by the work of Lord Todd and his colleagues' (Crick, 198–9). Ironically Todd had chosen to work on nucleic acids because they were puzzling chemical compounds, not because (as became clear after 1940) they were genetic materials.

By the mid-1950s the traditional techniques of degradation and synthesis that had guided Todd's elucidation of molecular structures had started to be outflanked by new, quicker physical methods of X-ray crystallography and various forms of spectroscopy, as well as by molecular orbital theory. While Todd was receptive to the advantages of these methods he did not find them congenial, commenting in 1974 that had such techniques existed in the 1920s he would have chosen to be a biologist, not a chemist. Such techniques took the joy and fascination of chemical thought away. Most of Todd's work was published in *Nature* and the *Journal of the Chemical Society*, with occasional forays into the *Biochemical Journal*. He was always scrupulous and generous in his collaborative papers, generally placing his name last rather than first.

He was never 'very interested in what other [chemists] do' and 'always wanted to be out in front' (Todd, 'Chemistry of life'). Under Todd's post-war direction Cambridge became filled with international co-workers, including (unusually during the cold war) Russian students.

Todd retired from his Cambridge chair to make way for a younger person in 1971, but continued as master of Christ's College (a position he had held since 1963) until 1978. The eighteen Manchester co-workers who moved to Cambridge with Todd formed the Toddler's Club in 1971 and met for a reunion dinner every May thereafter. Todd declined the offer of becoming vice-chancellor of the University of Cambridge on his retirement, but was proud to accept the position of becoming the first chancellor of the University of Strathclyde in 1965. He remained in this honorary position until 1991, and was always delighted to draw pints of beer in the students' bar, named the Lord Todd.

Statesman of science Together with Perkin, Robinson, and Ingold, Todd was among the most creative of twentieth-century British organic chemists. However, although he continued to supervise and publish chemical work up to his retirement, from 1957 onwards he became essentially a statesman of science. Once the war had ended his services were increasingly sought by outside bodies and he served on many committees. In 1946, at the instigation of his former Frankfurt and Oxford friend Bertie Blount, who was in charge of chemical research in the British zone of occupation, Todd was asked by the Foreign Office to visit Germany to help put German science back on its feet. He played an important part in ensuring that the great chemical reference aids of Beilstein and Gmelin stayed in German publishers' hands. In the same year, the Worshipful Company of Salters reactivated its Institute of Industrial Chemistry and invited Todd to help in its post-war efforts to encourage students towards industrial careers. He served as master of the livery from 1961 to 1962. Todd had established close contacts with chemical industry since his postgraduate days, advising on ICI's dyestuffs group research committee from 1939 to 1949 and acting as a director of Fison's Ltd between 1963 and 1978.

Through the influence of his father-in-law, Sir Henry Dale, who had served on the scientific advisory committee to the war cabinet, Todd joined its peacetime successor in 1947, the Advisory Council on Scientific Policy. His membership stimulated an interest in the relations between science, government, and industrial development that increasingly dominated his career. Although his membership under the chairmanship of Sir Henry Tizard officially ended in 1951, he was made Tizard's successor a year later. A knighthood followed in 1954, a life peerage in 1962 (when he chose the motto *Faire sans dire* for his arms and Trumpington as his territorial designation, since he lived in this Cambridge parish), and the Order of Merit in 1977. He took enormous pleasure in the fact that his wife could claim that both her father and husband had been Nobel laureates, presidents of the Royal Society, and holders of the Order of Merit.

Todd resigned from the advisory council in 1964, fore-seeing correctly that the Labour victory in the 1964 election would lead to changes in science policy with which he fundamentally disagreed. (He had never been close to his former Manchester colleague, the physicist Patrick Blackett, whose socialist views on the organization of science became approved Labour policy.) Nevertheless, having previously been a leading member of the inquiry under Sir Burke Trend into the organization of the civil service that called for the creation of a minister of science and improvements in the ways of delivering scientific advice to government, Todd agreed to serve as chairman of a royal commission on medical education, which ran from 1965 to 1968 and which recommended the transformation of the medical curriculum and an expansion in the numbers of both doctors and medical schools. With the return of a Conservative government in the 1980s Todd agreed to serve as chairman of the advisory council's successor, the parliamentary and scientific committee, and filled the post from 1983 to 1986.

Todd's brilliant performance as a government scientist and his fame as a Nobel prizewinner led to many other calls on his time outside the Cambridge laboratory. He was a governor of the United Cambridge Hospitals from 1969 to 1974. In 1950 he had been made a trustee of the Nuffield Foundation and he was its chairman from 1973 to 1979. During his time as a trustee the foundation was persuaded to fund the great radio telescope at Jodrell Bank, and to underwrite the Nuffield science teaching projects that transformed school science curricula in the 1960s. Todd was a trustee of the Ciba Foundation from 1963. His valuable experience with such philanthropic organizations also led to his appointment as a trustee of the Croucher Foundation of Hong Kong, and he was its president from 1988 until his death. In 1955 Todd was appointed a member of the International Union of Pure and Applied Chemistry, serving as its president in 1963–5, and in 1957 he participated in the discussions with Sir Winston Churchill and the fund-raising that led to the creation of Churchill College, Cambridge; he became an honorary fellow of the college in 1971. By some ruthless chairmanship of the syndics of Cambridge University Press between 1971 and 1975, Todd also successfully steered the press away from certain bankruptcy to commercial success.

The highest honour that British science can bestow, the presidency of the Royal Society, came in 1975. During his period of office, which ended in 1980, Todd succeeded in making the society much more international in outlook. He also used his four presidential orations to express his strongly held views on science policy—science and freedom of enquiry (1976 and 1978), his abhorrence of the way university expansion had occurred in the wake of the Robbins report (1977), and his dismay at the breakdown of the dual-support system of university research funding, which he had always supported (1979). He had already adumbrated some of these themes in a hard-hitting presidential address, 'A time to think', delivered to the British Association in 1970. Primarily stressing Britain's need to train more young people as technicians rather than as academics, this lecture attracted left-wing demonstrators dressed as nuclear corpses outside Durham Cathedral, where it was delivered.

Todd was awarded the Davy (1949), royal (1955), and Copley (1970) medals of the Royal Society. Honorary degrees were conferred upon him by more than twenty universities, including Glasgow, Edinburgh, Manchester, Leicester, London, Kiel, Strasbourg, Madrid, Harvard, Yale, California, Melbourne, Sydney, Adelaide, Aligarh, Hokkaido, and Hong Kong. He was a visiting professor at Caltech (1935), the University of Chicago (1948), Sydney (1950), and the Massachusetts Institute of Technology (1954). He was an honorary member of most national chemical societies and many science academies, and received medals from several of them, including the Lomonosov medal (1986) of the USSR Academy of Sciences. He was particularly pleased to be made an honorary fellow of the Royal College of Physicians in 1975. He served as president of the Science Masters' Association (1956), the Chemical Society (1960–62), and the Society of Chemical Industry (1981–2).

In the aftermath of the award of a Nobel prize it was inevitable that Todd should be invited to lecture at conferences all over the world, and many of his published papers and addresses became repetitious as the contents were recycled for different audiences. Nevertheless, he continually showed skill in writing historical reviews, such as the shrewd Royal Society memoir of Robinson (written with Sir John Cornforth in 1976), and lectures for important occasions, where he was free to state his Olympian views on education, industry, and many other matters that his long experience in the corridors of power gave him the authority to pronounce upon. In 1983 he published an entertaining and thoughtful autobiography, *Time to Remember*.

Despite a constant, hectic round of daily research supervision, lecturing, overseas travelling (which he loved), and chairing meetings, Todd's health remained good. A gall-bladder operation in 1949 was taken with equanimity (he had successfully synthesized cholesterol, he told Robinson, who was initially fooled by this wordplay). He took a heart attack in 1970 more seriously, and ceased chain-smoking. Although he had played tennis well as a young man, his mature recreations were fishing, golf, and gardening, coupled with drinking and debating with his large circle of academic, industrial, and political friends. Quick-witted, impulsive, and indefatigable, Todd was an unashamed élitist and patrician. His politics were firmly to the right of centre and he did not suffer fools gladly. Tony Benn, who sat next to him at a degree luncheon at Strathclyde University in 1969, noted that Todd was 'an impossibly arrogant and vain man' (*The Guardian*, 15 Jan 1997). Known as Lord Todd Almighty by undergraduates, his staff, and colleagues at Cambridge, he was the subject of innumerable witty limericks, such as:

Doesn't it strike you as odd
That a commonplace fellow like Todd
Should spell, if you please,

His name with two D's
When one is sufficient for God?
(*The Times*, 22 Jan 1997)

He was a master of committee management, commenting that 'it is the chairman's job to commit, not to committee'.

Todd stood well over 6 feet 6 inches tall, slim in build, and with an imposing head of initially blond and latterly snow-white hair. He naturally dominated any group, a dominance enhanced by a deep, gruff voice and compelling Glaswegian accent. Usually impeccably dressed in a pinstriped suit, Todd was easily mistaken for a city businessman. Both diffident and arrogant in character, he avoided the press and media when possible, despite asserting unpopular or controversial views that attracted their attention (for example, that comprehensive education was bound to mean a lowering of educational standards). Privately he was an affable, sociable man, and he and his wife were proud to have entertained every undergraduate who attended Christ's College. Lady Todd was the perfect complement to her husband: shy, modest, and retiring, where he was extrovert, masterful, and gregarious. Following her death in 1987, Barbara Mann, one of his 'Toddlers', who had acted as his Cambridge secretary since 1944, cared for Todd.

Todd died from heart disease and pneumonia at Midfield Lodge Nursing Home, Cambridge Road, Oakington, Cambridgeshire, on 10 January 1997. He was survived by his son and two daughters. His ashes were buried in the master's garden of Christ's College. A memorial service was held at St Margaret's Church, Westminster, London, on 16 July 1997.   W. H. BROCK

Sources A. R. Todd, *A time to remember: the autobiography of a chemist* (1983) · 'Chemistry of life: an interview with Lord Todd', *Chemistry in Britain*, 10 (1974), 207–14 · D. M. Brown and H. Kornberg, *Memoirs FRS*, 46 (2000), 515–32 · A. Eschenmoser, 'Lord Todd, an appreciation', *Orden pour le mérite für Wissenschaften und Künste*, 27 (1997), 31–7 · J. Mason, 'Address at the memorial service for Lord Todd, 16 July 1997', *Royal Society News* (Oct 1997) · J. G. Buchanan, 'Lord Todd', *Advances in Carbohydrate Chemistry and Biochemistry*, 55 (1999), 1–13 · R. J. Paradowski, 'Todd', *The Nobel prize-winners: chemistry*, ed. F. N. Magill (1990), 2.666–79 · P. Melius, 'Alexander Robertus Todd', *Nobel laureates in chemistry, 1901–1992*, ed. L. K. James (1993), 399–405 · H. Kornberg, 'Lord Todd', *Nuffield Foundation report for 1996* (1996), 10–11 · J. Maddox, 'Alexander Todd', *Nature*, 385 (1997), 492 · J. Baddiley, 'Lord Todd, 1907–97', *Chemistry in Britain*, 33/4 (1997), 70 · 'Lord Todd', *Interdisciplinary Science Reviews*, 22 (1997), 7–9 · *Daily Telegraph* (14 Jan 1997) · *The Guardian* (15 Jan 1997), 13 · *The Times* (15 Jan 1997) · *The Times* (18 Jan 1997) · *The Times* (22 Jan 1997) · *The Times* (18 July 1997) · *The Independent* (16 Jan 1997) · *The Scotsman* (16 Jan 1997) · WWW · *Debrett's Peerage* (1990), 1203 · *Burke, Peerage* · Lord Todd and J. W. Cornforth, 'Robert Robinson, 13 September 1886 – 8 February 1975', *Memoirs FRS*, 22 (1976), 415–527 [obit. of R. Robinson] · H. Chick, M. Hume, and M. Macfarlane, *War on disease: a history of the Lister Institute* (1971) · R. W. Clark, *A biography of the Nuffield Foundation* (1972) · F. H. Portugal and J. S. Cohen, *A century of DNA* (1977) · F. H. C. Crick, 'DNA, a cooperative discovery', *Annals of New York Academy of Science* (1995), 198–9 · A. Benn, *Office without power: diaries, 1968–72* (1988) · d. cert.
Archives CAC Cam., official papers · CUL, papers relating to work as chairman of the Royal Commission on Medical Education · priv. coll., personal papers | CAC Cam., trustees' meeting papers · ICL, corresp. with Lord Jackson · RS, collection of offprints |FILM Nobel Institute, Stockholm, 1957 Nobel prize ceremony |SOUND BL NSA, performance recording
Likenesses A. Newman, bromide print, 1978, NPG · W. E. Narraway, oils, 1979, RS · M. Noakes, oils, *c*.1979, Nuffield Foundation, London · K. Ingvarsson, photograph, 1989, NPG [*see illus.*] · N. Sinclair, bromide print, 1993, NPG · photograph, repro. in *Daily Telegraph* · photograph, repro. in *The Times* (15 Jan 1997) · photograph, repro. in *The Guardian* · photograph, repro. in *The Independent* · photograph, repro. in *The Scotsman*
Wealth at death £1,762,561: probate, 6 May 1997, *CGPLA Eng. & Wales*

Todd, Alpheus (1821–1884), librarian and constitutional historian in Canada, the son of Henry Cooke Todd, an author, was born in London on 30 July 1821. He emigrated with his family to York, Upper Canada, in 1833, and the following year, when York was incorporated as Toronto, produced an *Engraved Plan of the City of Toronto*. This work brought him to the notice of the lawyer Robert Baldwin Sullivan, who helped him gain employment in the library of the house of assembly of Upper Canada in 1835, and in 1836 he became assistant librarian. Keenly interested in British parliamentary practice and its relevance to Canada, he published *The Practice and Privileges of the Two Houses of Parliament* (1840), which was officially adopted for the use of Canadian members, who hitherto had had no such guide. In 1841 Todd was made assistant librarian to the assembly of the united province of Canada, and subsequently was appointed constitutional adviser to both houses of the legislature, a task for which his intimate knowledge of parliamentary precedent made him admirably suited. In 1856 he visited Europe to restock the library, which had suffered two serious fires. His canny buying there and his subsequent additions left the library with 55,000 volumes by 1865. On his return from Europe in 1856 he was made chief librarian. In 1867 he was appointed librarian at Ottawa to the dominion parliament, an office which he held until his death, judiciously stocking and efficiently organizing the library.

Todd's most important published work was *On Parliamentary Government in England* (2 vols., 1867–9), which met with acclaim at the time and soon ran to further editions and foreign-language translations. He sought to vindicate the power of the monarch and saw the rising tide of democracy with considerable foreboding. His work was extensively used in Britain and its dominions and in the development of parliamentary institutions in nineteenth-century Japan. Todd was special adviser in 1873 to the governor-general, Lord Dufferin, to whom he dedicated *Parliamentary Government in the British Colonies* (1880), which extended his study of the granting of responsible government by Britain to its possessions, particularly Canada, and in which he again stressed the continuing role of the crown, and therefore the governor-general.

In 1845 Todd married Sarah Anne St John. They had a daughter and four sons, one of whom, Arthur Hamlyn, edited second editions of his father's two main works and left an unpublished life of him. Todd was a keen student of the Bible and in 1837 entered the ministry of the Catholic Apostolic church. He was dissuaded from giving up his secular appointment only by the arguments of the church authorities themselves. From 1874 he had charge of the apostolic congregation at Ottawa, and at one point during this time of a second in the United States.

In 1881 Todd was made honorary LLD of Queen's College, Kingston, and was created CMG. He died suddenly at Ottawa on 22 January 1884. Of humble parentage and largely self-taught, he influenced the practice of government over much of the British empire through his meticulously researched publications.

H. R. TEDDER, rev. ELIZABETH BAIGENT

Sources DCB, vol. 11 · *Toronto Weekly Mail* (24 Jan 1884) · *The Globe* [Toronto] (23 Jan 1884) · E. R. Cameron, 'Alpheus Todd', *Canadian Bar Review*, 3 (1925), 440–47

Todd, Anthony (*bap.* 1718, *d.* 1798), foreign secretary of the Post Office, was born at Bridge End Farm, Frosterley, in co. Durham, and baptized at Stanhope, co. Durham, on 20 February 1718; he was the second son and fourth child of Thomas Todd (*bap.* 1677, *d.* 1765/6), farmer, and his wife, Eleanor Todd (*d.* 1773), of Dalton-le-Dale, co. Durham. His parents, who may have been related, since they had the same surname, worked Bridge End Farm and were near neighbours of Ferdinando Craggs, brother of the postmaster-general James Craggs (1657–1721). The Westgarth family, which enjoyed close connections with the Post Office, also lived nearby.

Todd was probably educated at Wolsingham grammar school but from about 1732 he was trained in Post Office business by Charles Westgarth (*d.* 1733), clerk of the west road. John Westgarth, a clerk in the foreign office of the Post Office, subsequently gave him instruction in that organization's handling of diplomatic correspondence and overseas mail, and in its interception of suspicious items. In 1738 Todd was appointed to the foreign office, and in 1747 was made second clerk to George Shelvocke (1702–1760), secretary of the Post Office. Such pluralism was unusual but arose from the upsurge of secret service business following the Jacobite rising of 1745. Todd was the obvious successor as foreign secretary of the Post Office when John Lefebure died in January 1752. This made him responsible for supervising the opening and copying of foreign correspondence, liaison with the deciphering branch to deal with intercepted items in code, and making recommendations to be laid before the king. As such he was in regular contact with the secretaries of state and the first lord of the Treasury. He enjoyed an annual income of about £850 but only £200 of this was official salary, the rest being secret service money. Todd soon recognized the existing system's over-reliance upon a small and ageing staff and made two recommendations, which were accepted by George II in 1754. These resulted in the appointment of a fourth copying clerk and the instruction of two young trainees in the arts of engraving forged seals and of opening and deciphering correspondence. Todd's foresight paid considerable dividends during the Seven Years' War, and in 1762 he was awarded a gift of £500 for his services to the late king. At the same time his official salary was increased by £100 a year.

On 12 June 1758 Todd married Ann Robinson (*d.* 1765), the daughter and heir of Christopher Robinson (*d.* 1762) of Appleby, Westmorland, resident surveyor in the Post Office. Her first cousin was the influential John Robinson, Treasury secretary under Lord North. The marriage brought Todd £5000, with which he purchased an estate of about 150 acres at Walthamstow, Essex. His father-in-law's death in 1762 brought him property in the City of London and at Sandal, Yorkshire, as well as £9000 in trust for his family. His wife gave birth to three daughters between 1761 and 1765 but the family's very happy home life came to an abrupt end when the third birth destroyed her health, and she died on 7 August. The youngest child survived her mother by only two months.

When Shelvocke died in March 1760 Pitt supported Todd for the resulting vacancy of secretary of the Post Office but Newcastle chose Henry Potts. Todd despised Potts and did everything in his power to undermine him but ministerial changes transformed his fortunes. In December 1762, several months after Bute succeeded Newcastle at the Treasury, Potts was dismissed. Todd replaced him but remained foreign secretary, which gave him unprecedented control over the Post Office and the secret and private offices. His annual income was now nearly £2000 and between 1763 and 1765 he carefully built up his own connection. All the existing Post Office clerks were retired or transferred and the department became filled with his own dependants. His relations with the board were excellent and he claimed credit for the Franking Act of 1765.

When Rockingham took office in July 1765 joint postmaster-general Lord Hyde informed Grantham that Todd was 'experienced, able, active, obliging and honest' (PRO, 30/8/64) and he was confirmed as foreign secretary within days. However, Rockingham's dismissal of the secretaries of state and the postmasters-general left Todd 'in a violent funk' (*Eglinton MSS*, 390) and on 19 July the new ministers restored Potts as secretary to the Post Office. Todd was obliged to withdraw to the secret office and to bear the loss of half his income. On Potts's sudden death, on 1 January 1768, Todd was immediately reappointed by the Chatham ministry to his old position, while again remaining foreign secretary.

For the next fifteen years Todd remained at the zenith of his influence and prestige. He enjoyed the confidence of successive postmasters-general, not least that of Francis Dashwood, eleventh Baron Le Despencer. With his backing Todd introduced several important innovations; in particular the collection of letters from London receiving houses was improved in 1769, the system of expresses was reformed in 1770, and a 'penny post office' was established in Dublin in 1773. Le Despencer supported Todd's determination to protect the office from excessive political interest. Demands from MPs to appoint their local postmasters and a number of patronage requests from Lord North were all turned down. In return Todd looked after the joint postmaster-generals' interests and dependants, while continuing to advance his own increasingly powerful connection.

The American War of Independence diverted attention

from reform to government service. Todd's robust health enabled him to endure a necessarily arduous workload. He was frequently at his desk until 3 a.m. and became renowned in the office for telling hilarious jokes designed to keep up everybody's spirits. Rising costs, the loss of forty boats, and serious damage to others hampered communication with the army in America but Todd's efforts successfully maintained a fleet for service. He also guarded against waste and fraud and promptly reverted to a peacetime establishment in 1783. His activities brought him highly lucrative rewards. He was worth at least £60,000 in 1782, with an annual income approaching £4000, over half of which was derived from poundage on packet expenditure.

In 1782 Todd secured a brilliant marriage for his second and only surviving daughter, Eleanour (1762–1856), to James, Viscount Maitland (1759–1839), son of the seventh earl of Lauderdale and at that time MP for Newport. Lauderdale, who had amassed substantial debts, accepted Todd's offer of £30,000, and the marriage took place at Walthamstow on 15 August 1782. On his wedding day Maitland was promised £1000 for each child of the marriage, and to Todd's delight a grandson, later the ninth earl, was born on 12 February 1784. A further eight siblings followed.

Todd's new son-in-law provided a valuable link to Charles James Fox, while the successful careers of his own friends gave him similar contact with the younger Pitt and his supporters. Todd considered himself 'above being of any one party whatever' (Lauderdale MSS, priv. coll. 26 July 1782) but several new factors began to threaten his influence. As the movement for economical reform gathered pace there were repeated Treasury inquiries and his poundage fees were strongly criticized. Burke's act of 1782, which substantially reduced the annual total of secret service money, resulted in Todd receiving less than £2000 for the secret office, compared with the previous £7100. In addition the government now required a daily service with the continent for intelligence purposes. Outport merchants also demanded faster posts. Motivated by a desire for increased revenue and greater efficiency William Pitt became interested in the plans of John Palmer (1742–1818) to use coaches to secure faster inland posts. Todd, who favoured mail carts, resorted to a variety of spoiling tactics to prove Palmer's scheme impracticable, including attempts to impose unworkable timetables, publication of partial revenue statistics, and the running of mail carts in direct competition. The foreign secretary, the marquess of Carmarthen, also clashed with Todd over appointments and salaries within the secret office. In 1786 Pitt persuaded Todd to drop his opposition to Palmer's scheme, and in return Pitt supported Todd against Carmarthen and forced Lord Tankerville, one of the postmasters-general, to resign over a minor issue, in August 1786. Tankerville was unwilling to go quietly and his kinsman Charles Grey took up his case in the Commons in May 1787, by demanding an investigation into abuses in the Post Office. When Pitt agreed to refer this to the existing commission for inquiry into fees in the public offices Todd embarked on defensive action. In July 1787 he resigned as foreign secretary, in favour of his nephew John Maddison (1741–1808), which effectively secured the latter's endowment for life. The commission's report, published at the end of May 1788, was unsparing in its criticism, and Todd was explicitly blamed for permitting the sailing packets to be wastefully run and his poundage was roundly denounced. It was clearly easier for his critics to recommend the abolition of sinecures, including the foreign secretaryship, and the replacement of fees and perquisites by salaries, than to grapple with the genuine administrative problems or to acknowledge Todd's previous valuable reforms.

In the late 1780s Todd, now over seventy, began to suffer ill health and thereafter made little effort to influence policy. When the new establishment of 1793 suppressed the controller-general's place Todd was once more left unrivalled in the office. He now enjoyed an annual salary of £1000 and a further £400 a year as compensation for perquisites; he was also allowed to retain his existing shares in the packets. Most of the work in the office was already being undertaken by Francis Freeling (1764–1836), the resident surveyor, who was made joint secretary in 1797, when the octogenarian Todd was no longer able to attend. The board allowed him to remain at home in Walthamstow on full salary, an arrangement that was shortly afterwards condemned by a Commons' committee as unwarrantable and extravagant indulgence. The joint postmasters-general ignored these criticisms but ordered Todd to sell his share in the *Grantham* packet boat.

On 18 April 1798 Todd's growing infirmities convinced him that he should draw up his will, in which the bulk of his estimated £80,000 fortune was bequeathed in trust for his daughter and grandchildren. He died at his house at Walthamstow on 8 June 1798. In the Post Office he continued to be remembered as 'a man of singular abilities and generally beloved' (Ackermann, 2.234). Freeling succeeded as secretary and remained in office until 1836.

PATRICK WOODLAND

Sources K. Ellis, *The Post Office in the eighteenth century: a study in administrative history* (1958) • H. Robinson, *Britain's Post Office* (1953) • B. Kemp, *Sir Francis Dashwood: an eighteenth-century independent* (1967) • *GM*, 1st ser., 54 (1784), 154 • *GM*, 1st ser., 68 (1798), 541 • *GM*, 1st ser., 68 (1798), 720 • *The Jenkinson papers, 1760–1766*, ed. N. S. Jucker (1949) • *Memoirs of a highland lady: the autobiography of Elizabeth Grant of Rothiemurchus*, ed. J. M. Strachey (1898) • R. Ackermann, *Microcosms of London*, 3 vols. (1904), 2.234 • GEC, *Peerage* • IGI • J. Ehrman, *The younger Pitt*, 1: *The years of acclaim* (1969) • HoP, *Commons, 1754–90* • L. B. Namier, *The structure of politics at the accession of George III*, 2nd edn (1957) • J. Norris, *Shelburne and reform* (1963) • *Reports on the manuscripts of the earl of Eglinton*, HMC, 10 (1885)
Archives BL, Add. MSS Aukland, 34413–34414; Hardwicke, 35413; Liverpool, 38201–38204, 38339, 38357; Newcastle, 32731–32735; Wallis, 32499; Willes, 24321, 32253–32309; 45518–45523 • Bodl. Oxf., Dashwood MSS, C.13 • Bodl. Oxf., North MSS • PRO, Chatham papers, 30/8 • PRO, material on secret activities, state papers, esp. FO 83/5; HO 33/1–4; 42/206–14; 79/1–4 • PRO, Treasury letter-books, official corresp. relating to General Post Office

Todd, Barbara Euphan (1897–1976), writer, was born at the vicarage, Arksey, near Doncaster, Yorkshire, on 9 January 1897, the daughter of Thomas Todd, vicar of Arksey, and his wife, Alice Maud Mary, *née* Bentham. Educated at St Catherine's School, Bramley, Guildford, Surrey, she left school in 1914, and during the First World War worked on the land and served as a voluntary aid detachment nurse. Since childhood she had written stories and poems, and after the war her work was published in a number of magazines. She made a name as a contributor and reviewer for *Punch*, using as a pseudonym her second forename Euphan. She wrote poems about children in a style highly reminiscent of A. A. Milne, which were received with great admiration and later collected in two volumes suitably illustrated by Ernest Shepard. On 5 November 1932 she married Commander John Graham Bower (1886–1940), a retired naval officer who had been in the Submarine Service and received the DSO; the son of Sir Graham John Bower, formerly colonial secretary of Mauritius, he was the divorced husband of Doris Violet Coghlan-White. Bower too was a writer, and they sometimes collaborated, he using the pseudonym Klaxon. Both liked dogs and enjoyed the English countryside and its customs, settling in the Berkshire village of Blewbury. They had no children.

In 1936 Todd published *Worzel Gummidge, or, The Scarecrow of Scatterbrook*. Her eponymous hero, with his turnip head, a body that had seen better days, and his habit of retreating into his trademark 'sulks' at the appearance of adults, became one of the most popular literary characters of the 1930s. The period between the wars was rich in immortal literary characters for children, and the appeal of 'this moody disagreeable boggart' seems to lie in those very qualities, at a time when children's fiction still reflected a degree of civility and respectability almost unimaginable today (Crouch, 62). Gummidge is rude, dirty, and innocent of the rules that govern adult society, and he gives the protected city children who befriend him the chance to be the same. He is an unreliable ally, timing his sulks so that adults are confronted with an inanimate scarecrow, two guilty children, and the evidences of his latest wrongdoing, but he is kind-hearted, well-intentioned, and wholeheartedly on the side of the country and its wildlife. Todd created memorable subsidiary characters, notably the motherly Earthy Mangold who marries the eternally lovesick Gummidge, the morose Hannah Harrow, and the cheerful Little Upsidaisy, whose collective exploits eventually filled ten books. Todd wrote other books but the ones featuring Gummidge, with his imperturbable logic and country sayings 'stands to reason', 'ooh aye', and 'humans is daft', were the only ones to achieve lasting fame. This occurred partly because a wide variety of media distributed the Gummidge stories. The original book was serialized on BBC *Children's Hour* and it

was chosen to be the first title in Puffin paperbacks, the high-quality children's series launched by Penguin in 1941. A television series, *Worzel Gummidge Turns Detective*, was made in 1953.

Todd, a widow since 1940, continued to write, publishing her last book in 1972, and played an active role in village life, where she was known for her excellent conversation. She died of chronic bronchitis at the Donnington Hayes Nursing Home, Donnington, Berkshire, on 2 February 1976. A second television series, freely adapted from the Worzel Gummidge books by Keith Waterhouse and Willis Hall and starring Jon Pertwee as the scarecrow, ran between 1978 and 1981, giving new life to Todd's most famous creation. By the 1980s, a generation that had grown up with the character used the term 'Worzel Gummidge' to denote anybody of untidy appearance.

Todd's career as an author spanned a half-century of immense change in the world of children's writing. The quaintness of her poems dates them irretrievably, and the Gummidge stories are beginning to look old-fashioned, although the original Worzel Gummidge book has remained in print. It is possible that the idea of Worzel Gummidge, the dirty and disreputable child/man with his sharp tongue and his confident and utterly misplaced logic, will survive the books and continue its existence in the territory of children's classics.

ELIZABETH J. MORSE

Sources *The Times* (14 Feb 1976), 16 · T. Chevalier, ed., *Twentieth-century children's writers* (1989) · H. Carpenter and M. Prichard, *The Oxford companion to children's literature* (1984) · B. Doyle, *The who's who of children's literature* (1968) · M. Crouch, *Treasure seekers and borrowers: children's books in Britain, 1900–1960* (1962) · M. Fisher, *Who's who in children's books* (1975) · M. Fisher, *Intent upon reading*, rev. edn (1964) · D. Pringle, *Imaginary people: a who's who of fictional characters*, 2nd edn (1996) · b. cert. · m. cert. · d. cert. · *WWW* [John Graham Bower] · *CGPLA Eng. & Wales* (1976)
Wealth at death £51,422: probate, 1976, *CGPLA Eng. & Wales*

Todd, Sir Charles (1826–1910), astronomer and meteorologist, was born in Islington, London, on 7 July 1826, the eldest son of Griffith Todd (1799–1878), a grocer of Greenwich, and his wife, Mary Parker (b. 1804). Educated in Greenwich until the age of fourteen Todd was then employed as supernumerary computer at the Greenwich Royal Observatory, and soon showed ability in mathematics and as an observer. In 1848 he became assistant astronomer at Cambridge University observatory where, in charge of the great Northumberland equatorial telescope, he was one of the early observers of the planet Neptune, discovered in 1846. With the same telescope he made one of the first attempts at astronomical photography, taking a daguerreotype picture of the moon. He also assisted with the determination by telegraphy of the difference in longitude between Cambridge and Greenwich.

In 1854 Todd returned to Greenwich as superintendent of the galvanic apparatus for the transmission of time signals, working closely with the Electric Telegraph Co. and with C. V. Walker, an electrical engineer who was a pioneer experimenter with submarine cables. During this time Todd became fascinated with the new communication technology of the telegraph. In 1855, in response to a request from the South Australian government, the astronomer royal, G. B. Airy, recommended Todd to the Colonial Office for the post of observer and superintendent of that colony's electric telegraph. Appointed on 10 February 1855, Todd married eighteen-year-old Alice Gillam Bell (1836–1898) in the Baptist Chapel at Cambridge on 5 April and they sailed for Australia on 29 July, accompanied by a technical assistant, Edward Charles Cracknell, and his wife. They arrived in Adelaide on 4 November.

In South Australia, Todd encountered the only existing private telegraph, a short line from the city of Adelaide to its port. He immediately set up a government line over the same route, which opened on 21 February 1856. Its rapid success led the government to purchase and dismantle the private line. In July 1856 Todd negotiated, on behalf of the South Australian government, with Samuel McGowan, Victoria's telegraph superintendent, for an intercolonial line connecting Adelaide and Melbourne. After returning on horseback along the 300 miles of the South Australian route from Portland to Adelaide he brought the telegraph service into use in July 1858. Meanwhile telegraph systems had been developing in the adjoining colonies of New South Wales and the island of Tasmania. Supported by their respective heads of government an Adelaide–Melbourne link opened in July 1858 with connections to Sydney in October, and via submarine cable to Launceston and Hobart (though only for one year) in 1859–60. By the time the line reached Brisbane, Queensland, in 1861, there were 110 telegraph stations connected to the network in the four mainland colonies.

As early as 1859, in request from Sir Richard MacDonnell, governor of South Australia, Todd had prepared a proposal to be submitted to the colonial secretary for a line to cross the continent from Adelaide to Port Darwin, in the extreme north. His preparation was helped by the exploration of the interior by John McDougall Stuart, although as late as 1869 Todd regarded a submarine cable via the west coast or off Queensland to be the more practical route. By this time the British Australia Telegraph Company (later the Eastern Extension Co.) was planning a cable from Singapore via Java to Port Darwin, where a connection could be made to an Australian land line, thus uniting Australia telegraphically with the rest of the world.

In January 1870 the telegraph and postal departments of South Australia amalgamated. Todd was appointed postmaster-general, a title normally reserved for government ministers. In April that year he reported in favour of an overland line linking Port Augusta to Port Darwin in the Northern Territory, and only recently acquired by South Australia. Legislation was hurried through the South Australian parliament in June 1870, and the colony bore the entire cost of laying the line, across nearly 2000 miles of mostly unknown country, under Todd's supervision. Communication with Britain was achieved on 21 October 1872; celebratory banquets were held three

weeks later, Todd was made CMG, and became an Australian hero. Between 1874 and 1877 a line spanning the continent from east to west practically completed the Australian system, which finally extended over 5000 miles.

Although Todd's major preoccupations until the late 1870s were with telegraphy and with his onerous duties administering South Australia's post and telegraph service, he gave increasing attention to his other two great preoccupations: astronomical and meteorological observations. From 1860 he had lived at the observatory in Adelaide. In 1868 he confirmed his suspicions that the fixing of the longitude 141° meridian boundary between New South Wales and South Australia was inaccurate (actually it was 2⅓ miles to the east of the original boundary). He subsequently made observations of Venus (1874 and 1882), establishing a temporary station at Wentworth in New South Wales. As a fellow of the Royal Astronomical Society (from 1864) he published a series of notes on the phenomena of Jupiter's satellites in the society's *Monthly Notices*.

By the late 1870s Todd had become well known as one of a small number of pioneering meteorologists in the Australian colonies. After corresponding with H. C. Russell in Sydney and R. L. J. Ellery in Melbourne, Todd met them (and also James Hector from New Zealand) at intercolonial meteorological conferences in 1879 and 1881, when they agreed on standard procedures and protocols for their regular weather reports, making use of the extensive network of telegraph stations throughout the Australasian colonies. This co-operative ethos was challenged after a third intercolonial meeting in 1888, attended by the abrasive Clement Wragge, the Queensland meteorologist based in Brisbane—about the time these meteorologists had the confidence to issue weather forecasts. Wragge confidently issued forecasts for all the Australian colonies from his self-styled 'Chief Weather Bureau' Thereafter, Todd engaged in private and public disputes with Wragge about the accuracy of their respective weather forecasts for South Australia throughout the 1890s.

Todd attended more of the many technological intercolonial conferences held in colonial Australasia than any other technocrat: twenty post and telegraph meetings, three gatherings of meteorologists, and conferences of surveyors and electricity experts. He exercised immense influence as the most experienced, persuasive, and versatile departmental head who accompanied ministers to these gatherings: as, for example, in 1893, when he persuaded the colonial ministers to endorse his preferred model of one standard time zone for the whole continent (based on Adelaide time) rather than the three time zones in the draft recommendation—although the three zones were subsequently introduced in the Australian colonies two years later. Todd's knighthood in 1893 marked the high point of his influence in technological matters in the colonial, intercolonial, and imperial circles in which he operated.

Driven by his goal of serving South Australia's interests, Todd, in the late 1880s and 1890s, provided technical advice to his political masters in South Australia to help undermine or delay the Pacific cable scheme, which was a threat to his colony's commercial interests through the overland telegraph's links with Eastern's cable monopoly into Australia. He was the key technical figure in Australia who collaborated with Eastern in its perennial divide and rule policy, culminating in the laying of the Cape cable from South Africa to Western Australia and to Adelaide in 1900, thus seriously dividing the Australian colonies at the time of their federation.

In 1866, during his only visit to Britain from Australia, the University of Cambridge made Todd an honorary MA. He was elected fellow of the Royal Society in 1889, and was also a fellow of the Royal Meteorological Society and of the Society of Electrical Engineers. He died at his summer home, Esplanade, Sea-Wall, Semaphore, near Adelaide, on 29 January 1910, and was buried at North Road cemetery, Adelaide, on 31 January.

H. P. HOLLIS, rev. K. T. LIVINGSTON

Sources State Library of South Australia, Adelaide, Royal Geographical Society of Australasia (SA) Library, G. W. Symes MSS • G. W. Symes, 'Todd, Sir Charles (1826–1910)', AusDB, 6.280–82 • G. W. Symes and B. J. Ward, 'Charles Todd and the overland telegraph', Proceedings of the Royal Geographical Society of Australasia, South Australian Branch, 81 (1980–81), 59–72 • K. T. Livingston, The wired nation continent: the communication revolution and federating Australia (1996) • R. W. Home and K. T. Livingston, 'Science and technology in the story of Australian federation: the case of meteorology, 1876–1908', Historical Records of Australian Science, 10 (1994–5), 109–27 • A. Moyal, Clear across Australia: a history of telecommunications (1984) • J. Jenkin, The Bragg family in Adelaide: a pictorial celebration (1986) • P. Taylor, An end to silence: the building of the overland telegraph line from Adelaide to Darwin (1980) • A. Moyal, Invention and innovation: the historian's lens (1986) • F. Clune, Overland telegraph: the story of a great Australian achievement and the link between Adelaide and Port Darwin (1955) • m. cert. • The Advertiser [Adelaide] (31 Jan 1910), 6–7
Archives NRA, corresp., diaries, notebooks, and papers • State Library of South Australia, Adelaide, Mortlock Library of South Australia, state records | National Archives of Australia, Adelaide, postmaster-general's department of meteorology • National Archives of Australia, Melbourne, McGowan MSS • NRA, letters to H. Y. L. Brown • Public Record Office, Laverton, Victoria, Ellery MSS • RAS, letters to Royal Astronomical Society • Royal Geographical Society of Australasia Library, Adelaide, Symes MSS
Likenesses lithograph, repro. in Sydney Mail (14 July 1877), supplement • photographs, repro. in Taylor, End to silence

Todd, Dorothy Annie [Ann] (1907–1993), actress, was born on 24 January 1907 at Crumley House, Hartford, near Northwich, Cheshire, the daughter of Scottish parents, Thomas Todd, a clerk in an alkali works, and his wife, Constance, née Brooke. Her brother was the playwright Harold Brooke. She was educated at St Winifred's boarding-school in Eastbourne and studied at the Central School of Speech Training and Dramatic Art, with the aim of teaching drama herself. She changed her mind after her début, in January 1928, as a fairy in Yeats's The Land of Heart's Desire at the Arts Theatre, and she appeared later that year as Lady Prudence Willowby in Wodehouse's A Damsel in Distress at the New Theatre. Many roles, few memorable, quickly followed: between 1929 and 1939 there were almost twenty parts at a dozen West End theatres. By the time of her appearance in The Man in Half-moon Street at the

New (1939), as a younger woman in love with an older man with a past, she had moved from the froth of the early 1930s to more serious work.

Throughout the decade Todd was equally busy in films, making her début in the melodrama These Charming People (1931), from Michael Arlen's play, followed by Keepers of Youth and The Ghost Train (both 1931, from plays by Arnold Ridley). The Water Gypsies (1932), from A. P. Herbert's novel, was her first showcase role, and she played Drummond's (Ralph Richardson's) kidnapped wife in The Return of Bulldog Drummond (1934). On 6 December 1933 she married Victor Neill Malcolm, an engineer and the grandson of Lillie Langtry, with whom she had a son. Further films included the costly science-fiction epic Things to Come (1936), from H. G. Wells's novel, a version of Edgar Wallace's The Squeaker (1937), Poison Pen (1939), and Ealing's melodrama Ships with Wings (1941). Most were routine ingénue roles, but Todd impressed as the neurotic wife of the squire (Ralph Richardson) in South Riding (1938). She also starred in the first ever British television serial, Ann and Harold (BBC, 1938). Having divorced Malcolm, on 27 October 1939 she married the writer Nigel Trevithick Tangye (1909–1988), with whom she had a daughter. Back on stage Todd was a lively Peter Pan (1942) at the Winter Garden, then scored her biggest success in Lottie Dundass (1943), an all-woman production at the Vaudeville, followed by a fine performance as a murderess, Madeleine Smith, in The Rest is Silence (1944) at the Prince of Wales. Although her brief time on screen in Perfect Strangers (1945) was praised by critics, Todd became an international star overnight with her film performance as the emotionally disturbed pianist Francesca Cunningham in the psychological drama The Seventh Veil (1945). The scene in which her Svengali-like guardian (James Mason) smashed his cane down on the keyboard at which Todd played became particularly notorious; she was suddenly in great demand. Blonde, with almost sphinx-like features, high cheekbones, and deep-set blue eyes, she had a glacial beauty. She signed, with Rank, what was at the time the biggest contract offered to a British actress. A Hollywood career, however, failed to materialize: she had the lesser female role in Hitchcock's talky, stodgy The Paradine Case (1947), and the brooding So Evil my Love (1948, and made in England), though good, was not popular. At home The Passionate Friends (1949) was a sensitive, entertaining, romantic drama; having divorced Tangye, she then married the film's director, David *Lean (1908–1991), on 21 May 1949. He directed her in Madeleine (1950, a reprise of her 1944 stage role), which was not a success, and The Sound Barrier (1952), in which she again appeared with Ralph Richardson, this time as his daughter. She and Lean divorced in 1957. Facial injuries sustained during an assault and robbery led to Todd's making fewer films; Losey's Time without Pity (1956) had been a sombre drama, Taste of Fear (1961) was a good Hammer thriller, and The Fiend (1971) was disturbing horror. Her last films were Preminger's unexciting spy film The Human Factor (1979) and the confusing thriller The McGuffin (1985).

In the 1950s, though, Todd was busy again on the stage.

She reprised her role in *The Seventh Veil* (1951) at the Prince's Theatre, but, oddly, it was not successful. She played Lady Macbeth at the 1954 Edinburgh festival with the Old Vic company, and played it again, along with roles in *Love's Labour's Lost*, *The Taming of the Shrew*, and *Henry IV*, parts 1 and 2, in its 1954–5 season. She was Jennifer Dubedat in a revival of *The Doctor's Dilemma* (1956) at the Saville and made her Broadway début, at the Cort Theatre, as Davina Mars in *The Four Winds* (1957). Her final stage appearance was at the Yvonne Arnaud Theatre, Guildford, as Florence Lancaster in a favourite play, Coward's *The Vortex* (1965). Thereafter she forged a new career as a documentary filmmaker, narrating, directing, and producing a series of travelogues, or 'diary documentaries' as she called them. Often made in exotic locations, they included *Free in the Sun* (Australia), *Thunder in Heaven* (Nepal), *Thunder of Silence* (Jordan), *Thunder of the Kings* (Egypt), and *Thunder of the Gods* (Greece).

Todd's autobiography, *The Eighth Veil* (1980), was 'an intelligent account of a varied, if not always happy, life' (*The Times*, 19). In 1989 Durham University awarded her an honorary DLitt. In her later years she made frequent radio and television appearances. Away from acting she enjoyed writing, painting, and gardening. Following a stroke, Todd died on 6 May 1993 at Chelsea and Westminster Hospital, London.   ROBERT SHARP

Sources *The Times* (7 May 1993), 19 · *The Independent* (7 May 1993), 22 · *The Guardian* (7 May 1993), 12 · *The Guardian* (18 May 1993), 17 · www.uk.imdb.com, 31 Aug 2001 · I. Herbert, ed., *Who's who in the theatre*, 1 (1981) · *Daily Telegraph* (8 May 1993) · b. cert. · m. certs. · d. cert.
Likenesses photographs, Hult. Arch.
Wealth at death £155, 637: probate, 1993, *CGPLA Eng. & Wales*

Todd, Elliott D'Arcy (1808–1845), army officer in the East India Company, was born on 28 January 1808 in Bury Street, St James's, London, the third and youngest son of Fryer Todd, accountant, of Chancery Lane, a Yorkshire gentleman of good family and originally wealthy. His mother was Mary Evans, the 'Mary' of Samuel Taylor Coleridge. His father lost his money by speculation, the home was broken up, and Elliott D'Arcy Todd, when three years old, came under the care of his maternal uncle, William Evans, of the East India Company's home establishment. He was educated at Ware, Hertfordshire, and in London, and, through his guardian's influence, entered the company's military college, Addiscombe College, in 1822, passing out in December 1823.

Todd was commissioned second lieutenant in the Bengal artillery on 18 December 1823, landed at Calcutta on 22 May 1824, and was stationed at the artillery headquarters at Dum-Dum until the rainy season of 1825, when he was posted to the 4th company 3rd battalion of foot artillery at Cawnpore. His company joined Lord Combermere's army for the second siege of Bharatpur. When the place was taken on 18 January 1826 Todd received a subaltern's share of the prize money amounting to £250, and the same year he was posted to the 1st troop 2nd brigade of the horse artillery; but, on promotion to first lieutenant on 28 September 1827 he reverted to the foot artillery. He was

posted in 1828 to a horse artillery troop at Mathura. In January 1829 he moved to Karnal, where bad health compelled him to go on sick leave to the hills.

On 2 March 1831 Todd was transferred to the 1st troop 1st brigade horse artillery. He studied Persian with such success that the Indian government, who, among their efforts to enable the shah of Persia to maintain his independence, had decided in 1833 to send British officers to instruct the Persian army, selected Todd to serve with the regular Persian troops under Colonel Pasmore, and to be artillery instructor. He embarked at Calcutta on 7 August, and arrived at Tehran on 28 March 1834. After the death of Shah Fatteh Ali and the accession of Muhammad Shah, a firman was issued on 31 July 1835 placing all matters connected with artillery in Todd's hands.

Todd took great pains in drilling the artillery at Tehran, and received from the shah the second class of the order of the Lion and Sun. Sir Henry Ellis, British minister at Tehran, was much impressed by a critical paper by Todd on Burnes's *Military Memoir on the Countries between the Caspian and the Indus*. Ellis wrote to Lord Auckland, the governor-general, urging the necessity of a political agent at Kabul, and recommending Todd.

In the autumn of 1836 Todd was at Tabriz as military secretary to Major-General Sir Henry Lindesay Bethune, commanding the Persian legion trained by British officers, but when Bethune declined to accompany the shah's troops beyond Khorasan and returned to Tehran, Todd was sent, in January 1837, by John McNeill (1795–1883), British minister, to travel by the shores of the Caspian, Ghilan, and Rudbar, to Qazvin, and thence to Tehran. For his report on this route he received a complimentary letter from Palmerston. He was granted the local rank of major while specially employed on service in Persia. In March 1838 Todd accompanied the British minister to the Persian camp before Herat, where he arrived on 6 April. Todd was employed by McNeill to negotiate with the Heratis, and, as it was the first time a British officer had appeared in Herat in full uniform, 'a vast crowd went out to gaze at him' (Kaye, *History*, 1.256). The negotiations failed, and in May Todd carried dispatches from McNeill to Lord Auckland. He travelled as an Englishman, but in Afghan dress and without baggage, and his route was by Kandahar, Kabul, and Peshawar. He arrived at Simla on 20 July, having accomplished the ride in sixty days.

On 1 October 1838 Todd was appointed political assistant and military secretary to William Hay Macnaghten, the British envoy and minister to Shah Shuja. He was promoted to be brevet captain on 18 December 1838. He arrived with Sir John Keane's army at Kandahar in April 1839. Eldred Pottinger was the political agent at Herat, but it was decided to send Todd on a special mission to negotiate a treaty with Shah Kamran, whose chief minister, or wazir, was Yar Muhammad, of whom Kaye has written 'of all the unscrupulous miscreants in Central Asia, Yar Mahommed was the most unscrupulous' (*History*, 1.218). The mission left Kandahar in June, and arrived at Herat on 25 July. A treaty was concluded with the Shah Kamran, by which he was allowed 25,000 rupees a month on certain conditions, one of which was that he should have no communication with Persia without the consent of the British envoy. A committed Christian, Todd loathed the slave trade and the cruelties of the Herati government. M. E. Yapp has suggested that 'a more cynical, less scrupulous unambitious man might have been a better envoy at Herat' (Yapp, 364). Todd favoured British annexation of Herat, but Auckland refused it. After Pottinger's departure for Kabul in September 1839 things went on smoothly at Herat for some months. One of the objects of the mission was to try to stop the slave trade by the central Asian peoples. In this traffic Yar Muhammad, the khan of Khiva, and the Turkoman peoples towards the Caspian were the chief offenders. In December 1839 Todd, on his own responsibility, sent Captain James Abbott, one of his assistants, on a friendly mission to the khan of Khiva to mediate between him and the Russians who were advancing on Khiva, and to negotiate for the release of the enslaved Russian captives. Todd's action was approved. Later, again on his own initiative, he sent Richmond Shakespear to Khiva to negotiate the release of the Russians sold into slavery, which Shakespear accomplished to the number of 416 captives.

Early in April 1840 Todd received, through the British chargé d'affaires at Erzurum, a letter which the wazir, Yar Muhammad, had written in January in the name of Shah Kamran to the Persian Shah Mahommed; Kamran declared himself the faithful servant of the Persian monarch, and stated that he merely tolerated the British at Herat from expediency. Kamran and his people had been saved from starvation by British aid, and had received over 10 lakhs of rupees from the Indian government. The act of treachery was, however, pardoned by the governor-general.

On 27 January 1841 Todd was formally gazetted political agent at Herat. From the time of his first arrival at Herat in 1839 he had desired to introduce into Herat a contingent of Indian troops under British officers. Early in 1841 Kamran and his minister proposed to agree to their introduction on condition that £20,000 was paid down and the monthly subsidy increased. It soon, however, became clear to Todd that Yar Muhammad and his master had no intention of admitting any contingent into Herat. Todd, apparently misunderstanding private instructions from Macnaghten, provoked a rupture with the Herati government. He refused to pay the subsidies. Yar Muhammad demanded more money, then expelled the mission. After submitting to indignities short of personal violence, Todd withdrew the mission on 9 February 1841 to Kandahar, without first receiving permission to do so.

Auckland was so exasperated by the withdrawal of the mission, which he believed jeopardized his policy, that, without waiting for Todd's explanations, he removed Todd from the political department and ordered him to rejoin his regiment as a subaltern. Todd was shocked by this. Macnaghten wrote to comfort him that his conduct had been admirable and that he had told Auckland so. But Auckland, angry and bitter at Todd's conduct at Herat, was obdurate. Todd ceased to be political agent and military

secretary to the envoy at Kabul on 24 March 1841, and gave over charge of the Herat political agency on 24 April, when he was posted to the Bengal artillery. Before joining he went to Calcutta, and had an interview with Auckland, but without result.

Todd joined his regiment at Dum-Dum in March 1842, having been appointed to command no. 9 light field battery on 2 February. He was promoted to be captain in the Bengal artillery on 13 May 1842, and on 22 August of the following year he married Marian, eldest daughter of Surgeon Backshall Lane Sandham of the 16th lancers. It was a brief marriage. On 27 September 1845 he was given the command of the 2nd troop of the 1st brigade of the horse artillery. His wife died on 9 December, and Todd left to take part in the First Anglo-Sikh War. At sunset on 21 December 1845 Todd's troop was ordered forward at the battle of Ferozeshahr. He placed himself in front of the troop, and was giving orders to advance when his head was taken off by a roundshot. His remains were buried on the field of battle.   R. H. VETCH, *rev.* JAMES LUNT

Sources J. W. Kaye, *Lives of Indian officers*, 2 (1867) • J. W. Kaye, *History of the war in Afghanistan*, 3rd edn, 3 vols. (1874) • G. Pottinger, *The Afghan connection* (1983) • B. P. Hughes, *The Bengal horse artillery, 1800–1861* (1971) • J. A. Norris, *The First Afghan War, 1838–1842* (1967) • J. Abbott, *Narrative of a journey from Heraut to Khiva, Moscow, and St Petersburg*, 2 vols. (1843) • P. Macrory, *Signal catastrophe: the story of a disastrous retreat from Kabul, 1842* (1966) • P. Hopkirk, *The great game: on secret service in high Asia* (1990) • H. M. Vibart, *Addiscombe: its heroes and men of note* (1894) • M. E. Yapp, *Strategies of British India: Britain, Iran and Afghanistan, 1798–1850* (1980)
Archives BL OIOC, Thomas MS
Likenesses C. G., line engraving, 1842, NPG; repro. in Hughes, *Bengal horse artillery*, facing p. 33

Todd, Henry John (*bap.* 1763, *d.* 1845), Church of England clergyman and literary scholar, baptized at Britford near Salisbury on 13 February 1763, was the son of Henry Todd (*b.* 1733/4), curate of that parish from 1758 to 1765, and his wife, Mary, *née* Smith. Admitted as a chorister of Magdalen College, Oxford, on 20 July 1771, he was educated at its school and proceeded to the college, matriculating on 15 October 1779; he graduated BA on 20 February 1784. Soon afterwards he became fellow–tutor and lecturer at Hertford College, and he took his MA on 4 May 1786. The previous year he had been ordained a deacon; he served as curate at East Lockinge, Berkshire, and in 1787 he was ordained priest.

In his early preferment Todd was greatly indebted to family connections. His paternal aunts presented him to his first living, the perpetual curacy of St John and St Bridget, Beckermet, in Cumberland. More advantageous was his father's long-standing friendship with Bishop Horne, then dean of Canterbury, who secured Todd a minor canonry in the cathedral while exempting him from the necessity of residing on his living. This patronage was given oblique acknowledgement in Todd's service as Horne's biographer, including him in his first published work of 1793, *Some Account of the Deans of Canterbury*. Its accompanying 'catalogue of the MSS in the Church Library' revealed Todd's scholarly métier, anticipating his later archival work at Lambeth. By 1792 Todd had become chaplain to Robert, eleventh Viscount Kilmorey, and James, second earl of Fife. Some time before that date Todd married Anne Dixon (1765/6–1844). The union produced eight daughters, the baptisms of several of whom between 1792 and 1801 are recorded in the registers of Canterbury Cathedral. Todd's literary ambitions brought him to the attention of Archbishop Moore, assuring him a succession of livings in the gift of the dean and chapter of Canterbury: a sinecure rectory at Ogarswick (1791–2) was followed by the vicarage at Milton, near Canterbury, which Todd held until 1801. Of greater significance was his association with the family of the eccentric antiquary Francis Egerton, to whom Todd dedicated the work which established his literary reputation. This was an edition of *Comus* (1798), which made extensive use of the important Bridgewater manuscript.

The patronage of Canterbury culminated in Todd's presentation to the rectory of All Hallows, Lombard Street, London, in November 1801, and with this advancement Todd took up residence in the capital. His arrival coincided with the publication of his *chef d'oeuvre*, an edition of Milton's poetical works. In addition to Todd's own copious annotations and judicious selection from previous commentaries, the work included for the first time extracts from Stillingfleet's projected edition, together with criticism solicited from the family of Thomas and Joseph Warton. Republished on four subsequent occasions, it remained the standard edition for fifty years. The first volume, a thorough biographical study of Milton, revised in 1809 and 1826, was published separately and enjoyed an equal measure of success. For his labours Todd was rewarded with the handsome sum of £200, and his newfound celebrity was acknowledged with his elevation as a fellow of the Society of Antiquaries in 1802. His reputation firmly established, Todd next set to work on an edition of Spenser, for which he received 'a very liberal sum' (Nichols, *Illustrations*, 7.59). Published in 1805, its reception was more equivocal, being 'severely but justly' appraised by Scott in the *Edinburgh Review* (*GM*, 25.322). In April 1803 he became chaplain to John William, seventh earl of Bridgewater, who shared Todd's antiquarian interests. William commissioned Todd to write a study of his inheritance, the privately printed *History of the College of Bonhommes at Ashridge* (1812), which contained Todd's reflections on the Gothic style.

After the publication of his work on Spenser, Todd focused his interests mainly on the archiepiscopal library at Lambeth, where he became keeper of manuscripts (or records) and embarked upon his next major project—a study of Bishop Walton and his circle's work on the polyglot Bible. By 1807 Todd had been appointed librarian and chaplain to Archbishop Manners-Sutton; this testified as much to Todd's churchmanship as to his personal merits, since the prelate's chaplains 'were all High Churchmen' (Nockles). This favourable association saw an appreciable change in Todd's fortunes, with his appointment to a rectory at Coulsdon (1807) followed by the vicarage of Addington (1812), both in Surrey. In December 1812 he was created royal chaplain-in-ordinary, a position which he retained until his death.

The depth of Todd's philological erudition, first witnessed in his Milton, was further demonstrated with the publication of a new edition of Johnson's dictionary in 1818. The same year saw Todd's promotion as one of the six preachers in Canterbury Cathedral and the first occasion on which his learning was brought to bear on theological matters, with the publication of *Original Sin, Free-Will and other Doctrines, as Maintained by our Reformers*, the first of a series of writings which sought to defend the Church of England against a background of Roman Catholic and dissenting agitation. In the preface Todd expressed his dismay at the prevalence of erroneous doctrines of justification, which he identified as an animating force behind the 'Great Rebellion'. For the next ten years Todd found himself engaged in various polemical writings, albeit of a scholarly hue. His next publication, *Vindication of our Authorised Translation and Translators of our Bible* (1819), answered the searching criticisms of its writers and their Caroline successors made by the Hebraist John Bellamy, who had published a new rendering of scripture in 1817. Todd's patient, largely philological exegesis, which sought to justify and explain their methods, revealed the depth of his study of Walton and his circle.

In 1818 Todd was presented by the earl of Bridgewater to the valuable rectory of Settrington in Yorkshire, where he took up residence. Except for occasional visits to London, which ill health made increasingly rare, he lived at the rectory for the next twenty-five years. Here, he established 'a tolerable collection of old books' and a 'formidable body of tracts … their number being some thousands … commenc[ing] about 1540' (MS Bodl. Oxf., 1004, fol. 26r). He sustained a prodigious output in the next decade which culminated with his biography of Cranmer. His immediate efforts were concentrated on seeing through the press the fruits 'of the years passed delightfully in Lambeth Library': his *Memoirs of Bishop Brian Walton, with Notices of his Coadjutors on the London Polyglot Bible* (1821). In the polemical preface to the memoir, Todd drew comparison between the 'Great Rebellion' and the present, and offered further unfavourable commentary on Bellamy's work. A companion volume, consisting of associated manuscripts deposited at Lambeth by the antiquarian Carlyle, appeared in 1823. Todd's scholarly labours were rewarded in 1824 with his election to the Royal Society of Literature.

The same year saw Todd engaged with a more formidable antagonist, the most illustrious of Manners-Sutton's protégés, Christopher Wordsworth, master of Trinity College, Cambridge, whose robust assertion of Charles I's authorship of *Eikon basilike* Todd set out to repudiate in his *Letter to the Archbishop of Canterbury on the Authorship of the Icon basilike* (1824). Wordsworth's vituperative reply, characterized by Todd as his opponent's 'verbosa et grandis Epistola', left its target apparently unscathed, remarking with genial contempt how the head of house had 'fired away his useless ammunition' (MS Bodl. Oxf., 1004, fol. 54r). Todd's more considered response, the baldly titled

Bishop Gauden the Author of the Icon basilike, further Shown in Answer to Dr Wordsworth, appeared in 1829; it hardly aimed to conciliate, with pointed epigraphs culled from Hooker warning of 'glozening delusion'; and Milton's portrait of Belial condemning:

> high words that bear
> Semblance of worth, not substance.

More significant was Todd's contribution to the debate which followed recent Roman Catholic accounts of the English Reformation: *Cranmer's defence of the true and Catholick doctrine of the sacrament* [1550], *with* [an] *introduction vindicating his character from Lingard and others* (1825). The 'vindication' was published separately the following year and was followed in 1827 by Todd's dissection of his principal opponent's spirited defence, *Reply to Lingard's Vindication of his History of England Concerning Cranmer*. He broadened the controversy the next year with *Of Confession and Absolution, and the Secrecy of Confession*, which sought to clarify the Church of England's position against the misrepresentation of Roman Catholic apologists.

In 1830 Todd was appointed by the archbishop to the prebendal stall of Husthwaite in York Cathedral. The following year his two-volume *Life of Archbishop Cranmer* appeared; in essence a more compendious contribution to the continuing debate on the foundations of the established church. On 2 November 1832 Todd was installed in the archdeaconry of Cleveland, an office in the gift of the archbishop. With characteristic industry, in the following year he saw through the press *Collections Relating to the Benefices in the Archdeaconry of Cleveland*. Todd remained active into his eighth decade, contributing to the convocation debate (1837) and publishing an appreciative selection from verse renderings of the Psalms in 1839. His last published work, *On Clerical Societies* (1841), was typically robust in its advice; warning clergy of the dangers of opening dialogue with dissenters and exhorting them to 'show the wisdom as well as the duty of obedience … to Episcopal rule' and to 'maintain the well-founded conviction of the Apostolical constitution, and of the validity and importance of the Litany and Articles' (H. J. Todd, *On Clerical Societies*, 2).

Todd's writings may conveniently be divided into those of literary, theological, and antiquarian interest, so long as it is borne in mind that his erudite philological and historical flair remained conspicuous irrespective of his chosen field of enquiry. Indubitably, his edition of Milton was Todd's *opus magnum*, a significant feat of scholarship which remained authoritative for fifty years. The foundations of Todd's methodology, selecting commentary and annotation from earlier editors complemented by the fruits of his own research, was familiar to his contemporaries, who thus designated him an 'illustrator' of literature. It is a procedure which broadly anticipates that of the variorum editions of twentieth-century scholarship. In his literary taste and judgement Todd was a confirmed Augustan; a follower of Pope and Gray rather than Wordsworth and Coleridge. His lack of sympathy with prevailing ideas helps to explain the unfavourable notice of one grudging obituarist, who complained that Todd's 'turn of

mind was not poetical' and expressed bafflement that he had dared 'to put a step into the regions of Parnassus'. The Romantic belief in the prerogative of poets as literary critics is confirmed with the concluding remark that Todd 'should have left Milton and Spenser to Southey and Scott' (*GM*, 25.323). The more measured appraisal of the historian of Milton's editors remains authoritative:

> Todd is a very industrious follower of the line of research pursued by Warton. While he added much to the material of his subject he contributed little to its method, and so must be classed rather among the useful than the great editors. (Oras)

The same authority concludes that the most important and original component of Todd's edition was his thorough survey of the poet's sources.

Any strict distinction between Todd's historical and theological writings is unsatisfactory and would have been incomprehensible to their author who, as an expositor of the Church of England, was at once priest and scholar, controversialist and historian. Todd's work on Cranmer was as much an account of the identity of the Church of England, offering a corrective to the nascent Roman Catholic historiography of Lingard, Butler, and Milner, as it was a biography. In his theological writings a common thread is Todd's endeavour to demonstrate the origins of the eucharistic teaching of the high-church party in the writings of the founders of the English Reformation, while at the same time downplaying the influence of Calvin in their deliberations. In this, his keen opposition to any toleration of protestant and Roman Catholic dissent and his reverence for the Restoration high-churchmen, together with his friends Routh and Oxlee he was one of a 'short file' of clerics who continued to give eloquent voice to the teachings of the Augustan Church of England on the eve of the Great Reform Bill. Yet the imperatives of scholarship were never subordinated to the expediency of party: Todd's meticulous and decisive contribution to the debate on a cherished high-church myth, the king's supposed authorship of *Eikon basilike*, proved that. Nor was he a bigot: his firm convictions on the preservation of the confessional *status quo* did not prevent his forming warm friendships with dissenters, most notably the publisher Charles Dilley, who left Todd a substantial legacy.

Of Todd's character his writings reveal only an unremarkable outline which may be summarized as fastidious, thorough, and, in the proper Augustan sense, polite. More revealing and attractive glimpses are afforded in his letters to the younger and importunate antiquary Edmund Barker, whom Todd indefatigably but fruitlessly attempted to lure to Settrington. Here emerges the stoic valetudinarian, the gentle but teasing wit, and the tireless, ever solicitous scholar. Two likenesses of Todd exist: one a sketch 'stealthily painted by a lady'; the second a handsome portrait in oils by Joseph Smith dated 1822, currently in the possession of Magdalen College School, showing its subject in clerical attire.

Todd died on 24 December 1845 at the rectory at Settrington; he was predeceased by his wife who died on 14

April 1844. He was buried in the chancel of the church where a monument of plain white marble commemorates both husband and wife. A stained-glass window was put by the clergy in the tower at the west end of the church. The beneficiaries of Todd's will included St Bee's College, where his father had been a pupil and which received his copy of Walton's polyglot Bible, and the antiquary Philip Bliss, who received copies of Todd's scarce Lambeth manuscript catalogues. His important collection of books relating to Milton had been donated to Magdalen College some years earlier. To his unmarried daughters he left 'many volumes from his library' (*GM*, 25.659). The sum of £50 was left to the poor of Settrington.

D. A. BRUNTON

Sources *GM*, 2nd ser., 21 (1844), 669 · *GM*, 2nd ser., 25 (1846), 322–4, 659 · Nichols, *Illustrations*, 6.620, 681–6; 7.54, 58–9 · Nichols, *Lit. anecdotes*, 2.672; 4.192 · Bodl. Oxf., MS Bodley 1004 · A. Oras, *Milton's editors and commentators from Patrick Hume to Henry John Todd, 1695–1801* (1931) · J. R. Bloxam, *A register of the presidents, fellows ... of Saint Mary Magdalen College*, 8 vols. (1853–85), vol. 1, pp. 177–91; vol. 2, pp. 111–12 · *Fasti Angl.* (Hardy), 3.149, 195 · *Literary Gazette* (24 Jan 1846), 88–9 · P. B. Nockles, *The Oxford Movement in context: Anglican high churchmanship, 1760–1857* (1994) · IGI
Archives BL, letters to Philip Bliss, Add. MSS 34568–34581 · Bodl. Oxf., letters to Edmund Henry Barker, MS Bodley 1003
Likenesses J. Smith, oils, 1822 (after sketch), Magdalen College School, Oxford · J. Smith, oils, *c*.1840–1853, Magd. Oxf. · miniature

Todd, Hugh (*c*.1657–1728), Church of England clergyman and antiquary, born at Blencow in Cumberland, was the eldest son of Thomas Todd, rector of Hutton in the Forest in the same county, who was ejected by Cromwell's sequestrators and imprisoned at Carlisle. Educated at Queen's College, Oxford, he matriculated on 29 March 1672, graduated BA in 1677, and was elected fellow of University College the following year. Proceeding MA in 1679, he became chaplain to Thomas Smith, bishop of Carlisle, in 1684 and vicar of Kirkland, Cumberland, in which county he resided for the rest of his life. In 1685 he was collated prebendary of Carlisle and presented to the vicarage of Stanwix, resigning that living in 1688 when Richard Graham, Viscount Preston, a staunch tory with Jacobite leanings, presented him to the rectory of Arthuret. Eleven years later Bishop Smith asked him to accept the vicarage of Penrith as well, and he held both livings in plurality until his death. Within a few months of taking up his Penrith parish, he married on 30 May 1700 Lucy Dalston (d. 1733), the eldest daughter of the late Christopher Dalston who had been lieutenant-governor of Carlisle in 1697.

Todd accumulated the degrees BD and DD in 1692 and was a man of wide intellectual interests. He contributed to Moses Pitt's *English Atlas*; assisted John Walker in his *Sufferings of the Clergy*, John Stevens in his additions to Dugdale's *Monasticon*, and Henry Wharton in his *Anglia sacra*; furnished Edmund Gibson with information for his 1698 edition of Camden's *Britannia*, and provided Edward Bernard with an account of several Cumbrian manuscript collections for his two-volume catalogue of English and Irish manuscripts, published in Oxford in 1697. As well as these contributions to the works of others he delivered papers to the Royal Society, translated into English works from Latin and Greek, and published several poems. Above all, however, he was a keen antiquary with a particular interest in the ecclesiastical history of his native county. His manuscript writings included 'An historical description of the bishoprick of Carlisle', the consummation of a lifetime's research, but which in spite of an ambition to that end, he never published 'for the most obvious of all reasons, namely waiting for further materials' (Nicolson and Burn, 1.iii). Although the local historian Benjamin Nightingale considered in 1911 that the value of Todd's work was diminished by his ecclesiastical bias and carelessness in his facts and dates (Nightingale, 1.437), this and Todd's other manuscripts relating to the city, diocese, and cathedral of Carlisle were sources which local ecclesiastical writers relied upon until the twentieth century.

A resolute high-church tory, Todd was frequently in controversy with the forceful William Nicolson, who became bishop of Carlisle in 1702. Their initial animosity predated Nicolson's shift from tory to whig, and was originally due to jealousy between fellow antiquaries and probably also to professional rivalry. After several rather petty squabbles, he and the absentee dean, Francis Atterbury, questioned the bishop's right of visitation, insisting that the cathedral statutes upon which Nicolson relied were invalid. On 6 February 1708 the court of common pleas upheld their contention, but not before Todd had been excommunicated by his diocesan. It was, however, a pyrrhic victory, for the ecclesiastical establishment, alarmed by the limitations placed upon episcopal authority, hastened to secure a parliamentary bill to re-establish their right of visitation. After its passage the sentence of excommunication was removed.

A generous benefactor and an energetic cleric, Todd undertook extensive improvements to the church at Arthuret in 1700, and St Andrew's, Penrith, was almost entirely rebuilt during his incumbency. Bibliophile as well as antiquary (he had a library of some 800 volumes among which were many fine editions) he was also, with Bishop Smith and Arthur Savage, one of those who towards the end of the seventeenth century re-established the dean and chapter library which had perished amid the disasters of the siege of Carlisle in 1644–5. Todd was buried at St Mary's Abbey, Carlisle, on 13 September 1728. His personal estate was valued at £1229 16s. All his books and manuscripts were sold by his widow in accordance with instructions contained in her late husband's will.

DAVID J. W. MAWSON

Sources B. Nightingale, *The ejected of 1662 in Cumberland and Westmorland: their predecessors and successors*, 1 (1911), 436–8, 487–8 · S. Jefferson, *The history and antiquities of Leath ward in the county of Cumberland* (1840), 479–81 · J. E. Prescott, ed. and trans., *The statutes of the cathedral church of Carlisle*, 2nd edn (1903), 6–9 · J. R. Magrath, ed., *The Flemings in Oxford*, 1, OHS, 44 (1904), 145, 260, 310; 2, OHS, 62 (1913), 115, 125, 162 · R. W. Dixon, 'The chapter library of Carlisle', *Transactions of the Cumberland and Westmorland Antiquarian and Archaeological Society*, 2 (1875–6), 312–36 · D. Mawson, 'Dr Hugh Todd's account of the diocese of Carlisle', *Transactions of the Cumberland and Westmorland Antiquarian and Archaeological Society*, [new ser.,] 88 (1988), 207–24 · D. Mawson, 'The library of an eighteenth century cleric—Dr Hugh Todd (c.1657–1728)', *Transactions of the Cumberland and Westmorland Antiquarian and Archaeological Society*, [new ser.,] 97 (1997), 153–72 • J. Nicolson and R. Burn, *The history and antiquities of the counties of Westmorland and Cumberland*, 1 (1777), iii • *The London diaries of William Nicolson, bishop of Carlisle, 1702–1718*, ed. C. Jones and G. Holmes (1985) • probate inventory, 1728, Cumbria AS • parish registers, 1728, Carlisle, St Mary's

Archives Cumbria AS, Carlisle, literary papers and corresp. | Bodl. Oxf., collections relating to history of diocese of Carlisle • Bodl. Oxf., letters to Humphrey Wanley • Cumbria AS, Carlisle, dean and chapter MSS

Wealth at death £1229 16s.—personal estate: probate inventory, 28 Nov 1728, Cumbria AS, P 1728

Todd, James Henthorn (1805–1869), biblical scholar, was born in Dublin on 23 April 1805, the eldest son of Charles Hawkes Todd (1782–1826), professor of surgery at the Royal College of Surgeons in Ireland, and his wife, Eliza (1786–1862), daughter of Colonel Bentley. Robert Bentley *Todd was his younger brother. Todd entered Trinity College, Dublin, on 6 November 1820, and graduated with honours in 1824; he took his BA in 1825. A year later his father died, leaving him the eldest of a family of fifteen who had very little money. He stayed in Trinity College, where he took pupils and edited the *Christian Examiner*, a church periodical aimed at placing the debate between the established Church of Ireland and the Roman Catholic church on a more historical and learned footing. Thereafter he believed it to be his mission to improve the condition of the established church in Ireland and to promote greater learning among the clergy and greater knowledge of church history among the people.

Todd was elected a fellow of Trinity College in 1831 and in the same year took deacon's orders. From this time until he became senior fellow in 1850 he was one of the most popular tutors in Trinity. He was conservative, a high-churchman (in doctrine rather than ritual), and disliked but accepted reform of the college. In 1832 he took priest's orders and wrote a brief history of the university for the *University Calendar* of 1833. Many years later he revised this history, and included it as the introduction to his published *List of Graduates of the University* (1866). He graduated BD in Dublin in 1837 and DD in 1840.

In 1833, through contacts made via Samuel Roffey Maitland, Todd began to write for the *British Magazine*, an English church periodical just started under the editorship of Hugh James Rose. His contributions, all of which defended protestant ascendancy, included papers on Wyclif, on church history, and on the Irish church questions of the day. Around this time the Irish national education system had been started by Archbishop Whately. This was intended to be non-denominational, but many members of the established church, including Todd, felt that the scripture lessons issued by the commissioners favoured Roman Catholics. In order to alert the people in England to what he saw as the true state of affairs, Todd published a fictional letter from the pope to his clergy, advocating the line of action already pursued. This letter, entitled *Sanctissimi domini nostri Gregorii papae XVI epistola ad archiepiscopos et episcopos Hiberniae … translated from the original Latin* (1836) may have been intended as a joke (the same tactic had been used against the Oxford Tractarians not long before), but the published 'letter' was taken as genuine by some protestants at a meeting at Exeter Hall, where it raised tensions considerably. Todd publicly announced himself as the author, and was severely criticized for his conduct which he attempted to justify in a preface to a second edition, published the same year.

In 1838 and 1839 Todd was the Donnellan lecturer in Trinity College. Choosing as his subject the biblical prophecies relating to Antichrist, he attacked the view then held by many Irish protestant clergy, that the pope was the Antichrist of Revelation, arguing that despite much corruption the Roman Catholic church still maintained the essential truths of Christianity. Todd's lectures were published as *Discourses on the Prophecies Relating to Antichrist in Daniel and St Paul* (1840). In the same spirit of calm and learned discussion of theological differences, he also started a society at Trinity College for the discussion of religious history, and published a small volume entitled *The search after infallibility: remarks on the testimony of the fathers to the Roman dogma of infallibility* (1848), long before the issue of papal infallibility was defined by the Roman Catholic church at the First Vatican Council (1869–70).

In 1843 Todd joined with Edwin Richard Quin, Lord Adare (afterwards third earl of Dunraven), W. Monsell (Lord Emly), William Sewell, and others, to found St Columba's College at Rathfarnham, near Dublin. The school was conducted on Anglican church principles. Unusually for an established school, it taught Irish as well as classics to would-be ordinands. Having also been treasurer of St Patrick's Cathedral, Dublin, since 1837, Todd was made precentor, the second dignitary of the cathedral, in 1864. He turned his attention first to restoration work on the building and then to the improvement of choral services.

In 1849 Todd was made regius professor of Hebrew at the University of Dublin and in 1852 he was appointed librarian at Trinity College. The library had long been neglected, but Todd, with the assistance of John O'Donovan and Eugene O'Curry, classified and arranged the large collection of Irish manuscripts held there. He spent what money the board of Trinity College allowed him in buying rare books, and left the library's holding more than quadrupled, as well as catalogued: 'his greatest monument is the printed catalogue' (McDowell and Webb, 278). Todd made Trinity College Library and manuscript room a world-class library for scholars. His numerous gifts to the university museum included mummy crocodiles and ancient Scandinavian almanacs. He also compiled a *Catalogue of Graduates*, since updated.

Todd's most substantial contribution to scholarship was in Irish studies, his work on which was centred mainly at the Royal Irish Academy. Elected a member of the academy in 1833, Todd was involved in its activities from the beginning. He procured transcripts or syntheses of Irish manuscripts held abroad, particularly at the Bibliothèque Royale, Brussels. He was the academy's honorary secretary from 1847 to 1855, and president for five years from 1856. As president he sought to raise the profile of Irish antiquities, and to promote scholarship in the field of

Irish literature. In 1840 he founded the Irish Archaeo-logical Society, which published a number of rare manu-scripts and volumes. Todd was also an energetic honorary secretary of the society, and contributed a number of pub-lications to its proceedings, including *The Irish Version of the Historia Brittonum of Nennius* (1847), the *Martyrology of Don-egal* (1864), edited in conjunction with William Reeves, and the *Liber hymnorum, or, Book of Hymns of the Ancient Church of Ireland* (2 vols., 1855 and 1869). Todd was very widely consulted about works relating to Irish literature and history, and was said to have been second only to Archbishop Ussher in his knowledge of, and help in devel-oping the discipline of, Irish studies.

About 1860, the same year in which he was given an *ad eundem* degree by the University of Oxford, Todd was asked by a London publisher to write the lives of the arch-bishops of Armagh. The publishing firm collapsed when the first volume, dealing with the life of St Patrick, was in press, and it was brought out independently in 1864 as *St Patrick, Apostle of Ireland*. In addition Todd published the text of two medieval Irish manuscripts in the Rolls Series as *Cogadh Gaedhel re Gallaibh: the war of the Gaedhil with the Gaill, or, The invasions of Ireland by the Danes and other Norse-men* (1867).

Todd was one of the best-known Irishmen of his day, consulted both by statesmen and theologians. During his life he advised and corresponded with Lord John George de la Poer Beresford, W. E. Gladstone, Lord Brougham, John Henry Newman, and E. B. Pusey. In politics he was conservative but independent-minded. He wanted the maintenance of the Anglican establishment at the univer-sity. However, according to R. B. McDowell and D. A. Webb, 'the rigidity with which he maintained as principles opin-ions … disqualified him from statesmanship even on a small scale; as Provost he would have been disastrous' (p. 278). Notwithstanding, his contributions to Irish litera-ture and to the development of Trinity College Library into a manuscript library of worldwide importance can-not be overestimated. Archdeacon Cotton once referred to Todd as the 'Sine qua non of every literary enterprise in Dublin' (ibid., 525–6).

Todd died, unmarried, in his home, Silveracre, Rath-farnham, co. Dublin, on 28 June 1869, and was buried in the churchyard of St Patrick's Cathedral. After his death the Todd lectureship of the Celtic languages was estab-lished in his memory with the help of the Royal Irish Academy.   E. M. TODD, *rev.* SINÉAD AGNEW

Sources Boase, *Mod. Eng. biog.* · A. J. Webb, *A compendium of Irish biography* (1878) · Ward, *Men of the reign*, 888 · *The Times* (29 June 1869), 12 · *The Times* (30 June 1869), 12 · Burtchaell & Sadleir, *Alum. Dubl.* · *N&Q*, 5th ser., 6 (1876), 362, 433, 477 · R. B. McDowell and D. A. Webb, *Trinity College, Dublin, 1592–1952: an academic history* (1982) · H. Cotton, *Fasti ecclesiae Hibernicae*, 2 (1848), 125, 418 · Alli-bone, *Dict.* · C. A. Cameron, *History of the Royal College of Surgeons in Ireland* (1886)

Archives NL Ire., corresp. · NRA, priv. coll., corresp. relating to St Columba's College · TCD, corresp. and papers | BL, letters to Philip Bliss, Add. MSS 34572–34579, *passim* · BL, corresp. Sir Fred-erick Madden, Egerton MSS 2841–2848, *passim* · Bodl. Oxf., corresp. with Sir T. Phillipps · PRO NIre., letters to Lord Dunraven · Pusey Oxf., corresp. with E. B. Pusey; MS commentary of Ezekiel · TCD,

corresp. with Beresford · U. Edin. L., letters to David Laing · U. Edin. L., letters to James Halliwell-Phillipps
Likenesses S. Smith, oils, NG Ire.

Todd, Lawrie. *See* Thorburn, Grant (1773–1863).

Todd, Robert Bentley (1809–1860), physician and physi-ologist, was born in Dublin on 9 April 1809, the second son of Charles Hawkes Todd (1782–1826), professor of anat-omy and surgery at the Royal College of Surgeons in Ire-land, and his wife, Eliza Bentley (1786–1862), daughter of a colonel in the Indian army. His father was a distinguished surgeon and teacher, an editor of the *Dublin Hospital Reports*, and a dedicated administrator and president of the college. Robert was one of nine sons and six daugh-ters; all of his brothers went into the professions—three into medicine, three into the church (one of these was James Henthorn *Todd; 1805–1869), and two into law, with one a solicitor and one a barrister.

Todd received his primary education at a local day school and from a private tutor, the Revd W. Higgins, later the bishop of Derry. Medicine, to which Todd so whole-heartedly devoted his life, was not his first choice as a car-eer: he entered Trinity College, Dublin, in January 1825 planning to study law. However, when his father died in March 1826 at the early age of forty-three he left his large family with very little money. Todd was obliged to become an apprentice at the Richmond Hospital, Dublin, where his father had been surgeon and had taught. He graduated with a BA from Dublin University in 1829 and was already living in Charlotte Street, London, when he became a licentiate of the Royal College of Surgeons in Ireland in 1831.

Todd's background as a member of the Anglo-Irish pro-fessional establishment and his Irish liberal and medical education served him well in London. The Irish medical schools were among the most innovative and brilliant in Europe at that time, and in 1826, precisely when Todd was taking up his medical studies, Robert Adams and Richard Carmichael, two of the luminaries of Irish medicine of their generation, established the Richmond school of medicine and surgery at the hospital. Todd also studied under Robert James Graves from whom, he later said, he imbibed his taste for physiological inquiry. Physiology was only beginning to be taught in London in the 1830s but the Irish College of Surgeons had had a chair in anat-omy and physiology since the end of the eighteenth cen-tury. Todd appreciated that the improvements in the microscope made in the 1820s provided the technology to move beyond the gross anatomy of the early physiolo-gists. He accurately predicted that microscopic anatomy and organic chemistry, accompanied by careful observa-tion of symptoms during life, would form the basis for future medical progress, and he therefore dedicated him-self to becoming a 'physiological physician'.

Todd had planned to spend a year studying in Paris but on receiving an offer to teach anatomy and physiology at one of the private schools of medicine, the Aldersgate School, he settled in London. He immediately began plan-ning to study for academic medical degrees, and attended

Robert Bentley Todd (1809–1860), by Maull & Polyblank

Oxford briefly; he received his MA in 1832, his BM in 1833, and his DM in 1836. Already in 1832 he was projecting his *Cyclopaedia of Anatomy and Physiology*. He travelled to Paris in 1833, and made the acquaintance of some of the great French scientists whom he recruited as contributors to the venture. In the same year he became a member of the Royal College of Physicians of London.

In 1834 Todd left the Aldersgate School and joined a physician and two surgeons from the Westminster Hospital, London, in establishing a new private school, where he taught for the next two years. Todd and his colleagues put up approximately £3000 to buy a building for this school, an indication that Todd had already established a successful private practice. During these years he became physician to the Western Dispensary and the Royal Infirmary for Children. In 1835 the first volume of *The Cyclopaedia* (5 vols., 1835–59) was published, establishing Todd as a leading physiologist, and in August of 1836 he was elected to the chair of physiology and general morbid anatomy at King's College, London. A few months later, on 20 December, he married Elizabeth, daughter of the late J. H. Hart, of Tenerife, at Hemple, near Hull; they had four children.

A man of boundless energy and a fine administrator, Todd immediately began major changes in the medical school at King's. Medical education in the 1830s was largely private and students were not required to attend lectures or take examinations until their final qualifying tests, which many failed. They lived in rooms all over the city 'in the midst of its bustle and gaiety', and 'exposed to all its temptations', as Todd wrote in 1837 in a series of articles proposing a radical reform of medical education (Todd, 11.337–8). In Todd's view the existing system trained the future medical practitioners of England to be radical in politics, indifferent in religion, and half-informed in professional matters. Todd and his colleagues at King's believed that religious education was key to developing the moral and mental habits which would make medical students respectable and useful both in their professional work and in society at large. At the same time Todd stressed the importance of a sound scientific and clinical education. He believed that students should want to acquire knowledge for its own sake; grasping first principles and thinking for themselves rather than simply learning facts by memory in order to pass exams, as was then the practice. Todd started a system of keeping attendance records at lectures, and, working with the clergy at King's, he introduced a residential collegiate system, modelled on that at Oxford and Cambridge; this was the first such medical college in England; in 1842 Todd became its first dean. He also was responsible for establishing the first scholarships for medical students in England.

The King's medical school had no clinical facilities when Todd arrived in 1836. Todd's conviction that clinical teaching was the only way to gain practical medical knowledge led, in 1840, to the establishment of the first King's College Hospital, situated in the former St Clement Danes poorhouse in Portugal Street. An accomplished fundraiser, Todd was also instrumental in building the second King's College Hospital, a model building which opened in 1861. By the 1850s Todd had achieved his goal of making King's both a leading clinical and academic medical school. Its students had a physiology laboratory, received their entire education within the college, wore caps and gowns, and were alone eligible to be clinical clerks, dressers, physician's assistants, and house surgeons to the hospital. These positions were awarded by examination, and could not be bought or achieved through apprenticeship as was still common practice elsewhere.

Todd's belief that a clinical hospital served the dual purpose of teaching academic medicine and providing the best possible care for the patients led him to undertake a second major and lasting reform, that of nursing. In 1848 a group of prominent Anglicans, whom Todd had recruited, established the first training school for nurses. The school, which became known as St John's House, took the form of an Anglican sisterhood and was based on the same principles as Todd's reforms of medical education. The school was residential and supervised by older, more educated persons. The sisters of St John's House were upper-class women—'ladies'—who received systematic training together with the working-class nurses in various teaching hospitals. Once trained, the sisters supervised and taught the pupil nurses, providing both religious education and practical bedside training, while doctors gave lectures on medical subjects.

By 1856 St John's House was able to take on the whole of

the nursing at King's College Hospital. The new nursing service was unique in England and immensely successful. It became the model for nursing reforms in the 1860s and 1870s. St John's House was to be the main inspiration for Florence Nightingale's school, which opened at St Thomas's Hospital in 1860; Sister Mary Jones, 'Lady superintendent' of St John's House from 1853 to 1868, became one of her principal mentors and dearest friends.

As with Todd's medical reforms, the aim of this seminal nursing reform was to improve the character of the working-class women who traditionally provided hospital nursing services by giving them systematic, professional education, and allowing them to achieve a better social position. For the lady nurses the goal was to provide a legitimate field of labour, either full-time or part-time. Socially it was a very radical move, for upper-class women lost their status as ladies if they worked at a regular job. It was also quite revolutionary for ladies to take the same training and work side by side in the wards with the working-class nurses. However, this nursing reform was characteristic of Todd and the broad-churchmen at King's, who fostered education for women and a corporate view of society. It is noteworthy that one of Todd's daughters, Bertha Jane *Johnson, who married the Revd Arthur Johnson, was one of the most active members in the circle that established the women's colleges at Oxford. She was the first principal of Oxford home students from 1893 to 1921.

Todd became a fellow of the Royal College of Physicians in 1837, a fellow of the Royal Society in 1839, a fellow of the Royal College of Surgeons in 1844, and one of the first physicians to King's College Hospital. At the Royal College of Physicians he gave the Goulstonian lectures in 1839, the Croonian lectures in 1842, and the Lumleian lectures in 1849–50. Todd was a great clinical lecturer as well as an internationally known researcher and a leading medical practitioner in London. In 1853 his growing private practice forced him to resign his chair. In order to keep his services, King's rescinded the rule that a physician to the hospital must be a college professor.

Todd's associates spoke of the enormous workload which he was able to carry and always mentioned his kindness and generosity. Sir William Bowman called him his 'loved and honoured friend and workfellow', describing him as having a fine countenance, excellence of heart and life, and as a man who was warmly loved by his students (W. Bowman, BMJ, 2, 1866, 190–91; The Times, 6 Feb 1860). Apart from the work which he constantly encouraged and supported among others, Todd's own contributions to medical knowledge were significant. In his time cerebro-vascular accidents were thought to be the cause of all paralyses. Todd demonstrated that epileptic seizures often caused a paralysis from which the patient could recover completely, within a matter of days ('Todd's paralysis'). He introduced the concept of afferent and efferent nerves and identified astereognosis, the inability to recognize objects or shapes by touch. Todd was also the first to describe hypertrophic cirrhosis of the liver and the first to describe tabes dorsalis, defining locomotor ataxia as a distinct clinical entity and connecting it with the lesions in the posterior columns of the spine.

Todd was also a leader in the movement which did away with the old depleting therapies of scant diets, bleeding, salivating, purging, and vomiting. Rather he advocated upholding the vital powers with food and stimulants. In his later years he considered alcohol the natural food of the nervous system and prescribed it with increasing enthusiasm—sometimes as much as 30 ounces of brandy a day. This practice was heavily criticized by many of his colleagues, and may explain why a man so pre-eminent in his own time was later largely forgotten. Some thought that he lost more patients than other doctors as a result, while the medical students at King's thought he was dosing himself with large quantities of brandy to bolster himself against the strains of his extensive private practice.

Todd was a prolific writer. His letters and lectures appeared frequently in the medical press and he published three volumes of clinical lectures. The five-volume Cyclopaedia of Anatomy and Physiology was considered his magnum opus, and it was still thought the most important work of its kind in England in the 1890s. The Physiological Anatomy and Physiology of Man, which he wrote together with William Bowman, was published between 1845 and 1857. It was the first text in physiology to describe the histology of the organs and tissues of the body in such minute detail, and its lucid style and fine microscopical detail immediately made it the standard authority in England and abroad.

Because of failing health Todd resigned as physician to King's College Hospital in December 1859. Six weeks later, on 30 January 1860, he died at his London consulting rooms in Brook Street, following multiple attacks of haematemesis. The post-mortem revealed advanced cirrhosis of the liver and congested and enlarged kidneys. Todd was buried on 4 February in Kensal Green cemetery, with more than two hundred of his former pupils following his coffin to the grave. His colleagues commissioned a marble statue of him which stands in front of the third King's College Hospital at Denmark Hill. Todd was survived by his wife and four children; their youngest child and only son, James Henthorn Todd (1847–1891) was educated at Eton College and at Worcester College, Oxford. He served in the Bombay civil service.

CAROL HELMSTADTER

Sources King's Lond., King's College Hospital Archives · LMA, St John's House, St Thomas's Hospital Archives · The Lancet (11 Jan 1824), 71 · The Lancet (21 March 1824), 388–93 · The Lancet (15 April 1826), 87–8 · The Lancet (20 Sept 1856), 332 · The Lancet (11 Feb 1860), 151 · The Lancet (25 Feb 1860), 198–9 · The Lancet (3 March 1860), 232 · L. S. Beale, On medical progress: in memoriam R. B. Todd (1870) · The Times (6 Feb 1860) · The Times (25 April 1927) [obit. of B. J. Johnson] · N. McIntyre, King's College Hospital Gazette, 35 (1956), 79–91, 184–98 · C. Helmstadter, 'Robert Bentley Todd, St John's House and the origins of the modern trained nurse', Bulletin of the History of Medicine, 67 (1993), 282–319 · J. B. Lyons, 'The neurology of Robert Bentley Todd', Historical aspects of the neurosciences, ed. F. C. Rose and W. F. Bynum (1982), 137–50 · 'Farewell address of Dr Todd', Medical Times and Gazette (26 March 1853), 322–4 · The collected papers of Sir W. Bowman, ed. J. Burdon-Sanderson and J. W. Hulke, 1 (1892), xvi–xviii; 2

(1892), 78–9 · R. B. Todd, 'The education of medical students', *British Magazine*, 11 (1837), 335–8, 460–63 · R. B. Todd, 'The education of medical students', *British Magazine*, 12 (1837), 95–100, 337–41 · C. A. Cameron, *History of the Royal College of Surgeons in Ireland* (1886) · *GM*, 2nd ser., 8 (1837), 201 · *CGPLA Eng. & Wales* (1860)
Archives King's College Hospital, London, case notes of patients who were under Todd's care; minute books · LMA, St John's House, St Thomas's Hospital Archives, administrative minute books
Likenesses T. H. McGuire, lithograph, 1848, RCP Lond., BM · M. Noble, marble bust, 1860, RSCE · M. Noble, marble statue, 1860, King's College Hospital, London · A. Zobel, mezzotint, 1860 (after D. T. Blakiston), RCP Lond. · Benson & Co., lithograph (*Halls and past surgeons and physicians of King's College Hospital, London*), Wellcome L. · J. H. Lynch, lithograph (after E. Armitage), BM · Maull & Polyblank, photograph, NPG [*see illus.*] · etching (after photograph by Maull & Polyblank), repro. in F. C. Rose and W. F. Bynum, eds., *Historical aspects of the neurosciences* (1982), 139
Wealth at death under £14,000: probate, 20 Feb 1860, *CGPLA Eng. & Wales*

Todd, Sweeney [*called* the Demon Barber of Fleet Street] (*supp. fl.* **1784**), legendary murderer and barber, may have his source in a murder reported in the *London Chronicle* of 2 December 1784. It related that a 'Journeyman Barber that lives near Hyde Park-corner, who had been a long time past jealous of his wife, but could no way bring it home to her' had shaved a gentleman who boasted of having had 'certain favours' from a young woman who lived nearby. 'The Barber concluding it to be his wife, in the height of his frenzy cut the Gentleman's throat from ear to ear, and absconded'. The story was reprinted in the *Annual Register* for 1784–5. The murderer's fate is unreported.

In 1823 a publication called *The Tell-Tale* published the story of a barber in the rue de la Harpe, Paris, who murdered a gentleman visiting from the country and then had the victim's body turned into pies by his next-door neighbour, a patissier. The story was reprinted in 1841, and was supposedly based on a case in France about twenty years earlier, but also resembled a French ballad about a fourteenth-century barber who likewise murdered his victims before having them turned into pies. The legend of the murderous barber may have played on a fear of cannibalism in urban centres; in a crowded city consumers could not see where their meat was coming from. This had been demonstrated by the hysterical reaction to the publication of a broadsheet by James *Catnach in London in 1818, which claimed that a butcher was selling human meat in his shop; a butcher, Thomas Pizzey, whose shop in Clare Market was besieged by a mob clutching Catnach's claims, successfully sued Catnach for malicious libel. In 1843 Charles Dickens, in *Martin Chuzzlewit*, had Tom Pinch wonder whether his friend John Westlock was 'afraid I have strayed into one of those streets where the countrymen are murdered; and that I have been made meat-pies of, or some horrible thing' (Dickens, 576). Whether or not this was a common apprehension of visitors to London it provided a commercial opportunity to a publisher associated with sensational fiction, Edward Lloyd. *Lloyd's Penny Atlas* (vol. 2, no. 97, 1844) included a story called 'Joddrel, the Barber, or, Mystery unravelled', about a French-Irish barber in London, Lewis Joddrel of Bishopsgate, whose neighbours realize that many of his customers disappear.

The bodies are discovered with stakes through their heads, but there is no mention of their flesh having been intended for human consumption.

On 21 November 1846 Lloyd began serializing *The String of Pearls* in *The People's Periodical and Family Library*. The eighteen-part serial has usually been attributed to Thomas Peckett *Prest, but Helen Smith has argued persuasively that it was actually the work of James Malcolm *Rymer. It was set in 1785, suggesting that the author may have read the newspaper account of the murdering barber of 1784. The story concerned Sweeney Todd, a barber in Fleet Street (the name may have been borrowed from Samuel Todd, a pearl-stringer who lived near Fleet Street in the 1830s) who murders wealthy clients for their valuables by throwing them from their chairs through a trapdoor into a cellar. (The device may have been borrowed from Thomas Deloney's late sixteenth-century prose work *Thomas of Reading*.) Todd's neighbour Mrs Lovett then cuts up the bodies to make them into pies. Todd apparently murders a customer, Mark Ingestre, for a string of pearls, but fails to account for the loyalty of Ingestre's lover Johanna or Ingestre's miraculous survival, which frightens him into confessing his crimes. Before the serial had ended a stage version of *The String of Pearls* had begun a long run at the Britannia Theatre, Hoxton, on 1 March 1847, almost certainly dramatized by George Dibdin Pitt. There Todd gained his stage catchphrase, 'I've polished him off' (Kalikoff, 25), which entered the English language. Edward Lloyd published an enlarged *The String of Pearls* as a stand-alone 'penny-blood' serial during 1850. Both the preface to the 1850 edition and the bills for Pitt's play insisted that the Todd story was based on fact. A further serial, which embellished the details of Pitt's version, and was possibly written by Charlton Lea, was published by Charles Fox in 1878, by which time Todd had become 'the Demon Barber of Fleet Street'.

By 1878 it had become widely accepted that Sweeney Todd was a historical person. A correspondent to *Notes and Queries* wrote that he could 'trace this credulity back (by report, of course) for at least seventy years' but that he had:

> searched in vain the various editions of the *Newgate Calendar*, the cognate *Malefactors' Register*, the Old Bailey Sessions papers, numerous collections of romances of London, London legends, the late Walter Thornbury's *Old Stories Retold, &c.*, but can find no trace of such a prosecution, or of any crime bearing resemblance to this one.   (*N&Q*, 5th ser.)

The exception was the sixteenth-century case of the cannibal Sawney *Beane, who, he suggested, may have been the original of the Todd legend. The story of Sweeney Todd was returned to several times in *Notes and Queries*, where correspondents usually turned to Pitt's play and concluded that the character was entirely fictitious. However, the legend gained further embellishments. 186 Fleet Street became established as Todd's residence, an identification encouraged by the discovery of human bones under the cellar during building work in the late nineteenth century, supposedly those of Todd's victims. An alternative explanation was that the cellar of 186 Fleet

Street had been built across the old vaults of St Dunstan-in-the-West.

Todd remained part of popular culture in the twentieth century and was the subject of several cinema films, most notably *Sweeney Todd, the Demon Barber of Fleet Street* (1935), starring Tod Slaughter, who also frequently played Todd on the stage. Theatre productions continued to claim that the story had a historical basis. The programme of one stage version, *Todd*, performed in New York in 1924, claimed that Todd was born in Stepney on 26 October 1756 and was tried for murder on 29 January 1802, citing (falsely) the *Newgate Calendar*, although there was no factual basis for these statements. By the 1930s 'the Sweeney' had become cockney rhyming slang for the Metropolitan Police's flying squad, and in the 1970s it provided the name for a television drama series about two flying-squad detectives. Malcolm Arnold composed a ballet, *Sweeney Todd*, in 1959. The story was reinterpreted for the late twentieth-century stage in 1968 by Christopher Bond, who presented Todd as a victim of society, robbed of his wife and daughter by a lustful and corrupt judge, who returned to London after many years to take a gruesome revenge. This version was adapted into the musical *Sweeney Todd, the Demon Barber of Fleet Street*, with music and lyrics by Stephen Sondheim and book by Hugh Wheeler, which opened in New York in 1979 and in London in the following year. The original productions of the musical won several awards. It was frequently revived, particularly in the United States. Although Bond declared that 'Sweeney Todd is pure fiction' (Sondheim, Wheeler, and Bond, xl), a belief persists that Todd existed, and Peter Haining has written several books arguing that Todd should be regarded as a historical figure. Todd is perhaps best described as a personification of early nineteenth-century fears of the anonymity of urban life built around some recorded events and older fictional or legendary sources.

MATTHEW KILBURN

Sources P. Haining, *The mystery and horrible murders of Sweeney Todd, the Demon Barber of Fleet Street* (1979) · B. Kalikoff, *Murder and moral decay in Victorian popular literature* (1986) · H. R. Smith, *New light on Sweeney Todd, Thomas Peckett Prest, James Malcolm Rymer and Elizabeth Caroline Grey* (2002) · *Annual Register* (1784–5), 208 · *London Chronicle* (2 Dec 1784) · N&Q, 5th ser., 10 (1878), 227 · N&Q, 9th ser., 7 (1901), 508; 8 (1901), 131, 168, 273–4, 348; 9 (1902), 345–6 · N&Q, 11th ser., 1 (1910), 468; 7 (1913), 426 · L. James, *Print and the people, 1819–1851* (1976) · M. Anglo, *Penny dreadfuls and other Victorian horrors* (1977) · S. Sondheim, H. Wheeler, and C. G. Bond, *Sweeney Todd, the Demon Barber of Fleet Street* (1991) · C. G. Bond, *Sweeney Todd, the Demon Barber of Fleet Street* (1974) · C. Dickens, *Martin Chuzzlewit*, ed. M. Cardwell (1982), 568, 576 · 'Star archive: Tod Slaughter', www.britishpictures.com/stars/Slaught.htm, 27 Sept 2002 · www.sondheim.com/shows/sweeney_todd, 10 Sept 2002 · private information (2004) [H. R. Smith]

Todhunter, Isaac (1820–1884), mathematician and historian of mathematics, was born on 23 November 1820 in Rye, Sussex, the second son of George Todhunter (*c.*1792–1825), Congregationalist minister, and his wife, Mary Hume (*c.*1790–1860). His father's death in 1825 left the family in reduced financial circumstances, and his mother opened a school for girls at Hastings. Todhunter, who as a child was 'unusually backward' (Macfarlane, 134), was

sent to a school in the same town kept by Robert Carr, and subsequently to one newly opened by a Mr J. B. Austin from London, by whose influence Todhunter's career was largely determined. About 1835 Todhunter moved with Austin to a school in Peckham where he became assistant master. While thus occupied, he managed to attend evening classes at University College, London, where he had for his instructors Thomas Hewitt Key, Henry Malden, George Long, James Joseph Sylvester, and Augustus De Morgan. He always held himself greatly indebted to all of them, but especially to the last, for whom his admiration was 'unbounded'. It was from this 'venerated master and friend' (Macfarlane, 142) he derived 'that interest in the history and bibliography of science, in moral philosophy and logic, which determined the course of his riper studies' (Mayor, 3). In 1842 Todhunter graduated BA, obtained a mathematical scholarship in the University of London, and, on proceeding MA two years later, obtained the gold medal awarded for that examination, as well as prizes for Greek and Hebrew. Concurrently with these studies, from 1841 he filled the post of mathematical master in a large school at Wimbledon.

On 4 May 1844, acting on De Morgan's advice, Todhunter entered St John's College, Cambridge. In 1848 he gained the senior wranglership and the first Smith's prize, as well as the Burney prize. In the following year he was elected fellow of his college (the delay probably being due to his nonconformist background). From this time he was mainly occupied as college lecturer and private tutor, and in the compilation of the numerous mathematical treatises, chiefly educational, by which he became widely known. Of these, his *Euclid* (1st edn, 1862) attained an enormous circulation and several editions, while his expositions of algebra (1858), trigonometry, plane and spherical (1859), mechanics (1867), and mensuration (1869), all became standard textbooks, remaining so until the beginning of the twentieth century. They secured a vast readership, were adopted by the Indian government, and were translated into Urdu and other oriental languages.

Todhunter was elected FRS on 5 June 1862, was a candidate for the Sadleirian professorship (to which Arthur Cayley was elected) in 1863, and became a member of the London Mathematical Society on 18 June 1866, in the second year of its existence. In 1864 he resigned his fellowship on his marriage, on 13 August, to Louisa Anna Maria (1832/3–1918), eldest daughter of Captain George Davies RN (at that time head of the Cambridge county constabulary force). In 1871 he won the Adams prize for his 'Researches on the calculus of variations'. Perhaps his most original work, it deals with the abstruse question of discontinuity in solution. In the same year he was elected a member of the council of the Royal Society, on which he served for two years. *The Conflict of Studies and other Essays* appeared in 1873, containing his views on many issues concerning education. In 1874 he was elected an honorary fellow of his college.

Todhunter's life was mainly that of a studious recluse, and his publications were the outcome of great research and industry which enabled him to acquire a wide acquaintance with general and foreign literature. Besides being a sound Latin and Greek scholar, he was also familiar with French, German, Spanish, Italian, Russian, Hebrew, Arabic, Persian, and Sanskrit. He was well versed in the history of philosophy, and was one of the chief founders of the moral science examination at Cambridge, acting as examiner in 1863–5. He was also responsible for editing posthumous works by two other prominent scientific figures: in 1865, the second edition of Boole's *Treatise on Differential Equations* and, eleven years later, the literary and scientific correspondence of William Whewell.

Todhunter is also remembered for his many valuable contributions to the history of mathematics. These were lengthy histories of the calculus of variations (1861), probability (1865), the theories of attraction and the figure of the earth (2 vols., 1873) and elasticity (2 vols., 1886–93), a posthumous publication completed by Karl Pearson. They remain valuable reference books to this day, although Todhunter's literary style hardly makes them light reading.

Todhunter's habits and tastes were singularly simple, and to a gentle, kindly disposition he added a high sense of honour, a warm sympathy with all that was calculated to advance the cause of genuinely scientific study in the university, and a love of animals, especially birds and cats. However, he had little love for art and no ear for music: 'He used to say he knew two tunes; one was "God save the Queen", the other wasn't; the former he recognized by the people standing up' (Macfarlane, 137). An affection of the eyes in 1880 proved the forerunner of an attack of paralysis which eventually prostrated him. He died on 1 March 1884, at his home, 6 Brookside, Trumpington Road, Cambridge. His widow, four sons, and a daughter survived him.   J. B. MULLINGER, *rev.* ADRIAN RICE

Sources J. E. B. M. [J. E. B. Mayor], 'In memoriam: Dr Todhunter', *Cambridge Review*, 5 (1883–4), 228–30, 245–7, 260–65; pubd separately (1884) • *The Eagle*, 13 (1885), 94–8 • E. J. R., *PRS*, 37 (1884), xxvii–xxxii • A. Macfarlane, *Lectures on ten British mathematicians of the nineteenth century* (1916), 134–46 • Venn, *Alum. Cant.* • W. Johnson, 'Isaac Todhunter, 1820–1884: textbook writer, scholar, coach and historian of science', *International Journal of Mechanical Sciences*, 38 (1996), 1231–70
Archives St John Cam., papers | CUL, letters to Sir George Stokes • RAS, letters to Royal Astronomical Society • RS, corresp. with Sir John Herschel • Trinity Cam., letters to J. I. Hammond • Trinity Cam., notebooks relating to W. Whewell • UCL, college corresp.
Likenesses E. R. Mullins, marble bust, St John Cam. • G. J. Stodart, print (after photograph), St John Cam. • T. C. Wageman, watercolour drawing, Trinity Cam. • four photographs, St John Cam. • medallion portrait, St John Cam.
Wealth at death £81,330 7s. 0d.: probate, 21 April 1884, *CGPLA Eng. & Wales*

Todhunter, John (1839–1916), playwright and poet, was born on 30 December 1839 at 19 Sir John Rogerson's Quay, Dublin, the eldest of the five surviving children of Thomas Harvey Todhunter (1799–1884), timber merchant, and his wife, Hannah Harvey (1806–1857), a cousin, and daughter of Joseph Massey Harvey, also a timber merchant, both members of the Society of Friends. He was educated in Quaker schools in Dublin, and later in Mountmellick, Queen's county, and York. Apprenticed to importing firms from the age of sixteen, he left that employ to study medicine at Trinity College, Dublin, taking his BA in 1867, MB and MCh in 1868, and MD in 1871, and studying in Vienna and Paris. He was assistant physician at Cork Street Fever Hospital in Dublin until 1874, but in 1870 also succeeded his friend and confidant Edward Dowden as professor of English literature at Alexandra College for Women. In 1872 he published an aesthetic treatise, *A Theory of the Beautiful*, to favourable comment in British and German intellectual circles. He contributed to the *Cornhill Magazine* under Thackeray's editorship.

Todhunter's marriage to Katharine Gresley Ball (*d.* 1871), daughter of Robert Ball, on 18 May 1870, ended with her death the following year in childbirth. Their son, Arthur, survived only until 1874. After experiencing this dual blow Todhunter resigned from the Society of Friends, ceased to practise medicine, and moved to London to pursue the artistic life. He was described by friends during this period as a large imposing man of sallow complexion and melancholic disposition. Although determined at first to become a painter like his college friend John Butler Yeats, Todhunter found himself gradually in London's Irish literary orbit, helping to found the Irish Literary Society and becoming a member of the Gaelic League, but also joining the Rhymers' Club, the Sette of Odd Volumes, and the Order of the Golden Dawn, along with his friend's son, William Butler Yeats, then an emerging poet.

On 12 July 1879, Todhunter married Dora Louisa, *née* Digby (1853?–1935). They had three children, Edith (1880–1946), John Reginald Arthur (1885–1968), and Margery Dorothea (1887–1968).

Todhunter's earliest literary success came with the publication of *The Banshee and other Poems* in 1888, which contains his most anthologized poem, 'Aghadoe', known to generations of Irish schoolchildren. It was, however, in the theatre that he would make his lasting literary contribution, initially with the staging of his verse play, *Helena in Troas*, in Hengler's Circus in 1886. Herbert Beerbohm Tree played a leading role and the newly wed Constance Wilde a minor one. Edward Godwin provided its elaborately authenticated stage design. Todhunter's most popular play, *A Sicilian Idyll*, a verse pastoral, was first performed in 1890 in the theatre in the model suburb and artists' colony at Bedford Park, Chiswick, where he lived.

In 1893 Todhunter's next theatrical success abandoned verse in an effort to keep pace with changing popular taste. *The Black Cat*, an Ibsenite prose play, was praised as avant-garde by William Archer. In the following year a fellow adept in the Order of the Golden Dawn, Florence Farr Emery, an actress, undertook with Todhunter and Annie Horniman to mount a season at the Avenue Theatre. Todhunter's *A Comedy of Sighs* (1894) was a play similarly constructed to *The Black Cat*, but with a contrived happy ending which avoided the earlier play's Hedda-esque suicide. Yeats's *Land of Heart's Desire* served as the curtain-raiser (in the event a disastrous choice, and unable to be heard by the audience). However, it was Todhunter's, not Yeats's, play that was replaced on the bill, by Shaw's *Arms and the Man*, a development that helped to launch that playwright's career. *A Comedy of Sighs* has an additional place in theatrical history in that the poster that advertised the production was an early commission for Aubrey Beardsley. It defied the convention that theatre posters be mostly typographic information. Beardsley's poster for the Yeats–Todhunter double bill, in vivid teal blue and lime green (considered a ghastly combination of colours at the time), featured a 'wanton' pre-Raphaelite beauty, and drew as much attention as the plays.

After the failure of *A Comedy of Sighs* Todhunter, who had enjoyed nearly two decades of literary success, seems to have withdrawn from public life. His considerable means provided a comfortable income. He is likely to have suffered from senility in his later years, and died after a long illness on 25 October 1916 at his home, Orchardcroft, 3 The Orchard, Bedford Park, Chiswick. He was cremated at Golders Green.

Todhunter experimented with many genres, writing a biography of Patrick Sarsfield and translating Goethe's *Faust* and Heine's *Book of Songs*. He provided the libretto for an oratorio, *The Legend of Stauffenberg*, which was composed by J. C. Culwick and performed to acclaim in Dublin in 1890, and another (unpublished and unperformed) for a children's opera *Pat in Fairyland*.

John Todhunter's literary achievement is, at its highest level, worthy. Most of his writing does not sustain that degree of attainment, but is a valuable record of the artistic taste of his era. His close connection with the Yeats family and minor role in the Irish literary revival earn him a secure place in literary history, as does the significance of his aesthetic, literary, and social affiliations in *fin de siècle* London. CHRISTINA HUNT MAHONY

Sources *The collected letters of W. B. Yeats*, 1, ed. J. Kelly and E. Domville (1986) · W. M. Murphy, *Prodigal father* (1978) · B. Cleeve, ed., *Dictionary of Irish writers*, 1 (1966) · B. J. P. McDermott, 'John Todhunter, MD, a minor figure in Anglo-Irish literature', MA diss., University College Dublin, 1968 · D. J. Moriarty, 'John Todhunter: child of the coming century', PhD diss., University of Wisconsin, Madison, 1979 · 'John Todhunter, MD, an account of his life', Religious Society of Friends, Dublin, Cup B, nos. 65–118 · H. Jackson, *The eighteen nineties* (1913); repr. (1976) · J. Johnson, *Florence Farr: Bernard Shaw's new woman* (1975) · R. S. Harrison, *A biographical dictionary of Irish Quakers* (1997) · H. Boylan, *A dictionary of Irish biography*, 2nd edn (1988) · m. cert. (1870) · d. cert.

Archives priv. coll., family papers · U. Reading L., corresp. and papers, MS 202.1–5 | Religious Society of Friends, Dublin, pedigree, John Todhunter of Cumberland and his descendants · TCD, corresp. with Edward Dowden, MS 3147–3154a, nos. 1–1132 · U. Leeds, Brotherton L., letters to Bram Stoker

Likenesses H. M. Paget, portrait, NG Ire. · J. Yeats, pencil sketch (*Portrait of Dr Todhunter at a calumet*), U. Reading

Wealth at death £8750 1s. 6d.: probate, 18 Jan 1917, CGPLA Eng. & Wales

Toft, Albert Arthur (1862–1949), sculptor, was born on 3 June 1862 in Hunters Lane, Handsworth, Birmingham, the son of Charles Toft (1832–1909) and his wife, Rosanna Reeves. He came from a family of Staffordshire pottery artists; his father was Wedgwood's principal modeller

Albert Arthur Toft (1862–1949), by unknown photographer, 1923 [in his studio, with the statue *Army*, unfinished]

from 1876 to 1888, and Albert himself served an apprenticeship there. Toft studied at the government schools of art at Hanley and Newcastle under Lyme, and in 1881 won a scholarship to the National Art Training School (later Royal College of Art), South Kensington. He was one of the earliest of Edward Lantéri's long line of outstanding sculpture students, winning silver medals in his second and third years.

Despite receiving offers to return to modelling for pottery, Toft gave priority to sculpture and, in doing so, 'passed through lean and trying years … much might be written concerning his struggles' (Reddie, 23). His earliest Royal Academy exhibits were reliefs, medallions, and portrait busts, the most important being that of W. E. Gladstone (1888; National Liberal Club, London). Modelled from the life, it was 'regarded by the family as his best portrait-bust' (Hamer, 396). Several ideal sculptures followed, including *Fate Led* (1892; Walker Art Gallery, Liverpool), *Spring* (1897; original model purchased for City of Birmingham Museum and Art Gallery), and *The Spirit of Contemplation* (1901; bronze, 1903, Laing Art Gallery, Newcastle upon Tyne). All three portray young nude women and possess characteristic New Sculpture qualities of naturalism in modelling and spiritual reverie in mood.

Commissions followed for commemorative portrait statuary, including monuments to Queen Victoria at Leamington Spa, Nottingham, and South Shields, and to

Edward VII at Birmingham and Warwick. Toft's allegorical reliefs are often more impressive than his actual statues. An example is the *Queen Victoria* statue (1905; Victoria Embankment, Nottingham), which is described by Susan Beattie as appearing 'almost superfluous to the complex fantasy explored below' (Beattie, 206). The *Charity* relief on the pedestal, framed by climbing roses, reflects the influence of Toft's friend Alfred Gilbert. Further major works include the Welsh memorial to the Second South African War (1910; Cathays Park, Cardiff) and four allegories representing the armed services (1923–4; Centenary Square, Birmingham). They comprise monumental seated bronze figures, which harmoniously complement the nearby Hall of Memory and attest to the vigour of the New Sculpture long after its supposed decline. In his Royal Fusiliers memorial, Holborn (1922; another version, Flers, France), Toft featured an alert soldier, bayonet fixed and ready for action.

Toft's early training in ceramics is indicated in his frequent use of terracotta, whose increasing unfashionableness he regretted. About 1913 he was commissioned to design the Royal Doulton slip-cast figure of W. S. Penley as *Charlie's Aunt*, a work that reveals his witty versatility. A notable work in yet another medium is Toft's coronation medal of George V and Queen Mary (1911); on the reverse, the dramatic use of lines to denote the ship of state again attests to Gilbert's influence. Although Toft regularly exhibited at the Royal Academy over many years (1885–1947), he was not elected to its membership. This was probably due to the abundance of talented sculptors slightly senior to Toft when his career was at its height. He was, however, elected to the Art Workers' Guild (1891) and to a fellowship of the Royal Society of British Sculptors (1938). Toft died in a nursing home, at 22 Downview Road, Worthing, Sussex, on 18 December 1949. He was married, and had at least one child, a daughter. His work is represented in the Tate collection; the Walker Art Gallery, Liverpool; Birmingham City Art Gallery; and the Laing Art Gallery, Newcastle upon Tyne. His public statuary is in many cities and towns in England and Wales.

Toft's temperament was described as 'warm and genial' (Reddie, 23), qualities which he displayed towards Gilbert following the latter's resignation from the Royal Academy and bankruptcy. Perhaps Toft's greatest claim to enduring significance is his book *Modelling and Sculpture* (1911; reprinted 1949). Less detailed and more accessible to the layman than Lantéri's *Modelling*, the text is clear and commonsensical, if conservative. In it, Toft celebrates 'the renaissance of the sculptor's art in Great Britain' (Toft, 19) and stresses the significance of Italian Renaissance sculpture and the legacy of Alfred Stevens in bringing this about.   MARK STOCKER

Sources A. Toft, *Modelling and sculpture: a full account of the various methods and processes employed in these arts* (1911); repr. (1949) • M. H. Spielmann, *British sculpture and sculptors of to-day* (1901) • A. Reddie, 'Albert Toft: sculptor', *The Studio*, 66 (1915–16), 18–28 • J. Hamer, 'Our rising artists: Mr Albert Toft', *Magazine of Art*, 25 (1900–01), 393–7 • S. Beattie, *The New Sculpture* (1983) • G. T. Noszlopy, *Public sculpture of Birmingham* (1998) • B. Read, *Victorian sculpture* (1982) • *The Times* (c.22 Dec 1949) • J. Glaves-Smith, ed., *Reverie, myth, sensuality: sculpture in Britain, 1880–1910* (1992) [exhibition catalogue, Stoke-on-Trent City Museum and Art Gallery, 26 Sept–29 Nov 1992, and Cartwright Hall, Bradford, 12 Dec 1992–7 March 1993] • A. Borg, *War memorials: from antiquity to the present* (1991) • R. Dorment and others, *Alfred Gilbert: sculptor and goldsmith* (1986) [exhibition catalogue, RA, 21 March – 29 June 1986] • J. Darke, *The monument guide to England and Wales* (1991) • J. Quérée, *Royal Doulton: illustrated with treasures from New Zealand and Australia* (1993) • J. Newman, S. Hughes, and A. Ward, *Glamorgan* (1995) • P. Attwood, *Artistic circles: the medal in Britain, 1880–1918* (1992) [exhibition catalogue] • Graves, *RA exhibitors* • b. cert. • d. cert.
Archives RA, M. H. Spielmann MSS
Likenesses A. Toft, self-portrait, drawing, 1901, repro. in *Magazine of Art*, 23 (1901) • photograph, c.1905, repro. in Toft, *Modelling and sculpture* • photograph, c.1922, repro. in Noszlopy, *Public sculpture of Birmingham* • photograph, 1923, Birmingham Central Library [see illus.] • H. Leslie, silhouette, NPG
Wealth at death £16,367 18s. 2d.: probate, 4 March 1950, CGPLA Eng. & Wales

Toft [*née* Denyer], **Mary** (bap. **1703**, d. **1763**), the 'rabbit-breeder', daughter of John and Jane Denyer, was baptized at Godalming, Surrey, on 21 February 1703. She married Joshua Toft, a journeyman clothier, about 1720. They had three children, Mary, Anne, and James. Joshua, who followed a trade in which many, including himself, were chronically underemployed, provided little income for his family. Mary, an illiterate, was of small stature, with a healthy, strong constitution, and a sullen temper.

In August of 1726 Mary miscarried. On 27 September 1726 Mary, her husband, and her mother-in-law cut up a cat, removed its innards, inserted the backbone of an eel into the cat's intestines, and placed the creation in Mary's reproductive tract. Mary sent for a neighbour, Mary Gill, and after her arrival complained of great pains, feigned a brief labour, and was delivered of a 'monster'. The 'monster' was taken to John Howard, a surgeon practising midwifery in nearby Guildford. Howard claimed he would be convinced that 'the monster' was an actual birth product only if the 'monstrous head' was delivered. Mary obliged, and after a few days, was delivered of the head of a rabbit. Mary recalled that earlier, when five weeks pregnant, she was startled by a rabbit while working in the hop fields. Immediately she desired the rabbit for a meal, but was unable to catch the animal. Her cravings were further increased by a dream about rabbits, yet her longings remained unfulfilled. Four months later, she claimed to have been delivered of a strange misshapen piece of flesh. She made a similar delivery some three weeks later, at which time Howard was called.

As soon as Mary Toft was delivered of her first whole rabbit-headed monster, she fell into labour once again. By early November, with Howard in attendance, she was producing almost a rabbit a day. Toft was moved to Guildford so that Howard could more closely monitor the situation, and she soon gave birth to her ninth rabbit. Howard preserved the delivered products, all still births, in spirits, kept notes on the deliveries, and recorded the progress of events. Toft's case soon gained more than casual notice. Nathanael St Andre, surgeon and anatomist to the royal household, and Samuel Molyneux, private secretary to

Mary Toft (*bap.* 1703, *d.* 1763), by John Faber junior (after John Laguerre)

the prince of Wales, took particular interest in this case. On 15 November they visited Howard, examined Toft, and witnessed her delivery of the fifteenth rabbit. After carefully comparing the pieces obtained from a series of deliveries, St Andre was convinced of their authenticity, and he prepared an account of the matter which was subsequently published on 3 December as *A Short Narrative of an Extraordinary Delivery of Rabbits, Perform'd by Mr John Howard Surgeon at Guilford.*

The Toft incident soon appeared in the periodical press, and Mary became the general talk of the town in London. George I dispatched Cyriacus Ahlers, surgeon to his majesty's German household, to investigate the matter. Ahlers arrived in Guildford on 20 November, and delivered part of a rabbit from Toft. Ever suspicious, Ahlers returned to London on 21 November and reported to the king that the births were a hoax. His published account, *Some Observations Concerning the Woman of Godlyman,* appeared on 8 December 1726. In an effort to resolve the controversial reports, George I dispatched the eminent London physician and man-midwife, Sir Richard Manningham, together with St Andre and Phillupus van Limborch, a surgeon and man-midwife, to Guildford to review the situation and return with Toft who had, by this time, been delivered of a total of seventeen rabbits.

Toft reached London on 29 November, and was lodged in Lacy's Bagnio in Leicester Fields, where assorted members of the medical profession gathered to watch her next production. Although Toft underwent a series of violent contractions, no more rabbits were delivered. Besieged by a succession of men, including Manningham, the surgeon

and anatomist James Douglas, justice of the peace Sir Thomas Clarges, the duke of Montagu, and Lord Baltimore, and threatened with 'a very painful experiment' to uncover any secret, Toft confessed her imposture on 7 December. Charged as a 'notorious and vile cheat', she was sent to Bridewell in Tothill Fields on 9 December.

At least fifteen pamphlets and songs appeared following Toft's disclosure, satirizing what was portrayed as a mass delusion. Among these were: by a 'Gentleman at Guilford', *The wonder of wonders, or, A true and perfect narrative of a woman near Guilford in Surrey, who was delivered lately of seventeen rabbets and three legs of a tabby cat* (1726); *Doctors in labour: a philosophical enquiry into the wonderful coney-warren, lately discovered at Godalmin near Guilford in Surrey* (1726); *The Sooterkin Dissected* (1726); T. Brathwaite, *Remarks on a short narrative of an extraordinary delivery of rabbets, perform'd by Mr. John Howard, surgeon at Guilford* (1726); *The Doctor's in Labour, or, A New Whim Wham from Guildford* (1726); R. Manningham, *An exact diary of what was observ'd during a close attendance upon Mary Toft, the pretended rabbet-breeder of Godalming in Surrey* (1726); J. Douglas, *An Advertisement Occasion'd by some Passages in Sir R. Manningham's Diary* (1727); *St. A–D–E's Miscarriage: a Full and True Account of the Rabbit Woman* (1727); Lemuel Gulliver, *The Anatomist Dissected, or, The Man-Midwife Finely Brought to Bed* (1727); *Much ado about nothing, or, A plain refutation of all that has been written or said concerning the rabbit-woman of Godalming* (1727); *The Discovery, or, The Squire Turned Ferret* (1727); and *St Andre's Miscarriage* (1727). Many of these works depicted Toft's surgical and medical attendants as gullible and credulous.

Toft was also parodied in several engravings, including William Hogarth's *The cunicularii, or, The wise men of Godliman in consultation* and, later, the second version of his engraving *Credulity, superstition, and fanaticism* (1762), as well as in a Drury Lane play. Toft's account continued to spark interest, most notably in Alexander Pope's poem, the *Dunciad* (1728), which revolves around a woman who proliferated monsters, and in the Daniel Turner–James Blondel controversy over the power of the maternal imagination. The case against Toft was dropped, and she returned to Godalming. Charles, second duke of Richmond, occasionally showed Mary as a spectacle or curiosity at his residence in Godalming. She was reportedly charged with receiving stolen 'fowles' in 1740. Toft died in Godalming, and was buried there on 13 January 1763.

PHILIP K. WILSON

Sources D. Todd, *Imagining monsters: miscreations of the self in eighteenth-century England* (1995) · S. A. Seligman, 'Mary Toft: the rabbit breeder', *Medical History,* 5 (1961), 349–60 · L. Cody, '"The doctor's in labour, or, A new whim wham from Guildford"', *Gender and History,* 4 (1992), 172–96 · L. Lewis Wall, 'The strange case of Mary Toft (who was delivered of sixteen rabbits and a tabby cat in 1726)', *Medical Heritage,* 1 (1985), 199–212 · parish register (baptism), Godalming, Surrey, 21 Feb 1703 · parish register (burial), Godalming, Surrey, 13 Jan 1763 · *The several depositions of Edward Costen, Richard Stedman, John Sweetapple, Mary Peyton, Elizabeth Mason, and Mary Costen: relating to the affair of Mary Toft, of Godalming in the county of Surrey, being deliver'd of several rabbits* (1727)

Archives LUL, Harry Price collection · U. Glas., Douglas MSS

Likenesses W. Hogarth, engraving, 1726 (*Cuniculari*), BL · J. Laguerre, engraving, *c.*1726, BL · line engraving, pubd 1810,

NPG • J. Faber junior, engraving (after J. Laguerre), NPG [*see illus.*] • W. Hogarth, engraving (*Credulity, superstition, and fanaticism*), BL • Hogarth, two etchings, Wellcome L. • Maddocks, stipple (after J. Laguerre), BM, NPG; repro. in J. Caulfield, *Portraits, memoirs, and characters of remarkable persons*, 4 vols. (1819–20) • stipple, Wellcome L. • stipple with watercolour, Wellcome L.

Tofte [Tafte], **Robert** (*bap.* 1562, *d.* 1619/20), poet and translator, was baptized in the parish of St Magnus the Martyr, London, on 15 January 1562, the younger son of William Tofte, a fishmonger (*d.* 1563) and his wife, Mary, the daughter of John Cowper, fishmonger and alderman for the ward of Bridge Without. The family seems to have originally been in the wool trade in the Guildford area. C. A. O. Fox claims he was the Robert Tafte (aged nineteen) who matriculated at Exeter College, Oxford, on 24 November 1581. He could also be the Robert Tafte, gentleman, who was paid for carrying official letters to Sir Edward Stafford, ambassador to France, in October 1590. Tofte did at times use the spelling Tafte for his name (Williams, 286). It seems he never married, and had a private income.

Tofte travelled around Italy from March 1591 to June 1594, and showed a keen interest in things Italian, which resulted in a manuscript, 'Discourse of the five laste Popes' (now Lambeth MS 1112). Although he took a dispassionate interest in Roman Catholic theology and church organization, he remained firmly protestant. He also became very familiar with the conventions of pastoral poetry. Renaissance pastoral depicted love and other pleasures in an idealized country setting, while often commenting on contemporary events, both public and private, and like the medieval courtly love poem it was a safe cover for declaring one's passion for an unattainable lady. Before Tofte left Italy he began *Laura*, a collection of short pastoral poems, and a short sonnet sequence 'moste parte conceived in Italie, and some of them brought foorthe in England'.

On his return to Britain in 1594 Tofte was embroiled in a lawsuit before the court of queen's bench over the banking arrangements for his trip. Tofte claimed that he had paid William Garraway, a London merchant, £45 16*s.* 8*d.* for bills of exchange that were to be cashed in Venice for 200 ducats. But Garraway's agent refused to honour the bills. Tofte sought damages of £100 for loss of credit. It is not known how the matter was resolved. In 1597 he published *Laura*, dedicating it to Lady Lucy Percy, the daughter of the eighth earl of Northumberland, and *Two Tales Translated out of Ariosto*. At this time he was living in the inns of court, but in 1598 he took rooms in Mistress Goodall's house near Barnard's Inn in Holborn. That year he published a translation of Matheo Maria Boiardo's *Orlando inamorato*, and his most important work, *Alba*, a cycle of poems on unrequited love dedicated to Anne Herne, the wife of Sir Edward Herne and sister of Sir John Brooke, to whom one of the prefatory poems is written. It is now extremely rare, and was edited in 1880 by Alexander Grosart.

Like Philip Sidney's *Astrophil*, *Alba* is probably autobiographical. It seems that Alba was a young married woman of the Caryll family with whom Tofte was infatuated. Grosart suggests she was Mary Caryll, the daughter of Sir Thomas Caryll of Bentone, Sussex. She married Sir Richard Molyneux of Sefton, who became Viscount Molyneux of Mayborough. She seems to have led Tofte on for many years before finally dropping him. Even the forematter of *Alba* observes pastoral convention: the last eight of its lyrics are arranged in the form of the song contest common in classical pastoral (cf. Virgil, *Eclogues* III, V, and VII). A number of these poems play on Tofte's nickname, Robin Redbreast. *Alba* is also notable for a reference to Shakespeare's *Love's Labour Lost*, in which Tofte saw a parallel to his own predicament.

In March 1599 came *Of Mariage and Wiving: an Excellent, Pleasant and Philosophicall Controversy*, Tofte's translation of Ercole Tasso's *Dello ammogliarsi piacevole*, in which Tasso argues against marriage and his brother, Torquato, defends it. This book was burnt at Stationers' Hall on 4 June 1599 under the provisions against satire. Another work on a similar theme, *The Bachelor's Banquet* (1603), a version of *Les quinze joies de mariage*, was probably by Tofte, and promised, in its full title, discourses on 'the variable humours of women, their quicknesse of wittes, and unsearchable deceits'. By this time it seems Tofte was acquiring a reputation for misogyny. His next work appeared in 1608, *Ariosto's Satyres*, published under the name of Gervais Markham, which Tofte bitterly resented. In the preface to his *Blazon of Jealousie* (1615) he writes:

> I had thought for thy better contentment to have inserted (at the end of the Booke) the disastrous fall of three noble Roman Gentlemen, overthrowne thorow jealousie, in their Loves; but the same was, with Ariosto's Satyres (translated by mee out of Italian into English Verse, and Notes upon the same) Printed without my consent or knowledge, in another man's name.

The publisher reissued the book in 1611, without the name of the translator. Tofte's other translations are *Honours Academie* (1610), from the French of Nicolas de Montreux, and Benedetto Varchi's *Blazon of Jealousie* published 'with special notes' in 1615.

Tofte was buried at St Andrew's, Holborn, on 24 January 1620. His long will specifically excludes 'my kinnesfolkes whose underserved unkyndenes and ingratitude towardes me hath estranged my harte from them'. Apart from the poor of the parish and certain friends, the beneficiaries of his will are a network of cousins belonging to the Urrie family of Thorlie, Isle of Wight, and the Day family of West Drayton, Middlesex. Tofte left a considerable estate, bequeathing about £750 in cash and almost the same amount in personal effects.   L. G. KELLY

Sources F. B. Williams, 'Robert Tofte', *Review of English Studies*, 13 (1937), 282–96; 405–24 • R. Tofte, *Alba*, ed. A. Grosart (1880) • C. A. O. Fox, *Notes on William Shakespeare and Robert Tofte* (privately printed, 1957)

Wealth at death approx. £1500; incl. cash and legacies to cousins: Tofte, *Alba*

Tofts, Catherine (*d.* 1756), singer, 'took her first Grounds of Musick here in her own Country' (Cibber, 226), but although she was to become the first English prima donna, her background and teachers are unknown. She appeared in eight subscription concerts at Drury Lane and Lincoln's Inn Fields theatres between 30 November 1703 and 14 March 1704, missing a concert on 14 December because of 'a great Cold' (*Daily Courant*, 21 Dec 1703). On each occasion she sang several songs in Italian and English and on 18 January she was also advertised as singing Pallas in John Weldon's *The Judgment of Paris*. A songsheet of 'Fly swift ye hours' by Henry Purcell was published as 'Sung by Mrs. Tofts in the Subscription Musick'. (At this time the title 'Mrs' does not indicate that she was married.) On 8 February 1704 a letter from Mrs Tofts was printed in the *Daily Courant*, expressing surprise and annoyance that her former servant, Ann Barwick, had 'committed a Rudeness last night at the Play-house, by throwing of Oranges, and hissing when Mrs. l'Epine the Italian Gentlewoman Sung'. The two singers were supported by different political factions, the whigs favouring 'British Tofts', and the tories 'fam'd L'Epine' (*Diverting Post*, 9–16 June 1705), but there is no evidence of personal animosity between them.

On 16 January 1705 at Drury Lane, Mrs Tofts took the title role in the first English opera in the Italian style, Thomas Clayton's *Arsinoe*, and a year later in the even more successful *Camilla* (Bononcini, arranged by Haym), the part with which she became identified. On 4 March 1707 she sang in Clayton's *Rosamond*, which had a libretto by Joseph Addison, and on 1 April in *Thomyris* (pasticcio, arranged by Pepusch). The arrival of the castrato Valentini led to opera performances in a mixture of Italian and English. Mrs Tofts, singing in English, had leading roles in *Love's Triumph* (26 February 1708), *Pyrrhus and Demetrius* (14 December 1708), and *Clotilda* (2 March 1709). The actor Colley Cibber never forgot 'the Beauty of her fine proportion'd Figure, and the exquisitely sweet, silver Tone of her Voice, with that peculiar, rapid Swiftness of her Throat' (Cibber, 226). She earned a reputation for avarice and pride and was repeatedly involved in disputes over pay, costume, and conditions. In March 1709 Charles Dering wrote that her benefit would raise 'a vast deal' and that she had been selling kisses at a guinea a time at the duke of Somerset's, where 'some took three, others four, others five kisses' (Milhous and Hume, *Register*, 437). Then on 26 May *The Tatler* reported 'the Distresses of the unfortunate *Camilla*, who has had the ill Luck to break before her Voice' (*The Tatler*, 26 May 1709). The details that follow have generally been interpreted as meaning that she had a nervous breakdown and Sir John Hawkins claimed that her mental problems returned later in her life. She never sang again in England. Anthony Hammond encountered her in the Netherlands *en route* for Hanover in July 1711 and by December she was in Venice. The following April the *Daily Courant* reported that she was much applauded there for her singing in grand private concerts. In September 1716 Alexander Cunningham wrote from Venice: 'As for Mr Smith he is soe much in Love wt Mrs Tofts, that he is fitt for nothing at present' (Levey, 352). This was Joseph *Smith (1673/4?–1770), a successful businessman and later British consul in Venice who was to become a patron of Canaletto and a collector of fine books and paintings, many of which are now in the Royal Collection. The date of his marriage to Catherine Tofts is unknown, but she was travelling under the name of Smith when Hammond met her in 1711; Hawkins, in his *History of Music*, states that Mrs Tofts travelled to Venice after marrying Smith. The Smiths lived in style in the Palazzo Balbi on the Grand Canal and a villa at Mogliano. It is likely that they had a son, since there is a tombstone for John Smith (1721–1727) in a church near their palazzo. She died early in 1756 and her husband erected a fine memorial to her in the protestant cemetery of San Nicolò del Lido.

OLIVE BALDWIN and THELMA WILSON

Sources E. L. Avery, ed., *The London stage, 1660–1800*, pt 2: *1700–1729* (1960) • *Daily Courant* (30 Nov 1703) • *Daily Courant* (14 Dec 1703) • *Daily Courant* (21 Dec 1703) • *Daily Courant* (4 Jan 1704) • *Daily Courant* (18 Jan 1704) • *Daily Courant* (1 Feb 1704) • *Daily Courant* (8 Feb 1704) • *Daily Courant* (21 Feb 1704) • *Daily Courant* (22 Feb 1704) • *Daily Courant* (7 March 1704) • *Daily Courant* (14 March 1704) • *Daily Courant* (25 April 1712) • M. Sands, 'Mrs. Tofts, 1685?–1756', *Theatre Notebook*, 20 (1965–6), 100–13 • C. Cibber, *An apology for the life of Mr. Colley Cibber* (1740) • J. Milhous and R. D. Hume, eds., *Vice Chamberlain Coke's theatrical papers, 1706–1715* (1982) • J. Milhous and R. D. Hume, eds., *A register of English theatrical documents, 1660–1737*, 1 (1991) • *The Tatler* (24–6 May 1709) • *The Spectator* (26 March 1711) • *The Spectator* (29 July 1712) • E. W. White, 'The rehearsal of an opera', *Theatre Notebook*, 14 (1959–60), 79–90 • M. Sands, 'The rehearsal of an opera', *Theatre Notebook*, 19 (1964–5), 30–31 • *Diverting Post* (24 Feb–3 March 1705) • *Diverting Post* (9–16 June 1705) • *Diverting Post* (23–30 June 1705) • *Diverting Post* (Feb 1706) • *Miscellanies in verse* (1727) • R. G. Schafer, 'Mrs Tofts goes abroad', *Huntington Library Quarterly*, 25 (1961–2), 69–70 • M. Levey, 'Marco Ricci and "Madama Smit"', *Burlington Magazine* (1962), 351–2 • J. Hawkins, *A general history of the science and practice of music*, 5 (1776) • *The life of Mr. Thomas Betterton* (1710) • P. Danchin, ed., *The prologues and epilogues of the eighteenth century: a complete edition* (1990–), vol. 1 • *N&Q*, 10th ser., 4 (1905), 221–2, 282–4, 383–4 • *The complete letters of Lady Mary Wortley Montagu*, ed. R. Halsband, 3 (1967)

Togodumnus (*d.* AD 43). *See under* Roman Britain, British leaders in (*act.* 55 BC–AD 84).

Toland, John (1670–1722), freethinker and philosopher, was born on 30 November 1670 on the peninsula of Inishowen, co. Donegal, Ireland. Although his parents are unknown, he supposedly was the illegitimate son of a Roman Catholic priest and was probably baptized Seán Eoghain (Sean Owen, John's John). He later wrote that he had been baptized Janus Junius, a play on his name that recalled both the Roman two-faced god Janus and Junius Brutus, reputed founder of the Roman republic. Appealing to his ability to read ancient Gaelic texts, he claimed a respected Irish ancestry, probably descent from the Uí Tuathalláin family, traditional historians and bards for the once powerful O'Neills.

Education and early years While still a child Owen of the Books (as Toland was known) developed a critical attitude toward his religious upbringing. At the age of sixteen he rejected Catholicism, 'the insupportable Yoke of the most Pompous and Tyrannical *Policy* that ever enslav'd Mankind under the name or shew of Religion' (J. Toland, *An Apology for Mr. Toland*, 1697, 16). Supported by Presbyterian sponsors who hoped that he would become a minister, he attended Redcastle School in Londonderry and in 1687 enrolled in the University of Glasgow. In 1689 he moved from Glasgow to the University of Edinburgh where he received the MA degree in 1690. In Edinburgh he seems to have had his first involvement with secret societies (probably the Rosicrucians). Soon afterwards he travelled to London where he tutored in the household of a wealthy widow and met prominent figures such as Daniel Williams 'the Presbyterian Pope'. Impressed by the young Irishman, Presbyterians in London sent him to the universities of Leiden and Utrecht to study under Friedrich Spanheim the younger. From Spanheim he learned exegetical techniques of biblical criticism developed by Baruch Spinoza, Pierre Bayle, and Richard Simon.

At the Rotterdam house of the English Quaker merchant Benjamin Furly, Toland met the Dutch remonstrant theologians Philip van Limborch and Jean Le Clerc, who wrote letters of introduction for him to John Locke. They described Toland as a 'freespirited ingenious man' and an 'excellent and not unlearned young man … frank, gentlemanly, and not at all of a servile character' (Daniel, 7). In the summer of 1693 he returned to London; a few months later he moved to Oxford to work at the Bodleian Library on an Irish dictionary and a dissertation proving that the Irish had been a colony of the Gauls. To the Ashmolean Museum curator Edward Lhuyd, Toland seemed arrogant but he impressed others (including the antiquary John Aubrey) as a promising scholar. He borrowed money from Locke, exchanged ideas about their manuscripts, and came to know Locke's closest friends, such as John Freke and James Tyrrell. In 'The fabulous death of Atilius Regulus' he questioned the reliability of classical texts, and in his manuscript of 'Christianity not mysterious' he combined a Lockean theory of meaning with strategies of biblical criticism learned from Spanheim. Locke's *Reasonableness of Christianity* (1695) seems to have been in part a response to points raised by Toland.

In conservative Oxford, Toland's coffee-house polemics quickly gained him a reputation as 'a man of fine parts, great learning, and little religion' (Daniel, 8). After the vice-chancellor ordered him out of the city, he retired to London and anonymously published *Two Essays Sent in a Letter from Oxford*. In *Two Essays* he introduced the materialist cosmology to which he would appeal for the rest of his life, arguing that fossils could have been shaped in rock by a 'plastic power' that contains the seeds of all forms of matter.

Christianity not Mysterious Toland was but twenty-five when his most famous work, *Christianity not Mysterious*, anonymously appeared late in 1695 (with a 1696 imprint). In it he argued that no tenets of true Christianity could be contrary to or above human reason, for if they were they would be unintelligible. This contradicted Locke who, in the *Essay Concerning Human Understanding* (1690), had argued that revealed truths (for example, about the divinity of Christ) may be above but are not contrary to reason. Toland countered that once a truth is divinely revealed, it is no longer beyond human comprehension; it is neither contrary to reason nor above reason. An unintelligible belief could not be an object of faith because no believer can assent to a doctrine without understanding what it

would mean to hold that belief. He concluded that the so-called mysteries of Christianity are not essential to the faith at all but are either puzzles that can be solved or ploys by which priests exercise control over others.

The book immediately caused a furore and was presented to the grand jury of Middlesex. A second edition appeared in late summer 1696 identifying its author. In early 1697 Toland returned to Ireland and introduced himself to Locke's friend William Molyneux. Molyneux wrote to Locke that he had found Toland a 'candid free-thinker and a good scholar' but that clerical animosity and Toland's practice of conducting theological disputes in taverns made it awkward to be seen with him (Sullivan, 7). Apparently Toland had hoped to offer his scholarly and linguistic skills to the new lord chancellor, John Methuen. But in Dublin his book was denounced from the pulpit as a Socinian attack against the divinity of Christ, and Peter Browne, provost of Trinity College, Dublin, blasted him for reducing faith to mere knowledge. In September it was condemned by the Irish House of Commons and Toland was ordered to be arrested. Before the order could be carried out, he retreated to London and spent the next five years defending his 'juvenile thoughts' and 'unadvised expressions' (as he called them). In a self-deluded bid to stand in the general election for a borough in London, he sought to clear his name in 1702 by resolving 'never hereafter to intermeddle in any religious controversies' (J. Toland, *Vindicius liberius*, 1702, 5).

None of this notoriety was missed by patrons attracted to his learning and free-spirited method of inquiry. Anthony Ashley Cooper, third earl of Shaftesbury, shared Toland's interest in antiquity, philosophy, religion, and opposition to superstition. It was probably through Shaftesbury that Toland met the leader of the 'country' forces in the House of Commons, Robert Harley, later first earl of Oxford. Harley saw in Toland an advocate for traditional whig causes supporting religious toleration for dissenters and the protestant succession. Other whigs, such as John Holles, first duke of Newcastle, and Sir Robert Clayton, director of the Bank of England and mayor of London, commissioned Toland to prepare biographies and editions to show how Commonwealthsmen Algernon Sidney, Denzil Holles, Edmund Ludlow, John Milton, and James Harrington were models of public religion and civic virtue. With Ludlow's *Memoirs* in particular, Toland took great liberties, changed its tone, improved its style, added his own reflections, and eliminated thousands of words written by the civil war republican. His portrait of Ludlow provided a model for both the notorious Calves-Head Club and for aristocratic whigs, and it united radical thinkers such as John Phillips, Matthew Tindal, and William Stephens, with members of the Grecian Club such as John Trenchard and Walter Moyle, and 'Roman' whigs like Shaftesbury, Harley, and Robert Molesworth. In the *Militia Reform'd* and *The Danger of Mercenary Parliaments* (both 1698) he endorsed the effort of Harley's country party coalition of Jacobite tories and republican whigs to prevent William's standing army from entering England. In his life of John Milton (1698) he argued that the *Eikon basilike* was not written by Charles I, as claimed, but by his chaplain, Gauden, and he added that many ancient writings, both secular and religious, were forgeries. When he was accused of doubting the authenticity of the Christian scriptures, he displayed his scholarly and exegetical abilities in *Amyntor* (1699) with a list of more than seventy spurious gospels, epistles, and acts attributed by early Christian writers and church fathers to Christ, Mary, and the apostles. Always seeking to portray himself as a defender of the faith, Toland turned even seemingly academic disputes about religion into opportunities for political alliances and, prompted by Harley and Shaftesbury, drew those themes together in *The Art of Governing by Partys* and *Paradoxes of State* (1702).

Pleased by Toland's justification of the protestant succession in *Anglia libera* (1701), Harley requested that the Irishman be selected as a secretary to the embassy of Hanover under Charles Girard, second earl of Macclesfield. Toland had the honour to present the Act of Settlement and a copy of his book to the Electress Sophia, who in turn introduced him to the court in Berlin and to her daughter, Sophie Charlotte, queen of Prussia. Amused by his wit, impressed by his knowledge of ten languages, and attracted by his good looks, the queen liked to walk and converse with Toland for hours at a time. In turn, he presented her with his rare copy of Giordano Bruno's *Expulsion of the Triumphant Beast*.

In 1702 Toland returned to Berlin where, in numerous discussions in the presence of the queen, he and G. W. Leibniz began a philosophical exchange that would last for years. Although Leibniz expressed doubts about Toland's manners, he respected the young man's intellect and even wrote a brief reply to *Christianity not Mysterious*, which Toland received with great pleasure. Toland's suggestions that Leibniz pay special attention to the works of Bruno were generally ignored, but his promotion of the Italian thinker gained Toland notoriety for his knowledge of rare books and manuscripts containing heterodox doctrines.

While passing through Holland on this second trip to Germany, Toland provided Pierre Bayle with a materialistic account of the soul that Bayle incorporated into the second edition of his *Dictionary*. He also met Baron von Hohendorf, chief lieutenant to Prince Eugène of Savoy, commander of the armies of the Austrian Habsburgs, who commissioned him to increase the prince's library of rare and clandestine works. It was especially in this context that Toland encouraged the widespread study of Bruno in clandestine circles.

After his return to England Toland set to work on *Letters to Serena* (Queen Sophie Charlotte). In it he diagnosed the origin and force of prejudices and superstitions, argued that motion was essential to matter, and rejected Spinoza's ahistorical account of motion and Newton's reliance on divine agency. When the book was published in 1704, followers of Newton (notably Samuel Clarke) quickly recognized the political and religious implications of Toland's attack on Newtonian physics in that it indicated how individuals did not need external, whether monarchical, clerical, or spiritual, inspiration to act.

Political propagandist After Harley became secretary of state in 1704, Toland expected to receive a more stable income than that provided by the occasional political piece commissioned by Harley. But Harley continued to rely on Toland merely as a source of information about intrigues on the continent and as a propagandist. Using the Quaker leader William Penn as an intermediary, Sidney Godolphin (the lord treasurer) had Toland compose *The Memorial of the State of England* (1705) to show how occasional religious conformity contributed to a stable commonwealth. Such commissions were hardly enough to support Toland, so Penn appealed to Harley on his behalf. Toland assured Harley that he had broken off the 'tattling and mean acquaintances' of his coffee-house days and publicly presented himself as a staunch supporter of the Church of England (Sullivan, 24). Although Harley remained aloof, Toland continued to supply him with confidential reports and to procure additions to his library.

In 1707 Toland returned to the continent. In Düsseldorf, desperate for money, he accepted a commission to write *The Declaration Lately Published by the Elector Palatine* (1707), in which he explained the elector's claim to have the right to curtail religious liberty, even if that meant the submission of protestants to Catholics. He next travelled to Hanover and Berlin and then on to Vienna where his knowledge of Bruno and hermetic texts was appreciated as nowhere else. He wintered in Prague at a convent of Irish Franciscans who attested to his ancestry and his scholarly credentials for Gaelic research. Early in 1708 he returned to Berlin where, despite his charm, he upset members of the court by claiming more privilege than his status warranted. In addition, he irritated Leibniz by drawing little distinction between superstition and true religion.

On his way back to England, Toland learned that Harley had been forced out of office, so without much prospect for fortune in England, he remained in Holland. His research turned to showing how primitive (especially Celtic) Christianity was not characterized by pomp or austere submission to a set of papist doctrines. Instead, he suggested, ancient Christianity celebrated fellowship, freedom of conscience, and egalitarian social virtues. Furthermore he imagined hermeneutic strategies for retrieving those ideals from centuries of institutionalized superstition. Some of this work he dedicated to his friend and fellow freethinker, Anthony Collins, in *Adeisidaemon* ('The unsuperstitious man'; 1709). He expanded on this research in *Nazarenus* (1718), in which he proposed that the ancient Celtic beliefs revealed in an Irish manuscript of the four gospels captured the true spirit of Christianity, Judaism, and Islam. In *Reasons for Naturalizing the Jews* (1714), he even went so far as to suggest that Jews should be afforded the same rights as other citizens of the nation.

After Harley's return to power in the tory government of October 1710, Toland still believed that Harley was primarily committed to the protestant succession and Queen Anne. So Toland returned to England early in 1711, supported by Harley with work and a house at Epsom. When

Harley was almost killed in an assassination attempt in March 1711, enemies of Toland spread a false rumour that the assassin was one of his correspondents. But Harley's affections for Toland (for whatever they were worth) had dissipated by then, and his concerns were less with maintaining whig ideals than with securing peace with the French. Toland knew this and shortly thereafter became an informer to Harley's political opponents.

For the next two years Toland's lifelong interests in religious toleration and civil liberty were the focus of his writings. When those principles seemed to have been thoroughly ignored in the government's negotiation of a commercial treaty with France in the peace of Utrecht (1713), he declared his final break with Harley in his bitter work *The Art of Restoring* (1714). Because Toland had been a close friend and dependant of Harley, his explicit attack confirmed the suspicions of many Englishmen that Harley (now Lord Oxford) no longer supported the ideals of the protestant succession. Toland's book went through ten printings in less than a year, which provided him with the financial independence he needed to compose his equally popular treatise on whig political theory, *The State Anatomy of Great Britain* (1717).

Pantheist In 1718 Toland published the results of his earlier work on biblical criticism and turned his attention to a projected monumental study of the druids. He was fascinated by the secretive activities of the ancient Irish, and in his *Tetradymus* (1720) and *Pantheisticon* (1720) he examined how the distinction between esoteric and exoteric doctrines function in religion and philosophy. His interest in the topic had appeared as early as in his *Letters to Serena*, and he had appropriated the term *pantheist* in his *Socinianism Truly Stated* from Joseph Raphson, who had referred to *panthei* and *pantheismus* in *De spatio reali, seu, Ente infinito* (1697). Like Raphson, Toland describes pantheists as those who think of God as the omnipresent space in which all material and immaterial distinctions are intelligible. God is not simply matter but that which is prior to all distinction, including the distinction between the material and immaterial. Because God is the matrix for all discernment, he is eminently accessible to every speaker and can hardly be considered mysterious. Pantheists tolerate promiscuous communication, therefore, because it is the means by which identity and differentiation first appear. In his *Origines Judaicae* (1709), Toland associated pantheists with Spinozists because their methodological toleration required that they limit philosophical discussion to what can be observed, namely, bodies in motion. He concluded that, if life itself is nothing more than such motion, then the adoption of a pantheistic attitude toward the universe and God would provide a tranquil temperament and peace of mind.

In the financial collapse of the South Sea Company in 1720, Toland lost what little money he had been given by his friend Robert Molesworth, by then Viscount Molesworth. The following year his already frail health declined further, aggravated by the polluted air of London. Although he moved out of the city to Putney his condition did not improve appreciably. Afflicted with kidney stones

and apparently drinking heavily, he became bedridden at Christmas 1721. On 11 March 1722 in the cluttered room of a carpenter's house, he died surrounded by piles of his books and manuscripts stacked on the floor. According to one account he told those around him 'I thank you for your care, but I am poisoned by a physician' (Sullivan, 39). It is also said that when asked, immediately before he died, whether he wanted anything, he replied he wanted only death. And after bidding those around him farewell, he simply said that he was going to sleep—an attitude that Voltaire greatly admired.

Toland was buried two days later in Putney churchyard, but because of his poverty no gravestone marks the spot. The Latin epitaph he composed for himself concluded: 'His spirit is joined with its ethereal father from whom it originally proceeded; his body likewise yielding to nature is laid again in the lap of its mother. But he's frequently to rise himself again, yet never to be the same Toland more … If you would know more of him, search his writings' (Daniel, 13–14).

Because Toland's life and writings were filled with challenges to propriety, he generated great hostility. By making reason a criterion of knowledge and faith, he raised doubts about the legitimacy of beliefs and texts and continued to prompt responses from apologists throughout the eighteenth century. His criticism of arbitrary power and his widely read editions of Sidney, Ludlow, Milton, and Harrington had, for many, the unsettling effect of bringing together republican and classical ideals. In the long term it provided a foundation for the whig intellectual tradition that influenced Maximilien Robespierre, Benjamin Franklin, Thomas Jefferson, and Thomas Paine. On the continent Toland's blend of polemics and toleration, his defence of liberty, and critique of religious excess, attracted Voltaire and other Enlightenment figures. According to Denis Diderot and the baron d'Holbach, his doctrine of the essential activity of matter undermined the simplistic distinction between matter and spirit that had burdened metaphysics since Descartes. Freemasons throughout Europe appropriated his clandestine practices and pantheist philosophy as models for responding to surreptitious efforts to impose ways of thinking and social order. In recent years the ground-breaking bibliographic work of Giancarlo Carabelli has opened up new prospects for research on Toland. Several major studies of his life and thought have been published since then, culminating in 1996 with a flurry of books and articles on the tercentenary of the publication of *Christianity not Mysterious*. Because of Toland's interest in challenging the bounds of propriety, he has been the object of work in hermeneutics, deconstruction, and post-structuralism. Not surprisingly, the assessment of his importance in understanding the political and religious intrigues of the early eighteenth century still provokes controversy.

STEPHEN H. DANIEL

Sources R. Sullivan, *John Toland and the deist controversy* (1982) • S. Daniel, *John Toland: his methods, manners, and mind* (1984) • G. Carabelli, *Tolandiana: materiali bibliografici per lo studio dell'opera e della fortuna de John Toland* (1975) • G. Carabelli, *Errata, addenda e indici*

(1978) · P. McGuinness, A. Harrison, and R. Kearney, eds., *John Toland's 'Christianity not mysterious': text, associated works and critical essays* (1997) · A. Santucci, ed., *Filosofia e cultura nel settecento britannico*, 1: *Fonti e connessioni continentali: John Toland e il deismo* (Bologna, 2000) · G. Brykman, ed., *John Toland (1670–1722) et la crise de conscience européenne* (1995) · R. Evans, *Pantheisticon: the career of John Toland* (1991) · C. Giuntini, *Panteismo e ideologia repubblicana: John Toland (1670–1722)* (1979) · P. Des Maizeaux, 'Some memoirs of the life and writings of Mr Toland', *A collection of several pieces of Mr John Toland*, ed. [P. Des Maizeaux] (1726), iii–xcii · E. Ludlow, *A voyce from the watch tower*, ed. A. B. Worden, CS, 4th ser., 21 (1978)
Archives BL, corresp. and MSS, Add. MSS 4295, 4465 · Bodl. Oxf., copy of Martin's *Western islands of Scotland* with MS notes and additions | Österreichische Nationalbibliothek, Vienna, Autographen XLV; MSS 10325, 10390 · Bodl. Oxf., MSS Rawl. · LPL, Gibson MSS · PRO, Shaftesbury MSS
Likenesses engraving, 1701 (of Toland?), AM Oxf. · drawing, repro. in Daniel, *John Toland*
Wealth at death see Des Maizeaux, 'Some memoirs'

Tolansky, Samuel (1907–1973), physicist, was born on 17 November 1907 at Newcastle upon Tyne, the second child in the family of two boys and two girls of Barnet Turlausky (the name was changed to Tolansky some time before 1912), a tailor, and his wife, Moise Chaiet. His parents, of Lithuanian Jewish origin, had recently migrated from Odessa. For the first ten years of Tolansky's life the family was very poor, and although there was some amelioration later, his progress beyond primary education depended on winning scholarships. He attended Rutherford College (a secondary school) from 1919 to 1925, when college scholarships enabled him to enter Armstrong College, Newcastle, then part of Durham University. He obtained a first-class degree in 1928 and then spent a year in the education department. He received a prize as the best student of the year (one of eight awards which he won at Armstrong College) but decided to undertake research work rather than become a teacher.

Tolansky was a research student under the spectroscopist W. E. Curtis at Newcastle from 1929 to 1931. He gained a travelling scholarship to study at Berlin under L. C. H. F. Paschen (the leading spectroscopist of that time) and an 1851 Exhibition scholarship gave him two years under Alfred Fowler at Imperial College, London. Between 1929 and 1934 he published twenty-one papers, a substantial contribution to high resolution spectroscopy. In 1934 Tolansky was appointed assistant lecturer at Manchester University under W. L. Bragg. He was subsequently promoted lecturer (1937), senior lecturer (1945), and reader (1946). In 1947, at the age of thirty-nine, he became professor of physics at Royal Holloway College, London, and held this post until his death. In 1935 he married Ottilie (Ethel) Pinkasovich (d. 1977), whose father, Salomo, was *Obercantor* at the Alte Synagoge in Berlin and a singer of international repute. They had a son and a daughter.

Tolansky's researches were in spectroscopy, in surface microtopography by multiple beam interferometry, and in diamond physics. He also made a contribution to the examination of moon dust where his prediction of the presence of tektites (small glassy spheres) was abundantly justified. Although the work on moon dust was a very small part of his total contribution to science it made him widely known to the general public.

Surface topography was the main work of Tolansky's life. In spectroscopy he had used methods previously known, but in microtopography he was the leader and many others followed. He began with Newton's rings, irregularities in which revealed surface defects of 200 nm in depth (1 nm = 10^{-9} metre). This limit did not change much until in 1943 Tolansky evaporated metal on to the surfaces, producing highly reflecting films which gave multiple beam interference. He obtained very sharp fringes, and steps on a surface of only 1.5 nm were observed. The most important part of his work on diamonds was the discovery of many small but important features on the surfaces of natural diamonds, synthetic diamond, and diamonds which had been etched or cleaved, though he made contributions to other aspects of diamond physics.

Tolansky was a kindly man, never known to speak ill of anyone. He was witty but without malice and he could enjoy a joke against himself. He always retained a deep feeling for the Jewish religion. He had wide interests in history, music, and art, and it must have given him much happiness that his wife was recognized as a distinguished artist and his son became a professional musician. Apart from his interest in music generally he gave much time to the study of Jewish music in a historical context, and had original ideas on the interpretation of musical instructions in the Psalms.

It was no accident that many of the photographs chosen for reproduction in Tolansky's scientific papers were of considerable artistic merit. His book *The History and Use of Diamond* (1962) was finely illustrated with well-chosen portraits of historical people wearing diamonds, and of diamonds in settings of great beauty. His capacity for prolonged work was profound. He examined tens of thousands of small diamonds under a microscope, looking for rare shapes. He published more than 250 papers and sixteen books.

Tolansky was elected FRS in 1952, a fellow of the Royal Astronomical Society in 1947, an honorary member of the American Association for the Advancement of Science in 1966, and honorary fellow of the Royal Microscopical Society in 1970. He died in London on 4 March 1973.

R. W. DITCHBURN, *rev.* ISOBEL FALCONER

Sources R. W. Ditchburn and G. D. Rochester, *Memoirs FRS*, 20 (1974), 429–55 [photograph, bibliography] · personal knowledge (1986) · private information (1986) · CGPLA Eng. & Wales (1973)
Archives LUL, corresp. and papers · Royal Holloway College, Egham, Surrey, corresp. and papers | University of Bristol Library, corresp. with Sir Charles Frank
Likenesses M. Rample-Cope, photograph, RS; repro. in Ditchburn and Rochester, *Memoirs FRS*, facing p. 429
Wealth at death £38,189: probate, 1973, CGPLA Eng. & Wales

Told, Silas (1711–1778), schoolmaster and prison visitor, was born at the Lime Kilns in Bristol on 3 April 1711 of 'very creditable' parentage. His father, a physician like his paternal grandfather, lost money invested in the building of a wet dock and died at sea. His mother was the daughter of Captain Thomas Suckabitch or Sucksbury of Topsham. He was admitted at age eight to the charity school founded by Edward Colston, where he had a vision of eternal bliss after nearly drowning. In 1725 he went to sea as an apprentice to Moses Lilly, captain of the merchantman *Prince of Wales*. The hazards of the voyages he experienced and his harsh treatment at the hands of those under whom he served are described in his autobiography, *An Account of the Life, and Dealings of God with Silas Told* (1786), a second edition of which appeared in 1790 under the title, *The Life of Mr. Silas Told, Written by himself*. After several transatlantic crossings and voyages to west Africa and the Mediterranean, he and his fellow crewmen were press-ganged into the navy; but he was fortunate to serve under a humane, Christian captain. In 1736 he was discharged, two years after marrying Mary Verney (*c*.1713–1744), and found employment first at a charity school at Stapleford Tawney, Essex, then as a clerk, and eventually as bookkeeper to a London builder. Under the influence of one of the young bricklayers, Charles Caspar Graves, Told reluctantly went to hear John Wesley preach at Short's Gardens and the Foundery Chapel, where he was convinced of sin and attached himself to the Methodists, despite family opposition. Following his wife's death, he was persuaded to take charge of the charity school at the Foundery. Wesley described him as 'a man of good understanding, although not much indebted to education' (*Life*, preface). His temporal circumstances were improved by a second marriage, the details of which are unknown. For about three years he suffered bouts of spiritual anguish until convinced of the forgiveness of his sins while walking alone in the fields one morning. Influenced by Wesley's sermon on Matthew 25: 43, he began to visit prisoners in Newgate and other London gaols and to accompany condemned felons to the gallows at Tyburn. He maintained this ministry for many years and Wesley thought 'no man for this hundred years has been so successful in that melancholy office' (*Journal*, 6.221). Told died in December 1778 and was buried in London on the 20th.   JOHN A. VICKERS

Sources *The life of Mr Silas Told, written by himself*, 2nd edn (1790) · *The journal of the Rev. John Wesley*, ed. N. Curnock and others, 8 vols. (1909–16), vol. 6, p. 221

Toledo, John of (d. **1275**), abbot of L'Épau and cardinal, was according to Matthew Paris and the Winchester annalist of English birth. Possibly he acquired his toponym from residence at the schools of Toledo, which were frequented by English scholars in the early thirteenth century. Paris reports that he was personal physician to Pope Innocent IV; but the necrology of Santa Giuliana of Perugia, a nunnery founded by Cardinal John, described him as a theologian. His life is obscure until his appointment as the first abbot of L'Épau, in the county of Maine, founded in 1228 by Queen Berengaria, the widow of Richard I. L'Épau received its first monks from Cîteaux in 1229, so John had presumably taken the Cistercian habit at the mother house. In the spring of 1241 he was involved in the catastrophe that overtook other prelates on their way to the general council, who were intercepted and arrested by the Pisan fleet on the instructions of the emperor, Frederick

II. Along with the abbots of Cîteaux and Clairvaux, he was imprisoned at Pisa and later at Tivoli and San Germano. On his release in 1243 he made his way to the papal curia, where he was retained by Innocent IV and, having resigned his abbatial office, on 28 May 1244 he was created cardinal-priest of the title of San Lorenzo-in-Lucina. Later that summer he accompanied the other cardinals who followed Pope Innocent in his flight from Italy to the security of Lyons, and he resided there until the return of the curia to Rome in 1251.

For over thirty years John of Toledo was in a position of power and influence at the curia, and he was constantly used by his countrymen, and by the Cistercian order, as a channel to papal favour. English proctors sent to the curia on the king's business were constantly referred to him for help and advice. The numerous English clerks who were at some time retained in his household as chaplains included members of notable ministerial families, like Master Roger Lovel, king's proctor, and William of Lexinton, as well as men who were to achieve high preferment in the church, such as Richard of Gravesend, the future bishop of Lincoln. Through the cardinal's patronage they obtained papal provision to benefices in the English church. To the Cistercians, John of Toledo was known as the White Cardinal—the protector in fact, if not by official title, of his own order. His role was recognized by the Cistercian general chapter which, on his elevation to the cardinalate in 1244, commanded every priest of the order to say a mass for him, and later decreed the observance of his anniversary in perpetuity. In 1245 he attended a meeting of the general chapter in person, and provided an *inspeximus* of all the order's papal privileges. He gave invaluable support to the plans of his compatriot Stephen of Lexinton, abbot of Clairvaux, to impose a system of studies on the order with, at its apex, a college for monks studying theology at the University of Paris. The chapter act of 1245 decreeing schools of theology for monks in every province was expressly issued by papal command and on the advice of Cardinal John, and endorsements of the privileges for the new college show that he was active in promoting the enterprise. He was also an enlightened patron and benefactor of women religious. At Rome he established a new Cistercian convent for reformed prostitutes at San Pancrazio on the Janiculum, and he founded and endowed Cistercian nunneries at Perugia and Viterbo.

During the pontificates of Innocent IV and Alexander IV, John of Toledo formed the nucleus of a pro-English group of cardinals at the Roman curia, united in a desire to further the ambitions of the English royal dynasty in Italy as a counter to the imperial claims of the Hohenstaufen. On two occasions he rendered important political services to the English court. In 1261, when Henry III was trying to rid himself of the baronial council imposed on him by the provisions of Oxford, Cardinal John assisted the royal proctors to obtain the king's absolution from his oath to abide by the provisions. He favoured the offer of the Sicilian crown to Henry's son Edmund; and he gave his energetic support to Henry's brother, Richard of Cornwall, on the latter's election to the empire in 1257. In the spring of 1261 he exerted all his powers in unsuccessful efforts to procure Earl Richard's election to the senatorial office at Rome, emptying his treasury and giving away his household silver, as he wrote sadly, in the earl's cause. Anxious to pre-empt the claims of King Manfred of Sicily, the Hohenstaufen candidate for the senatorship, Cardinal John wrote to Richard urging him to hasten to Rome if he wished to wear the imperial crown.

The death of Pope Alexander IV on 25 May of the same year, and the election of the French cardinal Jean Pantaleone as Urban IV, put an end to these hopes. Urban turned to France for assistance against the Hohenstaufen. John of Toledo was raised to the cardinal-bishopric of Porto by the new pope on 24 December 1261; but in the ensuing pontificate his political influence was much diminished. He continued, however, to promote the interests of the Cistercians, whose general chapter he personally attended in 1273. He died at San Germano on 13 July 1275 and was probably buried at the church of San Lorenzo-in-Lucina in Rome. Apart from a number of his letters, no literary work of his has been identified with any certainty. Medical treatises ascribed to him in late medieval copies, including a *Liber de sanitate corporis* and a short treatise *De pleurisi*, and an astrological letter, are probably the work of Johannes Hispanus, an earlier medical scholar who was also known as John of Toledo.

C. H. LAWRENCE

Sources Rymer, *Foedera*, new edn, vol. 4/1 · P. Chaplais, ed., *Diplomatic documents preserved in the Public Record Office*, 1 (1964) · *CEPR letters* · *Les registres d'Innocent IV*, ed. E. Berger, 4 vols. (Paris, 1884–1921) · *Les registres d'Alexandre IV*, ed. C. Bourel de la Roncière and others, 3 vols. (Paris, 1895–1959) · J. Guiraud, ed., *Les registres d'Urbain IV* (1901–30) · A. Largadier, *Die Papsturkunden des Staatsarchivs Zürich* (1963) · *Gallia Christiana in provincias ecclesiasticas distributa*, 14, ed. B. Hauréau (1870) · J. M. Canivez, ed., *Statuta capitulorum generalium ordinis Cisterciensis*, 1–2 (1933–4) · H. Denifle and A. Chatelain, eds., *Chartularium universitatis Parisiensis*, 1 (Paris, 1889) · *Paris, Chron.*, vols. 4–5 · *Ann. mon.*, vols. 2, 4 · A. O. Anderson and M. O. Anderson, eds., *The chronicle of Melrose* (1936) · *Ryccardi di Sancto Germano notarii chronica*, ed. G. H. Pertz, MGH Scriptores Rerum Germanicarum, [53] (1864) · H. Grauert, 'Meister Johann von Toledo', *Sitzungsberichte der Königlichen Bayerischen Akademie der Wissenschaften*, phil. hist. Klasse (1901), 111–325 · A. P. Bagliani, *Cardinali di curia e 'familiae' cardinalizie dal 1227 al 1254*, 2 vols. (1972) · F. Bock, 'Le trattive per la senatoria di Roma e Carlo d'Angio', *Arcivio della Società Romana di Storia Patria*, 78 (1955), 69–105 · J. B. Mahn, *L'ordre cistercien et son gouvernement* (1951)
Archives Biblioteca Ricardiana, Florence, MS LIII, 19 · Universitätsbibliothek, Munich, MSS Clm 480

Toler, John, first earl of Norbury (1745–1831), judge and politician, was born at Beechwood, co. Tipperary, on 3 December 1745, the youngest son of Daniel Toler (d. 1754x6) and Letitia Otway (d. 1794), the Tolers being a Cromwellian family who came originally from Norfolk. He was educated at Trinity College, Dublin, where he graduated BA in 1761 and MA in 1766. Admitted to Lincoln's Inn on 19 March 1761 he was called to the bar in Michaelmas 1770. On 2 June 1778 Toler married Grace (d. 21 July 1822), daughter of Hector Graham; they had two sons and two daughters. His father, on his deathbed, was said to have given him a case of silver mounted pistols and charged him 'never to omit the valour of an Irish gentleman in resorting to his weapons' (Sheil, 85–6). Whatever may have been the truth of that story Toler certainly demonstrated throughout his career a readiness to challenge those with whom he clashed to a duel.

Toler's political career began in 1776, when he was returned to the Irish House of Commons as MP for Tralee. He made clear his support for the government from the beginning and was duly advanced in his profession to the rank of king's counsel in 1781. In 1783 he was returned for the borough of Philipstown in King's county, his elder brother Daniel (d. 1796) having been returned at the same time for Tipperary. He represented Gorey, East Wexford, from 1790 to 1800. Toler was vehement in his opposition in parliament to the proposals for reform urged by Grattan and others, which included their proposals for the relaxation of the laws against Catholics. He was further rewarded for his loyalty to the government on 12 August 1789, when he was appointed solicitor-general. One of his first actions in post was to oppose a motion by Grattan deprecating the sale of places and peerages by the viceroy.

Toler was a jovial figure, on the short side and increasingly corpulent, with a ribald and sometimes seriously misplaced sense of humour. He was also remarkably belligerent, even by the parliamentary standards of the era. In 1792 he in turn was challenged, by James Napper Tandy, secretary of the United Irishmen, to a duel which never took place, Tandy being imprisoned for contempt by the Commons. Tandy was notoriously ugly and, commenting on his election as secretary, Toler said that it was odd that they had been unable 'to set a better *face* on the matter' (*DNB*), a characteristic example of the wit for which Toler was renowned.

Toler fell out of favour with the government when the liberal-minded Earl Fitzwilliam became viceroy in 1794, but the prime minister, William Pitt, only agreed to his being removed from the post of solicitor-general on the condition that another place would be found for him. Fitzwilliam was recalled after spending less than two months in Dublin, Toler's fortunes were restored, and his zealous denunciations of measures for Catholic relief handsomely rewarded. His wife was created a peeress of Ireland in her own right on 7 November 1797 with the title of Baroness Norwood of Knockalton, co. Tipperary; on 10 July 1798 Toler was appointed attorney-general, and he was sworn of the privy council on 2 August.

During and after the rising of 1798 Toler conducted some of the most important prosecutions in person with a ferocity which was unusual even by the standards of the time. In the most celebrated of the trials with which he was concerned, that of the brothers Sheares, his efforts to secure a conviction were helped by the fact that one of the counsel appearing for the brothers, Leonard McNally, was secretly in the pay of Dublin Castle and had disclosed one of the defence's legal strategies to Toler and his team, who were thus well prepared with their replying arguments. When the case had been at hearing for over fifteen hours one of the defence counsel, John Philpot Curran, who was described as 'fainting with exhaustion', pleaded for an adjournment, which was successfully opposed by Toler. The brothers were convicted and executed the following day, and Toler's anxiety that the sentence should be carried out as quickly as possible may have been due to his concern that the lord chancellor, Lord Clare, might be disposed to extend clemency to the brothers.

In the aftermath of the rising Toler was responsible for legislation which gave the viceroy a discretionary power to suspend the Habeas Corpus Act and establish martial law. These services and his support for the Act of Union in 1800 led to his appointment as chief justice of the court of common pleas on 20 December 1800. He was elevated to the peerage as Baron Norbury of Ballyorenode, co. Tipperary, nine days later.

Toler had a poor reputation as a lawyer. As an advocate his style blended buffoonery with portentous gravity. These features of his personality moved Lord Clare to his reported comment: 'Make him a bishop or an archbishop but not a judge' (DNB). Such misgivings as to Toler's fitness for office were amply justified by his conduct on the bench. His liking for coarse humour and his constant altercations with leading counsel, notably O'Connell, resulted in his court's frequently being crowded to capacity. His jocular approach was even evident when those before him were being sentenced to death. One contemporary account said contemptuously that his performances 'were greatly preferred, in the decline of the Dublin stage, to any theatrical exhibition' (Sheil, 97). It was not suggested that he was corrupt in the ordinary sense. In civil suits, however, he almost invariably found for the plaintiff and this was attributed by his critics to the fact that, at that time, the judge and the registrar were paid an additional fee if there was a decree in favour of the plaintiff. There were reported to be two bags underneath Norbury's desk, one of silver coins for himself and one of copper coins for his registrar.

As it happened, in the most celebrated trial over which he presided, that of Robert Emmet, Norbury was not at his worst. Before reaching his famous peroration—'let no man write my epitaph' (Phillips, 359–61)—Emmet had sought to justify his leadership of the abortive foray in the streets of Dublin in terms which the judges were bound to regard as treasonable. Yet he was given considerable latitude by them and when Norbury eventually intervened he did so in reasonably measured terms. He expressed the concern of the judges that the 26-year-old Emmet, whose father had been physician to the viceroy and whose elder brother, Christopher, had been a most highly regarded member of the Irish bar until his early death, should have been associated in so desperate an enterprise, and his dismissive comment on Emmet's followers as lower class riff-raff is hardly surprising for its time. It has even been said, although there is no authoritative confirmation of the suggestion, that he was moved to tears by Emmet's plight as he passed the death sentence.

The most serious threat to Norbury's continued tenure of office resulted not from his behaviour in court but from the discovery and publication of a letter sent to him some years previously from William Saurin, then attorney-general. In the letter Saurin had urged Norbury, when travelling on circuit, to encourage in private the members of the grand juries to resist the campaign for Catholic emancipation. The letter was found on Ormond Quay in Dublin by a young Catholic attorney and then came into O'Connell's possession. The latter wrote indignantly to Earl Grey, the prime minister, that the letter was 'clear evidence of a conspiracy to pervert the judicial character into an engine of calumny and bigotry' (Correspondence of Daniel O'Connell, 2.402). O'Connell enlisted the support of Henry Brougham, then a member of the House of Commons, in raising the matter there but it was brushed aside by the chief secretary for Ireland, Sir Robert Peel, who said that he thought the manner in which the letter was published baser than its contents. Norbury was infuriated by Brougham's actions and was reported to have said: 'I will resign to demand satisfaction. That Scottish Brougham wants to be made acquainted with an Irish stick' (DNB)—another fair sample of the excruciating puns on which Norbury's reputation as a wit apparently rested. The chance finding of the letter on Ormond Quay was said to have been the result of Norbury having put it, along with other papers, in the stuffing of an armchair that had been sent to be upholstered, but this may be apocryphal.

Although he survived that episode Norbury's behaviour on the bench led to increasing pressure for his removal. In 1825 O'Connell presented a petition to parliament calling for his removal on the ground that he had fallen asleep during a murder trial and was unable to give any account of the evidence when his notes were called for (he was then aged eighty). Again Norbury survived but when Canning became prime minister in 1827 he was at last induced to retire. However, his departure was smoothed by his advancement in the peerage as Viscount Glandine and earl of Norbury, together with a retiring pension of £3046. These titles were created with a special remainder in favour of Norbury's second son, Hector John (d. 1839), in consequence of the poor mental health of his eldest son, Daniel (d. 1832), second Baron Norwood in succession to his mother and later second Baron Norbury. O'Connell, in his private correspondence, described the departing chief justice as 'a sanguinary buffoon', who had been 'bought off the bench by a most shameful traffic' (Correspondence of Daniel O'Connell, 3.323).

In private life Norbury was an amiable person, given to singing and declaiming poetry; he knew much of Shakespeare and Milton by heart. He was also reputed to be an excellent landlord and a kindly and thoughtful employer. In contrast O'Connell regarded Norbury's behaviour as a judge as symptomatic of the worst features of the post-Union Irish judiciary. It was not simply that his hostility towards Catholic emancipation remained undiminished; even in an age when there was a more relaxed attitude towards idiosyncratic behaviour by judges Norbury was conspicuous for his eccentricity. He died at Cabra, near Dublin, on 27 July 1831.   RONAN KEANE

Sources R. L. Sheil, *Sketches, legal and political*, ed. M. W. Savage, 1 (1855), 85–118 · C. Phillips, *Recollections of Curran and some of his contemporaries*, 2nd edn (1822), 239–53 · H. Grattan, *The speeches of the Right Honourable Henry Grattan*, ed. H. Grattan, 2 (1822), 363; 3 (1822), 347 · *The correspondence of Daniel O'Connell*, ed. M. R. O'Connell, 8 vols., IMC (1972–80), vol. 2, pp. 399–41, 402–4; vol. 3, p. 323 · W. J. Fitzpatrick, *Secret service under Pitt* (1892), 125, 158, 312 · *DNB* · W. E. H. Lecky, *A history of England in the eighteenth century*, 8 vols. (1879–90), vol. 7, pp. 86–7 · F. E. Ball, *The judges in Ireland, 1221–1921*, 2 (1926), 237 · *Mr Gregory's letter-box, 1813–30*, ed. I. A. Gregory (1898), 128, 130–31 · R. R. Madden, *The United Irishmen: their lives and times*, 2 (New York, 1916), 255–7 · W. Russell, *Eccentric personages* (1865), 257–67 · *The trial of Robert Emmet esq taken in shorthand by a professional gentleman* (1803) · NA Ire., Norbury MSS · GEC, *Peerage*, new edn, 9.565–6 · Burke, *Peerage* (1999) · W. P. Baildon, ed., *The records of the Honorable Society of Lincoln's Inn: admissions*, 1 (1896)
Archives NA Ire., corresp. · PRO NIre., corresp. | BL, corresp. with Robert Peel, Add. MS 40206 · PRO NIre., corresp. with John Foster
Likenesses etching with watercolour, pubd 1811, NG Ire. · attrib. J. J. Russell, oils, King's Inns, Dublin · black and red chalk with white highlights on paper, NG Ire. · coloured etching, NPG · stipple, BM · stipple, NG Ire.
Wealth at death £3046 p.a. from pension after 1827

Tolfrey, William (*bap.* 1777?, *d.* 1817), orientalist, was probably baptized on 27 October 1777 at St Swithin London Stone, London, the son of William and Susannah Tolfrey. He was apparently educated in England. In 1794 he went to Calcutta, where his father then lived, and obtained at first some subordinate post in a public office, but soon afterwards relinquished this for an ensigncy in the 76th (foot) regiment. His military career was creditable. Promoted to the 74th regiment, he served in the Anglo-Mysore War under General George Harris and in the Maratha campaigns of 1803–4. He was distinguished also in the battle of Assaye.

In 1805 Tolfrey sold his commission, and, visiting an uncle, Samuel Tolfrey, in Ceylon, obtained a post in the civil service of the island in 1806. In 1813 he was assistant commissioner of revenue and commerce, and shortly afterwards his proficiency in Sinhalese obtained him the post of chief translator to the resident at Kandy. On the arrival of Sir Robert Brownrigg as governor in 1812, a Bible society was started, and with other scholars Tolfrey undertook the revision of the old Sinhalese translation of the Bible made by the Dutch. The work was printed under the direction of the Colombo Auxiliary Bible Society between 1817 and 1820. Struck by the unduly colloquial character of the original edition Tolfrey had decided on the course of first translating each verse into classical Pali. It was probably this that led him to attempt the translation of the whole New Testament into Pali, a work which he had nearly completed at the time of his death. It was subsequently printed, but as a literary production it was of no great or lasting value. Tolfrey was, however, probably the first Englishman to study Pali, the most important of the languages of Buddhism, and he merits recognition as a pioneer. Benjamin Clough used his materials for the compilation of his Pali grammar, printed in Colombo in 1824, which was the only work of the kind for some thirty years.

Tolfrey died in Ceylon on 4 January 1817. He appears to have been unmarried at the time of his death: his sole executor was his mother, and after leaving legacies to his servants, he bequeathed the residue of his personal estate to the Colombo Auxiliary Bible Society. A monument was erected to his memory in the church of St Peter in the fort of Colombo.   CECIL BENDALL, *rev.* J. B. KATZ

Sources *Ceylon Government Gazette* (11 Jan 1817) · *Ceylon Almanac* (1814) · J. Selkirk, *Recollections of Ceylon … with an account of the Church Missionary Society's operations* (1844), 94 · B. Clough, *A compendious Pali grammar* (1824) · PRO, PROB 11/1631, fols. 264–5 · *IGI*
Wealth at death see will, PRO, PROB 11/1631, fols. 264–5

Tolkien, John Ronald Reuel (1892–1973), writer and philologist, was born on 3 January 1892 in Bloemfontein, Orange Free State, the elder son of Arthur Reuel Tolkien (1857–1896) and his wife, Mabel (1870–1904), daughter of John Suffield. His father and mother both came from Birmingham, but Arthur Tolkien had left England in 1889, and by 1892 was manager of the Bloemfontein branch of the Bank of Africa.

Early life and education J. R. R. Tolkien's early life bears witness to continuing emotional distress and insecurity, coupled with precocious and idiosyncratic intellectual development. His mother returned to England on a visit in 1895 with her two sons (Tolkien's younger brother Hilary was born on 17 February 1894), expecting her husband to join them later. But Arthur Tolkien died of rheumatic fever in Bloemfontein on 15 February 1896, leaving only a few hundred pounds in shares as support for his widow. For a time Mabel Tolkien economized by teaching her sons herself, and by setting up home in the hamlet of Sarehole, now part of the King's Heath suburb of Birmingham but at that time still outside the city. When her elder son, aged eight, passed the entrance examination for King Edward's School, Birmingham, then located in the city centre, she was obliged to move into town, living in one rented house after another. Her financial situation was not eased by her conversion to Roman Catholicism in 1900, which caused an estrangement from some members of her family; and on 14 November 1904 she too died young, of diabetes, leaving her sons as wards of Father Francis Morgan of the Birmingham Oratory. He arranged for the boys to be boarded, first with a distant relative of theirs and then with an acquaintance of his own. But Tolkien experienced a further painful separation when, at the age of sixteen, he fell in love with a fellow lodger, Edith Bratt (1889–1971), daughter of Frances Bratt, of Wolverhampton, a fatherless girl three years older than himself. When his guardian learned of the relationship, the pair were separated and Tolkien was obliged to promise not to communicate with Edith until he came of age—a promise he kept to the letter.

Meanwhile Tolkien's school-life was unusually happy and successful. He had sympathetic teachers, showed special aptitude for languages, and was introduced, or introduced himself, to Old and Middle English, Old Norse, and Gothic. He also formed strong friendships with other members of an unofficial school literary society. In December 1910 he won an exhibition to Exeter College,

John Ronald Reuel Tolkien (1892–1973), by John Wyatt, 1968

Oxford, and went up to the university in 1911 to read honour moderations in classics. In 1913 he achieved only a second class, largely because of the time he had spent on Germanic languages outside the syllabus, and was allowed to change to the honours school of English, a large part of which was concerned with linguistic and philological study. Tolkien's tutor was Kenneth Sisam (1887–1971), but he was taught also by the Yorkshire philologist Joseph Wright. He found this course of study much more congenial, and achieved a first in his finals in 1915. He had also, just after midnight on his twenty-first birthday, while on vacation from Oxford, written again to Edith Bratt, the pair becoming engaged very soon after.

The war and early academic career On graduation, however, Tolkien followed his younger brother into the army, being commissioned into the Lancashire Fusiliers. He and Edith were married on 22 March 1916, but in June that year Tolkien was sent to France, to join the 11th battalion of the fusiliers as a signals officer. From July to October his regiment took part in the battle of the Somme, including the fighting in the battle's later stages around the Schwaben Redoubt. One of Tolkien's closest friends from school was killed at the very start of the battle, on 1 July, and another late in 1916. Tolkien, however, succumbed to trench fever on 27 October, and was returned to England the following month.

Tolkien remained in poor health for the rest of the war, and was not sent back to France. At the armistice he returned to Oxford, and worked for a time on the staff of the *New English Dictionary* under Henry Bradley. In 1920 he received the appointment of reader in English language at the University of Leeds, and could perhaps feel that—married, securely employed, with his first son, John, born in November 1917 and his second, Michael, in October 1920—he was experiencing domestic stability for the first time since babyhood. The Tolkien family was completed with the birth of a third son, Christopher, in November 1924, and a daughter, Priscilla, in June 1929.

Tolkien's professional career in the 1920s was also extremely successful. With the encouragement of his head of department at Leeds, George S. Gordon, he built up the language side of the English department until it rivalled literature in popularity with undergraduates. There was a plan, which came to nothing, for him to edit a volume or volumes of *Vorstudien* as part of a revitalization of the *Dictionary of National Biography* (H. C. G. Matthew, *Leslie Stephen and the 'New Dictionary of National Biography'*, 1995, 10). The University of Leeds made him a professor in 1924. In 1925, in collaboration with a junior colleague, E. V. Gordon (1896–1938), he brought out an edition of the Middle English poem *Sir Gawain and the Green Knight* which opened new fields of study and which remained standard, in revised form, throughout the twentieth century. Also in 1925 Tolkien was elected to the Rawlinson and Bosworth chair of Anglo-Saxon at Oxford, defeating his former tutor Kenneth Sisam in a close vote.

After this, Tolkien's academic career in some respects began to lose impetus. He produced a ground-breaking article on the early Middle English work *Ancrene wisse* in 1929, and his British Academy lecture of 1936, 'Beowulf: the monsters and the critics', is accepted as a turning point in the study of the poem. However, the Tolkien and Gordon edition of *Pearl*, intended as a follow-up to their edition of *Gawain*, appeared in 1953 only under the editorship of E. V. Gordon's widow, Ida L. Gordon (*b*. 1907). Tolkien's own edition of one manuscript of the *Ancrene wisse* did not appear until 1962, and then without the linguistic apparatus that had been hoped for. His Oxford lectures on *Beowulf* and the Old English poem *Exodus* did eventually reach print as editions, or partial editions, but only posthumously, compiled by others from his notes. He published little academically after 1940. Yet this was not a case of laziness, or lack of inspiration (though Tolkien was aware of such accusations). Rather, his undoubted philological brilliance had been diverted into fiction.

From *Beowulf* to *The Hobbit* With hindsight, one can see that a continuing theme in Tolkien's academic work was the conviction that literature and language are not divisible. The division was both temperamental and structural in many English faculties, but Tolkien remained convinced that, just as early works of literature illuminated the history of the language, so the history of language was a vital part of literature. The two aspects of language and literature were inextricably entwined, and a full appreciation of 'English', in its widest sense, necessitated a consideration of both. In his own mind Tolkien had accordingly been constructing both the story cycle which was to become *The Silmarillion*, and the imagined languages in which those stories would have been told, Quenya and Sindarin. The cycle was set in a developed form of the world of early Germanic mythology, inhabited by dragons and werewolves, dwarves and heroes, but centred on Tolkien's imagined history of the elves, seen as a race older than and in many respects superior to humanity. Quenya and Sindarin are elvish languages, whose philological relationship complements the complex sequence of tales about their speakers and the humans (and other beings) who interact with them. Tolkien had begun to write the legends and the languages down as early as 1915, in both prose and verse, but little of this work reached print during his lifetime. It did, however, create a setting for the first of Tolkien's works of fiction to be published, *The Hobbit* (1937).

In this Tolkien invented an entirely new mythological race of 'hobbits' who, like their representative Bilbo Baggins, are solid, respectable, anachronistically English, and, as appears when Bilbo is sent off by the wizard Gandalf to help recover the lost treasure of the dwarves from the dragon Smaug, capable of unsuspected resource. *The Hobbit* began as an amusement for the Tolkien children, and reached print rather unexpectedly, a typescript of it having been shown to Stanley Unwin by a former pupil of Tolkien's. Once published, however, it was an equally unexpected success. Unwin pressed Tolkien for a sequel.

The Lord of the Rings Tolkien accordingly, without abandoning hopes for his largely written but unfinished *Silmarillion*, began work on what was to become *The Lord of the Rings*. This tale 'grew in the telling', to use his own phrase, both in length and in the age of its intended audience; much of it was read serially, as it was composed, to the Oxford group known as the Inklings, which centred on Tolkien's close friend and colleague C. S. Lewis, whose support and enthusiasm in the years of composition Tolkien found invaluable.

The new work began with the Ring, which in *The Hobbit* Bilbo had found by accident and used for its gift of invisibility, passing to Bilbo's nephew Frodo, and also being discovered by Gandalf to be the long-lost One Ring, once the foundation of the evil power of Sauron, and with the potential to become so again. The Ring is too dangerous to be used; no possible recipient can be trusted to resist its allure, not even Gandalf; there is nowhere it can be kept safe. Frodo is obliged to take the Ring into the heart of Sauron's own country, Mordor, and there cast it into the Cracks of Doom and destroy it. This anti-quest, undertaken to throw something away, not regain it, is the heart of a story which also gives a complete picture, maps and chronicles included, of Tolkien's imagined Middle-earth and the peoples and languages within it.

The Lord of the Rings eventually appeared in print in three volumes between July 1954 and October 1955. Reaction was sharply divided. Although Tolkien received favourable and perceptive reviews from Lewis and from W. H. Auden, who had attended his Oxford lectures, many reviews were hostile, sometimes bitterly so, a critical response which has remained familiar. However, and in spite of the work's at that time unclassifiable nature, it sold extraordinarily well, as did the much-reissued *Hobbit*. The latter became an enormously successful children's book, with over thirty million copies sold, while *The Lord of the Rings* has sold many more. Both have been translated into almost all major European languages. *The Lord of the Rings* furthermore made a major change in public literary taste, creating a wave of imitations. 'Heroic fantasy' remains one of the most commercially successful literary genres and has had a significant impact upon the entertainment industry, from electronic games to movies. Animated versions of *The Hobbit* and *The Lord of the Rings* appeared in the late 1970s, while the film adaptations of the three volumes of *The Lord of the Rings*, directed by Peter Jackson and released in successive years (2001–3), proved among the most popular motion pictures of all time. All are developments wholly unimagined either by Tolkien or by his early critics.

Later academic career and death Tolkien's academic career continued largely unaffected by this popular success. In 1945 he moved to the Merton chair of English language and literature at Oxford, holding it until he retired in 1959. He was appointed CBE in 1972, and received honorary doctorates from Liège, Dublin, Nottingham, and Oxford, and honorary fellowships at both Exeter College and Merton College, Oxford. While his minor works of fiction, his translations, his early poems, and some academic essays were now eagerly published or republished, he brought out no further major work. In his later years he was much pursued by admirers. He lived for a time outside Oxford, but after the death of Edith Tolkien on 29 November 1971, he returned to live in rooms provided by Merton College. He died not long after, in Bournemouth, on 2 September 1973, of a chest infection associated with a gastric ulcer. Both Tolkien and his wife were buried at Wolvercote cemetery outside Oxford.

Reputation and achievement Tolkien's fiction has proved enduringly popular, and has indeed remained the focus of a considerable publishing industry, both in itself and through many marketing 'spin-offs'. The deep and abiding hostility shown to Tolkien's fiction by many literary critics meanwhile has no doubt several roots, among them refusal to accept the crossing of the language–literature divide, and anger that a professor of language should have succeeded so spectacularly in attracting public attention. A third cause may be the anti-modernism which Tolkien displayed on several levels. Although, or perhaps because, the standard image of the 'great writer' between the wars involved dandyism, contempt for the bourgeoisie, and disrespect for convention of all kinds, Tolkien, like his friend C. S. Lewis, made a point of entirely conventional dress and behaviour. Many photographs of him survive, several of them from the later years showing him lighting or smoking his pipe. Tolkien also remained a devout Catholic to the end of his life, going so far as to insist, in a letter of 2 December 1953 to a Jesuit friend, Robert Murray, that although *The Lord of the Rings* contains no overt reference to Christianity at any point, and very little to religion, it nevertheless remains 'a fundamentally religious and Catholic work'. His fiction predates but is in close sympathy with the environmentalist concerns of the Green movement.

Since Tolkien's death the complex genesis of his fiction has been shown by the eventual publication in 1977 of *The Silmarillion*, and then of his *Unfinished Tales* (1980), and the twelve-volume *History of Middle-Earth* (1983–96), all edited by Tolkien's third son, Christopher. A volume of his *Letters* has also appeared (1981), edited by Humphrey Carpenter, while his minor fictions, many of his drawings, paintings, and poems, and some of his academic essays have also been printed, reprinted, and collected in many ways.

It may finally be said that Tolkien did several things which might not have been thought possible. As a late English counterpart to such figures as the German philologist Jacob Grimm (1785–1863) or the Dane Nikolai Grundtvig (1783–1872) he showed the continuing vitality of traditional philology and the way in which it could be made to appeal to a national and international audience. He also created a mythological mediation between the Catholic Christianity in which he was a devout believer and the motifs of pre-Christian Germanic story. He furthermore, in an unheroic or anti-heroic age, succeeded in generating acceptable and inspiring images of heroism, drawing both on the ancient world of literature and the modern one of his own life-experience. His work combines atavism and contemporary relevance in ways which no one could have predicted (and which many continue to deny), but which have proved unforgettable to hundreds of millions of readers.   T. A. SHIPPEY

Sources H. Carpenter, *J. R. R. Tolkien: a biography* (1977) • H. Carpenter, ed., *The letters of J. R. R. Tolkien* (1981) • T. A. Shippey, *The road to Middle-earth* (1982); new edn (1992) • W. G. Hammond and D. A. Anderson, *J. R. R. Tolkien: a descriptive bibliography* (1993) • *DNB*
Archives Bodl. Oxf., maps and MSS • NRA, corresp. and papers • Wheaton College, Illinois, Marion E. Wade Center | BL, letters to Michael Tolkien, Add. MS 71567 • HarperCollins archive • U. Reading, Allen and Unwin archive | SOUND BBC audio and film archives
Likenesses photographs, 1955–c.1972, Hult. Arch. • B. Swanwick, pencil and wash, 1966–7, NPG • J. Wyatt, photograph, 1968, NPG [see illus.]
Wealth at death £190,577: probate, 20 Dec 1973, *CGPLA Eng. & Wales*

Tollemache, Elizabeth. *See* Murray, Elizabeth (*bap.* 1626, *d.* 1698).

Tollemache, Lionel Arthur (1838–1919), writer and man of leisure, was born on 28 May 1838, the second son of John Tollemache (1805–1890), benevolent landlord and affable tory politician, and Georgina Louisa, *née* Best, first wife and first cousin, who died on 18 July 1846. The other surviving son of this first marriage, Wilbraham, inherited the title of Baron Tollemache of Helmingham, which had been conferred upon John in 1876.

As a younger son Lionel played no part in the management of the extensive Tollemache estates. Nor did he share his father's politics: he always described himself as a 'staunch Whig'. Yet he was proud of his family and sufficiently close to his father to be called upon to accompany him and his second bride, Minnie Duff, on their honeymoon. There were no fewer than twenty-four sons of this second marriage, of whom only twelve survived, along with one daughter. Tollemache considered his father to be 'the grandest specimen of a country gentleman that our generation has seen or is likely to see'.

The pattern of Tollemache's life was shaped as much by physical misfortune as by family inheritance. Handicapped by a stammer, he suffered an accident in childhood which left him slightly lame. His eyesight was weak, and for many years before his death he was completely blind. There was something extraordinary, therefore, about his vast knowledge of books, including novels. He had a prodigious memory. He also came to rely on conversation.

There was nothing unusual, however, about Tollemache's education, given his family background. He was sent to Harrow School in 1850, and from there was awarded one of two scholarships to Balliol. In 1860, after being granted permission to dictate his answers to an amanuensis, he was placed in the first class in *literae humaniores*. He subsequently quoted frequently from the classics, using them as reference points in his depiction and analysis of the culture of his own time. His bent was speculative—he was interested in science and, above all, in the possible shapes of the future, as well as in history—but he savoured anecdotes about his contemporaries, and set out to be a Boswell for a selected few of them.

After reading inconclusively for the bar Tollemache turned in 1868 to writing for London periodicals, including the *Fortnightly Review*, going on to collect and add to them in two privately printed volumes which he offered to a number of open libraries. *Stones of Stumbling* (1884) dealt with philosophical and theological issues: its title was chosen to avoid offence to his evangelical father. *Safe Studies* (1883) dealt with people and less controversial ideas. Both volumes were published and advertised at cost price in 1891. They included Boswellian dialogues in the vein of Abraham Hayward and character sketches which pointed to, rather than avoided, contradictions. Two of the Oxford characters, Mark Pattison and Benjamin Jowett, were the subject of whole volumes in 1885 and 1895. Later in life Tollemache published two volumes of personal recollections, *Old and Cold Memories* (1908) and *Nuts and Chestnuts* (1911).

On 25 January 1870 Tollemache married Beatrix Lucia Catherine, the youngest daughter of William Tatton Egerton, Baron Egerton of Tatton, a Cheshire neighbour and neighbour of the Gladstones. A writer herself, she was in sympathy with his literary aspirations. The most remarkable of his books was his *Talks with Mr. Gladstone*, which appeared in June 1898, one month after Gladstone's death. Tollemache first met Gladstone in Oxford on 28 January 1857, but thereafter they met infrequently until more regular talks began at Biarritz in 1891. Gladstone, though cautious on some topics, unburdened himself a good deal to Tollemache, noting: 'he in particular is a very interesting person'. For health reasons Tollemache spent much of his life across the channel, and Biarritz, where he first met Pattison, was one of the aged Gladstone's frequent retreats. Tollemache was fascinated by longevity, and the talks were broad enough to encompass most topics, including religion. Immediate politics were avoided. The *St James's Gazette* called the volume 'the most interesting book of the year. It is of lasting value to historians' (Briggs, ix).

Tollemache's life was shorter than Gladstone's, but he reached the age of eighty and died at Dunrozel on 29 January 1919. The couple was childless; his widow died on 24 December 1926. **ASA BRIGGS**

Sources Burke, *Peerage* · L. A. Tollemache, *Gladstone's Boswell: late Victorian conversations*, ed. A. Briggs (1984) · Gladstone, *Diaries* · *CGPLA Eng. & Wales* (1919)
Archives BL, letters to W. E. Gladstone, Add. MSS 44515–44525, *passim*
Wealth at death £17,549 4s. 7d.: probate, 16 April 1919, *CGPLA Eng. & Wales*

Tollemache, Ralph William Lyonel Tollemache- (1826–1895), Church of England clergyman and bestower of eccentric names, was born on 19 October 1826, the eldest son of the Hon. and Revd Hugh Francis Tollemache (1802–1890), rector of Harrington, Northamptonshire, and his wife, Matilda, the daughter of Joseph Hume. His father was the fourth son of Baron Huntingtower of Buckminster and a close connection of the family of the earls of Dysart. Tollemache was educated at Uppingham School and at Peterhouse, Cambridge, whence he took his BA (1850) and MA (1854). He was ordained a deacon in Manchester in 1849 and priest in Lincoln in 1850, whereupon he became rector of South Wytham, Lincolnshire, a living he held until his death. He served as a JP for Lincolnshire. In 1863 he was declared bankrupt; he had been in dispute with his first wife's trustees since 1859, and accumulated debts of nearly £4000. He was discharged on 26 June 1868.

On 15 February 1853 Tollemache married his cousin Caroline (1828–1867), the daughter of the Hon. Felix Thomas Tollemache, of Tongswood, Kent, and a niece of the earl of Dysart. His second wife, whom he married on 22 February 1869, was Dora Cleopatra Maria Lorenza (d. 1929), the daughter of Colonel Ignacio Antonio de Orellana y Revest of the Spanish army. Tollemache's life is noteworthy, insofar as it can be ascertained, solely for the series of extraordinary names which he bestowed upon the fourteen children of these two marriages. The children of his first marriage had relatively modest names—Granville Grey Marchmont Manners Plantagenet (1858–1891), for example, and Evelyne Clementina Wentworth Cornelia Maude (b. 1856). But with his second marriage Tollemache's naming frenzy exploded. He surely deserves commemoration as the father of the gloriously named Lyulph Ydwallo Odin Nestor Egbert Lyonel Foedmag Hugh Erchenwyne Saxon Esa Cromwell Orma Nevill Dysart

Plantagenet (b. 1876), of Lyonella Fredegunda Cuthberga Ethelswytha Ideth Ysabel Grace Monica de Orellana Plantagenet (1882–1952), of Lyunulph Cospatrick Bruce Berkeley Jermyn Tullibardine Petersham de Orellana Dysart Plantagenet (1892–1966), and of Leone Sextus Denys Oswolf Fraudatifilius Tollemache-Tollemache de Orellana Plantagenet (1884–1917). Tollemache himself took an additional Tollemache for his own surname in 1876. In 1908 his seventh child and fifth son, Leo de Orellana (1879–1914), ungratefully renounced by deed poll the names of Quintus Tollemache Tollemache Plantagenet.

Tollemache died on 5 October 1895. His eldest son, Lyonel Felix Carteret Eugene (1854–1952), succeeded his cousin the fifth earl of Dysart in a family baronetcy.

K. D. REYNOLDS

Sources E. Lodge, *Peerage, baronetage, knightage and companionage of the British empire*, 81st edn, 3 vols. (1912) · Burke, *Peerage* (1939) · Burke, *Peerage* (1967) · Venn, *Alum. Cant.* · *The Times* (8 Oct 1895) · E. D. H. Tollemache, *The Tollemaches of Helmingham and Ham* (1949) · *The Times* (29 June 1859–27 June 1868)
Wealth at death £1619 19s. 7d.: probate, 18 Jan 1896, *CGPLA Eng. & Wales*

Tollemache [Tolmach, Talmach, Talmash], **Thomas** (c.1651–1694), army officer, was the second surviving son of Sir Lionel Tollemache, baronet (1624–1669), and his wife, Lady Elizabeth *Murray, from 1655 countess of Dysart and afterwards also duchess of Lauderdale (bap. 1626, d. 1698). It was rumoured that his mother had been Cromwell's mistress and that he was Oliver's son. According to Lord Dartmouth, Tollemache 'had a peculiar sort of vanity in desiring it should be understood' (*Burnet's History*, 4.228). Nevertheless, Sir Lionel was in no doubt that he was his own son and made ample provision for him in his will.

Tollemache was brought up at Helmingham in Suffolk and according to the inscription on his monument 'His natural abilities and first education were improved by his travels into foreign nations, where he spent several years, in the younger part of his life, in the observation of their genius, customs, politicks and interests'. Tollemache had returned to England by 1668 when he was admitted as a fellow commoner on 22 May to Queens' College, Cambridge. Entering the Inner Temple in the same year he was later created MA by Queens' in 1669.

Early military career Soon afterwards Tollemache joined the army, and by 1673 was serving as a captain in Cologne. He was commissioned into the Coldstream Guards on 16 January 1678 as a captain, but served for most of the year in Flanders as the lieutenant-colonel of a regiment raised by his cousin, Lord Alington. The regiment returned to England in early 1679 and was disbanded in April, freeing Tollemache to rejoin the Coldstreamers in May. In 1680 Tollemache was posted with a detachment of Coldstream Guards to the English outpost of Tangier, then under threat from the Moors. On 18 September he volunteered to command the advance guard in the successful but bloody attempt to recover the Pole Fort and later in the month he negotiated a temporary treaty with the Moors. On 27 October 1680 he took part in the garrison's last and

Thomas Tollemache (*c.*1651–1694), by unknown artist

most successful battle in which he and Percy Kirke were praised for having 'behaved themselves like brave and gallant men' (*A Particular Relation*). Tollemache arrived back in England from Tangier on 26 November 1680. In June 1682 he fought a duel, following which he lost his commission in the guards and returned to Tangier as a volunteer.

Supporter of William III Back in England by 1685 Tollemache was given the lieutenant-colonelcy of the newly raised Royal Regiment of Fusiliers, but in April 1686 he resigned his commission in protest at the admission of Catholics into the army. He was a leading member of the Treason Club, a group of youngish would-be politicians and officers led by Henry Wharton and Lord Colchester who met in the Rose tavern in Covent Garden with the purpose of encouraging and assisting an armed intervention by William of Orange. In March 1688 Tollemache was made the colonel of an English regiment in the pay of the Dutch government and sailed to the Netherlands, from where he kept in touch with his fellow conspirators in England. In November 1688 he returned as part of William's invasion force. His regiment formed the advance guard on the march from Torbay to London and occupied the Tower on 19 December 1688. In that same month he was appointed governor of Portsmouth and in January 1689 he was, through the influence of Henry Wharton, elected to parliament as the member for Malmesbury.

Tollemache was rewarded for his service to William III on 1 May 1689 by being made colonel of the Coldstream Guards. He was posted with his regiment to von Waldeck's allied army in Flanders where he played an important part in the victory at Walcourt (15 August 1689). After spending the winter in England, Tollemache returned to Flanders in spring 1690 to command the six British battalions that had been left there. In the summer he was ordered to join von Waldeck's army, but could not leave Ghent until money arrived from England to pay the debts incurred over the winter. In consequence he and his command missed the battle of Fleurus (21 June 1690). He spent the rest of the campaign in Flanders and in October 1690 commanded the battalions sent to winter in Brussels, after which he returned to England. He was promoted to major-general on 20 December and was ordered back to Flanders.

Ireland In May 1691 Tollemache was recalled to join the campaign in Ireland. He arrived in Dublin in June and joined Ginckel's army during the attack on Athlone. The Irish army had dug in on the west bank of the Shannon and had broken the bridge that separated them from the English. Tollemache proposed a simple but daring plan in which a few hundred armoured men would wade through the river to seize the bridgehead on the other side and hold it long enough for planks to be laid across the broken span so that the infantry could charge across the bridge. Ginckel was anxious to try any solution and, desperate though it was, Tollemache's plan was adopted.

To Tollemache's disappointment he was not allowed to put his own plan into action because the major-generals commanded in strict rotation, and Major-General Hugh Mackay refused to relinquish his turn. Mackay thought Tollemache's plan 'defied all the rules of law and policy' (Mackay, 144) as once the English troops had seized the town the whole Irish army, which was camped on the far side of Athlone, would drive them straight out again. On the day of the assault, 30 June 1691, Tollemache took part as a volunteer. He was carried through the river by his grenadiers and was the fifth man into the breach. The Irish were driven out of Athlone within the hour and the expected counter-attack never came. The French general of the Irish army, St Ruth, had ignored advice to tear down Athlone's western defences, and the English found themselves protected from the Irish by the town's walls.

On 12 July 1691 Tollemache commanded an infantry division in the centre of Ginckel's army at Aughrim. The Irish infantry attacked Ginckel's centre by crossing the bog that divided the two armies. Tollemache raced to support 'with some fresh men, he gave orders for our broken regiments to halt, and face about, which they did' (Story, 132). The Irish were chased back across the bog and eventually defeated in the bloodiest battle of the war.

Tollemache served in the short investment of Galway (19–29 July 1691) where his bravery and diligence were again praised. In a successful attack on the outworks it was noted that 'Major General *Talmash* would needs go a Volunteer as he usually did when it was not his turn to command' (Story, 163). He also took part in the siege of Limerick, and on 16 September 1691 supervised the construction of a pontoon across the Shannon and established a bridgehead through which most of the army later marched. After the Irish surrender of 3 October 1691 he remained behind as governor of Limerick. Once all the

Irish troops had marched out he left for Dublin, on 9 November, and returned to England.

Flanders and England Amid rumours that he was going to resign his commission in disgust at the preference given to William's Dutch officers over his British ones, Tollemache was summoned to a two hour private interview with the king 'who is extremely satisfied with his conduct of matters' (Luttrell, *Brief Historical Relation*, 2.338). On 23 January 1692, the same day on which he was sworn in as the member of parliament for Chippenham, Tollemache was promoted to lieutenant-general. He accompanied the Coldstream Guards to Flanders in March, but in May he was ordered back to England to take command of the army to oppose the threatened invasion by James II's Franco-Irish army. Once the danger had been averted by the destruction of the French fleet off La Hogue (19–24 May 1692) he returned to Flanders and served in the battle of Steenkerke (3 August 1692), where, although the French were victorious, 'our foot [were] brought off by the great conduct of lieutenant general Talmach' (ibid., 2.528). In the parliamentary debate on Steenkerke (23 November 1692) several members complained that the Dutchman Count Solms had been promoted over the better qualified Tollemache. Lord Colchester, the one-time chairman of the Rose tavern Treason Club, asserted that 'There is not a braver man in the world than General Tollemache' (*Parliamentary Diary of Narcissus Luttrell*, 255).

In September 1692 Tollemache was made governor of Dixmunde where he commanded a force of 12,000 men and foiled a French attempt to cut him off from Dunkirk and, in December, a threat to take both Dixmunde and Furnes. He arrived back in England on 22 December 1692. In March 1693 he took over as governor of the Isle of Wight in the king's absence, and in April was granted the rents for three years of almost 13,000 acres of forfeited land in Ireland. He returned to Flanders that month and in May he commanded the British troops outside Ghent. At the battle of Landen (29 July 1693) he played an important part in resisting the French attacks and had a horse killed under him.

On 11 December 1693 Tollemache addressed parliament in favour of the increased army estimates for 1694.

> It may be thought that I, having no estate, am ready to put the nation to a great charge; but I do declare I am as weary of war as any person and as desirous to have an end of it. And although I cannot answer for the success of the war, yet if the House will enable the king to come into the field with a good army, they may be able to preserve Flanders. (Grey, 364)

In spring 1694 Tollemache was commanded to lead an expedition to Brest, the home of the French Atlantic Fleet. The expedition was plagued by delays and by 1 May it was common knowledge that he was to lead an expedition 'to plunder the French seaside towns' (Luttrell, *Brief Historical Relation*, 3.304). In early May, Louis dispatched the engineer Vauban to Brest to improve the defences. Not only did the French know of his plans for Brest, but Tollemache knew of the French preparations for his reception before he left Spithead. He wrote to Whitehall for further instructions but did not receive a reply before his departure at the end of the month. He also wrote to his brother, Lord Huntingtower, to say that he had been 'resolv'd to goe Live in the country the rest of my life, but my ill fortune will not let me alone, and now I am ingag'd more than ever, I must say much against my will' (Tollemache, 81). He expected, he wrote, to return in a month and then to be posted back to Flanders.

Camaret Bay The English fleet anchored in Camaret Bay on 7 June 1694. The French were found to be 'much better prepared on all sides, with Mortars, Guns and Men, than we expected' (Caermarthen, 15). A council of war was called for the next morning, and Tollemache outlined his plans to land troops on the Quélern peninsula under covering fire from the fleet. Once the defences had been overrun on the south side of the Goulet, the narrow stretch of water that connects the Rade de Brest to Camaret Bay, the fleet would be able to pass through the Goulet and bombard Brest. According to Burnet 'the Council and Officers were all against making the attempt; but *Talmash* had set his heart so much upon it, that he could not be diverted from it' (*Burnet's History*, 4.227).

It took all morning of 8 June 1694 for Lord Carmarthen to position his ships and Tollemache was not able to give orders for the landing until noon, by which time it was clear that the fire from the warships was ineffectual against the French defences. He nevertheless sent towards the landing beach a flotilla of small boats led by his major-general, Lord Cutts. As the boats neared the shore they were met by heavy fire; the assault stalled, and in the moment of hesitation Tollemache had his boat rowed to within shouting distance of that carrying Cutts. 'My lord,' shouted Tollemache, 'is this following of orders? Do you see how the boats are in disorder? Pray, my lord, let us land in as good order as we can' (Childs, *William III*, 233). Cutts sent some of his men after his commanding officer, but remained afloat. To set an example Tollemache reached the shore, and with Captain Nathaniel Green and nine men made it to the cover of a large rock. Any further advance was prevented by the 150 French musketeers positioned further up the beach. Tollemache led his second wave of 150 grenadiers against this position. Most of his men were shot down, and he was shot in the thigh. He retreated until a further 200 men were landed, and led a second attack, but again the fire from the batteries and the musketeers was too fierce and most of them did not make it back to cover. Tollemache called for more men to land, but was persuaded to retreat to the boats once a body of French cavalry appeared along the shore. He was lifted into a boat and, still under heavy fire, was rowed to safety. Three hundred soldiers were lost in the raid.

Tollemache held one last council of war in which it was decided that the fleet should return to England. He reached Plymouth on the *Dreadnought* on 11 June 1694, where he was seen by surgeons. The prognosis was good, but in the afternoon of 12 June his leg

> was to a prodigious bigness swell'd from the Wound up to the Groyne, & so downward to the Anckle. ... Cap Green told him he fear'd it was death, the generall answer'd God's will

be done, I beleeve the same ... and about 7 a Clock hee dyed in Captn Green's Armes being sensible to the last. (Tollemache, 80)

'Before he died the general asserted it was impossible to have served their majesties better unless he had been obeyed, because none of the general officers landed with him' (*CSP dom.*, 184).

Tollemache was 'much lamented' (Luttrell, *Brief Historical Relation*, 3.329), and although it was planned to bury him in Westminster Abbey his wish to be buried at home was respected. On 30 June 1694 he was laid in the family vault at Helmingham where an elaborate memorial was erected and still stands. Tollemache never married, but left in his will provision for his son 'Lt-Coll Wilkins's ensign, commonly called Thomas Tolmach'.

Reputation At his funeral Tollemache was described as 'a true Englishman' (Brady, 23). Bishop Burnet remembered him as 'a brave and generous man, and a good officer, very apt to animate and encourage inferior officers and soldiers, but he was much too apt to be discontented and to turn mutinous' (*Burnet's History*, 4.228). Tollemache's family and supporters were left with the unpleasant suspicion that he had died in consequence of 'the envy of some of his pretended friends' (memorial) who had either warned the French of the attack or had failed him in its execution. Whatever the truth of those suspicions it is clear that at Camaret Bay Tollemache had again defied those laws of war and policy referred to by Mackay, and had sacrificed himself and his men in an attack on a strong and well-prepared position. 'I am indeed extremely affected with the loss of poor Tollemache', wrote King William when he received the news, 'although I do not approve of his conduct, yet I am of opinion that his too ardent zeal to distinguish himself induced him to attempt what was impracticable' (*Private and Original Correspondence of ... Shrewsbury*, 199). PIERS WAUCHOPE

Sources memorial, St Muary's Church, Helmingham, Suffolk · *Bishop Burnet's History of his own time: with the suppressed passages of the first volume*, ed. M. J. Routh, 6 vols. (1823), vol. 4 · *A particular relation of the late success of his majesties forces at Tangier against the Moors* (1680) · E. D. H. Tollemache, *The Tollemaches of Helmingham and Ham* (1949) · J. C. R. Childs, *The British army of William III, 1689–1702* (1987) · J. C. R. Childs, *The Nine Years' War and the British army, 1688–1697: the operations in the Low Countries* (1991) · J. Carswell, *The descent on England: a study of the English revolution of 1688 and its European background* (1969) · N. Luttrell, *A brief historical relation of state affairs from September 1678 to April 1714*, 2–3 (1857) · *The parliamentary diary of Narcissus Luttrell, 1691–1693*, ed. H. Horwitz (1972) · A. Grey, ed., *Debates of the House of Commons, from the year 1667 to the year 1694*, new edn, 10 (1769) · *A journal of the late motions and actions of the confederate forces against the French in the United Provinces and Spanish Netherlands* (1690) · W. Sawle, *An impartial relation of all the transactions between the army of the confederates and that of the French king ... with a more particular aspect of the battle of Fleury* (1691) · H. Mackay, *Memoirs of the war carried on in Scotland and Ireland*, ed. J. M. Hog and others, Bannatyne Club, 45 (1833) · H. Murtagh and M. O'Dwyer, eds., *Athlone besieged: eyewitness and other contemporary accounts of the sieges of Athlone*, Old Athlone Society (1991) · *Private and original correspondence of Charles Talbot, duke of Shrewsbury*, ed. W. Coxe (1821) · *CSP dom.*, 1694–5 · W. A. Shaw, ed., *Calendar of treasury books*, 10, PRO (1935) · G. Story, *A continuation of the impartial history of the wars of Ireland* (1693) · P. Osborne, Lord Caermarthen, *A journal of the Brest expedition by the Lord marquiss of Caermarthen* (1694) · N. Brady, *A sermon preached at Helmingham in Suffolk June 30th 1694 at the funeral of L. Gen. Tolmach* (1694) · will, PRO, PROB 11/421, sig. 162 · B. D. Henning, 'Tollemache, Hon. Thomas', HoP, *Commons, 1660–90*, 3.576 · *DNB*

Archives Grantham, Lincolnshire, family archives **Likenesses** G. Kneller, oils, 1688, Buccleuch estates, Selkirk · marble effigy on monument, 1694, St Mary's Church, Helmingham, Suffolk · H. Houbraken, engraving (after G. Kneller), repro. in T. Birch, *The heads of illustrious persons of Great Britain engraved by Mr Houbraken and Mr Vertue* (1756) · G. Kneller, oils, Ham House, London · portrait, Helmingham Hall, Suffolk [*see illus.*] **Wealth at death** comfortable

Toller, Sir Samuel (1764–1821), lawyer in India, was born on 10 November 1764, the eldest son of Thomas Toller (1732–1795), dissenting minister, and his wife, the daughter of Samuel Lawrence, dissenting minister. Thomas Toller was the youngest child of Hugh Toller, attorney, of Taunton; he attended Mile End Academy, Middlesex, was ordained in 1754, and in 1760 became a pastor at Monkwell Street Chapel, London, succeeding his deceased father-in-law. Following a quarrel with another pastor, he left about 1775, ministered in Hoxton, and died on 3 March 1795.

Samuel Toller was educated at Charterhouse School, Smithfield, London, from March 1775 to April 1782. He was admitted at Lincoln's Inn on 27 March 1781, and called to the bar. In 1793 Toller married Miss Cory of Cambridge, sister of Robert Towerson Cory, master of Emmanuel College, Cambridge, from 1797 to 1835; they had at least one child.

In March 1812 Toller was appointed advocate-general at Madras, and was subsequently knighted. He published two valued legal works: *The Law of Executors and Administrators* (1800; 7th edn by Francis Whitmarsh, 1838; 2nd American edn by T. F. Gordon, 1824; 3rd American edn by E. D. Ingraham, 1834) and *Treatise of the Law of Tithes: Compiled in Part from some Notes of Richard Wooddeson* (1808; 3rd edn, 1822).

Toller died in India on 19 November 1821, on his way to Bangalore, where he was going for his health.

E. I. CARLYLE, rev. ROGER T. STEARN

Sources A. Kippis, *A sermon preached ... upon occasion of ... the death of the Revd T. Toller* (1795) · *GM*, 1st ser., 63 (1793), 1050 · *GM*, 1st ser., 65 (1795), 260, 298, 345, 408 · *GM*, 1st ser., 82/1 (1812), 287 · *GM*, 1st ser., 88/1 (1818), 272 · *GM*, 1st ser., 92/1 (1822), 641 · W. P. Baildon, ed., *The records of the Honorable Society of Lincoln's Inn: admissions*, 1 (1896), 499 · [R. L. Arrowsmith], ed., *Charterhouse register, June 1769–May 1872* (1964), 333 · Venn, *Alum. Cant.* · Allibone, *Dict.* · M. R. Watts, *The dissenters: from the Reformation to the French Revolution* (1978)

Tollet, Elizabeth (1694–1754), poet, was born on 11 March 1694, the daughter of George *Tollet (d. 1719) and Elizabeth, née Cook (1659/60–1702). Her father was a central influence in her early intellectual development; she probably spent her first seven or eight years in his residence in York Buildings, then lived with him in his house in the Tower of London into her adulthood. Early on, he, 'observing her extraordinary Genius, gave her so excellent an Education, that besides great Skill in Music, and Drawing, she spoke fluently and correctly the *Latin, Italian,* and

French Languages; and well understood History, Poetry, and the Mathematicks' (preface to Tollet, *Poems*, i).

George Tollet was well acquainted with a number of the most prominent members of the intelligentsia of the day, including Samuel Pepys, John Evelyn, Edmond Halley, Isaac Newton, and Robert Harley, first earl of Oxford, whom Elizabeth Tollet praises in her poem 'To my Brother at St. John's College in Cambridge'. John Duncombe's biographical note on Elizabeth Tollet in John Nichols's *Select Collection of Poems* (1780) states that 'Sir Isaac Newton honoured both [George Tollet] and his daughter with his friendship, and was much pleased with some of her first essays' (6.64n.). From 1699 until his death in 1727 Newton was master of the mint, which was then within the precincts of the Tower of London. Although Elizabeth likely presented these 'first essays' to him during her years in the Tower, the family's acquaintance with Newton might date as far back as 1693, when, in preparation for a projected national lottery, Samuel Pepys corresponded with Newton and George Tollet on the nature of probabilities.

Elizabeth Tollet seems to have attained considerable literary proficiency even as a teenager, since Thomas Parnell's poem 'To a Young Lady, on her Translation of the Story of Phoebus and Daphne, from Ovid'—published initially in Steele's *Poetical Miscellanies* (December 1713)—is almost certainly in praise of Tollet's poem 'Apollo and Daphne', which must therefore have been written by 1713, when she could have been no older than nineteen. In 1724 a book of her poetry appeared anonymously—*Poems on Several Occasions. With Anne Boleyn to King Henry VIII. An Epistle*—published in London by John Clarke. Eighty-four pages in length, the slim duodecimo volume contains, in addition to the long title poem, several imitations of Horace, Ovid, and Virgil; a handful of Latin verse; poems to friends, such as the harpsichordist Elizabeth Blackler, and poems on famous contemporary writers such as William Congreve, Alexander Pope, Anne Finch, countess of Winchilsea, and Lady Mary Wortley Montagu, as well as other poems demonstrating striking artistic and intellectual range. Especially interesting to recent scholars is Tollet's poem 'Hypatia', a polemic of nearly 200 lines in which Tollet has the 'Shade' of the ancient female mathematician–philosopher Hypatia argue—against 'Tyrant Custom'—that women have the right to better education and to freedom of intellectual enquiry of diverse kinds—including scientific, classical, and theological. References to the inappropriateness of 'L——s' Spleen' and the inadequacy of '*Toland*'s Praise' in line 14 suggest Tollet's poem is in part a response to Thomas Lewis's *History of Hypatia* (1721) and the substantial third section, 'Hypatia', of John Toland's *Tetradymus* (1720).

Evidence from book subscription lists suggests Tollet probably lived in the Tower for some years after her father's retirement to Betley, Staffordshire. At his death in 1719 he left her 'a handsome Fortune' (preface to Tollet, *Poems*, i): this included an annuity of £250, among other legacies. She later lived in Stratford, Essex, where she was associated with 'the Stratford-le-Bow school', and spent her last years in Westham (now West Ham), Essex. She

died, unmarried, on 1 February 1754 and was buried in All Saints, West Ham, on 11 February. Her epitaph, now worn beyond legibility, once claimed

> Religion, Justice, and Benevolence,
> Appeared in all her Actions;
> And her Poems, in various Languages,
> Are adorn'd with extensive Learning,
> Applied to the best Purposes.
> (Toldervy, 2.230)

Clues to the contents of her library may be found in her poems, her will, book subscription lists (as indexed in the *Biography Database* CD-ROM), and Hodgson's *Catalogue of the Betley Hall Library* (1923).

William Cole described Tollet as 'a little, crooked woman, but a sharp wit' (Nichols, *Illustrations*, 8.584), but no portraits appear to be extant.

During her lifetime several of Tollet's poems were circulated in manuscript, and some saw periodical and miscellany publication, but it seems it was only after her death that any poem appeared under her name in print. Tollet's writings were entrusted to her chief executor, Colonel Richard King. She had in her will stated that she wanted posthumous publication of 'my Writings in Verse together with those already printed by Mr. Clark at the Royal Exchange that they may be published entire and without mixture of other Hands those in prose being wrote for private use'. At 238 pages, a considerably expanded edition of her poems, bearing the same title as that of the 1724 edition, appeared in 1755. In this posthumous volume, ascribed to 'Mrs. Elizabeth Tollet' by the title-page, there are many additional poems, including several concerning further contemporary artists or intellectuals such as Charles Jervas, Dr John Woodward, and Isaac Newton; over thirty renderings of psalms into English verse; as well as a 'musical drama' entitled 'Susanna; or, Innocence Preserv'd', which elaborates the apocryphal story of Susanna and the Elders from the Old Testament. The book also includes further Latin verses, and several poems which draw on recent scientific thought in their theological argumentation, the most elaborate of these being 'The Microcosm'. The text of the 1755 Clarke edition was later reissued by the publisher Thomas Lownds *c*.1756–60.

Tollet's work was anthologized by Henry Dell, in whose *Select Collection of the Psalms of David* (1756) Tollet, with twenty-nine psalm renderings, is by far the most well-represented author, by John Duncombe in John Nichols's *Select Collection of Poems* (1780), and by Robert Southey (1807), Alexander Dyce (1825), and Frederic Rowton (1848), among others. She was rediscovered by Roger Lonsdale and included in his influential 1980s anthologies of eighteenth-century verse, since when scholars such as Isobel Grundy in *Halcyon* and Deborah Baker Wyrick in the *Dictionary of Literary Biography* have called for Tollet's 'reinscription' into literary history, citing her importance as an early feminist and overlooked poetic voice of the period; and Tollet's work has been further and quite widely anthologized.　MICHAEL LONDRY

Sources register, St Martin-in-the-Fields, City Westm. AC [baptism], vol. 8, fol. 53*r* · E. Hinchliffe, *Barthomley: in letters from a former rector to his eldest son* (1856) · J. Craig, *The mint: a history of the London mint from A.D. 287 to 1948* (1953) · *Private correspondence and miscellaneous papers of Samuel Pepys, 1679–1703*, ed. J. R. Tanner, 2 vols. (1926) · R. Ollard, *Pepys: a biography* (1974) · *The correspondence of Isaac Newton*, ed. H. W. Turnbull, 3 (1961) · *Collected poems of Thomas Parnell*, ed. C. Rawson and F. P. Lock (1989) · will, 1718–19, Staffs. RO, D3272/1/22/10/1 [George Tollet, father] · Nichols, *Illustrations* · parish register, All Saints, West Ham, Essex RO, Chelmsford, D/P 256/1/3 · W. Toldervy, ed., *Select epitaphs*, 2 vols. (1755) · J. A. Cannon and F. Robinson, *Biography database, 1680–1830*, 1st ser. (1995–9) [CD-ROM] · E. Tollet, *Poems* (1755), preface · will, PRO, PROB 10/2150 · R. Lonsdale, ed., *Eighteenth-century women poets: an Oxford anthology* (1989) · I. Grundy, 'Against the Dead Poets Society: non-Augustan, non-Romantic, non-male poets', *Halcyon: A Journal of the Humanities*, 15 (1993), 181–97 · D. Baker Wyrick, 'Elizabeth Tollet', *Eighteenth-century British poets: first series*, ed. J. Sitter, DLitB, 95 (1990) · P. Fara, *History of Science*, 40 (2002)

Wealth at death annuity of £250; specific bequests totalled over £1770; gave £1000 and majority of books to nephew George Tollet, the Shakespearian critic; residue of her estate to his younger brother Charles Tollet of Deptford Yard: will, PRO, PROB 10/2150

Tollet, George (*d.* 1719), mathematician and naval administrator, is said to have lived to 'a very advanced age' (*St Margaret's*, 74), but his birth date and parentage are not known. He had at least three brothers—John, Thomas, and Charles. Much evidence suggests that his brother Thomas was the composer Thomas *Tollet thought to have died in 1696. George Tollet was also musical, owned a violin made by Nicolò Amati, and may have composed 'Tollet's Ground' and other works sometimes attributed to Thomas. In 1683 Tollet became a founder member of the Dublin Philosophical Society—a sister organization to the Royal Society—and would become one of its more active members: his experiments and presentations, as well as his correspondence with other scientists, including Edmond Halley, are often remarked upon in its minute book, which records his election to the position of treasurer on 2 November 1685. Several members of the Dublin society remained important contacts after Tollet moved to England, perhaps most notably William King (later archbishop of Dublin), with whom Tollet maintained an extensive correspondence spanning more than two decades, much of which survives in the library of Trinity College, Dublin (amid TCD, MSS 1995–2008).

Several of Tollet's contributions to the Dublin society's meetings involved applied mathematics—he presented papers on gunnery and on longitude, for example—but particularly striking, in light of his later attention to the education of his daughter Elizabeth, is his presentation of a young Irish prodigy. William Molyneux reported to Edmond Halley in a letter of 6 April 1685:

> several of our meetings have been employed by a young mathematical female in this place, bred up by one Mr Tollet, a teacher of mathematics, and a most excellent learned man in that kind. The child is not yet eleven, and yet she hath given sufficient proofs of her learning in arithmetic, the most abstruse parts, algebra, geometry, trigonometry plane and spherical, the doctrine of the globes, chronology, and on the violin plays anything almost at sight. (Gilbert, 2.177)

She was also deemed proficient in geography and astronomy.

In 1688 Tollet moved to England. Luttrell's parliamentary diary reports that Tollet was chosen secretary to the 'commissioners for taking the public accounts' in March 1691; was made 'comptroller of the foreign post office in the room of Mr Brocket' in May 1697; took a post at 'the custome house' in November 1697; and in June 1700 was made 'secretary of the excise, worth £500 per annum' (Luttrell, 2.192; 4.219, 306, 661). Not mentioned in Luttrell's diary, but noted by both Hinchliffe and Speake, is Tollet's appointment as accountant-general of Ireland, granted in December 1691.

Tollet's marriage to Elizabeth Cook (1659/60–1702) had taken place by at least 1690. There seems to have been considerable strife in the marriage. In a letter to William King of 24 November 1692 Tollet remarks how 'deeply sown' is 'ye seed of contention' (TCD, MSS 1995–2008/246). Elizabeth died at the age of forty-two on 6 February 1702, and was buried in St Martin-in-the-Fields, as her epitaph records, 'with two of their nine Children; a third lyeth near this grave' (Le Neve, 46). Apart from their daughter Elizabeth *Tollet, the poet (*b.* 11 March 1694), only two other children of the nine survived into adulthood: George (*b.* 17 Dec 1696) and Cook (*b.* 1 April 1698).

A letter from Tollet to Samuel Pepys the diarist and navy official, dated 8 February 1694, is headed 'Office of Accounts in York Buildings', and it seems likely that Tollet had his residence as well as his office in these 'comfortable mansions' in London (*Private Correspondence*, 1.90, 267; 2.2). But by 1702 the family had moved to the Tower of London, and on 11 February 1702 Tollet was appointed an extra commissioner to the navy with a salary of £500 per annum. It was perhaps through his work with the Navy Board that he became acquainted with that other famous diarist and navy official of the period, John Evelyn, at whose funeral in 1706 at Wotton he was a pallbearer. On 3 December 1708 George Tollet was granted a coat of arms. The Tollets' residence in the Tower continued well beyond the father's employment with the navy, which ended on 16 November 1714: the family 'certainly resided there' in

> the early part of the reign of George I, during the imprisonment of the celebrated Robert Harley, Earl of Oxford, who, in gratitude to Mr. Tollet, for his kindness to him when in confinement, presented him with a gilt cup, with the Tower engraved upon it, which has descended as an heir loom. (Hinchliffe, 188–9; will, Staffs. RO, D3272/1/22/10/1)

For the initial part of his imprisonment in 1715 Oxford had in fact stayed at the Tollets' residence.

Tollet wrote his will on 9 June 1718 in the Tower, and later that year retired to the small market town of Betley in Staffordshire to live in Betley Hall, which, with surrounding properties in Betley and Audley, he had recently purchased from Randle Egerton, esquire. He died within about a year of the move, and was buried on 5 November 1719 in St Margaret's Church, Betley. The Tollets and their descendants remained prominent in Betley and surrounding areas for nearly two centuries.   MICHAEL LONDRY

Sources *St Margaret's Church, Betley, Staffordshire: monumental inscriptions*, South Cheshire Family History Society (1998) · K. T. Hoppen, *The common scientist in the seventeenth century: a study of the*

Dublin Philosophical Society, 1683–1708 (1970) · minute and register book of the Dublin Philosophical Society, 1684–93, BL, Add. MS 4811 · G. Tollet, letters to W. King, TCD, Lyons collection, MSS 1995–2008 · J. T. Gilbert, *A history of the city of Dublin*, 3 vols. (1861) · C. McNeill, ed., *The Tanner letters*, IMC (1943) · parish register, London, St Martin-in-the-Fields, vol. 8, City Westm. AC [baptisms: George Tollet and Cook Tollet, children] · E. Hinchliffe, *Barthomley: in letters from a former rector to his eldest son* (1856) · R. Speake, ed., *Betley: a village of contrasts* (1980) · J. Le Neve, *Monumenta Anglicana*, 5 vols. (1717–19) · *Private correspondence and miscellaneous papers of Samuel Pepys, 1679–1703*, ed. J. R. Tanner, 2 vols. (1926) · J. M. Collinge, *Navy Board officials, 1660–1832* (1978) · J. J. Howard, ed., *Miscellanea genealogica et heraldica*, 2nd ser., 3 (1890) · will, 1718–19, Staffs. RO, D3272/1/22/10/1 · E. Hamilton, *The backstairs dragon: a life of Robert Harley, earl of Oxford* (1969) · P. W. L. Adams, ed., *Betley parish register, 1538–1812*, Staffordshire Parish Registers Society (1916) · G. Tollet, letter to Mr Collins, 1675, RS, MS EL. T.45 · N. Luttrell, *A brief historical relation of state affairs from September 1678 to April 1714*, 6 vols. (1857) · R. Ollard, *Pepys: a biography* (1974)

Archives TCD, letters to W. King

Wealth at death At death he possessed Betley Hall and surrounding properties in Betley and Audley, Staffordshire, and an annuity of £400, the selling of which he estimated would realize £8000. He bequeathed an annuity of £250 to his daughter Elizabeth and, after other specific legacies, the residue of his estate went to his eldest son, George Tollet: George Tollet's will, 1718–19

Tollet, George (*bap.* 1725, *d.* 1779), literary critic, son of George Tollet (*b.* 1696) and Elizabeth or Isabel (*née* Oates), was baptized on 29 September 1725 in Kirk Braddan, Isle of Man. He was probably a student at Eton College by 1742. Tollet matriculated from King's College, Cambridge, on 17 December 1744, and appears to have been in residence at King's from Michaelmas 1744 to Nativitatis 1748. He was admitted to Lincoln's Inn on 2 July 1745, and was called to the bar by the inn on 19 June 1751.

A bachelor, Tollet lived for the latter decades of his life in Betley Hall, in the small town of Betley, Staffordshire; he had inherited the house and surrounding properties from his father. In 1754 Tollet inherited the bulk of the library of his aunt Elizabeth Tollet, the poet, and subsequently enlarged it with his own acquisitions. He contributed fifteen notes to the 1773 edition of Shakespeare by Samuel Johnson and George Steevens, and over four hundred to the ten-volume 1778 edition. In Arthur Sherbo's assessment, this makes Tollet

> one of the greatest single contributors to the commentary on Shakespeare in the eighteenth century, always excepting the editors of the various editions. His notes are on all the plays of the accepted canon except *Julius Caesar, Titus Andronicus* (which many thought uncanonical), and *Romeo and Juliet* (hardly bachelor fare). (Sherbo, *Shakespeare's Midwives*, 51)

Sherbo laments that Tollet's scholarship has frequently been overlooked by recent Shakespearian critics, and asserts that his work 'richly deserves' greater attention (ibid., 66).

Tollet's dissertation on the so-called Betley Window, a painted glass window from his house in Betley, thought to depict Morris dancers and May day festivities, has inspired much comment from scholars of Shakespeare, folklore, and early English painted glass. This dissertation was first printed in the 1778 edition of Shakespeare by Johnson and Steevens (5.425–34), and a manuscript version addressed

to George Steevens is held by the Bodleian Library (Bodl. Oxf., MS Percy c. 4., 62*r*–65*v*). The window itself is now in the Victoria and Albert Museum, London. Tollet's copy of Elizabeth Tollet's *Poems on Several Occasions* (1755)—now at Smith College Library, Massachusetts—is enriched by extensive annotation in his hand, and constitutes an important source of evidence for the poetry and life of his aunt.

Tollet died in October 1779, probably on the 21st or 22nd, at Betley. He was buried there, at St Margaret's Church. William Cole, who had been a contemporary of Tollet at King's College, described him as 'a shy, reserved man, and of no genteel appearance or behaviour' (Nichols, *Illustrations*, 8.584), but no portraits have been located.

MICHAEL LONDRY

Sources parish register, Kirk Braddan, Manx National Heritage Library, Douglas, Isle of Man, MHML 0073/1/2 · R. A. Austen-Leigh, ed., *The Eton College register, 1698–1752* (1927) · bursar's particular books, 1744/5–1747/8, King's Cam., KCAR/3/1/146–149 · W. P. Baildon, ed., *The records of the Honorable Society of Lincoln's Inn: admissions*, 1 (1896) · W. P. Baildon, ed., *The records of the Honorable Society of Lincoln's Inn: the black books*, 3 (1899) · will, 1750–54, PRO, PROB 10/2150 [Elizabeth Tollet] · *A catalogue of the Betley Hall library formed during the eighteenth century by Elizabeth Tollet … and George Tollet* (1923) [sale catalogue, Hodgson & Co., London, 19–20 April 1923] · A. Sherbo, *Shakespeare's midwives: some neglected Shakespeareans* (1992) · A. Sherbo, 'The library of George Tollet, neglected Shakespearean', *Studies in Bibliography*, 34 (1981), 227–38 · G. N. Brown, *This old house: a domestic biography* (1987) [Betley, near Crewe, Cheshire: Betley Court Gallery] · probate of will and associated documents, 1779–96, Staffs. RO, D3272/1/22/10/2 · Nichols, *Illustrations*, vol. 8 · E. Hinchliffe, *Barthomley: in letters from a former rector to his eldest son* (1856) · P. W. L. Adams, ed., *Betley parish register, 1538–1812*, Staffordshire Parish Registers Society (1916) · will (clerk's transcript), 1779, PRO, PROB 11/1079, quire 320 · G. Baker, papers relating to Sir George Baker's treatment of George Tollet (1725–1779), 1779, Wellcome L., MS 7737/1–3 · register, St Martin-in-the-Fields, City Westm. AC, vol. 8, fol. 129*r* [baptism, father]

Archives Bodl. Oxf., dissertation on the figures depicted on the Betley Window, MS Percy c. 4, 62*r*–65*v* · Bodl. Oxf., notes concerning Staffordshire history, MS Gough. Staffs. 4., 99*r*–109*r* · Smith College, Northampton, Massachusetts, MS corrections and marginalia in Elizabeth Tollet's *Poems on several occasions* (1755), 825 T579

Wealth at death Betley Hall and surrounding properties; extensive library; annuity of £100, which was to be sold upon his death; specific legacies totalled well over £600; Betley Hall and associated properties inherited by younger brother, Charles Tollet: will (clerk's transcript) 1779, PRO, PROB 11/1079, quire 320

Tollet, Thomas (*d.* 1696?), musician and composer, is first known in 1669 when, along with two men who were perhaps his brothers, John Tollet (possibly the John 'Tallat' who had married an Ann Bates in Dublin in 1665, the earliest reference to the family name in Dublin) and George *Tollet (*d.* 1719), he is listed as one of the ten Dublin city musicians; a Charles Tollet was also appointed to the city musicians in 1677. Thomas, John, and Charles were again named as Dublin city musicians in 1688. Between 1673 and 1687 Christ Church, Dublin, purchased violins and music (unspecified except in one reference to '3 anthems') on a number of occasions from 'Mr Tollett' or 'the Tolletts', indicating that they ran a family music business alongside their activities as musicians. Richard, a son of 'Thomas Tallet, gent. and his wife Esther', was buried at St Michan's

Church, Dublin, in 1680, and a second, unnamed child in 1684.

Some instrumental music by both Thomas and George Tollet, included in a manuscript collection dating from the 1660s and 1670s and associated with the twenty-four violins of the English royal court, indicates professional links with England at this period. Thomas Tollet moved to London probably in 1688 or 1689 and there composed incidental music for the theatre including *Love or Money* (January 1690?), *The Marriage-Hater Match'd* (1692), and *The Virtuous Wife* (1694?), all by Thomas D'Urfey and given at Drury Lane. Tollet also wrote music for *Henry the Second* (by J. Bancroft, 1692), *The Volunteers* (T. Shadwell, 1692), *The Cheats* (J. Wilson, c.1693), *The Lover's Luck* (T. Dilke, 1695), and *The Generous Enemies* (J. Corye, 1696?). As a composer Tollet has been described as 'a reasonably competent follower of Purcell, though his music is unenterprising' (Holman, 'Tollett, Thomas').

Tollet published an instruction book, *Directions to Play on the French Flageolet* (now lost), in London in 1694. A number of shorter instrumental pieces by him survive, including 'The queen's farewell' written on the death of Queen Mary in 1694. It is likely that George Tollet composed some of the music attributed to Thomas Tollet including 'Tollett's ground', which first appeared in John Playford's *The Division Viol* (10th edn, 1685, and later edns) and remained popular into the eighteenth century. The fact that, unlike Thomas, John, and Charles Tollet, he was no longer a Dublin city musician in 1688 may be explained by his having developed his interest in mathematics if, as seems probable, he can be identified with the George Tollet who later became a commissioner of the navy and died in 1719. Tollet was sworn in as a member of the royal private musick in March 1695 but must have died (presumably in London) not long before 2 September 1696, when his place was taken by John Eccles.   BARRA R. BOYDELL

Sources P. Holman, 'Tollett, Thomas', *New Grove*, 2nd edn, 25.553–4 · J. T. Gilbert and R. M. Gilbert, eds., *Calendar of ancient records of Dublin*, 19 vols. (1889–1944); 4 (1894), 476–7; 5 (1895), 148, 475–6 · B. Boydell, *Music at Christ Church before 1800: documents and selected anthems* (1999), 136–9 · P. Holman, *Four and twenty fiddlers: the violin at the English court, 1540–1690* (1993), 321–2 · T. Warner, *An annotated bibliography of woodwind instruction books, 1600–1830* (1967), 4 · H. F. Berry, ed., *The registers of the church of S. Michan, Dublin, 1636–1700* (1909), 236, 274 · *Index to the act or grant books, and to original wills, of the diocese of Dublin to the year 1800* (1895), 831 · C. McNeill, ed., *The Tanner letters*, IMC (1943), 496 · index to prerogative wills, 1536–1858, NA Ire., XX3, 352; XX11, 30 · M. Tilmouth, 'Tollett, Thomas', *New Grove*

Tolley, Cyril James Hastings (1895–1978), golfer, was born at 138 Breakspears Road, Deptford, London, on 14 September 1895, the only child (there was previously a son who was stillborn) of James Thomas Tolley, a coffee merchant's clerk, and his wife, Christiana Mary Pascall. His delicate health as a boy of nine prompted his parents to move to Eastbourne, where he learned his golf and attended St George's preparatory school. As he was still supposed to be in frail health, his schooling was continued privately but he was fit enough to join up in the First World War. He obtained the rank of major in the

Royal Tank Corps, was awarded the MC for leading his tank on foot in the early mist of the battle of Cambrai, and was taken prisoner in November 1917. At twenty-six, therefore, he was older than the average freshman when he went up to University College, Oxford, in 1919.

It was during his years in the university side that Tolley became known as one of the best and most famous players in the history of amateur golf. The first notice of his ability came when he went to Muirfield in 1920 during his first summer term at Oxford and, despite being almost completely out of practice, won the amateur championship. This established him as a leading figure who quickly became an automatic choice for any international team at a time when international golf was just becoming fashionable. He played in the first Walker cup match against the United States in 1922 and continued to play in the cup, with the exception of 1928 and 1932, until 1934. On three occasions his foursomes partner was Roger Wethered, a contemporary at Oxford and a great friend, whose name was invariably linked with Tolley's.

Although he never finished higher than equal eighteenth in the open championship, Tolley showed how considerable his powers could be by winning the French open on two occasions (1924 and 1928) against a field of strong professionals, including some of the best of the Americans. He won the amateur championship for a second time in 1929 at Sandwich but his championship successes scarcely do him justice. On his best days he reached magnificent proportions. There seemed no reason why a swing of rhythmic beauty should ever hit the ball anything but straight; and it rarely did. His demeanour and general game had an unmistakably majestic air and he possessed the capacity for holing long putts, an act made more impressive by his habit, as Bernard Darwin wrote, 'of walking after the still moving ball with a view to picking it out. Occasionally, the ball disobeyed this imperious behest but very often it submitted.'

On the other hand, Tolley's sturdy build, given an impression of even greater imperturbability by his pipe smoking, concealed the fact that he was a highly strung person, who, like Bobby Jones, could suffer agonies. He could be temperamental, not always giving of his best and not always trying to. He lacked the competitive instinct of many champions who regarded every opponent as one to be beaten. Wethered wrote in a tribute after his death (*Times*, 26 May 1978): 'The unpredictable aspects of Cyril's character … sprang from a peculiar sensitivity and at the same time a dramatic element in his temperament. … He was a better player against a redoubtable opponent than against a poorer golfer.' As an example of this dramatic element, he cited the time Tolley paid his caddie the winner's tip before holing his winning putt in the 1920 amateur championship but he added: 'It was, I am sure, the unexpected and contradictory sides of his nature, combined with his benevolence and kindness, that made him such a lovable and enjoyable companion as well as such an entertaining partner at golf.'

One of Tolley's greatest matches ended in defeat. Defending his title in the amateur championship of 1930,

Tolley met Bobby Jones in a renowned match in the fourth round at St Andrews. He eventually stymied himself and lost at the nineteenth. Having cleared his greatest hurdle, Jones went on to complete the coveted 'grand slam'. But whereas Jones, a good six years' Tolley's junior, retired from competitive golf later that same year, Tolley reached the semi-final again in 1950 at the age of fifty-four, thus demonstrating his natural genius for the game. Nearly all the honours of golfing office befell him. He was captain of the Oxford and Cambridge golfing society (1946–8) and of the Royal and Ancient golfing club in 1948. He worked periodically as a stockbroker but after the Second World War became active in politics, and stood as a Liberal at Hendon South in 1950. He was not elected but, unlike many of his party, saved his deposit. He was treasurer of the London Liberal Party for one year and served from 1958 to 1962 as a Conservative councillor at Eastbourne, where he died on 18 May 1978. In 1924 he wrote *The Modern Golfer*. In addition to golf, he played bowls and croquet and was also a keen apiarist and philatelist. He was not married.   DONALD STEEL, *rev.*

Sources B. Darwin, *Golf between two wars* (1944) · D. Steel and P. Ryde, eds., *The Shell international encyclopaedia of golf* (1975) · *The Times* (20–26 May 1978) · b. cert. · *CGPLA Eng. & Wales* (1978)
Wealth at death £65,762: probate, 11 Aug 1978, *CGPLA Eng. & Wales*

Tolmie, Frances (1840–1926), folklorist, was born on 13 October 1840 at Uignish Farm, Duirinish, near Loch Dunvegan in the Isle of Skye, the daughter of John Tolmie (1797–1844) and Margaret MacAskill (*b.* 1808). Her Tolmie ancestors had had a long association with the MacLeod chiefs at Dunvegan. Her mother came from the island of Eigg, and she brought with her a rich store of Gaelic traditional song. Tolmie's family on both sides were involved in farming as tacksmen, and in various professional activities. She grew up in a bilingual family, in close touch with the traditional song culture, but with English dominating the educational sphere.

In 1854 Frances Tolmie's brother John was inducted as minister of Strontian in Ardnamurchan, Argyll, and his widowed mother, with the three youngest of her family, moved there to look after his household. Here Frances acquired a new tutor, a Miss Whyte from Edinburgh, who added music to the curriculum. In 1856 her brother took up the charge of Bracadale in Skye; at this stage Frances Tolmie seems to have tutored herself in reading Gaelic.

Tolmie spent from 1857 to 1858 in Edinburgh, studying English, French, Italian, and music. She returned to Skye in 1858, and soon after this she seems to have begun noting down the words and tunes of Gaelic songs. Some elderly female friends possessed a store of older songs, and Tolmie had been used to hearing a wide variety of songs at the 'tweed waulkings' (the process of shrinking tweed by pounding it on a trestle table) and also sung as accompaniment to such tasks as milking, churning, and rowing boats.

The years 1862–6 were again spent in Edinburgh, where Tolmie became governess to the two daughters of Thomas Constable of the Edinburgh publishing firm. It was there that she read two recent Gaelic publications, Thomas McLauchlan's imperfect edition (1862) of the Book of the Dean of Lismore and J. F. Campbell's *Popular Tales of the West Highlands* (1860–62). These works stimulated her interest in the heroic ballads, some of which she was to record from oral renditions when she returned to Skye; she also recorded songs in North Uist in 1870.

In 1873–4 Tolmie spent two terms at Merton Hall School in Cambridge; this was followed by a long stay (1874–95) at Coniston in the Lake District, as companion to an older woman, Harriette Rigbye, whom she accompanied on European travels. On her return to Scotland, Tolmie lived in Oban and Edinburgh, and came into contact with Keith Norman MacDonald, author of the Gesto collection of Gaelic songs, with George Henderson, and with Alexander Carmichael. She contributed songs to two later editions of the Gesto collection, and Henderson and Carmichael were both influential in turning her attention again to her collection of songs. Henderson, via an intermediary friend, recommended Frances to Lucy Broadwood, secretary of the Folk-song Society, and this was to lead to Frances Tolmie's seminal work, published in the *Journal of the Folk-Song Society* for 1911.

Frances Tolmie listed the works that appeared in this 1911 collection in her journal, with dates and other details, often including the names of the singers. The dates at which she heard the songs range from 1843–4 ('an early nursery memory') to 1908, while the songs themselves were sixteenth-century or later. The locations given for the hearing of the songs are predominantly on Skye, although a number are said to have originated on Eigg; locations that appear less frequently are Moidart, North Uist, Mull, and Barra. The singers were almost always women, sometimes employed by the Tolmie family, sometimes neighbours or acquaintances.

The collection contains 105 songs, including cradle and nursery songs, vocal dance songs, and labour songs. Gaelic texts and English translations are given (sometimes reduced texts if they had been printed already, as in Gesto), with staff notation of the melodies, and some background notes by George Henderson on historical and literary matters. Annie G. Gilchrist provided a short section on the modal system, and Lucy Broadwood another on the Gaelic scale system, adding their individual classifications to the song texts. Altogether this treatment resulted in the most detailed and illuminating collection of Gaelic song in print at that date. Frances Tolmie acknowledged her admiration for Patrick McDonald's *Highland Vocal Airs*, published in 1784, and knew of various collections of song texts, such as Archibald Sinclair's *An t-Oranaiche* (1876–9); some extensive collections, such as James McLagan's, still remained largely in manuscript form. The collection remains an important landmark in Gaelic song studies.

From 1905 to 1915 Frances Tolmie lived in Edinburgh; subsequently she returned to Skye to live at Dunvegan. Here she was visited by old friends and young people interested in her work on Gaelic song; she occasionally played the piano and sang in public. She died at Kilchoan Cottage, Dunvegan, Duirinish, Skye, on 31 December 1926 and was buried on the island.   DERICK S. THOMSON

Sources E. Bassin, *The old songs of Skye: Frances Tolmie and her circle* (1977) · F. Tolmie, 'Notes and reminiscences', *Journal of the Folk-song Society*, 16 (1911)
Archives priv. coll. | Cecil Sharp House, London, Lucy Broadwood MSS
Likenesses photographs, repro. in Bassin, *Old songs*
Wealth at death £4438 5*s*.: confirmation, 7 March 1927, *CCI*

Tolpuddle Martyrs [Dorchester Labourers, Six Men of Dorset] (*act.* **1834–*c*.1845**), agricultural labourers and trade unionists from the village of Tolpuddle in Dorset, became famous as victims of injustice, whose sentences of transportation caused a public outcry in 1834. **James Brine** (1813–1902), **James Hammett** (1811–1891), George *Loveless (1797–1874), **James Loveless** (1808–1873), **John Standfield** (1813–1898), and **Thomas Standfield** (1789–1864) all lived and worked in Tolpuddle, where they were arrested on the morning of 24 February 1834. They were marched in chains to Dorchester on charges of being present at an initiation ceremony where illegal oaths were administered during a meeting of a friendly society of agricultural labourers. This trade union had been formed in 1833, largely on George Loveless's initiative, in an attempt to resist wage cuts by local farmers. Evidence against the trade unionists was gathered by a spy who attended a meeting of the society in Thomas Standfield's cottage in December 1833, and the six men were made an example of to deter the further spread of union activity in the area. James Hammett was not present on the occasion in question, and seems to have been arrested in place of his brother John. The family connections within the group were such that one woman in the village, Diana Standfield, was wife of one of those arrested (Thomas Standfield), mother of another (John Standfield), and a sister of two of the others (the brothers George and James Loveless). Brine and Hammett were Anglicans, but the other four martyrs were all Methodists. George and James Loveless were local preachers, and George believed that he had been victimized as much for his Methodism as for his trade unionism.

The men were held in Dorchester gaol until the opening of the spring assizes, and were tried in the county court at Dorchester on 17 March 1834, where the jury found them guilty; they were subsequently sentenced to transportation for seven years. After their conviction, the group was split up: George Loveless was taken ill and moved to a prison hospital, while the others were transferred to Portsmouth, and thence to Plymouth, before setting sail for Australia on 11 April. After four months at sea, they reached Sydney in August 1834, and were assigned as convict labour to various employers in New South Wales, walking long distances to reach the farms where they were to work. Meanwhile, George Loveless was finally judged well enough to travel in early April, and was kept in a prison hulk at Portsmouth for six weeks before boarding a ship bound for Van Diemen's Land, where he landed on 4 September and was put to work on a government farm.

In England, agitation against the sentences began almost as soon as they were pronounced, and the outcry over the injustice of the case won the support of high-profile radical figures, including Daniel O'Connell, Fergus

THE RETURNED "CONVICTS."

JAMES BRINE, Aged 25.   THOMAS STANFIELD, Aged 51.   JOHN STANFIELD, Aged 25.   JAMES LOVELESS, Aged 29.

GEORGE LOVELESS, Aged 41.

Tolpuddle Martyrs (*act.* 1834–*c*.1845), by unknown engraver, (pubd 1838) [the five who returned from Australia in March 1838: left to right, above) James Brine, Thomas Standfield, John Standfield, and James Loveless; and (centre, below) George Loveless]

O'Connor, and William Cobbett. Less than a month after the trial the men were already being referred to as 'martyrs'. Petitions and demonstrations were organized, notably a mass gathering at Copenhagen Fields, from where thousands of protesters marched peacefully across London to Whitehall. Under the pressure of this campaign, the home secretary, Lord John Russell, granted the men conditional pardons in June 1835, followed by full pardons in March 1836. News of the full pardons reached Sydney at the end of August 1836, but the men were not informed directly and found out about them only by chance, remaining in assigned labour long after they should have been freed. George Loveless obtained a free passage at the end of January 1837, and was the first of the martyrs to return to England. He had already been back in England for two months by the time his brother, James Brine, and the two Standfields left Sydney in September, finally reaching Plymouth in March 1838, two full years after they had been granted free pardons. James Hammett remained in Australia until March 1839, having been on an assault charge when the others left Sydney; he was thus the last to return to England, in August 1839.

The men were greeted with heroes' receptions on their return, attending processions, public dinners, and speaker meetings. A committee had been formed to support the men's families in their absence, and the London Dorchester Committee continued to raise funds to help establish the martyrs on farms of their own. In September 1837 George Loveless published a pamphlet, *The Victims of Whiggery*, which became an important text at Chartist meetings. Following the success of *The Victims of Whiggery*, the Dorchester Committee brought out *A narrative of the sufferings of Jas. Loveless, Jas. Brine, and Thomas and John Standfield … displaying the horrors of transportation, written by themselves*, which was published in 1838, with the profits going towards the fund.

The Dorchester Committee raised enough money to obtain leaseholds on two farms in Essex, at Tilegate Green and Greensted, and the families moved there in August 1838, though their infamy assured them an unfriendly welcome from much of the local community. None of the men seems to have had much record of radical politics before the arrests, but following their return to England they took more political stances, establishing a Chartist association in Greensted, meetings of which were held in the Lovelesses' home, and which were the subject of complaints to the magistrate. The martyrs remained in Essex for several years, during which time the family connections were strengthened, as James Brine married Thomas Standfield's daughter Elizabeth. When Hammett at last arrived back in England, he and his wife and son moved to the Greensted farm, though in 1841 they returned to settle in Tolpuddle, where Hammett took up work in the building trade.

In the mid-1840s the remaining five martyrs and their families emigrated to the province of Ontario, Canada, escaping the prejudice which they had encountered in Essex. The Brines left England in 1844, and began farming in Huron county. The Lovelesses settled near London, where George Loveless took out a mortgage on a farm of 100 acres and his brother James became the sexton of North Street Methodist Church. George Loveless later moved to another farm in Siloam and helped to build the Methodist church there. The Standfields emigrated in 1846 and also settled in London township. John Standfield built a home called Dorset Hall and had a successful career as a storekeeper and hotelier, holding local public office and establishing a choir. In their new lives in Canada the men were determined to make a fresh start, and the story of their transportation remained a secret which they kept even from their younger children. All five men survived into old age, and all except James Loveless owned land in Canada. Thomas Standfield spent his later years living with his daughter Elizabeth, and died in 1864. James Loveless had three children, was widowed and later remarried, and died in 1873; he was buried in the Methodist cemetery in London, Ontario. George Loveless died in 1874, six years after the death of his wife; they had five children. The couples Thomas and Diana Standfield and George and Betsy Loveless were buried in adjoining plots in Siloam cemetery. John Standfield died in 1898, at the age of eighty-five, surviving his wife who had died fifteen years before; the couple had seven children, and were buried at Mount Pleasant cemetery in London, Ontario. The last survivor of the group was James Brine, who died in 1902. He had eleven children, eight of whom were born in Canada. He was buried in St Mary's cemetery in Blanshard township, Perth county, Ontario.

James Hammett, the only one of the martyrs to return to Tolpuddle, was widowed twice, in 1860 and 1870, and married for a third time; he had seven children with his first wife. In 1875 he found himself briefly in the limelight once more, when the National Agricultural Labourers' Union presented him with an illuminated address and a gold watch to commemorate his service to the cause of trade unionism. His final years were less happy, as his sight deteriorated, and he chose to go into the workhouse at Dorchester so as not to be a burden on his family. He died there in 1891, and was buried in the churchyard at Tolpuddle.

The case of the Dorchester Labourers, who were increasingly referred to as the Tolpuddle Martyrs, acquired an important place in the mythology of the trade-union movement, within Britain and on an international level. There were various schemes to commemorate the episode from the early years of the twentieth century onwards. Memorials were erected in Tolpuddle itself in the form of an arch outside the Methodist church (1912), a commemorative seat (1934), and a row of six cottages for retired agricultural workers, built and maintained by the Trades Union Congress (TUC) and each bearing the name of one of the martyrs (1934). A Labor Memorial Park was dedicated to the memory of the martyrs in London, Ontario, in 1969. The men's story was dramatized on stage and on radio in the 1930s, and the TUC organized a major commemoration in 1934 for the hundredth anniversary of the trial. The labour movement in Britain has held annual rallies in Tolpuddle since 1934 to celebrate these most famous of its early pioneers, who are also commemorated in a museum in the village.   C. V. J. GRIFFITHS

Sources *The book of the martyrs of Tolpuddle, 1834–1934*, Trades Union Congress General Council (1934) • J. Marlow, *The Tolpuddle Martyrs* (1971) • J. Loveless, J. Brine, T. Standfield, and J. Standfield, *A narrative of the sufferings of Jas. Loveless, Jas. Brine, and Thomas and John Standfield, four of the Dorchester labourers; displaying the horrors of transportation, written by themselves, with a brief description of New South Wales, by George Loveless* (1838) • G. Loveless, *The victims of whiggery* (1837) • G. Loveless, *The church shown up* (1838) • M. M. Firth and A. W. Hopkinson, *The Tolpuddle Martyrs* (1934) • files on 1934 commemoration, U. Warwick Mod. RC, TUC archive, MSS 292/1.91 and 1.92 • C. V. J. Griffiths, 'Remembering Tolpuddle: rural history and commemoration in the inter-war labour movement', *History Workshop Journal*, 44 (1997), 145–69
Archives U. Warwick Mod. RC, TUC archive, material relating to the case and its subsequent commemoration
Likenesses engraving, pubd 1838, Mitchell L., NSW [*see illus.*] • engraving, repro. in Marlow, *The Tolpuddle martyrs*, facing p. 32

Tom Nefyn. *See* Williams, Thomas (1895–1958).

Tom of Ten Thousand. *See* Thynne, Thomas (1647/8–1682).

Tomas ab Ieuan ap Rhys (*c*.1510–*c*.1560), poet, was the son of Ieuan ap Rhys Brydydd, and the grandson of the late fifteenth-century master poet Rhys Brydydd and a cousin to the more famous Lewis Morgannwg (*fl.* 1520–1565). He belonged to the leading family of traditional bards in the district of Tir Iarll in upper Glamorgan; however, he lived in Tythegston, not very far from Bridgend. Little is known about his life, but his earliest work undoubtedly predates the dissolution of the monasteries, and in one of his compositions he sang the praises of the abbey of Margam. Another of his *cwndidau* (short religious songs or carols), which contain many scriptural references, is a metrical version of the parable of the sower. He states in one of his poems that he had been imprisoned in the town of Kenfig, but the circumstances surrounding his incarceration are far from clear.

In general Tomas's work, which occasionally reflects personal and contemporary social problems, reveals that, notwithstanding his family connections and some instruction in the bardic craft, he did not have a firm grasp of the traditional bardic lore, while the poem he sang on the *cywydd* metre to the rood in Llangynwyd shows that he did not adhere, as did the professional bards, to the conservative standards of the literary language. Nevertheless, he was anxious not to be classed with the lower-grade itinerant poetasters and minstrels, who had gained a reputation for the composition of satirical verses. When his wife, of whom nothing is known, sent him 'to gather seed-corn in the Vale', he was enjoined never to satirize under any circumstances.

Even so, Tomas readily adopted in his poetry the style and metres of the inferior grade of bards and minstrels, and freely used colloquial and dialectal forms, which the master poets consistently eschewed. Moreover, he employed these metres not only in his *cwndidau*, but

also—and this is rather unusual—in the panegyrics and elegies he sang to members of such leading county families as the Herberts, the Stradlings, and the Gamages. Another interesting feature of his work is the opposition it expresses to protestantism, as well as the evidence it provides for the poet's great sense of loss as a result of the destruction of the old Catholic faith and its time-honoured ceremonies. Not surprisingly, he was overjoyed at the accession of Queen Mary in 1553, whom he compared with the Blessed Virgin.

The elegy which Tomas's friend and pupil, the gentleman-poet Hopcyn Tomas Phylip (*d.* 1597) of Gelli'r-fid, Llandyfodwg, sang to him shows that he also instructed the younger generation of *cwndidwyr* who came after him. It refers to his great learning, to his profound knowledge of the scriptures, to his understanding of astrology, and to his grasp of the work of the heraldic bards, who recorded the genealogies and coats of arms of the Welsh gentry. Obviously he had received much of the instruction that was imparted to the professional poets, to whose rigorous linguistic and metrical standards, nevertheless, he did not generally adhere in his own work.

Tomas ab Ieuan ap Rhys also composed prophetic verses (*daroganau*) not only in the traditional measures employed by the professional bards, but also in the metre called *triban Morgannwg*, the earliest surviving examples of which occur in his work. Indeed, it was as a vaticinator, even more than as an author of *cwndidau*, that he became renowned in Glamorgan. It was probably the reputation he had acquired in this connection that later prompted Edward Williams (Iolo Morganwg; 1747–1826) to fabricate so many remarkable stories about him.   C. W. LEWIS

Sources L. J. Hopkin-James and Cadrawd [T. C. Evans], *Hen gwndidau, carolau, a chywyddau* (1910), ix–liv, 1–51, 282–3 • NL Wales, Llanover MS E4 • R. H. Morris, ed., 'Parochialia', *Archaeologia Cambrensis*, suppl. (1911), 126–7 [see also various in suppls. for 1909–11] • Cadrawd [T. C. Evans], *History of Llangynwyd parish* (1887), 177–9 • G. J. Williams, *Traddodiad llenyddol Morgannwg* (1948), 116–18, 121–4, 138–43, 178–9 [also references in the index] • C. W. Lewis, 'The literary tradition of Morgannwg down to the middle of the sixteenth century', *Glamorgan county history*, ed. G. Williams, 3: *The middle ages*, ed. T. B. Pugh (1971), 449–554, esp. 526–34 • G. Williams, *The Welsh church from conquest to Reformation* (1962), 334, 417–18, 423, 509 • G. Williams, 'Yr hanesydd a'r canu rhydd cynnar', *Grym tafodau tân: ysgrifau hanesyddol ar grefydd a diwylliant* (1984), 140–63 • T. Parry, *A history of Welsh literature*, trans. H. I. Bell (1955), 164–91, esp. 175–8 [incl. appx on the twentieth century] • T. Williams, ed., *Iolo manuscripts* (1848), 201–3, 615–17 • T. H. Parry-Williams, *Canu rhydd cynnar* (1932) • J. Loth, *La métrique galloise*, 3 vols. (1900–02), 1.64–5, 68–71, 89–90, 95–7, 99–100 • J. Morris-Jones, *Cerdd dafod, sef, Celfyddyd barddoniaeth Gymraeg* (1925), 312, 327–8, 334, 337–8, 339–40 • *Geiriadur prifysgol Cymru: a dictionary of the Welsh language*, 1 (1950–67), 643, *s.v.* 'cwndid'

Tomás de Santa María. *See* Gage, Thomas (1603?–1656).

Tombes, John (1602–1676), clergyman and ejected minister, was born at Bewdley, Worcestershire, and was baptized in the parish of Ribbesford (which included Bewdley) on 10 October 1602, the son of Edward Tombes, a dyer. His mother's identity is unknown, but he had at least one elder sister. He probably attended Bewdley grammar school. On 23 January 1618 he matriculated at Magdalen Hall, Oxford, where he was a batteler, and was admitted BA on 12 June 1621, MA on 16 April 1624, and BD in Trinity term 1631. An accomplished linguist, he was the favourite pupil of the Hebraist William Pemble, and reputedly had the Greek Testament 'almost memoriter' (*Brief Lives*, 2.258). In 1623 he succeeded Pemble as catechism lecturer at Magdalen Hall, and while preparing a lecture in 1627 began to doubt the scriptural basis for infant baptism. During this period he was ordained and appointed a lecturer at St Martin Carfax, where his preaching was much admired, particularly by puritans. He 'was soon taken notice of' both for his intellectual ability and for his potential to 'doe a great deale of mischiefe to the Church of England' (*Brief Lives*, 2.258).

In 1630 Tombes became a preacher at Worcester, and on 17 November 1630 was instituted vicar of Leominster, Herefordshire. At about this time he married Elizabeth Scudder (1613–1633), daughter of the puritan divine Henry Scudder. Elizabeth died on 15 December 1633, leaving an only daughter, Elizabeth (*d.* 1658). Tombes had remarried by 1636, when his only son, John, was born on 26 November.

Tombes was highly regarded in Leominster until he became actively involved with the county's parliamentarian and presbyterian minority. His 'disusing the ceremonies' in December 1640 'nettled the ignorant and superstitious' (*Portland MSS*, 3.76), as did his participation in a puritan survey of Herefordshire clergy in early 1641. Early in 1642 he organized resubscription to the protestation oath and promoted a pro-parliamentary petition. By early August, the 'barbarous rage and impetuous violence of people' forced Tombes, his wife, and children to flee Herefordshire (J. Tombes, *Fermentum Pharisaeorum*, 1643, sig. A2v).

'After much wandring up and down' (Tombes, *Apology*, 6), Tombes was appointed lecturer at All Saints, Bristol, on 4 January 1643. During the next few months he published the sermons *Iehovah iireh* and *Fermentum Pharisaeorum* in support of his party's cause. He also had a momentous dispute with an antipaedobaptist which further undermined his belief in infant baptism, and left him resolved to go to London in order to 'consider that matter more full' (ibid., 6). However, in mid-July 1643 royalist advances forced him and his family to escape from Bristol by sea to Milford Haven.

Tombes eventually arrived in London on 22 September 1643, and by January 1644 was convinced of the case against infant baptism. By July he had presented a Latin 'Exercitation' on the scriptural evidence to the Westminster assembly, hoping in vain to have his arguments considered 'in a faire Scholastike way' (Tombes, *Apology*, 15). He also drew up a detailed manuscript 'Examen' of a sermon by Stephen Marshall published in August 1644 in defence of infant baptism, which was delivered to Marshall on 9 December and followed by a 'friendly conference' between the two men on 30 December 1644

(ibid., 11). During 1644 Tombes had been rector of St Gabriel Fenchurch but, his parishioners having become 'disaffected' (ibid., 10), he lost his position. On the understanding that he would not preach his antipaedobaptist opinions, he was appointed at the end of January 1645, apparently through Marshall's influence, to be master of the Temple where, as preacher to its two inns of court, he would not need to baptize infants. In May 1645 Tombes agreed to a copy of his 'Examen' being sent to New England by the Baptist Henry Jessey. He still, however, received no response from the assembly to his arguments, and on 15 December 1645 he published as *Two Treatises* an English translation of his 'Exercitation', and the 'Examen'. Numerous attacks on Tombes swiftly appeared in print, including one by Marshall dedicated to the assembly; in August 1646 Tombes defended himself in *An Apology or Plea for the Two Treatises*, but, in spite of presenting his writings to Cromwell, he was removed from the Temple.

Tombes returned during 1646 to his native Bewdley as curate of the town's chapel of ease. On 12 September 1646 he was also appointed rector of Ross, Herefordshire. He now devoted himself to the work which 'the Lord hath alotted me', the recovery of believers' baptism (J. Tombes, *Antipaedobaptism*, 3 vols., 1652–7, vol. 1, sig. A2r). At Bewdley, while retaining his parish role, he founded a small Baptist congregation, training some of its members for the Baptist ministry. On 1 January 1650 his celebrated public debate on baptism with Richard Baxter took place in Bewdley chapel, lasting from nine in the morning until five at night. Tombes was acknowledged to be the better disputant, but the numerous followers of each side at last 'fell by the eares, hurt was donne' (*Brief Lives*, 2.259). Tombes and Baxter were to maintain an uneasy relationship for the next twenty years, 'not enemies though antagonists' (Keeble and Nuttall, 1.416).

Perhaps as a result of this debate, Tombes left Bewdley during 1650, and by October 1651 had returned to his vicarage at Leominster, where he was to remain until 1662. He was also appointed master of St Catherine's Hospital, Ledbury, on 12 April 1649, a commissioner for approbation of public preachers in 1654, and an assistant to the Herefordshire commission on 29 September 1657. During this period Tombes participated in several other public debates on baptism, including a formal disputation with Henry Savage at the annual Oxford Act in 1652; he also disputed against Quakers, encountering George Fox in 1657. He published accounts of some of these debates, but his major work of the 1650s was the three-part *Antipaedobaptism* (1652, 1654, 1657), an exhaustive analysis of the arguments of his numerous opponents. He continued to foster Baptist congregations, but was gradually returning to his earlier belief that separation was not justifiable. It was to promote protestant unity that in 1659 he invited Baxter to contribute prefaces to *Romanism Discussed* (1660) and the anti-Quaker *True Old Light Exalted* (1660).

In 1660 Tombes 'willingly submitted' (Wood, *Ath. Oxon.*, 3.1063) to the Restoration, and published *A Serious Consideration* in defence of taking the oath of supremacy. For this and other works on the same subject he received a yearly pension of £50 through the influence of Clarendon, whom he had known at Magdalen Hall. None the less, his opposition to infant baptism made his ejection under the Act of Uniformity inevitable; in September 1662 Herbert Croft, bishop of Hereford, reported that 'the proud Anabaptist Toms, than whom I never knew a prouder' had refused subscription (Bodl. Oxf., MS Tanner 48, fol. 41).

On 4 September 1661 Tombes had married his third wife, the widow Elizabeth Combs, by licence at St Edmund's, Salisbury, and after his ejection he settled in her parish. With his characteristic blend of conservatism and radicalism, he regularly attended the parish church and received communion, while adhering to his tenet on infant baptism 'by going out of the Church whilst that office was performing and returning in again when it was ended' (*Calamy rev.*, 488). He was on good terms both with Seth Ward, bishop of Salisbury, and with local nonconformists. After the declaration of indulgence in 1672 his house was licensed as a presbyterian meeting-place, and he sometimes preached, 'though seldome & to few' (Keeble and Nuttall, 2.138).

Although Tombes continued 'every where disputing for his old opinion concerning paedobaptisme' (Keeble and Nuttall, 2.138), he accommodated his publications to the new regime, attacking Fifth Monarchists in *Saints No Smiters* (1664), separatists in *Theodulia* (1667), both dedicated to Clarendon, and Socinians in *Emmanuel, or, God-Man* (1669). His last work was *Animadversiones in librum Georgii Bulli* (1676), a Calvinist contribution to the controversy over Bull's *Harmonia apostolica* (1670).

Tombes was 'but a little man, neat limbed, a little quick searching eie, sad, gray'. Although a formidable disputant, he was charitable to his opponents and was generally acknowledged to be 'as great a divine as most we had' (*Brief Lives*, 2.260, 259). But as Tombes himself recognized, those 'usefull to uphold a Party, are the men esteemed' (Tombes, 3). He was alienated from presbyterians by his antipaedobaptism, and from most Baptists, even while being widely perceived as 'the great Ringleader of that Sect', by his acceptance of an established church (BL, Add. MS 63054, fol. 194r. 2). His reputation both in his own time and subsequently has suffered as a result.

John Tombes made his will on 6 May 1676 and died on 22 May at Salisbury, survived by his wife, Elizabeth. He was buried on 25 May in St Edmund's churchyard. He left an extensive library of controversial writings and 'Godly english Treatises' (PRO, PROB 11/351, fol. 331v); his epitaph, composed by himself, describes him simply as 'a constant preacher of God's word' (*Brief Lives*, 2.260).

JULIA J. SMITH

Sources Wood, *Ath. Oxon.*, new edn · *Brief lives, chiefly of contemporaries, set down by John Aubrey, between the years 1669 and 1696*, ed. A. Clark, 2 vols. (1898) · J. Tombes, *An apology or plea for the two treatises* (1646) · *Calendar of the correspondence of Richard Baxter*, ed. N. H. Keeble and G. F. Nuttall, 2 vols. (1991) · *Calamy rev.* · parish register, St Edmund, Wilts. & Swindon RO · parish register, Ribbesford, Worcestershire, Worcs. RO · will, PRO, PROB 11/351, sig. 96 · J. Eales, *Puritans and roundheads: the Harleys of Brampton Bryan and the outbreak of the English civil war* (1990) · *History from marble, compiled in the reign of Charles II by Thomas Dingley*, ed. J. G. Nichols, 2 vols., CS, 94, 97 (1867–8) · P. J. Anderson, 'Letters of Henry Jessey and John Tombes to the churches of New England, 1645', *Baptist Quarterly*, 28 (1979–80), 30–40 · Foster, *Alum. Oxon.* · J. R. Burton, *A history of Bewdley* (1883) · *The manuscripts of his grace the duke of Portland*, 10 vols., HMC, 29 (1891–1931), vol. 3 · will, PRO, PROB 11/233, sig. 195 [Henry Scudder]

Archives American Antiquarian Society, Worcester, Massachusetts, Baptist papers, letter to J. Cotton and J. Wilson · BL, Portland MSS, letters to Sir R. Harley and S. Gower, Loan 29/121; 29/172; 29/173 · DWL, corresp. with Richard Baxter

Tombs, Sir Henry (1824–1874), army officer, son of Major-General John Tombs (1777–1848), Bengal cavalry, and his wife, Mary (1791/2–1876) *née* Remington, came of a family settled since the fifteenth century at Long Marston, Gloucestershire, and was born at sea on 10 November 1824. He entered the East India Company's military college, Addiscombe, in 1839, and was commissioned second lieutenant, Bengal artillery, on 11 June 1841. He arrived at Calcutta on 18 November 1841 and was posted to the foot artillery at Dum-Dum. In August 1842 he went with a detachment to the upper provinces. On 1 March 1843 he was posted to the 3rd company, 5th battalion of artillery, at Saugor; on 23 November he went to the 6th company, 6th battalion, at Jhansi, and took part in the Gwalior campaign. He arrived with the force called the 'left wing' under Major-General Sir John Grey at Badli-ki-sarai on 28 December 1843, and next morning marched to Panniar, where the Marathas were defeated; he was mentioned in dispatches.

On 15 January 1844 Tombs was promoted first lieutenant, and on 1 March he was appointed to the horse artillery at Ludhiana. He served in the First Anglo-Sikh War (1845–6) in the 1st troop, 1st horse artillery brigade. This troop had suffered so severely from fever, prevalent at Ludhiana, that it was at first contemplated that the whole troop be left behind, but on the evening of 13 December 1845 Tombs brought the good news to the barracks that four guns were to march at daybreak next day, leaving the other two and the sick troopers behind. They first marched to Bassian (28 miles), then, on 16 December, to Wadni, where the governor shut the gates and refused supplies until the British forces were got into position, when he submitted. After a short march on 17 December, and a long and tedious one of 21 miles the following day, Mudki was reached, and, while the camp was being formed, the alarm was given and the battle began. Tombs's troop was hotly engaged, and its captain, Dashwood, died of his wounds. At the battle of Ferozeshahr on 21 December, Tombs was with his troop at headquarters, and engaged in the attack on the southern face of the Sikh entrenchment.

In the operations of January 1846, including the action of Badiwal (21 January), and culminating in the battle of Aliwal on 28 January, Tombs was acting aide-de-camp to Sir Harry George Wakelyn Smith, and was mentioned in dispatches. He served in the second Sikh or Punjab campaign as deputy assistant quartermaster-general of the artillery division, and was at the action of Ramnagar on 22 November 1848, at the battle of Chilianwala on 13 January 1849, and at the crowning victory of Gujrat on 21 February.

Sir Henry Tombs (1824–1874), by unknown photographer

He was mentioned in dispatches and was recommended for a brevet majority as soon as he attained the rank of captain.

Tombs was employed on special duty in 1849 and 1850. On 12 March 1850 he was appointed a member of the special committee of artillery officers at Ambala. On 30 October he was appointed adjutant and quartermaster of the 2nd brigade, horse artillery, and on 13 November adjutant of the Ambala division of artillery. On 30 November 1853 he was transferred to the foot artillery. He was promoted captain in the Bengal artillery on 25 July 1854, and brevet major for his services in the field on 1 August. On 27 November 1855 he returned to the horse artillery.

On the outbreak of the Indian mutiny in 1857 Tombs was at Meerut commanding the 2nd troop, 1st horse artillery brigade, and on 27 May moved with the column of Brigadier-General Archdale Wilson to co-operate with a force which the commander-in-chief was bringing down from Ambala. On approaching Ghazi-ud-din-Nagar, on the left of the River Hindan, on the afternoon of 30 May, the heat being very great, the column was attacked by the rebels. The iron bridge spanning the Hindan was held, and Tombs dashed across it with his guns and successfully turned the right flank of the enemy, who were repulsed. Tombs's horse was shot under him during this action, and again in that of the following day, when the village of Ghazi was cleared. He marched with Wilson on 5 June to Baghpat, crossed the Jumna, and joined the Ambala force under Sir Henry Barnard at Panipat on 7 June.

The combined forces marched from Alipur on 8 June, and Tombs, with his troop, was detached to the right with a force under Brigadier-General Hope Grant to cross the Jumna Canal, and so get in rear of the enemy at Badli-ki-sarai. The rebels fought desperately, but the British bayonet carried the day, and the cavalry and horse artillery converted the enemy's retreat into a rout. Tombs had two horses shot under him.

Tombs served all through the siege of Delhi. On 17 June he commanded a column which captured the *idgah* battery and took a 9-pounder gun. This battery was on the south-west of Paharipur, opposite the curtain between the Lahore gate and Garstin bastion; it was enclosed in a fort, and threatened to enfilade the British position. Tombs had two horses shot under him, and was slightly wounded. Sir Henry Barnard, the same evening at the staff mess, thanked Tombs for his gallantry, and proposed his health. Lord Roberts later wrote:

> The hero of the day was Harry Tombs … an unusually handsome man and a thorough soldier … As a cool, bold leader of men Tombs was unsurpassed … He was somewhat of a martinet, and was more feared than liked by his men until they realised what a grand leader he was.   (Roberts, 96)

Tombs also commanded a column in the action of 19 June under Hope Grant.

On 9 July 1857 Tombs went to the aid of Lieutenant James Hills (later Sir James Hills-Johnes) of Tombs's troop, who was attacked by some rebel cavalry while he was posted with two guns on picquet duty at 'the mound' to the right of the camp. Tombs ran through with his sword a sowar who was on the point of killing Hills: both Tombs and Hills received the VC.

Tombs commanded the artillery of the force under Brigadier-General John Nicholson at the battle of Najafgarh on 25 August 1857, when the enemy endeavoured to intercept the siege-train coming from Ferozepore, and were defeated. He commanded no. 4 battery, of ten heavy mortars, during the Delhi siege operations in September, and he commanded the horse artillery at the assault on 14 September, when he was wounded. He was promoted brevet lieutenant-colonel on 19 January, and was made a CB, military division, on 22 January 1858 for services at the siege of Delhi.

In March 1858 Tombs, in command of the 2nd troop of the 1st brigade of Bengal horse artillery, joined the artillery division, under Sir Archdale Wilson, of Sir Colin Campbell's army assembled at the Alambagh for the attack on Lucknow. He took part in the siege and capture of the city, and was mentioned in general orders. Tombs commanded his troop in the operations for the subjugation of Rohilkhand with the force under Brigadier-General Walpole. He left Lucknow on 7 April for Malaon, and, after the unsuccessful attack on Ruilja, took part on the 22nd in the action at Aliganj, when the enemy were driven across the river and four guns were captured. On 27 April, Tombs, with this force, joined that of the commander-in-chief and marched on Shahjahanpur, which was found evacuated; on 3 May he was united with the troops commanded by Major-General R. Penny at Miranpur Katra, on 4 May arrived at Faridpur, a day's march from Bareilly, and on 5 May took part in the battle of Bareilly.

On 15 May, Tombs and his troop marched with the commander-in-chief's force to the relief of Shahjahanpur, and took part in the action of 18 May. On 24 May he commanded the artillery in a force under Brigadier-General Jones against Muhamdi, out of which the rebels were driven, and the force returned to Shahjahanpur on 29 May. He took part also in an expedition against Shahabad on the night of 31 May, returning to Shahjahanpur on 4 June, when, the rebels having been driven out of Rohilkhand, the field force to which Tombs was attached was broken up. Tombs was promoted on 20 July 1858 brevet colonel, and was praised by Lord Panmure, the secretary of state for war, in the House of Lords in proposing a vote of thanks to the army.

Tombs was promoted lieutenant-colonel, Royal Artillery, on 29 April 1861, and was appointed to the 2nd brigade. From 16 May 1863 he was appointed a brigadier-general to command the artillery brigade at Gwalior. In 1865 he received a good-service pension. In 1864 he commanded the force which recaptured Dewangiri in Bhutan, for which campaign he was on 14 March 1868 made a KCB. After the Bhutan expedition he returned to his duties as brigadier-general commanding the artillery at Gwalior. He was promoted major-general on 11 March 1867. Tombs married, on 1 March 1869, Georgina Janet, youngest daughter of Admiral Sir James *Stirling; after his death, she married on 19 December 1877 Captain Herbert Stewart. On 30 August 1871 Tombs was appointed to command the Allahabad division of the army, and was transferred to the Oudh division on 24 October 1871. He became a regimental colonel of artillery on 1 August 1872. He was obliged to resign his command on account of ill health, and returned to England on sick leave. He died at Newport, Isle of Wight, on 2 August 1874.

At news of Tombs's death Lord Napier of Magdala issued a general order expressing regret at the loss of so distinguished an officer.   R. H. VETCH, rev. ROGER T. STEARN

Sources BL OIOC · War Office records, PRO · LondG · H. M. Vibart, Addiscombe: its heroes and men of note (1894) · F. W. Stubbs, ed., History of the organization, equipment, and war services of the regiment of Bengal artillery, 1–2 (1877) · V. C. P. Hodson, List of officers of the Bengal army, 1758–1834, 4 (1947) · G. B. Malleson, History of the Indian mutiny, 1857–1858: commencing from the close of the second volume of Sir John Kaye's History of the Sepoy War, 3 vols. (1878–80) · E. J. Thackwell, Narrative of the Second Seikh War, in 1848–49 (1851) · The Times (6 Aug 1874) · The Times (7 Aug 1874) · The Times (12 Aug 1874) · J. E. W. Rotton, The chaplain's narrative of the siege of Delhi (1858) · Lord Roberts [F. S. Roberts], Forty-one years in India, 31st edn (1900) · C. Hibbert, The great mutiny, India, 1857 (1978) · R. B. Smith, Life of Lord Lawrence, 2 vols. (1883) · T. A. Heathcote, The military in British India: the development of British land forces in south Asia, 1600–1947 (1995) · P. Moon, The British conquest and dominion of India (1989) · Boase, Mod. Eng. biog. · Dod's Peerage (1878)

Likenesses Swain, wood-engraving (after photograph by Grillet and Co.), repro. in Roberts, Forty-one years in India, facing p. 84 · engraving, repro. in ILN, 21 (1857), 460 · engraving, repro. in The Graphic, 10 (1874), 171 · photograph, NPG [see illus.] · two woodcuts, NPG

Wealth at death under £4000 in England: probate, 22 Aug 1874, CGPLA Eng. & Wales

Tomes, Sir Charles Sissmore (1846–1928). *See under* Tomes, Sir John (1815–1895).

Tomes, Sir John (1815–1895), dental surgeon, eldest son of John Tomes (1791–1864), farmer, and his wife, Sarah (1792–1870), daughter of William Baylies of Welford in Gloucestershire, was born at The Sands, Weston-on-Avon, in Gloucestershire, on 21 March 1815. After attending schools in Stratford upon Avon and Evesham, Tomes was articled in 1831 to Thomas Furley Smith, a medical practitioner in Evesham. In 1836 he began medical studies in London at King's College and the Middlesex Hospital, then temporarily united; although unqualified, he was house surgeon to the Middlesex Hospital between 1839 and 1840. He did not take his final examinations but, advised by Sir Thomas Watson (1792–1882) and James Moncrieff Arnott, Tomes decided to become a dental surgeon, and in 1840 he commenced practice at 41 Mortimer Street (later Cavendish Place) in central London. From 1840 to 1843 he was dental surgeon at King's College Hospital and from 1843 to 1874 he practised at the Middlesex Hospital. On 15 February 1844 Tomes married Jane Sibley (1823–1904), daughter of Robert Sibley, architect; of their two sons only the younger survived.

In 1838, while Tomes was still a student, his first paper was given to the Royal Society. Presented by Thomas Bell, this was on the microscopical structure of teeth and was the earliest detailed histological investigation on the subject to be published by an English author. For twenty years Tomes continued to study the histology of bone and dental tissues; several anatomical structures are named after him. He published widely in medical, dental, and scientific journals, and on 6 June 1850 he became a fellow of the Royal Society, where his most important papers were presented. Tomes also developed the more modern type of forceps adapted to the necks of individual teeth, and in 1845 patented the 'dentifactor' for carving ivory to fit irregular surfaces and to facilitate the making of dentures, for which he received the Isis gold medal of the Society of Arts. He introduced a number of technical innovations, devised new instruments, and made other improvements in operative dental surgery. In 1845 he delivered a course of lectures at the Middlesex Hospital which marked a new era in dentistry. These were published in 1848, and his System of Dental Surgery in 1859. This remained a standard work for fifty years. It reached a fifth edition in 1906 and was also published in France and America. When ether became available in 1847 he administered it for dental extractions and acted as anaesthetist for surgical operations at the Middlesex Hospital.

Entry to the dental profession was, in the mid-nineteenth century, haphazard, with no specific qualification available. After two unsuccessful attempts in 1843 and 1855, Tomes was one of several practitioners who, with the support of Arnott, persuaded the Royal College of Surgeons in 1858 to institute a licence in dental surgery (LDS). Having first belatedly qualified as a member of the Royal College of Surgeons, Tomes was appointed one of the first examiners. The establishment of a qualification ensuring fitness to practise gave encouragement to those who wished for statutory organization of dental practice, and eventually, after years of discussion, the Dental Reform Committee was set up in 1875. With others, notably James Smith Turner, Tomes, as chairman of the committee, pressed the government to enforce stricter regulation of dental practice, and the Dentists' Act of 1878 established a dentists' register under the control of the General Medical Council. The success of the Dental Reform Committee, which had proved the value of co-operation between dentists, led to the formation of the British Dental Association in 1880. Tomes was its first president. He was also a founder member of the Odontological Society and president in 1862 and 1875.

In 1876 Tomes retired to Upwood Gorse, Caterham, Surrey. He was elected an honorary fellow of the Royal College of Surgeons in 1883, and was knighted in 1886. On his golden wedding anniversary he was presented by his fellow dentists with an inkstand and a sum of money which endowed a prize bearing his name to be awarded triennially by the Royal College of Surgeons for researches in the field of dental science. Tomes died on 29 July 1895 at his home, Upwood Gorse, and was buried at St Mary's, Upper Caterham, on 1 August.

Tomes began to practise dentistry when it was a trade; he left it a well-equipped profession. He showed that a dentist was capable of the highest kind of scientific work—that of original observation. In addition he had considerable technical skills and a practical mind.

Tomes's younger son, **Sir Charles Sissmore Tomes** (1846–1928), dental surgeon, was born in London on 6 June 1846. Educated at Radley College and Christ Church, Oxford, he gained the only first-class honours in natural sciences in 1866. He then studied at King's College and the Middlesex Hospital, London, and qualified LDS and MRCS in 1869. He then joined his father's practice. On 12 November 1873 he married Elizabeth (Lizzie) Eno Cook (d. 1935) of New York, and a daughter was born in 1876. Tomes lectured at the Dental Hospital, Leicester Square, and for fourteen years was an examiner for the LDS. He published many papers on histology and comparative dental anatomy, and his collection of specimens enriched the Odontological Society museum, where he was curator from 1874 to 1880. He also compiled its first catalogue. He was president of the Odontological Society in 1887 and of the British Dental Association in 1894. His *Manual of Dental Anatomy, Human and Comparative* (1876) achieved eight editions. He edited and enlarged the second and subsequent editions of John Tomes's *System of Dental Surgery*. In 1878 Charles Tomes became a fellow of the Royal Society. From 1899 to 1920 he was crown nominee to the General Medical Council, and he was also its treasurer and chairman of its dental committee. In 1898 he was elected fellow of the Royal College of Surgeons and in 1909 he received an honorary LLD from the University of Birmingham; in 1919 he received a knighthood. Under the name of Charles Sissmore he painted in oils and watercolours, at least once exhibiting at the Royal Academy. He died on 24 October

1928 at his home, Mannington Hall, Aylsham, Norfolk, bequeathing £2000 to the Royal College of Surgeons, which endowed two annual eponymous lectures.

E. MURIEL COHEN

Sources Z. Cope, *Sir John Tomes: a pioneer of British dentistry* (1961) • *Journal of the British Dental Association*, 16 (1895), 462–92 • *British Journal of Dental Science*, 38 (1895), 747–9 • I. M. Tomes, 'Pedigree of the Tomes family', 1987, Warks. CRO • A. Hill, *The history of the reform movement in the dental profession in Great Britain during the last twenty years* (1887) • R. A. Cohen, 'The development of dental histology in Britain', *British Dental Journal*, 121 (1966), 59–71 • *The advance of the dental profession: a centenary history, 1880–1980*, British Dental Association (privately printed, London, 1979) • Z. Cope, *The Royal College of Surgeons of England: a history* (1959) • *BMJ* (10 Aug 1895), 396–7 • *Nature*, 52 (1895), 396 • C. Schelling, *Personal recollections of Sir Charles Tomes and others* (1936) • *British Dental Journal*, 49 (1928), 1230–32, 1364–6 • *Dental Record*, 48 (1928), 689–91 • *British Dental Journal*, 50 (1929), 165 [details of will of Charles Sissmore Tomes]
Archives Warks. CRO, corresp. and papers
Likenesses C. H. H. Macartney, oils, 1880, British Dental Association, London • C. H. H. Macartney, oils, in or before 1884, Royal Society of Medicine, London • G. Bayes, bronze bust, British Dental Association, London • O. E. Galsworthy, double portrait, oils (with Charles Sissmore Tomes), RCS Eng. • G. Meinster, oils, RSCE
Wealth at death £52,157 6s. 1d.: probate, 18 Oct 1895, CGPLA Eng. & Wales • £208,899 11s. 0d.—Charles Sissmore Tomes: probate, 15 Dec 1928, CGPLA Eng. & Wales

Tomkins, Charles (1757–1823). See under Tomkins, Peltro William (1759–1840).

Tomkins, Giles (b. after 1587, d. 1668). See under Tomkins, Thomas (1572–1656).

Tomkins, John (1586–1638). See under Tomkins, Thomas (1572–1656).

Tomkins, John (c.1663–1706), Quaker preacher and biographer, was born to Quaker parents. His father died when he was very young but his mother, who married again, ensured that he received a religious education, and he helped her in her business. He assisted the poor and the sick, and he became a good preacher.

Tomkins's collection of Quaker biographies, *Piety promoted, in a collection of dying sayings of many of the people called Quakers. With a brief account of some of their labours in the gospel and sufferings for the same*, was the first and a very influential example of an important Quaker form that continued into the twentieth century in the *Annual Monitor*. Tomkins wrote the first three parts of *Piety Promoted* (1701, 1702, and 1706) and the series continued to be expanded throughout the eighteenth century. It was reprinted in various forms until 1856 and was translated into Latin and French. Later contributors included Joseph Gurney Bevan and John Kendal. Tomkins's own brief biography appears in part 5 (1721). His other works include pieces on prayer and the Bible.

Tomkins, who was married and had children, died at Maryland Point, Stratford by Bow, Middlesex, on 12 July 1706.   CHARLOTTE FELL-SMITH, rev. EMMA MAJOR

Sources J. Tomkins and J. Field, *Piety promoted … in five parts* (1721), 423–6 • W. C. Braithwaite, *The second period of Quakerism*, ed. H. J. Cadbury, 2nd edn (1961), 174, 420 • J. Whiting, ed., *A catalogue of Friends' books: written by many of the people called Quakers* (1708) •

ESTC · J. Smith, *Bibliotheca anti-Quakeriana, or, A catalogue of books adverse to the Society of Friends* (1873), 747

Tomkins, Martin (d. **1755**), Presbyterian minister and religious writer, was born in the late seventeenth century, possibly in Abingdon, Berkshire, but little is known about his early life. He appears to have been closely related to Hardinge Tomkins, an attorney of note and clerk to the Company of Fishmongers, who may even have been his brother. In 1699 he travelled with Nathaniel Lardner to the Netherlands to study at the University of Utrecht, and met Daniel Neal there, but his name does not appear on the university's register of students. On 8 September 1702 he was admitted to the University of Leiden. In the following year he returned to England, accompanied by Lardner and Neal, and in 1707 he was appointed minister to the Presbyterian congregation in Church Street, Stoke Newington. At first his ministry was successful but it later became apparent that he differed from his congregation on important doctrinal subjects. Suspected of entertaining Arian views he was dismissed in July 1718, after which he published a defence of his opinions and of his right to hold views that differed from Trinitarian orthodoxy, in a pamphlet entitled *The Case of Martin Tomkins* (1719).

Tomkins did not again settle as a pastor of a congregation but he did preach occasionally. When, for instance, William Whiston met him 'about 1720' he was living at Burtonwood, Essex, and lodging with Mr Barber, the dissenting minister there, who 'invited him sometimes to preach for him' (Whiston, 295). Later he lived in Hackney, where he attended the ministry of John Barker, an uncompromising Trinitarian. Although in general Tomkins approved Barker's public ministrations he was dissatisfied with the Trinitarian doxologies that Barker preached at the close of his prayers. During this later period of his life Tomkins was engaged primarily in writing theological works against trinitarianism. The first of these, published anonymously in 1723 as an answer to Isaac Watts's *The Christian Doctrine of the Trinity*, was entitled *A sober appeal to a Turk or an Indian concerning the plain sense of scripture relating to the Trinity*. A second edition appeared in 1748 with additional tracts in answer to Watts's and Daniel Waterland's criticisms of his first edition. In 1732 he published *Jesus Christ the Mediator between God and Man*, a work in which he again argued against Christ's divinity. His most significant work was inspired by his distaste for John Barker's use of Trinitarian doxologies and entitled *A calm enquiry whether we have any warrant from scripture for addressing ourselves in a way of prayer or praise directly to the Holy Spirit* (1738). This was much admired by anti-Trinitarians and, according to Joshua Toulmin, 'contributed very much to the disuse of the Trinitarian doxology amongst the dissenters' (Toulmin, xvii). This was Tomkins's last major publication. He died, probably in Hackney, in 1755.

E. I. CARLYLE, *rev.* M. J. MERCER

Sources J. Toulmin, 'Life of Daniel Neal', in D. Neal, *The history of the puritans or protestant nonconformists*, ed. J. Toulmin, new edn, 1 (1822), xvii–xviii · *GM*, 1st ser., 77 (1807), 823, 999, 1014 · W. Wilson, *The history and antiquities of the dissenting churches and meeting houses in London, Westminster and Southwark*, 4 vols. (1808–14), vol. 2, pp. 44–

5 · T. S. James, *The history of the litigation and legislation respecting Presbyterian chapels and charities in England and Ireland between 1816 and 1849* (1867), 43, 97, 156–7, 690, 718 · W. Whiston, *Memoirs of the life and writings of Mr William Whiston: containing memoirs of several of his friends also* (1749), 294–5 · W. Robinson, *The history and antiquities of the parish of Stoke Newington* (1820), 216–17 · Allibone, *Dict.*, 3.2429 · *Theological Repository*, 3 (1771), 257 · E. Peacock, *Index to English speaking students … at Leyden* (1883)

Tomkins, Nathaniel (**1599–1681**). *See under* Tomkins, Thomas (1572–1656).

Tomkins, Oliver Stratford (1908–1992), bishop of Bristol and ecumenist, was born on 9 June 1908 in Hangchow (Hangzhou), China, the son of the Revd Leopold Charles Fellows Tomkins (1874–1943), Congregational minister, and his wife, Mary Katie Stratford (1867–1945). His father was a missionary with the Congregationalist London Missionary Society, but in 1920, after training at Westcott House, Cambridge, he was ordained as an Anglican priest. Oliver Tomkins's Congregational and Anglican upbringing, together with his father's ecumenical sympathies, were important early influences. He was educated at Trent College, Nottingham, where he was introduced to the Student Christian Movement (SCM). He went on to Christ's College, Cambridge, where he read history and theology (1928–32) and became president of the Cambridge SCM. There he made friends with others who were also to become leaders of the twentieth-century ecumenical movement, including Lesslie Newbigin and Kathleen Bliss.

From 1933 to 1940 Tomkins was the assistant general secretary of the SCM and from 1937 to 1940 he was editor of its magazine, the *Student Movement*. He trained for the priesthood at Westcott House, Cambridge, and was ordained deacon in 1935 and priest in 1936. During this period he visited universities and was concerned to make the Church of England take students seriously. He worked closely with J. H. Oldham, a major figure in the 'life and work' stream of the ecumenical movement, and acted as secretary to Oldham's group of British thinkers known as the Moot, through which he met major international and national figures, including T. S. Eliot. Tomkins recognized early on the necessity for lay leadership in the life of the churches and the ecumenical movement. During these years he met, and on 27 September 1939 married, Ursula Mary Dunn (b. 1913), who was working as an SCM secretary. She was the daughter of the Revd William Alexander Dunn, vicar of Kingswood, Surrey. They had three daughters, Monica (b. 1941), Ruth (b. 1946), and Deborah (b. 1948), and one son, Stephen (b. 1943).

With the outbreak of the Second World War the work of the SCM diminished, and the bishop of Sheffield invited Tomkins to become vicar of Holy Trinity, Millhouses, where he served from 1940 to 1945, acting also as an examining chaplain to the bishop. In these years he established a close working relationship with the local Methodist church and set up joint study groups and a shared magazine. This was a time for Tomkins to test out at the parish level his vision of ecumenism.

In October 1944, while attending the funeral of Archbishop William Temple, Tomkins met Willem A. Visser 't Hooft, who was to become the inspirational first general secretary of the World Council of Churches (WCC). Visser 't Hooft invited him to join the staff of the 'World Council of Churches in process of formation'. Tomkins joined the Geneva staff in 1945, and in 1948 he became the secretary of the faith and order commission and an associate general secretary of the WCC. From the inauguration of the WCC at the first assembly in Amsterdam, in 1948, to the third world conference on faith and order in Lund, in 1952, Tomkins was constantly travelling from country to country, meeting church leaders and laying a firm foundation and clear direction for the faith and order movement. He drafted what came to be known as the Lund principle, that the churches should ask themselves 'whether they should not act together in all matters except those in which deep differences of conviction compel them to act separately' (N. Lossky, ed., *Dictionary of the Ecumenical Movement*, 1991, 633). In 1949 he published *The Wholeness of the Church*, and in 1959 *Intercommunion*. These were important contributions to the developing understanding of the visible unity of the church and the steps that might be taken on the way to that unity.

In 1953 Tomkins returned to England to serve as warden of Lincoln Theological College and canon and prebendary of Lincoln Cathedral. After a life based on Geneva, with its concern for rebuilding a post-war Europe and its worldwide mission, he found life at Lincoln insular and the habits of the college somewhat inward-looking. Tomkins and his wife were nevertheless able to move the college on, and they welcomed wives of ordinands into the life of the college. Throughout his time at Lincoln, Tomkins served as chairman of the working committee of the WCC's faith and order commission. It was in this capacity that he chaired the fourth world conference on faith and order in Montreal, a conference noted for its breakthrough on the understanding of the relation between scripture, tradition, and traditions. This was to be crucial for the future direction of the ecumenical movement, providing the basic method for formulating ecumenical convergence statements. He also chaired with consummate patience the Church of England's commission on intercommunion.

Tomkins was consecrated bishop on 6 January 1959 and went to the see of Bristol, where he remained until his retirement in 1975. During this time he encouraged the ecumenical movement to take root in the diocese, and Bristol became one of the leading dioceses for advancing relations between the churches at the local level. Tomkins established good working relationships with both the free churches and the Roman Catholic church; he encouraged the Bristol Council of Churches; he helped to establish the south-west ecumenical congress; and he pioneered the establishment of areas of ecumenical experiment, where two or more churches shared a degree of worship, life, and mission. His book *Guarded by Faith* (1970) summed up his own beliefs and showed the importance Tomkins

attached to the teaching ministry of a bishop. In 1964 he chaired the Nottingham faith and order conference, which expressed the hope for the reunion of the churches in England by Easter 1980. During this time he maintained close links with the WCC: he went as a delegate to the general assembly in Uppsala in 1968, and served on the central committee from 1968 to 1975. He was concerned that the agenda of faith and order, one of the three founding streams of the WCC, was losing its central importance as attention became focused on matters of social witness and the controversial programme to combat racism.

Tomkins retired in 1975, and he and his wife, Ursula, moved to Worcester. He remained active, teaching for a term at Westcott House, Cambridge, leading retreats, and working as an assistant bishop in the diocese. He took an active interest in the Movement for the Ordination of Women, writing an influential essay, *A Fully Human Priesthood* (1984). During his retirement he also wrote *Prayer for Unity* (1987). He died of cancer in Esher, Surrey, on 29 October 1992, and was buried in Bristol Cathedral on 9 November. He was survived by his wife and their four children. A memorial service was held at St Margaret's Church, Westminster, on 21 January 1993.

Tomkins was an internationally respected and influential leader in the ecumenical movement, as well as a much loved bishop in the Church of England. He was committed to a vision of the visible unity of the church and to moving by steps and stages towards that end. He was able to hold together relations at the world level with those at the very local. He was a wise and kind man. One free church leader commented: 'he commended the concept of episcopacy so graciously for his was an episcopacy rooted in service and fellowship' (personal knowledge). He had qualities essential for an ecumenist. He was a good listener and could understand the views of others, he sought always to reconcile, he was given to friendship, and, above all, he was a man of prayer, concerned for wholeness and holiness.   MARY TANNER

Sources *The Independent* (2 Nov 1992) · *The Independent* (5 Dec 1992) · *The Guardian* (2 Nov 1992) · *The Times* (3 Nov 1992) · *The Times* (22 Jan 1993) · L. Stevenson, 'Oliver Stratford Tomkins, his contribution to the contemporary movement of the churches towards unity', PhD diss., University of Dublin, 1987 · M. Cleasby, ed., *Oliver Tomkins by his friends* (1995) · A. Hastings, *Oliver Tomkins* (2001) · *WWW*, 1991–5 · personal knowledge (2004) · private information (2004) · m. cert.
Archives GL, corresp. with Hodder & Stoughton · LPL, papers relating to Catholic Ecumenical Federation and to intercommunion · LPL, papers relating to World Council of Churches
Likenesses photograph, repro. in *The Independent* (2 Nov 1992) · photograph, repro. in *The Times* (3 Nov 1992)
Wealth at death £6334: probate, 21 Jan 1993, *CGPLA Eng. & Wales*

Tomkins, Peltro William (1759–1840), engraver and draughtsman, was born on 10 October 1759 in St Pancras, Middlesex, and baptized there on 15 October 1759, a younger son of William *Tomkins (*c*.1732–1792), landscape painter, and his wife, Susanna Callard. He entered the Royal Academy Schools in 1775, aged fifteen, and was taught to engrave by Francis Bartolozzi, a connection proudly proclaimed by Tomkins on many plates. After 1781, working chiefly in stipple, he engraved a large number of plates for a variety of publishers. The designers he interpreted were principally contemporaries such as William Redmore Bigg, Henry Bunbury, William Hamilton, Angelica Kaufmann, and Thomas Stothard. He was one of the principal engravers employed by Thomas Macklin for his *British Poets* and produced a fine interpretation of Henry Fuseli's *Prince Arthur's Vision* (1788) for the first number. He married Lucy Jones on 2 June 1787 and raised a large family, including a daughter, Emma, who practised as an artist and married Samuel Smith, an engraver.

Tomkins gave drawing lessons to the daughters of George III, and in 1793 he was appointed historical engraver to Queen Charlotte. He engraved Princess Elizabeth's designs for illustrations to Sir J. Bland Burgess's poem 'The Birth and Triumph of Love'. In 1793 he joined his brother J. F. Tomkins, trading as P. W. Tomkins & Co. at his print shop, 49 New Bond Street, a business continued until 1823. They financed ambitious works, notably an illustrated edition of James Thomson's *Seasons* (1797), with engravings by Tomkins and Bartolozzi after designs by William Hamilton. This was arguably the most magnificent book to be illustrated with stipple engravings. Two much later ventures, *The British Gallery of Pictures* (1818–20), with text by Henry Tresham, and *Engravings of the … Marquis of Stafford's Collection of Pictures* (1818), with text by William Young Ottley, were less successful. Tomkins suffered a heavy financial loss and was compelled to obtain a private act of parliament (57 Geo. III c. lxi) authorizing him to dispose by lottery of the watercolour drawings from which he had worked, together with the unsold impressions of the plates (many already coloured), the whole being valued at £150,000. The first prize consisted of 291 pictures, representing the entire collection of the marquess of Stafford. Before the lottery could take place the letterpress and apparatus for captioning the prints was lost in a fire and Tomkins was obliged to seek a second act (1 Geo. IV c. lxxxix) to extend the date of drawing the tickets until 31 March 1821. His last work was a series of three plates (1834–40) from copies by Harriet Whitshed of paintings discovered at Hampton Court. Tomkins died on 22 April 1840 at his home, 25 Osnaburgh Street, St Pancras, and was buried on 28 April at St Pancras Church.

Charles Tomkins (1757–1823), painter and etcher, was born in London on 7 July 1757, the elder brother of Peltro William Tomkins. He exhibited at the Royal Academy from 1773 to 1779. In 1776 he gained a premium from the Society of Arts for a view of Millbank, and he subsequently practised as a topographical and antiquarian draughtsman and aquatint engraver and publisher. A drawing of London from Wandsworth Hill was engraved and published in 1786. In 1791 he published, from 2 Rathbone Place, *Eight Views of Reading Abbey*, with text by himself; this was reissued in 1805 with twenty-three additional views of churches originally connected with the abbey. In 1796 he published *A Tour to the Isle of Wight*, with eighty aquatint plates, and in 1805 a set of illustrations to

Petrarch's sonnets, which he dedicated to the duchess of Devonshire. With Francis Jukes he engraved Cleveley's two pictures of the advance and defeat of a floating battery at Gibraltar (1782); he also drew and engraved the plates to the *British Volunteer* (1799) and a plan view of the sham fight of the St George's volunteers in Hyde Park in the same year. Many of his watercolour drawings are in the Crowle copy of Pennant's *London*, in the British Museum print room. He died in 1823.

TIMOTHY CLAYTON and ANITA McCONNELL

Sources D. Alexander, 'Tomkins family', *The dictionary of art*, ed. J. Turner (1996) · *GM*, 2nd ser., 14 (1840), 105 · E. Edwards, *Anecdotes of painters* (1808); facs. edn (1970) · T. Dodds, *History of English engravers*, BL, Add. MS 33406, fols. 38–43 · parish register, St Pancras, 28 April 1840 [burial] · d. cert. · parish registers, St Clement Danes, City Westm. AC, 2 June 1787 [marriage]

Tomkins, Thomas (1572–1656), composer, was born at St David's, Pembrokeshire, the son of Thomas Tomkins (*c*.1545–1627) of Lostwithiel, Cornwall, vicar-choral of St David's Cathedral, and his first wife, Margaret Pore (*d. c*.1583). In 1577 his father became organist and master of the choristers at St David's, but by 1594 he had moved to Gloucester as a minor canon. In the meantime Tomkins senior had married his second wife, Anne Hargest, with whom he had three other sons who subsequently also became notable musicians—John Tomkins, Giles Tomkins [see below], and Robert Tomkins.

Little is known of Thomas Tomkins's early musical education. He was educated at home, and probably gained his knowledge of the rudiments as a treble at St David's. It would appear that at some stage before he was appointed organist of Worcester Cathedral in 1596 he studied with William Byrd, the most significant composer of the Elizabethan era. Regrettably, the dedication of his madrigal 'Too much I once lamented', from the *Songs of 3. 4. 5. & 6. Parts* (1622), 'To my ancient and much reverenced master, William Byrd' is ambiguous as to the specific nature of their relationship. The 1607 citation of his Oxford BMus degree notes that he had been '14 years student in music': this would place the beginning of his formal instruction in 1593. In 1597 Tomkins married Alice Hassard (*c*.1563–1642), widow of his predecessor as organist at Worcester, Nathaniel Patrick. Their son Nathaniel Tomkins [see below] was born in 1599, and they also had a daughter, Ursula.

Tomkins's investigation of music theory must have been significantly enhanced by the publication of Thomas Morley's *A Plain and Easy Introduction to Practical Music* (1597). He worked through Morley's treatise carefully, making a number of marginal annotations to his copy that betray a fascination with theoretical aspects of music. His interest in theoretical abstractions was complemented by antiquarian zeal. He became the owner of an important manuscript source of English liturgical organ music dating back to the Marian period (BL, Add. MS 29996), into which he subsequently copied a variety of later pieces in different genres by more up-to-date composers such as Byrd and John Bull along with some pieces of his own. More extensive than this composite manuscript is a holograph source (Bibliothèque Nationale, Paris, MS Rés. 1122) which includes a significant number of Tomkins's own keyboard pieces. Many of the works contained in this manuscript bear precise dates (unusual for this period); remarkably, most were composed when he was approaching eighty years of age. This manuscript also contains two lists of keyboard pieces by Tallis, Byrd, and Bull among others, including some comments on the relative merits of the latter two. Byrd's work is singled out 'for Substance' (clearly an acknowledgement of Byrd's senior position among contemporary English composers), while Bull's is described as 'for the Hand', a comment inspired no doubt by its typically virtuosic technical demands, and not necessarily to be interpreted as a derogatory judgement. Tomkins's own keyboard works draw upon the techniques of both composers.

Clearly Tomkins's compositional gifts had made some impact in the capital by the turn of the century, since Morley included the madrigal 'The fauns and satyrs tripping' in his famous anthology *The Triumphs of Oriana* (1601) alongside the work of more established court composers. Tomkins may well have become attached to the court in some capacity shortly thereafter, dividing his time, like a number of his contemporaries, between a cathedral post (at Worcester) and the occasional demands of the Chapel Royal. The cheque book of the Chapel Royal contains no entry relating to Tomkins's actual appointment as a gentleman in ordinary, though he had been elected by 29 June 1620, when his signature appears in a record of a vestry meeting. Evidently he had been connected with the court in some capacity for about a decade before this: his anthem 'Know ye not' was clearly intended for the funeral of Prince Henry in 1612.

In 1621 Tomkins succeeded Edmund Hooper as an organist of the Chapel Royal, where his colleagues included Orlando Gibbons (senior organist) and Nathaniel Giles (master of the choristers). Both men were dedicatees the following year of madrigals in Tomkins's *Songs of 3. 4. 5. & 6. Parts* (1622), a collection in which each piece bears a specific dedication, giving quite a detailed impression of the composer's social circle during the first quarter of the century. This included, in addition to colleagues such as Gibbons and Giles, the composers John Coprario, John Danyel, William Heather (soon to become the first professor of music at Oxford), and William Byrd, the poet Phineas Fletcher, and the anthologist Thomas Myriell, in whose manuscript collection, 'Tristitiae remedium' (1616), Tomkins's best-known anthem, 'When David heard', is to be found. Following Gibbons's early death in 1625, Tomkins presumably became senior organist (although this is not specifically recorded) and was responsible, along with Giles, Heather, and John Stevens, for Charles I's coronation music. In 1628 he was the victim of an embarrassing administrative error by the bishop of Bath and Wells, who had drawn up a document appointing Tomkins 'Composer in Ordinary of the King's Musick' in succession to Alfonso Ferrabosco the elder at a salary of £40 per annum; this had to be hastily revoked when it was discovered that the position had previously been promised to Ferrabosco's son.

From about 1635 Tomkins's appearances at the Chapel Royal probably became less frequent. Although he enjoyed a long retirement, it cannot have been especially happy owing to a combination of personal and national misfortunes. Following the death of his wife, Alice, on 29 January 1642, Tomkins seems to have become increasingly involved in cathedral affairs at Worcester, a deepening involvement in a familiar environment from which he perhaps drew spiritual comfort amid the increasingly turbulent political scene. However, even that solace was short-lived. In 1646 Worcester surrendered to the parliamentary forces and cathedral services were effectively discontinued, although Tomkins (an ardent royalist) continued to reside in the cathedral close until 1654, when he moved to the nearby village of Martin Hussingtree to live with his son, Nathaniel. There he died in early June 1656, and was buried on 9 June.

Contemporaries considered Tomkins a worthy but not especially outstanding or idiosyncratic composer. It is perhaps significant that while seventeenth-century portraits of Bull and Gibbons survive in the Oxford music faculty there is none of Tomkins. His musical output is conservative in style. The keyboard pieces dating from the last decade of his life could easily have been composed sixty or more years earlier and include a relatively large quantity of pieces known as In nomine, a genre that had largely died out with Byrd (although some very late and uncharacteristic examples occur in the work of Purcell towards the end of the seventeenth century). While his instrumental music is significant, Tomkins's lasting contribution to English music lies in the field of church music. His particular forte was perhaps the verse anthem, a type of sacred vocal music for the Anglican rite that alternates 'full' and 'solo' choral groupings with organ accompaniment. His madrigals do not depart significantly from this 'serious' idiom and seem to avoid the Italianate influences that had been so prominent in the work of the previous generation led by Thomas Morley. His main contribution to the various instrumental repertories was undoubtedly in the realm of stylized dance music, especially the pavan and galliard. This music was clearly for private purposes, a fact reflected in the relatively narrow distribution of manuscript sources, mostly emanating from the west country (with which the composer maintained lifelong associations).

Tomkins's son **Nathaniel Tomkins** (1599–1681), Church of England clergyman and musician, was born in Worcester and studied at Balliol College, Oxford, graduating BA on 20 April 1619 and proceeding MA on 3 February 1622 and BD on 13 March 1629. On 15 May that year he was appointed canon of Worcester Cathedral by Bishop William Laud, for whom he had apparently acted as an agent against Bishop John Williams of Lincoln. In his *Memorial* (1693) of Williams, John Hacket claimed that:

Mr N. T., a musician and a Divine—one that could make better music upon an organ than upon a text ... had leave to use the whole [of Williams's] house, to go into the bishop's bedchamber, or study ... [he] transcribed some letters which he found and sent them to an enemy [Laud].   (Vining)

Tomkins became rector of St Martin's, Worcester, in 1633 and of Broadway, Worcestershire, in 1637. Ejected in 1646, he was sequestered before 1650. Restored to St Martin's in 1660, he also became rector of Todenham, Gloucestershire, that year and of Upton-on-Severn from 1663. He was probably the editor of his late father's *Musica Deo sacra* (1668), of which he was inspecting proof sheets as early as 1665. None of his own music survives. He died at Martin Hussingtree on 20 October 1681.

Thomas Tomkins's half-brother **John Tomkins** (1586–1638), organist, was born at St David's. A scholar of King's College, Cambridge, he served as organist there from 1606 to 1619, and graduated MusB on 6 June 1608. He later served as organist of St Paul's Cathedral (1619), gentleman-extraordinary of the Chapel Royal (1625), and gentleman ordinary of the chapel (1627). He was appointed organist of the Chapel Royal for the state visit to Scotland in 1633 (jointly with his brother Giles). Married, he was father of Thomas *Tomkins (1637/8–1675). He died in London on 27 September 1638, and was buried in St Paul's. References to John (as Thomalin) are found in the poetry of Phineas Fletcher, a contemporary at King's; an elegy on his death by William Lawes appeared in the latter's *Choice Psalmes* (1648).

John's brother **Giles Tomkins** (b. after 1587, d. 1668), musician, was also born at St David's. Organist of King's College, Cambridge, between December 1624 and June 1626, he was thereafter master of the choristers at Salisbury Cathedral (1629), musician for the virginals in the king's musick (1630), organist with the Chapel Royal during the Scottish visit of 1633, and musician for lutes, viols, and voices (from at least 1641). His court appointments, which were all renewed at the Restoration, were held concurrently with his duties at Salisbury, where he seems to have been mainly living in the 1660s. He was buried there on 4 April 1668. By his will dated 20 March and proved on 24 May by his eldest son, Thomas (b. 1631), he left legacies to his three sons and two daughters from his first marriage, his second wife, Elizabeth, and their son William, and his organ books to Salisbury Cathedral.

The third son of the elder Thomas Tomkins's second marriage, Robert Tomkins (b. after 1587, d. in or after 1641), viol player and composer, was appointed musician for the consort of the king's musick on 28 March 1628. He was listed in the lord chamberlain's accounts for 1630 (with a salary of £46 per annum) and with his brother Giles was one of the musicians for lutes, viols, and voices from 1641. Probably he died during the Commonwealth, since the Restoration account books make no further reference to him, naming in his place Henry Hawes. All that remains of his musical output are three verse anthems, although the texts for five others survive in the Chapel Royal anthem book.   JOHN IRVING

Sources D. Stevens, *Thomas Tomkins* (1957) · B. Rose, 'Thomas Tomkins, 1575?–1656', *Proceedings of the Royal Musical Association*, 82 (1955–6), 89–105 · J. Irving, *The instrumental music of Thomas Tomkins, 1572–1656* (1989) · I. Atkins, *The early occupants of the office of organist and master of the choristers of the cathedral church of Christ and the Blessed Virgin Mary, Worcester* (1918) · D. R. A. Evans, 'Thomas Tomkins and the prince of Wales', *Welsh Music*, 7/4 (1983), 57–69 · J. Irving, 'Consort playing in mid-17th-century Worcester: Thomas Tomkins and the Bodleian partbooks Mus. Sch.E.415–18', *Early Music*, 12 (1984), 337–44 · A. Ashbee, ed., *Records of English court music*, 9 vols. (1986–96) · J. Irving, 'Thomas Tomkins's copy of Morley's *A plain and easy introduction to practical music*', *Music and Letters*, 71 (1990), 483–93 · D. R. A. Evans, 'The life and works of John Tomkins', *Welsh Music*, 6/4 (1980), 56–62 · P. Vining, 'Nathaniel Tomkins: a bishop's pawn', *MT*, 133 (1992), 538–40 · A. Ashbee and D. Lasocki, eds., *A biographical dictionary of English court musicians, 1485–1714*, 2 vols. (1998) · Foster, *Alum. Oxon.* · Wood, *Ath. Oxon.*, new edn

Tomkins, Thomas (1637/8–1675), Church of England clergyman, was born in Aldersgate Street, London, the son of John *Tomkins (1586–1638) [*see under* Tomkins, Thomas (1572–1656)], organist of St Paul's and gentleman of the Chapel Royal, and his wife, Margaret, daughter of Sylvanus Griffith, dean of Hereford Cathedral. Thomas's family connections—notably his uncles, the musicians Thomas *Tomkins (1572–1656) and Giles *Tomkins (b. after 1587, d. 1668) [*see under* Tomkins, Thomas (1572–1656)], as well as his father who died when he was an infant—lay firmly within the world of the Caroline church and court. He 'was educated in virtue and learning from the cradle' by his cousin Nathaniel *Tomkins (1599–1681) [*see under* Tomkins, Thomas (1572–1656)], canon of Worcester Cathedral and a protégé of Archbishop Laud (Wood, *Ath. Oxon.*, 3.1046). Both Nathaniel and his father, the elder Thomas Tomkins, organist at Worcester, were ejected from their places by the parliamentarian authorities in 1646.

Tomkins matriculated from Balliol College, Oxford, on 12 May 1651, graduating BA on 13 February 1655 and proceeding MA on 6 July 1658. He was elected fellow of All Souls College, Oxford, in 1656, was university proctor in 1663, was incorporated at Cambridge in 1664, and proceeded BD at Oxford in 1665 and DD on 15 May 1675. At the Restoration he distinguished himself as a zealous royalist and churchman. He has been described as one of a stable of pamphleteers whom Gilbert Sheldon, bishop of London and later archbishop of Canterbury, sought to mould popular opinion against any possibility of comprehension within the Church of England or toleration of dissent. Tracts written by Tomkins, George Stradling, Samuel Parker, and others 'were tailored to suit the secular political terrain upon which these issues were fought' (Spurr, 48). In 1660 he published *The Rebels' Plea, or, Mr Baxter's Judgement Concerning the Late Wars*, in which he criticized with considerable force Baxter's theory of the constitution, as well as his defence of particular actions of parliament. This was followed the next year by *Short strictures, or, Animadversions on so much of Mr Crofton's 'Fastning St Peters bonds' as concern the reasons of the University of Oxford concerning the covenant*, a pamphlet which Hugh Griffith in *Mr Crofton's Case Soberly Considered* termed 'frivolous, scurrilous and invective'.

On 11 April 1665 Tomkins was admitted rector of St Mary Aldermary, London, and about the same time was appointed chaplain to Archbishop Sheldon and employed as an assistant licenser of books; with his move to London he resigned his fellowship at All Souls. In this capacity he nearly refused to licence *Paradise Lost* because he thought treasonable the lines:

As when the Sun, new risen,
Looks through the horizontal, misty air,
Shorn of his beams, or from behind the moon,
In dim eclipse, disastrous twilight sheds
On half the nations, and with fear of change
Perplexes monarchs:
(J. Milton, *Paradise Lost*, I)

This is Tomkins's main claim on the interest of posterity, and the cause of no little censure, although he overcame his misgivings and granted his imprimatur some time before 20 August 1667.

On 18 July 1667 Tomkins was appointed rector of Great Chart in Kent, and in the same year published a pamphlet entitled *The Inconveniences of Toleration*. On 8 November 1669 he was installed chancellor and prebendary at Exeter, and three weeks later, on 30 November, was instituted rector of Lambeth, Surrey, all of which preferments he held until his death, resigning his two former livings. The Lambeth living came, according to Wood, because Archbishop Sheldon 'valued him so much that he kept him many years chaplain in his house, and resolving never to part with him, made him rector of Lambeth' (Wood, *Ath. Oxon.*, 3.1046). In 1672 Tomkins added a further living when he was instituted rector of Monks Risborough, Buckinghamshire.

Tomkins's career as licenser and polemicist continued. On 2 July 1670 he licensed Milton's *Paradise Regained* and *Samson Agonistes*. In 1675 he published *The modern pleas for comprehension, toleration, and the taking away the obligation to the renouncing of the covenant considered and discussed*. Another edition appeared in 1680 with the title *The new distemper, or, The dissenter's usual pleas for comprehension, toleration and the renouncing of the covenant, consider'd and discuss'd*.

Tomkins died at Exeter on 20 August 1675, aged thirty-seven, and was buried in the chancel of the church at Martin Hussingtree, Worcestershire, the parish where his cousin Nathaniel lived. A memorial plaque celebrated him as a staunch defender of the Church of England 'contra schismatices' (Wood, *Ath. Oxon.*, 3.1047). Administration of his estate was granted to his brother John. Besides his polemical writings he composed some commendatory verses prefixed to Edmund Elys's *Dia pomata* (1665). He is sometimes said to have edited *Musica Deo sacra at ecclesiae Anglicanae* (1668), composed by his uncle Thomas, in spite of there being 'no proof that this eminent and learned divine had any great knowledge of music or deep interest in it' (Stevens, 69). Nathaniel, the elder Thomas's son, is a more likely candidate.

E. I. CARLYLE, *rev.* SEAN KELSEY

Sources Wood, *Ath. Oxon.*, new edn, 3.1046–48 · O. Manning and W. Bray, *The history and antiquities of the county of Surrey*, 3 (1814), 519 · D. Masson, *The life of John Milton*, 7 vols. (1859–94), vol. 6, pp. 506, 514–15, 616, 651 · D. Stevens, *Thomas Tomkins, 1572–1656* (1957) ·

J. Spurr, *The Restoration Church of England, 1646–1689* (1991), 48 · Foster, *Alum. Oxon.* · A. Ashbee and D. Lasocki, eds., *A biographical dictionary of English court musicians, 1485–1714*, 2 (1998), 1083–8 · *Fasti Angl., 1541–1857*, [Ely] · administration, PRO, PROB 6/50, fol. 3r **Wealth at death** see administration, Sept 1675, PRO, PROB 6/50, fol. 3r

Tomkins, Thomas (1743–1816), writing-master, of whose birth, upbringing, or early life nothing is known, eventually kept a boarding-school in Foster Lane, Cheapside, London, where he taught writing and accounts to 'Young Gentlemen for Trades, Merchts. for Counting Houses and the Public Offices' (Heal, 108) and he was said to have been an excellent teacher.

Tomkins's known work as a writing-master was not extensive; he published only two engraved copy-books and both of these appeared in the early part of his career. The first was entitled *The Beauties of Writing* (1777), an expensive volume which sold for 15s., and this was quickly followed by *Alphabets Written for the Improvement of Youth* (1779); both contained a combination of plain and decorative writing exercises in a variety of styles. Apart from these copy-books, published in his own name, the mainstay of Tomkins's career was in producing ornamental penmanship for other people. Occasionally, he worked for publishers executing decorative titles for luxury publications such as Thomas Macklin's Bible (1800) or Rudolph Ackermann's *Microcosm of London* (1808–10). In contrast to the work of early eighteenth-century writing-masters little of Tomkins's work was either intended for publication or ever engraved. Instead he specialized in producing unique presentation certificates and decorative transcripts of important texts and public addresses. Between 1776 and 1816 he was employed by the corporation of London to embellish the honorary freedoms that they distributed and it was through this channel that Tomkins's work was acclaimed by no less noble figures than Prince Leopold of Saxe-Coburg-Saalfeld and the dukes of Kent, Sussex, and Gloucester. He also transcribed the Royal Academy's annual addresses to the king and queen, turning these texts into highly refined examples of penmanship which his obituarist praised for their 'boldness of design, inexhaustible variety, and elegant freedom' (*GM*, 280). In 1806 and 1807 Tomkins also turned his hand to authorship and his *Poems on Various Subjects* (1807) was successful enough to go through several editions.

In fact Tomkins's life is characterized less by his achievements as a penman than by his dogged determination that calligraphy should be recognized as one of the sister arts and that, consequently, he should be honoured with a place in the Royal Academy. Despite Isaac D'Israeli's rather censorious view that this belief rendered him 'the vainest of all Writing Masters' (D'Israeli, 436) a number of entries in Joseph Farington's diaries reveal how well liked Tomkins actually was. Of course, as a calligrapher he was never given the opportunity to run for the Royal Academy, but his involvement in a number of benevolent schemes, including the scheme to erect a monument to commemorate the engraver William Woollett, in 1796, led to his being invited to several of the Royal Academy's annual dinners. A naturally good humoured and sociable man, Tomkins was friends with celebrities such as Samuel Johnson and Sir Joshua Reynolds. Indeed, when Reynolds completed Tomkins's portrait in 1789 he refused to take any more than £80 from 'a brother artist' (Heal, 109). According to one of Reynolds's first biographers, this compliment was extended when Reynolds, who signed few of his works, offered to give Tomkins '"a specimen of *my* writing", and immediately, [and] with the utmost freedom, wrote with his brush on the reverse of the canvas, "J. Reynolds, pinx.," 1789' (*Sunday Times*, 22 April 1928; portrait in the Guildhall, London). After suffering a long and painful illness, Tomkins died in September 1816 at his house in Sermon Lane, Doctors' Commons, London.

LUCY PELTZ

Sources *GM*, 1st ser., 86/2 (1816), 292–3 · Farington, *Diary* · A. Heal, *The English writing-masters and their copy-books, 1570–1800* (1931) · I. D'Israeli, *Curiosities of literature*, 14th edn, 3 vols. (1849) · *GM*, 1st ser., 86/2 (1816), 280–81 · *Engraved Brit. ports.* · A. Davies and E. Kilmurray, *Dictionary of British portraiture*, 4 vols. (1979–81) · W. T. Whitley, letter to the editor, *Sunday Times* (22 April 1928) · W. T. Whitley, *Artists and their friends in England, 1700–1799*, 2 vols. (1928)
Archives BM, embellished copy of Macklin's Bible | RA, MS sheet in presentation copy of T. Tomkins, *The beauties of writing exemplified* (1808) · RA, MS: a prize-winners' roll of gold and silver medallists, 1811
Likenesses J. Reynolds, oils, 1789, Guildhall Art Gallery, London · C. Turner, mezzotint, 1805 (after J. Reynolds) · F. Chantrey, marble bust, 1816, BM; plaster cast, AM Oxf. · S. W. Reynolds, mezzotint (after J. Reynolds), BM · L. Schiavonetti, line engraving (after G. Englehart), BM; repro. in T. Tomkins, *Rays of genius*, 2 vols. (1806) · J. Scott., mezzotint (after J. Reynolds), NPG

Tomkins, William (c.1732–1792), landscape painter, was first recorded on 7 July 1757 as the father of Charles *Tomkins (1757–1823) [see under Tomkins, Peltro William], topographical painter and engraver, and on 15 October 1759, on the baptism of his second son, Peltro William *Tomkins (1759–1840), also an engraver and draughtsman. The date of his marriage to their mother, Susanna Callard, is not known.

Tomkins first exhibited at the Free Society of Artists in 1761 and was awarded the second premium for a landscape by the Society of Arts in 1763. His reputation rests on his paintings in the manner of Claude (a number of whose works he copied) of gentlemen's seats, mainly in the west and north of England. He was promoted and patronized by Edward Walter of Stalbridge, Dorset, and his other patrons included the Parkers of Saltram House, Devon. Seven works by Tomkins remain in the Saltram collection, including five views of the environs of the house. He was paid £10 10s. for two pictures in 1785 but his work at Saltram began earlier, as accounts also record payments of £20 in 1778 for cleaning pictures and £31 10s. in June 1779 for 'Tomkins to pay Zucchi' (*The Saltram Collection*, 67). James Duff, second Earl Fife, was another important patron, for whom Tomkins painted a group of twelve landscapes. A number of his works were engraved for William Angus's and William Watt's sets of views of seats of the nobility and gentry, published in 1787 and 1779–86 respectively.

Tomkins exhibited at the Free Society of Artists (1761–4),

at the Incorporated Society of Artists (1764–8), and at the Royal Academy (1769–90). He was elected an associate of the Royal Academy in 1771. He died at his house in Queen Anne Street, London, on 1 January 1792.

DEBORAH GRAHAM-VERNON

Sources *DNB* · Waterhouse, *18c painters* · *The Saltram collection*, National Trust (1967) · M. H. Grant, *A chronological history of the old English landscape painters* (1947)

Tomkinson, Michael (1841–1921), carpet manufacturer, was born on 29 May 1841 at his father's house in the High Street, Kidderminster, the elder son of Michael Tomkinson (1810–1886), draper, and his wife, Sarah, daughter of James Grigg of Blakebrook, Kidderminster.

Tomkinson was educated at Bridgens Hall School, Bridgnorth, and King Charles I's Grammar School, Kidderminster. He commenced work at the age of fourteen as a clerk in a local hand-loom carpet factory. He was later employed in Schoolbred's drapery and soft furnishing shop in Tottenham Court Road, London, and on returning to Kidderminster by a carpet, rug, and yarn merchant.

In 1869 Tomkinson went into partnership with William Adam (1828–1898) in Kidderminster, founding the business which was to transform the manufacture of Axminster carpeting and make it a familiar object in middle-class homes. Tomkinson and Adam produced a variety of handmade carpets and rugs but their speciality was chenille Axminsters, woven by a process which had been patented by Adam's former employer, James Templeton of Glasgow. The firm established an international reputation by displaying its products at exhibitions in Europe and the USA, and by 1876 some 800 people were employed.

On 13 September 1871 Tomkinson married Ann Porritt (1850–1920), daughter of Matthew Porritt Stonehouse of Wakefield, worsted spinner. They lived in Kidderminster, for the last forty years of their married life at Franche Hall. There were twelve surviving children, the two eldest sons, Herbert and Gerald, becoming partners in the firm.

Tomkinson took a major new initiative in 1878 when he visited the USA and purchased the United Kingdom rights to Halcyon Skinner's spool Axminster power-loom, which wove a pile fabric imitating the luxurious hand-tufted Axminster carpets. Five other British firms were granted licences by Tomkinson and Adam and together they formed the Royal Axminster Manufacturers' Association which successfully maintained prices, permitting comfortable profit margins, until 1893. Tomkinson became its chairman, retaining the position for over forty years.

In the production of chenille Axminster carpeting a leading position was achieved by means of Adam's power-loom patented in 1880–82. Licences were given to three other firms and prices and profit levels protected by the formation of the Axminster Manufacturers' Association. The expiry of Skinner's patent and the perfection of alternative power-looms during the 1890s led to increased competition and a marked reduction in chenille and spool Axminster prices. Demand soared and the manufacture of Axminster carpeting became the largest sector of the carpet industry, and Tomkinson and Adam continued to expand. The firm employed 1300 people by 1907 and it ranked as the fourth largest firm in the industry. The firm's success owed much to Tomkinson's leadership and commercial acumen, while Adam seems to have confined himself to technical and production matters.

Tomkinson was prominent in local government. He sat on Worcestershire county council from its formation, became an alderman in 1892, and was a long-standing chairman of the finance committee. A member of Kidderminster borough council for thirty-five years, he also held office as mayor seven times between 1887 and 1913. As chairman of the library committee, he was mainly responsible for raising funds to build the borough library. He was a JP, and also served as a deputy lieutenant and high sheriff for Worcestershire.

A number of other good causes in Kidderminster attracted Tomkinson's time and energy. He was for many years chairman of the Kidderminster board of guardians, as well as treasurer of the Workmen's Club, a governor of the grammar school, and a trustee of Kidderminster Infirmary and Children's Hospital. In 1916 he was made an honorary freeman of the borough. An Anglican and a churchwarden, Tomkinson collected rare books and manuscripts, and he acquired a national reputation as a collector of Japanese ivories and lacquer work. This interest was reflected in *A Japanese Collection*, published in 1898; he was also an active member of the Japan Society. He enjoyed fishing and shooting on his country estate at Chilton, Cleobury Mortimer, and was a keen gardener, creating a notable rose garden at Franche Hall.

Tomkinson died at Franche Hall on 28 June 1921 after a brief illness. The funeral was held at Wolverley church, Worcestershire, where he was buried on 2 July 1921.

JAMES NEVILLE BARTLETT

Sources J. N. Bartlett, *Carpeting the millions: the growth of Britain's carpet industry* (1978) · *Kidderminster Shuttle* (12 April 1873) · *Kidderminster Shuttle* (8 Jan 1876) · *Kidderminster Shuttle* (13 May 1876) · *Kidderminster Shuttle* (23 March 1878) · *Kidderminster Shuttle* (14 May 1892) · *Kidderminster Shuttle* (23 Feb 1895) · *Kidderminster Shuttle* (1903) [special industrial number] · *Kidderminster Shuttle* (2 July 1921) · *Kidderminster Times* (10 July 1920) · note to his mother, Dec 1852, Archives of Tomkinsons Ltd, Kidderminster · letter from Pemberton Talbot, 1866, Archives of Tomkinsons Ltd, Kidderminster · Royal Axminster Manufacturers' Association minute book, 1878–94, notes of a speech given 7 July 1920, Archives of Tomkinsons Ltd, Kidderminster · b. cert. · b. certs. of wife and brother · m. cert. · d. cert. · Tomkinson & Adam price list, October 1869, Worcestershire County Museum, Hartlebury

Archives Tomkinsons Ltd, Kidderminster | Worcestershire County Museum, Hartlebury

Likenesses A. Hacker, oils, Kidderminster Public Library

Wealth at death £214,487 12s. 2d.: probate, 29 Oct 1921, *CGPLA Eng. & Wales*

Tomkinson, Thomas (1631–*c*.1710), Muggletonian, was the son of Richard Tomkinson and his wife, Ann (*d*. 1661/2), of Sladehouse in the parish of Ilam, Staffordshire. He came from a family of substantial tenant farmers long settled in the parishes of Ilam and Blore Ray. Tomkinson may have acquired his considerable learning from the library belonging to the estate of his namesake Thomas Tomkinson, who was buried at Blore Ray on 25 December 1640.

The future Muggletonian 'procured a library of presbyterian books' (*DNB*) and he also borrowed books (including St Augustine's *City of God* and the works of the Anglican apologist Henry Hammond) from his landlord, Thomas Cromwell, fourth Baron Cromwell and first earl of Ardglass, at Throwley Hall. On his mother's death in late 1661 or early 1662, Tomkinson's father made over his affairs to him, and boarded with his son as a lodger. Shortly after Tomkinson married 'a good virtuous maid' (whose name he does not record), who brought with her a marriage portion of £120 so that Tomkinson was able to pay his father for his cattle (BL, Add. MS 42505, fol. 2*v*). Tomkinson established himself as a factor and remained in Staffordshire until at least 1681. That year proved expensive for him when he lost £140, partly through damages awarded against him for a squib against his local minister whom he accused of popery, partly through the failure of a chapman in London with whom he traded.

In February 1652 God spoke to John Reeve, co-founder of Muggletonianism, and told him (on three successive mornings) that he and his cousin Lodowicke Muggleton, were the 'Two Last Witnesses' revealed in chapter 11 of the book of Revelation. Ten days afterwards Tomkinson had a visionary experience, suffering wonderful things in his sleep, when 'things were made plain to me and I beheld wonders inexpressible' (Tomkinson, 'Christian converte'). Yet Tomkinson did not hear about God's commission until nearly a decade later, remaining until then 'a most zealeous prespeterian' (BL, Add. MS 42505, fol. 4*v*). It was through reading the writings of Lawrence Clarkson that Tomkinson was able to tie up his own previous revelation with the principles of the new Muggletonian religion. His mother, who had shared her son's presbyterian commitment, followed her son into the new faith. She found hardest to give up her old presbyterian practice of praying to God, an issue over which Muggleton had broken with Reeve: Muggleton (and Tomkinson enthusiastically endorsed his position) denied that God took 'immediate notice' of his creatures.

Tomkinson's conversion was in 1661 but it would be another three years before he was fully committed to Muggletonianism, and blessed by Muggleton. During these three years Tomkinson pursued the prophet with detailed questions—he later praised Muggleton's patience in answering these doubts. He might not have been too pleased to know of Muggleton's comment to a third party: 'what a great deale of paine to please the unsatisfied fancye of one particular man' (BL, Add. MS 60171, fol. 373). To some exquisite rhapsody of doubts from Tomkinson in 1664 comes the prophet's revealingly brusque reply: 'Nothing venture, nothing have' (BL, Add. MS 60171, fol. 406). But by August of that year a believer, Ellen Sudbury, is welcoming him to the fold, and is also excited by news of his wife's growing interest. Just before his marriage Tomkinson had gone up to London to see Muggleton, leaving Staffordshire on May day 1662. He later acknowledged that he had occasionally attended church 'to please an old father and a young wife', until

1674 (BL, Add. MS 42505, fol. 2v). His father remained hostile to his son's new belief. Muggleton in 1666 wrote to Tomkinson that his wife would lose nothing by committing herself to the faith 'if she hold out to the End' (Delamaine, 180). Tomkinson's daughter, Anne (there was also a son, Thomas), was blessed by Muggleton on 10 July 1684.

The Tomkinson conversion was thus not straightforward: his enlightenment had preceded his discovery of his new religion; the occasional conformity he himself had practised (although he claimed, on the other side, to have made over twenty converts) would find dubious echoes in the behaviour of his brother-in-law and sister, who avoided persecution in 1682 by pretending to be papists. But it was, in the end, a prize worth having. Muggleton recognized this, however belatedly, when he used his authority (rarely exercised in this manner) to prevent Tomkinson from emigrating in 1674 to avoid persecution. When Tomkinson did turn up in court to pay a fine, Archdeacon Cook overheard him explaining to a Quaker where his doctrines were wrong. The sequel was a happy one. Cook was reported to have said 'if hee have no worse principles than this hee is not to be blamed'. So Tomkinson and a friend paid a 20s. fine each, while two Baptists were fined £16. Tomkinson said 'they never knew how I came off for our business was private' (Tomkinson, 'Christian converte').

Clarkson had been Tomkinson's introduction to Muggletonianism. Although personally disgraced in 1661 for challenging Muggleton's leadership, Clarkson was not ideologically disgraced. When one of Tomkinson's cavils prior to conversion had been whether the man Jesus knew he was God while on earth, Muggleton referred (this was in 1664) to the authority of Clarkson for support (BL, Add. MS 60171, fol. 404). Clarkson had been emphatic that God did not take 'immediate notice' of men and women, and Tomkinson followed Clarkson and Muggleton on this. In 1664 he wrote a concordance of Reeve's and Muggleton's writings, and scriptural references in support of the Muggleton/Clarkson doctrine were inserted (BL, Add. MS 60189, fol. 1v). The debate acquired new urgency in 1671 when Muggleton's denial of 'immediate notice' became the basis of a rebellion against his leadership, led principally by William Medgate and Walter Buchanan. Tomkinson was present at the debate between Muggleton and Buchanan and believed that Muggleton won it hands down: 'I was wonderfully satisfied at the prophets doctrine concerning God not taking notice of every particular Action that is done' (Tomkinson, 'Christian converte'). But he acknowledged in his 'Zions Sonnes' of 1679 that he himself had initially been tempted by the rebels' principles. The temptation had not lasted; he was boasting indeed in a letter to believers in Ireland in 1674 that he had enjoyed ten years 'without the least Doubt' in the faith (BL, Add. MS 60180, fol. 12).

Nobody would prove better in communicating such certainties than Tomkinson. He was the ablest of all Muggletonian writers in his age—perhaps in the religion's history. His greatest work was *Truth's Triumph* (published 1823). He wrote it in 1676; in April 1679 his fellow believer Alexander Delamaine wrote to him to say how much Muggleton had approved of it; in 1690 Tomkinson made additions to the manuscript; and he dedicated it to Muggleton on 9 August 1691. He does not add to the doctrines of Reeve and Muggleton, but they are presented in a sophisticated manner and backed by references to scholarly sources. What is clear in this work, and in others, is his explicit admiration for Thomas Hobbes. They shared reverence for magistracy, belief in mortalism and materialism, respect for Job, and contempt for free will and the Trinity.

Tomkinson was to have a pivotal role in the publication of Muggleton's autobiography in 1699, *The Acts of the Witnesses*. Muggleton had been known to be working upon the manuscript for some time but would not let anybody see it. But two weeks before his death (in 1698), he put it into the hands of Tomkinson. Tomkinson had ended his own 1692 work, *The Harmony of the Three Commissions, or, None but Christ* (published 1757), with a desperate postscript, lamenting internal strife within the movement. In the dedicatory epistle with which Tomkinson now prefaced the publication of Muggleton's posthumous memoirs the same sombre note was struck: there was no salvation for the believers who professed to own Reeve, and yet who would not acknowledge Muggleton. The 1671 scars had therefore not healed: they would even persist into Victorian Muggletonianism. But no man had done more to prevent this happening than Tomkinson. He died about 1710 in London, where he had settled some time after 1681.

WILLIAM LAMONT

Sources *DNB* · T. Tomkinson, 'Truth's triumph', 1676–90, BL, Add. MS 60190 · T. Tomkinson, 'Zions sonnes', 1679, BL, Add. MS 60193 · T. Tomkinson, The harmony of the three commissions, or, None but Christ, 1692, BL, Add. MS 60195 · T. Tomkinson, 'The Christian converte', 1692, BL, Add. MS 60206, fols. 35–74 · T. Tomkinson, 'The white divell uncased', 1704, BL, Add. MS 60197 [second recension] · T. Tomkinson, 'Discourse upon the epistle by Jude', 1704, BL, Add. MS 60198 · C. Hill, B. Reay, and W. Lamont, *The world of the Muggletonians* (1983) · L. Muggleton, *The acts of the witnesses*, ed. T. L. Underwood (1999) · *The works of John Reeve and Lodowicke Muggleton*, ed. J. Frost and I. Frost, 3 vols. (1832) · J. Peat, ed., *A stream from the tree of life* (1758) · A. Delamaine, ed., *A volume of spiritual epistles* (1755) · J. Frost and I. Frost, eds., *Supplement to the book of letters* (1831) · J. Frost, ed., *Sacred remains* (1856)

Tomkis [Tomkys], **Thomas** (*b. c.*1580, *d.* in or after 1615), playwright, the son of John *Tomkys (*d.* 1592), entered Trinity College, Cambridge, in 1597, was admitted scholar in 1599, and was granted his BA in 1600. In 1602 he was elected minor fellow, and two years later earned an MA; he became a major fellow the same year. Tomkis has been remembered by posterity as the author of two academic plays, both written and probably performed at Cambridge. The first, entitled *Albumazar*, was performed on the evening of 9 March 1615, in Trinity College hall, which was designed for theatrical use as well as for dining. (The hall was built by Thomas Nevile, master from 1593 to 1615, and included a demountable stage and galleries. It was the site of numerous royal visits.) Among the spectators were James I, Prince Charles, and various courtiers who had converged on the university for several days. The party was entertained by a different play each evening. One of these was written by Samuel Brookes, who eventually became master of Trinity College; another by Phineas Fletcher, admitted to King's College in 1600.

Albumazar, an adaptation of Giambattista della Porta's *L'astrologo* (printed in Venice in 1606), was performed in English by the members of Trinity College. In the college account book the senior bursar noted that Tomkis received £20 'for his paines in penning and ordering the English Commedie at our masters appoyntment' (Nelson, *Cambridge*, 1.527). The play was attributed to Tomkis on the title-page of two 1615 printings, and this was verified in an account of the royal visit in a manuscript by Sir Edward Dering (CUL, Add. MS 2677, art. 1, fol. 3). *Albumazar* was improperly identified by John Dryden in his prologue to a 1668 revival at Lincoln's Inn Fields as the model for Ben Jonson's *Alchemist* (1610). In the nineteenth century there was some speculation that the play was written by William Shakespeare, a theory that has been thoroughly dismissed (Rimbault, 259–60; Wright, 155).

The subject matter of Tomkis's play—a satire on astrology—apparently made the piece a great success. *Albumazar* was entered in the London Stationers' register on 28 April 1615 and printed almost immediately. However, the gossipmonger John Chamberlain remarked that 'there was no great matter in it more than one good clown's part' (Chambers, 3.498). The play was printed twice in 1615 and reprinted in 1634 and 1668, as well as numerous times throughout the eighteenth and nineteenth centuries. The first quarto was printed again in 1944, followed by another reprint in 1977. *Albumazar* retained its theatrical attractiveness throughout the eighteenth century, being performed at Drury Lane in 1744, 1747, and 1748. Subsequently the actor David Garrick made alterations and performed in his new version (also at Drury Lane) on 19 October 1773. This version was also published.

Although falsely ascribed to Antony Brewer (*fl.* 1630–1655) a second Tomkis play was correctly identified by Sir John Harington early in the seventeenth century: 'The combat of lingua' as written by 'Thom[as] Tomkis of Trinity colledge in Cambridge' (BL, Add. MS 27632, fol. 30). The play was probably also performed in Cambridge. Here Tomkis seems again to have been influenced by an Italian model; 'Lingua' is a farcical presentation of a struggle between personifications of the tongue and the five senses, all which are identified by their Latin names.

G. C. Moore Smith supported 1602 as a possible date for the composition of 'Lingua', on the theory that a compliment to Queen Psyche is really meant for Queen Elizabeth; however, other critics do not find this evidence convincing. There is also another myth, that Oliver Cromwell acted in 'Lingua', his young nephew performing the role of Small Beer. This led F. G. Fleay to suggest that the play formed part of Cromwell's entertainments for King James at Hinchinbrook on 27–9 April 1603. There is no evidence, however, to suggest that this was the case (Nelson, *Cambridge*, 2.942). A third theory, proposed by Frederick Boas,

dated the play later, to shortly before the time of publication, because of certain similarities with passages in *Macbeth*.

The play was entered into the Stationers' register on 23 February 1607 as 'A Commedie called Lingua', and an anonymous printing followed soon thereafter in the same year. Here the play was entitled *Lingua, or, The Combat of the Tongue, and the Five Senses*. Four other dated printings followed in 1617, 1622, 1632, and 1657, along with one undated printing. So popular was *Lingua* during its time that it was translated as *Speculum aestheticum* (1613) by Johannes Rhenanus for Maurice of Hesse-Cassel. Rhenanus probably accompanied Prince Otto to England in 1611.

In addition E. K. Chambers identified a later, doubtful play that was supposedly written by Tomkis: *Pathomachia, or, The Battle of Affections* (1630). In a running title, as well as in Bodleian Library manuscript (MS Eng. misc. e. 5), the same play is identified as *Love's Load-Stone*. The piece, which contains two references to 'Madame Lingua', appears to be from about 1616 (Chambers, 3.499). It is not known when Tomkis died. He has frequently been confused with Thomas Tomkins (*d.* 1656), the musician, and his son John (1586–1638); however, there is no known relationship between these families.   S. P. CERASANO

Sources E. K. Chambers, *The Elizabethan stage*, 4 vols. (1923) · A. H. Nelson, *Early Cambridge theatres: college, university, and town stages, 1464–1720* (1994) · *DNB* · A. H. Nelson, ed., *Cambridge*, 1 (1989) · E. F. Rimbault, 'Albumazar, a comedy: the Tomkins family', *N&Q*, 3rd ser., 9 (1866), 259–60 · W. A. Wright, 'Albumazar', *N&Q*, 3rd ser., 12 (1867), 155

Tomkys, John (*d.* 1592), Church of England clergyman, was a native of Bilston, near Wolverhampton, the son of Richard Tomkys, who seems to have been a person of some substance, since his 'ancestors' were buried in Wolverhampton church. Although he was credited with an MA by his employers at Shrewsbury, no record of a university education has survived. However, a dedicatory epistle acknowledges that he was maintained in his studies by a Staffordshire neighbour, Sir Richard Pipe, lord mayor of London, whose sons Humfrey and Samuel, Tomkys remembered in his will with gifts of religious books. This education may conceivably have taken Tomkys to Switzerland, whether or not as a Marian exile, since he published translations from French and Latin of works by the Zürich reformer Heinrich Bullinger and dedicated the first of these to his diocesan, Thomas Bentham, who had ministered in the English congregation at Geneva. In a dedication to Robert Dudley, earl of Leicester, Tomkys recalls serving 'at his spiritual table' 'in the county of Stafford where I was born' (Tomkys, *A Sermon Preached the 26 Day of May 1584*, 1586).

Nothing more is known of Tomkys's career until in 1582 he left Bilston for Shrewsbury, where he succeeded Edward Bulkeley as 'public preacher'. His appointment was backed by Sir George Bromley, elder brother of Sir Thomas Bromley, lord chancellor, who was Shrewsbury's recorder. Bulkeley had been paid the large salary of £72, raised partly from voluntary contributions, partly from the revenues of Shrewsbury School, to which the tithes of the two principal parish churches were appropriated. With the arrival of Tomkys, the town assembly attempted to place this burden on the entire rateable community. Tomkys was also incumbent of the royal peculiar of St Mary's, Shrewsbury, and as such styled himself 'Her Majesties Stipendiary Minister'. In reality he was employed by the town. The peculiar conveyed the right to hold a consistory court, an asset which was leased from Shrewsbury School. Here Tomkys announced seventy-nine visitation articles, which may be called, *à la* Geneva, the ecclesiastical ordinances of Shrewsbury, enforcing stringent requirements in respect of church attendance and sabbath observance, and forbidding various 'notorious sins'. Evidently the arrival on the scene of Tomkys represented a tightening of the ratchet of reformation in what was already a protestant town with some aspirations towards godliness. Tomkys published his own catechism dedicated to 'Christian parents and godly householders', and attempted to purge St Mary's Church of its stone altar and other superstitious images. That these, and especially the altar, had survived until this late date is remarkable, raising questions about the thoroughness of Reformation processes in pre-Tomkys Shrewsbury. A fortnight after these acts of iconoclasm, the earl of Leicester paid a notable civic visit and Tomkys published the sermon he preached on the occasion, the only sermon preached before the earl to have been printed.

The tight discipline enforced by Tomkys, with the backing of a magistracy dominated by the company of the drapers (and Tomkys lived in the guildhall of the drapers), met with spirited resistance. This clustered around the symbol of the shearmen's tree, a kind of maypole erected in celebration of their annual midsummer feast by the members of a trade and company, many of whose members were effectively dependent on the drapers for employment. Tomkys in his sermons began the campaign against the tree, and in 1591, when the younger drapers defied an order forbidding the setting up of the tree 'in superstitious order' (Somerset, 252) and were involved in a legal *cause célèbre*, he was subjected to the shaming ritual of a charivari. Three years later, further trouble over the tree led to a murder and the execution of two young apprentices, in circumstances which included Anglo-Welsh tension and something of a craft, if not class, war, as well as the religious and moral issues at stake.

But Tomkys had died before this, on 23 June 1592, in Shrewsbury, where a day later he was buried, his death, according to a local chronicler, much lamented 'of the perfect protestants' of the town (Leighton, 324). He had buried his wife (her name is unknown) in 1584 and now asked to be buried beside her, but not for any 'superstitious' reason, and he forbade ringing, alms giving, and 'entertaining of friends' at his funeral (Mander, 69–83). His son Thomas *Tomkis, who was a scholar at Trinity College, Cambridge, wrote the comedy *Albumazar*, which was performed before James I and appeared in nine editions between 1615 and 1634. It is unlikely that so perfect a protestant, not to say puritan, as his father would have

approved of such a thing. Tomkys himself published his catechism, *A Briefe Exposition of the Lordes Prayer* (1585), his sermon preached on 26 May 1584 (1586), and, translated from Bullinger, *A most Excellent Sermon of the Lordes Supper* (c.1577) and *A most Godly and Learned Discourse of the Woorthynesse … of the Holy Scripture* (1579).

PATRICK COLLINSON

Sources P. Collinson, 'The shearman's tree and the preacher: the strange death of merry England in Shrewsbury and beyond', *The Reformation in English towns*, ed. P. Collinson and J. Craig (1998), 205–20 · A. B. Somerset, ed., *Records of early English drama: Shropshire* (1994) · W. A. Leighton, ed., 'Early chronicles of Shrewsbury, 1372–1603', *Transactions of the Shropshire Archaeological and Natural History Society*, 3 (1880), 239–352 · B. Coulton, 'The establishment of protestantism in a provincial town: a study of Shrewsbury in the sixteenth century', *Sixteenth Century Journal*, 27 (1996), 307–35 · H. Owen and J. B. Blakeway, *A history of Shrewsbury*, 2 vols. (1825) · 'Will of John Tokys … public preacher of God's word in the town of Salop', ed. G. P. Mander, *The Wolverhampton antiquary*, 1 (1933), 69–83 · Shrewsbury School Library, Hotchkiss MS 1 · Shrewsbury assembly minutes, 1554–83, Shrops. RRC, MS 3365/76 · T. C. Mendenhall, *The Shrewsbury drapers and the Welsh wool trade in the XVI and XVII centuries* (1953)
Wealth at death see Mander, *Wolverhampton antiquary*, 1

Tomlin, Thomas James Chesshyre, Baron Tomlin (1867–1935), judge, was born at Combe House, Canterbury, Kent, on 6 May 1867, the elder son of George Taddy Tomlin (d. 1877), a barrister, and his wife, Alice (d. 1930), daughter of the Revd William John Chesshyre of Barton Court, Canterbury. He was educated at Harrow School and at New College, Oxford, where he obtained a first class in jurisprudence (1889) and a second class in the BCL examination (1891). He was called to the bar by the Middle Temple in 1891, and was subsequently (1892) called *ad eundem* by Lincoln's Inn, where he was elected a bencher in 1918. On 18 July 1893 he married Marion Olivia (b. 1867/8), elder daughter of Colonel William Garrow Waterfield CSI; they had three sons and two daughters.

Tomlin read as a pupil of R. J. Parker and continued as Parker's 'devil' until Parker was appointed to the bench in 1906. While he was Parker's devil, Tomlin's practice was only moderate. On Parker's elevation to the bench, however, the bulk of his very large practice came to him. In drafting pleadings and in advising on evidence he had few equals. He had both technical skill and a wide knowledge of the law. In court he was greatly admired for his clarity of exposition.

Tomlin was appointed junior equity counsel to the Board of Inland Revenue, the commissioners of woods and forests, the charity commissioners, the Board of Trade in foreshore cases, and the Board of Education in charity matters. To the surprise of the profession he was not offered the post of junior equity counsel to the Treasury when C. H. Sargant was elevated to the bench in 1913. Instead he took silk in the same year. As a king's counsel he was successful from the outset and commanded a large practice in the Chancery Division as well as an extensive appellate practice before the House of Lords and the privy council.

In 1923, on Sargant's promotion to the Court of Appeal,

Tomlin was appointed a judge of the Chancery Division and received the customary knighthood. In 1929 he was appointed a lord of appeal in ordinary without having served as a lord justice in the Court of Appeal—a course for which at that time precedents could be found only in the cases of Lord Blackburn and Lord Parker of Waddington. He was created a life peer (11 February 1929) and became Baron Tomlin. A few days earlier he had been sworn of the privy council and he became a member of the judicial committee.

Tomlin's appointment to the bench had been widely predicted and was universally welcomed. He proved himself to be an admirable judge. He was learned and, while quick and intolerant of irrelevance, was always courteous. He was not a silent judge, but liked to engage counsel in argument. His interruptions were always well directed and never gave the impression of a closed mind. He was equally successful as a lord of appeal. His personal charm secured the goodwill of his fellow law lords and he earned their respect by his learning, industry, and skill of statement. When he differed from the majority he took his points firmly but always courteously.

Tomlin's judgments and opinions were marked by learning, clear thinking, and lucidity of statement. The point at issue was always made clear and the right solution was often made to appear obvious. He is probably best remembered for the leading speech which he delivered for the majority in *Inland Revenue Commissioners* v. *Duke of Westminster* (1936), which contains his often cited defence of tax avoidance:

> Every man is entitled if he can to order his affairs so that the tax attaching under the appropriate Acts is less than it otherwise would be. If he succeeds in ordering them to secure this result, then, however unappreciative the Commissioners of Inland Revenue or his fellow taxpayers may be of his ingenuity, he cannot be compelled to pay an increased tax.   (ibid., 19)

Tomlin was remarkably versatile. At the bar he had handled few patent cases; as a judge he showed remarkable qualities in trying them. His success as a patent judge attested the correctness of his view that the best tribunal for such cases is the legal, not the scientific, mind. His decisions were admirable. A good judge often contributes to the improvement of legal practice as well as to the elucidation of the law. Among Tomlin's lasting contributions to legal procedure are his directions on the proper role of expert witnesses in a patent action (see *British Celanese* v. *Courtaulds*, 1935). He has gained immortality of a kind by devising and giving his name to the form of the order to be used when proceedings are settled by agreement. The 'Tomlin order', as it is still known, remains in general use more than sixty years after its author's death.

Tomlin's mind struck those who knew him best as being the incarnation of pure common sense, a quality which is rarer than might be supposed. He never seemed to leave the firm ground of fact. He had little speculative interest in the history and philosophy of the law. His principal interest lay in the correct disposal of the case before him.

Tomlin was the joint editor of the seventh and eighth editions of Lindley on partnership. In later life he undertook the chairmanship of several commissions. In 1923 he became chairman of the Royal Commission on Awards to Inventors and continued in that office until the commission was wound up in 1933. In 1925 he became chairman of the Child Adoption Committee; in 1926 chairman of the University of London commissioners; and in 1928 chairman of the Home Office advisory committee on the Cruelty to Animals Act. From 1929 to 1931 he was chairman of the important royal commission on the civil service. The commission was required to report on the structure and organization of the civil service, the conditions of service, and retirement. The MacDonnell commission (1912–15) had dealt with much the same subject but the civil service had in the meantime undergone considerable change. Its functions had been extended; the position of women had been altered materially; new methods of wage negotiation had been introduced; and there had been dislocation of normal methods of recruitment. The report was a valuable reasoned document. Much matter, some of which involved considerable detail, was adequately dealt with, but on some important matters, in particular the position of women and equal pay, the commission failed to reach agreement, to Tomlin's disappointment.

Tomlin was elected an honorary fellow of New College in 1929 and received the honorary degree of LLD from the universities of London, Toronto, and Columbia. He was president of the Harrow Association from 1933 until his death. He was a distinguished freemason, being appointed to the rank of past junior grand warden in 1929. Tomlin died in harness, of peritonitis and appendicitis, in a nursing home at 11 Ethelbert Road, Canterbury, on 12 August 1935, and was buried at Ash, Kent. He was survived by his wife, two daughters, and the youngest of his three sons, the sculptor Stephen Tomlin (1901–1937). His eldest son, Anthony, died in New Zealand in 1917, and his middle son, (George) Garrow, was killed in a flying accident in 1931.   LORD MILLETT

Sources DNB · *The Times* (14 Aug 1935) · personal knowledge (1949) [DNB] · personal knowledge (2004) · *The Times* (14 Dec 1931) · 'Judges, law officers ... memoranda', *Law reports: appeal cases* (1935), vii · GEC, *Peerage* · b. cert. · m. cert. · d. cert. · *CGPLA Eng. & Wales* (1935)
Wealth at death £82,880 4s. 9d.: probate, 30 Sept 1935, CGPLA Eng. & Wales

Tomline, Sir George Pretyman, fifth baronet (1750–1827), bishop of Winchester and political adviser, was born George Pretyman at Bury St Edmunds, Suffolk, on 9 October 1750, the eldest son of George Pretyman (1722–1810), landowner and wool dealer, and his wife, Susan (1720/21–1807), daughter of John Hubbard of Bury St Edmunds. A family document claims that the Pretyman pedigree can be traced back to 1362 (Suffolk RO, HA119/T108/45/19), and the family had owned land in Suffolk for many generations. Pretyman's father served as

Sir George Pretyman Tomline, fifth baronet (1750–1827), by John Jackson, exh. RA 1824

one of the capital burgesses of the corporation of Bury St Edmunds.

The young Pretyman was educated at Bury St Edmunds grammar school and matriculated from Pembroke College, Cambridge, in 1768. His mathematical abilities were recognized by the award of the Smith prize and by his status as senior wrangler. He graduated BA in 1772 and MA in 1775. He became a fellow of Pembroke in 1773, and was ordained deacon in the diocese of Norwich on 14 August 1774 and priest in the diocese of Peterborough two years later. When William Pitt the younger was sent as an undergraduate to Pembroke at the age of fourteen, Pretyman became his tutor, confidant, and friend, thus establishing the connection to which, as he frequently admitted, he owed his advancement in the church. He continued to play a part in university affairs, and assisted Pitt in his unsuccessful candidature for the university constituency in the general election of 1780. He served as university moderator in 1781. In 1782 he secured his first ecclesiastical preferment, the sinecure rectory of Corwen, Merioneth. Further preferment rapidly followed. In 1784 he was made a canon of Westminster and was created DD by Cambridge; in 1785 he became rector of Sudbourn-cum-Offord and was elected a fellow of the Royal Society.

The appointment of Pitt as prime minister in December 1783 and his success in the general election the following spring gave Pretyman access to political influence. Pitt appointed him to what was in effect the post of private secretary, although he avoided use of that term lest it hinder Pretyman's career in the church. 'Mr Pitt has given me very good Apartments in his house, where I am to eat, drink & sleep just as I please', wrote Pretyman (n.d., Tomline MS, HA119/T108/45/25). Pitt made full use of his mathematical skills, seeking his advice as to the details of financial policy, notably the sinking fund. Pretyman secured his reward when at the age of thirty-six he became bishop of Lincoln. Pitt had to overcome the resistance of George III, who regarded Pretyman's elevation as a party appointment. The *Gentleman's Magazine* subsequently repeated the familiar story that the king declared of Pretyman: 'Too young, too young—can't have it!' but that when Pitt replied, 'Oh, but please your Majesty, had it not been for Dr P. I should not have been in the office I now hold', the king yielded: 'He shall have it, Pitt—he shall have it, Pitt!' (*GM*, 201). He was consecrated on 11 March 1787 and in the same month was installed as dean of St Paul's. Although Pretyman no longer resided at Downing Street after moving to the bishop's residence at Buckden Palace, Huntingdonshire, he remained on terms of the closest friendship with Pitt, who frequently wrote to 'my dear bishop' to solicit his counsel about senior ecclesiastical appointments. According to George Rose, the secretary to the Treasury, who knew both men well, Pretyman's advice weighed heavily with his patron.

Pretyman married, on 3 September 1784, Elizabeth (*d.* 1826), eldest daughter of Thomas Maltby of Germains, Buckinghamshire; they had three sons. Elizabeth Pretyman's intellectual gifts are evident in her letters to her husband and he took her fully into his confidence over ecclesiastical and political matters. His letters to her form a valuable commentary on significant aspects of public life. After dining with some of his clergy during one of his regular three-yearly visitations, he confided to his wife: 'these public dinners and suppers are dreadful things' (n.d., Tomline MS, HA119/T108/45/1). He was none the less a conscientious diocesan, who conducted eleven visitations during his thirty-three years as bishop of Lincoln. His obituarist tactfully observed: 'Though to the inferior clergy there was unquestionably something over-awing in his presence, arising from their conscientiousness of his superior attainments, yet it was impossible not to admire the courtliness of his manners and the benevolence of his sentiments' (*GM*, 204). He was a loyal, albeit usually silent, supporter of Pitt's ministry in the House of Lords, although duties in his large diocese frequently kept him from London. However, he frequently visited Pitt and was accordingly well informed on public affairs, including the regency crisis of 1788–9. In 1789, preaching the 30 January sermon before the House of Lords, Pretyman showed that he shared Pitt's whiggish opinions by denouncing Charles I and praising those who had resisted him. During the late 1790s he advised Pitt over war finance and proposals for reform of the tithe laws. In 1800 he played an important part in devising Pitt's abortive 'ecclesiastical plan' which featured a scheme to augment clerical livings and to introduce a revised system of episcopal jurisdiction.

Pretyman strongly deplored Pitt's resignation in March 1801 and disagreed with his patron's willingness to countenance Catholic emancipation as a concomitant of the

Act of Union with Ireland. He disapproved of Addington's administration and on more than one occasion urged a reluctant Pitt to return to office. He began to evince a severe anti-Catholicism, warning Pitt to avoid provoking the king by demanding full liberty to enact Catholic emancipation. Pretyman told Pitt in February 1801 that 'in thinking of the Cath. of Ireland he was not to forget the Protestants of England—that there was still, & ought to be, a great Prejudice in this Country against Popery' (Tomline MS, HA119/T108/45/1). His personal friendship with Pitt was unaffected by this difference of policy and in 1801 he took a tactful lead in raising a subscription among Pitt's friends for the relief of the latter's debts; he himself contributed £1000.

Pretyman was already a man of financial substance and in 1803 his family fortune was consolidated when, apparently to his surprise, he inherited a mansion house and a large estate at Riby in Lincolnshire from Marmaduke Tomline. The latter was not a blood relation, and Pretyman estimated that he had not met him more than five or six times. He exulted to his wife that this new property was 'worth two thousand pounds a year!!' (23 June 1803, Tomline MS, HA119/T108/45/1). From this time he took the name Tomline. A further bequest from James Hayes in 1821 brought him several farms in Suffolk which had previously belonged to the Pretyman family.

Until the later 1790s Pretyman had not been noted as a theologian. However, in 1799 he published his two-volume *Elements of Christian Theology*, a work dedicated to Pitt and designed for Anglican ordinands. Its lucidity and accessibility earned it considerable popularity and it reached a twelfth edition in 1818. Several reprints and abridgements were made subsequently and the *Elements* remained in print well into the second half of the nineteenth century. He endeavoured to repudiate the Calvinist interpretation of article 17, arguing that God gave man free agency to accept or reject His offer of salvation and that He foresaw who would accept and who would reject the offer. This, he claimed, was the only sense in which predestination could be reconciled with the attributes of a loving deity. A pamphlet based on this section of the *Elements* appeared in 1822 under the title *A Scriptural Exposition of the Seventeenth Article*. Armed with something approaching a scholarly reputation, Tomline was a serious candidate for the archbishopric of Canterbury on the death of John Moore on 18 January 1805. Pitt had returned to office in 1804 after the renewal of war with France and the dissolution of Addington's ministry. Although he had previously made a tentative agreement with George III that the primacy should be conferred upon Charles Manners-Sutton, bishop of Norwich, Pitt vigorously promoted Tomline's case. The king, however, viewed Pitt's advocacy as importunity, suspected a threat to one of his remaining prerogatives, and insisted on retaining the presentation in his own hands. The ultimate appointment of Manners-Sutton led Pitt to consider resignation and was a bitter disappointment to Tomline and to his wife.

Tomline was present during Pitt's last days in January 1806 and attended him on his deathbed; after his death Tomline took on the role of custodian of his memory. He preached a eulogistic memorial sermon and undertook Pitt's biography. The result was a two-volume work published in 1821 which took the story to 1793; a second edition followed in 1822. Tomline was heavily criticized in several reviews for an excessive dependence on published sources; he also exaggerated Pitt's devotion to the Church of England. His account of Charles James Fox's questionable conduct at the time of the Anglo-Russian negotiations of 1791 involved him in a prolonged controversy with Fox's friend Robert Adair. Although Tomline compiled a further volume, it was never published, apparently as a result of the strictures directed against its predecessors. Pitt's death had removed him from political influence; he respected Lord Grenville but did not share his pro-Catholic sympathies and was relieved at the dismissal of Grenville's 'Talents' ministry in March 1807.

Tomline returned to theological writing and in 1811 he consolidated and extended the message of many of the charges to his clergy in *A Refutation of Calvinism*. He assembled a formidable collection of quotations from the fathers to demonstrate their opposition to Calvinist doctrines and, in chapter 6, argued from detailed evidence that the opinions of many heretics resembled Calvinism. He concluded: 'Our Church is not Lutheran—it is not Calvinistic—it is not Arminian—It is Scriptural: it is built upon the Apostles and Prophets, Jesus Christ himself being the chief corner-stone' (3rd edn, 1811, 590). The *Refutation* achieved considerable success, reaching an eighth edition in 1823, and provoked replies of a high quality, notably from Thomas Scott. In 1812 Tomline strongly denounced the Catholic claims, asserting that 'Protestantism is an essential part of the British Constitution' (G. Tomline, *A Charge Delivered to the Diocese of Lincoln*, 1812, 10); he was strongly attacked in ripostes from the Unitarian John Disney and the latitudinarian Sydney Smith. Although Tomline shared with the older generation of high-churchmen a keen interest in patristic scholarship and an 'eirenicism towards continental Protestantism' (Nockles, 156), his aggressive assertion of the protestant nature of Anglicanism tended to distinguish him from them.

In 1813 Tomline declined the bishopric of London on the death of John Randolph, as he was uneasy about the heavy responsibilities which that diocese would have involved. In July 1820, however, he was nominated bishop of Winchester and was enthroned by proxy on 27 October. He then resigned the deanery of St Paul's. In February 1823 his claim to a Nova Scotia baronetcy, originally conferred by Charles I upon Sir Thomas Pretyman, and dormant since 1749, was confirmed. Although for the rest of his life he was styled Sir George Pretyman Tomline, his descendants relinquished any claim to the title.

Tomline died of apoplexy at Kingston Hall, near Wimborne, Dorset, on 14 November 1827 and was buried in Winchester Cathedral on 28 November. His wife had died on 13 June 1826. He had few qualms about pluralism and also used his influence to advance members of his family in the church. His brother John became archdeacon of Lincoln, his second son George became chancellor of Lincoln and prebendary of Winchester, and his third son Richard became precentor of Lincoln. His eldest son, William Edward, was MP for, successively, Christchurch, Truro, and Minehead. Tomline himself in public created an impression of aloof dignity. James Green's portrait shows him as refined, scholarly, and rather austere. In sympathetic company, however, he was capable of genial informality and he was a devoted husband and parent. He earned the respect of men of such different opinions as Samuel Parr. Particularly from 1806 he was a strong supporter of the existing order in church and state. His influence in the defence of both was considerable.

G. M. DITCHFIELD

Sources Tomline MSS, Suffolk RO, Ipswich · Venn, *Alum. Cant.* · *GM*, 1st ser., 98/1 (1828), 201–4 · Burke, *Gen. GB* (1939) · S. H. Cassan, *The lives of the bishops of Winchester*, 2 vols. (1827) · *Fasti Angl., 1541–1857*, [Lincoln] · *Fasti Angl., 1541–1857*, [Ely] · *Fasti Angl., 1541–1857*, [Canterbury] · G. Pellew, *The life and correspondence of … Henry Addington, first Viscount Sidmouth*, 3 vols. (1847) · *The later correspondence of George III*, ed. A. Aspinall, 5 vols. (1962–70) · Earl Stanhope [P. H. Stanhope], *Life of the Right Honourable William Pitt*, 4 vols. (1861–2) · *The diaries and correspondence of the Right Hon. George Rose*, ed. L. V. V. Harcourt, 2 vols. (1860) · J. Ehrman, *The younger Pitt*, 1: *The years of acclaim* (1969) · J. Ehrman, *The younger Pitt*, 2: *The reluctant transition* (1983) · J. Ehrman, *The younger Pitt*, 3: *The consuming struggle* (1996) · P. B. Nockles, *The Oxford Movement in context: Anglican high churchmanship, 1760–1857* (1994) · J. J. Sack, *From Jacobite to conservative: reaction and orthodoxy in Britain, c. 1760–1832* (1993) · *DNB* · GEC, *Baronetage*
Archives BL, draft biography of William Pitt the Younger thought to be by subject, Add. MS 70827 · BL, drafts of biography of William Pitt, Add. MSS 45107–45108 · CKS, corresp. · Suffolk RO, Ipswich, corresp. and papers | BL, corresp. with Lord Grenville, Add. MS 59003 · BL, letters to Lord Hardwicke, Add. MSS 35641–35753, *passim* · BL, corresp. with earls of Liverpool, Add. MSS 38220–38300, 38474, 38571 · BL, corresp. with George Rose, Add. MS 42773 · CKS, corresp. with William Pitt and others · NMM, letters to Sir John Orde · Pembroke Cam., letters to W. Hughes
Likenesses J. Jackson, oils, exh. RA 1824, bishop's palace, Wolvesey, Winchester [*see illus.*] · R. Cooper, stipple (after H. Edridge), BM, NPG; repro. in *Contemporary Portraits* (1814) · J. Green, oils, bishops' house, Lincoln · H. Meyer, stipple (after J. Jackson), BM, NPG · C. Thomas, line engraving (after W. H. Brown), BM; repro. in *The Senator* (1791)
Wealth at death £200,000 personal effects: *GM*, 204 · land in Lymington, Boldre, Pennington, and Milford in Hampshire; also estate and house at Riby, Lincolnshire: will, PRO, PROB 11/1733, fol. 218v

Tomlins, Elizabeth Sophia (1763–1828), novelist, was born in London, the eldest of four daughters and second of (at least) five children born to Thomas Tomlins, esq. (*d.* 1815), a solicitor and clerk of the Painter–Stainers' Company, and his wife, about whom nothing is known. One of her nephews was the publisher and playwright Frederick Guest *Tomlins (1804–1867), who later succeeded his grandfather and uncle to the clerkship of the company.

With her elder brother, Sir Thomas Edlyne *Tomlins (1762–1841), Tomlins co-published her first known work, *Tributes of Affection: with a Slave and other Poems*, by 'A Lady and her Brother'. The collection includes sonnets, ballads, birthday pieces, and trifles, one of which provides a slight

description of the woman herself. 'To Eliza; Gardening', signed by her brother ('E') and dated 1790, mourns the waste of her maidenly personal attractions, a 'beauty and talent' later corroborated by her obituary in the *Gentleman's Magazine* in 1828. As a poet she is best known for 'The Slave' (signed 'S'), with its twin themes of personal liberty and politics in which the 'noble' slave Quashi, on the point of gaining freedom, chooses suicide over revenge. Reflecting the political climate in England, other anti-slavery poems in the collection include 'Wilberforce' and the closing poem, 'To the House of Commons, on their Vote for the Abolition of the Slave-Trade, April 2, 1792', signed by her brother. Eschewing the feminine tradition of writing exclusively of the personal, Tomlins's contributions incorporate the classical mode, along with a ballad trilogy of love, betrayal, and death, 'Connal' (1782), 'Mary' (1783), and 'Athol' (1784), published also in 'Dr. Langhorne's collection' (*GM*, 1st ser., 98).

As a novelist Tomlins's style shifted from early sentimentalism and didacticism to a post-1797 realism about deprivations of economics and personal freedom facing the working woman. Her first novel, *The Conquests of the Heart: a Novel. By a Young Lady* (1785), is a highly romanticized biography of a Jamaican friend, the subject of two poems, 'To R. N.' and 'To the same Friend'. The introduction to *Tributes of Affection* indicates that Tomlins and he ('R. N.') collaborated on the novel. During the same period Tomlins wrote *The Victim of Fancy* (1787), published also as *La victime de l'imagination, ou, L'enthousiaste de Werther*, whose Goethe-inspired heroine Theresa Morven acts out her life (and death) like a character in the current fiction, such as Sophia Lee's *The Recess*, on which she feeds. Between 1780 and 1827 other writings included a translation of the history of Napoleon Bonaparte and many periodical essays (*GM*, 1st ser., 98). During the gap between her early and later canon (after 1797), Tomlins subsumed her personal 'advantages' to her 'severe' father's directives; she assumed the duties of governess to his 'innumerable' children, in addition to attending his professional desk which she 'actually superintended' during the final seven years of his life (ibid.).

Rosalind de Tracey (1798) and an earlier novel, *Memoirs of a Baroness* (1792), while conventionally moralistic, also insert portrayals of the marginalized, especially the poor working woman. In a defence of the novel genre Tomlins claims to promote 'fortitude in affliction' (*Rosalind de Tracey*, vi) and female friendship. Tomlins's novels feature the lone female character who ventures haplessly into public commercialized space. Like the Baroness D'Alantun, Rosalind undergoes abduction and violence in London, a venue for Tomlins's true-to-life vignettes of working women, such as governesses, and women lacemakers dying in squalid conditions as they ply their trade to bedeck the rich.

After her father's death in 1815 Tomlins moved to The Firs, a family cottage in Chalden, Surrey, with three sisters and their mother. Returning to her 'fascination' with poetry, she had commenced a poem of 'considerable length', but, after falling from a pony on 7 August 1828, she died at Chalden in an 'apparent fainting fit' on 8 August 1828 (*GM*, 1st ser., 98), and was buried in the parish church there on 15 August.   POLLY STEVENS FIELDS

Sources *GM*, 1st ser., 98/2 (1828), 471 · *GM*, 2nd ser., 16 (1841), 321–2 [obit. of Sir T. E. Tomlins] · Blain, Clements & Grundy, *Feminist comp.*, 1086–7 · J. Todd, ed., *A dictionary of British and American women writers, 1660–1800* (1984) · Allibone, *Dict.* · K. Povey, 'Elizabeth Sophia Tomlins', *N&Q*, 154 (11 Feb 1928)

Tomlins, Frederick Guest (1804–1867), journalist, was born in August 1804. Little is known of his family or education. He married on 3 May 1829 Jane Vasey. His career began with contributions to periodicals such as Henry Hetherington's *Poor Man's Guardian* in 1831. In 1834 he became associated with Thomas Mayhew in the publication of the Penny National Library, for which he edited, among other works, the *Variorum History of England from Rapin to Hume* (1836). For a long time afterwards he was in the employment of Whittaker & Co., publishers, London, as publishing clerk and literary assistant to George Byrom Whittaker. Soon after Whittaker's death in 1847 Tomlins commenced business as a publisher in Southampton Street, Strand, London, and there issued his own periodicals, *The Self-Educator* and *The Topic*, which, however, were not very successful. He next opened a shop for new and second-hand books in Great Russell Street, Bloomsbury, near the British Museum, but after a while he abandoned business for literary pursuits.

Tomlins was well acquainted with Shakespeare and Shakespearian literature; he founded the Shakespeare Society in 1840 and acted as the society's secretary for the twelve years of its existence. His interest in the theatre dated back to his childhood, when he had seen Edmund Kean appear in the role of Shylock in *The Merchant of Venice* at the Drury Lane Theatre in January 1814; this interest led him to publish various works on drama: *The Past and Present State of Dramatic Art and Literature* (1839) and, in 1841, *A brief view of the English drama, with suggestions for elevating the present condition of the art, The Nature and State of the English Drama*, and *The Relative Value of Acted and Unacted Drama*. Tomlins also tried his hand at writing his own tragedy, *Garcia, or, The Noble Error*, which was produced at the Sadler's Wells Theatre in December 1849. From 1850 to his death he acted as the dramatic and fine-art critic of the *Morning Advertiser*. For a while he was also sub-editor, and later proprietor, of *Douglas Jerrold's Weekly Newspaper*. In 1865 he became the political editor of the *Weekly Times*, to which he contributed a series of letters signed Littlejohn, and was also editorially connected with *The Leader* soon after it started.

On the death of his uncle, in 1864, Tomlins succeeded him as clerk of the Painter–Stainers' Company, an office which had been held by his grandfather. Tomlins died at the Painter–Stainers' Hall, Little Trinity Lane, Queenhithe, London, where he had been living, on 21 September 1867, and was buried at St Peter's Church, Croydon, on 27 September. He was survived by his wife and a daughter, who married a cousin in the merchant navy and subsequently went to Australia with her husband.

NILANJANA BANERJI

Sources *The Era* (29 Sept 1867) · *The Bookseller* (30 Sept 1867) · Allibone, *Dict.* · D. Griffiths, ed., *The encyclopedia of the British press, 1422–1992* (1992) · Ward, *Men of the reign* · *Men of the time* (1865) · *DNB*
Archives U. Edin. L., corresp. with James Halliwell-Phillipps
Wealth at death under £600: probate, 29 Oct 1867, *CGPLA Eng. & Wales*

Tomlins, Sir Thomas Edlyne (1762–1841), legal writer, was born in London on 4 January 1762, the eldest son of Thomas Tomlins (d. 1815), solicitor and clerk to the Company of Painter–Stainers. Elizabeth Sophia *Tomlins (1763–1828) was his sister. The family was descended from the Tomlins of the neighbourhood of Ledbury in Herefordshire and of Hereford. Thomas Edlyne was admitted a scholar at St Paul's School on 21 September 1769. He matriculated from Queen's College, Oxford, on 27 October 1778, and was called to the bar by the society of the Inner Temple in Hilary term 1783.

For some years Tomlins was editor of the *St James's Chronicle*, a daily newspaper, and on 30 May 1801 he was appointed counsel to the chief secretary for Ireland. In the same year he became parliamentary counsel to the chancellor of the exchequer for Ireland, a post which he retained until the union of the British and Irish treasuries in 1816. He was knighted at Wanstead House on 29 June 1814, on the recommendation of the duke of Wellington. In 1818 he was appointed assistant counsel to the Treasury. In Hilary term 1823 he was elected a bencher of the Inner Temple, and in 1827 he filled the office of treasurer to the society. In January 1831, on the whigs' coming into office, he retired from his post in the Treasury. He died a widower on 1 July 1841 at St Mary Castlegate, York.

Tomlins was a prolific writer. Among other works, he wrote *A Familiar Explanation of the Law of Wills and Codicils* (1785), a clear account of the subject for the layman, which reached a seventh edition in 1819. His new edition of Giles Jacob's *Law Dictionary* (1797) was equally successful, and he produced further editions, under his own name, until 1838.

Sir Thomas's nephew, **Thomas Edlyne Tomlins** (1804–1872), legal writer and antiquary, was the son of Sir Thomas's brother Alfred Tomlins, a clerk in the Irish exchequer office, Paradise Row, Lambeth. He entered St Paul's School on 6 February 1811, and was admitted to practice in London as an attorney in the Michaelmas term of 1827.

Tomlins's legal publications included a popular law dictionary (1838) and an edition of Sir Thomas Littleton's *Treatise of Tenures* (1841). As an antiquary he translated the *Chronicles* of Jocelin of Brakelond (1844) and published an account of the environs of Islington (1844).

E. I. CARLYLE, *rev.* JONATHAN HARRIS

Sources *GM*, 2nd ser., 16 (1841), 321–2 · R. B. Gardiner, ed., *The admission registers of St Paul's School, from 1748 to 1876* (1884), 145, 241 · Foster, *Alum. Oxon.* · Holdsworth, *Eng. law*, 12.176, 395–6 · Holdsworth, *Eng. law*, 15.274–5 · Boase, *Mod. Eng. biog.* · Allibone, *Dict.*
Archives Inner Temple, London | BL, legal opinions and corresp. with Robert Peel, Add. MSS 40198–40378, *passim* · Lincoln's Inn, London, extracts from Clerkenwell cartularies

Tomlins, Thomas Edlyne (1804–1872). *See under* Tomlins, Sir Thomas Edlyne (1762–1841).

Tomlinson [*née* Bamford], **Annie** (1870–1933), journalist and co-operator, was born at 26 Ashworth Street, Rochdale, Lancashire, on 29 June 1870, the daughter of Samuel Bamford (1848–1898), wool sorter and from 1875 editor of the *Co-operative News*, and his wife, Elizabeth Maskew (1846–1923). Annie's younger brother, William (1873–1921), became sub-editor, and on Samuel's death, editor of the *Co-operative News*. The family moved to Manchester, where Annie was educated at Manchester High School for Girls. She benefited from her parents' advanced attitudes, enjoying, according to Lucy Sugar, a 'magnificent freedom … both in education, social life, speech, and broad thought' (*Co-operative News*, 13).

After attending a meeting addressed by Margaret Llewelyn Davies, the general secretary of the Women's Co-operative Guild (WCG), Annie Bamford undertook a lifetime commitment to the WCG, which built on her strong understanding of co-operation. Enthusiastic and energetic, at twenty-two she became secretary of the north-western section of the WCG, a position she held for more than ten years. She was also secretary of the Manchester, Downing Street, branch, and helped establish Manchester's Levenshulme branch. A prolific and popular speaker, 'fluent and vigorous', she was much in demand at guild meetings.

In 1901 Annie Bamford met Charles Ernest Tomlinson (*b.* 1874/5), a journalist, when they both covered the WCG annual congress in Blackpool; he was the son of Charles Henry Tomlinson, a marine engineer. They married shortly afterwards, on 5 March 1904, and Charles demonstrated an equal commitment to co-operation, becoming editor of *Millgate Monthly*, then foreign editor for Co-operative Wholesale Society publications. As companions and partners, their marriage was built on shared ideals and interests, and in keeping with the vision of marriage prominent within WCG literature.

Annie Tomlinson's own journalistic career began through assisting her father and brother at the *Co-operative News*, and filing regular reports in the 'Notes for women' section of the *Manchester and Salford Co-operative Herald*. In 1904 she became editor of 'Women's corner', a column in *Co-operative News* started twenty years earlier by Alice Acland, and she retained the editorship until her death, when she was succeeded by (Charlotte) Mary Stott. During her period as an editor, the number of co-operative publications aimed at women and children expanded: *Our Circle*, 'for young people' (1907); sixteen pages for women's issues in the *Millgate Monthly* (1918); *Women's Outlook* (1919); followed by *Sunshine Stories* and *Sunshine Annual*.

As a journalist and editor Annie Tomlinson was staunchly loyal to the WCG, 'capable of championing their cause in every way' (*Co-operative News*, 12). Committed to equality for women 'in all directions', she actively supported the WCG over suffrage and divorce law reform. This loyalty was vitally important during the divorce law reform controversy of 1914–18, when the Co-operative Union withheld the WCG's annual grant. 'Women's corner' regularly included articles on divorce law reform and

self-government, despite pressure from the instigators of the controversy, Salford Catholic Federation. Under her editorial influence, articles on pioneering and controversial women appeared in *Women's Outlook*. Her humour, enthusiasm, and sympathetic character contributed to her popularity among guildswomen. She encouraged links with women co-operators abroad, attended international guild congresses, and was credited with founding a co-operative guild in Czechoslovakia. She also served on the committee of the North-Western Co-operative Convalescent Homes. She died at her home, 24 Clevedon Road, Blackpool, on 6 April 1933, and was buried in Rochdale cemetery on 10 April; she was survived by her husband. JACQUELINE BURNETT

Sources *Co-operative News* (15 April 1933) · *Women's Outlook* (29 April 1933) · Women's Co-operative Guild, BLPES, Coll. misc. 0268, vol. 8/89, fol. 123 · b. cert. · m. cert. · Rochdale cemetery records · *Annual reports* [Women's Co-operative Guild] · G. Scott, *Feminism and the politics of working women* (1998) · G. Scott, 'Working out their own salvation', *New views of Co-operation*, ed. S. Yeo (1988) · *Catholic Federationist* · *Forgetting's no excuse: the autobiography of Mary Stott* (1989)
Wealth at death £8540 2s. 7d.: administration, 10 May 1933, CGPLA Eng. & Wales

Tomlinson, Charles (1808–1897), science teacher and writer, was born on 27 November 1808 in Tottenham, Middlesex, the younger son of Charles Tomlinson. His father sought to better his condition by enlisting in 1810 but, after serving in Holland, died on the way to India, leaving a widow in straitened circumstances to raise Charles and his elder brother, Lewis (1806–1880). The boys went first to a dame-school then to a large day school for boys. Charles's first employment was in the office of Joseph Woods, architect of the Corn Exchange. He next worked on transcribing *Pepys's Diary*, and afterwards was for some years in a lawyer's office. During this time he went to evening classes at the London Mechanics' Institute to study science, and also learned French. Lewis meanwhile maintained himself as a clerk at Wadham College, Oxford, graduated BA in 1829, took holy orders and became classics master in a school in Berkshire. When a vacancy arose in 1830 Charles joined him, teaching elementary Latin and French. A few years later Lewis obtained a curacy near Salisbury, and with his brother founded a school in the city where Charles taught modern languages and experimental science. At this time the brothers married the sisters of one of their students: Charles married Sarah Windsor (d. 1872), and Lewis married her elder sister, Maria (d. 1880).

Charles continued to improve his knowledge of science by attending lectures at University College, London, and elsewhere. Articles he contributed to popular science journals were, with others, reissued in 1838 as *The Student's Manual of Natural Philosophy*, which enjoyed a rapid sale and encouraged him in 1848 to leave Salisbury and settle in London. His connection with Parker's publishing house brought Tomlinson into contact with various men of science, among them Sir William Snow Harris, with whom he collaborated on the development of lightning conductors for ships. He gave editorial assistance to the chemist

William Thomas Brande, and to John Frederick Daniell, who was preparing a new edition of his *Meteorology*. When Daniell died in 1845 Tomlinson and William Allen Miller saw it into print. Tomlinson's wife, who was from an evangelical family, assisted him in all his work, and also wrote books of a moral and religious persuasion for the Society for Promoting Christian Knowledge.

Being by this time a familiar figure at King's College, London, Tomlinson was appointed lecturer in experimental science at King's College School. He took a large house in Hampstead Road where some of the scholars boarded, bringing a family atmosphere to his childless marriage. Tomlinson continued to write on a broad range of scientific and literary topics, but regarded his *Cyclopedia of Useful Arts* (1852, enlarged edition 1866) as his major production, coming as it did in the aftermath of the 1851 exhibition when industry and manufacture were advancing rapidly. In addition, his investigation of the behaviour of camphor, and other light and heavy fluids when added to water, led to important theories concerning surface tension of liquids.

Tomlinson's sight worsened in the late 1850s and by 1860, despite a visit to a celebrated German oculist, he was blind in one eye. He nevertheless remained active, being elected to the council of the British Association for the Advancement of Science in 1864, and in the same year to fellowship of the Chemical Society. In 1867 he was elected fellow of the Royal Society, serving for many years on its library committee. He retired from teaching in 1866 and moved to Highgate where he continued his experiments in a laboratory fitted up in his house. After several months' illness his wife died in 1872. In his later years Tomlinson turned to literature and the study of poetry, and from 1878 to 1880 he held the Dante lectureship at University College, London. Lewis and Maria Tomlinson both died in 1880 and their daughter Mary moved to Highgate to care for her uncle, who at seventy-three was still mentally and physically active and insisted on her learning to play chess. Latterly he was more frequently ill, and died at his home, 7 North Road, on 15 February 1897. He was buried at Highgate cemetery alongside his wife.

E. I. CARLYLE, rev. ANITA McCONNELL

Sources *The Times* (16 Feb 1897), 12d · *Biograph and Review*, 6 (1881), 265–70 · M. Tomlinson, *The life of Charles Tomlinson* (1900) · RS
Likenesses photograph, 1887, repro. in Tomlinson, *Life*, frontispiece
Wealth at death £10,912 8s. 3d.: probate, 5 April 1897, *CGPLA Eng. & Wales*

Tomlinson, David Cecil MacAlister (1917–2000), actor, was born on 7 May 1917 at Rosedene, St Andrew's Road, Henley-on-Thames, Oxfordshire, the son of Clarence Samuel Tomlinson, a solicitor, and his wife, Florence Elizabeth Sinclair-Thomson. Later in life he learned that his father, instead of staying at his London club during the week, as he claimed, had been living with his mistress in Chiswick, with whom he had seven children. Tomlinson was educated at Tonbridge School in Kent. There followed a period in the Grenadier Guards, but he bought himself out after sixteen months; he then worked for a time as a clerk at

David Cecil MacAlister Tomlinson (1917–2000), by Daniel Farson, 1953 [in his dressing room at the Lyric Theatre while appearing in *The Little Hut*]

Shell-Mex in London while seeking work in the theatre. After appearing in some amateur productions he found a temporary home with Folkestone repertory theatre, in bit parts and sometimes as stage manager: his first professional, non-speaking part was in Barrie's *Quality Street*. He then joined John Gielgud's company, where he was understudy for Alec Guinness. His London début was in *The Merchant of Venice*, and this was followed by parts in lighter plays, including *George and Margaret* and *A Quiet Wedding*. The director Anthony Asquith spotted him as the bridegroom on tour in the latter and offered him the part of the best man in the film version (1940). He had made his film début that year in a minor musical, *Garrison's Follies*. He played in several other films, including *Pimpernel Smith* (1941), before war service intervened. Already a qualified pilot, Tomlinson joined the RAF, spending part of his service as a flying instructor in Canada and ending the war as a flight lieutenant.

After the war Tomlinson returned to the screen in Asquith's *The Way to the Stars* (1945) as PO 'Prune' Parsons, and between 1946 and 1949 he made a further eighteen films. Many were light comedies in which he played dimwits or buffoons, an amiable duffer or an endearing ditherer, with 'bewildered and lugubrious features, full mouth drawn down in harmless but permanent perplexity' (*The Guardian*, 26 June 2000). He was a boffin who sacrifices himself in the attempt to perfect radar in *School for Secrets* (1946), a mill owner's pampered son in *Master of Bankdam* (1947), and was very good in *Miranda* (1948); but it was his performance as a young viscount who, to avoid army service, stands for parliament as a Labour Party candidate, only to be beaten by his own butler, in *The Chiltern Hundreds* (1949), that really established him as a star.

In 1950 Tomlinson was back in the theatre, in the three-hander *The Little Hut* with Robert Morley and Joan Tetzel; it enjoyed a long run at the Lyric. (Morley became a lifelong friend, and they once co-owned a racehorse.) He appeared in another hit, *All for Mary* (1954–5), with Kathleen Harrison at the Duke of York's, although their film version (1955) failed. He returned to the stage occasionally, and usually successfully, until the mid-1970s. On 17 May 1953 he married Audrey Freeman (*b*. 1931/2), an actress. They had four sons. In 1956 he was in court, charged with reckless flying, after his Tiger Moth crashed near his home in Mursley, Buckinghamshire.

On screen, Tomlinson was amusing in the exciting, true-life story of escape from Stalag Luft 3, *The Wooden Horse*, and played the brother who mysteriously disappears in *So Long at the Fair* (both 1950). He had his first top billing in *Castles in the Air* (1952), and played J in the curiously flat *Three Men in a Boat* (1956). *Carry on Admiral* (1957) was a vigorous but dated farce, but another broad farce, *Up the Creek* (1958), in which he played a scatterbrained rocket-mad naval officer opposite Peter Sellers, another long-time friend, was much better. Styles in British films were changing, but after playing Lord Fellamar in *Tom Jones* (1963) Tomlinson's career was given a new boost when Walt Disney, who had seen him in *Ring of Truth* (1959) at the Savoy, cast him in *Mary Poppins* (1964). Tomlinson hit all the right notes in a finely judged performance as the very proper London banker George Banks, a stern father who runs his house like clockwork until melted by the charm of a magical nanny (Julie Andrews) and the joys of kite flying. The film was hugely successful, won five Oscars, and became an evergreen family favourite.

Most of Tomlinson's remaining films were aimed primarily at a family audience. Again for Disney, he appeared in *The Love Bug* (1969) as the villainous Thorndyke trying to sabotage Herbie, the Volkswagen with a mind of its own, and in *Bedknobs and Broomsticks* (1971) he sang and danced with animated characters in a musical fantasy. Two films he made with the director Lionel Jeffries, *Wombling Free* (1977) and *The Water Babies* (1978), were much less successful. He made his final film, *The Fiendish Plot of Dr Fu Manchu*, in 1980. This was also Peter Sellers's last film, an unfunny swansong for two distinguished screen careers.

Though he was often a professional idiot on screen, Tomlinson invested wisely, and he retired to spend much more time with his family, though he was still often seen at first nights and film premières. He wrote his autobiography, *Luckier than most*, in 1990. Away from acting he was fond of ornithology and antiques, and was an active fund-raiser in aid of autism, helping to found Somerset Court, the first residential home in Europe specifically for autistic adults. Tomlinson died, after a series of strokes over several months, at Beaumont House, Beaumont Street, Westminster, on 24 June 2000.   ROBERT SHARP

Sources *The Times* (26 June 2000) · *Daily Telegraph* (26 June 2000) · *The Independent* (26 June 2000) · *The Guardian* (26 June 2000) · *The Guardian* (5 July 2000) · *The Scotsman* (27 June 2000) · *WWW* · www. uk.imdb.com, 9 Feb 2001 · www.obits.com, 9 Feb 2001 · b. cert. · m. cert. · d. cert.
Archives Bodl. Oxf., letters to J. W. Lambert

Likenesses D. Farson, photograph, 1953, Hult. Arch. [*see illus.*] · photograph, 1964, repro. in *The Times* · photograph, 1969, repro. in *The Scotsman* · photograph, repro. in *Guardian* (26 June 2000)
Wealth at death £2,595,981—gross; £2,590,457—net: probate, 26 April 2001, *CGPLA Eng. & Wales*

Tomlinson, George (1890–1952), politician, was born on 21 March 1890 in the industrial village of Rishton, Lancashire. He was the son of John Wesley Tomlinson, a weaver, and his wife, Alice Varley, also a weaver prior to marriage. George was the youngest of four children; he had two brothers and a sister.

The Tomlinsons were a thrifty, hard-working family struggling to survive on the small wages paid to late Victorian textile workers. George was educated at Rishton Wesleyan school, where slates not exercise books were the norm and where his high spirits led to frequent beatings. By the age of twelve he had become a 'half-timer', spending half his time at school and the remainder of his day at the local mill. A year later he followed in his father's footsteps when he was taken on full-time at the mill, earning 5*s*. for a 56-hour week.

In adolescence Tomlinson developed his own views on the issues that were most widely discussed at home and in the workplace—religion, politics, and cricket. His horizons were extended by avid reading, for which he was reprimanded at work. His mother remonstrated that 'them books just put ideas into year 'ead', something he reflected on in later life. '*Dear* soul, she didn't know that that was what books are for' (Blackburn, 30). After much study he became a Methodist lay preacher, though he was unsuccessful when applying for full-time ministry.

Politics, which like his father he regarded as inseparable from Christianity, became increasingly important in Tomlinson's life. He joined the Independent Labour Party, was elected to the local urban district council, and became at the age of twenty-two president of the Rishton District Weavers' Association. The latter post marked him out as a young man of potential. It provided him with opportunities to develop a highly effective speaking style: witty, yet with serious intent, and delivered in a rich Lancashire accent.

Tomlinson's political prospects were greatly set back, however, by the outbreak of the First World War. As a Christian pacifist he denounced the 'imperialist' conflict from both platform and pulpit, and when his appeal for exemption from military service was upheld he was ordered to find employment of national importance away from home. For three years he worked as an agricultural labourer near Manchester, trying to maintain a wife and young daughter back in Rishton on meagre wages. In 1914 he had married Ethel Pursell, a fellow mill worker, who was to be a loving companion for the remainder of his life; there were no other children.

During the inter-war years Tomlinson gradually established himself in local politics. He was elected to Farnworth urban district council, becoming chairman of the education committee (1928), and in 1931 he was returned as a member of Lancashire county council. Education was his area of particular interest, and in 1934 he became vice-president of the Association of Education Committees. He secured the Labour nomination for the parliamentary constituency of Farnworth, and at a by-election in January 1938 he increased the party's majority in defeating his National Conservative opponent, Felix Ryan. He held the Farnworth seat until his death.

Tomlinson adapted quickly to life as a back-bench MP in the House of Commons. He became a popular and highly regarded speaker, making frequent interventions in debates on agriculture, education, and the textile industry—issues on which he spoke with humour and sincerity, as well as with knowledge based on his working life and his experience in local government.

Tomlinson's qualities were recognized when in February 1941 he was appointed as joint parliamentary secretary at the Ministry of Labour and National Service in Churchill's wartime coalition. This meant working for Ernest Bevin, whom Tomlinson later called the greatest man he ever met, a figure who made an incalculable contribution to Britain's war effort on the home front. Bevin, in turn, had a high regard for 'young George', as he called him, making him responsible for the welfare of merchant seamen, the transference of textile workers to munitions, and the resettlement of disabled workers. Tomlinson was given much of the credit for a new employment act designed to assist the disabled, which was approved by the House of Commons in 1944.

After Labour's landslide election victory in 1945, the new prime minister, Attlee, promoted Tomlinson by making him minister of works. Although he established good relations with his civil servants and worked conscientiously, this first experience of running a department proved frustrating. He lamented that he had been put in charge of building materials when 'there weren't any'. House building had virtually ceased during the war. Materials and labour remained in short supply, and Tomlinson had to shoulder the blame for the government's tardiness in undertaking its emergency housing scheme. His difficulties were compounded by being outside the cabinet and having to defer to the Ministry of Health, which retained control over the long-term housing programme.

In February 1947 Attlee decided that Tomlinson was worthy of a place in the cabinet following the death of the minister of education, Ellen Wilkinson. This fulfilled for Tomlinson his highest political ambition. Unlike some who regarded the position simply as a stepping stone to higher office, Tomlinson relished the chance of becoming minister of education. In his eyes, the education department offered the ideal means of giving young people the type of opportunities he had been denied in his early life, and over the next few years he brought great application and enthusiasm to the job.

The framework for policy when Tomlinson went to the ministry had largely been determined by the passage of the 1944 Education Act, which had received cross-party support during the wartime coalition as a key feature of post-war reconstruction. The act proposed that, instead of the majority of children attending elementary schools from age five to fourteen, every child over the age of eleven should have access to free secondary education, hitherto confined to a mostly fee-paying élite. Two of the most urgent priorities, if the act were to be made a reality, were to provide adequate school buildings and to find ways of recruiting and training sufficient qualified teachers. Both of these problems had been exacerbated by the war and by the pledge, contained in the act, to raise the school-leaving age from fourteen to fifteen.

In spite of opposition at a time of economic hardship, Ellen Wilkinson had secured cabinet agreement to go ahead with the raising of the leaving age shortly before her death. Tomlinson's task was to provide an extra 400,000 school places by autumn 1948, a challenge he met by assuming close personal control of the building programme while working harmoniously with local education authorities. The steady increase of new places and the rapid increase in the output of trained teachers proved to be two of Tomlinson's most notable achievements.

Despite progress on these and other policy issues, such as the provision of school meals and free milk, Tomlinson's record has been criticized by distinguished historians such as Kenneth Morgan and Brian Simon. The central charge is that Attlee's government, with its massive parliamentary majority, missed a chance to bring about decisive change in education. No attempts were made to integrate the independent schools into the state sector, and, in spite of pressure from party activists, especially teachers, there was little government support for the common, or comprehensive, secondary school. Instead Tomlinson promoted a tripartite system—grammar schools, secondary moderns, and technical schools—which perpetuated the deep class divisions in British society.

Other writers take a more sympathetic view. Peter Gosden notes that government priorities were locked into place when Tomlinson took over, notably with the decision to raise the school-leaving age. This, together with a steep rise in the post-war birth rate, left him no choice but to focus on increasing school places. His success in this must be set against the enormous physical and financial problems facing Britain in the aftermath of war, highlighting the minister's considerable resolve in defending his department in relation to other social services. Educational expenditure continued to rise after 1947, though the rate of increase slowed down, and the priority Tomlinson secured for education was not maintained when the Conservatives returned to power in the 1950s.

On the issue of tripartitism, this too was strongly embedded in ministry thinking by 1947. There was a rising feeling among Labour educationists that the introduction of comprehensives was vital if hierarchical structures were to be broken down. But there was an equally strong belief that the real advance had been secured with the passage of the 1944 act. The pressing need was to make a reality of the vision of secondary education for all—to confront the difficult task of ensuring that every child over the age of eleven received schooling of a length and quality that had not been known before the war.

For Tomlinson, comprehensives were suitable on an experimental basis, particularly in scattered rural districts. But he regarded a wholesale move to the common school as unnecessary and financially prohibitive. It was widely hoped that it would be possible to achieve 'parity of esteem' between different types of secondary schools, catering for children according to their ages, aptitudes, and abilities. Only later, when the new system became operational, did it become apparent that parity of esteem was an elusive goal. While the prestigious grammar schools were highly sought after by middle-class families, the majority of working-class children languished in the markedly inferior secondary moderns.

Tomlinson's final months at the ministry were overshadowed by illness. He underwent a major operation for cancer from which he never fully recovered, writing his election address for the general election of October 1951 on hospital notepaper. He secured a comfortable majority at Farnworth, but the Conservatives' national victory sealed his departure from office and his return to the opposition back-benches. Tomlinson's poor health meant he was able to make only one speech in the new parliament, and he was never able to fulfil his ambition of retiring to a cottage in Blackpool with his wife. After his death in Manor House Hospital, Golders Green, on 22 September 1952, Attlee paid him a warm tribute as a fine servant of the labour movement and a 'great human being', a man of enormous charm, vitality, and good sense.

KEVIN JEFFERYS

Sources F. Blackburn, *George Tomlinson* (1954) · *DNB* · *The Times* (23 Sept 1952) · K. O. Morgan, *Labour in power, 1945–1951* (1984) · B. Simon, *Education and the social order, 1940–1990* (1991) · P. H. J. H. Gosden, *Education in the Second World War: a study in policy and administration* (1976) · R. Barker, *Education and politics, 1900–1951: a study of the labour party* (1972)
Archives FILM BFI NFTVA, current affairs footage · BFI NFTVA, documentary footage · BFI NFTVA, news footage
Likenesses W. Stoneman, photograph, 1945, NPG · photographs, Hult. Arch.

Tomlinson, Henry Major (1873–1958), journalist and novelist, was born at 41 Paynton Street, Poplar, London, on 21 June 1873, the eldest in the family of three sons and one daughter of Henry Tomlinson, cooper, and his wife, Emily Major, daughter of a master gunner in the navy. His father became a foreman at the West India Dock, and as a boy Tomlinson became familiar with ships and seamen and the lure of the sea. After his father's death in 1886 he was taken from school and placed in a City shipping office as a clerk at a wage of 6s. a week. He knew poverty and remembered it all his life; but with his mother's encouragement he soon began to read widely, especially in the history of travel and navigation, and in time he turned to the study of geology, to which he added botany, zoology, and mineralogy. In 1894 he was considered as a possible geologist for the Jackson–Harmsworth polar expedition, but, much to his disappointment, was advised that his health would not stand the strain. On 26 December 1899 he married Florence Margaret (b. 1873/4), a dressmaker, daughter of Thomas Hammond, ship's chandler. They had one son and two daughters.

Tomlinson grew increasingly restive in his office occupation although his frequent opportunities for visiting the ships and the docks were a source of inspiration for much of his future writing; the docklands were, he said, 'his university' (*The Times*, 6 Feb 1958, 10). It was not until 1904, however, that, after an office quarrel, he applied for a job with the radical *Morning Leader*, a paper to which he had already contributed. He was engaged as a reporter, and his love of the sea was soon turned to good account by his editor, Ernest Parke, who sent him to live for several weeks, in midwinter, with a fleet of trawlers on the Dogger Bank, followed by an assignment to the naval manoeuvres. Parke later made him still happier by sending him, ostensibly as ship's purser, on a voyage to Brazil and 2000 miles up the Amazon and Madeira rivers in the first English steamer to make that passage. His first book, *The Sea and the Jungle*, followed from this in 1912. The beauty of the prose and the descriptive writing showed Tomlinson to be a new author of unusual quality, and the book appeared in many subsequent editions. Tomlinson was also at this time contributing to the *English Review* edited by Ford Madox Hueffer (later Ford).

When the *Morning Leader* was amalgamated with the *Daily News* in 1912 Tomlinson stayed on as a leader writer; he became a war correspondent in Belgium and France in August 1914 and was official correspondent at British general headquarters in France in 1914–17. It was in France in 1917 that Tomlinson met H. W. Massingham, who later offered him the post of assistant editor of *The Nation*, where he remained until 1923.

In this time Tomlinson's renown as a writer grew. He was at his best with the 'evocative power' of his travel sketches and personal reflections in collections such as *Old Junk* (1918), *Waiting for Daylight* (1922), and *Gifts of Fortune* (1926). He travelled widely, and while *London River* (1921) was a moving book of memories and contemplations on the theme nearest his heart, *Tidemarks* (1924) took the reader to the islands and straits of the Dutch East Indies. His first novel, *Gallions Reach* (1927), which was awarded the Femina Vie Heureuse prize, was acclaimed as an important work on both sides of the Atlantic. Yet, although Tomlinson was a born descriptive writer, he was not a born novelist. His fiction was criticized for containing too many of his own 'strict, moral notions', and that he lacked the 'detachment to be either a good critic or a good novelist' (Swinnerton, 166). His next book, *All Our Yesterdays* (1930), a story of the First World War, demonstrated clearly that he was more of a poet, journalist, philosopher, and student of humanity, than an inventor of plot and fictional character.

Tomlinson continued to produce novels until the end of his life. His writings became increasingly permeated by a hatred of war—specifically proclaimed in *Mars His Idiot* (1935)—but they also showed a redeeming belief in the supreme value of individual personality. Tomlinson's political views were based on the fact that 'he still believes in the opposition of virtue and vice'. In his novels he was said to preach 'old-fashioned Liberalism' (Swinnerton, 165). Although his later work was somewhat uneven, he still demonstrated his talent as an essayist in collections such as *The Turn of the Tide* (1945), while *A Mingled Yarn* (1953), a series of autobiographical sketches, showed him at his characteristic best in reminiscence and description. In his last book, *The Trumpet Shall Sound* (1957), the story of the impact of the blitz on an English family, Tomlinson put into words the emotional experiences of many who lived through the Second World War.

Tomlinson was short of stature. His appearance was memorably described by J. Middleton Murry: 'quiet, weary, sad, with his unforgettable face, carved and weather-beaten like the figure heads of the sailing ships under whose bowsprits he walked and dreamed as a boy' (Havighurst, 275). He suffered from deafness caused by a football accident in early youth and aggravated by gunfire on the western front. This handicap led people to think of him as a shy man, but he had many friends and a fine sense of humour. A keen naturalist, Tomlinson loved walking, and even in his later years thought nothing of taking long walks through the unspoiled Dorset countryside where he spent each summer.

Tomlinson received the honorary degree of LLD from Aberdeen in 1949. He died at St George's Hospital, London, on 5 February 1958 and was buried in the churchyard at Abbotsbury, Dorset. His wife survived him.

DEREK HUDSON, *rev.* MARC BRODIE

Sources *The Times* (6–7 Feb 1958) · H. M. Tomlinson, *A mingled yarn: autobiographical sketches* (1953) · F. Swinnerton, *The Georgian literary scene: a panorama* (1935) · F. Swinnerton, *Figures in the foreground: literary reminiscences, 1917–40* (1963) · private information (1971) · A. F. Havighurst, *Radical journalist: H. W. Massingham* (1974) · D. Griffiths, ed., *The encyclopedia of the British press, 1422–1992* (1992) · WWW · b. cert. · d. cert.
Archives U. Reading L., corresp. · Yale U., Beinecke L., papers
Likenesses P. Evans, ink drawing, 1926, BM · R. Murry, oils, 1927, NPG · H. Coster, photographs, NPG · photograph, repro. in *The Times* (6 Feb 1958)
Wealth at death £1396 11s. 8d.: probate, 31 March 1958, CGPLA Eng. & Wales

Tomlinson, Kenelm [Kellom] (*b. c.*1693, *d.* in or after 1754?), dancing-master and choreographer, about whose birth and parentage nothing is known, was apprenticed to the respected London dancing-master Thomas Caverley from 1707 until 1714. He also studied under René Cherrier of Drury Lane Theatre. Tomlinson's manuscript workbook (now in the National Library of New Zealand) records the treatises and dance repertoire that he studied as an apprentice and also contains six theatrical dances that he created for Lincoln's Inn Fields theatre in 1716 and 1721. Though there is no evidence that Tomlinson himself ever appeared on stage his writings refer to two of his students—John Topham and Miss Francis—who both went on to distinguished stage careers. He also wrote theatrical dances for Diane Schoolding (later Mrs Anthony Moreau), Marie Sallé, and her brother (*The Submission*, 1716), and 'a New Ball Dance', which was performed on stage by M. Villeneuve and Mme Delagarde in 1743.

Tomlinson is best remembered for his ballroom *danses à deux* and for his treatise *The Art of Dancing*, which is now the major primary source for the study of early eighteenth-century English dance in the *belle danse* style. Six of his annual ball-dances were reissued as a set in 1720, dedicated to the 'Ladies, who have done Honour to this Art … by making it a Branch of Education', and for all their beauty and sophistication these dances are clearly pedagogic in intent. His treatise *The Art of Dancing*, begun in 1724, was published in 1735; its thirty-seven illustrative plates of dancers, step notation, and the entire ballroom minuet were the work of seven engravers, including Gerard Van der Gucht, George Vertue, Henry Fletcher, and George Bickham, to designs drawn by Tomlinson himself. The plates alone were considered 'proper Furniture for a Room or Closet … if put in Frames' and sold at 2 guineas a set, plus another half guinea for the text (*Art of Dancing*, bk 1, introduction to plates). Tomlinson's treatise is important as the most detailed description of the dance forms and steps current in England by the 1730s, as one of very few eighteenth-century manuals to describe theatrical as well as social dance, and for giving a unique insight into the circles in which Tomlinson was moving; this it achieved by naming in its subscription list 179 patrons, pupils, and professional colleagues, including 33 peers, 107 members of the gentry, and 22 of the leading dancers of the day. The work went to a second edition in 1744, which, like the first edition, was dedicated to Catherine Belasyse, Viscountess Fauconberg.

Tomlinson married Mary Alston of Aldgate at St Benet Paul's Wharf on 25 July 1717. No record of their having any children has been found but the marriage on 22 February 1782 of 'Kellom Tomlinson, Bachelor, and Mary Bestland, widow' at Portsmouth (parish register, St Mary Portsea) may indicate at least one descendant. According to Musgrave's *Obituary* Tomlinson may have died in or soon after 1754 but no burial or probate records have been found.

JENNIFER THORP

Sources K. Tomlinson, *The art of dancing explained by reading and figures* (1735) · *Six dances compos'd by Mr Kellom Tomlinson* (1720) · J. Shennan, ed., *A workbook by Kellom Tomlinson* (1992) · H. Bromley, *A catalogue of engraved British portraits* (1793) · Highfill, Burnim & Langhans, *BDA*, 15.21–3 · W. A. Littledale, ed., *The registers of St Bene't and St Peter, Paul's Wharf, London*, 2, Harleian Society, register section, 39 (1910) · W. Musgrave, *Obituary prior to 1800*, ed. G. J. Armytage, 3, Harleian Society, 46 (1900), 6.104 · W. Musgrave, ed., 'A general catalogue of engraved portraits', 1777, BL, Add. MSS. 25393–25395 [BL, Add. MS 25395] · R. Petre, 'Six new dances by Kellom Tomlinson: a recently discovered manuscript', *Early Music*, 18 (1990), 381–92
Archives NL NZ, MS workbook
Likenesses F. Merellon La Cave, engraving, 1754 (after R. van Bleeck, 1716), BL, music collections; repro. in Tomlinson, *Art of dancing*

Tomlinson [Thomlinson], **Matthew, appointed Lord Tomlinson under the protectorate** (*bap.* 1617, *d.* 1681), parliamentarian army officer and politician, was baptized at St Michael-le-Belfry, York, on 24 September 1617, two months after the death of his father, John Thomlinson. When Matthew was nine his mother, Eleanor, daughter of Matthew Dodsworth, married Thomas Coventry.

In 1642 Tomlinson was one of the gentlemen of the inns of court who enlisted under Sir Philip Stapleton in the earl of Essex's company of life guards. In spring 1645 he was

Matthew Tomlinson, appointed Lord Tomlinson under the protectorate (*bap.* 1617, *d.* 1681), by unknown artist, *c.*1650

campaigning in Oxfordshire. He had become a major and eventually took over command of Sir Robert Pye's troop of horse as colonel in 1647. His importance in the New Model Army was indicated in June 1647 when he was chosen to present the army's remonstrance to the House of Commons. He and his regiment were among those who arrived in London in August 1647, and the following October he participated in the debates at Putney over the future settlement of the kingdom. However, he was never conspicuous in political debate. His continuing importance in the army was shown in 1648. On 28 November he was one of those charged with justifying the army's fresh descent on London. Soon afterwards he commanded the troop which guarded Charles I during his trial (to which Tomlinson had been appointed as one of the judges, but had declined to sit) and attended the king to the scaffold. Charles acknowledged the courtesy with which he had been treated by Tomlinson, giving him a golden toothpick and case.

Tomlinson saw renewed fighting in the summer of 1649, quelling trouble in Kent. In 1650 he and his regiment joined Cromwell in Scotland. They were present at the battle of Worcester on 3 September 1651. Residual legal expertise may explain his inclusion by the Rump Parliament among the members of the Hale commission, set up to recommend reforms in the law. With the end of the Long Parliament, in May 1653, he was named to the council of state, and was then co-opted into Barebone's Parliament. His services were already exploited on a number of financial committees. Tomlinson made substantial purchases of crown land during the interregnum. He bought

in 1653 Ampthill Great Park, Bedfordshire, for £6140 and the following year part of the manor of Dyndathway, Anglesey, for £2754. He also bought Lincoln dean and chapter lands for, in all, £1671.

In August 1654 Tomlinson was included in the council which was to help Charles Fleetwood govern Ireland. Soon Fleetwood was effectively superseded by Henry Cromwell. Tomlinson was out of sympathy with what he—and others—regarded as the more conservative tenor of the administration, as it sought to widen its appeal among local civilians. Nevertheless outward courtesies were maintained, with Henry Cromwell knighting Tomlinson on 24 November 1657. Shortly afterwards, he was named to the other house of the Westminster parliament, but his duties in Ireland prevented his attendance. His sympathies with the opponents of the Cromwellian protectorate led to his reappointment to the successor government in Ireland as a parliamentary commissioner in July 1659. He collaborated with another proponent of 'the good old cause', Edmund Ludlow. He was toppled when a more conservative group seized Dublin Castle in December 1659, and was returned as a prisoner to England. At risk because of these sympathies, after Charles II's return he was imprisoned but not tried. For the rest of his life he was unobtrusive. In 1669 he was noted as pleading for religious toleration for protestant nonconformists. He had married well: his wife, Pembroke (*d.* 1683), daughter of Sir William Brooke, was an heir to the Cobham estates. They had two daughters, Jane (*d.* 1703) and Elizabeth (*d.* 1692). Tomlinson died at East Malling, Kent, on 3 or 5 November 1681 and was buried in the parish church there.

TOBY BARNARD

Sources C. H. Firth and G. Davies, *The regimental history of Cromwell's army*, 2 vols. (1940) • A. Clarke, *Prelude to Restoration in Ireland* (1999) • B. Worden, *The Rump Parliament, 1648–1653* (1974) • Greaves & Zaller, *BDBR*, 246–7 • T. C. Barnard, *Cromwellian Ireland: English government and reform in Ireland, 1649–1660* (1975) • *DNB* • A. Woolrych, *Commonwealth to protectorate* (1982) • *Dugdale's visitation of Yorkshire, with additions*, ed. J. W. Clay, 1 (1899), 202–3 • I. Gentles, 'The debentures market and military purchases of crown land, 1649–1660', PhD diss., U. Lond., 1969

Likenesses portrait, *c.*1650, unknown collection; copyprint, NPG [*see illus.*] • D. Mytens, oils

Tomlinson, Nicholas (1764–1847), naval officer, third son of Captain Robert Tomlinson RN, was from March 1772 on the books of the *Resolution*, guardship at Chatham, of which his father was first lieutenant. In 1776 he transferred to the *Thetis*, in which he made two voyages to St Helena and served on the North American station. In March 1779 he joined the *Charon*, with Captain John Luttrell, third earl of Carhampton, a friend of his father; he served as Luttrell's aide-de-camp in the capture of Omoa. Continuing in the *Charon* with Captain Thomas Symonds, he was present at the capture of the French privateer *Comte d'Artois* and the defence and surrender of Yorktown.

Tomlinson returned to England through an exchange of prisoners in December 1781, and on 23 March 1782 was made lieutenant in the *Bristol*, which went with convoy to the East Indies. In April 1783, a few days after the *Bristol's* arrival in Madras Roads, Tomlinson volunteered to go to the help of the Indiaman *Duke of Athol* and was on her when she was blown up with the death of nearly two hundred men. Tomlinson escaped with his life, but was severely injured. In the *Bristol* he was at the fifth action between Suffren and Sir Edward Hughes off Cuddalore; in September 1784 he was appointed to the *Juno* and in her returned to England in 1785.

From 1786 to 1790 Tomlinson served in the sloop *Savage* on the coast of Scotland. He then, with a recommendation from Lord Hawke, joined the Russian navy and had command of a Russian ship of the line, which he resigned on the imminence of the war between England and France in the beginning of 1793. In July he was appointed to the British *Regulus* (44 guns), which ill health compelled him to leave after a few months, but in July 1794 he was appointed to command the gunboat *Pelter*, in which he performed a variety of enterprising actions along the French coast, for one of which—the cover of the retreat of a party of French royalists after the failure of the expedition at Quiberon—he was publicly thanked by Sir John Borlase Warren on the quarterdeck of the *Pomone* in July 1795. He married, in 1794, Elizabeth, second daughter and coheir of Ralph Ward of Forburrows, near Colchester, and had a large family.

On 30 November 1795 after brief appointments to the *Glory* (98 guns) and the gun-vessel *Vesure* Tomlinson was promoted to the command of the sloop *Suffisante*, in which, in the following May, he captured the French brig *Revanche*; and through the summer he took or destroyed several privateers, armed vessels, storeships, and traders, for which the Committee for Encouraging the Capture of French Privateers voted him a piece of plate valued at £50, as did the court of directors of the Royal Exchange Assurance; and on 12 December 1796 he was advanced to post rank. In the following year, being unable to get employment from the Admiralty, he fitted out a privateer in which he made several rich prizes; but being reported to the Admiralty as having used the private signals to avoid being overhauled by warships, his name was struck off the list of post captains on 20 November 1798. After a determined effort to obtain reinstatement he was permitted in 1801 to serve as a volunteer in the fleet going to the Baltic with Sir Hyde Parker, and being favourably reported on by him was restored to his rank in the navy, with seniority, on 22 September 1801.

From July 1803 to June 1809 Tomlinson commanded the sea fencibles on the coast of Essex; in the summer of 1809 he fitted out and commanded a division of fireships for operations in the Scheldt. On returning to England he resumed the command of the fencibles until they were broken up early in 1810. In that year he successfully fought a legal case brought against him by the Navy Board for conniving at uttering a false receipt connected with the repair of the *Pelter* in 1795. He had no further employment, but was put on the retired list of rear-admirals on 22 July 1830; he was transferred to the active list on 17 August 1840 and was promoted vice-admiral on 23 November 1841. He died at his house near Lewes on 6 March 1847. Two

of his brothers also served in the navy and retired with the rank of commander after the war. Philip died in 1839, Robert at the age of eighty-five in 1844.

J. K. LAUGHTON, *rev.* ROGER MORRISS

Sources *The Tomlinson papers, selected from the correspondence and pamphlets of Captain Robert Tomlinson RN and Vice-Admiral Nicholas Tomlinson*, ed. J. G. Bullocke (1935) · J. Marshall, *Royal naval biography*, 2/1 (1824), 437 · O'Byrne, *Naval biog. dict.* · *Navy List*
Archives NMM
Likenesses Page, stipple, BM, NPG; repro. in *Naval chronicle* (1811)

Tomlinson, William (*fl.* 1650–1696), religious writer, was probably from the North Riding of Yorkshire, and may have been the person of this name who matriculated as a sizar at Trinity College, Cambridge, in Michaelmas term 1632 and graduated BA in 1637. According to George Fox, Tomlinson was a priest (by which he meant an Anglican clergyman) before becoming a Quaker. Tomlinson served as a lieutenant in Colonel Thomas Saunders's regiment of horse, but he claimed that he was dismissed in 1650 for opposing Saunders's views when the regiment was at Derby. However, when Tomlinson unsuccessfully sought reinstatement in June 1659, Saunders insisted he had voluntarily relinquished his commission, claiming to be lame and unable to participate in the campaign against the Scots.

In or before 1653 Tomlinson became a Quaker. In the first of his many tracts, *A Word of Reproof to the Priests or Ministers* (1653; 3rd edn., 1656), he castigated the Church of England's clergy as deceivers who boast of their ministry and sacraments while disdaining and persecuting others. The kings of the earth, he averred, commit fornication with the clergy because of their close relationship. Three years later, in a broadside entitled *A Bosome Opened to the Jews*, he added his voice to those urging the readmission of Jews to England. When James Nayler was tried by parliament in December 1656, Tomlinson, Fox, and Robert Rich submitted statements pertaining to the case. Tomlinson challenged parliament to define and prove the alleged blasphemy, for embracing Christ was not such an offence. In seeking to kill God's enemies, he warned, the MPs were in reality slaying his children. The statements were published as *Copies of some few of the papers given unto the house of parliament in the time of James Naylers tryal there* (1656). The following year Tomlinson published *Seven Particulars*, which opened with a powerful condemnation of those who oppress the poor, not least by charging exorbitant rents. Such oppressors, he proclaimed, are the pharaohs and taskmasters of the earth. He also denounced capital punishment for theft, the importance attributed to one's ancestry, compulsory tithes, and the persecution of Quakers who proclaimed their message of the inner light in traditional churches.

At the Restoration Tomlinson was imprisoned in the North Riding for refusing to take an oath. In *A Word of Information to them that Need it* (1660) he denounced episcopacy as unscriptural and the Book of Common Prayer as replete with evil. 'A Cup of Fornication', by which he meant 'a Pack of mens Inventions and Traditions', is spreading through the nations, intoxicating them (pp. 18–19). About the same time he wrote *A Position Concerning Persecution* (1660?), arguing that any religion which persecutes those who follow their consciences is an abomination. From Beaudesert, Warwickshire, on 30 August 1669, Sir Bryan Broughton reported to Joseph Williamson that Tomlinson, whom he described as a former eminent officer, had warned that civil war would ensue if people were not free to attend conventicles. In *An Awakening Voice to the Papists* (1673) Tomlinson accused the Catholic church of espousing doctrines and practices from the bottomless pit and labelled the pope 'that Man of Sin' (p. 27). His next work, *An Epistle to the Flock* (1674), reminded fellow Friends of the need to expel those whose religion was only formal; Quakers must walk in the light, not merely talk about it. In May 1675 Fox wanted Tomlinson to found a school to teach languages and botany, apparently in conjunction with the schoolmaster and botanist Thomas Lawson, but nothing came of this. Tomlinson renewed his attack on the Catholics in 1679, when he published *The principles of the papists … plainly demonstrated by the scriptures to be most erroneous and wicked*. He followed this in 1684 with *A Synopsis, or Short View of Essential Christianity in Part*, which reflects the Quakers' interest in the primitive church. The Catholics again occupied his attention, this time in *Innovations of Popery* (1689). The Finch manuscripts contain a letter dated 10 June 1690 from William III to the earl of Nottingham, directing him to do as he saw fit with a petition from Tomlinson to the countess of Derby. Tomlinson's final tract (and the last that is known of him), *A Short Work, but of the Greatest Concern*, was published in 1696. In his later years Tomlinson continued to manifest the stridency that characterized some of the earliest Friends, as reflected by the fact that in the 1670s and 1680s six of his tracts were edited or rejected by his colleagues.   RICHARD L. GREAVES

Sources CSP dom., 1658–9, 378; 1668–9, 465 · *Narrative papers of George Fox*, ed. H. J. Cadbury (1972) · J. Besse, *A collection of the sufferings of the people called Quakers*, 2 (1753), 102–3 · Venn, *Alum. Cant.* · W. C. Braithwaite, *The second period of Quakerism*, ed. H. J. Cadbury, 2nd edn (1961) · *Report on the manuscripts of Allan George Finch*, 5 vols., HMC, 71 (1913–2003), vol. 2, p. 292 · B. G. Reay, 'Tomlinson, William', Greaves & Zaller, *BDBR*, 3.247 · W. Tomlinson, *A word of reproof to the priests or ministers* (1653)

Tomos, Josua. *See* Thomas, Joshua (d. 1759).

Tompion, Thomas (*bap.* 1639, *d.* 1713), horologist and maker of scientific instruments, was baptized on 25 July 1639 at Northill, Bedfordshire, the eldest of three surviving offspring of Thomas Tompion (d. 1665), a blacksmith, and his wife, Margaret, of Ickwell, a hamlet in the parish of Northill. Nothing is known of his childhood but it is likely that he watched his father at work with the hammer and anvil and that he eventually practised forging metal under his tuition. Apart from this experience it is not known if he was ever formally apprenticed or how he learned the skills which brought him fame. He is believed to have left Ickwell before his father's death in 1665 because the blacksmithing business was continued by the younger son James.

Early work and innovation The nature of even Tompion's earliest recorded commissions bespeaks a pioneering

Thomas Tompion (*bap.* 1639, *d.* 1713), by Sir Godfrey Kneller, *c.*1685–90

craftsman of unparalleled versatility. In 1671 he cast a church bell of 4 cwt, in 1674 he made a turret clock for the Tower of London and a quadrant for the Royal Society, and, in 1675, he made a longcase clock with a dead-beat escapement for Sir Jonas Moore and a balance-spring watch for Charles II. By about 1680 he had produced the first of a group of two-train grande-sonnerie clocks whose workmanship is finer and more complex than that of any earlier English timepiece recorded.

Tompion is first recorded in London early in 1671 when he occupied one of the first post-fire houses to be rebuilt in Water Lane, a narrow byway running south towards the Thames from Fleet Street. After a search of his premises by Clockmakers' Company officials in July 1671 he was admitted to the company as a brother at the next quarter court on 4 September and he bought his freedom on 20 April 1674. Soon after, he enrolled the first of at least twenty-four apprentices bound during his career.

In the same year he became acquainted with two most influential men, both enthusiastic supporters of the advancement of scientific knowledge, Robert Hooke (1635–1703), curator of experiments for the Royal Society, and the mathematician Sir Jonas Moore (1627–1679), who took up residence at the Tower upon his appointment as surveyor-general of the ordnance in 1669. Hooke kept a diary which contains many references to Tompion and the projects they worked on, to social meetings, and topics they discussed. He first employed Tompion on behalf of the society to make a quadrant (with telescopic sights supplied by Cock) to demonstrate his criticism of the method of naked-eye astronomical observation. Tompion made other fine mathematical instruments and barometers. His 'quicksilver weatherglass' was advertised in the *Royal*

Almanac of 1677, which suggests that his was one of the first shops to offer mercury barometers for sale. Three fine barometers survive in the Royal Collection, two having been made for William III.

It was presumably Moore who commissioned Tompion to make the 'extraord^y Clock for the new Tower over the powder rooms' installed in the latter half of 1674, and early in 1675 he made for Moore a longcase clock which had a dead-beat escapement—one of the earliest recorded instances of its use—which stood in his dining-room. This was the first of at least three escapements, the others being another dead-beat design for clocks, and a 'virgule' for watches, which Tompion inexplicably chose to abandon, and their great potential lay dormant until the 1720s when George *Graham (*c.*1673–1751) modified the designs.

In 1675 when Huygens wrote from Paris of his invention of a watch with a balance-spring, Hooke indignantly reminded the Royal Society of his lectures on the subject delivered some years earlier, and a rough draft of his patent application of about 1660 survives to prove his previous involvement. There is no evidence, however, that he had achieved the use of a spiral spring and Huygens clearly deserves credit for that crucial advance. With a view to obstructing the patent application being sought for Huygens's invention, Hooke, accompanied by Moore and Tompion, was received in audience by the king to plead his case. In the event neither party was granted exclusive rights but Charles evidently ordered Hooke to produce a watch of his design and, with Moore's encouragement, Hooke commissioned Tompion to work on it. It is said to have been signed 'Robert Hooke inven. 1658. T. Tompion fecit 1675' but neither this, nor any of the small number believed to have been made and similarly signed, is known to have survived; James, duke of York, and Prince Rupert are both believed to have owned examples and two were made for the dauphin. Tompion soon abandoned its unnecessarily complicated escapement—it had two balances geared together—in favour of a single balance.

This important new advance still required some regulating device, and the standard method adopted by the majority of British makers of verge and cylinder movements from the late 1670s until the nineteenth century incorporated a pinion and a toothed rack with curb-pins. This device is known as 'Tompion regulation' but although he was among the first to use it, it cannot be shown that he was the inventor. The introduction of a successful balance-spring, with its controlling influence improving accuracy, served to encourage and enable further experimentation in movement design and in manufacturing methods.

At the beginning of 1676 Tompion moved his business and household into more extensive premises on the west side of Water Lane at the corner of the junction with Fleet Street (the site, no. 67 Fleet Street, is now identified by a blue plaque). His cotenant for the ensuing eight years, Jasper Braem, was a cabinet maker and inlayer of marquetry and there can be little doubt that he was responsible for many of the fine longcases of this period containing Tompion movements and dials; it is not inconceivable that he also made cases for other clockmakers and he may even have offered other items of furniture for sale in Tompion's shop. Braem was the first of several cotenants to share the property with Tompion but none of later date has yet been shown to have had horological leanings. Tompion traded from these premises for the rest of his life and his successor, Graham, remained until 1720 when he moved the business to the north side of Fleet Street.

Also in 1676, Tompion was commissioned by Moore to make a pair of year-going timepieces for the newly built Royal Observatory at Greenwich, which served John Flamsteed (1646–1719), the first astronomer royal, during his 35-year incumbency. Using these in harness with other instruments, including a quadrant that Tompion helped to make, Flamsteed was able to determine that the periods of the sun's successive crossings of the meridian are not regular but follow the table of equation which he had calculated. He also established that the earth revolves at a constant rate (a finding which was not challenged until the twentieth century), and he compiled a catalogue of 3000 stars, and tables of planetary motions and timings of Jupiter's moons. Both clocks have survived though their dead-beat escapements have been converted to recoil for domestic use. One has been in the British Museum since 1927, the other was returned to the observatory in 1994. Each dial bears the inscription: 'Sr Jonas Moore Caused this Movement With great Care to be thus Made A^o 1676 by Tho Tompion'.

Tompion's outstanding group of two-train grande-sonnerie clocks, the first of which was probably made in the late 1670s, incorporated a new type of striking mechanism termed rack and snail, which allowed the time to be determined, by bells, at any time upon pulling a cord; it was of particular use in bedrooms during hours of darkness. Perhaps inspired by an early Tompion quarter-repeating mechanism which utilized a six-step snail (but no rack), it was devised by the Revd Edward Barlow alias Booth (1639–1719). These were also the first table-clocks to have a pendulum suspension spring of flat steel strip whose use enabled another new device, rise-and-fall regulation, which allowed the owner to adjust the clock's rate simply by moving a hand on the dial.

Tompion went to some lengths, especially during the period 1675–90, to keep new designs secret by preventing easy access to the movements of the first retail models. Several early examples had secret locking bolts securing their movements within the cases, while other cases had no back door so that not even the back plate could be seen. Similarly, the earliest repeating watch movements were locked into their cases by secret latches.

Retailing and wealth The prestigious commissions of the 1670s enhanced Tompion's reputation and the fact that during this period he was occasionally obliged to buy in movements from other makers to be finished for retail in his own shop is evidence of his failure to satisfy all demands for his wares. It was probably this inability which encouraged the adoption of a rudimentary form of mass production of clocks and watches to ensure a steady supply of standard models for retail. Their cases, dials, and movements were almost certainly made in batches to await selection for assembly and sale and by the early 1680s as many as 100 to 150 watches and fifteen to twenty clocks were being retailed each year, figures which remained surprisingly consistent throughout his career. Increased production was not accompanied by a reduction in the quality of workmanship but rather the opposite. Improvements in manufacturing methods, the continual modernization of machinery, and the honing of individual skills all enabled greater precision in both production and performance and Tompion's business continued to offer the largest selection of items of the best quality. Most of Tompion's apprentices can be identified in the records of the Clockmakers' Company and while some are known to have remained in his employment after they were made free they could never have constituted a large enough body to account for the prolific output. Other employees and workshops were undoubtedly involved but very little is known of the network of selected artisans which would have developed as his business grew, persons he employed on his own premises as journeymen and work-masters, and elsewhere as outworkers. Between 1676 and 1691, for instance, Nathaniel Delander's workshop in Old Bailey supplied Tompion with well over a thousand watch-cases.

From about 1680 by far the greater number of items sold were standard stock items, timepiece watches, eight-day table clocks and timepieces, and thirty-hour, eight-day, or month-going longcase clocks. With most of this work delegated to others Tompion would have acted as overseer and probably spent time on unusual commissions, experimenting with and improving designs, and personally serving prestigious customers. He also employed a clerk, probably from the early 1680s, who would have dealt with accounts as well as serving in the shop. By the 1690s Tompion was a wealthy man. In June 1694 he bought £1000 worth of Bank of England stock (he was one of the first subscribers), and the 1695 assessment on marriages, etc., classed him as an individual with personal estate worth not less than £600 or real estate worth not less than £50 per year. He also invested money in the Million Bank, to the tune of £1500 by 1704. For small business transactions he employed, at least from 1702, the services of Sir Richard Hoare, banker, at the nearby sign of the Golden Bottle, Temple Bar. In 1684 he was excused from serving as steward to the Clockmakers' Company when he claimed he was sick and busy altering his house, but he kept his word and served the following year instead. In 1691 he was elected to the court of assistants and later served as junior warden (1700), renter warden (1701), senior warden (1702), and finally master in 1703.

Apart from his earlier role in the introduction of the balance-spring Tompion was at the forefront in improving other aspects of watch design. When Edward Barlow applied for a patent for repeating watches, Tompion made the watch produced in court in March 1687, but James II

ruled in favour of one made by Daniel Quare who countered Barlow's claim, Tompion's watch having two separate push-pieces while Quare's had just one. By about 1689 Tompion had developed a standard retail model which was of sturdier and more reliable construction than those of his contemporaries.

A deficiency of early watches with cases pierced to allow the sound of a bell to escape was their tendency to clog with dust and fluff. Tompion was probably the first maker to introduce a protective ring to encircle the movement, and about 1704 he began covering the balance-cock with a cap. It was not until ten years later, however, that these components were combined, probably by Graham or Quare, to form a dust-cap which effectively enclosed the movement; this became a standard component of the English watch.

In 1695, in conjunction with Booth and William Houghton, Tompion patented (no. 344) the first watch escapement to incorporate a horizontal escape wheel acting directly on a single balance arbor (the type later named virgule), whereby both the contrate and crown wheels were eliminated. The venture was not successful and production was soon abandoned (one incomplete movement was noted as part of his sixth recorded series) but George Graham returned to the idea thirty years later to achieve a substantial result—the cylinder escapement. In common with other leading London watchmakers Tompion began about 1710 to use diamond endstones for the balance-pivots of most repeating watches and of a few timepieces, to reduce friction and wear.

Tompion's record system It is possible that during Tompion's career well over a hundred employees contributed to the production and retail of those items bearing his name, working to the high standards which he himself set. This resulted in a uniformity in workshop procedures—a house style—which prevents any positive identification of an individual's work, and even Tompion's hand is unrecognizable in all but the earlier pre-standardization items. It was inevitable that such an output would soon necessitate a record system to ensure easy identification of items, and serial numbers, undoubtedly linked to ledger records, were placed on most of the standard watches and clocks.

At least six individual numbered series were begun, some of which were later merged together. The first was for all types of watch being produced at the time the series started about 1681. In 1683–94 the numbers were often coded. After Tompion's death in 1713 the series was continued by Graham and after his death in 1751 Colley used it until the 1760s. The second series, for spring-driven clocks, begun about 1682, and that for weight-driven clocks, probably begun at the same time, were merged together by about 1686. The series included all types of clock except a small number of special commissions, chiefly those for royal residences, and turret clocks. Graham continued the series, apparently until his death, although several late unnumbered examples are recorded. A series for repeating watches, begun about

1688 soon after their introduction, was continued by Graham and then Colley until about 1760. A fifth series, for clockwatches and alarm-watches, began about 1692, and from that time series 1 was used exclusively for timepieces. Graham continued series 5 but abandoned it about 1720, perhaps when he moved the business, whereupon these watches were included in the timepiece or the repeater series. The sixth series was for watches with the Tompion–Houghton–Booth virgule escapement, begun about 1695 but abandoned almost immediately.

The cases of several longcase clocks dating from about 1700 have been found to bear a secondary number, quite separate from Tompion's serial number, which may relate to a new case-maker's own records. No business records (other than a small number of sales receipts) are known to have survived and not a single manuscript in Tompion's hand is recorded. His signature appears on many documents, however, chiefly relating to Clockmakers' Company matters.

Royal patronage Tompion's goods were more costly than those of his contemporaries and his customers were chiefly from the highest and wealthiest ranks of society, from the royal household to the nobility and gentry. Though he was never appointed royal clockmaker Tompion enjoyed royal patronage. Apart from the early balance-spring watch Hooke also refers to a striking clock made for Charles II, but it was during the 1690s that Tompion produced his finest royal commissions. William III's extravagance allowed the clockmaker free rein and several clocks were supplied with movements displaying the very best of his mechanical genius. Their cases, of matching quality, were almost certainly designed in collaboration with Daniel Marot, William's versatile designer of interior and exterior decorative features from wallpaper to gardens. The finest examples include the spring-driven year-going Mostyn Tompion, an ebony, silver, and gilt bracket-clock (now in the British Museum), a silver-cased travelling-clock whose movement (stolen from a private collection during the 1980s) has a dial-operated mechanism which allows for the choice of pendulum or balance control, a walnut year-going equation longcase timepiece at Kensington Palace, and the so-called 'record Tompion', named after an early twentieth-century sale price, a walnut three-month longcase clock now owned by the Colonial Williamsburg Foundation, Virginia, USA. In addition he supplied three finely cased barometers, two of which now hang at Hampton Court, the other at Kensington Palace.

When Tompion petitioned Queen Anne for payment of William's unsettled debts she replied that she had 'no occasion for his clocks and watches' (State Papers, privy purse, 1703, PRO T 29/14, fol. 92). And yet Treasury accounts show that Tompion was employed upon work both for Anne and her husband, George, prince of Denmark. At Buckingham Palace is another year-going equation timepiece which is believed to have been made in 1703 for George, and he may also have owned the exceptional small silver and gilt travelling-clock with grande-sonnerie striking, quarter-repeat, and alarm, and choice of balance or pendulum control, now in the British Museum.

Tompion's reputation spread beyond Britain and among those who owned one of his clocks or watches were Carl XI of Sweden, Philip V of Spain, Cosimo III, Tsar Peter the Great, Karl, landgrave of Hesse-Cassel, and the dauphin. Some of the pieces were diplomatic gifts but others were probably ordered by ambassadors in London on behalf of their sovereigns. Peter the Great obtained his clock, a 'pendulum clock contrived to bear the motions of the sea', from the cabin of Admiral Sir John Norris during a dinner party held on board the *Ranelagh* in 1715. When the tsarina presented him with a diamond-studded snuff-box Norris felt obliged to part with the clock, along with some chairs, when they were admired by the tsar. Other adventurous works include an extraordinary month-going miniature boxwood longcase day and night clock with ting-tang quarter-strike, Roman notation hour-strike, and, to illuminate pierced dial numerals, oil lamps which are snuffed out automatically at a pre-set time. Also worthy of note is the group of complex three-train grande-sonnerie clocks like that given to Cosimo III, grand duke of Tuscany, by William III, and probably one of the items which the king failed to pay for. Tompion's reputation was such that watches fraudulently inscribed with his name were being made in the Netherlands and Switzerland at the end of the seventeenth century, and they could also be bought in Rome. Tompion published several editions of tables of equation as well as instructions, in English and French, for regulating watches.

The Tompion family Other members of the Tompion family were associated with him in London. Margaret, his sister, may have accompanied him when he moved to St Bride's about 1671; that was her address when she married one Stephen Kent in 1674. She was widowed after just three years, before the birth of a third daughter, and later lived in Thomas's house, possibly as his housekeeper, with two surviving daughters, Eleanor and Margaret. She predeceased Thomas but her burial has not been traced.

Tompion's nephew, Thomas junior, was apprenticed in the Clockmakers' Company to Charles Kemp, probably one of Tompion's workmen, in April 1694. He was freed in 1702 but none of his work has been positively identified and it is clear that he did not have the character to emulate his uncle, under whose will he was excused debts, inherited the Ickwell property, and had a moderate sum invested on his behalf. It was all to no avail; he went on trial at the Old Bailey with his wife, Anne, in November 1720 for stealing 11 guineas, and was described as of bad character and was alleged to have run a brothel for a number of years.

In December 1694 Tompion's niece Margaret Kent married Edward Banger, a Tompion apprentice of west country extraction bound in 1687 and freed in July 1695. About 1701 Tompion took Banger into a partnership which failed about 1708. Banger left and was scathingly denied any bequest in Tompion's will made five years later. He continued in the trade and several clocks and watches bearing his name alone are recorded; he died intestate and was buried at St Botolph without Bishopsgate on 12 December 1719. The burial of Margaret Banger, generously provided for under Tompion's will, has not been traced.

Thomas's niece Elizabeth (b. 1687) was just seventeen when she married George Graham, aged about thirty-one, in London in 1704. Graham had been apprenticed in July 1688 to a London clockmaker, Henry Aske, was made free in September 1695, and probably joined Tompion as a journeyman soon after. The marriage and Graham's character, highly commendable by all accounts, led Tompion to take Graham into partnership about 1711 and this arrangement lasted until Tompion's death.

Final years and influence It is not known when Tompion ceased practical work. He resorted to Bath, presumably finding the waters beneficial to an ailment, and the Pump Room's fine equation timepiece presented by him about 1709 is believed to have been in gratitude. He died on 20 November 1713 and was accorded the honour of burial in Westminster Abbey on 25 November, in the centre of the nave. In 1751 Graham was interred in the same grave and his name added to Tompion's stone. In his will dated 21 October 1713 Tompion named Graham and former cotenant Michael Tesmond as executors. He made bequests to relatives and friends but the business and the residue of his personal estate passed to George and Elizabeth Graham.

No description of Tompion's physical stature or of his personality is known but Kneller's half-length portrait of him wearing buttoned jacket and neck-scarf, probably painted in the late 1680s, shows him with an open, honest, genial face with full lips and clear skin, with shoulder-length hair, or perhaps a wig, with locks and curls.

Several factors account for Tompion's extraordinary rise to the forefront of London's horological community within only a decade of setting up business in 1671. Primarily, it must have been his metalworking skills together with his innovative reappraisal of all aspects of his trade which appealed to the likes of Hooke and Moore, but his success also owes something to the favourable circumstances existing at the time of his appearance in the City, ten years after the Restoration and the formation of the Royal Society, and five years after the great fire. London's rebuilding and repopulation were advancing fast and science and commerce were demanding better timekeepers from a trade which, like the City, was in the throes of drastic change. The pendulum had been introduced only twelve years earlier, the recoil escapement had just been conceived, and the balance-spring for watches was about to divert every watchmaker's thoughts. The time was ripe for experimentation and the stage was set for a surge in pioneering work.

Tompion's association with Hooke and Moore afforded him the opportunity to express his skills, ideas, and potential, and as a consequence, and more importantly to one with high aspirations, the opportunity to come to the notice of élite and influential members of society, and so to establish a reputation. One key to his great success lay in his business acumen, that is, in his ability to capitalize on that reputation by organizing batch production to meet demand. The serial numbers on surviving items are the only evidence of the ledger accounting system, whatever its nature, used to keep a check on production. Tompion's primary aims, even in cheaper items, were durability and accuracy, with the work being executed in as substantial or delicate a manner as was required. His appreciation of metals and their qualities, of the uses of springs, of efficiently profiled gearing, and of neat and precise finishing all resulted in the production of mechanisms of better and more reliable quality than any which preceded them. From his contributions grew a tradition of highest quality workmanship which was passed on by Graham to a third generation which included the likes of Thomas Mudge (1715–1794).

The business ran under Tompion's name (including the partnership periods) for forty-two years during which time about 800 clocks and 5000 watches of various description and function were sold, as well as dozens of scientific instruments—quadrants, barometers, pocket dials, and horizontal garden sundials. His business set the highest standards and doubtless he took great pride in the fact that none of his contemporaries achieved such consistently fine quality in such a wide range of products. His sobriquet 'the father of English watchmaking' was well-merited.

JEREMY LANCELOTTE EVANS

Sources R. W. Symonds, *Thomas Tompion: his life and work* (1951) · *The diary of Robert Hooke … 1672–1680*, ed. H. W. Robinson and W. Adams (1935); repr. (1968) · F. G. Emmison, ed., *Bedfordshire parish registers*, 13 (1936) · parish rate books for London, St Bride, and London, St Dunstan, GL · parish registers, London, St Bride, and London, St Dunstan, GL · Clockmakers' Company court minutes, GL [renter wardens' accounts] · C. E. Atkins, ed., *Register of apprentices of the Worshipful Company of Clockmakers of the City of London* (privately printed, London, 1931) · S. E. Atkins and W. H. Overall, *Some account of the Worshipful Company of Clockmakers of the City of London* (privately printed, London, 1881) · W. Derham, *The artificial clockmaker* (1696) · F. Baily, *An account of the Revd John Flamsteed, the first astronomer-royal* (1835) · J. B. Penfold, 'The marriages of George Graham and Edward Banger', *Horological Journal*, 94 (1952), 798–800 · D. Howse and B. Hutchinson, 'The Tompion clocks at Greenwich and the dead-beat escapement', *Antiquarian Horology and the Proceedings of the Antiquarian Horological Society*, 7 (1970–72), 18–34, 114–33 · D. Howse and V. Finch, 'John Flamsteed and the balance spring', *Antiquarian Horology and the Proceedings of the Antiquarian Horological Society*, 9 (1974–6), 664–75 · G. H. Baillie, *Clocks and watches: an historical bibliography* (1951) · C. Jagger, *Royal clocks* (1983) · H. A. Lloyd, 'The one and only Edward East', *Horological Journal*, 92 (1950), 296–8, 370–77 · Johan Horrins [J. Harrison], *Memoirs of a trait in the character of George III … authenticated by official papers and private letters* (1835), appx 6, n. · *LondG* (5 April 1683) [advertisement] · State Papers, privy purse, 1703, PRO, T29/14, fol. 92 · J. L. Evans, 'The numbering of Tompion's watches—series and system', *Antiquarian Horology and the Proceedings of the Antiquarian Horological Society*, 14 (1983–4), 585–97 · 'The diary of Robert Hooke', *Early science in Oxford*, ed. R. T. Gunther, 10: *The life and work of Robert Hooke, part 4* (1935), 69–265 · N. Goodison, *English barometers, 1680–1860*, rev. edn (1985)

Likenesses G. Kneller, oils, c.1685–1690, British Horological Institute, Upton Hall, Newark, Nottinghamshire [see illus.] · J. Smith, mezzotint (after G. Kneller), BM, NPG; repro. in Symonds, *Thomas Tompion*

Wealth at death over £1000: will

Tompkins, (Granville) Richard Francis (1918–1992), businessman, was born on 15 May 1918 at 93 Sussex Road,

(Granville) Richard Francis Tompkins (1918–1992), by unknown photographer

Upper Holloway, London, the son of Richard Tompkins and his wife, Ethel May, *née* Feargus. His father was then a mineral-water maker's motorman, but afterwards became a taxi-driver, and was finally employed in his son's publishing business. On leaving London county council's Pakeman Street School in 1932, Tompkins worked as a laundry delivery man and filling station attendant before becoming a van salesman in 1934. In 1938 he became an engineering draughtsman, which work he continued as a reserved occupation during the Second World War. On 29 August 1942 he married Valerie Margaret (*b.* 1921), daughter of Ernest Try, engine-fitter; together they had two daughters.

In 1945 Tompkins bought an old printing machine for £50, repaired it, and set up as a printer. He later diversified into direct mail advertising and pre-addressed envelopes. However, his stature in business history and his great fortune rested alike on his far-reaching innovations in British retailing. On holiday in the USA during the mid-1950s he noticed motorists queuing for service at certain petrol stations to which they had been enticed by trading stamps. These small, brightly coloured, and immediately recognizable stamps were given by retailers to consumers, mainly at supermarkets or garages, as incentives to spend. The more a consumer spent, the more stamps were given out; these could be redeemed for gifts at special centres. Although an earlier attempt to introduce trading stamps in Britain had failed, Tompkins saw them as a sensible extension of his printing business and resolved to make the effort again. He bought the brand name of Green Shield for £50 from a man operating a luggage company of that name, and in 1958 started the Green Shield Trading Stamp Co. Ltd, with himself as chairman and managing director.

British retailers initially doubted that trading stamps or the accompanying gifts would generate enough customer loyalty to justify Tompkins's scheme. Indeed, some chambers of commerce discouraged retailers from joining in a project that might disturb the equilibrium of high street sales. Tompkins persevered, and within five years had attracted enough adherents to his scheme to provoke a competitive foray in Britain by the US company, Sperry and Hutchinson. After the Fine Fare supermarket chain, controlled by Garfield Weston, adopted these rival pink trading stamps, Jack Cohen of Tesco in October 1963 contracted with Green Shield. Ultimately Tompkins beat his competitors in a colourful trading war that confirmed Green Shield's hegemony. For the rest of the 1960s only a few supermarket retailers, notably Lord Sainsbury, withstood the rage. Sainsbury believed that the costs to the retailer of purchasing trading stamps, which were represented as 2.5 per cent of turnover, should instead be reckoned at 16 per cent of gross margins, for the stamps entailed considerable handling costs. Sainsbury predicted that stamp trading would raise prices and thus depress demand. It was certainly widely believed in the petrol trade that individual garages raised prices in order to pay for stamp schemes. The Distributive Trades Alliance was mobilized by Sainsbury against Green Shield partly because trading stamps disrupted the system of retail price maintenance: simultaneously the intervention of suppliers such as Imperial Tobacco and the Distillers Company threatened to envelop Tompkins in a skein of litigation. As a result Edward Heath was roused in 1964 to introduce legislation abolishing retail price maintenance.

Trading stamps had an important secondary effect on British consumer attitudes in the last third of the twentieth century. Green Shield issued catalogues displaying in pictures and describing textually the gifts that could be exchanged for trading stamps. These catalogues crucially accustomed British consumers to shopping by catalogue. Mail-order business significantly expanded in consequence.

The use of catalogues meant that Green Shield's stamp exchange centres did not require large display areas to exhibit their wares and could be much smaller than traditional shops. Drawing on his immense profits from Green Shield, Tompkins capitalized on this feature by launching in 1973 the Argos retailing chain. At Argos customers could consult illustrated catalogues and then order goods stored on the premises: there was no display requiring a large floor area. Argos operated on a cash basis, and its premises were seen by Tompkins more as distribution outlets than as traditional shops. They were moderately successful, but the limited choice of wares in Argos catalogues combined with the outlet sites gave the chain a somewhat downmarket image. Tompkins sold this business to BAT Industries for £35 million in 1979.

Rampant inflation under the Heath and Callaghan governments of the 1970s ruined the trading stamps business. Customers preferred retailers to offer cash discounts to offset the effects of rising prices and depleted incomes. At the instigation of the young Tesco managing director, Ian MacLaurin, Cohen's company resolved in June 1977 to discontinue trading stamps. When Leslie Porter, Tesco's chairman, telephoned Tompkins with the news, the latter observed that twelve months' notice of cancellation was required; Porter had to remind him that the rolling notice period only applied to Green Shield's side of the contract, and that Tesco's fixed renewal date was only a week away. Green Shield's business shrivelled after this. In addition to the effects of inflation, consumers had become bored with stamps, and were satiated with Green Shield's promotional glasses, bowls, and such like. The company ceased issuing stamps in 1983 at a time when Tompkins was enduring a serious bout of illness.

In October 1986, encouraged by lower inflation, Tompkins revived the trading stamp concept with a launch in February 1987. Investing up to £10 million of his own money, Tompkins had the stamps redesigned and had thirty-three showrooms converted into Green Shield redemption centres. Some 2500 shops, together with Mobil and Total petrol stations, signed up with Green Shield, but supermarkets were never attracted, and in August 1991 the venture was abandoned.

Tompkins's first marriage ended in divorce, and on 3 October 1970 he married Elizabeth Nancy (b. 1937), freelance model, and daughter of Walter Harry Duke, bank manager; they had one daughter. Tompkins himself was a decent, straightforward, eager, and pleasant man. Among other charitable acts he endowed the Tompkins Foundation in 1980. He was a City liveryman, and together with his second wife received several decorations from the sovereign military orders of Malta during the 1980s. He was created CBE a few months before his death from stomach cancer, on 6 December 1992, at his home, 7 Belgrave Square, Westminster. RICHARD DAVENPORT-HINES

Sources *The Times* (9 Dec 1992) • *The Times* (29 Dec 1992) • *The Times* (16 May 1963) • *The Times* (30 Oct 1986) • *The Times* (5 April 1987) • *The Economist* (22 June 1963) • *The Economist* (10 Sept 1964) • b. cert. • m. cert. • d. cert.
Likenesses photograph, News International Syndication, London [*see illus.*] • photographs, Hult. Arch.
Wealth at death £34,894,513: probate, 7 April 1993, *CGPLA Eng. & Wales*

Tompson [Thompson], **John** (*fl.* 1382), Carmelite theologian, was born, it is claimed, in the village of Thompson in Norfolk and joined the order at Blakeney. He is probably to be identified with the *Johannes Tempsthone, informator* who signed the cartulary at Bishop's Lynn on 30 April 1378. The title *informator* indicates that he was teaching Latin to the younger students there. He pursued his studies at Oxford, and was BTh by 1382, when he attended the council convened at Blackfriars, London, on 17 May and 27 June to condemn the theological teaching of John Wyclif. He continued lecturing at Oxford where he incepted as DTh, but his later career is unclear. He seems to have returned to lecture for some years in the studium for Carmelite students at Norwich and possibly ended his days at Blakeney, for Bale does not list him among those buried in Norwich.

Tompson appears to have been a notable teacher, especially on the scriptures, as well as a successful preacher. In view of his presence at the Council of Blackfriars he was probably one of the group of Carmelite theologians at Oxford who vigorously opposed Wyclif's theology. Bale, who saw many of his works in the library at Norwich, listed his lectures on Ecclesiastes, St John's gospel, and the moral teaching of the Bible, all of which he recorded with their incipits and noted that each was accompanied by an index. Tompson also composed four books of sermons, and collections of extracts from *De mirabilibus mundi* and John Ridevall's work on Fulgentius. The only work by Tompson that possibly survives is a collection of extracts from Nicholas Trevet on Ovid's *Metamorphoses*, recorded with the same incipit as a similar work preserved in Merton College, Oxford (MS 85, fols. 111–123v).

Giovanni Grossi, in his *Viridarium* (*c.*1400), mistakenly called John Tompson 'John Campston', and this confused later historians (Pits, Villiers, and others), who have called him Campsen or Campscon, or who have created two separate individuals. RICHARD COPSEY

Sources Bodl. Oxf., MS Bodley 73 (SC 27635), fols. 56–56v, 71v, 113, 197v, 199v–200 • BL, Harley MS 3838, fols. 81v–82, 196–196v • 'Johannis Grossi: Tractatus de scriptoribus ordinis Carmelitarum', *De scriptoribus scholasticis saeculi XIV ex ordine Carmelitarum*, ed. B. M. Xiberta (Louvain, 1931), 42–53, esp. 49 • Emden, *Oxf.* • A. Little, 'Corrodies at the Carmelite friary of Lynn', ed. E. Stone, *Journal of Ecclesiastical History*, 9 (1958), 8–29, 9, 17n • Bale, *Cat.*, 1.489–90 • *Commentarii de scriptoribus Britannicis, auctore Joanne Lelando*, ed. A. Hall, 2 (1709), 401 • J. Pits, *Relationum historicarum de rebus Anglicis*, ed. [W. Bishop] (Paris, 1619), 449, 526 • A. Bostius, 'Speculum historiale', *Milano Bibl. Brera AE*, xii.22 [n.d., before 1491], 570 • C. de S. E. de Villiers, *Bibliotheca Carmelitana*, 2 vols. (Orléans, 1752); facs. edn, ed. P. G. Wessels (Rome, 1927), vol. 1, p. 808; vol. 2, pp.127–8 • D. Wilkins, ed., *Concilia Magnae Britanniae et Hiberniae*, 3 (1737); repr. (Brussels, 1964), 158 • Bodl. Oxf., MS Selden supra 41, fol. 174v
Archives Merton Oxf., MS 85, fols. 111–123v

Tompson, Richard (*d.* 1693), art dealer and printseller, had a shop at The Sun in Bedford Street, London. He is first recorded as publisher of a broadside in 1656, and in 1659 as a picture dealer. In 1669 he acted as co-publisher of Alexander Browne's *Ars pictoria*. Between about 1674/5 and 1686 he and Browne jointly conducted auctions of paintings, prints, and drawings, which seem to have been the first regular art auctions in London. He acted as 'crier' at the auction of Lely's paintings in 1682, and as a print dealer he sold prints to Robert Hooke between 1674 and 1676.

In 1666 Tompson published *The Infants Jesus and John Baptist Embracing*, an engraving by Arnold de Jode after Van Dyck; it was dedicated to Peter Lely who owned the painting and is described as Tompson's 'fautor' (patron). This helps to explain why he published thirty-seven mezzotints after Lely's paintings; they can be dated to the late 1670s, appearing before the comparable series issued by Browne. Tompson himself was not a printmaker, and his plates were made by Jan van Somer, Jan Vandervaart, Robert Williams, and others. In the early 1680s he published jointly with Edward Cooper three large plates by Peter Vandrebanc after Antonio Verrio's frescoes in Windsor Castle, as well as mezzotints by William Faithorne the younger and John Smith. Tompson dedicated a plate to Samuel Cooper. The posthumous sale of his collection of old master prints was advertised in the *London Gazette* of 5 October 1693. The spelling of his name varies: the earlier documents call him Thomson, while on the mezzotints he used Tompson. ANTONY GRIFFITHS

Sources Wing, *STC*, F2253 · J. C. Smith, *British mezzotinto portraits*, 3 (1880), 1366–81 · A. Laing, 'Sir Peter Lely and Sir Ralph Bankes', *Art and patronage in the Caroline courts: essays in honour of Sir Oliver Millar*, ed. D. Howarth (1993), 107–31, 123 · A. Griffiths, 'Early mezzotint publishing in England: Peter Lely, Tompson and Browne', *Print Quarterly*, 7 (1990), 130–45 · A. Griffiths and R. A. Gerard, *The print in Stuart Britain, 1603–1689* (1998), 231–4, 248 [exhibition catalogue, BM, 8 May – 20 Sept 1998] · *LondG* (5 Oct 1693)
Likenesses F. Place, mezzotint (after G. Soest), BM

Toms, Peter (*bap.* 1726, *d.* 1777), painter and herald, was baptized on 3 July 1726 at St Andrew, Holborn, London, the son of the engraver William Henry Toms (*c.*1700–*c.*1758) of Union Court, Holborn, and his wife, Rachael. Toms's father took on several apprentices, including John Boydell, who later noted that he was 'a very passionate man & committed many extravagances while his phrenzy lasted' (Farington, *Diary*, 4.1415). As a young man Peter Toms was apprenticed to the portrait painter Thomas Hudson, and in 1746 was appointed Portcullis pursuivant by the College of Arms. In November 1748 he appeared in a list of London's leading artists, being described by the *Universal Magazine* (vol. 2) as an 'eminent painter'. Toms was by now presumably employed as a portraitist, although no works by him are known. From 1749 he worked in London as a specialist painter of costume in other artists' portraits ('drapery painter'), following the death that year of the leading practitioner Joseph van Aken. It has plausibly been suggested that he was the unnamed artist mentioned by Lord Bath as working for Thomas Hudson, Allan Ramsay, and Joshua Reynolds in 1761 (Hudson, 53). Ramsay was certainly employing him in 1754 (Smart, 62). It was at one time also claimed that Toms worked for Gainsborough, although this would appear unlikely (Whitley, 2.279), especially as he was then based in Bath. From about 1755 Toms was employed as a drapery painter by Joshua Reynolds, for whom he worked until the early 1760s. In return for painting the draperies on a full-length portrait Toms received 15 guineas from Reynolds (Farington, *Diary*, 4.3238). According to Edwards, although he does not say when, Toms's price for painting 'the draperies, hands, &c.' of a whole-length portrait was 20 guineas; for a small 'three-quarter' length (30 × 25 in.), 3 guineas (Edwards, 55). Among other works Toms has been credited with painting the draperies in Reynolds's *Lady Elizabeth Keppel* (1761–2; priv. coll.) and *Master Thomas Lister* (*c.*1764–5; Bradford City Art Galleries and Museum). In the opinion of Reynolds's pupil James Northcote, Toms was a very good drapery painter, although his painting method

> did not exactly harmonise with the style of Sir Joshua's heads, as it was heavy and wanted freedom, so that his work had too much the appearance of having been done with a stamp, as the paper-hangings for rooms are executed. (Northcote, 2.28)

Their relationship was at times strained, as when Toms refused to replace the formal dress he had painted in a female portrait with the 'rural habit' required by Reynolds, telling him, 'you ought to be more explicit when you give the picture into my hands' (ibid., 2.29). Toms was evidently eccentric, Boydell recalling how he 'would strip himself & rub his body furiously from a notion that the

circulation of the blood was stopping: at other times would lay in bed many days together believing himself to be much disordered' (Farington, *Diary*, 4.1415). About 1763 Toms travelled to Dublin with the earl of Northumberland, lord lieutenant of Ireland, in an attempt to revive his own portrait career. However, he returned shortly afterwards, working intensively from 1763, or possibly 1764, as a drapery painter for Francis Cotes. It was during this time that he presumably also worked for Benjamin West (Edwards, 54). In 1768 Toms was elected a founder member of the Royal Academy, possibly because of his close professional relationship with Reynolds, Cotes, and West. He exhibited three works there between 1769 and 1771, an 'allegorical picture', an unidentified portrait, and a painting of wild plants. At this time he was living in Wimpole Street, around the corner from Francis Cotes, who had a grand residence in Cavendish Square. In June 1769 Toms witnessed Cotes's will. The death of Cotes, the following summer, apparently affected Toms deeply; he became increasingly depressed and turned to drink for solace. In 1772 Toms offered to sell his position at the College of Arms for £500, noting that he then earned between £30 and £40 per annum from the post, which he treated as a sinecure, plus £15 from the rental of his college apartments (Wagner, 409). In the event he retained the post until his death. Some time during the 1770s, while intoxicated, Toms attempted to commit suicide by cutting his throat. He survived for several years, dying on new year's day 1777 at his lodgings in Rathbone Place. His studio materials, prints, and drawings were auctioned by Gerrard later the same month. It is not known whether he married, although he was survived by a daughter, who was eighteen years old at his death (Whitley, 1.279).

MARTIN POSTLE

Sources E. Edwards, *Anecdotes of painters* (1808); facs. edn (1970), 53–5 · J. Northcote, *The life of Sir Joshua Reynolds*, 2nd edn, 2 vols. (1818) · Farington, *Diary* · A. Wagner, *Heralds of England: a history of the office and College of Arms* (1967) · C. R. Leslie and T. Taylor, *Life and times of Sir Joshua Reynolds*, 2 vols. (1865) · J. E. Hodgson and R. A. Eaton, 'The Royal Academy in the last century', *Art Journal*, new ser., 10 (1890), 114 · W. T. Whitley, *Artists and their friends in England, 1700–1799*, 2 vols. (1928) · D. Hudson, *Sir Joshua Reynolds: a personal study* (1958) · E. M. Johnson, *Francis Cotes* (1976) · E. G. Miles, *Thomas Hudson, 1701–1779* (1979) · N. Penny, ed., *Reynolds* (1986) [exhibition catalogue, RA, 16 Jan – 31 March 1986] · A. Smart, *Allan Ramsay: painter, essayist, and man of the Enlightenment* (1992) · *IGI*
Likenesses J. Zoffany, group portrait, oils (*Royal Academicians*, 1772), Royal Collection

Tomson, Arthur Graham (1859–1905), landscape painter and art critic, was born on 15 March 1859 at High Street, Chelmsford, Essex, sixth child of Whitbread Tomson (1825/6–1876), banker, and his wife, Elizabeth Maria Cremer (*d.* in or before 1904). After attending a preparatory school at Ingateston in Essex he continued his education at Uppingham School before studying at the academy of painting at Düsseldorf. On his return to England in 1882 he began to exhibit paintings at the Royal Academy and New Gallery, and from 1889 with the New English Art Club (NEAC). A staunch advocate of impressionism, he won praise for his evocative handling of colour, light, and atmosphere and for accurate images imbued with poetic effects. Moonrise and dawn were particularly congenial to his talents, as in the pastel *Moonrise on the Marsh: Picardy* (exh. NEAC 1889) or *Under the Downs* (exh. NEAC 1893), a twilight scene. Yet he achieved a wide range of effects. The small canvas *Stack-Making* (exh. NEAC 1891) vigorously handles monumental forms and distant spaces in the presence of blazing light, while *Apple Blossom* (Manchester City Galleries) subtly counterpoints light with shade, delicate blossoms with barnyard fowl, and a farmhouse sheltered by trees. Tomson's work has been compared to Edward Stott's landscapes, but Jean-François Millet was an abiding influence.

In October 1886 Tomson eloped to Cornwall with the poet Rosamund Armytage, later known as Rosamund Marriott *Watson (1860–1911), daughter of Benjamin Williams Ball, who was legally separated from her husband at the time. After Rosamund's divorce Arthur married her on 21 September 1887; their son Graham, known as Tommy to family and friends, was born the following month. The Tomsons settled in London in 1888, and husband and wife often collaborated, she (under the pseudonym Graham R. Tomson) writing essays for magazines on the landscapes he painted, he illustrating her edited collection *Concerning Cats* (1892).

Tomson also wrote poetry (published in *The Painter-Poets* of 1890) and fiction (*Many Waters*, 1904). But his best writing was on art. Tomson delighted in controversy as a critic, and the writer Elizabeth Pennell, who with her husband the etcher and writer Joseph Pennell became a lifelong friend, called him a 'spirited revolutionary' (Pennell, *Nights*, 202). With Francis Bate, secretary of the New English Art Club, Tomson edited the short-lived *Art Weekly* (February–July 1890), and his gift for gleeful polemic is evident in his attack on the Royal Academy in *Studio* (May 1893).

In 1893 Tomson was active in the Allahakbarries, the cricket team organized by James Barrie, which often practised in the grounds of the Tomsons' house in St John's Wood Road, Marylebone. Amusement turned to disaster when Tomson's wife left him for another member of the team, the Australian novelist H. B. Marriott Watson, in 1894. His divorce finalized in 1896, Tomson continued to exhibit with the NEAC and in April 1898 he became art critic for the *Morning Leader* under the pseudonym N. E. Vermind. On the 14th of that same month he married Agnes Mary Hastings (*b.* 1869/70), a clergyman's daughter and descendant of Warren Hastings, with whom he had a daughter, Marjorie (*b.* 23 Jan 1899). By 1900 they had moved to Dorset; Tomson subsequently contributed essays and drawings of Dorset subjects to the *Art Journal*. But he later told Elizabeth Pennell that the move to the country left him depressed and ruined his career. In 1903 Tomson published *Jean-François Millet and the Barbizon School*. He died of tuberculosis on 14 June 1905 at Silverdale, Salehurst, Sussex. He was buried in Steeple churchyard, near Wareham. Neither a retrospective show at the Baillie Gallery in 1906 nor his widow's bequest of paintings to the Victoria and Albert Museum and Manchester City Galleries could mend the obscurity into which he had fallen.

F. W. GIBSON, *rev.* LINDA K. HUGHES

Sources L. Cong., manuscript division, Pennell MSS · J. L. Waltman, 'The early London journals of Elizabeth Robins Pennell', PhD diss., U. Texas, 1976 · E. R. Pennell, *Nights: Rome and Venice in the aesthetic eighties, London and Paris in the fighting nineties*, 2nd edn (1916) · b. cert. · m. certs. · divorce certificate · d. cert. · A. Tomson, 'A first impression of the Royal Academy, 1893', *The Studio*, 1 (1893), 77–8 · A. Tomson, *Jean-François Millet and the Barbizon school* (1903) · G. R. Tomson, 'Picardy for painters, and others', *Longman's Magazine* (Sept 1888), 524–30 · *The Academy* (27 April 1889), 294 · *Scottish Art Review* (May 1889), 353 · *Scots Observer* (4 May 1889), 661 · R. A. M. S. [R. A. M. Stevenson], 'The New English Art Club', *Pall Mall Gazette* (24 Nov 1893) · 'Probate, divorce, and admiralty division: *Armitage v. Armitage and Tomson*', *The Times* (1 Feb 1887) · [J. Barrie], *Allahakbarries C. C.* (1893) [privately printed] · 'The journalist', *The Bookman*, 14 (1898), 10–12, esp. 11 · Wood, *Vic. painters*, 2nd edn · A. Thornton, *Fifty years of the New English Art Club, 1886–1935* (1935) · *Art Journal*, new ser., 25 (1905), 259 · Graves, *Artists*, 3rd edn · *CGPLA Eng. & Wales* (1905) · *Banker's Magazine*, 36 (1876), 474–5, 763
Archives L. Cong., manuscript division, Pennell MSS
Likenesses F. Hollyer, photograph, repro. in *Baillie Gallery memorial exhibition catalogue* (1906)
Wealth at death £6820 14*s.*: probate, 30 June 1905, *CGPLA Eng. & Wales*

Tomson, Giles (1553–1612), bishop of Gloucester, was born in London, the son of Giles Tomson, a grocer. He attended Merchant Taylors' School from 1564, and went up in 1571, as an exhibitioner, to University College, Oxford, where he graduated BA in 1575 and proceeded MA in 1578; he was incorporated at Cambridge the same year. He became a fellow of All Souls College, Oxford, in 1580, served as university proctor in 1586, and received his BD in 1590. At Elizabeth I's visit to Oxford in 1592 he distinguished himself by determining the natural philosophy disputation with 'a very learned and discreet speach' (Nichols), which from the queen's viewpoint probably also had the great merit of brevity. In the same year Tomson acquired the living of Pembridge in Herefordshire, and in 1594 a canonry in Hereford Cathedral from Bishop Westfaling. It appears that he never married. Some time in the late 1590s he became chaplain to Queen Elizabeth, preaching before her in the Lenten sermons of 1598 and 1599. He received his DD in 1602 and the plum deanery of Windsor in February 1603. Over the next nine years he often presided at chapter meetings at Windsor where he handled estate business and administered discipline to errant clerks and poor knights, one of whom accused him in 1608 of oppressive government. He remained a royal chaplain on the accession of James I.

In January 1604 Tomson attended the Hampton Court conference, though there is no record of his contribution. At the meeting it was agreed that a new translation of the Bible be prepared and Tomson was appointed to a team of eight Oxford theologians helping with the Greek versions of the gospels, Acts, and Revelation. Tomson was a 'good friend' of the poet John Davies, who praised his lively conversation and claimed that in Tomson's face 'witt, and pietie doth shine' (*Microcosmos*, 1603, sig. Nn2*ir*); John Manningham attended a court sermon that Tomson preached in April 1603, noting that he used 'a sounding laboured artificiall prounciacion' (*Diary of John Manningham*) as Tomson, it seems, commented tartly on the scramble for position with the imminent arrival of the new king.

Tomson continued to preach at the Jacobean court and, though his patrons remain obscure, in 1611 he earned the bishopric of Gloucester. He was consecrated on 9 June at Lambeth, having received permission to retain the deanery of Windsor for a year after his consecration; he died at Windsor Castle almost to the day, on 14 June 1612, not yet having visited his diocese. He was buried in Bray chapel at St George's Chapel, Windsor, with a monument depicting him, half-length, in the pulpit.   KENNETH FINCHAM

Sources PRO, PROB 11/120/63 · Foster, *Alum. Oxon.* · *Fasti Angl.* (Hardy) · Wood, *Ath. Oxon.*, new edn, 2.850–51 · J. Nichols, *The progresses and public processions of Queen Elizabeth*, new edn, 3 (1823), 156–7 · P. E. McCullough, *Sermons at court: politics and religion in Elizabethan and Jacobean preaching* (1998) [incl. CD-ROM] · A. W. Pollard, ed., *Records of the English Bible: the documents relating to the translation and publication of the Bible in English, 1525–1611* (1911); repr. (1974), 52–3 · S. Bond, ed., *The chapter acts of the dean and canons of Windsor: 1430, 1523–1672* (1966) · S. M. Bond, ed., *The monuments of St George's Chapel, Windsor Castle* (1958) · *The diary of John Manningham of the Middle Temple, 1602–1603*, ed. R. P. Sorlien (Hanover, NH, 1976)

Likenesses monument, St George's Chapel, Windsor, Bray chapel; repro. in Bond, *Monuments*

Wealth at death exact sum unknown: will, PRO, PROB 11/120/63

Tomson, Laurence (1539–1608), administrator, was born in Northamptonshire. In 1553 he entered Magdalen College, Oxford; he graduated BA six years later. He was subsequently elected a fellow of the college and proceeded MA in 1564. The college granted him permission to pursue his studies abroad, and in May 1565 Tomson left Oxford to begin his travels in Europe. He may well have spent time studying in Geneva before joining the embassy of Sir Thomas Hoby dispatched in March 1566 to France, where presumably he remained until the ambassador's death in July. From France, Tomson travelled to Germany, and matriculated at the University of Heidelberg in March 1568. Aside from the fact that he resigned his fellowship from Magdalen in 1569, little is certainly known of his movements over the next three years. However, the epitaph on Tomson's monument at Chertsey in Surrey states that he also journeyed to Russia, Sweden, Denmark, and Italy. By November 1572 he was living under the protection of the puritan earl of Huntingdon in Leicester.

It is hardly surprising that Tomson, well educated, cosmopolitan, and with a command of twelve languages, soon found his way into the service of Sir Francis Walsingham. Probably early in 1575 he was appointed Walsingham's secretary, in which capacity he was to serve for the next fifteen years. He accompanied the minister and William Broke, tenth Lord Cobham, to the Netherlands in June 1578. His role in this embassy was solely secretarial and indeed he never received an ambassadorial appointment. Nevertheless he was actively involved in England's foreign affairs. As well as drafting foreign correspondence for Walsingham, he wrote a Latin treatise, presumably for

his master, on the history of the trading disputes that existed between the Merchant Adventurers and the Hanseatic League, and in 1580 travelled to Boulogne to interview a papal agent regarding the activities of Esmé Stewart, duke of Lennox, in Scotland. In addition to his work as Walsingham's secretary and agent Tomson sat in parliament, first as MP for Melcombe Regis between 1578 and 1587, and latterly as the representative for Downton between 1588 and 1590. Upon Walsingham's death in 1590 he withdrew from public life to Laleham in Middlesex, where he died on 4 April 1608. He was survived by his wife, Jane, whom he had married before October 1579.

Tomson, whether scholar, civil servant, or politician, consistently displayed throughout his life a deep interest in and commitment to the puritan religion. It is likely that Laurence Humphrey, president of Magdalen and a well-known puritan himself, may have helped to shape the younger man's religious sympathies. In addition to Humphrey, Tomson's correspondents in the years after he left Oxford included the outspoken puritan leader Anthony Gilby; his name has also been associated with other dissidents, including Francis Hastings and Thomas Cartwright. In tandem with William Davison, Elizabeth's resident ambassador in the Low Countries, he supported Walter Travers, a puritan chaplain to the Merchant Adventurers, when the company sought to depose him. Before Davison returned to England in May 1579, Tomson gave him further help by supplying him with the names of two puritan ministers, whom he believed might be suitable to serve the English congregation in Antwerp. Among his activities as an MP Tomson sat on the committee appointed in 1584 to examine the quality of ministers chosen by John Whitgift and to consider the petitions of those so far excluded by the archbishop. The following year he attended a further committee concerned with revising the bill for the introduction of the Geneva prayer book. He also devoted considerable time to the translation of theological works. Best known are his translation from Latin of Beza's 1576 New Testament and his English translation, *The Sermons of Calvin on St Paul's Epistles to Timothie and Titus*. Yet for all Tomson's commitment to the puritan faith he was, to paraphrase Backus, more of a moderator than a pioneer. Although he possessed vociferous puritan friends, sat on government committees dealing with contentious religious issues, and translated other people's theological commentaries, it would seem that his considerable intelligence was equalled by his sense of caution.   LUKE MACMAHON

Sources Wood, *Ath. Oxon.*, new edn, vol. 2 · HoP, *Commons, 1558–1603*, 3.511–12 · I. Backus, 'Laurence Tomson (1539–1608) and Elizabethan puritanism', *Journal of Ecclesiastical History*, 28 (1977), 17–27 · P. Collinson, *The Elizabethan puritan movement* (1967) · monument, Chertsey church, Surrey · DNB

Tomson, Richard (*fl.* 1582–1600), merchant, may possibly have been the son of Robert Tomson of Andover and Seville, but is more likely to have had his roots in Norfolk. If so, he can probably be identified with Richard Tomson of

Yarmouth, nephew of John Thomson of Sheringham, whose mother was from Antwerp and who was engaged for some years in trade with the Mediterranean. In 1582 he was involved in litigation with the Turkey Company. He was part owner of the *Jesus of London*, which had been confiscated by a merchant rival and taken to Algiers; in 1583 he went there to ransom the prisoners. For four years (1585–9) he was a frequent correspondent with Walsingham. He spoke French and German, wrote in a vivid and fluent prose style, and may have been related to Laurence Tomson, Walsingham's secretary. He was involved in negotiations with Spain (1585–6) for the release of English prisoners in Dunkirk, and told Walsingham of the troop movements of Alessandro Farnese, duke of Parma. In January 1588 he was in Flanders, where he was solicited by Spaniards to deliver a large quantity of iron ordnance and cables from England, for which he was promised a monthly pension for life. Knowing that the ordnance was for equipping the projected armada, he refused the offer and informed Walsingham so that he could prevent its export. He later wrote to Burghley that 'no true-hearted Englishman will prefer filthy lucre before the public benefit of his country' (Tomson to Burghley, 3 April 1593 *CSP dom.*, *1581–1603*, ccxliv, 116).

In the summer of 1588 Tomson was lieutenant of the *Margaret and John*, a merchant ship involved against the armada, and wrote to Walsingham a long report from the Isle of Walcheren (30 July), giving particulars of his encounters with the Spaniards, especially the capture of the galleon of Don Pedro de Valdes during the night after the first battle, and the boarding of the *San Lorenzo*, which had keeled over in Calais harbour. But for Tomson it would not be known what occurred on the only occasion during the armada's passage when one of the combatants boarded and captured an enemy ship. He occupied her for one and a half hours, finally making off when the robbing of a French deputation provoked a loud protest from the guns of the castle at Calais. He was engaged (1588–9) in a lengthy negotiation with Parma over the ransom terms for the release of armada prisoners, and wrote regularly to Walsingham about this, and the possibility of replacing Spanish authority in Flanders. By 1591–2 he was corresponding with Burghley about the Catholic League's activities in France and Parma's projected march to aid them. He informed Burghley (1592) of Spanish preparations at Ferrol for a new armada against the British Isles.

It is possible that Tomson was the interloper charged by the Barbary Company (1596) with supplying Mawlay Ahmad, king of Morocco, with oars, lances, and firearms, in return for almonds, dates, molasses, and indigo; in vain the company asked Burghley to ban Tomson's imports into England. He traded in partnership with Gilbert Sootherne, who died in Morocco (1599), and protested to Robert Cecil that he was being deprived of his goods in Sootherne's possession, but despite a pressing letter from Elizabeth to the king his goods do not appear to have been released. Tomson is finally discovered writing to Cecil (1599–1600) about contradictory reports of a new Spanish armada and slanderous talk against Cecil which he overheard in a Suffolk inn while *en route* for his home in Norfolk. He may have been the Captain Tomson with the notorious pirate Peter Eston in 1611–12, but the name is too common to make identification certain.

BASIL MORGAN

Sources CSP for., 1584–93 · CSP dom., 1581–1603 · H. de Castries, *Les sources inédites de l'histoire du Maroc, 1 série, Dynastie Sa'dienne: archives et bibliothèques d'Angleterre*, 1–2 (1918–25), 101–3, 115, 139–41, 147–8 · T. S. Willan, *Studies in Elizabethan foreign trade* (1959) · *Calendar of the manuscripts of the most hon. the marquis of Salisbury*, 10, HMC, 9 (1904), 83 · G. M. Thomson, *Sir Francis Drake* (1972) · W. Graham, *The Spanish armadas* (1972) · J. K. Laughton, ed., *State papers relating to the defeat of the Spanish Armada, anno 1588*, 2 vols., Navy RS, 1–2 (1894) · M. Lewis, *Armada guns* (1961) · M. Lewis, *The Spanish armada* (1960)

Tone, Matilda (1769/70–1849). *See under* Tone, (Theobald) Wolfe (1763–1798).

Tone, William Theobald Wolfe (1791–1828). *See under* Tone, (Theobald) Wolfe (1763–1798).

Tone, (Theobald) Wolfe (1763–1798), Irish nationalist and political writer, was born in Dublin on 20 June 1763, probably at 27 St Bride Street, the eldest son of Peter Tone (d. 1805), a successful coach-builder, and his wife, Margaret Lamport (d. 1818). The Tones had sixteen children, but only five others survived: William (1764–c.1799), Matthew (1771–1798), Mary (c.1779–c.1800), Arthur (b. 1782; last heard of in 1812), and Fanny (c.1784–1792). As the eldest in this close-knit family, Tone took his family responsibilities very seriously. He had Matthew, Arthur, and Mary accompany him at various stages of his life in exile in America and France, giving a home to Mary and finding employment for his brothers. All the children had an adventurous streak, the boys sharing a fascination with military life: Arthur ran away to sea at the age of twelve and William left home when he was sixteen to enlist in the East India Company.

Early life In the 1760s and early 1770s the Tones were a relatively wealthy middle-class family, living at 44 Stafford Street close to the heart of fashionable Dublin, with property interests elsewhere in Dublin and in co. Kildare. In the late 1770s, however, Peter Tone's business declined, and the family moved out of Dublin to their home at Bodenstown, co. Kildare. This was part of the estate of the distinguished barrister and politician Theobald Wolfe, Tone's godfather and namesake. In 1789 Peter Tone lost all the family property after lengthy and expensive litigation with his elder brother Jonathan (d. 1792) over rightful ownership.

Tone's father was ambitious for his eldest son, and from an early age the boy was educated at private schools with the object of entering university in Dublin; his father stepped in to curb his waywardness, which almost certainly would have caused him to run away from home to embrace a military career. Tone entered Trinity College, Dublin, in February 1781. Much as at school, he was deemed a highly talented but scarcely diligent student, and he was suspended from college for a year because of his involvement in a duel in which a fellow student was

(Theobald) Wolfe Tone (1763–1798), by unknown artist

killed. Much of his 'sabbatical' was spent on amateur dramatics and a romantic liaison with a married woman, Eliza Martin, the wife of Richard Martin, MP for Jameston, co. Leitrim. Though there is much self-mockery in his journals about his appearance, we know that women found him attractive. He was 5 feet 8 inches in height, and while this was considered tall for the age, his slight frame created the impression of smallness. He had brown hair, a smallish, oval-shaped face, deep-set dark eyes, a large nose, and a sallow complexion: 'a slight, effeminate-looking man, with a hatchet face, long aquiline nose, rather handsome and genteel looking, with lank, straight hair', as he is described in a contemporary account (Walsh, 152–3). Another account thought the posthumous portrait by his daughter-in-law depicted him as far too passive, failing to capture:

> the small grey glancing eye of the original … According to my recollection of him he was a *very* slender, angular *rapid* moving man, a thin face, sallow and pockmarked, eyes small, lively bright … laughed and talked fast with enthusiasm about music and other innocent things … wise he could not be but he had not a foolish look—too lively and smart for that.   (TCD, MS 873/38, Sir Philip Crampton to Dr R. R. Madden, 3 May 1843)

Tone returned to university in 1783, chastened by his suspension, and had earned a glowing reputation by the time of his graduation in February 1786, most notably for his performances in the college historical society. At Trinity, Tone mixed with and befriended many who were to become statesmen and public leaders. He was being groomed to enter Ireland's political élite, and the next stage was training as a barrister at the Middle Temple in London (1787–9). But since there was little required of the students but dining regularly in hall, Tone turned to writing. He collaborated in writing a satirical *roman-à-clef*, *Belmont Castle* (1790), and produced a detailed plan for a British military colony on the Sandwich Islands (Hawaii), for which he tried unsuccessfully to elicit the support of the British prime minister, William Pitt.

While still a student at Trinity, Tone eloped with and married, on 21 July 1785, the sixteen-year-old Martha or Matilda Witherington, for which he earned the lifelong enmity of most of her family and that of their relative, the future lord chancellor of Ireland, John FitzGibbon, earl of Clare. **Matilda Tone** (1769/70–1849), as she was known after Tone renamed her Matilda in 1785, was the daughter of William Witherington, a Dublin woollen draper, and the granddaughter of a Church of Ireland clergyman by the name of Fanning. The couple had four children: Maria (1786–1803), **William Theobald Wolfe Tone** (1791–1828), Francis (1793–1806)—all of whom died of tuberculosis, a particular scourge of the Tone family—and Richard (1794–1795), who died in infancy. Early marriage and the decline in his family's fortune added to Tone's natural impatience as he embarked on his career as a barrister in 1789. The Irish legal profession was a recognized route to political preferment. But it required years of deference to and cultivation of the Irish protestant ascendancy to get anywhere, and the Irish bar was most definitely an appendage of the political establishment. Tone had some early success in attracting the patronage of the powerful whig family the Ponsonbys, but soon railed at the way they expected him to act as a hack writer in their cause—besides which he had by then started to make a name for himself as a talented political writer.

Political writer, 1790–1792 In 1789–90 Tone had sat in the public gallery of the Irish House of Commons as a heated electoral campaign was waged by the newly formed Irish whig party against placemen and corruption in government. Thus inspired, he produced, in March 1790, a pro-whig pamphlet, *A Review of the Conduct of Administration during the Last Session of Parliament*. Even this early, Tone's thinking had gone beyond the traditional whig programme of combating excessive executive power to stating the eighteenth-century classical republican idea of government as a trust, with power ultimately lying with the people. Inspired by the modest success of the pamphlet, Tone addressed another cause of the moment in the follow-up, *Spanish war!: An enquiry how far Ireland is bound of right to embark on the impending contest on the side of Great Britain* (July 1790). Though also inspired by debates in the Irish parliament, this was a much more independent work than the *Review* and his first analysis of the connection between Britain and Ireland. It called for Irish politicians to take an independent stance on the war issue and bemoaned Ireland's lack of separate national standing. Although in 1790 such ideas were already being aired by others, Tone's pamphlet was deemed dangerous, and he attributed its lack of success to a fearful bookseller suppressing it.

It was while attending the parliamentary debates in

1790 that Tone met and befriended Thomas Russell. Theirs was to be a very special and close friendship, and Russell was the main figure in Tone's celebrated journals. Indeed these were begun by Tone as a form of friendly rivalry with Russell, and they stand as testimony to the quick wit for which Tone was already celebrated during his time at Trinity. He was noted for being able to find the apt and wittiest quote for any situation, and the journals reveal a retentive mind and an impressive command of eighteenth-century ideas and writings. He was also a competent flautist; he packed his flute on his travels and made a special pilgrimage to a famous music store in the Netherlands while acting as United Irish agent to France after 1796. 'I admired him for the brilliancy and great variety of his conversation, the gay and social cast of his disposition', wrote a fellow barrister, William Sampson, traits which are amplified in his personal writings (*Memoirs*, 262).

Although Russell did not write with Tone's facility, he was a man of advanced opinions, particularly on religious toleration, and he had a marked influence on Tone's thought. An army officer, he was posted to Belfast in September 1790 and from there also introduced Tone to the thinking of the northern dissenters. It was Russell who wrote asking Tone to compile resolutions for a political club to be established in Belfast on the anniversary of the fall of the Bastille, 14 July 1791. These became the founding resolutions for the Society of United Irishmen, but it was the covering letter which was to receive most attention, for it fell into the hands of government and (since it declared Tone's preference for a separation from England) was later used by FitzGibbon to denounce Tone as a traitor. Tone's resolutions were at first rejected by the Belfast reformers (because of their implied demand for Catholic emancipation) and, irritated by such double standards among these self-styled reformers, he produced his most mature political work to date: *An Argument on Behalf of the Catholics of Ireland* (August 1791).

Tone's *Argument* was addressed to protestants (though more specifically the Ulster Presbyterians) who were radicals in politics but resistant to granting Catholics equal rights. In it he reiterated his complaint that Ireland was not recognized as a nation in its own right. The reason for this was the form of government, but the Irish tolerated it because of their own divisions. Thus had earlier reformers failed in their campaigns because government had been able to play upon their fears of the Catholics. He now thought such fears redundant in the newly secularized world created by the French Revolution. In the 1790s only Thomas Paine's *Rights of Man* gained a larger readership in Ireland than Tone's pamphlet, and it impacted on Presbyterians and Catholics alike. The Presbyterians dropped their reservations and invited Tone to Belfast in October 1791 to help found the Society of United Irishmen. The Catholics totally reformed their conservative Catholic Committee to reflect the new radicalism, and in 1792 Tone was invited to join their campaign for Catholic rights as their agent and secretary. He had found his métier as a talented political writer. He always prepared his ground by

detailed research, then wrote up his findings quickly, so that there is an immediacy and directness which sets his writings apart from the often torpid style of his contemporaries. Between 1791 and 1792 (the peak of his career as a political writer for both the United Irishmen and the Catholic Committee) he was recognized by both as their most talented propagandist.

It was with Tone's two-week visit to Belfast in October 1791 that his journals opened. These are a witty, often self-mocking account of Tone's and Russell's activities in the town, their late-night socializing at clubs, coteries, and the theatre intermixed with the political discussions associated with the foundation of the Society of United Irishmen. A typical eighteenth-century man of letters, Tone was as fascinated by new technology as by the play of ideas, and he was impressed by Belfast. It was the middle-class capital of Ireland, its largely Presbyterian business class stoking the developments which were already making Ulster the most prosperous province in the country. His growing distrust of aristocracy and privilege was deepened by his Ulster experience, for Belfast was a closed borough, its local government, like central government, monopolized by Ulster's landed (and largely Anglican) class.

Political activist, 1791–1794 The United Irish Society was finally inaugurated in Belfast on 14 October on the basis of Tone's slightly modified July resolutions. The *Declaration and Resolutions of the Society of United Irishmen of Belfast* reiterated many of Tone's arguments and formulated them into three objectives: a union among all the people of Ireland to counter the huge weight of English influence in the country; a radical reform of parliamentary representation as 'the sole constitutional mode' by which such influence can be countered; and the inclusion of Irishmen of 'every *religious* persuasion'. Tone and Russell then returned to Dublin as effective ambassadors for the north and inaugurated the Dublin Society of United Irishmen on 9 November on the same principles. Tone's *Argument* had been the decisive impetus in convincing the radicals that no reform could be achieved without also addressing Catholic grievances, and, although Tone continued to write on behalf of the United Irish Society and served for short spells early in 1792 as its chairman and secretary, it was in the cause of winning political rights for the Catholics that he devoted most of his efforts for the next three years.

In the leaders of the Catholic Committee, notably wealthy merchants such as John Keogh and Richard McCormick, Tone discovered the same middle-class community of interest against the Anglican political establishment which he so admired in Belfast. That Anglican ascendancy had conducted a vitriolic attack on the Catholic leaders in the parliamentary debates of February 1792, when the Catholics' petition for relief was rejected by a huge majority. In April Tone was invited to become agent and assistant secretary to the Catholic Committee, and for the rest of the year his energies were devoted to organizing national elections to a Catholic Convention to petition for Catholic rights. He accompanied John Keogh on a number of campaigning trips to win support, most notably to the north, where he was considered the bridge to the Presbyterians. A year after his resolutions had been defeated on 14 July 1791, he returned again to Belfast for Bastille day celebrations, this time as a Catholic agent. Knowing of continued opposition to immediate Catholic relief from a number of leading reformers, Tone's address of 1792 was much more conciliatory than that of 1791, and was accepted. But two visits to Rathfriland, co. Down, in July and August, to defuse growing sectarian conflict there, aroused considerable resentment from the local gentry, and on the second visit the delegates were all but run out of the town.

Throughout that summer it was Tone who conducted the publicity side of the Catholic Committee's campaign, responding to a series of letters in the northern press and, most notably, confronting leading members of the ascendancy who, through the country's grand juries, issued bigoted statements against Catholic relief. The statements declared that the Catholics were acting unconstitutionally and that a protestant ascendancy had been established by the revolution of 1688; with a superciliousness which infuriated the newly confident Catholic leaders, they denounced the Catholic leaders for not behaving sufficiently humbly. These addresses were badly written and a gift to someone like Tone. In a series of ripostes published in the press under the *nom de plume* Vindex, he assumed the character of the ordinary man (a favourite device of his) and showed the concept of a protestant ascendancy to be a pretence for unaccountable power and corruption. The ascendancy campaign backfired badly, and as a result the Catholics' cause attracted additional support from reforming protestants.

The object of all the campaigning, the Catholic Convention, opened in Dublin on 3 December, with 233 elected delegates. It was the first national body of lay Catholics to meet in over a century, and Tone's diary is the fullest account we have of the internal debates. While it highlights tensions between the more traditional conservatism of leading Catholics and the new radicalism of the age, the latter won the day because of the Irish administration's undisguised expectations that Catholics should behave submissively. The convention voted to go over Dublin Castle's authority and present their petition directly to the king. Tone was one of the delegation who travelled to London via Belfast, where his special relationship with the northerners was applauded by the crowds, who cheered the delegates and accompanied their carriage out of the town. In January 1793 they were well received by the king and the home secretary, Henry Dundas, who privately was trying to overcome the Irish ascendancy's resistance to Catholic emancipation. But war broke out between Britain and France in the following month. The political class on which the governance of Ireland depended was in mutinous mood, and the Catholic Relief Act of April 1793 fell short of Catholic expectations. Although the franchise (removed in 1728) was restored, the right to sit in parliament was rejected, and the tone of the debate was so anti-Catholic that the concessions were robbed of much of their conciliatory effect. The fragile unity of the Catholics fell apart, and Tone openly accused Keogh of having compromised their cause in London. But worse was to come, as the war crisis brought an immediate clampdown on the activities of the reformers and the arrest of a number of the United Irish leaders.

Tone was seriously disillusioned and spoke to Russell about emigrating to America. He had totally neglected his friends and family for much of the past year in his service to the Catholic Committee and 'muzzled' his own radicalism for fear of harming the Catholics by association. He had argued the Paineite principle that people had the right to vote for the laws by which they were governed, and he had admitted privately his belief that Ireland might fare better as an independent nation. But he was no doctrinaire, and in a broadside written on behalf of the United Irishmen in March 1793 he argued: 'we have no right to force men to be free'. 'If a nation wills a bad government, it ought to have that government' (PRO, HO 100/34/111). Indeed, given the reputation which he was to acquire as the 'father' of Irish republicanism, Tone's response of July 1793 to FitzGibbon's public revelation of his 1791 letter to Russell speaks volumes for his constitutionalism, even this late. FitzGibbon used it to argue that the Catholic elections of 1792 had been organized by Tone to induce the lower orders to rebel. But, far from feeling in any way threatened, Tone went immediately to press to denounce what he considered a particularly dishonourable use of a private letter. A desire to reduce England's influence on Ireland's government was not treason, he argued; it had been the core of the parliamentary patriot movement in the 1780s and latterly of the whigs. Certainly there was no sign of Tone's contemplating active republicanism at this stage, and, as the United Irish Society continued to fall apart, he stopped attending and decided reluctantly to return to his career as a barrister.

The emergence of a revolutionary, 1794–1795 In April 1794 Tone became involved with a French agent, William Jackson, and his future was changed decisively. Archibald Hamilton Rowan was one of a tiny handful of landed gentry in the otherwise middle-class United Irish Society, and, like his class, he tended to act with an irresponsibility which even Tone (who admired him) criticized. Even so, his arrest, trial, and imprisonment in January 1794 for distributing an address deemed seditious by the authorities was a terrible shock to the reformers, still unattuned to the brutal new realities of a government crackdown in time of war. Tone met Jackson while visiting Rowan in prison. On 14 April, at Rowan's request, Tone did what he had so often done before: he produced a paper on the state of Irish public opinion, in which he restated his belief that Ireland was governed by a protestant aristocracy in the interests of England. But now he thought there would be a popular revolt, led by the Ulster Presbyterians, if France invaded and disclaimed any idea of conquest. It is difficult to know what to make of this undoubtedly militant statement, for Tone had been a voice of restraint in recent months in the United Irish Society. Nor is it clear that he was apprised of Jackson's motivation (though Rowan was) when he wrote the paper, and, when told on 16 April about

Jackson's real identity and invited to travel to France as an Irish agent, he quickly backtracked and insisted on Rowan's burning the document. But Rowan had taken copies, and these were sent to France by Jackson. They were intercepted in the post and Jackson was arrested on 28 April.

What happened next is a remarkable insight into how Tone was viewed by the authorities, for, although he later admitted that he expected to be hanged, he was permitted to make a compact with government, giving a full account of his dealings with Jackson and an undertaking to leave the country, in return for immunity. He refused to compromise others (a refusal made easier by the escape and flight of Rowan on 1 May) and he withdrew entirely to the country for the rest of the year. He was regarded by the authorities as a nuisance, a talented tool in the hands of others, rather than a dangerous conspirator, and Dublin Castle was more anxious to get rid of him than to make an example of him. Indeed, in the early months of 1795, with the prospect of a more liberal regime under the new whig lord lieutenant, Earl Fitzwilliam, it even looked as if Tone might be rehabilitated, and he was invited back as agent by the Catholic Committee and accompanied another delegation to London that March. But the recall of Fitzwilliam, the introduction of a more hard-line regime under his successor, Earl Camden, and, most of all, the trial of Jackson on 23 April 1795 revealed Tone's immunity to be less secure than he supposed. It was the first occasion on which his involvement was made public, and there was an outcry. It was made clear to him that, if he did not speedily fulfil his agreement of quitting the country, he risked being tried for treason. Within weeks Tone had assigned the family cottage in Kildare over to his cousin, resigned from the bar, and made ready to leave for America. There is a real sense of danger in the rushed preparations, and many old friends rallied around. The Catholic Committee in particular raised all the outstanding payment owing to him, and, after settling his debts, he was left with £796 to start his new life. But, having rejected the idea of becoming a secret agent to France a year earlier, this is exactly what Tone now agreed to do.

The situation in Ireland had dramatically deteriorated on Fitzwilliam's recall and the radicals now despaired of achieving reform constitutionally. Russell was already involved in reorganizing the United Irishmen in northeast Ulster on a more secretive basis and clearly had a major impact on Tone's thinking in these weeks of unreality. In Dublin some leading Catholics and United Irishmen were taking a similar line and asked Tone to negotiate military assistance from France. He, Matilda, their children, his sister Mary, and his brother Arthur arrived in Belfast on 21 May 1795, from where they took ship for America on 12 June. Given the sense of danger and haste surrounding his departure from the south, the send-off which he and his family received in Belfast both testifies to the special esteem with which he was regarded there and amply justifies the warmth with which he speaks of the town and its people in his writings. There was a round of farewell social gatherings and a special subscription which raised some £1500 for Tone and his family. One gathering acquired particular significance both for Tone and the future nationalist tradition. During a large family picnic to the deer park just north of Belfast, Tone and a group of United Irish friends, including Russell, Henry Joy McCracken, Samuel Neilson, and Robert Simms, ascended the Cave Hill to its highest point, McArt's Fort, and there made 'a most solemn obligation … never to desist in our efforts, until we had subverted the authority of England over our country, and asserted her independence' (W. T. W. Tone, 1.127–8). In Irish nationalist tradition this is seen as the symbolic moment when modern Irish republicanism was born, testimony to the influence which Tone's journals and autobiography would later acquire, for his is the only account of the incident. Many in Ireland had felt Tone's treatment far exceeded his crime, and there can be no doubt that the militant republicanism for which he is best known was something of an accident of timing. Certainly the French revolutionary wars had made treasonable ideas which would not have been considered so a few years earlier, and Tone was able to operate unnoticed in France for almost two years because of this perception of him as hardly dangerous. Even so his character predisposed him to the revolutionary career on which he now embarked. 'The genius of Wolfe Tone', wrote David Plunket, the son of his friend and the future lord chancellor William Conyngham Plunket, 'was accompanied by its full share of eccentricity. His mind, powerful and impulsive, rushed at its object without looking to consequences, and foiled in one direction charged with double energy in another' (Plunket, 1.60–61).

The Tone family arrived in the United States on 1 August 1795 and took up residence in its new capital, Philadelphia. On 10 August Tone had his first audience with the French minister to Philadelphia, Pierre Adet, and over the next three days he wrote two statements, outlining the nature of the help the United Irishmen were seeking from France. But as Adet took his time in responding, Tone set about finding a home for his family. He eventually opted for Princeton, New Jersey, and seemed to be contemplating permanently taking up the life of a farmer. But reminders from his United Irish friends in Ireland about his undertaking sent him back to Adet in November, by which time the French minister was more responsive, and he approved his mission to the French government. Moreover, Tone was deeply unhappy in America. He found its people uncultured, overconfident, and materialistic, its climate too hot, its countryside unnatural. Neither he nor Matilda were keen to bring up their children among people whom he described as 'boorish and ignorant … uncivil and uncouth' (Elliott, *Wolfe Tone*, 267). His witty irreverence disappeared from his writings, as he recognized how much he missed the friendship he had known in Ireland. Although he, like the other United Irish leaders, had eulogized America as the first land of liberty, he found even its politics disappointing. The pro-British, anti-French federalists were in the ascendant. They were the party of big money and executive power, and Tone moved instead in the circle of their political opponents, the democratic republicans. Through the republicans he gained an introduction to France, through their representative in Paris, the future American president James Monroe. He sailed from New York on 1 January 1796, having acquired a false passport under the pseudonym James Smith. Matilda fully supported his decision and, so as not to dissuade him, kept the fact that she was pregnant again secret until after he had set sail.

Mission to France, 1796   Tone arrived at Le Havre on 2 February 1796 and reached Paris ten days later. He was fortunate in the timing of his arrival, for France was seeking revenge on England after its support for the French royalists in recent hostilities. Even so, Tone's success as a secret diplomat in France was remarkable, and other foreign revolutionaries demanding French help were not generally so well received. Tone secured his entrée to the French foreign ministry through Monroe. But he quickly sensed the divisions which bedevilled the regime then in power, the Directory, and resented having to deal with subalterns. On 24 February he accordingly took his case to the very top, in a private audience with the director charged with war policy, Lazare Carnot, and through him the Irish campaign was brought to the heart of French military strategy. It was, as ever, Tone's ability as a political writer which won the French over. His memorials on the Irish situation, written in February and making their way through the relevant French ministries over the next two months, outlined how France might use Ireland to combat her main enemy. They told of the alliance between Catholics and dissenters in the United Irishmen. But France must send a large enough force to prevent a civil war. The object was to attain Irish independence, and the French general should issue a manifesto disavowing all idea of conquest, offering protection to property and religion, and inviting the people to establish a national convention which would then form a government. It was a revolution Tone sought, not an insurrection, and he convinced the Directory that an Irish rising prior to a French invasion should be avoided. There is much in Tone's French writings about the need to minimize bloodshed. Although he had not condemned the execution of Louis XVI in 1793—thinking it 'necessary' if regrettable—in Paris he saw the places associated with the excesses of the terror and shuddered. 'If we have a republic in Ireland, we must build a Pantheon, but we must not, like the French, be in too great a hurry to people it' (TCD, MS 2048/21; W. T. W. Tone, 2.40–41).

Tone was short of money and lacked the friendship and sociability on which he had thrived in Ireland, and his early Paris journals lack the wit of his Irish ones. But the success of his mission had transformed his life by the summer and brought him a new set of friends. Foremost among these was France's top republican general, Lazare Hoche, fresh from his victory over civil war in the west and being courted by Carnot to accept command of an Irish invasion force. Tone was called to the seat of the Directory, the Luxembourg Palace, on 12 July to meet with

him. Tone would have been pleased with the communications between Hoche and the Directory after their meeting, for he had clearly won his case about Ireland's independence guaranteeing France an ally in her war against England. There would be no question about Ireland's being retained as a French conquest. Over the next days plans for the Irish invasion force were drawn up and Tone was made an adjutant-general in the French army. He had requested such a commission as a way of ensuring treatment as a prisoner of war. 'I was willing to encounter danger, as a soldier, but … I had a violent objection to being hanged as a traitor' (TCD, MS 2049/27; W. T. W. Tone, 2.71). But it was also the fulfilment of a lifetime's ambition, and he was to prove a good soldier, even though he had feared resentment from other French officers at such obvious inexperience and over-promotion. At Rennes, where he arrived to participate in the invasion preparations on 20 September, he lodged with Hoche and the other officers and was enthralled by the camaraderie of military life.

It was in the interval between his appointment and departure for the west that Tone wrote the document on which much of his future reputation was based: his 'Memorandums, relative to my life and opinions', or autobiography. This—with the seventeen notebooks of his journals—was published thirty years later as *The Life of Theobald Wolfe Tone*. It was undoubtedly influenced by the situation in which he found himself in the summer of 1796. His mission had succeeded beyond his wildest dreams, and there is a sense of destiny in the autobiography not present in his journals. There are many similarities between it and the propaganda he had been writing for France in preparation for the anticipated invasion of Ireland. In it his youthful rejection by Pitt, the haughtiness of the aristocratic faction in Ireland, his admiration for the Catholic Committee and the Ulster Presbyterians (whom together he envisaged forming Ireland's new government) came together in his 'theory', a theory which he now believed had motivated him since 1791:

> To subvert the tyranny of our execrable Government, to break the connection with England, the never-failing source of all our political evils, and to assert the independence of my country—these were my objects. To unite the whole people of Ireland, to abolish the memory of all past dissensions, and to substitute the common name of Irishman in the place of the denominations of Protestant, Catholic and Dissenter—these were my means.   (TCD, MS 2046/41v)

This was to become the most quoted passage in modern Irish history.

In the summer of 1796 Tone compiled the various proclamations for the invasion and was also charged with recruiting among the English and Irish prisoners of war. But preparations for the departure of the invasion force were frustratingly slow. The naval command prevaricated, and sufficient supplies were proving difficult to find. News reaching Tone of the deteriorating situation in Ireland and the arrests of most of his friends, including Russell, intensified his frustration, and he persuaded Hoche to dispatch a secret agent to Ireland to let them know of the forthcoming invasion and urge them to do all in their power to defer the trials. The fleet finally sailed from Brest on 15 December, carrying 14,450 troops, 41,644 stand of arms, and a supply of uniforms and cockades for the Irish expected to join them, and the Directory, fired by the successful passage of such a large expedition through an intensified British blockade, ordered a follow-up expedition of 17,000 men. Tone sailed on board the *Indomptable*, the largest ship in the expeditionary force. But the fleet encountered bad weather, and the frigate carrying Hoche and the naval commander (and all the printed addresses which Tone had composed for distribution in Ireland) was blown off course. The remainder of the fleet arrived at Bantry Bay in south-west Ireland on 22 December and Tone spent the evening preparing new addresses. But a storm blew up that night and over the next few days decimated the fleet. In the early days of 1797 fifteen of the original forty-three ships limped back to France. 'England', commented Tone, 'has not had such an escape since the Spanish Armada' (W. T. W. Tone, 2.266). And so indeed it was, for the British navy and defence forces had been taken totally by surprise, and even this failed attempt caused a major political and economic crisis in Britain and Ireland.

Life in the French army, 1797–1798 Tone was rescued from his despair only by the return of Hoche. He greeted Tone like a long-lost friend, assured him that he had not abandoned the Irish project, and invited him to join his staff with his new posting on the Rhine. Tone arrived at Cologne on 7 April 1797, but was denied his first taste of active service by urgent family concerns. His family had arrived in Hamburg in January after a protracted and stormy passage from America which had left Matilda extremely ill; she seems to have miscarried the baby she was carrying at the end of 1796. He secured leave from Hoche and travelled to Groningen in the Netherlands, where the family joined him on 7 May. His journals of his journey there show an impressive knowledge of the history and society of the countries through which he passed and a thirst for further information. He disliked the public display of Catholicism during Holy Week in Cologne—directing a characteristic enlightenment attack on friars, monks, and convents—and preferred the simpler practice of Dutch protestantism. Indeed the Dutch (Batavian) Republic he thought the model of good government. To this he attributed the country's commercial prosperity and the benefits it brought to the populations of northern Europe. He extolled the cleanliness of the Netherlands, comparing the country with the 'slovenliness' of Ireland, which he attributed to its poverty. The journal also reveals a tough attitude to governing systems. Tone thought republican government should be strong government, even supporting censorship of opposition press.

But although it took Tone some time to recognize it, his own mission to France steadily fell apart after the Bantry Bay failure. Hoche remained totally committed to another expedition, and his headquarters in Germany became the effective centre for continuing negotiations. It was from there that Tone was sent in June to bring back a new United Irish agent, Edward Lewins. He was a colleague from early United Irish and Catholic Committee campaigning in Dublin, and Tone remained loyal and supportive, despite signs over the next year that Lewins was not as active in his mission as he should have been. They agreed that Lewins should continue the negotiations in Paris which Tone had started, while Tone would work with any expedition to be sent to Ireland. In July 1797 this involved Tone's relocating to the Texel in the Netherlands, where France's Dutch ally had taken up the Irish invasion scheme, while Hoche would accompany another force apparently preparing in Brest. In July, however, Hoche became the scapegoat in a thwarted coup attempt which, if successful, would have seen him installed as the new war minister. He became demoralized by the bitter press attacks which followed, and when Tone arrived at Hoche's headquarters at Wetzlar, on 12 September, he found him in the advanced stages of tuberculosis. Two days later he died, aged twenty-nine, Tone being one of a handful of confidants who attended his deathbed. Hoche had been a good friend to Tone—as well as his most influential supporter—and his coterie of republican generals continued such support and friendship. But they lacked Hoche's stature and influence, and his loss left the way clear for the rise of his most bitter rival, Napoleon Bonaparte, for whom republican causes were anathema.

The threatened coup in France finally came about in September (the *coup d'état* of Fructidor) and removed from power nearly all the officials with whom Tone had negotiated, most notably Carnot. Tone—who had returned to Paris after Hoche's death—felt he and Lewins were having to start from scratch, and even though they secured audiences with Bonaparte himself, among others, they were receiving little more than generalized statements of support. The truth was that the post-Fructidorean 'second' Directory had adopted a much tougher policy towards foreign revolutionaries of only helping those who helped themselves. There would be no more expeditionary forces sent until the Irish had staged a rising. But Tone and Lewins, ignorant of this sea change in policy, continued to urge the United Irishmen to reserve their strength until the French arrived. That strength was steadily eroded through 1797 and early 1798, and the leadership was weakened by internal disagreement over the issue of rising before or after the French arrived.

The fallout from this split soon affected Tone's mission, as competing agents began to arrive on the continent from mid-1797. Many of the newer arrivals in France now gravitated to a Paris grouping led by the veteran patriot Napper Tandy, which was increasingly hostile towards Tone and Lewins. Indeed Tandy's public posturing and egotism betrayed Tone's activities in France to the British government for the first time since his arrival in 1796. Although he had made great personal sacrifices in pursuit of his mission, he now found himself the object of petty intrigue and was particularly hurt by accusations that he had sacrificed his country's interest to his own. He had always prided himself on his sense of honour and integrity—and indeed was recognized for such when he was in Ireland—and saw his personal sacrifices as part of his republican credentials. The only reward which he sought was in the reputation and gratitude of his countrymen, and the thought of being denied these preoccupied him throughout the early months of 1798. It was something of a relief to be posted to Rouen in April, where preparations were being made to invade England. In fact Bonaparte had already abandoned an English invasion in favour of his ill-fated Egyptian expedition, and Tone was ordered to Le Havre as adjutant to the commanding general defending the town against British bombardment.

By then Tone thought there was little chance of an Irish expedition, and reports coming through of the deteriorating situation in Ireland, mounting arrests, including those of nearly all his friends, the death of Lord Edward Fitzgerald, the declining state of Russell in prison, all fed a new desperation in his writings. He was not a naturally vengeful person, but he now wrote of avenging these 'martyrs of liberty', and of confiscating the property of the gentry (which he had rejected in the past). On 17 June he learned that a rising had finally broken out in Ireland, and he was recalled to Paris, where the news had reactivated the Directory's plans to invade. But, with the bulk of the army in Egypt, preparations were rushed and piecemeal. Several small forces were to land at different points on the Irish coast, and Tone was sent to join the main force of 8000 men preparing at Brest under one of Hoche's friends, General Hardy. Once again he was sent by the marine minister to recruit among the Irish and British prisoners of war, and on 1 August he arrived at Brest, where he joined Hardy on board the flagship *Hoche* (74 guns). But it was not until 16 September that the fleet finally sailed, and Tone knew that Britain had full knowledge of its movements and of his own presence on board, for they had been reported in the press. It is clear from his correspondence that he had no hope of its succeeding, but, as his son William recalled, he felt it his duty to accompany it. He told Matilda that 'he knew his life was gone', and he signed over to her full power of attorney. The fleet was tracked along the Irish coast by the British navy, and, on 12 October, as it was buffeted by a storm within sight of its Lough Swilly destination, it was attacked. Battle raged all day and Tone commanded one of the batteries. It was sinking when finally captured. The *Hoche* was to have been taken to Portsmouth, but it was blown off course by the continuing storm and only finally brought back to Lough Swilly on 31 October.

Final days, October–November 1798 Tone was reported to be among the first to step on shore. He had hoped his rank in the French army would have been respected, and he protested to the Irish commanders, to Dublin Castle, and to the French official charged with overseeing the exchange of prisoners of war at being treated like a common criminal and chained in Derry gaol. There was nothing insincere in this. He did expect death. But over the past two years he had been a French officer and by all accounts a good one. Having at first sought such a commission precisely to cover the perilous situation in which he now found himself, he had ended up assuming the persona of a French soldier and had insisted on wearing full dress uniform as he was brought a prisoner to Dublin.

Tone was imprisoned in the royal barracks and tried by a military court on 10 November. Charges of treason were read. He objected to the word 'traitorously' and read out an explanation of his actions. He spoke of the sacrifices he had made in a cause for which he was now ready to lay down his life, explaining how he tried to end the religious divisions in Ireland, and that when his friends abandoned him the Catholics had stood by him. He spoke of his pride in winning the esteem of his comrades in the French army and regretted the atrocities which had occurred in Ireland: 'I have attempted to establish the independence of my country; I have failed in the attempt; my life is in consequence forfeited' (PRO, HO 100/79/95–97). And he requested the death of a soldier by firing squad. He spent the following day writing final letters to Matilda, his father, his friends, and Matilda's brother and sister, asking them to take care of her. He learned of his fate that evening. He would be hanged publicly at 1 p.m. the following day, apparently at the insistence of some of his old opponents. But Lord Lieutenant Cornwallis had rejected the request that his head be struck off and publicly displayed. Tone wrote a final letter thanking his gaoler for having acted towards him like an officer and that night cut his own throat. He had written frequently in his journals of his horror of the shame of hanging and had admired the self-discipline of classical figures such as Cato in choosing suicide as an honourable end. He died on 19 November 1798, and his remains were given over to his family immediately following a coroner's inquest. His body was taken from the house of his relatives, the Dunbavins, at 52 High Street, where his parents had been living in straitened circumstances, and was buried at the family plot in Bodenstown on 21 November. His entire wealth on death—which he asked to be divided between his father and his wife—consisted of £50, a gold watch, and his trunk of clothes.

After Tone's death his widow, Matilda, remained in France, where she brought up her three remaining children with the help of a pension, belatedly granted by the Napoleonic government, due to her as the widow of a general in the French army. The only child to survive into adulthood, William, was educated at the cavalry school of St Germain and became a naturalized citizen. He fought in the Napoleonic army as lieutenant and aide-de-camp to General Bagneres and supported Bonaparte after his escape from Elba; he resigned his commission following the restoration of the monarchy in 1815. In July 1816 Matilda married a long-term friend and benefactor, Thomas Wilson (d. 1824), a Scottish radical who had been well liked by Tone, at the British embassy in Paris. She and her new husband and her son hoped to settle in Ireland, but the Irish administration refused to allow them to return. Instead they embarked for America and settled at Georgetown. William studied law in New York and briefly served in the artillery before pursuing a career in the War Office. In 1825 he married Catherine Sampson, the daughter of William Sampson (1764–1836), an old Dublin friend of his parents; they had one daughter, Grace Georgiana.

William died on 10 October 1828 and was buried on Long Island. Matilda survived into old age and died in 1849, aged eighty.

In 1826 Matilda and William published Tone's journals and writings. They formed the basis of the cult which by the twentieth century had turned Tone into the most influential inspiration of modern Irish nationalism and republicanism. But the cult had a slow gestation, coming to full maturity only with Fenianism's and Sinn Féin's promotion of the cult of the martyred dead. The tradition of republican speeches at his grave in Bodenstown began during the 1798 centenary celebrations: Patrick Pearse in his 1913 speech pronounced Tone's 1796 'theory' as encompassing 'the entire philosophy of Irish nationalism', particularly its 'blood sacrifice' tradition. But nationalists of all hues look back to Tone as their founding father, many groupings, besides republicans, paying annual pilgrimages to his grave. Today there is no sizeable town in the Irish Republic without a street named after him.   MARIANNE ELLIOTT

Sources W. T. W. Tone, *Life of Theobald Wolfe Tone*, 2 vols. (Washington, DC, 1826) • M. Elliott, *Wolfe Tone: prophet of Irish independence* (1989) • M. Elliott, *Partners in revolution: the United Irishmen and France* (1982) • TCD, Madden MS 873 • TCD, college historical society, MUN Soc/Hist.4–10, 40–41, 49–50, 57 • college muniments, TCD, MUN V/5/3–4, 9, 16, 27, 35, 46, 47, 86 • *The writings of Theobald Wolfe Tone, 1763–98*, ed. T. W. Moody, R. B. McDowell, and C. J. Woods, 1: *Tone's career in Ireland to June 1795* (1998) • W. T. W. Tone, *Life of Theobald Wolfe Tone*, ed. T. Bartlett (1998) • J. E. Walsh, *Sketches of Ireland sixty years ago* (1847) • *Memoirs of William Sampson* (NY, 1807) • D. Plunket, ed., *The life, letters and speeches of Lord Plunket*, 2 vols. (1867) • N. J. Curtis, 'Matilda Tone and virtuous republican femininity', *The women of 1798*, ed. D. Keogh and N. Furlong (1998), 26–48 **Archives** NL Ire., corresp. and papers • NL. Ire., letters, MS 3212 • TCD, autobiography, corresp., diaries, and papers, 2041–2050 and 3805–3809 | Archives du Ministère des Affaires Étrangères, Paris, Corr. Pol. Ang, 582–593 • Archives Nationales, Paris, AF III 186ᵃ⁻ᵇ, AF IV 1671, BB⁴103 • priv. coll., Dickason MSS, family papers • Rouen, Archives départementales de la Seine et Maritime, 1Mi 54–71, Hoche papers **Likenesses** portrait, 1798, repro. in *Walker's Hibernian Magazine* (Oct 1798) • C. A. Tone, miniature, repro. in Elliott, *Wolfe Tone*, frontispiece • death mask, TCD • miniature, NG Ire. [*see illus.*] • portrait (in volunteer uniform), NG Ire.; repro. in Madden, *United Irishmen* **Wealth at death** £50; gold watch; trunk of personal items: TCD, MS 872/145, Nov 1798; Elliott, *Wolfe Tone*, 471–2, notes 34–5, 51

Tong, William (1662–1727), Presbyterian minister and nonconformist tutor, was born on 24 June 1662, the son of William Tong, chapman, of Worsley in the parish of Eccles, Lancashire. His father died when Tong was young. Studying originally for the law, Tong through his mother's influence turned to the ministry, and entered the academy of Richard Frankland, then at Natland, on 2 March 1681. He was Frankland's most distinguished student. Early in 1685 he was licensed to preach, and began his ministry in Shropshire. 'He frequently preached to the poor people in the country, when he knew not but at the end of the sermon he might exchange the pulpit for a prison' (Newman, 34). For two years he served the families of Thomas Corbet of Stanwardine and Rowland Hunt of Boreatton as chaplain, thereby becoming acquainted with Philip Henry. He preached occasionally in the chapel of

Cockshut, parish of Ellesmere, Shropshire, using a small part of the Book of Common Prayer, until threatened with prosecution. Efforts were also made to persuade him to conform, including, later, by the dean of Chester. Tong first met Philip Henry's son Matthew, then a student in London, in May 1686. They formed a friendship broken only by Matthew's death in 1714.

With the publication of James II's declaration of indulgence in April 1687, the leading dissenters in Chester began to encourage preaching in public again. They chose Matthew Henry to be their minister, but since he was still a student in London they invited Tong 'to preach to them till he [Henry] came among them' (Henry, fol. 7r). Tong stayed for about three months, 'preaching with great acceptance' and 'their numbers did daily increase, so that they found it necessary to provide a larger place' even before Henry came to Chester (Newman, 36). At Chester, Tong fell ill with what was feared to be consumption, but he recovered and went first to Wrexham as a supply, but after a few months settled at Knutsford. There he helped establish a new meeting following divisions in the parish over the appointment of a public minister. He was ordained on 4 November 1687 at Warrington. While he was at Knutsford the present meeting-house was built (it was opened in 1689), but early in 1690 he moved to Coventry and was co-pastor first with Thomas Showell (d. 1694), then with Joshua Oldfield (1656–1729), who also conducted an academy, and finally with Matthew Warren. At Coventry, Tong maintained an active evangelical ministry, and 'continued long a burning and shining light, diffusing holy light and heat not only in that city, but in the country round about'. Such was his zeal that, in addition to the duties to his own congregation, he frequently preached in the surrounding villages and market towns, and by his serious lively preaching 'laid the foundation of several societies of protestant dissenters in those places, where there were none before' (Newman, 36–7).

When Frankland died in 1698 Tong was among those considered as his successor, but the academy closed. Tong is usually seen as Oldfield's assistant and successor in the academy at Coventry, but Vincent Carter received a grant of £10 from the Presbyterian Fund in April 1696, while 'under the instruction of Mr Tonge of Coventry' (DWL, MS OD 68, p. 41). When Oldfield became minister at Southwark, London, in 1699, the whole business of the academy fell on Tong.

On the death of Nathaniel Taylor in April 1702, Tong was elected minister of the Presbyterian congregation meeting at Salters' Hall, Canon Street, London, after Josiah Chorley and Matthew Henry had declined an invitation. The congregation was the wealthiest and most charitable in London. In 1705 Tong succeeded John Howe as one of the Tuesday morning Merchant lecturers at Salters' Hall. With the deaths of more senior ministers, Tong undertook an increasingly important role in the public affairs of the dissenters. He was a member of the Presbyterian Fund board from 1703 until his death, and represented the Presbyterians on the Committee of the Three Denominations after it was revived following the accession of George I. As a consequence he was generally present on those occasions when dissenters addressed the throne. He was named by Dr Daniel Williams (*d.* 1716) as one of the original twenty-three trustees of his charity. He was also one of the first distributors of the English *regium donum* for poor ministers and their dependants in 1723.

Tong had considerable antiquarian interests. He corresponded with, and in May 1697 visited, Ralph Thoresby, the Leeds antiquary. He included the antiquary Humfrey Wanley, a native of Coventry, among his friends. His historical interests were certainly influenced by his part in defending dissent in the controversy over schism instigated by the publication of his friend Matthew Henry's *Brief Enquiry* in 1689. Tong's *Defence of Mr. M. H's Brief Enquiry into the Nature of Schism* (1693) included 'A brief historical account of nonconformity'. He asked Thoresby for a copy of 'the Lancashire gentlemen's petition in favour of the Puritan preachers in Queen Elizabeth's reign' in June 1697, but it is clear his antiquarian interests were wider than dissent. He gave Thoresby a copy of Sampson Erdswicke's manuscript 'survey of Staffordshire' and was attempting to buy Dr Cuerden's manuscript 'Antiquities of Lancashire' with the intention of 'dressing them up' for publication (*Letters of Eminent Men*, 1.287). Pressure of business increasingly prevented Tong from pursuing his historical interests. When Henry Sampson, the nonconformist historian, died in July 1700 his widow promised to preserve his papers. Unfortunately she sent them to Tong, who 'is a fit man, if he had leisure to make a good improvement of them; but his hands are so full of other business, that it will be lost labour to send them to him' (ibid., 1.400). By January 1709 Sampson's collection had been split: part was held by Edmund Calamy, the rest was still with Tong, where Thoresby 'was troubled to find them in such confusion, and so incomplete' (*Diary*, 2.36). Nevertheless Tong's contributions to nonconformist history were among his most important published works. His best-known work was the *Account* (1716) of his friend Matthew Henry.

Tong took a prominent part on the orthodox side in the 1718 Exeter controversy and in the Salters' Hall debate the following year. His advice was sought by a number of ministers in Devon alarmed at the growth of heterodoxy in the south-west. When the London ministers met at Salters' Hall in early 1719 to debate the issues, Tong was a leading figure demanding subscription to a declaration in favour of the Trinity. He wrote the introduction to the *Doctrine of the Blessed Trinity Stated & Defended* (1719), published with three other subscribing ministers. He was an attractive figure, a man of learning, free from sectarian feeling, charitable, and 'an utter enemy to all real persecution, and thought that every man who did not hold principles destructive of the civil peace, ought to enjoy full liberty of conscience in matters of religion' (Newman, 39–40). It is not known whether he was married. He died in London on 21 March 1727. DAVID L. WYKES

Sources J. Newman, *A funeral sermon, occasion'd by the death of the late Reverend Mr William Tong, who departed this life March 21st, 1726/7: aged sixty-five: preach'd at Salters Hall, April 2d, 1727* (1727) · W. Tong, *An account of the life and death of Mr. Matthew Henry, minister of the gospel at Hackney, who dy'd June 22, 1714 in the 52d year of his age* (1716) · M. Henry, 'A short account of the beginning and progress of our congregation', 1710, Ches. & Chester ALSS, Records of the Matthew Henry Chapel, Chester, Chapel Book, D/MH/1, fol. 7r · A. Gordon, ed., *Cheshire classis: minutes, 1691–1745* (1919), 208 · F. Nicholson and E. Axon, *The older nonconformity in Kendal* (1915), 556 · G. E. Evans, *Record of the provincial assembly of Lancashire and Cheshire* (1896), 31, 77 · W. D. Jeremy, *The Presbyterian Fund and Dr Daniel Williams's Trust* (1885), 2, 13, 33, 105 · W. Wilson, *The history and antiquities of the dissenting churches and meeting houses in London, Westminster and Southwark*, 4 vols. (1808–14), vol. 2, pp. 20–32 · E. Calamy, *An historical account of my own life, with some reflections on the times I have lived in, 1671–1731*, ed. J. T. Rutt, 2nd edn, 2 (1830), 41, 465, 486, 493 · Presbyterian Fund board minutes, vol. 2, 5 Feb 1695–4 June 1722, DWL, MS OD68, fols. 41, 77, 90 · Presbyterian Fund board rough minutes, 1696–1708, 8 Jan 1699, DWL, MS OD163 · [J. Hunter], ed., *Letters of eminent men, addressed to Ralph Thoresby*, 1 (1832), 287, 313, 334–5, 355–6, 399–400, 403–4 · *Diary of Ralph Thoresby*, ed. J. Hunter, 2 vols. (1832), vol. 2, pp. 23, 25, 36 (15, 20 Jan, 4 Feb 1709) · DNB

Archives W. Yorks. AS, Leeds, Yorkshire Archaeological Society, Thoresby MSS

Likenesses J. Simon, mezzotint (after J. Wollaston), BM, NPG · oils, DWL

Tonge, Israel (1621–1680), informer and Church of England clergyman, was born in Tickhill, near Doncaster, on 11 November 1621, the son of Henry Tong of Holtby, Yorkshire, the minister of that parish. Tonge was educated locally in Doncaster until he went to University College, Oxford, on 3 May 1639. He graduated BA (14 March 1643), proceeding MA (6 July 1648). Tonge claimed that he did not wish to bear arms against the king, and on the outbreak of the civil war he retired to the country to become a schoolmaster at Churchill in Oxfordshire. It was there that he honed his teaching skills that were later to be so much admired by John Aubrey. Aubrey stated that Tonge had adopted, with no sense of irony considering Tonge's later career, the Jesuit methods of teaching, and added to them his own pictorial method of teaching using drawings and Latin verse, breaking up the teaching into two-hour sessions with play for the boys in between. Tonge may also have begun his interest in gardening, alchemy, and chemistry at this time. Aubrey claimed that at his death Tonge left 'two manuscript tomes in folio of alchymie [and that his] excellency lay there' (*Brief Lives*, 2.261–2). Tonge was also said to have left numerous manuscripts on chemistry, which were subsequently lost.

Civil war and Restoration In 1678 Tonge was to claim that he had been 'in armes with & for his Majestie in Oxfordshire, took the Oxfordshire oath or anticovenant, [and] continued all the warre in his majesties quarter' (Tonge, 44). With the close of the first civil war, however, Tonge returned to the university and became a fellow there. In 1649, seeking both marriage and a rectory, he obtained both from Edward Simpson, the rector of Pluckley in Kent, whose daughter, Jane, he married that year. In 1656 Tonge was made a doctor of theology, and in 1657, following the birth of his son, Simpson, he took up a fellowship at the newly constituted Cromwellian College at Durham. There he taught grammar until its closure in 1659. With the Restoration, Tonge was forced to seek other outlets for his talents. He briefly returned to schoolmastering in

Islington at an academy for girls, but in 1660, through the assistance of his 'honoured patron', Colonel Edward Harley, Tonge became a chaplain to the garrison at Dunkirk (BL, Add. MS 4365, fol. 24). When Dunkirk was sold to the French in 1661 Tonge obtained further ecclesiastical preferment from Harley at Leintwardine in Herefordshire. On 26 June 1666 he was given the rectory of St Mary Staying in London, but this burnt down during the great fire of London, and with this catastrophe his mind appears to have become permanently disturbed.

Tonge became obsessive about the Jesuits, whom he blamed for his own losses as well as those of the nation. In his anti-papal fervour he was somewhat extreme, although many of his ideas were perhaps more typical of the English of the day than historians once believed. While homeless, Tonge took a position as chaplain to the garrison at Tangier. It was claimed by some that Tonge was finally expelled from Tangier after two years because he sowed 'discord in the garrison' (Warner, 1.193). Whatever the truth of this, on his return to England Tonge became rector at St Michael's, Wood Street, London, which he subsequently held jointly with a rectory at Aston in Herefordshire from 1672 to 1677.

Introduced to Oates In 1675 Tonge fell in with Sir Richard Barker and his wife; Barker, a physician who was violently anti-Catholic, became his mentor. Tonge himself noted that he was very hospitably received into 'theire family where he continued & had of the knight, besides his diet and lodging, considerable summes of mon[e]y & other great encouragements in his studies' (Tonge, 1). These studies were anti-Catholic, and as a result Barker gave Tonge the rectory at 'Avon Dossett' (Avon Dassett in Warwickshire), although Tonge was to claim that 'illegall practices' prevented him taking the post (ibid.). This only added to Tonge's already growing paranoia and fear of the Jesuits over these years. Barker also became a patron of Samuel Oates and his son Titus about this time, and it was at Barker's home in the Barbican in London in 1677 that Israel Tonge met Titus Oates for the first time. Tonge became a useful sounding board for Oates to exercise his prejudices, as well as a source of money. By now Tonge, although supremely convinced of his own literary abilities, believed that a Jesuit plot, mainly centred around his translation of a work by Nicolas Perrault (published in 1679 as *The Jesuits Morals*), prevented him from publishing his work. As he continued to strive against publishers, plotters, and their agents Tonge claimed he could obtain 'neither ... favour or right in any cause he had in hand for his support & settlement' (ibid., 3). Together with Oates he now planned to write a series of pamphlets against the Catholics, but his co-author, after agreeing, promptly disappeared to France. How much Tonge was aware of Oates's actual activities at the English College at St Omer, or indeed encouraged them, is now difficult to say. Tonge later claimed that he had encouraged Oates to go to St Omer to learn more about Jesuit intrigue, while others maintained that it was really Tonge and not Oates who lay behind the construction of the plot, but at the time Tonge was merely puzzled by Oates's disappearance. Moreover

there seems little doubt that Tonge remained throughout the weaker character in the partnership.

Oates's final failure at St Omer and his expulsion from the college eventually brought him back to London in July 1678. Once there he enthralled Tonge with tales of Jesuit intrigue and his own daring actions in tormenting the Catholics in their very den. Indeed he pandered to Tonge's vanity by claiming that he had been sent back to kill the feared author of the (then unpublished) 'Jesuits morals' for £50, that there had actually been a popish plot since 1639, and it 'still held on & [was] generally true according to what Dr Tonge had described it in his ... booke of the Royall Martyr' (Tonge, 5). A suitably flattered Tonge subsequently demanded that Oates write down all he knew of the plot. In the meantime Tonge had moved into William Lambert's house at Vauxhall with Christopher Kirkby, a former assistant in Charles II's scientific experiments. Kirkby had bragged that he had access to the king. This was unfortunate, for it was at this time that Oates, still claiming to be fearful of his life, finally consented to give a copy of the forty-three articles detailing the plot and a number of assassination attempts allegedly made upon Charles II to Tonge. To give added mystery to the affair Oates agreed to leave them behind the wainscot in Barker's house. By 12 August 1678 Tonge had retranscribed the articles and was keen to give a copy to Charles II. Tonge told Kirkby of the articles and the plot, and Kirkby agreed to approach the king. On 13 August 1678 Kirkby finally warned Charles II of the threat to his life, and on the same day both Tonge and Kirkby had an interview with the king. Charles II subsequently left the investigation to his first minister, the earl of Danby, and seems never to have believed the story related by either Tonge or Oates.

Revealing the plot At this point Tonge was keen to keep Oates's name secret, and throughout Danby's investigations into the plot Tonge remained reluctant to expose his source. Instead, Tonge, with his sense of self-importance, sought to make himself the middleman between Oates and the government. Both Oates, still unwilling to reveal himself, and Danby agreed to this for a time, but Danby soon tired of the intrigue. Suspecting Tonge was merely mad, and after six weeks unable to come to the real intelligencer, he began to see the plot as nonsense. Others learning of Tonge's comings and goings began to agree. Gilbert Burnet claimed that Tonge approached him with news of the plot, and when he afterwards enquired at the secretary of state's office they dismissed Tonge as a man only 'making discoveries ... [in the hope that he would] get himself to be made a dean' (*Burnet's History*, 2.156). At this point the conspirators began to fear that Danby would drop them altogether, and so Oates chose to invent some actual correspondence to sustain the plot. These crude forgeries, with their 'ill spelling of names, and other suspitious marks', were then sent to Father Bedingfield, the duke of York's confessor, at Windsor (PRO, PC2/66, 392). They detailed more of the plot, although instead of being intercepted by Danby at the Post Office as had originally been planned, the letters actually reached a puzzled Bedingfield, who promptly took them to the duke of York. James now demanded an investigation, the very thing Tonge had actually wished for, and it was this that ultimately brought the Popish Plot into the public domain.

Tonge, who remained unaware of the investigation, was fearful that Oates would fly from the imaginary assassins he now claimed were pursuing him. As a result Tonge continued to seek further ways to bring the plot to public notice. Initially Tonge brought Oates to the home of Sir Joseph Williamson, the secretary of state, in order to get Oates's testimony sworn before a legal authority; Williamson, however, snubbed the pair. Tonge 'at a losse … advised with some very honourable friends about such a Justice as he might trust with soe weighty a business. They after some consideracion com[m]ended Sir Edmond Bury Godfrey' to him (Tonge, 35). This act was, indirectly, to lead to Godfrey's own mysterious death in September 1678. Ironically, on the same day as Oates swore his second oath before a sceptical Godfrey, Tonge was himself brought before the privy council to relate his tale. While the councillors remained merely amused at Tonge's rambling statements, they were considerably more impressed when Oates himself came before them and narrated his story with growing confidence. Oates, rather than Tonge, now became the 'saviour of the nation', and it was Oates who consequently took the main reward for revealing his spurious plot.

Although Tonge was afterwards lodged in Whitehall and given a pension suitable to his needs as the man 'to whose memory the nation is not a little indebted', his role in the crisis that unfolded was considerably less than that of Oates (CSP dom., 1680–81, 106). Tonge went before the House of Commons a number of times and was commended for his part in discovering the plot, but he had neither Oates's abilities as a liar or his partner's brazen nature to carry him further. As a result little reward came Tonge's way. His attempt to oust Obadiah Walker from the mastership of University College on the grounds of Catholicism did succeed, but Tonge did not, as he had planned, occupy the place in his stead. Instead he was finally allowed to print his rambling pamphlets on the plot, and these later works show some of the increasing inanities concerning Catholicism that he now inflicted on his readers. The works that most explain his thought include *Jesuits Assassins* (1680), in which Tonge tried his hand at anagrams and verse, alongside a history of the cruelties of the Jesuits. In the *New Design of Papists Detected* (1679) he argued that the Jesuits only protested their innocence because in the Catholic sense 'the Crime they suffered for were no Treason, because the King was deposed by the Pope [their master] and consequently, so far from needing a Pardon … [their actions] were a matter of merit' (Tonge, 6). The oddest of Tonge's works, however, remains *The Northern Star* (1680), a collection of prophecies 'collected out of my slender stock' and designed as 'Paper-Bullets in my Countrymen's Mouths' (sig. B2r). These pamphlets have little merit in general. Tonge's prose style, where it was not manic, remained turgid and generally unreadable. He tended to regurgitate earlier authors on the Jesuit menace and confirm both his and his readers' abiding prejudice against papists. To many contemporaries, Tonge's prose seems to have become even more muddled than his mind.

Final months At length Oates stole his former mentor's glory, while the elder man was pushed to one side. The arrival of William Bedloe and Miles Prance, among a multitude of other informers, left Tonge with only a minor role to play. For a time he seems to have become completely intoxicated by the general public acceptance of his long-held beliefs in a Jesuit plot. Bishop Burnet, visiting Tonge in Whitehall, found him 'so lifted up, that he seems to have lost the little sense he had' (*Burnet's History*, 2.162). In 1679, however, Tonge quarrelled with Oates and came, it was said, to have a very bad opinion of his erstwhile protégé. Tonge subsequently withdrew from association with Oates. As a result, although he appeared before the House of Commons on 21 March 1679 to relate his part in the discovery of the plot and retained his genuine belief that he would have been one of its main victims, no one required him to be a witness in the trials that followed Oates's revelations, and he was left to wallow in his literary efforts.

The activities of his son, Simpson, whom his father had abandoned in Simpson's youth because of his debauchery and his attempt to join the Catholic church, also distressed Tonge and left him 'Ruined in my name and reputation' (Stowe MS 746, fol. 40). Simpson Tonge was to claim in August 1680 that his father and Oates had concocted the plot between them, but his assertions were discounted mainly because of his own blatant inability to tell the truth. Following the misfiring of his accusations that Sir Edward Dering had corresponded with the papal nuncio Tonge became subject to a 'very dangerous sicknesse [and] deserted of all' in November 1680 (ibid., fol. 40). He died, 'sunk in my disease', at the home of Stephen College, the protestant agitator and pamphleteer, near Bridewell Ditch, London, on 18 December 1680; he was aged fifty-nine (ibid.). Tonge was buried in the churchyard of his former parish, St Mary Stayning, on 23 December 1680.

It was said that Israel Tonge still persisted on his deathbed in his belief of the plot's truthfulness as well as his own integrity in its discovery. This belief was likely to have been genuine, as he remained yet another dupe of Oates and besotted by ideas of Jesuit conspiracy. His brother John, who was a captain in the army, quickly seized control of the doctor's papers after his death, including his journal, and most of these documents fell into the hands of the government. They reveal that in the early stages of the plot Tonge had an almost blind faith in Oates's revelations and maintained enough of his egotism to claim that both he and his literary endeavours were central to the Popish Plot. ALAN MARSHALL

Sources I. Tonge, 'Journal of the plot, 1678', *Diaries of the Popish Plot*, ed. D. G. Greene (New York, 1977) · BL, Stowe MS 746, fols. 35, 38, 40 · BL, Add. MSS 4279, fol. 280; 4365, fols. 23–4 · *Brief lives,*

chiefly of contemporaries, set down by John Aubrey, between the years 1669 and 1696, ed. A. Clark, 2 vols. (1898) · *The life and times of Anthony Wood*, ed. A. Clark, 5 vols., OHS, 19, 21, 26, 30, 40 (1891–1900) · W. Winstanley, *Poor Robins dream, or, The visions of Hell* (1681) · PRO, PC 2/66 · *Burnet's History of my own time*, ed. O. Airy, new edn, 2 vols. (1897–1900) · J. Warner, *The history of English persecution of Catholics and the presbyterian plot*, ed. T. A. Birrell, trans. J. Bligh, 2 vols., Catholic RS, 47–8 (1953) · *CSP dom.*, 1680–81
Archives PRO, state papers, journal of Popish plot | PRO, SP 29 Charles II

Tonkin, Thomas (*bap.* 1678, *d.* 1741/2), antiquary and Cornish scholar, was born at Trevaunance, St Agnes, Cornwall, and baptized in the parish church there on 26 September 1678, the eldest son of Hugh Tonkin (1652–1711), landowner, and his first wife, Frances (1662–1691), daughter of Walter Vincent of Trelevan, near Tregony. His father served as vice-warden of the stannaries in 1701 and as sheriff of Cornwall in 1702. Tonkin matriculated from Queen's College, Oxford, on 12 March 1694, and was entered as a student at Lincoln's Inn on 20 February 1695. At Oxford he struck up friendships with Edmund Gibson, afterwards bishop of London, and, importantly for his future interests, with Edward Lhuyd, whose work has been regarded as the foundation of modern Celtic linguistic studies. Tonkin corresponded with Lhuyd between 1700 and 1708, when Lhuyd was working on aspects of the Cornish language.

Tonkin returned to Cornwall about 1700 and devoted himself to research into the history, topography, and genealogy of Cornwall. He is said to have become fluent in Welsh as well as Cornish. He married Elizabeth (*d.* 1739), daughter of James Kempe of the Barn, near Penryn, about 1710, although no exact date has been verified. It is reported that they had several children but the male line became extinct on the death of their third son, also named Thomas Tonkin.

Tonkin, at the time of his father's death, became faced with financial difficulties. He had discovered that his father and grandfather had spent large sums on improvements to their estates, especially on the erection of a quay at Trevaunance Porth, in Trevaunance Cove, to ship ore from the local mines. By 1710 Tonkin had spent a further £6000 on the quay's upkeep and he made attempts to raise money by seeking a patent for a weekly market and fairs at St Agnes but this was stopped by local opposition and he fell into debt. The quay at Trevaunance Cove was destroyed through lack of repair in 1730. Tonkin fell into the hands of a creditor and he lost a lawsuit against him and with it his family estates at Trevaunance. His later years were spent at his wife's estate in Gorran parish.

Partly through the influence of his in-laws, Tonkin won a by-election to represent the borough of Helston in the House of Commons from 12 April 1714 until 5 January 1715. However, he preferred to devote his time to academic pursuits. In 1737 he made a preliminary announcement of the publication of a three-volume history of Cornwall, priced at 3 guineas. He also planned to publish a collection of writings in Cornish, together with his own translations. Neither of these projected works was published; his lack of finances seemed the principal stumbling-block. His wife died at Pol Gorran, in Gorran parish, on 24 June 1739. Tonkin died at Gorran and was buried in the local church on 4 January 1742.

It is unfortunate that Tonkin's lifelong collection of material on the topography, natural history, parochial history, and language of Cornwall was never published during his lifetime. In spite of this, his contribution in gathering the literary fragments of the dying Cornish language played a major part in saving it from oblivion. In a letter to Lhuyd, in which he criticized the poor standard of William Hals's Cornish dictionary, *An Lhadymer ay Kernou*, Tonkin commented that the Cornish language, at that time, was reduced to a small area of Cornwall. Moreover, the language had become corrupted and even native speakers were illiterate in it. At his death, Tonkin's manuscripts were bequeathed to his family. In 1761 the Cornish scholar Dr William Borlase managed to get access to Tonkin's manuscripts, of which he found nine volumes, and made a list of them, subsequently printed in the *Journal of the Royal Institution of Cornwall* (vol. 6, no. 21). On the death of Tonkin's niece Miss Foss in 1780, the manuscript of his 'History of Cornwall' became the property of Lord de Dunstanville, who published an edition of Richard Carew's *Survey of Cornwall* (1602), *with Notes Illustrative of its History and Antiquities by Thomas Tonkin* (1811). Lord de Dunstanville subsequently allowed Davies Gilbert to edit and embody the Tonkin manuscript in his *Parochial History of Cornwall: Founded on the Manuscript Histories of Mr Hals and Mr Tonkin* (4 vols., 1838). The manuscript was passed from Lord de Dunstanville to Sir Thomas Phillips and sold by Sothebys to a Mr Quaritch in 1898. Several owners seemed then to possess sections, and many of them, such as W. C. Borlase, had the good sense to donate them to the museum of the Royal Institution of Cornwall.

Because of its now fragmentary manuscript nature, and its incorporation into other works, Tonkin's major contribution to the study of Cornish historiography and Cornish linguistics has often been overlooked. The value of his collections was, however, well understood by the late eighteenth-century Cornish historian Richard Polwhele, who described Tonkin as 'one of the most enlightened antiquaries of his day' (Polwhele, 1.182).

PETER BERRESFORD ELLIS

Sources H. L. Douch, 'Thomas Tonkin: an appreciation of a neglected Cornish historian', *Journal of the Royal Institution of Cornwall*, new ser. 4 (1961–4), 145–80 · R. Polwhele, *The history of Cornwall*, 7 vols. (1803–8); repr. with additions (1816), vol. 1, pp. 182, 203–6; vol. 5, pp. 8–14 · W. Pryce, *Archaeologia Cornu-Britannica* (1790), 225–6 · P. A. S. Pool, *The death of Cornish (1600–1800)* (privately printed, Penzance, 1975) · W. P. Courtney, *The parliamentary representation of Cornwall to 1832* (1889), 48 · P. Beresford Ellis, *The history of the Cornish language and its literature* (1974), 105–6, 111–13, 115, 122, 136–7 · H. Jenner, 'The Cornish manuscript in the provincial library at Bilbao in Spain', *Journal of the Royal Institution of Cornwall*, 21 (1922–5), 421–37 · Boase & Courtney, *Bibl. Corn.*, 1.31, 25, 318; 2.536, 727–8, 888, 897; 3.1190, 1195, 1346 · *DNB*
Archives BL, collections relating to Cornwall and Devon, Add. MS 33420 · BL, some of Tonkin's Cornish notes, Add. MS 29763 [transcript] · Provincial Library of Bilbao, MSS · Royal Institution

of Cornwall, Truro, antiquarian and natural history notes, transcripts, etc.

Tonks, Henry (1862–1937), artist and art teacher, was born in Solihull, Warwickshire, on 9 April 1862, the fifth among the eleven children of Edmund Tonks and his wife, Julia, *née* Johnson. The family, of Dutch descent, owned a brass foundry in Birmingham. Tonks attended Clifton College, Bristol, from 1877 to 1880 and then studied medicine at the London Hospital, Whitechapel. In 1887 he was the house surgeon of Sir Frederick Treves; he was elected FRCS in 1888 and appointed senior medical officer at the Royal Free Hospital. In 1892 he became demonstrator in anatomy at the London Hospital medical school.

A visit to Dresden in 1886 revived his interest in great paintings, and Tonks studied in his spare time with Fred Brown at the Westminster School of Art. Brown led a development of art education towards the idea of French impressionism represented by the New English Art Club (NEAC). Tonks first showed with the NEAC in 1891 and began his association with the advanced painters of his time, J. McNeil Whistler, John Singer Sargent, Walter Sickert, and George Clausen, as well as the writers D. S. MacColl and George Moore. They recreated in pure colour the way light creates a fleeting, momentary impression. In 1892 Brown was appointed Slade professor of fine art at University College, London, and he appointed Tonks his assistant professor with Philip Wilson Steer.

Tonks used his anatomical knowledge to teach life drawing as a swift and intelligent activity. He referred his students to old master drawings at the British Museum and taught his pupils to draw the model at the size it was seen, measured at arm's length (sight size), which enabled them continually to correct the drawing for themselves, against a physical object. He said 'to live with a bad drawing is to live with a lie'. Many of Tonks's ideas on drawing informed John Fothergill in 'The principles of teaching drawing at the Slade School', in *The Slade* (1907). The Slade produced a remarkable generation of artists in the 1890s, among them Harold Gilman, Spencer Frederick Gore, Augustus John, Gwen John, and Percy Wyndham Lewis. Subsequent generations included working-class students such as Stanley Spencer. Mark Gertler, David Bomberg, and Isaac Rosenberg were all funded by Jewish educational charities before 1914.

Tonks was a gifted caricaturist, and Roger Fry and Clive Bell were his targets. Some caricatures and an extensive correspondence are in a private collection formerly belonging to Mary Hutchinson, who was a close friend of Tonks. He portrayed their circle, and his affection for Mary, in *Saturday Evening at The Vale* (1929; priv. coll.). Fry was a symbolist painter, who after contact with Gertrude Stein and Bernard Berenson became curator of European paintings at the Metropolitan Museum of Art in New York. Tonks's scepticism of Fry's scholarship surfaced when Fry returned to London in 1910 as joint editor of the *Burlington Magazine* and published 'The bushman artists of South Africa'. Tonks objected to Fry's discussion of living human beings as stone-age artists. Many Slade students joined

Henry Tonks (1862–1937), self-portrait, 1909 [*Portrait of the Artist*]

Fry's influential circle, and Tonks was characterized as a reactionary critic of Cézanne.

Tonks was an attractive but austere figure. One of his students, Helen Lessore, recalled that 'physically he was a towering, dominating figure, about 6ft. 4in. tall, lean and ascetic looking, with large ears, hooded eyes, a nose dropping vertically from the bridge like an eagle's beak and quivering camel-like mouth' (Morris, 8). For him the arts were a moral activity that entailed social responsibility. He often quoted Goethe: 'All eras in a state of decline and dissolution are subjective; on the other hand all progressive eras have an objective tendency' (ibid.). Tonks's letters in the Hone collection at the University of Texas, Austin, contrast his fears on the outbreak of the First World War with the enthusiasm of Wyndham Lewis for the machine age. In *The Ark* (1916; BM) Tonks caricatured the ship of the American millionaire Henry Ford in which Ford travelled to Europe in 1915 to publicize his view that America should remain neutral. Ford's notorious comment that 'History is more or less bunk' epitomized Tonks's worst fears of industrial progress (Morris, 39). With the outbreak of war Tonks went back to medicine, first with war prisoners at a camp hospital in Dorchester, and then at Hill Hall, Essex, where he made pastel drawings of Auguste Rodin and his wife (Tate collection), who were among the refugees there. In 1915 he worked as an orderly near the Marne and with a British ambulance unit, organized by the historian G. M. Trevelyan, in Italy. In 1916 he was commissioned lieutenant in the Royal Army Medical Corps and began visiting Sir Harold Gillies's unit in

Cambridge, making pastel drawings of facial war wounds that were eventually published in Gillies's book *Plastic Surgery of the Face* (1930); the drawings were later acquired by the Royal College of Surgeons (Army Dental Museum, Aldershot, Surrey). In 1918 Tonks was appointed official war artist, and he went back to France with John Sargent. The realism of *Advanced Clearing Station in France: 1918* (1918/19; IWM) and Sargent's *Gassed* (1918; IWM) stirred many at the Royal Academy's 'War Artists' exhibition in 1919. That year Tonks went to Russia with the British expeditionary force.

Brown retired in 1918 and Tonks was offered the Slade professorship. He deferred to Sickert, whom he felt was a better artist, but Sickert declined. His friendship with Sickert and Steer was wittily captured in *Sodales—Mr Sickert and Mr Steer* (1930; Tate collection). Another generation of students included Sir Thomas Monnington, president of the Royal Academy, Sir William Coldstream, Helen Lessore, and the American Philip Evergood. The teaching of Tonks and Sickert was the foundation on which figurative painting rested in Britain throughout the twentieth century through the continuing influence and example of Spencer, Bomberg, and Coldstream, and Helen Lessore's Beaux Arts Gallery in London.

Tonks was offered a knighthood on his retirement in 1930, which he declined. He continued to confront the 'Art Boys' over Fry's disastrous restoration of the Mantegna murals at Hampton Court and his controversial attribution of a portrait of Henry VIII to Hans Holbein the younger. He wrote articles for *The Times* (2 March 1932, 4 May 1933, and 10 July 1934), and continued to paint and entertain. Important paintings by Tonks were acquired by Birmingham City Art Gallery, Manchester City Art Gallery, the Ashmolean Museum, Oxford, and the Tate Gallery. Tonks was only the second living British artist to be honoured by a retrospective exhibition at the Tate Gallery, in 1936. The exhibition showed the three phases of Tonks's work: his earlier impressionist figures in sun-lit interiors and images of women in summer gardens; the war paintings; and his late domestic interiors of his close circle of friends. He died at his home in The Vale, Chelsea, on 8 January 1937. A memorial exhibition of his work was held at Barbizon House, London, in June that year.

LYNDA MORRIS

Sources J. Hone, *The life of Henry Tonks* (1939) · L. Morris, ed., *Henry Tonks and the art of pure drawing* (1985) · J. Fothergill, 'The art of drawing', *Encyclopaedia Britannica*, 11th edn (1910–11) · *CGPLA Eng. & Wales* (1937)
Archives Ransom HRC, papers | Harvard U., Houghton L., letters to Sir William Rothenstein · Tate collection, letters to Rodney J. Burr · U. Glas. L., letters to D. S. MacColl
Likenesses G. C. Beresford, photographs, 1902–22, NPG · W. Orpen, group portrait, oils, 1909 (*Homage to Manet*), Man. City Gall. · H. Tonks, self-portrait, oils, 1909, Tate collection [see illus.] · G. C. Beresford, photograph, c.1918 · J. S. Sargent, pencil and ink drawing, 1918, FM Cam. · E. H. Thompson, ink and wash caricature, 1923, NPG · T. Monnington, pencil drawing, 1937, Slade School of Fine Art, London · W. Roberts, group portrait, oils, c.1961–1962 (*The vorticists at the Restaurant de la Tour Eiffel: spring 1915*), Tate collection · H. M. Campbell, pencil drawing, Man. City Gall. · G. W. Lambert, double portrait, pencil drawing (Percy Grainger), NPG · D. G. MacLaren, watercolour caricature (*Some members of the New English Art Club*), NPG · J. Mansbridge, etching, NPG · W. Orpen, group portrait, oils (*The selecting jury of the New English Art Club, 1909*), NPG · H. Tonks, self-portraits, pencil drawings, NPG
Wealth at death £17,005 0s. 3d.: probate, 10 April 1937, *CGPLA Eng. & Wales*

Tonna [*née* Browne], **Charlotte Elizabeth** (1790–1846), writer and social reformer, was born on 1 October 1790 in Norwich, the daughter of Michael Browne, who was the rector of St Giles's Church and minor canon of Norwich Cathedral. Her father was also a staunch tory, and this family background, in addition to the paranoid political atmosphere of the Napoleonic era, probably caused her hostility to Roman Catholicism and her political Conservatism. She also lost her hearing at the age of ten and as a result became fascinated with imaginative literature, especially Shakespeare. Later in life she came to see this fascination as sinful because it served no useful, religious purpose, but her early reading in drama, poetry, and fiction provided excellent preparation for her future writing career.

Charlotte Elizabeth married an army officer, Captain George Phelan (*d*. 1837), and eventually accompanied him to his estate in Ireland. She developed a sincere affection for the Irish people but at the same time grew increasingly severe and evangelical in her religious convictions. She began publishing religious tracts through the Dublin Tract Society, using the name Charlotte Elizabeth. In 1824 she separated from her abusive husband and returned to England; she lived at first with her brother, Captain John Browne, at Clifton, where she met the evangelical writer Hannah More. She continued to write tracts such as *Conformity: a Tale* (1841) and *Falsehood and Truth* (1841) for children and the lower classes, and didactic fiction on subjects that interested her. Her stay in Ireland had only intensified her antipathy towards the Catholic church, since she saw it as the means by which the Irish people were enslaved in ignorance and superstition, a view she professed in her novel *Derry* (1833). In contrast, her attitude towards Judaism was more complex. In her novel *Judah's Lion* (1843) she argued that the Jews could fulfil their religion only by recognizing Jesus Christ, but she also recognized them as recipients of God's covenant. There is some evidence to suggest, however, that she eventually abandoned this conversionist attitude towards Judaism and devoted her efforts towards fighting antisemitism. In July 1844, for example, she presented a petition, signed by many of her influential friends (such as Lord Shaftesbury), to Tsar Nicholas I on behalf of his 'oppressed and burdened Jewish subjects' (Rubinstein, 14).

After Phelan's death Charlotte Elizabeth on 5 February 1841 married Lewis Hippolytus Joseph *Tonna (1812–1857), a religious writer twenty years younger than herself, who encouraged her literary efforts. She was prolific as a writer and editor, publishing continuously and editing the *Christian Lady's Magazine* from 1834 to 1846, *The Protestant Annual* in 1840, and the *Protestant Magazine* from 1841 to 1846.

During the 1840s Tonna became convinced that industrialism threatened the physical and spiritual welfare of the poor, and she attacked the factory system in *Helen Fleetwood* (serialized 1839–40), *The Wrongs of Woman* (serialized 1843–4), and the anonymous, non-fictional *Perils of the Nation* (1842). Tonna died of breast cancer at Ramsgate on 12 July 1846, leaving a legacy of many literary works and active involvement with social causes, much of which is documented in her *Personal Recollections* (1841). Some of these causes, like her anti-Catholicism, are offensive to modern readers, but Tonna was also indefatigable in her support of the poor and oppressed. She wrote poetry and one novel, *The System* (1827), exposing the evils of slavery, but found an even more passionate voice in support of factory reform. Tonna's best works, *Helen Fleetwood* and *The Wrongs of Woman*, contain moving portrayals of physical and emotional suffering that are used to evoke audience sympathy. Tonna's contributions to social reform literature and her use of the *Christian Lady's Magazine* as a forum to influence politics through her female readers mark her as a significant nineteenth-century figure, especially for other women social reform writers, such as Harriet Beecher Stowe (who wrote the introduction for her collected works in 1844) and Elizabeth Gaskell. The rise of more formalist standards in literary criticism caused Tonna to fade quickly from literary history, however, and her work was almost entirely ignored until the women's movement created new interest in women's literature.

MARY LENARD

Sources C. E. Tonna, *Personal recollections* (1841) · C. E. Tonna, *Works of Charlotte Elizabeth, with introduction by Mrs. H. B. Stowe* (1845) · J. Kestner, *Protest and reform: the British social narrative by women* (1985) · DNB · B. Kanner and I. Kovacevic, 'Blue book into novel: the forgotten industrial fiction of Charlotte Elizabeth Tonna', *Nineteenth-Century Fiction*, 25 (1970), 152–73 · I. Kovacevic, *Fact into fiction* (1975) · C. Krueger, *The reader's repentance* (1992) · L. Cazamian, *The social novel in England, 1830–1850* (1903); M. Fido, trans. (1973) · M. Fryckedstedt, 'Charlotte Elizabeth Tonna and the *Christian Lady's Magazine*', *Victorian Periodicals Review*, 14 (1981), 43–51 · E. Koweleski, 'The heroine of some strange romance: the *Personal recollections* of Charlotte Elizabeth Tonna', *Tulsa Studies in Women's Literature*, 1 (1982), 141–53 · J. Kestner, 'Charlotte Elizabeth Tonna's *The wrongs of women*: female industrial protest', *Tulsa Studies in Women's Literature*, 2 (1983), 193–214 · M. Fryckedstedt, 'The early industrial novel: *Mary Barton* and its predecessors', *Bulletin of the John Rylands University Library*, 63 (1980), 11–30 · M. Lenard, 'Deathbeds and didacticism: Charlotte Elizabeth Tonna and Victorian social reform literature', *Silent voices: forgotten novels by Victorian women writers*, ed. B. Ayres (2002) · M. Lenard, *Preaching pity: Dickens, Gaskell and sentimentalism in Victorian culture* (1999) · H. L. Rubinstein, 'A pioneering philosemite: Charlotte Elizabeth Tonna (1790–1846) and the Jews', *Transactions of the Jewish Historical Society*, 35 (1996–8), 103–18
Archives Ransom HRC, Wolff collection
Likenesses F. Croll, stipple and line engraving, NPG; repro. in *Hogg's Instructor* · S. Friend?, engraving, repro. in Tonna, *Works of Charlotte Elizabeth*

Tonna, Lewis Hippolytus Joseph (1812–1857), protestant controversialist, was born on 3 September 1812 at Liverpool, where his father was vice-consul for Spain and consul for the kingdom of the Two Sicilies. His mother was the daughter of Major H. S. Blanckley, consul-general in the Balearic Islands. In 1828 he was at Corfu as a student when the death of his father left him to fend for himself.

He found work as an interpreter, with the rating of 'acting schoolmaster', on board the *Hydra*, then in the Gulf of Patras. In January 1831 he was transferred to the *Rainbow* with Sir John Franklin, and in October 1833 to the *Britannia*, flagship of Vice-Admiral Sir Pulteney Malcolm. Tonna returned to England in 1835 and the following year obtained—apparently through Malcolm's influence—the post of assistant director and, from 1845 until his death, of secretary of the Royal United Service Institution. He acquired a mastery of many foreign languages, including French, Italian, and Greek, and was elected both fellow of the Society of Antiquaries and, in 1855, fellow of the Royal Geographical Society.

On 5 February 1841 Tonna married the widow of Captain George Phelan, Charlotte Elizabeth Browne (1790–1846), the well-known writer of a wide range of popular protestant literature [*see* Tonna, Charlotte Elizabeth]. Tonna shared her religious sentiments and he, too, was the author of numerous small books and pamphlets, almost all on religious and controversial subjects, written from an uncompromisingly ultra-protestant point of view. In 1848 he married Mary Anne, daughter of Charles Dibdin the younger, who survived him. There were no children of either marriage. He died in London on 2 April 1857.

J. K. LAUGHTON, *rev.* STEPHEN GREGORY

Sources GM, 3rd ser., 2 (1857), 95–6 · Boase, *Mod. Eng. biog.* · ships' paybooks, etc., PRO · D. M. Lewis, ed., *The Blackwell dictionary of evangelical biography, 1730–1860*, 2 vols. (1995) · *Annual Register* (1858), 301 · m. cert.

Tonneys, John (*d.* 1514), prior of the Austin friars, London, and grammarian, was a native of Norfolk and received his early education at the Augustinian friary in Norwich. It was probably here that he entered the order. He is said by Blomefield to have become prior of the Norfolk house *c*.1478, but this date has been disputed. Tonneys prepared for the priesthood at the Oxford convent, and was ordained there on 25 May 1485. He was sent to Cambridge for his further education, and began his studies for the doctorate of divinity there in 1501–2. On 16 July 1503 Tonneys was elected vicar-general of the English province for the next general chapter. In July 1505 he was elected prior provincial of the order for a three-year term. But although he was re-elected prior provincial for life in August 1508, in April 1510 he was forced to resign the *magisterium* by the prior-general, Egidio da Viterbo, on the grounds that he had accepted the office without permission, and contrary to the order's regulations.

Tonneys duly resigned and called for a new chapter, but by the end of 1510 his fortunes had turned. He was appointed vicar-general and 'reformer' of the English province on 24 September, and was once more appointed prior provincial on 22 November. The prior-general also created a new position for him; Tonneys was made 'director of all houses of studies in England' (Roth, *English Austin Friars*, 129). He thereby became responsible for the appointment of regents and professors of both the *studia provincialia* and the *studia generalia*; he also had the authority to place student-friars where he saw fit, and to compel their priors to pay for the students' upkeep. Tonneys's learning made him an appropriate choice for the position. He studied Greek, and Bale told Leland that he had seen a Greek letter by him. Bale attributes ten works to Tonneys, including sermons, lectures, letters, *collectanea*, verses, and *Rudimenta grammatices* said to have been printed by Richard Pynson; none of these is extant. In May 1513 Tonneys became prior of the Augustinian friary in London. He died in 1514 and was buried in his London convent. In the same year the prior-general decided that Tonneys's possessions should be given to the London convent. They included 100 pieces of silver, and in July 1522 an inquiry was held into their disposal—the money had been spent without permission by Master Edmond Bellond, the convent's prior.

VICTORIA CHRISTINE APPEL

Sources F. X. Roth, *The English Austin friars, 1249–1538*, 2 (1966) · F. X. Roth, *Sources for a history of the English Austin friars* [1958–61], 33–108 · Emden, *Cam.*, 590–91 · *DNB* · Bale, *Cat.*, 1.630–31 · F. Blomefield and C. Parkin, *An essay towards a topographical history of the county of Norfolk*, 5 vols. (1739–75), vol. 4, p. 91

Wealth at death 100 pieces of silver: Roth, *English Austin friars*

PICTURE CREDITS

Te Rauparaha (d. 1849)—Alexander Turnbull Library, National Library of New Zealand, Te Puna Matauranga o Aotearoa

Teddeman, Sir Thomas (c.1620–1668)—© National Maritime Museum, London, Greenwich Hospital Collection

Tedder, Arthur William, first Baron Tedder (1890–1967)—The Imperial War Museum, London

Tedder, Henry Richard (1850–1924)—from the collection of the Athenaeum, London

Tegetmeier, William Bernhardt (1816–1912)—© National Portrait Gallery, London

Telford, Thomas (1757–1834)—Institution of Civil Engineers; photograph National Portrait Gallery, London

Tempest, Dame Marie (1864–1942)—© Elizabeth Banks; collection National Portrait Gallery, London

Temple, Emily Mary, Viscountess Palmerston (1787–1869)—Broadlands; photograph © National Portrait Gallery, London

Temple, Frederick (1821–1902)—by kind permission of the Lord Bishop of London and the Church Commissioners of England. Photograph: Photographic Survey, Courtauld Institute of Art, London

Temple, Georgina Cowper-, Lady Mount-Temple (1821?–1901)—The Collection of Pictures, Helmingham Hall. Photograph: Photographic Survey, Courtauld Institute of Art, London

Temple, Henry John, third Viscount Palmerston (1784–1865)—© National Portrait Gallery, London

Temple, Olive Susan Miranda (1880–1936)—private collection; photograph National Portrait Gallery, London

Temple, Sir Richard, third baronet (1634–1697)—unknown collection; photograph Sotheby's Picture Library, London / National Portrait Gallery, London

Temple, Richard, first Viscount Cobham (1675–1749)—© National Portrait Gallery, London

Temple, Sir Richard, first baronet (1826–1902)—© National Portrait Gallery, London

Temple, Sir William, baronet (1628–1699)—© reserved

Temple, William (1881–1944)—The de László Foundation / His Grace the Archbishop of Canterbury and the Church Commissioners. Photograph: Photographic Survey, Courtauld Institute of Art, London

Temple, William Francis Cowper-, Baron Mount-Temple (1811–1888)—© National Portrait Gallery, London

Templer, Sir Gerald Walter Robert (1898–1979)—© Harold Speed; Royal Society of Portrait Painters

Tenducci, Giusto Ferdinando (c.1735–1790)—The Barber Institute of Fine Arts, the University of Birmingham

Tenison, Thomas (1636–1715)—© Copyright The British Museum

Tennant, Charles (1768–1838)—© National Portrait Gallery, London

Tennant, Sir Charles, first baronet (1823–1906)—private collection; © reserved in the photograph

Tennant, Margery Mary Edith Josephine Pia (1869–1946)—© reserved

Tennant, Stephen James Napier (1906–1987)—© Cecil Beaton Archive, Sotheby's

Tennant, William (1784–1848)—Scottish National Portrait Gallery

Tenniel, Sir John (1820–1914)—© National Portrait Gallery, London

Tennyson, Alfred, first Baron Tennyson (1809–1892)—Museum of the History of Photography, Bradford; Science & Society Picture Library

Tennyson, Emily Sarah, Lady Tennyson (1813–1896)—from the Tennyson Research Centre, Lincoln. By permission of Lincolnshire County Council

Tennyson, Hallam, second Baron Tennyson (1852–1928)—© National Portrait Gallery, London

Tenzing Norgay [Sherpa Tenzing] (1914–1986)—The Royal Geographical Society, London

Ternan, Ellen Lawless (1839–1914)—V&A Images, The Victoria and Albert Museum

Terriss, Ellaline (1871–1971)—© National Portrait Gallery, London

Terriss, William (1847–1897)—© National Portrait Gallery, London

Terry, Edward O'Connor (1844–1912)—© National Portrait Gallery, London

Terry, Dame Ellen Alice (1847–1928)—© National Portrait Gallery, London

Terry, Marion Bessie (1852?–1930)—© National Portrait Gallery, London

Terry, Sir Richard Runciman (1864–1938)—© National Portrait Gallery, London

Tertis, Lionel (1876–1975)—© National Portrait Gallery, London

Teulon, Samuel Sanders (1812–1873)—RIBA Library Photographs Collection

Te Wherowhero, Potatau (c.1775–1860)—Alexander Turnbull Library, National Library of New Zealand, Te Puna Matauranga o Aotearoa

Tewson, Sir (Harold) Vincent (1898–1981)—© National Portrait Gallery, London

Thackeray, William Makepeace (1811–1863)—© National Portrait Gallery, London

Thelwall, John (1764–1834)—© National Portrait Gallery, London

Thesiger, Frederic Augustus, second Baron Chelmsford (1827–1905)—© National Portrait Gallery, London

Thesiger, Frederic John Napier, first Viscount Chelmsford (1868–1933)—© Sir Gerald Kelly

Thicknesse, Ann (1737–1824)—Cincinnati Art Museum, Bequest of Mary M. Emery

Thicknesse, Philip (1719–1792)—© National Portrait Gallery, London

Thirlwall, (Newell) Connop (1797–1875)—© National Portrait Gallery, London

Thistlewood, Arthur (bap. 1774, d. 1820)—© National Portrait Gallery, London

Thom, John Hamilton (1808–1894)—© National Portrait Gallery, London

Thomas of Lancaster, second earl of Lancaster, second earl of Leicester, and earl of Lincoln (c.1278–1322)—© Bodleian Library, University of Oxford

Thomas, (Walter) Brandon (1848–1914)—V&A Images, The Victoria and Albert Museum

Thomas, David Alfred, first Viscount Rhondda (1856–1918)—© National Portrait Gallery, London

Thomas, Dylan Marlais (1914–1953)—© National Museums and Galleries of Wales

Thomas, (Philip) Edward (1878–1917)—© National Portrait Gallery, London

Thomas, Freeman Freeman-, first marquess of Willingdon (1866–1941)—© National Portrait Gallery, London

Thomas, Sir George Alan, seventh baronet (1881–1972)—© National Portrait Gallery, London

Thomas, George Holt (1870–1929)—Royal Aeronautical Society Library

Thomas, Herbert Samuel (1883–1966)—© National Portrait Gallery, London

Thomas, Hugh Hamshaw (1885–1962)—© reserved

Thomas, James Henry (1874–1949)—© National Portrait Gallery, London

Thomas, John [Pencerdd Gwalia] (1826–1913)—© National Portrait Gallery, London

Thomas, John Godfrey Parry (1884–1927)—Getty Images – MacGregor

Thomas, Margaret Haig, suo jure Viscountess Rhondda (1883–1958)—© National Portrait Gallery, London

Thomas, (William) Miles Webster, Baron Thomas (1897–1980)—© National Portrait Gallery, London

Thomas, Ronald Stuart (1913–2000)—© John Hedgecoe; collection National Portrait Gallery, London

Thomas, Sir (Thomas) Shenton Whitelegge (1879–1962)—© National Portrait Gallery, London

Thomas, Sidney Gilchrist (1850–1885)—© National Portrait Gallery, London

Thomas, Thomas George, Viscount Tonypandy (1909–1997)—© Jane Bown

Thomas, (Lewis John) Wynford Vaughan- (1908–1987)—Getty Images – Haywood Magee

Thomason, Sir Edward (bap. 1769, d. 1849)—© National Portrait Gallery, London

Thompson, Sir Benjamin, Count Rumford in the nobility of the Holy Roman empire (1753–1814)—courtesy of the Fogg Art Museum, Harvard University Art Museums. Bequest of Edmund C. Converse. Photograph: © President and Fellows of Harvard College

Thompson, D'Arcy Wentworth (1829–1902)—© National Portrait Gallery, London

Thompson, Edward John (1886–1946)—© National Portrait Gallery, London

Thompson, Sir Edward Maunde (1840–1929)—© National Portrait Gallery, London

Thompson, Edward Palmer (1924–1993)—© Steve Pyke; collection National Portrait Gallery, London

Thompson, Sir (John) Eric Sidney (1898–1975)—photograph reproduced by courtesy of The British Academy

Thompson, Flora Jane (1876–1947)—Henry Westbury

Thompson, Francis Joseph (1859–1907)—© National Portrait Gallery, London

Thompson, George Donisthorpe (1804–1878)—© National Portrait Gallery, London

Thompson, Sir Henry, first baronet (1820–1904)—© Tate, London, 2004

Thompson, Henry Yates (1838–1928)—© National Portrait Gallery, London

Thompson, Jean Helen (1926–1992)—© reserved; News International Syndication; photograph National Portrait Gallery, London

Thompson, Lydia (1836?–1908)—© National Portrait Gallery, London

Thompson, Muriel Annie (1875–1939)—F.A.N.Y. Archives, London

Thompson, Pishey (1785–1862)—Lincolnshire County Council - Boston Library

Thompson, Thomas Perronet (1783–1869)—© National Portrait Gallery, London

Thompson, William (1793–1854)—© National Portrait Gallery, London

Thompson, William (1805–1852)—© National Portrait Gallery, London

Thompson, William [Bendigo] (1811–1880)—© National Portrait Gallery, London

Thompson, William Hepworth (1810–1886)—The Master and Fellows, Trinity College, Cambridge

Thoms, William John (1803–1885)—© National Portrait Gallery, London

Thomson, Sir Adam (1926–2000)—Scottish National Portrait Gallery

Thomson, Alexander [Greek Thomson] (1817–1875)—from Dr Ronald McFadzean, The life and work of Alexander Thomson (1979)

Thomson, Allen (1809–1884)—reproduced with the kind permission of the Royal College of Surgeons of Edinburgh

Thomson, Anthony Todd (1778–1849)—Wellcome Library, London

Thomson, Arthur (1858–1935)—Wellcome Library, London

Thomson, Charles Poulett, Baron Sydenham (1799–1841)—© National Portrait Gallery, London

Thomson, James (1700–1748)—Yale Center for British Art, Paul Mellon Collection

Thomson, James (1786–1849)—© National Portrait Gallery, London

Thomson, James (1834–1882)—© National Portrait Gallery, London

Thomson, John (1765–1846)—in the collection of the Royal College of Surgeons of Edinburgh; photograph courtesy the Scottish National Portrait Gallery

Thomson, Joseph (1858–1895)—© National Portrait Gallery, London

Thomson, Sir Joseph John (1856–1940)—Cavendish Laboratory, University of Cambridge, UK

Thomson, Roy Herbert, first Baron Thomson of Fleet (1894–1976)—from the Thomson Family Collection

Thomson, Thomas (1768–1852)—Scottish National Portrait Gallery

Thomson, Thomas (1773–1852)—Wellcome Library, London

Thomson, Sir William (1678–1739)—Guildhall Art Gallery, Corporation of London

Thomson, William (1819–1890)—© National Portrait Gallery, London

Thomson, William, Baron Kelvin (1824–1907)—Master and Fellows of Peterhouse, Cambridge

Thorburn, Grant (1773–1863)—© National Portrait Gallery, London

Thoresby, Ralph (1658–1725)—© National Portrait Gallery, London

Thornborough, John (1551?–1641)—© National Portrait Gallery, London

Thorndike, Dame (Agnes) Sybil (1882–1976)—© Estate of Bertram Park / Camera Press; collection National Portrait Gallery, London

Thorne, William James (1857–1946)—© Science & Society Picture Library; photograph National Portrait Gallery, London

Thorneycroft, (George Edward) Peter, Baron Thorneycroft (1909–1994)—© National Portrait Gallery, London

Thornhill, Sir James (1675/6–1734)—© National Portrait Gallery, London

Thornton, Alicia (fl. 1804)—© National Portrait Gallery, London

Thornton, Anne Jane (b. 1817)—© National Portrait Gallery, London

Thornton, Henry (1760–1815)—© National Portrait Gallery, London

Thornton, Robert John (1768–1837)—photograph by courtesy Sotheby's Picture Library, London

Thornton, Samuel (1754–1838)—Ashmolean Museum, Oxford

Thornton, Thomas (1751/2–1823)—photograph by courtesy Sotheby's Picture Library, London

Thornycroft, Sir (William) Hamo (1850–1925)—© National Portrait Gallery, London

Thornycroft, Sir John Isaac (1843–1928)—© National Portrait Gallery, London

Thornycroft, Mary (1809–1895)—© Leeds Museums & Galleries (Henry Moore Institute Archive)

Thornycroft, Thomas (1815–1885)—© Leeds Museums & Galleries (Henry Moore Institute Archive)

Thorold (fl. c.1100)—by special permission of the City of Bayeux

Thorpe, John (1682–1750)—© National Portrait Gallery, London

Threlfall, Sir Richard (1861–1932)—© National Portrait Gallery, London

Thring, Edward (1821–1887)—© National Portrait Gallery, London

Thring, Henry, Baron Thring (1818–1907)—© National Portrait Gallery, London

Throckmorton, Sir John Courtenay, fifth baronet (1753–1819)—Coughton Hall, The Throckmorton Collection (The National Trust). Photograph: Photographic Survey, Courtauld Institute of Art, London

Throckmorton, Sir Nicholas (1515/16–1571)—© National Portrait Gallery, London

Thrower, Percy John (1913–1988)—Jon Blau / Camera Press

Thurloe, John (bap. 1616, d. 1668)—© National Portrait Gallery, London

Thurlow, Edward, first Baron Thurlow (1731–1806)—The Royal Collection © 2004 HM Queen Elizabeth II

Thursfield, Sir James Richard (1840–1923)—© National Portrait Gallery, London

Thynne, Henry Frederick, sixth marquess of Bath (1905–1992)—© Eve Arnold / Magnum Photos; collection National Portrait Gallery, London

Thynne, Joan, Lady Thynne (bap. 1558, d. 1612)—reproduced by permission of the Marquess of Bath, Longleat House, Warminster, Wiltshire, Great Britain

Thynne, Sir John (1512/13–1580)—reproduced by permission of the Marquess of Bath, Longleat House, Warminster, Wiltshire, Great Britain. Photograph: Photographic Survey, Courtauld Institute of Art, London

Thynne, Thomas (1647/8–1682)—reproduced by permission of the Marquess of Bath, Longleat House, Wiltshire, Great Britain. Photograph: Photographic Survey, Courtauld Institute of Art, London

Thynne, Thomas, third Viscount Weymouth and first marquess of Bath (1734–1796)—reproduced by permission of the Marquess of Bath, Longleat House, Warminster, Wiltshire, Great Britain. Photograph: Photographic Survey, Courtauld Institute of Art, London

Tichborne, Sir Henry, third baronet (bap. 1624, d. 1689)—private collection

Tickell, Thomas (1685–1740)—reproduced by permission of the Provost and Fellows of the Queen's College, Oxford

Tiddy, Reginald John Elliott (1880–1916)—© National Portrait Gallery, London

Tierney, George (1761–1830)—© National Portrait Gallery, London

Tilak, Bal Gangadhar (1856–1920)—© National Portrait Gallery, London

Tillemans, Peter (c.1684–1734)—Norwich Castle Museum & Art Gallery

Tillett, Benjamin (1860–1943)—© National Portrait Gallery, London

Tilley, Cecil Edgar (1894–1973)—© National Portrait Gallery, London

Tilley, Vesta (1864–1952)—V&A Images, The Victoria and Albert Museum

Tillotson, John (1630–1694)—reproduced by kind permission of His Grace the Archbishop of Canterbury and the Church Commissioners. Photograph: Photographic Survey, Courtauld Institute of Art, London

Tilman, Harold William (1898–1977x9)—The Royal Geographical Society, London

Tiltman, John Hessell (1894–1982)—private collection

Tinbergen, Nikolaas (1907–1988)—Godfrey Argent Studios / Royal Society

Tipper, Constance Fligg (1894–1995)—MMP Cambridge

Tippett, Sir Michael Kemp (1905–1998)—© Michael Ward / National Portrait Gallery, London

Titchmarsh, Edward Charles (1899–1963)—© National Portrait Gallery, London

Titmuss, Richard Morris (1907–1973)—© National Portrait Gallery, London

Tizard, Sir Henry Thomas (1885–1959)—© National Portrait Gallery, London

Todd, Alexander Robertus, Baron Todd (1907–1997)—Kristinn Ingvarsson, Iceland

Todd, Robert Bentley (1809–1860)—© National Portrait Gallery, London

Toft, Albert Arthur (1862–1949)—reproduced by permission of Birmingham Library Services

Toft, Mary (bap. 1703, d. 1763)—© National Portrait Gallery, London

Tolkien, John Ronald Reuel (1892–1973)—© National Portrait Gallery, London

Tollemache, Thomas (c.1651–1694)—The Collection of Pictures, Helmingham Hall. Photograph: Photographic Survey, Courtauld Institute of Art, London

Tolpuddle Martyrs (act. 1834–c.1845)—Mitchell Library, State Library of New South Wales

Tombs, Sir Henry (1824–1874)—© National Portrait Gallery, London

Tomline, Sir George Pretyman, fifth baronet (1750–1827)—by kind permission of the Bishop of Winchester and the Church Commissioners

Tomlinson, David Cecil MacAlister (1917–2000)—Getty Images – Daniel Farson

Tomlinson, Matthew, appointed Lord Tomlinson under the protectorate (bap. 1617, d. 1681)—© National Portrait Gallery, London

Tompion, Thomas (bap. 1639, d. 1713)—by courtesy of the British Horological Institute Limited; original on display at the Upton Hall Time Museum, Upton, Newark, Nottinghamshire; photograph © National Portrait Gallery, London

Tompkins, (Granville) Richard Francis (1918–1992)—© News International Syndication; photograph National Portrait Gallery, London

Tone, (Theobald) Wolfe (1763–1798)—National Gallery of Ireland

Tonks, Henry (1862–1937)—© Family of the artist / Tate, London, 2004

Oxford dictionary of
national biography